Lecture Notes in Artificial Intelligence   3809

Edited by J. G. Carbonell and J. Siekmann

Subseries of Lecture Notes in Computer Science

Shichao Zhang   Ray Jarvis (Eds.)

AI 2005: Advances in Artificial Intelligence

18th Australian Joint Conference on Artificial Intelligence
Sydney, Australia, December 5-9, 2005
Proceedings

 Springer

Series Editors

Jaime G. Carbonell, Carnegie Mellon University, Pittsburgh, PA, USA
Jörg Siekmann, University of Saarland, Saarbrücken, Germany

Volume Editors

Shichao Zhang
University of Technology, Sydney
Faculty of Information Technology
Broadway, NSW 2007, Sydney, Australia
E-mail: zhangsc@it.uts.edu.au

Ray Jarvis
Monash University
Department of Electrical and Computer Systems Engineering
Victoria 3800, Melbourne, Australia
E-mail: Ray.Jarvis@eng.monash.edu.au

Library of Congress Control Number: 2005936732

CR Subject Classification (1998): I.2, F.4.1, H.3, H.2.8, F.1

ISSN   0302-9743
ISBN-10   3-540-30462-2 Springer Berlin Heidelberg New York
ISBN-13   978-3-540-30462-3 Springer Berlin Heidelberg New York

This work is subject to copyright. All rights are reserved, whether the whole or part of the material is concerned, specifically the rights of translation, reprinting, re-use of illustrations, recitation, broadcasting, reproduction on microfilms or in any other way, and storage in data banks. Duplication of this publication or parts thereof is permitted only under the provisions of the German Copyright Law of September 9, 1965, in its current version, and permission for use must always be obtained from Springer. Violations are liable to prosecution under the German Copyright Law.

Springer is a part of Springer Science+Business Media

springeronline.com

© Springer-Verlag Berlin Heidelberg 2005
Printed in Germany

Typesetting: Camera-ready by author, data conversion by Scientific Publishing Services, Chennai, India
Printed on acid-free paper   SPIN: 11589990   06/3142   5 4 3 2 1 0

Preface

The 18th Australian Joint Conference on Artificial Intelligence (AI 2005) was held at the University of Technology, Sydney (UTS), Sydney, Australia from 5 to 9 December 2005.

AI 2005 attracted a historical record number of submissions, a total of 535 papers. The review process was extremely selective. Out of these 535 submissions, the Program Chairs selected only 77 (14.4%) full papers and 119 (22.2%) short papers based on the review reports, making an acceptance rate of 36.6% in total. Authors of the accepted papers came from over 20 countries. This volume of the proceedings contains the abstracts of three keynote speeches and all the full and short papers. The full papers were categorized into three broad sections, namely: AI foundations and technologies, computational intelligence, and AI in specialized domains.

AI 2005 also hosted several tutorials and workshops, providing an interacting mode for specialists and scholars from Australia and other countries. Ronald R. Yager, Geoff Webb and David Goldberg (in conjunction with ACAL05) were the distinguished researchers invited to give presentations. Their contributions to AI 2005 are really appreciated.

It was a great pleasure for us to organize this event. However, we could not have done it without the valuable help of many colleagues around the world. First, we would like to thank the Program Committee members and referees for their extremely hard work and timely return of their comprehensive reports. Without them, it would have been impossible to make decisions and to produce such high-quality proceedings on time. Second, we would like to acknowledge the contributions of all the authors of the 535 papers submitted. Thanks to Mr. Yanchang Zhao for his contribution in helping us manage the paper reviewing process. We are indebted to Dr. Aizhong Lin, Ms. Li Liu and Mr. Zhenxing Qin for maintaining CyberChair and for managing the paper submission and reviewing process. Thanks also go to Dr. Debbie Zhang for organizing the poster session.

Thanks to the general Co-chairs, Tharam Dillon and Paul Compton, for their guidance and especially to the Organizing Chair, Jie Lu, for looking after everything for the conference to run smoothly.

We wish to thank the following for their financial contributions to the success of this conference: Air Force Office of Scientific Research (AFOSR), Asian Office of Aerospace Research and Development (AOARD). AFOSR/AOARD support is not intended to express or imply endorsement by the U.S. Federal Government. The Faculty of Information Technology at the University of Technology, Sydney, was also the financial sponsor for this event.

December 2005   Ray Jarvis
Sydney   Shichao Zhang

Organization

AI 2005 was hosted and organized by the University of Technology, Sydney, Australia. The conference was held at the Carlton Crest Hotel, Sydney, from 5 to 9 December 2005.

Conference Committee

Conference General Co-chairs
   Prof. Tharam Dillon (University of Technology, Sydney)
   Prof. Paul Compton (University of New South Wales)
Program Committee Co-chairs
   Dr. Shichao Zhang (University of Technology, Sydney)
   Prof. Ray Jarvis (Monash University)
Organizing Committee Chair
   A/Prof. Jie Lu (University of Technology, Sydney)
Sponsorship Chair
   Prof. John Debenham (University of Technology, Sydney)
Publicity Chair
   Dr. Hussein Abbass (University of New South Wales)
Workshop Chair
   A/Prof. Brijesh Verma (Central Queensland University)
Tutorial Chair
   Dr. Fei Liu (La-Trobe University)
Web-Master
   Dr. Aizhong Lin (University of New South Wales)

Program Committee

Hussein Abbass, Australia
David Albrecht, Australia
Leila Alem, Australia
James Bailey, Australia
Mike Bain, Australia
Nick Barnes, Australia
Mohammed Bennamoun, Australia
Mike Brooks, Australia
Longbing Cao, Australia
Steve Cassidy, Australia
Qingfeng Chen, Australia
Wanli Chen, Australia
William Cheung, Hong Kong, SAR China
Shu-Chuan Chu, Taiwan
Vic Ciesielski, Australia
Honghua Dai, Australia
John Debenham, Australia
Lance Fung, Australia
Michael Georgeff, Australia
Raj Gopalan, Australia
Guido Governatori, Australia
Xuetao Guo, Australia
Qing He, PR China
Tim Hendtlass, Australia
Philip Hingston, Australia
Jun Hu, PR China
He Huang, PR China

Andrew Jennings, Australia
Huidong Jin, Australia
Graham Kendall, UK
Shamim Khan, Australia
Jong-Hwan Kim, Korea
Irwin King, Hong kong
Michelle Kinsman, Australia
Vincent Lee, Australia
Chris Leckie, Australia
Chunsheng Li, PR China
Jinyan Li, Singapore
Wei Li, Australia
Xiaodong Li, Australia
Yuefeng Li, Australia
Aizhong Lin, Australia
Li Lin, Australia
Jie Lu, Australia
Jingli Lu, Australia
Xudong Luo, UK
Cara MacNish, Australia
Frederic Maire, Australia
Bob McKay, Australia
Matthew Mitchell, Australia
Abhaya Nayak, Australia
Douglas Newlands, Australia
Ann Nicholson, Australia
Kok-Leong Ong, Australia
Mehmet Orgun, Australia
Lin Padgham, Australia
Maurice Pagnucco, Australia
Adrian Pearce, Australia
Mikhail Prokopenko, Australia
Zhenxing Qin, Australia
Bernard Rolfe, Australia
Muhammad Sarfraz, Saudi Arabia
Ruhul Sarker, Australia
Abdul Sattar, Australia
Zhiping Shi, PR China

Zhongzhi Shi, PR China
Goh Ong Sing, Malaysia
Simeon J. Simoff, Australia
Joaquin Sitte, Australia
John Slaney, Australia
Liz Sonenberg, Australia
Eric Soubeiga, UK
David Squire, Australia
Markus Stumptner, Australia
Kaile Su, PR China
Ah Chung Tsoi, Australia
Toby Walsh, Australia
Chao Wang, Australia
Dianhui Wang, Australia
Jiaqi Wang, Australia
Kewen Wang, Australia
Lipo Wang, Singapore
Ruili Wang, New Zealand
Geoff West, Australia
Janet Wiles, Australia
Graham Williams, Australia
Mary-Anne Williams, Australia
Wayne Wobcke, Australia
Kok Wai WONG, Singapore
Boris Wu, Australia
Fengjie Wu, Australia
Zhuoming Xu, PR China
Ying Yang, Australia
Dingrong Yuan, PR China
Chengqi Zhang, Australia
Guangquan Zhang, Australia
Jilian Zhang, PR China
Minjie Zhang, Australia
Yan Zhang, Australia
Zili Zhang, Australia
Yanchang Zhao, Australia
Ingrid Zukerman, Australia

Referees

Rukshan Athauda
Quan Bai
David Billington
Tim Cleaver
Lavindra deSilva
David Dowe
Hongjian Fan
Sarah George
Vadim Gerasimov
Ying Guo
Peter Hebden
Hong Hu
Jian Alan Huang
Ri Huang
Geoff James
Xiaonan Ji
Yinjie Jia
Ryan Kelly
Angel Kennedy
Michael Kirley
Rex Bing Hung Kwok
Eric Lam
Henry Lee
Jiaming Li
Kevin Sin Yee Lee
Li Li
Qingyong Li
Xiaodong Li
Xin Li
Yanrong Li
Yong Liang
Weiqiang Lin
Mingzhe Liu
Wei Liu
Elsa Loekito
Gordon Lowe
Ping Luo
Yuval Marom
Kim Marriott

Bernd Meyer
Ajmal Mian
Vineet Nair
Jiarui Ni
Michael Niemann
Bhavna Orgun
Udaya Parampalli
Laurence Park
Mira Park
Dan Popescu
Iyad Rahwan
Sid Ray
Sebastian Sardina
Rolf Schwitter
Tatiana Semenova
Chuan Shi
Andy Song
Tele Tan
Roger Ting
Peter Tischer
Ronny Tjahyadi
Richard Thomas
Vu Binh Tran
Charles Twardy
Bao Quoc Vo
Jiaqi Wang
Mei Wang
Jie Wu
Zhili Wu
Hui Yang
Shan Yin
Hongchuan Yu
Yiming Zeng
Huaifeng Zhang
Sulan Zhang
Xiaofeng Zhang
Zhiyong Zhang
Zheng Zheng

Table of Contents

Invited Talks

K-Optimal Pattern Discovery: An Efficient and Effective Approach to Exploratory Data Mining
Geoffrey I. Webb 1

Providing Semantics for the WEB Using Fuzzy Set Methods
Ronald R. Yager 3

Little Models, Big Results
David E. Goldberg 4

PART I: AI Foundations and Technologies

Logic and Reasoning

Model Updating CTL Systems
Yulin Ding, Yan Zhang 5

Model Checking for PRS-Like Agents
Wayne Wobcke, Marc Chee, Krystian Ji 17

A Fibred Belief Logic for Multi-agent Systems
Chuchang Liu, Maris A. Ozols, Mehmet A. Orgun 29

Inconsistency-Based Strategy for Clarifying Vague Software Requirements
Kedian Mu, Zhi Jin, Ruqian Lu 39

Conditioning Graphs: Practical Structures for Inference in Bayesian Networks
Kevin Grant, Michael C. Horsch 49

Reasoning with the Outcomes of Plan Execution in Intentional Agents
Timothy William Cleaver, Abdul Sattar, Kewen Wang 60

Tie Breaking in Clause Weighting Local Search for SAT
Valnir Ferreira Jr., John Thornton 70

Syntactic and Semantic Disambiguation of Numeral Strings Using an N-Gram Method
Kyongho Min, William H. Wilson, Yoo-Jin Moon 82

Machine Learning

Locating Regions of Interest in CBIR with Multi-instance Learning Techniques
Zhi-Hua Zhou, Xiao-Bing Xue, Yuan Jiang 92

Ensemble Selection for SuperParent-One-Dependence Estimators
Ying Yang, Kevin Korb, Kai Ming Ting, Geoffrey I. Webb 102

Global Versus Local Constructive Function Approximation for On-Line Reinforcement Learning
Peter Vamplew, Robert Ollington 113

Any-Cost Discovery: Learning Optimal Classification Rules
Ailing Ni, Xiaofeng Zhu, Chengqi Zhang 123

Preprocessing Time Series Data for Classification with Application to CRM
Yiming Yang, Qiang Yang, Wei Lu, Jialin Pan, Rong Pan, Chenhui Lu, Lei Li, Zhenxing Qin 133

Combining Contents and Citations for Scientific Document Classification
Minh Duc Cao, Xiaoying Gao 143

Machine Learning Approach to Realtime Intrusion Detection System
Byung-Joo Kim, Il Kon Kim 153

Structural Abstraction Experiments in Reinforcement Learning
Robert Fitch, Bernhard Hengst, Dorian Šuc, Greg Calbert, Jason Scholz 164

A Hybrid Adaptive Multi-objective Memetic Algorithm for 0/1 Knapsack Problem
XiuPing Guo, ZhiMing Wu, GenKe Yang 176

Game Theory

Probability Estimation in Error Correcting Output Coding Framework Using Game Theory
Mikhail Petrovskiy 186

Evaluation of Strings in Computer Go Using Articulation Points Check and Seki Judgment
  Hyun-Soo Park, Kyung-Woo Kang 197

The Value of Stealth in the Game of Chess
  Peter Smet, Don Gossink, Greg Calbert 207

Robotic Technology

Coordinated Collision Avoidance of Multiple Biomimetic Robotic Fish
  Dandan Zhang, Long Wang, Guangming Xie, Weicun Zhang 215

The Virtual Room Inhabitant – Intuitive Interaction with Intelligent Environments
  Michael Kruppa, Lübomira Spassova, Michael Schmitz 225

Evaluating Techniques for Resolving Redundant Information and Specularity in Occupancy Grids
  Thomas Collins, J.J. Collins, Mark Mansfield, Shane O'Sullivan 235

PART II: Computational Intelligence

Data Mining

Analyzing Security Protocols Using Association Rule Mining
  Qingfeng Chen, Yi-Ping Phoebe Chen 245

Redundant Association Rules Reduction Techniques
  Mafruz Zaman Ashrafi, David Taniar, Kate Smith 254

Construction Algorithm of Principal Curves in the Sense of Limit
  Lianwei Zhao, Yanchang Zhao, Siwei Luo, Chao Shao 264

Collateral Missing Value Estimation: Robust Missing Value Estimation for Consequent Microarray Data Processing
  Muhammad Shoaib B. Sehgal, Iqbal Gondal, Laurence Dooley 274

Neural Networks

Using Neural Networks to Support Early Warning System for Financial Crisis Forecasting
  Kyong Joo Oh, Tae Yoon Kim, Hyoung Yong Lee, Hakbae Lee 284

A Neural Network Based Methodology for Performance Evaluation of
Parallel Systems
  Sırma Yavuz 297

Fuzzy Theory and Algorithms

Decomposition and Resolution of Fuzzy Relation Equations (II) Based
on Boolean-Type Implications
  Yanbin Luo, Chunjie Yang, Yongming Li, Daoying Pi 308

Applying a Fuzzy Trust Model to E-Commerce Systems
  Stefan Schmidt, Robert Steele, Tharam Dillon, Elizabeth Chang 318

Emotion-Based Crowd Simulation Using Fuzzy Algorithm
  Eun-Young Ahn, Jae-Won Kim, No-Yoon Kwak, Sang-Hoon Han ... 330

Evolutionary Computing

A Genetic Algorithm for Job Shop Scheduling with Load Balancing
  Sanja Petrovic, Carole Fayad 339

A Co-evolutionary Particle Swarm Optimization-Based Method for
Multiobjective Optimization
  Hong-yun Meng, Xiao-hua Zhang, San-yang Liu 349

The Effect of Mutation on the Accumulation of Information in a
Genetic Algorithm
  John Milton, Paul Kennedy, Heather Mitchell 360

Linear Genetic Programming for Multi-class Object Classification
  Christopher Fogelberg, Mengjie Zhang 369

Evolutionary Design of Fuzzy Classifiers Using Information Granules
  Do Wan Kim, Jin Bae Park, Young Hoon Joo 380

Constrained Optimization by the ε Constrained Hybrid Algorithm of
Particle Swarm Optimization and Genetic Algorithm
  Tetsuyuki Takahama, Setsuko Sakai, Noriyuki Iwane 389

Web Intelligence

Automated Information Mediator for HTML and XML Based Web
Information Delivery Service
  *Sung Sik Park, Yang Sok Kim, Gil Cheol Park, Byeong Ho Kang,
  Paul Compton* 401

Agent-Based Middleware for Web Service Dynamic Integration on
Peer-to-Peer Networks
  Aizhong Lin, Piyush Maheshwari 405

Towards User Profiling for Web Recommendation
  Guandong Xu, Yanchun Zhang, Xiaofang Zhou 415

A Controlled Natural Language Layer for the Semantic Web
  Rolf Schwitter 425

GaXsearch: An XML Information Retrieval Mechanism Using Genetic
Algorithms
  K.G. Srinivasa, S. Sharath, K.R. Venugopal, Lalit M. Patnaik 435

Decision Making

A New Approach on ρ to Decision Making Using Belief Functions
Under Incomplete Information
  Yuliang Fan, Peter Deer 445

A Hybrid Recommendation Approach for One-and-Only Items
  Xuetao Guo, Guangquan Zhang, Eng Chew, Steve Burdon 457

Exchange Rate Modelling Using News Articles and Economic Data
  Debbie Zhang, Simeon J. Simoff, John Debenham 467

Adaptive Utility-Based Scheduling in Resource-Constrained Systems
  David Vengerov 477

PART III: AI in Specialized Domains

Pattern Recognition

New Feature Extraction Approaches for Face Recognition
  Vo Dinh Minh Nhat, Sungyoung Lee 489

EBGM with Fuzzy Fusion on Face Recognition
  Jialiang Liu, Zhi-Qiang Liu 498

Robust License Plate Segmentation Method Based on Texture Features
and Radon Transform
  *Jun Kong, Xinyue Liu, YingHua Lu, Xiaofeng Zhou,
  Qiushi Zhao* 510

An Adaptive Selection of Motion for Online Hand-Eye Calibration
Jing Zhang, Fanhuai Shi, Yuncai Liu 520

Scene Boundary Detection by Audiovisual Contents Analysis
Joon-sik Baek, Soon-tak Lee, Joong-hwan Baek 530

k-Nearest Neighbors Associative Memory Model for Face Recognition
Bai-ling Zhang, Yuan Miao, Gopal Gupta 540

A New Spectral Smoothing Algorithm for Unit Concatenating Speech Synthesis
Sang-Jin Kim, Kyung Ae Jang, Hyun Bae Han, Minsoo Hahn 550

New Fuzzy Skin Model for Face Detection
Moon Hwan Kim, Jin Bae Park, Young Hoon Joo 557

Kernel Nonparametric Weighted Feature Extraction for Classification
Bor-Chen Kuo, Cheng-Hsuan Li 567

Iterative Training Techniques for Phonetic Template Based Speech Recognition with a Speaker-Independent Phonetic Recognizer
Weon-Goo Kim, MinSeok Jang, Chin-Hui Lee 577

Active Visual Learning and Recognition Using Incremental Kernel PCA
Byung-joo Kim 585

Automated Scene Understanding for Airport Aprons
James Ferryman, Mark Borg, David Thirde, Florent Fusier, Valéry Valentin, François Brémond, Monique Thonnat, Josep Aguilera, Martin Kampel 593

Semantic Correlation Network Based Text Clustering
Shaoxu Song, Chunping Li 604

Time-Varying Prototype Reduction Schemes Applicable for Non-stationary Data Sets
Sang-Woon Kim, B. John Oommen 614

Agent Technology

Multi-agent System Simulating Tumoral Cells Migration
Lynda Dib, Zahia Guessoum, Noël Bonnet, Mohamed T. Laskri 624

An Intelligent Agent-Based Framework for Collaborative Information
Security
   M.H. Kuo 633

Agents, Information and Trust
   John Debenham, Carles Sierra 643

Modelling Partner's Behaviour in Agent Negotiation
   Jakub Brzostowski, Ryszard Kowalczyk 653

Insurance Services in Multi-agent Systems
   Yuk-Hei Lam, Zili Zhang, Kok-Leong Ong 664

Dynamic Team Forming in Self-interested Multi-agent Systems
   Quan Bai, Minjie Zhang 674

N-Learning: A Reinforcement Learning Paradigm for Multiagent
Systems
   Mark Mansfield, J.J. Collins, Malachy Eaton, Thomas Collins 684

Preferences of Agents in Defeasible Logic
   *Mehdi Dastani, Guido Governatori, Antonino Rotolo,
   Leendert van der Torre* 695

MAHIS: An Agent-Oriented Methodology for Constructing Dynamic
Platform-Based HIS
   Chunsheng Li, Li Liu 705

3D Game Engine for Real-Time Facial Animation
   Hye Won Pyun 715

AI Applications

Intelligent 3D Video Avatar for Immersive Telecommunication
   *Sang-Yup Lee, Ig-Jae Kim, Sang C. Ahn, Myo-Taeg Lim,
   Hyoung-Gon Kim* 726

A Lagrangian Heuristic for Winner Determination Problem in
Combinatorial Auctions
   Andrew Lim, Jiqing Tang 736

Moving Cast Shadow Detection and Removal for Visual Traffic
Surveillance
   *Jeong-Hoon Cho, Tae-Gyun Kwon, Dae-Geun Jang,
   Chan-Sik Hwang* 746

A Hidden Markov Model and Immune Particle Swarm
Optimization-Based Algorithm for Multiple Sequence Alignment
  Hong-Wei Ge, Yan-Chun Liang 756

Design of Intelligent Security Management System Using
Simulation-Based Analysis
  Jang-Se Lee, Dong Seong Kim, Jong Sou Park, Sung-Do Chi 766

Neighborhood Re-structuring in Particle Swarm Optimization
  *Arvind S. Mohais, Rui Mendes, Christopher Ward,
  Christian Posthoff* 776

PART IV: Short Papers

Understanding the Pheromone System Within Ant Colony Optimization
  Stephen Gilmour, Mark Dras 786

Model Checking Sum and Product
  H.P. van Ditmarsch, J. Ruan, L.C. Verbrugge 790

The Proof Algorithms of Plausible Logic Form a Hierarchy
  David Billington 796

A Maximum Entropy Model for Transforming Sentences to Logical Form
  Minh Le Nguyen, Akira Shimazu, Hieu Xuan Phan 800

An Information-Theoretic Causal Power Theory
  Lucas R. Hope, Kevin B. Korb 805

A Fixed-Point Semantics for Plausible Logic
  David Billington 812

Applying Indiscernibility Attribute Sets to Knowledge Reduction
  Hong-Ru Li, Wen-Xiu Zhang 816

Dempster Conditioning and Conditional Independence in Evidence
Theory
  Yongchuan Tang, Jiacheng Zheng 822

Case-Based Conflict Resolution in Multi-agent Ship Design System
  Kyung Ho Lee, Kyu Yeul Lee 826

Reduced MDP Representation of a Logistical Planning Problem Using
Petri-Nets
  Sanjeev Naguleswaran, Sarah L. Hickmott, Langford B. White 830

Structure-Based Algorithms for Computing Preferred Arguments of
Defeasible Knowledge Bases
  Quoc Bao Vo 834

Solving Job-Shop Scheduling Problems by a Novel Artificial Immune
System
  Hong-Wei Ge, Liang Sun, Yan-Chun Liang 839

Agent-Based Ontology Mapping Towards Ontology Interoperability
  Li Li, Yun Yang, Baolin Wu 843

Dynamic Negative Selection Algorithm Based on Match Range Model
  Jungan Chen, Feng Liang, Dongyong Yang 847

A Virtual Prolog Approach to Implementing Beliefs, Desires and
Intentions in Animat Agents
  K.A. Hawick, H.A. James, C.J. Scogings 852

Obstacle Avoidance and Path Planning Based on Flow Field for
Biomimetic Robotic Fish
  Jinyan Shao, Guangming Xie, Long Wang, Weicun Zhang 857

A Facial Control Method Considering Internal Emotion of Sensibility
Robot
  Hiroshi Shibata, Masayoshi Kanoh, Shohei Kato, Hidenori Itoh 861

An Object Store Model for Diagnosing Java Programs
  Rong Chen, Franz Wotawa 865

A Multi-exchange Heuristic for a Production Location Problem
  Yunsong Guo, Yanzhi Li, Andrew Lim, Brian Rodrigues 871

The Car-Sequencing Problem as n-Ary CSP – Sequential and Parallel
Solving
  Mihaela Butaru, Zineb Habbas 875

Normalized Gaussian Networks with Mixed Feature Data
  Shu-Kay Ng, Geoffrey J. McLachlan 879

A Comparative Study for WordNet Guided Text Representation
  Jian Zhang, Chunping Li 883

Application of Bayesian Techniques for MLPs to Financial Time Series
Forecasting
  Andrew Skabar 888

An Incremental Nonlinear Dimensionality Reduction Algorithm Based on ISOMAP
  Lukui Shi, Pilian He, Enhai Liu 892

Robust Speaker Identification Based on t-Distribution Mixture Model
  Younjeong Lee, Hernsoo Hahn, Youngjoon Han, Joohun Lee 896

Inducing Sequential Patterns from Multidimensional Time Series Data
  Chang-Hwan Lee 900

Fitness Approximation in Estimation of Distribution Algorithms for Feature Selection
  Haixia Chen, Senmiao Yuan, Kai Jiang 904

Automatic Feature Selection for Classification of Health Data
  Hongxing He, Huidong Jin, Jie Chen 910

BP Learning and Numerical Algorithm of Dynamic Systems
  Jiuzhen Liang, Hong Jiang 914

Ant Colony Optimization Combining with Mutual Information for Feature Selection in Support Vector Machines
  Chunkai Zhang, Hong Hu 918

A Preliminary MML Linear Classifier Using Principal Components for Multiple Classes
  Lara Kornienko, David W. Albrecht, David L. Dowe 922

Content-Based Classification of Music Using VQ-Multifeature Clustering Technique
  Won-Jung Yoon, Kyu-Sik Park 927

Individual Clustering and Homogeneous Cluster Ensemble Approaches Applied to Gene Expression Data
  Shirlly C.M. Silva, Daniel S.A. de Araujo, Raul B. Paradeda, Valmar S. Severiano-Sobrinho, Marcilio C.P. de Souto 930

Joint Spatial and Frequency Domains Watermarking Algorithm Based on Wavelet Packets
  Yinghua Lu, Wei Wang, Jun Kong, Jialing Han, Gang Hou 934

Hybrid Agglomerative Clustering for Large Databases: An Efficient Interactivity Approach
  Ickjai Lee, Jianhua Yang 938

Constructing Multi-resolution Support Vector Regression Modelling
Hong Peng, Zheng Pei, Jun Wang 942

Revised Entropy Clustering Analysis with Features Selection
Ching-Hsue Cheng, Jing-Rong Chang, I-Ni Lei 946

IC^2: An Interval Based Characteristic Concept Learner
Pramod K. Singh 950

A Comparative Study for Assessing the Reliability of Complex Networks Using Rules Extracted from Different Machine Learning Approaches
Douglas E. Torres D., Claudio M. Rocco S. 954

Machine Learning for Time Interval Petri Nets
Vadim Bulitko, David C. Wilkins 959

Model Based Abnormal Acoustic Source Detection Using a Microphone Array
Heungkyu Lee, Jounghoon Beh, June Kim, Hanseok Ko 966

Improving the Mobile Phone Habitat - Learning Changes in User's Profiles
Robert Bridle, Eric McCreath 970

A Stigmergy Based Approach to Data Mining
Manu De Backer, Raf Haesen, David Martens, Bart Baesens 975

Mining Domain-Driven Correlations in Stock Markets
Li Lin, Dan Luo, Li Liu 979

Selective Data Masking Design in Intelligent Knowledge Capsule for Efficient Data Mining
JeongYon Shim 983

On a Mathematical Relationship Between the Fixed Point and the Closed Itemset in Association Rule Mining
Tian-rui Li, Da Ruan, Tianmin Huang, Yang Xu 989

A Data Mining Approach in Opponent Modeling
Remedios de Dios Bulos, Conirose Dulalia, Peggy Sharon L. Go, Pamela Vianne C. Tan, Ma. Zaide Ilene O. Uy 993

Automated Design and Knowledge Discovery of Logic Circuits Using a Multi-objective Adaptive GA
Shuguang Zhao, Licheng Jiao, Min Tang 997

Mining with Constraints by Pruning and Avoiding Ineffectual Processing
  Mohammad El-Hajj, Osmar R. Zaïane 1001

Rough Association Mining and Its Application in Web Information
Gathering
  Yuefeng Li, Ning Zhong 1005

Intrusion Detection Using Text Mining in a Web-Based Telemedicine
System
  J.J. García Adeva, J.M. Pikatza, S. Flórez, F.J. Sobrado 1009

Web Usage Mining Using Evolutionary Support Vector Machine
  Sung-Hae Jun 1015

Optimization of Genetic Algorithm Parameters for Multi-channel
Manufacturing Systems by Taguchi Method
  A. Sermet Anagun, Feristah Ozcelik 1021

UAV Controller Design Using Evolutionary Algorithms
  Sergey Khantsis, Anna Bourmistrova 1025

River Flow Forecasting with Constructive Neural Network
  Mêuser Valença, Teresa Ludermir, Anelle Valença 1031

A Novel License Plate Location Method Based on Neural Network and
Saturation Information
  Yinghua Lu, Lijie Yu, Jun Kong, Canghua Tang 1037

Verification and Validation of Artificial Neural Network Models
  Fei Liu, Ming Yang 1041

A Simulation Based Multi-criteria Scheduling Approach of
Dual-Resource Constrained Manufacturing Systems with Neural
Networks
  Ozlem Uzun Araz 1047

Quantitative Analysis of the Varieties of Apple Using Near Infrared
Spectroscopy by Principal Component Analysis and BP Model
  Yong He, Xiaoli Li, Yongni Shao 1053

Identification and Control of ITU Triga Mark-II Nuclear Research
Reactor Using Neural Networks and Fuzzy Logic
  Ramazan Coban, Burhanettin Can 1057

Differential Evolution Algorithm for Designing Optimal Adaptive
Linear Combiners
  Nurhan Karaboga, Canan Aslihan Koyuncu 1063

A Comparison of Evolutionary Methods for the Discovery of Local
Search Heuristics
  Stuart Bain, John Thornton, Abdul Sattar 1068

Evolutionally Optimized Fuzzy Neural Networks Based on Fuzzy
Relation Rules and Evolutionary Data Granulation
  *Sung-Kwun Oh, Hyun-Ki Kim, Seong-Whan Jang,
  Yong-Kab Kim* 1075

Evolving While-Loop Structures in Genetic Programming for Factorial
and Ant Problems
  Guang Chen, Mengjie Zhang 1079

Evolutionary Optimisation of Distributed Energy Resources
  Ying Guo, Jiaming Li, Geoff James 1086

Can Evolutionary Computation Handle Large Datasets? A Study into
Network Intrusion Detection
  Hai H. Dam, Kamran Shafi, Hussein A. Abbass 1092

Automatic Loop-Shaping of QFT Controllers Using GAs and
Evolutionary Computation
  Min-Soo Kim, Chan-Soo Chung 1096

Investigating the Effect of Incorporating Additional Levels in
Structured Genetic Algorithms
  Angelos Molfetas 1101

Accelerating Real-Valued Genetic Algorithms Using Mutation-with-
Momentum
  Luke Temby, Peter Vamplew, Adam Berry 1108

A Fuzzy Inference Method for Spam-Mail Filtering
  Jong-Wan Kim, Sin-Jae Kang, Byeong Man Kim 1112

Genetically Optimized Hybrid Fuzzy Polynomial Neural Networks
Based on Polynomial and Fuzzy Polynomial Neurons
  Sung-Kwun Oh, Hyun-Ki Kim 1116

Multi-item Fuzzy Inventory Model with Three Constraints: Genetic
Algorithm Approach
  Jafar Rezaei, Mansoor Davoodi 1120

Fuzzy Attribute Implications: Computing Non-redundant Bases Using Maximal Independent Sets
Radim Bělohlávek, Vilém Vychodil 1126

Fuzzy Classifier with Bayes Rule Consequent
Do Wan Kim, Jin Bae Park, Young Hoon Joo 1130

Identification of T–S Fuzzy Classifier Via Linear Matrix Inequalities
Moon Hwan Kim, Jin Bae Park, Weon Goo Kim, Young Hoon Joo 1134

An Adaptive Fuzzy c-Means Algorithm with the L_2 Norm
Nicomedes L. Cavalcanti Júnior, Francisco de A.T. de Carvalho 1138

Design of Information Granules-Based Fuzzy Systems Using Clustering Algorithm and Genetic Optimization
Sung-Kwun Oh, Keon-Jun Park, Witold Pedrycz, Tae-Chon Ahn 1142

A Personalized Recommendation System for Electronic Program Guide
Jin An Xu, Kenji Araki 1146

An Effective Recommendation Algorithm for Clustering-Based Recommender Systems
Taek-Hun Kim, Sung-Bong Yang 1150

An Intelligent Decision Making System to Support E-Service Management
Gülçin Büyüközkan, Mehmet Şakir Ersoy, Gülfem Işıklar 1154

OWL, Proteins and Data Integration
Amandeep S. Sidhu, Tharam S. Dillon, Elizabeth Chang, Baldev S. Sidhu 1158

Web Site Improvements Based on Representative Pages Identification
Sebastían A. Ríos, Juan D. Velásquez, Hiroshi Yasuda, Terumasa Aoki 1162

Unsupervised Bilingual Word Sense Disambiguation Using Web Statistics
Yuanyong Wang, Achim Hoffmann 1167

Optimal Production Policy for a Two-Stage Production System Under Lumpy Demand
Ding-zhong Feng, Mitsuo Yamashiro 1173

A Preliminary Investigation of a Linguistic Perceptron
  Sansanee Auephanwiriyaku 1180

Skeleton Driven Limb Animation Based on Three-Layered Structure
  Jiarong Yu, Jiaoying Shi, Yongxia Zhou 1187

Answer Set Programming for Distributed Authorization: The Language,
Computations, and Application
  Shujing Wang, Yan Zhang 1191

Multiagent Architecture (BlueAgents) with the Dynamic Pricing and
Maximum Profit Strategy in the TAC SCM
  David Han 1195

Agent-Based Plot Planning for Automatic Generation of Computer
Animation
  Wei Tang, Lei Zheng, Chunnian Liu 1199

Mobile Agent Migration: An Optimal Policy
  Salah El Falou, François Bourdon 1204

Human Action Understanding Using Motion Verbs in WordNet
  Miyoung Cho, Dan Song, Junho Choi, Pankoo Kim 1209

Partitional Approach for Estimating Null Value in Relational Database
  Jia-Wen Wang, Ching-Hsue Cheng, Wei-Ting Chang 1213

A Robust Face Recognition System
  Ying-Han Pang, Andrew Teoh Beng Jin, David Ngo Chek Ling 1217

Resampling LDA/QR and PCA+LDA for Face Recognition
  Jun Liu, Songcan Chen 1221

Curvature Based Range Face Recognition Analysis Using Projection
Vector by Subimage
  Yeunghak Lee, Ik-Dong Kim 1225

Multiple Face Tracking Using Kalman Estimator Based Color SSD
Algorithm
  *Kyunghwan Baek, Byoungki Kim, Sangbum Park, Youngjoon Han,
  Hernsoo Hahn* 1229

Target Word Selection for Korean Verbs Using a Bilingual Dictionary
and WordNet
  Kweon Yang Kim, Byong Gul Lee, Dong Kwon Hong 1233

A Color Image Segmentation Algorithm by Using Region and Edge
Information
  Yuchou Chang, Yue Zhou, Yonggang Wang, Yi Hong 1237

Recognition of Passports Using FCM-Based RBF Network
  Kwang-Baek Kim, Jae-Hyun Cho, Cheol-Ki Kim 1241

A Vision System for Partially Occluded Landmark Recognition
  Quoc V. Do, Peter Lozo, Lakhmi C. Jain 1246

Diversity Control in GP with ADF for Regression Tasks
  Huayang Xie 1253

Some Propositions of Information Fusion for Pattern Recognition with
Context Task
  Michal Wozniak 1258

A Personal Locating System Using the Vision-Based Augmented Reality
  J.B. Kim, J.M. Lee, H.S. Jun 1262

Fast Candidate Generation for Template Matching Using Two 1-D
Edge Projections
  Jong-Eun Ha, Dong-Joong Kang 1267

Finding Similar Patterns in Microarray Data
  Xiangsheng Chen, Jiuyong Li, Grant Daggard, Xiaodi Huang 1272

A Stereo Matching Using Variable Windows and Dynamic Programming
  Won-Pyo Dong, Yun-Seok Lee, Chang-Sung Jeong 1277

Detection of Auto Programs for MMORPGs
  Hyungil Kim, Sungwoo Hong, Juntae Kim 1281

Automated Classification of Dementia Subtypes from Post-mortem
Cortex Images
  David Cornforth, Herbert Jelinek 1285

Metrics for Model Selection in Consumer Finance Problems
  Debjit Biswas, Babu Narayanan, Ramasubramanian Sundararajan... 1289

Microcontroller Based Temperature Control of Oven Using Different
Kinds of Autotuning PID Methods
  Emine Doğru Bolat, Kadir Erkan, Seda Postalcıoğlu 1295

Aggregation of Preferences Based on FSAM
  Dae-Young Choi 1301

A Novel Particle Swarm Optimization for Constrained Optimization Problems
Xiangyong Li, Peng Tian, Min Kong 1305

A Framework for Relational Link Discovery
Dan Luo, Chao Luo, Chunzhi Zhang 1311

IPQDA: A Software Tool for Intelligent Analysis of Power Quality Disturbances
Aini Hussain, Azah Mohamed, Mohd Hanif Md Saad, Mohd Haszuan Shukairi, Noor Sabathiah Sayuti 1315

Bio-inspired Control of Dexterous Manipulation
Rosana Matuk Herrera, Fabio Leoni 1319

A Lagrangian Relaxation Based Heuristic for Solving the Length-Balanced Two Arc-Disjoint Shortest Paths Problem
Yanzhi Li, Andrew Lim, Hong Ma 1323

Optimizing Coupled Oscillators for Stability
David Newth, Markus Brede 1327

A Novel Approach for Vendor Combination Selection in Supply Chain Management
Ding-zhong Feng, Mitsuo Yamashiro, Lei-lei Chen 1331

A Robust SVM Design for Multi-class Classification
Minkook Cho, Hyeyoung Park 1335

Author Index 1339

K-Optimal Pattern Discovery: An Efficient and Effective Approach to Exploratory Data Mining

Geoffrey I. Webb

Faculty of Information Technology, Monash University, Vic, 3800, Australia
webb@infotech.monash.edu.au
http://www.csse.monash.edu.au/~webb

Abstract. Most data-mining techniques seek a single model that optimizes an objective function with respect to the data. In many real-world applications several models will equally optimize this function. However, they may not all equally satisfy a user's preferences, which will be affected by background knowledge and pragmatic considerations that are infeasible to quantify into an objective function.

Thus, the program may make arbitrary and potentially suboptimal decisions. In contrast, methods for exploratory pattern discovery seek all models that satisfy user-defined criteria. This allows the user select between these models, rather than relinquishing control to the program. Association rule discovery [1] is the best known example of this approach. However, it is based on the minimum-support technique, by which patterns are only discovered that occur in the data more than a user-specified number of times. While this approach has proved very effective in many applications, it is subject to a number of limitations.

- It creates an arbitrary discontinuity in the interestingness function by which one more or less case supporting a pattern can transform its assessment from uninteresting to most interesting.
- Sometimes the most interesting patterns are very rare [3].
- Minimum support may not be relevant to whether a pattern is interesting.
- It is often difficult to find a minimum support level that results in sufficient but not excessive numbers of patterns being discovered.
- It cannot handle dense data [2].
- It limits the ability to efficiently prune the search space on the basis on constraints that are neither monotone nor anti-monotone with respect to support.

K-optimal pattern discovery [4,5,11,14,15,17-20] is an exploratory technique that finds the k patterns that optimize a user-selected objective function while respecting other user-specified constraints. This strategy avoids the above problems while empowering the user to select between preference criteria and to directly control the number of patterns that are discovered. It also supports statistically sound exploratory pattern discovery [8]. Its effectiveness is demonstrated by a large range of applications [5-10,12,13].

References

1. Agrawal, R., Imielinski, T., Swami, A.N.: Mining Association Rules between Sets of Items in Large Databases. In Proc. 1993 ACM SIGMOD Int. Conf. Management of Data, Washington, D.C. (1993) 207-216.
2. Bayardo, Jr., R.J., Agrawal, R., Gunopulos, D.: Constraint-Based Rule Mining in Large, Dense Databases. Data Mining and Knowledge Discovery, 4 (2000) 217-240.
3. Cohen, E., Datar, M., Fujiwara, S., Gionis, A., Indyk, P., Motwani, R., Ullman, J.D., Yang, C.: Finding Interesting Associations without Support Pruning. In Proceedings Int. Conf. Data Engineering, (2000) 489-499.
4. Han, J., Wang, J., Lu, Y., Tzvetkov, P.: Mining Top-K Frequent Closed Patterns without Minimum Support. In Int. Conf. Data Mining (2002) 211-218.
5. Hellström,T.: Learning Robotic Behaviors with Association Rules. WSEAS transactions on systems. ISBN 1109-2777 (2003).
6. Eirinaki, M., Vazirgiannis, M., Varlamis, I.: SEWeP: using site semantics and a taxonomy to enhance the Web personalization process. In Proc. KDD-2003: the SIGKDD Conference of Knowledge Discovery and Datamining, ACM Press, New York (2003) 99-108.
7. Jiao, J., Zhang, Y.: Product portfolio identification based on association rule mining. Computer-Aided Design 37 (2005) 149-172
8. McAullay, D., Williams, G.J., Chen, J., Jin, H.: A Delivery Framework for Health Data Mining and Analytics. Australian Computer Science Conference (2005) 381-390.
9. Mennis, J., Liu, J.W.: Mining association rules in spatio-temporal data: an analysis of urban socioeconomic and land cover change. Transactions in GIS, 9 (2005) 13-18.
10. Raz, O.: Helping Everyday Users Find Anomalies in Data Feeds, Ph.D. Thesis - Software Engineering, Carnegie-Mellon University (2004).
11. Scheffer, T., Wrobel, S.: Finding the Most Interesting Patterns in a Database Quickly by Using Sequential Sampling. Journal of Machine Learning Research 3 (2002) 833-862.
12. Siu, K.K.W., Butler, S.M., Beveridge, T., Gillam, J.E., Hall, C.J., Kaye, A.H., Lewis, R.A., Mannan, K., McLoughlin, G., Pearson, S., Round, A.R., Schultke, E., Webb, G.I., Wilkinson, S.J. Identifying markers of pathology in SAXS data of malignant tissues of the brain. Nuclear Instruments and Methods in Physics Research A (In Press).
13. Tsironis L., Bilalis N., Moustakis V.: Using inductive Machine Learning to support Quality Management. In Proc. 3rd Int. Conf. Design and Analysis of Manufacturing Systems, Tinos Island, University of Aegean (2001).
14. Webb, G. I.: Discovering associations with numeric variables. In Proc. 7th ACM SIGKDD Int. Conf. Knowledge Discovery and Data mining. ACM Press, (2001) pp 383-388.
15. Webb, G. I.: OPUS: An efficient admissible algorithm for unordered search. Journal of Artificial Intelligence Research. 3 (1995) 431-465.
16. Webb, G. I.: Preliminary investigations into statistically valid exploratory rule discovery. In Proc. Australasian Data Mining Workshop (AusDM03), University of Technology, Sydney (2003) 1-9.
17. Webb, G. I., Butler, S., Newlands, D:. On detecting differences between groups. In Proc. KDD-2003: The SIGKDD Conference of Knowledge Discovery and Datamining, ACM Press, (2003) pp. 256-265.
18. Webb, G. I., Zhang, S. K-Optimal-Rule-Discovery. Data Mining and Knowledge Discovery, 10 (2005) 39-79.
19. Webb, G. I.: Efficient search for association rules. In Proc. KDD-2000: the SIGKDD Conf. Knowledge Discovery and Datamining, ACM Press, New York (2000) 99-107.
20. Wrobel, S.: An Algorithm for Multi-relational Discovery of Subgroups. In Proc. Principles of Data Mining and Knowledge Discovery, Springer, Berlin (1997) 78-87.

Providing Semantics for the WEB Using Fuzzy Set Methods

Ronald R. Yager

Director, Machine Intelligence Institute,
Iona College, New Rochelle, NY 10801
yager@panix.com

Abstract. We discuss the emerging applications of fuzzy logic and related technologies within the semantic web. Using fuzzy sets, we are able to provide an underlying semantics for linguistic concepts. We show how this framework allows for the representation of the types of imprecision characteristic of human conceptualization. We introduce some of the basic operations available for the representation and subsequent manipulation of knowledge. We illustrate the application of soft matching and searching technologies that exploit the underlying semantics provided by using fuzzy sets. We look at question-answering systems and point out how they differ from other information seeking applications, such as search engines, by requiring a deduction capability, an ability to answer questions by a synthesis of information residing in different parts of its knowledge base. This capability requires appropriate representation of various types of human knowledge, rules for locally manipulating this knowledge and framework for providing a global plan for appropriately mobilizing the information in the knowledge base to address the question posed. In this talk we suggest tools to provide these capabilities. We describe how the fuzzy set based theory of approximate reasoning can aid in the process of representing knowledge. We discuss how protoforms can be used to aid in deduction and local manipulation of knowledge. The concept of a knowledge tree is introduced to provide a global framework for mobilizing the knowledge in response to a query.

Little Models, Big Results

David E. Goldberg

117 Transportation Building MC-238,
Department of General Engineering,
104 S. Mathews Ave., Urbana IL 61801,
University of Illinois at Urbana-Champaign
deg@uiuc.edu

Abstract. Artificial intelligence and artificial life are nothing if not ambitious. The creation of an artificial intellect or life form is a daunting task, and daunting tasks seem to call for pulling out all the stops and using the biggest, baddest analytical tools on the block. Indeed over many, many years, AI and A-Life have thrown a plethora of sophisticated mathematical and computational techniques at solving the important problems of AI and AL, but the track record is mixed, and many of the knotty problems are problems still. This talk suggests a simpler approach to penetrating the complexity of AI and AL. In particular, a methodology of little models, using facetwise analyses, dimensional analysis, and a procedure of patchquilt integration are suggested to construct models that are especially useful in the design of AI and AL that works. The little modeling methodology is illustrated with a case study drawn from the development of competent and efficient genetic algorithms, including models of population size, run duration, and market share, and the race, and other examples are given from current work in the development of a simplified quantitative organizational theory (SQOT). The talk concludes by suggesting specific ways to adopt these techniques to advance the agendas of AI and AL.

Model Updating CTL Systems

Yulin Ding and Yan Zhang

School of Computing & Information Technology,
University of Western Sydney,
Kingswood, N.S.W. 1797, Australia
{yding, yan}@cit.uws.edu.au

Abstract. Minimal change is a fundamental principle for modelling system dynamics. In this paper, we study the issue of minimal change for Computational Tree Logic (CTL) model update. We first consider five primitive updates which capture the basic update operations in the CTL model. Based on these primitive updates, we then define the minimal change criteria for CTL model update and develop formal algorithms that embed the underlying minimal change principle. We also present the well known microwave oven scenario to demonstrate our update algorithms. Our work presented in this paper can be viewed as the first formalization towards an integration of model checking and model updating for system modification.

1 Introduction

Over the last few years, automated formal verification tools, such as model checkers, have shown their ability to provide a thorough automatic error diagnosis in complex designs. Currently, the state of the art model checkers are SMV [3], NuSMV [4] and Cadence SMV [10], which employ SMV specification language for both CTL and Lineal Temporal Logic (LTL) model checking, and SPIN [8], which uses Promela specification language for on the fly LTL model checking. Also, the MCK [6] model checker has enhanced currently in use model checkers by the inclusion of an added knowledge operator to check the knowledge of semantics of a Kripke model.

Along with model checking, error repair has begun to employ a formal methods approach. Buccafurri et al. [2] used abductive model revision techniques, repairing errors in concurrent programs. They aim at using techniques and concepts from model checking by combining them with AI principles. In the paper of Harris and Ryan [7], model checking is formalized with a belief updating operator $\diamond$ to satisfy classical proposition knowledge update KM postulates $U1$-$U8$.

The update of the knowledge base has been extensively studied. Winslett [11] was a pioneer of the update of the knowledge base and used series update and minimal change methods for databases. Recently, the update of the knowledge base is enhanced by the modality update by Baral and Zhang [1]. They discussed knowledge update and its minimal change, based on modal logic $S5$. Both the update of the knowledge base and the knowledge update are currently at the theoretical research stage.

Ding and Zhang [5] employed a formal approach called LTL model update for system modification, which is the first step of the theoretical integration of model checking and knowledge update. The LTL model update modifies the existing LTL model of an abstracted system to automatically correct the errors occurring within this model. In this paper, we extend the work of Ding and Zhang [5] from LTL model update to CTL model update and introduce minimal change rules for CTL model update as the main contribution. As preparation for implementation of CTL model update in the next stage, we have designed algorithms based on minimal change rules for CTL model update.

This paper is organized as follows: Section 2 reviews CTL syntax and semantics. Section 3 analyzes five types of primitive updates: PU1 to PU5 for CTL model update. Section 4 introduces minimal change rules. Section 5 designs algorithms for CTL model update. Section 6 presents a microwave example to demonstrate algorithms from the previous section. Finally, the paper concludes with Section 7.

2 CTL Syntax and Semantics

Definition 1. *[3] Let AP be a set of atomic propositions. A Kripke model M over AP is a three tuple $M = (S, R, L)$ where*
  1. *S is a finite set of states.*
  2. *$R \subseteq S \times S$ is a transition relation.*
  3. *$L : S \to 2^{AP}$ is a function that assigns each state with a set of atomic propositions.*

Definition 2. *[9] Computation tree logic (CTL) has the following syntax given in Backus naur form:*

$$\phi ::= \top \mid \bot \mid p \mid (\neg\phi) \mid (\phi \wedge \phi) \mid (\phi \vee \phi) \mid \phi \to \phi \mid AX\phi \mid EX\phi$$
$$\mid AG\phi \mid EG\phi \mid AF\phi \mid EF\phi \mid A[\phi \cup \phi] \mid E[\phi \cup \phi]$$

where p is any propositional atom.

A CTL formula is evaluated on a Kripke model M. A path in M from a state s is an infinite sequence of states $\pi \stackrel{def}{=} [s_0, s_1, s_2, \cdots, s_{i-1}, s_i, s_{i+1}, \cdots]$ such that $s_0 = s$ and the relation (s_i, s_{i+1}) holds for all $i \geq 0$. We write $(s_i, s_{i+1}) \subseteq \pi$ and $s_i \in \pi$. For simplicity, we donate $(pre(s_i), s_i) \in R$, where $s_{i-1} = pre(s_i)$, and $(s_i, succ(s)) \in R$, where $s_{i+1} = succ(s_i)$. If we express the above path as $\pi = [s_0, s_1, \cdots, s_i, \cdots, s_k, \cdots]$ and $i < k$, We denote that s_i is earlier than s_k as $s_i < s_k$.

Definition 3. *[9] Let $M = (S, R, L)$ be a Kripke model for CTL. Given any s in S, we define whether a CTL formula ϕ holds in state s. We denote this by $M, s \models \phi$. Naturally, the definition of the satisfaction relation $\models$ is done by structural induction on all CTL formulas:*

  1. *$M, s \models \top$ and $M, s \not\models \bot$ for all $s \in S$.*
  2. *$M, s \models p$ iff $p \in L(s)$.*
  3. *$M, s \models \neg\phi$ iff $M, s \not\models \phi$.*
  4. *$M, s \models \phi_1 \wedge \phi_2$ iff $M, s \models \phi_1$ and $M, s \models \phi_2$.*

5. $M, s \models \phi_1 \vee \phi_2$ iff $M, s \models \phi_1$ and $M, s \models \phi_2$.
6. $M, s \models \phi_1 \rightarrow \phi_2$ iff $M, s \not\models \phi_1$, or $M, s \models \phi_2$.
7. $M, s \models AX\phi$ iff for all s_1 such that $s \rightarrow s_1$ we have $M, s_1 \models \phi$.
8. $M, s \models EX\phi$ iff for some s_1 such that $s \rightarrow s_1$ we have $M, s_1 \models \phi$.
9. $M, s \models AG\phi$ holds iff for all paths $s_0 \rightarrow s_1 \rightarrow s_2 \rightarrow \cdots$, where s_0 equals s, and all s_i along the path, we have $M, s_i \models \phi$.
10. $M, s \models EG\phi$ holds iff there is a path $s_0 \rightarrow s_1 \rightarrow s_2 \rightarrow \cdots$, where s_0 equals s, and for all s_i along the path, we have $M, s_i \models \phi$.
11. $M, s \models AF\phi$ holds iff for all paths $s_0 \rightarrow s_1 \rightarrow s_2 \rightarrow \cdots$, where s_0 equals s, there is some s_i such that $M, s_i \models \phi$.
12. $M, s \models EF\phi$ holds iff there is a path $s_0 \rightarrow s_1 \rightarrow s_2 \rightarrow \cdots$, where $s_i = s$, and for some s_i along the path, we have $M, s_i \models \phi$.
13. $M, s \models A[\phi_1 \cup \phi_2]$ holds iff for all paths $s_0 \rightarrow s_1 \rightarrow s_2 \rightarrow \cdots$, where s_0 equals s, that path satisfies $\phi_1 \cup \phi_2$, i.e. there is some s_i along the path, such that $M, s_i \models \phi_2$, and, for each $j < i$, we have $M, s_j \models \phi_1$.
14. $M, s \models E[\phi_1 \cup \phi_2]$ holds iff there is a path $s_0 \rightarrow s_1 \rightarrow s_2 \rightarrow \cdots$, where s_0 equals s, that path satisfies $\phi_1 \cup \phi_2$, i.e. there is some s_i along the path, such that $M, s_i \models \phi_2$, and, for each $j < i$, we have $M, s_j \models \phi_1$.

3 CTL Model Update

Definition 4. *(CTL Model Update) Given a CTL Kripke model $M = (S, R, L)$ and a CTL formula ϕ, $\mathcal{M} = (M, s_0) \not\models \phi$, where $s_0 \in S$. An update of $\mathcal{M}$ with ϕ, is a new CTL Kripke model $\mathcal{M}' = (M', s_0')$, where $M' = (S', R', L')$ and $s_0' \in S'$, such that $\mathcal{M}' \models \phi$.*

3.1 Types of CTL Model Update: Primitive Updates

The operations to update the CTL model can be decomposed as five types which are compatible with simple modifications given in [5]. We name them as primitive updates: PU1, PU2, $\cdots$, PU5. Each primitive update is defined in its simplest way: one operation at a time.

PU1: Adding a relation only
Given $M = (S, R, L)$, its updated model $M' = (S', R', L')$ is the result of M having only added a new relation, iff $S' = S$; $L' = L$;
$R' = R \cup \{(s_{ar}, s_{ar2}) | (s_{ar}, s_{ar2}) \notin R, s_{ar} \in S, s_{ar2} \in S\}$.

PU2: Removing a relation only
Given $M = (S, R, L)$, its updated model $M' = (S', R', L')$ is the result of M having only removed an existing relation, iff $S' = S$; $L' = L$;
$R' = R - \{(s_{rr}, s_{rr2}) | (s_{rr}, s_{rr2}) \in R, s_{rr} \in S, s_{rr2} \in S\}$.

PU3: Substituting a state and its associated relation(s) only
Given $M = (S, R, L)$, its updated model $M' = (S', R', L')$ is the result of M having only substituted an existing state and its associated relation(s), iff there is a bijective mapping m between S and S', which makes

A. $\forall \pi = [s_0, s_1, \cdots, s_i, s_{i+1}, \cdots] \in M$, $\exists \pi' = [s'_0, s'_1, \cdots, s'_i, s'_{i+1}, \cdots] \in M'$
such that $m(s_i) = s'_i$, where $i = 0, 1, \cdots$;
B. $\forall \pi' = [s'_0, s'_1, \cdots, s'_i, s'_{i+1}, \cdots] \in M'$, $\exists \pi = [s_0, s_1, \cdots, s_i, s_{i+1}, \cdots] \in M$
such that $s_i = m^{-1}(s'_i)$, where $i = 0, 1, \cdots$;
$S' = S \cup \{s_{ss}|s_{ss} \notin S, s_{ss} \in S'\} - \{s_i|s_i \in S, s_i \notin S'\}$;
$R' = R \cup \{(s_{i-1}, s_{ss})(s_{ss}, s_{i+1})|s_{i-1} \in S, s_{i-1} \in S', s_{i+1} \in S, s_{i+1} \in S'\}$
$\quad -\{(s_{i-1}, s_i), (s_i, s_{i+1})\}$;
$L': \to 2^{AP}$, where $\forall s \in S'$, if $s \in S$, then $L'(s) = L(s)$, else
$L'(s_{ss}) = \tau(s_{ss})$, where τ is the truth assignment related to s_{ss},

where the associated relations of s_i (or s_{ss}) are its incoming and outgoing relations.

PU4: Adding a state and its associated relation(s) only
Given $M = (S, R, L)$, its updated model $M' = (S', R', L')$ is the result of M having only added a new state and its associated relation(s), iff
$S' = S \cup \{s_{as}|s_{as} \notin S, s_{as} \in S'\}$;
$R' = R \cup \{(s_{as-1}, s_{as})(s_{as}, s_{as+1})|s_{as-1} \in S, s_{as-1} \in S', s_{as+1} \in S, s_{as+1} \in S'\}$;
$L': \to 2^{AP}$, where $\forall s \in S'$, if $s \in S$, then $L'(s) = L(s)$, else
$L'(s_{as}) = \tau(s_{as})$, where τ is the truth assignment related to s_{as},

where the associated incoming and outgoing relations of s_{as} are added.

PU5: Removing a state and its associated relation(s) only
Given $M = (S, R, L)$, its updated model $M' = (S', R', L')$ is the result of M having only removed an existing state and its associated relation(s), iff
$S' = S - \{s_{rs}|s_{rs} \in S, s_{rs} \notin S'\}$;
$R' = R - \{(s_{rs-1}, s_{rs}), (s_{rs}, s_{rs+1})|s_{rs-1} \in S, s_{rs-1} \in S', s_{rs+1} \in S, s_{rs+1} \in S'\}$;
$L' : S' \to 2^{AP}$, since $S' \subseteq S$, $\forall s \in S'$, such that $L'(s) = L(s)$,

where the associated relations of s_{rs} are supposed to be its incoming and outgoing relations.

These primitive updates are atomic operations in CTL model update. The added or substituted states in PU3 and PU4 should also be atomic and minimal. The atomic features of the update are the foundation of minimal change rules described in later sections.

3.2 Examples for Combinations of Primitive Updates

One kind of combination is that each primitive update is repeated a few times within an updated model. Besides this, which is relatively simple, the combinations of different primitive updates could result in $C_2^5 + C_3^5 + C_4^5 + C_5^5 = 26$ possible cases. We give a couple of examples to illustrate combinations of primitive updates.

Case A: Combing PU1, PU2 and PU3
Given $M = (S, R, L)$, its updated model $M' = (S', R', L')$ is the result of M having added a new relation, removing an existing relation and substituting an existing state and its associated relations with a new state and its associated relations, iff

$S' = S \cup \{s_{ss}|s_{ss} \notin S, s_{ss} \in S'\} - \{s_i|s_i \in S, s_i \notin S'\}$;
$R' = R \cup \{(s_{ar}, s_{ar2})|(s_{ar}, s_{ar2}) \notin R, s_{ar} \in S, s_{ar} \in S', s_{ar2} \in S, s_{ar2} \in S'\}$
$\cup \{(s_{i-1}, s_{ss})(s_{ss}, s_{i+1})|s_{i-1} \in S, s_{i-1} \in S', s_{i+1} \in S, s_{i+1} \in S'\}$
$- \{(s_{rr}, s_{rr2})|(s_{rr}, s_{rr2}) \in R, s_{rr} \in S, s_{rr} \in S', s_{rr2} \in S, s_{rr2} \in S'\}$
$- \{(s_{i-1}, s_i), (s_i, s_{i+1})|s_{i-1} \in S, s_{i-1} \in S', s_{i+1} \in S, s_{i+1} \in S'\}$;
$L':\to 2^{AP}$, where $\forall s \in S'$, if $s \in S$, then $L'(s) = L(s)$, else
$L'(s_{ss}) = \tau(s_{ss})$, where τ is the truth assignment related to s_{ss}.

For the intermediate model $M'' = (S'', R'', L'')$ which is a result from M having substituted a state only (or "a result from M' having removed the new relation just added in PU1 and having added the existing relation just removed in PU2"), there is a bijective mapping m between S and S'', which makes

A. $\forall \pi = [s_0, s_1, \cdots, s_i, s_{i+1}, \cdots] \in M$, $\exists \pi'' = [s_0'', s_1'', \cdots, s_i'', s_{i+1}'', \cdots] \in M''$ such that $m(s_i) = s_{ss}$, where $i = 0, 1, \cdots, s_i \in \pi$ and $s_{ss} \in \pi''$;

B. $\forall \pi'' = [s_0'', s_1'', \cdots, s_i'', s_{i+1}'', \cdots] \in M''$, $\exists \pi = [s_0, s_1, \cdots, s_i, s_{i+1}, \cdots] \in M$ such that $s_i = m^{-1}(s_{ss})$, where $i = 0, 1, \cdots, s_{ss} \in \pi''$ and $s_i \in \pi$;

Example 1. In Fig. 1, M_1 is a resulting model by updating M with PU1, PU2 and PU3 in case A. During the update, a new relation (s_0, s_2) is added to M which belongs to PU1; an existing relation (s_1, s_2) is removed from M which belongs to PU2; an existing state s_3 is substituted with s_3' and its associated relations (s_2, s_3) and (s_3, s_0) are substituted with (s_2, s_3') and (s_3', s_0) respectively, which belongs to PU3.

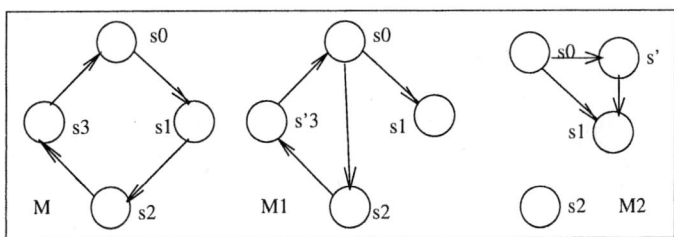

Fig. 1. The illustration of combinations of primitive updates

Case B: Combing PU2, PU4 and PU5

Given $M = (S, R, L)$, its updated model $M' = (S', R', L')$ is the result of M having added a new state, removing an existing relation and removing a state with its associated relations, iff

$S' = S \cup \{s_{as}|s_{as} \notin S, s_{as} \in S'\} - \{s_{rs}|s_{rs} \in S, s_{rs} \notin S'\}$;
$R' = R \cup \{(s_{as-1}, s_{as})(s_{as}, s_{as+1})|s_{as-1} \in S, s_{as-1} \in S', s_{as+1} \in S, s_{as+1} \in S'\}$
$-\{(s_{rs-1}, s_{rs})(s_{rs}, s_{rs+1})|s_{rs-1} \in S, s_{rs-1} \in S', s_{rs+1} \in S, s_{rs+1} \in S'\}$
$- \{(s_{rr}, s_{rr2})|(s_{rr}, s_{rr2}) \in R, s_{rr} \in S, s_{rr} \in S', s_{rr2} \in S, s_{rr2} \in S'\}$;
$L':\to 2^{AP}$, where $\forall s \in S'$, if $s \in S$, then $L'(s) = L(s)$, else
$L'(s_{as}) = \tau(s_{as})$, where τ is the truth assignment related to s_{as}.

Example 2. In Fig. 1, M_2 is a resulting model by updating M with PU2,PU4 and PU5 in case B. During the update, an existing relation (s_1, s_2) is removed from M which belongs to PU2; a new state s' and its associated relations (s_0, s') and (s', s_1) are added to M, which belongs to PU4; and an existing state s_3 and its associated relations (s_2, s_3) and (s_3, s_0) are removed, which belongs to PU3.

4 Minimal Change

The minimal change rules are based on the minimal difference of the same type of primitive updates. We do not compare minimal change with different primitive updates, because in that circumstance, primitive updates need to be quantified for comparison, which is left for future work. Thus, the minimal change in this paper is a partial order.

Given any two sets X and Y, the *symmetric difference* between X and Y is denoted as $Diff(X, Y) = (X - Y) \cup (Y - X)$.

For two updated models from the same original model with the same type of primitive updates, the change of an updated model is more than the change of another, if the first change contains the second change. To capture this principle, the notation $Diff_{PUi}(M, M')$ is used, where PUi could be any primitive update within PU1-PU5 in section 3.1. PU1 and PU2 are counted by changes in relations between M and M': $Diff_{PUi}(M, M') = (R - R') \cup (R' - R)$, where $i = 1, 2$; PU3, PU4 and PU5 are counted by changes in states between M and M': $Diff_{PUj}(M, M') = (S - S') \cup (S' - S)$, where $j = 3, 4, 5$. S, S', R and R' are defined in PU1-PU5 in section 3.1. The total difference between the original model M and the updated model M' is $Diff(M, M') = (Diff_{PU1}(M, M'), Diff_{PU2}(M, M'), \cdots, Diff_{PU5}(M, M'))$, which contains the difference of each of the five primitive updates. If the change of a primitive update $Diff_{PUi}(M, M')$ in $Diff(M, M')$ is empty, it means there is not this type of primitive update PUi during the update process.

Definition 5. *(Closeness Ordering) Given three CTL Kripke models $M = (S, R, L)$, $M_1 = (S_1, R_1, L_1)$ and $M_2 = (S_2, R_2, L_2)$,*

1. the difference between M and M_1 is as close to the difference of M and M_2, denoted as $Diff(M, M_1) \preceq Diff(M, M_2)$, iff
$\forall i (i = 1, \cdots, 5)$ $Diff_{PUi}(M, M_1) \subseteq Diff_{PUi}(M, M_2)$, such that

2. M_1 is as close to M as M_2, denoted as $M_1 \leq_M M_2$, iff
$Diff(M, M_1) \preceq Diff(M, M_2)$.

$M_1 <_M M_2$, if $M_1 \leq_M M_2$, but $M_2 \not\leq_M M_1$.

Definition 6. *(Admissible Update) Given a CTL Kripke model M and a CTL formula ϕ, an update of M with ϕ, denoted as $Update(M, \phi)$, is called admissible, if any resulting model M_1, obtained from $Update(M, \phi)$, has the following properties:*

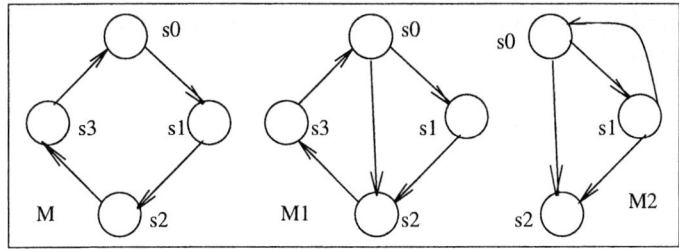

Fig. 2. The illustration of minimal change rules

1. $M_1 \models \phi$;
2. There does not exist a resulting model M_2 from other update of M with ϕ, such that $M_2 \models \phi$ and $M_2 <_M M_1$.

Example 3. In Fig. 2, model M is updated in two different ways. M_1 is a resulting model after M is updated by applying PU1. M_2 is another resulting model after M is updated by applying PU1 and PU5. We have
$Diff_{PU1}(M, M_1) = \{(s_0, s_2)\}$, $Diff_{PU1}(M, M_2) = \{(s_1, s_0), (s_0, s_2)\}$, such that $Diff_{PU1}(M, M_1) \subset Diff_{PU1}(M, M_2)$;
$Diff_{PU5}(M, M_1) = \emptyset$, $Diff_{PU5}(M, M_2) = \{s_3\}$, such that $Diff_{PU5}(M, M_1) \subset Diff_{PU5}(M, M_2)$; we have
$Diff(M, M_1) \prec Diff(M, M_2)$, such that $M_1 \leq_M M_2$ and M_1 is the resulting model of admissible update.

5 Algorithms for CTL Model Update

The purpose of CTL model update and its minimal change is to design algorithms which can be used in practice for the CTL model updater. The major tasks for the CTL update algorithms are to code the principles of characterizations based on our minimal change rules in section 4 for semantic features of the CTL Kripke model in Definition 3. For example, the characterization for EF to achieve minimal change is to perform either PU3 or PU4 once on any path of a model as described in the function UPDATE$_{EF}$, which calls the main function CTL*UPDATE to reach function UPDATE$_p$. PU3 is performed in the function UPDATE$_p$. To achieve minimal change update in the characterization for AG in the function UPDATE$_{AG}$, either PU2 and PU5 or PU3 are applied for different circumstances. In this function, PU2 and PU5 are for deleting the relation or state after the initial state respectively; PU3 is for substituting all states in a model which do not satisfy required properties.

We design the algorithms in the form of pseudo-code and the manner of recursive calls. We only list the main function CTL*UPDATE and its five subfunctions, which are needed by the microwave oven example in section 6, and omit other functions due to space limitation. The new pseudo-code for CTL model update is designed to be compatible with the SAT algorithms for CTL model checking as presented in [9,3]. This compatibility makes our algorithms more standard and portable for later integration of the CTL model updater into the CTL model checker.

> function CTL*UPDATE($\mathcal{M},\phi$) /* $\mathcal{M} \not\models \phi$. Update $\mathcal{M}$ to satisfy ϕ. */
> INPUT $M = (S, R, L)$, $\mathcal{M} = (M, s_0)$, where $s_0 \in S$ and $\mathcal{M} \not\models \phi$;
> OUTPUT $M' = (S', R', L')$, $\mathcal{M}' = (M', s'_0)$, where $s'_0 \in S'$ and $\mathcal{M}' \models \phi'$;
> { case
> ϕ is $\bot$: return $\{M\}$;
> ϕ is atomic p : return $\{\text{UPDATE}_p(\mathcal{M},p)\}$;
> ϕ is $\neg\phi_1$: return $\{\text{UPDATE}_\neg(\mathcal{M},\phi_1)\}$;
> ϕ is $\phi_1 \vee \phi_2$: return $\{\text{CTL*UPDATE}(\mathcal{M},\phi_1) \text{ or } \text{CTL*UPDATE}(\mathcal{M},\phi_2)\}$;
> ϕ is $\phi_1 \wedge \phi_2$: return $\{\text{UPDATE}_\wedge(\mathcal{M},\phi_1,\phi_2)\}$;
> ϕ is $EX\phi_1$: return $\{\text{UPDATE}_{EX}(\mathcal{M},\phi_1)\}$;
> ϕ is $AX\phi_1$: return $\{\text{UPDATE}_{AX}(\mathcal{M},\phi_1)\}$;
> ϕ is $EF\phi_1$: return $\{\text{UPDATE}_{EF}(\mathcal{M},\phi_1)\}$;
> ϕ is $AF\phi_1$: return $\{\text{UPDATE}_{AF}(\mathcal{M},\phi_1)\}$;
> ϕ is $EG\phi_1$: return $\{\text{UPDATE}_{EG}(\mathcal{M},\phi_1)\}$;
> ϕ is $AG\phi_1$: return $\{\text{UPDATE}_{AG}(\mathcal{M},\phi_1)\}$;
> ϕ is $E(\phi_1 \cup \phi_2)$: return $\{\text{UPDATE}_{EU}(\mathcal{M},\phi_1,\phi_2)\}$;
> ϕ is $A(\phi_1 \cup \phi_2)$: return $\{\text{UPDATE}_{AU}(\mathcal{M},\phi_1,\phi_2)\}$;
> }
>
> function UPDATE$_p(\mathcal{M},p)$ /* $\mathcal{M} \not\models p$. Update s_0 to satisfy p. */
> {
>   PU3 is applied:
>   1. $s'_0 := s_0 \cup \{p\}$;
>   2. $S' := S - \{s_0\} \cup \{s'_0\}$;
>   3. $R' := R - \{(s_0, s_i) \mid \forall s_i = succ(s_0)\} \cup \{(s'_0, s_i) \mid \forall s_i = succ(s_0)\} -$
> $\{(s_j, s_0) \mid \forall s_j = pre(s_0)\} \cup \{(s_j, s'_0) \mid \forall s_j = pre(s_0)\}$;
>   4. $L': S' \to 2^{AP}$, where $\forall s \in S'$, if $s \in S$, then $L'(s) = L(s)$;
>   else $s = s'_0$, and
> $L'(s'_0) := \tau(s'_0)$, where τ is the truth assignment related to s'_0;
>   5. $\mathcal{M}' := (M', s'_0)$, where $M' = (S', R', L')$ and $s'_0 \in S'$;
>   6. return $\{\mathcal{M}'\}$;
> }
>
> function UPDATE$_\neg(\mathcal{M},\phi)$ /* $\mathcal{M} \not\models \phi$. Update $\mathcal{M}$ to satisfy ϕ. */
> { case
> ϕ is $\neg p$:   1. $s'_0 := s_0 - \{p\}$;
>   2.— 6. are the same as those in the function UPDATE$_p(\mathcal{M},p)$;
> ϕ is $\neg(\phi_1 \vee \phi_2) = \neg\phi_1 \wedge \neg\phi_2$: return$\{\text{UPDATE}_\wedge(\mathcal{M},\neg\phi_1,\neg\phi_2)\}$;
> ϕ is $\neg(\phi_1 \wedge \phi_2) = \neg\phi_1 \vee \neg\phi_2$: return $\{\text{UPDATE}_\neg(\mathcal{M},\phi_1) \text{ or } \text{UPDATE}_\neg(\mathcal{M},\phi_2)\}$;
> ϕ is $\neg EX(\phi_1) = AX(\neg\phi_1)$: return$\{\text{UPDATE}_{AX}(\mathcal{M},\neg\phi_1)\}$;
> ϕ is $\neg AX(\phi_1) = EX(\neg\phi_1)$: return$\{\text{UPDATE}_{EX}(\mathcal{M},\neg\phi_1)\}$;
> ϕ is $\neg EF(\phi_1) = AG(\neg\phi_1)$: return$\{\text{UPDATE}_{AG}(\mathcal{M},\neg\phi_1)\}$;
> ϕ is $\neg AF(\phi_1) = EG(\neg\phi_1)$: return$\{\text{UPDATE}_{EG}(\mathcal{M},\neg\phi_1)\}$;
> ϕ is $\neg EG(\phi_1) = AF(\neg\phi_1)$: return$\{\text{UPDATE}_{AF}(\mathcal{M},\neg\phi_1)\}$;

ϕ is $\neg AG(\phi_1) = EF(\neg\phi_1)$: return$\{$UPDATE$_{EF}(\mathcal{M},\neg\phi_1)\}$;
ϕ is $\neg E(\phi_1 \cup \phi_2)$: return$\{$UPDATE$_{\neg EU}(\mathcal{M},\phi_1,\phi_2)\}$;
ϕ is $\neg A(\phi_1 \cup \phi_2) = E[\neg\phi_2 \cup (\neg\phi_1 \wedge \neg\phi_2)] \vee EG\neg\phi_2$:
 return$\{$UPDATE$_{EU}(\mathcal{M},\neg\phi_2,\neg\phi_1 \wedge \neg\phi_2)$ or UPDATE$_{EG}(\mathcal{M},\neg\phi_2)\}$;
}

function UPDATE$_\wedge(\mathcal{M},\phi_1,\phi_2)$/*$\mathcal{M}\not\models \phi_2 \wedge \phi_2$. Update $\mathcal{M}$ to satisfy $\phi_1 \wedge \phi_2$.*/
{ 1. $\mathcal{M}'$ =CTL*UPDATE(CTL*UPDATE($\mathcal{M},\phi_1),\phi_2$);
2. if $\mathcal{M}' \models \phi_1 \wedge \phi_2$, then return $\{\mathcal{M}'\}$; else $\mathcal{M}'$ =UPDATE$_\wedge(\mathcal{M}',\phi_1,\phi_2)$;
}

function UPDATE$_{EF}(\mathcal{M},\phi)$ /*$\mathcal{M}\not\models EF\phi$. Update $\mathcal{M}$ to satisfy $EF\phi$. */
{ 1. Select a state s_i on a path $\pi = [s_0, s_1, \cdots]$, such that $(M, s_i) \not\models \phi$;
2. Update the state s_i with minimal change rules:
 2.1. PU3 is applied:
  return $\{$CTL*UPDATE$(\mathcal{M}_i,\phi)\}$;/* where $\mathcal{M}_i= (M, s_i)$ */
 2.2. PU4 is applied:
  $S' := S \cup s_{as}$, where $s_{as} \notin S, \in S'$;
  $R' := R \cup \{(s_{as-1}, s_{as}), (s_{as}, s_{as+1})\}$,
   where $s_{as-1} \in S, s_{as-1} \in S', s_{as+1} \in S, s_{as+1} \in S'$;
  $L' :\to 2^{AP}$, where $\forall s \in S'$, if $s \in S$, then $L'(s) = L(s)$, else
  $L'(s_{as}) :=\tau(s_{as})$, where τ is the truth assignment related to s_{as};
  return$\{\mathcal{M}'\}$;
}

function UPDATE$_{AG}(\mathcal{M},\phi)$ /* $\mathcal{M}\not\models AG\phi$. Update $\mathcal{M}$ to satisfy $AG\phi$. */
{ 1. If $\mathcal{M}_0= (M, s_0) \not\models \phi$, then PU3 is applied to s_0, such that
 $\mathcal{M}':=$CTL*UPDATE$(\mathcal{M}_0,\phi)$;
2. else {
2.1. Select a path $\pi = [s_0, s_1, \cdots]$, where $\exists s_i \in \pi$ such that
 $\mathcal{M}_i= (M, s_i) \not\models \phi$;
2.2. select a s_i, such that $\nexists s_j < s_i$ with $(M, s_j) \not\models \phi$, then
 2.2.1. PU2 is applied to delete relation $(pre(s_i), s_i)$, then
 $S' := S$;
 $R' := R - \{(pre(s_i), s_i)\}$;
 $L' := L$, since only a relation is removed;
 or
 2.2.2. PU5 is applied to delete s_i and its associated relations, then
 $S' := S - \{s_i\}$;
 $R' := R - \{(pre(s_i), s_i), (s_i, succ(s_i))\}$,
  where if associated relations of s_i are 2;
 $L': S' \to 2^{AP}$, since $S' \subseteq S$, $\forall s \in S'$, such that $L'(s) := L(s)$;
 or
 2.3. PU3 is applied: $\mathcal{M}':=$CTL*UPDATE$(\mathcal{M}_i,\phi)$;
  }
3. if $\mathcal{M}'\models AG\phi$, then return $\{\mathcal{M}'\}$; else $\mathcal{M}'$=UPDATE$_{AG}(\mathcal{M}',\phi)$;
}

6 A Case Study – The Microwave Oven Example

We present a case study to illustrate features of our CTL model update approach. For a microwave oven scenario [3], we assume that the processes of a microwave oven include both a normal heat process and a faulty process. For the normal process, no error occurs. The oven is closed to heat food. For the faulty process, the oven will not heat food after it is started. The purpose of model checking is to identify that a faulty process exists. The purpose of model updating, on the other hand, is to correct the original model which contains the faulty process. Fig. 3 gives the Kripke structure for this Microwave oven. $s_1, s_2, \cdots, s_7$ are states of this system. The path $s_1 \rightarrow s_2 \rightarrow s_5 \rightarrow s_3$ is the faulty process. The path $s_1 \rightarrow s_3 \rightarrow s_6 \rightarrow s_7 \rightarrow s_4$ is a normal heat process.

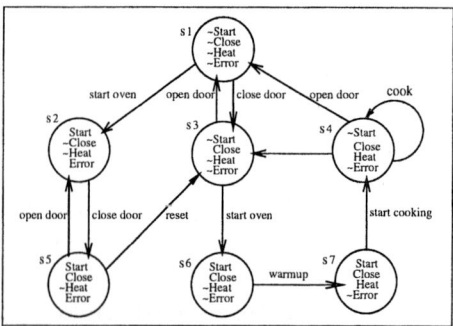

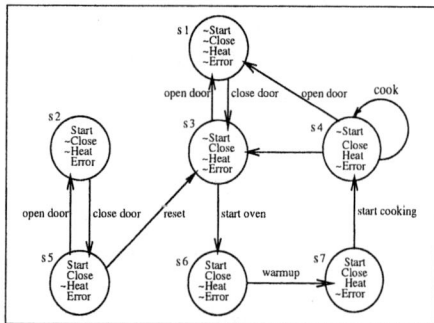

Fig. 3. The Original CTL Kripke Structure of a Microwave Oven

Fig. 4. The Updated Microwave Oven Model with Primitive Update PU2

The formal definition of the Kripke structure of the microwave oven is given:
$M = (S, R, L)$, where $S = \{s_1, s_2, s_3, s_4, s_5, s_6, s_7\}$, $R = \{(s_1, s_2), (s_2, s_5), (s_5, s_2), (s_5, s_3), (s_3, s_1), (s_1, s_3), (s_3, s_6), (s_6, s_7), (s_7, s_4), (s_4, s_4), (s_4, s_3)(s_4, s_1)\}$,
$AP = \{Start, Close, Heat, Error\}$,
L assigns states $s_1, s_2, s_3, s_4, s_5, s_6$ and s_7 in M with $\{\neg Start, \neg Close, \neg Heat, \neg Error\}$,
$\{Start, \neg Close, \neg Heat, Error\}, \{\neg Start, Close, \neg Heat, \neg Error\}$,
$\{\neg Start, Close, Heat, \neg Error\}, \{Start, Close, \neg Heat, Error\}$,
$\{Start, Close, \neg Heat, \neg Error\}, \{Start, Close, Heat, \neg Error\}$ respectively.

The CTL formula $\neg EF(Start \land EG \neg Heat)$ is checked. From the model checking, The loop path π containing states $\{s_1, s_2, s_5, s_3\}$ satisfies $EG \neg Heat$ with starting state s_1. The states on this loop which satisfy $Start$ are states s_2 and s_5. Thus, states satisfying $EF(Start \land EG \neg Heat)$ are s_2 and s_5. We need the Kripke structure not to have any state which satisfies $EF(Start \land EG \neg Heat)$. The result of the model checking is that the microwave oven system described by the Kripke structure does not satisfy the given specification. Thus, we need to update the system to satisfy the specification. We use our algorithms in the previous section to update this Kripke structure. This also serves to check the correctness of our algorithms.

Step 1: in the function CTL*UPDATE($\mathcal{M},\phi$), the function UPDATE$_\neg$($\mathcal{M},\phi$) is called. In our case, ϕ is $\neg EF(Start \wedge EG\neg Heat)$.

Step 2: in the function UPDATE$_\neg$($\mathcal{M},\phi$), our case is "ϕ is $\neg EF(\phi_1) = AG(\neg\phi_1)$", where ϕ_1 is $(Start \wedge EG\neg Heat)$, it returns UPDATE$_{AG}$($\mathcal{M},\neg(Start \wedge EG\neg Heat)$).

Step 3: in the function UPDATE$_{AG}$($\mathcal{M},\neg(Start \wedge EG\neg Heat)$), update for AG has three equal minimal changes:

a. PU2 is one option of different minimal changes to update the microwave model. In this case, relation (s_1,s_2) is deleted, such that $\mathcal{M}'= (M',s_1) \models \neg EF(Start \wedge EG\neg Heat))$. The resulting model is shown as Fig. 4.

b. PU5 is another option. In this case, state s_2 and relations (s_1,s_2), (s_2,s_5) and (s_5,s_2) are deleted, such that $\mathcal{M}'= (M',s_1) \models \neg EF(Start \wedge EG\neg Heat))$. The resulting model is shown as Fig. 5.

c. PU3 is the third option to substitute s_2 and s_5 with new states s'_2 and s'_5 respectively. The function UPDATE$_{AG}$($\mathcal{M},\neg(Start \wedge EG\neg Heat)$) calls the main function CTL*UPDATE($\mathcal{M},\neg Start \vee \neg EG\neg Heat$). This function will return CTL*UPDATE($\mathcal{M},\neg Start$) or CTL*UPDATE($\mathcal{M},\neg EG\neg Heat$) for the case $\phi_1 \vee \phi_2$. For simplicity, we choose the former one. In this case, we need to update the atomic proposition $Start$ in states s_2 and s_5 of path π with $\neg Start$ instead, then no states on path π have the specification $EF(Start \wedge EG\neg Heat))$. That is $\mathcal{M}'= (M',s_1) \models \neg EF(Start \wedge EG\neg Heat))$. The resulting model is shown as Fig. 6.

The above three resulting models are all minimally changed from the original model and are admissible. They are not interchangeable with each other due to our minimal change rules in this paper.

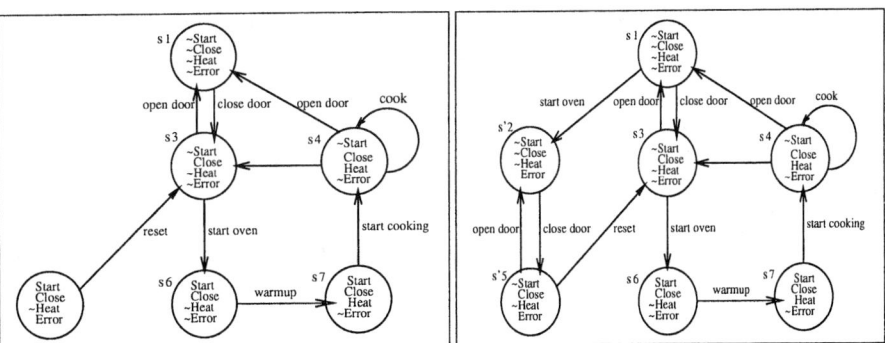

Fig. 5. The Updated Microwave Oven Model with Primitive Update PU5

Fig. 6. The Updated Microwave Oven Model with Primitive Update PU3

7 Conclusions and Future Work

This paper has analyzed the CTL model and then introduced minimal change rules for CTL model update. The CTL model update is decomposed into five primitive updates PU1-PU5, which can capture the simplest and atomic update features. The primitive updates form the foundation of minimal change rules. The minimal change rules are defined on the bases of minimal differences between the original model and its resulting model with the same type of primitive updates. We have developed algorithms for CTL model update which satisfy our minimal change rules. We have also demonstrated the microwave oven example to show the practical usage of our algorithms for CTL model update.

Our work presented in this paper is a further development of work in Ding and Zhang in [5], which dealt with LTL model update and did not propose formal algorithms. Above all, our work in this paper is a foundation for our next stage of research: implementing a CTL model update compiler, which is called the CTL model updater. This updater will perform the automatic model update function. The original model before this updater is supposed to be checked by a model checker such as SMV. Our model updater will automatically correct errors identified by a model checker. The updated model should satisfy the required features such as EF and AG in Definition 3. Our goal is to develop a general approach that integrates both model checking and model updating for automatic system modification.

References

1. Baral, C. and Zhang, Y. (2005). Knowledge updates: semantics and complexity issues. *Artificial Intelligence* 164 (2005) 209-243.
2. Buccafurri, F., Eiter, T., Gottlob, G. and Leone, N. (1999). Enhancing model checking in verification by AI techniques. *Artificial Intelligence* 112(1999) 57-104.
3. Clarke, E. Jr. et al. (1999). *Model Checking*, The MIT press, Cambridge, Massachusetts, London, England.
4. Cimatti, A. et al. (1999). NUSMV: a new symbolic model verifier. In *Proceedings of the 11th International Conference on Computer Aided Verification*. Vol. 1633 in LNCS. Pp.495-499.
5. Ding, Y. and Zhang, Y. (2005). A logic approach for LTL system modification. In *Proceedings of the 15th International Symposium on Methodologies for Intelligent Systems* (ISMIS 2005). LNAI3488. Pp. 436-444.
6. Gammie, P. and van der Meyden, R.(2004). MCK-Model checking the logic of knowledge. In *the Proceeding of the 16th International Conference on Computer Aided Verification.* Pp. 479 - 483.
7. Harris,H. and Ryan,M. (2003). Theoretical foundations of updating systems. In *the Prodeeding of the 18th IEEE International Conference on Automated Software Engineering.* Pp.291-298.
8. Holzmann, G. (2003). *The SPIN Model Checker: Primer and Reference Manual.* Addison-Wesley Professional.
9. Huth, M. and Ryan, M. (2000). *Logic in Computer Science: Modelling and Reasoning about Systems.* University Press, Canbridge.
10. McMillan,K. and Amla,N. (2002). Automatic abstraction without counterexamples. Cadence Berkeley Labs, Cadence Design Systems.
11. Winslett, M. (1990). *Updating Logical Databases.* Cambridge University Press.

Model Checking for PRS-Like Agents

Wayne Wobcke[1], Marc Chee[1], and Krystian Ji[1,2]

[1] School of Computer Science and Engineering,
University of New South Wales, Sydney NSW 2052, Australia
{wobcke, marcchee, krystianj}@cse.unsw.edu.au
[2] National ICT Australia, University of New South Wales,
Sydney NSW 2052, Australia
krystian.ji@nicta.com.au

Abstract. The key problem in applying verification techniques such as model checking to agent architectures is to show how to map systematically from an agent program to a model structure that not only includes the possible behaviours of the agent in its environment, but which also captures appropriate mental notions, such as belief, desire and intention, that may be used by the designer to reason about the agent. In this paper, we present an algorithm providing a mapping from agent programs under a simplified PRS-type agent architecture to a reachability graph structure extended to include representations of beliefs, goals and intentions, and illustrate the translation with a simple "waypoint following" agent. We conclude with a brief discussion of the differences between the internal (operational) notion of intention used in the architecture and the formal (external) notion of intention used in the modelling.

1 Introduction

The issues of specification and verification of agent programs are of critical importance in developing reliable software agents. This paper is concerned with applying model checking techniques to agents built using PRS-type agent architectures. The PRS-style architecture is useful for a class of applications requiring the agent to achieve a balance between reactivity to changes in the environment, and deliberation to exhibit goal-directed behaviour. This balance, which is partly under the programmer's control and partly pre-defined by the architecture, accounts for much of the complexity of designing and reasoning about agent programs for this architecture. Because of the inherent intricacy of this computational model, methodologies and tools for building agents of this type are an important step towards making this paradigm more widely adopted.

The PRS-style architecture operates with notions of belief, desire and intention, and is accordingly described as a "BDI architecture". However, using logical versions of idealized concepts of belief, desire and intention to model this architecture is inadequate for validating agent programs, because these idealized concepts do not match their specific meanings as used in the architecture. Rather, the "PRS-like" agent uses a plan library to store pre-defined plans for achieving goals, explicit beliefs to represent information about the environment that guides the selection of actions both in response to events and to refine plans, and various strategies for action execution to realize commitments to the chosen plans. Specification and verification of PRS-type agent programs requires a formal model of *these* mental notions, and then for these attitudes to be derived, in specific cases, in a principled way, from the execution models of agent programs implemented within the architecture. So, while Rao and Georgeff [13] presented a model checking algorithm for their BDI logic, they did not address the central question of generating these models from agent programs in the first place.

Recently, there have been some efforts to apply model checking to classes of systems that include some characteristics of agency. In the work of Bordini *et al.* [1], AgentSpeak(L) agent programs, Rao [10], are coded in PROMELA for verification using the SPIN model checker; however, the meaning of the belief, goal and intention modalities is not captured semantically, but instead specific beliefs, goals and intentions of the agent are encoded as extra state information in SPIN models. Under this approach, there is thus no way to answer the question of whether these mental notions are modelled correctly in the semantics, nor even to determine all but the simplest logical properties of these notions so as to check whether they satisfy intuitively correct properties. On the other hand, in the work of van der Meyden and Shilov [15], Penczek and Lomuscio [8] and Raimondi and Lomuscio [9], model checking techniques are applied to a class of distributed programs in a principled way, but these models involve only the knowledge modality (and this understood in the way specific to Fagin *et al.* [4]), so the agents do not have the complexity of PRS-type agents (do not have beliefs, desires and intentions).

Our aim in this paper is to develop a technique for applying model checking for PRS-type agents. The key problem is to show how any agent program executing within the architecture can be mapped onto a semantic structure that can be generated computationally and that includes not only the possible behaviours of the agent in a potentially highly nondeterministic environment, but faithfully captures the mental states (beliefs, desires and intentions) of the agent at any time in its execution. Inevitably, in contrast to the logical formalisms developed in previous work, e.g. Cohen and Levesque [3], Rao and Georgeff [11, 14], Wooldridge [19], these mappings must incorporate architecture-specific aspects both in the definition of the possible execution paths of an agent program and in how mental notions are realized in agents implemented in the architecture.

This paper is organized as follows. We first briefly summarize the PRS-like agent architecture. Then the main part of the paper consists of a description of how the execution structures of an agent program can be represented in a reachability graph. We give an algorithm for computing a reachability graph for any PRS-like agent program from a given initial configuration, then an example of this construction for a simple "waypoint following" agent. The example shows how the behaviour of the agent in changing its intentions in response to events in the environment is modelled.

This work is part of a larger project aimed towards developing sound logical foundations and computational tools for understanding and reasoning about the family of PRS-like agent architectures. This project includes development of a precise operational semantics that synthesizes a number of properties common to various PRS-like architectures, Wobcke [16], and the development of formal approaches to the semantics of the mental notions employed in this type of architecture, Wobcke [17], extended to belief update and the modelling of success and failure through action attempts, Wobcke [18]. To make this paper self-contained, many of the formal details must be omitted: the reader is referred to this earlier work for such details.

2 PRS-Like Agent Architectures

The class of agent architectures studied in this paper are the *PRS-like* architectures as defined in Wobcke [16], which is supposed to cover PRS (Procedural Reasoning System), Georgeff and Lansky [5], and variants such as UM-PRS, C-PRS, AgentSpeak(L), dMARS, JAM and JACK Intelligent Agents™. The agent's computation cycle can be conveniently described with reference to the simplified interpreter shown in Figure 1, adapted from Rao and Georgeff [12]. In this abstract interpreter, the system state consists of sets of beliefs B and intentions I. Each element of I is a partially executed hierarchical plan. Each cycle of this simplified interpreter runs as follows. The process begins with the external event (if there is one) triggering instances of pre-existing plans from the plan library (the belief set is used to test the context conditions of these plans): one selected plan is then added to the intention structure. The plans in the set of intentions that are applicable in the current state (i.e. the precondition of the next action in the plan body is believed to hold) constitute the options available to the agent in that state. The agent selects one such plan for execution, involving, if the next action in this plan is of the form *achieve* γ, selecting an instance of a plan from the plan library whose postcondition logically implies γ and whose precondition and context are believed, and updating the set of intentions accordingly. The agent then attempts the next action in the chosen plan, updating the intention structure appropriately in the case of a test action. After making a new observation and revising beliefs, the set of current intentions is further updated, first by removing those plans that are believed to have successfully completed (whose postcondition is believed), then by dropping those believed to be im-

```
Abstract BDI Interpreter:
  initialize-state(B, I);
  do
     get-external-event(e);
     new-options := trigger-plans(e, B);
     selected-option := select-option(new-options);
     update-intentions(selected-option, I);
     selected-intention := select-intention(I);
     execute(selected-intention);
     update-intention(selected-intention, I);
     get-observation(o);
     update-beliefs(o, B);
     drop-successful-plans(B, I);
     drop-impossible-plans(B, I)
  until quit
```

Fig. 1. Abstract BDI Interpreter

possible to complete (whose termination condition is believed). For the very first cycle, we can assume the agent has no plans and some arbitrary set of beliefs.

The internal states of the agent are pairs $\langle B, I \rangle$ where B is the set of beliefs and I is the set of intentions (partially executed hierarchical plans). We assume a finite propositional language $\mathcal{L}$ for representing the beliefs of the agent, and the agent's belief set B at any time is assumed to be a consistent set of literals of $\mathcal{L}$. The conditions of each plan in the plan library are also formulae of $\mathcal{L}$, and the body of each plan is a program. The language of programs consists of a set of atomic programs, including special actions *achieve* γ (where γ is a formula of $\mathcal{L}$) and an "empty" program Λ, and conditional and iterative statements **if** α **then** π **else** ψ and **while** α **do** π (where α is a formula of $\mathcal{L}$ and π and ψ are programs). Note that the tests in these statements are tests on the agent's beliefs, not on the state of the environment.

The agent's selection mechanisms are constrained as follows:

- Given a set of options triggered by an event (whose precondition and context are believed), the function select-option returns a randomly selected element of maximal priority within that set;
- Given a set of intentions, the function select-intention returns a randomly selected element of maximal priority in the subset of this set of plans which are applicable (whose preconditions are believed) in the current state; moreover, if a plan is chosen to break a tie, as long as its execution is believed successful, it continues to be chosen on future cycles until it terminates.

The functions for belief and intention update are as follows. For simplicity, it is assumed that the observations on each cycle correspond to a consistent set of literals L. Then the belief revision function can be defined as the function that removes the complement $\bar{l}$ of each literal l in L from the belief set B (if it is contained in B) and then adds each (now consistent) literal l of L to B. The only subtlety with the intention update function is in defining which plans may be dropped as achieved or infeasible. We take it that on failure, only whole plans can be dropped, and on success, only whole plans or the initial actions of any plan can be dropped (if an action of the form *achieve* γ is dropped, the achieve action and all its subplans are removed from the intention structure). Dropping a subplan leaves the achieve subgoal that resulted in the plan's selection as the next step to be executed in that hierarchical plan.

3 Reachability Graphs for PRS-Like Agents

In this section, we show how the execution of a PRS-like agent is modelled using reachability graphs. A reachability graph is a structure representing a class of program executions that also has the flavour of a mathematical model, in that formulae (including modal and temporal formulae) can be evaluated at nodes in the graph. Reachability graphs are used as the representation underlying the SPIN model checker, Holzmann [7], and are particularly appropriate for PRS-like agents because computing the entire state space is impractical. A reachability graph essentially represents a simulation of multiple executions of a program, with nodes in the graph corresponding to execution states, and transitions in the graph corresponding to atomic action execution. These executions all start with a given initial configuration, so only a portion of the entire state space (those states "reachable" from the starting configuration) are explored. Once a reachability graph is constructed, evaluating the truth of formulae is relatively straightforward, e.g. SPIN includes an algorithm for evaluating Linear Temporal Logic formulae with respect to the execution paths of distributed reactive systems. However, applying the reachability graph method for PRS-like agents is more complicated, because not only do program executions need to be modelled, but the beliefs, goals and intentions of the agent need to be represented in the graph structure. Moreover, the execution of an agent program depends on the mental states of the agent: first, because the evaluation of tests in conditional and iterative statements depends on the agent's beliefs, and second because the intentions of the agent influence which actions the agent will eventually perform. Thus there is a close interaction between the agent's program execution and its mental states.

The nodes of the reachability graph, the *execution states*, must be related systematically to the internal (operational) states of the PRS-like interpreter, yet cannot be identical to those states (as in the work of Bordini *et al.* [1]) because this would leave the important intentional notions unformalized. On the other hand, execution states cannot be identical to environment states, because the reachability graph construction algorithm relies on termination through eventually revisiting execution states, so all the information relevant to the execution state must be used when identifying execution states. Our approach is to distinguish between the information explicitly associated with a node in the reachability graph and the information used for identifying execution states, which is also represented in the graph but not as information explicitly encoded in states. The explicit information in an execution state is just the state of the environment together with any event that occurs at that state.

A single reachability graph may contain multiple computation trees, corresponding to different starting states – these are "possible worlds" the agent could be inhabiting (*actual worlds*). A reachability graph may also contain "possible worlds" corresponding to the beliefs of the agent in states in actual worlds (*belief-alternative worlds*). As in the work of Raimondi and Lomuscio [9], the beliefs of the agent are represented using a serial, transitive, Euclidean accessibility relation b between execution states (this means that the agent's beliefs can be no more fine-grained than the model of the environment). Intentions are modelled in a more complex manner, following our analysis of intention as actions the agent will eventually successfully perform in all actual worlds considered possible by the agent. Some reduction of this nature is necessary if model checking techniques, which construct only execution paths, are to capture a notion of intention. Intentions in reachability graphs are represented using a reflexive, symmetric, transitive accessibility relation a and a boolean i: for any execution state, the a-related states (actual alternatives) are those corresponding to execution states indistinguishable by the agent given its current set of intentions (accordingly, those states in alternative actual worlds in which its intentions must be capable of being fulfilled), and i defines which execution states in a world result from successful action attempts. Execution states in reachability graphs are identified only if they have the same environment state and event, the same set of execution states related under b and a, and the same value of i. This embodies a Markov assumption in that the co-evolution of the agent/environment must be identical for execution states identified using this definition.

Our action semantics is inspired by the computation tree semantics for Propositional Dynamic Logic, Harel [6]. The basic idea is to define a relation $\mathcal{R}_\pi$ for each program π which enables the execution of each program to be modelled as the set of all its execution structures (actual worlds with associated belief-alternative worlds), the arcs in each tree corresponding to individual performances of atomic actions together with the effect of making an observation (it is further assumed that the agent's observations are all accurate and at least include whether the postcondition of the action holds). It is assumed that each atomic action π is defined as a binary relation R_π on states of the environment (with $R_\pi \subseteq R_{attempt\ \pi}$), and that the occurrence of events in states of the environment is independent of history and dependent only on the chosen action. To model belief revision, special actions *observe* α are used, where α is a conjunction of literals in the language of beliefs $\mathcal{L}$. The relation $R_{observe\ \alpha}$ is defined to respect the operational definition of belief revision (and so is deterministic). Transitions in belief-alternative worlds correspond only to the execution of actions of the form *observe* α.

Our logical language makes use of a formula $do(\pi)$ which is true at an execution state iff the program π is the action about to be executed by the agent at that state. A state in a reachability graph satisfies a formula $do(\pi)$ if the subgraph emanating from that state is isomorphic to an execution structure in $\mathcal{R}_\pi$ (i.e. are the ways of executing π in that state), taking into account the belief alternatives of the states. The semantics of action must distinguish between doing an action and attempting to do an action, as the PRS-like agent cannot guarantee success. For this, the language of programs includes special actions of the form *attempt* π; typically an execution state satisfies $do(attempt\ \pi)$ while what the agent intends is $do(\pi)$ (a successful attempt to do π).

In our work on the formal semantics of PRS-like agents, we developed a logical language of beliefs and intentions called **ADL** (Agent Dynamic Logic) for reasoning about BDI agents, based on both Rao and Georgeff's **BDI-CTL** [11], which extends **CTL** (Computation Tree Logic) with modal operators for modelling beliefs, desires (goals) and intentions, and **PDL** (Propositional Dynamic Logic), which includes modal operators corresponding to program terms. The following definition gives the satisfaction conditions of **ADL** formulae in reachability graphs. For any reachability graph G, let $\mathcal{I}(G)$ be the subgraph of G that contains only those transitions of G corresponding to successful action executions and their associated observe actions ($\forall$ quantifies over all paths emanating from a state, $\Diamond$ is "eventually" with respect to a given path).

Definition 1. *An execution state σ in a reachability graph satisfies a BDI formula as follows.*

$\sigma \models_G B\alpha$ *if $\sigma' \models_G \alpha$ whenever $b(\sigma, \sigma')$*
$\sigma \models_G I\pi$ *if $\sigma' \models_{\mathcal{I}(G)} \forall \Diamond do(\pi)$ whenever $a(\sigma, \sigma')$*
$\sigma \models_G G\gamma$ *if $\sigma \models_G I(achieve\ \gamma)$*

4 Reachability Graph Construction

In this section, we provide an algorithm for the generation of a reachability graph for an arbitrary PRS-like agent program. The algorithm effectively carries out a breadth-first search of the execution states, beginning with a given set of initial execution states (a-related alternatives), and their sets of epistemic alternatives (b-related alternatives). The basic idea of the algorithm is that, at each execution state in the graph, for each possible action the agent could attempt at that state and for each possible outcome of executing that attempt (including a possible new event), the search explores a new execution state and its belief-alternative states. The algorithm keeps track of execution states already visited, and terminates when no new execution states are discovered (which is not guaranteed in general, since there can be infinitely many steps in iterative programs and expansions of hierarchical plans).

A high-level description of the general reachability graph construction algorithm is shown in Figure 2. The a-related alternatives of a state are called "intention alternatives" in this description of the algorithm.

```
Reachability Graph Construction:
  create initial (intention alternative) states and their belief alternatives
  do
    for each new state in the graph
      for each action the agent can attempt in that state
        create a copy of the state and its belief alternatives to represent this choice
        for each possible outcome and observation for the action attempt
          create a new state and its belief alternatives for this outcome
          mark the new state a success state iff it satisfies the action's postcondition
          if an event can occur in this new state
            for each maximal priority applicable plan triggered by this event
              create a new state and its belief alternatives for this outcome
                with this event and the resulting new set of intentions
    set two states to be intention alternatives if they are both successors of intention alternatives
      and are both indexed by the same set of intentions
  until no new states are generated
```

Fig. 2. High-Level Reachability Graph Construction Algorithm

The detailed reachability graph construction algorithm is shown in the appendix. As in the high-level description, the algorithm simulates all possible execution paths of the BDI interpreter in a breadth-first search, keeping track of repeated execution states. The variables Σ_i in the algorithm are used to record the new execution states generated at each level of the search, and the algorithm terminates if there are no new states discovered. The algorithm takes two parameters: S, the set of possible initial environment states, which become the initial states in the alternative actual worlds of the agent, i.e. these states are initially all a-related alternatives of one another, and B, the initial set of beliefs of the agent, which generate a set of b-related alternative states for each initial environment state. The execution states in the algorithm are denoted $\sigma_{\{s,e,B,I\}}$ for those in actual worlds and $\sigma_{\{s,s',e,B,I\}}$ for those in belief alternatives, i.e. execution states are indexed by s (the state of the environment), s' (the possible state of the environment in a belief alternative of s), e (any event occuring at the state, ϵ if there is no event), B (the agent's set of beliefs) and I (the agent's set of intentions). Two execution states are identified only if all of these are the same.

As the reachability graph construction algorithm proceeds, a number of relations are computed that represent the structure of the graph. The relation R defines the transitions between execution states, while the accessibility relations b and a represent the belief alternatives and the actual (intention) alternatives. The b and a relations of the R-successors of an execution state σ are defined in terms of the successors of the states

b and a-related to σ. The boolean i is true iff an execution state is the result of a successful action attempt (which is determined by whether the state of the environment satisfies the action's postcondition).

The algorithm makes use of two selection functions from the PRS-like agent interpreter: options and intentions return the set of plans and the set of intentions that could be chosen by the interpreter's functions select-option (the maximal priority applicable plans triggered by an event) and select-intention (the maximal priority applicable plans possible to be executed). But whereas the agent will choose randomly one of the outputs of these functions in any particular execution, the reachability graph includes execution paths for all of them (intuitively, the agent program must work for all possible outputs of these functions). The algorithm also makes use of the functions update-intention, drop and revise. The function update-intention computes the continuations of the program (a test statement is replaced by one reflecting the outcome of the test, an action *achieve* γ is replaced by the continuation of one of its expansions). The functions drop and revise implement the agent's intention and belief revision functions: drop removes from the intentions any successfully completed action or subplan (one whose postcondition is believed) or any infeasible subplan (one whose termination condition is believed); revise implements the agent's belief revision function. Note that all these functions are independent of the particular agent program.

5 Example

In this section, we illustrate the reachability graph construction algorithm through an example "waypoint following" agent. The waypoint agent has a simple task: it must visit four waypoints, numbered 1–4, in order, whilst not running out of fuel. There is fuel at locations 1 and 3 though this knowledge is not explicit in the agent's beliefs. Rather, the agent is constructed to have refuelling plans, as shown in Figure 3 for the fuel at location 1 (the agent also has two plans similar to $Refuel_1$ and $Refuel_2$ for the fuel at location 3). The agent is capable of carrying out the actions $visit_i$ and $refuel$; the refueling plans are used in response to a $warn$ event in order to direct the agent to a fuel depot where a refuel action is attempted.

The agent always has knowledge of its position, represented as beliefs at_i and $\neg at_j$ ($j \neq i$), and each $visit_i$ action includes a correct observation of the agent's position. The agent initially has no belief about the fuel level, but after a $refuel$ action, correctly observes the state of the fuel tank, represented as a belief $full$ ($= \neg empty$) or $empty$.

An issue that must be addressed in applying model checking to any agent system is the specification of the action semantics, including the transition relations $\mathcal{R}_\pi$ for each atomic action and the specification of when events may occur in the environment. For now, we specify this informally for the waypoint agent. For simplicity, the $visit_i$ and $refuel$ actions always succeed, except that on occasion (here only at location 3) a $warn$ event occurs. A $warn$ event can therefore occur even after a refueling action (the $refuel$ action may not provide enough fuel to offset the warning).

The reachability graph construction algorithm must be supplied an initial configuration representing the agent's beliefs and the possible initial states of the environment: in this example, the agent starts at location 1 (and believes this) and has a full fuel tank

Main
priority: 0
pre: *true*
trigger: *start*
context: *true*
body: $visit_1; visit_2; visit_3; visit_4$
post: $v_1 \wedge v_2 \wedge v_3 \wedge v_4$

Refuel$_1$
priority: 1
pre: *true*
trigger: *warn*
context: at_1
body: *refuel*
post: *full*

Refuel$_2$
priority: 1
pre: *true*
trigger: *warn*
context: $\neg at_1$
body: $visit_1; refuel$
post: *full*

Fig. 3. Waypoint Agent Plans

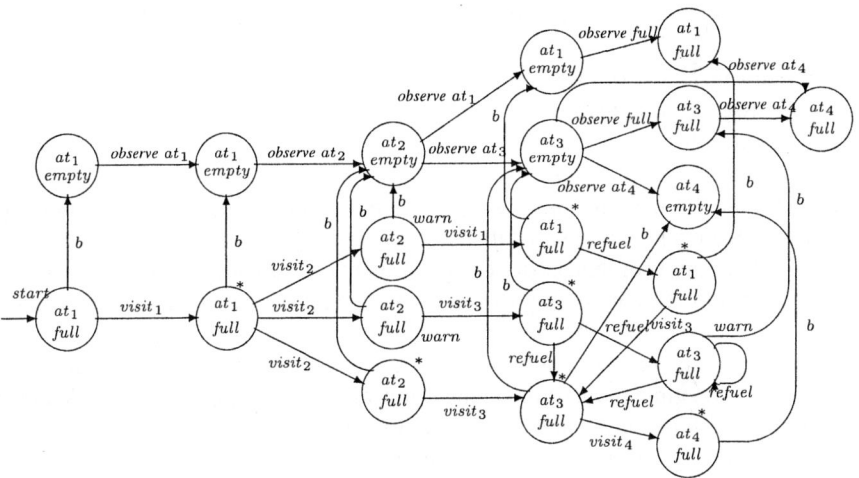

Fig. 4. Waypoint Agent Reachability Graph

(though does not believe this). Thus the initial execution state in the reachability graph has two b-related alternatives (one where the tank is *full* and one where it is *empty*), but just one a-related alternative (the agent would perform very poorly were it in a world where it had no fuel initially).

A portion of the reachability graph for the waypoint agent is shown in Figure 4 (in the diagram, a and b-related links between a state and itself are omitted, and states resulting from successful executions are marked with $*$). The actions labelling the transitions correspond to an atomic action formula π such that $do(\pi)$ is satisfied at the state.

The following lists some examples of the kind of properties of the agent that could be tested using such a graph:

$\forall \Box (full \Leftrightarrow \mathbf{B} full)$
$\forall \Diamond at_4$
$\forall (\mathsf{I} visit_i \, \mathcal{U} \, at_i)$
if $warn \in \sigma$ then $\sigma \models \forall (\mathsf{I} refuel \, \mathcal{U} \mathbf{B} full)$

The first two formulae are not satisfied at the initial state of the graph, the second since the agent may become stuck handling an infinite sequence of fuel warnings. This points to one complicated aspect of event handling in the PRS-like architecture. The third and fourth properties represent the persistence of intentions.

6 Conclusion

This paper has provided a formalization of the execution model of a family of BDI agents based on the PRS architecture, and shown how precise notions of belief and intention can be represented in reachability graphs, structures that are suitable for applying model checking algorithms to this class of agents. By clarifying the mental notions underlying this class of agents and by systematically relating these notions to the operational behaviour of the agent interpreter, a more robust methodology underpinning the verification of complex BDI agents is made possible. Moreover, the approach enables a precise semantic theory of PRS-like agents based on these notions to be defined, allowing agent program designers to reason logically about the mental states of the agents with confidence that this reasoning faithfully represents the behaviour of the agent.

However, the (external) notion of intention as encoded in reachability graphs and BDI models differs from the agent's (internal) notion in that there can be actions that occur in the agent's intention structures that are not *intentions* as defined in these models. A simple example of this occurs when the agent has adopted a number of plans that are not compatible (i.e. it is not possible to execute all the agent's plans to successful completion, even when no adverse events occur in the world). In such a case, the theory says that the agent does not really "intend" to execute those plans; it only intends to execute the compatible parts of the plans. Thus the notion of intention encoded in the reachability graph is more a notion of commitment (the agent intends those actions it is "committed" to performing), whereas the notion of intention used in the architecture is something weaker again (the agent is not even committed to carrying out its "intentions"). It remains to be seen whether this notion of intention, which is clearly much simplified from Bratman's original theory [2], is useful from the agent programmer's point of view. However, our work presents, for the first time, one way of precisely capturing this complex mental notion in semantic structures that are amenable to verification techniques.

Acknowledgements

This work is funded by an Australian Research Council Discovery Project Grant. Krystian Ji is supported by a UNSW International Postgraduate Research Scholarship and a scholarship from NICTA, National ICT Australia Ltd. National ICT Australia is funded through the Australian Government's *Backing Australia's Ability* initiative, in part through the Australian Research Council.

References

1. Bordini, R.H., Fisher, M., Pardavila, C. & Wooldridge, M. (2003) 'Model Checking AgentSpeak.' *Proceedings of the Second International Joint Conference on Autonomous Agents and Multiagent Systems*, 409–416.
2. Bratman, M.E. (1987) *Intention, Plans, and Practical Reason.* Harvard University Press, Cambridge, MA.
3. Cohen, P.R. & Levesque, H.J. (1990) 'Intention is Choice with Commitment.' *Artificial Intelligence*, **42**, 213–261.
4. Fagin, R., Halpern, J.Y., Moses, Y. & Vardi, M.Y. (1995) *Reasoning About Knowledge.* MIT Press, Cambridge, MA.
5. Georgeff, M.P. & Lansky, A.L. (1987) 'Reactive Reasoning and Planning.' *Proceedings of the Sixth National Conference on Artificial Intelligence (AAAI-87)*, 677–682.
6. Harel, D. (1979) *First-Order Dynamic Logic.* Springer-Verlag, Berlin.
7. Holzmann, G.J. (1997) 'The Model Checker SPIN.' *IEEE Transactions on Software Engineering*, **23**(5), 279–295.
8. Penczek, W. & Lomuscio, A. (2003) 'Verifying Epistemic Properties of Multi-agent Systems via Bounded Model Checking.' *Proceedings of the Second International Joint Conference on Autonomous Agents and Multiagent Systems*, 209–216.
9. Raimondi, F. & Lomuscio, A. (2004) 'Verification of Multiagent Systems via Ordered Binary Decision Diagrams: An Algorithm and Its Implementation.' *Proceedings of the Third International Joint Conference on Autonomous Agents and Multiagent Systems*, 630–637.
10. Rao, A.S. (1996) 'AgentSpeak(L): BDI Agents Speak Out in a Logical Computable Language.' in Van de Velde, W. & Perram, J.W. (Eds) *Agents Breaking Away.* Springer-Verlag, Berlin.
11. Rao, A.S. & Georgeff, M.P. (1991) 'Modeling Rational Agents within a BDI-Architecture.' *Proceedings of the Second International Conference on Principles of Knowledge Representation and Reasoning (KR'91)*, 473–484.
12. Rao, A.S. & Georgeff, M.P. (1992) 'An Abstract Architecture for Rational Agents.' *Proceedings of the Third International Conference on Principles of Knowledge Representation and Reasoning (KR'92)*, 439–449.
13. Rao, A.S. & Georgeff, M.P. (1993) 'A Model-Theoretic Approach to the Verification of Situated Reasoning Systems.' *Proceedings of the Thirteenth International Joint Conference on Artificial Intelligence*, 318–324.
14. Rao, A.S. & Georgeff, M.P. (1998) 'Decision Procedures for BDI Logics.' *Journal of Logic and Computation*, **8**, 293–343.
15. van der Meyden, R. & Shilov, N.V. (1999) 'Model Checking Knowledge and Time in Systems with Perfect Recall (Extended Abstract).' in Pandu Rangan, C., Raman, V. & Ramanujam, R. (Eds) *Foundations of Software Technology and Theoretical Computer Science: 19th Conference.* Springer-Verlag, Berlin.
16. Wobcke, W.R. (2001) 'An Operational Semantics for a PRS-like Agent Architecture.' in Stumptner, M., Corbett, D. & Brooks, M. (Eds) *AI 2001: Advances in Artificial Intelligence.* Springer-Verlag, Berlin.
17. Wobcke, W.R. (2002) 'Modelling PRS-like Agents' Mental States.' in Ishizuka, M. & Sattar, A. (Eds) *PRICAI 2002: Trends in Artificial Intelligence.* Springer-Verlag, Berlin.
18. Wobcke, W.R. (2004) 'Model Theory for PRS-Like Agents: Modelling Belief Update and Action Attempts.' in Zhang, C., Guesgen, H.W. & Yeap, W.K. (Eds) *PRICAI 2004: Trends in Artificial Intelligence.* Springer-Verlag, Berlin.
19. Wooldridge, M.J. (2000) *Reasoning About Rational Agents.* MIT Press, Cambridge, MA.

Appendix. Reachability Graph Construction Algorithm

Reachability Graph Construction:
$\Sigma_0 := \{\}$;
for each $s \in S$ **do**
  e := generate-event(s);   % ϵ if no event
  for each $\iota \in$ options(trigger-plans(e, B)) **do**
    $I := \{\iota\}$;
    create $\sigma_{\{s,e,B,I\}}$ and add to Σ_0;
    set $i(\sigma_{\{s,e,B,I\}}) = false$;
    set $b(\sigma_{\{s,e,B,I\}}, \sigma_{\{s,e,B,I\}})$ if $s \models B$;
    create $\sigma_{\{s,s',e,B,0\}}$ for each $s' \neq s$, $s' \models B$;
    set $i(\sigma_{\{s,s',e,B,0\}}) = false$;
    set $b(\sigma_{\{s,e,B,I\}}, \sigma_{\{s,s',e,B,0\}})$ for each $s' \models B$;
set $a(\sigma_{\{s,e,B,I\}}, \sigma_{\{s',e',B,I\}})$ for each $\sigma_{\{s,e,B,I\}}, \sigma_{\{s',e',B,I\}} \in \Sigma_0$;
$i := 0$;
do
  $\Sigma_{i+1} := \{\}$;
  for each new $\sigma_{\{s,e,B,I\}} \in \Sigma_i$ **do**
    Π := intentions(B, I);   % $\{env\}$ if no intention
    replace $\sigma_{\{s,e,B,I\}}$ by $|\Pi|$ copies $\sigma^{\pi}_{\{s,e,B,I\}}$ of itself;   % split state to represent choices
    set $i(\sigma^{\pi}_{\{s,e,B,I\}}) = i(\sigma_{\{s,e,B,I\}})$;
    for each $\sigma_{\{s,s',e,B,i\}}$ such that $b(\sigma_{\{s,e,B,I\}}, \sigma_{\{s,s',e,B,i\}})$ **do**
      set $b(\sigma^{\pi}_{\{s,e,B,I\}}, \sigma_{\{s,s',e,B,i\}})$;
    set $a(\sigma^{\pi}_{\{s,e,B,I\}}, \sigma^{\psi}_{\{s,e,B,I\}})$ for each such $\sigma^{\pi}_{\{s,e,B,I\}}, \sigma^{\psi}_{\{s,e,B,I\}}$;
    for each $\pi \in \Pi$ **do**
      for each initial primitive action a of π (or of an expansion of an initial action *achieve* γ) **do**
        for each $(s, s') \in \mathcal{R}_{attempt\ a}$ **do**
          o := observation(s', *attempt a*);   % observation associated with action
          B' := revise(B, o);
          I' := drop(B', update-intention(I));   % update due to test or *achieve* γ expansion
          create $\sigma_{\{s',\epsilon,B',I'\}}$ and add to Σ_{i+1};
          set $R(\sigma^{\pi}_{\{s,e,B,I\}}, \sigma_{\{s',\epsilon,B',I'\}})$;
          set $i(\sigma_{\{s',\epsilon,B',I'\}})$ according to whether $s' \models post(a)$;   % intend success
          set $b(\sigma_{\{s',\epsilon,B',I'\}}, \sigma_{\{s',\epsilon,B',I'\}})$ if $s' \models B'$;
          for each $\sigma_{\{s,s',e,B,i\}}$ such that $b(\sigma_{\{s,e,B,I\}}, \sigma_{\{s,s',e,B,i\}})$ **do**
            s'' := revise(s', o);
            create $\sigma_{\{s',s'',\epsilon,B',i+1\}}$ for each $s'' \models B'$;
            set $R(\sigma_{\{s,s',e,B,i\}}, \sigma_{\{s',s'',\epsilon,B',i+1\}})$;
            set $i(\sigma_{\{s',s'',\epsilon,B',i+1\}}) = false$;
            set $b(\sigma_{\{s',\epsilon,B',I'\}}, \sigma_{s',s'',\epsilon,B',i+1\}})$ for each $s'' \neq s'$, $s'' \models B'$;
          e' := generate-event(s', *attempt a*);   % ϵ if no event
          if $e' \neq \epsilon$
            for each $\iota \in$ options(trigger-plans(e', B')) **do**
              I' := drop(B', update-intention(I)) $\cup \{\iota\}$;
              create $\sigma_{\{s',e',B',I'\}}$ and add to Σ_{i+1};
              set $R(\sigma^{\pi}_{\{s,e,B,I\}}, \sigma_{\{s',e',B',I'\}})$;
              set $i(\sigma_{\{s',e',B',I'\}}) = false$;   % unexpected events are unintended
              set $b(\sigma_{\{s',e',B',I'\}}, \sigma_{s',e',B',I'\}})$ if $s' \models B'$;
              for each $\sigma_{\{s,s',e,B,i\}}$ such that $b(\sigma_{\{s,e,B,I\}}, \sigma_{\{s,s',e,B,i\}})$ **do**
                s'' := revise(s', o);
                create $\sigma_{\{s',s'',e',B',i+1\}}$ for each $s'' \models B'$;
                set $R(\sigma_{\{s,s',e,B,i\}}, \sigma_{\{s',s'',e',B',i+1\}})$;
                set $i(\sigma_{\{s',s'',e',B',i+1\}}) = false$;
                set $b(\sigma_{\{s',e,B',I'\}}, \sigma_{s',s'',e',B',i+1\}})$ for each $s'' \neq s'$, $s'' \models B'$;
set $a(\sigma_{\{s,e,B,I\}}, \sigma_{\{s',e',B',I'\}})$ if $I = I'$ for each $\sigma_{\{s,e,B,I\}}, \sigma_{\{s',e',B',I'\}} \in \Sigma_{i+1}$
    that are both R-successors of a-related states;
$i := i + 1$
until no new states are generated

A Fibred Belief Logic for Multi-agent Systems

Chuchang Liu[1], Maris A. Ozols[1], and Mehmet A. Orgun[2]

[1] Information Networks Division, Defence Science and Technology Organisation,
PO Box 1500, Edinburgh, SA 5111, Australia
[2] Department of Computing, Macquarie University, Sydney, NSW 2109, Australia

Abstract. To introduce a temporal dimension to a belief logic, we consider a powerful technique called fibring for combining belief logics and temporal logics. In a fibred belief logic, both temporal operators and belief operators are treated equally. This paper in particular discusses a combination of a belief logic called Typed-Modal Logic with a linear-time temporal logic. We show that, in the resulting logic, we can specify and reason about not only agent beliefs but also the timing properties of a system. With this logical system one is able to build theories of trust for the description of, and reasoning about, multi-agent systems.

1 Introduction

Multi-agent systems (MASs for short) consist of a collection of agents that interact with each other in dynamic and unpredictable environments. Agents communicate with one another by exchanging messages, and they have the ability to cooperate, coordinate and negotiate with each other to achieve their objectives. In order to develop theories to specify and reason about various aspects of multi-agent systems, many researchers have proposed the use of modal logics such as belief logics [2,4] and logics of knowledge [3,6]. Many of such formalisms have successfully been used for dealing with some particular aspect of agents that they address, but they generally ignore the other aspects. As multi-agent systems operate in dynamic environments, there is also a need to model the evolution of multi-agent systems through time.

In order to introduce a temporal dimension to a belief logic, Liu *et al.* [9] have proposed a temporalized logic called TML^+, which provides a logical framework for users to specify the dynamics of trust and model evolving theories of trust for multi-agent systems. However, in TML^+ there are certain restrictions on the use of temporal and belief operators because of the hierarchical combination of belief and temporal logics used. Temporal operators can never be within the scope of a belief operator, hence we cannot express a statement asserting that some agent believes an event to happen at some time, e.g., the logic does not have a formula such as $\mathbf{B}_{john}$ **first** $holds(bob, k)$, which could be used to express an assertion that *john* believes that at the initial time *bob* holds the key k. Such kind of assertions are often needed, for example, in analysing stream authentication protocols. We therefore consider a more powerful combination technique called fibring [5] that treats temporal operators and belief operators equally.

This paper in particular discusses a combination of a belief logic called Typed-Modal Logic with a linear-time temporal logic. We show that, in the resulting logic, we can specify and reason about not only agent beliefs but also the timing properties of a system. With this logical system one is able to build theories of trust for the description of, and reasoning about, multi-agent systems.

2 Two Logics: SLTL and TML

This section gives a brief introduction to the logics Simple Linear-time Temporal Logic (SLTL) and Typed Modal Logic (TML).

2.1 SLTL: Simple Linear-Time Temporal Logic

SLTL offers two operators, **first** and **next**, which refer to the initial moment and the next moment in time respectively. The collection of moments in time is the set of natural numbers with its usual ordering relation $<$. Let $\mathcal{P}$ be a set of countably many propositional symbols. We define $\mathcal{L}_{sltl}$ as the smallest set of temporal propositional formulae of SLTL such that:

- $\mathcal{P} \subset \mathcal{L}_{sltl}$;
- If A is in $\mathcal{L}_{sltl}$, then $\neg A$, **first** A and **next** A are in $\mathcal{L}_{sltl}$; and
- If A and B are in $\mathcal{L}_{sltl}$, so $A \wedge B$ is, too.

From here on, we assume that connectives $\vee, \rightarrow$ and $\leftrightarrow$ are derived from the primitive connectives in each logic as usual.

We define the global clock as the increasing sequence of natural numbers, i.e., $\langle 0, 1, 2, \ldots \rangle$, and a local clock is an infinite subsequence of the global clock.

Definition 1 (time models). *A time model for the logic SLTL has the form* $\mathbf{c} = \langle C, <, \nu \rangle$, *where* $C = (t_0, t_1, t_2, \ldots)$ *is a clock,* $<$ *is the usual ordering relation over* C *as mentioned above, and* ν *is an assignment function, that is, a binary function giving a value* $\nu(t, q) \in \{true, false\}$ *for any time point* t *in* C *and any atomic formula* q.

We write $\mathbf{c}, t \models A$ to stand for "A is true at time t in the model $\mathbf{c}$". Then the semantics definition for the temporal operators with the notion of satisfaction in SLTL is given as follows:

- $\mathbf{c}, t_i \models$ **first** A iff $\mathbf{c}, t_0 \models A$.
- $\mathbf{c}, t_i \models$ **next** A iff $\mathbf{c}, t_{i+1} \models A$.
- satisfaction in the model $\mathbf{c} = (C, <, \nu)$ is defined as satisfaction at some time point on C.

A minimal axiomatic system for the propositional temporal logic consists of the following axioms (axiom schemata):

A0. all classical tautologies.   A1. $\triangledown(\textbf{first } A) \leftrightarrow \textbf{first } A$.
A2. $\triangledown(\neg A) \leftrightarrow \neg(\triangledown A)$.   A3. $\triangledown(A \wedge B) \leftrightarrow (\triangledown A) \wedge (\triangledown B)$.

where $\triangledown$ stands for **first** or **next** in any axiom schema. Apart from the generic substitution rule, this axiomatic system has two rules of inference as follows:

MP. From $\vdash A$ and $\vdash A \to B$ infer $\vdash B$. (Modus Ponens)
TG. From $\vdash A$ infer $\vdash$ **first** A and $\vdash$ **next** A. (Temporal Generalisation)

The soundness and completeness of the axiomatisation system for SLTL with respect the class $\mathcal{C}$ consisting of all local clocks are straightforward [8].

2.2 TML: Typed Modal Logic

We assume that there are n agents $a_1, \ldots, a_n$ and, correspondingly, n modal operators $\mathbf{B}_1, \ldots, \mathbf{B}_n$ in the logic, where $\mathbf{B}_i$ ($1 \leq i \leq n$) stands for "agent a_i believes that". Let Φ_0 be a set of countably many atomic formulae of the first-order logic with typed variables. We define $\mathcal{L}_{tml}$ as the smallest set of well-formed formulae (wffs) of the logic TML such that:

- $\Phi_0 \subset \mathcal{L}_{tml}$;
- if φ is in $\mathcal{L}_{tml}$, so are $\neg \varphi$ and $\mathbf{B}_i \varphi$ for all i ($1 \leq i \leq n$);
- if φ and ψ are in $\mathcal{L}_{tml}$, then $\varphi \wedge \psi$ is in $\mathcal{L}_{tml}$; and
- if $\varphi(X)$ is in $\mathcal{L}_{tml}$ where X is a free variable, then $\forall X \varphi(X)$ is, too.

We assume that in TML all the wffs are correctly typed. We also assume the fixed-domain approach to quantification.

A *classical Kripke model* for the logic is defined as $\mathbf{m} = \langle S, R_1, \ldots, R_n, \pi \rangle$, where S is the set of states or possible worlds; and each R_i, $i = 1, \ldots, n$, is a relation over S, R_i, called the *possibility relation* according to agent a_i, is defined as follows: R_i is a non-empty set consisting of state pairs (s, t) such that $(s, t) \in R_i$ iff, at state s, agent a_i considers the state t possible; and π is the *assignment function*, which gives a value $\pi(s, q) \in \{true, false\}$ for any $s \in S$ and atomic formula q. We write $\mathbf{m}, s \models \varphi$ to stand for "φ is true at the state s in the model $\mathbf{m}$" or "φ holds at s in $\mathbf{m}$". The semantics definition for the belief operators with the notion of satisfaction in TML is given as follows:

- $\mathbf{m}, s \models \mathbf{B}_i \varphi$ iff, for all t such that $(s, t) \in R_i$, $\mathbf{m}, t \models \varphi$.
- A formula φ is satisfiable in a model $\mathbf{m}$ if there exists $s \in S$ such that $\mathbf{m}, s \models \varphi$.

In preparation for fibring the logic TML with the temporal logic SLTL, we now consider monadic models for TML defined as follows:

Definition 2 (monadic models). *A monadic model for TML has the form* $\mathbf{m} = \langle S, R_1, \ldots, R_n, \pi, u \rangle$, *where* $(S, R_1, \ldots, R_n, \pi)$ *is a classical model for TML and* $u \in S$ *is called the actual world.* φ *is satisfiable in the monadic model* $\mathbf{m}$ *if and only if* $\mathbf{m}, u \models \varphi$.

We define $\mathcal{K}_{tml}$ as a class of monadic models of the form $\langle S, R_1, \ldots, R_n, \pi, u \rangle$, for which the set of states is assumed to be

(1) $S = \{x \mid \exists R_{i_1} \ldots R_{i_k} \, uR_{i_1} \circ \ldots \circ R_{i_k} x, R_{i_1}, \ldots, R_{i_k} \in \{R_1, \ldots, R_n\}\}$,

where $R_i \circ R_j$ represents the relative product (or composition) of R_i and R_j, defined in the usual manner. Furthermore, using the notation **m** for a model in $\mathcal{K}_{tml}$, we write $\mathbf{m} = \langle S^{(\mathbf{m})}, R_1^{(\mathbf{m})}, \ldots, R_n^{(\mathbf{m})}, \pi^{(\mathbf{m})}, u^{(\mathbf{m})} \rangle$. Thus, we can make assumptions:

(2) if $\mathbf{m}_1 \neq \mathbf{m}_2$, then $S^{(\mathbf{m}_1)} \cap S^{(\mathbf{m}_2)} = \emptyset$.
(3) $\mathbf{m}_1 = \mathbf{m}_2$ iff $u^{(\mathbf{m}_1)} = u^{(\mathbf{m}_2)}$.

Assumption (2) indicates that all sets of possible worlds in $\mathcal{K}_{tml}$ are all pairwise disjoint, and that there are infinitely many isomorphic (but disjoint) copies of each model; assumption (3) means that a model in $\mathcal{K}_{tml}$ can in fact be identified by the actual world in it.

The axiom set of TML consists of the following axiom schemata:

B0. all axioms of the classical first-order logic[11].
B1. $\mathbf{B}_i(\varphi \to \psi) \land \mathbf{B}_i\varphi \to \mathbf{B}_i\psi$ for all i ($1 \leq i \leq n$).
B2. $\mathbf{B}_i(\neg\varphi) \to \neg(\mathbf{B}_i\varphi)$ for all i ($1 \leq i \leq n$).
B3. $\forall X \mathbf{B}_i\varphi(X) \to \mathbf{B}_i\forall X\varphi(X)$ for all i ($1 \leq i \leq n$).

The rules of inference in this logic are:

I1. From φ and $\varphi \to \psi$ infer ψ. (Modus Ponens)
I2. From $\forall X\varphi(X)$ infer $\varphi(Y)$. (Instantiation)
I3. From $\varphi(X)$ infer $\forall X\varphi(X)$. (Generalisation)
I4. From φ infer $\mathbf{B}_i\varphi$ for all i ($1 \leq i \leq n$). (Necessitation)

The soundness and completeness of the axiomatisation system for TML, consisting of axioms B0-B3 and rules I1-I4, can be proved in a standard pattern [7].

3 FL: Fibred Logic

The Fibred Logic (FL) is obtained through the use of fibring technique for combining the logic TML with the logic SLTL. Let $\mathcal{O} = \{\mathbf{B}_1, \ldots, \mathbf{B}_n, \mathbf{first}, \mathbf{next}\}$ be the set of modal connectives of FL, then we have

Definition 3 (syntax). *Let Φ_0 be a set of countably many atomic formulae of the (typed) first-order logic, then $\mathcal{L}_{fl}$ as the smallest set of well-formed formulae (wffs) of the logic FL is defined by the following formation rules:*

1. $\Phi_0 \subset \mathcal{L}_{fl}$;
2. *if φ is in $\mathcal{L}_{fl}$, so are $\neg\varphi$ and $\triangledown \varphi$ for all $\triangledown \in \mathcal{O}$;*
3. *if φ and ψ are in $\mathcal{L}_{fl}$, then $\varphi \land \psi$ is in $\mathcal{L}_{fl}$; and*
4. *if $\varphi(X)$ is in $\mathcal{L}_{fl}$ where X is a free variable, then $\forall X\varphi(X)$ is, too.*

We assume that in FL all the wffs are correctly typed.

This paper discusses the fibred semantics in the case of the Kripke monadic models for TML using a single, global time model for SLTL. Following Gabbay [5], we define the fibred semantics for TML as follows:

A Fibred Belief Logic for Multi-agent Systems   33

Definition 4 (sfm models). $\langle W, W_t, W_b, R_0, R_1, \ldots, R_n, \pi, \mathbf{F}, w_0 \rangle$ *is called a simplified fibred model or a smf model, where*

1. W *is a set of worlds,* $w_0 \in W_t \cup W_b$
2. $W_b \subseteq W$, *and* W_t *is a set of natural numbers, we also have* $W_t \subseteq W$.
3. *For* $s \in W_b$, *let* $S^{(s)} = \{x \mid sR_{i_1} \circ \ldots \circ R_{i_k} x,$ *for some* $R_{i_1}, \ldots, R_{i_k} \in \{R_1, \ldots, R_n\}\}$, *then (1) For all* $s \in W_b$, $S^{(s)} \cap W_t = \emptyset$; *(2) For all* $s, r \in W_b$, *if* $s \neq r$, *then* $S^{(s)} \cap S^{(r)} = \emptyset$; *and (3)* $W = (\bigcup_{s \in W_b} S^{(s)}) \cup W_t$.
4. $R_0 = \{(x,y) \mid x, y \in W_t \ \& \ x < y,$ *for all* $x, y \in W\}$.
5. *For all* $u \in W_t$, *the model* $\mathbf{c} = (C, R_0, \pi^{(\mathbf{c})})$ *satisfies the condition that* $u \in W_t$ *iff* u *is a time point in the clock* C, *and is in the semantics of SLTL*.
6. *For each* $u \in W_b$, *the model* $\mathbf{m}^{(u)} = (S^{(u)}, R_1 \lfloor S^{(u)} \times S^{(u)}, \ldots, R_n \lfloor S^{(u)} \times S^{(u)}, u, h \lfloor S^{(u)})$ *is in the semantics of* $\mathcal{K}_{tml}$ *of the logic TML*.
7. $\mathbf{F}$ *is the fibred function consisting of two folds,* $\mathbf{F}_b$ *and* $\mathbf{F}_t$. *It satisfies the following conditions: (1) For all connectives* $\triangledown \in \mathcal{O}$ *and all worlds* $w \in W$,

$$\mathbf{F}(\triangledown, w) = \begin{cases} \mathbf{F}_t(w) & \text{if } \triangledown \text{ is \textbf{first} or \textbf{next}} \\ \mathbf{F}_b(w), & \text{otherwise}. \end{cases}$$

(2) If $x \in S^{(u)}$ *and* $u \in W_b$, *then* $\mathbf{F}_b(x) = x$; *If* $x \in W_t$, *then* $\mathbf{F}_b(x) \in W_b$; *If* $x \in W_t$, *then* $\mathbf{F}_t(x) = x$; *and If* $x \notin W_t$, *then* $\mathbf{F}_t(x) \in W_t$.

Definition 5 (semantics). *Given a model* $\langle W, W_c, W_b, R_0, R_1, \ldots, R_n, \pi, \mathbf{F}, w_0 \rangle$. *Then the semantics of formulas in the model for the logic FL is defined inductively as follows: For any* $w \in W$,

1. *for any atomic formula* q, $w \models q$ *iff* $\pi(w, q)$ *has the true value "true"*.
2. $w \models \neg \varphi$ *iff it is not the case that* $w \models \varphi$.
3. $w \models (\varphi \wedge \psi)$ *iff* $w \models \varphi$ *and* $w \models \psi$.
4. $w \models \forall X \varphi(X)$ *iff, for all* $d \in \mathcal{T}$, $w \models \forall X \varphi(d)$, *where* $\mathcal{T}$ *is the type of* X.
5. $w \models \triangledown \varphi$ *iff* $\mathbf{F}(\triangledown, w) \models \triangledown \varphi$.
6. $w \models \mathbf{first} \ \varphi$ *when* $w \in W_t$ *iff* $\min\{t \mid t \in W_t\} \models \varphi$.
7. $w \models \mathbf{next} \ \varphi$ *when* $w \in W_t$ *iff* $\min\{t \mid w R_0 t\} \models \varphi$.
8. $w \models \mathbf{B}_i \varphi$ *when* $w \notin W_t$ *and* $1 \leq i \leq n$ *iff, for all* s *such that* $w R_i s$, $s \models \varphi$, *assuming* $s \in S^{(\mathbf{m})}$ *and* $\mathbf{m} \in \mathcal{K}_{bl}$.

With the sfm model $\langle W, W_c, W_b, R_0, R_1, \ldots, R_n, \pi, \mathbf{F}, w_0 \rangle$ we say that it satisfies the formula φ iff $w_0 \models \varphi$. Furthermore, $\mathbf{m} = \langle W, W_c, W_b, R_0, R_1, \ldots, R_n, \pi, \mathbf{F} \rangle$ is called a *regular fibred semantics model* for the logic FL. We say φ is valid in the model $\mathbf{m}$, and written as $\mathbf{m} \models \varphi$, if, for all $w_0 \in W_t \cup W_b$, the model $\langle W, W_c, W_b, R_0, R_1, \ldots, R_n, \pi, \mathbf{F}, w_0 \rangle$ satisfies φ; φ is satisfied in the model $\mathbf{m}$ if, for some $w_0 \in W_t \cup W_b$, the model $\langle W, W_c, W_b, R_0, R_1, \ldots, R_n, \pi, \mathbf{F}, w_0 \rangle$ satisfies φ. Let $\mathcal{K}_{fl}$ be the set of regular fibred semantics models which defines the fibred logic FL, then we say φ is valid in the logic FL if, for all $\mathbf{m} \in \mathcal{K}_{fl}$, $\mathbf{m} \models \varphi$.

The axiom set of FL consists of the following axiom schemata:

F0. all axioms of classical first-order logic[11].
F1. $\triangledown(\varphi \to \psi) \wedge \triangledown\varphi \to \triangledown\psi$, for all $\triangledown \in \mathcal{O}$.
F2. $\triangledown(\varphi \wedge \psi) \leftrightarrow (\triangledown\varphi) \wedge (\triangledown\psi)$, for all $\triangledown \in \mathcal{O}$.
F3. $\forall X(\triangledown\varphi(X)) \to \triangledown(\forall X\varphi(X))$, for all $\triangledown \in \mathcal{O}$.
F4. $\mathbf{B}_i(\neg\varphi) \to \neg(\mathbf{B}_i \varphi)$ for all i ($1 \leq i \leq n$).
F5. **first**$(\neg\varphi) \leftrightarrow \neg($**first** $\varphi)$.　　F6. **next**$(\neg\varphi) \leftrightarrow \neg($**next** $\varphi)$.
F7. **first**(**first** $\varphi) \leftrightarrow$ **first** φ.　　F8. **next**(**first** $\varphi) \leftrightarrow$ **first** φ.

The rules of inference for the logic FL are:

R1.　From φ and $\varphi \to \psi$ infer ψ.　　　　　　　　(Modus Ponens)
R2.　From $\forall X\varphi(X)$ infer $\varphi(Y)$.　　　　　　　　　(Instantiation)
R3.　From $\varphi(X)$ infer $\forall X\varphi(X)$.　　　　　　　　　(Generalisation)
R4.　From φ infer $\triangledown\varphi$ for all $\triangledown \in \mathcal{O}$.　　　　　　(Necessitation)

The soundness for the logic FL depends on the soundness theorems for logics TML and SLTL, and is not difficult to prove. The completeness theory for FL can be proved by the techniques used in [5].

4　Application of the Logic FL

In this section, we propose a method for building a theory of trust to specify the TESLA protocol, a multicast stream authentication protocol developed by Perrig et al. [12]. In TESLA, the process for verifying data packets received to be authentic depends on trust of the receiver in the sender, and belief on whether an intruder can have prior knowledge of a key before it is published by the protocol.

4.1　The Formalization of TESLA

We consider a basic scheme for the TESLA Protocol, called the PCTS scheme, in which each message M_i is sent in a packet P_i, along with additional authentication information [1,12]. The sender issues a signed commitment to a key that is only known to itself. To send message M_i, the sender uses that key to compute a MAC (Message Authenticating Code) on a packet P_i, and later discloses the key in packet P_{i+1}, which enables the receiver (or receivers, when multiple receivers are involved) to verify the commitment and the MAC of packet P_i. A successful verification will imply that packet P_i is authenticated and trusted. We assume that, apart from the initial contact messages between the sender and the receiver, for all $i \geq 2$, the packet P_i from the sender to receiver has the standard form $\langle D_i, MAC(K'_i, D_i)\rangle$, where K's are keys, $D_i = \langle M_i, f(K_{i+1}), K_{i-1}\rangle$, $K'_j = f'(K_j)$ for $j \geq 1$, and f and f' are two different pseudo-random functions.

In a threat model, we assume that the intruder has the ability to capture, drop, resend, delay, and alter packets, can access to a fast network with negligible delay, and can perform efficient computations, such as computing a reasonable number of pseudo-random function applications and MACs with negligible delay.

Nonetheless, the intruder cannot invert a pseudo-random function with non-negligible probability.

With the purpose of making the logic FL appropriate for specifying the protocol, we restrict the time model of FL to guarantee that the time interval between any moment and its next moment in time has the same length, 1 unit time. This restriction matches the special timing property that the TESLA scheme satisfies: *the sender sends packets at regular time intervals*. The assumption makes our discussion simple without harming its correctness.

We now establish a specific theory that describes the behavior or functions of the protocol with the scheme PCTS. The basic types involved in such a theory include: (1) *Agents*: A, B, S, R, I; (2) *Messages*: X, Y, D, D'; and (3) *Keys*: K, K_1, K_2. Here S, R, I are intended to stand for the sender, the receiver, and the intruder, respectively. In the case when there are multiple receivers, we may have $R_1, R_2, \ldots$ in the type *Agents*.

Through an analysis of the TESLA protocol, we specify a theory consisting of four modules, M_{sr} (*send-receive mode specification*), M_{mk} (*message receiving and knowledge gained*), M_{ms} (*message sending*), and M_{ar} (*authentication hentication rules*). Several predicates are used to express the axioms in each module. Their meanings are intuitive and hence not discussed here.

Send-receive mode specification depends on what kind of mode is adopted. We first consider a simple mode called the *zero-delay mode*, which is based on two assumptions: (1) Zero time is spent between sending a message and receiving this message, i.e., the sending time of a packet P_i is equal to the receiving time of the packet on the synchronized receiver's clock, for any P_i; and (2) the packet rate is assumed to be 1 (i.e., 1 packet per unit time). With this mode, module M_{sr} consists of the following axiom schemata:

Z1. $sends(S, R, X) \rightarrow receives(R, X)$.
Z2. $sends(S, R, \langle D, MAC(f'(K), D) \rangle) \leftrightarrow \textbf{next } sends(S, R, X) \wedge K \in X$.

The first rule says that, if the sender sends the receiver a message, then the receiver will receive the message at the same time; and the second one says that the sender sends the receiver a message packet with a singed commitment to a key if it will send the receiver a packet containing that key at the next moment in time. Zero-delay mode is an idealized mode. However, generally the time spent between sending and receiving messages cannot be zero. Considering this point, we give the definition of send-receive modes by introducing a generic form.

Definition 6 (time intervals). *For a send-receive mode, there is a time interval with packet arrival, denoted as $[min, max]$, such that, for every packet P_i,*

$$sends(S, R, P_i) \rightarrow \textbf{next}^{(t)} \ receives(R, P_i), \ min \leq t \leq max.$$

Definition 6 indicates that any packet sent by the sender must arrive at a moment between the min and max moments.

Definition 7 (time distance of sending). *Let $d = 1/r$, where r is the packet rate (i.e., number of packets sent per unit time). We call d the time distance of sending between two packets.*

Note that a send-receive mode is in fact determined based on the time interval of packet arrival and the time distance of sending.

Definition 8 (send-receive modes). $m([u,v],d)$ *is a* send-receive mode *of the PCTS scheme of TESLA or, simply, a* mode *if* $u,v,d \in \mathcal{N}$, *the set of all natural numbers, and* $u \leq v$, *where* $[u,v]$ *is regarded as the time interval of this mode, and d is the time distance of sending with it. Furthermore, we say that* $m([u,v],d)$ *is a* safe *mode if* $v < d$.

Thus, we have the following generic rules to specify the mode $m([u,v],d)$:

G1. $sends(S,R,X) \rightarrow \mathbf{next}^{(u)}\ receives(R,X) \vee \ldots \vee \mathbf{next}^{(v)} receives(R,X)$.
G2. $sends(S,R,\langle D, MAC(f'(K),D)\rangle) \leftrightarrow \mathbf{next}^{(d)}\ sends(S,R,X) \wedge K \in X$.

These rules are definitely determined when u,v and d are definitely given. For example, within the mode $m([2,3],4)$, we have

S1. $sends(S,R,X) \rightarrow \mathbf{next}^{(2)}\ receives(R,X) \vee \mathbf{next}^{(3)} receives(R,X)$.
S2. $sends(S,R,\langle D, MAC(f'(K),D)\rangle) \leftrightarrow \mathbf{next}^{(4)}\ sends(S,R,X) \wedge K \in X$.

Modules M_{mk}, M_{ms}, and M_{ar} are are fixed and applied for any mode. Due to space limitation, all these modules are listed below without explanations.
M_{mk} **(message receiving and knowledge gained):**

G3. $receives(A, \langle X,Y \rangle) \rightarrow receives(A,X) \wedge receives(A,Y)$.
G4. $receives(A,X) \rightarrow knows(A,X)$.
G5. $knows(A,K) \rightarrow knows(A,f(K)) \wedge knows(A,f'(K))$.
G6. $knows(A, \{X\}_{SK(B)}) \rightarrow knows(A,X)$.
G7. $knows(A,K) \wedge knows(A,X) \rightarrow knows(A,MAC(K,X))$.
G8. $knows(A,X) \rightarrow \mathbf{next}\ knows(A,X)$.

where $SK(B)$ is the private key of agent B and its corresponding public key can be known by anybody, so we have G8.
M_{ms} **(Message sending):**

G9. $sends(A,B,\langle X,Y \rangle) \rightarrow sends(A,B,X) \wedge sends(A,B,Y)$.
G10. $sends(A,B,X) \rightarrow has\_sent(A,B,X)$.
G11. $has\_sent(A,B,X) \rightarrow \mathbf{next}\ has\_sent(A,B,X)$.

M_{ar} **(Authentication rules):**

G12. $is\_auth(\langle X, MAC(f'(k),D)\rangle) \leftrightarrow$
     $\qquad verify\_success(f(K)) \wedge verify\_success(MAC(f'(K),D))$.
G13. $is\_auth(X) \rightarrow has\_been\_auth(X)$.
G14. $\mathbf{B}_R\ has\_been\_auth(X) \rightarrow \mathbf{next}\ \mathbf{B}_R\ has\_been\_auth(X)$.
G15. $receives(R, \langle X, MAC(f'(K),D)\rangle) \wedge \mathbf{B}_R\ \neg has\_sent(S,R,K) \rightarrow$
     $\qquad \mathbf{B}_R\ arrived\_safe(\langle X, MAC(f'(K),D)\rangle)$.
G16. $arrived\_safe(X) \rightarrow has\_arrived\_safe(X)$.
G17. $\mathbf{B}_R\ has\_arrived\_safe(X) \rightarrow \mathbf{next}\ \mathbf{B}_R\ has\_arrived\_safe(X)$.
G18. $\mathbf{B}_R\ verify\_success(f(K)) \leftrightarrow \mathbf{B}_R\ has\_arrived\_safe(\langle X, MAC(f'(K),D)\rangle)$
     $\qquad \wedge knows(R,K) \wedge \mathbf{B}_R\ has\_been\_auth(\langle D', MAC(f'(K),D')\rangle) \wedge f(K) \in D'$.
G19. $\mathbf{B}_R\ verify\_success(MAC(f'(K),D)) \leftrightarrow$
     $\qquad \mathbf{B}_R\ has\_arrived\_safe(\langle X, MAC(f'(K),D)\rangle) \wedge$
     $\qquad knows(R,K) \wedge MAC(f'(K),X) = MAC(f'(K),D)$.

Thus, we have obtained a theory $\mathbf{T} = \mathrm{M}_{sr} \cup \mathrm{M}_{mk} \cup \mathrm{M}_{ms} \cup \mathrm{M}_{ar}$ to specify the PCTS scheme of TESLA given in Section 4.1, where $\mathrm{M}_{sr} = \{\mathrm{G1}, \mathrm{G2}\}$, $\mathrm{M}_{mk} = \{\mathrm{G3}, \ldots, \mathrm{G8}\}$, $\mathrm{M}_{ms} = \{\mathrm{G9}, \mathrm{G10}, \mathrm{G11}\}$, and $\mathrm{M}_{ar} = \{\mathrm{G12}, \ldots, \mathrm{G19}\}$.

4.2 Mechanizing Theories for the Correctness Analysis

The correctness condition for a given TESLA scheme should guarantee the authenticity of the received messages.

Definition 9 (correctness condition). *The local correctness for a TESLA scheme to the receiver R who receives messages from the sender S means that, if R has verified that a packet is authentic, then the packet was indeed sent by S. That is,*

$$\forall X \ (\mathbf{B}_R \ \mathit{has\_been\_auth}(X) \land \mathit{has\_sent}(A, R, X) \rightarrow A = S).$$

Further, the (global) correctness for the TESLA scheme means that the local correctness for the scheme to all receivers holds.

The theory discussed above is based on a time model where the clock is regarded as the synchronized receiver's clock (correspondingly to the global clock). It provides a basis for the receiver to verify stream messages received through the PCTS scheme of the TESLA protocol if the scheme with its send-receive mode satisfies the correctness condition.

In order to prove that the scheme satisfies the security property required, or to show that it does not satisfy the correctness condition, we need to mechanize the theory describing the behaviour of the protocol in an appropriate proof system such as the SMV model checker [10].

Based on the theory developed above, we can show that the PCTS scheme with the mode $m([u, v], d)$ mode is secure if $m([u, v], d)$ is a safe mode. We can also show that the PCTS scheme with an unsafe mode, e.g, the mode $m([1, 4], 2)$, provides chances for the intruder to attack the system. Consider the case: assume that packets P_i and P_{i+1} are sent out by the sender at time t and at $t + 2$), respectively. The intruder, I, first intercepts P_i at $t + 2$ and then, at $t + 3$, again intercepts P_{i+1} when it arrives. By creating a packet P'_i, instead of P_i, using key K_i in packet P_{i+1}, I masquerades as the sender send packet P'_i to the receiver. The attach will be successful if P'_i reaches the receiver at $t + 4$.

5 Conclusion

With the logic FL, we use a simple case of the fibred semantics arising from Kripke models with a single global time model. However, it is not difficult to extend it by considering other different time models. Such extensions would be needed when one wants to deal with, for instance, different local clocks for multi-agent systems.

We have discussed an application of the logic FL in analysing the TESLA protocol. Our analysis has shown that the PCTS scheme of TESLA with a safe send-receive mode is secure given that the correctness condition is satisfied. Since the modular structure makes it easy for the user to modify a theory, we believe that our approach can be easily extended such that it is also suitable for other schemes of the TESLA protocol, and for other stream authentication protocols.

Acknowledgements

The work presented in this article has been supported in part by an Australian Research Council (ARC) Discovery Project grant.

References

1. P. Broadfoot and G. Lowe. Analysing a stream authentication protocol using model checking. In *Proc. of the 7th European Symposium on Research in Computer Security (ESORICS)*, 2002.
2. M. Burrows, M. Abadi, and R. M. Needham. A logic of authentication. *ACM Transactions on Computer Systems*, 8(1):18–36, 1990.
3. E. Clarke, S. Jha, and W. Marrero. A machine checkable logic of knowledge for specifying security properties of electronic commerce protocols. In *Proc. of the Workshop on Formal Methods and Security Protocols*, 1998.
4. N. Durgin, J. Mitchell, and D. Pavlovic. A compositional logic for proving security properties of protocols. *Journal of Computer Security*, 11(2003):677–721.
5. Dov M. Gabbay. *Fibring Logics*. Oxford University Press, Oxford, 1999.
6. J. Y. Halpern and Y. Moses. A guide to completeness and complexity for modal logics of knowledge and belief. *Artificial Intelligence* **54**, pages 319–379, 1992.
7. G. E. Hughes and M. J. Cresswell. *A New Introduction to Modal Logic*. Routledge, 1996.
8. C. Liu and M. A. Orgun. Dealing with multiple granularity of time in temporal logic programming. *Journal of Symbolic Computation*, 22:699–720, 1996.
9. C. Liu, M. Ozols, and M. A. Orgun. A temporalised belief logic for specifying the dynamics of trust for multi-agent systems. In *Proc. of the Ninth Asian Computer Science Conference 2004*, LNCS, Vol. 3321, pages 142–156. Springer, Dec. 2004.
10. K. L. McMillan. Symbolic model checking - an approach to the state explosion problem. PhD thesis, SCS, Carnegie Mellon University, 1992.
11. E. Mendelson. *Introduction to Mathematical Logic*. Fourth Edition. International Thomson Publishing, 1997.
12. A. Perrig, R. Canetti, J. D. Tygar, and D. Song. Efficient authentication and signing of multicast streams over lossy channels. In *IEEE Symposium on Security and Privacy*, pages 56–73, May 2000.

Inconsistency-Based Strategy for Clarifying Vague Software Requirements

Kedian Mu[1], Zhi Jin[1,2], and Ruqian Lu[1,2]

[1] Institute of Computing Technology,
Chinese Academy of Sciences, Beijing 100080, P.R. China
[2] Academy of Mathematics and System Sciences,
Chinese Academy of Sciences, Beijing 100080, P.R. China

Abstract. It seems to be inevitable to confront vague information about customer's needs during the software requirements stage. It may be desirable to record and clarify the vague information to avoid missing real requirements. In this paper, we provide an inconsistency-based strategy to handle vague information in the framework of Annotated Predicate Calculus. This strategy permits the stakeholder to describe the different vague information using statements with different levels of belief, where each level of belief is determined by the degree of vagueness. By checking consistency of the union of vague requirements and clear requirements, we then heighten the level of belief in uncontroversial vague requirements. We also lower the levels of belief in requirements involved in undesirable inferences and leave them to be articulated in some following stage. To support this, Annotated Predicate Calculus is used to represent the requirements specification. In particular, we present a special *belief semilattice*, which defines truth values appropriate for representing the strength of analyst's belief in the truth of requirements statements.

1 Introduction

It seems to be inevitable to confront vague information about customer's needs during the early requirements stage. As the first stage of software development, software requirements elicitation just starts with some disorganized observations to related domains and fragmented descriptions for customer's demand in many cases. Incomplete nature of information available at this stage makes clarifying vague descriptions be a difficult task. To make matters worse, vagueness may result in difficulties in the following stages of software development. For example, vague descriptions may lead to uncertainty in decision during the design stage. Most software developers view vague information as undesirable. But most also recognize that it may be desirable to record and clarify vague information to avoid missing real software requirements.

A systematic approach to managing vague information can help solve many problems during the requirements stage. Clarifying vague information draws attention to problem areas, which means you can use vagueness-clarifying as a tool to

- mine the customer's real needs,
- direct the communication between the analysts and the customer,
- improve the analysts' shared understanding, and
- assist with identification of inconsistency.

However, to turn vagueness-clarifying into a tool, a framework for representing and clarifying vague information must be provided in the process of requirements elicitation.

Currently, techniques for formalizing requirements specifications are underdeveloped. Some approaches touch on this topic. In particular, since most software developers recognize that their requirements specifications are frequently inconsistent, paraconsistent logics have been paid much attention recently [1,2,3,4,5,6,7,8]. However, existing approaches have only focused on clear requirements statements. None of these techniques provide a direct framework for representing vague requirements information.

A complete representation of the vague requirements statement should focus on both the statement and the stakeholder's belief in that. As usual in vague information processing, the stakeholder's belief in vague requirements statements plays an important role in handling vague requirements. It affects decision on identifying appropriate vagueness-handling actions in practice.

To address this, we present an inconsistency-based strategy for clarifying vague requirements. Informally speaking, we have different levels of belief in requirements statements with different degrees of vagueness. By checking consistency of requirements specification, the uncontroversial vague requirements statement could be viewed as clear requirements statements. That is, we may heighten the level of belief in uncontroversial vague requirements statements. We also lower the levels of belief in requirements that result in inconsistencies, and leave them to be articulated in some following stage. The inconsistency arising in requirements specification plays an important role in the process of vague requirements clarification. It is viewed as a trigger to modify the levels of stakeholder's belief in requirements.

To support this strategy, we use a form of paraconsistent logic, called Annotated Predicate Calculus(abbr. **APC**) [9], to formalize the requirements specifications. The syntax and the semantics of **APC** is based on classical logic, except that the atomic formulas (e.g. $l:r$) are constructed from classical atomic formulas (e.g. l) by appending to them values (e.g. r) drawn from a belief semilattice. Informally, an annotation, r, represents strength of reasoner's belief in the truth of the statements annotated with r. Thus, it provides a promising tool to represent requirements statements with different levels of belief.

The rest of this paper is organized as follows. Section 2 applies **APC** to representing requirements specifications by defining a special belief semilattice. Section 3 presents an inconsistency-based strategy for clarifying vague information in the framework of **APC**. In section 4, we illustrate the strategy with an example. Finally, we conclude this paper in section 5.

2   Representing Requirements in APC

For several reasons, Annotated Predicate Calculus provides a promising logical tool to represent requirements statements. Firstly, *epistemic* embedding has been shown to be a suitable tool for analyzing inconsistent classical theories [9]. It means that we can embed clear requirements statements into **APC**. Secondly, we may also define some special belief semilattice (abbr. *BSL*) appropriate to vague requirements statements. For instance, we may introduce truth value t_p(*It is possible to be true*) in *BSL*. The lower levels of belief in vague requirements statements may distinguish the vague information from clear requirements statements. Thirdly, it is shown in [9] that **APC** could be applied in nonmonotonic reasoning. It may provide a technical basis for potential modification of requirements specification.

Now, we define a special *BSL*, which defines the truth values appropriate for representing vague information. As usual in **APC**, *BSL* is an upper semilattice with the following properties [9]: (1) It contains at least the following four distinguished elements: $\mathbf{t}$(true), $\mathbf{f}$(false), $\top$(contradiction), and $\bot$ (unknown); (2) For every $s \in BSL$, $\bot \leq s \leq \top$($\leq$ is the semilattice ordering); (3)$lub(\mathbf{t},\mathbf{f}) = \top$, where *lub* denotes the least upper bound.

Generally, the truth value appropriate for vague information should be viewed as a relative measure of degree of its vagueness. In fact, it is difficult to measure the degree of vagueness based on numerical values in many cases. We may just differentiate vague information based on several qualitative levels of vagueness, such as "*possible*", "*very possible*", and "*certain*".

We may define different *BSL* according to the levels of vagueness we used in practice. For example, we may define 7-valued *belief semilattice* $\mathcal{L}^p$ and 10-valued *belief semilattice* $\mathcal{L}^{pv}$, as shown in figure 1. As usual, the meanings of the values $\top$, $\mathbf{t}$ and $\mathbf{f}$ are *inconsistent*, *true*, and *false*, respectively. The other truth values are explained below.

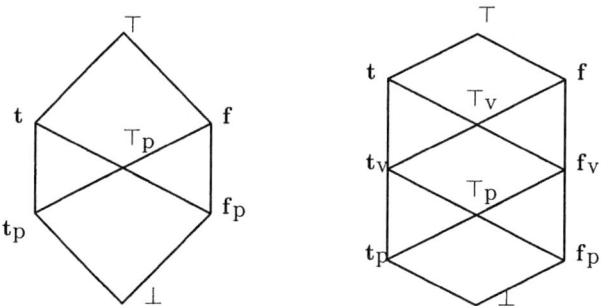

Fig. 1. 7-valued *BSL* and 10-valued *BSL*

In general case, the meaning of the value $\bot$ is *undefined* or *unknown*. But in this paper, the value $\bot$ is explained as *To Be Determined*(abbr. *TBD*). Informally, the value t_p signifies that *it is possible to be true*. The value f_p signifies that *it is possible to be false*. The value $\mathbf{t_V}$ signifies that *it is very possible to be true*. The value $\mathbf{f_V}$ signifies that *it is very possible to be false*. Finally, the value $\top_\mathrm{P}$ signifies that *it is possible to be inconsistent*, and the values $\top_\mathrm{V}$ signifies that *it is very possible to be inconsistent*.

Just for convenience, 7-valued *belief semilattice* $\mathcal{L}^p$ is adopted as the *BSL* used in this paper. It is the simplest *BSL* appropriate for representing vague information. The goal of our strategy is to translate the requirements specification into **APC** and to clarify vague information based on reasoning with specifications.

Clear requirements statements. Clear requirements statements could be translated into classical logic [3]. Moreover, classical formulas could be embedded in **APC** by *epistemic embedding*. That is, given a classical clause, its positive literals are embedded using the truth value $\mathbf{t}$, and its negative literals are embedded using the truth value $\mathbf{f}$. For example, under *epistemic embedding*, $\{\alpha \vee \gamma, \neg \alpha \vee \neg \beta\}$ is embedded in **APC** as $\{\alpha : \mathbf{t} \vee \gamma : \mathbf{t}, \alpha : \mathbf{f} \vee \beta : \mathbf{f}\}$.

Vague requirements statements. Vague requirements statements could be translated into formulas with annotations drawn from $\mathcal{L}^p$. A particular thing is that there is at least an annotation drawn from $\{\mathbf{t_p}, \mathbf{f_p}\}$ in each formula. We also use formulas with the annotation $\bot$ to represent the *TBD* requirements. We give the following example to illustrate the representation of requirements statements.

Example 1. Consider the following statements about customer's needs.
- stakeholder A: *If a user's application for borrowing a book is judged to be valid, then the book should be reserved for the user.*
- stakeholder B: *In many cases, if a book is reserved for a user, then the user should borrow the book.*
- stakeholder C: *At present, there is no consensus that a user with an overdue book should be notified.*

Obviously, the information provided by A could be represented by

$$Valid(User, Apply, Book) : \mathbf{t} \rightarrow Reserve(User, Book) : \mathbf{t}$$

The information provided by B and C is vague. But it is not difficult to get the following representation of the information provided by B.

$$Reserve(User, Book) : \mathbf{t} \rightarrow Borrow(User, Book) : \mathbf{t_p}$$

The information provided by C may be viewed as *TBD*. It may be represented as follows:

$$Borrow(User, Book) : \mathbf{t} \wedge Overdue(Book) : \mathbf{t} \rightarrow Notify(User, Book) : \bot$$

Further, each requirements statement can be viewed as an annotated formula of the form $\varphi \rightarrow \psi$. φ and ψ are called *antecedent* and *consequent* of the requirements statement, respectively. We use Δ_C and Δ_V to stand for a set of clear requirements statements and a set of vague requirements statements, respectively. Finally, we use $\Delta_\bot$ to denote a set of *TBD* requirements. In the rest of this paper, we use Δ to denote $\Delta_C \cup \Delta_V$ if no confusion arises.

3 Clarifying Vague Requirements

To clarify vague requirements, we need to distinguish "good" requirements from "problematical" requirements. Informally speaking, the "good" requirements statements should be free from undesirable inferences. The gist of our approach is to heighten the level of stakeholder's belief in "good" vague information and to lower the level of stakeholder's belief in "problematical" requirements. We start clarification of vague requirements with the following definitions.

Definition 1. *Let Δ be a set of annotated formulas. Then*

$$\mathsf{INC}(\Delta) = \{\Gamma \subseteq \Delta | \Gamma \models \alpha : r, r \in \{\top, \top_p\}\},$$
$$\mathsf{CON}(\Delta) = \{\Gamma \subseteq \Delta | \Gamma \not\models \alpha : r, r \in \{\top, \top_p\}\},$$
$$\mathsf{MC}(\Delta) = \{\Phi \in \mathsf{CON}(\Delta) | \forall \Psi \in \mathsf{CON}(\Delta), \Phi \not\subset \Psi\},$$
$$\mathsf{MI}(\Delta) = \{\Phi \in \mathsf{INC}(\Delta) | \forall \Psi \in \mathsf{INC}(\Delta), \Psi \not\subset \Phi\},$$

where $\models$ is the logical entailment relation in $\mathbf{APC}$.

Actually, $\mathsf{CON}(\Delta)$ is the set of consistent subsets of Δ. $\mathsf{INC}(\Delta)$ is the set of inconsistent subsets of Δ. $\mathsf{MC}(\Delta)$ is the set of maximally consistent subsets of Δ; $\mathsf{MI}(\Delta)$ is the set of minimally inconsistent subsets of Δ. Furthermore, we can consider a maximally consistent subset of a specification as capturing a "plausible" or "coherent" view on the specification. Notice that we focus on $\top_p$ as well as $\top$ in the definition of inconsistent subset. This means that both clear inconsistency and vague inconsistency are paid attention.

Another particular thing is that we could identify the potential inconsistency, which will be resulted from the transformation of vague requirements into clear requirements. For example, if $\alpha : \mathbf{t} \in \Delta$ and $\alpha : \mathbf{f}_p \in \Delta$, then we could get final conclusion $\Delta \models \alpha : \mathbf{t}$ since $\mathbf{f}_p < \mathbf{t}$ in $\mathcal{L}^p$. But if we transform the vague requirements statement into clear requirements statement $\alpha : \mathbf{f}$, then inconsistency $\alpha : \top$ appears in Δ. However, the identification of potential inconsistency could be viewed as a prediction of the results to clarifying vague information.

Definition 2. *Let Δ be a set of annotated formulas. Then*

$$\mathsf{PINC}_{t \wedge f_p}(\Delta) = \{\Gamma \in \mathsf{CON}(\Delta) | \Gamma \models \alpha : t,\ \Gamma \models \alpha : f_p\},$$
$$\mathsf{PINC}_{f \wedge t_p}(\Delta) = \{\Gamma \in \mathsf{CON}(\Delta) | \Gamma \models \alpha : f,\ \Gamma \models \alpha : t_p\},$$
$$\mathsf{PINC}(\Delta) = \mathsf{PINC}_{t \wedge f_p}(\Delta) \cup \mathsf{PINC}_{f \wedge t_p}(\Delta)$$

Essentially, $\mathsf{PINC}(\Delta)$ is the set of consistent subsets of Δ that may result in potential inconsistencies. We call it the set of potential inconsistent subsets of Δ.

Definition 3. *Let Δ be a set of annotated formulas. Then*

$$\mathsf{MPI}(\Delta) = \{\Phi \in \mathsf{PINC}(\Delta) | \forall \Psi \in \mathsf{PINC}(\Delta), \Psi \not\subset \Phi\},$$
$$\mathsf{PFREE}(\Delta) = \Delta - \bigcup_{\Phi \in \mathsf{MI}(\Delta) \cup \mathsf{MPI}(\Delta)} \Phi$$

MPI(Δ) is the set of minimal potential inconsistent subsets of Δ, while PFREE(Δ) is the subset of Δ that is free from both inconsistency and potential inconsistency. However, PFREE(Δ) could be viewed as the reflection of all the "really uncontroversial" information in Δ. In contrast, the set $\bigcup_{\Phi \in \mathsf{MI}(\Delta) \cup \mathsf{MPI}(\Delta)} \Phi$ can be viewed as the collection of "problematical" information in Δ.

For a specification Δ, it is more meaningful to act on the requirements statements involved in the problematical inferences. First, we define two kinds of action appropriate for this purpose.

Definition 4. (Confirming). *Let Δ be a set of requirements statements. For every $\phi \in \Delta$, its confirmation is defined as ϕ^c, where ϕ^c is constructed by*

- *replacing each annotation t_p in ϕ by t;*
- *replacing each annotation f_p in ϕ by f.*

Proposition 1. *Let Δ be a set of requirements statements. For each $\varphi \to \psi \in \Delta$, $(\varphi \to \psi)^c \leftrightarrow \varphi^c \to \psi^c$.*

Definition 5. (Degrading). *Let Δ be a set of requirements statements. For every requirements statement $\varphi \to \psi \in \Delta$, its degradation is defined as $\varphi \to \psi^d$, where ψ^d is constructed by replacing each annotation in ψ by $\bot$.*

Essentially, confirming a vague requirements statement is to heighten the level of stakeholder's belief in the statement. In contrast, degrading a requirements statement is to lower the level of stakeholder's belief in that. Either action is triggered by undesirable inferences, i.e., inconsistency or potential inconsistency.

The main goal of our approach is to clarify some vague information based on the results of reasoning with requirements specifications. Informally, we can adopt a meta-level approach to prescribe vagueness-clarifying strategies of the form

- *Being involved in (potential) inconsistency implies Degradation;*
- *Being free from inconsistency implies Confirmation.*

In detail, the inconsistency-based strategy for clarifying vague requirements can be described as follows.

Let $\Delta = \Delta_C \cup \Delta_V$ be a set of requirements statements. Let Δ_0 be the set of relevant facts to model certain scenarios with regard to Δ. We may choose the following actions to improve the requirements statements.

- *Confirming Vague Requirements.* For $\varphi \to \psi \in \Delta_V$, if $\varphi \to \psi \in \mathsf{PFREE}(\Delta \cup \Delta_0)$, then we view it as a clear requirements statement, that is, we replace $\varphi \to \psi$ with its confirmation $\varphi^c \to \psi^c$ in the requirements specification;
- *Degrading Problematical Requirements.* For $\varphi \to \psi \in \Delta$, if $\varphi \to \psi \notin \mathsf{PFREE}(\Delta \cup \Delta_0)$, then we view it as a *TBD* requirements, that is, we replace $\varphi \to \psi$ with its degradation $\varphi \to \psi^d$ in the requirements specification.

Notice that the inconsistency-based strategy is cautious. All the requirements statements involved in undesirable inferences will be transformed into *TBD* requirements. It means that these requirements will be pending currently. In fact, if there is adequate domain knowledge, we may identify the "likely" sources of undesirable inferences. Further, we may only degrade the requirements statements in the "likely" sources. Briefly speaking, we may adapt the inconsistency-based strategy to the different processes of requirements elicitation in practice.

4 Case Study

Our motivation for using inconsistency-based strategy is to clarify the vague information about customer's needs. For the following example of requirements elicitation, we will view the clear requirements statements as being correct and not subject to the modification of vague information. This will allow us to focus our attention on identification of real requirements from vague information.

Example 2. Consider the requirements for a computer-aided airline ticket reservation system. The requirements document for the system-to-be contains information such as the following:

- **Clear Information**
    - A valid order is confirmed by the client and the demand information (Date, Flight, Destination) is correct.
    - On receipt of an order for reserving a ticket, if the order is judged to be valid, then the available ticket should be reserved for the client and the client should be notified.
    - On receipt of an order for reserving a ticket, if the order is judged not to be valid, then the client should be notified to reorder.
    - On receipt of an order for reserving a ticket, if the order is judged to be valid but no ticket is available, then the ticket should not be reserved for the client and the client should be notified.
- **Vague Information**
    - On receipt of an order for reserving a ticket, if the order is judged to be valid but no ticket is available, then it **would be better** to recommend the client an other available flight to the same destination.
    - **Generally**, the client should pay for the reserved ticket.
    - **It'd better** allow the client to cancel his reservation.
    - **Maybe** only the failure in reservation needs notification.

For the clear information in the requirements document, we can translate them into the following set of annotated formulas, Δ_C. Note, Person, Ticket, Date, Destination, Flight, Ticket1 are variable symbols, and Failure, Reorder are constant symbols.

(i) $Confirm(Person, Ticket) : \mathbf{t} \wedge Correct(Date, Destination, Flight) : \mathbf{t}$
$$\leftrightarrow Valid(Person, Ticket) : \mathbf{t};$$

(ii) $Order(Person, Ticket) : \mathbf{t} \wedge Valid(Person, Ticket) : \mathbf{t}$
$\wedge Available(Ticket) : \mathbf{t}$
$\rightarrow Reserve(Person, Ticket) : \mathbf{t} \wedge Notify(Person, Ticket) : \mathbf{t};$

(iii) $Order(Person, Ticket) : \mathbf{t} \wedge Valid(Person, Ticket) : \mathbf{f}$
$\rightarrow Notify(Person, Reorder) : \mathbf{t};$

(iv) $Order(Person, Ticket) : \mathbf{t} \wedge Valid(Person, Ticket) : \mathbf{t}$
$\wedge Available(Ticket) : \mathbf{f}$
$\rightarrow Reserve(Person, Ticket) : \mathbf{f} \wedge Notify(Person, Failure) : \mathbf{t};$

We also translate the vague information into the following annotated formulas:

(v) $Order(Person, Ticket) : \mathbf{t} \wedge Valid(Person, Ticket) : \mathbf{t}$
$\wedge Available(Ticket) : \mathbf{f} \wedge Available(Ticket1) : \mathbf{t}$
$\wedge Samedestination(Ticket, Ticket1) : \mathbf{t}$
$\rightarrow Recommend(Person, Ticket1) : \mathbf{t_p};$

(vi) $Reserve(Person, Ticket) : \mathbf{t} \rightarrow Pay(Person, Ticket) : \mathbf{t_p};$

(vii) $Reserve(Person, Ticket) : \mathbf{t} \wedge Cancel(Person, Ticket) : \mathbf{t}$
$\rightarrow Pay(Person, Ticket) : \mathbf{f_p};$

(viii) $Reserve(Person, Ticket) : \mathbf{t} \rightarrow Notify(Person, Ticket) : \mathbf{f_p}.$

Let Δ_V be the set of these formulas. Consider the set of relevant facts, Δ_0 :

(ix) $Order(Alice, HU7802/Beijing/31May) : \mathbf{t};$

(x) $Confirm(Alice, HU7802/Beijing/31May) : \mathbf{t};$

(xi) $Correct(31May, Beijing, HU7802) : \mathbf{t};$

(xii) $Available(HU7802/Beijing/31May) : \mathbf{t};$

(xiii) $Cancel(Alice, HU7802/Beijing/31May) : \mathbf{t};$

(xiv) $Order(Bob, HU7803/Zurich/28May) : \mathbf{t};$

(xv) $Confirm(Bob, HU7803/Zurich/28May) : \mathbf{t};$

(xvi) $Correct(28May, Zurich, HU7803) : \mathbf{t};$

(xvii) $Available(HU7803/Zurich/28May) : \mathbf{f};$

(xviii) $Available(HU7809/Zurich/28May) : \mathbf{t};$

(xix) $Samedestination(HU7803/Zurich/28May, HU7809/Zurich/28May) : \mathbf{t}$

From $\Delta \cup \Delta_0$, we can generate the following inconsistency from (i), (ii), (vi), (vii), (ix), (x), (xi), (xii), and (xiii):

$Pay(Alice, HU7802/Beijing/31May) : \top_\mathbf{p},$

and also generate a potential inconsistency from (ix), (x), (xi), (xii), (ii), and (viii):

$Notify(Alice, HU7802/Beijing/31May) : \mathbf{t},$
$Notify(Alice, HU7802/Beijing/31May) : \mathbf{f_p};$

Thus, PFREE($\Delta \cup \Delta_0$) consists of the three formulas (iii), (iv), and (v).

According to the inconsistency-based strategy, the vague description (v) could be confirmed as a clear requirements statement:

(v) $Order(Person, Ticket) : \mathbf{t} \wedge Valid(Person, Ticket) : \mathbf{t}$
$\wedge Available(Ticket) : \mathbf{f} \wedge Available(Ticket1) : \mathbf{t}$
$\wedge Samedestination(Ticket, Ticket1) : \mathbf{t}$
$\rightarrow Recommend(Person, Ticket1) : \mathbf{t};$

By adding this statement to Δ_C, we get a new set of clear requirements Δ'_C.

The problematical vague requirements (vi),(vii), and (viii) will be degraded as *To Be Determined*, and then $\Delta'_\perp$ contains:

(vi) $Reserve(Person, Ticket) : \mathbf{t} \rightarrow Pay(Person, Ticket) : \perp;$
(vii) $Reserve(Person, Ticket) : \mathbf{t} \wedge Cancel(Person, Ticket) : \mathbf{t}$
$\rightarrow Pay(Person, Ticket) : \perp;$
(viii) $Reserve(Person, Ticket) : \mathbf{t} \rightarrow Notify(Person, Ticket) : \perp.$

It means that we should pay attention on the vague information (vi),(vii), and (viii). Suppose after some negotiation with customers, we get another set of vague descriptions Δ''_V from $\Delta'_\perp$ as follows:

(vi) $Reserve(Person, Ticket) : \mathbf{t} \wedge Cancel(Person, Ticket) : \mathbf{f}$
$\rightarrow Pay(Person, Ticket) : \mathbf{t_p};$
(vii) $Reserve(Person, Ticket) : \mathbf{t} \wedge Cancel(Person, Ticket) : \mathbf{t}$
$\rightarrow Pay(Person, Ticket) : \mathbf{f_p};$

At present, neither inconsistency nor potential inconsistency appears in the $\Delta''_V \cup \Delta'_C$. Consequently, we have mined the following clear requirements from original vague descriptions:

(vi) $Reserve(Person, Ticket) : \mathbf{t} \wedge Cancel(Person, Ticket) : \mathbf{f}$
$\rightarrow Pay(Person, Ticket) : \mathbf{t};$
(vii) $Reserve(Person, Ticket) : \mathbf{t} \wedge Cancel(Person, Ticket) : \mathbf{t}$
$\rightarrow Pay(Person, Ticket) : \mathbf{f}.$

5 Conclusions

We have presented an inconsistency-based strategy to clarify vague requirements in the framework of Annotated Predicate calculus. According to this strategy, requirements statements are translated into formulas in Annotated Predicate Calculus with an appropriate truth values lattice. By checking consistency of requirements specifications, we then modify the levels of belief in requirements statements. That is, we heighten the level of belief in the vague requirements statements that are free from both inconsistency and potential inconsistency. We also lower the levels of belief in the requirements statements involved in undesirable inferences.

The overwhelming majority of previous work on representing requirements specifications has only focused on clear requirements statements. It is difficult to apply them to handle vague requirements statements. In contrast, Annotated Predicate Calculus with BSL defined in this paper is appropriate for representing vague requirements statements as well as clear requirements statements.

The strategy we have described in this paper is cautious. We degrade all the requirements statements involved in undesirable inferences and transform them into TBD requirements. However, if there is adequate domain knowledge, then we may adapt the inconsistency-based strategy to the different processes of requirements elicitation in practice.

Acknowledgements

This work was partly supported by the National Natural Science Foundation of China (No.60233010 and No.60496324), the National Key Research and Development Program (Grant No. 2002CB312004) of China, the Knowledge Innovation Program of the Chinese Academy of Sciences and MADIS of the Chinese Academy of Sciences.

References

1. Spanoudakis, G., A.Finkelstein: Reconciling requirements: a method for managing interference, inconsistency and conflict. Annals of Software Engineering **3** (1997) 433–457
2. Spanoudakis, G., A.Zisman: Inconsistency management in software engineering: Survey and open research issues. In S.K.Chang, ed.: Handbook of Software Engineering and Knowledge Engineering. World Scientific Publishing Co. (2001) 329–380
3. Hunter, A., B.Nuseibeh: Managing inconsistent specification. ACM Transactions on Software Engineering and Methodology **7** (1998) 335–367
4. Lamsweerde, A., E.Letier: Handling obstacles in goal-driven requirements engineering. IEEE Transactions on Software Engineering **26** (2000) 978–1005
5. Bowman, H., M.Steen, E.Boiten, J.Derrick: A formal framework for viewpoint consistency. Formal Methods in System Design **21** (2002) 111–166
6. Easterbrook, S., M.Chechik: 2nd international workshop on living with inconsistency. Software Engineering Notes **26** (2001) 76–78
7. Easterbrook, S., M.Chechik: A framework for multi-valued reasoning over inconsistent viewpoints. In Harrold, M., Schafer, W., Muller, H., eds.: Proceedings of International Conference on Software Engineering (ICSE'01), Toronto, Canada (2001) 411–420
8. Chechik, M., Devereux, B., S.Easterbrook: Efficient multiple-valued model-checking using lattice representations. In Larsen, K.G., Nielsen, M., eds.: Proceedings of the International Conference on Concurrency Theory. Volume 2154 of LNCS., Aalborg, Denmark, Springer (2001) 21–24
9. Kifer, M., Lozinskii, E.L.: A logic for reasoning with inconsistency. Journal of Automated Reasoning **9** (1992) 179–215

Conditioning Graphs: Practical Structures for Inference in Bayesian Networks

Kevin Grant[1] and Michael C. Horsch[1]

Dept. of Computer Science, University of Saskatchewan, Saskatoon, SK, S7N 5A9
kjg658@mail.usask.ca, horsch@cs.usask.ca

Abstract. Programmers employing inference in Bayesian networks typically rely on the inclusion of the model as well as an inference engine into their application. Sophisticated inference engines require non-trivial amounts of space and are also difficult to implement. This limits their use in some applications that would otherwise benefit from probabilistic inference. This paper presents a system that minimizes the space requirement of the model. The inference engine is sufficiently simple as to avoid space-limitation and be easily implemented in almost any environment. We show a fast, compact indexing structure that is linear in the size of the network. The additional space required to compute over the model is linear in the number of variables in the network.

1 Introduction

When programmers wish to use a Bayesian network in their applications, the standard approach is to store the entire network, as well as an inference engine to compute posteriors from the model. Algorithms based on junction-tree message passing [7] or variable elimination [5,12] have a high space requirement and are difficult to code. Furthermore, application programmers not wishing to implement their own version of inference must import large general-purpose libraries. There are few algorithms which can be simply implemented in limited space.

To overcome some of these difficulties, Darwiche and Provan developed Query-DAGs [4]. A Query-DAG (or Q-DAG) is a data structure that represents the desired posterior probabilities as an arithmetic equation (in graphical form) parameterized by evidence variables. Computing probabilities involves setting the appropriate evidence variables, and updating the graph, which involves a minimal set of multiplications and summations. That is, the Bayesian network is "compiled out;" the result is a structure consisting only of node pointers, floating point numbers and boolean variables, easily implementable on any machine. The evaluator for Q-DAGs is a small set of rules composed of elementary computational operations, such as pointer referencing, arithmetic operations, and variable modification. Together with its evaluation engine, a Q-DAG is self-contained. However, the size of a Q-DAG may be exponential in the size of the network it is derived from.

The technique of *conditioning* [2,8,9] for probabilistic inference requires only linear space. However, cutset conditioning [9] requires an implementation of the message-passing algorithm, which is non-trivial to program. Recursive conditioning [2] is an inference engine that is easy to implement. However, it lacks the desirable properties of Q-DAGs; namely, a run-time structure with the details relevant to a specific query compiled away.

To overcome this problem, we present *conditioning graphs*. Conditioning graphs combine the linear space requirements of conditioning with the simplicity of Q-DAGs. Its components consist of simple node pointers and floating point values; no high-level elements of Bayesian network computation are included. As well, the evaluator for conditioning graphs is very simple: evaluating each node requires a series of arithmetic operations over floating point values.

The remainder of this paper is structured as follows. Section 2 gives some necessary background, and introduces *elimination trees*, which are the basis for conditioning graphs. Section 3 presents conditioning graphs, and demonstrates their construction from elimination trees. Section 4 shows how to optimize a structure when application-specific information is known. Section 6 outlines current and future research.

2 Elimination Trees

We denote a random variable with capital letters (eg. X, Y, Z), and sets of variables with boldfaced capital letters $\mathbf{X} = \{X_1, ..., X_n\}$. Each random variable V has an associated domain $\mathcal{D}(V) = \{v_1, ..., v_k\}$. An instantiation of a variable is denoted $X = x$, or x for short. A *context*, or instantiation of a set of variables, is denoted $\mathbf{X} = \mathbf{x}$ or $\mathbf{x}$. Given a set of random variables $\mathbf{V} = \{V_1, ..., V_n\}$ with domain function $\mathcal{D}$, a Bayesian network is a tuple $\langle \mathbf{V}, \mathbf{\Phi} \rangle$. $\mathbf{\Phi} = \{\phi_{V_1}, ..., \phi_{V_n}\}$ is a set of distributions with a one-to-one correspondence with the elements of $\mathbf{V}$. Each $\phi_{V_i} \in \mathbf{\Phi}$ is the conditional probability of V_i given its parents in the network (called *conditional probability tables* or CPTs). That is, if π_{V_i} represents the parents of V_i, then $\phi_{V_i} = P(V_i | \pi_{V_i})$. A variable in a Bayesian network is said to be *conditionally independent* of its non-descendents given its parents. This allows the joint probability to be factorized as:

$$P(\mathbf{V}) = \prod_{i=1}^{n} P(V_i | \pi_{V_i}) \ . \tag{1}$$

Figure 1 shows an example of a Bayesian network, and the CPTs associated with each variable, which we use as a running example.

A common inference problem in Bayesian networks is to compute posterior probabilities, which is NP-hard [1]. However, several algorithms give tractable run-times in many cases. The class of algorithms of interest is conditioning, specifically, recursive decomposition. Recursive decomposition [3,8,11] partitions a network by conditioning on a subset of its variables (such a subset of variables is deemed a *cutset*). Each of these components can be decomposed again, until each component in the final product is a single variable (with its associated distribution). Figure 2(a) shows a recursive decomposition for the *Fire* example.

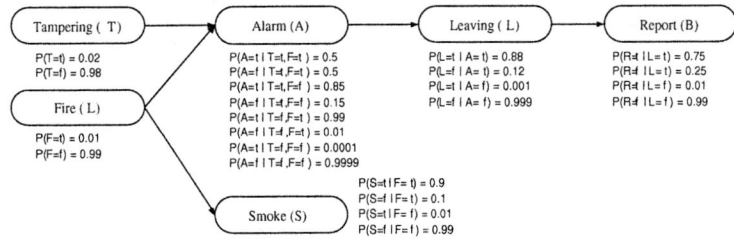

Fig. 1. The *Fire* Bayesian network (taken from Poole et al. [10])

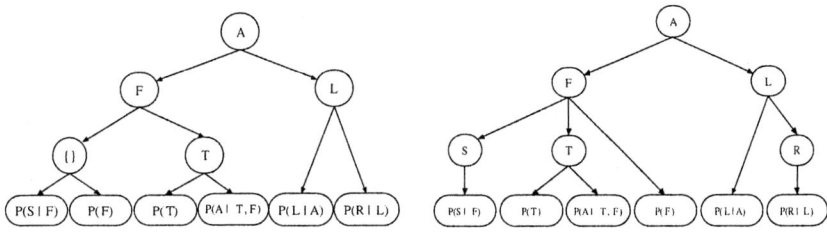

(a) A recursive decomposition of the *Fire* network

(b) An elimination tree for the *Fire* network

Fig. 2. Two decompositions of the *Fire* network

We begin by introducing elimination trees, which are another type of recursive decomposition. An *elimination tree* is a tree whose leaves and internal nodes correspond to the CPTs and variables of a Bayesian network, respectively. The tree is structured such that all CPTs containing variable V_i in their domain are contained in the subtree of the node labeled with V_i. Figure 2(b) shows a possible elimination tree for the *Fire* network.

There are two primary differences between elimination trees and other recursive decompositions (such as recursive conditioning [3]). The first is that the size of a cutset at any variable is restricted to exactly one variable. The other difference is that each variable of the Bayesian network must appear in a cutset, whereas leaf variables typically do not appear in the cutsets of recursive conditioning structures. These restrictions allow for simple low-level implementation, which is one of the goals of this project.

Elimination trees have a close correspondence with elimination algorithms [5,12]. The algorithm for building an elimination tree parallels variable elimination, where an internal node represents the marginalization of its variable label, and the children of the node represent the distributions that would be multiplied together. Thus, an internal node is labeled with a variable, but represents a distribution. Figure 3 gives a simple algorithm for constructing an elimination tree from a Bayesian network $\langle V, \Phi \rangle$. In the algorithm, we use $dom(T)$ to represent the union of all CPT domains from the leaves of T's subtree.

Notice that the algorithm in Figure 3 returns a set of trees, rather than a single tree. In the event that the network is not connected, the number of

```
elimtree(⟨V, Φ⟩)
    T ← {}
    for each ϕ ∈ Φ do
        Construct a leaf node T_ϕ containing ϕ
        Add T_ϕ to T
    for each V_i ∈ V do
        Select the set T_i = {t ∈ T|V_i ∈ dom(t)}
        Remove T_i from T
        Construct a new internal node t_i whose children are T_i
        Label t_i with V_i, and add it to T
    return T
```

Fig. 3. The code for generating an elimination tree from a Bayesian network

```
P(T, c)
    if T is a leaf node
        return ϕ_T(c)
    elseif V_T is instantiated in c
        Total ← 1
        for each T' ∈ ch_T
            Total ← Total * P(T', c)
        return Total
    else
        Total ← 0
        for each v_T ∈ dom(V_T)
            Total ← Total + P(T, c ∪ {v_T})
        return Total
```

Fig. 4. The code for processing an elimination tree given a context.

disconnected components will correspond to the number of trees returned by *elimtree*. For the following discussion, we consider the case where the elimination tree is a single tree. Cases where multiple trees occur are examined in Section 4.

To calculate probabilities from an elimination tree, we define algorithm $\mathcal{P}$ (see Figure 4). $\mathcal{P}$ takes as parameters a node from an elimination tree and a context, and returns a distribution. We use the following notation: if T is a leaf node, then ϕ_T represents the CPT at T. If T is an internal node, V_T represents the variable labeling T, and ch_T represents its children.

The following theorem specifies the relationship between the probabilities of interest and the algorithm $\mathcal{P}$. Its correctness follows from the correctness of the other recursive decomposition algorithms. A proof of the theorem can be found in Grant and Horsch [6].

Theorem 1. *Given a Bayesian network* $\langle V, \Phi \rangle$ *and an associated elimination tree* T:

$$P(x_q|c) = \alpha \mathcal{P}(T, \{x_q\} \cup c) \qquad (2)$$

where $\alpha = P(c)^{-1}$ *is a normalization constant.*

The major advantage of recursive decompositions (and conditioning in general) is the linear space property of the algorithm. It is summarized in the following theorem, whose proof is also found in Grant and Horsch [6].

Theorem 2. *Given a Bayesian network and an corresponding elimination tree T, $\mathcal{P}(T, \boldsymbol{C} = \boldsymbol{c})$ makes $\boldsymbol{O}(n \exp(d))$ recursive calls and requires $\boldsymbol{O}(d)$ space, where d is the height of the elimination tree.*

Theorem 2 demonstrates the relationship between the depth of the tree and the complexity of the algorithm $\mathcal{P}$. The depth of the tree is a consequence of the order in which the variables are selected from the *elimtree* algorithm. Choosing an ordering that optimizes the depth of the tree is an open problem.

There are several optimizations that can be made to this structure. However, we first consider some implementation details for elimination trees - one that provides minimal indexing. Further optimization will be considered in subsequent sections.

3 Conditioning Graphs

In this section, we will give a low-level representation for a Bayesian network as an elimination tree, and a compact efficient implementation of the algorithm $\mathcal{P}$.

We implement $\mathcal{P}$ as a depth-first traversal. When we reach a leaf node, we need to retrieve the parameter that corresponds to the context. To do this, we assume that each CPT is stored as a linear array of parameters. Indexing a CPT assumes an ordering of its variables and the domain values of each variable. Let $\{C_1, ..., C_k\}$ be an ordering of the variables in a CPT. C_i is the *ith* variable in the ordering, and c_i is an integer specifying the $c_i th$ value of C_i's domain, where $0 \leq i < m$. We calculate the index of a context $\{c_1, ..., c_k\}$ as follows:

$$index(c_1, ..., c_k) = \sum_{i=1}^{k} c_i m^{k-i} . \tag{3}$$

A more efficient version of this function is the Horner form of the polynomial:

1. $index([]) = 0$
2. $index([c_1, ..., c_i]) = c_i + m(index([c_1, ..., c_{i-1}]))$

For any given ordering of the variables, we can index into a CPT using this function. If we choose an ordering that is consistent with the path from root to leaf in the elimination tree, then we can index the CPTs as the context is constructed, as we traverse the tree. However, to make the associations between variables and distributions, we require a second set of arcs at each internal node, referred to here as *secondary pointers* (call the original pointers *primary pointers*). The secondary arcs are added according to the following rule: *there is an arc from an internal node A to leaf node B iff the variable X associated with A is contained in the domain of the CPT associated with B*. The number of secondary arcs emitting from a node with variable V is equivalent to $|ch_V|+1$, where ch_V refers to the number of arcs emitting from V in the Bayesian network. Cumulatively, the number of secondary arcs in the entire structure is $e+n$, where e is the number of arcs in the original network.

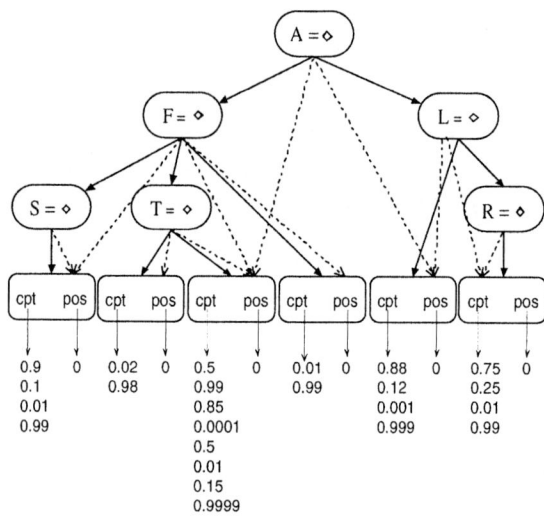

Fig. 5. The conditioning graph

An example of the final structure is shown in Figure 5. We refer to this structure as a *conditioning graph*, as the secondary arcs destroy its tree properties. Note that at each leaf, we store the CPT as an array of values, and the index as an integer variable, which we call *pos*. In each internal node, we store a set of primary pointers (from the elimination tree), a set of secondary pointers, and an integer representing the current value of the node's variable.

We maintain one global context over all variables, denoted as g. Each variable V_i is instantiated in g to a member of $\mathcal{D}(V_i) \cup \{\diamond\}$. The symbol $\diamond$ (borrowed from Darwiche and Provan [4]) is a special symbol that means the variable is unobserved. Initially, all nodes are assigned $\diamond$ in g, as no variables have been instantiated. To calculate $P(E_1 = e_1, ..., E_k = e_k)$, we set $E_i = e_i$ in g for $i = 1$ to k. While performing the algorithm, when conditioning a node to $V_i = v_i$, we set $V_i = v_i$. To 'uncondition' the variable (after conditioning on all values from its domain), we set $V_i = \diamond$ in g.

Figure 6 shows an implementation of $\mathcal{P}$. Note that we use dot notation to refer to the members of the variables. For a leaf node N, we use $N.cpt$ and $N.pos$ to refer to the CPT and its current index, respectively. For an internal node N, we use $N.primary$, $N.secondary$, and $N.value$ to refer to the variables primary children, secondary children, and variable value, respectively. The member *value* at each internal node can also represent the input from the programmer. To set

```
Query(N)
    if N is a leaf node
        return N.cpt[N.pos]
    else if N.value ≠ ⋄
        for each S' ∈ N.secondary do
            S'.pos ← S'.pos * m + N.value
        Total ← 1
        for each P' ∈ N.primary do
            Total ← Total * Query(P')
        for each S' ∈ N.secondary do
            S'.pos ← S'.pos/m
        return Total
    else
        Total ← 0
        for i ← 0 to m − 1 do
            N.value = i
            Total ← Total + Query(N)
        N.value = ⋄
        return Total
```

Fig. 6. The process algorithm

evidence $V = v_i$, the programmer would have to set $N.value$ to the appropriate value for the node N labeled with variable V.

The algorithm assumes that all variables are of size m. Extending conditioning graphs to variables of various sizes is easily accomplished with a little extra storage. If a node stores the size of its variable (as an integer value *size*) then we can replace all instances of m with $N.size$ in the algorithm, and it can handle multi-sized variables. A more interesting case is when the variables have sizes that are powers of two (eg. binary models). In this case, our multiplications and divisions become shift operations, which is much more efficient. In fact, if our secondary pointers can refer directly to their corresponding bits in the indexing variables, then shifting becomes unnecessary altogether, as does the requirement that the entries in the CPTs be ordered according to the global ordering (although they must be ordered according to some ordering). This optimization could be useful in some particular hardware implementations.

4 Sensor Models

It is well known that one can condition a Bayesian network on the evidence before performing inference. This reduces network connectivity, resulting in smaller cutset widths, and eliminates the evidence nodes from the CPTs, resulting in fewer marginalizations. If we know that some set of variables will always be observable, we can likewise modify the conditioning graph to be more efficient. This is a realistic situation: in any application, there typically exists at least a small subset of variables that are always observable. Examples of these include monitor output in medical patient monitoring, and sensor values in car diagnosis. We refer to these variables that can always be observed as *sensor variables*.

Considering the *Fire* model, suppose we know in advance that we will always be able to observe the state of the fire alarm, and whether or not there is smoke present (both are easily accomplished using sensors). Hence, our set of sensor variables is $\boldsymbol{E} = \{S, A\}$. We construct the elimination tree by removing $\boldsymbol{E}$ from the set of variables, and building the elimination tree over the variables that remain; all the CPTs are included in the tree. Essentially, this constructs a tree that does not marginalize S or A. See Figure 7(a). A conditioning graph is constructed from the elimination tree as before, with secondary arcs from each internal node to the appropriate leaf nodes. As well, the variables in $\boldsymbol{E}$ are included in the conditioning graph, with secondary arcs pointing to the appropriate leaf nodes, but they are not connected to the tree structure with any primary arcs. Figure 7(b) shows the resulting structure.

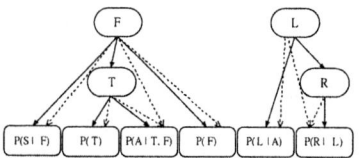
(a) The new conditioning graph. Note that *Alarm* and *Smoke* are never marginalized.

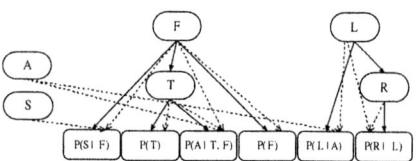
(b) The new conditioning graph, with nodes for *Alarm* and *Smoke*.

Fig. 7. The new conditioning graph, utilizing the evidence optimization. Note that for space consideration, we use the CPT notation, rather than listing the array of values explicitly.

There are definite benefits to this separation of the evidence nodes from the conditioning graph. Leaving $\boldsymbol{E}$ out of the elimination tree may result in several distinct trees, each of which is smaller than if they were included. Computing $P(x_q|e)$ only requires processing the component containing X_q in its nodes. Thus, even though our conditioning graph is static at run-time, we are able to "prune" away irrelevant parts of the model during compilation. Note that this requires a pointer from each variable X_q to its corresponding elimination tree, but these pointers require only linear space to store. There are other advantages. Reducing the conditioning graph by leaving out the observable variables may reduce its depth, which can produce exponential speedup when computing probabilities. Plus, as long as the evidence remains the same, we need only process the relevant elimination tree to handle multiple queries.

5 Query Variables

In variable elimination, it is well known that eliminating barren variables can improve the time it takes to process a query. Also, any nodes in the Bayesian

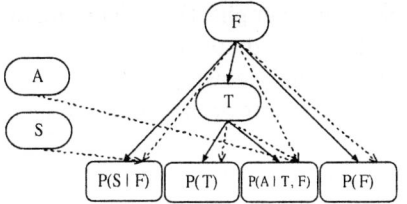
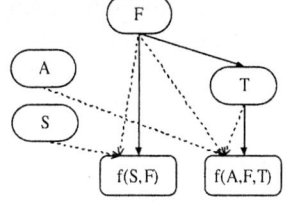

(a) The conditioning graph, leaving out *Report* and *Leaving*

(b) The conditioning graph, with leaf nodes for each internal node compacted

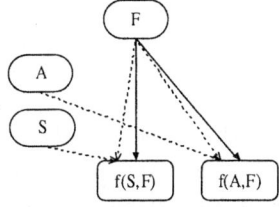
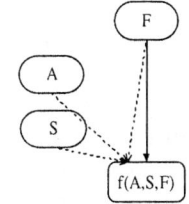

(c) The conditioning graph, with *Tampering* marginalized out

(d) The final conditioning graph

Fig. 8. Optimizing the conditioning graph

network that are d-separated from the query can be removed. These optimizations can also be used in conditioning graphs, if it is known in advance which variables will be queried, and which variables will be evidence variables. For example, if we knew that variables *Report* and *Leaving* would never be queried or observed, then that portion of the network need not even be stored. This eliminates approximately 33% of the space required for storage. Figure 8(a) shows the new structure.

If an internal node in a conditioning graph has several leaf nodes, the distributions can be multiplied at compile time, and the single distribution made the only child of the node. This will reduce the number of multiplications during inference, but has the potential to increase the space requirement of the problem. Thus it should only be performed if this increase in size is acceptable. On the other hand, it is possible that this operation may decrease the space required to store the conditioning graph.

From our previous example, we see that the internal node associated with *Tampering* has two leaf nodes, whose CPTs correspond to $P(A|T,F)$ and $P(T)$. Multiplying these two CPTs produces a factor over $\{A,T,F\}$, with 8 values. This operation does not add to the space requirements (in fact, it reduces them). Similarly, the node for *Fire* has two leaf nodes that can be multiplied with the same effects. Figure 8(b) shows the conditioning graph after these two optimizations are performed. Note that the size of the network and the number of operations necessary has been reduced.

We can take this optimization one step further considering that we know of variables that will never be observed or queried. If a subtree in the elimination tree contains only variables that will never be queried or observed, then we can compact that subtree into a single leaf node at compile time. This amounts to doing partial elimination, before we condition, and storing an intermediate distribution, rather than all CPTs from the original network. Once again, this step has the potential to increase the space requirements of the conditioning tree. However, we can calculate the size of the leaf node without actually performing the computation. This allows us to decide beforehand whether such an absorption is acceptable given our current size restrictions.

Continuing with the example, suppose that the need to query the *Tampering* node is now eliminated, and assume that it is not observable. Hence, we can multiply all of its children (there's only one in this example), and marginalize out the tampering variable. Figure 8(c) shows the system after we perform this step. Note that we have reduced the depth of the tree, decreasing our complexity by a factor of m (2, in this case). As well, the *Fire* variable now has two leaf nodes, that can be compacted without increasing the space complexity. Figure 8(d) shows the final product, an extremely small, efficient version of the original problem. In fact, we have reduced it to a simple lookup, given the values of the evidence and query. Note that such a reduction is not always possible, but it can reduce considerable portions of the network given the right variable ordering.

6 Conclusions and Future Work

This paper presents conditioning graphs, a low-level representation of inference in Bayesian networks. Conditioning graphs allow for Bayesian computation without storing the original model, or a large inference algorithm. We demonstrate their construction and operation, generate complexity results for their operation, and elicit some optimizations to improve their performance.

The system described in this paper is a generalization of conditioning over an elimination tree. Our work is inspired by the work on recursive conditioning [3] and adaptive conditioning [11]. However, rather than storing the original model and a complex inference engine, the abstraction converts the network to a very simple structure that allows us to compute posterior probabilities using a very simple, very small algorithm. The space required for storage and inference (over and above the storage for the parameters of the Bayesian network) is linear in the size of the model.

This paper presents the preliminary stages of this research project. Orderings considered good for standard inference are not necessarily good for the conditioning graphs. For example, consider a Bayesian network that is a chain of n variables. Summing out the variables in the order of the chain represents an optimal ordering in standard inference, but it represents the worst-case time complexity for the conditioning graph. Finding an optimal variable ordering is NP-hard, and the research community resorts to heuristics in many cases. Perhaps the nature of the problem may suggest heuristics that are tailored towards shallow conditioning graphs.

In our model, many values may be recomputed several times. Darwiche has demonstrated in his dtrees how simple caching procedures can increase the time performance of the algorithms exponentially, if the space is available. The caching procedure is somewhat involved, so porting it directly to conditioning graphs is not obvious, but marks an available area of research.

References

1. G. F. Cooper. The computational complexity of probabilistic inference using Bayesian Inference. *Artificial Intelligence*, 42:393–405, 1990.
2. A. Darwiche. Any-space probabilistic inference. In *Proceedings of the Sixteenth Conference on Uncertainty and Artificial Intelligence*, pages 133–142, 2000.
3. A. Darwiche. Recursive Conditioning: Any-space conditioning algorithm with treewidth-bounded complexity. *Artificial Intelligence*, pages 5–41, 2000.
4. A. Darwiche and G. Provan. Query dags: A practical paradigm for implementing belief network inference. In *Proceedings of the 12th Annual Conference on Uncertainty in Artificial Intelligence (UAI-96)*, pages 203–210, San Francisco, CA, 1996. Morgan Kaufmann Publishers.
5. R. Dechter. Bucket elimination: A unifying framework for reasoning. *Artificial Intelligence*, 113(1-2):41–85, 1999.
6. K. Grant and M. Horsch. Conditioning Graphs: Practical Structures for Inference in Bayesian Networks. Technical Report 2005-04, Dept. of Computer Science, University of Saskatchewan, Saskatoon, SK, Canada, 2005.
7. S. Lauritzen and D. Spiegelhalter. Local computations with probabilities on graphical structures and their application to expert systems. *Journal of the Royal Statistical Society*, 50:157–224, 1988.
8. S. Monti and G. F. Cooper. Bounded recursive decomposition: a search-based method for belief-network inference under limited resources. *Int. J. Approx. Reasoning*, 15(1):49–75, 1996.
9. J. Pearl. *Probabilistic Reasoning in Intelligent Systems: Networks of Plausible Inference*. Morgan Kaufmann Publishers Inc., 1988.
10. D. Poole, A. Mackworth, and R. Goebel. *Computational Intelligence* . Oxford University Press, 1998.
11. F. Ramos, F. Cozman, and J. Ide. Embedded Bayesian Networks: Anyspace, Anytime Probabilistic Inference. In *AAAI/KDD/UAI Workshop in Real-time Decision Support and Diagnosis Systems*, 2002.
12. N. Zhang and D. Poole. A Simple Approach to Bayesian Network Computations. In *Proc. of the Tenth Canadian Conference on Artificial Intelligence*, pages 171–178, 1994.

Reasoning with the Outcomes of Plan Execution in Intentional Agents

Timothy William Cleaver, Abdul Sattar, and Kewen Wang

Institute for Integrated and Intelligent Systems (IIIS),
Griffith University,
PMB 50, GCMC 9726, Australia
Tim.Cleaver@student.griffith.edu.au,
{a.sattar, k.wang}@griffith.edu.au

Abstract. Intentional agents must be aware of their success and failure to truly assess their own progress towards their intended goals. However, our analysis of intentional agent systems indicate that existing architectures are inadequate in this regard. Specifically, existing systems provide few, if any, mechanisms for monitoring for the failure of behavior. This inability to detect failure means that agents retain an unrealistically optimistic view of the success of their behaviors and the state of their environment. In this paper we extend the solution proposed in [1] in three ways. Firstly, we extend the formulation to handle cases in which an agent has conflicting evidence regarding the causation of the effects of a plan or action. We do this by identifying a number of policies that an agent may use in order to alleviate these conflicts. Secondly, we provide mechanisms by which the agent can utilize its failure handling routines to recover when failure is detected. Lastly, we lift the requirement that all the effects be realized simultaneously and allow for progressive satisfaction of effects. Like the original solution these extensions can be applied to existing BDI systems.

Keywords: Agents; AI architectures; and Reasoning about Actions and Change.

1 Introduction

An agent is a program or process that can balance time critical reactive behavior with temporally extended goal directed conduct based on its incomplete and dynamic knowledge of the environment in which it is situated. Intentional agents are a sub-set of these programs that are modeled using the mental attitudes of belief, desire and intention. In order to execute purposeful behavior an intentional agent needs to reason about the success and failure of its past endeavors. In order to be reasoned with, instances of success and failure must be monitored for and detected within the environment. Observing the environment for indications of success and failure are interlinked. Signs of success imply the absence failure and those of failure the absence of success. However, the absence of failure does not imply success nor does the absence of success imply failure. Existing models of intentional behavior focus on the verification of success without regard to detecting failure. Consequently, these formalisms assume failure whenever success is unable to be verified. Given the non-equivalence between failure and the absence of success we believe that this assumption is invalid and that instances of failure must be detected independently.

Failure is manifest in two ways: failure to complete and failure to produce the desired outcomes. Intentional agents monitoring for failure must critic their own behavior with these sources of failure in mind. Auditing for failure to complete is less challenging than checking for instances where behaviors do not produce their intended effects. For instance, detecting the failure of an action to complete can be achieved using proprioception. Similarly, detecting the failure of a plan to complete can be reduced to detecting the failure of one of the sub-goals of the plan. Monitoring for the failure of a particular behavior to produce its desired outcomes is more complicated. The success or failure of an action or plan is not necessarily immediately apparent. There may be a temporal delay between the time at which the action is completed and the time at which its effects become observable. Additionally, the effect for which an action or plan was executed may itself not be directly observable, but, there may be aspects of the environment which are syntactically unrelated to the intended effect which when observed provide evidence for asserting that the action or plan has produced or will not produce the intended effect.

In this paper we take AgentSpeak(L) as the prototypical BDI-like system. We review the extensions to the semantics and syntax of AgentSpeak(L) proposed in [1]. Next we provide further extensions to these semantics to utilize the failure handling components of the architecture, to deal with conflicting evidence regarding the outcome of the execution of an action or plan and to facilitate the progressive satisfaction of effects. Following this we then compare this approach to how other existing BDI-like architectures handle success and failure in their reasoning cycles. We conclude this study with a brief discussion on the merits of our approach and further research issues.

2 AgentSpeak Extended to Reason with Success and Failure

In [1], a number of extensions where made to the AgentSpeak(L) language syntax and semantics. The syntax was modified so that each plan had a definition of the effects expected and required as a result of executing said plan:

Definition 1.

$$l \to te : ct \leftarrow h.es$$

where:

l : is a label for plan specified as a predicate [1]
te : is the trigger of the plan ("+!l", "-!l", "+?l", "-?l", "+l" or "-l" where l is a literal)
ct : is the context (represented as a set of literals and internal actions) that must be a consequence of the agents beliefs for the plan to be applicable for handling the trigger te
h : is a sequence of goals (achieve, test and action [both internal and external]) that must be executed in order to handle the trigger te
es : are a set of effects where each effect is defined according to Definition 2

---
[1] This is a syntactic addition made in [2].

However, rather than specifying these effects (es) as simply a set of literals that must become a consequence of the agents beliefs, each effect was specified as a compound entity.

Definition 2.

$$effect\_name : \langle\{succ\_cond_0, ..., succ\_cond_n\}, \{fail\_cond_0, ..., fail\_cond_m\}\rangle$$

where the name provided a means by which to refer to the effect as a whole, the success conditions ($succ\_cond_0, ..., succ\_cond_n$) were conditions on the belief base that indicated that the event ($effect\_name$) had successfully resulted from the plans execution and the failure conditions ($fail\_cond_0, ..., fail\_cond_n$) indicated, upon becoming a consequence of the agents beliefs, that the effect would not be realized as a result of plan execution.

The semantics were modified from those of [3] to include an additional data store in the agents circumstance, replacement of the rules for handling the case when a plan has finished executing and additional rules for the monitoring of the effects of the plan. More specifically the circumstance C of an agent was redefined as the following tuple:

$$\langle I, E, A, R, Ap, P_\iota, \iota, \rho, \varepsilon \rangle$$

where:

$I, E, A, R, Ap, \iota, \rho, \varepsilon$ retain their original definitions.
P_ι represents the intentions which have plans that have completed execution, for which the outcome of the effects of the plan are unknown.

The additional data store (P_ι) allowed an agent to keep the intended means once completed until the agent has evidence that either the effects have eventuated or are not going to.

The first rule proposed (Rule 1') replaced Rule 1 of [3]. When the selected intention was a single empty intended means then it was removed from the set of active intentions (C_I) and placed in the set of paused intentions (P_ι). Similarly, the second rule (Rule 2') replaced Rule 2. This rule moved the selected intention from the set of active intentions to the set of paused intentions whenever the selected intention was a stack with a depth of at least one and its top most plan had completed all its sub-goals.

Rule 1': New Clear empty intentions (empty plan)

$$\text{ClrInt}_1 \frac{}{\langle ag, C \rangle \to \langle ag, C' \rangle} \sharp C_\iota = [l \to head \leftarrow .es]$$

where:

$C'_\iota = \_$
$C'_I = C'_I - \{C_\iota\}$
$P'_\iota = P_\iota \cup \{C_\iota\}$

Rule 2': New Clear empty intentions (completed goal)

$$\text{ClrInt}_2 \frac{}{\langle ag, C \rangle \to \langle ag, C' \rangle} \sharp C_\iota = i' \left[l' \to head' \leftarrow at; h'.es' \right] [l \to head \leftarrow .es]$$

where:

$$C'_\iota = \_$$
$$C'_I = C_I - \{C_\iota\}$$
$$P'_\iota = P_\iota \cup \{i' \, [l' \to head' \leftarrow h'.es']\}$$

Whenever the selected intention (C_ι) had a depth of more than 1 ($i' \, [l' \to head' \leftarrow !at; h'.es'] \, [l \to head \leftarrow .es]$), this rule removed the completed plan from the top of C_ι, removed the goal (at), added the remaining intention ($i' \, [l' \to head' \leftarrow h'.es']$) to the set of paused intentions (P_ι) and removed C_ι from the set of active intentions.

Additional rules were then provided that allowed the agent to reason about the fulfillment of the effects of plans whose execution was complete. This was done using the following rule (Rule 3).

Rule 3: Processing Incomplete Intended Means

$$\text{ProcIncIM} \frac{\text{CompIMs}(P_\iota) \neq \{\}}{\langle ag, C \rangle \to \langle ag, C' \rangle} \sharp P_\iota \neq \{\}$$

where:

$$P'_\iota = P_\iota - \{\text{CompIMs}(P_\iota)\}$$
$$C'_I = C_I \cup \{\text{UpdInts}(\text{CompIMs}(P_\iota))\}$$

which was dependent on Definition 3[2], which filters P_ι and extracts those intended means that have no effects outstanding.

Definition 3.

$$\text{CompIMs}(bs, P_\iota) = \{p \, | \, p \in P_\iota \wedge \text{CompIM}(bs, p) = true\}$$

that, in turn, was dependent on Definition 4. Definition 4 stated that an intended means was complete when it had no outstanding effects remaining.

Definition 4.

$$\text{CompIM}(bs, [l \to te : ct \leftarrow h.effects]) = \begin{cases} true & \text{if } \begin{pmatrix} \forall x | x \in effects \\ x \in \text{FinEffect}(bs, effects) \end{pmatrix} \\ false & otherwise \end{cases}$$

In order to generate the set of finished effects (**FinEffect**()) the following definition was required:

Definition 5.

$$\text{FinEffect}(bs, efs) = \left\{ \langle \{succ\}, \{fail\} \rangle \,\middle|\, \begin{array}{l} \langle \{succ\}, \{fail\} \rangle \in efs \wedge \\ (\exists x.x \in succ \wedge bs \models x) \vee \\ (\exists y.y \in fail \wedge bs \models y) \end{array} \right\}$$

Definitions 3, 4 and 5 and Rule 3 allowed an agent to retain all its completed plans until it had an evidence that all of the effects of its plan have been realized in the environment. Further definitions (Definition 6) were required in order update the completed intended means and return the intention to the active set of intentions for further processing:

---

[2] In which bs is the set of literals that make up the agents beliefs.

Definition 6.

$$\mathbf{UpdInts}(I) = \{i' \mid i' \in I \wedge \mathbf{UpdInt}(i') \neq \emptyset\}$$

which relied on the following to define what it is to update a single intention:

Definition 7.

$$\mathbf{UpdInt}(i) = \begin{cases} i'\,[l' \to head' \leftarrow h'.effects'] & if\ i = \begin{matrix} i'\,[l' \to head' \leftarrow at;\, h'.effects'] \\ [l \to head \leftarrow .effects] \end{matrix} \\ [l' \to head' \leftarrow h'.effects'] & if\ i = \begin{matrix} [l' \to head' \leftarrow at;\, h'.effects'] \\ [l \to head \leftarrow .effects] \end{matrix} \\ \emptyset & otherwise \end{cases}$$

3 Updating Effects

As we have indicated, there are number of outstanding issues that the above extensions do not address. The primary cause of these inadequacies lies in the definition of the function that updates the effects of the intended means (**UpdateEffects()**). Firstly, in the existing formalism, this function only updates the effects component of the intended means returning this updated set. However, this precludes the function from returning whether the plan has failed in generating all the intended outcomes. To correct this we redefine **UpdateEffects()** to return a tuple containing the updated effect set and a Boolean variable indicating whether the plan is still valid. Secondly, the existing **UpdateEffects()** function has no way to deal with conflicting evidence for the success and failure of a particular effect. We have identified a number of different policies an agent may use to handle this conflict and present **UpdateEffects()** functions encapsulating each policy.

Firstly, we have a **pessimistic effect update** mechanism which causes a plan to fail upon any effect failure regardless of indications of success for the same effect.

Definition 8 (Pessimistic Effect Update).

$UpdateEffects(bs, es) =$
$$\begin{cases} \langle \top, \emptyset \rangle & if\ \forall \langle s, f \rangle . \langle s, f \rangle \in es \wedge \exists x.x \in s \wedge bs \models x \\ \langle \top, es' \rangle & if\ es' = es - \{\langle s, f \rangle \mid \langle s, f \rangle \in es \wedge \exists x.x \in s \wedge bs \models x \wedge \forall y.y \in f \wedge bs \not\models y\} \\ \langle \bot, es \rangle & if\ \exists \langle s, f \rangle . \langle s, f \rangle \in es \wedge \exists x.x \in f \wedge bs \models x \end{cases}$$

Secondly, we have an **optimistic effect update** that causes a plan to fail only if there is an effect for which there is indication of failure with no corresponding indication of success. In other words, an effect is said to have been realized provided there is evidence for it. Any indications of failure are ignored in the light of an indication of success.

Definition 9 (Optimistic Effect Update).

$UpdateEffects(bs, es) =$
$$\begin{cases} \langle \top, \emptyset \rangle & if\ \forall \langle s, f \rangle . \langle s, f \rangle \in es \wedge \exists x.x \in s \wedge bs \models x \\ \langle \top, es' \rangle & if\ es' = es - \{\langle s, f \rangle \mid \langle s, f \rangle \in es \wedge \exists x.x \in s \wedge bs \models x\} \\ \langle \bot, es \rangle & if\ \exists \langle s, f \rangle . \langle s, f \rangle \in es \wedge \exists x.x \in f \wedge bs \models x \wedge \forall y.y \in s \wedge bs \not\models y \end{cases}$$

Thirdly, we have **relative effect update** in which an effect is seen as successfully caused if it has strictly more indicators of success than there are failure; an effect is seen as failing to have been caused if it has strictly more indications of failure than there are of success; and is ignored if the number of indications of success and failure are equal.

Definition 10 (Relative Effect Update).

$UpdateEffects(bs, es) =$
$$\begin{cases} \langle \top, \emptyset \rangle & \text{if } \forall \langle s, f \rangle . \langle s, f \rangle \in es \land \exists x . x \in s \land bs \models x \\ \langle \top, es' \rangle & \text{if } es' = es - \{\langle s, f \rangle \mid \langle s, f \rangle \in es \land |\{x \mid x \in s \land bs \models x\}| > |\{y \mid y \in f \land bs \models y\}|\} \\ \langle \top, es \rangle & \text{if } \forall \langle s, f \rangle \in es \mid \{x \mid x \in s \land bs \models x\}| = |\{y \mid y \in f \land bs \models y\}| \\ \langle \bot, es' \rangle & \text{if } \exists \langle s, f \rangle . \langle s, f \rangle \in es \land |\{x \mid x \in s \land bs \models x\}| < |\{y \mid y \in f \land bs \models y\}| \end{cases}$$

Finally, given that the **relative effect update** can potentially leave an intention in the set of suspended intentions indefinitely, we propose the **pessimistic relative effect update** and the **optimistic relative effect update** to alleviate this problem. The **optimistic relative effect update** process considers the effect to have successfully been realized even if the evidence for success is equal to that for failure. The **pessimistic relative effect update** asserts failure given equal evidence for both success and failure.

Definition 11 (Pessimistic Relative Effect Update).

$UpdateEffects(bs, es) =$
$$\begin{cases} \langle \top, \emptyset \rangle & \text{if } \forall \langle s, f \rangle . \langle s, f \rangle \in es \land \exists x . x \in s \land bs \models x \\ \langle \top, es' \rangle & \text{if } es' = es - \{\langle s, f \rangle \mid \langle s, f \rangle \in es \land |\{x \mid x \in s \land bs \models x\}| > |\{y \mid y \in f \land bs \models y\}|\} \\ \langle \bot, es' \rangle & \text{if } \exists \langle s, f \rangle . \langle s, f \rangle \in es \land |\{x \mid x \in s \land bs \models x\}| <= |\{y \mid y \in f \land bs \models y\}| \end{cases}$$

Definition 12 (Optimistic Relative Effect Update).

$UpdateEffects(bs, es) =$
$$\begin{cases} \langle \top, \emptyset \rangle & \text{if } \forall \langle s, f \rangle . \langle s, f \rangle \in es \land \exists x . x \in s \land bs \models x \\ \langle \top, es' \rangle & \text{if } es' = es - \{\langle s, f \rangle \mid \langle s, f \rangle \in es \land |\{x \mid x \in s \land bs \models x\}| >= |\{y \mid y \in f \land bs \models y\}|\} \\ \langle \bot, es' \rangle & \text{if } \exists \langle s, f \rangle . \langle s, f \rangle \in es \land |\{x \mid x \in s \land bs \models x\}| < |\{y \mid y \in f \land bs \models y\}| \end{cases}$$

Given these new, more powerful versions of the **UpdateEffects()** we need to modify the rules that utilize this function in order to integrate with the agents failure handling facilities. We replace Rule 3 with Rule 3' which allows us to capture the case where the intended means has produced all its intended effects. This rule returns the intentions in P_ι to the active intentions (C_I) once all the effects that their top most plan can cause have been shown to have been successfully caused.

Rule 3': Processing Successful and Complete Intended Means

$$\textbf{ProcIncIM}_1 \frac{\textbf{UpdateEffects}(bs, es) = \langle \top, \emptyset \rangle}{\langle ag, C \rangle \rightarrow \langle ag, C' \rangle} \sharp i\,[l \rightarrow te : ct \leftarrow h.es] \in P_\iota$$

where:

$P'_\iota = P_\iota - \{i\,[l \rightarrow te : ct \leftarrow h.es]\}$
$C'_I = C_I \cup \{i\,[l \rightarrow te : ct \leftarrow h.es]\}$

However, should any effect fail to be caused by the execution of the plan then the plan has failed. In order to integrate with the failure handling process of the architecture we then add an event to the set of events indicating the failure of the plan to handle the event for which it was intended. The following rule accomplishes this by reversing the sign of the triggering event of the plan, generating an event from the reversed trigger and adding this to the set of events:

Rule 4: Processing Failed Intended Means

$$\text{ProcIncIM}_2 \frac{\text{UpdateEffects}(bs, es) = \langle \bot, es' \rangle}{\langle ag, C \rangle \rightarrow \langle ag, C' \rangle} \sharp i\, [l \rightarrow te : ct \leftarrow h.es] \in P_\iota$$

where:

$P'_\iota = P_\iota - \{i\, [l \rightarrow te : ct \leftarrow h.es]\}$

$$C'_E = \begin{cases} C_E \cup \{+t\} & \text{if } te = -t \text{ (where } l \text{ is a literal)} \\ C_E \cup \{-t\} & \text{if } te = +t \text{ (where } l \text{ is a literal)} \\ C_E \cup \{+!t\} & \text{if } te = -!t \text{ (where } l \text{ is a literal)} \\ C_E \cup \{-!t\} & \text{if } te = +!t \text{ (where } l \text{ is a literal)} \\ C_E \cup \{+?t\} & \text{if } te = -?t \text{ (where } l \text{ is a literal)} \\ C_E \cup \{-?t\} & \text{if } te = +?t \text{ (where } l \text{ is a literal)} \end{cases}$$

The above rules (3' & 4) allow us to reason about a plan successfully causing all of its listed effects and plans for which an effect failed to be realized. However, we are still required to handle the case where one or more effects have been realized successfully but not all have. We need a rule that allows us to update our representation of effects to reflect those that have been realized. The rule below is designed to facilitate this:

Rule 5: Processing Successful but Incomplete Intended Means

$$\text{ProcIncIM}_3 \frac{\text{UpdateEffects}(bs, es) = \langle \top, es' \rangle}{\langle ag, C \rangle \rightarrow \langle ag, C' \rangle} \sharp i\, [l \rightarrow te : ct \leftarrow h.es] \in P_\iota$$

where:

$P'_\iota = (P_\iota - \{i\, [l \rightarrow te : ct \leftarrow h.es]\}) \cup \{i\, [l \rightarrow te : tc \leftarrow h.es']\}$

Rules (3'-5) are applied iteratively to all of the intentions in the suspended intention set (P_ι). In this way the effects of all plans executed are monitored based on whether the effects for which they were executed are realized. By updating the outstanding effects remaining to succeed we allow a variable temporal delay between the completion of the executing plan and those effects for which it was executed. The choice of which particular effect update operator is the most appropriate is domain dependent. However, we consider the **pessimistic relative effect update** operator to be the most appealing given its complete yet conservative nature.

By adopting the above rules and incorporating them into the AgentSpeak(L) framework the architecture depicted in Figure 1 results. The primary additions[3] are the data store: "Incomplete Intended Means" and the one new process: "Update Effects"

---

[3] Highlighted here in black.

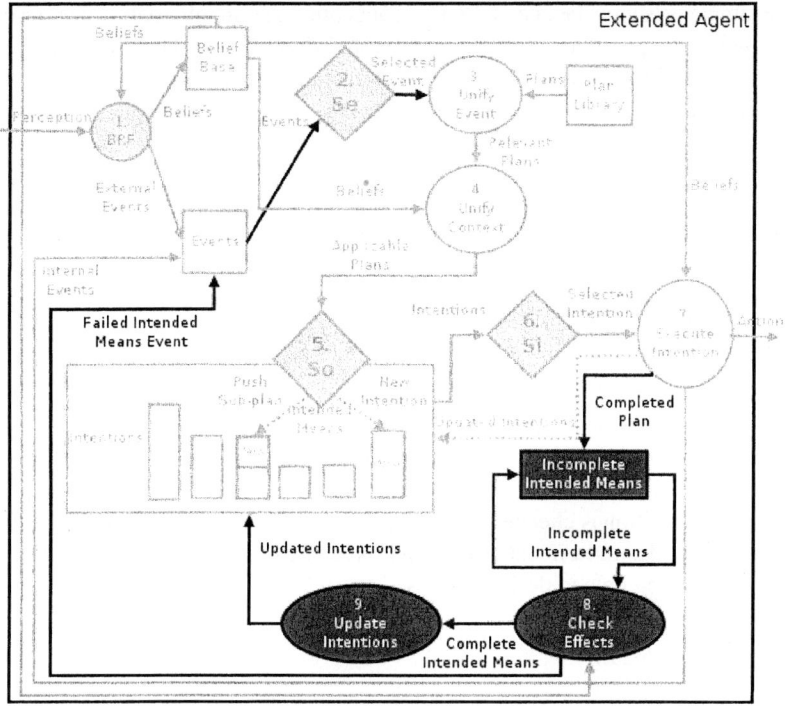

Fig. 1. Extended Architecture

(process 8). Process 8 represents the application of rules (3'-5) to all intentions in the suspended intention set (P_ι). The new architecture now supports the requirements of success and failure outlined in the introduction. As a result we claim that the new architecture allows an agent to reason more completely with success and failure which in turn means that the agent retains a more detailed and accurate view of its progress towards its intended goals.

4 Related Work

C-PRS[4, 5] represents the first implementation of the PRS architecture (the first intentional (BDI-like) architecture). Plans are represented as graphs with the labels of each arc indicating the sub-goal to be achieved for the arc to be successfully traversed. Failure is detected when a primitive action fails to execute successfully, or any sub-goals of a plan are unsuccessful. The system does not detect whether a plan or action has actually achieved the effect for which it was executed, this is simply assumed.

UM-PRS[6] is a C++ implementation of PRS completed at the University of Michigan. The unique aspect of this implementation lies in the application to which it was put: Robot Vehicle Control. However, the methods by which failure is detected remains equivalent to those used in C-PRS [4, 5].

The above systems lacked a strong conceptualization of goals, plan priorities/ utilities and some procedural constructs (parallel execution). These were the primary issues that JAM[7] aimed to address. However, failure detection, as in UM-PRS, remained unchanged from the original specification.

Like UM-PRS, dMARS[8, 9] is a re-implementation of PRS using C++. However, unlike the above systems, it utilizes a more powerful procedure for the detection of failure. Plans are extended to have maintenance/in-conditions. Maintenance conditions are expressed as formula ranging over the beliefs of the agent with operators for disjunction, conjunction, true and false. If this formula becomes false at any time during the execution of the plan then the plan has failed. Again, this mechanism facilitates the detection of whether a plan completes but does not allow an agent to monitor whether the intended effects were realized.

JACK[10, 11] is a Java implementation derived from the dMARS architecture. In addition to the extensions made in the dMARS system, JACK extends the representation of plans to include a post-condition. Like the in-condition of dMARS, the post-condition is represented as a set of formula ranging over the beliefs of the agent. However, the post-condition is checked only once the plan has been completed in an attempt to guarantee that desired effects of the plan have been realized. Failure is assumed in the absence of being able to detect success.

5 Conclusion

In order for an agent to maintain a synchronicity between its behaviour and the environment it needs methods by which it can assess the performance of its past endeavours. This synchronicity is necessary lest the agent act in a way that is independent of the environment in which it is embedded. Traditionally, BDI systems have lacked such monitoring facilities. More specifically, the solution to this issue proposed in [1] is limited in a number of fundamental ways. Firstly, an agent was unable to reason with conflicting evidence about the causation of the effects of a plan or action. Secondly, upon the detection of the failure of a plan to cause its intended effects the agent was provided with no mechanism by which to recover. Lastly, all the effects of a plan or action were required to be sensed and recognised simultaneously. This precluded the progressive satisfaction of effects. Consequently, we extended the approach proposed in [1] in a number of ways so as to remedy these limitations. The existing semantic rules for processing completed intended means were reformulated. Rules to handle intended means that had failed to cause their listed effects were added. Rules to update the outstanding effects in cases in which only a sub-set of the effects have been realized were introduced. The **UpdateEffects()** function was generalized so as to embed a number of policies for resolving conflicting evidence for the satisfaction and failure of an effect. As a result, an agent implementing these semantics is able to handle conflicting evidence, recognize the progressive satisfaction of the effects of plans and actions, and utilize its failure recovery mechanisms upon detecting the failure of plans or actions to cause their intended effects.

However a number of issues remain. Firstly, given the current plan adoption policy utilized by this class of agents, it is impossible to determine which particular effects are relevant for the given goal. We require that a plan cause all of its listed effects successfully for the plan to be considered successful. This is unrealistic in that only the effect for which the plan was executed is of relevance. This issue will be the primary focus of our future research. Secondly, the approach proposed seems to be computationally expensive. Our future work will also involve an investigation to gain a better understanding of the cost of this approach. Outstanding issues aside, we believe that this paper provides an initial insight into an area that has been ignored within intentional agents and agents in general for too long.

Acknowledgments

We would like to hereby thank the Smart Internet Cooperative Research Centre (SIT-CRC) for their funding of this work. We would also like to express our thanks for the feedback of Wayne Wobcke and Vineet Nair.

References

[1] Cleaver, T., Sattar, A., Wang, K.: Reasoning about success and failure in intentional agents. In: Proceedings of the 2005 Pacific Rim International Workshop on Multi-Agents. (2005)
[2] Bordini, R., Bazzan, A., Jannone, R., Basso, D., Vicari, R., Lesser, V.: Agentspeak(XL): Efficient Intention Selection in BDI Agents via Decision-Theoretic Task Scheduling. In: Proceedings of the first International Joint Conference on Autonomous Agents and Multi-Agent Systems. (2002) 1294–1302
[3] Bordini, R., Moreira, A.: Proving BDI properties of agent-oriented programming languages: The asymmetry thesis principles in agentspeak(l). Annals of Mathematics and Artificial Intelligence **42** (2004) 197–226
[4] Georgeff, M., Ingrand, F.: Decision-making in an Embedded Reasoning System. In: Proceedings of the eleventh International Joint Conference on Artificial Intelligence. (1989) 972–978
[5] Ingrand, F., Chatila, R., Alami, R., Robert, F.: PRS: A High Level Supervision and Control Language for Autonomous Mobile Robots. In: Proceedings of the IEEE International Conference on Robotics and Automation. (1996)
[6] Lee, J., Huber, M., Kenny, P., Durfee, E.: UM-PRS: An Implementation of the Procedural Reasoning System for Multi-robot Applications. In: Proceedings of the AIAA/NASA Conference on Intelligent Robots in Field, Factory, Service, and Space. (1994) 842–849
[7] Huber, M.: JAM: A BDI-Theoretic Mobile Agent Architecture. In: Proceedings of the third International Conference on Autonomous Agents. (1999) 236–243
[8] d'Inverno, M., Kinny, D., Luck, M., Wooldridge, M.: A Formal Specification of dMARS. Agent Theories, Architectures and Languages (1997) 115–176
[9] d'Inverno, M., Luck, M., Georgeff, M., Kinny, D., Wooldridge, M.: The dMARS Architecture: A Specification of the Distributed Multi-Agent Reasoning System. Autonomous Agents and Multi-Agent Systems **9** (2004) 5–53
[10] Busetta, P., Rönnquist, R., Hodgson, A., Lucas, A.: Jack Intelligent Agents - Components for Intelligent Agents in Java. AgentLink News Letter (1999)
[11] Howden, N., Rönnquist, R., Hodgson, A., Lucas, A.: Jack Intelligent Agents - Summary of an Agent Infrastructure. In: Proceedings of the fifth International Conference on Autonomous Agents. (2001)

Tie Breaking in Clause Weighting Local Search for SAT

Valnir Ferreira Jr. and John Thornton

Institute for Integrated and Intelligent Systems,
Griffith University, PMB50 Gold Coast Mail Centre, QLD 9726
{v.ferreira, j.thornton}@griffith.edu.au

Abstract. Clause weighting local search methods are widely used for satisfiability testing. A feature of particular importance for such methods is the scheme used to maintain the clause weight distribution relevant to different areas of the search landscape. Existing methods periodically adjust clause weights either multiplicatively or additively. Tie breaking strategies are used whenever a method's evaluation function encounters more than one optimal candidate flip, with the dominant approach being to break such ties randomly. Although this is acceptable for multiplicative methods as they rarely encounter such situations, additive methods encounter significantly more tie breaking scenarios in their landscapes, and therefore a more refined tie breaking strategy is of much greater relevance. This paper proposes a new way of handling the tie breaking situations frequently encountered in the landscapes of additive constraint weighting local search methods. We demonstrate through an empirical study that when this idea is used to modify the purely random tie breaking strategy of a state-of-the-art solver, the modified method significantly outperforms the existing one on a range of benchmarks, especially when we consider the encodings of large and structured problems.

1 Introduction

Local search methods are of considerable interest to the AI community due to their ability to efficiently find solutions to combinatorial problems that are beyond the reach of complete search methods. The satisfiability (SAT) problem is of significant practical and theoretical interest as many application domains can be formulated in this way. The SAT problem consists of finding an assignment for the Boolean variables in a propositional formula that makes the formula true. Typically, local search methods for SAT work by iteratively changing (flipping) the value of one Boolean variable in the problem in order to minimise an evaluation function that maps any given variable assignment to the number of unsatisfied clauses under this assignment. This heuristic is followed until a satisfying assignment is found (all clauses are satisfied) or until either a maximum run-time or number of flips is reached.

Clause weighting local search methods (CWLS) modify a basic local search by having individual weights assigned to all clauses in the problem, thus dynamically changing the evaluation function and the search landscape as the search progresses. As a consequence, successful CWLS methods need efficient ways to adjust clause weights, so they can maintain the clause weight distribution relevant to the context in which they are searching. To this end, most methods can be divided into those that adjust weights multiplicatively, and those that do so additively. Multiplicative methods use floating point clause weights and increase/decrease multipliers that give the clause weight distribution a much finer granularity. Additive methods, on the other hand, assign integer values to clause weights and increase/decrease amounts, resulting in a coarser weight distribution.

Since their introduction [1,2], several improvements have been proposed to CWLS methods, such as DLM [3] and SAPS [4]. While DLM uses additive weighting, SAPS adjusts clause weights multiplicatively. Recently, the pure additive weighting scheme (PAWS) was introduced [5] and shown to give significant performance improvements over SAPS on a range of challenging SAT problems from the SATLIB[1] and DIMACS[2] libraries, as well as on a set of SAT-encoded random binary CSPs from the phase transition region.

2 Tie Breaking and Search Landscapes

Consider a search landscape L for an instance π, $L(\pi) := (S, N, g)$, where S is the space of all candidate solutions, N is a given neighbourhood relation, and g is an evaluation function. Now consider the following definitions of landscape position taken from [6]. For a position $s \in S$ the following functions determine the number of upwards, sideways, and downwards flips from s to its direct neighbours[3], respectively: $upw := \#\{s' \in N(s) \mid g(s') > g(s)\}$, $sidew := \#\{s' \in N(s) \mid g(s') = g(s)\}$, and $down := \#\{s' \in N(s) \mid g(s') < g(s)\}$; and the following landscape positions of interest: $SLMIN(s) :\Leftrightarrow downw(s) = sidew(s) = 0$, and $LMIN(s) :\Leftrightarrow downw(s) = 0 \wedge sidew(s) > 0 \wedge upw(s) > 0$.

It is well known that multiplicative methods encounter negligible numbers of tie breaking situations in their search landscapes [7,5] due to the finer granularity of their clause weight distributions. Furthermore, by not taking equal-cost flips, multiplicative methods make no distinction between strict local minima ($SLMIN$) and local minima ($LMIN$), treating such positions as generic local minima. Specifically, SAPS randomly breaks ties amongst cost-improving flips, but if the candidate flips are either cost-increasing, or equal-cost, then it performs a random walk step with 1% probability by randomly selecting a variable for flipping from the domain of all variables in the problem.

In contrast, additive methods such as DLM and PAWS tend to encounter significantly more $LMIN$ positions in their landscapes, and hence having an efficient mechanism to deal with such positions appears to be of crucial importance for their performance. Additionally, they distinguish between $SLMIN$ and $LMIN$,

---

[1] http://www.satlib.org
[2] http://dimacs.rutgers.edu/Challenges/Seventh/PC
[3] A neighbour s' of s is a position that differs from s on at most one variable assignment.

and execute an equal-cost flip strategy whenever the latter is encountered. Like SAPS, PAWS also randomly breaks ties amongst cost-improving and equal-cost flips, but in the equal-cost case it will take such a flip with 15% probability, otherwise it will adjust the clause weights[4]. It never takes a cost-increasing flip.

This work's main motivation is to investigate an alternative way for breaking the ties frequently encountered in the landscapes of additive CWLS methods. After observing that a vast proportion of flips are randomly selected from a list of tied candidates, we hypothesise that the performance of these methods can be significantly enhanced by replacing the purely random tie breaking mechanism with one that also incorporates a heuristic that considers information about the landscape being searched. This paper reports on the implementation of this idea on a state-of-the-art additive CWLS method. We will demonstrate that our resulting method is able to significantly outperform the original one on a range of benchmark SAT problems.

3 Random Versus Heuristic Tie Breaking

Figure 1 shows the PAWS method extended to accommodate heuristic tie breaking (HTB). Of interest here are its two parameters: P_{flat} (line 17) and WDP (line 25). The former controls the probability with which PAWS takes an equal-cost flip, while the latter determines the number of weight increases (line 24) allowed before a weight decrease takes place (lines 25-26). In practice only WDP has its value set on a problem-per-problem basis, whereas a P_{flat} setting of 0.15 was found to generally work well for all problems [5]. PAWS is suitable as a host method as it achieves state-of-the-art performance for satisfiable SAT instances, and because it represents the purest implementation of an additive CWLS method. As a result, the insights gained from this study are sufficiently general and thus can be of practical relevance for the design of new methods.

In a preliminary study only partially reported here, we developed twenty alternatives to PAWS's purely random strategy for breaking ties of *equal-cost* candidate flips (Figure 1 lines 17-22). We chose to initially only deal with equal-cost flips for two reasons. Firstly, recent methods' reliance on purely random tie breaking mechanisms to achieve current levels of performance has meant that little attention has been given to the investigation of novel heuristic-based alternatives for dealing with equal-cost flips. Secondly, as the setting of P_{flat} regulates the frequency of equal-cost flips, we were able to place an upper bound on the usage of candidate heuristics without having to introduce and tune a new parameter.

We implemented each alternative tie breaking heuristic and tested the resulting method using a diverse problem set. The experimental conditions were identical to those reported later in the main part of this study. Control data was obtained by running the unmodified PAWS under the same conditions.

---

[4] Both SAPS's random walk and PAWS's equal-cost probabilities are parameters in the corresponding algorithms, but are in practice set to 0.01 and 0.15, respectively.

```
PAWS+HTB procedure
1.  begin
2.      generate random starting point
3.      for each clause c_i do set clause weight w_i ← 1
4.      while solution not found and not terminated do
5.          best ← ∞
6.          for each literal x_ij in each false clause f_i do
7.              Δw ← change Σw in f_i caused by flipping x_ij
8.              if Δw < best then L ← x_ij and best ← Δw
9.              else if Δw = best then L = L ∪ x_ij
10.         end for
11.         if best < 0 then
12.             if HTB and probability ≤ 1-P_flat then
13.                 call BOCM procedure
14.             else
15.                 randomly flip x_ij ∈ L
16.             end if
17.         else if best = 0 and probability ≤ P_flat
18.             if HTB then
19.                 call TB procedure
20.             else
21.                 randomly flip x_ij ∈ L
22.             end if
23.         else
24.             for each false clause f_i do w_i ← w_i + 1
25.             if # times clause weights increased % WDP = 0 then
26.                 for each clause c_i | w_i > 1 do w_i ← w_i - 1
27.             end if
28.         end if
29.     end while
30. end
```

Fig. 1. The pure additive weighting scheme extended to accommodate heuristic tie breaking for equal-cost and cost-improving flips. This pseudo-code corresponds to the HTB method used in our empirical study.

In order to estimate the performance variation arising from the introduction of each candidate heuristic, we computed the average median run-time for PAWS and each of the variants across all problems. A measure of variation in performance was then calculated as a percentage of PAWS's performance, and a ranking of candidate heuristics was obtained based on this measure. Scores for the best, median, and worst performing heuristics were 86.25%, 94.87%, and 110.18%, respectively. The main idea behind our best performing heuristic, TB (Figure 2(a)), lies on biasing the selection towards those candidates appearing in clauses that have been most rarely weighted during the search. For example, consider the CNF formula: $(a \vee \neg b \vee c) \wedge (\neg a \vee \neg b \vee c) \wedge (a \vee b \vee c) \wedge (a \vee \neg b \vee \neg c)$, the corresponding clause weight $C_w = \{3,3,3,4\}$, and number of weight updates distributions $C_{wu} = \{10, 20, 10, 10\}$; and a complete candidate solution $S = \{a := false, b := true, c := false\}$.

In this example, only the first clause is falsified, so when selecting a literal to flip, PAWS calculates Δw for each literal appearing in it (Figure 1 line 7): $\Delta w = \{a := 0, \neg b := 0, c := 1\}$. At this point, PAWS would then randomly

```
TB procedure
1.  begin
2.    best ← ∞
3.    for each x_ij ∈ L
4.      for each true clause c_i in which x_ij appears
5.        thisValue += #WeightUpdates_ci
6.      end for
7.      if thisValue < best then
8.        L' ← x_ij and best ← thisValue
9.      else if thisValue = best then
10.       L' = L' ∪ x_ij
11.     end if
12.   end for
13.   if # candidate literals in L' > 1 then call BOCM
14.   else return x_ij ∈ L'
15. end
```
(a) TB

```
BOCM procedure
1.  begin
2.    best ← 0
3.    for each literal x_ij in L' do
4.      if clauseMake_ij > best then
5.        L" ← x_ij and best ← clauseMake_ij
6.      else if clauseMake_ij = best then
7.        L" = L" ∪ x_ij
8.      end if
9.    end for
10.   randomly flip x_ij ∈ L"
11. end
```
(b) BOCM

Fig. 2. TB and BOCM

break the tie amongst the two best candidates a and $\neg b$ with 15% probability, given this is an equal cost flip.

However, if TB is used, then the tie breaking is biased towards the selection of those flips that appear in clauses that are (a) currently satisfied, and (b) have had their weight updated the least number of times during the search. Continuing with our example, the tie-breaker value for the two tied candidates is calculated (Figure 2(a) lines 4-6), resulting in the tie being broken in favour of a, as its tie-breaker value (20) is smaller than that of the other candidate (30). Although space limitations preclude us from discussing the other candidate heuristics in detail, we note that in some of the less successful variants the bias favoured the candidate flips with the *highest* tie breaking value. We also tested versions that took into account both satisfied and *unsatisfied* clauses in their tie breaking computation. If after using TB there was still a tie between a and $\neg b$, then BOCM (the procedure shown in Figure 2(b) for breaking ties on *clauseMake*[5]) would have been used and the tie would have been broken in favour of the candidate that, if flipped, would satisfy the greater number of clauses. Any remaining ties would be broken at random.

For all heuristics tested, we observed that the number of flips resulting from heuristic tie breaking amounted to an average of approximately 3% of all search flips. This corresponds to a reduction of the same magnitude in the number of random flips performed by the host method. Therefore, the most striking finding of this preliminary study was that the reduction in the number of random flips resulted in a relatively larger improvement in overall performance when we consider our best performing heuristics.

Hence, we investigated the effects of allowing the *heuristic-to-random* flip ratio to increase by extending heuristic tie breaking to cost-increasing flips. In

---

[5] *clauseMake* refers to a data structure introduced in the Walksat framework [8] and now commonly used in CWLS methods that counts how many clauses would be made true for any given variable flip.

an initial attempt to implement this, the TB heuristic was used to break ties of cost-improving flips as well, with probability 1-P_{flat}. However, the improvement in performance in terms of number of flips as observed for several problems compared poorly against the decrease in run-time performance brought about by the additional computational overheads. In other words, obtaining a further decrease in randomness in this fashion proved to be too expensive.

In an alternative implementation, BOCM was used in place of TB for cost-improving flips (maintaining the 1-P_{flat} setting), while continuing to use TB for breaking ties of equal-cost flips. TB remained the chosen heuristic for equal-cost flips because when we tested BOCM as a standalone heuristic for this purpose, its performance was inferior to the performance obtained while using TB. Finally, as we observed that TB's usage of BOCM was almost negligible at 0.02%, we decided to switch TB's BOCM off in our resulting method.

As a result, we obtained a competitive method with which to test our hypothesis that an increase in the heuristic-to-random flip ratio can result in significant performance improvements for additive CWLS methods. We call this resulting method PAWS with heuristic tie breaking, or HTB, and use the empirical study reported next to compare its performance against the unmodified PAWS.

4 Empirical Study

4.1 Problem Set and Parameter Setting

Our diverse test set draws problems from four different domains: uniform random 3-SAT, SAT-encoded graph colouring, parity learning, and planning. The -med and -hard instances from the original SATLIB sets flat100, flat200, uf100 and uf250 correspond to the median and hardest instances from these sets as found in a previous study [5] . From DIMACS we use the two most difficult graph colouring problems (g125.17 and g250.29) and the median and hardest 16-bit parity learning problems (par16-2-c and par16-3-c). For the random 3-SAT problems, 3 sets of problems (400, 800 and 1600 variable sets) were generated from the 4.3 clause-to-variable ratio hard region. To these sets, the f400, f800, and f1600 problems from DIMACS were added and determined the median and hardest instances, resulting in the 6 random 3-SAT problems (f400, f800 and f1600 -med and -hard). A range of random binary CSPs (also from the accepted hard region) were generated and transformed into SAT instances using the multi-valued encoding procedure described in [9]. These problems were divided into 4 sets of 5 problems each according to the number of variables (v) the domain size (d) and the constraint density (c) from the originating CSP, which resulted in the 30v10d40c, 30v10d80v, 50v15d40c, and 50v15d80c problem sets from which the hardest problem in each set was chosen. We obtained three sets of balanced quasigroup with holes (BQWH) problems with orders 30, 33, and 36, sampled from the backbone phase transition region ($number\,of\,holes/N^{1.55} = 1.7$) suggested in [10], and using the encoding method proposed in [11][6]. We then selected the

---

[6] The authors would like to thank Duc Nghia Pham for generating these instances.

easy, median, and hard instances used in this study according to the number of flips (averaged from 20 runs) taken by PAWS to find a solution.

PAWS and HTB only require the WDP parameter to be set in practice, as P_{flat} can be treated as a constant and for all experiments reported here was set to the suggested 0.15. The PAWS WDP settings were taken from [12], except the settings for the BQWH problems, found according to the same thorough empirical evaluation used for finding the optimal HTB WDP settings for each problem.

4.2 Testing for Significance

Local search run-times on the same problem can vary greatly due to different starting points and subsequent randomised decisions. For this reason, empirical studies have traditionally reported statistics like mean, median and standard deviation obtained from many runs on the same problem to ascertain one algorithm's superiority over another. As the standard deviation is only informative for normally distributed data, and local search run-time and run-length distributions are usually not normally distributed, the non-parametric Wilcoxon rank-sum test can be used to measure the confidence level of these assertions. The test requires that the run-times or number of flips from two sets of observations A and B be sorted in ascending order, and that observations be ranked from 1 to n. Then, the sum of the ranks for distribution A is calculated and its value used to obtain, using the normal approximation to the Wilcoxon distribution, the z value giving the probability P that the null hypothesis $H_0 : A \geq B$ is true.

The Wilcoxon values presented below the mean time and number of flips for each problem in Tables 1 and 2 give the probability P that the null hypothesis $A \geq B$ is true, where A is the distribution of the run-times (or number of flips) that has the smaller rank-sum value. We record the P value against distribution A, and take $P < 0.05$ to indicate with an asterisk that A is *significantly* less than B. Significant performance difference is granted if the Wilcoxon test on run-times *and* number of flips is significant for $P < 0.05$. Using run-time and flips in combination allows us to capture any significant performance degradation in run-time arising from the introduction of the heuristic tie breaking that would otherwise be missed if we only used the Wilcoxon test on the distribution of flips.

5 Results and Analysis

All statistics were obtained from 1,000 runs (100 runs for the bqwh-33-384-hard and bqwh-36-440-med and -hard) with a 20 million flip cut-off (50 million for 50v15d40c, and 250 million for all BQWH problems). We used a Sun supercomputer with 8 Sun Fire V880 servers, each with 8 UltraSPARC-III 900 MHz CPU and 8 GB memory per node.

An initial inspection of Tables 1 and 2 reveals two interesting results. Firstly, HTB was significantly better on sixteen problems, whereas PAWS gave significantly better performance on five. Secondly, all five problems where PAWS was

Table 1. Random instances

	HTB					PAWS				
	WDP	% Solved	Mean Time (secs)	Flips	Random Flips %	WDP	% Solved	Mean Time (secs)	Flips	Random Flips %
Random 3-SAT										
uf100-hard	20	100.0	0.01	2,838	24.48%	15	100.0	0.01 (0.1339)	2,795 (0.2925)	51.01%
uf250-med	18	100.0	0.03	6,940	33.14%	15	100.0	0.02 (*0.0054)	5,604 (0.0029)	64.31%
uf250-hard	27	100.0	0.93 (*0.0000)	234,333 (*0.0000)	33.71%	18	100.0	1.26	319,366	64.67%
f400-med	17	100.0	0.16	38,007	36.36%	9	100.0	0.14 (*0.0447)	36,359 (0.2993)	61.62%
f400-hard	19	100.0	4.98 (*0.0084)	1,112,995 (*0.0024)	41.96%	11	100.0	5.95	1,363,548	71.35%
f800-med	15	100.0	0.90	180,202	47.30%	9	100.0	0.62 (*0.0000)	125,647 (*0.0000)	74.31%
f800-hard	17	100.0	8.27	1,801,078	40.38%	10	100.0	4.99 (*0.0000)	1,089,711 (*0.0000)	68.59%
f1600-med	18	100.0	4.56	859,664	45.37%	10	100.0	2.28 (*0.0000)	461,533 (*0.0000)	69.07%
f1600-hard	17	97.8	18.61 (*0.0000)	3,795,765 (*0.0000)	42.79%	11	98.1	29.59	4,752,810	79.20%
Random Binary CSPs										
30v10d80c	12	100.0	0.10	11,808	39.14%	7	100.0	0.08 (*0.0010)	10,323 (*0.0076)	59.94%
30v10d40c	9	100.0	0.19 (0.3219)	23,913 (0.3671)	39.54%	5	100.0	0.19	24,130	64.11%
50v15d80c	9	100.0	2.88	195,496	43.93%	7	100.0	2.24 (*0.0000)	155,804 (*0.0000)	64.61%
50v15d40c	8	98.6	178.36 (*0.0000)	11,406,521 (*0.0000)	46.82%	6	95.4	216.33	13,556,479	72.73%

superior are randomly generated instances shown in Table 1. Should our analysis be restricted to the arguably more relevant domain of structured encodings shown in Table 2, then HTB is significantly better in twelve problems, whereas PAWS fails to give significant performance improvements over HTB on any of the twenty-six structured problems. Our results also show the number of random flips as a percentage of the total number of flips, performed by each method on each problem. HTB used approximately 18% less random flips, on average, across the whole problem set.

These observations indicate that the reduction in the number of random flips introduced by HTB may not be as useful for random problems, i.e., randomly generated search landscapes may be more efficiently searched by a method that utilises proportionally more random flips. However, the significant performance improvement afforded by the heuristic tie breaking method on the two largest random problems, 50v15d40c and f1600-hard, suggests that in addition to problem structure, problem size also plays a significant part in determining the usefulness of heuristic tie breaking for additive CWLS methods.

For all but three problems in our test set, heuristic tie breaking resulted in an increase in the optimal setting of WDP. Therefore, the additional computational overhead caused by the introduction of heuristic tie breaking is compensated by the less frequent clause weight updates. Whether these higher settings are indicative of a desirable increase in the robustness of the WDP settings is not yet clear to us, and is therefore an issue that requires further investigation.

When comparing performance, it is also relevant to show that one method can frequently give higher solution probabilities than the other. Such probabilistic domination can be ascertained by visually inspecting a plot of the runtime distribution (RTD) data for the different methods on any given problem.

Table 2. Structured instances

	HTB					PAWS			
	WDP	% Solved	Mean Time (secs)	Flips	Random Flips	WDP	% Solved	Mean Time (secs)	Flips	Random Flips %
Blocks World										
bw_large.a	35	100.0	0.02	3,133	29.66%	34	100.0	0.02 (0.3835)	3,066 (0.2809)	52.64%
bw_large.b	60	100.0	0.31 (0.4179)	43,163	29.10%	50	100.0	0.30	41,985 (0.4336)	56.16%
bw_large.c	6	100.0	7.71 (*0.0000)	898,743 (*0.0000)	49.82%	5	100.0	10.06	1,211,756	66.00%
bw_large.d	5	100.0	13.88 (*0.0001)	1,270,084 (*0.0014)	56.76%	4	100.0	16.90	1,501,005	72.47%
AIS, Logistics, Par										
ais10	70	100.0	0.12 (*0.0195)	17,595 (*0.0319)	25.64%	52	100.0	0.15	20,211	41.25%
ais12	80	100.0	1.08 (0.1204)	123,640 (*0.0060)	28.14%	148	100.0	1.12	137,461	36.11%
logistics.c	∞	100.0	0.04 (*0.0001)	6,375 (*0.0042)	32.47%	∞	100.0	0.05	6,676	51.22%
logistics.d	∞	100.0	0.26 (*0.0148)	20,263 (*0.0001)	40.43%	∞	100.0	0.27	21,531	60.54%
par16-2-c	39	98.9	15.95 (*0.0003)	4,051,732 (*0.0000)	66.74%	36	98.5	18.13	4,845,096	76.40%
par16-3-c	39	99.4	15.26	3,879,903	66.29%	40	98.9	14.10 (0.1112)	3,711,505 (0.2967)	77.26%
Graph Colouring										
flat100-med	20	100.0	0.02 (*0.0000)	7,699 (*0.0000)	45.51%	16	100.0	0.03	9,462	69.91%
flat100-hard	35	100.0	0.10	33,940 (0.3395)	47.34%	46	100.0	0.10 (0.3807)	34,822	63.08%
flat200-med	16	100.0	0.46 (*0.0016)	134,334 (*0.0000)	56.66%	9	100.0	0.57	183,618	74.82%
flat200-hard	78	100.0	10.80	3,270,296 (0.3608)	47.94%	74	99.8	10.52 (0.4595)	3,261,605	66.15%
g125.17	10	100.0	12.87 (0.1190)	674,462 (*0.0008)	54.92%	4	100.0	12.78	737,912	66.36%
g250.29	11	100.0	33.17	324,516 (*0.0056)	62.29%	4	100.0	30.23 (*0.0046)	353,746	70.98%
QWH										
bqwh-30-332-easy	4	100.0	1.69 (*0.0207)	292,089 (*0.0027)	59.10%	3	100.0	1.92	347,602	67.75%
bqwh-30-332-med	5	100.0	15.18 (0.2773)	2,317,550 (0.1618)	66.02%	4	100.0	16.08	2,509,285	74.09%
bqwh-30-332-hard	5	100.0	118.06 (0.1442)	17,301,209 (*0.0485)	67.46%	4	100.0	122.50	18,534,584	74.86%
bqwh-33-384-easy	5	100.0	23.62 (0.1262)	3,672,471 (*0.0399)	64.97%	4	100.0	24.72	3,970,927	73.05%
bqwh-33-384-med	4	100.0	55.66 (*0.0000)	10,199,421 (*0.0001)	58.00%	4	100.0	83.14	11,719,052	75.67%
bqwh-33-384-hard	5	98.0	301.25 (*0.0494)	39,903,182 (*0.0366)	69.81%	4	98.0	371.90	50,428,307	76.75%
bqwh-36-440-easy	4	100.0	41.73 (*0.0000)	6,857,439 (*0.0000)	61.91%	3	99.8	54.13	9,566,874	69.56%
bqwh-36-440-med	4	100.0	286.585 (0.1925)	45,866,880 (0.0929)	63.24%	3	100.0	339.58	59,211,063	72.12%
bqwh-36-440-hard	4	80.0	560.55 (0.1464)	91,481,218 (*0.0065)	62.01%	3	66.0	608.76	105,869,465	70.18%

If these RTDs do not cross then the method whose RTD appears to the left of the other probabilistically dominates for *all* solution probabilities [6]. In practice, we normally relax this definition to allow for some crossing for low solution probabilities, i.e., $P \leq 0.1$. The RTD in Figure 3 (left) is an example of probabilistic domination for all probabilities $P > 0.05$.

Run-time and run-length distribution (RLD) plots are also useful for detecting erratic run-time behaviour. For example, the RTD in Figure 3 (right) reveals that although HTB dominates PAWS for all $0.05 \leq P < 0.95$, the crossing of the distributions at $P = 0.95$ indicates that PAWS was faster on the 3 longest runs sampled. This could be a symptom of search stagnation on HTB's behalf. Stagnation invariably arises from poor search diversification. As additive methods rely on the strong use of random flips to diversify their search [13], any changes

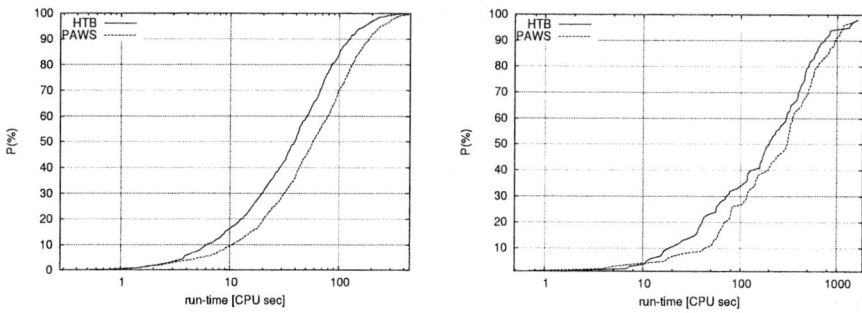

Fig. 3. Run-time behaviour analysis of HTB and PAWS using the RTDs for problems bqwh-33-384-med (left) and -hard (right)

likely to result in a substantial reduction in the number of random flips must also consider adjustments to the method's diversification strategy. In our host method, effective diversification relies on an adequate equal-cost flip strategy. Consequently, we see two possible ways to address this problem in the HTB method. One is to fine-tune the setting of P_{flat}. Another, to replace PAWS's equal-cost strategy with the random-walk mechanism typically found in implementations of less randomised multiplicative CWLS methods. We continue to work on this problem and intend to report on our findings in forthcoming work.

As pointed out earlier, we initially considered using the TB heuristic for breaking the ties of cost-improving flips as well, but opted for using BOCM because it offered less computational overheads while still delivering a method suitable for the goals of our study. However, given HTB's performance in our empirical evaluation, we became interested in investigating whether we could obtain further gains by handling tied cost-improving flips with a more sophisticated heuristic. Using HTB, we replaced BOCM with TB for handling equal-cost flips, naming the resulting method HTB+.

Figure 4 shows the performance of this method on the largest blocks world problem. As expected, the run-time performance (Figure 4 (left)) is impaired by the additional computational overheads, although this is only the case for solu-

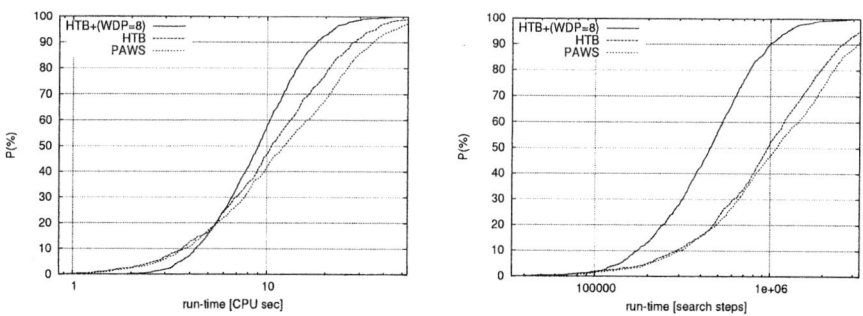

Fig. 4. RTD and RLD analysis of PAWS, HTB, and HTB+ on bw_large.d, 1,000 runs

tion probabilities below 25%. For higher solution probabilities (i.e. longer runs), this difference is noticeably outweighted by the method's superior performance.

An RLD analysis (Figure 4 (right)) shows that HTB+ clearly dominates both HTB and PAWS for all solution probabilities above 5%, solving 80% more instances than either of the other two methods within 1 million flips. Similar results were also observed on the RTDs and RLDs for the bw_large.c problem, as well as on several BQWH instances. This evidence suggests that it is worthwhile investigating the use of more sophisticated heuristic tie breaking techniques, although a more thorough investigation in this direction is needed before any conclusive findings can be reached.

6 Conclusion

This study advances our understanding of the usefulness of heuristic tie breaking for the performance of constraint weighting local search methods. We have used an empirical study to demonstrate that when heuristic tie breaking is used in combination with the random tie breaking mechanism of an existing state-of-the-art solver, the resulting method gives significant performance improvements, especially for the large and structured search spaces.

Our proposed approach is conceptually simple, and does not require the use of any additional parameters. Our findings therefore serve to motivate the adoption of heuristic tie breaking as a worthwhile avenue to be explored for the further development of additive CWLS methods.

References

1. Morris, P.: The breakout method for escaping from local minima. In: Proceedings of the 11th National Conference on Artificial Intelligence (AAAI'93), Washington, D.C., MIT Press (1993) 40–45
2. Selman, B., Kautz, H.: Domain-independent extensions to GSAT: Solving large structured satisfiability problems. In: Proceedings of the International Joint Conference on Artificial Intelligence (IJCAI'93), Chambery, France, Morgan Kaufmann (1993) 290–295
3. Wah, B., Shang, Y.: Discrete lagrangian-based search for solving MAX-SAT problems. In: Proceedings of the 15th International Joint Conference on Artificial Intelligence (IJCAI'97), Nagoya, Japan, Morgan Kaufmann (1997) 378–383
4. Hutter, F., Tompkins, D., Hoos, H.: Scaling and probabilistic smoothing: Efficient dynamic local search for SAT. In: Proceedings of CP-02. Volume 2470 of LNCS., Ithaca, New York, Springer Verlag (2002) 233–248
5. Thornton, J., Pham, D.N., Bain, S., Ferreira Jr., V.: Additive versus multiplicative clause weighting for SAT. In: Proceedings of the 20th National Conference on Artificial Intelligence (AAAI'04), San Jose, California, MIT Press (2004) 191–196
6. Hoos, H.H., Stützle, T.: Stochastic Local Search: Foundations and Applications. Morgan Kaufmann, San Francisco, California (2005)
7. Schuurmans, D., Southey, F.: Local search characteristics of incomplete SAT procedures. In: Proceedings of the 1tth National Conference on Artificial Intelligence (AAAI'00), Austin, TX, MIT Press (2000) 297–302

8. Selmann, B., Kautz, H.A., Cohen, B.: Noise strategies for improving local search. In: Proceedings of the 12th National Conference on Artificial Intelligence (AAAI'94), Seattle, WA, AAAI Press (1994) 337–343
9. Prestwich, S.: Local search on sat-encoded CSPs. In: Proceedings of the 6th International Conference on Theory and Applications of Satisfiability Testing (SAT 2003), Portofino, Italy, Springer (2003)
10. Achlioptas, D., Gomes, C., Kautz, H., Selman, B.: Generating satisfiable problem instances. In: Proceedings of the 17th National Conference on Artificial Intelligence (AAAI'00), Austin, TX, MIT Press (2000) 256–261
11. Kautz, H., Ruan, Y., Achlioptas, D., Gomes, C., Selman, B., Stickel, M.: Balance and filtering in structured satisfiable problems. In: Proceedings of the International Joint Conference on Artificial Intelligence (IJCAI'01), Seattle, Morgan Kaufmann (2001) 351–358
12. Thornton, J.: Clause weighting local search for SAT. Journal of Artificial Intelligence Research (to appear)
13. Tompkins, D., Hoos, H.: Warped landscapes and random acts of SAT solving. In: Proceedings of the Eighth International Symposium on Artificial Intelligence and Mathematics - AMAI, AI&M 2004, Fort Lauderdale, Florida (2004)

Syntactic and Semantic Disambiguation of Numeral Strings Using an N-Gram Method

Kyongho Min[1], William H. Wilson[2], and Yoo-Jin Moon[3]

[1] School of Computer and Information Sciences, AUT,
Auckland, New Zealand
kyongho.min@aut.ac.nz
[2] School of Computer Science and Engineering, UNSW,
Sydney, Australia
billw@cse.unsw.edu.au
[3] Department of Management Information Systems, HUFS,
YongIn, Kyonggi, Korea
yjmoon@hufs.ac.kr

Abstract. This paper describes the interpretation of numerals, and strings including numerals, composed of a number and words or symbols that indicate whether the string is a SPEED, LENGTH, or whatever. The interpretation is done at three levels: lexical, syntactic, and semantic. The system employs three interpretation processes: a word trigram constructor with tokeniser, a rule-based processor of number strings, and n-gram based disambiguation of meanings. We extracted numeral strings from 378 online newspaper articles, finding that, on average, they comprised about 2.2% of the words in the articles. We chose 287 of these articles to provide unseen test data (3251 numeral strings), and used the remaining 91 articles to provide 886 numeral strings for use in manually extracting n-gram constraints to disambiguate the meanings of the numeral strings. We implemented six different disambiguation methods based on category frequency statistics collected from the sample data and on the number of word trigram constraints of each category. Precision ratios for the six methods when applied to the test data ranged from 85.6% to 87.9%.

1 Introduction

Some NLP systems aim to understand a document that is composed of sentences. Each sentence is composed of words, numerals, symbols, and punctuation marks. Thus NLP systems process a sequence of characters (i.e. strings) at three levels: lexical, sentential, and textual. Dale [4] discussed various types of tokens NLP systems need to process in real world text. One of these token types is the complex numeral token such as "25-12-92", "1994-95", or "20-strong".

Strings that signify DATE (e.g. "09.03.05"), SPEED (e.g. "250km/h"), and QUANTITY ("21 voters"), etc. are frequently used in real world text. In current NLP systems, such strings are recognised as either a numeral (number, e.g. "25 players") or as a named entity (money, e.g. "$2.5 million"). However, ambiguity of interpretation can arise for such strings at the lexical level: for example, the numeral string "21" can on the surface be interpreted as any of the following - (a) QUANTITY in "survey of

21 voters"; (b) DAY in a date expression (e.g. "September 21"); or (c) AGE in "he turns *21* today", at the lexical level. We called these types of numeral strings *separate* numeral strings because the numeral strings are separate from its modified words. Some numeral strings would not be ambiguous because they have affixed meaningful units, and they are called *affixed* numeral strings (e.g. speed in "his serve of *240km/h*") in this paper.

For the separate numeral strings, some structural patterns (e.g. DAY) or syntactic functional relationships (e.g. QUANTITY as a modifier of a head noun) would be useful for interpretation of the numeral strings. However, the affixed numeral strings require the understanding of some meaningful units such as SPEED ("km/h" in "250km/h") and LENGTH ("m" in "a 10m yacht").

Past research has rarely studied the understanding of varieties of numeral strings. The ICE-GB grammar [7] treated numerals as one of cardinal, ordinal, fraction, hyphenated, etc. Maynard et al. [6] used semantic categories for named entity recognition (e.g. date, time, money, percent, etc.) using a tokeniser, a gazetteer, and hand-crafted rules. For Japanese text processing, a rule-based method [9] has been employed. Morphological analysis, POS tagging, and chunking methods were employed to extract and interpret numeral strings in [1].

Polanyi and van den Berg [8] studied anaphoric resolution of quantifiers and cardinals using a quantifier logic framework. A HMM [12] was employed to recognise and classify names, times, and numerical quantities with surface sub-features, word features, and semantic features like FourDigitNum (e.g. 1990) were used to pick a year form, and similarly for containsDigitAndSlash (e.g. "11/9/89"), and SuffixTime (e.g. "a.m.") [2, 11]. FACILE [3] in MUC used a rule-based named entity recognition system incorporating a chart-parsing technique and semantic categories such as PERSON, ORGANISATION, DATE, TIME, etc.

Unlike other systems based on machine learning algorithms with an annotated corpus, we implemented a rule-based numeral interpretation system that combines a tokeniser, rule-based processing of number strings, and disambiguation of meanings based on word trigram constraints (i.e. from the left and right neighbours of a numeral string). The rule-based number processing system analyses affixed numeral strings that have their own meaningful semantic affixes (e.g. the speed unit in "24km/h") using syntactic rules (e.g. speed → number + length-unit + slash + time-unit). After processing the separate numeral strings, the best meaning of each numeral string is disambiguated by word trigram constraints.

In the next section, the categories and rules used in this system will be described. In section 3, we will describe the understanding process for both separate and affixed numeral strings, in more detail. Section 4 will describe experimental results obtained with this algorithm, and discussion and conclusions follow.

2 Syntactic-Semantic Categories and Syntactic Rules

In this section, semantic and syntactic categories and syntactic rules used to parse numeral strings in real text are described.

This system used both syntactic and semantic categories to understand both separate and affixed numeral strings, because a separate numeral string like "20" in "20 pages" can be understood by itself or with reference to a structural relationship to adjacent strings as in "on September 20 2003". The separate numeral string "20" in "20 pages" can be recognised as QUANTITY to modify the noun "pages". However, knowledge of the specific DATE pattern representation in "on September 20 2003" is needed to understand "20" as DAY. This is even clearer with "7/12/2003" which can mean July 12, 2003 (US) or 7 December, 2003 (e.g. in Australia and New Zealand). Thus semantic categories including DAY, MONTH, and YEAR were used for date representation.

We used 40 syntactic (e.g. NUMBER, QUANT, etc.) and semantic categories (e.g. (MONEY, DATE, etc.) (Table 1). For example, the category FMNUMBER (ForMatted Number) means numbers that include commas every 3 digits to the left of the unit digit for ease of reading, as in "*5,000* peacekeepers."

Table 1. Some Categories and their examples

Category	Example	Category	Example
Age	"mature *20-year-old* contender"	Scores	"a narrow *3-6* away loss to Otago"
Date	"*20.08.2003*"	Range	"for *20-30* minutes"
Year	"by September *2026*"	Plural	"putting a *43-man* squad"
Day	"August *11*"	Number	"*8000* of the Asian plants"
Daytime	"between *9:30am* and *2am*"	Fmnumber	"took command of *5,000* peacekeepers"
Money	"spend *US$1.4* billion"	Ordinal	"a cake for her *18th* birthday"
Name	"Brent crude *LCOc1*"	Quant	"survey of *801* voters"
Temperature	"temperatures still above *40C*"	Phone-number	"ph: (09) 917 1234"

The lexicon used for this system includes symbol tokens (e.g. "(", ")"), lexical words (e.g. "year"), and semantic units (e.g. "km", "m", "h", etc.). For example, the lexical information for "km" is (LU (Length Unit)) with its meaning KILOMETER.

The system uses 64 context-free rules to represent the structural form of affixed numeral strings. Each rule describes relationships between syntactic/semantic categories of the components (e.g. a character or a few characters and a number) produced by token analysis of the affixed string. Each rule is composed of LHS (left hand side), RHS (right hand side), and constraints on the RHS.

The context free rules are based on deep tokenisation of affixed strings. Affixed numeral strings (e.g. "240km/h serve" and "a 10m yacht") require knowledge of their expression formats (e.g. speed → number ("240") + length-unit ("km") + slash ("/") + time-unit ("h")) for understanding. For example, the string "240km/h" is tokenized into "240" + "km" + "/" + "h", and "8.2μmol/L" might be split as ("8.2") + "μmol" + "/" + "L". The tokeniser considers embedded punctuation and special symbols. Some examples of deep tokenisation are as follows:

"($12.56)" → "(" + "$" + "12" + "." + "56" + ")"
"20.08.2003" → "20" + "." + "08" + "." + "2003"
"1980s" → "1980" + "s"

The context-free rules are used to interpret deeply tokenized affixed numeral strings and some examples are as follows:

DATE1 → **LHS**: DATE
RHS: (DAY DOT MONTH DOT YEAR)
Constraint: ((LEAPDATEP DAY MONTH YEAR)) - the well-formedness of DATE (e.g. "08.12.2003") is verified using the constraint (LEAPDATEP DAY MONTH YEAR).

SPEED1 → **LHS**: SPEED
RHS: (NUMBER LU SLASH TU)
Constraint: ((SPEED-AMOUNT-P NUMBER)) – if the number is an integer (e.g. "240") or a decimal fraction (e.g. "15.8").

With the context-free rules, the syntactic structure of deeply tokenised affixed numeral strings is processed.

3 Interpretation Method

The numeral string interpretation algorithm is composed of two processes: a rule-based interpretation module, called ENUMS (English NUMber understanding System), which employs a CFG augmented by constraints, and a category disambiguation module to select the best category for an ambiguous numeral string using a word trigram.

3.1 Numeral String Interpretation

After tokenising the string, dictionary lookup and a rule-based numeral processing system based on a simple bottom-up chart parsing technique [5] are invoked. Special forms of numbers (e.g. "03" in a time, day, etc.) are not stored in the lexicon. Thus if the substring is composed of all digits, then the substring is assigned to several possible numeric lexical categories. For example, if a numeral string is "03", then the string is assigned to SECOND, MINUTE, HOUR, DAY, MONTH, and BLDNUMBER (signifying digits after a decimal point, e.g. "0.03"). If the numeral string is "13" or higher, then the category cannot be MONTH (and similarly for DAY). However, "13" can be used as a quantifier (e.g. "13 books").

Non-numeral strings in a deeply tokenized numeral string (e.g. "km", "/", and "h" in "240km/h") are processed by dictionary lookup as mentioned above, and the lexical categories used are necessarily more semantic than in regular parsing. For example, the string "m" has three lexical categories: LU (Length Unit) - METER (e.g. "a 10m yacht"), MILLION (e.g. "$1.5m"), and TU (Time Unit) - MINUTE (e.g. "12m 10s" - 12 minutes and 10 seconds).

After lexical processing of substrings, an agenda-based simple bottom-up chart parsing is applied with 64 context-free rules augmented by constraints. For example, the rule to process dates of the form "28.03.2003" is DATE → (DAY DOT MONTH DOT YEAR) with the constraint (LEAPYEARP DAY MONTH YEAR), which checks whether the date is valid. An inactive phrasal constituent DATE1 with its RHS, (DAY1 DOT1 MONTH1 DOT2 YEAR1), would be produced and the constraint (i.e. LEAPYEARP) would be applied to verify the well-formedness.

3.2 Category Disambiguation Based on Word-Trigram Constraints

After the rule-based parsing step, word trigrams are used to disambiguate the syntactic/semantic categories of numeral strings. Disambiguation of categories is based on constraints manually encoded by studying sample data, and each constraint is based on morpho-syntactic/semantic features of the word trigrams. The features are syntactic categories (e.g. NOUN, VERB, etc.), punctuation marks (e.g. period, comma, etc.), number features (e.g. singular, plural), heuristic features (e.g. year-range (1000 ~ 2200)), and semantic patterns (e.g. "January" for Month).

Different types of constraints used for disambiguation of numeral strings are:

1. Constraints based on syntactic/subcategorical features:
   - Quant: e.g. "for *1800* vessels"
     (and (preposition-p left-wordgram ("for"))
           (plural-noun-p right-wordgram ("vessels")));
2. Constraints based on punctuation features:
   - Age: e.g. "Lee, *41*, has"
     (and (comma-p left-wordgram ("Lee,"))
           (capital-letter-p left-wordgram ("Lee,"))
           (comma-p numeral-string ("41,")));
3. Constraints based on semantic features:
   - Day: e.g. "on July *7* to discuss"
     (and (month-p left-wordgram ("July"))
           (valid-day-p left-wordgram numeral-string ("July" "7")));
4. Constraints based on heuristic features:
   - Year: e.g. "by September *2026*."
     (and (month-p left-wordgram ("September"))
           (>= numeral-string ("2026") 1000)
           (<= numeral-string ("2026") 2200));
5. Constraints based on pattern matching between left/right wordgram:
   - Scores: e.g. "a narrow 3-6 away loss"
     (and (score-left-pattern left-wordgram ("narrow" "win" "lose" etc.))
           (score-right-pattern right-wordgram, ("away" "defeat" etc.)));

The contextual information, expressed in word trigrams, is applied to disambiguating multiple categories that resulted from the numeral string interpretation process. We implemented six heuristic methods to compare their effectiveness. Method-1 and Method-2 are based on the number of wordgram constraints such as QUANT (22 constraints) > NUMBER (8) > YEAR (7) > AGE (5) > DAY (4) > RANGE (3) > DAYTIME (2) > LENGTH (1) > SCORES (1).

Table 2. Frequency of categories obtained from a sample dataset (*886 numeral strings)

Category	Frequency	Category	Frequency	Category	Frequency
Quant	200	Age	35	Ordinal	13
Money	186	Plural	32	Length	12
Date	81	Day	32	Name	9
Year	80	Daytime	21	Range	6
Number	64	Fmnumber	19	Cent	5
Floatnumber	59	Scores	19	Area	3

(*Another eight categories have 1 or 2 occurrences in the sample dataset)

The six Methods we implemented are as follows:

- Method-1 (M1): The categorical constraints were sequentially applied to ambiguous categories of the interpreted numeral string in descending order of the number of word trigram constraints. Thus the category QUANT with 22 constraints was applied first. If the word trigram of a numeral string satisfies any of the QUANT constraints, then the category of the numeral string is disambiguated as QUANT. If no constraint of this category is satisfied, then the category with the next most constraints is applied to the numeral string. If no categorical constraint is satisfied, then the first category of the multiple categories of the numeral string is selected.
- Method-2 (M2): Method-2 is the same as Method-1 but the categorical constraints were sequentially applied in ascending order of the number of constraints. Thus the category SCORES is applied first. Then the category with the next fewest constraints is applied and so on.
- Method-3 (M3): Method-3 applies categorical constraints in a sequence determined by the frequency of hand-classified categories in a sample dataset (see Table 2). Categorical constraints for the most frequently tagged category in the sample dataset (namely QUANT) were applied first. If the first category's constraints were satisfied, then the numeral string is considered to be disambiguated successfully. Otherwise the next category's constraints were applied and so on. If no constraints were satisfied, then the most frequently tagged category was selected.
- Method-4 (M4): Method-4 is based on rarity of hand-classified categories in a sample dataset. Thus the categorical constraints with the least common category in the sample dataset (namely AREA) were applied first. If this category's constraints were not satisfied, then categorical constraints of the next rarest category (namely CENT > RANGE > NAME etc.) were applied in order until any category's constraints were satisfied.
- Method-5 (M5): Method-5 collects all categories whose categorical constraints are all satisfied. For example, if all and only the constraints for QUANT and NUMBER were satisfied, then these two categories are collected. Using the annotation frequency of the two categories (e.g. QUANT and NUMBER) collected from a sample dataset, the category with more frequent annotation is selected as the best. If no categorical constraints were satisfied, then the most frequent category in the sample dataset (namely QUANT) is selected.
- Method-6 (M6): Method-6 is similar to Method-5. Categories satisfying all their constraints are collected, but then the least frequent category, not the most frequent, is selected. If no category satisfies all its constraints, then the least frequent category overall (namely DAY) is selected.

4 Experimental Results

We implemented our system in Common LISP with IDE. We collected online newspaper articles for 9 days across topics such as national, international, sports, economy, etc., and annotated all numeral strings manually. A sample dataset of 91 articles was used to build disambiguation rules for the categories of numeral strings. The remaining 287 articles (test data) were used to test the system. Among the 48498 words in the sample data, 886 numeral strings (1.8% of total strings, or 10 numeral strings on average for each article) were found. For the test data, 3251 out of 144030 words (2.2% of total strings, or 11 numeral strings on average for each article) were identified as numeral strings (Table 3). The sample dataset contained 21.4% of the total collection of numeral strings (886 out of 4173).

Table 3. Data size and portion of numeral strings

Data Name	Total Articles	Total Strings	Total Numerals
Sample	91 (24.1%)	48498 (25.2%)	886 (1.8%)
Test	287 (75.9%)	144030 (74.8%)	3251 (2.3%)
Total	378	192528	4173 (2.2%)

The proportion of numeral strings belonging to each category in both sample and test data were QUANT (826 of 3251 - 20.0%), MONEY (727 - 17.6%), DATE (380 - 9.2%), YEAR (378 - 9.1%), NUMBER (300 - 7.3%), SCORES (224 - 5.4%), and FLOATNUMBER (8.0%) in order.

Table 4. Recall/Precision/F-measurement Ratios (%) for the Six Methods on the Test Data

Ratio	Method-1	Method-2	Method-3	Method-4	Method-5	Method-6
Recall	78.9	80.2	75.8	74.5	77.1	77.6
Precision	85.6	87.9	87.7	85.8	86.8	86.3
F-measure	82.1	83.9	81.3	79.7	81.6	81.7

Table 4 shows the recall/precision/F-measurement ratios (balanced F-measurement) for the six methods. Method-2 shows the best recall ratios (80.2%), and also the best precision (87.9%) and F-measurement (83.9%). The sample data showed 85.9% to 90.2% on the F-measurement ratio while the test data showed 79.7% to 83.9%, using disambiguation rules manually extracted from the sample data, which covers 25.2% of both sample and test strings.

Table 5 shows F-measurement ratios for selected categories for the six methods on the test data. Affixed numeral strings (e.g. Floatnumber, Fmnumber, Money, Range, Scores) showed big differences in F-measurement performance (0% to 99.4%). The result for separate numeral strings (e.g. Age, Day, Number, Quant, Year) also showed big differences in performance (40.2% to 89.2%). The performance for the Range category is poor because of numeral strings like "$US5m-$US7m" and "10am-8pm", that are not covered by our CFG yet. NUMBER in Table 5 showed poor results because manually encoded word trigram constraints could not cover its occurrences in test data and the constraints were based on ambiguous lexical categories (e.g. "in" – preposition, adverb, or noun).

Table 5. Selected Categories' F-measurement Ratios (%) for the Six Methods

Category	F-measurement (%)					
	M1	M2	M3	M4	M5	M6
C1: Age	79.0	79.0	79.0	74.1	59.3	59.3
C2: Day	81.4	81.4	82.0	82.0	76.3	74.1
C3: Number	50.9	58.2	40.2	40.2	54.4	51.9
C4: Quant	84.3	87.2	77.6	79.2	84.4	87.3
C5: Year	71.6	89.2	87.2	75.5	88.6	78.7
C6: Floatnumber	97.6	97.6	97.6	93.6	96.9	96.9
C7: Fmnumber	99.2	99.2	99.2	99.2	99.2	99.2
C8: Money	99.4	99.5	99.3	99.3	99.3	99.3
C9: Range	37.9	42.9	0.0	0.0	0.0	39.4
C10: Scores	83.3	83.6	86.9	86.6	86.6	83.3

Figure 1 shows the precision ratios of selected categories on the test data; their performance ranged from 0% (C9 in Method-3) to 100% (C2 in Method-2, etc.). The best average precision ratio across 10 categories is 85.3%, obtained by Method-2, and the worst average precision ratio is 76.7%, obtained with Method-4.

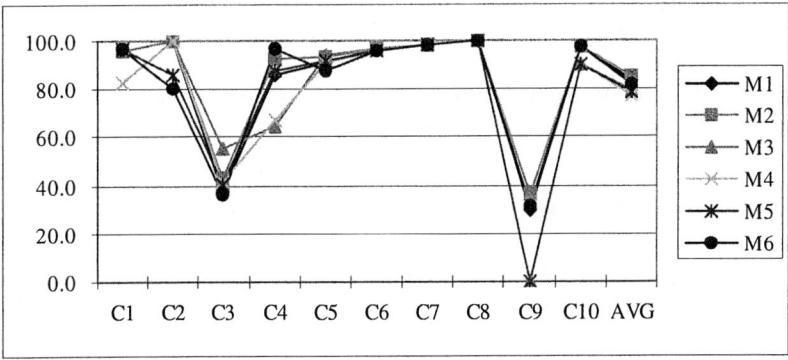

Fig. 1. Precision Ratios (%) of Categories (C1 to C10 in Table 6) for the Six Methods

Figure 2 shows the recall ratios of selected categories on the test data and their performance ranged from 0% (C9 in Method-3) to 100% (C7 in Method-1, etc.). The best recall ratio across 10 categories is 81.7%, obtained with Method-2, and the worst average recall ratio is 71.0%, obtained with Method-4.

Figures 1 and 2 show that interpretation and disambiguation of two categories (NUMBER = C3 and RANGE = C9) were very difficult. In the case of NUMBER, it is difficult to distinguish from other categories (e.g. AGE, DAY, QUANT). For RANGE, some numeral strings were not processed properly because there are different types of RANGEs such as range of Money (e.g. "$US5m-$US7m"), range of Daytime (e.g. "9am-5pm"), etc. Compared to other separate numeral strings, the system interpreted QUANT category better than YEAR and NUMBER, because the disambiguation module for the QUANT category has more word-trigram constraints (22 constraints for QUANT, 8 for NUMBER, and 7 for YEAR).

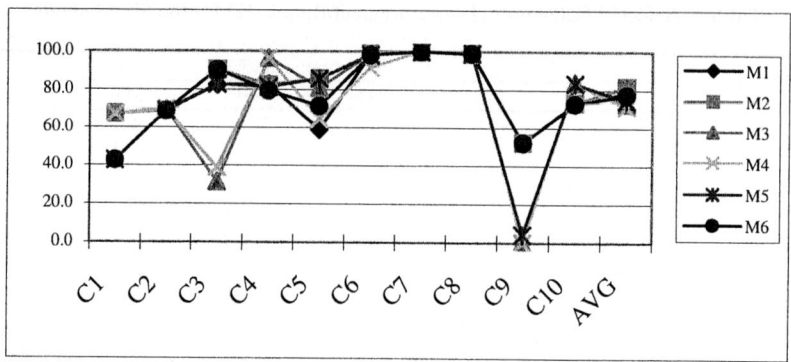

Fig. 2. Recall Ratios (%) of Categories (C1 to C10 in Table 6) for the Six Methods

For disambiguation processes Method-5 and Method-6, 2213 (53.5%) of the 4137 numeral strings were ambiguous after numeral string processing and word trigram-based constraints were applied. Of these, 746 (33.7%) satisfied no constraint, 1271 (57.4%) satisfied one constraint, 185 (8.4%) satisfied two constraints, and 11 (0.5%) satisfied three constraints. "Satisfied no constraint" means that no categorical word-trigram constraint applied to the numeral string, because some categories, like QUANT and NUMBER, had few word-trigram constraints available. This part of the system needs further development.

5 Discussion and Conclusions

It is not easy to compare our system to other Named Entity recognition systems directly because the target recognition of named entities is different. Other systems in MUC-7 [3] focused on general recognition task of named entities including person, location, money, date and organisation. The systems in MUC-7 were trained by using the necessary training corpus with document preprocessing (e.g. tagging and machine learning). However, our system focused on understanding of varieties of numeral strings more deeply and had no training phase. The manually annotated constraints from sample data (25%) were used for disambiguation of categories. Performances of MUC-7 systems were more than 90% in precision. Our system correctly interpreted 87.9% of numeral strings. The precision ratio for the MONEY category was more than 99% in our system. The precision ratios for DAY ranged from 80.4% to 100% depending on implemented methods in this paper.

Further rules and lexical information are required to process more numerals in real world text (see [4]). For better disambiguation, more fine-grained disambiguation constraints based on word trigrams would be required. Currently syntactic categories of both left and right wordgram of each numeral string are used. The major problem of the use of syntactic category is lexical ambiguity (e.g. "in" could be a preposition, adverb, or noun). In addition, the extension of this system to other data, like biomedical corpora [10], is needed to test effectiveness of our approach.

In conclusion, separate and affixed numeral strings are frequently used in real text. However, there seems to be no system that interprets varieties of numeral strings systematically; they are frequently treated as either numerals or nominal entities. In this paper, we have analysed the numeral strings at lexical, syntactic, and semantic levels with word trigram contextual information. The system was composed of a tokeniser with word trigram constructor, numeral string processor that includes token analysis and a simple bottom-up chart parser with context-free rules augmented by constraints, and a disambiguation module based on word trigrams. The numeral string interpretation system successfully interpreted 87.9% of test data with manually encoded word trigram constraints extracted from 21.4% of numeral strings in both sample and test data. The system could be scaled up to cover more numeral strings by extending lexicon and rules.

References

1. Asahara, M., Matsumoto Y.: Japanese Named Entity Extraction with Redundant Morphological Analysis. Proceedings of HLT-NAACL 2003. (2003) 8-15
2. Bikel, D., Schwartz, R., Weischedel, R.: An Algorithm that Learns What's in a Name. Machine Learning. 34 (1999) 211-231
3. Black, W., Rinaldi, F., Mowatt, D.: FACILE: Description of the NE system used for MUC-7. Proceedings of Message Uunderstanding Conference (MUC)-7. (1998)
4. Dale, R.: A Framework for Complex Tokenisation and its Application to Newspaper Text. Proceedings of the second Australian Document Computing Symposium. (1997)
5. Earley, J.: An Efficient Context-Free Parsing Algorithm. CACM. 13(2) (1970) 94-102
6. Maynard, D., Tablan, V., Ursu, C., Cunningham, H., Wilks, Y.: Named Entity Recognition from Diverse Text Types. Proceedings of Recent Advances in NLP. (2001)
7. Nelson, G., Wallis, S., Aarts, B.: Exlporing Natural Language - Working with the British Component of the International Corpus of English, John Benjamins, The Netherlands. (2002)
8. Polanyi, L., van den Berg, M.: Logical Structure and Discourse Anaphora Resolution. Proceedings of ACL99 Workshop on The Relation of Discourse/Dialogue Structure and Reference. (1999) 10-117
9. Siegel, M., Bender, E. M.: Efficient Deep Processing of Japanese. Proceedings of the 3rd Workshop on Asian Language Resources and International Standardization. (2002)
10. Torii, M., Kamboj, S., Vijay-Shanker, K.: An investigation of Various Information Sources for Classifying Biological Names. Proceedings of ACL2003 Workshop on Natural Language Processing in Biomedicine. (2003) 113-120
11. Wang, H., Yu, S.: The Semantic Knowledge-base of Contemporary Chinese and its Apllication in WSD. Proceedings of the Second SIGHAN Workshop on Chinese Language Processing. (2003) 112-118
12. Zhou, G., and Su, J. Named Entity Recognition using an HMM-based Chunk Tagger. Proceedings of ACL2002. (2002) 473-480

Locating Regions of Interest in CBIR with Multi-instance Learning Techniques

Zhi-Hua Zhou, Xiao-Bing Xue, and Yuan Jiang

National Laboratory for Novel Software Technology,
Nanjing University, Nanjing 210093, China
{zhouzh, xuexb, jiangy}@lamda.nju.edu.cn

Abstract. In content-based image retrieval (CBIR), the user usually poses several labelled images and then the system attempts to retrieve all the images relevant to the target concept defined by these labelled images. It may be helpful if the system can return relevant images where the *regions of interest* (ROI) are explicitly located. In this paper, this task is accomplished with the help of multi-instance learning techniques. In detail, this paper proposes the CkNN-ROI algorithm, which regards each image as a *bag* comprising many instances and picks from positive bag the instance that has great chance to meet the target concept to help locate ROI. Experiments show that the proposed algorithm can efficiently locate ROI in CBIR process.

1 Introduction

With the rapid increase of the volume of digital image collections, content-based image retrieval (CBIR) has attracted a lot of research interests in recent years [5]. Here the main difficulty lies in the gap between the high-level image semantics and the low-level image features, due to the rich content but subjective semantics of an image. Although much endeavor has been devoted to bridging this gap [4][11], it remains an unsolved problem at present. Nevertheless, many good CBIR systems have already been developed.

In CBIR, the user usually poses several labelled images, i.e. positive or negative images corresponding to a target concept, in the query and relevant feedback process, and the CBIR system attempts to retrieve all the images relevant to the target concept from the image database. It is noteworthy that although the user feeds whole images to the system, usually he or she is only interested in some regions in these images, i.e. *regions of interest* (ROI). In applications involving the scan of huge volume of images to detect suspect areas, such as to some medical or military purposes, it may be valuable if the ROI can be identified and exhibited when the retrieved images are presented to the user. Even in common CBIR scenarios, considering that the system usually returns a lot of images, explicitly showing the ROI may be helpful because it could help the user recognize the images he or she really wants more quickly. Unfortunately, at present few CBIR systems can return retrieved images where the ROI has been located.

In this paper, the CkNN-ROI algorithm is proposed to address the problem of locating ROI in CBIR. CkNN-ROI regards each image as a *bag* comprising many instances. The labelled positive or negative images provided by the user are regarded respectively as positive or negative training bags. For every image in the database, CkNN-ROI determines whether or not it is a positive bag with the help of some adjacent training bags, and if the image is a positive bag then the instance which has the biggest chance to meet the target concept is picked out while its corresponding image region is regarded as ROI. Experiments show that this algorithm can locate ROI in the CBIR process with high efficiency.

The rest of the paper is organized as follows. Section 2 briefly introduces multi-instance learning and its application in CBIR. Section 3 proposes the CkNN-ROI algorithm. Section 4 reports on the experiments. Finally, Section 5 concludes and raises several issues for future work.

2 Multi-instance Learning and CBIR

In *multi-instance learning* [10], the training set is composed of many *bags* each contains many instances. A bag is positively labelled if it contains at least one positive instance and negatively labelled otherwise. The task is to learn something from the training bags for correctly labelling unseen bags. This task is difficult because unlike supervised learning where all the training instances are labelled, here the labels of the individual instances are unknown. It is obvious that if a whole image is regarded as a bag while its regions are regarded as instances, then the problem of determining whether an image is relevant to a target concept can be viewed as a multi-instance problem. Therefore, multi-instance learning has great potential in tasks involving image analysis.

Maron and Ratan [3] applied multi-instance learning techniques to natural scene classification. In their work each image was initially smoothed using a Gaussian filter and subsampled to an 8×8 matrix of *color blobs* where each blob was a 2×2 set of pixels within the 8×8 matrix. Then, different *bag generators* were used to transform various configurations of blobs of each image, such as *rows*, *single blob with neighbors* (SBN), *two blobs with no neighbors*, etc., into instances of the corresponding bag. Finally, the Diverse Density algorithm [2] was used to learn the target concept. Although natural scene classification is different from CBIR, this work gave some illumination on the application of multi-instance learning techniques to CBIR.

Yang and Lozano-Pérez [7] first applied multi-instance learning techniques to CBIR. They transformed color images into gray-scale images at first. Then, they divided each image into many overlapping regions. Regions with low variances were thrown out and each of the remaining ones was smoothed and subsampled to a low-resolution $h \times h$ matrix. Through concatenating these elements, an h^2-dimensional feature vector was generated. After subtracting the mean of the feature vector from it and then dividing it by its standard deviation, a new h^2-dimensional feature vector was obtained, which was used to describe the corresponding instance. Finally, a variation of the weighted correlation statistic was utilized to measure the similarity between feature vectors, and the Diverse Density algorithm was employed to learn the target concept. It is worth noting that this bag generator requires converting color images into gray-scale images, therefore it is not suitable to the process of color images.

Zhang et al. [9] enhanced Maron and Ratan's SBN bag generator [3] through exploiting a variety of image processing techniques such as wavelet transformation. They used this bag generator to convert the images to bags and employed the EM-DD algorithm [8], a variant of the Diverse Density algorithm which utilizes the EM technique, to learn the target concept. It is noteworthy that besides boolean labels, they also tried real-valued labels for each bag indicating how well the corresponding image meets the target concept.

Zhou et al. [13] developed the bag generator ImaBag, which was derived from an SOM-based image segmentation technique. Here the pixels in each image were clustered based on their color and spatial features by an SOM neural network, and then the clustered blocks were merged into a specific number of regions. Each region was represented with a feature vector formed by its mean R, G, B values, which was regarded as an instance in the bag corresponding to the image. Then the Diverse Density algorithm was used to learn the target concept.

3 CkNN-ROI

It can be seen from Section 2 that among current multi-instance learning algorithms, the Diverse Density algorithm and its variants have already been used in CBIR. This is not strange because Diverse Density is the first practical multi-instance learning algorithm, which employs gradient ascent with multiple starting points to search for the point with the maximum *diverse density* in the feature space [2]. The *diverse density* at a point is defined to be a measure of how many different positive bags have instances near that point, and how far the negative instances are from that point. It is obvious that the Diverse Density algorithm can be used to locate ROI because after training process the point with maximum diverse density in the feature space is identified, therefor for a positive image bag the instance closest to that point should be the one corresponding to ROI. In fact, this property has already been exploited in Maron and Ratan's work on natural scene classification [3].

However, the Diverse Density algorithm suffers from huge time cost. In order to get the concept point, i.e. the point with the maximum diverse density in the feature space, this algorithm has to perform gradient-based optimizations starting from every instance in every positive bags. Suppose the training set contains m positive bags and each positive bag contains l instances. Then the total number of gradient-based optimizations required by the Diverse Density algorithm is $(m \times l)$. In natural scene classification such a time cost is tolerable because all the classes of the natural scenes are known when the the image database is constructed. Therefore, the concept points for different classes can be pre-computed and a new image can be quickly classified through computing its distances to different concept points. However, in CBIR the classes that may occur are not known when the image database is constructed, because the possible target concepts the user may query for may be infinite. Thus, the concept point can only be computed after the user provides labelled images. Since the gradient-based optimizations have to be executed online, the retrieval process will be time-consuming, which might not be acceptable because usually the user wants to get the retrieval results as soon as possible.

Based on the above recognition, nearest neighbor algorithms [1] appear to be better choices because they only involve the computation of distances while the distances between training examples can be pre-computed. Actually, there is a nearest neighbor style multi-instance learning algorithm, i.e. Citation-kNN [6]. This algorithm borrows the notion of *citation* and *reference* of scientific literatures in the way that a bag is labelled through analyzing not only its neighboring bags but also the bags that regard the concerned bag as a neighbor. In computing the distances between different bags, the *minimal Hausdorff distance* is employed, as shown in Eq. 1 where A and B are two different bags, i.e. $A = \{a_1, a_2, \cdots, a_m\}$ and $B = \{b_1, b_2, \cdots, b_h\}$ while a_i ($1 \leq i \leq m$) and b_j ($1 \leq j \leq h$) are the instances.

$$\text{Dist}(A, B) = \MIN_{\substack{1 \leq i \leq m \\ 1 \leq j \leq h}} (\text{Dist}(a_i, b_j)) = \MIN_{a \in A} \MIN_{b \in B} \|a - b\| \qquad (1)$$

The Citation-kNN algorithm achieved the best performance on the *Musk* data, a popular benchmark test for multi-instance learning algorithms, at the time it was proposed [6]. Recently, Zhou et al. [12] developed a variant of Citation-kNN for a web mining task through modifying the minimum Hausdorff distance for text features and obtained success. This demonstrates the great application potential of the k-NN style multi-instance learning algorithms. However, up to now such kind of algorithms have not been applied to tasks involving image analysis, while the CkNN-ROI algorithm described below is the first attempt to introduce them into CBIR.

In fact, the Citation-kNN algorithm can be directly applied to CBIR without any modification. However, this algorithm can not locate ROI by itself. Therefore, the CkNN-ROI algorithm is proposed, which works in two steps.

In the first step, the label of a new bag is determined in the same way as that of Citation-kNN. That is, for a given new bag, its r-nearest neighboring training bags (r-*references*) as well as the training bags (c-*citers*) which regard the new bag as its c-nearest neighbor are identified according to Eq. 1, and then the label of the new bag is determined by voting among these training bags.

In the second step, if the new bag is deemed as negative then nothing will be done because a negative image should contain no ROI corresponding to the target concept; otherwise the following process is executed. For each instance in the new bag, its k-nearest neighboring training bags can be identified according to Eq. 1 through regarding the concerned instance as a bag containing only one instance. Each of these training bags contributes a score to the estimation of the chance for the instance to meet the target concept. Intuitively, the closer the positive bags while the farther the negative bags, the bigger the chance.

Table 1. Pseudo-code describing the CkNN-ROI algorithm

Algorithm: CkNN-ROI
 Input: New bag B^*, training set T, parameters to set: r, c, k
 Output: Instance of B^* corresponding to ROI
 Process: Labelling Step:
     1) Find B^*'s r-nearest bags in T according to Eq. 1. Add them to R.
         $p \leftarrow$ the number of positive bags in R
         $n \leftarrow$ the number of negative bags in R
     2) Find all bags in T whose c-nearest bags contain B^* according to Eq. 1. Add them to C.
         $p \leftarrow p +$ the number of positive bags in C
         $n \leftarrow n +$ the number of negative bags in C
     3) If $p > n$ then goto Locating Step; otherwise B^* is negative which contains no ROI. Exit.
 Locating Step:
     1) For each instance in B^*, find its k-nearest bags in T according to Eq. 1 through regarding the instance itself as a bag. Add them to Ω. Compute $Score$ according to Eq. 2.
     2) Find the instance, say I^*, having the biggest $Score$.
     3) Return I^*.

Therefore, an exponential distance is employed and the equation for computing the score is empirically developed as shown in Eq. 2, where B^* is the new bag while I_v^* is its vth instance, $\Omega = \{k$-nearest neighboring training bags of $I_v^*\}$, I_{ij} is an instance of B_i, $class(B_i)$ returns $+1$ if B_i is positive and -1 otherwise, $\|\cdots\|_2$ is the l_2-norm.

$$Score_v = \sum_{i: B_i \in \Omega} (-1)^{class(B_i)} \exp\left(-\left(\min_{I_{ij} \in B_i} \|I_v^* - I_{ij}\|_2\right)^2\right) \quad (2)$$

The instance with the biggest score is deemed as a positive instance corresponding to the target concept, while its corresponding image region is regarded as the ROI. The pseudo-code of the CkNN-ROI algorithm is shown in Table 1.

Note that the first step of the CkNN-ROI algorithm reassembles the Citation-kNN algorithm, which has computed the distances between all the instances. Therefore, the computational cost of the CkNN-ROI algorithm is only slightly bigger than that of the Citation-kNN algorithm, where the additional cost lies in directly putting the existing $\min_{I_{ij} \in B_i} \|I_v^* - I_{ij}\|_2$ values into Eq. 2 and then picking out the instance with the biggest $Score$. Moreover, the distances between all the different training bags can be pre-computed when the image database is constructed. Therefore, comparing to Diverse Density, CkNN-ROI can be much more efficient, which is desirable in CBIR because the user can get the retrieval results much more quickly.

4 Experiments

An image database consisting of 500 COREL images is used in the experiments, which includes 100 images from each of the five image types: *castle, firework, mountain, sunset*, and *waterfall*. Here each image type corresponds to a target concept to be retrieved. A training set comprising 50 images is created by randomly choosing 10 images from each of the five image types. The remaining 450 images constitute a test set. The training-test partition is randomly generated for ten times where the generated training sets are not overlapped, and the average statistics is recorded.

The CkNN-ROI algorithm is compared with Diverse Density. For CkNN-ROI, the parameters r and c are set to 3 and 5, respectively, which is the recommended parameter setting of Citation-kNN [6]; the parameter k is set to 3, which has not been finely tuned. For Diverse Density, the *single point scaling* concept is adopted [2]. Both algorithms are facilitated with the same bag generator, i.e. the SBN presented by Maron and Ratan [3]. Images are first filtered and subsampled to 8×8. Then an SBN is defined as the combination of a single blob with its four neighboring blobs (up, down, left, right). The sub-image is described as a 15-dimensional vector, where the first three features represent the mean R, G, B values of the central blob and the remaining twelve features correspond to the differences in mean color values between the central blob and other four neighboring blobs respectively. Therefore, each image bag is represented by a collection of thirty-six 15-dimensional feature vectors obtained by using each of the blobs not along the border as the central blob. Note that in order to locate ROI more precisely, here 1 × 1 blob is used instead of 2 × 2 blob used in [3]. Fig. 1 illustrates the bag generator.

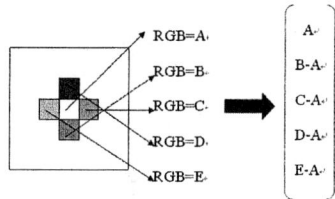

Fig. 1. The SBN bag generator

The experiments are performed on a machine with Intel Pentium III 533Hz CPU, 384MB memory, and Windows XP operating system. The average time cost per query is compared, as shown in Table 2.

Table 2 shows that the CkNN-ROI algorithm is about 45,234 ($= 14,475/0.32$) times faster than the Diverse Density algorithm in dealing with CBIR queries. The process time of CkNN-ROI, i.e. 0.32 second per query, is a very good record even in the context of state-of-the-art CBIR systems. Note that if the image database is larger, the distances between more bags should be pre-computed,

Table 2. Comparison on the average time cost per query

	Diverse Density	CkNN-ROI
Time(second)	14,475	0.32

but fortunately the online process time of CkNN-ROI will only increase linearly as well as Diverse Density. While even on the relatively small experimental image database, the process time of Diverse Density, i.e. 14,475 seconds per query, is unbearable because it is difficult to anticipate such a patient user who will wait more than 4 hours for a query! This discloses the fact that even though the Diverse Density algorithm could obtain good retrieval results, it could hardly be really used in CBIR dues to its overwhelmingly low efficiency.

Fig. 2 shows the precision-recall graphs of the retrieval performance of CkNN-ROI and Diverse Density on the target concepts. Note that each point shown in the graphs is the average result of 10 queries of the same type. This figure shows that the performance of CkNN-ROI is comparable to that of Diverse Density on three target concepts, i.e. *castle*, *firework*, and *waterfall*; while apparently worse than that of Diverse Density on two target concepts, i.e. *mountain* and *sunset*.

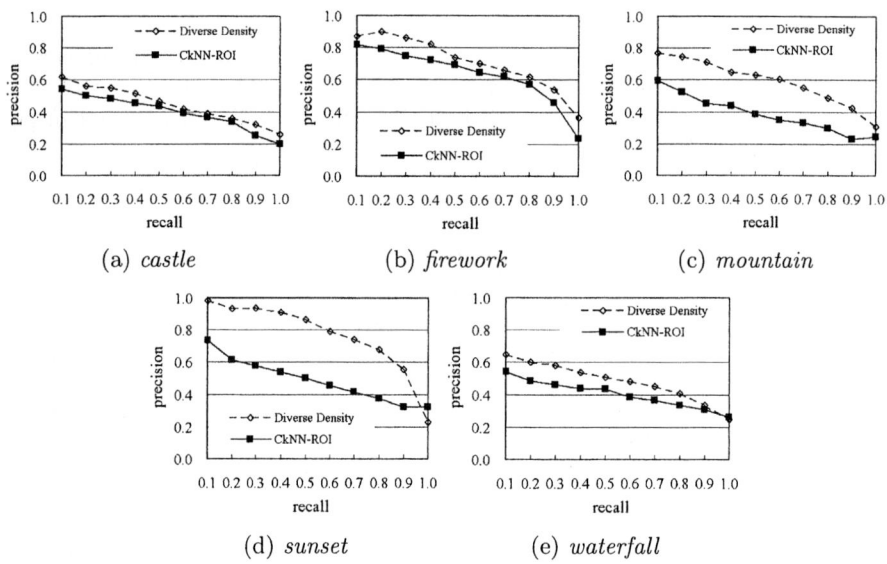

Fig. 2. Precision-recall graphs for different target concepts

The ROI locating ability of CkNN-ROI and Diverse Density are also compared. In detail, ROI of each image is manually marked in advance. Then, for each relevant image in the database, if the ROI returned by the algorithm is covered by the real ROI then it is recorded as a success. Note that here whether

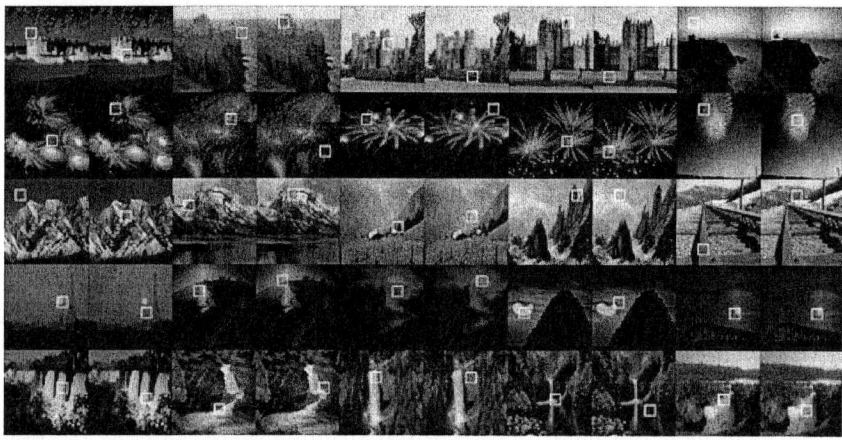

Fig. 3. The ROI located by Diverse Density and CkNN-ROI. Each row shows five pairs of example images on the target concepts *castle, firework, mountain, sunset,* and *waterfall,* respectively. In each pair the first image is obtained with Diverse Density while the second one is obtained with CkNN-ROI.

Table 3. Comparison on the success ratio of ROI locating

Target Concept	Diverse Density	CkNN-ROI
castle	0.668	0.608
firework	0.719	0.484
mountain	0.678	0.712
sunset	0.386	0.074
waterfall	0.767	0.409

an image is relevant to the target concept or not is determined by its real label, therefore in this way the ROI locating performance and the retrieval performance can be separately evaluated. The ratio of the number of successes against the total number of relevant images on each target type is computed and compared in Table 3. Fig. 3 shows some example images with located ROI.

Table 3 shows that the ROI locating performance of CkNN-ROI is worse than that of Diverse Density on *firework, sunset,* and *waterfall,* while comparable or better on *castle* and *mountain*. This is not difficult to explain because the bag generator used here mainly considers color information, therefore the instances can be viewed as some kind of color patterns. Diverse Density attempts to find a color pattern shared by all the positive bags but no negative bags, and uses this pattern to locate ROI; while CkNN-ROI attempts to evaluate each color pattern through finding its k nearest neighboring bags that have similar color patterns, and the more positive bags among these k bags, the more likely the concerned color pattern is regarded as ROI. So, CkNN-ROI is a local method while Diverse Density is a somewhat global method. If the image semantics is strongly coupled with a specific color pattern, then all the positive bags do share some specific color patterns, and in this case Diverse Density should perform better than CkNN-ROI; while if the image semantics is not strongly coupled with a specific color pattern, then it is difficult to find out a color pattern shared by all the positive bags, and in this case CkNN-ROI may perform better.

In fact, Fig. 3 confirms that when the image semantics is strongly coupled with a specific color pattern, such as on *firework*, *sunset*, and *waterfall*, the ROI locating performance of Diverse Density is apparently better than that of CkNN-ROI. While when the image semantics is not strongly coupled with a specific color pattern, such as on *castle* and *mountain*, the ROI locating performance of CkNN-ROI can be comparable to or even better than that of Diverse Density.

Overall, experiments reported in this section reveal that the efficiency of CkNN-ROI is far better than that of Diverse Density, the retrieval performance and ROI locating performance of CkNN-ROI are often worse than that of Diverse Density, but on many target concepts the performance of CkNN-ROI can be comparable or better. Moreover, considering that Diverse Density can hardly be really used in CBIR systems due to its overwhelmingly high time cost, CkNN-ROI seems like a better choice.

5 Conclusion

CBIR has been widely investigated in the past years. Although many CBIR systems have been developed, few of them can return relevant images where the ROI has been located. On the other hand, although multi-instance learning techniques have been introduced into CBIR, kNN style multi-instance algorithms have not been utilized. In this paper, these two issues are addressed by the CkNN-ROI algorithm, which is a new variant of Citation-kNN and could locate ROI in CBIR with high efficiency.

The experiments reported in this paper are performed on a relatively small image database and a small number of target concepts. Experiments on more images and more target concepts will be performed and reported in the future. Moreover, in the current version of CkNN-ROI, only one ROI can be located in each image and marked with a constant framework. It will be more helpful if all the ROI can be located and marked with a framework that can be with arbitrary shape. This is an interesting issue to be explored in the future.

It is noteworthy that CkNN-ROI is far from a flawless solution to the problem of ROI locating. Nevertheless, it is anticipated that this work might help raise the interest in applying kNN style multi-instance learning algorithms to tasks involving image analysis, and more importantly, arouse investigation on the problem of ROI locating in CBIR.

Acknowledgement

This work was supported by the National Science Foundation of China under the Grant No. 60473046, the Jiangsu Science Foundation under Grant No.

BK2005412, and the National 973 Fundamental Research Program of China under the Grant No. 2002CB312002.

References

1. Dasarathy, B.V.: Nearest Neighbor Norms: NN Pattern Classification Techniques. IEEE Computer Society Press, Los Alamitos, CA (1991)
2. Maron, O., Lozano-Pérez, T.: A framework for multiple-instance learning. In: Jordan, M.I., Kearns, M.J., Solla, S.A. (eds.): Advances in Neural Information Processing Systems, Vol. 10. MIT Press, Cambridge, MA (1998) 570–576
3. Maron, O., Ratan, A.L.: Multiple-instance learning for natural scene classification. In: Proceedings of the 15th International Conference on Machine Learning, Madison, WI (1998) 341–349
4. Rui, Y., Huang, T.S., Ortega, M., Mehrotra., S.: Relevance feedback: a power tool for interactive content-based image retrieval. IEEE Transactions on Circuits and Systems for Video Technology 8 (1998) 644–655
5. Smeulders, A.W.M., Worring, M., Santini, S., Gupta, A., Jain, R.: Content-based image retrieval at the end of the early years. IEEE Transactions on Pattern Analysis and Machine Intelligence 22 (2000) 1349–1380
6. Wang, J., Zucker, J.-D.: Solving the multiple-instance problem: a lazy learning approach. In: Proceedings of the 17th International Conference on Machine Learning, San Francisco, CA (2000) 1119–1125
7. Yang, C., Lozano-Pérez, T.: Image database retrieval with multiple-instance learning techniques. In: Proceedings of the 16th International Conference on Data Engineering, San Diego, CA (2000) 233–243
8. Zhang, Q., Goldman, S.A.: EM-DD: an improved multi-instance learning technique. In: Dietterich, T.G., Becker, S., Ghahramani, Z. (eds.): Advances in Neural Information Processing Systems, Vol. 14. MIT Press, Cambridge, MA (2002) 1073–1080
9. Zhang, Q., Yu, W., Goldman, S.A., Fritts, J.E. Content-based image retrieval using multiple-instance learning. In: Proceedings of the 19th International Conference on Machine Learning, Sydney, Australia (2002) 682–680
10. Zhou, Z.-H.: Multi-instance learning: a survey. Technical Report, AI Lab, Computer Science & Technology Department, Nanjing University, Nanjing, China, Mar. 2004
11. Zhou, Z.-H., Chen, K.-J., Jiang, Y.: Exploiting unlabeled data in content-based image retrieval. In: Boulicaut, J.-F., Esposito, F., Giannotti, F., Pedreschi, D. (eds.): Lecture Notes in Artificial Intelligence, Vol.3201. Springer, Berlin (2004) 525–536
12. Zhou, Z.-H., Jiang, K., Li, M.: Multi-instance learning based web mining. Applied Intelligence 22 (2005) 135–147
13. Zhou, Z.-H., Zhang, M.-L., Chen, K.-J.: A novel bag generator for image database retrieval with multi-instance learning techniques. In: Proceedings of the 15th IEEE International Conference on Tools with Artificial Intelligence, Sacramento, CA (2003) 565–569

Ensemble Selection for SuperParent-One-Dependence Estimators

Ying Yang, Kevin Korb, Kai Ming Ting, and Geoffrey I. Webb

School of Computer Science and Software Engineering,
Faculty of Information Technology,
Monash University, VIC 3800, Australia
{Ying.Yang, Kevin.Korb, Kaiming.Ting, Geoff.Webb}@Infotech.Monash.edu.au

Abstract. SuperParent-One-Dependence Estimators (SPODEs) loosen Naive-Bayes' attribute independence assumption by allowing each attribute to depend on a common single attribute (superparent) in addition to the class. An ensemble of SPODEs is able to achieve high classification accuracy with modest computational cost. This paper investigates how to select SPODEs for ensembling. Various popular model selection strategies are presented. Their learning efficacy and efficiency are theoretically analyzed and empirically verified. Accordingly, guidelines are investigated for choosing between selection criteria in differing contexts.

1 Introduction

One-Dependence Estimators (ODEs) provide a simple, yet powerful, alternative to Naive-Bayes classifiers (NB). As depicted in Figure 1, an ODE is similar to an NB except that each attribute is allowed to depend on at most one other attribute in addition to the class. Both theoretical analysis and empirical evidence have shown that ODEs can improve upon NB's accuracy when its attribute independence assumption is violated (Sahami, 1996; Friedman, Geiger, & Goldszmidt, 1997; Keogh & Pazzani, 1999). A SuperParent-One-Dependence Estimator (SPODE) is an ODE where all attributes depend on the *same* attribute (the *superparent*) in addition to the class (Keogh & Pazzani, 1999). Averaged One-Dependence Estimators (AODE) ensembles all SPODEs that satisfy a minimum support constraint (Webb, Boughton, & Wang, 2005) and estimate class conditional probabilities by averaging across them. This ensemble has demonstrated very high prediction accuracy with modest computational requirements.

This paper addresses how to select SPODEs for ensembling so as to minimize classification error. A data sample of m attributes can potentially have m SPODEs, each alternatively taking a different attribute as the superparent.

Finding answers to this SPODE selection problem is of great importance. Its solution will further improve classification accuracy while reducing classification time, albeit at a cost in additional training time.

The paper adopts the following notation. The training data D have n instances. Each instance $\mathbf{x} < x_1, x_2, \cdots, x_m, c >$ is composed of one class label c and m attribute values x_i ($i \in [1, m]$). Each attribute X_i ($i \in [1, m]$) takes v_i

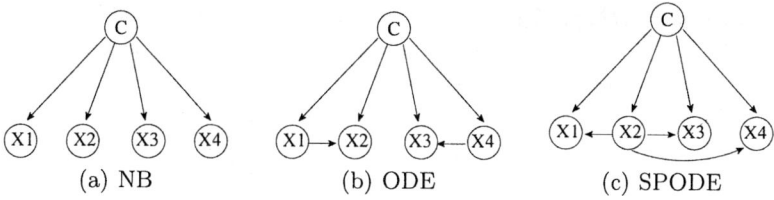

Fig. 1. Examples of NB, ODE and SPODE. Assuming there are four attributes $X_1 \cdots X_4$ and one class C. An arc points from a parent to a child.

distinct nominal values. Numeric values will be discretized beforehand. The parents of X_i are referred to by $\Pi(i)$.[1] ϕ_{ir} is the r-th joint state (jointly instantiated values) of the parents of X_i. $|\phi_i|$ is the number of joint states of X_i's parents.

2 SuperParent-One-Dependance Estimators (SPODE)

A SPODE requires all attributes to depend on the *same* attribute, namely the *superparent*, in addition to the class (Keogh & Pazzani, 1999). A SPODE with superparent X_p will estimate the probability of each class label c given an instance $\mathbf{x}$ as follows. Denote the value of X_p in $\mathbf{x}$ by x_p.

$$P(c\,|\,\mathbf{x}) = P(c,\mathbf{x}) \,/\, P(\mathbf{x}) = P(c,x_p,\mathbf{x}) \,/\, P(\mathbf{x}) = P(c,x_p) \times P(\mathbf{x}\,|\,c,x_p) \,/\, P(\mathbf{x})$$
$$= (P(c,x_p) \times \prod_{i=1}^{m} P(x_i\,|\,c,x_p)) \,/\, P(\mathbf{x}). \qquad (1)$$

Since the equality (1) holds for every SPODE, it also holds for the mean over any subset. An ensemble of k SPODEs corresponding to the superparents $X_{p_1}, \cdots, X_{p_k}$ estimate the class probability by averaging their results as follows.

$$P(c\,|\,\mathbf{x}) = \frac{\sum_{i=1}^{k} P(c,x_{p_i}) \times \prod_{j=1}^{m} P(x_j\,|\,c,x_{p_i})}{k} \,/\, P(\mathbf{x}). \qquad (2)$$

Averaged One-Dependence Estimators (AODE) (Webb et al., 2005) uses an ensemble of all SPODEs except for those who have less than 30 training instances. This simple selection criterion has offered surprisingly good performance, delivering competitive prediction accuracy together with improved efficiency in comparison to TAN (Friedman et al., 1997) and SP-TAN (Keogh & Pazzani, 1999). However, one should expect that selecting *out* poorly predictive SPODEs would both improve classification accuracy and speed, which is the goal of this paper.

---

[1] For a SPODE, the class is the root and has no parents. The superparent has a single parent: the class. Other attributes have two parents: the class and the superparent.

3 Selecting SPODEs

The general problem for model selection is, given training instances, how to decide which the best explanatory model(s) is within some model space. Given m attributes, the model space here consists of m SPODEs, each appointing one superparent. To select SPODEs, two key factors are the ordering metric and the stopping criterion. The former orders each SPODE on merit. The latter decides when SPODEs of sufficient merit are no longer to be found for the ensemble.

Five ordering metrics are studied here, including popular information-theoretic metrics and accuracy-based empirical metrics: Minimum Description Length (MDL), Minimum Message Length (MML), Leave One Out (LOO), Backward Sequential Elimination (BSE), and Forward Sequential Addition (FSA). The stopping criterion coupled with each metric may vary.

3.1 Information-Theoretic Metrics

Information-theoretic metrics provide a combined score for a proposed explanatory model and for the data given the model: $I(D|h)+I(h)$, where h is a SPODE and D are the training data. All such metrics aim to find a balance between goodness of fit ($I(D|h)$) and model simplicity ($I(h)$), and thereby achieve good modeling performance without overfitting the data.

The first term, $I(D|h)$, is shared by information-theoretic metrics and is:[2]

$$I(D|h) = n(\sum_{i=1}^{m+1} H(X_i) - \sum_{i=1}^{m+1} H(X_i, \Pi(i)))$$

where $H(X_i) = -\sum_{j=1}^{v_i} P(X_i = x_{ij}) \log P(X_i = x_{ij})$ is the entropy of X_i; and $H(X_i, \Pi(i)) = H(X_i) - H(X_i|\Pi(i)) = \sum_{j \leq v_i} \sum_{m \leq |\phi_i|} P(x_{ij}, \phi_{ir}) \log \frac{P(x_{ij}, \phi_{ir})}{P(x_{ij})P(\phi_{ir})}$ is the mutual information between X_i and its parent variables.[3]

Minimum Description Length (MDL). Suzuki (1996) developed MDL for learning Bayesian networks and calculates $I(h)$ as follows. For any root node X_i (where $\Pi(i) = \emptyset$), the product term on the right should be replaced by 1.

$$I_{MDL}(h) = \frac{1}{2} \log n (\sum_{i=1}^{m+1} (v_i - 1) \prod_{j \in \Pi(i)} v_j).$$

MDL is proportional to both Akaike's information criterion (AIC) (Akaike, 1974) and the Bayesian information criterion (BIC) (Schwarz, 1978), which respectively calculate $I(h)$ by $2(\sum_{i=1}^{m+1}(v_i - 1) \prod_{j \in \Pi(i)} v_j)$ and $\log n(\sum_{i=1}^{m+1}(v_i - 1) \prod_{j \in \Pi(i)} v_j)$. Hence, as our interest lies only in ordering the models, the analysis and evaluation of MDL here also represent those of AIC and BIC.

---

[2] For uniformity, X_i represents the class variable when $i = m + 1$.
[3] Generally the log base does not matter and this paper assumes natural logs (base-e).

Minimum Message Length (MML). MML rather than MDL is strictly efficient for encoding Bayesian networks. Also, it is a basic principle of MML that there is a relation between the precision of estimated parameters and the volume of data. So the MML score for $I(h)$ takes the data volume into account:[4]

$$I_{MML}(h) = \log(m+1)! + C_2^{m+1} - \log(m-1)! + \sum_{i=1}^{m+1} \frac{v_i - 1}{2}(\log \frac{\pi}{6} + 1)$$

$$- \log \prod_{i=1}^{m+1} \prod_{j=1}^{|\phi_i|} \frac{(v_i - 1)!}{(S_{ij} + v_i - 1)!} \prod_{l=1}^{v_i} \alpha_{ijl}!$$

where S_{ij} is the number of training instances where the parents $\Pi(i)$ take their joint j-th value, and α_{ijl} is the number of training instances where X_i takes its l-th value and $\Pi(i)$ take their j-th joint value. For any root X_i, $|\phi_i|$ should be treated as 1 and every instance should be treated as matching the parents for the purposes of computing S_{ij} and α_{ijl}.

3.2 Accuracy-Based Empirical Metrics

In contrast to theoretic metrics, empirical metrics select individual SPODEs, or their ensembles, strictly on how well they perform in predictive tests.

Leave One Out (LOO). LOO scores each individual SPODE with superparent X_p by its error on leave-one-out cross validation in the training data. Given this SPODE, LOO loops through the training data n times, each time training the SPODE from $(n-1)$ instances and using it to classify the remaining 1 instance. The misclassifications are summed and averaged over n iterations. The resulting classification error rate is taken as the metric value of the SPODE.

Backward Sequential Elimination (BSE). BSE starts with including every SPODE. It then uses hill-climbing search to iteratively eliminate SPODEs whose individual exclusion most lowers the classification error. In each iteration, suppose the current ensemble is $E_{current}$ involving k SPODEs. BSE eliminates each member SPODE in turn from $E_{current}$ and obtains an ensemble E_{test} of size $(k-1)$. It then calculates the leave-one-out error of E_{test}.[5] The E_{test} which yields the lowest error is retained and the corresponding eliminated SPODE is permanently deleted from the ensemble. The same process is applied to the new SPODE ensemble of size $(k-1)$ and so on, until the ensemble is empty. The order of the elimination produces a ranking order for SPODEs.

---

[4] C_2^{m+1} is combination of 2 out of $(m+1)$. See Chapter 8 (Korb & Nicholson, 2004) for details. Discrepancies between this and Korb and Nicholson's chapter in the first part of the formula are due to the restriction here to SPODEs, rather than the full range of Bayesian networks.

[5] A SPODE ensemble does classification by Formula 2.

Forward Sequential Addition (FSA). FSA begins with an empty ensemble. It then uses hill-climbing search to iteratively add SPODEs most helpful for lowering the ensemble's classification error. In each iteration, suppose the current ensemble is $E_{current}$ with k SPODEs. FSA in turn adds each candidate SPODE, one that has not been included into $E_{current}$, and obtains an ensemble E_{test} of size $(k+1)$. It then calculates the leave-one-out accuracy of E_{test}. The E_{test} who obtains the lowest error is retained and the corresponding added SPODE is permanently included into the ensemble. The same process is applied to the new SPODE ensemble of size $(k+1)$ and so on, until every SPODE has been included. The order of addition produces a ranking order for SPODEs.

3.3 Stopping Criterion

For MDL, MML and LOO, the lower its metric value, the higher priority is given to using a SPODE. The stopping criterion used here is the mean value of a metric over all candidate SPODEs. SPODEs whose metric values are lower than the mean will be included in the ensemble, while those of higher values will not.

For BSE, the process produces m SPODE ensembles, from size m to 1. Each ensemble is the one that achieves the lowest classification error among all ensembles of its size. Across these m ensembles, the one with the lowest classification error, E_{min}, gives the stopping point. Following the reverse order of the elimination order, one should first include the last SPODE to be eliminated and so on until the ensemble reaches the set of SPODEs that delivered E_{min}.

For FSA, the stopping criterion is similar to BSE's, being the ensemble that achieves the lowest classification error during the addition process. The difference is that one should follow the addition order to include SPODEs until the ensemble reaches the set of SPODEs that delivered E_{min}.

4 Time Complexity Analysis

Assume that the number of training instances and attributes are n and m. The average number of values for an attribute is v. The number of classes is c.

4.1 Training Overhead

MDL. The complexity of calculating $I(D|h)$ is $O(mv^2c)$. The dominating part is from $H(X_i, \Pi(i))$ which iterates through each value $(O(v))$, and then each joint value of the superparent and the class $(O(vc))$. The complexity of calculating $I(h)$ is $O(m)$.[6] Since the selection repeats for each attribute $(O(m))$, the overall complexity is $O(m * (mv^2c + m)) = O(m^2v^2c)$.

---
[6] Although MDL has an extra loop $\prod_{j \in \Pi(i)} v_j$, in case of SPODE, $|\Pi(i)|$ is of maximum value 2 (the superparent and the class). Hence it can be treated as a constant and does not increase the order of the complexity.

MML. The dominating complexity of MML for SPODEs is from $\prod_{i=1}^{m+1} \prod_{j=1}^{|\phi_i|} \frac{(v_i-1)!}{(S_{ij}+v_i-1)!} \prod_{l=1}^{v_i} \alpha_{ijl}!$. MML iterates through each attribute $(O(m))$; and then each joint value of the superparent and the class $(O(vc))$ for which two factorials are calculated $(O(v) + O(\frac{n}{vc}))$. On top of that it loops through each attribute value $(O(v))$ for which a third factorial is calculated $(O(\frac{n}{v^2 c}))$. Hence the complexity is $O(m * vc * (v + \frac{n}{vc}) * v * \frac{n}{v^2 c}) = O(mn(v + \frac{n}{vc}))$. This repeats for each attribute $(O(m))$ and the overall complexity is hence $O(m^2 n(v + \frac{n}{vc}))$.

LOO. To classify an instance, a SPODE will multiply the conditional probability of each attribute value given each class label and one (constant) superparent value. This results in $O(mc)$. To do leave-one-out cross validation, the classification will repeat n times. Hence the complexity is $O(mcn)$. This repeats for each attribute $(O(m))$ and the overall complexity is hence $O(m^2 cn)$.

BSE. The hill climbing procedure of reducing a SPODE ensemble of size m to 0 will render a complexity of $O(m^3)$. In the first round, it alternatively eliminates each of m SPODEs, each time testing a SPODE set of size $(m-1)$. In the second round, it alternatively eliminates each of $(m-1)$ SPODEs, each time testing a SPODE set of size $(m-2)$. Following this line of reasoning, the total number of SPODE evaluations is $m(m-1)+(m-1)(m-2)+\cdots+2*1+1*0 = O(m^3)$. As explained for LOO, to test each SPODE by leave-one-out cross validation will incur complexity of $O(mcn)$. As a result, the overall complexity is $O(m^4 cn)$.

FSA. The hill climbing procedure of increasing a SPODE ensemble from empty to size m will render a complexity of $O(m^2)$. In the first round, it alternatively adds each of m SPODEs, each time testing a SPODE set of size 1. In the second round, it alternatively adds each of $(m-1)$ SPODEs, each time testing a SPODE set of size 2. Following this line of reasoning, the total number of SPODE evaluations is $m*1+(m-1)*2+\cdots+2*(m-1)+1*m = O(m^2)$. As explained for LOO, to test each SPODE by leave-one-out cross validation will incur complexity of $O(mcn)$. As a result, the overall complexity is $O(m^3 cn)$.

4.2 Classification Overhead

Each selection metric leads to a linear combination of SPODEs. Hence, each metric's classification time complexity is of the same order $O(m^2 c)$, resulting from an $O(mc)$ classifying algorithm applied over an $O(m)$ sized ensemble.

5 Experiments

Experiments are conducted to find out the classification efficacy and efficiency for each selection metric.

5.1 Design and Results

Experimental data involve a comprehensive suite of 41 often-used data sets from the UCI machine learning repository (Blake & Merz, 2004). The statistics of each data set are presented in Table 2 in Appendix. To test a selection strategy, a 3-fold cross validation is conducted. Each candidate selection metric selects SPODEs according to evidence offered by the training data, and uses the resulting SPODE ensemble to classify the test data.

The classification error rate on each data set produced by each selection metric is presented in Table 2 in Appendix. The resulting win/lose/draw record of each metric compared against each other metric is presented in Table 1. A binomial sign test can be applied to each record to suggest whether the wins are by chance or systematic. The training time and classification time of each metric on each data set are presented in Table 3 in Appendix.

Table 1. Win-lose-draw record of each method in column compared against each in row. A **bold face** indicates that the wins against losses are statistically significant using a two-tailed binomial sign test at the critical level 0.05, and hence the corresponding method has a systematic (instead of by chance) advantage over its counterpart.

	NB	AODE	MDL	MML	LOO	FSA	BSE
NB	0/0/41	10/27/4	13/25/3	11/27/3	9/26/6	8/28/5	8/29/4
AODE	**27/10/4**	0/0/41	17/14/10	11/19/11	10/22/9	10/24/7	11/25/5
MDL	**25/13/3**	14/17/10	0/0/41	11/16/14	13/20/8	8/25/8	10/25/6
MML	**27/11/3**	19/11/11	16/11/14	0/0/41	17/19/5	12/24/5	13/21/7
LOO	**26/9/6**	**22/10/9**	20/13/8	19/17/5	0/0/41	9/23/9	10/24/7
FSA	**28/8/5**	**24/10/7**	**25/8/8**	**24/12/5**	23/9/9	0/0/41	13/11/17
BSE	**29/8/4**	**25/11/5**	**25/10/6**	21/13/7	**24/10/7**	11/13/17	0/0/41

5.2 Observations and Analysis

Selection Makes a Difference. Compared with AODE, all selection metrics except MDL win more often than not across the 41 data sets. LOO, FSA and BSE achieve win/lose/tie records of 22/10/9, 24/10/7 and 25/11/5 respectively, all of which are statistically significant at the 0.05 critical level according to the binomial sign test. This suggests that their advantages over AODE are systematic rather than due to chance. Hence model selection for SPODEs is advisable.

MML Is More Effective Than MDL. Among the information-theoretic metrics, MML wins against MDL more often than not. It also achieves lower arithmetic and geometric mean error than MDL. Compared with AODE, MML outperforms AODE with a win/lose/tie record of 19/11/11. By contrast, MDL loses to AODE (and so also AIC and BIC). The plausible explanation lies in MML providing a more efficient encoding of network structure, as well as taking the precision of its parameter estimates more seriously.

Empirical Metrics Are More Effective Than Theoretic Metrics. All three empirical metrics outperform their theoretic counterparts. Compared with the most effective theoretic metric MML, FSA achieves a win/lose/draw record of 24/12/5, BSE of 21/13/7 and LOO of 19/17/5. A possible reason is that not only do empirical metrics consider interactions among the class, the superparent and other attributes within the model, they also consider the interaction's impact on the classification accuracy. When selecting a classifier it is always desirable to optimize the thing that one wants to optimize, that is, the accuracy.

Measuring Ensembles Outperforms Measuring Single SPODEs. MDL, MML and LOO measure each individual SPODEs in isolation.[7] BSE and FSA measure a SPODE ensemble as a whole. FSA and BSE outperform the best theoretic metric MML with their win/lose/tie records being 24/12/5 and 21/13/7 respectively. They also outperform their empirical peer LOO with the win/lose/tie records being 23/9/9 and 24/10/7. Most of these wins are statistically significant at the 0.05 critical level. The reason is that the eventual classification task is carried out by a team of SPODEs. A SPODE that achieves high accuracy in isolation does not necessarily mean it is the most valuable one to include in an ensemble. Measuring the collective merit of a SPODE ensemble directly assesses what one is trying to learn, giving better results.

Metrics Have Different Training Efficiencies. For training efficiency, MDL is faster than MML while LOO is faster than FSA and BSE. Metrics that measure SPODE ensembles (FSA and BSE) are slower than those that measure individual SPODEs (MDL, MML and LOO) because the former need evaluate different aggregations of individual SPODEs.

All Metrics Are Fast for Classification. For classification efficiency, every selection metric is equally fast. In many real-world scenarios, classification efficiency is more important than training efficiency. The experimental results suggest that when training time is not taken into consideration, high classification accuracy and high classification efficiency are not necessarily exclusive. This observation suggests that metrics like FSA and BSE hold considerable promise as practical, accurate and feasible selection strategies.

6 Conclusion

An ensemble of SuperParent-One-Dependence-Estimators (SPODEs) retains the simplicity and direct theoretical foundation of naive Bayes while alleviating the limitations of its attribute independence assumption. In consequence it delivers effective classification with modest computational overhead (Webb et al., 2005). This paper focuses on how to select SPODEs for ensembling so as to further improve their classification accuracy. Popular information-theoretic metrics like MDL and MML, and accuracy-based empirical metrics like LOO, BSE and FSA have been applied for model selection.

---

[7] Note that the information-theoretic metrics can be extended to apply to ensembles rather than individual models. To do so is a future work.

Evidence obtained from theoretical analysis and empirical trials suggests that appropriate selection of the SPODEs to be included in an ensemble can further improve classification accuracy. Empirical metrics that involve testing SPODEs' classification performance on training data can outperform theoretic metrics at a cost of higher training time overhead. Metrics that measure the ensemble as a whole can outperform metrics that measure SPODEs in isolation, also at a cost of higher training time overhead. For classification time, various selection criteria all produce a linear combination of SPODEs. Hence, they have the same order of time complexity for classification.

As a result, if the training time is limited, it is suggested to employ MML, LOO, FSA and BSE in that order. If the training time is not a concern, FSA and BSE are metrics of choice among alternatives studied here.

Acknowledgement

This research was supported by Australian Research Council grant DP0556279.

References

Akaike, H. (1974). A new look at the statistical model identification. *IEEE Transactions on Automatic Control, AC-19*, 716–23.

Blake, C., & Merz, C. J. (2004). UCI repository of machine learning databases. [Machine-readable data repository]. University of California, Department of Information and Computer Science, Irvine, CA.

Friedman, N., Geiger, D., & Goldszmidt, M. (1997). Bayesian network classifiers. *Machine Learning, 29*(2-3), 131–163.

Keogh, E., & Pazzani, M. (1999). Learning augmented Bayesian classifiers: A comparison of distribution-based and classification-based approaches. In *Proceedings of the International Workshop on Artificial Intelligence and Statistics*, pp. 225–230.

Korb, K., & Nicholson, A. (2004). *Bayesian Artificial Intelligence*. Chapman & Hall/CRC, Boca Raton, FL.

Sahami, M. (1996). Learning limited dependence Bayesian classifiers. In *Proceedings of the Second International Conference on Knowledge Discovery and Data Mining*, pp. 334–338 Menlo Park, CA. AAAI Press.

Schwarz, G. (1978). Estimating the dimension of a model. *Annals of Statistics, 6*, 461–5.

Suzuki, J. (1996). Learning Bayesian belief networks based on the MDL principle: an efficient algorithm using the branch and bound technique. In *Proceedings of the International Conference on Machine Learning*, pp. 463–470.

Webb, G. I., Boughton, J., & Wang, Z. (2005). Not so naive Bayes: Averaged one-dependence estimators. *Machine Learning, 58*(1), 5–24.

Appendix

Table 2. Data sets and classification error (%)

Data Set	Size	Att	NB	AODE	MDL	MML	LOO	FSA	BSE
adult	48842	14	16.2	14.8	14.7	14.8	14.7	14.0	14.0
anneal	898	38	4.1	3.5	3.5	3.5	3.1	3.0	2.4
balance-scale	625	4	24.3	27.5	25.8	24.3	27.2	24.0	24.0
bands	1078	36	28.4	27.8	26.5	26.2	27.5	26.7	27.5
bcw	699	9	2.7	3.4	3.0	3.6	3.3	3.0	3.0
bupa	345	6	42.9	42.9	42.9	42.9	42.9	42.9	42.9
chess	551	39	13.1	12.2	12.7	13.2	12.0	11.1	11.8
cleveland	303	13	16.5	17.2	17.2	17.5	16.8	17.2	16.8
crx	690	15	13.9	12.8	12.9	13.2	13.0	13.9	12.9
echo74	74	6	24.3	25.7	23.0	23.0	24.3	23.0	23.0
german	1000	20	26.4	26.0	26.9	27.1	26.2	25.3	25.5
glass	214	9	23.4	22.9	22.9	22.4	22.9	22.9	22.4
heart	270	13	17.0	16.7	15.9	16.3	16.7	17.4	17.4
hepatitis	155	19	14.8	14.2	13.5	13.5	15.5	15.5	14.8
horse-colic	368	21	23.9	21.5	22.0	20.9	21.5	20.7	20.9
house-votes-84	435	16	9.9	6.2	5.7	5.7	5.5	4.8	6.0
hungarian	294	13	16.3	16.3	16.3	16.3	16.3	16.0	16.0
hypo	3772	29	1.9	2.0	2.2	2.2	1.9	1.2	1.2
ionosphere	351	34	9.7	9.7	10.3	8.8	9.4	9.7	9.1
iris	150	4	5.3	6.0	6.0	6.0	6.0	6.0	6.0
kr-vs-kp	6393	36	12.3	8.8	8.8	8.6	7.0	5.4	5.3
labor-neg	57	16	14.0	10.5	10.5	10.5	12.3	12.3	14.0
led	1000	7	26.6	26.7	26.3	26.2	26.8	26.8	26.8
letter-recognition	20000	16	26.1	12.1	13.9	12.3	11.7	11.4	11.3
lyn	296	18	15.5	13.5	12.2	12.8	12.2	12.2	12.2
mfeat-mor	2000	6	32.0	31.5	31.5	31.4	30.5	30.7	30.8
musk1	476	166	18.9	18.3	17.2	17.4	18.3	16.6	16.0
new-thyroid	215	5	7.0	7.0	8.4	8.4	8.4	6.5	6.5
pendigits	10992	16	12.6	2.6	3.0	2.6	2.7	2.6	2.6
pid	768	8	25.0	24.7	25.0	24.5	24.6	24.9	24.7
post-operative	90	8	30.0	27.8	32.2	26.7	28.9	28.9	28.9
promoters	106	57	9.4	17.9	15.1	16.0	15.1	9.4	9.4
ptn	339	17	52.2	53.4	52.8	52.8	53.4	52.2	54.3
sign	12546	8	36.3	28.9	28.5	28.5	28.6	28.0	28.1
sonar	208	60	26.9	26.0	27.4	28.8	26.9	27.4	28.8
soybean	683	35	11.3	7.6	7.8	7.6	7.5	7.5	8.2
thyroid	9169	29	11.7	8.3	8.7	8.3	8.3	7.9	8.0
ttt	958	9	29.1	25.3	25.5	25.5	26.6	25.6	25.3
vehicle	846	18	39.7	31.3	31.7	31.3	30.9	31.3	31.6
vowel-context	990	11	42.3	28.4	32.8	30.7	26.4	24.1	24.1
wine	178	13	2.2	2.8	2.8	2.8	2.2	3.9	3.9
Arithmetic Mean	-	-	19.9	18.1	18.2	17.9	18.0	17.4	17.5
Geometric Mean	-	-	20.0	18.2	18.3	18.0	18.0	17.5	17.6

Table 3. Training and classification time (milliseconds)

Data Set	Training Time					Classification Time				
	MDL	MML	LOO	BSE	FSA	MDL	MML	LOO	BSE	FSA
adult	3,320	11,630	12,640	133,530	114,240	580	570	670	450	460
anneal	240	360	1,650	78,220	53,290	40	20	40	40	40
balance-scale	20	30	20	60	70	30	0	30	20	10
bands	90	580	1,150	37,380	30,110	20	10	40	40	10
bcw	50	50	70	440	500	30	10	20	20	30
bupa	10	40	20	50	70	10	0	0	0	10
chess	40	670	1,120	50,380	40,780	30	40	40	30	20
cleveland	10	50	140	590	1,070	20	30	40	20	10
crx	60	130	400	3,060	1,770	30	10	40	20	10
echo74	10	10	20	20	30	0	0	0	0	10
german	10	430	450	8,340	6,770	20	60	20	40	20
glass	20	80	50	190	150	10	0	0	10	10
heart	20	90	70	600	470	20	10	10	10	10
hepatitis	20	60	80	810	1,350	0	0	0	10	20
horse-colic	30	110	220	3,390	2,920	0	20	10	40	10
house-votes-84	20	90	140	1,730	1,410	30	20	10	20	20
hungarian	20	50	80	870	560	10	20	10	20	20
hypo	260	5,080	4,280	181,750	126,870	110	250	180	90	80
ionosphere	220	470	670	18,340	16,090	10	10	20	10	10
iris	20	0	10	20	0	10	10	20	0	0
kr-vs-kp	350	3,510	5,590	224,960	169,020	310	120	90	80	80
labor-neg	10	20	30	150	270	0	10	0	10	0
led	20	80	80	760	610	30	40	10	30	30
letter	4,290	11,930	21,790	1,282,030	760,180	3,440	5,650	3,830	4,300	4,180
lyn	60	40	80	1,630	1,420	10	10	10	10	0
mfeat-mor	230	270	270	1,130	950	60	60	50	60	40
musk1	1,220	11,040	138,540	18,842,398	15,084,140	380	170	340	60	50
new-thyroid	0	30	40	20	50	10	10	10	0	20
pendigits	2,050	3,820	8,250	252,520	165,620	610	780	780	840	830
pid	40	70	120	360	340	10	30	20	10	20
post-operative	10	0	30	40	30	10	0	0	0	0
promoters	290	370	1,190	34,050	37,250	10	10	0	0	0
ptn	90	80	200	10,230	6,470	50	30	40	20	20
sign	770	3,260	1,520	6,750	6,010	140	280	120	140	160
sonar	160	600	1,390	106,300	72,010	40	20	30	10	20
soybean	540	660	2,260	594,910	252,010	230	260	360	130	100
thyroid	1,090	6,540	15,470	2,591,640	1,302,000	3,920	750	1,340	680	910
ttt	10	100	60	640	480	20	10	30	20	30
vehicle	110	300	390	8,550	5,790	40	40	50	10	30
vowel-context	300	360	400	3,960	2,940	50	70	40	40	20
wine	30	60	60	440	370	0	10	0	10	0
Arithmetic Mean	394	1,540	5,391	597,152	445,524	253	230	204	179	179

Global Versus Local Constructive Function Approximation for On-Line Reinforcement Learning

Peter Vamplew and Robert Ollington

School of Computing, University of Tasmania, Private Bag 100, Hobart,
Tasmania 7001, Australia
Peter.Vamplew@utas.edu.au

Abstract. In order to scale to large state-spaces, reinforcement learning (RL) algorithms need to apply function approximation techniques. Research on function approximation for RL has so far focused either on global methods with a static structure or on constructive architectures using locally responsive units. The former, whilst achieving some notable successes, has also failed on some relatively simple tasks. The locally constructive approach is more stable, but may scale poorly to higher-dimensional inputs. This paper examines two globally constructive algorithms based on the Cascor supervised-learning algorithm. These algorithms are applied within the sarsa RL algorithm, and their performance compared against a multi-layer perceptron and a locally constructive algorithm (the Resource Allocating Network). It is shown that the globally constructive algorithms are less stable, but that on some tasks they achieve similar performance to the RAN, whilst generating more compact solutions.

1 Introduction

Reinforcement learning (RL) addresses the problem of an agent interacting with an environment. The agent repeatedly observes the current state, selects and executes an action, and receives a scalar reward. The agent must learn a mapping from state-to-action to maximise the long-term reward. One way to do this is to learn the expected return, either per state or per state-action pair. Many algorithms for learning these values are based on the use of temporal differences (TD) [1] where the value of the current state is used to update the estimated value of previous states. For problems with small state-spaces the values can be stored in a table, but as the dimensionality of the state increases, the storage requirements become impractical. In addition learning slows, as tabular algorithms only learn about states which the agent has experienced. For such tasks function approximation must instead be used to estimate the values. Function approximators require less storage and can generalise from experienced states to similar states that are yet to be visited, hence increasing the rate of learning.

Two main approaches to function approximation have been explored in the RL literature. Global approximators such as neural networks have been applied successfully to a range of problems, such as elevator control [2] and backgammon [3]. However this success has failed to be replicated on other, similar tasks. The second approach is to use local approximators such as CMACs [4] or radial-basis functions [5]. The local approach has been shown to be more stable and more amenable to formal analysis, but may scale less well to higher-dimensional state spaces [6].

Several sources have argued for constructive approaches to function approximation in RL. [7] showed that function approximators are prone to overestimation of values when used with RL algorithms, and argued that approximators with a bounded memory are less likely to overcome this systematic bias than those with an unbounded memory. [3] suggests the use of Cascor networks to avoid the need to completely retrain the system when new input features are added. More generally constructive algorithms are suited to tasks which require building on previously knowledge.

Within the localised approximator research, there has been significant exploration of constructive approximators. [8] adapted the Resource Allocating Network (RAN) to RL, whilst [9] explored the use of constructive Sparse Distributed Memories. In contrast the use of constructive global approximators for RL has been minimal. This style of system has been widely used for supervised learning, with Cascade-Correlation (Cascor) [10] being a widely adopted algorithm. Cascor has been shown to equal or outperform fixed-architecture networks on a wide range of supervised learning tasks [10, 11]. Despite this, the only previous work using a Cascor network for RL appears to be that of [12, 13], which will be discussed in Section 3.

2 Constructive Learning Algorithms

Constructive neural networks can be categorised on whether their hidden neurons are locally or globally responsive. This section will describe one algorithm of each type, which are used as the basis for the RL systems described in Sections 3 and 4.

2.1 Cascade Networks

Cascor is a globally-constructive algorithm. A Cascor net starts with each input connected to every output, with no hidden neurons. The network is trained to minimise the MSE on a set of training examples. The error is monitored, and if it fails to fall sufficiently over recent training epochs the decision is made to add a new hidden neuron. A pool of candidates is created, connected to all inputs and any prior hidden neurons. Candidates are trained to maximise the correlation between their activation and the error on the training set. The candidate with the highest correlation is added to the net, its input weights are frozen, and it is connected to the outputs with random weights. Training of output weights and candidates continues to alternate until a suitable solution is found or a maximum network size is reached.

2.2 Resource Allocating Networks

As with Cascor, a RAN [14] starts from a minimal architecture containing just input and output neurons. During training the RAN adds hidden units which use a locally-responsive gaussian activation function. When a new input pattern is presented to the network, it is tested against two novelty criteria. If the distance between this pattern and the centre of the closest hidden neuron exceeds a threshold, and the network's error on this input exceeds an error threshold, then a new hidden neuron is added to the network, with its parameters determined from the current input. The centre of the gaussian is set to the current input, and the width is set to a percentage of the distance to the centre of the nearest existing hidden neuron. The weight of the connection from the new neuron to each output is set to equal the current error at that output. If the current input does not meet the novelty criteria, then the weights of the output neurons and the centres of the hidden neurons are trained using gradient descent.

The RAN has two potential advantages over Cascor. First the direct initialisation of the hidden neuron parameters is potentially much faster than the training of candidates. This is of benefit in online learning as it may allow more rapid improvements in performance. Second the localised response of the RAN's neurons may be of benefit in problems with discontinuities in the output. However the RAN's single hidden-layer architecture prevents it forming the higher-level feature detectors available in Cascor. In addition the localised nature of the RAN's neurons means that many more neurons may be required to solve a given problem. So it is not clear *a priori* which of these architectures will be best suited for RL value approximation.

3 Adapting Cascor to Online RL

Several features of Cascor prevent it from being applied directly to online RL. [12, 13] modified the RL process to allow direct use of the Cascor algorithm. They propose a learning algorithm with two alternating stages. Initially the agent executes actions, and stores the input and the TD target value in a cache. Once the cache is full, a Cascor network is trained on the cached examples. Following training the cache is cleared and the algorithm returns to cache-filling. Results are reported for tic-tac-toe, car-rental and backgammon tasks. The results for the first two tasks are promising, but poor for the backgammon task. In addition, this approach may not be suitable in real-time tasks due to the time requirements of the training phase.

In contrast we modified Cascor to allow direct incorporation into existing online RL algorithms. For this paper we used the sarsa algorithm [15], but the cascade network should be equally applicable to other TD-based algorithms. As in [15] we use a separate single-output network for each action.

3.1 Choice of Cascade Algorithm, and Weight Update Algorithm

Several authors have shown that Cascor, whilst effective for classification, is less successful for regression due to the correlation term driving hidden unit activations to their extreme values, making it difficult to produce a smoothly varying output [16, 17]. Learning state values is a regression task, and so Cascor may not be the best algorithm for this case. Several variants of Cascor have been proposed to address this issue [16, 18, 19]. We have used the Cascade2 [18] and Fixed Cascade Error (FCE) [19] algorithms. Cascade2 trains candidates to directly minimise the residual error and simultaneously trains output weights for each candidate which are also transplanted to the main network when a new hidden node is added. FCE remains closer to the original Cascor algorithm, but uses a different objective function to be maximised which avoids the problems resulting from using the correlation term.

Whilst several weight update algorithms can be used in the cascade training process, most implementations use Quickprop [20]. Quickprop uses an estimate of the second derivative of the error to produce faster training. However it is designed for batch-training, and can not readily be adapted to online training. Therefore for these experiments steepest-descent backpropagation was used instead. This was also used for the multi-layer perceptron and RAN results reported here, to ensure that any differences in results were due to the architectural aspects of the networks.

3.2 Serial Versus Parallel Training of Candidates

In supervised learning, the cascade training process alternates between training the output weights, and training the candidates. This approach which we will call 'serial training' facilitates the training of the candidates by ensuring that the problem facing them is static, as the main net does not change during candidates training. However serial training has serious disadvantages for on-line learning. During training of the output weights, the agent interacts with the environment whilst also adjusting its behaviour. However during candidate training the agent is still interacting with the environment, but the candidate weight adjustments do not alter the agent's policy until a new hidden neuron is added, so the agent is interacting with the environment whilst following a fixed, sub-optimal policy which may significantly impact on its online performance. [12, 13] address this issue by caching data to use in off-line training. The time required to fill the cache will be much smaller than the time spent training the network and therefore this approach reduces the regret due to following a static, non-optimal policy, but it does not produce a truly on-line algorithm.

For this reason we have used parallel candidate training. After each time-step the TD error δ_{TD} is calculated. The eligibility traces and weights associated with the output neuron are updated, as shown in equations 1 and 2, where w_i is the weight of the connection from the ith input/hidden neuron to the output neuron, e_i is the eligibility trace for that connection, I_i is the output of the ith input/hidden neuron, λ is the trace decay rate and α is the learning rate.

$$e_i' = \lambda e_i, \text{ if this action was not the most recently selected} \quad (1)$$

$$e_i' = I_i + \lambda e_i, \text{ if this action was the most recently selected}$$

$$\Delta w_i = \alpha \delta_{TD} e_i' \quad (2)$$

In parallel, eligibility trace and weight updates are performed for candidate neurons. For Cascade2, the input and output weights for the candidates are trained to reduce the residual error, by minimising the following term (where w_c is the output weight for the candidate neuron, and o_c is the current activation of the candidate neuron):

$$\delta_c = \delta_{TD} - w_c o_c \quad (3)$$

For FCE the candidates are trained to maximise the value of the following function:

$$C_{FE} = \left(\delta_{TD} - \overline{\delta_{TD}}\right) p_c \quad (4)$$

3.3 Patience Testing Across Multiple Networks

In Cascor, the output error is accumulated during training, and tested against a patience threshold to decide whether to add a new node. In sarsa the same error (δ_{TD}) is used for all networks so basing patience tests on this term would result in the same topology for all networks. The function to be learnt may vary in complexity between the different actions, and so each net should be able to independently determine its own topology. One means to achieve this is to weight the δ_{TD} term based on its relevance to each action, which will depend on how recently that action has been selected. A replacing eligibility trace e_n is maintained for each net, and the following weighted error term is used in the patience testing process (where P is the number of episodes in the patience period, and t_E is the number of time-steps in episode E):

$$\frac{\sum_{E=1}^{P}\sum_{t=1}^{t_E} \delta_{TD}^2 e_n}{\sum_{E=1}^{P}\sum_{t=1}^{t_E} e_n} \quad (5)$$

If this value fails to improve sufficiently on the value from the previous patience period then a candidate will be selected to add to the network. The candidate with the lowest value for the metric in equation 6 is selected to be added to the main network.

$$\sum_{E=1}^{P}\sum_{t=1}^{t_E}\delta_C^2 e_n \qquad (6)$$

3.4 The Cascade-Sarsa Algorithm

Combining all of the issues discussed in Sections 3.1 to 3.3 yields the cascade-sarsa algorithm, as shown in Figure 1. The Cascade2 and FCE variants differ only in the calculation of the eligibility traces.

```
P_last = +∞
while (!finished training) do
{
    P_current = 0
    for P learning episodes
    {
        clear all eligibility traces
        while (! end of the episode)
        {
            observe the current state of the environment
            calculate the output of each network
            select an action a e-greedily based on networks' outputs
            Q_t = output of network a
            if this action is not the first in the episode
                δ_TD = r + γQ_t - Q_t-1
                for each network
                    update output weights to minimise δ_TD
                    update candidate weights
                    recalculate network activations
                Q_t-1 = output of network a
            update eligibility traces for all weights in all networks
            execute action a and observe the reward r
            update Pcurrent as per equation 5
        }
    }
    if P_current > patience-threshold * Plast
        select best candidate (per equation 6) and add to the network
        P_last = +∞
    else
        P_last = P_current
}
```

Fig. 1. The Cascade-sarsa algorithm

4 Adapting the RAN to Online RL

Unlike Cascor, the RAN was designed for on-line function approximation and so requires little modification for use in RL. As with the Cascade networks, a separate RAN was created for each possible action. As discussed in Section 3.3 it is preferable for each net to be free to determine its own topology. Therefore we maintain a replacing eligibility trace for each network, and weight the TD error by this trace when testing an input pattern against the error threshold. It is important to note that this weighted error is only used for this purpose; all weight updates are calculated based on the original unweighted TD error.

[5] reported that training the centres of existing hidden neurons via gradient-descent as in the original supervised RAN was found to be detrimental in a RL context. Our experience agreed with this observation, and therefore in these experiments the centres of neurons were fixed once added to the network, with only the output weights subject to gradient-descent training.

5 Experimental Method

The constructive RL algorithms described in Sections 3 and 4 were compared against a multi-layer perceptron on three problems from the RL literature - Acrobot, Mountain-Car and Puddleworld [4, 21] (see Figure 2). These problems were chosen as [21] reports that a MLP was unable to learn a suitable policy on any of these tasks.

The Acrobot is a two-link robot, able to apply torque only at the joint between the links. The task is to raise the tip to a designated height above the first joint. The system is described by four continuous variables - the joints' angular positions and velocities. As the positions are cyclical, each position is encoded by a pair of inputs storing the sine and cosine of the angle, to avoid discontinuities in the input [22]. This results in a total of six input neurons for this task. There are three actions - exerting positive torque, negative torque or no torque. A penalty of -1 is received on all steps on which the goal-state is not reached.

The Mountain-Car task requires a car to escape from a valley. The engine is less powerful than gravity, and so the car must reverse up the left of the valley to build enough potential energy to escape. The inputs are the car's current position and velocity, and there are three actions - full throttle forward, full throttle backward, and zero throttle. The penalty structure is the same as for the Acrobot task.

Puddleworld is a two-dimensional environment. The agent starts at a random state and has to reach the goal. It receives its current coordinates as input, and selects between four actions (left, right, up or down) which move 0.05 units (plus a small amount of gaussian noise) in the desired direction. The penalty structure is the same as for the other tasks, with an additional penalty if the agent is within a puddle.

Four styles of network were applied to each problem - a multi-layer perceptron with a single hidden layer, Cascade2, FCE and RAN. All networks used linear activation functions for their output neurons. For each problem, multiple trials were run for each network to find appropriate values for the parameters (the learning rate α and eligibility trace decay factor λ; the number of hidden nodes for the MLP; the patience period length for the cascade networks; and the error and distance thresholds for the RAN). A fixed patience threshold of 0.95 was used for all cascade network trials. For each set of parameters 20 networks were trained, with different initial weights. Each network was trained over 1000 episodes, using ε-greedy selection. ε was set to 0.2 for the Puddleworld and Mountain-Car tasks, and to a lower value of 0.05 for the Acrobot task as non-optimal actions can have a greater effect in this task [4]. Episodes ended either when the goal state was reached, or after a maximum number of time-steps (a limit of 1000 steps was used for Mountain-Car and Puddleworld and 500 for Acrobot). No discounting was used.

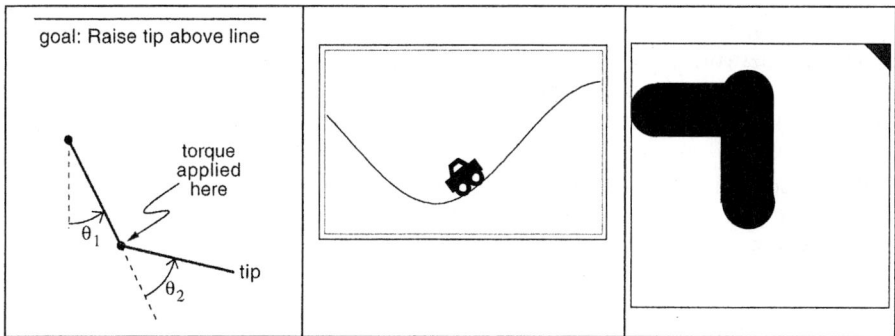

Fig. 2. (a) Acrobot (from [23, p. 271]) (b) Mountain-Car. The goal is to escape from the right-hand edge of the valley. (c) Puddleworld. The goal is the triangle in the top-right corner.

For each trial the on-line performance was assessed via the mean reward received per episode. Whilst on-line performance is an important measure of the performance of an on-line learning algorithm, it has the potential to be misleading as the choice of the number of episodes over which to measure performance introduces a source of bias. Therefore the quality of the final policy learnt by each network was also measured, in two ways. The first was the mean on-line reward received over the final 50 episodes of training - this will be called the final on-line reward. The second approach was to measure the network's off-line performance by running a further set of episodes after training, using strictly greedy selection and no learning.

6 Results and Discussion

Table 1 shows the mean results achieved by each network type, over the 20 networks trained using the best parameter set found for that type of network. In line with the findings of [21], the fixed-architecture network found these tasks difficult, faring poorly on all tasks in on-line and particularly off-line performance. In contrast the RAN performed well on all three benchmarks for both the on-line and off-line measures. However this performance was only achieved by choosing parameters which allowed the RAN to create a very large number of hidden neurons. The Acrobot task which had the highest input dimensionality also resulted in the largest network as every trial added the maximum allowed 200 neurons.

The performance of the two cascade constructive algorithms was less consistent. Both Cascade2 and FCE were competitive with RAN on the Acrobot and Mountain-Car tasks, and due to the use of globally-responsive neurons were able to achieve this performance using far fewer resource. However both cascade algorithms failed on the Puddleworld, failing to match even the relatively poor on-line results of the MLP.

Some insight into the inconsistent performance of the cascade algorithms is given by examining the policies required for each task. The decision boundaries in the Mountain-Car and Acrobot tasks are primarily linear, and hence the cascade algorithms perform well as the candidates can readily learn to improve the value approximation. In contrast Puddleworld requires the networks to form localised regions within the input space, which can not be achieved by a single hidden neuron. In contrast the RAN's localised neurons can readily adjust the estimate in just the relevant regions of the input-space. Even the MLP is better suited to this problem than the cascade networks. As it trains multiple hidden neurons simultaneously, they can collectively produce the necessary localised change in the system's output, although clearly from the results this process is slower and less accurate than that of the RAN.

Table 1. Results on the Acrobot, Mountain-Car and Puddleworld tasks, for the best parameter set found for each style of network. The results are the means over 20 trials from different starting weights.

		MLP	Cascade2	FCE	RAN
Acrobot	Parameters	$\lambda = .8$, $\alpha = 0.005$	$P = 40$, $\lambda = 1$, $\alpha = 0.001$	$P = 60$, $\lambda = 1$, $\alpha = 0.0005$	$E = 2$, $\lambda = 0.8$, $\alpha = 0.01$
	Hidden nodes	10.0	8.5	5.3	200.0
	On-line (all episodes)	-260.1	-122.0	-122.4	-120.1
	On-line (final)	-165.3	-108.0	-108.6	-111.0
	Off-line	-290.7	-103.4	-96.7	-102.4
Mountain-Car	Parameters	$\lambda = 0.8$, $\alpha = 0.001$	$P = 60$, $\lambda = 1$, $\alpha = 0.001$	$P = 20$, $\lambda = 1$, $\alpha = 0.001$	$E = 2$, $\lambda = 1$, $\alpha = 0.001$
	Hidden nodes	12.0	5.4	19.1	150.0
	On-line (all episodes)	-216.4	-91.5	-91.7	-87.6
	On-line (final)	-157.5	-83.0	-86.6	-74.1
	Off-line	-319.2	-77.4	-98.7	-91.4
Puddleworld	Parameters	$\lambda = .6$, $\alpha = 0.01$	$P = 80$, $\lambda = .9$, $\alpha = 0.001$	$P = 40$, $\lambda = 1$, $\alpha = 0.001$	$E = 2$, $\lambda = 0.7$, $\alpha = 0.001$
	Hidden nodes	12.0	4.7	4.0	129.7
	On-line (all episodes)	-163.9	-335.2	-435.8	-158.6
	On-line (final)	-103.5	-193.0	-255.5	-61.7
	Off-line	-406.9	-299.8	-301.6	-48.4

7 Conclusion and Future Work

The function approximation abilities of neural networks should make them valuable for use in RL, but fixed-architecture nets have been found to be unreliable when trained using TD methods. Previous work has suggested the use of constructive function approximators, with the majority of algorithms using locally-responsive units. This paper has presented two constructive algorithms using globally-responsive units. It has been shown that for some problems these globally-constructive algorithms can provide similar performance to a locally-constructive algorithm (the RAN), whilst producing far more compact solutions. However the Puddleworld task exposed major failings in the globally-constructive algorithms as they struggle to deal with localised discontinuities in the value function.

Generating compact solutions is a potentially useful feature of globally constructive methods, as it offers the possibility of scaling more effectively to problems with high input dimensionality. However these benefits can only be realised if the weakness of these algorithms on problems such as Puddleworld can be overcome. We intend to attack this problem in two ways. One approach is to modify the cascade algorithm to encourage the formation of groups of neurons which together function as a locally-responsive unit. A second approach is to modify a locally-constructive method to allow less localised units where they would prove useful.

References

1. Sutton, R.S. (1988). Learning to predict by the methods of temporal differences, Machine Learning, Vol. 3, pp 9-44.
2. Crites, R.H. and Barto, A.G. (1996), Improving Elevator Performance Using Reinforcement Learning, NIPS-8.
3. Tesauro, G. J. (1995), Temporal difference learning and TD-Gammon, Communications of the ACM. 38(3), pp.58-68.
4. Sutton R.S. (1996). Generalisation in reinforcement learning: Successful examples using sparse coarse coding. In Touretzky D.S., Mozer M.C., & Hasselmo M.E. (Eds.). Advances in Neural Information Processing Systems: Proceedings of the 1995 Conference (1038-1044). Cambridge, MA: The MIT Press.
5. Kretchmar, R. M. and C. W. Anderson (1997). Comparison of CMACs and RBFs for local function approximators in reinforcement learning. IEEE International Conference on Neural Networks.
6. Coulom, R. (2002). Feedforward Neural Networks in Reinforcement Learning Applied to High-dimensional Motor Control. ALT2002, Springer-Verlag.
7. Thrun, S. and Schwartz, A. (1993), Issues in Using Function Approximation for Reinforcement Learning, Proceedings of the Fourth Connectionist Models Summer School, Hillsdale, NJ, Dec 1993.
8. Anderson, C. W. (1993). Q-learning with hidden unit restarting. Advances in Neural Information Processing Systems.
9. Ratitch, B. and D. Precup (2004). Sparse Distributed Memories for On-Line Value-Based Reinforcement Learning. ECML.
10. Fahlman, S. E. and Lebiere, C. (1990). The Cascade-Correlation Learning Architecture. in Touretzky, D.S., Advances in Neural Information Processing II, Morgan Kauffman.

11. Waugh, S.G. (1995), Extending and benchmarking Cascade-Correlation, PhD thesis, Department of Computer Science, University of Tasmania
12. Rivest, F. and D. Precup (2003). Combining TD-learning with Cascade-correlation Networks. Twentieth International Conference on Machine Learning, Washington DC.
13. Bellemare, M.G., Precup, D. and Rivest, F. (2004), Reinforcement Learning Using Cascade-Correlation Neural Networks, Technical Report RL-3.04, McGill University.
14. Platt, J. (1991). "A Resource-Allocating Network for Function Interpolation." Neural Computation 3: 213-225.
15. Rummery, G. and M. Niranjan (1994). On-line Q-Learning Using Connectionist Systems. Cambridge, Cambridge University Engineering Department.
16. Adams, A. and S. Waugh (1995), Function Evaluation and the Cascade-Correlation Architecture, IEEE International Conference on Neural Networks. pp. 942-946.
17. Hwang, J.-H., S.-S. You, et al. (1996). "The Cascade-Correlation Learning: A Projection Pursuit Learning Perspective." IEEE Transactions on Neural Networks 7(2): 278-288.
18. Prechelt, L. (1997). Investigation of the CasCor Family of Learning Algorithms, in Neural Networks, 10 (5) : 885-896.
19. Lahnajarvi, J. J.T., Lehtokangas, M.I., Saarinen, J.P.P., (2002). Evaluation of constructive neural networks with cascaded architectures, in Neurocomputing 48: 573-607.
20. Fahlman, S. E. (1988) "Faster-Learning Variations on Back-Propagation: An Empirical Study", Proceedings of the 1988 Connectionist Models Summer School
21. Boyan, J.A. and Moore, A.W. (1995), Generalization in reinforcement learning: Safely approximating the value function, NIPS-7.
22. Adams, A and Vamplew, P (1998), "Encoding and Decoding Cyclic Data", The South Pacific Journal of Natural Science, Vol 16, pp. 54-58
23. Sutton, R. and Barto, S. (1998), Reinforcement Learning, MIT Press

Any-Cost Discovery: Learning Optimal Classification Rules

Ailing Ni, Xiaofeng Zhu, and Chengqi Zhang

Department of Computer Science, GuangXi Normal University, Guilin, 541004, China
Faculty of Information Technology, University of Technology Sydney, Australia
zynal13@163.com, chengqi@it.uts.edu.au

Abstract. Fully taking into account the hints possibly hidden in the absent data, this paper proposes a new criterion when selecting attributes for splitting to build a decision tree for a given dataset. In our approach, it must pay a certain cost to obtain an attribute value and pay a cost if a prediction is error. We use different scales for the two kinds of cost instead of the same cost scale defined by previous works. We propose a new algorithm to build decision tree with null branch strategy to minimize the misclassification cost. When consumer offers finite resources, we can make the best use of the resources as well as optimal results obtained by the tree. We also consider discounts in test costs when groups of attributes are tested together. In addition, we also put forward advice about whether it is worthy of increasing resources or not. Our results can be readily applied to real-world diagnosis tasks, such as medical diagnosis where doctors must try to determine what tests should be performed for a patient to minimize the misclassification cost in certain resources.

1 Introduction

Existing machine learning and data mining algorithms depend strongly on the quality of the data. And the data quality has been very important yet challenging. However, the data is often incomplete in real-world applications. There are two major kinds of the incompleteness of the data: one is missing, that is to say, the data exist but it is missing now; the other is absent, namely, there was not any data originally. To the former, there are many methods to patch up the missing data; the latter, e.g., in medical diagnosis, to obtain the value of an attribute need cost and part of examination is expensive. So to those people who have not enough money to perform the expensive examination, the attribute value cannot be obtained but be absent. It is unmeaning and unreasonable if we patch up the absent value. From the perspective of classical decision tree learning criterion, these incomplete data is disadvantageous for the classification right-ratio. But from the view of reality, the presence of these absent data is because of limited resources. And most of the resources are limited, so the absent data is inevitably. That is to say, the absent data is an important strategy. So we hope there is a method, which can select the most proper attributes to test according to the limited resources, and let some attributes' value absent.

It is enjoyment that some experts has begun to research the test cost and the misclassification cost [1][2][3][4][5][7][8]. They considered not only the misclassification cost but also test cost instead of the right ratio of the classification or expect to achieve a balance between the test cost and the misclassification cost. [2][5] proposed a new method to build a cost-sensitive decision tree to minimal the total cost(the test cost and the misclassification cost). Ling et al. also proposed several strategies to obtain the optimal total cost in [5]. But in their work, the test cost and the misclassification cost have been defined on the same cost scale, such as the dollar cost incurred in a medical diagnosis. For example, the test cost of attribute A1 is 50 dollars, the A2 is 20 dollars, the cost of false positive is 600 dollars, and the cost of false negative is 800 dollars.

But in fact, the same cost scale is not always reasonable. For sometimes we may meet difficulty to define the multiple costs on the same cost scale. It is not only a technology issue, but also a social issue. For example, in medical diagnosis, how much money you should assign for a misclassification cost? So we need to involve both of the two cost scales.

In this paper, we use two different cost scales for test costs and misclassification costs. That is to say, the scale of test cost is dollars but the misclassification cost just is a relative value. For making the best use of limited resources, note that there are possibly hints about information of classification confining within different resources hidden in the database with absent values. So we propose a new method to obtain an optimal result confining within different resources in absent data. In addition, the same money has different effects at different stage. We also put forward advice about whether it is worthy of increasing resources or not.

The rest of the paper is organized as follows. In Section 2, we review the related work. In Section 3, we first introduce some simple conceptions that used in this paper. In Section 4, we present the process and the method of building decision tree. The strategy of dealing with the discount is introduced in Section 5. Then we show the results of the experiments in Section 6. Finally we conclude the work in Section 7.

2 Review of Previous Work

More recently, researchers have begun to consider both test and misclassification costs[1][2][3][4][5][7][8]. The objective is to minimize the expected total cost of tests and misclassifications. Turney [6] analyzed a whole variety of costs, such as misclassification costs, test costs, active learning costs, computation cost, human-computer interaction cost, etc, in which, the first two types of costs are the misclassification costs and the test costs.

In Zubek [7], the cost-sensitive learning problem is cast as a Markov Decision Process (MDP), and an optimal solution is given as a search in a state space for optimal policies. For a given new case, depending on the values obtained so far, the optimal policy can suggest a best action to perform in order to both minimize the misclassification and the test costs. Their research adopts an optimal search strategy, which may incur very high computational cost to conduct the search. In contrast, we adopt the local search using a polynomial time algorithm to build a new decision trees.

Similar in the interest in constructing an optimal learner, Greiner [8] studied the theoretical aspects of active learning with test costs using a PAC learning framework.

Turney [4] presented a genetic algorithm to build a decision tree to minimize the cost of tests and misclassification. Our algorithm also build a decision tree, and it is expected to be more efficient because of some special strategies.

Ling et al. [5] propose a new decision tree learning program that uses minimal total cost of tests and misclassifications as the attribute split criterion. They also propose several test strategies to handle the missing value in the test data. But in their tree, it assumes both the test cost and the misclassification cost have been defined on the same scale, such as the dollar cost incurred in a medical diagnosis.

In our work, we address the problems above by building an any-cost sensitive decision tree by involving two kinds of cost scales and null branch strategy, which make the best use of given specific resources and minimize the misclassification cost. We also present a new strategy to deal with the discount. In addition, we also put forward advice about whether it is worthy of increasing resources or not.

3 Conception

Decision tree is one of the classical classifier. ID3 algorithm is one method to build decision tree proposed by Quinlan. It uses the Gain as a measurement to select attributes for splitting to build a decision tree. Later Quinlan use the Gain Ratio instead of Gain in the C4.5 for avoiding partial to an attribute with many values.

1) Gain Ratio

$$\text{GainRatio}(A,T) = \text{Gain}(A,T)/\text{SplitInfo}(A,T) \tag{1}$$

where, Gain(A,T) is the information brought by condition attribution A in T, namely Gain Ratio. The information brought by the attribute will be larger when the Gain Ratio is larger. The Gain(A,T) obtained by the following equation:

$$\text{Gain}(A,T) = \text{Info}(T) - \text{Info}(A,T)$$

where, $\text{Info}(T) = -(p_1 * \log_2(p_1) + p_2 * \log(p_2) + \cdots + p_n * \log_2(p_n))$, p_i is the percentage of the i-th value of decision attribute in all object T.

$\text{Info}(A,T) = \sum_{i=1}^{n} |T_i|/|T| * \text{Info}(T_i)$, where, $|T|$ is the number of all object. $|T_i|$ is the number of the object that value of the attribute A is the i-th value.

The definition of SplitInfo(A) in equation(1) is:

SplitInfo(A,T)=I(|T$_1$|/|T|, |T$_2$|/|T|, …, |T$_m$|/|T|), where, it assumes that the condition attribute A has m values, the number of the ith value is Ti, so

$\text{SplitInfo}(A,T) = -(|T_1|/|T| * \log_2 |T_1|/|T| + \cdots + |T_m|/|T| * \log_2 |T_m|/|T|)$

So when the Gain Ratio of an attribute is larger, it has more information.

2) Misclassification Cost and Test Cost

If there is an error in a test, it must pay the misclassification cost. Further more, the costs are different when the errors are different. For example, if a case is positive (illness) but it is predicted to be negative (no illness), he will pay the cost of medicine, on the contrary, he may pay his life. The former error is false negative (FN), the latter is false positive (FP). In reality, if we consider a patient (positive) as a healthy man (false negative), maybe he will lost of his life. On the contrary (false positive), he may pay the cost of medicine, etc. So in general, the cost is different, and in our experiment, we think that the cost of false negative (FN) is larger than the cost of false positive (FP),that is to say, FN > FP. at the same time, we think either TP(illness is predicted correctly)cost or TN(no illness is predicted correctly) cost is zero.

In previous work, the cost of the two kinds of error and the test cost are presented with the same scale. But in fact, people own different sum of money may have different idea about the misclassification cost. For instance, haves may hope to reach the highest right ratio and consider nothing about money, while have-nots may hope to reach an acceptable right ratio because of his limited money. So the relation between the test cost and the misclassification cost is varying from people to people. In this paper, we present the cost of FP and FN in relative value, which can be given by experts. The relative value only implies that the relation between FP and FN. It has no relation with money. For instance, if FP/FN is 600/800, it is only show that, in experts view, the cost of false negative is 1.33 multiples of the cost of false positive. So it is the same with 3/4.

Test cost is obtained by the knowledge of domains. For medical diagnosis, the test cost can be obtained from the hospital, and generally, it has the same scale with the money, such as dollar, etc.

3) The Bias of Experts
People who have domain knowledge (such as the doctor in the medical diagnosis) always have some bias about some special test because of their knowledge and experience. So here the expert of the domain can present the bias about attributes w_i, which is the bias of the i-th attribute. If he has no idea about the bias, the default bias is 1 to all attributes.

4 The Method and the Process of Building Decision Tree

1) Selecting the Attributes for Splitting
In the early method of decision tree, the right ratio of classification is most important. It uses the fewest attributes to obtain the highest right ratio of the classification. So the Gain (in ID3) and the Gain Ratio (in C4.5) are the criteria for selecting attributes for splitting in building decision tree. But in our view, we hope to obtain optimal results when the cost of the false positive and the false negative are different, and the resources are limited. So only using the Gain or the Gain Ratio is not properly. In our strategy, the criteria for selecting attributes for splitting Performance is equal to the return (the Gain Ratio multiply the total misclassification cost reduction) divided by the investment (test cost). That is to say, we select the attribute that it has larger Gain Ratio, lower test cost. In addition, it can decrease the misclassification cost sooner. The Performance defined as follows:

$$\text{Performance}(A_i)' = (2^{\text{GainRatio}(A_i, T)} - 1) * \text{Redu\_Mc}(A_i) / (\text{TestCost}(A_i) + 1) \qquad (2)$$

where, GainRatio(Ai,T) is the Gain Ratio of attribute A_i, TestCost(Ai) is the test cost of attribute Ai. Redu_Mc(A_i) is the decrease of misclassification cost brought by the attribute A_i.

$$\text{Redu\_Mc}(A_i) = Mc - \sum_{i=0}^{n} Mc(A_i)$$

where, Mc is the misclassification cost before testing the attribute A_i. If an attribute A_i has n branches, $\sum_{i=0}^{n} Mc(A_i)$ is the total misclassification cost after splitting on A_i.

For examples in a positive node, the Mc = fp * FP, fp is the number of negative examples in the node, FP is the misclassification cost for false positive. On the contrary, for examples in a negative node, the Mc = fn * FN, fn is the number of positive examples in the node, FN is the misclassification cost for false negative.

Thinking of the bias of experts, we have the following equation:

$$\text{Performance}(A_i)' = (2^{\text{GainRatio}(A_i,T)} - 1) * \text{Redu\_Mc}(A_i) / (\text{TestCost}(A_i) + 1) * W_i \quad (3)$$

So equation (3) is the criterion for selecting attribute for splitting to build a decision tree. We select the attribute A, when Performance(A) = max(Performance(A_i)), i is from 1 to m. m is the number of attributes.

2) Building Tree

We will deal with the data, in which there are absent values. For example, in medical diagnosis database, some test is absent because of the restriction of money. It assumes that there will be the same situation, that is to say, there must be someone who has not enough money to finish all the tests in the future. So it is necessary that we make the best use of his limited resources to reduce the misclassification cost. Our goal is to build a decision tree using the data with absent values for finding the optimal attributes to test confined by the limited resources. Material process is as follows:

First, according to the equation (3), we select the optimal attribute. If some of the attributes' Performance are the same, the criterion to select test attribute should be follow in priority order: 1) the bigger Redu_Mc; 2) the bigger test cost. For our goal is to minimize the misclassification cost.

Second, we split a node into k+1 child-nodes with an attribute that was selected according to the above criterion, where, k is the value's number of the splitting attribute, 1 is a branch whose value is null. That is to say, there is a null branch to gather those cases whose value of splitting attribute is null. We use this null node strategy to achieve the goal that making the best use of the limited resources. In the process of building tree, we select the attribute that it has the highest ratio of performance to cost. So the splitting attribute in the parent node may has the higher test cost than the splitting attribute in the children node of the decision tree. When we test a case with limited resources, the left resources will decrease because of the test cost. If the leaving resource is not enough to test the next attribute, the test will not be done, so the test cost of the attribute is zero. But if we use the null embranchment, we can let the case enter the child node along the null embranchment. The splitting attribute in the children may be cheap enough to be test. So we can make the best use of the limited resources to obtain more information to decrease the misclassification cost. For simplicity, we will build a simple decision tree with the following simple dataset(Table1) which has seven attributes(A1,A2,...,A7), one class label(d) and six cases(e1,e2,...,e6), where, the symbol "*" denotes absent values. The test cost of the seven attributes in Table 1 is given in Table 2.

Table 1.

	A1	A2	A3	A4	A5	A6	A7	d
e1	3	1	2	1	1	*	2	1
e2	1	2	2	2	1	2	*	1
e3	*	*	*	1	*	*	1	0
e4	2	*	1	*	2	*	*	0
e5	*	2	2	2	2	3	2	0
e6	*	*	2	*	1	*	1	1

Table 2. Seven attributes and their test costs

attribute	A1	A2	A3	A4	A5	A6	A7
test cost	30	50	20	30	20	70	40

First of all, we use the equation(3) to select the splitting attribute A2. For A2 has two values,:1,2 and a absent value, the root node has three branches. Then we use the same method to split each node if it isn't a leaf node. Figure 1 is the decision tree with the dataset in Table 1.

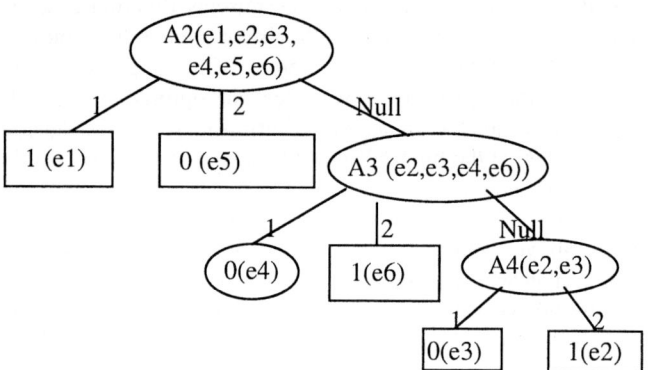

Fig. 1.

In the following, we will illustrate the efficiency of the null branch in the decision tree. If there is a new case that we will use the decision tree to classify its label. And it assumes that there is only 40 dollars. From table 1, we know that the test cost of A2 needs 50 dollars. Obviously the resources are not enough to perform A2. If there is no null branch, the test can only stop in the internal node A2, the left resources will be waste. But if we have null branch, we don't do the test A2 and we along the null branch and enter the test of A3. We also know from the table 1 that the test cost of A3 is 20 dollars. For we have 40 dollars left which is bigger than 20, the test of A3 will be done. So we can obtain more information by the null branch. The misclassification cost will be decreased, too.

The condition of stopping building tree is similar to the C4.5. That is to say, when one of the following two conditions is satisfied, the process of building tree will be stopped: a). all the cases in one node are positive or negative; b). all the attributes are run out of. Because different people have different resources, so we build tree with all attributes. When the resources are enough and the case does not reach a leaf node, more tests will be done to decrease the misclassification cost. If the resource is used up and the case does not reach a leaf node, the case will stop in an internal node. And the criterion for judging whether an internal node is positive or not is as follows.

3) The Criterion for Judging the Class of a Node

For a node, P denotes the node is positive and N denotes the node is negative. The criterion is as follows:

$$\begin{cases} P & \text{if} \quad p*FN > n*FP \\ N & \text{if} \quad p*FN < n*FP \end{cases}$$

where, p is the number of the positive case in the node, while n is the number of negative case. FN is the cost of false negative, and FP is the cost of false positive. If a node including positive cases and negative cases, we must pay the cost of misclassification no matter what we conclude. But the two costs are different, so we will choice the smaller one. Here we consider that the cost of the right judgment is 0. For example, there is a node including 20 positive cases and 24 negative cases, and if the cost of the false positive and false negative is the same, the node will be considered negative. But in our view, they are different, such as FN is 800 and FP is 600, the node will be considered positive because 16000 is larger than 14400.

5 Dealing with the Discount

In practice application, it maybe cheaper when we do some test together. For example, if we perform two kinds of blood test at the same time, the total cost may be smaller than we test them separately. This kind of cost was presented by P. Turney. He calls it Conditional Test Cost [6].

In our strategy, we group the tests together as a new attribute if the test cost of all these tests is discount when they are test at the same moment. The values of the new attribute are the combination of the values of the original attributes. Such as, there are two attributes A1 (1,2), A2 (1,2,3) grouped together. The values of the new attribute(including A1 and A2) are {(1,1) (1,2) (1,3) (2,1) (2,2) (2,3)}, so we can mark them as (1,2,3,4,5,6). The test cost is group discount.

After dealing with the discount attributes, we can use the strategy of building tree illustrated in part 3 to build tree. But the difference is that all the attributes included in the new attribute should be deleted from the candidate attributes if the new attribute had been selected for splitting. When we think of the discount, the number of attributes is n+1, n is the true number of attributes, and 1 is the new attribute. For example, if the attribute A2 (cost: 50 dollars), and A3 (20 dollars) are grouped together, the total test cost is 60 dollars. The new attribute is A8. So, in a decision tree, the attributes A2 and A3 may appear in different nodes or in the same node, e.g. A8.

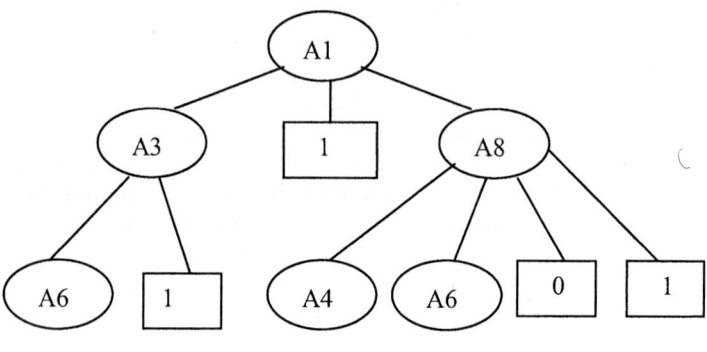

Fig. 2.

Figure 2 is part of a decision tree. It assumes that attribute A1 has three values, A2 and A3 have 2 values. As a result, A8 has 4 values. We can see that the attribute A2 and A3 may be grouped together or appear individually. Whether they are grouped together or not depends on the equation (3).

6 Experiments

We use the Mushroom dataset from the UCI Machine Learning Repository in the experiment. For test examples, a certain ratio of attributes are randomly selected and marked as unknown to simulate test cases with absent values. The test cost and the misclassification cost of the dataset are unknown. So we simply assign certain values as dollars for these test costs. This is reasonable because we compare the relative performance of the two strategies under the same costs. We choose randomly the test costs of all attributes to be some values between $10 and $100. The misclassification cost is set to 600/800(600 for false positive and 800 for false negative). Note that here the misclassification cost is only a relative value. It has different scales with test costs.

For finding out the influence of the null branch in the decision tree, we compared the misclassification costs brought by the two kinds of decision tree, one has the null branch and the other has no null branch. The decision tree with no null branch keeps examples with missing values in internal nodes, and does not build branches for them during tree building. When classifying a test example, if the tree encounters an attribute whose value is unknown, then the class probability of training examples falling at the internal node is used to classify it.

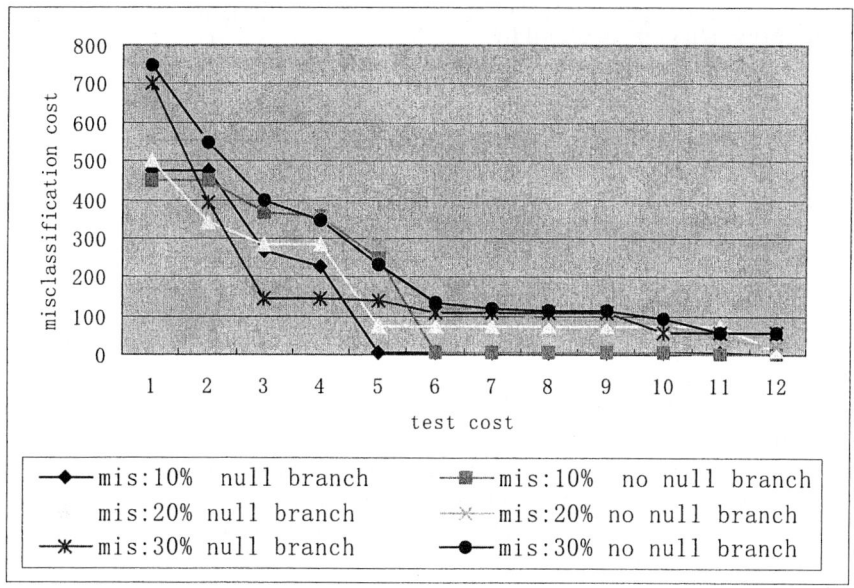

Fig. 3.

From the Figure 3, we can conclude the following results:

First, with the increasing resources, at the most of the situations, the misclassification cost of the null branch strategy decreases sooner than the no null branch strategy. This is because the null branch can make the best use of the limited resources. As a result, the misclassification cost is smaller. But we also find from the results in the Figure 3 that the difference is not obvious on occasion. The primary reason is that the null branch has no use when the cost of the attribute in the children node is more expensive comparing to the parent node, and the null branch has no effect.

Second, with the sum of the resources increasing, we conclude from the experiments that the misclassification cost is decreasing. But at the same time, we noted that the slope is different when the sum of resource is different. That is to say, the speed of the decreasing is not the same. And the speed is sooner when the sum of the resource is fewer. When the sum of the resource is larger than a certain value, the decrease of misclassification cost is very little. So in reality application, we can put forward some advices. For example, we will advise a patient to test the next attribute if the test can decrease the misclassification cost a lot by paying a little test cost. On the contrary, we will advise a patient not to do the next test. If we want to give a piece of advice to a patient, we must know the next test cost and the misclassification cost after the next test. The test cost is static, so we can get it directly. But the misclassification cost is different for the different values of the next attribute. We can count the average misclassification cost (Ave_Mc) for all the child nodes of the next test according to the following equation

$$Ave\_Mc = (1/n) * \sum_{j=1}^{n} Mc(child_i)$$

where n is the number of the child of the next attribute. Mc (child$_i$) is the misclassification cost of the i-th child node, it was defined in the Section 4.

As a result, we can present the average misclassification cost, the misclassification cost now and the test cost to the patient, and then put forward the advice.

7 Conclusion and Future Work

In this paper, we have proposed a decision tree learning algorithm to minimize the misclassification cost with any given resources and built an any-cost sensitive decision tree by involving two kinds of cost scales. We have also considered possible discount on tests performed in groups of attributes. In addition, we have put forward a piece of advice according to the decision tree. We have experimentally evaluated the proposed approach, and demonstrated it is efficient and promising.

In our future work, we plan to apply our algorithms to medical data with real costs. We also plan to incorporate other types of costs in our decision tree learning and test strategies.

References

1. Cost-Sensitive Decision Trees with Multiple Cost Scales. Zhenxing Qin, Shichao Zhang, and Chengqi Zhang. AI 2004, pp.380-390, 2004.
2. Test-Cost Sensitive Naive Bayes Classification. Xiaoyong Chai, Lin Deng and Qiang Yang, Charles X. Ling. Proceedings of The IEEE International Conference on Data Mining (ICDM'2004),2004.
3. "Missing is Useful": Missing Values in Cost-sensitive Decision Trees. IEEE Transactions on Knowledge and Data Engineering, Shichao Zhang, Zhenxing Qin, Charles X.Ling, Shengli Sheng
4. Cost-Sensitive Classification: Empirical Evaluation of a Hybrid Genetic Decision Tree Induction Algorithm, Turney, P. D. Journal of Artificial Intelligence Research. 2, (1995): 369-409.
5. Decision Trees with Minimal Costs. Charles X. Ling, Qiang Yang, Jianning Wang, Shichao Zhang. Proceedings of the 21th International Conference on Machine Learning(ICML), Banff, Canada, 2004.
6. Types of Cost in Inductive Concept Learning. P. Turney. Proceedings of the Cost-Sensitive Learning Workshop at the 17th ICML-2000 Conference, Standford, CA.
7. Pruning improves heuristic search for cost-sensitive learning. Zubek, V.B., and Dietterich, T. 2002. In Proceedings of the Nineteenth International Conference of Machine Learning, 20-35,Sydney, Australia; Morgan Kaufmann.
8. Learning Cost-Sensitive Active Classifiers. Russell Greiner, Adam J. Grove. Artificial Intelligence, Volume: 139, Issue: 2, August, 2002.

Preprocessing Time Series Data for Classification with Application to CRM

Yiming Yang[1], Qiang Yang[2], Wei Lu[1], Jialin Pan[1], Rong Pan[2], Chenhui Lu[1], Lei Li[1], and Zhenxing Qin[3]

[1] Software Institute, Zhongshan University,
Guangzhou, Guangdong Province, China
yangym@gsta.com, sinno@sohu.com, luwei00@hotmail.com,
lncsri07@cs.zsu.edu.cn
[2] Department of Computer Science, Hong Kong University of Science and Technology,
Clearwater Bay, Kowloon Hong Kong, China
qyang@cs.ust.hk, panrong@cs.ust.hk
[3] Faculty of Information Technology, University of Technology,
Sydney PO Box 123, Broadway NSW 2007 Australia

Abstract. We develop an innovative data preprocessing algorithm for classifying customers using unbalanced time series data. This problem is directly motivated by an application whose aim is to uncover the customers' churning behavior in the telecommunication industry. We model this problem as a sequential classification problem, and present an effective solution for solving the challenging problem, where the elements in the sequences are of a multi-dimensional nature, the sequences are uneven in length and classes of the data are highly unbalanced. Our solution is to integrate model based clustering and develop an innovative data preprocessing algorithm for the time series data. In this paper, we provide the theory and algorithms for the task, and empirically demonstrate that the method is effective in determining the customer class for CRM applications in the telecommunications industry.

Keywords: Classification of time series data for Telecommunications Applications.

1 Introduction

With massive industry deregulation across the world, telecom customers are facing a large number of choices in services. As a result, an increasing number of customers are switching service providers from one institution to another. This phenomenon is called customer "churning" or "attrition", which is a major problem for these companies to keep profitable. It is highly important for these companies and institutions to identify the likely customers who churn and formulate plans to combat the problem.

In machine learning and data mining research, the customer churning problems have been addressed in the framework of cost-sensitive classification and ranking [10,5,6,12]. For example, this was the central theme of the KDDCUP-98 competition [1]. However, the direct marketing problem in telecommunication industry pose some new challenges. Similar to the traditional problem formulation, the data in the telecommunications industry are also highly unbalanced with only 5% of customers who actually churn. However, unlike the KDDCUP-98 problem, the telecom data is sequential in nature, where the elements of the sequences are multi-dimensional in nature and the sequences themselves are uneven. With sequential data, many traditional methods for ranking and classification cannot be directly applied.

In this paper, we formulate the above problem as one of classification of time series data. This problem is difficult due to several issues. First, these data are unbalanced, where the positive data that correspond to churning customers represent less than 5% of the population total. Second, each data record is a time series consisting of monthly bills. From the bills we can also extract a large number of features. Furthermore, these time series are of different lengths, some are quite long, while others are short. Third, it is not clear when the customers have churned, given the bill. It may happen that some customers may have already switched their main business to a competitor, while retaining some remaining minor activity with the company in question. These problems make it difficult to design a classification algorithm for identifying escaping customers using the traditional methods. We model the problem as a two class sequential classification problem. We focus on how to transform the uneven data set into one that can be applied to directly by any classification algorithms. Thus, our contribution is in the area of data preparation.

In particular, we consider those customers who churned as positive class, and those who do not churn as negative data. We design an innovative method that combines clustering and classification under the framework of maximum likelihood estimation (MLE). Our general approach includes two major steps: first we compute clusters using model-based clustering algorithms. Then, we refine the clusters by injecting the class information, allowing the clusters to refine themselves to suite the need for classification. We then apply the computed models to future data. Through extensive experiments, we have found our algorithm to be very effective on a large scale data set.

Our main contribution in this work consists of the following. First, we transform the variable-length time series data to fixed-dimension vectors using an innovative model-based clustering algorithm. Then, we then test a number of classification algorithms on the transformed data to test their effectiveness in the transformation method. Finally, we report the result from a real and large sized CRM dataset.

2 Problem Statement and Related Work

2.1 Problem Statement

We first define a time-series classification problem. For this problem, we are given a set S of sequences, where each sequence S_i consists of elements $p_i, i =$

$1, 2, \ldots, n$, and each element p_i consists of a (large) collection of attribute-value pairs $\langle (a_j = v_j), j = 1, 2, \ldots, k \rangle$. In our CRM problem, each p_i is a monthly bill. Each sequence is also associated with a class label $C_l, l = 1, 2, \ldots, m$; for our discussion, we consider a two class problem $(+, -)$, where the positive class $+$ means the customer is known to have churned. Our objective then is to obtain classify test sequences S_{test} such that some optimization criterion is satisfied. For example, one such criterion is the accuracy measure. However, as we will show later in the paper, a more useful measure is the *area under the ROC curve (AUC)* [9].

In our CRM example, a sequence can be a consecutive series of monthly bills from a customer $S_i = p_1 p_2 \ldots p_n$, where $p's$ are the telecom services that a user used in a certain month. Examples of the services include long distance service, local service, call forwarding service, and so on. Each service element in p_i is a vector of real values $\langle e_1, e_2, \ldots, e_k \rangle$, where each e_i is the dollar amount paid by the customer in the corresponding month. If we use discrete integer numbers as an identifier to denote the individual services, the top-level sequences from a *service log* is exemplified in Table 1. A much longer (and uneven) sequence can be obtained using the individual phone calls made by a customer, where each phone call is represented by its duration, services used, cost, time of day and many other factors.

Table 1. Sequences from a service log with class labels

Index	Service Sequence	Class
1	17 2 17 16 16 16	+
2	16 27 27 16 19 18	-
3	20 20 23 23 24 17 17 16 16 16	+
4	16 16 17 17 17 16 16	+
5	16 1 2 6 26	+
6	15 16 27 21 27 19 16	-

In this work, the measure that we optimize is area under the ROC curve. The AUC can be calculated by the formula [7] $AUC = \frac{\sum_{i=1}^{n_0}(r_i - i)}{n_0 n_1}$, where n_0 and n_1 are the number of positive and negative examples respectively, and r_i is the position of the ith positive example.

2.2 Related Work

In data mining and knowledge discovery, learning about sequences has captured the special attention of many researchers and practitioners. Many techniques and applications have been explored in the past, including modelling using Finite State Automata [3,8], Markov Model-based classification and clustering for Web mining [4,11]), association-rule based methods for market-basket analysis ([2]). Of these past work, user-behavior mining has been a central focus of much research and applications. Because it is difficult to provide labelled information manually for massive databases and Web-based systems, many researchers have turned to applying unsupervised learning on sequence data, using methods such as *sequence clustering*.

In clustering, Web researchers such as Cadez et al. ([4]) grouped user behaviors by first-order Markov models. These models are trained by an EM algorithm. These clustering algorithms reveal insight on users' Web-browsing behavior through visualization.

Classification of unbalanced data has been a major task in KDD. For example, a famous benchmark dataset is the the KDDCUP-98 dataset [1] which was collected from the result of the 1997 Paralyzed Veterans of America fundraising mailing campaign. This data set is unbalanced in the sense that about 5% of records are responders. The majority of the competitive methods ranks customers by their estimated probability to respond. Such works include [10]. Recognizing the inverse correlation between the probability to respond and the amount of donation, a trend is to apply cost-sensitive learning, in which false positive and negative costs are considered together with the probability estimates. [5] proposed the MetaCost framework for adapting accuracy-based classification to cost-sensitive learning by incorporating a cost matrix C(i; j) for misclassifying true class j into class i. [13] examined the more general case where the benefit depends not only on the classes involved but also on the individual customers. [9] studied AUC as a general metric for measuring the performance of a cost-sensitive classification problem, and showed that AUC has a better discriminate ability than accuracy in general.

Despite the similarity to our work, all the above methods are designed for data that are not sequential in nature. Furthermore, they are aimed at maximizing only the classification accuracy or related measures (such as maximal profit), rather than producing a good ranking of the customers. In this work, we focus instead on optimizing AUC for ranking sequences, which is a novel problem and a much harder one as compared to the special cases when the sequence lengths are one. The most important feature of our work is that we apply a novel data preprocessing method that transforms the data into equal-length vectors which include the temporal features in the data. The transformation allows any standard classification methods to be used, include hidden-Markov models, 1-class and multi-class SVM, as well as Bayesian methods. In this paper, we present an additional contribution, that is, standard maximum likelihood method can in fact outperform more sophisticated methods such as SVM and boosting methods. This is surprising to us, but is yet another evidence that "simple is beautiful."

3 Time-Series Data Transformation for Classification

3.1 Overview

The telecom time-series classification problem has many general features common to all sequence classification problems. Because the data come from a large number of different customers, some data sequences are long, consisting over 20 months of billing data, while others are short, consisting of perhaps only three or four months of billing data. Furthermore, each data item in a time series is a multi-dimensional vector, instead of just a single number as in some stock-market analysis data sets. These problems pose particular difficulties for many time series analysis methods, because most standard classification methods such as decision trees, maximum likelihood and SVM methods require that the input data be consist of equal length vectors of attribute-values pairs.

Our general approach is to follow a two-step process. In the first step, we transform the data into a equal-length vectors. A key issue is how to maintain as much key temporal information as we can. To this end, we will apply a model based clustering method to help us transform the data. In the second step, we apply and compare different standard classification methods to achieve high levels of the AUC metric.

3.2 Data Transformation Through Model Based Clustering

Our algorithm is shown in Table 2. As shown in the table, we partition the positive-class and negative-class training data into two sets: DB_+ and DB_-. We then apply a model-based clustering algorithm to build separate sets of clusters within each partition. In particular, we build p_+ number of clusters from the positive data set DB_+ and p_- number of clusters from DB_-. This is done in Step 2. The details on how to build the clusters are given in the next subsection. Then, in Step 4, the algorithm loops through all training examples. In each iteration, every datum is measured against all clusters in terms of the maximum likelihood of the sequence belonging to that clusters. This measurement generates a number of probability measures, one for each cluster. The result is a new vector $vector_i$, which has a dimension of $p_+ + p_-$. This transformed data is then saved in the set of all vectors $Vectors$, which is returned as the newly transformed data set.

Below, we consider each step of the algorithm in detail.

Table 2. Model based clustering for transforming the input data

	Time-Series Transformation Algorithm ClusterTrans($TrainDB, p_+, p_-$)
Input:	Training database $TrainDB$, numbers of clusters p_+ and p_-;
Output:	transformed training data $Vectors$;
Steps	Algorithm
1	Partition $TrainDB$ into a positive subset DB_+ and a negative subset DB_-;
2	$Clusters_+ = ModelBasedClustering(DB_+, p_+)$;
	$Clusters_- = ModelBasedClustering(DB_-, p_-)$;
3	$Model = (Clusters_+, Clusters_-)$; Vectors=$\{\}$;
4	For each input datum $seq_i \in TrainDB$, do
5	$\quad vector_i = maxlikelihood(seq_i, Model)$;
6	$\quad Vectors = Vectors \cup vector_i$;
7	end For
8	Return $Vectors$;

3.3 Model-Based Clustering

Step 2 of the ClusterTrans algorithm builds clusters from the positive-class or negative class input data. However, each customer record is a complex structure, which may contain both categorical or continuous data. As an example, consider two sessions from users *u1* and *u2* in Table 3. The attribute 'age' is a numerical feature, while 'gender', 'service', 'weekday', 'month' are categorical features. Finally, 'duration' is a range feature. Our first task in applying the model based clustering algorithm is to convert these data into discrete states. We first discretize all numerical attributes to discrete attributes. This can be done in various ways using some standard supervised or unsupervised discretization algorithms. In this work, we take all customer bill data and performed clustering analysis in this space. This returns N states: $S_i, i = 1, 2, \ldots, n$, where n is a parameter which we can fine tune later [1].

Table 3. Example of Telecom Record, two sessions: u1 and u2 only. (The 'time' is the seconds from 1970-01-01 00:00:00. We removed private content to protect privacy. Column 'Duration' is measured in seconds.)

user	service	age	gender	time	duration	weekday
u1	S2	36	1	...6589	109	5
u1	S2	36	1	...6631	19	5
u1	S2	36	1	...6658	80	5
u2	S1	29	1	...5806	37	1
u2	S5	29	1	...9720	20	3
u2	S3	29	1	...9903	56	4
u2	S5	29	1	...1848	85	5

From the obtained state information, each customer data sequence is then transformed into a state-transition sequence $s_1, s_2, \ldots$. We apply a EM-based clustering algorithm to general p_+ or p_- clusters from each data DB_+ or DB_-, respectively. Suppose that there are n states in Markov models and k Markov chains inside each cluster. Suppose the prior state distribution is $Pr(s_i) = a_i$, and the state-transition matrix is:

$$\vec{v}_p = \begin{pmatrix} a_1 \\ a_2 \\ \ldots \\ a_n \end{pmatrix}, T_p = \begin{pmatrix} t_{11} t_{12} \ldots t_{1n} \\ t_{21} t_{22} \ldots t_{2n} \\ \ldots \\ t_{n1} t_{n2} \ldots t_{nn} \end{pmatrix} \quad (1)$$

where t_{ij} is the transition probability in each cluster of transferring from a state s_i to s_j. We have:

$$a_i = \frac{\sum_{t=1}^{t=k} I(c_t = i)}{k} \quad (2)$$

---

[1] In our experiment, we applied SOM-based clustering algorithm to obtain the states. Other clustering algorithms can also be used.

and

$$t_{ij} = \frac{\sum_{t=1}^{t=k}\sum_{s=1}^{s=i_t-1} I(c_{ts}=i, c_{t(s+1)}=j)}{\sum_{t=1}^{t=k}\sum_{s=1}^{s=i_t-1} I(c_{ts}=i)} \qquad (3)$$

where $I(x) = 1$ if x is true and 0 otherwise. With these input data, we can then train a mixture Markov model with K clusters of the form:

$$p(v|\theta) = \sum_{k=1}^{K} p(c_k|\theta) p_k(v|c_k, \theta) \qquad (4)$$

where $p(c_k|\theta)$ is the marginal probability of the kth cluster and $\sum_{k=1}^{K} p(c_k|\theta) = 1$, $p_k(v|c_k, \theta)$ is the statistical model describing the behavior for users in the kth cluster, and θ denotes the parameters of the model. Here, $v = v_1 v_2 ... v_L$ is an arbitrarily long sequence of feature vectors. We assume that each model component is a first-order Markov model, described by

$$p_k(v|c_k, \theta) = p(v_1|\theta_k^I) \prod_{i=2}^{L} p(v_i|v_{i-1}, \theta_k^T) \qquad (5)$$

where θ_k^I denotes the parameters of the probability distribution over the initial feature vectors among users in cluster k, and θ_k^T denotes the parameters of the probability distributions over transitions from one feature vector to the next in a cluster k. This model captures the order of users' requests, including their initial requests and the dependency between two consecutive requests.

4 Classifying and Ranking Sequences Using the Mixture Model

After the preceding algorithm, we now have a collection of $K = p_- + p_+$ clusters; in this paper, we set p_+ to be one. For any given time series seq, we can then compute the probability distribution over the K clusters, and represent this distribution as a vector $V = \langle p_1, p_2, \ldots, p_K \rangle$. We can use this method to transform all training and testing data into K-dimensional vectors. Each p_i can be calculated using Equation ??. This probability measure for the new data sequence v is then used to rank among all test sequences. This will generate a ranked list. In the experiment, we will compute the AUC measure on the list for comparison, using the ground truth values.

During the testing phase, we can now apply any standard classification and ranking algorithm to each input data sequence. We apply the following methods.

Maximum Likelihood Method and SVM method This method, which is essentially a naive Bayesian method, is the simplest among all methods we consider. In particular, we first convert a test data sequence seq_i into a vector form: $s_1 \rightarrow s_2 \rightarrow \ldots \rightarrow s_k, s_k \in States\{1, ...n\}$. This generates a vector V_i of size K, where K is the number of clusters. We can then calculate the probability of this sequence in the positive and negative Markov models, respectively as $prob\_p$ and $prob\_n$. If $prob\_p \geq prob\_n$, then predict that the customer is escaping with class ($Y = 1$); otherwise predict the customer as staying with ($Y = 0$). For each decision, we can obtain the value of false positive FP and false negative FN. Furthermore, Using $prob\_p$ and $prob\_n$, we calculate a ranking score for the customer:

$$Score = \frac{prob\_p}{prob\_p + prob\_n} \quad (6)$$

We then sort all test data set based on the value of $Score$, and calculate the final AUC value of generated list. With the SVM method, we use the distance to the boundary to measure the ranking.

5 Experimental Setup and Analysis

Our experiments were designed to test the effectiveness of the data transformation algorithm in terms of its ability to distinguish positive (churning) and negative customers, measured on the AUC measure. We obtained a large amount of data from the telecom company to form our training and testing sets. Below, we discuss our experimental set up, the testing results of the clustering module and the ranking module.

We randomly chose 20,000 customers from a telecom company's database. This database contains 96% of non-attritors (negative class) and 4% of known attritors (positive class). Each customer is associated with a sequence of service records and bills. The sequences are variable in lengths, consisting monthly service records and bills for the customer that range anywhere from 4 to 24 (i.e., two years). We split the data into 10 folds in a cross-validation test.

We test the algorithm on AUC-based ranking measure. In our first test, we compared our proposed Maximum Likelihood (MLE) method with the performance of a number of other classification algorithms, including SVM, Boosting (with Naive Bayesian as the base classifier), and K-nearest neighbor algorithm (where K is set to be 10). Our goal is to establish that MLE with performs the best among all algorithms, due to our data preprocessing algorithm *Cluster-Trans*. In this paper, we only have space to describe our results of comparing with 2-class SVM.

Our empirical test varied the number of states as a result of clustering in the vector space, where each multidimensional vector is a representation of a customer bill at a time point. When the number of states is large, the transitions from a state to another is more evenly distributed, and the preprocessing through *Cluster-Trans* will have more difficulty. The result is shown in Figure 1. As can be seen from the figure, the AUC figures for all classification algorithms follow a downward trend. The MLE algorithm is a clear winner, for all state numbers.

This is because our MLE-based algorithm when coupled with the *Cluster-Trans* data transformation can take advantage of the knowledge about AUC measures much better. This result is further confirmed when we varied the number of clusters. We can also see that the MLE in fact performs very robustly

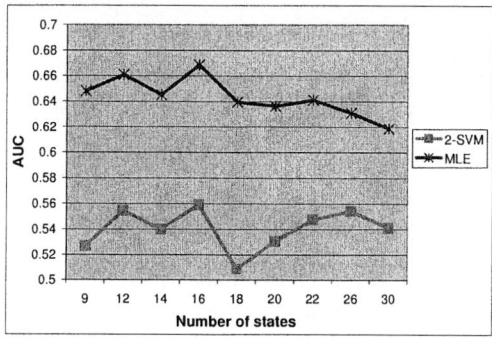

Fig. 1. Comparing two different algorithms with changing number of states

when the number of clusters change from small to large. Thus, one advantage of our preprocessing algorithm is that the resultant data set can be used to train a robust classifier for customer ranking. This effect is demonstrated in a test where we increased the percentage of positive data. This is in contrast to when the data consists of the raw customer data, such as for KDDCUP 1998, when the performance of classifiers are highly dependent on the composition of the training data [12].

6 Conclusions

Sequence ranking is critical for many CRM applications such as customer churning behavior classification. A major problem for this research is how to resolve the many sequences which are ambiguous in that they confuse between positive and negative instances during classification. In this paper, we have presented a novel method to solving this problem. Our solution is to employ a model based clustering algorithm and repeated filter out negative instances that do not contribute to the optimization of the AUC measure.

In the future, we plan to expand the preprocessing component to including the classification algorithms as well, to consider what the best combination is for a given classification algorithm. We also plan to test our algorithms for other multi-dimensional time series data.

Acknowledgement

We thank Ping Huang, Ian Li, George Li and Hui Wang for valuable comments. Qiang Yang and Rong Pan are supported by a Hong Kong RGC Central Allocation grant CA03/04.EG01(RGC HKBU 2/03C), and all other authors are also supported by Zhong Shan University.

References

1. http://kdd.ics.uci.edu/databases/kddcup98/kddcup98.html. 1998.
2. Rakesh Agrawal and Ramakrishnan Srikant. Mining sequential patterns. In Philip S. Yu and Arbee S. P. Chen, editors, *Eleventh International Conference on Data Engineering,* pages 3–14, Taipei, Taiwan, 1995. IEEE Computer Society Press.
3. Jose Borges and Mark Levene. Data mining of user navigation patterns. In *The Workshop on Web Usage Analysis and User Profiling (WEBKDD'99),* pages 31–36, San Diego, CA, August 1999.
4. Igor Cadez, David Heckerman, Christopher Meek, Padhraic Smyth, and Steven White. Visualization of navigation patterns on a web site using model-based clustering. In *Knowledge Discovery and Data Mining,* pages 280–284, March 2000.
5. P. Domingos. Metacost: A general method for making classifiers cost sensitive. In *Proceedings of the Fifth International Conference on Knowledge Discovery and Data Mining,* pages 155–164. AAAI Press, 1999.
6. C. Elkan. The foundations of cost-sensitive learning. In *Proceedings of the 17th International Joint Conference on Artificial Intelligence,* pages 973–978, 2001.
7. D. J. Hand and R. J. Till. A simple generalisation of the area under the ROC curve for multiple class classification problems. *Machine Learning,* 45:171–186, 2001.
8. Mark Levene and George Loizou. A probabilistic approach to navigation in hypertext. *Information Sciences,* 114(1–4):165–186, 1999.
9. C. X. Ling, J. Huang, and H. Zhang. AUC: a statistically consistent and more discriminating measure than accuracy. In *Proceedings of 18th International Conference on Artificial Intelligence (IJCAI–2003),* pages 329–341, 2003.
10. C.X. Ling and C. Li. Data mining for direct marketing - specific problems and solutions. In *Proceedings of Fourth International Conference on Knowledge Discovery and Data Mining (KDD–98),* pages 73–79, 1998.
11. Padhraic Smyth. Clustering sequences with hidden markov models. In Michael C. Mozer, Michael I. Jordan, and Thomas Petsche, editors, *Advances in Neural Information Processing Systems,* volume 9, page 648. The MIT Press, 1997.
12. Ke Wang, Senqiang Zhou, Qiang Yang, and J.M.S. Yeung. Mining customer value: from association rules to direct marketing.*Journal of Data Mining and Knowledge Discovery,* 2005.
13. B. Zadrozny and C. Elkan. Learning and making decisions when costs and probabilities are both unknown. *In Proceedings of the seventh ACM SIGKDD international conference on Knowledge discovery and data mining (SIGKDD01),* pages 204–213, San Francisco, CA, USA, 2001.

Combining Contents and Citations for Scientific Document Classification

Minh Duc Cao and Xiaoying Gao

School of Mathematics, Statistics & Computer Science,
Victoria University of Wellington,
P.O. Box 600, Wellington, New Zealand
{minhduc, xgao}@mcs.vuw.ac.nz

Abstract. This paper introduces a classification system that exploits the content information as well as citation structure for scientific paper classification. The system first applies a content-based statistical classification method which is similar to general text classification. We investigate several classification methods including K-nearest neighbours, nearest centroid, naive Bayes and decision trees. Among those methods, the K-nearest neighbours is found to outperform others while the rest perform comparably. Using phrases in addition to words and a good feature selection strategy such as information gain can improve system accuracy and reduce training time in comparison with using words only. To combine citation links for classification, the system proposes an iterative method to update the labellings of classified instances using citation links. Our results show that, combining contents and citations significantly improves the system performance.

1 Introduction

With the increasing volume of scientific literature nowadays, classification of scientific documents is becoming more and more important in research communities. A system of automatic paper classification and recommendation would be very helpful for scientists in their daily research work. Conference organisers, librarians and journal publishers would find such a system considerably useful in dealing with an enormous number of papers submitted and published. It is obvious that, manual categorisation of those documents is very time consuming and often makes unnecessary errors. Thus, it is essential to develop a scientific papers classification system that can work automatically and adaptively.

Much of effort from research community has devoted to the field of document classification (aka. *text categorisation* or *topic identification*). In early 1960s, Borko and Bernick [1] developed two systems to show the possibility of scientific literature classification. Their methods were purely based on statistical analysis of document content. In the 1990s, document classification using machine learning became an active research area. The machine learning approaches are reported to gain an accuracy comparable to human experts while no human intervention is required [2]. The most important methods in machine learning such as nearest centroid [3], k-nearest neighbours [4], naive Bayes [5], maximum entropy [6], neural networks [7], support vector machines [8] and decision trees [9], mainly exploit information from content of documents for topic identification.

Scientific papers, different from general documents, do not exist in isolation but are linked together by a citation link network. Link analysis has been intensively researched in information retrieval, especially after the birth of the World Wide Web. Brin and Page [10] exploited hypertext mining for PageRank, the technology behind the success of Google. Recently, Getoor et al. [11] applied the relational model [12] for link mining and Craven and Slattery [13] proposed combining statistical text analysis with a relational learner such as FOIL [14].

1.1 Goals

To our knowledge, there has not been much research that combines the content-based statistical approach with citation-based approaches for scientific paper classification. The primary goal of our research is to investigate the integration of document contents and citation structure for improving categorisation accuracy. Our scientific paper classification system first applies one of the content-based classification as a starting point. The system then exploits citation structure by iteratively updating labellings using connected documents.

To apply a content-based classification method, there are a number of research issues involved, for example, which classification method and what features can be used effectively, and what dimensionality reduction method (feature selection) is suitable for scientific paper classification. Our secondary goal is to compare and evaluate various classification methods, examine the effectiveness of using a feature selection method, and explore the possibility of using phrases as features.

1.2 Structure

The paper is organised as follows. Section 2 introduces the background of content-based statistical classification and Section 3 describes the data set used in our experiments. Section 4 describes several common classification algorithms namely k-nearest neighbours, nearest centroid, naive Bayes and decision trees, and presents our comparison results for those methods. The section also describes feature selection methods we used for content-based classification. Section 5 describes our work on combining the content-based approach with citation structure exploitation in classification. We then sum up our work in Section 6.

2 Background

The main task of machine learning approach for document classification is to train a classifier from a set of manually labelled documents called the *training set*. The training process gleans discriminative characteristics of documents in each category and encodes them into the classifier. The trained classifier is evaluated on another labelled set of documents called the `test set`. The output of the classifier on each document in the test set is compared with its true label to determine the accuracy of the classifier.

In the initial process of document classification, each document is converted to a numeric feature vector $d_i = \langle w_1^i, w_2^i ... w_{|\tau|}^i \rangle$, where τ is a set of features and w_j^i is the weight of feature j in document i. The most common document representation is *bag of words* model in which each unique word used in the corpus corresponds to a feature and the weight w_j^i reflects the number of occurrences of word j in document i.

A variety of machine learning algorithms have been proposed for document classification. Instance-based methods such as k-nearest neighbours and nearest centroid rely on the topics of the training examples that are similar to the document to be classified [2]. A naive Bayes classifier [5] computes the likelihood of a document belonging to a category using Bayes' theorem. Decision trees classifier [9] builds a tree in which leaves are labelled by categories, and categorises a document by locating it to a leaf. Several others such as neural networks, support vector machines [8], maximum entropy [6] and inductive logic programming [15,16] have also been proposed and reported achieving reasonable performance. Section 4 investigates some common methods for scientific papers classification.

Using all words for features inevitably results in a large size of the feature vector and thus it takes the system very long to learn the classifier. In fact, study from [17] shows that, using only a subset of highly *informative* words would significantly reduce the feature space dimensionality without losing any accuracy. Some simple feature selection methods include removing of topic-neutral words such as *the, a, an, that* etc and *stemming* [18], that is, considering words having the same root like *report, reporting* and *reported* as one feature. More advanced techniques for feature space dimensionality reduction employ a measurement of the *informativeness* of words and get the best informative words for classification features. Among them are document frequency thresholding, information gain, mutual information, χ^2 statistic and term strength [17]. Section 4 details the feature selection methods used in our experiments.

3 Data Set

For experiments throughout this study, we use Cora, a real world scientific paper corpus collected by McCallum et al [19]. We select a subset of 4330 papers in seven subjects of machine learning: case based, probabilistic methods, learning theory, genetic algorithms, reinforcement learning, neural networks and rule learning. The proportion of papers in each topic ranges from 7% in rule learning topic to 32% in neural network topic. These papers are connected by a network of 12260 citation links. For each experiment, we randomly select 40% of the papers from each of the seven categories for training a classifier, and use the rest as the test set to evaluate the classifier. Ten runs are performed and the average results are reported for each of the experiment.

4 Evaluation of Content-Based Classification Approaches

In this section, we describe our investigation of the content-based classification approach by applying a number of statistical classification algorithms and some feature selection methods in a real world scientific paper corpus.

4.1 Machine Learning Methods

The four algorithms we used are k nearest neighbours, nearest centroid, naive Bayes and decision tree. The output of the classification of each unknown document d_i is called a *labelling* of the document, which is a vector $V_i = (c_1, c_2, ..., c_m)$ where m is the number of categories/classes and c_k is the weight of category k. The document is assigned to the category which has the highest weight.

K Nearest Neighbours Method. The k nearest neighbours (kNN) method [4] is an example of instance-based (or sometime called memory-based) classification strategy. The idea behind the kNN method is relatively simple. The classifier simply "remembers" feature vectors of all documents in the training set. To rank categories of an unknown document d_i, the classifier selects k (a predefined number) nearest (most similar) documents to the input document, and assign the weight of each category to the sum of the similarity scores of selected nearest documents in that category.

In our experiment, we use cosine distance between two feature vectors to measure the similarity between two documents. We choose $k = 10$, which is found to perform the best on our dataset. We also apply *noisy pruning* [4], a process to remove those documents that tend to misclassify from training database. This pruning process does not only increase the accuracy of classification, but also improves the classifying time as the training set is reduced.

Nearest Centroid Method. The nearest centroid (NC) classification method [3] is similar to kNN method above. The difference is that, for each category, the classifier only need to "remember" a *centroid* vector representing that category. The centroid vector of each category is computed as the mean of feature vectors of all documents belonging to that category in the training set. The classifier ranks category weights of each unknown document by the similarity scores of that document to the centroids of those classes/categories.

Naive Bayes Method. The naive Bayes (NB) approach [5] applies Bayes theorem to estimate the probability of a class given a test document based on the assumption that words are independent given the category. The learning process in NB classification is to learn the parameters of a probabilistic model from the training data. Our work uses the *multinomial mixture* model [20], which estimates the probability of a word given a class as the counting of the occurrences of that word in the class, divided by the total number of all words in the class. To prevent zero probability from happening, the *Laplace smoothing* is employed by adding one into the counting.

Decision Tree Method. A text decision tree (DT) classifier [9] is a tree in which internal nodes are labelled by features and leaves are labelled by categories. The decision tree is trained and constructed by selected features from the training set that can decide the category of a document. The common technique of measuring the influence of a feature on the classification of a document uses information gain, an entropy-based measurement [9]. The weight of those features in the feature vector of a document will recursively direct the document to traverse the tree until a leaf is reached. The label associated with that leaf will be assigned to the document.

4.2 Feature Selection

In general document classification, a word in the corpus dictionary corresponds to a feature. In a large corpus of documents, the size of feature space dimensionality could be millions. Performing classification in a feature space with such a big dimensionality would become infeasible. The general methods for feature selection include removal of less informative features and introducing new features which have good information for classification. The informative level of words is measured based on corpus statistics, and features are generally removed by thresholding some quantity measurements. We use *information gain* [21], an entropy based measurement to determine the informativeness of features.

The use of phrases as features in text documents has been described as "not uniformly encouraging" by Sebastiani[2]. Lewis [22] argues that, although phrases have superior semantic quality, they have inferior statistical quality. However, it is observable that, many terminologies are in compound words, and they are sources of information to identify topics of papers. Our experiment explores the use of phrases in addition to words and finds a promising result when combining phrases. Phrases are first added into the corpus dictionary as terms, and then a dimensionality reduction strategy like information gain is performed.

4.3 Evaluation and Comparison

The results from our evaluation are shown in Table 1. It is noticeable from the table that, among those classifiers, kNN outperforms others despite being simple. The other three obtain a similar accuracy. However, the penalty of the kNN method is that, it theoretically requires long classifying time as the unknown document has to be compared with all of training samples. Therefore, if a document classification system has a large training corpus, other alternatives are recommended.

The second observation from our experiment is that, in all classifiers, feature space dimensionalities reduction using information gain can remove up to 98% of words without losing any accuracy. Particularly, in kNN algorithm, when 95% of the words are removed, the accuracy increases to 78% compared with 76% of all words used. Figure 1 shows the accuracy of the kNN method against the percentage of terms removed using information gain. This observation is consistent with work from Yang and Perdersen [17].

Table 1. Performance summary of classification methods

Classifiers	kNN	NC	NB	DT
Use all words	76%	72%	73%	72%
Use IG(remove 95% words)	78%	73%	74%	72%
Add Phrases and IG	80%	74%	76%	74%

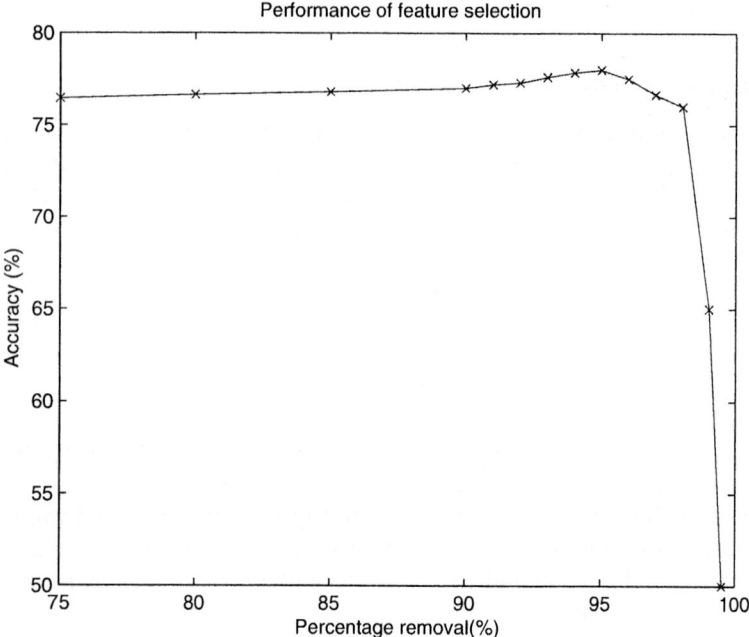

Fig. 1. Accuracy using information gain feature selection

The last row of Table 1 shows the performance of the four classifiers described above when phrases are added to features and information gain feature selection method is used. Phrases are constructed by any two consecutive words and added to feature set, making the number of dimensionalities 20 times higher. The information gain feature selection method is used to remove of 99.5% of the total terms. The strategy is found to improve accuracy of all classification methods used, particularly, for kNN the accuracy improves to 80%.

5 Combining Contents with Citation Links

In scientific paper domain, the connectivity is clearly a source of information for topic identification. Chakrabarti et al. [23] explored the combining of words from neighbouring documents (i.e. documents having links to or from) into the feature vector of a document. Their work on a patent database and a web page collection shows that the naive use of text form neighbouring documents even degrades classification accuracy. Their explanation for the decrease is that link information is noisy and the distribution of terms from neighbouring document is not sufficiently similar to the distribution of the "true" class. However, they reported that category information from neighbouring documents is helpful.

5.1 Updating Labellings Using Citations

In this section, we present a method to integrate the link structure information to improve classification accuracy. It is observable that there is a correlation among topics of documents connected by citation links. Therefore, incorporation of category information from connected documents (citing or cited papers) would be more evident for identifying the topic of a paper.

As described in the content-based classification in Section 4, the output of statistical content-based classification is a labelling $V_i = (c_1, c_2, ..., c_m)$ in which c_k is the likelihood (weight) of that paper in class k. If the topic of a paper is known as category k, c_k is set to maximum $c_k = 1.0$, and other weights are set to zero. We denote the statistical labelling resulted from a content-based classifier as V_i^{CF}. In order to incorporate the content-based classification and the citation information, the labelling of the document i is a function of its statistical labelling and labellings from its connected paper:

$$V_i = F(V_i^{CF}, \{V_j\})$$

where V_js are the labellings of the set of documents j having connections with document i and F is a function representing the incorporation.

However, the labellings of all connected documents j may not be available prior to the computation of labelling of document i. In our model, we first assign the labelling of each document to the statistical labelling as a starting point $V_i^0 = V_i^{CF}$, then iteratively update it with labellings from connected documents. We use a simple linear function F to present the incorporation. The classification of paper i at iteration $k+1$ is updated by the last iteration labellings of all the papers j that are connected to paper i:

$$V_i^{k+1} = F(V_i^k, V_j^k) = \frac{(\eta \Sigma_j V_j^k + V_i^k)}{\mu}$$

η is a parameter that reflects the influence of linked papers and μ is the normalised factor to ensure $\Sigma_i^m c_i = 1$. The updating procedure is performed iteratively until the classifications of all documents in the corpus become stable, i.e. the change of labellings is small enough.

5.2 Results and Discussion

This section presents results from our classification system after the labellings update is performed. To get the starting point, we use the best statistical classifiers found in Section 4, in which phrases are added to features and information

Table 2. Performance of Combination Classifiers

Classifiers	kNN	NC	NB	DT
Add Phrases and IG	80%	74%	76%	74%
Labelling Update	84%	78%	80%	77%

gain feature selection method is used. On our experiment on citation structure we use update parameter $\eta = 0.2$.

Generally, the system takes less than 10 iterations to converse and produces better results than using content only. Table 2 displays the accuracy of the system of each classification method before and after combining with the citation network. As can be seen from the table, the accuracy of the system is significantly improved by the labelling update process regardless of what statistical algorithm used for the starting point. In most cases, about another 4% of accuracy is gained.

The labelling update method, despite being simple, is helpful for scientific paper classification in a document corpus. This shows that, apart from content, the connectivity in scientific document is also a source of information that could be helpful for automatic topic identification of scientific papers.

6 Conclusions

We have developed a system for scientific paper classification utilising both text statistical features and citation information. Our system first applies a content-based classification and then iteratively updates the labellings of unknown documents using citations.

Our evaluation of statistical classification methods shows that k-nearest neighbours classification algorithm has a better performance than nearest centroid, naive Bayes and decision tree algorithms. We also applied a dimensionality reduction strategy using information gain and found that the information gain feature selection method can get rid of the majority of words from the corpus without sacrificing any performance, even gaining some performance improvement. Our experiment also shows that phrases have some contribution to the classification accuracy if they are used in conjunction with an appropriate feature selection method.

On our investigation of combining citation links with document content for classification, we found that the combination results in a better classification performance. The labellings of papers computed from the statistical classification are iteratively updated. The process normally converses after a small number of passes, and significantly improves the accuracy of the scientific paper classification system.

In future work, we will investigate the use of more effective models of the citation structure to improve the system performance. We will investigate the belief propagation techniques from graphical model to model the citation network. We will also study ways of learning the parameters of the model from training data.

Acknowledgments. We would like to thank Dr. Mengjie Zhang for supervising this work and providing many helpful comments for writing the paper.

References

1. Borko, H., Bernick, M.: Automatic document classification. J. ACM **10** (1963) 151–162
2. Sebastiani, F.: Machine learning in automated text categorization. ACM Computing Surveys **34** (2002) 1–47
3. Han, E.-H., Karypis, G.: Centroid-Based Document Classification: Analysis and Experimental Results. Principles of Data Mining and Knowledge Discovery (2000) 424–431
4. Witten, I.H., Frank, E.: Data Mining, Practical Machine Learning Tools and Techniques with Java Implementations. Morgan Kaufmann Publishers (2000)
5. Lewis, D.D.: Naive (Bayes) at forty: The independence assumption in information retrieval. In Nédellec, C., Rouveirol, C., eds.: Proceedings of ECML-98, 10th European Conference on Machine Learning. Number 1398, Chemnitz, DE, Springer Verlag, Heidelberg, DE (1998) 4–15
6. Nigam, K., Lafferty, J., McCallum, A.: Using maximum entropy for text classification. In: IJCAI-99 Workshop on Machine Learning for Information Filtering. (1999) 61–67
7. Wiener, E., Pedersen, L.O., Weigend, A.S.: A neural network approach to topic spotting. In: Proc. of the Symposium on Document Analysis and Information Retrieval. (1995) 317–332
8. Joachims, T.: Text categorization with support vector machines: learning with many relevant features. In Nédellec, C., Rouveirol, C., eds.: Proceedings of ECML-98, 10th European Conference on Machine Learning. Number 1398, Chemnitz, DE, Springer Verlag, Heidelberg, DE (1998) 137–142
9. Mitchell, T.: Machine Learning. McGraw-Hill (1997)
10. Brin, S., Page, L.: The anatomy of a large-scale hypertextual Web search engine. Computer Networks and ISDN Systems **30** (1998) 107–117
11. Getoor, L., Friedman, N., Koller, D., Taskar, B.: Learning probabilistic models of link structure. J. Mach. Learn. Res. **3** (2003) 679–707
12. Taskar, B., Segal, E., Koller, D.: Probabilistic classification and clustering in relational data. In Nebel, B., ed.: Proceeding of IJCAI-01, 17th International Joint Conference on Artificial Intelligence, Seattle, US (2001) 870–878
13. Craven, M., Slattery, S.: Relational learning with statistical predicate invention: Better models for hypertext. Mach. Learn. **43** (2001) 97–119
14. Quinlan, J.R.: Learning logical definitions from relations. Mach. Learn. **5** (1990) 239–266
15. Cohen, W.: Learning to classify English text with ILP methods. In: Advances in Inductive Logic Programming, IOS Press (1996) 124–143
16. Junker, M., Sintek, M., Rinck, M.: Learning for text categorization and information extraction with ILP. In Cussens, J., ed.: Proceedings of the 1st Workshop on Learning Language in Logic, Bled, Slovenia (1999) 84–93
17. Yang, Y., Pedersen, J.O.: A comparative study on feature selection in text categorization. In Fisher, D.H., ed.: Proceedings of ICML-97, 14th International Conference on Machine Learning, Nashville, US, Morgan Kaufmann Publishers, San Francisco, US (1997) 412–420

18. Porter, M.F.: An algorithm for suffix stripping. Readings in Information Retrieval (1997) 313–316
19. McCallum, A.K., Nigam, K., Rennie, J., Seymore, K.: Automating the construction of internet portals with machine learning. Information Retrieval **3** (2000) 127–163
20. McCallum, A., Nigam, K.: A comparison of event models for naive Bayes text classification. In: AAAI-98 Workshop on Learning for Text Categorization. (1998)
21. Lewis, D.D., Ringuette, M.: A comparison of two learning algorithms for text categorization. In: Proceedings of SDAIR-94, 3rd Annual Symposium on Document Analysis and Information Retrieval, Las Vegas, US (1994) 81–93
22. Lewis, D.: An evaluation of prasal and clustered representation of text categorisation tasks. In: Proceedings of SIGIR-92, 15th ACM International Conference on Reseach and Deveplopment in Information Retrieval. (1992) 289–297
23. Chakrabarti, S., Dom, B., Indyk, P.: Enhanced hypertext categorization using hyperlinks. In: SIGMOD '98: Proceedings of the 1998 ACM SIGMOD international conference on Management of data, New York, NY, USA, ACM Press (1998) 307–318

Machine Learning Approach to Realtime Intrusion Detection System*

Byung-Joo Kim[1] and Il Kon Kim[2]

[1] Youngsan University Dept. of Network and Information Engineering,
150, Junam-ri, Ungsang-eup, Yangsan-si, Kyoungnam 626-847, Korea
phone: +82-55-380-9447
bjkim@ysu.ac.kr

[2] Kyungpook National University Department of Computer Science, Korea
ikkim@knu.ac.kr

Abstract. Computer security has become a critical issue with the rapid development of business and other transaction systems over the internet. Recently applying artificial intelligence, machine learning and data mining techniques to intrusion detection system are increasing. But most of researches are focused on improving the classification performance of classifier. Selecting important features from input data lead to a simplification of the problem, faster and more accurate detection rates. Thus selecting important features is an important issue in intrusion detection. Another issue in intrusion detection is that most of the intrusion detection systems are performed by off-line and it is not proper method for realtime intrusion detection system. In this paper, we develop the realtime intrusion detection system which combining on-line feature extraction method with Least Squares Support Vector Machine classifier. Applying proposed system to KDD CUP 99 data, experimental results show that it have remarkable feature feature extraction and classification performance compared to existing off-line intrusion detection system.

Content Areas: machine learning, data mining, knowledge discovery, industrial applications of AI.

1 Introduction

Computer security has become a critical issue with the rapid development of business and other transaction systems over the internet. Intrusion detection is to detect intrusive activities while they are acting on computer network systems. Most intrusion detection systems(IDSs) are based on hand-crafted signatures that are developed by manual coding of expert knowledge. These systems match activity on the system being monitored to known signatures of attack. The major problem with this approach is that these IDSs fail to generalize to detect new attacks or attacks without known signatures. Recently, there has been an

---

* This study was supported by a grant of the Korea Health 21 R&D Project, Ministry of Health & Welfare, Republic of Korea (02-PJ1-PG6-HI03-0004).

increased interest in data mining based approaches to building detection models for IDSs. These models generalize from both known attacks and normal behavior in order to detect unknown attacks. They can also be generated in a quicker and more automated method than manually encoded models that require difficult analysis of audit data by domain experts. Several effective data mining techniques for detecting intrusions have been developed[1][2][3], many of which perform close to or better than systems engineered by domain experts.

However, successful data mining techniques are themselves not enough to create effective IDSs. Despite the promise of better detection performance and generalization ability of data mining based IDSs, there are some difficulties in the implementation of the system. We can group these difficulties into three general categories: accuracy(i.e., detection performance), efficiency, and usability. In this paper, we discuss accuracy problem in developing a real-time IDS. Another issue in IDS is that it should operate in real-time. In typical applications of data mining to intrusion detection, detection models are produced off-line because the learning algorithms must process tremendous amounts of archived audit data. These models can naturally be used for off-line intrusion detection. Effective IDS should work in real-time, as intrusions take place, to minimize security compromises. Elimination of the insignificant and/or useless inputs leads to a simplification of the problem, faster and more accurate detection result. Feature selection therefore, is an important issue in intrusion detection.

Principal Component Analysis(PCA)[4] is a powerful technique for extracting features from data sets. For reviews of the existing literature is described in [5][6][7]. Traditional PCA, however, has several problems. First PCA requires a batch computation step and it causes a serious problem when the data set is large i.e., the PCA computation becomes very expensive. Second problem is that, in order to update the subspace of eigenvectors with another data, we have to recompute the whole eigenspace. Finial problem is that PCA only defines a linear projection of the data, the scope of its application is necessarily somewhat limited. It has been shown that most of the data in the real world are inherently non-symmetric and therefore contain higher-order correlation information that could be useful[8]. PCA is incapable of representing such data. For such cases, nonlinear transforms is necessary. Recently kernel trick has been applied to PCA and is based on a formulation of PCA in terms of the dot product matrix instead of the covariance matrix[9]. Kernel PCA(KPCA), however, requires storing and finding the eigenvectors of a $N \times N$ kernel matrix where N is a number of patterns. It is infeasible method when N is large. This fact has motivated the development of on-line way of KPCA method which does not store the kernel matrix. It is hoped that the distribution of the extracted features in the feature space has a simple distribution so that a classifier could do a proper task. But it is point out that extracted features by KPCA are global features for all input data and thus may not be optimal for discriminating one class from others[9]. In order to solve this problem, we developed the realtime intrusion detection system. Proposed real time IDS is composed of two parts. First part is used for on-line feature extraction. To extract on-line nonlinear features, we propose a new feature extraction method which overcomes the problem of memory requirement of KPCA by on-line eigenspace update method incorporating with an adaptation of kernel function. Second part is used for classification. Extracted features are used as input for classification. We take Least Squares Support Vector Machines(LS-SVM)[10] as a classifier. LS-SVM is reformulations to the standard Support Vector Machines(SVM)[11]. Paper is composed of as follows. In Section 2 we will briefly explain the on-line feature extraction method. In Section 3 KPCA is introduced and to make KPCA on-line, empirical kernel map method is is explained. Proposed classifier combining LS-SVM with proposed feature extraction method is described in Section 4. Experimental results to evaluate the performance of proposed system is shown in Section 5. Discussion of proposed IDS and future work is described in Section 6.

2   On-Line Feature Extraction

In this section, we will give a brief introduction to the method of on-line PCA algorithm which overcomes the computational complexity and memory requirement of standard PCA. Before continuing, a note on notation is in order. Vectors are columns, and the size of a vector, or matrix, where it is important, is denoted with subscripts. Particular column vectors within a matrix are denoted with a superscript, while a superscript on a vector denotes a particular observation from a set of observations, so we treat observations as column vectors of a matrix. As an example, A_{mn}^i is the ith column vector in an $m \times n$ matrix. We denote a column extension to a matrix using square brackets. Thus $[A_{mn}b]$ is an $(m \times (n+1))$ matrix, with vector b appended to A_{mn} as a last column.

To explain the on-line PCA, we assume that we have already built a set of eigenvectors $U = [u_j], j = 1, \cdots, k$ after having trained the input data $\mathbf{x}_i, i = 1, \cdots, N$. The corresponding eigenvalues are Λ and $\bar{\mathbf{x}}$ is the mean of input vector. On-line building of eigenspace requires to update these eigenspace to take into account of a new input data. Here we give a brief summarization of the method which is described in [12]. First, we update the mean:

$$\bar{x}' = \frac{1}{N+1}(N\bar{x} + x_{N+1}) \qquad (1)$$

We then update the set of eigenvectors to reflect the new input vector and to apply a rotational transformation to U. For doing this, it is necessary to compute the orthogonal residual vector $\hat{h} = (Ua_{N+1} + \bar{x}) - x_{N+1}$ and normalize it to obtain $h_{N+1} = \frac{h_{N+1}}{\|h_{N+1}\|_2}$ for $\| h_{N+1} \|_2 > 0$ and $h_{N+1} = 0$ otherwise. We obtain the new matrix of Eigenvectors U' by appending h_{N+1} to the eigenvectors U and rotating them :

$$U' = [U, h_{N+1}]R \qquad (2)$$

where $R \in \mathbf{R}_{(k+1) \times (k+1)}$ is a rotation matrix. R is the solution of the eigenproblem of the following form:

$$DR = R\Lambda' \qquad (3)$$

where Λ' is a diagonal matrix of new Eigenvalues. We compose $D \in \mathbf{R}_{(k+1)\times(k+1)}$ as:

$$D = \frac{N}{N+1}\begin{bmatrix} \Lambda & 0 \\ 0^T & 0 \end{bmatrix} + \frac{N}{(N+1)^2}\begin{bmatrix} aa^T & \gamma a \\ \gamma a^T & \gamma^2 \end{bmatrix} \quad (4)$$

where $\gamma = h_{N+1}^T(x_{N+1} - \bar{x})$ and $a = U^T(x_{N+1} - \bar{x})$. Though there are other ways to construct matrix D[13][14], the only method ,however, described in [12] allows for the updating of mean.

2.1 Eigenspace Updating Criterion

The on-line PCA represents the input data with principal components $a_{i(N)}$ and it can be approximated as follows:

$$\hat{x}_{i(N)} = Ua_{i(N)} + \bar{x} \quad (5)$$

To update the principal components $a_{i(N)}$ for a new input x_{N+1}, computing an auxiliary vector η is necessary. η is calculated as follows:

$$\eta = \left[U\hat{h}_{N+1}\right]^T (\bar{x} - \bar{x}') \quad (6)$$

then the computation of all principal components is

$$a_{i(N+1)} = (R')^T \begin{bmatrix} a_{i(N)} \\ 0 \end{bmatrix} + \eta, \quad i = 1, \cdots, N+1 \quad (7)$$

The above transformation produces a representation with $k+1$ dimensions. Due to the increase of the dimensionality by one, however, more storage is required to represent the data. If we try to keep a k-dimensional eigenspace, we lose a certain amount of information. It is needed for us to set the criterion on retaining the number of eigenvectors. There is no explicit guideline for retaining a number of eigenvectors. Here we introduce some general criteria to deal with the model's dimensionality:

- Adding a new vector whenever the size of the residual vector exceeds an absolute threshold;
- Adding a new vector when the percentage of energy carried by the last eigenvalue in the total energy of the system exceeds an absolute threshold, or equivalently, defining a percentage of the total energy of the system that will be kept in each update;
- Discarding Eigenvectors whose Eigenvalues are smaller than a percentage of the first Eigenvalue;
- Keeping the dimensionality constant.

In this paper we take a rule described in second. We set our criterion on adding an Eigenvector as $\lambda'_{k+1} > 0.7\bar{\lambda}$ where $\bar{\lambda}$ is a mean of the λ. Based on this rule, we decide whether adding u'_{k+1} or not.

3 On-Line KPCA

A prerequisite of the on-line eigenspace update method is that it has to be applied on the data set. Furthermore on-line PCA builds the subspace of eigenvectors on-line, it is restricted to apply the linear data. But in the case of KPCA this data set $\Phi(x^N)$ is high dimensional and can most of the time not even be calculated explicitly. For the case of nonlinear data set, applying feature mapping function method to on-line PCA may be one of the solutions. This is performed by so-called *kernel-trick*, which means an implicit embedding to an infinite dimensional Hilbert space[11](i.e. feature space) F.

$$K(x,y) = \Phi(x) \cdot \Phi(y) \tag{8}$$

Where K is a given kernel function in an input space. When K is semi positive definite, the existence of Φ is proven[11]. Most of the case, however, the mapping Φ is high-dimensional and cannot be obtained explicitly. The vector in the feature space is not observable and only the inner product between vectors can be observed via a kernel function. However, for a given data set, it is possible to approximate Φ by empirical kernel map proposed by Scholkopf[15] and Tsuda[16] which is defined as $\Psi_N : \mathbf{R}^d \to \mathbf{R}^N$

$$\begin{aligned}\Psi_N(x) &= [\Phi(x_1)\cdot\Phi(x),\cdots,\Phi(x_N)\cdot\Phi(x)]^T \\ &= [K(x_1,x),\cdots,K(x_N,x)]^T\end{aligned} \tag{9}$$

A performance evaluation of empirical kernel map was shown by Tsuda. He shows that support vector machine with an empirical kernel map is identical with the conventional kernel map[17]. The empirical kernel map $\Psi_N(x_N)$, however, do not form an orthonormal basis in $\mathbf{R}^N$, the dot product in this space is not the ordinary dot product. In the case of KPCA, however, we can be ignored as the following argument. The idea is that we have to perform linear PCA on the $\Psi_N(x_N)$ from the empirical kernel map and thus diagonalize its covariance matrix. Let the $N \times N$ matrix $\Psi = [\Psi_N(x_1), \Psi_N(x_2),\ldots,\Psi_N(x_N)]$, then from equation (9) and definition of the kernel matrix we can construct $\Psi = NK$. The covariance matrix of the empirically mapped data is:

$$C_\Psi = \frac{1}{N}\Psi\Psi^T = NKK^T = NK^2 \tag{10}$$

In case of empirical kernel map, we diagonalize NK^2 instead of K as in KPCA. Mika shows that the two matrices have the same eigenvectors $\{u_k\}$[17]. The eigenvalues $\{\lambda_k\}$ of K are related to the eigenvalues $\{k_k\}$ of NK^2 by

$$\lambda_k = \sqrt{\frac{k_k}{N}} \tag{11}$$

and as before we can normalize the eigenvectors $\{v_k\}$ for the covariance matrix C of the data by dividing each $\{u_k\}$ by $\sqrt{\lambda_k N}$. Instead of actually diagonalize the covariance matrix C_Ψ, the IKPCA is applied directly on the mapped data

$\Psi = NK$. This makes it easy for us to adapt the on-line eigenspace update method to KPCA such that it is also correctly takes into account the centering of the mapped data in an on-line way. By this result, we only need to apply the empirical map to one data point at a time and do not need to store the $N \times N$ kernel matrix.

4 Proposed System

In earlier Section 3 we proposed an on-line KPCA method for nonlinear feature extraction. Feature extraction by on-line KPCA effectively acts a nonlinear mapping from the input space to an implicit high dimensional feature space. It is hoped that the distribution of the mapped data in the feature space has a simple distribution so that a classifier can classify them properly. But it is point out that extracted features by KPCA are global features for all input data and thus may not be optimal for discriminating one class from others. For classification purpose, after global features are extracted using they must be used as input data for classification. There are many famous classifier in machine learning field. Among them neural network is popular method for classification and prediction purpose.

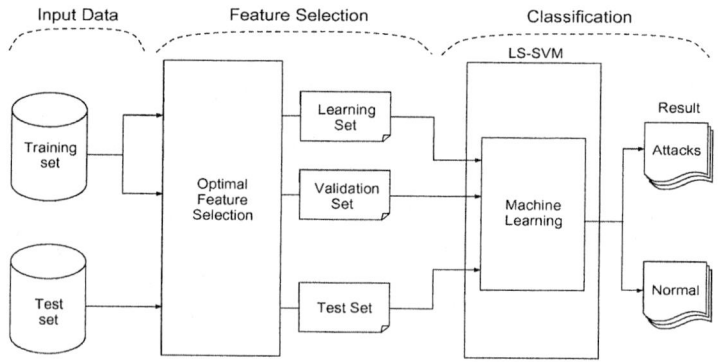

Fig. 1. Overall structure of realtime based IDS

Traditional neural network approaches, however have suffered difficulties with generalization, producing models that can overfit the data. To overcome the problem of classical neural network technique, support vector machines(SVM) have been introduced. The foundations of SVM have been developed by Vapnik and it is a powerful methodology for solving problems in nonlinear classification. Originally, it has been introduced within the context of statistical learning theory and structural risk minimization. In the methods one solves convex optimization problems, typically by quadratic programming(QP). Solving QP problem requires complicated computational effort and need more memory requirement. LS-SVM overcomes this problem by solving a set of linear equations in the problem formulation. LS-SVM method is computationally attractive and easier to extend than SVM. The overall structure and main components of proposed system is depicted in Figure 1. Proposed real time IDS is composed of two parts. First part is used for on-line feature extraction. To extract on-line nonlinear features, we propose a new feature extraction method which overcomes the problem of memory requirement of KPCA by on-line eigenspace update method incorporating with an adaptation of kernel function. Second part is used for classification. Extracted features are used as input for classification. We take Least Squares Support Vector Machines(LS-SVM)[19] as a classifier.

5 Experiment

To evaluate the classification performance of proposed realtime IDS system, we use KDD CUP 99 data[18]. The following sections present the results of experiments.

5.1 Description of Dataset

The raw training data(kddcup.data.gz) was about four gigabytes of compressed binary TCP dump data from seven weeks of network traffic. This was processed into about five million connection records. Similarly, the two weeks of test data yielded around two million connection records. A connection is a sequence of TCP packets starting and ending at some well defined times, between which data flows to and from a source IP address to a target IP address under some well defined protocol. Each connection is labeled as either normal, or as an attack, with exactly one specific attack type. Each connection record consists of about 100 bytes. Attacks fall into four main categories:

- DOS: denial-of-service, e.g. syn flood;
- R2L: unauthorized access from a remote machine, e.g. guessing password;
- U2R: unauthorized access to local superuser (root) privileges, e.g., various "buffer overflow" attacks;
- Probing: surveillance and other probing, e.g., port scanning.

It is important to note that the test data(corrected.gz) is not from the same probability distribution as the training data, and it includes specific attack types not in the training data. This makes the task more realistic. The datasets contain a total of 24 training attack types, with an additional 14 types in the test data only.

5.2 Experimental Condition

To evaluate the classification performance of proposed system, we randomly split the the training data as 80% and remaining as validation data. To evaluate the classification accuracy of proposed system we compare the proposed system to

SVM. Because standard LS-SVM and SVM are only capable of binary classification, we take multi-class LS-SVM and SVM. A RBF kernel has been taken and optimal hyper-parameter of multi-class SVM and LS-SVM[20] was obtained by 10-fold cross-validation procedure. In [19] it is shown that the use of 10-fold cross-validation for hyper-parameter selection of SVM and LS-SVMs consistently leads to very good results.

In experiment we will evaluate the generalization ability of proposed IDS on test data set since there are 14 additional attack types in the test data which are not included int the training set. To do this, extracted features by on-line KPCA will be used as input for multi-class LS-SVM. Our results are summarized in the following sections.

5.3 Evaluate Feature Extraction Performance

Table 1 gives the result of extracted features for each class by on-line KPCA method.

Table 1. Extracted features on each class by on-line KPCA

Class	Extracted features
Normal	1,2,3,5,6,7,8,9,10,11,12,13,14,16,17,18,20,21,22,23,25,27,29,30,31,32,34,37,38,39,41
Probe	3,5,6,23,24,32,33,38
DOS	1,3,6,8,19,23,28,32,33,35,36,38,39,41
U2R	5,6,15,16,18,25,32,33,38,39
R2L	3,5,6,24,32,33,34,35,38

Table 2. Performance of proposed system using all features

Class	Accuracy(%)	Training Time(Sec)	Testing Time(Sec)
Normal	98.55	5.83	1.45
Probe	98.59	28.0	1.96
DOS	98.10	16.62	1.74
U2R	98.64	2.7	1.34
R2L	98.69	7.8	1.27

Table 2 shows the results of the classification performance and computing time for training and testing data by proposed system using all features. Table 3 shows the results of the classification performance and computing time for training and testing data by proposed system using extracted features. We can see that using important features for classification gives similar accuracies compared to using all features and reduces the train, testing time. Comparing Table 2 with Table 3, we obtain following results. The performance of using the extracted features do not show the significant differences to that of using all features. This means that proposed on-line feature extraction method has good

Table 3. Performance of proposed system using extracted features

Class	Accuracy(%)	Training Time(Sec)	Testing Time(Sec)
Normal	98.43	5.25	1.42
Probe	98.63	25.52	1.55
DOS	98.14	15.92	1.48
U2R	98.64	2.17	1.32
R2L	98.70	7.2	1.08

performance in extracting features. Proposed method has another merit in memory requirement. The advantage of proposed feature extraction method is more efficient in terms of memory requirement than a batch KPCA because proposed feature extraction method do not require the whole N × N kernel matrix where N is the number of the training data. Second one is that proposed on-line feature extraction method has similar performance is comparable in performance to a batch KPCA.

5.4 Suitable for Realtime IDS

Table 2 and Table 3 show that using extracted features decreases the training and testing time compared to using all features. Furthermore classification accuracy of proposed system is similar to using all features. This makes proposed IDS suitable for realtime IDS.

5.5 Comparison with SVM

Recently SVM is a powerful methodology for solving problems in nonlinear classification problem. To evaluate the classification accuracy of proposed system it is desirable to compare with SVM.

Generally the disadvantage of incremental method is their accuracy compared to batch method even though it has the advantage of memory efficiency. According to Table 4 and Table 5 we can see that proposed method has better classification performance compared to batch SVM. By this result we can show that proposed realtime IDS has remarkable classification accuracy though it is worked by incremental way.

Table 4. Performance comparison of proposed method and SVM using all features

	Normal	Probe	DOS	U2R	R2L
Proposed method	98.76	98.81	98.56	98.92	98.86
SVM	98.55	98.70	98.25	98.87	98.78

Table 5. Performance comparison of proposed method and SVM using extracted features

	Normal	Probe	DOS	U2R	R2L
Proposed method	98.67	98.72	98.56	98.88	98.78
SVM	98.59	98.38	98.22	98.87	98.78

6 Conclusion and Remarks

Second one is that proposed on-line feature extraction method has similar performance is comparable in performance to a batch KPCA.

This paper was devoted to the exposition of a new technique on realtime IDSs . To develop this system, we made use of empirical kernel mapping with incremental learning by eigenspace approach. Proposed on-line KPCA has following advantages. Firstly, The performance of using the extracted features do not show the significant differences to that of using all features. This means that proposed on-line feature extraction method has good performance in extracting features. Secondly, proposed method has merit in memory requirement. The advantage of proposed feature extraction method is more efficient in terms of memory requirement than a batch KPCA because proposed feature extraction method do not require the whole N × N kernel matrix where N is the number of the training data. Thirdly, proposed on-line feature extraction method has similar performance is comparable in performance to a batch KPCA though it works incrementally.

Our ongoing experiment is that applying proposed system to more realistic world data to evaluate the realtime detection performance.

References

1. Eskin, E. :Anomaly detection over noisy data using learned probability distribution. In Proceedings of the Seventeenth International Conference on Machine Learning (2000) 443-482
2. Ghosh, A. and Schwartzbard, A. :A Study in using neural networks for anomaly and misuse detection. In Proceedings of the Eighth USENIX Security Symposium, (1999) 443-482
3. Lee, W. Stolfo, S.J. and Mok, K.:A Data mining in workflow environments. :Experience in intrusion detection. In Proceedings of the 1999 Conference on Knowledge Discovery and Data Mining, (1999)
4. Tipping, M.E. and Bishop, C.M. :Mixtures of probabilistic principal component analysers. Neural Computation 11(2) (1998) 443-482
5. Kramer, M.A.:Nonlinear principal component analysis using autoassociative neural networks. AICHE Journal 37(2) (1991) 233-243
6. Diamantaras, K.I. and Kung, S.Y.:Principal Component Neural Networks: Theory and Applications. New York John Wiley & Sons, Inc (1996)
7. Kim, Byung Joo. Shim, Joo Yong. Hwang, Chang Ha. Kim, Il Kon.: On-line Feature Extraction Based on Emperical Feature Map. Foundations of Intelligent Systems, volume 2871 of Lecture Notes in Artificial Intelligence (2003) 440-444

8. Softky, W.S and Kammen, D.M.: Correlation in high dimensional or asymmetric data set: Hebbian neuronal processing. Neural Networks vol. 4, Nov. (1991) 337-348
9. Gupta, H., Agrawal, A.K., Pruthi, T., Shekhar, C., and Chellappa., R.:An Experimental Evaluation of Linear and Kernel-Based Methods for Face Recognition," accessible at http://citeseer.nj.nec.com.
10. Suykens, J.A.K. and Vandewalle, J.:Least squares support vector machine classifiers. Neural Processing Letters, vol.9, (1999) 293-300
11. Vapnik, V. N.:Statistical learning theory. John Wiley & Sons, New York (1998)
12. Hall, P. Marshall, D. and Martin, R.: On-line eigenalysis for classification. In British Machine Vision Conference, volume 1, September (1998) 286-295
13. Winkeler, J. Manjunath, B.S. and Chandrasekaran, S.:Subset selection for active object recognition. In CVPR, volume 2, IEEE Computer Society Press, June (1999) 511-516
14. Murakami, H. Kumar.,B.V.K.V.:Efficient calculation of primary images from a set of images. IEEE PAMI, 4(5) (1982) 511-515
15. Scholkopf, B. Smola, A. and Muller, K.R.:Nonlinear component analysis as a kernel eigenvalue problem. Neural Computation 10(5), (1998) 1299-1319
16. Tsuda, K.:Support vector classifier based on asymmetric kernel function. Proc. ESANN (1999)
17. Mika, S.:Kernel algorithms for nonlinear signal processing in feature spaces. Master's thesis, Technical University of Berlin, November (1998)
18. Accessable at http://kdd.ics.uci.edu/databases/kddcup99
19. Gestel, V. Suykens, T. J.A.K. Lanckriet, G. Lambrechts, De Moor, A. B. and Vandewalle, J.:A Bayesian Framework for Least Squares Support Vector Machine Classifiers. Internal Report 00-65, ESAT-SISTA, K.U. Leuven.
20. Suykens, J.A.K. and Vandewalle, J.:Multiclass Least Squares Support Vector Machines. In Proc. International Joint Conference on Neural Networks (IJCNN'99), Washington DC (1999)

Structural Abstraction Experiments in Reinforcement Learning

Robert Fitch[1], Bernhard Hengst[1], Dorian Šuc[1], Greg Calbert[2], and Jason Scholz[2]

[1] National ICT Australia, University of NSW, Australia
{robert.fitch, bernhard.hengst, dorian.suc}@nicta.com.au
[2] Defence Science and Technology Organization, Salisbury SA, Australia
{greg.calbert, jason.scholz}@dsto.defence.gov.au

Abstract. A challenge in applying reinforcement learning to large problems is how to manage the explosive increase in storage and time complexity. This is especially problematic in multi-agent systems, where the state space grows exponentially in the number of agents. Function approximation based on simple supervised learning is unlikely to scale to complex domains on its own, but structural abstraction that exploits system properties and problem representations shows more promise. In this paper, we investigate several classes of known abstractions: 1) symmetry, 2) decomposition into multiple agents, 3) hierarchical decomposition, and 4) sequential execution. We compare memory requirements, learning time, and solution quality empirically in two problem variations. Our results indicate that the most effective solutions come from combinations of structural abstractions, and encourage development of methods for automatic discovery in novel problem formulations.

1 Introduction

When specifying a problem such as learning to walk, learning to manipulate objects or learning to play a game as a reinforcement learning (RL) problem, the number of states and actions is often too large for the learner to manage. It is straightforward to describe the state of a system using several variables to represent the various attributes of its components. Similarly, individual system component actions can be used to describe a joint action vector. However, this approach very quickly leads to an intractable specification of the RL problem. A tabular state-action representation requires storage proportional to the product of the size of all the state and action variables, leading to intractable storage and time complexity.

Function approximation can often help by generalizing the value function across many states. Function approximation is based on supervised learning. Gradient descent methods, such as artificial neural networks and linear function approximation are frequently used in RL for this purpose [1]. However, there are reasons to believe that simple function approximation will not scale to larger, more complex, problems.

Some problems may have structure and regularities that are not readily apparent and difficult to learn in one step [2]. Learning may be made tractable by the right problem decomposition and by learning in stages, reusing and combining previously learnt concepts. Learning in complex environments proceeds at the "frontier of receptivity" where new tasks can only be learnt once component child tasks have been learnt [3].

Our objective in this paper is to explore several structural abstraction methods and to study their effect on storage requirements, learning time and the quality of the solution for one problem with two different levels of inter-dependency. The contribution of this paper is to give a systematic description and experimental evaluation of a collection of known structural abstractions that can be used in a wide variety of RL problems. Our motivation comes in part from the desire to develop tractable decision systems for complex multi-agent games, and secondly to gain insight for automating the modelling process.

Our experiments in this paper are based on a task that requires two taxis acting together to pickup and deliver two passengers on the 5×5 grid. This task is chosen because it is intuitive and small enough so that we can still compute the optimal solution, yet it is complex enough to make it challenging to demonstrate various abstractions.

The formalisms underpinning the experiments in this paper are those of Markov decision problems (MDPs) and model reductions expressed as homomorphic mappings. The latter are important in establishing whether one system is a model of another and which properties of the original system the model retains [4]. The abstractions we will explore are symmetry reductions, multi-agent decompositions, hierarchical decompositions, sequential execution and some combinations.

In the rest of this paper we will first introduce the two-taxi task as our working example and summarize the formalisms. We then in turn describe the various structural abstractions of the problem including related work. In each case we discuss the computing requirements in relation to solution quality for the taxi task and comment on the scaling potential.

2 The Two-Taxi Problem

Taxi problems have been used by several researchers in related work. They have analogues in other problems, such as logistic problems involving transporters and cargo. We have taken two taxis [5] working jointly to pick up and deliver two passengers on the 5×5 grid shown in Figure 1.

The objective is to deliver both passengers in the minimum number of steps. At each time step a taxi can take a navigation action and attempt a move one position North, South, East or West. These actions are stochastic. With 92.5% probability they move the taxi in the intended direction and with 7.5% probability they move the taxi randomly in one of the other three directions. Other actions available are to pickup passenger one, pickup passenger two, put down its passenger or stay. Taxis can only carry one passenger at a time. A move

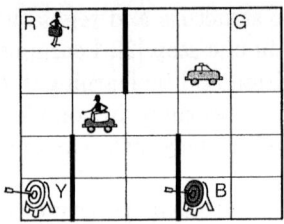

Fig. 1. The two-taxi Problem

into a barrier or the grid boundary is counted as one step and results in the taxi staying where it is. There are four special locations marked R, G, Y, B that represent the possible source and destination locations of the passengers. At the commencement of every episode each passenger is located at random on one of the special locations and each taxi is located at random anywhere on the grid. Each passenger must be picked up by one of the taxis and put down at his or her destination location, even if the source and destination locations are the same. If a passenger is waiting to be picked up and both taxis are at this location then a joint action by both taxis to pick up the passenger results in only one taxi being successful.

We consider two versions of the problem, with and without taxi collisions. Without collisions the taxis are able to occupy the same cell and pass each other without impediment. With collisions the taxis cannot occupy the same cell nor can they pass each other in the sense that they cannot occupy each other's former cell following a joint action. A move resulting in a collision leaves the taxi locations unchanged. Initial taxi positions on the same cell are disallowed with collisions, although passengers can have the same pickup and destinations locations.

3 Modelling Formalisms

We now introduce RL, its application to the two-taxi task and abstractions formalized as homomorphisms.

3.1 RL Problem Formulation

Underlying RL is the Markov decision problem framework. We consider a system modelled at a base level by a set of states. At each time-step the system transitions from state to state depending on an input action to the system and generating a real-valued reward. We can describe a Markov decision problem (MDP) as a tuple $< S, A, T, R, S_0 >$ where S is the finite set of states, A is the finite set of actions, $T : S \times A \times S \rightarrow [0,1]$ is the transition function giving the probability of moving from one state to another after taking a particular action, $R : S \times A \times R \rightarrow [0,1]$ is the probability of receiving a reward when taking an action, and $S_0 : S \to [0,1]$ is the starting state distribution giving the probability of starting in each state. The Markov property requires that the states and actions can be defined so that the probabilities are independent of the history of transitions and rewards. In addition we assume the probabilities are independent of time, i.e. stationary. An MDP includes an optimality criterion, usually to maximize a function of the sum of future rewards. The objective is to find an optimal policy $\pi : S \to A$ providing the action to take in any state to optimize the value function. A semi-MDP is a generalization of an MDP where actions can be *extended*, taking several time steps to complete.

Specifying the two-taxi problem above as an MDP we proceed to define the state $s \in S$ by the variables $(t_1, t_2, p_1, p_2, d_1, d_2)$, where t_1 and t_2 each specify the respective taxi location as one of the 25 grid values, p_1 and p_2 indicate the location of the passengers at either one of the four pickup locations, riding in either taxi or delivered, and d_1 and d_2 each specify one of the four destinations of the respective passengers. The total number of possible collision-free states is therefore $25 \times 25 \times 7 \times 7 \times 4 \times 4 = 490,000$. The actions $a \in A$ are defined by the variables (a_1, a_2) representing the simultaneous joint actions of the two taxis. There are eight actions available per taxi giving a joint action set of 64. At each time step we specify a joint reward of -1 until both passengers are delivered. Maximizing the sum of future rewards achieves our objective to minimize the number of steps to complete the task.

We assume the learner can fully observe the state, but that the transition and reward functions are not known beforehand. We use simple *Q-learning* [6] to learn the optimal policy as our base case. Q-learning involves updating an action-value function stored as a *Q-table* with one entry for each state action pair. The update performed after each step is called a *Bellman backup* and given by $Q(s,a) \leftarrow (1-\alpha)Q(s,a) + \alpha(r + \gamma \max_{a'} Q(s',a'))$, where the system has transitioned from s to s' after taking action a and receiving reward r. The discount rate for future rewards is γ and set to 1.0 in our experiments. The learning rate is α. It is well known that given sufficient exploration of all states and actions and suitable reduction in the learning rate the action-value function will converge to its optimal value, Q^*, and the optimal policies are $\pi^*(s) = argmax_a Q^*(s,a)$. While there are many speedup techniques such as prioritized sweeping and eligibility traces, we have used this simple form of RL with $\alpha = 0.1$ in all our experiments for consistency. Our exploration policy is ϵ-greedy with ϵ generally set to 10%. All performance is measured using greedy policies. We are primarily interested in comparing learning efficiency with various model abstractions and have found that similar relationships hold for any setting of α and adequate exploration.

3.2 Abstractions as Homomorphisms

The idea of an abstraction is to simplify the representation of a system in such a way that the problem of interest can be solved more efficiently. Ideally we would like a model to perfectly preserve the system characteristics of interest so that we only need to solve the simplified model and the solution is guaranteed to be a solution for the original system. A useful algebraic formalism for modelling abstractions is a homomorphism. We are particularly interested in homomorphisms in the framework of MDPs and semi-MDPs. A homomorphic mapping from a system to a model means that if we perform an action or temporally extended action in a system state then the resultant model state is the same whether we map the resultant system state to the model or whether we first map the system state and (extended) action to the model and perform the model action. State transition homomorphisms by themselves do not guarantee that the reduced model is relevant to the problem at hand. An MDP homomorphism ensures relevancy by also mapping the reward function and thus preserving the implicit goal specification. A useful exposition of MDP and semi-MDPs is given by Ravindran [7].

4 Abstraction Classes

We study several exact and approximate model abstractions (homomorphisms) and apply them to the two-taxi problem. The results are shown in Table 1 and Figure 2 and are explained in this section.

The base case Q-table size for the collision-free two-taxi problem is 490,000 states × 64 actions = 31,360,000 entries. With collisions the base case Q-table size is 30,105,600 as taxis cannot occupy the same state. We have calculated the optimal solution using dynamic programming for both base cases. Q-learning on the base case takes over four billion time steps to converge. We have defined convergence to be the number of time-steps required for the mean of the results to be within 5% of its final value. Q-learning oscillates slightly short of optimal performance with the learning rate α fixed at 0.1 (see Table 1, "Base Case"). For the base case and other abstractions we have found that the mean converged average steps per episode over multiple runs has a standard deviation of less than 0.06.

4.1 Symmetry

Symmetries in MDPs arise when states, actions or a combination of both can be mapped to an equivalent reduced MDP that has less states and actions. For example, if two actions have identical transition and reward probability functions between any two states then one action can be eliminated. An example of a problem with state symmetry is learning to exit similar rooms that differ only in color. More general symmetries often arise where state-action pairs are mapped together both with different states and actions from the original in the reduced model [8]. We call these forms of symmetry simple state-action symmetries. Another class of symmetry that overlaps the class of simple state-action symmetry is bisimulation homogeneity [9]. In bisimulation homogeneity the states of a problem can be partitioned into blocks such that the inter-block transition probabilities and reward probabilities are constant for all actions. An example of model reduction using this type of symmetry is the elimination of an irrelevant random variable in a state description.

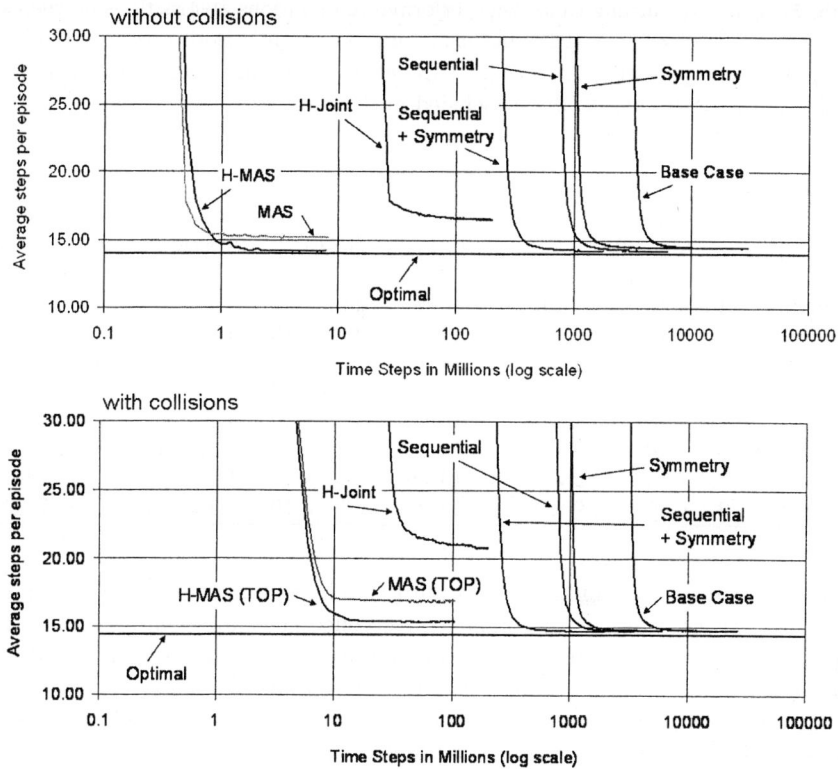

Fig. 2. Two-taxi task results: without collisions (top) and with collisions (bottom)

The taxi problem exhibits simple state-action symmetry assuming homogeneity of taxis and passengers. In one form of symmetry two different navigation actions by the taxis can be interchanged without affecting the solution whenever both taxis occupy the same location. If the taxis are at different locations and they are interchanged the two situations are also symmetrical and can be mapped to the same abstract state. The second mapping will not reduce the states if both taxis are on the same cell, a situation that can only arise in the collision-free problem. Similarly, swapping passenger-destination pairs can be exploited as a state-action symmetry abstraction, as can swapping both taxis and passengers. Specifically, state $(t_1, t_2, p_1, p_2, d_1, d_2)$ with action (a_1, a_2) is symmetrically equivalent to $(t_2, t_1, p_1, p_2, d_1, d_2)$, (a_2, a_1) where p_1 and p_2 need to be adjusted whenever the passengers are in the taxis. Similar homomorphic state-action mappings can be defined for a passenger swap and for both a taxi and passenger swap providing a 4-to-1 state reduction mapping when taxi and passenger-destination locations differ.

The above abstraction reduces the two-taxi problem without collisions to 131,950 states compared to 490,000 for the base case. The approximately 3.7-fold reduction in the number of states in the reduced model leads to a commensurate

Table 1. Memory, learning times and performance of various abstractions on the two-taxi tasks for *collision free* (left) and *with collisions* (right). Both cases use the same abstractions, except with MAS and H-MAS, where it the case *with collisions* also the position of the other taxi (TOP) is included in the state.

	COLLISION FREE			WITH COLLISIONS		
	MEMORY ($|Q|$)	STEPS TO CONVERGE	CONVERGED AVE. STEPS PER EPISODE	MEMORY ($|Q|$)	STEPS TO CONVERGE	CONVERGED AVE. STEPS PER EPISODE
OPTIMAL	3.1×10^7	DP	14.06	3.0×10^7	DP	14.46
BASE CASE	3.1×10^7	4.4×10^9	14.46	3.0×10^7	4.2×10^9	14.80
SYMMETRY	8.4×10^6	1.5×10^9	14.45	7.2×10^6	1.3×10^9	14.82
MAS	4.2×10^3	7×10^5	15.18	1.0×10^5	9×10^6	16.90
H-JOINT	2.7×10^5	3.4×10^7	16.56	2.0×10^5	4.6×10^7	20.78
H-MAS	5.7×10^3	9×10^5	14.24	1.1×10^5	1×10^7	15.41
SEQUENTIAL	7.8×10^6	1.2×10^9	14.26	7.5×10^6	1.1×10^9	14.76
SEQ.+SYM.	2.1×10^6	3.9×10^8	14.27	1.8×10^6	3.5×10^8	14.75

speedup in learning as illustrated in Figure 2. The symmetries also apply to the taxi task with collisions with similar convergence speedup results. These state and action abstractions are an exact homomorphism of the original MDP and therefore converge to an optimal policy of the original problem.

For the general collision-free task involving n taxis on a size k grid with m passengers and l special locations the number of states is $k^n \cdot (l+n+1)^m \cdot l^m$. This can be shown to abstract to $C_n^{k+n-1} \cdot C_m^{(l+n+1)l+m-1}$ states[1], when taxis and passengers are indistinguishable.

An approach to generalizing exact symmetries is to consider approximate symmetries. A bounded parameter Markov decision process [10] can be used to bound the error when inter-block transitions and rewards probabilities are not constant but constrained to a range of values. Symmetries will only take us so far in model reduction. We will now turn to another type of structural abstraction.

4.2 Multiagency

Modelling a system as a simultaneous interaction of multiple autonomous agents can be a significant abstraction [11]. When a problem is specified using a multi-dimensional action description, it is natural to attempt this type of decomposition.

In multi-agency the overall homomorphism is approximated by combining independent homomorphic mappings for each agent. One of the major issues is the abstraction of the global reward signal for each agent so that their combined behavior is in the common good [12]. If the actions of all the agents are independent and the global reward is the sum of the rewards for each agent then the multi-agent homomorphism is exact and will produce an optimal solution.

---

[1] C_k^n (n choose k) $= n!/(k!(n-k)!)$.

This total decomposition is rare for interesting problems and does not hold for either version of the two-taxi task. For optimal performance the taxis need a coordinated strategy for picking up passengers and need to avoid each other when collision is possible.

One homomorphic approximation arbitrarily pre-allocates one passenger to each taxi. Each agent receives the global reward. Effectively we have defined two reduced MDPs (one for each agent) that together comprise the two-taxi problem. When the two agents are identical we can additionally apply symmetry from Section 4.1 and use only one MDP for both agents. This not only saves storage space, but transfers learning between the two agents. The actions per taxi can be reduced by one as they now do not need to specify which passenger is to be picked up. This means that only $25 \times 6 \times 4$ states and 7 actions are required to be modelled reducing the number of table entries to 4,200 compared to the original 31,360,000. The reduced MDP in effect solves Dietterich's original single taxi problem.

The joint action policy required for the original MDP is formed by combining the actions from the reduced MDP, primed respectively with the two sets of agent states. Each taxi agent models the world by focussing on its passenger and ignores the other agent and passenger. It is rewarded for delivering its passenger.

Figure 2 shows the results for a multi-agent system (MAS) learner with the above abstraction using the fixed allocation policy. Fixing the allocation of the taxis to passengers is clearly suboptimal. We can do better if we learn a joint dispatch strategy as a higher level decision task as described in the next section.

For the case with collisions, the previous model of the partially observable environment from the point of view of one taxi is now inadequate. Collisions depend on the other taxi that cannot be observed. The model is no longer Markov and the homomorphism fails. When the outcome for one agent depends on the actions of the others then it is necessary to include extra state information to try to retain the individual agent homomorphic mappings[2]. To address this situation we have included the other taxi's position (TOP) as an integral part of the state description for each agent. This is an approximation, modelling the other agent's movements as stochastic. The resulting reduced model requires the least amount of storage in our experiments with collision and produces reasonably good results as shown in Figure 2 MAS (TOP). The abstraction also requires us to dispatch the taxis to a fictitious passenger pickup location after they complete their mission to avoid each taxi inadvertently blocking the other.

The requirement for a better dispatching policy and Dietterich's original decomposition of the single taxi problem suggest we can do better by turning to another form of structural abstraction – hierarchical decomposition.

---

[2] However, even when all information is taken into account and the individual agent models are exact, if agents behave greedily the overall abstraction may only be approximate and produce suboptimal solutions. This effect is well known as Voter's Paradox, or the Tragedy of the Commons, and has consequences such as Braess Paradox [13] where more options can reduce overall performance.

4.3 Task Hierarchies

A problem may be able to be decomposed into a task hierarchy in which each parent task can choose to execute any of its child subtasks. Dietterich introduced the MAXQ decomposition to compactly represent a value function over a task hierarchy with reusable subtasks [5]. The whole task hierarchy is a semi-MDP homomorphism that maps child task policies to temporally extended actions at the root node. The homomorphism is in general approximate in that a task hierarchy may constrain the policies available in the original problem. Indeed, each parent task in the hierarchy can be interpreted as a sub-model of the problem using a semi-MDP homomorphism where child policies are mapped as the parent's abstract actions. Learnt from the bottom up, a task hierarchy implements the "frontiers of receptivity" [3] in a multi-layered learning paradigm.

One such task hierarchy decomposes the two-taxi problem into two levels of subtasks as shown in Figure 3. The lower level navigation subtasks with states (t_1, t_2) and actions (a_1, a_2) has the objective of jointly moving the taxis to the four special locations. As the actions are joint they can handle collisions. The joint navigation subtasks terminate when both taxis have reached their designated special locations. If the taxis are interpreted as separate agents then this model implicitly implements the concurrent action model T_{all} termination scheme [14]. The termination scheme requires agents to terminate simultaneously and is clearly suboptimal. However, forced synchrony reduces the number of sub-MDPs and abstract actions required in the hierarchy. Sixteen sub-MPDs are needed at level one for the collision-free problem and 12 with collisions, representing the various termination combinations at the four special locations for the two taxis.

The level two dispatch subtask uses states (p_1, p_2, d_1, d_2) and policies from level one generating 108 and 144 abstract actions on the task with and without collisions respectively. These represent the combination of pickup and putdown actions upon termination of the sub-MDPs. We have used a semi-automatic version of the HEXQ algorithm [15] for our implementation. Results are labelled "H-Joint" in Table 1 and Figure 2 and show about two orders of magnitude savings in both memory and learning time but are clearly suboptimal as expected. The HEXQ algorithm constructs the task hierarchy while learning but its variable-wise decomposition does not produce a multi-agent decomposition. The large number of abstract actions makes execution expensive. This type of joint action hierarchy could be abstracted further by using symmetry as discussed in Section 4.1 but this was not implemented.

Our second hierarchical abstraction is shown in Figure 3 and builds on the multi-agent abstraction from the previous section. In this three-level task hierarchy the level one subtasks are the individual taxi agents performing the whole delivery task. We only use one Q-table for both taxis as discussed in Section 4.2. The second level tasks represent the various dispatching options for the two taxis. There are four options altogether allocating each taxi to deliver both passengers or one or the other. In the event that one taxi is to deliver both passengers, the level two tasks learn the best order of delivery. This problem is akin

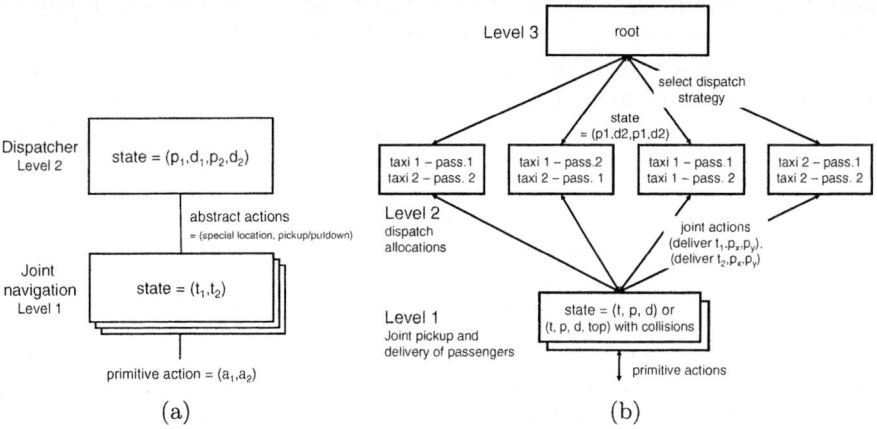

Fig. 3. Dispatcher and joint navigation task hierarchy (H-Joint) is shown in (a); (b) shows three-level hierarchy using multi-agent travelling salesman dispatcher and whole delivery task at lower level (H-MAS)

to a multi-agent travelling salesman problem (TSP) in which each city needs to be visited by one agent only. A city visit corresponds to a passenger pickup and delivery. The root task simply chooses one of the dispatch strategies.

The result are depicted in Figure 2 and Table 1 as H-MAS and H-MAS(TOP). This task hierarchy gives near optimal results for the collision-free version of the problem. It is suboptimal because, due to stochastic drift, it is possible that the optimal dispatch decision should be switched prior to pickup but is locked in by the second level controller in the hierarchy. We conjecture to be able to improve the results, achieving optimality in this case, by using hierarchical greedy execution (polling) [16,5].

The H-MAS structural abstractions combine hierarchy, multi-agency and symmetry and achieve the best resource effectiveness with and without collisions. Interestingly, storage can be reduced further by more than a factor of four and learning time by at least a factor of two by decomposing the level one subtask in Figure 3 into three levels as for the original taxi task [5], creating a five level hierarchical decomposition for the two-taxi task.

4.4 Sequential Execution

The idea behind sequential execution is to "simulate" the concurrent action of the agents by timesharing their execution. This means that the agents act one at a time as far as the learner is concerned, but are assumed to be able to execute jointly in a real world.

This is a semi-MDP homomorphism in which one joint action is mapped to a two-step temporally extend action. The advantage is that the number of actions is the sum rather than the product of the number of actions of the agents. In effect we are assuming that the problem can be approximated with a reduced action set with joint actions $(a_1, stay)$ and $(stay, a_2)$.

With and without collisions, this reduces the memory use and learning time by about a factor of four and achieves near optimal results. In combination with symmetry we achieve the multiplicative benefit of both abstractions. These results are labelled "Sequential" and "Seq.+Sym." in Table 1 and Figure 2.

5 Automatic Discovery of Abstractions

One of the major lessons from implementing these abstractions, even on this relatively simple example, is the difficulty in manually specifying the various decompositions. For example, the symmetry abstractions require both states and actions to be mapped together, but it is not straightforward to specify the complete homomorphic mapping in Section 4.1. Whenever the user provides an abstraction we are effectively providing background information to the learner and this must be manually tailored for each problem. Both these issues motivate automating the discovery of structural abstractions.

Our approach to automation would try to exploit any structure in a problem by searching for symmetry, multi-agent and hierarchical abstractions. We may, for example, be able to find sub-models that are well defined homomorphisms covering parts of the whole problem. These sub-models may be able to be found by simultaneously exploring the projected spaces defined by subsets of state-action variables and testing for Markov transitions and rewards. The sub-models become the building blocks for a search for even more abstract models at a higher level. In this way it is envisaged that a task hierarchy could be shaped from the bottom up to solve the problem efficiently.

6 Discussion and Future Work

This paper presents classes of abstraction useful for scaling up RL and points towards promising future work in two directions – the manual use of structural abstractions, and their automatic discovery. Our experimental results show that the performance gains of single abstractions can be further improved through their combination. Our best results combine symmetry, task hierarchy and multi-agency. We have already indicated a clear opportunity for improving these results in Section 4.3 and believe there are further model reduction and scaling opportunities available. The model of the other agent (TOP) in our implementation uses a global position variable. We conjecture that it is possible to parsimoniously use only a "window of influence" for the TOP model, possibly a deictic representation, that would reduce memory requirements significantly. Further, given the correspondence to multi-agent TSP, this logistic problem should scale tractably with good results using many vehicles and cargo in much larger simulations.

The expected gains from abstractions depend on the degree of system coupling. In the experiments we found that increasing interdependency reduces the number of reachable states because of the added constraints but also creates less opportunity for abstraction.

The experiments and forgoing reasoning give some hope that we can scale RL to larger problems by using manually defined abstractions. The unifying framework of treating model reduction as a homomorphism suits and supports structural abstraction well. Our experiments also indicate the feasibility of developing methods for automatic discovery of abstractions as outlined in Section 5. We are currently exploring both of these approaches in complex domains such as battle-space simulations.

References

1. Sutton, R.S., Barto, A.G.: Reinforcement Learning: An Introduction. MIT Press, Cambridge, Massachusetts (1998)
2. Clark, A., Thornton, C.: Trading spaces: Computation, representation, and the limits of uninformed learning. Behavioral and Brain Sciences **20** (1997) 57–66
3. Utgoff, P.E., Stracuzzi, D.J.: Many-layered learning. In: Neural Computation, MIT Press Journals (2002)
4. Ashby, R.: Introduction to Cybernetics. Chapman & Hall, London (1956)
5. Dietterich, T.G.: Hierarchical reinforcement learning with the MAXQ value function decomposition. Journal of Artificial Intelligence Research **13** (2000) 227–303
6. Watkins, C.J.C.H.: Learning from Delayed Rewards. PhD thesis, King's College (1989)
7. Ravindran, B., Barto, A.G.: SMDP homomorphisms: An algebraic approach to abstraction in semi markov decision processes. In: Proc. of the Eighteenth International Joint Conference on Artificial Intelligence (IJCAI 03). (2003) 1011–1018
8. Ravindran, B., Barto, A.G.: Model minimization in hierarchical reinforcement learning. In: Fifth Symposium on Abstraction, Reformulation and Approximation (SARA 2002). LNCS, Springer Verlag (2002) 196–211
9. Dean, T., Givan, R.: Model minimization in markov decision processes. In: AAAI/IAAI. (1997) 106–111
10. Givan, R., Leach, S.M., Dean, T.: Bounded-parameter markov decision processes. Artificial Intelligence **122** (2000) 71–109
11. Crites, R.H., Barto, A.G.: Elevator group control using multiple reinforcement learning agents. Machine Learning **33** (1998) 235–262
12. Wolpert, D., Tumer, K.: An introduction to collective intelligence. Technical Report NASA-ARC-IC-99-63, NASA Ames Research Center, CA (1999)
13. Braess, D.: Über ein Paradoxon der Verkehrsplanung. Unternehmensforschung **12** (1968) 258–268
14. Rohanimanesh, K., Mahadevan, S.: Learning to take concurrent actions. In: NIPS. (2002) 1619–1626
15. Hengst, B.: Discovering hierarchy in reinforcement learning with HEXQ. In Sammut, C., Hoffmann, A., eds.: Proceedings of the Nineteenth International Conference on Machine Learning, Morgan-Kaufman (2002) 243–250
16. Kaelbling, L.P.: Hierarchical learning in stochastic domains: Preliminary results. In: Machine Learning Proceedings of the Tenth International Conference, San Mateo, CA, Morgan Kaufmann (1993) 167–173

A Hybrid Adaptive Multi-objective Memetic Algorithm for 0/1 Knapsack Problem

XiuPing Guo, ZhiMing Wu, and GenKe Yang

Department of Automation, Shanghai Jiaotong University, Shanghai 200030,
Shanghai, P.R. China
{gxp, ziminwu, gkyang}@sjtu.edu.cn

Abstract. A hybrid adaptive memetic algorithm for a multi-objective combinatorial optimization problem is proposed in this paper. Different solution fitness evaluation methods are hybridized to achieve global exploitation and exploration. At each generation, a wide diversified set of weights are used to search across all regions in objective space, and each weighted linear utility function is optimized with a simulated annealing. For a broader exploration, a grid-based technique is employed to discover the missing nondominated regions on existing tradeoff surface, and a Pareto-based local perturbation is used to reproduce additional good individuals trying to fill up the discontinuous areas. For better stability and convergence of the algorithm, the procedure is made dynamic and adaptive to online optimization conditions based upon a function of improvement ratio. Experiment results show the effectiveness of the proposed method on multi-objective 0/1 knapsack problems.

1 Introduction

The general multi-objective problem (MOP) can be formulated as:

$$
\begin{aligned}
\text{max} \quad & \mathbf{f}(\mathbf{x}) = \{f_1(\mathbf{x}), f_2(\mathbf{x}), ..., f_n(\mathbf{x})\} \\
\text{s.t.} \quad & g_c(\mathbf{x}) \leq 0 \quad c = 1, 2, ..., r \\
& \mathbf{x} = (x_1, x_2, ..., x_m) \in X
\end{aligned}
\quad (1)
$$

where solution $\mathbf{x}$ is a vector of decision variables, X is the space of feasible solutions, point $\mathbf{f}(\mathbf{x})$ is objective vector of $\mathbf{x}$, and g_c is constraint.

For any two solutions $\mathbf{a}, \mathbf{b} \in X$, $\mathbf{a}$ is said to dominate $\mathbf{b}$ (written as $\mathbf{a} \succ \mathbf{b}$) iff

$$\forall i = \{1, 2, ..., n\} : f_i(\mathbf{a}) \geq f_i(\mathbf{b}) \ \land \ \exists i = \{1, 2, ..., n\} : f_i(\mathbf{a}) > f_i(\mathbf{b}) \ . \quad (2)$$

Correspondingly, $\mathbf{f}(\mathbf{a}) \succ \mathbf{f}(\mathbf{b})$ if $\mathbf{a} \succ \mathbf{b}$. A solution $\mathbf{x} \in X$ is called efficient if there is no $x' \in X$ that dominates $\mathbf{x}$. The objective vector of an efficient solution is called nondominated. The set of all efficient solutions is called Pareto-optimal set. The image of the Pareto-optimal set in objective space is called Pareto front.

One alternative for fitness evaluation in MOP is aggregating all objectives into a single scalar value using the weighted linear utility function defined as:

$$s(\mathbf{f}, \lambda) = \sum_{i=1}^{n} \lambda_i f_i(\mathbf{x}) \ . \tag{3}$$

where weight vector $\lambda=(\lambda_1,\lambda_2,...,\lambda_n)$ meeting the condition: $\forall i \ \ \lambda_i \geq 0, \sum_{i=1}^{n} \lambda_i = 1$.

Another alternative for fitness assignment is called Pareto-based evaluation, in which a vector containing all objective values represents the fitness, and dominance relationship is used to determine the survival probability of candidates.

A good many single objective metaheuristics based on local search such as tabu search and simulated annealing have been adapted to MOP by using aggregation functions. Recently, the number of Pareto-based multi-objective evolutionary algorithms (MOEAs) has increased tremendously, such as [3], [4], [5], [6] and [7]. Presently, some multi-objective memetic algorithms or called multi-objective genetic local search that incorporate local search into evolutionary algorithms have been devised to improve results obtained with these methods. Studies [7], [8], [9] and [10] have indicated that the memetic algorithms have high search capability to efficiently find near Pareto-optimal solutions.

Multi-objective 0/1 knapsack problems (MOKP) represent a class of real-world applications. Given n knapsacks and m items, it is formulated as [6]:

$$\begin{aligned}\texttt{max} \quad & \mathbf{f}(\mathbf{x}) = \{f_1(\mathbf{x}), f_2(\mathbf{x}), ..., f_n(\mathbf{x})\} \\ \texttt{s.t.} \quad & \sum_{j=1}^{m} w_{i,j} \cdot x_j \leq c_i, \quad i=1,2,...,n \ .\end{aligned} \tag{4}$$

where $\forall i=1,2,...,n$: $f_i(\mathbf{x})=\sum_{j=1}^{m} p_{i,j} \cdot x_j$, $p_{i,j}$ is the profit of item j according to knapsack i, $w_{i,j}$ is the weight of item j according to knapsack i, c_i is the capacity of knapsack i, $\mathbf{x}=(x_1,x_2,...,x_m) \in \{0,1\}^m$, $x_j=1$ iff item j is selected.

In this study, we propose a hybrid adaptive multi-objective memetic algorithm (HAMOMA) for MOKP. This algorithm employs the weighted linear utility functions and Pareto dominance to perform fitness evaluation in local search and recombination phases respectively, and uses a simulated annealing (SA) to optimize each of the utility functions. The aims for doing so are: using a wide diversified set of weights to exploit the nondominated solutions dispersed over objective space; employing a grid-based technique corporated with a Pareto-based incrementing strategy to enhance the local search ability as well as achieve a broader exploration. To obtain better robustness of the algorithm, the procedure is made self-adjusted based on an online feedback improvement ratio.

The rest of this paper is organized as follows: Section 2 describes the proposed algorithm. The computational experiments and comparisons with the state-of-the-art methods, M-PAES [7], MOGLS [10], SPEA [6], SPEA2 [13] and NSGA-II [3], on the test instances are presented in Section 3. Section 4 offers conclusions.

2 Hybrid Adaptive Multi-objective Memetic Algorithm

HAMOMA is a population-based metaheuristic where each generation consists of two phases: local search first and recombination second. Two archives are needed in HAMOMA: one is an internal archive functioned to hold nondominated solutions generated during the local search, another is an external archive served as a memory for storing all nondominated solutions found during optimization.

```
Procedure: SA (x, λ, IA, iter(ir))
Input: x-solution to be improved; λ-weight vector; IA-
       internal archive; iter(ir)-the iterations number
       at each temperature in current generation g ;
Output: x-improved solution
Begin
   Set temperature: T_k ← T_0, k ← 0   //T_0 :initial temperature
   Set IA as empty and Place x into IA: IA ← φ, IA ← x
   Do
      Do
        Mutate x to generate a feasible neighbor solution x_1
        If ( Δs = ∑_{i=1}^{n} λ_i(f_i(x) - f_i(x_1)) ≤ 0 ) {Accept x_1 (x ← x_1)
                                                  and Update IA with x_1}
        Else If (exp(-Δs/T_k) > random[0,1) ) {Accept x_1 (x ← x_1)}
        k++
      While ( k < iter(ir) )
      Update temperature: T_{k+1} ← γT_k   //γ : cooling rate
   While ( T_k > T_end )               // T_end : end temperature
   Return x
End Begin
```

Fig. 1. Local Search Procedure

2.1 Local Search with Simulated Annealing

Generally, a given weight vector induces a privileged search direction on the Pareto front. We use a wide diversified set of weights to exploit the dispersed solutions. At each generation, for each individual x in population is associated with a randomly selected weight vector λ, as presented in Fig.1, the utility function s of x is maximized using the SA, where the archive IA is updated and a mutant is accepted if the utility function is improved, otherwise, it is accepted with an acceptance probability $\exp(-\Delta s/T_k)$.

Noticed that the iterations number $iter$ in Fig.1 is made self-adjusted based on a function of an improvement ratio ir. The ir at generation g is defined as:

$$ir(g) = \frac{|\{\mathbf{f(a)} \in nd(g); \exists \mathbf{f(b)} \in nd(g-1) : \mathbf{f(a)} \succ \mathbf{f(b)}\}|}{|nd(g)|} \quad . \tag{5}$$

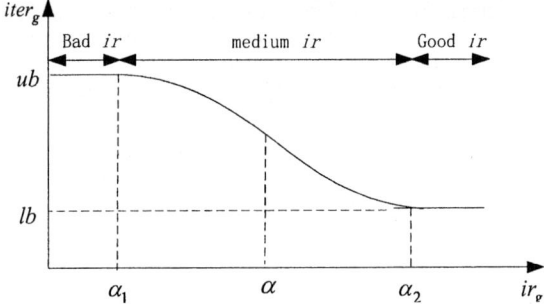

Fig. 2. Number of iterations $iter_g$ at each temperature versus improvement ratio ir

where $nd(g)$ and $nd(g-1)$ are respectively the sets of all nondominated solutions hold in the external archive at generations g and $(g-1)$. With the evolution proceeding, ir decreases gradually towards a small value close to zero, as indicates a bigger room for further improvement at the initial stage and lower probability of producing new nondominated solutions at the final stage. For better ir, it is essential to tune the local search to reproduce more "fitter" individuals, especially as the approximation approaches to the Pareto front. Thereby, the number $iter$ of local exploration at each temperature in the SA should follow the reverse trend of ir along the evolution, as shown in Fig.2, the $iter$ at generation g is determined as:

$$iter_g(ir) = \begin{cases} ub, & 0 \leq ir < \alpha_1; \\ ub - 2(ub\text{-}lb)(\frac{ir-\alpha_1}{g})^2, & \alpha_1 \leq ir < \alpha; \\ lb + 2(ub\text{-}lb)(\frac{ir+1-\alpha_2-g}{g})^2, & \alpha \leq ir \leq \alpha_2; \\ lb, & \alpha_2 < ir \leq 1. \end{cases} \quad (6)$$

where ir is the improvement ratio at generation g, α_1 and α_2 are the fuzzy boundaries of "Bad ir" and "Good ir" states, α is a satisfactory level for ir, ub and lb are respectively the upper and lower bounds of $iter$. For a stable ir, $ir(g)$ is taken as the average ir value of the last l generations, i.e., $ir(g)=(1/l)\sum_{i=g+1-l}^{g} ir(i)$.

2.2 Recombination with Pareto Dominance

Recombination serves as an elitist in HAMOMA. We use crossover to recombine the distinct local optima found by the SA, and use a grid-based method of local perturbation called GBLP for further exploration. GBLP works via dividing n dimensional objective space occupied by the members of the external archive into $G_1 \times G_2 \times \cdots \times G_n$ grids, where G_k, $k=1,2,...n$, represents the grids number in the kth objective dimension. The location of each individual in the grids is found in the way as used in [14]. The density of a grid is defined as the number of individuals dwelling in it. For a broader exploration, the parents selected by a tournament are perturbed to generate incrementing individuals. The tournament

```
Procedure: Recombination(Pop,EA,np(ir))
Input: Pop-resulted population in local search phase;
       np(ir)-the perturbation number per parent in GBLP
       at current generation g; EA-external archive;
Output: Pop-resulted population for new generation;
Begin         //applying Pareto dominance
  Perform simple crossover for individuals randomly selected
  from population EA∪Pop , updating EA as necessary
  Set r←0
  Do
    Draw a parent y by the tournament selection from EA
    Perform GBLP with np(ir) number of perturbation for y,
    updating EA as necessary and returning a set pc ⊄ EA
    If ( pc =∅) {Use tournament selection to select a new
                 child c from EA}
    Else  {Select a child c∈ pc with the lowest density}
    Place c back into Pop
    r++
  While (r<popsize)
  Return Pop
End Begin
```

Fig. 3. Recombination Procedure

selection is solely based on the density of an individual's location, i.e., the parents located in the less crowded regions have higher probability to be perturbed as compared to those located in the more crowded regions. Each of the selected parents is perturbed with an extension of mutation, in which more than one child are produced per parent. For the MOKP with n knapsacks and m items, a solution is encoded as m-digit chromosome $\mathbf{x}=\{x_s:s=1,2,...,m\}\in\{0,1\}^m$, where s is coding index, $s=1$ denoting the most significant index and $s=m$ representing the least significant index of the chromosome. For increasing the perturbation probability within the parents' neighborhood rather than outside the neighborhood, the genes of $\mathbf{x}$ are sorted (decreasing) according to the ratio [6]:

$$\max_{i=1}^{n}\{\frac{p_{i,j}}{w_{i,j}}\}, j=1,2,...,m,$$

and the perturbation probability P_s for the gene x_s of $\mathbf{x}$ is determined by a sigmoid function [15], which makes the more significant a digit in $\mathbf{x}$, the lower it perturbation probability in GBLP. The number of perturbation np per parent at generation g is made dynamic and adaptive to the feedback improvement ratio, following the same trend defined by the function (6). Empirically, the lower and upper bounds of np are set as 10 and 50 respectively, and the lower and upper bounds of P_s are set as 0.03 and 0.8 respectively.

Fig.3 presents the recombination procedure, in which a certain number of crossovers are performed firstly on the individuals selected at random from the union set of Pop and all members of EA. Secondly the GBLP is used to perturb each of the parents selected from EA, reproducing the perturbed children set

pc, whose members are not dominated by any point in EA. If pc is not empty, the child with the lowest location density is placed back into Pop, otherwise, the tournament selection is used to select a new offspring from EA to join Pop.

2.3 HAMOMA Scheme

Based on the presentation above, the HAMOMA can be depicted as an adaptive feedback control scheme (see in Fig.4). Fig.5 presents the HAMOMA procedure.

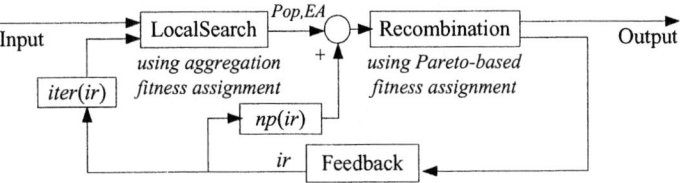

Fig. 4. Adaptive feedback control scheme for HAMOMA

```
Procedure: HAMOMA(popsize, γ , T₀ , T_end ,gen)
Input: popsize-population size;
       gen-the number of HAMOMA generations;
Output: EA-all generated nondominated solutions;
Begin
  Generate random initial population Pop of solutions
  Set internal and external archives empty: IA ← φ , EA ← φ
  Put all nondominated individuals of Pop into EA
  Set g ← 0
  Do
    Calculate iter_g(ir) and np_g(ir) at current generation g
    For (each individual x ∈ Pop )
      Draw at random a weight vector λ
      Perform local search SA (x ,λ ,IA , iter_g(ir))
      Place improved solution x back into Pop
      Update EA with IA : EA ← EA ∪ IA
    EndFor
    Recombination (Pop, EA , np_g(ir))
    g++
  While (g<gen)
End Begin
```

Fig. 5. HAMOMA Procedure

3 Numerical Experiments

The HAMOMA was implemented in C++ builder and all experiments have been performed on a notebook with Celeron(R) CPU 2.40 GHz and 512 M memory.

In this study, we use the same set of MOKP instances that were used in [6]. The instances have 2, 3 and 4 objectives and 250,500,and 750 items, denoted as 2-250, 2-500, 2-750, 3-250, 3-500, 3-750, 4-250, 4-500, 4-750.

The instances and the approximations to the Pareto front generated by SPEA, SPEA2 and NSGA-II are available on the web-site [11]. The results of SPEA2 and NSGA-II are available only for instances with 750 items. The results of MOGLS [10] to the same set of instances are available on the web-site [12]. The results of M-PAES on the same set of instances were generated with the same parameters as set in [7].

One of the performance metrics used here is the coverage of two sets. Let A and B are two approximations. The coverage metric $\tilde{C}$ [2] is defined as:

$$\tilde{C}(A, B) = \frac{|\{\mathbf{f}(\mathbf{b}') \in B; \exists \mathbf{f}(\mathbf{a}') \in A : \mathbf{f}(\mathbf{a}') \succ \mathbf{f}(\mathbf{b}')\}|}{|B|}. \tag{7}$$

The value $\tilde{C}$ is in the interval [0,1]. In general, $\tilde{C}(A,B) \neq \tilde{C}(B,A)$, both should be considered independently.

As the second performance metric, we use the front spread (FS) [1] to measure the size of the objective space covered by an approximation. A larger FS value is preferable. Let the approximation A be the image of the solutions set S. The metric FS of A is defined as:

$$FS(A) = \sqrt{\sum_{i=0}^{n-1} \max_{(\mathbf{x}^0, \mathbf{x}^1) \in S \times S} \{(f_i(\mathbf{x}^0) - f_i(\mathbf{x}^1))^2\}}. \tag{8}$$

where n is the number of objectives, $f_i(\mathbf{x}^0)$ and $f_i(\mathbf{x}^1)$ are the objective values of solutions x^0 and x^1.

The proposed algorithm was run 30 times with different random seeds on each instance, for generations 10 using the population sizes described in Table 1. In this table are described, for each instance, lower bound (lb) and upper bound (ub) of $iter$ in the SA, grids number G_i in the ith objective dimension, and the average computational time, in second (sec), consumed by the HAMOMA is reported at the last column.

The mutation rate was set as $4/L$ (where L is the number of bits in the chromosome) for all instances, but the mutation rate is $1/L$ in GBLP. An intensive experiment was performed to find good combination of parameters, and the

Table 1. Parameter values in our HAMOMA and execution time for each test instance

Instance	Popsize	lb	ub	G_1	G_2	G_3	G_4	Time(sec)
2-250	10	500	700	8	8	-	-	27
2-500	10	700	900	8	8	-	-	66
2-750	10	900	1100	8	8	-	-	107
3-250	15	800	1000	16	16	16	-	92
3-500	15	1000	1200	16	16	16	-	152
3-750	15	1000	1200	16	16	16	-	208
4-250	15	1000	1200	32	32	32	32	180
4-500	20	1000	1200	32	32	32	32	372
4-750	15	1000	1200	32	32	32	32	421

other parameters in HAMOMA for each instance were set as follows: $\alpha_1=0.001$, $\alpha_2=0.9$, $l=2$, $\alpha=0.5$, and the parameters in the local searcher SA were chosen as: $T_0=0.0001$, $T_{end}=0.000001$ and $\gamma=0.95$.

The comparison results based on the $\tilde{C}$ metric are presented in Figs.6 and 7. A simple version of box plots is used to visualize the distribution of the $\tilde{C}$ samples. From Fig.6, we can see that HAMOMA obviously outperforms MOGLS and M-PAES. For each instance, the HAMOMA approximation dominates a large percentage of the points generated by MOGLS and M-PAES, while the MOGLS and M-PAES fronts respectively dominate a rather small portion of the HAMOMA fronts, especially for the instances with four objectives.

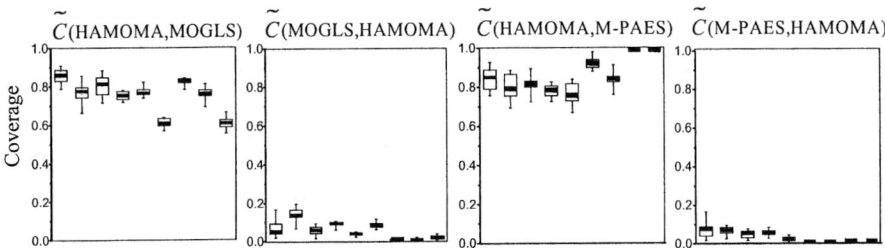

Fig. 6. Box plots based on the $\tilde{C}$ metric of nine instances. In each chart, the three box plots to the left associate with two knapsacks and (from left to right) 250,500 and 750 items. Correspondingly, the three middle box plots associate with three knapsacks and the three to the right with four knapsacks.

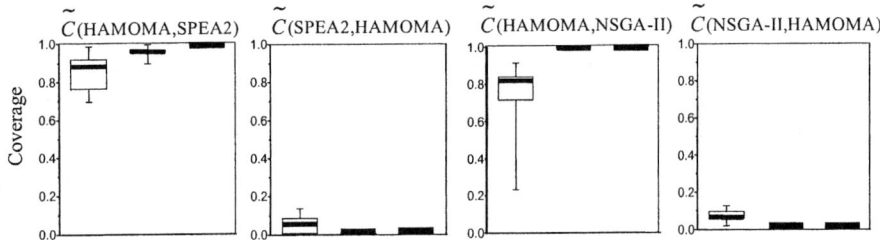

Fig. 7. Box plots based on the $\tilde{C}$ metric of three instances with 750 items. The three box plots associated with two, three and four knapsacks (from left to right).

Compared with SPEA2 and NSGA-II for instances with 750 items, Fig.7 shows that for instances with three and four objectives, the coverage metric indicates clear advantage of HAMOMA over SPEA2 and NSGA-II, whose fronts are dominated by the HAMOMA fronts by nearly 100%.

Figs.8 (a) and (b) present the fronts generated by HAMOMA, MOGLS, SPEA and SPEA2 for instance 2-750. Clearly, the fronts obtained by HAMOMA are closer to the Pareto front.

The results concerning the *FS* metric are reported in Table 2, which presents the average *FS* values for the approximations generated by the given algorithms.

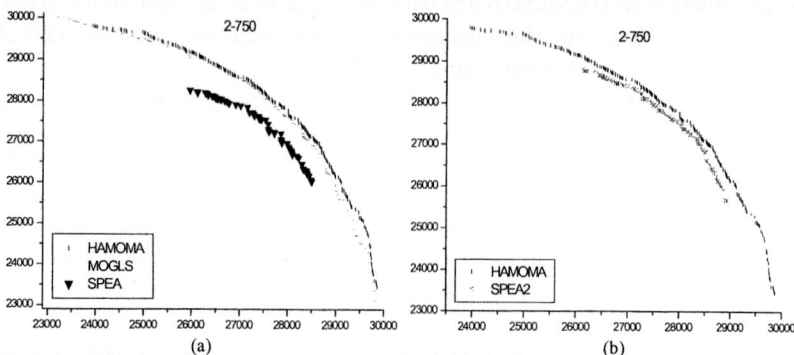

Fig. 8. Approximations obtained by particular algorithms

Table 2. Comparison of given algorithms: Front Spread (*FS*)

Instance	HAMOMA	MOGLS	M-PAES	SPEA2	NSGA-II
2-250	3250	3465	2577	-	-
2-500	4844	5346	3868	-	-
2-750	8300	8935	6514	4220	2897
3-250	4283	4437	2998	-	-
3-500	7629	7763	3565	-	-
3-750	10511	11260	4940	5796	6119
4-250	4342	4857	2593	-	-
4-500	8693	8282	4391	-	-
4-750	12256	13498	4617	8549	9982

Table 2 shows that HAMOMA obtains more diversified solutions compared to M-PAES for all instances in that it achieves larger *FS* values, but as is not the case when compared with MOGLS in terms of the *FS* metric. For instances with 750 items, Table 2 gives clear evidence that the proposed method outperforms SPEA2 and NSGA-II according to the *FS* values.

4 Conclusions

In this paper, we proposed a hybrid adaptive multi-objective memetic algorithm (HAMOMA) for the MOKP. In order to achieve a global exploitation and exploration, the aggregation functions are hybridized with the Pareto dominance to perform the fitness evaluation. The algorithm is implemented by using a simulated annealing combined with the use of a population, crossover and a grid-based local perturbation. For a good robustness of the algorithm, the procedure is self-adjusted based on the online improvement ratio.

To illustrate the effectiveness of HAMOMA on the MOKP, we compared it with several prominent algorithms. The computational results reveal that, for all tested instances, the proposed algorithm is completely superior to M-PAES, SPEA2, NSGA-II on the metrics of the coverage and front spread. Although HAMOMA is a little inferior to MOGLS based on the front spread for most of instances, it obviously outperforms MOGLS in the sense of Pareto optimality.

In future work, the performance of the proposed method to other problem domains would be investigated, and comparison between HAMOMA and other recently proposed memetic algorithms should be performed.

References

1. P.A.N.Bosman and D.Thierens. The balance between proximity and diversity in multiobjective evolutionary algorithms. *IEEE Trans. on Evolutionary Computation.*,(7):174-188, 2003.
2. J.E.Fieldsend, R.M.Everson and S.Singh. Using unconstrained elite archives for multiobjective optimization. *IEEE Trans. on Evolutionary Computation.*, (7):305-323, 2003.
3. K.Deb, A.Pratap, S.Agarwal and T.Meyarivan. A fast and elitist multiobjective genetic algorithm: NSGA-II. *IEEE Trans. on Evolutionary Computation.*,(6):182-197, 2002.
4. J.D.Knowles and D.W.Corne. The Pareto archived evolution strategy: a new baseline algorithm for Pareto multiobjective optimization. *Proceedings of the 1999 Congress on Evolutionary Computation.*, 98-105, 1999.
5. Shu Min Yang, Dong Guo Shao and Yang Jie Luo. A novel evolution strategy for multiobjective optimization problem. *Applied Mathematics and Computation.*, 1-24, 2005.
6. E.Zitzler and L.Thiele. Multiobjective evolutionary algorithms: a comparative case study and the strength Pareto approach. *IEEE Trans. on Evolutionary Computation.*,(3):257-271, 1999.
7. J.D.Knowles and D.W.Corne. M-PAES: a memetic algorithm for multiobjective optimization. *Proceedings of the 2000 Congress on Evolutionary Computation.*,325-332, 2000.
8. H.Ishibuchi and T.Murata. A multi-objective genetic local search algorithm and its application to flowshop scheduling. *IEEE Trans. Syst., Man. & Cybern.*, (28):392-403, 1998.
9. H.Ishibuchi, T.Yoshida and T.Murata. Balance between genetic search and local search in memetic algorithms for multiobjective permutation flowshop scheduling. *IEEE Trans. on Evolutionary Computation.*, (7):204-223, 2003.
10. A.Jaszkiewicz. Genetic local search for multiple objective combinatorial optimization. *European J. of Oper. Res.*, (137):50-71, 2002.
11. Http://www.tik.ee.ethz.ch/ ziztler/testdata.html
12. Http://www-idss.cs.put.poznan.pl/ jaszkiewicz/mokp
13. E.Zitzler, M.Laumanns and L.Thiele. SPEA2: Improving the strength pareto evolutionary algorithm. *TIK-Report 103,Switxerland.*, 2001.
14. G.G.Yen and L.Haiming. Dynamic multiobjective evolutionary algorithm: adaptive cell-based rank and density estimation. *IEEE Trans. on Evolutionary Computation.*, (7):253-274, 2003.
15. K.C.Tan, T.H.Lee and E.F.Khor. Evolutionary algorithms with dynamic population size and local exploration for multiobjective optimization. *IEEE Trans. on Evolutionary Computation.*,(5): 565-588, 2001.

Probability Estimation in Error Correcting Output Coding Framework Using Game Theory

Mikhail Petrovskiy*

Computer Science Department of Lomonosov Moscow State University,
Building 2, MSU, Vorobjovy Gory, Moscow, 119992, Russia
Phone: +7 095 9391789, Fax: +7 095 9391988
michael@cs.msu.su

Abstract. This paper is devoted to the problem of obtaining class probability 0estimates for multi-class classification problem in Error-correcting output coding (ECOC) framework. We consider the problem of class prediction via ECOC ensemble of binary classifiers as a decision-making problem and propose to solve it using game theory approach. We show that class prediction problem in ECOC framework can be formulated as a matrix game of special form. Investigation of the optimal solution in pure and mixed strategies is resulted in development of novel method for obtaining class probability estimates. Experimental performance evaluation on well-known benchmark datasets has demonstrated that proposed game theoretic method outperforms traditional methods for class probabilities estimation in ECOC framework.

1 Introduction

This paper is devoted to the problem of estimating class probabilities in Error-correcting output coding (ECOC) framework. ECOC has been reported as one of the most powerful techniques for solving *multi-class classification problem* [1,2,3,7,9,11,12]. This technique is a generalization of well-known *one-against-one* and *one-against-rest* approaches. In ECOC framework the original multi-class classification problem is decomposed into several binary sub-problems that are then being solved independently. In many applications ECOC methods have demonstrated the ability to improve the generalization performance of traditional binary [3,9,11] and multi-class [1,2,7,12] supervised learning algorithms. There are three main stages in ECOC framework: *coding, learning* and *decoding*. On the coding stage the original multi-class problem is decomposed into fixed number of *individual binary sub-problems*. This decomposition is encoded by so called *coding matrix*. It associates with each binary sub-problem two subsets of "positive" and "negative" classes that have to be separated solving this particular binary sub-problem. On the learning stage all binary sub-problems are solved independently using one of standard supervised learning algorithms. As a result, an *individual binary classifier* is trained for each sub-problem. Finally, on decoding stage to classify new data one needs to apply all individual binary classifiers and combine their outputs using a *decoding rule*.

---

* Research is supported by RFBR grant # 03-01-00745.

Many real-world applications require posteriori *class probability estimations* instead of simple class label prediction. This problem has to be solved on the decoding stage [2,6,7,11,12]. Existing methods are based on the idea of transformation from probabilistic outputs of individual binary classifiers into class probabilities. There are two main approaches: *least squares approach* [2,12], which assumes that this transformation is explicitly defined by the coding matrix, and *paired comparisons approach* [6,7,11] based on some models of pairwise class probabilities comparisons. Existing methods have several important drawbacks. They are applicable to probabilistic individual classifiers only. They are approximate and computationally expensive. Some of them are based on empirical assumptions about relationship between probabilistic outputs of individual classifiers and class probabilities. We discuss it in Section 2 in details. To avoid weaknesses of the existing methods we propose a novel method for probability estimation in ECOC framework based on mathematical apparatus of game theory [5]. It is described in Section 3. Section 4 presents the results of experimental performance evaluation of our method on several well-known benchmark datasets. Finally, in Section 5 the conclusions are formulated.

2 Probability Estimation Methods in ECOC Framework

Let us consider the *deterministic* and *probabilistic* problem statements for multi-class classification problem. Assume that we are given a training set $Z = \{x_i, y_i\}_{i=1}^n \in X \times Y$, which consist of n labeled *instances* x_i from some domain X, *class* labels y_i belong to the domain $Y = \{1,...,k\}$, $k>2$. In the deterministic case the learning algorithm uses the training set Z to generate a classifier or single hypothesis $f : X \rightarrow Y$, where f belongs to some hypothesis space F. In the probabilistic case the goal of the learning algorithm is to estimate the *distribution* over classifiers $P(f(x) = y | Z)$. It means that for any given x instead of single prediction $y=f(x)$ the probabilistic algorithm computes posteriori class probabilities $\overline{p}(x)$ according to some $P(y | x)$:

$$\overline{p}(x) = \{p_j(x)\}_{j=1}^k, \text{ where } p_j(x) = P(y = j | x) \text{ and } \sum_{j=1}^k p_j(x) = 1 \text{ for all } x. \quad (1)$$

Usually, to construct a final predictor from a distribution $P(f(x) = y | Z)$ a Bayes optimal rule is used $f_{bayes}(x) = \arg\max_{j \in \{1,...,k\}} p_j(x)$.

Let us now return to multi-class classification problem in ECOC framework. Using ECOC approach the original k-class problem is converted into l binary classification sub-problems. The main idea of ECOC approach is to associate each class $y \in Y$ with a row of coding matrix $M \in \{-1,0,1\}^{k \times l}$, so called *codeword*. In this case each column of coding matrix M defines a single binary classification problem. All instances x_i from the original training set, initially labeled by y_i, are included in *s-th* binary sub-problem with new (mapped) label $M(y_i, s) \neq 0$. Thus, for each *s-th* binary sub-problem we have three sets of classes defined: "positive" classes

$I_s^+ = \{y \mid y \in Y \wedge M(y,s) = 1\}$, "negative" classes $I_s^- = \{y \mid y \in Y \wedge M(y,s) = -1\}$ and "ignored" classes $I_s^0 = \{y \mid y \in Y \wedge M(y,s) = 0\}$. After the coding stage completed the learning algorithm is applied to each individual binary problem. It separates "positive" classes from "negative". As a result l binary classifiers are trained and l hypothesizes $f_1,...,f_l$ are generated such that $f_s : X \to Y_{bin}$. The output domain Y_{bin} is specific for the learning algorithm. It can be $\{0,1\}$ for hard-level (pure Boolean) classifiers, or $\Re$ for soft-level (e.g. for large margin classifiers [9]). Moreover, the output of individual binary classifiers can be probabilistic:

$$r_s = P(f_s(x) \in I_s^+ \mid f_s(x) \in I_s^+ \wedge f_s(x) \in I_s^-). \tag{2}$$

To classify new data x in ECOC framework one has to apply all binary classifiers and obtain a vector of predicted values $\bar{f}(x) = (f_1(x),...,f_l(x))$. To predict class label y these values $\bar{f}(x)$ are combined together using some decoding rules [13]. The simplest and the most widely used decoding method is choosing a class r minimizing the Hamming or Minkowski [13] distance between r-th codeword in coding matrix M and $\bar{f}(x)$. But such decoding rules don not provide a tool for estimating posteriori class probabilities (1). Existing methods for probability estimation in ECOC are based on the idea of mapping the probabilistic output of individual classifiers (2) into class probabilities (1). Some learning algorithms, for example, Naïve Bayes [7] and Decision Trees [2,7,12] can directly produce probabilistic outputs (2). For others the special techniques to obtain probabilities from real-valued outputs $\bar{f}(x)$ have been proposed, e.g. a sigmoid model for large-margin classifiers [4]. One of the first methods for probability estimation in ECOC was proposed in [12]. It was based on the assumption that the coding matrix M explicitly defines a transformation between spaces from original probabilistic outputs to class probabilities:

$$\bar{r}(x) = M^T \bar{p}(x), \text{ subject to } \sum_{j=1}^{k} p_j(x) = 1, \; p_j(x) \geq 0 \text{ for all } j \text{ and } x. \tag{3}$$

But usually, system of linear equations (3) is inconsistent and the least squares method can be used to find an approximate solution of (3) [12]. More sophisticated version of this method was developed in [2]. All methods involving *least square approach* are called LS-ECOC methods. An alternative is so called *paired comparisons* approach. It is based on paired comparisons methods developed in statistics [10]. To demonstrate the idea we have chosen as an example the method proposed in [11] and implemented in popular SVM library LIBSVM [14]. It is a generalization of Bradley-Terry model, where the individual pairwise comparisons are extended to group paired comparisons:

$$P(I_s^+ \text{ beats } I_s^-) = \sum_{j \in I_s^+} p_j \Big/ \sum_{j \in I_s^+ \cup I_s^-} p_j. \tag{4}$$

Estimating class probabilities via generalized Bradley-Terry model leads to the following optimization problem (negative log-likelihood minimization) [11]:

$$\min_{\vec{p}} \left[-\sum_{s=1}^{l} \left(r_s \log(q_s^+ / q_s) + (1-r_s) \log(q_s^- / q_s) \right) \right], \text{ subject to } \sum_{j=1}^{k} p_j = 1, p_j \geq 0, \quad (5)$$

where $q_s = \sum_{j \in I_s^+ \cup I_s^-} p_j$, $q_s^+ = \sum_{j \in I_s^+} p_j$, $q_s^- = \sum_{j \in I_s^-} p_j$ for all s.

There are several other variations on this theme in [6,7]. All these methods exploit the idea that class probabilities are related by (4) and lead optimization problems similar to (5). Though paired comparison methods demonstrated good performance on benchmark tests and in some applications [11], they can be criticized for using heuristic assumptions and approximations both in models formulations and in solving algorithms.

3 Our Game Theoretic Approach

In this section we formulate our new method for class probability estimation in ECOC framework. It is based on game theoretic mathematical apparatus. Before going into further details let us introduce some basic definitions and facts from game theory [5], which we will need below. The *normal* (or *strategic*) form of two-person zero-sum game is given by a triplet (S_1, S_2, A). S_1 and S_2 are nonempty sets of strategies available for Player 1 and Player 2 correspondingly. A is a real-valued function $A: S_1 \times S_2 \to \Re$. It associates with every pair of strategies the value a, which is a *gain* of Player 1 and in the same time the *loss* of Player 2. When S_1 and S_2 are finite sets the function A can be represented as a matrix $[a_{ij}]$, where column (row) indices are enumerated strategies of Player 2 (Player 1). The value a_{ij} is Player 1 gain (Player 2 loss) in the case if Player 1 selects i-th strategy and Player 2 selects j-th strategy. Such game is called *matrix game*. Matrix A is called a *payoff matrix* (or *loss matrix* for Player 2). The goal of Player 1 is to select the strategy maximizing his/her gain. The goal of Player 2 is inverse. Let (S_1, S_2, A) be a two-person zero-sum game [5]. The strategies $s_1^* \in S_1$ and $s_2^* \in S_2$ are *equalizing pure strategies* if $A(s_1^*, s_2) \geq A(s_1^*, s_2^*) \geq A(s_1, s_2^*)$ for all $s_1 \in S_1$ and $s_2 \in S_2$. It means that if Player 1 selects the strategy $s_1^* \in S_1$ he/she has a guaranteed *lower gain* $V_G = A(s_1^*, s_2)$, no matter what Player 2 does. Similarly, if Player 2 selects the strategy $s_2^* \in S_2$ he/she has a guaranteed *upper loss* $V_L = A(s_1, s_2^*)$, no matter what Player 1 does. The point $(s_1^*, s_2^*) \in S_1 \times S_2$ is called a *saddle point* and $A(s_1^*, s_2^*)$ is the *value of the game*.

Saddle Point Theorem [5]. *Matrix game* (S_1, S_2, A) *has a saddle point* (i_0, j_0) *if and only if* $\min_j \max_i a_{ij} = \max_i \min_j a_{ij} = a_{i0,j0}$.

If the matrix game satisfies the conditions of the theorem the *optimal strategies* for both players exist and they are defined by a saddle point (i_0, j_0) (i_0-th strategy is optimal for Player 1, j_0-th strategy is optimal for Player 2). In this case the matrix game has a solution in *pure strategies*. Unfortunately, very seldom a matrix game has the saddle point and in this case game theory recommends finding a solution in *mixed strategies*. They are defined as probabilistic distributions over pure strategies. For the matrix game (S_1, S_2, A) with $m \times n$ matrix A the set of mixed strategies Q of Player 1 and P of Player 2 are represented as following probability vectors:

$$Q = \{q = (q_1, ..., q_m) : q_i \geq 0, \sum_{i=1}^{m} q_i = 1\}, P = \{p = (p_1, ..., p_n) : p_j \geq 0, \sum_{j=1}^{n} p_j = 1\}. \quad (6)$$

It means that q_i is a probability of Player 1 selects *i-th* pure strategy and p_j is a probability of Player 2 selects *j-th* pure strategy. In this case the payoff (loss) is considered as *average payoff* (*average loss*) and it is equal to $q^T A p = \sum\sum a_{ij} q_i p_j$. Thus, we come to the game *(Q,P,A)*, for which *saddle point* and *game value* are defined as follows. The mixed strategies $q^* \in Q$ and $p^* \in P$ are *optimal mixed strategies* if $q^{*T} A p \geq q^{*T} A p^* \geq q^T A p^*$ for all $q \in Q$ and $p \in P$. The point $(q^*, p^*) \in Q \times P$ is called a *saddle point for mixed strategies* and the value $q^{*T} A p^*$ is called the *value of the game in mixed strategies*. The pure strategy can be considered as a mixed strategy, where all components except one are equal to zero.

Matrix Game Main Theorem [5]. *Every matrix game has a solution in mixed strategies.*

In general case for any given matrix game A the value of the game V and the solutions in mixed strategies can be found as a solution of a linear programming problem [5]. For Player 2 this problem is formulated as follows:

$$\min V, \text{ subject to } \sum_i p_i = 1, \sum_i a_{ji} p_i \leq V, p_j \geq 0. \quad (7)$$

For Player 1 the optimization problem is dual to (7).

3.1 Formulation of ECOC Decoding Problem as a Matrix Game

Let us consider the ECOC decoding problem with k classes and l binary individual classifiers trained with respect to decomposition defined by some coding matrix $M \in \{-1, 0, 1\}^{k \times l}$. The task is to estimate posteriori class probabilities (1) for a given data x combining the outputs of individual binary classifiers. The key idea of our approach is to consider the ECOC decoding problem as a decision-making problem and solve it using the apparatus of matrix games. We consider Player 1 as an *environment* or *uncontrolled factor* that has semantic "unobserved class of x". There are k possible states for uncontrolled factor. t-th state means "x belongs to class t". Player 2 is a multi-class classifier that has k *alternatives*, where r-th alternative stands for "assign x to class r". To formulate a matrix game we need to define for each pair "*selected alternative*"-"*unknown factor state*" the value of loss $\Delta L(r \mid t)$. It can be defined as an *additional (or conditional) loss* that we have in the case when real class of x is t, but x is assigned to class r. It is zero if x is assigned correctly, i.e. $\Delta L(t \mid t) = 0$. As a result, we obtain the following matrix game $(\{1, ..., k\}, \{1, ..., k\}, \Delta L)$ with square loss matrix $\Delta L \in [0, \infty]^{k \times k}$ having zero diagonal ($\Delta L(t \mid t) = 0$ for all t):

$$\begin{array}{c|ccccc}
 & 1 & \ldots & r & \ldots & k \\
\hline
1 & \Delta L(1|1) & \ldots & \Delta L(r|1) & \ldots & \Delta L(k|1) \\
\ldots & \ldots & \ldots & \ldots & \ldots & \ldots \\
t & \Delta L(1|t) & \ldots & \Delta L(r|t) & \ldots & \Delta L(k|t) \\
\ldots & \ldots & \ldots & \ldots & \ldots & \ldots \\
k & \Delta L(1|k) & \ldots & \Delta L(r|k) & \ldots & \Delta L(k|k)
\end{array} \qquad (8)$$

We need to solve a game with matrix (10) taking the part of Player 2. By this formulation, finding optimal solution means assigning given data x to the class r to minimize possible additional loss in case of misclassification. Before going into discussion how to find the optimal solution let us explain how to construct the loss matrix using individual classifiers outputs $\bar{f}(x)$ and coding matrix M.

We propose to calculate the value of additional loss $\Delta L(r|t)$ as a combination of losses produced by s individual binary classifiers with respect to codewords r and t from the coding matrix M. We start with introduction of *loss function for individual binary classification problem* as a function $L: X \times \{-1,1\} \times \Re \rightarrow \Re_0^+$, such that $L(x, y, f(x))$ describes the cost of assigning a pattern $x \in X$ to the class $y \in \{-1,1\}$, when the predicted value for x is $f(x)$. Here we use traditional loss function definition in classification context with restriction to binary classification problem. Many standard loss functions, including 0-1 binary, soft-margin, logistic, exponential and others [3,9] satisfy this definition and can be used in our approach. With probabilistic loss function $L(x, y, f(x)) = -\ln P(y | f(x))$ we can handle probabilistic output of individual binary classifiers exactly in the same way as real-valued and Boolean binary classifiers. For these purposes we take the probabilistic output (2) of s-th individual binary classifier $r_s(x) = P(y | f_s(x))$ and calculate the loss as $L(x, y, r_s(x)) = -\ln r_s(x)$. Thus, in our approach we can use any individual binary classifiers, including hard-level, real-valued and probabilistic.

Now we can define the *total loss for class r* as a sum over all binary sub-problems with respect to the coding matrix M:

$$L_{class}(x, r, M, \bar{f}(x)) = \sum_{s \in \{i | M(r,i) \neq 0\}} L(x, r, f_s(x)) . \qquad (9)$$

Note, that definition (9) is the same as loss-based distance definition in [3]. Now let us define the *additional loss* $\Delta L(r|t)$ of class r with respect to class t. The idea is simple: we have to calculate loss for class r, but consider only those binary sub-problems that have opposite coding in class t: $M(r,s) \neq M(t,s)$. Besides, losses from binary sub-problems with zero codes $M(t,s) = 0$ should be ignored, because for real class t the decision of s-th individual binary sub-problem is insufficient. Thus, in formula (9) we should take the sum over those indices s, such that $M(r,s) * M(t,s) = -1$:

$$\Delta L(r|t) = L_\Delta(x, r, t, M, \bar{f}(x)) = \sum_{s \in \{i | M(r,i)*M(t,i)=-1\}} L(x, r, f_s(x)) . \qquad (10)$$

It is obvious that according to (10) $\Delta L(t|t) = 0$ for all t. Using (10) we calculate $\Delta L(r|t)$ for all $r,t \in \{1,...,k\}$ and construct corresponding matrix game (8).

3.2 Solving ECOC Decoding Problem as a Matrix Game

To apply our method for a given ECOC decoding problem we need to calculate additional losses (10), then formulate the game with matrix (8) and solve it in pure or mixed strategies. Let us consider under what conditions what type of strategy exists, how the solution can be found, and what is its semantic. We start with investigation of the case when the *deterministic solution* exists. Assume that matrix game (8) has a unique solution in pure strategies. It means that there exists such class r that choosing it we always obtain the minimal additional loss. In this case we have no uncertainty in our decision and have to choose class r with probability 1. In other words, the class probability estimation in this case is as follows:

$$p_r(x) = 1, \quad p_j(x) = 0 \text{ for all } j \neq r. \qquad (11)$$

Before formulating the conditions on existence of the *deterministic solution* (11) we need to establish some additional conditions on the coding matrix M and loss function for individual binary sub-problems L. We concern the loss functions L such that:

$$L(x,1,z) + L(x,-1,z) > 0 \text{ for all } z \text{ and } x. \qquad (12)$$

It is easy to check that soft-margin, exponential, logistic, binary and many other loss functions satisfy this property. Besides, we claim that matrix M satisfy the property:

$$\forall i \forall j \exists s_0 : M(i, s_0) = -M(j, s_0) \neq 0. \qquad (13)$$

It means that for each pair (i,j) of codewords in the coding matrix M, there exsists at least one index s_0 such that which s_0-th binary sub-problem contains class i in $I_{s_0}^+$ and j in $I_{s_0}^-$, or vise verse. In other words, there must be at least one binary sub-problem s_0 separating classes i and j. All practically useful coding matrices do satisfy this property [13].

Theorem 1. *In ECOC framework consider k-class classification problem with l binary classifiers trained with respect to decomposition defined by a coding matrix $M \in \{-1,0,1\}^{k \times l}$ satisfying (13). Then for a given pattern x class r is a deterministic solution (11) if and only if the total loss (9) is equal to zero. The loss function for individual binary sub-problem L used in (9) should satisfy property (12).*

Lemma 1. *Matrix game (10) has a pure strategy saddle point in column r if and only if $\Delta L(r|i) = 0$ for all i.*

Proof: Matrix game (8) has a zero diagonal: $\Delta L(i|i) = 0$ for all i. Thus lower value of the game $\max_i \min_j \Delta L(j|i)$ is always zero. According to the Matrix Game Saddle

Point Theorem the saddle point exists if and only if the lower value of the game is equal to the upper value $\min_j \max_i \Delta L(j|i)$, and in our case they both are to be equal to zero. But $\min_j \max_i \Delta L(j|i) = 0$ if and only if there exists such r that $\max_i \Delta L(r|i) = 0$. It is true if and only if $\Delta L(r|i) = 0$ for all i. ∎

Lemma 2. *If a coding matrix M satisfies (13), a loss function for binary classification problem L satisfies (12) and a matrix game (8) has a pure strategy saddle point in some column r then there are no other saddle points in any other column $j \neq r$.*

Proof: Assume that it is not true and matrix game (8) has a second saddle point in some column $j \neq r$. It follows from Lemma 1 that in this case $\Delta L(r|i) = 0$ and $\Delta L(j|i) = 0$ for all i. Since the latter equalities are true for all i we obtain that $\Delta L(r|j) = \Delta L(j|r) = 0$. It follows from (10) that in this case $L(x, M(r,s), f_s(x)) = 0$ and $L(x, M(j,s), f_s(x)) = 0$ for all s, where $M(r,s) * M(j,s) = -1$. According to condition (13) there exists at least one binary sub-problem s_0 such that $M(r, s_0) = -M(j, s_0) \neq 0$. As long as $M(j, s_0)$ and $M(r, s_0)$ are not zeros, corresponding binary losses must be equal to zero: $L(x, M(j, s_0), f_{s0}(x)) = L(x, M(r, s_0), f_{s0}(x)) = 0$. But, it means that $L(x, 1, f_{s0}(x)) = L(x, -1, f_{s0}(x)) = 0$ and it contradicts to condition (12). ∎

Proof of Theorem 1: According to conditions of the theorem, there is class r, such that its total loss (9) is zero. $L_{class}(x, r, M, \bar{f}(x)) = 0$ if and only if $L(x, M(r, s), f_s(x)) = 0$ for all s where $M(r, s) \neq 0$. It follows from (10) that in this case $L_\Delta(x, r, t, M, \bar{f}(x)) = \Delta L(r|t) = 0$ for all t. Finally, applying Lemma 1 we get that it is necessary and sufficient condition for matrix game (8) to have a saddle point in the column r. The uniqueness of class r follows from Lemma 2. Thus, we have a deterministic solution – class r. ∎

In practice, Theorem1 let us to reduce the amount of computations. We can calculate total losses for all classes and check if the deterministic solution (11) exists. If there is no deterministic solution we always can solve (8) in mixed strategies. The semantic of this solution for ECOC decoding problem is the following. If we have optimal solution in mixed strategies we have a probability distribution over available pure strategies guaranteeing us minimal additional loss in average. In our case j-th pure strategy stands for "assign x to class j". Thus, the mixed strategy solution explicitly identifies class probabilities (1) and stands for "assign x to class j with probability $p_j(x) = P(y = j | x)$", where $p_j(x)$ are defined by (6). Mixed strategies can be found as a solution of linear programming problem (7). In our case it has the following form:

$$\min V, \quad \sum_{j=1}^{k} p_j = 1, \sum_{j} \Delta L(i \mid j) p_j \leq V, \quad p_j \geq 0 \text{ for all } j. \tag{14}$$

Solving (14) we obtain $\{p_j\}_{j=1}^{k}$ - the class probability estimates (1) for given x. As a result, the *novel* method for class probabilities estimation in ECOC framework is formulated. It finds the deterministic solution in conditions of Theorem 1. If conditions of Theorem 1 are not satisfied it computes class probability estimates (1) as a solution of the linear programming problem (14). Problem (14) has dimensionality k, where loss matrix (8) is calculated using formula (10). The final deterministic class prediction can be obtained using Bayes rule: $f_{bayes}(x) = \arg\max_{j \in \{1,...,k\}} p_j(x)$. We denote or method below as MG-ECOC that stands for "Matrix Game - ECOC".

4 Experiments

In this section we present the results of experimental performance evaluation. We compared least-squares method (LS-ECOC) [12], generalized Bradley-Terry model method (BT-ECOC) [11] and our matrix game method (MG-ECOC) for class probabilities estimation in ECOC. In our method the following loss functions were used: binary (bin), soft margin (soft), exponential (exp) and probabilistic (prob). We selected several popular multi-class benchmark datasets from LIBSVM repository [14]: *dna*, *satimage*, *shuttle* and *letter*. All attribute values in all datasets (except dna) were scaled to [-1,1]. As a base binary classifier we used support vector machines (SVM) with RBF kernel from LIBSVM package. We used the experimental setup and SVM parameters estimation procedures the same as described in [8]. We run each series of experiments with four different coding matrices: "1vs1" one-against-one approach, "1vsAll" one-against-others approach, "dense" ECOC decomposition – coding matrix does not contain zeros, "sparse" ECOC decomposition – coding matrix may contain zeros. For "dense" and "sparse" ECOC matrices the random codes generation approach described in [11] was used. The code length was $[10\log_2 k]$ for "dense" and $[15\log_2 k]$ for "sparse" decompositions. SVM decision function $f(x)$ is real-valued. Thus, in our MG-ECOC method we can use $f(x)$ "as is" in soft-margin $L(x, y, f(x)) = \max(0, 1 - yf(x))$ and exponential $L(x, y, f(x)) = \exp(-yf(x))$ loss functions. To model hard-level 0-1 output we used $sign(f(x))$. To model the probabilistic output (2) for our method with probabilistic loss function and for LS-ECOC and BT-ECOC methods we used a sigmoid model [4] with sigmoid parameters estimation procedure implemented in LIBSVM [14].

Analyzing experimental results we can contend that for every experimental run the developed game theoretic method with properly chosen loss function outperforms, or at least performs not worse than traditional least squares and Bradley-Terry methods. Besides, our method with soft-margin loss functions demonstrated the best performance in average over all experiments.

Table 1. Experimental results: accuracy. Column "total wins" contains the number of experimental series, where a method outperforms the others

	Decomposition	LSECOC	BTECOC	MGECOC (bin)	MGECOC (soft)	MGECOC (exp)	MGECOC (prob)
dna	1vs1	67.79%	**94.69%**	94.60%	**94.69%**	94.60%	94.52%
Satimage	1vs1	61.9%	90.5%	90.35%	90.3%	90.25%	**90.75%**
Shuttle	1vs1	91%	99.86%	**99.92%**	**99.92%**	**99.92%**	99.83%
Letter	1vs1	86.56%	96.9%	97.02%	97%	**97.06%**	96.96%
dna	1vsAll	**94.77%**	**94.77%**	94.42%	**94.77%**	**94.77%**	**94.77%**
Satimage	1vsAll	90 %	90 %	89.1%	**90.1%**	**90.1%**	90%
Shuttle	1vsAll	99.89%	99.89%	**99.9%**	99.89%	99.89%	99.87%
Letter	1vsAll	96.84%	96.84%	93.72%	**96.88%**	**96.88%**	96.84%
dna	Dense	**94.77%**	**94.77%**	94.42%	**94.77%**	**94.77%**	**94.77%**
Satimage	Dense	87.65%	**90.1%**	89.8%	**90.1%**	**90.1%**	**90.1%**
Shuttle	Dense	**99.9%**	99.89%	**99.9%**	**99.9%**	99.89%	93.73%
Letter	Dense	96.32%	96.94%	96.84%	96.86%	96.88%	**96.94%**
dna	Sparse	60.78%	94.60%	94.60%	**94.69%**	94.60%	94.44%
Satimage	Sparse	88.2%	**90.4%**	90.25%	90.05%	90.15%	**90.4%**
Shuttle	Sparse	98.37%	99.87%	99.89%	**99.9%**	99.89%	95.85%
Letter	Sparse	83.2%	96.94%	96.7%	**96.94%**	95.58%	96.88%
total wins	-	3	5	3	**11**	7	6

5 Conclusions

In this paper we considered the problem of obtaining class probabilities via ECOC ensemble of binary classifiers. We have discussed that existing methods for class probability estimation in ECOC framework has several significant weaknesses. To avoid them we have developed new method based on mathematical apparatus of game theory. Unlike other existing methods, our method does not require individual probability estimates for binary sub-problems and can work with any binary classifiers, including real-valued, pure Boolean and probabilistic. It is parameter-free. It provides accurate class probability estimates, which can be found as a solution of a linear programming problem of dimensionality k, where k is a number of classes. Finally, the experimental performance evaluation on well-known benchmark datasets has demonstrated that our method outperforms traditional methods for class probability estimation in ECOC framework.

References

1. Dietterich, T. G., Bakiri, G.: Solving multi-class learning problems via error-correcting output codes. Journal of Artificial Intelligence Research, 2, (1995), pp. 263–286.
2. Ghaderi, R., Windeatt, T. Least squares and estimation measures via error correcting output code. In 2nd Int. Workshop Multiple Classifier Systems, Lecture notes in computer science, Springer-Verlag, (2001), pp. 148–157.
3. Allwein, E.L., Schapire, R.E., Singer, Y.: Reducing multiclass to binary: A unifying approach for margin classifiers. In: Journal of Machine Learning Research,2000(1), pp.113-141.

4. Platt, J.: Probabilistic Outputs for Support Vector Machines and Comparison to Regularized Likelihood Methods. In Adv. in Large Margin Classifiers. MIT Press, (1999), pp.61–74.
5. Fudenberg, D, Tirole, J.,: Game Theory. MIT Press, 1991.
6. Dekel, O., Singer, Y.: Multiclass Learning by Probabilistic Embeddings. NIPS 2002, pp.945-952.
7. Zadrozny, B., Elkan, C.: Obtaining calibrated probability estimates from decision trees and naive bayesian classifiers. ICML proceedings, 2000, pp. 609–616..
8. Lin, K.-M., Lin, C.-J. A study on reduced support vector machines, Neural Networks, IEEE Transactions on 14 (6) (2003) pp. 1449 - 1459.
9. Schapire, R.E. Using output codes to boost multiclass learning problems. ICML proceedings, (1997), pp. 313–321.
10. David, H. A.: The method of paired comparisons. Oxford University Press, New York, second edition, 1988.
11. Huang, T.-K., Weng, R., Lin, C.-J.: A Generalized Bradley-Terry Model: From Group Competition to Individual Skill. NIPS 2004.
12. Kong E.B., Diettrich, T.G.: Probability estimation via error-correcting output coding. In Int. Conf. of Artificial Intelligence and soft computing, Banff,Canada, 6 pages, 1997.
13. Windeatt, T.m Ghaderi, R. Coding and decoding strategies for multi-class learning problems. Information Fusion, (2003), 4(1): 11-21.
14. Chang, C.-C., Lin, C.-J. LIBSVM: a library for support vector machines, 2001.Software available at http://www.csie.ntu.edu.tw/~cjlin/libsvm.

Evaluation of Strings in Computer Go Using Articulation Points Check and Seki Judgment

Hyun-Soo Park[1] and Kyung-Woo Kang[2]

[1] Department of Computer Information Technology,
Kyungdong College of Techno-Information, 224-1, Buho, Hayang, Kyungpook, Korea
hspark@kdtc.ac.kr
[2] Department of Computer and Communication Engineering, Cheonan University, 115,
Anseo-dong, Cheonan 330-704, Choongnam, Korea
kwkang@infocom.chonan.ac.kr

Abstract. The purpose of this paper is to judge life and death in computer Go using Articulation Point Check(APC), Seki judgment and rules. To make static analysis possible, the researchers define a String Graph (SG) and judge the life and death of the strings using the rules. To judge the life and death of the strings, the researchers will adopt the APC Rule because it will judge life and death according to the numbers of the junctures. The researchers also suggest that Seki Rules be applied to judge Seki. By excluding Stones and using a String Graph (SG), the researchers postulate the use of SR (String Reduction), ER (Empty Reduction), ET (Edge Transformation) Rules, or CG (Circular Graph) in judging life and death. In addition, the DESR (Dead Enemy Strings Reduction) Rule was used when the dead enemy Stones were involved. Moreover, the SCSR (Same Color String Reduction) Rule was used when the dead enemy and Stones were empty and abridged. If our forces were involved in, the researchers abridged the String Graph by using SCSR (Same Color String Reduction) Rule and judged whether it was ASG(Alive String Graph) or not. The data that were used in the experiment were 31 IGS counted items among the Computer Go Test Collection composed of 11,191 points and 1,123 strings. The division of points and strings yielded 100% accuracy.

1 Introduction

The research on artificial intelligence has been focused on expert systems, written text and voice recognition, strategic games, and natural language processing. Especially the intelligence games that have focused on human intellectual ability have yielded very solid research findings. From the traditional games to high level ones, the data about these games are available at this moment.

Chess, which is a Western strategic game, can beat human beings by using game trees, pattern recognition, and knowledge base. The scope of research has been extended to Go, which has wider problem ranges than those of Chess. The problem scope of Chess is 10^{40}, whereas that of Go is 10^{761}. The spatial difference between Go and Chess has made it possible for Go to be the focus of investigation. The artificial intelligence techniques that are related to computerized Go are evaluation function, heuristic search, machine learning, automatic knowledge generation, mathematical morphology, and cognitive science.

David B. Benson[1] defined safe (unconditionally alive) by using graphic theory in his research on static analysis. The collection of strings is unconditionally alive when two strings have different vital domains in the collective strings. His research proves that safety and unconditional life are in the same position on the game board.

In addition, Landman calculated various eye-spaces values by using the Bargo model. Popma and Allis[3] also suggested 'X life', meaning alive, after passing X number. Wolf sought to solve the life or death problem by adopting tree searches.

Martin Miller[2] devised an exchange method by attaching to unconditional safety, raised the chain patterns, and extended the notion to the chain. He[4] also evaluated the whole Go board combining evaluation obtained from his program (Explorer) heuristically. His research focused on stability by using static rules and local searches in a game.

Ken Chen[7] and Zhixing Chen offered a method utilizing tree searches effectively in Go Intellect and Hand Talk. They used static analysis by investigating the contexts which surround the inner group. By looking at eye-spaces whose primary concern is whether to take enemy Stones or not, they tried to provide the fundamental solution for the geometrical increase in Go's game trees. Finally, Thore Graepel[8] depicts position information for the sake of learning by using the Common Fate Graph (CFG), considering Go in the perspective of machine learning.

In addition to the above-mentioned studies, a study needs to be conducted in judging life and death on the computer by using graphs and rules. In this paper, the researchers[5] evaluate static stability by using string graphs and rules. A String Graph (SG) depicts the relationships between strings and empty spaces graphically. From a string graph (SG), one can identify strings' lives and deaths intuitively, via static evaluation. Also, this paper will expound the String Graph's (SG) definition and expression. Also, the definition of the situation where Stones are involved or not, and the articulation point and Seki rules will be offered. Fig. 1 represents a block diagram that this paper suggests.

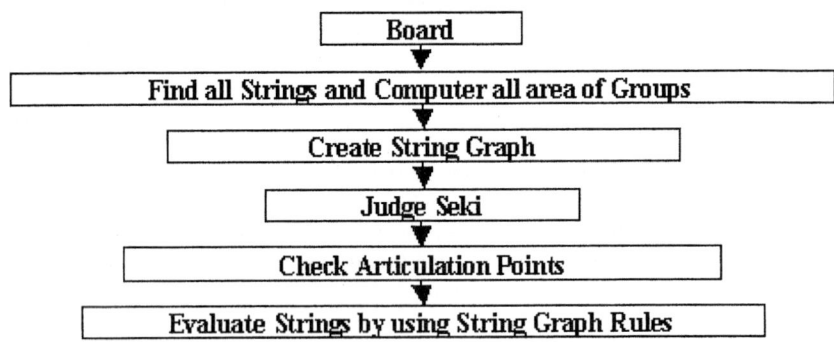

Fig. 1. A Suggested Block Diagram

What makes this study different from the conventional static analysis is that the suggested method evaluates the living status by using graphs which represent strings and groups. The primary concern of the experiment was to detect the accurateness of points and strings. The results of the experiment indicate that this study yields better results than those of Miller's study, which used static rules and searches.

In this paper, in section 2, the researchers will expound on the String Graph (SG) and Rules. Also, the management of articulation points, rules and Seki evaluation will be explained in detail. In section 3, the effectiveness of the suggested method will be shown through the experiment and analysis. Finally, in section 4, the summary and the limitation of the suggested method will be the focus of the discussion. Also suggested will be a direction for future studies in this field.

2 The String Graph (SG) Rules

A string is a basic element which will be eliminated when the Stone is dead on a Go board. Stones on the Go board are represented as board graphs which have two-dimensional grid structures. Board graphs can be defined as undirected graphs, that is $G_B = (V,E)$, $G_B \in G_U$. In this paper, the relationships among strings are represented by graphs. By defining the relationships among the strings of our forces, neighbor empty points, and enemy strings, the researchers believe that the process of static analysis will be more elaborate and accurate.

Definition 1. A String Graph (SG) can be defined as follows:

$SG = (V, E)$
$V = \{BS, WS, ES\}$, $BS, WS, ES \in String$,
$E : \{e_d, e_u\}$,
e_d : Regarding optional vertex v_i and v_j, if v_i includes v_j, v_i is directed edge of v_j. Therefore, $e_d = (v_i, v_j)$.
e_u : Regarding optional vertex v_i and v_j, if v_i is near v_j, v_i and v_j are undirected edge. Therefore, $e_u = (v_i, v_j)$.

In this paper, black strings are represented as the BS vertex, and white strings as the WS vertex respectively. The ES vertex represents empty clusters which are included in the strings which are black and white, and the neighboring empties also represent the ES vertex. The String Graph, $SG = (V, E)$ is composed of a limited V and a limited E collection. Each edge shows the order of the vertex. In a SG, vertices can be expressed as $v_1, v_2, ...$, and edge as $e_0, e_1, e_2, ...$ respectively. A SG consists of a directed and undirected graph. The undirected edge depicts the adjacency relationship between two vertexes, and the directed edge indicates the inclusion relationships. That is to say, if no empty string includes empty strings or other strings, they can be represented as the directed edge.

Definition 2. If an optional dot belongs to the strings not as an empty string, the dot is in the realm of the inner domains of the strings. If e_d, which is a directed edge, includes not an optional string but other strings, it can be expressed as a directed edge. The left column of Fig. 2 is a case where ES1 is included by BS1. In addition, the right column of Fig. 2 expresses a SG, which is a directed edge.

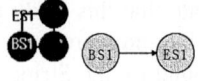 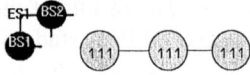

Fig. 2. An Example of A Directed Edge   **Fig. 3.** An Example of The Undirected Edges

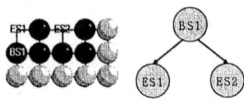

Fig. 4. The Elements of An Alive String Graph (ASG)

Also, an undirected edge can be expressed as e_u if optional strings are near other strings. In other words, if strings and empty points are near other strings and empty points, they are depicted as an undirected edge. In the left-hand column of Fig. 3, ES1 and BS1 are in the neighboring situation, and the right Fig. represents the left one as SG. ES1 is also near BS1 and BS2. In Fig. 4, the left Fig. shows a string which is alive with two eyes, and the right one is represented as a SG.

In this paper, the distinctions are made between two cases where Stones are included or not. According to Stones' inclusion or exclusion, rules will be defined and the static analysis will be conducted in turn.

2.1 The Articulation Point Management Rules

Rule 1. APC: Articulation Point Check

An optional string includes an empty string that has empty points. An optional string is alive if the internal empty string has less than five empty points and more than two articulation points. Also, if the internal empty string has six empty points and zero or two more articulation points, an optional string is alive. If the articulation point is one (rokumoku nakade), it is dead. And if the numbers of empty points exceed seven, it is absolutely alive except nanamoku nakade. If the numbers of empty points exceed eight, regardless of the numbers of articulation points, it will be alive, on the condition that the string includes exclusively only one side.

If an enemy holds the next turn, one can say that life will be guaranteed if the numbers of the articulation points in empty string are more than two. These articulation points make eyes. If there is only one eye, it becomes a vital part where the one who places the Stone first is alive. Therefore, how many articulation points exist in the empty strings is an essential issue.

Let us imagine that there are many enemies but no articulation points. If there are six empties and zero or two or more articulation points, it is alive. If there is one, it is death. And if there are more than seven empties, it is absolutely alive except nanamoku nakade. In this rule, only one side belongs to the string. magari-shimoku is alive, whereas bent four in the corner is dead because it has two sides.

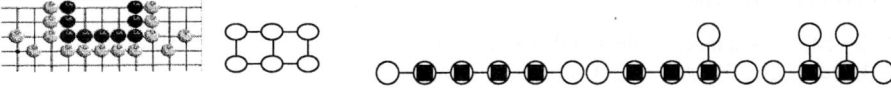

Fig. 5. 0-An Example of An Articulation Point

Fig. 6. Examples of Articulation Points

In Fig. 5, although the articulation point is zero, it is alive. The two points in the middle are fork. Fig. 6 is an exemplary case where there are six empties and more than two articulation points. Because the articulation points are more than two, it is alive. Fig. 7 is an example of rokumoku nakade. In rokumoku nakade, there is one articulation point. So it is dead.

Fig. 7. One Articulation Point in rokumoku nakade   **Fig. 8.** One Articulation Point in nanamoku nakade

The right-hand column of Fig. 8 is called nanamoku nakade. The numbers of empty points are seven, and if the enemy is located in the articulation point, it is the same as rokumoku nakade. If an enemy takes the articulation point, it will be eventually led to death.

2.2 The Evaluation of Seki

We represent the strings to BG where the status is Seki. Fig. 9 exemplifies a case where black and white are Seki. In Seki, both sides are alive, whereas empty point is not area. In this paper, Seki is judged by using a SG and an articulation point.

   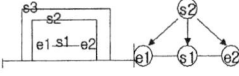

Fig. 9. An Example of Seki   **Fig. 10.** One Example of Seki Depicted by a SG

In Fig. 10, s1 and s2 are one string and form one group (OSOG: One String and One Group). S3 does not need to be OSOG, but it has the same color as s1.

Among Sekis which can occur from the other side, in this paper, Seki will be accepted only if it meets the following condition:

Rule 2. JOS: Judgment of Seki

Condition: a. S2 are completely surrounded by S3 without external empty points.
b. S1, which is OSOG is included in S2 and is enemy of S2.
c. There are two empties(e1 and e2) in S2.

Procedure of Evaluation:

A. S4 can be created by putting down the same color Stone of S1 on e1.
B. If S4 is alive by APC, tag1 = true or if not, tag1 = false.
C. S5 can be created by laying down the same color Stone of S1 on e2.
D. If S5 is alive by APC, tag2 = true or if not, tag2 = false.
E. If tag1 and tag2 are all true, S1 and S2 are Seki, e1 and e2 are not area of both.
   If not, S1 is alive, but S2 is dead. e1 and e2 belong to S1's territory.

In Fig. 11, blacks include whites and whites include blacks' other strings. Blacks and whites are dead once they are laid down. They are judged as Seki according to the evaluation of Seki. If there are many Stones, the evaluation of Seki yields a very effective result. If one wants to judge whether it is Seki or not, if one does not use Seki judgment procedures suggested here, one has to use a game tree which costs too much. Fig. 12 shows the results of no Seki obtained from Seki judgment procedures.

 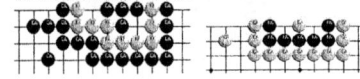

Fig. 11. An Example of Seki   **Fig. 12.** Examples of No Seki

2.3 Rules Which Do Not Include Stones

The status, which does not include Stones is a basic form. Fig. 4's exemplifies a case where ES1 and ES2 are completely included in BS1, which means life is guaranteed. This is unconditionally alive. Fig. 4 is a prototype of a living string. This graph is defined as an Alive String Graph (ASG). ASG has at least two directed edges.

Rule 3. SR: String Reduction
If an empty point is located between the same color vertexes, the vertexes with the same color and one can be reduced to a new vertex. This new vertex is called LV (Link Vertex). LV contains color characteristics that originated prior to the reduction.

Rule 4. ER: Empty Reduction
When SR (String Reduction) occurs, neighboring empty vertexes can be reduced into new empty vertexes.

Rule 5. ET: Edge Transformation
When ER (Empty Reduction) occurs, if ES has a single color vertex and an undirected edge, the undirected edge must be converted into a directed edge.

Rule 6. CG: Circular Graph
Graph G_{SG} which has the limited sequence where vertexes and undirected edges are coexistent ($v_0, e_1, v_1, e_2, \ldots, v_{k-1}, e_k, v_k$ are walk, trail and closed) is called a Circular graph, which means it is alive. But, the sequence of $f(v_i) = f(v_j)$, $0 \leq i, j \leq k$, The continuity of e is considered as one of e, $v \in \{WS, BS\}$, $e \in \{ES\}$.

2.4 Rules Which Include Stones

Rule 7. DESR: Dead Enemy Strings Reduction
If a dead enemy is included in a string, and it is near the included empty, a neighboring empty and a dead enemy are reduced into an empty string.

Rule 8. SCSR: Same Color String Reduction
If an optional string that is included in the same color string is close to two empty strings, an optional string will be reduced to it. Therefore, the result graph is ASG.

2.5 The Evaluation of the Stability of Strings

The evaluating method of the stability of strings using a String Graph (SG) is done by the adoption of a SG and the rules. The following diagram summarizes the procedures of the evaluating method of the stability of a string. The evaluating method of the stability of a string by using a SG is done by using Rule 1's articulation point methods. Strings which can not be judged alive by APC can be judged as ASG, CA and can not be judged as ASG, KJ by utilizing the SG Rules.

```
Procedure EvaluatingTheStabilityofStringsUsingSG()
Begin
  if S is OSOG and n(S)≥ 6 then {
    if S is Seki then
       S.stab = BG;
    else {
       if IntArea(S) ≥ 8 then S.stab = CA;
       if IntArea(S) == 7 then {
         if IsnotApricot7(S) then
            S.stab = CA;
         else
            S.stab = KK;
       }//end of if IntArea(S)
       if IntArea(S) == 6 then {
         if NAP(IntArea(S))==0 or NAP(IntArea(S)) ≥ 2 then
            S.stab = CA;
         else
            S.stab = KK;
         if IntArea(S) ≤ 5 then {
            if NAP(IntArea(S)) ≥ 2 then
               S.stab = CA;
            else
               S.stab = KK;
         }//end of if IntArea(S)
    }//end of else
  }//if S is OSOG and n(S) ≥ 6
  if the Stability of S is not changed then {
    if SG(IntArea(S)) is ASG then
       S.stab = CA;
    else
       S.stab = KJ;
  }//end of if the Stability of S is not changed
End//end of Begin
```

The above-mentioned procedure can process all of the strings which are positioned on the input board. If function IntArea receives input from OSOG (One String is One Group), it will output the numbers of empty point in the inner realm. In addition, function IsnotApricot7 identifies whether it is nanamoku nakade or not. If it is not nanamoku nakade, the stability of this string becomes CA. Moreover, function NAP outputs the numbers of articulation points.

First of all, This Procedure will process on the condition that it be OSOG to most of the strings, and the number of Stones which belong to the string should be more than six. If the string is proved to be Seki from the judgment procedure, the stability will have a BG value. Otherwise, the stability will be judged by APC. Regarding other strings to which these procedures can't be applied, the previously mentioned rules will also be applicable. By using these rules, the possibility of an ASG or a SG will be tested according to the situation of the string's realm and enemy Stones. If an optional string is determined to be CA, no more evaluation will be available.

```
Procedure EvaluationUsingSG()
Begin
   Find all strings and Compute all area of groups;
   Call EvaluateStabilityofStringUsingSG();
   Remove strings if the stability is KK or KJ;
   Update strings and groups information;
   Call EvaluateStabilityofStringUsingSG;
   Compute score, white_score, and black_score;
End //end of Begin
```

Evaluation Using SG depicts a procedure of the evaluation of stability of strings by using a String Graph. This procedure obtains information from other strings and a group, identifies the group's domain, and evaluates all strings through evaluating the stability of strings by using a SG. In addition, KK or KJ strings which are almost dead or have low stability, are considered to be dead and eliminated. Evaluating the stability of strings by using a SG will be reevaluated to include all of the strings. Each realm will be calculated from the white and black group, and the whole score will be counted by using Komi.

3 The Analysis of an Experiment

The experiment concerning the evaluating method of the stability of strings by using a String Graph (SG) was conducted by adopting IGS_31_counted problems in a Computer Go Test Collection at www.cs.ualberta.ca/~mmueller. These problems include 31 games tested by amateur Go players. They were performed complete score. This experiment on the evaluating method of the stability of strings investigates 31 games' final stability.

The data include 31 points (361 = 11,191) and 1,123 strings. The purpose of this experiment is to evaluate the stability and the accuracy of the territory. The accuracy of empty point is excluded because the points are included. Table 1 shows the comparison between the results of Miller's study and our suggested method. The suggested method yields 100 percent accuracy in terms of sorting in points and strings. This result indicates that the suggested method in this study is very effective.

The best result from Miller's study in point sorting is 92 %, whereas the suggested method yields 100%. (a) of Fig. 13 is an example where the suggested method is applied. 'CA' represents the case where strings' stability is alive, whereas 'KJ' symbolizes its death. And the numbers on the Go board means their numbers in a group.

Table 1. A comparison between Miller's and current study

Method	Points		Strings	
	Accuracy	%	Accuracy	%
Benson	1886	16	103	9
Müller Static	2481	22	168	14
Müller Search	2954	26	198	17
String Graph	11,191	100	1,123	100

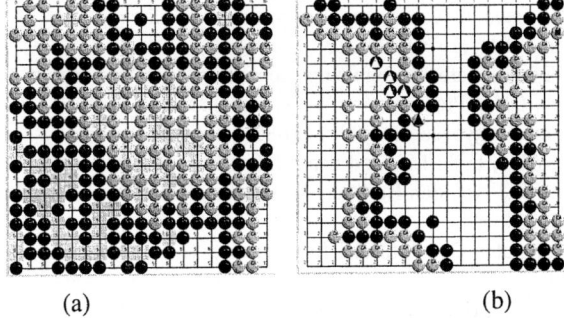

(a)   (b)

Fig. 13. (a) The evaluation results of the game 4   (b) The evaluation results of the game 9

(b) of Fig. 13 shows the worst result of Miller's method where there is 0% point sortings. However, the suggested method yields a 100 % accuracy result. The territory which belongs to a group was numbered according to a group. The territory which does not have numbers is an empty point which does not belong to any group. However, the problem of the suggested method is that strings with the same color and the strings broken by an enemy can not be included in any group.

4 Conclusion

To conduct static analysis, the researchers have defined a String Graph (SG) and judged life or death by using rules. In the experiment, the researchers used the IGS_31_counted problems among Computer Go Test Collections. The results indicate that there are 11,191 points and 1,123 strings. The evaluation of points and strings shows 100% accuracy. To judge the strings' life or death, the numbers of articulation points have been the primary concern of the study and the APC (Articulation Point Check) Rule has been used. To judge Seki, the Seki evaluating rule is suggested. By using a String Graph (SG), SR (String Reduction), ER (Empty Reduction), and ET (Edge Transformation) rules are suggested where Stones are not included. In addition, the life or death of a CG (Circular Graph) has been judged. When the Stones are included, if the enemy Stones are dead, the dead enemy Stones and empty spaces are reduced by using the DESR (Dead Enemy Strings Reduction) Rule. When our forces were included, the researchers reduced them by using the SCSR (Same Color String Reduction) Rule and judged whether they are ASG or not. The problem of the suggested method goes back to that of reading strategies. The remaining problems are the strings broken by an enemy, unended gang fights, a stone supplement, and oi-otoshi. The suggested method can be used in the last stages of a game. Moreover, it could be used in minimizing the depth of exploration when the localized judgment of life or death is made by evaluation function.

References

1. Benson, D.B.: Life in the game of Go, Information Sciences, Vol. 10, pp 17-29, ISSN 0020-0255. Reprinted in Computer Games,(Ed. D.N.L.Levy), Vol. II, Springer-Verlag, New York, N.Y. ISBN, (1976) 203-213
2. Muller, M.: Playing it safe: Recognizing secure territories in computer Go by using static rules and search. Game Programming Workshop in Japan '97(Ed. H. Matsubara), Computer Shogi Association, Tokyo, Japan (1997) .80-86
3. Popma, R. and Allis, L.V.: Life and death refined. Heuristic Programming in Artificial Intelligence 3(Eds. H.J. van den Herik and L.V.Allis), Ellis Horwood Ltd., Chichester, England. ISBN 157-164
4. Muller, M.: Computer Go. Artificial Intelligence, Vol. 134, Nos. 1-2, ISSN 0004-3702 (2002) 145-179
5. H. S. Park, D. H. Lee, H. J. Kim.: Static Analysis of String Stability and Group Territory in Computer Go, Journal of the Institute of Electronics Engineers of Korea, Vol. 40CI, No.6, Nov, (2003) 77-86
6. H. S. Park, J. G. Lim, J. C. Lee.: Research On Solving Life-Death Problems Using Heuristic Function in Paduk, Proceedings of 21st KISS Spring Conference, Vol.21, No.1 (1994) 233-236
7. K. Chen and Z. Chen: Static analysis of life and death in the game of Go, Information Sciences 121, 1999.
8. T. Graepel, M. Goutrie, M. Kruger, R. Hervrich: Learning on graphs in the game of Go, In International Conference on Artificial Neural Networks (ICANN-01), Vienna, Austria, 2001.

The Value of Stealth in the Game of Chess

Peter Smet, Don Gossink, and Greg Calbert

Command and Control Division,
Defence Science Technology Organisation (DSTO),
PO Box 1500, Edinburgh 5111, Australia
{peter.smet, don.gossink, greg.calbert}@dsto.defence.gov.au

Abstract. We have modified the rules of chess to create a game of imperfect information. By introducing hidden pieces into the game, we have been able to gauge the effect of uncertainty on playing strength. The addition of a hidden white piece led to white winning between 63%-89% of its games. The advantage gained from an invisible piece is dependent on both the type of piece that is hidden, and the search depth at which games are played. Greater search depths increase the value of hidden pieces, although diminishing returns were noted at increased depths. The advantage of a hidden piece is typically greater than the effect of an equivalent extra piece. In this sense, information superiority gained via stealth is a more powerful advantage than additional material. The results indicate that uncertainty arising from hidden pieces profoundly influences outcomes in the game of chess.

1 Introduction

"War is not unlike chess. But in war, you do not have a clear view of the other side of the board"

General Chuck Horner [6].

We have previously quantified the advantages of search depth, extra material and extra mobility in the game of chess [2]. We now examine the effect of hidden pieces on win percentages in chess. Uncertainty adds an extra dimension to the game, and a concomitant increase in complexity. While chess has an average branching factor of 35, in hidden chess this factor is multiplied by the number of squares the invisible piece may occupy [1]. Assuming the hidden piece could occupy any one of 8 squares, the branching factor increases to $35 \times 8 = 280$. For an average game in which each player moves 50 times the entire game tree will consist of 280^{100} nodes. Games of imperfect information necessitate a strategy for coping with uncertainty, and in this sense are more indicative of strategies and decisions required in real-world situations.

2 Method

The effects of uncertainty on chess skill were examined by using computer agents to play against each other. Uncertainty was introduced using a variant of chess in which white was given a single piece that remained invisible to black throughout the game.

The invisible piece was either a knight, bishop, rook, or queen, and was always located on the queen side of the board at the start of the game. Hidden pawns were not used, since it can be trivially shown that the number of possible squares a hidden pawn can occupy is limited to at most two.

The standard rules of chess were modified to cope with illegal moves. These typically occur when black attempts to move "through" an obstructing hidden piece, or unknowingly exposes it's king to check [1]. In our trials, it was legal to leave the king in check, allowing it to be captured on the next move. The "stealth checkmate" rule allows hidden pieces to place the king in check without giving away their location, so maximizing the advantage of stealth. All other illegal moves were handled by retracting the move and forfeiting that player's turn. The implications of these rule modifications are discussed in a later section.

Games were scored according to the rules of the International Chess Federation. A player scores one point for a win, and half a point for a draw. No points are awarded for a loss [3]. A game was declared a draw if the number of moves exceeded 500, or by stalemate [2]. To neutralize the first move advantage that white traditionally has [4], black and white alternate in opening games.

All agents were stochastic in their move selection. This enabled us to examine conditions over thousands of games, and so produce valid statistical inferences. All legal moves were scored, and a random move selected from all of the equally ranked highest-scoring moves. Random numbers were generated using a linear congruential algorithm [5], seeded from the system clock at the start of each set of trials.

White used a straightforward minimax algorithm with a look ahead of 2, 4, or 6 ply. The evaluation function examined material only, using a standard set of weightings [2]. A queen is valued at 9 units, a rook at 5, bishops and knights at 3. Pawns are worth one unit. Hidden pieces were valued one point higher than their visible equivalents. Board position scoring was achieved as follows: the summed value of the adversary's pieces was subtracted from the summed value of the player's pieces.

Black used an extended version of minimax, incorporating uncertainty about the hidden piece's location. For each square that the hidden piece could be positioned, black "places" the piece there, and performs a full-depth search for that potential starting configuration. Scores are computed for all possible starting configurations, and the *lowest* of these scores becomes the score assigned to the position being evaluated. Black therefore assumes that white has placed the hidden piece where it will maximize white's advantage. Although based on a pessimistic playing style, the algorithm is optimal given best play by the adversary.

During game play, black continually updates it's representation of which squares the hidden piece may potentially occupy. The list of potential squares changes whenever a) the hidden piece is moved, b) a square in the list is occupied or traversed by a visible piece, or c) the hidden piece captures another piece.

The statistical analysis was conducted as follows. Variance was calculated according to the binomial theorem, $\sigma^2 = (p \times q)/n$. Where, p is the probability of white winning, q is the probability of white losing $(1-p)$, and n represents the number of games played. A modified maximum likelihood estimate is used to calculate p, where $p = (w + (0.5 \times d))/n$, and w and d represent the number of wins and draws respectively.

3 Results

The results show that having a single invisible piece has a powerful effect on chess playing strength. The advantage ranges from 63% to 89%, and is dependent on both search depth and the type of hidden piece (Figure 1). The value of the hidden pieces can be ranked as follows: queen > rook > knight > bishop. This is similar to the ranking of the pieces in standard chess, with the exception that a bishop is generally recognised as somewhat more powerful than the knight. This discrepancy may be due to higher levels of uncertainty associated with the knight. Knights are typically moved earlier in the game than bishops, and their movement cannot be blocked by intervening pieces. The potential number of squares a hidden knight may occupy is therefore likely to be larger than that for a bishop. We suspect the added uncertainty of a knight's location translates to errors in black's play.

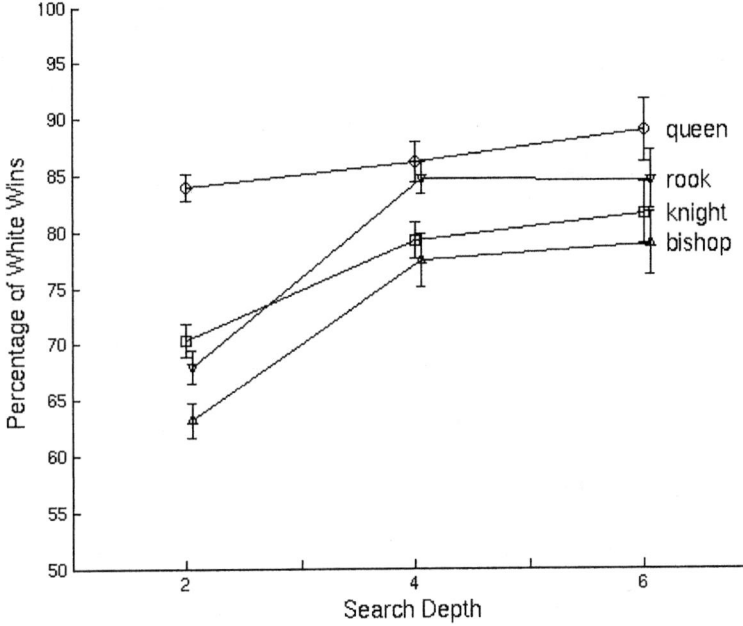

Search Depth	Knight	Bishop	Rook	Queen
2	70.30 ±1.45%(1000)	63.20 ±1.53%(1000)	68.00 ±1.48%(1000)	83.90 ±1.19%(1000)
4	79.17 ±1.63%(624)	77.43 ±2.36%(319)	84.73 ±1.43%(658)	86.18 ±1.78%(380)
6	81.59 ±2.77%(201)	78.97 ±2.83%(214)	84.60 ±2.56%(204)	88.98 ±2.88%(127)

Fig. 1. Chess playing strength assessed when white has a single invisible piece. The proportion of white wins ± the standard deviation for 2, 4, and 6 ply look ahead is shown. Numbers in brackets represent the total number of games played for that trial condition.

Games played at greater search depths amplify the advantage of an invisible piece. It should be noted that search depth was increased symmetrically, so that white and black were always matched on look ahead level. When search depth was increased from 2 to 4 ply, there was an average improvement of 10.5% in the proportion of wins for white. Increasing the search depth further, from 4 ply to 6 ply, produced only a marginal improvement, of less than 3%. The diminishing returns at 6 ply may be attributable to the high percentage of wins already apparent at 4 ply. The 82% mean win result for white at 4 ply leaves little room for improvement at greater search depths. The trials indicate that the advantage of stealth is not absolute, and depends on the skill level of the match. Deeper search allows agents to exploit their opponents' uncertainty to a greater extent, so maximizing the advantage of the hidden piece.

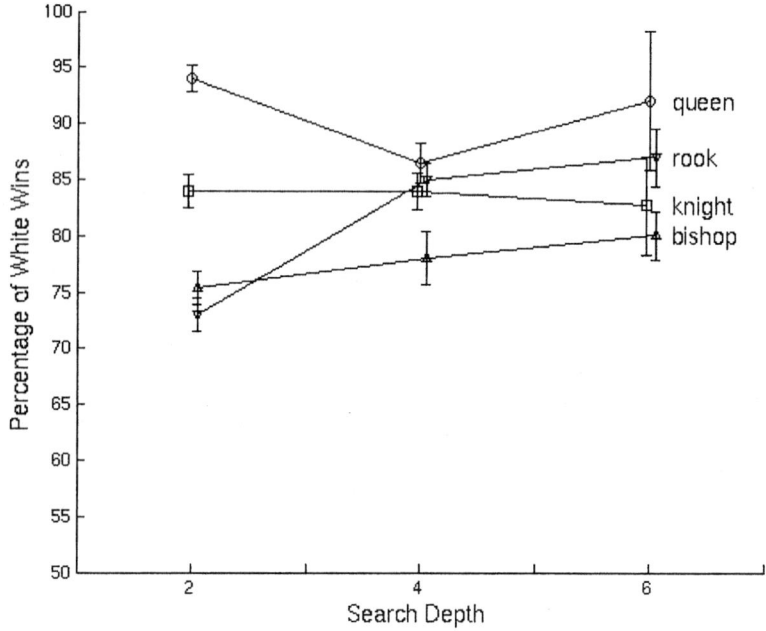

Search Depth	Knight	Bishop	Rook	Queen
2	83.95 ±1.45%(1000)	75.35 ±1.53%(1000)	73.00 ±1.48%(1000)	94.00 ±1.19%(1000)
4	84.00 ±1.63%(624)	78.00 ±2.36%(319)	85.00 ±1.43%(658)	86.40 ±1.78%(380)
6	82.70 ±4.30%(75)	80.03 ±2.13%(353)	87.00 ±2.56%(204)	92.10 ±6.2%(28)

Fig. 2. Chess playing strength with a single invisible white piece, this time using a strategy aimed at maximizing the opponent's uncertainty. Numbers in brackets represent the total number of games played for that trial condition.

A second series of trials were performed, in which white attempted to maximize black's uncertainty. For these trials, the move selection algorithm was modified. Each time the invisible piece could be moved, it was, given that no superior alternative moves were available. This change had a dramatic impact on win proportions, as shown in figure 2. Using a 2-ply lookahead, the algorithm to maximize uncertainty improved win proportions by over 10%, from 71.35% to 81.58%. At 4 and 6-ply, the effect was far less dramatic, typically lifting wins by only a few percent. In the case of the hidden queen, the algorithm actually seemed to perform slightly *worse* at higher search depths. Even under these conditions, the maximum uncertainty algorithm still performed as well as the normal move-selection algorithm. It is not immediately clear why an invisible queen should produce results such as these. One possibility is that the pessimistic strategy for coping with uncertainty becomes overly pessimistic as the search space increases. Such a scenario occurs when a hidden queen with many possible positions is combined with a deep search ply. Selecting the lowest-scoring move from 10,000 positions, for example, will yield a more defensive, conservative move than one selected from only 100 positions. The issue of optimistic versus pessimistic strategies to cope with uncertainty is further explored in the discussion.

4 Discussion

4.1 The Advantage of Stealth Relative to Material

For comparative purposes, we here refer to our previous results of chess games where one player begins with an extra piece [2]. The effects of stealth are generally stronger than comparable material advantages (Figure 3). When averaged across all search depths, an invisible knight gives a 77% winning advantage. By comparison, an extra knight delivers only a 63% advantage [2]. Similarly, an invisible bishop wins 73% of the time, compared to 68.7% for an extra bishop. For the rook, the invisible piece wins 79% of games, relative to 74.7% for the extra piece. The queen is an exception, with the extra queen providing a greater advantage (93%) than the hidden queen (86.4%). The queen is the most powerful piece on the board, at 9 points nearly twice as strong as the rook. Our trials suggest that a single stealth piece can potentially outplay a 3-5 point material disadvantage, but not a 9 point difference.

4.2 Maximizing the Effects of Stealth

It should be emphasized that our measure of stealth advantage is a conservative one. White does not attempt to maximize black's uncertainty. This could be achieved by moving the hidden piece early and often, and would extend white's advantage. Furthermore, our agents use a limited evaluation function, which only examines material. Previous investigators have modified the chess engine, GNU Chess, to play hidden chess. The evaluation function in that study was sophisticated, and included a feature to maximize the opponent's uncertainty regarding the location of the hidden piece. Under these conditions, the player with the hidden piece won between 89%-93% of the time [1]. While these results are suggestive, they are not directly comparable to our work, as all drawn games were discarded from their analysis.

Our estimate of stealth is conservative in another way. Black's strategy is to envisage and analyse all board positions corresponding to possible locations of the hidden piece. This results in an exponentially increased search space. By allowing both players to search to a given depth, we are effectively allowing black to search many more board positions than white. If search is restricted by either time or the number of board positions examined, rather than by depth, black would face a overwhelming disadvantage. Under such conditions, invisibility effectively limits the search horizon of an opponent. Our earlier work has shown that searching even one ply less than your opponent results in the loss of 85%-98% of all games [2, see also 7].

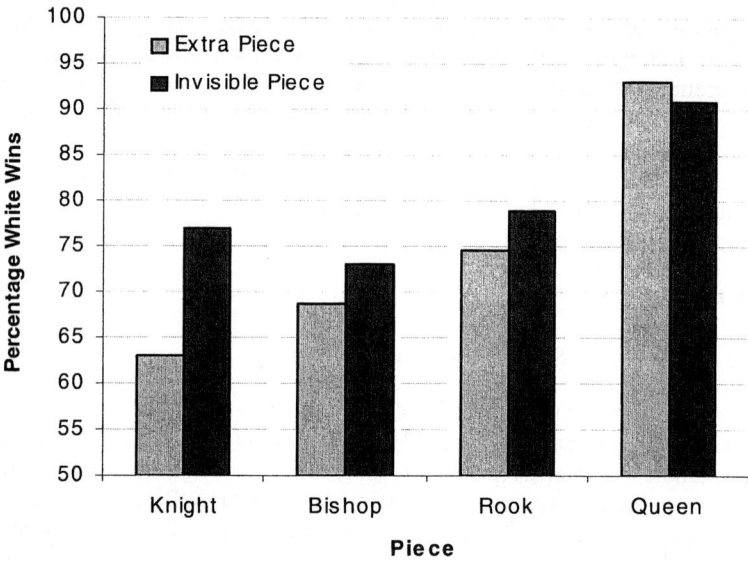

Fig. 3. A comparison of the relative advantage of extra pieces versus hidden pieces. Win proportions were averaged across 2, 4 and 6 ply games. Data pertaining to Material advantages from [2].

4.3 Pessimistic Versus Optimistic Strategies for Coping with Uncertainty

The strategy black used to combat uncertainty was a pessimistic one. It is assumed that of all possible places the hidden piece could occupy, it will be in the one most advantageous to white (and therefore most damaging to black). A situation in which a single hidden piece may be positioned on any of three squares is like playing against three "virtual" pieces, and having to deal with the piece in the strongest position. In this sense, stealth adds strength by adding "virtual" material to the board, which must be reckoned with. We ran some preliminary trials comparing the pessimistic strategy to an optimistic one. The optimistic agent assumed the hidden white piece was located on the square most favourable to black. These trials showed the optimistic strategy fared at least 6% worse than the pessimistic one (data not shown). The value of uncertainty is therefore not attributable to the negative strategy of black, since alternative strategies perform worse. Uncertainty forces the player to assume a conservative posture, however, giving the player with hidden material a strong advantage.

4.4 The Effect of Illegal Moves on Tempo and Game Outcomes

As outlined in the methods, we modified the rules of chess so that illegal moves led to the forfeit of a turn. This rule prevents players from using illegal moves to obtain "free" information about the state of the board. The rule however, also has side effects on tempo. Under some circumstances, white will be allowed to play more moves than black. Could the advantage of stealth be wholly or partially attributable to the gain in tempo white gets from turns forfeited by black? We calculated what effect the forfeit rule had on the outcome of the trials. We determined the average frequency of illegal moves across all trials to be 0.34%. This corresponds to one extra move each 295 moves, or less than one extra move per game. Our previous study has shown that one extra turn per 100 gives no advantage at 2 ply, and a 9% to 12% advantage at 4 and 6 ply. Using an exponential curve fitted to this data set, we extrapolate that an extra move every 295 moves will result in advantage of around 0.06%. We therefore feel confident that the advantage of stealth has nothing to do with decreased tempo resulting from lost turns.

5 Conclusions

We have shown that uncertainty arising from hidden pieces significantly affects chess performance, lending a powerful advantage to the player with the hidden pieces. The extent of this advantage is dependent on the type of hidden piece, and the search depth at which games are played. At 6 ply look ahead, the advantage of an invisible piece ranged from 79%-89%. In general, greater search depths leverage more advantage from hidden pieces, although there are signs of diminishing returns at increased depths. The advantage of a hidden piece is normally greater than the effect of an extra equivalent piece, and in this simple sense, stealth is a more powerful advantage than material. It must be emphasized that our estimate of the effects of stealth are conservative, in that our agents did not exploit stealth maximally. The results indicate that hidden states, and the associated uncertainty, profoundly influence outcomes in the game of chess.

References

1. Bud, A.E., Albrecht, D.W., Nicholson, A.E., and Zukerman, I.: Information-Theoretic advisors in Invisible Chess. Game Theoretic and Decision Theoretic Agents. Papers from the 2001 AAAI Symposium. Technical Report SS-01-03. AAAI Press. pp.6-15. Menlo Park, CA, USA. (2001).
2. Smet, P., Calbert, G., Scholz, J.B., Gossink, D., Kwok, H.W., and Webb, M.: The Effects of Material, Tempo and Search Depth on Win-Loss Ratios in Chess. Lecture Notes in Computer Science, vol 2903, pp 501-510. (2003).

3. http://www.fide.com/official/handbook.asp?level=EE101/ Article 11: scoring (2000).
4. Sonas, J.: The sonas rating formula - better than Elo?, http://www.chesscenter.com/t wic/event/sonas/sonasrat.html (2003).
5. Knuth, D.E.: The Art of Computer Programming, Volume 2. Seminumerical algorithms, Addison-Wesley, Reading Mass., ISBN 0-201-03822-6 (1981).
6. Tom Clancy and Chuck Horner.: Every Man a Tiger pp 361 Berkley Books, New York (1999).
7. Thompson, K.: Computer Chess Strength. In: Clarke, M.R.B. (ed.): Advances in Computer Chess, Pergamon (1982) 55-56.

Coordinated Collision Avoidance of Multiple Biomimetic Robotic Fish

Dandan Zhang[1], Long Wang[1], Guangming Xie[1], and Weicun Zhang[2]

[1] Intelligent Control Laboratory, Center for Systems and Control,
Department of Mechanics and Engineering Science,
Peking University, Beijing 100871, P.R. China
twinkleice@pku.edu.cn
[2] Automation Department,
University of Science and Technology Beijing,
Beijing 100083, P.R. China

Abstract. This paper presents a novel reactive collision avoidance method among multiple biomimetic robotic fish with kinematic constraints. Based on successfully developing a robotic fish prototype, we step further to study navigation problem of robotic fish in dynamic water environments. Considering the nonholonomic properties and the inherent kinematic constraints of the robotic fish, limit cycle approach is employed with which the robotic fish can avoid one another smoothly and efficiently. The effectiveness of the proposed method is verified through experiments conducted with three robotic fish.

1 Introduction

It is well-known that a fish in nature propels itself by coordinated motion of the body, fins, and tail, so as to achieve tremendous propulsive efficiency and excellent maneuverability. From the perspective of engineering science, fish is a prototype of a distinguished autonomous underwater vehicle. Taking advantage of progress in robotics, control technology, artificial intelligence, hydrodynamics of fish-like swimming, new materials, sensors, and actuators, emerging research has been focused on developing novel fish-like vehicles, to imitate the locomotion mechanism of fish in nature to get favorable efficiency, maneuverability and low noise performance. Research on robotic fish has become a hot topic [1]-[7].

We have developed several radio-controlled, multi-link robotic fish of different forms and functionalities (shown in Fig. 1), each propelled by the flexible posterior body and the oscillatory tail. In this paper, we study robotic fish navigation problem in unstructured and dynamic environment.

Robot navigation is concerned with driving a robot to the destination along a collision free path to perform a given task. In general, the navigation methods can be classified into two categories: global navigation, which is based on a prior known environment information; reactive navigation, which is based on real-time sensory information. Global navigation methods include roadmap approach, cell decomposition approach, artificial potential field approach, electrostatic potential field and the magnetic field method, etc [8]. These methods can be understood well from the theoretical

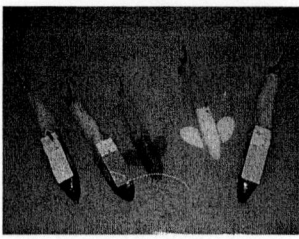

Fig. 1. Robotic fishes of different forms and functionalities

aspect, but the computational cost is expensive, so they are not applicable in dynamic environments. In reactive navigation, the robot makes decision on the real time sensory information. The low computational cost allows this approach suitable to be used in unknown or dynamic environment. Examples of this approach include: Potential Fields [9], Vector Field Histogram [10], behavior-based method [11], fuzzy logic [12] and the Nearness Diagram Navigation [13]. Reactive navigation approach is effective in many dynamic scenarios, but most research on this method considers the robot as a point with holonomic properties. For the robotic fish, due to the particular propulsive mechanism, the translational velocity and the rotational velocity are not independent but coupled with each other. In addition, the robotic fish cannot move reversely or stop immediately in the water environment due to the inertial drift. Because of the particular kinematic characteristics of robotic fish and the complexity of the underwater environment, few navigation methods in the literature can be applied to robotic fish navigation directly. New navigation methods are required to be exploited for the robotic fish.

In this paper, we propose a new reactive collision avoidance method for robotic fish navigation in unstructured and dynamic environment. Considering the nonholonomic properties and the inherent kinematic constraints of the robotic fish, limit cycle approach is proposed, with which the robotic fish can avoid one another smoothly and efficiently. Experiments performed by three robotic fish demonstrate the effectiveness of the proposed method.

The paper is organized as follows. In section 2, the robotic fish prototype is presented. In section 3, we describe our collision avoidance method in detail. Experimental results are given in section 4. Section 5 concludes the paper.

2 Robotic Fish Prototype

2.1 Simplified Propulsive Model of the Robotic Fish

Our designed robotic fish takes carangiform movement. Barrett et al. has presented a relative swimming model for RoboTuna (carangiform) in [6], and the undulatory motion is assumed to take the form of a propulsive travelling wave which is described by:

$$y_{body}(x,t) = [(c_1 x + c_2 x^2)][\sin(kx + \omega t)]. \tag{1}$$

In (1), y_{body} is the transverse displacement of the fish body, x the displacement along the main axis, k the body wave number ($k = 2\pi/\lambda$), λ the body wave length, c_1 the linear wave amplitude envelope, c_2 the quadratic wave amplitude envelope, and ω the body wave frequency ($\omega=2\pi f$).

For simplification, we consider the discrete form of travelling wave (1), which is described by:

$$y_{body}(x,i) = [(c_1 x + c_2 x^2)][\sin(kx \pm \frac{2\pi}{M} i)], \qquad (2)$$

where i denotes the index of the sequences, M is the body wave resolution, representing the discrete degree of the overall travelling wave.

3 Coordinated Collision Avoidance

3.1 Kinematic Constraints of the Robotic Fish

Due to the particular propulsive mechanism, the translational velocity v and the rotational velocity ω of the robotic fish are not independent, but coupled with each other. Typical coupling relations of them under different oscillatory frequencies of the tail are shown in Fig. 2. We use the following equation to describe the relations:

$$\omega = F(v, frequency). \qquad (3)$$

Equation (3) is called *inherent constraints* of the robotic fish. Any control input pair of (v, ω) shall satisfy the *inherent constraints*.

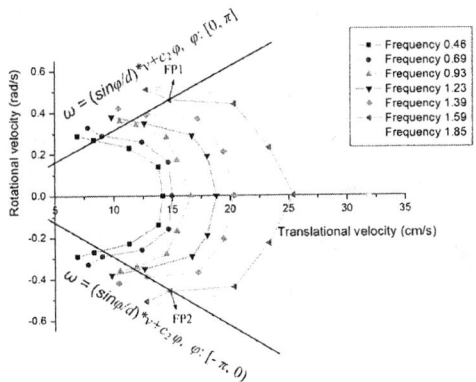

Fig. 2. Relations between the translational velocity and the rotational velocity under different oscillatory frequencies

3.2 Limit Cycle Approach for Collision Avoidance

Next we discuss how collisions among multiple robotic fish are avoided. For simplification, The shape of the fish is described as an ellipse in the two dimensional plane. First we give one important lemma.

Poincaré-Bendixson Theory:
If D is an annulus-shape bounded absorbing region, $D \subset R^2$, and contains no equilibria, then D contains at least one periodic orbit. (A bounded region D on the phase plane is absorbing if no trajectories leave it.)

3.3 Limit Cycle Approach

Considering the following nonlinear system in the fish frame:

$$\dot{\bar{x}} = \lambda(\mu\bar{y} + \gamma\bar{x}(r^2 - \bar{x}^2 - \mu^2\bar{y}^2)) \\ \dot{\bar{y}} = \lambda(-\frac{1}{\mu}\bar{x} + \gamma\bar{y}(r^2 - \bar{x}^2 - \mu^2\bar{y}^2)), \tag{4}$$

where γ, λ, μ, r are positive parameters. In order to prove the ellipse $\bar{x}^2 + \mu^2\bar{y}^2 = r^2$ is the limit cycle of system (4), we use the following Lyapunov function:

$$V(\bar{x}, \bar{y}) = \bar{x}^2 + \mu^2\bar{y}^2, \tag{5}$$

such that:

$$\dot{V}(\bar{x}, \bar{y}) = 2\lambda\gamma(r^2 - \bar{x}^2 - \mu^2\bar{y}^2)(\bar{x}^2 + \mu^2\bar{y}^2) \\ = 2\lambda\gamma(r^2 - V(\bar{x},\bar{y}))V(\bar{x},\bar{y}). \tag{6}$$

We can see $\dot{V}(\bar{x},\bar{y}) < 0$ when $V(\bar{x},\bar{y}) > r^2$, while $\dot{V}(\bar{x},\bar{y}) > 0$ when $V(\bar{x},\bar{y}) < r^2$. This shows the following annulus-shape region

$$B = \{\alpha 1 \le V(\bar{x},\bar{y}) \le \alpha 2, |0 < \alpha 1 < r^2, \alpha 2 > r^2\} \tag{7}$$

is absorbing. It is also bounded and free of equilibrium points, since the unique equilibrium point is $(0,0)$. According to Poincaré-Bendixson Theory, B contains at least one periodic orbit. Since this argument is adaptive for any $0 < \alpha 1 < r^2$, and $\alpha 2 > r^2$, when $\alpha 1$, $\alpha 2$ get close to r^2, region B shrinks to the ellipse $V(\bar{x},\bar{y}) = r^2$. Thus we get the limit cycle in the fish frame (shown in Fig. 3):

$$V(\bar{x},\bar{y}) = r^2 \implies \bar{x}^2 + \mu^2\bar{y}^2 = r^2. \tag{8}$$

The convergence speed of $(\bar{x}, \bar{y})$ toward the limit cycle can be tuned by the constant γ. Fig. 3 (a) shows the fast convergence condition with $\gamma = 0.001$, and Fig. 3 (b) shows the slow convergence condition with $\gamma = 0.0001$. From Fig. 3 we can see the trajectory from any point $(\bar{x}, \bar{y})$ moves toward and converges to the limit cycle clockwise when close. The counterclockwise condition can be derived by the following system (shown in Fig. 4):

$$\dot{\bar{x}} = \lambda(-\mu\bar{y} + \gamma\bar{x}(r^2 - \bar{x}^2 - \mu^2\bar{y}^2)) \\ \dot{\bar{y}} = \lambda(\frac{1}{\mu}\bar{x} + \gamma\bar{y}(r^2 - \bar{x}^2 - \mu^2\bar{y}^2)). \tag{9}$$

Since the trajectory from any point $(\bar{x}, \bar{y})$ inside the limit cycle moves outward the cycle (thus away the center point of the cycle), and the trajectory from any point $(\bar{x}, \bar{y})$ outside the limit cycle approaches the cycle by aparting the center point distances (determined by the cycle), the limit cycle provides a method for collision avoidance among multiple robotic fish.

Shown in Fig. 6, the shape of the obstacle fish body is described by an ellipse, and the safe region is defined by a concentric safe ellipse. When another fish is in the safe region, by the limit cycle approach, it will move away the obstacle fish toward the safe ellipse. Let θ denote the orientation of the fish, (x_0, y_0) the center point of the fish. With the following transformation we get the expression of system (4) in the original frame:

$$x = \cos\theta(\bar{x} + x_0) - \sin\theta(\bar{y} + y_0) \\ y = \sin\theta(\bar{x} + x_0) + \cos\theta(\bar{y} + y_0), \tag{10}$$

such that:
$$\dot{x} = \cos\theta \dot{\tilde{x}} - \sin\theta \dot{\tilde{y}}$$
$$\dot{y} = \sin\theta \dot{\tilde{x}} + \cos\theta \dot{\tilde{y}}. \qquad (11)$$

Let v denote the translational velocity of the fish in the original frame, α the direction of the motion. The kinematic model of the robotic fish is described by:
$$\dot{x} = v\cos\alpha$$
$$\dot{y} = v\sin\alpha \qquad (12)$$
$$\frac{\dot{y}}{\dot{x}} = \tan\alpha.$$

Substituting (11) into (12) we get:
$$v = \sqrt{\dot{\tilde{x}}^2 + \dot{\tilde{y}}^2}$$
$$\alpha = \arctan\frac{\dot{\tilde{y}}}{\dot{\tilde{x}}} + \theta. \qquad (13)$$

By tuning the value of λ, we can adjust the magnitude of v to get arbitrary speed values. Advantages of the limit cycle approach are listed below:

1) Since the control inputs of the robotic fish are the translational velocity v and the orientation angle α instead of the rotational velocity ω, we eliminate the trouble of treating the tackled coupling between v and ω in collision avoidance.

2) It is an efficient reactive collsion avoidance approach, and the fish can avoid the obstacle with the safety distances and appropriate direction without moving far away from the obstacle.

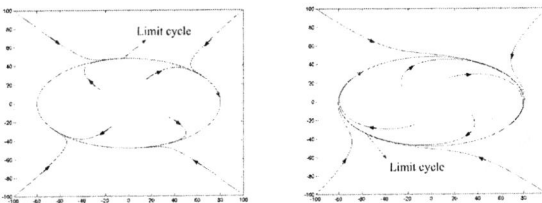

(a) Fast convergence with $\gamma = 0.001$ (b) Slow convergence with $\gamma = 0.0001$

Fig. 3. Phase portrait of limit cycle (clockwise)

3.4 Applying Limit Cycle Approach in Multiple Robotic Fish Collision Avoidance

Next we employ three robotic fish for discussion. To apply the limit cycle approach in the coordinated collision avoidance, we employ the "situated-behavior" method (similar to the *situated-activity* paradigm (see [14])) to divide the environment into a set of *exclusive* and *complete* situations, and for each situation, a behavior is elaborately designed to solve the situation associated problem individually. The advantage of employing this method is that it is a "divide and conquer" strategy, which reduces the task difficulty; in addition, the real-time *behavior coordination problem* need not to be taken into consideration, since the situations are complete and exclusive.

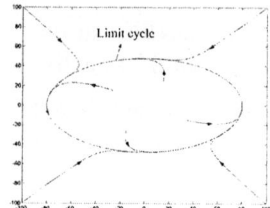

Fig. 4. Phase portrait of limit cycle (counterclockwise)

Situations. Here we discuss only the situations for fish 1. The situations for other fish are similar. We use a decision tree to define the set of situations according to the relative locations of the robotic fish. The decision tree is traversed through binary decision rules according to several criteria. As shown in Fig. 5, the inputs of the decision tree are the goal location information and sensory information from the overhead camera, including the ID information, the location and orientation information of the fish. The current situation is identified according to the input information. The decision tree is traversed through binary decision rules according to the following four criteria.

Criterion 1: Obstruction criterion. This criterion classifies the situations into the following two categories according to whether fish 1 is obstructed by another fish:

(1) Nobs (not obstructed) situation: Fish 1 is not obstructed by any other fish;
(2) OBS (obstructed) situation: otherwise.

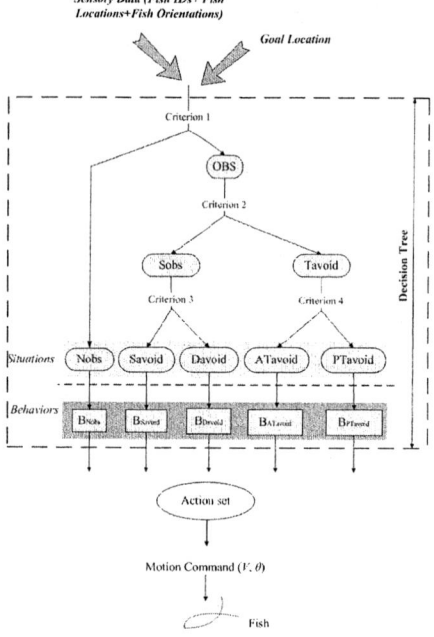

Fig. 5. Situations of coordinated collision avoidance

Criterion 2: Obstacle fish number criterion. This criterion divides OBS situation into the following two situations:

(1) Sobs (single obstructed) situation: Fish 1 is obstructed by only one fish;

(2) Tavoid (trap avoiding) situation: Fish 1 is obstructed by other two fish simultaneously (shown in Fig. 7 (d)).

Criterion 3: Dual avoiding criterion. This criterion classifies Sobs situation into the following two situations according to whether fish 1 and the other fish are obstructed by each other:

(1) Savoid (single avoiding) situation: Fish 1 is obstructed by the other fish but not an obstacle for that fish (shown in Fig. 7 (a));

(2) Davoid (dual avoiding) situation: Fish 1 and the other fish are obstructed by each other (shown in Fig. 7 (b) (c)).

Criterion 4: Active avoiding criterion. According to whether fish 1 has the highest priority among fish in Tavoid situation (here the priorities of the fish are arranged according to their IDs), this criterion divides Tavoid situation into the following two situations:

(1) ATavoid (active trap avoiding) situation: Fish 1 has the highest priority;

(2) PTavoid (passive trap avoiding) situation: Otherwise.

We only care the leaf nodes of the decision tree: Nobs, Savoid, Davoid, ATavoid, PTavoid. Obtained through a binary decision tree, these five situations are exclusive and complete.

Behaviors associated with the situations. First we define a *normal behavior*.

normal behavior: If the goal direction is to the right of the obstacle direction, and the path of the fish to the goal location is obstructed by the safe ellipse of the obstacle fish, shown in Fig. 6 (a), the fish moves toward the limit cycle counterclockwise; while if the goal direction is to the left of the obstacle direction, and the path of the fish to the goal location is obstructed by an obstacle fish, the fish moves toward the limit cycle clockwise, shown in Fig. 6 (b).

1) B_{Nobs}: Fish 1 approaches the goal location directly.

2) B_{Savoid}: Fish 1 avoids the obstacle fish with *normal behavior* (shown in Fig. 7 (a)).

3) B_{Davoid}: The two fish avoids each other with the same limit cycle direction (both clockwise, or both counterclockwise). If fish 1 is prior to the other fish, it avoids the other fish with *normal behavior*; otherwise it avoids the other fish with the direction opposite to *normal behavior* (shown in Fig. 7 (b) (c)).

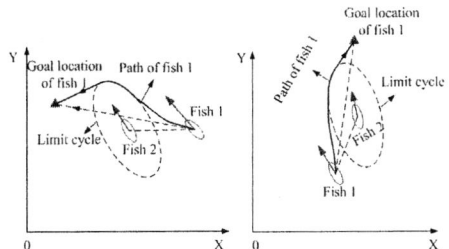

(a) Avoiding fish counterclockwise (b) Avoiding fish clockwise

Fig. 6. Normal behavior

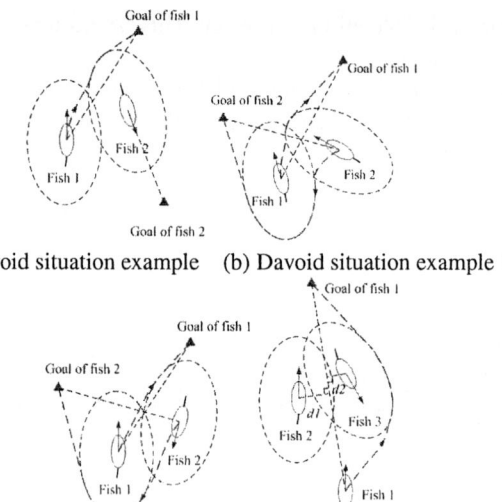

(a) Savoid situation example (b) Davoid situation example 1

(c) Davoid situation example 2 (d) ATavoid situation example

Fig. 7. Situations and associated behavior design

4) $B_{ATavoid}$: In Tavoid situation, it is possible for fish 1 to get stuck in a local minima with *normal behavior*. For example, in Fig. 7 (d), fish 1 is avoiding fish 2 counterclockwise; however, since it is also obstructed by fish 3, then it will avoid fish 3 clockwise. Thus fish 1 will get stuck between fish 2 and fish 3. $B_{ATavoid}$ is to avoid this situation. Let l denote the line from fish 1 to Goal of fish 1, and fish i ($i \in (2,3)$) represent the fish with the shorter distance to line l. Fish 1 avoids fish i with direction opposite to *normal behavior*, until the local trap situation is eliminated (shown in Fig. 7 (d)).

$B_{PTavoid}$: Fish 1 avoids the fish in ATavoid situation with the same limit cycle direction to overcome conflicts.

4 Experimental Results

To evaluate the proposed collision avoidance method, two types of experiments are performed in a swimming pool with size 3200 mm ×2200 mm ×700 mm (length × width × depth). The ID information and the posture information (including location and orientation) of the fish are recognized by an overhead camera. The sensory range of each fish is 200 cm (although we employ an overhead camera as the unique sensory for obtaining the environment information, to constitute a local navigation method, we utilize only partial vision information for each fish). The goal locations of the fish are marked by blue poles. If a fish is within a distance of 20 cm (determined by the size of the fish and the blue pole) to the goal location, we state that the fish has reached its goal location.

In experiment I, we evaluate the coordinated collision avoidance between two robotic fish. We assume the long axis of the safe ellipse is 127 cm, and the short axis 76cm. The experiment scenarios are shown in Fig. 8. In Fig. 8 (a), the two robotic fish

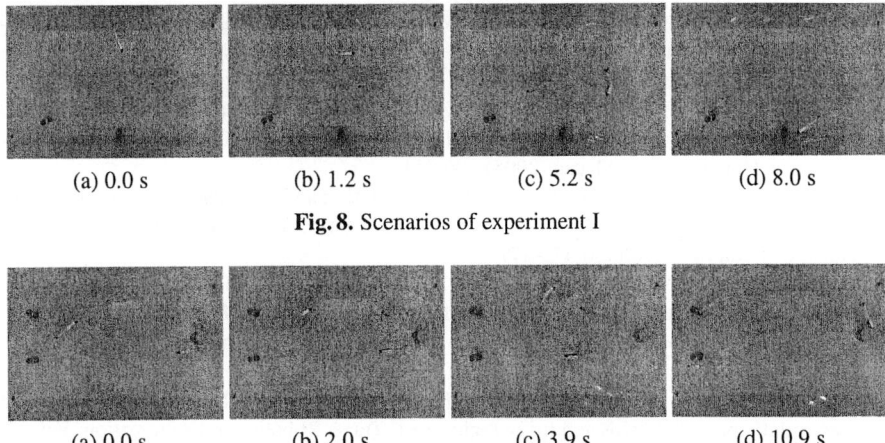

(a) 0.0 s   (b) 1.2 s   (c) 5.2 s   (d) 8.0 s

Fig. 8. Scenarios of experiment I

(a) 0.0 s   (b) 2.0 s   (c) 3.9 s   (d) 10.9 s

Fig. 9. Scenarios of experiment II

start out moving to their goal locations. Meanwhile, the fish detect that they are obstructed by each other. So they avoid each other by performing B_{Davoid} both clockwise (shown in Fig. 8 (b)). At 5.2 s, the two fish have got safe. At 8.0 s, they have reached their goal locations successfully (shown in Fig. 8 (d)).

In experiment II, we employ three robotic fish to verify the ability to overcome local minima of the proposed collision avoidance method. The experiment scenarios are shown in Fig. 9. After the three fish start, fish 3 senses that it is obstructed simultaneously by fish 1 and fish 2 (shown in Fig. 9 (a)). To avoid getting trapped between these two fish, fish 3 performs $B_{ATavoid}$ since it is the only fish in Tavoid situation. Shown in Fig. 9 (b), fish 3 avoids the orange-pink fish with direction opposite to *normal behavior*. At 3.9 s, the Tavoid situation has been eliminated (shown in Fig. 9 (c)). At 10.9 s, the three robotic fish have reached their goal locations successfully (shown in Fig. 9 (d)).

5 Conclusion

We have presented a novel collision avoidance method for multiple robotic fish. Considering the inherent kinematic constraints of the robotic fish, we employ limit cycle approach for coordinated collision avoidance among the robotic fish. This approach allows the robotic fish to avoid one another smoothly and efficiently, and also eliminates the local minima problem. Experimental results demonstrate the effectiveness of the proposed method.

References

1. J. Yu, and L. Wang: Parameter optimization of simplified propulsive model for biomimetic robot fish. In Proc. IEEE Int. Conf. Robotics and Automation. Barcelona, Spain (2005) 3317-3322
2. J. Yu, L. Wang, and M. Tan: A Framework for Biomimetic Robot Fish's Design and Its Realization. In Proc. of American Control Conference. Portland, USA (2005) 1593-1598

3. D. Zhang, Y. Fang, G. Xie, J. Yu and L. Wang: Coordinating Dual-mode Biomimetic Robotic Fish in Box-pushing Task. Lecture Notes in Artificial Intelligence. Vol. 3630. Springer-Verlag, Berlin Heidelberg (2005) 815-824
4. Y. Fang, J. Yu, R. Fan, L. Wang, and G. Xie: Performance Optimization and Coordinated Control of Multiple Biomimetic Robotic Fish. In Proc. IEEE Int. Conf. Robotics and Biomimetics. Hongkong and Macau (2005) 206-211
5. J. Yu, Y. Fang, W. Zhao, and L. Wang: Behavioral Design and Strategy for Cooperative Multiple Biomimetic Robot Fish System. In Proc. IEEE Int. Conf. Robotics and Biomimetics. Hongkong and Macau (2005) 472-477
6. D. Barrett, M. Triantafyllou, D. K. P. Yue, M. A. Grosenbaugh, and M. J. Wolfgang: Drag reduction in fish-like locomotion. J. Fluid Mech. Vol. 392. (1999) 183-212
7. M. Sfakiotakis, D. M. Lane, and J. B. C. Davies: Review of fish swimming modes for aquatic locomotion. IEEE J. Oceanic Eng. Vol. 24. (1999) 237-252
8. N. C. Tsourveloudis, K. P. Valavanis and T. Hebert: Autonomous vehicle navigation utilizing electrostatic potential fields and fuzzy logic. IEEE Trans. Robotics and Automation. Vol. 17. (2001) 490-497
9. W. Tianmiao and Z. Bo: Time-varing potential field based "perception-action" behaviors of mobile robot. In Proc. IEEE Int. Conf. Robotics and Automation. (1992) 2549-2554
10. J. Borenstein and Y. Koren: The vector field histogram-fast obstacle avoidance for mobile robots. IEEE Trans. Robotics and Automation. Vol. 7. (1991) 278-288
11. A. Taliansky and N. Shimkin: Behavior-based navigation for an indoor mobile robot. In The 21st IEEE Convention of Electrical and Electronic Engineers in Israel. (2000) 281-284
12. T.E. Mora and E.N. Sanchez: Fuzzy logic-based real-time navigation controller for a mobile robot. In Proc. IEEE Int. Conf. Intelligent Robots and Systems. Vol. 1. (1998) 612-617
13. J. Minguez and L. Montano: Nearness Diagram (ND) Navigation: Collision Avoidance in Troublesome Scenarios. IEEE Trans. Robotics and Automation. Vol. 20. (2004) 45-59
14. R. C. Arkin: Behavior-Based Robotics. Cambridge, MA: MIT Press (1999)

The Virtual Room Inhabitant – Intuitive Interaction with Intelligent Environments

Michael Kruppa, Lübomira Spassova, and Michael Schmitz

Saarland University, Stuhlsatzenhausweg B. 36.1,
66123 Saarbrücken, Germany
{mkruppa, mira, schmitz}@cs.uni-sb.de

Abstract. In this paper we describe a new way to improve the usability of complex hardware setups in Intelligent Environments. By introducing a virtual character, we facilitate intuitive interaction with our Intelligent Environment. The character is capable of freely moving along the walls of the room. The character is aware of the users position and orientation within the room. In this way, it may offer situated assistance as well as unambiguous references to physical objects by means of combined gestures, speech and physical locomotion. We make use of a steerable projector and a spatial audio system, in order to position the character within the environment.

Keywords: Intelligent Environments, Life-like Characters, Location-Aware Interaction.

1 Introduction

Intelligent Environments physically combine several different input and output devices. These devices are spread all over the environment, and some may even be hidden in the environment. Furthermore, Intelligent Environments often offer a variety of different devices or combinations of devices capable of fulfilling a specific task. However, users in Intelligent Environments are often unaware of the different possibilities offered by the environment. Hence, in order to optimize the users benefit in the Intelligent Environment, it is necessary to find an interaction metaphor which pro-actively informs users about the technology hidden in the environment and services available to the user. The solution discussed in this paper uses a virtual character, capable of roaming on an arbitrary surface in an Intelligent Environment, in order to maximize the usability of the Intelligent Environment as a whole. As Towns et al.[1] have shown, virtual characters capable of performing judicious combinations of speech, locomotion and gestures are very effective in providing unambiguous, realtime advice in a virtual 3D environment. The goal of the project discussed in this paper, is to transfer the concept of *deictic believability*[1] of virtual characters in virtual 3D worlds to the physical world, by allowing a virtual character to "freely" move within physical space. The idea of a Virtual Room Inhabitant (VRI) is to allow the character to appear as an expert within the environment which is always available and aware of the state of each device. Our concept of a virtual character "living" within the Intelligent Environment, and thus playing the role of a host, allows both novice and advanced users to efficiently interact with the different devices and services integrated within the Intelligent Environment. The character is capable of welcoming a first time visitor and its main purpose is to explain the setup of the environment and to help users while interacting with the Intelligent Environment. Furthermore, the character is aware of the users position and orientation and is hence capable of positioning itself accordingly.

In a next step, we will enable the character to suggest a number of devices to be used, in order to fulfill a certain task for the user. In case several users are interacting with the Intelligent Environment simultaneously, the character will also be able to support users in sharing devices, and in doing so, it will maximize the benefit of all users.

2 Related Work

In the last few years, the number of projects dealing with Intelligent Environments has increased significantly. While many of these projects focused on the technical setup of these environments (see [2] and [3]), the demand for innovative, functional user interfaces for Intelligent Environments has constantly risen and thus became a central point within this research area. In [4], the authors stated their vision of an Intelligent Workspace, consisting of a network of agents, capable of organizing the combined usage of many different devices to maximize the benefit of all users. The proposed agent network allows the system to dynamically react on changing hardware setups within the environment (see [5]).

The importance of integrating additional dimensions, like geographical information as well as the state and position of each user, within the information space of an Intelligent Environment is discussed in [6]. Knowing a user's position and orientation may help to identify optimal devices or device combinations when performing a specific task within the Intelligent Environment.

The importance and effectiveness of virtual characters capable of performing deictic believable gestures, in order to provide problem-solving advices, has been discussed in a number of publications (e.g. [7], [1]). These virtual characters have proven to decrease efficiently the ambiguity of references to virtual objects within the virtual environment.

In our approach, we combine the idea of a network of agents with the geographical (i.e. positional) information derived from our outdoor/indoor navigation system [8]. Furthermore, we introduce a virtual character in our scenario, which is capable of giving unambiguous references to physical objects by means of speech, gestures and physical locomotion.

3 Realization

In order to realize our vision of a life-like character "living" in our Intelligent Environment, several software/hardware components were combined (see

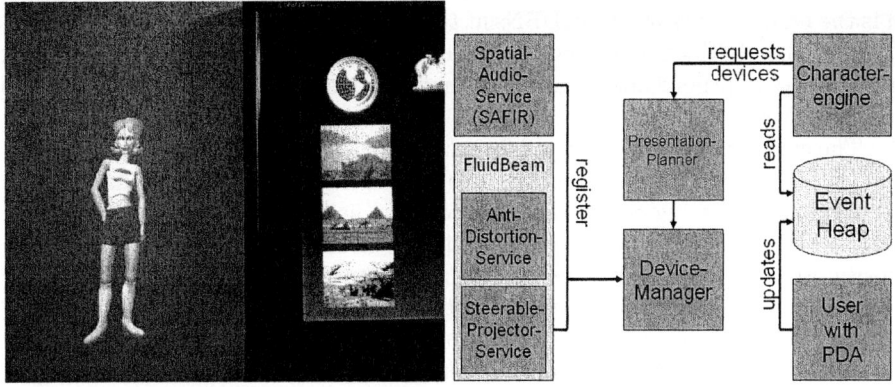

Fig. 1. The VRI besides a plasma-screen and the VRI system components

Figure 1). Each device has to be registered on our device manager as a service. The device manager, in combination with a presentation manager, grants access to all registered devices. In this way, we are able to share our devices between several applications running simultaneously. The remote access mechanism is realized with Java Remote Method Invocation[1] objects, which allow arbitrary applications to control remote devices as if they were locally connected.

We use two kinds of senders to detect user positions: Infrared beacons (IR beacons) and active Radio Frequency Identification tags (RFID tags). Most positioning systems equip the user with infrared batches or RFID tags and put respective sensors at the wall or ceiling to detect the presence and/or proximity of a user. In our approach the beacons and tags are mounted at the ceiling and the user carries a Personal Digital Assistant (PDA) with integrated sensors (the standard infrared port of the PDA and a PCMCIA active RFID reader card).

A received (or sensed) tag or beacon indicates that a user is near the location of the respective sender[2] (in case of the Infrared Beacons, which need a direct line of sight, the orientation of the user/PDA is also determined). The active RFID tags have a memory of 64 bytes of which 56 bytes can be freely used (read and write). We use this memory to store the coordinate of the tag. Each IR beacon is combined with one RFID tag that provides the coordinates of the beacon and the tag itself. When a tag or beacon is sensed by the PDA a Geo Referenced Dynamic Bayesian Network (geoDBN[9]) is instantiated ("induced") and associated with the coordinate that is stored in its memory.

The position of the user is then calculated from the weighted combination of the coordinates at which geoDBNs exist:

$$UserPos_t = \sum_{i=1}^{n} \alpha \ w(\text{GeoDBN}[i]) \ \text{Coord}(\text{GeoDBN}[i]).$$

---

[1] http://java.sun.com/products/jdk/rmi/
[2] Or near a coordinate that lies in the area of the sender or receiver.

n is the number of existing geoDBNs at time t ($n \geq$ *NumberOfReceivedSenders$_t$*), (Coord(GeoDBN[i])) is the coordinate and w(GeoDBN[i]) the weight of the ith geoDBN. α is a normalization factor that ensures that the sum of all weights multiplied with α is one.

The calculated position is then forwarded by the PDA via wireless LAN to an Event Heap, a tuplespace infrastructure that provides convenient mechanisms for storing and retrieving collections of type-value fields [10]. On this Event Heap, we collect all kinds of information retrieved within the environment (i.e. user positions, interactions with the system). Our central component, the character engine, monitors the Event Heap and automatically reacts according to changing user positions.

The Virtual Room Inhabitant implementation combines a character engine with a spatial audio system and a steerable projector, to allow the character to freely move within the room (i.e. move along the walls of the room). These three main parts of our implementation will be explained in detail in the following subsections. However, we will start with a short description of the setup of our Intelligent Environment.

3.1 The Instrumented Room

The testbed for our VRI implementation is an instrumented room with various types of devices. There is an instrumented desk, i.e. an ordinary table on which an interface is projected. The user is able to interact with the interface by means of a ceiling-mounted camera that is able to recognize simple gestures such as activating projected buttons. Another application in this environment is the Smart Shopping Assistant, consisting of a Smart Shelf and a Smart Shopping Cart. The assistant recognizes which products are taken out of the shelf or put into the shopping cart using RFID-technology and gives the user information about them or suggests recipes that can be cooked with the chosen products. A spatial audio system (SAFIR) and a steerable projector and camera unit (Fluid Beam) are integrated in the instrumented room and enable the realization of the VRI. Both systems are described in detail below in this paper. IR beacons and RFID tags are attached to the ceiling to allow for an accurate positioning service within the room.

3.2 Character Engine

The character engine consists of two parts, namely the character engine server (CE-server) written in Java and the character animation, which was realized with Macromedia Flash MX[3]. These two components are connected via an XML-Socket-Connection. The CE-server controls the Flash animation by sending XML commands/scripts. The Flash animation also uses the XML-Socket-Connection to send updates on the current state of the animation to the CE-server (i.e. whenever a part of an animation is started/finished). The character animation

---

[3] http://www.macromedia.com/software/flash/

itself consists of ~9000 still images rendered with Discreet 3D Studio Max[4] which were transformed into Flash animations. To cope with the immense use of system memory, while running such a huge Flash animation, we divided the animation into 17 subparts. While the first consists of default and idle animations, the remaining sixteen are combinations of character gestures, like for example: shake, nod, look behind, etc. Each animation includes a lip movement loop, so that we are able to let the character talk in almost any position or while performing an arbitrary gesture. We have a toplevel movie to control these movie parts. Initially, we load the default movie (i.e. when we start the character engine). Whenever we have a demand for a certain gesture (or a sequence of gestures), the CE-server sends the corresponding XML script to the toplevel Flash movie which than sequentially loads the corresponding gesture movies.

The following is a short example of an XML script for the character engine:

```
<VRI-script>
    <script>
        <part>gesture=LookFrontal sound=welcome1.mp3</part>
        <part>gesture=Hips sound=welcome2.mp3</part>
        <part>gesture=swirl sound=swirlsound</part>
    </script>
    <script>
        <part>gesture=LookFrontal sound=cart.mp3</part>
        <part>gesture=PointDownLeft sound=cart2.mp3</part>
        <part>gesture=swirl sound=swirlsound</part>
    </script>
    <script>
        <part>gesture=PointLeft sound=panel.mp3</part>
        <part>gesture=swirl sound=swirlsound</part>
    </script>
</VRI-script>
```

Each script part is enclosed by a script tag. After a script part was successfully performed by the VRI animation, the CE-server initiates the next step (i.e. moves the character to another physical location by moving the steerable projector and repositioning the voice of the character on the spatial audio system, or instructs the VRI animation to perform the next presentation part). In order to guarantee for a smooth character animation, we defined certain frames in the default animation as possible exit points. On these frames, the character is in exactly the same position as on each initial frame of the gesture animations. Each gesture animation also has an exit frame. As soon as this frame is reached, we unload the gesture animation, to free the memory, and instead continue with the default movie or we load another gesture movie, depending on the active XML script.

In addition to its animation control function, the CE-server also requests appropriate devices from the presentation planner. Once access to these devices

---

[4] http://www4.discreet.com/3dsmax/

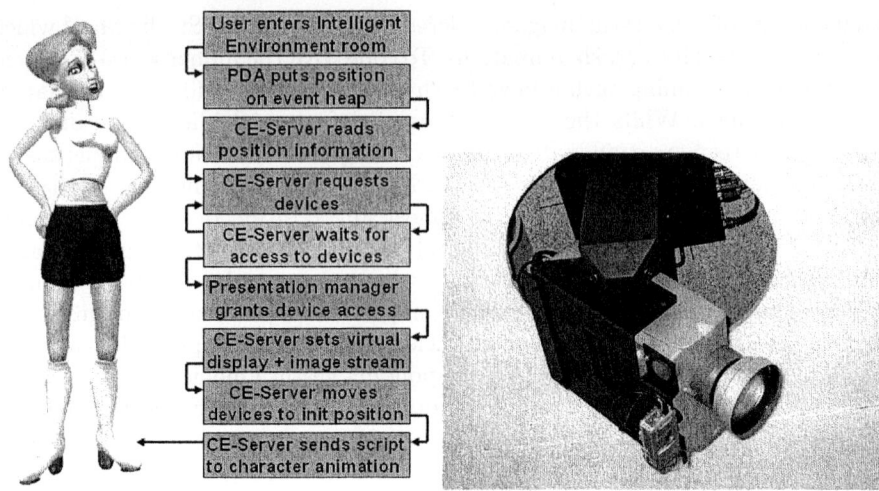

Fig. 2. System initialization steps for the VRI and the steerable projector

has been granted, the CE-server controls the spatial audio device, the steerable projector and the anti distortion software. The two devices, together with the anti distortion software are synchronized by commands generated by the CE-server, in order to allow the character to appear at any position along the walls of the instrumented room, and to allow the origin of the character's voice to be exactly where the character's visual representation is. Presentations within our Intelligent Environment are triggered by the user's movements within our lab. Our users are equipped with a PDA which is used for an outdoor/indoor navigation task. The indoor positional information, retrieved by the PDA, is forwarded to our Event Heap. On this heap, we store/publish all kinds of information which might be important for services running within the Intelligent Environment. As soon as a user enters the instrumented room, the CE-server recognizes the according information on the Event Heap. In a next step, the CE-server requests access to the devices needed for the VRI. Given access to these devices is granted by the presentation manager (otherwise the server repeats the request after a while), the CE-server generates a virtual display on the anti distortion software and starts a screen capture stream, capturing the character animation, which is then mapped on the virtual display (details will be explained below). It also moves the steerable projector and the spatial audio source to an initial position.

As a final step, the CE-server sends an XML script to the character animation, which will result in a combination of several gestures, performed by the character while playing synchronized MP3 files (synthesized speech) over the spatial audio device. The whole initialization process is indicated in figure 2.

3.3 Steerable Projector and Camera Unit (Fluid Beam)

A device consisting of an LCD projector and a digital camera placed in a movable unit is used to visualize the virtual character (see figure 2). The movable unit

(Moving Yoke) is mounted on the ceiling of the Instrumented Environment and can be rotated horizontally (pan) and vertically (tilt). In this way it is possible to project at any walls and desk surfaces in the Instrumented Environment. The digital camera can provide high resolution images or a low resolution video stream which are used to recognize optical markers or simple gestures.

As the projection surfaces are usually not perpendicular to the projector beam, the resulting image would appear distorted. In order to correct this distortion we apply a method described in [11]. It is based on the fact that projection is a geometrical inversion of the process of taking a picture given that the camera and the projector have the same optical parameters and the same position and orientation (see figure 3). The implementation of this approach requires an exact 3D model of the Instrumented Environment, in which the projector is replaced by a virtual camera. Both the intrinsic (i.e. field of view) and the extrinsic (i.e. position and orientation) parameters of the virtual camera must match those of the given projector.

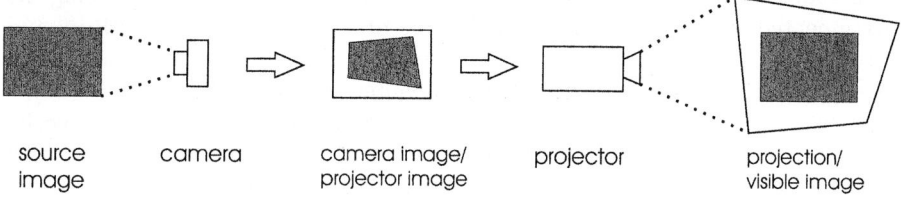

Fig. 3. Distortion correction using the virtual camera method

In this way we create a kind of virtual layer covering the surfaces of the Instrumented Environment on which virtual displays can be placed. This layer is visible only in the area that is currently illuminated by the projector beam. Thus the steerable projector serves as a kind of virtual torch making the virtual displays visible when it is moved in the appropriate direction. The displays are implemented as textured surfaces in the 3D model of the environment on which images, videos and live video streams can be displayed.

The VRI is created as a live video stream texture on a virtual display. Thus it can be animated in real time by the character engine. By moving the virtual display in the 3D model and an appropriate movement of the steerable projector the character appears to "hover" along the walls of the room.

3.4 Spatial Audio

The synthesized speech of the VRI generates audio output that could be played by any device with audio rendering capabilities. For such purposes we developed a Spatial Audio Framework for Instrumented Rooms (SAFIR, [12]) that runs as a service in our environment and allows applications to concurrently spatialize arbitrary sounds in our lab. The CE-server sends the generated MP3 files and the coordinates of the current location of the character to the spatial audio system, which positions the sounds accordingly. The anthropomorphic interface obviously appears more natural with the speech being perceived from the same direction as the projection is seen. This is particularly helpful in situations when other applications clutter up the acoustic space with additional audio sources at the same time: The spatial attributes of the audio output of the virtual character allow the user to associate the speech with the projection of the avatar more easily. Furthermore it automatically directs the user's attention to the position of the character when it appears outside the user's field of vision.

4 Application Example

To test our VRI, we integrated it within a shopping and navigation demo running at our lab. In this scenario, users are given a PDA and perform a combined indoor/outdoor navigation task. The idea is, to lead the users to an airport ground and upon entering the airport facilities, to guide them towards certain duty free shops until the departure time is close. In our demonstration setup, these shops are represented by different rooms in our lab, one of them being the instrumented room. The VRI plays the role of a host, welcoming visitors and introducing them to the components of the instrumented room. In figure 1, the VRI is standing beside a display that is mounted on one of the walls.

As soon as a user enters the room, the character appears on the wall nearby the entrance to welcome the user. Next step of the demonstration setup would be to interact with the smart shopping assistant mentioned in section 3.1. The demo involves the instrumented shelf, recognizing if products are removed, a shopping cart that also detects items placed into it, a tablet PC (mounted on the cart) presenting proactive shopping support to the user and a wall-mounted display showing additional product recommendations.

As the user approaches the shelf, the VRI introduces these devices step by step and describes the interaction possibilities given to the user. While explaining the demo, the VRI moves along the walls, in order to appear next to the objects it is talking about.

To conclude the shopping demo, the VRI is triggered once more to notify users about the immediate boarding of their flight. It appears alongside the exit of the room, points to it and instructs the user to proceed to the boarding gate.

5 Conclusions/Future Work

In summary, this paper has presented the design, implementation and application of the VRI, a new interaction metaphor for Intelligent Environments. By introducing a life-like character in our Intelligent Environment, we support users while interacting with various different devices and services. In a first step, the character is used to explain the technology in our instrumented room to new users. Since the character is capable of moving freely along the walls of the room, it may offer situated information to the users. By integrating sensor technology (i.e. PDAs, Infrared Beacons and RFID-Tags), the system may estimate the position of the user in the room and react accordingly.

While in the first phase of the project, we concentrated on the technical realization of the VRI, in the second phase we will focus on the behavior and interactivity of the character.

In a next step, we will integrate a speech recognizer which is capable of analyzing audio signals streamed from a PDA via wireless LAN to a server (based on the approach described in [13]).

To adapt the character's behavior to the user, we will integrate a combination of an interaction history and external user model. While the interaction history will allow the character engine to adapt the presentations by relating to previously presented information, the external user model (which will be available for specific services on the internet) will allow the system to adapt to general preferences shared by the user with the system (for example, a user might prefer to always use the headphones attached to his PDA when in a public situation, instead of a public audio system).

To further improve the flexibility of the approach, we will also allow the character to migrate from the environment to the users PDA (this technology has already been used in a former project and is well established, see [14]). In this way, the character will be capable of presenting personalized information to the user, while others are in the same room. Additionally, the character on the PDA will be able to guide users to different locations, in situations (i.e locations), where the character is unable to move along the walls(as discussed in [15]).

The VRI has been successfully tested during many different presentations and has been welcoming almost every visitor coming to our lab ever since it has been installed. We believe, that the VRI is a promising first step towards an intuitive interaction method for Intelligent Environments.

Acknowledgments

We would like to thank Peter Rist, who designed the life-like character used in this project. We would also like to thank the FLUIDUM research group for providing the hardware used to realize the VRI project.

References

1. Towns, S.G., Voerman, J.L., Callaway, C.B., Lester, J.C.: Coherent gestures, locomotion, and speech in life-like pedagogical agents. In: IUI '98: Proceedings of the 3rd international conference on Intelligent user interfaces, ACM Press (1998) 13–20
2. Coen, M.: Design principles for intelligent environments. In: AAAI/IAAI. (1998) 547–554
3. Kidd, C., Orr, R., Abowd, G., Atkeson, C., Essa, I., MacIntyre, B., Mynatt, E., Starner, T., Newstetter, W.: The aware home: A living laboratory for ubiquitous computing research. In: Cooperative Buildings. (1999) 191–198
4. Hanssens, N., Kulkarni, A., Tuchinda, R., Horton, T.: Building agent-based intelligent workspaces. In: Proceedings of ABA Conference. (2002) To Appear.

5. Coen, M., Phillips, B., Warshawsky, N., Weisman, L., Peters, S., Finin, P.: Meeting the computational needs of intelligent environments: The metaglue system. In: Proceedings of MANSE'99, Dublin, Ireland (1999)
6. Brumitt, B., Meyers, B., Krumm, J., Kern, A., Shafer, S.: Easyliving: Technologies for intelligent environments. In: HUC. (2000) 12–29
7. Lester, J.C., Voerman, J.L., Towns, S.G., Callaway, C.B.: Deictic believability: Coordinated gesture, locomotion, and speech in lifelike pedagogical agents. Applied Artificial Intelligence **13** (1999) 383–414
8. Baus, J., Krüger, A., Wahlster, W.: A Resource-Adaptive Mobile Navigation System. In: IUI2002: International Conference on Intelligent User Interfaces, New York, ACM Press (2002) 15–22
9. Brandherm, B., Schwartz, T.: Geo referenced dynamic Bayesian networks for user positioning on mobile systems. In: Submitted to the 2005 International Workshop on Location- and Context-Awareness. (2005)
10. Johanson, B., Fox, A.: The event heap: A coordination infrastructure for interactive workspaces. In: Proceedings of the Workshop on Mobile Computing Systems and Applications. (2002)
11. Pinhanez, C.: The everywhere displays projector: A device to create ubiquitous graphical interfaces. Lecture Notes in Computer Science (2001)
12. Schmitz, M.: Safir: Spatial audio framework for instrumented rooms. In: Proceedings of the Workshop on Intelligent and Transparent Interfaces, held at Advanced Visual Interfaces 2004, Gallipoli, Department of Computer Science, Saarland University, Germany (2004)
13. Müller, C., Wittig, F.: Speech as a source for ubiquitous user modeling. In: Website of the Workshop on User Modelling for Ubiquitous Computing at UM 2003, "http://www.di.uniba.it/~ubium03/" (2003)
14. Kruppa, M., Kruger, A., Rocchi, C., Stock, O., Zancanaro, M.: Seamless personalized tv-like presentations on mobile and stationary devices in a museum. In: Proceedings of the 2003 International Cultural Heritage Informatics Meeting. (2003)
15. Kruppa, M.: Towards explicit physical object referencing. In: Proceedings of 10th international conferernce on User Modeling, Springer (2005) 506–508

Evaluating Techniques for Resolving Redundant Information and Specularity in Occupancy Grids

Thomas Collins[1], J.J. Collins[1], Mark Mansfield[1], and Shane O'Sullivan[2]

[1] Department of Computer Science and Information Systems,
University of Limerick, Limerick, Ireland
[2] Dublin Software Lab, IBM, Mulhuddart, Dublin 15, Ireland
Tel. +35361 202783
Thomas.Collins@ul.ie

Abstract. In this paper we consider the effect that techniques designed to deal with the problems of redundant information and erroneous sensory data have on the results of robotic mapping. We accomplish this by evaluating several configurations of these techniques using identical test data. Through evaluating the results of these experiments using an extensible benchmarking suite, that our group has developed, we outline which technique yields the greatest environmental representational gain.

1 Introduction

The performance of an autonomous mobile robot in acquiring a meaningful spatial model of its operating environment depends greatly on the accuracy of its perceptual capabilities. As it operates in the environment the robot gathers sensory information and subsequently incorporates this into a representation of the environment. The field that is concerned with such issues is known as robotic mapping.

The traditional approach to recovering such information is based on the use of a tessellated 2D grid known as an *Occupancy Grid* (OccGrid) [1]. OccGrids store fine grained qualitative information regarding which areas of the robots operating environment are occupied and which are empty. Specifically each individual cell in the grid records a certainty factor relating to the confidence that the particular cell is occupied.

In mobile robotics one of the most popular sensors used is ultrasonic sonar due to its low cost, its speed of operation and ease of use. These sensors report relative distances between the unit and obstacles located within its perceptual cone. This means that an obstacle, if detected, may be located somewhere within the sonar cone at the distance specified. However, despite their advantages, sonars are prone to error in measurement due to such factors as wave reflection and absorption etc. This introduces uncertainty into the map building process which can reduce the overall quality of the maps created. Catering for such ambiguity is the reason that robotic mapping is such a difficult problem[2].

We present a comprehensive analysis of the effect that techniques designed to deal with the problems of redundant information and erroneous sensory data have on robotic mapping. Specifically we consider:

- Pose Buckets[3]
- Feature Prediction[4]
- Neural Network based specular reading detection[5]

Pose buckets are a means of dealing with redundant information that were originally developed by Konolige as part of his MURIEL mapping paradigm [3]. Feature prediction and neural network based specular reading detection are both means of dealing with the problem of erroneous readings which may be received during operation. These techniques are expanded on in the following section.

We use four standard mapping paradigms, [1,3,5,6], augmented with the techniques mentioned above, as the basis for our experimentation. The paradigms are evaluated using identical testbed data and benchmarks from a suite which we have specifically designed for empirical evaluation of robotic mapping. This allows the determination of which paradigm-technique combination provides a mobile robot with the greatest environmental representational ability.

2 Occupancy Grid Mapping and Techniques for Dealing with Uncertainty

2.1 Occupancy Grid Mapping

The problem of robotic mapping is that of acquiring a spatial model of a robots environment. An occupancy grid is a tessellated grid with each individual cell in the grid recording a certainty factor relating to the confidence that the particular cell is occupied. For the purposes of the evaluation outlined herein we utilise four established mapping paradigms which we modify so as to incorporate the various techniques. The specific paradigms are:

- Moravec and Elfes - 1985, probabilistic framework[1]
- Matthies and Elfes - 1988, Bayesian framework [6]
- Thrun - 1993, neural network based approach [5]
- Konolige - 1997, enhanced Bayesian framework [3]

The following provides a brief overview and analysis of these. For further information the reader is referred to the relevant publications.

Moravec and Elfes - 1985: this paradigm generates two intermediate models, an empty map *Emp* and an occupied map *Occ*, which are subsequently integrated to form a final map. The sensory beam uses a binary classification with cells being in either the free area or the surface (occupied) area. A two dimensional Gaussian sensor model is used to calculate the probability of the cell being empty if it is in the free area and likewise for cells in the occupied area. The map update used by this paradigm is heuristic in nature with the probability of a cell being empty integrated into *Emp* and likewise the probability of a cell being occupied being integrated into the *Occ* map. Finally the *Emp* and *Occ* maps are combined into a single representation with a thresholding step where the larger value for each cell is chosen for inclusion in the map. The first limitation with this paradigm comes from the fact that specular reflection is not considered. Specular reflection occurs when the sensory beam reflects of multiple surfaces and then either returns or does not return to the emitter, causing an erroneous reading in either case.

Matthies and Elfes - 1988: used the same sensory model as Moravec and Elfes for the purposes of sensor interpretation in their paradigm. However they did develop a more rigorous Bayesian based map updating formula which replaces the heuristic method from Moravec and Elf's - 1985 approach. There are two main disadvantages to using the Bayesian update formula. Firstly a single update can change the occupancy value of a cell drastically which means that cell values can fluctuate. The second disadvantage is that once a cell has converged to certainty i.e. either 0 or 1 the occupancy value cannot be changed.

Thrun - 1993: this method outlines an occupancy grid mapping paradigm which utilises neural networks (NN). The sensory interpretation aspect of this algorithm is implicitly defined in the *sensor interpretation network* which reports values in the range <0...1> for the sensory readings that it is presented with. Certainty values relating to these readings are determined through the second network, the *confidence network*. In this case the map update procedure is similar to that in Matthies and Elf's - 1988 approach. For reasons of tractability the network is not trained to convergence, as to do so would encode environmental characteristics in addition to sensory characteristics in the network.

Konolige - 1997: also uses a sensory model which separates the model into occupied and empty sections. However in this case an identical formula is used for both with a probabilistic profile determining whether a cell is in the free or occupied part of the sensory beam. He also introduced 'Pose Buckets' as a means of dealing with redundant information and tackled the problem of specular sensory information through probabilistic inference. For purposes of updating the map Konolige's method combines the probability of the cell being occupied and empty using a logarithmic technique.

One issue with this approach is the way in which specularity estimation is applied to individual cells. Specifically if a cell is very confident of the specularity of a sonar reading then this should be propagated to all cells in the sonar beam not just the cell itself as there is a great deal of inter-dependence between cells in a sonar beam. Also when a sonar reading is given a high probability of specularity the effect of that reading on the map should be reduced. Also it would be desirable if both the free and occupied segments of the beam were considered by the paradigm.

2.2 Techniques for Dealing with Uncertainty During Mapping

The previous section outlined standard robotic mapping paradigms. However for all paradigms unreliability of information obtained from sensors is a major issue characterised by two problems:

- *Redundant Information* The assumption is made that each fresh sensor reading gives new information, whereas the actual case may be that the information is simply repetition of what has been previously sensed, resulting in a biased view of the world.
- *Specular Reflection* The energy emitted from a sensory device is scattered off a surface before returning to the sensor or is reflected at a wide angle and subsequently never returns to the device which results in the sensor reporting incorrect readings.

Currently in the domain there exists very little quantative information regarding the tackling of such issues. Therefore in this paper we empirically evaluate techniques developed to address these problems. Specifically we consider two techniques designed to deal with the specular reflection problem, Feature Prediction (FP) and a Neural Network based technique (NN). We also consider the problem of redundant information through Konolige's Pose Buckets (PB).

2.3 Removing Redundant Information

When dealing with OccGrid mapping, a simplifying assumption of conditional independence is made. This states that each cell in a map has no effect on other cells, and that each sensory reading received is independent of all other readings. Using the concept of conditional independence, a map is constructed by taking sensor readings from many different positions and angles. However there often arises the case where the robot is stationary. The issue with this scenario is that no new information is being added to the map after the first reading was obtained from the position. Each successive reading is clearly not independent of the one that came before, it is, in fact, conceptually the same.

PB's were designed to deal with this issue. They utilise an OccGrid map which has a dual representation. Each constituent cell of the map represents both the occupancy of the area and the 'pose' of readings that have effected that cell. This variable is set to true when the first reading from a particular pose is received, and all following readings from that pose for the particular cell are subsequently discarded.

The main issue with PB's is that it is conceivable that due to their manner of dealing with received sensory readings, i.e. accept the first reading received as being illustrative of the true state of the environment, some useful information could be discarded. However work recently completed within the group, [7], addressed this problem and it is this enhanced version of PB's that we utilise.

2.4 Dealing with Erroneous Sensor Readings

Feature Prediction: is a method for detecting specular sonar readings. During operation FP uses three models of the environment, a sonar map, a local map and a global map. The sonar map is a model which contains features, which are essentially line segments, that have been extrapolated from the current sonar readings set. The local map maintains a set of features that have been estimated from previous readings, but only from the area withing the immediate vicinity of the robot. The process of reconciling the sonar and local map requires the estimation of a confidence value for each sensor reading. This confidence value is used by the Bayes filter when integrating the reading set into the global map. More information of FP can be found in [4,7] .

Using Neural Networks: in [5], Thrun outlines an OccGrid mapping approach which utilises neural networks (NN). In this approach a network known as the *sensor interpretation network (R)* is used to compute the occupancy values for each individual cell in the overall map and a separate network, known as the *confidence network (C)*, is used to calculate a confidence estimation for each sensory reading received.

As can be appreciated there are similarities between this approach to the detection of erroneous readings and FP. However FP works on the macro level, considering a world centric view of the current situation whereas the neural network based approach considers a more robot centric view. Therefore, in theory, both techniques are complimentary.

The NN approach operates as follows. In relation to a cell of interest the network is presented with the following inputs:

- The four sensor readings closest to the cell of interest $< x, y >$
- The relative angle, θ, to the cell of interest
- The relative distance, d, to the cell of interest

The network is trained using the classic Back-Propagation algorithm to output a scalar in the range `<0,1>` which is an error estimate relating to the particular reading r. The training examples used during training consist of the inputs outlined earlier and the desired, error value for the particular reading that is being dealt with in that particular instance.

As the confidence network estimates the expected error relating to a particular reading the confidence in the reading is low if the output from the network is high and vice versa. It is straight forward to use this error estimate as a means of registering specular readings.

As mentioned, the aim of this paper is to consider the effect that techniques designed to deal with the problems of redundant information and erroneous sensory data have on the results of robotic mapping. Toward this end the three techniques were incorporated into the four mapping approaches outlined in section 2.1 to arrived at augmented versions of these approaches. These augmented mapping versions were subsequently used as the experimental basis.

3 Benchmarking Techniques

The purpose of this paper is to determine which technique, or combination of techniques is the most effective in the context of robotic mapping. To actually determine this, maps generated using the techniques must be evaluated.

Toward this end we use an extensible suite of benchmarks which allow for the empirical evaluation of map building paradigms [8]. This suite includes utilising techniques from image analysis, techniques specifically developed for the evaluation of OccGrid maps in addition to techniques designed to evaluate the usability of a generated map by a robot.

1. *Correlation*: As a generated map is similar to an image it is possible to use a technique from image analysis known as *Baron's cross correlation coefficient* [9] as a basis for evaluating the map. With this metric a higher percentage indicates that the map being tested has a high degree of similarity to an ideal map of the environment.
2. *Map Score*: This is a technique originally proposed by Martin and Moravec in [10] which calculates the difference between a generated map and an ideal map of the environment. The lower the percentage difference the greater the similarity between the two maps.
3. *Map Score of Occupied Cells* This metric is similar to the previous one but only tests those cells in the map that are occupied. This metric addresses the weakness in the first map score metric where mapping paradigms which over-specify free space could achieve a better score than maps which identify obstacles more accurately.
4. *Path Based Analysis*: We use a voronoi diagramming technique of which there are two categories
   - The degree to which the paths created in the generated map would cause the robot to collide with an obstacle in the real world, and are therefore invalid. These are known as *false positives*.
   - The degree to which the robot should be able to plan a path from one position to the another using the generated map, but cannot. These are known as *false negatives*.

Obtaining an overall score:

$$CLS_{\text{map} \in M} = \frac{D_{\text{map}} P_{\text{map}}}{\Sigma(D_{\text{map}} P_{\text{map}})} \quad (1)$$

where

$$D_{\text{map}} = \frac{CT - \text{MapScore}_{all} * CT - \text{MapScore}_{occ} * B_n}{\Sigma(CT - \text{MapScore}_{all} * CT - \text{MapScore}_{occ} * B_n)}$$

and

$$P_m = \frac{(\text{FP}) * (CT - \text{FN})}{\Sigma((\text{FP}) * (CT - \text{FN}))}$$

In the above, CLS is the overall classification score obtained M is the overall set of maps in an experiment subset, map is a particular map within the set of maps M, CT is a normalising constant that accounts for the inverse benchmark relationships, MapScore_{all} is the result from the *Map Score* metric applied to all cells in the applicable map, MapScore_{occ} is the result from the *Map Score* metric applied to the occupied cells in the maps, B_n is the result obtained from *Correlation*, FP is the result obtained from the *False Positive* path analysis metric and FN is the result obtained from the *False Negative* path analysis metric. This rule combines the normalised certainty factors from the five benchmarks in a manner that is consistent with the differing orientations of the benchmarking techniques.

4 Results

The experimentation carried out consisted of testing the four basic mapping paradigms with identical data obtained from three test runs in two test environments. To fully determine the contribution that the techniques have on the mapping process we ran a number of experiments which used combinations of the techniques. In total eight configurations were utilised, table 1.

Table 1. Combinations of techniques

Reference	FP	PB	NN
Config 1	N	N	N
Config 2	Y	N	N
Config 3	Y	N	Y
Config 4	Y	Y	N
Config 5	N	Y	N
Config 6	N	N	Y
Config 7	N	Y	Y
Config 8	Y	Y	Y

Table 2. Experiment Results

Key	Reference	ME85	ME88	K97	T93
A	Config 1	0.42	0.47	0.52	0.42
B	Config 2	0.54	0.55	0.61	0.48
C	Config 3	0.54	0.55	0.60	0.48
D	Config 4	0.64	0.51	0.62	0.52
E	Config 5	0.47	0.47	0.63	0.44
F	Config 6	0.46	0.63	0.54	0.44
G	Config 7	0.44	0.55	0.56	0.43
H	Config 8	0.64	0.51	0.60	0.48

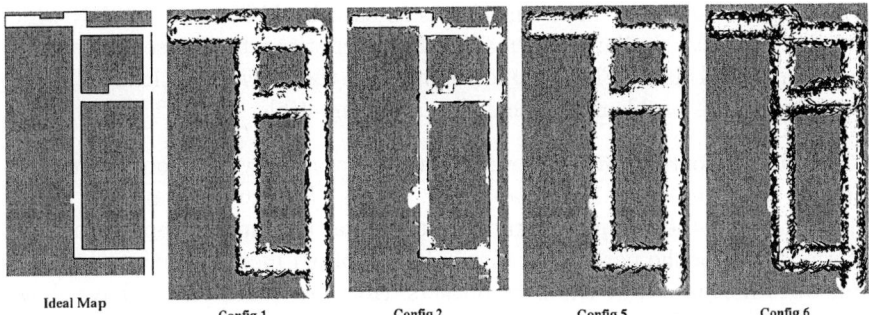

Fig. 1. Ideal map 24m x 44m and some illustrative maps generated during experimentation

Each of the four mapping paradigms was configured according to table 1 and used to generate a number of OccGrid maps. This means that the results presented in this paper are obtained from analysing a total of 192 OccGrid maps.

Table 2 presents the overall results from the experimentation. Therein ME85 represents the augmented version of Moravec and Elfes 1985 mapping paradigm and ME88, K97, T93 represent the augmented versions of Matthies and Elfes, Konoligie's and Thrun's techniques from 1988, 1997 and 1993 respectively. Figure 1 present some illustrative maps generated by Konolige's method using configurations one, two, five and six from table 1 in addition to an ideal map of the environment, which is provided for reference.

5 Analysis

The results outlined in the previous section originated from experiments aimed at evaluating the overall contribution made by the various extensions to the robotic mapping paradigm. In the following, as per table 2 ME85 refers to the augmented version of Moravec and Elfes 1985 paradigm [1], ME88 refers to the augmented version of Matthies and Elfes 1988 paradigm [6], K97 to the augmented version of Konoligie's 1997 paradigm [3] and T93 to the augmented version of Thruns 1993 paradigm [5] mapping paradigms which were used as the basis for the experimentation outlined herein. The following analysis considers the results from the context of the overall classification that we are evaluating i.e. sensory reading critique through FP and NN and redundant information filtering through PB.

Reading Confidence Estimation: the experimental configurations from table 1 that involved determining a confidence estimate were configurations two, three, six which relate to the results in table 2 - B,C and F. As the results show the use of FP on its own, the use of FP in conjunction with NN based confidence estimation and the use of NN based confidence estimation on its own all promoted more of a general improvement in the K97 and ME85 mapping paradigms than in the ME88 or the T93 paradigms. This can be attributed to the fact that there is a conceptual similarity in the mechanisms used by ME88 and T93NN which cause them to have similar performance characteristics when presented with filtered operational data. These trends show that these two drastically differing approaches to the problem of specularity are compatible.

Redundant Information Filtering: on this occasion we are considering configuration five from table 1 and table 2 E. When PB were used on their own in conjunction with the mapping paradigms there was an improvement in the overall performance of the paradigms. Again K97 profited more from the removal of redundant information by the pose buckets. However as the results have shown K97's performance in relation to false negative paths was poor. This is because, while PB's believe both free-space and occupied readings equally they ensure that there is at most a difference of one reading between the number of free and occupied readings from any given position. The reason for this is that K97's slight favouring of occupied space over empty space will effect the ability of the the free space readings from altering the incorrect occupied readings registered with the pose buckets.

Reading Confidence Estimation in conjunction with Redundant Information Filtering: in this case we are considering configurations four and seven i.e. table 2 - D and G. When FP and PB were used together there was a slightly better performance than the case where PB were used in conjunction with the NN based confidence estimation. This shows that PB are more compatible with algorithmic rather than a learned means of critiquing sensory readings. This is because of the overlap in their performance. However FP maintains an explicit historical record which serves as the basis for determining the erroneous readings which the NN based paradigm does not. This means that FP is slightly more subtle in its removal of readings due to its historical perspective whereas the network based paradigm is more harsh i.e. there exists the possibility that the NN based paradigm will regard more readings as erroneous that the algorithmic method due to its temporally localised nature.

Using all extensions: here we are considering configuration eight from table 1 and table 2 - H. When all three extensions were used together the overall result was that the performance was similar to the case where only FP and PB were used. This is because while FP and NN based confidence estimation do perform essentially the same job FP can be slightly more subtle than the NN based paradigm to reading critique. Essentially this means that when both techniques are used in conjunction with PB the FP will catch any readings that the NN based paradigm missed which means that FP is the dominant reading critique mechanism. Therefore the results are similar in this case to the scenario where the NN based paradigm was not used. However as can be seen the performance for all mapping paradigms has improved when compared to the configuration where we do not use any of the extensions, as shown in table 2 A.

6 Conclusion

In this paper we have presented an analysis of algorithmic extensions, which are designed to deal with the problems of redundant information and erroneous sensory data in robotic mapping. We have outlined a benchmarking suite developed to allow empirical evaluation of such maps and used it to evaluate the impact of the extensions. Our results have shown that Feature Prediction, Pose Buckets and Neural Network Based reading critique all serve to enhance the performance of the mapping process resulting in the creation of accurate and usable maps of a robots operating environment. However, as the results have shown, the neural network based enhancement has a negligible impact on the overall performance of the paradigms.

References

1. Moravec, H., Elfes, A.: High resolution maps from wide angle sonar. In: Proceedings of the 1985 IEEE International Conference on Robotics and Automation. (1985)
2. Thrun, S.: Robotic mapping: A survey. In Lakemeyer, G., Nebel, B., eds.: Exploring Artificial Intelligence in the New Millenium. Morgan Kaufmann (2002)
3. Konolige, K.: Improved occupancy grids for map building. Autonomous Robots (1997) 351–367
4. O'Sullivan, S., J.J.Collins, Mansfield, M., Haskett, D., Eaton, M.: Linear feature prediction for confidence estimation of sonar readings in map building. In: Proceedings Ninth International Symposium on Artificial Life and Robots, Oita, Japan (2004)
5. Thrun, S.: Exploration and model building in mobile robot domains. In: Proceedings of IEEE International Conference on Neural Networks,, Seattle, Washington, USA, IEEE neural Network Council (1993) 175–180
6. Matthies, L., Elfes, A.: Integration of sonar and stereo range data using a grid-based representation. In: Proceedings of the 1988 IEEE International Conference on Robotics and Automation. (1988)
7. O'Sullivan, S.: An empirical evaluation of map building methodologies in mobile robotics using the feature prediction sonar noise filter and metric grid map benchmarking suite. Master's thesis, University of Limerick (2003)
8. Collins, J., O'Sullivan, S., Mansfield, M., Eaton, M., Haskett, D.: Developing an extensible benchmarking framework for map building paradigms. In: Proceedings Ninth International Symposium on Artificial Life and Robots, Oita, Japan (2004)
9. Baron, R.J.: Mechanisms of human facial recognition. In: International journal of man machine studdies. Volume 15. (1981) 137–178
10. Martin, M.C., Moravec, H.: Robot evidence grids. Technical Report CMU-RI-TR-96-06, Robotics Institute, Carnegie Mellon University, Pittsburgh, PA (1996)

Analyzing Security Protocols Using Association Rule Mining

Qingfeng Chen and Yi-Ping Phoebe Chen

School of Information Technology,
Deakin University, Melbourne, VIC 3125, Australia
{qifengch, phoebe}@deakin.edu.au

Abstract. Current studies to analyzing security protocols using formal methods require users to predefine authentication goals. Besides, they are unable to discover potential correlations between secure messages. This research attempts to analyze security protocols using data mining. This is done by extending the idea of association rule mining and converting the verification of protocols into computing the frequency and confidence of inconsistent secure messages. It provides a novel and efficient way to analyze security protocols and find out potential correlations between secure messages. The conducted experiments demonstrate our approaches.

1 Introduction

The rapid growth of electronic commerce (e-commerce) has played an important role in global economy but it also poses big challenge to the security of e-commerce. Although a variety of security protocols have been developed to guarantee secure transactions, they are often error-prone and vulnerable.

Formal methods such as theorem proving [1,7,8] and model checking [2] have been successfully used to verify security protocols. They model the behavior of a protocol by formalizing message generating, sending and receiving, and implement rigorous deduction using inference rules. Ideally, it requires analyzers have clear ideas about what the suspectable problem is. However, the traditional approaches are confronted with many difficulties in dealing with multiple authentication goals. On the other hand, secure messages from sender, receiver and the third party are often inconsistent in a hostile environment for the communication block, message lost and/or malicious attacks. Missing and spurious data are a prevalent phenomenon in transaction databases. Moreover, there possibly exist correlations between secure messages, which imply potential security flaws. For example, if a message is encrypted by key k, k is needed to decrypt this message. Identifying the associations can thus assist us in analyzing security protocols. Nevertheless, this is lacking in current approaches.

Data mining techniques have recently emerged as a means of identifying patterns and trends from large quantities of data. Among them, association rule mining is a popular summarization and pattern extraction algorithm to identify correlations between items in transactional databases [3,4,5]. This paper extends the original idea to *mining secure messages*.

- First, the missing message should be considered. For example, $A' = \{password_2, expiration\ date\}$, $A = \{expiration\ date, password_1, name\}$, A and A' are different itemsets for $name$ is missing in A'.
- If two corresponding items are not identical, they are viewed as inconsistent items. For example, the $password_2$ in A' is not identical with $password_1$ in itemset A, so they are inconsistent.

If messages in itemset A were lost or tampered in a transaction T, it would lead to the decrease of the number of occurrences of this itemset, and in this way, the support and confidence of this rule will decrease. And thereby, it is reasonable to say this transaction is insecure if its support and confidence are too low.

This paper presents how to use association rule mining to analyze security protocols and discover potential associations between secure messages. The freshness and dynamics properties of secure messages are validated in the preprocessing for correct and efficient data mining. Experiments are conducted to analyze a *purchase request* transaction in SET [9].

The rest of this paper is organized as follows. Some basic concepts are presented in Section 2. The problem definition is stated in Section 3. Section 4 presents how to analyze security protocols using association rule mining. Finally, we conclude this paper in Section 5.

2 Basic Concepts

Suppose $\mathcal{L}$ denotes a set of proposition formulae formed in the usual way from a set of atom symbols $\mathcal{A}$. In particular, $\mathcal{A}$ can contain α and $\neg \alpha$ for some atom α. $\wedge, \neg$ and $\rightarrow$ denote logical connectives. We use X, Y and P for principals, CA for Certificate Authority, and $m, \alpha \in \mathcal{A}$ for messages in general. Let k be a key and $Cert(X)_{CA}$ be X's certificate signed by CA. $K_p(X)$ and $K^{-1}(X)$ represent X's public/private pair respectively; $S(m, k)$ presents the signed message m by key k.

The following rules are derived from BAN logic [1] to authenticate the freshness of secure messages and validity of principal's public key.

(1) *Generation Rule.* If message m is generated by X, X must know m.

$$\frac{generates(X, m)}{knows(X, m)}$$

(2) *Delivery Rule.* If X knows message m and sends m to receiver Y, Y can see the message m.

$$\frac{knows(X, m) \wedge sends(X, Y, m)}{sees(Y, m)}$$

(3) *Public Key Rule.* If Y sees a message m encrypted by X's private key $K^{-1}(X)$, Y believes this message is sent by X.

$$\frac{sees(Y, S(m, K^{-1}(X)))}{sends(X, Y, S(m, K^{-1}(X)))}$$

This rule ascertains the originator of messages in terms of the belief in the association between public keys and principals. Nevertheless, Y has not yet believed this message for its freshness needs to be further confirmed.

(4) *Belief Rule.* X generates message m and sends it to Y. If Y sees this message and m is fresh, Y believes X in the message m.

$$\frac{sends(X,Y,m) \land sees(Y,X,m) \land fresh(m)}{believes(Y,X,m)}$$

This rule represents that Y believes that the message m from principal X is not a replay. The timestamp has been proved to be useful to ensure the freshness of secure messages [6].

(5) *Certificate Rule1.* If CA_2's certificate is signed with CA_1's private key, and Y verifies CA_2's public key using CA_1's public key, Y believes CA_2's public key.

$$\frac{signs(CA_1, CA_2, Cert(CA_2)_{CA_1}) \land verify(Y, CA_2, K_p(CA_2))}{believes(Y, CA_2, K_p(CA_2))}$$

(6) *Certificate Rule2.* If X's certificate is signed with CA_2's private key, and Y verifies X's public key, principal Y believes X's public key.

$$\frac{signs(CA, X, Cert(X)_{CA}) \land verify(Y, X, K_p(X))}{believes(Y, X, K_p(X))}$$

These rules ensure the belief in message freshness and the validity of principal's public keys. Accordingly, a supporting relation $\models$ is given below where D_S, D_R and D_T represent transaction databases from *sender*, *receiver* and *the third party* respectively.

(1) $D_S \models \alpha$ iff D_S knows α, and α is *fresh*;
(2) $D_R \models \alpha$ iff D_R believes α, and α is *fresh*;
(3) $D_T \models \alpha$ iff D_T believes α, and α is *fresh*;
(4) $D \models K_p(X)$ iff D authenticates X's public key $K_p(X)$.

However, the integrity of secure messages cannot be guaranteed in a hostile environment. This leads to inconsistent secure messages in different transaction databases. For example, $D_S \models \alpha$ and $D_R \models \neg \alpha$ represents a pair of inconsistent messages.

3 Problem Definition

Traditional analysis of security protocols requires users to predefine authentication goals. However, without careful inspection, some latent problems are too implicit to be detected. If there are many goals, the analysis will become even more difficult. On the other hand, unlike the well-defined market basket data, secure messages have properties of freshness and dynamics. The former is a prerequisite to protect secure messages from replay attacks and is usually realized using timestamp [6]. And the latter confirms the message is really derived from the sender and received by whom it claims to be. Therefore, it is necessary to verify the freshness and dynamics of secure messages before going to data mining. Nevertheless, the integrity of secure messages cannot be absolutely protected by only freshness and dynamics.

Actually, missing and spurious messages happen very often in transactions for the potential communication block, message lost and/or block cipher. This affects the integrity of secure messages and leads to inconsistent data in different sources. For example, a user's password can be maliciously tampered in a transaction. On the other hand, there may be potential correlations between secure messages. For example, an encrypted message by key k is related to the message m and key k. Any attacks on m or k may have an effect on its security. Hence, we can observe that the potential correlations are useful to discover hidden problems that are difficult to be detected using traditional approaches.

In this article, the original idea of association rule mining is extended to analyze security protocols. During a transaction, if the item A were lost or tampered, it will lead to the decrease of the number of occurrences of this item, and in this way, the degree of support and confidence for corresponding rules will decrease too. It is reasonable to say a transaction is insecure if the corresponding rule is not a rule of interest. Additionally, the discovered association rules can uncover some potential correlations between inconsistent secure messages, which imply potential security flaws in security protocols. The analysis of security protocols is hence converted into computing the frequency and confidence of inconsistent secure messages.

4 Association Rule Mining for Inconsistent Secure Messages

For simplicity, only data security such as authentication and integrity is considered in this article. Also, it assumes that messages are fresh, generated and sent by the sender and received and seen by whom it claims to be, and principal's public keys are valid. The details can be found in [1,8] and will not be mentioned here.

4.1 The Basics of Association Rule Mining

An association rule is an implication of the form, $A \rightarrow B$, where A and B are itemsets, and $A \cap B = \emptyset$ [3]. *Support* for a rule $A \rightarrow B$ is the percentage of transactions in D that contains $A \cup B$, defined as $supp(A \cup B)$; and *confidence* for a rule $A \rightarrow B$ is defined as $conf(A \rightarrow B) = supp(A \cup B)/ supp(A)$.

According to the support-confidence framwork in [4], a rule $A \rightarrow B$ is of interest if $supp(A \cup B) \geq minsupp$ and $conf(A \rightarrow B) = \geq minconf$. Due to

Piatetsky-Shapiro's argument, the rule $A \to B$ can be extracted as a valid rule of interest if $|\frac{supp(A \cup B)}{supp(A)*supp(B)} - 1| \geq mininterest$, where *minsupp*, *minconf* and *mininterest* are specified by users or experts. The identification of rules consists of two phases: (1) extracting all frequent itemsets; and (2) generating rules in terms of discovered frequent itemsets.

4.2 Mining Inconsistent Secure Messages

Data preprocessing is needed to convert secure messages to the form of items. Suppose $D = \{D_1, \cdots, D_n\}$ is a set of transaction databases. Each database consists of a collection of secure messages. Let $I = \{x \mid x \in D_i, 1 \leq i \leq n\}$ be a set of items. $A \subseteq I$ and $B \subseteq I$ are itemsets. A rule $A \to B$ has *support*, s in the set of transaction databases if $s\%$ of transaction databases contains $A \cup B$. The association rule has *confidence*, c in the set of transaction databases if $c\%$ of transaction databases containing A also contains $A \cup B$.

Example 1. To register an account, a cardholder needs to fill out the registration form issued by *CA* with information such as the *cardholder's name, date of birth, expiration date* and *account billing address*. Let $I = \{cardholder's\ name,\ date\ of\ birth,\ expiration\ date,\ account\ billing\ address\}$ be the set of items. Hence we can say $\{cardholder's\ name,\ date\ of\ birth\}$ and $\{expiration\ date,\ account\ billing\ address\}$ are itemsets as usual.

Suppose a transaction $T = D_1 \cup D_2 \cup \ldots \cup D_n$ comprises n transaction databases, in which D_i ($1 \leq i \leq n$) may be sender, receiver or the third party. Let φ be a public key. If D_i contains φ and believes its freshness or validity, itemset φ has local support from D_i, namely $D_i \models \varphi$. The global support of itemset φ actually integrates the local support from all databases in T.

Definition 1. *Suppose D_i, $1 \leq i \leq n$, is a database in T. Let φ be an itemset and $\varphi(D_i) = \{D_i\ in\ T \mid D_i\ contains\ \varphi\}$. Let the global support of φ be $supp(\varphi)$.*

$$supp(\varphi) = \sum_{i=1}^{n} |\varphi(D_i)|/|T| \qquad (1)$$

An association rule is the implication $\chi: A \to B$, where $A \cap B = \emptyset$. Therefore, the confidence of the rule $A \to B$ is

$$conf(A \to B) = \frac{\sum_{i=1}^{n} |\chi(D_i)|/|T|}{supp(A)} \qquad (2)$$

Example 2. In an online booking, a user needs to fill out a form with *credit card number, key k, amount* and *address*. They are encrypted and sent to merchant *Y*. Initially, *Y* needs to authenticate the received message via the third party such as financial institutions. Suppose $D_1 = \{card\_number,\ k,\ amount,\ address\}$, $D_2 = \{card\_number,\ k,\ amount\}$ and $D_3 = \{card\_number,\ k,\ address\}$ are transaction databases. Let $minsupp = 50\%$, $minconf = 60\%$ and $mininterest = 0.07$. We have $supp(\{card\_number, k, amount\}) = 2/3 > 0.5$, $supp(\{card\_number, k\}) = 1 > 0.5$, $supp(\{amount\}) = 2/3 > 0.5$, $conf(\{card\_number, k\} \rightarrow \{amount\}) = 2/3 > 0.6$ and $|\frac{supp(card\_number,k,amount)}{supp(card\_number,k)*supp(amount)} - 1| < mininterest$. Hence $\{card\_number, k\} \rightarrow \{amount\}$ is not a valid rule of interest.

The derived rule also indicates that this transaction is unreliable and insecure and the occurrence of lost and tampered messages is high. The lower the inconsistency between secure messages is, the higher the support and confidence of association rules are.

In particular, keys are unlike the general secure messages for their confidentiality. For example, in public-key cryptography, each principal has a pairs of keys: a public key and a private key. Usually, the former is known to everyone but the latter is only known by the holder. Nobody can forge his signature without knowledge of his/her private key. Therefore, for each public/private key pair, *private key* and *public key* are viewed as identical items when computing support or confidence.

Example 3. For example, suppose $A = \{K_p(X), password\}$ and $A' = \{K^{-1}(X), password\}$ are two itemsets. A and A' are hence viewed as identical itemsets.

As mentioned above, if secure messages in an itemset were lost or tampered or public/private key pairs were not counterpart it would lead to the decrease of occurrence of the itemset. The degree of support and confidence on relevant rules will decrease too. Therefore, if an association rule is not a rule of interest it is natural to say that the corresponding transaction is insecure.

Definition 2. *Suppose $D \in \{D_S, D_R, D_T\}$ are transaction databases, and A and B are two itemsets of T, $A \subseteq D$, $B \subseteq D$ and $A \cap B = \emptyset$.*

1. $belief(A \rightarrow B) = $ "*secure*", *if* $supp(A \cup B) \geq minsupp$, $conf(A \rightarrow B) \geq minconf$ *and* $|\frac{supp(A \cup B)}{supp(A)*supp(B)} - 1| \geq mininterest$;
2. $belief(A \rightarrow B) = $ "*insecure*", *otherwise*.

The belief in $A \rightarrow B$ indicates the degree of reliability of transaction T. The parameters including $minsupp$, $minconf$ and $mininterest$ can be regulated to achieve different levels of security. Consequently, the verification of protocols can be converted into measuring the *support* and *confidence* of corresponding association rules. Therefore, it provides a novel way to analyze security protocols.

4.3 Experiments

The transaction here illustrates a customer orders some commodities from electronic storefronts via e-commerce system based on SET protocol. It starts with the *cardholder* who holds a payment card. The *third parties* here include the financial institution and the processor of transactions. SET aims at providing confidentiality of information, ensuring payment integrity, and authenticating both merchants and cardholders.

The selected data correspond to the *purchase request* in the protocol. When the cardholder sends purchase request he should have approved the contents and terms. In addition, the cardholder will have selected a payment card (*PC*) as the means of payment. The order starts when the cardholder software requests a copy of the gateway's certificate.

1. The cardholder C verifies the merchant's and payment gateway's certificates from merchant and holds these certificates for later use.
2. The cardholder generates Order information (*OI*) and Payment instructions (*PI*). The cardholder software generates a digital signature on concatenating *OI* and *PI* and encrypts the signature using a random symmetric encryption key k. The cardholder account number $Acct(C)$ and k are encrypted by the Payment Gateway's key exchange key $K_p(P)$. Finally, C sends them to the merchant M.
3. M verifies the cardholder signature certificates and the signature on *OI* and *PI*. After processing *OI*, M generates a purchase response message, including the merchant signature certificate and confirmation of receiving cardholder's order, and digitally signs it. The response is then sent to C.
4. C verifies the merchant's signature certificate and digital signature.

The transmitted message in above transaction mainly include *OI*, *PI*, k, $Acct(C)$, $K^{-1}(P)$, $K_p(P)$, $K^{-1}(M)$, $K_p(M)$ $K^{-1}(C)$ and $K_p(C)$. D_C, D_M, D_{T_1} and D_{T_2} represent transaction databases from *Cardholder*, *Merchant* and *Third parties* respectively. Table 1 presents the data of them.

Table 1. Purchase Request in SET

	OI	*PI*	$K(C)$	$K(M)$	$K_p(P)$	k	$Acct(C)$
D_C	*OI*	*PI*	$K^{-1}(C)$	$K_p(M)$	$K_p(P)$	k	$Acct(C)$
D_M	*OI*	¬*PI*	$K_p(C)$	$K^{-1}(M)$	null	null	null
D_{T_1}	*OI*	*PI*	$K_p(C)$	$K_p(M)$	null	null	null
D_{T_2}	¬*OI*	*PI*	$K_p(C)$	$K_p(M)$	null	null	null

In Table 1, ¬ represents the message can be missing or tampered. *null* means the message is encrypted and unknown to the transaction database. For example, the message including $K_p(P)$, k and $Acct(C)$ is actually sent to payment gateway for authentication. Therefore, they are unknown to D_M, D_{T_1} and D_{T_2}. On the other hand, this transaction focuses on authenticating *OI* and *PI*. The irrelevant itemsets are thus pruned from identifying association rules.

FP-tree algorithm [5] is used to discover frequent patterns (frequent itemsets) here. Let $minsupp = 50\%$, $minconf = 60\%$ and $mininterest = 0.07$. For simplicity, we use $K(X)$ to represent X's Public/Private key pairs below.

According to Table 1, we have $supp(K(C) \cup K(M)) = 4/4 = 1 > minsupp$, $supp(K(C) \cup K(M) \cup OI \cup PI) = 2/4 = 0.5 \geq minsupp$, $conf(K(C) \cup K(M) \rightarrow OI \cup PI) = 2/4 < minconf$; $supp(K(C) \cup K(M) \cup OI) = 3/4 > minsupp$,

$supp(PI) = 3/4 > minsupp$, $conf(K(C) \cup K(M) \cup OI \to PI) = 2/3 > minconf$ and $|\frac{supp(K(C),K(M),OI,PI)}{supp(K(C),K(M),OI)*supp(PI)} - 1| = 0.11 > mininterest$; $supp(K(C) \cup K(M) \cup PI) = 3/4 > minsupp$, $supp(OI) = 3/4 > minsupp$, $conf(K(C) \cup K(M) \cup PI \to OI) = 2/3 > minconf$ and $|\frac{supp(K(C),K(M),OI,PI)}{supp(K(C),K(M),PI)*supp(OI)} - 1| = 0.11 > mininterest$. This transaction is insecure for $K(C) \cup K(M) \to OI \cup PI$ is not a rule of interest. Another two rules indicate the potential correlation between $\{K(C), K(M), PI\}$ and $\{OI\}$, and between $\{K(C), K(M), OI\}$ and $\{PI\}$, which in fact imply latent flaws in security protocols. Although there are other association rules they are ignored here. From the observation, association rule mining can complement the analysis of security protocols and discover potential associations between secure messages.

5 Conclusions

The increasingly complicated security protocols challenge the traditional formal approaches to analyze security protocols. Besides, inconsistent secure messages have been prevalent in electronic transactions for the hostile environments. This paper presents how to use association rule mining to analyze security protocols. The freshness and dynamics of secure messages and principal's public key are taken into account before extracting frequent patterns. Derived association rules assist in not only measuring the reliability of transactions but also discovering potential correlations between secure messages. Experiments demonstrate our approaches are novel and promising in analyzing security protocols.

Acknowledgements

The work reported in this paper was partially supported by the Australian Research Council's Discovery Project Grants DP0559251.

References

1. Burrows M., Abadi M., Needham R., A logic for Authentication, *ACM Transactions on Computer Systems*, 8(1), pp 18-36, February 1990.
2. Heintze N., Tygar J., Wing J., and Wong H., Model Checking Electronic Commerce Protocols, *Proceedings of the 2nd USENIX Workshop on Electronic Commerce*, pp 147-164, Oakland, California November, 1996.
3. Chengqi Zhang and Shichao Zhang., Association Rule Mining: Models and Algorithms, LNAI 2307, Springer-Verlag, Germany 2002.
4. Agrawal R., Imielinski T., and Swami A., Database mining: A performance perspective. *IEEE Transaction. Knowledge and Data Eng*, 5(6), pp 914-925, 1993.
5. Han J., Pei J. and Yin Y., Mining frequent patterns without candidate generation, *Proceedings of the ACM SIGMOD International Conference on Management of Data*, pp 1-12, 2000.

3 Proposed Methods

Most of the association rule mining algorithms use support and confidence to specify the range and precision of an association rule [2]. Earlier researchers emphasize the importance for considering these threshold values when dealing with redundant rules [3, 8, 12 and 13]. Therefore in our proposed methods we also consider confidence and support value of each rule before we discard any redundant rule. All of our proposed methods verify subset of each antecedent and consequence itemset to identify redundant rules. Thus, it is not only able to find redundant rules but also never forces to drop any higher confidence or interest rule while eliminating redundant rules. Since we divide all discovered association rules into two groups and then find redundant rules each of them. Therefore, for better understanding here in the following figure 2 we are showing a sample dataset 2(a), all frequent itemsets 2(b) and rules 2(c) that have 50% support and 60% confidence and later we will refer this figure to find redundant rules.

Database

Transaction	Items
1	A C T W
2	C D W
3	A C T W
4	A C W
5	A C D T W
6	A W

(a)

Frequent Itemsets ($min\_sup = 50\%$)

Support	Items
100%(6)	W
83%(5)	A, AW, C, CW
67%(4)	AC, ACW
50%(3)	AT, ATW, TW, ACT, CT, CTW, ACTW,T

(b)

Rules	Freq. Itemset	Supp.	Conf.	Rules	Freq. Itemset	Supp.	Conf.	Rules	Freq. Itemset	Supp.	Conf.
A → C	AC	67	80	TW → AC	ACTW	50	100	W → A	AW	83	83
C → A	AC	67	80	T → ACW	ACTW	50	100	T → C	TC	50	100
AC → T	ACT	50	75	AC → W	ACW	67	100	CT → W	CTW	50	100
AT → C	ACT	50	100	AW → C	ACW	67	80	TW → C	CTW	50	100
CT → A	ACT	50	100	A → CW	ACW	67	80	T → CW	CTW	50	100
T → AC	ACT	50	100	CW → A	ACW	67	80	C → W	CW	83	100
ACT → W	ACTW	50	100	C → AW	ACW	67	80	W → C	CW	83	83
ACW → T	ACTW	50	75	T → A	AT	50	100	T → W	TW	50	100
AC → TW	ACTW	50	75	AT → W	ATW	50	100	A → T	AT	50	60
ATW → C	ACTW	50	100	TW → A	ATW	50	100	C → T	CT	50	60
AT → CW	ACTW	50	100	T → AW	ATW	50	100	CW → T	CTW	50	60
CTW → A	ACTW	50	100	A → W	AW	83	100	C → TW	CTW	50	60
CT → AW	ACWT	50	100	C → ATW	ACTW	50	60	AW → T	ATW	50	60
A → CTW	ACTW	50	60	AW → CT	ACTW	50	60	A → TW	ATW	50	60
C → AT	ACT	50	60	A → CT	ACT	50	60	CW → AT	ACTW	50	60

(c)

Fig. 2. Sample dataset, frequent itemset and rules

3.1 Rules with Multiple Consequence Items

In this section, we will find redundant rules that have multiple items in the consequence. For example, consider a rule $A \rightarrow B\ C$ has 2 items in the consequent. Suppose if two rules such as $A \rightarrow B$ and $A \rightarrow C$ also satisfy user specified support and confidence. However consequent itemset of the latter rules are the proper subset of consequent itemset of the former rule. For simplicity, we named rules that have multiple items in the consequence, here in this case A→B C as *proper* rule, and rules that have subset of consequent itemset A→B and A→C as *sub-consequence* rule.

Since both proper and sub-consequence rules satisfy user specified confidence and express the same meaning because of the following facts: (1) the antecedent of those rules are the same and (2) consequent of each sub-consequence rule is a proper subset of consequent of the proper rule. Thus, one set of rules become redundant in the presence of the other. To find which set of rules we should consider as redundant, we propose the following analogies:

3.1.1 Total Dominance

The itemset of proper and it corresponding sub-consequence rules not always have the same support thus the confidence of those groups of rules may not be the same. If a proper rule rules dominates its sub-consequence rules in both support and confidence then that proper rule is known as total dominance rule or vice versa. Though both proper and sub-consequent rules have the same antecedent itemset but the sub-consequence rules have minimal items in the consequent thus here only the sub-consequence rules dominate its proper rule in support and confidence. Since the sub-consequence rules have higher support and confidence than the proper rule hence the proper rule is considered as redundant.

Example: Suppose a proper rule W→A C and its sub-consequence rules W→A and W→C as shown in figure 2. As we can see from figure 2, both sub-consequence rules W→A and W→C have higher support and confidence than the proper rule W→A C. Since sub-consequence rules express the same meaning of the proper rule and both W→A and W→C also has higher support and confidence than the corresponding proper rule, consequently the proper rule is considered as redundant.

3.1.2 Partial Dominance

A proper rule may have up to n number of sub-consequence rules. If several sub-consequence rules but not all dominates its corresponding proper rule in confidence value, then we called these sub-consequence rules as *partial dominance* rules. Similar to total dominance, here we consider proper rules as redundant mainly because of several sub-consequence rule rules have a higher support than the proper rule, thus, those sub-consequence rules that have higher confidence. Therefore it is more appropriate to consider proper rule as redundant.

Example: From the figure 2 let us consider a proper rule A W→C T, and its corresponding sub-consequence rules, A W→T and A W→C. Despite all of these rules has a common antecedent itemset but the support and confidence of these rules are not equal. For example, the sub-consequence rule A W→C has a higher support and confidence than its proper rule A W→ C T, whereas the other sub-consequence rule, that is, A W→T has equal support and confidence to A W→C T. Since the sub-consequence rules are sufficient to express the meaning of its proper rule and at least one of the sub-consequence rules dominates its proper rule both in support and confidence. Therefore, the proper rule A W→ C T is considered as redundant.

3.1.3 Indifference Dominance

In many times we come across sub-consequence and proper rules that have the same support and confidence. Since proper rule and its corresponding sub-consequence have the same meaning thus one group of rule become redundant in the presence of the other. Here in this case we consider the sub-consequence rules as redundant because the proper rule summarizes the knowledge of several sub-consequence rules. Thus consider as more informative than sub-consequence rules.

Example: Similar to our previous example, let us first find a proper and its sub-consequence rules that fall into an indifference category, from figure 2. Let us consider a proper rule $T \rightarrow A\ C$ and its corresponding sub-consequence rules $T \rightarrow A$ and $T \rightarrow C$. Each of these rules not only has the same antecedent itemset but also has the same support and confidence. Since all rules have the same support and confidence, the proper rule is sufficient to convey the meaning of its sub-consequence rules thus we keep only the proper rule.

3.2 Rules with Multiple Antecedent Items

Association rule mining algorithms produce many rules that have common consequent itemset but different antecedent itemset. Indeed many of those antecedent itemsets are proper subset of others rules. For example, suppose three rules such as "*C $\rightarrow$ Database*", "*Java $\rightarrow$ Database*" and "*C, Java $\rightarrow$ Database*" satisfies user specified support and confidence. All three rules have the same consequent itemset however the antecedent itemset of former two rules is a proper subset of the latter rule. For simplicity, we name the group of rules that has subset antecedent itemset as *sub-antecedent* rules in this case "*C $\rightarrow$ Database*" and "*Java $\rightarrow$ Database*" and the other group as *proper rule* that is "*C, Java $\rightarrow$ Database*" in this case. Since the proper rule has n number of items in the antecedent, therefore each sub-antecedent rule set satisfies the following properties:

1. $\forall\ A' \subseteq A$, where A' is the antecedent itemset of sub-antecedent rule and A is antecedent itemset of the proper rule.
2. Union of antecedent itemset of sub-antecedent rules is the antecedent itemset of the proper rule.

The proper rule and its corresponding sub-antecedent rules have the same consequent itemset therefore in the presence of a proper rule the corresponding sub-antecedent rules become redundant or vice versa. Thus, it is necessary to remove one of the groups in the presence of the other group. To find which group of rules to be consider as redundant, we propose a similar type of analogies based on the support and confidence as state in the section 3.1.

3.2.1 Total Dominance

The total dominance rules are those rules that either dominates its sub-antecedent or proper rules in confidence. In general, the proper rule dominates its corresponding sub-antecedent rules when all itemset of those rules have equal support but the antecedent itemsets of sub-antecedent rules have higher support than the antecedent itemset of proper rule. The sub-antecedent rules dominate a proper rule when itemset of the sub-antecedent rules have higher support than itemset of the proper rule.

Since the proper or sub-antecedent rules could dominate other thus we keep only that group of rules that dominate the other in confidence. For example, if the proper rule dominates sub-antecedent rules then we only keep proper rule and exclude all sub-antecedent rules or vice versa. The rationale is that the confidence of a rule measures its interestingness, and here the rules that dominate the other always have higher confidence.

Example: The dataset we use here is small, we could find only a proper rule A C→T that dominates its sub-antecedent rules that is A→T and C→T totally in confidence as shown in the figure 2. Despite all itemsets of the sub-antecedent and proper rules have an equal support, but the confidence of the proper rule is higher. It is because the antecedent of proper rule has a lower support than the antecedent of the sub-antecedent rules.

3.2.2 Partial Dominance

The supports of all sub-antecedent rules are not equal, and therefore it is often found that sub-antecedent rules of a proper rule have different confidence value. If confidence value of any sub-antecedent rules dominates its proper rule, this implies that itemset of sub-antecedent rule not only have a higher confidence but also itemset of these rules appear in the dataset higher number of times. Hence it is more appropriate to keep those sub-antecedent rules. However, if the proper rule dominates some of the sub-antecedent rules and remaining sub-antecedent and the proper rules have equal confidence. Then, it is obvious that we should keep proper rules and discard sub-antecedent rules.

Example: The sub-antecedent rules such as A→C, W→C as shown in the figure 2 dominates its proper rule A W→C in the confidence value. The itemset of rule W→C has higher support and confidence than the proper rule A W→C, whereas the remaining sub-consequence rule A→C and proper rule A W→C both have equal support and confidence. Consequently, rule A W→C is considered as redundant in the presence of rules A→C and W→C. On the other hand, the proper rule A C W→T has three sub-antecedent rules such as A W→T, C W→T and A C→T. The proper rule A C W→T has higher confidence than first two sub-antecedent rules and remaining sub-antecedent rule and it have the equal confidence. Thus we can conclude in this case the proper rule partially dominates its sub-antecedent rules. Subsequently we keep only the proper rule and discard all sub-antecedent rules.

3.2.3 Indifference Dominance

If the sub-antecedent and its corresponding proper rule have an equal confidence then we called those sub-antecedent and proper rules as indifference dominate rules. Since the sub-antecedent rules express the same meaning of its proper rule or vice versa, thus, we can either keep the sub-antecedent rules or its corresponding proper rules.

Example: Consider the sub-antecedent rules A→W, C→W and proper rule A C→W shown in figure 2. Since all rules have equal confidence and the meaning of one group of rules can be exchanged by the other. However if we consider the support of those rules then we found the both itemset of sub-antecedent rules have higher support than the support of its corresponding proper rule itemset. Thus the proper rule A C→W is discarded and all sub-antecedent rules are kept.

4 Performance Study

We have done performance study on our proposed methods to conform our analysis of its effectiveness in eliminating redundant rules. We have chosen four datasets for this performance study. First two datasets were taken from the UC Irvine Machine Learning Dataset Repository [9]. The pumsb* datasets contain the census data with each transaction representation to answers to census questionnaires. The connect-4 dataset represents the different state of a game. The T10I4D100K is synthetic dataset, which mimic the transactions in a retailing environment and generated using IBM data generator. Finally, the BMS-Web-View-1 is a real world dataset contains several months worth of click stream data from an e-commerce web site and publicly available by Blue Martini Software [10]. It is worth to mention that many association rule mining algorithms [7, 13] had used all of these datasets as a benchmark.

In the following experiments we examine the level of redundancy (i.e. redundant rules) present in the resultant rule set. The benchmark for measuring the level of redundancy is referred to the redundancy ratio [3] and is defined as follows:

$$\text{Redundancy Ratio } (\partial) = \frac{\text{Total Rules Generated}(T)}{\text{Essential Rules } (E)} \ldots \ldots \ldots \quad (1)$$

$$\text{Essential Rules } (E) = T - R \ldots \ldots \quad (2)$$

where R is the total number of redundant rules present in the resultant rule set.

To find redundancy ratio, at first we use those datasets to generate frequent itemsets using the frequent itemset generation algorithm [11]. After generating frequent itemsets we use these itemsets for rule generation purpose. To generate association rules, we choose a publicly available traditional association rule

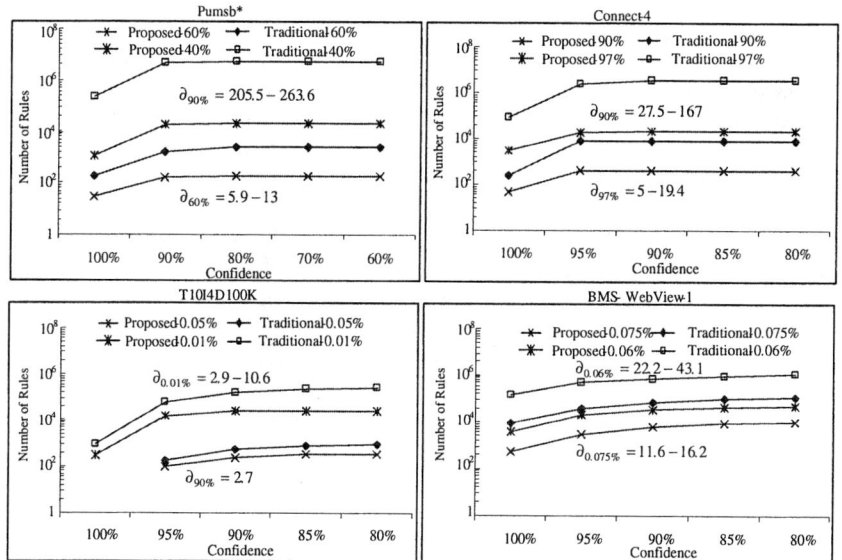

Fig. 3. Number of rule Proposed vs. Traditional

generation program [11]. Finally, we compare our proposed methods with the traditional approaches, and the results are as shown in figure 3.

Figure 3 compares the total number of rules generated by the traditional methods with our proposed methods. It also depicts the redundancy ratio. From the above graphs, it is clear that the proposed methods reduce the total number of rules drastically. It generates 2.7 to 263 times less number of rules compared with the traditional approach. The number of rules increases as the confidence decreases. In dense datasets, the curve indicating the number of rules and it becomes straight line after 90% confidence because most of the rules have above 90% confidence thus we could not found any additional rules though we decrease the confidence.

Since the traditional approach considers all possible subsets of a frequent itemsets as antecedent of a rule, it produces a large number of rules in all datasets regardless of the support threshold. However, our proposed methods verify every rule with a set of rules in order to find redundant rule. Therefore it only generates fewer rules from each frequent itemset. In addition, the total number of rules grows as the support threshold decreases, and subsequently the proposed methods reduce more number of redundant rules when the support thresholds are low.

The proposed methods reduce not only the number of redundant rules when the rules are generated from frequent itemsets but also reduce the redundant rules when the rules are generated from FCI. As mentioned in the section 2 that the FCI generates less number of itemsets than frequent itemset approach.

Table 1. Comparison between our proposed methods vs. the closed framework

Dataset	Support & Confidence	Proposed (no. of rules)	Closed (no. of rules)
connect-4	97%	314	1116
	90%	6116	18848
pumbs_star	60%	162	192
	40%	10087	13489
T40I10D100K	0.5%	574	1231
	0.1%	33500	86902

To confirm our claim that the proposed methods reduce redundant rules when the rules are generated from FCI, we conduct further experiments whereby our proposed methods generate rules from FCI. We compare our result with closed framework [7, 13] as shown in Table 1. From the table it is clear that the proposed method generate less number of rules than the closed framework. This is because the closed framework generates rules based on the concepts such as adjacent, up-arcs and down-arcs etc. Nevertheless these concepts fail to find redundant rules that have slightly different representations. In contrast our proposed methods rigorously check every single rule with a set of rules and hence we are able to remove more number of redundant rules.

5 Conclusion

In this paper we examine various reasons that cause redundancy problem in association rule mining. We have also proposed several methods to eliminate redundant rules. The proposed methods rigorously verify every single rule with a set of rules and eliminate redundant rules. Consequently it generates smaller number of rules from any given frequent itemsets compared to all traditional approaches. The experimental evaluation also suggests that the proposed methods not only theoretically eliminates redundant rules but also reduces such rules from real datasets.

References

1. Rakesh Agrawal, Tomasz Imielinski and Ramakrishnan Srikant "Mining Association Rules between Sets of Items in Large Databases", *In the proc. ACM SIGMOD*, 207-216, 1993.
2. Mohammed Javeed Zaki, "Parallel and Distributed Association Mining: A Survey", *IEEE Concurrency*, pp. 14-25, October-December 1999.
3. Charu C. Aggarwal and Philip S. Yu, "A new Approach to Online Generation of Association Rules". *IEEE TKDE*, **13**(4):527- 540.
4. Bing Liu, Minqing Hu and Wynne Hsu "Multi-Level Organization and Summarization of the Discovered Rules". *In the proc. KDD*, pp. 208-217, 2000.
5. Bing Liu, Wynne Hsu and Yiming Ma, "Pruning and Summarize the Discovered Associations". *In the proc. ACM SIGMOD*, pp. 125 134, San Diego, CA, August 1999.
6. Mika Klemettinen, Heikki Mannila, Pirjo Ronkainen, Hannu Toivonen and A. Inkeri Verkamo, "Finding Interesting Rules from Large Sets of Discovered Association Rules" *In Proc.CIKM*, pp. 401-407, 1994.
7. Mohammed Javed Zaki, "Generating non-redundant association rules" *In Proceeding of the ACM SIGKDD*, pp.34-43, 2000.
8. Bing Liu, Wynne Hsu and Yiming Ma, "Mining Association Rules with Multiple Minimum Supports". *In the proc. KDD*, pp. 337-341, 1999.
9. C. L. Blake and C. J. Merz. UCI Repository of Machine Learning Databases, University of California, Irvine, Dept. of Information and Computer Science, www.ics.uci.edu/~mlearn/MLRepository.html, 1998.
10. Ron Kohavi and Carla Brodley and Brian Frasca and Llew Mason and Zijian Zheng "KDD-Cup 2000 organizers report: Peeling the onion", *SIGKDD Explorations*, **2**(2):86-98, 2000, http://www.ecn.purdue.edu/KDDCUP/
11. Bart Goethals, Frequent Pattern Mining Implementations, University of Helsinki-Department of Computer Science, http://www.cs.helsinki.fi/u/goethals/software/.
12. Yves Bastide and Nicolas Pasquier and Rafik Taouil and Gerd Stumme and Lotfi Lakhal, "Mining Minimal Non-redundant Association Rules Using Frequent Closed Itemsets" *In Proc. 1st International Conference of Computational Logic*, **1861**:972, 2000.
13. Mohammed Javed Zaki, "Mining Non-Redundant Association Rules", *Data Mining and Knowledge Discovery*, vol. 9, 223-248, 2004.

Construction Algorithm of Principal Curves in the Sense of Limit

Lianwei Zhao[1], Yanchang Zhao[2], Siwei Luo[1], and Chao Shao[1]

[1] School of Computer and Information Technology, Beijing Jiaotong University,
Beijing 100044, China
lw_zhao@126.com
[2] Faculty of Information Technology, University of Technology, Sydney, Australia
yczhao@it.uts.edu.au

Abstract. Principal curves have been defined as self-consistent, smooth, one-dimensional curves which pass through the middle of a multidimensional data set. They are nonlinear generalization of the first Principal Component. In this paper, we take a new approach by defining principal curves as continuous curves based on the local tangent space in the sense of limit. It is proved that this new principal curves not only satisfy the self-consistent property, but also are the unique existence for any given open covering. Based on the new definition, a new practical algorithm for constructing principal curves is given. And the convergence properties of this algorithm are analyzed. The new construction algorithm of principal curves is illustrated on some simulated data sets.

1 Introduction

Finding low-dimensional manifold embedded in the high-dimensional space is a fundamental problem in the field of data mining, pattern recognition and computer vision. The research on this problem started as linear, and then as nonlinear parametric model, at last generated to the nonlinear non-parametric model. Meantime, there bring many mathematic problems, such as theory foundation, approximation algorithm and so on. Principal Curves are the nonlinear generalization of first principal components, and have been defined as smooth one-dimensional curves, which pass through the middle of a multidimensional data set. Although the description is intuitional, there are different definitions about the middle of data distribution. Principal curves were firstly introduced by Hastie and Stuetzle [1], and have been defined as satisfying the self-consistency property (HSPC). Tharpey and Flury[2] generalize the concept of self-consistency to random vectors, and then construct a unified theoretical basis for principal components, principal curves and surfaces, principal points, principal variables, and other statistical methods, and show the relationships between the various method. Tibshirani[3] gives an alternative definition of principal curves based on a mixture model, then carry out the estimation through EM algorithm. This model, however, has inducted parameters, and can not give the method to remove the bias of estimation, and in practice it does not satisfy the property of self-consistency. Kégl et al. [4] provide a new definition for principal curves with bounded length, and show that such curves exist for any distribution with bounded second moment. They also give an algorithm to implement the proposals, and calculate rates of convergence of the estimators. Due to the length constraint, the treatment does not encompass the case of classical principal component analysis. Delicado[5] introduces a new definition of principal curves based on the principal oriented points, proves the existence of principal curves passing through these points, and then proposes an algorithm to find the principal curves, but all the arguments are based on conditional expectation and variance. Chang[6] proposes an unified model as probabilistic principal surface (PPS) to address a number of issues associated with current algorithms using a manifold oriented covariance noise model, based on the generative topographical mapping (GTM), which can be viewed as a parametric formulation of SOM. In the past twenty years, the research on the principal curves around the middle property of data distribution has got excited progress, however, there are some open problems. For example, the existence of principal curves cannot be guaranteed for any distributions, and theoretical analysis is not as straightforward as with parametric models due to its nonparametric formulation. Duchamp and Stuetzle[7,8], José L. Martínez-Morales[9] study the differential geometry property of principal curves in the plane, find that the largest and the smallest principal components are extrema of the distance of expected distance from the data points, but all the principal curves are saddle points. This means that cross-validation can not be used to choose the complexity of principal curves estimates. By solving differential equation, they find that there are oscillating solutions and principal curves will not be unique. These conclusions indicate that the middle of data distribution lacks the sufficient theoretic support.

Therefore, we must turn back to consider the problem of nonlinear generalizations. There are two different ways in technology: one is that we can assume the data set obey some kind of distribution, and then find the statistical distribution model which is the best of the intrinsic structures describing this distribution. Manifold fitting, principal curves and GTM are the representative algorithms. Another is to transform the input data space, and then computer the linear component, such as kernel PCA. Principal component analysis is a widely used tool in multivariate data analysis for purposes such as dimension reduction and feature extraction. Now that principal curves are the nonlinear generalization of principal components, they can be used for reference more idea from linear PCA. PCA can be used to project the high-dimensional observed data to low-dimensional principal subspace, and the preconditions is that data set can be embedded in the global linear or approximation linear low-dimensional sub-manifold. So if the sub-manifold is nonlinear, PCA can not preserve the local information. Eliminating the statistical redundancy among the components of high-dimensional data with little information loss, is the main goal of finding low-dimensional representation. So in this problem, although the data distribution is nonlinear in global, can we think it as linear in local? And is it feasible in theoretic and algorithm?

In the following of this paper, we firstly introduce definition and construction algorithm of HSPC and discuss the property of self-consistency in Section 2. Then in Section 3, according to the relationship between the local tangent space and principal components, a new definition of principal curves is given in the sense of limit. We also prove that this principal curves satisfy the self-consistency property, and the existence of that curves for any given open covering. Based on this definition, a constructing algorithm of principal curves is proposed in Section 4. Our experimental results on simulate data sets are given in Section 5. Conclusions are provided in the last section.

2 Definition of HSPC and Self-consistency Property

2.1 Definition and Construction Algorithm of HSPC

Problem Description: Considering multivariate random variable $X = (X_1, X_2, \cdots, X_p)$ in R^p with density function $p_X(x)$ and a random sample from X, named $x_1, x_2, \cdots, x_n$, then how to find a one-dimensional smooth curves $f(\lambda)$, which pass through the middle of X?

The first principal component can be viewed as the straight line which best fits the clouds of data. Principal curves were firstly introduced by Hastie to formalize the notion of curves passing through the middle of a dataset.

Definition 1 (HSPC): Let $f(\lambda)$ be smooth curves in R^p, parametrized by $\lambda \in R$, and for any $\lambda \in R$, let projection index $\lambda_f(x)$ denote the largest parameter value λ for which the distance between x and $f(\lambda)$ is minimized, i.e., $\lambda_f(x) = \sup_\lambda \{\lambda : \|x - f(\lambda)\| = \inf_\mu \|x - f(\mu)\|\}$. Then principal curves are the curves satisfying the self-consistency property $E(X | \lambda_f(X) = \lambda) = f(\lambda)$.

Hastie has proved that the project index should be a random variable, and found the principal curves have the same property as principal component. But according to this definition, HSPC cannot be the self-intersecting curves. Given the density function of X, HS principal algorithm for constructing principal curves is given in the following:

Step 1: Set $f^{(0)}(\lambda)$ be the first principal component line for X, and set $j = 1$;

Step 2: Define $f^{(j)}(\lambda) = E(X | \lambda_{f^{(j)}}(X) = \lambda)$;

Step 3: Compute $\lambda_{f^{(j)}}(x) = \max\{\lambda : \|x - f^{(j)}(\lambda)\| = \min_\mu \|x - f^{(j)}(\mu)\|\}$, for all $x \in R^d$;

Step 4: Compute $\Delta(f^{(j)}) = E\|(X - f^{(j)}(\lambda_{f^{(j)}}(X))\|$. If $|\Delta(f^{(j)}) - \Delta(f^{(j-1)})| < threshold$, then stop. Otherwise, let $j = j+1$ and go to Step 2.

In practice, the distribution of X is often unknown, but the data set consisting of n samples from X is known, so the expectation in step 2 can be substituted by a smoother or non-parametric regression estimation.

2.2 Self-consistency Property

In HSPC, self-consistency is introduced to describe the property that each point on the smooth curves is the mean of all points projected onto it. Self-consistency is the fundamental property of principal curves, and then is generalized to define the self-consistent random vectors.

Definition 2: A random vector Y is self-consistent for X if each point in the support of Y is the conditional mean of X, namely $E(X|Y) = Y$.

For jointly distributed random vectors Y and X, the conditional mean $E(Y|X)$ is called the regression of Y on X. For the regression equation $Y = f(X) + \varepsilon$, where X is m-dimensional random variable, $f(\cdot)$ a function from R^m to R^n, ε is a n-dimensional random vector independent of X, and $E(\varepsilon) = 0$. Then $E(Y|f(X)) = f(X)$, that is, $f(X)$ is self-consistent for Y.

In practice, because we only have the finite data set, so the point projected on the principal curves is only one at most. Therefore Hastie introduces the conception of neighborhood and defines the point as conditional expectations of data set projected in the neighborhood. This definition also agrees with the mental image of a summary.

3 Definition of Principal Curves Based on Local Tangent Space

Consider $f(\lambda)$ is continuously differentiable curve, where $\lambda \in \text{supp}(\lambda)$. A Taylor series approximation about λ_0 is $f(\lambda) = f(\lambda_0) + J_f(\lambda_0)(\lambda - \lambda_0) + O(\|\lambda - \lambda_0\|^2)$, where $J_f(\lambda_0)$ is the Jacobian matrix. The tangent space of $f(\lambda)$ on λ_0 will be spanned by the column vectors of $J_f(\lambda_0)$. So the points in the neighborhood of $f(\lambda_0)$ can be approximated by $f(\lambda) \approx f(\lambda_0) + J_f(\lambda_0)(\lambda - \lambda_0)$. A new definition of principal curves is presented in the following:

Definition 3: Let $f(\lambda)$ be a smooth curves in R^p, parametrized by $\lambda \in R$. For any $\lambda \in R$, a cluster of neighborhood $\{B(\lambda_1, \delta_1), B(\lambda_2, \delta_2), \cdots, B(\lambda_k, \delta_k)\}$ is an open covering of λ, where $\lambda_i \in \lambda, i = 1, 2, \cdots, k$, ξ_i is the local tangent space vector of $f(\lambda)$ in the $B(\lambda_i, \delta_i)$. Let $P_{\xi_i}(x), x \in B(\lambda_i, \delta_i)$ be the projection on the ξ_i. If $\lim_{\delta \to 0} \sum_{i=1}^{k} P_{\xi_i}(x) \delta_i$ is existent, then $f(\lambda) = \lim_{\delta \to 0} \sum_{i=1}^{k} P_{\xi_i}(x) \delta_i$ is the principal curves, and satisfies the self-consistency property, where $\delta = \max_{i=1,2,\cdots,k} \{\delta_i\}$.

Some remarks on the above definition is given in the following.

a). Definition of principal curves is in the sense of limit.

Supposed random samples $x_1, x_2, \cdots, x_n$ is iid, and embedded on the smooth manifold M in R^p, and $x = f(\lambda)$, $\lambda \in R^m$, where, $m \ll p$. The mean of samples is $\bar{x}$, the covariance matrix is $Cov(X) = \frac{1}{n}\sum_{i=1}^{n}(x_i - \bar{x})(x_i - \bar{x})^T$. Wanli Min et al.[11] have proved that the eigenvectors of $Cov(X)$ can construct the tangent space of manifold M on $\bar{x}$. This indicates that the local tangent space can be approximated by the eigenvectors of the covariance matrix of samples, and in each local neighborhood, the topology structure can be preserved.

So for any $\lambda_i \in \lambda, i = 1, 2, \cdots, k$, its tangent vector can be approximated by the first eigenvectors ξ_i of covariance matrix of data points in the $B(\lambda_i, \delta_i), i = 1, 2, \cdots, k$.

So we have $\sum_{i=1}^{k} P_{\xi_i}(x)\delta_i \approx \sum_{i=1}^{k} J_f(\lambda_i)\delta_i$

Because $J_f(\lambda_i) = \frac{f(\lambda) - f(\lambda_i)}{\lambda - \lambda_i} - \frac{O(\|\lambda - \lambda_i\|^2)}{\lambda - \lambda_i}$, $\lim_{\lambda \to \lambda_0} J_f(\lambda_i) = \lim_{\lambda \to \lambda_0} P_{\xi_i}(x)$ is existent.

Then $\lim_{\delta \to 0}\sum_{i=1}^{k} P_{\xi_i}(x)\delta_i = \lim_{\delta \to 0}\sum_{i=1}^{k} J_f(\lambda_i)\delta_i = \int_{\lambda} J_f(\lambda)d\lambda = f(\lambda)$, where $\delta = \max_{i=1,2,\cdots,k}\{\delta_i\}$.

b). Satisfying the self-consistency property

Self-consistency is the fundamental property of principal curves, in the following we will show how this definition satisfying this property.

Suppose for given any neighborhood $B(\lambda_i, \delta_i)$, P is the orthogonal projection from R^p to its q linear subspace M. If $Y_i = (I - P)E(X_i) + PX_i$ is self-consistency for X_i, then M is spanned by the q eigenvectors of $Cov(X_i)$. If $P = \xi\xi'$, where ξ is the first principal components of $Cov(X_i)$, the $Y_i = (I - \xi\xi')E(X_i) + \xi\xi' X_i$ is self-consistency for X_i.

For any point $f(\lambda^*)$ on the $f(\lambda)$, $\{B(\lambda_1, \delta_1), B(\lambda_2, \delta_2), \cdots, B(\lambda_k, \delta_k)\}$ is an open covering for λ, so there exist a $\lambda_i \in \lambda, i = 1, 2, \cdots, k$, $f(\lambda^*) \in Y_i \subset B(\lambda_i, \delta_i)$, satisfying $E(X | \lambda_f(X) = \lambda^*) = f(\lambda^*)$. Therefore, $f(\lambda)$ is self-consistency.

c). For any given covering, there exists a principal curves which minimizes LRE

Suppose random vector X and Y, for any function g, $E\|X - E(X | Y)\| \leq E\|X - g(Y)\|$. Taking g to be the identity, then $E\|X - E(X | Y)\| \leq E\|X - Y\|$. Thus if $Y = E(X | Y)$, Y is local optimal for approximating X.

For the observed data sets, in every neighborhood $B(\lambda_i, \delta_i), i = 1, 2, \cdots, k$, the local reconstruction error LRE ($LRE_{ki} = \sum_{x_{ij} \in B(\lambda_i, \delta_i)} \|x_{ij} - \hat{x}_{ij}\|_2^2$) is minimal if and only if $\hat{x}_{ij} = \bar{x} + \xi_h \xi_h^T (x_{ij} - \bar{x})$, where ξ_k is the eigenvectors of the input covariance matrix corresponding to its largest eigenvalue.

Hence, for any given open covering, there exist curves which minimize the local reconstruction error.

4 Construction Algorithm of Principal Curves

In this section, we give a construction algorithm of principal curves based on the local tangent space, according to Definition 3. The algorithm of construct principal curves is described as following.

Step 1: Let neighborhood $\{B_k(\lambda_1,\delta_1), B_k(\lambda_2,\delta_2),\cdots,B_k(\lambda_k,\delta_k)\}$ be an open covering for sample;

Step 2: For the sample points $x_{i1}, x_{i2},\cdots,x_{in}$ in $B_k(\lambda_i,\delta_i), i=1,2,\cdots k$, compute the $E_{ki}(x)$, $Cov_{ki}(x)$, and $V_{kij}=(v_{i1},v_{i2},\cdots,v_{ij})$;

Step 3: Let $V_{ki}=\min\{V_{(k-1)l}{}^T v_{im}\}, m=1,\cdots,j$, where $V_{(k-1)l}$ denotes the principal eigenvector of covariance matrix of sample points in $B_{k-1}(\lambda_l,\delta_l)$, and $B_k(\lambda_i,\delta_i) \subset B_{k-1}(\lambda_l,\delta_l)$. Compute the projection of data point x_{ki} on V_{ki}, and reconstruction $\hat{x}_{ki}$;

Step 4: Connect $\hat{x}_{ki}$, and use the method for local smooth interpolation;

Step 5: Compute global reconstruction error GRE_k. If $GRE_k - GRE_{k-1} <$ threshold, then stop. Otherwise, let $k = k+1$, and go to Step 1.

Note about the convergence properties of this algorithm in the following:
For every $LRE_{ki} \geq 0$, the global least reconstruction error is

$$GRE_k = \sum_{i=1}^{k} LRE_{ki} = \sum_{i=1}^{k} \sum_{x_{ij} \in B(\lambda_i,\delta_i)} \left\|x_{ij} - \hat{x}_{ij}\right\|_2^2 = \sum_{i,j}\left\|x_{ij} - \bar{x} + \xi_h \xi_h^T (x_{ij} - \bar{x})\right\|_2^2, \text{ then}$$

$$GRE_k - GRE_{k-1} = \sum_{i,j}\left\|x_{ij} - \bar{x} + \xi_h \xi_h^T (x_{ij} - \bar{x})\right\|_2^2 - \sum_{i,j}\left\|x_{ij} - \bar{x} + \xi_{h-1} \xi_{h-1}^T (x_{ij} - \bar{x})\right\|_2^2$$

$$\leq \sum_{i,j}\left(\left\|x_{ij} - \bar{x} + \xi_h \xi_h^T (x_{ij} - \bar{x}) - x_{ij} + \bar{x} - \xi_{h-1} \xi_{h-1}^T (x_{ij} - \bar{x})\right\|_2^2\right)$$

$$= \sum_{i,j}\left(\left\|(\xi_h \xi_h^T - \xi_{h-1} \xi_{h-1}^T)(x_{ij} - \bar{x})\right\|_2^2\right)$$

For any continuous differential function $f(\lambda)$ and $\lambda_0 \in \text{supp}(\lambda)$, where λ is a compact subset of R., $B(\lambda_0,\delta_k)$ and $B(\lambda_0,\delta_{k-1})$ are two neighborhood of λ_0, and $B(\lambda_0,\delta_{k-1}) \subset B(\lambda_0,\delta_k)$. For any $\lambda_1 \in B(\lambda_0,\delta_k)$ and $\lambda_2 \in B(\lambda_0,\delta_{k-1})$,

$$\lim_{\lambda_1 \to \lambda_0} \left|\frac{f(\lambda_1)-f(\lambda_0)}{\lambda_1 - \lambda_0} - \frac{f(\lambda_2)-f(\lambda_0)}{\lambda_2 - \lambda_0}\right| = \left|\xi_k - \xi_{k-1}\right| = 0$$

Therefore, $GRE_k - GRE_{k-1} \to 0$.

5 Experimental Results

To test the algorithm presented above, we conducted experiments on several artificial data sets. Consider a random sample $x_1, x_2, \cdots, x_n$ from a multi-dimensional random variable X, suppose that a nonlinear curves is a good summary of the structure of the distribution of X and we try to recovering the curves from the observed samples $x_1, x_2, \cdots, x_n$.

5.1 Experiments on Continuous Function Without Noise

Consider $y = \sin(x), x \in [-2,2]$, the number of selected points is 400, and the number of neighborhood is 1, 2, 3, 10, respectively. In Fig. 1, we illustrate several stages of the principal curve constructing. And the result is promising, when k=10, we can see that the principal curves constructed with the proposed algorithm have approximated to the origin continuous functions.

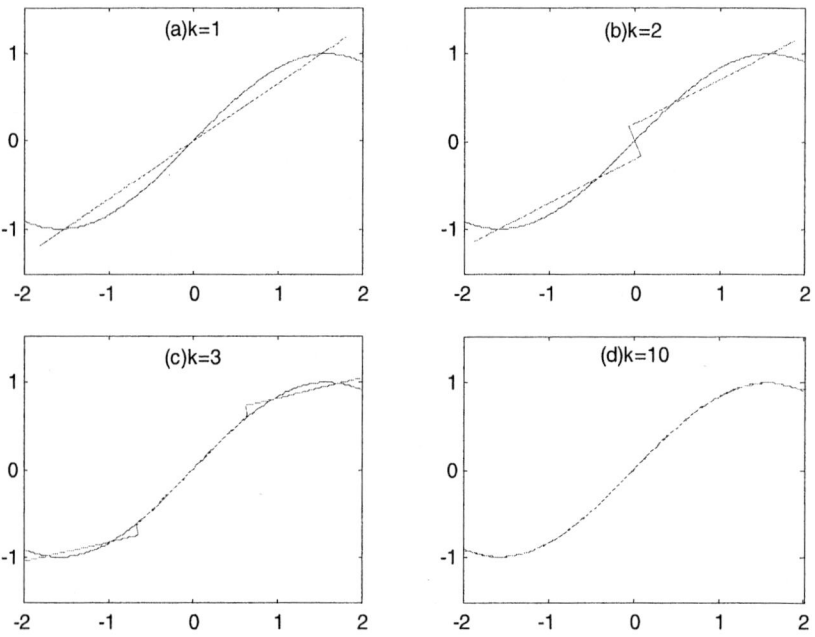

Fig. 1. Principal Curves. The data was generated by continuous function (sinusoid): (a)k=1, (b)k=2, (c)k=3, (d)k=10.

5.2 Experiments on Gaussian Distributions

Consider the two independent Gaussian distribution and randomly selected 100 points. We get the principal curves with k=2 and 5, as Fig. 2 shows. From these results, we can see the principal curves approximate to the principal component.

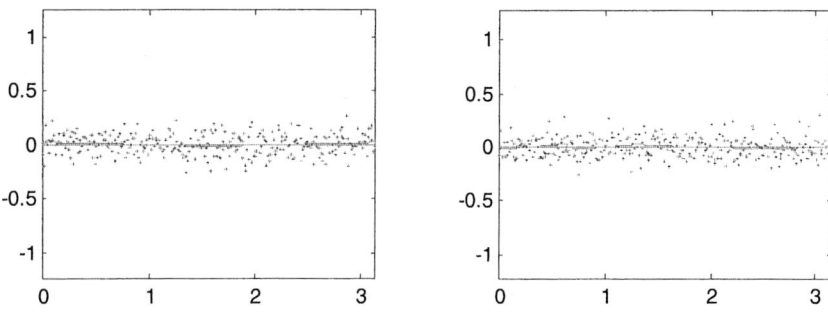

Fig. 2. The Principal Curves from elliptical distribution, with k=2(left) and k=5(right) respectively

5.3 Experiments on Continuous Function with Noise

Consider the $x = \sin\theta, y = \cos\theta, \theta \in [0, \pi]$, randomly select 200 points, and add independent Gaussian noise $\varepsilon_i \sim N(0, 0.1)$. Let k=1,2,4,40 respectively and we illustrate several stages of the principal curve constructing in fig. 3. The result is also promising, when k=40, we can see that the principal curves constructed with the proposed algorithm have approximated to the origin continuous functions with noise.

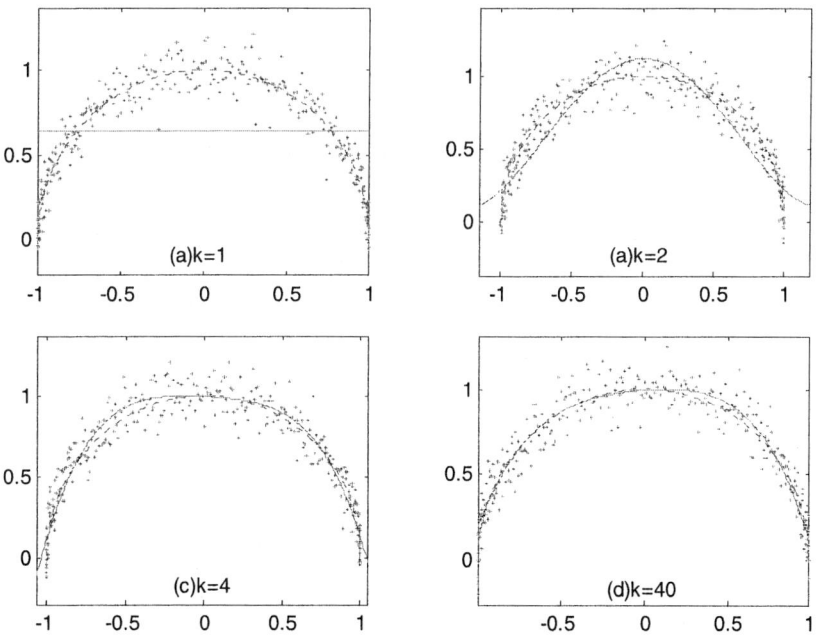

Fig. 3. The Principal Curves. The data was generated by adding independent Guassian noise on a half circle (a)k=1, (b)k=2, (c)k=4, (d)k=40.

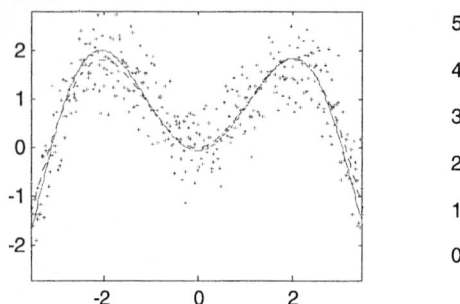 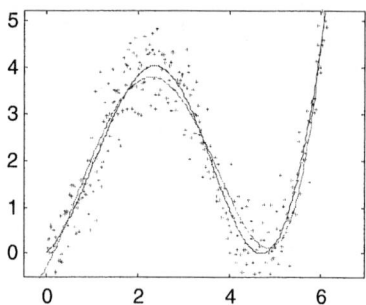

Fig. 4. The Principal Curves. The data was generated by adding independent Guassian noise on continuous function.

And in the fig.4, we give other two experiments results. Due to limited space we cannot present exhaustive experimental results but just some illustrations here.

6 Conclusions

For high-dimensional random vector, it is very important to find an approximation whose support is a low-dimensional manifold. Principal curves can be regard as one dimension principal manifold, and have been used for dimension reduction and pattern classification. In this paper based on the local tangent space, we give a new definition of principal curves in the sense of limit, and prove it is self-consistency. We also show for any given open covering, this principal curves exists. According to the definition, we give a construction algorithm of principal curves. Experimental results show that we can approximate to the true principal curves. In this paper we suppose the domain of principal curves is compact set and can be covered by finite open covering. How to find an open covering for more complex data set will be future work.

Acknowledgements

The research is supported by national natural science foundations of China (60373029).

References

1. Hastie T and Stuetzle W. Principal Curves. Journal of the American Statistical Association. 1989,84: 502-516.
2. Tarpey T and Flury B. Self-consistency: A fundamental concept in statistics. Statistical Science. 1996,11 (3): 229-243.
3. Tibshirani R. Principal Curves Revisited. Statistics and Computation. 1992,2:183-190.
4. Kégl B, Krzyzak A, Linder T and Zeger K. Learning and design of principal curves. IEEE Trans. on Pattern Analysis and Machine Intelligence. 2000,22 (3): 281-297.
5. Delicado P. Another Look at Principal Curves and Surfaces. Journal of Multivariate Analysis.2001,77:84-116.

6. Chang Kui-yu and Joydeep Ghosh. A Unified Model for Probabilistic Principal Surfaces. IEEE Trans. on Pattern Analysis and Machine Intelligence. 2001,23(1):22-41.
7. Duchamp T and Stuezle W. Geometric Properties of Principal Curves in the Plane. Robust Statistics. Data Analysis, and Computer Intensive Methods. 1995:135-152.
8. Duchamp T and Stuetzle W. Extremal Properties of Principal Curves in the Plane. Annals of Statistics. 1996,24 (4): 1511-1520.
9. José L. Martínez-Morales. Extremal Properties of Principal Embeddings. J. Math. Pures Appl.1999,78: 913-923.
10. Zhang Junping and Wang Jue. An Overview of Principal Curves. Chinese Journal of Computers. 2003,26(2):129-146.
11. Min Wanli, Lu Ke, He Xiaofei. Locality Pursuit Embedding. Pattern Recognition, 2004,37: 781-788.
12. Jos Koetsier, Ying Han, Colin Fyfe. Twinned principal curves, Neural Networks. 2004,17: 399-409.
13. Kambhatla N and Leen T.K. Dimension reduction by local principal component analysis. Neural Computation.1997, 9: 1493-1516.

Collateral Missing Value Estimation: Robust Missing Value Estimation for Consequent Microarray Data Processing

Muhammad Shoaib B. Sehgal, Iqbal Gondal, and Laurence Dooley

Faculty of IT, Monash University, Churchill VIC 3842, Australia
{Shoaib.Sehgal, Iqbal.Gondal, Laurence.Dooley}
@infotech.monash.edu.au

Abstract. Microarrays have unique ability to probe thousands of genes at a time that makes it a useful tool for variety of applications, ranging from diagnosis to drug discovery. However, data generated by microarrays often contains multiple missing gene expressions that affect the subsequent analysis, as most of the times these missing values are ignored. In this paper we have analyzed how accurate estimation of missing values can lead to better subsequent gene selection and class prediction. *Collateral Missing Values Estimation* (CMVE), which demonstrates superior imputation performance compared to *Bayesian Principal Component Analysis* (BPCA) Impute, *K-Nearest Neighbour* (KNN) algorithm, when estimating missing values in the BRCA1, BRCA2 and Sporadic genetic mutation samples present in ovarian cancer by exploiting both local/global and positive/negative correlation values. CMVE also consistently outperforms, in terms of classification accuracies, BPCA, KNN and *ZeroImpute* techniques. The imputation is followed by gene selection using fusion of *Between Group to within Group Sum of Squares* and *Weighted Partial Least Squares* where *Ridge Partial Least Square* algorithm is used as a class predictor.

1 Introduction

Microarrays have has wide range of applicability from diagnosis to drug discovery due to their ability to probe tens or thousands genes at a time [1, 2]. Despite this however, microarray data frequently contains missing values due to spotting problems, slide scratches, blemishes on the chip, hybridization error, image corruption or simply dust on the slide [3]. These missing values affect subsequent inference from: gene selection, class prediction and data dimension reducing techniques such as *Between Group to within Group Sum of Squares* (BSS/WSS) [4], *Neural Networks* (NN), *Support Vector Machines* (SVM), *Principal Component Analysis* (PCA) and *Singular Value Decomposition* (SVD) [5, 6]. Different strategies to solve the problem of missing data can be adopted. The simplest method is to repeat the process, though this is seldom feasible for economic reasons or ignoring those samples, containing missing values, though this again is not recommended due to limited number of samples available. The best strategy is to attempt to accurately estimate the missing values. Normally missing values are replaced with zero values which doesn't take advantage of data correlations, so leading to errors in the subsequent analysis [7]. However, if the correlation between data is exploited then the missing value prediction error can be significantly reduced [8].

Besides this, the number of samples m in microarray data is relatively much less than the number of genes n per sample (usually in thousands) that makes most of the classical class prediction methods to perform poorly and they overfit to the training data [9]. For example, FLD function in *Fisher Linear Discriminant* (FLD) Analysis is singular when $m < n + 2$ [10]. In spite of this if the genes are included for class prediction by classifiers; it includes the associated noise of the data resulting in lower prediction accuracy. This problem can be solved if feature selection is applied to the data.

Most feature selection algorithms are dimension reduction techniques, for example PCA [1] and SVD, do not consider class discrimination while converting data to Eigen space resulting in lower class prediction accuracy. Alternatively, univariate algorithms are used, for example; t-test, signal to noise ratio [11], BSS/WSS [4], *Significance Analysis of Microarray* (SAM) [12] which are either made for binary class response or they consider each relevant gene individually which selects the genes which are highly correlated which it introduces redundancy [13]. The problem can be avoided if multivariate gene selection is applied to simultaneously consider multiple genes and class information, hence reducing redundancy of covariate genes and keeping the class discrimination intact. However, if multivariate method is coupled with class prediction accuracy then it is highly dependent on learning method [13]. Therefore, a suitable strategy is required which can predict the missing values and also can minimize the problems in feature selection techniques.

In this paper we have proposed an innovative solution to the aforementioned problems by applying the recently introduced *Collateral Missing Value Estimation* (CMVE) algorithm [14] that not only guarantees lower prediction error than *Bayesian PCA* (BPCA), *ZeroImpute* and *K Nearest Neighbour* (KNN), but has also increased the classification accuracy for the range of missing values from 1-20% for multiclass ovarian cancer data [15]. To select significant genes, a two fold strategy is applied which uses both univariate and multivariate methods by stacking both algorithms. The p discriminant genes are first selected by univariate BSS/WSS to gain the advantage of model independence and then redundant genes are removed by *Weighted Partial Least Square Method* (WPLS). The other benefit of applying BSS/WSS prior to WPLS is that it reduces computational time by selecting a smaller search space for WPLS. For classification *Ridge Partial Least Squares* (RPLS) is applied by regressing significant genes with ridge penalty [16]. The motivation to employ RPLS came from its better prediction ability than other classification algorithms for multi-class microarray data.

The rest of the paper is organized as follows: Section 2 briefly presents methods for Imputation, Gene Selection and Classification used in this paper. Section 3 analyzes empirical results while conclusions are drawn is Section 4.

2 Review of Gene Selection, Missing Value and Classification Algorithms

The following convention is adopted throughout this paper to present Imputation, Gene Selection and Classification techniques. $Y \in \mathbb{R}^{m \times n}$ is assumed to be the gene expression matrix, where m is the number of genes and n is the number of samples. In Y, every gene I is represented by $g_I \in Y$, so Y in n experiments is organized as:-

$$Y = \begin{bmatrix} g_1^T \\ \vdots \\ g_m^T \end{bmatrix} \in \mathbb{R}^{m \times n}. \quad (1)$$

A missing value in gene I for sample J is expressed as:-

$$Y(I,J) = g_I(J) = \Xi. \quad (2)$$

Following three Sections outline the Collateral Missing Value Estimation, BSS/WSS Gene Selection and RPLS Class Prediction techniques.

2.1 Collateral Missing Value Estimation

Collateral Missing Value Estimation (CMVE) algorithm estimates missing values using multiple estimation matrices with *Least Square Regression* (LS), *Non Negative LS* and *Linear Programming* (LP), by regressing k-ranked covariate genes $\partial \in \mathbb{R}^{k \times n}$. CMVE imputes missing values by merging three estimation matrices Φ_1, Φ_2 and Φ_3, computed using LS, NNLS and LP. To estimate Φ_1 for g_{IJ}, LS regression method [17] is used. LS regression problem for $Y \in \mathbb{R}^{m \times n}$ be expressed as:-

$$\Phi_1 = \varsigma + \rho Y + \xi, \quad (3)$$

where ξ is the error term that minimizes the variance in the LS model, ς and ρ are unknown coefficients obtained by minimizing least square error. To estimate Φ_2 and Φ_3 CMVE finds a linear combination of models that best fit ∂ and g_I using NNLS algorithm such as:-

$$\Phi_2 = \sum_{i=1}^{k} \phi + \eta - \sum_{i=1}^{k} \xi^2, \quad (4)$$

$$\Phi_1 = \frac{\sum_{i=1}^{k} (\phi^T \times g_I)}{k} + \eta, \quad (5)$$

where ϕ is the vector that minimizes ξ_0 in (6), η is the normal residual and ξ is the actual residual. The objective function in NNLS minimizes, using linear programming techniques, the prediction error ξ_0 so that:-

$$\xi, \phi, \eta = \min(\xi_0), \tag{6}$$

that is $\min(\xi_0)$ is a function that locates the normal vector ϕ with minimum prediction error ξ_0 and residual η. The value of ξ_0 in (6) is obtained from:-

$$\xi_0 = \max(SV(\beta.\phi - g_I^T)), \tag{7}$$

where SV are the singular values of the difference vector between the dot product β and prediction coefficients ϕ with the gene expression g_1^T. The final estimate χ for Ξ is formed using:-

$$\chi = \Upsilon.\Phi_1 + \Delta.\Phi_2 + \Lambda.\Phi_3, \tag{8}$$

where probabilities where $\Upsilon=\Delta=\Lambda= 0.33$ ensures an equal weighting to the respective estimates Φ_1, Φ_2 and Φ_3. The rationale for this choice is that as each estimate is highly data dependent, it avoids any bias towards one particular estimate [8]. CMVE derives its superior imputation performance over BPCA and KNN by considering both local/global and positive correlations [14], coupled together with a unique self-correcting error property, which guards against the danger of a wildly initial predictions of the missing values [14].

2.2 Between Group to Within Group Sum of Squares

This gene selection method identifies those genes which have large inter-class variations while concomitantly having small intra-class variations. For any gene I in $Y \in \mathbb{R}^{m \times n}$ BSS/WSS is calculated as follows:-

$$BSS(I)/WSS(I) = \frac{\sum_{t=1}^{T} \sum_{q=1}^{Q} F(L_t = q)(\bar{Y}_{ql} - \bar{Y}_I)^2}{\sum_{t=1}^{T} \sum_{q=1}^{Q} F(L_t = q)(Y_{It} - \bar{Y}_{ql})^2}, \tag{9}$$

where T is the size of a training sample, Q is the number of classes *and $F(\bullet)$* is a Boolean function which results in 1 if the condition is true, and zero otherwise, $\bar{Y}_J$ denotes the average expression level of gene I across all samples and $\bar{y}_{ql}$ is the average expression level of gene I across all samples belonging to class q. The genes G are ranked from highest to lowest BSS/WSS ratios to form significant gene expression matrix ϑ. The first p genes are then selected from ϑ for subsequent class prediction. It is followed by Weighted Partial Least Square (WPLS) to eliminate correlated genes from p. The motivation to select genes using BSS/WSS and then WPLS is that BSS/WSS does not select multiple genes simultaneously and hence account for dependency between the genes. Also, BSS/WSS ignores the model uncertainty by predicting set of relevant genes and then predicting relevant class [18]. WPLS accounts for model uncertainty by considering class prediction accuracy. However, if only WPLS is used then selected genes are highly dependent on prediction model [13]. Another reason for employing BSS/WSS is that the gene to sample ratio is reduced, so resulting in a shorter convergence time for WPLS.

2.3 Ridge Partial Least Squares

Ridge Partial Least Squares (RPLS) method uses *Partial Least Squares* (PLS) with the *Penalized Logistic Regression* (PLR) for class prediction. To apply PLS for class prediction, class labels are replace by a pseudo-response variable that has expected value in linear relationship with the covariates because PLS can only handle continuous responses. Therefore, in order to extend PLS to Generalized Linear Models, RPLS replaces pseudo-response variable Z^∞ at the convergence of *Iterative Reweighted Least Square* (RIRLS) algorithm with ridge penalty. The other advantage of choosing Z^∞ is that this allows the combination of a regularization and dimension-reduction step. RPLS comprises of three major steps:-

1- Pseudo-response variable Z^∞ and weighted matrix W^∞ are computed using:-

$$(Z^\infty, W^\infty) = RIRLS(L, Y, \lambda), \tag{10}$$

where λ is some positive real constant which is calculated by minimizing the *Bayesian Information Criterion* (BIC) [19] and L is a set containing discrete class labels.

2- Matrices Z^∞ and W^∞ are then used to compute $\hat{\alpha} \in \mathbb{R}^{p+1}$ by WPLS method using:-

$$\hat{\alpha}^{PLS,\kappa} = WPLS(Z^\infty, Y, W^\infty, \kappa), \tag{11}$$

where Y is the input matrix and κ is a positive integer which determines number of iterations.

3- Finally, class response is determined using *Linear Logistic Discrimination* (LLD). In LLD the conditional class probability of response L for a given data Y is:-

$$P(L = 1 | Y = y; \hat{\alpha}), \tag{12}$$

where parameter $\hat{\alpha} \in \mathbb{R}^{p+1}$ is estimated using (11) and p are number of predictor genes determined using BSS/WSS (Section 2.2). The probability P in (12) is computed using:-

$$P(L = 1 | Y = y; \hat{\alpha}) = h([1 \ y]\hat{\alpha}), \tag{13}$$

where $h(\eta) = 1/[1+exp(-\eta)]$. The quantity $h([1 \ y]\hat{\alpha})$ is a linear predictor. The log-likelihood of the observations for the parameter $\hat{\alpha}$ is given by:-

$$l(\hat{\alpha}) = \sum_{i=1}^{n} \{L_i \hat{v}_i(\hat{\alpha}) - \ln[1 + \exp(\hat{v}_i(\hat{\alpha}))]\}, \tag{14}$$

which for all $1 \leq i \leq n, \hat{v}_i(\hat{\alpha}) = (Z\hat{\alpha})_i$ and $Z = [\Upsilon_n \ Y]$ of size $n \times (p+1)$ and Υ_n is the column matrix of size n. The class label L is 1 if $\wp > 1-\wp$ and zero otherwise where

$$\wp = h([1 \ y]\hat{\alpha}). \tag{15}$$

3 Results Analysis

Well tested, ovarian cancer microarray data [20] was used as a test data in all the experiments. The motivation to use this data set is that cancer data contains up/down regulated genes and hence are difficult to predict using estimation algorithms [5]. The data set contained 18, 16 and 27 samples of BRCA1, BRCA2 and sporadic mutations (neither BRCA1 nor BRCA2) respectively. Each data sample contained logarithmic microarray data of 6445 genes. To quantitatively evaluate the performance of CMVE imputation technique, the following *imputation error* and *classification error* estimation measures were employed.

3.1 Imputation Error Measure

For the comparison of different imputation techniques, between 1% and 20% of the values were randomly removed from the BRCA1, BRCA2 and Sporadic dataset samples and the *Normalized Root Mean Square* (NRMS) imputation error ξ computed as:-

$$\xi = \frac{RMS(Y - Y_{est})}{RMS(Y)}, \tag{16}$$

where Y is the original data matrix and Y_{est} is the estimated matrix using either CMVE, BPCA or KNN. The advantage of using (16) for error estimation is that $\xi=1$ for zero imputation [5].

Different values of k were tested for both KNN and CMVE, with $k=10$ exhibiting the best results. The plots in Fig. 1(a-e) show the NRMS error in estimating randomly introduced missing values from 1% to 20% for BRCA1, BRCA2 and Sporadic datasets. The results confirm that CMVE performed better than BPCA and KNN (see Fig. 1(a-e)). It is also obvious from the graphs that CMVE exhibited improved robustness at higher missing values, with the reason for these improvements being traced back to the reason explained in Section 2.1, that CMVE exploits the relationship between gene expression values more effectively than BPCA and KNN by considering both global and local, as well as positive and negative data correlations.

3.2 Classification Error Measure

Missing values inevitably affect classification accuracy and gene selection, yet many classifiers only use zero imputation [8]. Our cross validation results show that with the proper estimation of missing values, the gene selection and classification accuracy can be significantly improved [12, 14]. So, for the proof of concept, an alternative way is to test imputation methods by randomly removing values from the data and testing the impact on decision making techniques such as gene selections and classification.

The estimation results in Fig. 2(a-f) confirm that CMVE consistently perform better than BPCA, KNN and *ZeroImpute*. The overall classification accuracy by CMVE (See Fig. (f)) clearly shows higher classification accuracy for the range of missing values from 1-20% when values are imputed using CMVE as compared to other estimation algorithms. The reason for this better performance is that CMVE exploits all

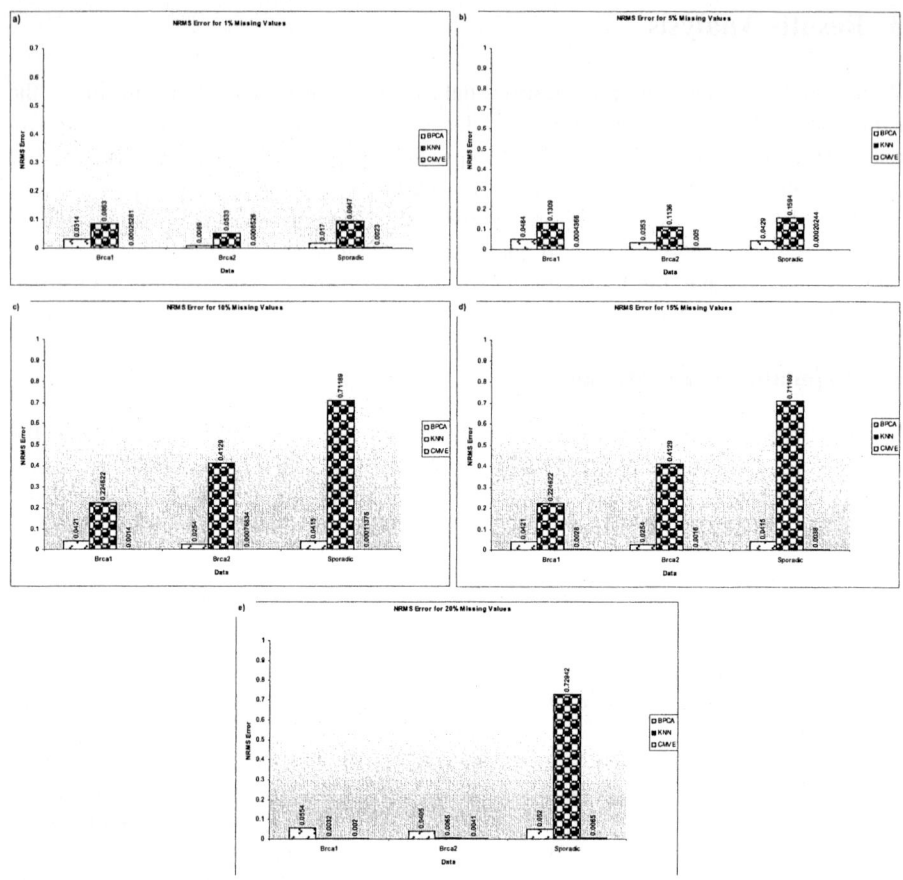

Fig. 1. NRMS Error for KNN, BPCA and CMVE for 1-20% Missing Values

types of correlation structure of the data as compared to KNN that only considers positive correlations, BPCA that only considers global correlation and *ZeroImpute* that doesn't consider any correlation.

Results in Fig. 2 (a-f) also draw attention to some interesting observation, RPLS followed by gene selection step, performed better when *ZeroImpute* was used as compared to KNN (See Fig. 2(f)). Because the data between classes was more separable and thus easier to classify, that is zero values actually improved separability. The other reason of poor performance of KNN is that if smaller k is used by KNN it increases the variance of the data leading to false selection of significant genes, however large value of k increases bias and leads to coarse estimates. In practice however, for the vast majority of datasets, zero imputation will not improve separability because for instance, if a particular gene has missing values, for both classes to be classified, *ZeroImpute* results in the same value, namely zero [5]. This means the gene has same value for both classes despite some genes being more significant than others. Also, BPCA performed better than KNN and *ZeroImpute* due to better estimation of missing values because of considering both positive and negative correlations [14].

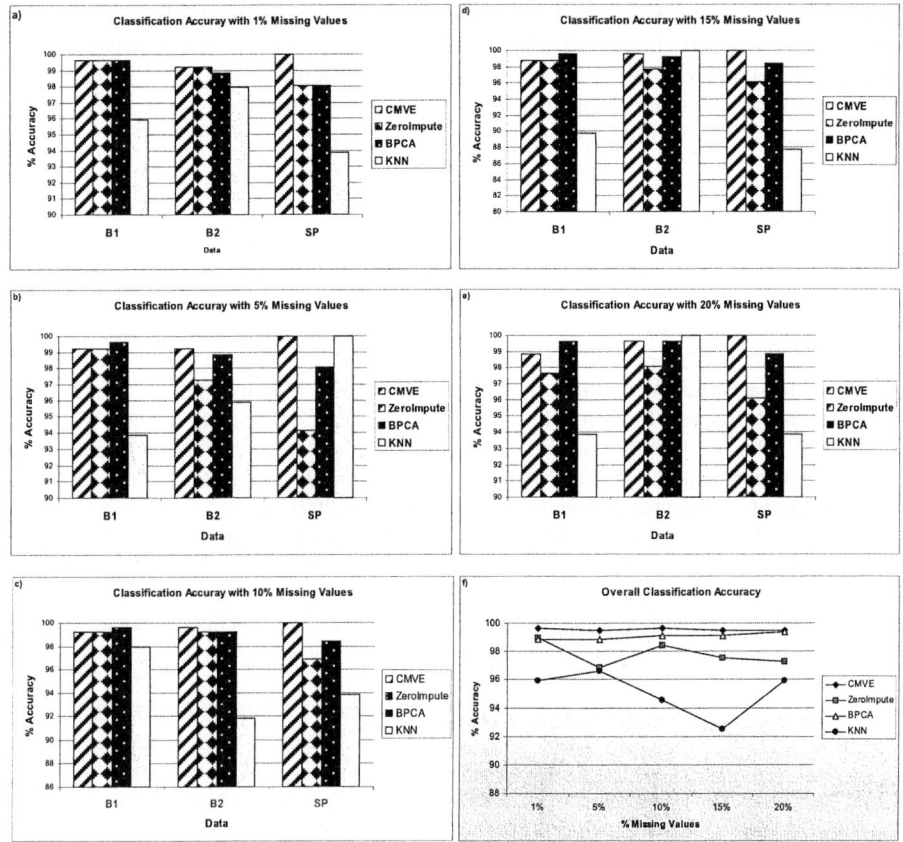

Fig. 2. Class Prediction Accuracy using CMVE, BPCA, KNN and *ZeroImpute* to estimate between 1% and 20% Missing Values

For this reason, it is always better to exploits all sort of correlation structure for estimation in the data.

4 Conclusions

This paper has presented a new *Collateral Missing Value Estimation* (CMVE) algorithm for accurate missing value estimation which leads to better gene selection and classification. CMVE has demonstrated superior imputation performance compared to the *Bayesian Principal Component Analysis* (BPCA), *K Nearest* Neighbour (KNN) algorithm and *ZeroImpute* methods, for estimating randomly missing values over the probability range from 0.01 to 0.2 in the BRCA1, BRCA2 and Sporadic genetic mutation samples present in ovarian cancer. Experimental results also reveal that CMVE consistently outperformed BPCA, KNN and *ZeroImpute* techniques in terms of their classification accuracies by exploiting all types of correlations between the data. The *Ridge Partial Least Squares* (RPLS) classifier was applied for the class prediction followed by the fusion of genes selection method, *Between Group to within Group*

Sum of Squares (BSS/WSS) and *Weighted Partial Least Square* (WPLS), and these afforded consistently improved classification performance for all experiments on ovarian cancer microarray data, when used in combination with CMVE. The results also corroborate the theoretical basis for the better performance of CMVE which means it can be successfully applied to any correlated data.

References

[1] M. S. B. Sehgal, I. Gondal, and L. Dooley, "Statistical Neural Networks and Support Vector Machine for the Classification of Genetic Mutations in Ovarian Cancer," *IEEE Symposium on Computational Intelligence in Bioinformatics and Computational Biology (CIBCB)'04, USA.*, pp. 140-146, 2004.

[2] A. Bhattacharjee, W. G. Richards, J. Staunton, C. Li, S. Monti, P. Vasa, C. Ladd, J. Beheshti, R. Bueno, M. Gillette, M. Loda, G. Weber, E. F. Mark, E. S. Lander, W. Wong, B. E. Johnson, T. R. Golub, D. J. Sugarbaker, and M. Meyerson, "Classification of human lung carcinomas by mRNA expression profiling reveals distinct adenocarcinoma subclasses," presented at Proc. Natl. Acad. Sci, USA, 2001.

[3] S. Oba, M. A. Sato, I. Takemasa, M. Monden, K. Matsubara, and S. Ishii, "A Bayesian Missing Value Estimation Method for Gene Expression Profile Data," *Bioinformatics*, vol. 19, pp. 2088-2096, 2003.

[4] S. Dudoit, J. Fridlyand, and T. P. Speed, "Comparison of discrimination methods for the classification of tumors using gene expression data," *Journal of the American Statistical Association*, pp. 77-78, 2002.

[5] M. S. B. Sehgal, I. Gondal, and L. Dooley, "K-Ranked Covariance Based Missing Values Estimation for Microarray Data Classification," *IEEE Hybrid Intelligent Systems (HIS)'04, Japan*, vol. 00, pp. 274-279, 2004.

[6] E. Acuna and C. Rodriguez, "The treatment of missing values and its effect in the classifier accuracy," *Classification, Clustering and Data Mining Applications*, pp. 639-648, 2004.

[7] O. Troyanskaya, M. Cantor, G. Sherlock, P. Brown, T. Hastie, R. Tibshirani, D. Botstein, and R. Altman, "Missing Value Estimation Methods for DNA Microarrays," *Bioinformatics*, vol. 17, pp. 520-525, 2001.

[8] M. S. B. Sehgal, I. Gondal, and L. Dooley, "A Collateral Missing Value Estimation Algorithm for DNA Microarrays," *2005 IEEE International Conference on Acoustics, Speech, and Signal Processing (ICASSP), USA*, pp. 377-380, 2005.

[9] M. S. B. Sehgal, I. Gondal, and L. Dooley, "Support Vector Machine and Generalized Regression Neural Network Based Classification Fusion Models for Cancer Diagnosis," *IEEE Hybrid Intelligent Systems (HIS)'04, Japan*, pp. 49–54, 2004.

[10] A. Antoniadis, S. Lambert-Lacroix, and F. Leblanc, "Effective dimension reduction methods for tumor classification using gene expression data," *Bioinformatics*, vol. 19 no. 5, pp. 563-570, 2003.

[11] T. R. Golub, D. K. Slonim, P. Tamayo, C. Huard, M. Gaasen-beek, J. P. Mesirov, H. Coller, M. L. Loh, J. R. Down-ing, M. A. Caligiuri, C. D. Bloomfield, and E. S. Lan-der, "Molecular classification of cancer: class discovery and class prediction by gene expression monitoring," *Science*, pp. 286(5439):531-537, 1999.

[12] P. Broët, A. Lewin, S. Richardson, C. Dalmasso, and H. Magdelenat, "A mixture model-based strategy for selecting sets of genes in multiclass response microarray experiments," *Bioinformatics*, vol. 20, pp. 2562 - 2571, 2004.

[13] X. Liu, A. Krishnan, and A. Mondry, "An Entropy-based gene selection method for cancer classification using microarray data," *BMC Bioinformatics*, vol. 6:76, 2005.
[14] M. S. B. Sehgal, I. Gondal, and L. Dooley, "Collateral Missing Value Imputation: a new robust missing value estimation algorithm for microarray data," *Bioinformatics*, vol. 21(10), pp. 2417-2423, 2005.
[15] I. Hedenfalk, D. Duggan, Y. Chen, M. Radmacher, M. Bittner, R. Simon, P. Meltzer, B. Gusterson, M. Esteller, O. P. Kallioniemi, B. Wilfond, A. Borg, and J. Trent, "Gene-expression profiles in hereditary breast cancer," *N. Engl. J. Med*, pp. 22; 344(8):539-548, 2001.
[16] G. Fort and S. Lambert-Lacroix, "Classification using partial least squares with penalized logistic regression," *Bioinformatics*, vol. 21, pp. 1104-1111, 2005.
[17] M. Harvey and C. Arthur, "Fitting models to biological Data using linear and nonlinear regression," Oxford University Press, 2004.
[18] K. Y. Yeung, R. E. Bumgarner, and A. E. Raftery, "Bayesian Model Averaging: development of an improved multi-class, gene selection and classification tool for microarray data," *Bioinformatics*, vol. 21 no.10, pp. 2394-2402, 2005.
[19] X. Zhou, X. Wang, and E. R. Dougherty, "Gene Selection Using Logistic Regressions Based on AIC, BIC and MDL Criteria," *New Mathematics and Natural Computation*, vol. 1, pp. 129-145, 2005.
[20] A. J. Amir, C. J. Yee, C. Sotiriou, K. R. Brantley, J. Boyd, and E. T. Liu, "Gene Expression Profiles of Brca1-Linked, Brca2-Linked, and Sporadic Ovarian Cancers," *Journal of the National Cancer Institute*, vol. 94 (13), 2002.

Using Neural Networks to Support Early Warning System for Financial Crisis Forecasting

Kyong Joo Oh[1], Tae Yoon Kim[2], Hyoung Yong Lee[3], and Hakbae Lee[4]

[1] Dept. of Information and Industrial Engineering, Yonsei University, Seoul, Korea
johanoh@yonsei.ac.kr
[2] Dept. of Statistics, Keimyung University, Daegu, Korea
tykim@yonsei.ac.kr
[3] Dept. of Management Engineering, Korea Advanced Institute of Science and Technology, Seoul, Korea
leemit@kgsm.kaist.ac.kr
[4] Dept. of Statistics, Yonsei University, Seoul, Korea
hblee@yonsei.ac.kr

Abstract. This study deals with the construction process of a daily financial condition indicator (DFCI), which can be used as an early warning signal using neural networks and nonlinear programming. One of the characteristics in the proposed indicator is to establish *an alarm zone* in the DFCI, which plays a role of predicting a potential financial crisis. The previous financial condition indicators based on statistical methods are developed such that they examine whether a crisis will be break out within 24 months. In this study, however, the alarm zone makes it possible for the DFCI to forecast an unexpected crisis on a daily basis and then issue an early warning signal. Therefore, DFCI involves daily monitoring of the evolution of the stock price index, foreign exchange rate and interest rate, which tend to exhibit unusual behaviors preceding a possible crisis. Using nonlinear programming, the procedure of DFCI construction is completed by integrating three sub-DFCIs, based on each financial variable, into the final DFCI. The DFCI for Korean financial market will be established as an empirical study. This study then examines the predictability of alarm zone for the financial crisis forecasting in Korea.

1 Introduction

Financial crises that have swept across many developing countries in the 1990s, e.g. the Asian crisis in 1997, have imposed severe economic and social costs on the inflicted financial markets and threatened the stability of the international monetary system. Since these financial crises begin in the shape of a foreign exchange crisis, a variety of theoretical and empirical works have been done to search for early warning signals from various financial variables [2, 3]. Most of these works, however, have focused on long term prediction (e.g., a possible crisis within two years) based on financial variables observed over a rather "long period of time," which implies loss of vast, useful information that comes directly from dynamic daily movements of financial markets. This study is intended to utilize such daily-basis dynamic information in searching for early warning signals of crisis. For this purpose, the *daily financial condition indicator* (DFCI), which monitors the financial markets on a daily basis with the purpose of providing early warning signs, is introduced, and its construction procedure is discussed.

Traditionally, the studies on financial crises have concentrated on the fundamentals of financial market since it was believed that the weak fundamentals of financial market eventually induce crises [1, 5, 6]. However, recent crises have evidently shown another style, i.e., a crisis may develop without a significant deterioration in the fundamentals of financial market since it is often self-fulfilling under complicated situations and uncertainty of financial market [7, 13]. This new perspective of a financial crisis highlights the importance of financial variables observed daily in studying crises. The stock price index (SPI), foreign exchange rates (FER) and interest rates (INT) are major financial variables that reflect daily dynamic movements of the financial markets. In addition, Kim et al. [4] demonstrated neural networks (NN) are more efficient in monitoring the situation of financial market and providing early warning signals than other artificial intelligence (AI) tools, such as neuro-fuzzy model and inductive learning. In this study, therefore, all these three major daily financial variables are considered to construct a DFCI using NN and nonlinear programming (NLP).

One of characteristics in the proposed indicator is to establish *an alarm zone* in the DFCI, which plays a role of predicting a potential financial crisis. The previous financial condition indicators based on statistical methods [2, 3] are developed such that they examine whether a crisis will break out within 24 months. In this study, however, the alarm zone makes it possible for the DFCI to forecast an unexpected crisis daily and then issue an early warning signal. To give a specific illustration of DFCI construction, a DFCI is constructed for the Korean financial market, which experienced a severe financial crisis in 1997. This study then examines the predictability of alarm zone for financial crisis forecasting.

This study consists of five sections. Following Section 1, the introduction, in Section 2 discusses the detailed procedure of DFCI construction, and Section 3 explains the DFCI construction case study for the Korean financial market. The conclusion is given in Section 4.

2 Model Specification

In this section, we discuss the DFCI construction procedure, which consists of three phases. Its basic architecture, integrating NN and NLP, is given by Figure 1. As an NN algorithm in this study, BPN is introduced, which is the most widely used one suitable for nonlinear data analysis in science, engineering, finance and other fields [8, 10, 11]. For DFCI construction, BPN is used to train sub-DFCIs based on each of the three financial variables. In financial time series analysis, NLP provides more accurate and less ambiguous results [9], which means that NLP can be useful in financial time series forecasting [12]. Using NLP, therefore, the procedure of DFCI construction is completed by integrating three sub-DFCIs, based on each financial variable, into the final DFCI.

Throughout this study, we classify the conditions of financial market into three phases according to the level of its volatilities: (i) the stable period (SP), (ii) the unstable period (UP), (iii) the crisis period (CP). In our model, SP, UP and CP are

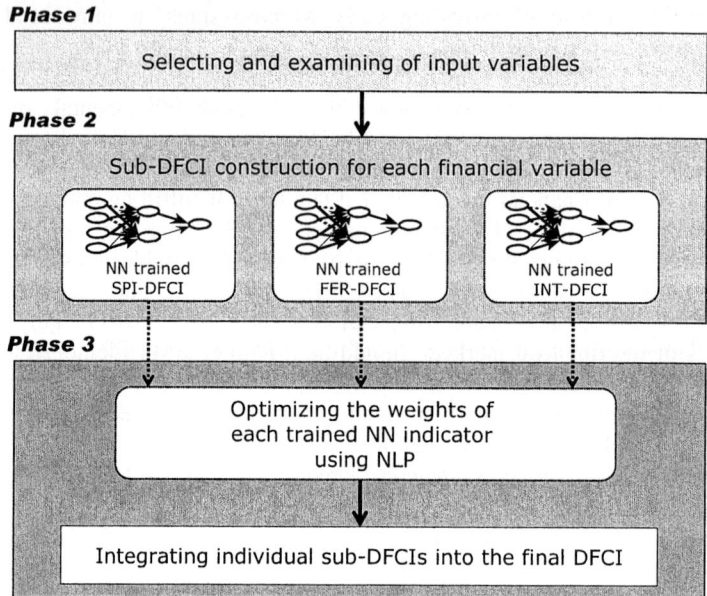

Fig. 1. DFCI construction architecture

denoted by 1, 2 and 3, respectively. SP is literally a stable period while UP is a phase, which is characterized by a sudden increase of volatility and rapid swings in market sentiment and plays a role of *an alarm zone* mentioned in Section 2.2. In CP, the financial market recognizes the occurrence of the crisis and adapts itself to the crisis. Since these three phases or patterns are structurally different from each other, they are considered as a pattern set to be classified and thus serve as a basis of the DFCI. The terms "stable, unstable and crisis" are used as descriptive terminologies to describe the financial market responses to the given conditions of financial market.

2.1 The Construction Process of the DFCI

The DFCI is established by the following phases: In Phase 1, input variables for each index are selected appropriately. Using NN, then, three sub-DFCIs are constructed in Phase 2 while they are integrated into the final DFCI using NLP in Phase 3.

Phase 1: Selecting and examining of input variables. Input and target data for each financial variable should be selected with due consideration paid to the final task that an individual sub-DFCI is to perform. Indeed, the selection of input and target variables should be viewed as the model construction process, through which SP, UP and CP could be defined such that each of them has its own distinctive feature. Thus, it is crucial to select a set of proper input variables which could measure the volatility level of the financial market and sensitively detect its changes. This is an essential phase for defining an individual sub-DFCI successfully. Transformation of the original daily financial variables (SPI, FER and INT) and expert opinion always prove quite useful in this phase.

Phase 2: Sub-DFCI Construction for Each Financial Variable. In this phase, NN is designed and trained to develop a sub-DFCI for each financial variable. The design stage of working with NN involves a number of aspects: designing the network structure, selecting neuron transfer functions, selecting a method for updating the weights and a training cessation scheme. After being trained on the given training data, each sub-DFCI is to be tested and adjusted by applying it to test data and checking its performance. Performance will be measured as a degree of consistency between the output of each sub-DFCI and the real development of financial market. If performance achieves a desired level, each NN will be labeled as the sub-DFCI for each financial variable.

Phase 3: Integrating Individual Sub-DFCIs into the Final DFCI. In this phase, using NLP, the individually trained NNs (or sub-DFCIs) are combined into the final DFCI as follows:

$$DECI_t = w_1 S_t + w_2 F_t + w_3 I_t, \quad t = 1, 2, \ldots, n \tag{1}$$

where w_1, w_2 and w_3 are weights, and S_t, F_t and I_t are the trained sub-DFCIs for the SPI, FER and INT, respectively. Note that S_t, F_t and I_t take on values 1, 2, or 3. Finding the optimal weights is resolved by NLP. For this, it is essential to define an objective function $E(w)$ and then find an optimal way to produce the desired final DFCI. Indeed, the objective function $E(w)$ under consideration is defined as:

$$E(w) = \sum_{t=1}^{n} (w_1 S_t + w_2 F_t + w_3 I_t - 2)^2 \tag{2}$$

which is minimized over $w_1, w_2, w_3 \geq 0$ satisfying $w_1 + w_2 + w_3 = 1$. Of course, '2' in (2) means the objective function is constructed such that *the alarm zone* probes into the condition of financial market.

2.2 The Role of the Alarm Zone in DFCI

There is no clear classified consensus about the definition of a financial crisis. However, we establish our definition in terms of volatility. These three phases or patterns are used as an output. The UP above, usually occurring just prior to a crisis, could be interpreted as a phase through which the financial market makes a transition from a stable condition to a crisis. Often, it is called a grey zone where self-correcting mechanisms of the financial market deteriorate [4]. In this study, it is defined *an alarm zone*. There is no consensus about how long it lasts, but it is usually expected to be a very short period because of an abrupt reversal of market sentiment. In the meantime, an alarm zone may shift to either a stable condition or a crisis. In other words, even though the financial market reaches an alarm zone, it may get back to a stable one through recovery or reform measures. One of the main contributions of the DFCI developed here is that the crisis trained DFCI is able to provide a decision as to whether the financial market has entered an alarm zone and hence an appropriate warning signal. Thus, an alarm zone can allow DFCI to perform the role of forecasting an unexpected crisis. The role of the alarm zone is evaluated by applying the DFCI to real data, and examining its performance which might be measured by matching its final output signal with the event of financial market at that time.

3 An Empirical Study

The Korean financial crisis that occurred in late 1997 and persisted for over a year brought massive bankruptcies in financial and industrial systems. It was a quite new experience for Korea, which had become accustomed to a steady growth track until then. This unprecedented and peculiar crisis brought large scale changes to the Korean financial market, and since then much attention has been focused on the study of financial crisis. Especially, much effort has been made to build an early warning system on a long-term basis. However, one on short-term basis is strongly demanded by quite a few members of the Korean financial market since there is a strong argument that the crisis that the financial market had experienced was abrupt and unexpected, i.e., seemingly not a result of long term aggravation of financial market. Indeed, such demand is partially met by the early warning system based on the Korean stock price index (KOSPI) by Kim et al. [4] whose construction steps will be helpful here. Throughout this section, the variable names given in Table 1 are used.

Table 1. Input variables considered

Variable name	Numerical formula	Description
IND	x_t	Index or Rate
DRF	$p_t = \dfrac{x_t - x_{t-1}}{x_{t-1}}$	Daily rise and fall rate
MA(m)	$\overline{p}_{m,t} = \dfrac{1}{m} \sum_{i=t-(m-1)}^{t} p_i$	m-day moving average
MV(m)	$s^2_{m,t} = \dfrac{1}{m} \sum_{i=t-(m-1)}^{t} (p_i - \overline{p}_{m,t})^2$	m-day moving variance

The KOSPI 200, Korea won/U.S. dollar exchange rate, and Korea Treasury bill rate with 3-year maturity are considered as the three major financial variables. In order to establish training data with a set of proper input variables, the movements of 1997 financial markets are examined closely. A rough look at the three major variables (IND, Figure 2) in 1997 reveals that all three variables appear to change their movements around October 1997. To check structural changes of three variables during the crisis, DRF p_t is calculated. The main reason for choosing p_t is that it actively responds to the increased instability or volatility of the financial market due to the potential crisis, which would lead to a sudden increase of frequency and amplitude of p_t. As expected, such a phenomenon is easy to notice in Figure 3 (See

Appendix). Around October or November of 1997, indeed, there was a strong signal of a volatility increase in each DRF movement. Note that, in December 1997, Korea was officially put in the IMF (International Monetary Fund) financial rescue program.

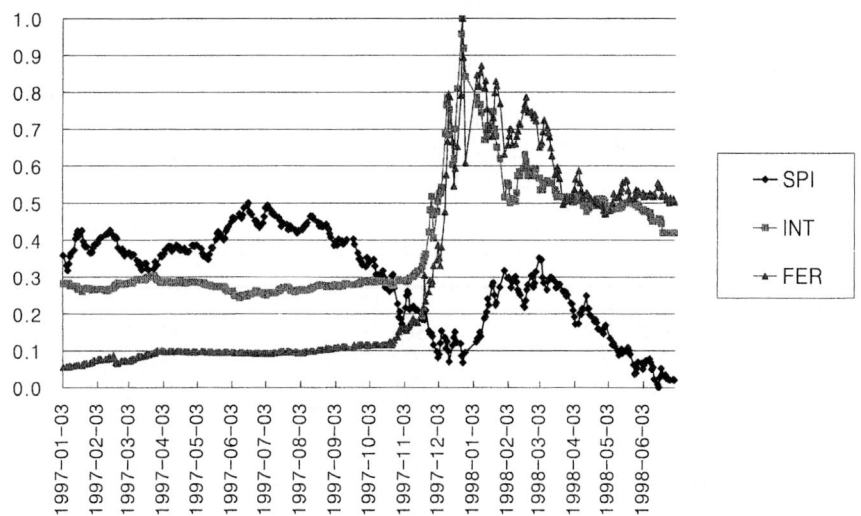

Fig. 2. Korea stock price index, foreign exchange rates and interest rates of 1997, which are scaled from 0 to 1

To investigate DRF further, its 5-day moving average $\overline{p}_t$, (MA(5)) and 5-day moving variance s_t^2 (MV(5), Figure 4 (See Appendix), another measure of volatility) are studied for each variable. A rather short period of 5 days was chosen here for the moving average to take into account the visibly clear non-stationarity of DRF from Figure 3 (See Appendix). Figure 4 (See Appendix) shows that all three MV(5)'s have sudden increases in around October 1997.

To construct the training data, the 1997 and the early 1998 period, during which Korea experienced the crisis, is considered. Since a sudden increase of moving variance s_t^2 is a signal of the volatility increase, UPs are first established around that point. In fact, a UP for each financial variable is established as Set. 19 – Oct. 21 for SPI, Oct. 27 – Nov. 30 for FER, and Nov. 13 – Dec. 12 for INT, each of which contains the point of sudden volatility increase. SP and CP are established before and after a UP, respectively, which gives training data sets for each variable as in Table 2. The length of the periods for each variable is adjusted and corrected such that its training error rate is optimized. It is interesting to observe that the signal in s_t^2 (sudden increase in volatility) for each variable appears in the order of SPI, FER and INT in 1997. This confirms that the stock market responds quickly to the condition changes of financial market while the exchange rate and bond market are slow in responding. In addition to the main input variables (IND, DRF and MV(m)), which are basically introduced by Kim et al. [4], MA(m) ($m = 5, 20, 60, 120$ or 240) are considered (it would make more sense to have the m-day moving average, a past history, instead of having just current daily data as input variables), and among them, some variables are heuristically selected such that the resulting NN is well fitted to the training data set (Figure 5 (See Appendix)). Input and output variables selected are shown in Table 3 where SP, UP and CP are encoded by 1, 2 and 3, respectively. Note that training is done for the well-known BPN. The number of hidden layers of NN used for SPI ranges from 2 to 4 while those for FER and INT range from 3 to 7. As an activation function, the logistic function is used with the learning rate, momentum and initial weights given by 0.1, 0.1 and 0.3, respectively.

Table 2. Specific dates of SP, UP and CP for training data

Index	SP	UP	CP
SPI	Apr. 22, 97 – Sep. 18, 97	Sep. 19, 97 – Oct. 21, 97	Oct. 22, 97 – Mar. 10, 98
FER	Jul. 1, 97 – Oct. 26, 97	Oct. 27, 97 – Nov. 30, 97	Dec. 1, 97 – Mar. 20, 98
INT	Aug. 21, 97 – Nov. 12, 97	Nov. 13, 97 – Dec. 12, 97	Dec. 13, 97 – Mar. 16, 98

Table 3. List of input and output variables for each sub-DFCI

	Input Variables	Output Variable
DFCI (SPI)	IND, DRF, MA(5), VA(5)	SP: 1
DFCI (FER)	DRF, MA(5), VA(5), MA(20), VA(20), MA(60), VA(60)	UP: 2
DFCI (INT)	DRF, MA(5), VA(5), MA(20), VA(20), MA(60), VA(60)	CP: 3

Table 4. The coefficients obtained for three sub-DFCI

	Coefficients
SPI	0.4959
FER	0
INT	0.5041

The Individually trained NN (sub-DFCI) is applied to the period other than the training data set. The overall classification results of each sub-DFCI are given in Figure 6 (See Appendix), which shows that the sub-DFCI for SPI has higher fluctuations than other variables. Indeed, in Figure 6 (See Appendix), the sub-DFCI of SPI moves quickly between the patterns. We combine the three trained sub-DFCIs into the final DFCI by NLP. Table 4 shows coefficients obtained for the three sub-DFCIs when they are integrated by NLP. It is noticed that FER contributes the least among the three major financial variables, which was somewhat anticipated since FER in 1997 was largely controlled by the policy authority.

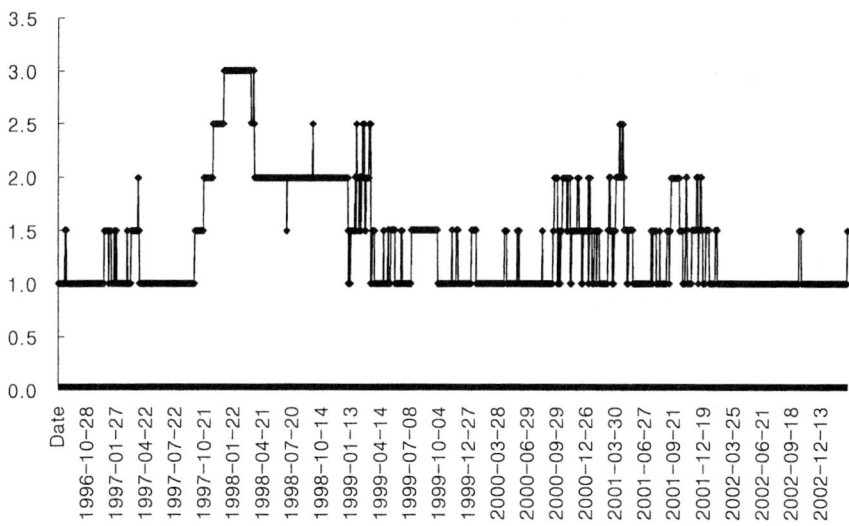

Fig. 7. The final DFCI from May 1996 to March 2003

In the reflection on the periods having "2" (i.e., UP) or more values at which *the alarm zone* operates, in Figure 7, the Korean financial market suffered a severe recession and went through strong financial reform programs during the 1997 – 1998 crisis periods. As a result of successful reform programs coupled with the steady U.S. and world financial expansion, it returned to a stable condition in the early 1999. Note that the Korean financial market is typically opened. In 1999, however, it bumped into trouble due to the severe liquidity shortage of Daewoo, one of the major Korean conglomerates. In 2000, the Korean financial market faced more severe difficulty due to liquidity problems of Hyundai Engineering & Construction Co., Hyundai Investment & Trust Co., and Hynix Semiconductor Co., which together constitute the gigantic Korean conglomerate enterprise. Then, the slump of the real U.S. financial market started in 2001, and on Sep. 11 of that year, terrorists attacked the World Trade Center in New York City, U.S. In 2002, external condition of financial became worse due to increased tension between North Korea and the U.S. When one examines the behaviors of the DFCI with respect to the difficulties of financial market that Korea experienced, one may note that the DFCI produces meaningful and adequate warning signals, i.e., UP. Thus, it is obvious that the DFCI explains the Korean financial market well and *the alarm zone* operates responsively for predicting some crisis status.

4 Conclusion

The financial crises in many parts of the world for the 1990s sparked interest in establishing financial condition indicators. However, most indicators developed so far measure only the present condition instead of forecasting the future status of financial market. Although some indicators can provide notification of a crisis in advance, they do not issue the warning signals abruptly since they are built on a long-term basis. Thus, these indicators are ineffective for forecasting the future state of financial market. In order to overcome this problem, this study suggests a DFCI to involve an alarm zone which allows it to forecast ongoing crises responsively. Early warning signals are produced daily by establishing the DFCI that provides a signal for potential crisis based on its daily monitoring of major financial variables (e.g., the stock price index, exchange rate, and interest rate). Three sub-DFCIs are constructed using NN, and then they are integrated to build up the final DFCI using NLP. Then, the usefulness of *the alarm zone* is evaluated by matching the final output signals with the events of financial market in test data, which also becomes the performance of the DFCI. An empirical study is done for the Korean financial market which had experienced a financial crisis in 1997. It turns out that the DFCI is desirable for the Korean financial market and *the alarm zone* plays an important role in improving the performance of the DFCI.

Acknowledgment

This work was supported by Yonsei University Research Fund of 2005.

References

1. Eichengreen, B., Rose, A., Wyplosz, C.: Exchange Market Mayhem: The Antecedents and Aftermath of Speculative Attacks. Economic Policy **21** (1995) 249-312.
2. Frankel, J.A., Rose, A.K.: Currency Crashes in Emerging Markets: An Empirical Treatment. Journal of International Economics **41** (1996) 351-366.
3. Kaminsky, G., Reinhart, C.M.: The Twin Crises: The Causes of Banking and Balance-of-Payments Problems. American Economic Review **89** (1999) 473-500.
4. Kim, T.Y., Oh, K.J., Sohn, I. Hwang, C.: Usefulness of Artificial Neural Networks for Early Warning System of Financial Crisis. Expert Systems with Applications **26** (2004) 585-592.
5. Krugman, P.: A Model of Balance-of-Payments Crises. Journal of Money, Credit and Banking **11** (1979) 311-325.
6. Obstfeld, M.: Rational and Self-fulfilling Balance-of-Payments Crises. American Economic Review **76** (1986) 72-81.
7. Ozkan, F.G., Sutherland, A.: Policy Measures to avoid a Currency Crisis. Economic Journal **105** (1995) 510-519.
8. Patterson, D.W.: Artificial Neural Networks. Prentice Hall, New York (1996).
9. Powell, J.G., Premachandra, I.M.: Accommodating Diverse Institutional Investment Objectives and Constraints using Non-linear Goal Programming. European Journal of Operational Research **105** (1998) 447-456.
10. Rosenblatt, F.: Principles of Neurodynamics. Spartan, New York (1962).
11. Rumelhart, D.E., Hinton, G.E., Williams, R.J.: Learning Internal Representations by Back Propagation. In: Rumelhart, D.E., McClelland, J.L., PDP Research Group (eds.): Parallel Distributed Processing, Vol. 1. MIT Press, Cambridge (1986).
12. Seppälä, J.: The Diversification of Currency Loans: A Comparison between Safety-First and Mean-Variance Criteria. European Journal of Operational Research **74** (1994) 325-343.
13. Velasco, A.: Financial and balance of payments crises: A Simple Model of the Southern Cone Experience. Journal of Development Economics **27** (1987) 263-283.

Appendix: Figures 3 to 6

(a) Stock price index

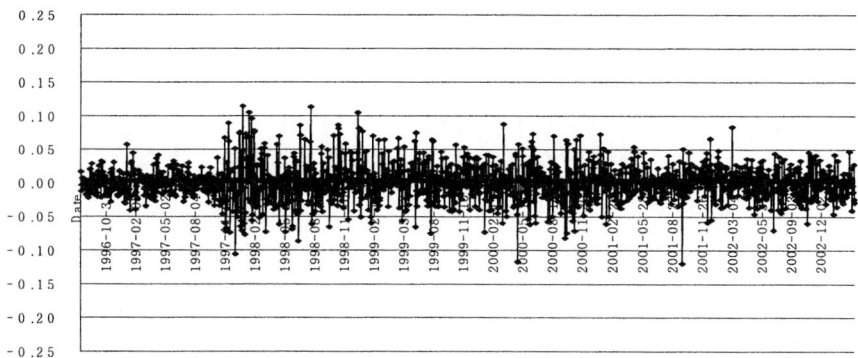

(b) Foreign exchange rates

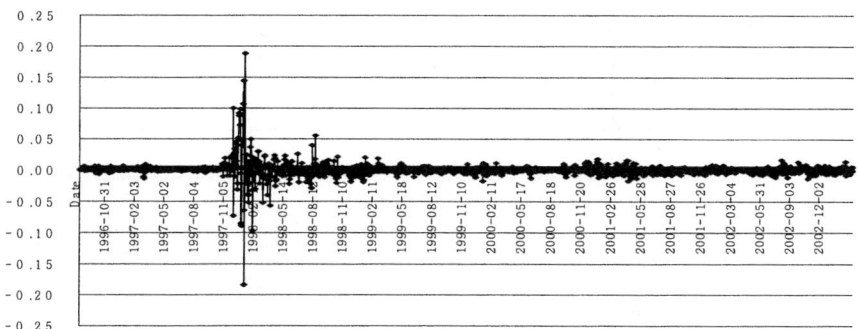

(c) Interest rates

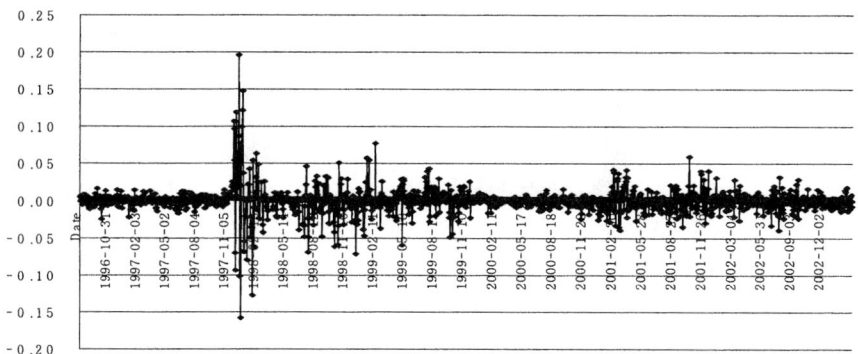

Fig. 3. Daily rise and fall rate, p_t, from May 1996 to March 2003

294   K.J. Oh et al.

(a) Stock price index

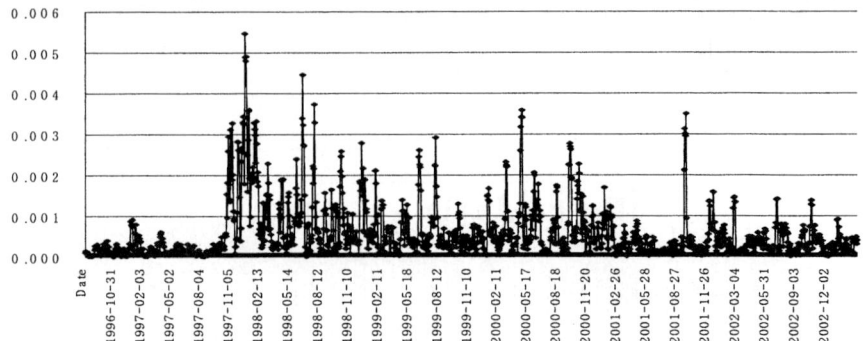

(b) Foreign exchange rates

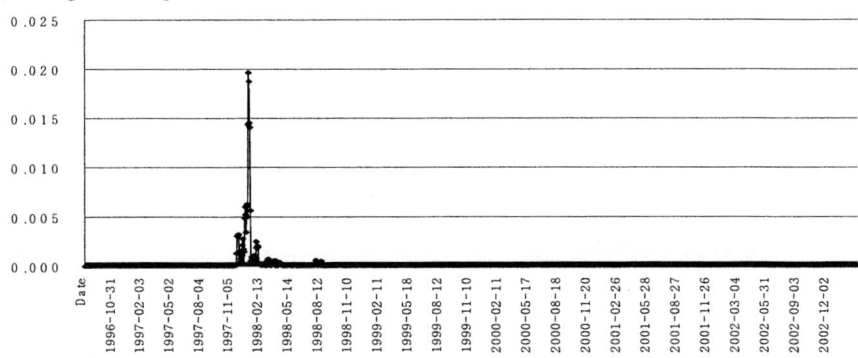

(c) Interest rates

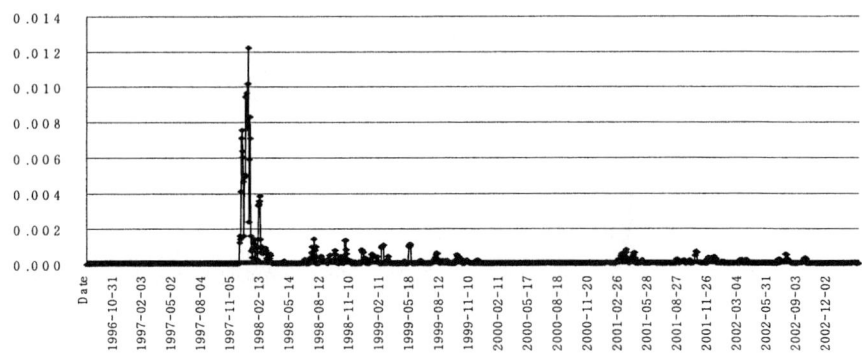

Fig. 4. 5-day moving variance of daily rise and fall rate, s_t, from May 1996 to March 2003

(a) Stock price index

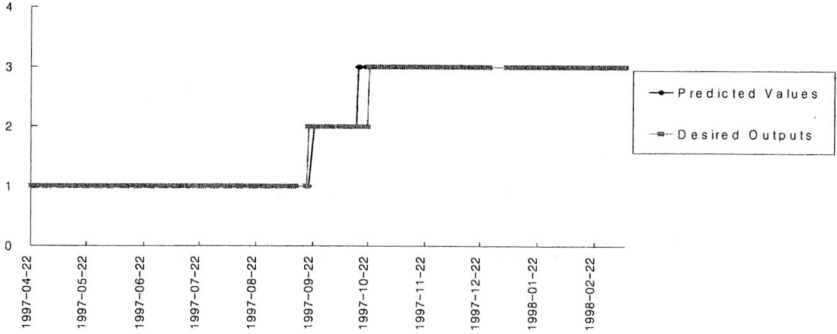

(b) Foreign exchange rates

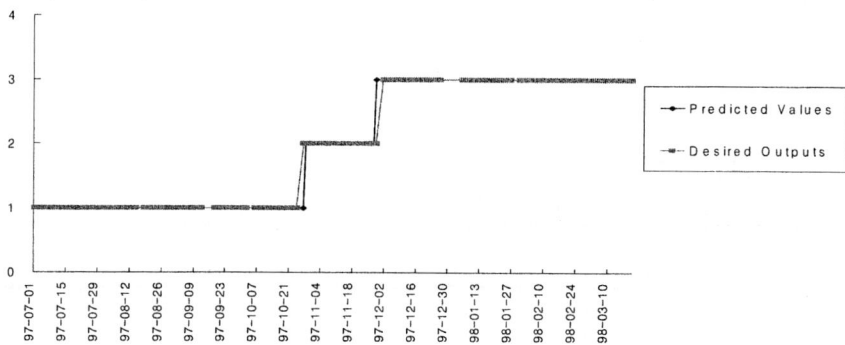

(c) Interest rates

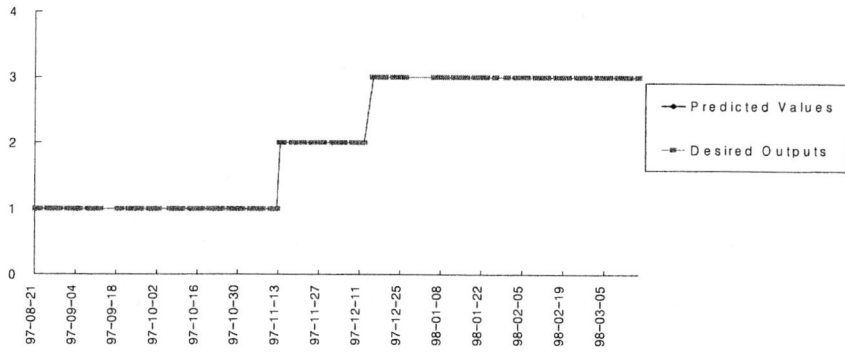

Fig. 5. Classification results of individual sub-DFCI for each training dataset (1, 2 and 3 denotes SP, UP and CP, respectively)

(a) Stock price index

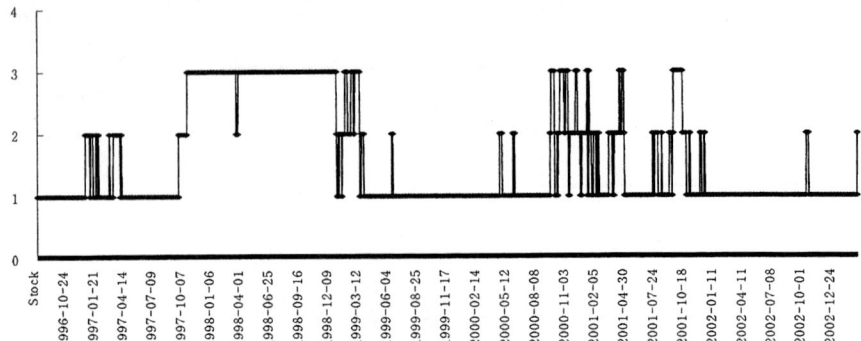

(b) Foreign exchange rates

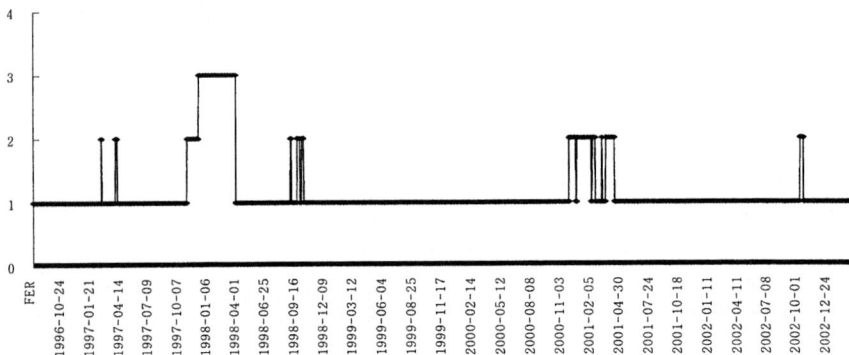

(c) Interest rates

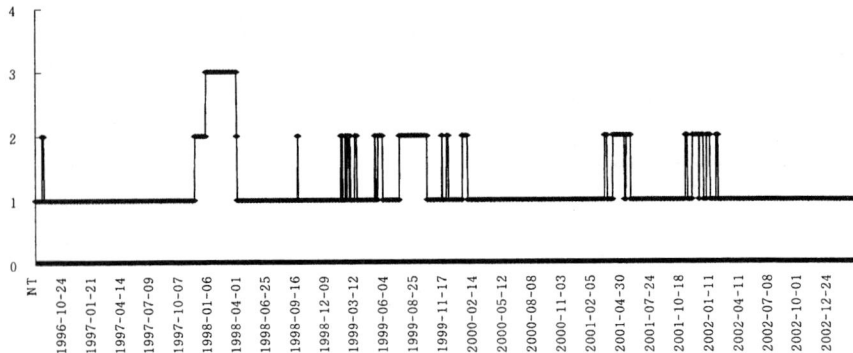

Fig. 6. Classification results of individual sub-DFCI from May 1996 to March 2003

A Neural Network Based Methodology for Performance Evaluation of Parallel Systems

Sırma Yavuz

Yıldız Technical University, Computer Engineering Department,
34349 Beşiktaş, İstanbul, Turkey
`sirma@ce.yildiz.edu.tr`

Abstract. In this study we propose a method using multi layer perceptron (MLP) neural networks to evaluate and predict the performance of parallel systems and report our findings. Artificial neural networks may provide a good alternative to conventional methods in terms of identifying the contribution of individual system and application parameters to performance. Neural network models presented here are used to predict the computational and communication performance of parallel applications running on different platforms. Two applications are considered: the first one is a 2-Dimensional Fast Fourier Transform (FFT) application that requires intensive data exchange between processors, which is valuable for communication performance tests and the second one is a Monte Carlo application which can be classified as a typical floating-point application. There are two types of data used to train, validate and test the neural network models. A large portion of the input data composed from real measurements taken on SunSparc workstations. To enhance the available data, results obtained by modeling some unavailable systems into PACE (the Performance Analysis and Characterization Environment) have been also included.

1 Introduction

Performance evaluation and modeling of parallel systems is a complex task, requiring consideration of various interrelated architectural and application parameters. With the diversity of architectural approaches and rapid advances in communication infrastructure, it can be very difficult and sometimes impossible to predict and validate the contributions of these factors. On the other hand, artificial neural networks may provide an excellent alternative to conventional techniques with their ability to capture many kinds of relationships [8].

Conventional performance evaluation techniques include benchmarking, analytical modeling and simulation [7,11]. Each of these methods has their advantages as well as limitations. Analytical models are very powerful but their applicability is not universal. In order to be traceable, they do simplifying assumptions about the architecture and application characteristics that may not reflect the accurate representation of reality. While simulation tools allow designers to understand the system beyond analytical models can provide, they are expensive to run and still do not replace real measurements. These difficulties have led to the use of benchmark programs to characterize and evaluate parallel computer performance. Although they are very popular, their reliability has been widely discussed over the past two decades [9]. The common methodologies used in benchmarking and the pitfalls encountered are explained in [2].

MLPs are the most widely used class of neural networks for diverse applications, including financial forecasting, process control in manufacturing, speech and image recognition [1,12]. This study explores the possibility of using MLPs in performance evaluation of parallel systems that would allow an in-depth examination of architectural and application parameters affecting performance.

2 Specifications of the Test Platforms and Applications

Two applications have been used to collect the data to train, validate and test the neural network models.

The first application is a two-dimensional convolution operation, which performs Fast Fourier Transform (FFT) on a 2D data array (image), does a multiplication between this array and a filter array, and then performs an inverse FFT. This operation can be expressed as:

$$F(i,j) = W * I(i,j) \qquad (1)$$

where I is the input image, F is the output image, and '*' is the convolution operator. W is the convolution weighting function (kernel), and (i, j) indicates the data element. If we define the size of the rectangular kernel as R x S, the convolution can be written as in equation 2.

$$F(i,j) = \sum_{p=-R}^{R} \sum_{q=-S}^{S} W(p-q) * I(i-p, j-q) \qquad (2)$$

The second parallel application studied here, calculates European option prices using Monte Carlo simulation techniques. Monte Carlo methods are effective for pricing some financial derivatives, especially when the price cannot be calculated analytically because it depends on the historical movement of underlying variables [6]. The set of trajectories were divided equally among the processors, and the results reported back to a master:

- each processor calculates the trajectories of asset prices ,
- the master sums the individual results,
- each slave obtains the sum from the master and calculate local error,
- and the master sums the individual errors.

The accuracy of the resulting price is primarily a function of the number of Monte-Carlo trials performed.

Specifications of the workstations and the networks, some of which are also used as the neural network inputs, are given in Table 1 and Table 2. To utilize

Table 1. Specifications of existing and modeled architectures

	SparcStation 5	Ultra 1	Ultra 10	Sun Blade 1000 Model 1750/1900	Hp Server rx4610
Architecture	MicroSPARC II	UltraSPARC I	UltraSPARC II i	UltraSPARC III	Itanium IA-64
CPU Clock Rate	170 MHz	143 MHz	300/333 MHz	750/900 MHz	733/800 MHz
Main Memory	64 Mb	64 Mb	128 Mb	1 Gb	8 Gb
Functional Units	Integrated FPU 1 IU	3 FPU 4 IU 2 ALU	3 FPU 4 IU 2 ALU	3 FPU 4 IU 2 ALU	2 double,1 single precision FMAC
Pipeline Stages	5 Stage Pipeline can issue up to 4 instructions per cycle	9 Stage Pipeline can issue up to 4 instructions per cycle	9 Stage Pipeline can issue up to 4 instructions per cycle	14 Stage Pipeline can issue up to 4 instructions per cycle	10 Stage Pipeline can issue up to 6 instructions per cycle

Table 2. Specifications of modeled networking products

Network Type	Product	Theoretical Bandwidths or Transfer Rates
Ethernet	SunSwift PCI Adapter	10 Mbps or 100 Mbps
Fast Ethernet	Sun Fast Ethernet PCI Adapter	10 Mbps or 100 Mbps
FDDI	Sun FDDI/P Adapter	supports up to 100 Mbps
Gigabit Ethernet	Sun GigaSwift UTP Adapter	1000 Mbps (full duplex)
Myrinet	M2M-PCI32 from Myricom	Each link is capable of full bi-directional 1.2 GBit/s

the network of workstations as a parallel resource, MPICH, a complete implementation of the Message Passing Interface MPI, has been used [3,14].

The data used in this study contains actual measurements taken on SunSparc workstations connected by an Ethernet network, as well as estimations obtained by modeling the unavailable systems into PACE.

The PACE methodology, which has been developed at Warwick, is based on a layered framework that separates out the software and hardware system components through the use of a parallelization template [13]. PACE is a performance modeling approach that allows cross-platform comparisons to be easily undertaken. Reusable hardware and communication models can be interchanged for experimental analysis. The results obtained by PACE are reasonably accurate, within 10 percent of actual measurements.

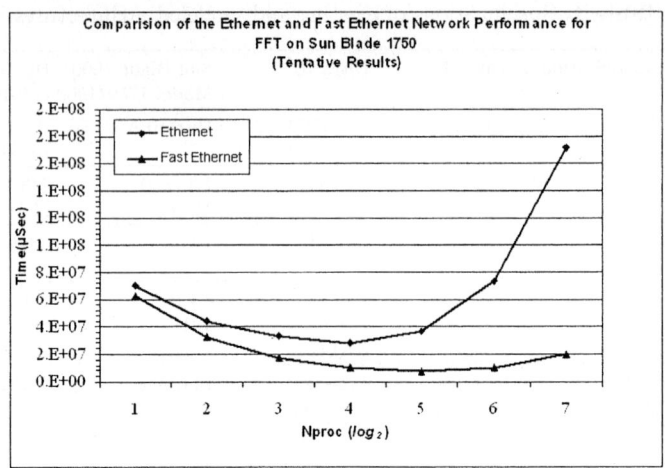

Fig. 1. Comparision of the Ethernet and Fast Ethernet Network Performance for FFT on Sun Blade 1750

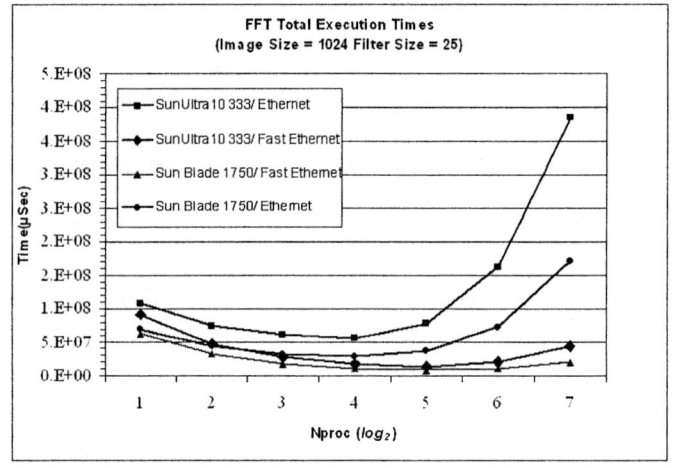

Fig. 2. Total execution times for FFT application (Image Size=1024 Filter Size=25)

Part of the results, containing both real measurements and tentative results obtained using PACE, are given in Fig. 1 and Fig. 2.

Fig. 1 shows the time spent on communication for FFT application, due to intensive communication required by this application the underlying communication medium gains great importance. A slow communication platform may turn parallelization into an inefficient task, where performance of the clustered computers is invalid (Fig. 2). On the other hand, for Monte Carlo Application, the floating point operation power of the underlying architectures gains importance.

The models presented here aim to serve as a performance analysis tool that can capture the effects of interrelated system and application parameters to each other. Neural network models similar to the ones presented here, may help users in different ways like identifying the optimum number of processors for their specific application or choosing the extra FPU over a higher CPU clock rate.

3 Neural Network Models

The model presented in this study is a multi-layer feed-forward network that is used with the back propagation algorithm. Back-propagation involves performing computations backwards through the network to determine the gradient of the cost function. Then the weights are adjusted in the direction of the negative gradient. The mechanism by which weights are updated is known as training algorithm. The selected training algorithm is the Levenberg-Marquardt [4,15], which is one of the most often used non-linear curve fitting methods. Fig. 3 shows the architecture of the models used for computational and communication performance prediction. The activation function for the hidden units is the tanh function defined as:

$$f(x) = \frac{2}{1 + e^{-2x}} - 1 \qquad (3)$$

while the output activation function is the logsig function defined as:

$$f(x) = \frac{1}{1 + e^{-x}} \qquad (4)$$

The hardware and application parameters used as network inputs to predict the computational performance are:

- Number of Processors: Number of processors on the network running the target application, it is between 2 and 512.
- CPU Speed: The CPU speed of the microprocessors running the application.
- Problem Size: For the FFT application: 'Image size' and 'Filter Size', for the Monte Carlo application : 'Number of Varietes' and 'Number of Trials' determine the problem size.
- Number of Integer Operations: The number of integer arithmetic operations in the application, identified from the C codes of the application, expressed as a function of problem size and number of processors.
- Number of Floating Point Operations: The number of integer arithmetic operations in the application, identified from the C codes of the application, expressed as a function of problem size and number of processors.

For communication performance prediction model, the inputs of the neural network are:

- Number of Processors
- CPU Speed
- Problem Size

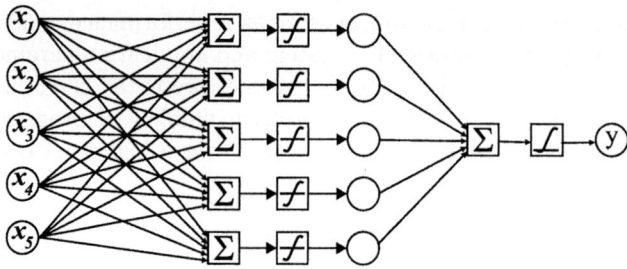

Fig. 3. NN model used for computational and communication performance prediction

- Number of MPI Communication Calls: The number of MPI point-to-point communication calls in the application, determined dynamically as a function of inputs.
- Network Bandwidth: The maximum rate at which the interconnection network can propagate information once the message enters the network.

4 Data Processing

4.1 Checking for Randomness and Outliers

The quality of the predicted sequence is important to train the network properly and for the success of the prediction task. Very often in data sets, samples that do not comply with the general behavior or model of the data exist. Such data samples, which are extremely different from or inconsistent with the remaining set of data, are called outliers [5].

In order to check for outliers, the lower and upper quartiles of the distribution data were calculated:

- Q_1 (Lower Quartile) = The 25th percentile
- Q_2 (Median) = The 50th percentile
- Q_3 (Upper Quartile) = The 75th percentile

The 25th percentile is a value that splits the data set in two subsets that each one contains 25% and 75% of the mass of the samples respectively. The 50th percentile is the median of the data set. Any value in the data set, that is greater than $Q_3+3(Q_3-Q_1)$ or lower than $Q_1-3(Q_3-Q_1)$, is called an extreme outlier. There were no outliers in the data sets presented in this study.

Randomness, also means unpredictability of future events based on past events. In the literature there are a number of tests that can be used to prove whether a sequence is random or not. These tests are divided into two major categories empirical and theoretical tests. In this study, the training and test data sets have been verified for randomness, using the 'Run' test [10].

4.2 Pre-processing and Post-processing of Data

Theoretically, a neural network can be used to map the raw input data directly to required output data. But in practice, it is almost always beneficial, sometimes critical to apply pre-processing to the input data before they are fed to a network. There are many techniques and considerations relevant to data pre-processing. Since the choice of pre-processing algorithms depends on the application and the nature of the data, the range of possibilities is vast.

In our case, min-max normalization was used, to squash the data values to the intervals [0, 1]. The advantage of this method is that it preserves all relationships of the data values exactly.

Post-processing covers any process that is applied to the output of the network. As with pre-processing, it is entirely dependent on the application. Sometimes it is just the reverse process of data pre-processing, as it is in this study.

4.3 Organization of the Data Sets

There are four sets of data presented in this study. They are subdivided into training, validation, and test sets. Organization of the data sets, and the amount of data points in each set are given in Table 3. Each set contains data points, belonging to different systems for different problem sizes. This is necessary to prevent data redundancy, and to ensure a proper training and testing process.

Table 3. Organization of the data sets

	Data set 1	Data set 2	Data set 3	Data set 4
Total Number of Data	250	100	275	300
Number of Training Data	150	60	190	220
Number of Validation Data	17	16	22	27
Number of Test Data	83	24	63	53

5 Results

To train a network and measure how well it performs, an error function (or cost function) must be defined. The weights of the network are updated in the direction that makes the error function minimum. The mean square error (mse), one of the most common error functions, is used in this study. The mean square errors are calculated by the program using the equation 5, where $t(k)$ is the target value, $a(k)$ is the output of the neural network at kth point and Q is the number of elements in the data set.

$$mse = \frac{1}{Q}\sum_{k=1}^{Q} e(k)^2 = \frac{1}{Q}\sum_{k=1}^{Q} (t(k) - a(k))^2 \qquad (5)$$

The training set is given as $[p_1, t_1][p_2, t_2]\ldots[p_q, t_q]$ where $[p_q]$ is an input to the network, and $[t_q]$ is the corresponding target output. As each input is applied to the network, the network output is compared to the target. The error is calculated as the difference between the target output t and the network output a. Weights are adjusted to minimize the average of the sum of these errors.

Table 4. Results for selected data sets

Dataset	Training Performance (mse)	Network Testing Performance (mse)	Average Error (%)	Standard Deviation
1	6.538E-11	5.950E-10	0.91852	1.17
2	1.932E-11	3.204E-11	0.61109	0.72
3	6.741E-10	2.393E-08	1.82467	2.61
4	1.354E-07	1.418E-07	0.19110	0.13

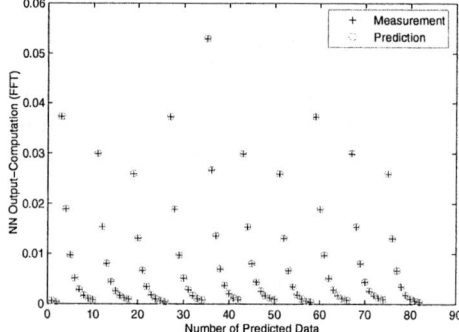

Fig. 4. Performance of the computation prediction model for FFT application (Dataset1)

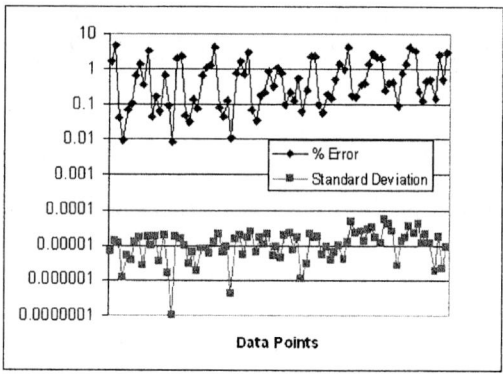

Fig. 5. Percentage errors and standard deviations for computation prediction model using points in Dataset 1

Also average percentage errors and the standard deviations are calculated for each data set using the equation 6 and equation 7, where Q is the number of elements in the data set. The results are given in Table 4.

$$Avg.Error(\%) = \frac{1}{Q} \sum_{i=1}^{Q} \frac{|measurement_i - prediction_i|}{measurement_i} x100\% \qquad (6)$$

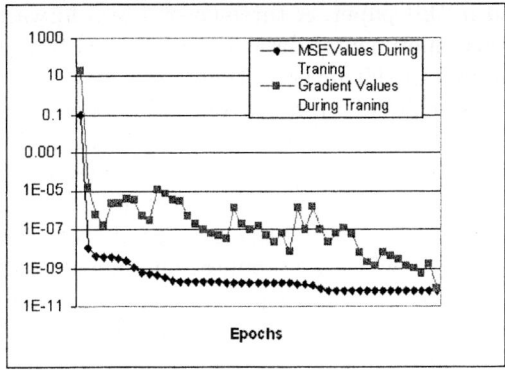

Fig. 6. Changes in mean squared error and gradient values during training for FFT application (Dataset 1)

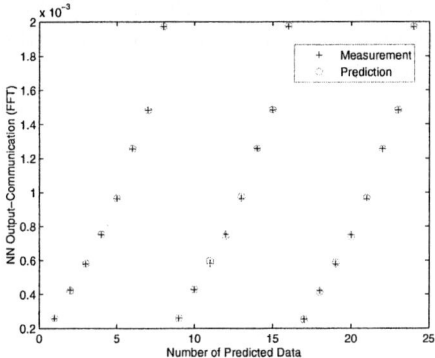

Fig. 7. Performance of the communication prediction model for FFT application (Dataset 2)

$$Stdev = \sqrt{\frac{\sum_{i=1}^{Q}(Error(\%)_i - Avg.Error(\%))^2}{Q-1}} \qquad (7)$$

Fig. 4 shows the network performance for Dataset 1. Fig. 5 shows the resulting percentage errors and the standard deviations for Dataset 1, in logarithmic scale. Fig. 6 shows the changes in mean squared error and gradient values during training for the same data set.

Fig. 7 shows the actual and predicted result for the communication prediction model, using Dataset 2.

6 Conclusions

A novel approach making use of neural network models to predict the performance of FFT and Monte Carlo applications on parallel systems has been developed and presented in this paper. A three-layered feed-forward NN is used and trained by using the experimental data. Four different training,validation and test sets have been used in this investigation.

The accuracy rates achieved are very promising. In particular, the predictions are within approximately 5% of measured execution times. Almost a perfect fit between measurements and predictions have been achieved in most cases.

However, determination of the presented neural network inputs requires a level of effort, in terms of identifying the number of operations and number of MPI communication calls, which are application dependent. These parameters have been expressed as a function of problem size and number of processors, after an in-depth analysis of target application's source codes.

Recurrent Neural Networks which are functionally dynamic are more powerful than feedforward networks and may produce more consistent results.

In future studies, extracting fuzzy rules from the available data to combine with neural networks will be valuable as well. The obtained rules may reveal more insight into the data that generated the model, providing a better understanding of system dynamics to identify the effects of individual parameters to performance. The fusion of neural networks and fuzzy logic in neurofuzzy models can provide learning as well as readability.

References

1. Chunrong Yuan, Niemann, H. : An appearance based neural image processing algorithm for 3-D object recognition. Proceedings of International Conference on Image Processing, p. 344 - 347, vol.3. (2000)
2. Dongarra J.J., Martin J., and Worlton J.: Computer Benchmarking Paths And Pitfalls. IEEE Computer 24 : 38-43(1987)
3. Gropp W.,Lusk E., and Skjellum A.: Using MPI: Portable Parallel Programming with the Message Passing Interface.Scientific and Engineering Computation Series. The MIT Press; 2nd edition (1999)
4. Hagan M. and Menhaj M.: Training Feedforward Networks with the Marquardt Algorithm. IEEE Transactions on Neural Networks, Vol. 5, No. 6, pp. 989-993. (1994)
5. Han J. and Kamber M.: Data mining concepts and techniques. Academic Press, San Francisco (2001)
6. Jackel P.: Monte Carlo Methods in Finance. John Wiley & Sons Ltd., England (2002)
7. Jain R.: The Art of Computer Systems Performance Analysis - Techniques for Experimental Design, Measurement, Simulation and Modelling. John Wiley & Sons Ltd. (1991)
8. Jain Anil K., Mao J., Mohiuddin K. M.: Artificial Neural Networks: A Tutorial. IEEE Computer 29(3): 31-44 (1996)
9. John L. K.: More on finding a single number to indicate overall performance of a benchmark suite. ACM SIGARCH Computer Architecture News, v.32 n.1, March (2004)
10. Knuth E. D.: The art of computer programming. 2 nd edn, Addison-Wesley (1981)
11. Lilja David J.: Measuring computer performance: a practitioner's guide, Cambridge University Press, New York, NY. (2000)

12. Neji Z., and Beji F.M.: Neural Network and Time Series Identification and Prediction. IEEE INNS-ENNS International Joint Conference on Neural Networks (IJCNN'00) 4, Italy (2000)
13. G.R.Nudd, D.J. Kerbyson, E.Papaefstathiou, J.S.Harper, S.C.Perry, D.V.Wilcox. PACE: A toolset for the performance prediction of parallel and distributed systems. Journal of High Performance and Scientific Applications, (1999)
14. Pacheco Peter S.: Parallel Programming with MPI. Morgan Kaufmann, (1997)
15. Reed R. D. and Marks R. J.: Neural Smithing: Supervised Learning in Feedforward Artificial Neural Networks. MIT Press (1999)

Decomposition and Resolution of Fuzzy Relation Equations (II) Based on Boolean-Type Implications*

Yanbin Luo[1], Chunjie Yang[1], Yongming Li[2], and Daoying Pi[1]

[1] National Laboratory of Industrial Control Technology,
Zhejiang University, Hangzhou 310027, China
luoyanbin008@yahoo.com.cn, cjyang,dypi@iipc.zju.edu.cn
[2] Institute of Fuzzy Systems, College of Mathematics and Information Sciences,
Shaanxi Normal University, Xi'an 710062, China
liyongm@snnu.edu.cn

Abstract. The problem of solving fuzzy relation equations (II) based on Boolean-type implications is studied in the present paper. Decomposition of fuzzy relation equations (II) based on Boolean-type implications is first presented in a finite case. Then, the solution existence of fuzzy relation equations (II) based on Boolean-type implications is discussed, and for nice Boolean-type implications, some new solvability criteria based upon the notion of "solution matrices" are given. It is also shown that for each solution **a** of a fuzzy relation equation (II) based on Boolean-type implication, there exists a minimal solution $\mathbf{a}_*$ of this equation, such that $\mathbf{a}_*$ is less than or equal to **a**, whenever the solution set of this equation is nonempty. The complete solution set of fuzzy relation equation (II) based on Boolean-type implication can be determined by all minimal solutions of this equation. Finally, an effective method to solve fuzzy relation equations (II) based on Boolean-type implications is proposed.

1 Introduction

The concept of composite fuzzy relation equations(FREs) and their solutions originated by Sanchez [7]. Since then, much of the research on sup $-t$ composition FREs have been done [1,2,7,8]. Min-implication composition FRE based on a Boolean-type implication (which contains R-implication, S-implication and Ql-implication) is another important type of FREs, which was first studied by Miyakoshi and Shimbo [6] for R-implication. The importance of min-implication FRE has been shown in [3,4,5]. Min-implication composition fuzzy relation equations based on Boolean-type implications have the following two cases:

(I) Given $A = (a_{ij})_{n \times m}$, $B = (b_{ij})_{n \times k}$, determine $X = (x_{ij})_{m \times k}$, such that

$$A \circ^{\theta} X = B. \tag{1}$$

---

* This work is sponsored by the 973 program of China under grant No.2002CB312200, the National Science Foundation of China under grant No.60474045, the Scientific Research Foundation for the Returned Overseas Chinese Scholars, State Education Ministry, Zhejiang Province and Zhejiang University.

(II) Given $R = (r_{ij})_{m \times k}$, $B = (b_{ij})_{n \times k}$, determine $X = (x_{ij})_{n \times m}$, such that
$$X \circ^\theta R = B. \tag{2}$$

The algebraic properties of Boolean-type implications θ determine that we have to discuss the resolution problem of the two types of fuzzy relation equations respectively. We have studied the problem of solving min-implication fuzzy relation equations (I), which the implication is any R-implication [3] or S-implication [4], and have also got better research results. In the present paper, we shall discuss the resolution problem of min-implication composition fuzzy relation equations (II) based on Boolean-type implications. For the remainder of this paper, all fuzzy relation equations (FREs) denote min-implication composition fuzzy relation equations (II) based on Boolean-type implications.

The structure of the rest of this paper is organized as follows. In Section 2, we give a brief review of Boolean-type implications, and some notations used in this paper are also given. Then, the decomposition of FREs is presented. In Section 3, we discuss the simple equations of θ-implications. Some solvability criterion of FREs is studied in Section 4. In Section 5, the complete solution set of FREs is obtained based on an effective method to find the minimal solution set, and some examples are presented in Section 6 to illustrate the methods in this paper. Conclusions are given in Section 7.

2 Boolean-Type Implications and Decomposition of FREs Based on Boolean-Type Implications

In this paper, we assume that the universe of discourse is a finite set. Suppose that $X = \{x_1, x_2, \cdots x_n\}$, $Y = \{y_1, y_2, \cdots, y_m\}$, $N_n = \{1, 2, \cdots, n\}$, let $F(X)$ denote the set of all of fuzzy subsets in X, $A \in F(X)$, $B \in F(Y)$, and $R \in F(X \times Y)$.

Definition 1. *Let P is a poset, two binary operators T_θ and θ in P are called adjoined operators, if the following three conditions are satisfied:*

(i) $T_\theta : P \times P \to P$ is monotonic increasing,

(ii) $\theta : P \times P \to P$ is non-increasing about the first variable, and non-decreasing about the second variable,

(iii) $T_\theta(a, b) \leq c$ iff (if and only if) $a \leq b\theta c$, $a, b, c \in P$.

Then θ is called residual implication, in short form, R-implication.

Definition 2. *Let s be a triangle co-norm, h be a negation. Define θ: $[0,1]^2 \to [0,1]$ as follows*
$$a\theta b = s(h(a), b), \forall a, b \in [0, 1], \tag{3}$$
then θ is called Strong implication, in short form, S-implication.

Definition 3. *Let s be a triangle co-norm, t be the dual triangle norm of s, i.e, $t(a, b) = h(s(h(a), h(b)))$, h be a negation, define θ: $[0,1]^2 \to [0,1]$ as follows*
$$a\theta b = s(h(a), t(a, b)), \forall a, b \in [0, 1], \tag{4}$$
then θ be called a Quantum logic implication, in short form, Ql-implication.

The true values of the above three types of implications are just the same under the two-value logic, so they are also called *Boolean-type implications*.

For a fuzzy relation equation

$$A \circ^\theta R = B \tag{5}$$

where A, R, B are $n \times m$ matrix, $m \times k$ matrix and $n \times k$ matrix, respectively. Eq.(5) can be decomposed as the set of n simpler fuzzy relation equations:

$$\mathbf{a} \circ^\theta R = \mathbf{b} \tag{6}$$

where $\mathbf{a}_{1 \times m}$ and $\mathbf{b}_{n \times 1}$ are the row vector of A and the column vector of B, respectively. Let $\eta(R, \mathbf{b})$ be the solution set of Eq.(6), i.e. $\eta(R, \mathbf{b}) = \{\mathbf{a} : \mathbf{a} \circ^\theta R = \mathbf{b}\}$.

Eq.(6) can be further decomposed as a system of k fuzzy relation equations:

$$\mathbf{a} \circ^\theta \mathbf{r} = b \tag{7}$$

where $\mathbf{r}_{m \times 1}$ be a column vector of R, $b \in [0,1]$. Let $\eta(\mathbf{r}, b)$ be the solution set of Eq.(7), i.e. $\eta(\mathbf{r}, b) = \{\mathbf{a} : \mathbf{a} \circ^\theta \mathbf{r} = b\}$.

It is easily observed that Eq.(5) has a solution iff the k equations of form (6) have at least one solution for all row vectors $\mathbf{b}$ of B, and that Eq.(6) has a solution for an $\mathbf{a}$ iff all the n equations of form (7) have at least one common solution for $\mathbf{a}$.

Definition 4. *Let $R = (a_{ij})_{m \times k}$, $B = (b_{ij})_{n \times k}$, θ be any R-implication, define the θ-composition of B and R^{-1} as follows*

$$\theta(B, R^{-1})(i, j) = \inf_{t \in N_k} (b_{it} \theta r_{tj}).$$

For any R-implication, Miyakoshi obtained the following result in [6].

Proposition 1. *For any R-implication θ, $\eta(R, \mathbf{b}) \neq \emptyset$ iff $\theta(\mathbf{b}, R^{-1}) \in \eta(R, \mathbf{b})$ and $\theta(\mathbf{b}, R^{-1})$ is the greatest solution.*

For Eq.(7), Baets got the following result in [1].

Proposition 2. *Let θ be any nice Boolean-type implication, then $\eta(\mathbf{r}, b) \neq \emptyset$ iff $\sup\{x : x\theta \mathbf{r} \geq b\}$ is the greatest solution.*

3   Equations of θ-Implications

The resolution problem of Eqs. (5) and Eq. (6) can be converted into the resolution of Eq.(7), so we first consider the simple equation of the form

$$x\theta r = b, \tag{8}$$

where $r, b \in [0,1]$ are given, Eq. (8) is actually a special case of Eq. (7), $n = m = 1$.

Definition 5. *Let θ be a R-implication. θ is called a nice R-implication (NR-implication) if θ is continuous with respect to the first variable, i.e. $\forall r \in [0,1]$, the function $x\theta r : [0,1] \to [0,1]$ is continuous.*

Remark 1. Let $f: [0,1] \to [0,1]$ be a monotone decreasing function. From elementary analysis, we know that, f is continuous iff $f: [0,1] \to [f(1), f(0)]$ is a surjective function.

Due to the above remark, θ is an NR-implication iff for any $r \in [0,1]$, the function $x\theta r : [0,1] \to [r,1]$ is a surjective function.

It is a routine to prove the following proposition.

Proposition 3. *Let θ be a R-implication, T_θ is its corresponding t-norm. If T_θ is continuous in $[0, 1]$, then θ is an NR-implication.*

Definition 6. *Let θ be an S-implication. If the function $f(x) = x\theta r$ is continuous, then θ is called a nice S-implication (NS-implication).*

Due to the above remark, θ is an NS-implication iff for any $r \in [0,1]$, the function $x\theta r : [0,1] \to [r,1]$ is surjective.

We can easily obtain the following result.

Proposition 4. *Let θ be an S-implication. If both the corresponding triangle co-norm s and the negation h are all continuous, then θ is an NS-implication.*

Remark 2. Both NR-implications and NS-implications are called nice Boolean-type implications.

Now, we give a solvability criterion for Eq. (8).

Proposition 5. *Let θ be a nice Boolean implication, and $a, b, x \in [0,1]$. The equation $x\theta r = b$ has a solution for x iff $r \leq b$.*

For a general Boolean-type implication we can give the following result.

Theorem 1. *Let θ be a Boolean-type implication, and $r \in [0,1]$. If the image set of the function $x\theta r : [0,1] \to [0,1]$ is denoted by $I(r)$, then the equation $x\theta r = b$ has a solution iff $b \in I(r)$.*

Proof. If the equation $x\theta r = b$ has a solution for x iff there exists a $x_0 \in [0,1]$, such that $x_0 \theta r = b$ iff $b \in I(r)$. □

Let $r \hat{\otimes}^\theta b$ and $r \check{\otimes}^\theta b$ denote the maximal solution and the minimal solution of Eq.(8), respectively (if they exist), i.e.

$$r \hat{\otimes}^\theta b = \sup\{x \in [0,1] : x\theta r = b\},$$

$$r \check{\otimes}^\theta b = \inf\{x \in [0,1] : x\theta r = b\}.$$

Based on the above notation, the maximal solution operator (max-SO) $\hat{w}$ and the minimal solution operator (min-SO) $\check{w}$ are defined as follows

$$\hat{w}_\theta(r,b) = \begin{cases} r\hat{\otimes}^\theta b, & r \leq b \\ 1, & r > b, \end{cases} \tag{9}$$

$$\check{w}_\theta(r,b) = \begin{cases} r\check{\otimes}^\theta b, & r \leq b \\ 0, & r > b. \end{cases} \tag{10}$$

For the convenience of denoting the minimal solution matrix, we define the following operator

$$w_{min}(a,b) = \begin{cases} 0, & a < b \\ b, & a \geq b. \end{cases} \tag{11}$$

Some useful properties of Max-SO and Min-SO for any Boolean-type implication are provided in the following.

Lemma 1. *Let $r, b \in [0,1]$, and θ be any nice Boolean-type implication. Then $\check{w}_\theta(r,b)\theta r \geq b$.*

Lemma 2. *Let $r, b \in [0,1]$, and θ be any nice Boolean-type implication. Then $\hat{w}_\theta(r,b) \geq \check{w}_\theta(r,b)$.*

4 Resolution of FREs Based on Boolean-Type Implications

In this section we mainly discuss some conditions for the existence of the solution of Eq. (6). We have known Eq. (6) has a solution iff k equations of form (7) have a common solution, so we establish the following lemma.

Lemma 3. *Let $\mathbf{a} \circ^\theta \mathbf{r} = b$ be a fuzzy relation equation of form (7). Then $\eta(\mathbf{r},b) \neq \emptyset$ iff there exists $j \in N_m$, such that $b \in I(r_j)$.*

Proof. If $\eta(\mathbf{r},b) \neq \emptyset$, then there exists a row vector $\mathbf{a}$, such that $\mathbf{a} \circ^\theta \mathbf{r} = b$. Thus there exists $j \in N_m$ such that $a_j \theta r_j = b$. From Theorem 1, we have $b \in I(r_j)$. On the other hand, if there exists $j \in N_m$ such that $b \in I(r_j)$, then there exists a scalar $a_j \in [0,1]$ such that $a_j \theta r_j = b$. We construct a row vector $\mathbf{a}$ with $a_i = 0$ for $i \neq j$. Obviously, $\mathbf{a} \in \eta(\mathbf{r},b)$. So, $\eta(\mathbf{r},b) \neq \emptyset$. □

Corollary 1. *Let $\mathbf{a} \circ^\theta \mathbf{r} = b$ be a fuzzy relation equation of form (7) and θ be a nice Boolean-type implication. Then $\eta(\mathbf{r},b) \neq \emptyset$ iff there exists $j \in N_m$, such that $r_j \leq b$.*

Corollary 2. *Let $\mathbf{a} \circ^\theta \mathbf{r} = b$ be a fuzzy relation equation of form (7). If there exists $j \in N_m$ such that $r_j = 0$, then $\eta(\mathbf{r},b) \neq \emptyset$.*

Based on the above conditions for existence of the solution of Eq. (7), we can easily get the conditions for existence of the solution of Eq. (6).

Theorem 2. Let $a \circ^\theta R = b$ be a fuzzy relation equation of form (6). If for any $i \in N_k$, there exists $j \in N_m$ such that $b_i \in I(r_{ji})$ and $b_l \notin I(r_{jl}), \forall l \in N_k - \{i\}$, then $\eta(R, b) \neq \emptyset$.

Proof. Define $\mathbf{a} = [a_j]^{-1}$ as follows:

$$a_j = \begin{cases} r_{ji} \hat{\otimes}^\theta b_i, & \exists i \in N_k, b_i \in I(r_{ji}) \text{ and } b_l \notin I(r_{jl}), \forall l \in N_k - \{i\} \\ 0, & \text{otherwise,} \end{cases} \quad (12)$$

for $j = 1, 2, \cdots, m$.

From (12), we have $\forall i \in N_k, j \in N_m$ such that $b_i \in I(r_{ji})$ and $b_l \notin I(r_{jl})$, $\forall l \in N_k - \{i\}$,

$$a_j \theta r_{ji} = (r_{ji} \hat{\otimes}^\theta b_i) \theta r_{ji} = b_i. \quad (13)$$

For the other case, $\forall i \in N_k, j \in N_m$ such that $b_i \notin I(r_{ji})$, or $b_i \in I(r_{ji})$ and $\exists l \in N_k - \{i\}$ such that $b_l \in I(r_{lj})$, from (13), one obtains

$$a_j \theta r_{ji} = 0 \theta r_{ji} = 1. \quad (14)$$

So, from (13) and (14), we get

$$a_j \theta r_{ji} = \begin{cases} b_i, & 1 \theta r_{ji} \leq b_i \\ 1, & \text{otherwise,} \end{cases}$$

for any $i = 1, 2, \cdots, k$, and consequently $\inf_{j \in N_m}(a_j \theta r_{ji}) = b_i$ holds for any $i \in N_k$. So, $\mathbf{a} \circ^\theta R = \mathbf{b}$, that is, $\eta(R, \mathbf{b}) \neq \emptyset$. □

Corollary 3. Let $a \circ^\theta R = b$ be a fuzzy relation equation of form (6). If for any $i \in N_k$, there exists $j \in N_m$ such that $r_{ji} \leq b_i$ and $r_{jl} \geq b_l, \forall l \in N_k - \{i\}$, then $\eta(R, b) \neq \emptyset$.

Corollary 4. Let $a \circ^\theta R = b$ be a fuzzy relation equation of form (6). If for any $i \in N_k$, there exists $j \in N_m$ such that $r_{ji} = 0$ and $r_{jl} = 1, \forall l \in N_k - \{i\}$, then $\eta(R, b) \neq \emptyset$.

In the following, based on the solution matrices we propose a sufficient and necessary condition for the existence of the solution of the fuzzy relation equation of form (6).

Definition 7. Let $a \circ^\theta R = b$ be a fuzzy relation equation of form (6), and θ be a nice Boolean-type implication. The matrix $(\bar{\Gamma}_{ij})_{k \times m}$ is called a mean solution matrix (mean-SM) of the fuzzy relation equation, where

$$\bar{\Gamma}_{ij} = \breve{w}_\theta(r_{ji}, b_j), \forall i \in N_k, \forall j \in N_m.$$

The matrix $(\hat{\Gamma}_{ij})_{k \times m}$ is called the maximal solution matrix (max-SM) of the fuzzy relation equation, where

$$\hat{\Gamma}_{ij} = \hat{w}_\theta(r_{ji}, b_j), \forall i \in N_k, \forall j \in N_m.$$

The matrix $(\check{\Gamma}_{ij})_{k \times m}$ is called the minimal solution matrix (min-SM), where

$$\check{\Gamma}_{ij} = w_{min}(\inf_{l \in N_m} \hat{\Gamma}_{il}, \bar{\Gamma}_{ij}), \forall i \in N_k, \forall j \in N_m.$$

Theorem 3. *Let $a \circ^\theta R = b$ be a fuzzy relation equation of form (6). If $\eta(r_{\cdot j}, b_j) \neq \emptyset$, $\forall j \in N_k$, then $\hat{\Gamma}_{\cdot j} \in \eta(r_{\cdot j}, b_j)$, $\bar{\Gamma}_{\cdot j} \in \eta(r_{\cdot j}, b_j)$, $\forall j \in N_k$, where $\hat{\Gamma}$ and $\bar{\Gamma}$ are the max-SM and the mean-SM, and $r_{j \cdot}$ and $r_{\cdot j}$ are the jth row and jth column of the matrix R, respectively.*

Proof. Since $\eta(r_{\cdot j}, b_j) \neq \emptyset$, from Lemma 3, one obtains there exists $i \in N_m$ such that $r_{ij} \leq b_j$. Thus, $\hat{\Gamma}_{ji} = r_{ij} \hat{\otimes}^\theta b_j$ and $\bar{\Gamma}_{ji} = r_{ji} \check{\otimes}^\theta b_j$, it follows that $\hat{\Gamma}_{ji} \theta r_{ij} = b_j$ and $\bar{\Gamma}_{ji} \theta r_{ij} = b_j$. On the other hand, let $\forall r, b \in [0,1]$, since θ is a nice Boolean-type implication, it follows from Lemma 1 that $\check{w}_\theta(r, b) \theta r \geq b$. Again, it follows from that $\hat{w}_\theta(r, b) \theta r \geq b$. So, $\hat{\Gamma}_{ji} \theta r_{ij} \geq b_j$ and $\bar{\Gamma}_{ji} \theta r_{ij} \geq b_j$. Hence, $\inf_{i \in N_m}(\hat{\Gamma}_{ji} \theta r_{ij}) = b_j$ and $\inf_{i \in N_m}(\bar{\Gamma}_{ji} \theta r_{ij}) = b_j$, $\forall j \in N_k$. This means that $\hat{\Gamma}_{\cdot j} \in \eta(r_{\cdot j}, b_j)$ and $\bar{\Gamma}_{\cdot j} \in \eta(r_{\cdot j}, b_j)$, $\forall j \in N_k$. □

Corollary 5. *Let $a \circ^\theta r = b$ be a fuzzy relation equation of form (7). If $\eta(r, b) \neq \emptyset$, then $\check{\Gamma} \in \eta(r, b)$.*

Theorem 4. *Let $a \circ^\theta R = b$ be a fuzzy relation equation of form (6). The following properties are equivalent:*
(i) $\eta(R, b) = \emptyset$; (ii) $\exists j \in N_k$ such that $\check{\Gamma}_{\cdot j} = 0$ and $b_j \neq 1$.

Proof. (i)⇒(ii): If $\eta(R, \mathbf{b}) = \emptyset$, then there are the following two cases:
(a) $\exists j \in N_k$, $\eta(r_{\cdot j}, b_j) = \emptyset$, and $b_j \neq 1$, then $\forall i \in N_m$, $r_{ij} > b_j$, $\bar{\Gamma}_{\cdot j} = 0$, so, $\check{\Gamma}_{\cdot j} = 0$; (b) $\eta(r_{\cdot j}, b_j) \neq \emptyset$, $\forall j \in N_k$. Since $\eta(R, \mathbf{b}) = \emptyset$, if $\hat{\mathbf{a}} \notin \eta(R, \mathbf{b})$, then there exists $j \in N_k$ such that $\hat{\mathbf{a}} \notin \eta(r_{\cdot j}, b_j)$. It follows from Theorem 3 that $\hat{\Gamma}_{\cdot j} \in \eta(r_{\cdot j}, b_j)$ and $\bar{\Gamma}_{\cdot j} \in \eta(r_{\cdot j}, b_j)$. Therefore, from Lemma 3, we have $\exists i \in N_m$ such that $r_{ij} \leq b_j$. Then, for any $i \in N_m$ such that $r_{ij} \leq b_j$, one obtains $\hat{a}_i = \inf \hat{\Gamma}_{\cdot i} \leq \hat{\Gamma}_{ji} = r_{ij} \hat{\otimes}^\theta b_j$. Furthermore, $\bar{\Gamma}_{\cdot j} \leq \hat{\Gamma}_{\cdot j}$ and $\hat{a}_i \notin \eta(r_{ij}, b_j)$. Hence, $\hat{a}_i < r_{ij} \check{\otimes}^\theta b_j = \bar{\Gamma}_{ji}$. It follows that $\check{\Gamma}_{\cdot j} = w_{min}(\hat{\mathbf{a}}, \bar{\Gamma}_{\cdot j}) = 0$. While for any $i \in N_m$ such that $r_{ij} > b_j$, we have $\bar{\Gamma}_{ji} = 0$. Therefore, $\check{\Gamma}_{\cdot j} = w_{min}(\hat{\mathbf{a}}, \bar{\Gamma}_{\cdot j}) = 0$.

(ii⇒i): If $\check{\Gamma}_{\cdot j} = 0$, there are the following two cases:
(a)$\bar{\Gamma}_{\cdot j} = 0$; (b)$\bar{\Gamma}_{\cdot j} \neq 0$, and $\hat{a}_i < \bar{\Gamma}_{ji}$, $\forall i \in N_m$. If $\bar{\Gamma}_{\cdot j} = 0$, since $b_j \neq 1$, it follows that $\bar{\Gamma}_{\cdot j} \theta r_{\cdot j} = 0 \theta r_{\cdot j} = 1 \neq b_j$. It means that $\bar{\Gamma}_{\cdot j} \notin \eta(r_{\cdot j}, b_j)$. Thus, it follows from Theorem 3 that $\eta(r_{\cdot j}, b_j) = \emptyset$. So, $\eta(R, \mathbf{b}) = \emptyset$. If $\bar{\Gamma}_{\cdot j} \neq 0$ and $\hat{a}_i < \bar{\Gamma}_{ji}$, $\forall i \in N_m$, then $\forall i \in N_m$ such that $\bar{\Gamma}_{ij} \neq 0$, we have $\hat{a}_i < \bar{\Gamma}_{ij} = r_{ij} \check{\otimes}^\theta b_j$. Hence, $\hat{a}_i \theta r_{ij} > \bar{\Gamma}_{ji} \theta r_{ij} = (r_{ij} \check{\otimes}^\theta b_j) \theta r_{ij} = b_j$, it follows that for any $i \in N_m$, $\hat{a}_i \theta r_{ij} > b_j$. Thus, $\inf_{i \in N_m}(\hat{a}_i \theta r_{ij}) > b_j$. Therefore, $\hat{\mathbf{a}} \notin \eta(R, \mathbf{b})$, that is, $\eta(R, \mathbf{b}) = \emptyset$. □

5 Complete Solution Set of the FRE Based on Boolean-Type Implications

Let $\mathbf{t} = \inf \hat{\Gamma}$, that is, $\mathbf{t} = (t_1, t_2, \ldots, t_m)$, where $t_i = \inf_j \hat{w}_\theta(r_{ij}, b_j), \forall i \in N_m$. The following lemma gives another solvability criterion of the fuzzy relation equation of form (6).

Lemma 4. *(i) The fuzzy relation equation of form (6) has a solution iff $\mathbf{t} \circ^\theta R \leq \mathbf{b}$. (ii) If the fuzzy relation equation of form (6) has a solution, then $\mathbf{t}$ is the greatest solution.*

Proof. (i) "If" part. Since $\inf_{i\in N_m}(t_i\theta r_{ij}) = \inf_{i\in N_m}(\inf_j \hat{w}_\theta(r_{ij},b_j)\theta r_{ij}) \geq \inf_{i\in N_m}(\hat{w}_\theta(r_{ij},b_j)\theta r_{ij}) = b_j$, then, the inequality $\mathbf{t} \circ^\theta R \geq \mathbf{b}$ always holds. So, $\mathbf{t} \circ^\theta R = \mathbf{b}$. "Only if" part. Assume that $\mathbf{a} = (a_1,a_2,\ldots,a_m)$ is a solution of the fuzzy relation equation of form (6), then $a_i\theta r_{ij} \geq b_j, \forall i \in N_m$. Hence, $\hat{w}_\theta(r_{ij},b_j) \geq a_i$, it follows that $t_i \geq a_i$. Therefore, $\inf_i(t_i\theta r_{ij}) \leq \inf_i(a_i\theta r_{ij}) = b_j$, that is, $\mathbf{t} \circ^\theta R \leq \mathbf{b}$.

(ii) The proof of "Only if" part of (i) also shows that if the equation (6) has a solution, then $\mathbf{t}$ is the greatest solution. □

The following theorem shows that the complete solution set of the fuzzy relation equation of form (6) is determined by its greatest solution and minimal solutions.

Theorem 5. *Let $\mathbf{a}\circ^\theta R = \mathbf{b}$ be a fuzzy relation equation of form (6). If $\eta(R,\mathbf{b}) \neq \emptyset$, then for any $\mathbf{a} \in \eta(R,\mathbf{b})$, there is a minimal element $\mathbf{a}_*$ in $\eta(R,\mathbf{b})$ such that $\mathbf{a} \leq \mathbf{a}_*$, and the minimal set of the solution set $\eta(R,\mathbf{b})$ is a finite set.*

Proof. It follows from Lemma 4 that $\mathbf{t}$ is the greatest solution. Define $N(j) = \{i \in N_m : t_i\theta r_{ij} = b_j\}, \forall j \in N_k$. Then, $N(j) \neq \emptyset$. Let $E_t = \{f \subseteq N_m : \forall j \in N_k, f \cap N(j)$ contains at least one element$\}$. Then E_t is a finite poset under the subset inclusion. Let F be the subset of E_t including all minimal elements of E_t. Hence, F is finite and for any $f \in E_t$ there exists $g \in F$ such that $g \subseteq f$, and the elements of F are not comparable with each other(in other words, the elements of F don't contain each other). For any $f \in E_t$, construct $\mathbf{a}_f = (a_{1*}, a_{2*}, \ldots, a_{m*})$ as follows,

$$a_{i*} = \begin{cases} \sup\{r_{ij}\check{\otimes}^\theta b_j : i \in N(j)\}, & i \in f \\ 0, & \text{otherwise.} \end{cases} \qquad (15)$$

In the following we show that $M = \{\mathbf{a}_f : f \in F\}$ satisfies the conditions of the theorem.

First, for any $f \in E_t$, we prove $\mathbf{a}_f$ is a solution of the equation (6). If $b_j = 1$, then for any $i \in N(j), t_i = 0$. In this case, $a_{i*} = 0$. Thus, $\inf_i(a_{i*}\theta r_{ij}) = 1 = b_j$. If $b_j < 1$, then there exists $i_0 \in N_m$ such that $t_{i_0}\theta r_{i_0 j} = b_j$, so, $i_0 \in N(j)$. In this case, $\inf_i(a_{i*}\theta r_{ij}) \leq a_{i_0*}\theta r_{i_0 j} = (\sup\{r_{ij}\check{\otimes}^\theta b_j : i \in N(j)\})\theta r_{i_0 j} \leq (r_{i_0 j}\check{\otimes}^\theta b_j)\theta r_{i_0 j} = b_j$. On the other hand, since $i \in N(j)$, that is, $t_i\theta r_{ij} = b_j, r_{ij}\check{\otimes}^\theta b_j \leq t_i$. We have $a_{i*} = \sup\{r_{ij}\check{\otimes}^\theta b_j : i \in N(j)\} \leq \sup\{t_i : i \in N(j)\} = t_i$. Hence, $\inf_i(a_i\theta r_{ij}) \geq \inf_i(t_i\theta r_{ij}) = b_j$. Therefore, $\mathbf{a}_f = (a_{1*}, a_{2*}, \ldots, a_{m*})$ is a solution of the equation (6).

Second, for $f_1, f_2 \in E_t$, if $f_1 \subseteq f_2$, then it is obvious that $\mathbf{a}_{f_1} \leq \mathbf{a}_{f_2}$ from the definition of $\mathbf{a}_f$.

Third, for any solution $\mathbf{a} \in \eta(R,\mathbf{b})$, we shall prove there is $f \in F$ such that $\mathbf{a} \leq \mathbf{a}_f$. Let $N'(j) = \{i \in N_m : a_i\theta r_{ij} = b_j\}$, then $N'(j) \neq \emptyset$ and $N'(j) \subseteq N(j)$. Construct $E_a = \{f \subseteq N_m : \forall j \in N_k, f \cap N'(j)$ contains at least one element$\}$, then it is obvious that $E_a \subseteq E_t$. We show that for any $f \in E_a, \mathbf{a} \leq \mathbf{a}_f$, then there is $f \in F$ such that $\mathbf{a} \leq \mathbf{a}_f$. If $i \in f, \forall f \in E_a$, then $a_i\theta r_{ij} = b_j, \forall i \in N'(j)$. So, $a_i \geq r_{ij}\check{\otimes}^\theta b_j$. It follows that $a_i \geq \sup\{r_{ij}\check{\otimes}^\theta b_j : i \in N(j)\} = a_{i*}$. Therefore, $\mathbf{a} \geq \mathbf{a}_f, \forall f \in E_a$.

Fourth, we show that $M = \{\mathbf{a}_f : f \in F\}$ is the minimal subset of the solution set $\eta(R, \mathbf{b})$ of the equation (6). The left is only shown that all elements of M aren't comparable with each other. Since F is minimal, for any $f_1, f_2 \in F$, there exist $i_1 \in f_1$ and $i_2 \in f_2$ such that $i_1 \notin f_2, i_2 \notin f_1$. In this case, the i_2th coordinate of $\mathbf{a}_{f_1}$ is 0, and the i_1th coordinate of $\mathbf{a}_{f_2}$, While both the i_1th coordinate of $\mathbf{a}_{f_1}$ and the i_2th coordinate of $\mathbf{a}_{f_2}$ aren't equal to 0. This means that $\mathbf{a}_{f_1}$ and $\mathbf{a}_{f_2}$ aren't comparable. Therefore, M is the minimal subset of the solution set $\eta(R, \mathbf{b})$ of the equation (6). □

In fact, the proof of Theorem 5 provides us a method of calculating all minimal solutions when the fuzzy relation equation of form (6) has a solution, and we present it in the following:

Step 1 Calculate the greatest solution $\mathbf{t}$.
Step 2 Calculate $N(j)$, for any $j \in N_k$, where $N(j) = \{i \in N_m : t_i \theta r_{ij} = b_j\}$.
Step 3 Calculate the solution matrix $\hat{\Gamma} = (\hat{\Gamma}_{ij})$.
Step 4 Calculate the set E_t and the minimal subset F of the set E_t, where $E_t = \{f \subseteq N_m : \forall j \in N_k, f \cap N(j) \text{ contains at least one element}\}$, F is the minimal subset of E_t as a poset under subset inclusion.
Step 5 Calculate the set $M = \{\mathbf{a}_f : f \in F\}$ as in (15) giving the set of the minimal solutions of Eq.(6).

6 Some Examples

In this section we mainly introduce some numerical examples to illustrate the methodologies proposed in this paper.

Example 1. $R = \begin{pmatrix} 0.7 & 0.5 & 1 & 0.5 \\ 0.5 & 0.2 & 0.7 & 0.6 \\ 1 & 0.8 & 0.3 & 0 \end{pmatrix}, \mathbf{b} = \begin{pmatrix} 0.8 & 0.8 & 0.9 & 0.8 \end{pmatrix}$.

Let $\forall a, b \in [0, 1]$, and S-implication θ be the Kleene-Dienes implication $R_K(a, b) = (1 - a) \vee b$. Noting that

$$\check{w}_\theta(a, b) = \begin{cases} 1 - b, & a \leq b \\ 0, & a > b \end{cases}, \hat{w}_\theta(a, b) = \begin{cases} 1 - b, & a \leq b \\ 1, & a > b \end{cases}.$$

Calculate $\hat{\Gamma}$ as:

$$\hat{\Gamma} = \begin{pmatrix} 0.2 & 0.2 & 1 \\ 0.2 & 0.2 & 0.2 \\ 1 & 0.1 & 0.1 \\ 0.2 & 0.2 & 0.2 \end{pmatrix},$$

Then, $\mathbf{t} = (0.2, 0.1, 0.1)$, it is easy to verify that $\mathbf{t}$ is a solution of this equation, and thus the greatest solution. We calculate $\bar{\Gamma}$ and $\check{\Gamma}$ as:

$$\bar{\Gamma} = \begin{pmatrix} 0.2 & 0.2 & 0 \\ 0.2 & 0.2 & 0.2 \\ 0 & 0.1 & 0.1 \\ 0.2 & 0.2 & 0.2 \end{pmatrix}, \check{\Gamma} = \begin{pmatrix} 0.2 & 0.2 & 0 \\ 0.2 & 0.2 & 0.2 \\ 0 & 0.1 & 0.1 \\ 0.2 & 0.2 & 0.2 \end{pmatrix}.$$

Then $N(1) = \{1\}, N(2) = \{1\}, N(3) = \{2,3\}$ and $N(4) = \{1\}$. In this case, $E_t = \{\{1,2\},\{1,3\}\}$ and $F = \{\{1,2\},\{1,3\}\}$. The solution corresponding to the set $\{1, 2\}$ is $(0.2, 0.1, 0)$, and the solution corresponding to the set $\{1, 3\}$ is $(0.2, 0, 0.1)$. Therefore, the minimal solution set is $M = \{(0.2, 0.1, 0), (0.2, 0, 0.1)\}$ and the complete solution set is $\eta(R, \mathbf{b}) = \{(0.2, 0.1, [0, 0.1]), (0.2, [0, 0.1], 0.1)\}$.

7 Conclusions

We have discussed the resolution problem of the fuzzy relation equation (I) based on R-implication [3] or S-implication [4]. In the present paper, the resolution problem of the fuzzy relation equation (II) is studied. The general decomposition of fuzzy relation equations (II) based on Boolean-type implications is first given in a finite case. Then, the solution existence of fuzzy relation equations (II) based on Boolean-type implications is studied, and for nice Boolean-type implications, some new solvability criteria based upon the notion of "solution matrices" are discussed. Finally, an effective method is given to solve the fuzzy relation equation (II) based on Boolean-type implications by introducing the notation of "solution matrices", and the minimal solution set of the fuzzy relation equation (II) is also presented.

References

1. De Basets, B.: Analytical solution methods for fuzzy relational equations. In: Dubois, D., Prade, H. (Eds.): Fundamentals of fuzzy sets. The handbooks of fuzzy sets series. vol. 1. Kluwer Academic Publishers, Dordrecht (2000) 291-340
2. Dubois, D., Prade, H.: Fuzzy sets in approximate reasoning, Part 1: Inference with possibility distributions. Fuzzy Sets Syst. **100 supplement** (1999) 73-132.
3. Luo, Y., Li, Y.: Decomposition and resolution of θ-Fuzzy relation equations based on R-implications. Fuzzy Syst. Math. **4** (2003) 81-87 (in Chinese)
4. Luo, Y., Li, Y.: Decomposition and resolution of min-implication fuzzy relation equations based on S-implications. Fuzzy Sets Syst. **148** (2004) 305-317
5. Li, Y., Shi, Z., Li, Z.: Approximation theory of fuzzy systems based upon genuine many valued implications-MIMO cases. Fuzzy Sets Syst. **130** (2002) 159-174
6. Miyakoshi, M., Shimbo, M.: Solutions of composite fuzzy relational equations with triangular norms. Fuzzy Sets Syst. **16** (1985) 53-63.
7. Sanchez, E.: Resolution of composite fuzzy relation equations. Inform. Contr. **30** (1976) 38-48.
8. Stamou, G. B., Tzafestas, S. G.: Fuzzy relation equations and fuzzy inference systems: an inside approach. IEEE Trans. Syst., Man, Cybern.-Part B. **29** (1999) 694-702.

Applying a Fuzzy Trust Model to E-Commerce Systems

Stefan Schmidt[1], Robert Steele[1], Tharam Dillon[1], and Elizabeth Chang[2]

[1] University of Technology, Sydney, PO Box 123 Broadway,
NSW 2007, Australia
{sschmidt, rsteele, tharam}@it.uts.edu.au
[2] Curtin University of Technology, Perth, GPO Box U1987,
WA 6845, Australia
e.chang@curtin.edu.au

Abstract. Moving towards automated service selection, contract negotiation, and contract fulfillment remains a promising vision for E-commerce systems. Trust is one of the main reasons why this vision is not put into practice in current E-commerce systems. Various theoretical models and technical concepts are in place to facilitate crucial factors such as system interoperability or communication-level security. However, proven models, to measure social values such as trustworthiness, reputation or credibility of service consumers and service providers in loosely coupled, distributed E-commerce systems, are the missing factors which prevent the adoption of automated service interaction. This paper demonstrates the application of our Fuzzy trust model in an E-commerce platform. We apply an exemplary business scenario to demonstrate the usage of our Fuzzy trust model.

1 Introduction

Intelligent agents are designed to act on behalf of users in multi-agent systems such as E-commerce markets; therefore, they need to mimic various abilities of the human mind. One characteristic of computational logic, however, represents its precision and certainty, which is contrary to the reasoning based on approximations and uncertainties applied by human beings. Hence, the interaction process between two agents should imitate the conventions of human behavior and thus needs to emulate reasoning based on tolerance and approximations. Fuzzy logic represents an excellent concept to close the gap between human reasoning and computational logic [3].

Variables like trustworthiness, credibility, and reputation imply subjectivity as well as uncertainty and they cannot be measured as crisp values; however, their calculation is still highly desirable. Fuzzy logic represents a mathematical approach to deal with uncertainty in the decision-making process by using imprecise numbers (fuzzy numbers) to express the membership to a context [2]. In the context of trust measurement for autonomous agent interactions, one is interested in processing this imprecise input to calculate the degree of trust in surrounding agents [1, 5].

In automated and unsupervised E-commerce platforms, where agents collaborate to reach owner-defined goals, the measurement and computation of trust is a key building block upon which all business interaction scenarios rely [10]. The credibility and reputation values can not be stored at a central repository in a truly distributed network where agents access various E-commerce platforms to achieve their goals. So if either party wants to access the credibility and reputation values of a particular peer-agent, it needs to broadcast a reputation request and processes the received information together with its private information and policies to compute an overall trust value. This distributed knowledge can then be used to evaluate the trustworthiness of potential business partners.

Our Fuzzy trust model [4] assigns public reputation and credibility values to all agents. Only agents, which possess sufficient credibility and reputation values, are qualified to receive peer opinions. These opinions facilitate the evaluation of trustworthiness values of eligible future negotiation partners. Service provider agents use this information to assess the risks when dealing with service consumer agents. For example, a service provider agent may offer a service consumer agent more attractive payment options if the service consumer agent possesses outstanding credibility and reputation values. A service consumer agent can accumulate these credibility and reputation values through continuous truthful and accurate trustworthiness reports.

This paper demonstrates the application of our Fuzzy trust model [4] in an E-commerce platform. We have chosen a business scenario to highlight the usage of our Fuzzy trust evaluation module, the business interaction module and the credibility adjustment module by describing an exemplary service selection and review process. Furthermore, the evolvement of credibility records for neighboring agents is examined and discussed.

2 Background

The measurement of trust is currently not satisfactorily reflected in multi-agent environments and needs further exploration [11]. We claim that the provision of sophisticated trust evaluation methods for distributed environments can overcome the current restraints for a wider acceptance of electronic and mobile commerce applications.

The importance of trust and reputation measurement between autonomous agents or services is widely recognized [6, 12, 13, 15] among researchers. For instance, Sycara [12] and Kollingbaum et al. [13] addressed this problem by introducing a third party which acts as trusted and certificate authority to guarantee the identity of agents and services. This approach may be suitable for semi-autonomous behavior within an E-commerce platform where agent-owners initially trust this central third-party authority node. However, in truly distributed systems where agents access multiple E-commerce platforms to accomplish their goals, a centrally trusted authority service is not realizable.

Another approach is the rating of a partner after the completion of a transaction following the ebay.com model [15]. This model relies on the availability of a central registry in which the global rating for each agent is openly accessible. This simple approach may work well in environments such as online communities or weblogs, but it has several weaknesses when applied to automated electronic and mobile commerce environments. A globally computed trustworthiness value, for example, is easily attackable by adding an infinite number of fake ratings to the global value. Furthermore, for the sake of fairness every agent would have to comply to the same regulations on how to rate its peers in a system with a central registry. This approach would not allow personalized and subjective interpretations and calculations of values for trustworthiness and credibility.

We claim that only the individual computation of trustworthiness and credibility values of one agent for another agent can fulfill the demand for security in multi-agent networks. These individual calculations can still use information provided by external sources such as peer nodes or registries, but the evaluation and processing of those information should be based on the individual settings of each agent-owner.

More recent contributions to the evaluation of trust and reputation using Bayesian networks [14] and fuzzy logic concepts [1, 5, 7] provided a starting point to improve the modeling capabilities of social networks. However, these models lack the individual trustworthiness and credibility computation as well as an integrated model which adjusts and reviews its parameters after the completion of a business interaction. They also do not recognize individual security requirements of agent-owners sufficiently.

Our proposed Fuzzy trust model enables intelligent agents to autonomously build a distributed trust network while reflecting the dynamic nature of trust. This paper demonstrates this capability in a business scenario by describing different stages of the trust building and trust development process.

3 Fuzzy Trust Model

We apply our proposed Fuzzy trust model [4] to an E-commerce system where autonomous agents collaborate in order to achieve their given goals. The model is composed of three modules which are designed to gradually build a trust network which will enable consumer agents to discover, select and evaluate service providers. On the other side, service providing agents will be able to evaluate the trustworthiness of service consumer agents. Figure 1 depicts this context for both, service consumer agents and service provider agents.

The agent to be assessed for trustworthiness is called Reputation Queried Agent. The agent assessing the Reputation Queried Agent's trustworthiness is called Trusting Agent. Peer agents which share information about their past experiences with the Requesting Agent are called Recommending Agents. Following [8, 9] we define trust as the Requesting Agent's belief in the Recommendation Queried Agent's willingness and capability to behave as expected by the Requesting Agent in a given context at a given time slot. We use the notion trustworthiness as a measure to quantify the trust level the Requesting Agent has in the Recommendation Queried Agent in a given context at a given time slot.

In our model, service consumer agents and service provider agents have strong incentives to report truthful and accurate trustworthiness values. Good reputation and credibility values lead to more business interactions for service provider agents since service consumer agents base their service selection on a trust evaluation process. This process depends on opinions, delivered by peer agents, about the service provider. On the other hand, service consumer agents also have public reputation and credibility values allocated to them. Moreover, service provider agents could use this information to assess the operative risks of dealing with service consumer agents. It allows them, for example, to offer a service consumer agent more attractive payment options if the service consumer agent possesses outstanding credibility and reputation values.

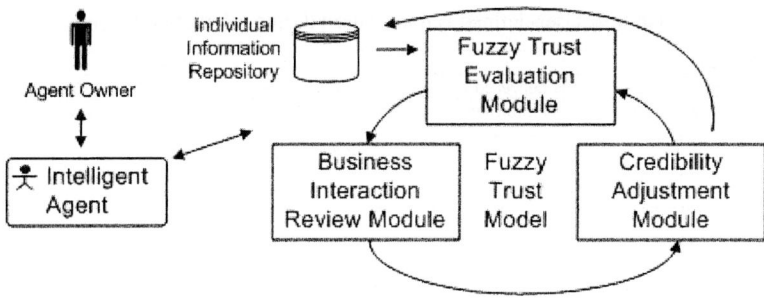

Fig. 1. Fuzzy Trust Model Lifecycle

Furthermore, our model only allows those agents with sufficient credibility and reputation values to receive peer opinions, which facilitate the evaluation of trustworthiness for eligible future negotiation partners. For both sides, the credibility and reputation values are not stored at a central repository but rather shared over the distributed network in the form of peer-opinions. So, if either party wants to access the credibility and reputation values of a particular peer-agent, it broadcasts a reputation request and processes the received information together with its private information and policies to compute an overall trust value.

4 Applying the Fuzzy Trust Model

The following example demonstrates the usage of our model for the development of an information repository consisting of credibility and trustworthiness values about the Recommendation Queried Agent. Besides a one-off setting where the agent-owner defines several values and policies, three major phases are defined by our proposed model [4]; trustworthiness evaluation, business interaction review, and credibility value adjustments.

As a business scenario, we have chosen the classic book buying example. The agent-owner specifies his requirements as follows:

Table 1. Context of the book-buying example

Context	Requirement Specification	Influence
Topic	Trust and Reputation in Service Oriented Architectures	4.5
Format	Hard-cover book	3.5
Delivery	Within 3 days	3
Price	< 20 USD	3
Payment	Defined in Policy Table (see Table 2.)	5

4.1 User Defined Settings

The agent-owner is required to define a set of variables and policies needed by the Trusting Agent at several stages of its trust calculations (see Table 2 and Table 3). The configuration of these parameters is a one-off task and mostly reflects the individual security requirements of the agent-owner. For example, it is necessary to specify the rate of decay ($N = 5$ years $= 1760$ days) which is used during the calculation of the Weighted Trustworthiness Value (WTV).

Table 2. User-defined variables used during calculation process

Variable	Value
Rate of decay (D) for Opinions delivered by Recommending Agents:	D = 5 years = 1760 days
Weight for internal and external information sources:	$W_I / W_E = 0.4 / 0.6$
Importance of negative, neutral and positive fuzzy variables:	$\{W_-; W_0; W_+\} = \{-1; 0.1; 1\}$
Tolerance (ε) for credibility adjustment:	$\varepsilon = 15\% = 0.15$

Moreover, the agent-owner is required to specify the consequent block of the 27 rules (see for the Fuzzy rule base, which is to be used by the Trusting Agent during the trust evaluation process. Also, percentage intervals for all trustworthiness levels as well as policies, which restrain the actions of the software agent in different situations are defined. Furthermore, the specification of weights used after the defuzzification process for internal and external information needs to be defined as well as the importance of negative, neutral and positive fuzzy variables used in the defuzzification process (see Table 3).

Table 3. User-defined Variables and Policies

Trust-worthiness Level	Percentage Intervals (User defined)	User-defined Policies (for Interaction with Recommendation Queried Agent)	
Level -1 (unknown agent)	n/a	No interaction, but opinions used for trustworthiness estimation (used for future trustworthiness evaluations)	
Level 0	0-19%	No interaction, agent is untrustworthy	
Level 1	20-39%	Exchange of uncritical information or services	
Level 2	40-59%	Exchange of goods, or information or services.	of low value ($0-$10) (consult agent-owner about payment options)
Level 3	60-79%		of medium value ($0-$20) (no credit card disclosure, use Cheque)
Level 4	80-89%		of high value ($0-$70) (no credit card disclosure, use Cheque)
Level 5	90-100%		no limitations

Note, that the trustworthiness value will be in the interval [W_-, W_+], therefore, we need to scale this number to the interval [0,5] to comply with the trustworthiness levels defined in [8, 9].

4.2 Example

In this section, we demonstrate our Fuzzy Trust model in an E-commerce scenario. We assume that a Trusting Agent A_T found another service or agent that can satisfy its demand as specified in Table 1. It is able to assess the reputation of the discovered service or agent sufficiently for the given timeslot and/or context. The Trusting Agent determines the trustworthiness of the Recommendation Queried Agent from, both, its own information repository, and through the broadcast of a ReputationRequest.

Following the lifecycle of our trust model, the Trusting Agent is able to evaluate the trustworthiness of the Reputation Queried Agent sufficiently, engage into a business interaction upon sufficient evaluation results, review the business interaction after its completion, and adjust the credibility and trustworthiness of all involved entities.

The Trustworthiness Evaluation Module

Although, the Trusting Agent possesses information about the Recommendation Queried Agent, he broadcasts a ReputationRequest (see Table 4) to strengthen and/or update his confidence in the Recommendation Queried Agent's trustworthiness prediction for the following business interaction:

Table 4. ReputationRequest and ReputationResponses for Scenario 2

	ReputationRequest:
A_T:	[Agent-ID:5688, Agent-ID:4820, Context{Book Retail}]
	ReputationResponses:
A_1:	[Agent-ID:8988, Agent-ID:4820, Context{Book Retail}, '2005-04-25', 0, 10, 6.5]
	... {15 opinions omitted}
	[Agent-ID:8988, Agent-ID:4820, Context{Book Retail}, '2004-01-12', 0, 10, 3.6]
A_2:	[Agent-ID:4564, Agent-ID:4820, Context{Book Retail}, '2004-01-06', -6, 6, 3.4]
	... {9 opinions omitted}
	[Agent-ID:4564, Agent-ID:4820, Context{Book Retail}, '2005-03-26', -6, 6, 4.5]
A_3:	[Agent-ID:2199, Agent-ID:4820, Context{Book Retail}, '2004-10-15', -10, 10, 5]
	... {3 opinions omitted}
	[Agent-ID:2199, Agent-ID:4820, Context{Book Retail}, '2005-03-26', -10, 10, 6.87]
A_4:	[Agent-ID:5633, Agent-ID:4820, Context{Book Retail}, '2004-10-25', -1, 1, 0.3]
	... {24 opinions omitted}
	[Agent-ID:5633, Agent-ID:4820, Context{Book Retail}, '2005-06-03', -1, 1, 0.334]

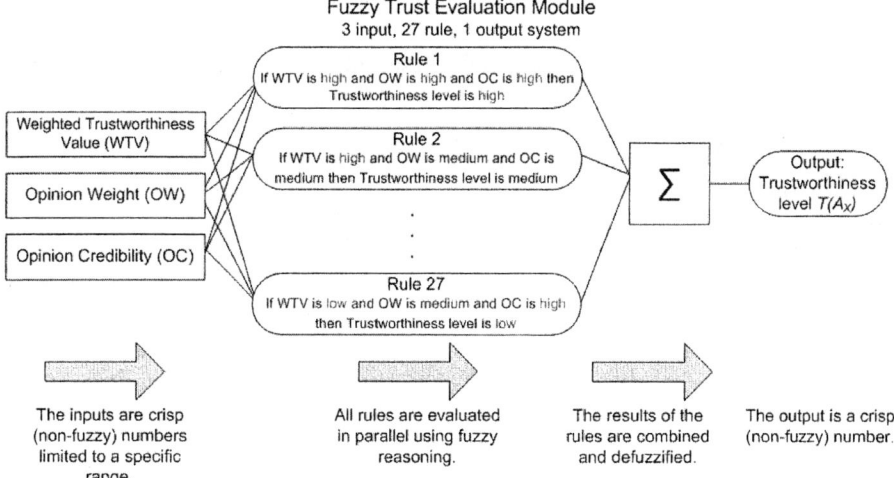

Fig. 2. Conceptual trust model a using fuzzy system [16]

In the following, we demonstrate the Fuzzy trust evaluation procedure depicted in Figure 2 step by step for this module.

Using the previously defined user settings the Trusting Agent can immediately start its calculations:

Step 1: Calculate WTV using expression [4] $WTV = \dfrac{\sum_{s=1}^{S}\left[e^{\frac{-(n-m)}{D}} \cdot \left(\dfrac{t_{val} - t_{min}}{t_{max} - t_{min}} \cdot 5\right)\right]}{S}$:

WTV(A_1) = 3.275; WTV(A_2) = 3.889; WTV(A_3) = 2.679; WTV(A_4) = 2.145

Step 2: The maximum number of opinions provided by Recommending Agents will be taken as maximum value for t_3, $t_1 = 0$, and $t_2 = \dfrac{t_3}{2}$. The range for the input and output variables for WTV and OC are static in the interval [0,5].

For example, A_1 has supplied 17 opinions in his ReputationResponse, hence we define: OW(A_1){t_1=0, t_2=8.5, t_3=17};
OW(A_2){t_1=0, t_2=5.5, t_3=11};
OW(A_3){t_1=0, t_2=2.5, t_3=5};
OW(A_4){t_1=0, t_2=13, t_3=26};

Step 3: For each fuzzy rule we apply the fuzzy operation 'AND' which calculates the intersection between the three membership function outputs. The opinion credibility (OC) of a Recommending Agent is pulled from existing records of the Trusting Agent. For example: Calculation for rule 1:
$FR_1 = \min\{WTV_0(x), OW_-(y), OC_0(z)\} = \min\{0.736, 0.5, 0.84\} = 0.5$

Step 4: For each fuzzy rule we apply the implication method which is x^2. For example: Calculation for rule 1: $FR_1 = 0.5^2 = 0.25$.

Step 5: We group the rules according to the three output fuzzy sets ('negative', 'neutral', 'positive') sum them and calculate the square root:

$FR_-^\sim = \sqrt{\sum(FR_-^2)} = 0.326$;

$FR_0^\sim = \sqrt{\sum(FR_0^2)} = 0.736$;

$FR_+^\sim = \sqrt{\sum(FR_+^2)} = 0.696$

Step 6: We multiply each of the results from step 4 with the group weights W_-, W_0 and W_+, and scale the results from the output interval of [-1,1] to the new output interval [0,5]:

$T(A_1) = \left(\dfrac{FR_-^\sim W_- + FR_0^\sim W_0 + FR_+^\sim W_+}{FR_-^\sim + FR_0^\sim + FR_+^\sim} + 1\right) * 2.5 = \left(\dfrac{0.326 \cdot -1 + 0.736 \cdot 0.1 + 0.696 \cdot 1}{0.326 + 0.736 + 0.696} + 1\right) * 2.5 = 3.131$

$T(A_2) = 3.876$;

$T(A_3) = 2.267$;

$T(A_4) = 2.045$;

Using these values as well as its own trustworthiness value for the Recommendation Queried Agent of 3.432, the Trusting Agent can then compute the overall output trust value:

$$OTV(A_T) = W_E \cdot \frac{\sum_{n=1}^{N} T(A_n)}{N} + W_I \cdot T_T = 0.4 \cdot \left(\frac{3.131 + 3.876 + 2.267 + 2.045}{4}\right) + 0.6 \cdot 3.432 = 3.191$$

The final decision of the Requesting Agent regarding his interaction with the Trusted Agent depends on the user-defined interaction policies (see Table 3). In our scenario, the OTV value corresponds to 63.82%, and, thus, the trustworthiness level is 3: 'Largely Trustworthy' which limits the Trusting Agent to interactions defined by the agent-owner for this specific trustworthiness level. Hence the Trusting Agent is allowed to exchange goods, or information, or services of medium value. Furthermore, the Trusting Agent is not allowed to disclose any credit card details to the Trusted Agent during the payment process but must instead use Cheques.

Business Interaction Review Module

After the business interaction with the Trusted Agent the Trusting Agent reviews the performance and Quality of Service (QoS) of the delivered goods or services. The Trusting Agent uses CCCI metrics [8, 9] to ensure a fair and precise review process:

Step 1: Record expected and actual behaviour of the Trusted Agent and determine the clarity and commitment of each criterion:

Table 5. Expected and Actual Business Outcomes

Context	Expected Behavior	Actual Behavior	Commitment	Influence	Clarity
Topic	Trust and Reputation in Service Oriented Architectures	Creating a Network of Trust for Web Services Presentation	2.5	4.5	3
Format	Hard-cover book	PDF File	1.5	3.5	5
Delivery	Within 3 days	After 2 days	5	3	4.5
Price	< 20 USD	9.95 USD	5	3	4
Payment	Cheque payment	Cheque payment	4.5	5	3

Step 2: Calculate the relative correlation value:

$$RC = \frac{\sum_{C=1}^{N} Commit_{criterion(c)} \cdot Clarity_{criterion(c)} \cdot Influence_{criterion(c)}}{5 \cdot \sum_{C=1}^{N} Max\_Clarity_{criterion(c)} \cdot Max\_Influence_{criterion(c)}}$$

$$RC = \frac{2.5 \cdot 4.5 \cdot 3 + 1.5 \cdot 3.5 \cdot 5 + 5 \cdot 3 \cdot 4.5 + 5 \cdot 3 \cdot 4 + 4.5 \cdot 5 \cdot 3}{5 \cdot (4.5 \cdot 3 + 3.5 \cdot 5 + 3 \cdot 4.5 + 3 \cdot 4 + 5 \cdot 3)} = 0.7133 = 71.33\%$$

The calculation result for the relative correlation confirms that the actual behaviour of the Trusted Agent was significantly better than the expected value of 63.81%.

Credibility Adjustment Module

Our Fuzzy trust model [4] proposes a credibility adjustment method that allows the reinforcement of the agent credibility for opinions close to the actual outcome of the business interaction and the penalisation of agent credibility for opinions differing from the actual business outcome (see Figure 3). The introduction of a tolerance ε helps to determine, whether the credibility value is to be increased for opinions within the pre-defined tolerance, or decreased for those outside.

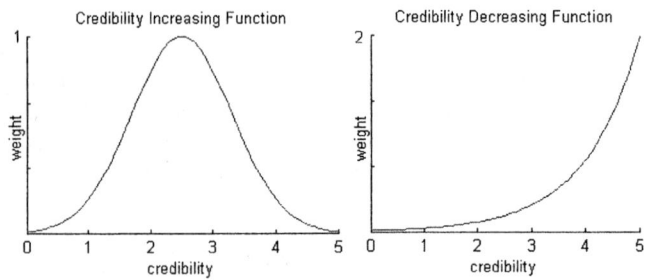

Fig. 3. Functions for credibility increase, credibility decrease

The Trusting Agent can now adjust the credibility values for its Recommending Agents in the following way:

Step 1: Translate the Relative Correlation value into the trustworthiness value range: 0.7133 * 5 = 3.566.

Step 2: Calculate the relative correlation between the opinions delivered by the Recommending Agents and the actual outcome of the business interaction with the Trusted Agent. By comparing the outcome with the user-defined tolerance of 15% it, furthermore, determines whether the credibility of each agent should be increased or decreased:
A_1: 3.131/3.566 = 0.878 → **increase** credibility
A_2: 3.876/3.566 = 1.087 → **increase** credibility
A_3: 2.267/3.566 = 0.636 → **decrease** credibility
A_4: 2.045/3.566 = 0.574 → **decrease** credibility

Step 3: Compute the mean, standard deviation and variance from all delivered opinions:

$$\sigma^2 = \frac{1}{N}\sum_{n=1}^{N}\left(\frac{t_n - t_{min}}{t_{max} - t_{min}} - \frac{1}{N}\sum_{n=1}^{N}\frac{t_n - t_{min}}{t_{max} - t_{min}}\right)^2 = 0.638$$

Step 4: Calculate of the new credibility values for each Recommending Agent:
$OC(A_1)_{new} =$

$$OC_{old} + \left(1 - \frac{\sigma}{OC_{max}}\right) \cdot \frac{1}{\sqrt{2\pi\sigma^2}} e^{\frac{-(OC_{old} - \bar{x})^2}{2\sigma^2}} = 3.455 + \left(1 - \frac{0.799}{5}\right) \cdot \frac{1}{\sqrt{\pi \cdot 0.638}} e^{\frac{-(3.455 - 3.678)^2}{2 \cdot 0.638}} = 4.026$$

$OC(A_2)_{new} = 3.183$

$$OC(A_3)_{new} = OC_{old} + \left(1 - \frac{\sigma}{OC_{max}}\right) \cdot \left[\left(-\frac{e^{OC_{old}}}{e^{OC_{max}}}\right) \cdot 2\right] = 3.018 + \left(1 - \frac{0.799}{5}\right) \cdot \left[\left(-\frac{e^{3.018}}{e^5}\right) \cdot 2\right] = 2.786$$

$$OC(A_4)_{new} = 3.289$$

5 Evolution of Peer Credibility Records

We examined the development of the credibility values for the Recommending Agents using data from several credibility adjustment cycles recorded during model tests. These cycles result from business interactions within a pre-defined context. Taking into consideration that Recommending Agents follow their own agenda, they might deliberately provide false information. For example, they could deliver correct opinions when the profit or impact of the business interaction is small. A false opinion, however, could be deliberately provided if the Recommending Agent was able to gain a considerable advantage.

Our credibility adjustment model reflects this consideration by providing separate functions for increasing and decreasing the credibility values of Recommending Agents. Our model determines that the reduction of credibility values is greater if the trustworthiness review calculations have a negative outcome than vice-versa. Figure 4 depicts the development of credibility values during our tests.

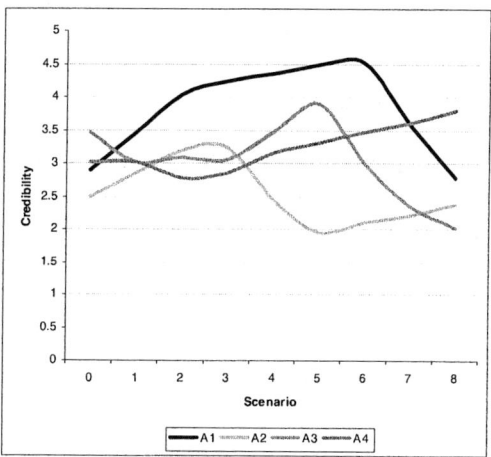

Fig. 4. Development of credibility values

6 Conclusion and Future Work

The ability of an autonomous agent to calculate trustworthiness and credibility values for its peer agents is crucial for the success of automated interactions in multi-agent environments. The characteristics of fuzzy logic to model uncertainty along with the capability to allow individual perceptions of trust, makes it an excellent methodology to mimic social behaviour in multi-agent environment such as an E-commerce market. This paper demonstrated our Fuzzy trust model which quantifies and formalises human perception of trust in a realistic business scenario.

We have shown, how external information, received from peer agents, can be taken into account when evaluating a Trusted Agent. Also, our model provided a mechanism to weight the data set delivered by a Recommending Agent with the individual credibility value for that agent. The Trusting Agent maintains credibility records of the Recommending Agents to help prevent possible attacks such as the delivery of false information or cyclic dishonesty. In addition, we accounted for past experiences between the Recommending Agents and the Trusted Agent.

In summary, we examined that during several test-runs our overall model has performed as expected. Both, trustworthiness values and credibility records mature over time, hence increasing the confidence and precision of our model. Future work will validate our model in a large sized e-commerce environment to assess the framework accuracy on a long-term basis. Eventually, our model can be incorporated into existing E-commerce markets as a key building block where autonomous agents interact by imitating human social behaviour.

References

1. Del Acebo E., de la Rosa, J., L., A Fuzzy System Based Approach to Social Modeling in Multi-Agent Systems, in Proceedings of the first international joint conference on Autonomous agents and multiagent systems, Bologna Italy, 2002.
2. Berthold, M., R.; Hand, D., J., Intelligent Data Analysis, In Chapter 9: Fuzzy Logic p. 321 – 350, Berlin, Springer, 2003
3. Zadeh, L. A., Fuzzy logic, neural networks, and soft computing, in Communications of the ACM archive, Volume 37, Issue 3 Pages: 77 – 84, March 1994
4. Schmidt, S., Steele, R., Dillon, T., Chang, E. Building a Fuzzy Trust Network in Unsupervised Multi-Agent Environments. Invited paper to the special session on Trust, Agia Napa, Cyprus, 2005
5. Castelfranchi, C., Falcone, R., Pezzulo, G., Trust in Information Sources as a Source for Trust: A Fuzzy Approach, in Proceedings of the second international joint conference on Autonomous agents and multiagent systems, Melbourne Australia, 2003.
6. Yang, S., Hsieh, J., Lan, B., Chung, J., Composition and evaluation of trustworthy Web Services, EEE05 international workshop on Business services networks, Hong Kong, 2005
7. Sabater, J., Sierra, C., Reputation and Social Network Analysis in Multi-Agent Systems, in Proceedings of the first international joint conference on Autonomous agents and multiagent systems, Bologna Italy, 2002.
8. Chang, E., Dillon, T., Hussain, F.K., Trust and Reputation for Service-oriented Environments, John Wiley & Sons, to appear Oct. 2005, ISBN: 0-470-01547-0
9. Hussain, F.K., Chang, E., Dillon, T., Trustworthiness and CCCI Metrics for Assigning Trustworthiness in P2P Communication., in Intl. J. Computer Systems Science and Eng. vol. 19, no. 4, pp. 95-112, 2004
10. Patrick, A. S., Building trustworthy software agents, in Internet Computing, IEEE, Volume 6, Issue 6 Nov.-Dec, Pages: 46 - 53,. 2002
11. Huhns, M.N., Buell, D.A., Trusted autonomy, in Internet Computing, IEEE, Volume 6, Issue 3 May-June, Pages: 92 - 95, 2002
12. Sycara, K., Multi-agent Infrastructure, agent discovery, middle agents for Web services and interoperation Multi-agents systems and applications, Springer-Verlag New York, Inc., Pages: 17-49, 2001

13. Kollingbaum, M. J., Norman, T. J., Supervised interaction: creating a web of trust for contracting agents in electronic environments, in Proceedings of the first international joint conference on Autonomous agents and multiagent systems: part 1, Bologna, Italy, Pages: 272 – 279, 2002
14. Wang, Y., Vassileva, J., Bayesian Network-Based Trust Model, in Proceedings of the IEEE/WIC International Conference on Web Intelligence (WI'03)
15. Resnick, P., Zeckhauser, R., Trust Among Strangers in Internet Transactions: Empirical Analysis of eBay's Reputation System. The Economics of the Internet and E-Commerce. Advances in Applied Microeconomics, 11, 2002
16. The MathWorks, Fuzzy Logic Toolbox for Mathlab Documentation, Available at:http://www.mathworks.com/access/helpdesk/help/ toolbox/ fuzzy/ (Accessed: 2004, September 16)

Emotion-Based Crowd Simulation Using Fuzzy Algorithm

Eun-Young Ahn[1], Jae-Won Kim[2], No-Yoon Kwak[1], and Sang-Hoon Han[3]

[1] Div. of Information and Communication Engineering, Cheonan University, 115 Anseo-Dong
Cheonan-City, Chungcheongnam-Do 330-704, Rep. of Korea
{ahnyoung, nykwak}@cheonan.ac.kr
[2] Dept. Mechanical Engineering, Sunmoon University,100 Kalsan ri, Tangjeong myeon,
Asan si, Chungnam, Rep. of Korea
jwk@sunmoon.ac.kr
[3] Dept. of Information Security, Korea National College of Rehabilitation & Welfare,
5-3 JangAn-Dong, Pyung Taek-Si, Gyeong Gi-Do, Rep. of Korea
hansh@dgu.ac.kr

Abstract. The present investigation is concerned with the crowd simulation in game or virtual reality and proposes new methodology dealing with emotion of the NPC (Non-Player Character) for increasing the reality of the behavior and action of crowd. The behavior of NPC depends on the individual disposition, which forms the properties of the crowd. The reorganization of the crowd is possible by meeting and parting according to the properties of NPC. In order to apply human emotion to the virtual characters, a number of factors and rules for identification of the status of emotion are considered. Fuzzy theory is used for the ambiguous description of the human emotion. The fuzzy functions and rules are designed to determine the conditions of emotion and reasonable inference is introduced to decide the control value of character's actions like as speed and his direction. The proposed model is validated by the present experiments embodying more natural simulation of crowd behaviors.

1 Introduction

Crowd simulation has been a main topic in the province of computer animation and game. The terminology of crowd means the cluster of peoples in motion or gathering and the simulation for the activities of the crowd in the virtual domain or computer animation is called crowd simulation [1~3].

The initial work was done by Reynolds (1987) and his investigation suggested a characteristic model concerning on the movements of herd of animals. Remarkable work on the crowd's activities is carried out by Lloyd et al. (1997) and Brogan and Hodgins proposed a model for the collective behavior[4][5]. More recently, Schweiss et al. (1999) showed a real-time control method for the crowds[6]. In addition, their group presented a rule-based architecture for controlling crowds (1999)[7][8].

However, the prior works didn't focus on individual characteristic of a member in the crowd. The main emphasis lies on the design of the emotion-based decision rules for generating the behavior patterns of the NPCs who have different one from the crowd's conduct. Two factors are considered for the decision of the individual's response; one is temper of prior properties and the other disposition of posterior character. Fuzzy theory is adopted for the depiction of human emotion because it is proper to illustrate ambiguous heuristic expression.

2 Design of Crowd's Behaviors

Designs of behavior patterns for both each NPC in the crowd and its leader are considered using the emotion-based control rules for the behaviors of it.

2.1 General Rule for the Behaviors of NPCs

General rule for behaviors of NPCs is applied only for the case of the members are in the recognition region [1, 7]. Figure 1 shows the general rules for controlling the behavior of a character by using flocking algorithm including separation, alignment, cohesion, and avoidance regulations. In details, separation rule keeps a proper distance between individuals. Consistency for the direction and moving speed of a unit cell with neighboring cells is governed by alignment rules and avoidance regulation prevents each individual to collide against the others defined as an opponent or a member in other flocks. Cohesion has a role of gathering members into unique crowd.

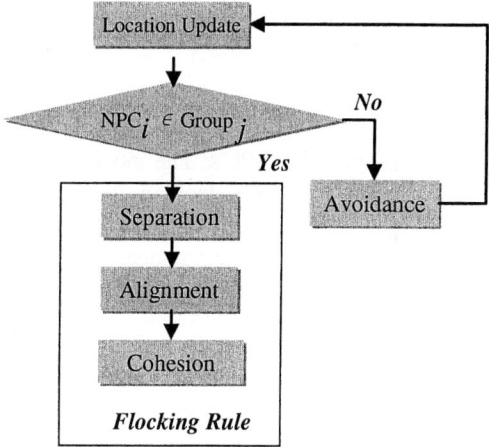

Fig. 1. General rule pfor controlling behaviors of NPCs

Overall property of multitude means the motion of the crowd and a movement of a member in the flock is defined as its local attribute that is a main factor to decide a character of the flock in this work. The human feeling denotes subjectively restless emotion caused by doing activities. Human's emotion is an essential element to decide a reaction against the surroundings. Emotion depends on the feeling governed by disposition. Many parameters including physical fatigue degree of each member affect human emotion. Only the level of physical fatigue due to the complexity of a passage is considered in the present investigation. Figure 2 explains the extended rules of NPC's behaviors taking account of the emotion of each emotion.

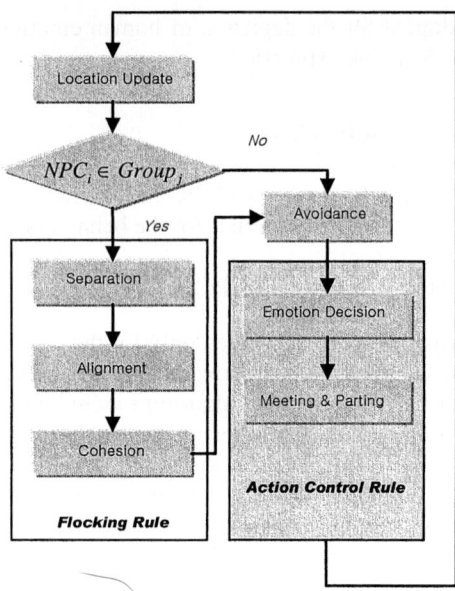

Fig. 2. Emotion-based action control for NPC. Adding action control rule, individual control for NPCs is possible according to those emotion status.

According to the model based on emotion, the feeling is so close to the character of human that it is treated as a property of NPC's. The mood varies with physical situation of each member and it is quantitatively decided depending on the complication level of a passage. More complex path decreases the disposition level because the fatigue strength is increased with the intricate passage. The relationship between the disposition and emotion is qualitatively defined using the present regulation for emotion-decision.

2.1.1 Definition of Factors Setting Up Emotion

Dichotomous distinction is not enough to define the status of emotion. Fuzzy inference is a useful tool to present the status of emotion which is a heuristic element. The fuzzy inference is an operational method where the input value is converted an element of a fuzzy set and defuzzied for the final output value. In the present fuzzy set, two input values involve both the disposition and feeling that become membership function. In this paragraph, the fuzzy operation is defined for the settlements of the status of feeling and fuzzy regulations.

(1) Decision of the disposition
The mood level is fixed when the NPC is generated. The levels are distinguished in five states from very active to very passive. Equation (1) adopts a triangular membership function and the operational results are displayed in Figure 3.

$$U_{tr}(x) = \begin{cases} \dfrac{1}{(r-p)}(x-r)+1 & p < x \leq r \\ -\dfrac{1}{(q-r)}(x-r)+1 & r < x \leq q \end{cases} \quad (1)$$

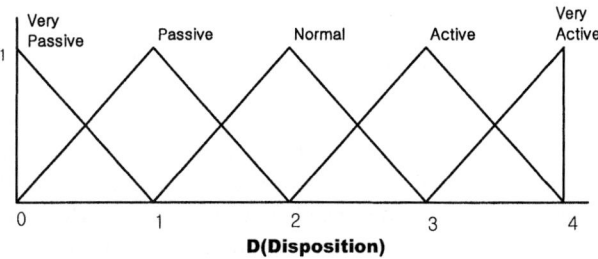

Fig. 3. Member function for disposition which consist of 5 fuzzy terms (Very Passive, Passive, Normal, Active, Very Active)

(2) Decision of feeling
Fuzzy terms for the definition of feeling is represented by "very good", "good", "not bad", and "bad", respectively. Figure 4 denotes the membership function for the feeling, by using equation (1). As stated above, the state of the feeling of each NPC depends on the complexity of a path that is measured as the frequency of the contact between it and obstacles. However, the contact is not realized due to the presence of the avoidance condition. Consequently, the fatigue level of each NPC is quantitatively fixed by a weighting factor, which is increased when obstacles appear in a prefixed range.

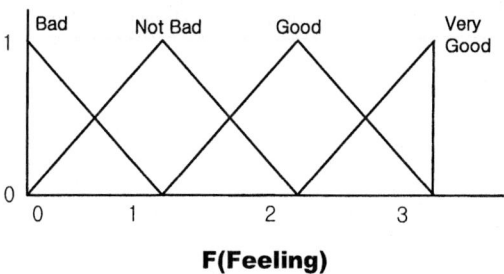

Fig. 4. Member function for feeling which consist of 4 fuzzy terms (very good, good, not bad, bad)

In practice, the level of the feeling increase when there is no stress caused by contact with hindrances. The weighting factor changes with the status of the neighbors (see algorithm 1).

```
Procedure Decide_Feeling_Index()
{
    if (Being obstacle in the concerned region ≡ TRUE)
        if ( Collision ≡ TURE ) then
            Feeling_index += α
        else if ( reasonable time passed ≡ TRUE )
            Feeling_index -= β
}
```

Algorithm 1. Deciding feeling index

(3) Matrix for behavior rules

Fuzzy regulation includes inferential predictions of the states of emotion from the membership functions of the feeling and disposition. For example, the introvert in very good feeling keeps a proper distance between the others. However, the introvert in bad feeling keeps a longer distance from the others of NPCs in a group. Those are typical fuzzy regulations for the behavior control.

Fuzzy terms for the feeling and the disposition are summarized as the matrix in Table 1 that defines the behavior patterns of NPCs. As shown in the table, the extravert in very good mood becomes active and positive states for moving other flocks. In contrast to the extrovert, the introvert hesitates to move toward the other crowds and keeps a proper distance with the other groups.

Table 1. Matrix for Fuzzy Control Rule

Feeling \ Dispostion	Very Active	Active	Normal	Passive	Very Passive
Very Good	Changeable	Changeable	Normal	Normal	Normal
Good	Changeable	Normal	Normal	Distant	Distant
Not Bad	Normal	Normal	Distant	Distant	Far
Bad	Normal	Normal	Distant	Far	Far

(4) Action of NPCs

The decision of the moving patters of NPCs is possible by the defuzzification. The process converts the fuzzy values in the set into crisp ones. Table 2 shows defuzzifier for the moving patterns. The emotion degree is calculated from the possibility distributions by using equation (2) which adopts the method of the center of gravity. The defuzzification makes the degree of the feeling digitize and the quantitative level become a reference value for the control of NPC's behaviors.

$$Degree = \frac{u[i] \times u(i, Degree)}{u[i]}$$

$$where, \ u[i] = \sum_{i=1}^{20} MIN(Dispostion, Feeling) \quad (2)$$

$$u(i, Degree) = Degree \ of \ i\_th \ rule$$

Table 2. Defuzzifier

Range of Movement	Action	Control value
Other Group	Move to other group(C)	2.0
Same Group	Keep **Far** distance(F)	1.3
Same Group	Keep **Distant** distance(D)	1.2
Same Group	Keep **Normal** distance(N)	1.0

Dichotomous distinction is not enough to define the status of emotion. Fuzzy inference is a useful tool to present the status of emotion which is a heuristic element. The fuzzy inference is an operational method where the input value is converted an element of a fuzzy set and defuzzied for the final output value.

In the present fuzzy set, two input values involve both the disposition and feeling that become a membership function. In this paragraph, the fuzzy operation is defined for the settlements of the status of feeling and fuzzy regulations.

```
Procedure Emotion-based Reorganization Rule()
{
    N_NPC ≡ Find_Neighbor(NPC_i ∈ Crowd_m)

    if (N_NPC ∈ Crowd_{n, m≠n} AND N_NPC ≡ Leader_NPC)
        if (Direction and Destination of NPC_i is same with N_NPC)
            if ( Property of NPC_i ≡ Changeable)
            {
                Delete NPC_i from the list of Crowd_m
                Insert  NPC_i from the list of Crowd_n
            }
}
```

Algorithm 2. Emotion-based Reorganization Rule

2.1.2 Rules of Crowd Reorganization

The NPCs in the crowds within the same passage and destination are free to alternate between flocks. And this locomotion of the NPCs enhances the reality of the depiction of the multitudes[4]. The reorganization is performed by exchange of members including leaders of crowds. According to the reorganization, frequent transition of members is happened to neighboring crowds with the same passages. The restriction managing is necessary to restrain the movement between the multitudes and the requirement is accomplished by introducing the regulation of feelings decision which admits a NPC in positive emotion state to transfer to other crowds. Consequently, the NPC in positive emotional state can move toward the other flock with the same passage of its crowd <algorithm 2>.

2.2 Behavior Patterns of NPC Leader

A locomotion-rule for a leader NPC is represented in this paragraph. In general, the leader NPC has a property of moving toward fixed destination and path is different from NPCs that follow the behavior-rule shown in Fig. 2. In addition, the reorganization rule is not applied to the leader NPC because the leader NPC is basic unit for being crowds.

Passing point is assigned by generating coordinates in a random manner. The coordinates for the passing point is informed to a leader NPC and used for the determination of the magnitude and the direction of transfer vector. At this time, the state of the feeling of a leader NPC adjusts the speed of the moving. The weighting factor on the feeling of the leader NPC controls the moving speed as depicted in <algorithm 3>.

```
Procedure Motion_Rule_for_ Leader_NPC ()
{
    if (Reach Target Location)   then
            Delete the Crowd
    else {
        // Deciding direction and seep
        Direction = Target_location – Leader_NPC
        N_direction = Normalize(Direction)
        Velocity = NORMAL_SPEED * Degree
        Movement = N_direction * Velocity

        LocationUpdate(Movement)
    }
}
```

Algorithm 3. Motion Rule of Leader NPC

3 Experiments and Results

For the validation of the proposed method, the crowd simulation is processed. Microsoft Visual C++ 6.0 and Microsoft DirectX 9.1 SDK are used. User friendly environment is implemented for enhanced freedom of observations. The information of the destination can be supplied to leaders and generates various virtual environments for the verifications for the present simulation model.

A large number of crowds with characters whose emotions are adjustable by the inference result of the emotion follow their leader. Five groups are considered for the trial execution and each crow is composed of five NPCs. Below two figures show the feasibility of suggested method, controlling the behavior of each member in the crowds and reorganizing of crowds according to the result of inference of emotion. Figure 5 illustrates the context in which the two groups meet casually and move toward the same goal. In that case, the moving speed of NPCs in the crowd will be decreased because of increase crowdedness. The two groups shall separate each other some time later because that the leader will select the different path each other. By general behavior rule, the crowds should have static a member. But by adopting proposed method, an aggressive member of the crowd has a chance to move to neighbor group if its emotional status is 'Changeable'. In addition, moving speed will increase since the complexity between members decrease. Figure 6 illustrates the result of

Emotion-Based Crowd Simulation Using Fuzzy Algorithm   337

Fig. 5. Simulation for controlling individual behavior of a member NPC following theleader NPC(woman). This illustrates the two groups moving toward the same goal. An aggressive member of the crowd has a chance to move to the neighbor group if its status of emotion is 'Changeable'.

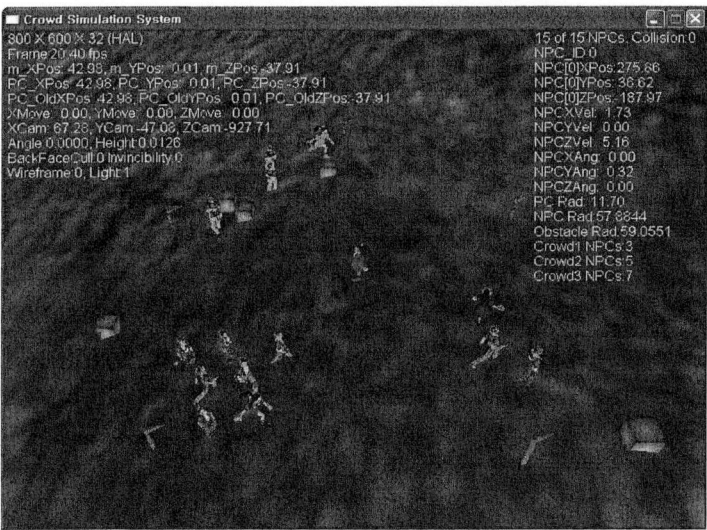

Fig. 6. Reorganization of crowd. This illustrates the result of adopting the reorganization rule. In the case of the situation as depict in Fig. 5(two crowds are moving toward the same goal and the member of the crowd get 'Changeable' status), they change their group if some requirements are satisfied.

adopting the reorganization rule. In the case of the situation as depict in Fig. 5, they change their group if some requirements are satisfied. Consequently, dynamic reorganization is realized. In the figure, we can perceive the dynamic change for the number of crowd by NPC's property.

As demonstrated above, it is possible to generate enrich patterns of NPC's behaviors and describe the crowds naturally by the present emotion based simulations. Moreover, the present optimal technique could be extended its application to the area of both the virtual reality and game.

4 Conclusions and Further Works

The present investigation proposes the emotion-based reorganization model for crowd simulation that enhances the reality of it. A few of rules for the application of human emotion to the NPC are constituted and utilized for the actual transfer of NPC's in a crowd toward other multitudes.

The theory of fuzzy inference is adopted for the decision of the status of human emotion. The fuzzy logic is designed with the membership functions for selection of the defined emotions. It is found that the illustration of the crowd becomes more realistic with the emotional characters that have sentimental properties.

Acknowledgement

This paper is financially supported by the grant of RRC-ACCT and CAERIS(RIS-05-04).

References

1. Reynolds, C. W. "Steering Behaviors For Autonomous Characters", Proceeding 1999, Game Development Conference(GDC'99). Miller Freeman Game Group, San Francisco, California, pp.763-782, 1999
2. Tsai-Yen Li, Ying-Jiun Jeng, Shih-I Chang, "Simulating Virtual Human Crowds with a Leader-Follower Model", Computer Animation, 2001. The Fourteenth Conference on Computer Animation. Proceeding, 7-8 Nov. 2001, pp.93-102, 2001
3. Dohan Kim, "An Event-Driven Approach to Crowd Simulation with Example Motions", Computer Science Technical Report, Kaist, 22 Jan, 2003
4. Benford, S. D., Greenhalgh, C. M. and Lloyd, D. "Crowded Collaborative Virtual Environments", Proceeding 1997 ACM Conference on Human Factors in Computing Systems(CHI'97), Atlanta, Georgia, US, March 22-27, 1997
5. Brogan, D. and Hodgins, J. "Group Behaviors for Systems with Significant Dynamics", Autonomous Robots, 4, 137-153. 1997
6. E. Schweiss, S. R. Musse, F. Garat, D. Thalmann, "An Architecture to Guide Crowds Using a Rule-Based Behaviour System" Proceeding, Agents 1999.
7. Reynolds, C. W. "Flocks, Herds, and Schools: A Distributed Behavioral Model", Proceeding Computer Graphics (SIGGRAPH'87), Vol.21, No.4, pp.25-34, July, 1987
8. S. R. Musse, F. Garat, D. Thalmann, "Guiding and Interacting with Virtual Crowds in Real-time, Proceeding Eurographics Workshop on Animation and Simulation '99(CAS'99), Milan, Italy, Springer, Wien, pp.23-34, 1999

A Genetic Algorithm for Job Shop Scheduling with Load Balancing

Sanja Petrovic and Carole Fayad

School of Computer Science and Information Technology,
University of Nottingham, Jubilee Campus, Wollaton Road, Nottingham NG8 1BB, UK
{sxp,cxf}@cs.nott.ac.uk
http://www.cs.nott.ac.uk/~sxp,~cxf

Abstract. This paper deals with the load-balancing of machines in a real-world job-shop scheduling problem with identical machines. The load-balancing algorithm allocates jobs, split into lots, on identical machines, with objectives to reduce job total throughput time and to improve machine utilization. A genetic algorithm is developed, whose fitness function evaluates the load-balancing in the generated schedule. This load-balancing algorithm is used within a multi-objective genetic algorithm, which minimizes average tardiness, number of tardy jobs, setup times, idle times of machines and throughput times of jobs. The performance of the algorithm is evaluated using real-world data and compared to the results obtained with no load-balancing.

Keywords: Job shop scheduling, fuzzy logic and fuzzy sets, genetic algorithms, lot-sizing, load balancing.

1 Introduction

In a job shop-scheduling problem, a set of jobs, where each job consists of a chain of operations, has to be processed on a set of machines (Pinedo, 2002). Each machine can process one operation at a time. Each operation needs to be processed during an uninterrupted period of a given length on a given machine. There is a good deal of research that considers different issues of theoretical or practical nature that appears in scheduling. This paper is focused on the issue of load balancing.

Load-balancing is in use in many scheduling applications, but mostly in those pertinent to parallel, distributed, and network-based computer systems (Kranzlmuller, 2003). However, load balancing in shop scheduling has not been fully investigated yet. The aim is to equally spread the load on machines in such a way as to maximize machine utilization while minimizing the total job throughput time. This can be achieved by transferring jobs from heavily to lightly loaded machines so that no machines are idle while there are other jobs waiting to be processed (Zomaya & Tei 2001). Moon et al. (2004) investigated assignment of jobs to relevant machines and allocation of machines to operators in order to minimize the unbalance of the workloads among operators. However, regardless of the nature of the application, there seems to be an ongoing interest in genetic algorithms for the implementation of load balancing (Greene, 2001). Lee (2004) developed a genetic algorithm for the load balancing in a distributed system. Wang & Fu (2002) proposed a genetic algorithm for machine load balancing in an advanced manufacturing shop floor.

In the research described in this paper, we investigate a complex real-world job shop scheduling problem in a printing company. In order to satisfy customer demands, the company often split jobs into lots and tries to deliver them on time. In this paper, we describe a genetic algorithm, which aims to allocate these lots to machines taking into consideration load balancing of the machines. The developed algorithm is used within a multi-objective fuzzy genetic algorithm for job shop scheduling (Fayad and Petrovic, 2005), (Petrovic et al, 2005). The benefits of using load balancing of machines in scheduling are discussed.

The paper is organized as follows. In Section 2, the job shop problem is introduced together with the objectives and constraints. Section 3 illustrates the job shop scheduling algorithm, while Section 4 describes the genetic algorithm for load balancing. The real-world scheduling problem in a printing company is explained in Section 5 with experimental results obtained on real-world data, followed by conclusions in Section 6.

2 Problem Statement

The job shop scheduling problem considered in this research consists of N jobs $J_1,...,J_j,...,J_N$ which have to be scheduled on a set of M machines $M_1,...,M_i,...,M_M$. Machines are grouped into W working centres $W_1,...,W_c,...,W_C$. A working centre W_C consists of identical and non-identical machines. Identical machines denote machines, which have the same characteristics. Each job J_j is assigned a release date r_j, i.e., the date when the job can start its processing and a due date d_j, i.e., the date when the job is due to finish its processing. The processing of job J_j on machine M_i is referred to as operation represented by the order pair (i,j), with the processing time denoted by p_{ij}. Precedence constraints are imposed on the order of operation processing. Operation processing times are imprecise due to machine and human factors. For example, we can estimate that the processing time of an operation is not shorter than a, not longer than c, but most likely it takes b time units. Due dates are also imprecise, allowing the scheduler to express his/her dissatisfaction with the jobs that are tardy, i.e., jobs that cannot meet their due dates.

Jobs are of different types and are grouped into F families on the basis of their processing requirements. Changing of operations that belong to different families of jobs to be processed on the machine incur reconfiguration and/or cleaning of the machine which leads to setup time/cost. Batching refers to scheduling of operations that belong to the same family, one after the other, in order to minimize the setup time/cost.

Very often it is not possible to meet the due date for all the jobs. In order to deliver at least part of the job to the customer, the scheduler can decide to split the job into lots. In addition, it is allowed to overlap processing of lots of the same operation on the machines of the same work-centre, which reduces throughput time, i.e., time that the job spends on the shop floor.

Each operation is allocated to a machine from the specified work-centre, before the sequencing of operations on the machine takes place. Different objectives can be used in machine allocation, for example to load *mostly* one machine, to balance the load of the machines, to randomly allocate the machines, etc.

The scheduling problem is formulated as the problem of generating a non-preemptive sequence of operations of N jobs on M machines with the following objectives:

(I) to minimise the average tardiness of jobs in schedule s

$$AT(s) = \frac{1}{n}\sum_{j=1}^{N} w_j T_j \qquad (1)$$

where $T_j = \max(C_j - d_j, 0)$ is the tardiness of job J_j, C_j is the completion time of job J_j and w_j is the relative importance of job J_j.

(II) to minimise the number of tardy jobs in schedule s

$$NT(s) = \sum_{j=1}^{N} u_j, \text{ where } u_j = \begin{cases} 1 & \text{if } T_j > 0 \\ 0 & \text{otherwise} \end{cases} \qquad (2)$$

(III) to minimise the total setup time in schedule s

$$ST(s) = \sum_{t=1}^{T}\sum_{f=1}^{F} aX_{ft}, \qquad (3)$$

where T is the total number of periods within the planning horizon

$$X_{ft} = \begin{cases} 1 & \text{if processing of the operation of the family } f \text{ in period } t \text{ requires setup} \\ 0 & \text{otherwise} \end{cases}$$

where a is a parameter with a constant value that represents time units required for the setup.

(IV) to minimise the total idle time of machines where the idle time is defined as time within the planning horizon during which the machines are used neither for processing of jobs nor for setup

$$IT(s) = T \cdot M - \left(\sum_{t=1}^{T}\sum_{f=1}^{F} aX_{ft}\right) - \left(\sum_{i=1}^{M}\sum_{j=1}^{N} p_{ij}\right) \qquad (4)$$

(V) to minimise the total throughput time defined as the total time that jobs spend on the shop floor

$$TT(s) = \sum_{j=1}^{N}(C_j - s_j); \quad j = 1,...,N \qquad (5)$$

where s_j is the time when job J_j starts its processing.

3 Job Shop Scheduling Algorithm

A sequential algorithm consisting of three phases is developed for the described job shop scheduling problem.

Phase 1. Lots determination: for each job a decision whether to split it up into lots is made together with the size of lots.

Phase 2. Machine allocation: a machine is allocated to each operation/lot of each job.

Phase 3. Sequencing of each machine: for each machine, a sequence of operations/lots allocated to it is determined.

The focus of this paper is on phase 2. Phases 1 and 3 will be described briefly in the remainder of this section while the description of machine load balancing will be given in Section 4.

A fuzzy *if-then* rule-based system was developed which decides on splitting-up of jobs and the size of each lot. Initially, lots are of the same size. Fuzzy if-then rules determine the *change of the lot* expressed by the linguistic variables, (*Large Negative, Medium Negative, Small, Medium Positive* and *Large Positive*) using the values of linguistic variables *workload of the shop floor, size of the job*, and the *urgency of the job*. The developed rule-based system for lot sizing is given in detail in (Petrovic et al, 2005).

A fuzzy multi-objective genetic algorithm was developed for sequencing of jobs on machines, where each operation/lot has predefined machines to be operated on (Fayad & Petrovic, 2005). Imprecise processing times of operations and due dates are modeled by fuzzy sets. Satisfaction grades are introduced for each objective to reflect the decision maker preferences to the achieved values of the objectives. Values of the objectives are mapped into satisfaction grades, which take values from the interval [0, 1], where 0 represents full dissatisfaction and 1 full satisfaction with the achieved objective value. An average of the satisfaction grades of all objectives is used as the fitness function F in the developed genetic algorithm to evaluate the quality of solutions (schedules).

4 Genetic Algorithm for Load Balancing

A genetic algorithm was developed to search for machine allocations of each work-centre to lots of jobs, which balances work-loads of machines. A genetic algorithm is an iterative search procedure, which was successfully used in a variety of combinatorial optimization problems (Reeves, 1995). A genetic algorithm maintains iteratively a population of solutions, each solution being represented by a chromosome. The fitness of the solution is determined by the value of the objective function achieved by the solution. The solutions with higher fitness have better chances to survive to the next generation. The solutions are changed from generation to generation by applying crossover operators, which combine two chromosomes to obtain offsprings and mutation operator, which modifies a single chromosome. The main characteristics of the developed genetic algorithm are described below.

<u>Initialisation:</u> The algorithm which generates initial solutions distinguishes two cases: when the number of lots of a job is smaller or equal, and larger than the number of machines. In the first case, lots of a single job to be processed in the work-centre are allocated in a random order to the identical machines in such a way so that no machine processes more than one lot of the same job. In the second case, the lots are allocated to the different identical machines. When all machines are used in allocation, then for each remaining lot, the current workload of the machines is calculated and the machine of the lowest workload is chosen.

<u>Chromosome representation:</u> Each chromosome represents allocation of lots to machines using two layers, shown in Figure 1. First layer contains job identification number and the number of lots the job is split into. The number of lots determines the

number of elements in the second layer. Each element in the second layer consists of 2 parts: identification of the lot and the machine the lot is allocated to.

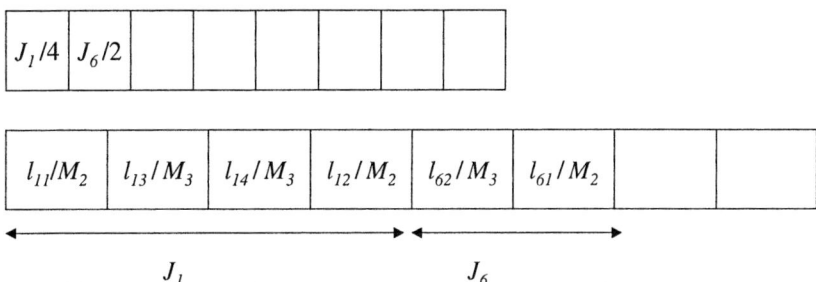

Fig. 1. An example of a two-layered chromosome in the load balancing GA

Fitness function: It evaluates the quality of the allocation of the machines represented by chromosomes. It measures the dispersion of the load of machines from the average load. It is calculated using the following expression:

$$TSD_c = \sum_{i=1}^{P_c} (AW_c - WL_i)^2 \qquad (6)$$

where P_c is the number of identical machines in the work-centre W_c, AW_c is the average load of the machines in this work-centre, while WL_i is the workload of machine M_i in the work-centre W_c. The rational behind this definition of the fitness function is that if all the machines have the load equal or close to the average load then the machines in the work-centre are well balanced.

Mutation operator: It modifies the solution, i.e., allocation of lots of a randomly chosen job to machines. If the job is split into lots, then the mutation operator chooses randomly a point in the sub-chromosome in the second layer representing the machines and swaps the two machines across the selected point. If the job is not split into lots (i.e., number of lots is equal to 1), then the allocated machine is replaced with a randomly chosen identical machine, if it exists.

Crossover operator: The combination of two chromosomes produces an offspring which does not preserve the existence of all the machines from the parent chromosomes and it would require a complex repair. Therefore, the crossover operator is not implemented.

Selection operator: A roulette-wheel-selection technique is used for selection of chromosomes to survive to the next iteration.

5 A Real-World Scheduling Problem

The developed algorithm for job shop scheduling with lots, batching and load balancing was tested on real-world data provided by a printing company Sherwood Press Ltd, UK. There are 18 machines on the shop floor, grouped in 8 work-centres, for Printing, Cutting, Folding, Card-inserting, Embossing and Debossing, Gathering and Finishing which contains Stitching and Trimming, Packaging and Handwork. Although, all the jobs have to be processed in pre-determined work-centres, the route of processing is not the same for all of them. Each job is described by the following data: identification of the job, the processing route of the job, uncertain processing times of all the operations on required machines, required quantity of the items, family of the job, release date, uncertain due date, and the priority of the job described by linguistic terms. The planning horizon T is given in minutes. In order to satisfy customers, the company splits up large jobs into lots. Setup time/cost occurs only on the printing machines when the jobs of different families, which require different colours are scheduled for printing one after the other. Therefore batching can take place only on these machines.

Each work-centre has a number of machines, some of them being identical. Work-centres are listed in Table 1 together with their machines. Single machines in the work-centre and identical machines (shaded in grey) are given respectively in the upper and lower parts of the row representing the work-centre.

Table 1. Work-centres and their machines

Work-centre	Non-identical machines
	Identical machines
Printing	K3
	K4 & K5
Cutting	Polar1 and Polar2
Folding	H&H Folder
	Longford1 and Lognford2
	MBO1 and MBO2
Card-inserting	Hunkler
Embossing and debossing	Sanwa, Propak
	Platen 1 and Platen 2
Gathering and finishing and trimming	Muller GST
Packaging	Flowrapper
Handwork	

Operations/lots can be allocated to machines in different ways. We run experiments using four ways of allocations:

SP: Allocation of lots used in Sherwood that usually loads one machine in the work-centre. Raw data are used without taking into consideration changes of machine allocation that occasionally take place on the shop floor.
GALB: Allocation produced by the developed genetic algorithm, which performs load balancing with the described initialization
GALBR: Same as *GALB* but using random initialization of the genetic algorithm
RD: Random allocation of lots to appropriate machines

The algorithm was developed using Visual C++ and the testing was performed in a Windows XP environment on a PC Pentium 2 GHz with 512 MB of RAM. Population size is 50 chromosomes. Mutation probability is 0.4, while the algorithm stops after 500 generations. The algorithm was run 5 times and the results obtained using real-world data for one month planning horizon discretised homogeneously into one minute unit time periods, are given in Table 2. This specific month was chosen because it was considered to be rather busy with 158 jobs and a *workload* of 5120125 required items.

Table 2 presents best values of the fitness function (the average satisfaction grades of all objectives) of the genetic algorithm for scheduling using 4 different ways of machines loading and the corresponding values of the satisfaction grades of the objective functions given in (1)-(5) together with the makespan C_{max} which is the time when the last job finishes its processing.

Table 2. Performance of schedules using 4 different ways of machine loading

Machine allocation methods	F	C_{max} (minutes)	S_{AT}	S_{NT}	S_{ST}	S_{IT}	S_{TT}
SP (Best)	0.54	**31614**	**0.43**	0.74	**0.26**	0.38	**0.85**
SP (Average)	0.53	31854	0.42	0.62	0.35	0.37	0.85
GALB (Best)	**0.6**	**27150**	**0.46**	1	**0.22**	**0.45**	**0.9**
GALB (Average)	0.59	27639	0.45	0.96	0.22	0.45	0.88
GALBR (Best)	**0.61**	**27974**	**0.46**	0.68	**0.29**	**0.39**	**0.87**
GALBR (Average)	0.6	28056	0.45	0.89	0.29	0.43	0.87
RD (Best)	0.59	**28718**	**0.45**	0.87	**0.32**	**0.43**	**0.86**
RD (Average)	0.58	29262	0.45	0.9	0.29	0.44	0.87

The results show that load balancing (both *GALB* and *GALBR*) does improve objectives related to tardiness (*AT*, *NT*) because jobs do not wait to be processed on a single machine, but all identical machines are used. In addition, idle time of machines and total throughput time of jobs are reduced by load balancing.

Although the best and average values of fitness function of *GALB* were slightly worse than those of *GALBR*, it obtained better value of both objectives the idle times

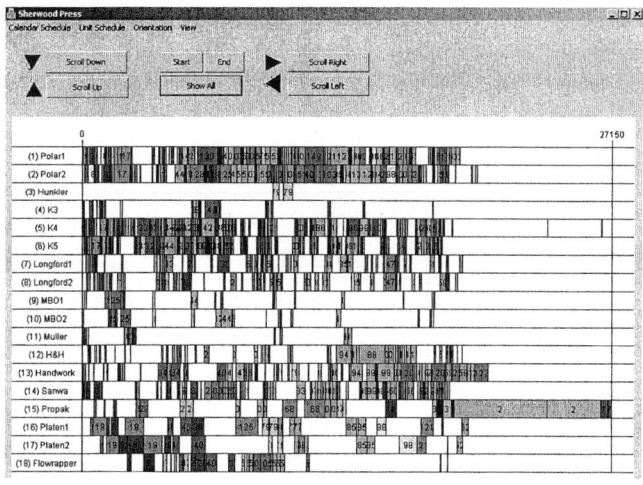

Fig. 2. Best schedule obtained by using *GALB* algorithm

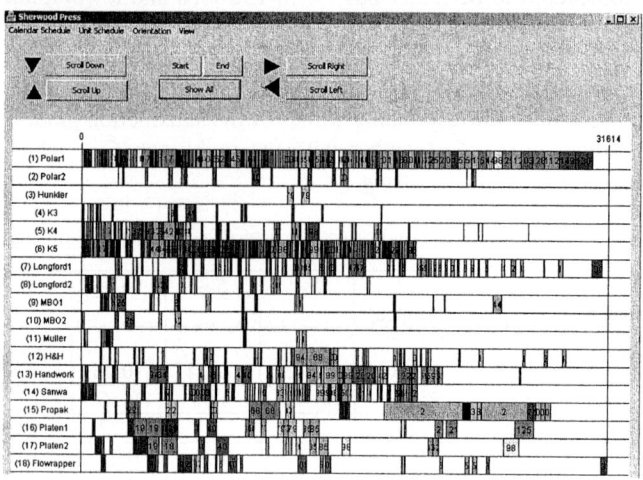

Fig. 3. Best schedule obtained by using *SP* algorithm

of machines and the total throughput time of jobs and produced schedules of better (shorter) makespan C_{max}. Also, *GALB* algorithm has produced a schedule with no tardy jobs.

Figures 2 and 3 represent Gantt charts of the best schedule obtained by *GALB* and by *SP*, respectively. Good load balancing algorithm of machines (*GALB*) lead to *similar* completion times of jobs on all machines within each work-centre. Consequently, the achieved makespan of the *GALB* schedule is better (27150 minutes obtained using *GALB* as opposed to a considerably *larger* makespan of 31614 minutes obtained using *SP*).

Table 3 shows the average utility of identical machines over the given planning horizon. It can be observed that *GALB* balances the workload of the identical machines. For example, it balances most obviously Polar1 and Polar2, and K5 and K4, while SP loads much more machines Polar1 and K5. The conclusion can be drawn that when

Table 3. Average machine utility for the best solution obtained using *GALB* and *SP*

Identical machines	Load balancing with *GALB* (in minutes)	Load balancing with *SP* (in minutes)
K4	14739	8471
K5	12977	19245
Polar1	16060	29906
Polar2	16848	3002
Longford1	6415	9140
Lognford2	7219	4494
MBO1	2229	3490
MBO2	2922	1661
Platen 1	8790	8940
Platen 2	8055	7905

lots of single jobs are processed in parallel on identical machines, it leads to a better overall utility of machines compared to the machine utility where no load balancing has been applied

6 Conclusion

This paper deals with the problem of load-balancing of identical machines in a job shop scheduling problem, where jobs are split into lots.

A genetic algorithm was developed which allocates lots to machines, with the objective to minimize the difference between the load of each machines. This genetic algorithm generates a machine allocation, which serves as an input to the fuzzy multi-objective genetic algorithm for job shop scheduling. The objectives considered are to minimize average tardiness, number of tardy jobs, setup times, idle times of machines and throughput times of jobs.

The performance of the algorithm is evaluated with numerical experiments provided by the printing company. The experiments prove that the load balancing improves the relevant objectives, namely the objectives related to tardiness, better utilization of the machines and better throughput of the jobs.

Acknowledgments

The authors would like to thank the Engineering and Physics Science Research Council (EPSRC), UK, Grant No. GR/R95319/01 for supporting this research. We also acknowledge the support of our industrial collaborator Sherwood Press Ltd, Nottingham, and Martin Geiger for supplying the software for the visualization of the schedule.

References

Fayad, C. and Petrovic, S., "A Genetic Algorithm for Real-World Job Shop Scheduling", in Ali, M. and Esposito, M., (Eds.), Innovations in Applied Artificial Intelligence, LNAI-3533, the 18th International Conference on Industrial and Engineering Applications of Artificial Intelligence and Expert Systems, 22-25 June, Bari, Italy. 2005.

Greene, W, "Dynamic Load-Balancing via a Genetic Algorithm," 13th IEEE International Conference on Tools with Artificial Intelligence (ICTAI'01), Dallas, US, (2001) 121-129.

Kranzlmuller, D., 'Scheduling and Load Balancing,' Fifth International Conference on Parallel Processing and Applied Mathematics, Czestochowa, Poland, LNCS-3019, Springer Verlag, (2003).

Lee, S. and Lee, D., "GA based adaptive load balancing approach for a distributed system", in Zhang, J. and HeJ-H; FuY. (Eds), Computational and Information Science, Kralov, Poland, LNCS 3314, Springer-Verlag, (2004) 182-7.

Moon, D.H., Kim, D.K. and Jung J.Y., An Operator Load-Balancing problem in a Semi-Automatic Parallel Machine Shop, Computers & Industrial Engineering 46 (2004) 355-362.

Petrovic S., Fayad C. and Petrovic D., "Job Shop Scheduling with Lot-Sizing and Batching in an Uncertain Real-World Environment," 2nd Multidisciplinary Conference on Scheduling: Theory and Applications (MISTA), 18-21 July, NY, USA (2005).

Pinedo, M., Scheduling Theory, Algorithms, and Systems, Prentice Hall, Second Edition, (2002).

Reeves, C., Genetic Algorithms and Combinatorial Optimisation: Applications of Modern Heuristic Techniques, In V.J. Rayward-Smith (Eds), Alfred Waller Ltd, Henley-on-Thames, UK (2005).

Zomaya, A. and Teh, Y.H., Observations on Using Genetic Algorithms for Dynamic Load-Balancing, IEEE Transactions on Parallel and Distributed Systems, 12 9 (2001) 899-911.

Wang, T and Fu Y., "Application of An Improved Genetic Algorithm for Shop Floor Scheduling," Computer Integrated Manufacturing Systems, 8 5 (2002) 392-420.

A Co-evolutionary Particle Swarm Optimization-Based Method for Multiobjective Optimization

Hong-yun Meng[1], Xiao-hua Zhang[2], and San-yang Liu[1]

[1] Dept.of Applied Math. XiDian University, Xian, China
{mhyxdmath, lsy}@hotmail.com
[2] Institute of Intelligent Information Processing, XiDian University, Xian, China
mzhangh@hotmail.com

Abstract. A co-evolutionary particle swarm optimization is proposed for multiobjective optimization (MO), in which co-evolutionary operator, competition mutation operator and new selection mechanism are designed for MO problem to guide the whole evolutionary process. By the sharing and exchange of information among particles, it can not only shrink the searching region but maintain the diversity of the population, avoid getting trapped in local optima which is proved to be effective in providing an appropriate selection pressure to propel the population towards the Pareto-optimal Front. Finally, the proposed algorithm is evaluated by the proposed quality measures and metrics in literatures.

1 Introduction

Co-evolutionary algorithm[1,2] is an extension of standard evolutionary algorithm in which the fitness of evolving solutions depends on the state of other, coevolving individuals rather than a fixed evaluation function. Co-evolutionary search involves either one or more populations. Generally, co-evolutionary algorithm can be grouped in two categories: cooperation and competition. Studies have found that a balance of cooperation and competition is necessary to prevent evolutionary algorithms from getting trapped in local minima. Particle Swarm Optimization (PSO) first introduced by Kennedy and Eberhart [3, 4], is a relatively recent heuristic algorithm that can be likened to the behavior of a flock of birds or the sociological behavior of a group of people. PSO seems to be particularly suitable for MO problems mainly because of the high speed of convergence that it presents for single objective problems. Recently, there have been several recent proposals to extend PSO to deal with multiobjective problem [5-11]. But there exist some shortcomings in PSO. On the one hand, the fitness is defined in advance, and in fact the fitness should adapt with the environment. On the other hand, the existing evolution model only notices the competition among individuals, and neglects the ability of cooperation among them. The cooperation and competition exist simultaneously in fact. In this paper, a co-evolutionary particle swarm optimization is proposed for multiobjective optimization (CMOPSO) to shrink the searching region, quicken approximation and avoid getting trapped in local optima.

2 Basic Concepts and Particle Swarm Optimizers

2.1 Basic Concepts

Let X be the n-dimensional search space and $f_i(x)$ ($i=1,2,\cdots,k$) be k objective functions defined over X. MO problem can be stated as finding a $x^* = (x_1^*, x_2^*, \cdots, x_n^*) \in X$ that optimizes(without loss of generality we consider only the minimization case) the vector function $F(x) = (f_1(x), f_2(x), \cdots, f_k(x))$.

Definition 1 (Pareto Dominance): Let $u = (u_1, u_2, \cdots, u_k)$ and $v = (v_1, v_2, \cdots, v_k)$ be two vectors. Then, u dominates v if and only if $u_i \leq v_i, i=1,2,\cdots,k$, and $u_i < v_i$ for at least one component. This property is known as Pareto Dominance and it is used to define the Pareto optimal points. A solution x of the MO problem is said to be Pareto optimal if and only if there does not exist another solution y such that $F(y)$ dominates $F(x)$. The set of all Pareto optimal solutions of an MO problem is called Pareto Optimal Set and we denote it with $P(F, X)$. The set $PF(F, X) = \{F(x) \mid x \in P(F, X)\}$ is called Pareto Front.

Definition 2 (Extreme Point Set of the Pareto Front): The Extreme Point Set $PFS(F, X)$ of the Pareto Front is defined as $PFS(F, X) = \bigcup_{i=1}^{k} PFS_i(F, X)$, here

$$PFS_i(F, X) = \{(f_1(x), \cdots f_k(x)) \mid f_i(x) = m_i, \nexists y, F(y) \preceq F(x), y, x \in P(F, X)\}$$

where $m_i = \min_{z \in P(F,X)} f_i(z), i = 1, \cdots, k$.

2.2 Particle Swarm Optimizers (PSO)

In the standard PSO, the update of the particles is accomplished according to the following equations. Equation (1) calculates a new velocity for each particle (potential solution) based on its previous velocity v, the particle's best location $x^\#$, and the population global best location x^*. Equation (2) updates each particle's position in solution hyperspace.

$$\begin{cases} \overline{v} = v + c_1 r_1 (x^\# - x) + c_2 r_2 (x^* - x) & (1) \\ \overline{x} = x + w\overline{v} & (2) \end{cases}$$

w is also called constriction factor, c_1, c_2 are two coefficients; r_1 and r_2 are two random numbers in [0, 1].This process can be illustrated in Fig.1. Easy to see, the updating process is a course in essence learning from $x^\#$ and x^*. Obviously, the location chosen as $x^\#$ and x^* will influence the converging velocity, even the uniformity and wide extension of the whole particle swarm. In the standard PSO, new particles are produced only by v, $x^\#$ and x^*, and there is no sharing of information among other particles in the population, except that each particle can access the global best. For MOP, we argue that such sharing of information among all the individuals in a population is crucial in order to introduce the necessary selection pressure to propel the population moving towards the true Pareto-optimal Front. On the other hand, from the definition 2, all the Pareto optimal lies in the hyper-rectangle constituted by extreme points of the Pareto Front.

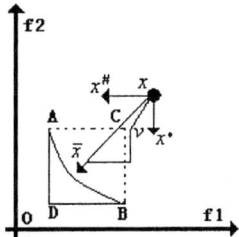 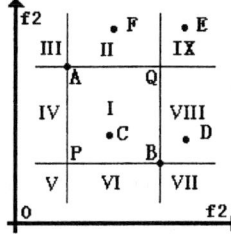

Fig. 1. Updating process of particle   **Fig. 2.** Distribution of particles in objective space

Take a two-objective continuous numeric optimization problem in Fig.2. Assume A and B are two extreme points of the Pareto Front, and then all the Pareto optimal solutions are in the rectangle ADBC. The searching domain will quickly be reduced if the extreme points can be obtained at the initial stages. In addition, a large number comparison experiments on test functions in [12] with MOPSO [5] and NSGA-II [6] were carried out both with and without extreme points in the initial stages under the same conditions. From the comparison, it is easy to find that the extreme points play a more important role in multiobjective particle swarm optimization than in NSGA-II. The reason is that the extreme points of the Pareto Front in the NSGA-II are only regarded as common Pareto optimal, so they do not take the role of guidance. However, it is a pity that the extreme points are usually unknown at the initial stages. In order to find these points early, several particle swarms are used and the concept of co-evolutionary is taken to exploit the Pareto Front and its extreme points of the Pareto Fronts.

3   Co-evolutionary Multiobjective Particle Swarm Optimization

In this paper, $k+1$ populations $PoP_i (i=1,\cdots,k+1)$ of PSOs are involved in the CMOPSO to solve multiobjective problem, where k is the number of objective functions. $PoP_i (i=1,\cdots,k)$ is named as cooperation swarms, which is used to explore the extreme point set $PFS_i(F, X)$. While PoP_{k+1} is called evolutionary population and its function is to find the Pareto optimal set $P(F, X)$. And the size of cooperation population N_i is less than that of PoP_{k+1}. Here, $lbest_i^j$ record the best position for the j-th particle in PoP_i (denoted as $PoP_i(j)$). While $gbest_i$ record the position of the best particle that gives the best fitness in PoP_i ($i=1,\cdots,k+1$) with the size of M_i, and $M_{k+1} \gg M_i (i = 1, \cdots, k)$. In addition, it is obvious that $gbest_i$ can be used as an approximation for Extreme Point Set of the Pareto Front.

3.1 Updating the Best Location of $lbest_i^j$ and $gbest_i$

As mentioned before, particle swarm $PoP_i (i = 1, \cdots, k)$ is used to explore the extreme point set of the whole Pareto Front, so the locations of $lbest_i^j$ and $gbest_i$ with smaller function value in $i-th$ objective function should be kept as soon as possible. The updating method for them in this paper is as follows.

If $f_i(lbest_i^j) > f_i(PoP_i(j))$, then $lbest_i^j$ is replaced by $PoP_i(j)$;

If $f_i(lbest_i^j) = f_i(PoP_i(j))$ and $F(lbest_i^j) \succeq F(PoP_i(j))$, $lbest_i^j$ is replaced by $PoP_i(j)$; otherwise, choose one from $F(lbest_i^j)$ and $F(PoP_i(j))$ randomly as $lbest_i^j$ ($j = 1, \cdots, N_i$); Otherwise $lbest_i^j$ is kept invariable.

Let $T_i = \{x \mid f_i(x) = m_i, \nexists z \in PoP_i \cup gbest_i, F(z) \prec F(x)\}$, in which $m_i = \min f_i(y)$, $y \in PoP_i \cup gbest_i$. If $|T_i| \le M_i$, then $gbest_i$ is replaced by T_i, otherwise, cluster on T_i and select M_i particles from T_i to replace $gbest_i$. The function of clustering is mainly to keep the uniformity and diversity of $gbest_i$.

For swarm PoP_{k+1}, the method for updating $lbest_{k+1}^j$ and $gbest_{k+1}$ is in the following. If $F(lbest_{k+1}^j) \succeq F(PoP_{k+1}(j))$, replace $lbest_{k+1}^j$ by $PoP_{k+1}(j)$. If $F(lbest_{k+1}^j)$ and $F(PoP_{k+1}(j))$ can not be compared, then select one randomly from $F(lbest_{k+1}^j)$ and $F(PoP_{k+1}(j))$ as $lbest_{k+1}^j$. The aim of $gbest_{k+1}$ is to keep the Pareto optimal solutions with a uniformly distributed and well extended Pareto Front. Define

$$T_{k+1} = \{x \mid x \in PoP_{k+1} \cup gbest_{k+1}, \nexists y \in PoP_{k+1} \cup gbest_{k+1}, F(y) \prec F(x)\}.$$

If $|T_{k+1}| \le M_{k+1}$, replace $gbest_{k+1}$ with T_{k+1}, or cluster on T_{k+1} and select M_{k+1} particles to replace $gbest_{k+1}$.

3.2 Co-evolutionary Operator

In this paper, the evolution process of swarms PoP_i is independent. The sharing of information among swarms does help to expand the searching regions, and the difference among particles can maintain the diversity of the whole population. In addition, such sharing of information has two sides in this paper. On the one hand, the swarm PoP_{k+1} can provide useful information for swarms $PoP_i (i = 1, \cdots, k)$ to search extreme point set. The main step is as follows. Let $M_i = gbest_i \cup PoP_{k+1} \cup gbest_{k+1}$, $Q_i = \{x \mid f_i(x) = m_i, \nexists z \in M_i, F(Z) \prec F(x)\}$, where $m_i = \min_{y \in M_i} f_i(y)$. If $|Q_i| > M_i$, then cluster on Q_i and select M_i particles to replace $gbest_i$. On the other hand, the information among $gbest_i$ can also provide guidance for PoP_{k+1}. In this paper, $gbest_{k+1}$ will be updated with the information of $gbest_i (i=1,\cdots,k)$. The main step for this is in the following.

Let $H_{k+1} = \left\{ x \mid \exists y, F(y) \prec F(x), x, y \in \bigcup_{i=1}^{k+1} gbest_i \right\}$, if $|H_{k+1}| > M_{k+1}$, then cluster on H_{k+1} and select M_{k+1} particles to substitute for $gbest_{k+1}$.

3.3 Competition Mutation Operator

From the definition 2, the approximation Pareto optimal solutions set T_{k+1} are all in the hyper-rectangle constituted by $gbest_i (i \leq k)$, while non-Pareto optimal solutions, $L_{k+1} = \{F(x) \mid x \in PoP_{k+1} \cup gbest_{k+1}, x \notin T_{k+1}\}$, are out of the hyper-rectangle. As a case for $k = 2$ (in Fig.2), assume A and B are two extreme points of Pareto Front, the objective space is divided into nine parts (I、II、III、IV、V、VI、VII、VIII、IX) by A and B, T_{k+1} is in rectangle APBQ, while L_{k+1} is in the regions of II、VIII、IX. As is known to all, in the standard PSO, all the particles are updated according to equation (1) and (2), the performance of each particle and competition between particles are neglected. For example, particles located at the position A, B, C in Fig.2 need take local exploitation, while particles at the position such as F, E, and D need be explored globally to maintain the diversity of population.

Based on the above analysis, the classical updating method and competition mutation operator are taken to produce new particles. As in Fig.2, particles located in hyper-rectangle are updated by the equation(1) and (2) with smaller w, while for particles like F、E、D, mutation is done on them, and other particles in $PoP_i (i=1,\cdots,k)$ are updated with the classical method.

Suppose the suit of duality $(x,v) = ((x_1,v_1),\cdots,(x_n,v_n))$, $x = (x_1, x_2, \cdots, x_n)$ is a candidate solution, and its current velocity is $v = (v_1, v_2, \cdots, v_n)$, n is the dimension of search space. The range of x_i is $[xl_i, xu_i]$ and v_i is $[vl_i, vu_i]$. The mutation is in the following. First, an integer z is given randomly between 1 and n, then compute $d = \min\{|x-xl_z|, |xu_z - x|\}$. Finally, a random position in $[x-\alpha d, x+\alpha d]$ is chosen for x_z, in which α is related to the number of generation. So is for v_z.

3.4 Selection Method for Global Optimum Position

At present, random and constrained methods are common-used. The former has the advantage of low computation but followed by the lack of guidance during the searching. While more attention is paid to approximating, wide range and the computation in the latter. Based on the above reasons, a combination of random and constrained selection is taken in the following.

First, a random number r_1 is given in $[0,1]$. If r_1 is bigger than a given threshold T, then random selection is taken. Otherwise constrained selection is taken as follows.

In the constrained selection, hyper-rectangle HT is constructed according to the approximation set $gbest_i \, (i=1,\cdots,k)$. Then HT is divided uniformly with step ε, at the same time the set $gbest_{k+1}$ is divided into L subsets $gbest_{k+1}^i$. When selecting the optimum position, an integer number r_2 in $[1,L]$ is given randomly, and one particle is taken from $gbest_{k+1}^{r_2}$ as the global optimum position.

For cooperation population $PoP_i \, (i=1,\cdots,k)$, the optimum positions are chosen randomly.

3.5 Stopping Condition

If $gbest_i \, (i=1,\cdots,k)$, as the approximation of the extreme point set of cooperation population $PoP_i \, (i=1,\cdots,k)$, has no more improvement in several generations, the PSO on them will be stopped, while the PSO for population PoP_{k+1} still continues according to fixed probability p_m.

3.6 CMOPSO Algorithm

The main steps of CMOPSO can be summarized in the following:
1. Initialize the population PoP_i with the size of N_i, and empty archive with size of M_i for $gbest_i$ $(i=1,\cdots,k+1)$. Let $lbest_i = PoP_i$.
2. Calculate the objective functions and evaluate each particle of $PoP_i, i=1,\cdots,k+1$.
3. Update the optimum position of $lbest_i$ and $gbest_i$, $i=1,\cdots,k+1$.
4. Update $gbest_i \, (i=1,\cdots,k+1)$ with co-evolutionary operators.
5. Update each particle in PoP_i ($i=1,\cdots,k+1$) by (1),(2) and Competition Mutation Operator.
6. While the stopping conditions is satisfied, output $gbest_{k+1}$, else, go to 2.

4 Performance Metrics

In order to allow a quantitative assessment of the performance of a multiobjective optimization algorithm, several quality measures have been used or proposed in the literatures. Generational distance (GD) [13] is used to measure the closeness of the Pareto Front generated to the true Pareto-optimal Front. Schott [14] proposed Spacing (SP) to measure the range (distance) variance of neighboring vectors in the found nondominated solution set. Error ratio(ER) was proposed by Van Veldhuizen[15] to indicate the percentage of solutions(from the nondominated vectors found so far) that are not members of the true Pareto optimal set.

ε-Error ratio(ER_ε). The definition of ER is as $ER = (\sum_{i=1}^{n} e_i)/n$, where n is the number of non-dominated vectors found so far, $e_i = 0$ if vector x_i is a member of the

Pareto optimal set, and $e_i = 1$, otherwise. It should then be clear that $ER = 0$ indicates that all the vectors generated by our algorithm belong to the Pareto optimal set of the problem. However, there exists error during the computation, and it is impossible that the comparison between two solutions is identical. Hence, ε-Error ratio is given in this paper. In the new metric, if the Euclidean distance(in the objective space) between the solution in found and a real Pareto optimal set is less than a given positive value ε, then $e_i = 0$, otherwise, $e_i = 1$. The definition expression of ε-ER is as the same as ER. It should be pointed out the smaller ER_ε is wished.

Well-Extended of the Found Nondominated Solution Set. To measure well-extended of the Pareto optimal set, we present a new measure described as follows. (1) Construct reference solution set $P_r = \{F_1^1, \cdots, F_k^1\}$, in which each element is called reference solution and $F_i^1 = (L_1, \cdots, L_{i-1}, U_i, L_{i+1}, \cdots, L_k)$, here $U_i = \max_{x \in P(F,X)} f_i(x)$ $L_i = \min_{x \in P(F,X)} f_i(x)$ (2) Define the distance between a reference solution $p_r \in P_r$ to set P as $d_r^P = \min\{d(p_r, p) \mid p \in P\}$. A smaller d_r^P means P have a better well extended Pareto frontier. Hence, the extension of P is defined to be $EX = \sqrt{\sum(d_r^P)^2}/k$, where k is the number of the objective functions. From the metric, the smaller the value of EX, the well extended for the found nondominated solution set.

5 Experiments

To validate our approach, we performed both quantitative (adopting four performance measures) and qualitative comparisons (plotting the Pareto Fronts produced). Four test functions ZDT1, ZDT3, ZDT4 and ZDT6 were used [12]. These functions are considered to be difficult. Fig.3 shows the Pareto Front produced by CMOPSO, NSGAII, and MOPSO with the median GD. The evolutionary population size of CMOPSO was set to 100. The size of each cooperation population is 20. c_1 and c_2 were set to 2.0. w was linearly decreased from 0.6 to 0.2 over time. The NSGA-II was run using a population size of 80, a crossover rate of 0.9, tournament selection, and a mutation rate of 1/k, where k is the dimension of decision variables. MOPSO used a population of 100 particles, a repository size of 100 particles, a mutation rate of 0.05, and 30 divisions for the adaptive grid. In all the following examples, we report the results obtained from performing 30 independent runs of each algorithm compared, and the source codes of NSGAII and MOPSO are from URL: http://delta.cs.cinvestav.mx/~ccoello/ EMOO/EMOOsoftware.html. The total number of fitness function evaluations for each function was set to 3360, 4160, 20960 and 8160, respectively.

6 Results and Discussion

From Fig.3, it is easily found that the Pareto Fronts produced by the proposed algorithm are all below those of other's. In addition, we can also find from the Fig. 3

that the Pareto Fronts of the three algorithms are similarity in ZDT1 and ZDT3, while for ZDT4 and ZDT6, CMOPSO outperforms well than the other two. In the four test functions, ZDT 4 and ZDT6 are more difficult to achieve a well distributed nondominated Front since the Pareto Front is either multimodal or non-uniformly distributed. However, CMOPSO performs well on both of them.

In Table1, (a), (b), (c) and (d) show the comparison of results among the three algorithms considering the metrics previously described. According to the metric measures given in the Section 4, with respect to the improved Error ration(ER), ε-Error ratio(ER_ε), the average performance of CMOPSO outperforms the other two, which means that the percentage of all the vectors generated by our algorithm belong to the Pareto optimal set of the problem is higher than the other two. As for the Generational distance (GD), it was found that the average performance of the CMOPSO was the best with respect to GD except for ZDT3, however, the GD value of the CMOPSO (0.0020) is very close to that of NSGA-II (0.0013), but the graphical solutions show that the MOPSO is able to cover the entire Pareto Front of the problem

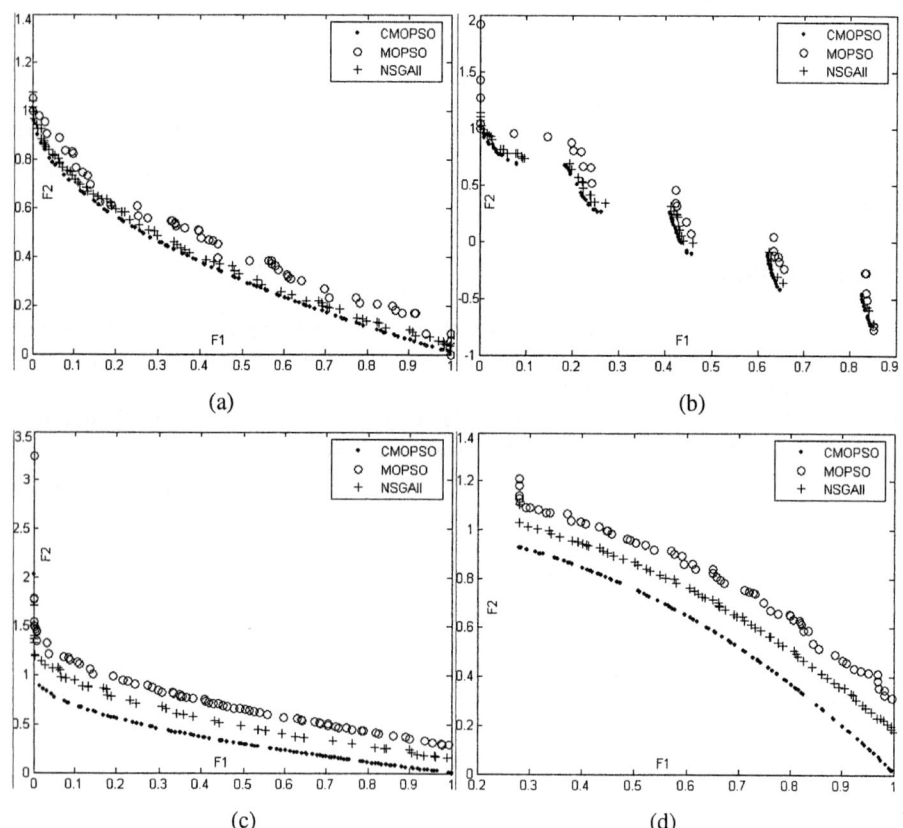

Fig. 3. Pareto Fronts for different test functions with three algorithms. (a) Fronts for ZDT1. (b) Fronts for ZDT3. (c) Fronts for ZDT4. (d) Fronts for ZDT6.

Table 1. Comparison of results between our approach(denoted by CMOPSO), MOPSO and NSGA-II for ZDT1, ZDT3, ZDT4 and ZDT6 are in (a), (b), (c) and (d)

(a)

	Test Function ZDT1			
		CMOPSO	MOPSO	NSGA-II
ER_E	Worst	0.9500	0.9677	0.9125
	Best	0.0000	0.8571	0.5250
	Average	0.3930	0.9256	0.7425
	Median	0.3200	0.9216	0.7500
	Std.Dev.	0.6470	0.9745	0.9093
GD	Worst	0.0004	0.0106	0.0018
	Best	0.0000	0.0010	0.0002
	Average	0.0001	0.0041	0.0004
	Median	0.0001	0.0037	0.0004
	Std.Dev.	0.0001	0.0023	0.0003
SP	Worst	0.3881	0.4578	0.4250
	Best	0.2216	0.2192	0.2121
	Average	0.2945	0.3521	0.3131
	Median	0.2938	0.3644	0.3017
	Std.Dev.	0.0551	0.0701	0.0743
EX	Worst	0.0659	0.0517	0.0757
	Best	0.0003	0.0134	0.0218
	Average	0.0343	0.0264	0.0394
	Median	0.0322	0.0294	0.0368
	Std.Dev.	0.0157	0.0142	0.0133

(b)

	Test Function ZDT3			
		CMOPSO	MOPSO	NSGA-II
ER_E	Worst	0.8276	0.9545	0.8085
	Best	0.1020	0.4474	0.2373
	Average	0.3596	0.8008	0.6182
	Median	0.3482	0.8574	0.6248
	Std.Dev.	0.8329	0.8576	0.8795
GD	Worst	0.0299	0.0560	0.0041
	Best	0.0000	0.0013	0.0003
	Average	0.0020	0.0193	0.0013
	Median	0.0003	0.0118	0.0008
	Std.Dev.	0.0062	0.0158	0.0010
SP	Worst	0.5969	0.7028	0.6203
	Best	0.2915	0.2943	0.2299
	Average	0.4302	0.4737	0.4314
	Median	0.4446	0.4446	0.4403
	Std.Dev.	0.1013	0.1248	0.1072
EX	Worst	0.0762	0.2151	0.8866
	Best	0.0000	0.0000	0.0559
	Average	0.0151	0.1489	0.1909
	Median	0.0000	0.1371	0.1250
	Std.Dev.	0.0233	0.0141	0.2075

(c)

	Test Function ZDT4			
		CMOPSO	MOPSO	NSGA-II
ER_E	Worst	0.8367	1.0000	1.0000
	Best	0.0000	0.8125	0.0500
	Average	0.2356	0.9932	0.8419
	Median	0.0739	1.0000	1.0000
	Std.Dev.	0.7031	0.9658	0.6731
GD	Worst	0.1822	2.8105	0.6398
	Best	0.0000	0.0010	0.0028
	Average	0.0139	0.5608	0.1356
	Median	0.0002	0.3077	0.0478
	Std.Dev.	0.0437	0.6143	0.1623
SP	Worst	0.7287	1.3331	0.7541
	Best	0.1886	0.0235	0.2476
	Average	0.3045	0.4659	0.4178
	Median	0.2763	0.4258	0.4155
	Std.Dev.	0.1220	0.2163	0.1105
EX	Worst	0.1508	2.3747	0.9713
	Best	0.0000	0.0507	0.0126
	Average	0.0243	0.7984	0.2965
	Median	0.0052	0.7274	0.1989
	Std.Dev.	0.0435	0.4925	0.2630

(d)

	Test Function ZDT6			
		CMOPSO	MOPSO	NSGA-II
ER_E	Worst	1.0000	1.0000	1.0000
	Best	0.0000	1.0000	0.9750
	Average	0.2134	1.0000	0.9896
	Median	0.0204	1.0000	0.9875
	Std.Dev.	0.6899	1.0000	0.9907
GD	Worst	0.0031	0.0237	0.0116
	Best	0.0000	0.0091	0.0053
	Average	0.0002	0.0165	0.0074
	Median	0.0000	0.0164	0.0071
	Std.Dev.	0.0006	0.0047	0.0013
SP	Worst	0.3549	0.3614	0.3461
	Best	0.1758	0.1631	0.1681
	Average	0.2750	0.2589	0.2539
	Median	0.2732	0.2559	0.2488
	Std.Dev.	0.0581	0.0673	0.0586
EX	Worst	0.1196	0.4055	0.2437
	Best	0.0061	0.2196	0.1605
	Average	0.0679	0.3173	0.1909
	Median	0.0743	0.3150	0.1881
	Std.Dev.	0.0357	0.0511	0.0185

and lower than the others. For SP, CMOPSO does well (except for ZDT6) than NSGA-II and MOPSO, but with a lower standard deviation, which indicates the proposed algorithm performs well in the uniformity of the found nondominated solution set. As for the well-extended of the found nondominated solution set, CMOPSO performs well than the other two except for ZDT1. However, graphical results again indicate that the CMOPSO can cover the full Pareto Front. Based on the above analysis, we can conclude that CMOPSO presented the best results in most functions (except for GD in ZDT3, SP in ZDT6, EX in ZDT1). Also, it is important to notice the approximation of CMOPSO was clearly superior to the other two approaches adopted in our comparative study. Thus, this indicates that CMOPSO was able to obtain a good number of points of the true Pareto set and a good approximation of all the test functions used in this paper. In addition, during the experiments, too many Pareto optimal solutions are superposed and the diversity of population for MOPSO and NSGA-II is lost.

7 Conclusion

In the proposed approach, co-evolutionary operator, competition mutation operator and selection mechanism are designed, and quantitative and qualitative comparisons have shown that the proposed algorithm has an average performance highly competitive with respect to some of the best multiobjective evolutionary algorithms known to date and is relatively easy to implement. In addition, further work will be done on the application of CMOPSO to the problems with more than two objectives and real-world MO problems.

References

1. Rosen, C., et al. New methods for competitive coevolution. Evolutionary Computation, 1997,5(1): 1-29.
2. Angeline, P. J. & Pollack, J. B. (1993); Competitive environments evolve better solutions for complex tasks. In: Forrest, S. (ed.), *Proceedings ICGA 5*. Morgan Kaufmann, pp. 264–270.
3. Kennedy J, Eberhart R. Particle swarm optimization. Proc. IEEE Int. Conf. On Neural Networks. Perth, 1995. 1942-1948.
4. Eberhart R, Kennedy J. A new optimizer using particle swarm theory. Proc. 6th Int.Symposium on Micro machine and Human Science. Nagoya, 1995.39-43.
5. Coello C.C., Pulido G.T. and Lechuga M.S... Handling Multiple Objectives with Particle swarm optimization. IEEE Trans. On Evolutionary Computation, 8(3), 2004, 256-279.
6. Coello C.C. and Lechuga M.S., MOPSO: A proposal for multiple objective particle swarm optimization. In Proc. Congr. Evolutionary Computation(CEC'2002),vol.1, Honolulu, HI, May 2002,1051-1056.
7. Fieldsend J.E. and Singh S., A multiobjective algorithm based upon particle swarm optimization, an efficient data structure and turbulence. In Proc. 2002 U.K. Workshop on Computational Intelligence, Birmingham, U.K., Sept.2002,37-44.
8. Mostaghim S. and Teich J., Strategies for finding good local guides in Multiobjective Particle Swarm Optimization (MOPSO). In Proc. 2003 IEEE Swarm Intelligence Symp., Indianapolis,IN,Apr.2003,26-33.

9. Parsopoulos K.E. and Vrahatis M.N. Particle swarm optimization method in multiobjective problems. In Proc. 2002ACM Symp. Applied Computing (SAC'2002), Madrid, Spain, 2002,603-607.
10. Deb, K.: Multi-Objective Optimization using Evolutionary Algorithms, John Wiley & Sons, Chichester, UK (2001).
11. Deb K, Pratap A, Agrawal S, Meyarivan T. A Fast Elitist Non-Dominated Sorting Genetic Algorithm for Multi-Objective Optimization: NSGA-II. IEEE Trans. On Evolutionary Computation, 6(2), 2002, 182-197.
12. Zitzler E. Evolutionary Algorithms for Multi-objective Optimization: Methods and Applications.Ph.D. Thesis, Swiss Federal Institute of Technology (ETH), Zurich, Switzerland, November, 1999.
13. D.A.Van Veldhuizen and G.B. lamont. Multiobjective Evolutionary Algorithm Research: A history and analysis. Dept. Elec.Comput.Eng.,Graduate School of Eng., Air Force Inst.Technol.,Wright-Patterson AFB, OH.Tech.Rep.TR-98-03,1998.
14. J.R.Schott. Fault tolerant design using single and multicriteria genetic algorithm optimization.M.S. thesis,Dept.Aeronautics and Astronautics, Massachusetts Inst.Technol.,Cambridge,MA,May,1995.
15. D.A.Van Veldhuizen. Multiobjective evolutionary algorithms: Classifications, analyzes, and new innovations. Ph.D. dissertation, Dept. Elec. Compt. Eng., Graduate School of Eng., Air Force Inst.Technol., Wright-Patterson AFB,OH,May,1999.

The Effect of Mutation on the Accumulation of Information in a Genetic Algorithm

John Milton[1], Paul Kennedy[1], and Heather Mitchell[2]

[1] Faculty of Information Technology, University of Technology Sydney, Sydney, Australia
UTS, PO Box 123, Broadway, Australia 2007 (Ph:0421042234)
milton77@bigpond.net.au
[2] School of Economics, Finance and Marketing, Royal Melbourne Institute of Technology, Melbourne, Australia

Abstract. We use an information theory approach to investigate the role of mutation on Genetic Algorithms (GA). The concept of solution alleles representing information in the GA and the associated concept of information density, being the average frequency of solution alleles in the population, are introduced. Using these concepts, we show that mutation applied indiscriminately across the population has, on average, a detrimental effect on the accumulation of solution alleles within the population and hence the construction of the solution. Mutation is shown to reliably promote the accumulation of solution alleles only when it is targeted at individuals with a lower information density than the mutation source. When individuals with a lower information density than the mutation source are targeted for mutation, very high rates of mutation can be used. This significantly increases the diversity of alleles present in the population, while also increasing the average occurrence of solution alleles.

Keywords: Evolutionary computing, genetic algorithm, mutation, information theory.

1 Introduction

Genetic Algorithms (GA) are optimisation algorithms based on the principles of biological evolution. GA are applicable to optimisation of a wide range of computer-based problems because they do not assume that the problem to be optimised is differentiable or convex. GA are population based search methods which are not easily distracted by local minima or maxima and generally find useful solutions quickly. Potential solutions to problems are encoded on an artificial genome (analogous to the biological DNA) and populations of genomes are tested and bred together (combining genetic material with crossover and mutation of genes) so that solutions that more completely optimise the problem flourish and weaker solutions die out. GA are relatively straightforward to program but understanding how they work is challenging and has been a major research goal for some decades.

Early work on evolutionary algorithms occurred in the late 1950s and early 1960s. Fraser [1], Box [2] and Bremermann [3] described artificial evolution systems. In the 1970s, Holland [4], Rechenberg [5] and others further developed evolutionary algorithms. The basic approach to GAs were developed in Goldberg [6], Mitchell [7] and extended by Goldberg [8]. These provided a basic foundation for understanding the operation of GAs and gave some guide to their construction. Other related approaches in evolutionary computation are genetic programming (eg. Koza [9]) and real valued GAs, Rechenberg, [5] and, Schwefel [10].

However even with this work, a rigorous approach to optimal GA design, akin to electronic circuit design or mechanical engineering designs, has not been achieved. Arguably the main step in this direction has been the building block hypothesis, which describes how, using crossover and selection, partial solutions of varying fitness (building blocks) are assembled into an optimal solution [4],[6].

While building blocks are on the surface convincing and may well form an important function in GA success, they are still not universally accepted as the key attribute of a GA [11],[12],[13]. Additionally, GA operators such as mutation are universally accepted to maintain diversity in the population. Yet it is not clear whether mutation is, on average, beneficial to the efficient operation of a GA or whether alternative methods of maintaining diversity in the GA may be superior.

Information theory is characterised by a quantitative approach to the notion of information. It provides a framework to understand how information can be transmitted and stored compactly and the maximum quantity of information that can be transmitted through a channel [14]. Information theory introduces the ideas; information measure, information sources, entropy and rate distortion. The language used to describe information sources and the symbols they generate, provide a new perspective on a GA population and the dynamics at work as the population becomes structured and accumulates information.

Information theory is frequently used in papers on GAs to describe and analyse the problem to be optimised and many authors have been influenced by ideas derived from information theory as evidenced by the large number of references to information theory texts. However, few authors appear to have explicitly applied an information-theoretic approach to the analysis of GA parameters such as population size, mutation rate or selection pressure. Exceptions are Bala [15], who used an independent ranking of each feature with an information theory based entropy measure (infomax) to estimate which features are the most discriminatory, and Araujo [16] who employs a distance measure for fitness evaluation derived from information theory.

This paper uses an information theoretic approach to show when mutation is beneficial and how it should be applied to maximise this benefit. The concept of solution alleles representing information in the GA and the associated information density of the population will be introduced. Using these concepts it will be shown that mutation applied indiscriminately across the population has, on average, a detrimental effect on the accumulation of solution alleles within the population and that mutation is only beneficial when targeted at individuals with a lower information density than the mutation source.

Section 2 introduces relevant information theory, the idea of information in a GA population and defines the idea of information density. Section 3 analyses the effect of mutation on a population's information density. In particular the probability of gaining or losing information is examined. Section 4 repeats the Section 3 analysis using a form of mutation often described as 'bit flipping'. Section 5 discusses and compares the information gain of these two forms of mutation and suggestions for further work. Section 6 provides concluding remarks.

2 Information Density

Borrowing from information theory, an information source is defined as an algorithm, that generates symbols in a stationary stochastic sequence. A memoryless information source is one where the symbols are statistically independent [14]. For the purposes of this study we assume that the initial population of a GA is constructed using a memoryless information source, which randomly generates symbols and places them into positions (loci) belonging to individuals. Each of these individuals represents a possible solution to the problem.

One or more optimum solutions to the problem to be solved will exist. For the purpose of this paper we arbitrarily choose one of these solutions to represent the ideal solution, we can define ideal alleles as those symbols in appropriate loci which form the ideal solution. These ideal alleles will be regarded as information contained within the population.

Unless the information source has special knowledge of the problem, these ideal alleles will occur at the rate $1/A$ in the initial population; where A is the number of possible alleles at each locus. A will be referred to as the coding order (binary, octal, hexadecimal or other) and does not vary from loci to loci. Hence the frequency of ideal alleles in the initial population will equal $1/A$ and will be referred to as the information density ρ_0 of the initial population. ie $\rho_0=1/A$.

Diversity is the variation of symbols (alleles) present in the population. The initial population is the most diverse population that can be generated as it is produced by a memoryless information source. As a GA discards low performing individuals, alleles will be lost and the diversity of symbols in the population will decrease. Generally this is useful as the relative frequency of high performing individuals and their constituent alleles will increase. However, the loss of alleles changes the relative frequency of symbols in the population and hence applies a bias to the GA and ultimately a reduction in the size of the solution space that is searched. If this happens prematurely, then the GA may lose paths to the ideal solution.

The most common way to re-introduce alleles is by randomly selecting a locus in a randomly selected individual and changing that allele to another symbol. This process is called mutation and has the effect of maintaining diversity of symbols in the population. Mutation is the main technique used to maintain diversity in GAs.

Since an ideal allele represents information, mutation is a form of information loss or gain. The population will gain information if the mutation operator changes an incorrect allele into an ideal allele. The population will lose information if the reverse occurs. The mutation operator also requires an information source, typically this is the same source as the one used to generate the initial population.

3 Mutation Analysed

Mutation is the result of random processes that may be modelled using information theoretic approaches. Information theory provides a language and framework for understanding the source of symbols used to generate populations and can be adapted to examine the effect of mutation on those populations.

A common form of mutation is to randomly select a locus in a randomly selected individual and change that allele to any symbol produced by the memoryless information source. In this section the probability of information loss or gain due to this type of mutation will be quantified.

To find the probability that a mutation operation, on a genome of length L and with A symbols available to each locus, gains or loses information, first consider the probability of a gain in information, P_{gain}.

The probability of a gain in information is given by the joint probability of:

- selecting an individual with exactly λ ideal alleles,
- selecting a non-ideal allele for mutation, within that individual, and
- mutating this non-ideal allele to an ideal allele.

Assuming ideal alleles are randomly distributed, and ρ_g is the information density of the population at generation g; then the probability of selecting for mutation an individual with exactly λ 'ideal' alleles at generation g, will be given by the binomial probability $P_g(\lambda|L,\rho_g)$. The probability that an incorrect allele within this individual is selected for mutation is $(1-\lambda/L)$. Because the initial information source of the population equals the mutation source, and recalling an initial assumption that all loci have the same coding order, then the probability that the mutation source generates an ideal allele at any loci is $1/A$.

Hence:

$$P_{gain} = \sum_{\lambda=0}^{L} P_g(\lambda | L, \rho_g).[1-\tfrac{\lambda}{L}].\tfrac{1}{A}$$

Noting that $\Sigma P_g(\lambda.P_g(\lambda|L,\rho_g))=1$, gives

$$P_{gain} = \frac{1}{A}.\left[1 - \frac{1}{L}\sum_{\lambda=0}^{L} \lambda.P_g(\lambda | L, \rho_g)\right] \quad (1)$$

P_{gain} is the probability that the number of ideal alleles in the mutated individual will rise by 1 allele as a result of a single mutation event. There are two other transition probabilities. P_{loss} is the probability that the number of ideal alleles in the mutated individual will fall by 1 allele and P_{none} for no change in the number of ideal alleles.

P_{loss} is a joint probability that is found in a similar way as P_{gain}. Hence:

$$P_{loss} = \left[1 - \frac{1}{A}\right].\frac{1}{L}\sum_{\lambda=0}^{L} \lambda.P_g(\lambda | L, \rho_g) \quad (2)$$

Equations (1) and (2) are equal when the population's information density is equal to the information density of the mutation source, that is $\rho_g=1/A$. This occurs only during the initial generation or when strong selection pressure returns the population's information density to the initial level of ρ_0.

Sometimes mutation will replace an ideal allele with an ideal allele or an incorrect allele with an incorrect allele. This P_{none} causes neither loss nor gain and is related to the neutral drift investigated by Shipman [17]. P_{none} transitions may allow larger areas of a search space to be explored with no detriment, but may also represent a processing inefficiency as there is a danger of prolonged periods of random drift.

To find P_{none}, we need to calculate the joint probability of:

- selecting an individual with exactly λ ideal alleles,
- selecting a non-ideal allele for mutation, within that individual, and
- mutating this non-ideal allele to a non-ideal allele;

combined with the joint probability of:

- selecting an individual with exactly λ ideal alleles.
- selecting an ideal allele for mutation, within that individual, and
- mutating this ideal allele to an ideal allele.

Taking these joint probabilities into account we can then find P_{none}.

$$P_{none} = \sum_{\lambda=0}^{L} \lambda.P_g(\lambda|L,\rho_g).\frac{1}{L}.\frac{1}{A} + \sum_{\lambda=0}^{L} P_g(\lambda|L,\rho_g).[1-\frac{\lambda}{L}].[1-\frac{1}{A}]$$

$$P_{none} = 1 - \frac{1}{A} + [\frac{2}{A}-1].\frac{1}{L}.\sum_{\lambda=0}^{L} \lambda.P_g(\lambda|L,\rho_g) \qquad (3)$$

As all transition probabilities must sum to one, equations (1), (2), and (3) sum to one.

For information to accumulate on average, $P_{gain} - P_{loss}$ must be greater than 0. Substituting the probabilities of gaining and losing information as defined by (1) and (2) then simplifying gives

$$\frac{1}{A} - \frac{1}{L}.\sum_{\lambda=0}^{L} \lambda.P_g(\lambda|L,\rho_g) > 0 \qquad (4)$$

Due to selection, when $g>0$, the average information density of the population (the second term in equation 4) will be greater than the information density of the mutation source (the first term in equation 4). Therefore equation (4) is not satisfied for $g>0$ and, on average, information accumulates only if the information density of the population falls below the information density of the mutation source $1/A$, for example when the population has experienced strong selection pressure.

4 An Alternative Mutation Mechanism – Symbol Flipping

Another common form of mutation is symbol flipping (bit flipping for binary coding order). This form of mutation replaces the allele with any symbol other than the current symbol. While this form of mutation is different from the one described above, it does not produce ideal alleles at a higher rate.

The conditions for information gain here are the same as in Section 3. However, the probability of mutating a non-ideal to an ideal allele is different. In this case we start with an incorrect allele and we do not replace it with itself. Hence there are $A-1$ choices (instead of A choices) in this mutation scheme and only one of them is the ideal allele.

Proceeding as before, we get a probability of gain:

$$P_{gain} = \frac{1}{[A-1]} \cdot \left[1 - \frac{1}{L} \sum_{\lambda=0}^{L} \lambda P_g(\lambda | L, \rho_g) \right] \quad (5)$$

and a probability of loss:

$$P_{loss} = \frac{1}{L} \sum_{\lambda=0}^{L} \lambda P_g(\lambda | L, \rho_g) \quad (6)$$

In the case of loss, there is no A term because we start with an ideal allele and we do not replace it with itself. So the probability it is replaced with an incorrect allele is one.

We now calculate P_{none} in a similar way to Section 3.

$$P_{none} = \sum_{\lambda=0}^{L} P_g(\lambda | L, \rho_g) \cdot [1 - \tfrac{\lambda}{L}] \cdot \frac{[A-2]}{[A-1]}$$

$$P_{none} = \frac{[A-2]}{[A-1]} \left[1 - \frac{1}{L} \sum_{\lambda=0}^{L} \lambda P_g(\lambda | L, \rho_g) \right] \quad (7)$$

As before the transition probabilities in equations (5), (6), and (7) sum to one.

Again, for information to accumulate on average, $P_{gain} - P_{loss}$ must be greater than 0. Substituting the probabilities of gaining and losing information as defined by equations (5) and (6) then simplifying gives:

$$\frac{A}{[A-1]} \left[\frac{1}{A} - \frac{1}{L} \sum_{\lambda=0}^{L} \lambda P_g(\lambda | L, \rho_g) \right] > 0 \quad (8)$$

However, as noted in Section 3, after the first generation $g>0$, the average information density of the population (the third term in equation 8) will be greater than the information density of the mutation source (the second term in equation 8). Therefore equation (8) is not satisfied for $g>0$ and, on average, information accumulates only if the information density of the population falls below the information density of the mutation source $1/A$, for example when the population has experienced strong selection pressure.

5 Discussion

For mutation to provide an average gain in information, the information density of the mutation source $1/A$ must be greater than the information density of the population λP.

$$\frac{1}{A} > \lambda P = \frac{1}{L} \cdot \sum_{\lambda=0}^{L} \lambda . P_g (\lambda \mid L, \rho_g)$$

On average, there is no change in information density when $1/A = \lambda P$, and an average loss when $1/A < \lambda P$.

Comparing the two mutation operators can be done by inspection of equations (4) and (8). As explained above, both operators are detrimental to the progress of the GA when the population's information density λP exceeds $1/A$. However, the information gain or loss due to symbol flipping, is accelerated by the term

$$\frac{A}{[A-1]}$$

Hence the effect of symbol flipping is accelerated when compared to the Section 3 mutation operator. The difference is most pronounced for binary coding order $A=2$ and diminishes as the coding order is increased.

5.1 Why Use Mutation at all?

Mutation is, on average, detrimental to a GA information density because, after the first generation, the average information density of the population is greater than that of the mutation source. Why then is mutation used in GAs with good effect? Mutation promotes diversity and helps delay convergence. Mutation re-introduces lost alleles. Sometimes, the new alleles are ideal alleles. When this occurs, selection locks in the gained alleles.

The analysis in Sections 3 and 4 refers to the average effect over many individuals and/or generations. When small amounts of mutation are followed closely by selection, damage is minor and on the occasions where ideal alleles arise, they are quickly locked in by selection before further detrimental mutation reverses their benefit.

A high mutation rate is more likely to behave as described in Sections 3 and 4. Hence high mutation rates are more detrimental than low mutation rates. This is why GAs have been more successful when using very low mutation rates.

5.2 Targeting Mutation to Add Information

Mutating alleles selected at random from the population is, on average, detrimental to the information density of a population. However, the analysis in Sections 3 and 4 suggests that an approach which targets individuals with a lower information density than the mutation source will, on average, improve the information density of that individual and hence the population overall.

To target mutation at individuals with an information density less than the mutation source in this way, it is first necessary to rank all individuals in the population. Next we must identify the threshold separating high scoring individuals, having information density greater than the mutation source, from low scoring individuals, with information density less than that of the mutation source. This threshold is the critical selection threshold.

Individuals with rank above the critical selection threshold are retained in the population (without mutation). Individuals below this threshold can either be selected for deletion (and replacement with newly produced individuals) or have randomly selected loci mutated. Either method is straightforward, although replacement by newly generated individuals has a more significant effect on the diversity of symbols in the population because more alleles are replaced. This increased diversity assists the GA since diversity provides alternative paths to a solution.

Replacement of individuals with rank below the critical threshold benefits the population because the average number of ideal alleles in the deleted individuals is less than the average number of ideal alleles reintroduced by the new individuals. The challenge is to accurately identify the critical selection threshold. This will be addressed in future work.

6 Conclusion

It has been shown that mutation applied indiscriminately across the population has, on average, a detrimental effect to the population's information density and therefore the accumulation of ideal (solution) alleles. This is because, as a GA increases the information density of the population, it quickly exceeds the information density of the mutation source. This increases the probability that mutation will replace ideal alleles with non-ideal alleles.

The analysis described here suggests that when mutation is targeted specifically at individuals with an information density less than the mutation source, then significant amounts of mutation can be applied, which both increases the average occurrence of ideal alleles in the population and also improves the population's diversity.

References

1. Fraser, A. S. (1957) Simulation of genetic systems by automatic digital computers. Australian Journal of Biological Science, 10, 484-491.
2. Box, G. E. P. (1957) Evolutionary operation: a method of increasing industrial productivity. Applied Statistics, Vol. 6, 81-101.

3. Bremermann, H. J., Rogson, M. and Salaff, S. (1966) Global properties of evolution processes. In Natural Automata and Useful Simulation, pp. 3-41, Eds. Pattee, H. H., Edlsack, E. A., Fein, L., and Callahan, A. B., Spartan Books, Washington DC.
4. Holland, J.: Adaptation in natural and artificial systems. University of Michigan Press, Ann Arbor, MI:, MIT Press, Cambridge, MA, (1975)
5. Rechenberg, I.: Evolutionsstrategie: Optimierung Technischer Systeme nach Prinzipien der iologischen Evolution. Frommann-Holzboog, Stuttgart (DE) (1973)
6. Goldberg, D.: Genetic Algorithms in Search Optimization and Machine Learning. Addison Wesley (1989)
7. Mitchell, M.: An Introduction to Genetic Algorithms. MIT Press (1999)
8. Goldberg, D.:The Design of Innovation: lessons from and for competent genetic algorithms. Kluwer Academic Publishers (2002)
9. Koza, J.: Genetic programming: on the programming of computers by means of natural selection. MIT Press Cambridge, MA, USA (1992)
10. Schwefel, H.: Numerical Optimization of Computer Models. New York: John Wiley & Sons (1981)
11. Beyer, H.: An alternative explanation for the manner in which genetic algorithms operate. Elsevier Science, Biosystems, vol. 41, no. 1, (1997) pp. 1-15 (15)
12. Stephens, C., Waelbroeck, H.: Schemata evolution and building blocks. Evolutionary Computation 7(2): (1999) 109-124
13. Whitley, D.: An overview of evolutionary algorithms: practical issues and common pitfalls. Information and Software Technology 43, (2001) 817-831
14. Van der Lubbe, J.: Information Theory. Cambridge University Press (1997)
15. Bala, J., Huang, J., Vafaie, H., DeJong, K.,Wechsler, H.: Hybrid Learning Using Genetic Algorithms and Decision Trees for Pattern Classification. IJCAI conference, Montreal (1995) 19-25
16. Araujo, D., Lopes, H., Freitas, A.: A Parallel Genetic Algorithm for Rule Discovery in Large Databases. Proceedings IEEE Systems, Man and Cybernetics Conf., Tokyo v. III, (1999) 940-945
17. Shipman, R., Shackleton, M., Ebner, M., Watson, R.: Neutral Search Spaces for Artificial Evolution: a lesson from life' : Artificial Life: Proceedings of Seventh International Conference on Artificial Life. MIT Press: Cambridge, MA. (2000)

Linear Genetic Programming for Multi-class Object Classification

Christopher Fogelberg and Mengjie Zhang

School of Mathematics, Statistics and Computer Sciences
Victoria University of Wellington, P. O. Box 600, Wellington, New Zealand
{fogelbchri,mengjie}@mcs.vuw.ac.nz

Abstract. Multi-class object classification is an important field of research in computer vision. In this paper basic linear genetic programming is modified to be more suitable for multi-class classification and its performance is then compared to tree-based genetic programming. The directed acyclic graph nature of linear genetic programming is exploited. The existing fitness function is modified to more accurately approximate the true feature space. The results show that the new linear genetic programming approach outperforms the basic tree-based genetic programming approach on all the tasks investigated here and that the new fitness function leads to better and more consistent results. The genetic programs evolved by the new linear genetic programming system are also more comprehensible than those evolved by the tree-based system.

1 Introduction

Image classification tasks occur in a wide variety of problem domains. While human experts can frequently accurately classify the data manually, such experts are typically rare or too expensive. Thus computer based solutions to many of these problems are very desirable.

Genetic Programming (GP) [1, 2] is a promising approach for building reliable classification programs quickly and automatically, given only a set of examples on which a program can be evaluated. GP uses ideas analogous to biological evolution to search the space of possible programs to evolve a good program for a particular task.

While showing promise, current GP techniques frequently do not give satisfactory results on difficult classification tasks, particularly multi-class classification (tasks with more than two classes). There are at least two limitations in currently used GP *program structures* and *fitness functions* that prevent GP from finding acceptable programs in a reasonable time.

The programs that GP evolves are typically tree-like structures [3], which map a vector of input values to a single real-valued output[4, 5, 6]. For classification tasks, this output must be mapped into a set of class labels. For binary classification problems, there is a natural mapping of negative values to one class and positive values to the other class. For multi-class classification problems, finding the appropriate boundaries on the number line to separate the classes is very difficult. Several new translations have recently been developed in the interpretation of the single output value of the tree-based GP [4, 7, 8], with differing strengths in addressing different types of problem. While these translations have achieved better classification performance, the evolution is still slow and the evolved programs are hard to interpret, particularly for more difficult problems or problems with a large number of classes.

In solving classification problems, GP typically uses the classification accuracy, error rate or a similar measure as the fitness function [5, 7, 8], which approximates the true fitness of an individual program. Given that the training set size is often highly limited, such an approximation frequently fails to accurately estimate the classification of the true feature space.

1.1 Goals

To address the problems above, this paper aims to investigate an approach to the use of linear genetic programming (LGP) and a new fitness function for multi-class object classification problems. This approach will be compared with the basic tree-based GP (TGP) approach on three image classification tasks of increasing difficulty. Specifically, we are interested in:

- Whether the LGP approach outperforms the basic TGP approach on these object classification problems in terms of classification performance.
- Whether the genetic programs evolved by LGP are more comprehensible.
- Whether the new fitness function improves the classification performance over the existing fitness function.

2 LGP for Multi-class Object Classification

2.1 LGP Overview

This work used register machine LGP (hereafter just LGP) [2], where an individual program is represented by a sequence of register machine instructions, typically expressed in human-readable form as C-style code.

Prior to any program being executed, the registers which it can read from or write to are zeroed. The features representing the objects to be classified are loaded into predefined registers. The program is executed in an imperative manner and represents a *directed acyclic graph* (DAG). This is different from tree-based GP which represents a tree. Any register's value may be used in multiple instructions during the execution of the program.

2.2 Multi-class Output Interpretation

An LGP program often has only one register interpreted in determining its output [9, 2]. This configuration can be easily used for regression and binary classification problems as in the tree-based GP.

In this work, we use LGP for multi-class object classification problems. We want an LGP program to produce one output for each class. Thus, instead of using only one register as the output, we use multiple registers each corresponding to one class. The winner-takes-all strategy is then used and the class represented by the register with the largest value is considered the class of the input object by that genetic program.

This program output representation for the different classes is very similar to a feed forward neural network classifier [10]. However, the structure of such an LGP program is more flexible than that of the feed forward neural network.

2.3 Evolutionary Operators

We used reproduction, crossover and mutation as genetic operators. In reproduction, the best programs in the current generation are copied into the next generation without any change.

We used two different forms of mutation [11] in this work. *Macromutation* involves the replacement of an entire instruction with a randomly generated one. *Micromutation* changes only either the destination register, a source register or the operation. These operations can cause dramatic changes in the DAG that a program represents [12].

In the crossover operator, we randomly choose a section from each of the two parents, then swap them to produce offspring. If a newly produced program is longer than the maximum length allowed, then an instruction is randomly selected and removed until the program can fit into the maximum length. This is similar to two-point crossover in GAs[13], but the two sections chosen from the parents can have different lengths here.

2.4 The Old Fitness Function and the Hurdle Problem

Given that the size of the training set must be finite, any fitness function can only be an approximation to an program's true fitness. This can lead to problems such as overfitting, where a program's true fitness is sacrificed for fitness on the training set. In a multi-class object classification problem, a program's true fitness is the fraction of the feature space it can correctly classify. A good fitness function is one which accurately estimates this fraction.

A typical fitness function for classification problem is the *error rate* of a program classifier. This was also used in our early experiments. While it performed reasonably well, this fitness function frequently fails to accurately estimate the fraction of the feature space correctly classified by a program.

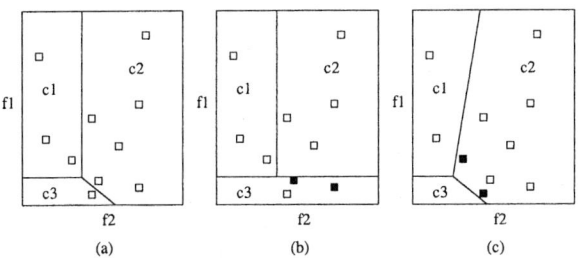

Fig. 1. The hurdle problem. Solid objects are misclassified

Figure 1 shows a simple classification problem with two features. Figure 1(a) shows the true feature space — feature vectors of class c1 objects always appear in the fraction of the feature space denoted "c1", and similarly for the fractions denoted "c2" and "c3". Figure 1(b) shows that program1 misclassifies two objects of c2 as c3. This program has an error rate of 18% (2/11). Figure 1(c) shows that program2 misclassifies one object from class c3 and one object from class c1 as c2. This program also has an error rate of 18% and will be treated the same as the program1. program2 actually approximated the true fitness more accurately than program1, but the fitness function cannot accurately reflect this difference.

We call this problem *the hurdle problem*. It occurs when (any two) classes have a very complex boundary in the feature space. In such a situation, it is easy to classify the bulk of fitness cases for one class correctly, but learning to recognise the other class often initially comes only at an equal or greater loss of accuracy in classifying the first class. This creates a strong selection pressure against making the classification boundary in the feature space more complex and GP with such a fitness function often cannot surmount the hurdle.

2.5 The Decay Curve Fitness Function

To address the hurdle problem, we introduced a new fitness function, the *decay curve fitness function* to estimate true fitness more accurately. The new fitness function uses an *increasing penalty* for each of the M_c misclassifications of some class c, as shown in equation 1.

$$f_{decay} = \sum_c \sum_{i=0}^{M_c} \alpha^{\beta i} / N \qquad (1)$$

The values of α and β are determined through empirical search. We used a fitness function with $\alpha > 1$ to approximate the true fitness so that the penalty of later misclassifications increased exponentially. N is the number of training examples.

Obviously, as α approaches 1.0 and β approaches 0.0, the curve becomes progressively flatter and more similar to a traditional fitness function (error rate in this case).

3 Experiment Design and Configuration

3.1 Data Sets

Experiments were conducted on three different image data sets providing object classification problems of increasing difficulty. Examples are shown in figure 2.

The first data set (figure 2a) was generated to give well defined objects against a relatively clean background. The pixels of the objects were produced using a Gaussian generator with different means and variances for each class. Four classes of 600 small objects (150 for each class) were used to form the classification data set. The four classes are: dark circles (*class1*), light circles (*class2*), dark squares (*class3*), and light squares (*class4*). This data set is referred to as *shape*. The objects in class1 and class3, and in class2 and class4 are very similar in the average values of pixel intensities, which makes the problem reasonably difficult.

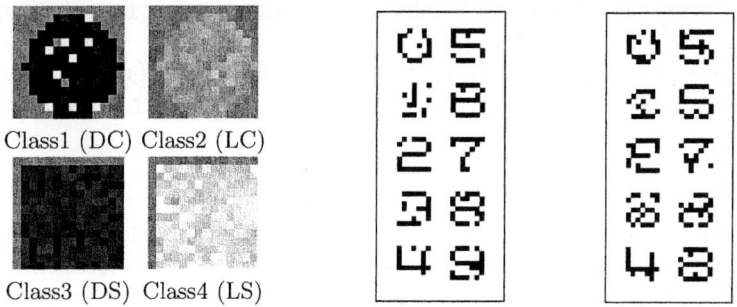

Fig. 2. Image data sets. (a) shape; (b) digit15; (c) digit30

The second and third data sets are two digit recognition tasks, each consisting of 1000 digit examples. Each digit is represented by a 7×7 bitmap image. In the two tasks, the goal is to automatically recognise which of the 10 classes (0, 1, 2, ..., 9) each bitmap belongs to. Note that all the digit patterns have been corrupted by noise. In the two tasks (figure 2 (b) and (c)), 15% and 30% of pixels, chosen at random, have been flipped. In data set 2 (*digit15*), while some patterns can be clearly recognised by human eyes such as "0", "2", "5", "7", and possibly "4", it is not easy to distinguish between "6", "8" and "3". The task in data set 3 (*digit30*) is even more difficult — human eyes cannot recognise majority of the patterns, particularly "8", "9" and "3", "5" and "6", and even "1", "2" and "0". In addition, the number of classes is much greater than that in task 1, making the two tasks even more difficult.

3.2 Primitive Sets

Terminals. In the *shape* data set, we used eight features extracted from the objects and an random number as the terminal set. The eight features are shown in figure 3.

For the two digit data sets, we used the raw pixels as the terminal sets, meaning that the feature vector of each object has 49 values. The large number of terminals makes these tasks more difficult, but we expect that the GP evolu-

Feature	LGP Index	Description
f1	cf[0]	mean brightness of the entire object
f2	cf[1]	mean of the top left quadrant
f3	cf[2]	mean of the top right quadrant
f4	cf[3]	mean of the bottom left quadrant
f5	cf[4]	mean of the bottom right quadrant
f6	cf[5]	mean of the centre quadrant
f7	cf[6]	standard deviation of the whole object
f8	cf[7]	standard deviation of centre quadrant

Fig. 3. Terminal set for the *shape* data set

tionary process can automatically select those highly relevant to each recognition problem.

Functions. The function set for all the three data sets was {+, -, *, /, if}. Division (/) was protected to return 0 on a divide-by-zero. if executes the next statement if the condition is true.

3.3 Parameters and Termination Criteria

The parameter values used for the LGP system for the three data sets are shown in table 1. Evolution is terminated at generation 50 unless a successful solution is found, in which case the evolution is terminated early.

Table 1. Parameter values for the LGP system for the three data sets

parameter name	shape	digit15	digit30	parameter name	shape	digit15	digit30
pop_size	500	500	500	macromutation_rate	30%	30%	30%
max_program_length	15	35	35	micromutation_rate	30%	30%	30%
reproduction_rate	10%	10%	10%	α	1.2	1.2	1.2
crossover_rate	30%	30%	30%	β	0.24	0.24	0.24

3.4 TGP Configuration

The LGP approach developed in this work was compared to the basic TGP approach [3]. In TGP, the ramped half-and-half method was used for initial generation and mutation[2]. The proportional selection mechanism and the reproduction, crossover and mutation operators [3] were used in the learning and evolutionary process. The program output was translated into a class label according to the static range selection method [4].

The TGP system used the same terminal sets, function sets, fitness function, population size and termination criteria for the three data sets as the LGP approach. The reproduction, mutation, and crossover rates used were 10%, 30%, and 60%, respectively. The program depth was 3–5 for the shape data set, and 4–6 for the two digit data sets. All single experiments were repeated 50 times. The average results are presented in the next section.

The program depths above in TGP were derived from the LGP program lengths based on a heuristic. An LGP instruction typically consists of one or two arguments and an operation, each corresponding to a node in a TGP program tree. Considering that each TGP operation might be used by its children and/or parents, an LGP instruction roughly corresponds to 1.5 tree nodes. Assuming each non-leaf node has two children (or more for some functions), we can calculate the expressive capacity of a depth-n TGP in LGP program instructions.

4 Results and Discussion

4.1 Classification Performance

Classification Accuracy. Table 2 shows a comparison between the LGP approach developed in this work and the standard TGP approach for the three object classification problems.

Table 2. Classification accuracy of the LGP and TGP on the three data sets

Data set	Method	Training Set Accuracy % ($\mu \pm \sigma$)	Test Set Accuracy % ($\mu \pm \sigma$)
shape	LGP	100.00 ± 0.00	99.91 ± 0.17
	TGP	85.04 ± 16.49	84.41 ± 17.17
digit15	LGP	68.02% ± 4.16%	62.48% ± 5.03%
	TGP	52.60% ± 6.65%	51.80% ± 6.85%
digit30	LGP	55.22% ± 3.49%	51.04% ± 4.26%
	TGP	41.15% ± 5.03%	35.00% ± 6.17%

On the shape data set, our LGP approach always generated a genetic program which successfully classified all objects in the training set. These 50 program classifiers also achieved almost perfect classification performance on the unseen objects in the test set. On the other hand, the TGP approach only achieved about 85.04% and 84.41% accuracy on the training and the test sets, respectively. In addition, the LGP approach resulted in a much smaller standard deviation than the TGP approach. This shows that the LGP method is more stable and more reliable than the TGP approach on this problem. These results suggest that the LGP approach greatly outperforms the TGP approach on this data set in terms of the classification accuracy.

The classification results on the two digit data sets show a similar pattern to those on the shape data set. In both cases, the LGP approach achieved a higher average value and a lower standard deviation of the classification accuracy on the test set than the corresponding TGP approach. The improvements are quite considerable, suggesting that the LGP approach is better than the TGP approach for these multi-class object classification problems.

Training Efficiency. Inspection of the number of generations used reveals that the LGP approach is more efficient than the TGP approach in finding a good genetic program classifier for these object classification problems. For example, in the shape data set, the $\mu \pm \sigma$ of the number of generations for the LGP approach was 16.46 ± 10.22, which was much smaller than the corresponding number for the TGP approach (41.22 ± 14.11).

4.2 Comprehensibility of the Evolved Genetic Programs

To check whether the genetic programs evolved by the LGP approach are easy to interpret or not, we use a typical evolved program which perfectly classified all objects for the shape data set as an example. The code of the evolved genetic program is shown in figure 4 (left). Note that structural introns are commented using //. The DAG representation of the simplified program is shown in figure 4 (right) after the introns are removed.

In this program, the array cf (cf[0] to cf[7]) are the eight feature terminals (f1, ..., f8) as described in figure 3 and the register array r (r[0] to r[3]) correspond to the four class labels (class1, class2, class3, class4). Given an object, the feature values and the register values can be easily calculated and the class of the object can be simply determined by taking the register

```
//r[1] = r[1] / r[1];
//r[3] = cf[0] + cf[5];
//if(r[3] < 0.86539)
//r[3] = r[3] - r[1];
r[0] = 0.453012 - cf[1];
//r[3] = r[2] * cf[5];
r[1] = r[0] * 0.89811;
if(cf[6] < cf[1])
r[2] = 0.453012 - cf[3];
r[3] = cf[4] - 0.86539;
```

Fig. 4. A sample program evolved by LGP

with the largest value. For example, given the following four objects with different feature values:

	cf[0]	cf[1]	cf[2]	cf[3]	cf[4]	cf[5]	cf[6]	cf[7]
Obj1 (class1):	0.3056	0.3458	0.2917	0.2796	0.3052	0.1754	0.5432	0.5422
Obj2 (class2):	0.6449	0.6239	0.6452	0.6423	0.6682	0.7075	0.1716	0.1009
Obj3 (class3):	0.2783	0.3194	0.2784	0.2770	0.2383	0.2331	0.2349	0.0958
Obj4 (class4):	0.8238	0.7910	0.8176	0.8198	0.8666	0.8689	0.2410	0.1021

we can obtain the following register values and classification r[] for each object example.

Object	True-Class	r[0]	r[1]	r[2]	r[3]	Classified-Class
Obj1	class1	**0.1474**	0.13240	0.0000	-0.5602	class1
Obj2	class2	-0.1919	**-0.1723**	-0.1893	-0.1972	class2
Obj3	class3	0.1747	0.1569	**0.1760**	-0.6271	class3
Obj4	class4	-0.3708	-0.3330	-0.3668	**0.0012**	class4

As can be seen from the results, this genetic program classified all the four object examples correctly. Examining the program and features used suggests that the genetic programs evolved by LGP are quite comprehensible.

Further inspection of this program reveals that only four of eight features were selected from the terminal set. This suggests that the LGP approach can automatically select features relevant to a particular task. The DAG representation of the program (figure 4b) shows that the LGP approach can co-evolve sub-programs together each for a particular class and that some terminals and functions can be reused by different sub-programs.

On the other hand, a program evolved by the TGP approach can only produce a single value, which must be translated/interpreted into a set of class labels. A typical genetic program evolved by the TGP approach is:

```
(* (- (+ (/ f1 -0.268213) (/ -0.828695 f6))
      (/ (/ f7 f6) (+ -0.828695 f5)))
   (* (- (/ f1 f5) (/ f5 f6))
      (+ (- f4 -0.828695) (+ f1 f2))))
)
```

This program used almost all the features and it is not clear how it does the classification. Such programs are more difficult to interpret for multi-class classification problems.

4.3 Impact of the New Fitness Function

To investigate whether the new fitness function is helpful in reducing the hurdle problem, we used the shape data set as an example to compare the classification performance between the new fitness function and the old fitness function (error rate).

When doing experiments, we used a slightly different setting in program size. Notice that the frequency of the hurdle problem will drop as the program size is increased, although it is not eliminated. Hence the LGP programs in the assessment of the new decay curve fitness function use a program length 10, which is still long enough to express a solution to the problem — solutions have been found when the maximum length is 5. In TGP the tree depths are left at 3–5. These limits are likely to be representative of the situation when a much more difficult problem is being addressed. In such tasks, the maximum depth which is computationally tractable with existing hardware may also be so short relative to the problem's difficulty that the hurdle problem is a major issue.

Table 3 shows the classification results of the two fitness functions using both the TGP and the LGP methods for the shape data set. For the TGP method, the new fitness function led to a very significant improvement on both the training set and the test set. For the LGP method, the classification accuracy was also improved using the new fitness function, but the improvement was not as significant. This was mainly because the LGP method with the old fitness function already performed quite well (98.76%) due to the power of LGP. When using either the old or the new fitness functions, the LGP method always outperformed the TGP method. This is consistent with our previous observation.

Table 3. A comparison of the two fitness functions on the shape data set

Method	Fitness Function	Training Accuracy ($\mu \pm \sigma$)	Test Accuracy ($\mu \pm \sigma$)
TGP	old	77.31% ± 6.74%	77.14% ± 6.68%
	new	85.04% ± 16.49%	84.41% ± 17.17%
LGP	old	98.90% ± 4.98%	98.76% ± 5.04%
	new	99.97% ± 0.11%	99.90% ± 0.25%

Further inspection of the results using the TGP method on the shape data set shows that only 6 of the 50 runs using the old fitness function had a test or training accuracy greater than 75%. When those 6 runs are excluded, the μ and σ becomes 74.95% ± 0.0019% on the training set and 74.86% ± 0.0024% on the test set. These figures indicate how solid the hurdle actually is in situations where the problem is at the limit of a GP configuration's expressiveness. By using the new decay curve fitness function, 36 of the 50 runs finished with test and training accuracies greater than 75%.

5 Conclusions

The goal of this paper was to investigate an approach to the use of LGP and a new fitness function for multi-class object classification problems. This approach was compared with the basic TGP approach on three image data sets providing object classification problems of increasing difficulty. The results suggest that the LGP approach outperformed the TGP approach on all tasks in terms of classification accuracy and evolvability.

Inspection of the evolved genetic programs reveals that the programs evolved by the LGP approach are relatively easy to interpret for these problems. The results suggest that the LGP approach can automatically select features relevant to a particular task, that the programs evolved by LGP can be represented as a DAG, and that the LGP approach can simultaneously sub-programs together, each for a particular class.

A comparison between the old fitness function and the new fitness function has also highlighted the nature of the fitness function as an approximation to the true fitness of a problem. The results show that the new fitness function, with either the TGP approach or the LGP approach, can bring better and more consistently accurate results than the old fitness function.

Although developed for multi-class object classification problems, we expect that this approach can be applied to other multi-class classification problems.

References

1. Koza, J.R.: Genetic Programming. MIT Press, Campridge, Massachusetts (1992)
2. Banzhaf, W., Nordin, P., Keller, R.E., Francone, F.D.: Genetic Programming – An Introduction; On the Automatic Evolution of Computer Programs and its Applications. Morgan Kaufmann, dpunkt.verlag (1998)
3. Koza, J.R.: Genetic Programming II: Automatic Discovery of Reusable P rograms. Cambridge, Mass. : MIT Press, London, England (1994)
4. Loveard, T., Ciesielski, V.: Representing classification problems in genetic programming. In: Proceedings of the Congress on Evolutionary Computation. Volume 2., IEEE Press (2001) 1070–1077
5. Tackett, W.A.: Recombination, Selection, and the Genetic Construction of Computer Programs. PhD thesis, Faculty of the Graduate School, University of Southern C alifornia, Canoga Park, California, USA (1994)
6. Zhang, M., Ciesielski, V.: Genetic programming for multiple class object detection. In Proceedings of the 12th Australian Joint Conference o n Artificial Intelligence, Springer-Verlag (1999) 180–192 (LNAI Volume 1747).
7. Zhang, M., Ciesielski, V., Andreae, P.: A domain independent window-approach to multiclass object detection using genetic programming. EURASIP Journal on Signal Processing **2003** (2003) 841–859
8. Zhang, M., Smart, W.: Multiclass object classification using genetic programming. In Applications of Evolutionary Computing, EvoWorkshops2004. Volume 3005 of LNCS., Springer Verlag (2004) 369–378
9. Oltean, M., Grosan, C., Oltean, M.: Encoding multiple solutions in a linear genetic programming chromosome. In Proceedings of 4th International Conference on Computational Science, Part III. Springer-Verlag (2004) 1281–1288

10. Rumelhart, D.E., Hinton, G.E., Williams, R.J.: Learning internal representations by error propagation. In Parallel distributed Processing, Explorations in the Microstructure of Cognition, Volume 1: Foundations. The MIT Press (1986)
11. Brameier, M., Banzhaf, W.: A comparison of genetic programming and neural networks in medical data analysis. Reihe CI 43/98, Dortmund University (1998)
12. Brameier, M., Banzhaf, W.: Effective linear genetic programming. Technical report, Department of Computer Science, University of Dortmund, Germany (2001)
13. Goldberg, D.E.: Genetic Algorithms in Search, Optimization, and Machine Learning. Addison-Wesley, Reading, MA (1989)

Evolutionary Design of Fuzzy Classifiers Using Information Granules

Do Wan Kim[1], Jin Bae Park[1], and Young Hoon Joo[2]

[1] Yonsei University, Seodaemun-gu, Seoul 120-749, Korea
TEL: +82-2-2123-2773
{dwkim, jbpark}@yonssei.ac.kr
[2] Kunsan National University, Kunsan, Chunbuk 573-701, Korea
TEL: +82-63-469-4706
yhjoo@kunsan.ac.kr

Abstract. A new GA-based methodology using information granules is suggested for the construction of fuzzy classifiers. The proposed scheme consists of three steps: selection of information granules, construction of the associated fuzzy sets, and tuning of the fuzzy rules. First, the genetic algorithm (GA) is applied to the development of the adequate information granules. The fuzzy sets are then constructed from the analysis of the developed information granules. An interpretable fuzzy classifier is designed by using the constructed fuzzy sets. Finally, the GA are utilized for tuning of the fuzzy rules, which can enhance the classification performance on the misclassified data (e.g., data with the strange pattern or on the boundaries of the classes).

1 Introduction

There are two fundamental areas in the classification problem: feature selection and pattern classification. In dealing with the feature selection and/or the pattern classification, it is quite promising to utilize the knowledge of the domain experts. Since Zadeh suggested the fuzzy set in 1965 [3], the fuzzy theory has been regarded as a resolution of a mathematical modelling of the intuitive human knowledge [1, 2]. With this technical point of view, various construction methods of fuzzy classifiers have been proposed [4–11]. A table look up scheme was studied to generate the fuzzy rules for the fuzzy classifier directly [5], or by using the genetic algorithm (GA) [6]. Abe *et al.* designed several fuzzy classifiers from the various information granules to express the characteristics of the fuzzy classifiers by considering the shapes of the information granules [4, 8].

Generally, the construction process of the fuzzy classifier consists of the following three stages: (i) selecting the information granules, (ii) constructing the fuzzy sets associated with the information granules, and (iii) tuning the fuzzy rules. In Stage (i), it is important to optimally select the information granules from the feature spaces because the performance of the fuzzy classifier highly depends on the choice of the information granules. Unfortunately, dividing the feature space into the optimal information granules is generally known to be a complex and mutually associated problem. An approach to resolve this difficulty is to generate the activation and the inhibition hyperboxes, recursively [8]. However, it generates too many ones to analyze information granules easily as well as to show the pattern visually. In Stage (ii), the fuzzy sets produced by information granules should fulfill two requirements: the fuzzy sets should exhibit a large degree of overlapping, and the fuzzy sets should describe the context of the information granule. Wu *et al.* proposed a construction technique of the fuzzy sets via the α-cut and the similarity degree [12]. However, when all the fuzzy sets for a feature are overlapped, some of the fuzzy sets are merged into one. Consequently, they may be irrelevant to the patten classification because all classes are represented by only one fuzzy set. In Stage (iii), the tuning of the fuzzy rules constructed from the previous stages is necessary to appropriately deal with the misclassified data (to improve the classification performance). Although Abe *et al.* proposed a tuning method of the slope of the membership function [4], their techniques neither consider the overfitting nor the outlier problem.

Motivated by the above observations, this paper aims at improving the performance of the fuzzy classifier by resolving the above-mentioned problems. To this end, we propose a GA-based construction method of the fuzzy classifier. In order to determine optimal information granules, the GA, which has been shown to be a flexible and robust optimization tool [13], are used in Stage (i). An efficient fuzzy sets constructing technique based on the α-cut and the similarity degree is then proposed in Stage (ii) to extract, merge, and reduce the fuzzy sets from the developed information granules, which produces a set of human interpretable classification rules in the form of the multi-inputs and multi-outputs (MIMO) Takagi-Sugeno (T-S) fuzzy model. In Stage (iii), in order to decrease the number of the misclassified data, the GA is also used to tune parameters of the obtained fuzzy sets and to newly generate additional fuzzy rules.

2 Preliminaries

2.1 Fuzzy Classifier Model

To perform the classification, the MIMO T-S fuzzy system is designed by

$$R_i : \text{IF } x_1 \text{ is } A_{i1} \text{ and } \ldots \text{ and } x_N \text{ is } A_{iN} \\ \text{THEN the class is } i\text{: } (y_{i1} = \xi_{i1}, \ldots, y_{iL} = \xi_{iL}) \quad (1)$$

where $x_j, j \in \mathcal{I}_N = \{1, 2, \ldots, N\}$, is the jth feature; $R_i, i \in \mathcal{I}_L = \{1, \ldots, L\}$, is the ith fuzzy rule; $y_{ih}, (i, h) \in \mathcal{I}_L \times \mathcal{I}_L$, is the hth singleton output in the ith rule; $\xi_{ih} \in [0, 1]$ is a real constant value; and $A_{ij}, (i, j) \in \mathcal{I}_L \times \mathcal{I}_N$, is the fuzzy set to be determined from the information granules. Here, we initially equate the number of the classes to the one of the fuzzy rules, and set the ith output of the ith fuzzy rule R_i, y_{ii} as a maximum so that the fuzzy rule R_i can well describe the ith class. By using product inference engine, singleton fuzzifier, and center average defuzzifier, the global output of the hth class inferred from the T-S fuzzy system (1) is represented by $y_h = \sum_{i=1}^{L} \theta_{A_i}(x) y_{ih}$, where $\theta_{A_i}(x) = \frac{\prod_{j=1}^{N} A_{ij}(x_j)}{\sum_{i=1}^{L} \prod_{j=1}^{N} A_{ij}(x_j)}$ and

$A_{ij}(x_j) \in [0,1]$ is the membership function value of the linguistic variable x_j on the fuzzy set A_{ij}. The global output y_h implies the confidence measure of each class. The predicted class is computed as $y = \max_{h \in \mathcal{I}_L} y_h$

2.2 Information Granules

Information granules are a tool that can effectively describe the input-output pattern from the given data. Figure 1 shows an example of information granule in 2 dimensional case, where '*' denotes given data and the rectangle means the information granule or the hyperbox.

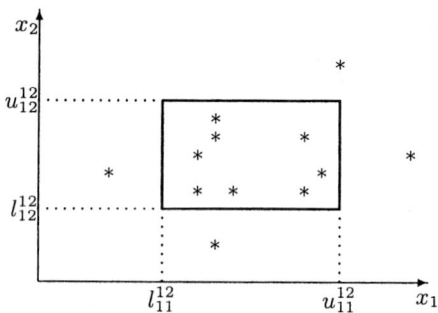

Fig. 1. Example of information granules in 2 dimensional case. *: the given data; the rectangle: the information granule.

Remark 1. To determine the optimal fuzzy region in the supervised learning, the information granules should satisfy the following requirements as much as possible:

(i) The information granules should cover as many data as possible so that the density of the data within the information granules is made as high as possible [14].
(ii) There should be the minimum overlaps among the information granules because each information granule should describe different characteristics in the given data.
(iii) One information granule should cover one class within the admissible limits so that the fuzzy sets extracted from an information granule describe a class on several feature spaces.

3 Classification Using Information Granules

3.1 Optimization of Information Granules Using the GA

In order to obtain the fuzzy classifier with low complexity, we concentrate on determining the information granules subjected to the number of the class regions without generating the additional information granules.

Obviously according to Remark 1, the information granules should be developed such that the following objectives are fulfilled:

$$\text{Maximize}_{1\le m<n\le N}\quad J_1^{mn} = \frac{\Lambda^{mn}}{D}$$

$$\text{Minimize}_{1\le m<n\le N}\quad J_2^{mn} = \frac{\sum_{i=1}^{L}\Omega_i^{mn}}{\Lambda^{mn}}$$

$$\text{Maximize}_{1\le m<n\le N}\quad J_3^{mn} = \prod_{i=1}^{N}\frac{\Psi_i^{mn}}{\Omega_i^{mn}} \quad (2)$$

$$\text{Maximize}_{1\le m<n\le N}\quad J_4^{mn} = \sum_{i=1}^{L}\frac{\Omega_i^{mn}}{\text{area}(l_{ij}^{mn}, u_{ij}^{mn})}$$

where the superscript 'mn' denotes a 2 dimensional feature space with x_m and x_n. Throughout this paper, it fulfills $1 \le m < n \le N$. J_1^{mn} is the covering rate; J_2^{mn} is the overlapping rate; J_3^{mn} is the classification performance; J_4^{mn} is the density rate, and D is the number of the given data; Λ^{mn} is the number of the data covered by all information granules in the mnth feature space; Ω_i^{mn} is the number of the data covered by the ith information granule in the mnth feature space; Ψ_i^{mn} is the largest data number of the intersections among the class regions and the ith information granule and area$(l_{ij}^{mn}, u_{ij}^{mn})$ is the area of the ith information granule to be searched, where l_{ij}^{mn} and u_{ij}^{mn} are the left-lower and the right-upper vertex of the ith hyperbox in the mnth feature space, respectively. The multi objectives function for the mnth feature space can be written as

$$\text{Minimize}_{1\le m<n\le N}\quad J^{mn} = \frac{J_2^{mn}}{J_1^{mn} J_3^{mn}} + \frac{\nu_1}{J_4^{mn}} \quad (3)$$

where ν_1 is a positive scalar to adjust the weight between the two terms in (3).

The GA represents the searching variables of the given optimization problem (3) as the chromosome that contains one or more sub-strings. In this case, the searching variables are l_{ij}^{mn} and u_{ij}^{mn}. A convenient way to convey the searching variables into a chromosome is to gather all searching variables associated with all information granules in the mnth feature space, and to concatenate the strings as follows:

$$\mathcal{G}^{mn} = \{(l_1^{mn}, u_1^{mn}), \ldots, (l_N^{mn}, u_N^{mn})\}$$
$$\mathcal{G} = \left\{\mathcal{G}^{12}, \mathcal{G}^{13}, \mathcal{G}^{23}, \ldots, \mathcal{G}^{(n-2)(n-1)}, \mathcal{G}^{1n}, \ldots, \mathcal{G}^{(n-1)n}, \mathcal{G}^{1(n+1)}, \ldots, \mathcal{G}^{(N-1)N}\right\} \quad (4)$$

where $\mathcal{G}^{mn}$ is the parameter substring of the mnth feature space in a chromosome and $\mathcal{G}$ denotes a chromosome.

Initial population is made up with initial individuals to the extent of the population size. To efficiently perform the optimization, the search spaces in

GA should be reduced as much as possible. In this case, we utilize the following constraints on the search spaces.

$$\mathcal{S}(\mathcal{G}^{mn}) \subset \mathcal{F}^{mn} \qquad (5)$$

$$\mathcal{S}(l_{ij}^{mn}, u_{ij}^{mn}) \subset \mathcal{C}_i^{mn} \qquad (6)$$

where $\mathcal{S}(\mathcal{G}^{mn})$ and $\mathcal{S}(l_{ij}^{mn}, u_{ij}^{mn})$ are the search space for the sub-string and the ith information granule, respectively, $\mathcal{F}^{mn}$ implies the mnth feature space, and $\mathcal{C}_i^{mn}$ denotes the ith class region.

Since the GA originally searches the optimal solution so that the fitness function value is maximized, it is necessary to map the objective function (3) to the fitness function formed by

$$f(J^{mn}) = \frac{J_1^{mn} J_3^{mn}}{J_2^{mn}} + \frac{J_4^{mn}}{\nu_1} \qquad (7)$$

The best chromosome $\widehat{\mathcal{G}}_t$ is composed of the best sub-chromosomes $\widehat{\mathcal{G}}_t^{mn}$ with the highest fitness values $\widehat{f}_t^{mn}$ at the tth generation as follows:

$$\widehat{\mathcal{G}}_t = \left\{ \widehat{\mathcal{G}}_t^{12}, \widehat{\mathcal{G}}_t^{13}, \widehat{\mathcal{G}}_t^{23}, \ldots, \widehat{\mathcal{G}}_t^{(n-2)(n-1)}, \widehat{\mathcal{G}}_t^{1n}, \ldots, \widehat{\mathcal{G}}_t^{(n-1)n}, \widehat{\mathcal{G}}_t^{1(n+1)}, \ldots, \widehat{\mathcal{G}}_t^{(N-1)N} \right\}$$

where $t \in \mathcal{I}_T = \{1, 2, \ldots, T\}$ is the genetic process generation number. Then, the best overall fitness value in the mth generation can be written as

$$\widehat{f}_t = \sum_{1 \le m < n \le N} \widehat{f}_t^{mn}$$

3.2 Construction of Fuzzy Sets

The α-cut operation and the similarity measurement are utilized for extracting, merging, and removing the fuzzy sets. In the mnth feature space, the fuzzy sets A_{ij}^{mn} extracted from L information granules are represented by:

$$A_{ij}^{mn}(x_j) = \begin{cases} \frac{x_j - a_{ij}^{mn}}{|b_{ij}^{mn} - a_{ij}^{mn}|} & \text{if } a_{ij}^{mn} \le x_j < b_{ij}^{mn} \\ \frac{c_{ij}^{mn} - x_j}{|c_{ij}^{mn} - b_{ij}^{mn}|} & \text{if } b_{ij}^{mn} \le x_j < c_{ij}^{mn} \\ 0 & \text{otherwise} \end{cases} \qquad (8)$$

where l_{ij}^{mn} and u_{ij}^{mn} denote the left-lower and the right-upper vertices of the ith information granule on the horizontal x_j-axis, and $b_{ij}^{mn} = \frac{l_{ij}^{mn} + u_{ij}^{mn}}{2}$, respectively. The parameters a_{ij}^{mn} and c_{ij}^{mn} in (8) are computed from the α-cut operation $\left(A_{ij}^{mn}\right)_\alpha = \{x_j \in U_j | A_{ij}^{mn}(x_j) \ge \alpha\}, U_j = [x_{j\min}, x_{j\max}], \alpha \in [0, 1]$ of a fuzzy set A_{ij}^{mn} as follows:

$$a_{ij}^{mn} = b_{ij}^{mn} - \frac{b_{ij}^{mn} - l_{ij}^{mn}}{1 - \alpha}$$

$$c_{ij}^{mn} = b_{ij}^{mn} + \frac{u_{ij}^{mn} - b_{ij}^{mn}}{1 - \alpha}$$

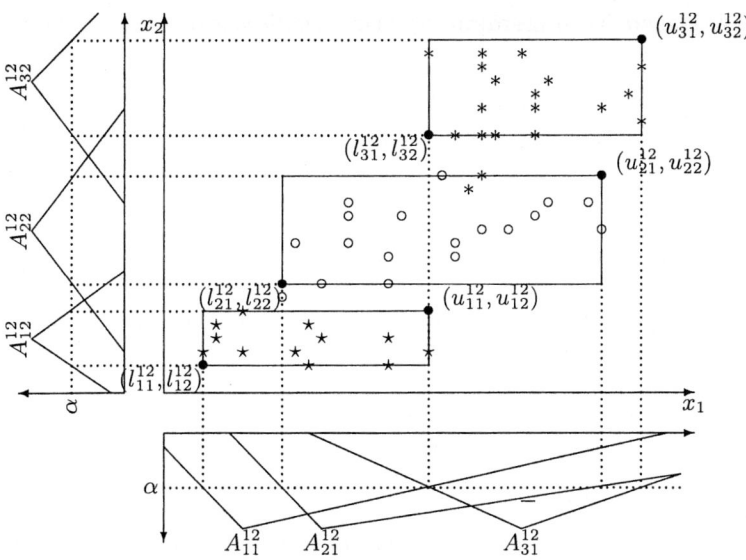

Fig. 2. Example of the fuzzy sets extraction with $L = 3$ and $N = 2$. $\star$: data included in class 1, $\circ$: data included in class 2, and $\ast$: data included in class 3.

Figure 2 shows an example of extracting the fuzzy sets with $L = 3$ and $N = 2$. The fuzzy sets A_{ij}^{mn} extracted from the mnth feature spaces are merged into one fuzzy set A_{ij} with the following parameters:

$$a_{ij} = b_{ij} - \frac{b_{ij} - l_{ij}}{1 - \alpha}$$
$$c_{ij} = b_{ij} + \frac{u_{ij} - b_{ij}}{1 - \alpha}$$
(9)

where $b_{ij} = \frac{1}{n-1} \sum_{1 \leq m < n \leq N} b_{ij}^{mn}$, $l_{ij} = \frac{1}{n-1} \sum_{1 \leq m < n \leq N} l_{ij}^{mn}$, and $u_{ij} = \frac{1}{n-1} \sum_{1 \leq m < n \leq N} u_{ij}^{mn}$.

There are a lot of methods to measure the similarity between two distinct fuzzy sets [15, 16]. In this study, the set-theoretic operation-based similarity measurement [10, 12]

$$S((\cdot)_\alpha, (\cdot\cdot)_\alpha) = \frac{|(\cdot)_\alpha \cap (\cdot\cdot)_\alpha|}{|(\cdot)_\alpha \cup (\cdot\cdot)_\alpha|}$$

is applied to removing the similar fuzzy sets, where $|\cdot|$ denotes the cardinality of a set. Therefore, if the fuzzy set $A_{\tilde{i}j}$ satisfies the following condition inequality, it is removed.

$$\sum_{i=1, i \neq \tilde{i}}^{N} S\left((A_{ij})_\alpha, (A_{i'j})_\alpha\right) \geq \beta$$
(10)

where $\beta \in [0, 1]$ denotes a real constant value.

3.3 GA-Based Management of Misclassification

It is necessary to tune the fuzzy classifiers constructed in the previous subsection for the classification performance improvement on the data that lie into the overlaps of the classes, and the strange pattern unlike the well classified data such as outliers. This subsection proposes a GA-based management technique for misclassification, which consists of the tuning process of the obtained fuzzy rules and the generation process of additional fuzzy rules.

To decrease risk due to overfitting, the following constraints are imported:

$$A_{ij}(x_j) = \begin{cases} \Delta A_{ij}(x_j; \Delta a_{ij}, b_{ij}, \Delta c_{ij}) & \text{if overalps exist in } C^i \\ A_{ij}(x_j; a_{ij}, b_{ij}, c_{ij}) & \text{otherwise} \end{cases}$$

$$y_{ih} = \begin{cases} \Delta y_{ii} & \text{if overalps exist in } C^i \\ y_{ih} & \text{otherwise} \end{cases} \quad (11)$$

$$L' \in [0, \bar{L}]$$

where $\bar{L} \in \mathbb{Z}^+$ and L' means the number of fuzzy rules to be newly generated, C^i denotes the ith class region, and $\Delta(\cdot)$ symbolizes the tuning of $(\cdot)$ to be determined from the GA-based technique that will be discussed in this subsection. Considering (8) and (11), and tuning its cutting level α_{ij} for A_{ij} produce

$$A_{ij}(x_j) = \begin{cases} \frac{x_j - \Delta a_{ij}}{|b_{ij} - \Delta a_{ij}|} & \text{if } \Delta a_{ij} \leq x_j < b_{ij} \\ \frac{\Delta c_{ij} - x_j}{|\Delta c_{ij} - b_{ij}|} & \text{if } b_{ij} \leq x_j < \Delta c_{ij} \\ 0 & \text{otherwise} \end{cases} \quad (12)$$

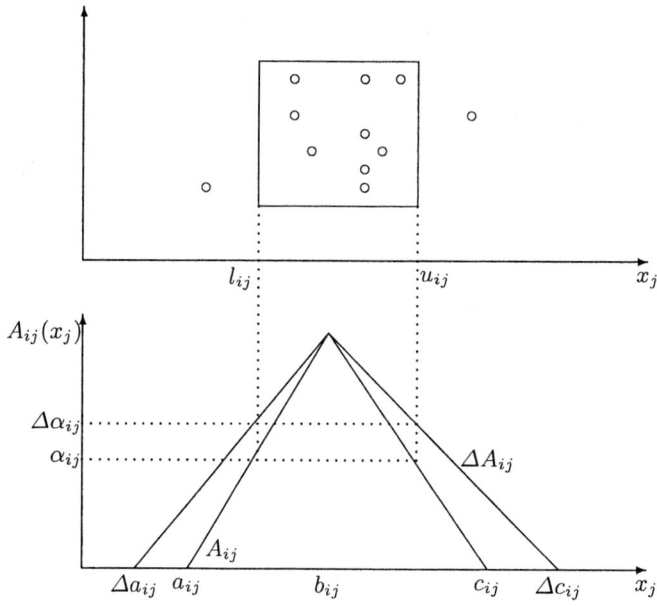

Fig. 3. The fuzzy set ΔA_{ij} tuned by changing α_{ij}

where $\Delta a_{ij} = b_{ij} - \frac{b_{ij}-l_{ij}}{1-\Delta\alpha_{ij}}$, $\Delta c_{ij} = b_{ij} + \frac{u_{ij}-b_{ij}}{1-\Delta\alpha_{ij}}$. Figure 3 illustrates an example of the tuned fuzzy set $\Delta \tilde{A}_{ij}$.

Now, we can design the final fuzzy system by adding the following supplementary fuzzy rules to the fuzzy classifier (1).

$$R_{i'} : \text{IF } x_1 \text{ is } A_{i'1} \text{ and } \ldots \text{ and } x_N \text{ is } A_{i'N}$$
$$\text{THEN the class is misclassification: } (y_{i'1} = \xi_{i'1}, \ldots, y_{i'L} = \xi_{i'L}) \quad (13)$$

where $\xi_{i'h} \in [-1,1]$. By using product inference engine, singleton fuzzifier, and center average defuzzifier, the hth global output of the final fuzzy classifier (1) and (13) is represented as

$$y_h = \underbrace{\sum_{i=1}^{L} \theta_{A_i}(x) y_{ih}}_{(1)} + \underbrace{\sum_{i'=1}^{L'} \theta_{A_{i'}}(x) y_{i'h}}_{(13)} \quad (14)$$

where $\theta_{A_i}(x) = \frac{\prod_{j=1}^{N} A_{ij}(x_j)}{\sum_{i=1}^{L}\prod_{j=1}^{N} A_{ij}(x_j) + \sum_{i'=1}^{L'}\prod_{j=1}^{N} A_{i'j}(x_j)}$,

$\theta_{A_{i'}}(x) = \frac{\prod_{j=1}^{N} A_{i'j}(x_j)}{\sum_{i=1}^{L}\prod_{j=1}^{N} A_{ij}(x_j) + \sum_{i'=1}^{L'}\prod_{j=1}^{N} A_{i'j}(x_j)}$. The predicted class $\hat{y}$ is decided by the maximum of (14).

Naturally, the objective of the resulting fuzzy classifier (14) is that the classification performance should be as high as possible. Furthermore, it is desired to reduce the number of the additional fuzzy rules from the viewpoints of hardware implementation and computation resource. The following objective functions should be maximized and minimized, respectively:

$$\text{Maximize} \quad J_5 = \frac{1}{D} \sum_{d=1}^{D} \delta(\hat{y}(x_d) - (\text{class of } x_d))$$

$$\text{Minimize} \quad J_6 = \bar{L}$$

where $\delta(\cdot)$ is the Dirac delta function. The fitness function to be maximized via the GA is then

$$f(J_5, J_6) = J_5 + \nu_2 \frac{1}{J_6 + \lambda}$$

where λ is the coefficient to prevent the large fitness function value.

The GA is again applied to optimally tune (α_{ij}, ξ_{ih}) and the parameters introduced in (13). At the same time, to identify the number of the supplementary fuzzy rules, h is also tuned. The chromosome $\tilde{\mathcal{G}}$ is organized as

$$\tilde{\mathcal{G}} = \{\alpha_{11}, \ldots, \alpha_{1N}, \ldots, \alpha_{L1}, \ldots, \alpha_{LN}, \xi_{11}, \ldots, \xi_{1L}, \ldots, \xi_{(L-1)1}, \ldots, \xi_{LL},$$
$$a_{11}, b_{11}, c_{11}, \ldots, a_{1N}, b_{1N}, c_{1N}, \ldots, a_{L'1}, b_{L'1}, c_{L'1}, \ldots, a_{L'N},$$
$$b_{L'N}, c_{L'N}, \xi_{11}, \ldots, \xi_{1L}, \ldots, \xi_{(L'-1)1}, \ldots, \xi_{L'L}, L'\} \quad (15)$$

4 Conclusions

In this paper, the GA-based method for constructing the fuzzy classifier has been proposed. The advantages of the proposed method are threefold: First, although the number of the information granules equals to the number of the classes, the information granules developed by the GA accomplish the satisfactory fuzzy region. Second, the procedure of constructing the fuzzy sets from the information granules provides an effective tool for the feature selection and the pattern classification. Finally, as we additionally generate the fuzzy rules for the misclassification management, the final fuzzy classifier can describe the misclassified data. Therefore, the proposed method provides the selection of the information granules as well as the solution to the two major problems: the feature selection and the pattern classification.

References

1. Joo Y. H., Hwang H. S., Kim K. B., and Woo K. B.: Linguistic model identification for fuzzy system. Electron. Letter **31** (1995) 330-331
2. Joo Y. H., Hwang H. S., Kim K. B., and Woo K. B.: Fuzzy system modeling by fuzzy partition and GA hybrid schemes. Fuzzy Set and Syst. **86** (1997) 279-288
3. Zadeh L. A.: Fuzzy sets. Informat. Control **8** (1965) 338-353
4. Abe S. and Thawonmas R.: A fuzzy classifier with ellipsoidal regions. IEEE Trans. Fuzzy Systems **5** (1997) 358-368
5. Wang L. X. and Mendel J. M.: Generating fuzzy rules by learning from examples. IEEE Trans. Syst., Man, Cybern. B. **22** (1992) 1414-1427
6. Ishibuchi H., Nozaki K., Yamamoto N., and Tanaka H.: Selecting fuzzy if-then rules for classification problems using genetic algoritms. IEEE Trans. Fuzzy Systems **3** (1995) 260-270
7. Thawonmas R. and Abe S.: A novel approach to feature selection based on analysis of class regions. IEEE Trans. Syst., Man, Cybern. B. **27** (1997) 196-207
8. Abe S. and Lan M. S.: A method for fuzzy rules extraction directly from numerical data and its application to pattern classification. IEEE Trans. Fuzzy Systems **5** (1995) 358-368
9. Lee H. M., Chen C. M., Chen J. M., and Jou Y. L.: An efficient fuzzy classifier with feature selection based on fuzzy entropy. IEEE Trans. Syst., Man, Cybern. B. **3** (1997) 426-432
10. Roubos H. and Setnes M.: Compact transparent fuzzy models and classifiers through iterative complexity reduction. IEEE Trans. Fuzzy Systems **9** (2001) 516 - 524
11. Shi Y., Eberhart R., and Chen Y.: Implementation of evolutionary fuzzy systems. IEEE Trans. Fuzzy Systems **7** (1999) 109-119
12. Wu T. P. and Chen S. M.: A new method for constructing membership functions and fuzzy rules from training examples. IEEE Trans. Syst., Man, Cybern. B. **29** (1999) 25-40
13. Goldberg D. E.: Genetic algorithms in searh, optimization, and machine learning. Addison-Wesley publishing company, Inc., (1989)
14. Pedrycz W. and Bargiela A.: Granular clustering: a granular signature of data. IEEE Trans. Syst., Man, Cybern. B. **32** (2002) 212-224
15. Chen S. M., Yeh M. S., and Hsiao P. Y.: A comparison of similarity measures of fuzzy values. Fuzzy Sets Syst. **72** (1995) 79-89
16. Young V. R.: Fuzzy subsethood. Fuzzy Sets Syst **77** (1996) 371-384

Constrained Optimization by the ε Constrained Hybrid Algorithm of Particle Swarm Optimization and Genetic Algorithm

Tetsuyuki Takahama[1], Setsuko Sakai[2], and Noriyuki Iwane[1]

[1] Hiroshima City University, Hiroshima 731-3194, Japan
takahama@its.hiroshima-cu.ac.jp
http://www.chi.its.hiroshima-cu.ac.jp/~takahama/eng
[2] Hiroshima Shudo University, Hiroshima 731-3195, Japan
setuko@shudo-u.ac.jp

Abstract. The ε constrained method is an algorithm transformation method, which can convert algorithms for unconstrained problems to algorithms for constrained problems using the ε level comparison that compares search points based on the constraint violation of them. We proposed the ε constrained particle swarm optimizer εPSO, which is the combination of the ε constrained method and particle swarm optimization. The εPSO can run very fast and find very high quality solutions, but the εPSO is not very stable and sometimes can only find lower quality solutions. On the contrary, the εGA, which is the combination of the ε constrained method and GA, is very stable and can find high quality solutions, but it is difficult for the εGA to find higher quality solutions than the εPSO. In this study, we propose the hybrid algorithm of the εPSO and the εGA to find very high quality solutions stably. The effectiveness of the hybrid algorithm is shown by comparing it with various methods on well known nonlinear constrained problems.

1 Introduction

Constrained optimization problems, especially nonlinear optimization problems, where objective functions are minimized under given constraints, are very important and frequently appear in the real world. In this study, the following optimization problem (P) with inequality constraints, equality constraints, upper bound constraints and lower bound constraints will be discussed.

$$(\text{P}) \quad \text{minimize} \quad f(\boldsymbol{x}) \tag{1}$$
$$\text{subject to} \quad g_j(\boldsymbol{x}) \leq 0, \ j = 1, \ldots, q$$
$$h_j(\boldsymbol{x}) = 0, \ j = q+1, \ldots, m$$
$$l_i \leq x_i \leq u_i, \ i = 1, \ldots, n,$$

where $\boldsymbol{x} = (x_1, x_2, \cdots, x_n)$ is an n dimensional vector, $f(\boldsymbol{x})$ is an objective function, $g_j(\boldsymbol{x}) \leq 0$ and $h_j(\boldsymbol{x}) = 0$ are q inequality constraints and $m - q$ equality constraints, respectively. Functions f, g_j and h_j are linear or nonlinear real-valued functions. Values u_i and l_i are the upper bound and the lower bound of x_i, respectively. Also, let the feasible space in which every point satisfies all constraints be denoted by $\mathcal{F}$ and the search space in which every point satisfies the upper and lower bound constraints be denoted by $\mathcal{S}\,(\supset \mathcal{F})$.

There exist many studies on solving constrained optimization problems using evolutionary computations[1, 2] and particle swarm optimization[3]. These studies can be classified into several categories according to the way the constraints are treated as follows:

(1) Constraints are only used to see whether a search point is feasible or not[4]. Approaches in this category are usually called death penalty methods. In this category, the searching process begins with one or more feasible points and continues to search for new points within the feasible region. When a new search point is generated and the point is not feasible, the point is repaired or discarded. In this category, generating initial feasible points is difficult and computationally demanding when the feasible region is very small.

(2) The constraint violation, which is the sum of the violation of all constraint functions, is combined with the objective function. The penalty function method is in this category[5, 6, 7, 8, 9, 10]. In the penalty function method, an extended objective function is defined by adding the constraint violation to the objective function as a penalty. The optimization of the objective function and the constraint violation is realized by the optimization of the extended objective function. The main difficulty of the penalty function method is the selection of an appropriate value for the penalty coefficient that adjusts the strength of the penalty.

(3) The constraint violation and the objective function are used separately. In this category, both the constraint violation and the objective function are optimized by a lexicographic order in which the constraint violation precedes the objective function. Deb[11] proposed a method in which the extended objective function that realizes the lexicographic ordering is used. Takahama and Sakai proposed the α constrained method[12] and ε constrained method[13], which adopt a lexicographic ordering with relaxation of the constraints. Runarsson and Yao[14] proposed the stochastic ranking method in which the stochastic lexicographic order, which ignores the constraint violation with some probability, is used. These methods were successfully applied to various problems.

(4) The constraints and the objective function are optimized by multiobjective optimization methods. In this category, the constrained optimization problems are solved as the multiobjective optimization problems in which the objective function and the constraint functions are objectives to be optimized[15, 16, 17, 18]. But in many cases, solving multiobjective optimization problems is a more difficult and expensive task than solving single objective optimization problems.

It has been shown that the methods in the third category have better performance than methods in other categories in many benchmark problems. Especially, the α and the ε constrained methods are quite new and unique approaches to constrained optimization. We call these methods *algorithm transformation* methods, because these methods does not convert objective function, but convert an algorithm for unconstrained optimization into an algorithm for constrained optimization by replacing the ordinal comparisons with the α level and the ε level comparisons in direct search methods. These methods can be applied to various unconstrained direct search methods and can obtain constrained optimization algorithms. We showed the advantage of the α constrained methods by applying the methods to Powell's method[12], nonlinear simplex method[19,20], genetic algorithms (GAs)[21] and particle swarm optimization (PSO)[22].

Recently, we proposed the ε constrained method and the ε Constrained Particle Swarm Optimizer(εPSO)[13], which is the combination of the ε constrained method and PSO. In the εPSO, the agent or point which satisfies the constraints will move to optimize the objective function and the agent which does not satisfy the constraints will move to satisfy the constraints, naturally. The εPSO can run very fast and find very high quality solutions, but the εPSO is not very stable and sometimes can only find lower quality solutions. On the contrary, the εGA, which is the combination of the ε constrained method and GA, is very stable and can find high quality solutions, but it is difficult for the εGA to find higher quality solutions than the εPSO. In this study, we propose the hybrid algorithm of the εPSO and the εGA to obtain the algorithm that can find very high quality solutions stably. The effectiveness of the hybrid algorithm is shown by comparing it with various methods on some well known problems mentioned in [2], where the performance of many methods in all categories were compared.

2 The ε Constrained Method

2.1 Constraint Violation and ε Level Comparison

In the ε constrained method, constraint violation $\phi(\boldsymbol{x})$ is defined. The constraint violation can be given by the maximum of all constraints or the sum of all constraints.

$$\phi(\boldsymbol{x}) = \max\{\max_j\{0, g_j(\boldsymbol{x})\}, \max_j |h_j(\boldsymbol{x})|\} \qquad (2)$$

$$\phi(\boldsymbol{x}) = \sum_j ||max\{0, g_j(\boldsymbol{x})\}||^p + \sum_j ||h_j(\boldsymbol{x})||^p \qquad (3)$$

where p is a positive number.

The ε *level comparison* is defined as an order relation on a pair of objective function value and constraint violation $(f(\boldsymbol{x}), \phi(\boldsymbol{x}))$. If the constraint violation of a point is greater than 0, the point is not feasible and its worth is low. The ε level comparisons are defined basically as a lexicographic order in which $\phi(\boldsymbol{x})$ precedes $f(\boldsymbol{x})$, because the feasibility of $\boldsymbol{x}$ is more important than the minimization of $f(\boldsymbol{x})$. This precedence can be adjusted by the parameter ε.

Let f_1 (f_2) and ϕ_1 (ϕ_2) be the function values and the constraint violation at a point $\boldsymbol{x}_1$ ($\boldsymbol{x}_2$), respectively. Then, for any ε satisfying $\varepsilon \geq 0$, ε level comparison $<_\varepsilon$ and $\leq_\varepsilon$ between (f_1, ϕ_1) and (f_2, ϕ_2) is defined as follows:

$$(f_1,\phi_1) <_\varepsilon (f_2,\phi_2) \Leftrightarrow \begin{cases} f_1 < f_2, & \text{if } \phi_1,\phi_2 \leq \varepsilon \\ f_1 < f_2, & \text{if } \phi_1 = \phi_2 \\ \phi_1 < \phi_2, & \text{otherwise} \end{cases} \quad (4)$$

$$(f_1,\phi_1) \leq_\varepsilon (f_2,\phi_2) \Leftrightarrow \begin{cases} f_1 \leq f_2, & \text{if } \phi_1,\phi_2 \leq \varepsilon \\ f_1 \leq f_2, & \text{if } \phi_1 = \phi_2 \\ \phi_1 < \phi_2, & \text{otherwise} \end{cases} \quad (5)$$

In case of $\varepsilon = \infty$, the ε level comparison $<_\infty$ and $\leq_\infty$ are equivalent to the ordinal comparison $<$ and $\leq$ between function values. Also, in case of $\varepsilon = 0$, $<_0$ and $\leq_0$ are equivalent to the lexicographic order in which the constraint violation $\phi(x)$ precedes the function value $f(x)$.

2.2 The Properties of the ε Constrained Method

The ε constrained method converts a constrained optimization problem into an unconstrained one by replacing the order relation in direct search methods with the ε level comparison. An optimization problem solved by the ε constrained method, that is, a problem in which the ordinary comparison is replaced with the ε level comparison, $(P_{\leq_\varepsilon})$, is defined as follows:

$$(P_{\leq_\varepsilon}) \quad \text{minimize}_{\leq_\varepsilon} \; f(x), \quad (6)$$

where minimize$_{\leq_\varepsilon}$ means the minimization based on the ε level comparison $\leq_\varepsilon$. Also, a problem (P^ε) is defined that the constraints of (P), that is, $\phi(x) = 0$, is relaxed and replaced with $\phi(x) \leq \varepsilon$:

$$(P^\varepsilon) \quad \begin{aligned} &\text{minimize} \; f(x) \\ &\text{subject to } \phi(x) \leq \varepsilon \end{aligned} \quad (7)$$

It is obvious that (P^0) is equivalent to (P).

For the three types of problems, (P^ε), $(P_{\leq_\varepsilon})$ and (P), the following theorems are given based on the ε constrained method[13].

Theorem 1. *If an optimal solution (P^0) exists, any optimal solution of $(P_{\leq_\varepsilon})$ is an optimal solution of (P^ε).*

Theorem 2. *If an optimal solution of (P) exists, any optimal solution of $(P_{\leq_0})$ is an optimal solution of (P).*

Theorem 3. *Let $\{\varepsilon_n\}$ be a strictly decreasing non-negative sequence and converge to 0. Let $f(x)$ and $\phi(x)$ be continuous functions of x. Assume that an optimal solution x^* of (P^0) exists and an optimal solution $\hat{x}_n$ of $(P_{\leq_{\varepsilon_n}})$ exists for any ε_n. Then, any accumulation point to the sequence $\{\hat{x}_n\}$ is an optimal solution of (P^0).*

Theorem 1 and 2 show that a constrained optimization problem can be transformed into an equivalent unconstrained optimization problem by using the ε level comparison. So, if the ε level comparison is incorporated into an existing unconstrained optimization method, constrained optimization problems can be solved. Theorem 3 shows that, in the ε constrained method, an optimal solution of (P^0) can be given by converging ε to 0 as well as by increasing the penalty coefficient to infinity in the penalty method.

3 The ε Constrained Hybrid Algorithm of PSO and GA

In this section, a hybrid algorithm, which is defined by combining the ε constrained method with particle swarm optimization and genetic algorithm, is proposed.

3.1 Particle Swarm Optimization PSO

PSO[23] was inspired by the movement of a group of animals such as a bird flock or fish school, in which the animals avoid predators and seek foods and mates as a group. PSO imitates the movement to solve optimization problems and is considered as a probabilistic multi-point search method like GAs. For PSO is based on such a very simple concept, it can be realized by primitive mathematical operators. It computationally is very efficient, runs very fast, and requires few memories. PSO has been applied to various application fields.

Searching procedures by PSO can be described as follows: A group of agents optimizes a certain objective function $f(\cdot)$. At any time t, each agent i knows its current position x_i^t. It also remembers its private best value until now $pbest_i$ and the position x_i^*. Moreover, every agent knows the best value in the group until now $gbest$ and the position x_G^*.

$$pbest_i = \min_{t=1,\cdots,k} f(x_i^t), \quad x_i^* = \arg \min_{t=1,\cdots,k} f(x_i^t) \tag{8}$$

$$gbest = \min_i pbest_i, \quad x_G^* = \arg \min_i f(x_i^*) \tag{9}$$

The modified velocity v_i^{k+1} of each agent can be calculated by using the current velocity v_i^k and the difference among x_i^k, x_i^* and x_G^* as shown below:

$$v_{ij}^{k+1} = w v_{ij}^k + c_1 \, rand \, (x_{ij}^* - x_{ij}^k) + c_2 \, rand \, (x_{Gj}^* - x_{ij}^k) \tag{10}$$

where $rand$ is a random number in the interval $[0, 1]$. The parameters c_1 and c_2 are called *cognitive* and *social* parameters, respectively, and they are used to bias the agent's search towards its own best previous position and towards the best experience of the group. The parameter w is called *inertia weight* and it is used to control the trade-off between the global and the local searching ability of the group.

Using the above eq. (10), a certain velocity that gradually get close to the agent best position x_i^* and the group best position x_G^* can be calculated. The position of agent i, x_i^k, is replaced with x_i^{k+1} as follows:

$$x_i^{k+1} = x_i^k + v_i^{k+1} \tag{11}$$

3.2 Hybrid Algorithm of PSO and GA

In the hybrid algorithm, solutions are represented by agents $\{x_1, x_2, \cdots, x_N\}$ for PSO and individuals $\{y_1, y_2, \cdots, y_M\}$ for GA as shown in Fig. 1, where N and M are the number of agents and individuals, respectively. In each iteration,

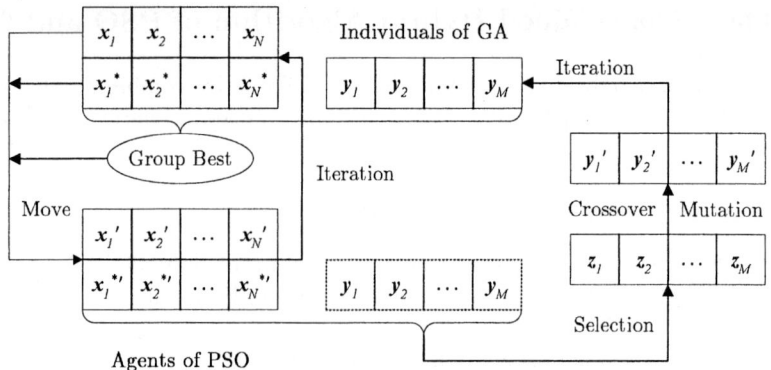

Fig. 1. Flow of hybrid algorithm

PSO process and GA process are performed. In the PSO process, every agent x_i moves using the private best x_i^* and the group best z^* that is taken from all agents and individuals ($z^* = \arg\min_{i,k}\{f(x_i^*), f(y_k)\}$). After then, in the GA process, M parents are selected from all agents (new $x_i^* = x_i^{*\prime}$) and individuals (y_k), and crossover and mutation operation is applied to the parents.

The hybrid algorithm is equivalent to the εPSO if the number of individuals $M = 0$, and is equivalent to the εGA if the number of agents $N = 0$.

In this study, M individuals are selected from $N+M$ individuals using linear ranking selection, and uniform crossover and Gaussian mutation with large and small sigma decreasing over generations or iterations are adopted.

$$y'_{kj} = y_{kj} + (u_j - l_j) \times \begin{cases} \sigma_{\text{small}} \; N(0,1) \; \text{w.p.} \; P_{\text{small}} \\ \sigma_{\text{large}} \; N(0,1) \; \text{w.p.} \; P_{\text{large}} \end{cases} \quad (12)$$

$$\sigma_{type}(t) = \sigma_{type}(0) \exp(-\alpha_\sigma t / T) \quad (13)$$

where y_{kj} and y'_{kj} are the value of the j-th decision variable in the k-th individual before and after mutation, u_j and l_j are the upper and lower bound, P_{small} and P_{large} are mutation rate for small sigma and larger sigma, $type$ is small or large where $\sigma_{\text{small}}(0) < \sigma_{\text{large}}(0)$, and T is the maximum number of iterations.

The pseudo-code of the algorithm is given in Fig. 2.

```
Initialize X={x_i}, Y={y_k}
z*=arg min_< f(z), z ∈ X ∪ Y
for(t=1;t ≤ T;t++) {
 // PSO phase
 for(each agent i in X) {
  Update x_i with group best being z*
  if(f(x_i) <_ε f(z*)) z*=x_i
 }
 // GA phase
 Z=Select individuals from X ∪ Y
```

```
 for(each pair z_p,z_q in Z) {
  Crossover z_p,z_q with crossover rate
  for(each individual z_k in z_p,z_q) {
   for(each dimension z_ki in z_k)
    Mutate z_ki with P_small, P_large
   if(f(z_k) <_ε f(z*)) z*=z_k;
  }
 }
 Y=Z
}
```

Fig. 2. Pseudo-code of the proposed hybrid algorithm

4 Solving Nonlinear Optimization Problems

4.1 Test Problems and Experimental Conditions

In this study, three problems are tested: Himmelblau's problem, welded beam design problem and pressure vessel design problem, which are solved by various methods and compared in [2]. In the following, the results except for the hybrid algorithm, the εPSO, and the εGA are taken from [2].

The parameters for the ε constrained method are as follows: The constraint violation ϕ is given by the square sum of all constraints ($p=2$) in eq. (3). The ε level is assigned to 0, i.e. $\varepsilon(t) = 0$ ($0 \leq t \leq T$). This means that problems are solved using a lexicographic order in which the constraint violation precedes the objective function. The parameters for PSO are: The number of agents $N=20$ for the εPSO, 10 for the hybrid algorithm, and 0 for the εGA, $w^0 = 0.9$, $w^T = 0.4$. The initial velocity is **0**. The maximum velocity is set to the range of each dimension $(u_i - l_i)$. The parameters for GA are: The number of individuals $M=0$ for the εPSO, 10 for the hybrid algorithm, and 20 for the εGA, maximum expected value of linear ranking selection is 2.0, crossover rate is 0.5, mutation rate $P_{\text{small}} = P_{\text{large}} = 0.5$, $\sigma_{\text{small}}(0) = 0.01$, $\sigma_{\text{large}}(0) = 0.1$ and $\alpha_\sigma = 2.3$. The maximum number of iterations $T = 249$ (5,000 evaluations) and $T = 2499$ (50,000 evaluations). For each problem, 30 independent runs are performed.

4.2 Himmelblau's Nonlinear Optimization Problem

Himmelblau's problem was originally given by Himmelblau[24], and it has been used as a benchmark for several GA-based methods that use penalties. In this problem, there are 5 decision variables, 6 nonlinear inequality constraints and 10 boundary conditions.

This problem was originally solved using the Generalized Reduced Gradient method (GRG)[24]. Gen and Cheng[25] used a genetic algorithm based on both local and global reference. The problem was solved using death penalty[2] in the first category and various penalty function approaches in the second category such as static penalty[5], dynamic penalty[6], annealing penalty[7], adaptive penalty[8] and co-evolutionary penalty[9]. Also, the problem was solved using MGA (multiobjective genetic algorithm)[17] in the forth category.

Experimental results on the problem are shown in Table 1. The columns labeled Best, Average, Worst and S.D. are the best value, the average value, the worst value and the standard deviation of the best agent in each run, respectively. The good approaches were the hybrid algorithm, the εPSO, the εGA, MGA and Co-evolutionary penalty method. Note that the hybrid algorithm, the εPSO, the εGA, MGA and other penalty based approaches performed only 5,000 function evaluations while Co-evolutionary penalty method performed 900,000 function evaluations.

The hybrid algorithm showed better performance than the εPSO on all values, the εGA on the best and average values, MGA on all values, and Co-evolutionary penalty on all values (in case of 50,000 evaluations). The εPSO found higher quality solution than the εGA, but the stability which is indicated

Table 1. Result of Himmelblau's problem

Algorithm	Best	Average	Worst	S.D.
hybrid (5,000)	-31016.8002	-30952.2531	-30855.6951	38.8166
hybrid (50,000)	-31025.5168	-31023.9699	-31012.5285	2.6167
εPSO (5,000)	-31011.9988	-30947.3262	-30762.8890	55.8631
εGA (5,000)	-30987.1366	-30945.5421	-30904.1387	19.9409
GRG[24]	-30373.949	N/A	N/A	N/A
Gen[25]	-30183.576	N/A	N/A	N/A
Death[2]	-30790.271	-30429.371	-29834.385	234.555
Static[5]	-30790.2716	-30446.4618	-29834.3847	226.3428
Dynamic[6]	-30903.877	-30539.9156	-30106.2498	200.035
Annealing[7]	-30829.201	-30442.126	-29773.085	244.619
Adaptive[8]	-30903.877	-30448.007	-29926.1544	249.485
Co-evolutionary[9]	-31020.859	-30984.2407	-30792.4077	73.6335
MGA[17]	-31005.7966	-30862.8735	-30721.0418	73.240

by the standard deviation is lower than the εGA. The hybrid algorithm found much better solutions more stably than the εPSO. So, the hybrid algorithm is the best method which can find very good solutions efficiently. It found the objective value -31016.8002 in 5,000 evaluations and -31025.5168 in 50,000 evaluations that could not be found by other methods and found high quality solutions very stably for this problem. Also, the hybrid algorithm ran very fast and the execution time for solving this problem was only 0.0151 seconds (5,000 function evaluations) using notebook PC with 1.3GHz Mobile Pentium III.

4.3 Welded Beam Design

A welded beam is designed for minimum cost subject to constraints on shear stress (τ), bending stress in the beam (σ), buckling load on the bar (P_c), end deflection of the beam (δ) and side constraints[26]. There are 4 design variables: weld thickness $h(x_1)$, length of weld $l(x_2)$, width of the beam $t(x_3)$, thickness of the beam $b(x_4)$. The problem has 7 inequality constraints.

Experimental results on the problem are shown in Table 2. The good approaches were the hybrid algorithm, the εPSO, the εGA, MGA and Co-evolutionary penalty method. Note that Co-evolutionary penalty method performed 900,000 function evaluations.

The hybrid algorithm showed better performance than the εPSO on all values except for the best value, the εGA on all values except for the standard deviation, MGA on all values, and Co-evolutionary penalty on all values (in case of 50,000 evaluations). The εPSO found very higher quality solution than the εGA, but the stability is lower than the εGA. The hybrid algorithm found higher quality solutions on average more stably than the εPSO. So, the hybrid algorithm is the best method which can find very good solutions efficiently. The hybrid algorithm found the objective value 1.7268 in 5,000 evaluations and 1.7249 in 50,000 evaluations that could not be found by other methods, and found high quality solutions very stably for this problem. Also, the εPSO ran very fast and the

Table 2. Result of welded beam design

Algorithm	Best	Average	Worst	S.D.
hybrid (5,000)	1.7268	1.7635	1.9173	0.0463
hybrid (50,000)	1.7249	1.7251	1.7270	0.0006
εPSO (5,000)	1.7258	1.8073	2.1427	0.1200
εGA (5,000)	1.7852	1.8236	1.9422	0.0329
Death[2]	2.0821	3.1158	4.5138	0.6625
Static[5]	2.0469	2.9728	4.5741	0.6196
Dynamic[6]	2.1062	3.1556	5.0359	0.7006
Annealing[7]	2.0713	2.9533	4.1261	0.4902
Adaptive[8]	1.9589	2.9898	4.8404	0.6515
Co-evolutionary[9]	1.7483	1.7720	1.7858	0.0112
MGA[17]	1.8245	1.9190	1.9950	0.0538

execution time for solving this problem was only 0.0154 seconds (5,000 function evaluations).

4.4 Pressure Vessel Design

A pressure vessel is a cylindrical vessel which is capped at both ends by hemispherical heads. The vessel is designed to minimize total cost including the cost of material, forming and welding[27]. There are 4 design variables: thickness of the shell $T_s(x_1)$, thickness of the head $T_h(x_2)$, inner radius $R(x_3)$, length of the cylindrical section of the vessel not including the head $L(x_4)$. T_s and T_h are integer multiples of 0.0625 inch, which are the available thickness of rolled steel plates, and R and L are continuous. The problem has 4 inequality constraints.

This problem was solved by Sandgren[28] using Branch and Bound, by Kannan and Kramer[27] using an augmented Lagrangian Multiplier approach. Also, the problem was solved by Deb[29] using Genetic Adaptive Search (GeneAS) in the third category.

In the hybrid algorithm, to solve this mixed integer problem, new decision variable x'_1 and x'_2 are introduced and the value of x_i, $i = 1, 2$ is given by the multiple of 0.0625 and the integer part of x'_i. Experimental results on the problem are shown in Table 3. The good approaches were the hybrid algorithm, the εPSO, the εGA, MGA and Co-evolutionary penalty method. Note that the hybrid algorithm, the εPSO, the εGA and MGA performed 50,000 function evaluations, Co-evolutionary penalty method performed 900,000 function evaluations, and other penalty based approaches performed 2,500,000 function evaluations.

The hybrid algorithm showed better or equivalent performance than the εPSO on all values. It showed better performance than the εGA on the best and average values, MGA on all values except for the worst value, and Co-evolutionary penalty on all values except for standard deviation even in case of 50,000 evaluations. So, the hybrid algorithm is very good method which can find very good solutions efficiently. The hybrid algorithm and the εPSO found the objective value 6059.7143 in 50,000 evaluations that could not be found by other methods, and found high quality solutions on average for this problem. Also, the

Table 3. Design of pressure vessel

Algorithm	Best	Average	Worst	S.D.
hybrid (50,000)	6059.7143	6112.6750	6410.0868	91.4934
εPSO (50,000)	6059.7143	6154.4386	6410.0868	132.6205
εGA (50,000)	6074.6305	6172.9887	6335.7302	72.0513
Sandgren[28]	8129.1036	N/A	N/A	N/A
Kannan[27]	7198.0428	N/A	N/A	N/A
Deb[29]	6410.3811	N/A	N/A	N/A
Death[2]	6127.4143	6616.9333	7572.6591	358.8497
Static[5]	6110.8117	6656.2616	7242.2035	320.8196
Dynamic[6]	6213.6923	6691.5606	7445.6923	322.7647
Annealing[7]	6127.4143	6660.8631	7380.4810	330.7516
Adaptive[8]	6110.8117	6689.6049	7411.2532	330.4483
Co-evolutionary[9]	6288.7445	6293.8432	6308.1497	7.4133
MGA[17]	6069.3267	6263.7925	6403.4500	97.9445

hybrid algorithm ran very fast and the execution time for solving this problem was 0.1221 seconds (50,000 function evaluations).

5 Conclusions

Particle swarm optimization is a fast and an efficient optimization algorithm for unconstrained problems. We have proposed the εPSO, which is the combination of the ε constrained method and PSO, for constrained problems. In this study, we proposed the hybrid algorithm of PSO and GA to obtain high quality solutions stably. By applying the hybrid algorithm to three constrained optimization problems, it was shown that the algorithm could find much better solutions that had been never found by other methods for all problems and find better solutions on average for all problems. It was shown that the hybrid algorithm was an efficient and stable optimization algorithm.

Also, we showed the advantage of the ε constrained method. In the penalty function method, feasible points can be found by increasing the penalty coefficient towards infinity in a theoretical sense, although it is difficult to do so computationally. In the ε constrained method, feasible points can be found by letting the ε level to 0 or decreasing the ε level to 0, and this is easy to do computationally. If the constraints at a point aren't satisfied, the constraint violation is minimized, and the point will become feasible. In feature, we will apply the ε constrained method to other direct search methods, and define other type of hybrid algorithms. Also, we will apply the hybrid algorithm including the εPSO and the εGA to various application fields.

Acknowledgments

This research is supported in part by Grant-in-Aid for Scientific Research (C) (No. 16500083,17510139) of Japan society for the promotion of science.

References

1. Michalewicz, Z., Nazhiyath, G.: GENOCOP III: A co-evolutionary algorithm for numerical optimization problems with nonlinear constraints. In: Proc. of the 2nd IEEE International Conference on Evolutionary Computation. Volume 2., Perth, Australia (1995) 647–651
2. Coello, C.A.C.: Theoretical and numerical constraint-handling techniques used with evolutionary algorithms: A survey of the state of the art. Computer Methods in Applied Mechanics and Engineering **191** (2002) 1245–1287
3. Coath, G., Halgamuge, S.K.: A comparison of constraint-handling methods for the application of particle swarm optimization to constrained nonlinear optimization problems. In: Proc. of IEEE Congress on Evolutionary Computation, Canberra, Australia (2003) 2419–2425
4. Hu, X., Eberhart, R.C.: Solving constrained nonlinear optimization problems with particle swarm optimization. In: Proc. of the Sixth World Multiconference on Systemics, Cybernetics and Informatics, Orlando, Florida (2002)
5. Homaifar, A., Lai, S.H.Y., Qi, X.: Constrained optimization via genetic algorithms. Simulation **62** (1994) 242–254
6. Joines, J., Houck, C.: On the use of non-stationary penalty functions to solve nonlinear constrained optimization problems with GAs. In: Proc. of the First IEEE Conference on Evolutionary Computation, Orlando, Florida (1994) 579–584
7. Michalewicz, Z., Attia, N.F.: Evolutionary optimization of constrained problems. In: Proc. of the 3rd Annual Conference on Evolutionary Programming, Singapore (1994) 98–108
8. Hadj-Alouane, A.B., Bean, J.C.: A genetic algorithm for the multiple-choice integer program. Operations Research **45** (1997) 92–101
9. Coello, C.A.C.: Use of a self-adaptive penalty approach for engineering optimization problems. Computers in Industry **41** (2000) 113–127
10. Parsopoulos, K.E., Vrahatis, M.N.: Particle swarm optimization method for constrained optimization problems. In Sincak, P., Vascak, J., et al., eds.: Intelligent Technologies — Theory and Application: New Trends in Intelligent Technologies. Volume 76 of Frontiers in Artificial Intelligence and Applications. IOS Press (2002) 214–220
11. Deb, K.: An efficient constraint handling method for genetic algorithms. Computer Methods in Applied Mechanics and Engineering **186** (2000) 311–338
12. Takahama, T., Sakai, S.: Tuning fuzzy control rules by the α constrained method which solves constrained nonlinear optimization problems. Electronics and Communications in Japan **83** (2000) 1–12
13. Takahama, T., Sakai, S.: Constrained optimization by ε constrained particle swarm optimizer with ε-level control. In: Proc. of the 4th IEEE International Workshop on Soft Computing as Transdisciplinary Science and Technology (WSTST'05), Muroran, Japan (2005) 1019–1029
14. Runarsson, T.P., Yao, X.: Stochastic ranking for constrained evolutionary optimization. IEEE Transactions on Evolutionary Computation **4** (2000) 284–294
15. Camponogara, E., Talukdar, S.N.: A genetic algorithm for constrained and multiobjective optimization. In: 3rd Nordic Workshop on Genetic Algorithms and Their Applications, Vaasa, Finland (1997) 49–62
16. Surry, P.D., Radcliffe, N.J.: The COMOGA method: Constrained optimisation by multiobjective genetic algorithms. Control and Cybernetics **26** (1997) 391–412

17. Coello, C.A.C.: Constraint-handling using an evolutionary multiobjective optimization technique. Civil Engineering and Environmental Systems **17** (2000) 319–346
18. Ray, T., Liew, K., Saini, P.: An intelligent information sharing strategy within a swarm for unconstrained and constrained optimization problems. Soft Computing – A Fusion of Foundations, Methodologies and Applications **6** (2002) 38–44
19. Takahama, T., Sakai, S.: Learning fuzzy control rules by α-constrained simplex method. System and Computers in Japan **34** (2003) 80–90
20. Takahama, T., Sakai, S.: Constrained optimization by applying the α constrained method to the nonlinear simplex method with mutations. IEEE Trans. on Evolutionary Computation (to appear)
21. Takahama, T., Sakai, S.: Constrained optimization by α constrained genetic algorithm (αGA). Systems and Computers in Japan **35** (2004) 11–22
22. Takahama, T., Sakai, S.: Constrained optimization by the α constrained particle swarm optimizer. Journal of Advanced Computational Intelligence and Intelligent Informatics **9** (2005) 282–289
23. Kennedy, J., Eberhart, R.C.: Swarm Intelligence. Morgan Kaufmann, San Francisco (2001)
24. Himmelblau, D.M.: Applied Nonlinear Programming. McGrow-Hill, New York (1972)
25. Gen, M., Cheng, R.: Genetic Algorithms & Engineering Design. Wiley, New York (1997)
26. Rao, S.S.: Engineering Optimization. third edn. Wiley, New York (1996)
27. Kannan, B.K., Kramer, S.N.: An augmented lagrange multiplier based method for mixed integer discrete continuous optimization and its applications to mechanical design. Journal of mechanical design, Transactions of the ASME **116** (1994) 318–320
28. Sandgren, E.: Nonlinear integer and discrete programming in mechanical design. In: Proc. of the ASME Design Technology Conference, Kissimine, Florida (1988) 95–105
29. Deb, K.: GeneAS: A robust optimal design technique for mechanical component design. In Dasgupta, D., Michalewicz, Z., eds.: Evolutionary Algorithms in Engineering Applications. Springer, Berlin (1997) 497–514

Automated Information Mediator for HTML and XML Based Web Information Delivery Service[*]

Sung Sik Park[1], Yang Sok Kim[1], Gil Cheol Park[2], Byeong Ho Kang[1], and Paul Compton[3]

[1] School of Computing, University of Tasmania,
Hobart, Tasmania 7001, Australia
{sspark, yangsokk, bhkang}@utas.edu.au
[2] School of Information & Multimedia, Hannam University
133 Ojung-Dong, Daeduk-Gu, Daejeon 306-791, Korea
gcpark@mail.hannam.ac.kr
[3] School of Computer Science and Engineering
University of New South Wales, Sydney, Australia
compton@cse.unsw.edu.au

Abstract. The World Wide Web (Web) was not designed to 'push' information to clients but for clients to 'pull' information from servers (providers). This type of technology is not efficient in prompt information delivery from changing sources. Recently, XML-based 'RSS', or 'Weblog', has become popular, because they simulate real time information delivery using automated client pull technology. However, this is still inefficient because people have to manually manage large quantities of Web information, causing information overflow. Secondly, most current Web information still uses HTML instead of XML. Our automated information mediator (AIMS) collects new information from both traditional HTML sites and XML sites and alleviates the information overload problem by using narrowcasting from the server side, and information filtering from the client side using Multiple Classification Ripple-Down Rules (MCRDR) knowledge acquisition for document classification. The approach overcomes the traditional knowledge acquisition problem with an exception based knowledge representation and case based validation and verification. By employing this approach, the system allows domain experts, or even naive end users to manage their knowledge and personalize their agent system without help from a knowledge engineer.

1 Introduction

Nowadays a new XML based internet information delivery approach, known as RSS (RDF Site Summary), has been introduced to overcome pull based internet information delivery limitations. The RSS aggregator programs are set up to periodically check for new information from the user subscribed feeds. New <item> elements in the feeds are reported as new information. The RSS service can save a tremendous amount of time and mitigates information overloads by using an automated client pull

---
[*] This work was supported by a grant No. R12-2003-004-00010-0 from Ministry of Commerce, Industry and Energy, Korea.

and user defined subscription mechanism. For this reason, it is regarded as a next generation information delivery method.

However, current RSS services have two significant limitations: Firstly, like push service, the current RSS service can suffer an information overload problem because the current RSS service mainly focuses on timely information dissemination, not on personalized information delivery. Although RSS service sites provide categorized RSS feeds, the number of articles, even in a specific category, usually exceeds human information processing capability, and still contains lots of irrelevant information. Therefore, information overflow is an unavoidable problem in the current RSS service. Secondly, the current RSS service can be applied only to XML based RSS Web sites. Though the number of the RSS supporting Web sites increases rapidly, they are still a small portion of the whole of Web information. Until now, most of the Web information has been provided by HTML based information. In this research we focus on a method to overcome these limitations. Our system has been implemented to monitor both HTML based Web pages and XML based RSS Web pages. Therefore, our system can provide more complete information provision than that of current RSS service. To alleviate the information overflow problem, we employed the MCRDR (Multiple Classification Ripple-Down Rules) based document classification method, because this method supports incremental knowledge acquisition according to the changes of classification context.

2 MCRDR Document Classification System

We used the Multiple Classification Ripple-Down Rules (MCRDR) knowledge acquisition method to implement the document classification system. This strategy reduces the difficulty of knowledge acquisition by using an exception-based knowledge representation scheme and case-based validation [1-3]. Each rule has a condition part, a conclusion part, and a cornerstone case(s). Conditions are keywords, and conclusions are folders. Cornerstone cases are the cases that are used in rule creation processes and they are important in the new rule validation process of the MCRDR system. Each child rule is an exception of parent rule. A classification recommendation (conclusion) is provided by the last rule satisfied in a pathway. All children of a satisfied parent rule are evaluated, allowing for multiple conclusions. The main benefit of the MCRDR system is that a domain expert can easily maintain his/her classification knowledge incrementally. The main difference between our approach and typical machine learning approach is that the training of the MCRDR system is an on going process, unlike machine learning based classification systems. Our prior research results show that the highly accurate classification knowledge base can be constructed within a very short time – about 20 hours training. More detailed explanations about the MCRDR document classification approach are in [4, 5].

3 AIM (Automated Information Mediator) Framework

We propose an Automated Information Mediator framework, called AIM, as illustrated in **Fig. 2**. The AIM operates in client-server architecture and is implemented with C++ program language and uses MySQL database. The MCRDR based document classification system is used in the server and client system with different purposes.

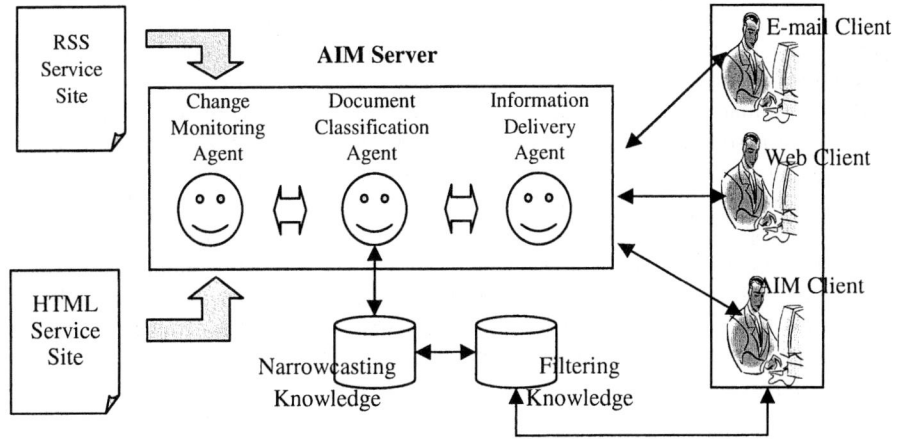

Fig. 2. AIM System Framework

The AIM server collects new information by applying different schemes to XML based RSS Web sites and HTML based Web sites. The AIM server collects new information by applying the following algorithm:

(1) Fetch the HTML or XML source from the target Web site
(2) Parse the HTML or XML source to extract all hyperlinks for HTML Web pag e monitoring and <item>s for RSS monitoring.
(3) At a certain time later (T_1), do (1) and (2) to get hyperlinks and <item>s
(4) Then the AIM server decides whether hyperlink or <item> element is new inf ormation or not.

A domain expert uses the MCRDR document classification system to construct a narrowcasting knowledge base. After the system is trained, it automatically classifies collected information by using this knowledge. End users can receive new information by subscribing specific categories or specific information sources which are managed by the domain expert with the AIM Server. Therefore, the AIM server acts as a mediator between original information providers and end users. End users can also manage incoming information by using the MCRDR document classification system. Each user's personal classification knowledge is used to classify new information from the AIM server automatically.

4 Empirical Experiment

We conducted an empirical experiment to examine the AIM server's mediating activities. Ten honours and masters students in the School of Computing at the University of Tasmania participated in the experiment, which was executed over one month. The students acted as domain experts, selecting monitoring Web sites (information source) and training the MCRDR classification system. In total 122 web pages were monitored from 95 Web sites. On average, 1,950 articles per domain were collected and 621 articles were classified as relevant articles (31.9%). The number of monitored articles and its average number in each domain varied greatly. The content usage rate (number of classified articles / number of monitored articles) of each domain varied greatly; the minimum rate was 8.0% and maximum rate was 100%. The rate was determined by the domain expert's narrowcasting strategy. A lower rate was obtained when the domain expert wanted to dispose of large quantities of irrelevant information before narrowcasting, whereas a higher rate was obtained when the domain expert wanted to cast most collected information because he/she regarded it as very relevant information for the end user. This does not mean, however, that a narrow information specification is better than a broad specification. Rather, it indicates that a domain expert's information management strategy differs from domain experts. In total 1,263 rules were created by the students and the average number of rules for each domain was 126. The number of rules needed, depends on the characteristics of the domain and the style of classification.

5 Conclusion

In this research, we illustrated an automated information mediator system for HTML and XML-based Web information delivery service. By applying our framework, we can overcome current RSS service limitations. The evaluation results presented, indicate that this approach provides a workable solution to the problem of providing timely personalized information from the Web.

References

1. Compton, P. and R. Jansen, *A philosophical basis for knowledge acquisition.* Knowledge Acquisition, 1990. **vol.2, no.3**: p. 241-258.
2. Compton, P., et al. *Ripple down rules: possibilities and limitations.* in *6th Bannf AAAI Knowledge Acquisition for Knowledge Based Systems Workshop.* 1991. Banff, Canada.
3. Kang, B., P. Compton, and P. Preston. *Multiple Classification Ripple Down Rules : Evaluation and Possibilities.* in *9th AAAI-Sponsored Banff Knowledge Acquisition for Knowledge-Based Systems Workshop.* 1995. , Banff, Canada, University of Calgary.
4. Kim, Y.S., et al. *Adaptive Web Document Classification with MCRDR.* in *International Conference on Information Technology: Coding and Computing ITCC 2004.* 2004. Orleans, Las Vegas, Nevada, USA.
5. Park, S.S., Y.S. Kim, and B.H. Kang. *Web Document Classification: Managing Context Change.* in *IADIS International Conference WWW/Internet 2004.* 2004. Madrid, Spain.

Agent-Based Middleware for Web Service Dynamic Integration on Peer-to-Peer Networks

Aizhong Lin and Piyush Maheshwari

School of Computer Science and Engineering,
The University of New South Wales,
Sydney NSW 2052, Australia
{alin, piyush}@cse.unsw.edu.au

Abstract. Performing business processes normally requires dynamic and casual collaborations among enterprises that are not centrally controlled. Enterprise application integration and Peer-to-Peer computing provide a solution to the business processes. Web service integration and agent-based middleware constitute the paradigms to implement enterprise application integration on Peer-to-Peer networks because of the loosely-coupled property of Web services and the autonomous, adaptive, and interactive properties of agents. Previous Web service integration researches focused on Web service integration based on client/server network architecture. However, along with the highly demands of Web service quality, Web services are not always provided on client/server networks. This research aims to construct an agent-based middleware for Web service dynamic integration on Peer-to-Peer networks to pursue the integration of optimal quality of Web services for enterprise application integration. The paper introduces the agent-based middleware including the formalization, Web service dynamic integration model, agent reasoning model, and the application.

1 Introduction

Performing business processes normally require dynamic and casual collaborations among enterprises that are not centrally controlled. A well-know scenario specified in [1] is an example of these business processes. A travel organizer to serve a university staff member who is going to attend a conference includes connecting an airline service to buy a flight ticket; a hotel service to book a room; a car rental service to rent a car, and a credit card service to pay all expenses. The airline company agency, hotel, car rent company, and the credit card company collaborate dynamically and casually with the travel organizer. After the process instance is performed, all those collaboration channels are disconnected. When starting another travel instance, the organizer may contact other airline, hotel, car rent, and credit card companies.

Enterprise Application Integration (EAI) and Peer-to-Peer (P2P) computing provide a solution to these business processes. Web Service Integration (WSi) and Agent-based Middleware (AbM) constitute the paradigms to implement EAI on P2P networks. Because of the loose coupling properties of Web services, their integration naturally meets the requirements of dynamic and casual collaboration among enterprises. P2P computing provides the easiest scalable network architecture for Web service deployment, publication, and interoperation. Agents, which are situated in

P2P networks and monitoring Web services, provide critical information for choosing most qualified Web services to be integrated.

Previous Web service integration projects [2, 3, 4, 5] rarely concerned the Web services deployed and published in P2P networks. On the other hand, previous P2P applications [6, 7, 8, 9, 10, 11, 12] seldom supported Web services sharing or interoperation. However, along with the highly demands of Web service quality improvement, Client/Server architecture will not be the solo network architecture for Web service deployment and publication. P2P architecture provides another option. Two reasons motivate that the Web services are deployed and published in peers: (1) not all business relationships among the enterprises are able to be established in Client/Server; and (2) the Web services involved in WSi are required to have the optimal quality determined by the Web service availability, reliability, security, efficiency, and fees.

This research aims to construct an agent-based middleware (AbM) for Web service dynamic integration (WSDI) on P2P networks to pursue the integration of optimal quality of Web services. This paper introduces the AbM and the application.

2 Formalization

2.1 Web Service Integration/Composition

Web service integration composites individual Web services to achieve business process goals. Here four atomic integration types are defined in which s_1 and s_2 are two Web services:

- *sequence* $(s_1 \rightarrow s_2)$:   Web service s_2 follows the Web service s_1
- *parallel* $(s_1 \wedge s_2)$:   Web service s_1 and s_2 are executed simultaneously without any order
- *option* $(s_1 \vee s_2)$:   Web service s_1 and s_2 are executed alternatively
- *aggregation* $(s_1 \rightleftharpoons s_2)$:   Web service s_2 are invoked by Web service s_1

Using these atomic types and "(" and ")", multi-x (multi-sequence, multi-parallel, multi-option, and multi-aggregation) types can be obtained:

- *multi-sequence*: $s_1 \rightarrow s_2 \rightarrow s_3 \rightarrow \ldots \rightarrow s_m$
- *multi-parallel*: $s_1 \wedge s_2 \wedge s_3 \wedge \ldots \wedge s_m$
- *multi-option*: $s_1 \vee s_2 \vee s_3 \vee \ldots \vee s_m$
- *multi-aggregation*: $s_1 \rightleftharpoons (s_2 \wedge s_3 \wedge \ldots \wedge s_m)$ and $s_1 \rightleftharpoons (s_2 \vee s_3 \vee \ldots \vee s_{m'})$

2.2 Web Service Quality

The *quality* of a Web service s_i, denoted by sq, is a 5-tuple, i.e., $sq(s_i) = (sav(s_i), sre(s_i), sla(s_i), sse(s_i), sfe(s_i))$. Where

- *Web service availability* (sav: $0 \leq sav \leq 1$): It is determined by the available rate of a Web service. A Web service is defined "available" if it can be discovered and invoked.

- *Web service reliability (sre: $0 \leq sre \leq 1$)*: It is determined by the success rate of a Web service. A Web service is defined "success" if it provides the expected result.
- *Web service latency (sla)*: It is determined by the Web service average processing time of invocations. The Web service latency is a negative parameter of the Web service *efficiency* and the Web service quality.
- *Web service security (sse: $0 \leq sse \leq 1$)*: It is determined by that the security level (encryption, hashing, authentication, https, X509, ...) the Web service can support divided by the number of levels.
- *Web service fee (sfe)*: It is the average fee payment for Web service executions. The Web service fee is a negative parameter of the Web service quality. It is required when using a commercial or industrial Web service. The Web service provided by Google search engine is one of such kind Web services.

Web service availability, reliability, latency, security, and fee are called Web service quality attributes in which availability, reliability, and security are positive whilst latency and fee are negative. The Web service quality difference, denoted by dsq, is calculated by following formula [13]

$$dsq(s_1, s_2) = \sum_{a \in pos} (a_{s_1} - a_{s_2}) + \sum_{a \in neg} (\frac{1}{a_{s_1}} - \frac{1}{a_{s_2}})$$

where:
- a is an attribute of the Web service quality,
- $a \in pos$ means all attributes belong to positive parameters , and
- $a \in neg$ means all attributes belong to negative parameters
- s_1 and s_2 are two Web services,

2.3 Web Service Dynamic Integration

As the number of Web services providing a given functionality may be large and constantly changing, a Web service in a composition pattern to achieve a business process goal may be replaced with another Web service at execution time rather than design time to optimize the quality of the business process performance.

Web service dynamic integration (WSDI) is a process to replace Web services with other better quality Web services in an integration patterns at execution time to optimize the quality of business process performance.

3 Web Service Dynamic Integration Model

Web service dynamic integration focuses on replacing some Web services in a integration pattern with better quality Web services at execution time. As an example illustrated in Figure 1, a Web service integration pattern to achieve a business process goal "book_travel_package" is:

$$(s_1 \wedge s_2 \wedge s_3) \rightarrow s_4,$$

where:
- s_1: a Web service provides flight fare booking
- s_2: a Web service provides hotel room booking

- s_3: a Web service provides car rent booking
- s_4: a Web service provides credit card payment

Suppose to each s_i ($1 \leq i \leq 4$), a number of Web services $\{s_{i,1}, s_{i,2}, ..., s_{i,m_i}\}$ can provide the same functionalities of s_i. An agent ag_i is assigned the tasks to monitor the option set of Web services $\{s_{i,1}, s_{i,2}, ..., s_{i,m_i}\}$ and responsible for choosing one Web service with the best quality from the option set before a process instance is performed. The Web service are deployed and published in peers of P2P networks. The agent perceives the joining peers and Web services and the removing of the existing peers or Web services.

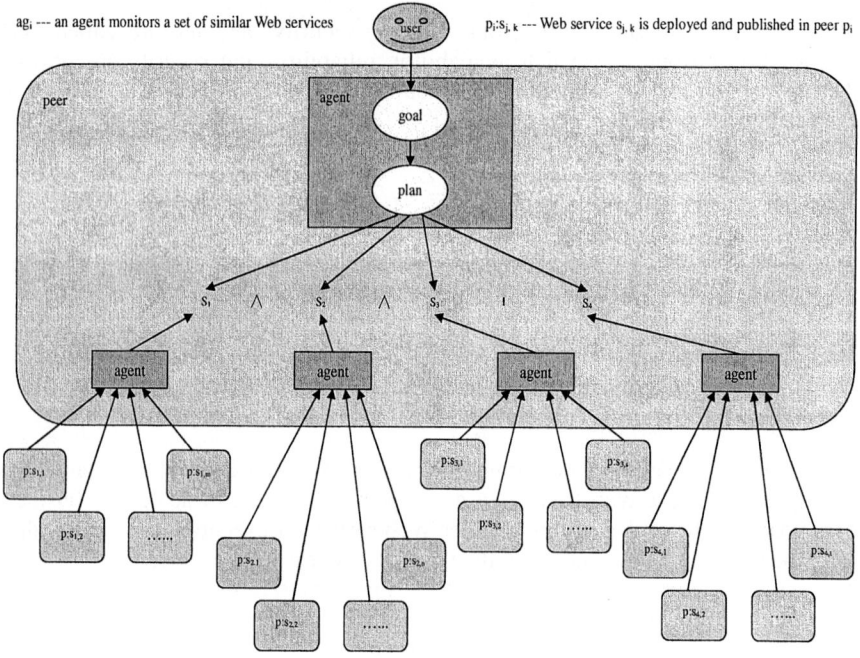

Fig. 1. The Web service dynamic integration model

4 The Agent Conceptual Reasoning Model

Agents are naturally goal-driven software components that employ reactive and proactive (goal-driven) architectures to achieve goals. Figure 2 illustrates these architectures. In Figure 2, the small cycle (Environment->Event->EBA rules-> Action->Environment) describes the reactive architecture. The large cycle (Environment->Event->EBG rules->Goal->Plan->Action->Environment) describes the goal-driven flow chart. Concepts such as event, belief, Event-Belief-Action (EBA) rules and Event-Belief-Goal (EBG) rules are used. They are all defined formally in previous section as well as following BNF.

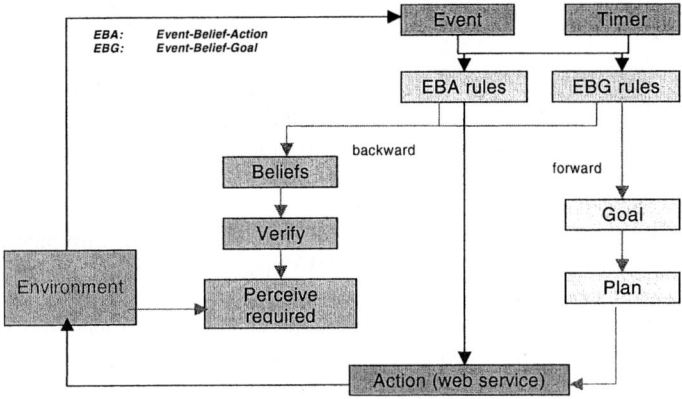

Fig. 2. The goal-driven agent architecture

```
agent           ::= [events] [beliefs] rules [goals] [plans] actions [interactions]
events          ::= (event)*
event           ::= "@"literal";"
beliefs         ::= (belief)*
belief          ::= "%"belief_literal";"
belief_literal  ::= literal | "!"literal
goals           ::= (goal)*
goal            ::= "?"literal";"
actions         ::= (action)*
action          ::= ">"literal";"
Interactions    ::= (interaction)*
Interaction     ::= "<"literal";"
rules           ::= (EBArule)* | (EBGrule)*
EBArule         ::= "when" "(" events ")" "if" "(" (beliefs | "true") ")" "then" action
EBGrule         ::= "when" "(" events ")" "if" "(" (beliefs | "true") ")" "then" (goal_name | plan_literal)+
plans           ::= (plan)*
plan            ::= "#"plan_name ":"goal_name "(" plan_literal ")"
plan_name       ::= identifier
goal_name       ::= identifier
plan_literal    ::= (action)+ | ("<service>" literal "</service>")+
                    "<sequence>" plan_literal "</sequence>" |
                    "<parallel>" plan_literal "</parallel>" |
                    "<option>" plan_literal "</option>"
literal         ::= formula | "!"formula
formula         ::= identifier ["(" terms ")"]
terms           ::= term ("," term)*
term            ::= formula | identifier | string | number
identifier      ::= (["a"-"z"] | ["A"-"Z"])+ (
                                              ["a"-"z"] |
                                              ["A"-"Z"] |
                                              ["0"-"9"] |
                                              ["_"]
                                             )*
string          ::= "\"" (["A"-"Z"])(
                                     ["a"-"z"] |
                                     ["A"-"Z"] |
                                     ["0"-"9"] |
                                     ["_", "/", " ",",",".","."]
```

From the BNF of the agent plan, we know it is specifically defined for Web service integration. In current stage, three atomic Web service integration types (sequence and parallel) are considered.

5 The Application

The well-know scenario --- Travel Use Case --- is presented in below and an AbM is designed in Figure 3 to achieve the scenario business process goals.

A travel company provides a travel application to achieve the travelers' goals. For example, the travel application works for travelers to book best suit complete travel packages: plane tickets, hotels, and car rental.

Service providers (airlines, hotel chains, car rentals, and credit card payment), each of which exist in a peer in a Peer-to-Peer (P2P) business relationships, are providing Web services to query their offerings and perform reservations.

Software agents (or agents for simple) work on behalf of the travel application and Web service provider peers to interact with each other to choose the best suitable services from the P2P network for the travel application. Due to the loosely coupled-nature of Web services, the travel application does not need to have a priori agreements with Web service providers. This allows the travel application to have access to more services, offering more options to its customers to make their customers benefited, and the service providers can offer their services broadly and easily and therefore earning more benefits for themselves.

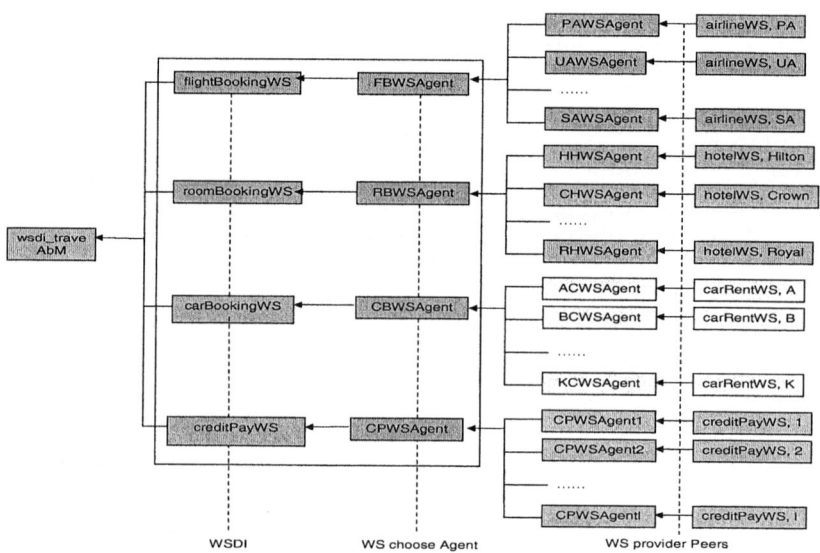

Fig. 3. The architecture of the WSDI travel application

We use three computers (two in a private network and the other one in the Internet), which are connected as a P2P network, to test the application. In each computer twelve peers are installed. In total thirty six peers, thirty peers provide airline_WS (twelve peers), hotel_WS (ten peers), and car_rent_WS (eight peers). The other six peers provide credit_card_payment_WS. In this experiment, peers are set randomly joining or leaving the P2P network, and Web services are set randomly joining or leaving peers respectively. We focus on testing following properties:

- P2P network refreshing time
- Web service discovery time
- Web service collection (in which all Web services are similar to each other) forming time
- Web service choosing time
- Web service invocation time
- Web service integration pattern (business process) execution time

The average times of the properties after one hundred times of the prototype executions are given in following Table 1. They tell us that Web service dynamic integration over P2P networks is feasible and acceptable.

Table 1. The average times of properties based 100 times of prototype execution

Testing Properties	Average Time (milliseconds)
Network refresh time	3312
WS discovery time	425
WS collection forming time	1168
WS choosing time	324
WS invocation time	698
WSIP execution time	1847

6 Related Work

This research integrates a couple of new technologies (P2P, Web service, Agent, and Middleware) into a project. Large amount of related work is found from the journals and Internet.

P2P applications and research systems are becoming more and more popular in sharing resources over the Internet. They are classified into three categories (1) Centralized P2P: the centralized P2P network normally owns a server to register the identifier (IP addresses or domain names) of all joined peers. When sharing a resource, a peer gets the identifier of a destination peer from the server and then establishes a direct communication channel. The representative of the centralized P2P is Napster [1]; (2) Pure distributed P2P: in pure distributed P2P, each peer possesses a partial group of identifiers of all joined peers using a Distributed Hash Table (DHT) [4]. When locating a resource, a peer firstly retrieve its local DHT and has the ability to propagate the request to other peers when it fails to locate the resource. The representatives of this category are Gnutella [2], Freenet [3], and Chord [4]; (3) Hybrid P2P: the hybrid P2P is the combination of the centralized P2P and pure distributed P2P. A hybrid P2P has some super peers that store the identifiers of sub networks. Meanwhile, a super peer has a DHT to record a partial group of identifiers of all other super peers. The representatives of this category are SBARC [25] based on PAST [5], Kazaa [6], and JXTA [19]. In these popular P2P applications or research systems, none of them treats Web services as the shared resources. Our research is going to fill the gap.

Since WSDL [8] is specified, Web service integration becomes feasible. In the early work, IBM and Microsoft provided WSFL [9] and XLANG [10] respectively for specifying Web service flows. Based on WSFL and XLANG, they cooperatively published the Business Process Execution Language --- BPEL4WS [11-12] --- A language to specify Web service flow for business processes. Meanwhile, other Web service flow specifications such as BPML [13], WSCI [14], and WS-CDL [15] are also provided. Web service dynamic composition (or integration) is also the major research theme in the Web service integration research area. Most of the researches about dynamic integration suggest "quality-driven" [16], i.e., choosing the best quality Web services to be composed to achieve business goals. To do this, [16] and [17] provide the Web service quality models. The authors argue that the Web service quality is determined by the Web service execution fee, efficiency, availability, reliability, and reputation. [17] proposess Web service security to be an important attribute to determine Web service quality, but its security definition is difficult for dynamic computation. [18] defines Inverse rules for Web service dynamic discovery.

Intelligent agent technology has been exploited in Web service dynamic integration. DAML-S (also called OWL-S in the recent version) [26] is a Web service language which has the direct connection with "planning" of Web service composition. DAML-OIL (the language used to build DAML-S) [27] supports logic expression using Description Logic [28]. PDDL [29] is another language that supports planning of Web service integration. Furthermore, SWORD [30] is a developer toolkit for building composite Web services using rule-based plan generation. Other research projects such as [31] and [32] also stress the uses of agents in Web service integration. Such previous work is mainly focused on "planning" of Web services. Our project employs agents to monitor Web services availability, reliability, efficiency, security, payment, and reputation for Web service quality computation. Based on the obtained/measured quality, the most suitable Web service will be chosen from a Web service option.

7 Conclusion and Future Work

A good advertisement for AbM might be "delegate a business process goal to the AbM, the AbM will automatically and autonomously achieve the goal on your behalf by employing the best quality of Web services that purely distributed". With the usage of AbM, application developers can save precious time by asking agents to retrieve the large number of Web services and understand their usages. Furthermore, AbM provides optimal efficiencies for enterprise application integration that implements the casual and dynamic collaboration among enterprises for achieving business process goals.

The current implementation of the AbM is a prototype that is constructed based on a number of existing open source projects such as JXTA and AXIS. The integration of the projects is not seamless. At moment, the prototype can support only one application --- organizing travel. In future, a seamlessly integrated AbM platform will be generated to support business process applications on P2P networks. In addition, the new platform will provide more agents to enable the AbM to support more applications with better Web service efficiency, availability, reliability, and security.

Acknowledgement

This work is jointly funded by the Australian Research Council and Microsoft Research Asia (ARC Linkage Project LP0453880).

References

[1] Web service use case: Travel reservation. http://www.w3.org/2002/06/ws-example
[2] Liangzhao Zeng , Boualem Benatallah , Marlon Dumas , Jayant Kalagnanam , Quan Z. Sheng, Quality driven web services composition, Proceedings of the twelfth international conference on World Wide Web, May 20-24, 2003, Budapest, Hungary
[3] Efficient Delivery of Web services. http://citeseer.ist.psu.edu/cache/papers/cs/32175/ http:zSzzSzeuropa.nvc.cs.vt.eduzSz~mouradzSzmourad.ouzzani.pdf/ouzzani04efficient.pdf
[4] Snehal Thakkar, Craig A. Knoblock, and José Luis Ambite. A View Integration Approach to Dynamic Composition of Web Services. http://www.isi.edu/info-agents/papers/thakkar03-p4ws.pdf
[5] Wil M.P. van der Aalst, Marlon Dumas, Arthur H.M. ter Hofstede. Analysis of Web services composition languages: The case of BPEL4WS. http://is.tm.tue.nl/research/patterns/ download/bpel_er.pdf
[6] http://www.napster.com.
[7] http://gnutella.wego.com.
[8] http://freenet.sourceforge.com.
[9] I. Stoica, R. Morris, D. Liben-Nowell, D. Karger, M. F. Kaashoek, F. Dabek, and H. Balakrishnan. Chord: A scalable peer-to-peer lookup protocol for Internet applications. IEEE/ACM Transactions on Networking, 11(1):17-32, Feb. 2003.
[10] A. Rowstron and P. Druschel, "Storage management and caching in PAST, A large-scale, persistent peer-to-peer storage utility," in SOSP, Banff, Alberta, Canada, pp. 188–201, Oct. 2001.
[11] http://www.kazaa.com.
[12] A. Rowstron and P. Druschel. Pastry: Scalable, decentralized object location, and routing for large-scale peer-to-peer systems. In IFIP/ACM Middleware, Nov. 2001.
[13] Ouzzani, M.; Bouguettaya, A.. Efficient Access to Web Service, IEEE Internet Computing, 2004
[14] P. Maheshwari, T. Nguyen, and A, Erradi, QoS-based message-oriented middleware for Web services, Proceedings of the WISE 2004 Web Services Quality Workshop, LNCS 3307, Brisbane, Australia, November 21, 2004, pp. 241-251.
[15] http://www.jxta.org
[16] http://ws.apache.org/axis/
[17] http://ws.apache.org/juddi/
[18] Zhiyong Xu and Yiming Hu. SBARC: A Supernode Based Peer-to-Peer File Sharing System. http://www.ececs.uc.edu/~oscar/papers/zyxu_sbarc.pdf
[19] WSDL specification. http://www.w3.org/TR/wsdl20/. 2004
[20] WSFL Specification. http://www-306.ibm.com/software/solutions/webservices/pdf/WSFL.pdf
[21] XLANG Specification. http://www.gotdotnet.com/team/xml_wsspecs/xlang-c/default.ht
[22] Fank Leymann. Business Processes in a Web Services World: A Quick Overview of BPEL4WS. http://www-106.ibm.com/developerworks/library/ws-bpelwp. 2002
[23] BPML Specification. http://xml.coverpages.org/bpml.html

[24] WSCI Specification. http://www.w3.org/TR/wsci/
[25] WS-CDL Specification. http://www.w3.org/TR/2004/WD-ws-cdl-10-20041217/
[26] R. A. Brooks. Intelligence without reason. Proceedings of the Twelfth International Joint Conference on Artificial Intelligence (IJCAI-91), pp569-595. Sydney, Australia, 1991.
[27] M. E. Bratman. Intentions, Plans, and Practical Reason. Harvard University Press, Cambridge, MA, 1987.
[28] A. Rao and M. Georgeff. BDI agents from theory to practice. Technical report, Technical Note 56, AAII, 1995.
[29] T. Finin, M. J. Labroux. KQML as an agent communication language; in: Bradshaw, J. (Ed.): Software Agents; Menlo Park 1995.
[30] FIPA specification. Agent Communication Language. http://www.fipa.org/specs/fipa00003/OC00003A.html
[31] http://www.w3.org/TR/owl-ref/
[32] D. Connolly, F. van Harmelen, I. Horrocks, D. L. McGuinness, P. F. Patel-Schneider, and L. Stein. DAML+OIL (March 2001) Reference Description. W3C Note 18, December 2001. http://www.w3.org/TR/daml+oil-reference
[33] G. D. Giacomo, M. Lenzerini. A Uniform Framework for Concept Definitions in Description Logics. Journal of Artificial Intelligence Research 6 (1997) 87-110
[34] M. Ghallab et al. PDDL-The Planning Domain Definition Language V. 2. Technical Report, report CVC TR-98-003/DCS TR-1165, Yale Center for Computational Vision and Control, 1998.
[35] S. R. Ponnekanti and A. Fox. SWORD: A developer toolkit for building composite web services. In Proceedings of the 11th International World Wide Web Conference, 2002
[36] C. Preist, C. Bartolini, A. Byde. Agent-based service composition through simultaneous negotiation in forward and reverse auctions. Proceedings of the 4th ACM conference on Electronic commerce. June 2003.
[37] J. J. Bryson, D. Martin, S. I. McIlraith, and L. A. Stein. Agent-based composite services in daml-s: The behavior-oriented design of an intelligent semantic web. In Ning Zhong, Jiming Liu, and Yiyu Yao, editors, Web Intelligence. Springer, 2002.

Towards User Profiling for Web Recommendation

Guandong Xu[1], Yanchun Zhang[1], and Xiaofang Zhou[2]

[1] School of Computer Science and Mathematics,
Victoria University, PO Box 14428, VIC 8001, Australia
{xu,yzhang}@csm.vu.edu.au
[2] School of Information Technology & Electrical Engineering,
University of Queensland, Brisbane QLD 4072, Australia
zxf@itee.uq.edu.au

Abstract. Collaborative recommendation is one of widely used recommendation systems, which recommend items to visitor on a basis of referring other's preference that is similar to current user. User profiling technique upon Web transaction data is able to capture such informative knowledge of user task or interest. With the discovered usage pattern information, it is likely to recommend Web users more preferred content or customize the Web presentation to visitors via collaborative recommendation. In addition, it is helpful to identify the underlying relationships among Web users, items as well as latent tasks during Web mining period. In this paper, we propose a Web recommendation framework based on user profiling technique. In this approach, we employ *Probabilistic Latent Semantic Analysis* (PLSA) to model the co-occurrence activities and develop a modified k-means clustering algorithm to build user profiles as the representatives of usage patterns. Moreover, the hidden task model is derived by characterizing the meaningful latent factor space. With the discovered user profiles, we then choose the most matched profile, which possesses the closely similar preference to current user and make collaborative recommendation based on the corresponding page weights appeared in the selected user profile. The preliminary experimental results performed on real world data sets show that the proposed approach is capable of making recommendation accurately and efficiently.

1 Introduction

In recent years, the massive influx of information onto World Wide Web has facilitated user, not only retrieving information, but also discovering knowledge. However, Web users usually suffer from the information overload problem due to the fact of significantly increasing and rapidly expanding growth in amount of information on the Web. One approach addressed to the information overload is the recommendation system, which aims to help users locate more needed or preferred information. Typically, Web recommendation system focuses on the processes of identifying Web users or objects, collecting information with respect to users' preference or interests as well as adapting its service to satisfy the users' needs. In short, Web recommendation can be used to provide better quality service and application of Web to users during their browsing period.

To-date, the problem of recommending appropriate items from data repository to users has been extensively studied and two paradigms named content-based filtering and collaborative filtering systems have emerged. Content-based filtering systems such as WebWatcher [8], try to recommend items that are similar to those visited by a given user in the past, whereas collaborative filtering systems intend to identify user category whose taste or preference is close enough to the given user and recommend items that are historically rated by them [6]. The former often utilizes traditional information filtering and information retrieval methods, while the latter employs user correlation or nearest-neighbor algorithm. Especially, the collaborative filtering technique has been gradually adopted in the context of Web recommendation applications and has achieved great success as well [5, 9] in recent years.

Web usage mining technique, which exploits data mining methods, such as k-Nearest Neighbor algorithm (*kNN*) [5], Web user or page clustering [4, 11, 12], association rule mining [1] and sequential pattern mining technique [2], to create model based on the analysis of usage data, has been used in building Web recommendation system recently. With the usage pattern knowledge discovered in Web usage mining process, Web recommendation system can generate usage-based user profiles as the representatives of the aggregate user behaviors for collaborative recommendation. As a result, a variety of research communities have addressed this topic and Web usage mining is becoming a potential approach for Web recommendation. To reveal the underlying relationships among Web objects, *Latent Semantic Analysis* (LSA) technique has been incorporated into Web usage mining process. Some LSA-based algorithms are developed for Web recommendation [13, 14].

In this paper, we propose a Web recommendation framework based on user profiling technique. The usage pattern knowledge, in the form of user profile derived from Web usage mining, is combined into Web recommendation system to improve the efficiency of recommendation by predicting user-preferred content and customizing the presentation. During pattern discovery stage, probabilistic inference method based on *Probabilistic Latent Semantic Analysis* (PLSA) model, a variant of LSA, is exploited to model the underlying relationships among the co-occurrence activities and identify the latent task model in terms of latent semantic factor. Through Web user session clustering, we create user profiles as the representatives of usage patterns. To make Web recommendation, we match the current active user activity against such discovered patterns to find the most like-minded user category, in turn, determine the potentially interested pages as recommendation set based on the visited probabilities exhibited by such type of users. We demonstrate the effectiveness of the proposed technique through experiments performed on real world data sets. The evaluation results show that the usage-based approach is more applicable in comparison with some traditional techniques.

The rest of the paper is organized as follows. In section 2, we introduce the Web usage mining process, especially we focus on how to model Web co-occurrence activities based on PLSA. We present the algorithms for discovering usage-based user profiles and latent factors in section 3. In section 4, we propose the Web recommendation framework upon user profiling approach. We conduct preliminary experiments on two real world datasets, implement some comparisons against the traditional work in section 5, conclude and outline future work in section 6.

2 Usage-Based User Profiling with PLSA

As discussed above, Web recommendation is the ultimate goal of Web usage mining conducted on the data collected at the Web log servers of a specific Web site. This whole procedure usually consists of three steps, i.e. data collection and preprocessing, pattern mining as well as knowledge application. Figure 1 depicts the whole process.

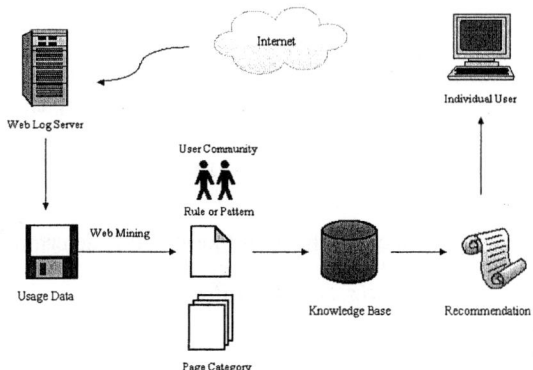

Fig. 1. The process of Web Mining and Web Recommendation

2.1 Usage Data Representation

Prior to introducing user profiling technique, we briefly discuss the issue with respect to construction of usage data. In general, the exhibited user access interests may be reflected by the varying degrees of visits on different Web pages during one session. Thus, we can represent a user session as a weighted page vector visited by the user during a period. In this paper, we use the following notations to model the co-occurrence activities of Web users and pages:

- $S = \{s_1, s_2, \cdots s_m\}$: a set of m user sessions.
- $P = \{p_1, p_2, \cdots p_n\}$: a set of n Web pages.
- For each user, the navigational session is represented as a sequence of visited pages with corresponding weights: $s_i = \{a_{i,1}, a_{i,2}, \cdots a_{i,n}\}$, where $a_{i,j}$ denotes the weight for page p_j visited in s_i user session. The corresponding weight is usually determined by the number of hit or the amount time spent on the specific page. Here, we use both of them to construct usage data from two real world data sets.
- $SP_{m \times n} = \{a_{i,j}\}$: the ultimate usage data in the form of weight matrix with dimensionality of $m \times n$.

2.2 PLSA Model

The PLSA model is based on a statistic model called aspect model, which can be utilized to identify the hidden semantic relationships among general co-occurrence activities. Similarly, we can conceptually view the user sessions over Web pages space as co-occurrence activities in the context of Web usage mining to discover the latent usage pattern. For the given aspect model, suppose that there is a latent factor space $Z = \{z_1, z_2, \cdots z_k\}$ and each co-occurrence observation data $<s_i, p_j>$ is associated with the factor $z_k \in Z$ by varying degree to z_k.

Based on these assumptions and Bayesian rule, we calculate the probability of an observed pair $<s_i, p_j>$ by adopting the latent factor variable z_k as:

$$P(s_i, p_j) = \sum_{z_k \in Z} P(z_k) \bullet P(s_i | z_k) \bullet P(p_j | z_k) \quad (1)$$

Following the likelihood principle, the total likelihood is determined as

$$L_i = \sum_{s_i \in S, p_j \in P} m(s_i, p_j) \bullet \log P(s_i, p_j) \quad (2)$$

where $m(s_i, p_j)$ is the element of the session-page matrix corresponding to session s_i and page p_j.

In order to maximize the total likelihood, we make use of *Expectation Maximization* (EM) algorithm to perform maximum likelihood estimation of $P(z_k)$, $P(s_i | z_k)$, $P(p_j | z_k)$ in latent variable model [3]. The executing of E-step and M-step is repeating until L_i is converging to a local optimal limit, which means the estimated results can represent the final probabilities of observation data. It is easily found that the computational complexity of this algorithm is $O(mnk)$, where m is the number of user session, n is the number of page, and k is the number of factors.

3 Discovery of Latent Factors and Usage-Based User Profiles

As we discussed in section 2, the estimated probabilities quantitatively measure the underlying relationships among Web users, pages as well as latent factors (i.e. tasks). Therefore, it is reasonable to identify the latent factors and discover the related usage-based access patterns upon probability inference process. In this section, we propose how to derive the aforementioned usage information.

3.1 Characterizing Latent Factor

First, we discuss how to capture the latent factor associated with user navigational behavior. This aim is to be achieved by characterizing the "dominant" pages that contribute significantly to the factor. Note that $p(p_j | z_k)$ represents the conditional occurrence probability over the page space corresponding to a specific factor, whereas $p(z_k | p_j)$ reflects the conditional probability distribution over the factor space corresponding to a specific page. Thus, we may choose the pages whose conditional probabilities $p(z_k | p_j)$ and $p(p_j | z_k)$ are both greater than a predefined threshold to form "dominant" page set. Exploring the contents of these pages would result in characterizing the semantic meaning of each factor. In section 4, we will present various examples of latent factors as well as those "dominant" pages derived from two real data sets.

3.2 Building Usage-Based User Profiles

Note that the set of $P(z_k | s_i)$ is conceptually representing the probability distribution over the latent factor space for a specific user session s_i, we, thus, construct the session-factor matrix based on the calculated probability estimates, to reflect the relationship between Web users and latent factors, which is expressed as follows:

$$s_i' = (b_{i,1}, b_{i,2}, ..., b_{i,k}) \qquad (3)$$

where $b_{i,s}$ is the occurrence probability of session s_i on factor z_s. In this way, the distance between two session vectors may reflect the exhibited navigational behavior similarity. We, therefore, define their similarity by applying well-known *cosine* similarity as:

$$sim(s_i', s_j') = (s_i', s_j') / (\|s_i'\|_2 \bullet \|s_j'\|_2) \qquad (4)$$

where $(s_i', s_j') = \sum_{m=1}^{k} b_{i,m} b_{j,m}$, $\|s_i'\|_2 = \sqrt{\sum_{m=1}^{k} b_{i,m}^2}$, $\|s_j'\|_2 = \sqrt{\sum_{m=1}^{k} b_{j,m}^2}$

With the page similarity measurement (4), we propose a modified k-means clustering algorithm [13] to partition user sessions into corresponding clusters. As each user session is represented as a weighted page vector, it is reasonable to derive the centroid of cluster obtained as the usage pattern in the form of user profile. In this work, we compute the mean vector to represent the centroid. The algorithm for clustering user sessions and constructing user profiles is as follows:

Algorithm 1. Building User Profiles

Input: the set of conditional probabilities $P(z_k | s_i)$

Output: A set of user session clusters $SCL = \{SCL_1, SCL_2, \cdots, SCL_p\}$ and a set of user profiles $PF = \{PF_1, PF_2, \cdots, PF_p\}$

1. For all user sessions, employ the modified k-means clustering algorithm and output a set of usage-based session clusters $SCL = \{SCL_t\}$.
2. for each user session cluster, calculate the centroid of cluster as

$$Cid_t = 1/|SCL_t| \bullet \sum_{s_i \in SCL_t} s_i' \qquad (5)$$

where $|SCL_t|$ is the number of sessions in the cluster.

3. Treat the centroid of generated cluster as the aggregate user profile, and sort the normalized weights in a descending order to reflect the relative "significance" contributed by the corresponding pages within the selected user profile, i.e.

$$PF_t = \{<p_1^t, w_1^t>, <p_2^t, w_2^t>, \cdots, <p_n^t, w_n^t>\} \qquad (6)$$

where $w_j^t = 1/|SCL_t| \cdot \sum_{s_i \in SCL_t} a_{i,j}$, $w_1^t > w_2^t > \cdots > w_n^t$, and $p_j^t \in P$

4. Output $PF = \{PF_t\}$.

4 Using PLSA for Web Personalization

Generally, we recommend Web items to users in customized or preferred style based on analysis of their interests exhibited by individual or groups of users. In this work, we adopt the model-based technique in our Web recommendation framework. We consider the usage-based user profiles generated in section 3.2 as the aggregated representatives of common navigational behaviors exhibited by all individuals in same particular user category. For a newly coming active user session, we utilize *cosine* function to measure the similarity between it and discovered user profile. We, then, choose the closest profile, which shares the highest similarity with the current user session, as the matched pattern to current user. Finally, we generate the top-N recommendation pages based on the historically visited probabilities of pages by other users in the selected profile. The detailed procedure is as follows:

Algorithm 2. Web Recommendation Based on user profiling
Input: An active user session and a set of user profiles
Output: The top-N recommendation pages
1. The active session and the profiles are to be simplified as n-dimensional weight vectors s_a, s_p instead of page-weight pair vector over the page space that is generated from algorithm 3 within a site, i.e. $s_p = [w_1^p, w_2^p, \cdots, w_n^p]$, where w_i^p is the significance weight contributed by page p_i in this profile, similarly $s_a = [w_1^a, w_2^a, \cdots w_n^a]$, where $w_i^a = 1$, if page p_i is already accessed, and otherwise $w_i^a = 0$.

2. Measure the similarities between the active session and all derived usage profiles, and choose the maximum one out of the calculated similarities as the most matched pattern:

$$sim(s_a, s_p^{mat}) = \max_j(sim(s_a, s_p^j)) = \max_j((s_a \bullet s_p)/\|s_a\|_2 \|s_p\|_2) \qquad (7)$$

3. Incorporate the selected profile s_p^{mat} with the active session s_a, then calculate the recommendation score $rs(p_i)$ for each page p_i:

$$rs(p_i) = w_i^{mat}, \ w_i^{mat} \in s_p^{mat} \tag{8}$$

Thus, each page in the profile will be assigned a recommendation score between 0 and 1. Note that the recommendation score will be 0 if the page is already visited in the current session.

4. Sort the calculated recommendation scores in step 3 in a descending order, i.e. $rs = (w_1^{mat}, w_2^{mat}, \cdots, w_n^{mat})$, and select the N pages with the highest recommendation scores to construct the top-N recommendation set:

$$REC(N) = \{p_j^{mat} \mid rs(p_j^{mat}) > rs(p_{j+1}^{mat}), j = 1, 2, \cdots N, p_j^{mat} \in P\} \tag{9}$$

5 Experiments and Evaluations

In order to evaluate the effectiveness of the proposed method based on PLSA model and explore the discovered latent semantic factor, we have conducted preliminary experiments on two real world data sets.

5.1 Data Sets

The first data set we used is downloaded from KDDCUP Web site (www.ecn.purdue.edu/KDDCUP/). After data preparation, we have setup an evaluation data set including 9308 user sessions and 69 pages, where every session consists of 11.88 pages in average. We refer this data set to "KDDCUP data". In this data set, the number of Web page hits by the given user determines the element in session-page matrix associated with the specific page in the given session.

The second data set is from a academic Website log files[10]. The data is based on a 2-week Web log file during April of 2002. After data preprocessing stage, the filtered data contains 13745 sessions and 683 pages. The entries in the usage data correspond to the amount of time (in seconds) spent on pages during a given session. For convenience, we refer this data as "CTI data".

5.2 Latent Factors Based on PLSA Model

We conduct experiments on the two data sets to extract the latent factors via identifying "dominant" page set. Here, we present the experimental results of the derived latent factors from two real data sets based on PLSA model respectively. Table 1 illustrates one example out of the derived factors extracted from the KDDCUP data set as well as the "dominant" page set, whose probabilities are over the predefined threshold, whereas Table 2 presents the example out of those from CTI data set. From these tables, it is easily concluded that the factor #6 in KDDCUP data set reflects the scenario involving in online shopping process, whereas the factor #13 stands for activity of searching postgraduate program information.

Table 1. Example of laten factor and its associated pages from KDDCUP

Factor	Page #	Content	Pgae #	Content
# 6 online shopping process	27	main/login2	50	account/past_orders
	32	main/registration	52	account/credit_info
	42	account/your_account	60	checkout/thankyou
	44	checkout/expresCheckout	64	account/create_credit
	45	checout/confirm_order	65	main/welcome
	47	account/address	66	account/edit_credit

Table 2. Example of laten factor and its associated pages from CTI

Factor	Page #	Content	Pgae #	Content
# 13 Postgrad-program	386	/News	588	/Prog/2002/Gradect2002
	575	/Programs	590	/Prog/2002/Gradis2002
	586	/Prog/2002/Gradcs2002	591	/Prog/2002/Gradmis2002
	587	/Prog/2002/Gradds2002	592	/Prog/2002/Gradse2002

5.3 Evaluation Metric of User Session Clusters and Web Recommendation

In order to evaluate the quality of clusters derived from PLSA-based approach, we adopt one specific metric, named the *Weighted Average Visit Percentage* (WAVP) [8]. This evaluation method is based on assessing each user profile individually according to the likelihood that a user session, which contains any pages in the session cluster, will include the rest pages in the cluster during the same session. Suppose T is one of session set within the evaluation set, and for s specific cluster C, let T_c denote a subset of T whose elements contain at least one page from C, the WAVP is computed as:

$$WAVP = \left(\sum_{t \in T_c} \frac{\vec{t} \bullet \vec{C}}{|T_c|} \right) \bigg/ \left(\sum_{p \in PF} wt(p, pf) \right)$$

On the other hand, we exploit a metric called *hit precision* [7] to measure the precision in the context of top-N recommendation. Given a user session in the test set, we extract the first j pages as an active user session to generate a top-N recommendation set via the procedure described in section 4. Since the recommendation set is in descending order, we then obtain the rank of $j+1$ page in the sorted recommendation list. Furthermore, for each rank $r > 0$, we sum the number of test data that exactly rank the rth as $Nb(r)$. Let $S(r) = \sum_{i=1}^{r} Nb(i)$, and $hitp = S(N)/|T|$, where $|T|$ represents the number of testing data in the whole test set. Thus, $hitp$ stands for the hit precision of Web recommendation.

In order to compare our approach with other existing methods, we implement a baseline method that is based on the clustering technique [11]. This method is to

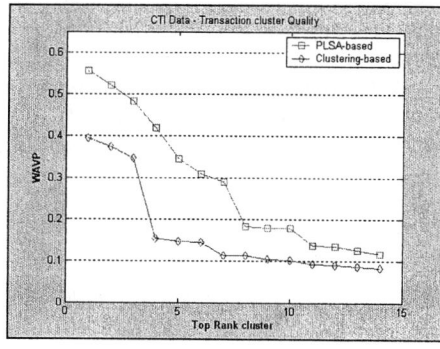 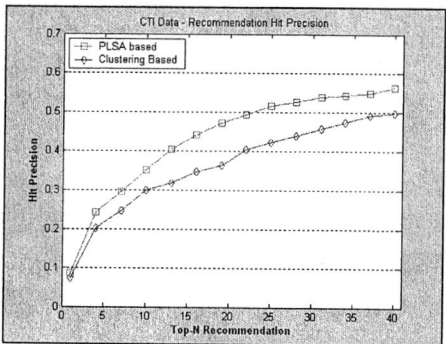

Fig. 2. *WAVP* comparison for CTI   **Fig. 3.** *Hitp* comparison for CTI

generate usage-based session clusters by performing k-means clustering process on usage data explicitly. Then, the cluster centroids are treated as the aggregated access patterns.

Figures 2 and 3 depict the comparison results of *WAVP* and *hitp* coefficient performed on CTI dataset using the two methods discussed above respectively. The results demonstrate that the proposed PLSA-based technique consistently overweighs standard clustering-based algorithm in terms of *WAVP* and *hit precision* parameter. In this scenario, it can be concluded that our approach is capable of making Web recommendation more accurately and effectively against the conventional method. In addition to recommendation, this approach is able to identify the hidden factors why such user sessions or Web pages are grouped together in same category.

6 Conclusion and Future Work

In this paper, we have developed a Web recommendation framework incorporating user profiling technique based on PLSA model. With the proposed probabilistic method, we can measure the co-occurrence activities (i.e. user sessions) in terms of probability estimations to capture the underlying relationships among Web users, pages as well as latent tasks. Analysis of the estimated probabilities leads to build up usage-based user profiles and identify the hidden factors associated with the corresponding interests or patterns as well. The discovered usage patterns in the forms of user profiles is used to make collaborative recommendation, in turn, lead to improve the precision and effectiveness of Web recommendation. We have demonstrated the efficiency of our technique through preliminary experiments performed on the real world datasets and comparisons with other existing work.

Our future work will focus on the following issues: we intend to identify the primitive task of active user and incorporate Web page categories to predict user potentially visited pages, and implement more experiments to validate the scalability of our approach.

References

1. R. Agarwal, C. Aggarwal and V. Prasad, *A Tree Projection Algorithm for Generation of Frequent Itemsets*, Journal of Parallel and Distributed Computing, 61 (1999), pp. 350-371.
2. R. Agrawal and R. Srikant, *Mining Sequential Patterns*, in P. S. Y. a. A. S. P. Chen, ed., *Proceedings of the International Conference on Data Engineering (ICDE)*, IEEE Computer Society Press, Taipei, Taiwan, 1995, pp. 3-14.
3. A. P. Dempster, N. M. Laird and D. B. Rubin, *Maximum likelihood from incomplete data via the EM algorithm*, Journal Royal Statist. Soc. B, 39 (1977), pp. 1-38.
4. E. Han, G. Karypis, V. Kumar and B. Mobasher, *Hypergraph Based Clustering in High-Dimensional Data Sets: A Summary of Results*, IEEE Data Engineering Bulletin, 21 (1998), pp. 15-22.
5. J. Herlocker, J. KONSTAN, A. BORCHERS and J. RIEDL, *An Algorithmic Framework for Performing Collaborative Filtering*, Proceedings of the 22nd ACM Conference on Researchand Development in Information Retrieval (SIGIR'99), Berkeley, CA., 1999.
6. J. L. Herlocker, J. A. Konstan, L. G. Terveen and J. T. Riedl, *Evaluating collaborative filtering recommender systems*, ACM Transactions on Information Systems (TOIS), 22 (2004), pp. 5 - 53.
7. X. Jin, Y. Zhou and B. Mobasher, *A Unified Approach to Personalization Based on Probabilistic Latent Semantic Models of Web Usage and Content*, Proceedings of the AAAI 2004 Workshop on Semantic Web Personalization (SWP'04), San Jose, 2004.
8. T. Joachims, D. Freitag and T. Mitchell, *Webwatcher: A tour guide for the world wide web*, The 15th International Joint Conference on Artificial Intelligence (ICJAI'97), Nagoya, Japan, 1997, pp. 770-777.
9. J. Konstan, B. Miller, D. Maltz, J. Herlocker, L. Gordon and J. Riedl, *Grouplens: Applying Collaborative Filtering to Usenet News*, Communications of the ACM, 40 (1997), pp. 77-87.
10. B. Mobasher, *Web Usage Mining and Personalization*, in M. P. Singh, ed., *Practical Handbook of Internet Computing*, CRC Press, 2004.
11. B. Mobasher, H. Dai, M. Nakagawa and T. Luo, *Discovery and Evaluation of Aggregate Usage Profiles for Web Personalization*, Data Mining and Knowledge Discovery, 6 (2002), pp. 61-82.
12. M. Perkowitz and O. Etzioni, *Adaptive Web Sites: Automatically Synthesizing Web Pages.*, Proceedings of the 15th National Conference on Artificial Intelligence, AAAI, Madison, WI, 1998, pp. 727-732.
13. G. Xu, Y. Zhang and X. Zhou, *A Latent Usage Approach for Clustering Web Transaction and Building User Profile*, The First International Conference on Advanced Data Mining and Applications (ADMA 2005), Springer, Wuhan, china, 2005, pp. 31-42.
14. G. Xu, Y. Zhang and X. Zhou, *Using Probabilistic Semantic Latent Analysis for Web Page Grouping*, 15th International Workshop on Research Issues on Data Engineering: Stream Data Mining and Applications (RIDE-SDMA'2005), Tokyo, Japan, 2005.

A Controlled Natural Language Layer for the Semantic Web

Rolf Schwitter

Centre for Language Technology, Macquarie University,
Sydney, NSW 2109, Australia
schwitt@ics.mq.edu.au

Abstract. In this paper, I will show how a controlled natural language can be used to describe knowledge for the Semantic Web and discuss the formal properties of this language. At the first glance, the proposed controlled natural language looks like full English and can therefore be easily written and understood by non-specialists. However, its built-in grammatical and lexical restrictions, which are enforced by an intelligent authoring tool, guarantee that the language can be directly translated into description logic programs, i.e. the intersection of an expressive description logic with function-free logic programs. The controlled natural language can be used to make assertional and terminological statements as well as to specify rules for reasoning with the resulting assertional and terminological knowledge.

1 Introduction

The Semantic Web is based on the idea of having well-defined data on the Web linked in such a way that this data can be processed by computers to solve well-defined problems by performing well-defined operations. So far, a lot of effort has been put into the design of various standards by the W3C to extend the current Web to achieve this goal [13], but little attention has been paid to the so-called people axis where the Semantic Web is tailored for people, and not only for computers [10]. Even worse and somehow incomprehensible, it has been suggested, since the early days of the Semantic Web, that people should make an extra effort to understand computers, instead of asking computers to understand people's language [3].

It is true that full natural language is difficult to process for computers because of its inherent ambiguity and because of its expressive power which turns out to be one of the biggest stumbling blocks when it comes to machine processability. However, well-defined subsets of natural language (i.e. controlled natural languages) with clear grammatical and lexical restrictions can be used to describe a piece of knowledge in an unambiguous and precise way, if the authors are supported by an intelligent authoring tool that guarantees the compliance of the input with the controlled language standard [6,15].

Such a controlled natural language needs to fulfill at least three requirements to serve as a useful interface layer to the Semantic Web. Firstly, the controlled language should allow for expressing assertional and terminological statements as well as rules which can then be used for making inferences over the assertional and terminological knowledge. Secondly, the controlled language should be easy to write and read for humans without the need to memorise the grammatical and lexical restrictions of the language. Thirdly, the expressive power of the controlled language should be equivalent to a subset of first-order logic, in the ideal case a combination of description logic and clausal logic. In this paper, I will lay out the design of a controlled natural language that meets these requirements.

The reminder of this paper is organised as follows: In Section 2, I will give an overview of current Semantic Web ontology languages, describe their most important constructors and discuss research results that point out that the layering of these languages results in a number of problems. In Section 3, I will show that description logic programs offer a way out of these problems and provide a sound formal basis for language layering and for the design of a controlled natural language. In Section 4, I will introduce the controlled natural language by example and demonstrate how assertional, terminological and conditional statements can be expressed in a straightforward way in this language. In Section 5, I will discuss how the writing process of this controlled natural language is supported by an intelligent authoring tool. In Section 6, I will show how the controlled natural language is translated into the underlying representation language and then subsequently processed by a forward chaining model generator. In Section 7, I will talk about different reasoning tasks and their rendering in controlled natural language. Finally, in Section 8, I will conclude and summarise the advantages of the presented approach.

2 Semantic Web Ontology Languages

The most important ontology languages designed for the Semantic Web are currently RDF Schema [4] and the Web Ontology Language OWL [14]. The strategy of the W3C is to layer these ontology languages on top of RDF using XML as common syntax for the exchange and processing of metadata. RDF itself is based on the idea of identifying things on the Web via URI references and expressing statements about resources in terms of simple properties and property values, whereas each statement consists of a subject, a predicate, and an object. RDF models statements as nodes (for subjects and objects) and arcs (for predicates) in a graph. The vocabulary of such a graph is the set of names which occur as the subject, predicate or object of any triple in the graph [11].

2.1 RDFS

RDFS is a light-weight ontology language that was developed as the lowest layer of the Semantic Web languages. RDFS extends RDF to include larger vocabularies with more semantic constraints [4]. The most basic constructors of RDFS are used for the organisation of these vocabularies in typed hierarchies: subclass and subproperty relationships, domain and range restrictions, and instances of classes. Apart from these basic constructors, full RDFS provides more powerful constructors that allow for meta-modelling and reification. It has been shown that these constructors lead to semantic problems, if the full power of RDFS is used to define the subsequent language layers and that the vocabulary needs to be strictly partitioned to be useful for these layers [2].

2.2 OWL

In comparison to RDFS, OWL adds more vocabulary for describing properties and classes: for example, specific relations between classes, cardinality, equality, richer typing of properties, characteristics of properties, and enumerated classes. OWL comes in three increasingly expressive layers that are designed for different groups of users: OWL Lite, OWL DL, and OWL Full [14]. If the RDFS vocabulary is strictly partitioned as required above, then a strict language inclusion relationship holds between RDFS, OWL Lite and OWL DL. However, no inclusion holds between OWL DL and OWL Full because of the lack of reification in OWL DL and OWL Lite. OWL Lite and OWL DL are syntactic variants of description logic languages, whereas OWL Full cannot be translated into a description logic language (since entailment in OWL Full is undecidable in the general case). Checking class membership and instance retrieval (ABox reasoning) is very expensive in most description logic reasoners and alternatives to description logic have been investigated. One way to solve this problem is to use a subset of description logic, translate it into function-free logic programs and rely on well-known deductive database techniques for reasoning [5].

3 Description Logic Programs

It has been argued that the intersection of description logic with logic programs can provide a straightforward computational pathway for reasoning and interoperability on the Semantic Web [7,8,9]. In particular, the description logic programming language L_0 has been identified as the maximal intersection of the expressive description logic $SHOIN$ (the language underlying OWL DL) and function-free logic programs (Datalog) [17]. This intersection does not allow arbitrary negation, disjunction in the head of rules or existential quantification. At first sight, this looks like a serious restriction, but it turns out that most of the ontologies developed for the Semantic Web fall under this fragment [17].

There exist restricted variants of OWL Lite and OWL DL (called OWL Lite⁻ and OWL DL⁻) that can be translated directly into Datalog. The RDFS subset of OWL Lite⁻ corresponds to the RDFS subset of OWL Lite and provides the same basic constructors (as introduced above). Apart from that OWL Lite⁻ allows for expressing complete class definitions, class and property equivalence, inverse and symmetric properties, transitive properties, and universal value restriction. OWL DL⁻ adds very limited expressivity to OWL Lite⁻ and allows for specifying classes based on the existence of particular property values and for restricting the first argument of the subclass property via existential value restriction or enumerated classes [5].

In contrast to the unrestricted versions of OWL Lite and OWL DL, the restricted variants stay within a well-established logic programming framework, allow the combination with rules languages and provide the basis for layering more expressive languages.

4 Towards a Controlled Natural Language Layer

Let us now work towards a controlled natural language that has the same formal properties as the description logic programming language L_0. The user should be able to express statements and rules directly in controlled natural language using simple approved syntactic constructions that are familiar from full English. The semantic correspondence between the controlled natural language and the formal language is then guaranteed by a bi-directional translation.

Instead of writing the following assertional statement in OWL:

```
<owl:Thing rdf:ID="MarkHoyer"/>

<owl:Thing rdf:about="#MarkHoyer">
   <rdf:type rdf:resource="#Professor"/>
</owl:Thing>
```

the user should be able to express the same information in controlled natural language:

```
Mark Hoyer is a professor.
```

Here the subject 'Mark Hoyer' identifies the resource of the statement, the predicate 'is' identifies the property of the statement and the object 'professor' identifies the value of the statement. The namespaces for these names are not displayed here but are handled by the authoring tool that supports the writing process of the controlled natural language (see Section 5).

4.1 Assertional Statements in Controlled Natural Language

Assertional statements in controlled natural language will most likely be used by non-specialists who want to annotate a Web page with machine-processable information. The syntactic structure for making assertional statements consists of simple subject-predicate-object patterns and well-defined variations of these patterns, for example:

```
Ben Vermeer is a senior lecturer.
Ben Vermeer teaches COMP248 and COMP349.
Sharon Long who is trained by Mark Hoyer is a student.
```

The first statement is a simple one and consists of a single subject-predicate-object pattern. The second statement is a compound one and can (in principle) be split up into two simple statements by distributing the verb (i.e. the property):

Ben Vermeer teaches COMP248. Ben Vermeer teaches COMP349.

The third statement is a complex one that uses a relative sentence plus a passive construction. This statement corresponds to the following two simple statements:

Sharon Long is a student. Mark Hoyer trains Sharon Long.

As we will see in the next section, the relation between the active construction *trains* and the passive construction *is trained by* can be specified via a terminological statement that uses the *inverse of* constructor.

4.2 Terminological Statements in Controlled Natural Language

Terminological statements will most probably be used by knowledge engineers in order to construct an ontology. Terminological statements speak about classes, properties, instances of classes, and various kinds of relationships between instances, classes and properties. For example, the following statement

The property 'teach' has the type 'object property'.

talks about the *'teach'* property and assigns the type *'object property'* to it. This defines the property *'teach'* as a binary relation between instances of classes. The same terminological statement can be written in an abbreviated form:

'teach' has the type 'object property'.

The property *'teach'* can be further restricted by specifying its range and domain, for example:

'teach' has the domain 'academic staff member'.
'teach' has the range 'student'.

This allows us to relate instances of the class *'academic staff member'* to instances of the class *'student'*. More elaborate constructors are available that allow us to specify additional restrictions on classes and properties, for example:

'teach' has the equivalent property 'give lessons to'.
'train' is a subproperty of 'teach'.
'train' is the inverse of 'be trained by'.
'professor' is a subclass of 'academic staff member'.
'senior lecturer' is a subclass of 'academic staff member'.
'PhD student' is a subclass of 'student'.
'COMP248' has the equivalent class 'Language Technology'.

This terminological knowledge is used by the model generator for reasoning purposes as well as by the authoring tool to guide the writing process of assertional statements.

4.3 Conditional Statements in Controlled Natural Language

As already mentioned, the description logic programming language L_0 allows us to work with rules. These rules have the form of conditional sentences and can be used to specify class and property hierarchies, to describe property characteristics, and to indicate property restrictions. Constructing these rules is the task of a software engineer and not of a layperson.

Here is a rule in controlled natural language that specifies the formal meaning of the subclass relationship:

```
If C1 is a subclass of C2 and C2 is a subclass of C3
   then C1 is a subclass of C3.
```

This rule guarantees, for example, that if 'assistant professor' is a subclass of 'professor' and 'professor' is a subclass of 'academic staff member', then 'assistant professor' is a subclass of 'academic staff member'. Additionally, we need a rule that makes sure that an individual takes the class hierarchy into account:

```
If C1 is a subclass of C2 and E has the type C1
   then E has the type C2.
```

This rule ensures, for example, that if 'professor' is a subclass of 'academic staff member' and 'Mark Hoyer' has the type 'professor', then 'Mark Hoyer' has the type 'academic staff member'.

The following rule is an example of a property characteristic and specifies the formal meaning of the inverse property:

```
If E has the property P1 whose value is V
   and the property P2 is the inverse of P1
   then V has P2 whose value is E.
```

This rule says, for example, that if 'Mark Hoyer' has the property 'train' whose value is 'Sharon Long' and the property 'be trained by' is the inverse of 'train', then 'Sharon Long' has the property 'be trained by' whose value is 'Mark Hoyer'.

The following terminological statements define that the inverse property is a symmetric property and that the subject position and object position of the inverse property are realised by individuals:

```
'inverse of' has the type 'symmetric property'.
'inverse of' has the domain 'object property'.
'inverse of' has the range 'object property'.
```

Additional rules are required here that specify the behavior of the symmetric property and restrict its domain and range.

5 Writing in Controlled Natural Language

Writing in controlled natural language is supported by a intelligent text editor. This editor can be used either to write an assertional specification, to construct an ontology or to build an axiomatic rule set. The user does not need to learn the restrictions of the controlled natural language explicitly, since he is guided by a look-ahead mechanism while the text is written [16].

For an assertional specification, the user first selects the ontologies he wants to work with via a menu. Thereby the text editor becomes "ontology-aware", guides the writing process via look-ahead categories and deals with namespaces. Let's imagine that the user wants to express the assertional statement:

```
Ben Vermeer teaches COMP248.
```

The editor first displays a look-ahead category for the subject position:

[ProperNoun]

After entering the name 'Ben Vermeer', the editor displays further look-ahead categories (partially) derived from the syntactic information available in the grammar and from the terminological knowledge:

[who — is — has — org:teaches — edu:teaches — ...]

The user can now select the approved words from a context menu. In our example, the user has to choose between 'org:teaches' and 'edu:teaches', since there are two properties available with the same name defined in different namespaces. The property 'teaches' takes either instances of the class *'unit'* or of the class *'student'* as its range. After selecting the suitable option, the look-ahead editor asks for the value of the statement.

6 Processing Controlled Natural Language

Specifications written in controlled natural language are translated via a bi-directional Definite Clause Grammar (DCG) into a set of range-restricted clauses that can be processed directly by a forward chaining model generator [12]. These clauses (as well as facts) are uniformally represented in an implicational rule format. The following DCG rules

```
sentence(C1-C2) -->
  proper_noun(N,S),
  verb_phrase(a,_,N,S,C1-C2),
  ['.'].

verb_phrase(a,-,N,S,C1-[true--->term(S,V,O)|C2]) -->
  verb(N,V),
  noun_phrase(a,N,O,C1-C2).
```

illustrate how the rule (= fact)

```
true ---> term(['Mark','Hoyer'],rdf:[type],[professor]).
```

is built up via unification while the sentence

```
Mark Hoyer is a professor.
```

is parsed. This is a very simple example but the grammar can deal with more complex sentences. For instance, the following sentence

```
Ben Vermeer who is a senior lecturer teaches COMP248 and COMP349.
```

consisting of a relative sentence and a coordinated constituent is translated into three rules (= facts):

```
true ---> term(['Ben','Vermeer'],org:[teach],['COMP248']).
true ---> term(['Ben','Vermeer'],org:[teach],['COMP349']).
true ---> term(['Ben','Vermeer'],rdf:[type],[senior, lecturer]).
```

A terminological statement such as

```
'teach' has the domain 'academic staff member'.
```

results in a similar translation:

```
true ---> term(org:[teach],rdfs:[domain],[academic,staff,member]).
```

And finally a conditional statement, such as

```
If P1 is a subproperty of P2 and P2 is a subproperty of P3
   then P1 is a subproperty of P3.
```

is translated into the following rule (clause):

```
term(P1,rdfs:[subPropertyOf],P2), term(P2,rdfs:[subPropertyOf],P3)
   ---> term(P1,rdfs:[subPropertyOf],P3).
```

The model generator takes such clauses as input and tries to generate a finite satisfying model (for details see [1]).

7 Reasoning in Controlled Natural Language

Given a number of assertional and terminological statements about the domain and a complete rule set that describes the meaning of the constructors, the model can be generated incrementally by performing forward chaining. Since the resulting model contains new information of the form:

```
term([Mark,Hoyer],rdf:[type],[academic,staff,member]).
```

It is straightforward to extract all entailed assertional statements and use the bi-directional DCG to render the output in controlled natural language, for example:

```
Mark Hoyer is an academic staff member.
Mark Hoyer gives lessons to Sharon Long.
Mark Hoyer teaches Sharon Long.
Mark Hoyer trains Sharon Long.
```

Not only can all entailed assertional statements be generated in this way, but also all terminological statements that are entailed, for example:

```
'Language Technology' has the type 'unit'.
'COMP248' has the type 'unit'.
'Language Technology' has the equivalent class 'COMP248'.
'give lessons to' has the range 'student'.
'give lessons on' has the range 'unit'.
'be trained by' is the inverse of 'train'.
```

The generated model can directly be used to answer questions in controlled natural language, for example:

```
Who trains Sharon Long?
Is Mark Hoyer an academic staff member?
Does Ben Vermeer teach Language Technology and COMP349?
```

Such questions are first translated into the implicational rule format (= negated clauses), then solution(s) are looked up in the model, and answers are generated in controlled natural language.

8 Conclusions

In this paper, I presented a controlled natural language for the Semantic Web that can be unambiguously translated into description logic programs, i.e. the intersection of an expressive description logic with function-free logic programs. In contrast to OWL, the controlled natural language cannot only be used for making assertional and terminological statements but also for describing axiomatic set of rules. Non-specialists can immediately use this language to annotate Web pages with machine-processable knowledge without the need to formally encode this information. Knowledge experts and software engineers can use this language to specify ontologies in domain-related terms and to define rules for reasoning. Note that the users of this controlled natural language do not need to remember the grammatical and lexical restrictions of the language, since these restrictions are enforced by an intelligent authoring tool that guides the writing process. In short: This controlled natural language does not require people to make an extra effort to understand computers as it is the case with formal languages designed for the Semantic Web, but asks computers to understand a well-defined subset of people's language.

Acknowledgments

The research reported here is supported by the Australian Research Council, Discovery Project DP0449928. The author would also like to thank Marc Tilbrook for working on the look-ahead text editor.

References

1. S. Abdennadher, F. Bry, N. Eisinger, T. Geisler. 1995. The Theorem Prover Satchmo: Strategies, Heuristics, and Applications (System Description). *Research Report PMS-FB-1995-3*, May, Institute for Informatics, Ludwig Maximilians University, Munich, Germany.
2. G. Antoniou and F. van Harmelen. 2004. *A Semantic Web Primer*. MIT Press.
3. T. Berners-Lee. 1998. What the Semantic Web isn't but can represent. <http://www.w3.org/DesignIssues/>, September 17.
4. D. Brickley, R. V. Guha. 2004. RDF Vocabulary Description Language 1.0: RDF Schema. *W3C Recommendation*, 10 February 2004.
5. J. de Bruijn, A. Polleres, R. Lara, D. Fensel. 2004. WSML Deliverable, D20.1 v0.2, OWL$^-$. *WSML Working Draft*, May 25.
6. N. E. Fuchs, U. Schwertel, R. Schwitter. 1999. Attempto Controlled English - Not Just Another Logic Specification Language. Vol. 1559 of *LNCS*, Springer.
7. B. N. Grosof, I. Horrocks, R. Volz, S. Decker. 2003. Description logic programs: Combining logic programs with description logic. In: *Proceedings of the Twelfth International World Wide Web Conference (WWW 2003)*, pp. 48–57.
8. I. Horrocks, P. F. Patel-Schneider. 2003. Three theses of representation in the semantic web. In: *Proceedings of the Twelfth International World Wide Web Conference (WWW 2003)*, pp. 39–47.
9. I. Horrocks, P. F. Patel-Schneider. 2004. A proposal for an OWL rules language. In: *Proceedings of the Thirteenth International World Wide Web Conference (WWW 2004)*, pp. 723-731.
10. M. Marchiori. 2004. Towards a People's Web: Metalog. In: *Proceedings of the IEEE/WIC/ACM International Conference on Web Intelligence (WI 2004)*, IEEE Press, pp. 320-326.
11. F. Manola and E. Miller. 2004. RDF Primer. *W3C Recommendation*, 10 February 2004.
12. R. Manthey and F. Bry. 1988. Satchmo: a theorem prover implemented in prolog. In: E. Lusk and R. Overbeek, (eds.), *Proceedings of CADE-88*, vol. 310 of LNCS, Springer, 415–434.
13. E. Miller, R. Swick, D. Brickley, B. McBride, J. Handler, G. Schreiber, D. Connolly. 2005. Semantic Web. *W3C, Technology and Society, Semantic Web Activity*, 19 August 2005.
14. M. K. Smith, C. Welty, D. L. Mc Guinness. 2004. OWL Web Ontology Language. Guide. *W3C Recommendation*, 10 February 2004.
15. R. Schwitter, A. Ljungberg, D. Hood. 2003. ECOLE – A Look-ahead Editor for a Controlled Language. In: *Controlled Translation, Proceedings of EAMT-CLAW03*, May 15-17, Dublin City University, Ireland, pp. 141–150.
16. R. Schwitter and M. Tilbrook. 2004. Controlled Natural Language meets the Semantic Web. In: A. Asudeh, C. Paris, S. Wan (eds.), *Proceedings of the Australasian Language Technology Workshop 2004*, Macquarie University, pp. 55-62.
17. R. Volz. 2004. Web Ontology Reasoning with Logic Databases. *PhD thesis*, AIFB, Karlsruhe.

GaXsearch: An XML Information Retrieval Mechanism Using Genetic Algorithms

K.G. Srinivasa[1], S. Sharath[2], K.R. Venugopal[1], and Lalit M. Patnaik[3]

[1] Department of Computer Science and Engineering,
University Visvesvaraya College of Engineering, Bangalore - 560001, India
kgsrinivas@msrit.edu, venugopalkr@gmail.com
[2] Infosys Technologies, Bangalore, India
sharathsrinivas@gmail.com
[3] Microprocessor Applications Laboratory, Indian Institute of Science, India
lalit@micro.iisc.ernet.in

Abstract. The XML technology, with its self-describing and extensible tags, is significantly contributing to the next generation semantic web. The present search techniques used for HTML and text documents are not efficient to retrieve relevant XML documents. In this paper, Genetic Algorithms are presented to learn about the tags, which are useful in indexing. The indices and relationship strength metric are used to extract fast and accurate semantically related elements in the XML documents. The Experiments are conducted on the DataBase systems and Logic Programming (DBLP) XML corpus and are evaluated for precision and recall. The proposed GaXsearch outperforms XSEarch [1] and XRank [2] with respect to accuracy and query execution time.

1 Introduction

Extensible Markup Language (XML) has been recognized as a standard for describing the data format and its meaning. The user defined tags associate semantics with the contents of XML documents. Hence, XML is a medium for interoperability over the Internet. With these advantages, the amount of data that is being published on the Web in the form of XML is growing enormously and many naive users find the need to search over large XML document collections. The keyword query is a search technique that does not require the users to know the structure of the underlying data. There is no need to learn complex query languages to discover knowledge. Thus, the keyword search over XML documents in the present context is of significant importance.

Genetic algorithms (GA) is an extremely effective technique for searching enormous, possibly unstructured solution spaces. The solutions are represented by *chromosomes* which are strings of *alleles*. The recombination of chromosomes creates new strings with alleles taken from the parent chromosomes. Since solutions are evolved by trying out answers and combining the answers that work best, the technique is particularly well-suited to solving problems where the solution space is large. The human search strategy which is efficient for small documents, is not viable when performing search over enormous amounts of data. Hence, making search engines cognizant of a search strategy using GA can help in fast and accurate search over large document collections.

Search engines for XML can be classified into two general categories: Database-oriented and information retrieval-oriented. In the database approach [3], the XML documents are decomposed and stored in relational database. However, query processing becomes expensive since, in many cases, an excessive number of joins is required to recover information from the fragmented data. A structured declarative query is supported by XQuery [4], which is analogous to SQL queries over relational databases. In Information Retrieval, GAs have been used in several ways [5] but in a different context. GAs have been used to modify user queries [6] and for automatic retrieval of keywords from documents. In [7], GA has been used for mining of HTML structures. The algorithm learns the important factors of HTML tags through a series of queries. Keyword search over XML documents is supported by XRANK [2] and XSEarch [1]. These keyword search techniques have elaborate ranking schemes. The simplicity of the search queries i.e., keywords make these techniques suitable for naive users. But, precision and recall values tend to suffer and the extensive ranking function employed acts as an overhead during query execution.

Contributions: We have explored the possibility of Retrieval and ranking of XML fragments based on keyword queries. GAs are used for learning tag information. A measure of distance metric between the keywords among the XML documents is proposed. Genetically learned tag information is used to retrieve semantically interconnected document fragments.

2   XML Data Model and Query Semantics

In this section, we briefly describe the XML data model and the keyword query semantics for search over XML documents.

Data Model: The XML document can be considered as a directed, node-labeled *data graph* $G = (X, E)$. Each node in X corresponds to an XML element in the document and is characterized by a unique *object identifier*, and a *label* that captures the semantics of the element. Leaf nodes are also associated with a sequence of keywords. E is the set of edges which define the relationships between nodes in X. The edge $(l, k) \in E$, if there exists a directed edge from node l to node k in G. The edge $(l, k) \in E$ also denotes that node l is the parent of node k in G. Node l is also the ancestor of node k if a sequence of directed edges from node l leads to node k. An example XML document tree is shown in Figure 1.

Query Semantics and Results: Let the XML document tree be called τ. Let x be an interior node in this tree. We say that x directly satisfies a search term k if x has a leaf child that contains the keyword k and x indirectly satisfies a keyword k if some descendent of x directly satisfies the search term k. A search query $q = \{k_1, k_2, ...k_m\}$ is satisfied by a node x iff x satisfies each of $k_1, k_2, ...k_m$

either directly or indirectly. For example, in the XML tree shown in Figure 2, *inproceedings(1)* satisfies the search term *Vipin* and the search term *Vipin 1979* but not the term *Vipin 1980*.

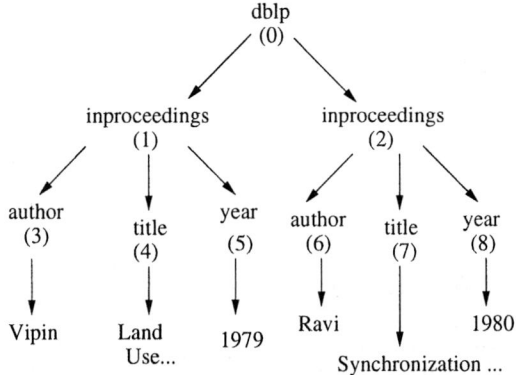

Fig. 1. Example XML Document Tree

We say that $R = \{x_1, x_2, ...x_l\}$ is a search result consisting of l nodes if,

1. Each node in the set $\{x_1, x_2, ...x_l\}$ satisfies at least one term from $\{k_1, k_2, ...k_m\}$.
2. $\{x_1, x_2, ...x_l\} \in \tau$.
3. The set of nodes $\{x_1, x_2, ...x_l\}$ shall be semantically relevant.

Semantically related nodes are nodes that appear in the same context; for example, an author and the title of his book having the *inproceedings* ancestor node.

3 Genetic Learning of Tags

XML documents include extensible tags for formatting the data. The tags represent the semantics of the data and thus can contribute to improve the accuracy of keyword search. Making use of GAs to learn the tag information has two advantages. First, when the same keyword appears more than once in the XML document with different semantics (different tags), the knowledge learnt from the GA is used to rank the search results. Hence, the results that are more relevant to the user queries are better ranked than the other results. Second, separate indices can be built for both the frequently and less frequently searched tags. Thus the indices are smaller in size and hence manageable.

Consider a training set with n documents. Let $q = \{q_1, q_2, ...q_m\}$ be a collection of typical user queries where q_i represents the ith query and m is the total number of queries. The chromosome is represented as $j = \{j_1, j_2, ...j_l\}$ where j_i denotes the weight of the tag i, l is the total number of distinct tags appearing in the document corpus which can be determined from the Document Type Definition (DTD) of the corpus. Thus, a tag weight is associated with each of the distinct tags appearing in the document collection. A real coded GA making use of selection, recombination and mutation operators is used for learning the tag information in GaXsearch, and is explained in Table 1.

Table 1. Genetic Algorithms for Learning Tab Information

Begin

1. Initialize the population P_i by assigning random tag weights to $j = \{j_1, j_2, ...j_l\}$.
2. for gen = 1 : maximum generation limit, do
   (a) Order the tags by their decreasing weights and select the top k tags. Let $S_{tag} = \{t_1, t_2, ...t_k\}$ represent the selected tags.
   (b) Evaluate fitness using Equation 1.
   (c) For the population P_i perform a selection with *stochastic universal sampling* as the selection operator.
   (d) Perform *intermediate recombination* on the selected individuals of the population P_i.
   (e) Perform mutation on the individuals of the population P_i.
3. Next.

End

The selection operator tries to improve the quality of the future generations by giving individuals with higher fitness, a greater probability of getting copied into the next generation. Here the assumption is that parents with higher fitness values generate better Offspring. The fitness function used in the GA is given by,

$$fitness = \alpha * (\sum_{i=1}^{N} \frac{freq(i, S_{tag})}{rank(i)}) + (1 - \alpha)N \qquad (1)$$

where N is the number of documents retrieved with a specific tag configuration, S_{tag} is the set of top k tags with highest tag weights. $freq(i, S_{tag})$ is the frequency of occurrence of the terms of the query $q = \{q_1, q_2, ...q_m\}$ within the tags in S_{tag} in the ith retrieved document. The retrieved documents are ranked according to the frequency of occurrence of the terms. The $rank(i)$ denotes the rank of the ith retrieved document provided the document is also classified as relevant by the user. α is a parameter that is used to the express the degree of user preference for accuracy of the search results or the total number of documents that are retrieved. The selection operator used in the algorithm is *stochastic universal sampling* and the recombination operator is intermediate recombination. A real valued mutation operation is also applied in the algorithm to explore new regions and make sure that good genetic material is never lost.

The result of the GA is the classification of tags as either frequently used or occasionally used. This precise categorization helps in maintaining separate indices for the information within the tags. The information within the frequently used tags is stored in an index called Most frequently used Index (MFI) and the information within the occasionally used tags is stored in an index called Less frequently used Index (LFI). The problem can be generalized to create many indices, prioritized according to the frequency of their usage.

4 Search Algorithm

The response to a search over an XML document is not the document in its entirety but only semantically related and relevant document fragments. In this section we discuss the identification schemes and semantic relationship between nodes in the XML tree. An algorithm to retrieve and rank the results is also discussed.

Identification Scheme: The granularity of search over XML documents is not at the document level, but at the node level in the XML document tree. Hence, an identification scheme for the nodes in the document tree is required. This is accomplished by encoding the position of each node in the tree as a data value before storing it in an index. Given the identification values of the nodes, the scheme must also be able to reconstruct the original XML tree. An identification scheme called Hierarchical Vector for Identification (hvi) is derived.

Let x be a node in the XML document tree τ. Then the Hierarchal Vector for Identification of x is given by, $hvi(x) = [\tau id(x)p(x)sj(p)]$, Here, τ_{id} is the unique identification number assigned to the XML document tree τ, and $p(x)$ is a vector which is recursively defined as, $p(x) = [p(parent(x))s_j(parent(p(x)))]$ and $s_j(p)$ denotes the jth sibling of the parent p. With this identification scheme, each node captures its absolute position within the whole document. The hvi of a node identifies itself and all its ancestors. The hvi of various nodes in two XML documents are shown in Figure 2(a) and 2(b).

Theorem 1: Let $\tau_1, \tau_2, ...\tau_n$ represent the XML document trees of the documents with identification numbers $(1, 2, 3,...n)$, where n is the number of documents. Then, $\{\exists x_i \in \{\tau_1, \tau_2, ...\tau_n\} \wedge \exists x_j \in \{\tau_1, \tau_2, ...\tau_n\}$, such that $x_i \neq x_j, hvi(x_i) \neq hvi(x_j)\}$, that is, there exist no two distinct nodes among all the XML documents in the collection, such that they have the same hvi.

Proof: Case 1: Consider that the two nodes x_i and x_j are present in different documents. i.e., $x_i \in \tau_i$ and $x_j \in \tau_j$ such that $\tau_i \neq \tau_j$. Since $\tau_i \neq \tau_j$, $\tau_{id}(x_i) \neq \tau_{id}(x_j)$ therefore, $hvi(x_i) \neq hvi(x_j)$.

Case 2: Consider that the two nodes x_i and x_j are present in the same document. that is, $\{x_i, x_j\} \in \tau$. Since both the nodes are in the same XML document $\tau_{id}(x_i) = \tau_{id}(x_j)$. But, since $x_i \neq x_j$ (from the statement of the theorem) and $\{x_i, x_j\} \in \tau$ there exist two possibilities $p(x_i) = p(x_j)$ or $p(x_i) \neq p(x_j)$. If $p(x_i) \neq p(x_j)$ then $hvi(x_i) \neq hvi(x_j)$. If $p(x_i) = p(x_j)$ then x_i and

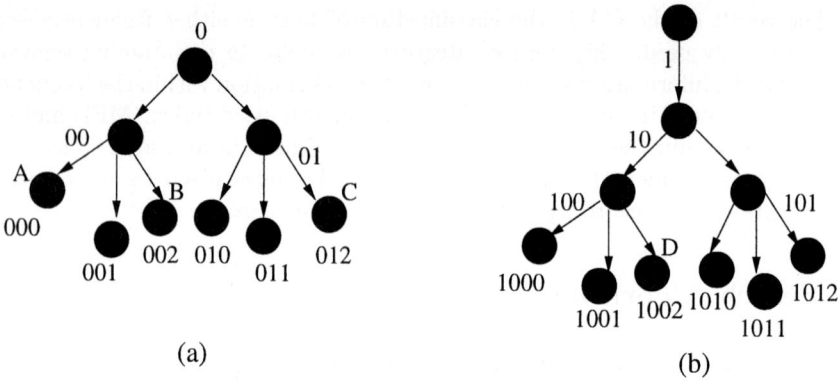

Fig. 2. Semantic Interconnection

x_j represent different siblings of the same parent; therefore $hvi(x_i) \neq hvi(x_j)$. Thus, each element of all the XML documents in the document collection is assigned a unique identifier. From Figure 2(a) and 2(b), it can be observed that there are no two nodes with the same hvi values. The same is true for a collection of n documents.

Relationship Strength: Let $hvi(x_i)$ and $hvi(x_j)$ represent the *hvi* of two distinct nodes x_i and x_j, existing in the XML document tree τ. The length of the longest common prefix(*lcp*) for both the *hvi* is denoted as $lcp(x_i, x_j)$. Consider two keywords k_1, k_2. The relationship strength between these two keywords, denoted as $RS(k_1, k_2)$ is defined as, $RS(k_1, k_2) = lcp(x_i, x_j)$, such that x_i directly satisfies k_1 and x_j directly satisfies k_2. The condition that the node should *directly satisfy* the keyword ensures that only those nodes satisfying the keyword and also having the longest length of their identification vectors (*hvi*), are selected while evaluating the Relationship Strength(RS). This is important because a node and all its ancestors satisfy a keyword, but a true measure of RS is represented only by the node which directly satisfies the keyword.

Consider two keywords k_1 and k_2 such that x_i directly satisfies k_1, x_j directly satisfies k_2. If $x_i \in \tau_i$ and $x_j \in \tau_j$ such that $\tau_i \neq \tau_j$, then $RS(k_1, k_2) = lcp(x_i, x_j) = 0$, since they do not share a common prefix. Thus a Relationship Strength value of zero indicates unrelated keywords (keywords in different documents). If $\tau_i = \tau_j$ and both the keywords are directly satisfied by the same node i.e., $x_i = x_j$, then $RS(k_1, k_2) = lcp(x_i, x_j) = length(hvi(x_i)) = RS_{max}$. Thus Relationship Strength values of two keywords can take integer values in the range of $[0 : RS_{max}]$ based on their occurrence and proximity in the XML document. The concept of Relationship Strength can be extended to a query $q = \{k_1, k_2, ...k_m\}$ consisting of m terms. For example, in the document trees in Figure 2(a) and 2(b), the nodes A and B have a common prefix of length two. Thus, they have a RS value of two; similarly nodes A and C have an RS value of one. Whereas, nodes A and D have an RS value zero since they belong to different document trees.

Semantic Interconnection: In terms of the XML document tree, two nodes are semantically interconnected if they share a common ancestor and this ancestor is not the root of the document tree. As an illustration, consider the XML document tree in Figure 1. The keywords *Vipin* and 1979 have a common ancestor, *inproceedings*(1). Thus, they are semantically interconnected. Whereas the keywords *Vipin* and 1980 have a common ancestor, *dblp*(0), which is the root of the document tree. Hence, the two keywords are not semantically connected.

Theorem 2: Two keywords k_1 and k_2 are semantically interconnected if and only if, $RS(k_1, k_2) > level_i + 1$, where $level_i$ is the first such level in the document tree where the degree of the node is greater than one.

Proof: Consider $level_i = 0$. The document tree is as shown in Figure 2(a). Since $level_i = 0$, $RS(k_1, k_2) > 1$. If $RS(k_1, k_2) > 1$, then there exist two nodes x_i, x_j that directly satisfy k_1, k_2 and with Hierarchical Vectors for Identification $hvi(x_i)$ and $hvi(x_j)$, such that $lcp(x_i, x_j) \geq 2$. Thus the two keywords have at least two common ancestors and of these only one can be the root of the document tree. The two keywords k_1, k_2 share at least one common ancestor apart from the root, hence they are Semantically Interconnected. For $level_i > 0$, the document tree is as shown in Figure 2(b).

For example, in the XML document tree in Figure 2(a), since $level_i = 0$, RS must be greater than one for the nodes to be semantically relevant. The nodes A and B have an RS value of two and are semantically relevant. Whereas, nodes A and C have an RS value of one, and hence are not semantically relevant. The RS can also be used to rank the semantically interconnected keywords. The semantically interconnected keywords with higher RS values are the more relevant results and hence are better ranked than those having lesser RS values. The architecture to compute semantically related results from the Most Frequently used Index (MFI) and Less Frequently used Index (LFI) is shown in Figure 3.

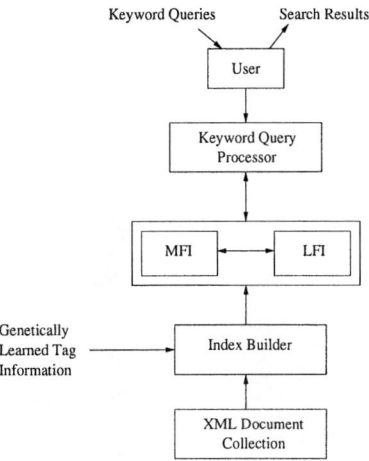

Fig. 3. Architecture of GaXsearch

The search algorithm first checks the length of the keyword query. If the query consists of a single term, a search over the MFI is performed. If the search is not successful, the algorithm continues search over the LFI. A failure to retrieve results from both MFI and LFI implies that the term is not found. The same technique is extended when searching with queries having more than one term. The only change is that, at each stage the semantic interconnection of the results is checked. Only semantically interconnected nodes are considered as the search results.

5 Performance Studies

In this section, we analyze the efficiency, and accuracy of GaXsearch, which is implemented in Java, via experiments on real data. The real data are XML files from the DBLP database [8]. The experiments were carried out on a Pentium IV, with a CPU of 2GHZ and 512 MB of RAM, running the Windows XP operating system.

Genetic Learning of Tags: The GA used in GaXsearch takes a small number of user queries and the documents adjudged as relevant by the user as inputs. The input queries are sampled randomly from a large collection of user queries. Weights are associated with tags and. The GA tries to explore all possible tag combinations and finds the best tag combination which satisfies the maximum number of queries. This is used to build the MFI and LFI. As the generation continues, the weights of the tags in the XML document are adjusted. The adjustments are such that maximum number of relevant results are retrieved. The DBLP XML database has a large number of distinct tags (about 30). The evolution of these tag weights with the generations of the GA is shown in Figure 4. Due to space constraints the evolution of all the tags cannot be represented; so we illustrate the evolution in the weights of only six tags: $<author>$, $<title>$, $<year>$, $<pages>$, $<booktitle>$, and $<url>$. The average tag weight represents the average of the weights assigned to all the tags in the document.

The weight of a tag, when compared to the average weight of all tags in the document, is a measure of the importance of the tag within the document.

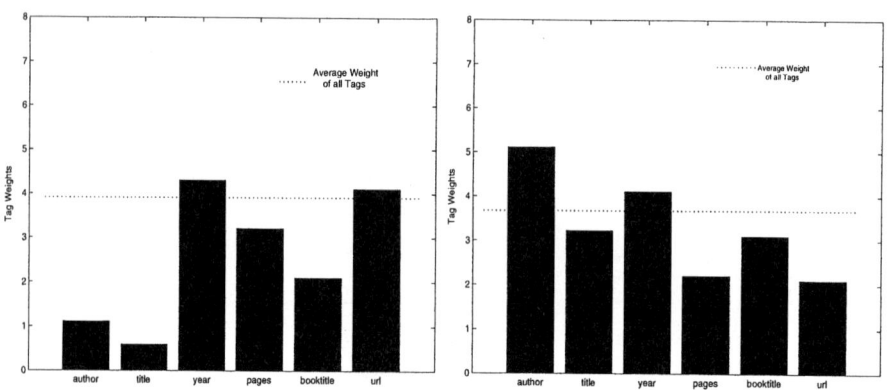

Fig. 4. (a): Tag weights at the start of GA; (b): Tag weights at termination

Figure 4(a) shows the random tag weights assigned to the tags at the start of GA. As the generations continue, the user queries are evaluated and the tag weights are adjusted so as to obtain maximum fitness values. The tag weights after the termination of GA are the real measure of the importance of tags, and are as shown in Figure 4(b). For the DBLP dataset, based on randomly sampled user queries, tags like $<author>$, $<title>$, $<year>$, and $<booktitle>$ are classified as important. The tags like $<pages>$, $<url>$, $<cite>$, and $<ee>$ failed to classify as important.

Query Performance: We now evaluate the performance of keyword queries over a subset of the DBLP XML corpus, using GaXsearch. Here, we compare the performances of a search using a normal index and a search using MFI and LFI. A normal index is one which stores all the XML tag information within a single flat index structure. For large XML collections, such an index becomes huge and is difficult to manage. In contrast, the MFI has an index size which is much smaller, but still is capable of satisfying a majority of the user queries. During experimentation, the normal index which we built from the subset of the DBLP XML document had a size of 51.8 MB. The same document was indexed into two separate partitions by making use of the knowledge learnt from GA. The two partitions, MFI and LFI, had sizes of 20.4 MB and 31.6 MB respectively. In addition to this, MFI was capable of satisfying about 70% of the user keyword queries and for the remaining 30% of the queries, search had to be continued with LFI.

The query execution time is shown in Figure 5(a) and Figure 5(b). The query execution time depends upon several factors like the number of terms in the search query, the desired number of search results and the frequency of occurrence of the keywords. We experimented with variations in all these factors and found that the frequency of occurrence of keywords was the main factor which decided the query execution time. Terms like *database*, *conference*, *technique* had very high frequency of occurrence in the DBLP document, and search queries involving these terms took longer to execute.

Precision and Recall: Precision of the search results is the proportion of the retrieved document fragments that are relevant. Relevance is the proportion of relevant document fragments that are retrieved. For precision and recall, we compare GaXsearch with XSEarch [1] and the naive results. Naive results are those which satisfy the search query, but are not semantically interconnected. All these techniques yield perfect recall i.e., all relevant documents are retrieved and the precision values vary. This is because of the factor that apart from the relevant results, some irrelevant results are also retrieved. The precision values of GaXsearch are found to be higher than those of XSEarch and naive approaches, when compared with the DBLP XML dataset. The small loss in precision occurs when the same keywords are present in both the MFI and LFI and the intention of the user is to retrieve information from the LFI. In such cases, the algorithm has already retrieved the results from the MFI, it will not continue search over the LFI. The possibility of such an event is quite rare, and hence GaXsearch manages to exhibit high precision values.

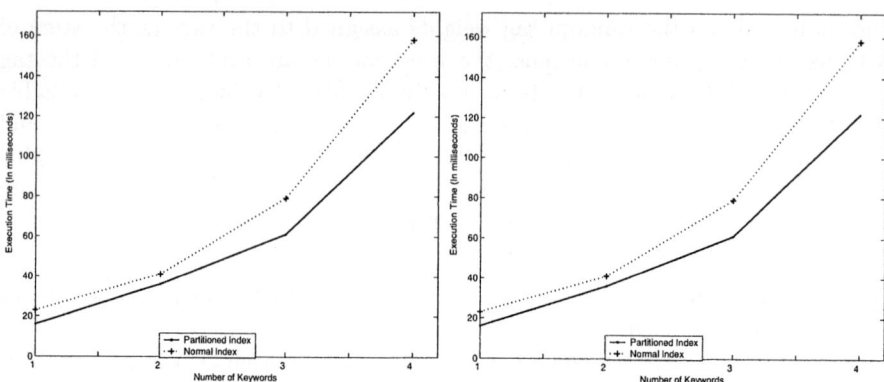

Fig. 5. (a): Low frequency of occurance of keywords; (b): High frequency of occurence of keywords

6 Conclusions

We have proposed a framework for information retrieval from XML documents that uses tag information to improve the retrieval performance. Genetic Algorithms, which are efficient for search in large problem spaces, are used to learn the significance of the tags. The notations for relationship strength and semantic relationship help in efficient retrieval of semantically interconnected results as well as ranking the search results based on the proximity of the keywords. Experiment on real data show that the GaXsearch is accurate and efficient.

References

1. Cohen S, Mamou J, Kanza Y, Sagiv Y, *XSEarch: A Semantic Search Engine for XML*, VLDB 2003, pp. 45-56.
2. L Guo, et. al., *XRANK: Ranked Keyword Search over XML Documents*, SIGMOD 2003.
3. R Luk, et. al., *A Survey of Search Engines for XML Documents*, SIGIR Workshop on XML and IR, 2000.
4. World Wide Web Consortium *XQUERY: A Query Language for XML W3c* Working Draft, http://www.w3.org/XML/Query.
5. J Yang and R R Korfhage, *Effects of Query Term Weights Modification in Annual Document Retrieval: A Study Based on a Genetic Algorithm* In Proceedings of the Second Symposium on Document Analysis and Information Retrieval, 1993, pp. 271-285.
6. J Yang, R R Korfhage, and E Rasmussen, *Query improvement in Information Retrieval using Genetic Algorithms: A Report on the Experiments of the TREC project*, Proceedings of the First Text Retrieval Conference (TREC-1), 1993, pp. 31-58.
7. S Kim, B T Zhang *Genetic Mining of HTML Structures for effective Web Document Retrieval*, Applied Intelligence, Vol. 18, 2003, pp. 243-256.
8. DBLP XML Records http://acm.org/ sigmoid/dblp/db/index.html, Feb 2001.

A New Approach on ρ to Decision Making Using Belief Functions Under Incomplete Information

Yuliang Fan and Peter Deer

School of Information and Communication Technology,
Griffith University, Gold Coast Campus,
PMB 50 Gold Coast Mail Centre, Queensland 9726, Australia
{y.fan, p.deer}@griffith.edu.au

Abstract. This paper discusses an expected utility approach on ρ to decision making under incomplete information using the belief function framework. In order to make rational decisions under incomplete information, some subjective assumptions often need to be made because of the interval representations of the belief functions. We assume that a decision maker may have some evidence from different sources about the value of ρ, and this evidence can also be represented by a belief function or can result in a unique consonant belief function that is constrained by the evidence over the same frame of discernment. We thus propose a novel approach based on the two-level reasoning Transferable Belief Model and calculate the expected utility value of ρ using pignistic probabilities transformed from the interval-based belief functions. The result can then be used to make a choice between overlapped expected value intervals. Our assumption is between the strongest assumption of a warranted point value of ρ and the weakest assumption of a uniform probability distribution for an unwarranted ρ.

1 Introduction

We are regularly confronted in our daily life with situations where we must make decisions based on incomplete information. Reasoning about actions and making decisions under uncertainty and scarce resources is also central to solving difficult problems in artificial intelligence. Traditionally, when uncertainty is represented by probabilities, the utility maximization approach can be used to make decisions under uncertainty. However, the traditional approach does not work when uncertainties cannot be represented by probabilities or when *a prior* probability distributions about the values of the quantity of interest are not available [1]. Dempster-Shafer theory of belief functions, developed by Glenn Shafer [2] based on earlier work of Arthur Dempster [3], provides an alternative approach to handling uncertainties in decision making problems. One of the main advantages over the probability theory is its ability to express partial or total ignorance. However, to make rational decisions under uncertainty is somewhat complicated in Dempster-Shafer theory because of its interval representation of belief. In order to compare different interval representations of different actions, one should collect more information until the intervals no longer overlap and the choice becomes clear. However, sometimes one is forced to choose without further information. Thus some subjective assumptions often need to be made in order to be able to compare the interval representations. Various authors have expressed preference for different assumptions under the belief function framework [5][7][8][9].

Strat [6] presented a different approach using expected value (utility) interval and introduced a parameter ρ to make a decision to the specified problem. However his approach needs a warranted point evaluation about the value of ρ in order to calculate the expected utility value of the problem. Based on Strat's approach, Schubert [10] proposed another approach, which applies a uniform probability distribution to ρ from the perspective of the nonspecificity of a set. Schubert argues that it is sufficient to assume a uniform probability distribution for ρ to be able to discern the most preferable choices. However, when two or more interval lengths of ρ are equal, it is often difficult to make a choice without having additional information.

In this paper, we illustrate Strat's approach of decision making when uncertainties are represented in terms of belief functions. In order to illustrate the process, we first discuss the examples under the probability framework and then change the situation and show how decisions can be made using belief functions. We then present an alternative approach based on interval-based belief functions using transferable belief model [9] to the problem proposed. We assume that if there is no warranted evidence available about the value of ρ, the decision maker may have some partial knowledge about the value of ρ. We can thus still make a rational decision under incomplete information.

In section 2 we discuss decision making problems under uncertainty using probabilities and belief functions with different assumptions. In Section 3 we show an alternative approach on ρ to the proposed problem. We show that a rational decision can be made under the partial knowledge assumption. A numerical example will be given in Section 4. Finally, conclusions are drawn in Section 5.

2 Related Work and Theory Elements

2.1 Decision Making Using Probabilities

Probability theory allows us to make rational decisions under uncertainty, i.e. when the uncertain states of nature are represented by probability distributions, and each possible state is assigned a value or utility, then the best decision is the one that yields the greatest expected utility.

Consider Strat's example of Carnival wheel [6] as follows:

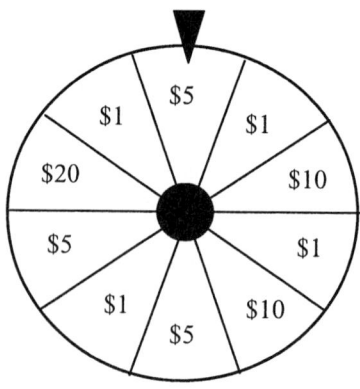

Fig. 1. Carnival wheel No.1

This wheel has ten equal sectors. Each sectors is labelled with a dollar amount as shown. Four sectors are labelled $1, three sectors $5, two $10, and one $20. The question is how much are you willing to pay to spin this wheel and receive the amount shown in the sector that stops at the top?

To answer the question, we need to calculate the expected utility value of the game. We assume that the monetary value here is directly proportional to utility because of the small dollar amount involved.

We have four possible outcomes ($1, $5, $10, $20) and the related uncertainties are represented by the following probability distribution:
$$P(\$1) = 0.4, \ P(\$5) = 0.3, \ P(\$10) = 0.2, \ \text{and} \ P(\$20) = 0.1.$$
The expected value $E(x)$ is:

$$E(x) = \sum_{x \in \theta} xP(x) = 0.4(\$1) + 0.3(\$5) + 0.2(\$10) + 0.1(\$20) = \$5.90$$

where θ is the set of possible outcomes. The result shows that one should not play the game by paying more than $5.90 fee.

2.2 Decision Making Using Belief Functions

Let us consider another situation where the information about sections is not complete as shown in Figure 2. [6]. Carnival wheel No.2 is divided into ten equal sectors. Four sectors are labelled $1, two sectors $5, two $10, and one $20. However, for one sector the label of dollar amount is hidden from the view. With a $5.90 fee, will you still play the game?

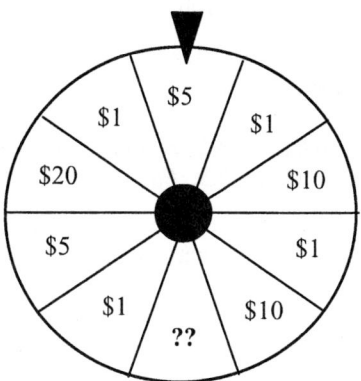

Fig. 2. Carnival wheel No.2

Since a complete prior probability distribution is not available in this situation, one has to use belief functions to represent uncertainties. Let θ denote a finite non-empty set called the *frame of discernment*, its power set, 2^θ, is the set of all subsets of propositions of interest. A function $m: 2^\theta \to [0,1]$ is called a *basic probability assignment* (bpa) if: $m(\emptyset) = 0; \ \sum_{A \subseteq \theta} m(A) = 1.$ where $\emptyset$ is the *empty set*, $m(A)$ represents the exact amount of belief committed to the proposition represented by the subset A of θ. Any subset A that satisfies $m(A) > 0$ is called a focal element of θ. A *belief function* is then a function Bel: $2^\theta \rightarrow [0,1]$, induced by m, defined as: $Bel(\phi) = 0$; $Bel(\theta) = 1$; $Bel(A) = \sum_{B \subseteq A \neq \phi} m(B)$, for all $A \subseteq \theta$. $Bel(A)$ represents the amount of support given to A. A *plausibility function* is a function $Pl: 2^\theta \rightarrow [0,1]$, defined as: $Pl(A) = \sum_{B \cap A \neq \phi} m(B) = 1 - Bel(\neg A)$, for all $A \subseteq \theta$. $Pl(A)$ represents the potential amount of support that could be given to A. There exists a belief interval between $Bel(A)$ and $Pl(A)$ which represents the uncertainty on the occurrence of event A as shown in Figure 3.

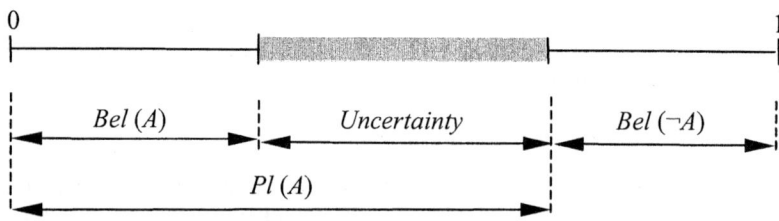

Fig. 3. Uncertainty in belief function representation

Consider the situation of carnival wheel in Figure 2., the bpa over the frame of discernment $\theta = \{\$1, \$5, \$10, \$20\}$ of the problem is:

$m(\$1) = 0.4$, $m(\$5) = 0.3$, $m(\$10) = 0.2$, $m(\$20) = 0.1$, and $m(\theta) = 0.1$.

The corresponding beliefs and plausibilities for the four outcomes are:

$Bel(\$1) = 0.4$, $Bel(\$5) = 0.2$, $Bel(\$10) = 0.2$, $Bel(\$20) = 0.1$,
$Pl(\$1) = 0.5$, $Pl(\$5) = 0.3$, $Pl(\$10) = 0.3$, $Pl(\$20) = 0.2$.

If one has to make a decision based on the expected value, then how to eliminate these belief intervals is of interest. Different assumptions were thus made trying to resolve these ambiguities.

Dubois and Prade [7] assume that the probabilities for the possible values of the hidden sector should be evenly distributed based on the generalized insufficient reason principle or equivalently the maximum entropy principle. The expected value under this assumption will be:

$$E(x) = \sum_{x \in \theta} xP(x) = 0.425(\$1) + 0.225(\$5) + 0.225(\$10) + 0.125(20) = \$6.30$$

Another assumption is that the probability distribution for the value of the hidden sector should be the same as the known distribution of the visible sector, hence the expected value will be $6.

Different with the above assumptions, Strat [6] introduces a concept called *expected value interval* (EVI), $[E_*, E^*]$, where

$$E_*(x) = \sum_{A_i \subseteq \theta} \inf(A_i) m(A_i)$$
$$E^*(x) = \sum_{A_i \subseteq \theta} \sup(A_i) m(A_i) \quad (2.1)$$

$\inf(A_i)$ and $\sup(A_i)$ are the smallest and largest element in the set $A_i \subseteq \theta$.

He then calculates a single value for the expected value for the outcomes of the game by resolving ambiguity in the problem through the choice of a parameter, ρ, that defines the probability that ambiguity will be resolved as favourable (to the decision maker) as possible. Which means $(1-\rho)$ represents the probability that ambiguity will be resolved as unfavourable as possible. He proves that by introducing this value the expected utility value of the problem will be:

$$E(x) = E_*(x) + \rho[E^*(x) - E_*(x)] \quad (2.2)$$

This distinguished point can then be used as the basis for comparison of several choices when their respective EVIs overlap.

For the Carnival wheel No.2, the expected value is $E(x) = E_* + \rho[E^* - E_*] = 5.50 + 1.90\rho$.

However, a warranted ρ is not always available. Schubert [10] thus assumes a uniform probability distribution for ρ derived from the perspective of nonspecificity of a set. For example, given two EVIs, $[E_{1*}, E_1^*]$ and $[E_{2*}, E_2^*]$, he tries to calculate the value of ρ_{12}:

$$\rho_{12} = \frac{E_{1*} - E_{2*}}{(E_2^* - E_{2*}) - (E_1^* - E_{1*})} \quad (2.3)$$

A choice will be considered preferable for the maximum interval length of ρ.

However, under the uniform probability distribution assumption, it is not always the case that one can differentiate between choices. For example, of choice1 [0.5, 0.6] and choice2 [0.4, 0.7], $\rho_{12} = 0.5$, they will be equally preferable because of the same length of ρ, which is not appropriate.

We propose an alternative ρ approach to the problem. Our assumption is between the strongest assumption of a warranted point value of ρ and the weakest assumption of a uniform probability distribution for an unwarranted ρ. We show that one can make rational decisions under the partial knowledge about ρ.

3 An Alternative Approach

We show an alternative approach that is different with the current approaches. We assume that the decision maker has some partial knowledge about ρ. We argue that this assumption is reasonable when the decision maker has no hard evidence about the point value of ρ, but still has some knowledge about the distribution of ρ, for example the percentile values, from some sources.

We apply the Transferable Belief Model (TBM) [9][11] to the continuous interval space to calculate the value of p. We can thus get the expected utility value to the problem and make the choice.

3.1 Credal and Pignistic Levels of TBM

Transferable Belief Model is an important milestone of Dempster-Shafer theory. It is the axiomatic justifications of Dempster-Shafer theory of belief functions. The TBM provides a model for the representation of quantified beliefs. It is based on the assumption that beliefs manifest themselves at two mental levels: the 'credal' level where beliefs are entertained and the 'pignistic' level where beliefs are used to make decisions.

At the credal level, Smets defends that beliefs are represented by belief functions. When a decision must be made, the beliefs held at the credal level induce a probability function at the pignistic level. This probability function is called the pignistic probability function.

In the TBM, the pignistic and credal levels are distinct which implies that the justification for using probability functions at the credal level does not hold anymore [12].

3.2 Pignistic Probability Transform

When a decision must be made, one uses the expected utility theory, which implies the need to construct a probability function on θ. This can be achieved by the so-called pignistic transformation [9][11] that transforms a belief function into a probability function, which is the pignistic probability and denoted by BetP.

The value of the pignistic probability is given by:

$$BetP(A) = \sum_{B \in \theta} \frac{|A \cap B|}{|B|} \frac{m(B)}{1 - m(\phi)} \qquad (3.1)$$

where |A| denotes the number of propositions in the set A.

It is justified that the function BetP so obtained is indeed a probability function [11]. Decisions are then achieved by computing the expected utilities of the acts using BetP as the probability function needed to compute the expectations.

3.3 Discounting

Sources of information may have different reliability. It could be interesting to have a way to weight the potentials by their reliability. Intuitively, to discount a bpa function by α means to move a total of mass α from the focal elements of θ to the whole space θ. Suppose an agent believes at level 1-α that the source is reliable, and α it is not, then the belief m^{α} on θ becomes:

$$Bel^{\alpha}(A) = (1-\alpha)Bel(A) \quad \forall A \subseteq \theta$$
$$Bel^{\alpha}(\theta) = \alpha + (1-\alpha)Bel(\theta) \qquad (3.2)$$

This is called the discounting by Shafer [2]. Note that combination and discounting do not commute, so the order with which they are applied is important.

Applying discounting to different sources can effectively avoid the possible conflict among different pieces of evidence.

3.4 Principle of Minimal Commitment

The principle of minimal commitment consists in selecting the least committed belief function in a set of equally justified belief functions. It is also at the core of the TBM. The principle formalizes the idea that one should never give more support than justified to any subset of θ.

Duibios and Prade [13] have proposed three solutions to order belief functions according to the 'strength' of belief they represent. The intuitive idea is that the smaller the focal elements, the stronger the beliefs. Let m_1 and m_2 be the two bpa's on θ,

pl – ordering. If $pl_1(A) > pl_2(A)$ for all $A \subseteq \theta$, we say that m_1 is pl–less committed than m_2.

q – ordering. If $q_1(A) > q_2(A)$ for all $A \subseteq \theta$, we say that m_1 is q–less committed than m_2.

s – ordering. If m_1 is a specialization of m_2, we say that m_1 is s–less committed than m_2.

where $pl(A)$ and $q(A)$ are the respective plausibility function and commonality function of A over θ.

In practice it is difficult to find both s–order and pl–order. Dubois et al [14] has proved that a q–least committed isopignistic belief function is a consonant belief function, its element is unique. The set of belief functions on θ which pignistic transformation equals to the constraints $BetP$ is called the set of isopignistic belief functions induced by the constraints. A belief function is called a consonant belief function when all its focal elements are nested.

3.5 Decision Making on Interval-Based Belief Functions

Suppose the decision maker has some information about ρ from more than two independent sources. We consider two quantified subjective data types possibly available in practice. The first type is the direct quantified belief (distribution) elicited from subjective assessments. These assessments are based on the interval values, which mean the basic probability assignments are given to different interval values based on unit interval [0, 1].

The second data type that we may get from subjective assessments is of percentile values. agents usually give assessments in the form of 5%, 50%, and 95% (or 5% and 95%) percentiles of a subjective distribution in many real problems. It is a meta-probability distribution. These meta-probabilities are also pignistic probabilities [15].

As the evidence combination of direct belief assessments is more obvious, we thus mainly focus on how to deal with assessments in forms of percentile values.

If there are more than two independent pieces of evidence about the value of ρ, we need to combine these evidences and get a combined distribution. However, it is often difficult to combine probability distributions directly using Bayesian theorem without having more information about *a priori* probability and *likelihood* functions [4]. While Dempster-Shafer theory provides an important mechanism (Dempster's rule of combination) for combining belief functions from independent sources. Thus we first need to build a unique consonant belief function distribution under the constraint of the available meta-probability distribution for each independent pieces of evidence based on the Principle of Minimal Commitment [14]. Then Dempster's rule of combination [2] can be used to calculate the combined belief functions.

If m_1 and m_2 are two basic probability assignments on the same frame of discernment θ, then the combined $m_1 \oplus m_2$ is a function $m_1 \oplus m_2: 2^\theta \to [0,1]$ such that

$$m_1 \oplus m_2(A) = \begin{cases} 0 & \text{if } A = \phi \\ \dfrac{1}{1-k} \sum_{X \cap Y = A} m_1(X) m_2(Y) & \text{if } \phi \neq A \subseteq \theta \end{cases} \quad (3.3)$$

where k is defined as

$$k = \sum_{X \cap Y = \phi} m_1(X) m_2(Y) \quad (3.4)$$

which measures the extent of conflict between the two evidences. The discussion on how to manage the possible conflicts encountered when applying Dempster's rule of combination to the evidence is out of the scope of this paper.

As we try to calculate the expected value of the p based on the combined belief functions of p. We again need to transform the beliefs at credal level into probabilities at pignistic level using *pignistic transformation* Equation (3.1), this *pignistic* probability distribution ($BetP(x)$) can then be used to make the decision.

For a traditional probability distribution, we calculate the expected values as follows:

$$\mu_x = \sum_{x \in X} x \cdot f(x) \text{ for the discrete probability distribution, and}$$

$$\mu_x = \int_{-\infty}^{\infty} x f(x) dx \text{ for the continuous probability distribution}$$

However for the interval-based belief functions, to calculate the expected utility, we need to build a probability density function (pdf) from the above $BetP(x)$.

Let $I(x, [a, b])$ be an indicator function, which is defined as:

$$I(x,[a,b]) = \begin{cases} 1 & \text{if } x \in [a,b] \\ 0 & \text{otherwise} \end{cases} \quad (3.5)$$

where $0 \leq a < b \leq 1$. The pignistic probability density function can thus be defined as:

$$\begin{aligned} BetP(x) = &\, BetP([a_1,b_1])I(x,[a_1,b_1])/(b_1 - a_1) + \\ &\, BetP([a_2,b_2])I(x,[a_2,b_2])/(b_2 - a_2) + \\ &\, \ldots + BetP([a_i,b_i])I(x,[a_i,b_i])/(b_i - a_i) \end{aligned} \quad (3.6)$$

We can then calculate the expected value as follows:

$$\mu_E = \int_0^1 xBetP(x)dx$$

$$= \int_0^1 x \sum_{i=1}^{n} BetP([a_i,b_i]) \frac{I(x,[a_i,b_i])}{(b_i-a_i)} dx$$

$$= \sum_{i=1}^{n} BetP([a_i,b_i]) \int_0^1 x \frac{I(x,[a_i,b_i])}{(b_i-a_i)} dx$$

$$= \sum_{i=1}^{n} BetP([a_i,b_i]) \int_{a_i}^{b_i} \frac{x}{(b_i-a_i)} dx \qquad (3.7)$$

$$= \sum_{i=1}^{n} BetP([a_i,b_i])(\frac{1}{b_i-a_i}) \int_{a_i}^{b_i} x dx$$

$$= \sum_{i=1}^{n} BetP([a_i,b_i]) \frac{(a_i+b_i)}{2}$$

where n is the number of focal sets.

Thus the expected utility value of the EVI to the problem becomes:

$$E(x) = E_* + \sum_{i=1}^{n} BetP([a_i,b_i]) \frac{(a_i+b_i)}{2} [E^* - E_*] \qquad (3.8)$$

which can be used to make decisions.

4 An Example

Let us consider an example with two choices whose expected utility intervals are as follows:

Choice 1: $[E_{1*}, E_1^*] = [0.5, 0.6]$,
Choice 2: $[E_{2*}, E_2^*] = [0.4, 0.7]$.

Suppose a warranted point value of ρ is not available, and the uniform probability distribution assumption is also unable to differentiate the two choices.

However, a decision maker has some partial knowledge about ρ from two sources, S1 and S2, i.e. some percentile values. Assume that the first percentile values on ρ from S1 based on [0, 1] are:

$$x_{5\%} = 0.5, \ x_{50\%} = 0.7, \ x_{95\%} = 0.8,$$

It means: $BetP([0, 0.5]) = 0.05$; $BetP([0.5, 0.7]) = 0.45$; $BetP([0.7, 0.8]) = 0.45$; $BetP([0.8, 1.0]) = 0.05$. We try to build the consonant belief distribution on [0, 1] that induces these *BetP*s.

A mass given to interval [a, b] is spread equally on the interval, so the divider for the mass becomes (b-a).

The mass given to the whole interval [0, 1] must be such that $BetP([0, 0.5]) = 0.05$. The mass given to [0, 1] is spread equally on the interval [0, 1] by pignistic transformation. Thus value $m([0, 1]) = 2 * 0.05 = 0.1$, which explains the 0.05 given to [0, 0.5] and is compatible with the other data.

Thus we get the first mass, and the $BetP([0, 0.5])$ is fully satisfied, and does not need to be considered again.

The next constraint to be satisfied is the $x_{95\%} = 0.8$. The [0.8, 1] interval already received a probability of $m([0, 1])*0.2 = 0.02$, we assume that the unexplained (0.05-0.02)=0.03 must be from the largest left intervals available, that is [0.5, 1.0], thus the we can calculate the $m[0.5, 1] = 0.03*0.5/0.2 = 0.075$.

Hence we have satisfied two constrains.

The next constraint is $BetP([0.5, 0.7]) = 0.45$. As we are looking for the consonant belief function, thus the next largest unexplained interval is [0.5, 0.8], it must be that it will justify the unclaimed mass left, which is $(0.45 - 0.02 - 0.03) = 0.4$, thus $m([0.5, 0.8]) = 0.4 * 0.3 / 0.2 = 0.60$.

The last constraint is $BetP([0.7, 0.8]) = 0.45$. It should justify all the masses allocated to the left unexplained intervals.

Therefore the result bpas are:

$m([0, 1]) = 0.1$, $m[0.5, 1] = 0.075$, $m([0.5, 0.8]) = 0.60$, $m([0.7, 0.8]) = 0.225$.

It is a q–least committed belief function, as we put the masses as high as possible (on the largest possible intervals), the proof for the method has been justified by Dubois et al [14][16].

Suppose the decision maker gets the second percentile values from S2:

$$x_{5\%} = 0.4, \quad x_{50\%} = 0.6, \quad x_{95\%} = 0.9,$$

In the same way we can obtain the q–least committed consonant belief function which adequately represents the belief induced by these constraints.

The results are:

$m([0, 1]) = 0.125$, $m[0.4, 1] = 0.225$, $m([0.4, 0.9]) = 0.50$, $m([0.4, 0.6]) = 0.150$.

We try to combine these two pieces evidence.

Suppose the decision maker assigns the level of 0.8 to S1, and fully trust S2.

According to the Equation (3.2) the discounted bpas for each pieces of evidence are:

$m_1([0, 1]) = 0.28$, $m_1[0.5, 1] = 0.06$, $m_1([0.5, 0.8]) = 0.48$, $m_1([0.7, 0.8]) = 0.18$.
$m_2([0, 1]) = 0.125$, $m_2[0.4, 1] = 0.225$, $m_2([0.4, 0.9]) = 0.50$, $m_2([0.4, 0.6]) = 0.150$.

By using Dempster's rule of combination (Equation 3.3 and 3.4), we get the combined belief distribution:

{([0, 1], 0.036), ([0.4, 1], 0.0647), ([0.5, 1], 0.0216), ([0.4, 0.9], 0.1439), ([0.5, 0.9], 0.0308), ([0.5, 0.8], 0.4193), ([0.4, 0.6], 0.0432), ([0.7, 0.8], 0.1572), ([0.5, 0.6], 0.0832)}.

By using pignistic transformation (Equation 3.1), we get a new $BetP$ distribution transformed from the above combined belief distribution:

$BetP([0.5, 0.6]) = 0.2998$, $BetP([0.7, 0.8]) = 0.3522$, $BetP([0, 0.5]) = 0.0792$,
$BetP([0.6, 0.7]) = 0.1950$, $BetP([0.8, 1.0]) = 0.0739$.

Based on the above pignistic probability distribution, we can thus calculate the expected value of ρ using Equation (3.7) to make the decision.

$$\rho_E = \sum_{i=1}^{n} BetP([a_i, b_i]) \frac{(a_i + b_i)}{2}$$

$$= BetP([0.5, 0.6]) \times (0.5+0.6)/2 + BetP([0.7, 0.8]) \times (0.7+0.8)/2$$
$$+ BetP([0, 0.5]) \times (0+0.5)/2 + BetP([0.6, 0.7]) \times (0.6+0.7)/2$$
$$+ BetP([0.8, 0.9]) \times (0.8+0.9)/2$$
$$= 0.6384$$

Thus,

$E_1(x) = E_{1*} + \rho_E [E_1^* - E_{1*}] = 0.5638$,
$E_2(x) = E_{2*} + \rho_E [E_2^* - E_{2*}] = 0.5915$.

Therefore we prefer Choice 2 to Choice 1 based on the partial knowledge about ρ.

5 Conclusion

We have demonstrated the decision making problems under incomplete information using the belief function framework. To make a rational decision under the interval representation of beliefs, some subjective assumptions are needed to order the different belief intervals especially when they are overlapped. Between the strongest assumption of point value and the weakest possible assumption of a uniform probability distribution about ρ, we assume that a decision maker may have some partial knowledge about ρ. We show how the transferable belief model can be used on the interval-based belief functions, and can thus calculate the expected value of ρ by reasoning at two different levels under incomplete information. Based on this value, we can compute the distinguished point of the EVIs of the specified problem and make the decision. We argue that by using this approach we can avoid the possible decision difficulties under the uniform probability distribution assumption and make decisions without the need for a warranted value of ρ.

Acknowledgement

The authors would like to thank Philippe Smets for his great help and also acknowledge the support from the School of Information and Communication Technology of Griffith University.

References

[1] Dubois, D. and Prade, H. (1994), "Possibility theory and data fusion in poorly informed environments," *Control and Engineering Practice*, vol. 2, no. 5, pp. 811-823.
[2] Shafer, G.. (1976), *A Mathematical Theory of Evidence*, Princeton University Press, Princeton, NJ.
[3] Dempster, A. P. (1968), "A generalisation of Bayesian inference (with discussion)," *Journals of the Royal Statistical Society B*, vol. 30, pp. 205-232.

[4] Clemen, R. T. and Winkler, R. L. (1999), "Combining Probability Distributions From Experts in Risk Analysis," *Risk Analysis*, vol. 19, no. 2, pp. 187-203.
[5] Lesh, S. A. (1986), *An evidential theory approach to judgement-based decision making*, PhD thesis, Dept. of Forestry and Environmental Studies, Duke University.
[6] Strat, T. M. (1994), "Decision Analysis Using Belief Functions," *Advances in the Dempster-Shafer Theory of Evidence*, edited by R.R. Yager, M. Fedrizzi, and J. Kacprzyk, John Wiley and Sons. New York, NY.
[7] Dubois, D. and Prade, H. (1982), "On several representations of an uncertain body of evidence," *Fuzzy Information and Decision Process*, edited by M. M. Gupta and E. Sanchez, North-Holland, Amsterdam, pp. 167-181.
[8] Nguyen, H. T. and Walker, E. A. (1994), "On Decision Making Using Belief Functions," *Advances in the Dempster-Shafer Theory of Evidence*, edited by R.R. Yager, M. Fedrizzi, and J. Kacprzyk, John Wiley and Sons. New York, NY.
[9] Smets, P. and Kennes, R. (1994), "The transferable belief model," *Artificial Intelligence*, vol. 66, pp. 191-234.
[10] Schubert, J. (1995), "On ρ in a Decision-Theoretic Apparatus of Dempster-Shafer Theory," *International Journal of Approximate Reasoning*, vol. 13, pp. 185-200.
[11] Smets, P. (2002), "Decision Making in a Context where Uncertainty is Represented by Belief Functions," *Belief Functions in Business Decisions*, edited by R. Srivastava and T. J. Mock, Physica-Verlag, Heidelberg, Germany, pp. 17-61.
[12] Dubois, D., Prade, H. and Smets, P. (1996), "Representing partial ignorance," *IEEE System Machine and Cybernetic*, vol. 26, pp. 361-377.
[13] Dubois, D. and Prade, H. (1986), "The principle of minimum specificity as a basis for evidential reasoning," *IPMU*, pp. 75-84.
[14] Dubois, D., Prade, H., and Smets, P. (2001), "New semantics for quantitative possibility theory." *Proceedings of the Second International Symposium on Imprecise Probabilities and Their Applications*, Ithaca, NY, USA. pp. 152-161.
[15] Smets, P. (1998), "Probability, Possibility, Belief: Which and Where," *Handbook of Defeasible Reasoning and Uncertainty Management Systems*. Gabbay D. and Smets P. (Series eds). P. Smets (Vol. eds.), vol. 1, Quantified Representation of Uncertainty and Imprecision, Kluwer, Doordrecht, pp. 1-24.
[16] Dubois, D. and Prade, H. and Smets, P. (2003), "A definition of subjective possibility," *Operations Research and Decisions*, vol. 4, pp. 7-22.

A Hybrid Recommendation Approach for One-and-Only Items

Xuetao Guo[1], Guangquan Zhang[1], Eng Chew[1], and Steve Burdon[2]

[1] Faculty of Information Technology, University of Technology Sydney,
PO Box 123 Broadway, NSW 2007, Australia
{xguo, zhangg, engchew}@it.uts.edu.au
[2] Faculty of Business, University of Technology Sydney,
PO Box 123 Broadway, NSW 2007, Australia
steve.burdon@uts.edu.au

Abstract. Many mechanisms have been developed to deliver only relevant information to the web users and prevent information overload. The most popular recent developments in the e-commerce domain are the user-preference based personalization and recommendation techniques. However, the existing techniques have a major drawback – poor accuracy of recommendation on one-and-only items – because most of them do not understand the item's semantic features and attributes. Thus, in this study, we propose a novel Semantic Product Relevance model and its attendant personalized recommendation approach to assist Export business selecting the right international trade exhibitions for market promotion. A recommender system, called Smart Trade Exhibition Finder (STEF), is developed to tailor the relevant trade exhibition information to each particular business user. STEF reduces significantly the time, cost and risk faced by exporters in selecting, entering and developing international markets. In particular, the proposed model can be used to overcome the drawback of existing recommendation techniques.

1 Introduction

The rapid growth of web information results in the difficulty of locating relevant information from the seas of information, much of which is irrelevant for users. This difficulty in locating relevant information is commonly referred to as information overload. In order to protect web users from the problem of information overload, many mechanisms have been developed to assist web users to separate relevant information from those irrelevant ones. As the Internet has become an increasingly critical information sources, many websites attempt to develop unique support features for users to encourage repeat visits. One of these features is personalization, which may deliver the adaptive services to individual user. Recently IDC, International Data Company (http://www.idc.com), forecasts 212% annual growth in personalization applications over the next decade [3]. With personalized services and products becoming more easily accessible on the Internet, the interest on personalization is accordingly growing. Many practitioners and researchers are investigating into various issues of personalization. Indeed, the Fifth Annual Accenture eGovernment study

[1] indicates that personalization in E-government is emerging as one of the five key trends. The personalization of E-government services can be seen as an evolution of the intentions-based approach. Current personalization efforts engage in greater segmentation. So far, some evidence of personalization in governments' approaches to online service has been found. However, implementation appears to be in its infancy.

A recommender system is one of the most popular applications of personalization techniques and it refers to the systems which aim at filtering out the uninterested items (or predicting the interested ones) automatically on behalf of the users according to their personal preferences. In the past ten years, recommender systems have been used in various applications. However, recommender system has received less attention in E-government service applications.

In this study, we propose the semantic product relevance model and the attendant personalized recommendation approach to help the businesses choose the right trade exhibitions. As a result, a recommender system prototype, named Smart Trade Exhibition Finder (STEF), is developed to tailor the relevant trade exhibition information to each particular business user's preferences. STEF helps organizations find the most appropriate trade exhibition, conference, industry or government business trade delegations to meet their specific needs. It, therefore, helps exporters reduce the time, cost and risk involved in selecting, entering and developing international markets. Also, the outcome of this study is expected to significantly overcome the drawback of existing recommendation techniques.

2 Related Works

Personalization is experiencing widespread adoption in the commercial areas such as E-commerce and web development. Three types of personalization service applications have been identified:

- *Adaptive websites* [10] modify the content and structure of a site to suit an individual user. Designing a complex website so that it readily yields its information is a difficult task. Kohrs and Merialdo [8] presented a method to create the adaptive websites by Collaborative Filtering. Zhu et al. [17] proposed a method to construct the link hierarchy of a website using web log file.
- *Personalized search* [11] tailors the search results to the individual user's needs. In the area of personalized web search, Liu et al. [9] proposed a novel technique to learn user profiles from users' search histories. Then the user profiles are used to improve retrieval effectiveness in web search. Pretschner and Gauch [12] presented an ontology-based personalized search approach.
- *Peer-to-peer recommender system* [6] has the capacity to guarantee the delivery of the right information to the right user at the right time. Through peer-to-peer recommendation, customers automatically receive different levels of treatment based on past behavior. From this perspective, personalization can have the same meaning as recommendation systems. Recommender systems provide personalized recommendations based on users' preferences.

Various approaches for recommender systems have been developed. Previous research efforts show that most existing recommender systems adopt two types of techniques: *content-based approach* and *collaborative filtering* (CF) approach [15]. A content-based approach relies mainly on content and relevant profiles to offer recommendations. CF approach offers recommendation based on the similarity of groups users. In the content-based approach, it recommends web objects that are similar to what the user has been interested in the past. In CF-based approach, one identifies users whose tastes are similar to those of the given user and recommends items they have liked. CF has been known to be the most popular recommendation technique. It has been used in a number of different applications such as recommending web pages, movies, articles and products. User-based and item-based techniques have been identified in CF research community. A major problem with user-based approach is the lack of scalability and sparsity. The complexity of computation increases linearly with the user and rating number. In contrast, item-based CF is used to deal with the scalability problems in the traditional CF algorithms. Item-based CF avoids the bottleneck in user-user computations by first considering the relationships among items. Item-based CF has been shown to achieve prediction accuracies that are comparable to or even better than user-based CF algorithms [15]. Item-based CF algorithms still suffer from the problems associated with data sparsity, and they still lack the ability to provide recommendations or predictions for new or recently added items.

The content-based and CF-based recommendation techniques have strengths and weaknesses. A common thread in recommender system research is the need to combine recommendation techniques to achieve peak performance. The combination of different techniques is called hybrid approach. Many researchers have chosen to combine content-based and CF techniques in different ways. For example, Fab proposed by Balabanovic and Shoham [4] is the first hybrid recommender system using meta-level hybrid technique, which uses the model generated by one as the input for another. In Fab, user-specific selection agents perform content-based filtering to maintain a term vector model that describes the user's interest. Collection agents use the models from all users to gather new pages from the web. Condliff et al. [7] use a two-stage Bayesian mixed-effects scheme: a content-based naïve Bayes classifier is built for each user and then the parameters of the classifiers are linked across different users using regression. GroupLens proposed by Sarwar et al. [16] employs feature augmentation hybrid technique to improve email filtering with simple agent implementation. This hybrid technique implements a set of filterbots using specific criteria, such as the number of spelling errors and the size of included messages. Then these bots contributes ratings to the database of rating used by the CF part of the recommender system. Feature augmentation hybrid systems include two recommenders and the first one has an influence over the second. In the feature augmentation hybrid, the features used by the second recommender include the output of the first one. However, the data representations of the existing hybrid types are usually are only suitable for resolving their specific problems. There are a number of areas where the space of hybrid recommendation is not fully explored.

3 Recommendation Approach and Implementation

3.1 Problem Description

International trade fairs, conferences and trade missions have become a relatively important promotion tool for exporters and industrial firms. It is vital that the government help companies choose the right vehicle. The individual needs will vary between making contact with suppliers, potential suppliers, customers and alliance partners and ascertaining the best match of these needs to potential channels. For instance, the Australian Trade Commission (Austrade) is the Australian government agency that helps Australian companies develop international markets. Organizing trade exhibition participation and helping more Australian companies succeed in export are the important tasks conducted by Austrade (http://www.austrade.gov.au). However, Austrade can only offer the simple database match functions from their online service websites. On the other hand, although recommender system techniques have gained successful applications in E-commerce domain, most of them do not understand the item's semantic features and attributes. This can result in a poor accuracy of prediction. In addition, without the benefit of deeper semantic knowledge about the underlying domain, a recommendation system can not handle heterogeneous and complex objects based on their properties and relationships, nor can these systems possess the ability to automatically explain or reason about the user models or user recommendations [2]. For instance, a trade exhibition event is a one-and-only item and it may include many sections, for example, China's 95th Canton Fair, includes sections like clothes, manufactured goods, food and much more. Each user has special desires about the section of trade exhibition when he/she provides a rating of interest or preference.

3.2 Semantic Product Relevance Model

Semantic information about an item consists of the attributes, the item's relationship to other items, and other meta-information. Semantic similarity among objects and entity classes has been a considerable study in the past few years. Usually, attributes describe different types of distinguishing features of a class. These attributes provide the opportunity to capture details about classes, and their values describe the properties of individual objects (i.e. instance of a class) [13]. For example, some of attributes of a trade exhibition are time, city, product and fee. On the other hand, product taxonomy plays an important role in presenting online information and may affect the results. Product taxonomy is used for identifying similar products and grouping them together, by specifying the level of aggregation provided by the marketers or domain experts.

In this study, by combining the semantic similarity and product taxonomy approaches, we propose the semantic product relevance (SPR) model to conduct the semantic-based product relevance analysis. Fig. 1 shows an example of the SPR model. The SPR model allows domain experts to provide a weight of product relevance by a defined product relevance degree. In the approach, we represent a particular product's relevance to product category by a hierarchical concept tree [5] with weights associated with each concept, thereby reflecting relevance of concepts to offer suggestions. The SPR model provides more expressive semantics than the most existing recommendation approaches. For example, a cosmetic exporter wants to find trade fair information in relevance to cosmetics. Domain experts can define a range of trade fairs related to it according to product taxonomy, such as, health, chemical, beauty, fashion, and gift. The scale is presented from 1 (lowest relevance level) to 5 (highest relevance level), and any missing rating can be presented as 0. The scales 3, 4, 5, 3 and 3, shown in Figure 1, denote the respective relevance degrees with product category – health, chemical, beauty, fashion, and gift.

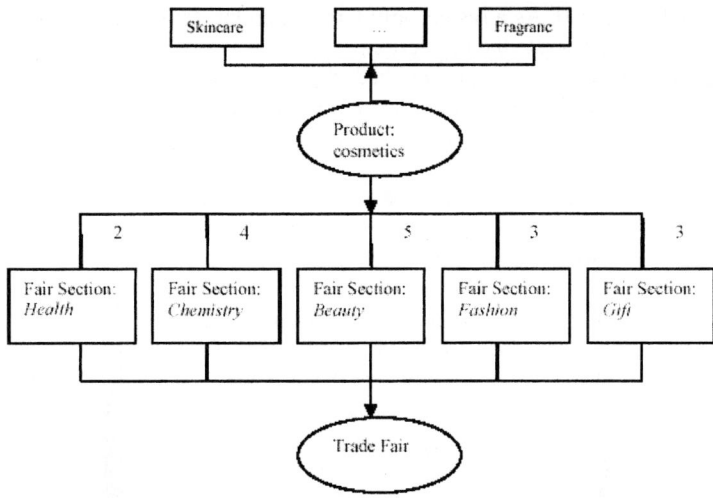

Fig. 1. An example of semantic product relevance model

3.3 Recommendation Generation and Implementation

A recommender system suggests the relevant items to each particular user. The items can be products or information according to domain of system application. For example, the items refer to the products in the e-commerce recommendation, and the websites in the web navigation recommendation.

Our approach looks into the set of items and computes how similar the items are to target item i and then selects k most similar items $\{i_1, i_2, i_3, ...i_k\}$. The recommendation is generated through the following steps. The first step computes the similarity of two items i_p and i_q, here $p, q \in N$. Many measures can be used to compute the similarity between items. In this step, the correlation-based similarity measure is employed in order to take into account the variances in user ratings. We denote the rating similarity between two items i_p and i_q as $Isim(i_p, i_q)$. The second step performs semantic similarity analysis on target product and product category. There are a list of M products $J = \{j_1, j_2, ..., j_M\}$ and N items $I = \{i_1, i_2,...,i_N\}$. Each matrix $a=m \times n$ present the semantic relevance scale of the mth product with the nth item. The semantic similarity measure $SemSim(i_p, i_q)$, for two items i_p and i_q, is computed using the standard vector-based cosine similarity. In the third step, we integrate the two similarity measures to get $TotalSim(i_p, i_q)$ as their linear combination, the formula is shown as follow:

$$TotalSim(i_p, i_q) = \beta * I_{sim}(i_p, i_q) + (1-\beta) * SemSim(i_p, i_q) \quad (1)$$

Here, β is a semantic combination parameter specifying the weight of semantic similarity in the integrated measure. We choose the proper value by performing sensitivity analysis for particular data sets in our experimental section. In the final step, we select a set of k most similar items to the target item and generate a predicted value for the target item. In order to compute predicted ratings value and generate recommendations, we use the weighted sum approach. If user does not express any ratings on item

i, then we define $r_{ai} = 0$. As a result, only k most similar items (k nearest neighbors of item i_k) are used to generate the prediction.

As a data collect interface and test bed, the recommender system STEF is implemented in Microsoft Visual Studio 6.0 environment with ASP programming language. The example of system interface is showed in Fig. 2.

Fig. 2. An example of system interface

4 Experiments and Results

A recommender system STEF has been developed as the test bed. Totally 300 trade exhibition shows are selected from the website as the experiment samples:

- Australian Trade Commission: http://www.austrade.gov.au,
- Australia Exhibition and Conference: http://www.aec.net.au/.

The data was collected between January 2004 and January 2005. This study first determines the sensitivity of different parameters, and obtains the optimum value of these parameters, then uses them in the experiments.

To measure the accuracy of recommendations, the standard *Mean Absolute Error (MAE)* is the most widely used metric in recommendation research. *MAE* is calculated by the deviation of prediction from the actual rating, shown in formula. Specifically, for item i, we have an actual rating a_i and a prediction rating p_i. We first compute the absolute error between them, and then calculate the average absolute error of all rating-prediction pairs for all the n rating-prediction pairs as *MAE*.

$$MAE = \frac{\sum_{i=1}^{n} |a_i - p_i|}{n} \quad (2)$$

To evaluate the quality of the recommendation set, recall and precision have been widely used to evaluate the quality of the recommendations. In this study, the combination metric called *F1*, shown in formula (3), which gives equal weight to both recall and precision, is used for our quality experiments to represent the effects of combining precision and recall. Here, we compute *F1* for each individual user, and calculate the average value to use as our metric.

$$F1 = \frac{2 \times recall \times precision}{recall + precision} \qquad (3)$$

Neighbourhood size was reported to have a significant impact on the recommendation quality [14]. To determine the optimum neighbourhood size, we perform an experiment through varying the number of neighbours and computing the corresponding *MAE* and *F1*. Then optimum neighbour size is obtained through considering both the value of *MAE* and *F1*. The experimental results about the impact of neighbourhood number on *MAE* and *F1* are shown in Fig. 3 and Fig. 4 respectively. The two figures indicate that the size of neighbourhood size has an effect on the accuracy and quality of recommendations. Fig. 3 shows that when a neighbourhood size is bigger than 30 business neighbours, the curve tends to be flat. Therefore, the neighbourhood size 30 is the optimum value for having a minimum *MAE*. In Fig. 4, the neighbourhood size 50 is the optimum value to obtain maximum *F1*. Finally, the average value 40 is selected as the optimum choice of neighbourhood size.

Also, β has an impact on the performance of recommendation. The following experiments determine the optimum β value. The experimental results about the impact of β value on *MAE* and *F1* are shown in Fig. 5 and Fig. 6 respectively. The two figures show that β value does have an effect on the accuracy and quality of recommendations. In Fig. 5, it indicates that 0.3 is the optimum value for having minimum *MAE*. In Fig. 6, it is observed that 0.5 is the optimum value to obtain a maximum *F1*. Finally, 0.4 is selected as the optimum choice of β.

To compare whether the proposed approach works better than the others, an experiment is conducted to test the accuracy of recommendation among content-based, CF and hybrid approaches. The results are shown in Table 1.

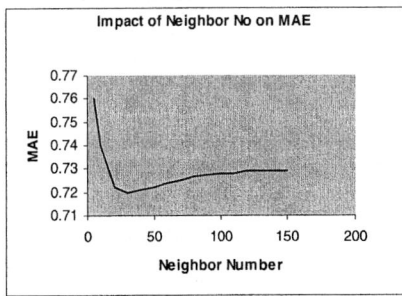
Fig. 3. Impact of neighbor number on recommendation accuracy MAE

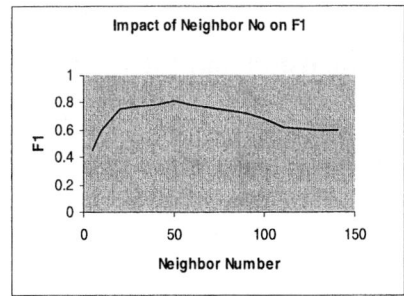
Fig. 4. Impact of neighbor number on recommendation quality F1

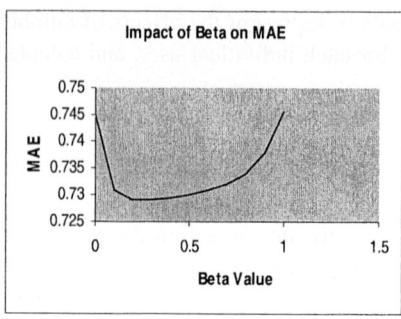 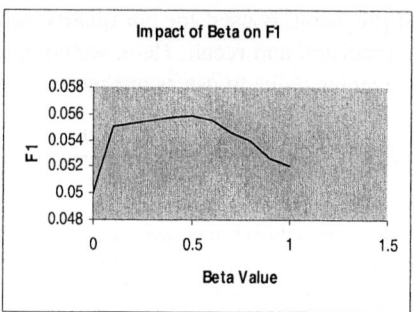

Fig. 5. Impact of Beta on recommendation accuracy MAE

Fig. 6. Impact of Beta on recommendation quality F1

The Table 1 shows that, based on our data set, hybrid approach proposed in our study has lower *MAE* (0.71) than the traditional content-based and CF-based approaches. This achieves the best MAE value in the existing recommender systems. Also, the pure SPR-based approach can achieve the worst accuracy of recommendation because of inadequate data about items and inadequate consideration on users' preference. According to the experiment results, it is concluded that a hybrid approach by combining items' semantic information and the traditional item-based CF approach may achieve better accuracy of recommendation than the content-based and CF-based approaches. For a recommender system, prediction accuracy MAE has been used as the most important evaluation measure of recommendation performance. Thus, in this study, we conducted the comparison of different approaches based on MAE only.

Table 1. Comparison of different recommendation approaches on MAE

	Content-based	CF-based	Pure SPR-based	Hybrid
MAE	0.86	0.83	0.89	0.71

5 Conclusion and Further Study

In this study, we proposed a novel recommendation approach, integrating semantic information with item-based CF recommendation approaches, to overcome the weakness of the existing recommendation techniques. The study demonstrated a recommender system STEF which is able to recommend relevant trade exhibitions to exporters for the improvement of product export and international business. The experimental results have shown that the hybrid approach used in STEF has a better accuracy of recommendation than the traditional content-based and CF-based approaches. The system has achieved the best MAE value to the best of our knowledge. Although our approach is developed in the E-government service domain, the other recommendation applications are able to use the mechanism developed in this study. For example, an e-commerce application can conduct a recommendation according to the features of particular products. In addition, to further validate the current experimental results, the data sets in the test bed will be expanded to cover conferences and trade delegations to significantly improve its usefulness to potential exporters. The further study will concentrate on the performance evaluation of our approach in various different application domains. We will also extend the evaluation study to include frequently used recommendation data sets.

References

[1] Accenture, "eGovernment leadership: high performance, maximum value," Fifth Annual Accenture eGovernment Study, Available at http://www.accenture.com/xdoc/en/industries/government/gove_egov_value.pdf., 2004.
[2] C. C. Aggarwal, J. Wolf, K. Wu, and P. S. Yu, "Horting hatches an egg: an new graph-theoretic approach to collaborative filtering," presented at Proceedings of the 15th ACM SIGKDD International Conference on Knowledge Discovery and Data Mining, San Diego, CA, USA, 1999.
[3] D. L. Amoroso and B. A. Reinig, "Personalization management systems: minitrack introduction," presented at Proceedings of the 37th Annual Hawaii International Conference on System Sciences (HICSS'04), Big Island, Hawaii, 2004.
[4] M. Balabanovic and Y. Shoham, "Fab: content-based collaborative recommendation," *Communications of the ACM*, vol. 40, pp. 66 - 72, 1997.
[5] Y. H. Cho and J. K. Kim, "Application of web usage mining and product taxonomy to collaborative recommendations in e-commerce," *Expert Systems with Applications*, vol. 26, pp. 233-246, 2004.
[6] Comm.ACM, "Special issue on recommender system," *Communications of the ACM*, vol. 40, pp. 5, 1997.
[7] M. Condliff, D. D. Lewis, D. Madigan, and C. Posse, "Bayesian mixed-effects models for recommender systems," presented at Proceedings of the SIGIR'99 Workshop on Recommender Systems: Algorithms and Evaluation, Berkeley, CA, 1999.
[8] A. Kohrs and B. Merialdo, "Creating user-adapted websites by the use of collaborative filtering," *Interacting with Computers*, vol. 13, pp. 695-716, 2001.
[9] F. Liu, C. Yu, and M. Weiyi, "Personalized web search for improving retrieval effectiveness," *IEEE Transactions on Knowledge and Data Engineering*, vol. 16, pp. 28-40, 2004.
[10] M. Perkowitz and O. Etzioni, "Towards adaptive Web sites: conceptual framework and case study," *Artificial Intelligence*, vol. 118, pp. 245-275, 2000.
[11] J. Pitkow, H. Schutze, T. Cass, R. Cooley, D. Turnbull, A. Edmonds, E. Adar, and T. Breuel, "Personalized search," *Communications of the ACM*, vol. 45 (9), pp. 50-55, 2002.
[12] A. Pretschner and S. Gauch, "Ontology based personalized search," presented at Proceedings of the 11th IEEE International Conference on Tools with Artificial Intelligence, Chicago, Illinois, 1999.
[13] M. A. Rodriguez and M. J. Egenhofer, "Determining semantic similarity among entity classes from different ontologies," *IEEE Transactions on Knowledge and Data Engineering*, vol. 15, pp. 442-456, 2003.
[14] B. Sarwar, G. Karypis, J. Konstan, and J. Riedl, "Analysis of recommendation algorithms for E-commerce," presented at Proceedings of the 2nd ACM Conference on Electronic Commerce, Minneapolis, Minnesota, USA, 2000.

[15] B. Sarwar, G. Karypis, J. Konstan, and J. Riedl, "Item-based collaborative filtering recommendation algorithm," presented at Proceedings of the 10th International World Wide Web Conference, Hong Kong, China, 2001.
[16] B. Sarwar, J. Konstan, A. Borchers, J. Herlocker, B. Miller, and J. Riedl, "Using filtering agents to improve prediction quality in the GroupLens research collaborative filtering system," presented at Proceedings of the 1998 ACM Conference on Computer Support Cooperative Work, Seattle, WA, USA, 1998.
[17] J. Zhu, J. Hong, and J. G. Hughes, "PageCluster: mining conceptual link hierarchies from Web log files for adaptive Web site navigation," *ACM Transactions on Internet Technology*, vol. 4, pp. 185-208, 2004.

Exchange Rate Modelling Using News Articles and Economic Data

Debbie Zhang, Simeon J. Simoff, and John Debenham

Faculty of Information Technology, University of Technology, Sydney
{debbiez, simeon, debenham}@it.uts.edu.au

Abstract. This paper provides a framework of using news articles and economic data to model the exchange rate changes between Euro and US dollars. Many studies have conducted on the approach of regressing exchange rate movement using numerical data such as macroeconomic indicators. However, this approach is effective in studying the long term trend of the movement but not so accurate in short to middle term behaviour. Recent research suggests that the market daily movement is the result of the market reaction to the daily news. In this paper, it is proposed to use text mining methods to incorporate the daily economic news as well as economic and political events into the prediction model. While this type of news is not included in most of existing models due to its non-quantitative nature, it has important influence in short to middle terms of market behaviour. It is expected that this approach will lead to an exchange rate model with improved accuracy.

1 Introduction

Exchange rates prediction is one of the most challenging applications of modern time series forecasting. Despite a large amount of research being done in the area, economists know remarkably little about exchange rate regimes [1]. Meese and Rogoff [2] in their well-known paper showed that fundamentals (economic index) dictated by monetary models do not outperform a naive model of no changes in the out-of-sample forecast of nominal exchange rates. After over twenty years of research since the publication of the Meese-Rogoff studies, their findings remain very robust. Although the structural models do not deliver a better forecasting performance than a random walk model, there is evidence on the ability of the structural models to correctly predict the direction of change. Among the enormous amount of empirical models, the sticky price monetary model of Dornbusch and Frankel remains the workhorse of policy-oriented analysis of exchange rate fluctuations [3], which can be expressed as follows:

$$s_t = \beta_0 + \beta_1 \hat{m}_t + \beta_2 \hat{y}_t + \beta_3 \hat{i}_t + \beta_4 \hat{\pi}_t + \mu_t \qquad (1)$$

where s is the changes of interest rate during each sampling period; m and y denote the logarithm of the money value and real GDP respectively; i and π are the interest and inflation rate, respectively; $\hat{\bullet}$ denotes the inter-country difference of the corresponding variable; μ is the error term.

While models based on fundamentals have performed reasonably well in explaining exchange rate development in the long term, economists have little success in predicting exchange rate in short and middle term movement. The general consensus of the poor performance of the traditional empirical models using economic fundamentals to account for exchange rate developments on short to medium term is caused by the irrationality of the market participants, bubbles, and herd behaviour, which are hard to be captured in econometric models.

Recent literature shows that news about fundamentals has played an important role in creating market dynamics. Prast and De Vor [4] have studied the reaction of investors in foreign exchange markets to news information about the euro area and the United States on days of large changes in the euro-dollar exchange rates. Unlike the traditional models, daily changes in the euro/dollar rate on news about economic variables in the United States and the euro area, and the variables capturing news in the two economies were used in the regression model, which is:

$$E_t = \alpha + \sum_{i=1}^{8} \beta_i D_i + \varepsilon \quad (2)$$

where E_t is the percentage daily change in the euro-dollar exchange rate; D_{1-8} represent the following variables: 1 - real economy, euro area; 2 - inflation, euro area; 3 - change in official interest rate, ECB; 4 - statements/political events, euro area; 5 - real economy, United States; 6 - inflation, United States; 7 - change in official interest rate, United States; 8 - statements/political events, United States. It has been found that there is strong correlation between exchange rate daily movement and the market participants' responses to the daily economy news and political events.

More recent research has confirmed that news has statistically significant effects on daily exchange rate movement. Ehrmann and Fratzscher [5] have evaluated the overall impact of macro news by analysing the daily exchange rate responses using similar regression models with news variables. Three key results were found. Firstly, the news about fundamentals can explain relatively well the direction, but only a much smaller extent to the magnitude of exchange rate development. Secondly, news about US economy has a larger impact on exchange rates than news about the euro area. Thirdly, higher degree of market uncertainty will lead to more significant effects of news releases on exchange rate movements.

The above findings motivated the research reported in this paper. By using the text mining techniques, the manual process of identification and classification of positive and negative news can be automated. As the correlation between news and currency exchange rate has only been identified recently, there is not much work reported in this area. Eddelbüttel [6] and Wong [7] both tried to use the keywords in news headlines to forecast intraday currency exchange rate movements. Eddelbüttel used a set of keywords to identify the relevant news and sorted them into three groups: "All", "DEM" and "USD". Then the number of news pieces in three groups are calculated and used as the variable in the GARCH(1,1) model for prediction. The news analysis is restricted to the counting of the number of relevant news headlines to avoid qualitative judgement about "good" and "bad" news. Wong etc. proposed a prediction model based on the occurrence of keywords in news titles. The keywords in the news title are identified by selecting the words with the highest weighting values. A set of rules for predicting the exchange rate movement direction from the keywords in the news titles are generated. These over simplified approaches only utilise news information to a very limited extent. In this paper, a more sophisticated text mining approach for news filtering and classification is presented. An empirical model based on macroeconomic data and the results of new classification is proposed. The system structure and implementation issues are also provided.

2 News Filtering and Classification Based on Text Mining

Before incorporating the news effect into an exchange rate model, it is important to identify the relevant news and classify them into "good" or "bad" news category, that would have opposite impact on the market behaviours. This section describes the training process of news filtering and classification.

2.1 Data Collection and Pre-processing

News articles used in the prediction model are retrieved from online news sources. Prior to the processing, the news articles used for training are manually classified into two groups: news affect exchange rate (target corpus) and other news (generic corpus). Choosing the news articles in the target corpus is crucial for the process since the target corpus contains the underlying knowledge of what factors affect exchange rate movement. Much research has studied the factors that affect currency exchange rate, which can be macroeconomic data, statements by central bankers and politicians and political events that affect macroeconomics. Therefore, only the news that is relevant to these is chosen.

To improve the process efficiency and avoid noise distraction, stop words in the target corpora are replaced by a stop word symbol but are not removed completely to avoid incorrect word co-occurrence. Porter stem algorithm is also applied to remove the common morphological and inflexional endings from words in the documents.

2.2 Automatical Keyword Extraction

Text mining operations are mainly based on the frequency of keywords. The goal of this step is to generate the best set of keywords that can distinguish news documents related to exchange rate from other news documents. To reduce the calculation complexity and increase the processing efficiency, the number of keywords are kept to the minimum amount but are still a good approximation of the original document set in its full space. There are two types of keyword frequencies used in this paper: term frequency and document frequency. The term frequency is calculated by the number of times a term appears in the corpora. The document frequency is the number of the documents that contain this term in the corpora.

Keywords are not restricted to single words, but can be phrases. Therefore, the first step is to identify phrases in the target corpus. The phrases are extracted based on the assumption that two constituent words form a collocation if they co-occur a lot [8].

Once the phrases have been extracted, the key terms are extracted amongst the single words except stop words and phrases in the target corpus. The generic corpus as the background filter. The distribution of terms in the target corpus and the generic corpus are compared. The terms in the target corpus that stand out are considered as the features of the corpus, indicating that these terms are domain-specific terminology.

Dunning [9] suggested the log likelihood ratio (LLR) Chi-square statistic test is effective in determination of domain-specific terms. Vogel [10] also reported that LLR had a greater ability to differentiate the importance of a term in a domain than other methods such as information gain (IG) or mutual information (MI).

The likelihood ratio for a hypothesis is the ratio of the maximum value of the likelihood function over the subspace represented by the hypothesis to the maximum value of the likelihood function over the entire parameter space. In this case, the null hypothesis H_0 is formulated to test the distribution of a term is the same in the generic corpus and target corpus. H_a measures the actual distribution of the term in the whole data set. The log likelihood ratio for this test is:

$$-2\log\left(\frac{H_0\left(p;k_1,n_1,k_2,n_2\right)}{H_a\left(p_1,p_2;k_1,n_1,k_2,n_2\right)}\right) \quad (3)$$

The binomial distribution of the log likelihood statistic is given by:

$$\begin{aligned}-2\log\lambda &= 2\left[\log L\left(p_1,k_1,n_1\right)+\log L\left(p_2,k_2,n_2\right)\right.\\ &\quad\left.-\log L\left(p,k_1,n_1\right)-\log L\left(p,k_2,n_2\right)\right]\end{aligned} \quad (4)$$

where $\log L(p,n,k) = k\log p + (n-k)\log(1-p)$,
k_1 and k_2 are the document frequency of a term in the target corpus and generic corpus respectively,
n_1 and n_2 are the size of the target corpus and generic corpus respectively,
$p_1 = \frac{k_1}{n_1}$, $p_2 = \frac{k_2}{n_2}$, and $p = \frac{k_1+k_2}{n_1+n_2}$.

The method scores the terms based on the difference in the percentage of documents containing the term in the target and generic corpus. It does not distinguish whether the difference is caused by the term occurring more or less in the target corpus. As in this research that only the terms significant in the target corpus are concerned, a simple condition is added to the ranking equation so the terms are significant in the generic corpus are filtered out:

$$\frac{p_1}{p_2} \geq 1 \qquad (5)$$

2.3 News Relevance Classification

The news relevance classification is divided into two steps: the first step is to identify the news that has potential to cause movement in exchange rates, the second step is to identify the news that is Euro and/or US dollar related.

The exchange rate related news can be separated from other news based on the key terms extracted from the previous section, which often well represent the characteristics of the data set. In this case, a modified k-Means classification algorithm, which is particular suitable for this case, is chosen as being computationally simple and efficient. The centroid of the target corpus and the maximum Euclidean distance in the training data are calculated. The maximum distance is used as the threshold to determine if the data belongs to a target cluster.

News related to exchange rate may not be discussing Euro and US dollar currencies, which is further identified by using the frequency of the words of currency and country names it contains.

2.4 Positive and Negative News Classification

It is important to further classify the relevant news into "positive news" and "negative news" categories, as news in different groups have entirely different effects on the market behaviour.

Recent studies show that the effect of the news is the combined effect of market expectation and the news itself. A piece of news could have positive or negative impact to the market depending on the market expectation. Therefore, unlike some studies that define good and bad news by its immediately effect to the market, in this research, the news is defined to be good or bad according to its fundamental effect to the market. The market expectation is incorporated into the model in a later stage. For example, a news about US increased its interest rate is defined to be positive news to US dollars.

The task of identifying "good" and "bad" news of exchange rate is not straight forward since both groups of news use similar set of keywords. For example, the following two pieces of news have exactly same set of words, but one is considered to be positive and the other is considered to be negative to the appreciation of US dollars:

1. The interest rate has gone up. The US dollar has gone down.
2. The interest rate has gone down. The US dollar has gone up.

The positive and negative news can use similar set of key terms, which causes great difficulties in the classification. However, the sequences of the key terms can represent the meaning of sentences better, which is well illustrated in the previous example. Therefore, a term is defined as the sequence of key terms in a sentence, which is used as the input features for the positive and negative news classification. The feature vectors of the above example can be represented as:

Table 1. Example of feature vector representation for "good"/"bad" news classification

features	document 1	document 2
interest rate up	1	0
interest rate down	0	1
US dollar down	1	0
US dollar up	0	1

However, using key term sequence as classification features leads to a high dimensional vector space with sparsely distributed elements, which causes difficulty in separating instances into classes (subspaces). Therefore, the discriminant analysis is implemented to combine features of the original data in a way that most effectively discriminates between classes [11]. The discriminant analysis is to project the documents onto a lower dimensional subspace of the original vector space. After the projection, instances in the same class are tightly grouped, but well separated from the other clusters. Also, with a smaller set of input features, the complexity of the classification is reduced and the calculation efficiency can be greatly improved.

Again, the document collection with n documents and m features in cluster i represented by a term (key term sequence) frequency document matrix. In this application, there are two clusters - "good" news and "bad" news.

$$A_i = [a_1 a_2 \cdots a_{n_i}] \in \Re^{m \times n_i} \qquad (6)$$

An optimal linear transformation G^T can be found such that the Euclidean distance between the clusters is maximised while the distance between instances within each cluster is minimised:

$$G^T \in \Re^{l \times m} : a_j \in \Re^{m \times 1} \to y_j \in \Re^{l \times 1}, 1 \leq j \leq n_1 + n_2 \qquad (7)$$

To measure the cluster quality, scatter matrices are formulated based on the distance of each instance to the centroid. The scatter matrix within cluster and between clusters are defined as the following equations:

$$S_w = \sum_{i=1}^{2} \sum_{j \in n_i} (a_j - c^i)(a_j - c^i)^T \qquad (8)$$

$$S_b = \sum_{i=1}^{2} \sum_{j \in n_i} (c^i - c)(c^i - c)^T = \sum_{i=1}^{2} n_i (c^i - c)(c^i - c)^T \qquad (9)$$

The scatter matrices of the transformed feature vectors are as follows:

$$S_w^Y = G^T S_w G, \quad S_b^Y = G^T S_b G \qquad (10)$$

The closeness of the instances with the cluster and the separation between clusters can be calculated from the scatter matrices as trace(S_w^Y) and trace(S_b^Y) respectively.

The transformation matrix G^T is calculated by maximising the value of trace $S_w^Y (S_b^Y)^{-1}$ that approximates the maximisation of $trace(S_w^Y)$ and minimisation of $trace(S_b^Y)$. The numerical algorithm for this optimisation problem presented in [11] is adapted.

After the G^T being calculated, the k-Means classification algorithm can be applied to classify the transformed feature vectors y_j into "good" and "bad" news categories.

3 The Econometric Model of Exchange Rate Responding to News and Economic Data

This research focuses on using text mining methods to incorporate the information in the news articles into a currency prediction model. As euro/dollar exchange rate will be used as the testing case, the empirical model presented by Galati and Ho to study the news effect on economic data particular for euro/dollar exchange rate is chosen [12]. In this work, the above model is modified to incorporate a news index (I_{news}), which reflects the news effect on exchange rate. The regression equation has the following form:

$$\Delta \ln S(t) = \alpha_0 + \alpha_i x_i(t) + \beta I_{news} + \varepsilon \qquad (11)$$

where x_i represent the economic data variables which include: US non-farm payrolls, US unemployment rate, US employment cost index, US durable goods orders, NAPM manufacturing, NAPM non-manufacturing, US advance retail sales, US industrial production, US CPI, Ifo index, Germany unemployment rate, Germany industrial production, INSEE industrial trends, Germany CPI and EU 11 PPI.

4 System Structure and Implementation Issues

The system is designed as a multi-agent system, as shown in figure 1.

The user interface module is the accessing point to the system, which is shown in Figure 2. The exchange rate data and the news articles are displayed on the main page. There are three major menu items: "Data", "Training" and "Prediction Model" on the menu bar. Each of these menu items controls one of the agents in the system.

"Data" menu item allows the user to set the data sources (URLs) and schedule the download frequency and time for the data extraction agent. Since users

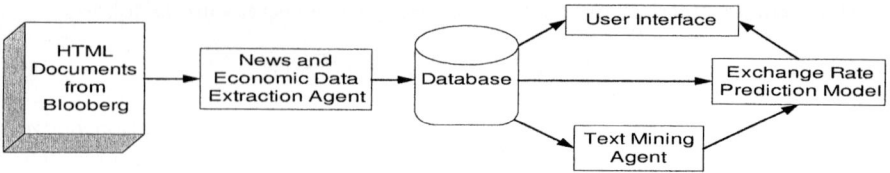

Fig. 1. The structure of the exchange rate prediction system

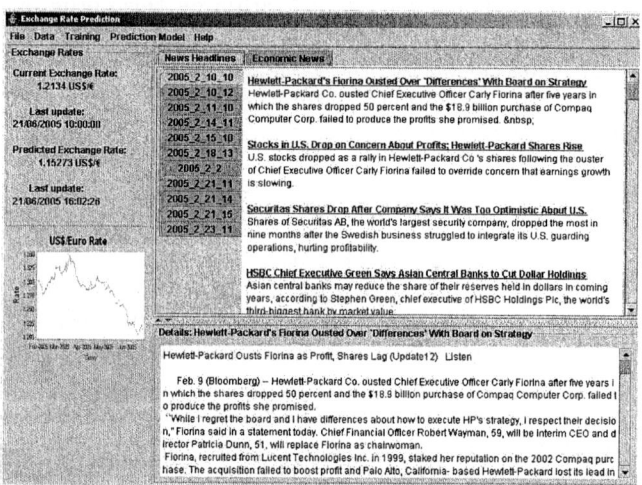

Fig. 2. User interface

are allowed to set the data sources, the template of the HTML files retrieved from the data source is unknown. Therefore, flexible methods to extract the data from HTML tags are required. Extracting the news articles from HTML file is not a simple task since each web site has different layout and format. A generic news extraction and validation algorithm was developed to solve this problem [13]. Extracting the economic data from HTML files is relative simple since data are always held in HTML tables. A program was developed to search these tables by using keywords.

"Training" menu item is designed to execute the operations provided by the text mining agent. It contains a pull-down menu list with five options: "Select Good/Bad News", "Keyword Generation", "News Relevancy Training", "Good/Bad News Training" and "Automatic Training". Each of the menu item executes one of the training step described in section 2.

Once the training process is completed, the above classification system can be used to classify "live" news articles online, as shown in the following algorithm:

```
Input: news article tt (String)

Output: news category n (integer 0<=n<=2)
        when n=0, unrelated news
        when n=1, positive news
        when n=2, negative news
   const
        currency keywords US_Euro (String[])
        currency keywords Non_US_Euro (String[])
   var
        generated from "Keyword Generation":
            key terms kw (String[])
        generated from "News Relevancy Training":
            centroid C (float[])
            threshold T (float)
        generated from "Good/Bad News Training":
            key term sequences ks (String[])
            transformation matrix G_T (float[][])
            "good" news centroid g_C (float[])
            "bad" news centroid b_C (float[])

Begin:  apply stem algorithm to tt
        replace all words in tt to a word symbol except words in kw
        calculate the frequency of the key terms kw in tt
        d := the distance to the relevance news data set centroid C
        if d > T
            n = 0 (unrelated news), return;
        calculate the frequency of currency keywords US_Euro
        calculate the frequency of currency keywords Non_US_Euro
        compare the average frequency of US_Euro and Non_US_Euro
        if average frequency Non_US_Euro > average frequency US_Euro
            n = 0 (unrelated news), return;
        remove all quotations in tt except """, ",", "?", "."
        A := calculated key term sequence ks frequency in tt
        Y := G_T * A
        d_good = distance of Y to "good" news data set centroid g_C
        d_bad = distance of Y to "bad" news data set centroid b_C
        if d_good > d_bad
            n = 2 (negative news), return;
        else
            n = 1 (positive news), return;
End.
```

The exchange rate prediction model is generated offline by a Matlab program. The "Prediction model" menu item allows users to input the regression parameters of the model. At the end of each day, a prediction value is calculated based on the number of "good"/"bad" news documents of the day and the current economic data.

5 Conclusions

A novel approach to an exchange rate prediction model using news articles and economical data has been developed. This paper focuses on the aspects of theoretical development and system structure design. A comprehensive case study is being conducted to evaluate the system.

References

1. Rose, A.K.: Exchange rate regimes and stability: Where do we stand? Technical Report Unpublished working report, U.C. Berkeley. (2004)
2. Meese, R., Rogoff, K.: Empirical exchange rate models of the seventies. do they fit out of sample? Journal of International Economics **14** (1983) 3–24
3. Dornbusch, R.: Expectations and exchange rate dynamics. Journal of Political Economy **84** (1976) 1161–1176
4. Prast, H.M., de Vor, M.P.H.: Investor reactions to news: a cognitive dissonance analysis of the euro-dollar exchange rate. European Journal of Political Economy **21** (2005) 115–141 TY - JOUR.
5. Ehrmann, M., Fratzscher, M.: Exchange rates and fundamentals: new evidence from real-time data. Journal of International Money and Finance **24** (2005) 317–341 TY - JOUR.
6. Eddelbttel, D., McCurdy, T.: The impact of news on foreign exchange rates: evidence from high frequency data. Technical report, University of Toronto (1998)
7. Peramunetilleke, D., Wong, R.K.: Currency exchange rate forecasting from news headlines. Aust. Comput. Sci. Commun. **24** (2002) 131–139
8. Manning, C.D., Schutze, H.: Foundations of statistical natural language processing. MIT Press, Cambridge, Mass. (1999) Christopher D. Manning, Hinrich Schutze. 24 cm.
9. Dunning, T.: Accurate methods for the statistics of surprise and coincidence. Computational Linguistics **19** (1994) 61–74
10. Vogel, D.: Using generic corpora to learn domain-specific terminology. In: The Ninth ACM SIGKDD International Conference on Knowledge Discovery and Data Mining (Workshop on Link Analysis for Detecting Complex Behavior), Washington, DC, USA (2003)
11. Berry, M.W.: Survey of text mining : clustering, classification, and retrieval. Springer, New York (2003)
12. Galati, G., Ho, C.: Macroeconomic news and the euro/dollar exchange rate. Technical Report 105, Bank for International Settlements (2001)
13. Zhang, D., Simoff, S.: Informing the curious negotiator: Automatic news extraction from the internet. In: Australasian Data Mining Conference, Cairns, Australia (2004)

Adaptive Utility-Based Scheduling in Resource-Constrained Systems

David Vengerov

Sun Microsystems Laboratories, UMPK16-160,
16 Network Circle, Menlo Park, CA 94025
david.vengerov@sun.com

Abstract. This paper addresses the problem of scheduling jobs in soft real-time systems, where the utility of completing each job decreases over time. We present a utility-based framework for making repeated scheduling decisions based on dynamically observed information about unscheduled jobs and system's resources. This framework generalizes the standard scheduling problem to a resource-constrained environment, where resource allocation (RA) decisions (how many CPUs to allocate to each job) have to be made concurrently with the scheduling decisions (when to execute each job). Discrete-time Optimal Control theory is used to formulate the optimization problem of finding the scheduling/RA policy that maximizes the average utility per time step obtained from completed jobs. We propose a Reinforcement Learning (RL) architecture for solving the NP-hard Optimal Control problem in real time, and our experimental results demonstrate the feasibility and benefits of the proposed approach.

1 Introduction

The classical real-time scheduling problem is that of deciding on the order in which the currently unscheduled jobs should be executed by a single processor, with no possibility of processor sharing. In the case of *hard real-time systems*, each job is characterized by an execution time and a deadline. A *soft real-time system* is the one where each job receives some utility as a function of its completion time. The concept of scheduling jobs based on Time Utility Functions (TUFs) was first introduced by Jensen in [3], where the objective of maximizing the total utility accrued by the system over time was used. The utility accrual (UA) paradigm is a generalization of the deadline scheduling in hard real-time systems. An important benefit of the UA paradigm is that it allows one to optimize the *productivity* of the system: average utility from completed jobs per unit of time ([4]).

Recently, the originator of the UA paradigm E. D. Jensen has co-authored a paper [9], which claims to present the only scheduling algorithm that can handle arbitrarily shaped TUFs and multi-unit resource constraints (multiple resource types, each having multiple units). This algorithm is based on the idea that since the future is unpredictable, it is best to use the "greedy" strategy of inserting as many "high utility" jobs into the schedule as early as possible. While it is a reasonable heuristic for a resource-constrained environment, it is possible to develop algorithms that do try to predict the future and hence can perform better than the greedy strategy.

The Optimal Control Theory addresses the problem of finding a policy that maximizes a possibly discounted sum of future rewards and hence can be used to address the scheduling problem within the UA paradigm. The discrete-time optimal control problem, also known as the Markov Decision Problem (MDP), can be solved using dynamic programming if the system model is known and the number of possible system states is small. Neither of these conditions is satisfied in the real-world scheduling systems, and the Reinforcement Learning methodology ([1, 6]) was developed as a formal extension of dynamic programming to the case of unknown system models and large state spaces. We are not aware of any attempts of using the Optimal Control or the MDP formulation for solving the real-time scheduling problem within the UA paradigm, for a single CPU or a multi-CPU environment.

This paper addresses the above shortcomings by presenting a general MDP framework and algorithms for solving scheduling problems within the UA paradigm in the multi-CPU environment. The key feature of the proposed scheduling approach is approximation of the value function that computes the expected long-term productivity of the machine (average utility per time step obtained from all completed jobs) as a function of its current state, which is accomplished using the Reinforcement Learning methodology. Once an approximation to this value function is obtained, any scheduling decisions can be made that modify the current machine state with the goal of increasing its state value.

The experimental results implementing the above utility-based scheduling approach are presented, which demonstrate a consistent increase in machine productivity over the standard scheduling approach in the UA domain. This benchmark approach is the one lying at the heart of the algorithms presented in [2, 5, 9], suitably extended to handle multi-CPU jobs contending for a limited number of CPUs.

2 Problem Formulation

Each job arriving into the system requires a certain number of CPUs to be executed at the maximum rate but can be executed with fewer CPUs at a slower rate. The final job utility decays as its waiting+execution time increases. Then, if only a small number of CPUs are idle in the system, a question arises whether a new job that ideally requires more CPUs should still be scheduled, receiving a small final utility due to its prolonged execution time. Alternatively, the scheduler can wait until more CPUs become available to ensure a smaller execution time, while risking to have a long waiting time for this job and a low final utility once again. Another possible resource management decision in such a situation is to suspend some of the currently running jobs or compact them to a smaller number of CPUs (extending the execution time of each job) and free up enough CPUs for the waiting job to be executed at a fast rate.

This paper presents a novel utility-based scheduling framework capable of adequately resolving the tradeoffs mentioned above. An overview of the considered problem is given below. More details will be given in section 4. The job execution time, if assigned the required number of CPUs, varies among the jobs but is assumed to be known (this assumption is not necessary in order for the scheduling policies to work – job execution times can be random and knowing only the mean execution time for each job would suffice).

The *unit* utility of each job is a decreasing function of the job completion time, which includes the job waiting time. The *final* utility of each job is its unit utility multiplied by $K*L$, where K is its desired number of CPUs and L is its *ideal* execution time if the job were to receive K CPUs. The $K*L$ factor is introduced to reflect the assumption that the larger and the longer jobs should receive the same scheduling priority as the smaller and the shorter jobs – to make the scheduler indifferent between scheduling one job requiring K CPUs and having the ideal execution time L and scheduling $K*L$ jobs each of which requires one CPU and has an ideal execution time of one unit of time.

The jobs are assumed to arrive randomly into the system. The goal is to continually schedule incoming jobs onto the system and to decide how many CPUs should be allocated to each job so as to maximize average system productivity (final utility from all completed jobs) per time step.

3 Solution Methodology

3.1 Overview

The basic scheduling algorithm uses the best-fit technique: the machine selects the next job to be scheduled which has the tightest fit for this machine (will have the fewest free CPUs remaining after the job is scheduled). If there is a tie among the jobs that provide the best fit to the available resources, then the highest unit utility job gets scheduled. In addition to this basic scheduling algorithm, this paper considers two types of utility-based policies, which apply if the machine cannot fit any of the currently waiting jobs.

The first *preemption* policy decides whether one or several of the jobs currently running on that machine should be temporarily suspended in order to allow one of the waiting jobs to be scheduled with all the desired CPUs. The suspended jobs are placed in the waiting queue and can be resumed from the place they left off. The second *oversubscribing* policy decides whether any of the currently waiting jobs should be "squeezed" into the remaining free CPUs even if there are fewer of them than the job ideally desires.

Both of these policies make scheduling decisions by selecting the job configuration that provides the best starting point for machine's future operations in terms of maximizing the expected *long-term utility* (value) from all jobs completed in the future. Thus, the key component of the proposed scheduling framework is the possibility of learning the value function for a machine based on the state of its resources, the jobs it is executing and the jobs waiting to be scheduled. Once such a value function is obtained, any kind of scheduling decisions can be considered (not just preemption and oversubscribing), which can now be driven by maximization of the machine's state value following the scheduling decision.

Any kind of parameterized value function approximation can be used in the proposed scheduling framework, since the only criterion for its compatability with the reinforcement learning methodology for tuning its parameters is function differentiability with respect to each tunable parameter. As a demonstration, a parameterized fuzzy rulebase will be used in this paper to approximate machine value functions.

3.2 Value Function Approximation

A fuzzy rulebase is a function f that maps an input vector $x \in \Re^K$ into a scalar output y. This function is formed out of fuzzy rules, where a fuzzy rule i is a function f_i that maps an input vector $x \in \Re^K$ into a scalar p^i. The following common form of the fuzzy rules is used in this paper:

- Rule i: IF (x_1 is S_1^i) and (x_2 is S_2^i) and ... (x_K is S_K^i) THEN (p^i),

where x_j is the jth component of x, S_j^i are the input labels in rule i and p^i are the output coefficients. The degree to which the linguistic expression (x_j is S_j^i) is satisfied is given by a *membership function* $\mu : \Re \to \Re$, which maps its input x_j into a degree to which this input belongs to the fuzzy category described by the corresponding label. The output of the fuzzy rulebase $f(x)$ is a weighted average of p^i:

$$y = f(x) = \frac{\sum_{i=1}^{M} p^i w^i(x)}{\sum_{i=1}^{M} w^i(x)}, \quad (1)$$

where M is the number of rules and $w^i(x)$ is the weight of rule i. The product inference is commonly used for computing the weight of each rule: $w^i(x) = \prod_{j=1}^{K} \mu_{S_j^i}(x_j)$. Note that if the membership functions $\mu()$ are kept constant and only the output coefficients p^i are tuned, then the fuzzy rulebase becomes equivalent to a linear combination of basis functions – a well known statistical regression model. If the membership functions are tuned as well, then the above form of the fuzzy rulebase was proven to be a universal function approximator [8], just like a multi-layer perceptron neural network. However, tuning the membership functions requires a nonlinear learning algorithm, which is much harder to set up and use. In practice, tuning the output coefficients p^i is often sufficient to come up with a good policy, and for simplicity of exposition this approach is taken in this paper.

As a simple demonstration of the proposed scheduling framework, we use the following variables for evaluating the *value* of machine state at any point in time: x_1 = CPU-weighted average unit utility of the currently running jobs, x_2 = the expected time remaining until any of the currently running jobs is completed, x_3 = the number of free CPUs on the machine.

These variables are used as inputs to the fuzzy rulebase, which outputs the *value* $V(x)$ of the state x: the *long-term* utility per time step that the machine expects to obtain in the future when starting from the state x. A description of the reinforcement learning algorithm for updating the rulebase parameters p^i so that the rulebase output in fact approximates $V(x)$ will be given in section 3.4. Each input variable x_j to the fuzzy rulebase was softly classified into two fuzzy categories: small (S) and large (L), thereby creating 8 fuzzy rules. The weight w^i of each fuzzy rule is the product of the degrees to which every precondition is satisfied. The membership functions μ, which compute these degrees, have the following form:

- degree to which (x_1 is S_1): $\mu_{S_1}(x_1) = 1 - x_1$
- degree to which (x_1 is L_1): $\mu_{L_1}(x_1) = x_1$
- degree to which (x_2 is S_2): $\mu_{S_2}(x_2) = 1 - x_2/MaxJobLength$
- degree to which (x_2 is L_2): $\mu_{L_1}(x_2) = x_2/MaxJobLength$
- degree to which (x_3 is S_3): $\mu_{S_3}(x_3) = (N - x_3)/N$
- degree to which (x_3 is L_3): $\mu_{L_3}(x_3) = x_3/N$,

where N is the maximum number of CPUs on the machine and $MaxJobLength$ is the maximum length of a job that can be scheduled on this machine. The final output of the fuzzy rulebase is computed according to equation (1).

3.3 Value-Based Job Scheduling Algorithm

The preemption policy can be invoked at any point of time for deciding whether or not one or several of the jobs currently running on the machine should be preempted in order to allow one of the waiting jobs to be scheduled with all the desired CPUs. The oversubscribing policy can be used for deciding whether or not any of the currently waiting jobs should be "squeezed" into a smaller number of available CPUs than initially requested by the job (oversubscribing the machine).

Given an architecture for approximating the value of machine's state (which can still be in the process of being tuned), the following general steps are used by the scheduling algorithm:

1. Schedule jobs onto the free CPUs without any preemption or oversubscribing using any traditional scheduling approach such as best-fit scheduling.

If any jobs are still waiting and there are some free CPUs on the machine, perform the following steps:

2. Compute the variables x_1, x_2, and x_3 for the current machine state.

3. Use the computed x_j as inputs to the fuzzy rulebase to compute V_0 – the long-term expected utility (average utility per time step) that can be obtained by the machine if none of the currently waiting jobs are scheduled.

If the preemption policy is enabled, the scheduling algorithm performs the following two steps for every waiting job i:

4. Compute the alternate possible machine state in terms of new values for x_1, x_2, and x_3 that would arise if job i were forcefully scheduled, preempting enough jobs to fit itself, in the order of increasing *remaining utility*. The remaining utility of each running job is its expected unit utility at completion divided by the expected time remaining to completion. If job i needs to preempt a job with

a higher remaining unit utility than its own in order to fit itself (e.g. if all the currently running jobs have high remaining unit utilities), then it is eliminated from further consideration for forceful scheduling.

5. If job i qualifies for forceful scheduling, use the newly computed x_j in the fuzzy rulebase to compute V_1^i – the long-term expected utility that can be obtained by the machine if job i were forcefully scheduled.

6. Let $MaxV1 = \max_i(V_1^i)$

7. If $MaxV1 > V_0$ then preempt enough lowest-utility jobs and schedule the job with the highest V_1^i onto the machine; otherwise, do not preempt any jobs and do not schedule any of the currently waiting jobs.

If the oversubscribing policy is also enabled, the scheduling algorithm performs the following two steps for every job i that is still waiting to be scheduled:

8. Compute the alternate machine state in terms of the variables x_1, x_2, and x_3 that would result if job i were scheduled onto the free CPUs, oversubscribing the machine.

9. Use the newly computed x_j in the fuzzy rulebase to compute V_2^i – the expected long-term benefit of oversubscribing the machine with the job i.

10. Let $MaxV2 = \max_i(V_2^i)$

11. If $MaxV2 > V_0$ then oversubscribe the machine with the job that has the highest V_2^i; otherwise do not oversubscribe.

3.4 Reinforcement Learning Algorithm for Tuning Value Functions

We first describe the general mathematical context of the Markov Decision Problem (MDP) where reinforcement learning (RL) algorithms can be used. An MDP for a single agent (decision maker) can be described by a quadruple (S, A, R, T) consisting of:

- A finite set of states S
- A finite set of actions A
- A reward function $r : S \times A \times S \to \Re$
- A state transition function $T : S \times A \to PD(S)$, which maps the agent's current state and action into the set of probability distributions over S.

At each time t, the agent observes the state $s_t \in S$ of the system, selects an action $a \in A$ and the system changes its state according to the probability distribution specified by T, which depends only on s_t and a_t. The agent then receives a real-valued reward signal $r(s_t, a_t, s_{t+1})$. The agent's objective is to find a stationary policy $\pi : S \to A$ that maximizes expectation of either a discounted sum of future rewards or the average reward per time step starting from any initial state, which are the two most popular optimization criteria.

For a stationary policy π, the average reward per time step is defined as:

$$\rho^\pi = \lim_{T \to \infty} \frac{1}{T} \sum_{t=0}^{T-1} r(s_t, \pi(s_t), s_{t+1}), \qquad (2)$$

The optimal policy π^* from a class of policies Π is defined as $\pi^* = \operatorname*{argmax}_{\pi \in \Pi} \rho^\pi$. The *value* of a state s under a policy π in the average reward case is defined as:

$$V^\pi(s) = E[\sum_{t=0}^\infty (r(s_t, \pi(s_t), s_{t+1}) - \rho^\pi)|s_0 = s]. \tag{3}$$

If $V^\pi(s)$ is known, then a higher average reward can be obtained by a new policy π' that takes greedy actions with respect to the values $V^\pi(.)$:

$$\pi'(s) = \operatorname*{argmax}_a E[r(s, \pi(s), s_{t+1}) - \rho^\pi + V^\pi(s_{t+1})], \tag{4}$$

where $E[.]$ denotes expected value. A well-known procedure for iteratively approximating $V^\pi(s)$ is called *temporal difference* (TD) learning. Its simplest form is called TD(0):

$$V^\pi(s_t) \leftarrow V^\pi(s_t) + \alpha_t(r(s_t, \pi(s_t), s_{t+1}) - \rho_t + V^\pi(s_{t+1}) - V^\pi(s_t)), \tag{5}$$

where α_t is the learning rate and ρ_t is updated as:

$$\rho_t = (1 - \alpha_t)\rho_t + \alpha_t r(s_t, \pi(s_t), s_{t+1}). \tag{6}$$

The above iterative procedure converges as long as the underlying Markov chain of states encountered under policy π is irreducible and aperiodic and the learning rate α_t satisfies $\sum_{t=0}^\infty \alpha_t = \infty$ and $\sum_{t=0}^\infty \alpha_t^2 < \infty$ [7]. For example, $\alpha_t = 1/t$ satisfies this conditions.

The temporal differencing approach based on assigning a value to each state becomes impractical when the state space becomes very large or continuous, since visits to any given state become very improbable. In this case, a function approximation architecture needs to be used in order to generalize the value function across neighboring states. Let $\hat{V}(s, p)$ be an approximation to the optimal value function $V^*(s)$ based on a linear combination of basis functions with a parameter vector p: $\hat{V}(s,p) = \sum_{i=1}^M p^i \phi^i(s)$, where $p = (p^1, p^2, ..., p^M)^T$ and $\phi(s,a) = (\phi^1(s), \phi^2(s), ..., \phi^M(s))^T$. The parameter updating rule in this case becomes (executed for all parameters simultaneously):

$$p_{t+1}^i = p_t^i + \alpha_t \frac{\partial}{\partial p^i}[r(s_t, a_t, s_{t+1}) - \rho_t + \hat{V}(s_{t+1}, p_t) - \hat{V}(s_t, p_t)]^2$$

$$= p_t^i + \alpha_t[r(s_t, a_t, s_{t+1}) - \rho_t + \hat{V}(s_{t+1}, p_t) - \hat{V}(s_t, p_t)]\frac{\partial}{\partial p^i}\hat{V}(s_t, p_t)$$

$$= p_t^i + \alpha_t[r(s_t, a_t, s_{t+1}) - \rho_t + \hat{V}(s_{t+1}, p_t) - \hat{V}(s_t, p_t)]\phi(s_t), \tag{7}$$

where $\phi(s_t)$ is a vector of all basis functions and the average reward estimate is updated as in equation (6). The above iterative procedure is also guaranteed to converge to the correct state values if certain additional conditions are satisfied [7]. The most important ones are that the basis functions $\phi^i(s)$ are linearly independent and that the states for update are sampled according to the steady-state distribution of the underlying Markov chain for the given policy. Note that the scheduling algorithm of section 3.3 occasionally changes the machine state to a "better" state, from which the state evolution proceeds. While no theoretical convergence results are available for this scenario, our positive experimental results suggest its feasibility.

We use equation (7) for updating parameters p^i of the fuzzy rulebase approximation to the state value function, with $\phi^i(s)$ being the normalized weight of each fuzzy rule i: $\frac{w^i(s)}{\sum_{i=1}^{M} w^i(s)}$. The parameters of the fuzzy rulebase are updated when the machine state is changed due to a job being preempted. The parameters are also updated when any of the currently running jobs are finished and the machine is not oversubscribed, which indicates that the decision of not doing anything was made at the last decision point. The parameters of the fuzzy rulebase are also updated when a resource-starved job is finished, which indicates that the decision of oversubscribing the machine was made at the last decision point. The above heuristic for timing the parameter updates was necessary to account for the fact that scheduling decisions cannot be made at every time step – they occur at random time intervals. However, the MDP framework still applies to such an environment (if the state vector summarizes all relevant system information), since visitations to a certain set of states (e.g. the states where scheduling decisions can be made) by an ergodic Markov chain also evolve as a Markov chain.

4 Simulation Results

Performance of adaptive utility-based policies for oversubscribing and preemption was evaluated using a Grid simulator developed in collaboration with the DReAM team at the Sunnyvale Ranch of Sun Microsystems. The test results demonstrated a consistent increase in machine productivity over non-adaptive policies when either one of the utility-based policies was deployed and adaptively tuned using the RL methodology, with the maximum productivity obtained when both policies were deployed and tuned simultaneously. The benefit of this approach was found to increase as the job arrival rate (system load) increased and more jobs became available for scheduling. Furthermore, sensitivity analysis of performance results to the shape of the Time Utility Functions showed that performance increases as utility functions become more convex.

The experimental results are summarized in Figures 2 and 3. They present the case of 3 machines with 24 CPUs each – the maximum machine size currently used in the Sunnyvale Ranch. A larger number of machines was not necessary since the utility-based scheduling framework allows each machine to adapt its value function completely independently of the number of other machines present. The machines in our experiments sequentially executed the algorithm described in section 3.3.

The number of CPUs required for each job was sampled from a random uniform distribution on [4, 20] and the ideal job execution time was sampled from a random uniform distribution on [5, 10]. The unit utility of each job as a function of the total completion time (TUF) was equal to 1 between t = 0 and t = "ideal execution time L" and then decayed to 0 at t = 2L, as shown

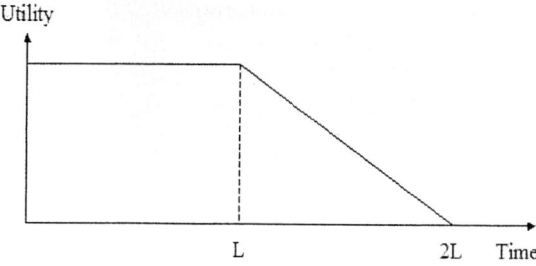

Fig. 1. Time Utility Function (TUF) used by the jobs, where L is the "ideal execution time"

in Figure 1. Jobs arrived stochastically in a Poisson manner. For simplicity, we assumed that the job execution time is given by $L \frac{N_I}{\min(N_A, N_I)}$, where N_I is the ideal number of CPUs requested by the job, L is the ideal execution time if the job were given N_I CPUs and N_A is the number of CPUs actually allocated to the job. Any other dependence on the number of assigned CPUs could have been used, since our scheduling algorithms do not use this information explicitly. All results are given over a test period of 2000 time steps and are averaged over 50 experiments, so that performance difference for between all policies would be statistically significant.

Figure 2 shows performance of various scheduling policies for the job arrival rate of 0.15, evaluating the total productivity of 3 machines (total final utility of all completed jobs), in terms of 1000 utility units. The first row corresponds to the best-fit scheduling policy with no preemption or oversubscribing. Whenever there is a tie among jobs that provide the best fit to the available CPUs, the job with the highest expected final utility gets scheduled first, in the spirit of the best known scheduling algorithms [2,5,9].

The second row corresponds to the strategies of "aggressive" oversubscribing, preemption, and combined preemption-oversubscribing policies. Each of these policies uses best-fit scheduling as described above, and if no jobs can be scheduled during some time step but some jobs are waiting, an aggressive policy oversubscribes the machine by scheduling a job with fewer than desired CPUs, tries to forcefully schedule a job (preempting, if possible, some of the lower-valued currently running jobs as explained in section 3.3), or considers preemptive scheduling followed by oversubscribing, depending on the exact policy used. The smallest of the waiting jobs is scheduled by an "aggressive" policy, which showed better results than scheduling the job with the highest unit utility (which would get "squeezed" to a larger extent or would preempt more jobs).

The third row corresponds to the utility-based oversubscribing, preemption, and combined preemption-oversubscribing policies. These policies make their decisions based on maximizing the value of machine state as explained in section 3.3. Prior to testing a utility-based policy, parameters of the utility function approximation architecture $V(x)$ were adjusted for 20000 time steps using the reinforcement learning equation (7) starting from $p^i = 0$.

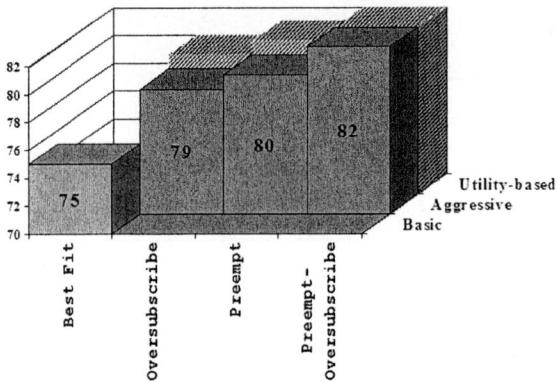

Fig. 2. Machine productivity for various policies and a job arrival rate of 0.15

As an example, the following vector of output fuzzy rulebase parameters defines the value function learned by the preemption-oversubscribing policy in one set of experiments: $\mathbf{p}=(-0.97, -0.25, -0.86, -0.39, 0.48, -0.85, 4.03, 0.19)$. By relating the above output parameter values with the fuzzy rules described in section 3.2, we can see that all else being equal, the machine state value (expected average utility from jobs completed in the future) increases as the first input variable (average CPU-weighted utility of the currently running jobs) increases, the second variable (the expected time remaining until any of the currently running jobs completes its execution) increases, and the third variable (number of free CPUs on the machine) decreases. While this pattern corresponds to our prior expectations, the actual numbers learned with RL allow one to trade off relative changes in each of these variables (e.g. deciding whether a certain increase in the first variable outweighs a certain decrease in the second variable, etc.).

The arrival rate of 0.15 used in Figure 2 corresponds to a low-stressed system, where on average 12% of jobs would expire in the best-fit policy without getting scheduled (would miss their hardest deadline). Figure 3 shows the sensitivity of the utility-based preemption-oversubscribing policy to the shape of job TUFs for the arrival rate of 0.3, corresponding to a high-stressed system where on average 41% of jobs would expire in the best-fit policy. For comparison, productivity of the best-fit policy and of the aggressive preemption-oversubscribing policy are given.

Figure 2 shows that the aggressive preemption-oversubscribing policy is optimal for a low-stressed system (the optimal utility-based policy learned with RL makes similar decisions and achieves similar performance). This makes sense because if a job is waiting at some point of time and fewer CPUs than this job desires are available, then the probability of a smaller job arriving in the near future to fill these CPUs is low (because of the low job arrival rate), and hence forcefully scheduling this job or oversubscribing the machine is better than doing nothing. However, for high job arrival rates, the probability of a smaller job arriving in the near future is high enough that waiting might be the best course

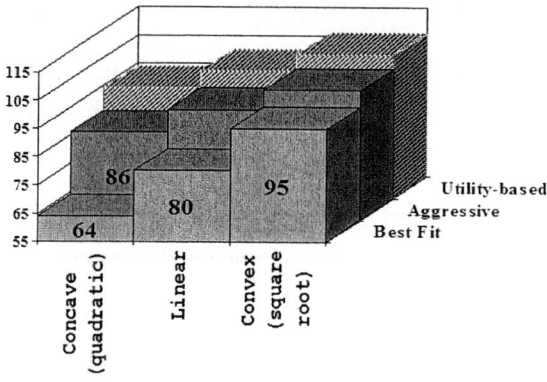

Fig. 3. Sensitivity of productivity to the shape of TUFs for job arrival rate of 0.3

of action in some situations. Correspondingly, Figure 3 shows that the utility-based policy trained with RL learns the situations (system states) when waiting is preferred and hence outperforms both fixed policies.

5 Conclusions

This paper presents a utility-based approach for scheduling jobs in a computing facility and demonstrates the feasibility of tuning parameters of the utility functions with reinforcement learning. Many other details can be added to the basic scheduling framework described in this paper. However, the central idea of scheduling jobs so as to maximize the state value of a server or a computing facility is general enough to be used in various scheduling environments: a massively-parallel supercomputer, a data center, a Grid computing facility, etc.

The utility-based policy learning framework allows each machine to adjust its policies independently of other machines, the performance results presented in this paper are expected to hold for any number of machines. The Time Utility Functions used in this paper not only allow each user to encode its Quality of Service preferences, but also provide a natural optimization objective (total utility of all completed jobs) for any algorithms that perform automatic tuning of scheduling policies. In some environments it might be preferable to ensure that every submitted job gets executed in a fair manner, which can be achieved by *increasing* the utility of each job as it waits in the queue, as opposed to decreasing it.

The presented utility-based scheduling framework can be easily extended to the multi-project domain, where different projects have different priorities. In that case, a job from a higher-priority project would automatically preempt enough of the lower-priority jobs to fit itself (preempting those with lowest remaining utility first), and the utility-based preemption and oversubscribing policies would be invoked only for arbitrating between unscheduled jobs of the same priority.

Acknowledgement

The author would like to thank Declan Murphy and Ilya Gluhovsky from Sun Microsystems for helpful comments and corrections to this paper.

References

1. D. Bertsekas and J. Tsitsiklis, *Neuro-Dynamic Programming*, Athena Scientific, 1996.
2. R. K. Clark. "Scheduling Dependent Real-Time Activities," Ph.D. Dissertation, Carnegie Mellon University, CMU-CS-90-155, 1990.
3. E.D. Jensen, C.D. Locke, and H. Tokuda. "A time driven scheduling model for real-time operating systems," In Proceedings IEEE Real-Time Systems Symposium, pp. 112-122, 1985.
4. J. Kepner, "HPC Productivity Model Synthesis," *International Journal of High Performance Computing Applications: Special Issue on HPC Productivity.* J. Kepner (editor), vol. 18, no. 4, Winter 2004 (November).
5. P. Li, B. Ravindran, H. Wu, E. D. Jensen. "A Utility Accrual Scheduling Algorithm for Real-Time Activities With Mutual Exclusion Resource Constraints," The MITRE Corporation Working Paper, April 2004.
6. R.S. Sutton and A. G. Barto. *Reinforcement Learning: An Introduction.* MIT Press, 1998.
7. J. N. Tsitsiklis and B. Van Roy. "Average Cost Temporal-Difference Learning," *Automatica*, Vol. 35, No. 11, November 1999, pp. 1799-1808.
8. L.-X. Wang. "Fuzzy systems are universal approximators," In Proceedings of the IEEE International Conference on Fuzzy Systems (FUZZ-IEEE '92), pp. 1163-1169, 1992.
9. H. Wu, B. Ravindran, E. D. Jensen, and U. Balli. "Utility Accrual Scheduling Under Arbitrary Time/Utility Functions and Multiunit Resource Constraints," *IEEE Real-Time and Embedded Computing Systems and Applications*, August 2004, To appear.

New Feature Extraction Approaches for Face Recognition*

Vo Dinh Minh Nhat** and Sungyoung Lee**

Kyung Hee University, South of Korea
{vdmnhat, sylee}@oslab.khu.ac.kr

Abstract. All the traditional PCA-based and LDA-based methods are based on the analysis of vectors. So, it is difficult to evaluate the covariance matrices in such a high-dimensional vector space. Recently, two-dimensional PCA (2DPCA) and two-dimensional LDA (2DLDA) have been proposed in which image covariance matrices can be constructed directly using original image matrices. In contrast to the covariance matrices of traditional 1D approaches (PCA and LDA), the size of the image covariance matrices using 2D approaches (2DPCA and 2DLDA) are much smaller. As a result, it is easier to evaluate the covariance matrices accurately and computation cost is reduced. However, a drawback of 2D approaches is that it needs more coefficients than traditional approaches for image representation. Thus, 2D approach needs more memory to store its features and costs more time to calculate distance (similarity) in classification phase. In this paper, we develop a new image feature extraction methods called *two-stage 2D* subspace approaches to overcome the disadvantage of 2DPCA and 2DLDA. The initial idea of *two-stage 2D* subspace approaches which consist of *two-stage* 2DPCA and *two-stage* 2DLDA is to perform 2DPCA or 2DLDA twice: the first one is in horizontal direction and the second is in vertical direction. After the two sequential 2D transforms, the discriminant information is compacted into the up-left corner of the image. Experiment results show our methods achieve better performance in comparison with the other approaches with the lower computation cost.

Index Terms: Principle component analysis (PCA), Linear Discriminant Analysis (LDA), Face Recognition.

1 Introduction

PRINCIPAL component analysis (PCA), also known as Karhunen-Loeve expansion, is a classical feature extraction and data representation technique widely used in the areas of pattern recognition and computer vision. Within this context, Turk and

---

* This research was supported by the MIC (Ministry of Information and Communication), Korea, under the ITRC(Information Technology Research Center) support program supervised by the IITA (Institute of Information Technology Assessment).
** Corresponding Authors. Vo Dinh Minh Nhat (vo_dinhminhnhat@yahoo.com), and SungYoung Lee (sylee@oslab.khu.ac.kr).

Pentland [1] presented the well-known Eigenfaces method for face recognition in 1991. Since then, PCA has been widely investigated and has become one of the most successful approaches in face recognition. However, PCA could not capture even the simplest invariance unless this information is explicitly provided in the training data. It also cannot make full use of pattern separability information like the Fisher criterion, and its recognition effect is not ideal when the size of the sample set is large.

The Fisherface method [4] combines PCA and the Fisher criterion [9] to extract the information that discriminates between the classes of a sample set. It is a most representative method of LDA. Nevertheless, Martinez et al. demonstrated that when the training data set is small, the Eigenface method outperforms the Fisherface method [7]. Should the latter be outperformed by the former? This provoked a variety of explanations. Liu et al. thought that it might have been because the Fisherface method uses all the principal components, but the components with the small eigenvalues correspond to high-frequency components and usually encode noise [11], leading to recognition results that are less than ideal. In line with this theory, they presented two enhanced Fisher linear discrimination (FLD) models (EFMs) [11] and an enhanced Fisher classifier [12] for face recognition. Their experiential explanation lacks sufficient theoretical demonstration, however, and EFM does not provide an automatic strategy for selecting the components. Chen et al. proved that the null space of the within-class scatter matrix contains the most discriminative information when a small sample size problem takes place [13]. Their method is also inadequate, however, as it does not use any of the information outside the null space. In [5], Yu et al. propose a direct LDA (DLDA) approach to solve this problem. It removes the null space of the between-class scatter matrix firstly by doing eigen-analysis. Then a simultaneous diagonalization procedure is used to seek the optimal discriminant vectors in the subspace of the between-class scatter matrix. However, in this method, removing the null space of the between-class scatter matrix by dimensionality reduction would indirectly lead to the losing of the null space of the within-class scatter matrix which contains considerable discriminative information. Rui Huang [10] proposed the method in which the null space of total scatter matrix which has been proved to be the common null space of both between-class and within-class scatter matrix, and useless for discrimination, is firstly removed. Then in the lower-dimensional projected space, the null space of the resulting within-class scatter matrix is calculated. This lower-dimensional null space, combined with the previous projection, represents a subspace of the whole null space of within-class scatter matrix, and is really useful for discrimination. The optimal discriminant vectors of LDA are derived from it. In [14], a common vector for each individual class is obtained by removing all the features that are in the direction of the eigenvectors corresponding to the nonzero eigenvalues of the scatter matrix of its own class. The common vectors are then used for recognition. In their case, instead of using a given class's own scatter matrix, they use the within-class scatter matrix of all classes to obtain the common vectors.

However, all the previous traditional PCA-based and LDA-based methods are based on the analysis of vectors. So, it is difficult to evaluate the covariance matrices in such a high-dimensional vector space. Recently, two-dimensional PCA (2DPCA) [15] and two-dimensional LDA (2DLDA) [16] have been proposed in which image covariance matrices can be constructed directly using original image matrices. In contrast to the covariance matrices of traditional 1D approaches (PCA and LDA), the size of the image covariance matrices using 2D approaches (2DPCA and 2DLDA) are much smaller. As a result, it is easier to evaluate the covariance matrices accurately and computation cost is reduced. However, a drawback of 2D approaches is that it needs more coefficients than traditional approaches for image representation. Thus, 2D approach needs more memory to store its features and costs more time to calculate distance (similarity) in classification phase. In this paper, we develop a new image feature extraction methods called *two-stage 2D* subspace approaches to overcome the disadvantage of 2DPCA and 2DLDA. The initial idea of *two-stage 2D* subspace approaches which consist of *two-stage* 2DPCA and *two-stage* 2DLDA is to perform 2DPCA or 2DLDA twice: the first one is in horizontal direction and the second is in vertical direction. After the two sequential 2D transforms, the discriminant information is compacted into the up-left corner of the image. The remainder of this paper is organized as follows: In Section 2, the traditional PCA and LDA methods are reviewed. 2DPCA, 2DLDA and the proposed methods are described in Section 3. In Section 4, experimental results are presented for the ORL face image databases to demonstrate the effectiveness of our methods. Finally, conclusions are presented in Section 5.

2 PCA and LDA

One approach to coping with the problem of excessive dimensionality of the image space is to reduce the dimensionality by combining features. Linear combinations are particular, attractive because they are simple to compute and analytically tractable. In effect, linear methods project the high-dimensional data onto a lower dimensional subspace.

Suppose that we have N sample images $\{x_1, x_2, ..., x_N\}$ taking values in an n-dimensional image space. Let us also consider a linear transformation mapping the original n-dimensional image space into an m-dimensional feature space, where $m < n$. The new feature vectors $y_k \in \mathbb{R}^m$ are defined by the following linear transformation:

$$y_k = W^T x_k \qquad (1)$$

where $k = 1, 2, ..., N$ and $W \in \mathbb{R}^{n \times m}$ is a matrix with orthonormal columns.

Different objective functions will yield different algorithms with different properties. PCA aims to extract a subspace in which the variance is maximized. Its objective function is as follows:

$$W_{opt} = [w_1 w_2 ... w_m] = \arg\max_W \left| W^T S_T W \right| \qquad (2)$$

with the total scatter matrix is defined as

$$S_T = \sum_{k=1}^{N}(x_k - \mu)(x_k - \mu)^T \qquad (3)$$

and $\mu \in \mathbb{R}^n$ is the mean image of all samples.

The optimal projection $W_{opt} = [w_1 w_2 ... w_m]$ is the set of n-dimensional eigenvectors of S_T corresponding to the m largest eigenvalues.

While PCA seeks directions that are efficient for representation, Linear Discriminant Analysis seeks directions that are efficient for discrimination. Assume that each image belongs to one of c classes $\{C_1, C_2, ..., C_c\}$. Let N_i be the number of the samples in class $C_i (i = 1, 2, ..., c)$, $\mu_i = \frac{1}{N_i} \sum_{x \in C_i} x$ be the mean of the samples in class X_i, $\mu = \frac{1}{N} \sum_{i=1}^{N} x_i$ be the mean of all samples. Then the between-class scatter matrix S_b is defined as

$$S_b = \frac{1}{N} \sum_{i=1}^{c} N_i (\mu_i - \mu)(\mu_i - \mu)^T = \frac{1}{N} \Phi_b \Phi_b^T \qquad (4)$$

and the within-class scatter matrix S_w is defined as

$$S_w = \frac{1}{N} \sum_{i=1}^{c} \sum_{x_k \in C_i} (x_k - \mu_i)(x_k - \mu_i)^T = \frac{1}{N} \Phi_w \Phi_w^T \qquad (5)$$

In LDA, the projection W_{opt} is chosen to maximize the ratio of the determinant of the between-class scatter matrix of the projected samples to the determinant of the within-class scatter matrix of the projected samples, i.e.,

$$W_{opt} = \arg\max_W \frac{|W^T S_b W|}{|W^T S_w W|} = [w_1 w_2 ... w_m] \qquad (6)$$

where $\{w_i | i = 1, 2, ..., m\}$ is the set of generalized eigenvectors of S_b and S_w corresponding to the m largest generalized eigenvalues $\{\lambda_i | i = 1, 2, ..., m\}$, i.e.,

$$S_b w_i = \lambda_i S_w w_i \quad i = 1, 2, ..., m \qquad (7)$$

3 Two-Dimensional PCA, Two-Dimensional LDA and Our Proposed Approaches

In 2D approach, the image matrix does not need to be previously transformed into a vector, so a set of N sample images is represented as $\{X_1, X_2, ..., X_N\}$ with $X_i \in \mathbb{R}^{kxs}$. The total scatter matrix is defined as

$$G_T = \sum_{i=1}^{N}(X_i - \mu_X)(X_i - \mu_X)^T \tag{8}$$

with $\mu_X = \frac{1}{N}\sum_{i=1}^{N} X_i \in \mathbb{R}^{kxs}$ is the mean image of all samples. $G_T \in \mathbb{R}^{kxk}$ is also called image covariance (scatter) matrix.

A linear transformation mapping the original kxs image space into an mxs feature space, where $m < k$. The new feature matrices $Y_i \in \mathbb{R}^{mxs}$ are defined by the following linear transformation:

$$Y_i = W^T(X_i - \mu_X) \in \mathbb{R}^{mxs} \tag{9}$$

where $i = 1, 2, ..., N$ and $W \in \mathbb{R}^{kxm}$ is a matrix with orthonormal columns. In 2DPCA, the projection W_{opt} is chosen to maximize $tr(W^T G_T W)$. The optimal projection $W_{opt} = [w_1 w_2 ... w_m]$ with $\{w_i | i = 1, 2, ..., m\}$ is the set of n-dimensional eigenvectors of G_T corresponding to the m largest eigenvalues.

In 2DLDA, the between-class scatter matrix S_b is re-defined as

$$S_b = \frac{1}{N}\sum_{i=1}^{c} N_i (\mu_{C_i} - \mu_X)(\mu_{C_i} - \mu_X)^T \tag{10}$$

and the within-class scatter matrix S_w is re-defined as

$$S_w = \frac{1}{N}\sum_{i=1}^{c}\sum_{X_k \in C_i}(X_k - \mu_{C_i})(X_k - \mu_{C_i})^T \tag{11}$$

with $\mu_X = \sum_{i=1}^{N} X_i \in \mathbb{R}^{kxs}$ is the mean image of all samples and $\mu_{C_i} = \frac{1}{N_i}\sum_{X \in C_i} X$ be the mean of the samples in class C_i.

Similarly, a linear transformation mapping the original kxs image space into an mxs feature space, where $m<k$. The new feature matrices $Y_i \in \mathbb{R}^{mxs}$ are defined by the following linear transformation :

$$Y_i = W^T(X_i - \mu_X) \in \mathbb{R}^{mxs} \qquad (12)$$

where $i=1,2,...,N$ and $W \in \mathbb{R}^{kxm}$ is a matrix with orthonormal columns. And the projection W_{opt} is chosen with the criterion same as that in (6).

After a transformation by 2DPCA or 2DLDA, a feature matrix is obtained for each image. Then, a nearest neighbor classifier is used for classification. Here, the distance between two arbitrary feature matrices Y_i and Y_j is defined by using Euclidean distance as follows :

$$d(Y_i, Y_j) = \sqrt{\sum_{u=1}^{k}\sum_{v=1}^{s}(Y_i(u,v)-Y_j(u,v))^2} \qquad (13)$$

Given a test sample Y_t, if $d(Y_t, Y_c) = \min_j d(Y_t, Y_j)$, then the resulting decision is Y_t belongs to the same class as Y_c.

The 2D approach can eliminate the correlations between image columns and compress the discriminant information optimally into a few of columns in horizontal direction. However, it disregards the correlations between image rows and the data compression in vertical direction. So, its compression rate is far lower than 1D approach and more coefficients are needed for the representation of images. This must lead to a slow classification speed and large storage requirements for large-scaled databases. In this section, we will suggest a way to overcome the weakness of 2DPCA and 2DLDA. Our idea is simple, just to perform 2DPCA or 2DLDA twice: the first one is in horizontal direction and the second is in vertical direction (note that any operation in vertical direction can be equivalently implemented by an operation in horizontal direction by virtue of the transpose operation of matrix). Specifically, given image X_i, we obtain its feature matrix Y_i after the first 2DPCA or 2DLDA transform. Then, we transpose Y_i and input Y_i^T into 2DPCA or 2DLDA, and the resulting feature matrix Z_i could be obtained. This process is illustrated in Fig. 1.

Detailed implementation of *two-stage* 2DPCA or 2DLDA can be summarized as follow

Step 1. Horizontal 2DPCA or 2DLDA

- Given training images X_i with $i=1..N$, calculate the total scatter matrix, or between-class scatter matrix and within-class scatter matrix by (8), (10), (11).

- After first transformation by 2DPCA or 2DLDA, a feature matrix is obtained for each image $Y_i = W_{1opt}^T X_i$ with $W_{1opt} = [w_1 w_2 ... w_m]$ is the optimal projection.

Step 2. Vertical 2DPCA or 2DLDA
- Similarly, input Y_i^T into 2DPCA or 2DLDA, and the resulting feature matrix $Z_i = W_{2opt}^T Y_i^T$ could be obtained.

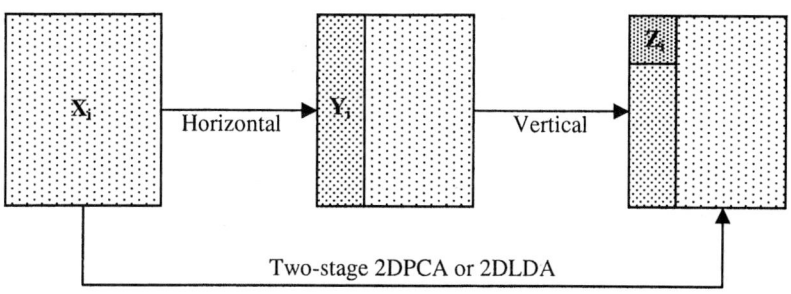

Fig. 1. The illustration of *two-stage* 2DPCA or 2DLDA

4 Experimental Results

This section evaluates the performance of our propoped algorithms *two-stage* 2DPCA and *two-stage* 2DPCA with the following algoriths : Eigenfaces (PCA) , Fisherfaces (LDA), Direct LDA [5], 2DPCA and 2DLDA based on using ORL face database. In the ORL database, there are ten different images of each of 40 distinct subjects. For some subjects, the images were taken at different times, varying the lighting, facial expressions (open / closed eyes, smiling / not smiling) and facial details (glasses / no glasses). All the images were taken against a dark homogeneous background with the subjects in an upright, frontal position (with tolerance for some side movement).

In our experiments, we tested the recognition rates with different number of training samples. $k(k = 2, 3, 4, 5)$ images of each subject are randomly selected from the database for training and the remaining images of each subject for testing. Since the number of projection vectors, has a considerable impact on the results of the different algorithms, we choose the value that corresponds to the best classification result on the image set consisting of the first k images of each subject as its optimal value. In all of the experiments, the nearest neighbor algorithm under the Euclidean distance is employed to classify the test images. For each value of k, 30 runs are performed with different random partition between training set and testing set. *Table 1* shows the average recognition rates (%) of different approaches with ORL database, while *Table 2* show us the performances of those approaches in terms of computation time.

Table 1. Comparison of the average error rates (%) of different approaches on the ORL database

k	2	3	4	5	6
Eigenfaces - PCA	82.46	89.27	92.73	95.24	96.11
Fisherfaces - LDA	79.47	86.84	90.37	91.89	93.93
Direct LDA	80.94	89.19	92.71	95.46	96.97
2DPCA	85.05	90.18	93.89	96.18	97.11
Two-stage 2DPCA	**86.02**	**90.89**	**94.36**	**97.80**	**98.20**
2DLDA	87.41	92.34	95.54	96.12	96.70
Two-stage 2DLDA	**89.14**	**93.56**	**96.87**	**97.36**	**98.15**

Table 2. The average CPU time (s) consumed for training and testing, the top recognition rates (%) and the corresponding number of samples of seven methods. (CPU : PIV 2.4 GHz, RAM 512M)

k	2	3	4	5	6
Eigenfaces - PCA	27.59	37.70	52.34	36.08	32.15
Fisherfaces - LDA	16.18	32.71	44.08	68.96	81.09
Direct LDA	15.59	15.61	15.31	17.61	17.31
2DPCA	0.50	1.10	1.25	1.39	1.52
Two-stage 2DPCA	**0.35**	**0.90**	**1.16**	**1.19**	**1.31**
2DLDA	0.58	1.21	1.34	1.45	1.63
Two-stage 2DLDA	**0.41**	**0.98**	**1.22**	**1.34**	**1.49**

We can see that our methods achieve the better recognition rate compared to the other approaches with a lower computation cost.

5 Conclusions

New 2DPCA-based and 2DLDA-based methods for face recognition have been proposed in this paper. The proposed methods can outperform the other methods in terms of both recognition rate and computation cost. The initial idea of *two-stage* 2DPCA or *two-stage* 2DPCA is to perform 2DPCA or 2DLDA twice: the first one is in horizontal direction and the second is in vertical direction. After the two sequential transforms, the discriminant information is compacted into the up-left corner of the image. The effectiveness of the proposed approaches can be seen through our experiments based on ORL face databases.

References

1. M. Turk, A. Pentland : Eigenfaces for face recognition. *Int. J. Cog. Neurosci.*, vol. 3, (1991) 71–86.
2. W. Zhao, R. Chellappa, P.J. Phillips: Subspace Linear Discriminant Analysis for Face Recognition. Technical Report CAR-TR-914, Center for Automation Research, University of Maryland, 1999.

3. D. L. Swets, J. J. Weng: Using discrimination eigenfeatures for image retrieval. *IEEE Trans. Pattern Anal. Machine Intell.*, vol. 18 (1996) 831–836.
4. P. N. Belhumeur, J. P. Hespanha, D. J. Kriegman: Eigenfaces vs. fisherface: Recognition using class specific linear projection. *IEEE Trans. Pattern Anal. Machine Intell.*, vol. 19 (1997) 711–720.
5. H. Yu, J. Yang: A direct LDA algorithm for high-dimensional data with application to face recognition. *Pattern Recognit.*, vol. 34 (2001) 2067–2070.
6. M. Loog, R. P. W. Duin, R. Haeb-Umbach: Multiclass linear dimension reduction by weighted pairwise fisher criteria. *IEEE Trans. Pattern Anal. Machine Intell.*, vol. 23 (2001) 762–766.
7. A. M. Martinez, A. C. Kak: PCA versus LDA. *IEEE Trans. Pattern Anal. Machine Intell.*, vol. 23 (2001) 228–233.
8. D. H. Foley, J. W. Sammon: An optimal set of discrimination vectors. *IEEE Trans. Comput.*, vol. C-24 (1975) 281–289.
9. [9] R. A. Fisher, "The use of multiple measurements in taxonomic problems," *Ann. Eugenics*, vol. 7, pp. 178–188, 1936.
10. Rui Huang, Qingshan Liu, Hanqing Lu, Songde Ma: Solving the small sample size problem of LDA. Pattern Recognition, 2002. Proceedings. 16th International Conference on , Vol 3 (2002) 29 – 32.
11. C. Liu, H. Wechsler: Robust coding scheme for indexing and retrieval from large face databases. *IEEE Trans. Image Processing*, vol. 9 (2000) 132–137.
12. Chengjun Liu, Wechsler H.: A shape- and texture-based enhanced Fisher classifier for face recognition. *IEEE Trans. Image Processing*, vol. 10 (2001) 598–608.
13. L. Chen, H. M. Liao, M. Ko, J. Lin, G. Yu: A new LDA-based face recognition system which can solve the small sample size problem. Pattern Recognit., vol. 33 (2000) 1713–1726.
14. Cevikalp, H., Neamtu, M., Wilkes. M., Barkana, A.: Discriminative common vectors for face recognition. Pattern Analysis and Machine Intelligence, IEEE Transactions on , Vol. 27 (2005) 4 – 13.
15. Jian Yang, Zhang, D., Frangi, A.F., Jing-yu Yang: Two-dimensional PCA: a new approach to appearance-based face representation and recognition. Pattern Analysis and Machine Intelligence, IEEE Transactions on , Vol. 26 (2004) 131 – 137
16. Ming Li, Baozong Yuan : 2D-LDA: A statistical linear discriminant analysis for image matrix. Pattern Recognition Letters, Vol. 26, Issue 5 (2005) 527-532.
17. "The ORL face database" http://www.uk.research.att.com/facedatabase.html.

EBGM with Fuzzy Fusion on Face Recognition

Jialiang Liu and Zhi-Qiang Liu

The University of Melbourne, Australia
jiall@cs.mu.oz.au

Abstract. Elastic Bunch Graph Matching (EBGM) is regarded as a successful method to perform recognition on 2D face images. It employs an indiscriminate, part-separated aggregation method to conclude the overall recognition from local recognition results on face parts. Supported by the experimental evidence from cognitive research, we consider the human face recognition is an aggregation process that combines the local recognitions together in a inter-dependent and collective manner rather than a indiscriminate and part-separated process. This paper presents a improved EBGM face recognition system with the use of fuzzy fusion techniques (fuzzy measure and fuzzy integral) as the collective aggregation method. Experimental result shows the EBGM with fuzzy fusion produces better recognition performance over the original EBGM.

1 Introduction

Over the years in literature of face recognition, two main trends of approach have emerged in research of simulating the computational model of human face recognition. One is global expert approach that treats face as a whole to extract global features to form the compact representation of the face. This global representation will then be used to determine if two faces are similar. Principle Component Analysis (PCA) [1] is an representative in this approach. PCA treats a face image as a high dimensional vector. Using eigenvector projection it compress the vector into a low dimensional vector as the representation of the face. Recognition then can proceed utilizing the similarity definition based on these global features produced by global expert. Another is a local expert approach that performs local similarity recognition in salient nodes of a face, then the overall recognition is concluded from the resulting multi-source recognition contributed locally. Elastic Bunch Graph Matching (EBGM) [2] is considered as a successful method in this approach. EBGM applies Gabor wavelet frequency filters to a face image, and generate filtered coefficients in local salient points (eyes , nose, etc). Local recognitions are performed based on the similarities of local filtered coefficients, then the overall recognition is simply the sum of recognition from local experts plus the spatial similarity of the topography structure of the salient points. It appears that EBGM has slight advantage over PCA as EBGM incorporate local recognition (local similarity of filtered coefficients in each salient point) and a minimum global recognition (the similarity of topographical structure of salient points) together to produce a overall recognition.

The current aggregation of local recognitions in EBGM treats each local expert in each salient position indiscriminately, this strategy disregards the fact of different distribution of importance from local experts in different salient positions. For instance, the similarity in the eye may have more distinctive importance than the similarity in the hair during the course of human face recognition. One might suggest a weighted operator could be adopted. It can be seen that both the indiscriminate and simple weighted aggregation decompose the face into parts, and the overall recognition relies on the independent recognition of the separated local parts and their spatial arrangement. We argue that this part-separated recognition has a limited performance for recognizing homogeneous objects such as face that has the same basic component parts in the same basic spatial arrangement. In fact, the local parts of the face should not be treated separately and the local recognition should be dependent on each other. To emphasize the inherent relationships between local recognitions, we propose the use of fuzzy fusion technique as the aggregation method.

Fuzzy integral of information fusion has long been a useful tool for pattern recognition. A decision can be expressed as an aggregation of a set of evidence sources with different distribution of importance that supports or rejects that decision. Applying it in the EBGM case, the evidence sources will be the local recognitions in different salient positions, and the degree of importance of each evidence source can be learned from training samples. The final decision whether two face images belong to the same person is based on this multi-sources fuzzy integration.

2 The System

2.1 EBGM

EBGM applies Gabor wavelet transform to face image to obtain Jet values. A Jet is described as the set of 40 $\mathcal{J}_j$, each defined as convolution with image $\mathcal{I}(\boldsymbol{x})$:

$$\mathcal{J}_j(\boldsymbol{x}) = \int \mathcal{I}(\boldsymbol{x})\psi_j(\boldsymbol{x}-\boldsymbol{x}')d^2\boldsymbol{x}' \qquad (1)$$

with a family of Gabor kernels:

$$\psi_j(\boldsymbol{x}) = \frac{f_j^2}{\sigma^2}exp(-\frac{f_j^2 x^2}{2\sigma^2})[exp(i\boldsymbol{f}_j\boldsymbol{x}) - exp(-\frac{\sigma^2}{2})]$$

spatial frequencies:

$$\boldsymbol{f}_j = \begin{pmatrix} f_{jx} \\ f_{jy} \end{pmatrix} = \begin{pmatrix} f_\nu cos\varphi_\mu \\ f_\nu sin\varphi_\mu \end{pmatrix}, f_\nu = 2^{-\frac{\nu+2}{2}}\pi, \varphi_\mu = \mu\frac{\pi}{8}, \sigma = 2\pi$$

index:

$$j = \mu + 8\nu, \nu = 0, ..., 4, \mu = 0, ..., 7.$$

The convolution result $\{\mathcal{J}_j = a_j exp(i\phi_j)\}_{j=1,..,40}$ is a set of 40 complex coefficients that contain information in different spatial frequency bandwidth for one image point $\boldsymbol{x}$. A sparse collection of such jets in obvious salient nodes together with the topographical relations of these salient positions constitutes a Graph structure that represents an object such as a face. For a probe image graph $\mathcal{G}$ and a template image graph $\mathcal{G}'$ with salient nodes $x_1, x_2, ..., x_n$ and the edge vectors between two nodes $\Delta x_1, \Delta x_2, ..., \Delta x_e$, the definitions of Jet Similarity in node x_i is

$$S(\mathcal{J}_{x_i}, \mathcal{J}'_{x_i}) = \frac{\sum_{j=1}^{40} a_j a'_j \cos(\phi_j - \phi'_j - \boldsymbol{d}\boldsymbol{f_j})}{\sqrt{\sum_{j=1}^{40} a_j^2 \sum_{j=1}^{40} a'^2_j}} \quad (2)$$

(where $\boldsymbol{d}$ is the estimated displacement of a node with jet value $\mathcal{J}$ and a node with jet value $\mathcal{J}'$), and Graph Similarity

$$S(\mathcal{G}, \mathcal{G}') = \frac{1}{n}\sum_{i=1}^{n} S(\mathcal{J}_{x_i}, \mathcal{J}'_{x_i}) - \frac{\tau}{e}\sum_{i=1}^{e} \frac{(\Delta x_i^{\mathcal{G}} - \Delta x_i^{\mathcal{G}'})}{(\Delta x_i^{\mathcal{G}'})} \quad (3)$$

(where τ determines the relative importance of jet information and topographical structure) defines the similarity between two face images represented by these two Graphs.

EBGM comprises of three main stages:

- FBG Construction, a FBG (Face Bunch Graph) structure containing a rich set of Jets corresponded to the predefined salient nodes (eyes, nose, etc.) in a variety of face training samples is constructed. The FBG serves as a representation of faces in general.
- Face Location and graph extraction, A Displacement Estimation algorithm (DE) utilized the FBG as a general face template is adopted to locate salient nodes (eyes, nose, etc.) in the unknown probe image. The DE algorithm can be applied iteratively until sub-pixel accuracy is achieved. The graph structure corresponded to the located face is extracted.
- Matching, The graph structure extracted will then be matched with the graph template in face database using the graph similarity definition 3.

2.2 Fuzzy Measure and Fuzzy Integral

Fuzzy measure has been introduced by Sugeno [6] in order to extend probability measure by relaxing the additivity property.

Definition 1: Suppose X is a set, a function $g: 2^X \to [0,1]$ with

- $g(\emptyset) = 0$, $g(X) = 1$,
- $g(A) \leq g(B)$ if $A \subset B$

is called a fuzzy measure. Based on this definition, g_λ measure can be defined to specify the non-addictive relationship between two fuzzy sources. For over-addictive, we have the following property:

for all $A, B \subset X$ and $A \cap B = \emptyset$,
$g(A \cup B) = g(A) + g(B) + \lambda g(A)g(B)$

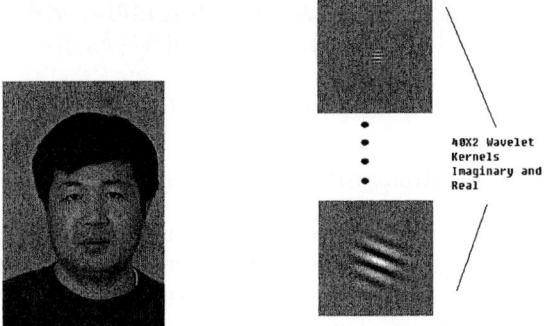

Fig. 1. Original Image convoluted with 40 × 2 (real and imaginary) kernels

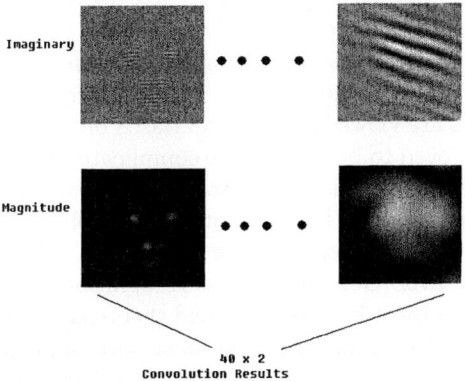

Fig. 2. Convolution Result Images

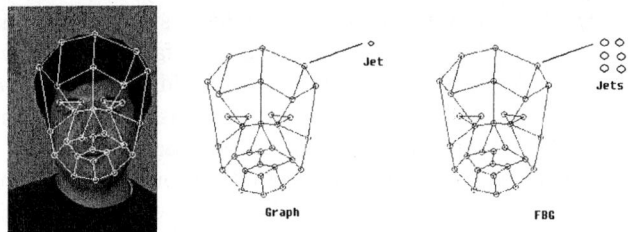

Fig. 3. Face graph and FBG structure based on jet coefficients extracted from convoluted result images

The notion of fuzzy integral is the logical continuation of the notion of fuzzy measure.

Definition 2: Let X be a set and $h : X \to [0,1]$ be a function. The Sugeno fuzzy integral over $A \subseteq X$ of the function h with respect to a fuzzy measure g is defined by

$$\int_A h(x) \circ g(\cdot) = sup_{E \subseteq X}[min(min_{x \in E}(h(x), g(A \cap E)))]$$
$$= sup_{\alpha \in [0,1]}[min(\alpha, g(A \cap F_\alpha))]$$

$$where F_\alpha = \{x \mid h(x) \geq \alpha\}$$

2.3 Fuzzy Integral Recognition with Multiple Jet Similarity Sources

Why Fuzzy Integral. The Jet Similarity value of a salient node (left eye, for instance) serves as a local expert to describe how similar the left eyes of two faces are. Global information comprises of many of these local similarities to indicate the similarity of two objects. This is a classic multi-sources recognition process. The current Graph Similarity definition in equation 3 treats each recognition source (Jet Similarity in each salient node defined in equation 2) indiscriminately. One will intuitively suggested that a person can be recognized more based on the recognition of the eyes rather than the recognition the ears. So a weighted operator can be applied as the aggregator. However, a simple weighted approach implicitly assumes the multiple evident sources are independent of one another, their effects are viewed as additive. Based on cognitive research, human face recognition is proved to be much more complicate than simple additive combination of individual recognition of separated local parts such as eye, nose, etc. Tim Valentine [7] argues that the computations involved in human face recognitions are not part of a general purpose recognition system used to recognize objects at the basic level. General purpose recognition relies on the perceptual decomposition of the object into its parts and their spatial arrangement, and the additive summation of recognitions from local parts and their spatial arrangement. This part-additive process is ideal for basic level recognition because at that level objects either differ primarily in the parts that they have or have significant difference in the spatial arrangement of its parts (a part is missing, for instance). In contrast to basic level objects, human faces share a similar configuration, having the same basic parts in the same basic spatial arrangement. Basic level recognition can only tell if we are looking at a face, but not whose face it is. We consider that the poor performance of part-additive recognition is due to the fact that it does not address the inherent relationships between recognitions of local parts. It rather treats the local recognition independently.

The fact that some elements of local recognition sources may have tighter relationship than others is not considered in the simple weighted additive process. This is not justifiable in real world cases, the importance of the combined recognition of both eyes is higher than the sum of importance associated with the recognition of left eye and right eye alone. To address the problem, a non-additive fuzzy measure can be adopted to characterize the importance of multiple recognition sources, and respectively fuzzy integral is used as a synthetic classifier. While still based on individual local recognitions, the fuzzy fusion approach emphasizes more in the collective prospect of the recognition. It conforms to the evidence that human face recognition is not a separated process involving isolated eye recognition, ear recognition, etc, but rather a collective process involving eye recognition, ear recognition, etc together. Also as the difference of spatial arrangement of parts in different faces is insignificant, we can simply abandon the rather ineffective similarity comparison of spatial structure.

The Recognition Process. The recognition process is given. The FBG construction, face location and graph extraction remain the same as the original EBGM. In the matching stage, the simple indiscriminate integration is replaced by the fuzzy fusion aggregation. Formally, to determine how similar of two face graphs $\mathcal{G}$ and $\mathcal{G}'$ extracted from the second stage, the Jet Similarities $h(x_1) = S(\mathcal{J}_{x_1}, \mathcal{J}'_{x_1}), h(x_2) = S(\mathcal{J}_{x_2}, \mathcal{J}'_{x_2}), ..., h(x_n) = S(\mathcal{J}_{x_n}, \mathcal{J}'_{x_n})$ with x_n indexing salient node in a face are calculated according to equation 2 and rearrange so that $h(x_1) \geq h(x_2) \geq ... \geq h(x_n)$, each salient node is associated with a fuzzy density g^i representing the degree of importance of the similarity in x_i salient node towards the final recognition. In a later section we will explain how to decide the degree of importance (fuzzy density) through learning. A Sugeno fuzzy integral e can be computed by

$$e = max_{i=1}^{n}[min(h(x_i), g(A_i))] \qquad (4)$$

where $A_i = \{x_1, x_2, ...x_i\}$ and $g(A_i)$ are computed recursively as:

$$g(A_1) = g(\{x_1\}) = g^1$$

$$g(A_i) = g^i + g(A_{i-1}) + \lambda g^i g(A_{i-1}), for 1 \leq i \leq n$$

The value of λ can be found from equation

$$\lambda + 1 = \prod_{i=1}^{n}(1 + \lambda g^i)$$

The calculated fuzzy integral e represents the degree of similarity of the two face graphs.

The following is the interpretation of the fuzzy integral face recognition. Suppose the recognition object, the probe face graph is evaluated from the point of view of a set of sources A. These sources are the jet similarities $h(x_i) = S(\mathcal{J}_{x_i}, \mathcal{J}'_{x_i}), i = 1, 2, ..n$ in salient nodes (eyes, nose, etc) between this probe face graph and the template face graph. So $h(x_i)$ denotes the decision for the matching process when $i \in A$ source is considered and let g^i denote the degree of importance of this source. The quantity $min_{i \in A} h(x_i)$ is considered as the best security decision that the set of jet similarities in A provides. $g(A)$ expresses the grade of importance of this set of sources. The value obtained from comparing these two quantities in terms of the min operator is interpreted as the grade of agreement between the real possibilities of matchness (how much of matchness between probe face and template face based on the evidence of jet similarities in sources A), $h(x_i)$ and the expectations of matchness (how much they should match between probe face and template face based on our expectation in sources A) $g(A)$. Hence fuzzy integration is interpreted as searching for the maximal grade of agreement between the evidence and the expectation from the set of

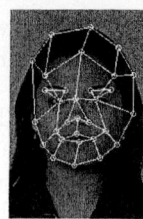 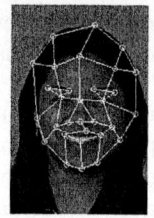 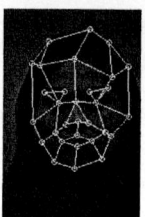

Fig. 4. Face images belonged to the same person with normal expression (*fa* and *ba* image), smiling expression (*fb* and *bj* image) and under darker illumination (*bk* image). The graphs in the images were generated automatically utilizing DE algorithm and FBG structure.

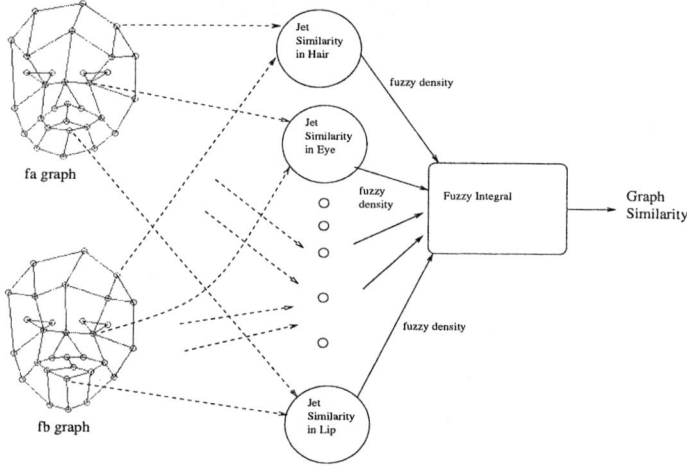

Fig. 5. The fuzzy integral recognition process

local group recognitions involved the subsets of salient nodes. An instance of a local group recognition is the recognition based on the jet similarities and fuzzy densities involving only the salient nodes of left-eye, left-inner-eyebrow and left–outer-eyebrow.

Fuzzy Density Learning Process. A key issue remains unsolved in the application of fuzzy integrals - the determination of fuzzy density values interpreted as the relative importance of information sources to be combined. The performance of fuzzy integral application critically depends on the fuzzy densities assigned. Here we explain two alternative fuzzy density learning approaches that can learn the relative importance of sub-classifiers via training process.

Discriminative Power Learning: To determine which salient node recognition is more important in the recognition process, we need to know which salient node recognition produce more discriminative power in the training, that is, the recognition in a salient node has more discriminative power and should be assigned more weight if its jet similarity value is larger when comparing two face images belong to the same class (same person's faces in different environment or in different expression), and smaller when comparing two face images belong to different classes (different person's faces in different environment or in different expression).

Suppose there are two groups of training face images, ϕ and ϕ'. Each has m number of face images with alternative expression (or in different lighting), belonging to the same set of persons. So an image graph $\mathcal{G}_k^\phi$ is the graph extracted from a face image in group ϕ with normal expression belong to the kth person, while $\mathcal{G}_k^{\phi'}$ is the graph extracted from a face image in group ϕ' with smiling expression belong to the same kth person. The fuzzy density for x_i salient node can be defined as

$$g^i = \frac{1}{m}\sum_{k=1}^{m} S(\mathcal{J}_{x_i}^{\mathcal{G}_k^\phi}, \mathcal{J}_{x_i}^{\mathcal{G}_k^{\phi'}})$$

$$-\frac{1}{m(m-1)}\sum_{k=1}^{m}\sum_{l=1,l\neq k}^{m} S(\mathcal{J}_{x_i}^{\mathcal{G}_k^\phi}, \mathcal{J}_{x_i}^{\mathcal{G}_l^{\phi'}}) \qquad (5)$$

Performance Power Learning: In the area of multi-classifiers recognition, an sub-classifier is regarded as more important and should be assigned more weight if the recognition performance solely based on this sub-classifier outperforms other sub-classifiers in the training. Following the same notations as above, we have performance measurement η_i defined as the measurement of how close to the correct matching (that is, how well the recognition performance) the matching solely based on the ith sub-classifier is. The individual sub-classifier would be the jet similarity of a salient node in the current context. In the training process of matching the face image in group ϕ belonged to the kth person with the template face images in group ϕ', if the jet similarity in ith salient node $S(\mathcal{J}_{x_i}^{\mathcal{G}_k^\phi}, \mathcal{J}_{x_i}^{\mathcal{G}_k^{\phi'}})$ is the nth largest value out of all $S(\mathcal{J}_{x_i}^{\mathcal{G}_k^\phi}, \mathcal{J}_{x_i}^{\mathcal{G}_l^{\phi'}})$, $l = 1, 2, ..k..m$, then performance measurement $\eta_i^k = \frac{m-(n-1)}{m}$ expresses the measure of how close to the correct matching using the jet similarity in ith salient node. Simply concluded the performance measurements from all the training samples, the fuzzy density for x_i salient node is defined as

$$g^i = \frac{\sum_{k=1}^{m} \eta_i^k}{m} \qquad (6)$$

Some interesting observations can be draw in relation to cognitive research of learning for human face recognition. As we argued in the previous section, human face recognition is not a simple additive combination of individual recognitions of separated local parts. Instead, it is a collective process involving the inherent relationships between recognition of local parts. The inherent relationships are refered to as relational features by Tim Valentime. We suggest that an important form of relational features are the relative importance of recognition of local parts, that is, the fuzzy densities. The ratios of distances between parts of the face are also regarded as relational features by some researchers. As we mentioned before, faces are homogeneous objects that have the same component parts in the same basic spatial arrangement, and also due to our poor understand of how human brain encodes spatial informations, the inclusion of the distance ratios or spatial data of face parts is rather insignificant and ineffective. So fuzzy densities is our primary relational features in the current context. The recognition performance critically depends on the learning of fuzzy densities. It analogies the critical importance of relational features in human face recognition. The understanding of relative importance or relation feature is an expertise humans possessed and learned throughout childhood with massive amounts of practice. The concept of expertise explains why people often experience difficulties in recognizing other race faces. The lack of practice means the relative importance relationships or relational features can not be learned properly and used effectively, and that people must rely largely on the ineffective, isolated part recognitions.

3 Experiments and Results

The goal of our experiments is to compare the performance of the following recognition methods: non-weighted original EBGM, simple weighted EBGM and fuzzy integral EBGM. The face images we used in our experiments were taken from FERET database [3] provided by the US Defense Advanced Research Products Agency (DARPA). FERET database provides grayscale images with human heads in different pose, expression and lighting.

Our experiments used various template and target image galleries from FERET with faces of different expression and illumination. Each image set contains 180 faces with just one image per subject (person). We also compare the two alternative fuzzy density (or weight) learning methods.

3.1 Experiment Procedure

In the experiments described below, original images from FERET were normalized to grayscale images with a format of 256×256 pixels. There are 180 subjects (persons). Each subject has three frontal images in three galleries with different expression or different lighting. Images with normal expression are in template gallery ba. Images with alternative expression to ba are in target gallery bj. Images with normal expression but taken under different lighting are in target gallery bk.

50 ba images were arbitrarily chosen as the training images to construct the FBG structure. For each of these 50 training images, a set of (31 in our experiments) fiducial points in salient positions (left eye, right eye, top lip, bottom lip, etc) were manually marked and edge between node positions were labeled. Gabor wavelet transform was then applied to provide the jets for these 31 node positions and a graph structure for each image was generated. All 50 trained jets generated from transform for one particular salient node were stacked together to form a jet stack. The collection of such jet stacks in salient nodes together

with the topographical relations of these salient positions constitutes the FBG structure. The FBG combines information from these 50 faces as the jet stack in each of the 31 salient node in FBG covers 50 possible local variations in the appearance of faces. So the FBG can serve as a representation of faces in general. The more training images, the more variations our FBG can cover. But a larger FBG will cost more computations.

Once the FBG was built, it then can be used as a template for face extraction in the rest of ba, bj and bk images.

First, given a unknown image, Gabor wavelet transform was applied, a number of graphs were extracted from each location of a square lattice with a spacing of 4 pixels in the unknown image. With the jets information in FBG and the extracted graph, utilizing the similarity definition 3, we were able to tell if the graph was extracted from the face position. Once the face location is approximately found, salient node positions in the face need to be accurately located. Again, the jets of a jets stack in a FBG salient node can serve as templates to locate the salient node in the probe image. The displacement estimation algorithm estimates the displacement between the current guessing position and the actual salient position by calculating the difference between the jet extracted from the current guessing position and the closest jet in the corresponding FBG salient position. Adopting a gradient descent style refinement process, the guess position can be refined with the newly calculated displacement. Finally the actual salient positions (eye, nose, etc) can be accurately located by applying this process iteratively.

Follow the process described above, the face graphs in gallery ba, bj and bk were accurately extracted automatically. With the graphs representing the face images in ba, bj and bk all available, we then were able to compare the recognition performance.

First we carefully selected another set of approximate 50 well-extracted face graphs from each group ba, bj and bk. Based on the training graphs set in ba and bj, the weights or the fuzzy densities for the recognitions between ba and bj with the two different learning methods - Discriminative Power and Performance Power can be calculated. Similarly, the weights or the fuzzy densities for the recognition between ba and bk with the two different learning methods can be calculated.

In our experiments, the Original EBGM method uses the original graph similarity definition 3. The simple Weighted EBGM method also adopts the same formula 3 with the modification of applying a weight factor to each individual jet similarity. The Fuzzy Integral EBGM calculates the degree of similarity of two face graphs with the fuzzy integral definition 4. The weight factors for the simple Weighted EBGM and the fuzzy densities for the Fuzzy Integral EBGM were learned from the training process described above.

3.2 Results

Recognition results are shown in table 1. As we can observe from the result table, in both cases of recognition with different expression and different lighting,

Table 1. Performance Results

Template gallery	Target gallery	Recognition Method	Training Method	Percent Correct %
ba 130 images	bj 130 images	Original EBGM	/	93.9
		Simple Weighted EBGM	Discriminative Power	94.5
			Performance Power	95.0
		Fuzzy Integral EBGM	Discriminative Power	98.9
			Performance Power	98.9
ba 130 images	bk 130 images	Original EBGM	/	86.26
		Simple Weighted EBGM	Discriminative Power	85.7
			Performance Power	89.5
		Fuzzy Integral EBGM	Discriminative Power	91.7
			Performance Power	93.4

- *ba*: frontal images with normal expression
- *bj*: frontal images with alternative expression to ba
- *bk*: frontal images corresponding to ba, but taken under different lighting

the simple weighted EBGM system performed slightly better than the original EBGM system and the EBGM system with fuzzy fusion demonstrated the best performance in all three. The experiment results conform to the cognitive evidence that human face recognition is not an isolated and simple part-additive recognition, but rather an inherently collective and non-additive fuzzy recognition.

It is also shown that the Performance Power learning method produces a better set of weights or fuzzy densities that results in better recognition performance in general. The different learning methods resulting in different performances reflects the fact that humans recognize face more accurately if they possess a better understanding of the face relational features learned from practices.

4 Conclusions

Fuzzy Integral is considered as a valid information fusion method. Elastic Bunch Graph Matching has been a success in face recognition. In this paper, we presented an improved face recognition system based on the combination of these two. We argued that the combined system reflects and simulates more closely to the nature of human face recognition process. Experiments have shown that the combined system achieves a better performance compared to the original system.

Acknowledgments

The authors would like to acknowledge the suggestions from Dr Leslie Kitchen and Jun Liu.

References

1. Turk, M. and Pentland, A. *Eigenfaces for recognition*, Journal of Cognitive Neuroscience 1991
2. L.Wiskott, J-M. Fellous, N. Kruger, and C. von der Malsburg, *Face Recognition by Elastic Bunch Graph Matching*, Technical Report IR-INI96-08, 1996.
3. P.J. Phillips, H. Moon, P Rauss and S.S. Rizvi, *The FERET Evaluation Methodology for Face-Recognition Algorithms*, Proc. First Int'l Conf. Audio and Video-Based Biometric Person Authentication, 1997.
4. X.B. Li, Z.Q. Liu and K.M.Leung, *Detection of Vehicles from Traffic Scenes Using Fuzzy Integral.* Pattern Recognition.
5. H.Tahani and J.M.Keller. *Information fusion in computer vision using the fuzzy integral* Fuzzy Measure Theory 1992
6. M.Sugeno *Fuzzy Measure and Fuzzy Integrals: a Surey* Fuzzy Automation and Decision Processes Amsterdam: North Holland 1977.
7. Valentine T. *Cognitive and computational aspects of face recognition: Explorations in face space* London: Routledge, 1995
8. Fleet, D.J. and Jepson, A.D *Computation of component image velocity from local phase information* International Journal of Computer Vision 1990
9. Jones, J and Palmer, L. *An Evaluation of the two dimensional Gabor filter model of simple receptive fields in cat striate cortex* Journal of Neurophysiology 1987
10. Brunelli, R. and Poggio, T. *Face recognition: Features versus Templates* IEEE Transactions on Pattern Analysis and Machine Intelligence 1993
11. N.Ahuja, and D.Kriegman. *Face Recognition using kernel eigenfaces* Proc. IEEE Int. Conf. Imaging Processing, 2000
12. and H.Wechsler. *Evolutionary pursuit and its application to face recognition* IEEE Trans. Pattern Anal. Machine Intell 2000
13. and B.K.Low *Face detection: A survey* Comput. Vision Imaging Understanding 2001
14. and G.Sommer *Wavelet network for face processing* J. Opt. Soc. Amer. A 2002
15. J.Wu, S.Lu, H.L.Toh *Face recognition with radial basis function (rbf) neural networks* IEEE Trans. Neural Networks 2002

Robust License Plate Segmentation Method Based on Texture Features and Radon Transform

Jun Kong[1], Xinyue Liu[1], YingHua Lu[1,2], Xiaofeng Zhou[1], and Qiushi Zhao[1]

[1] Computer School, Northeast Normal University, Changchun, Jilin Province, China
[2] Computer School, Jilin University, Changchun, Jilin Province, China
{kongjun, liuxy581, luyh, zhouxf594, zhaoqs522}@nenu.edu.cn

Abstract. A robust method for plate segmentation in a License Plate Recognition system is presented in this paper, the proposed approach is designed to work in a wide range of acquisition conditions, including unrestricted scene environments, lighting conditions, viewing points and camera-to-car distance. Experiments have been preformed to prove the robustness and accuracy of the approach. The experiment results show that almost 96.2% of input images are correctly segmented on the average. Because our algorithm has fast speed and needs little memory space, it can be used in real time system.

1 Introduction

Intelligent Transportation Systems (ITS) combining electronics, information, communication, network technologies and so on are developed to improve traffic problems. Automatic license plate recognition (LPR) is an essential application in ITS, and many methods have been developed in recent years. License Plate Recognition can basically be divided into two main steps: segmentation of plate area and character recognition. Since the result of recognition is directly dependent on the former step, plate segmentation is particularly important. It is a challenging task to segment plate area from an image successfully, because the image may be composed of a great variety of objects and be affected by illumination, noises, weather conditions and perspective variations. All these variable environment conditions result in a complex scene, where plate area is embedded within such scene and difficult to be located and identified. Another reason causes it difficult is the position of the camera. In some applications, such as access control system, cameras are typically fixed in a place and thus the scene features (perspective, distance, background, etc.) are easily predictable and the size of plate is almost fixed. But in other applications, the position of the camera and the scene are not predictable, this leads to a wide range of plates size as well as the plates that are out of shape due to the angle of view.

Currently, there have been many different approaches for license plate localization, such as edge detection [1, 2], morphological operations [3, 4], artificial neural network [5], fuzzy maps [6], vector quantization [7] and color-based analysis [8, 9], etc. Edge-based approach is normally simple and fast. However, it is too sensitive for the noises, resulting in the unwanted edges. Morphology has been known to be robust to noise signals, but this method cannot be used independently. Neural networks need a large memory space and considerable amount of samples for training and computing time, so it can't satisfy the requirement in real time LPR system. Color-based analysis is another method for searching special color area over image. But when the vehicle's color is similar to the plate's color (especially black and white), the approach has certain difficulty in finding plate area.

Considering the fact that spatial variation in the license plate region is much more frequent and has more characteristics than in the background due to the existence of the characters in the plate, our algorithm proposed accurately localizes the license plate using linear window checking, Vertical-cutting and applying some simple prior knowledge of the license plate, such as the character number, the aspect ratio, the size of the area and the density of the plate. The algorithm can be found to work very well, robustly and in real time even when applied to images in skew, distorted or noisy conditions.

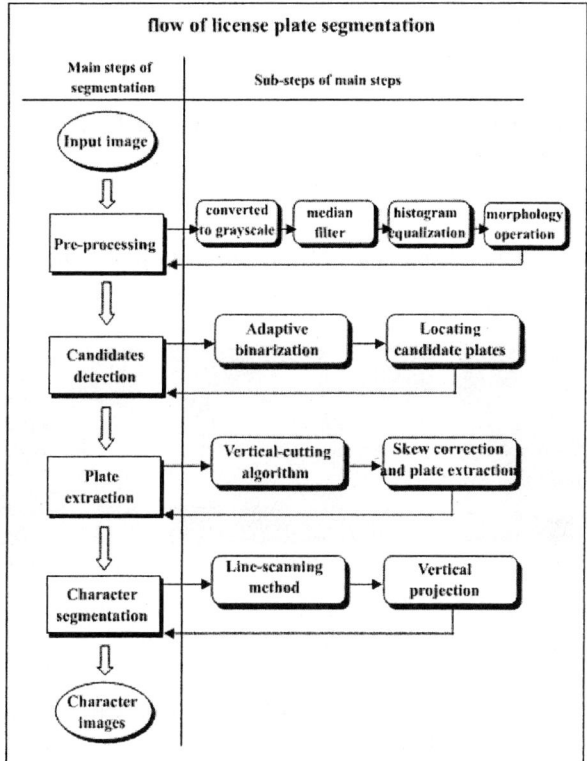

Fig. 1. The flowchart of our license plate segmentation method

A four-stage search process is proposed in the paper: preprocessing, candidate region detecting using the linear window checking, plate extracting using some prior knowledge of vehicle license plate as well as applying Radon transform to do skew correction, following with the character segmenting. A flowchart of our approach is shown in Fig. 1. In the Section 2, we will describe the algorithm in detail. The experiment results are given in Section 3. Conclusion and future research are presented in Section 4.

2 License Plate Segmentation

2.1 Preprocessing

Firstly, preprocess the image using a median filter (a 3×3 template in our study) after the input image being converted from RGB image to grayscale. The reason for choosing median filter is that it can eliminate insular noise but meanwhile keep intact the edge information of characters. Secondly, histogram equalization is used to enhance the contrast of the image. Then morphological top-hat operation and bottom-hat operation are performed on the grayscale image respectively.

Morphological processing [4] is a useful method to compensate illumination variations. The morphological opening of the image A by structuring element B, denoted $A \circ B$, is simply erosion of A by B, followed by dilation of the result by B:

$$A \circ B = (A \ominus B) \oplus B. \tag{1}$$

The morphological closing of A by structuring element B, denoted $A \bullet B$, is dilation followed by erosion:

$$A \bullet B = (A \oplus B) \ominus B. \tag{2}$$

where $\ominus$ donates erosion operation and $\oplus$ donates dilation operation. The structuring element used is diamond.

(a)　　　　　　　　　　(b)　　　　　　　　　　(c)

Fig. 2. (a) The input grayscale image. (b) The result image after median filtering and histogram equalizing. (c) The enhanced image after morphological operating.

Subtracting the opened image from the original is called top-hat transformation. A similar operation, bottom-hat transformation, is defined as the closing of the image minus the original image. After that, we subtract the result of bottom-hat transformation from top-hat transformation for enhancing image further. This method yields generally superior results. See Fig. 2.

2.2 Candidate Region Detecting

2.2.1 Adaptive Binarizing of the Enhanced Image
This step is the most important step because all the later works directly depend on it. Firstly, we use the Otsu method [10] to determine the threshold. Generally, it could

receive a satisfactory result in our study. However, considering the algorithm should be robust to deal with images in various conditions, we try to make the algorithm decide an appropriate threshold automatically according to the information contained by the image through an iterative selection-verification process [11] in case the global threshold method fails. Every time it fails to result in a better threshold value (which means there is no result returned in Section 2.2.2), the current value is decreased and increased by 1 unit respectively to restart another search process until it finally finds the candidate plates. Here the step sets 5 units instead of 1 unit so as to accelerate the whole process but with little impact on the result. See Fig. 3. (a).

(a)　　　　　　　　　　　　　　(b)

Fig. 3. (a) The binary image. (b) Three candidate zones extracted from grayscale image.

2.2.2 Candidate Plate Detecting Using Linear Window Checking

This step detects all the zones in the image that might contain plate. The method of candidate region detecting is based on the texture features of the image, in other words, considering the fact that spatial variation or transient differences of the binary image in the license plate region are much more frequent than rest areas of the car or other background. But due to the complex scene, the result we get may include several candidate zones. Linear window checking algorithm is described as follows:

Step 1. Computing the sum of transient differences in each linear window for the input image $f(x,y)$ of size $w \times h$.

For $j = 1: h-1$
　For $i = 1: w - W_{search} - 1$

$$C_{sum} = \sum_{k=i}^{i+W_{search}} f(k,j) - f(k+1,j) \cdot \quad (3)$$

where (i, j) is the start coordinate of the linear window, W_{search} is the search width of the window.

Step 2. With the window slipping, the sum of transient differences within the linear window is recorded into a variable C_{sum}.

If $(C_{sum} > C)$, set $F_{line}^i = 1$, else set $F_{line}^i = 0$

where C is a given threshold (a setting value is 15).

Step 3. Add up the consecutive rows marked F_{line} as 1 line by line, then store the amount of consecutive rows into a variable L.

For $i = 1: h\text{-}1$

If $F_{line}^i = 1$ ($i=m, m+1\ldots n$), set

$$L = \sum_{i=m}^{n} F_{line}^i \qquad (4)$$

Step 4. If ($L > L_{sum}$), set $Y_{end}^q = i$ and $Y_{start}^q = i - L$. $q=1, 2\ldots$

where L_{sum} is a given threshold (a setting value is 20), q is the amount of the candidate zones. Extract these regions as candidates according to array Y_{start} and Y_{end} from the grayscale image for the requirement of edge detection in the Section 2.3.1.

After applying the above steps, we might get several candidate zones. The results are shown in Fig. 3. (b).

2.3 Vehicle License Plate Extracting

2.3.1 Finding Real Plate Region from Candidates

After several candidate zones have been obtained using the method mentioned in previous subsections, it is necessary to extract real license plate. Based on the observation that the edge pixels are usually rich and distribute evenly in the real license plate region, edge detection method is used on candidate zones to detect the edge of plate. Then Vertical-cutting algorithm combined with some prior knowledge of vehicle license plate is preformed to locate real plate region.

2.3.1.1 Edge Detection. There are many methods for performing edge detection. Some of the common ones are Sobel, Laplacian of a Gaussian (Log), Roberts, Canny and Prewitt operator. In this paper, the gradient of the image is obtained using the Sobel operator. After edge detecting, the edge of the plate and the contours of characters are emerged clear from the zone that contains the plate while other zones have rarely consecutive edges because most of them contain irregular noise of background. Fig. 4. (a) shows the results of edge detection for three candidate zones.

(a) (b)

Fig. 4. (a) The results of edge detection for three candidate zones. (b) The real license plate detecting using Vertical-cutting algorithm.

2.3.1.2 Vertical-Cutting Algorithm.
Based on the observation that the gradient changes are more frequent in the plate area, the left and right boundary of the license plate can be located by using Vertical-cutting algorithm as follows:

Step 1. Locate the middle row in candidate zone from the result of edge detection.

$$i = (H_{candidate} + 1)/2. \qquad (5)$$

where the row number i is obtained as a integer, $H_{candidate}$ is the height of the candidate zone.

Step 2. Record transient column numbers on this row.

$$C_{transient} = |f(i, j) - f(i, j+1)|. \qquad (6)$$

where $f(i, j)$ is the pixel value at (i, j), $j=1, 2...W_{candidate}$. $W_{candidate}$ is the width of the candidate zone. If $C_{transient}=1$, then record the column number j into array A_n, that is, $A_n^k = j$, where n is the size of the array, k is the sequence number in the array.

Step 3. Calculate the difference of each adjacent column in the array A_n, namely, the distance between the adjacent transient columns.

$$B^k = A_n^{k+1} - A_n^k. \qquad (7)$$

where $k=1,2...n-1$

Step 4. For $k=1:n-1$
    If $B^k < H_{plate}$, set $A_n^{k+1}, A_n^k \in S_i$
    else set $i=i+1$

where H_{plate} is an adjustable parameter, and a setting value is the height of the plate in our study. S_i is a set and the subscript i denotes the number of sets and its original value is 1.

Step 5. If the amount of elements of the set S_i is closest to $T_{changes}$ (a given threshold value is 12), the smallest column number in this set is the left boundary of plate and the biggest column number is the right boundary.

In most cases, the license plate regions can be located successfully after the above algorithm, but sometimes, more than one rectangle regions may be obtained from those candidate zones. Hence combining Vertical-cutting algorithm with some features or prior knowledge of license plate to find the real plate region can get better result.

With the important information from the real plate region, some features of region such as the aspect ratio (R), the area size (A) and the density (D) of region are adopted in our study. Let R denote the region of rectangles with width W and height H, then $R = W/H$ and $A = W \times H$. Let N denote the number of the object pixels in the rectangles, then $D = N/(W \times H)$. The values of those parameters are set after testing multiple images, and regions that satisfying the restriction conditions are selected. On the average, only one region can satisfy all those conditions, which means the real plate region is located successfully. The result is shown in Fig. 4. (b).

2.3.2 Radon Transform to Do Skew Correction and Plate Extraction

This step determines the angle of the plate edge with respect to the vertical and horizontal in the supplied image. We use the Radon transform in order to find lines in the image, and return the angle of the most visible one, after skew correction according to the angle, extract the plate accurately.

The Radon transform is an important topic in integral geometry which deals with the problem of expressing a function on a manifold in terms of its integrals over certain sub-manifolds. These transform is able to transform two dimensional images with lines into a domain of possible line parameters, where each line in the image will give a peak positioned at the corresponding line parameters. As we know, the projection of two dimensional function $f(x,y)$ is it's line integral on certain direction. The two dimensional line integral of $f(x,y)$ on vertical direction is the projection of $f(x,y)$ on x axis; The two dimensional line integral of $f(x,y)$ on horizontal direction is the projection of $f(x,y)$ on y axis. Fig. 5. (a) show the horizontal and vertical projection of a simple two dimensional function.

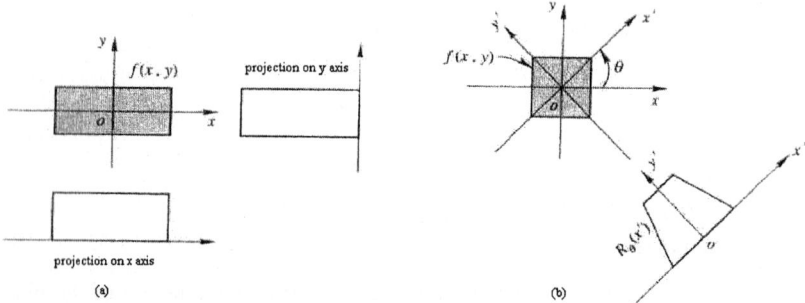

Fig. 5. (a) The horizontal and vertical projection of a simple two dimensional function. (b) The method of Radon transform.

We can calculate the projection of a function along any angle θ, in other words, Radon transform can be preformed at any angle. Fig. 5. (b) show the theory of Radon transform. The formula of Radon transform is given as following:

$$R\theta(x') = \int_{-\infty}^{\infty} f(x'\cos\theta - y'\sin\theta, x'\sin\theta + y'\cos\theta)dy'. \tag{8}$$

where $\begin{bmatrix} x' \\ y' \end{bmatrix} = \begin{bmatrix} \cos\theta & \sin\theta \\ -\sin\theta & \cos\theta \end{bmatrix} \begin{bmatrix} x \\ y \end{bmatrix}$.

In our study, Radon transform is used to draw parallel lines along the plate's horizontal edges to detect the angle of them relatively to the horizontal and rotate the image with the angle. Then, extract the plate according to the parallel lines. The result is shown in Fig. 6.

Fig. 6. (a) Angle detecting using Radon transform. (b) Rotated result according to the angle.

2.4 Character Segmenting

After the plate is extracted, the characters of license plate will be segmented using the vertical projection method. The idea is: "Assign value 1 to character pixels (foreground color) and 0 to background pixels. If we add up every column of the image, we will obtain a vector (projection). Minima in this vector will allow us to discover gaps between characters". For gaining the better result, we need to remove the white rims around the character that exist probably in the binary image using line-scanning checking method. The method is described as follows:

Locating a horizontal line in the middle of the image, which is named start-line, checks the image from start-line to the top line until the amount of white pixels of any line are not more than a setting value T, then this line is identified as the top boundary. In a similar way, the bottom boundary can also be identified. Checking the image from the left vertical column to right until the amount of white pixels of any column are not more than a setting value P, this column is identified as the left boundary. The right boundary identified is similar to the left boundary, but checking the image from the right to left. According the top, bottom, left and right boundary we can remove the white rims and obtain a clear image that only contains some characters. The result is shown in Fig. 7. (a).

In addition, as the noise exists, there are connections between characters in the projection image. In our actual operation, we elevate the horizontal axis several units upper in order to distinguish every peak clearly, otherwise may connect at the bottom.

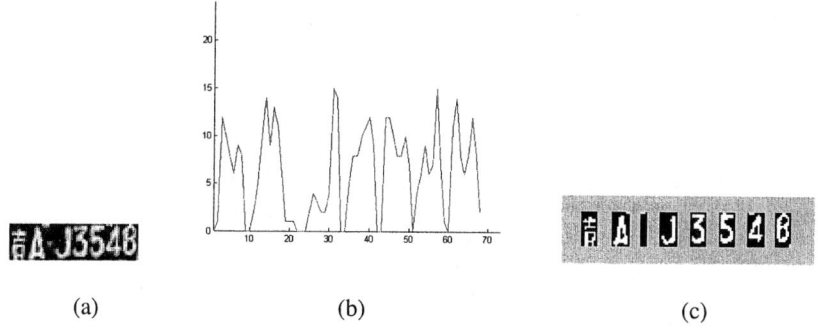

Fig. 7. (a) The plate region. (b) The projection result. (c) The segmented characters.

3 Experiment Results

Our algorithm was tested with 315 natural RGB images of size 640×480. The images contained different background including people, other vehicles, buildings, trees and so on. In some images the vehicle license plates were at an inclination, distorted or noisy to a different extent. These conditions will demonstrate the robustness of our algorithm.

In the experiment on locating license plates stage, 315 images were tested. Of which, 12 images have been failed; the license plates location rate of success is 96.2%. Sources of the failure can be classified into two major categories: 1) existence of other text regions which are very similar to license plates. 2) Unclear boundary or weak gradient information from the plate area. In the experiment on segmenting characters stage, 303 images, from which license plates have been successfully extracted, were used. Of which, 5 images have been failed to segment characters in the images; the characters segmentation rate of success is 94.6%. It can be due to the nuts and bolts within the plate and too many connections between characters.

The implementation of the algorithm is quite fast and can be realized in real time. Generally, the processing time of one color image is not more than 100ms. Performance is carried out on PIV 1800MHz/256RAM. What's more, although it is mainly aimed at Chinese vehicle license plate, it can be easily extended to other area license plate detection with trivial modifications in the setting of some parameters. And also it is easy to be extended to fit cases where multi license plates may be present in one single image.

Table 1. The experiment results of the proposed algorithm

Total images	Candidates	Correct	Error	Reject	Character segmentation
315	916	303	10	2	298
(%)		96.2	3.17	0.63	94.6

4 Conclusion and Future Research

A robust license plate segmentation scheme is presented in this paper. The main three stage of this approach is designed to deal with images taken under various real world conditions. In the first stage, the license plate candidate zones are located based on adaptive binarization and a slip linear window checking. In the second stage, the candidates are examined to verify whether it contains the real license plate by introducing a Vertical-cutting algorithm combined with the prior knowledge of the license plate. In the last stage, Radon transform to do skew correction.

The shortcoming of our method is mainly due to bad quality of input image during the acquisition stage, or unclear detection or extraction of the edges. Nevertheless, the algorithm presents good results on our database, and it is fast and relatively robust to variations of the background and different kinds of vehicle. Based on the experimental results, the performance of the proposed approach is promising. Future researches are directed to improve the performance of the system.

References

1. Hongliang Bai, Junmin Zhu, Changping Liu: A fast license plate extraction method on complex background, Intelligent Transportation Systems Proceedings (2003). IEEE Volume 2, 12-15 Oct (2003) 985 - 987
2. R.C. Gonzalez and R.E. Woods: Digital Image Processing. 2nd Ed. Prentice-Hall, N. J (2002)
3. Jun-Wei Hsieh, Shih-Hao Yu, Yung-Sheng Chen: Morphology-based License Plate Detection from Complex Scenes, 16th International Conference On Pattern Recognition (2002) 176-179
4. Fernando Martin, Maite Garcia, Jose Luis Alba: New Methods for Automatic Reading of VLP's, Signal Processing Pattern Recognition and application (2002)
5. M.Raus, L.Kreft: Reading car license plates by the use of artificial neural networks, Circuits and Systems Proceedings (1995). Proceedings of the 38th Midwest Symposium on Volume 1, 13-16 Aug (1995) 538-541
6. Shyang-Lih Chang, Li-Shien Chen, Yun-Chung Chung, Sei-Wan Chen: Automatic license plate recognition, Intelligent Transportation Systems, IEEE Transactions on Volume 5, Issue 1, March (2004) 42-53
7. Stefano Rovetta, Rodolfo Zunino: License-plate localization by using vector quantization (1999). International Conference on Acoustics, Speech and Signal Processing (1999)
8. Xu Jianfeng, Li Shaofa, Chen Zhibin, Robotics: Color analysis for Chinese car plate recognition, Intelligent Systems and Signal Processing (2003)
9. Eun Ryung Lee, Pyeoung Kee kim, Hang Joon Kim: Automatic recognition of a Car License Plate Using Color Image Processing, Proceeding of International Conference on Image Processing (1994) 301-305
10. N. Otsu: A Threshold Selection Method from Gray Level Histogram, IEEE Transactions on Systems, Man, and Cybernetics, SMC-9 (1979) 62-66
11. Guangzhi Cao, Jianqian Chen, Jingping Jiang: An adaptive approach to vehicle license plate localization, Industrial Electronics Society (2003). The 29th Annual Conference of the IEEE Volume 2, 2-6 Nov (2003)1786 - 1791

An Adaptive Selection of Motion for Online Hand-Eye Calibration

Jing Zhang, Fanhuai Shi, and Yuncai Liu

Inst. Image Processing and Pattern Recognition,
Shanghai Jiao Tong University, Shanghai 200240, P.R. China
{zhjseraph, fhshi, whomliu}@sjtu.edu.cn

Abstract. As the robot makes unplanned movement, online hand-eye calibration determines the relative pose between the robot gripper/end-effector and the sensors mounted on it. With noisy measurements, hand-eye calibration is sensitive to small rotations in real applications. Moreover, degenerate cases such as pure translations have no effect in hand-eye calibration. This paper proposes an adaptive motion selection algorithm for online hand-eye calibration, which can adaptively set the thresholds of motion selection according to the characteristics of the unplanned motion sequence. It is achieved by using polynomial-regression to predict the relationship between RMS of calibration error and thresholds. Thus, this procedure leads to an adaptive method of motion selection. It can adapt itself to online hand-eye calibration in various applications. Experiments using simulated data are conducted and present good results. Experiments using real scenes also show that the method is promising.

1 Introduction

The goal of this paper is to improve the accuracy of online hand-eye calibration. We focus on the algorithm of adaptively setting the thresholds of "motion selection"[11], which is a method to exclude degenerate motions and small rotations during online hand-eye calibration. It is achieved by selecting the motions until the selected satisfy the given thresholds. Using this method, one can get "good" motions for online hand-eye calibration. The aim of this paper is to refine the method and give an adaptive algorithm to set the thresholds.

The calibration of robotic hand-eye relationship is a classical problem in robotics. Algebraically, the problem is known to lead to a linear homogeneous equation in the unknown pose matrix X, namely $A \cdot X = X \cdot B$ [1]-[7], where A is the rigid motion of the robot gripper and B is the corresponding camera motion. A, B and X are all homogeneous transformation 4×4 matrices. Because most hand-eye calibration methods are iterative, they are not fit for online computation. Andreff et al.[9][10] and Angeles et al.[8] first introduce the method of online implementation of hand-eye calibration. Whichever method is used, 2 motions with non-parallel rotation axes are necessary to determine the hand-eye transformation. The algebraically and geometrically analysis on hand-eye calibration can be seen in [2][3]. But when we make online hand-eye calibration, we cannot know the movements of the robot beforehand. And also, we cannot do motion plan in advance. So, there are maybe degenerate cases in the motion sequence, which can ruin the result. To solve this problem, Shi et al. [11] first introduced the concept of "motion selection", which try to select the "effective" motions for hand-eye calibration and has greatly decreased the error of online hand-eye calibration.

In [11], Shi et al. make motion selection according to the following observations in [2]:

Observation 1: The RMS (root mean square) error of rotation from gripper to camera is inversely proportional to the sine of the angle α between the interstation rotation axes;
Observation 2: The rotation and translation error are both inversely proportional to the interstation rotation angle β;
Observation 4: The distance between the robot gripper coordinate centers at different stations d is also a critical factor in forming the error of translation.

If one motion fulfill the three constrain, the algorithm will regard it as an "effective" one and do calibration. Otherwise, the algorithm will combine it with its following motion until the synthesized movement satisfies the thresholds. Then they use those effective movements to do calibration. Using this method, not only can one avoid the degenerate cases, but also the small rotations to decrease the calibration error. However, the algorithm in [11] sets the thresholds of α, β, d by experience, which may not adapt to the requirements of different applications.

In this paper, we propose an adaptive algorithm to set the thresholds of motion selection in online hand-eye calibration. The remainder of this paper decomposes as follows. Section 2 describes the objective problem. Then, detailed algorithm of adaptive motion selection for online hand-eye calibration is presented in Section 3. Section 4 conducts some simulated and real experiments to validate the proposed algorithm.

2 Problem Formulation

In this section, we first give a simple description of the algorithm in Shi[11], which is the foundation of our method. Then we describe the problem we attempt to solve.

We use upper-case boldface letters for matrices, e.g. X, and lower-case boldface letters for 3-D vectors, e.g. x. The angle between two vectors is denoted by $\angle(x, y)$. The $\|\cdot\|$ means the Frobenius norm of a vector or a matrix. Rigid transformation is represented with a 4×4 homogeneous matrix X, which is often referred to as the couple (R, t). At the i-th measurement, the camera pose with respect to reference object is denoted by homogeneous matrix P_i, and the recorded gripper pose relative to robot base is homogeneous matrix Q_i.

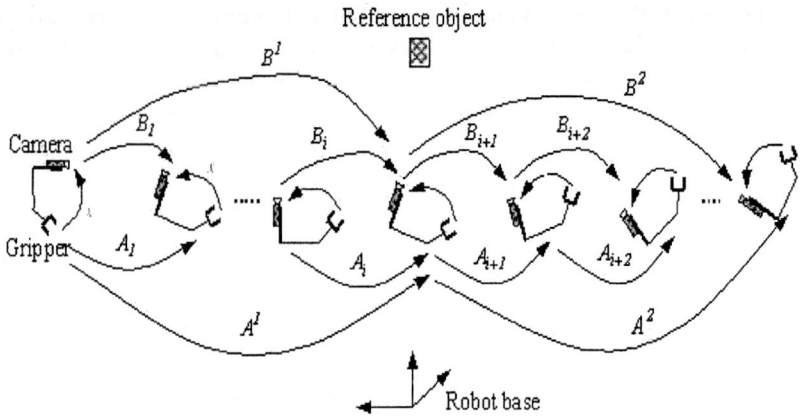

Fig. 1. Algorithm of motion selection for online hand-eye calibration

The usual way to describe the hand-eye calibration is by means of homogeneous transformation matrices. We denote the transformation from gripper to camera by $X = (R_x, t_x)$, the i-th motion matrix of the gripper by $A_i = (R_{a,i}, t_{a,i})$, and the i-th motion matrix of the camera by $B_i = (R_{b,i}, t_{b,i})$. As a rotation matrix R can be expressed as a rotation around a rotation axis k by an angle , the relations between θ, k and R are given by Rodrigues theorem[13]. Moreover, R_a and R_b have the same angle of rotation [1]. We can rewrite R_a and R_b as $Rot(k_a, \theta)$ and $Rot(k_b, \theta)$ respectively. Motion selection is to sequentially find the pairs of consecutive motions(A_i, B_i) and (A_{i+1}, B_{i+1}) for hand-eye computation from sampled motion series[11].

In Ref. [11], the following golden rules are used for motion selection:

Rule 1: Try to make $\angle(k_{a,i}, k_{a,i+1})$ (which is equal to $\angle(k_{b,i}, k_{b,i+1})$ [2]) large, the minimal threshold is set to be α_0 ;
Rule 2: Try to make θ_i large, the minimal threshold is β_i ;
Rule 3: Try to make $\|t_{a,i}\|$ small, the maximal threshold is d_0 .

The i-th sampled hand-eye pose and motion are denoted by (P_i, Q_i) and (A_i, B_i) respectively in this section. (A', B') and (A'', B'') are selected motion pairs for calibration (see Fig. 1). For A' and A'', the rotation axis, rotation angle and translation are denoted by (k'_a, θ'_a, t'_a) , $(k''_a, \theta''_a, t''_a)$ respectively.

At the beginning of the calibration process, they need to estimate (A', B'). The (A', B') is first recovered from (P_1, Q_1) and (P_2, Q_2). If $\theta' \geq \beta_0$ and $\|t'_a\| \leq d_0$, they claim that the (A', B') has been found. Or else, they continue to compute (A', B') from (P_1, Q_1) and (P_3, Q_3) and judge the value θ' and $\|t'_a\|$ in the same way as before. Repeat this procedure until θ' and $\|t'_a\|$ fulfill the given conditions. Here, they assume that the first (A', B') is estimated from (P_1, Q_1) and (P_i, Q_i). After (A', B') has been found, another motion pair (A'', B'') can be sought starting from (P_i, Q_i) and (P_{i+1}, Q_{i+1}) in the similar way as that of

(A', B'), but the constrained conditions are changed to be $\theta' \geq \beta_0$ and $\|t'_a\| \leq d_0$ and $\angle(k'_a, k''_a) \leq \alpha_0$. When both motion pairs are found, they can make one calibration using the method of Andreff [10].

In the next calibration, they take the last motion pair (A'', B'') as the new motion pair (A', B'), and then continue to seek for new (A'', B'') from the successive sampled series and make a new hand-eye calibration in the same way as before.

The above is the motion selection procedure in [11]. But α_0, β_0 and d_0 in this algorithm are set by experience, which is not robust to different situations, as the movements of robot gripper vary with applications. So, in order to improve the robustness and accuracy of the method of online hand-eye calibration by using motion selection, we should set the threshold adaptively to different applications. For this aim, we propose an adaptive motion selection algorithm to do online hand-eye calibration.

3 Adaptive Selection of Motion for Online Hand-Eye Calibration

3.1 Main Algorithm

In our algorithm, we use $sin(\alpha)$ instead of α as the threshold of sine of the angle between the interstation rotation axes, which is derived from *observation 1* in [2]. At the beginning of the process, we just set the average value of $sin(\alpha), \beta, d$ of the first N movements as the initial thresholds.

$$(sin(\alpha_0), \beta_0, d_0) = \frac{1}{N}(\sum_{n=1}^{N} sin(\alpha_n), \sum_{n=1}^{N} \beta_n, \sum_{n=1}^{N} d_n) \tag{1}$$

One can set N according to the application. Such as, if you can predict that the motion number will be large, N may be set larger than 5. Then the initial threshold may reflect the characteristics of the motion sequence better. Otherwise, N may be set smaller than 5 to fulfill the requirement of threshold prediction. But as our algorithm is adaptive according to local characteristic, the influence of the value of N is not remarkable. Then, we use the initial thresholds to do motion selection and calibration for five times. In each calibration, we will compute the RMS of rotation and translation and modifying the thresholds by multiplying $sin(\alpha_0), \beta_0$ a parameter larger than 1 and multiplying d_0 a parameter less than 1. During this process, if we cannot do one calibration for more than certain number motions, such as five in our algorithm, we will simply reduce $sin(\alpha_0), \beta_0$ and increase d_0 by multiplying parameters.

After we have done five calibrations, we begin to adaptively set the thresholds of $(sin(\alpha), \beta, d)$ using polynomial-regression method. In the subsequent calibration, we take the last motion pair (A'', B'') as the new motion pair (A', B'), and then continue to seek for new (A'', B'') from the successive sampled series using the new thresholds. And make a new hand-eye calibration in the same way as before.

The corresponding algorithm is as follows:

Main Algorithm

1. $N \leftarrow 5$, Compute the initial thresholds of $sin(\alpha_0), \beta_0, d_0$, using Eq(1);
2. $i \leftarrow N+1$, $start \leftarrow i$, $interval \leftarrow 5$, $calibNo \leftarrow 0$;
3. $A' = Q_5^{-1}Q_i$, $B' = P_5^{-1}P_i$;
4. Compute θ' and t'_a from A';
5. if $\theta \geq \beta_0$ and $\|t'_a\| \leq d_0$, then go to 8;
6. if $i - start \leq interval$, then $i \leftarrow i+1$, go to 3; (Sample one more motion)
7. if $\theta' < \beta_0$, then $\beta_0 \leftarrow \beta_0 \times 0.8$, if $\|t'_a\| > d_0$, then $d_0 \leftarrow d_0 \times 1.2$, $i \leftarrow i+1$, $start \leftarrow i$, goto 3;
8. $j \leftarrow i+1$, $start \leftarrow j$ (Begin to search for A'');
9. $A' = Q_i^{-1}Q_j$, $B' = P_i^{-1}P_j$;
10. Compute $\angle(k'_a, k''_a), \theta''$ and t''_a from A' and A'';
11. if $sin(\angle(k'_a, k''_a)) \geq sin(\alpha_0)$ and $\theta' \geq \beta_0$ and $\|t''_a\| \leq d_0$, then go to 14;
12. if $j - start \leq interval$, then $j \leftarrow j+1$, go to 9; (Sample one more motion)
13. if $sin(\angle(k'_a, k''_a)) \leq sin(\alpha_0)$, then $sin(\alpha_0) \leftarrow sin(\alpha_0) \times 0.8$
    if $\theta' \leq \beta_0$, then $\beta_0 \leftarrow \beta_0 \times 0.8$
    if $\|t''_a\| \geq d_0$, then $d_0 \leftarrow d_0 \times 1.2$
    $j \leftarrow j+1$, $start \leftarrow j$, go to 9;
14. Make one hand-eye calibration using the method in Andreff[10], compute RMS of rotation and translation, save the value of $(sin(\alpha_0), \beta_0, d_0)$, $calibNo \leftarrow caliNo + 1$;
15. if $calibNo \geq 5$, then use $AlgorithmI, II, III$ respectively to predict the next set of thresholds; Else $sin(\alpha_0) \leftarrow sin(\alpha_0) \times 1.2, \beta_0 \leftarrow \beta_0 \times 1.2, d_0 \leftarrow d_0 \times 0.8$;
16. $A' \leftarrow A'', B' \leftarrow B''$;
17. $i \leftarrow j, j \leftarrow j+1$, go to 9 for next calibration.

3.2 The Algorithm to Adaptively Set the Thresholds

From the observations in [2] we can see that $(sin(\alpha_0), \beta_0, d_0)$ affect the accuracy of hand-eye calibration. So we use polynomial-regression [12] to simulate the relationship between $(sin(\alpha_0), \beta_0, d_0)$ and RMS of rotation and translation. In the following paragraph, we will represent RMS of rotation error as $rmsR$ and RMS of translation error as $rmsT$. Because the polynomial-regression needs at least four sets of data to insure the reliability, we do five calibrations at first. We normalized the five sets of $rmsR$ and $rmsT$. They are divided by the maximum value of them respectively. The mathematical model to evaluate the error and thresholds is given by polynomial regression model [12] as depicted by the following equation:

$$y = b_0 + b_1 \times x + b_2 \times x^2 + b_3 \times x^3 \qquad (2)$$

where x is $rmsR$ or $rmsT$, y is threshold, b_0, b_1, b_2, b_3 is constants to be determined.

The anterior four sets of normalized $rmsR$ and $rmsT$ and four sets of $(sin(\alpha_0), \beta_0, d_0)$ are used to compute the constants of polynomial-regression.

After we have got three cubic curves of $(sin(\alpha_0), \beta_0, d_0)$ respectively, we use the fifth set of normalized $rmsR$ and $rmsT$ to predict the new value of $(sin(\alpha_0), \beta_0, d_0)$. Using the new thresholds, we will do a next calibration in the same way as before.

To fulfill the requirement of least-square, b_1, b_2, b_3 must satisfy the following equations:

$$\begin{cases} L_{11} \times b_1 + L_{12} \times b_2 + L_{13} \times b_3 = L_{10} \\ L_{21} \times b_1 + L_{22} \times b_2 + L_{23} \times b_3 = L_{20} \\ L_{31} \times b_1 + L_{32} \times b_2 + L_{33} \times b_3 = L_{30} \end{cases} \quad (3)$$

where
$L_{11} = \sum(x - \bar{x}_1)^2, L_{12} = L_{21} = \sum(x - \bar{x}_1)(x^2 - \bar{x}_2), L_{10} = \sum(x - \bar{x})(y - \bar{y}),$
$L_{22} = \sum(x^2 - \bar{x}_2)^2, L_{13} = L_{31} = \sum(x - \bar{x}_1)(x^3 - \bar{x}_3), L_{20} = \sum(x^2 - \bar{x}^2)(y - \bar{y}),$
$L_{33} = \sum(x^3 - \bar{x}_3)^2, L_{23} = L_{32} = \sum(x^2 - \bar{x}_2)(x^3 - \bar{x}_3), L_{30} = \sum(x^3 - \bar{x}_3)(y - \bar{y}),$
$\bar{x}_1 = \frac{1}{4}\sum x, \bar{x}_2 = \frac{1}{4}\sum x^2, \bar{x}_3 = \frac{1}{4}\sum x^3, \bar{y} = \frac{1}{4}\sum y,$
$b_0 = \bar{y} - b_1 \times \bar{x}_1 - b_2 \times \bar{x}_2 - b_3 \times \bar{x}_3$

The corresponding algorithm is as follows. In these algorithms, $alfaMin$, $betaMin$ are the minimum value that $sin(\alpha_0), \beta_0$ should satisfy respectively, $dMax$ is the maximum value that d_0 should satisfy. One can estimate them using *Observation 1,2,4* in [2] according to the requirement of application.

By the detailed analysis on *Observation 1* in [2], we note that $sin(\alpha_0)$ affecting the RMS of rotation error. So we use $rmsR$ to predict $sin(\alpha_0)$.

Algorithm I

1. Using the four normalized $rmsR$ as x, anterior four $sin(\alpha_0)$ as y to compute the constants b_0, b_1, b_2, b_3 of the cubic curve of $sin(\alpha_0)$, that is

$$\begin{bmatrix} 1 & rmsR_1 & rmsR_1^2 & rmsR_1^3 \\ 1 & rmsR_2 & rmsR_2^2 & rmsR_2^3 \\ 1 & rmsR_3 & rmsR_3^2 & rmsR_3^3 \\ 1 & rmsR_4 & rmsR_4^2 & rmsR_4^3 \end{bmatrix} \times \begin{bmatrix} b_0 \\ b_1 \\ b_2 \\ b_3 \end{bmatrix} = \begin{bmatrix} sin(\alpha_0)_1 \\ sin(\alpha_0)_2 \\ sin(\alpha_0)_3 \\ sin(\alpha_0)_4 \end{bmatrix} \quad (4)$$

2. Using the fifth normalized $rmsR$ as x_{new} to compute the new value of $sin(\alpha_0)$, that is

$$sin(\alpha_0)_{new} = b_0 + b_1 \times rmsR_5 + b_2 \times rmsR_5^2 + b_3 \times rmsR_5^3 \quad (5)$$

3. $if\ sin(\alpha_0)_{new} \leq 0, then\ sin(\alpha_0) = abs(sin(\alpha_0)_{new})$
   $if\ sin(\alpha_0)_{new} \leq alfaMin, then\ sin(\alpha_0) = alfaMin$
   $if\ sin(\alpha_0)_{new} \geq 1, then\ sin(\alpha_0) = 0.9$

By the detailed analysis on *Observation 2* in [2], we note that $beta_0$ affecting both rotation and translation error. So we use $rmsR$ and $rmsT$ to predict $beta_0$.

Algorithm II

1. Using the four normalized $rmsR$ as x, anterior four β_0 as y to compute the constants b_0, b_1, b_2, b_3 of the cubic curve of β_0;
2. Using the fifth normalized $rmsR$ as x_{new} to compute the new value $\beta_1 = y_{new}$;
3. Using the four normalized $rmsT$ as x', anterior four β_0 as y' to compute the constants b'_0, b'_1, b'_2, b'_3 of the second cubic curve;
4. Using the fifth normalized $rmsT$ as x'_{new} to compute the new value $\beta_2 = y'_{new}$;
5. $while\ abs(\beta_1) > 360, \beta_1 = abs(\beta_1) - 360$;
   $if\ \beta_1 > 180, then\ \beta_1 = 360 - \beta_1$,
   $while\ abs(\beta_2) > 360, \beta_2 = abs(\beta_2) - 360$;
   $if\ \beta_2 > 180, then\ \beta_2 = 360 - \beta_2$;
6. $\beta_0 = (3 \times \beta_1 + \beta_2)/4, if\ \beta_0 < betaMin, then\ \beta_0 = betaMin$ (for the reason that RMS of rotation has a more important effect on the value of $beta_0$ than translation).

By the detailed analysis on Observation 4 in [2], we note that d_0 affecting the RMS of translation error. So we use rmsT to predict.

Algorithm III

1. Using the four normalized $rmsT$ as x, anterior four d_0 as y to compute the constants b_0, b_1, b_2, b_3 of the cubic curve of d_0;
2. Using the fifth normalized $rmsT$ as x_{new}, to compute the new value of d_{0new};
3. $if\ d_{0new} < 0, d_0 = 10; if\ d_{0new} > dMax, d_0 = 150$;

One can see that all three algorithms are linear, so the new method don't need extra computational time.

4 Experiments

In this section, experiments on synthetic data and real scenes are carried out to validate our algorithm. As Shi [11] did comparison to traditional hand-eye online calibration, like in Andreff[9][10], we just do experiments to compare the performance between our method and the method in Shi[11].

4.1 Simulated Data

The motivation of the simulated experiments is to test the performance of the new method for random motions.

The simulation is conducted as follows: we establish a consecutive random motion series with 500 hand stations Q_i. We add uniformly distributed random noise with relative amplitude of 0.1% on the rotation matrix and of 1% on the translation vector. We assume a hand-eye setup and compute the camera pose P_i, to which we also add uniformly distributed random noise as before.

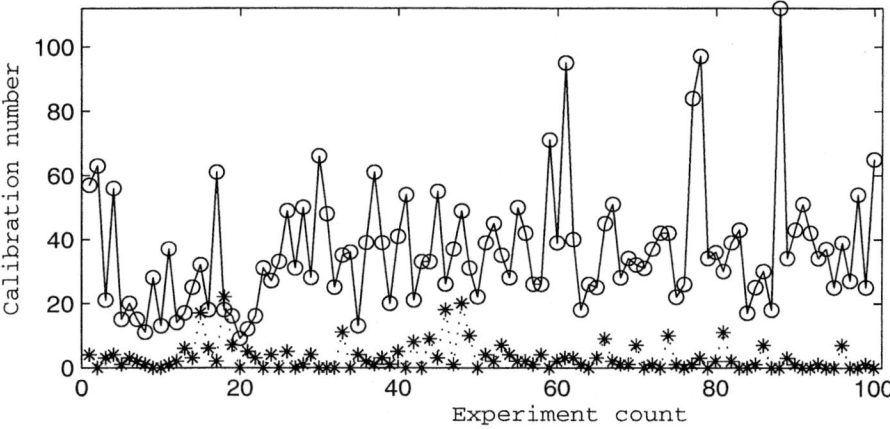

Fig. 2. Calibration number in 100 experiment, where the solid with label "O" denote our method and the dotted with label "*" denote the method in Ref.[11]

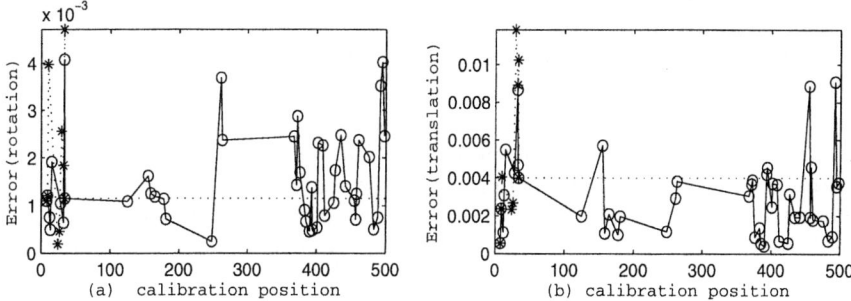

Fig. 3. RMS of the errors in the rotation matrix and the RMS of the relative errors $\|t - \hat{t}\|/\|t\|$ in the translation, where the solid with label "O" denote our method and the dotted with label "*" denote the method in Ref.[11]

We did 100 experiments and recorded the calibration number each time. To compare the performance, we make additional experiments by using the method of Shi [11] and use the same random consecutive motion series each time. We also record the 100 result of calibration number. The thresholds in the method of Shi [11] are set by the average value of the first five motions. Fig. 2 shows the results of the test. It can be seen that by using our method we can do much more calibrations than that of the method in Ref. [11]. Using our method, the average number of calibration is 36.4300. Using the method in Ref. [11], it is only 3.12 and it cannot do calibration at all in 29 instances of 100 tests. We also give a result of RMS of the errors in the rotation matrix and the RMS of the relative errors $\|t - \hat{t}\|/\|t\|$ in the translation of one of the 100 experiments. The result is shown in Fig.3. One can see that the accuracy of our method is about equal to the method in Ref[11]. Using our method, it can do 45 calibrations, but using the method in Ref[11], the times is only 9.

4.2 Real Scenes

We also demonstrate the foregoing algorithm on a real setup composed of an infrared marker and a pair of CCD cameras (Watec-902B (CCIR)), which are attached to the end-effector of a 6-DOF robot (MOTOMAN CYR-UPJ3-B00). After the stereo rig is precisely calibrated, we mount an infrared filter on each camera. Thus, we get an infrared navigation system with stereoscopic vision. Without loss of generality, we compute the hand-eye transformation between the left camera and the gripper.

Table 1. Results of the real experiment

	stations	Times of calibration
Our method	35	7
Method in Ref[11]	35	1

In the real test, the aim is to prove the adaptability of the proposed algorithm to translation and compare the performance of our method and the method of Shi [11]. The robot is fixed on a workbench and the moving cameras observe the static infrared mark. We move the gripper to 35 locations. Each time, the gripper is moved closer to the mark than the previous one. For every time instant, gripper pose Q_i can be read from robot controller and the pose of reference object P_i relative to the camera can be solved by binocular vision. As the camera pose can be computed, we adopt Algorithm Main in the real experiment. We perform the hand-eye calibration using the similar methods as in the synthetic experiments. The different point is the computation of RMS of rotation error and translation error. In each calibration, we let $A_i X - X B_i = \begin{bmatrix} \Delta R_{3\times 3} & \Delta T_{3\times 1} \\ 1 & 0 \end{bmatrix}$ where the 3×3 matrix $\Delta R_{3\times 3}$ take the responsibility of rotation error and the 3×1 vector $\Delta T_{3\times 1}$ take the responsibility of translation error. Although they are not the real error of rotation and translation, the change of them can reflect the change of real couple and so take the responsibility.

In this situation, as our method is adaptive, the thresholds can be changed according to the characteristic of the motion. Although the translation become larger and larger, it still can do calibration. But the thresholds of the method of Shi [11] cannot be changed. So it only did few calibrations in this situation.

The experiment results of times of calibration are shown in Table 1. One can see that our method makes more calibrations than the method in Ref. [11].

5 Conclusion

In this paper, we propose an algorithm of adaptive motion selection for online hand-eye calibration, which can not only avoid the degenerate cases in hand-eye calibration, but also increase the calibration number by adaptively modify the thresholds according to the characteristics of motion sequence. So it is robust to different applications. Experimental results from simulated data and real setup show that the method can greatly increase the performance of online hand-eye calibration.

References

1. Y. C. Shiu and S. Ahmad, Calibration of wrist-mounted robotic sensors by solving homogeneous transform equations of the form AX = XB, IEEE Trans. Robot. Automat., vol. 5, pp. 16-29, Feb. 1989.
2. R. Y. Tsai and R. K. Lenz, A new technique for fully autonomous and efficient 3d robotics hand/eye calibration, IEEE Trans. Robot. Automat., vol. 5, pp. 345-358, 1989.
3. H. Chen. A screw motion approach to uniqueness analysis of head-eye geometry. in Proc. IEEE Int. Conf. on Computer Vision and Pattern Recognition, Maui, Hawaii, USA, pp. 145-151, June 1991.
4. C. Wang. Extrinsic calibration of a robot sensor mounted on a robot. IEEE Trans. Robot. Automat., 8(2):161-175, Apr. 1992.
5. Hanqi Zhuang and Yui Cheung Shiu, A Noise-Tolerant Algorithm for Robotic Hand-Eye Calibration With or Without Sensor Orientation Measurement. IEEE Trans. on System, Man and Cybernetics, 23(4):1168-1175,1993.
6. R. Horaud and F. Dornaika,Hand-eye calibration, Int. J. Robot. Res., 14(3):195-210, 1995.
7. K. Daniilidis.Hand-eye calibration using dual quaternions. Int. J. Robot. Res., 18(3):286-298, 1999.
8. J. Angeles, G. Soucy and F. P. Ferrie,The online solution of the hand-eye problem, IEEE Trans. Robot. Automat., vol. 16, pp. 720-731, Dec. 2000.
9. N. Andreff, R. Horaud and B. Espiau,On-line hand-eye calibration, in Proc. Int. Conf. on 3-D Digital Imaging and Modeling, pp. 430 - 436, Oct. 1999.
10. N. Andreff, R. Horaud, and B. Espiau,Robot hand-eye calibration using structure-from-motion, Int. J. Robot. Res., 20(3):228-248, 2001.
11. F.H. Shi, J.H.Wang and Y.C.Liu,An Approach to Improve Online Hand-Eye Calibration. In Proc. of IbPRIA 2005, LNCS 3522, pp.647-655, 2005.
12. Regression Analysis, Numeral Statistic group, Chinese Academy of ScienceBeijing-Science Press1974.
13. S. Ma and Z. Zhang, Computer Vision, 2nd edition. Beijing : Science Press, 1998. ch.6.

Scene Boundary Detection by Audiovisual Contents Analysis

Joon-sik Baek[1], Soon-tak Lee[1], and Joong-hwan Baek[2]

[1] Multimedia Retrieval Lab. in School of Electronics and Communication Engineering,
Hankuk Aviation University
waterbat@mail.hangkong.ac.kr, stlee@telechips.com
[2] School of Electronics and Communication Engineering, Hankuk Aviation University
jhbaek@mail.hangkong.ac.kr

Abstract. Scene boundary detection is an essential research in content-based video summary, retrieval, and browsing. In this paper, we present an efficient and robust scene extraction algorithm. The proposed algorithm consists of three stages. The first stage is shot boundary detection, and the second stage is the musical scene boundary detection through detection of musical shot. In the last stage, scene detection among non-musical shots is accomplished. In order to detect musical shots, audio categorization is accomplished on audio clips that are divided into visual shot unit. Then low level audio features are calculated for categorization of audio clips. Finally, the parts of video which are containing music component are discriminated on the assumption that the shots in a scene contain same background music. In scene change detection among non-musical shots, distance matrix among shots is calculated based on visual information and time distances between each shot. To provide a reasonable limitation of time distance, variable length time-window method is proposed. The scene boundaries are detected by using shot clustering and scene formation.

1 Introduction

In content-based video summary, retrieval and browsing, video parsing and structuring is an essential research. However, the video structuring based on shot level could not fairly well represent the event-based semantics of video. Moreover, the number of shots in one video is too large to manage efficiently. Therefore, video retrieval which reflects user's preference cannot be satisfied by shot level video summary. To overcome such problems, more sophisticated video summary methods have been proposed. One of them is scene-based video structuring.

Several researches have focused on visual similarity of video sequence. In [3], shot grouping based on visual similarity was proposed. To calculate visual similarity, color histogram and MPEG-1 motion vector is used. The color histogram has been most widely used in both shot boundary detection and scene segmentation technique.

However, by using only video information, the accuracy of scene boundary detection is poor.

In [7], Kuo proposed a scene level video segmentation method based on both audio and video information. For audio analysis, they used zero-crossing rate, short-time energy contour, spectrum flux, line spectrum pair (LSP), band periodicity, noise

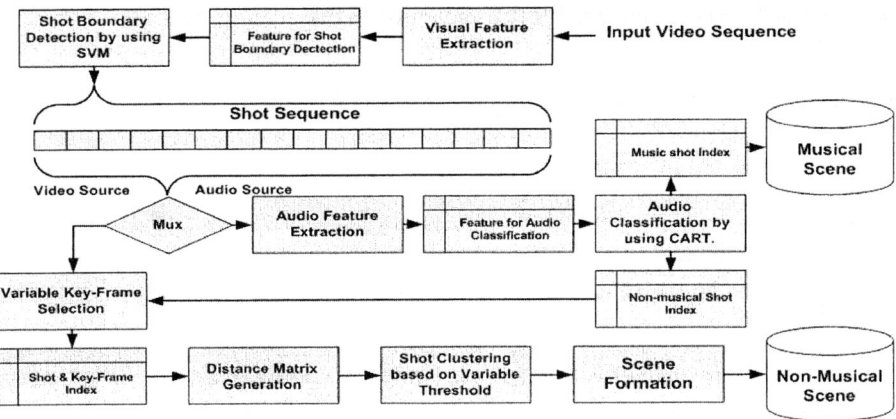

Fig. 1. The flow chart of presented method is described. The input video is separated into video part and audio part.

frame ratio, and band energy distribution for speech and non-speech discrimination and for detail classification of non-speech category.

In this paper, we present a robust and efficient content-based video summary technique on scene level by using both video and audio data. The proposed technique consists of three stages; splitting video sequence into shot unit, scene extraction through musical shot detection, and scene boundary detection among non-musical shots. In the first stage, distances of color histogram and differences from block matching between consecutive frames are calculated for detection of abrupt changes. SVM is used to detect shot boundary. In the second stage, we extract musical scenes which are containing background music on the assumption that shots in a scene contain same background music. In this paper, features which have foundation in fundamental frequency and RMS are calculated to detect music component, and then shots are classified into two categories; musical shot and non-music shot. Classification tree is used for classification method in this stage. In the last stage, key-frame selection for comparison among detected shots is accomplished. By using selected key-frames, distance matrix based on visual information among shots is extracted with variable length time-window method. By applying this algorithm, temporal distance restriction in visual distance extraction procedure is available.

The whole procedure is described in Fig. 1, and this paper is organized as follow. Feature extraction for shot boundary detection and classification is discussed in Section 2. In section 3, musical scene detection by using audio source is discussed. In section 4, shot clustering with variable length time-window method is represented. Experiment evaluation results are given in Section 5.

2 Shot Change Detection by Using SVM

In this section, we propose an efficient and robust shot boundary detection algorithm which is used as a pre-procedure of scene boundary detection. Feature extraction based on pixel, histogram, and block comparison is discussed in Section 2.1. In Section 2.2, SVM which is used for classification is described.

2.1 Visual Feature for Dissimilarity Measure Between Frames

Features which calculated by using pixel difference and histogram comparison are excellent for detection of abrupt shot change. The luminance component is used for the pixel difference calculation. To compare histograms, two kinds of histograms are used; one is global histogram which uses all the components of HSV and the other is local histogram which uses only luminance component. Global histogram and local histogram contain 10-bins on H, S, and V, and 10-bins on only V respectively. In local histogram comparison, a frame is uniformly segmented into 16 sub-blocks, and then only 8 blocks which have the biggest similarity is used. By ignoring the others, partial motions of several objects are ignored. The local histogram comparison is described in Eq. (1).

$$LH_m = \frac{1}{8}\sum_{i=0}^{7} \min[LHB_i] \quad (1)$$

$$where, LHB_j = \frac{1}{2|BS|}\sum_{k=0}^{B}|H_m(k,j) - H_{m-1}(k,j)|, 0 \le j \le 16$$

In block based comparison, a frame is uniformly segmented into 16 sub-blocks, and then similarity between corresponding blocks is calculated. To compare blocks, only the luminance component is used. The procedure of the block based comparison is shown *below*.

$$LLR_m = \sum_{i=0}^{r} W_i \quad (2)$$

$$where, W_i = \begin{cases} 1, & LHR_j \ge Th \\ 0, & otherwise \end{cases}, and\ LHR_j = \frac{\left\{\frac{\sigma_{m,j}^2 + \sigma_{m-1,j}^2}{2} + \left(\frac{\mu_{m,j} - \mu_{m-1,j}}{2}\right)^2\right\}^2}{\sigma_{m,j}^2 \times \sigma_{m-1,j}^2}$$

2.2 Shot Change Detection by Using SVM

Consider the problem of separating a set of training examples belonging to two classes, $(x_i; y_i)_{1 \le i \le N}$ where each example $x_i \in R^d$ being features which are calculated in Section 2.1, belongs to a class labeled by $y_i = \{-1, 1\}$ which are shot boundary and non-shot boundary respectively. Once a kernel $K(X_i, X_j)$ satisfying Mercer's condition has been chosen, an optimal separating hyperplane will be constructed in the mapping space. In this paper, we use Gaussian radial basis function (RBF) kernel and Polynomial kernel, which is defined in Eq. (3) and (4), since they were observed to perform better than the other. Performance comparison between these two kernel functions is described in Section 5.1.

$$K_{Gaussian}(x,y) = \exp\left(-\rho \parallel x - y \parallel^2 \right) \qquad (3)$$

$$K_{Polynomial}(x,y) = \left(\langle x, y \rangle + c\right)^2 \qquad (4)$$

3 Musical Scene Detection by Audio Analysis

In [7][8], they categorized audio into several classes, and then the intersection of each component is regarded as a scene boundary. However, the intersection of audio categories, such like transition silence to dialog or silence to environmental sound, could not be a suitable clue of scene change. Therefore, in this paper, we present more suitable rule for scene boundary detection by using audio analysis. If a shot contains background music, most of all shots in a scene which includes corresponding shot have same background music in general. So, we can detect certain scene boundaries by detecting music component in each shot.

In Section 3.1, we discuss about the relative characteristic between music and non-music component. Feature selection is described in Section 3.2, and classification procedure and description about CART is presented in Section 3.3.

3.1 Audio Characteristic of Music, and Non-music Component

Since voice and music component are the most important contents of audio source, volume is relatively louder than another kinds of audio. However, in consideration of compactness characteristic of audio, voice has less compact sound than music due to the syllable. On the other hand, volume of environmental sound is smaller than voice and music components, because it is an additional component which is captured during a filming. However, there are several cases which the volume of environmental sound is louder than music or voice. To discriminate between these kinds of sounds and music, analysis of frequency components is essentially required.

3.2 Features Based on RMS and Fundamental Frequency for Music Detection

In this paper, we use statistical values of RMS and fundamental frequency (FuF) of short time audio source for analysis of the sound characteristic. All audio features are extracted from each shot which is segmented in Section 2. By using the shift-window method, RMS and FuF are calculated from every window, and then statistical values of extracted features in each shot are calculated.

RMS efficiently and easily represents volume of audio signals, and computational cost is relatively low. But the number of windows in each shot is different according to the length of corresponding shot, and a proper method which integrates various number of RMS in a shot into fixed number of representations is required. The average volume level and the sound compactness could be efficiently represented by mean and variance of audio signal power respectively. The representations of mean and variance of RMS are shown *below*, and $x_{i,j}(k)$ is the k-th sample in the i-th window of the j-th shot.

$$\mu_{rms}(j) = \frac{1}{n}\sum_{i=1}^{n} P(i,j), \quad \sigma_{rms}^2(j) = \frac{1}{n}\sum_{i=1}^{n}\left[P(i,j) - \mu_{rms}(j)\right]^2 \tag{5}$$

$$\text{where, } P(i,j) = \sqrt{\frac{1}{m}\sum_{k=1}^{m} x_{i,j}^2(k)}$$

Since most of all environmental sounds are similar to noise or appeared intermittently, FuF of environmental sound is lower than that of music component, and variance is relatively large. But mean and variance are not enough to fully represent frequency characteristic. That is because several redundantly high fundamental frequency components increase average level of fundamental frequency. In [7], Tong and Jay used zero ratio of fundamental frequency by using a fixed threshold. However, decision of the proper threshold is difficult due to the frequency characteristics of specific musical instruments. In this paper, we use more flexible clipping method of fundamental frequency. That is clipping by using sigmoid function. Mean and variance of clipped fundamental frequency are used for audio features, and described below.

$$\mu_{Fu}(j) = \frac{1}{n}\sum_{i=1}^{n} Fu_C(i,j), \quad \sigma_{Fu}^2 = \frac{1}{n}\sum_{i=1}^{n}\left[Fu_C(i,j) - \mu_{Fu}(j)\right]^2 \tag{6}$$

$$\text{where, } Fu_C(i,j) = \frac{1}{1+\exp[\alpha \times Fu(i,j) + \beta]}, \quad \beta \leq 0, 1 \leq \alpha$$

$Fu(i,j)$ represents the fundamental frequency of i-th window in j-th shot. By using clipping function based on sigmoid function, we prevent the increase of fundamental frequency average level due to several redundantly high fundamental frequency components.

3.3 Shot Categorization by Using Classification Tree

Classification tree consists of the root node, links or branches, and terminal or leaf nodes. It follows tree-growing methodology known as CART and is grown through the splitting and pruning process. In splitting process, each node chooses a feature decreasing the impurity as much as possible in the descendent node and splits the data into subsets by the selected feature. Entropy, *Gini*, and misclassification impurity functions are generally used as the function to measure the impurity. We measure impurity using Gini impurity function that is generalized the variance impurity function useful in the two classes case. In this stage, four features which are mean and variance of RMS and clipped fundamental frequency are used for classification. As mentioned *above*, two desired classes are musical shot and non-musical shot respectively.

4 Scene Change Detection Based on Visual Similarity

In spite of musical scene extraction, most parts of video are remained. Therefore, another scene extraction method is necessary to extract non-musical scene. In previous research, shot clustering method with time restriction has been accomplished to extract scene. The most difficult one, however, is the decision of several parameters due to the various characteristic of shots. In this section, we propose a flexible threshold making which is robust to variation of shot characteristic.

The previous method is briefly described in Section 4.1. In Section 4.2, we discuss the enhancement of the previous method by using variable length time-window method.

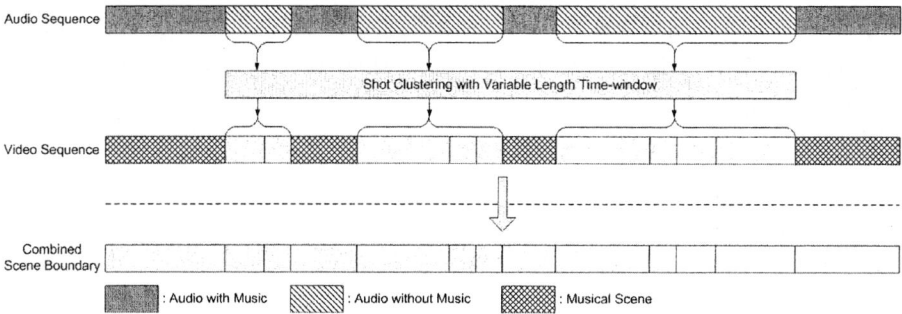

Fig. 2. The combination of the results from the video analysis and audio analysis is described

4.1 Shot Clustering with Time Restriction [1]

In previous works, they used key-frame selection and the time-window method to reduce computational cost. The static number of key-frames in a shot could not fully represent the contents of corresponding shot. To overcome this problem, various key-frame selection method has been accomplished.

In general, the number of shots included in a scene or the length of a scene has limitation in time domain. Therefore, if the time distance of two shots is over than general length, the probability which they are included in same scene is low even though their visual similarity is high. By using time-window method, the similarity between two shots which are far from each other would be ignored. After the distance matrix based on visual similarity is calculated, shot clustering is performed.

4.2 Variable Length Time-Window Method

The previous time-window method [1] is shown *below*.

$$d(S_i, S_j) = \begin{cases} d_K(S_i, S_j), & T_b(S_j) - T_e(S_i) \leq Th_T \\ 1, & otherwise \end{cases}, \quad i < j \quad (7)$$

where, $d_K(S_i, S_j)$ is the similarity between two shots S_i and S_j, and $T_b(S)$ and $T_e(S)$ represent start time and end time of the shot S respectively. The variable length time-window $Th_T(S_i, S_j)$ could be defined like shown below.

$$Th_T(S_i, S_j) = Th_B + \omega_S \cdot \left\{ \omega_C \cdot \frac{1}{\left[\sum_{k=1}^{j-i}\left[d(S_i, S_{i+k}) - \mu_{d(S_i, S_j)}\right]\right]^2} + \omega_R \cdot R(\gamma) \right\}, i < j \quad (8)$$

$$\text{where, } \mu_{D(S_i, S_j)} = \frac{1}{j-i} \sum_{k=1}^{j-i} d(S_i, S_{i+k})$$

Th_B is basis time length and decided experimentally. ω_S, ω_S, and ω_R are constants for scaling and $R(\gamma)$ is ratio of the number of shots which are most similar to S_i. $R(\gamma)$ is described like below.

$$R(\gamma) = \frac{n\left[C_{i,j}(\gamma)\right]}{j-i}, \; C_{i,j}(\gamma) = \left\{S_k \mid d(S_i, S_k) \le \gamma\right\} \quad (9)$$

$$\text{where, } d(S_i, S_{i+k}) = \min_{f_n \in S_i, f_m \in S_{i+k}} D(f_n, f_m)$$

$n(C)$ represents the number of units in set C and $D(f_n, f_m)$ is the color-histogram intersection [2] between two frames. Variable length time-window lengthens its window size if characteristic of shots in a window is similar to each other, and vice versa.

5 Experimental Result

As a sample data set, two color films which have 25 fps are used; one is used for training, and the other is used for test. There are 135,000 and 79,500 frames respectively, at a spatial resolution of 160× 120. These video have each audio source which is digitized at 44.1 KHz with 16-bit precision in mono sound. In Section 5.1, we discuss performance of shot boundary detection. The experiment of musical scene extraction and the improvement of shot clustering with variable length time-window method for non-musical shots is described in Section 5.2.

5.1 Performance of Shot Boundary Detection

To convert non-linearly separable input space to linearly separable feature space, two kinds of kernel functions were used. One is radial basis function, the other is polynomial function. For a training sample set, 2472 shot boundaries and 5210 couples of successive frames were used for positive and negative sample set respectively. With fully trained SVM, 732 positive samples and 1493 negative samples were tested to examine performance. Performance of each kernel function is varied according to the change of parameter value, and described in Fig. 3. The optimal performance of shot boundary detection by using each kernel function is shown as Table 1.

Most of all miss classification is occurred due to the shot change in dialog scene. In this case, color distribution of background is similar between two successive frames, and camera composition is focused on actor's face in general. Hence, visual dissimilarity between such shots is very small. In case on false detection, most general problem is abrupt and rapid appearance of object.

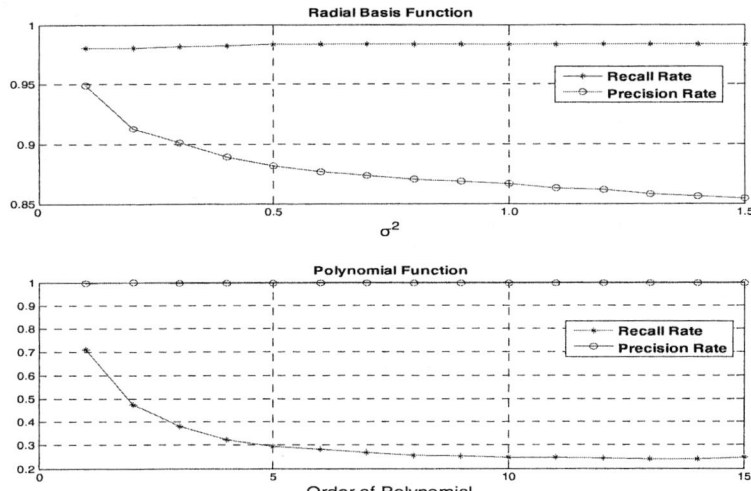

Fig. 3. Recall and precision ratio of shot boundary detection by using each kernel function

Table 1. Performance of shot boundary detection

Kernel function	# of Detected shot boundaries	Performance	
		Recall rate	Precision Rate
Radial Basis Function	771	0.98	0.949
Polynomial Function	625	0.71	0.996

5.2 Result of Shot Clustering with Variable Length Time-Window and Musical Scene Detection

For audio analysis, 249 audio clips which are containing music and 483 audio clips which are non-music are used for positive and negative sample set respectively. Due to the insufficiency of samples, classification tree was trained by using 10-fold cross validation. Performance of audio analysis described in Table 2.

To confirm the improvement by using variable length time-window, shot clustering with fixed length time-window method is accomplished on same sample set. We set fixed length of time-window as 110 sec. Results from both of them are described in Table 3. In this experiment, we prefer over-segmentation to less-segmentation. That is because less-segmentation directly means the loss of information.

Table 2. Performance of audio analysis

Category	# of samples	Recall Rate	Precision Rate
Shot with Music	249	84.36%	82.20%
Shot without Music	483	92.74%	95.24%

Table 3. Scene boundary detection result comparison. As a test video sample, '*Love Letter*' is used. ( ) is incorrect detection, and **italic** is musical scene which is extracted by audio analysis. FL, VL, and Au mean fixed length time-window, variable length time-window, and audio analysis respectively.

Location	Duration (h:mm:ss)	Scene number FL	Scene number VL & Au
Hill	0:00:20 ~ 0:02:57	1~(4)	1~(2)
Funeral(a)	0:02:57 ~ 0:04:02	(5)	(3)
Funeral (b)	0:04:02 ~ 0:05:41	6	4
In a car	0:05:41 ~ 0:06:37	7~9	5~7
Ichuki(m)'s Living Room	0:06:37 ~ 0:07:06	10~11	8~9
Ichuki(m)'s Room	0:07:06 ~ 0:10:30	12~22	10~13
Landscape of town	0:10:30 ~ 0:10:46	23	14
Ichuki(f)'s home(a)	0:10:46 ~ 0:11:25	24	15~16
Ichuki(f)'s home(b)	0:11:25 ~ 0:12:52	25~(28)	17~(19)
Ichuki(f)'s home(a)	0:12:52 ~ 0:15:16	(29)~30	(20)~21
Ichuki(f)'s room	0:15:16 ~ 0:16:44	31~34	**22~23**
Workroom	0:16:44 ~ 0:22:19	35~36	24
Ichuki(f)'s home	0:22:19 ~ 0:22:44	37	25
Library	0:22:44 ~ 0:28:30	43~44	26~27
Cafeteria	0:28:30 ~ 0:31:44	45~(46)	28
Way to Workroom2	0:31:44 ~ 0:32:26	(47)	29
Workroom2	0:32:26 ~ 0:33:13	(47)~48	30~32
Ichuki(f)'s yard	0:33:13 ~ 0:33:27	49~50	33~34
Ichuki(f)'s Living room	0:33:27 ~ 0:33:47	51	35
Recollection in hospital	0:33:47 ~ 0:35:32	52~(59)	36~40
Ichuki(f)'s yard	0:35:32 ~ 0:40:44	(60)~62	**41~42**
Ichuki(f)'s room	0:40:44 ~ 0:41:10	63	43
Road	0:41:10 ~ 0:43:00	64~67	**44**
Ichuki(m)'s room	0:43:00 ~ 0:47:49	68~72	45~50
High school classroom	0:47:59 ~ 0:53:51	73~80	**51~53**

6 Conclusions

Existing content-based video summary which is used for shot boundary detection is not proper to provide a meaningful unit of video. Through this proposed method, more precise and meaningful content-based video summary has been available. Scene boundary detection is still incorrect in comparison with the accuracy of shot boundary detection. Existing method used shot clustering with fixed parameters. However, due to the variety of video, fixed parameters could not be robust and precise in general video. Hence we proposed variable length time-window method. Experimental result shows that this method provides more precise result. An advantage of scene boundary detection is that audio source is available. We could detect another clue of scene boundary by using audio source, since background music plays a great roll in representation an atmosphere of video. In general, background music is fully contained in a scene. Therefore, we utilized several low level audio features to detect music component in a shot. The number of over-segmented scenes has been reduced by using proposed method and combination rule. However, combination rule between results from video and audio analysis is still poor. To maximize the efficiency of audio analysis, more robust and reasonable rule is required.

Acknowledgement. This research was supported by the Internet information Retrieval Research Center (IRC) in Hankuk Aviation University. IRC is a Regional Research Center of Kyounggi Province, designated by ITEP and Ministry of Commerce, Industry and Energy.

References

1. Minerva Yeung; Boon-Lock Yeo: Segmentation of Video by Clustering and Graph Analysis. Computer Vision and Image Understanding, vol. 71, no. 1. (1998) 94-109
2. Yeung, M.M.; Bede Liu: Efficient matching and clustering of video shots. Image Processing, 1995. Proceedings., International Conference on vol. 1. (1995) 338 - 341
3. Yong-Moo Kwon; Chang-Jun Song; Ig-Jae Kim: A new approach for high level video structuring. Multimedia and Expo, 2000. ICME 2000. 2000 IEEE International Conference on vol. 2, no. 30. (2000) 773-776
4. Ba Tu Truong; Venkatesh, S.; Dorai, C.: Scene extraction in motion pictures. Circuits and Systems for Video Technology, IEEE Transactions on vol. 13, Issue. 1. (2003) 5-15
5. S.B. Hong; W.Nah; J.H. Baek: Abrupt Shot Change Detection Using Multiple Features and Classification Tree. IDEAL 4th International Conference on Intelligent Data Engineering and Automated Learning 2003, LNCS 2690. (2003) 553-560
6. Richard O. Duda, Peter E. Hart, David G. Stork, Pattern Classification 2nd edition, Wiley Interscience, (2001) 259-265
7. Tong Zhang; C.-C. Jay Kuo,: Audio content analysis for online audiovisual data segmentation and classification Speech and Audio Processing. IEEE Transactions on Volume 9, Issue 4. (2001) 441 – 457
8. Lie Lu; Hong-Jiang Zhang; Hao Jiang: Content analysis for audio classification and segmentation Speech and Audio Processing, IEEE Transactions on Volume 10, Issue 7. (2002) 504 – 516

k−Nearest Neighbors Associative Memory Model for Face Recognition

Bai-ling Zhang[1], Yuan Miao[1], and Gopal Gupta[2]

[1] School of Computer Science and Mathematics,
Victoria University, VIC 3011, Australia
{bailing.zhang, Yuan.Miao}@vu.edu.au
[2] School of Computer Science and Software Engineering,
Monash University, VIC 3800, Australia
Gopal.Gupta@csse.monash.edu.au

Abstract. Associative memory (AM) models for human faces recognition have been previously studied in psychology and neuroscience. A kernel based AM model (KAM) has been recently proposed and demonstrated with good recognition performances. KAM first forward transforms input space to a feature space and then reconstructs input from the kernel features. For a given subject, KAM uses all of the training samples to build the model, regardless what a query face image will be. This not only keeps unnecessary overhead for model building when the number of smaples is large, but also makes the model not robust when there are outliers in the training samples, for example, from occlusions or illumination. In this paper, an improved associative memory model is investigated by combining the KAM with the k−Nearest Neighbors classification algorithm. Named as k−Nearest Neighbors Associative Memory (kNN-AM), the model takes into account the closeness between a query face image and the training prototype face images. A modular scheme of applying the proposed kNN-AM to face recognition was discussed. As a multi-class classification problem, face recognition can be carried out by simply comparing which associative memory model best describe a given query face image. Results of extensive experiments on several well-known face database show that the kNN-AM has very satisfactory recognition accuracies.

1 Introduction

Face recognition has been one of the most active research topics due to its wide spectrum of applications. In recent years, considerable progress has been made on face recognition and some other related problems such as face detection and tracking.

Given a set of subjects' face images as training samples, a face recognition system is supposed to identify a specific subject by an unknown face image. A subject to be identified from a facial image represents a class and face recognition system must determine whether or not an instance face image belongs to a given class. One of the difficulties is that only a few of sample face images available for a given subject, which is known as *small sample size* (SSS) problem. The existing practice, the "1-out-of-N" encoding scheme, assigns different codes to the subjects for just one classfier. The performance of "1-out-of-N" encoding, however, is often unsatisfactory.

To solve the SSS problem in face recognition, a memory-based system is preferable. In a memory-based system, recall of a stored pattern can be accomplised by providing a distorted version of samples as a probe or query. Design of a memory-based system for face images can be based on neural schemes for pattern storage and retrieval, such as the corrleation memory [Kohonen 1972], which can recall one of the original patterns it has learnt by reconstructing a query pattern.

The role of linear AM models in face recognition has been extensively investigated in psychovisual study [Abdi et al 1997, O'Toole 1995, Valentin et al 1997]. Linear AM models share the limitations of Eigenface method [Turk and Pentland 1991], due to their similar eigen-decompositions. For example, eigenface and linear AM models usually give high similarities indiscriminately for two images from a single person or from two different persons.

To improve the performance of linear associative memory models, a kernel based model, called Kernel Auto-associative Memory (KAM), was proposed in [Zhang 2004], which nonlinearly maps the data into a high dimensional feature space through operating a kernel function with input space. For a given subject, KAM builds the model from all of the training samples, which not only keeps excess overhead for model building when there are relatively large number of smaples, but also makes the model not robust when there are outliers in the training samples, for example, from occlusions or illumination.

In this paper, we propose an improved KAM model for face recognition by taking the closenee between query face image and the training samples into account. Instead of taking all the training samples in establishing the memory model, the new KAM model first finds the k nearest neighbors for a given query face image and then construct the corresponding KAM with the selected examples. Experiments show that the kNN-AM gives high recognition performance.

2 Kernel Associative Memory as Computational Model of Faces

2.1 Previous Studies on Kernel Associative Memory

Let H_k be a *reproducing kernel Hillbert space* and $k(\cdot, \cdot)$ be a positive-definite function in H_k. The inner product in H is defined by

$$< k_x, k_t > = k(x, t) ,$$

and $k(\cdot, \cdot)$ is called the *reproducing kernel* for H_k.

Let F_b be a linear mapping function from H_k to the input space E^N. The principle of kernel associative memory is to perform auto-associative mapping via the kernel feature space, i.e., reconstructing patterns from their counterparts in H_k [Zhang 2005]:

$$\hat{\mathbf{x}} = F_b^{(m)}(\Phi(\mathbf{x})), \qquad \text{for } \mathbf{x} \in \text{class } m$$

where $\Phi(\mathbf{x}) = k(\mathbf{x}, \cdot)$ represents the feature in functional form in H_k and the subscript b denotes the function for reverse mapping.

When the patterns to be reproduced are multidimensional, F_b will be composed of a set of functions $\{f_{b_n}\}$, each corresponding to an element of the output space: $F_b = [f_{b_1}, \cdots, f_{b_N}]^T$. Consider an element function f_{b_n} and omit the element label n, the function in linear form is

$$\hat{x} = f_b(\Phi(\mathbf{x})) = <\beta_\phi, \Phi(\mathbf{x})>,$$

Here $\hat{x}$ represents an element of the output vector $\hat{\mathbf{x}}$, and β_ϕ is a vector in the feature space. Suppose the vector β_ϕ can be spanned by the images of M training samples:

$$\beta_\phi = \sum_{i=1}^{M} b_i \Phi(\mathbf{x}_i),$$

then the linear function f_b can be written as

$$\hat{x} = <\sum_{i=1}^{M} b_i \Phi(\mathbf{x}_i), \Phi(\mathbf{x})> = \sum_{i=1}^{M} b_i k(\mathbf{x}_i, \mathbf{x}) = \mathbf{b}^T \mathbf{k}$$

where $\mathbf{b} = [b_1, \cdots, b_M]^T$ is the vector of expansion coefficients, and $\mathbf{k} = [k(\mathbf{x}_1, \mathbf{x}), \cdots, k(\mathbf{x}_M, \mathbf{x})]^T$ represents the vector of kernel products. So the complete output vector $\hat{\mathbf{x}}$ is

$$\hat{\mathbf{x}} = B\mathbf{k}, \tag{1}$$

where $B = [b_1, \cdots, b_N]$ denotes the collection of linear projections for each output element. Given a set of samples, for example, $(\mathbf{x}_1, \mathbf{x}_2, \cdots, \mathbf{x}_M)$ for training, we can first compute the kernel product vectors $(\mathbf{k}_1, \mathbf{k}_2, \cdots, \mathbf{k}_M)$. The desired output can be expressed as

$$X = BK, \tag{2}$$

where X is the matrix with each column an example pattern, $X = (\mathbf{x}_1, \mathbf{x}_2, \cdots, \mathbf{x}_M)$, and K represents the matrix with each column a corresponding kernel product vector, $K = (\mathbf{k}_1, \mathbf{k}_2, \cdots, \mathbf{k}_M)$.

In [Zhang 2004] we proposed a simple method of learning the projection matrix B by finding a matrix that minimizing the empirical square error $\sum_i ||\mathbf{x}_i - B\mathbf{k}_i||^2$, which gives us a minimization result:

$$B = XK^+ \tag{3}$$

where K^+ is the pseudo-inverse of the matrix K: $K^+ = (K^T K)^{-1} K^T$.

2.2 An Improved Kernel Associative Memory Model

Suppose that we have C class sample set $\{\mathbf{x}_i^{(j)}\}, j = 1, \cdots, C;\ i = 1, \cdots, N_j$, where $\mathbf{x}_i^{(j)}$ is the ith sample of the jth class, and N_j is the number of the samples in the jth class. Let $\mathbf{x}$ be the query sample. Suppose $\mathbf{x}_{N(1)}^{(j)}, \mathbf{x}_{N(2)}^{(j)}, \cdots, \mathbf{x}_{N(k)}^{(j)}$ are the k nearest neghbors of the query $\mathbf{x}$ in the jth class, then a kernel assciative memory can be modelled as a composite mapping based on the selected samples:

$$\begin{aligned}\hat{\mathbf{x}}^{(j)} &= T(\mathbf{x}_l^{(j)}, \mathbf{x}) \\ &= T_2(T_1(\mathbf{x}_l^{(j)}, \mathbf{x})) \quad l \in N(k),\ j = 1, \cdots, C\end{aligned} \quad (4)$$

where T_1 and T_2 are non-linear and linear transformations respectively. The nonlinear processing can be written as the following kernel transform, $T_1 : R^N \to R^k$, which is performed on $\mathbf{x}$ to obtain $\mathbf{y}_l^{(j)}$, where $\mathbf{y}_l^{(j)}$ is defined as

$$y_l^{(j)} = k(\mathbf{x}, \mathbf{x}_l^{(j)}) = \exp(-\frac{||\mathbf{x} - \mathbf{x}_l^{(j)}||}{2\sigma^2}), \quad l \in N(k),\ j = 1, \cdots, C \quad (5)$$

where $||\cdot||$ is the L_2 norm. The kernel transformation k is then followed by a linear transformation:

$$\hat{\mathbf{X}}^{(j)} = \mathbf{B}\mathbf{Y}^{(j)}, \quad j = 1, \cdots, C \quad (6)$$

where $\hat{\mathbf{X}}^{(j)}$ is an $N \times N_j$ matrix for jth class whose lth column is $\mathbf{x}_l^{(j)}$, $\mathbf{Y}^{(j)}$ is an $k \times N_j$ matrix whose lth column is $\mathbf{y}_l^{(j)}$, and $\mathbf{B}$ is an $N \times k$ matrix with similar meaning as given in Eq.(3).

For the jth class, the distance between the query sample $\mathbf{x}$ and the recalled $\hat{\mathbf{x}}^{(j)}$ is given by

$$d(\mathbf{x}, \hat{\mathbf{x}}^{(j)}) = ||\mathbf{x} - \hat{\mathbf{x}}^{(j)}||, \quad j = 1, \cdots, C \quad (7)$$

For face recognition, the closeness between the query image $\mathbf{x}$ and jth kNN-AM face model can also be measured by the cosine of the angle between the vectors $\hat{\mathbf{x}}^{(j)}$ and $\mathbf{x}$, i.e.,

$$\cos(\hat{\mathbf{x}}^{(j)}, \mathbf{x}) = \frac{\mathbf{x}^T \hat{\mathbf{x}}^{(j)}}{||\hat{\mathbf{x}}^{(j)}|| \cdot ||\mathbf{x}||}, \quad j = 1, \cdots, C \quad (8)$$

with cosine of 1 indicating a perfect reconstruction of the query image.

In the above kNN-AM for faces modelling, an important issue is about an appropriate selection of the σ value in Eq.(5), which should be properly related to the relative proximity of the test data to the training data. When applying to face recognition, an average of the similarities (in L_2 norm sense) between the query image and every training samples from the k−nearest neighbors can be calculated as σ value.

3 A Practical Face Recognition Scheme

3.1 Facial Features from Wavelet Transform

Face recognition always involves choosing a suitable representation for images. In practice, plain pixel intensity or low resolution "thumb-nail" representation is often used, which is not an efficient one. Another popular method of face representation attempts to capture and define the face as a whole and exploit the statistical regularities of pixel intensity variations. Principal component analysis (PCA) is a typical method, by which faces are represented by a linear combination of weighted eigenvectors, known as eigenfaces [Turk and Pentland 1991]. In practice, however, the representation capability from PCA is very limited.

Wavelet based image representation has many advantages. In recent years, extensive works have been made in applying Gabor wavelets to face recognition, which seem to be the most probable candidate from facial feature extraction point of view. But Gabor functions are both nonorthogonal and complex which makes the computation of wavelet coefficients difficult and expensive. A more practical way is with a dyadic or wavelet filter bank. Converging evidence in neurophysiology and psychology is consistent with the notion that the human visual system analyses input at several spatial resolution scales [Valentin 1999]. By spatial frequency analysis, an image is represented as a weighted combination of basis functions, in which high frequencies carry finely detailed information whereas low frequencies carry coarse, shape-based information.

There are several implementations of wavelet filter based algorithms. In a tree structured algorithm, a wavelet and a scaling filter are used to decompose an image into 4 subbands denoted by LL, HL, LH, HH. The subbands LH and HL record the changes of the image along horizontal and vertical directions, respectively. The HH band shows the high frequency component of the image. Second level decomposition can then be conducted on the LL subband. Figure 1 shows a two-level wavelet decomposition of an image of size 200×150 pixels. The wavelet subband LL is a coarser approximation to the original image, which is insensitive to minor changes in facial appearance, lighting and occulusion. In the following, the Daubechies wavelet will be applied for image decomposition.

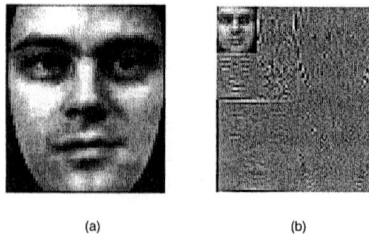

(a) (b)

Fig. 1. (a). An original image with resolution 192×128; (b) the 2-level wavelet decomposition

3.2 The Overall Face Recognition System

The face recognition system consists of a set of separate kNN-AM models, each offering a categorization of faces of the respective subject. In the model building stage, we assign a separate kNN-AM model to each subject. For a specific kth person, let the set of training images be $\mathbf{x}_1^{(k)}, \mathbf{x}_2^{(k)}, \cdots, \mathbf{x}_N^{(k)}$, $k = 1, \cdots, C$, where N is the number of training images for the kth person and C the number of subjects. We first calculated an average face. Then a set of mean-centered vectors $\mathbf{x}_i$ is obtained by subtracting each input image from the average face. After applying an L-level wavelet transform to decompose the reference images, a collection of LL subband image representations for each subject is saved. Then k nearest neighbour training samples for each subject are selected and used to construct a kNN-AM model.

When an unknown image $\mathbf{x}$ is presented, it is substracted by the average face and a caricature image is obtained. Then, an L-level WT is applied to transform the caricature image. The LL subband coefficient is represented as a query. The query image is then applied to all kNN-AM models to yield respective estimations, and a dissimilarity measurement between the query image and a recalled image is performed to determine which of the recalled best match the query. Given the query $\mathbf{A}$ and a recalled result $\mathbf{B}$, the dissimilarity measure $\rho(A, B)$ is defined as $\cos(\mathbf{A}, \mathbf{B})$ as in Eqn. (8).

4 Experimental Results

We conducted experiments to compare the proposed kNN-AM with some other well-known methods, e.g., the eigenface technique [Turk and Pentland 1991] and ARENA [Sim et al 1999], using two representative face database, the FERET standard facial databases (Release2)[Phillips et al 1999] and the AR face database (http://rvl1.ecn.purdue.edu/~aleix/aleix_face_DB.html).

As there are only a few of training examples available, the transformation variancies are difficult to capture. One efficient approach for tackling the issue is to augment the training set with some synthetically-generated face images. In all of the experiments, we synthesize images by some simple geometric transformations, particularly rotation and scaling. In the experiments, 10 synthetic images from each raw training image are generated by making small, random perturbations to the original image: rotation (up to $+5^o$ and -5°) and scaling (by a factor between 95% and 105%).

4.1 Experiments with FERET Datasets

FERET2, the second release of the FERET, consists of 14,051 8-bit grayscale images of human heads with views ranging from frontal to left and right profile, and the database design took into account variable factors such as different expressions, different eyewears/hairstyles, and different illuminations.

Our experimental data consists of a subset of FERET images with 119 persons and 927 images. There are more than 5 frontal or near-frontal images for

Fig. 2. Top row: samples from the FERET dataset; Bottom row: the corresponding normalized images

each subject. The images were imposed on face masks. Figure 2 shows four faces from the FERET dataset and the corresponding pre-processed images. For each subject, we use 50% of images to construct the corresponding kNN-AM model and the remaining images for testing the recognition performance.

We apply wavelet transform to get LL subband representations. A 2 level decomposition results in 2-dimensional LL subband coefficients with size of 38×33. As a comparison, we also experimented with low-resolution image representation, with each face image being down-sampled by bilinear methods to a size of 38×33.

As Eigenfaces are still widely used as baseline for face recognition, we evaluated a variant of the methods, called PCA-nearest-neighbour [Sim et al 1999]. Basic Eigenfaces compute the centroid of weight vectors for each person in the training set, by assuming that each person's face images will be clustered in the eigenface space. While in PCA-nearest-neighbour, each of the weight vectors is individually stored for richer representation. When a query image is presented, it first transforms into the eigenspace and the weight vector will be compared with memorized patterns, then a nearest-neighbour (NN) method will be employed to locate the closest pattern class (person identity). From the face images dataset, the first n eigenvectors were chosen to construct a subspace. After several trial of different n from 20 to 30 until without obvious effect on the recognition performance, we use $n = 25$.

Another face recognition method we compared in the experiments is a recently proposed simple nearest-neighbor based template matching, termed ARENA [Sim et al 1999]. ARENA employs reduced-resolution images and similar to PCA, every training pattern was memorized. A L_0 distance from the query image to each of the stored images in the database is computed, and the label of the best match is returned.

We then assessed the performance of the kNN-AM using the FERET face dataset. For each query face image, a kNN-AM is created for each subject by the selected k nearest samples $\{\mathbf{x}_n\}$, which is specified by matrix B and variance σ. The constructed kNN-AM models recognize the query face by picking the optimal response.

To evaluate the recognition performance, we adopted the methodology called cumulative match scores proposed in [Phillips 1999]. In this method, an identification is regarded as correct if the true object is in the top n matchs. In the left of Figure 3, the cumulative match scores of differenct algorithms are illustrated. The number n is plotted along the horizontal axis, and the vertical axis is the percentage of correct matches. Here kNN-AM exhibits obvious evidence of superiority in performance over the other two methods. Particularly, when only a small sample set is available, kNN-AM performs better with wavelets LL subband representation than with reduced-resolution images. From the simulation results we can see that the Eigenface method and ARENA again show a similar performance as their scores are very close, particularly with reduced-resolution images.

The recognition accuracy can be enhanced by rejecting some query face images based on some thresholds. Denote the largest similarity score ρ_j and second largest score ρ_i. A face image is rejected from recognition if $\rho_j/\rho_i \leq \eta$, where η is a predefined threshold. The recognition accuracy will be increased by tuning the threshold larger. In the right of Figure 3, we illustrate the accuracy versus the rejection rate which results from equally varying η from 0.01 to 0.1. From the simulations we see that for the FERET faces the highest recognition accuracy is achieved from the kNN-AM, which is over 99.5% accuracy vis a rejection rate of 20%. For the rejected faces, more sophisticated methods could be pursued for further analysis.

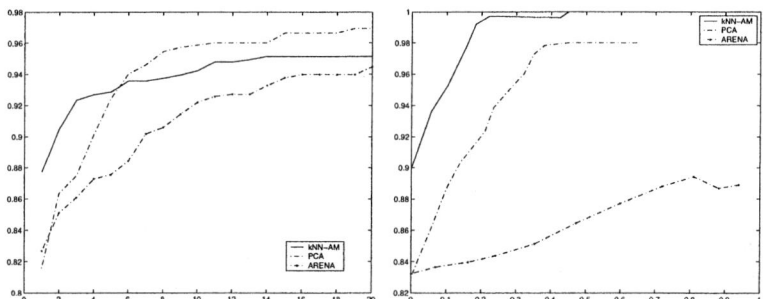

Fig. 3. Left: the cumulative match scores (CMS) for the comparison of Eigenface, ARENA and kNN-AM. Right: Accuracy comparison of Eigenface, ARENA and kNN-AM.

4.2 Experiments with AR Database

AR face databse from Purdue University consists of over 3200 color images of the frontal images of faces of 126 subjects. There are 26 different images for each subject. For each subject, these images were recorded in two different sessions separated by two weeks, each session consisting of 13 images. All images were taken by the same camera under tightly controlled conditions of illumination and viewpoint. Each image in the database consists of a 768 × 576 array of pixels, and each pixel is represented by 24 bits of RGB color values. For illustration, some images are shown in the top of Fig.4.

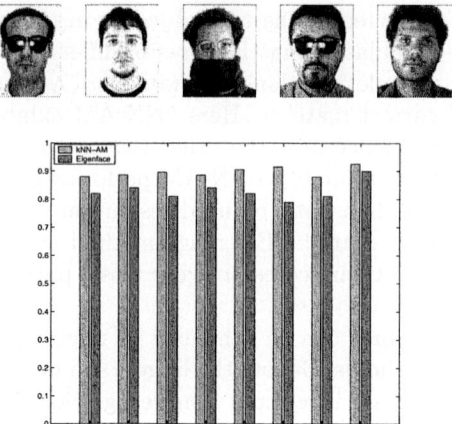

Fig. 4. Top: Sample face images from the AR face database. Bottom: average recognition accuracies from the eight AR face databases.

Similar experiments were carried out to evaluate the performance of our proposed method. All the images are decomposed by one level wavelet transform yielding an LL subband image of size 52 × 43. For each of the eight databases, 10 experiments were conducted for both the kNN-AM scheme and the Eigenface method with downsized image (52 × 43) as the facial feature. The comparison of the averaged recognition performances is illustrated in the bottom of Figure 4, which again showing the superiority of the kNN-AM.

5 Conclusions

In this paper a new associative memory model is introduced for face recognition, which builds a KAM model for the k nearest neighborhood around the query face image. The recognition system gives the likelihood that the query is from the corresponding class by calculating the matching scores. The kNN-AM method not only takes high-order statistical features into account through mapping input space into high-dimensional feature space, but also focus on the nearest neighbour prototypes of the query face image instead of all the prototypes for each subject. As a result, the generalisation capability of KAM is improved and a corresponding face recognition scheme thus benefits. The performance of the proposed scheme has been demonstrated on two standard databases, namely, FERET abd AR face database, showing that the kNN-AM model is efficient in recognition accuracy.

References

[Abdi 1997]   Abdi, H., Valentin, D.,and O'Toole,A. J.(1997). A generalized autoassociator model for face processing and sex categorization: From principal components to multivariate analysis. In D.S.Levine, & W.R.Elsberry (eds.) *Optimality in biological and artificial networks?*. Mahwah (N.J.): Erlbaum. pp.317-337.

[Kohonen1972] Kohonen,T. (1972). Correlation matrix memories. *IEEE Trans. Computers*, 21:353-359.

[Mallat 1989] Mallat,S. (1989). A theory of multiresolution signal decomposition: the wavelet representation. *IEEE Trans. Pattern Anal. Mach. Intell.*, 11:674-693.

[O'Toole et al 1995] O'Toole,A. J., Abdi, H., Deffenbacher,K. A., and Valentin,D. (1995) A perceptual learning theory of the information in faces. in T.Valentin, (Ed.) *Cognitive and Computational Aspects of Face Recognition*, London: Routledge. pp.159-182.

[Phillips, 1999] Phillips, P.(1999). The FERET Evaluation Methodology for Face-Recognition Algorithms *IEEE Transactions on Pattern Analysis and Machine Intelligence*

[Sim et al 1999] Sim, T., Sukthankar, R., Mullin, M., and Baluja, S.(1999). High-performance memory-based face recognition for visitor identification. *Technical Report* JPRC-TR-1999-001-1.

[Turk, 1991] Turk, M. and Pentland,A.(1991). Eigenfaces for Recognition. *Journal of Cognitive Neuroscience*, 3:71-86.

[Valentin et al 1996] Valentin,D. and Abdi,H.(1996). Can a linear autoassociator recognize faces from new orientations? *Journal of the Optical Society of America* , A13:717-724.

[Valentin et al 1997] Valentin,D., Abdi,H., Edelman,B. and Posamentier,M. (1997). What represents a face: a computational approach for the integration of physiological and psychological data. *Perceptron*, 26:1271-1288.

[Valentin, 1999] Valentin,D.(1999). Face-Space Models of Face Recognition. in *Computational, geometric, and process perspectives on facial cognition: Contexts and challenges*, Hillsdale, New Jersey: Lawrence Erbaum Associates Inc.

[Vapnik, 1998] Vapnik, V. N. (1998). *Statistical Learning Theory*. Wiley Series on Adaptive and Learning Systems for Signal Processing, Communications and Control. Wiley, New York

[Zhang, 2004] Zhang, B. et al (2004) *Face Recognition by Applying Wavelet Subband Representation and Kernel Associative Memory* IEEE Transactions on Neural Networks, pp 166-177, Jan. 2004

[Zhang, 2005] Zhang, H., W.Huang, Z.Huang and B.Zhang (2005) *A Kernel Autoassociator Approach to Pattern Classification* IEEE Transactions on System, Man and Cybernetics - B, VOL. 35, NO. 3, 2005

A New Spectral Smoothing Algorithm for Unit Concatenating Speech Synthesis

Sang-Jin Kim[1], Kyung Ae Jang[2], Hyun Bae Han[3], and Minsoo Hahn[1]

[1] Speech and Audio Info. Lab., Information and Communications Univ., Korea
{sangjin, mshahn}@icu.ac.kr
[2] Spoken Language Research Team, Service Development Lab., KT, Korea
kajang@kt.co.kr
[3] U-City Planning Center, U-City Planning Department, KT, Korea
sunshine@kt.co.kr

Abstract. Speech unit concatenation with a large database is presently the most popular method for speech synthesis. In this approach, the mismatches at the unit boundaries are unavoidable and become one of the reasons for quality degradation. This paper proposes an algorithm to reduce undesired discontinuities between the subsequent units. Optimal matching points are calculated in two steps. Firstly, the Kullback-Leibler distance measurement is utilized for the spectral matching, then the unit sliding and the overlap windowing are used for the waveform matching. The proposed algorithm is implemented for the corpus-based unit concatenating Korean text-to-speech system that has an automatically labeled database. Experimental results show that our algorithm is fairly better than the raw concatenation or the overlap smoothing method.

1 Introduction

A corpus-based unit concatenating text-to-speech (TTS) system generates continuous speech by selecting and concatenating proper speech segments from a large speech database[1]. Because of its high output speech quality, this technique is presently most popular. The technique, however, depends highly on a speech database having labeled and clustered segments. The output speech is generated with subsequently selected best segments from the sufficiently large speaker-dependent database. If there are ideal units that perfectly fit target units, and the database is large enough to hold the ideal units, the system could yield ideal, i.e., human speaker-like results. The size of the database, however, is generally constrained. Besides, when the input text contains unseen contexts not included in the database, substitutions of unseen units cause mismatches on the concatenation boundaries[2]. Even though the size of the database is large enough, the discontinuities still may occur and they degrade the synthesized speech quality. Thus, we need a spectral smoothing to reduce this kind of undesired mismatches. In this paper, we propose a spectral smoothing method with its usefulness. Firstly, spectral smoothing is introduced in Section 2 and the proposed algorithm is described in Section 3. Experiments and test results are following in Section 4 while conclusion and summary are given in Section 5.

2 Spectral Smoothing

If a speech database is so well segmented and large enough to cover all the possible target units, a special algorithm wouldn't be required and just the raw concatenation of the units would generate high quality speech outputs. However, spectral discontinuities at the unit transition commonly happen in a unit concatenating speech synthesis. Since the number of the candidate units is limited, sudden transitions in the joints are not unusual. If an appropriate smoothing technique is applied, the results will be similar to the ideal cases, even though the boundaries can still have mismatches. Several studies introduced smoothing techniques but were developed mostly for the voice transformation or the prosody modification[3][4].

Chappell and Hansen examined some smoothing algorithms and showed the mean opinion score (MOS) results in their work[3]. Raw concatenation, optimal unit coupling, waveform interpolation, the LP technique (pole shifting and LSF interpolation), and the continuity effect are tested. According to their results, only the optimal coupling algorithm is better than raw concatenation, which means that the most signal processing algorithms usually degrade the concatenated speech quality. In this paper, we didn't consider those algorithms except optimal coupling. Chappell and Hansen also addressed that spectral smoothing tends to perform best when the original spectra are similar to each other such as in speech coding and unit concatenating synthesis with a large or a specially-designed database[3].

2.1 Optimal Coupling Technique

In the optimal coupling technique, the matching point of each unit is searched to fit best with the subsequent unit by utilizing an objective measure for the spectral mismatch[5]. This algorithm is simple and easy to implement. In addition, it doesn't introduce any additional artifact because there is no modification on the speech. How-ever, the optimal coupling technique needs exhaustive calculations to search the best joint.

2.2 Proposed Spectral Smoothing Algorithm

The proposed spectral smoothing algorithm is basically motivated by the optimal coupling technique. However, it introduced predefined matching regions to reduce the searching time. The algorithm consists of the detailed steps as follow:

– Intensity smoothing,
– Spectral matching,
– Phone environment checking,
– Waveform matching,
– Overlap windowing.

The whole system procedure is shown in Fig. 1 and each block is described in detail.

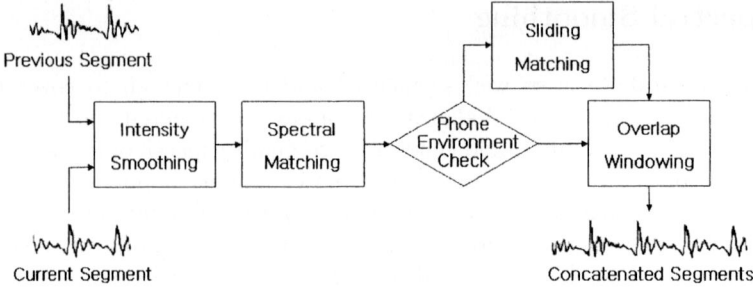

Fig. 1. Proposed spectral smoothing algorithm

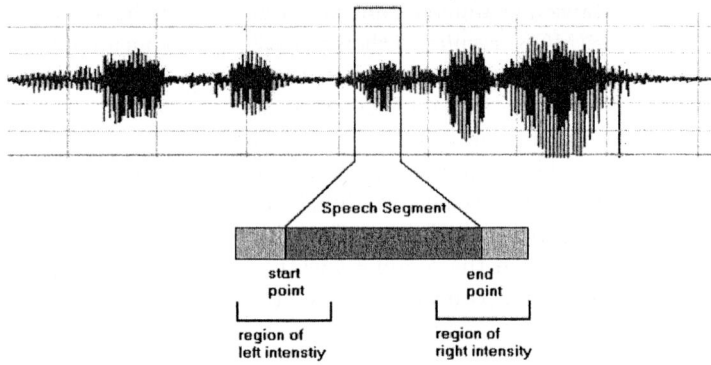

Fig. 2. A smoothing example of a speech unit with extra samples

Intensity Smoothing. Since the selected units to be concatenated are taken from the different speech utterances, intensities of the unit boundary are usually different. Even though the unit selection algorithm considers the intensity difference as the joint cost function, the difference, in many cases, needs to be smoothed. Firstly, the correlation between the left intensity of the current unit and the right intensity of the previous unit is calculated as,

$$Unit(n)_{correlation}^{intensity} = \frac{Unit(n-1)_{right}^{intensity}}{\sqrt{Unit(n-1)_{right}^{intensity} \times Unit(n)_{left}^{intensity}}} . \quad (1)$$

Each unit in the database is segmented to have extra samples outside both the start and the end points of the labeled segment as shown in Fig. 2. The left and the right intensity are calculated with these extra samples and the intensity of the units in junctions will be normalized linearly by utilizing the above correlation.

Spectral Matching. Klabbers and Veldhuis showed that the symmetric Kullback-Leibler (SKL) distance could effectively calculate the spectral discontinuities since spectral peaks were more emphasized than valleys[6][7]. Audible spectral differences mostly come from sudden changes in the frequency, so we

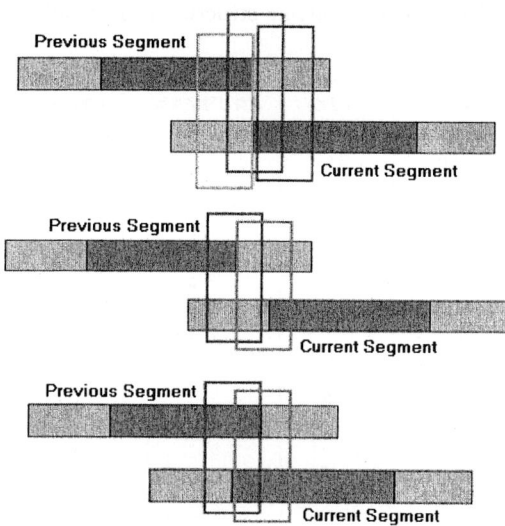

Fig. 3. Spectral matching calculation regions with the SKL distance

utilized the SKL distance to reduce the spectral mismatches. The SKL distance is defined as,

$$D_{SKL}(P,Q) = \int (P(w) - Q(w))log(\frac{P(w)}{Q(w)})dw . \quad (2)$$

Here, P(w) and Q(w) are the power spectra of the candidate pair regions of the subsequent units as shown in Fig. 3. The matching region of the smallest distance would have the smallest spectral discontinuity, so this region should be interpolated. In addition, our technique searches only parts of the subsequent triphones as shown Fig. 3, and we can reduce the search time noticeably.

Phonetic Environment Checking. According to our experiments, spectral discontinuities are often detected at the concatenation boundaries. But, when a phoneme classified as velar or alveolopalatal one is followed by a vowel, we can hardly notice the discontinuity even with the raw concatenation technique. Hence, it is necessary to check the phonetic environments of the segments, and to decide whether to concatenate the following segment with or without any signal processing. Hence, we applied some phonetic rules constructed by observing our Korean database. Table 1 shows the consonant structure in Korean.

Waveform Matching. Even though a boundary is spectrally well-matched, it doesn't guarantee the well synchronized pitch concatenation. If the both segments are voiced ones, the overlap range of them should be matched more precisely. Since we already know the spectral matching range, we can find the pitch synchronous matching point by means of the unit sliding as shown in Fig. 4. One pitch of the unit sliding is sufficient. In case of unvoiced sounds, however, no sliding is required.

Table 1. Consonants structure in Korean[8]

	Bilabial (양순음)	Alveolar (치경음)	Alveolopalatal (치경경구개음)	Velar (연구개음)	Glottal (성문음)
Plosive (파열음)	ㅂ p ㅍ p^h ㅃ p*	ㄷ t ㅌ t^h ㄸ t*		ㄱ k ㅋ k^h ㄲ k*	
Fricative (마찰음)		ㅅ s ㅆ s*			ㅎ h
Affricate (파찰음)			ㅈ tɕ ㅊ tɕ^h ㅉ tɕ*		
Nasal (비음)	ㅁ m	ㄴ n		ㅇ ŋ	
Lateral (설측음)		ㄹ l			

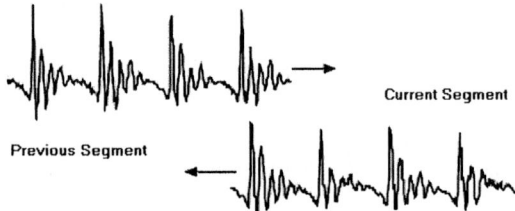

Fig. 4. Sliding for optimal matching point search

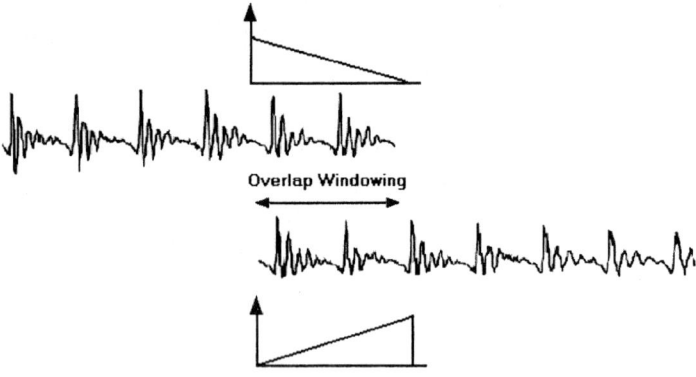

Fig. 5. Triangular windowing for overlap

Overlap Windowing. If the units are manually well-labeled, and the boundaries of the connected units are well-matched with each other, the raw con-

Table 2. MOS and CCR test results

smoothing method	test sentence	MOS	CCR[a] vote		
			Better	Similar	Worse
raw concatenation	database	3.08	N/A	N/A	N/A
	newspaper	2.78	N/A	N/A	N/A
overlap smoothing	database	3.36	5	2	3
	newspaper	3.14	5	3	2
proposed smoothing	database	3.45	6	2	2
	newspaper	3.27	5	3	2

[a] Included are the number of votes for better and worse than raw concatenation.

catenation will generate high quality speech outputs. If the units, however, are labeled automatically just like our TTS system, the system will produce better results with the overlap windowing technique as shown in Fig. 5. One or two pitch periods of overlap is found to be sufficient.

3 Experimental Results

Since direct comparisons are required to check the usefulness of our proposed algorithm, we used not only the conventional MOS test on a scale from 1 to 5 but also the comparison category rating (CCR) method which is an ITU recommendation[9]. In the CCR test, two different speech samples are presented to the listeners in the random order. The listeners then compare the quality of the second speech to that of the first, and give one of seven relative degrees. They are much better(3), better(2), slightly better(1), about the same(0), slightly worse(-1), worse(-2), and much worse(-3). In our work, we used only three degrees of better, about same, and worse. Three difference concatenation methods are tested on our corpus-based Korean TTS system. The speech database of our TTS system has about 160,000 triphone units sampled at 16 KHz with 16 bit resolution, and labeled automatically. Ten listeners tested ten sentences. Five out of the ten are from the database sentences, and the others are randomly selected from a newspaper. The simple overlap-add technique is used as the overlap smoothing method. The CCR tests are performed among the raw concatenation, the overlap smoothing, and the proposed smoothing techniques. The results are summarized in Table 2. In Table 2, we can see that the smoothing methods produce better results than the raw concatenation. The MOS test shows that our proposed smoothing technique outperforms the overlap smoothing one for both the intra-database and the newspaper sentences.

4 Conclusion

In this paper, we proposed a new spectral smoothing algorithm to reduce spectral discontinuities at the unit concatenation boundaries for unit concatenating TTS systems. We utilized spectral matching and waveform matching techniques subsequently for optimal matching, and overlap windowing for smooth interpolation of the consecutively concatenated synthesis units. The spectral matching with the SKL distance and the phonetic environment check can reduce the searching time of the optimal concatenating point. When the proposed algorithm is applied to our TTS system, the final speech outputs are smoother and more natural to listen. The test results show that the algorithm works well even with our automatically labeled speech database, and showed better results than the raw concatenation or the simple overlap smoothing technique. Our algorithm is also believed to be useful for a limited or small size data-base inevitable for the embedded TTS systems.

References

1. Hunt, A.J., Black, A.W.: Unit Selection in a Concatenative Speech Synthesis System using a Large Speech Database. Proc. IEEE ICASSP. (1996) 959–962.
2. Low, P.H., Vaseghi, S.: Synthesis of Unseen Context and Spectral and Pitch Contour Smoothing in Concatenated Text to Speech Synthesis. Proc. IEEE ICASSP. (2002) 469–472.
3. Chappell, D.T., Hansen, J.H.L.: A Comparison of Spectral Smoothing Methods for Segment Concatenation based Speech Synthesis. Speech Communication, Vol. 36. Elsevier Science (2002) 343–374.
4. Pfister, B.: High-Quality Prosodic Modification of Speech Signals. Proc. ISCLP. (1996) 2446–2449.
5. Conkie, A.D., Isard, S.: Optimal Coupling of Diphones. Progress in Speech Synthesis. Springer. Chapter 23. (1997) 293–304.
6. Klabbers, E., Veldhuis, R.: On the Reduction of Concatenation Artifacts in Diphone Synthesis. Proc. ICSLP. (1998) 1983–1986.
7. Klabbers, E., Veldhuis, R.: Reducing Audible Spectral Discontinuities. IEEE Transactions on Speech and Audio Processing. (2001) 39–51.
8. Shin, Ji-Young : Understanding of Korean Speech (printed in Korean), Hankook-Moonwha-sa. Korea. (2000).
9. Huang, X., Acero, A., Hon, H. : Spoken Lagnuage Processing. Prentice Hall. (2001) 840–842.

New Fuzzy Skin Model for Face Detection

Moon Hwan Kim[1], Jin Bae Park[1], and Young Hoon Joo[2]

[1] Department of Electrical and Electronic Engineering, Yonsei University,
Seodaemun-gu, Seoul 120-749, Korea
jmacs@control.yonsei.ac.kr
jbpark@yonsei.ac.kr

[2] School of Electronic and Information Engineering, Kunsan National University,
Kunsan, Chonbuk 573-701, Korea
yhjoo@kunsan.ac.kr

Abstract. We discuss the face detection method by using skin information. Skin color has proven to be a useful and robust cue for face detection, localization and tracking. Numerous techniques for skin color modelling and recognition have been proposed during several past years. In this paper we propose a new fuzzy skin model for face detection and its identification method. The fuzzy skin model comprise of the fuzzy rules with color information. The membership function and structure of fuzzy rule are identified by the proposed linear matrix inequality method. Experimental results demonstrate successful face detection.

1 Introduction

Face detection and tracking has been the topics of extensive research for several past decades. Many heuristic and pattern-recognition based strategies have been proposed for achieving robust and accurate face detection. Among feature-based face detection methods, ones using skin color as a detection cue, have gained strong popularity. Color allows fast processing and is highly robust to geometric variations of the face pattern. When building a system, that uses skin color as a feature for face detection, researcher usually faces three main problems. First, what colorspace to choose, second, how exactly skin color distribution should be modeled, and finally, what will be the way of processing of color segmentation results for face detection. This paper covers the first two questions, leaving the third for another discussion.

The answer of the first question is not easy. Various colorspace can be used to build the face detection system: RGB, normalized RGB, hue saturation intensity (HSI), tint saturation lightness (TSL), YCrCb, and perceptual uniform colorspace [1,2,3,5,6]. One of them, however, HSI color space has the intuitiveness of the colorspace components and explicit discrimination between luminance and chrominance properties and these properties made these colorspaces popular in the works on skin color segmentation. In this paper, we use HSI colorspace to build system.

The second question asks how to model the skin color. The skin color modeling method can be classified into three classes: Explicitly defined skin model [18], nonparametric skin distribution model [14, 4], and parametric skin distribution model [15, 16, 17]. The explicitly defined skin model describes the skin information as specific range of color space. The obvious advantage of this method is simplicity of skin detection rules that leads to construction of very rapid face detection. The main difficulty achieving high recognition rates with this method is to find both good colorspace and adequate decision rules empirically. The key idea of the non-parametric skin modelling methods is to estimate skin color distribution from the training data without deriving an explicit model of the skin color. There are two clear advantages of the non-parametric methods. At first, it is fast in training and usage. Second, it is theoretically independent to the shape of skin distribution. The disadvantages are that it needs much storage space and is inability to interpolate or generalize the training data. The most popular histogram-based non-parametric skin models require much storage space and their performance directly depends on the representativeness of the training images set. The need for more compact skin model representation for certain applications along with ability to generalize and interpolate the training data stimulates the development of parametric skin distribution models. The disadvantage of parametric skin distribution models is that this model operates in colorspace chrominance plane, ignoring the luminance information and it is not easy to select and identify skin distribution model.

To overcome the limitation of conventional skin distribution model, in this paper, we propose a new fuzzy skin color model and its identification method. The proposed skin model takes less storage space than non-parametric method and uses all information and colorspace and is identified automatically by using linear matrix inequality (LMI) based fuzzy clustering method. The fuzzy skin color model consists with T-S type fuzzy rules. The pixel HSI information in the color image converted to membership degree of fuzzy model and are determined whether the pixel is skin region or not. The LMI based fuzzy clustering method determines the structure and membership functions in the fuzzy model. The consequent parameters are also identified as LMI optimization method.

The organization of this paper is as follows. Section 2 presents the fuzzy skin model and it identification method. Simulation results are given in Section 3. Finally, the paper is concluded in Section 4.

2 Fuzzy Skin Model for Face Detection

2.1 Colorspace Selection

In the sense of color images, to obtain a 2D image from a 3D scene, typical CCD color cameras have three classes of sensors (Red, Green and Blue). Each sensor is sensitive to a specific range of frequencies, and provides, for each pixel within the images, three scalar values that are dependent on the spectral distribution of incident energy. The 3D space defined by the sensor values is know as RGB-cube [21].

However, RGB color space is needed to convert another color space in order to represent color as perceptual variables such that hue, saturation and lightness. In this paper, we convert original RGB color image to new HSI color image.

2.2 Structure of Fuzzy Skin Model

Generally, it is not easy to recognize the skin color in give image because skin color changes depend on personality and illumination condition. However the skin color should be detected by using some kinds of filter in order to extract the facial region. To solve this difficulty we proposed fuzzy color filter for the detection of skin color. The fuzzy color filter is based on fuzzy inference system. The vague skin colors are represented as fuzzy sets and memorized in fuzzy rules. The structure of fuzzy rule is represented as,

$$R_i : \text{IF } x_1 \text{ is } M_{i1} \text{ and } \ldots \text{ and } x_3 \text{ is } M_{i3} \qquad (1)$$
$$\text{THEN } y_i(x) = a_i, i = 1, \ldots, l$$

where $\{x_1, x_2, x_3\} \in \mathbb{R}$ is the pixel of HSI color image, $M_{i1}, \ldots, M_{i3}$ are the antecedent fuzzy sets, $y_i(x)$ is the consequent output of the ith rule, $x = [x_1, \ldots, x_3]^T \in F \subset \mathbb{R}^3$ is the input feature vector, F is the feature vector set, and a_i is the consequent parameter and mean the weight for rule i. The output of the fuzzy rule system is inferred by following equations:

$$Y(x) = \frac{\sum_{i=1}^{l} h_i(x) a_i}{\sum_{i=1}^{l} h_i(x)} \qquad (2)$$

$$h_i(x) = \prod_{j=1}^{3} \mu_{M_{ij}}(x_j) \qquad (3)$$

where $h_i(x)$ is the firing strength of the ith rule and $\mu_{M_{ij}}(x_j) \in \mathbb{R}[0,1]$ is the membership degree of the jth feature of the ith rule. The membership function is defined as,

$$\mu_{M_{ij}} = e^{-\frac{(c_j^i - x_j)^2}{v_j^i}} \qquad (4)$$

where c_j^i is the center and v_j^i is the width of the jth feature of the ith rule. For computational convenience, the output $Y(x)$ can be represented as following matrix equation:

$$Y(x) = H^T A \qquad (5)$$

where

$$H = \begin{bmatrix} d_1(x) \\ \vdots \\ d_i(x) \\ \vdots \\ d_l(x) \end{bmatrix}, \quad A = \begin{bmatrix} a_1 \\ \vdots \\ a_i \\ \vdots \\ a_l \end{bmatrix} \qquad (6)$$

$$d_i = \frac{h_i(x)}{\sum_{j=1}^{l} h_j(x)}. \qquad (7)$$

Finally, the final output of fuzzy color filter $\hat{Y}(x)$ is calculated as

$$\hat{Y}(x) = \alpha u(Y(x) - Y_{min}). \qquad (8)$$

where α is the offset value for gray image, $u(x)$ is the unit step function, and Y_{min} is minimum value of $Y(x)$. Therefore, if $Y(x)$ is greater than Y_{min}, the final output has α. Adjusting Y_{min}, we can change robustness of skin color filter.

2.3 Identification of Fuzzy Skin Model

In this subsection, we discuss on identification of fuzzy skin model via the new LMI based clustering method. The proposed clustering method can determine rule structure and parameters of membership function in the antecedent simultaneously. In this paper, the membership function and rule structure of T-S fuzzy classifier are determined via LMI based fuzzy clustering directly. In the proposed clustering method, the number of cluster becomes the number of fuzzy rule and the membership functions in each rule are treated as fuzzy cluster function. This clustering method represents membership degree of cluster as output of firing strength instead of simple fuzzy set.

Consider a finite set of input features $X = \{x^1, x^2, \ldots, x^{N_d}\}, \forall x^k \in F$ as being classification data. x^i is ith input feature set containing HSI pixel information. N_d means the number of whole pixels. The problem is to perform a partition of this collection of elements as N_c fuzzy cluster, where N_c is a given number of cluster. The end result of LMI based fuzzy clustering can be expressed by as partition matrix U such that

$$U = [u_{ij}]_{i=1,\ldots,N_c, j=1,\ldots,N_d} \qquad (9)$$

where u_{ij} is a crisp numerical value in $[0,1]$ and expresses the membership of element x^j belongs to the ith cluster. partition matrix has following two constraints,

$$\sum_{i=1}^{N_c} u_{ij} = 1 \quad \text{for all } j = 1, 2, \ldots, N_d \qquad (10)$$

$$0 < \sum_{j=1}^{N_d} u_{ij} < N_d \quad \text{for all } i = 1, 2, \ldots, N_c \qquad (11)$$

In addition, we need cluster additional membership matrix W to determine partition of data. The membership matrix W can be defined as

$$W = [w_{ij}]_{i=1,\ldots,N_c, j=1,\ldots,N_d} \qquad (12)$$

where w_{ij} is the firing strength of element x^j belongs to the ith cluster,

$$w_{ij} = \prod_{k=1}^{n} e^{-\frac{(m_k^i - x_k^j)^2}{\sigma_k^i}} \qquad (13)$$

After membership matrix is calculated, the partition matrix is updated by using membership degree

$$u_{ik} = 1, i = 1, 2, \ldots, N_c \qquad (14)$$

$$k = \arg_j \max_{\forall j \in C_i, \sum_{h=1}^{N_c} u_{hj} = 0} w_{ij} \qquad (15)$$

where C_i is the set of data belongs to class of the ith cluster.

When partition matrix is updated, the width and center of membership function is updated via LMI optimization method. The center m_k^i is simply update by averaging x_k^j belongs the ith cluster. The widths update can be denoted as identifying membership function satisfying following two constraints,

$$\tau_i(x^k) = 1, \quad x^k \in C_i \qquad (16)$$
$$\tau_i(x^k) = 0, \quad x^k \notin C_i \qquad (17)$$

For computational convenience, the parameters of $\tau_i(x^k)$ can be reformulated as follows:

$$\tau_i(x^k) = e^{-\frac{(c_1^i - x_1^k)^2}{v_1^i}} \times e^{-\frac{(c_2^i - x_2^k)^2}{v_2^i}} \times e^{-\frac{(c_3^i - x_n^k)^2}{v_n^i}}$$

$$= e^{-\sum_{j=1}^{3} \frac{(c_j^i - x_j^k)^2}{v_j^i}}$$

$$= e^{-(x^k - c_i)^T V_i (x^k - c_i)} \qquad (18)$$

$$= e^{-(e^k)^T V_i (e^k)} \qquad (19)$$

where $V_i = \text{diag}\left(\frac{1}{v_1^i}, \ldots, \frac{1}{v_3^i}\right)$ is the diagonal matrix containing the widthes of the Gaussian membership functions of the ith cluster, and $c_i = [c_1^i, \ldots, c_3^i]$ represents center values of the membership function of the ith cluster. Then we could formulate following minimization problem to identify membership function.

Problem 1. When element x^k belongs to C_i is is given, determine widths V_i of membership functions of the i th cluster for T–S fuzzy skin model, such as the following constraints are satisfied:

$$\underset{V_i}{\text{Minimize}} \quad \gamma \quad \text{subject to}$$

$$V_i > 0 \tag{20}$$

$$(e^k)^T V_i (e^k) < \gamma, \quad x^k \in C_i \tag{21}$$

$$(e^k)^T V_i (e^k) < \frac{1}{\gamma}, \quad x^k \notin C_i \tag{22}$$

Theorem 1. *If element x^k belongs to C_i is is given, widths V_i of membership functions of the i th cluster for T–S fuzzy skin model is determined by solving the following GEVPs,*

$$\underset{V_i}{\text{Minimize}} \quad \gamma \quad \text{subject to}$$

$$V_i > 0 \tag{23}$$

$$\begin{bmatrix} \gamma & \star \\ (e^k)^T V_i(e^k) & \gamma \end{bmatrix} > 0, \quad x^k \in C_i \tag{24}$$

$$\begin{bmatrix} \gamma(e^k)^T V_i(e^k) & \star \\ 1 & \gamma \end{bmatrix} > 0, \quad x^k \notin C_i \tag{25}$$

where $\star$ denotes the transposed element matrix for the symmetric position.

Proof. The proof is omitted due to page limitation.

Theorem 1 represents GVEP for ith cluster to identify width of membership functions.

In addition, we should consider rule reduction method. it means the combining similar cluster into one cluster. To check similarity of two cluster, the distance between two cluster is defined as

$$\rho(i,j) = \|c_i - c_j\| \max\{\sum_{k=1}^{n} \frac{v_k^i}{v_k^j}, \sum_{k=1}^{n} \frac{v_k^j}{v_k^i}\}. \tag{26}$$

The clusters in the system are checked the distance between other cluster.

we consider the ith cluster is similar and should be merged when the distance between other clusters is smaller than δ_i which is defined as

$$\delta_i = \underset{k=1,\ldots,3}{\max} \left\{ \frac{1}{n(C_i)} \sum_{\forall x_k^j \in C_i} (x_k^j)^2 - \left(\frac{1}{n(C_i)} \sum_{\forall x_k^j \in C_i} (x_k^j) \right)^2 \right\}. \tag{27}$$

The cluster combining is performed by update partition matrix. When $\rho(i,j) < \delta_i$ satisfied and the classes of the cluster i and j are same, the partition information of the ith cluster are transferred to the the jth cluster,

$$u_{jk} = u_{ik}, k = 1, \ldots, N_d. \tag{28}$$

Finally, the stoping criterion is needed to end up clustering procedure. The stopping condition is based on the partition matrix. Here is two condition to terminate clustering procedure,

$$S_k = N_d \tag{29}$$
$$S_{k-1} = S_k \tag{30}$$

where S_k is the the sum of all partition matrix $\sum_{j=1}^{N_d} \sum_{i=1}^{N_C} u_{ij}$ in the kth iteration. If one of two condition is satisfied, the clustering procedure will be ended.

After parameters of membership functions in the antecedent part is determined, the consequent parameters should be identified. Assume that the parameters of antecedent is completely determined. With Given H and x we could formulated following key equation,

$$Y_d = H^T A, \quad \forall x \in F \tag{31}$$

where Y_d is desired output of the class and is determined as one of index of class. Finally, by finding A satisfying (31), we could get desired output Y_d. Notice that (31) can be converted LMI optimization problem directly. Theorem 3 shows the GEVP for determining A in the consequent part.

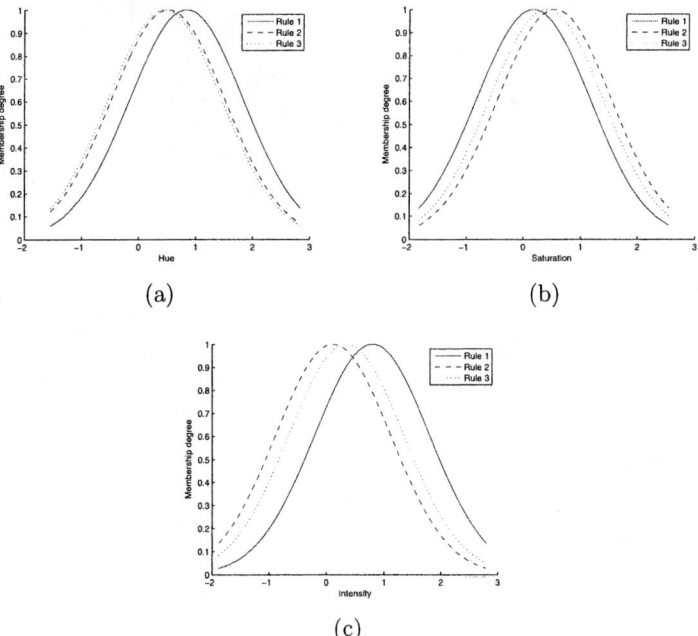

Fig. 1. Identified membership function of fuzzy skin model

Theorem 2. *If x, Y_d, and H are given, consequent parameter A of the proposed T–S fuzzy skin model are determined by solving the following GEVP*

$$\underset{A}{\text{Minimize}} \quad \gamma \quad \text{subject to}$$

$$\begin{bmatrix} \gamma & \star \\ Y_d - H^T A & \gamma \end{bmatrix} > 0, \quad \forall x \in F. \tag{32}$$

Proof. The proof is omitted due to lack of space.

3 Experimental Results

In this paper, we acquire the 24bit color target images by using CCD camera with 320 × 240 size. The target image contains the front head and shoulder images. The sample images used to train the fuzzy color filter are obtained from the skin images of three people under 4 different illuminations. To determine the structures and parameters, LMI based fuzzy clustering method is applied. The initial number of cluster is 20. After clustering, 20 cluster reduced to 3. Figure 1 represents the identified membership function of fuzzy skin model. The identified consequent parameters is described as,

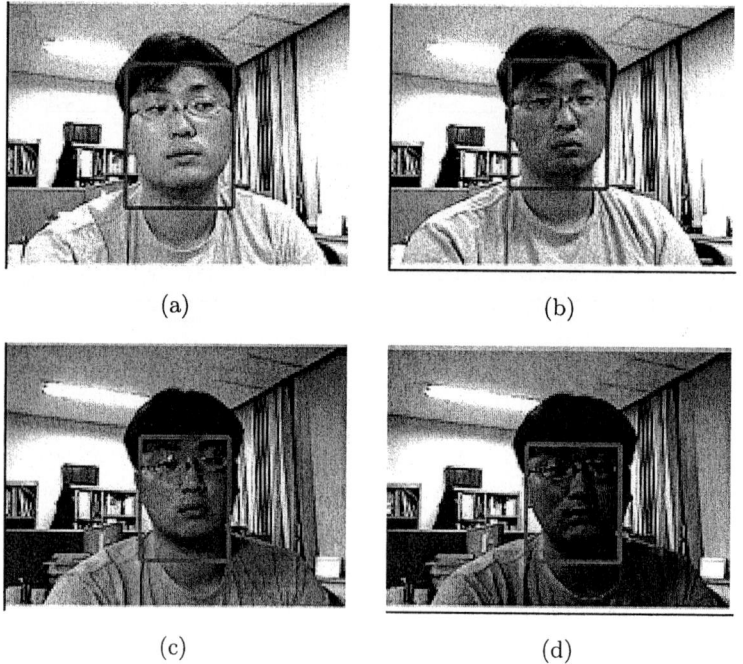

Fig. 2. Facial region detection under various illumination. a) high illumination. (b) normal illumination. (c) low illumination. (d) very low illumination.

Illumination condition	No. of correctly extracted image
High illumination	20
Normal illumination	20
Low illumination	19
Very low illumination	18

$$A = \begin{bmatrix} 1.7846 \\ -4.1184 \\ 3.3663 \end{bmatrix}.$$

In order to test the robustness for illumination variation, additional 80 images with four different illumination conditions are used in simulation. Under each illumination condition, 20 pictures are acquired. Figure 2 shows the target image and the extracted facial region with various illuminations. Table 1 shows the performance under various illumination. From simulation results, we can confirm the robustness and superiority of the proposed method.

4 Conclusion

In this paper we propose a new fuzzy skin model for face detection. The fuzzy skin model comprise of the fuzzy rules with color information. The membership function and structure of fuzzy rule are identified by the proposed LMI based clustering method. The consequent parameters are identified via LMI optimization method. Finally, the performance of proposed system is evaluated.

Acknowledgement

This work is supported by a proejct "Ubiquitous Robotic Companion (URC)," and was funded from the Ministry of Information and Communications (MIC) Republic of Korea.

References

1. Brand J. and Mason J.: A comparative assessment of three approaches to pixellevel human skin-detection. In Proc. of the International Conference on Pattern Recognition. **1** (2000) 1056-1059.
2. Jones M. J. and Reheg J. M.: Statistical color models with application to skin detection. In Proc. of the CVPR 99 **1** (1999) 274-280.
3. Brown D., Craw I., and Lewthwaite J.: A som based approach to skin detection with application in real time systems. In Proc. of the British Machine Vision Conference. (2001)
4. Zarit B. D., Super B. J., and Quek F. K. H.: Comparison of five color models in skin pixel classification. In ICCV99 Intl Workshop on recognition, analysis and tracking of faces and gestures in Real-Time systems. (1999) 58-63.

5. Soriano M., Huovinen S., Martinkauppi B., and Laaksonen M.: Skin detection in video under changing illumination conditions. In Proc. 15th International Conference on Pattern Recognition. **1** (2000) 839-842.
6. Oliver N., Pentland A., and Berard F.: Lafter: Lips and face real time tracker. In Proc. Computer Vision and Pattern Recognition. (1997) 123-129.
7. Yang J., LU W., and Waibel A.: Skin-color modeling and adaptation. In Proceedings of ACCV. (1998) 687-694.
8. Mckenna S., Gong S., and Raja Y.: Modelling facial colour and identity with gaussian mixtures. Pattern Recognition 31, **12** (1998) 1883-1892.
9. Sigal L., Sclaroff S., and Athitsos V. x: Estimation and prediction of evolving color distributions for skin segmentation under varying illumination. In Proc. IEEE Conf. on Computer Vision and Pattern Recognition. **2** (1998) 152-159.
10. birchfield S.: Elliptical head tracking using intensity gradients and color histograms. In Proceedings of CVPR 98. (1998) 232-237.
11. Jordao L., Perrone M., Costeira J., and Santos-Victor J.: Active face and feature tracking. In Proceedings of the 10th International Conference on Image Analysis and Processing (1999) 572-577.
12. Terrillon J.-C., Shirazi M. N., Fukamachi H., and Akamatsu S.: Comparative performance of different skin chrominance models and chrominance spaces for the automatic detection of human faces in color images. In Proc. of the International Conference on Face and Gesture Recognition, (1999) 54-61.
13. Phung S. L., Bouzerdoum A., and Chai D.: A novel skin color model in ycbcr color space and its application to human face detection. In IEEE International Conference on Image Processing (ICIP2002), **1** (1999) 289-292.
14. Chen Q., Wu H., and Yachida M.: Face detection by fuzzy pattern matching. In Proc. of the Fifth International Conference on Computer Vision. (1995) 591-597.
15. Hsu R.-L., Abdel-Mottaleb M., and Jain A. K.: Face detection in color images. IEEE Trans. Pattern Analysis and Machine Intelligence **5** (2002) 696-706, .
16. Yang M.-H. and Ahuja N.: Detecting human faces in color images. In International Conference on Image Processing (ICIP). **1** (1998) 127-130.
17. Lee J. Y.and Yoo S. I.: An elliptical boundary model for skin color detection. In Proc. of the 2002 International Conference on Imaging Science, Systems, and Technology. (2002).
18. Peer P., Kovac J., and Solina F.: Human skin colour clustering for face detection. In submitted to EUROCON 2003 - International Conference on Computer as a Tool, (2003)
19. Garcia C. and Tziritas G.: Face Detection Using Quantized Skin Color Regions Merging and Wavelet Packet Analysis. IEEE Trans. Multimedia. **1** (1999) 264-277.
20. Montseny E., Sobrevilla P., Romani S.: A fuzzy approach to white blood cells segmentation in color bone marrow images. IEEE International Conference on Fuzzy Systems. **1** (2004) 173-178.
21. Pratt W. Digital Image Processing. John wiley and Sons. (1978)

Kernel Nonparametric Weighted Feature Extraction for Classification

Bor-Chen Kuo[1] and Cheng-Hsuan Li[2]

[1] Graduate School of Educational Measurement and Statistics,
National Taichung University,
140 Min-Shen Road, Taichung, Taiwan, R.O.C.
kbc@mail.ntctc.edu.tw
[2] Department of Applied Math.,
National Chung Hsing University,
250 Kuo-Kuang Road, Taichung, Taiwan, R.O.C.
u4815977@yahoo.com.tw

Abstract. Usually feature extraction is applied for dimension reduction in hyperspectral data classification problems. Many researches show that nonparametric weighted feature extraction (NWFE) is a powerful tool for extracting hyperspectral image features and kernel-based methods are computationally efficient, robust and stable for pattern analysis. In this paper, a kernel-based NWFE is proposed and a real data experiment is conducted for evaluating its performance. The experimental result shows that the proposed method outperforms original NWFE when the size training samples is large enough.

1 Introduction

In the recent years, many researches [1], [2], [3] show that kernel-based methods are computationally efficient, robust and stable for pattern analysis. The main ideal of kernel-based methods is to map the input data from the original space to a convenient feature space by a nonlinear mapping where inner products in the feature space can be computed by a kernel function without knowing the nonlinear mapping explicitly and linear relations are sought among the images of the data items in the feature space.

For hyperspectral data classification problems, small training sets usually result in the Hughes phenomenon (Hughes, 1968) and singularity problems (Landgrebe, 2003). Traditionally, feature extraction (FE) or feature selection (FS) techniques are applied to overcome this problem. In recent study [4], Kuo and Landgrebe show that nonparametric weighted feature extraction (NWFE) outperform linear discriminant analysis (LDA, [5]), nonparametric discriminant analysis (NDA, [5]) for extracting features from hyperspectral images. In this paper, a kernel-based NWFE is proposed and a real data experiment is conducted for evaluating its performance.

This paper is organized as follows. Section 2 we give a brief review the formulations of NWFE. In Section 3 we discuss the concept of the kernel method. We present the formulations and processes of kernel nonparametric weighted feature extraction in Section 4. In Section 5 we use a trick to deal with kernel matrix and experimental results are presented in Section 6. Finally, some concluding remarks are given in Section 7.

2 Nonparametric Weighted Feature Extraction

To begin with, we partition a data set of N samples into L classes and $x_1^{(i)},...,x_{N_i}^{(i)}$ are the samples in class i, $i=1,...,L$, $N=N_1+\cdots+N_L$. Let P_i denote the prior probability of class i and $\text{dist}(x,z)$ be the Euclidean distance from x to z.

Nonparametric weighted feature extraction (NWFE) is used for dimension reduction in classification problems. The main ideals of NWFE are putting different weights on every sample to compute the "weighted means" and defining new nonparametric between-class and within-class scatter matrices. The between-class scatter matrix S_b^{NW} and the within-class scatter matrix S_w^{NW} are defined as

$$S_b^{NW} = \sum_{i=1}^{L} P_i \sum_{\substack{j=1 \\ j \neq i}}^{L} \sum_{\ell=1}^{N_i} \frac{\lambda_\ell^{(i,j)}}{N_i} (x_\ell^{(i)} - M_j(x_\ell^{(i)}))(x_\ell^{(i)} - M_j(x_\ell^{(i)}))^T \qquad (1)$$

and

$$S_w^{NW} = \sum_{i=1}^{L} P_i \sum_{\ell=1}^{N_i} \frac{\lambda_\ell^{(i,i)}}{N_i} (x_\ell^{(i)} - M_i(x_\ell^{(i)}))(x_\ell^{(i)} - M_i(x_\ell^{(i)}))^T \qquad (2)$$

where the scatter matrix weight $\lambda_\ell^{(i,j)}$ is defined by

$$\lambda_\ell^{(i,j)} = \frac{\text{dist}(x_\ell^{(i)}, M_j(x_\ell^{(i)}))^{-1}}{\sum_{t=1}^{N_i} \text{dist}(x_t^{(i)}, M_j(x_t^{(i)}))^{-1}} \qquad (3)$$

and the

$$M_j(x_\ell^{(i)}) = \sum_{k=1}^{N_j} w_{\ell k}^{(i,j)} x_k^{(j)}, \quad w_{\ell k}^{(i,j)} = \frac{\text{dist}(x_\ell^{(i)}, x_k^{(j)})^{-1}}{\sum_{t=1}^{N_j} \text{dist}(x_\ell^{(i)}, x_t^{(j)})^{-1}} \qquad (4)$$

denotes the weighted mean with respect to $x_\ell^{(i)}$ in class j.

The scatter matrix weight $\lambda_\ell^{(i,j)}$ will be closed to 1 if the distance between $x_\ell^{(i)}$ and $M_j(x_\ell^{(i)})$ is small. Otherwise, $\lambda_\ell^{(i,j)}$ will be closed to 0. Similarity the weight $w_{\ell k}^{(i,j)}$ for computing weighted means will be closed to 1 if the distance between $x_\ell^{(i)}$ and $x_k^{(j)}$ is small. Otherwise, $w_{\ell k}^{(i,j)}$ will be closed to 0. NWFE proposes the "weighted mean" [see (4)] and using weighted between- and within-class vector. The separability of classes in a data set can be measured by S_b^{NW} and S_w^{NW}.

The goal of NWFE is to find a linear transformation $A \in R^{d \times p}$, $p \leq d$, which maximizes the between-class scatter and minimizes the within-class scatter. The columns of A are the optimal features by optimizing the Fisher criteria, i.e.,

$$A = \arg\max_A \text{tr}((A^T S_w^{NW} A)^{-1} A^T S_b^{NW} A) \cdot \qquad (5)$$

This maximization is equivalent to find eigenvalues λ and eigenvectors v for the generalized eigenvalue problem

$$S_b^{NW} v = \lambda S_w^{NW} v.$$

3 The Kernel Trick

It is easier for classification if data is distributed sparser. Generally speaking, High dimensionality (the number of spectral bands) potentially provides better class separability. The strategy of kernel method is to embed the samples from original space R^d into a feature space $\mathscr{H}$, a Hilbert space with higher dimensionality, where the patterns can be discovered as linear relations and we can compute the inner product of samples in the feature space directly from the original data items using a kernel function. This is based on the fact that for any kernel function $\kappa: R^d \times R^d \to R$ satisfying the characterization of kernels [1], there is a nonlinear mapping $\phi: R^d \to \mathscr{H}$, a Hilbert space, such that

$$\kappa(x,z) = <\phi(x), \phi(z)>$$

where $x, z \in R^d$. Since κ satisfies the characterization of kernels, the kernel matrix $K = [\kappa(x_i, x_j)]_{1 \leq i, j \leq N}$ of κ with respect to data set $\{x_1, ..., x_N\}$ is positive semi-definite.

There are some widely used kernel functions as the linear kernel

$$\kappa(x,z) = <x,z>,$$

the polynomial kernel

$$\kappa(x,z) = (<x,z>+1)^r, \quad r \in Z^+,$$

and the RBF (Gaussian) kernel

$$\kappa(x,z) = \exp\left(\frac{-\|x-z\|^2}{2\sigma^2}\right), \quad \sigma \in R - \{0\}.$$

If we use the linear kernel, the feature mapping ϕ is identity map, that is, ϕ is linear. Otherwise, the feature mapping can be nonlinear. One important ideal for using kernel method is without knowing the nonlinear mapping explicitly.

4 Kernel Nonparametric Weighted Feature Extraction

Let κ be a kernel function and ϕ be the corresponding feature mapping from original space to feature space $\mathscr{H}$. Put the samples $\phi(x_1^{(i)}),...,\phi(x_{N_i}^{(i)})$ into X_i^T, i.e.,

$$X_i^T = [\phi(x_1^{(i)}),...,\phi(x_{N_i}^{(i)})], \quad i=1,...,L,$$

and
$$X^T = [X_1^T, ..., X_L^T].$$

The kernel matrix K with respect to κ on samples is XX^T.

The between-class scatter matrix S_b^{KNW} and the within-class scatter matrix S_w^{KNW} using NWFE in the feature space $\mathscr{H}$ are

$$S_b^{KNW} = \sum_{i=1}^{L} P_i \sum_{\substack{j=1 \\ j \neq i}}^{L} \sum_{\ell=1}^{N_i} \frac{\lambda_\ell^{(i,j)}}{N_i} (\phi(x_\ell^{(i)}) - M_j(\phi(x_\ell^{(i)})))(\phi(x_\ell^{(i)}) - M_j(\phi(x_\ell^{(i)})))^T \quad (6)$$

and

$$S_w^{KNW} = \sum_{i=1}^{L} P_i \sum_{\ell=1}^{N_i} \frac{\lambda_\ell^{(i,i)}}{N_i} (\phi(x_\ell^{(i)}) - M_i(\phi(x_\ell^{(i)})))(\phi(x_\ell^{(i)}) - M_i(\phi(x_\ell^{(i)})))^T \quad (7)$$

where the scatter matrix weight $\lambda_\ell^{(i,j)}$ is defined by

$$\lambda_\ell^{(i,j)} = \frac{\operatorname{dist}(\phi(x_\ell^{(i)}), M_j(\phi(x_\ell^{(i)})))^{-1}}{\sum_{t=1}^{N_i} \operatorname{dist}(\phi(x_t^{(i)}), M_j(\phi(x_t^{(i)})))^{-1}} \quad (8)$$

and the

$$M_j(\phi(x_\ell^{(i)})) = \sum_{k=1}^{N_j} w_{\ell k}^{(i,j)} \phi(x_k^{(j)}), \quad w_{\ell k}^{(i,j)} = \frac{\operatorname{dist}(\phi(x_\ell^{(i)}), \phi(x_k^{(j)}))^{-1}}{\sum_{t=1}^{N_j} \operatorname{dist}(\phi(x_\ell^{(i)}), \phi(x_t^{(j)}))^{-1}} \quad (9)$$

denotes the weighted mean with respect to $\phi(x_\ell^{(i)})$ in class j. Suppose that $\Lambda^{(i,j)} = \operatorname{diag}\{\frac{\lambda_1^{(i,j)}}{N_i}, ..., \frac{\lambda_{N_i}^{(i,j)}}{N_i}\}$ and

$$W^{(i,j)} = \begin{bmatrix} w_{11}^{(i,j)} & \cdots & w_{1N_j}^{(i,j)} \\ \vdots & & \vdots \\ w_{N_i 1}^{(i,j)} & \cdots & w_{N_i N_j}^{(i,j)} \end{bmatrix}.$$

The within-class scatter matrix S_w^{KNW} becomes

$$\begin{aligned} S_w^{KNW} &= \sum_{i=1}^{L} P_i (X_i^T \Lambda^{(i,i)} X_i - X_i^T \Lambda^{(i,i)} W^{(i,i)} X_i \\ &\quad - X_i^T W^{(i,i)^T} \Lambda^{(i,i)} X_i + X_i^T W^{(i,i)^T} \Lambda^{(i,i)} W^{(i,i)} X_i) \\ &= X^T (W_1 - W_2 - W_2^T + W_3) X, \end{aligned} \quad (10)$$

where

$W_1 = \operatorname{diag}\{P_1 \Lambda^{(1,1)}, ..., P_L \Lambda^{(L,L)}\}$,
$W_2 = \operatorname{diag}\{P_1 \Lambda^{(1,1)} W^{(1,1)}, ..., P_L \Lambda^{(L,L)} W^{(L,L)}\}$, and
$W_3 = \operatorname{diag}\{P_1 W^{(1,1)^T} \Lambda^{(1,1)} W^{(1,1)}, ..., P_L W^{(L,L)^T} \Lambda^{(L,L)} W^{(L,L)}\}$.

Let $W = W_1 - W_2 - W_2^T + W_3$. Then $S_w^{KNW} = X^T W X$. The between-class scatter matrix S_b^{KNW} becomes

$$S_b^{KNW} = \sum_{i=1}^{L} P_i \sum_{\substack{j=1 \\ j \neq i}}^{L} (X_i^T \Lambda^{(i,j)} X_i - X_i^T \Lambda^{(i,j)} W^{(i,j)} X_j$$

$$- X_j^T W^{(i,j)^T} \Lambda^{(i,j)} X_i + X_j^T W^{(i,j)^T} \Lambda^{(i,j)} W^{(i,j)} X_j)$$

$$= X^T (B_1 - B_2 - B_2^T + B_3) X - X^T W X,$$

where

$$B_1 = \text{diag}\{ P_1 \sum_{j=1}^{L} \Lambda^{(1,j)}, \ldots, P_L \sum_{j=1}^{L} \Lambda^{(L,j)} \},$$

$$B_2 = \begin{bmatrix} P_1 \Lambda^{(1,1)} W^{(1,1)} & \cdots & P_1 \Lambda^{(1,L)} W^{(1,L)} \\ \vdots & & \vdots \\ P_L \Lambda^{(L,1)} W^{(L,1)} & \cdots & P_L \Lambda^{(L,L)} W^{(L,L)} \end{bmatrix}, \text{ and}$$

$$B_3 = \sum_{i=1}^{L} P_i \text{ diag}\{ W^{(i,1)^T} \Lambda^{(i,1)} W^{(i,1)}, \ldots, W^{(i,L)^T} \Lambda^{(i,L)} W^{(i,L)} \}.$$

Let $B = B_1 - B_2 - B_2^T + B_3$. Then $S_b^{KNW} = X^T (B - W) X$.

From above process (5) becomes

$$A = \arg\max_{A} \text{tr}((A^T X^T W X A)^{-1} A^T X^T (B-W) X A) \cdot \tag{11}$$

Since our reduced space is a subspace of span of all training samples in $\mathcal{H}$, we can express A in dual form, i.e.,

$$A = X^T \tilde{A}$$

where $\tilde{A} \in R^{N \times p}$. Then the (11) is equivalent to the following optimization

$$A = \arg\max_{\tilde{A}} \text{tr}((\tilde{A}^T K W K \tilde{A})^{-1} \tilde{A}^T K (B-W) K \tilde{A}) \cdot \tag{12}$$

5 Eigenvalue Resolution

Let us use the eigen-decomposition of the kernel matrix K, a symmetric matrix, i.e.,

$$K = P \Gamma P^T,$$

where Γ is the diagonal matrix of all eigenvalues of K and P is a orthogonal matrix. Substituting K in (12), we have

$$\text{tr}((\tilde{A}^T K W K \tilde{A})^{-1} \tilde{A}^T K (B-W) K \tilde{A}) = \text{tr}((\tilde{A}^T P \Gamma P^T W P \Gamma P^T \tilde{A})^{-1} \tilde{A}^T P \Gamma P^T (B-W) P \Gamma P^T \tilde{A}).$$

Let us proceed to variable modification using U such that

$$U = \Gamma P^T \tilde{A}.$$

Then the problem (12) is equivalent to

$$U = \arg\max_{U} \operatorname{tr}((U^T(P^TWP)U)^{-1} U^T(P^T(B-W)P)U) \cdot \qquad (13)$$

Therefore the process of find $\tilde{A}$ can be divided into two parts. The first step is to find the eigenvalues λ and eigenvectors u for the following generalized eigenvalue problem

$$P^T(B-W)Pu = \lambda P^T W P u.$$

The extracted p features are the p eigenvectors with largest p eigenvalues of the following matrix:

$$(P^T W P)^{-1} P^T (B-W) P. \qquad (14)$$

Here the $P^T WP$ is regularized by

$$0.5\,(P^T WP) + 0.5\,\operatorname{diag}(P^T WP). \qquad (15)$$

Hence we can build U. After U is calculated, we compute $\tilde{A}$ by

$$\tilde{A} = P\Gamma^{-1} U. \qquad (16)$$

We finally compute the projection of a point $\phi(z)$ by

$$A^T \phi(z) = \tilde{A}^T X \phi(z) = \tilde{A}^T \begin{bmatrix} \phi(x_1)^T \\ \vdots \\ \phi(x_N)^T \end{bmatrix} \phi(z) = \tilde{A}^T \begin{bmatrix} \kappa(x_1, z) \\ \vdots \\ \kappa(x_N, z) \end{bmatrix}.$$

KNWFE procedure is summarized in the following steps:

1) Compute the distances between each pair of sample points in the feature space and form the distance matrix.
2) Compute $w_{\ell k}^{(i,j)}$ using the distance matrix and get the matrix $W^{(i,j)}$.
3) Compute the scatter matrix weight $\lambda_\ell^{(i,j)}$ and get the matrix $\Lambda^{(i,j)}$.
4) Compute B, W and hence $S_b^{KNW} = X^T(B-W)X$, $S_w^{KNW} = X^T W X$.
5) Do eigen-decomposition for K, i.e., $K = P\Gamma P^T$.
6) Extract features by solving $P^T(B-W)Pu = \lambda P^T WPu$.
7) Compute $\tilde{A}$ and the projections of test points.

6 Experimental Results

In this section, only real data experiment results are displayed. The design of Experiment is to compare the multiclass classification performance of using NWFE and KNWFE (with different kernel functions) features applied to quadratic Bayes normal (qdc), 1NN, and Parzen classifiers. Here we use a dataset: the Washington, DC Mall as an urban site in the experiment. There are seven classes and the performances of two training data sets with 40 and 100 training samples in every class are evaluated. There are 191 bands in the DC Mall image data, and every 20-th band, which begins from the first one, are selected for the 10 bands case. At each situation, 10 random training and testing data sets are generated for computing the testing sample accuracies of algorithms. In this paper, we use the linear kernel (Linear K), polynomial kernel with degree 1 to 3 (Poly K-1 to Poly K-3), and the RBF kernel (RBF K), where σ is the mean of variances in every band of training samples.

The results of experiment are displayed in Fig. 1-3. Here L indicates the number of classes, N_i is the number of training samples in each class, and p is the number of features extracted by NWFE or KNWFE. These figures show the following.

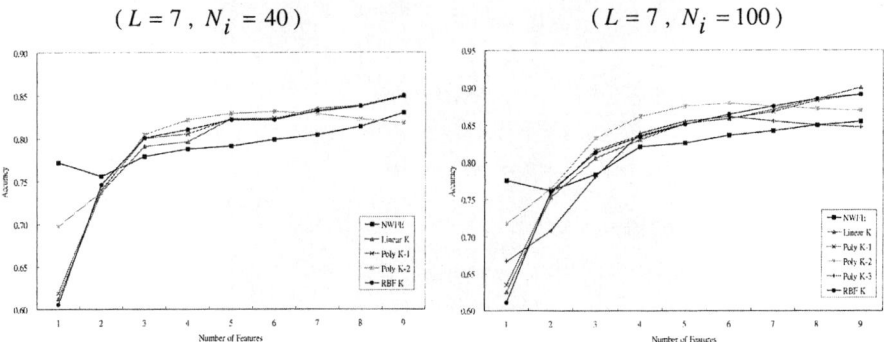

Fig. 1. Mean of accuracies using 1-9 features (DC Mall, Quadratic Bayes Normal Classifier)

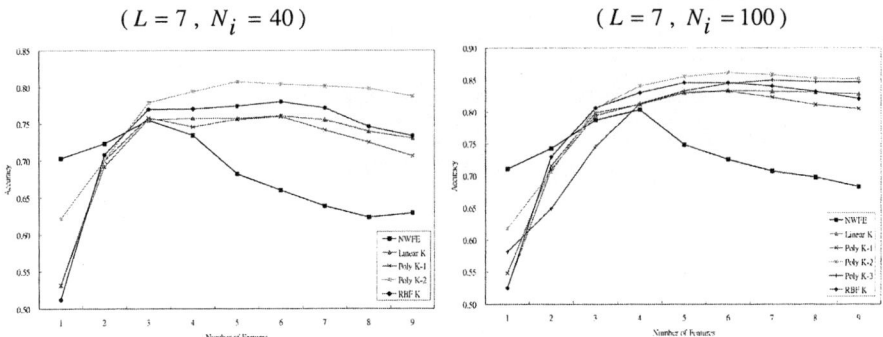

Fig. 2. Mean of accuracies using 1-9 features (DC Mall, 1NN Classifier)

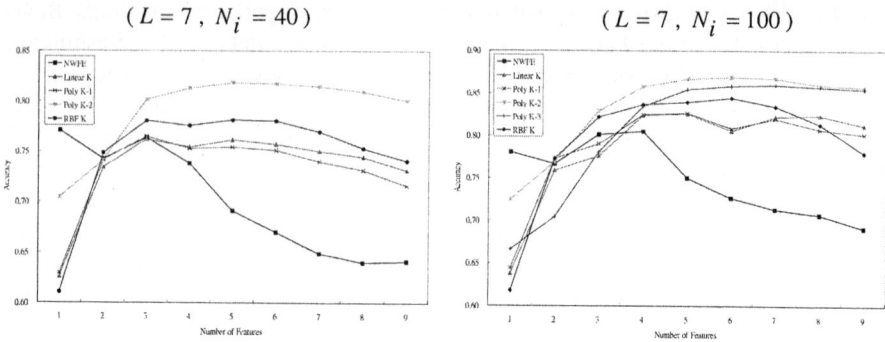

Fig. 3. Mean of accuracies using 1-9 features (DC Mall, Parzen Classifier)

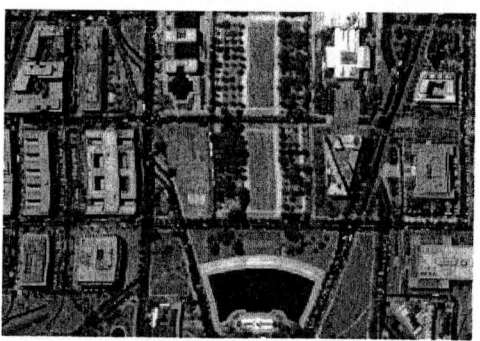

Fig. 4. Simulated grayscale IR image of a portion of the DC dataset

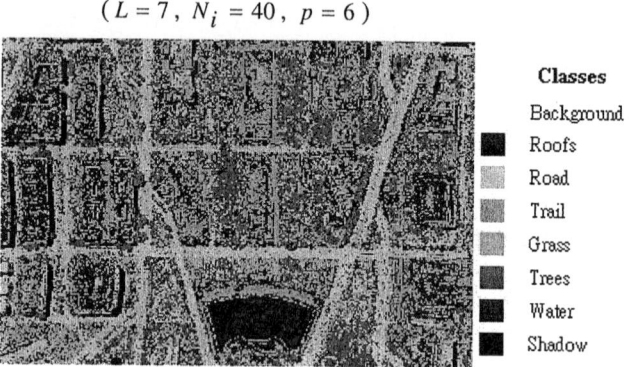

Fig. 5. Thematic map resulting from the classification of the area of Fig. 4 using NWFE features and quadratic Bayes normal classifier

1) The performances of all three classifiers with KNWFE features are better than those of classifiers with NWFE features.
2) The polynomial kernel with degree 2 outperforms other kernel functions in 1NN and Parzen cases.
3) Among three classifiers, quadratic Bayes normal classifier has the best performance. The best classification accuracy is 0.9 and obtained by qdc classifier with 9 features extracted by KNWFE with linear kernel in the case of $N_i = 100$.
4) Comparing Fig. 5 and 6, one sees that the performance of KNWFE is better than that of NWFE in almost in all classes.

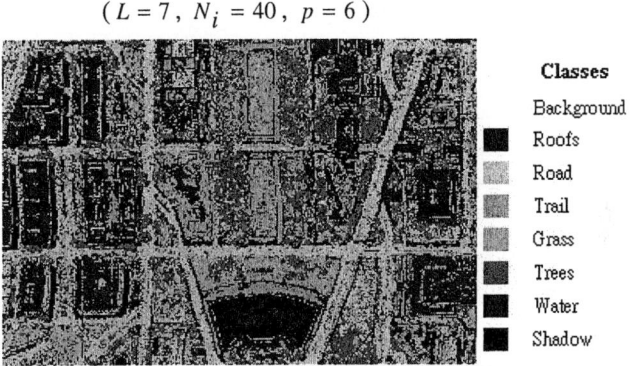

Fig. 6. Thematic map resulting from the classification of the area of Fig. 4 using KNWFE features and quadratic Bayes normal classifier

7 Conclusion

In this paper, we proposed a new kernel-based nonparametric weighted feature extraction. In particular, we have analyzed and compared NWFE and KNWFE both theoretically and experimentally. From theoretical point of view, NWFE is a special case of KNWFE with linear kernel and the result of a real hyperspectral image shows that the average classification accuracy of applying KNWFE is better than that of applying NWFE. In conclusion, we can state that, in our case study, the use of KNWFE is more beneficial and yielding better results than NWFE.

References

1. John Shawe-Taylor and Nello Cristianini, *Kernel Methods for Pattern Analysis.* Cambridge: 2004.
2. Farid Melgani, and Leorenzo Bruzzone, "Classification of hyperspectral remote sensing images with support vector machines," *IEEE Trans. Geosci. Remote Sens.*, vol. 42, no. 8, pp.1778-1790, August 2004.

3. Gustavo Camps-Valls and Lorenzo Bruzzone, "Kernel-based methods for hyperspectral image classification," *IEEE Trans. Geosci. Remote Sens.*, vol. 43, no. 6, pp.1351-1362, June 2005.
4. Bor-Chen Kuo and David A. Landgrebe, "Nonparametric weighted feature extraction for classification," *IEEE Trans. Geosci. Remote Sens.*, vol. 42, no. 5, pp.1096-1105, May 2004.
5. K. Fukunaga, *Introduction to Sataistical Pattern Recognition*. San Diego, CA: Academic, 1990.
6. G. Baudat and F. Anouar, "Generalized discriminant analysis using a kernel approach", *Neural computation*, 12(2000), pp.2385-2404.
7. G. F. Hughes, "On the mean accuracy of statistical pattern recognition," *IEEE Trans. Inform. Theory*, vol. IT-14, pp. 55-63, Jan. 1968.
8. R. P. W. Duin, "PRTools, a Matlab Toolbox for Pattern Recognition," [Online]. Available: http://www.ph.tn.tudelft.nl/prtools/, Aug. 2002.

Iterative Training Techniques for Phonetic Template Based Speech Recognition with a Speaker-Independent Phonetic Recognizer

Weon-Goo Kim[1], MinSeok Jang[2], and Chin-Hui Lee[3]

[1] School of Electronic and Information Eng., Kunsan National Univ.,
Kunsan, Chonbuk 573-701, Korea
Biometrics Engineering Research Center
wgkim@kunsan.ac.kr
[2] Dept. of Computer Information Science, Kunsan National Univ.,
Kunsan, Chonbuk 573-701, Korea
msjang@kunsan.ac.kr
[3] School of Electrical and Computer Eng., Georgia Institute of Technology,
Atlanta, Georgia 30332, USA
chl@ece.gatech.edu

Abstract. This paper presents a new method that improves the performance of the speaker specific phonetic template based speech recognizer with the speaker-independent (SI) phoneme HMMs. Since the phonetic template based speech recognizer uses only the phoneme transcription of the input utterance, the performance of the system is worse than that of the speaker dependent system due to the mismatch between the training data and the SI models. In order to solve these problems, a new training method that iteratively estimates the phonetic templates and transformation vectors for the adaptation of the SI phoneme HMMs is presented. The phonetic class based and codebook-based stochastic matching methods are used to estimate the transformation vectors for speaker adaptation. Performance evaluation using the speaker dependent recognition experiments performed over actual telephone line showed a reduction of about 40% in the error rates when compare to the conventional speaker specific phonetic template based speech recognizer.

1 Introduction

Voice dialing, in which a spoken word or phrase can be used to dial a phone number, has been successfully deployed in telephone and cellular networks and is gaining user acceptance. Typically the voice dialing is based on speaker dependent system in which each speaker can easily define his/her own personal repertory containing the set of command or keywords that will be used later on to automatically dial the phone number. The set up of such a system is usually based on two sessions. In an enrollment session, the user pronounces each of the word or phrase several times and provides the system with their associated phone number. The model is generated and saved for recognition. In a recognition session, after claimed identity of the user is verified, the user pronounces a phrase and the system automatically dials the associated phone number.

As the popularity of this service increases, the requirements of data storage and access for performing speech recognition become crucial. To overcome this problem, methods that use the speaker-specific phonetic templates or phonetic base-form for each label were presented [1–5]. The advantage of these approaches are that the only information that need to be stored for each speaker is the phonetic string associated with each speaker's words or phrase from speech in terms of speaker independent (SI) sub-word acoustic units (phones), resulting in substantial data reduction. However, this method has two drawbacks. The first one is that a large amount of phoneme recognition errors are generated using SI phoneme HMMs. The other is that the performance of the system is worse than that of the speaker dependent (SD) system since SI models are used.

In this paper, a new method that jointly estimates the transformation function (bias) and transcriptions for the speaker adaptation from training utterances is presented to improve the performance of the personal voice dialing system using SI phoneme HMMs. In training process, the biases and transcriptions are estimated iteratively from the training data of each user with maximum likelihood approach to the stochastic matching using SI phoneme models and then saved for recognition. In recognition process, after SI phoneme models are transformed using speaker specific bias vectors, input sentence is recognized. Experimental result shows that the proposed method is superior to the conventional method using transcriptions only and the storage space for bias vectors for each user is small.

2 Iterative Training of Phonetic Transcription Based Voice Dialing System

A new method that jointly estimates the transformation function (bias) and transcriptions for the speaker adaptation from training utterances is presented to improve the performance of the personal voice dialing system using SI phoneme HMMs. The concept of the proposed system is shown in Fig. 1. There are two kinds of sessions, enrollment and test. In an enrollment session, a user need to repeat a name for two or three times, then input a telephone number associated with the name. The joint estimation stage consists of two pass, recognizer and adaptation. The first pass is standard decoding which produce the phoneme transcription as well as the state segmentation necessary for the estimation of SI phoneme model biases. During the second pass, model biases are estimated using stochastic matching method to generate the new set of HMMs. This process is iterated several times until achieving convergence and then final transcriptions and biases of each user are saved into the database. In a test session, the user just needs to utter the name. For telephone, the identity can be obtained from caller ID or from user's input. After SI phoneme HMMs are adapted using bias vectors, decoder recognize the input speech with transcriptions and adapted SI phoneme HMMs.

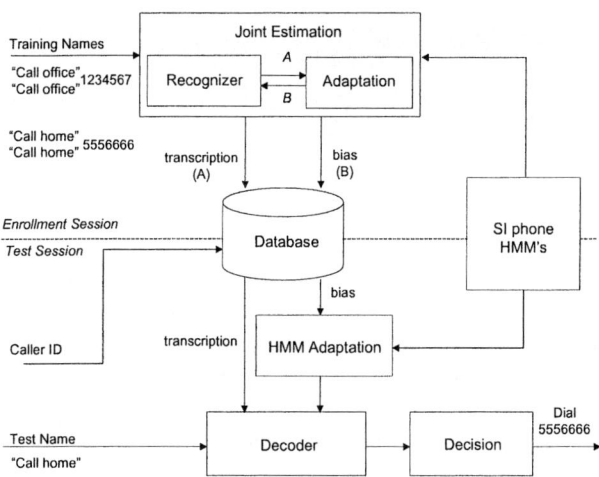

Fig. 1. The phonetic template based speech recognizes with iterative training techniques

The maximum likelihood technique to the stochastic matching for speaker adaptation can be applied as follows [6,7]. Consider a sequence of feature vector $Y = \{y_1, y_2, \ldots, y_T\}$ and a set of speaker independent phoneme HMMs Λ_X. The transformation G_η with parameters η maps Λ_X into the transformed model Λ_Y so that

$$\Lambda_Y = G_\eta(\Lambda_X) . \tag{1}$$

One Approach to decreasing the mismatch between Y and Λ_X is to find parameters η and the phoneme sequence W that maximize the joint likelihood of Y and W. Thus, we need to find η' such that

$$(\eta', W') = \arg\max_{(\eta,W)} p(Y, W|\eta, \Lambda_X) = \arg\max_{(\eta,W)} p(Y|W, \eta, \Lambda_X) P(W) . \tag{2}$$

This joint maximization over the variables η and W in (2) can be done iteratively by keeping η fixed and maximizing over W, and then keeping W fixed and maximizing over η. Under the assumptions, the structure of Λ_Y remains the same as that of Λ_X. The mean $\boldsymbol{\mu_y}$ of each mixture component in adapted SI HMMs are derived by adding the bias $\boldsymbol{\mu_b}$ to the mean $\boldsymbol{\mu_x}$ of the corresponding mixture components in SI HMMs , i.e.,

$$\boldsymbol{\mu_y} = \boldsymbol{\mu_x} + \boldsymbol{\mu_b} . \tag{3}$$

The transformation vector or bias $\boldsymbol{\mu_b} = \{\mu_1, \mu_2, \ldots, \mu_D\}$ can be obtained by maximum likelihood estimate, such that

$$\mu_{b_i} = \frac{\sum_{t=1}^{T}\sum_{n=1}^{N}\sum_{m=1}^{M}\gamma_t(n,m)\frac{y_{t,i}-\mu_{m,n,i}}{\sigma_{n,m,i}^2}}{\sum_{t=1}^{T}\sum_{n=1}^{N}\sum_{m=1}^{M}\frac{\gamma_t(n,m)}{\sigma_{n,m,i}^2}}, \quad i=1,\ldots,D \quad (4)$$

and

$$\gamma_t(n,m) = \begin{cases} \frac{w_{n,m}N[y_t;\mu_{n,m},C_{n,m}]}{\sum_{j=1}^{M}w_{n,m}N[y_t;\mu_{n,m},C_{n,m}]}, & \text{if } s=n \\ 0, & \text{otherwise} \end{cases} \quad (5)$$

where N and M are the number of state and mixtures of HMM, D is the dimension of the feature vector, $\mu_{n,m}$, $C_{mn,m}$ are the mean and variance vector corresponding to mixture m in state n, $w_{n,m}$ is the probability of mixture m in state n, N is the normal distribution and s is the state sequence corresponding to the input utterance.

The proposed method in enrollment session consists of three steps:

1. Multiple transcription hypothesis of the input utterance and state segmentations are obtained using SI phoneme HMMs.
2. The transformation vectors (bias) are estimated using stochastic matching method.
3. SI phoneme models are adapted with the transformation vectors.
4. Step 2 and 3 are iterated until adaptation becomes sufficiently precise and then multiple transcriptions and bias vector are saved into database.

In a test session, the user just needs to utter the name. For telephone, the identity can be obtained from caller ID or from user's input. After SI phoneme HMMs are adapted using bias vectors, decoder recognize the input speech with transcriptions and adapted SI phoneme HMMs.

3 Experimental Results

3.1 Database and System Setup

The experimental database consists of 10 speakers, 5 males and 5 females speaking 15 name entries repeated 13 times by each speaker over a period of several weeks [8]. The database evaluation is on a worst-case situation where all the names are "Call ", e.g. "Call office", "Call home", "Call mom", etc. This means that about a half of the contents are the same. Many names are very short in about 1 second, which makes the recognition even more difficult. This database was collected over the telephone network using digital telephone interface. The input speech was sampled at 6.67kHz and saved as 8bit μ-law PCM format. In training, three utterances of each name recorded in one session were used to train a name model. In testing, ten utterances from each speaker collected from 5 different sessions were used to evaluate the recognition performance.

The sampled input speech was pre-emphasized using a first-order filter with a coefficient of 0.97, and the analysis frames were 30-ms width with 20-ms overlap. A 39-dimensional feature vector was extracted based on tenth order LPC analysis. The feature corresponds to a 12-dimensional cepstrum vector, 12-dimensional delta-cepstrum vector, 12-dimensional delta-delta-cepstrum vector, a normalized log energy, a delta log energy and a delta-delta log energy.

The SI phoneme models were trained using the database collected over the telephone network. SI phoneme HMMs consist of 41 phoneme HMMs and a silence HMM. The phoneme HMM models are left-to-right HMMs and each phoneme HMM have 3 or 5 states consisting of 10 continuous Gaussian mixture components and a silence model has one state consisting of 256 continuous Gaussian mixture components.

3.2 Performance of Baseline System

We first conduct baseline experiments to study the effect of speaker adaptation. The base line system is SD voice dialing system using speaker-specific phonetic templates (transcription) and SI phoneme HMMs. Although this kind of system can in substantially reduce storage space, a large amount of phoneme recognition errors are generated using SI phoneme HMMs, especially at the front and end of the input utterance. One way to reduce the phoneme recognition errors is to use the end point detection method. Voice dialing experiment was conducted with and without processing the end point detection method. Table 1 gives the percentage word error rates for voice dialing with and without processing the end point detection method. As expected, using end point detection method reduces percentage word error rates from 4.2% to 3.8% since some of phoneme recognition errors are eliminated.

Table 1. Performance comparison of the baseline system with or without endpoint detection

	with endpoint detection	without endpoint detection
Error rate(%)	3.8	4.2

3.3 Performance of the Iterative Training Techniques

In order to evaluate the performance of proposed system, transformation vector (bias) and transcriptions for the speaker adaptation are estimated iteratively by using the stochastic matching method. Two kinds of stochastic matching methods, phonetic class based and codebook-based, are used to estimate the biases. In the phonetic class based stochastic matching, multiple biases are used according to the phonetic classes. The number of bias is selected according to the acoustic phonetic class. Table 2 shows the number of bias according to the phonetic class. When a bias is used, all of phonemes have a common transformation vector. When two biases, one is for all of phoneme models and the other is for a silence model. When three biases, the phonetic classes consist of vowels, consonants and a silence. When nine biases, the phonetic classes consist of silence, vowel, diphthongs, semivowels, stops, etc. when 14 biases, the phonetic classes are silence, front vowel, mid vowel, back vowel, diphthongs, liquids, glides, voiced stops, unvoiced stops, etc. When 42 biases, the phonetic classes are all

Table 2. The number of bias according to the phonetic class for phonetic class based stochastic matching

number of bias	phonetic class
1	no phonetic class
2	silence and speech
3	silence, vowel and consonants
9	silence, vowel, diphthongs, semivowels, stops, ...
14	silence, {front, mid, back} vowel, diphthongs, liquids, glides, {voiced, unvoiced} stops, ...
42	silence and all phones
180	all of SI HMM states

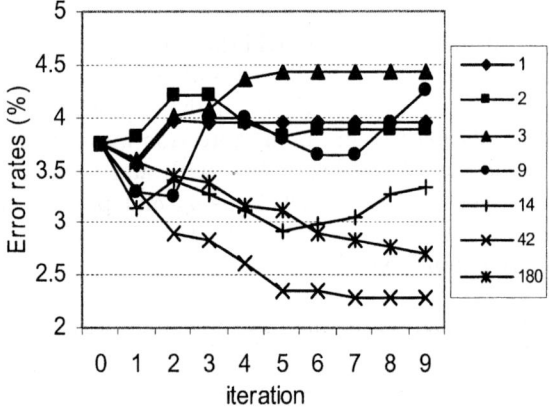

Fig. 2. Performance of the voice dialing system using speaker adaptation algorithm according to the phonetic class(the number of transformation vector: 1, 2, 3, 9, 14, 42, 180)

phonemes and a silence. When 180 biases, it is equal to the number of states of all phoneme HMMs.

Fig. 2 shows the percentage word error rates and convergence speed of the algorithm according to the number of transformation vector. As seen in Figure 2, the performance of proposed system did not enhanced when the number of transformation vector is fewer than 9. However, error reduction could be achieved when the number of transformation vector is more than 14. When 42 transformation vectors are used, the best performance (2.3% word error rate) could be achieved. It corresponds to about a 40% reduction in word error rate as compared to the performance of the baseline system.

In the codebook-based stochastic matching, the concept of "tying" among model parameters is used in determining the number of biases. Different degrees of tying control the size of the codebook and consequently the number of biases used. The codebook could range in size from one entry, which applies a global

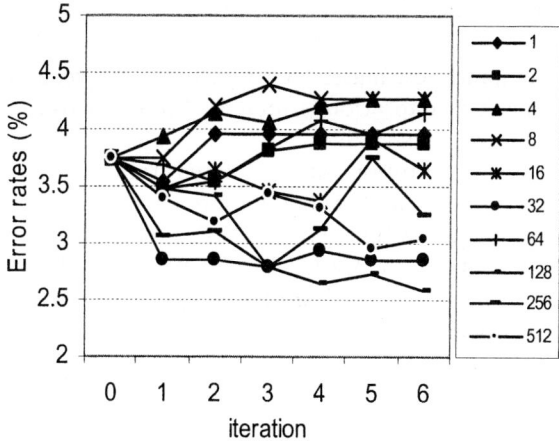

Fig. 3. Performance of the voice dialing system using speaker adaptation algorithm according to the codebook size(the number of transformation vector: 1, 2, 4, 8, 16, 32, 64, 128, 256, 512)

Table 3. Performance comparison of the proposed speaker adaptation method with conventional ones

Type of system	Baseline	Baseline with bias	Proposed system	Ideal case	SD system
Error rate(%)	3.8	3.3	2.3	2.3	1.8

bias to entire SI HMMs, to as many entries as the number of mixture components available. The codebook is constructed by clustering the set of mean vectors of mixture components for SI HMMs using the Lloyd algorithm with a Euclidean distance. Figure 3 illustrates the effect of varying the codebook size(i.e., the number of biases utilized) from one to 512 on the recognition performance. This experiment seems to indicate that a codebook size of 32 and beyond produce error reduction. Using a codebook size of 128, 2.6% word error rate could be achieved.

Table 3 shows the performance comparison of the proposed method with the conventional methods. The error rate of baseline system is 3.8%. The error rate of system adapted with the transformation vector only(i.e., transcriptions are not updated) is 3.3%. This shows that adaptation with the transformation vector only could reduce the error rate. The error rate of proposed system in which the transformation vectors and the transcriptions for the speaker adaptation are estimated iteratively is 2.3%. This is the same error rate of ideal case in which correct transcriptions are assumed to be known. Finally, the error rate of SD HMMs is 1.8%. Although this is the lowest, large amount of storage space are required.

4 Conclusion

A new method that jointly estimates the transformation vectors and the transcriptions for the speaker adaptation is presented in order to improves the performance of the personal voice dialing system in which SI phoneme HMMs are used. The biases and transcriptions are estimated iteratively from the training data of each user with maximum likelihood approach to the stochastic matching using SI phoneme models. Two kinds of stochastic matching methods, phonetic class based and codebook-based, are used to estimate the biases. Experimental result shows that the performance of proposed system corresponds to about a 40% reduction in word error rate, when compared to the performance of the baseline system.

Acknowledgement

This work was supported by the Korea Science and Engineering Foundation (KOSEF) through the Biometrics Engineering Research Center (BERC) at Yonsei University.

References

1. Jain, N., Cole, R. Barnard, E.: Creating Speaker-Specific Phonetic Templates with a Speaker-Independent Phonetic Recognizer: Implications for Voice Dialing. Proc. of ICASSP'96 (1996) 881–884
2. Fontaine, V., Bourlard, H.: Speaker-Dependent Speech Recognition Based on Phone-Like Units Models-Application to Voice Dialing. Proc. of ICASSP'97 (1997) 1527–1530
3. Ramabhadran, B., Bahl, L.R., deSouza, P.V., Padmanabhan, M.: Acoustic-Only Based Automatic Phonetic Baseform Generation. Proc. of ICASSP'98 (1998) 2275–2278
4. Shozakai, M.: Speech Interface for Car Applications. Proc. of ICASSP'99 (1999) 1386–1389
5. Deligne, S., Mangu, L.: On the use of Lattices for Automatic Generation of Pronunciations. Proc. of ICASSP'03 (2003) 204–207
6. Zavaliagkos, G., Schwartz, R., Makhoul, J.: Batch, Incremental and Instantaneous Adaptation Techniques for Speech Recognition. Proc. of ICASSP'95 (1995) 676–679
7. Sankar, A., Lee, C.H.: A Maximum-Likelihood Approach to Stochastic Matching for Robust Speech Recognition. IEEE Trans. on Speech and Audio Processing, Vol. 4. (1996) 190–202
8. Sukkar, R.A., Lee, C.H.: Vocabulary Independent Discriminative Utterance Verification for Non-keyword Rejection in Subword based Speech Recognition. IEEE Trans. on Speech and Audio Processing, Vol. 4. (1996) 420–429

Active Visual Learning and Recognition Using Incremental Kernel PCA

Byung-joo Kim

Youngsan University Dept. of Network and Information Engineering, Korea
bjkim@ysu.ac.kr

Abstract. Eigenspace models are a convenient way to represent set of images with widespread applications. In the traditional approach to calculate these eigenspace models, known as batch PCA method, model must capture all the images needed to build the internal representation. This approach has some drawbacks. Since the entire set of images is necessary, it is impossible to make the model build an internal representation while exploring a new object. Updating of the existing eigenspace is only possible when all the images must be kept in order to update the eigenspace, requiring a lot of storage capability. In this paper we propose a method that allows for incremental eigenspace update method by incremental kernel PCA for vision learning and recognition. Experimental results indicate that accuracy performance of proposed method is comparable to batch KPCA and outperform than APEX. Furthermore proposed method has efficiency in memory requirement compared to KPCA.

Content Area: Vision, robotics.

1 Introduction

Object recognition is a key task in machine vision. In the context of robot vision, object recognition techniques are applied in order to identify or classify these objects. Let us consider the following scenario: A camera is mounted on a robot which explores a object and builds an internal representation in terms of eigenspace-based method. Eigenspace methods are then used to build a compact representation of the set of images. Updating of the existing eigenspace is only possible when all the images must be kept in order to update the eigenspace, requiring a lot of storage capability. To overcome these problems, some authors proposed methods that build the eigenspace model incrementally. The basic idea behind these algorithms are to start with an initial eigenvectors and associated eigenvalues and update the eigenspace in order to represent new acquired data. By this result there is no need to build the eigenspace from scratch at each time when a new image is added to the eiegnspace. Another problem of batch PCA is that it only defines a linear projection of the data, the scope of its application is necessarily somewhat limited. It has been shown that most of the data in the real world are inherently non-symmetric and therefore contain higher-order correlation information that could be useful[1]. PCA is incapable of representing such data. For such cases, nonlinear transforms is necessary. Recently kernel trick has been applied to PCA and is based on a formulation of PCA in terms of the dot product matrix instead of the covariance matrix[2]. Kernel PCA(KPCA), however, requires storing and finding the eigenvectors of a $N \times N$ kernel matrix where N is a number of patterns. It is infeasible method for when N is large. This fact has motivated the development of incremental way of KPCA method which does not store the kernel matrix. In this paper we propose a method that allows for incremental eigenspace update method by incremental kernel PCA for vision learning and recognition. Paper is composed of as follows. In Section 2 we will briefly explain the incremental PCA method. In Section 3 KPCA is introduced and to make KPCA incrementally, empirical kernel map method is explained. Experimental results to evaluate the performance of proposed method is shown in Section 4. Discussion of proposed method and future work is described in Section 5.

2 Incremental PCA

In this section, we will give a brief introduction to the method of incremental PCA algorithm which overcomes the computational complexity of standard PCA. Before continuing, a note on notation is in order. Vectors are columns, and the size of a vector, or matrix, where it is important, is denoted with subscripts. Particular column vectors within a matrix are denoted with a superscript, while a superscript on a vector denotes a particular observation from a set of observations, so we treat observations as column vectors of a matrix. As an example, A_{mn}^i is the ith column vector in an $m \times n$ matrix. We denote a column extension to a matrix using square brackets. Thus $[A_{mn}b]$ is an $(m \times (n+1))$ matrix, with vector b appended to A_{mn} as a last column.

To explain the incremental PCA, we assume that we have already built a set of eigenvectors $U = [u_j], j = 1, \cdots, k$ after having trained the input images $x_i, i = 1, \cdots, N$. The corresponding eigenvalues are Λ and $\bar{x}$ is the mean of input image. Incremental building of eigenspace requires to update these eigenspace to take into account of a new input image. Here we give a brief summarization of the method which is described in [12]. First, we update the mean:

$$\bar{x}' = \frac{1}{N+1}(N\bar{x} + x_{N+1}) \qquad (1)$$

We then update the set of eigenvectors to reflect the new input image and to apply a rotational transformation to U. For doing this, it is necessary to compute the orthogonal residual vector $\hat{h} = (Ua_{N+1} + \bar{x}) - x_{N+1}$ where a_{N+1} is principal component and normalize it to obtain $h_{N+1} = \frac{h_{N+1}}{\|h_{N+1}\|_2}$ for $\| h_{N+1} \|_2 > 0$ and $h_{N+1} = 0$ otherwise. We obtain the new matrix of eigenvectors U' by appending h_{N+1} to the eigenvectors U and rotating them :

$$U' = [U, h_{N+1}]R \qquad (2)$$

where $R \in \mathbf{R}_{(k+1) \times (k+1)}$ is a rotation matrix. R is the solution of the eigenspace of the following form:
$$DR = R\Lambda' \qquad (3)$$
where Λ' is a diagonal matrix of new eigenvalues. We compose $D \in \mathbf{R}_{(k+1) \times (k+1)}$ as:
$$D = \frac{N}{N+1} \begin{bmatrix} \Lambda & 0 \\ 0^T & 0 \end{bmatrix} + \frac{N}{(N+1)^2} \begin{bmatrix} aa^T & \gamma a \\ \gamma a^T & \gamma^2 \end{bmatrix} \qquad (4)$$
where $\gamma = h_{N+1}^T(x_{N+1} - \bar{x})$ and $a = U^T(x_{N+1} - \bar{x})$. Though there are other ways to construct matrix D[4][5], the only method, however, described in [3] allows for the updating of mean.

2.1 Updating Image Representations

The incrementl PCA represents the input image with principal components $a_{i(N)}$ and it can be approximated as follows:
$$\hat{x}_{i(N)} = U a_{i(N)} + \bar{x} \qquad (5)$$
To update the principal components $a_{i(N)}$ for a new image x_{N+1}, computing an auxiliary vector η is necessary. η is calculated as follows:
$$\eta = \left[U \hat{h}_{N+1} \right]^T (\bar{x} - \bar{x}') \qquad (6)$$
then the computation of all principal components is
$$a_{i(N+1)} = (R')^T \begin{bmatrix} a_{i(N)} \\ 0 \end{bmatrix} + \eta, \quad i = 1, \cdots, N+1 \qquad (7)$$

The transformations described above yield a model that represents the input images with the same accuracy as the previous one, therefore we can now discard the old subspace and the coefficients that represent the image in it. x_{N+1} is represented accurately as well, so we can safely discard it. The representation of all $N+1$ images is possible because the subspace is spanned by $k+1$ eigenvector. Due to the increase of the dimensionality by one, however, more storage is required to represent the data. If we try to keep a k-dimensional eigenspace, we lose a certain amount of information. In order to balance the storage requirements with the level of accuracy, it is needed for us to set the criterion on retaining the number of eigenvectors. There is no explicit guideline for retaining a number of eigenvectors. Here we introduce some general criteria to deal with the model's dimensionality:

- Adding a new vector whenever the size of the residual vector exceeds an absolute threshold;
- Adding a new vector when the percentage of energy carried by the last eigenvalue in the total energy of the system exceeds an absolute threshold, or equivalently, defining a percentage of the total energy of the system that will be kept in each update;

- Discarding eigenvectors whose eigenvalues are smaller than a percentage of the first eigenvalue;
- Keeping the dimensionality constant.

In this paper we take a rule described in second. We set our criterion on adding an eigenvector as $\lambda'_{k+1} > 0.7\bar{\lambda}$ where $\bar{\lambda}$ is a mean of the λ. Based on this rule, we decide whether adding u'_{k+1} or not.

3 Incremental KPCA

A prerequisite of the incremental eigenspace update method is that it has to be applied on the data set. Furthermore incremental PCA builds the subspace of eigenvectors incrementally, it is restricted to apply the linear data. But in the case of KPCA this data set $\Phi(x^N)$ is high dimensional and can most of the time not even be calculated explicitly. For the case of nonlinear data set, applying feature mapping function method to incremental PCA may be one of the solutions. This is performed by so-called *kernel-trick*, which means an implicit embedding to an infinite dimensional Hilbert space[6](i.e. feature space) F.

$$K(x,y) = \Phi(x) \cdot \Phi(y) \tag{8}$$

Where K is a given kernel function in an input space. When K is semi positive definite, the existence of Φ is proven[7]. Most of the case ,however, the mapping Φ is high-dimensional and cannot be obtained explicitly. The vector in the feature space is not observable and only the inner product between vectors can be observed via a kernel function. However, for a given data set, it is possible to approximate Φ by empirical kernel map proposed by Scholkopf[8] and Tsuda[9] which is defined as $\Psi_N : \mathbf{R}^d \rightarrow \mathbf{R}^N$

$$\begin{aligned}\Psi_N(x) &= [\Phi(x_1) \cdot \Phi(x), \cdots, \Phi(x_N) \cdot \Phi(x)]^T \\ &= [K(x_1,x), \cdots, K(x_N,x)]^T\end{aligned} \tag{9}$$

A performance evaluation of empirical kernel map was shown by Tsuda. He shows that support vector machine with an empirical kernel map is identical with the conventional kernel map[9]. The empirical kernel map $\Psi_N(x_N)$,however, do not form an orthonormal basis in $\mathbf{R}^N$, the dot product in this space is not the ordinary dot product. In the case of KPCA ,however, we can be ignored as the following argument. The idea is that we have to perform linear PCA on the $\Psi_N(x_N)$ from the empirical kernel map and thus diagonalize its covariance matrix. Let the $N \times N$ matrix $\Psi = [\Psi_N(x_1), \Psi_N(x_2), \ldots, \Psi_N(x_N)]$, then from equation (9) and definition of the kernel matrix we can construct $\Psi = NK$. The covariance matrix of the empirically mapped data is:

$$C_\Psi = \frac{1}{N}\Psi\Psi^T = NKK^T = NK^2 \tag{10}$$

In case of empirical kernel map, we diagonalize NK^2 instead of K as in KPCA. Mika shows that the two matrices have the same eigenvectors $\{u_k\}$[10]. The eigenvalues $\{\lambda_k\}$ of K are related to the eigenvalues $\{k_k\}$ of NK^2 by

$$\lambda_k = \sqrt{\frac{k_k}{N}} \tag{11}$$

and as before we can normalize the eigenvectors $\{v_k\}$ for the covariance matrix C_Ψ of the data by dividing each $\{u_k\}$ by $\sqrt{\lambda_k N}$. Instead of actually diagonalize the covariance matrix C_Ψ, the incremental KPCA is applied directly on the mapped data $\Psi = NK$. This makes it easy for us to adapt the incremental eigenspace update method to KPCA such that it is also correctly takes into account the centering of the mapped data in an incremental way. By this result, we only need to apply the empirical map to one data point at a time and do not need to store the $N \times N$ kernel matrix.

4 Experiment

To evaluate the performance of accuracy on eiegnspace update for incremental data we take nonlinear data. The disadvantage of incremental method is their accuracy compared to batch method even though it has the advantage of memory efficiency. So we shall apply proposed method to a simple toy data which will show the accuracy and memory efficiency of incremental KPCA compared to APEX model proposed by Kung[11] and batch KPCA. Next we will use images from the Columbia Object Image Library(COIL-20). The set is consisted of images of 20 objects rotated about their vertical axis, resulting in 72 images per objects. We used these images for testing the performance of incremental KPCA.

4.1 Toy Data

To evaluate the eigenspace update accuracy and memory efficiency of incremental KPCA compared to APEX and KPCA we take nonlinear data used by Scholkoff[8]. Totally 41 training data set is generated by:

$$y = x^2 + 0.2\varepsilon : \ \varepsilon \ from \ N(0,1), x = [-1,1] \tag{12}$$

First we compare feature extraction ability of incremental KPCA to APEX model. APEX model is famous principal component extractor based on Hebbian learning rule. Applying toy data to incremental KPCA we finally obtain 2 eigenvectors. To evaluate the performance of two methods on same condition, we set 2 output nodes to standard APEX model.

In table 1 we experimented APEX method on various conditions. Generally neural network based learning model has difficulty in determining the parameters; for example learning rate, initial weight value and optimal hidden layer node. This makes us to conduct experiments on various conditions. $\parallel w \parallel$ is norm of weight vector in APEX and $\parallel w \parallel = 1$ means that it converges stable minimum. $cos\theta$ is angle between eigenvector of KPCA and APEX, incremental KPCA respectively. $cos\theta$ of eigenvector can be a factor of evaluating accuracy how much incremental KPCA and APEX is close to accuracy of KPCA. Table 1 nicely shows the two advantages of incremental KPCA compared to APEX: first, performance of incremental KPCA is better than APEX; second, the performance

Table 1. Performance evaluation of incremental KPCA(IKPCA) and APEX

Method	Iteration	Learning Rate	$\|w_1\|$	$\|w_2\|$	$\cos\theta_1$	$\cos\theta_2$	MSE
APEX	50	0.01	0.6827	1.4346	0.9993	0.7084	14.8589
APEX	50	0.05				do not converge	
APEX	500	0.01	1.0068	1.0014	0.9995	0.9970	4.4403
APEX	500	0.05	1.0152	1.0470	0.9861	0.9432	4.6340
APEX	1000	0.01	1.0068	1.0014	0.9995	0.9970	4.4403
APEX	1000	0.05	1.0152	1.0470	0.9861	0.9432	4.6340
IKPCA	100		1	1	1	1	0.0223

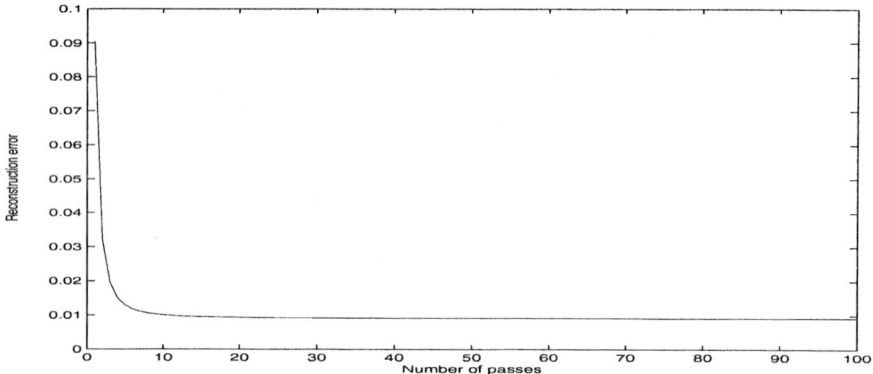

Fig. 1. Reconstruction error change by re-learning in incremental KPCA

of incremental KPCA is easily improved by re-learning. Another factor of evaluating accuracy is reconstruction error. Reconstruction error is defined as the squared distance between the image of x_N and reconstruction when projected onto the first i principal components.

$$\delta = |\Psi(x_N) - P_l\Psi(x_N)|^2 \qquad (13)$$

In here P_l is the first i principal component. The MSE(Mean Square Error) value of reconstruction error in APEX is 4.4403 whereas incremental KPCA is 0.0223. This means that the accuracy of incremental KPCA is superior to standard APEX and similar to that of batch KPCA. Figure 1 shows the MSE value change for reconstruction error by re-learning in incremental KPCA. Re-learning is similar meaning of epoch in neural network learning. We can see that the performance of incremental KPCA is easily improved by re-learning. Above results of simple toy problem indicate that incremental KPCA is comparable to the batch way KPCA and superior in terms of accuracy.

Next we will compare the memory efficiency of incremental KPCA compared to KPCA. In this experiments, incremental KPCA only needs D matrix and R matrix whereas KPCA needs kernel matrix. Table 2 shows the memory requirement of each method. Memory requirement of standard KPCA is 93 times more than incremental KPCA. We can see that incremental KPCA is more efficient in memory requirement than KPCA and has similar ability of eigenspace update accuracy. By this simple toy problem we can show that incremental KPCA has similar accuracy compare to KPCA and more efficient in memory requirement than KPCA.

Table 2. Memory efficiency of incremental KPCA compared to KPCA on toy data

	KPCA	IKPCA
Kernel matrix	41 X 41	none
R matrix	none	3 X 3
D matrix	none	3 X 3
Efficiency ratio	93.3889	1

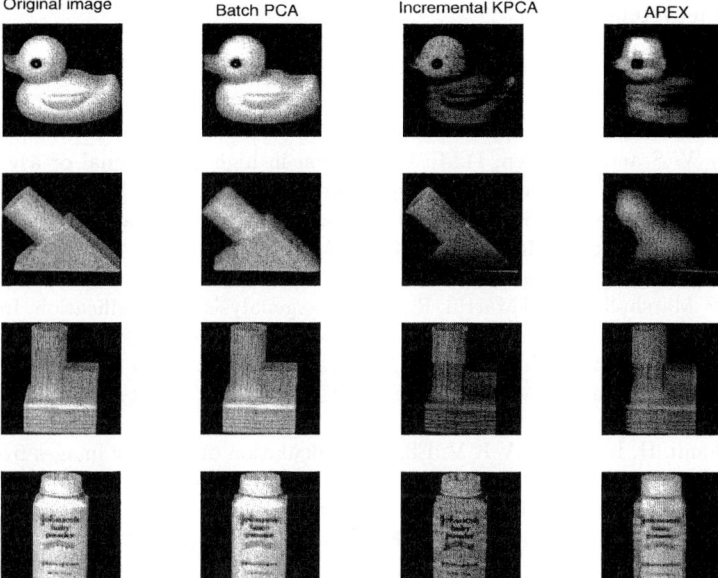

Fig. 2. Reconstructed image by incremental KPCA, APEX and batch PCA

4.2 Reconstruction Ability

To compare the reconstruction ability of incremental eigenspace update method proposed by Hall to APEX model we conducted experiment on image data. In this experiment we use COIL-20 data set. Applying this data to incremental eigenspace update method we finally obtain 31 Eigenvectors. As earlier experiment we set 31 output nodes to standard APEX method. Figure 2 shows the original data and their reconstructed images by incremental KPCA method, batch PCA and APEX respectively. The MSE(Mean Square Error) value of reconstruction error in APEX is 5.247 whereas incremental KPCA is 0.1426 and KPCA is 0.1247. This means that the accuracy of incremental KPCA is superior to standard APEX and similar to that of batch KPCA. We can see that reconstructed images by incremental KPCA update method is similar to original image and more clear compared to APEX method.

5 Conclusion and Remarks

In this paper, we discuss the problem of object recognition in robot vision. We use incremental KPCA method in order to represent images in a low-dimensional subspace. Proposed method allows discarding the acquired images immediately after the update. By experimental results we can show that incremental KPCA has similar accuracy compare to KPCA and more efficient in memory requirement than KPCA. This makes proposed model is suitable for robot vision and recognition system.

References

1. Softky, W.S and Kammen, D.M.: Correlation in high dimensional or asymmetric data set: Hebbian neuronal processing. Neural Networks vol. 4, Nov. (1991) 337-348
2. Gupta, H., Agrawal, A.K., Pruthi, T., Shekhar, C., and Chellappa., R.:An Experimental Evaluation of Linear and Kernel-Based Methods for Face Recognition," accessible at http://citeseer.nj.nec.com.
3. Hall, P. Marshall, D. and Martin, R.: On-line eigenanalysis for classification. In British Machine Vision Conference, volume 1, September (1998) 286-295
4. Winkeler, J. Manjunath, B.S. and Chandrasekaran, S.:Subset selection for active object recognition. In CVPR, volume 2, IEEE Computer Society Press, June (1999) 511-516
5. Murakami, H. Kumar.,B.V.K.V.:Efficient calculation of primary images from a set of images. IEEE PAMI, 4(5) (1982) 511-515
6. Vapnik, V. N.:Statistical learning theory. John Wiley & Sons, New York (1998)
7. Scholkopf, B. Smola, A. and Muller, K.R.:Nonlinear component analysis as a kernel eigenvalue problem. Neural Computation 10(5), (1998) 1299-1319
8. Tsuda, K.:Support vector classifier based on asymmetric kernel function. Proc. ESANN (1999)
9. Mika, S.:Kernel algorithms for nonlinear signal processing in feature spaces. Master's thesis, Technical University of Berlin, November (1998)
10. Diamantaras, K.I. and Kung, S.Y.:Principal Component Neural Networks: Theory and Applications. New York John Wiley & Sons, Inc (1996)

Automated Scene Understanding for Airport Aprons

James Ferryman[1], Mark Borg[1], David Thirde[1], Florent Fusier[2], Valéry Valentin[2], François Brémond[2], Monique Thonnat[2], Josep Aguilera[3], and Martin Kampel[3]

[1] Computational Vision Group, The University of Reading, UK
{J.Ferryman, M.Borg, D.J.Thirde}@reading.ac.uk
[2] ORION Team, INRIA Sophia-Antipolis, France
{Florent.Fusier, Valery.Valentin, Francois.Bremond, Monique.Thonnat}@sophia.inria.fr
[3] Pattern Recognition and Image Processing Group, Vienna University of Technology, Austria
{agu, kampel}@prip.tuwien.ac.at

Abstract. This paper presents a complete visual surveillance system for automatic scene interpretation of airport aprons. The system comprises two main modules — Scene Tracking and Scene Understanding. The Scene Tracking module is responsible for detecting, tracking and classifying the semantic objects within the scene using computer vision. The Scene Understanding module performs high level interpretation of the observed objects by detecting video events using cognitive vision techniques based on spatio-temporal reasoning. The performance of the system is evaluated for a series of pre-defined video events specified using a video event ontology.

1 Introduction

This paper describes work undertaken on the EU project AVITRACK. The main aim of this project is to automate the supervision of commercial aircraft servicing operations on the ground at airports (in bounded areas known as *aprons*). A combination of visual surveillance and video event recognition algorithms are applied in a decentralised multi-camera environment with overlapping fields of view (FOV) to track objects and recognise activities predefined by a set of servicing operations. Each camera agent performs per frame detection and tracking of scene objects, and the output data is transmitted to a central server where fused object tracking is performed. This tracking result is fed to a video event recognition module where spatial and temporal events relating to the servicing of the aircraft are detected and analysed. The system must be capable of monitoring and recognising the activities and interaction of numerous vehicles and personnel in a dynamic environment over extended periods of time, operating in real-time (12.5 FPS, 720 × 576 resolution) on colour video streams.

The tracking of moving objects on the apron has previously been performed using a top-down model based approach [10] although such methods are generally computationally expensive when applied to real time tracking. An alternative approach, bottom-up scene tracking, refers to a process that comprises the two sub-processes *motion detection* and *object tracking*; the advantage of bottom-up scene tracking is that it is more generic and computationally efficient compared to the top-down method.

Motion detection methods attempt to locate connected regions of pixels that represent the moving objects within the scene; there are many ways to achieve this including frame to frame differencing, background subtraction and motion analysis (e.g. optical flow) techniques. Background subtraction methods [9,7,13] store an estimate of the static scene, learnt from an initial period of observation, which is subsequently applied to find foreground (i.e. moving) regions that do not match the static scene.

Image plane based object tracking methods take as input the result from the motion detection stage and commonly apply trajectory or appearance analysis to predict, associate and update previously observed objects in the current time step. One such method, the Kanade-Lucas-Tomasi (KLT) feature tracker [8] combines a local feature selection criterion with feature-based matching in adjacent frames; this method has the advantage that objects can be tracked through partial occlusion when only a sub-set of the features are visible. Tracking algorithms have to deal with motion detection errors and complex object interactions; e.g. objects appear to merge together, occlude each other, fragment, undergo non-rigid motion, etc. Apron analysis presents further challenges due to the size of the vehicles tracked (e.g. the aircraft size is $34 \times 38 \times 12$ metres), therefore prolonged occlusions occur frequently throughout apron operations. The apron can also be congested with objects; this enhances the difficulty of associating objects with regions.

Video event recognition algorithms analyse tracking results spatially and temporally to automatically recognise the high-level activities occurring in the scene; for aircraft servicing analysis such activities occur simultaneously over extended time periods in apron areas. Recent work by Xiang *et al* [14] applied a hierarchical dynamic Bayesian network to recognise scene events; however, such models are incapable of recognising simultaneous complex scene activities in real-time over extended time periods. The approach adopted for AVITRACK [12] addresses these problems using cognitive vision techniques based on spatio-temporal reasoning, *a priori knowledge* of the observed scene and a set of predefined video events corresponding to the servicing operations to recognise. Previous work was performed on primitive video events; here the focus is on more complex video events corresponding to servicing operations on apron area.

Section 2 details the Scene Tracking module comprising per-camera motion detection, bottom-up feature-based object tracking and finally fused object tracking using the combined object tracking results from the camera agents. Section 3 describes the Scene Understanding module including both the representation of video events and the video event recognition algorithm itself applied to apron monitoring. Section 4 presents the results, while Section 5 contains the discussion and lists future work.

2 Scene Tracking

The Scene Tracking module is responsible for the per-camera detection and tracking of moving objects, transforming the image positions into 3D world co-ordinates, and fusing the multiple camera observations of each object into single world measurements.

2.1 Motion Detection

For detecting connected regions of foreground pixels, 16 motion detection algorithms were implemented for AVITRACK and evaluated quantitively on various apron sequences under different environmental conditions (sunny conditions, fog, etc.). The evaluation process is described in more detail in [1]. Of these algorithms, the colour mean and variance method was selected [13], after taking into account processing efficiency and sensitivity. This motion detector has a background model represented by a pixel-wise Gaussian distribution $N(\mu, \sigma^2)$ over the normalised RGB colour space. In addition, a shadow/highlight detection component based on the work of Horprasert *et al* [6], is used to handle illumination variability. The algorithm also employs a multiple background layer technique to allow the temporary inclusion into the background model of objects that become stationary for a short period of time.

2.2 Object Tracking

Real-time object tracking can be described as a correspondence problem of finding which object in a video frame relates to which object in the next frame. As the time interval between two frames is small, inter-frame changes are limited, allowing the use of temporal constraints and object features to simplify the correspondence problem.

The KLT algorithm considers features to be independent entities and tracks each of them individually. Therefore, it is incorporated into a higher-level tracking process that groups features into objects, maintain associations between them, and uses the individual feature tracking results to track objects, taking into account complex object interactions. For each object O, a set of sparse features S is maintained, with the number of features determined dynamically from the object size and a configurable feature density parameter ρ. The KLT tracker takes as input the set of observations $\{M_j\}$ identified by the motion detector, where M_j is a connected set of foreground pixels, with the addition of a nearest neighbour spatial filter of clustering radius r_c, i.e., connected components with gaps $\leq r_c$. A prediction P_i^t is then associated with one or more observations, through a matching process that uses the individual tracking results of its features S and their spatial and/or motion information, in a rule-based approach.

The spatial rule-based reasoning method is based on the idea that if a feature belongs to object O_i at time $t-1$, then it should remain spatially within the foreground region of O_i at time t. A match function f is defined which returns the number of tracked features of prediction P_i^t that reside in the foreground region of observation M_j^t.

The use of motion information in the matching process, is based on the idea that features belonging to an object should follow approximately the same motion (assuming rigid object motion). Affine motion models (solving for $w_t^T F w_{t-N} = 0$ [15]) are fitted to each group of k neighbouring features of P_i; then represented as points in a motion parameter space and clustering is performed to find the most significant motion(s) of the object. These motions are subsequently filtered temporally and matched per frame to allow tracking through merging/occlusion and identify splitting events.

2.3 Data Fusion

The data fusion module combines the tracking data seen by the individual cameras to maximise the useful information content of the scene being observed and hence achieve enhanced occlusion reasoning, a larger visible area and improved 3D localisation. Spatial registration of the cameras is performed using per camera coplanar calibration and the camera streams are synchronised temporally across the network.

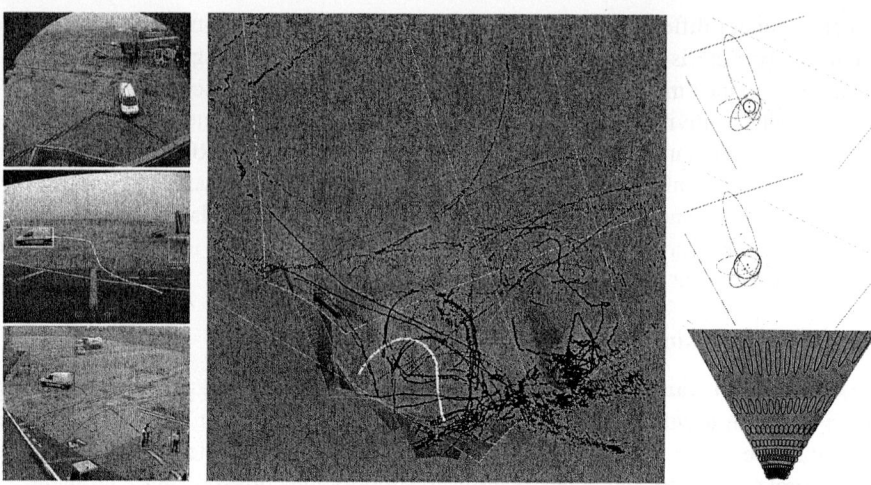

Fig. 1. (Left) Tracking results for 3 cameras for frame 9126 of sequence 21. (Middle) shows data fusion results on the ground-plane for the sequence (9600 frames) with the vehicle track shown in white. (Top-right) the fused observation (in black) for the vehicle (frame 9126) using the covariance accumulation method, (Middle-right) shows the result for covariance intersection. (Bottom-right) shows the sensory uncertainty field measured for camera 6.

The method for Data Fusion is based on a nearest neighbour Kalman filter approach [3] with a constant velocity model. The measurement noise covariance $\mathbf{R}$ is estimated by propagating a nominal image plane uncertainty Λ such that the measurement uncertainty in the world co-ordinate system is given by [4] i.e. $\mathbf{R}(x_w, y_w, z_w) = \mathbf{J}(x_c, y_c) \Lambda \mathbf{J}(x_c, y_c)^T$ where $\mathbf{J}$ is the Jacobian matrix found by taking the derivatives of the two mapping functions between the image and world co-ordinate systems. The measurement uncertainty field is shown in Figure 1 for camera 6; this estimate of uncertainty allows formal methods to be used to associate observations originating from the same measurement, as well as providing mechanisms for fusing observations into a single estimated measurement. For each object the measurement location and associated uncertainty is also dependent on the object dimensions; a bias is incorporated in the estimate using a heuristic method that includes the camera angle to the ground plane, object category and the measured object size.

In the association step a validation gate [3] is applied to limit the potential matches between existing tracks and observations. Matched observations are combined to find the fused estimate of the location and uncertainty of the object, this is achieved using *covariance accumulation* and *covariance intersection*. Covariance accumulation estimates the fused uncertainty $\mathbf{R}_{fused}$ for N matched observations as $\mathbf{R}_{fused} = \left(\mathbf{R}_1^{-1} + \ldots + \mathbf{R}_N^{-1}\right)^{-1}$. The covariance intersection method is conceptually similar to the accumulation except that the observation uncertainty covariances are weighted in the summation: $\mathbf{R}_{fused} = \left(w_1 \mathbf{R}_1^{-1} + \ldots + w_N \mathbf{R}_N^{-1}\right)^{-1}$, where $w_i = w_i' / \sum_{j=1}^N w_j'$ and $w_i' = 1/\text{Tr}(\mathbf{R}_i^c)$. $\mathbf{R}_i^c$ is the measurement uncertainty of the i'th associated observation (made by camera c); Covariance intersection therefore weights in favour of the sensors that have more certain measurements. The resulting fused observations are demonstrated in Figure 1; the covariance accumulation method results in a more localised estimate of the fused measurement than the covariance intersection approach. Remaining unassociated measurements are fused into new tracks, using a validation gate between observations to constrain the association and fusion steps. The track category is estimated as a weighted average over the fused observations; with each class probability modelled using a supervised 2-D Gaussian Mixture Model, representing object width and height in world co-ordinates.

3 Scene Understanding

The Scene Understanding module is responsible for the recognition of video events in the scene observed through video sequences. This module performs a high-level interpretation of the scene by detecting video events occurring in it. The method to detect video events uses cognitive vision techniques based on spatio-temporal reasoning, *a priori* knowledge of the observed environment and a set of predefined event models. A Video Event Recognition module takes the tracked mobile objects from the previously described modules as input, and outputs events that have been recognised.

The *a priori* knowledge is the knowledge about the observed empty scene. This includes the camera information, the vehicle models, the expected moving objects and the empty scene model (also called the static environment observed by the cameras) containing the contextual objects (e.g. equipment, zones of interest, walls, doors). Contextual objects are characterised by their 3D geometry (to provide an approximative shape) and by their semantics (to describe how they interact with mobile objects like persons or vehicles). The *a priori* knowledge also includes the set of event models defined by the domain experts using a video event description language described in [5].

3.1 Video Event Representation

The video event representation corresponds to the specification of all the knowledge used by the system to detect video events occurring in the scene. To allow experts in the aircraft activity monitoring to easily define and modify the video event models, the description of the knowledge is declarative and intuitive (in natural terms). Thus, the video event recognition uses the knowledge represented by experts through event models. The proposed model of a video event E is composed of five parts:

- a set of Physical Object variables corresponding to the physical objects involved in E: any contextual object including static object (equipment, zone of interest) and mobile object (person, vehicle, aircraft). The vehicle mobile objects can be of different subtypes to represent different vehicles (GPU, Loader, Tanker, Transporter).
- a set of temporal variables corresponding to the components (sub-events) of E
- a set of forbidden variables corresponding to the components that are not allowed to occur during the detection of E
- a set of constraints (symbolic, logical, spatial and temporal constraints including Allen's interval algebra operators [2]) involving these variables
- a set of decisions corresponding to the tasks predefined by experts that need to be executed when E is detected (e.g. activating an alarm or displaying a message)

CompositeState(Vehicle_Stopped_Inside_Zone,
PhysicalObjects((v1 : Vehicle), (z1 : Zone))
Components((c1 : PrimitiveState Inside_Zone(v1, z1))
     (c2 : PrimitiveState Vehicle_Stopped(v1)))
Constraints((c2 during c1)))

PrimitiveEvent(Enters_Zone,
PhysicalObjects((m1 : MobileObject), (z1 : Zone))
Components((c1 : PrimitiveState Outside_Zone(m1, z1))
     (c2 : PrimitiveState Inside_Zone(m1, z1)))
Constraints((c1 meet c2)))

Fig. 2. (Left) The model of the composite state for detecting when a vehicle stops inside a zone of interest. (Right) The model of the primitive event when a vehicle enters a zone of interest.

There are four types of video events: primitive state, composite state, primitive event and composite event. A state describes a situation characterising one or several physical objects defined at time t or a stable situation defined over a time interval. A primitive state (e.g. a person is inside a zone) corresponds to a vision property directly computed by the vision module. A composite state, as shown in Figure 2, corresponds to a combination of primitive states. An event is an activity containing at least a change of state values between two consecutive times (e.g. a vehicle leaves a zone of interest : it is inside the zone and then it is outside). A primitive event, as shown in Figure 2, is a change of primitive state values and a composite event is a combination of states and/or events.

3.2 Video Event Recognition

The video event recognition algorithm recognises which events are occurring in a stream of mobile objects tracked by the vision module. The algorithm to recognise a primitive state consists of two operations in a loop: (1) selection of a set of physical objects; then (2) verification of the corresponding atemporal constraints until all combinations of physical objects have been tested. Once a set of physical objects satisfies all atemporal constraints, the primitive state is said to be recognised. In order to facilitate primitive event recognition, event templates are generated for each primitive event, the last component of which corresponds to this recognised primitive state. The event template contains the list of physical objects involved in the primitive state. These physical objects partially instantiate the event template.

To recognise a primitive event, given the event template partially instantiated, the recognition algorithm selects (if needed) a set of physical objects matching the remaining physical object variables of the event model. It then looks back in the past for any previously recognised primitive state that matches the first component of the event model. If these two recognised components verify the event model constraints, the primitive event is said to be recognised. In order to facilitate composite event recognition, after each primitive event recognition, event templates are generated for all composite events, the last component of which corresponds to this recognised primitive event.

The recognition of composite states and events usually requires a search in a large space composed of all the possible combinations of components and objects. To avoid this combinatorial explosion, all composite states and events are simplified into states and events composed of at most 2 components through a stage of compilation in a preprocessing phase. Then the recognition of composite states and events is performed in a similar way to the recognition of primitive events. The video event recognition algorithm is based on the method of Vu *et al* [12].

3.3 Video Event Recognition for Apron Monitoring

In the Video Event Recognition module, *a priori* knowledge corresponds to apron zones of interest (access zones, stopping zones), aircraft and vehicle (e.g. GPU, Loader, Tanker and Transporter) models. Even if the handling operations on the apron are codified and controlled, some problems may occur while trying to build an accurate context of the scene. For example, access zones to aircraft can be at different positions according to the aircraft type. In some cases, one needs to detect a person getting out of a parked vehicle which does not always stop exactly at the same place. To solve these problems, dynamic properties are added to the *a priori* knowledge, by defining dynamic zones in the local coordinate system of vehicles. In order to effectively use dynamic context, accurate information is needed from the Scene Tracking modules for the orientation when a vehicle is parked. A transformation matrix is computed from local to global scene coordinate system and then dynamic zones are added to the context This is illustrated in Figure 3). This notion of dynamic context allows more complex scenarios to be defined in which mobile objects can directly interact with each other.

Fig. 3. (Left) Two dynamic zones (in blue) linked with the Loader and the Transporter vehicles involved in the event "Worker_Manipulating_Container" (event 26) detected. (Right) The Unloading operation involving 8 physical objects and 3 composite components with 2 constraints on the vehicle subtypes, 4 constraints on the zones of interest and 2 temporal constraints.

3.4 Predefined Video Events

Currently a set of 21 basic video events has been defined, including 10 primitive states, 5 composite states and 6 primitive events; these are used in the definition of video events representing the handling operations. The primitive states correspond to spatio-temporal properties related to persons and vehicles involved in the scene. Some examples include: a person is located inside a zone of interest, a person is close to a vehicle, a person has stopped, a vehicle is located inside a zone of interest, a vehicle is located outside a zone of interest, a vehicle is close to another vehicle, a vehicle has stopped, a vehicle is moving at a slow pace, and a vehicle is moving at a normal speed.

Using these primitive states, the following composite states have been modelled, such as: a person stays inside a zone of interest, a vehicle has arrived in a zone of interest, a vehicle has stopped in a zone of interest (as shown in Figure 2), a vehicle stays inside a zone of interest, and a vehicle is exceeding the speed limitation. The composite states have in turn been used to model primitive events, such as: a person enters a zone of interest, a person changes from a zone of interest to another, a person leaves a zone of interest, a vehicle enters a zone of interest (as shown in Figure 2), a vehicle change from a zone of interest to another, and a vehicle leaves a zone of interest. These states and events are used in the definition of the composite events (modelling behaviours) representing the apron operations.

Current work has been performed on video events involving (1) the GPU (Ground Power Unit) vehicle which operates in the aircraft arrival preparation operation, (2) the Tanker vehicle which operates in the refuelling operation and (3) the Loader and Transporter vehicles which are involved in the baggages loading/unloading operations. To recognise these operations 28 composite video events were defined, including 8 video events for the aircraft arrival preparation operation, 8 video events for the refuelling operation, and 12 video events for the unloading operation.

The aircraft arrival preparation operation (event 8) involves the GPU, its driver and 4 zones of interest. The system recognises that the GPU vehicle arrives in the ERA Zone (event 1), respecting the speed limit (event 2); then it enters (event 3) and stops (event 4) in the "GPU Access Area", the driver gets out of the vehicle (event 5) and deposits the chocks and stud at the location where the plane will stop (events 6 and 7). This operation, and another modelled one, the refuelling operation, are considered to be basic operations because they involve only one person and one vehicle.

The baggage unloading operation is more complex. It involves both a Loader and a Transporter vehicle, the conductor of the Loader, and a person working in the area. This operation is composed of the following steps: first, the Loader vehicle arrives in the ERA zone (event 17), enters its restricted area (event 18) and then stops in this zone (event 19); a dynamic zone is automatically added, at the rear of the Loader's stop position ("Loader_Arrival", event 20), where the Transporter will enter and stop. When the Transporter enters (event 21) and stops (event 22) in this zone ("Transporter_Arrival", event 23), another dynamic zone is automatically added to the context. The back of the Loader is then elevated (event 24) and the baggage containers are unloaded from the aircraft by the Loader conductor (event 25) one by one. The conductor unloads these containers into the dynamic zone of the Transporter where a worker arrives (event 26) and directs the containers (event 27) on to the Transporter.

4 Results

The Scene Tracking evaluation assesses the performance of the three core components (motion detection, object tracking and data fusion) on representative test data. The performance evaluation of the different motion detector algorithms for AVITRACK is described in more detail in [1]. It is noted that some objects are partially detected due to the achromaticity of the scene and the presence of fog causes a relatively high number of foreground pixels to be misclassified as highlighted background pixels resulting in a decrease in accuracy. Strong shadows also cause problems, often detected as part of the mobile objects. The performance evaluation of the tracking algorithm (representative results shown in Figure 1), is described in more detail in [11]. In is noted that some objects can produce a ghost which remains behind the previous object position. An object is integrated into the background when becomes stationary for an extended time period. In these cases, ghosts are created when stationary objects start to move again. Partial detection of objects can result in fragmentation in tracked objects with similar colour as the background. The Data Fusion module performs adequately given correctly detected objects in the Frame Tracker (a representative result is shown in Figure 1). The Data Fusion module incorporates uncertainty information in the location estimate of the observation and it is often an inaccurate location estimate that results in the failure of the data association step; a significant proportion of the localisation problems that occur in data fusion can be traced back to motion detection errors i.e. shadow, reflections etc.

The Scene Understanding evaluation has been performed on sequences for which the Scene Tracking module gives good results. Video event recognition has been tested on sequences involving the GPU (aircraft arrival preparation operation), the Tanker (refuelling operation) and the Loader and the Transporter vehicles (baggage unloading). Video events 1 to 4, involving a GPU, have been tested on a dataset of 4 scenes corresponding to 2x4 video sequences (containing from 1899 to 3774 frames and including one night sequence). These events are detected with a perfect True Positive rate. Video events 4 to 8, also involving a GPU, have been tested on 2 scenes corresponding to 2 video sequences because only one camera is available to observe these events.

The video events involving the Tanker have been tested on one scene (more than 15000 frames corresponding to about 30 minutes) showing the "Tanker Arrival" (event 13) and the driver of the Tanker extending the refuelling pipe to the aircraft (events 14 to 16). The "Unloading Baggage operation" involving the Loader (events 17 to 20, 24 and 25) and the Transporter (events 21 to 23) have been tested on one scene where the point of view allows full observation of the vehicle movements and interactions between the vehicles and people. Currently, the Scene Understanding evaluation is mainly qualitative and performed manually; the results of the evaluation are shown in Table 1. The goal is to give an idea of the performance of the Scene Understanding and to anticipate potential problems in event detection for apron monitoring. All video events are recognised correctly (49 TPs) without false alarms (0 FPs) and misdetection (0 FNs).

Table 1. Performance results of the Scene Understanding module for apron monitoring. TP = "Event exists in the real world and is well recognised", FN = "Event exists in the real world but is not recognised", FP = "Event does not exist in the real world but is recognised".

Vehicle type	Sequence	TP	FP	FN
GPU				
Events 1 to 4	4 scenes * 2 cam.	32	0	0
Events 4 to 8	2 scenes * 1 cam.	8	0	0
Tanker				
Events 9 to 13	2 scenes * 1 cam.	10	0	0
Events 14 to 16	1 scene * 1 cam.	3	0	0
Loader-Transporter				
Events 17 to 28	1 scenes * 1 cam.	12	0	0

These results are very encouraging but one has to keep in mind that situations where the vision module misdetects or overdetects mobile objects were not addressed.

5 Discussion and Future Work

The results are encouraging for both the Scene Tracking and Scene Understanding modules. The performance of multi-view object tracking provides adequate results; however, tracking is sensitive to significant dynamic and static object occlusion within the scene. Future work will address shadow supression and explicit occlusion analysis.

The Scene Understanding results show that the proposed approach is adapted to apron monitoring and can be applied to complex activity recognition. The main difficulty for apron monitoring is to model operations using *a priori* expert knowledge (49 video events already defined) and to recognise them all in parallel. The recognition of complex operations (e.g. "baggage unloading") involving people and vehicles gives good results and encourages us to continue with more complex operations, more interactions between people and vehicles. Another issue is incorporating uncertainty to enable recognition of events even when the Scene Tracking module gives unreliable output.

Acknowledgements

This work is supported by the EU, grant AVITRACK (AST3-CT-3002-502818).[1]

References

1. J. Aguilera, H. Wildernauer, M. Kampel, M. Borg, D. Thirde, and J. Ferryman. Evaluation of motion segmentation quality for aircraft activity surveillance. In *Proc. Joint IEEE Int. Workshop on VS-PETS, Beijing*, Oct 2005.
2. J. F. Allen. Maintaining knowledge about temporal intervals. In *Communications of the ACM*, volume 26 num 11, pages 823–843, Nov 1983.
3. Y. Bar-Shalom and X.R. Li. *Multitarget-Multisensor Tracking: Principles and Techniques*. YBS Publishing, 1995.
4. J. Black and T.J. Ellis. Multi Camera Image Measurement and Correspondence. In *Measurement - Journal of the International Measurement Confederation*, volume 35 num 1, pages 61–71, 2002.
5. M. Thonnat F. Brémond, N. Maillot and V. Vu. Ontologies for video events. In *Research report number 51895*, Nov 2003.
6. T. Horprasert, D. Harwood, and L.S. Davis. A statistical approach for real-time robust background subtraction and shadow detection. In *IEEE ICCV'99 FRAME-RATE Workshop*, 1999.
7. S. Jabri, Z. Duric, H. Wechsler, and A. Rosenfeld. Detection and location of people in video images using adaptive fusion of color and edge information. In *Proc. IAPR Internation Conference on Pattern Recognition*, pages 4627–4631, 2000.
8. J. Shi and C. Tomasi. Good features to track. In *Proc. of IEEE Conference on Computer Vision and Pattern Recognition*, pages 593–600, 1994.

---

[1] However, this paper does not necessarily represent the opinion of the EU, and the EU is not responsible for any use which may be made of its contents.

9. C. Stauffer and W.E.L. Grimson. Adaptive background mixture models for real-time tracking. In *Proc. International Conference on Pattern Recognition*, pages 246–252, 1999.
10. G. D. Sullivan. Visual interpretation of known objects in constrained scenes. In *Phil. Trans. R. Soc. Lon.*, volume B, 337, pages 361–370, 1992.
11. D. Thirde, M. Borg, V. Valentin, F. Fusier, J.Aguilera, J. Ferryman, F. Brémond, M. Thonnat, and M.Kampel. Visual surveillance for aircraft activity monitoring. In *Proc. Joint IEEE Int. Workshop on VS-PETS*, Beijing, Oct 2005.
12. V. Vu, F. Brémond, and M. Thonnat. Automatic video interpretation: A novel algorithm for temporal event recognition. In *IJCAI'03, Acapulco, Mexico*, Aug 2003.
13. C. R. Wren, A. Azarbayejani, T. Darrell, and A. Pentland. Pfinder: Real-time tracking of the human body. In *IEEE Transactions on PAMI*, volume 19 num 7, pages 780–785, 1997.
14. T. Xiang and S. Gong. On the structure of dynamic bayesian networks for complex scene modelling. In *Proc. Joint IEEE Int. Workshop on Visual Surveillance and Performance Evaluation of Tracking and Surveillance (VS-PETS)*, pages 17–22, Oct 2003.
15. G. Xu and Z. Zhang. *Epipolar Geometry in Stereo, Motion and Object Recognition: A Unified Approach*. Kluwer Academic Publ., 1996.

Semantic Correlation Network Based Text Clustering

Shaoxu Song and Chunping Li

School of Software, Tsinghua University, Beijing 100084, China
song-sx03@mails.tsinghua.edu.cn, cli@tsinghua.edu.cn

Abstract. Text documents have sparse data spaces, and nearest neighbors may belong to different classes when using current existing proximity measures to describe the correlation of documents. In this paper, we propose an asymmetric similarity measure to strengthen the discriminative feature of document objects. We construct a semantic correlation network by asymmetric similarity between documents and conjecture the power law feature of the connections distributions. Hub points which exist in semantic correlation network are classified by an agglomerative hierarchical clustering approach named SCN. Both objects similarity and neighbors similarity are considered in the definition of hub points proximity. Finally, we assign the rest text objects to their nearest hub points. The experimental evaluation on textual data sets demonstrates the validity and efficiency of SCN. The comparison with other clustering algorithms shows the superiority of our approach.

Keywords: Data Mining, Knowledge Discovery.

1 Introduction

Text clustering is a process of grouping a set of text objects into classes with high inner proximity. For text mining, data objects are always semi-structured or unstructured, like text and hypertext documents. Due to the high dimensionality and polysemy of words, the nearest distance neighbors of a document belong to different classes in some cases [1]. Methods, such as TFxIDF [2], try to strengthen the discriminative features of objects when describing the correlations between them. Instead of traditional proximity measures like distance, ROCK(RObust Clustering using linKs) [3] presents a concept of correlation that is based on links between data points. The notion of links between text documents helps us overcome the problem that some nearest neighbors belong to different classes. However, ROCK ignores the information about the closeness of two clusters while emphasizing on their inter-connectivity [4]. CHAMELEON [5] explores dynamic modeling in hierarchical clustering and it takes into account both the inter-connectivity and the closeness of the clusters.

In the specifical case of textual data, we should consider the discriminative feature of document objects in clustering. Current existing approaches (including CHAMELEON) can hardly deal with the special textual correlation. For example, some specialized articles may dedicate to one topic (i.e. *basketball*) in a single document, while some summarized articles may include several topics (i.e. *sports* including *basketball* and *football*) in one document. Traditional symmetric measures cannot tell the difference between summarized articles and specialized ones. On the other hand, *NIKE*, known as a famous sports sponsor, always be talked together with *football* and *basketball*. Although *NIKE* may not appear in a *sports* topic based article, *NIKE* and *sports* do have correlation with each other in common sense. Also it is hard to find this correlation by familiar methods.

In this paper, we construct a semantic correlation network in a more natural way. Asymmetric similarity is used for describing the correlation between documents and the semantic correlation of document topics are considered. Some recent researches in [6] analyze the scale-free features of semantic networks, such as WordNet [7]. We conjecture that the distributions of our topic based semantic correlation have the power law feature. Hub points are classified by an agglomerative hierarchical clustering approach. Those hub points connected with similar neighbors belong to the same cluster. Finally, we assign the rest text objects to their nearest hub points.

This paper is organized as follows. In Section 2 we briefly introduce the construction of semantic correlation network and some features. In Section 3 we propose our definition of text object proximity measure and an agglomerative hierarchical clustering approach based on hub points. Section 4 reports an experimental evaluation on real textual data and shows the quality of our approach. Finally, Section 5 is a summery of our study.

2 Semantic Correlation Network

In order to construct semantic correlation network, we need to define semantic correlation between documents. Many clustering investigations use a proximity measure of *dissimilarity*, *distance* or *similarity*. We firstly introduce the representation of documents. For most text clustering algorithms, documents are represented by *vector-space model*. In this model, each text document d is represented by a vector of weights of p terms:

$$d_i = (w_{i1}, \ldots, w_{ip}) \qquad (1)$$

where d_i is the vector of document i, w_{ik} is the weight of term k in document i. After transformed text documents to numeric vectors, *Euclidean Distance* and *Cosine Measure* are commonly used to measure the correlation of documents. In this paper, we use an asymmetric similarity measure in order to strengthen the discriminative feature of documents.

2.1 Document Correlation

Consider that the common terms of two documents d_i and d_j are s. If the weight of s in d_j is large, then the asymmetric similarity from d_i to d_j is high; and if the weight of s in d_i is small, then the asymmetric similarity from d_j to d_i is low. More precisely,

$$\vec{\phi}(d_i, d_j) = \sum_{k=1}^{p} |w_{ik} - |w_{ik} - w_{jk}|| \bigg/ \sum_{k=1}^{p} w_{jk} \qquad (2)$$

where $\vec{\phi}(d_i, d_j)$ is the direct similarity value from document d_i to d_j, w_{ik} is the weight value of term k in document d_i. Clearly, the similarity between documents is asymmetric (i.e., $\vec{\phi}(d_i, d_j) \neq \vec{\phi}(d_j, d_i)$).

Let us see the example in Section 1 again. Fig. 1 shows an asymmetric similarity description of the example case. Gray points denote articles, and directed links mean the asymmetric similarity between them. As mentioned above, the summarized article about *sports* may include more topic terms like *basketball* and *football*, while the specialized articles may contain less and specific topic terms. According to the asymmetric similarity definition, the similarity from summarized articles to specialized ones is higher than the reverse. The summarized articles stand out by setting a minimum similarity threshold.

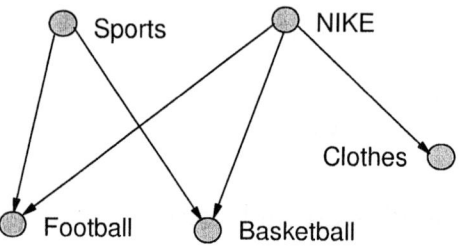

Fig. 1. Example of asymmetric similarity

2.2 Distribution Feature

We are interested in the structure of semantic correlation networks. A recent research [6] shows that semantic networks, such as WordNet, have a small world structure: they are sparse, exhibit short average path-lengths between objects as well as strong local clustering. This is a good information for topic based text clustering. In addition, the distributions of the number of connections follow power laws that suggests a hub structure similar to WWW [8]. In other words, a few objects have a very large number of connections to the others. The probability of observing a degree k can be described by:

$$P(k) \approx k^{-\gamma} \qquad (3)$$

where k means the number of connections, the exponent γ is always in the range of $2 < \gamma \leq 3$.

We construct the semantic correlation network by the asymmetric similarity between documents. Due to the sparsity of document term spaces, the network of correlation is also sparse. According to the definition of asymmetric similarity above, the summarized document d_m may have a larger similarity value to specialized document d_p than the reverse one. The discriminative features of documents have been strengthened, and it is easier to find the specialized documents by setting a minimum similarity threshold. This asymmetry feature induces that the summarized documents have more connections while the specialized ones have less. This phenomenon is quite similar to the features of small worlds. We conjecture that hub structure exists in our semantic correlation network and the summarized documents can be deemed to hub points. But we haven't proved that the distributions of asymmetric similarity connections follow power laws in this paper. Fig. 2 shows a simple example of semantic correlation network constructed by asymmetric similarity, where black points denote hub documents.

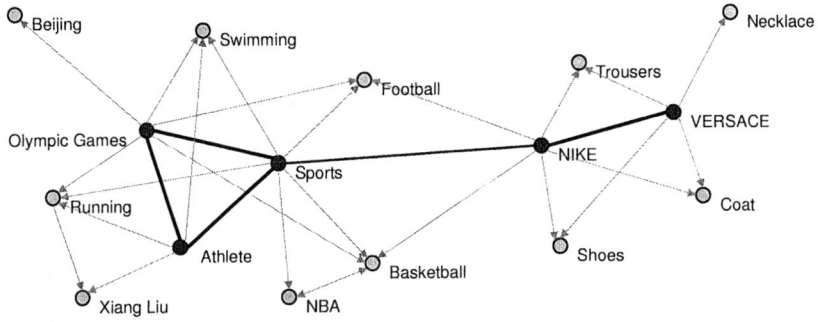

Fig. 2. Example of semantic correlation network

3 Clustering Algorithm

According to the hub documents(points), we can carry on clustering in a dynamical process. As shown in Fig. 2, clustering of hub points is processing at first, then we assign the rest text objects to their nearest hub points.

3.1 Proximity Measure

We assume that each document may be hub points and those hub points which have similar neighbors may belong to the same class. Distinct with traditional object similarity measure, we consider not only the similarity between objects but also the neighbors of them. All the similarity values from a hub point are represented by a sparse vector:

$$\Phi_i = \left(\overrightarrow{\phi}(p_i, p_1), \ldots, \overrightarrow{\phi}(p_i, p_k)\right) \quad (4)$$

where $p_1, \ldots, p_k$ mean all the points in the network, Φ_i stores the neighbors of hub point p_i. Obversely, Φ_i is a sparse vector. We can find the neighbor similarity of hub points by comparing their Φ_i vector. Just as using term similarity of documents to represent the document similarity, we use the neighbor similarity to compute the hub points proximity, i.e. $\vec{\phi}(\Phi_i, \Phi_j)$. The proximity of hub points can be defined by

$$\vec{\varphi}(p_i, p_j) = \frac{\vec{\phi}(\Phi_i, \Phi_j)\vec{\phi}(p_i, p_j)}{(n_i + n_j)^\gamma - n_i^\gamma - n_j^\gamma} \quad (5)$$

where p_i, p_j mean hub points that can be documents or clusters, n_i, n_j mean the number of documents in p_i, p_j, the exponent γ is a parameter in the range of $2 < \gamma \leq 3$. $\vec{\phi}(p_i, p_j)$ is the object similarity calculated by formula (2) and it denotes the sum of all similarity values from clusters p_i to p_j, i.e. $\sum_{d_q \in p_i, d_r \in p_j} \vec{\phi}(d_q, d_r)$, when points p_i and p_j are clusters.

3.2 Algorithm Description

We develop an agglomerative hierarchical algorithm, named SCN(Semantic Correlation Network based clustering). SCN algorithm performs clustering process based on the hub points of network. All the proximity values between hub points are described by a sparse matrix. The clustering analysis work is based on the strong components partition algorithm. The strong components of sparse matrix are dense, and the proximity between dense objects are high [9]. This partition analysis satisfies the principle of clustering that high inner proximity and low exterior proximity.

SCN clustering algorithm is presented as follows. In the first step of constructing similarity matrix M of p documents, formula (2) is used. Then we place each document in it's own initial cluster. In every iteration, formula (5) computes the proximity of hub points in the network. The core step is to find all strong components of sparse matrix P as new clusters. During the following iteration SCN reconstructs similarity matrix M by merging points in the same clustering. The iteration stops after k steps. The final work is a process of assigning the rest points to their nearest clusters.

SCN Clustering Algorithm

```
begin
  M := similarity matrix of all documents;
  C := initial clusters;
  repeat
    P := proximity matrix of hub points(C, M);
    C := strong components(P);
    M := merge similarity(C, M);
  until k iterations
  C := assign rest points to clusters;
end.
```

4 Experiments

This section reports an experimental evaluation of SCN clustering algorithm on real textual data sets. The experiments are performed on Xeon server with

2.8GHz clock speed and 1 GB main memory. The programs are implemented with java 1.5. Pre-classified documents are needed to test and compare cluster algorithms. We use two different data sets *RCV1* and *20Newsgroups*, which are widely used in text categorization.

4.1 Data Sets

RCV1. We work with the new version of Reuters corpus: Reuters Corpus Volume I (RCV1). It is an archive of over 800,000 manually categorized newswire stories recently made available by Reuters, Ltd. for research purposes. Topic codes are assigned to capture the major subjects of a story. They are organized in four hierarchical groups: CCAT (Corporate/Industrial), ECAT (Economics), GCAT (Government/Social), and MCAT (Markets). The sizes of these four categories are different. For further detail see [10]. We use 2000 documents which consist of 49% CCAT, 20% MCAT, 18% GCAT and 12% ECAT.

20Newsgroups. The 20 Newsgroups[1] (20Ng) data set, collected by Lang [11], contains about 20,000 articles. Each newsgroup represents one class in the classification task. Each article is designated to one or more semantic categories and the total number of categories is 20, all of them are about the same size. Most of the articles have only one semantic tag, however, about 7% of them have two and more ones. We chose 4 topic categories with 2000 documents in our experiments, i.e. "comp.graphics", "comp.sys.ibm.pc.hardware", "sci.crypt" and "sci.electronics".

4.2 Evaluation Criteria

We evaluate our method by the classification accuracy, which has also been used in [12] [13]. Kohonen et al. define the classification error as "all documents that represented a minority newsgroup at any grid point were counted as classification errors." Our classification accuracy is very similar to Kohonen's, but we count the correct documents instead of errors. The article is correct, if one of the original labels assigned by data set matches the cluster label. The accuracy is calculated by the proportion of the number of correct articles to the number of all input news articles.

4.3 Evaluation

Iterative Process. We observe the iterative process of hub points hierarchical clustering. Fig. 3 shows the observed result on *RCV1* and *20 Newsgroups* with both 2000 documents. From the right of the figure to the left, it shows the decrease of cluster numbers and the changes of accuracy in the iterative process. With the cluster number getting smaller, the accuracy drops sharply. It is reasonable, because the hub point clustering is neighbor based. Similar points are merged in every iteration, and the reliable neighbors of hub points reduce with

---
[1] The 20 newsgroups collection can be achieved at: http://kdd.ics.uci.edu/.

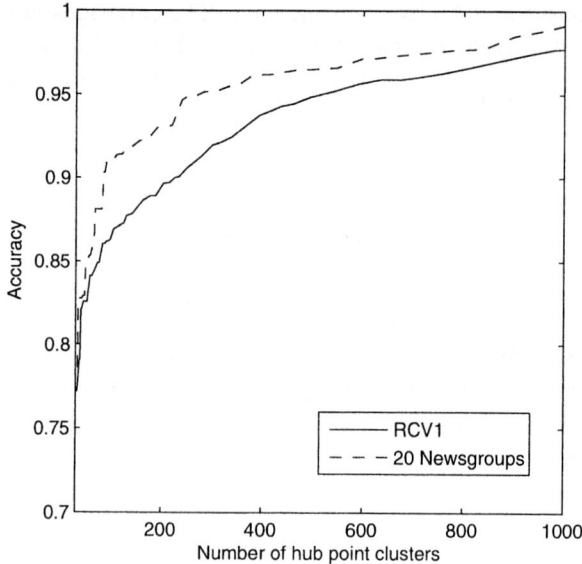

Fig. 3. Accuracy in different iterations

the decrease of total points(clusters). The clustering of hub points is poor at the end of iterative process. The rest points always can be those specialized documents which have low asymmetric similarity to others. It is the reason why we take a dynamical approach for assigning the rest points in the last step. Furthermore, the clustering of hub points shows higher accuracy on the *20 Newsgroups* data with similar class size.

Comparison with Other Approaches. This experiment was focused on evaluating the quality of SCN clustering algorithm. As a comparison with classical algorithm, we chose K-means and it's extension, i.e. Bisecting K-means (see [1][14]). Initial centroids were selected by randomly choosing K documents, so we ran the program 10 times and chose the best results. In Bisecting K-means, we chose the biggest cluster to partition in each iteration. For hierarchical approach, ROCK was compared with SCN. These algorithms were compared on both *RCV1* and *20Newsgroups*.

Table 1. Comparison of the accuracy among SCN, K-means, bisecting K-means (on RCV1 data), where $\gamma = 2.95$ in SCN

Number of Clusters	SCN	K-means	Bisecting K-means
9	0.707	0.628	0.591
15	0.770	0.638	0.595
30	0.815	0.698	0.602
43	0.830	0.722	0.608

Table 2. Comparison of the accuracy among SCN, K-means, bisecting K-means (on 20 Newsgroups data), where $\gamma = 2.85$ in SCN

Number of Clusters	SCN	K-means	Bisecting K-means
6	0.814	0.742	0.787
17	0.829	0.800	0.838
29	0.859	0.829	0.840
39	0.875	0.835	0.840

Table 3. Comparison among SCN and ROCK (on RCV1 data), where $\gamma = 2.95$ in SCN and $\theta = 0.02$ in ROCK

Number of Clusters	Accuracy		Iterations	
	SCN	ROCK	SCN	ROCK
9	0.707	0.664	81	1991
15	0.770	0.672	75	1985
30	0.815	0.806	66	1970
43	0.830	0.847	60	1957

Table 4. Comparison among SCN and ROCK (on 20 Newsgroups data), where $\gamma = 2.85$ in SCN and $\theta = 0.02$ in ROCK

Number of Clusters	Accuracy		Iterations	
	SCN	ROCK	SCN	ROCK
6	0.814	0.252	84	1994
17	0.829	0.772	63	1983
29	0.859	0.825	56	1971
39	0.875	0.922	52	1961

The comparison with partition algorithms is given in Table 1 and Table 2. From the table we can learn that SCN has a high accuracy on both *RCV1* and *20 Newsgroups*. SCN performs better than two others in different number of end clusters. Moreover, Bisecting K-means works even poorer than K-means on *RCV1* which has different class sizes, because it chooses the biggest cluster for division in each iteration. The validity superiority of SCN is outstanding especially on *RCV1*, while the time efficiency of SCN is poor in the comparison with partition algorithms.

We also compare SCN with an agglomerative hierarchical clustering algorithm, ROCK. The results are given in Table 3 and Table 4. As shown in these two tables, SCN achieves a high performance when dealing with smaller number of clusters, whereas the accuracy of ROCK drops quickly in small number of end clusters, especially on *20 Newsgroups*. This observation illustrates the validity of final assigning step in SCN. Furthermore, the efficiency of SCN is obvious when compared with ROCK. As traditional agglomerative hierarchical approach, ROCK merges two objects in each iteration and needs much more iterations than SCN. On the other hand, ROCK merges the most similar objects only, and the accuracy is high in each step when there are enough reliable neighbors. So it is the reason why ROCK achieves a better performance when the number of end clusters is large.

5 Conclusions

In this paper, we construct a semantic correlation network by the asymmetric similarity of documents. Asymmetric similarity strengthens the discriminative feature of summarized documents, and we conjecture that hub points exist in our semantic correlation network. The SCN clustering algorithm is developed based on the hub points. Both the objects similarity and neighbors similarity are considered in the proximity measure of hub points. SCN algorithm performs clustering analysis of hub points in an agglomerative hierarchical way. Then the rest points are assigned to their nearest hub points.

Our experimental evaluation on real text data sets demonstrates that SCN yields a better cluster quality than classical partition algorithm. Furthermore, SCN uses a strong components partition strategy, which shows better performance than ROCK. Our study achieves a natural description of document correlation, semantic correlation network, which shows superiority in text clustering. However, some inherent defects still exist, like the evidence of power law distribution in semantic correlation network. We hope to improve them in the future work by using more sophisticated approaches.

Acknowledgments. This work was supported by Chinese 973 Research Project under grant No. 2004CB719401.

References

1. Steinbach, M., Karypis, G., Kumar, V.: A comparison of document clustering techniques, In KDD 2000 Workshop on Text Mining (2000)
2. Salton, G.: Automatic text processing: the transformation, analysis, and retrieval of information by computer. Addison-Wesley (1989)
3. Guha, S., Rastogi, R., Shim, K.: ROCK: a robust clustering algorithm for categorical attributes. Information Systems, Vol. 25, **5** (2000) 345–366
4. Han, J., Kamber, M.: Data mining: concept and techniques. Morgan Kaufmann Publishers (2001)
5. Karypis, G., Han, E. H., Kumar, V.: Chameleon: hierarchical clustering using dynamic modeling. IEEE Computer, Vol. 32, **8** (1999) 68–75
6. Steyvers, M., Tenenbaum, J.: Small worlds in semantic networks. Unpublished manuscript (2001)
7. Fellbaum, C. (Ed.).: WordNet: an electronic lexical database. MIT Press (1998)
8. Barabási, A. L., Albert, R.: Emergence of scaling in random networks. Science, 286 (1999) 509–512
9. Pissanetzky, S.: Sparse matrix technology. London: Academic Press (1984)

10. Lewis, D. D., Yang, Y., Rose, T., Li, F.: RCV1: a new benchmark collection for text categorization research. Journal of Machine Learning Research **5** (2004) 361–397
11. Lang, K.: NewsWeeder: Learning to filter netnews. In Proceedings of the 12th International Conference on Machine Learning, ICML'95 (1995) 331–339
12. Kohonen, T., Kaski, S., Lagus, K., Salojärvi, J., Honkela, J., Paatero, V., Saarela, A.: Self organization of a massive document collection. In IEEE Transactions on Neural Networks, Vol. 11, **3** (2000) 574–585
13. Wermter, S., Hung, C.: Selforganising classification on the Reuters news corpus. The 19th International Conference on Computational Linguistics (COLING 2002), Taipei, Taiwan (2002) 1086–1092
14. Larsen, B., Aone, C.: Fast and effective text mining using linear-time document clustering. In Proc. of the 5th ACM SIGKDD Int. Conf. on Knowledge Discovery and Data Mining (1999) 16–22

Time-Varying Prototype Reduction Schemes Applicable for Non-stationary Data Sets[*]

Sang-Woon Kim[1] and B. John Oommen[2]

[1] *Senior Member, IEEE*, Dept. of Computer Science and Engineering,
Myongji University, Yongin 449-728 Korea
kimsw@mju.ac.kr
[2] *Fellow of the IEEE*, School of Computer Science, Carleton University,
Ottawa, ON, K1S 5B6, Canada
oommen@scs.carleton.ca

Abstract. All of the Prototype Reduction Schemes (PRS) which have been reported in the literature, process *time-invariant* data to yield a subset of prototypes that are useful in nearest-neighbor-like classification. In this paper, we suggest two time-varying PRS mechanisms which, in turn, are suitable for two *distinct* models of non-stationarity. In both of these models, rather than process all the data as a whole set using a PRS, we propose that the information gleaned from a previous PRS computation be enhanced to yield the prototypes for the current data set, and this enhancement is accomplished using a LVQ3-type "fine tuning". The experimental results, which to our knowledge are the first reported results applicable for PRS schemes suitable for non-stationary data, are, in our opinion, very impressive.

Keywords : Prototype Reduction Schemes (PRS), Time Varying Samples (TVS), Nonstatinoary Environments, Hybrid-type Prototype Reduction.

1 Introduction

Over the past five decade numerous families and avenues of statistical Pattern Recognition (PR) systems have been developed. The general model of computation has been the following: The system is provided with a set of data represented in terms of its features. Using these so-called "training samples", the system builds a classifier which is, for example, of a parametric form, or the non-parametric form. Subsequently, data to be tested is provided, and the quality of the classifier is measured by quantifying the accuracy by which these samples are classified. We emphasize, though, that traditionally, all classifiers assume that the training samples and their underlying distribution are stationary.

---

[*] The first author was partially supported by KOSEF, the Korea Science and Engineering Foundation, and the second author was partially supported by NSERC, Natural Sciences and Engineering Research Council of Canada.

In this paper, we suggest two time-varying PRS mechanisms which can be utilized for applications involving non-stationary data. Such data is typical of video and multimedia applications, in which the objects to be recognized move in space, or change with time. In particular, we propose two methods to tackle non-stationarity, which, in turn, are suitable for two *distinct* models of non-stationarity. In the first model, we assume that the data points obtained at discrete time steps, are individually perturbed in the feature space, because of *noise in the measurements* or features. In the second model, however, we assume that, at discrete time steps, new data points, which are themselves generated due to a non-stationarity in the *parameters* of the feature space, are available. The solution we advocate is the following : In both of these cases, rather than process all the data as a whole set using a PRS to yield a "time-varying set of prototypes", we propose that the information gleaned from a previous PRS computation be enhanced to yield the prototypes for the current data set, and this enhancement is accomplished using an LVQ3-type "fine tuning".

In non-parametric pattern classification which use the Nearest Neighbour (NN) or the $k-$NN rule, each class is described using a set of sample prototypes, and the class of an unknown vector is decided based on the identity of the closest neighbour(s) which are found among all the prototypes. To reduce the number of training vectors, various PRSs have been reported in the literature - two excellent surveys are found in [1], [3]. Rather than embark on yet another survey of the field, we mention here a *few* representative methods of the "zillions" that have been reported. One of the first of its kind is the Condensed Nearest Neighbour (CNN) rule [8]. The reduced set produced by the CNN, however, customarily includes "interior" samples, which can be completely eliminated, without altering the performance of the resultant classifier. Accordingly, other methods have been proposed successively, such as the Reduced Nearest Neighbour (RNN) rule [7], the Prototypes for Nearest Neighbour (PNN) classifiers [2], the Selective Nearest Neighbour (SNN) rule [17], two modifications of the CNN [18], the Edited Nearest Neighbour (ENN) rule [5], and the non-parametric data reduction method [6]. Besides these, in [19], the Vector Quantization (VQ) and the Bootstrap [9] techniques and Support Vector Machines (SVM) [11] have also been reported as being extremely effective approaches to data reduction.

In selecting prototypes, vectors near the boundaries between the classes have to be considered to be more significant, and the created prototypes need to be adjusted towards the classification boundaries so as to yield a higher performance. Based on this philosophy, we recently proposed a new hybrid approach that involved two distinct phases, namely, selecting and adjusting [14], [15]. To overcome the computational burden for "large" datasets, we also proposed a recursive PRS mechanism in [16]. In [16], the data set is sub-divided recursively into smaller subsets to filter out the "useless" internal points. Subsequently, a conventional PRS processes the smaller subsets of data points that effectively sample the entire space to yield *subsets* of prototypes – one set of prototypes for each subset. The prototypes, which result from each subset, are then coalesced, and processed again by the PRS to yield more refined prototypes. In this manner, prototypes which are in the interior of the Voronoi boundaries, and are thus ineffective in the classification, are eliminated at the subsequent invocations of the PRS. As a result, the processing time of the PRS is *significantly* reduced.

2 Prototype Reduction Schemes for Non-stationary Data

2.1 Models of Non-stationarity

Let us suppose that at time 't' the system is presented with a data set $S_i(t)$, which represents the samples of class ω_i as measured at 't'. The jth sample in this set is $x_{i,j}(t)$. We propose the following two models for capturing non-stationarity.

Noisy Measurement Non-stationarity. In this model of non-stationarity we assume that the sample $x_{i,j}$ is obtained by a noisy perturbation on the sample at time 't'. This perturbation can be perceived as the inclusion of some additional noise[1] $\theta_1(t+1)$, and thus we write:

$$x_{i,j}(t+1) = x_{i,j}(t) + \theta_1(t+1), \quad (1)$$

$$S_i(t+1) = \bigcup x_{i,j}(t+1). \quad (2)$$

Typically, each data point $x_{i,j}(t+1)$ is in the neighbourhood of $x_{i,j}(t)$ as shown in Figure 1(a). We present an example for the two-dimensional data set referred to as "Random", which is generated randomly with a uniform distribution, but with irregular decision boundaries [16]. In this case, the points are generated uniformly, and the assignment of the points to the respective classes is achieved by *artificially* assigning them to the region they fall into, as per the manually created "irregular decision boundary". The set of just 10 sample vectors is generated for the samples of the Class '1' (which are represented by '*' in the picture) and the same number of 10 sample vectors for points of Class '2' (which are represented by '·' in the picture).

To demonstrate the properties of the mechanism, after generating the $x_{i,j}(t)$, $i = 1, 2, j = 1, \cdots, 10$, samples, we again generate "time-varying" points, $x_{i,j}(t+1)$, $i = 1, 2, j = 1, \cdots, 10$, using the model of non-stationarity, which are represented by '⊗' and '⊙', respectively. Observe that in this example, the discriminant function also changes with time, but is essentially a perturbed variation of the discriminant function at the previous time instant.

Noisy Parameter Non-stationarity. This is a more fundamental model of non-stationarity, in which the data at time '$t+1$' is not just generated from perturbing the data at time 't'. Rather, in this second model, the *entire* set at time '$t+1$' is obtained, as it were, by being generated by a random sample generator, whose *parameters* are perturbed versions of the *parameters* from 't'.

---
[1] $\theta_1(\cdot)$ and $\theta_2(\cdot)$ refer to the noise generation random variables associated with Models 1 and 2 respectively.

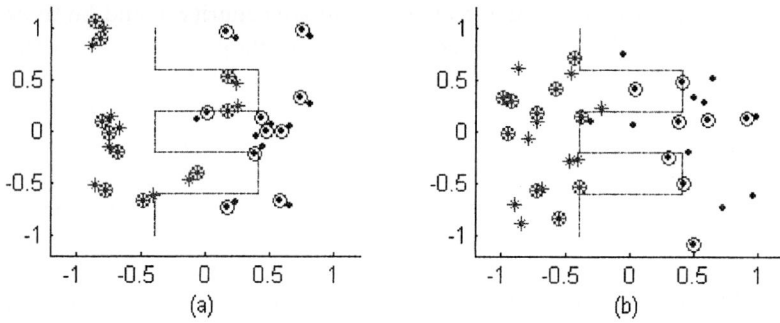

Fig. 1. *Two* Non-stationarity models. (a) "Noisy Measurement Model" samples. (b) "Noisy Parameter Model" samples. The details of the figure are found in the text.

To show how this model works, let us suppose that at time 't' the system is presented with a data set $S_i(t)$, which represents the samples of class ω_i as measured at 't'. Again, the jth sample in this set is $x_{i,j}(t)$. In this model of non-stationarity, we assume that the entire sample set $S_i(t+1)$ is obtained by a noisy perturbation on the sample set $S_i(t)$ at time 't'. This perturbation can be perceived as the inclusion of some additional noise, $\theta_2(t+1)$ (which is typically a vector) on the *parameters* of the distribution of $S_i(t)$. Thus we write:

$$Parameters[S_i(t+1)] = Parameters[S_i(t)] + \theta_2(t+1). \tag{3}$$

We again present an example for the two-dimensional data set referred to as "Random", which is generated randomly with a uniform distribution, but with irregular decision boundaries. Typically, in this case, the data point $x_{i,j}(t+1)$ need not be in the neighbourhood of $x_{i,j}(t)$ as shown in Figure 1(b), although the parameters (the mean and the covariance) at time '$t+1$' are perturbed versions of the same parameters at time 't'.

2.2 Schema for the Proposed Solutions

As mentioned earlier, in this paper we deal with the non-parametric model of PR. Thus, we seek to attain to the classification by a nearest-neighbour-like decision rule. In this setting, the most naive method to handle non-stationarity is to not consider any variation at all[2]. In this case, the prototypes[3] obtained from $S_i(0)$ are used to achieve the classification at all future time instants. Thus, if $P_i(0)$ is the set of prototypes representing class ω_i, the classification is achieved by a nearest-neighbour-like decision rule involving $P_i(0)$, for all i, and for all t.

---

[2] Pattern recognition systems which use traditional PRS methods would, typically, resort to such a philosophy.

[3] Throughout this section, we assume that the user has access to any of the previously mentioned PRSs. Thus, s/he may choose to use the CNN, the PNN, the HYB or any "pet" PRS scheme from the ones mentioned earlier to yield his/her current prototypes. Our intention is to enhance the prototypes obtained by invoking *this* PRS, by incorporating the information in $S(t+1)$.

A more sophisticated method to handle non-stationarity would be to update $P_i(t)$ from the samples of the classes currently available. Thus, when the new set of data $S_i(t+1)$ is available, the system would invoke a PRS afresh for the new data, and effectively treat the problem as a brand new pattern classification problem. Thus, if $P_i(t)$ is the set of prototypes representing class ω_i, at time t, at time $t+1$ the classification is achieved by a nearest-neighbour-like decision rule involving $P_i(t+1)$, for all i, where the latter is obtained by performing a PRS on $\bigcup S_i(t+1)$. We believe that this is an expensive strategy. Furthermore, we believe that any "intelligent" system must be capable of utilizing the information in $P_i(t)$ in its effort to compute $P_i(t+1)$. This is what we attempt to accomplish here by invoking an LVQ3-type scheme[4].

2.3 Updating PRS for the Noisy Measurement Non-stationarity

For the Noisy Measurement Non-stationarity, we propose that the new prototypes at time $t+1$ be obtained by fine-tuning the prototypes $\{P_i(t+1)\}$ by invoking an LVQ3-type enhancement on $\{P_i(t)\}$. This fine-tuning is achieved by moving the prototypes in the feature space without invoking a PRS on $S_i(t+1)$. Thus, the set $S_i(t+1)$ is directly presented to the existing prototypes, $P_i(t)$, and they, in turn, are migrated so as to optimize the recognition accuracy of the testing samples. The fine-tuning *Adjusting* is performed as $P_i(t+1) \leftarrow P_i(t) \bigotimes S_i(t+1)$, $(t = 0, 1, \cdots, T-1)$, which means that the prototype subset $P_i(t)$ was adjusted with the time-variant data set measured at time $t+1$, $S_i(t+1)$, using an LVQ3-type algorithm after selecting initial prototypes, $P_i(0)$, from a given data set, $S_i(0)$, by using a conventional PRS method.

2.4 Updating PRS for the Noisy Parameter Non-stationarity

For updating PRS for the Noisy Parameter Non-stationarity, we have two methods as follows: (1) Using the same PRS method applied to the Noisy Measurement Non-stationarity, and (2) Using a new PRS method in which the prototypes are obtained from adjusting the previous prototypes, $P(t)$, with the current ones, $P(t+1)$, not with $S(t+1)$.

In the second method itemized above, the new prototypes at time $t+1$ are obtained by two steps: First, we obtain crude values of $\{P_i(t+1)\}$ for every class i, and then we fine-tune these crude prototypes $\{P_i(t+1)\}$ by invoking an LVQ3-type enhancement on $\{P_i(t)\}$. This fine-tuning is done by moving the prototypes at time t in the feature space by using the information found in the crude values, $P_i(t+1)$ and not the entire set $S_i(t+1)$. Thus, the crude set $P_i(t+1)$ is directly

---

[4] Unfortunately, space does not permit us to describe *how an LVQ3-type updating can be achieved*, but we refer the reader to [10], where this process is described in detail. In LVQ3, the updating rules ensure that the code-book vectors continue to approximate the respective class distributions, and simultaneously enhance the quality of the classification boundary. However, the more crucial issue is that of determining the parameters of the LVQ3, and this is described, in detail, in [14], [15] and [16].

presented to the existing prototypes, $P_i(t)$, and they, in turn, are migrated so as to optimize the recognition accuracy of the testing samples.

3 Experimental Verification

Experimental Data. The *time-varying* PRS has been tested fairly extensively, and compared with many conventional PRSs on both real and artificial data sets. The time-varying data sets consist of *four* subsets which have been generated randomly with two kinds of non-stationary data models, *Model 1* and *Model 2*. In our experiments, the two data sets "Non_normal 2" and "Non_normal 3" (in short, "Non2" and "Non3"), were generated with different sizes of testing and training sets of cardinality 500 and 5,000 respectively. The data sets "Arrhythmia" (in short, "Arrh") and "Adult4" (in short, "Adul"), which are real benchmark data sets, are cited from the UCI Machine Learning Repository [12].

The data set named "Non_normal", first of all, was generated from a mixture of four 8-dimensional Gaussian distributions as follows: $p_1(x) = \frac{1}{2}N(\mu_{11}, I_8) + \frac{1}{2}N(\mu_{12}, I_8), p_2(x) = \frac{1}{2}N(\mu_{21}, I_8) + \frac{1}{2}N(\mu_{22}, I_8)$, where $\mu_{11} = [0, 0, \cdots, 0]$, $\mu_{12} = [6.58, 0, \cdots, 0]$, $\mu_{21} = [3.29, 0, \cdots, 0]$ and $\mu_{22} = [9.87, 0, \cdots, 0]$. In these expressions, I_8 is the *8*-dimensional *Identity* matrix [9], [19]. The "Arrh" data set contains 279 attributes, 206 of which are real-valued and the rest are nominal. In our experiments, the nominal features were replaced by zeros. The aim of the PR exercise was to classify the feature into one of the 16 groups. In our case, in the interest of uniformity, we merely attempted to classify the total instances into two categories, namely, "normal" and "abnormal". The "Adul" data set was extracted from a census bureau database [12]. The aim of the PR task here is to separate people by incomes into two groups. Each sample vector has fourteen attributes. The total number of samples is 33,330. Due to time considerations, however, we randomly selected 8,336 samples - approximately 25 % of the set.

The above artificial and real-life benchmark data sets are used to generate their four *time-varying* data sets, $S(t)$, $t = 1, \cdots, 4$, using the two kinds of non-stationary data models, namely, the Noisy Measurement Non-stationarity and the Noisy Parameter Non-stationarity. In the Noisy Measurement Non-stationarity (which is refereed to Model '1' in the experimental results of next sections), their four *time-varying* data sets are generated as follows: At first, we calculate the variance, Var, of a given data set, $S(0)$. Then, we randomly generate its first *time-varying* data set, $S(1)$ as: $S(1) \leftarrow S(0) + Var * (1 + rand)$; Here, the function *rand* is to generate an array of random numbers whose elements are normally distributed with mean 0 and variance 1. Finally, we repeat the above procedures to generate *time-varying* data sets $S(t+1)$ from $S(t)$, $t = 1, \cdots, T$.

In the Noisy Parameter Non-stationarity (which is referred to as Model '2' in the experimental results), the four *time-varying* data sets are generated as follows: At first, for every class i, we calculate the mean and standard deviation, μ_i and σ_i, of a given data set, $S(0)$. Then, we randomly generate its first *time-varying* data set, $S(1)$ as: $\mu_i \leftarrow \mu_i * (1 + rand)$; $\sigma_i \leftarrow \sigma_i * (1 + rand)$; $S(1) \leftarrow Normal(\mu_i, \sigma_i)$, where the *Normal* is a function to generate Normal (Gaussian) random numbers with the μ_i and the σ_i. Finally, we repeat the above procedures to generate *time-varying* data sets $S(t+1)$ from $S(t)$, $t = 1, \cdots, T$.

In the above data sets, all of the vectors were normalized using their standard deviations. Also, for every class i, the data set for the class was randomly split into two subsets, $S_{i,T}(t)$ and $S_{i,V}(t)$ of equal size. One of them was used for choosing initial code-book vectors and training the classifiers as explained earlier, and the other subset was used in the validation (or testing) of the classifiers. The roles of these sets were later interchanged.

In this case, we employed just three PRSs, namely the CNN[5], PNN and HYB[6] so as to evaluate the strengths and weaknesses of the current algorithms.

The LVQ3 Parameters. In the proposed method, the $P(t+1)$ is obtained by adjusting $P(t)$ using an LVQ3-type algorithm with $S(t+1)$, where the LVQ3 parameters such as the related window width, w, the relative learning rate, ϵ, the learning rate, α and the number of iteration steps, η, play an important role in the classification task. In this experiment, the optimal or near-optimal parameters of w^*, ϵ^*, α^* and η^* were determined by repeating the "pseudo-testing" [14], [15], [16] by adjusting the Δw, $\Delta \epsilon$, $\Delta \alpha$ and setting $\eta = 100$. The LVQ3 parameters employed for the *proposed* PRS algorithms for the "Non2", "Non3", "Arrh" and "Adul", are omitted here, but can be found in [13].

The Classification Accuracy. We report below the classification accuracy rates of the *proposed* PRS algorithms for some "Medium-sized" time-varying data sets. Table 1 shows the experimental results of the conventional CNN and the proposed CNN for the time-varying "Artificial" and "Real-life" data sets, namely, "Non2", "Non3", "Arrh" and "Adul" in succession. In the table, the first column, '1' and '2', is the results for the "Noisy Measurement Model" and the "Noisy Parameter Model", respectively. Also, the first row for each model, that is, $P(t)$, is the number of prototype vectors extracted from the data sets of $S_T(t)$ and $S_V(t)$, $t = 0, \cdots, 4$, respectively. Finally, the abbreviations *Ex1*, *Ex2* and *Ex3* are evaluation methods for the classification accuracy employed in this experimentation. In *Ex1*, the prototypes $P(0)$ of the source data set $S(0)$, are constantly used as the prototypes of the four "Non-stationary" data sets,

---

[5] It appears from the literature that the CNN method by Hart is not the *best* competitor for prototype selection in terms of both accuracy *and* effectiveness. We have chosen this method over the methods surveyed in [1], [3] because of its relative simplicity and ease of implementation.

[6] Here, we employed SVM [11], as a *pre-processing* PRS of the HYB method. As is well known, the SVM does reduce the set of prototypes, but not for the nearest neighbor method. This means that the set of prototypes, which are also the *support vectors* obtained through the SVM method could be absolutely useless with 1-NN. All the other methods considered in this paper are supposed to select a reference set suitable for the 1-NN method. Indeed, from this perspective, SVM belongs to a completely different group! Thus, although it is, in one sense, inappropriate for testing it as a basic PRS method, it has advantages if it is used recursively. This is the rationale for including it in our test suite.

Table 1. The classification accuracy rates (%) of the time-varying CNN for the artificial and real-life data sets, "Non2", "Non3", "Arrh" and "Adul" in succession. Here, the "1" and "2" in the first column represent the "Model 1" and "Model 2" of each data set. The two Acc's of $Original$ set refer to the results when the source training and valuation sets, $S_T(0)$ and $S_V(0)$, are then interchanged. Also, the Acc's of Non-$stationary$ data sets are the classification accuracies (%) for the corresponding data sets, $S_T(t)$ and $S_V(t)$, $t = 1, \cdots, 4$, respectively. The results reported in the final column, $\overline{Acc}$, are the average Acc rates (%). Then, the two 'integer' numerics of the $P(t)$ row of each data set, are the numbers of prototypes extracted from the data sets of $S_T(t)$ and $S_V(t)$, $t = 0, \cdots, 4$, respectively. Finally, the abbreviations $Ex1$, $Ex2$ and $Ex3$ are evaluation methods for the classification accuracy employed in this experimentation.

# of Model	Eval Meth	Acc of Original Set	Acc of Non-stationary Data Sets				
			$S_T(1), S_V(1)$	$S_T(2), S_V(2)$	$S_T(3), S_V(3)$	$S_T(4), S_V(4)$	$\overline{Acc}$
Non2	$P(t)$	64, 66	64, 83	73, 107	105, 112	103, 118	
1	$Ex1$	92.60, 91.20	90.20, 90.20	86.00, 84.20	82.80, 78.20	77.00, 74.20	82.85
	$Ex2$	92.60, 91.20	91.60, 90.20	90.00, 89.40	89.00, 88.80	88.40, 88.80	89.53
	$Ex3$	92.60, 91.20	93.00, 93.00	92.40, 90.40	90.40, 90.60	89.00, 89.00	90.98
	$P(t)$	64, 66	169, 150	236, 217	246, 216	237, 241	
2	$Ex1$	92.60, 91.20	72.00, 70.00	60.60, 57.00	52.80, 53.60	53.80, 53.20	59.13
	$Ex2$	92.60, 91.20	82.80, 80.20	71.60, 73.20	70.60, 69.00	67.40, 65.60	72.55
	$Ex3$	92.60, 91.20	81.60, 84.80	74.20, 78.80	72.60, 75.60	70.80, 72.00	76.30
Non3	$P(t)$	503, 477	5000, 5000	5000, 5000	5000, 5000	5000, 5000	
1	$Ex1$	91.74, 91.88	89.44, 90.84	85.82, 87.22	80.12, 81.10	75.26, 76.66	83.31
	$Ex2$	91.74, 91.88	90.48, 90.80	89.20, 89.44	86.90, 87.02	85.40, 85.72	88.12
	$Ex3$	91.74, 91.88	89.78, 90.80	87.46, 88.68	85.54, 85.96	85.26, 84.28	87.22
	$P(t)$	503, 477	5000, 5000	5000, 5000	5000, 5000	5000, 5000	
2	$Ex1$	91.74, 91.88	73.30, 73.42	60.08, 59.18	54.96, 54.38	52.50, 52.76	60.07
	$Ex2$	91.74, 91.88	81.46, 81.64	75.54, 76.20	72.02, 71.40	70.14, 69.58	74.75
	$Ex3$	91.74, 91.88	82.48, 84.48	81.82, 81.24	78.34, 78.94	78.68, 76.00	80.25
Arrh	$P(t)$	31, 31	34, 33	27, 31	40, 44	40, 42	
1	$Ex1$	95.58, 97.79	87.61, 95.58	78.32, 93.36	67.70, 78.32	61.95, 67.26	78.76
	$Ex2$	95.58, 97.79	93.81, 92.04	91.59, 95.13	89.82, 92.92	88.50, 90.71	91.81
	$Ex3$	95.58, 97.79	98.67, 99.12	98.23, 97.79	96.90, 96.02	97.79, 96.46	97.62
	$P(t)$	31, 31	31, 33	34, 37	55, 25	37, 31	
2	$Ex1$	95.58, 97.79	80.53, 80.53	64.16, 65.49	57.97, 62.83	58.85, 57.08	65.93
	$Ex2$	95.58, 97.79	95.13, 93.36	92.04, 84.96	87.61, 84.96	92.48, 81.42	89.00
	$Ex3$	95.58, 97.79	99.56, 98.67	99.12, 97.79	98.23, 97.35	96.46, 92.04	97.40
Adul	$P(t)$	743, 737	772, 766	837, 818	831, 797	841, 850	
1	$Ex1$	91.10, 91.55	91.48, 91.65	93.16, 91.94	93.57, 92.06	94.22, 92.27	92.54
	$Ex2$	91.10, 91.55	90.19, 88.65	89.25, 89.11	89.23, 88.55	88.48, 89.08	89.07
	$Ex3$	91.10, 91.55	92.35, 91.19	93.50, 92.25	93.45, 92.95	93.78, 92.78	92.78
	$P(t)$	743, 737	592, 536	581, 655	645, 615	638, 665	
2	$Ex1$	91.10, 91.55	93.23, 92.01	94.55, 90.69	94.91, 93.57	94.88, 90.52	93.05
	$Ex2$	91.10, 91.55	89.92, 88.34	88.75, 87.62	88.67, 88.31	87.43, 87.45	88.31
	$Ex3$	91.10, 91.55	93.09, 93.98	94.43, 93.62	94.53, 93.98	94.62, 94.43	94.09

$S(t)$, $t = 1, \cdots, 4$. Then, in *Ex2*, the prototypes $P(t)$ at time t are extracted directly from the corresponding data set $S(t)$ using a conventional PRS algorithm. Finally, *Ex3* is obtained using the "*time-varying*" PRS proposed in this paper.

Consider the results for the '1' model of the "Non2" data set. First of all, the training 500 samples and the testing 500 samples, namely, $S_T(0)$ and $S_V(0)$, were reduced into 64 and 66, points respectively. Also the first non-stationary data sets, $S_T(1)$ and $S_V(1)$, were condensed into 64 and 83 points, respectively. Also, the prototypes of the other non-stationary subsets, namely, $S_T(t)$ and $S_V(t)$, $t = 2, 3, 4$, are 73 and 107 ($t = 2$), 105 and 112 ($t = 3$), and 103 and 118 ($t = 4$), respectively. The resulting averaged classification accuracies, $\overline{Acc}$, of the *Ex1*, *Ex2* and *Ex3*, which have been calculated from the *eight* Acc's of the corresponding non-stationary data sets, are $82.85, 89.53$, and 90.98%, respectively.

For the PNN and HYB methods[7], the same accuracy characteristics can be observed for both Models '1' and '2'. From these considerations, we can see a comparison of the results obtained with the *Ex1*, *Ex2* and *Ex3* methods. The comparison demonstrates that the prototype vectors of the *non-stationary* data sets can be extracted efficiently by employing the proposed philosophy. Indeed, such accuracy results are also typical of all the data sets used.

The Time Complexity. We report below the time complexity of the *proposed* PRS algorithms. Consider the PNN method for the *four* data sets, namely, "Non2", "Non3", "Arrh" and "Adul". First of all, for Model '1', the averaged CPU-times for the *Ex2* and *Ex3* are 0.30 and 0.01 *minutes*, 315.69 and 4.79 *mins*, 1.05 and 0.02 *mins*, and 394.58 and 1.09 *mins*, respectively. Then, for Model '2', the averaged CPU-times for the *Ex2* and *Ex3* are 0.35 and 0.01 *mins*, 428.54 and 4.72 *mins*, 1.01 and 0.02 *mins*, and 184.23 and 1.10 *mins*, respectively. For both Models '1' and '2' in the HYB method, the same characteristics can be observed from the results of the *four* data sets. From these considerations[8], the reader should observe that the proposed philosophy of *Ex3* needs less time than that of *Ex2* in the cases of the PNN and HYB methods.

4 Conclusions

In this paper we have proposed a mechanism applicable for the non-stationary data sets. In the proposed time-varying PRS method, the prototypes of the non-stationary data versions of a given data set, can be obtained by adjusting the *previous* prototypes with the *current* non-stationary data set using an LVQ3-type algorithm. The proposed method was tested on both artificial and real-life benchmark time-varying data sets, and compared with a few representative conventional methods. The experimental results for small and medium-sized non-stationary data sets demonstrate that the proposed algorithm can improve

---

[7] The experimental results of the PNN and HYB methods for the "Non2", "Non3", "Arrh" and "Adul" data sets are omitted here, but can be found in [13].
[8] The time for using the CNN as the kernel is excessive and so is not included here. The results of the HYB method is also omitted here, but can be found in [13].

the reduction rate of the conventional PRSs such as the CNN, PNN and HYB methods, and that their classification accuracies are comparable, although they require almost the same or less CPU-times.

References

1. J. C. Bezdek and L. I. Kuncheva, "Nearest prototype classifier designs: An experimental study", *Int'l., J. of Intell. Syst.*, vol. 16, no. 12, pp. 1445 - 1473, 2001.
2. C. L. Chang, "Finding prototypes for nearest neighbour classifiers", *IEEE Trans. Computers*, vol. C-23, no. 11, pp. 1179 - 1184, Nov. 1974.
3. B. V. Dasarathy, *Nearest Neighbour (NN) Norms: NN Pattern Classification Techniques*, IEEE Computer Society Press, Los Alamitos, 1991.
4. B. V. Dasarathy, "Minimal Consistent Set (MCS) identification for optimal nearest neighbor decision systems design", *IEEE Trans. Systems, Man, and Cybernetics*, vol. 24, no. 3, pp. 511 - 517, Mar. 1994.
5. P. A. Devijver and J. Kittler, "On the edited nearest neighbour rule", *Proc. 5th Int. Conf. on Pattern Recognition*, pp. 72 - 80, Dec. 1980.
6. K. Fukunaga and J. M. Mantock, "Nonparametric data reduction", *IEEE Trans. Pattern Anal. and Machine Intell.*, vol. PAMI-6, no. 1, pp. 115 - 118, Jan. 1984.
7. G. W. Gates, "The reduced nearest neighbour rule", *IEEE Trans. Inform. Theory*, vol. IT-18, pp. 431 - 433, May 1972.
8. P. E. Hart, "The condensed nearest neighbour rule", *IEEE Trans. Inform. Theory*, vol. IT-14, pp. 515 - 516, May 1968.
9. Y. Hamamoto, S. Uchimura and S. Tomita, "A bootstrap technique for nearest neighbour classifier design", *IEEE Trans. Pattern Anal. and Machine Intell.*, vol. PAMI-19, no. 1, pp. 73 - 79, Jan. 1997.
10. http://cochlea.hut.fi/research/som_lvq_pak.shtml
11. http://svm.research.bell−labs.com/SVMdoc.html
12. http://www.ics.uci.edu/mlearn/MLRepository.html.
13. S.-W. Kim and B. J. Oommen, "Time-Varying Prototype Reduction Schemes Applicable for Non-stationary Data Sets". *Pattern Recognition*.
14. S. -W. Kim and B. J. Oommen, "Enhancing prototype reduction schemes with LVQ3-type algorithms", *Pattern Recognition*, vol. 36, no. 5, pp. 1083 - 1093, 2003.
15. S. -W. Kim and B. J. Oommen, "A Brief Taxonomy and Ranking of Creative Prototype Reduction Schemes", *Pattern Analysis and Applications*, vol. 6, no. 3, pp. 232 - 244, December 2003.
16. S. -W. Kim and B. J. Oommen, "Enhancing Prototype Reduction Schemes with Recursion : A Method Applicable for "Large" Data Sets", *IEEE Trans. Systems, Man, and Cybernetics - Part B*, vol. SMC-34, no. 3, pp. 1384 - 1397, June 2004.
17. G. L. Ritter, H. B. Woodruff, S. R. Lowry and T. L. Isenhour, "An algorithm for a selective nearest neighbour rule", *IEEE Trans. Inform. Theory*, vol. IT-21, pp. 665 - 669, Nov. 1975.
18. I. Tomek, "Two modifications of CNN", *IEEE Trans. Syst., Man and Cybern.*, vol. SMC-6, no. 6, pp. 769 - 772, Nov. 1976.
19. Q. Xie, C.A. Laszlo and R. K. Ward, "Vector quantization techniques for nonparametric classifier design", *IEEE Trans. Pattern Anal. and Machine Intell.*, vol. PAMI-15, no. 12, pp. 1326 - 1330, Dec. 1993.

Multi-agent System Simulating Tumoral Cells Migration

Lynda Dib[1], Zahia Guessoum[2,3], Noël Bonnet[3], and Mohamed T. Laskri[1]

[1] University Badji Mokhtar, Computer science department, BP12 Annaba, Algeria
diblynda@yahoo.fr
[2] LIP6, University of Paris 6
Zahia.Guessoum@lip6.fr
[3] CReSTIC, University of Rheims

Abstract. The migration of tumoral Cells through the biological barrier constitutes the major dynamic event of tumoral invasion. This article presents the CellMigration system that we have realized under multi-agent platform (oriented object) DIMA. CellMigration simulates the migratory behaviour of tumoral Cells in describing the specific factor called AMF, the molecules of adhesion "integrine" and molecules of dissociation "protease"...

1 Introduction

If the cells are generally rather home bird, the desire may sometimes lead them to see else where. In order to study the behaviour of cellular populations, the biologists often use the microscopy-video. This study is based on samples and need enough time. On the other side, the sample modification to change the parameters is impossible. This work is inscribed in a multi-agent platform which aims are the modelisation and simulation of cellular populations. The observed collectives behaviours will be then confronted by the biologists to the observations and to the quantitative data results obtained in video-microscopy. This step allows refining the biologic models existed notably in tumoral invasion. Several models have been proposed for the study of the cellular behaviour as the model of automaton cellular [2], the based agent model [4] and the mathematical model [5]. In our approach, we propose CellMigration a multi-agent model of cellular populations that offers a very powerful tool to study the behaviour of cells and their interactions. CellMigration simulates the loss of adhesion between cells in the presence of dissociation molecules "protease" then, the secretion of *AMF* factor[1] by tumoral cells themselves which stimulate the formation of pseudopodia extensions before the migration of the whole cell, and finally, it stimulates the surface protein "integrine" responsible for the motility accretion of malignant cells and their invasion to the other tissue forming the metastases. This article is organized as follows: In the first section, we describe the suggested model for the realization of CellMigration system. In the second section will be devoted to the results obtained by the system.

---

[1] Factor : is a molecule secreted by the cell.

2 Multi-agent CellMigration System

The complexity of the biological system necessitates an appropriate type of simulation. For the realization of our system, we suggested to use the multi-agent system because they have properties adapted to the representation of knowledge of biological domain. The CellMigration conception goes through many steps necessitating the biological domain knowledge.

2.1 OntoCell

OntoCell is a cellular ontology that we constructed in order to represent knowledge of cellular biology [5]. Hence, OntoCell represents the concepts of cellular bases, their components, their behaviours and their interactions. It serves as a base of knowledge in the CellMigration system. The OntoCell is out of the scope of this paper, so its will not be described here.

2.2 Cellular Migration Modelisation

2.2.1 Model of the System

Our model defines a cell population by a population of AgentCell in interaction in their environment. In this model, every cell, represented by an agent *'AgentCell'*, observes and interacts with the others and try to adapt at all changes in the environment a function of its internal and external context of its current state and, this, in the aim to grow, to survive and to collaborate with all other AgentCells in its population for the realization of a common task. The environment represented by a particular class *'Environment'*, evolves dynamically to every change of cellular state. It contains a cell population, represented by a vector *'VCell'*, a certain number of molecules and resources for the cellular survival (sugar, k+...) represented by another vector *'Vmol'*. At every resource and molecule a certain number of characteristics, represented by the variables, are pre-calculated such as: *'RC'* (Rate of Concentration), antiquates the existing actual quantity of a resource or molecule in the environment. The *RC* may be increased *'TCA'* or decreased *'TCD'*. *'SeuilMin'*, *'SeuilMax'*, express a minimal, maximal limit of a resource or molecule concentration, in the environment that won't be clear. In addition to these concepts, we find another very important entity in the simulated environment; it's the extra cellular matrix. It is modelled by a simple variable and represented, in the window of study, by a straight line and thickening. This extra cellular matrix serves to support at the polarised cells and the interstitial tissue. It forms a frontier with the conjunctive tissue and plays a primordial role in the cellular migration being the first rampart against tumoral invasion.

2.2.2 Model of the Cell

A cell (AgentCell) is principally defined by a group of characteristics represented by the variables (*numCell, free, extMem....*) a position *'pos'*, and a group of junctions that the cell establishes with their neighbours in the environment. (see figure1).

In CellMigration, these junctions are modelled by the class *'Junction'* and represented, in the window of study, by a single black link (see figure2). The behaviour of the cell is described according to its *normal or abnormal state*.

1. Behaviour of a healthy cell in a *"normal"* functioning: an adult healthy tissue in a normal functioning is constituted of cells in different states (*differentiated* : the cell is functioning or is maturating, *proliferated* : the cell is in cycle, *quiescent* : the cell is latent growing toward the differentiation or the proliferation according to the present factors or *dead* : the end of the cell life).
2. Behaviour of tumoral cell in *"abnormal"* functioning: the cell become abnormal when it escapes to all regulations. A tumoral adult tissue in abnormal functioning is constituted of cells in different states: *benign tumours* in which the cells look like normal cells remaining confined in the safe tissues and *malignant tumour*: habitually less good differentiated with the cells of benign tumours. They do not remain located because they invade the environment tissue and get ready to proliferate of their original site in order to form metastases.

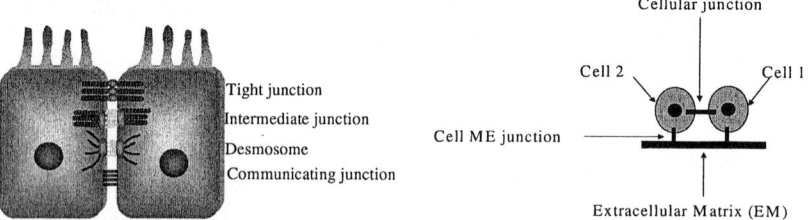

Fig. 1. Biological Cell/Cell Junctions **Fig. 2.** Cellular Junctions in CellMigration

2.3 Simulation of CellMigration

The tumoral invasion constituted the major characteristics of malignant tumours that they distinguish benign tumours.

2.3.1 Generation of Safe AgentCells Population
The union makes strength; this is the word order in the healthy cells. In CellMigration, they are characterized by the alignment of oriented cells and joined by different communication junctions. The simulator follows the following process:

Initially, a set of identical cells is created forming thus a healthy tissue. Every AgentCell is activated, be in a normal state, has a position in the window of study and establishes some physical links with its neighbouring. At the end, a healthy tissue in "normal" working is generated.

2.3.2 Generation of Tumoral AgentCells Population
After a time T, only one modified cell appears in the tissue. The system chooses randomly a normal cell "$AgentCell_k$" to be transformed in a tumoral one. After a time T', $AgentCell_k$ begins to proliferate and to give other tumoral cells forming a mass. The benign tumour is located and controlled, while these cells remain grouped and don't invade the surrounding tissues. In CellMigration, these cells look like the normal cells and they stay enclosed in their good tissue.

2.3.3 Generation of a Cancer

These tumoral cells become progressively malignant by secretion of the AMF factor, while generating the membrane extensions to be able to displace on the extra cellular matrix then to invade it. The malignant tumours don't stay located and encapsulated. They displace to invade the surrounding tissues. In CellMigration these cells have differentiated minus those benign tumoral cells. They separate the some of others by destruction of their junctions, give out membrane extensions, and then they begin their displacement on extra cellular matrix and invade it.

2.3.4 Cancerous Cells Movement

Cancerous cells movement is an abnormal cellular behaviour. It is conditioned by the detection of certain factors at the environmental level, so that the molecule of dissociation *'protease'*; that conducts to the destruction of cellular junctions. The migration in our system is realized by the following steps:

Step1: Dissociation Cellular Link (Pre-invasive Phase): The cellular destruction to its communicating junctions leads to a migratory state (displacement) of the cell which can lead to cancer. This destruction is done by the dissociation of the inter-AgentCell link or the dissociation of the AgentCell and extra cellular matrix link, (figure 3).

When the AgentCell destructs its links, it goes through normal state to a free state. Arriving at this state, AgentCell can start its displacement on the extra cellular matrix and cross it to invade other neighbouring tissue. As, it goes through the free state to the cancerous state.

Step2: cellular displacement (invasive phase): It is the sticking of cells in extra cellular matrix (figure 4, case A). This behaviour is realized by the three following phases:

First phase: the cell forms a great *lamellipode* and a queue retraction. These two events are important in the migratory movement (figure 4, case B).

Second phase: the displaying of the cell depends on specific cellular receptors: the molecule of adherences *'integrine'*. The initial adherence thanks to lamellipodia is followed by the anchorage of the cell on the substratum. This anchorage is mediated by many fascicules of *'integrine'* situated at the extremity of the *'actin'* fibbers (figure 4, case C).

Third phase: Once the cell leaves the site E0 and arrives at a level E1 it lets back a remain, marking its trajectory on the extra cellular matrix (see figure 4, case D).

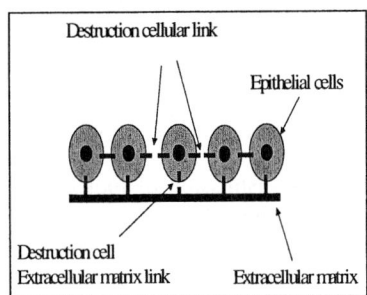

Fig. 3. Cellular Dissociation

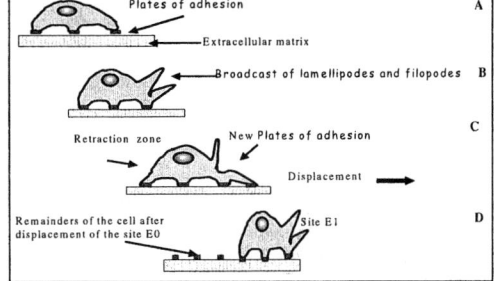

Fig. 4. AgentCell in a displacement state

The agents used in CellMigration are, at a time, reactive and communicating. They are programmed and regrouped under a package form in the platform presented here after.

3 Experimentation

Our multi-agent CellMigration system has been implemented in the DIMA environment [1]. The behaviour of DIMA regroups the classes that can be re-used and/or adapted to construct agents easily. For our system, we have used a framework of communication that integrates an ATN framework (Augmented transition Network). The ATN is an automaton that represents the agent behaviour. It is formed of transitions. Each of them is defined by a condition and an action. If the condition is verified, the agent does the corresponding action and changes the state. These signatures are the Java methods that must be implemented. It is from the characteristics of the normal cells and the cancerous cell, that the ATN concerning the normal cell and the cancerous cell has been achieved (figure 5).

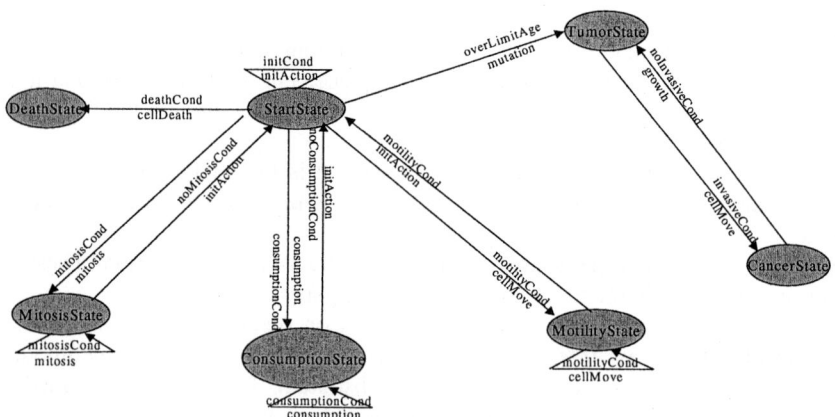

Fig. 5. Behaviour Automaton of an autonomous cell

The life cycle, represented by the method step() in DIMA, of the AgentCell is defined in the class lead like the passage of the state at an other by transition if all the conditions are reunited:

```
public void step(){CurrentState =
            curretntState.crossTransition(this);}
```

The interactions between AgentCells are made by the transmission of molecules. In our system these interactions are implemented by the messages.

The AgentCell sender look for knowing if a neighbouring AgentCell accepts to be linked. According to its attributes, it will answer "yes" or "no" (see figure 6).

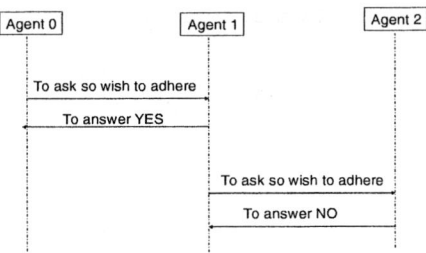

Fig. 6. Interactions diagram between cells

A message corresponds to a method of the AgentCell class. It has the following form.

```
public void adhesionAsk(AgentCell){ }
```

The communicating AgentCell reads its box to letters and treat messages that he received:

```
public void preActivity(){ ReadMailBox(); }
```

The DIMA method of the message has been redefined in CellMigration. Contrary to distributed SAM which communication is based on a service of naming (supplied by a middleware), in our system, the communication is managed by the environment. Through the identity of the AgentCell receiver, its address is recovered to send its message:

```
public void sendMessage (AbstractAgent agentId,Message m)
{CommunicationComponent com=new CommunicationCompnent (agen-
tId);
  m.setSender(this.getIdentifier());
  m.setReceiver(agentId.getIdentifier());
  com.sendMessage( (mC.getAddress(agentId)),m);
}
```

The simulator inherits the properties of the *ProactiveComponentsManager* from DIMA. As its name indicates, this class permits to manage the proactive components, therefore agents activated during the simulation. The simulator can be:

- interrupted, so agents are deactivated, by the *stopAll()* method in which each proactive agent has its value attribute alive put at false,
- activated while activating the proactive objects (*startAllSimulator() method*) like a threads.

```
for ( i = 0 ;i < proactiveObjects ; i++)
{ProactiveComponent pao=(ProactiveComponent) pv.elementAt(i);
ProactiveComponentEngine paoEngine=new ProactiveComponentEn-
gine(pao);
paoEngine.startUp();
}
```

- is recaptured while reactivating all the proactive objects present in the milieu, through the *reStartAll()* method,
- the progression of n step with the *startAllWithStep()* method.

```
for ( i = 0 ;i < stepNumber ; i++)
 {for ( j = 0 ;j < proactiveObjects ; j++)
  {ProactiveComponent pao=ProactiveComponent)pv.elementAt(i);
   if (pao.isActive()){ pao.step(); }
   else{pv.removeElement(pao); }}}
```

- the progression step by step : variant of n step ,n to the value 1,
- stop completely with the *killAll()* method and the simulation interface is then redrawn empty and the agents are withdrawn from the environment.

4 Discussion

To validate CellMigration, we have carried on many experimentations to evaluate different parameters so that the number of invasive Cells, tumoral AgentCells, and the AgentCells that die. For each simulation we have considered the following parameters:

- the simulation is initialised with the AgentCell number=100.
- initially, all AgentCell are in the *StartState* (normal state).
- the molecules (factors) exist in the environment *(Factor=true)*.
- the molecule dissociation (protease) exist in the environment *(Protease=true)*.
- the molecule of adherence (integrine) exist in the environment *(Integrine=true)*.

4.1 Evaluation of the AgentCell Number

The first test carries on the evaluation of invasive AgentCells number, knowing that these last are in different states, during the simulations times.

On the figure 7, we remark the evolution of the AgentCells number. This number is almost constant at the beginning of the simulation then it starts to grow. This can be explained by the cellular renewal (mitosis) that progress by the increase of the AgentCells numbers in the time.

4.2 Evaluation of the Tumour

This second test is carried on the evaluation of tumoral AgentCells number, during the simulations times. The figure 8 shows the evolution of tumoral AgentCell number during the simulations. This number is almost constant at the beginning of simulations. It decreases then increases slightly with the progression of simulation time.

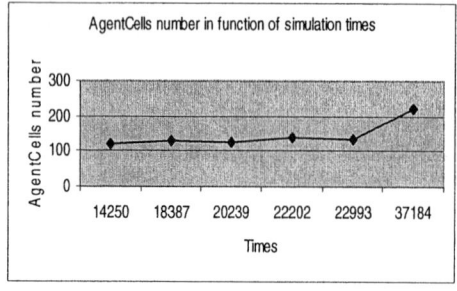

Fig. 7. Evolution of AgentCells number

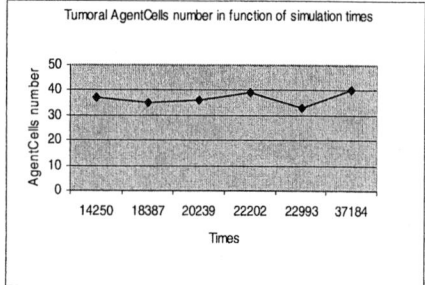

Fig. 8. Evolution of tumoral AgentCells

4.3 Evaluation of Invasion

The third test is carried on the evaluation of invasive AgentCells number during the simulations times. The figure 9 shows that the invasive AgentCells number is almost in continued progression, during the simulations times, until a very determined number. This is explained by the fast proliferation and no controlled invasive AgentCells.

4.4 Evaluation of the Mortality

This fourth test is carried on the evaluation of AgentCells number that dies after mitosis. On the figure 10, we notice that the death rate of AgentCells in the beginning simulation is in decrease. Arriving to a time 'T' this rate starts to grow. This phenomenon is explained that initially, the AgentCell are young and in cycle so to do not die. With the time progression this same AgentCell starts to grow old on that act the probability of mortality believes with the time.

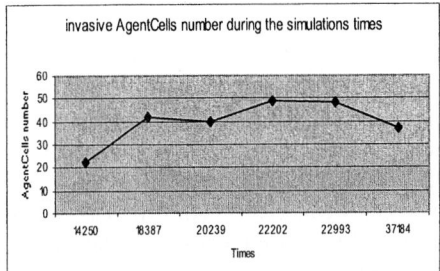
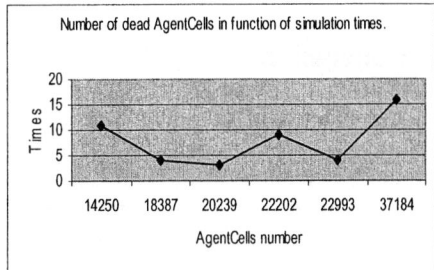

Fig. 9. Evolution of invasive AgentCells   **Fig. 10.** Evolution of AgentCells that dies

4.5 Evaluation of the Mitosis and the Consumption

This test is carried on the evaluation of AgentCells number in mitosis or consumption. On figure 11, we notice two phases respectively in the proliferation and the consumption:

– the first phase corresponds to the progression of the young AgentCells number in mitosis or in consumption until a very determined value. This can be explained by the progression of AgentCells number during simulation. So, we can say that, if the probabilities that these AgentCells proliferate or consumes the resources existing in the environment are bred than the probability of mortality decreases.
– the second phase corresponds to the regression of the AgentCells number in mitosis or in consumption. This, is explained by the ageing of the AgentCells during the time. Thus, the probability is that these AgentCells proliferate and consume resources of the environment will be decreased and this leads to the growth of the mortality of AgentCells numbers.

4.6 Motility Evaluation

The last test is carried on the evaluation of the AgentCells number in mortality. On the figure12, we remark the slight progression of the AgentCells number in motility

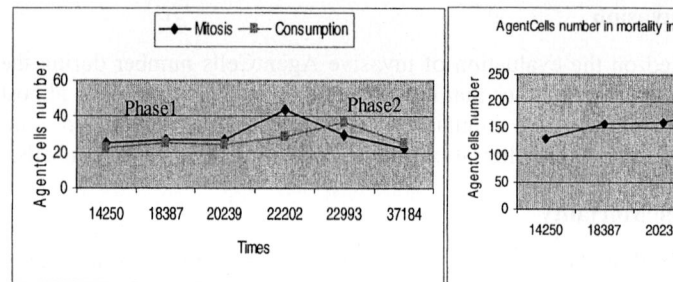

Fig. 11. Evolution of AgentCells in mitosis or consumption

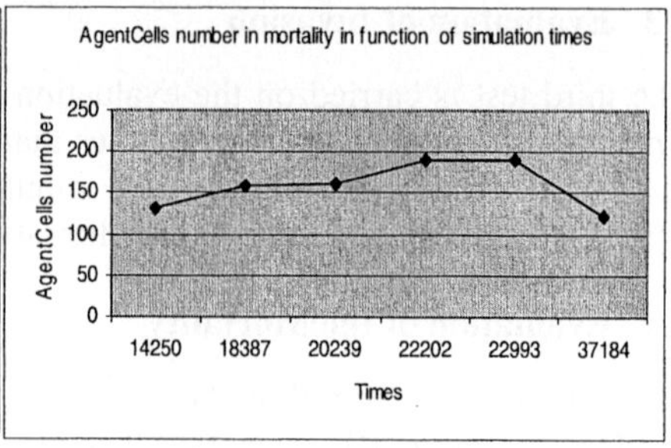

Fig. 12. Evolution of AgentCells in motility

until a value most determined then this progression remain constant a short moment to start regressing.

5 Conclusion

In this article, we presented the CellMigration system that we have realized under multi-agent platform DIMA. CellMigration permits to model and to simulate the migratory behaviour of tumoral Cells. In this system the cell is either a healthy or a cell contaminated of a benign tumour and whether a cancerous cell. This last can be free, clear extra cellular matrix, invade new site and to cause metastases. The simulation achieved by our system reflects the reality of the biologic nature.

The objective of *CellMigration* is to be a virtual world of this cellular biology helping its specialists to better understand, to good interpret and to warn changes of cell states according to its actual intern state and to the state of its environment. From CellMigration, the evolution of a cellular population in the time is calculated (under a form of a sequence of simulated images). The biologic phenomena studied are: the cellular migration, the adherence, the shape and the deformation in relation with the function.

References

1. Guessoum Z., Meurisse T., Briot J. P., Modular construction of adaptive agents and systems multi-agents in DIMA. Submitted to TSI, thematic Number,: Environment of development of systems multi-agent, 2002.
2. Noël Bonnet, *member,* Manuela Matos, Myriam Polette, Jean-Marie Zahm, Béatrice Nawrocki, Raby, and Philippe Birembaut : A density-based cellular automaton model for studying the clustering mechanism of non invasive cells.
3. Yuri Mansurya, Thomas S. Deisboecka. Simulating 'structure–function' patterns of malignant brain tumours. ScienceDirect, elsevier, Physica A 331 (2004) 219 – 232
4. Yuri Mansurya, Thomas S. Deisboecka. Simulating the time series of a selected gene expression profile in an agent-based tumour model. Physica D 196 (2004) 193–204
5. L. Dib, OntoCell: An ontology of Cellular Biology, Journal of Computer Science 1 (3): 445-449, 2005.

An Intelligent Agent-Based Framework for Collaborative Information Security

M.H. Kuo

Department of Information Management,
Chaoyang University of Technology,
Taichung County, Taiwan
mhk@mail.cyut.edu.tw

Abstract. In this paper we proposed a framework for collaborative intelligent agents in a distributed environment to execute sound security strategies to protect information resources. First, the intelligent agent based Duty Reliable Center in the framework uses group decision method to determine a global information threat level. Then local agent employs the threat level and applies the Bayes' decision procedure to calculate expected loss of its all possible actions, and choices an action among them with minimum expected loss to protect its information resources. The model enables an agent to choose among alternatives in an optimal fashion, taking into account the worth of acquiring prior information to reduce the uncertainty. Because system operations are distributed, hackers are unlikely to wreck the whole system. Thus, it is expected to yield information security cost-effective solutions.

1 Introduction

Traditional information security methods usually use passive mechanisms such as encryption, authentication, firewall, system guards, etc. to protect information resources. These methods are "static" that cannot detect possible information attacks before they really happen. They passively use pre-defined filtering rules to blockade illegal network access. For example, firewalls do not inspect the contents of information packets. If a valid application contains viruses or worms, they will not be able to detect the attacks. Furthermore, firewalls or system guards are unable to stop hackers who use denial-of-service techniques to attack network. Besides these two drawbacks, firewalls or system guards are ineffective in detecting internal attacks [1].

Compared with firewalls or system guards, Intrusion Detection System (IDS) is an IT technique that can detect network intruders or crackers on its own initiative. Many current intrusion detection systems are based on Denning's intrusion detection model [2], that audits records, network packets, or any other observable activities as the basis for detecting abnormalities in the system or checking them with traces and signals of known intrusion patterns. S. Kumar divided the methodology into two categories [3]:

(1). Misuse Intrusion Detection : uses well-defined intrusion patterns to check if a user was hacker or cracker. These intrusion patterns can be installed into the system in advance.

(2). Anomaly Intrusion Detection : builds statistical profiles of the activities from network users' activity records. It regards activities that differ remarkably from normal use as intrusions, i.e. the user could be a hacker or cracker.

Each method has its own drawbacks. The misuse intrusion detection method will not work against new or unknown forms of attack. The anomaly intrusion detection method is ineffective in detecting inside attacks. Thus, any intrusion detection system that employs only one of these methods will have a limited range of intrusions it can detect. An intrusion detection system that intends to avoid these handicaps usually involves parallel employment of both techniques. Unfortunately, the system will become very large and operate slowly. In addition, IDS is usually installed in an intrusion server. To protect the intranet, it needs momentarily to check, analyze and store the activities of network users alone. The so-called "Client-Server protection mechanism" will become a big burden of the network because it generates much extra communication information between IDS and application systems.

Many previous research works have been proposed using software agent technologies that attempt to provide IDS a balance between security requirements, system flexibility and adaptability [4-6]. More recently, the study of Hegazy et al. [7] proposed a multi-agent based framework for intrusion detection. The framework includes four main modules: the sniffing module, the analysis module, the decision module and the reporting module. The sniffing module is responsible for gathering packets from the network. The analysis module is responsible for analyzing the packets. The decision module is responsible for taking actions relevant to the severity of the detected attack. The reporting module generates reports and logs. Even the proposed framework for solving IDS problems is still at its infant stage, it represents a step towards a complete multi-agent based system for networking security. Helmer et al. [8] designed and implemented an intrusion detection system prototype based on lightweight mobile agents (agents that accomplish their essential tasks with minimal code). The agents in the system travel between monitored systems in a network of distributed systems, obtain information from data cleaning agents, classify and correlate information, and report the information to a user interface and database via mediators. Their system allows runtime addition of new capabilities to agents, and thus provides a convenient mechanism for implementing a new form of communication in IDS. Lang et al. [9] proposed an automatic intrusion response system based on mobile agents. The system can generate a response plan automatically based on the intrusion report from the intrusion detection system, and implement the response plan automatically.

Even previously discussed works have provided abilities to tackle IDS drawbacks, they have not discussed or resolved the following three questions:

(1) Information security devices or systems (IDS, firewall, system guards, etc.) are usually very expensive that are not always affordable for an ordinary enterprise. How can an allied enterprise/organization that has not installed any security device or system in a coalition environment (such as in a supply chain environment) obtain information protection?

(2) How can an allied enterprise/organization in the coalition environment get information attack warning from other allied member and take action to protect its information resources before it suffers an attack?
(3) What is the optimal strategy for an allied enterprise/organization to choose an action among alternatives to protect its information resources when it suffers an attack?

Bearing these questions in mind, in this paper we proposed an intelligent agent-based collaborative information security framework (ACISF) that dynamically integrates all distributed information security facilities to achieve efficiently collaborative information security.

2 The Intelligent Agent-Based Framework for Collaborative Information Security

Basically, ACISF is composed of many enterprise/organization network systems. These network systems are called "allied members". Each allied member is installed with three kinds of agents. They are inspection agent, messaging agent and mediating agent. The functions of each agent are described as follows:

(1). *Inspection Agent*
Inspection agent is installed in a local allied member, always monitors possible information attack and evaluates the threat value according to the following criteria:

Let $(M_1, M_2, \ldots, M_n)$ be a set of profile and $(S_1, S_2, \ldots, S_n)$ be the respective deviations, then we define the threat value τ as :

$$\tau = \sqrt{\frac{r_1 S_1^2 + r_2 S_2^2 + \cdots + r_n S_n^2}{n}} \qquad (1)$$

where
$1 \geq r_i > 0$ is the reliability of ith deviation (be adjustable).

(2). *Mediating Agent*
Mediating agent is an intelligent agent installed in a local allied member. The function of mediating agent is according to the role it played in ACISF. There are two candidate roles it may play, namely "ordinary ACISF member" and "Duty Reliable Center (DRC)":

<u>Ordinary ACISF Member</u>
When the allied member is an ordinary ACISF member, the mediating agent analyzes inspection agent's information attack reports, delivers attack information (threat value τ) to the DRC, and takes corresponding actions according to the network system's security policy.

For convenience of determining the information threat level and taking corresponding actions, the mediating agent uses (2) to define a local threat level:

$$l = \begin{cases} 1 & \text{if } 0.0 < \tau \le 0.2 \\ 2 & \text{if } 0.2 < \tau \le 0.4 \\ 3 & \text{if } 0.4 < \tau \le 0.6 \\ 4 & \text{if } 0.6 < \tau \le 0.8 \\ 5 & \text{if } 0.8 < \tau \le 1.0 \end{cases} \quad (2)$$

Then it uses the threat level to determine a corresponding action. For example, when it finds a level-1 information attack, it increases in incident monitoring and looks for patterns across a wide range of variables, but doesn't stop any information activities. But when it finds that a level-5 information attack has happened it immediately stops all information activities (such as disconnects extranet and intranet service, stops application systems, implements information system damage assessment and damage systems repair/reload etc.). The system's default threat level is zero ($l = 0$), meaning that no information attack has happened. Other attack threat levels and their corresponding actions are given in table 1. Note that the actions in table 1 can be different from system to system.

Table 1. The threat level and its corresponding actions

Threat level	Action	Description
$l = 0$	a0	Do nothing.
$l = 1$	a1	Increase in incident monitoring and look for patterns across a wide range of variables.
$l = 2$	a2	Disconnect extra network connection/ services.
$l = 3$	a3	Disconnect extra network connection/ services, and stop database services.
$l = 4$	a4	Disconnect extra network connections/ services, stop application systems, and disconnect partial intra network connection/ services.
$l = 5$	a5	Disconnect all information activities.

Duty Reliable Center (DRC)
When the allied member is the Duty Reliable Center (DRC), the mediating agent accepts other ACISF allied members' information threat reports (through messaging agent), uses these reports to determine the whole framework's global threat level and warns all ACISF allied members of information attack. The criterion of global threat value at time t is determined as follows:

$$\Gamma_t = \frac{\sum_{j=1}^{n}(\tau_{(j,i)} \times w_j)}{m} \quad (3)$$

where
$\tau_{(j,i)}$: the threat value reported by the jth allied member.
$0 < w_j \le 1$: the weight of jth allied member.
n : the number of allied members suffer information attack.
m : the total number of ACISF allied members.

Similar to equation (2), the DRC determines the global threat level at time t as follows:

$$L_t = \begin{cases} 1 & if\ 0.0 < \Gamma_t \leq 0.2 \\ 2 & if\ 0.2 < \Gamma_t \leq 0.4 \\ 3 & if\ 0.4 < \Gamma_t \leq 0.6 \\ 4 & if\ 0.6 < \Gamma_t \leq 0.8 \\ 5 & if\ 0.8 < \Gamma_t \leq 1.0 \end{cases} \qquad (4)$$

(3). Messaging Agent
Messaging agent is a mobile agent dispatched by a mediating agent mandatory constantly reporting attack information to the DRC (when it is an ordinary ACISF member) or warning all ACISF allied members that there are information attacks (when the member is the DRC). The characteristics of mobile agent make it ideal for executing tasks in a distributed environment. For example, using mobile agent to deliver information will reduce the proposed framework's network load. In a distributed client/server system, tasks can be executed only if some effective communication protocol is followed. It implies that multiple interactions exist on the network, since all the temporary data during the execution must be transmitted between the client and the server. A mobile agent can reduce the load and solve unsteadiness on the network based on its abilities such as pro-activity and portability. It means that operations on the network can be more efficient and stable.

3 Evaluating the Weight of Local Security System

In equation (3), the global threat value depends on two factors that are the total number of allied members suffered from information attack, and the allied member's weighted information threat value. The first factor is determined according to the nature of information attack. But the second factor, the allied member's information threat value, is determined according to the profile deviations produced by the member's information security system (firewall, IDS, etc). However, different security system may generate different profile deviations for a certain kind of information attack. The result is that some members will overestimate the strength of information attack, while some will underestimate it. The global threat level thus becomes unreliable. To avoid this from happening, we multiply each allied member's information threat value by a weight to balance the bias. But the problem is how to determine the weight?

In our daily life, people usually believe that the public opinion is "the most accurate". From the group decision point of view, this concept is an essential element in reaching a consensus on a decision or decision-related task, although discussion or debate could happen in the decision process. Based on this concept, we proposed an iteration procedure to evaluate each allied member's weigh.

Let ξ be the average information threat values of those allied members which to have suffered information attacks in $\bar{t}$, i.e.

$$\xi = \frac{\sum_{i=1}^{n} w_i * \tau_{(i,j)}}{n}, \qquad (5)$$

and η_j be the difference between ξ and the jth allied member's weighted information threat value, i.e.,

$$\eta_j = \xi - w_j * \tau_{(j,i)} \qquad (6)$$

Then, the weight w_j of the jth allied member is determined using following iteration algorithm:

Weight determination algorithm
Set $k=0$, $w_{j,0} = 1$,
While any $\eta_j \geq \varepsilon$, do:
{
$\quad w_{j,k+1} = w_{j,k} + \eta_{j,k+1}$, $j=1,2,\ldots n$
$\quad k=k+1$
}

4 The Decision Strategy of Local Agent

Since an agent is software program that can't make decision on its own, therefore we need to provide it some strategies to make rational decision. For this, we apply Bayes' decision procedure to let the mediating agent choose among alternatives in an optimal fashion. The Bayes' decision procedure tells the decision maker to select that action which minimizes the expected loss. The expected loss is evaluated with respect to the prior distribution, which is defined over the possible states of nature.

Suppose that the mediating agent has r possible information security actions in respect of DRC's information attack warning. Then the expected loss of each action is defined as follows:

$$Eloss(a_i) = \sum_{j=0}^{5} loss(a_i, l_j) p(l_j), \; i=1,\ldots, r \qquad (7)$$

where

$loss(a_i, l_j)$: the loss function of the ith action in respect of l_j level of information attack.

$p(l_j)$: the probability of the local member suffers a l_j level of information attack.

Using the Bayes' decision procedure leads the mediating agent selecting the action with minimum expected loss to protect its information resources; that is,

$$Action = Min(Eloss(a_i)) \qquad (8)$$

It is interesting to speculate as to whether the mediating agent could have improved upon this expected loss rather than just following the DRC's warning and taking corresponding action. It can be shown that the mediating agent cannot significantly improve its position by using (7) because $p(l_j)$ in (7) is a prior distribution that depends upon the experience or intuition of the local member. However, if some experimentation is possible, the data derived from this experimentation should be incorporated into the decision-making process. In other words, the mediating agent could take DRC warning into account to improve its decision-making. Thus we rewrite equation (7) to be (9) as follows,

$$Eloss(a_i) = \sum_{j=0}^{5} loss(a_i, l_j) p(l_j | L) , i=1,\ldots,r \qquad (9)$$

where

$p(l_j | L)$: the conditional distribution (posterior distribution) of local member has suffered a l_j level of information attack, given an L level of global information attack.

According to the Baye's rule, we also rewrite equation (9) as (10)

$$Eloss(a_i) = \sum_{j=1}^{r} loss(a_i, l_j) p(l_j | L) = \sum_{j=1}^{r} loss(a_i, l_j) \left(\frac{p(L|l_j) p(l_j)}{\sum_{k=0}^{5} p(L|l_k) p(l_k)} \right) \qquad (10)$$

where

$p(l_j)$: the prior distribution of l_j that depends upon the experience or intuition of the local member. Here we let it be the ratio of m times of l_j level information attack to n times of total information attack, i.e. $p(l_j) = m/n$.

$p(L|l_k)$: a prior distribution that there is an L level of global information attack, given a l_k level of threat.

5 Experimental Results

Software agents in ACISF are written using IBM Aglets. Five inter-connected network systems A, B, C, D, E that are installed with Symantec's NetProwler, Anti-Hacker's SIDS (Smart Intrusion Detection System), Symantec Norton Firewall, ZoneAlarm, and Macafee Firewall respectively.

First, we use Doorknob Rattling (DR), SYN Flooding (SYN), IP Spoofing (IPS) and Denial of Service (DoS) to "drill" the ACISF and apply the weight determination algorithm to evaluate their security system's weights which are w_A:1.0538, w_B:0.9499, w_C:0.9963, w_D:0.9283, w_E:0.9433 respectively. Next, we simulate hackers using DR, SYN, IPS and DoS to randomly attack five inter-connected network systems. In table 2, the first column shows the Nth attack, the upper part of column 2~6 shows each local member's threat value (τ) and its corresponding threat level (l_j), and the lower part shows the member's posterior distribution of l_j level of information attack, given an L level of global information threat. The last column shows the global threat level.

Table 2. Information attack simulation (partial result)

N^{th}	l_a (tool,τ) / $P(l_a\|L)$	l_b (tool, τ) / $P(l_b\|L)$	l_c (tool, τ) / $P(l_c\|L)$	l_d (tool, τ) / $P(l_d\|L)$	l_e (tool, τ) / $P(l_e\|L)$	L
1	4 (IPS,τ=0.75) p(0/4)=0.00 p(1/4)=0.00 p(2/4)=0.00 p(3/4)=0.00 p(4/4)=1.00 p(5/4)=0.00	3 (DR,τ=0.41) p(0/4)=0.00 p(1/4)=0.00 p(2/4)=0.00 p(3/4)=1.00 p(4/4)=0.00 p(5/4)=0.00	5 (DoS,τ=0.94) p(0/4)=0.00 p(1/4)=0.00 p(2/4)=0.00 p(3/4)=0.00 p(4/4)=0.00 p(5/4)=1.00	3 (SYN,τ=0.57) p(0/4)=0.00 p(1/4)=0.00 p(2/4)=0.00 p(3/4)=1.00 p(4/4)=0.00 p(5/4)=0.00	3 (SYN,τ=0.56) p(0/4)=0.00 p(1/4)=0.00 p(2/4)=0.00 p(3/4)=1.00 p(4/4)=0.00 p(5/4)=0.00	4
2	2 (DR,τ=0.35) p(2/0)=0.00 p(2/1)=0.00 p(2/2)=1.00 p(2/3)=0.00 p(2/4)=0.00 p(2/5)=0.00	3 (SYN,τ=0.55) p(0/2)=0.00 p(1/2)=0.00 p(2/2)=0.00 p(3/2)=1.00 p(4/2)=0.00 p(5/2)=0.00	2 (DR,τ=0.38) p(0/2)=0.00 p(1/2)=0.00 p(2/2)=1.00 p(3/2)=0.00 p(4/2)=0.00 p(5/2)=0.00	4 (IPS,τ=0.79) p(0/2)=0.00 p(1/2)=0.00 p(2/2)=0.00 p(3/2)=0.00 p(4/2)=1.00 p(5/2)=0.00	3 (SYN,τ=0.56) p(0/2)=0.00 p(1/2)=0.00 p(2/2)=0.00 p(3/2)=1.00 p(4/2)=0.00 p(5/2)=0.00	2
25	0 (NULL,τ=0.00) p(0/3)=0.05 p(1/3)=0.00 p(2/3)=0.19 p(3/3)=0.12 p(4/3)=0.64 p(5/3)=0.00	3 (DR,τ=0.41) p(0/3)=0.06 p(1/3)=0.00 p(2/3)=0.00 p(3/3)=0.59 p(4/3)=0.12 p(5/3)=0.24	2 (DR,τ=0.38) p(0/3)=0.24 p(1/3)=0.00 p(2/3)=0.12 p(3/3)=0.24 p(4/3)=0.18 p(5/3)=0.21	4 (IPS,τ=0.79) p(0/3)=0.06 p(1/3)=0.00 p(2/3)=0.00 p(3/3)=0.34 p(4/3)=0.30 p(5/3)=0.30	5 (DoS,τ=0.96) p(0/3)=0.00 p(1/3)=0.00 p(2/3)=0.00 p(3/3)=0.46 p(4/3)=0.47 p(5/3)=0.07	3
26	5 (DoS,τ=0.93) p(0/4)=0.00 p(1/4)=0.00 p(2/4)=0.00 p(3/4)=0.06 p(4/4)=0.56 p(5/4)=0.38	5 (DoS,τ=0.95) p(0/4)=0.00 p(1/4)=0.00 p(2/4)=0.00 p(3/4)=0.47 p(4/4)=0.28 p(5/4)=0.25	5 (DoS,τ=0.94) p(0/4)=0.06 p(1/4)=0.00 p(2/4)=0.06 p(3/4)=0.12 p(4/4)=0.27 p(5/4)=0.48	5 (DoS,τ=0.97) p(0/4)=0.00 p(1/4)=0.00 p(2/4)=0.00 p(3/4)=0.29 p(4/4)=0.33 p(5/4)=0.38	3 (DR,τ=0.41) p(0/4)=0.01 p(1/4)=0.00 p(2/4)=0.00 p(3/4)=0.69 p(4/4)=0.30 p(5/4)=0.00	4

Note: (1) NULL: Not attacked.
(2) The entity with gray color background means that the local member did not suffer information attack before the DRC's N^{th} warning.

For example, the entries in upper part of column 2~6 of the third row (the 25th attack) are each allied member's threat values and their corresponding information threat levels which are 0 (τ=0.00), 3 (τ=0.41), 2 (τ=0.38), 4 (τ=0.79) and 5 (τ=0.96) respectively. By applying equation (3), the global threat value is determined as following:

$$\Gamma_t = \frac{\sum_{j=1}^{n}(\tau_{(j,i)} \times w_j)}{m} = (0.41*0.9499+0.38*0.9963+0.79*0.9283+0.96*0.9433)/5 = 0.4814$$

According to equation (4), it is a level-3 global threat.

Using data in table 2 and the Baye's rule we can calculate the posterior distributions of each local member suffers an l_j level of information attack, given an L level of global information threat.

At the local site, allied member's agent will employ the global threat level and apply the Bayes' decision procedure (described in previous section) to calculate expected loss of its all possible actions, and chooses an action among them with minimum expected loss to protect its information resources. For example, suppose that allied member C has six possible information security actions in respect of different information attack, and each action's corresponding loss is defined in Table 3. When it receives the DRC's 26th global information attack warning ($L=4$), it applies equation (10) to calculate each action's expected loss (table 4). According to equation (8), it finds that action 5 has the minimum expected loss $-189. Therefore, it selects **a5** in advance to protect its information resources. Later, it suffers a level 5 attack. Thus an expected saving of $700 (see the entity in the last raw, last column in table 3) is obtained by using the Bayes' procedure.

Table 3. Loss function for allied member C

Threat / Action	Level 0	Level 1	Level 2	Level 3	Level 4	Level 5
a0	0	100	200	500	1000	1500
a1	100	0	100	400	800	1400
a2	200	100	0	300	700	900
a3	300	200	100	-200	200	600
a4	500	400	300	0	-500	300
a5	800	700	600	300	-200	-700

Note: If the problem is formulated in terms of gains, a gain can be termed as a negative loss.

Table 4. Member C's expected loss for each action

Action (a_i)	$loss(a_i,l_j)*p(l_j|L)$						$Eloss(a_i)$
	Level 0	Level 1	Level 2	Level 3	Level 4	Level 5	
a0	0	0	14	75	330	570	989
a1	7	0	7	60	264	532	870
a2	14	0	0	45	231	342	632
a3	21	0	7	-30	66	228	292
a4	35	0	21	0	-165	114	170
a5	56	0	42	45	-66	-266	-189

6 Conclusion

This paper has proposed an agent-based collaborative information security framework (ACISF) that dynamically integrates all distributed information security facilities to achieve efficiently collaborative information security. The prototype of the proposed framework has been developed using IBM Aglets, and primitive experimental results are given in section 5. In conclusion, the benefits of the new model are follows:

(1) The ACISF provides a warning mechanism for allied members to take action to protect their information resources before they suffer information attacks.
(2) The decision model in the ACISF enables an allied system's agent to choose among alternatives in an optimal fashion, taking into account the worth of acquiring prior information to reduce the uncertainty.
(3) Because the ACISF uses a "dual protection strategy" to protect its DRC and it is a distributed architecture, hackers are unlikely to wreck the whole framework.
(4) Based on the agent characteristics such as autonomy, reactivity, adaptability, and mobility, it reduces the load on the network.

Even the proposed model is expecting to yield information security cost-effective solutions; we do not claim that the allied members in ACISF thereafter wouldn't suffer any information attack damage. We must say that the main purpose of the proposed model is to let allied member in the ACISF avoid or reduce damages as much as possible when it suffers an information attack.

References

1. Kenny Hung, Network System Intrusion and Protection, Unalis Publish, (2000)
2. D. E. Denning, "An Intrusion-Detection Model", *IEEE Transactions on Software Engineering*, Vol. SE-13. No. 2 (1987), 222-232
3. S. Kumar, Classification and Detection of Computer Intrusions, Purdue University Ph.D. Dissertation, (1995)
4. Guy G. Helmer, Johnny S. K., Vasant Honavar, and Les Miller, "Intelligent Agents for Intrusion Detection," *IEEE* Information Technology Conference (1998 September) 121-124
5. Eugene H. Spafford and Diego Zamboni, "Intrusion Detection Using Autonomous Agents," *Computer Networks*, 34 (2000) 547-570
6. K. Boudaoud, H. Labiod, R. Boutaba and Z. Guessoum, "Network Security Management with Intelligent Agents," *IEEE Security Management (1)* (2000) 579-592
7. Hegazy, I.M.; Al-Arif, T.; Fayed, Z.T.; Faheem, H.M., "A multi-agent based system for intrusion detection," *Potentials, IEEE* , Volume: 22 , Issue: 4 (2003) 28 – 31
8. Helmer, Guy; Wong, Johnny S.K.; Honavar, Vasant; Miller, Les; Wang, Yanxin, "Lightweight agents for intrusion detection," *Journal of Systems and Software*, Volume: 67, Issue: 2, (2003) 109-122
9. Bo Lang; Junhe Liu; Jiudan Zheng; "The research on automated intrusion response system based on mobile agents," The 8th International Conference on *Computer Supported Cooperative Work in Design*, Volume: 1, (2004) 344 -347

Agents, Information and Trust

John Debenham[1] and Carles Sierra[2]

[1] Faculty of Information Technology, UTS, NSW, Australia
debenham@it.uts.edu.au
http://www-staff.it.uts.edu.au/~debenham/
[2] IIIA, CSIC, UAB, 08193 Bellaterra, Catalonia, Spain

Abstract. Trust measures the relationship between commitment and perceived execution of contracts, and is the foundation for the confidence that an agent has in signing a contract. Negotiation is an information exchange process as well as a proposal exchange process. A rich decision model for intelligent agents involved in multi issue negotiations is described. The model, grounded on information theory, takes into account the aspects of trust and preference to devise mechanisms to manage dialogues. The model supports the design of agents that aim to take 'informed decisions' taking into account that which they have actually observed.

1 Introduction

A negotiating agent, α, uses ideas from information theory to evaluate its negotiation information. If its opponent, β, communicates information, the value of that communication is the decrease in uncertainty in α's model of β. One measure of this decrease in uncertainty is *Shannon information* [10], or negative entropy. If α communicates information it evaluates that information as its expectation of the resulting decrease in β's uncertainty about α. Any such decrease in uncertainty is seen against the continually increasing uncertainty in information because information integrity necessarily decays in time. Information theory may also be used to measure features of inter-agent relationships that extend beyond single negotiations — for example, the sharing of information in a trading pact or relationship, and the strength of trading networks that form as a result of such information sharing. α uses entropy-based inference — both maximum entropy inference and minimum relative entropy inference — to derive probability distributions for that which it does not know in line with the following principle.

Information Principle. α's information base contains only observed facts — in the absence of observed facts, α may speculate about what those facts might be. For example in competitive negotiation, β's utility, deadlines, and other private information will never be observable — unless β is foolish. Further, β's motivations (such as being a utility optimizer) will also never be observable. So in competitive negotiation β's private information is "off α's radar" — α does not contemplate it or speculate about it.

We assume that the interactions between agents are made within the framework of an infrastructure that fixes ontology and meaning, for instance an Electronic Institution [1]. Thus, no differences in the observation of illocutions have to be assumed. Moreover, we assume that the role of a player is public information that can be observed — this is the case for instance if we are within an electronic institution framework. However, the perception of the execution of a contract is subjective in the sense that two deviations of behaviour can be perceived differently by two different agents. We will therefore assume that each agent is equipped with a perception function (noted in this paper as Observe($\cdot$)) that determines which contract execution has actually occurred. Trust measures the relationship between commitment and execution of contracts. More precisely, between signed contracts and *perceived* execution of contracts. In this way, a natural way to base our modelling of trust is on a conditional probability, P^t, between contracts given a context e as:

$$P^t(\text{Observe}(\alpha, b')|\text{Accept}(\beta, \alpha, (a, b)), e)$$

where every contract execution represents a point in that distribution.[1] A concrete relation between a signed contract and the perception of an executed one.

2 Trust and Negotiation

Trust is a multi-faceted concept that has received increasing attention recently [11,12,13,6]. In the context of negotiation, trust represents a general assessment on how 'serious' an agent is about the negotiation process, i.e. that his proposals 'make sense' and he is not 'flying a kite', and that he is committed to what he signs. A lack of trust may provoke agents to breakdown negotiations, or to demand additional guarantees to cover the risk of potential defections. Therefore, in any model of trust the central issue is how to model expectations about the actual outcome at contract execution time. Contracts, when executed, may, and frequently do, yield a different result to what was initially signed. Goods may be delivered late, quality may be (perceived) different from the contract specification, extra costs may be claimed, etc. So the outcome is uncertain to some extent, and trust, precisely, is a measure of how uncertain the outcome of a contract is. Naturally, the higher the trust in a partner the more sure we are of his or her reliability. Trust is therefore a *measure of expected deviations of behaviour* along a given dimension, and in many cases for a given value (region) in that dimension (e.g. I might trust you on low-priced contracts but not on high-priced ones). In this sense, the higher the trust the lower the expectation that a (significant) deviation from what is signed occurs.

Rhetorics in a negotiation context represents the use of language constructs to persuade the oponent to accept our proposals. Agents use rhetorics because they want to change their opponents' preferences or their opponents' view of

---
[1] To simplify notation in the rest of the paper we will denote $P^t(\text{Observe}(\alpha, b')|\text{Accept}(\beta, \alpha, (a, b), e)$ as $P^t(b'|b, e)$.

them. Rhetorical constructs are intimately linked to *social structure* and *time*. The *amount* and the *persistence* of preference change induced by a rhetorical construct depends strongly on the distance in some social scale between the speaker and the hearer. The larger the distance the bigger the impact. The closer, the longer the effect. A Nobel Prize winner is able to change *a lot* our views on a certain subject although getting convinced by a peer on some matter usually has *longer* impact [9].

Another dimension that is very important in the analysis of dialogues is ontology. The contents of illocutions determine whether our assumptions about the opponent's model of the problem are correct. New values can be added to a dimension by a simple question: "Have you got yellow plastic crocodiles?". A simplifying solution is to start any negotiation process by fixing a common ontology. Alternatively, we can use ontology clarifying dialogues and then be ready to modify our models during the dialogue.

3 A Negotiation Language

Agent α is negotiating with an opponent β. They aim to strike a deal $\delta = (a, b)$ where a is α's commitment and b is β's. (Where a or b might be empty.) We denote by A the set of all possible commitments by α, and by B the set of all possible commitments by β. The agents have two languages, $\mathcal{C}$ for communication (illocutionary based) and $\mathcal{L}$ for internal representation (as a restricted first-order language).[2]

In this paper we assume that the illocution particle set is:

$$\iota = \{\text{Offer}, \text{Accept}, \text{Reject}, \text{Withdraw}, \text{Inform}\}$$

with the following syntax and informal meaning:

- Offer(α, β, δ) Agent α offers agent β a deal $\delta = (a, b)$ with action commitments a for α and b for β.
- Accept(α, β, δ) Agent α accepts agent β's previously offered deal δ.
- Reject$(\alpha, \beta, \delta, [info])$ Agent α rejects agent β's previously offered deal δ. Optionally, information explaining the reason for the rejection can be given.
- Withdraw$(\alpha, \beta, [info])$ Agent α breaks down negotiation with β. Extra *info* justifying the withdrawal may be given here.
- Inform$(\alpha, \beta, [info])$ Agent α informs β about *info*.

The accompanying information, *info*, can be of two basic types: (i) referring to the process (plan) used by an agent to solve a problem, or (ii) data (beliefs) of the agent including preferences. When negotiating, agents will therefore try

---

[2] It is commonly accepted since the works by Austin and Searle that illocutionary acts are actions that succeed or fail. We will abuse notation in this paper and will consider that they are predicates in a first order logic meaning 'the action has been performed'. For those more pure-minded an alternative is to consider dynamic logic.

to influence the opponent by trying to change their processes (plans) or by providing new data.

Following the extensive literature on preferences, preferences are divided into two classes:

Quantitative. These preferences are usually called *soft constraints* (hard constraints are particular cases of soft constraints). A soft constraint associates each instantiation of its variables with a value from a partially ordered set. One natural interpretation of this value is the probability of choice. In general, preferences can be expressed as values within a semi-ring $\langle A, +, \times, 0, 1 \rangle$ such that A is a set and $0, 1 \in A$; $+$ is commutative, associative with 0 as its unit element; $\times$ is associative, distributes over $+$, 1 is its unit element, and 0 is its annihilating element. Given a semi-ring $\langle A, +, \times, 0, 1 \rangle$, an ordered set of variables $V = \{v_1, ..., v_n\}$ and their corresponding domains $D = \{D_1, ..., D_n\}$ a soft constraint is a pair $\langle f, con \rangle$ where $con \subseteq V$ and $f \colon D^{|con|} \to A$ with the following intuitive meaning: $f(d_1, \ldots, d_n) = \kappa$ means that the binding $x_1 = d_1, \ldots, x_n = d_n$ satisfies the constraint to a level of κ.[3]

Qualitative. In many domains it is difficult to formulate precise numerical preferences, and it is more convenient to express preference relations between variable assignments: "I prefer red cars to yellow cars". The usual way to represent this relationship formally is $v = a > v = a'$, or simpler $a > a'$, meaning that we prefer the assignment of variable v to a than to a'. Also, in case of an absolute preference for a particular value in a domain, that is, when our preference is $\forall x \neq a.v = a > v = x$ we can simply write $v = a$ or just a. Also, in many cases preference relations depend on the values assigned to other variables (configuring what is called a Conditional Preference Net (CP-net) [2]). "If they serve meat, I prefer red wine to white wine". A conditional preference can be represented as $v_1 = c \colon v_2 = d > v_2 = d'$ (or again $c \colon d > d'$) meaning that we prefer d to d' in the context where c is the case. In general, any DNF over value assignments could be used as the condition. And also, other comparatives than '=' could be used.

Finally, it seems natural that the constraints have an associated certainty degree representing their degree of truth. We thus propose the following content language expressed in BNF: ($info \in \mathcal{L}$):

info	::=	*unit*[**and** *info*]
unit	::=	$K\|B\|soft\|qual\|cond$
K	::=	**K**(*WFF*)
B	::=	**B**(*WFF*)
soft	::=	**soft**($f, \{V^+\}$)

---

[3] As we use maximum entropy inference we have to make the simplifying assumption that domains of quantitative constraints must be finite. This means that continuous domains must be represented as a finite set of intervals, further the way in which those intervals are chosen affects the outcome. This is sometime cited as a weakness of the maximum entropy approach. In [3] it is argued to the contrary, that the choice of intervals represents our prior expectations in fine-grained detail.

```
qual          ::= V=D[>V=D]
cond          ::= If DNF Then qual
WFF           ::= any wff over subsets of variables {V}
DNF           ::= conjunction[ or DNF]
conjunction   ::= qual[ and conjunction]
V             ::= v₁|···|vₙ
D             ::= a|a'|b|···
f             ::= any function from the domains of subsets
                  of V to a set A. For instance a fuzzy set
                  membership function if A = [0,1]
```

4 Information-Based Negotiation

We ground our negotiation model on information-based concepts. *Entropy*, H, is a measure of uncertainty [10] in a probability distribution for a discrete random variable X: $H(X) \triangleq -\sum_i p(x_i) \log p(x_i)$ where $p(x_i) = P(X = x_i)$. Maximum entropy inference is used to derive sentence probabilities for that which is not known by constructing the "maximally noncommittal" [8] probability distribution.

Let $\mathcal{G}$ be the set of all positive ground literals that can be constructed using our language $\mathcal{L}$. A *possible world*, v, is a valuation function: $\mathcal{G} \to \{\top, \bot\}$. $\mathcal{V}|\mathcal{K} = \{v_i\}$ is the set of all possible worlds that are consistent with an agent's knowledge base $\mathcal{K}$ that contains statements which the agent believes are true. A *random world* for $\mathcal{K}$, $W|\mathcal{K} = \{p_i\}$ is a probability distribution over $\mathcal{V}|\mathcal{K}^a = \{v_i\}$, where p_i expresses an agent's degree of belief that each of the possible worlds, v_i, is the actual world. The *derived sentence probability* of any $\sigma \in \mathcal{L}$, with respect to a random world $W|\mathcal{K}$ is:

$$(\forall \sigma \in \mathcal{L}) P_{\{W|\mathcal{K}\}}(\sigma) \triangleq \sum_n \{ p_n : \sigma \text{ is } \top \text{ in } v_n \} \tag{1}$$

The agent's *belief set* $\mathcal{B} = \{\varphi_j\}_{j=1}^M$ contains statements to which the agent attaches a *given sentence probability* $B(\cdot)$. A random world $W|\mathcal{K}$ is *consistent* with $\mathcal{B}$ if: $(\forall \varphi \in \mathcal{B})(B(\varphi) = P_{\{W|\mathcal{K}\}}(\varphi))$. Let $\{p_i\} = \{\overline{W}|\mathcal{K}, \mathcal{B}\}$ be the "maximum entropy probability distribution over $\mathcal{V}|\mathcal{K}$ that is consistent with $\mathcal{B}$". Given an agent with $\mathcal{K}$ and $\mathcal{B}$, *maximum entropy inference* states that the *derived sentence probability* for any sentence, $\sigma \in \mathcal{L}$, is:

$$(\forall \sigma \in \mathcal{L}) P_{\{\overline{W}|\mathcal{K},\mathcal{B}\}}(\sigma) \triangleq \sum_n \{ p_n : \sigma \text{ is } \top \text{ in } v_n \} \tag{2}$$

From Eqn. 2, each belief imposes a linear constraint on the $\{p_i\}$. The maximum entropy distribution: $\arg\max_{\underline{p}} H(\underline{p})$, $\underline{p} = (p_1, \ldots, p_N)$, subject to $M+1$ linear constraints:

$$g_j(\underline{p}) = \sum_{i=1}^N c_{ji} p_i - B(\varphi_j) = 0, \quad j = 1, \ldots, M. \quad g_0(\underline{p}) = \sum_{i=1}^N p_i - 1 = 0$$

$c_{ji} = 1$ if φ_j is ⊤ in v_i and 0 otherwise, and $p_i \geq 0, i = 1, \ldots, N$, is found by introducing Lagrange multipliers, and then obtaining a numerical solution using the multivariate Newton-Raphson method. In the subsequent subsections we'll see how an agent updates the sentence probabilities depending on the type of information used in the update.

An important aspect that we want to model is the fact that beliefs 'evaporate' as time goes by. If we don't keep an ongoing relationship, we somehow forget how *good* the opponent was. If I stop buying from my butcher, I'm not sure anymore that he will sell me the 'best' meat. This decay is what justifies a continuous relationship between individuals. In our model, the conditional probabilities should tend to ignorance. If we have the set of observable contracts as $B = \{b_1, b_2, \ldots, b_n\}$ then complete ignorance of the opponent's expected behaviour means that given the opponent commits to b the conditional probability for each observable contract becomes $\frac{1}{n}$ — i.e. the unconstrained maximum entropy distribution. This natural decay of belief is offset by new observations.

We define the evolution of the probability distribution that supports the previous definition of decay using an equation inspired by pheromone like models [5]:

$$P^{t+1}(b'|b) = \kappa \cdot \left(\frac{1-\rho}{n} + \rho \cdot \left(P^t(b'|b) + \Delta^t P(b'|b) \right) \right) \tag{3}$$

where κ is a normalisation constant to ensure that the resulting values for $P^{t+1}(b'|b)$ are a probability distribution. This equation models the passage of time for a conveniently large $\rho \in [0, 1]$ and where the term $\Delta^t P(b'|b)$ represents the increment in an instant of time according to the last experienced event as the following possibilities show.

Similarity based. The question is how to use the observation of a contract execution c' given a signed contract c in the update of the overall probability distribution over the set of all possible contracts. Here we use the idea that given a particular deviation in a region of the space, *similar* deviations should be expected in other regions. The intuition behind the update is that if my butcher has not given me the quality that I expected when I bought lamb chops, then I might expect similar deviations with respect to chicken. This idea is built upon a function $f(x, y)$ that takes into account the difference between acceptance probabilities and similarity between the perception of the execution x of a contract y, that is a contract for which there was an Accept(β, α, y). Thus, after the observation of c' the increment of probability distribution at time $t+1$ is:

$$\Delta^t P(b'|b) = (1 - |f(c', c) - f(b', b)|) \tag{4}$$

where $f(x, y)$ is

$$f(x, y) = \begin{cases} 1 & \text{if } P^t(\text{Accept}(x)) > P^t(\text{Accept}(y)) \\ \text{Sim}(x, y) & \text{otherwise.} \end{cases}$$

and where Sim is an appropriate similarity function (reflexive and symmetric) that determines the indistinguishability between the perceived and the committed contract.

Entropy based. Suppose that outcome space is $B = (b_1, \ldots, b_m)$, then for a given b_k, $(P_\beta^t(b_1|b_k), \ldots, P_\beta^t(b_m|b_k))$ is the prior distribution of α's estimate of what β will actually execute if he contracted to deliver b_k. Suppose that α's evaluation space is $E = (e_1, \ldots, e_n)$ with evaluation function $\underline{v}$, then $\underline{v}(b_k) = (v_1(b_k), \ldots, v_n(b_k))$ is α's evaluation over E of what β contracted to do. Then α's expected evaluation of what β will deliver if β contracts to deliver b_k is:

$$\underline{v}_\beta(b_k) = \left(\sum_{j=1}^m P_\beta^t(b_j|b_k) \cdot v_1(b_j), \ldots, \sum_{j=1}^m P_\beta^t(b_j|b_k) \cdot v_n(b_j) \right).$$

Now suppose that α observes the event $(c'|c)$, α may wish to revise the prior estimate $\underline{v}_\beta(b)$ in the light of this observation to:

$$(\underline{v}_\beta(b) \mid (c'|c)) = g(\underline{v}_\beta(b), \underline{v}(c), \underline{v}(c')),$$

for some function g — the idea being, for example, that if the chicken, c', was tough then our expectation that the beef, b', will be tough should increase. The entropy based approach achieves this by estimating $\Delta^t P(b'|b)$ by applying the principle of minimum relative entropy — see Sec. 4. Let:

$$\left(P_{\beta,C}^t(b_j|b) \right)_{j=1}^n = \arg\min_{\underline{p}} \sum_{i=1}^n p_i \log \frac{p_i}{P_\beta^t(b_i|b)} \tag{5}$$

satisfying the n constraints C, and $\underline{p} = (p_j)_{j=1}^n$. Then:

$$\Delta^t P(b'|b) = P_{\beta,C}^t(b'|b) - P_\beta^t(b'|b) \tag{6}$$

The n constraints C are: $\sum_{j=1}^m P_\beta^t(b_j|b_k) \cdot v_i(b_j) = g_i(\underline{v}_\beta(b), \underline{v}(c), \underline{v}(c'))$, for $i = 1, \ldots, n$. This is a set of n linear equations in m unknowns, and so the calculation of the minimum relative entropy distribution may be impossible if $n > m$. In this case, we take only the m equations for which the change from the prior to the posterior value is greatest. That is, we attempt to select the most significant factors.

5 A Trust Model

"Trust" may have different significance in different contexts. Agents build and destroy trust by the way in which they execute their contractual commitments. If agent α who is committed to execute a actually executes a' then we distinguish two ways in which a and a' may differ. First, a' may be a variation of commitment a within the ontological context of the negotiation. Second, the contract variation may involve something outside the ontological context. A contract execution could involve variations of both of these types. In the following we are primarily interested in variations of the first type. Variations of the second type can be managed by reference to market data that together with entropy-based inference enables α to value such variations.

Trust as expected behaviour. Consider a distribution of expected contract executions that represent α's "ideal" for β, in the sense that it is the best that α could reasonably expect β to do. This distribution will be a function of β, α's trading history with β, anything else that α believes about β, and general environmental information including time — denote all of this by e, then we have $P_I^t(b'|b,e)$. For example, if it is unacceptable for the execution b' to be less preferred than the agreement b then $P_I^t(b'|b,e)$ will only be non-zero for those b' that α prefers to b. The distribution $P_I^t(\cdot)$ represents what α expects, or hopes, β will do. So if β commits to deliver 12 bottles of water then the probability of b' being a case of champagne could be low. Trust is the relative entropy between this ideal distribution, $P_I^t(b'|b,e)$, and the distribution of the observation of expected contract execution, $P_\beta^t(b'|b)$. That is:

$$T(\alpha,\beta,b) = 1 - \sum_{b' \in B(b)} P_I^t(b'|b,e) \log \frac{P_I^t(b'|b,e)}{P_\beta^t(b'|b)}$$

This defines trust for one, single commitment b — for example, my trust in my butcher if I order precisely seventeen lamb loin chops. It makes sense to aggregate these values over a class of commitments, say over those b' that satisfy some first-order formula $\Phi(\cdot)$. In this way we measure the trust that I have in my butcher for lamb cuts generally:

$$T(\alpha,\beta,\Phi) = 1 - \frac{\sum_{\{b \in B|\Phi(b)\}} P_\beta^t(b) \left[\sum_{b' \in B(b)} P_I^t(b'|b,e) \log \frac{P_I^t(b'|b,e)}{P_\beta^t(b'|b)} \right]}{\sum_{\{b \in B|\Phi(b)\}} P^t(b)}$$

where $P^t(b)$ is the probability of α signing a contract with β that involves the commitment b. Similarly, for an overall estimate of α's trust in β:

$$T(\alpha,\beta) = 1 - \sum_{b \in B} P^t(b) \left[\sum_{b' \in B(b)} P_I^t(b'|b,e) \log \frac{P_I^t(b'|b,e)}{P_\beta^t(b'|b)} \right]$$

Trust as expected acceptability. The notion of trust in the previous section Sec. 5 was expressed in terms of our expected behaviour in an opponent that was defined for each contract specification b. That notion requires that an ideal distribution, $P_I^t(b'|b,e)$, has to be specified for each b. The specification of ideal distributions may be avoided by considering "expected acceptability" instead of "expected behaviour". The idea is that we trust β if the acceptability of his contract executions are at or marginally above the acceptability of the contract specification, $P^t(\text{IAcc}(\alpha,\beta,\nu,(a,b)))$. Defining a function:

$$f(x) = \begin{cases} 0 & \text{if } x < P^t(\text{IAcc}(\alpha,\beta,\nu,(a,b))) \\ 1 & \text{if } P^t(\text{IAcc}(\alpha,\beta,\nu,(a,b))) < x < P^t(\text{IAcc}(\alpha,\beta,\nu,(a,b))) + \epsilon \\ 0 & \text{otherwise} \end{cases}$$

(or perhaps a similar function with smoother shape) for some small ϵ, then define:

$$T(\alpha, \beta, b) = \sum_{b' \in B} f(P^t(\text{IAcc}(\alpha, \beta, \nu, (a, b')))) \cdot P^t_\beta(b'|b)$$

$$T(\alpha, \beta, \Phi) = \frac{\sum_{\{b \in B | \Phi(b)\}} P^t(b) \cdot \sum_{b' \in B} f(P^t(\text{IAcc}(\alpha, \beta, \nu, (a, b')))) \cdot P^t_\beta(b'|b)}{\sum_{\{b \in B | \Phi(b)\}} P^t(b)}$$

$$T(\alpha, \beta) = \sum_{b \in B} P^t(b) \cdot \sum_{b' \in B} f(P^t(\text{IAcc}(\alpha, \beta, \nu, (a, b')))) \cdot P^t_\beta(b'|b)$$

Trust as certainty in contract execution. Trust is consistency in expected acceptable contract executions, or "the lack of expected uncertainty in those possible executions that are better than the contract specification". The idea here is that α will trust β more if variations, b', from expectation, b, are not random. The Trust that an agent α has on agent β with respect to the fulfilment of a contract (a, b) is:

$$T(\alpha, \beta, b) = 1 + \frac{1}{B^*} \cdot \sum_{b' \in B} P^t_+(b'|b) \log P^t_+(b'|b)$$

where $P^t_+(b'|b)$ is the normalisation of $P^t_\beta(b'|b)$ for those values of b' for which $P^t(\text{IAcc}(\alpha, \beta, \nu, (a, b'))) > P^t(\text{IAcc}(\alpha, \beta, \nu, (a, b)))$ and zero otherwise, $B(b)^+$ is the set of contract executions that α prefers to b,

$$B^* = \begin{cases} 1 & \text{if } |B(b)^+| = 1 \\ \log |B(b)^+| & \text{otherwise} \end{cases}$$

and β has agreed to execute b, and α systematically observes b'. Given some b' that α does not prefer to b, the trust value will be 0. Trust will tend to 0 when the dispersion of observations is maximal.

As above we aggregate this measure for those deals of a particular type, that is, those that satisfy $\Phi(\cdot)$:

$$T(\alpha, \beta, \Phi) = 1 + \frac{\sum_{\{b \in B | \Phi(b)\}} \sum_{b' \in B} \left[P^t_+(b', b) \log P^t_+(b'|b)\right]}{B^* \cdot \sum_{\{b \in B | \Phi(b)\}} P^t(b)}$$

where $P^t_\beta(b', b)$ is the joint probability distribution. And, as a general measure of α's trust on β we naturally use the normalised negative conditional entropy of executed contracts given signed contracts:

$$T(\alpha, \beta) = 1 + \frac{\sum_{b \in B} \sum_{b' \in B} \left[P^t_+(b', b) \log P^t_+(b'|b)\right]}{B^*}$$

6 Conclusion

Game theory tells α that she should accept a proposal if $s_\delta > m_\delta$ where s_δ is the surplus, $s_\delta = u(\omega) - u(\pi)$ and m_δ is the margin. This is fine if everything is certain. If it is not then game theory tells α to work with a random variable, S_δ, instead. Incidentally this means that α has to be certain about her uncertainty, but that is not the issue. This means that α can consider $P(S_\delta > m_\delta)$, and the standard deviation, $\sigma(S_\delta)$, is a measure of uncertainty in the process. Then α asks "how risk averse am I", and then is able to calculate $P((accept(\delta))$.

With uncertain information and decaying integrity, the "utility calculation" in the previous paragraph is a futile exercise. Instead we argue that it makes more sense to ask simply: "on the basis of what we actually know, what is the best thing to do?". We claim that α will be more concerned about the integrity of the information with which the decision is being made, than with an uncertain estimation of her utility distribution.

References

1. J. L. Arcos, M. Esteva, P. Noriega, J. A. Rodríguez, and C. Sierra. Environment engineering for multiagent systems. *Journal on Engineering Applications of Artificial Intelligence*, 18, 2005.
2. C. Boutilier, R. Brafman, C. Domshlak, H. Hoos, and D. Poole. CP-nets: A tool for representing and reasoning with conditional ceteris paribus preference statements. *Journal of Artificial Intelligence Research*, 21:135 – 191, 2004.
3. J. Debenham. Auctions and bidding with information. In P. Faratin and J. Rodriguez-Aguilar, editors, *Proceedings Agent-Mediated Electronic Commerce VI: AMEC*, pages 15 – 28, July 2004.
4. J. Debenham. Bargaining with information. In N. Jennings, C. Sierra, L. Sonenberg, and M. Tambe, editors, *Proceedings Third International Conference on Autonomous Agents and Multi Agent Systems AAMAS-2004*, pages 664 – 671. ACM, July 2004.
5. M. Dorigo and T. Stützle. *Ant Colony Optimization*. MIT Press, Cambridge, MA, 2004.
6. R. Falcone and C. Castelfranchi. The socio-cognitive dynamics of trust: Does trust create trust? In *Proceedings of the workshop on Deception, Fraud, and Trust in Agent Societies*, pages 55 – 72, 2001.
7. P. Faratin, C. Sierra, and N. Jennings. Using similarity criteria to make issue trade-offs in automated negotiation. *Journal of Artificial Intelligence*, 142(2):205–237, 2003.
8. E. Jaynes. *Probability Theory — The Logic of Science*. Cambridge University Press, 2003.
9. M. Karlins and H. Abelson. *Persuasion*. Crosby Lockwood and Son, 1970.
10. D. MacKay. *Information Theory, Inference and Learning Algorithms*. Cambridge University Press, 2003.
11. S. Ramchurn, C. Sierra, L. Godo, and N. Jennings. Devising a trust model for multiagent interactions using confidence and reputation. *International Journal of Applied Artificial Intelligence*, 18(9–10):91–204, 2005.
12. J. Sabater and C. Sierra. Reputation and social network analysis in multi-agent systems. In *Proceedings of the First International Conference on Autonomous Agents and Multi-Agent systems*, pages 475 – 482, 2002.
13. P. Yolum and M. Singh. Achieving trust via service graphs. In *Proceedings of the Autonomous Agents and Multi-Agent Systems Workshop on Deception, Fraud and Trust in Agent Societies*. Springer-Verlag, 2003.

Modelling Partner's Behaviour in Agent Negotiation

Jakub Brzostowski and Ryszard Kowalczyk

Faculty of Information and Communication Technologies,
Swinburne University of Technology, Hawthorn, Victoria 3122, Australia
{jbrzostowski, rkowalczyk}@it.swin.edu.au

Abstract. The paper proposes new approach for modelling negotiation partners and predictive decision-making. It is based on the prediction of negotiation partners behaviour from its previous offers in the current encounter. The approach allows the negotiating agent to asses different factors influencing other agent's behaviour during negotiation and make optimal decisions according to the prediction. It is tested in simple scenario and the results illustrating the comparison with random strategy selection are presented.

1 Introduction

Negotiation can be regarded as a distributed search through a space of potential agreements to find solution that satisfies requirements of all parties [4]. Negotiation has been studied in may fields such as: management, social sciences, decision and game theory, artificial intelligence and intelligent agents [8]. The intelligent agents offer capabilities that allow for automation of the negotiation process. However, agent negotiation faces many problems including agent's limited or uncertain knowledge about other agents and conflicting preferences. Apart from the communication protocols the agents require appropriate decision-making mechanisms allowing them to reach good agreements in a reasonable time (low communication cost). In order to be successful an agent needs to adapt to the behaviour of its partners and changing environment. The heuristic approach proposed by Faratin [3] employs an idea of tactics generated by decision functions. These mechanisms allow the agents for a limited adaptation to partner's behaviour to limited extent by the use of behaviour-dependant tactics. In the behaviour-dependant tactic an agent imitates its partner, i.e. makes concessions proportional to the partners concessions. However, in general when an agent has a number of tactics at its disposal it is difficult to determine what tactics to use and to what extent in terms of mixture of different factors such as: time and imitation. The problem of determining appropriate tactics and concessions may be regarded as a kind of optimization. Too large concessions may cause a low outcome of the negotiation for the agent and too small concessions may discourage the negotiation partner from making bigger concessions and as a result the partner may break the encounter. Therefore, highly adaptive decision-making mechanism is required. This mechanism should allow an agent to learn about negotiation partner during the current encounter from the previous offers in order to predict the partner's future behaviour and adapt to it.

A vast literature about learning for negotiation focuses mostly on learning from previous negotiations. The learning approaches for supporting the negotiation include Bayesian learning [11], Q-learning [2], case-based-reasoning [1] and evolutionary computation [10][9]. Those address an issue of learning from historical interactions with a little devotion to learning from the current encounter. Some interesting work of recent years [6][5] focus on analysis of negotiation scenarios involving various parameters of negotiation such as: deadlines and reservation values. However, this work assumes a simplified type of negotiation strategy, namely only the time-dependant strategy. It is more required to design a decision-making mechanism for negotiation agents that enables them to cope with more complex partners behaviour involving a mixture of different factors.

A learning approach based on regression was proposed by Hou [7] where the nonlinear regression analysis was applied to model the negotiation partners behaviour based only on previous offers. However, again the approach was proposed to cope only with pure tactics. The application of regression in modelling multi-factor behaviour would be extremely difficult because of many degrees of freedom of the model.

We propose to base prediction on simple difference methods. Although such modelling is rougher than regression, it is computationally more efficient and does not assume that the partner is using particular type of decision function. Our mechanism first estimates the extents to which different factors influence the behaviour of the modelled agent. It combines the separate predictions of contributions of different factors in order to predict the overall behaviour of the negotiation partner.

The remainder of the paper is organized as follows. In the second section we present a mechanism for predicting the values of contributions of different factors in partners behaviour. The third section describes the prediction mechanism for different factors. Fourth section presents an idea of semi-strategical reasoning based on the prediction results. In section 5 we present some experimental results and in section 6 the conclusions and future work are described.

2 The Estimation of Degrees of Various Factors Dependency

We will test our mechanism against an approach proposed by Faratin [3]. In that work three families of negotiation tactics were proposed: time-dependant, resource-dependant and behaviour-dependant. We can distinguish two main factors influencing the negotiation agent behaviour: time-dependency and behaviour dependency. In order to asses the extents to which an agent is behaviour-dependent and time-dependent we introduce the criteria as functions mapping a history of the previous offers in a given encounter of both parties to the interval $[0, 1]$. Such two criteria should answer the question to what extent the negotiation partner imitates behaviour of our agent and to what extent it responds to a time constraint imposed on the encounter. We propose to define these criteria as necessary conditions indicating that the modelled agent uses pure tactic (either behaviour-dependant or time-dependant). In other words we need to determine what is characteristic for an agent using time-dependant tactic (necessary condition) and use this feature as the time-dependency assessment criterion. Analogously for the behaviour dependency the corresponding criterion is required.

2.1 Time-Dependency

The time-dependent tactics usually use the polynomial or exponential functions. The characteristic feature of the whole family of such functions is the constant sign of their all derivatives. The information available about our negotiation partner is a sequence of the previous offers of the current encounter. Our aim is to determine the extent to which it is generated by a particular pure tactic. In other words we want to calculate the degree to which the sequence fits to a particular decision function corresponding to the pure tactic. If we assume that the decision function used for generation of a sequence of offers has its all derivatives with a constant sign then the differences of all the orders calculated for the sequence must also have constant signs. This is because the difference of n-th order approximates the n-th derivative of the function. Assuming that we have the sequence of partner offers: b_i of a length m the differences of different orders can be calculated as follows:

$$\Delta^1 b_i = b_{i+1} - b_i \qquad i \in \{1, 2, \ldots, m-1\}$$
$$\Delta^2 b_i = \Delta b_{i+1} - \Delta b_i \qquad i \in \{1, 2, \ldots, m-2\}$$
$$\Delta^3 b_i = \Delta^2 b_{i+1} - \Delta^2 b_i \qquad i \in \{1, 2, \ldots, m-3\}$$
$$\ldots$$
$$\Delta^{m-1} b_i = \Delta^{m-2} b_{i+1} - \Delta^{m-2} b_i \qquad i \in \{1\}$$

The necessary condition for being time-dependant will be fully satisifed if all the differences for each particular order k have the same sign:

$$\forall k \in \{1, 2, \ldots, m-1\} \quad \forall i, j \in \{1, 2, \ldots, m-k\} \quad sgn(\Delta^k b_i) = sgn(\Delta^k b_j)$$

In addition, we need a criterion determining the degree to which time-dependency is satisfied. First we introduce a subcriterion D_k for differences of a particular degree k. This subcreterion will be fully satisfied if all the differences are either negative or positive, and it will be fully violated if the means of the positive and negative values counterbalance each other. It means that the contributions of the positive and negative values are the same. If there is a dominance of one sign over the other then we obtain a partial degree of satisfaction. The higher the dominance the higher the degree of satisfaction. Therefore, the partial degree of satisfaction D^k for the difference of an order k may be introduced as an aggregate of the means of the positive values of the differences and the negative values of the differences as follows:

$$D_k = \frac{|\frac{\sigma_p^k}{m_p^k} + \frac{\sigma_n^k}{m_n^k}|}{Max\{|\frac{\sigma_p^k}{m_p^k}|, |\frac{\sigma_n^k}{m_n^k}|\}} \qquad (1)$$

where $\sigma_p^k = \sum_{\Delta_k b_i > 0} \Delta_k b_i$, $\sigma_n^k = \sum_{\Delta_k b_i < 0} \Delta_k b_i$. m_p^k and m_n^k are the amounts of the positive and negative values of $\Delta^k b_i$, respectively. The value of D_k is small if the absolute values of the averages: $|\frac{\sigma_p^k}{m_p^k}|, |\frac{\sigma_n^k}{m_n^k}|$ are close, which means the condition violation is high. The values D^k are then aggregated to the overall value of criterion satisfaction. This can be done by the use of a weighted sum. The weights are proportional to the extent of contribution of the differences $\Delta^k b_i$:

$$D_t = \sum_{k \leq m-1} w_k D_k$$

where w_k is calculated as follows:

$$w_k = \frac{Max\{|\sigma_p^k|, |\sigma_n^k|\}}{\sum_{j=1}^{m-1} Max\{|\sigma_p^j|, |\sigma_n^j|\}}$$

2.2 Behaviour-Dependency

The behaviour-dependant tactics usually imitate the partners behaviour. In order to be able to determine an extent to which an agent is behaviour-dependant we need to calculate a sequence of the relative first order differences. Assuming that we have a sequence of the last m offers of our agent: s_i and a sequence of the last m offers b_i of the modelled agent we calculate a sequence $r_i = \frac{\Delta^1 b_i}{\Delta^1 s_i}$. r_i describes a change of behaviour of the modelled agent in relation to the change of behaviour of our agent. We will define two subcreteria assesing the level of responsivenes of the modelled agent. First subcreterion will be based on the aggregate r of values of r_i. This aggregate can be an average or weighted sum of values of r_i

$$r = \sum_{i=1}^{m} w_i r_i$$

The weights w_i can be incresaing with the value of i if we decide that the more current values of r_i are more important than the older ones (lower i). If the value of r is higher than 1 then the modelled agent is highly responsive because it makes bigger concessions than our agent. If $r < 1$ than the agent is not highly responsive beacuse his concessions are smaller than ours. In the case of $r = 1$ we can say that the modelled agent is neutral because his concessions are equal to ours and. The first subcreterion should be a function $h : r \mapsto [0, 1]$ mapping the value of r into the degree of responsivenes and can be defined as follows:

$$D_1 = h(r) = Max[1, Min[0, 0.5r]]$$

The function h assigns the value 0.5 to the value of $r = 1$ beacuse in terms of fuzzy logic 0.5 means that the condition is satisfied and not satisfied to the same extent. For the values of r higher than 1 the level of satisfaction is bigger than 0.5 (more true than false) and for the values of r lower than 1 the level of satisfaction is lower than 0.5 (more false than true).

The second subcreterion can asses the level of trend in the sequence r_i in terms of monotonicity. We can measure the level of monotonicity D_2 by measuring the level of sign consistency for the differences Δr_i. This is done in the same way as in previous subsection (formula 1). The obtained values of creteria satisfaction D_1 and D_2 can be aggregated by the use of mean:

$$D_b = \frac{D_1 + D_2}{2}$$

3 Difference Method for Behaviour Prediction

As mentioned earlier the negotiation agents behaviour is influenced by a mixture of two factors: imitation and time. We propose to construct separate predictions for the imitative behaviour and time-depending behaviour, and then mix them together using the weights obtained in the previous section. The prediction will be a function that maps a history of m last offers of both parties H_m and our future offer s_{m+1} into a value of prediction of the next offer of the negotiation partner $\hat{b}_{m+1}$:

$$f : (H_m, s_{m+1}) \to \hat{b}_{m+1}$$

The obtained time-depending prediction f_t and imitation-depending prediction f_b are combined together in order to predict the overall offer of the negotiation partner as a response to our future offer s_{m+1}:

$$\hat{b}^t_{m+1} = f_t(H_m) \tag{2}$$

$$\hat{b}^b_{m+1} = f_b(H_m, s_{m+1}) \tag{3}$$

$$\hat{b}_{m+1} = f(H_m, s_{m+1}) = \\ = \frac{D_t}{D_t + D_b} \times \hat{b}^t_{m+1} + \frac{D_b}{D_t + D_b} \times \hat{b}^b_{m+1} \tag{4}$$

In order to obtain a prediction for l offers forward we perform the procedure recursively. The time-depending prediction will be stored: $\hat{H}^t_{m+1} = H^t_m \cup \{s_{m+1}, \hat{b}^t_{m+1}\}$ in order to be reused later ($H^t_m = H_m$). The overall prediction will also be stored: $\hat{H}_{m+1} = H_m \cup \{s_{m+1}, \hat{b}_{m+1}\}$. The prediction for the next step is performed recursively as follows:

$$\hat{b}^t_{m+2} = f_t(\hat{H}^t_{m+1}) \tag{5}$$

$$\hat{b}^b_{m+2} = f_b(\hat{H}_{m+1}, s_{m+2}) \tag{6}$$

where s_{m+2} is the offer of our agent in the next step of negotiation.

$$\hat{b}_{m+2} = f(\hat{H}_{m+1}, s_{m+2}) =$$
$$= \frac{D_t}{D_t + D_b} \times \hat{b}^t_{m+2} + \frac{D_b}{D_t + D_b} \times \hat{b}^b_{m+2} \quad (7)$$

This procedure can be repeated l times.

3.1 Time-Depending Prediction

In order to predict the partners behaviour succesfully we need to determine a level of the trend in its behaviour. In the previous section we focused on the level of time-dependency and in this section we want to determine a level of a particular type of time-dependent tactic in the quantitative sense. By a trend we mean the degree of concavity or convexity of the concession curve. In other words we need to asses if the negotiation partner is playing the linear, conceder or boulware tactics, and how strong are these tactics. This information is needed for determining the maximal order of the differences that should be taken into account in the prediction. In a case of the linear and conceder tactic only the first order difference will be taken into account because for the linear tactic all higher order differences are equal to zero and the conceder tactic is close to linear after a number of offers. The most important is the successful prediction of the boulware tactic because the most violent changes occur later in time for this tactic. For the prediction we use all the differences up to k-th order having the same sign as follows:

$$sgn(\Delta^1 b_i) = sgn(\Delta^2 b_i) = \ldots = sgn(\Delta^k b_i) \neq sgn(\Delta^{k+1} b_i)$$

The more differences are consistent in a sign the stronger boulware tactic of the opponent agent. The time-dependent prediction for the next step is calculated as follows (Figure 1):

$$\hat{b}_{m+1} = f_t(H_m) = b_m + \sum_{j=1}^{k} \Delta^j b_{m-j} \quad (8)$$

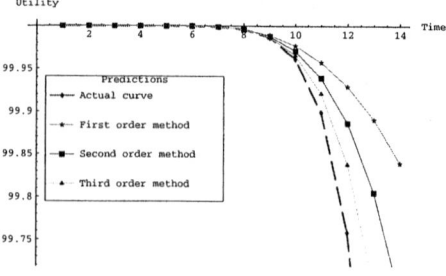

Fig. 1. Examples of different order predictions for boulware tactic

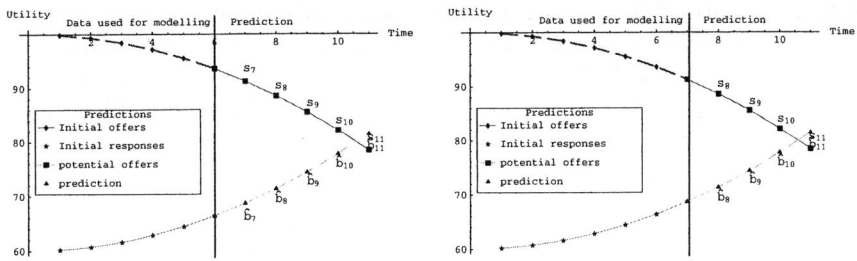

Fig. 2. An example of prediction as a response to sequence of potential offers in steps 7 and 8

where $\hat{b}_{m+1}$ is the prediction od the $m+1$ offer and k is index of the last difference consistent in sign. The formula 8 can be applied recursively in order to obtain the prediction for the next steps.

3.2 Imitation-Depending Prediction

For the imitation-depending prediction we construct a function that maps the history of negotiation and the next offer of our agent to the next offer of the modelled agent:

$$\hat{b}_{m+1} = f_b(H_m, s_{m+1})$$

This function is intended to predict how the modelled agent will respond to the offer s_{m+1} of our agent. The history H_m is constant but s_{m+1} is a variable in the function f_b. We use the second order Taylor's formula to construct the prediction as follows:

$$f_b(H_m, s_{m+1}) = b_m + \frac{\Delta b_{m-1}}{\Delta s_{m-1}}(s_{m+1} - s_m) + 0.5 \times \frac{\Delta r_{m-2}}{\Delta s_{m-1}}(s_{m+1} - s_m)^2$$

where $\frac{\Delta b_{m-1}}{\Delta s_{m-1}}$ is treated as an approximation of the first order derivative of the function f_b in a point s_m and $\frac{\Delta r_{m-2}}{\Delta s_{m-1}}$ is treated as an approximation of the second order derivative of the function f_b in a point s_m and $\Delta r_{m-2} = \frac{\Delta b_{m-1}}{\Delta s_{m-1}} - \frac{\Delta b_{m-2}}{\Delta s_{m-2}}$.

4 Semi-strategical Reasoning

In the previous sections we described the prediction methods and in this section we will present a mechanism combining the prediction with decision making. The prediction mechanism is able to predict our negotiation partner's overall response to our sequence of l offers: $s_{m+1}, s_{m+2}, \ldots, s_{m+l}$ in the form of a sequence $\hat{b}_{m+1}, \hat{b}_{m+2}, \ldots, \hat{b}_{m+l}$. Therefore, it is able to predict the outcome of the negotiation if according to our prediction it ends in l steps. Otherwise, the prediction about the last partner's offer $\hat{b}_{m+l}$ is treated as a temporary prediction of the negotiation outcome. The decision making process involves determining the optimal sequence of offers given the prediction model of the opponent agent. We discretize the space of each potential offer in each negotiation step and consider all sequences of offers. All the sequences in the discrete space are assessed by the use of our prediction mechanism and the sequence with highest utility is chosen. The first offer of the chosen sequence is proposed to the negotiation partner. After the counterpart has responded the whole mechanism can be reused for further decision making in the next steps of negotiation.

5 Results

We test our approach by simulating experimental negotiations with settings more advanced than in [3]. Our negotiation agent is playing against static strategies being mixtures of the time-dependant tactic and the behaviour-dependant tactic with various weights. The time-dependant tactics are divided into three groups of tactics:

- Conceder: $C = \{\beta \mid \beta \in \{2, 5, 8\}\}$
- Linear: $L = \{\beta \mid \beta \in \{1\}\}$
- Boulware: $B = \{\beta \mid \beta \in \{0, 3, 0.5, 0.7\}\}$

Two behaviour-dependant tactics are considered:

- Absolute Tit-For-Tat: a: $\delta \in \{1\}$ and $R(M) = 0$ (without random factor)
- Relative Tit-For-Tat: r: $\delta \in \{1\}$

The weights assigned to the tactics are divided into three groups:

- Small: $S = \{0.1, 0.2, 0.3\}$
- Medium: $M = \{0.4, 0.5, 0.6\}$
- Large: $L = \{0.7, 0.8, 0.9\}$

The resulting set of all 126 static strategies will be constructed as follow:

$$ST = (C \cup L \cup B) \times \{a, r\} \times (S \cup M \cup L)$$

In order to illustrate the performance of our approach we decompose the whole set ST into 18 groups of strategies:

$$\begin{aligned} ST = & (C \times \{a\} \times S) \cup (L \times \{a\} \times S) \cup (B \times \{a\} \times S) \cup \\ & \cup (C \times \{a\} \times M) \cup (L \times \{a\} \times M) \cup (B \times \{a\} \times M) \cup \\ & \cup (C \times \{a\} \times L) \cup (L \times \{a\} \times L) \cup (B \times \{a\} \times L) \cup \\ & \cup (C \times \{r\} \times S) \cup (L \times \{r\} \times S) \cup (B \times \{r\} \times S) \cup \\ & \cup (C \times \{r\} \times M) \cup (L \times \{r\} \times M) \cup (B \times \{r\} \times M) \cup \\ & \cup (C \times \{r\} \times L) \cup (L \times \{r\} \times L) \cup (B \times \{r\} \times L) \end{aligned} \quad (9)$$

Each group will be shortly denoted using only the first letters. For example:

$$CAS = C \times \{a\} \times S$$

In this paper we discuss results for simple scenarios. The buyer's $min^b \in \{10\}$, $max^b \in \{50\}$, $k^b \in \{0\}$, $t^b_{max} = 15$. We assume the full overlapping degree ($\Phi = 0$) of the seller's and the buyer's ranges. As in [3], $max^b - min^b = max^s = min^s$ and $k^s = k^b$. $min^s = min^b + \Phi * (max^b - min^b)$, $max^s = min^s + (max^b - min^b)$. We consider modelling without a communication cost and with a low communication cost ($comm \in \{0.01\}$) separately (cost $\tau(t) = tanh(t * comm)$). More complex scenarios, different behaviour-dependant tactics and different values of communication cost will be considered in future work. The prediction mechanism is used after six offers have been generated in order to provide the initial data for the modelling. For the first six offers our agent uses only time-dependent tactic slightly tougher ($\beta = 0.8$) than Linear tactic with some additional perturbations to explore the opponent's initial responses. The figures (3,4) illustrate the performance of the modelling approach. The lower parts of the bars in the chart represent the value of average utility of an agent playing against particular group of tactics using random strategy from ST. This means that all strategies from the set ST have been played against all strategies from particular subset (for instance: CSA) and the average utility is illustrated in a form of a lower part of a bar. The additional surplus over or under a bar illustrates the gain or loss respectively, in terms of utility obtained by substituting the random strategy choice by our prediction mechanism.

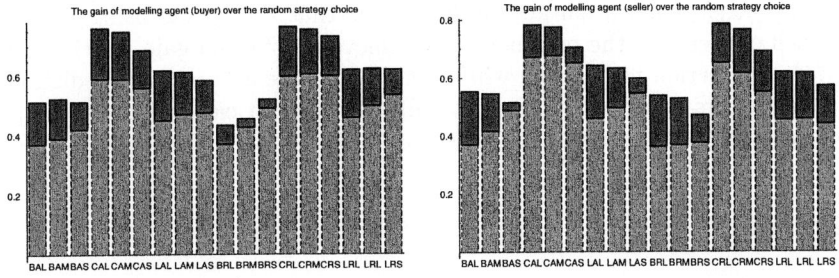

Fig. 3. The performance of prediction mechanism applied for the buyer and the seller

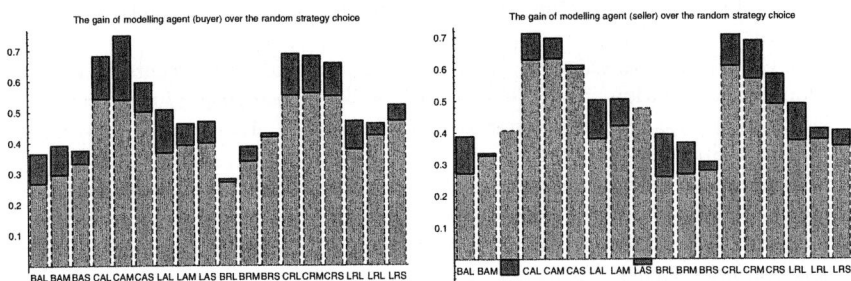

Fig. 4. The performance of prediction mechanism taking into account the communication cost applied for the buyer and the seller

From the bar charts (Figure 3), we can see that our mechanism outperforms the random strategy selection. For most of the strategies the gain is significant. However, in the cases of strategies with high contribution of behaviour-dependant tactic (BAS, BRS, etc.) the gains are relatively smaller. This is because the accuracy of the weights assessments (Section 3) still needs to be improved. Another reason for this is that using the behaviour-dependant tactic our partner imitates our behaviour what means that roughly his concession will not be bigger than ours and big gain is not possible in such a case.

After introducing low cost to the mechanism it still performs better than the random choice (Figure 4), although in some cases there is no gain or the gain is negative (BAS and LAS for the seller). The reason for it is the same as in the situation without cost. The results are not symmetric for the buyer and for the seller because of the use of Relative Tit For Tat tactic that does not work symmetrically.

6 Conclusions and Future Work

The paper proposes a new approach for negotiation agent modelling and predictive reasoning from the history of previous offers in a given encounter about the negotiation partner's attitude. This allows an agent to adapt to the partner and therefore, reaching better agreements. The initial experimentation and comparison with other negotiation approaches shows that the agents using proposed approach outperform the opponent and achieve substantial gain. In the future work the prediction mechanism will be improved (the accuracy of prediction of different factors contribution) and it will be tested in cases of more complex scenarios with other types of strategies.

References

1. Jakub Brzostowski and Ryszard Kowalczyk. On possibilistic case-based reasoning for selecting partners in multi-agent negotiation. In Geoff Webb and Xinghuo Yu, editors, *Proceedings of the 17th Australian Joint Conference on Artificial Intelligence*, volume 3339 of *Lecture Notes in Computer Science*, pages 694–705, Cairns, Australia, 2004. Springer.
2. H. L. Cardoso and E. Oliveira. Using and evaluating adaptive agents for electronic commerce negotiation. In *IBERAMIA-SBIA '00: Proceedings of the International Joint Conference, 7th Ibero-American Conference on AI*, pages 96–105, London, UK, 2000. Springer-Verlag.
3. P. Faratin. *Automated Service Negotiation Between Autonomous Computational Agents*. PhD thesis, University of Londodn, 2000.
4. P. Faratin, C. Sierra, and N. R. Jennings. *Negotiation among groups of autonomous computational agents*. University of Londond, 1998.
5. S. Fatima, M. Wooldridge, and N. R. Jennings. Comparing equilibria for game theoretic and evolutionary bargaining models. In *5th International Workshop on Agent-Mediated E-Commerce*, pages 70–77, 2003.

6. S. S. Fatima, M. Wooldridge, and N. R. Jennings. Optimal negotiation strategies for agents with incomplete information. In *ATAL '01: Revised Papers from the 8th International Workshop on Intelligent Agents VIII*, pages 377–392, London, UK, 2002. Springer-Verlag.
7. C. Hou. Modelling agents behaviour in automated negotiation. Technical Report KMI-TR-144, Knowledge Media Institute, The open University, Milton Keynes, UK, May 2004.
8. Guoming Lai, Cuihong Li, Katia Sycara, and Joseph Andrew Giampapa. Literature review on multi-attribute negotiations. Technical Report CMU-RI-TR-04-66, Robotics Institute, Carnegie Mellon University, Pittsburgh, PA, December 2004.
9. N. Matos, C. Sierra, and N. Jennings. Determining successful negotiation strategies: An evolutionary approach. In *ICMAS '98: Proceedings of the 3rd International Conference on Multi Agent Systems*, page 182, Washington, DC, USA, 1998. IEEE Computer Society.
10. J. Oliver. A machine learning approach to automated negotiation and prospects for electronic commerce, 1997.
11. D. Zeng and K. Sycara. Bayesian learning in negotiation. In Sandip Sen, editor, *Working Notes for the AAAI Symposium on Adaptation, Co-evolution and Learning in Multiagent Systems*, pages 99–104, Stanford University, CA, USA, 1996.

Insurance Services in Multi-agent Systems*

Yuk-Hei Lam[1], Zili Zhang[1,2], and Kok-Leong Ong[1]

[1] School of Information Technology, Deakin University,
Waurn Ponds, Victoria 3217, Australia
{yuk, zzhang, leong}@deakin.edu.au
[2] Faculty of Computer and Information Science,
Southwest China University, Chongqing 400715, China

Abstract. In a multi-agent environment, there is often the need for an agent to cooperate with others so as to ensure that a given task is achieved timely and cost-effectively. Present agent systems currently maximizes this through mechanisms such as trust and risk assessments. In this paper, we extend this mechanism by introducing the concept of insurance, in which the insurance agents act as a bridge between agents who require resources from others. Unlike traditional systems, agents purchase insurance so as to guarantee to have the requested resources during the task execution time and thus minimize the risk in task failure. The novelty of this proposal is that it ensures agents continuously to exchange resources and to seek maximum expected utility in a dynamic environment at the same time. Our experimental results confirm the feasibility of our approach.

1 Introduction

The nature of multi-agent system enables software agents to work together in order to solve the complicated tasks. Even though agents are considered mostly self-interested, they tend to form coalition for a particular task. Furthermore, it is often beneficial to cooperate with other agents [1,2]. However, it is very difficult for agents to discover or search the required resources[1] (e.g., manpower, platform access time, services such as a particular skill, etc.) in such virtual dynamic environments. Towards this, the directory services from FIPA Compliant Agent Platforms [3] and Retsina MAS [4] are proposed. The idea of directory services is to discover the agents and resources available in the system. The agents will use the directory services when they need resources from the system, and do not know who to contact. In this sense, the directory services only act as the yellow pages for advertisement purposes.

We consider that the major difficulty for agents in this case is not only limited to discovering the resources, but also negotiating the resources. We argue that negotiating for a particular resource provided by other unknown agents is a very

---

* This work is supported by Deakin University CRGS grant.
[1] We define resources as anything that agents are willing to share or exchange with other agents.

costly, time-consuming and difficult task, and often can not guarantee the result[2]. In addition, the self-interested agents will not give out resources free and often require a kind of reciprocation in a competitive environment. Currently, present agent systems solve this problem through mechanisms such as negotiation [5], trust and risk assessments [6,7]. In this paper, we extend this mechanism by introducing the concept of insurance. With the insurance concept in place, agents are guaranteed to have the requested resources in execution without any extra afford in negotiation and resources discovery.

In general, the insurance is defined as the pooling of fortuitous losses by transfer to an insurer, who agrees to indemnify insureds for such losses and render services connected with the risk [8]. In the real life, the concept of insurance provides significant benefits to the human society. Individuals, firms or corporations purchase insurance so as to protect themselves against risks and minimize the potential losses, thus relief their financial burden after a loss. In computing technology, multi-agent brokering system [9,10] and distributed systems [11,12] make use of insurance to facilitate their needs.

Inspired by the above, we put the concept of insurance into a new dimension in the multi-agent system with the fundamental work of insurance from Rothschild and Stilglitz [13]. Hence, the integrity of our insurance model can be ensured in a well-developed manner.

In our system, the insurers (insurance agents in our case) guarantee the availability of resources for the insured (insured agents in our case). The insurance agents act as the broker agents who are responsible for exchanging resources among the insured agents. In this sense, the insured agents are no longer suffer from lack of resources in execution or even require to search for extra resources. The main concept is that agents committed to pay premium so as to guarantee the insurance agents will "lend" the resources to them, in exchange of "returning" the resources in advance or in the future (premium paid).

The remaining sections of this paper are organized as follows: In the next section, we define the main concept of insurance and illustrate our concept with a practical example. We then discuss how agents reason about demanding and purchasing insurance in Section 3 and Section 4, respectively. In Section 5, we present the simulation results, and the conclusions are laid out in Section 6.

2 Insurance in Multi-agent Systems

We consider a set of self-interested agents, who occupied in a multi-agent system, are often required different resources in order to accomplish the task on time. Under the circumstances, we interpret the concept of insurance in the context of multi-agent system as the commitment between the insurance agent and the insured agent, in which both parties guarantee to provide the requested resources to others. In doing so, the insured agent is required to provide resource (either

---

[2] Failure can be caused by unable to allocate resources and/or failed to make an agreement with regards to the terms of negotiation.

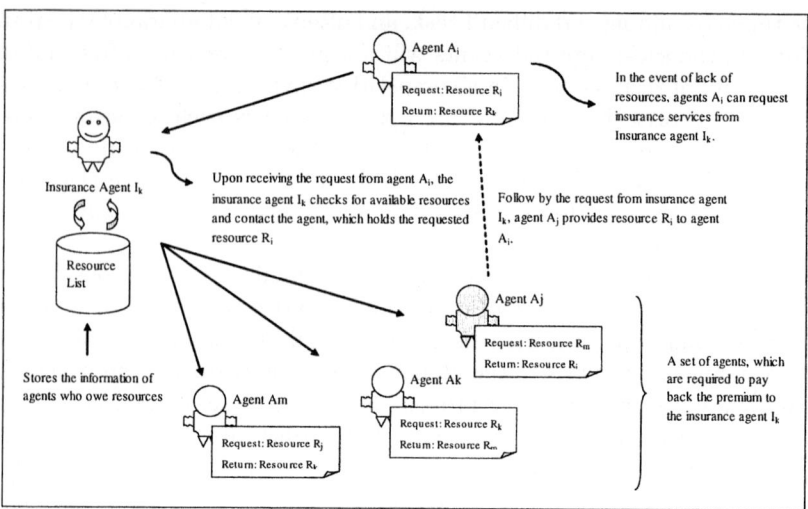

Fig. 1. Agent $\mathcal{A}_i$ purchases insurance through insurance agent $\mathcal{I}_k$. The insurance agent checks its available resources from the resources list and allocates the requested resource $\mathcal{R}_i$ to the Agent $\mathcal{A}_i$.

nominated or by request) to the insurance agent, in exchange of guaranteeing the requested resource can be used or accessed in a particular time.

Consider an agent $\mathcal{A}_i$ has the task $\mathcal{T}_i$ to accomplish as shown in Figure 1. After evaluation, agent $\mathcal{A}_i$ has found out that a resource $\mathcal{R}_i$ is needed for task $\mathcal{T}_i$. Since the task can not be completed without the required resource $\mathcal{R}_i$, then agent $\mathcal{A}_i$ must requests a resource $\mathcal{R}_i$ from other agents. In this case, agent $\mathcal{A}_i$ decides to purchase insurance as a way to guarantee the resources availability in execution. In order to be insured, agent $\mathcal{A}_i$ makes commitment with the insurance agent $\mathcal{I}_k$ that they both agree to exchange resources in favor to one another. Thus, agent $\mathcal{A}_i$ starts to propose that the resource $\mathcal{R}_k$ will be returned as the cost of premium[3]. At this stage, it is possible that the insured agents might deceit the insurance agents by refusing to pay the premium as promised. In this case, the insurance agents should apply some forms of trust mechanisms such as [14,15,16,17,18] to protect themselves against the potential fraud and deception. In this paper, we make assumption that the insurance agents have already assessed the agents' application before accepting it.

Once the resources exchange agreement is made, the insurance agent $\mathcal{I}_k$ checks the resources list, which contains all the available resources that can be transferred to other agents. If the requested resource is available (from agent $\mathcal{A}_j$ in this case), the insurance agent $\mathcal{I}_k$ will accept agent $\mathcal{A}_i$'s application and add its name to the resources list with the associated resources that agent $\mathcal{A}_i$ can provide in the later stage. In the mean time, the insurance agent $\mathcal{I}_k$ informs agent $\mathcal{A}_j$ to pay back the premium.

---

[3] The insurance agent $\mathcal{I}_k$, however, has the right to request agent $\mathcal{A}_i$ to provide a particular resource.

Follow by the request from the insurance agent $\mathcal{I}_k$, agent $\mathcal{A}_j$ contacts agent $\mathcal{A}_i$ and provides the resource $\mathcal{R}_i$ to agent $\mathcal{A}_j$ (as shown in dotted line). Once the task $\mathcal{T}_i$ is completed, agent $\mathcal{A}_i$ will inform the insurance agent $\mathcal{I}_k$ that it has received the requested resource. Then, the insurance agent $\mathcal{I}_k$ will erase the tuple of agent $\mathcal{A}_j$ in the resources list, indicating that agent $\mathcal{A}_j$ has no longer owed any premium.

3 Demand for Insurance

The concept of insurance provides significant benefits to both agents and systems. From agents' prospective, insurance guarantees the amount of resources available in a particular time. Second, insurance relieves the burden in searching for a particular resources as the insurance agents will allocate resources for them. Third, insurance enhances the credit of agents. Agents who purchase insurances are considered to be more trustworthy than the one without insurance. From the system's prospective, the failure rate in completing the task will be decreased. As a result, the system becomes more stable with a better throughput.

3.1 Income, Premium and Insurance Contract

Without loss of generality, we assume a multi-agent system operating in a networked environment with self-interested agents $\mathcal{A}_1, \ldots, \mathcal{A}_n$ that required to complete a set of tasks, $T = \mathcal{T}_1, \ldots, \mathcal{T}_m$, where $n \gg m$. Moreover, each agent owns a set of resources, $R = \mathcal{R}_1, \ldots, \mathcal{R}_k$, which is used for executing any given task. We further define that $\mathcal{I}_1, \ldots, \mathcal{I}_p$ be a set of insurance agents who provide insurance services in the system.

Based on the previous example, consider an agent $\mathcal{A}_i$ who is required to complete task $\mathcal{T}_i$. If agent $\mathcal{A}_i$ is lucky enough to avoid resources shortage and accomplish the task on time, it will be awarded a utility of income $U(\mathcal{A}_i, \mathcal{T}_i)$. In the event of failure, the agent will be penalized by deducting its utility of income by $\text{pen}(\mathcal{A}_i, \mathcal{T}_i)$. Therefore, the utility of income will be $U(\mathcal{A}_i, \mathcal{T}_i) - \text{pen}(\mathcal{A}_i, \mathcal{T}_i)$.

Definition 1. *The utility of income, notated as $\mathcal{S}$, is the set of possibilities after a task is carried out.*

Let $\mathcal{S}_1$ and $\mathcal{S}_2$ be the utility of income without and with accident, respectively. Considering there are only two possibilities, that is $\mathcal{S} = \{\mathcal{S}_1, \mathcal{S}_2\}$. Refer to the given example, the utility of income is

$$\mathcal{S} = \{U(\mathcal{A}_i, \mathcal{T}_i), U(\mathcal{A}_i, \mathcal{T}_i) - \text{pen}(\mathcal{A}_i, \mathcal{T}_i)\} \tag{1}$$

In order to avoid the failure of task, agents can insure themselves against the accident by paying a premium α_1 to an insurance agent $\mathcal{I}_i$, in return for which agents will be paid a compensation, $\hat{\alpha}_2$, if the resource shortage accident occurs.

Definition 2. *The insurance contract, notated as α, is the set of outcomes for agents who undertake the insurance. Let α_2 be the net compensation under insurance, where $\alpha_2 = \hat{\alpha}_2 - \alpha_1$. Therefore, the insurance contract can be described as the vector $\alpha = \{\alpha_1, \alpha_2\}$.*

With insurance, the utility of income becomes

$$\mathcal{S} = \{U(\mathcal{A}_i, \mathcal{T}_i) - \alpha_1, U(\mathcal{A}_i, \mathcal{T}_i) - \text{pen}(\mathcal{A}_i, \mathcal{T}_i) + \alpha_2\}. \qquad (2)$$

Definition 3. *Given that resources $\mathcal{R}_i$ needed to be paid back to insurance agent under the insurance contract, we compute the cost of premium towards agent as $\alpha_1 = U(\mathcal{A}_i, \mathcal{R}_i)$.*

The cost of premium depends on how critical the requested resource is and the importance of the task which uses the resource. For instance, if the requested resource is given out when agents are in an idle stage, then the cost of premium will be low. Alternatively, the cost will be high if the requested resource is used by critical task when requested.

3.2 Expected Utility

In game theory, the usage of expected utility enables agents to evaluate the expected gain in completing a task. Based on this nature, we incorporate the idea of expected utility with insurance in multi-agent systems. Let $\text{EU}(p, \mathcal{S}_1, \mathcal{S}_2)$ be the Von Neumann-Morgenstern Expected Utility [19], which is modified as

$$\text{EU}(p, \mathcal{S}_1, \mathcal{S}_2) = (1-p) \cdot U(\mathcal{S}_1) + p \cdot U(\mathcal{S}_2) \qquad (3)$$

where p is the probability of an accident. By incorporating Equations (1) and (2), the expected utility without and with insurance for agent $\mathcal{A}_i$ are

$$\begin{aligned}\text{EU}(p, \mathcal{S}_1, \mathcal{S}_2) = &(1-p) \cdot U(\mathcal{A}_i, \mathcal{T}_i) \\ &+ p \cdot (U(\mathcal{A}_i, \mathcal{T}_i) - \text{pen}(\mathcal{A}_i, \mathcal{T}_i))\end{aligned} \qquad (4)$$

and

$$\begin{aligned}\text{EU}(p, \mathcal{S}_1, \mathcal{S}_2) = &(1-p) \cdot (U(\mathcal{A}_i, \mathcal{T}_i) - \alpha_1) \\ &+ p \cdot (U(\mathcal{A}_i, \mathcal{T}_i) - \text{pen}(\mathcal{A}_i, \mathcal{T}_i) + \alpha_2)\end{aligned} \qquad (5)$$

respectively. In the above, the value of expected utility gives the agents an insight of how valuable the requested resource in comparison with the resource that will be given out as the cost of premium. Once the agent $\mathcal{A}_i$ estimates the expected utility of the task, then it must decides whether to purchase insurance.

4 Purchasing Insurance

We have so far considered the beneficial of the insurance concept in multi-agent systems. However, agents need not purchase insurance for every transaction. In fact, they must reason about the effectiveness of purchasing insurance in different circumstances.

4.1 Evaluation Based on Criticality of Task

From the resources management prospective, the rational agents need to consider whether it is affordable to pay back the premium in a particular time. Towards this, agent $\mathcal{A}_i$ first needs to define the degree of importance of the task, $\mathcal{T}_i \in \mathrm{T}$, in order to decide whether it should have the intention to purchase insurance.

Let $\mathrm{W}(\mathcal{A}_i, \mathcal{T}_i)$ be the weight that determines the degree of importance of the task $\mathcal{T}_i$ from agent $\mathcal{A}_i$'s perspective. The higher value of weight, the more critical the task is. Agents can adjust the value of weight dynamically. A task $\mathcal{T}_i$ is considered critical by agent $\mathcal{A}_i$ if $\mathrm{W}(\mathcal{A}_i, \mathcal{T}_i) >= \Theta(\mathcal{A}_i)$, where $\Theta(\mathcal{A}_i)$ is the weight threshold is determined by agent $\mathcal{A}_i$. On the other hand, a task $\mathcal{T}_i$ is considered non-critical if $\mathrm{W}(\mathcal{A}_i, \mathcal{T}_i) < \Theta(\mathcal{A}_i)$. Let $\mathrm{C}(\mathcal{A}_i)$ and $\mathrm{N}(\mathcal{A}_i)$ be the sets of critical tasks and non-critical tasks to agent $\mathcal{A}_i$ respectively, i.e.,

$$\mathrm{C}(\mathcal{A}_i) = \{\mathcal{T}_i \in \mathrm{T} \mid \mathrm{W}(\mathcal{A}_i, \mathcal{T}_i) >= \Theta(\mathcal{A}_i)\} \quad (6)$$

and

$$\mathrm{N}(\mathcal{A}_i) = \{\mathcal{T}_i \in \mathrm{T} \mid \mathrm{W}(\mathcal{A}_i, \mathcal{T}_i) < \Theta(\mathcal{A}_i)\} \quad (7)$$

where $\Theta(\mathcal{A}_i) \in [0, 1]$.

By defining the importance of the task and classify them into two groups: critical and non-critical, agent $\mathcal{A}_i$ can reason about whether it is affordable to pay back the premium. If the requested resource is not being used by any critical task at the time of premium return (i.e., $\mathcal{T}_i \in \mathrm{N}$), then agent $\mathcal{A}_i$ has sufficient evidence to prove that it has the ability to pay the premium at this stage.

4.2 Evaluation Based on Financial Aspects

The next step is to consider the act of purchasing insurance financially. From the financial prospective, agent $\mathcal{A}_i$ should only purchase insurance if it is beneficial. That is to maximize the expected utility stated in Equation (3). Nevertheless, we also consider that the value of expected utility will be affected by the agents' personal risk attitude.

In traditional Expected Utility theory [19], the shape of utility function determines the type of personal risk attitude. Risk neutral agents have a linear utility function. This type of agents expect that the utility should be equivalent to the actual cost at all time. Risk averse agents have a concave utility function as they rather pay more utility to avoid certain risk. Also, they tend to sacrifice more utility to avoid themselves from entering into the risky situation. Therefore, the utility of risk averse agents can get is less than the actual cost. If agents are risk seeking, they like to take risks with a convex utility function. Unlike risk averse agents, the utility gained is greater than the actual value. Following [20], the personal risk attitude of the agent $\mathcal{A}_i$ is given as:

$$\mathrm{RA}(\mathcal{A}_i) = \begin{cases} 0 < \mathrm{RA}(\mathcal{A}_i) < 1 & \text{if agent } \mathcal{A}_i \text{ is risk averse} \\ 1 & \text{if agent } \mathcal{A}_i \text{ is risk neutral} \\ 1 < \mathrm{RA}(\mathcal{A}_i) <= 2 & \text{if agent } \mathcal{A}_i \text{ is risk seeking} \end{cases} \quad (8)$$

and the resources cost for agent $\mathcal{A}_i$ to complete the task $\mathcal{T}_i$ using resources $\mathcal{R}_i$ equals to the cost of the premium, α_1, which is affected by different types of personal risk attitude:

$$\alpha_1 = \frac{\alpha_1^{\text{RA}(\mathcal{A}_i)}}{\text{RA}(\mathcal{A}_i)} \quad (9)$$

As we can observe, agents who do not like risky situations are more likely to purchase insurance as one of the ways to minimize risk. By applying Equation (5), an insurance contract α is worth $\text{EU}(p,\alpha) = (1-p) \cdot (U(\mathcal{A}_i, \mathcal{T}_i) - \alpha_1) + p \cdot (U(\mathcal{A}_i, \mathcal{T}_i) - \text{pen}(\mathcal{A}_i, \mathcal{T}_i) + \alpha_2)$. Based on the value of insurance contract and the personal risk attitude, agent $\mathcal{A}_i$ should consider purchasing insurance as there is a financial benefit to do so, such that

$$\text{EU}(p, \alpha) \geq \text{EU}(p, 0) \quad (10)$$

where $\text{EU}(p, 0) = \text{EU}(p, U(\mathcal{A}_i, \mathcal{T}_i), U(\mathcal{A}_i, \mathcal{T}_i) - \text{pen}(\mathcal{A}_i, \mathcal{T}_i))$.

5 Empirical Results

The objective of our experiments is to verify the effectiveness and benefits of applying insurance concept in multi-agent systems. Due to space limitation, we only report a summary of our results here. The full details can be obtained from [21].

In the first experiment, the effectiveness of the insurance concept in multi-agent systems is examined. Figure 2 shows the plot on the average success rate of agents to complete the allocated tasks. We can observe that the agents with insurance perform much better then the one without insurance in all cases: the average success rate is vary from 55% to 95% with no insurance in Figure 2(a), (b) and (c). Alternatively, the average success rate was increased at least 75% when insurance is in place.

The advantage of our proposal becomes obvious when there is a lack of resources in the system. In the worst case (Figure 2(c)), agents can achieved 55%

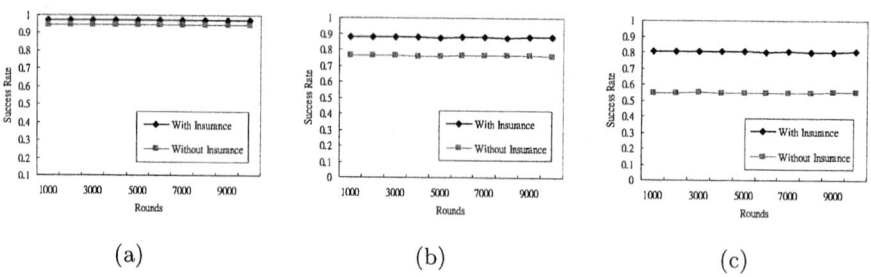

(a) (b) (c)

Fig. 2. Simulation results for the overall performance of agents under different ratios of resources shortage: (a) 10% of resources shortage occurrence; (b) 50% of resources shortage occurrence; (c) 90% of resources shortage occurrence

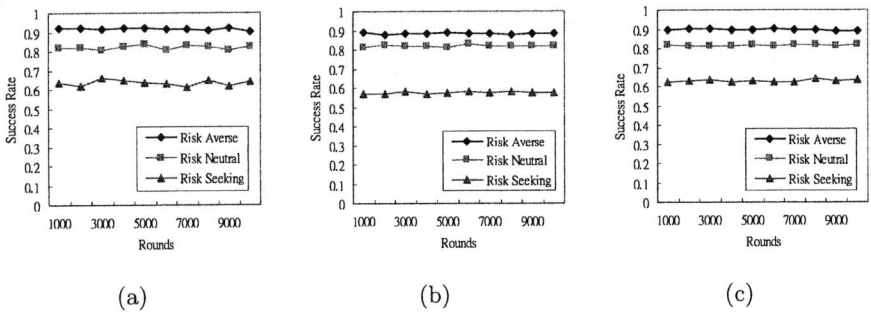

Fig. 3. Simulation results for the success rate of agents when the resources shortage problem occurs: (a) 10% of resources shortage occurrence; (b) 50% of resources shortage occurrence; (c) 90% of resources shortage occurrence

of average success rate with no insurance. Alternatively, 80% of average success rate is achieved when insurance is in place. Even though agents can reach a high average success rate without insurance in Figure 2(a), the overall success rate can still be improved (about 3%) with the help of insurance.

The aim of the second experiment is to examine how the risk attitude of agents affects the usage of insurance services. In this experiment, the performance of agents is evaluated under resources shortage environment only. The success rate is calculated only when the resources shortage occurs.

In Figure 3, we see that agents with different risk attitudes react differently when the lack of resources problems occur. For instance, we can observe that the risk averse agents are more likely to purchase insurance among the other two types (between 80% and 85% of buy rate) and therefore they rather pay more cost to avoid themselves from entering any risky situations. Hence, this type of agents maintain a high success rate (around 90%) as shown in Figure 3(a). The nature of risk seeking agents "encourage" gambling for more gain cost, so they are more likely to neglect the importance of insurance regardless the level of risk involved. Also, the experimental results have confirmed this finding: the insurance buy rate has dropped dramatically (between 12% and 22%) compared with the risk averse agents. As predicted, this type of agents receive a lower success rate (between 50% and 60% in most cases) when the lack of resources problems occur frequently in the system. The risk neutral agents take a balance between two types, with the 82% of success rate and between 60% and 65% of buy rate, respectively.

From the above experimental results, we can conclude that agents make use of insurance as one of the ways to improve the performance. In general, agents with insurance have more stable performance and they often can reach a higher success rate. Second, insurance concept works well in all different environments (from only 10% of resources to 90% resources available in the system): agents can still maintain a high success rate with insurance in all cases. From the experimental results, we expect that even the resources availability has suddenly dropped down dramatically, agents who purchase insurance can still maintain a high success rate (at least 90% for risk averse agents, 80% for risk neutral agents and 55% for risk seeking agents). Therefore, insurance concept helps to stabilize the performance of agents. In conclusion, insurance services enable better utilization of resources, thus increase the throughput of the whole system.

6 Conclusions

We consider intelligent agents working in an open multi-agent system, in which they are required to search resources in order to complete the task on time. However, agents often cannot guarantee that the requested resources can be accessed in execution time even with any comprehensive mechanisms such as negotiations and resources allocation. Towards this, the concept of insurance enables agents to use insurance services as a method to (i) allocate resources, (ii) guarantee the requested resources are available in the execution time, and (iii) increase the throughput.

In view of the above, the concept of insurance provides agents an alternative approach to allocating resources and to avoiding risky situations. With the personal risk attitude being explicit, agents are now more flexible in reasoning about whether to purchase insurance. From our initial simulation results, we believe we have shown the beneficial of applying the insurance concept in multi-agent systems and thus have evidence to support the feasibility of our proposal. Hence, our future work is to make further improvements to the existing insurance services, such as provide mechanism for insurance agents to reason about the trustworthiness of other agents as well as to enable different types of insurance agents in the system so as to provide different kinds of insurance services.

References

1. Breban, S., Vassileva, J.: A coalition formation mechanism based on inter-agent trust relationships. In: AAMAS '02, New York, NY, USA (2002) 306–307
2. Sandholm, T., Lesser, V.: Coalition Formation among Bounded Rational Agents. 14th International Joint Conference on Artificial Intelligence (1995) 662–669
3. Erdur, R., Dikenelli, O., Seylan, I., Gurcan, O.: An infrastructure for the semantic integration of fipa compliant agent platforms. In: AAMAS 2004. (2004) 1316–1317
4. Wong, H.C., Sycara, K.: Adding security and trust to multi-agent systems. In: Proceedings of Autonomous Agents '99 Workshop on Deception, Fraud, and Trust in Agent Societies. (1999) 149 – 161
5. Luo, X., Jennings, N.R., Shadbolt, N., fung Leung, H., man Lee, J.H.: A fuzzy constraint-based knowledge model for bilateral, multi-issue negotiations in semi-competitive environments. Artificial Intelligence **148** (2003) 53–102
6. He, M., Jennings, N.R., Leung, H.: On agent-mediated electronic commerce. IEEE Trans on Knowledge and Data Engineering **15** (2003) 985–1003
7. He, M., Leung, H., Jennings, N.R.: A fuzzy logic based bidding strategy for autonomous agents in continuous double auctions. IEEE Trans on Knowledge and Data Engineering **15** (2003) 1345–1363
8. Rejda, G.: Principles of Risk Management and Insurance (6th Edition). Addison-Wesley Educational Publishers Inc. (1998)

9. Jonker, C., Lam, R., Treur, J.: A multi-agent architecture for an intelligent website in insurance. In: CIA '99: Proceedings of the Third International Workshop on Cooperative Information Agents III. (1999) 86–100
10. Nunes, L., Oliveira, E.: Brokering in electronic insurance markets. The Interdisciplinary Journal of Artificial Intelligence and the Simulation of Behaviour **1** (2003)
11. Lai, C., Medvinsky, G., Neuman, B.: Endorsements, licensing, and insurance for distributed system services. In: In Proc. of the 2nd ACM Conf. on Computer and Comm. Security. (1994) 170–175
12. Millen, J., Wright, R.: Reasoning about trust and insurance in a public key infrastructure. In: 13th IEEE Computer Security Foundations Workshop. (2000) 16–22
13. Rothschild, M., Stiglitz, J.: Equilibrum in competitive insurance markets: An essay on the economics of imperfect information. The Quarterly Journal of Economics **90** (1976) 629–649
14. Carbone, M., Nielsen, M., Sassone, V.: A Formal Model for Trust in Dynamic Networks. In: Proc. Int. Conf. on Software Engineering and Formal Methods, Brisbane, Australia (2003)
15. Mui, L., Mohtashemi, M., Halberstadt, A.: A Computational Model of Trust and Reputation. In: Proc. 35th Hawaii Int. Conf. on System Sciences, Hilton Waikoloa Village (2002)
16. Ramchurn, S.D., Sierra, C., Godo, L., Jennings, N.R.: A Computational Trust Model for Multi-Agent Interactions Based on Confidence and Reputation. In: Proc. Int. Workshop of Deception, Fraud and Trust in Agent Societies, Melbourne, Australia (2003) 69–75
17. Xiong, L., Liu, L.: A Reputation-Based Trust Model for Peer-to-Peer e-Commerce Communities. In: Proc. IEEE Conf. on e-Commerce, Newport Beach (2003)
18. Yu, B., Singh, P.M.: An Evidential Model of Distributed Reputation Management. In: Proc. AAMAS, Bologna, Italy (2002) 294–301
19. Neumann, J.V., Morgenstern, O.: Theory of games and economic behavior. Princeton, Princeton Univ (1947)
20. Gardner, R.: Games for Business ad Economics. John Wiley and Sons, Inc. (1995)
21. Lam, Y., Zhang, Z., Ong, K.: Insurance services in multi-agent systems. Technical Report TRC05/11, School of Information Technology, Deakin University, http://www.deakin.edu.au/~yuk/TechReports/InsuranceModel05.pdf (2005)

Dynamic Team Forming in Self-interested Multi-agent Systems

Quan Bai and Minjie Zhang

School of Information Technology and Computer Science,
University of Wollongong, Wollongong,
NSW 2522, Australia
{qb92, minjie}@uow.edu.au

Abstract. As social entities, intelligent agents need to collaborate with others, regardless of whether they are cooperative or self-interested. The durations of agent collaborations can be long-term or "one-shot". Nowadays, many multi-agent system applications require the system to work in open and dynamic domains. In such dynamic environments, how long collaboration should be kept among particular agents are always a problem to be discussed. In this paper, we focus on general self-interested multi-agent systems and analyze the advantages and disadvantages that can be brought by one-shot teams and long-term teams. Furthermore, we present a mechanism that can enable agents to form teams with reasonable terms and objects.

Keywords: Multi-agent system, team formation, self-interested agent, dynamic team forming.

1 Introduction

A multi-agent system (MAS) is a collection of intelligent agents. An intelligent agent is a reactive, proactive, autonomous and social entity, which performs a given task using information gleaned from its environment [10]. Generally, agents of an MAS can be characterized by whether they are cooperative or self-interested [9]. However, due to the distributed nature of the problem to be solved or the limitations of agent abilities, both cooperative and self-interested agents will often need to collaborate with other agents to achieve their goals [1, 4].

Today, as MAS applications getting more and more complex, many multi-agent systems (MASs) need to work in open and dynamic domains [6, 14, 15]. Uncertainties of dynamic application domains obstruct coherent teamwork and bring more challenges for agent team forming. In dynamic environments, factors such as system constrains, resource availabilities, agent goals (especially for self-interested agents), etc. are all changeable, and the changing may directly bring the MAS to different situations. However, "there is no single type of organization that is suitable for all situations" [7]. Therefore, in many MAS applications, a dynamic team forming mechanism is needed to enable agents to automatically form and reform groups/teams according to the changing of the environment.

Toward challenges brought by open environments, a number of researchers try to find an optimal mechanism for dynamic team forming. Abdallah, Shehory and Tambe proposed mechanisms to form agent teams based on skills of agents that are required for task completion [1, 12, 13]. This kind of mechanisms is efficient for cooperative MASs. But in self-interested MASs, individual agents' willingness and goals are another important factor to be considered during team forming. The research on team formation for self-interested agents generally focuses on the problem of forming one-shot teams, which is also called short-term teams, for individual tasks. In this kind of mechanisms, agents come together when they need to handle some tasks, and their relationships will be terminated after tasks have been accomplished. Obviously, one-shot teaming will arouse frequent grouping and regrouping among agents, and unfortunately, each time grouping/regrouping will consume some communication, computation, etc. resources. To overcome the weakness of one-shot teaming, Rathod and desJardins proposed several stable-team forming strategies for self-interested MASs [11]. These strategies cite human organization styles (i.e. humans always tend to prefer working with people they know and trust) into MAS organization formations, and try to make self-interested agents form long-term relationships to cut team forming consumptions. However, for many self-interested MASs, agent goals or willingness are changeable and uncertain. A long-term relationship is very hard to be kept after the goals of team member agents are changed.

In this paper, we introduce a mechanism that enables self-interested agents to dynamically form teams. Agent goals/willingness, task requirements and system constraints are all considered in this mechanism. In addition, the mechanism can enable agents to form both one-shot and long-term teams according to the situation of the environment and individual agent goals. The rest of this paper is arranged as follows. In the second section, we introduce the MAS structures and some important definitions and assumptions that are related with the mechanism. In Section 3, we analyze the advantages, disadvantages and suitable areas of long-term and one-shot teams. In addition, we describe our team forming mechanism. Finally, the conclusions and further directions of this research are presented in Section 4.

2 System Architecture and Problem Definition

Various MAS applications may have different system structures. In this research, we set up the environment with the aim of demonstrating and analyzing the team forming mechanism. Hence, the system structure set up toward assisting agent communication and task allocation. We also make some simplifying assumptions and definitions to avoid adding the scheduling and task decomposing problems. Furthermore, we only employ elementary agents and task models in the MAS. However, these models are generic enough to be practical and applicable to a wide range of real applications. In this section, we introduce our assumptions, problem definitions and the system structures.

2.1 The System Architecture

Our MAS architecture is shown in Fig. 1. In this paper, we assume that all agents of the system are self-interested. Their goals are to achieve awards through accomplishing tasks which are sent by outside users. New tasks are published on the Task Board

(TB) of the system, and will be removed from TB after been taken by an agent or agent team (AT). Published tasks are accessible to all individual agents and agent teams (ATs) of the system. The agent number of the system can be dynamic. Agents can enter and leave the system according to their willingness. However, agents have to publish and remove their registration information on the Agent Board (AB) of the system before they enter and leave the system. The registration information records the skills and status (see Subsection 2.2) of an agent.

Agent abilities are limited. To perform tasks beyond its ability, an agent needs to collaborate with other agents through joining or forming a team. Each AT is composed by one (and only one) Team Leader (TL) and several Team Members (TMs). After an agent joins an AT, it can get payments from the AT and at the same time it needs to work for the AT for a certain period. The payment and serving term are described in the contract (see Definition 3) between the Team Member (TM) and the TL.

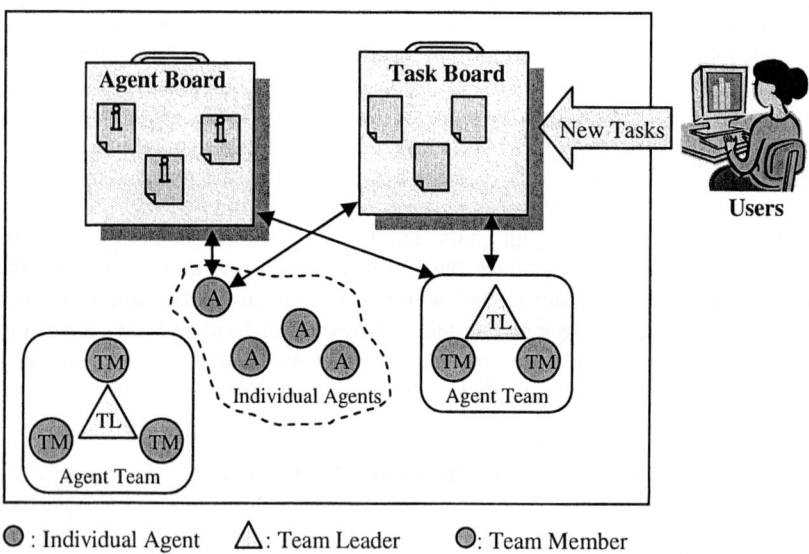

Fig. 1. The system architecture

2.2 Definitions and Assumptions

Before presenting the team forming mechanism, we need to give some important definitions and assumptions in this subsection.

Definition 1. Task. A task is formally defined as $t_i=<w_i, R_i'>$, where w_i is the reward gained by an agent/agent team if task t_i is accomplished by that agent/agent team; R_i' is the set of resources or skills, which are possessed by agents of the system, required by task t_i. A task can only be assigned to one agent or AT.

Definition 2. Agent. An agent is formally defined as $a_i=<g_i, R_i, s_i>$, where g_i is a set of individual goals of agent a_i; R_i is the skills and resources possessed by agent a_i; s_i is the status of a_i, where s_i includes three parameters: $s_i=(v_a, v_p, t)$. The meanings of v_a, v_p and t are listed in Table 1. s_i represents whether agent a_i is performing a task and participating an AT. Meanings of different s_i values are listed in Table 2.

Table 1. Parameters of s_i

Parameter	Meaning
v_a	Availability: presents whether an agent is performing a task; $v_a=0$ when the agent has no task (available); $v_a=1$ when the agent is performing a task (not available).
v_p	Position: presents whether an agent is an individual agent, TL or TM; $v_p=0$ when the agent is individual; $v_p=1$ when the agent is a TM of an AT; $v_p=2$ when the agent is a TL of an AT;
t	Contract Ending Time: see Definition 3

Table 2. Status of an agent

s_i value	Status of agent a_i
(0, 0, 0)	The agent is performing no task; has no AT (available).
(1, 0, 0)	The agent is performing a task; has no AT.
(0, 1, 0)	The agent has a one-shot contract as a TM and is performing no task.
(1, 1, 0)	The agent has a one-shot contract as a TM and is performing a task.
(0, 1, t)	The agent the TM of an AT for period t, and it is currently performing no task.
(1, 1, t)	The agent is the TM of an AT for period t, and it is currently performing a task.
(0, 2, 0)	The agent is the TL of an AT, and it is performing no task currently. (We assume that the TL cannot quit from its AT and let t value of a TL equal to 0.)
(1, 2, 0)	The agent is the TL of an AT, and it is performing a task currently.

Table 3. Payment types and explanations

Payment type	Explanations
Commission sc_{ij}	Payment that TM a_j can gain for each task completed by the AT, when a_j directly participates in the task.
Dividend sd_{ij}	Dividend that TM a_j can share for each task completed by the AT, when a_j does not actually participate in that task.

Definition 3. Contract. A Contract c_{ij} is an agreement between TL a_i and TM a_j. It can be defined as $c_{ij}=<t_{ij}, p_{ij}, S_{ij}>$, where t_{ij} is the contract ending time; p_{ij} is the penalty that the TL or TM has to pay (to the other side of the contract) if it breaks the

contract and terminates the cooperation relationship before t_{ij}; S_{ij} is a set of payment that a_j can gain through serving the AT. S_{ij} can be described as tuple $<sc_{ij}, sd_{ij}>$ (see Table 3 for explanations). For contracts between the TL and TM of a one-shot team, t_{ij}, p_{ij}, and sd_{ij} equal to 0.

Definition 4. Agent Team (AT). An Agent Team is a set of agents. It can be formally defined as $AT_i=<MS_i, TR_i>$, where MS_i is the set of agents that currently are TMs of AT_i; TR_i is the capacity of the whole AT.

In this paper, we assume that $TR_i = \sum_{j | a_j \in MS_i} R_j + R_i$, where R_i and R_j are resources possessed by the team leader and team members, respectively. In the other word, the capability of an AT is the sum of its TMs' capabilities and TL's capability. We also define that $\forall i \neq j : MS_i \cap MS_j = \Phi$, which means an agent can only participate in one AT.

Definition 5. Contributor Set (CS). A Contributor Set CS_{ij} ($CS_{ij} \subseteq MS_i$) of Agent Team AT_i is the set of agents that participate in performing task t_j, where t_j is a task of agent team AT_i. For a one-shot team, the CS equals to MS_i of the team (also refer to Definition 4).

Definition 6. Member Contribution (MC). For Agent Team AT_i, a Member Contribution mc_{ijk} is the contribution of agent a_k, where $a_k \in CS_{ij}$, in performing task t_j ($t_i=<w, R_i'>$). mc_{ijk} is equal to w/N, where N is the size of CS.

3 A Flexible Team Forming Approach

After presenting the system architecture and some important definitions, in this section, we will briefly introduce and compare the one-shot and long-term team forming strategies. Furthermore, we will present a flexible team-forming approach that can enable self-interested agents to select team-forming strategies and valuable team members automatically.

3.1 One-Shot Teams

One-shot team strategy is widely applied in many MAS applications. In this strategy, agents of the system do not have a team initially. When a task t_i is published in the TB, agents start to bid on the new task. The system facilitator will choose (or randomly select) a bidder to assign the task. After the agent bided the task successfully, it becomes a TL and starts to look for collaborators according to the task requirement R_i'. Finally, the AT will disband after t_i is accomplished.

Generally, the one-shot team strategy includes following processes. (Here, we only consider that the agents of the MAS cannot achieve the task individually.)

(1) The system facilitator of the MAS publishes a new task t_i ($t_i=<w_i, R_i'>$) on the TB;
(2) Agents, whose $g<w_i$ and $s=(0, 0, 0)$ bid on t_i;

(3) The system facilitator awards t_i to agent a_j ($a_j=<g_j, R_j, s_j>$). At the same time, a_j becomes the TL of agent team AT_j and modifies its s_j to (0, 2, 0). At this movement, $TR_j=R_j$;
(4) a_j searches the Agent Board to look for agents with status (0, 0, 0), which can provide the lacking resources R, where $R \subseteq (R_i' - R_i' \cap TR_j)$;
(5) a_j finds a required agent a_p, where $R_p \subseteq (R_i' - R_i' \cap TR_j)$;
(6) a_j sends a contract c_{jp} to a_p, where $sc_{jp} \leq (w_i - g_j) \cdot \#R_p / \#(R_i' - R_i)$ (#R is the size of set R);
(7) a_p accepts c_{jp} if $sc_{jp} \geq g_p$ or rejects c_{jp} if $sc_{jp} \leq g_p$;
(8) If c_{jp} is accepted by a_p, $TR_j = TR_j \cup R_p$, and a_p modifies its status to (0, 1, 0);
(9) Goes to Process (4) until $TR_j=R_i'$;
(10) AT_j starts to perform t_i; the TL and TMs of AT_j modify their statuses to (1, 1, 0) and (1, 2, 0), respectively;
(11) AT_j accomplishes t_i; agents of AT_j modify their statuses to (0, 0, 0) and are released from the team.

One-shot teams are suitable for dynamic MAS application domains. It always keeps loosely coupled relationships among agents as default. However, many dynamic applications are not that dynamic. For example, the new tasks may have some similarity, and their requirements might be similar (which means they may just need similar ATs). In this case, frequent grouping and regrouping are not very necessary, especially each time grouping will consume some system resources.

3.2 Long-Term Teams

Different from one-shot team forming, in long-term team forming strategy, the AT will not be dissolved after perform tasks. In the contrary, the TL of the team pays TMs some payments to keep the cooperation relationships, even if the TM does not contribute on the task accomplishment.

The long-term team strategy normally includes following processes.

(1) TL a_i finds several free agents, whose status value are (0, 0, 0), from the AB and send them contracts in order to form a team with them. Agents modify their statuses to (0, 1, t_{ij}) if they accept the contracts. In this case, agent team AT_i is formed successfully;
(2) TL a_i searches the TB for a suitable task and bids on task t_k ($t_k=<w_k, R_k'>$), where $R_k' \subseteq TR_i$ and $w_k \geq \sum_{jla_j \in MS_i} S_{ij} + g_i$ (also refer to Definition 1–4).
(3) If t_k is bided successfully, TL a_i assigns t_k to TM $a_p, a_q \ldots a_n$, where $R_p \cup R_q \cdots \cup R_n$ is the minimum set that satisfies $R_k' \subseteq R_p \cup R_q \cdots \cup R_n$. At the same time, $a_p, a_q \ldots a_n$ modify their statuses to (1, 1, t_{ip}), (1, 1, t_{iq}), ... (1, 1, t_{in}). Also, for this task performance, the Contributor Set CS_{ik} (refer to Definition 5) will be $\{a_p, a_q, \ldots, a_n\}$;
(4) $a_p, a_q \ldots a_n$ modify their statuses to (0, 1, t_{ip}), (0, 1, t_{iq}), ... (0, 1, t_{in}) after t_k is accomplished;

(5) TL a_i awards TM a_m, where $a_m \in AT_i$, with $(sc_{im}+sd_{im})$ if $a_m \in CS_{ik}$ and $(sc_{iq}+sd_{iq})$, and sd_{im} if $a_m \notin CS_{ik}$;

In addition, if the TL a_i or TM a_p wants to terminate the contract before the contract ending time (t_{ip}), they may process following two steps.

(1) a_i/a_p terminates c_{ip} with a_p/a_i, and pays p_{ip} to a_p/a_i;
(2) a_p is released from AT_i, and its status is modified to (0, 0, 0).

Hiring long-term teams can greatly reduce the system consumption caused by grouping and regrouping. However, most current long-term team forming strategies cannot figure out when agents should form long-term teams, which agents should be included in, and how long the relationships should be kept. For self-interested MAS applications, keeping unnecessary long-term cooperation relationships could be very dangerous and harmful for the overall performance of the system.

3.3 Team Member Evaluations and Flexible Team-Forming

From the comparison of last subsection, we can see that both long-term and one-shot teams have some advantages and disadvantages. One-shot teams are suitable for "ideal" dynamic tasks, i.e. requirements of various new tasks are totally different. On the other side, long-term teams possess advantages when tasks are "stable". In this subsection, we introduce an approach to enable agents to select a team style according to the task-requirement changing trend.

Obviously, TMs that are always contribute on performing tasks and can bring benefits to the team, are the most valuable members of an AT. These TMs should be kept into the team for a long term. In contrary, the AT should not include members that seldom contribute for the group for long periods.

In our approach, a TM is evaluated by two parameters: Utilization Rate (UR) ur_{Mk} and Sum Contribution (SC) sc_{Mk}. ur_{Mk} ($0 \leq ur_{Mk} \leq 1$) is the frequency that the TM has participated in the most recent M tasks of the AT. It can be calculated by Equation 1. sc_{Mk} is the total benefit that the TM has contributed to the AT in the most recent M tasks, it can be find out by using Equation 2.

$$ur_{Mk} = \sum_{k|a_k \in CS_{ij}}^{j|j\in[1,M]} \frac{1}{M} \qquad (1)$$

$$sc_{Mk} = \sum_{k|a_k \in CS_{ij}}^{j|j\in[1,M]} mc_{ijk} \qquad (2)$$

Here, we give a simple example. Suppose $t_1=<40, R_1'>$, $t_2=<50, R_2'>$ and $t_3=<60, R_3'>$ are the most recent three tasks accomplished by agent team AT_i. TMs that participate in these three tasks are $\{a_p, a_q\}$, $\{a_p, a_r\}$ and $\{a_p, a_q, a_s\}$, respectively. According to Equation 1 and 2, we can find out the UR and SC values of a_p, a_q, a_r and a_s are:

a_p: $ur_{3p}=3/3=1$; $sc_{3p}= 40/2+50/2+60/3=75$
a_q: $ur_{3q}=2/3$; $sc_{3p}= 40/2+0+60/3=50$
a_r: $ur_{3r}=1/3$; $sc_{3p}= 0+50/2=25$
a_s: $ur_{3s}=1/3$; $sc_{3p}= 0+0+60/3=30$

Comparing the UR and SC values of the four TMs of AT_i, we can see that a_p is the most important member of AT_i, it frequently participated in recent tasks and contributed the most benefit to the team. On the other hand, a_r and a_s seldom participated in recent tasks and do not contribute much to AT_i.

Table 4. Agent Evaluation

SC \ UR	High	Low
High	Can frequently participate in high award tasks;	Can participate in high award tasks; Not frequently be used.
Low	Can only participate in low award tasks; Frequently be used.	Can only participate in low award tasks; Seldom be used.

With UR and SC, the TL can evaluate the importance of an agent. Furthermore, the TL can make decision on which kind of relationship should be set up with the agent and which level payment should be included in the contract (see Table 4). The TL should keep long-term relationships with agents with high UR and SC, and the payments for these agents could be high. Agents with low UR will not contribute much to the team. Hence the TL should not include them in the AT. Agents with low sc_{Mk} and high ur_{Mk} values can only participate in low award tasks. So they can be included in the team for a long-term with low payments contracts. Finally, agents with high sc_{Mk} and low ur_{Mk} values can perform high award tasks. However, the MAS does not often have this kind of tasks. So the TL can set up one-shot cooperation with high commissions with these agents.

4 Conclusions and Future Work

As a social entity, an intelligent agent needs to collaborate with others in most multi-agent environments. However, the nature of such collaboration may vary in duration. Focused on challenges brought by dynamic application domains, many AI researchers suggest hiring long-term or one-shot team forming mechanisms in MASs. However, both of these two kinds of mechanisms have advantages and disadvantages. In this paper, we mainly focused on self-interested multi-agent systems and analyzed when the one-shot teams or long-term teams should be set up in the system. We also introduced a mechanism that can enable agents to automatically evaluate the importance of other agents; form teams with reasonable terms and objects according to the evaluation result.

The future work of this research is to extend the mechanism to more complex MAS organization structures. The agent organizations discussed in this paper are in simple team structures. However, in many MAS applications, more complex organization structures, such as holon [5] and congregation [3], need to be hired in the system. The next step of this research will be focused on developing mechanisms to make agents form these complex organizations automatically.

Acknowledgment

This research is supported by an International Linkage Grant from the Australian Research Council (contract number LX0346249) and a postgraduate scholarship from University of Wollongong.

References

1. Abdallah, S. and Lesser, V.: Organization-Based Cooperative Coalition Formation. Proceedings of the IEEE/WIC/ACM International Conference on Intelligent Agent Techonology, IAT, (2004) 162-168
2. Artikis, A. and Pitt, J.: A Formal Model of Open Agent Societies. Proceedings of the 5th International Conference on Autonomous Agents, ACM Press, (2001) 192–193
3. Brooks, C., Durfee, E. and Armstrong, A.: An Introduction to Congregating in Multiagent Systems. Proceedings of 4th International Conference on Multiagent Systems, (2000) 79-86
4. Decker, K. and Lesser, V.: Designing a Family of Coordination Algorithms. Proceedings of the 1st International Conference on Multi-Agent Systems, San Francisco, USA, (1995) 73-80
5. Fischer, K., Schillo, M. and Siekmann, J.: Holonic Multiagent Systems: The Foundation for the Organization of Multiagent Systems. Proceedings of the First International Conference on Applications of Holonic and Multiagent Systems (HoloMAS'03), LNAI 2744, Springer-Verlag, (2003) 71-80
6. Gerkey, B. and Mataric, M.: Multi-robot Task Allocation: Analyzing the Complexity and Optimality of Key Architectures. Proceedings of the IEEE International Conference on Robotics and Automation, Taibei, China, (2003) 3862–3868.
7. Horling, B. and Lesser, V.: A Survey of Multi-Agent Organizational Paradigms. Knowledge Engineering Review, (2005), at ftp://mas.cs.umass.edu/pub/bhorling/horling-paradigms.pdf (visited on 30/06/2005)
8. Huhns, M. and Stephens, L.: Multiagent Systems and Societies of Agents. Multiagent Systems: A Modern Approach to Distributed Artificial Intelligence. Gerhard Weiss (Eds.), MIT Press, Cambridge, Massachusetts, USA, (1999)
9. Lesser, V.: Cooperative Multiagent Systems: A Personal View of the State of the Art. IEEE Transactions on Knowledge and Data Engineering, Vol. 11(1), (1999) 133-142
10. Rao, A. and Georgeff, M.: An Abstract Architecture for Rational Agents. Proceedings of the Third International Conference on Principles of Knowledge Representation and Reasoning, San Mateo, USA, (1992) 439-449
11. Rathod, P. and desJardins, M.: Stable Team Formation among Self-interested Agents. AAAI Workshop on Forming and Maintaining Coalitions in Adaptive Multiagent Systems, San Jose, California, USA, (2004) 29-36

12. Shehory, O.: Methods for Task Allocation via Agent Coalition Formation. Artificial Intelligence Journal, Vol. 101(1–2), (1998) 165–200
13. Tambe, M.: Agent Architectures for Flexible, Practical Teamwork. Proceedings of the 14th National Conference on Artificial Intelligence, Providence, USA, (1997) 22–28
14. Tambe, M.: Towards Flexible Teamwork. Journal of Artificial Intelligence Research, Vol. 7, (1997) 83–124
15. Tambe, M.: Implementing Agent Teams in Dynamic Multi-agent Environments. Applied Artificial Intelligence, Vol. 12, (1998) 189–210

N-Learning: A Reinforcement Learning Paradigm for Multiagent Systems

Mark Mansfield, J.J. Collins, Malachy Eaton, and Thomas Collins

Department of Computer Science and Information Systems,
University of Limerick, Limerick, Ireland
mark.mansfield@ul.ie

Abstract. We introduce a novel reinforcement learning method for multiagent systems called N-learning. It has been developed to deal with the state space explosion caused by the presence of additional agents in an environment. N-learning is applied to a pursuit-evasion problem where a pursuer aims to calculate optimal policies for the interception of a deterministically moving evader, using an action selection component that can be realised through a number of techniques, and a heuristic reinforcement learning reward function. It is demonstrated that N-learning is able to outperform Q-learning at the pursuit-evasion task.

1 Introduction

Reinforcement Learning (RL) is a machine learning paradigm where an agent aims to improve at a task through interaction with the world. The agent learns to evaluate the utility of actions based on rewards received from the environment. Standard single-agent, tabular RL paradigms are typically defined for static environments with small state spaces. When other agents are added to a problem the size, and hence dimensionality, of the state space increases dramatically. Due to this, multiagent tasks may rapidly become intractable for Cartesian RL paradigms. Pursuit-evasion (PE) scenarios are among the most interesting multiagent systems (MAS) to study for a variety of reasons outlined by Cliff and Miller [6]. Among these reasons are that they provide insights into co-evolution, animal behaviour and neuroscience among other disciplines. They are of interest to the robotics community because successful pursuers or evaders require a tight integration of the sensory-motor loop due to a highly dynamic environment caused by the presence of an adversarial agent.

N-learning, a novel paradigm based on RL, has been applied to a PE task in a twenty five cell toroidal grid world. The evader moves deterministically around the grid world and the pursuer uses N-learning to learn optimal pursuit policies. The premise behind N-learning is that one-step lookahead can be used to find successful control strategies. In this work, one-step control is implemented using Q-learning or dynamic programming (DP). While this behaviour policy is used during training, an estimation policy, called the N-policy, is simultaneously updated off-line. Once the training phase is complete the pursuer is tested during a performance phase where the N-policy is used for control.

A significant strength of N-learning is that it does not need access to the full state signal in order to learn well. This means that the state space representation can have a lower dimensionality. Reducing the dimensionality of the state space as a means of tackling the state space explosion can lead to the phenomenon of perceptual aliasing, discussed in more detail later.

2   Reinforcement Learning

RL involves an agent improving at a task through interaction with the environment. It has been used to find solutions to tasks including chess [2], control optimisation [3], mobile robot control [9] and backgammon [12].

The tabular form of RL has an input vector which specifies the current state of the world. The goal of the agent is to associate the input vector with actions, in order to maximise an external reward signal. The mapping from state to action is known as a policy and the agent aims to learn the optimal policy; that is, the policy that maximises the expected discounted return denoted by:

$$V_t = \sum_{k=0}^{\infty} \gamma^k r_{t+k} \qquad (1)$$

where V_t is the expected discounted cumulative reward starting at time t, r_t is the reward received after the action selected at time t, and $0 \leq \gamma \leq 1$ is the discount parameter which makes future rewards less valuable than immediate ones.

2.1   Q-Learning

Q-learning [13] is a commonly used temporal difference RL method that uses equation 2 to update the value of state-action pairs.

$$Q(s_t, a_t) \leftarrow Q(s_t, a_t) + \alpha[r_{t+1} + \gamma max_a Q(s_{t+1}, a_{t+1}) - Q(s_t, a_t)] \qquad (2)$$

where s_t is the state at time t, a_t is the action executed in response to the sensation of t, r_{t+1} is the reward generated by the state transition caused by execution of a_t, s_{t+1} is the new state following the transition and $0 \leq \alpha \leq 1$ is the learning rate. Results for Q-learning applied to a PE problem specified in section 5 are provided, as a means of evaluating the performance of N-learning.

2.2   Dynamic Programming

DP is used to compute optimal value functions and policies given a perfect model of the environment in the form of a Markov Decision Process. DP obtains optimal policies by the iterative application of the Bellman optimality equation, shown in equation 3, to all state values.

$$V^\pi(s) = \sum_a \pi(s,a) \, \mathcal{P}^a_{ss'} [\mathcal{R}^a_{ss'} + \gamma V^\pi(s')] \qquad (3)$$

where $\pi(s,a)$ is the probability of taking action a in state s, s' represents the state at the next time step, $\mathcal{P}^a_{ss'}$ is the probability of taking action a in state s and transitioning to new state s', $\mathcal{R}^a_{ss'}$ is the reward received as a result of taking action a in state s and transitioning to new state s', and $\gamma V^\pi(s')$ is the discounted value of next state s' in the value function.

3 Multiagent Systems and Reinforcement Learning

The fundamental problem that MAS pose for tabular single agent RL methods is that they cause an explosion in the size of the state space. Suppose the task facing a learner in a single agent domain is to move to a designated goal cell in a twenty five cell grid world. A sufficient state signal, or input vector, in this case would be the agent's own position, giving twenty five distinct states. However, in the PE task described later, the input vector would necessarily include the position of the evader, leading to a large increase in the size of the state space that has to be represented by the value function. In this example there are now 25^2 distinct states.

Several attempts have been made to apply RL to MAS. Zhao and Schmidhuber [17] developed a technique called *incremental self-improvement* to simulate a continuous evolutionary race and show that agents could learn in continually changing environments. Ono et al [8] used a variant of Whitehead's modular RL architecture, [15], to allow four predators to surround an evader in a grid world. Nagayuki et al [7] consider a two-agent PE cooperation task where agents learn models of other agents to aid action selection. Their method extends an agent's Q-function to include the action set of other agents in the environment. Stone enabled a team of soccer playing robots to learn pass selection using TPOT-RL [10]. A pass is evaluated by a reward value from t_{lim} time steps into the future. The technique bears similarities to both temporal difference methods and Monte Carlo methods but is not strictly recognisable as either. M-Dyna-Q is proposed as an implementation of single agent Dyna-Q by Weiß [14] for cooperation in MAS.

3.1 Perceptual Aliasing in Multiagent Systems

Perceptual Aliasing (PA), a term first introduced by Whitehead and Ballard [16], occurs when an agent's internal representation of a problem domain is inconsistent with the true representation of the domain. It occurs when distinct situations that are indistinguishable from immediate perceptual input require different optimal actions from an agent. PA occurs because the mapping between world states and an agent's internal representation of the world can be many-to-many. A state in the real world, $s \in \mathcal{S}_{RW}$, may map to several internal states, $s \in \mathcal{S}_I$, or conversely many real world states could map to the same internally represented state.

Due to the fact that N-learning addresses the problem of state space explosion by reducing it's dimensionality, the problem of PA has been introduced. Empirical results in [4] show that the standard RL paradigms Sarsa and Q-learning do not cope well with perceptually aliased tasks.

In section 6, results for Q-learning applied to a PE task using incomplete, or partial, and full input vectors are reported and compared with results for N-learning, which only uses a partial input vector to learn it's value function. In a twenty five cell grid world with two agents, a partial input vector for the pursuer includes only it's own position, while the full input vector includes the position of both agents.

4 N-Learning

In this section N-learning is introduced, which has been developed to enable agents to learn in multiagent systems. The basic concept behind N-learning is to use a one-step lookahead behaviour policy to control an agent during training. Simultaneously, the agent learns an offline estimation policy to achieve the same task, based on state-action pairs visited during episodes.

4.1 N-Learning Algorithm

N-learning has two phases; the training phase and the performance phase. During the training phase the N-policy is learned. Control during training is implemented by a behaviour policy, which can be implemented using any desirable paradigm. In this work we have implemented N-learning with both a Q-learning and DP behaviour policy. The N-policy is learned based on the state-action pairs sampled during training contests. In the performance (testing) phase, the N-policy is used to control the learning agent. It is from this performance that results are derived.

Training phase:
Repeat for each training episode:
    For each time step of episode:
        Determine agent action by applying DP to an environmental model
            (a) Set the reward function:
                $\forall s' \in \mathcal{S}$: reward = 100 if the expected next state = s'
                else reward = 0
            (b) Set the transition function using feedback bias factor, $\mathcal{K}^a_s$,
                discussed in section 4.2
            (c) Carry out value iteration
                Output a deterministic policy , π, such that
                $\pi(s) = \arg\max_a \sum_{s'} \mathcal{P}^a_{ss'} \mathcal{K}^a_s [\, \mathcal{R}^a_{ss'} + \gamma V(s') \,]$
    Execute learning agent action as specified by DP
    Record state-action pair visited by learner
End episode
Update N Policy using record of state-action pairs visited

Performance phase:
   For each time step of episode:
      Determine and execute agent action by consulting N-policy
   End episode

Listing 1: The N-learning algorithm

The N-learning algorithm using a DP behaviour policy is shown in listing 1. It is clear to see how, during the training phase, the behaviour policy is used for control and then at the end of each episode the N-policy is updated. Steps (a), (b) and (c) are specific to the DP action selection mechanism and would need to be altered depending on the particular behaviour paradigm in use.

4.2 Feedback Loop

The purpose of the feedback loop from the N-policy is to improve the action selections of the behaviour policy. As contests proceed during the training phase, the N-policy is somewhat passive. It is updated but does not contribute to the control of the pursuer. This is wasteful because the N-policy value function implicitly encodes what has happened in previous training episodes. The relative values of state-action pairs in the N-policy indicate which ones have proved more valuable than others in the past. N-learning uses this information that is implicit in the N-value function to influence action selection in the behaviour policy. The exact implementation of the feedback loop is dependent on the behavioural policy in use.

Feedback Loop for DP Behaviour Policy. The N value function is used to perturb the state transition function, $\mathcal{P}^a_{ss'}$, for DP control during training. To do this a term called the *feedback bias factor*, $\mathcal{K}^a_s$, is introduced to equation 3:

$$V^\pi(s) = \sum_a \pi(s,a) \, \mathcal{P}^a_{ss'} \mathcal{K}^a_s [\mathcal{R}^a_{ss'} + \gamma V^\pi(s')] \qquad (4)$$

For each state, $\mathcal{K}^a_s$ is calculated for all actions from that state, based on their values in the N value function. The values for all actions from a state are summed and normalised to one, with any negative values being assigned a value of zero. This system biases the DP against state-action pairs that have a negative value in the N-value function. Exploration is implemented, with a given probability, by assigning random values to $\mathcal{K}^a_s$ for all actions from a state. As this exploration is implicit in the DP control mechanism, there is no need for explicit action selection exploration i.e. the action suggested by the DP control policy can be executed without the need for an exploration mechanism such as ϵ-greedy action selection for example.

Within the N-learning framework the DP action selection method poses three problems.

- Firstly, the computational requirements to carry out DP for each action selection are unnecessarily high.

- Secondly, the input to the DP action selection module is the position of both agents. Therefore, it may not be justifiable to say that N-learning only works with partial state information.
- Thirdly, a model of the environment is required

An alternative to DP for action selection is Q-learning, which has none of the three drawbacks listed above.

Feedback Loop for Q-Learning Behaviour Policy. The feedback loop works in a similar manner for the Q-learning behaviour policy. At the beginning of each episode the Q-values for all state action pairs are again altered using a *feedback bias factor* calculated from the corresponding values in the N value function according to equation 5.

$$Q(s,a) = \mathcal{K}_s^a Q(s,a) \tag{5}$$

The term $\mathcal{K}_s^a$ is calculated for each state action pair in a similar manner to the feedback bias factor for DP action selection. The behaviour policy is again biased against actions that have been proven to lead to long episodes in the past.

4.3 N-Learning Update

At the end of each training episode the N-policy is updated using a heuristic RL reward function. It is heuristic because knowledge of optimal behaviour in the domain is used to choose parameter values for the update. The update function is a type of RL reward function, but not the simple scalar function that is often encountered. A characteristic of RL is that it evaluates examples of behaviour using a reward function [1].

Once an episode is finished, the state-action pairs that were visited are updated based on the outcome of the episode. Each state-action pair that was sampled is updated according to equation 6.

$$N(s,a) = N(s,a) + \alpha(update\_target - N(s,a)) \tag{6}$$

The *update target* is determined by the reward function for the task in question. In the experiment of section 5 the goal of the agent is to learn a policy with the shortest episodes possible and so *update_target* is calculated as follows:

If $episode\_length = maximum\_length$, $update\_target = -1$, else:
$update\_target = \frac{10000}{ep\_length} * \frac{position}{ep\_length^{ep\_length}}$

where *ep_length* is the length of the training episode in question and *position* is the position the state-action pair was sampled in the episode i.e. the first, second, third etc. state-action pair visited in the contest. This update function is designed to reward the final state-action pairs visited in short contests most highly. In the next section the problem environment is described and in section 6 results for both Q-learning and N-learning when applied to the problem are presented.

5 Pursuit-Evasion Environment and Agent Dynamics

Contests take place in a 25 cell, square grid world. This is a toroidal grid meaning that the edges are wrap-around. The evader moves in a deterministic manner and can move one cell up, down, to the left or to the right on each time step. The evader's deterministic movement model and the three trajectories contained in it are shown in figure 1. The start position of the evader determines it's trajectory in a contest. The task for the learning agent, the pursuer, is to determine a policy that allows it to intercept the evader in the shortest number of moves possible. The pursuer has kinematic parity with the evader; but it can also remain in the same cell for a time step. This is a difficult environment for the pursuer to learn in because the grid can behave like a two dimensional open plane if the evader moves in a continuous straight line.

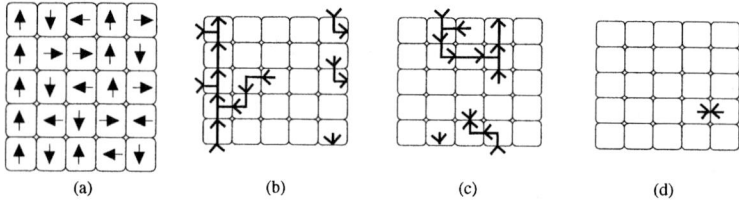

(a)   (b)   (c)   (d)

Fig. 1. The evader movement model with the three trajectories contained within it

Contests progress as follows. From their original positions, the agents select an action on each time step and move to a new cell simultaneously. If both agents are in the same cell after they move, then the contest is finished. If a contest lasts longer than ten time steps then it is terminated and a new one is started. Ten time steps was chosen as the termination time because it was calculated that an optimal pursuer should not take longer than four time steps to intercept the pursuer under any circumstance.

6 Results

Here results for Q-learning and N-learning when applied to the PE problem discussed in section 5 are presented. Results for Q-learning are based on a learning agent having access to either a *full* or *partial* state input vector. A full input vector includes the positions of both agents, while a partial input vector only takes into account the position of the pursuer. Table 1 shows the parameter settings for the N-learning and Q-learning experiments. 5,000 episodes was an arbitrary choice for the training time and no attempts were made to optimise parameters.

6.1 Q-Learning with a *Full* State Input Vector

For these Q-learning experiments, updates to state-action pairs were carried out using equation 2. In an n cell grid there are n^2 combinations of pursuer-evader

Table 1. Parameters for Q-learning and N-learning experiments

Parameter	Q-learning	N-learning
Training Episodes	5,000	5,000
Exploration Probability	0.2	0.2
Learning Rate	1/number of episodes experienced	0.01
Discount Parameter	1/time step in episode	Implicit in update
Rewards	Capture = 100, no capture = 0	Implicit in update

Table 2. Q-learning with *full* state input vector

Time steps to capture	Optimal Performance	Q Performance	Q Performance %Optimality	Q Cumulative %Optimality
1	125	88	70.4	70.4
2	200	200	100	88.62
3	200	200	100	92.95
4	100	98	98	93.76
Total	625	586	N/A	N/A

start position. This means that in a twenty five cell grid there are 625 start configurations. Table 2 shows how many of the 625 start configurations had ended after one, two, three and four time steps. Optimal pursuer performance can be calculated because of the deterministic movement pattern of the evader. The second column of table 2 shows how an optimal pursuer should perform. Column 3 shows how the Q-learner performed. The second last column indicates Q-learning performance as a % of optimal performance and the final column is the cumulative % of optimal performace over the four time steps. In any cases where the optimal path was not found, the paths found were suboptimal or were terminated because that took more than ten time steps to intercept the evader. It is clear from table 2 that the Q-learning performance is close to optimal when the learner has access to the full state signal. However, if the state space was increased or another agent was introduced to the environment then this method may become intractable.

6.2 Q-Learning with a *Partial* State Input Vector

From table 3, it can be seen that with a partial input vector the pursuer is able to find the optimal pursuit trajectory in just 51.7% of all start configurations. We suggest that this poor performance can be attributed to perceptual aliasing, as the Q value function is not of a suitable dimensionality to represent the state space accurately.

6.3 N-Learning Using a DP Behaviour Policy

Table 4 shows how the N-learning implementation with the DP action selection mechanism (NDP) performed on the PE task compared with optimal behaviour. NDP exhibits close to optimal behaviour and is better than Q-learning

Table 3. Q-learning with *partial* state input vector

Time steps to capture	Optimal Performance	Q-learning Performance	Q-learning Performance %Optimality	Q-learning Cumulative %Optimality
1	125	109	87.2	87.2
2	200	93	46.5	62.2
3	200	83	41.5	54.3
4	100	38	38	51.7
Total	625	323	N/A	N/A

Table 4. N-learning with DP behaviour policy

Time steps to capture	Optimal Performance	NDP Performance	NDP Performance %Optimality	NDP Cumulative %Optimality
1	125	125	100	100
2	200	196	98	98.77
3	200	193	96.5	97.9
4	100	93	93	97.12
Total	625	622	N/A	N/A

performance in section 6.1. NDP found the optimal path for all but three of the pursuer-evader start configurations and even these were only one move longer than the corresponding optimal paths. Reasons for this suboptimal performance could be that the update function needs to be improved, the training period is not long enough or the constant learning rate is unsuitable. Current investigations examine these areas in more detail.

6.4 N-Learning Using a Partial Q-learning Behaviour Policy

The behaviour policy for this N-learning implementation is the partial Q-learning action selection of section 6.2. As partial Q-learning only has the position of the

Table 5. N-learning using partial Q-learning behaviour policy

Time steps to capture	Optimal Performance	NPQ Performance	NPQ Performance %Optimality	NPQ Cumulative %Optimality
1	125	125	100	100
2	200	200	100	100
3	200	199	99.5	99.76
4	100	97	97	99.36
Total	625	621	N/A	N/A

pursuer as its input, it can be said that this N-learning architecture does indeed use a partial input vector. Results for N-learning with partial Q-learning (NPQ) action selection are shown in table 5.

It can be seen that NPQ and NDP have similar performance. This is a highly significant result because using NPQ, the entire N-learning architecture now learns effectively without a model of the environment and without a full input vector. It is also clear from results in tables 2 and 5 that NPQ performs as well as Q-learning with a full input vector i.e. the situation where there is no perceptual aliasing.

7 Conclusion

Further investigations into N-learning are currently being carried out concerning the convergence properties for N-learning and experiments involving non-deterministic evaders. In this paper the N-learning architecture was introduced, which has been developed in response to some of the difficulties posed to standard single agent paradigms by multiagent systems. The novel elements of this architecture have been discussed including the update heuristic and the feedback mechanism. Results have shown that N-learning is a promising concept that certainly warrants further investigation. There are several interesting opportunities for the further progress of N-learning including the possible introduction of function approximation techniques, so that N-learning can be tested outside the limited domain of grid worlds. The N-learning model is quite primitive and could quite feasibly be developed on-line as learning progresses, as is the case with Sutton's Dyna architecture [11], or with n^{th} order statistics in a similar manner to Ficici and Pollack [5].

Acknowledgment

This research has been funded by a postgraduate scholarship granted by the Irish Research Council for Science, Engineering and Technology, IRCSET.

References

1. Andrew G. Barto and Thomas G. Dietterich. Reinforcement learning and its relationship to supervised learning. In *Handbook of Learing and Approximate Dynamic Programming*. Wiley-IEEE Press, Cambridge, MA, USA, 2004.
2. Jonathan Baxter, Andrew Tridgell, and Lex Weaver. Learning to play chess using temporal differences. *Mach. Learn.*, 40(3):243–263, 2000.
3. Robert H. Crites and Andrew G. Barto. Improving elevator performance using reinforcement learning. In *Advances in Neural Information Processing Systems*, volume 8. The MIT Press.
4. P. Crook and G. Hayes. Learning in a State of confusion: Perceptual aliasing in grid world navigation. In *In Towards Intelligent Mobile Robots 2003 (TIMR 2003), 4 British Conference on (Mobile) Robotics, UWE, Bristol.*, 2003.

5. Sevan G. Ficici and Jordan B. Pollack. Statistical reasoning strategies in the pursuit and evasion domain. In *European Conference on Artificial Life*, pages 79–88, 1999.
6. Geoffrey F. Miller and Dave Cliff. Co-evolution of pursuit and evasion I: Biological and game-theoretic fouondations. Technical Report CSRP311, 1994.
7. Yasuo Nagayuki, Shin Ishii, and Kenji Doya. Multi-agent reinforcement learning: An approach based on the other agent's internal model. In *ICMAS '00: Proceedings of the Fourth International Conference on MultiAgent Systems (ICMAS-2000)*, page 215, Washington, DC, USA, 2000. IEEE Computer Society.
8. Norihiko Ono, Kenji Fukumoto, and Osamu Ikeda. Collective behavior by modular reinforcement learning animats. In *From animals to animats 4*, pages 618–624, Cambridge, MA, 1996. MIT Press.
9. W. Smart and L. Kaelbling. Effective reinforcement learning for mobile robots. In *In Proceedings of the IEEE International Conference on Robotics and Automation, pages 3404–3410, 2002. IEEE, Piscataway, NJ.*, 2002.
10. Peter Stone and Manuela M. Veloso. Team-partitioned, opaque-transition reinforced learning. In *RoboCup*, pages 261–272, 1998.
11. Richard S. Sutton. Planning by incremental dynamic programming. In *Proceedings of the Eighth International Workshop on Machine Learning*, pages 353–357. Morgan Kaufmann, 1991.
12. Gerald Tesauro. Temporal difference learning and td-gammon. *Commun. ACM*, 38(3):58–68, 1995.
13. Christopher J. Watkins. *Learning from delayed rewards*. PhD thesis, University of Cambridge, Cambridge, England, 1989.
14. Gerhard Weiß. Technical report fki-233-90: A multiagent framework for planning, reacting and learning. Technical report, D-80290 Munchen, Germany, 1999.
15. Steven Whitehead. Learning multiple goal behavior via task decomposition and dynamic policy merging. In Jonathan H. Connell and Sridhar Mahadevan, editors, *Robot Learning*. Kluwer Academic Publishers, Norwell, MA, USA, 1993.
16. Steven D. Whitehead and Dana H. Ballard. Learning to perceive and act by trial and error. *Mach. Learn.*, 7(1):45–83, 1991.
17. Jieyu Zhao and Juergen Schmidhuber. Incremental self-improvement for life-time multi-agent reinforcement learning. In Pattie Maes, Maja J. Mataric, Jean-Arcady Meyer, Jordan Pollack, and Stewart W. Wilson, editors, *Proceedings of the Fourth International Conference on Simulation of Adaptive Behavior: From animals to animats 4*, pages 516–525, Cape Code, USA, 9-13 1996. MIT Press.

Preferences of Agents in Defeasible Logic*

Mehdi Dastani[1], Guido Governatori[2], Antonino Rotolo[3], and Leendert van der Torre[4]

[1] Intelligent Systems Group, Utrecht University,
P.O.Box 80.089, NL-3508 TB Utrecht, The Netherlands
mehdi@cs.uu.nl
[2] School of ITEE, The University of Queensland
Brisbane QLD 4072, Australia
guido@itee.uq.edu.au
[3] CIRSFID, University of Bologna,
Via Galliera 3, I-40121 Bologna, Italy
rotolo@cirsfid.unibo.it
[4] CWI, Amsterdam, and Delft University of Technology,
Kruislaan 413, NL-1098 SJ Amsterdam, The Netherlands
torre@cwi.nl

Abstract. We are interested in programming languages for cognitive agents with preferences. We define rule-based agent theories and inference procedures in defeasible logic, and in this setting we discuss patterns of agent behavior called agent types.

1 Introduction

There are several rule-based approaches to programming cognitive agents [4,7,2]. In this paper we extend the Defeasible Logic (DL) approach. DL is a simple, efficient but flexible non-monotonic formalism able to deal with many different intuitions of non-monotonic reasoning and recently applied in many fields. Here we propose a non-monotonic logic of agency which extends the framework developed in [1]. DL is one of the most expressive languages of the type we are interested in, and in particular it has defined the largest set of patterns called agent types. Moreover, it is flexible to incorporate ideas from other languages which have not been introduced yet, such as extension generation and selection from BOID [4], or deliberation languages from 3APL [7,5].

However, it has two drawbacks. First, DL, as well as its rival rule based programming languages, is based on a uniform representation of rules, whereas in artificial intelligence and in practical reasoning other complex structures have been proposed. Most importantly, rule-based approaches are based on conditionals, whereas an alternative approach is based on comparative notions. Examples are preference logics and CP nets instead of logics of desires and goals, ordered disjunctions instead of default logics, betterness logics instead of logics of ideality, logics of sub-ideality in deontic logic, etc. Second, it is not immediate how DL can deal with complex actions discussed in action

---

* This work was partially supported by Australia Research Council under Discovery Project No. DP0558854 on "A Formal Approach to Resource Allocation in Web Service Oriented Composition in Open Marketplaces".

languages such as 3APL [7] and in recent incarnations of the BOID architecture [6]. In this paper we address the first drawback while the second is left for future research.

Some issues of agent programming languages should be addressed: how to detect and resolve conflicts that include such preferences, and which kind of agent types can be introduced to deal with preferences. Summarizing, we therefore contribute to cognitive agent programming languages by addressing the following research question: *How to use DL extended with graded preferences?* This question breaks down in the following sub-questions:

1. How to introduce graded preferences in DL?
2. How to detect and resolve conflicts using preferences?
3. How to define agent types based on preferences?

For the representation of preferences we use a variant of the $\otimes$ operator of [8] in DL, because it has several advantages over other comparative notions. First, it has already been integrated with a rule based formalism. Second, it has been applied to complicated problems in deontic logic, e.g., to the so-called contrary-to-duty reasoning. Third, it allows to clearly distinguish between conflicts and violations within a rule-based system. In fact, though these notions may conflate, conflicts and violations have in general to be kept separate. Suppose you have an agent doing A while an obligation states $\text{OBL}\neg A$. Since the logic for OBL is usually not reflexive, the scenario does not lead necessarily to a logical conflict but a violation: indeed, conflict-resolution strategies may require that $\text{OBL}\neg A$ is not overriden.

In this paper we focus on goal generation based on beliefs, desires, intentions and obligations. Our system is rule-based, and rules will allow to derive new motivational factors of an agent. We will divide the rules into rules for beliefs, desires, intentions, and obligations. Provability for beliefs will not generate goals, since in our view they concern agent's knowledge about the world: beliefs may contribute to derive goals (desires, intentions, and obligations), but they are not in themselves motivations for action.

The layout of this paper is as follows. In Section 2 we introduce agents with preferences in DL, and in Section 3 we show how to infer goal conclusions from rules with preferences. In Section 4 we discuss conflicts among rules and patterns called agent types.

2 Agents in Defeasible Logic

We focus on how mental attitudes and obligations jointly interplay in modeling agent deliberation and behavior. The formal language contains modal literals, and preferences (including literals as a borderline case).

Definition 1 (Language). *Let* $M = \{\text{BEL}, \text{DES}, \text{INT}, \text{OBL}\}$ *be a set of modal operators, and P a set of propositional atoms.*

- *The set of literals is defined as* $L = P \cup \{\neg p | p \in P\}$.
- *If q is a literal, $\sim q$ denotes the complementary literal (if q is a positive literal p then $\sim q$ is $\neg p$; and if q is $\neg p$, then $\sim q$ is p).*

- Given the set of literals and the modal operators BEL, DES, INT, and OBL, if l is a literal and X is a modal operator, then Xl and $\neg Xl$ are modal literals. Every literal l is an $\otimes$-expression. If $l_1,\ldots,l_n$ are literals then $l_1 \otimes \ldots \otimes l_n$ is an $\otimes$-expression. The goal language L_{goal} is the smallest set that contains literals, modal literals and $\otimes$-expressions.

For $X \in \{\text{BEL}, \text{INT}, \text{DES}, \text{OBL}\}$, we have that $\phi \rightarrow_X \psi$ is a *strict rule* such that whenever the premises ϕ are indisputable so is the conclusion ψ. $\phi \Rightarrow_X \psi$ is a *defeasible rule* that can be defeated by contrary evidence. $\phi \leadsto_X \psi$ is a *defeater* that is used to defeat some defeasible rules by producing evidence to the contrary.

Definition 2 (Rules). *A rule r consists of its* antecedent *(or body) $A(r)$ ($A(r)$ may be omitted if it is the empty set), an arrow ($\rightarrow$ for a strict rule, $\Rightarrow$ for a defeasible rule, and $\leadsto$ for a defeater), and its* consequent *(or head) $C(r)$. In addition the arrow is labelled either with a modal operator $X \in M$. If the arrow is labelled with BEL the rule is for belief, and similarly for the other modal operators.*

- Given a rule r, $A(r)$ is a set of literals or modal literals, and $C(r)$ is a literal with no occurrence of $\otimes$ for strict rules, an $\otimes$-expression for defeasible rules and defeaters.
- Given a set R of rules, we denote the set of all strict rules in R by R_s, the set of strict and defeasible rules in R by R_{sd}, the set of defeasible rules in R by R_d, and the set of defeaters in R by R_{dft}. $R[q]$ denotes the set of rules in R with consequent q. For some i, $1 \leq i \leq n$, such that $c_i = q$, $R[c_i = q]$ and $r_d^X[c_i = q]$ denote, respectively, the set of rules and a defeasible rule of type X with the head $\otimes_{i=1}^n c_i$.

Rules for beliefs are meant to constitute the reasoning core of the system. The purpose of goal generation is to derive the other modal literals. For example, the application of $p \Rightarrow_{\text{INT}} q$ permits to infer INTq. Accordingly, modalities do not occur in the consequents of rules to keep the system manageable.

Definition 3 (Defeasible agent theory). *A defeasible agent theory is a structure $D = (F, R^{\text{BEL}}, R^{\text{DES}}, R^{\text{INT}}, R^{\text{OBL}}, >)$ where F is a finite set of facts, R^{BEL} is a finite set of rules for belief, R^{DES} is a finite set of rules for desire, R^{INT} is a finite set of rules for intention, R^{OBL} is a finite set of rules for obligation, and $>$, the superiority relation, is a binary relation over the set of rules.*

The *superiority relation* $>$ says when one rule may override the conclusion of another rule. *Facts* are indisputable statements. Beside the superiority relation, which is used when we have contradictory conclusions, we can establish a preference over the conclusions by using the operator $\otimes$. Thus, the intuitive reading of a sequence like $a \otimes b \otimes c$ means that a is preferred, but if $\neg a$ is the case, then b is preferred; if $\neg b$ is the case, then the third choice is c.[1]

Definition 4 (Operators). *A preference operator $\otimes$ is a binary operator satisfying the following properties: (1) $a \otimes (b \otimes c) = (a \otimes b) \otimes c$ (associativity); (2) $\otimes_{i=1}^n a_i = (\otimes_{i=1}^{k-1} a_i) \otimes (\otimes_{i=k+1}^n a_i)$ where exists j such that $a_j = a_k$ and $j < k$ (duplication and contraction on the right).*

---

[1] A similar approach, but with a different motivation has been proposed in the context of logic programming by Brewka and co-worker in their logic of ordered disjunction [3].

The general idea of degree of preferences is that $\otimes$ formulas are interpreted as preference formulas like in [8] and are here extended to cover all motivational component: *for beliefs*, a construction such as $\neg SunShining \Rightarrow_{BEL} Raining \otimes Snowing$ says that the agent believes that it is raining, but if it is not raining then it is snowing as the sun is not shining; *for desires*, rule $TimeForHoliday \Rightarrow_{DES} GoToAustralia \otimes GoToSpain$ means that, if it is time for holiday, the agent has the primary desire to go to Australia, but, if this is not the case, her desire is to go to Spain; *for intentions*, rule $SunShining \Rightarrow_{INT} Jogging \otimes Walking$ says that the agent intends to do jogging if the sun is shining, but, if, for some other reasons, this is not the case, then she will have the intention to have a walk; *for obligations*, rule $Order \Rightarrow_{OBL} Pay \otimes PayInterest$ says that, if the agent sends her purchase order, then she will be obliged to pay, but, in the event this is not done, she will have to pay interest.

The $\otimes$ formulas are characterized by the following subsumption relation among rules, which is used in the following section to infer goals from an agent theory.

Definition 5. *Let* $r_1 = \Gamma \Rightarrow_X \bigotimes_{i=1}^m a_i \otimes b$ *and* $r_2 = \Gamma' \Rightarrow_X c$ *be two goal rules. Then* r_1 *subsumes* r_2 *iff* $\Gamma \cup \{\neg a_1, \ldots, \neg a_m\} = \Gamma'$, $c = e$ *and* $b = (e \otimes (\bigotimes_{k=1}^n d_k))$, $0 \leq n$.

The following example illustrates subsumption.

Example 1. $Order \Rightarrow_{OBL} Pay \otimes PayInterest$ subsumes $Order \Rightarrow_{OBL} Pay$. Moreover, $Order \Rightarrow_{OBL} Pay \otimes PayInterest$ subsumes $Order, \neg Pay \Rightarrow_{OBL} PayInterest$.

The following example illustrates the agent theory.

Example 2. (Running example) Suppose an agent desires an application server. She can buy two products from X or Y. In general she prefers X but, for working with Linux, she does not intend to order X's product. X requires a payment, within 2 days, of 300\$, otherwise X forbids to download the software. Y requires a payment of 600\$ within 1 day, or, as a second choice, a payment of 660\$. The agent, for some reasons, does not intend to pay to Y 660\$. Agent's financial resources amount to 700\$, which are available in 4 days. As facts, we also know that the agent is a Linux user. The following piece of theory is considered to derive the agent's goals.

$F = \{700\$In4days, UseLinux, DESApplserver\}$
$R = \{r_1 : 700\$In4days \Rightarrow_{BEL} \neg PayY600\$1days, \ r_2 : 700\$In4days \Rightarrow_{BEL} \neg PayX300\$2days,$
$\quad r_3 : DESApplserver \Rightarrow_{INT} OrderX \otimes OrderY, \ r_4 : UseLinux \Rightarrow_{INT} \neg OrderX$
$\quad r_5 : INTOrderY \Rightarrow_{INT} \neg PayY660\$, \ r_6 : INTOrderY \Rightarrow_{OBL} PayY600\$1days \otimes PayY660\$,$
$\quad r_7 : INTOrderX \Rightarrow_{OBL} PayX300\$2days \otimes \neg DownloadApplserverX\}$
$>= \{r_4 > r_3\}$

3 Goal Generation: Inference with Preferences

Proofs are based on proof tags $+\Delta$, $-\Delta$, $+\partial$ and $-\partial$. $+\Delta_X q$ means that q is provable using only facts and strict rules for X, $-\Delta_X q$ means that it has been proved that q is not definitely provable, $+\partial_X q$ means that q is defeasibly provable in D and $-\partial_X q$ means that it has been proved that q is not defeasibly provable.

Definition 6 (Proofs). *Given an agent theory D, a proof in D is a linear derivation, i.e, a sequence of labelled formulas of the type $+\Delta_X q$, $-\Delta_X q$, $+\partial_X q$ and $-\partial_X q$, where the proof conditions defined in the rest of this section hold.*

We start with some terminology. As explained in the previous section, the following definition states the special status of belief rules, and that an introduction of a modal operator corresponds to being able to derive the associated literal using the rules for the modal operator.

Definition 7. *Let $\# \in \{\Delta, \partial\}$, $X \in \{\text{DES}, \text{INTOBL}\}$, and $P = (P(1), \ldots, P(n))$ be a proof in D. A literal q is #-provable in P if there is a line $P(m)$ of P such that either*

1. *q is a literal and $P(m) = +\#_{\text{BEL}} q$ or*
2. *q is a modal literal Xp and $P(m) = +\#_X p$ or*
3. *q is a modal literal $\neg Xp$ and $P(m) = -\#_X p$;*

a literal q is #-rejected in P if there is a line $P(m)$ of P such that either

1. *q is a literal and $P(m) = -\#_{\text{BEL}} q$ or*
2. *q is a modal literal Xp and $P(m) = -\#_X p$ or*
3. *q is a modal literal $\neg Xp$ and $P(m) = +\#_X p$.*

The first type of tagged literals, denoted by Δ_X, correspond to strict rules. The definition of Δ_X describes just forward chaining of strict rules:

$+\Delta_X$: If $P(i+1) = +\Delta_X q$ then
(1) $q \in F$ or
(2) $\exists r \in R_s^X[q]$ $\forall a \in A(r)$ a is Δ-provable or
(3) $\exists r \in R_s^{\text{BEL}}[q]$ $\forall a \in A(r)$ Xa is Δ-provable.

$-\Delta_X$: If $P(i+1) = -\Delta_X q$ then
(1) $q \notin F$ and
(2) $\forall r \in R_s^X[q]$ $\exists a \in A(r)$: a is Δ-rejected and
(3) $\forall r \in R_s^{\text{BEL}}[q]$ $\exists a \in A(r)$ Xa is Δ-rejected.

For a literal q to be definitely provable we need to find a strict rule with head q, whose antecedents have all been definitely proved previously. And to establish that q cannot be proven definitely we must establish that for every strict rule with head q there is at least one of antecedent which has been shown to be non-provable. Condition (3) says that a belief rule can be used as a rule for a different modal operator in case all literals in the body of the rules are modalized with the modal operator we want to prove.

Conditions for ∂_X are more complicated since we have to consider ⊗-expressions that may occur in defeasible rules. We define when a rule is applicable or discarded. A rule for a belief is applicable if all the literals in the antecedent of the rule are provable with the appropriate modalities, while the rule is discarded if at least one the literals in the antecedent is not provable. For the other types of rules we have to take complex derivations into account called conversions [9]. We say there is a conversion from X to Y if a X rule can also be used as a Y rule. We have thus to determine conditions under which a rule for X can be used to directly derive a literal q modalized by Y. Roughly, the condition is that all the antecedents a of the rule are such that $+\partial_Y a$. We represent all allowed conversions by a conversion relation c (see next section for further interpretation of conversions in terms of agent types).

Definition 8. *Let a conversion relation c be a binary relation between $\{\text{BEL}, \text{INT}, \text{DES}, \text{OBL}\}$, such that $c(X,Y)$ stands for the conversion of X rules into Y rules.*

- A rule r in R^{BEL} is applicable iff $\forall a \in A(r)$, $+\partial_{\text{BEL}}a \in P(1..n)$ and $\forall Xa \in A(r)$, where X is a modal operator, $+\partial_X a \in P(1..n)$.
- A rule $r \in R_{sd}[c_i = q]$ is applicable in the condition for $\pm\partial_X$ iff
  1. $r \in R^X$ and $\forall a \in A(r)$, $+\partial a \in P(1..n)$ and $\forall Ya \in A(r)$ $+\partial_Y a \in P(1..n)$, or
  2. $r \in R^Y$ and $\forall a \in A(r)$, $+\partial_X a \in P(1..n)$.
- A rule r is discarded if we prove either $-\partial_{\text{BEL}}a$ or $-\partial_X a$ for some $a \in A(r)$.

Example 3. The belief rule $a, \text{INT}b \Rightarrow_{\text{BEL}} c$ is applicable if we can prove $+\partial_{\text{BEL}}a$ and $+\partial_{\text{INT}}b$.

Example 4. If we have a type of agent that allows a deontic rule to be converted into a rule for intention, $c(\text{OBL}, \text{INT})$, then the definition of applicable in the condition for $\pm\partial_{\text{INT}}$ is as follows: a rule $r \in R_{sd}[c_i = q]$ is applicable iff (1) $r \in R^{\text{INT}}$ and $\forall a \in A(r)$, $+\partial a \in P(1..n)$ and $\forall Xa \in A(r)$, $+\partial_X a \in P(1..n)$, (2) or $r \in R^O$ and $\forall a \in A(r)$, $+\partial_{\text{INT}}a \in P(1..n)$.

The second type of tagged literals, denoted by ∂, correspond to defeasible rules. Two cases of these tagged literals are distinguished: $+\partial_X$ to indicate positive defeasible provability for the modality X and $-\partial_X$ to indicate negative defeasible provability for the modality X. Proof conditions for $\pm\partial_X$ are thus as follows:

$+\partial_X$: If $P(n+1) = +\partial_X q$ then
(1) $+\Delta_X q \in P(1..n)$ or
  (2.1) $-\Delta_X {\sim} q \in P(1..n)$ and
  (2.2) $\exists r \in R_{sd}[c_i = q]$ such that r is applicable, and
    $\forall i' < i, -\partial_{\text{BEL}}c_{i'} \in P(1..n)$; and
  (2.3) $\forall s \in R[c_j = {\sim}q]$, either s is discarded, or
    $\exists j' < j$ such that $+\partial_X c_{j'} \in P(1..n)$, or
  (2.3.1) $\exists t \in R[c_k = q]$ s.t. r is applicable and
    $\forall k' < k, -\partial_{\text{BEL}}c_{k'} \in P(1..n)$ and $t > s$

$-\partial_X$: If $P(n+1) = -\partial_X q$ then
(1) $-\Delta_X q \in P(1..n)$) and either
  (2.1) $+\Delta_X {\sim} q \in P(1..n)$ or
  (2.2) $\forall r \in R_{sd}[c_i = q]$, either r is discarded or
    $\exists i' < i$ such that $+\partial_{\text{BEL}}c_{i'} \in P(1..n)$, or
  (2.3) $\exists s \in R[c_j = {\sim}q]$, such that s is applicable and
    $\forall j' < j, -\partial_X c_{j'} \in P(1..n)$ and
  (2.3.1) $\forall t \in R[c_k = q]$ either t is discarded, or
    $\exists k' < k$ such that $+\partial_{\text{BEL}}c_{k'} \in P(1..n)$ or $t \not> s$

For defeasible rules we deal with $\otimes$ formulas, and this is where the subsumption relation comes into the system. Roughly, a rule $a \Rightarrow_X b \otimes c$ is interpreted as two rules $a \Rightarrow_X b$ and $a, \neg b \Rightarrow_X c$. To show that q is provable defeasibly we have two choices: (1) We show that q is already definitely provable; or (2) we need to argue using the defeasible part of D. For this second case, three (sub)conditions must be satisfied. First, we require that there must be a strict or defeasible rule for q which can be applied (2.1). Second, we need to consider possible reasoning chains in support of $\sim q$, and show that $\sim q$ is not definitely provable (2.2). Third, we must consider the set of all rules which are not known to be inapplicable and which permit to get $\sim q$ (2.3). Essentially each such a rule s attacks the conclusion q. For q to be provable, s must be counterattacked by a rule t for q with the following properties: (i) t must be applicable, and (ii) t must be stronger than s. Thus each attack on the conclusion q must be counterattacked by a stronger rule. In other words, r and the rules t form a team (for q) that defeats the rules s. $-\partial_X q$ is defined in an analogous manner.

The purpose of the $-\partial_X$ inference rules is to establish that it is not possible to prove $+\partial_X$. This rule is defined in such a way that all the possibilities for proving $+\partial_X q$ (for example) are explored and shown to fail before $-\partial_X q$ can be concluded. Thus conclusions tagged with $-\partial_X$ are the outcome of a constructive proof that the corresponding positive conclusion cannot be obtained.

Goals are obtained as $+\partial_G$ or $+\Delta_G$, $G \in \{\text{DES}, \text{INT}, \text{OBL}\}$. As it was said, provability for beliefs does not generate goals, since beliefs concern agent's knowledge about the world.

Example 5. (Running example; continued) Let us assume that the agent is realistic, namely that beliefs override all motivational components (see Section 4). Below is the set C of all conclusions we get using the rules in R:

$$C = \{\neg PayY600\$1days, \neg PayX300\$2days, \text{INT}\,OrderY,$$
$$\text{INT}\neg OrderX, \text{INT}\neg PayY660\$\}$$

Since the agent desires an application server, from r_3, r_4, $r_4 > r_3$ and $\otimes$-elimination, we have $+\partial_{\text{INT}} OrderY$. This makes r_6 and r_5 applicable, while r_7 is not. However, the agent will have 700 \$ available within 4 days and so, since the agent is realistic, from r_1 we get $+\partial_{\text{BEL}} \neg PayY600\$1days$, which is a violation of the primary obligation in r_6. We would obtain $+\partial_{\text{OBL}} PayY660\$$, but this not the case since the theory does not provide criteria for resolving the conflict between this conclusion and that of r_5.

4 Goal Generation: Conflict Resolution and Agent Types

Classically, agent types are characterized by stating conflict resolution types in terms of orders of overruling between rules [4,9]. For example, an agent is *realistic* when rules for beliefs override all other components; she is *social* when obligations are stronger than the other components with the exception of beliefs. Agent types can be characterized by stating that, for any types of rules X and Y, for every r and r' such that $r \in R^X[c_i = q]$ and $r' \in R^Y[d_i = \sim q]$, we have that $r > r'$.

Let us assume to work with realistic agents, namely, with agents for which, for every r and r', $r \in R^{\text{BEL}}[c_i = q]$ and $r' \in R^Y[d_i = \sim q]$, $Y \in \{\text{DES}, \text{INT}, \text{OBL}\}$ we have that $r > r'$. Table 1 shows al possible cases and, for each kind of rule, indicates all attacks on it. Since we have defined four kinds of rules for generating goals, we have to analyze twelve combinations. (To save space, in Table 1 "s-" is an abbreviation for "strongly-".) Independent and strongly-independent agents are free respectively to adopt desires and intentions in conflict with obligations. For social and strongly-social agents obligations

Table 1. Agent Types: Attacks

$r_d^{OBL}[c_i = p]/r_d^{INT}[c_j = \sim p]$		$r_d^{OBL}[c_i = p]/r_d^{DES}[c_j = \sim p]$		$r_d^{INT}[c_i = p]/r_d^{DES}[c_j = \sim p]$	
$+\partial_{OBL}p \mid +\partial_{INT}\sim p$	s-independent	$+\partial_{OBL}p \mid +\partial_{DES}\sim p$	independent	$+\partial_{INT}p \mid +\partial_{DES}\sim p$	unstable
$+\partial_{OBL}p \mid -\partial_{INT}\sim p$	s-social	$+\partial_{OBL}p \mid -\partial_{DES}\sim p$	social	$+\partial_{INT}p \mid -\partial_{DES}p$	stable
$-\partial_{OBL}p \mid +\partial_{INT}\sim p$	s-deviant	$-\partial_{OBL}p \mid +\partial_{DES}\sim p$	deviant	$-\partial_{INT}p \mid +\partial_{DES}\sim p$	selfish
$-\partial_{OBL}p \mid -\partial_{INT}\sim p$	s-pragmatic	$-\partial_{OBL}p \mid -\partial_{DES}\sim p$	pragmatic	$-\partial_{INT}p \mid -\partial_{DES}\sim p$	slothful

override desires and intentions. For pragmatic and strongly-pragmatic, no derivation is possible and so the agent's generation of goals is open to any other course of action other than those specified in the rules considered. Stable and selfish agents are those for which, respectively, intentions override desires or the opposite. Unstable agents are free to adopt desires in conflict with intentions, while, for slothful agents, conflicting desires and intentions override each other[2].

This taxonomy can be enriched thanks to the role played by $\otimes$-expressions. In fact, in traditional rules-based systems, conflict-detection returns a boolean: either there is a conflict, or there is not. For $\otimes$ constructs, it seems that we may need a finer distinction. For example, we can have degrees of violation. Of course, if we define a conflict detection function that returns no longer booleans but a more complex structure (e.g., an integer that returns 0 if no violation, 1 if violation of primary obligation, 2 if violation of secondary obligation), then we have to write conflict resolution methods which can somehow deal with this. Section 3 provides criteria to solve conflict between rules including $\otimes$ constructions. In this perspective, the role of $\otimes$ can be made fruitful. In particular, the introduction of $\otimes$ is crucial if we want to impose some constraints on the number of violations in deriving a goals. Goal generation can be constrained, so that provability of a goal g is permitted only if getting g does not require more than n violations for each rule with g in the head:

Definition 9 (Violation constraint on goals). *Let n and X be an integer and a type of rule, respectively. A theory D will be n-X-constrained iff, given the definition of $+\partial$, for all literals q, $+\partial_X q$ iff (1) $i'' \leq n$; and (2) if $1 \leq j'' \leq j'$ and $s \in R_X$, then $j'' \leq n$; and (3) $k' \leq n$. Otherwise, $-\partial_X q$.*

Similar intuitions are applicable to directly constraint agent types, thus introducing graded agent types: e.g., for any two rules $r_1 : r_d^{OBL}[c_i = p]$ and $r_2 : r_d^{DES}[c_j = \sim p]$ we may reframe the type "social" of Table 1 stating that an n-social agent is such that

$$+\partial_{OBL}p / -\partial_{DES}\sim p \text{ iff } i \leq n$$

Thus the idea of agent type can also be generalized taking into account $\otimes$ constructs.

It is possible to integrate the above classifications by referring to the notion of conversion [9]. Conversions do not have a direct relation with conflict resolution because they simply affect the condition of applicability of rules. However, they contribute to define the cognitive profile of agents because they allow to obtain conclusions modalized by a certain X through the application of rules which are not modalized by X. According to this view, for example, we may have agent types for which, given $p \Rightarrow_{OBL} q$ and

---

[2] Table 1 covers only some agent types as it focuses on attacks that involve only two rules.

$+\partial_{INT}p$ we can obtain $+\partial_{INT}q$. Of course, this is possible only if we assume a kind of norm regimentation, by which we impose that all agents intend what is prescribed by deontic rules. This conversion, in particular, seems appropriate to characterize some kinds of social agent. Other conversions, which, on the contrary, should hold for all realistic agents are, for example, those that permit to obtain $+\partial_X q, X \in \{DES, INT, OBL\}$, from $p \Rightarrow_{BEL} q$ and $+\partial_X p$ [9]. Table 2 shows the conversions and specifies the agent types with respect to which each conversion seems to be appropriate. We assume to work at least with realistic agents. Since conversions are used only indirectly for conflict resolution but are conceptually decisive for characterizing agents, they provide criteria to specify new agent types. Not all conversion types make sense and so we consider only 9 of 12 cases. At which phase do agent types intervene in the treatment of conflicts? We argue that classic agent types, but also violation constraints and conversions, play their role mainly in the goal generation phase, because all these features mainly contribute to characterize the motivational profile of the agent.

Table 2. Conversions

$c(BEL, OBL)$	realistic	$c(BEL, INT)$	realistic	$c(BEL, DES)$	realistic
$c(OBL, DES)$	c-social	$c(OBL, INT)$	c-strongly-social	$c(DES, OBL)$	c-deviant
$c(INT, DES)$	c-stable	$c(DES, INT)$	c-selfish	$c(INT, OBL)$	c-strongly-deviant

Example 6 (Running example; continued). Suppose the agent be strongly-social and c-strongly-social, namely, that obligations override intentions and that we accept conversion $c(OBL, INT)$. So, we obtain the following additional goals:

$$\{OBLPayY660\$, INTPayY660\$\}$$

Since r_6 is now stronger than r_5, we obtain $OBLPayY660\$$, while the second goal is derived via r_6 and conversion $c(OBL, INT)$. This second means that we dropped the previous conclusion that the agent intended the opposite.

Assume now that the theory is also 0-X-constrained, for $X \in \{INT, OBL\}$. This means that no violation is permitted. If so, no new intention or obligation can be derived.

Finally, suppose the agent is realistic and 1-stable. Let us add to R_X the rule r' : $a \Rightarrow_{DES} \neg OrderY$, and to F the fact a. Thus we would obtain $DES \neg OrderY$, which is in conflict with the conclusion that can be obtained from r_3. Indeed this is the case since an intention overrides a conflicting desire only if the former is a primary intention.

5 Conclusions and Future Work

In this paper we study programming languages for cognitive agents with preferences. We define rule-based agent theories and inference procedures in defeasible logic using a variant of the $\otimes$ operator of [8] in DL for the representation of preferences, and inspired by the BOID architecture [6] separating conflict-detection from -resolution.

We show how to detect and resolve conflicts using preferences. Programming languages for cognitive agents need such fine-grained mechanisms to represent and resolve conflicts among rules for the interaction among mental attitudes – though ways to resolve conflicts must be described abstractly. We define agent types based on preferences. Agent programming languages must describe patterns of ways to deal with conflicts and more generally patterns of agent behavior. Such patterns have been called agent types. Traditional agent types are realistic and committed, other notions introduced before are stable, selfish, social and opportunistic. In this paper we distinguish twelve agent types for attacks and nine for conversions.

Agent programming languages have to distinguish between an abstract language that deals with interaction among mental attitudes, called a deliberation language, and low level procedures to deal with definitions of conflicts based on temporal and causal reasoning, resources, scheduling, and the like. In this paper we assumed that we can use the same deliberation language with preferences as has been used by Dastani and van der Torre [6].

The architecture for cognitive agents can be divided into modules: goal generation module and plan generation module. In this paper we confined ourselves only to the former. Plan generation can be achieved in a similar way. The the inference mechanism (based on defeasible logic) will be used to deduce sequence of actions (plans) that are required to achieve goals. Thus special rules that permit to infer plans must be devised if certain beliefs and goals are given or obtained via the goal generation module. This means that we have to introduce planning rules, where a planning rule has the following format $\phi_1, \ldots, \phi_n : \psi \Rightarrow_p \pi$. The intuition is that a planning rule can be applied if $\phi_1, \ldots, \phi_n$ are derivable from the agent's beliefs, and ψ is derivable from the agent's goals. In addition we have to devise proof conditions, similar in nature to that we have presented for goal generation, which enable us to deal with both complete plans and partial plans, and how to compose them. These issues are left as matter for future research.

References

1. G. Antoniou, D. Billington, G. Governatori, and M.J. Maher. A flexible framework for defeasible logics. In *Proc. AAAI-2000*, Menlo Park, CA, 2000. AAAI/MIT Press.
2. F.M.T. Brazier, B. Dunin Keplicz, N. Jennings, and J. Treur. Desire: Modelling multi-agent systems in a compositional formal framework. *Int. J. Coop. Inf. Syst.*, 6:67–94, 1997.
3. G. Brewka, S. Benferhat, and D. Le Berre. Qualitative choice logic. *Artificial Intelligence*, 157:203–237, 2004.
4. J. Broersen, M. Dastani, J. Hulstijn, and L. van der Torre. Goal generation in the BOID architecture. *Cog. Sc. Quart.*, 2(3-4):428–447, 2002.
5. M. Dastani, F. de Boer, F. Dignum, and J.-J. Meyer. Programming agent deliberation. In *Proc. AAMAS'03*. 2003.
6. M. Dastani and L.W.N. van der Torre. Programming BOID-plan agents: Deliberating about conflicts among defeasible mental attitudes and plans. In *Proc. AAMAS 2004*, New York, 2004. ACM.
7. M. Dastani, B. van Riemsdijk, F. Dignum, and J.-J. Meyer. A programming language for cognitive agents: Goal directed 3APL. In *Proc. ProMAS'03*. 2003.
8. G. Governatori and A. Rotolo. A Gentzen system for reasoning with contrary-to-duty obligations. In A. Jones and J. Horty, editors, *Proc. Δeon'02*, London, May 2002. Imperial College.
9. G. Governatori and A. Rotolo. Defeasible logic: Agency, intention and obligation. In A. Lomuscio and D. Nute, editors, *Proc. Δeon'04*, Berlin, 2004. Springer.

MAHIS: An Agent-Oriented Methodology for Constructing Dynamic Platform-Based HIS

Chunsheng Li[1] and Li Liu[2]

[1] College of Computer and Information Technology, Daqing Petroleum Institute,
Heilongjiang, 163318, China
`csli@pislab.com`
[2] Faculty of Information Technology, University of Technology, Sydney,
PO Box 123, Broadway, NSW 2007, Australia
`liliu@it.uts.edu.au`

Abstract. Hierarchical structure, reusable and dynamic components, and predictable interactions are distinct characteristics of hybrid intelligent systems (HIS). The existing agent-oriented methodologies are deficient in HIS construction because they did not take into account the characteristics of HIS. In this paper, we propose a Methodology for constructing Agent-based HIS (MAHIS). MAHIS consists of eight models: Hybrid Strategy Identification Model, Organization Model, Task Model, Agent Model, Expertise Model, Coordination Model, Reorganization Model, and Design Model. The Reorganization Model is the key model to support dynamic platform-based HIS. It consists of category role, group roles, virtual organization role, and dynamics rules. This model describes the characteristics of HIS with virtual organization, category, and group perspectives. Some previously developed agents can be reused by means of involving them in a new virtual organization dynamically. The output of the Reorganization Model is the specification of the dynamic platform which comprises middle agents and makes all agents and agent groups hierarchical and dynamic.

1 Introduction

Design and development of hybrid intelligent systems (HIS) are difficult because HIS has their own distinct characteristics, such as, the hierarchical structure of interrelated subsystems, the arbitrary primitive components of subsystems, the dynamic components of system, and the unpredictable interactions among these components [1]. In recent years, both researchers and practitioners have recognized the advantages of applying the agent-based paradigm for the development of HIS [2-4]. However, the number of deployed commercial agent-based hybrid intelligent applications is small. One of the reasons for this is the lack of practical methodologies for agent-based hybrid intelligent applications development. Even in the agent research field, although more than two dozens agent-oriented methodologies have been developed during the last decade [5], only a few complete and well-grounded methodologies have been proposed to the analysis and design of multi-agent systems so far [1]. Moreover, these methodologies are deficient in HIS construction because they did not take into account the characteristics of HIS. Although some researchers have considered this issue and attempted to propose agent-oriented methodologies for constructing HIS, there is no one methodology that can fully meet the requirements of the analysis and design of agent-based HIS [1].

In this paper, we have devised a Methodology for constructing Agent-based HIS (MAHIS for short). To avoid building MAHIS from scratch, we have followed the strategy which extends the existing well-known agent-oriented methodology in order to bridge the gap between the existing methodology and agent-based HIS construction. MAHIS has extended the capabilities of MAS-CommonKADS in agent-based HIS development. MAHIS consists of eight models: *Hybrid Strategy Identification Model, Organization Model, Task Model, Agent Model, Expertise Model, Coordination Model, Reorganization Model, and Design Model*. These models are grouped into three levels: *conceptualization, analysis,* and *design*. Both the *Hybrid Strategy Identification Model* and *Reorganization Model* are newly developed models rather than from MAS-CommonKADS. At the same time, some existing models have been improved accordingly. The *Reorganization Model* is the key model to support dynamic platform-based HIS. It consists of category role, group roles, virtual organization role, and dynamics rules. This model describes the characteristics of HIS with virtual organization, category, and group perspectives. Some previously developed agents can be reused by means of involving them in a new virtual organization dynamically. The output of the Reorganization Model is the specification of the dynamic platform which comprises middle agents and makes all agents and agent groups hierarchical and dynamic. MAHIS is suitable for constructing dynamic platform-based HIS. The 'platform-based HIS' means that all agents in a hybrid intelligent system are managed by a self-organized dynamic platform which comprises middle agents.

2 Outline of MAHIS

MAHIS attempts to direct users to develop their agent-based HIS from the descriptions of the problems which are needed to be solved to the output of the specifications which can be implemented directly. Two aspects of tasks have been done when we proposed MAHIS based on MAS-CommonKADS. The first one is to extend MAS-CommonKADS for bridging the gap between MAS-CommonKADS and the HIS construction. The second one is to cut out the redundant contents of MAS-CommonKADS because they are not suitable for constructing HIS, or they conflict with the extended parts.

The framework of MAHIS is presented in Figure 1. The conceptualization level includes the *Hybrid Strategy Identification Model* and the description of hybrid problem requirements. During this phase, an elicitation task to obtain a preliminary description of the hybrid problem is carried out. Based on the problem description, the hybrid strategy model adopted by the HIS is identified. The purpose to identify the hybrid strategy is to help other models to decide the architectural model of the HIS because the hybrid strategy adopted by a hybrid intelligent system decides the organizational structure and coordination mechanism of the system. The analysis level includes the *Organization Model, Task Model, Agent Model, Reorganization Model,*

Expertise Model, and *Coordination Model*. These models can be classified into two sublevels: context and concept. The context sublevel includes the *Organization Model*, *Task Model*, and *Agent Model*, which attempt to clarify the tasks, agents, organizational context, and environment. The concept sublevel includes the *Reorganization Model*, *Expertise Model*, and *Coordination Model*, which issue the conceptual descriptions of the knowledge applied in a task, the interactions between agents, and the hierarchical structure and the primitive members in each level. The design level only includes the design model which consists of four steps: architecture design, agent communication language (ACL) design, platform design, and application design.

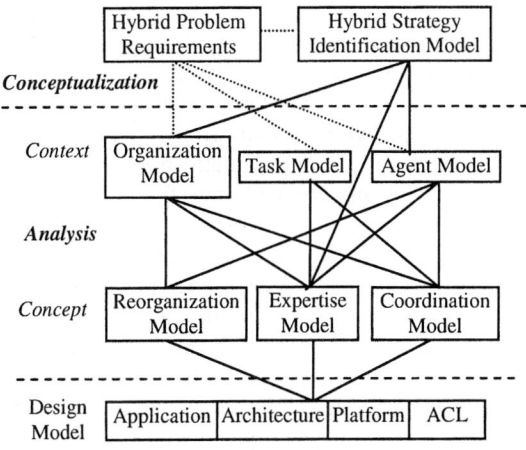

Fig. 1. Framework of the methodology

The hybrid problem to be solved is represented in the *Hybrid Problem Requirements*. The information in the *Hybrid Problem Requirements* can be used to develop the *Hybrid Strategy Identification Model, Organization Model, Task Model*, and *Agent Model*. The *Organization Model* supports the analysis of the major features of an organization in order to describe the organization into which the HIS is going to be introduced and the social organization of the agent society. The *Task Model* analyses the global task layout, its inputs and outputs, preconditions and performance criteria, as well as needed resources and competences. The *Agent Model* describes the agent characteristics: groups and hierarchy. The purpose of the *Expertise Model* is to explicate in detail the types and structures of the knowledge used in performing a task. The *Coordination Model* describes the conversations between agents: their interactions, protocols and required capabilities. The *Reorganization Model* is the key model to support platform-based HIS. It consists of category role, group roles, virtual organization role, and dynamics rules. This model describes the hierarchical, dynamic, reusable, and unpredictable characteristics of HIS with virtual organization, category, and group perspectives. The virtual organization (VO) in this paper is regarded as a running subsystem or application. The members of a VO include all agents for completing the task of the subsystem or application. An agent may belong to more than one VO at the same time. Some previously developed agents can be reused by means of involving them in a new VO dynamically. The output of the *Reorganization Model* is the specification of the dynamic platform which comprises middle agents and makes all agents and agent groups hierarchical and dynamic. The *Design Model* gives the technical system specification in terms of application, architecture, platform, and ACL to concretize the outputs of the reorganization, coordination, and expertise models. The output of the design model can be implemented based on the different developing environments.

3 Specification of MAHIS

A methodology should include three aspects of components: lifecycle process, technique set and modeling language [5]. A hybrid system development life cycle (HSDLC) for developing agent-based HIS have been proposed. The HSDLC consists of a set of activities, such as, hybrid technique and hybrid strategy analysis, agent categorization with hierarchical structure, platform development, and application development. Those activities are grouped into five process stages (procedures): conceptualization, analysis, design, implementation, and maintenance. The platform development and application development are separated for supporting dynamic addition and removal of agents and applications (projects), which make HSDLC support dynamic project management. While the models of MAHIS were proposed, some meta-model with well-known notations, such as AUML [6], use case of OOSE [7], MSC and HMSC [8], KQML [9], and DFD (Data Flow Diagraph) [10] have been adopted for representing the generated HIS. The contents and the formal presentation of the outputs of each model have been defined and made out. About the techniques, the methodology supports hybrid techniques which have been developed or will be developed and hybrid strategies. At the same time, some tools based on the meta-models can be employed to represent the notations.

3.1 Conceptualization Phase

The task of the conceptualization is to obtain a first description of the problem and to determine use cases which can help to understand informal requirements and to test the system. The method of use case modeling has the advantage of being formalized with *Message Sequence Charts*, which are used for modeling the proposed coordination model.

During the hybrid problem requirements phase, an elicitation task to obtain a preliminary description of the problem is carried out following a user-centered approach by determining some use case which can help us to understand informal requirements and to test the system. Use case are described using OOSE notation and the interactions are formalized with MSC (*Message Sequence Charts*) [8].

The hybrid strategy identification model consists of the following components: 1) an algorithm to indicate what intelligent techniques to be taken by the system according to the results of hybrid problem requirements; 2) an algorithm to indicate what hybrid strategy is adopted by the system based on the hybrid problem descriptions and the system's environment; 3) a mechanism to select hybrid technique relations; (4) a list of hybrid techniques adopted by the system; 5) a knowledge base to accumulate the knowledge used by the hybrid strategy identification model.

The inputs of this model are the hybrid problem requirements, environment statements, and knowledge. An environment provides the conditions under which entity exists. The environment consists not only of all the other entities, but also those principle and processes under which the agents exist and communicate. There is a knowledge base in this model, which supports intelligent techniques selection, hybrid strategy selection, hybrid technique relations selection, and the hybrid techniques proposing.

The outputs of this model include: (1) the statements of the selected intelligent techniques and hybrid technique relations; (2) the descriptions of the selected hybrid strategy; (3) the list of hybrid technique models adopted by the system. The statements of the selected intelligent techniques and hybrid technique relations will be used by organization model for helping to decide the categories and groups. The information about hybrid strategies not only affects the agent categorizing and grouping, but also helps developers to design the agent architecture and the group architecture. The descriptions of the selected hybrid strategy will be used by organization model and reorganization model for helping to analyze the agent categorizing, agent grouping, and dynamic rules. The hybrid technique models will be detailed (proposed) in expertise model.

3.2 Analysis Phase

The results of this phase are the requirements specification of the agent-based HIS through the development of the models described in Section 2, except for the hybrid strategy identification model and design model. These models are developed in a risk-driven way, and the steps are:

- Organization modeling: developing the organization model. The construction of these models in the analysis phase is done by means of worksheets.
- Task modeling: task decomposition and determination of the goals and ingredients of the tasks.
- Agent modeling: developing initial instance of the agent model for identifying and describing the agents.
- Coordination modeling: developing the coordination model for describing the interactions and coordination protocols between the agents.
- Knowledge Modeling: developing expertise model which includes the knowledge on the domain, the agents (knowledge needed to carry out the tasks and their proactive behavior) and the environment (beliefs and inferences of the world, including the rest of agents).
- Reorganization modeling: modeling the dynamic feature of agent-based HIS for dynamically organizing agents with hierarchical structure. In this case, three instances of the reorganization model are developed: agent categorizing (each category located in the different level of the hierarchical structure), agent grouping (primitive member of each category and group-based applications), and agent dynamics (coordination mechanism).

The organization model describes the organization in a structured, systems-like fashion. The organization model includes different aspects, such as organization structure, processes, staff, and resources. The idea is that in the model these components have to be filled in both for the current and the future situation. The inputs of this model are requirements, environment, and the outputs of the hybrid strategy identification model. The selected hybrid strategy and the list of the hybrid techniques of the hybrid strategy identification model will be processed and delivered to the reorganization model and the expertise model by this organization model.

The first part of the organization model focuses on problems and opportunities, as seen in the wider organizational context. The second part contains broad categories such as the organization's mission, goals, strategy, value chain, and external influencing factors. The last part involves the processes categorizing and grouping from the hierarchical structure point of view.

The rules to category and group the processes are expressed in the following steps:

Step 1: decide the process categories according to the selected hybrid strategy;

Step 2: decide the primitive members of each category according to the selected intelligent techniques and hybrid technique relations;

Step 3: describe the dynamics of the primitive members in each category.

Four kinds of graphical models are used to develop the organization model: use case notation of OOSE for representing the organization, MSC, packages of AUML, templates of AUML, or protocol diagrams for depicting the processes, DFD (Data-Flow Diagram) for describing the relationships between processes and resources, and HRD (Hierarchical Relationship Diagram) or extended deployment diagram of AUML for depicting the results of categorizing and grouping.

Tasks are decomposed following a top-down approach, and described in an 'and/or tree'. The description of a task includes its name, a short description, input and output ingredients, task structure, its control, frequency of application, preconditions and required capabilities of the performers. Some of the items in the task model, such as value, quality, and performance, refer directly to organizational considerations. Other items in the task model, notably dependency/flow, and time/control, have a natural link with other approaches to information-systems modeling.

Three kinds of graphical models are used to develop the task model: And/or tree for describing the tasks, DFD for representing the relationships between tasks, and state chart of AUML for describing the control relation with other tasks.

The purpose of the agent model is to understand the roles and competences that the various actors in the organization bring with them to perform a shared task. The information contained in the agent specification is for a large part a rearrangement of information already existing in previous worksheets. The agent has five attributes: name, type (human, new system agent or predefined system agent), role, position, category, and groups (agent groups the agent belongs to). Other constituents of the agent model are service, goal, reasoning capabilities, general capabilities, constraints, etc. Service is the facilities offered to the rest of agents to satisfy their goals. It can perform one task of the task model, and has five attributes: name, type, task, and ingredients. Goal is the objectives of the agents. The goal has the following attributes: name, description, type and ingredients. The goal can be satisfied according to the reasoning capabilities of the agent. Reasoning capabilities are the requirements on the agent's expertise imposed by the task assignment. These are realized by the expertise model. General capabilities are the skills (sensors and effectors to manipulate the environment) and languages the agent understands (agent communication language and knowledge representation language). Constraints are norms, preferences and permissions of the agent. The norms and preferences have special interest in the case of agent-based HIS.

Agents can be identified with the following strategies (or a combination of them):

- ✓ Analysis of the actors of the use cases defined in the conceptualization phase based on the descriptions of organization model and task model. The actors of the use cases and the tasks described in task model delimit the external agents of the system. Several similar roles (actors) can be mapped onto one agent to simplify the communication.
- ✓ Usage of heuristics. The agents can be identified determining whether there is some conceptual distance: knowledge distribution, geographical distribution, logical distribution or organizational distribution.
- ✓ The task and expertise models can help us to identify the necessary functions and the required knowledge capabilities, resulting in a preliminary definition of the agents. The goals of the tasks will be assigned to the agents.
- ✓ Application of the internal use cases technique. Taking as input the use cases of the conceptualization phase and some initial agents, we can think that each agent uses other agents, and can use these agents with different roles. The use case notation is extended for showing human agents (with the round head) and soft agents (with the squared head). When an agent needs to use an agent for a particular function, such an agent is looked for in the agent-library for reusing, combining in this way the top-down and bottom-up approach.
- ✓ The intelligent techniques and hybrid technique models. The intelligent techniques and hybrid technique models are important processes in agent-based HIS. They can be easily identified by following the outputs of the hybrid strategy identification model.

When the agents are identified, the textual template of the agent model should be filled in for each agent that includes its name, type, role, position, groups, a description, offered services, goals, skills, reasoning capabilities, general capabilities, norms, preferences, and permissions.

The activity diagram or state chart of the AUML can be used to develop the agent model. Specification of an agent protocol requires spelling out the detailed processing that takes place within an agent in order to implement the protocol. The state charts and activity diagrams can specify the internal processing of agents that are not aggregates.

The coordination model contains four constitutes: conversation, interaction, capabilities, and protocols. The conversation is a set of interactions in order to ask for a service or request or update information. It is distinguished by the name and the requested service name. The interaction is a simple interchange of messages. It has the following attributes: speech-act, agent communication language, knowledge representation language, synchronization, transmitter, receiver and ingredients. The capabilities are the skills and knowledge of the initiator of the conversation and the other participants. The protocol is a set of rules that govern the conversation. It defines the different states and interactions allowed.

The expertise model consists of the development of the application knowledge (consisting of domain knowledge, inference knowledge and task knowledge) and problem solving knowledge. The expertise model can be defined as following using CML (Conceptual Modeling Language).

Reorganization model is developed to describe the dynamic feature of HIS with virtual organization (VO), category, and group perspectives. This model shows the organizational relationships between agents for supporting dynamic addition and removal of agents in agent-based HIS. At the same time, this model has the ability to make the agents that are developed previously reusable. Because each agent can be dynamically involved in a new VO, the agents in the system are reorganized.

Reorganization model consists of four components: category role, group roles, VO role, and dynamics rules.

In agent-based HIS, agents are divided into several categories. Each category locates in a specific level in a hierarchical structure. The category role indicates these categories. A category is an instance of the category role. The following questions must be answered in the category role. How many categories must be divided? What is the type of members in each category like? What is the hierarchy between agent categories? What are the characteristics of the organizational structures organized the members for each category? The description of category role includes instances (categories), member type (one of the group roles), hierarchy, and structure type. However, it is conceptually wrong to think of a structure type as something that actually defines the organizational structure. Instead, in the design phase, the structure type should derive from the organizational structure that is explicitly chosen. The category role can be depicted in AUML class diagram.

For the purposes of dynamic addition and removal of agents, a member in a category may consist of more than one agent. The member of each category is an agent group, which is described in group role. An agent group is an instance of group role. Each category has its own group role. So the number of the group roles is not more than the number of categories. The agents in a group can coordinate to achieve their goal or they have closer relationships. Agent group roles describe the aforementioned features of an agent-based system. The following attributes must be described in each group role. What are the rules for grouping the agents? What category does the group role belong to? What is the organizational structure adapted in a group for organizing the agents? Are the agents in a group reusable? The description of each group role includes group role name, rules for grouping agents, instances of the group role, category belonged to, structure type, and reusability of the agents. The group roles can be depicted in AUML class diagram.

For reusing agent, an instance (so-called virtual organization) of the VO role may consist of more than one agent across all or some categories. A VO can be regarded as a subsystem or an application in the agent-based HIS. An agent may belong to more than one VO at the same time. When a VO registered into the system, its member may change dynamically. A VO may include all agents of a group or parts of its agents. The description of the VO role includes instances (VOs), VO member, and

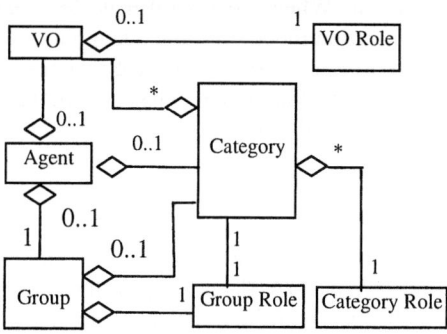

Fig. 2. Category, group, VO, and agent relationships

structure type. The VO roles can be depicted in AUML class diagram. Figure 2 shows relationships between category, group, VO, and agent using AUML class diagram.

Dynamics rules include two aspects of rules. The first one is about the interactions between categories. These rules indicate the coordination mechanism of the category role. The second one is about the operation mechanism of the VO. The dynamic ability of agent-based system is described in system dynamics rules. The following attributes must be described in dynamics rules. What is the coordination mechanism between categories? How to establish and maintain the mechanism for the dynamic addition and removal of groups in each category? What are the rules for reorganizing agents as a VO? How or when to initialize the agent-based HIS? The description of the dynamics rules includes category mechanism, group mechanism, reorganization mechanism, and initialization mechanism. The dynamics rules can be depicted using MSC, sequence diagram of AUML, or collaboration diagram of AUML.

3.3 Design Phase

This phase consist of four steps.

- ➤ **Step1:** Architecture design ---- The general architecture of a system is specified according to the structure and mechanism description in reorganization and coordination models. Because the hierarchical structure of agent categories and the organizational structures of agent groups and agents have been predefined in reorganization model, this step can therefore be carried out quickly.
- ➤ **Step 2:** Agent communication language ---- As we know, KQML is a popular ACL for transmitting messages between agents. KQML can be adopted in the agent-based system. However, for hybrid intelligent system it is not suitable to transmit shared information. According to the application, the practical ACL should be improved or enriched. ACL design is an important work which should be taken before design the platform and any application.
- ➤ **Step 3:** Platform design ---- The platform which supports the dynamic addition and removal of agents is designed in this step. When the platform is designed, hardware and software environment should be considered for the convenience of

system implementation. When the platform is designed, all the specifications described in reorganization model must be taken into account.

➢ **Step 4:** Application design ---- In the final step we take the ingredients from the analysis models (organization model, task model, agent model, coordination model, reorganization model) and map those onto the architecture and platform.

4 Conclusion

MAHIS has three distinct characteristics which are not covered by other agent-oriented methodologies. Firstly, MAHIS is suitable for constructing agent-based HIS as well as other open systems with hierarchical structure. Secondly, it supports the construction of agent-based systems with the ability of reorganization of agents. Finally, dynamic platform development is taken into account from the methodology point of view. The platform can dynamically organize all agents in a system. A dynamic platform has been developed by following MAHIS. The platform not only verified MAHIS in dynamic platform construction, but also can be used as infrastructure of agent-based HIS.

References

1. Zhang, Z. and Zhang, C., Agent-based hybrid intelligent systems, vol. 2938. Berlin, Germany: Springer, 2004.
2. Centeno-Gonzalez, J., Velasco, J. R., and Iglesias, C. A., "An agent-based operational model for hybrid connectionist-symbolic learning," presented at the International Work-Conference on Artificial and Natural Neural Networks, Alicante, Spain, 1999.
3. Khosla, R. and Dillon, T., Engineering intelligent hybrid multi-agent systems. Boston, USA: Kluwer Academic Publishers, 1997.
4. Li, C., Liu, L., and Song, Q., "A practical framework for agent-based hybrid intelligent systems," Asian Journal of Information Technology, vol. 3, pp. 107-114, 2004.
5. Sturm, A. and Shehory, O., "A framework for evaluating agent-oriented methodologies," in Agent-Oriented Information Systems, Lecture Notes in Computer Science 3030, P. Giorgini, B. Henderson-Sellers, and M. Winikoff, Eds. Berlin, Germany: Springer, 2003, pp. 94-109.
6. Bauer, B., Muller, J. P., and Odell, J. J., "Agent UML: a formalism for specifying multiagent interaction," in Agent-Oriented Software Engineering, Ciancarini, P. and Wooldridge, M., Eds. Berlin, Germany: Springer, 2001, pp. 91-103.
7. Iglesias, C. A., Garijo, M., Centeno-Gonzalez, J., and Velasco, J. R., "Analysis and design of multiagent systems using MAS-CommonKADS," presented at 4th International Workshop, ATAL '97, Providence, Rhode Island, USA, 1997.
8. Rudolph, E., Graubman, P., and Grabowski, J., "Tutorial on Message Sequence Charts," Computer Networks and ISDN Systems, vol. 28, pp. 1629-1641, 1996.
9. Finin, T., Labrou, Y., and Mayfield, J., "KQML as an agent communication language," in Software Agents, J. M. Brashaw, Ed.: AAAI Press/The MIT Press, 1997, pp. 291-316.
10. Mrhailaf, R. and Sahraoui, A., "DFD extended methods for specifying hybrid systems," presented at the International Conference on Systems, Man and Cybernetics, Le Touquet France, 1993.
11. Schreiber, G., Akkermans, H., Anjewierden, A., Hoog, R. d., Shadbolt, N., and Velde, W. v. d., Knowledge engineering and management: the CommonKADS methodology: MIT Press, 1999.

3D Game Engine for Real-Time Facial Animation

Hye Won Pyun

Broadcasting Technical Research Institute,
Korean Broadcasting System, Seoul, Korea
hyewon@kbs.co.kr

Abstract. For 3D game engine, we present facial animation method based on multiple face models. In order to overcome the heavy burden of geometry data management on game engine, we employ wire curve [22] which is a simple, intuitive interface to local deformation of complex geometric objects such as human face models. Given multiple face models, we first extract wire curves and deformation parameters from a facial model. In runtime, given an input of expression parameters, only the extracted wire curves are blended to create new expression. Then, the blended output of the wire curves is applied to the reference model of neutral expression. The resulting animation preserves the characteristic features of the multiple face models as well real-time performance. Our method promotes local deformation and non-uniform blending by making use of the power of wire curve.

Keywords: Real-time facial animation, multiple face models, local deformation, wire deformation.

1 Introduction

Creating lifelike characters on game engine is an interesting and challenging task. Especially, high quality facial animation breathes emotion and personality into newly created characters. Existing facial animation techniques in games are hampered by a lot of obstacles, such as limited resources and the requirement of real-time speed. Our goal is to achieve realistic and expressive facial animation with real-time performance for 3D game engine. We employ both multiple face models and wire curves.

Multiple face models, called templates, are widely used for facial animation of the conversational characters on desktop platforms.[1,2,4,7,9,17,18,20,24]. Each of these models reflects both a facial expression of different type and designer's insight to be a good guideline for animation. Those templates comprise a facial expression database from which we select appropriate face models to blend and to deform. However, a template consists of a set of vertices with few handles to control such geometric operations except the vertices themselves. It is almost impossible to keep all the vertices of multiple face models on mobile devices with limited resources. Furthermore, to achieve smooth local deformation and non-uniform blending without any tools, one would have to deal with every vertex of face models involved in these operations.

"Wires"[22] have become a popular tool for facial animation, due to its abstract representation and capability of local control on facial features such as eyes and a mouth. The basic idea of wire deformation is to locally deform the vertices of a facial feature according to the displacements of wire curves from their references together with deformation parameters (see Section 2.) Therefore, by deforming a wire curve, the features near the curve are also deformed accordingly. These features may be refined further with deformation parameters.

In order to abstractly represent the templates, we present a method to extract a set of wire curves and deformation parameters from a template. The extracted wire curves have replaced the templates. This lowers a heavy burden of a lot of template geometry data on 3D game engine with limited resources. In runtime, given the input of new expression parameter, the blended output of the extracted wire curves is applied to a reference template to create real-time facial animation. Our method not only provides handles for local deformation and non-uniform blending but also reduces the volume of the template database, by representing a template as a set of wire curves and deformation parameters characterizing its corresponding facial expression.

The remainder of the paper is organized as follows. We provide related work in Section 2. In Section 3, we give an introduction to the wire deformation technique. We present a formulation for extracting wire curves and deformation parameters in Section 4. In Section 5, we demonstrate how our technique can be used for facial animation. Finally, we conclude this paper in Section 6.

2 Related Work

Blending multiple face models with different expressions is popular for real-time facial animation [1,9,17,18,20]. Pighin et al.[17] captured face geometry and textures by fitting a generic face model to a number of photographs. Through transitions between captured face models of different expressions, they were able to generate expressive facial animation. Blanz et al.[1] and Pighin et al.[18] proposed an automatic face modeling technique by linearly blending a set of example faces from a database of scanned 3D face models. To avoid unlikely faces, they restricted the range of allowable faces with constraints derived from the example set. For local control on each facial feature, those approaches allow interactive segmentation of a face into a set of regions to assign a proper blending factor to every vertex. Joshi et al.[9] adopted an automatic segmentation method to learn the local deformation information directly from the multiple face models.

Other alternatives are based on deformation techniques. In free-form deformation(FFD)[21], control points of a parallelpiped-shaped lattice are manipulated to deform an object. Further extensions to FFD adopted lattices of arbitrary topology instead of regular lattices[3,5,15]. For direct control, Hsu et al.[8] computed the displacements of the control points from the movements of points on the surface of an object. Thalmann et al.[12] employed FFD to simulate the muscle action on the skin surface of a human face. Kahler et al.[10,11] and Terzopoulos et al.[14] proposed a physically-based method for skin and muscle deformation to enhance the degree of realism over purely geometric techniques. Williams[23] and Guenter et. al.[6] used facial motion data captured from real actors to deform face models. Marschner et al.[16] computed the displacements of control points for a specific face model from the movements of sample points on a face performer by solving a system of linear equations in the least squares sense.

Singh et al.[22] provided a more effective control metaphor based on wire deformation. A parametric curve called "wire curve" is used to define and directly control a salient deformable feature on a face model. Its basic idea is to locally deform geometry near the wire curve by manipulating the curve. Due to the capability of local control as well as direct manipulation, wire deformation is versatile for synthesizing facial expressions interactively.

3 Wire Deformation

Singh *et. al.* [22] proposed wire deformation as a simple, intuitive interface to deforming complex geometric objects such as human face models. In this section, we briefly summarize their deformation scheme.

Wire deformation is defined by a tuple $< W, R, f, r, s >$, where W and R denote parametric curves called wire and reference curves, respectively, and f, r, and s are deformation parameters to be explained later. Initially, W and R are coincident. By deforming the wire curve W, it is displaced from R. For a point $\mathbf{p}$ on an object M to deform, let $\mathbf{p}_R$ be its nearest point on R, and $\mathbf{p}_W$ the point on W corresponding to $\mathbf{p}_R$. That is, $\mathbf{p}_R$ and $\mathbf{p}_W$ have the same curve parameter value. When W is deformed, the point $\mathbf{p}$ is moved to $\mathbf{p}'$ as follows.

$$\mathbf{p}' = \mathbf{p} + (\mathbf{p}_W - \mathbf{p}_R)f(x). \tag{1}$$

Here, x is a function of R, $\mathbf{p}$, and the range parameter r. The x is proportional to the Euclidean distance from $\mathbf{p}_R$ to $\mathbf{p}$, that is normalized by r. The function f in Equation (1) is a monotonically decreasing function of x that satisfies $f(0) = 1$ and $f(x) = 0$ for $x \geq 1$. The wire deformation in Equation (1) can be enhanced further with a radial scaling parameter s, that is,

$$\mathbf{p}' = \mathbf{p} + (s-1)(\mathbf{p} - \mathbf{p}_R)f(x) + (\mathbf{p}_W - \mathbf{p}_R)f(x). \tag{2}$$

The scaling parameter s controls the movement of $\mathbf{p}$ in the direction of $\mathbf{p} - \mathbf{p}_R$ or its reverse. The second term of the right-hand side of Equation (2) is for scaling. To assure no scaling when $s = 1$, we have modified the original work. We also ignore the rotation term since rotations are rarely employed for deformation of face models.

Multiple wire curves can be used to better control the shape of the object. In their original work, Singh *et. al.* proposed three alternatives. For our purpose, we choose the one described below: Let $\Delta\mathbf{p}_j$ be the displacement of the point $\mathbf{p}$ when a wire curve W_j alone is applied. Given n wire curves $W_j, j = 0, 1, 2, \cdots, m$, the new position $\mathbf{p}'$ is obtained as follows:

$$\mathbf{p}' = \mathbf{p} + \frac{\sum_{j=0}^{m} \Delta\mathbf{p}_j f_j(x)^k}{\sum_{j=0}^{m} f_j(x)^k}. \tag{3}$$

Here, $f_j(x) = f(x(R_j, \mathbf{p}, r_j))$ where R_j and r_j are the reference curve and the range parameter corresponding to W_j. The localizing parameter k controls the influence of W_j and s_j on deformation. For example, as $f_j(x)$ approaches one (or $\mathbf{p}$ approaches R_j), the influence of W_j and s_j are more rapidly increasing with bigger k.

4 Wire Extraction

Suppose that we use m pairs of wire and reference curves, denoted by (W_j, R_j), $j = 0, 1, 2, \cdots, m$, to characterize the geometry of a facial expression template T deformed from the base model M by displacing their vertex positions. Then, our problem is:

> Given M and T, determine the curve pairs, $(W_j, R_j), j = 0, 1, 2, \cdots, m$ and deformation parameters, f, r, s, and k such that T can be obtained from M through wire deformation by using those curve pairs and parameters.

The reference curves $R_j(u), j = 0, 1, 2, \cdots, m$ characterize the features of the base face model M such as eyes and the mouth and thus are not dependent on a specific template T. The range parameter $r_j(u)$ is an attribute of the curve $R_j(u)$ defined along it for all u. The localizing parameter k is applied uniformly to every point on M regardless of T. Therefore, we assume that experienced designers specify R_j's, r_j's, and k interactively to reflect their intuition on M. Provided with R_j's and r_j's, $f(x(R_j, \mathbf{p}, r_j))$ is uniquely computed. Hence, we will be done if the radial scaling parameters s_j's and the wire curves W_j's are determined. Here, s_j is a useful parameter for expression exaggeration or attenuation. The cheek bulge for an exaggerated smile is a good example of a very much use of s_j.

Let $\mathbf{p}_i$ and $\mathbf{p}'_i, i = 0, 1, 2, \cdots, n$ be the vertices of M and its corresponding vertices of T. From equation (3),

$$\Delta\mathbf{p}_i = \frac{\sum_{j=0}^{m} f_{ij}(x)^k \Delta\mathbf{p}_{ij}}{\sum_{j=0}^{m} f_{ij}(x)^k}, i = 0, 1, 2, \cdots, n. \tag{4}$$

Here, $\Delta\mathbf{p}_{ij}$ is the displacement of $\mathbf{p}_i$ when only W_j is applied, $f_{ij}=f(x(R_j, \mathbf{p}_i, r_j))$, and $\Delta\mathbf{p}_i = \mathbf{p}'_i - \mathbf{p}_i$. From Equation (2),

$$\Delta\mathbf{p}_{ij} = (s_j - 1)f_{ij}(x)(\mathbf{p}_i - \mathbf{p}_{iR_j}) + f_{ij}(x)(\mathbf{p}_{iW_j} - \mathbf{p}_{iR_j}), \tag{5}$$

where $\mathbf{p}_i$, s_j, $\mathbf{p}_{iR_j}$, and $\mathbf{p}_{iW_j}$ are a vertex $\mathbf{p}_i$ on M, the scaling parameter of the reference curve R_j, the point on R_j closest to $\mathbf{p}_i$, and the point on W_j corresponding to $\mathbf{p}_{iR_j}$. As stated in the previous section, W_j and R_j are parametric curves. In particular, we employ cubic B-splines to represent them. Therefore, $(\mathbf{p}_{iW_j} - \mathbf{p}_{iR_j})$ can be expressed as follows:

$$(\mathbf{p}_{iW_j} - \mathbf{p}_{iR_j}) = \sum_{l=0}^{t_j} B_l(\mathbf{w}_{jl} - \mathbf{r}_{jl}), \qquad (6)$$

where $\mathbf{w}_{jl}$ and $\mathbf{r}_{jl}, l = 0, 1, 2, \cdots, t_j$ are the control points of wire and reference curves W_j and R_j, respectively, and $B_l, l = 0, 1, 2, ..., t_j$ are their basis functions.

From Equations (4), (5), and (6)

$$\Delta \mathbf{p}_i = \sum_{j=0}^{m} \frac{f_{ij}(x)^k}{\sum_{j=0}^{m} f_{ij}(x)^k}[(s_j-1)f_{ij}(x)(\mathbf{p}_i - \mathbf{p}_{iR_j}) + f_{ij}(x)\sum_{l=0}^{t_j} B_l(\mathbf{w}_{jl} - \mathbf{r}_{jl})]. \qquad (7)$$

Given $\mathbf{p}_i$, we can determine $\mathbf{p}_{iR_j}$ and its curve parameter value on R_j and thus B_l can be evaluated. The only unknowns on the right-hand side of Equation (7) is the control points $\mathbf{w}_{jl}$'s of the wire curve W_j and their scaling factor s_j's.

We are going to solve Equation (7) for s_j and W_j. In a special case, we can trivially get W_j. Suppose that R_j passes through a sequence of vertices on the base model M and also that only one wire curve is defined on M. Then, R_j and W_j become R_0 and W_0, respectively, since we have one wire curve. For vertex $\mathbf{p}_i$ on R_0, the first term of the equation vanishes since $\mathbf{p}_i - \mathbf{p}_{iR_0} = 0$. Moreover, $f_{i0}(x) = 1$ since the vertex $\mathbf{p}_i$ is on R_0. Therefore, Equation (7) is reduced to $\Delta \mathbf{p}_i = \mathbf{p}_{iW_0} - \mathbf{p}_{iR_0}$. That is, the displacement of vertex $\mathbf{p}_i$ is determined only by a single wire curve W_0. Therefore, W_0 can be computed from the vertices on the expression template T corresponding to those on M. However, multiple wire curves are generally defined on M for facial animation. The vertex $\mathbf{p}_i$ on M moves to a new position by the influence of multiple wire curves. Hence, even if R_j passes through the sequence of vertices on M, W_j can not be obtained from the same sequence of vertices on T corresponding to those on M.

Let

$$w_{ij} = (f_{ij}(x)^{k+1})/(\sum_{j=0}^{m} f_{ij}(x)^k),$$

$$\mathbf{c}_i = \sum_{j=0}^{m} w_{ij}(\mathbf{p}_i - \mathbf{p}_{iR_j}), \text{ and}$$

$$\mathbf{q}_{jl} = \mathbf{w}_{jl} - \mathbf{r}_{jl}, l = 0, 1, 2, \cdots, t_j.$$

Then, Equation (7) becomes

$$\Delta \mathbf{p}_i = \mathbf{c}_i + \sum_{j=0}^{m} w_{ij}((\mathbf{p}_i - \mathbf{p}_{iR_j})s_j + \sum_{l=0}^{t_j} B_l \mathbf{q}_{jl}), i = 0, 1, 2, \cdots, n. \qquad (8)$$

Here, q_{jl}'s and s_j's are the only unknowns. Rearranging Equation (8), we have a system of linear equations:

$$\sum_{j=0}^{m} w_{ij}(\mathbf{p}_i - \mathbf{p}_{iR_j})s_j + \sum_{j=0}^{m}\sum_{l=0}^{t_j} w_{ij} B_l \mathbf{q}_{jl} = \Delta \mathbf{p}_i - \mathbf{c}_i, i = 0, 1, 2, \cdots, n, \quad (9)$$

or

$$\mathbf{Bs} + \mathbf{Cq} = \mathbf{b}, \quad (10)$$

where

$$\mathbf{B} = \begin{bmatrix} w_{00}(\mathbf{p}_0 - \mathbf{p}_{0R_1}) & w_{01}(\mathbf{p}_0 - \mathbf{p}_{0R_2}) & \cdots & w_{0m}(\mathbf{p}_0 - \mathbf{p}_{0R_m}) \\ w_{10}(\mathbf{p}_1 - \mathbf{p}_{1R_1}) & w_{11}(\mathbf{p}_1 - \mathbf{p}_{1R_2}) & \cdots & w_{1m}(\mathbf{p}_1 - \mathbf{p}_{1R_m}) \\ \cdots & \cdots & \cdots & \cdots \\ w_{n0}(\mathbf{p}_n - \mathbf{p}_{nR_1}) & w_{n1}(\mathbf{p}_n - \mathbf{p}_{nR_2}) & \cdots & w_{nm}(\mathbf{p}_n - \mathbf{p}_{nR_m}) \end{bmatrix},$$

$$\mathbf{C} = \begin{bmatrix} w_{00}B_0 & w_{00}B_1 & \cdots & w_{00}B_{t_0} & w_{01}B_0 & w_{01}B_1 & \cdots & w_{01}B_{t_1} & \cdots & w_{0m}B_0 & w_{0m}B_1 & \cdots & w_{0m}B_{t_m} \\ w_{10}B_0 & w_{10}B_1 & \cdots & w_{10}B_{t_0} & w_{11}B_0 & w_{11}B_1 & \cdots & w_{11}B_{t_1} & \cdots & w_{1m}B_0 & w_{1m}B_1 & \cdots & w_{1m}B_{t_m} \\ \cdots & & & & & & & & & & & & \\ w_{n0}B_0 & w_{n0}B_1 & \cdots & w_{n0}B_{t_0} & w_{n1}B_0 & w_{n1}B_1 & \cdots & w_{n1}B_{t_1} & \cdots & w_{nm}B_0 & w_{nm}B_1 & \cdots & w_{nm}B_{t_m} \end{bmatrix},$$

$$\mathbf{q} = (\mathbf{q}_{00}\ \mathbf{q}_{01}\ \cdots\ \mathbf{q}_{0t_0}\ \mathbf{q}_{10}\ \mathbf{q}_{11}\ \cdots\ \mathbf{q}_{1t_1}\ \cdots\ \mathbf{q}_{m0}\ \mathbf{q}_{m1}\ \cdots\ \mathbf{q}_{mt_m})^T,$$
$$\mathbf{s} = (s_1\ s_2\ \cdots\ s_m)^T, \text{ and}$$
$$\mathbf{b} = (\Delta\mathbf{p}_0 - \mathbf{c}_0\ \Delta\mathbf{p}_1 - \mathbf{c}_1\ \cdots\ \Delta\mathbf{p}_n - \mathbf{c}_n)^T.$$

The vector $\mathbf{s}$ represents the radial scaling factors. Each element $\mathbf{q}_{il}$ of the vector $\mathbf{q}$ is the displacement of the control point $\mathbf{w}_{il}$ from $\mathbf{r}_{il}$. We can further simplify Equation (10), juxtaposing matrices $\mathbf{B}$ and $\mathbf{C}$:

$$\mathbf{A}\hat{\mathbf{q}} = \mathbf{b}, \quad (11)$$

where $\mathbf{A} = [\mathbf{B}|\mathbf{C}]$ and $\hat{\mathbf{q}} = (\mathbf{s}^T, \mathbf{q}^T)^T$. Solving Equation (11) for $\hat{\mathbf{q}}$, we can not only find the scaling factors but also extract all wire curves. The system given in Equation (11) is over-constrained, since the number of vertices in the face model M is much greater than the total number of control points for all reference (or equivalently wire) curves and their scaling factors. Therefore, we need to compute the least squares solution, that is,

$$\hat{\mathbf{q}} = (\mathbf{A}^T\mathbf{A})^+ \mathbf{A}^T \mathbf{b}. \quad (12)$$

$(\mathbf{A}^T\mathbf{A})^+$ is the pseudo inverse of $(\mathbf{A}^T\mathbf{A})$ obtained from its singular value decomposition [13,19]. The first m elements of $\hat{\mathbf{q}}$ give the scaling factors s_j's for the template T. Displacing the control points of the reference curves (or equivalently the initial wire curves) with the rest of elements, we finally compute the control points of all wire curves.

5 Experimental Results

For our experiments, we have built a base face model and its templates of different expression types. The base model consists of about 5,658 vertices and 10,201 triangles and the length of a main diagonal of its bounding box is about 24.384. The expression templates are derived by designers from the base model through displacing the vertices of the base model. As shown in Figure 1, we define 15 reference (and thus wire) curves lying on the base model. Each of reference and wire curves is a cubic B-spline and has four or more control points.

First, we show how well our wire extraction scheme works. In Figure 3, the original templates are arranged side by side with their corresponding reconstructed templates. In the first column (Figure 3 (a)), we give the original templates that have sad, happy, surprised and angry expressions from top to bottom, respectively. In the second column (Figure 3 (b)), we show the extracted wire curves on the reconstructed templates. The reconstructed templates are created by deforming the base model with the extracted curves and deformation parameters. In the third column (Figure 3 (c)), we get rid of the wire curves from the reconstructed templates in the second column to show them more clearly. We can observe that they are visually very similar.

Now, we exhibit the capability of wire curves for local deformation. With the wire curves and deformation parameters extracted, we can use them as a high level user interface to locally deform facial features such as eyes, lips, forehead, cheeks, and etc, instead of interactively manipulating every vertex involved in the deformation, individually. Figure 2 shows local deformation achieved with such

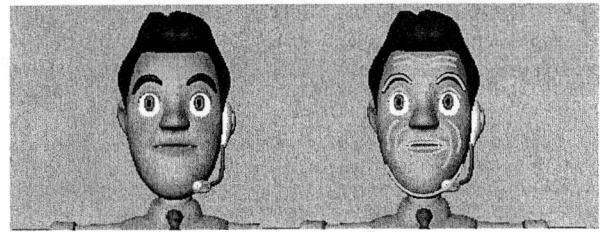

Fig. 1. The base facial model and its corresponding wire curves

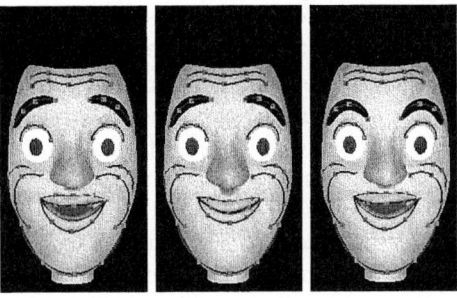

Fig. 2. The examples of high level user interface for local deformation

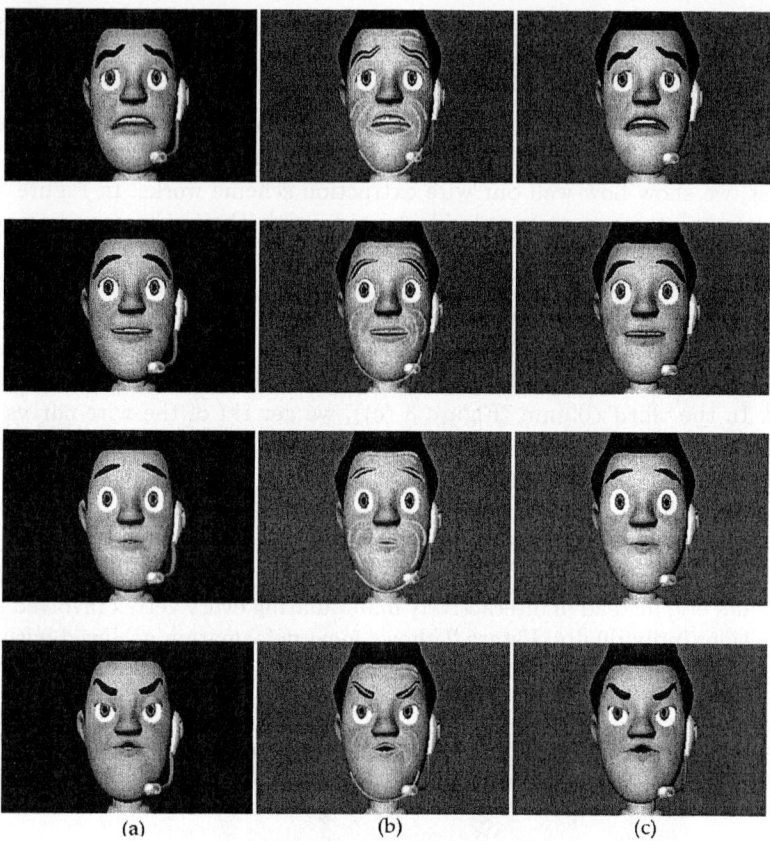

Fig. 3. The original face templates and their corresponding reconstructed face templates. (a) The original face templates with sad, happy, surprised, and angry expression (b) The extracted wire curves (c) The reconstructed face templates.

wire curves: The left figure shows a smiling expression and its corresponding wire curve configuration, the expression in the middle is obtained by manipulating mainly the wire curves that characterize the lips, and the expression on the right is obtained by deforming mainly the wire curves on eyebrows.

Finally, we demonstrate the ease of non-uniform blending with wire curves extracted. The upper row of Figure 4 shows the uniform blending of facial features, that is, uniform feature interpolation between two templates represented by image (1) and image (10), respectively. Each facial feature of the former is transited to that of the later at the same speed. The lower row gives an image sequence due to their feature-wise non-uniform blending. For this non-uniform blending, we use different blending functions for eyes and the mouth. Feature-wise non-uniform blending can hardly be achieved efficiently without an effective user-interface such as the wire deformation scheme. Figure 5 shows an example of uniform and non-uniform blending for another model.

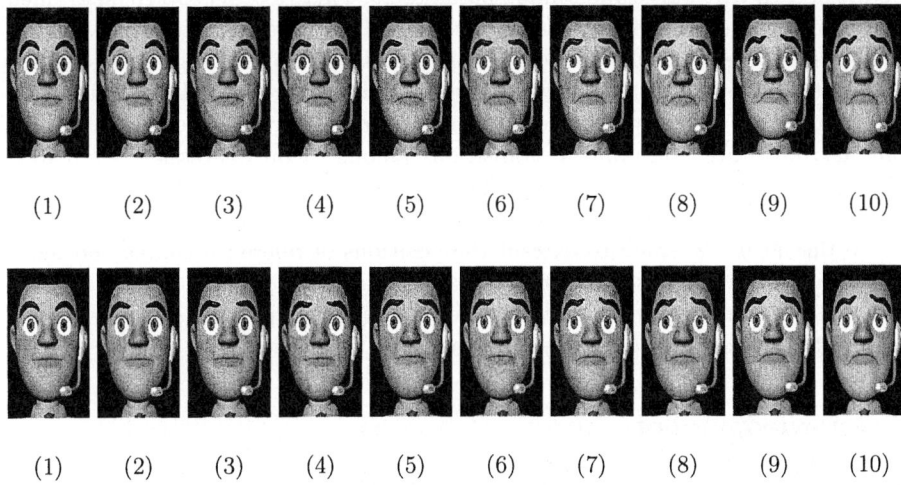

Fig. 4. Upper row: uniform blending. lower row: non-uniform blending.

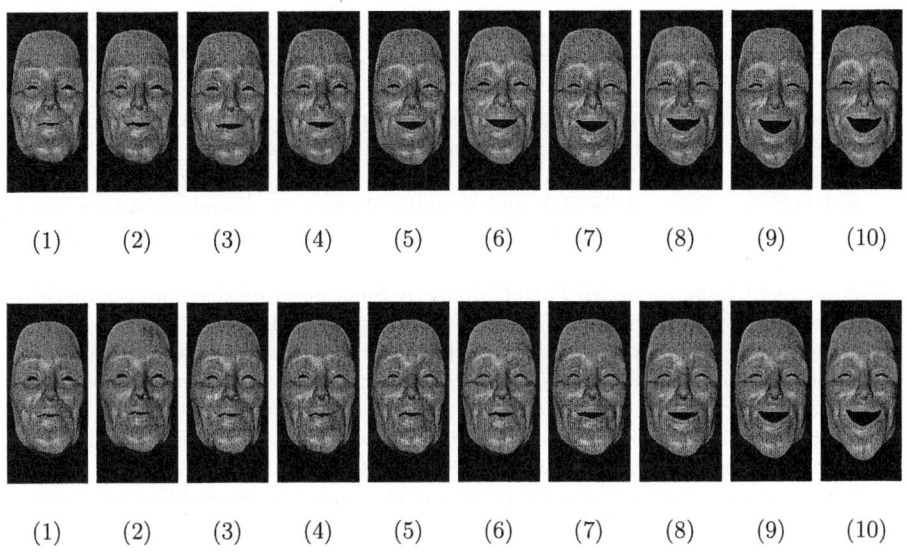

Fig. 5. Upper row: uniform blending. lower row: non-uniform blending.

6 Conclusion

In this paper, we present a method to extract a set of wire curves and deformation parameters from a face model regardless of its construction history. Given a pair of reference and face models with an identical topological structure, we formulate a system of linear equations of which the unknowns are the positions of control points of each wire curve and scaling parameters. This system is over-constrained since the number of vertices in the face models is much greater than that of unknowns. We extract the wire curves and parameters by solving the system for the least squares solution. The wire curves together with the scaling parameters, thus extracted, not only provide convenient handles for local geometry control but also facilitate non-uniform transitions among facial expression templates. The experimental results show the effectiveness of wire curve extraction and its usefulness.

In the future, we plan to extract the positions of reference curves and more deformation parameters. With the initial position of a reference curve interactively given by a designer, we will try to extract the best position of the reference curve that fits for a facial expression model and its reference.

Acknowledgement

This work was supported by the Korea Research Foundation Grant funded by Korea Government(MOEHRD, Basic Research Promotion Fund, KRF-2005-204-D00033).

References

1. Volker Blanz and Thomas Vetter. A morphable model for the synthesis of 3d faces. *SIGGRAPH 1999 Conference Proceedings*, pages 187–194, 1999.
2. Ian Buck, Adam Finkelstein, Charles Jacobs, Allison Klein, David H. Salesin, Joshua Seims, Richard Szeliski, and Kentaro Toyama. Performance-driven hand-drawn animation. *Symposium on Non Photorealistic Animation and Rendering*, pages 101–108, 2000.
3. Yu-Kuang Chang and Alyn P. Rockwood. A generalized de casteljau approach to 3d free-form deformation. *SIGGRAPH 94*, 28:257–260, 1994.
4. Erika Chuang and Chris Bregler. Performance driven facial animation using blendshape interpolation. *Stanford University Computer Science Technical Report, CS-TR-2002-02*, 2002.
5. Sabine Coquillart. Extended free-form deformation: A sculpturing tool for 3d geometric modeling. *SIGGRAPH 90*, 24:187–196, 1990.
6. Brian Guenter, Cindy Grimm, Daniel Wood, Henrique Malvar, and Frederic Pighin. Making faces. *SIGGRAPH 98 Conference Proceedings*, pages 55–67, 1998.
7. Adele Hars. Masters of motion capture. *Computer Graphics World*, pages 27–34, October 1996.
8. William M. Hsu, John F. Hugues, and Henry Kaufman. Direct manipulation of free-form deformation. *SIGGRAPH 92*, pages 177–184, 1992.
9. Pushkar Joshi, Wen C. Tien, Mathieu Desbrun, and Frederic Pighin. Learning controls for blend shape based realistic facial animation. *Eurographics/SIGGRAPH Symposium on Computer Animation*, 2003.
10. Kolja Kahler, Jorg Haber, and Hans-Peter Seidel. Geometry-based muscle modeling for facial animation. *Graphics Interface*, pages 37–46, 2001.
11. Kolja Kahler, Jorg Haber, and Hans-Peter Seidel. Reanimating the dead: Reconstruction of expressive faces from skull data. *SIGGRAPH 2003*, 2003.

12. Prem Kalra, Angelo Mangili, Nadia M. Thalmann, and Daniel Thalmann. Simulation of facial muscle actions based on rational free form deformations. *Eurographics 92*, 58:59–69, 1992.
13. Min Ho Kyung, Myung Soo Kim, and Sung Je Hong. A new approach to through-the-lens camera control. *CVGIP: Graphical Models and Image Processing*, 58(3):262–285, 1996.
14. Yuencheng Lee, Demetri Terzopoulos, and Keith Waters. Realistic modeling for facial animation. *SIGGRAPH 95 Conference Proceedings*, pages 55–62, 1995.
15. Ron MacCracken and Kenneth I. Joy. Free-form deformations with lattices of arbitrary topology. *SIGGRAPH 96*, 30:181–189, 1996.
16. Stephen R. Marschner, Brian Guenter, and Sashi Raghupathy. Modeling and rendering for realistic facial animation. *EUROGRAPHICS Rendering Workshop 2000*, pages 98–110, 2000.
17. Frederic Pighin, Jamie Hecker, Dani Lischinski, Richard Szeliski, and David H. Salesin. Synthesizing realistic facial expressions from photographs. *SIGGRAPH 98 Conference Proceedings*, pages 75–84, 1998.
18. Frederic Pighin, Richard Szeliski, and David Salesin. Resynthesizing facial animation through 3d model-based tracking. *International Conference on Computer Vision*, pages 143–150, 1999.
19. William H. Press, Saul A. Teukolsky, William T. Vetterling, and Brian P. Flannery. *Numerical recipes in C: Art of scientific computing*. Cambridge University Press, 2nd edition, 1992.
20. Hyewon Pyun, Yejin Kim, Wonseok Chae, Hyung Woo Kang, and Sung Yong Shin. An example-based approach for facial expression cloning. *Eurographics/SIGGRAPH Symposium on Computer Animation*, 2003.
21. Thomas W. Sederberg and Scott R. Parry. Free-form deformation of solid geometric models. *SIGGRAPH 86*, 20:151–160, 1986.
22. Karan Singh and Eugene Fiume. Wires: A geometric deformation technique. *SIGGRAPH 98 Conference Proceedings*, pages 299–308, 1998.
23. Lance Williams. Performance-driven facial animation. *SIGGRAPH 90*, 24:235–242, 1990.
24. Qingshan Zhang, Zicheng Liu, Baining Guo, and Harry Shum. Geometry-driven photorealistic facial expression synthesis. *Eurographics/SIGGRAPH Symposium on Computer Animation*, 2003.

Intelligent 3D Video Avatar for Immersive Telecommunication

Sang-Yup Lee[1,2], Ig-Jae Kim[1], Sang C. Ahn[1], Myo-Taeg Lim[2], and Hyoung-Gon Kim[1]

[1] Imaging Media Research Center, Korea Institute of Science and Technology,
Seoul, 136-791, Korea
{sylee, kij, ahn, hgk}@imrc.kist.re.kr
[2] School of Electrical Engineering, Korea University, Seoul, 136-701, Korea
mlim@korea.ac.kr

Abstract. Immersive telecommunication is a new challenging field that enables a user to share a virtual space with remote participants. The main objective is to offer rich communication modalities, as similar as those used in the face-to-face meetings like gestures, gaze awareness, realistic images, and correct sound direction. Moreover, natural full body interaction is presented as a tangible interface where people meet the cyber space. As a result, the user can be immersed and has interaction with virtual objects including remote participants. This would overcome the limitations both of the conventional video-based telecommunication and also the VR-based collaborative virtual environment approaches.

1 Introduction

Recently, immersive display rendering technologies, such as the CAVE system [1] have become popular in the virtual reality community. These generate high quality of visual immersion and can be used in a communication environment by being connected into a network for collaboration. Immersive tele-collaboration system with the CAVE allows geographically distributed users to work jointly at the same cyber space. The same world scene can be displayed for each participant with the correct user viewpoint by continuously tracking the movement of the participant eyes.

In the networked immersive virtual environment, users can share a virtual world with a high-quality sense of presence. However, it is necessary to transmit images of the users in order to show participants' images on a mutual display for natural communication. In the distributed virtual world with the network, synthetic 3D avatars have been used for this purpose. Although the user's positional relationship can be shared in virtual space with synthetic avatar, it is difficult to represent the realities of the exact human motion, facial expressions, and emotions using this technique. Over last few years, various research activities on 3D video avatar generation have been reported. 3D video avatar generation to support the dynamic rendering of participants is at the heart of immersive communication system because immersion relies mostly on visual experience in mixed reality, and it also enables more natural interactions with entities in virtual environments. 3D information can be retrieved using stereo camera which generates range images. Matusik[2] and Li [3] compute a visual hull from multiple camera views, using epipolar geometry, and generate a 3D textured model. Geometry information can also be retrieved by Voxel Coloring.

Recently the Systems Technology Division in Korea Institute of Science and Technology (KIST) is continuously researching and developing the core technology for the intelligent HCI. It has launched a project named "Tangible Space Initiative (TSI)." The art of TSI is based on the concept of tangible space where several real objects of physical environment are integrated into a computer generated virtual environment. Thus, the space creates a new kind of living environment for human which exceeds all the spatial and physical limits.

In order to interlink human user with tangible space, tangible interface is developed for providing a natural interface for users which allows them to obtain visual, aural and tactile senses. The sight is one of the important and the most used sense organ. To give an effective sensation to human's sight an immersive large display environment with high resolution is being developed. This kind of display covers almost the whole field of view. Thus it gives users a feeling of being immersed into the computer generated world and increases the sense of reality. Sound rendering is an important issue as well to merge real world in computer generated world. Generating a sound exactly like in the real world can give user more information about objects in the virtual world and therefore more sense of reality. Another important aspect to bridge the gap between users and cyber space is to integrate haptic feedback that gives users a physical sense. In this paper, we present an immersive and natural interface that allows a user to experience immersive telecommunication and the full body interaction with remote participants and virtual environment. The proposed immersive telecommunication system is implemented between the CAVE and Smart-Portal at KIST.

2 Immersive Telecommunication System

Both of the CAVE and Smart-Portal have multi-screen immersive projection environment that have four and three screens, respectively. CAVE is an emerging display paradigm superior to other display paradigms. A user is surrounded by the projected images generated by computers. The virtual camera view point is synchronized in space with the real user viewpoint and generated images are warped for the seamless display on the screen. This viewer-centric perspective of CAVE simulates an asymmetric perspective view from the current location of the viewer. Sensors continuously track viewer's position and send the information to the rendering system to maintain correct perspective. Currently, the CAVE consists of four square walls, each with the size of 260×260 centimeters, four projectors with rear projection, and SPIDAR[4] as a haptic device. The Smart-Portal is the CAVE-like spatially immersive display environment which has three screens - one at the front and one each on the left and right. The sizes of front and side screen are 700×240 and 600×240 centimeters, respectively. Seven projectors with front projection are used to display images and one ceiling projector is used for smart purposes, such as elimination of the shadows occurred from front projection-based displays, active illumination, or visualization of augmented information. Because of the wide multi-screen configuration, Smart-Portal provides an extremely wide field of view and effectively synthesizes a life-sized immersive VR environment.

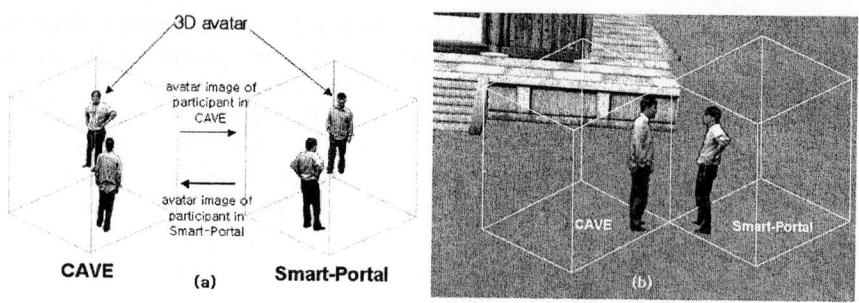

Fig. 1. Concept of immersive telecommunication system

Figure 1 shows the concept of immersive telecommunication system. In this immersive virtual environment, participants at remote locations experience natural communication using 3D video avatars (see Figure 1 (a)). Consequently, users have the sense of being in the same space and sharing the same world as shown in Figure 1 (b). Proposed immersive telecommunication system can be viewed as composed of three parts: a context acquisition system to obtain and represent the information of the participant and environment, such as 3D human shapes, motion data, and sound; a communication framework to handle various data; and a rendering system to make the local user feel as if he/she were present in the remote scene.

Figure 2 depicts the overview of the telecommunication system between CAVE and Smart-Portal. The context acquisition system consists of Avatar Server and Device Server. Avatar Server generates 3D video avatar with his/her speech, human motion, and volume information for interacting with virtual environment. Moreover, the intention of users is understood and expressed by using multimodal interface in Avatar Server. Device Server provides an interface to various interaction hardware devices, such as head tracker, 3D wand, keyboard, and haptic device. Especially, 3D information of the user's head is important for both rendering and avatar generation processes. A retro-reflective marker attached on the top of a participant's head is used so that it can be detected by the stereo IR camera easily for the sake of tracking participant's head in display environments. Vision based tracker is capable of obtaining 6 DOF tracking information at 30Hz.

Since the system is implemented on complex distributed environment with many heterogeneous subsystems, it requires an efficient communication framework to handle the data generated by Avatar Server as well as all other data streams common to most collaborative virtual environments. These include event and message-based communication, i.e., user-triggered modifications of the shared virtual scene; real-time audio for voice communication; and tracking data. This framework is named Networked Augmented Virtual Environment Real-time (NAVER)[5]. NAVER is designed to provide flexible, extensible, scalable reconfigurable framework for VR applications. In the NAVER, component nodes are classified into several categories according to its main function.

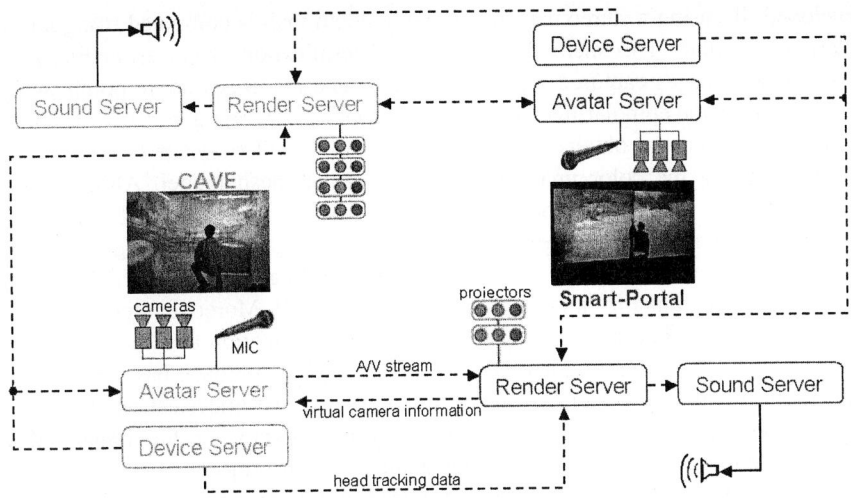

Fig. 2. Immersive Telecommunication System Overview

Our immersive telecommunication display environment is built with CAVE and Smart-Portal as mentioned before. Each display screen is large enough for life-size projection of remote participant's environment. The display surfaces are covered with a polarization-preserving fabric for the stereoscopic rendering. In addition to realistic graphics rendering and natural interaction, spatial sound enhances the sense of presence in virtual environments. The audio rendering system is designed for rendering dynamically moving sound sources (participants) in multi-speaker environments using 3D sound localization algorithm. Spatialized sound rendering is provided by a Sound Server that receives remote sound through network. In the 3D positioning stage of Sound Server, received audio stream is mixed onto several speaker channels by volume panning method. The volume panning method models a sound field with different intensities according to the direction of the virtual source.

3 Real-Time 3D Video Avatar

In order to realize a natural communication in the networked immersive environment, human images should be viewed on mutual displays. Although distributed virtual environments often use computer graphics-based avatars, natural interaction with a polygon-based avatar is limited due to the lack of reality. To overcome this drawback, an image based avatar has been developed, where the texture of the avatar is segmented from background and then augmented into virtual world through mapping video avatar on a two-dimensional billboard. The problem in augmenting video avatar into virtual world is caused by the fact that human's body has a 3D shape while the video image is 2D. Therefore, in generating a video avatar, it is important to create a geometric model to generate images from arbitrary viewpoint. To relieve these problems, 2.5D video avatar based on the Depth from Stereo (DfS) has been developed. By using a stereo camera system, a depth map is computed using a triangulation algorithm. This method requires the determination of corresponding pixels between two images captured by stereo camera. These corresponding points are determined along the epipolar line. Then the graphics workstation generates a triangular mesh model from the obtained depth map, and 2.5D video avatar is generated by texture mapping the color image onto the triangular mesh model. Although 2.5D avatar has depth information, there are some problems to apply it to real-time immersive telecommunication. The result of *DfS* is not robust due to lighting and camera conditions. Immersive displays currently have low lighting conditions which make the acquisition of high quality images from cameras difficult. Moreover stereo matching process is still the bottleneck for the real time implementation due to the computational complexity. Recently, Shape from Silhouette (*SfS*) approach has been successfully used in real time systems in order to compensate the imperfection of the 2.5D video avatar. The reconstructed result of this approach is known as the 'visual hull', an approximate model that envelopes the true geometry of the object.

The concept of the visual hull was introduced by Laurentini [6]. A visual hull has the properties that it always contains the object. The visual hull is not guaranteed to be the same as the original object since the concave surface regions can never be distinguished using silhouette information alone. Nevertheless, it is an effective method to reconstruct 3D avatar because surfaces of human model are generally convex.

In the suggested immersive telecommunication system, the avatar server has been developed in order to reconstruct the visual hull and send the result image to remote rendering server. The avatar server captures the images of the reference views in real-time with multiple video cameras, and also receives head tracking data from remote render server in order to generate the novel view of 3D avatar. The dynamic 3D visual hull reconstruction algorithm is implemented in three steps: 1) image processing to label object pixels, 2) calculating the volume intersection, 3) and rendering the visual hull. Because of computational complexity in volume intersection, we modify the plane-based volume intersection algorithm for GPU processing [7].

Technical difficulties for true bi-directional immersive telecommunication arise from the fact that the capture and display should take place at the same place. Immersive display environment generally has low lighting condition which makes the acquisition of high quality image difficult. In blue-c project [8], a synchronized stroboscopic light, shuttered projection screens, and shutter glasses are used to capture a vivid human image in immersive environments. But the system needs expensive hardware equipments and users must wear shutter glasses.

We developed a real-time robust method that provides a realistic avatar image using active segmentation [9] in immersive environments. Active segmentation method consists of optical IR-keying segmentation and active illumination (see Fig. 3). The texture of the segmented image is enhanced by illuminating only the human body with image-based active projectors, providing high quality realistic texture acquisition for live avatar while preserving user's immersive display environment. Fig. 4 shows result images of the various stages of the active segmentation processing.

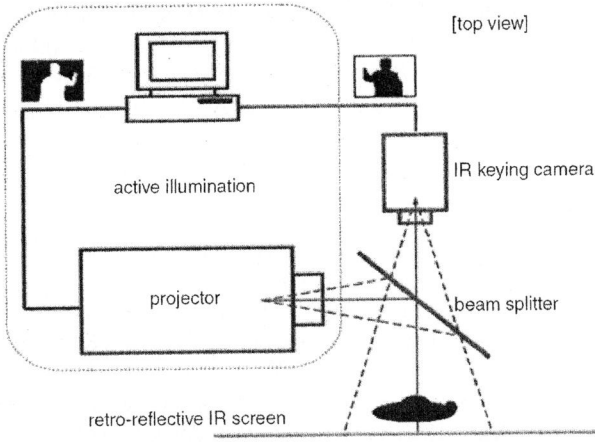

Fig. 3. Active illumination system with optical IR keying camera

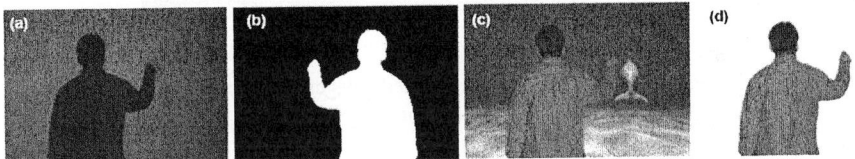

Fig. 4. Results of active segmentation: (a) a captured image from the IR camera in CAVE-like environment, (b) an input image of the projector, (c) a captured image from the color camera with proposed active illumination, (d) segmented image using active segmentation.

Figure 5 shows the reconstructed 3D video avatar by proposed algorithm when 3 video cameras are used. In this figure, white wire-frames represent the reference cameras. The 3D video avatar results can be used not only for rendering desired scene in a virtual world but also for volumetric effects and interaction. In order to integrate the avatar in a realistic way in a virtual scene we can apply shadows. These shadows help understanding relative object position in the virtual scene and increase immersion.

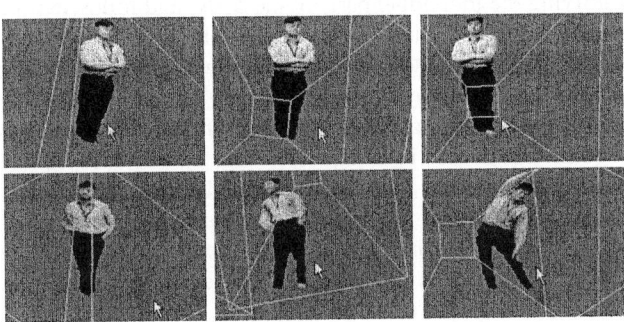

Fig. 5. 3D reconstructed images using multiple video cameras

We implemented our method to generate 3D guide in virtual heritage tour. Our scenario named "Heritage Alive" enables interactive group exploration of cultural heritage in tangible space. A 3D guide at remote space can fully control the scenario using natural interaction described in section 4. A view of the 3D guide is decoded to MPEG video and streamed to the Render Server that combines video image in virtual environment context using billboarding method (see Figure 6).

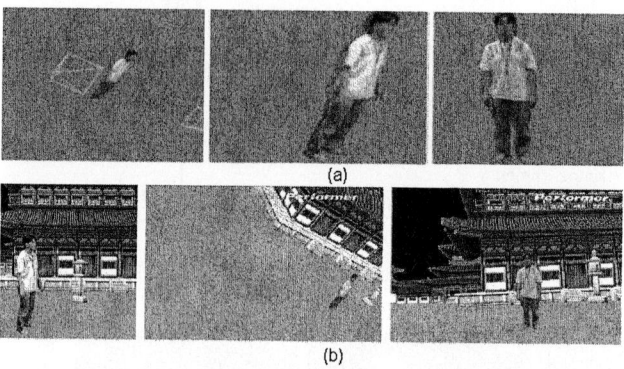

Fig. 6. 3D video avatar results : (a) 3D reconstructed images with respect to virtual camera direction (b) augmented 3D video avatar using billboarding

4 Natural Interface for Full Body Interaction

In order for an avatar to realize its function actively, it should behave appropriately to the environment and situation. Therefore, we should recognize intention and status of users in real-time. In this section, we describe Avatar Server more detail focusing on the natural interface mechanism. Avatar Server consists of avatar generator which provide a novel view 3D video avatar, physics engine which enable 3D video avatar to have dynamic behaviors in virtual world, motion capture for posture recognition, and inference engine which infers the user's intention by using speech and posture recognition (see Fig. 7).

Because the volume information of human body is extracted via the visual hull, we proceed by identifying the individual parts of the body, and following their movement from one frame to the next. This is a complex problem which requires knowledge about both the appearance and the dynamics of the objects being tracked. In our system, the appearance is modeled by several ellipsoids. The process used to match ellipsoids to groups of voxels is a variant of the well-known Expectation-Maximization (EM) algorithm which proceeds in 2 steps (see Fig. 8). For each voxel, we compute the distance to every ellipsoid using the Mahalanobis distance. Then, the voxel is assigned to the nearest ellipsoid. After Expectation step, the new means and covariances of each ellipsoid are estimated by using the set of voxels assigned to it. From the motion capture component in Avatar Server, we can generate motion information naturally which is used for posture recognition.

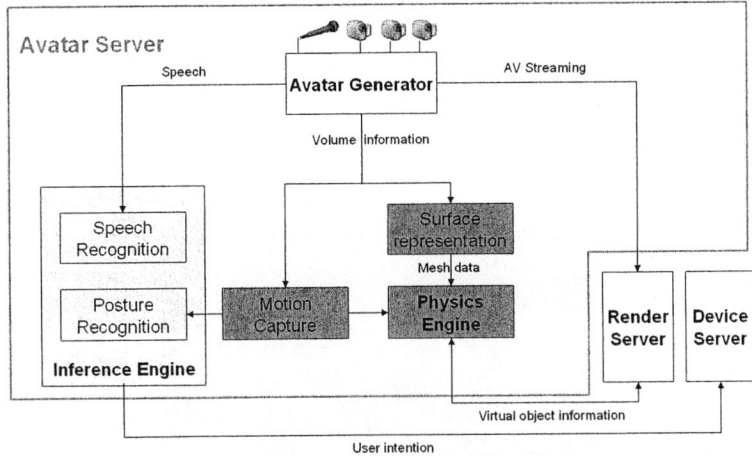

Fig. 7. Avatar Server Architecture

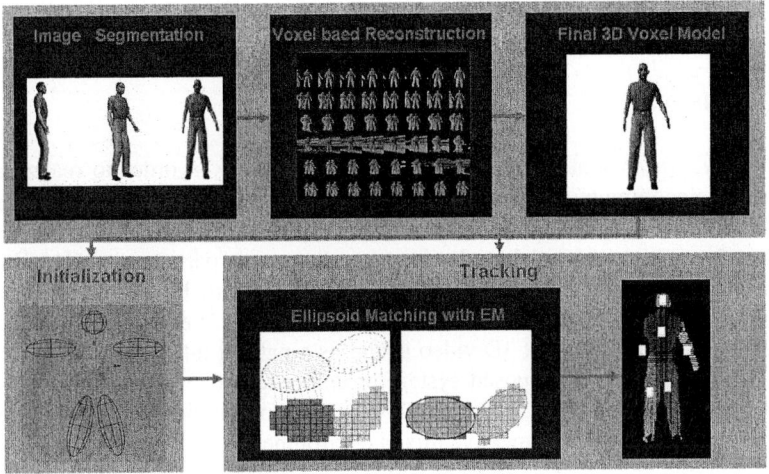

Fig. 8. Volume based motion tracking process

For generating 3D video avatar, the user is always viewed from a set of reference views. This assumption limits user's behavior and he/she cannot navigate freely in virtual space by himself. In order to compensate the behavior of avatar, inference engine is used for understanding the user's intention. User can issue a command to control his/her video avatar by saying "Up / Down / Left / Right / Front / Back", or by body posture.

Body posture is recognized by relative position and direction of body parts. Once the posture is recognized, it is converted to a command and sent to Device Server by network. Then, Render Server applies an appropriate action with respect to the dynamic shared state from the Device Server.

On the other hand, in order to interact with 3D virtual environment a triangulated surface from volume data is produced by the marching cube algorithm. The generated mesh model is well-suited to rendering with general graphics hardware, which is optimized for triangular mesh processing. It is used as an input data for physics simulation. Fig. 9 shows the results of physics simulation between 3D video avatar and virtual objects.

Fig. 9. Full body interaction with virtual objects using physics simulation

5 Conclusion

In this study, we presented a 3D video avatar technology in order to realize a high immersive telecommunication in the networked virtual world. Our system allows virtual environments to be truly immersive and enables interaction not only between the real and synthetic objects, but also between the remote participants. CAVE and its extension into a life-sized immersive environment, Smart-Portal, demonstrate the possibility of immersive telecommunication via network. We have presented a new method to build an intelligent 3D video avatar as a natural interface of telecommunication environment. The proposed system promises to move virtual world one step closer to our life by enabling real time 3D video telecommunication between the user and remote participants in immersive mixed environment.

References

1. Cruz-Neira, C., Sandin, D. J., DeFanti, T. A., Kenyon, R. V., & Hart, J. C. : The CAVE: Audio Visual Experience Automatic Virtual Environment. Communications of the ACM, Vol. 35, No. 6 (1992) 64-72
2. Matusik, W., Buehler, C., Raskar, R., Gortler, S., & McMillan, L. : Image-Based Visual Hulls. Proceedings of ACM SIGGRAPH 2000 (2000) 369-374
3. Li, M., Magnor, M., & Seidel, H. : Online Accelerated Rendering of Visual Hulls in Real Scenes. Journal of WSCG 2003, 11(2) (2003) 290-297
4. Sato, M : Development of String-based Force Display : SPIDAR. 8th International Conference on Virtual Systems and Multimedia. (2002)

5. Park, Y. D., Kim J. W., Ko, H. D., Choy, Y. C. : Dynamic Shared State management For Distributed Interactive Virtual Environment. Proceedings of the 14th international conference on artificial reality and telexistence (2004) 75-80
6. Laurentini, A. : The visual hull concept for silhouette-based image understanding. IEEE Trans. Pattern Anal. Machine Intell., 16(2) (1994) 150–162
7. Lee, S. Y., Kim, I. J., Ahn, S. C., Ko, H. D., Lim, M. T., Kim, H. G. : Real Time 3D Avatar for Interactive Mixed Reality. Proceedings of VRCAI 2004 (2004) 75-80
8. Markus, G., Stephan, W., Martin, N., Edouard, L., Christian, S., Andreas, K., Esther, K., Tomas, S., Luc, V. G., Silke, L., Kai, S., Andrew, V. M., & Oliver, S. : blue-c: A Spatially Immersive Display and 3D Video Portal for Telepresence. Proceedings of ACM SIGGRAPH 2003
9. Lee, S. Y., Kim, I. G., Ahn, S. C., Kim, H. G. : Active Segmentation for Immersive Live Avatar, IEE Electronics Letters (2004)

A Lagrangian Heuristic for Winner Determination Problem in Combinatorial Auctions

Andrew Lim[1,2] and Jiqing Tang[1]

[1] Dept of Industrial Engineering and Logistics Management,
Hong Kong Univ of Science and Technology,
Clear Water Bay, Kowloon, Hong Kong
[2] School of Computer Science & Engineering,
South China University of Technology,
GuangDong, PR China

Abstract. We present a Lagrangian-based heuristic LAHA for the Winner Determination Problem in Combinatorial Auctions. The algorithm makes use of the market computing power by applying subgradient optimization with variable fixing. A number of different bid ordering and selection rules are used in our heuristic. Moreover, an effective local search refinement procedure is presented at the end of our algorithm. We propose a new methodology PBP to produce realistic test problems which are computationally more difficult than CATS generated benchmarks. LAHA was tested on 238 problems of 13 different distributions. Among the 146 problems for which the optimum is known, LAHA found the optimum in 91 cases and produce on average 99.2% optimal solutions for the rest. Moreover, on the other 92 hard problems for which the optimum is not known, LAHA's solutions were on average 2% better than the solutions generated by CPLEX 8.0 in 30 minutes.

1 Introduction

Combinatorial Auctions usually lead to better resource allocations than traditional auctions since they allow bidders to place bids on combinations of items. However, the problem of how to identify the winning bids so as to maximize the seller's revenue is known to be $\mathcal{NP}$-Complete [11]. The problem has lately attracted much attention and a number of algorithms have been proposed [15, 6, 17, 10, 18, 9] in the literature.

In this paper we present a Lagrangian-based heuristic LAHA for the Winner Determination Problem. We compare the computational results against ILOG's state-of-the-art IP solver CPLEX 8.0 and a recent fast heuristic SAGII [9]. The rest of the paper is organized as follows. In the next section we define the problem and discuss its Lagrangian relaxation form. LAHA is described in Section 3 and experimental results is presented in Section 4. We conclude our work in Section 5.

2 The Lagrangian Relaxation of the Winner Determination Problem

Formally, the Winner Determination Problem (WDP) can be defined as follows. The auctioneer has a set of items $M = \{1, 2, \ldots, m\}$ for bid. The bidders have placed a number of bids $N = \{1, 2, \ldots, n\}$. Each bid j covers a subset I_j of items with a price of c_j. The WDP is to maximize the auctioneer's revenue by identifying a set of winning bids under the constraint that each item can be allocated to at most one such bid. The IP formulation of WDP is equivalent to a maximization Set Packing Problem:

$$\max \quad Z = \sum_{j=1}^{n} c_j x_j \tag{1}$$

$$\text{s.t.} \quad \sum_{j=1}^{n} a_{ij} x_j \leq 1, \forall i \in M \tag{2}$$

$$x_j \in \{0, 1\}, \forall j \in N \tag{3}$$

Here $a_{ij} = 1$ if item i is included in bid j, i.e., $i \in I_j$; $a_{ij} = 0$ otherwise. For notational convenience let $J_i = \{j \in N : a_{ij} = 1\}$ be the set of bids including item i. The density of the problem is defined as $d = \sum_{i \in M} \sum_{j \in N} a_{ij}/(nm)$.

Our heuristic is based on the Lagrangian relaxation of the IP formulation (1)-(3). We assume the reader is familiar with Lagrangian relaxation theory, see [5] for an introduction. Given a Lagrangian multiplier vector $\mu = (\mu_i) \in \mathcal{R}_m^+$, the Lagrangian Relaxation (LR) of WDP reads:

$$\max L(\mu) = \sum_{j=1}^{n} c_j x_j + \sum_{i=1}^{m} \mu_i (1 - \sum_{j=1}^{n} a_{ij} x_j) \tag{4}$$

$$\text{s.t.} \quad 0 \leq x_j \leq 1, \forall j \in N \tag{5}$$

If we use $c_j(\mu) = c_j - \sum_{i=1}^{m} a_{ij} \mu_i$ to denote the *Lagrangian cost* associated with each bid $j \in N$ for any Lagrangian multipliers μ, the objective function (4) becomes:

$$\max L(\mu) = \sum_{i=1}^{m} \mu_i + \sum_{j=1}^{n} c_j(\mu) x_j \tag{6}$$

Obviously, the optimal solution to LR for any given Lagrangian multiplier μ can be determined in linear time: set $x_j(\mu) = 0$ if $c_j(\mu) < 0$; $x_j(\mu) = 1$ if $c_j(\mu) > 0$; and $x_j(\mu)$ be either 0 or 1 when $c_j(\mu) = 0$. LR provides an upper bound for WDP and the Lagrangian Dual (LD) problem associated with the LR asks for a Lagrangian multiplier vector μ which minimizes the upper bound:

$$L_d = \min L(\mu) \tag{7}$$

$$\text{s.t.} \quad \mu \geq 0 \tag{8}$$

A commonly used technique for finding near optimal Lagrangian multipliers is *Subgradient Optimization*. The approach generates a sequence of $\mu^0, \mu^1, \ldots$ non-negative Lagrangian multiplier vectors in order to lower down the upper bounds. μ^0 is the initial value and μ^k can be determined from μ^{k-1} by using the following updating formula:

$$\mu_i^k = \max(\mu_i^{k-1} + \lambda \frac{L_B - L(\mu^{k-1})}{\|s(\mu^{k-1})\|^2} s_i(\mu^{k-1}), 0) \quad \forall i \in M \quad (9)$$

Here L_B is the best lower bound found so far, and $\lambda > 0$ is a given step-size parameter. $s(\mu) = (s_i(\mu))$ is the subgradient vector defined as:

$$s_i(\mu) = 1 - \sum_{j=1}^{n} a_{ij} x_j(\mu) \quad \forall i \in M$$

and $\|s(\mu)\| = \sqrt{\sum_{i=1}^{m} s_i(\mu)^2}$ is its norm.

We apply subgradient optimization in our heuristic. The Lagrangian cost $c_j(\mu)$ is used extensively in our bid ordering and selection heuristics.

3 A Lagrangian Heuristic

The main frame of our algorithm consists of 2 phases. The first phase is the subgradient phase, in which we aim at quickly finding near optimal Lagrangian multipliers. Several heuristics are applied in this phase in order to generate good feasible solutions. The second phase is the local search phase, in which we apply local search to furthur improve solution's quality.

3.1 Subgradient Optimization

In the classical Held-Karp approach of subgradient optimization, the step-size parameter λ is initialized with 2 and is halved whenever the bound does not improve for a number of $p(\lambda)$ consecutive iterations. Our algorithm starts with $\lambda = 1$. For every $p(\lambda)$ iterations, we compute the difference of the incumbent best upper bounds. If the improvement is greater than 1 in absolute value or 1% relatively, the same λ will be used for another $p(\lambda)$ iterations. Otherwise if the improvement is small, we keep the same λ for another 10 iterations. The value of λ is halved if there is no improvement at all. We set $p(\lambda) = 100$ for all λ except $\lambda = 1$ for which $p(1) = 150$. This decision is motivated by our observation that iterating more times at the beginning of the subgradient phase not only can speed up the convergence speed, but also help the exploration in the solution space, on which our heuristic methods rely. For the initial Lagrangian multiplier μ^0, we use the average price of each item, namely:

$$\mu_i^0 = \frac{\sum_{j \in J_i} \frac{c_j}{|I_j|}}{|J_i|}, \quad \forall i \in M$$

The subgradient phase ends as soon as λ becomes smaller than 0.01.

The initial lower bound L_B is calculated by *Enumerative Greedy*. First we sort the bids in decreasing order according to their price c_j. Then non-conflicting bids are added to the current solution one by one. However, different from the usual greedy methods, we will examine all the 2^8 possibilities of the first 8 non-conflicting bids. The rest of the bids will be added greedily. The same process is repeated by first sorting the bids with $c_j/|I_j|$ and L_B is set to the higher value from these two methods.

Put into the context of Combinatorial Auctions, the subgradient optimization can be considered as a market based method which makes use of market's self-adjusting power. The Lagrangian Multiplier μ can be interpreted as the price for items. For each bid $j \in N$, the Lagrangian cost $c_j(\mu) = c_j - \sum_{i=1}^{m} a_{ij}\mu_i$ gives its surplus. Obviously, we should only accept the bid $(x_j(\mu) = 1)$ when its surplus is positive $c_j(\mu) > 0$; otherwise the bid is turned back $x_j(\mu) = 0$. The subgradient $s_i(\mu) = 1 - \sum_{j=1}^{n} a_{ij}x_j(\mu)$ is used to denote the stock of item i. When more than one profitable bids request item i and it is out of stock $s_i(\mu) < 0$, we should increase the price for the item μ_i by using the updating formula (9); otherwise if item i is not allocated $s_i(\mu) = 1$, we have to lower down its price; $s_i(\mu) = 0$ indicates balanced supply and demand, in which case its price is not changed. The objective function (6) is used to estimate whether an overall good allocation has been reached.

3.2 Bids Ordering and Selection Heuristics

The first heuristic method used during the subgradient phase is *Stochastic Bid Selection*. Since the Lagrangian cost $c_j(\mu)$ can be considered as the surplus of the bids, we first sort the bids in decreasing order according to $c_j(\mu)$. Then for each unsatisfied bid which does not conflict with previous selected bids, it is accepted into the solution with probability 0.9. The procedure ends when no more bids are available and the last bid is guaranteed to be selected. The whole process is repeated for a number of 50 times. Then we rank the bids by $c_j(\mu)/|I_j|$ and run the selection algorithm again. We observe most of the best solutions found during the subgradient phase are from this heuristic method.

The second heuristic is based on the solutions $x(\mu)$ obtained from solving the LR, which is not necessarily feasible to the original WDP. This heuristic will try to adjust the solution and ensure its feasibility. Suppose $X = \{j : x_j(\mu) = 1\}$ is the optimal solution to the current LR. For each bid $j \in X$, we compute , the set of bids which share at least one common item with bid j. In order to remove the infeasibility, we choose the bid $j \in X$ which minimizes the function $c_j(\mu)/|T_j|$ and remove it from X. The step is repeated until X becomes feasible. At this time, the solution may still be augmented, so we would add non-conflicting bids greedily according to their price. The heuristic function $c_j(\mu)/|T_j|$ needs not to be computed from scratch every time. T_j can be updated dynamically whenever a bid j is removed from X. This speeds up the computation significantly.

For the sake of efficiency, the above two heuristics are only called sporadically so as to balance the computation time and the solution quality. Stochastic Bid Selection is called every iteration for $\lambda = 1$, once every 3 iterations for $\lambda = 0.5$ and once every 5 iterations for the rest small λ. The second heuristic is called every iteration when $\lambda < 1$.

As soon as the subgradient optimization ends, we start with the best Lagrangian multiplier μ^* to generate a sequence of multipliers in an attempt to explore the neighborhood of the near-optimal multipliers. To this end, we update the multipliers as in the subgradient phase, but with $\lambda = 0.02$, for a number of 10 times. We will apply all the heuristics described above every iteration, including the enumerative greedy with bids ranked by $c_j(\mu)/|I_j|$ and $c_j(\mu)$. This technique is akin to that used for Set Covering problem in [4].

3.3 Variable Fixing

During the subgradient optimization, we can obtain the Lagrangian cost $c(\mu)$ as well as an upper bound $L(\mu)$ by solving the LR. If the Lagrangian cost $c_j(\mu)$ satisfies $c_j(\mu) \geq L(\mu) - L_B$, then $x_j = 1$ in any better feasible solution; if $c_j(\mu) \leq -(L(\mu) - L_B)$, then $x_j = 0$ in any better feasible solution. In other words, bids can be fixed during the computation. The technique is called *variable fixing* [19] and was also used for Set Covering problem in [2, 3].

Table 1. Number of bids being fixed

Distribution	m	n	d	f_0	f_1
Random	400	2000	50%	1819.5	2.6
Weighted	400	2000	49.8%	1966.5	0
Uniform	100	500	3%	0.2	0
Decay	200	10000	1.6%	1219	0
Binomial 2	150	1500	20.5%	0	0
Binomial 4	30	3000	22.8%	2135.1	0
Exponential	30	3000	8.5%	2948.1	2.2

In Table 1, we tested 10 problem instances for each distribution. f_0 and f_1 are the average numbers of bids being fixed at 0 and 1 respectively after the subgradient optimization. The test problems used here are similar to those studied in [18, 6] and can be downloaded from the Internet [1].

For distributions like Random, Weighted Random and Exponential, more than 90% of the bids can be eliminated. On the other side, the bids can be fixed at 1 are very rare. For this reason, we only implemented the part that would fix bids at 0 in LAHA. We suggest the number of bids being fixed, i.e., $f_0 + f_1$ can be used to determine the hardness of the test instances. From Table 1 we can conclude immediately that all of the above test problems are easy except Uniform and Binomial 2.

3.4 Local Search Refinement

The solution we obtain at the end of the subgradient optimization phase is usually very close to the optimum, but in some cases it can be further improved. For this purpose, we have designed a simple local search algorithm for refining the solution. The neighborhood for a feasible solution X in our local search is defined as follows: first, we try to add a new bid $j \notin X$ into the solution X; this may entail removing some bids from X which conflict with j, and the solution becomes ; finally, we try to extend the solution by adding bids greedily according to their price. During the local search, we move from one solution X to another X' only if the revenue of second one is higher. If multiple moves exist, we will process and search all of them by saving them into a priority queue data structure. The local search stops as soon as no possible move can be found.

To make use of the information from the previous phase, we record the best 50 solutions found during the subgradient optimization and use them as the starting feasible solutions for the local search. In order to expedite the search process, we also limit the local search in a relatively small set of bids G_B by choosing them heuristically: first, we add all the bids in the top 50 solutions to G_B; then we sort the remaining bids by their price and add them to G_B until a pre-set number of bids has been reached. We set the maximum limit of $|G_B| = 1500$ in our algorithm. In order to test the effect of our local search refinement, we tested

Table 2. Results with and without local search refinement

Distribution	t_1	Sol_1	t_2	Sol_2
Uniform	2.06	98.57%	0.55	99.35%
Decay	43.39	98.71%	15.67	99.36%

10 problems from the Uniform and Decay distribution respectively. In Table 2, t_1 is the average time spent for the subgradient optimization and t_2 is the time for the local search refinement. Sol_1 and Sol_2 are the average solutions quality at the end of these two phases. We can see this refinement procedure improves the solution quality significantly in a relatively short computing time.

4 Computational Results

We tested LAHA extensively by applying various test problems. LAHA was able to produce high quality solutions for all problems within short computing time and the computational results were compared against the state-of-the-art IP solver CPLEX 8.0 and a hybrid heuristic SAGII [9].

4.1 Experimental Setup

All of our experiments were done on a 2.8 GHz Pentium 4 machine with 1.0 GB memory. LAHA was implemented in ANSI C++ and was compiled with GNU GCC 3.2 compiler. We did an extensive test to tune CPLEX's parameters before the experiments. However, because of the various natures and characteristics of our test instances, there is not a universal parameter setting which works best for all of them. After careful consideration, we decided to set the parameters as suggested in [7]:

1. Set *MIP strategy* to emphasize on "feasibility";
2. Set *MIP clique cut* generation strategy to "aggressively";
3. Set the *MIP branching direction* to explore the "up" branch first in the enumeration tree.

The default values were used for all the rest parameters. Since CPLEX was unable to solve some of the hard problems to optimality, we also enforced a time limit of 30 minutes.

We found the above setting for CPLEX worked especially well for the hard problems. It would give drastically better solutions than the default setting within the same amount of time. Table 3 shows the solutions generated by these two settings within 30 minutes for 5 hard problems chosen from the SAGII problem set.

Table 3. Solution quality of CPLEX with and without parameters tuning

Name	Solution default	Solution tuned	Boost
in101	67027.482	70098.078	4.58%
in102	65717.396	70766.106	7.68%
in103	64854.964	69402.363	7.01%
in104	68613.375	69477.633	1.26%
in105	65525.054	69777.727	6.49%

However, since this setting emphasizes on feasibility rather than optimality (i.e. CPLEX would generate more feasible solutions as it solves the problem), it might actually take a longer time to verify solutions's optimality on some of the problems.

4.2 On Test Problems

We tested on all the problem sets that we obtained from the literature. Moreover, we also propose a new methodology to generate realistic hard problems. The four test problem sets we used are:

1. **The Legacy Problem Set:** These distributions were first introduced in [16, 6]. Later they were also studied by [1]. We tested all 6 distributions of problems generated by Andersson[1]: **Random, Weighted Random, Uniform, Decay, Binomial** and **Exponential**.
2. **CATS Generated Problem Set:** The second problem set we tested is those generated by CATS [14, 13] (Combinatorial Auction Test Suite). We used the latest CATS 2.0 and tested LAHA on all of its distributions: **Paths, Regions, Arbitrary, Matching** and **Scheduling**.

---
[1] Andersson generated these problems in a slightly different way from Sandholm and Fujishima.

3. **The SAGII Problem Set:** These problems were generated by [8] according to the description in [12]. They were also tested in [9] by the SAGII heuristic. We find these test sets are realistic in the sense that they considered real auction factors such as bidder fairness, job's preference etc during the generation.
4. **The PBP Problem Set:** The fourth problem set is generated by our new methodology PBP (Proportional Bid Price). The price for each item is given by the number of bids including it multiplied by a random factor from 0.9 to 1.1. The price for each bid is given by the summation of its items' price multiplied by a random factor from 0.9 to 1.1. The coefficients a_{ij} are generated as in the Binomial Distribution. We found the problems generated by this scheme are computationally challenging.

4.3 Preliminary Results

We tested a number of 238 problems from the above 4 problem sets. The computational results are compiled in Table 4.

From the table we see LAHA performs well on all the problem distributions. For Random, Weighted Random, Binomial 2, Exponential and Scheduling distributions, it produced optimal solutions for all the problems. For Uniform, Decay, Binomial 4, Path and Matching distributions, LAHA produced solutions

Table 4. Computational results

Distribution	cases	CPLEX sol	time	LAHA sol	time	SAGII sol	time
Random	10	16143.8	5.4	16143.8 (100%)	15.4	15553.3 (96.1%)	30.9
Weighted	10	586833	2.9	586833 (100%)	25.4	586833 (100%)	32.3
Uniform	10	129050	28.7	128202 (99.3%)	2.6	110312 (85.5%)	5.5
Decay	10	196266	32.7	195016 (99.4%)	56.6	Not Available[#]	
Binomial 2	10	94792.7	223.3	94792.7 (100%)	8.1	94792.7 (100%)	6.4
Binomial 4	10	43426	5.4	43302.5 (99.7%)	5.6	41909 (96.5%)	16.0
Exponential	10	44723.8	0.3	44723.8 (100%)	0.8	42918 (96%)	26.7
Path	11	81.1	7.7	80.9 (99.8%)	37.7	68.9 (86.1%)	137.8
Regions-npv	11	12620.1*	335.3	12529.6 (99.4%)	13.4	11104.2 (88.7%)	20.3
Regions-upv	11	13329.7*	598.4	13258.5 (99.5%)	16.8	11909.3 (89.9%)	20.5
Arbitrary-npv	11	7053.9*	539.5	7017.1 (99.6%)	9.4	6320.8 (90.6%)	13.1
Arbitrary-upv	11	7597.5*	713.2	7495.5 (98.8%)	11.3	6838.9 (91.0%)	14.5
Matching	11	987.4	0.3	987.2 (99.9%)	12.5	794 (80.6%)	355.9
Scheduling	11	101	0.3	101 (100%)	25.3	100.9 (99.9%)	24.9
SAGII 1	10	69486.3*	1800	71195.7 (102.5%)	12.3	65324.1 (94%)	14.9
SAGII 2	10	86346*	1800	88193.3 (102.2%)	12.9	84207 (97.6%)	18.7
SAGII 3	10	75644.1*	1800	75644.1 (100%)	5.6	73653 (97.3%)	5.7
SAGII 4	10	82104*	1800	86758 (105.8%)	25.6	82549.9 (100.6%)	36.9
SAGII 5	10	101426*	1800	108214 (106.8%)	32.4	100665 (99.3%)	57.1
PBP	11	7116.2*	1003.9	7090.9 (99.5%)	3.6	6881.4 (96.9%)	3.8

[*] means the time limit is exceeded and some of the solutions may not be optimal.
[#] the SAGII can only handle problems with up to 3000 bids and items.

of high quality within reasonable amount of time. For the rest hard problems, notably for the SAGII problem set, LAHA's solutions were much better than those generated by CPLEX 8.0 in 30 minutes.

4.4 Anytime Performance on Hard Problems

We generated 10 hard Uniform problems size 500×2000 density 2% and compared the anytime performances of LAHA and CPLEX based on this problem set. Our results show that LAHA usually spent a little more than 20 seconds on each problem. However, for 9 out of the 10 problems, the solutions it generated are better than those generated by CPLEX in 30 minutes. From our extensive experiments, LAHA has better anytime performance than CPLEX on this distribution.

5 Conclusions

We propose a Lagrangian Relaxation based heuristic LAHA for Winner Determination Problem in Combinatorial Auctions. Some classical OR techniques, like Subgradient Optimization and Variable Fixing, are applied for the problem. We propose a number of improvements on the standard way of controlling the parameters of these techniques. Moreover, we invent some novel heuristics, like Enumerative Greedy and Stochastic Bid Selection, to quickly generate good allocations. We also present an efficient local search refinement procedure at the end of the algorithm.

We tested LAHA extensively on various problems in the literature. We suggest the number of fixed variables be used to estimate the real hardness of the test problems. In this sense, most of the previous problem distributions are easy. We also propose a new methodology to generate realistic test problems which turn out to be drastically more difficult than CATS generated benchmarks. LAHA is generally very fast at producing high quality solutions and it is especially efficient in handling with large scale hard problems. Among the 146 problems for which the optimum is known, LAHA found the optimum in 91 cases and produced on average 99.2% optimal solutions for the rest. Moreover, on the other 92 hard problems for which the optimum is not known, LAHA's solutions were on average 2% better than the solutions generated by CPLEX in 30 minutes. It is also shown that LAHA has significantly better anytime behavior than CPLEX on hard problems.

References

[1] A. Andersson, M. Tenhunen, and F. Ygge. Integer programming for combinatorial auction winner determination. *Proceedings of the fourth International Conference on Multi-Agent Systems(ICMAS00)*, pages 39–46, 2000.
[2] E. Balas and A. Ho. Set covering algorithms using cutting planes, heuristics, and subgradient optimization: a computational study. *Mathematical Programming*, 12:37–60, 1980.

[3] J. E. Beasley. An algorithm for set covering problem. *European Journal of Operational Research*, 31:85–93, 1987.

[4] A. Caprara, M. Fischetti, and P. Toth. A heuristic method for the set covering problem. *Operations Research*, 47(5):730–743, 1999.

[5] M. L. Fisher. The lagrangian relaxation method for solving integer programming problems. *Management Science*, 27(1):1–18, 1981.

[6] Y. Fujishima, K. Leyton-Brown, and Y. Shoham. Taming the computatoinal complexity of combinatorial auctions: optimal and approximate approaches. pages 548–553, 1999.

[7] O. Gűnlűk, L. Ladányi, and S. D. Vries. A branch-and-price algorithm and new test problems for spectrum auctions. *Management Science Special Issue - Electronic Markets*, 2004.

[8] Y. Guo, A. Lim, B. Rodrigues, and Y.Zhu. Heuristics for a brokering set packing problem. In *8th International Symposium on Artificial Intelligence and Mathematics (AIMA 2004)*, 2004.

[9] Y. Guo, A. Lim, B. Rodrigues, and Y.Zhu. A non-exact approach and experiment studies on the combinatorial auction problem. In *Thirty-Eight Hawaii International Conference on System Sciences (HICSS-38)*, 2005.

[10] H. H. Hoos and C. Boutilier. Solving combinatorial auctions using stochastic local search. In *Proceedings of American Association for Artificial Intelligence (AAAI 2000)*, 2000.

[11] R. Karp. Reducibility among combinatorial problems. *Complexity of Computer Computations*, pages 85–103, 1972.

[12] H. C. Lau and Y. G. Goh. An intelligent brokering system to support multi-agent web-based 4th-party logistics. *Proceedings of the 14th IEEE International Conference on Tools with Artificial Intelligence (ICTAI-02)*, 2002.

[13] K. Leyton-Brown, E. Nudelman, G. Andrew, J. McFaddan, and Y. Shoham. Boosting as a metaphor for algorithm design. *working paper*.

[14] K. Leyton-Brown, M. Pearson, and Y. Shoham. Towards a universal test suite for combinatorial auction algorithms. *ACM conference on Electronic Commerce (EC-00)*, pages 66–76, 2000.

[15] M.H. Rothkopf, A. Pekeč, and R.M. Harstad. Computationally manageable combinatorial auctions. *Management Science*, 44(8):1131–1147, 1998.

[16] T. Sandholm. An algorithm for optimal winner determination in combinatorial auctions. *Proceedings of the Sixteenth International Joint Conference on Artificial Intelligence (IJCAI-99)*, pages 542–547, 1999.

[17] T. Sandholm. Algorithm for optimal winner determination in combinatorial auctions. *Artificial Intelligence*, 135(1-2):1–54, 2002.

[18] T. Sandholm, S. Suri, A. Gilpin, and D. Levine. Cabob: A fast optimal algorithm for combinatorial auctions. *Proceedings of the Seventeenth International Joint Conference on Artificial Intelligence (IJCAI-01)*, pages 1102–1108, 2001.

[19] L.A. Wolsey. *Integer Programming*. John Wiley, 1998.

Moving Cast Shadow Detection and Removal for Visual Traffic Surveillance

Jeong-Hoon Cho, Tae-Gyun Kwon, Dae-Geun Jang, and Chan-Sik Hwang

School of Electronics & Electrical Engineering, Kyungpook National University,
1370 Sankyuk-dong, Puk-gu, Daegu, 702-701, Korea
silkroad@ee.knu.ac.kr

Abstract. Shadow detection and removal is important to deal with traffic image sequences. The shadow cast by a vehicle can lead to inaccurate object feature extraction and an erroneous scene analysis. Furthermore, separate vehicles can be connected through a shadow, thereby confusing an object recognition system. Accordingly, this paper proposes a robust method for detecting and removing an active cast shadow from monocular color image sequences. A background subtraction method is used to extract moving blobs in color and gradient dimensions, and YCrCb color space adopted to detect and remove the cast shadow. Even when shadows link different vehicles, each vehicle figure can be separately detected using a modified mask based on a shadow bar. Experimental results from town scenes demonstrate that the proposed method is effective and the classification accuracy is sufficient for general vehicle type classification.

1 Introduction

As the number of roads and vehicles continues to increase, problems with regulating speeding, illegal, and overloaded freight vehicles are generated, plus automatic toll systems are also needed. To solve these problems, surveillance and management systems using cameras have already been installed on many roads. However, the speed limit varies depending on the type of vehicle, which also needs to be classified to accurately regulate overloading and for automatic toll systems. Therefore, intelligent transportation systems based on vision-based monitoring have been developed that use image processing and recognition mechanisms [1-5]. As the images captured by the camera contain more information, such vision-based systems can be applied to diverse fields and are less expensive than systems that use a magnetic loop detector or Radio Frequency Identification (RFID) [6]. However, it is not easy to detect only the vehicle figure from the image, since it involves separating the image into the vehicle and the cast shadow. The vehicles can be classified based on their width and length of vehicle [7,8]. But these methods suffer from inaccurate features about the width, length, size, shape, and location of the vehicle because the region of the detected vehicle also contains its shadow. Although numerous shadow detection methods have been proposed, they all suffer from certain limitations that make them ineffective in a real outdoor environment. One method suggests removing the shadow using the properties of the cast shadow [9], where the pixels corresponding to the shadow are indicated based on calculating the shadow properties of the luminance, chrominance, and gradient density. As a result, separating the vehicle and the cast shadow using the indicator of pixels and edge information in the image produces a better performance than when using only the edge or luminance information. However, this method cannot remove a shadow connecting different vehicles, in which case it is apt to misrecognize the vehicles as a single large-size vehicle and make errors in the detection and feature extraction.

Accordingly, this paper proposes a robust shadow removal method that can split vehicles connected by a cast shadow and recognizes individual vehicles by removing not only the shadow created by a moving vehicle but also the shadow connecting several different vehicles. The remainder of this paper is organized as follows: Section 2 briefly outlines the vehicle classification system using a block diagram, then Section 3 deals with the methods used for vehicle detection and calculating the shadow confidence scores. Thereafter, Section 4 presents the proposed shadow removal algorithm for splitting multiple vehicles connected by a cast shadow, then experimental results with general road image sequences are presented in Section 5 to demonstrate the robustness of the proposed method in the case of a cast shadow. Finally conclusions are given in Section 6.

2 Concept and Methodology

Figure 1 is a flowchart explaining the proposed process for detecting and removing a cast shadow. The background image is generated from an input image sequence. A fast and accurate scoreboard-based algorithm for estimating a stationary background is adopted to create a stationary background image [10]. To extract the moving blobs from input sequences, background subtraction is used in color and gradient density dimensions [11-13]. A morphological operation and median filter are then employed to generate a binary image mask that contains the moving blob information. Since the extracted blob contains both the vehicle and its shadow, a shadow confidence score

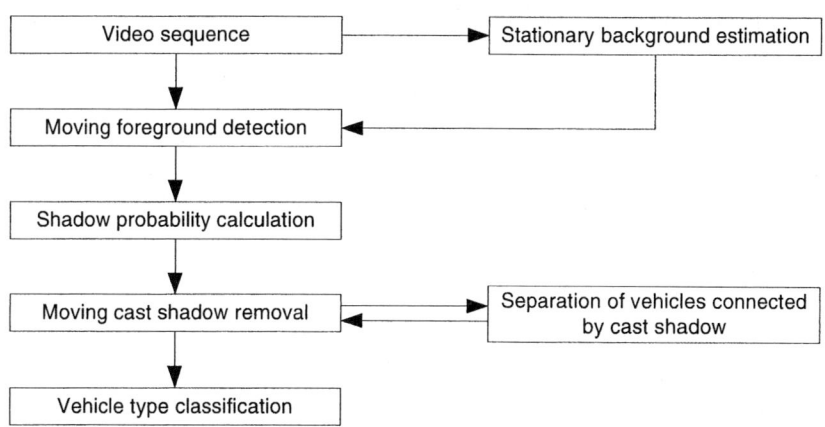

Fig. 1. Block diagram of proposed system

(SCS) is computed using the shadow properties of the luminance, chrominance, and gradient density to remove the shadow. As such, the SCS indicates which pixels in the extracted blob are part of the cast shadow region and which are part of the object region. Using the SCS and edge information for the input image, the vehicle is then separated from the cast shadow in a non-rigid form by applying a bounding convex hull. However, shadows linking different vehicles are not yet removed, and this type of shadow can produce an error, where several vehicles are mistakenly recognized as a single large vehicle. Thus, multiple vehicles connected by shadows are estimated using the lane width and large vehicle length, where the estimation is identified by the presence or absence of a shadow bar acquired by shadow features. Upon identifying vehicles connected by a cast shadow, a modified mask is generated using the shadow bar, then the shadow removal is performed recursively using the modified mask until there are no vehicles connected by a shadow. As a result, the connected vehicles are segmented and separated from the cast shadow.

3 Vehicle Detection and Shadow Confidence Score Calculation

3.1 Vehicle Detection

The vehicle detection extracts a moving blob based on subtracting the background from the input image and a background image. Given that the RGB color channels of the input image are R_f, G_f, B_f, and the RGB channels of the background are R_b, G_b, B_b, the maximum absolute value $Diff_c$ for an individual color channel is defined as follows:

$$Diff_c = \max\{|R_f - R_b|, |G_f - G_b|, |B_f - B_b|\} \quad (1)$$

The gradient density difference is also obtained in the same manner as below:

$$Diff_g = \max\{|GD_{Rf} - GD_{Rb}|, |GD_{Gf} - GD_{Gb}|, |GD_{Bf} - GD_{Bb}|\} \quad (2)$$

where the gradient density is defined as

$$GD(m,n) = \frac{1}{(2w+1)^2} \sum_{i=m-w}^{i=m+w} \sum_{j=n-w}^{j=n+w} |G_x(i,j) + G_y(i,j)| \quad (3)$$

$G_x(i, j)$ and $G_y(i, j)$ are the horizontal and vertical edge magnitudes using a laplacian gradient operator for pixel (i, j), and $2w+1$ is the size of the average window filter. The foreground mask can then be attained in accordance with equation (4) based on equations (1) and (2).

$$M(x,y) = \begin{cases} 1, & \text{if } Diff_c > T_1 \text{ or } Diff_g > T_2 \\ 0, & \text{otherwise} \end{cases} \quad (4)$$

Since the calculated foreground mask contains noise, due to the error in the background, a modified mask is generated using a morphological operation and median filtering. A more accurate mask is then generated by removing the holes in the blobs and very small blobs based on the determination that the very small blobs are not objects but noises.

3.2 Shadow Confidence Score Calculation

To calculate the shadow confidence scores, the input image and background image are converted from RGB to YCbCr color space, which is the most effective color space for shadow removal in traffic images [14,15]. Each SCS is calculated using the subtraction of the input image and background, and the shadow properties of the luminance, chrominance, and gradient density dimensions. The resulting SCS then indicates which pixels belong to the cast shadow region and which belong to the object region. Computing the luminance score (S_L) and chrominance score (S_C) is given by

$$S_L = \begin{cases} 1 & , \quad L_{diff}(x,y) \leq 0 \\ (T_L - L_{diff}(x,y))/T_L, & 0 < L_{diff}(x,y) < T_L \\ 0 & , \quad L_{diff}(x,y) \geq T_L \end{cases} \quad (5)$$

$$L_{diff}(x,y) = L_{fore}(x,y) - L_{back}(x,y), \qquad \forall(x,y) \text{ where } M(x,y) = 1 \quad (6)$$

where L_{diff} is the luminance difference between the input image and the background image, and L_{fore} and L_{back} is the luminance for the input image and background image, respectively. This is based on the property that the luminance of a cast shadow is lower than that of the background.

$$S_C = \begin{cases} 1 & , \quad C_{diff}(x,y) \leq T_{C1} \\ (T_{C2} - C_{diff}(x,y))/(T_{C2} - T_{C1}), & T_{C1} < C_{diff}(x,y) < T_{C2} \\ 0 & , \quad C_{diff}(x,y) \geq T_{C2} \end{cases} \quad (7)$$

$$C_{diff}(x,y) = |Cb_{fore}(x,y) - Cb_{back}(x,y)| + |Cr_{fore}(x,y) - Cr_{back}(x,y)|, \quad (8)$$
$$\forall(x,y) \text{ where } M(x,y) = 1$$

where C_{diff} is the magnitude of the chrominance difference between the input image and the background image, C_{fore} and C_{back} is the chrominance for the input image and background image, respectively, and T_{C1} and T_{C2} are the thresholds ($T_{C2} = T_{C1}*2$). This is based on the property that the chrominance of a cast shadow is identical or only slightly shifted when compared with the background. Computing the gradient density score (S_G) is given by

$$S_G = \begin{cases} 1 & , \quad GD_{diff}(x,y) \leq T_{G1} \\ (T_{G2} - GD_{diff}(x,y))/(T_{G2} - T_{G1}), & T_{G1} < GD_{diff}(x,y) < T_{G2} \\ 0 & , \quad GD_{diff}(x,y) \geq T_{G2} \end{cases} \quad (9)$$

$$GD_{diff}(x,y) = GD_{fore}(x,y) - GD_{back}(x,y), \qquad \forall(x,y) \text{ where } M(x,y) = 1 \quad (10)$$

where GD_{diff} is the gradient density difference between the input image and the background image, GD_{fore} and GD_{back} is the gradient density for the input image and background image, respectively, and T_{G1} and T_{G2} are the thresholds ($T_{G2} = T_{G1}*2$). This is based on the property that the difference in the gradient density between a cast shadow and the background is lower than the difference in the gradient difference between an object and the background. Finally, after the three scores, S_L, S_C, and S_G are calculated for the three difference dimensions, the total shadow confidence score S_{total} is computed by combining all three scores.

$$S_{total}(x,y) = S_L(x,y) \times S_C(x,y) \times S_G(x,y) \qquad (11)$$

S_{total} provides the indication of pixel to determine the cast shadow region. S_{total} within cast shadow region will be much higher than the score of vehicle.

3.3 Moving Cast Shadow Removal

All the pixels with a significant gradient level are detected using a canny edge detector within a blob in the mask. These pixels are denoted as E_1. The more shadow pixels estimated, the higher the luminance score, chrominance score, and gradient density score. As a result, the total shadow confidence score S_{total} for a shadow pixel is higher than that for an object pixel, and conversely the S_{total} for a vehicle region becomes lower. Therefore, a thresholding test is applied to E_1 to filter out the pixels with a high S_{total} using T_S. The threshold for identifying a cast shadow is denoted as T_S.

$$E_2(x,y) = \begin{cases} 0, & S_{total} \geq T_S \\ 1, & S_{total} < T_S \end{cases} \qquad (12)$$

As a result, E_2 does not include noise or edge pixels that do not belong to the vehicle. Subsequently, the cast shadow is removed from the mask and the vehicle object alone is detected by applying a convex hull to E_2. The cast shadow is then identified as the moving foreground excluding the object.

4 Proposed Shadow Removal Method

Multiple vehicles connected by a cast shadow are apt to be recognized as a single vehicle and induce errors in shadow removal and vehicle type classification procedures. Thus, to overcome these problems, a shadow bar is adopted to separate the shadow-connected vehicles. Figure 2 shows a flowchart of the proposed moving cast shadow detection and removal method. First, thresholds T_{width} and T_{length} to estimate whether vehicles are connected horizontally or vertically by a cast shadow are defined using the lane width and large vehicle length in the vehicle surveillance area. As a typical bus or truck is not wider in width than a road lane, it is assumed that a few vehicles are connected horizontally by a shadow upon detecting a large object exceeding T_{width}, then the presence of a shadow bar is investigated. However, an object with a width higher than T_{width} does not always mean vehicles connected by a cast shadow. For example, a very large vehicle with a width exceeding the road lane may be detected, or a long vehicle like a bus may change its lane. In this case, a single vehicle is recognized through the absence of a shadow bar. If T_{width} is set to too low, the computation is increased as the possibility of a connecting shadow will be investigated for most vehicles in image sequences. Conversely, if T_{width} is set too high, it will miss small vehicles connected by a shadow. Therefore, this paper defines T_{width} = *lane width* $\times 2 / 3$ and T_{length} = *large vehicle length* in the same manner. A shadow bar is a vertically or horizontally connected straight line that is assumed to consist of only cast shadow pixels within a blob in the mask, located in the shadow region between vehicles, and not part of the vehicles. A vertical shadow bar passes the cross point of extended lanes in parallel with the lane. A mask of vehicles connected by a

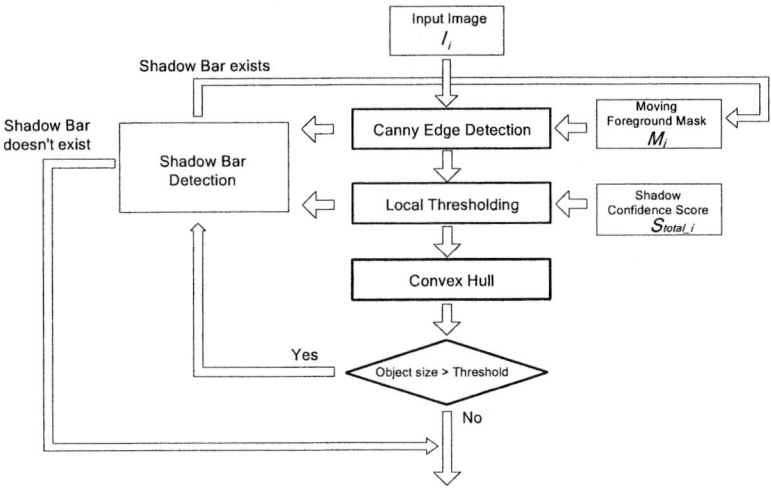

Fig. 2. Proposed moving cast shadow removal method

shadow is then separated by the line where the shadow bar is detected, and the shadow removal is performed recursively using a modified mask. Two properties are used to detect a shadow bar:

Property 1: The difference in the gradient density between a cast shadow and the background is lower than the difference in the gradient density between an object and the background.

Property 2: The shadow confidence score of a pixel in a cast shadow region is higher than that in an object region.

The shadow bar detection and cast shadow removal algorithm is:

(a) Read the input image I_i and generate mask M_i
(b) Generate the set of all possible bars $B_1,...,B_k$ in blob of M_i
(c) The cast shadow is removed from an object by applying a convex hull using S_{total_i} and E_2 in section 3.3
(d) When an object is estimated as multiple vehicles connected vertically or horizontally by a shadow using T_{width} and T_{length},
```
for j = 1 to k do {
    set tag = 1;
    for all (x, y) ∈ B_j do {
        if (S_total_i(x, y) < T_s ) or ( E_i(x, y) = 1) {
            tag = 0; break; } }
    if (tag = 1) {
        B_j is a shadow bar;
        Generate modified M_i using B_j and go to step (c); }
    if (j = k)
        Detected object is a large vehicle;
}
```

In the proposed method, edge information is acquired by applying a canny edge operator to the foreground image, as shown in Fig. 3(b). Fig. 3(c) depicts the object edges inside the mask. The boundary edges of the mask and lane edges are removed using the edges of the background. A vertical shadow bar can be generated between the vehicles in Fig. 3(c) based on Property 1. However, if a shadow bar is generated at a weak edge region within a vehicle, the opposite problem arises to the case when a shadow connects vehicles, as a single vehicle is segmented into several objects, resulting in errors in object recognition, classification, feature extraction and vehicle counting. Thus, to prevent such errors, Property 2 is adopted. As such, for the total shadow confidence score of the image in Fig. 3(d), all S_{total} for the shadow bar pixels must be higher than T_S in section 3.3. Shadow bars are investigated from the center of the mask to reduce the computation amount. When searching for a vertical shadow bar consisting of pixels satisfying property 1 and property 2, the first shadow bar is detected, as shown in Fig. 3(e). The mask is then separated based on the shadow bar and a convex hull applied to the modified mask to detect the shadow-free objects in Fig. 3(f).

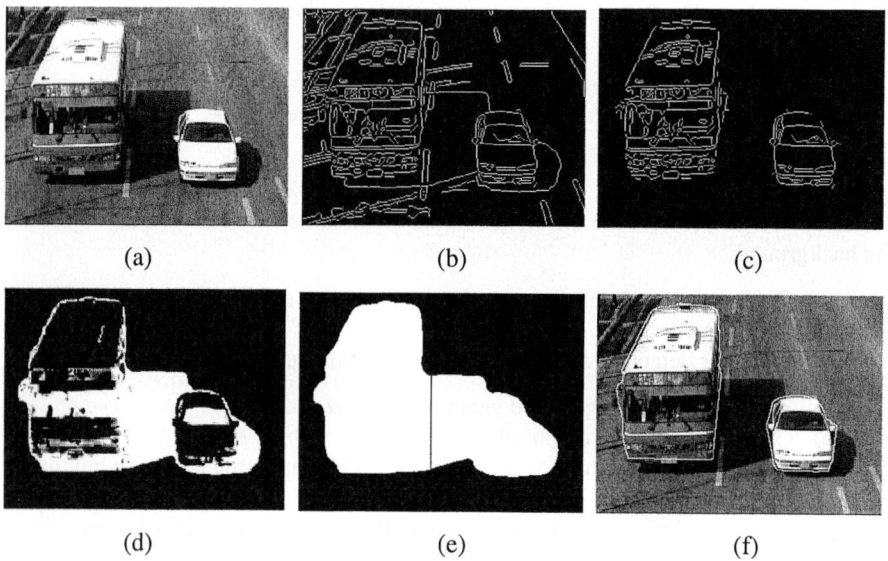

Fig. 3. Shadow removal procedure for vehicles connected by cast shadow

5 Experimental Results and Analysis

In the experiments, the frames were grabbed at a rate of 8 frames/s, the image size of the sequence scene was 320 × 240 pixels, and a passive shadow resulting from roadside trees grew significantly in the test video. Figure 4 shows the results of the vehicle detection and classification when using the SCS method and proposed method. The white boundary indicates the vehicle object detected by the computer, and the vehicle types estimated by the computer are also listed under the corresponding frames. Figure 4 (a) and (c) show two vehicles connected by a cast shadow vertically and horizontally, and the SCS method failed to classify the vehicle type correctly and missed one vehicle. In contrast, the proposed method detected each vehicle and correctly classified the vehicle type using a horizontal and vertical shadow bar.

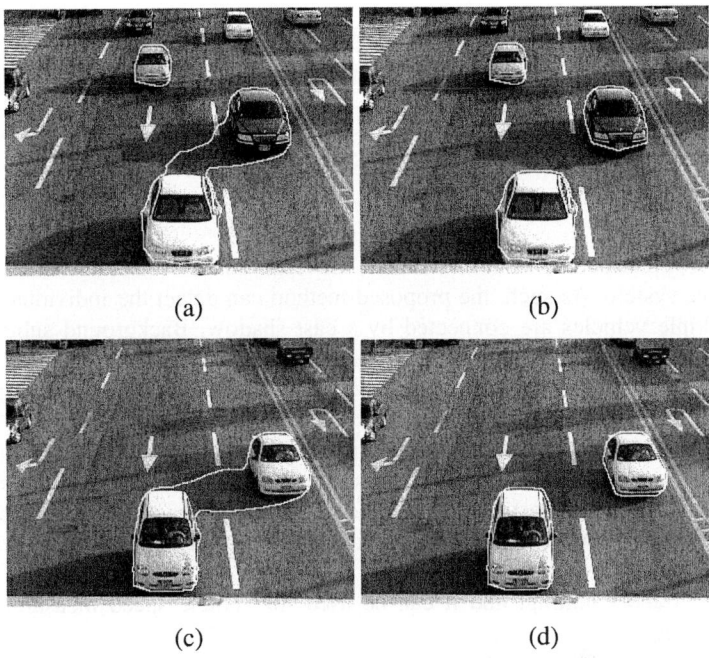

Fig. 4. Experimental results. (a) SCS method (large, small); (b) Proposed method (small, small, small, horizontal shadow bar); (c) SCS method (large); (d) Proposed method (small, small, vertical shadow bar).

Table 1 shows the results of the vehicle type classification when using the proposed method and SCS method. The features used for the classification were the length, width, area, and orientation of the vehicle, because the detected objects were non-rigid in form. "Missed detection" means the existence of a vehicle in the detecting area that was undetected by the algorithm. This mainly resulted from vehicles connected by a cast shadow. "False classification" means the false classification of the vehicle type in the detecting area, which mainly resulted from incomplete shadow removal from the vehicle or multiple vehicles connected by a cast shadow.

The experimental results demonstrated that the proposed method worked well under relatively light traffic conditions. However, under heavy traffic conditions, it is possible that the proposed method may mistake a vehicle as a larger one in the case of an occlusion that looks like different vehicles being connected in the input images. Thus, to reduce the effects of the occlusion, the angle of the camera over the road was set as high as possible and vehicles detected in the lowest area in the image. Furthermore, it is expected that a better performance could be acquired by combining the algorithms using consecutive frames.

Table 1. Results of vehicle detection and classification duing 63 minutes

	Missed detection rate	False classification rate	Correct classification rate
SCS method	6.5 %	13.9 %	86.1 %
Proposed method	0 %	1.8 %	98.2 %

6 Conclusion

This paper presented a robust method for cast shadow removal in a vehicle surveillance system. As such, the proposed method can detect the individual vehicles when multiple vehicles are connected by a cast shadow. Background subtraction is used to extract a moving blob in color and gradient dimensions, while a shadow confidence score is computed using the shadow properties in the luminance, chrominance, gradient density to remove a cast shadow in a non-rigid form. Multiple vehicles connected by a cast shadow are estimated using the lane width and large vehicle length, and identified by the presence of a shadow bar. Upon identifying vehicles connected by a cast shadow, a modified mask is generated using the shadow bar, and the shadow removal performed recursively using the modified mask. Experimental results demonstrate that the proposed method is efficient for classification and counting, and it can be used for vehicle speed measurement and vehicle tracking.

References

1. Ayland, N., Davies, P.: Automatic vehicle identification for heavy vehicle monitoring. In: Proc. of IEE International Conf. Vol. 2, p. 152-155, 1989.
2. Lipton, A.J., Fujiyoshi, H., Patil, R.S.: Moving target classification and tracking from real-time video. In: Proc. of IEEE Workshop Applications of Computer Vision. p. 8-14, 1998.
3. Cucchiara, R., Piccardi, M., Mello, P.: Image analysis and rule-based reasoning for a traffic monitoring system. IEEE Transactions on Intelligent Transportation Systems. Vol. 1, p. 119-130, 2000.
4. Foresti, G.L.: Object recognition an tracking for remote video surveillance. IEEE Transactions on Circuits and Systems for Video Technology. Vol. 9, p. 1045-1062, 1999.
5. Hongzan Sun, Tieniu Tan: Spatio-temporal segmentation for video surveillance. Electronics Letters. Vol. 37, p. 20-21, 2001.
6. Gajda, J., Sroka, R., Stencel, M., Wajda, A., Zeglen, T.: A vehicle classification based on inductive loop detectors. In: Proc. of IEEE International Conf. on Instrumentation and Measurement Technology. Vol. 1, p. 460-464, 2001.
7. Wu Yi-Ming, Ye Xiu-Qing, Gu Wei-Kang: A shadow handler in traffic monitoring system. In: Proc. of IEEE Conf. on Vehicular Technology. Vol. 1, p. 303-307, 2002.

8. Gupte, S., Masoud, O., Papanikolopoulos, P.: Vision-based vehicle classification. In: Proc. of IEEE Conf. on Intelligent Transportation Systems. Vol. 3, p. 46-51, 2000.
9. G.S.K. Fung, N.H.C. Yung, G.K.K. Pang, A,H.S. Lai: Towards detection of moving cast shadows for visual traffic surveillance. In: Proc. of IEEE International Conf. Vol. 4, p. 2505-2510, 2001.
10. Lai, A.H.S., Yung, N.H.C.: A fast and accurate scoreboard algorithm for estimating stationary backgrounds in an Image Sequence. In: Proc. of IEEE International symposium on Circuits and Systems, Vol. 4, p. 241-144, 1998.
11. Kilger, M.: A shadow handler in a video-based real-time traffic monitoring system. In: Proc. of IEEE Workshop on Applications of Computer Vision. Vol. 2, p. 11-18, 1992.
12. Su Zhang, Hanfeng Chen, Zheru Chi, Pengfei Shi: An algorithm for segmenting moving vehicles. In: Proc. of IEEE Conf. on Acoustic, Speech, and Signal Processing. Vol. 3, p. 369-372, 2003.
13. Zhou, Q., Aggarwal, J.K.: Tracking and classifying moving objects from Video. In: Proc. of IEEE International Workshop on PETS, 2001.
14. Gamba, P., Lilla, M., Mecocci, A.: A fast algorithm for target shadow removal in monocular colour sequences. In: Proc. of IEEE Conf. on Image Processing. Vol. 1, p. 436-447, 1997.
15. Kumar, P., Sengupta, K., and Lee, A.: A comparative study of different color spaces for foreground and shadow detection for traffic monitoring system. In: Proc. of IEEE International Conf. p. 100-105, 2002.

A Hidden Markov Model and Immune Particle Swarm Optimization-Based Algorithm for Multiple Sequence Alignment

Hong-Wei Ge and Yan-Chun Liang[*]

College of Computer Science, Jilin University, Key Laboratory of Symbol Computation and Knowledge Engineering of the Ministry of Education, Changchun 130012, China
ycliang@jlu.edu.cn

Abstract. Multiple sequence alignment (MSA) is a fundamental and challenging problem in the analysis of biologic sequences. In this paper, an immune particle swarm optimization (IPSO) is proposed, which is based on the models of the vaccination and the receptor editing in immune systems. The proposed algorithm is used to train hidden Markov models (HMMs), further, an integration algorithm based on the HMM and IPSO for the MSA is constructed. The approach is tested on a set of standard instances taken from the Benchmark Alignment database, BAliBASE. Numerical simulated results are compared with those obtained by using the Baum-Welch training algorithm. The results show that the proposed algorithm not only improves the alignment abilities, but also reduces the time cost.

1 Introduction

Computational biology is emerging as an important field for the computer science community with the development of the genome project. The acceleration in the accumulation of biological sequences is more and more great, which makes it challenging to search for sequence similarity by comparing many related sequences simultaneously. Multiple sequence alignment (MSA) is one of the most important techniques in the sequence comparison. Algorithms for multiple sequence alignment are commonly used to find conserved regions in biomolecular sequences, to construct family and superfamily representations of sequences, and to reveal evolutionary histories of species. Conserved sub-regions in DNA and protein sequences may represent important functions or regulatory elements. The profile or consensus sequences obtained from a multiple alignment can be used to characterize a family of species. An optimal sequence alignment can be computed by the methods based on dynamic programming, such as the Needleman-Wunsch algorithm for the global alignment [1], the Smith-Waterman algorithm for the local alignment [2], and so on. However, the running time increases rapidly with the increase of the number of sequences to be aligned. So many heuristics and approximation algorithms have been proposed [3, 4]. With the emerging of new techniques in the field of artificial intelligence, some newly developed methods have been introduced to address these problems in recent years,

---

[*] Corresponding author.

such as simulated annealing (SA) [5], genetic algorithm (GA) [6]. Besides these methods, a very general form of probabilistic model for sequences of symbols, called a hidden Markov model (HMM), has also been applied to MSA [7]. However, because the MSA is among the members of the class of hard NP-complete problems there remains much room for improvement in current techniques and exploitation of new efficient methods. In this paper, a novel algorithm for MSA based on an improved swarm intelligence method and an HMM is proposed. The critical and difficult problem for using HMM approach is how to set up a steady and reliable model by a finite training set, moreover, there is no known deterministic algorithm that can guarantee to find the optimally trained HMM with reasonable running time. The most widely used approach to train an HMM is based on statistics and re-estimation, such as Baum-Welch (BW) algorithm [8]. This paper proposes an immune particle swarm optimization to train the HMM. The proposed algorithm possesses the randomicity of stochastic optimization algorithms, which can be used to solve the optimization problem for non-linear systems; moreover, the proposed algorithm possesses the adaptive ability that enables the algorithm to solve machine learning problems.

2   Hidden Markov Models for Multiple Sequence Alignment

At an abstract level, molecular sequences are long strings of characters over an alphabet of size four for DNA and twenty for protein. Although each base position presents one of four or twenty states, the number of these positions is likely to vary, that is homologous nucleotide sequences or amino acid sequences may differ in length. This sequence length variation has led to the development of the algorithm for multiple sequence alignment, which is used to align these bases so that homologous residues among a set of sequences are aligned together in columns.

Consider N homologous sequences $S_1 = s_{11}s_{12}\cdots s_{1L_1}$, $S_2 = s_{21}s_{22}\cdots s_{2L_2}, \cdots,$ $S_N = s_{N1}s_{N2}\cdots s_{NL_N}$, where s_{nl} ($n \in [1,N], l \in [1, L_n]$) denotes a single nucleotide or amino acid, collectively called a residue. The set of valid residue types is denoted by Σ. During the evolutionary process, some residues may stay unchanged while some may change to other types. For simplicity, we regard conservation as matching to itself. In addition, some residues may be lost, or new residues may insert somewhere between or outside the preexisting sites. The final result of the series of mutational events (M for match, I for insert, and D for delete) is conveniently represented by a two-dimensional character matrix $A = (a_{ij})_{N \times M}$, where $a_{ij} \in \Sigma \cup \{-\}$. The null character '–' represents a space. Each row turns out to be a contemporary sequence if all null characters are removed. The gained alignment can be evaluated by different scoring systems. The multiple sequence alignment is combinatorial problem in nature because there are exponentially many ways of inserting spaces to form an alignment.

A hidden Markov model is a statistical model. Mathematically, an HMM is defined by specifying: a set of states $W = \{w_1, w_2, \cdots, w_n\}$, an alphabet $O = \{o_1, o_2, \cdots o_m\}$, transition probability matrix $(t_{ij})_{n \times n}$, $t_{ij} = P(w_j | w_i)$, ($1 \leq i, j \leq n$), which represents the transition probability from state w_i to state w_j; emission probability matrix $(b_{jk})_{n \times m}$, $b_{jk} = b_j(o_k) = P(o_k | w_j)$, ($1 \leq j \leq n, 1 \leq k \leq m$), which represents the emission probability of the letter o_k in the state w_j. The sum of the probabilities of all transitions going out of a state is 1, and the sum of all emission probabilities in each state is 1. A letter from the alphabet in a state is generated according to the emission probability, then a new state is chosen according to the transition probability and the cycle continues. An HMM can be represented by a graph in which the nodes correspond to the states, and arrows connect nodes for which there is a non-zero transition probability. An HMM for multiple sequence alignment is a state chain including matching (M), insertion (I) and deletion (D) in nature. The HMM structure used in this paper is the standard topology for the MSA problem as shown in Figure 1, in which the length of the HMM is 3.

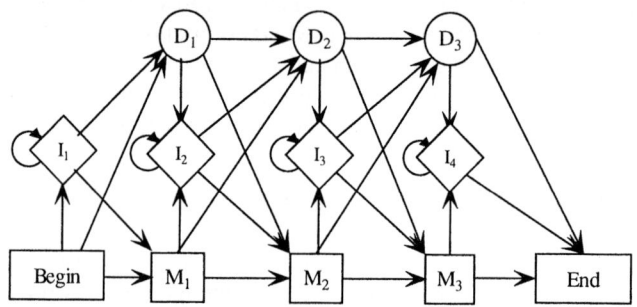

Fig. 1. An HMM structure for MSA

When applying HMMs to MSA, the sequence of observables is given in the form of some unaligned sequences of amino acids. Different sequences are generated with different probability. A sequence S is generated with probability $P(S|\lambda)$, where λ is the parameter set including all the transition and emission probabilities and determines an HMM model. The goal is to find the model parameter set λ^* such that it maximizes the probability $\prod_{k=1,2,\cdots,K} P(S_k | \lambda^*)$, where $S_1,\cdots,S_K$ are the sequences we try to align. The procedure of finding λ^* can be thought as training an HMM using the training set $\{S_1,\cdots,S_K\}$. The traditional training algorithm is based on the method of expectation maximization or generalized expectation maximization, such as Baum-Welch algorithm [8]. The core idea in these training algorithms is to update probability parameters using the way of recursion. The computation cost is enormous, and the computation complexity is $O(KN^2)$ at each training step, where K is the number of the sequences and N is the length of the HMM. These training algorithms are only guaranteed to converge to a local maximum in the parameter space. The main problem is that in most applications of interest the optimization surface is very complex and there are many local maxima which trap the model and prevent it from reaching a global maximum. Besides, Baum-Welch algorithm does not have the parameter for learning step, so it is easy to be affected by some isolated samples. In this paper, the models of vaccination and receptor editing in immune systems is introduced into particle swarm optimization (PSO). The new optimization algorithm is called IPSO, which is used to train HMM. It is prone to avoid getting into local maxima, and the most of the computing time is spent on the evaluation of candidate solutions.

3 Immune Particle Swarm Optimization Algorithm

Particle swarm optimization (PSO), originally developed by Kennedy and Elberhart [9], is a method for optimizing hard numerical functions on metaphor of social behavior of flocks of birds and schools of fish. It is an evolutionary computation technique based on swarm intelligence. A swarm consists of individuals, called particles, which change their positions over time. Each particle represents a potential solution to the problem. In a PSO system, particles fly around in a multi-dimensional search space. During its flight each particle adjusts its position according to its own experience and the experience of its neighboring particles, making use of the best position encountered by itself and its neighbors. The effect is that particles move towards the better solution areas, while still having the ability to search a wide area around the better solution areas. The performance of each particle is measured according to a predefined fitness function, which is related to the problem being solved and indicates how good a candidate solution is. The PSO has been found to be robust and fast in solving non-linear, non-differentiable, multi-modal problems. The mathematical abstract and executive steps of PSO are as follows.

Let the i th particle in a D-dimensional space be represented as $X_i = (x_{i1},\ldots,x_{id},\ldots,x_{iD})$. The best previous position (which possesses the best fitness value) of the i th particle is recorded and represented as $P_i = (p_{i1},\ldots,p_{id},\ldots,p_{iD})$, which is also called $pbest$. The index of the best $pbest$ among all the particles is represented by the symbol g. The location P_g is also called $gbest$. The velocity for the i th particle is represented as $V_i = (v_{i1},\ldots,v_{id},\ldots,v_{iD})$. The concept of the particle swarm optimization consists of, at each time step, changing the velocity and location of each particle towards its $pbest$ and $gbest$ locations according to Eqs. (1) and (2), respectively:

$$V_i(k+1) = wV_i(k) + c_1 r_1 (P_i - X_i(k))/\Delta t + c_2 r_2 (P_g - X_i(k))/\Delta t . \tag{1}$$

$$X_i(k+1) = X_i(k) + V_i(k+1)\Delta t . \tag{2}$$

where w is the inertia coefficient which is a constant in interval [0, 1] and can be adjusted in the direction of linear decrease [10]; c_1 and c_2 are learning rates which are nonnegative constants; r_1 and r_2 are generated randomly in the interval [0, 1]; Δt is the time interval, and commonly be set as unit; $v_{id} \in [-v_{max}, v_{max}]$, and v_{max} is a designated maximum velocity. The termination criterion for iterations is determined according to whether the maximum generation or a designated value of the fitness is reached.

The method described above can be considered as the conventional particle swarm optimization, in which as time goes on, some particles become inactive quickly because they are similar to the *gbest* and lost their velocities. In the following generations, they will have less contribution for their very low global and local search capability and this problem will induce the emergence of the prematurity. In this paper, an immune particle swarm optimization (IPSO) is proposed.

In immune systems, for immature B cells the receptor editing is stimulated by B-cell receptor and provides an important means of maintaining self-tolerance. The process of the receptor editing may diversify antibodies not only to jump local affinity optima, but also across the entire affinity landscape. It does make a significant contribution to affinity maturation by a slight modification on local affinity optima. The experiment of the receptor editing by the transgenic animal model show that at least 25% of peripheral B cells were observed to have undergone editing [11]. So we introduce the adaptive mechanism to improve the performance of PSO. Each particle is an antibody, and the fitness of the particle is corresponding to the affinity of the antibody. The inactive particles are recognized and 25% of them are edited after each given generation. Whether the algorithm is premature and some particles are inactive is judged by the following conditions. Define

$$\bar{f} = \frac{1}{n}\sum_{i=1}^{n} f_i, \qquad \sigma_f^2 = \frac{1}{n}\sum_{i=1}^{n}(f_i - \bar{f})^2 . \qquad (3)$$

Where f_i is the fitness value of the i th particle, n is the number of the particles in the population, $\bar{f}$ is the average fitness of all the particles, and σ_f^2 is the variance, which reflects the convergence degree of the population. Define

$$\tau^2 = \frac{\sigma_f^2}{\max\{(f_j - \bar{f})^2, (j=1,2,\cdots n)\}} . \qquad (4)$$

If τ^2 is less than a small given threshold, and the theoretical global optimum or the expectation optimum has not been found, the algorithm is considered to get into the premature convergence. Then we identify those inactive particles by using the inequality

$$\frac{f_g - f_i}{\max\{(f_g - f_j), (j=1,\cdots,n)\}} \leq \theta . \qquad (5)$$

where f_g is the fitness of the best particle *gbest* and θ is a small given threshold.

Then the best particle is retained and only one of them is retained if there are lots of the best. At the same time the inactive particles are chosen to perform receptor editing by using a Gauss random disturbance on them

$$P_{ij} = P_{ij} + \beta_{ij} \qquad (j=1,\cdots,D) . \qquad (6)$$

where P_{ij} is the j th component of the i th inactive particle; β_{ij} is a random variable and follow a Gaussian distribution with zero mean and constant variance 1, namely $\beta_{ij} \sim N(0,1)$. If the edited particle by the above rules is out of the domain of definition, an adjustment is made for β_{ij} by the method of dichotomy until the particle satisfies the given constraint.

Besides, a vaccination model based on immune systems is also designed to improve the algorithm performance. Similarly to the techniques of the vaccine inoculation, we take full advantage of some characteristic information and knowledge in the process of solving problem to distill vaccines, and then vaccinate some particles. After each given generation we distill vaccines from the best particle and vaccinate some particles by the adaptive vaccination probability. The process is designed as follows.

Let P_v be the vaccination probability, and relatively smaller P_v should be adopted for those better particles whose fitness values are higher than the average fitness of the population, whereas a relatively larger P_v should be adopted for those particles whose fitness values are lower than the average fitness. Let $\bar{f}/f_i = \mu$. The adaptive vaccination probability P_v can be expressed as

$$p_v = \frac{f_g - f_i}{f_g - \mu \bar{f}}, \quad \text{if } \mu \le 1; \qquad P_v = 1, \quad \text{if } \mu > 1. \tag{7}$$

Let the best particle $P_g = (p_{g1}, p_{g2}, \ldots, p_{gj}, \ldots, p_{gD})$, the vaccinated particle $X_i = (x_{i1}, x_{i2}, \ldots x_{ij}, \ldots, x_{iD})$, $\forall j$, assume that $p_{gj} \le x_{ij}$, otherwise exchange p_{gj} with x_{ij}. Let vectors $A = (a_1, a_2, \cdots, a_j, \cdots, a_D)$ and $B = (b_1, b_2, \cdots, b_j, \cdots, b_D)$ define the lower and upper bounds of the problem domain. For arbitrary particle X_k, $a_j \le x_{kj} \le b_j$, $j = (1,2,\cdots,D)$. Define

$$p_{gj}^* = x_{ij} + \frac{(x_{ij} - p_{gj})(b_j - x_{ij})}{x_{ij} - a_j}, \quad x_{ij}^* = p_{gj} - \frac{(x_{ij} - p_{gj})(p_{gj} - a_j)}{b_j - p_{gj}}. \tag{8}$$

It is easy to prove that

$$a_j \le x_{ij}^* \le p_{gj} \le x_{ij} \le p_{gj}^* \le b_j. \tag{9}$$

Let vector $Z_i = (z_{i1}, z_{i2}, \cdots, z_{ij}, \cdots, z_{iD})$ denote the particle generated by the vaccination operation. It can be obtained by the following rules:

$$z_{ij} = \begin{cases} \alpha a_j + (1-\alpha)p_{gj}, & \text{if } \mod(\theta,4) = 0 \\ Rom(\alpha p_{gj} + (1-\alpha)x_{ij}, \alpha p_{gj} + (1-\alpha)x_{ij}^*), & \text{if } \mod(\theta,4) = 1 \\ Rom(\alpha x_{ij} + (1-\alpha)p_{gj}, \alpha x_{ij} + (1-\alpha)p_{gj}^*), & \text{if } \mod(\theta,4) = 2 \\ \alpha x_{ij} + (1-\alpha)b_j, & \text{if } \mod(\theta,4) = 3 \end{cases}$$

$$j = (1,2,\cdots,D) \tag{10}$$

Where α is a real number generated randomly in the interval [0, 1], and θ is a nonnegative integer generated randomly. $Rom(x, y)$ is a random selection function, which represents select one randomly from x and y.

It is easy to obtain the following conclusions. When $\mod(\theta,4) = 0$, the generated z_{ij} satisfies that $a_j \le z_{ij} \le p_{gj}$; when $\mod(\theta,4) = 3$, z_{ij} satisfies that $x_{ij} \le z_{ij} \le b_j$;

when $\mod(\theta,4)=1$ or $\mod(\theta,4)=2$, z_{ij} satisfies that $a_j \le z_{ij} \le b_j$. Finally, the immune test is performed. If the produced particle is better than the original particle, replace the original by the produced.

4 Multiple Sequence Alignment Based on IPSO and HMM

The ordered components in the location vector of a particle are defined as all the transition probabilities and emission probabilities when using IPSO to train HMM for MSA. For the HMM profile shown in Fig.1, let N be the predetermined length of the HMM, which is taken as the average length of the sequences in the alignment problem, and |A| denotes the size of the alphabet. Without regard to the "begin" state and the "end" state, the location vector of a particle is a permutation with real encoding of $9N+3$ transition probabilities and $(2N+1)|A|$ emission probabilities, which spans a search space of $(2N+1)|A|+9N+3$ dimensions. When N is large enough, the number of the probability parameters is $49N$ for protein models and $17N$ for DNA models. So a particle corresponds to a determined HMM model, and the evaluation of a particle is also the evaluation for its corresponding HMM model. Before evaluating a particle all the probability parameters need to be normalized to satisfy that the sum of the probabilities of all transitions going out of a state is 1, and the sum of all emission probabilities in each state is 1. Then the most probable state sequence path for each sequence can be gained by using the Viterbi algorithm [12]. Afterwards, the sequences can be aligned according to the specific states in their paths. Finally, a gained alignment can be evaluated by a scoring system.

Let population size be m, and iteration generations be n. The operation of receptor editing is performed after each s generations, and the operation of vaccination is performed after each t generations. Then the whole evaluation times in the algorithm is about

$$k = \text{int}[nm(1+\frac{1}{4s}+\frac{p_v}{t})]. \qquad (11)$$

where int[·] is the truncation function.

Defines

$$\delta_i(t) = \max_{\pi_i(t)} P(\pi_i(t) | \lambda). \qquad (12)$$

In the Viterbi algorithm, where $\pi_i(t)$ is the prefix path to observe the partial sequence $X^1 \cdots X^t$ up to time t and state i at time t given the model λ. $\delta_i(t)$ is the probability relative to the most probable path. The variable is updated by the transmission mechanism similar to the forward algorithm.

For the match and insertion states,

$$\delta_i(t+1) = (\max_j \delta_j(t) t_{ji}) b_{ik}. \qquad (13)$$

For the deletion states,

$$\delta_i(t+1) = (\max_j \delta_j(t) t_{ji}). \qquad (14)$$

The alignment score, namely the fitness of a particle, is evaluated by a scoring system. In this paper, a modified version of the sum-of-pairs function [13] is adopted. Given a test alignment of N sequences consisting of M columns, the ith column of the alignment is denoted by $A_{i1}, A_{i2}, \cdots, A_{iN}$. For each pair of residues A_{ij} and A_{ik}, define p_{ijk} such that $p_{ijk}=1$ if residues A_{ij} and A_{ik} are aligned with each other in the reference alignment, otherwise $p_{ijk}=0$. The score S_i for the ith column is defined as:

$$S_i = \sum_{j=1, j \neq k}^{N} \sum_{k=1}^{N} p_{ijk} . \tag{15}$$

The *SPS* for the alignment is then:

$$SPS = \sum_{i=1}^{M} S_i \bigg/ \sum_{i=1}^{M_r} S_{ri} . \tag{16}$$

where M_r is the number of columns in the reference alignment and S_{ri} is the score S_i for the ith column in the reference alignment.

Thus far, the proposed algorithm for MSA can be described by the flow chart shown in Figure 2.

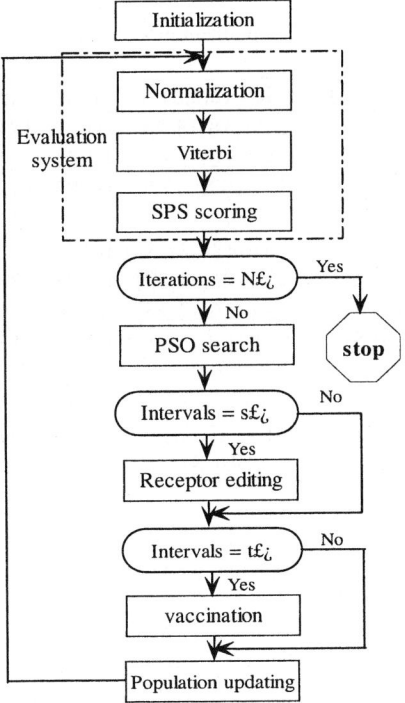

Fig. 2. The flow chart of the algorithm for MSA

5 Numerical Simulation Results

The performance of the proposed algorithm for MSA is examined by the benchmark problems from the BAliBASE alignment database. BaliBASE is available on the World Wide Web at http://bips.u-strasbg.fr/fr/Products/Databases/BAliBASE2. The database contains reasonably high-quality, well-documented alignments that have been confirmed using a variety of programs and by manual verification. The first version of BAliBASE contains 142 reference alignments, with a total of more than 1000 sequences. It is divided in five hierarchical reference sets by the length and similarity of the sequences in the core blocks and by the presence of insertions and N/C-terminal extensions. We select a total of twelve sequence sets from the reference sets, which are listed in Table 1. Some parameters in the simulated experiment are taken as: $m=30$, $c_1=1.9$, $c_2=0.8$, $w=0.5$, $s=50$, $t=30$, $n=1600$. Numerical simulated results are compared with those obtained by using the Baum-Welch training algorithm and listed in Table 1. The contents of the table include the name of each test problem (Name), the number of sequences (N), the length of sequences (LSEQ(m, n), m-minimum, n-maximum), the percentage sequence identity (Id%(a, b, c), a- average, b- minimum, c-maximum), the results gained by using the Baum-Welch algorithm (BW), the results gained by using IPSO training algorithm (IPSO), and the time cost (Time).

Table 1. The benchmark alignment problems and simulation results

Name	N	LSEQ(m, n)	Id%(a,b,c)	BW	Time(s)	IPSO	Time(s)
1aboA	5	(48,74)	<25%(18,14,26)	0.622	121.28	0.678	19.67
451c	5	(70,87)	20-40%(27,23,34)	0.321	159.73	0.557	25.01
9rnt	5	(96,103)	>35%(57,51,65)	0.783	178.78	0.845	34.15
kinase	5	(260,273)	<25%(20,17,25)	0.308	437.65	0.467	86.80
2cba	5	(237,259)	20-40%(26,22,33)	0.653	408.63	0.794	91.38
1ppn	5	(212,220)	>35%(46,41,59)	0.605	383.86	0.714	64.49
2myr	4	(340,474)	<25%(16,13,25)	0.236	589.71	0.472	81.86
1eft	4	(334,405)	20-40%(30,25,35)	0.728	512.34	0.754	84.93
1taq	5	(806,928)	>35%(40,35,50)	0.747	4278.93	0.889	256.13
1ubi	17	(76,97)	-(30,8,71)	0.267	853.42	0.438	132.10
kinase	18	(257,287)	-(32,17,73)	0.186	2119.87	0.347	160.88
1idy	27	(49,60)	-(19,1,81)	0.295	996.06	0.412	107.96

From the table it can be seen that each score of the twelve alignment results gained by using the IPSO is higher than that using the Baum-Welch algorithm. The average score gained by using the Baum-Welch algorithm is 0.479, whereas that gained by using the IPSO is 0.614, which is about 1.3 times of the Baum-Welch algorithm. On the other hand, the time cost of the proposed algorithm is much less than using the Baum-Welch algorithm. So it could be concluded that using the proposed IPSO-based algorithm to train HMM for solving MSA is superior to the Baum-Welch algorithm.

6 Conclusions

We propose an immune particle swarm optimization algorithm based on the models of the vaccination and the receptor editing in immune systems. In the IPSO, the operations of the vaccination and the receptor editing are designed. Further, the proposed algorithm is used to train hidden Markov models for multiple sequence alignment. Numerical results show that the proposed algorithm is effective for multiple sequence alignment.

Acknowledgements

The authors are grateful to the support of the National Natural Science Foundation of China (60433020), the science-technology development project of Jilin Province of China (20050705-2), and the doctoral funds of the Education Ministry of China (20030183060).

References

1. Du, Z. H., Lin, F.: Improvement of the Needleman-Wunsch algorithm. Lecture Notes in Artificial Intelligence, 2004, 3066: 792-797.
2. Zhang, F., Qiao, X. Z., Liu, Z. Y.: Parallel divide and conquer bio-sequence comparison based on Smith-Waterman algorithm. Science in China Series F-Information Sciences, 2004, 47 (2): 221-231.
3. Thompson, J.D., Higgins, D. G., Gibson, T. J.: CLUSTAL W: improving the sensitivity of progressive multiple sequence alignment through sequence weighting, position-specific gap penalties and weight matrix choice. Nucl. Acids Res, 1994, 22: 4673–4680.
4. Goto, O.: Optimal alignment between groups of sequences and its application to multiple sequence alignment. Comput. Appl. Biosci., 1993, 9: 361-370.
5. Williams, A., Gilbert, D. R., Westhead, D. R.: Multiple structural alignment for distantly related all beta structures using TOPS pattern discovery and simulated annealing. Protein Engineering, 2003, 16 (12): 913-923.
6. Shyu, C., Foster, J. A.: Evolving consensus sequence for multiple sequence alignment with a genetic algorithm. Lecture Notes in Computer Science, 2003, 2724: 2313-2324.
7. Edgar, R. C., Sjolander, K.: Sequence alignment and tree construction using hidden Markov models. Bioinformatics, 2003, 19 (11): 1404-1411.
8. Otterpohl, J. R.: Baum-Welch learning in discrete hidden Markov models with linear factorial constraints. Lecture Notes in Computer Science, 2002, 2415: 1180-1185.
9. Kennedy, J., Eberhart, R.: Particle swarm optimization. Proceedings of the IEEE International Conference on Neural Networks, Piscataway, NJ, USA: IEEE press, 1995, 4: 1942-1948.
10. Shi, Y., Eberhart, R.: A modified particle swarm optimizer. IEEE World Congress on Computational Intelligence, Piscataway, NJ, USA: IEEE press, 1998, 69-73.
11. Verkoczy, L. K., Martensson, A. S., Nemazee, D.: The scope of receptor editing and its association with autoimmunity. Current opinion in immunology, 2004, 16(6): 808-814.
12. Chao, C. C., Yao, Y. L.: Hidden Markov models for the burst error statistics of Viterbi decoding. IEEE Transactions on Communications, 1996, 44(12): 1620-1622.
13. Thompson, J., Plewniak, F., Poch, O.: A comprehensive comparison of multiple sequence alignment programs. Nucl. Acids. Res., 1999, 27 (13): 2682–2690.

Design of Intelligent Security Management System Using Simulation-Based Analysis

Jang-Se Lee[1], Dong Seong Kim[2], Jong Sou Park[2], and Sung-Do Chi[2]

[1] The Division of Information Technology Engineering, Korea Maritime University,
#1, Dongsam-dong, Youngdo-gu, Busan, 606-791, Korea
jslee@bada.hhu.ac.kr
[2] The Department of Computer Engineering, Hangkong University,
200-1, Hwajon-dong, Deokyang-gu, Koyang-city,
Kyonggi-do, 412-791, Korea
{dskim, jspark, sdchi}@mail.hangkong.ac.kr

Abstract. The objective of this paper is to propose an intelligent security management system using simulation based analysis, which is capable to monitor network status, evaluate vulnerabilities, generate defense strategies, and apply it to the network. To do this, we have employed the intelligent system design concept based on the advanced modeling and simulation environment for developing network security models and simulation-based evaluation of vulnerability as well as defense strategy. Our approach differs from others in that i) it is able to analyze vulnerabilities on node, link, and network in quantitative manner, ii) it can generate and apply defense strategies automatically, and iii) it supports a coherent design concept for intelligent security management system. A case study performed on a test bed will illustrate our techniques and demonstrate effectiveness of propose system.

1 Introduction

While the computing environment is getting powerful and the network dependence is getting increased because of the explosive usage of Internet, most systems linked by Internet are exposed in external intrusion so that the damage by cyber-attacks that exploits vulnerabilities is rapidly increased [1.2]. Accordingly, researches for various individual security techniques like as intrusion detection, authentication, and cryptology to solve vulnerabilities of Internet infrastructure is prevailing. Recently, the enterprise security management systems [2] are introduced for coherently combing those individual solutions [3], however, those systems are mainly focus on the heterogeneous integration so that it only provides API interface between security solution to interconnect them and supports static vulnerabilities of given network component. That means, the deep analysis of dynamically changing vulnerabilities based on the network states are not allowed.

To deal with this, we have employed the intelligent system design concept based on the advanced modeling and simulation environment for developing network security models and simulation-based evaluation of vulnerability as well as defense strategy. Our approach differs from others in that i) it is able to analyze vulnerabilities on node, link, and network in quantitative manner, ii) it can generate and apply defense strategies automatically, and iii) it supports a coherent design concept for intelligent security management system. A case study performed on a test bed will illustrate our techniques.

2 Background

2.1 Brief Descriptions on SES/MB Simulation Environment

System Entity Structure/Model Base (SES/MB) framework is a modeling and simulation environment providing the plan-generate-evaluate paradigm in system design and/or analysis [4,5]. It was proposed by Zeigler as a step toward marrying the dynamics-based formalism of simulation with the symbolic formalisms of AI [5]. It basically consists of a system entity structure (SES) and model base (MB).

Fig. 1 shows an approach to model base management that relies on the concept of system entity structure. The behaviors of primitive components of a real world system are specified by atomic models and saved in the model base. The structural knowledge of the system is represented as a system entity structure by means of an operation called entity structuring. The entity structured serves as a compact representation for organizing all possible hierarchical composition structures of the system. This separation of model composition structures from their behaviors may reduce the modeling complexity of real-world systems [4]. Hierarchical and modular simulation models may be constructed by applying the transformation operation to the system entity structure and model base.

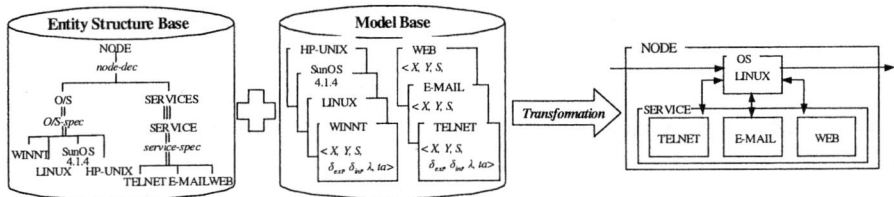

Fig. 1. SES/MB Framework Concept

2.2 Vulnerability Metrics

In our previous work [9], we have defined the vulnerability metrics of node, link, and network as follows.

2.2.1 Node Vulnerability

Node vulnerability includes the comprehensive vulnerability items that each network component currently and/or latently has. Every node on the network has a subset of the vulnerability items according to its own configurations, however, some vulnerability items are static (time-independent) and others are not (time-dependent). Thus, the simulation method are necessary for evaluating the later vulnerability items. The node vulnerability is defined by the arithmetic average of product of impact level by value of each vulnerability item. The node vulnerability of ith component, NV_i, is defined as follows;

$$NV_i = \Sigma(w_j \times vul_j) / \Sigma w_j \quad (1)$$

Where the w_j and vul_j represent the impact level and evaluated value of jth vulnerability item, respectively. The impact level represents how much damage the successful cyber-attack exploiting the corresponding vulnerability item will cost. The value is ranging from 0 to 1.

2.2.2 Link Vulnerability

Because of the diverse access path due to increased access points in worldwide Internet environment, the link vulnerability analysis is becoming essential. To deal with this, we have defined link vulnerability metric, LV_i, that has the value ranging from 0 to 1 as follows.

$$LV_i = n_{success} / n_{trial} \quad (2)$$

Where, the $n_{success}$ represents the number of successful attack scenarios and the n_{trial} denotes the number of attack scenarios injected into the target components from the attacker model.

2.2.3 Network Vulnerability

Network vulnerability denotes the total node vulnerability on a given network. Therefore, the network vulnerability may be simply obtained by taking the arithmetic means of node vulnerabilities. Thus, the ith network vulnerability, $NetV_i$, is defined as follows.

$$NetV_i = \Sigma(W_j \times NV_j) / \Sigma W_j \quad (3)$$

Where, the W_j represents the weight of importance of jth node about appropriate network.

2.3 Vulnerability Analysis Using SES/MB Simulation Environment

The vulnerability analysis methodology using SES/MB [9,10,11] is depicted in Fig 2. The 1st phase shows conceptual specification: the relationship such as partition, grouping and coupling of target network system can be described by System Entity Structure (SES). In 2nd phase, we generate not only the model of attackers and a analyzer but also model of each network components by using DEVS formalism, and store these model in Model Base(MB). In 3rd phase, simulation model is generated as the result of integrating stored model in MB according to the defined network structure by SES. Hereby, we can execute simulation for the various cyber attacks. Finally, 4th phase apply vulnerability metric to the result of simulation execution and it analyzes vulnerabilities of configuration components in quantitative manners.

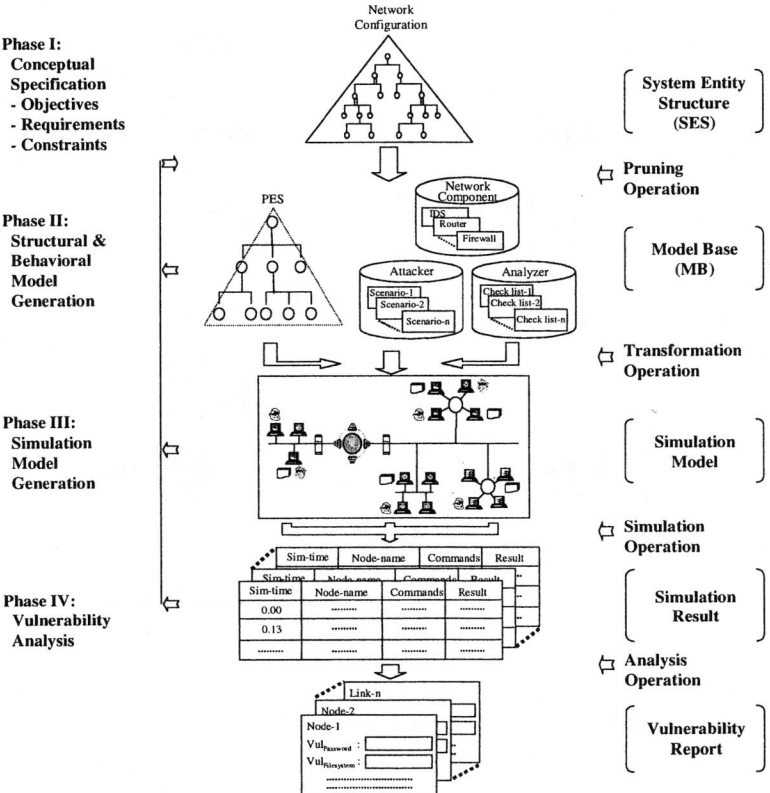

Fig. 2. Vulnerability Analysis Methodology based on Simulation

3 Intelligent Security Management System

3.1 Intelligent System Concept

An endomorphic modeling concept shows that the intelligent system must have the knowledge that is an objectives-driven model about the world to be controlled [4,5,8]. By analyzing the sensory data, it makes a decision based on the knowledge (i.e., by simulation on model) and then it sends a resulting control command to the real world [4,5,8,12,13]. Fig. 3 shows an endomorphic modeling concept applied to the intelligent security management systems.

Fig. 4 represents detailed design concept of the intelligent security management system. The intelligent security management system consists of Analyzer (*sense*), Planner (*decide*) and Defender (*act*) as well as simulator. The Analyzer first gathers every monitoring data from the real network and then performs the simulation via Planner to evaluate the vulnerabilities. An optimal defense strategy for minimizing the estimated vulnerabilities is decided by evaluating all possible defense strategies through the simulation on Defender via Planner.

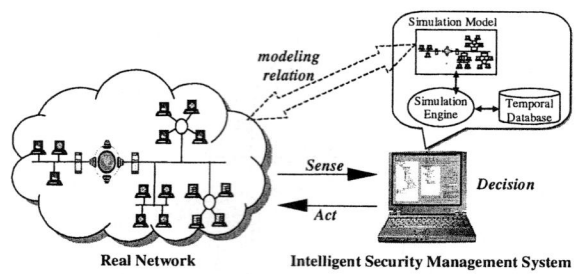

Fig. 3. Intelligent System Concept

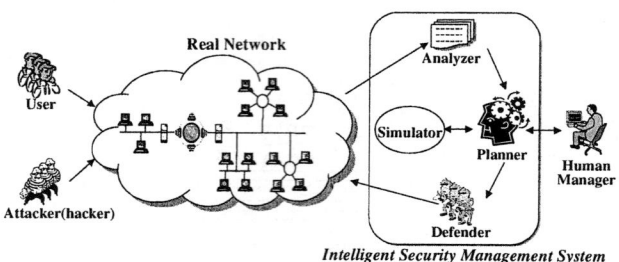

Fig. 4. Intelligent Security Management System

3.2 Design of Intelligent Security Management System

Proposed architecture of the simulation-based intelligent security management system is depicted in Fig. 5. The *Analyzer* first receives monitored information from *Security Agents* connected with security tools and then *Analyzer* sends monitored information to *simulator*. *Simulator* constructs the model structure of given network from the *MB* and initializes models. The *Simulator* performs simulation against cyber-attacks by

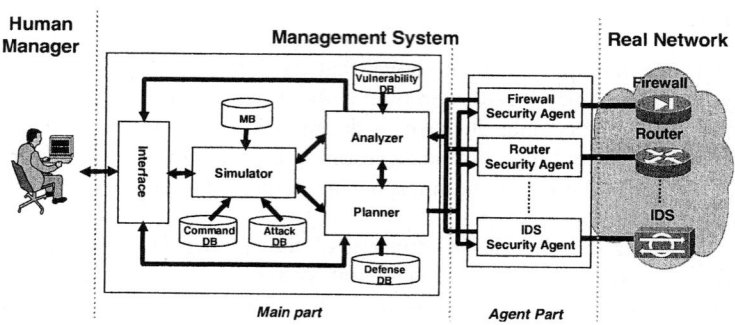

Fig. 5. The architecture of Intelligent Security Management System

means of *Attack DB* and *Command DB*, reports simulation result to the *Analyzer*. The *Analyzer* applies vulnerability metrics to the simulation result by using the *Vulnerability DB* and analyzes vulnerabilities of the components in quantitative manner. Continuously, *Planner* produces all possible defense strategies through the *Defense DB*, the pre-defined security policy from *Interface,* and the simulation result. It selects an optimal defense strategy by evaluating all strategies via *Simulator*. Finally, the optimal defense strategy is projected to the security tools through *Security Agents*.

Components composing the intelligent security management system in Fig. 5 are like as following;

- *Interface*: it supports the communication between human manager and proposed system.
- *Analyzer*: it is for analyzing the node, link, and network vulnerabilities using the simulation by *Simulator*.
- *Planner*: it generates the defense strategies according to the defense policy of human manager and decides an optimal defense strategy via *Simulator*.
- *Simulator*: it performs the simulation for evaluating the vulnerabilities and defense strategies.
- *MB*: it is a model base that contains DEVS models of given network components (see Fig. 6).

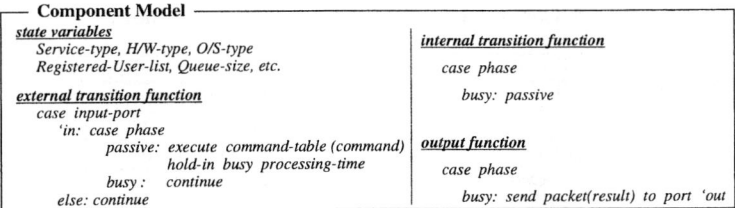

Fig. 6. Example of component model's DEVS representation

- *Command-DB*: it is a database of command, i.e., it is composed of condition for execution (pre-condition) and status after execution (post-condition) (see Table. 1).
- *Attack-DB*: it is a database of cyber-attack scenario composed by set of commands (see Table. 2).
- *Vulnerability-DB*: it is a database of vulnerability for analysis of vulnerabilities (see Table. 3).
- *Defense-DB*: it is a database of defense strategy for generating defense strategies (see Table. 4).
- *Security Agent*: it receives the monitoring information from the network through the connected security tool and transmits the defense strategy from the management system to its security tool.

Table 1. Pre/post-condition representation of Unix commands (partially-shown)

Command	Pre-condition	Output	Post-condition
cd	Check the file existence	Change work-directory	Change directory attributes
rm	"	Remove file entries	Change file attributes
chmod	"	Change the permission	Change permission attribute

Table 2. Attack scenario table (partially-shown)

Attack scenario #	Commands	Exploited vulnerability	Effected vulnerability
AS-1	showmount -e taget.host mount target.host:/usr/tmp cd /tmp ls -alg echo abcxyz:1234:10001:1::: >> passwd ls -alg su abcxyz echo attacker >> .rhosts	$Vul_{Filesystem}$ $Vul_{Userfile}$	$Vul_{Filesystem}$ $Vul_{Password}$ $Vul_{Userfile}$
AS-2	telnet taget.host User abcxyz 1234 umask 000 cd /tmp ln -s /.test .status.dce glance -j 1 -i 1 -m 1	Vul_{glance}	$Vul_{Userfile}$

Table 3. Component vulnerability table (partially-shown)

Category	Vulnerability item	Impact level (w_i)	Remarks
Fixed vulnerability	Vul_{Phf}	0.75	Phf CGI vulnerability
	Vul_{glance}	1.0	HP-UXB 1.0.2 glance vulnerability
Changeable vulnerability	$Vul_{Password}$	0.5	Password vulnerability
	$Vul_{Userfile}$	0.75	User file vulnerability

Table 4. Defense strategy table (partially-shown)

Related vulnerability	Defense strategy	Remarks
$Vul_{Password}$	Check the password file	Unsuitable setting of password
$Vul_{Userfile}$	Change the file permission	Unsuitable permission setting of User file
Vul_{glance}	Patch the O/S	Vulnerable old version O/S

4 Case Study

In order to demonstrate the applicability of proposed system, we have developed the simplified intelligent enterprise security management system under the Visual C++. The implemented system consists of a Manager and Security Agents for hosts and routers. The Manager deals with the network by analyzing vulnerabilities and generating defense strategy through the simulation with information obtained from every component on the network. The Security Agent for host monitors the host information and applies the defense strategy made by the Manager. The Security Agent for router controls router against link vulnerabilities of path. As shown in Fig. 7, we have established a test bed that is consisted of three routers, four hosts using Linux, and four hosts using Windows-2000. We also have implemented more than ten cyber attack scenarios for the vulnerability analysis.

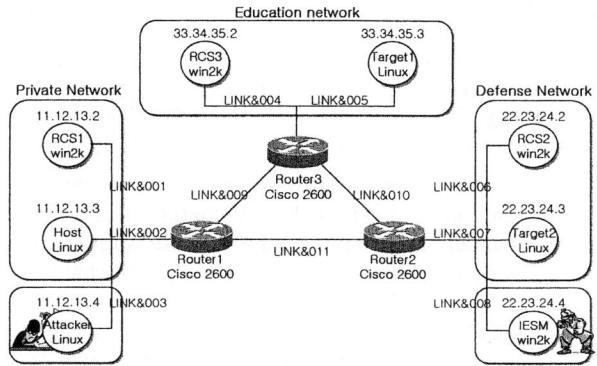

Fig. 7. Configuration of test-bed

Firstly, after we confirmed by real attack that vulnerabilities using error of configuration exist in the host composing the test bed, we executed the proposed management system. The system performed monitoring on the hosts by security agent. And it analyzed quantitatively that hosts have vulnerabilities such as error of configuration through result of simulation using cyber attack scenarios (see Table 5 'Vulnerability (Before)'), it generated strategies such as changing of configuration (see Table 6) and changing of access list of router. Table 5 shows vulnerability change on the test bed being analyzed by simulation. In this, 'Name' means a component's name composing the test bed, 'Category' means a type of vulnerability, and 'Vulnerability (Before)' and 'Vulnerability (After)' means quantitative vulnerabilities before applying defense and after applying defense respectively. As shown in the 'Vulnerability (After)', we can predict that the vulnerability of node, link and network is removed or decrease by applying generated strategies.

Table 5. Vulnerability change on the test bed (partially shown)

Name	Category	Vulnerability (Before)	Vulnerability (After)
Host	Node	0.11	0.00
Target-1	Node	0.67	0.33
Target-2	Node	0.56	0.00
Link&003	Link	0.79	0.53
Link&005	Link	0.82	0.53
Link&007	Link	1.00	0.00
Link&009	Link	0.79	0.53
Link&010	Link	1.00	0.00
Private Network	Network	0.07	0.00
Education Network	Network	0.33	0.16
Defense Network	Network	0.19	0.00

Table 6. Defense strategy for the Target 2(partially shown)

[NODE NAME : NetworkM&005]	
Os update : Linux Updated..!!	
Permission change [Setuid] :	
/home/islab/jslee/a	11s101101 => 111101101
/home/islab/jslee/prog1	11s101101 => 111101101
/home/islab/jslee/test	11s101101 => 111101101
Permission change [Execution] :	
/home/islab/jslee/agent	111101101 => 111101100
/home/islab/jslee/folder	111101101 => 111101100
/home/islab/jslee/sys_ls	111101101 => 111101100

On the basis of this, the system controlled hosts and routers by using security agents. Like this, proposed system can analyze vulnerabilities on node, link, and network in quantitative manner, and generate the defense strategy. Through this, we examined that security management on the test bed performed automatically and intelligently.

Fig. 8 shows screen copies of the management system. In Fig. 8, program menu consists of submenu for communication between security agents and intelligent network security management system, submenu for simulation, and submenu for displaying various result files produced by security management. The network information window provides detailed information about components composing a network. The component attribute window shows attributes of components selected by human manager. The processing information window shows processing status by executing menu or by performing simulation. The vulnerability analysis window shows result of vulnerability analysis on the node, link and network. And, the defense strategy window shows defense strategies against it.

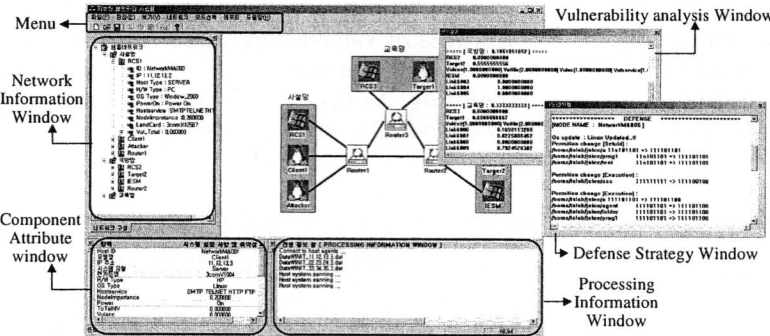

Fig. 8. Screen copies of Intelligent Security Management System

5 Conclusions

This paper proposed an intelligent security management system capable to monitor network status, evaluate vulnerabilities, generate defense strategies, and apply it to the network. To solve vulnerabilities of Internet infrastructure, researches for various individual security techniques is prevailing. Recently, the enterprise security management systems are introduced for coherently combing those individual solutions, however, those systems are mainly focus on the heterogeneous integration so that it only provides API interface between security solution to interconnect them and supports static vulnerabilities of given network component. That means, the deep analysis of dynamically changing vulnerabilities based on the network states are not allowed. To deal with this, we have employed the intelligent system design concept based on the advanced modeling and simulation environment for developing network security models and simulation-based evaluation of vulnerability as well as defense strategy. And we developed the simplified intelligent enterprise security management system under Visual C++ and demonstrated applicability of proposed system. Our approach differs from others in that i) it is able to analyze vulnerabilities on node, link, and network in quantitative manner, ii) it can generate and apply defense strategies automatically, and iii) it supports a coherent design concept for intelligent security management system. We leave here future further studied about refining for proposed system, agent for combining with individual security solutions.

References

1. T. A. Longstaff, Clyde Chittister, Rich Pethia, Yacov Y. Haimes, "Are We Forgetting the Risks of Information Technology", IEEE Computer, pp 43-51, December, 2000.
2. http://new.itfind.or.kr/KIC/etlars/industry/jugidong/1026/102603.htm", Dec., 2001.
3. H. Y. Ahn, "Enterprise Security Management: It's way to go", The 7th Network Security Workshop-Korea, Apr., 2001.
4. Zeigler, B.P., H. Praehofer, and T.G. Kim. Theory of Modeling and Simulation 2ed. Academic Press, 1999.
5. Chi, S.D. *Modeling and Simulation for High Autonomy Systems*, Ph.D. Dissertation, Dept. of Electrical and Computer Engineering, Univ. of Arizona, 1991.
6. S.D. Chi, J.S. Park, K.C. Jung and J.S. Lee, " Network Security Modeling and Cyber Attack Simulation Methodology", Lecture Notes in Computer Science 2119, 2001.
7. B.P. Zeigler, Multifacetted Modeling and Discrete Event Simulation, Academic Press, 1984.
8. B. P. Zeigler, Object-oriented Simulation with Hierarchical, Modular Models: Intelligent Agents and Endomorphic systems, Academic Press, 1990.
9. J.S. Lee, J.R. Jung, S.D Chi, "Vulnerability Measures for Network Vulnerability Analysis System", Proc. of 2002 IRC International Conference on Internet Information Retrieval, Korea, Nov., 2002.
10. S.D. Chi, J.S. Park and J.S. Lee, "A Role of DEVS Simulation for Information Assurance", Lecture Notes in Computer Science 2908, 2004.
11. J.S. Lee and S.D Chi, "Simulation-based Vulnerability Analysis", Computer Systems Science & Engineering (submitted).
12. B.P. Zeigler, "High Autonomy Systems: Concept and Models", AI, Simulation and Planning in High Autonomy Systems, IEEE Computer Society Press, 1990
13. S.D. Chi, "Model-Based Concept for Design of High Autonomy System", Journal of The Korean Institute of Electrical Engineering, Vol. 42, No. 3, 1993.

Neighborhood Re-structuring in Particle Swarm Optimization

Arvind S. Mohais[1], Rui Mendes[2], Christopher Ward[1], and Christian Posthoff[1]

[1] The University of the West Indies, St. Augustine, Trinidad
amohais@fsa.uwi.tt
[2] Universidade do Minho, Braga, Portugal
azuki@di.uminho.pt

Abstract. This paper considers the use of randomly generated directed graphs as neighborhoods for particle swarm optimizers (PSO) using fully informed particles (FIPS), together with dynamic changes to the graph during an algorithm run as a diversity-preserving measure. Different graph sizes, constructed with a uniform out-degree were studied with regard to their effect on the performance of the PSO on optimization problems. Comparisons were made with a static random method, as well as with several canonical PSO and FIPS methods. The results indicate that under appropriate parameter settings, the use of random directed graphs with a probabilistic disruptive re-structuring of the graph produces the best results on the test functions considered.

1 Introduction

Particle Swarm Optimization (PSO) [1,2] is an evolutionary algorithm inspired by social interaction. At each iteration, each particle imitates the behavior of its most successful neighbor. A particle's neighborhood is the set of other particles that it is connected to; it considers their experience when updating its velocity. The graph of inter-connections is called the neighborhood structure. Generally, neighborhood connections are independent of the positions occupied by particles. Two basic structures [1] are the 'global neighborhood', in which each particle is connected to all others and the 'local best' or 'ring', in which particles are connected in a circular manner, with each one being connected to the one on its left and the one on its right. More complex graphs have also been investigated. Mendes [3] studied various fixed graphs on 20 nodes with PSO and conjectured that an average degree of 4 might be suitable for the functions investigated. Using graphs to dictate the interactions between individuals of an evolutionary algorithm has also been used outside of PSO [4].

Dynamic neighborhoods, i.e. ones that change the structure of connections as the algorithm progresses have also been studied. Kennedy [5] investigated 'clustering', wherein after each iteration particles form fully connected clusters based on their search-space locations. Suganthan [6] studied the effect of starting with a sparsely connected graph and progressively adding edges during the run, with the aim of gradually shifting the focus from exploration to exploitation.

Mohais et al [7] performed a proof-of-concept study involving the random migration of edges in a randomly-generated graph, meaning that some edges were disconnected from one of their endpoints and randomly re-attached elsewhere.

This paper further studies random and dynamic neighborhoods. Different size populations, of uniform out-degree 5 were tested on six functions. Two types of probabilistic dynamism were considered: random edge migrations and complete graph re-structuring. These methods were also compared to some pre-defined static neighborhood structures, L-Best-1 (the ring), L-Best-2, and the von Neumann topology.

2 Particle Swarm Optimization

A Particle Swarm Optimizer is a set, or population, of n particles that evolves over time. At time t, the population is $Pop(t) = \{P_1(t), P_2(t), \ldots, P_n(t)\}$ where the ith particle is defined by $P_i(t) = (x_i(t), p_i(t), v_i(t), e_i(t))$. The current position in the d-dimensional search space is $x_i(t) \in \mathbb{R}^d$. $p_i(t) \in \mathbb{R}^d$ is the position visited in the past that had the best function evaluation. $v_i(t) \in \mathbb{R}^d$ is called the 'velocity', it is the speed and direction with which the particle is moving. $e_i(t)$ is the evaluation of $p_i(t)$ under the function being optimized, i.e. $e_i(t) = f(p_i(t))$.

Particles are connected to others in the population via a predefined topology. Common topologies are the ring and global topologies which are illustrated below ((a) and (b)). However there is no reason that an asymmetrical, or even randomly generated topology cannot be used (see (c)).

(a)
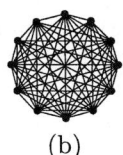
(b)
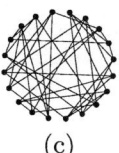
(c)

At each iteration, a new population is produced by allowing each particle to move stochastically toward its previous best position and at the same time toward the best of the previous best positions of all other particles to which it is connected. The following is an outline of a generic PSO.

1. Set the iteration counter, $t = 0$.
2. Initialize each $x_i(0)$ and $v_i(0)$ randomly. Set $p_i(0) = x_i(0)$.
3. Evaluate each particle and set $e_i(0) = f(p_i(0))$.
4. Let $t = t + 1$ and generate a new population, $P(t)$ by moving each particle i in $P(t-1)$ to a new position in the search space according to:
    (i) $v_i(t) = velocity\_update(t-1)$.
    (ii) $x_i(t) = x_i(t-1) + v_i(t)$.
    (iii) Evaluate the new position, $e = f(x_i(t))$. If it is better than the previous best, update the particle's previous best position. i.e if $e < e_i(t-1)$ then let $p_i(t) = x_i(t)$ and $e_i(t) = e$, else let $p_i(t) = p_i(t-1)$ and $e_i(t) = e_i(t-1)$.

The original PSO used the following velocity update equation

$$velocity\_update(t-1) = v_i(t-1) + r_1 c_1(p_i(t-1) - x_i(t-1)) \\ + r_2 c_2(p_g(t-1) - x_i(t-1))$$

where c_1 and c_2 are constants known as the 'individual' and 'social' constants respectively. They represent the weights accorded to the influence of the particle's personal memory, and the memory of it's neighborhood respectively. $r_1, r_2 \sim U(0,1)$. New values for r_1 and r_2 are selected for each dimension of the updated velocity vector as it is being computed. $p_g(t-1)$ is the previous best position of the particle in i's neighborhood that has the best previous best evaluation of all particles in that neighborhood at time $t-1$. In other words, $g = arg\{min\{e_j(t-1)|j \in N(i)\}\}$, where $N(i)$ is the neighborhood of particle i. Two variations on the velocity update equation are described below.

Constriction Factor PSO (Canonical). Clerc and Kennedy [8] introduced the use of a 'constriction factor' χ, into the velocity update equation.

$$velocity\_update(t-1) = \chi[v_i(t-1) + r_1 c_1(p_i(t-1) - x_i(t-1)) \\ + r_2 c_2(p_g(t-1) - x_i(t-1))]$$

A common configuration involves choosing $c_1 = c_2 = 2.05$ and $\chi = 0.729$.

Fully Informed PSO (FIPS). An approach that involves utilizing information from all members of particle i's neighborhood, $N(i)$, was proposed by Mendes et al [9]. Each member of $N(i)$ contributes to the new velocity. Mendes' formulation allows for weighted (possibly equal) contributions from each neighbor. With $\phi_{max} = c_1 + c_2$, the velocity update equation becomes,

$$velocity\_update(t-1) = \chi \left[v_i(t-1) + \frac{\sum_{k \in N(i)} U(0, \phi_{max})(p_k - x_t)}{|N(i)|} \right]$$

3 Random and Dynamic Neighborhoods

In this paper, directed graphs were used to represent neighborhoods. An edge from u to v was taken to mean that u will consider v as a neighbor, but not vice versa. Two parameters were used in the generation of a random neighborhood. The first was the size n of the neighborhood, and the other was the out-degree of each node (the number of outgoing edges). Based on preliminary experimental trials, a uniform out-degree of 5 was used. For each node, 5 different, randomly selected neighbors, were added to the node's neighborhood.

Two methods of modifying the structure of a neighborhood were considered. The first is called 'random edge migration' [7]. It involves randomly selecting a node with a neighborhood of size greater than 1, detaching one of its neighbors from it, and re-attaching that neighbor to some other randomly selected node that does not have a full neighborhood.

The second method is called a 'neighborhood re-structuring'. This is an entirely new method that involves a more abrupt type of dynamism in the neighborhood structure. Instead of there being small and gradual changes, this approach keeps the neighborhood structure fixed for an amount of time and then completely re-initializes it; essentially imposing a new random neighborhood structure on the population. Only the parameters of the neighborhood, i.e. size and out-degree, are kept fixed, the connections are completely changed.

4 Experimental Investigations

4.1 The Test Problems

The neighborhood structures and dynamic modification schemes described above along with standard schemes were tested on six optimization functions commonly used by researchers of PSO systems. The functions are given below. The Schaffer F6 function is 2 dimensional, all the others were in 30 dimensions except the Griewank function which was used in 10 dimensions since in practice this is harder to optimize than the 30-dimensional one.

Sphere	$\sum_{i=1}^{n} x_i^2$
Rosenbrock	$\sum_{i=1}^{n-1} 100(x_{i+1} - x_i^2)^2 + (x_i - 1)^2$
Ackley	$20 + e - 20\, e^{-0.2\sqrt{\frac{\sum_{i=1}^{n} x_i^2}{n}}} - e^{\frac{\sum_{i=1}^{n} cos2\pi x_i}{n}}$
Rastrigin	$\sum_{i=1}^{n} x_i^2 - 10\, cos2\pi x_i + 10$
Griewank	$1 + \frac{\sum_{i=1}^{n}(x_i - 100)^2}{4000} - \prod_{i=1}^{n} cos\frac{x_i - 100}{\sqrt{i}}$
Schaffer F6	$0.5 + \frac{sin(\sqrt{x_1^2 + x_2^2})^2 - 0.5}{(1 + 0.001(x_1^2 + x_2^2))^2}$

4.2 General Experimental Protocol

The experiments involved configuring a particular type of PSO, and testing it on each of the six optimization problems. Each configuration was tested 50 times on each function. At the end of each run, the global best function evaluation was recorded. Each run was allowed to run for a maximum of 20000 function evaluations. This is equivalent to using a population size of 20 for 1000 iterations. However, for different size populations, fewer or more iterations would result.

4.3 Experiment 1: Comparison of Random Dynamic Schemes

A first experiment compared the performance of re-structuring, migration and, static random neighborhoods. For all experiments an initial random neighborhood was generated; sizes ranged from 10 to 100 in steps of 5 and regardless of the size, each node was randomly assigned 5 neighbors. An out-degree of 5 was chosen because initial probing suggested it to be a good choice.

For the migration method, a probability parameter $p_m \in \{0.1, 0.2, \ldots, 1.0\}$ controlled how often an edge migration would occur. After each iteration, a decision was made whether or not to perform a random edge migration, based on the p_m value. Similarly, for re-structuring, after each iteration a decision was made whether or not to perform the operation based on a probability parameter $p_r \in \{0.01, 0.02, \ldots, 0.1\}$.

4.4 Results of Experiment 1

A first observation is that a distinctive shape is obtained when population size is plotted against mean best performance, regardless of whether the static method was a dynamic one was used. Figure 1 illustrates this, each plot contains overlays of the population size vs mean best performance plots of the static method, and all probabilities of the migration and re-structuring methods for a given function.

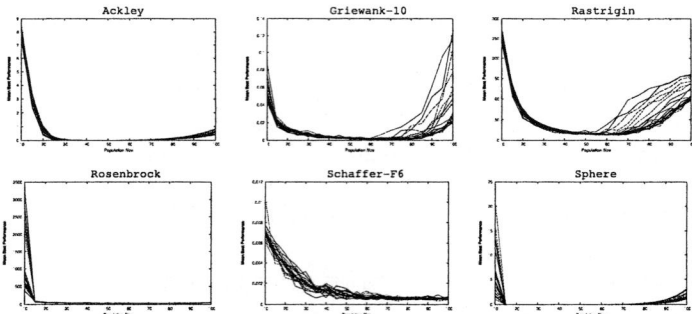

Fig. 1. Overlays of population size versus mean best performance plots for PSOs using random neighborhoods either statically or dynamically

Table 1 shows the top three configurations in each method, the migration configuration using a probability p_m is represented by 'mig-p_m' and the re-structuring configuration using a probability p_r is represented by 'rst-p_r'. The results are sorted by mean best performance.

4.5 Experiment 2: Comparison with Other Methods

A second experiment was performed to compare the best of these methods to a state-of-the-art variant of the PSO algorithm, as well as with some standard PSO configurations. Each PSO variant described below was tested using population sizes of 10, ..., 100 in steps of 5.

Table 1. Top 3 configurations, in terms of mean best performance, for each random neighborhood method (migration, re-structuring and static), given for each function

Popsize	Variant	Performance	Popsize	Variant	Performance
	Ackley			**Griewank-10**	
25	rst-0.10	1.32E-7 ± 3.23E-8	70	rst-0.04	4.96E-4 ± 6.69E-4
25	rst-0.09	1.65E-7 ± 4.69E-8	75	mig-0.8	5.63E-4 ± 5.28E-4
30	mig-0.5	1.06E-6 ± 1.53E-7	75	rst-0.01	6.30E-4 ± 5.93E-4
30	mig-0.7	1.29E-6 ± 1.87E-7	75	mig-0.5	6.82E-4 ± 5.97E-4
30	mig-0.1	1.48E-6 ± 3.81E-7	70	mig-0.3	7.22E-4 ± 6.81E-4
30	rst-0.05	1.52E-6 ± 2.24E-7	55	rst-0.02	8.87E-4 ± 9.25E-4
40	static	7.92E-5 ± 7.68E-6	85	static	1.54E-3 ± 6.84E-4
45	static	3.08E-4 ± 2.67E-5	60	static	1.76E-3 ± 1.21E-3
50	static	1.02E-3 ± 7.36E-5	65	static	2.12E-3 ± 1.34E-3
	Rastrigin			**Rosenbrock**	
65	mig-0.1	12.860 ± 1.234	45	rst-0.06	26.560 ± 0.192
65	mig-0.5	13.078 ± 1.053	50	mig-1.0	26.760 ± 0.084
60	mig-0.9	13.092 ± 1.076	50	rst-0.09	26.933 ± 0.130
60	rst-0.01	13.184 ± 1.141	55	rst-0.08	27.257 ± 0.118
55	rst-0.07	13.184 ± 1.086	45	mig-0.3	27.628 ± 2.358
60	rst-0.04	13.325 ± 1.157	65	mig-1.0	27.692 ± 0.067
65	static	13.580 ± 1.226	75	static	28.323 ± 0.084
60	static	13.603 ± 1.076	85	static	29.609 ± 0.162
55	static	14.657 ± 1.002	60	static	30.356 ± 4.274
	Schaffer-F6			**Sphere**	
75	rst-0.05	2.99E-4 ± 9.22E-5	20	rst-0.10	8.55E-15 ± 6.77E-15
95	mig-0.7	3.32E-4 ± 1.15E-4	20	rst-0.09	1.96E-14 ± 1.89E-14
75	rst-0.08	4.01E-4 ± 1.02E-4	20	rst-0.03	7.35E-14 ± 5.52E-14
80	rst-0.07	4.03E-4 ± 9.98E-5	20	mig-1.0	3.49E-13 ± 3.40E-13
90	mig-0.3	4.22E-4 ± 1.64E-4	25	mig-0.6	3.85E-13 ± 2.20E-13
90	mig-1.0	4.29E-4 ± 1.21E-4	25	mig-0.9	4.09E-13 ± 1.97E-13
100	static	4.32E-4 ± 1.13E-4	25	static	9.17E-12 ± 1.39E-11
95	static	5.62E-4 ± 2.25E-4	30	static	5.62E-11 ± 2.01E-11
70	static	5.65E-4 ± 1.92E-4	20	static	5.19E-10 ± 1.04E-9

It has been found that a PSO using FIPS with the von Neumann (a toroidal grid) neighborhood is usually a good choice for the optimization functions being considered. Thus, this was one of the PSO variants used for comparison in this experiment. Given a population size of n, the von Neumann neighborhood was configured into r rows and c columns, where r is the smallest integer less than or equal to $\sqrt{n}$ that evenly divides n and $c = n/r$. L-Best-1 and L-Best-2 were also tested with FIPS. The L-best-k topology consists of n nodes arranged in a ring, in which node i is connected to each node in $\{(i+j) \bmod n : j = \pm 1, \pm 2, \ldots, \pm k\}$. Some other standard PSO configurations were used; these were the canonical constriction factor PSO using the L-best-1, L-best-2 and von Neumann topologies. Finally the global neighborhood (gbest) was tested with the canonical PSO.

4.6 Results of Experiment 2

Table 2 summarizes the top performing configurations of the methods used for comparison. Only the best three methods out of the seven tested are shown. A prefix of 'fips' means FIPS was used, otherwise a canonical PSO was used; 'lb1', 'lb2' and 'von' stand for L-Best-1, L-Best-2 and von Neumann respectively.

Table 2. Top configurations in terms of mean best performance, of the schemes tested in experiment 2, given for each function. Only the best 3 are shown.

Popsize	Variant	Performance	Popsize	Variant	Performance
	Ackley			Griewank-10	
25	fips_lb2	2.83E-5 ± 3.80E-6	40	fips_lb2	4.82E-3 ± 2.53E-3
25	fips_von	2.92E-5 ± 5.19E-6	40	fips_von	5.40E-3 ± 3.15E-3
25	fips_lb1	5.64E-5 ± 1.33E-5	30	fips_lb1	8.04E-3 ± 2.90E-3
	Rastrigin			Rosenbrock	
30	fips_von	20.270 ± 1.843	40	fips_lb2	28.566 ± 2.225
30	fips_lb1	20.566 ± 1.530	55	fips_von	33.119 ± 3.811
30	fips_lb2	20.835 ± 2.070	40	fips_lb1	35.293 ± 7.976
	Schaffer-F6			Sphere	
35	von	3.81E-5 ± 4.61E-5	15	fips_lb2	1.94E-11 ± 2.94E-11
40	fips_lb1	3.81E-4 ± 1.73E-4	20	fips_von	6.31E-11 ± 4.17E-11
100	fips_lb2	4.86E-4 ± 1.78E-4	15	fips_lb1	2.02E-10 ± 2.52E-10

5 Analysis of Results

5.1 Methodology

When conducting experiments, it is necessary to follow a methodology that will validate the results. We often want to know if there is a significant difference between several approaches. The Wilcoxon rank-sum test is a non-parametric alternative to the two-sample t-test which is based solely on the order in which the observations from the two samples fall. It is valid for data from any distribution, Normal or not, and is much less sensitive to outliers than the two-sample t-test. When the assumptions of the two-sample t-test hold, the Wilcoxon test is somewhat less likely to detect a location shift than is the two-sample t-test. However, the losses in this regard are usually quite small [10].

We used Wilcoxon tests for two-sample comparisons and Kruskal-Wallis comparisons for 3 or more independent samples. The Kruskal-Wallis test is a non-parametric alternative to the one-way independent-samples ANOVA. Our results are presented using a symbolic encoding of the p-values, this improves readability and allows us to visually interpret the result of a test The p-values were coded as follows: **3** if $p < 0.01$; **2** if $0.01 \leq p < 0.05$; **1** if $0.05 \leq p < 0.1$ and - if $p \geq 0.1$

The standard cut-off for considering a p-value for a statistically significant difference is $p < 0.05$. For a single comparison, this indicates that the observed differences would occur by chance only 5% of the time. The probability of observing a sizable difference for one of the comparisons increases with the number of comparisons performed. For 20 independent comparisons, the probability of the observed differences occurring by chance increases to 64%. This is why it is important to correct the p-value of each test when performing multiple comparisons.

There are several p-value corrections that may be used. One of the simplest and common ones is the Bonferroni correction. It is very simple to apply: one simply multiplies each p-value by the number of tests performed. As a consequence, when performing 20 tests at a time, the highest accepted individual p-value is 0.0025. The main concern of this correction is to control the number of false positives. However, it does so at the expense of many false negatives.

The Bonferroni step-down (Holm) correction is very similar to the Bonferroni, but a little less stringent [11]. The p-values of of each test are ranked from the smallest to the largest. The smallest p-value is multiplied by the number of tests, t, the next by $t-1$, the one after that by $t-2$ and so on. Because it is a little less corrective as the p-value increases, this correction is less conservative. However, the family-wise error rate is very similar to the Bonferroni correction. We used the Holm correction in our analysis.

5.2 Discussion of the Results

The dynamic methods performed well, but different population sizes and dynamism probabilities are required in order to obtain such performance for different functions. The plots for Ackley, Griewank-10, Rastrigin and Sphere in figure 1 show that there is a basin-shaped region in which to find the best population size for these functions. Performance is best near the bottom of this basin; it is poor for small as well as for very large population sizes. The plots for all three random neighborhood methods follow the same general shape regardless of the probabilities used. Unfortunately, the widths and locations of these basins for the various functions are different. The Rosenbrock and Schaffer-F6 functions differ from this trend in that larger population sizes seem to give better performance.

Tables 1 and 2 suggest that the best configuration of re-structuring always generates the best performance in all functions. We performed pairwise two-tailed Wilcoxon tests using the Holm correction (table 3). This in conjunction with tables 1 and 2 shows that the best performance of re-structuring was indeed superior to the other methods on the Ackley, Rosenbrock and Sphere functions. It was better than the non-random methods on the Rastrigin function. On Griewank-10 it was better than the migration and static random methods, but no significant difference was found in comparison to the non-random methods. No significant difference was found with any of the other methods on Schaffer-F6.

Overall, the results suggest that using directed random graphs and dynamically changing the graph by probabilistic re-structuring improves the robustness of the algorithm in comparison to using non-random neighborhoods. Statistical evidence for this was obtained in 4 out of the 6 functions. We could not find a statistically significant difference for the other two. The results did not provide any indication of how to configure the random graphs or the rate of dynamism.

We decided to test for the importance of the effect of both the probability and population size parameters on the restructuring method. Table 4 shows the results of the two-sided Kruskal-Wallis tests of the effect of the probability of the restructuring method; the values were corrected using the Holm method. In most cases the difference is significant. The exceptions where the Schaffer function, Rosenbrock for all the population sizes below 50 and Griewank below 30. A similar test was conducted to account for the effect of population sizes, grouped by probability. As all p-values where below 0.01, we decided not to present the results in a table.

Table 3. Wilcoxon signed rank tests. The table compares re-structuring with other methods. von Neumann, L-Best-1 and L-Best-2 were used with FIPS.

	Wilcoxon Signed Rank Test of Re-Structuring Versus				
	Migration	Static	von Neumann	L-Best-1	L-Best-2
Ackley	3	3	3	3	3
Griewank-10	3	3	-	-	-
Rastrigin	-	-	3	3	3
Rosenbrock	3	3	3	3	3
Schaffer-F6	-	-	-	-	-
Sphere	3	3	3	3	3

Table 4. Kruskal-Wallis tests for the re-structuring method. Groupings consist of all probabilities for a given population size.

	Kruskal-Wallis Rank Sum Tests by Pop. Sizes																		
	10	15	20	25	30	35	40	45	50	55	60	65	70	75	80	85	90	95	100
Ackley	-	1	3	-	3	3	3	3	3	3	3	3	3	3	3	3	3	3	3
Griewank-10	-	-	-	-	-	3	3	3	-	3	3	3	3	3	3	3	3	3	3
Rastrigin	-	1	3	2	3	3	3	3	-	-	3	3	3	3	3	3	3	3	3
Rosenbrock	-	-	-	-	-	-	-	-	-	3	2	3	3	3	3	3	3	3	3
Schaffer-F6	-	-	-	-	-	-	-	-	-	-	-	-	-	-	-	-	-	-	-
Sphere	1	3	3	1	3	3	3	3	3	3	3	3	3	3	3	3	3	3	3

6 Conclusions

This paper looked at the effect of using random directed graphs with a uniform outdegree of five, in PSOs. Once generated at the beginning of the algorithm, the graphs were then either kept fixed throughout the run, or were modified during the run. Two forms of modification were considered; the first was a gradual type in which, probabilistically at each iteration, a randomly selected edge was moved in the graph (migration). The second was one in which the entire graph was re-initialized probabilistically (re-structuring) at each iteration. These methods were tested on a PSO using the fully informed neighborhood technique. Tests were performed using a benchmark of six optimization functions. The results were validated against commonly used and state of the art approaches in PSO.

The results indicate that probabilistic re-structuring is a good strategy for social topologies. On each function, our approach is never worse than any other, and in most cases it is the best. In most instances, statistical evidence was found to prove a clear superiority over the non-random methods. In two cases no such evidence was found; high p-values indicated that there was no statistical difference between re-structuring and the non-random methods. It was found that the interaction of population size and re-structuring probability affects the performance of the algorithm in most cases.

Previous studies show that that the correct choice of a specific fixed graph for use in PSO gives good results, but these graphs are difficult to code and to generalize. The fact that the random choice of social topologies works well indicates that there is no need for such fixed topologies. Further research is needed to improve these methods, especially to create rules about population sizes and dynamism probabilities. The reason for the performance of random dynamic topologies is an important outstanding question.

References

1. Kennedy, J., Eberhart, R.: Particle swarm optimization. In: Proc. of IEEE International Conference on Neural Networks, IEEE Press (1995) 1942–1948
2. Kennedy, J., Eberhart, R., Shi, Y.: Swarm Intelligence. Morgan Kaufmann (2001)
3. Mendes, R.: Population Toplogies and Their Influence in Particle Swarm Performance. PhD thesis, Universidade do Minho, Braga, Portugal (2004)
4. Ashlock, D., Smucker, M., Walker, J.: Graph based genetic algorithms. In: Proc. of the IEEE Congress on Evolutionary Computation, IEEE Press (1999) 1362–1368
5. Kennedy, J.: Stereotyping: Improving particle swarm performance with cluster analysis. In: Proc. of the IEEE Congress on Evolutionary Computation. (2000) 1507–1512
6. Suganthan, P.N.: Particle swarm optimiser with neighbourhood operator. In: Proc. of the IEEE Congress on Evolutionary Computation, IEEE Press (1999) 1958–1962
7. Mohais, A., Ward, C., Posthoff, C.: Randomized directed neighborhoods with edge migration in particle swarm optimization. In: Proc. of the 2004 IEEE Congress on Evolutionary Computation, IEEE Press (2004) 548–555
8. Clerc, M., Kennedy, J.: The particle swarm - explosion, stability, and convergence in a multidimensional complex space. IEEE Transactions on Evolutionary Computation **6** (2002) 58–73
9. Mendes, R., Kennedy, J., Neves, J.: The fully informed particle swarm: Simple, maybe better. IEEE Transactions on Evolutionary Computation **8** (2004) 204–210
10. Gouri K. Bhattacharyya, R.A.J.: Statistical Concepts and Methods. (May 1977)
11. Holm, S.: A simple sequentially rejective multiple test procedure. Scandinavian Journal of Statistics **6** (1979) 65–70

Understanding the Pheromone System Within Ant Colony Optimization

Stephen Gilmour and Mark Dras

Department of Computing, Macquarie University,
North Ryde, Australia 2109
{gilmour, madras}@ics.mq.edu.au

Abstract. Ant Colony Optimization (ACO) is a collection of meta-heuristics inspired by foraging in ant colonies, whose aim is to solve combinatorial optimization problems. We identify some principles behind the metaheuristics' rules; and we show that ensuring their application, as a correction to a published algorithm for the vertex cover problem, leads to a statistically significant improvement in empirical results.

1 Introduction

Ant Colony Optimization (ACO) is a collection of biologically inspired meta-heuristics for solving difficult combinatorial optimization problems (COPs); they were applied first to the Traveling Salesman Problem (TSP) [DG97] but since then to many other COPs. A general problem with many heuristic methods is the discovery of good parameter values. One approach is to systematically search the parameter space [DMC96]; another is to analyse the properties of the parameter space. The first strategy is interested in how to find the optimal parameters whereas the second strategy is interested in looking at what range of parameters will allow the system to work effectively. Although research has been done on what are good parameters for ACO algorithms, little research has been done as to how the ACO pheromone system actually works theoretically and what space the parameters can be selected from so that the system works effectively and efficiently. This paper is concerned with starting to explore the Ant Colony System (ACS) pheromone system in this direction. It is difficult to apply ACS to new problems when the variables within the problems do not correspond. Through our work we hope to give an understanding of how the ACS pheromone system should work so that translation between problems is less hit-and-miss.

2 ACS Pheromone System

ACO uses agents modelled on ants to find heuristic solutions to COPs. These agents communicate only indirectly by laying pheromone in the environment (*stigmergy*). The more pheromone a particular part of the environment contains, the more desirable that part of the environment becomes to the ants. This is how the ants find solutions.

The ACS pheromone system consists of two rules; one rule is applied whilst constructing solutions (local pheromone update rule) and the other rule is applied after all ants have finished constructing a solution (global pheromone update rule). These rules have different purposes. The purpose of the local pheromone update rule is to make "the visited edges less and less attractive as they are visited by ants, indirectly favouring the exploration of not yet visited edges. As a consequence, ants tend not to converge to a common path" [BDT99]. The purpose of the global pheromone update rule is to encourage ants "to search for paths in the vicinity of the best tour found so far" [BDT99]. Here, as an example, we look at the local pheromone update rule, which for the TSP is

$$\tau_{ij}(t) \longleftarrow (1-\rho) \cdot \tau_{ij}(t) + \rho \cdot \tau_0 \qquad (1)$$

where $\tau_{ij}(t)$ is the amount of pheromone on the edge (i,j) at time t; ρ is a parameter governing pheromone decay such that $0 < \rho < 1$; and τ_0 is the initial value of pheromone on all edges. Experimentally, the optimal value for ρ has been found to be 0.1 and a good formulation for τ_0 has been found to be $\tau_0 = \frac{1}{n \cdot L_{nn}}$, where n is the number of nodes in the graph, and L_{nn} is the length of the tour found by a nearest neighbour heuristic.

We now propose some properties for the local pheromone update rule. These are straightforward consequences of the rule definition above. It is possible to do the same for the global pheromone update rule; we give full details of our analysis and general approach in [GD05].

Property 1. *For every graph which contains a solution, since $L_{nn} \geq 1$ and $n \geq 2$, $0 < \tau_0 < 1$.*

Property 2. *For an edge (i,j) at time t, if $0 < \tau_{ij}(t) < 1$ then $0 < ((1-\rho) \cdot \tau_{ij}(t) + \rho \cdot \tau_0) < 1$.*

Property 3. *In the absence of the global pheromone update rule, for every edge (i,j), if $\tau_{ij}(t) > \tau_0$ then $\tau_{ij}(t+1) < \tau_{ij}(t)$.*

Property 4. *In the absence of the global pheromone update rule, for every edge (i,j), if $\tau_{ij}(t) < \tau_0$ then $\tau_{ij}(t+1) > \tau_{ij}(t)$.*

Property 5. *In the absence of the global pheromone update rule, for every edge (i,j), $\lim_{t \to \infty} \tau_{ij}(t) = \tau_0$*

3 Vertex Cover Problem

As one instance for analysis, [LDS04] give an ACS algorithm for the set covering problem. This algorithm fits the properties described here and in more detail in [GD05].

A second instance is the algorithm of Shyu et al [SYL04], an attempt to translate the Ant Colony System metaheuristic to the minimum weight vertex cover problem (MWVC problem). In the MWVC problem we want to find a subset of nodes within a graph such that every edge is covered by a node from this subset of nodes and such that the weight of the subset of nodes is minimised. The difficulty with this translation is that the MWVC problem contains two explicit parameters; the covering of all nodes and the minimisation of weight. This dual focus is not covered within Ant Colony System for the traveling salesman problem as it is only explicitly concerned with minimisation of weight. The forming of a cycle that visits every node occurs implicitly.

Because of this, Shyu et al have had to alter the traditional ACS rules so that they work for the MWVC problem; this has included slight alteration of the ACS pheromone rules. For example, in their new rule for the local pheromone update rule τ_0 is given as $\tau_0 = \frac{n(n-a)}{C}$, where n is the number of nodes within the graph; a is the number of nodes found in an initial approximation; and C is the total weight of the initial approximation.

However, their choices violate our proposed properties. The effect of these violations is that the local pheromone update rule will not encourage the shuffling of solutions to find new and better solutions and will encourage getting stuck in local minimums. Further, the amount of pheromone the global pheromone update rule is depositing will be significantly less than what the local pheromone update rule is depositing; this will cause the current best solution not to be reinforced but the pheromone will become lost among the noise from the local pheromone update rule. To correct this, as one example, we reformulate τ_0 as $\tau_0 = \frac{1}{n \cdot \sum_{j \in V'_{nn}} w(j)}$, where n is the number of nodes in the graph; $w(j)$ is the weight of node j; and V'_{nn} is the solution generated using a simple greedy algorithm.

4 Evaluation

We compared an implementation of the Shyu et al (SYL) algorithm with our own variant (GD). We ran both algorithms five times each on five different graphs, each with 400 nodes and 600 edges. We then repeated this with graphs containing 400 nodes and 800 edges. The weights on every edge were one. Each algorithm ran for 15 minutes. Results are in table 1.

As can be seen from these tables, our algorithm improved upon or equalled Shyu et al for every graph and in every run except one, where the difference was one node. We performed a paired t-test on the 25 pairs generated for the graphs with 600 edges and for the graphs with 800 edges; differences are statistically significant for both graph sizes ($p < 0.0001$).

5 Conclusion

The Ant Colony System metaheuristic is a useful approach for getting optimal or near-optimal solutions to difficult optimization problems. In this paper we have attempted to show that investigating the properties of the parameters in the

Table 1. Comparison on graphs with 400 nodes and 600 edges (top) and 400 nodes and 800 edges (bottom)

Graphs	1		2		3		4		5	
Algorithms	SYLH	GD	SYLH	GD	SYLH	GD	SYLH	GD	SYLH	GD
Runs										
1	215	212	212	208	215	214	211	210	211	210
2	209	208	213	210	213	212	214	215	212	210
3	211	211	220	213	216	215	214	208	212	211
4	209	205	208	201	210	207	218	215	203	200
5	211	203	211	209	213	212	210	209	213	212
Average	211	207.8	212.8	208.2	213.4	212	213.4	211.4	210.2	208.6
(SYL-GD)	3.2		4.6		1.4		2		1.6	

Graphs	1		2		3		4		5	
Algorithms	SYLH	GD	SYLH	GD	SYLH	GD	SYLH	GD	SYLH	GD
Runs										
1	225	222	229	223	226	220	230	226	228	225
2	221	218	228	227	227	224	229	223	229	227
3	227	225	227	217	223	219	220	220	228	227
4	226	225	223	222	232	224	221	220	227	224
5	228	223	229	223	220	219	232	226	227	223
Average	225.4	222.6	227.2	222.4	225.6	221.2	226.4	223	227.8	225.2
(SYL-GD)	2.8		4.8		4.4		3.4		2.6	

pheromone system for ACS, in addition to searching the parameter space, is important. Our empirical results show that a statistically significant improvement on a previous algorithm for the vertex cover problem is thereby possible.

References

[BDT99] Eric Bonabeau, Marco Dorigo, and Guy Theraulaz. *Swarm Intelligence From Natural to Artificial Systems*. A volume in the Santa Fe Institute studies in the science of complexity. Oxford University Press, 1999.

[DG97] Marco Dorigo and Luca Maria Gambardella. Ant colonies for the traveling salesman problem. *BioSystems*, 43:73–81, 1997.

[DMC96] Marco Dorigo, Vittorio Maniezzo, and Alberto Colorni. The Ant System: Optimization by a colony of cooperating agents. *IEEE Transactions on Systems, Man, and Cybernetics Part B: Cybernetics*, 26(1):29–41, 1996.

[GD05] Stephen Gilmour and Mark Dras. Understanding the Pheromone System within Ant Colony Optimmization. MS. Macquarie University, September 2005.

[LDS04] Lucas Lessing, Irina Dumitrescu, and Thomas Stützle. A Comparison between ACO Algorithms for the Set Covering Problem. *ANTS 2004, LNCS 3172*, pages 1–12, 2004.

[SYL04] Shyong Jian Shyu, Peng-Yeng Yin, and Bertrand M. T. Lin. An Ant Colony Optimization Algorithm for the Minimum Weight Vertex Cover Problem. *Annals of Operational Research*, 131:283–304, 2004.

Model Checking Sum and Product

H.P. van Ditmarsch[1], J. Ruan[1,*], and L.C. Verbrugge[2,**]

[1] University of Otago, New Zealand
{hans, jruan}@cs.otago.ac.nz
[2] University of Groningen, Netherlands
rineke@ai.rug.nl

Abstract. We model the well-known Sum-and-Product problem in a modal logic, and verify its solution in a model checker. The modal logic is public announcement logic. The riddle is then implemented and its solution verified in the epistemic model checker DEMO.

1 Introduction

The Sum-and-Product problem was first stated—in Dutch—in [1]:

A says to S and P: I have chosen two integers x, y such that $1 < x < y$ and $x + y \leq 100$. In a moment, I will inform S only of $s = x + y$, and P only of $p = xy$. These announcements remain private. You are required to determine the pair (x, y).
He acts as said. The following conversation now takes place:
1. P says: "I do not know it."
2. S says: "I knew you didn't."
3. P says: "I now know it."
4. S says: "I now also know it."
Determine the pair (x, y).

This problem is, that the agents' announcements *appear* to be uninformative, as they are about ignorance and knowledge and not about (numerical) facts, whereas *actually* they are very informative: the agents learn facts from the other's announcements. For example, the numbers cannot be 14 and 16: if they were, their sum would be 30. This is also the sum of 7 and 23. If those were the numbers their product would have been 161 which, as these are prime numbers, *only* is the product of 7 and 23. So Product (P) would have known the numbers, and therefore Sum (S)—if the sum had been 30—would have considered it possible that Product knew the numbers. But Sum said that he *knew* that Product didn't know the numbers. So the numbers cannot be 14 and 16. Sum and Product learn enough, by eliminations of which we gave an example, to be able to determine the pair of numbers: the unique solution of the problem is the pair (4, 13).

---
[*] Hans and Ji appreciate support from AOARD research grant AOARD-05-4017.
[**] Hans and Rineke appreciate support from the Netherlands Organization for Scientific Research (NWO).

Logical approaches to solve the problem are found in [2,3,4,5]. As far as we know, we are the first to use an automated model checker to tackle the Sum-and-Product problem.

In Section 2 we model the Sum-and-Product problem in public announcement logic. In Section 3 we implement the Sum-and-Product specification of Section 2 in DEMO and verify its epistemic features.

2 Public Announcement Logic

Public announcement logic is a dynamic epistemic logic and is an extension of standard multi-agent epistemic logic. Intuitive explanations of the epistemic part of the semantics can be found in [6]. We give a concise overview of the logic.

Language. Given are a set of agents N and a set of atoms Q. The language of public announcement logic is inductively defined as

$$\varphi ::= q \mid \neg\varphi \mid (\varphi \wedge \psi) \mid K_n\varphi \mid C_G\varphi \mid [\varphi]\psi$$

where $q \in Q$, $n \in N$, and $G \subseteq N$ are arbitrary. For $K_n\varphi$, read 'agent n knows formula φ'. For $C_G\varphi$, read 'group of agents G commonly know formula φ'. For $[\varphi]\psi$, read 'after public announcement of φ, formula ψ (is true)'.

Structures. An *epistemic model* $M = \langle W, \sim, V \rangle$ consists of a *domain* W of (factual) *states* (or 'worlds'), *accessibility* $\sim : N \to \mathcal{P}(W \times W)$, and a *valuation* $V : Q \to \mathcal{P}(W)$. For $w \in W$, (M, w) is an *epistemic state* (also known as a pointed Kripke model). For $\sim(n)$ we write $\sim_n$, and for $V(q)$ we write V_q.

Semantics. Assume an epistemic model $M = \langle W, \sim, V \rangle$.

$M, w \models q$ iff $w \in V_q$
$M, w \models \neg\varphi$ iff $M, w \not\models \varphi$
$M, w \models \varphi \wedge \psi$ iff $M, w \models \varphi$ and $M, w \models \psi$
$M, w \models K_n\varphi$ iff for all $v \in W : w \sim_n v$ implies $M, v \models \varphi$
$M, w \models C_G\varphi$ iff for all $v \in W : w \sim_G v$ implies $M, v \models \varphi$
$M, w \models [\varphi]\psi$ iff $M, w \models \varphi$ implies $M|\varphi, w \models \psi$

The group accessibility relation $\sim_G$ is the transitive and reflexive closure of the union of all access for the individuals in G: $\sim_G \equiv (\bigcup_{n \in G} \sim_n)^*$. Epistemic model $M|\varphi = \langle W', \sim', V' \rangle$ is defined as

$$W' = \{w' \in W \mid M, w' \models \varphi\}$$
$$\sim'_n = \sim_n \cap (W' \times W')$$
$$V'_q = V_q \cap W'$$

The dynamic modal operator $[\varphi]$ is interpreted as an epistemic state transformer. Announcements are assumed to be truthful, and this is commonly known by all agents. Therefore, the model $M|\varphi$ is the model M restricted to all the states where φ is true, including access between states. The dual of $[\varphi]$ is $\langle\varphi\rangle$: $M,w \models \langle\varphi\rangle\psi$ iff $M,w \models \varphi$ and $M|\varphi, w \models \psi$. Validity and logical consequence are defined in the standard way. For a proof system, see [7].

To give a specification of the Sum-and-Product problem in public announcement logic, first we need to determine the set of atomic propositions and the set of agents. Define $I \equiv \{(x,y) \in \mathbb{N}^2 \mid 1 < x < y \text{ and } x+y \leq 100\}$. Consider the variable x. If its value is 3, we can represent this information as the (truth of) the atomic proposition '$x = 3$'. Slightly more formally we can think of '$x = 3$' as a propositional letter x_3. Thus we create a (finite) set of atoms $\{x_i \mid (i,j) \in I\} \cup \{y_j \mid (i,j) \in I\}$. The set of agents is $\{S, P\}$; S and P will also be referred to as Sum and Product, respectively.

A proposition such as 'Sum knows that the numbers are 4 and 13' is described as $K_S(x_4 \wedge y_{13})$. The proposition 'Sum knows the (pair of) numbers' is described as $K_S(x,y) \equiv \bigvee_{(i,j)\in I} K_S(x_i \wedge y_j)$. Similarly, 'Product knows the numbers' is described as $K_P(x,y) \equiv \bigvee_{(i,j)\in I} K_P(x_i \wedge y_j)$. This is sufficient to formalize the announcements made towards a solution of the problem:

1. P says: "I do not know it": $\neg K_P(x,y)$
2. S says: "I knew you didn't": $K_S \neg K_P(x,y)$
3. P says: "I now know it": $K_P(x,y)$
4. S says: "I now also know it": $K_S(x,y)$

We can interpret these statements on an epistemic model $\mathcal{SP}_{(x,y)} \equiv \langle I, \sim, V \rangle$ consisting of a domain of all pairs $(x,y) \in I$ (as above), with accessibility relations $\sim_S$ and $\sim_P$ such that for Sum: $(x,y) \sim_S (x',y')$ iff $x+y = x'+y'$, and for Product: $(x,y) \sim_P (x',y')$ iff $xy = x'y'$; and with valuation V such that $V_{x_i} = \{(x,y) \in I \mid x = i\}$ and $V_{y_j} = \{(x,y) \in I \mid y = j\}$. The solution of the problem is represented by the truth of the statement

$$\mathcal{SP}_{(x,y)}, (4,13) \models \langle K_S \neg K_P(x,y)\rangle\langle K_P(x,y)\rangle\langle K_S(x,y)\rangle\top$$

or, properly expressing that $(4,13)$ is the only solution, by the model validity

$$\mathcal{SP}_{(x,y)} \models [K_S \neg K_P(x,y)][K_P(x,y)][K_S(x,y)](x_4 \wedge y_{13})$$

Note that announcement 1 by Product is superfluous in the analysis. The 'knew' in announcement 2, by Sum, refers to the truth of that announcement in the *initial* epistemic state, not in the epistemic state *resulting* from announcement 1, by Product.

3 The Epistemic Model Checker DEMO

Recently, epistemic model checkers have been developed to verify properties of interpreted systems, knowledge-based protocols, and various other multi-agent systems. The model checkers MCK [8] and MCMAS [9] have a temporal epistemic architecture, and exploration of the search space is based on ordered binary decision diagrams. The epistemic model checker DEMO, developed by Jan van

```
module SNP
where
import DEMO

pairs    = [(x,y)|x<-[2..100], y<-[2..100], x<y, x+y<=100]
numpairs = llength(pairs)
llength [] =0
llength (x:xs) = 1+ llength xs
ipairs = zip [0..numpairs-1] pairs

msnp :: EpistM
msnp = (Pmod [0..numpairs-1] val acc [0..numpairs-1])
  where
   val = [(w,[P x, Q y]) | (w,(x,y))<- ipairs]
   acc = [(a,w,v)|(w,(x1,y1))<-ipairs,(v,(x2,y2))<-ipairs,x1+y1==x2+y2 ]++
         [(b,w,v)|(w,(x1,y1))<-ipairs,(v,(x2,y2))<-ipairs,x1*y1==x2*y2 ]

fmrs1e = K a (Conj [Disj[Neg (Conj [Prop (P x),Prop (Q y)]),
          Neg (K b (Conj [Prop (P x),Prop (Q y)]))]| (x,y)<-pairs])
amrs1e = public (fmrs1e)
fmrp2e = Conj [(Disj[Neg (Conj [Prop (P x),Prop (Q y)]),
          K b (Conj [Prop (P x),Prop (Q y)]) ] )|(x,y)<-pairs]
amrp2e = public (fmrp2e)
fmrs3e = Conj [(Disj[Neg (Conj [Prop (P x),Prop (Q y)]),
          K a (Conj [Prop (P x),Prop (Q y)]) ] )|(x,y)<-pairs]
amrs3e = public (fmrs3e)

solution = showM (upds msnp [amrs1e, amrp2e, amrs3e])
```

Fig. 1. The DEMO program SNP.hs. Comment lines have been removed.

Eijck [10], is not based on temporal epistemics. DEMO is short for Dynamic Epistemic MOdelling. It allows modelling epistemic updates, graphical display of Kripke structures involved, and formula evaluation in epistemic states. DEMO is written in the functional programming language Haskell. The model checker DEMO implements the dynamic epistemic logic of [7]. For a comparative study of these three model checkers, on a different problem, see [11]. We have specified the 'Sum and Product riddle' in DEMO only. The verification of a comparable specification in MCK exceeds its computational power (and this is also to be expected for MCMAS), although clever restriction of variables might well bring such verification with reach.

Figure 1 contains the specification of the Sum and Product riddle in DEMO. The set $I \equiv \{(x,y) \in \mathbb{N}^2 \mid 1 < x < y \text{ and } x+y \leq 100\}$ is realized in DEMO as the list pairs = [(x,y)| x<-[2..100], y<-[2..100], x<y, x+y<=100]. A pair such as (4, 18) is not a proper name for a domain element. In DEMO, natural numbers are such proper names. Therefore, we associate each element in pairs with a natural number and make a new list ipairs = zip [0..numpairs-1] pairs. Here, numpairs is the number of elements in pairs, and the function zip pairs the i-th element in [0..numpairs-1] with the i-th element in pairs, and makes that the i-th element of ipairs.

The initial model msnp of the Sum-and-Product riddle (see Figure 1) is a multi-pointed epistemic model, that consists—this is the line msnp = (Pmod [0..numpairs-1] val acc [0..numpairs-1]) in the program—of a domain [0..numpairs-1], a valuation function val, an accessibility relation function acc, and [0..numpairs-1] points. As the points of the model are the entire domain, we may think of this initial epistemic state as the (not-pointed) epistemic model underlying it.

The valuation function val maps each state in the domain to the subset of atoms that are true in that state. This is different from our previous definition of a valuation V, but the correspondence $q \in \text{val}(w)$ iff $w \in V(q)$ is elementary. An element (w,[P x, Q y]) in val means that in state w, atoms P x and Q y are true. For example, given that (0,(2,3)) is in ipairs, P 2 and Q 3 are true in state 0, where P 2 stands for 'the smaller number is 2' and Q 3 stands for 'the larger number is 3'. These same facts were described in the previous section by x_2 and y_3, respectively, as that gave the closest match with the original problem formulation. In DEMO, names of atoms *must* start with capital P, Q, R.

The function acc specifies the accessibility relations. Agent a represents Sum and agent b represents Product. For (w,(x1,y1)) and (v,(x2,y2)) in ipairs, if their sum is the same: x1+y1==x2+y2, then they cannot be distinguished by Sum: (a,w,v) in acc; and if their product is the same: x1*y1==x2*y2, then they cannot be distinguished by Product: (b,w,v) in acc. Function ++ is an operation merging two lists.

Sum and Product's announcements are modelled as structures called 'singleton action models', generated by the announced formula (precondition) φ and an operation public. For our purposes it is sufficient to focus on that precondition.

Consider $K_S \neg \bigvee_{(i,j) \in I} K_P(x_i \wedge y_j)$, expressing that Sum says: "I knew you didn't." This is equivalent to $K_S \bigwedge_{(i,j) \in I} \neg K_P(x_i \wedge y_j)$. A conjunct $\neg K_P(x_i \wedge y_j)$ in that expression, for 'Product does not know that the pair is (i,j)', is equivalent to $(x_i \wedge y_j) \rightarrow \neg K_P(x_i \wedge y_j)$. The latter is computationally cheaper to check in the model, than the former: in all states but (i,j) of the model, the latter requires a check on two booleans only, whereas the former requires a check *in each of those states* of Product's ignorance, that relates to his equivalence class for that state, and that typically consists of several states. This explains that the check on $\bigwedge_{(i,j) \in I} \neg K_P(x_i \wedge y_j)$ can be replaced by one on $\bigwedge_{(i,j) \in I}((x_i \wedge y_j) \rightarrow \neg K_P(x_i \wedge y_j))$. Using a model validity, the check on $\bigvee_{(i,j) \in I} K_P(x_i \wedge y_j)$ (Product knows the numbers) can also be replaced, namely by a check $\bigwedge_{(i,j) \in I}((x_i \wedge y_j) \rightarrow K_P(x_i \wedge y_j))$. Using these observations, and writing an implication $\varphi \rightarrow \psi$ as $\neg \varphi \vee \psi$, the three problem announcements 2, 3, and 4 listed on page 792 are checked in DEMO in by the formulas fmrs1e, fmrp2e, and fmrs3e, respectively, as listed in Figure 1. The corresponding singleton action models are obtained by applying the function public, for example, amrs1e = public (fmrs1e).

The riddle is solved by updating the initial model msnp with the action models corresponding to the three successive announcements:

```
*SNP> showM (upds msnp [amrs1e, amrp2e, amrs3e])
==> [0]
[0]
(0,[p4,q13])
(a,[[0]])
(b,[[0]])
```

This function showM displays a pointed epistemic model with, on successive lines, point [0], domain [0]—after each update, states are renumbered starting from 0—, valuation (0, [p4,q13])—representing the facts P 4 and Q 13, i.e., the solution pair (4, 13)—, and accessibility relations (a, [[0]]) and (b, [[0]])—Sum and Product have full knowledge, as their access is the indentity. Intermediate results of the computation can also be given. For the complete output of such interaction, see www.cs.otago.ac.nz/staffpriv/hans/sumpro/.

References

1. Freudenthal, H.: (formulation of the sum-and-product problem). Nieuw Archief voor Wiskunde **3(17)** (1969) 152
2. McCarthy, J.: Formalization of two puzzles involving knowledge. In Lifschitz, V., ed.: Formalizing Common Sense : Papers by John McCarthy. Ablex series in artificial intelligence. Ablex Publishing Corporation, Norwood, N.J. (1990) original manuscript dated 1978–1981.
3. Plaza, J.: Logics of public communications. In Emrich, M., Pfeifer, M., Hadzikadic, M., Ras, Z., eds.: Proceedings of the 4th International Symposium on Methodologies for Intelligent Systems. (1989) 201–216
4. Panti, G.: Solution of a number theoretic problem involving knowledge. International Journal of Foundations of Computer Science **2(4)** (1991) 419–424
5. van der Meyden, R.: Mutual belief revision. In Doyle, J., Sandewall, E., Torasso, P., eds.: Proceedings of the 4th international conference on principles of knowledge representation and reasoning (KR), Morgan Kaufmann (1994) 595–606
6. Fagin, R., Halpern, J., Moses, Y., Vardi, M.: Reasoning about Knowledge. MIT Press, Cambridge MA (1995)
7. Baltag, A., Moss, L., Solecki, S.: The logic of public announcements, common knowledge, and private suspicions. Technical report, Centrum voor Wiskunde en Informatica, Amsterdam (1999) CWI Report SEN-R9922.
8. Gammie, P., van der Meyden, R.: MCK: Model checking the logic of knowledge. In Alur, R., Peled, D., eds.: Proceedings of the 16th International conference on Computer Aided Verification (CAV 2004), Springer (2004) 479–483
9. Raimondi, F., Lomuscio, A.: Verification of multiagent systems via ordered binary decision diagrams: An algorithm and its implementation. In: 3rd International Joint Conference on Autonomous Agents and Multiagent Systems (AAMAS 2004), IEEE Computer Society (2004) 630–637
10. van Eijck, J.: Dynamic epistemic modelling. Technical report, Centrum voor Wiskunde en Informatica, Amsterdam (2004) CWI Report SEN-E0424.
11. van Ditmarsch, H., van der Hoek, W., van der Meyden, R., Ruan, J.: Model checking russian cards. Electronic Notes in Theoretical Computer Science (2005) To appear; presented at MoChArt 05 (Model Checking in Artificial Intelligence).

The Proof Algorithms of Plausible Logic Form a Hierarchy

David Billington

School of Information and Communication Technology,
Nathan campus, Griffith University, Brisbane, Queensland 4111, Australia
d.billington@griffith.edu.au

Abstract. Plausible Logic is a non-monotonic logic with an efficient implementation. Plausible Logic has five proof algorithms, one is monotonic and four are non-monotonic. These five proof algorithms form a hierarchy. Ambiguity propagating proof algorithms are less risky than ambiguity blocking proof algorithms. The hierarchy shows that the benefit of using the riskier algorithms is that more formulas can be proved. Unlike previous Plausible Logics, the Plausible Logic in this paper is relatively consistent, checks for loops, can prove all its facts and all tautologies, and allows countably many formulas and rules to be considered.

1 Introduction

The Plausible Logics before 2003 (for example [2]), although able to prove more than the Plausible Logics after 2002, could not be shown to have the important property of relative consistency (see theorem 3.1). The Plausible Logic of [3], say PL03, was relatively consistent but could not check for loops, could not prove all its facts and all tautologies, and could manage only finitely many formulas and rules. The Plausible Logic of [1], say PL04, just added loop checking to PL03. However the Plausible Logic in this paper is relatively consistent, checks for loops, can prove all its facts and all tautologies, and allows countably many formulas and rules to be considered. All the major properties of PL04 have been proved for the logic in this paper.

Plausible Logic has five proof algorithms, one is monotonic and four are non-monotonic. Often a formula can be proved using some of the algorithms but not the others. So what is the relationship between these algorithms? The main result of this paper is to classify these five algorithms into a hierarchy. Unfortunately, in general, this hierarchy is not a chain (that is a tree with only one leaf), but a tree with two leaves. However under some reasonable conditions the hierarchy becomes a chain, but at the cost of making two of the proof algorithms the same.

The paper is organised into three sections. An intuitive understanding of Plausible Logic is provided in section 2. Some properties of Plausible Logic, including the hierarchy results, are presented in section 3.

2 Overview of Plausible Logic

This section provides an intuitive understanding of Plausible Logic.

The factual and defeasible information with which Plausible Logic reasons is represented by strict rules, plausible rules, defeater rules, and a priority relation on the rules. A rule which contains free variables is treated as a rule schema, and so regarded as an abbreviation for the set of ground instances of the rule. Thus Plausible Logic is essentially propositional. All rules have the form "finite-set-of-literals arrow literal".

Strict rules, for example $A \rightarrow l$, represent the aspects of a situation which are certain. If all the literals in A are proved then l can be deduced, no matter what the evidence against l is. So strict rules behave like material implication. An atomic fact is represented by a strict rule with an empty antecedent. For example, "Emma is an emu." is represented by $\{\} \rightarrow emu(emma)$.

More generally a clausal fact with n literals is represented by n strict rules. For instance, $\vee\{a, b, c\}$ is represented by the following three strict rules: $\{\neg b, \neg c\} \rightarrow a$, $\{\neg a, \neg c\} \rightarrow b$, $\{\neg a, \neg b\} \rightarrow c$. All factual information must first be transformed into a set Ax of clauses. Ax and all its resolvents form a set from which only the essential clauses are then converted into strict rules. For example, "Emus are birds." is thought of as the strict rule (schema) $emu(x) \rightarrow bird(x)$, which is transformed into the clause $\vee\{\neg emu(x), bird(x)\}$ which is then converted into the two strict rules $emu(x) \rightarrow bird(x)$ and its contrapositive $\neg bird(x) \rightarrow \neg emu(x)$. (If the antecedent of a rule is a singleton set then we often omit the set braces.)

Plausible rules, for example $A \Rightarrow l$, represent some of the aspects of a situation which are plausible. If all the literals in A are proved then l can be deduced provided that all the evidence against l has been nullified. So we take $A \Rightarrow l$ to mean that, in the absence of evidence against l, A is sufficient evidence for concluding l. For example, "Birds usually fly." is represented by $bird(x) \Rightarrow fly(x)$. The idea is that if we know that something is a bird, then we may conclude that it flies, unless there is other evidence suggesting that it may not fly.

A defeater rule, for example $A \rightsquigarrow \neg l$, is evidence against l. In the absence of other rules, $A \rightsquigarrow \neg l$ means that if A is not disproved then it is too risky to conclude l. Defeater rules are used to prevent conclusions which would be too risky. For example, "Sick birds might not fly." is represented by $\{sick(x), bird(x)\} \rightsquigarrow \neg fly(x)$. The idea is that a bird being sick is not sufficient evidence to conclude that it does not fly; it is only evidence against the conclusion that it usually flies. Another use for defeater rules is to cut chains of plausible rules which are too long. For instance, given $a \Rightarrow b$ and $b \Rightarrow c$ it may be too risky to conclude that c holds given that a holds. In which case we could add the defeater rule $a \rightsquigarrow \neg c$. The point is that adding $a \Rightarrow \neg c$ instead of $a \rightsquigarrow \neg c$ would be wrong, because accepting a is not a reason for accepting $\neg c$, indeed it is a weak reason for accepting c.

The priority relation, $>$, on the set of rules allows the representation of preferences among rules. The priority relation must be acyclic. Moreover only plausible rules can occur on the left of $>$; and strict rules must not occur on either side of $>$. For example consider the following (Tweety triangle) situation.

$R1$: $\{\} \rightarrow quail(Quin)$ [Quin is a quail.]
$R2$: $quail(x) \rightarrow bird(x)$ [Quails are birds.]
$R3$: $\neg bird(x) \rightarrow \neg quail(x)$ [Contrapositive of $R2$.]
$R4$: $bird(x) \Rightarrow fly(x)$ [Birds usually fly.]
$R5$: $quail(x) \Rightarrow \neg fly(x)$ [Quails usually do not fly.]

We want to conclude that usually Quin does not fly. But this can only be done if we prefer $R5$ to $R4$, hence we define $R5 > R4$.

Most non-monotonic logics do not distinguish between formulas proved using only factual information and those proved using defeasible information. Plausible Logic does. Indeed Plausible Logic distinguishes between formulas proved with each of five different proof algorithms. It does this by attaching the name of the algorithm to the formula being proved. The five algorithms are denoted by μ, α, π, β, and δ. So instead of proving $\neg fly(Quin)$ we actually prove $\lambda\neg fly(Quin)$, where $\lambda \in \{\mu, \alpha, \pi, \beta, \delta\}$. The μ algorithm is monotonic (μ for monotonic) and only uses the factual information. It is essentially classical propositional logic. The other four algorithms use all the available information and are non-monotonic.

An atom a is *ambiguous* if and only if neither a nor its negation, $\neg a$, can be proved. (This is a slight change from the more complicated definition of ambiguous in [4].) Suppose there is evidence for b. If a is ambiguous and a is evidence for $\neg b$ then what should be concluded about b? A logic is *ambiguity blocking* if it can conclude b; and it is *ambiguity propagating* if b is ambiguous, because the ambiguity of a has been propagated to b. So ambiguity propagation gives more reliable answers than ambiguity blocking.

The π algorithm propagates ambiguity (π for propagates). The β algorithm blocks ambiguity (β for blocks) and has been used in every Plausible Logic. The α algorithm is the conjunction (α for and) of the π and β algorithms, and the δ algorithm is the disjunction (δ for disjunction) of the π and β algorithms.

A plausible theory, $T = (R, >)$, consists of a set of rules R and its priority relation $>$, which may be empty. The task of proving a formula is done by a recursive function P called the proof function of T. The input to P is the proof algorithm to be used, the formula to be proved, and the empty set. The empty set is an initially empty storage bin into which is put all the literals which are currently being proved as P recursively calls itself. The purpose of this bin is to detect loops. The output of P is either $+1$, 0, or -1. Essentially we have a three valued logic in which $+1$ denotes proved, 0 denotes loops, and -1 denotes that there is a demonstration that the formula is not provable and does not generate a loop.

3 Some Properties of Plausible Logic

Many properties of Plausible Logic have been proved, but perhaps the most important is relative consistency. This is important because it shows that the deductive mechanism does not introduce any inconsistencies.

Theorem 3.1. (Relative Consistency)
If T is a plausible theory and all the facts of T are consistent then the set $T(+\lambda)$ of everything provable from T using λ is consistent.
End3.1.

The five proof algorithms form a hierarchy (see theorem 3.2). Most other non-monotonic logics have only one proof mechanism and so force the user to accept either the blocking or the propagation of ambiguity. With Plausible Logic the user can choose either sort of proof mechanism.

Theorem 3.2. (Hierarchy)
Let T be a plausible theory.
(1) $T(+\mu) \subseteq T(+\alpha) \subseteq T(+\pi) \subseteq T(+\delta)$.
(2) $T(+\mu) \subseteq T(+\beta)$.
End3.2.

Unfortunately β cannot be placed in the chain of theorem 3.2(1) unless there are extra conditions, as in the next result. Define λ to be *nice* iff whenever f is a clause or a dual-clause and B be a set of literals and $P(\lambda f, B) = +1$ then $P(\lambda \sim f, B) = -1$.

Theorem 3.3. (Nice Hierarchy)
Let T be a plausible theory.
(1) If β or δ is nice then $\beta = \delta$, and β and δ are nice.
(2) If β or δ is nice then $T(+\mu) \subseteq T(+\alpha) \subseteq T(+\pi) \subseteq T(+\beta) = T(+\delta)$.
End3.3.

Although niceness is just what is needed to insert β into the chain of theorem 3.2(1), it does so by effectively making β and δ the same.

References

[1] David Billington. A Plausible Logic which Detects Loops. In *Proceedings of the Tenth International Workshop on Nonmonotonic Reasoning*, pages 65-71, Whistler BC Canada, June 2004.

[2] David Billington and Andrew Rock. Propositional Plausible Logic: Introduction and Implementation. *Studia Logica* 67:243-269, 2001.

[3] D. Billington, A. Rock. Constructive Plausible Logic is Relatively Consistent. *Proceedings of the 16th Australian Conference on Artificial Intelligence*, 2003, Lecture Notes in Artificial Intelligence vol. 2903, 954-965. Springer 2003.

[4] Guido Governatori, Michael J. Maher, Grigoris Antoniou, and David Billington. Argumentation Semantics for Defeasible Logic. *Journal of Logic and Computation*, 14(5) (2004), 675-702. Oxford University Press 2004.

A Maximum Entropy Model for Transforming Sentences to Logical Form*

Minh Le Nguyen, Akira Shimazu, and Hieu Xuan Phan

Japan Advanced Institute of Science and Technology
{nguyenml, shimazu, hieuxuan}@jaist.ac.jp
http://www.jaist.ac.jp/ nguyenml
Japan Advanced Institute of Science, Nomi 1-8,
923-1292 Ishikawa, Japan

Abstract. We formulate the problem of transformation natural language sentences as the determination of sequence of actions that transforms an input sentence to its logical form. The model to determine a sequence of actions for a corresponding sentence is automatically estimated from a corpus of sentences and their logical forms with a MEM framework. Experimental results show that the MEM framework are suitable for the transformation problem and archived a comparable result in comparison with other methods.

1 Introduction

Semantic parsing has been an interesting problem in NLP as it would very likely be part of any interesting NLP applications, particularly those that would require translation of a natural language input to a specific command.

Transforming natural language sentence to its logical forms are subtasks of semantic parsing which refer to the process of mapping a natural language input (a sentence) to some meaning representation structures which are suitable for manipulation by a machine [1].

The task of transforming a natural language sentence to a logical form was formulated as the task of determining a sequence of actions that transforms the given input sentence to a logical form[2][3][4]. The main problem is how to learn a set of rules from the corpus. For that purpose the inductive logical programming approaches were proposed in the previous work. The obstacle of this approach (ILP) is that it is quite complex and slow to acquire parsers for mapping sentences to logical forms. The advantage of the ILP method is that we do not need to design features for learning a set of rules from corpus.

While statistical machine learning (SML) are applied successful to the domain of natural language processing[5], the application of it to the transforming problem has not been reported yet. In this paper, we investigate the performance of SML to the transforming problem by employing a kind of maximum entropy models with various feature sets. With the framework of MEM for transformation NL to logical form presented in this paper, we initially draw a novel

---

* The work on this paper was supported by a Monbukagakusho 21st COE Program.

application of using statistical machine learning to the difficult and challenging problem - the transformation task.

The rest of this paper are organized as follow: Section 1 introduces briefly the problem of transforming natural language to logical forms. Section 2 then describes the shift-reduce models to this problem. Section 3 proposes our method using maximum entropy models to the transforming natural language sentences to logical forms. Section 4 shows experiment results and Section 5 discusses the advantage of our methods and future works.

2 Shift-Reduce Model for Transforming NL to Logical Forms

We show the architecture of the shift-reduce model on transforming natural sentences to logical forms[2]. We use only one stack and five kinds of actions as follows.

- Shift: Simply push a word into stack
- Assign (X,Y): Assign a phrase X with a term Y
- Binds[X,Y],n_1, n_2, a_1, a_2: Unify the n_1th argument of the term X with the n_2th argument of term Y if X and Y are on stack having arity a_1 and a_2, respectively
- DROP(X,Y, a_1, a_2, n_2): Place the term Y in the n_2 argument of the term X to form a new conjunct if X comes before Y on the parse stack having arity a_1 and a_2, respectively.

To transform a sentence to a logical form using a shift-reduce model we have to determine a sequence of actions. One of method for solving the problem is to use machine learning to determine actions by learn automatically from a corpus of sentences and its logical forms. The initial CHILL system[2][3] used (inductive logic programming) ILP to learn Prolog control rules and employed deterministic parsing, using the learned rules to decide the appropriate parse action for each state.

3 Transforming NL to Logical Form with MEM

This section describes a novel method for transforming NL sentences to logical form under maximum entropy framework. First, we introduce the principle of maximum entropy models. Second, we describe the features using to transform NL sentences to logical forms by MEM as well as a method creating training examples for MEM.

3.1 Maximum Entropy Models

Maximum entropy models [6], do not make unnecessary independence assumptions. Therefore, we are able to optimally integrate together whatever sources of knowledge we believe to be potentially useful to the transformation task within the maximum entropy model. The maximum entropy model will be able to exploit these features which are beneficial and effectively ignore those that are irrelevant. We model the probability of a class c given a vector of features x according to the ME formulation:

$$p(c|x) = \frac{\exp[\sum_{i=0}^{n} \lambda_i f_i(c,x)]}{Z_x}$$

Here Z_x is the normalization constant, $f_i(c,x)$ is a feature function which maps each class and vector element to a binary feature, n is the total number of features, and λ_i is a weight for a given feature function.

3.2 Features

First, we convert a logical form to a tree structure in which a path of tree nodes started from the root to the leaf node and combines to a string.

As to the MEM model we incorporate the following set of templates which are used to generate set of features for the maximum entropy model.

- paction: previous action
- wi+i and wi-i: the word position
- s+i and s-i: the sub trees in the stack position
- The conjunctions between two sub tree in the stack position (i.e s+i&s+i+1) are used as features.
- stack-num: the number of elements in the stack
- s-arg+i and s-arg-i: the number of arguments within s+i and s-i
- s-p+i and s-p-i: the path tree information of each s+i and s-i. The path tree is either the first child node or the last child node.
- The conjunctions between the path tree information and the subtree are used (i.e s+i&s-p+i-1)
- We also consider part of speech (pos tags) of each words as linguistic information for our feature set. To obtained these syntactic information we used the Charniak's syntactic parser[7].

These template features are used to observer feature functions $f_i(x,c)$ from the training data. After that weight values λ_i will be estimated via a learning algorithm such as the L-BFGs algorithm [8].

4 Experimental Results

To illustrate our MEM model for transforming NL sentences to logical forms, we experimented it on the corpus of previous work[3] which includes 880 pairs of sentences and their logical forms. Here is an example about the corpus.

- answer(A,count(B,(city(B),loc(B,C), const(C,countryid(usa))),A))
- How many cities are there in the US?

4.1 Training Results

Generating all training data from corpus, we converted it to the format of maximum entropy model. To evaluate the training result we used the cross-validation test(10-fold), in which 880 pairs o f sentences and its logic form are obtained from the previous works[3]. After generating training examples we obtained approximately 8,210 training examples, using the L-BFGs estimation via maximum entropy model and ten-fold cross validation test, the average accuracy of the model is 84.2% after 50 routes of the L-BFGs algorithm [8]. This result shows that using statistical machine learning for transforming NL sentences to logical forms seems to be promising. It also claims that our implemented features are good for this task. We also use pos tags information as some more features for the MEM which described in the previous section. Using ten-folds cross validation test, the average accuracy of the model is 85.7% after 50 routes of the L-BFGs algorithm which results show that the syntactic information (i.e the pos tag information) is useful for the transformation task.

To training our model we implemented a maximum entropy model[1], and let it as a free open source code in C++.

4.2 Testing Results

We also used 10-fold cross-validation test for testing data. We evaluate the performance of our system using precession and recall as follows. Our goal is to compare the transformation output of our system with the gold-standard output[4]. Assuming that we obtain a transformation output and represent it to a tree. We call a correct node if it is in the gold-standard output.

$$precision = \frac{\#correct-nodes}{\#nodes-in-output-trees}$$
$$recall = \frac{\#correct-nodes}{\#nodes-in-gold-standard-trees}$$

With this evaluation score, we obtained the precision 0.88 and the recall 0.46 for without using pos tag features (MEM). We also obtained 0.89 precision and 0.46 recall for using pos tag features (MEM-pos). In both cases, the high precision means that our results usually are confident logical form and the number of nodes in an output is smaller than the number of nodes in the gold-standard output. The higher precision of MEM-pos comparing to MEM shows that syntactic information are necessary for the transformation task. The results also clearly indicated that using statistical machine learning for transforming logical is promising.

In the current time, we do not compare our results with the previous work directly because they has to use a [9] query system to compute the precision and recall score. However their results also reflect that the precision is high (87.75%) while the recall is not high (53.41%). In addition, our evaluation method described in this paper indicated that we could evaluate the transformation result independently with a query system.

---

[1] http://www.jaist.ac.jp/~hieuxuan/flexcrfs/flexcrfs.html

Table 1. Experiment results with GEOQUERY corpus

Method	Precision	Recall
MEM	0.88	0.49
MEM-pos	0.89	0.51

5 Conclusions

We have proposed a novel method of transforming NL sentence to logical form with statistical machine learning via maximum entropy models. Our contributions are selecting a number of useful features for transforming sentences to logical form under the MEM framework. Experimental results show that the MEM model is suitable for the transforming task. In addition, the technical presented in the paper also provides a general framework of using statistical learning for the transformation NL sentences to logical form task.

References

1. Allen, J. F. 1995. Natural Language Understanding (2nd Edition). Mento Park, CA: Benjaming/Cumming
2. J.M. Zelle and R.J. Mooney: Learning to parse database queries using inductive logic programming. In Proceedings of the Third teen National Conference on Artificial Intelligence, AAAI-96, 1050-1055.
3. L.R. Tang: Integrating Top-down and Bottom-up Approaches in Inductive Logic Programming: Applications in Natural Language Processing and Relation Data mining. Ph.D. Dissertation, Department of Computer Sciences, University of Texas, Austin, TX.
4. J.R. Mooney: Learning semantic Parsers: An Important but Under-Studied problem   AAAI 2004 Spring Symposium on Language Learning: An Interdisciplinary Perspective, pp. 39-44, Stanford, CA. March,
5. D.C. Manning and H. Schutze: Foundation of Statistical Natural Language Processing. Cambridge, MA: MIT Press.
6. A.L. Berger, V. J.D. Pietra, and S.A.D. Pietra, A maximum entropy approach to natural language proceesing. Computational Linguistic, 22(1):39-71.
7. E. Charniak: A Maximum-Entropy-Inspired Parser. 6th Applied Natural Language Processing Conference, April 29 - May 4, Seattle, Washington, USA, pp 132-139, 2000.
8. D.C. Liu and J. Nocedal. On the limited memory BFGS method for large-scale optimization. Mathematical Programing, 45: 503-528.
9. R.J. Kate, Y.W. Wong, R. Ge, and R.J. Mooney. Learning to Transform Naturalto Formal Languages, Pittsburgh, PA, pp. 1062–1068, July 2005.

An Information-Theoretic Causal Power Theory

Lucas R. Hope and Kevin B. Korb

School of Information Technology,
Monash University, Clayton, Victoria 3800, Australia
{lhope, korb}@csse.monash.edu.au

Abstract. A metric of causal power can assist in developing and using causal Bayesian networks. We introduce a metric based upon information theory. We show that it generalizes prior metrics restricted to linear and noisy-or models, while providing a metric appropriate to the full representational power of Bayesian nets.

1 Introduction

The causal interpretation of Bayesian networks has risen greatly in prominence since the development of causal discovery algorithms (Verma and Pearl, 1990; Spirtes et al., 2000; Neapolitan, 2004). However, the causal interpretation brings with it a host of difficulties, philosophical and technical, leading to various current research efforts, such as the attempt to couple the philosophical theories of probabilistic causality with causal Bayesian networks (e.g., Halpern and Pearl, 2001; Twardy and Korb, 2004).

Another long-standing research problem in philosophy and psychology has been to develop a formal theory of causal power. As causation comes in degrees, causal explanatory power — the normative attribution of an effect to one of its causes — ought also to come in degrees.

The development of a well-founded metric of causal power promises to be of wide interest: as a normative standard for assessing causal attributions; as an aid in designing Bayesian networks, by providing guidance in the interpretation of prototypes; for understanding and using probabilistic expert systems; and also for the growing collaboration between AI and philosophy of science, in understanding, for example, the nature of scientific explanation.

Here we review the best known prior theories, from I.J. Good (1961) to Cheng (1997), Glymour (2001) and Hiddleston (2005). A problem common to all of these theories is that they find their inspiration in simple linear (or additive) models of causality. Whereas simplicity can be an asset in developing a theory, it can be an impediment when attempting to generalize; this is the predicament of causal power theory. In particular, the transitive nature of causality in linear models has seduced some into thinking that causality is in general transitive. However, it is not, as Christopher Hitchcock (2001) and others have shown. In response, we offer an information-theoretic metric of causal power applicable to non-linear Bayesian networks, while also illustrating their application to linear models.

2 A History of Causal Power

2.1 Good's Causal Calculus

The first serious attempt to provide a formal theory of causal power is that of I.J. Good (1961). Good's formulation seems motivated by a desire for a theory analagous to circuit theory. Causal strength (Q) is analogous to conductivity, and he defines a kind of 'causal resistance' (R) to parallel circuit resistance. In circuits, resistors in series are additive; in turn, Good's causal resistance is additive along a causal chain. Conductivity and causal power, on the other hand, are additive in parallel. In circuits, conductivity is the reciprocal of resistance; similar to this, Good's causal strength and causal resistance are related thus: $e^{-R} + e^{-Q} = 1$.

Good's definition of causal strength for a direct causal link is $Q_{link}(E:C) = -\log \frac{1-p}{1-q}$,[1] where $p = P(e|c)$ and $q = P(e|\neg c)$. Good stipulates that Q_{link} be non-negative, so where the formula above would yield a negative value, it takes zero instead. Thus, c must promote e for Q_{link} to be non-zero. Good calls this formula "the weight of evidence against e, if c didn't happen."

The causal strength along a chain can be calculated by calculating total resistance and then converting this to causal strength:

$$Q(E:C) = -\log\left(1 - \prod_i \frac{p_i - q_i}{1 - q_i}\right) \tag{1}$$

where c and e are connected by a chain of n links indexed by i.

Good's theory has some nice properties; the analogy to circuit resistances in particular is mathematically pleasing, as is the use of information-theoretic ideas. However, there are some key objections. The first is that the theory is committed to the transitivity of causation, because of the additivity of resistances. Since causation in general is not transitive, this will often yield the wrong answer. Take, for example, Richard Neapolitan's case of finesteride Neapolitan (2004). Finesteride reduces testosterone levels (at least in rats); lowered testosterone levels can lead to erectile dysfunction. However, finesteride fails to reduce testosterone levels *sufficiently* for the follow-on erectile dysfunction to occur. Salmon (1980) also pointed out technical difficulties in Good's calculus which allow distinct causal chains with distinct end-to-end dependencies to be accorded the same end-to-end Q values, evidently misrepresenting the causal story.

2.2 Cheng's Power PC Theory

The starting point for the probabilistic theory of casuality is probabilistic contrast: $\Delta P_c = P(e|c) - P(e|\neg c)$.[2] In this case c is only a *prima facie* cause, since a common ancestor may be responsible for correlating two effects. Cheng's causal power theory attempts to overcome the limitations of *prima facie* causation.

---

[1] Good includes the context in his formula, which we leave implicit here.
[2] Suppes (1970) describes this as *prima facie causation*.

Generative Causes. Cheng's causal power theory begins with some very stringent requirements for causal structure. The covariation between the effect e and candidate cause c must be independent from any covariation of e and all other causes (grouped as a). Further, the occurence of c must itself be independent of a. This implies that either a and c occur independently, or else that all the causes of a are fixed.

Cheng then defines the theoretical entities p_c and p_a, respectively the causal powers of c and a to bring about e. The causal power of c for e is defined as the probability that c produces (or generates) e. Since under Cheng's assumptions e comes about either via c or via a, and nothing else, this leads to:

$$P(e) = P(c)p_c + P(a)p_a - P(c)P(a)p_c p_a \qquad (2)$$

(2) is used to calculate ΔP_c and then solved for p_c using the above assumptions to eliminate $P(a)$ and p_a, giving:

$$p_c = \frac{\Delta P_c}{1 - P(e|\neg c)} \qquad (3)$$

Cheng claims that this is an improvement on prior theory, such as Rescorla and Wagner (1972). Among other reasons, this is because it provides the 'correct' answer when e always occurs. If e always occurs, then p_c is undefined, rather than zero, as Rascorla and Wagner suggested. Undefined is supposedly correct because we should be unable to assess the causes of a universal event.

Preventative Causes. Cheng stipulates the same restrictive assumptions for preventative as for generative causes; the definitions are unchanged, except that p_c is labeled preventative, leaving a to be the only generative cause. Cheng says e is the combination of e produced by a with e *not being stopped* by c, and so:

$$P(e) = P(a)p_a(1 - P(c)p_c) \qquad (4)$$

This assumes that e being produced by a is independent of e being prevented by c, a rather strange assumption, as noted by Hiddleston (2005).

As with generative causes, (4) is used to find ΔP_c and then solved for p_c:

$$p_c = \frac{-\Delta P_c}{P(e|\neg c)} \qquad (5)$$

Analogously, this leaves preventative power for an impossible e undefined.

Problems. The main difficulty for Cheng's theory is that it is extremely limited in scope. It is only defined over binary variables; but worse, the independence assumptions and limits on interactions between causes guarantees a small range of applicability.

2.3 Hiddleston's Causal Powers

Hiddelston's analysis of causal powers is heavily influenced by Cheng's account (Hiddleston, 2005). However, he disagrees with Cheng's formulation of preventative causes. Recall Cheng's formula (4) for how e occurs when c is a preventative: $P(e) = P(a)p_a(1 - P(c)p_c)$. This means that e occurs only when a causes it and, independently, c fails to prevent it. But Hiddleston argues that preventers work by preventing particular causes, and so he suggests instead $P(e) = P(a)p_a(1 - P(c|a)p_{c,a})$ where $p_{c,a}$ is c's probability of preventing a's effect on e.

This difference between Cheng's and Hiddleston's accounts can be thought of as a difference between two kinds of preventative barriers against some generative powers. Cheng's is a uniform barrier against all possible generative causes, while Hiddleston's only shields against a specific cause.

3 Causal Information

Our measure of causal power combines information theory with causal interventions on causal networks (Pearl, 2000; Korb et al., 2004).[3]

Definition 1. Causal information *(CI) between a cause c and an effect e in the causal model g (or, causal power of c for e) is the mutual information (MI) between the two variables in an auxiliary model g^*, where g^* is the same as g, except the arcs between c and its parents have been cut (removed). c's distribution in g^* is set as its prior in g.*

Mutual information for the discrete case is (Cover and Thomas, 1991):

$$MI(X,Y) = \sum_{x \in X, y \in Y} p(xy) \log \frac{p(xy)}{p(x)p(y)} \qquad (6)$$

This has two relevant interpretations. The first is Kullback-Leibler (KL) divergence (or cross-entropy) between the joint probability and the product of the two marginal distributions. KL divergence takes the form

$$KL(p(X), q(X)) = \sum_{x \in X} p(x) \log \frac{p(x)}{q(x)} \qquad (7)$$

where p is taken to be the true distribution and q an approximation to p. KL is a measure of the expected information cost of using q to describe p. When X and Y are independent $p(xy) = p(x)p(y)$, so MI is the cost of assuming the two variables are independent when they may not be.

Another interpretation of mutual information is through the identity

$$MI(X,Y) = H(X) - H(X|Y)$$

---

[3] Space constraints force the removal of proofs to Hope and Korb (2005).

The entropy $H(X)$ is the expected length of an efficient code for X. $H(X|Y)$ is the same, given knowledge of Y. So, MI information measures the aid one variable gives to the task of describing the other. However, since MI is symmetric, it cannot directly measure an asymmetric causal power. By introducing interventions, justifying the cutting of arcs in Definition 1 (e.g., Pearl, 2000; Glymour, 2001; Korb et al., 2004), causal information introduces the correct asymmetry.

There is a direct relation between causal information and KL divergence:

Theorem 1. *The causal information of intervention $c \in C$ wrt E is:*

$$CI(C = c, E) = KL(p(E|c), p(E)) = \sum_{e \in E} p(e|c) \log \frac{p(e|c)}{p(e)} \quad (8)$$

in auxiliary model g^*.

This account has the immediate advantage of being defined in general, applying to any system for which we can find the underlying causal structure. (The causal structure is necessary in order to identify which arcs are to be cut under intervention, of course.) Thus, it applies to linear models, Cheng models and their extensions, and also to discrete variable models, and thus the full range of (causal) Bayesian networks, unlike any predecessors. In order to assess this account against its predecessors, however, we need to see how it applies to the simpler cases of linear and Cheng models.

4 Applications

4.1 Path Models

In application to linear models we turn to the theory of path models, which are a general method of treating linear Gaussian models. In particular, our causal power should agree with the correlation (r), as calculated by the method of Wright (1934). Hope and Korb (2005) found that MI between two (unit) normals is $-\log \sqrt{1-r^2}$, where r is the correlation between the two. Thus the mutual information is an increasing function of the magnitude of correlation, as we should expect and demand, since for linear models the causal information account of power is transitive, as is correlation.

4.2 Cheng Models

The particular feature which Cheng liked to emphasize was that her metric yielded "undefined" when the effect was impossible or necessary. Causal information is in such cases technically defined, but only because the standard convention in information theory is to treat $\log p/0$ as 0.

It is more interesting to see what causal information does with noisy-or models. Glymour (2001) noted that the assumptions Cheng applied to her models correspond to noisy-or models, which are probabilistic generalisations of the Boolean or-gate, where each parent of variable e has an independant chance of triggering it, namely p_c for parent c (expanded to p_{ce} when otherwise ambiguous). It is easiest to calculate using the probability that a cause will be inhibited: $q_i = 1 - p_i$. Let $pa(c)$ be the parents of c and $pa_T(c)$ be the subset containing those which are true, then,

$$p(e|pa(e)) = 1 - \prod_{i \in pa_T(e)} q_i \qquad (9)$$

The probability of e being false is the probability that all the inhibitors of the occurent causes activate. Since the inhibitors are assumed to be independent, this is the product of their individual probabilities, so the probability of e is just one minus this quantity.

Now we describe some results for networks which contain only noisy-or gates. We simplify by assuming that the causes under consideration are the only true parents; the results readily generalize. (For proofs see Hope and Korb, 2005.)

Theorem 2. *The total causal power of a noisy-or chain is the product of the powers of the individual links.*

Another result is that parallel non-interactive paths are additive, which we get by using the inclusion-exclusion principle (Comtet, 1974). We refer to this as 'IE-addition' and denote it by the operator $\oplus$. For two paths with powers p and q, $p \oplus q$ is defined as $p + q - pq$. The general definition is:

Definition 2.

$$\oplus_i p_i = \sum_{I \in \{1,\ldots,n\}^2} (-1)^{\text{even}(|I|)} \prod_{i \in I} p_i$$

where I is a subset of the power set of indices of the p_i, $|I|$ is its cardinality.

Theorem 3. *The causal power of a set of parallel noisy-or chains is IE-additive. That is, if c is connected to e by n distinct paths, then the total power is $p_1 \oplus p_2 \oplus \ldots \oplus p_n$.*

The causal information for Cheng models is easily derived as $CI(C = c, E) = -p_{ce} \log p(c)$, meaning that causal information is the causal power of c mediated by the information content of c.

5 Conclusion

Causal information is far better than the metrics offered previously:

- Since it is based upon mutual information measured over Bayesian networks, it is automatically as general as Bayesian networks, including coping with interactive causes.
- The simpler properties of prior analyses, such as transitivity and additivity of causal powers, reappear when appropriate, as in linear and noisy-or models.
- As mutual information applies to individual variables or sets of variables, causal information can immediately be applied to complexes of causes.

References

Cheng, P. W. (1997). From covariation to causation: A causal power theory. *Psych Rev 104*(2), 367–405.

Comtet, L. (1974). *Advanced Combinatorics*, Chapter 4, pp. 176–178.

Cover, T. M. and J. A. Thomas (1991). *Elements of Information Theory*. Wiley.

Glymour, C. (2001). *The Mind's Arrows*. MIT: MIT Press.

Good, I. J. (1961). A causal calculus. *Brit Jrn for Phil Sci 11*, 305–318.

Halpern, J. Y. and J. Pearl (2001). Causes and explanations: A structural-model approach — Part I: Causes. In J. Breese and D. Koller (Eds.), *UAI*, pp. 194–202.

Hiddleston, E. (2005). Causal powers. *Brit Jrn for Phil Sci 56*, 27–59.

Hitchcock, C. R. (2001). The intransitivity of causation revealed in equations and graphs. *JP 98*(6), 273–299.

Hope, L. R. and K. B. Korb (2005). Information-theoretic causal power. Technical Report 2005/176, Monash University.

Korb, K. B., L. R. Hope, A. E. Nicholson, and K. Axnick (2004). Varieties of causal intervention. In *PRICAI'04*, pp. 322–331.

Neapolitan, R. E. (2004). *Learning Bayesian Networks*. Prentice-Hall.

Pearl, J. (2000). *Causality*. Cambridge, UK: Cambridge.

Rescorla, R. A. and A. R. Wagner (1972). A theory of Pavlovian conditioning. In Black and Prokasy (Eds.), *Classical Conditioning II*, pp. 64–99.

Salmon, W. (1980). Probabilistic causality. *Pacific Phil Qtly 61*, 50–74.

Spirtes, P., C. Glymour, and R. Scheines (2000). *Causation, prediction and search: 2nd ed.* MIT.

Suppes, P. (1970). *A Probabilistic Theory of Causality*. Amsterdam.

Twardy, C. R. and K. B. Korb (2004). A criterion of probabilistic causality. *Philosophy of Science 71*, 241–62.

Verma, T. and J. Pearl (1990). Equivalence and synthesis of causal models. In *Uncertainty in Artificial Intelligence, 6*, pp. 462–470. Morgan Kaufmann.

Wright, S. (1934). The method of path coefficients. *Ann of Math Stat 5*, 161–215.

A Fixed-Point Semantics for Plausible Logic

David Billington

School of Information and Communication Technology,
Nathan campus, Griffith University,
Brisbane, Queensland 4111, Australia
d.billington@griffith.edu.au

Abstract. Plausible Logic is a non-monotonic logic with an efficient implementation, but no semantics. This paper gives Plausible Logic a fixed-point semantics, similar to the extensions of Reiter's Default Logic. The proof theory is sound but deliberately incomplete with respect to this semantics. This is because the semantics is an attempt to define what follows from a plausible theory, rather than merely giving a different characterisation of what is provable.

1 Introduction

The Plausible Logic used in this paper is the same as the one in [3], which is in this volume. So the reader is referred to [3] for an overview of Plausible Logic.

A logic usually has a syntax for representing information, a proof theory for deducing a formula from the represented information using an explicit set of syntactic inference rules, and a semantics which gives the set of formulas which follow from the represented information. Plausible Logic has a natural rule-based syntax, an efficient proof theory, but no semantics.

This paper provides Plausible Logic with a sound fixed-point semantics, similar to the extensions of Reiter's Default Logic [7]. The proof theory is sound but deliberately incomplete with respect to this semantics. This is because the semantics is an attempt to define what follows from a plausible theory, rather than merely giving a different characterisation of what is provable. As an example of the use of this semantics, we define a class of Default Logics which are equivalent to a class of Plausible Logics.

The paper has three sections. The fixed-point semantics is presented in section 2. Section 3 concludes the paper with a discussion and suggests directions for future work.

2 A Fixed-Point Semantics

We begin by introducing our notation in the familiar context of Reiter's Default Logic [7], so that the similarities between the fixed-point semantics of Default Logic and Plausible Logic are more obvious. *Frm* is the set of all propositional formulas in a given language, and $CnfFrm \subseteq Frm$ is the set of all conjunctive normal form formulas. A *default* d is a triple, which we shall write as $(p(d) : J(d) / c(d))$, such that

$p(d) \in Frm$, $J(d)$ is a finite subset of Frm, and $c(d) \in Frm$. The formula $p(d)$ is called the *prerequisite* of d, $J(d)$ is the set of *justifications* of d, and $c(d)$ is the *consequent* of d. A *default theory* is an ordered pair (Ax, D) such that Ax is a set of formulas, called *axioms*, and D is a countable set of defaults. If $N \subseteq D$ define $c(N) = \{c(d) : d \in N\}$. To aid readability we shall sometimes write cN for $c(N)$.

Let $DT = (Ax, D)$ be a default theory. Suppose $G \subseteq Frm$ and $F \subseteq Frm$. A default d is *F-applicable to* G iff $p(d) \in Cn(G)$ and for all j in $J(d)$, $\neg j \notin F$. Define $D(G, F) = \{d \in D : d \text{ is } F\text{-applicable to } G\}$. The *semantic function*, $\sum$, of DT is defined as follows. $\sum : \mathcal{P}(Frm) \to \mathcal{P}(Frm)$ and $\sum(F) = \cap\{G \in \mathcal{P}(Frm) : Ax \subseteq G, Cn(G) = G, \& cD(G, F) \subseteq G\}$. If $E \subseteq Frm$ then E is an *extension* of DT iff $\sum(E) = E$. This is just Reiter's definition expressed in our notation.

Now suppose $T = (R, >)$ is a plausible theory, $\lambda \in \{\alpha, \pi, \beta, \delta\}$, $G \subseteq Frm$, and $F \subseteq Frm$. The facts of T are denoted by $Ax(T)$. If $s \in R$ then $A(s)$ is the antecedent of s. A plausible rule r is (λ,F)-*applicable to* G iff $A(r) \subseteq Cn(G)$ and a condition which makes the result of applying r to G consistent, given F. Define $R(\lambda, G, F) = \{r \in R_p : r \text{ is } (\lambda,F)\text{-applicable to } G\}$. For ease of reading let $cR(\lambda, G, F) = c(R(\lambda, G, F))$. $cR(\lambda, G, F)$ is the set of consequents of plausible rules which should be accepted given λ, G and F.

The *semantic function of* T, *corresponding to* λ is denoted by $\sum_\lambda$, and is defined by $\sum_\lambda : \mathcal{P}(Frm) \to \mathcal{P}(Frm)$ and $\sum_\lambda(F) = \cap\{G \in \mathcal{P}(Frm) : Ax(T) \subseteq G, Cn(G) = G, \& cR(\lambda,G,F) \subseteq G\}$. Define E to be a λ-*extension* of T, iff $\sum_\lambda(E) = E$. Let $Ext(\lambda,T) = \{E : E \text{ is a } \lambda\text{-extension of } T\}$.

Suppose $F \subseteq Frm$. For each i in $\mathbb{N}$, (the set of non-negative integers), we define $\sum(\lambda, F, i)$ and hence $\sum(\lambda, F)$ as follows.
$\sum(\lambda, F, 0) = Cn(Ax(T))$.
$\sum(\lambda, F, i+1) = Cn(Ax(T) \cup cR(\lambda, \sum(\lambda, F, i), F))$.
$\sum(\lambda, F) = \cup\{\sum(\lambda, F, i) : i \in \mathbb{N}\}$.

Many familiar properties of default extensions are enjoyed by λ-extensions, as we see below.

Theorem 2.1. (λ-extensions)
Suppose T is a plausible theory, $\lambda \in \{\alpha, \pi, \beta, \delta\}$, $F \in \mathcal{P}(Frm)$, and $E \in Ext(\lambda,T)$.
(1) $\sum_\lambda(F) = \sum(\lambda, F)$.
(2) $F \in Ext(\lambda,T)$ iff $F = \sum(\lambda, F)$.
(3) $E = Cn(Ax(T) \cup cR(\lambda, E, E))$.
(4) If $Ax(T)$ is satisfiable then E is satisfiable.
(5) If $\{E, E^*\} \subseteq Ext(\lambda,T)$ and $E \subseteq E^*$ then $E = E^*$.
(6) $\sum(\pi, \{\})$ is the only π-extension of T.
End2.1.

The next result shows that (1) everything which is λ-provable, $T(+\lambda)$, is in all λ-extensions, and (2) providing the axioms are consistent, everything which is λ-disprovable, $T(-\lambda)$, is not in any λ-extension. Part (3) shows that μ-provability is sound and complete, and hence equivalent to classical propositional logic.

Theorem 2.1(4) and theorem 2.2(1) give an alternative proof of relative consistency (see [3]).

Theorem 2.2. (Soundness, and Completeness for μ)
Suppose T is a plausible theory and $\lambda \in \{\alpha, \pi, \beta, \delta\}$.
(1)(Soundness) $T(+\lambda) \subseteq CnfFrm \cap \cap Ext(\lambda, T)$.
(2) If $Ax(T)$ is consistent then $T(-\lambda) \cap \cup Ext(\lambda, T) = \{\}$.
(3) If $Ax(T)$ is consistent then $T(+\mu) = Cn(Ax(T)) \cap CnfFrm$.
End2.2.

3 Conclusion

The main purpose of a semantics of a logic is to formally define the meaning of the formulas. This is usually done by interpreting the formulas in some appropriate structure. The concepts of satisfaction and semantic consequence can then be defined. Semantic consequence can then be used to formally define the set of formulas which follow from a given set of formulas. In the case of Default Logic and Plausible Logic we take the intersection of all the (λ-)extensions to be the set of formulas which follow from the default or plausible theory. It is in this sense that the fixed-point semantics is a semantics.

Unlike Default Logic, Plausible Logic has a proof theory. So the set of all formulas provable from a plausible theory can be regarded as a set of formulas which following from that theory. Theorem 2.2(1) shows that these two ideas of "following from" do not conflict. In some logics (for example SLDNF-resolution for normal logic programs [5, section 16], and arithmetic [4, see section 3.5 for Godel's incompleteness theorem]) these two notions do not coincide. That is there are formulas which semantically follow from a theory but are not provable, in such cases the proof theory is said to be incomplete with respect to the semantics. In a logic which deals with negation and disjunction, like Plausible Logic, it is unlikely that a computationally useful proof theory will be complete. Examples show that the proof theory of Plausible Logic is indeed incomplete with respect to its fixed-point semantics. So the proof theory does not capture our intuition of what "follows from" a given theory. The desire to formally capture this intuition is the main motivation for developing a semantics for Plausible Logic. Thus it is required that the proof theory be incomplete with respect to this semantics. Although there would be little point in developing a semantics which made the proof theory complete, if such a semantics was desired then one could start by applying the methods in [6] which gave a sound and complete model-theoretic semantics for Defeasible Logic. Of course each time the proof theory was made more complete (see the next paragraph) the old model-theoretic semantics would no longer be sound.

The proof theory and the fixed-point semantics can be improved. Carefully increasing the completeness of the proof theory, without sacrificing efficiency, is the subject of further research. The fixed-point semantics is not fully satisfactory either. It is difficult to check if a formula is in the intersection of all the extensions of a plausible theory. More fundamentally it is not obvious that all the formulas which could be regarded as "following from" a plausible theory are in the intersection of all extensions. Both of these problems are the subject of continuing research.

Acknowledgments

The initial work on the fixed-point semantics was sparked by a conversation with Professor Donald Nute while visiting him in February 2004 at the Artificial Intelligence Center of the University of Georgia, USA. The trip was funded by the Australian Research Council's IREX grant X00001634.

References

[1] Grigoris Antoniou. *Nonmonotonic Reasoning*. MIT Press, 1997.
[2] Grigoris Antoniou and David Billington. Relating Defeasible and Default Logic. *Proceedings of the 14th Australian Joint Conference on Artificial Intelligence*, Lecture Notes in Computer Science 2256, 13-24. Springer, 2001.
[3] David Billington. The Proof Algorithms of Plausible Logic Form a Hierarchy. *Proceedings of the 18th Australian Conference on Artificial Intelligence*, AI2005, Lecture Notes in Artificial Intelligence, this volume. Springer 2005.
[4] Herbert B. Enderton. *A Mathematical Introduction to Logic*. Academic Press, 1972.
[5] John Wylie Lloyd. *Foundations of Logic Programming*, 2nd extended edition. Springer-Verlag, 1987.
[6] Michael J. Maher. A Model-Theoretic Semantics for Defeasible Logic. In H. Decker, J. Villadsen, and T. Waragai, eds., *Paraconsistent Computational Logic*, 67-80. Roskilde University, Roskilde, Denmark, 2002. This proceedings volume contains the papers presented at the ICLP 2002 workshop Paraconsistent Computational Logic, on July 27, in Copenhagen, Denmark, as part of the Federated Logic Conference (FLoC). Also available at http://arxiv.org/abs/cs.LO/0207086 and http://arxiv.org/pdf/cs.LO/0207086
[7] R. Reiter. A Logic for Default Reasoning. *Artificial Intelligence* 13 (1980), 81-132. Elsevier 1980.

Applying Indiscernibility Attribute Sets to Knowledge Reduction

Hong-Ru Li[1,2] and Wen-Xiu Zhang[1]

[1] Faculty of Science, Institute for Information and System Sciences,
Xi'an Jiaotong University, Xi'an, Shaan'xi 710049, P.R. China
lihongru1126@163.com
wxzhang@mail.xjtu.edu.cn
[2] Department of Mathematics and Information Sciences, Yan'tai University,
Yan'tai, Shan'dong 264005, P.R. China

Abstract. Knowledge reduction is one of the key problems of rough set theory. In this paper, we investigate some theoretical issues of the reduction of information systems and present a new reduction approach. A closure operator on the power set of attributes is defined. The relations between the closed sets determined by the closure operator and the indiscernibility attribute sets are then investigated. Based on the relations, we can determine a partition on the power of attributes by using the indiscernibility attribute sets. Consequently, the reducts of any subset of attributes in information systems can be derived.

1 Introduction

Rough set theory introduced by Pawlak [6] offers an effective mathematical approach to data mining and knowledge acquisition. In rough set view, the knowledge reduction of an information system is to find a minimal subset of attributes that enables the same classification of elements of the universe as the whole set of attributes. In recent years, knowledge reduction within the framework of rough set theory has been studied extensively from different perspectives [1,2,3,5,9]. A commonly used reduction method is to use the discernibility matrix and the discernibility formula [8]. In this paper, we consider the reduction problem of information systems from the viewpoint of classification. For any subset of attributes its reducts is defined based on a classification on the power set of attributes. Our focus here is to determine a partition in which the elements of each class make the same classification of elements of the universe. Based on the binary relations of objects and attributes, two equivalence relations on the universe and on the power set of attributes are introduced. A closure operator on the power set of attributes is then proposed. We discuss the properties of the closed sets determined by the closure operator and demonstrate the relationships between the closed sets and indiscernibility sets. According to the relations, we can determine the partition on the power set of attributes using only the indiscernibility attribute sets, from which a new reduction approach in information systems is obtained.

2 Preliminaries

For a set U, let $\mathcal{P}(U)$ be the powerset of U. If R is an equivalence relation on U, we use U/R to denote the family of all equivalence classes of R, i.e.,

$$U/R = \{ [x]_R;\ x \in U \}, \quad \text{where } [x]_R = \{ y \in U;\ (x,y) \in R \}.$$

Let S be a nonempty finite set with a binary operation $*$. An equivalence relation R on S is called a *congruence* on $(S, *)$ if R satisfies the condition: $\forall\, x, x', y, y' \in S$, if $(x, x') \in R$, $(y, y') \in R$, then $(x * y, x' * y') \in R$.

An *information system* is an quadruple $IS = (U, A, V, F)$, where

- $U = \{x_1, x_2, \cdots, x_n\}$ is a universe, the elements of U are called objects.
- $A = \{a_1, a_2, \cdots, a_m\}$ is a set of attributes.
- $V = \bigcup_{l=1}^{m} V_{a_l}$, V_{a_l} is a nonempty set of the values of attribute $a_l \in A$.
- $F = \{f_1, f_2, \cdots, f_m\}$ is a set of relationships between U and A, where $f_l : U \to V_l$, $(l = 1, \cdots, m)$, and F is called a description function of IS.

Definition 1. Let $IS = (U, A, V, F)$ be an information system, R a congruence on $\mathcal{P}(A)$. A set $D \in \mathcal{P}(A)$ is called a *R-independent element*, if D is a minimal element of the class $[D]_R$. The set of all R-independent elements in $\mathcal{P}(A)$ is denoted by $I(R)$.

Definition 2. Let $IS = (U, A, V, F)$ be an information system, R a congruence on $\mathcal{P}(A)$. $B, E \in \mathcal{P}(A)$, E is called a *reduct* of B, if E satisfies the conditions: (i) $E \in I(R)$; (ii) $E \subseteq B$; (iii) $(B, E) \in R$.

The set of all reducts of B is denoted by $\mathrm{RED}(R, B)$.

3 Closure Operator $C(R)$ and Its Properties

Theorem 1. *Let (U, A, V, F) be an information system and let*

$$\begin{aligned} R_B &= \{(x_i, x_j) \in U \times U;\ f_l(x_i) = f_l(x_j),\ a_l \in B \subseteq A\}, \\ R &= \{(B, D) \in \mathcal{P}(A) \times \mathcal{P}(A);\ R_B = R_D\}. \end{aligned} \qquad (1)$$

The following assertions are true:

(i) R_B *is an equivalence relation on* U; (ii) R *is a congruence on* $(\mathcal{P}(A), \cup)$.

Proof. (i) is evident. (ii) can be proved from the definition of congruence. $\square$

Theorem 2. *Let (U, A, V, F) be an information system, R a congruence on $(\mathcal{P}(A), \cup)$. For any $B \in \mathcal{P}(A)$, defined by*

$$C(R)(B) = \cup [B]_R. \qquad (2)$$

Then $C(R)$ is a closure operator on $(\mathcal{P}(A), \cup)$.

Proof. It is follows from Theorem 17 in [5]. □

Let $B \in \mathcal{P}(A)$. If B satisfies the condition: $C(R)(B) = B$, we say that B is a $C(R)$-closed set in $\mathcal{P}(A)$. The set of all $C(R)$-closed sets of $\mathcal{P}(A)$ is denoted by C_R. The following conclusions can be derived directly from above theorems.

Proposition 3. Let (U, A, V, F) be an information system. The relations R_B and R satisfy the following properties:

(i) $\forall B, D \subseteq A$, $B \subseteq D \Rightarrow R_D \subseteq R_B$;
(ii) $B \subseteq D \subseteq C(R)(B) \Rightarrow R_B = R_D = R_{C(R)(B)}$;
(iii) $\forall B, D \in \mathcal{P}(A)$, $(B, D) \in R \Rightarrow (B, B \cup D) \in R$;
(iv) $C_R = \{\cup [B]_R; \ [B]_R \in \mathcal{P}(A)/R\}$.

4 Indiscernibility Attribute Set and Its Properties

Definition 3. Let (U, A, V, F) be an information system. A set $B \subseteq A$ is called an *indiscernibility attribute set*, if there exists elements $x_i, x_j \in U$, such that $B = \{a_l \in A; \ f_l(x_i) = f_l(x_j)\}$.

Let (U, A, V, F) be an information system, we let

$$U/R_A = \{X_1, X_2, \ldots, X_k\}, \quad 1 \leq k \leq n. \tag{3}$$
$$G = \{G_{ij}; \ 1 \leq i, j \leq k\}, \tag{4}$$

where $G_{ij} = \{a_l \in A; \ f_l(X_i) = f_l(X_j)\}$. It is easy to see that G is the set of all indiscernibility attribute sets of $\mathcal{P}(A)$. By the definitions of classification [8] and $C(R)$-closed set, we can prove the following Lemmas.

Lemma 4. Let (U, A, V, F) be an information system. Then,

$$\emptyset \notin C_R \iff \exists B \in \mathcal{P}(A), \ \forall X_i, X_j \in U/R_A \text{ and } \forall a_l \in B, \ f_l(X_i) = f_l(X_j).$$

Lemma 5. Let (U, A, V, F) be an information system. Then

(i) $\emptyset \notin C_R$ implies $\emptyset \notin G$; (ii) $\emptyset \in C_R$ iff $\bigcap_{1 \leq i,j \leq k} G_{ij} = \emptyset$.

Lemma 6. Let (U, A, V, F) be an information system. Then each element of G is a $C(R)$-closed set in $(\mathcal{P}(A), \cup)$.

We now show the relationships between the $C(R)$-closed sets and the indiscernibility attribute sets. According to the relations, we may determine the partition $\mathcal{P}(A)/R$ by using the set G.

Theorem 7. Let (U, A, V, F) be an information system. Then

$$G = C_R \quad \text{or} \quad G \cup \emptyset = C_R. \tag{5}$$

Proof. Lemma 6 and the condition (iv) of Proposition 3 imply $G \subseteq C_R$.

Conversely, suppose $B \in C_R$ and $B \neq \emptyset$. For any $(x_i, x_j) \in R_B$, if there exists $D \subseteq A$ and $D \not\subseteq B$ such that $(x_i, x_j) \in R_D$, then $R_B \subseteq R_D$, and $R_B \subseteq R_B \cap R_D = R_{B \cup D}$. Since $B \subseteq B \cup D$ we have $R_{B \cup D} \subseteq R_B$ (see [8]). It follows that $R_B = R_{B \cup D}$. Thus, $\forall a_l \in B$, $a_l \in D \subset Co(B)$ holds, where $Co(B)$ denotes the complementary set of B. This is a contradiction. Hence, there exists at least one element $(x_s, x_t) \in R_B$ (suppose $x_s \in X_i, x_t \in X_j$) such that $\forall D \not\subseteq B$ ($D \subseteq A$), $(x_s, x_t) \notin R_D$. That is, for any $a_l \in A - B$, $f_l(X_i) \neq f_l(X_j)$. Thus we have $B = \{a_l \in A; f_l(X_i) = f_l(X_j)\} = G_{ij} \in G$. Therefore, when $\emptyset \notin C_R$, $G = C_R$; when $\emptyset \in C_R$ and $\emptyset \notin G$, $G \cup \emptyset = C_R$. □

5 Attribute Reduction

Theorem 8. *Let (U, A, V, F) be an information system,*

$$T(G) = \{(B, D) \in \mathcal{P}(A) \times \mathcal{P}(A); \forall G_{ij} \in G, B \subseteq G_{ij} \text{ iff } D \subseteq G_{ij}\}. \quad (6)$$

Then $R = T(G)$.

Proof. Since C_R is the set of all $C(R)$-closed sets in $(\mathcal{P}(A), \cup)$, if $G = C_R$, by Theorem 18 and Theorem 21 in [5] we have $R = K(C(R)) = T(C_R) = T(G)$. If $G \cup \emptyset = C_R$, then $(\emptyset, \emptyset) \in T(C_R)$ and $\forall B \in \mathcal{P}(A)$ $(B \neq \emptyset)$, $(\emptyset, B) \notin T(C_R)$. By (ii) of Lemma 5, $\emptyset \in C_R$ implies $\bigcap_{1 \leq i,j \leq k} G_{ij} = \emptyset$. Hence, there exists exactly one element $\emptyset \in \mathcal{P}(A)$ such that $\forall G_{ij} \in G$, $\emptyset \subseteq G_{ij}$. This implies $(\emptyset, \emptyset) \in T(G)$ and $\forall D \in \mathcal{P}(A)$ $(D \neq \emptyset)$, $(D, \emptyset) \notin T(G)$. It follows that $R = T(C_R) = T(G)$. □

To illustrate the proposed method we consider the following example.

Example. Let $IS = (U, A, V, F)$ be an information system. The data table of IS is given by Table 1.

Table 1. Description of IS

U	a_1	a_2	a_3
x_1	2	1	3
x_2	1	1	4
x_3	3	2	1
x_4	2	1	3
x_5	1	1	2
x_6	3	2	3

By Table 1 and (3), we can determine the partition of U as $U/R_A = \{X_1, \ldots, X_5\}$. where $X_1 = \{x_1, x_4\}$, $X_2 = \{x_2\}$, $X_3 = \{x_3\}$, $X_4 = \{x_5\}$, $X_5 = \{x_6\}$.

From Table 2 and equation (4), we have $G = \{\emptyset, \{a_2\}, \{a_3\}, \{a_1, a_2\}, A\}$.

Table 2. Indiscernibility matrix of IS

	X_1	X_2	X_3	X_4	X_5
X_1	A	$\{a_2\}$	$\emptyset$	$\{a_2\}$	$\{a_3\}$
X_2	$\{a_2\}$	A	$\emptyset$	$\{a_1,a_2\}$	$\emptyset$
X_3	$\emptyset$	$\emptyset$	A	$\emptyset$	$\{a_1,a_2\}$
X_4	$\{a_2\}$	$\{a_1,a_2\}$	$\emptyset$	A	$\emptyset$
X_5	$\{a_3\}$	$\emptyset$	$\{a_1,a_2\}$	$\emptyset$	A

For the sake of brevity, we let $\emptyset = 0$, $\{a_i\} = i$, $\{a_i, a_j\} = ij$, with $1 \leq i < j \leq 3$, and $A = 123$. Thus, $G = \{0, 2, 3, 12, A\}$.

Since $\emptyset \in G$, this implies $C_R = G$ (Theorem 7). Using equation (6) we have

$$R = \{(0,0), (1,1), (2,2), (3,3), (1,12), (12,1),$$
$$(13,23), (23,13), (13,A), (A,13), (23,A), (A,23)\}.$$
$$P(A)/R = \{\ \{0\},\ \{2\},\ \{3\},\ \{1,12\},\ \{13,23,A\}\ \}.$$

By definition 1, we can find the all R-independent elements in S as

$$I(R) = \{\ 0,\ 1,\ 2,\ 3,\ 13,\ 23\ \}.$$

Now we can determine the reducts of information system IS by the partition $\mathcal{P}(A)/R$. For example, the set 13 satisfies the conditions of definition 2 for the set A, i.e., $13 \in I(R)$, $13 \subseteq A$ and $(13, A) \in R$. Hence, $13 \in \text{RED}(R, A)$. Similarly, $23 \in \text{RED}(R, A)$. In fact, we can find the reducts of any subset of attributes by using the method, e.g.,

RED(R,A)={13,23}, RED(R,12)={1}, RED(R,3)={3}, etc.

6 Conclusion

This paper examined some theoretical issues of the reduction of information systems from the viewpoint of classifications. Based on the binary relations of objects and attributes in information systems, a closure operator $C(R)$ and indiscernibility attribute sets were defined and their properties were investigated. We presented a reduction method that employs the indiscernibility attribute sets to determine a partition of the power set of attributes. This method also offers some possibilities to further study classifications in information systems.

References

1. Chouchoulas, A., Halliwell, J., Shen, Q., On the implementation of rough set attribute reduction, Proc. 2002 UK Workshop on Computational Intelligence (2002) pp. 18-23
2. Jensen, R., Shen, Q., Fuzzy-rough attribute reduction with application to web categorization, Fuzzy Sets and Systems **141** (2004) 469-485

3. Kryszkiewicz, M., Comparative study of alternative type of knowledge reduction in inconsistent systems, International Journal of Intelligent Systems **16** (2001) 105-120
4. Mi, J.-S., Wu, W.-Z., Zhang, W.-X., Approaches to knowledge reduction based on variable precision rough set model, Information Sciences **159** (2004) 255-272
5. Novotný, M., Dependence Spaces of Information Systems, In: E. Orlowska(Ed.), Incomplete Informations: Rough Sets Analysis, Physica-Verlag (1998) pp, 193-246
6. Pawlak, Z., Rough sets, International Journal of Computer and Information Sciences **11** (1982) 341-356
7. Yao, Y.Y., Constructive and algebraic methods of the theory of rough sets, Journal of Information Sciences **109** (1998) 21-47
8. Zhang, W.-X., Leung, Y., Wu, W.-Z., Information Systems and Knowledge Discovery, Science Press, Beijing, 2003
9. Zhu, W., Wang, F.-Y., Reduction and axiomization of covering generalized rough sets, Information Sciences **152** (2003) 217-230

Dempster Conditioning and Conditional Independence in Evidence Theory

Yongchuan Tang[1] and Jiacheng Zheng[2],*

[1] College of Computer Science, Zhejiang University,
Hangzhou, Zhejiang Province, 310027, P.R. China
yongchuan@263.net
[2] College of Economics, Zhejiang University,
Hangzhou, Zhejiang Province, 310027, P.R. China
zjcheng@zj.com

Abstract. In this paper, we discuss the conditioning issue in D-S evidence theory in multi-dimensional space. Based on Dempster conditioning, Bayes' rule and product rule, which are similar to that in probability theory, are presented in this paper. Two kinds of conditional independence called weak conditional independence and strong conditional independence are introduced, which can significantly simplify the inference process when evidence theory is applied to practical application.

1 Introduction

In this paper, we develop conditioning and its related issue in D-S evidence theory [2,4]. We mainly concern the evidence theory defined in a multi-dimensional space. Firstly, some basic operations in evidence theory are introduced. Then, we show that product rule and Bayes' rule, which is similar to that in probability theory, are also held in evidence theory. Finally, we discuss some properties of two possible conditional independence–strong conditional independence and weak conditional independence in evidence theory.

2 Evidence Theory

In evidence theory, the basic objects are the variables $X, Y, \ldots$ having values on the finite domain $\Omega_X, \Omega_Y, \ldots$, respectively, and some random sets $\Sigma, \Gamma, \ldots$ defined on these domains. In this paper we just consider a class of special random sets whose focal elements have special forms [1]. For example, let Σ be random set on $X \times Y$, then each focal element associated with Σ has the form of $S \times T = (S, T)$ where $S \subseteq \Omega_X, T \subseteq \Omega_Y$.

Definition 1 (Dempster's Rule of Combination). *Let Σ and Γ be two random sets on a finite universe Ω_X. Then the conjunctive combination of Σ and Γ is a new random set, denoted as $\Sigma \oplus \Gamma$, having the following mass assignments,*

---

* Corresponding author. Tel: 86-571-87952639; Fax: 86-571-87953695

$$m_{\Sigma \oplus \Gamma}(S) = \frac{\sum_{E \cap F = S} m_\Sigma(E) m_\Gamma(F)}{N} \qquad (1)$$

for $\emptyset \neq S \subseteq \Omega_X$, where N is the normalization factor, defined as

$$N = 1 - \sum_{E \cap F = \emptyset} m_\Sigma(E) m_\Gamma(F). \qquad (2)$$

Definition 2 (Vacuous Extension). *Let Σ be a random set on a finite universe Ω_X, and Ω_Y be another finite universe. Then the vacuous extension of Σ from Ω_X to $\Omega_X \times \Omega_Y$ is a new random set $\Sigma^{\uparrow \{X,Y\}}$ defined on $\Omega_X \times \Omega_Y$, having the following mass assignments,*

$$m_{\Sigma^{\uparrow\{X,Y\}}}(S,T) = \begin{cases} m_\Sigma(S), & \text{if } T = \Omega_Y \\ 0, & \text{otherwise} \end{cases} \qquad (3)$$

for any $S \subseteq \Omega_X, T \subseteq \Omega_Y$.

Definition 3 (Conjunctive Combination). *Let Σ be a random set on Ω_X, and Γ be a random set on Ω_Y. Then the conjunctive combination of Σ and Γ is a new random set $\Sigma \oplus \Gamma$ defined on $\Omega_X \times \Omega_Y$,*

$$\Sigma \oplus \Gamma = \Sigma^{\uparrow\{X,Y\}} \oplus \Gamma^{\uparrow\{X,Y\}}. \qquad (4)$$

Definition 4 (Marginalization). *Let Σ be a random set on a finite universe $\Omega_X \times \Omega_Y$. Then the marginal $\Sigma^{\downarrow X}$ of Σ is a new random set defined on Ω_X, which has the following mass assignments,*

$$m_{\Sigma^{\downarrow X}}(S) = \sum_{T \subseteq \Omega_Y} m_\Sigma(S,T), \qquad (5)$$

for any $\emptyset \neq S \subseteq \Omega_X$.

So we use $m_{\Sigma^\downarrow}$ to represent the marginal mass distribution induced from the joint mass distribution m_Σ. Sometimes $\Sigma^\uparrow$ and $\Sigma^\downarrow$ are simplified as Σ when no confusion is involved.

3 Conditioning

In this section, we introduce conditioning in evidence theory [3,5,6]. We develop some uncertain reasoning mechanism in evidence theory, which is similar to the probability theory.

Definition 5 (Conditional Mass Distribution). *Let Σ be a random set on $\Omega_X \times \Omega_Y$, and E be a nonempty subset of Ω_X. Then, for any $F \subseteq \Omega_Y$, the conditional mass of F given E is defined as follows,*

$$m_\Sigma(F \mid E) = m_{(\Sigma \oplus E)^{\downarrow Y}}(F). \qquad (6)$$

Proposition 1. *Let Σ be a random set on $\Omega_X \times \Omega_Y$, and E be a nonempty subset of Ω_X. Then, for any $F \subseteq \Omega_Y$, the conditional mass of F given E is*

$$m_\Sigma(F \mid E) = \frac{1}{Pl_\Sigma(E)} \sum_{E_1 \cap E \neq \emptyset} m_\Sigma(E_1, F), \qquad (7)$$

whenever $Pl_\Sigma > 0$.

Definition 6 (Conditional Belief and Plausibility Measure). *Let Σ be a random set on $\Omega_X \times \Omega_Y$, and S be a subset of Ω_X. Then, for any nonempty subset $T \subseteq \Omega_Y$, the conditional belief measure $Bel_\Sigma(T \mid S)$ and plausibility measure $Pl_\Sigma(T \mid S)$ of T given S are defined as follows,*

$$Bel_\Sigma(T \mid S) = \sum_{F \subseteq \Omega_Y, F \subseteq T} m_\Sigma(F \mid S). \qquad (8)$$

$$Pl_\Sigma(T \mid S) = \sum_{F \subseteq \Omega_Y, F \cap T \neq \emptyset} m_\Sigma(F \mid S). \qquad (9)$$

Theorem 1 (Product Rule). *Let Σ be a random set on $\Omega_X \times \Omega_Y$, S and T be subsets of Ω_X and Ω_Y, respectively. Then*

$$Pl_\Sigma(T \mid S) = \frac{Pl_\Sigma(S,T)}{Pl_\Sigma(S)}. \qquad (10)$$

Corollary 1 (Bayes' Rule). *Let Σ be a random set on $\Omega_X \times \Omega_Y$, S and T be subsets of Ω_X and Ω_Y, respectively. Then*

$$Pl_\Sigma(S \mid T) = \frac{Pl_\Sigma(T \mid S) Pl_\Sigma(S)}{Pl_\Sigma(T)}. \qquad (11)$$

4 Conditional Independence

In order to simplify the computation, the independence or conditional independence are often assumed in practical application. In evidence theory, there exists at least two possible independence which should be distinguished.

Definition 7 (Weak Conditional Independence). *Let Σ be a random set on $\Omega_X \times \Omega_Y \times \Omega_Z$. Then X and Y are conditional independent given Z in the sense of plausibility measure Pl_Σ if, for any $S \subseteq \Omega_X$, $T \subset \Omega_Y$ and $R \subseteq \Omega_Z$, the following formula holds,*

$$Pl_\Sigma(S, T \mid R) = Pl_\Sigma(S \mid R) Pl_\Sigma(T \mid R). \qquad (12)$$

Proposition 2. *Formula (12) in the definition of weak conditional independence holds if and only if the following formula holds,*

$$Pl_\Sigma(S \mid T, R) = Pl_\Sigma(S \mid R). \qquad (13)$$

Definition 8 (Strong Conditional Independence). *Let Σ be a random set on $\Omega_X \times \Omega_Y \times \Omega_Z$. Then X and Y are strong conditional independent given Z in the sense of mass measure m_Σ if, for any $S \subseteq \Omega_X$, $T \subseteq \Omega_Y$ and $R \subseteq \Omega_Z$, the following formula holds,*

$$m_\Sigma(S, T \mid R) = m_\Sigma(S \mid R) m_\Sigma(T \mid R). \tag{14}$$

Although that $m_\Sigma(S,T) = m_\Sigma(T \mid S) m_\Sigma(S)$ doesn't hold in general. But we have the following conclusion.

Proposition 3. *Let Σ be a random set on $\Omega_X \times \Omega_Y \times \Omega_Z$. Then X and Y are strong conditional independent given Z in the sense of mass measure m_Σ if and only if, for any $S \subseteq \Omega_X$, $T \subseteq \Omega_Y$ and $R \subseteq \Omega_Z$, the following formula holds,*

$$m_\Sigma(S \mid T, R) = m_\Sigma(S \mid R), \tag{15}$$

5 Conclusions

Combination is a well-developed tool in D-S evidence theory. In this paper, we focus on another important tool–conditioning in evidence theory. We show that product rule and Bayes' rule can be induced from the conditioning defined in evidence theory. Hence, the evidence theory developed in this paper can be considered as the generalization of probability theory. The plausibility measure in evidence theory acts as the role of the probability measure in probability theory. And most properties in probability theory are held in evidence theory. We expect that these properties can guarantee the efficient application of evidence theory.

Acknowledgements

This work has been supported by Zhejiang Province Natural Science Foundation (No. Y104225), Department of Education of Zhejiang Province (No. 20040115), the National Natural Science Foundation of China (No. 60475025).

References

1. B. Ben Yaghlane, Ph. Smets and K. Mellouli, "Belief function independence: I. The marginal case," Journal of Approxiamte Reasoning 29 (2002) 47–70.
2. A. P. Dempster, "upper and lower probabilities induced by a multi-valued mapping," Ann. Mathematical Statistics, vol. 38, pp. 325–339, 1967.
3. J. Y. Jaffray, Bayesian updating and belief functions, IEEE Trans. Systems Man and Cybernetics 22(5) (1992) 1144–1152.
4. G. Shafer, *A Mathematical Theory of Evidences*, Princeton University Press, 1976.
5. M. Spies, Conditonal events, conditioning, and random sets, IEEE Trans. Systems Man and Cybernetics 24(12) (1994) 1755–1763.
6. Y. Tang, S. Sun and Y. Liu, Conditional evidence theory and its application in knowledge discovery, Lecture Notes in Computer Sciences 3007 (2004) 500–505.

Case-Based Conflict Resolution in Multi-agent Ship Design System

Kyung Ho Lee[1] and Kyu Yeul Lee[2]

[1] Inha University, Department of Naval Architecture & Ocean Engineering,
253 Yonghyun-dong Nam-gu Incheon 402-751 South Korea
kyungho@inha.ac.kr
[2] Seoul National University, Department of Naval Architecture & Ocean Engineering,
San 59 Silim-dong Kwanak-gu Seoul South Korea
kylee@snu.ac.kr

Abstract. In this paper, a basic architecture of implemented multi-agent ship design system is introduced briefly. And then several cases of conflicts occurred in designing process are described. Finally, conflict resolution method based on case-based reasoning (CBR) approach is presented. Through the help of the developed multi-agent ship design system, a designer can make decisions or resolve some conflicts easily based on the previous resolved similar cases.

1 Introduction

Recently, the enterprises are assigning design and production environments around the world in different areas. A serious problem of information exchange emerges as companies use traditional hardware and very distinct softwares appropriate to their field of expertise. To overcome the problem of low productivity due to the interruption of information, we need some tools to support information exchange or sharing between heterogeneous design systems. One of the solutions to solve this problem is multi-agent system.

This paper treats several topics such as a basic architecture of implemented multi-agent ship design system, several cases of conflicts occurred in ship designing process, conflict resolution method based on case-based reasoning (CBR) approach, and so on.

2 Multi-agent Ship Design System

Recently, Korean shipyards recognized the important of information exchange or sharing between these heterogeneous CAD systems. But it is impossible to unify these CAD systems as same one. Many researches have been tried to solve the problem. Currently, among the different researches performed, the knowledge sharing approach which introduces the concept of agent is receiving very much of the spotlight[1,2]. Through the adoption of agent-based system, we don't have to unify each model and tool in design system. Each system can exchange and share information through ACL (Agent Communication Language).

The multi-agent system is implemented which exchanges and shares information of the preliminary ship design process using the ACL according to this concept. The knowledge Query Manipulation Language(KQML)[1] is used as the outer language, the Prolog is used as the inner language and the CORBA as information channel, referred to as the standard distributed object environment, is used as the technique of exchanging the information in the distributed environment.

The preliminary ship design agent system is composed of several agents, such as 'user sub-agent' for taking requirements, 'principal dimension sub-agent', 'weight estimation sub-agent', and so on. And it is developed with the distributed object structure that is capable of communicating efficiently between agents using the CORBA. For this, the Caffeine function of the VisiBroker is used. And the design flow control is freely achieved using the inference function of the Prolog. The conversation module is added in order to use efficiently the KQML message and to exchange meaningful messages. Fig. 1 depicts the inner structure of the system. ACL Handler as a part of agent manages delivered message from other agent by way of CORBA. The system implemented in this study infers using the Prolog as the inner language, and implemented using the conversation module, the KQML handler and the CORBA.

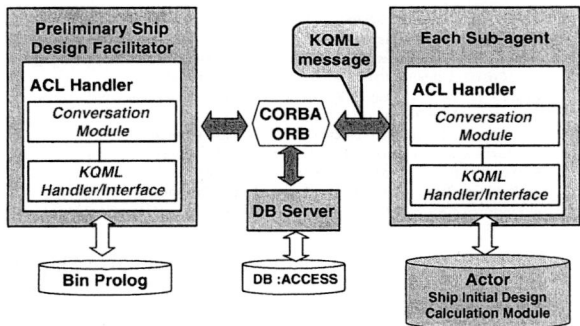

Fig. 1. Inner Structure of the Proposed Multi-agent System

An agent is operated in a JATLite 0.4 framework, and agent communication language (ACL) is transferred to KQML message handler by way of CORBA.

3 Case-Based Conflict Resolution

One of the most important problems to be solved in this multi-agent collaborative system is a conflict resolution. Most design tasks involve the management of conflict. Therefore, conflict resolution is a central issue for problems and technical approaches related to cooperative design[3].

In this section, the design conflicts and their resolution cases occurring in a multi-agent ship design system are extracted. Fig.2 depicts conflict problems in ship design process caused by different design notions of the related agents. That is, preliminary design agent wants to shorten the length of ship in an economic point of view. On the contrary, the hullform design agent prefers to lengthen the ship based on a performance viewpoint, such as low wave resistance, high speed, and so on. In the same manner, the machinery arrangement (MA) design agent has to arrange a great deal of machinery in the narrow space of ship engine room (E/R) located in the stern part of a ship. Hence the broader the engine room space, the better the viewpoint of layout. But the goal of the hullform design agent is a slender stern part of a ship in the viewpoint of performance. In addition, structural design agent is willing to arrange a bigger web frame in the viewpoint of strength. This makes an engine room space narrower. So many conflicts are occurring in the middle of the ship designing process caused by these different notions.

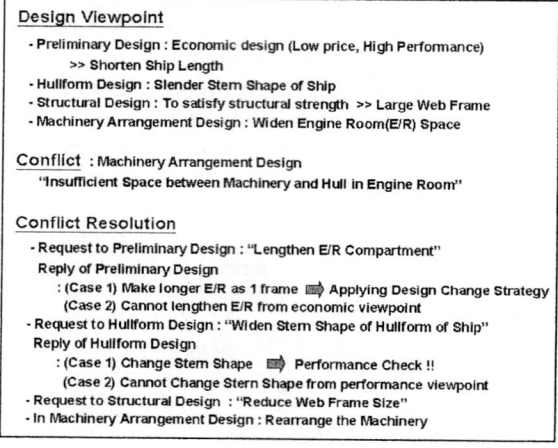

Fig. 2. Some Critical Design Conflicts Occurred in Collaborative Ship Design Process

There have been many attempts to resolve conflicts in diverse manners[4,5]. Of these attempts, the approach to resolve a current conflict problem based on previous similar cases is a very reasonable. In this section, the case-based conflict resolution approach is presented by using the conflicts described above.

In this paper, a case-based conflict resolution (CR) handler is developed to assist decision making in a cooperative preliminary ship design. This handler located in the facilitator perceives whether a conflict has occurred or not, based on the received information from agents. When a conflict has occurred, it is resolved promptly and the reply is transferred to related agents.

The following Fig.3 illustrates the concept of conflict resolution in machinery layout design of ship and collaboration in multi-agent ship design system.

4 Conclusions

In this paper, multi-agent ship design system is presented to support collaborative works for a ship design such as information exchange and sharing. This agent structure helps the heterogeneous systems exchange and share information each other.

The KQML is used as the outer language, the Prolog is used as the inner language and the CORBA, referred to as the standard distributed object environment, is used as the technique of exchanging the information in the distributed environment. In addition, conflict resolution strategy based on a CBR technique is also implemented. Especially conflict resolution handler plays an important role to detect conflicts in the middle of cooperative work and treat conflict problems in cooperation with CBR system. Through the help of the cooperation among design agents, facilitator, conflict resolution handler, and case-based system, a designer can be supported effectively in his/her decision-making based on similar previously resolved cases under the collaborative ship design environment.

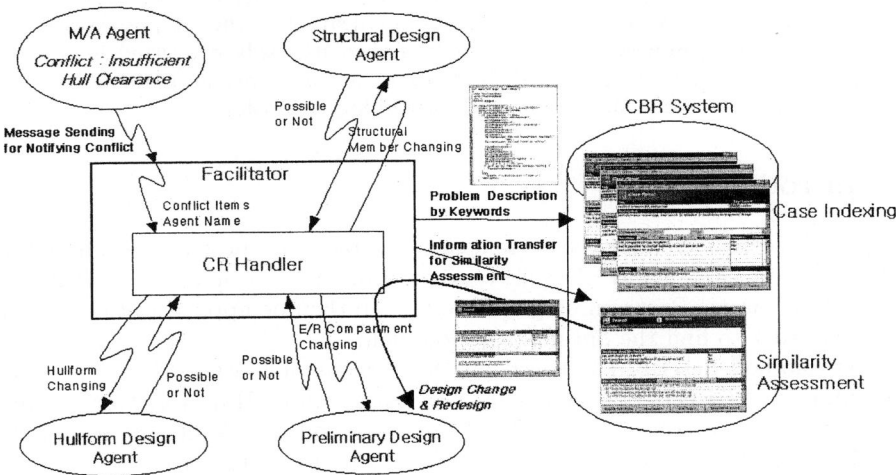

Fig. 3. Conflict Resolution Process for a Machinery Layout Design in the Developed System

Acknowledgement

This work is supported by Advanced Ship Engineering Research Center (R11-2002-104-08002-0) and INHA University.

References

1. Finin, T. & Wiederhold, G.: An Overview of KQML: A Knowledge Query and Manipulation Language, Technical Report, Logic Group, Computer Science Dept., Stanford University (1991)
2. Genesereth, M.R. & Ketchpel, S.: Software Agents, Communication of the ACM, 37(7) (1994)
3. Smith, Ian F.C.: Special Issue: Conflict Management in Design, AIEDAM. 9 (1995) 245-246
4. Klein, M.: Supporting Conflict Resolution in Cooperative Design Systems, IEEE Trans. on Stems, Man, and Cybernetics 21(6) (1991)
5. Sycara, K.: Negotiation Planning: An AI Approach, European Journal of Operational Research. 46 (1990) 216-234

Reduced MDP Representation of a Logistical Planning Problem Using Petri-Nets

Sanjeev Naguleswaran, Sarah L. Hickmott, and Langford B. White

National ICT Australia and School of Electrical and Electronic Engineering,
University of Adelaide, Australia

Abstract. This paper describes a method for unfolding a Predicate-net representation of a logistical planning problem, such that it possesses the Markov property. The problem can then be easily converted into a Markov Decision Process (MDP) which can be solved in a tractable manner using standard Dynamic Programming algorithms.

1 Introduction

This work seeks to reduce the state space of a planning problem, by unfolding a Petri-net in such a way that its configurations can be mapped to states of an MDP. Dynamic Programming techniques can then be applied to the reduced MDP in order to find the optimal solution plan.

The method described is based on the concept of Markov Nets [1], which are unfolded Petri-nets that posses the Markov property. However, Markov Nets are limited to representing automated processes, since they do not model the possibility of choosing between two actions required for planning.

Petri-nets are generally used for modelling and analysis of distributed systems and can be used to model a planning problem. The marking of a Petri-net is the mapping of tokens to places, and represents the state of the world. A Predicate Transition-net (PrT-net) is a high-level Petri-net formally defined in [2]. The planning problem described in this paper is represented as a PrT-net.

2 Reduced MDP Representation of Planning Problem

This section uses an example of a logistical planning problem to describe the mapping of a Petri-net to an MDP with reduced state space.

2.1 Unfolding a Petri-Net

The PrT-net representation of the planning problem can be unfolded into a labelled Occurrence Net (ON). The ON explicitly represents all possible runs, or configurations of the net. The nodes of the ON are labelled by the nodes of the original Petri-net. Detailed definitions of the concepts and algorithms for unfolding a low-level Petri-net are given in [3,4]. These form the basis for a method to unfold a high-level Petri-net described in [5].

2.2 2-Box, 2-Truck, 2-City Planning Problem

The 2-box, 2-Truck, 2-city planning domain involves moving boxes between cities, via trucks. A truck can only move one box at a time. The planning problem addressed here considers the situation where the two boxes are originally in city1 and the two trucks are in city2. The goal is to move both boxes to city2 with minimum cost. A PrT net representing this problem is shown in Figure 1(a). The place BiN(Box, City) contains tokens identifying the location of each Box. Similarly tokens in the place TiN(Truck, City) represent the location of the trucks. The place OnT(Box, Truck, City) represents the notion of a Box being on a Truck in a particular City. The actions Unload/Load(Box, Truck, City) unload/load the Box from the Truck in the specified City. The action Drive(Truck, City, City) takes the Truck from one City to the other.

The PrT-net is unfolded, as shown in Figure 1(b). A method of demarcating the unfolding of a net into layers possessing the Markov property is given in [1]. All combinations of local configurations in a layer are identified as runs. Each run is denoted by w_L^r, where the upper index r is the run number and lower index L denotes the layer. The possibility of not performing any run in a particular layer L is referred to as the w_L^0 run. The unfolding of the net is shown in Figure 1(b).

The cost of a run w on a layer L is the sum of the costs of all events contained in w. The occurrence of a run in a given layer is conditionally dependent on the occurrence of runs in previous layers.

In the example, in layer 1, the following additional runs derived from the combinations of local configurations are possible, but not depicted in Figure 1(b):

$$w_1^1 + w_1^3 = w_1^5, w_1^1 + w_1^4 = w_1^6, w_1^2 + w_1^3 = w_1^7, w_1^2 + w_1^4 = w_1^8.$$

The non-zero conditional probabilities of runs in each layer are now given. In layer 1, If the initial condition is β_0, then $p(w_1^i|\beta_0) = 1$, $i = 0..8$.

In layer 2,

$$p(w_2^0|w_1^j) = 1; j = 0..8,$$
$$p(w_2^1|w_1^j) = 1; j = 1,5,6,$$
$$p(w_2^2|w_1^j) = 1; j = 3,5,7,$$
$$p(w_2^3|w_1^j) = 1; j = 0..8.$$

In layer 3,

$$p(w_3^0|w_2^j) = 1; j = 0..3,$$
$$p(w_3^1|w_2^2) = 1,$$
$$p(w_3^2|w_2^1) = 1,$$
$$p(w_3^3|w_2^1) = 1,$$
$$p(w_3^4|w_2^3) = 1.$$

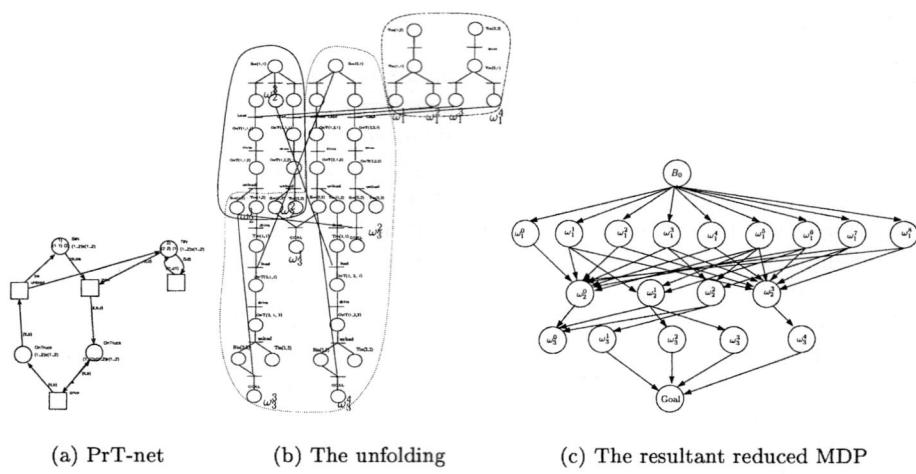

(a) PrT-net (b) The unfolding (c) The resultant reduced MDP

Fig. 1. The PrT-net, unfolding and Reduced MDP for the planning problem

An event e will only be a cut-off if the cost of reaching it is more expensive than the cost of reaching some other event e' with the same final state. All paths from this final state will thus be more expensive via e than e', so no path from e will ever be a minimum cost path to the goal. The implicit continuation of paths from event e can be neglected and the determination of layers, aggregation of runs as states, and mapping to an MDP can be processed as if it was the entire unfolding. It is possible to extend this method to stochastic problems with some additional conditions.

In the example the unfolding of the net is continued beyond the point at which the goal can first be reached, because there are other paths to the goal. The branches ending with truck1 in city2 (TiN(1,2)) can be continued without exceeding one of the costs necessary to reach the goal state, namely bringing a box using truck2 necessary to reach the goal state. The continuation of the unfolding of the net provides an alternative path to the goal state which appears further down the unfolding. The costs involved in the process are, cost of driving truck1, $c(T_1) = x$, cost of driving truck2, $c(T_2) = 3x$ and the combined cost of loading and unloading either of the trucks is y. Then the costs of each of the possible runs will be:

$$c(\omega_*^0) = \infty,$$
$$c(\omega_1^1) = x,\ c(\omega_1^2) = x,\ c(\omega_1^3) = 3x,\ c(\omega_1^4) = 3x,$$
$$c(\omega_1^5) = 4x,\ c(\omega_1^6) = 4x,\ c(\omega_1^7) = 4x,\ c(\omega_1^8) = 4x$$
$$c(\omega_2^1) = x + y,\ c(\omega_2^2) = 3x + y,\ c(\omega_2^3) = 0,$$
$$c(\omega_3^1) = x + y,\ c(\omega_3^2) = 3x + y,\ c(\omega_3^3) = 2x + y,\ c(\omega_3^4) = 2x + y.$$

The resultant MDP is shown in Figure 1(c). A total order has been imposed on the problem and therefore, the concurrent actions are ordered in a manner compatible with the Markov property. However, all required information for optimising the path to goal was preserved. The optimal solution can be extracted from the MDP using standard Dynamic Programming (DP) algorithms. The complexity of these algorithms are polynomial in the number of states. The state space of a relational MDP formulated directly from the problem specification would contain 2^{12} states. Therefore, the complexity savings in solving the smaller MDP is significant. The complexity of unfolding has not been properly analysed, although considerable work on reducing the complexity of unfolding is currently being undertaken[6][7].

3 Conclusion

A technique for converting a planning problem to a Petri-net model and analysing it as an MDP, by using and extending the concept of Markov Nets, was described in this paper. The resultant state-space of the MDP consisted of runs on layers of the net. This resulted in a significant reduction in the size of the state-space somewhat alleviating the problem of "state-space explosion" encountered in typical planning problems.

Further work on formalising the unfolding technique and the application of this technique to other standard planning domains and to stochastic problems is under investigation.

References

1. A. Benveniste, E. Fabre, S. Haar. Markov nets: Probabilistic models for distributed and concurrent systems - extended version. *Internal Report, IRISA, http://www.irisa.fr/distribcom/benveniste/ downloaded: November 2004*, 2003.
2. T. Murata, D. Zhang. A predicate-transition net model for parallel interpretation of logic programs. *IEEE Trans. on Software Engrg.*, 14:481–497, 1988.
3. J. Esparza, S. Romer, W. Vogler. An improvement of mcmillan's unfolding algorithm. *Formal Methods in System Design*, 20:285–310, 2002.
4. K. L. McMillan. A technique of a state space search based on unfolding. *Formal Methods in System Design*, 6:44–65, 1995.
5. V. Khomenko, M. Koutny. Branching processes of high level petri nets. *Proc. TACAS 2003, LNCS*, 2619, 2002.
6. M. Koutny V. Khomenko, W. Vogler. Towards an efficient algorithm for unfolding petri nets. *Proc. CONCUR 2001, LNCS*, 2154:366–380, 2001.
7. V. Khomenko K. Heljanko, M. Koutny. Parallelisation of the petri net unfolding algorithm. *Proc. TACAS 2002*, strony 372–385, 2002.

Structure-Based Algorithms for Computing Preferred Arguments of Defeasible Knowledge Bases

Quoc Bao Vo

School of Computer Science and Information Technology,
RMIT University, GPO Box 2476V, Melbourne, 3001, Australia
vqbao@cs.rmit.edu.au

Abstract. In this paper we present several efficient computational procedures for defeasible reasoning while the plausible and well-defined semantics, *viz. preferred models* and *stable models*, are not given up. The proposed algorithms exploit the structural information of defeasible knowledge bases to facilitate efficient computational models.

1 Introduction

Defeasible reasoning is considered as part of the core of common sense reasoning frameworks. Together with the conviction that common sense reasoning should be at heart of any construction of automated intelligent agents, this has motivated a great line of research in AI. However, most defeasible reasoning frameworks have often been plagued by heavy computational complexity. For instance, in the simple case of propositional logic, existing non-monotonic reasoning formalisms, e.g. default logic, autoepistemic logic, truth maintenance systems, etc. are computationally intractable. Results have been established that they are at least NP-complete (see e.g. [4,7,9]). The complexity of these formalisms gets even worse if one adopts the sceptical attitude towards the conclusions drawn by defeasible inferences.

Yet another problem, as it has always been one for the defeasible reasoning community, is the plausibility of the conclusions drawn by defeasible inference formalisms. The literature has witnessed quite a number of semantics proposed for various formalisms of defeasible reasoning, such as *extensions* for default theories [14], *expansions* for autoepistemic logic [11], *fix point* semantics for non-monotonic modal logics [10], *stable models* [6], *well-founded* semantics [5], *perfect models* [13], etc. for logic programs. Results have been established showing that under certain conditions standard semantics of non-monotonic and defeasible reasoning, i.e. extension, expansion and stable models are equivalent. However, even within a single formalism for defeasible reasoning, e.g. logic programming, several semantics are still competing and claiming their plausibility. For logic programs, we have stable model semantics, well-founded semantics, Kunen's 3-valued semantics, program completion-based semantics, perfect model semantics, etc. to name but a few.

In this paper, we pursue a general semantics for default knowledge bases which subsumes the stable model semantics. As a consequence, the computation is expected to be complex. We then introduce some algorithms that promise to work efficiently in the average cases by exploiting the structures of the defeasible knowledge bases.

2 Technical Framework

Throughout this paper we will follow the notations used in the answer set programming (ASP) paradigm [8] as well as those used in the argumentation-theoretic framework introduced by Bondarenko *et al.* [1]. We fix a set $\mathbf{P}$ of propositional symbols, called *atoms*, together with two additional symbols, i.e. $\top$, interpreted as true, and $\bot$, interpreted as false. A *literal* is an expression of the form A or $\neg A$, where A is an atom. (The symbol $\neg$ is called "classical negation".) The set of all literals is denoted by $\mathbf{P}^*$. We also use an operator *not* that plays a similar role to the negation-as-failure operator in logic programming. Specifically, the set $Ab \stackrel{def}{=} \{not\ L \mid L \in \mathbf{P}^*\}$ consists of the assumptions the reasoner can make in the absence of the contrary information. Given an assumption $not\ L \in Ab$, we define the contrary of $not\ L$, denoted by $\overline{not\ L}$, to be L. Obviously, L falsifies the assumption that L doesn't hold. We also define **arguments** to be subsets of $\mathbf{P}^* \cup Ab$.

Given an argument Ω, we define: $\Omega^+ \stackrel{\Delta}{=} \Omega \cap \mathbf{P}^*$ and $\Omega^- \stackrel{\Delta}{=} \Omega \cap Ab$. Also, relative to Ω, a member of Ω^+ is said to be **arguably** (or, **provably**) **true** while a member of Ω^- is **assumably false**.

Definition 1. *1. A rule element is a member of* $\mathbf{P}^* \cup Ab$*;*
2. A rule is an ordered pair

$$Head \leftarrow Body \qquad (1)$$

where $Head \in \mathbf{P}^*$ *and* $Body$ *is a finite set of rule elements;*
3. A (defeasible) knowledge base Π *is a set of rules.*

Given a rule r, we let $head(r)$ (resp. $body(r)$) denote the $Head$ (resp. the $Body$) of r. If $body(r) = \{L_1, \ldots, L_m, not\ L_{m+1}, \ldots, L_n\}$, then

- $body^+(r) \stackrel{\Delta}{=} \{L_1, \ldots, L_m\}$ containing the *pre-requisites* of r; and
- $body^-(r) \stackrel{\Delta}{=} \{not\ L_{m+1}, \ldots, L_n\}$ containing the *assumptions* of r.

Rule r is said to be *about* $head(r)$. A rule with an empty body is called a *unit rule*. A rule is *Horn* if it does not contain any assumption. A knowledge base is *Horn* if all its rules are Horn. Note that we omit the notion of *theories* in the formalisation of assumption-based frameworks here. A theory can be encoded as unit rules in this restricted representation of knowledge bases. Moreover, a knowledge base can be expanded or shrunk as information is added to (removed from) it. The added information is of course also in the form of rules. We denote by $lit(r)$ (resp. $r.elem(r)$ the set of literals (resp. rule elements) appearing in rule r.

Definition 2. Let Π be a knowledge base and $\Delta \subseteq Ab$ a set of assumptions. A *proof* based on Π wrt. Δ, abbreviated as (Π, Δ)-proof, is a sequence $(\beta_1, \ldots, \beta_m)$, where $m > 0$, such that for $i = 1, \ldots, m$: (i) $\beta_i \in \Delta$, or (ii) there exists $\beta_i \leftarrow \alpha_1, \ldots, \alpha_n$ in Π such that $\{\alpha_1, \ldots, \alpha_n\} \subseteq \{\beta_1, \ldots, \beta_{i-1}\}$.

A (Π, Δ)-proof $(\beta_1, \ldots, \beta_m)$ is said to be *for* α if $\beta_m = \alpha$. $L \in \mathbf{P}^*$ is a **consequence** of (Π, Δ), abbreviated as (Π, Δ)-consequence, iff there is a (Π, Δ)-proof for L. The set $\Delta \cup \{L \in \mathbf{P}^* \mid L \text{ is a consequence of } (\Pi, \Delta)\}$ is the **argument** wrt. (Π, Δ).

The above definition for knowledge bases is similar to definitions of normal logic programs. Therefore, notions such as stable models and well-founded models are applicable to knowledge bases. As with logic programs, not all knowledge bases have stable models. Bondarenko et al. [1] introduce a generalised version of stable models called preferred models. Their study is based on the properties of the set of assumptions accepted by a model. Given a knowledge base Π, a set of assumptions Δ **attacks** an assumption $not\ L$ iff L is a (Π, Δ)-consequence. And Δ attacks a set of assumptions Δ' iff there is some member of Δ' that is attacked by Δ. Now, relative to a given knowledge base Π, a set of assumptions Δ is **stable** if it does not attack itself and it attacks every assumption that is not a member of its. Bondarenko et al. [1] show that the above notion of stable sets of assumptions corresponds exactly with the stable models defined for logic programs (and extensions as defined for default logic). Another interesting notion is admissible sets of assumptions. An **admissible** set of assumptions Δ does not attack itself and is able to defend itself against all attacks against it, i.e. if some other set of assumptions attacks Δ then Δ attacks back at that set. To avoid trivial admissible sets of assumptions such as the empty set, the **preferred** sets of assumptions are considered: they are maximal (wrt set inclusion) admissible sets of assumptions. Since, relative to a knowledge base Π, every set of assumptions uniquely determines an argument, the notions of stability, admissibility and preferability are extended to arguments.

In order to exploit the structures of knowledge base for the sake of efficient inference, we appeal to the *inference graphs*, a formulation introduced by Pollock [12]. An *inference graph* is a labelled directed graph $\langle V, \mathcal{L}, \mathcal{I}, \mathcal{D} \rangle$ consisting of a finite set of nodes V representing the *steps of inference* (or *reasons*), and $\mathcal{L}$ is a set of labels which gives each justification of a node a unique name. Furthermore, $\mathcal{I}$(resp. $\mathcal{D}$) $\subseteq V \times V \times \mathcal{L}$ are the sets of labelled inference links (resp. defeat links) such that if $(\alpha_1, \beta_1, l), (\alpha_2, \beta_2, l) \in \mathcal{I} \cup \mathcal{D}$ then $\beta_1 = \beta_2$. Following Pollock [12], we call the labels of $\mathcal{L}$ the **justifications**.[1]

Our proposal is to keep knowledge bases at the core of a declarative representation while putting up equivalent inference graphs for the purpose of efficient reasoning.

3 Computing Preferred Arguments

As the nodes in an inference graph correspond to the atoms occurring in the associated knowledge base, it is desirable to compute interpretations over the set of steps of inference (i.e. nodes) of an inference graph. Pollock [12] introduces the notion of *status assignments* that assign the statuses of being $undefeated$, $defeated$ or $unknown$ to nodes of an inference graph. These statuses correspond to the associated atoms being provably true, assumably false, and unknown, respectively. Given a set of nodes W, a status assignment σ is *complete* regarding W if every node in W is assigned a status by

---

[1] Observe our generalisation from Pollock's original definition as we allow multiple justifications for steps of inference and defeaters being relative to particular justifications.

σ. A status assignment σ is *partial* wrt W if there is some node in W that is assigned *unknown* by σ. σ is *total* if it is complete and is not partial.

The two algorithms we propose to compute the preferred arguments of a given defeasible knowledge base are based on the following observations: The computational hardness of computing preferred (resp. stable) arguments is due to the set of non-Horn rules $\mathcal{NH}$ of the given defeasible knowledge base. Once the applicability of these rules is fixed, the preferred (resp. stable) arguments of the given knowledge base can be computed in polynomial time. There are two ways to fix the applicability of the non-Horn rules of a given defeasible knowledge base: (i) fixing the set of applicable non-Horn rules in advance (while regarding the rest of unapplicable), and verify whether the resulting argument meets the conditions of preferred arguments; and (ii) start with the acceptability status of the defeaters in the bodies of the non-Horn rules and proceed to assign the status for other nodes in the inference graph representing the given defeasible knowledge base.

In the former approach, the power set of $\mathcal{NH}$ is structured into a lattice whose top element is $\mathcal{NH}$ itself and bottom element is the empty set $\emptyset$. The relationship between the subsets of $\mathcal{NH}$ is the set-inclusion relation. The algorithm traverses the lattice from top to bottom using a breath-first search strategy: As soon as the set of non-Horn rules at the node it is visiting produces a preferred argument, it records this set and removes all descendants of this node (from the lattice) before continuing the search by visiting the next sibling of this node.

In the latter approach, the algorithm is based on the idea behind the proof procedure proposed by Davis, Putnam, Logemann, and Loveland (DPLL) [3,2] that checks for satisfiability of a set of propositional formulas. Essentially, the algorithm assigns acceptability, rejectability, and unknown statuses to the nodes from the corresponding inference graph and performs the propagation of these stautuses to other nodes. Details of the algorithms are discussed in the full paper.

References

1. A. Bondarenko, Phan M. Dung, Robert A. Kowalski, and Francesca Toni. An abstract, argumentation-theoretic approach to default reasoning. *AIJ*, 93:63–101, 1997.
2. Martin Davis, George Logemann, and Donald Loveland. A machine program for theorem-proving. *Communications of the ACM*, 5:394–397, 1962.
3. Martin Davis and Hilary Putnam. A computing procedure for quantification theory. *Journal of the ACM*, 7(3):201–215, 1960.
4. Charles Elkan. A rational reconstruction of nonmonotonic truth maintenance systems. *Artificial Intelligence Journal*, 43(2):219–234, 1990.
5. Allen Van Gelder, Kenneth A. Ross, and John S. Schlipf. The well-founded semantics for general logic programs. *Journal of the ACM*, 38(3):620–650, 1991.
6. Michael Gelfond and Vladimir Lifschitz. The stable model semantics for logic programming. In *Procs. of the 5th ICLP*, pages 1070–1080, 1988.
7. Henry A. Kautz and Bart Selman. Hard problems for simple default logics. *AIJ*, 49(1-3):243–279, 1991.
8. V. Lifschitz. Answer set programming and plan generation. *AIJ*, 138(1-2):39–54, 2002.
9. W. Marek and M. Truszczynski. Autoepistemic logic. *Journal of the ACM*, 38(3):588–619, 1991.

10. Drew V. McDermott and Jon Doyle. Non-monotonic logic I. *AIJ*, 13(1-2):41–72, 1980.
11. R. Moore. Semantical considerations on nonmonotonic logic. *AIJ*, 25(1):75–94, 1985.
12. John Pollock. *Cognitive Carpentry: A Blueprint for How to Build a Person.* MIT Press, London, 1995.
13. Teodor C. Przymusinski. Perfect model semantics. In *the Fifth International Conference and Symposium on Logic Programming*, Seattle, Washington, 1988.
14. Ray Reiter. A logic for default reasoning. *AIJ*, 13:81–132, 1980.

Solving Job-Shop Scheduling Problems by a Novel Artificial Immune System

Hong-Wei Ge, Liang Sun, and Yan-Chun Liang*

College of Computer Science, Jilin University, Key Laboratory of Symbol Computation and
Knowledge Engineering of the Ministry of Education, Changchun 130012, China
ycliang@jlu.edu.cn

Abstract. The optimization of job-shop scheduling is very important because of its theoretical and practical significance. This paper proposes an efficient scheduling method based on artificial immune systems. In the proposed method, the initial population is generated by a proposed scheduling initialization algorithm based on the G&T algorithm, and the models of the vaccination and receptor editing are designed to improve the immune performance. The approach is tested on a set of standard instances taken from the existing standard library. The simulation results validate the effectiveness of the proposed algorithm.

1 Introduction

The job-shop scheduling problem (JSSP) is a very important practical problem in both fields of production management and combinatorial optimization. Efficient methods for solving the JSSP have significant effects on profitability and product quality. Historically, the JSSP was primarily treated by exact optimization algorithms and some heuristic methods. Because the JSSP is among the worst members of the class of NP-complete problems, there remains much room for improvement in current techniques and exploitation of new efficient methods. In this paper, a new scheduling algorithm based on the principles of the artificial immune system (AIS) is proposed. The proposed algorithm is built on the principles of clonal selection, affinity maturation and the abilities of learning and memory.

2 A Novel AIS-Based Scheduling Algorithm

The job shop problem studied in the paper consists of scheduling a set of jobs on a set of machines with the objective to minimize the makespan. Each machine can handle at most one job at a time. Each job consists of a chain of operations to be processed in a specified sequence, on specified machines, and during an uninterrupted time period of given length. In solving the JSSP by the AIS, each antibody molecule is requested to represent a potential solution of the problem, and the corresponding problem is the antigen. In this paper, an operation-based representation is adopted, which uses an

---

* Corresponding author.

unpartitioned permutation with m-repetitions of job numbers. The antibody affinity degree with the antigen is evaluated by the following formulation

$$f_i = 100 \times opt/T_i. \qquad (1)$$

Where opt is the theoretical optimum makespan, T_i is the makespan corresponding to the ith antibody. The affinity function is linearly adjusted to avoid early convergence and ensure the variety of antibodies and the proportional model is used for the clonal selection in this paper.

2.1 Population Initialization Algorithm

In this paper, a novel scheduling initialization algorithm is proposed based on the algorithm of Giffler and Thompson. The brief outlineof the algorithm is as follows:

Step 1. Let the set A contain the first schedulable operation of each job. Let $s_{jm}=0$, for all the operation (j, m) in the set A, where s_{jm} is the earliest time at which the operation (j, m) can start.

Step 2. Calculate $t(A)=\min(s_{jm}+p_{jm})$, for all the operation $(j, m) \in A$, where p_{jm} is the processing time of the operation (j, m).

Step 3. Set up the set M, for all the operations, if $(j, m) \in A$, $s_{jm}< t(A)$, put the machine m into set M. Then set up the set G, randomly select a machine m^*, for all the operations $(j, m) \in A$, put the operation (j, m) into set G if it is processed on the machine m^*.

Step 4. For all the operations $(j, m^*) \in G$, calculate the earliest completed time of job j if the operation (j, m^*) is currently processed, let j^* denote the lastly completed job.

Step 5. Select the operation (j^*, m^*) from the set G and append it to the schedule.

Step 6. Delete the operation (j^*, m^*) from the set A, then subjoin its immediate successor into set A. Then update s_{jm} in the set A and return to step 2 until A is empty, namely all the operations are scheduled.

2.2 Vaccination and Mutation

In this section, a novel vaccination operation is proposed. We take full advantage of some characteristic information and knowledge in the process of solving problem to distill vaccines, and then vaccinate some antibodies. The process of vaccination is designed as follows. First, the antibody with the highest affinity is recognized, here called the best antibody, and then an antibody is selected for vaccination. Produce a vector of length $j \times m$ for the problem of j jobs and m machines which is randomly filled with elements of the set $\{0, 1\}$. This vector defines the order in which genes of the newly produced antibody molecule are drawn from the best antibody and the selected antibody, respectively. After a gene is drawn from one antibody and deleted from the other one, it is appended to the newly produced antibody molecule. This step is repeated until both the best and the selected antibody molecules are empty and the produced antibody contains all the genes involved. If the produced antibody is better than the original antibody, replace the original antibody by the produced. The mutation operations are completed by selecting several positions from the antibody molecule and permuting the genes on these positions randomly.

2.3 Receptor Editing

Due to the random characteristic of the mutation processes, a large proportion of mutating genes become non-functional or develop into harmful anti-self specificities. Those cells are eliminated by a programmed death process known as receptor editing. The proposed receptor editing model includes antibody introduction and gene shift.

If there is no improvement of the highest affinity degree for a certain number of generations, the two operations are performed. The antibody introduction is that a certain percentage of antibodies are randomly produced by the proposed initialization algorithm and replace the worst antibodies of the whole population. The process of the gene shift is described as follows. Randomly select some antibodies, for every selected antibody, randomly select a gene of the antibody molecule, make it move backwards in turn and once shift one position until it moves λ times, and then the λ new antibodies are produced. We replace the original antibody by the antibody with the highest affinity among the produced antibodies if it is better than the original.

2.4 Novel Artificial Immune Algorithm for JSSP

The outline of the proposed algorithm based on the AIS can be described as follows:

Step 1. Initialize n antibodies as an initial population.

Step 2. Calculate and adjust the affinity degree of each antibody.

Step 3. Select m antibodies from the population by the proportional selection model and clone them to a clonal library.

Step 4. Perform the mutation operation for each of the antibodies in the clone library.

Step 5. Randomly select r antibodies from the clonal library to perform the vaccination. Then replace the worst s antibodies in the population by the best s antibodies from the clonal library.

Step 6. Perform the operation of receptor editing if there is no improvement of the highest affinity degree for a certain number of generations G.

Step 7. Stop if the termination condition is satisfied, else repeat Step 2-Step 7.

3 Numerical Simulation Results

The performance of the proposed novel AIS-based algorithm for the JSSP is examined by using some test problems taken from the OR-Library [1]. Numerical experiments are performed on a PC with Pentium IV 1.4 GHz processor and 256MB memory. Some parameters in the AIS are taken as: $n=50$, $m=30$, $r=10$, $s=10$, $G=100$. The simulation results are compared with using the greedy randomized adaptive search procedure (GRASP) proposed in Reference [2].

Table 1 shows these simulated results. The BKS represents the value of the best known solution for each problem. From the table it could be concluded that the proposed novel AIS-based algorithm for solving JSSP is very superior by comparing the makespan and the time cost, especially for larger problems.

Table 1. Comparisons of the results between AIS and GRASP

Problem	Size	BKS	AIS	GRASP	AIS err(%)	GRASP err(%)	AIS time(s)	GRASP time(s)
la06	15×5	926	926	926	0.00	0.00	0.02	240
la07	15×5	890	890	890	0.00	0.00	0.17	250
la16	10×10	945	945	946	0.00	0.11	474	155310
la17	10×10	784	784	784	0.00	0.00	10.9	60300
la20	10×10	902	907	907	0.55	0.55	4.8	160320
la21	15×10	1046	1062	1091	1.53	4.30	321	325650
la24	15×10	935	967	978	3.42	4.60	773	64640
la25	15×10	977	982	1028	0.51	5.22	495	64640
la26	20×10	1218	1233	1271	1.23	4.35	1235	109080
la27	20×10	1235	1269	1320	2.75	6.88	1337	110090
la28	20×10	1216	1232	1293	1.32	6.33	553	110090
la29	20×10	1152	1196	1293	3.82	12.24	1882	112110
la31	30×10	1784	1784	1784	0.00	0.00	196	231290
la34	30×10	1721	1721	1753	0.00	1.86	8543	240380
la36	15×15	1268	1291	1334	1.81	5.21	840	115360
la39	15×15	1233	1250	1290	1.38	4.62	11200	115360
la40	15×15	1222	1242	1259	1.64	3.03	13300	123200

4 Conclusions

A promising AIS-based algorithm for job-shop scheduling problem is proposed. The simulation results are compared with using the GRASP algorithm. Numerical results show that the proposed algorithm not only improves the optimization performance, but also reduces the time cost, which provides an effective approach for solving scheduling problems.

Acknowledgements

The authors are grateful to the support of the NSFC of China (60433020), the science-technology development project of Jilin Province of China (20050705-2), and the doctoral funds of the Education Ministry of China (20030183060).

References

1. Beasley, J. E.: OR-Library: Distributing Test Problems by Electronic Mail. Journal of the Operations Research Society, 1990, 41 (11): 1069-1072.
2. Binato, S., Hery, W.J., Loewenstern, D.M., Resende., MG.C.: A GRASP for Job Shop Scheduling. Essays and Surveys in Metaheuristics, Kluwer Academic Publishers, Boston, 2001, 59–80.

Agent-Based Ontology Mapping Towards Ontology Interoperability

Li Li, Yun Yang, and Baolin Wu

Faculty of Information and Communication Technologies,
Swinburne University of Technology,
PO Box 218, Hawthorn, Melbourne, Australia 3122
{lli, yyang, bwu}@it.swin.edu.au

Abstract. Globalisation of business environments on the Web has given rise to the advent of similar ontologies in which dynamic ontology mapping is called in. Ontology mapping is necessary for ontology interoperability. In this paper, a novel agent-based ontology mapping is presented for agents to operate ontology mapping flexibly in a dynamic environment regardless heterogeneous platforms and different ontology representations. The mapping mechanism is discussed by having a close look at both inherent inter-processes of mapping tasks of an agent and relevant interaction processes. The interrelated processes of agents also enable agent-based ontology mapping to take ontology changes into account whenever needed. A mapping prototype is built for verification.

1 Introduction

Ontologies facilitate the interoperability between heterogeneous systems involved in commonly interested domain applications by providing a shared understanding of domain problems and a formalisation that makes ontologies machine-processable. An ontology is a formal description of a domain of discourse, intended for sharing among different applications, and expressed in a language that can be used for reasoning. It is known that any information system uses its own ontology, either implicitly or explicitly. The proliferation of Internet technology and globalisation of business environments, and tendency of different organisitions working together in order to solve a problem beyond individual capabilities and knowledge bring ontology mapping to the center of ontology related research. Besides, challenges arise from underlying ontologies evolving over time with the presence of changing environment such as the Web. All these may take place at unpredictable times, for unpredictable reasons, between unpredictable organisations. Agents in multi-agent systems (MAS) operate flexibly and rationally in an environment which are dynamic and heterogeneous, given that agents have abilities to perceive changes of environments and respond in a timely fashion [7]. A MAS perspective is thus suitable for tackling ontology mapping within and across the boundaries of organisations. The aim of this paper is to develop a novel agent-based ontology mapping mechanism to operate dynamic ontology mapping in order to achieve ontology interoperability.

Of the approaches of ontology mapping, some progresses [1,5,6] have been made already. In practice, most previous work have exploited only one form or another of ontology mapping in restrictive settings. We refer the reader to an excellent and thorough review [3] for a detailed discussion in this field. It is a great challenge to perform ontology mapping as flexible as possible by considering heterogeneous ontology sources (including heterogeneous platforms and different ontology representations) in a dynamic environment. To our best knowledge, ontology mapping on the fly through agent communications or interactions is a novel and feasible approach. It is better than current systems and tools which treat the environment of ontology mapping mainly static.

To this end, an agent-based ontology mapping mechanism based on our work [4] is developed. A key feature of our work is its flexibility and scalability; and its ability to perform ontology mapping dynamically. As actions of individual agents are based on interactions, any change of ontologies may be reflected in their interactions. Thus the proposed ontology mapping mechanism can be thought of also taking ontology changes or evolution into consideration.

This paper is organised as follows. Section 2 introduces the terminology of ontologies. Section 3 proposes our agent-based ontology mapping mechanism. Section 4 describes the prototype and the verification. And finally, Section 5 concludes our results.

2 Ontology Terminology

In this paper, we follow Gruber's best known ontology definition [2]. *An ontology is an explicit specification of a conceptualisation.* Within the ontology definition, we define an ontology $\mathcal{O}$ with a specific domain model, $\mathcal{T}$. Thus a conceptualisation Σ is a pair of $<\mathcal{C}, \mathcal{R}>$, where $\mathcal{C}$ represents a set of concepts, and $\mathcal{R}$ stands for a set of relations over these concepts. A specification is a pair of $<\Sigma, \Psi>$ to describe that Σ satisfies the axioms Ψ derived from the domain model.

There are many representations and languages[1] available for encoding an ontology, however to establish the notation of ontology used in a MAS internally for the task of ontology mapping, an Entity-Relation (E-R) data model is considered to encode an ontology, where concepts are regarded as classes. A typical concept class will have an identifier that distinguishes from others, and a set of attributes that describes the properties of the concept class. Then it is feasible to compare two concepts by looking at the identifier as well as the attributes. Below are definitions between two concept classes from two different ontologies. We assume that $\mathcal{O}_i$ and $\mathcal{O}_j$ are in the same domain, and c_i where $c_i \in \mathcal{O}_i$, c_j where $c_j \in \mathcal{O}_j$ are two different concepts.

Definition (*Equivalent*): Two concepts are semantically equivalent, i.e. $c_i \sim c_j$, if these two concepts: (1) have the same denotation names (e.g. labels); (2) are synonyms; or (3) their attributes are the same.

---
[1] There are many formal languages, such as RDF(s), OIL, DAML+OIL, or OWL for ontology representation. Intuitively, these languages differ in their terminologies and expressiveness. The ontologies that they model essentially share the same features.

Definition (*Inclusive*): Two concepts are semantically inclusive, i.e. $c_i \sqsubseteq c_j$ (e.g. c_i is a kind of c_j), if the attributes of one concept are also the attributes of the other.

Based on these definitions, we will define `ontology mapping` and `ontology interoperability` in the following.

Definition (*Ontology Mapping*): An mapping $\Re$ between two ontologies $\mathcal{O}_i$ and $\mathcal{O}_j$ exists, if $\exists c_i, c_j, \Re(c_i, c_j) \in \{equivalence, inclusion\}$.

Definition (*Ontology Interoperability*): Two ontologies $\mathcal{O}_i$ and $\mathcal{O}_j$ are interoperable, i.e. $\mathcal{O}_i \longleftrightarrow \mathcal{O}_j$, if there exists a mapping $\Re$ between these two ontologies.

3 Agent-Based Ontology Mapping Towards Ontology Interoperability

In our proposed framework [4], there are different kinds of agents to represent multiple perspectives of competing but coordinating organisations, and the distributed nature of the problems. Suppose an `ontology agent` (*OA*), which acts on behalf of the corresponding ontology, is in charge of ontology related tasks. It provides as much information of the ontology it acts on as possible. The *OA* operates over two structures: (1) the ontology structure (e.g. the ontology it acts on behalf of); and (2) the mapping result file. Besides, *OA*s act properly when triggered by different sources of driving-forces. For example, in a query module, an *OA* will dispatch a particular query request to other known *OA*s if it is unable to answer the query.

The `mapping agent` (*MA*) takes effect via the `interface agent` (*IA*) in the module of deciding whether existing ontologies come from the same domain or not; or in the module of ontology mapping through the *OA* and `thesaurus similarity agent` (*SA*) to acquire relevant information. The former module paves the way for deployment of rules in the latter. Actually, these rules are the little required prior knowledge (see **Definition (*Equivalent*)** & **Definition (*Inclusive*)**) in Section 2).

The `query agent` (*QA*) operates over the mapping results to investigate ontology-understandable of heterogeneous ontologies after executing ontology mapping. The query is done as follows: (1) if the query can be answered by a specified *OA*, then it terminates; (2) the specified *OA* dispatches the query to other relevant *OA*s if it is unable to answer the query; (3) the query module continues unless it runs out of candidates of *OA*s, or some *OA* can answer the query; (4) a dispatch path is found at the end if the query module ends with the query being answered, otherwise, no path found.

4 Prototype and Verification

We have developed an agent-based ontology mapping prototype by using the JADE platform (*http://jade.tilab.com/*). In order to facilitate multiple agents in the prototype to communicate with each other, a `meta-ontology` is built.

The feasibility of working together only comes after they can understand each other. Mapping needs to be done between pairs of ontologies. The **mapping** module in the prototype runs as follows:

(1) *Import* existing ontologies;
(2) *Develop* corresponding *OA* for each available ontology;
(3) *Develop* corresponding functionary agents (e.g *MA*);
(4) *Execute* the **mapping** module.

The above **mapping** module may loop between pairs of ontologies according to a corresponding scenario.

The verification such as **query** in distributed ontologies is conducted with the prototype. For the **query** module, we deliberately query a particular *OA* before/after ontology mapping. The experiments clearly show that a particular *OA* can instantly return corresponding concepts or **True/False** of the given propositions after running the **mapping** module. We believe that a query can be done given the graph (mapping) that is **weakly connected**.

5 Conclusions

In this paper, we have presented a novel agent-based ontology mapping to achieve ontology interoperability regardless heterogeneous environments and different ontology representations. The proposed mechanism allows flexible system organisation by also taking ontology evolution into consideration. Moreover, it is also in accordance with little prior knowledge needed but acquiring relevant knowledge directly from agent interactions during run-time.

References

1. Doan, A., Madhavan, J., Dhamankar, R., Domingos, P., and Halevy, A., Learning to Match Ontologies on the Semantic Web, *VLDB Journal*, Special Issue on the Semantic Web, 12(4), pp. 303-319, 2003.
2. Gruber, T. R., Toward Principles for the Design of Ontologies Used for Knowledge Sharing, KSL-93-04, http://ksl-web.stanford.edu/, 1993.
3. Kalfoglou, Y., and Schorlemmer, M., Ontology Mapping: The State of the Art, *Knowledge Engineering Review*, 18(1), pp. 1-31, 2003.
4. Li, L., Yang, Y., and Wu, B., Implementation of Agent-based Ontology Mapping and Integration, Technical Report, Swinburne University, http://www.it.swin.edu.au/personal/yyang/papers/2005TR-Li-1.pdf, 2005.
5. McGuinness, L. D., Conceptual Modelling for Distributed Ontology Environments, *Proc. of International Conference on Conceptual Structures*, pp. 100-112, 2000.
6. Noy, N. F., and Musen, M. A., The PROMPT Suite: Interactive Tools for Ontology Merging and Mapping, *International Journal of Human-Computer Studies*, 59(6), pp. 983-1024, 2003.
7. Wooldridge, M., *An Introduction to MultiAgent Systems*, John Wiley & Sons, ISBN 047149691X, 2002.

Dynamic Negative Selection Algorithm Based on Match Range Model

Jungan Chen[1], Feng Liang[1], and Dongyong Yang[2]

[1] Zhejiang Wanli University,
Ningbo, Zhejiang 315100, China
{friendcen21, liangf_hz}@hotmail.com
[2] Zhejiang University of Technology, No.6 District, Zhaohui Xincun,
Hangzhou, Zhejiang 310032, China
yangdy@ieee.org

Abstract. Dynamic Negative Selection Algorithm Based on Affinity Maturation (DNSA-AM) is proposed to generate dynamic detectors changed with nonselves. But it can not be adapted to the change of self because the match threshold is constant. In this work, a match range model inspired from T-cells maturation is proposed. Based on the model, an augmented algorithm is proposed. There is no match threshold but self-adapted match range. The proposed algorithm is tested by simulation experiment for anomaly detection and compared with DNSA-AM. The results show that the proposed algorithm is more effective than DNSA-AM with several excellent characters such as self-adapted match range and less time complexity.

1 Introduction

As a new area of soft computing, artificial immune system constructs the algorithms based on negative selection, immune network model, or clonal selection [1][2][3]. Negative Selection Algorithm (NSA) is applied to change detection [1], detection for time series data [4]. Several extensions are made and applied to network intrusion detection [5]. Real-valued NSA is combined with classification system and used to anomaly detection [6]. But NSA can not generate dynamic detectors changed with nonselves. Inspired from affinity maturation[5][7][8], Dynamic Negative Selection Algorithm Based on Affinity Maturation (DNSA-AM) is proposed by Wenjian L. and can be adapted to the change of nonself. In DNSA-AM, NSA is used to delete detectors which detect any selves [7].

Match rule is one of the most important components in NSA and DNSA-AM. There are several major types [5][9]. But no matter what kind of match rule, the match threshold (r) must be set at first. The value r is related to self data[1], so DNSA-AM can not be adapted to the change of self data.

In this work, a match range model inspired from T-cells maturation is proposed. With that, Dynamic Negative Selection Algorithm Based on Match Range Model (DNSA-MRM) is proposed. In DNSA-MRM,There is no match threshold but match range with selfmax,selfmin which is adapted to the change of selves.

2 The Model of the Dynamic Negative Selection Algorithm

T-cells maturation goes through two processes, positive and negative selection [9]. Positive selection requires T-cells to recognize self cells with lower affinity, while T-cells must not recognize self cells with higher affinity in negative selection. Based on this principle, there is a range between lower affinity and higher affinity. So a match range model with selfmin,selfmax is proposed in this work. *Selfmin* is the minimal distance between detector and selves. *Selfmax* is the maximal distance. The range between *selfmin* and *selfmax* is belonged to the self space. When the distance is bigger than *selfmax* or smaller than *selfmin*, a nonself is detected. By being set the value of selfmax and selfmin, one detector will not detect any selves because the distance between detector and selves is in the range between selfmax and selfmin. So NSA operator in DNSA-AM can be replaced by this operator which sets the value of selfmax and selfmin. With that, match range can be adapted to the change of self data because the value of selfmax and selfmin is evaluated by the self data.

```
1: Initialized the parameters and Detectors (detector population with PSize size)
2: While(haveAbnormal() and Generation < MaxGen) {
3:     Abnormal=getNextAbnormal()
4:     Do{  If(gen>MaxGen) break;
5:          AffinityEvaluation(Detectors, Abnormal)
6:          Children=GenerateNewDetectors(PSize*a,Detectors)
7:          Children= Children ∪ RandomNewDetectors(PSize * β)
8:          Evaluate selfmax and selfmin of Children
9:          AffinityEvaluation(Children, Abnormal)
10:         Detectors=select PSize detectors with higher affinity from {Children ∪ Detectors}
11:         If (Detect(Detectors,Abnormal)) { Abnormal is detected,break;}
12:         Else{ Abnormal.UndetectGen++;
13:             If (Abnormal.UndetectGen>MaxUndetectGen) {
                    Abnormal is taken as normal event,break; }}
14:         Generation++ ;
15:     } While(1) }
```

Fig. 1. Model of DNSA-MRM

Based on DNSA-AM and match range model inspired from T-cells maturation, DNSA-MRM shown in fig.1 is proposed. When abnormal is arrived (step 2~4), DNSA-MRM will be stimulated to response and detect this abnormal through affinity maturation (step 5~10) until abnormal is detected or taken as normal (step 11~13). In Fig.1, UndetectGen is defined as times failing to detect. Abnormal is taken as normal if Abnormal.UndetectGen is bigger than MaxUndetectGen. Step 5,9 evaluates the hamming distance between detector and abnormal, the fitness of detector is the hamming distance; Step6~10 simulate the affinity maturation. In step 6, the mutated number of bits is (the number of the bits in detector - affirnity)/2 and the number of children to be reproduced by a single parent are equal to the affinity of the parent. Step 7 is used to randomly generate detectors to avoid reaching local optimized value [3]. Step 8 is used to set the match range, so detector will not detect any self. Step 11~13 is used to detect abnormal. Abnormal will be taken as normal when it can not be detected within MaxUndetectGen generations.

3 Experiments for Anomaly Detection and Analysis

The objective of these experiments is to compare DNSA-MRM with DNSA-AM and investigate the self-adapted character of DNSA-MRM. The number of bits in detector is 64. a=0.95, β=1-a=0.05. PSize=200, MaxGen= MaxUndetectGen =250.

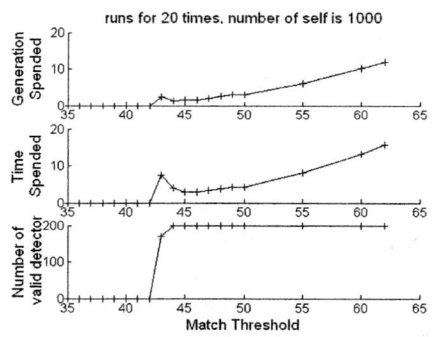
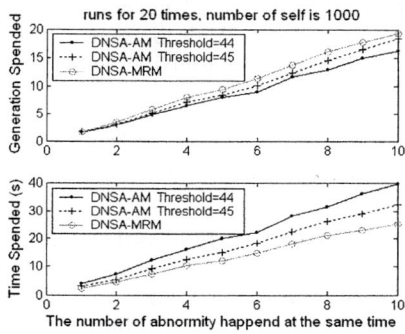

(a) Result of DNSA-AM with different match threshold

(b) Results of Generation Spended, Time Spended

Fig. 2. Comparison between DNSA-MRM and DNSA-AM

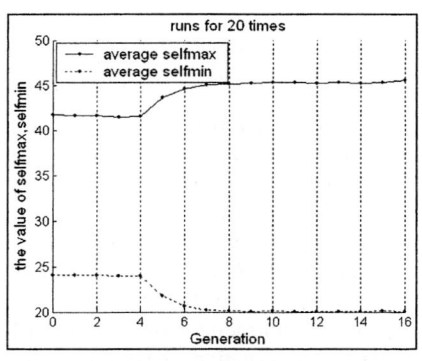
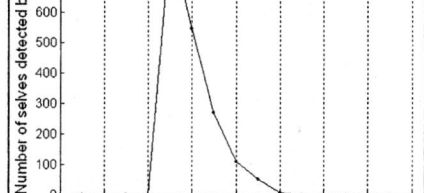

(a) Self-adapted Match Range

(b) Self-adapted False Positive

Fig. 3. Results of self-adapted character of DNSA-MRM

(1) Comparison between DNSA-MRM and DNSA-AM: Random generated string is used to simulation experiment just like [7]. The number of selves is 1000. To get the optimized match threshold of DNSA-AM, the number of abnormality is 1 and DNSA-AM runs for 20 times with different match threshold. The result is shown in fig.2 (a). It is shown that there is an optimized value r (44 or 45) to balance the generation spended and time spended. In this paper, the number of generations to detect the specific abnormalities is called generation spended.

Both DNSA-AM with optimized match threshold and DNSA-MRM runs for 20 times with different number of abnormalities. The result is shown in fig.2 (b). It is shown that time spended of DNSA-MRM is the smallest.

(2) Self-adapted character of DNSA-MRM: Random generated string is still used. The number of selves is 50 before the 5th generation and changed to 1000 after the 5th generation. DNSA-MRM runs for 20 times. Result is shown in fig.3. In fig.3 (a), the curve between the 5th generation and 10th generation shows the self-adapted process of match range. With the stimulation of abnormalities, old detectors are replaced by new detectors continually; False Positive is adapted to the change of nonselves in fig.3 (b).

4 Conclusions

In summary, the proposed algorithm DNSA-MRM is effective with self-adapted match range and less time complexity. Otherwise, with the stimulation of nonselves, DNSA-MRM will produce detectors with higher fitness. Some detectors will survive for a long time because of the stimulation of the same or similar nonselves repeatedly, so the patterns of nonselves will be remembered, which called 'memory' or 'learning' [5].However, there is one problem in DNSA-MRM. When data sets including both nonself and self data are send to detect, times of successful classification between nonself and self is really small. In human immune system, self cells have MHC marker to be identified as selves. So it is required to further research on this way.

References

[1] Forrest S., Perelson, A. S., Allen L., and Cherukuri R., Self-nonself Discrimination in a Computer, Proceedings of the 1994 IEEE Symposium on Research in Security and Privacy, Los Alamos, CA:IEEE Computer Society Press, 1994. Available at http://www.cs.unm.edu/~forrest/papers.html

[2] de Castro L. N. and Von Zuben F. J., aiNet: An Artificial Immune Network for Data Analysis, Book Chapter in Data Mining: A Heuristic Approach, H. A. Abbass, R. A. Sarker, and C. S. Newton (eds.), Idea Group Publishing, USA, Chapter XII, pp. 231-259, 2001

[3] de Castro L. N. and Von Zuben F. J., Learning and Optimization Using the Clonal Selection Principle, IEEE Transactions on Evolutionary Computation, Special Issue on Artificial Immune Systems, 6(3), pp. 239-251. 2002

[4] Dasgupta D., Forrest S.,Novelty Detection in Time Series Data using Ideas from Immunology. In Proceedings of The International Conference on Intelligent Systems, 1999.

[5] Hofmeyr S. A., An Immunological Model of Distributed Detection and its Application to Computer Security, PhD Dissertation, University of New Mexico, 1999.
[6] González F. and Dagupta D., Anomaly detection using real-valued negative selection.Genetic Programming and Evolvable Machines, 4(4), pp.383-403, 2003
[7] Wenjian L.,Research on Artificial Immune Model and Algorithms Applied to Intrusion Detection, PhD Dissertation, University of Science and Technology of China, 2003
[8] de Castro, Artificial Immune Systems and Their Applications, at the Brazilian Symposium on Neural Networks (SBRN'2000), 22-25th November, Rio de Janeiro/Brazil, 2000.
[9] Gonzalez F., A Study of Artificial Immune Systems applied to Anomaly Detection, PhD Dissertation, The University of Memphis, May 2003.

A Virtual Prolog Approach to Implementing Beliefs, Desires and Intentions in Animat Agents

K.A. Hawick, H.A. James, and C.J. Scogings

Computer Science, Massey University Albany,
North Shore 102-904, Auckland, New Zealand
{k.a.hawick, h.a.james, c.scogings}@massey.ac.nz
Tel: +64 9 414 0800, Fax: +64 9 441 8181

Abstract. Simulating a system of agents that navigate in a physical space is a challenging problem when the environment is sophisticated and the number of agents involved is large. We describe experiments in establishing a "virtual Prolog engine" in each agent in a simulation and the scalability and performance issues with such an approach. We report on experiments with a simple predator-prey animat model and discuss how this approach allows us to impart a degree of reasoning and intelligence to what are otherwise very simple animat agents.

Keywords: Animat agents; beliefs, desires and intentions; physical navigation and reasoning.

1 Introduction

The problem of representing per-agent knowledge in a multi-agent simulation system is not an easy one, especially if one considers the situation in which there are a very large number of independent agents. This problem is easily solvable if one makes the simplifying assumption that agents are homogeneous and they are "memory-less" agents. However, as soon as individual agents are enabled with a memory this problem becomes far more complex.

In this paper we consider the benefits and drawbacks of using a Prolog [5] or Prolog-like knowledge back-end for our agents and the various different configuration scenarios one can use when setting up such a system. We use the term "Virtual Prolog" simply to highlight the fact that we may or may not have embedded within our simulation system a commercial implementation of the Prolog engine, and that a single such engine may or may not be shared between all agents in our simulation.

We consider a general architecture for an animat agent. The animat encounters the environment in terms of other animats of a particular kind at particular locations during its travels. This, along with an internal notion of time, its own encoded behaviour (either learned or inherited), and a memory of where it has been in its own particular reference frame can combine to produce a decision on where to move next or what actions to perform. This idea is not new and forms the basic model for many robots and simulated life forms.

We consider the implementation issues of using a coded set of instructions or a logical reasoning engine as the core of the animat. We are especially interested in exploring the many-animat regime which is not yet economically feasible to explore for hardware robots with their own on-board computers. Finally, we are also interested in the interplay between different software coding and implementation styles – namely between mixing declarative knowledge base languages like Prolog with low-level encoded instructions or behaviours that can be acted upon with genetic algorithmic operations.

We have constructed a predator-prey model consisting of two distinct groups of animats: predators (known as "foxes") and prey (known as "rabbits"). The global environment is controlled by a number of fixed parameters, for example how long a fox takes to get hungry, at what age a rabbit will die of old age, etc. These parameters were established in order to provide a stable model that will continue for several thousand time-steps [7]. In our current simulation system, all species have the ability to perceive other animals up to a given radius; this perception radius is currently set to 80 pixels for foxes and 20 pixels for rabbits. Beyond that, nothing can be perceived. As our current simulation is "memoryless", knowledge of any animats that are identified as being nearby, but not close enough to take immediate action (i.e. prey being predated), is lost at the start of the next update cycle. We expect that the introduction of an animat memory will lead to interesting medium range interaction effects, such as prey actively avoiding predators, which will change the observed life-forms we have observed in previous studies [3]. We have conducted experiments with changing the order of priority of the rules [4]. These experiments do not qualify as genetic evolution experiments as every animat is an exact clone of its parents. The predator-prey model outlined above has resulted in some fascinating emergent behaviour in which animats formed clusters and spirals. This behaviour is analysed in [3]. However, interesting behaviours only occur when the model contains over 20,000 animats and is run for hundreds of time-steps. For this reason we are primarily interested in the run-time behaviour of readily accessible Prolog and Prolog-like systems when the knowledge base they have to maintain is of the order of 20,000 individual animats.

The BDI (Belief, Desire, Intention) [9] formalism is useful for representing the fully cognitive agent approach in which agents are able not only to store a searchable history, but are also able to formulate (or at least have specified) some sort of goals. This is a relatively well understood theory in AI and distributed AI [2]. Beliefs and intentions are relatively simple to express in our agent-based system: beliefs are based on an agent's perception of the environment, including similar and dissimilar types of animal and the physical environment; intentions are the rules invoked in response to the beliefs and desires of the animals. In a general case such as when simulating a large number of animats, desires (or goals) are possibly the hardest of all properties to express. For example, what does an animat predator (e.g. a fox) want? Does it want to keep its belly full? Does it want to reproduce as often as possible to increase the predator population? Even these two simplistic goals can be seen as conflicting: the more prey a predator eats the fewer there will be when it becomes hungry, and adding to the gene pool by reproducing will have the effect of introducing more competition for food. We find it convenient to distinguish between long-term goals and short-term goals. For example, the prey in our example system (e.g. a rabbit) may just want to eat or reproduce. These two goals may be considered to be a long-term goal while a short-term goal might be to not be eaten by a predator through the action of running away.

2 Declarative and Reasoning Engines

Prolog is a logic programming language built around the notion of first-order predicate calculus: facts, and relationships between different facts can be stated and queries can be posed using those relationships to prove or disprove statements. We have implemented a version of our simulation in Java for the purpose of graphical interactivity and Prolog experimentation. This allows us to implement an efficient multi-agent update algorithm (and graphical display) using Java and a knowledge representation back-end with Prolog. We anticipate that by combining both programming methodologies, we will be able to only use the most appropriate features of both systems, introducing few inefficiencies.

Consider the very simple case in which each of our 20,000 unique agents has moved only four times, encountering a different object at each step. If we only consider the predicates necessary to store knowledge of these objects, and each animat in the 20,000-strong system has encountered four objects, then this requires the Prolog reasoning system to be able to easily handle 80,000 predicates. Of course, this figure does not include the data necessary to represent an animat's internal state nor the animat's precise movement history. We use these figures as ball-park estimates of the predicates in our system for the purposes of testing.

We have considered two fundamental ways to link the simulation program manager with the Prolog engine: a) the factual database pertinent to a single animat is loaded and a move is generated. The facts are unloaded and facts relevant for the next animat are loaded into context. This way the prolog engine does not need to be concerned with an overly large database. There is however a latency that arises from the loading and unloading process. Because this approach uses a separate database of facts for each animat, it is a requirement that all facts (and rules) common to the system under consideration must be replicated inside each database. Depending on the complexity of the simulation system, this may be a considerable overhead.

Alternatively, one can load all facts into the same database and let the Prolog engine deal with the non-scalability. This is the second case under consideration: the database is loaded once and before each animat's state can be updated a filter must be imposed to only take into account the facts pertinent to that animat. This approach does have the distinct advantage that the more general logic production rules and system facts do not have to be replicated for each agent, but it does add a slight complexity to the way in which individual animats' knowledge must be stored in order to make them apply only to one agent.

We have also trialled CKIProlog [8] and JIProlog [1], Prolog-like libraries implemented completely in the Java programming language. The library implements a Prolog interpreter as a single first-class object; as such, one has the option of declaring a `Prolog` object inside either each animat *or* inside the simulation, this neatly implements the above two cases. Table 1 shows the representative times taken by the CKIProlog Java library to perform various simple operations on our multi-agent simulation systems. Times reported in the table are in milliseconds, as recorded on a dual-processor G4 Macintosh. It is worth noting that in order to create 100,000 Prolog interpreters (Model 1) it was necessary to increase the default memory size of the Java interpreter, thus making this approach slightly less attractive, although this overhead is slight compared with the time taken when using a single Prolog interpreter. Note that the time taken to query the single interpreter for 100,000 assertions took longer than over-night, so the query was cancelled. We have also considered semi-commercial packages such as Minerva [6] but as the style of programming was quite radically different from the existing C/C++/Java implementations we have not continued to use them.

Table 1. Time (ms) to perform simple actions using the CKIProlog Java library: creating Prolog interpreters, adding assertions to the Prolog engine, and querying the Prolog engine. The creation time is constant for the single Prolog interpreter as there is only ever one instantiated. The time to query the single interpreter for 100,000 assertions took longer than overnight so the query was cancelled.

number of animats	Prolog Interpreter per Animat			Single Prolog Interpreter		
	create	assert	query	create	assert	query
10	39	4	13	39	7	23
100	66	33	55	39	58	210
1,000	614	199	199	39	206	10582
10,000	1600	609	1587	39	7260	1067635
100,000	14736	8484	11202	39	1270826	

The overwhelming result from the experiments reported in table 1 is that while there is a considerable memory overhead in maintaining a separate Prolog engine for each animat in our Java implementation, it is significantly faster to assert new facts and search the existing knowledge base for only one animat. The memory saved by only maintaining a single Prolog engine is dwarfed by the amount of time that it takes to do a search when there are even 10,000 predicates in the system.

This agrees with our theory of optimising the most common case: that of having an animat decide what should be its next action based on its history. We are currently experimenting with a further hybrid approach of maintaining a small number of agents in the same Prolog engine so as to cut down on the amount of time spent in establishing the predicates and rules for the agents' physical systems. We anticipate this approach may also be useful when we update our model to pass on information to new 'young' animats created by parent reproduction in the process of model evolution.

3 Discussion and Conclusions

The convolution of declarative and reasoning engines in large-scale multi-agent simulation systems is an exciting area of research that we believe will show the way forward for many of the more complex problems facing researchers who wish to add more complexity into their simulations, while retaining their runtime efficiency.

There exist many off-the-shelf Prolog systems that allow the use of Prolog knowledge management and searching techniques with imperative languages without having to incur significant overheads such as swapping process contexts. Applications Programmer Interfaces are provided to many systems, and some, such as CKIProlog, are already implemented in an imperative language and accessible by native programming code.

We have shown in this paper that while it is logically more elegant to only have a single Prolog engine that stores all the facts for a given system, the explosion in run-time access when the number of individual agents numbers more than 1,000 makes this approach infeasible. While it is more expensive, in terms of memory overhead, it is more efficient to maintain a separate Prolog engine for each agent in the system. This new approach, incorporating Prolog with the existing Java/C/C++ code does not make the code any messier, although the model set-up time is increased because of the need to distribute out to all animats information on the physical bounds of their environment. Also somewhat tricky are the neighbour-checking routines that determine friend/foe proximity.

References

1. Chirico, U. "JIProlog 3.0.1". Available from http://www.ugosweb.com/jiprolog
2. Ferber, J. "Multi-Agent Systems An Introduction to Distributed Artificial Intelligence", Addison-Wesley, 1999, ISBN 0-201-36048-9.
3. Hawick, K.A., Scogings, C.J. and James, H.A. "Defensive Spiral Emergence in a Predator-Prey Model" in Proc. Complexity 2004, Cairns, Australia, December 2004.
4. Hawick, K.A., James, H.A. and Scogings, C.J. "Roles of Rule-Priority Evolution in Animat Models", To appear *Proc ACAL'05*, Sydney, 2005.
5. International Standards Organisation "Prolog Standards, ISO/IEC 13211-1:1995", 1995.
6. IF Computer. "MINERVA" Available from http://www.ifcomputer.co.jp/MINERVA
7. James, H.A., Scogings, C.J. and Hawick, K.A. "A Framework and Simulation Engine for Studying Artificial Life", in Research Letters in the Information and Mathematical Sciences, Vol 6, May 2004, pp143-155, ISSN 1175-2777. Available from http://iims.massey.ac.nz/research/letters/volume6/
8. van Otterloo, S. "CKI Prolog" Available from http://www.csc.liv.ac.uk/~sieuwert/programs.html
9. Rao, A.S. and Georgeff, M.P. "BDI Agents: From Theory to Practice", in Proc First Int Conf on Multi-Agent Systems (ICMAS-95), San Francisco, USA June, 1995.

Obstacle Avoidance and Path Planning Based on Flow Field for Biomimetic Robotic Fish

Jinyan Shao[1], Guangming Xie[1], Long Wang[1], and Weicun Zhang[2]

[1] Center for Systems and Control, Department of Mechanics and Engineering Science,
Peking University, Beijing 100871, P.R. China
jyshao@pku.edu.cn
[2] Automation Department, University of Science and Technology Beijing,
Beijing 100083, P.R. China

Abstract. This paper investigates the problem of obstacle avoidance and path planning for robotic fish. The swimming of the robot fish to avoid some obstacles is viewed as potential flow around the obstacles. Then the streamlines from the robot position to the target are chosen as the desired paths for the mobile robot to move to the destination. Since there are mature algorithms with high computational efficiency to establish flow field and figure out the streamlines based on fluid mechanics theory, our approach is practical for application. We conduct two example experiments to verify the effectiveness of the approach.

1 Introduction

One of the essential requirements for underwater mobile robots is to plan a safe and economic trajectory in its working environment. Thus, the problem of obstacle avoidance is one of the important issues in current robotics research. While there is a wide literature about obstacle avoidance and path planning for ground robots, a relatively little number of papers report the algorithms specifically designed for underwater applications. In addition, the specific characteristics of underwater robots do not allow a straightforward extension of most motion algorithms designed for land vehicles to underwater vehicles. In this paper, we present a novel framework for obstacle avoidance by viewing the underwater robot's movement as the flowing of fluid. Firstly, we put a point source at the location of the robot and a point sink at the destination and establish a flow field. Then the flow field can be solved based on theories in fluid dynamics and streamlines can be obtained. Finally, we choose streamlines as feasible paths for the robot to avoid obstacles and reach its destination.

2 Problem Formulation and Algorithm

For the sake of convenience, we focus on the 2-dimensional plane and irrotational motion of inviscid and incompressible fluid with closed boundary. As shown in figure 1 (a), we view the initial position of the robotic fish as a source from which the fluid flow around radially and uniformly, and the destination as a sink which conducts the surrounding fluid to flow into it. By applying the fluid dynamics theory, the fluid satisfies the following classical fluid mechanics equations [3].

$$div\ v = 0, \quad rot\ v = 0, \quad \frac{Dv}{Dt} = F_b - \frac{1}{\rho}\nabla p \tag{1}$$

and the boundary condition on the surface of the obstacle,

$$v \cdot n\ |_w = v_w \cdot n \tag{2}$$

where v is the velocity vector of the fluid. There are many mature algorithms to establish the flow field and figure out the streamlines, such as finite difference method, finite element method, and panel method. In panel method, the boundary of obstacle is supposed to be covered by finite small pieces, which are called panels. A point source with certain intensity is set on each panel. These point sources are used such that when it encounters the boundary of the object, the fluid shunts along the tangent of the object. It follows that the velocity vector of the fluid is tangent to the panel at the point source. For example, suppose there are m panels around the obstacle. Let (x_1,y_1), $(x_2,y_2)\cdots(x_m,y_m)$ denote the coordinates of the m point sources, and $\lambda_1, \lambda_2 \cdots \lambda_m$ be the intensity of the intensity of unit length on the panels. Denote (a_1,b_1), (a_2,b_2) the coordinates of the point source and the point sink, respectively. The velocity potential of the flow at the control point (x_i,y_i) on panel i is given by

$$\varphi(x_i,y_i) = \frac{Q}{2\pi}\ln r_1 - \frac{Q + \sum_{j=1}^{m}\lambda_j}{2\pi}\ln r_2 + \sum_{j=1}^{m}\frac{\lambda_j}{2\pi}\int_j \ln r_{ij} ds_j \tag{3}$$

where Q is the flowrate from the point source and $r_1 = \sqrt{(x_i - a_1)^2 + (y_i - b_1)^2}$, $r_2 = \sqrt{(x_i - a_2)^2 + (y_i - b_2)^2}$, $r_{ij} = \sqrt{(x_i - x_j)^2 + (y_i - y_j)^2}$. Moreover, denote n_i the outside normal vector of the panel i, and β_i tie inclination between the vector n_i and the x-axis, i = 1, 2, $\cdots$ m. The boundary condition on the obstacle's surface requires that the velocity on the normal direction of the control point must be zero, that is, $\frac{\partial}{\partial n_i}\varphi(x_i,y_i) = 0$, $i = 1,2,\cdots m$. Substituting (1) to (2), get

$$\frac{\lambda_i}{2} + \sum_{j\neq i}^{m}\frac{\lambda_j}{2\pi}\int_j \frac{\partial}{\partial n_i}(\ln r_{ij})ds_j = \frac{\partial}{\partial n_i}(\frac{Q + \sum_{j=1}^{m}\lambda_j}{2\pi}\ln r_2 - \frac{Q}{2\pi}\ln r_1) \tag{4}$$

Since the obstacle is known, the normal vector n_i at every control point is known as well. If we calculate the value of $\int_j \frac{\partial}{\partial n_i}(\ln r_{ij})ds_j$, we can obtain a set of m algebra equations for solving $\lambda_1, \lambda_2 \cdots \lambda_m$. Then, we can write down the following streamline equation

$$\psi = \frac{Q}{2\pi}\arctan\frac{y-b_1}{x-a_1} - \frac{Q + \sum_{j=1}^{m}\lambda_j}{2\pi}\arctan\frac{y-b_2}{x-a_2} + \sum_{j=1}^{m}\frac{\lambda_j}{2\pi}\arctan\frac{y-y_i}{x-x_i} \tag{5}$$

Another method is the finite element method which is an approximate method of solving differential equations of boundary. In this method, a continuous solving domain is divided into many small elements of convenient shapes. Choosing suitable points called "nodes" within the elements, the variable in the differential equation is written as a linear combination of appropriately selected interpolation functions and the values of the variable or its various derivatives specified at the nodes. Using variational principles or weighted residual methods, the governing differential equations are transformed into "finite element equations" governing all isolated elements. These local elements are finally collected together to form a global system of differential or algebraic equations with proper boundary and/or initial conditions imposed. We can't present the algorithm in detail due to space limitation.

3 Experiments and Results

We conduct the experiments in a lab environment, and figure 1 (b) shows the the experimental test-bed. The platform consists of four subsystems: robot fish subsystem, image capturing subsystem, decision making and control subsystem and wireless communication subsystem. The employed robotic fish is a 400mm long four-linked robotic fish and its characteristics can be found in [1] and [2].

Next, we show two examples to verify the flow field approach. In the first example, we put two convex obstacles in to the pond as shown in figure 2 (a). The initial position of the robot fish is at $(97, 70)$ and the final goal position is at $(350, 300)$. In the second example, as shown in figure 2 (b), we put a concave obstacle in another smaller pond with the initial as $(70, 175)$ and final positions as $(600, 175)$. The results show using the flow field method, the robot fish can successfully negotiate concave obstacles without sticking in local minima. Figures 2 (c) (d) indicate the trajectories of the robotic fish in the experiments.

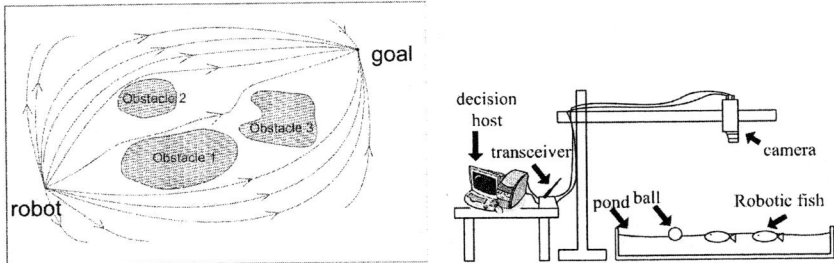

Fig. 1. (a) Problem formulation based on flow field. (b) Hardware platform for obstacle avoidance of multiple biomimetic robot fish.

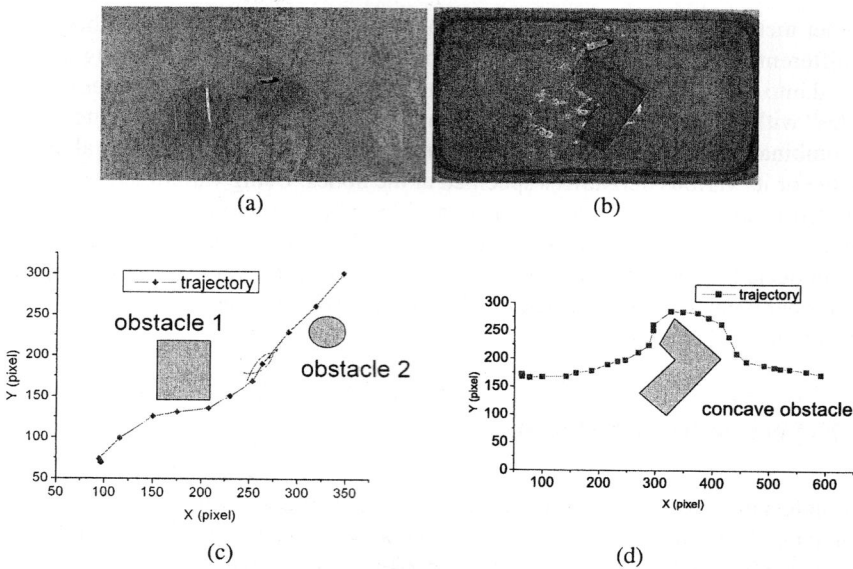

Fig. 2. (a) Two obstacles example. (b) The robot fish negotiates a concave obstacle. (c) The trajectory of the robot fish in example (a). (d) The trajectory of the robot fish in example (b).

4 Conclusions and Future Work

In this paper, the problem of obstacle avoidance and path planning for a bio-mimetic robot fish has been investigated. Based on the characteristics of the robot fish and the hydrodynamics, a novel approach based on flow field has been presented. In this approach, the movement of the robot fish avoiding obstacles is viewed as the flowing of certain fluid around the obstacles and a flow field is established. We take the streamlines connecting the initial position to the destination as the desired path for the mobile robot to move to its goal. The experimental results show the effectiveness and advantages of this approach. Future work includes figuring out the optimal streamline to the destination and exploiting the possible application of our approach in three dimensional space.

References

1. J. Yu, L. Wang, and M. Tan. A framework for biomimetic robot fishs design and its realization. Proceedings of American Control Conference, Portland, USA, 1593-1598, 2005.
2. J. Yu and L. Wang. Parameter optimization of simplified propulsive model for biomimetic robot fish. Proceedings of IEEE International Conference on Robotics and Automation. Barcelona, Spain, 3317- 3322, 2005.
3. J. D. Anderson, Computational Fluid Dynamics, McGraw-Hill Companies, Inc, 2002.

A Facial Control Method Considering Internal Emotion of Sensibility Robot

Hiroshi Shibata[1], Masayoshi Kanoh[2], Shohei Kato[1], and Hidenori Itoh[1]

[1] Nagoya Institute of Technology, Gokiso-cho, Showa-ku, Nagoya 466-8555, Japan
{shibata, shohey, itoh}@ics.nitech.ac.jp
[2] Chukyo University, 101 Tokodachi, Kaizu-cho, Toyota 470-0393, Japan
mkanoh@life.chukyo-u.ac.jp

Abstract. This paper presents a method that enable a domestic robot to show emotions with its facial expressions. The previous methods using built-in facial expressions were able to show only scanty face. To express faces showing complex emotion, mixed emotions and different strengths of emotions, more facial expressions are needed. We have therefore developed a system that converts emotions into "Ifbot" robot's facial expressions automatically. They are created from *emotion parameters*, which represent its emotions.

Content Areas: Entertainment and AI, robotics.

1 Introduction

We focused on the facial expressions as a mechanism that enable robot to express emotions to people. Facial expressions, as well as speech and gestures, play an important role when people express emotions during communication [1]. Facial expressions for robots are created by the intricate, coordinated movement of motors located eyes, eyelids, neck, and the others. Development of a method for interpolating or merging designed expressions would enable creation of many expressions showing several emotions. We investigated a mechanism for generating facial expressions that would enable robots to express several emotions. We developed a sensibility robot, the Ifbot [2,3], with facial expression mechanisms using emotions. Figure 1 shows Ifbot appearance. Ifbot is able to communicate with a person, showing its "emotions" through facial expressions and gestures. The method used for smooth connecting some facial expressions reflecting its "emotions" [3] is based on the methods of Ueki *et al.* [4]. While it can generate expressions showing simple emotions, it cannot generate ones showing mixed emotions or different strengths of emotions. We have overcome these by controlling Ifbot's face using *emotion parameters* that can be used to adjust the computation of its emotions such as anger and sadness.

2 Facial Expression Mechanism

The mechanism for controlling Ifbot's facial expressions have 10 motors and 101 LEDs (Figure 2). The motors actuate Ifbot's neck, both sides of the eyes,

Fig. 1. Front view of Ifbot

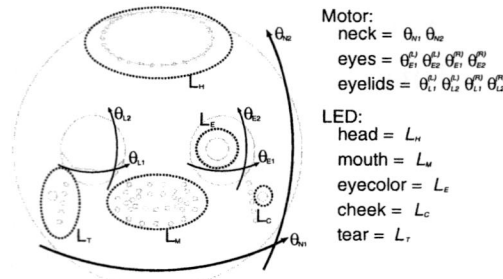

Fig. 2. Facial expression mechanisms of Ifbot

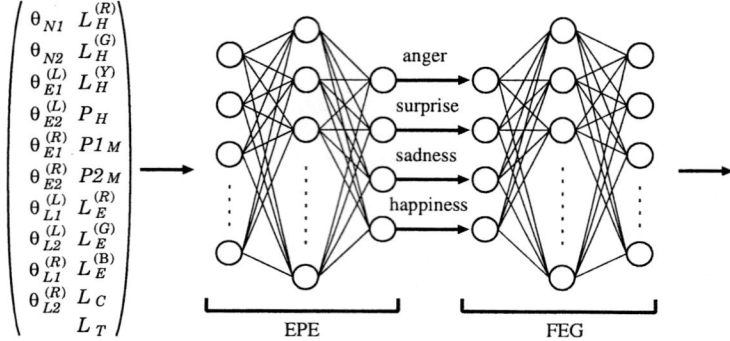

Fig. 3. Facial control system using emotion parameters

and both sides of the eyelids. The neck has two axes (θ_{N1}, θ_{N2}), and each side of the eyes has two axes (left: $\theta_{E1}^{(L)}$, $\theta_{E2}^{(L)}$; right: $\theta_{E1}^{(R)}$, $\theta_{E2}^{(R)}$). Each side of the eyelids has two axes (left: $\theta_{L1}^{(L)}$, $\theta_{L2}^{(L)}$; right: $\theta_{L1}^{(R)}$, $\theta_{L2}^{(R)}$). LEDs are located on head emitting three colors (orange, green, red), mouth emitting orange, eye emitting three colors (green, red, blue), cheeks emitting red, and tears emitting blue. These LEDs enable to express several emotions with these motors. Using this mechanism, Ifbot can communicate using various facial expressions.

3 Facial Control System

We propose a system shown in Figure 3. In this system, four emotions (anger, surprise, sadness, and happiness) comprising six basic emotions [5] are used as the emotion parameters[1]. The system has two neural networks: the emotional parameter extractor (EPE) extracts emotion parameters from facial expressions

---

[1] Disgust and fear tend to be confused with sadness because the facial expression mechanism of Ifbot is deformed and simplified based on human face. For example, Ifbot cannot furrow its brow. These two emotions are not used as emotion parameters.

of Ifbot and the facial expression generator (FEG) generates facial expressions using the emotion parameters. Training data is iteratively sent to their input and output layers at random. The EPE is trained by sending parameters for actuating facial mechanism to its input layer and by sending the emotion parameters for generating facial expression made from the actuating parameters to its output layer. The FEG learns by sending actuating parameters to the EPE and receiving emotion parameters in return. It sends the emotion parameters to its input layer and the actuating parameters same as sending to EPE input layer send to FEG output layer. We use the following vector as the parameters for actuating facial mechanism.

$$S = (\theta_{N1}, \theta_{N2}, \theta_{E1}^{(L)}, \theta_{E2}^{(L)}, \theta_{E1}^{(R)}, \theta_{E2}^{(R)}, \theta_{L1}^{(L)}, \theta_{L2}^{(L)}, \theta_{L1}^{(R)}, \theta_{L2}^{(R)},$$
$$L_H^{(R)}, L_H^{(G)}, L_H^{(Y)}, P_H, P1_M, P2_M, L_E^{(R)}, L_E^{(G)}, L_E^{(B)}, L_C, L_T). \tag{1}$$

where $\theta^{(\cdot)}$ are the motor outputs corresponding to $\theta^{(\cdot)}$ in Figure 2. The LEDs are patterns output from the LEDs for the head (red $L_H^{(R)}$, green $L_H^{(G)}$, orange $L_H^{(Y)}$, pattern P_H), eye color (red $L_E^{(R)}$, green $L_E^{(G)}$, blue $L_E^{(B)}$), cheeks (red L_C), and tears (blue L_T). The pattern for mouth LEDs describes ($P1_M, P2_M$).

4 Experiments

We investigated whether the actuating parameters output by the FEG corresponded to the input emotion parameters. We evaluated the facial expressions generated by the FEG subjectively. We divided the emotion parameters into five equal parts from 0 to 1 before inputting them to the FEG, which an emotion parameter was increased and the others were kept 0. The facial expressions generated by the FEG were shown to 20 people, who were asked to judge the

Table 1. Subjective judgement for angry face

—	Emotion parameters				Subjective scores			
Exp.	Ang	Sup	Sad	Hap	Ang.	Sup.	Sad.	Hap.
1	0.00	0	0	0	3.0	1.5	3.5	1.0
2	0.25	0	0	0	7.5	0.5	3.5	0.0
3	0.50	0	0	0	13.0	1.5	3.0	0.0
4	0.75	0	0	0	18.0	0.0	4.5	0.0
5	1.00	0	0	0	18.5	0.0	2.5	0.0

Table 2. Subjective judgement for surprised face

—	Emotion parameters				Subjective scores			
Exp.	Ang	Sup	Sad	Hap	Ang.	Sup.	Sad.	Hap.
1	0	0.00	0	0	3.0	1.5	3.5	1.0
6	0	0.25	0	0	6.5	5.5	7.0	0.0
7	0	0.50	0	0	3.0	6.0	5.5	0.5
8	0	0.75	0	0	0.0	18.5	0.0	3.0
9	0	1.00	0	0	0.0	19.0	0.0	2.5

Table 3. Subjective judgement for sad face

—	Emotion parameters				Subjective scores			
Exp.	Ang	Sup	Sad	Hap	Ang.	Sup.	Sad.	Hap.
1	0	0	0.00	0	3.0	1.5	3.5	1.0
10	0	0	0.25	0	2.0	0.5	11.5	0.0
11	0	0	0.50	0	1.0	1.0	17.5	0.0
12	0	0	0.75	0	0.0	0.5	19.0	0.0
13	0	0	1.00	0	0.0	0.0	19.5	0.0

Table 4. Subjective judgement for happy face

—	Emotion parameters				Subjective scores			
Exp.	Ang	Sup	Sad	Hap	Ang.	Sup.	Sad.	Hap.
1	0	0	0	0.00	3.0	1.5	3.5	1.0
14	0	0	0	0.25	2.5	2.5	2.5	1.0
15	0	0	0	0.50	0.0	0.5	2.0	12.5
16	0	0	0	0.75	0.0	2.5	1.5	14.0
17	0	0	0	1.00	0.0	3.0	2.0	12.5

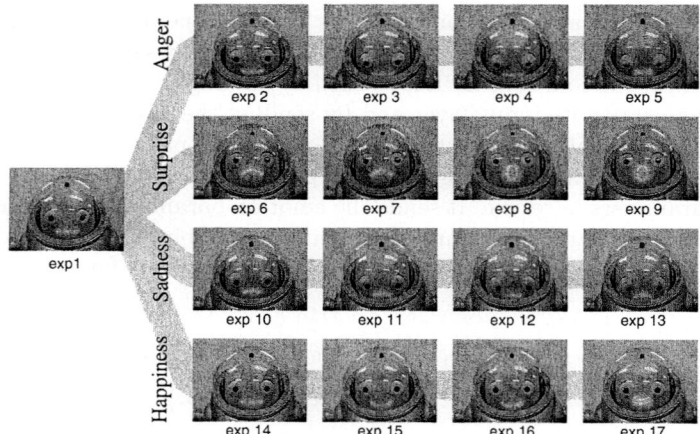

Fig. 4. Example output from facial expression generator

intensity of emotion for each expression. A score of 0 was given when the expression was judged not to show any emotion, 0.5 was given when the expression was judged to show weak emotion, 1 was given when the expression was judged to show strong emotion.

Tables 1-4 list summarize the results, and Figure 4 shows the sequence of facial expressions for each emotion. The maximum score was 20. The higher the score, the higher the intensity for the expression. As the emotion parameter was increased, the corresponding emotion score increased.

5 Conclusion

We have developed a system for showing a robot's "emotions" as facial expressions using two neural networks. The EPE extracts emotion parameters from the robot's facial expressions. The FEG generates facial expressions from the emotion parameters. Comparison of the EPE's output with the results of subjective judgement showed that it can reasonable well. A similar evaluation showed that the FEG can generate facial expressions reasonably well.

References

1. W. Von Raffler-Engel. *Aspects of nonverbal communication.* Loyola Pr, 1979.
2. Business Design Laboratory Co. Ltd. *Communication Robot Ifbot.* http://www.business-design. co.jp/en/product/001/ index.html.
3. M. Kanoh, S. Kato, and H. Itoh. Facial expressions using emotional space in sensitivity communication robot "ifbot". *IROS 2004*, pages 1586–1591, 2004.
4. N. Ueki and et al. Expression analysis/synthesis system based on emotion space constructed by multilayered neural network. *Systems and Computers in Japan*, 25(13):95–107, 1995.
5. Paul Ekman. *Unmasking the Face.* Prentice-Hall, 1975.

An Object Store Model for Diagnosing Java Programs

Rong Chen[1,2] and Franz Wotawa[3,*]

[1] College of Computer Science and Technology, Dalian Maritime University,
Linghai 1, 116026 Dalian, China
[2] Institute of Software Research, Zhongshan University
[3] Technische Universität Graz, Institut for Software Technology,
Inffeldgasse 16b/2, A-8010 Graz, Austria
{chen, wotawa}@ist.tugraz.at

Abstract. During the last decade many intelligent debugging tools have been developed to assist users to detect program errors in a software system. The tools based on formal verification reveal counterexamples in case a given program violates the specified properties. However, these counterexamples do not allow to locate the root cause sufficiently. In order to bridge the gap between counterexamples and root causes of failure we introduce a new model for localizing program errors. The model we use keeps track on object relations arising during program execution on the given counterexample. We have used the approach to isolate the errors in several small Java programs.

1 Introduction

During the last decade many intelligent debugging tools have been developed to assist users to detect program errors in a software system. For example, the Aspect system [8] catches errors of missing variables by checking code against abstract dependencies. The PREfix tool [2] finds path conditions under which null pointers arise. Using a powerful tailored theorem prover, the ESC [6] tool checks code against user-supplied annotations to find errors. Program verification tools [4] aid users to check whether a software system meets the properties. They detect program errors in various cases and reveal the violation of properties by providing the user with detailed counterexamples. However, there is still a long way to go when it comes to correct program errors, even with a detailed trace of a failure in hand.

Fault localization provides a way to aid users in moving from a trace of failure to an understanding of the error, and even perhaps to a correction of the error. The benefit of such a technique is that the error locations are highlighted and thus the error can be fixed quickly and cheaply in the coding process.

Several approaches have been proposed to localize program errors automatically. Among them are counterexample explanation [1,7], specification-assisted

---
* The work presented in this paper was funded by the Austrian Science Fund (FWF) P15265-N04, and supported by the National Natural Science Foundation of China (NSFC) Project 60203015.

error localization [5], delta debugging [12], and model-based software debugging (MBSD) [9]. Counterexample explanation identifies the root cause of a detected bug by examining the differences between an erroneous run and the correct run which is close to the erroneous one. In delta debugging [12] possible error locations are highlighted by conducting a modified binary search between a failing and a succeeding run of a program. In [5] the error of data structure inconsistency is localized by minimizing the distance between the error and its manifestation as observably incorrect behavior. The MBSD pinpoints bug locations by using a model-based diagnosis technique [10]. They handle the code very well and successfully localize the statements responsible for the faulty program behavior, but they diagnose data structure inconsistencies poorly because they cannot handle the structural properties and their implications very well.

In this paper we propose a model for diagnosing corrupted data structures. This model handles run-time object relations and their compile-time abstractions, and the first results reveal that it provides a quality diagnosis of data structure inconsistencies.

```
class LinkedList {                      void insert(Object v) {
  LinkedList next;                        LinkedList c = this;
  Object value;                           LinkedList p = this;
  ...                                     while (!c.nextIsEmtpy()&&(v>c.value)){
  LinkedList(Object o){                     p = c;
    next = null;                            c = c.next;
    value = o;                            }
  }                                       if (p.nextIsEmpty()||(v!=p.value)){
  boolean nextIsEmpty(){                    p.next = new LinkedList();
    return (this.next == null)              p = p.next;
  }                                         p.value = v;
  ...                                       p.next = c;
                                          }
                                        }
                                      }
```

Fig. 1. A Java example of *LinkedList*

2 Diagnosing Java Programs

To illustrate the process of diagnosing Java programs, we begin with the program error of data structure inconsistency in Section 2.1, then introduce our new model in Section 2.2 and explain how it is used to localize program errors in Section 2.3.

2.1 Data Structure Inconsistency

To illustrate data structure inconsistency, we use a Java program in Figure 1, which operates on a linked list. The list is implemented by the class *LinkedList* that provides methods to insert elements, remove elements, and reverse elements. This simple data structure comes with a structural constraint as follows:

Property 1. *List l is always acyclic.*

The code is truly simple. However we have already introduced a bug in the code. What can go wrong is that the *insert(v)* does not respect Property 1; it creates a cyclic list when it is ever called on a list with a single element.

Invoking the buggy *insert(v)* method on a list possibly corrupts the list. However, the corrupted list can grow further with new elements. So we have to wait even longer until the corrupted list manifests itself as observably incorrect behavior.

To see where it goes wrong, we write a *demo(b)* method in Figure 2(a), where the corrupted list *l* manifests itself as an infinite loop because the *size()* method is going through the entire list to calculate the length.

```
void demo(boolean b){
1. LinkedList l = new LinkedList(2);
2. if (b) {
   3. l.insert(20);
   4. l.insert(3);
   5. l.insert(5);
   }
/*@l.next.next.next.next!=l@*/
/*@¬ cyclic(l) @*/
6. l.size();
}
```

(a) The code

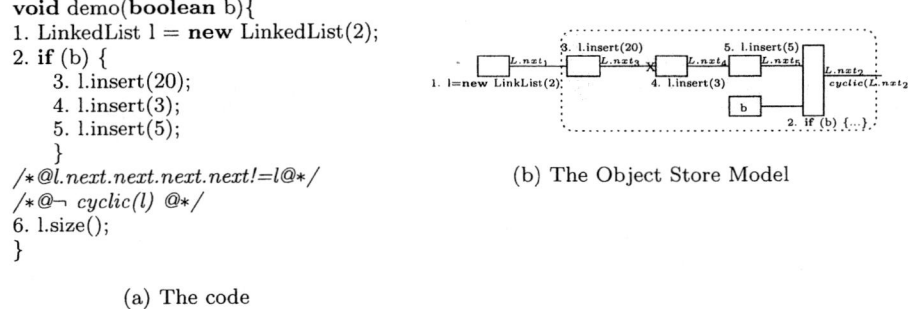

(b) The Object Store Model

Fig. 2. A Java example of *LinkedList*

Data structure inconsistencies become especially problematic because these errors do not manifest themselves as errors immediately but propagate the corrupted data to the distant code where they fail the program. The greater the distance, the longer the program executed in an incorrect state, the harder it is to find the root cause.

2.2 Object Store Model

Our approach on fault localization is a modification of the standard Model-Based Diagnosis [10]. Formally, a diagnosis system is a tuple $(SD, STMNTS, SPEC)$, where SD is a logical description of the program behavior, $STMNTS$ the set of statements, and $SPEC$ denotes the light-weighted specification of correctness. For instance, a test case specifies the input data and the expected output data. The program fault on the other hand is a set of system components, i.e., statements or expressions, which are responsible for the detected misbehavior.

To compile the program into models, we assume each syntactic entity has a function *buildOSM* which maps itself into a component, links its input ports, possibly propagate forwards static information, and returns its output connection. Statement by statement, we convert classes and methods successively and return a set of components defining the diagnosis system [3].

Similar to [9], the algorithm maps loops and method calls to hierarchic components with inner sub-models. The loop component contains two sub-models: M_C and M_B, where M_C denotes the sub-model of the loop condition, and M_B the sub-model of the loop body (represented as a nested if-statement[1])

To illustrate the resulting description, Figure 2(b) displays the graphical representation of the system description of the statements 1 ~ 5, where each statement is mapped to a component and L is abbreviated for *LinkedList*. Components are connected through variables that they manipulate. Moreover, connection $L.nxt_i$ is a relation variable which holds a set of object pairs accessed through the *next* field of the list l after statement i.

Definition 1 (Relation Variable)
A relation variable is a variable $T.f$, where f is a binary relation $f : T \to T'$. The value assigned to a relation variable is a set of pairs in the form (i_1, i_2) where i_1 and i_2 are of type T and T' respectively.

In this way, the program model is defined by the structure of a component network and behaviors of all components. While the structural part corresponds to syntactic entities, the behavior part implements the language semantics. Given the input data, the network is initialized, values are propagated forward through connections to the output of the network.

The test case runs the model in that input and output values are propagated forward and backward throughout the network. A contradiction is raised in the diagnosis system when (1) a variable gets two or more different values from different components, or (2) a relation variable's value violates a certain property. Since we implement a set of methods to perform a consistency checking on relation variables, we can check user-provided structural properties and thus detect a corrupted data structure.

Definition 2 (Object Store)
An Object Store is a collection of relation variables and their values.

2.3 Search for Bug Locations

The diagnosis process is a process of searching for possible bug locations by assuming how statements might behave. We represent the *correctness assumptions* about the behavior of statements in terms of predicates assigning appropriate modes to the statements. Formally, the diagnosis process is a searching process to find a set of assumptions that is consistent with the given specification:

Definition 3 (Mode Assignment)
A mode assignment for statements $\{S_1, ..., S_n\} \subseteq STMNTS$, each having an assigned set of modes ms and a default mode $default$ such that $default \in mc(S_i)$ for each $S_i \in STMNTS$, is a set of predicates $\{m_1(S_1), ..., m_n(S_n)\}$ where $m_i \in ms(S_i)$ and $m_i \neq default\ (S_i)$.

---

[1] The nesting size is obtained by computing all pairs shortest path in a dependency graph (see [11]).

Consider the *demo(b)* method, statements have the modes $\neg AB$ (not abnormal) and AB (abnormal), referring to the assumption of correct and incorrect behavior respectively. The goal of the diagnosing process is to find a set of assumptions that are consistent with the given specification.

Definition 4 (Diagnosis)
A set $\Delta \subseteq STMNTS$ is a diagnosis for a diagnosis problem $(SD, STMNTS, SPEC)$ iff $SD \cup SPEC \cup \{\neg AB(S) \mid S \in STMNTS \setminus \Delta\}$ is consistent.

A conflict is defined by a set of components causing the contradictions. For example, choosing $\neg AB$ mode as the default mode, we cannot assume all statements $1 \sim 5$ work correctly because the output list l_2 after statement 2 violates Property 1, i.e., $\neg cyclic(l)$ in Figure 2(b).

To diagnose the erroneous run [1, 2, 3, 4, 5], our approach starts from the last statement 5, go back through all statements [1, 2, 3, 4, 5], compute the witness $cyclic(l)$ at each statement, and thus to see where the data structure inconsistency actually originates. A contraction is thus raised at connection l_3, marked by X in Figure 2(b). This is because component *l.insert(20)* receives an acyclic list but sends a cyclic list. So we cannot assume statements 1, 2 and 3 work correctly at the same time. Thus we have three single fault diagnoses $\{AB$ $(1)\}$, $\{AB\ (2)\}$, and $\{AB\ (3)\}$. The diagnoses pinpoint the flaw in the *insert(v)* method, i.e., the list become cyclic when it is used to insert the second element. This is informative for the user, giving a hint on how the flaw could be corrected.

In contrast, the VBM is less informative. An assertion *l.next.next.next.next* $! = l$ is used to specify the expected behavior of the *demo(b)* method. Surely this assertion is violated. The VBM's diagnosis is that all statements 1, 2, 3, 4, 5 are possibly faulty because they influence the value of the assertion. Of course, the diagnosis is not false, but it obscures the original source of error.

3 First Results

To evaluate the Object Store model, several example programs have been created. The example programs implement a shape class and various data structures such as linked list, stack, tree, etc. (see Table 1), where the OA column shows the number of object accesses. All programs involve various control flows, virtual method invocation, and object-oriented language notations, such as multiple objects, class creations, instance method calls, class and instance variables, etc.

The diagnosis experiments are performed on example programs with a seeded fault. The results are summarized in Table 2, where it depicts the elapse time for modeling (M-G column), the elapsed time for computing diagnoses (T-D column), and the number of diagnosis (N-D column). The right column lists the result obtained by diagnosing with a VBM. Compared with the VBM, it is shown that the number of diagnosis candidates is reduced and all diagnosis candidates are in the VBM's diagnosis. So our model hits the original source of error sufficiently and accurately, directing attention to the root cause of a property violation.

Table 1. Benchmarks

Program	Main Methods	Lines [#]	OA [#]
LinkedList	insert, remove, join, reverse	58	20
Stack	push, pop, etc.	67	22
Shape	overlap, scaleBy, transpose, rotate	200	120
ExpressionTree	insert, remove, left, right, etc.	146	58

Table 2. Empirical results

Program	M-G [sec.]	T-D [sec.]	N-D [#]	VBM N-D
LinkedList	0.6	0.3	3	10
Stack	0.6	0.4	1	4
	0.9	0.4	2	4
Shape	2.3	0.3	1	5
ExpressionTree	7.2	2.5	4	9

4 Conclusion

In this paper, we present an Object Store model to diagnose data structure inconsistencies. Our approach hits both the structural properties and their implications by reasoning about object relations arising from the program execution. We have used the approach to isolate errors in several small Java programs to prove their principal applicability.

In the future, we will scale up to large examples and work on programs with exceptions, threads and recursive method calls.

References

1. T. Ball, M. Naik, and S.K. Rajamani. From symptom to cause: localizing errors in counterexample traces. In *Proc. of POPL*, pages 97–105. ACM Press, 2003.
2. William R. Bush, Jonathan D. Pincus, and David J. Sielaff. A static analyzer for finding dynamic programming errors. *Software Practice and Experience*, 30(7):775–802, 2000.
3. R. Chen, D. Koeb, and F. Wotawa. Exploring object relations for automated fault localization. Pacific Grove, California, USA, 2005.
4. E. Clarke, O. Grumberg, and D. Peled. *Model Checking*. The MIT Press, Cambridge, Massachusetts, 2000.
5. Brian Demsky and Martin Rinard. Automatic detection and repair of errors in data structures. *ACM SIGPLAN Notices*, 38(11):78–95, 2003.
6. David L. Detlefs, K. Rustan M. Leino, Greg Nelson, and James B. Saxe. Extended static checking. Technical Report SRC-RR-159, HP Laboratories, 1998.
7. A. Groce. Error explanation with distance metrics. In *TACAS*, volume 2988 of *Lecture Notes in Computer Science*. Springer, 2004.
8. Daniel Jackson. Aspect: Detecting Bugs with Abstract Dependences. *ACM TOSEM*, 4(2):109–145, 1995.
9. W. Mayer, M. Stumptner, D. Wieland, and F. Wotawa. Can ai help to improve debugging substantially? debugging experiences with value-based models. In *Proc. ECAI*, pages 417–421. IOS Press, 2002.
10. Raymond Reiter. A theory of diagnosis from first principles. *Artificial Intelligence*, 32(1):57–95, 1987.
11. D. Wieland. *Model-Based Debugging of Java Programs Using Dependencies*. PhD thesis, Vienna University of Technology, Institute of Information Systems (184), Nov. 2001.
12. Andreas Zeller and Ralf Hildebrandt. Simplifying and isolating failure-inducing input. *IEEE Transactions on Software Engineering*, 28(2), 2002.

A Multi-exchange Heuristic for a Production Location Problem

Yunsong Guo[1], Yanzhi Li[2], Andrew Lim[2,3], and Brian Rodrigues[4]

[1] School of Computing, National University of Singapore,
3 Science Drive 2, Singapore
isc10469@nus.edu.sg
[2] Department of IELM, Hong Kong University of Science and Technology,
Clear Water Bay, Hong Kong
{ieyanzhi, iealim}@ust.hk
[3] School of Computer Science & Engineering,
South China University of Technology, GuangDong, P.R. China
[4] Lee Kong Chian School of Business, Singapore Management University,
50 Stamford Road, Singapore
br@smu.edu.sg

Abstract. In this work, we develop a multi-exchange heuristic based on an estimation improvement graph embedded in a simulated annealing to solve a problem arising in plant location planning where tariff exemptions apply. The method is shown to be effective in experiments since it provides good solutions for problems of realistic size. It is superior to CPLEX in terms of time, and is able to provide solutions for large test problems.

Keywords: Search, heuristics, planning.

1 The n-Stage Production Planning Problem

In this paper we study a production location problem (PLP) as follows. A company manufactures a single product to sell in the market in country D, using production consisting of n stages, where one or more stages can occur in a given country.

Consider the value added rule for tariff elimination. All costs are defined for one unit of product, where a "unit" is generic and can mean a piece, carton etc., whose value, accrued up to stage k, is given by V_k, for $k = 1, ..., n$. Here V_k is an aggregate value of the product, which includes all the costs incurred up to the point k, with profit, or its "internationally recognized value" (IRV). Take A_{ki} to be the sum of the value adds in country i up to stage k. Here added value is calculated taking stages as wholes, or, alternatively, by adding value cumulatively. If stage k occurs in country i and stage $k + 1$ in country j, then the value add rule is applied as follows: if local value add in country i, A_{ki}, taken as a percentage of V_k is less than β_{kij}, tariff equal to α_{kij} is incurred. Here, β_{kij} is the threshold local content minimum required for tariff elimination for the product exported from country i to country j following stage k of its production, and α_{kij} is calculated as a percentage of its IRV; otherwise, the product is tariff free.

Let m be the number of countries, t_{kij} the unit transportation cost from country i to j, following stage k, where $k = 1,..,n;\ i,j = 1,..,m, m+1$ (where $m+1$ is country D) and $P_{kj} =$ the production cost incurred in stage k in country j, where $k = 1,..,n; j = 1,..,m$. Production cost here is a generic term, which includes costs such as raw material costs, labor costs, local production tax, facility cost, factory rental cost, etc.

The objective in the problem is to find an assignment of production stages to countries to minimize the total cost, including production cost, transportation cost and tariff, taking into consideration FTA tariff exemptions that apply between countries.

Such a problem can be proved NP-hard by reduction to the well-known 2-partition problem. We can formulate it as with integer programming(IP), while which is hard to solve with available commercial software such as ILOG CPLEX. Instead we propose a multi-exchange heuristic approach in the next section.

2 A Multi-exchange Heuristic Embedded in Simulated Annealing

A multi-exchange neighborhood local search is a variant of the very large-scale neighborhood (VLSN) search[1]. The approach we propose in this work is new in two aspects: (1) neighborhoods are searched with a heuristic using a constructed estimation improvement graph, whereas in traditional VSLN, exact improvement graphs are required[2]; (2) VLSN is embedded into a simulated annealing(SA)[5] framework. A standard SA procedure can be found in [3]. We embed VLSN in a SA framework. A geometric annealing scheme is used, with the constant C_0 taken to be 0.995, where a reheating mechanism is employed whenever an iteration cannot yield a new current solution. The reheating is geometrically defined by $Temperature = Temperature * (1 + \frac{(1-C_0)}{5})$.

2.1 Generating Initial Solutions

Let the array S of length n represent a solution where $S[i]$ is the index of country which stage i is assigned to, $1 \leq S[i] \leq m, 1 \leq i \leq n$. Two methods were used to generate the initial solution. The first is to randomly choose a country for a stage to be processed in, which serves as a comparison for the second method. The second is to use a weighted probability to assign a country index to every stage, by considering the stages 1 to n sequentially. Since there is no tariff cost or transportation cost involved in stage 1 of production, the total cost of stage 1, if assigned to country j, $1 \leq j \leq m$, can be estimated to be the production cost P_{1j}. This is an estimation since the effect of assigning country index to stage 1 on later decisions for stage 2 to stage n is not known. Define $Q_{1j} = \frac{1}{P_{1j}}$ and $Q_{total} = \Sigma_j Q_{1j}$ and assign j to stage 1 with probability $\frac{Q_{1j}}{Q_{total}}$. This is to increase the chance that stage 1 is processed in countries that have a smaller production cost. After stage 1 is assigned to a country, continue to decide country indices

A Multi-exchange Heuristic for a Production Location Problem   873

for stage 2 to n in a similar way, sequentially, except that the estimated cost for assigning country index j to stage k would, in addition, include transportation cost and tariff (if incurred) from the country where stage $(k-1)$ is processed. To decide a country index for the last stage, tariff and transportation cost to the destination is used.

2.2 Very Large-Scale Neighborhood Search

Neighborhood Structure. For a solution $\mathbf{S}$, define set C_j $1 \leq j \leq m$ by $C_j = \{i \mid S[i] = j, 1 \leq i \leq n\}$, which is the set of indexes of stages processed in country j. A cyclic exchange neighborhood move is to first select K different countries $i_1, i_2, ..., i_K$ such that $C_{i_j} \neq \emptyset$, for $j \in \{1, 2, .., K\}$. In each selected country j, $1 \leq j \leq K$, choose stage $t_j \in C_{i_j}$ and reassign stages t_1 to t_K to country C_{i_j}, $j = 1..K$ in a cyclic manner: $S[t_i] := S[t_{i+1}]$ for $i = 1...K-1$, and $S[t_K] := S[t_1]$. Consequently, C_j, $1 \leq j \leq m$ is changed accordingly and the changes take place simultaneously. It is clear that by the Kth-cyclic change, the number of neighborhood solutions is $(n/K)^K K!$ assuming the n stages are uniformly allocated in m countries, and in general, the number of neighborhood solutions $\mathcal{N}(\mathbf{S}) = \Omega(n^K)$. When K is allowed to vary linearly with n, the neighborhood size becomes exponential with n. In the algorithm developed here, K_{max} is fixed to be approximately 10% as large as n, and in each iteration of cyclic local move, K is selected randomly in the range $[2, K_{max}]$. A neighborhood in path exchange is very similar to the cyclic one in spite of the fact that path exchange does not select any stage in C_{i_K} to move to C_{i_1}.

Estimation Improvement Graph. Given a solution $\mathbf{S}$ and C_j, $1 \leq j \leq m$ defined in the previous sections, an *estimation improvement graph* is a directed graph $G(\mathbf{S}) = (V, E)$ in which the set of vertices V contains n nodes: v_k, $1 \leq k \leq n$ each representing a stage k in the solution $\mathbf{S}$. The arc set E represents the relationship between different stages, where there is a directed arc (k, l) from v_k to v_k if and only if $S[k] \neq S[l]$. The weight of each arc (k, l) is taken to be E_{kl} where:

$$E_{kl} = \begin{cases} P_{k,s[l]} - P_{l,s[l]}, & \text{if } k = 1 \text{ or } l = 1 \\ P_{k,s[l]} - P_{l,s[l]} + t_{k,s[k-1],s[l]} - t_{l,s[l-1],s[l]} + T_{k,S[k-1],[S[l]} - T_{l,S[l-1],S[l]}, & o.w. \end{cases}$$

This weight is designed to reflect the total cost change if we reassign stage k to country $S[l]$ and reassign stage l to some other country. It is easy to see that the above function E_{kl} can only be an estimation.

Probabilistic Selection of Cycles and Paths. Once the estimation improvement graph has been constructed, the algorithm will first randomly choose K countries C_{i_j}, $1 \leq j \leq K$. If it is a cyclic neighborhood move, $C_{i_j} \neq \emptyset$, for all $j \in \{1, 2, .., K\}$, while if it is a path exchange, $C_{i_K} = \emptyset$ is allowed. In the neighborhood search, a stage in C_{i_1} is chosen to be included as the first stage in the cycle/path as follows: Let the production cost P_{ji_1} be the indicator of the preference to choose stage j originally in C_{i_1} for all j such that $j \in C_{i_1}$.

Define $P_{total} = \Sigma_j P_{ji_1}$. Then stage $j \in C_{i_1}$ is selected by the cyclic neighborhood change with probability $\frac{P_{ji_1}}{P_{total}}$.

When a stage from country C_{i_1} is selected, one stage for each of the remaining $K - 1$ countries is selected sequentially to be used in the cyclic exchange move. Let the index of the selected stage from country C_{i_j} be l_j for $1 \leq j \leq K$. The selection of l_j is based on the value of l_{j-1} for $2 \leq j \leq K$. In the estimation improvement graph, there should be an arc from the node representing l_{j-1} to every node in C_{i_j} by definition. A negative arc weight indicates a potential improvement in solution quality if the exchange local move is made to contain the stages associated with this arc. Arc weights are modified in the following way: first, multiply these by -1 and then add a minimum positive number to the arcs to make all weights positive. This is to facilitate later calculations of probabilities used for selecting each stage in C_{i_j}. Let E'_{pq} be the modified arc weight from stage p to stage q and $Arc_{total} = \Sigma_{q \in C_{i_j}} E'_{l_{i-1}q}$ and select stage $q \in C_{i_j}$ in the cyclic exchange neighborhood move with probability $E'_{l_{i-1}q}/Arc_{totoal}$. If there is a cyclic exchange, when deciding stage from C_{i_K}, the cost from C_{i_K} to C_{i_1} is included by using the arc weight E_{ql_1} to determine the probability of selecting stage $q \in C_{i_K}$. If the local move is a path exchange, we do not need to select stage from C_{i_K} as this is unnecessary. When l_i for $i \in \{1, 2, ..K\}$ are fixed, cyclic/path exchange is performed to complete an iteration of the neighborhood search.

3 Experimental Analysis

Due to the lack of practical data we generated test cases based on several realistic concerns. We ran our algorithm to compare with results obtained by solving IP models with CPLEX9.0. The later provided optimal solutions or lower bounds given long enough time. It showed that for smaller test cases both approaches can reach optimum while for larger test cases our approach outperformed IP approach in shorter time. Due to the page limit, we omit the result. Interested readers may refer to [4] for further details.

References

[1] R.K. Ahuja, O. Ergun, J.B. Orlin, and A.P. Punnen. A survey of very large-scale neighborhood search techniques. *Discrete Applied Mathematics*, 123:75–102, 2002.
[2] R.K. Ahuja, J.B. Orlin, S. Pallottino, M.P. Scaparra, and M.G. Scutella. A multi-exchange heuristic for the single source capacitated facility location. *Management Science*, 50(6):749–760, June 2004.
[3] K. Dowsland. *Simulated annealing*, pages 20–69. Blackwell Scientific Publications, Oxford, 1993.
[4] Y. Guo, Y. Li, A. Lim, and B. Rodrigues. A multi-exchange heuristic for a production location problem. *working paper,http://ihome.ust.hk/~ieyanzhi/FTA2.pdf*, 2005.
[5] S. Kirkpatrick, C.D. Gelatt, and M.P. Vecchi. Optimization by simulated annealing. *Science*, 20:671–680, 1983.

The Car-Sequencing Problem as n-Ary CSP – Sequential and Parallel Solving

Mihaela Butaru and Zineb Habbas

LITA, Université de Metz,
UFR M.I.M., Ile du Saulcy, F-57045 Metz Cedex 1, France
{butaru, zineb.habbas}@univ-metz.fr

Abstract. The *car-sequencing* problem arises from the manufacture of cars on an assembly line (based on [1]). A number of cars are to be produced; they are not identical, because different options are available as variants on the basic model. The assembly line has different stations (designed to handle at most a certain percentage of the cars passing along the assembly line) which install the various options. Furthermore, the cars requiring a certain option must not be bunched together, otherwise the station will not be able to cope. Consequently, the cars must be arranged in a sequence so that the capacity of each station is never exceeded. The solving methods for constraint satisfaction problems (CSPs) [2], [3], [4] represent good alternatives for certain instances of the problem. Constraint programming tools [5], [6] use a search algorithm based on Forward Checking (FC) [7] to solve CSPs, with different variable or value ordering heuristics. In this article, we undertake an experimental study for the instances of the car-sequencing problem in CSPLib, encoded as an n-ary CSP using an implementation with constraints of fixed arity 5. By applying value ordering heuristics based on fail-first principle, a great number of these instances can be solved in little time. Moreover, the parallel solving using a shared memory model based on OpenMP makes it possible to increase the number of solved problems.

Keywords: Constraint satisfaction, heuristics, problem solving, scheduling.

1 The Car-Sequencing Problem Encoded as a CSP

The car-sequencing problem can be encoded as a CSP (see [2]) in which slots in the sequence are variables, cars to be built are their values. Following [8], the first step is to group the cars into classes, such that the cars in each class all require the same option. A matrix of binary elements of size the number of classes multiplied by the number of options specifies the present options in each class. We have to arrange the cars to produce into a sequence such that none of the *capacity constraint* is violated. These constraints are formalized q_i/p_i (i.e. the unit is able to produce at most q_i cars with the option i out of each sequence of p_i cars; this should be read q_i *outof* p_i). The constraints already stated are sufficient to express the problem; it seems that the only important thing about the options capacities is not to exceed them, and going *below* the capacity does not matter. This is not true: a certain number of cars requiring each option have to be fitted into the sequence, so that going below the capacity in one part of the sequence could make it impossible to avoid exceeding the capacity elsewhere. In [8], the authors suggest adding *implied constraints* in order to allow failures to be detected earlier than it would otherwise be possible.

2 Value Ordering Heuristics for Car-Sequencing Problem

The ordering of variables and values was studied by Smith [2]. More specifically, the effects of the *fail-first* and the *succeed-first* were tested for the car-sequencing problem. The fail-first principle consists in choosing a variable or a value which has the greatest pruning effect on the domains of the future variables, while the succeed-first principle consists in choosing the variable or the value that is likely to lead to a solution, and so reduces the risk of having to backtrack to this variable and try an alternative value. In [2] the author suggests that for the car-sequencing problem the variables should be assigned consecutively. In [9] we describe seven value ordering heuristics for this problem: $MaxUtil$, $MinCars$, $MaxOpt$, $MaxPQ$ based on fail-first priciple and $MinUtil$, $MaxCars$, $MinOpt$ based on succeed-first one.

3 Implementation Framework and Experimental Results

In our implementation, we generate the car-sequencing problem as an n-ary CSP with n variables (the slots in the sequence), d values (the cars to be built) and $m = n - 4$ constraints of fixed arity 5 are posted on any 5 consecutive variables. The relations corresponding to the constraints are explicitly built as valid tuples, generated respecting the capacity constraints for the options and the total production for each car. We implemented [10] five versions of n-ary FC algorithms (i.e. nFC0, nFC2, nFC3, nFC4, nFC5) which differ between them in the extent of look-ahead they perform after each variable assignment [4]. Due to our implementation, we can apply any of the developed algorithms, not only some algorithms specific to car-sequencing problem. Of course, we take into account the presence of the implied constraints in the problem. We present here the results corresponding to nFC2 algorithm, noticed as the best one. The heuristics in Section 2 are evaluated on two groups of instances of car-sequencing problem in the CSPLib[1]: the first group includes 70 instances of 200 cars, the second one contains 9 instances of 100 cars.

We also present in this paper our first results (see the full paper [9]) of parallel solving for car-sequencing problem, using the search tree distribution approach within a shared memory model (see [11] for details) based on OpenMP.

Our solver has been developed in C++ using a Unix CC compiler and executed on a SGI3800 machine of 768 R1400 processors 500 MHz. In the tables below, T_{max} is either the necessary time to solve the problem or, in the case of

---
[1] http://4c.ucc.ie/~tw/csplib/prob/prob001/data.txt

a unsolved problem, the maximum time spent to seek a solution (restricted to 900 seconds); D is the number of positions in the sequence which it was possible to affect; t_D is the necessary time to reach this depth; #nodes, #ccks and #BT counts respectively the number of visited nodes, constraint checks and backtracking to reach D; #OK is the number of solved problems solved; Y/N indicates if the problem was solved; T_g is the time CPU corresponding to the *guided* tasks allocation in the parallel execution (within the OpenMP environment, there is a *static*, *dynamic* or *guided* tasks allocation [12]; we present here only the last one, which performs better, even if with small differences, than the two others).

Tables 1, 2 give the results for the first group, while Tables 3, 4 give the results for the second group.

Table 1. Sequential results of $MaxUtil$ and $MaxPQ$ for the first group

	MaxUtil							MaxPQ					
Pb.	T_{max}	D	t_D	#nodes	#ccks	#BT	#OK	Pb.	T_{max}	D	t_D	#nodes	#ccks	#BT	#OK
60	3.15	200	3.15	200	525705	0	10	60	3.37	200	3.37	300	527670	100	10
65	3.97	200	3.97	200	805918	0	10	65	4.44	200	4.44	302	806229	102	10
70	4.70	200	4.70	200	1029707	0	10	70	4.91	200	4.91	268	1021358	68	10
75	5.65	200	5.65	200	1326867	0	10	75	5.75	200	5.75	257	1281343	57	10
80	6.82	200	6.82	200	1682611	0	10	80	6.91	200	6.91	239	1705391	39	10
85	8.35	200	8.35	200	2292852	0	10	85	8.24	200	8.24	226	2205163	26	10
90	10.73	200	10.73	200	3078951	0	10	90	10.93	200	10.93	240	3034675	40	10
Avg:	6.20	200	6.20	200	1534659	0	70	Avg:	6.36	200	6.36	261	1511647	61	70

Table 2. Parallel results of $nFC2$, $MinCars$ and $MaxOpt$ for the first group

	nFC2					MinCars					MaxOpt			
	Serial		Parallel			Serial		Parallel			Serial		Parallel	
Pb.	T_{max}	#OK	T_g	#OK	Pb.	T_{max}	#OK	T_g	#OK	Pb.	T_{max}	#OK	T_g	#OK
60	721.84	2	524.1	7	60	451.43	5	119.86	9	60	349.15	8	97.87	9
65	722.98	2	401.27	6	65	272.5	7	110.10	9	65	276.74	7	19.87	10
70	734.36	2	423.16	6	70	284.55	7	12.36	10	70	364.67	6	102.43	9
75	816.75	1	590.43	5	75	183.98	8	5.04	10	75	214.84	8	21.39	10
80	900	0	773.27	3	80	116.69	9	22.63	10	80	301.17	7	92.09	10
85	900	0	724.63	3	85	810.72	1	364.51	6	85	186.4	8	98.72	9
90	811.2	1	772.03	2	90	723.25	2	297.15	7	90	23.11	10	9.06	10
Avg: 800		8	Avg: 601	32		Avg: 406	39	Avg: 133	61		Avg: 245	54	Avg: 63	67

Table 3. Serial results of $MaxUtil$ and $MaxPQ$ for the second group

	MaxUtil							MaxPQ						
Pb.	T_{max}	D	t_D	#nodes	#ccks	#BT	Y/N	Pb.	T_{max}	D	t_D	#nodes	#ccks	#BT	Y/N
4_72	900	90	1	152	732450	62	N	4_72	900	91	320	41124	48467390	41033	N
6_76	900	70	2	398	652343	328	N	6_76	900	58	0	74	434567	16	N
10_93	900	75	6	406	2565764	331	N	10_93	900	76	34	2662	98008555	2586	N
16_81	155	100	155	35966	15391983	35866	Y	16_81	900	95	12	1664	2077529	1570	N
19_71	900	91	29	6559	3577762	6468	N	19_71	900	90	71	9162	12538120	9072	N
21_90	900	91	3	874	641208	783	N	21_90	900	88	7	1532	1133881	1444	N
36_92	900	70	2	387	682380	317	N	36_92	900	75	23	3653	3922874	3578	N
41_66	0.903	100	0.903	101	310180	1	Y	41_66	1.22	100	1.225	179	355985	79	Y
26_82	900	95	20	6412	2284875	6317	N	26_82	900	85	764	108937	110949640	108852	N
Avg:	717	87	24	5632	2982105	5545	2	Avg:	800	84	148	18775	21076505	18691	1

The results obtained showed the superiority of the fail-first strategy against a succeed-first one. Moreover, $MaxUtil$ and $MaxPQ$ solved all the instances of 200 variables. The same heuristics in [13] solved 12 respectively 51 instances. These problems were solved in little time (6 seconds on average), which can be justified by our encoding. The longest time (13 seconds) was spent for the

Table 4. Parallel results of $MaxUtil$, $MaxOpt$ and $MaxPQ$ for the second group

	$MaxUtil$					$MaxOpt$					$MaxPQ$			
Pb.	Serial		Parallel		Pb.	Serial		Parallel		Pb.	Serial		Parallel	
	T_{max}	Y/N	T_g	Y/N		T_{max}	Y/N	T_g	Y/N		T_{max}	Y/N	T_g	Y/N
4_72	900	N	2.009	Y	4_72	900	N	4.253	Y	4_72	900	N	2.324	Y
16_81	155.085	Y	65.241	Y	16_81	900	N	900	N	16_81	900	N	900	N
41_66	0.903	Y	0.9	Y	41_66	900	N	900	N	41_66	1.255	Y	1.2	Y
26_82	900	N	862.24	Y	26_82	900	N	900	N	26_82	900	N	900	N

instance 90_09, whereas with ILOG Solver the least powerful time exceeds 1 minute. For the second group, $MaxUtil$ solves the problems 16_81 and 41_66, while $MaxPQ$ solves the problem 41_66. For this group, [13] did not solve any instance. The parallel execution using a shared memory model based on OpenMP increased the number of solved problems for the first group, and all the problems known as satisfiable in the second one using $MaxUtil$, which remains the best heuristic because it is surprisingly backtrack-free.

References

1. Parrello, B.D., Kabat, W.C., Wos, L.: Job-shop schedulind using automated reasoning: a case study of the car-sequencing problem. Journal of Automated Reasoning **2** (1986) 1–42
2. Smith, B.M.: Succeed-first or fail-first: A case study in variable and value ordering. Report 96.26, University of Leeds (1996)
3. Régin, J.C., Puget, J.F.: A filtering algorithm for global sequencing constraints. Constraint Programming (1997) 32–46
4. Bessière, C., Meseguer, P., Freuder, C., Larossa, J.: On forward checking for non binary constraint satisfaction. Artificial Intelligence **141** (2002) 205–224
5. van Hentenryck, P.: Constraint Satisfaction in Logic Programming. MIT Press, Cambridge (1989)
6. Puget, J.F.: A c++ implementation of clp. In: Proceedings of SPICIS94 (Singapore International Conference on Intelligent Systems). (1994)
7. Haralick, R.M., Elliot, G.L.: Increasing the search efficiency for constraint satisfaction problems. Artificial Intelligence **14** (1980) 263–313
8. Dincbas, M., Simonis, H., van Hentenryck, P.: Solving the car-sequencing problem in constraint logic programming. In: Proceedings ECAI-88. (1988) 290–295
9. Butaru, M., Habbas, Z.: Sequential and parallel solving for the car-sequencing problem. Rapport interne 2005–101, Université de Metz, Laboratoire d'Informatique Théorique et Appliquée (2005)
10. Butaru, M., Habbas, Z.: Problèmes de satisfaction de contraintes n-aire: une étude expérimentale. In: Actes des Premières Journées Francophones de Programmation par Contraintes (JFPC05), Lens, France (8-10 Juin, 2005)
11. Butaru, M., Habbas, Z.: Parallel solving with n-ary forward checking: A shared memory implementation. In: Proceedings of the First International Workshop on OpenMP (IWOMP05), Eugene, Oregon, USA (June 1-4, 2005) to appear.
12. OpenMP Architecture Review Board: OpenMP Application Program Interface. (2005) http://www.openmp.org.
13. Boivin, S., Gravel, M., Krajecki, M., Gagné, C.: Résolution du problème de carsequencing à l'aide d'une approche de type fc. In: Actes des Premières Journées Francophones de Programmation par Contraintes (JFPC05), Lens, France (8-10 Juin, 2005)

Normalized Gaussian Networks with Mixed Feature Data

Shu-Kay Ng[1] and Geoffrey J. McLachlan[1,2]

[1] Department of Mathematics, University of Queensland,
Brisbane, QLD 4072, Australia
{skn, gjm}@maths.uq.edu.au
[2] Institute for Molecular Bioscience, University of Queensland,
Brisbane, QLD 4072, Australia

Abstract. With mixed feature data, problems are induced in modeling the gating network of normalized Gaussian (NG) networks as the assumption of multivariate Gaussian becomes invalid. In this paper, we propose an independence model to handle mixed feature data within the framework of NG networks. The method is illustrated using a real example of breast cancer data.

1 Introduction

Normalized Gaussian (NG) networks, such as the NG mixture of experts (NGME) nets [1], are of extensive interest due to their wide applicability, generalization capability, and the advantage of efficient learning via the expectation-maximization (EM) algorithm [2]; see for example [1,3,4]. For many applied problems in machine learning, there often involves both categorical and continuous feature variables [5]. With the mixed feature data, the input vector x_j on the j-th entity consists of q categorical variables in the vector x_{1j} in addition to p continuous variables represented by the vector x_{2j} for $j = 1, \ldots, n$, where n is the total number of observations. Problems are therefore induced in modeling the gating network with NG networks as the assumption of multivariate Gaussian becomes invalid when the data are mixed-mode. In this paper, we propose an independence model to handle mixed feature data within the framework of NG networks. The method is based on the NAIVE assumption that the categorical variables are independent of each other and of the continuous variables [6,7].

2 Generalized NGME and Learning Via the EM Algorithm

Normalized Gaussian networks softly partition the input space into, say M, regions by NG functions (the gating network)

$$\mathcal{N}_h(x; \pi, \alpha) = \pi_h f_h(x; \alpha_h) / \sum_{l=1}^{M} \pi_l f_l(x; \alpha_l) \qquad (h = 1, \ldots, M), \qquad (1)$$

where $\pi_h > 0$, $\sum_{h=1}^{M} \pi_h = 1$, and $f_h(x; \alpha_h) = \phi_h(x; \mu_h, \Sigma_h)$ denotes the multivariate Gaussian function for input vector x, with mean μ_h and covariance matrix Σ_h. The local units (experts) approximate the distribution of the output y_j within the partition. The final output of the NGME network is given by the summation of these local outputs weighted by the NG functions (1):

$$f(y_j|x_j; \Psi) = \sum_{h=1}^{M} \mathcal{N}_h(x_j; \pi, \alpha) f_h(y_j|x_j; \theta_h), \quad (2)$$

where Ψ is the vector of all the unknown parameters and $f_h(y_j|x_j; \theta_h)$ are local output densities, which are generally assumed to belong to the exponential family of densities [1,8]. The unknown parameter vector Ψ can be estimated by the maximum likelihood approach via the EM algorithm [1]. In contrast to the ME networks [8], the learning of NGME networks does not require both the selection of a learning rate and the iterative inner loop in the EM algorithm [1,4,8]. Under the independence assumption, $f_h(x_j; \alpha_h)$ in (1) can be written as

$$f_h(x_j; \alpha_h) = \prod_{i=1}^{q} g_h(x_{1ij}) \phi_h(x_{2j}; \mu_h, \Sigma_h) = \prod_{i=1}^{q} \prod_{v=1}^{n_i} \lambda_{hiv}^{\delta(x_{1ij}, v)} \phi_h(x_{2j}; \mu_h, \Sigma_h), \quad (3)$$

where the h-th conditional density of the i-th categorical variable x_{1ij} ($i = 1, \ldots, q$) in x_{1j}, $g_h(x_{1ij})$, is given by a multinomial distribution consisting of one draw on n_i distinct values with probabilities $\lambda_{hi1}, \ldots, \lambda_{hin_i}$, and where $\lambda_{hin_i} = 1 - \sum_{l=1}^{n_i-1} \lambda_{hil}$ and $\delta(x_{1ij}, v) = 1$ if $x_{1ij} = v$ and is zero otherwise ($v = 1, \ldots, n_i$). The vector of unknown parameters α_h thus consists of λ_{hiv} ($i = 1, \ldots, q; v = 1, \ldots, n_i - 1$), and the elements of μ_h and Σ_h ($h = 1, \ldots, M$).

To apply the EM algorithm to the generalized NGME networks, we introduce the indicator variables z_{hj}, where z_{hj} is one or zero according to whether y_j belongs or does not belong to the hth expert [4]. On the $(k+1)$th iteration, the E-step involves the calculation of $\tau_{hj}^{(k)}$

$$\tau_{hj}^{(k)} = \text{pr}_{\Psi^{(k)}}\{Z_{hj} = 1 | y_j, x_j\} = \frac{\pi_h^{(k)} f_h(x_j; \alpha_h^{(k)}) f_h(y_j|x_j; \theta_h^{(k)})}{\sum_{l=1}^{M} \pi_l^{(k)} f_l(x_j; \alpha_l^{(k)}) f_l(y_j|x_j; \theta_l^{(k)})} \quad (4)$$

for $h = 1, \ldots, M$, with $f_h(x_j; \alpha_h^{(k)})$ given by (3) based on the current estimate $\alpha_h^{(k)}$. In the M-step, the updated estimates of Ψ are obtained as follows:

$$\pi_h^{(k+1)} = \sum_{j=1}^{n} \tau_{hj}^{(k)}/n, \quad \lambda_{hiv}^{(k+1)} = \frac{\sum_{j=1}^{n} \tau_{hj}^{(k)} \delta(x_{1ij}, v)}{\sum_{j=1}^{n} \tau_{hj}^{(k)}},$$

$$\mu_h^{(k+1)} = \frac{\sum_{j=1}^{n} \tau_{hj}^{(k)} x_{2j}}{\sum_{j=1}^{n} \tau_{hj}^{(k)}}, \quad \Sigma_h^{(k+1)} = \frac{\sum_{j=1}^{n} \tau_{hj}^{(k)} (x_{2j} - \mu_h^{(k+1)})(x_{2j} - \mu_h^{(k+1)})^T}{\sum_{j=1}^{n} \tau_{hj}^{(k)}}.$$

For binary classification problems, $f_h(y_j|x_j; \theta_h)$ are assumed to be Bernoulli distribution of possible binary outcomes of "failure" and "success" [8]. That is,

$$f_h(y_j|x_j; \theta_h) = \left(\frac{\exp(w_h^T x_j)}{1 + \exp(w_h^T x_j)}\right)^{y_j} \left(\frac{1}{1 + \exp(w_h^T x_j)}\right)^{1-y_j}, \quad (5)$$

Table 1. Leave-one-out error rates for the breast cancer data

Method	Error rate
NGME network on continuous variables	29.5%
independence model on mixed variables	19.2%

where $\boldsymbol{\theta}_h = \boldsymbol{w}_h$. For notational convenience, we still present the mixed-mode input vector as $\boldsymbol{x}_j$ in (5). Indeed, the categorical variables are replaced by n_i-1 dummy variables and contribute to the local output via the linear predictor $\eta_{hj} = \boldsymbol{w}_h^T \boldsymbol{x}_j$; see [4]. The updated estimate of $\boldsymbol{\theta}_h^{(k+1)}$ is obtained by solving

$$\sum_{j=1}^{n} \tau_{hj}^{(k)} \partial \log f_h(\boldsymbol{y}_j|\boldsymbol{x}_j;\boldsymbol{\theta}_h)/\partial \boldsymbol{\theta}_h = \sum_{j=1}^{n} \tau_{hj}^{(k)} \left(y_j - \frac{\exp(\boldsymbol{w}_h^T \boldsymbol{x}_j)}{1+\exp(\boldsymbol{w}_h^T \boldsymbol{x}_j)} \right) \boldsymbol{x}_j = \boldsymbol{0}$$

for $h = 1, \ldots, M$, which are M sets of nonlinear equations each with unknown parameter vector $\boldsymbol{w}_h$.

3 A Real Example: Breast Cancer Data

We illustrate the method using an example of classifying breast cancer patients on the basis of the gene expression-profile vector of tumor samples and categorical variables of patient's clinical characterisitcs. The original data set [9] consists of 5000 gene expression profiles and 6 binary variables of clinical indicators from 78 sporadic lymph-node-negative breast cancer patients. With these patients, 44 remained metastasis free after a period of more than 5 years (good prognosis) and 34 patients had developed distant metastases within 5 years (poor prognosis). In this study, we work on the data set with 6 binary variables of clinical indicators and 5 continuous variables representing the top 5 "metagenes" ranked in terms of the likelihood ratio statistic described in [10]. We first apply the NGME network of [1] on the continuous variables to classify the patients into good and poor prognosis subgroups; see Eqt. (5). This preliminary analysis provides the initial estimates and the determination of the number of experts M for the generalized NGME network. In addition, the improvement of the generalized NGME network by using additional binary clinical indicators can be assessed. Such evaluation is based on the misclassification error rate using the "leave-one-out" method for cross-validation. The number of experts M is determined based on a frequentist analog of the "worth index" on model selection [11]. A NGME network with $M = 2$ experts is selected. The leave-one-out error rate is provided in Table 1. We then apply the generalized NGME networks to classify the patients, using the independence model, on the mixed feature data. From Table 1, it can be seen that the generalized NGME network significantly reduces the error rate by using additional binary clinical indicators.

4 Discussion

We have extended the NGME network to incorporate the independence model for tackling problems with mixed feature data. Although the independence assumption is likely to be unrealistic for many problems, it often performs surprisingly well in practice as a way of handling problems with mixed feature data [6,7]. One important reason is that the NAIVE method usually requires fewer parameters to be estimated and hence tends to have a lower variance for the estimates [6].

The error rates in Table 1 have been considered in a relative sense. However, caution should be exercised in interpreting these rates in an absolute sense. This is because the metagenes in the data set are determined using the expression profiles from the 78 cancer patients. Thus, the misclassification error rate is calculated without allowance for the selection bias [12]. The error rates given in Table 1 should therefore be interpreted as apparent error rates. An "external" cross-validation can be adopted to correct for the bias in estimating the error of a prediction rule [12].

References

1. Xu, L., Jordan, M.I., Hinton, G.E.: An alternative model for mixtures of experts. In: Cowan, J.D., Tesauro, G., Alspector, J. (eds.): Adv. in Neural Inf. Proc. Systems 7. MIT Press, Cambridge, Massachusetts (1995) 633–640
2. Dempster, A.P., Laird, N.M., Rubin, D.B.: Maximum likelihood from incomplete data via the EM algorithm. J. Roy. Stat. Soc. Ser. B **39** (1977) 1–38
3. Moody, J., Darken, C.J.: Fast learning in networks of locally-tuned processing units. Neural Comput. **1** (1989) 281–294
4. Ng, S.K., McLachlan, G.J.: Using the EM algorithm to train neural networks: Misconceptions and a new algorithm for multiclass classification. IEEE T. Neural Networ. **15** (2004) 738–749
5. McLachlan, G.J., Peel, D.: Finite Mixture Models. Wiley, New York (2000)
6. Hand, D.J., Yi, K.: Idiot's Bayes – not so stupid after all? Int. Stat. Rev. **69** (2001) 385–398
7. Titterington, D.M., Murray, G.D., Murray, L.S., et al.: Comparison of discrimination techniques applied to a complex data set of head injured patients. J. Roy. Stat. Soc. Ser. A **144** (1981) 145–175
8. Jordan, M.I., Jacobs, R.A.: Hierarchical mixtures of experts and the EM algorithm. Neural Comput. **6** (1994) 181–214
9. van't Veer, L.J., Dai, H., van de Vijver, M.J., et al.: Gene expression profiling predicts clinical outcomes of breast cancer. Nature **415** (2002) 530–536
10. McLachlan, G.J., Bean, R.W., Peel, D.: A mixture model-based approach to the clustering of microarray expression data. Bioinformatics **18** (2002) 413–422
11. Ng, S.K., McLachlan, G.J., Yau, K.K.W., Lee, A.H.: Modelling the distribution of ischaemic stroke-specific survival time using an EM-based mixture approach with random effects adjustment. Statist. Med. **23** (2004) 2729–2744
12. Ambroise, C., McLachlan, G.J.: Selection bias in gene extraction on the basis of microarray gene-expression data. Proc. Natl. Acad. Sci. USA **99** (2002) 6562–6566

A Comparative Study for WordNet Guided Text Representation

Jian Zhang and Chunping Li

School of Software, Tsinghua University, Beijing 100084, China
zjian03@mails.tsinghua.edu.cn
cli@tsinghua.edu.cn

Abstract. Text information processing depends critically on the proper text representation. A common and naïve way of representing a document is a bag of its component words [1], but the semantic relations between words are ignored, such as synonymy and hypernymy-hyponymy between nouns. This paper presents a model for representing a document in terms of the synonymy sets (synsets) in WordNet [2]. The synsets stand for concepts corresponding to the words of the document. The Vector Space Model describes a document as orthogonal term vectors. We replace terms with concepts to build Concept Vector Space Model (CVSM) for the training set. Our experiments on the Reuters Corpus Volume I (RCV1) dataset have shown that the result is satisfactory.

Keywords: Data mining, ontology, knowledge discovery.

1 Introduction

Text representation is critical in text classification tasks. During the last decades, a large number of methods have been developed for text classification and produced promising results. However, existing text classification systems typically use the bag-of-words model [1], where single word or word stem is used as features for representing document content. This model ignores the semantic relations between words. In addition, another difficulty of traditional methods is the high dimensionality of the feature space. Large numbers of features often make documents undistinguishable in higher dimensional spaces.

In this paper, we propose an approach for text representation by replacing terms with concepts. Concepts can be connected by using the WordNet hyper graph structure. We call the approach as Concept Vector Space Model (CVSM). We try to extract more abstract information for representing the training documents.

This paper is structured as follows. In Section 2 we briefly introduce some background research about WordNet, and describe some important items of WordNet. Section 3 introduces an approach for building CVSM as the representation of documents using WordNet. Experiments and evaluation are given in Section 4. Finally, we summarize our work in Section 5.

2 WordNet

The English WordNet [2] is an online lexical reference system whose design is inspired by current psycho-linguistic theories of human lexical memory. English nouns, verbs, adjectives, adverbs and multi-word expressions are organized into synonym sets or synsets, each representing one underlying lexical concept and linking these through semantic relations. The version 2.0 of WordNet comprises a total of 115,424 synsets, 79,685 noun synsets in it. WordNet includes the following important items. (1) *Unique beginner:* In WordNet, unique beginner is a noun synset with no hypernymy synsets. (2) *Lexicographer:* A decimal integer uniquely identifies a sense (synset) in WordNet. (3) *Concept chain:* Concept chain is a structure $\varsigma := (C,<)$ consisting of a set C, whose elements are concepts. These concepts are related to each other through hypernymy-hyponymy relation.

To date, there have been some attempts to use WordNet in text classification. Agirre and Rigau [3] attempt to disambiguate the words in a text using the idea of conceptual density in WordNet. Scott [4] discusses the use of hypernymy to represent text in terms of the synsets of its constituent words. These methods rely on making immediate decisions on word senses and retain only one sense per word.

In our work, we mainly consider the hypernymy-hyponymy relation between noun synsets. This kind of semantic relation can help us extract more generalized information of documents. And we consider all concepts of concept chains which are related to terms in documents and built by using WordNet.

3 Using WordNet for Text Representation

In order to use concept knowledge in text classification, we need to transform documents to numeric vectors. First of all, documents are represented by vector space model. Each document is represented by a vector of weights of terms:

$$d_i = (w_{i1}, \ldots, w_{in}) \qquad (1)$$

where d_i is vector of document i, w_{it} is weight of term t in document i. w_{it} is computed using a form of TF*IWF*IWF weighting developed by Roberto Basili [8], outperforms TF*IDF. So we adopt equation (2) to calculate term vectors.

$$w_{it} = n(t, i) * [\log_e(|D|/n(t))]^2 \qquad (2)$$

where $n(t, i)$ is the number of occurrence of term t in document i, and $|D|$ is the number of documents used in computing the inverse document frequency weight of term t. $n(t)$ is the number of documents in which term t occurs.

Here, we replace the terms with concepts in order to strengthen the semantic relations between terms. The weight of concept c, which occurs in the concept chain of term t, is computed by equation (3).

$$w_i(c) = w_{it} * \alpha * \beta^k \qquad (3)$$

where $w_i(c)$ is the weight of concept c which is one node of the concept chain to describe term t. Input parameter β is a decline factor in the range of $0< \beta <1$, which is used to limit the weight of concept and distinguish the levels of concept chain. k is the level position of concept c in the chain. α, computed by equation (4), is the inverse category frequency of concept c.

$$\alpha = \sqrt{\sqrt{\sum_{i=1}^{m}(T(c,i)-\tau(c)/m)^2} \Big/ \sum_{i=1}^{m}T(c,i)} \quad (4)$$

where $T(c, i)$ is the number of occurrence of concept c in document class i. m is the number of document class in training set. $\tau(c)$ is the number of occurrence of concept c in the whole training set. α is used to weaken the weight of quite high level concepts which are little useful for describing the characters of document classes.

4 Experiments and Results

We compare the performance of our text representation method against the performance achieved by text representation based on terms. We choose documents from Reuters Corpus Volume I (RCV1) dataset [5] to form our training and test sets. The documents are organized in four hierarchical groups: ECAT (Economics), CCAT (Corporate/Industrial), GCAT (Government/Social), and MCAT (Markets).

In Experiment 1, 1700 documents are chosen randomly from each category. 700 of 1700 documents from each category are randomly chosen as test set and the remaining 1000 formed the training set. We change the size of training set from 200 to 4000 documents and keep the size of test set unvaried. Some statistical information concerning the training set is described in Table 1. In Experiment 2, 27085 documents form training set [5], and test set is the same as that of Experiment 1.

We set decline factor $\beta = 0.5$ and adopt cosine measure based on concept vector space model to process text classification in our experiments.

We use precision, recall and F_1 measure [1][6] to evaluate the performance of CVSM text classifier. We describe the result of experiments as follows.

In Experiment 1, a comparative experiment measuring the performance against the size of training set is conducted using training sets of different sizes listed in Table 1. In Fig.1, when the size of training set increases from 200 to 4000, the accuracy of concept-based classifier increases from 85.11% to 88.36%, and the accuracy of term-based classifier increases from 45.36% to 60.86%. The accuracy of concept-based classifier is always higher than that of term-based classifier, but for the gradient of the

Table 1. Statistical information concerning the training set

	Training set	Size	Distinct Terms	Distinct Concepts
Experiment 1	A	200	3983	8060
	B	400	5880	9681
	C	800	9038	11364
	D	1600	12795	13030
	E	2000	14051	13509
	F	2400	15765	13939
	G	3200	18107	14487
	H	4000	19696	14894
Experiment 2	J	27085	46808	18931

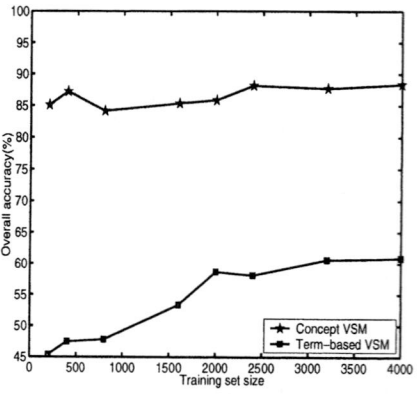

Fig. 1. Comparison of accuracy in training set from A to H

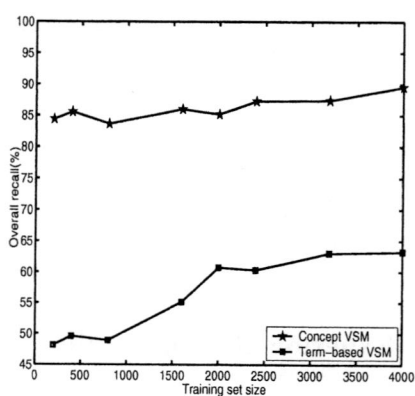

Fig. 2. Comparison of recall in training set from A to H

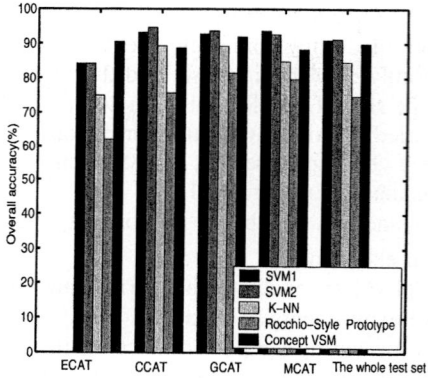

Fig. 3. Comparison of accuracy in training set J

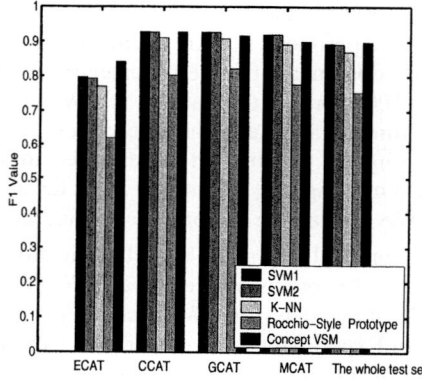

Fig. 4. Comparison of $F1$ measure in set J

accuracy, the latter is larger than the former. In Fig.2, the recall of concept-based classifier increases from 84.4% to 89.55%, and the recall of term-based classifier increases from 48.11% to 63.25%. Besides, when the size of training set increases from 200 to 1600, the difference between the number of concepts and the number of terms is smaller and smaller. In experiment 2, the difference is 27877.

In Experiment 2, we use training set J, 27085 training documents from RCV1 (the size of training set of any class is different). SVM1, SVM2, K-NN and Rocchio are used for performance comparison referred to [5]. Here, these algorithms are based on term vector space. A number of interesting observations can be made from the result in Fig.3 and Fig.4. First, compared with these term-based classifiers, the accuracy and F1 measure achieved by the concept vector space model are higher for test set of ECAT. Second, we see that, compared with these term-based classifiers, the overall F1 measure achieved by concept-based classifier increases from 75.38%, 87.05%, 89.18% and 89.35% to 89.94%, or a 14.56%, a 2.91%, a 0.76% and a 0.59% increase respectively.

5 Conclusions

In this paper, we develop a model for representing a document in terms of the synsets in WordNet. The model can extract more abstract information which can help improve the performance of classifier. Results show that the performance of concept-based classifier which uses concept vector space for representing documents is better than that of SVM classifier which uses term vector space. And when the size of training set becomes larger, using concept can reduce the dimensionality of feature space. In our future work, we will improve the model in more specialized domains.

Acknowledgments. This work was supported by Chinese 973 Research Project under grant No.2004CB719401.

References

1. Yang, Y.: An evaluation of statistical approaches to text category. Journal of Information Retrieval, Vol 1, No. 1/2, (1999) pages 67-88
2. Fellbaum Christians, ed. WordNet: an electronic lexical database. MIT Press, Map (1998)
3. Agirre, E. and Rigan, G.: Word sense disambiguation using conceptual density. In Proceedings of COLING'98.(1998)
4. Scott, Sam and Stan Matwin.: Text classification using the WordNet hypernyms. In Proceedings of the COLING/ACL Workshop on Usage of the WordNet in Natural Language Processing Systems, Montreal, (1998)
5. David, D.Lewis, Yang, Y., Fan Li (2004): RCV1: A new benchmark collection for text categorization research. Journal of Machine Learning Research 5 (2004) pages 361-397
6. Stephan, B., Andreas, H.: Boosting for text classification with semantic features. In Proceedings of the MSW 2004 Workshop at the 10th ACM SIGKDD Conference on Knowledge Discovery and Data Mining , Seattle, USA, (2004)

Application of Bayesian Techniques for MLPs to Financial Time Series Forecasting

Andrew Skabar

Department of Computer Science and Computer Engineering,
La Trobe University, Bundoora, 3083, VIC, Australia
a.skabar@latrobe.edu.au

Abstract. Bayesian learning techniques for MLPs are applied to the problem of forecasting the direction of change in daily close values of the Australian All Ordinaries Index. Predictions made over a 13 year out-of-sample period were tested against two null hypotheses—the null hypothesis of a mean accuracy of 0.5 (which is the expected accuracy if prices follow a random walk), and a null hypothesis which takes into account non-stationarity in the prices series. Results show that both null hypotheses can be rejected at the 0.005 level, but much more confidently in the case of the Bayesian approach as compared to an approach using conventional gradient descent based weight optimization.

1 Introduction

One of the main difficulties in applying MLPs to financial time series forecasting concerns the high level of noise in the data, and thus the danger of overfitting the network. An important issue concerns how to optimize model parameters such as the number of hidden units and regularization coefficient, so as to minimize the degree of overfitting on training data. One approach is to use an independent validation set to optimize these parameters; however, the difficulty here is how to select examples for the validation set: if validation examples are chosen to be adjacent to, but between, the training and test sets, any patterns found in the training data may have dissipated before the model is applied to the test data. Moreover, because the validation set is itself noisy, there will be considerable uncertainty in whether the parameter values are optimal. An alternative approach is to omit the validation set, and select parameters that provide the best results on the test data; but in this case we can never be sure that we have not simply optimized these parameters to the test set.

In contrast to gradient-descent based weight optimization methods, Bayesian learning techniques for MLPs [1, 2] do not attempt to find a single 'best' weight vector; but rather, they attempt to infer the posterior distribution of the weights, given the data. Samples can then be taken from this distribution, each sample representing a distinct MLP. Given some novel example, each of the sampled networks can be applied to the example, with the resulting prediction being the average prediction over the sample of networks weighted by the posterior probability of the network given the training data. This integrative approach allows Bayesian learning techniques to avoid many of the difficulties that conventional approaches have in avoiding overfitting.

2 Bayesian Learning Techniques for MLPs

Bayesian methods for MLPs infer the posterior distribution of the weights given the data. The predicted output corresponding to some input vector $\mathbf{x}^n$ is then obtained by performing a weighted sum of the predictions over all possible weight vectors, where the weighting coefficient for a particular weight vector depends on $p(\mathbf{w}|D)$. Thus,

$$\hat{y}^n = \int f(\mathbf{x}^n, \mathbf{w}) \, p(\mathbf{w} \mid D) \, d\mathbf{w} \tag{1}$$

where $f(\mathbf{x}^n, \mathbf{w})$ is the MLP output. The fact that $p(\mathbf{w}|D)$ is a probability density function allows us to express the integral in Equation 1 as the expected value of $f(\mathbf{x}^n, \mathbf{w})$ over this density:

$$\int f(\mathbf{x}^n, \mathbf{w}) p(\mathbf{w} \mid D) d\mathbf{w} = E_{p(\mathbf{w}|D)} \left[f(\mathbf{x}^n, \mathbf{w}) \right] \simeq \frac{1}{N} \sum_{i=1}^{N} f(\mathbf{x}^n, \mathbf{w}) \tag{2}$$

Thus, the integral can be estimated by drawing N samples from the density $p(\mathbf{w}|D)$, and averaging the predictions due to these samples. This process is known as *Monte Carlo* integration.

The density $p(\mathbf{w}|D)$ can be estimated using the fact that $p(\mathbf{w} \mid D) \propto p(D \mid \mathbf{w}) p(\mathbf{w})$, where $p(\mathbf{w} \mid D)$ is the likelihood, and $p(\mathbf{w})$ is the prior weight distribution. If the target values are binary, then the likelihood can be expressed as

$$p(D \mid \mathbf{w}) = \exp\left(-\left(-\sum_{n} \left\{ t^n \ln f(\mathbf{x}^n, \mathbf{w}) + (1-t)^n \ln(1 - f(\mathbf{x}^n, \mathbf{w})) \right\} \right) \right) \tag{3}$$

where, for the financial prediction problem, $t^n = 1$ if the close value for day $n+1$ is greater than that for day n (i.e., an upwards movement) and 0 otherwise (downwards movement). The prior weight distribution, $p(\mathbf{w})$, should reflect any prior knowledge that we have about the complexity of the MLP. To reflect the fact that we want it to be a smooth function, $p(\mathbf{w})$ is commonly assumed to be Gaussian with zero mean and inverse variance α, giving preference to weights with smaller magnitudes; i.e.,

$$p(\mathbf{w}) = \left(\frac{\alpha}{2\pi} \right)^{m/2} \exp\left(-\frac{\alpha}{2} \sum_{i=1}^{m} w_i^2 \right) \tag{4}$$

where m is the number of weights in the network [2]. However, we usually do not know what variance to assume for the prior distribution, and for this reason it is common to set a distribution of values. (The reader is referred to [2] for a detailed treatment of this). Because the prior depends on α, Equation 1 should be modified such that it includes the posterior distribution over the α parameters:

$$\hat{y}^n = \int f(\mathbf{x}^n, \mathbf{w}) \, p(\mathbf{w}, \alpha \mid D) \, d\mathbf{w} d\alpha \tag{5}$$

where

$$p(\mathbf{w}, \alpha \mid D) \propto p(D \mid \mathbf{w}) p(\mathbf{w}, \alpha) \tag{6}$$

Monte Carlo integration depends on the ability to obtain samples from the posterior distribution. The objective is to sample preferentially from the region where $p(\mathbf{w}, \alpha | D)$ is large. The Metropolis algorithm [3] achieves this by generating a sequence of vectors in such a way that each successive vector depends on the previous vector as well as having a random component; i.e., $\mathbf{w}_{new} = \mathbf{w}_{old} + \varepsilon$, where ε is a small random vector. Preferential sampling is then achieved using the criterion:

if $p(\mathbf{w}_{new} | D) > p(\mathbf{w}_{old} | D)$ accept

if $p(\mathbf{w}_{new} | D) < p(\mathbf{w}_{old} | D)$ accept with probability $\dfrac{p(\mathbf{w}_{new} | D)}{p(\mathbf{w}_{old} | D)}$ (7)

The difficulty in using the Metropolis algorithm to estimate the integrals for neural networks stems from the strong correlations in the posterior weight distribution; i.e., the great majority of the candidate steps generated in the random walk will be rejected as they lead to a decrease in $p(\mathbf{w}|D)$ [4]. The Hybrid Monte Carlo algorithm [5] reduces the random walk behaviour by using gradient information, which, in the case of MLPs, can be readily calculated.

3 Empirical Results

We applied the technique to predicting the direction of movement (*up* or *down*) of the closing value of the Australian All Ordinaries Index (AORD) for all trading days from November 1990 to December 2004. We are interested in the proportion of test examples for which the direction in movement is predicted correctly, and we refer to this as the *sign correctness proportion* (SCP). Input variables used were the relative change in close value from the previous day to the current day (r_1), and the 5, 10, 30 and 60 day moving averages (ma_5, ma_{10}, ma_{30}, ma_{60}). A prediction window period of 30 days was used in this study, with the training set for each 30-day prediction period consisting of data for the 200 trading days immediately preceding the test period. A total of 120 30-day predictions were made (*i.e.*, 3600 days), with the training and test windows advanced by 30 days after each 30-day prediction period. For Monte Carlo sampling we allowed a burn-in period of 1000 samples (to allow sampling to converge to the posterior distribution), following which we saved every tenth sample until a set of 100 samples was obtained. Each of the 100 samples was then applied to predicting the probability of an upwards change in the value of the index on the test examples, and the probabilities were then averaged over the 100 samples.

If the efficient markets hypothesis is correct, then we would expect the mean number of correct predictions to be 0.5. This suggests the following null hypothesis:

Null Hypothesis 1: H_0: $\mu = 0.5$ H_1: $\mu \neq 0.5$

The problem with a null hypothesis of a 0.5 mean is that it does not reflect the fact that there can be a general trend, over some extended period of time, for the value of the index to rise. A better approach is to compensate for any bias that may be present in the prediction model. This can be done by using the biased mean, defined as:

$$\mu_{bias} = [(x_a \times x_p) + ((1-x_a) \times (1-x_p))] / N \qquad (8)$$

where x_a and x_p represent the proportion of days in the test period for which the actual and predicted movements respectively are upwards, and N is the number of days in the prediction period. Here is the modified null hypothesis:

Null Hypothesis 2: $\quad H_0: \mu = \mu_{bias} \quad H_1: \mu \neq \mu_{bias}$

We tested the null hypotheses by performing a paired t-test of the samples obtained from each of the 120 30-day prediction periods, and then compared the mean proportion of days correctly predicted with the number of days expected to be correctly predicted, given the bias in the predictions. The results in Table 1 compare the performance of the Bayesian approach (labelled 'MCMC' in the table) with that of the gradient-descent approach using the Scaled Conjugate gradients (SCG) algorithm. Note that the reported results for SCG correspond to the best performance (i.e., smallest p-values) obtained from 10 trials, each using a different value for the weight regularization coefficient.

Table 1. Accuracies and paired t-test significance values for SCG compared with MCMC using $\alpha=1$

Method	Train. Acc.	Test. Acc.	p-value (Ho)	
			$\mu = 0.5$	$\mu = \mu_{bias}$
SCG	0.585	0.524	0.0048	0.0068
MCMC	0.571	0.528	0.0019	0.0011

The prediction accuracy on test data for MCMC is higher than that for SCG, however, note that the training accuracy for MCMC is *lower* than that for SCG. This adds support to the claim that the Bayesian approach is better at avoiding overfitting than are conventional weight optimization methods. It is also highly significant to note that the null hypotheses (particularly the second null hypothesis) is rejected much more confidently in the Bayesian case. In future work, we intend to test the approach on additional datasets, including international monetary exchange rates.

References

[1] MacKay, D.J.C. 1992, A practical Bayesian framework for backpropagation networks. In *Neural Computation*, 4(3), pp. 448-472.
[2] Neal, R.M., 1996, Bayesian Learning for Neural Networks, New York: Springer-Verlag.
[3] Metropolis, N.A., Rosenbluth, A.W., Rosenbluth, M.N., Teller & Teller, E., A.H., 1953, Equation of State Calculations by Fast Computing Machines. *Journal of Chemical Physics* 21(6), pp. 1087-1092.
[4] Bishop, C., 1995, Neural networks for pattern recognition, Oxford University Press, Oxford.
[5] Duane, S., Kennedy, A.D., Pendleton, B.J. & Roweth, D., 1987, Hybrid Monte Carlo. *Physics Letters B*. 195(2), pp. 216-222.

An Incremental Nonlinear Dimensionality Reduction Algorithm Based on ISOMAP[*]

Lukui Shi[1,2], Pilian He[2], and Enhai Liu[1]

[1] School of Computer Science and Engineering, Hebei University of Technology,
Tianjin 300130, China
[2] School of Electronic and Information Engineering, Tianjin University,
Tianjin 300072, China
`lkshi@eyou.com, plhe@tju.edu.cn`

Abstract. Recently, there are several nonlinear dimensionality reduction algorithms that can discover the low-dimensional coordinates on a manifold based on training samples, such as ISOMAP, LLE, Laplacian eigenmaps. However, most of these algorithms work in batch mode. In this paper, we presented an incremental nonlinear dimensionality reduction algorithm to efficiently map new samples into the embedded space. The method permits one to select some landmark points and to only preserve geodesic distances between new data and landmark points. Self-organizing map algorithm is used to choose landmark points. Experiments demonstrate that the proposed algorithm is effective.

1 Introduction

Dimensionality reduction is an important task to treat high-dimensional data. The goal of dimensionality reduction is to find the meaningful low-dimensional structures hidden in high-dimensional data. Two popular methods for dimensionality reduction are principal component analysis (PCA) and multidimensional scaling (MDS). They are both efficient to recover the true structure of data when handling a linear manifold. However, they have no way to discover complex nonlinear manifold structures [1]. Thus, it can be beneficial to consider nonlinear dimensionality reduction techniques.

In recent years, several unsupervised learning algorithms have been proposed to perform dimensionality reduction of low-dimensional nonlinear manifolds embedded in a high-dimensional space, such as ISOMAP [1], LLE [2], Laplacian eigenmaps [3] and so on. However, all these algorithms are only defined on training sets. They all do not map a new sample from the input space to the embedded space because they require a whole set as an input in order to project them into the embedded space.

In this paper, we proposed an incremental nonlinear dimensionality reduction algorithm based on ISOMAP for new samples. It only preserves the geodesic distances between new data and some landmark points selected from the training set.

---

[*] This work was supported by Science-Technology Development Project of Tianjin (No. 04310941R) and by Applied Basic Research Project of Tianjin (No. 05YFJMJC11700).

Experiments show that the extension to new samples is easy to implement, efficient to compute, and effective to map new samples into the low-dimensional space.

2 Review of ISOMAP

ISOMAP is a generalization of MDS. The main idea behind it is to replace Euclidean distances with an approximation of the geodesic distances on the manifold. The key of the method is to estimate the geodesic distances between points, which represent the shortest paths along the curved surface of the manifold. The algorithm is summarized as follows: (i) Construct the neighborhood graph. (ii) Estimate the geodesic distances between all pairs of points. (iii) Discover low-dimensional coordinates by applying MDS on the pairwise distance matrix. Details can be referred to [1].

3 An Incremental Nonlinear Dimensionality Reduction Algorithm

ISOMAP cannot project new data into the embedded space for it is stationary with respect to the data. Suppose that the set X contains N samples and that the dimension of the low-dimensional space doesn't grow after mapping a new point into it. To obtain the embedded coordinates of a new sample X_{N+1}, the simplest way is to execute ISOMAP again on the set containing all data in X and the new point X_{N+1}. During the procedure, the k nearest neighbors of each point must be updated and geodesic distances between all pairwise must be recomputed. However, the process has $O(N^3)$ time complexity [4]. In other words, the time complexity of computing the low-dimensional coordinates is $O(N^3)$ for each new sample. To improve the efficiency of mapping new data into the embedded spaces, we select some landmark points from the training set and only preserve geodesic distances between new samples and landmark points according to the idea of LDMS [4]. However, how many landmark points should be selected? The number n of landmark points and the dimension d of the embedded space should satisfy that $n \geq d+2$ [4]. The algorithm to obtain the low-dimensional coordinates of a new sample is as follows.

1) Select n ($n \ll N$) landmark points from the training set with a suitable way.

2) Search the k nearest neighbors of the new data in X and calculate geodesic distances between the new sample and landmark points based on the training set.

3) Merge landmark points and the new data into a set X', which has $n+1$ objects. One can run ISOMAP on X' and obtain the embedded coordinates of the new point.

Usually, one can randomly select some landmark points. However, it often occurs that landmark sets randomly selected don't represent the true topology of the manifold in the input space and will lead to worse results. Then how should one select landmark points? The criterion is that the low-dimensional embedding of the set can best preserve the geodesic distances among them in the input space. We propose to use clustering algorithms to gain landmark points. Here, the self-organizing map algorithm (SOM) [5] is used to determine landmark points. For high-dimensional data, SOM should be executed on the embedded coordinates instead of the original data to speed SOM. In section 4, experiments show that landmark sets decided with SOM can often better preserve the true topology of the manifold.

To map a testing point, the geodesic distances between it and landmark points need to be calculated. Suppose that the k nearest neighbors of all training objects is invariable while adding new data, which means that geodesic distances between training points are also not changed. Let the k nearest neighbors of the new data be $x_{k1}, x_{k2}, ..., x_{kk}$. According to Dijkstra's algorithm, the geodesic distances between the new data x_{N+1} and landmark points can be approximated with the following equation

$$d_G(x_{N+1}, x_i) = \min\{d(x_{N+1}, x_{k1}) + d_G(x_{k1}, x_i), ..., d(x_{N+1}, x_{kk}) + d_G(x_{kk}, x_i)\}, \quad (1)$$

where $d_G(i,j)$ and $d(i,j)$ is respectively the geodesic distance and Euclidean distance between pair of points (i,j). For the convenience of computing geodesic distances, we store the k nearest neighbor graph of the training set that is a $k \times n$ matrix.

In the algorithm, it takes $O(kN)$ time to search the k nearest neighbors of a new sample in the training set at most. The time complexity of estimating geodesic distances is $O(kn)$. The MDS eigenvalue calculation involves a full $n \times n$ matrix and has complexity $O(n^3)$. Therefore, the total time complexity of obtaining the low-dimensional coordinates of a new sample is $O(kN + n^3)$.

4 Experiments

In this section, we have evaluated the effectivity of the algorithm proposed. The algorithm was implemented in MATLAB6.5. All experiments have been run on a PC with 2.0GHz CPU. Experiments are done on Swiss roll data and the database of 698 synthetic face images. Both are used in [1] and available at http://isomap.stanford.edu. For a set X with N samples in a high-dimensional space, we split it into two disjoint subsets X_1 and X_2. The subset X_1 is used as the training set and X_2 as the testing set. Let $|X_1| = m$, then $|X_2| = N - m$. We apply the following steps to test the method.

1) We run ISOMAP on $X = X_1 \cup X_2$. Y_1 and Y_2 are respectively the low-dimensional embeddings of X_1 and X_2.
2) We use the incremental method to predict the embedded coordinates Y_2' of X_2.
3) We align Y_2 and Y_2'. The mean difference between them is defined as

$$\frac{1}{N-m}\sum_{i=1}^{N-m}\| y_i - y_i' \|^2 \quad (2)$$

The mean difference is computed for various m.

4) We compare the mean differences between results from selecting landmark points with SOM and the random method respectively.

Fig. 1 gives mean differences between results with ISOMAP and the incremental algorithm on two data sets for different m. The results with SOM to select landmark points are shown in the bottom curve. The results with the random method are given in the top one, which are the average of 100 random computations. Here, the neighborhood size and the number of landmark points are identical for two methods to choose landmark points. Experiments prove that results with SOM are usually better than those with the random method.

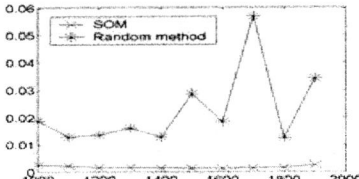
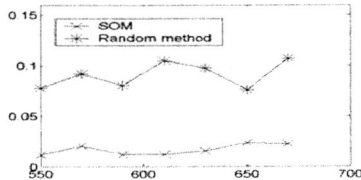

Fig. 1. Mean differences between the coordinates from ISOMAP and from the incremental algorithm on Swiss roll data (left) and synthetic face images (right) for different m. Top curve: randomly selecting landmark points. Bottom curve: selecting landmark points with SOM.

5 Conclusions

Several nonlinear dimensionality reduction algorithms can effectively find the low-dimensional embedding on a manifold. However, they all cannot directly map new samples into the embedded space. We proposed an incremental nonlinear dimensionality reduction algorithm. In the method, one can select some landmark points with SOM algorithm and only preserve geodesic distances between new data and landmark points. Experiments show that the proposed algorithm is efficient and accurate.

References

1. Tenenbaum, J. B., de Silva, V., Langford, J. C.: A Global Geometric Framework for Nonlinear Dimensionality Reduction. Science, Vol. 290, (2000) 2319-2323.
2. Roweis, S. T., Saul, L. K.: Nonlinear Dimensionality Reduction by Locally Linear Embedding. Science, Vol. 290, (2000) 2323-2326.
3. Belkin, M., Niyogi, P.: Laplacian Eigenmaps for Dimensionality Reduction and Data Representation. Neural Computation, Vol. 15, (2003) 1373–1396.
4. de Silva, V., Tenenbaum, J. B.: Global versus Local Methods in Nonlinear Dimensionality Reduction. In NIPS, Vol. 15, (2002) 705-712.
5. Kohonen, T., Self-organization and Associative memory, Spring-Verlag, 1984.

Robust Speaker Identification Based on t-Distribution Mixture Model

Younjeong Lee[1], Hernsoo Hahn[1], Youngjoon Han[1], and Joohun Lee[2]

[1] School of Electronic Engineering, Soongsil University, Dongjak-gu, Seoul, Korea
{youn, hahn, young}@ssu.ac.kr
[2] Dept. of Internet Broadcasting, Dong-Ah Broadcasting College, Anseong, Korea
vincelee21@naver.com

Abstract. To minimize the outliers' effects, in this paper, a new speaker identification scheme based on the t-distribution mixture model is proposed. Since the t-distribution provides a longer and heavier tailed alternative to the Gaussian distribution, the mixture model with multivariate t-distribution is expected to show more robust results than the Gaussian mixture model(GMM) in the cases where outliers exist. In experiments, we compared the performance of the proposed scheme with that of using the conventional GMM to show its robustness.

1 Introduction

The GMM, which is widely used for speaker identification and verification, suffers from outliers having non-linear distributions. The performance of speaker identification based on the GMM is degraded by atypical observations induced by various factors, such as irregular utterance variations in several sessions, the physical and psychological condition of the speaker, variation of vocal tract, microphones, additive background noise, and speaking styles, etc.[1,2,3]. Even in clean speech data, some frames of a speaker's test utterance can become more similar to another speaker's model than to his/her model[2]. That is, the performance of speaker identification depends on how properly handle error data, called outliers.

Hence, in this paper, to overcome the limitation of the GMM in handling outliers with non-Gaussian distribution, we propose to use the t-distribution mixture model. Since the t-distribution provides a longer-tailed alternative to the Gaussian distribution, the mixture model with multivariate t-distribution is expected to show more robust results than the GMM in the cases where outliers exist.

In the experiments, we confirmed that the t-distribution mixture model is more robust and shows higher performance than the conventional GMM and the GMM based on the frame pruning scheme, with the expense of small amount of additional computation burden.

2 Robust Speaker Identification Based on t-Distribution Mixture Model

To deal with the outliers, we propose to use the t-distribution mixture model. If the model is obtained from adjusting properly the degree of freedom of t-distribution mixture model, the abnormal data (outliers) in the Gaussian distribution can be included in the *t*-distribution, since the tail of *t*-distribution is heavier and longer than one of the Gaussian distribution.

For data sets containing outliers, the *t*-distribution mixture model is obtained from modifying the *d*-multivariate Gaussian function using the robust M-estimator of Huber[4] and the degree of freedom γ of chi-square random variable. The *d*-multivariate *t*-distribution probability is represented by the following form:

$$t(x_t \mid \lambda) = \sum_{i=1}^{M} \pi_i t_i(x_t) \tag{1}$$

where π_i is the mixture weights satisfying the constraint $\sum_{i=1}^{M} \pi_i = 1$, and $t_i(x_t)$ is the component densities defined by *t*-distribution with a mean vector μ_i and a covariance matrix Σ_i for *i*-th mixture, represented as follows:

$$t_i(x_t) = \frac{\Gamma\left(\frac{\gamma_i+d}{2}\right)|\Sigma_i|^{-1/2}}{(\pi \gamma_i)^{\frac{d}{2}} \Gamma\left(\frac{\gamma_i}{2}\right)\{1 + \delta(x_t, \mu_i; \Sigma_i)/\gamma_i\}^{\frac{1}{2}(\gamma_i+d)}}, \quad i = 1, \cdots, M, \tag{2}$$

where $\delta(x_t, \mu; \Sigma)$ is the Mahalanobis squared distance. Collectively, the parameters of speaker's density model are denoted as $\lambda = \{\pi_i, \mu_i, \Sigma_i, \gamma_i\}_{i=1}^{M}$. To estimate parameters form all sequences of *T*, the likelihood of *t*-distribution mixture model can be written as

$$P(X \mid \lambda) = \prod_{t=1}^{T} t(x_t \mid \lambda). \tag{3}$$

A posterior probability z_{ti} that x_t belongs to *i*-th component of mixture is represented by

$$z_{ti} = \frac{\pi_i t_i(x_t)}{\sum_{l=1}^{M} \pi_l t_l(x_t)} \tag{4}$$

and the conditional expectation u_{ti} given x_t represented by

$$u_{ti} = \frac{\gamma_i + d}{\gamma_i + \delta(x_t, \mu_i; \Sigma_i)}. \tag{5}$$

In Eq. (5), the degree of freedom γ_i is obtained from the nonlinear Gamma function [5,6,7]. Using the posterior probability z_{ti}, the parameter for the ML algorithm can be iterlatively estimated by the following EM algorithm.

$$\hat{\pi}_i = \frac{1}{T} \sum_{t=1}^{T} z_{ti} \tag{6}$$

$$\hat{\mu}_i = \frac{\sum_{t=1}^{T} z_{ti} u_{ti} x_t}{\sum_{t=1}^{T} z_{ti} u_{ti}} \tag{7}$$

$$\hat{\Sigma}_i = \frac{\sum_{t=1}^{T} z_{ti} u_{ti} (x_t - \mu_i)(x_t - \mu_i)^T}{\sum_{t=1}^{T} z_{ti}} \tag{8}$$

To construct the speaker's models for robust speaker identification in the training phase, each of S speakers, $\lambda_1,...,\lambda_S$, is represented by the t-distribution mixture model, respectively. Then, if a feature sequence of an unknown speaker's speech data is given, in the test phase, the speaker model $\hat{\lambda}$, which has the maximum log-likelihood among the database is selected as the unknown speaker's model.

$$\hat{\lambda} = \max_{1 \leq s \leq S} \frac{1}{T} \sum_{t=1}^{T} \log t(x_t | \lambda_s) \qquad (9)$$

In experiments shown in the following, the robustness of the t-distribution mixture model is proved by showing that its performance is superior to the GMM with frame pruning which is considered as a robust scheme in the speaker identification.

3 Experimental Results

To show the robustness of the proposed speaker identification based on the t-distribution mixture model, its performance is compared to that of the GMM with the alpha frame pruning. The GMM with the alpha frame pruning is a method in which the maximum likelihood is calculated by averaging the log-likelihood of the remaining frames after the $\alpha\%$ of lower frames are removed. Based on the assumption that the log-likelihood of the correct model in the speaker identification is higher than those of the fault models, the weights of the frames concerned with the outliers are set to zero. Therefore, the effect of outliers on the decision is minimized, where $\alpha = 0\%, 5\%$, and 10%, respectively. Here, the frame pruning with $\alpha = 0\%$ is same as the conventional GMM.

In our experiments, speech consisting of Korean sentences uttered 15 times each by 200 speakers (100 females and 100 males). Speaker models were trained using 10 utterances of each speaker. The remaining 5 utterances were used for test of the speaker identification. The speech data was sampled at 16 kHz and was parameterized using 25 MFCCs with 13 delta cepstrum.

Fig. 1 shows the speaker identification rates for the 4 algorithms. Fig. 1 shows that the performances of all algorithms are approaching to their best ones when M=19: 99.7% in the t-distribution mixture model, 98.8% in the conventional GMM, and

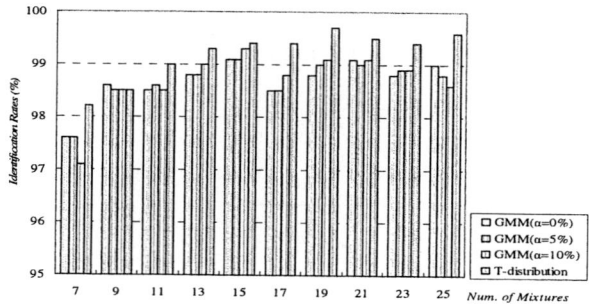

Fig. 1. The performance of speaker identification

99%, 99.1% in the GMM with the 5%, 10% frame pruning, respectively. As shown in Fig. 1, the proposed method with t-distribution shows better performance than the others do, in most range of the number of mixtures.

4 Conclusions

To properly handle the outlier problem, a robust speaker identification scheme using the t-distribution mixture model is proposed in this paper. The t-distribution has been expected as the possible solution since it provides a longer and heavier tailed alternative to the Gaussian distribution. To confirm that this expectation is correct, its performance has been compared with that of the GMM with a frame pruning which is considered as a robust method. In experiments, we proved that the performance of the proposed scheme is superior to that of the GMM in most cases.

Acknowledgement

This work was supported by the Soongsil University Research Fund.

References

1. Reynolds, D.A., Rose, R. :Robust text-independent speaker identification using Gaussian mixture speaker models, IEEE Trans. on SAP, 3(1), (1995) 72-82
2. Bessacier, L. and Bonastre, J.F.: Frame Pruning for speaker recognition, ICASSP98, (1998) 765-768
3. Lee, J., Rheem, J. and Lee, K. Y.: Robust Speaker Recognition Against Utterance Variations, LNCS2668, (2003) 624-630
4. Huber, P. J.: Robust Statistics. New York: Wiley, 1981
5. Peel, D., McLachlan, G.J. : Robust mixture modeling using the t-distribution, Statistics and computing, 10, (2000) 339-348
6. McLachlan, G.J. and Peel, D., : Finite Mixture Models, New York ;Wiley, 2000
7. Wang, H., Zhang, Q., Luo, B. and Wei, S. :Robust mixture modeling using multivariate t-distribution with missing information, Pattern Recognition Letters, 25, (2004) 701-710

Inducing Sequential Patterns from Multidimensional Time Series Data

Chang-Hwan Lee

Department of Information and Communications,
DongGuk University, Seoul, Korea 100-715
chlee@dgu.ac.kr

Abstract. Inducing sequential patterns from time series data is an important data mining problem. While most of the current methods are generating sequential patterns within a single attribute, this paper proposes a new method, using Hellinger entropy measure, for generating multi-dimensional sequential patterns. A number of theorems are proposed to reduce the computational complexity of the proposed method.

1 Introduction

Among many techniques in data mining, sequential pattern is a technique which can discover more meaningful information by considering time attribute, together with other traditional attributes. While most of the current sequential pattern methods are generating single-dimensional patterns [1] [3] [4], we propose a new method and thoroughly explore efficient methods for multi-dimensional sequential pattern mining with the use of Hellinger entropy measure. In addition, our method could calculate the significance of each sequential pattern as a numeric value, called H measure, and these sequential patterns are given in a sorted order based on this H measure.

The sequential patterns induced in this paper is represented as follows:

$$A = a \ \wedge B = b \ \wedge \ \cdots \ \rightarrow \ T = t \ \ with \ H$$

where A, B and T are attributes with a, b and t being values in their respective discrete alphabets. The H represent the *significance* of sequential pattern, respectively. The final sequential patterns generated from the database are sorted based on the H value. The database of our proposed method is in its first normal form. In case multiple items are purchased together, each of them is represented in different tuples with the same customer-id and time-id.

2 Contents of H Measure

The probability distribution of the target attribute changes when it is measured under certain conditions usually given as value assignments of other attributes. Therefore, it is a natural definition, in this paper, that the significance of a sequential pattern is interpreted as the degree of dissimilarity between a priori probability distribution and a posteriori probability distribution of the target attribute. This dissimilarity is defined as instantaneous information, which is the information content of the sequential pattern given that the left-hand side happens.

In this paper, we employ an entropy function, called Hellinger measure [2], as a tool for defining the information content of sequential pattern rules. In terms of the sequential patterns, let us interpret the event $A = a$ as the target concept to be learned and the event(possibly conjunctive) $B = b$ as the hypothesis describing this concept. The *information content* of the sequential pattern, using Hellinger measure, is defined as

$$\left[\sqrt{P(a|b)} - \sqrt{P(a)}\right]^2 + \left[\sqrt{1-P(a|b)} - \sqrt{1-P(a)}\right]^2 \qquad (1)$$

where $P(a|b)$ means the conditional probability of $A = a$ under the condition $B = b$ has happened beforehand.

Another criteria we have to consider is the *generality* of the sequential patterns. The left-hand side must occur relatively often for a pattern to be deemed useful. In this paper, we use $\sqrt{P(b)}$ to represent the probability that the sequential pattern will occur and, as such, can be interpreted as the measure of sequential pattern generality. As a result, by multiplying the generality with the information content of the sequential pattern rules, we have the following term

$$\sqrt{P(b)}\left[\left(\sqrt{P(a|b)} - \sqrt{P(a)}\right)^2 + \left(\sqrt{1-P(a|b)} - \sqrt{1-P(a)}\right)^2\right]$$

which possesses a direct interpretation as a multiplicative measure of the generality and information content of a given sequential pattern rule. In this paper, we call above multiplicative term as H *measure* of sequential patterns.

3 Boundaries of H Measure

Suppose we have a sequential pattern $B = b \to A = a$. We would like to specialize this sequential pattern by adding a condition $C = c$ so that we have a specialized sequential pattern $B = b \land C = c \to A = a$. For the sake of illustration, above sequential patterns are denoted as R_g and R_s, respectively. Suppose H_g and H_s are the H measures of the sequential patterns R_g and R_s, respectively. Our goal is to answer the question "Can we describe the bound of H_s in terms of H_g ?" In other words, is it possible to estimate the maximum value of H_s without knowing any information about attribute C ?

Consider that we are given a general sequential pattern whose H measure, H_g, is defined as

$$H_g = \sqrt{P(b)}\left[2 - 2\sqrt{P(a|b)P(a)} - 2\sqrt{(1-P(a|b))(1-P(a))}\right]$$

We try to calculate the bound of H_s. Given no information about C, we can state the following results.

Theorem 1. *If the H measure of a specialized pattern satisfies the following boundary:*

$$H_s \leq \max\{\sqrt{P(a|b)}\sqrt{P(b)}\left[2\sqrt{m} - 2\sqrt{P(a)}\right],$$
$$2\sqrt{P(b)} - \sqrt{1 - P(a|b)}\sqrt{P(b)}\left[2\sqrt{P(a)} + 2\sqrt{1 - P(a)}\right]\}$$

where m *represents the number of class in the target attribute, the general pattern discontinues specializing.*

Theorem 2. *If the conditional probability($P(a|b)$) of general pattern is 1, H measure of specialized pattern cannot be greater than that of general pattern. Therefore, the general pattern discontinues specializing.*

As a consequence of these theorems we note that the bound of specialized sequential pattern is achievable without further information about C. We can decide in advance that the specialized sequential pattern cannot be improved with respect to H Measure. This principle will be the basis for restricting the search space of the system.

Algorithm Description

The algorithm takes time series database in the form of discrete attribute vectors and generates a set of K sequential patterns, where K is a user-defined parameter.

The algorithm employs branch-and-bound with depth-first search over possible left-hand sides. The algorithm first generates all possible cases of first-order sequential patterns. The first-order sequential patterns are sequential patterns that have single value assignment in left-hand side. The algorithm proceeds then calculating the H measures of each first-order sequential patterns, finding K most informative sequential patterns in terms of H measure, and then placing these K sequential patterns in an ordered list, called BEST. The smallest H measure, that of the Kth element of BEST, is then defined as the running minimum H_*.

From that point onwards, new patterns which are candidates for inclusion in the sequential pattern set have their H measure compared with H_*. If greater than H_*, they are inserted in the list and the Kth sequential pattern is deleted. And H_* is updated with the value of the H measure of whatever sequential pattern is now Kth on the list. The algorithm systematically tries to specialize all first-order sequential patterns and terminates when it has determined that no more sequential patterns exist which can be specialized to achieve a higher H measure than H_*.

4 Experimental Results

In order to test the functionality of the algorithm proposed in this paper, we assumed an artificial transaction database. The database contains 14 attributes

Table 1. Multi-dimensional sequential patterns generated from the database

Sequential Patterns	Conf.	H
Price=20-29 → Item=P07	0.13137	0.00023
Gender=male & Item=P06 → Item=P02	0.11015	0.00021
Qty=1 → Item=P09	0.11800	0.00021
Item=P09 → Item=P01	0.11067	0.00019
SaleorNot=sale → Item=P00	0.11207	0.00017
Age=20-29 & Qty=over 5 → Item=P03	0.10592	0.00015

and 20,000 records. Data values are generated using random numbers. The entire data set is read and then 100 most informative sequential patterns were generated.

The topmost 6 sequential patterns from the first database is shown in Table 1. For each pattern in Table 1, its corresponding values for confidence(Conf.) and H measure are shown, and the resulting patterns are sorted based on their H measure values. The confidence means the number of transactions satisfying both left-hand side and right-hand side of the pattern divided by the number of transactions satisfying left-hand side only. The topmost pattern in Table 1 means that customers who purchased items (whatever the items are) of which price are between 20-29 later purchase item P07. This type of patterns can not be acquired from traditional sequential pattern methods. The 4th pattern shows a sequential pattern equivalent to the one generated from Apriori-like method. It illustrates that the functionality of our method includes that of traditional sequential pattern methods.

5 Conclusion

In this paper we have introduced a new method for generating multi-dimensional sequential patterns from transaction databases. We developed an information theoretic measure, called H measure, which becomes the criteria for selecting and sorting inductive sequential patterns generated. The boundary of the H measure is analyzed and two heuristics are developed to reduce the computational complexity of the system. The resulting sequential patterns generated from synthetic data sets show how the system generates multi-dimensional sequential patterns of data sets effectively.

References

1. R. Agrawal and R. Srikant, Mining *sequential patterns,* Int. Conf. on Data Engineering, 1995, pp. 3–14.
2. R. J. Beran, *Minimum hellinger distances for parametric models,* Ann. Statistics 5 (1977), 445–463.
3. B. Mortazavi-Asl Q. Chen U. Dayal J. Han, J. Pei and M-C. Hsu,*Freespan: Frequent pattern-projected sequential pattern mining,* Int. Conf. Knowledge Discovery and Data Mining (KDD00), 2000.
4. M. J. Zaki, Spade: *An ecient algorithm for mining frequent sequences,* Machine Learning 42 (2001), 31–60.

Fitness Approximation in Estimation of Distribution Algorithms for Feature Selection

Haixia Chen[1], Senmiao Yuan[1], and Kai Jiang[2]

[1] College of Computer Science and Technology, Jilin University,
Changchun 130025, China
hxchen2004@sohu.com
[2] The 45th Research Institute of CETC, Beijing 101601, China
kjiang2004@sohu.com

Abstract. Estimation of distribution algorithms (EDAs) are popular and robust algorithms that combine two technical disciplines of soft computing methodologies, probabilistic reasoning and evolutionary computing, for optimization problems. Several algorithms have already been proposed by different authors. However, these algorithms may require huge computation power, which is seldom considered in those applications. This paper introduces a "fast estimation of distribution algorithm" (FEDA) for feature selection that does not evaluate all new individuals by actual fitness function, thus reducing the computational cost and improve the performance. Bayesian networks are used to model the probabilistic distribution and generate new individuals in the optimization process. Moreover, fitness value is assigned to each new individual using the extended Bayesian network as an approximate model to fitness function. Implementation issues such as individual control strategy, model management are addressed. Promising results are achieved in experiments on 5 UCI datasets. The results indicate that, as population-sizing requirements for building appropriate models of promising solutions lead to good fitness estimates, more compact feature subsets that give more accurate result can be found.

1 Introduction

Feature selection (FS) is one of the most important issues in the community of data mining, machine learning, pattern recognition, etc[1]. There are two basic approaches to feature selection: wrapper approaches and filter approaches[2]. While wrappers give better results in terms of the accuracy of the final classifier, being a NP-hard problem, the selection process becomes more complex with the number of features and instances in the given task increasing.

Estimation of distribution algorithms (EDAs) are a quite recent topic in optimization techniques. Using different assumption of the joint probability distribution, different algorithms have been proposed and good results have been observed [1], [3], [4]. In the wrappers for feature selection optimization, the time to run EDAs is dominated by the 'slow-to-compute' fitness function evaluation. To compound the problem further, it is often necessary for EDAs to select a large population size for distribution estimation and use a large number of generations to obtain an acceptable solution and avoid premature convergence. For evolutionary algorithms models, there are two main ways to reduce the computational cost by integrating approximate models that exploit knowledge of past evaluation into the optimization: evolution control and surrogate approach [5]. As it is difficult to construct an approximate model that is globally correct due to the high dimensionality, ill distribution and limited number of training samples, it is found that the surrogate approach is likely to converge to a false optimum, which is an optimum of the approximate model, but not the one for the actual fitness function. Therefore, the evolution control approach is of more practical importance.

This paper introduces a "fast estimation of distribution algorithm" (FEDA) to deal with the computational overburden comes along with the wrapper approach for feature selection. It uses Bayesian Networks (BNs) to estimate the probability distribution of each generation. In addition, the BNs are extended as approximate models to assign fitness values. As those assigned fitness values are not the actual fitness values, the individual control strategy and model management strategy are proposed to find those informative individuals with high fitness values or in an unexplored region. The main aim of the approximate model is not only to assign fitness but also to find informative individuals for updating itself.

2 The FEDA for Feature Selection

The framework for FEDA can be summarized as follows. First, a group of individuals are initialized randomly. Then, individuals are selected according to the individual control strategy for actual evaluation and added into the population by steady-state strategy. In the first generation, as there is no model for fitness estimation, all individuals are controlled. Third, a Bayesian network are build from the population, fitness statistics of the selected population are collected according to the Bayesian network structure and used to extend the model. Last, new individuals are generated by sampling from the Bayesian network and sent to the approximate model for fitness assignment. The process terminates if the stopping criterion is meet. Otherwise, it goes to the second step for the next iteration.

Given dataset D with d features: $X = \{X_1, X_2, \cdots, X_d\}$. The purpose of the learning system is to induce a classifier c in the hypothesis space H that can best describe the dataset. Each individual in the search can be represented by a binary string of d bits, $s = \{s_i\}, s_i \in \{0,1\}, i = 1,...,d$, with each bit indicating whether a feature is present (1) or absent (0). And the aim of the wrapper is to select a feature subset s in the feature subset space S that satisfies $s = \arg\max_{c \in H, s' \in S}(P(c, s', D))$. Where $P(c, s, D)$ measures the performance of the classifier c with a feature subset s on the dataset D, and comprises the accuracy measure [1] and the 'parsimony' measure that indicates how many features and data acquirement and preparation cost we have managed to save.

Estimation of Distribution Algorithms (EDAs) replace the crossover and mutation operators in GAs by building a probabilistic model and sampling from the model. Bayesian networks are used in this paper as the probabilistic models. And the traditional Bayesian networks are extended to act as approximate models for fitness approximation so as to avoid additional cost in model building and to exploit the complicated expressive power of the Bayesian networks.

For every variable S_i of the population and each possible value s_i of the variable, let $f_c(s_i | \pi_i)$ denote the contribution of S_i at value s_i to the total fitness.

$$f_c(s_i | \pi_i) = f(s_i | \pi_i) - \sum_{s_i} p(s_i | \pi_i) f(s_i | \pi_i). \quad (1)$$

Where Π_i is the set of parent variables (nodes) that S_i has in the BN and π_i is its possible instantiation. $f(s_i | \pi_i)$ is average fitness of individuals with $S_i = s_i$ and $\Pi_i = \pi_i$. The fitness of an individual can be estimated as the sum of the average fitness and the contribution of every bit:

$$f_{est}(s) = \overline{f} + \sum_{i=1}^{d} f_c(s_i | \pi_i). \quad (2)$$

To accommodate this extension, the conditional probability table of BN is modified by adding two additional entries that represent $f_c(s_i | \pi_i)$ to each row.

2.1 Individual Control Strategy

The first problem comes along with FEDA is how should individuals be evaluated by the actual fitness function. There are two possibilities to combine the actual fitness function with the approximate fitness function. One is individual-based evolution control in which a certain number of individuals within a generation are evaluated with the actual fitness function. Another is generation-based evolution control, which means in every T generations, T' ($T' < T$) generations will be actually evaluated. We prefer individual control in FEDA because EDA evolves with a large population, and we want to find the near optimum as soon as possible. The problem now is to determine which and how many individuals should be evaluated/controlled by the actual fitness function. To this end, a strategy with four units is proposed.

1. Model Fidelity Test. The model fidelity factor is defined as:

$$\alpha = L_{max} / L_t(BN). \quad (3)$$

Where L_{max} is the maximum log likelihood of BN to the population. $L_t(BN)$ is the log likelihood for the current model. t denotes the number of iteration. $0 < \alpha \leq 1$.

2. Exploration. For each new sampled individual s, the probability for sampling it $\hat{p}(s)$ is calculated according to the current BN. If $\hat{p}(s) < 1/|S|$, then the individual is put into the exploration unit, otherwise it is sent to the exploitation unit that will be addressed below. For individual that is put into the exploration unit, its approximate fitness $\hat{f}_t(s)$ is calculated according to formula 2 and compared to the average fitness $\overline{f}_t$. If $\hat{f}_t(s) < \overline{f}_t$, then the individual is not controlled. Otherwise, the individual is evaluated by the actual fitness function.

3. Exploitation. For individuals in the exploitation unit, the best β percent is controlled. We call β the exploitation factor.

4. Random Control. For the rest individuals in the exploitation unit, random numbers between 0 and 1 are obtained. If the number is higher than min(α, η), then the individual is truly evaluated. η is the random factor that is less than 1.

The strategy is designed to find the unexplored region and the promising region. Individuals with low sampling probability imply two cases. For one thing, the individual is really not so good and should be eliminated from the evolutionary process. For another, the individual is in fact a good one but not in the current search region. The exploration unit tries to find the latter one. The approximate model gives a consistent answer indicating a really bad individual when it assigns a low approximate fitness to an individual with low probability. However, when an individual with low probability is assigned a high fitness, we may conclude that the approximate model itself doesn't confirm its decision. So the individual should be controlled. For individuals with high probability, as the current population gives enough information for model building, the approximate fitness is sound to a great degree and only a small percentage of individuals with highest approximate fitness should be actually evaluated. However, for small percentage value, the fitness values of most individuals in the population will be estimated. Such an approach might affect the selection process and cause the population converges to a sub-optimum point. To make up for this, the random control unit demands at least some additional true evaluations will occur to every generation according on the fidelity of the model.

2.2 Model Management Strategy

Another problem comes along with FEDA is whether all or just the fraction of actually evaluated individuals should be used for model update. Due to the high dimensionality, ill distribution and limited number of training samples, it is very difficult to construct an approximate model that is globally correct. In fact, it is of more practical importance to build an approximate model that represents the promising individuals step by step. The individual control strategy described above can be viewed as a good filter for actively selecting the most informative individuals for model update.

With no prior knowledge, the evolutionary process often starts with a population generated according to uniform distribution. So the approximate model is often of poor quality at the beginning of the search. With more promising individuals are found by exploration and exploitation, the model quality also improves as the evolutionary search proceeds. Thus, another general rule for model management is that the model should be updated with more controlled individuals at the beginning. After a certain number of generations, the model becomes much more reliable and the control frequency can reduce. The individuals that will be controlled in each generation are determined by three factors, α, β and η. α is determined online by the performance of the model. η is used jointly with α to ensure at least some individuals are controlled. Only β can be controlled easily. We let it decreases with the evolutionary process. Those controlled individuals replace the ones with the lowest fitness values in the father population. In this way, only individuals that are thought as informative, promising are introduced into the individual pool.

3 Experiments

Experiments were carried out on the German, soybean, chess, anneal and mushroom datasets from UCI repository [7]. We used a population with 2000 individuals. The search finished when no improvement was found in two consecutive generations or when a maximum of 20 generations was reached. Exploitation factor β decreased from 0.1 to 0.05 with step length 0.01, and kept constant in the following generations. Random factor $\eta = 0.95$. For each individual, a naive Bayes (NB) classifier was constructed. We compared FEDA with FSS-EBNA[1].

Fig. 1 shows the best fitness value as a function of the number of true evaluations for German dataset. Similar results were observed for the other datasets. It is noted that FEDA can achieve better results with less actual evaluation than FSS-EBNA. About 60% actual evaluations are saved by introduction of the approximate model. Furthermore, FEDA can find better results than FSS-EBNA. It seems contradictory as FSS-EBNA takes more actual evaluations. We think the individual control strategy and model management strategy can answer for this. In FSS-EBNA all the new generated individuals are evaluated by the actual fitness function and enter into the next generation. However, in FEDA, only individuals that meet the individual control strategy are controlled. The model fidelity test, exploration, exploitation, and random control units in the individual control strategy help to find informative individuals. That is, the strategy actively finds those individuals that help most. It is like a filter that rejects those useless individuals from model building. As we can only build a local model in practice, the active learning implied by the strategy helps to find better models. It is also noted that we take a pessimistic termination criterion in the compare. As FEDA takes less actual evaluations, we hope it can evolve more and find better results given the same time as FSS-EBNA.

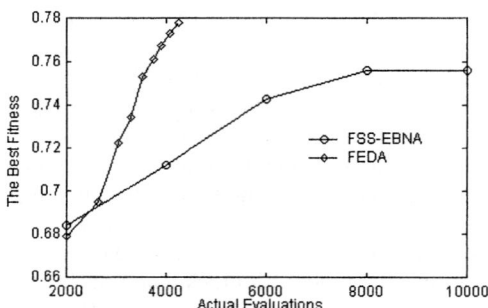

Fig. 1. The best fitness value as a function of the number of actual evaluations for FEDA and FSS-EBNA

Fig. 2 illustrates the accuracy and size of the final optimal feature subset for the five datasets averaged over 30 runs. In each run, the performance of the algorithm is determined by five-fold cross validation on the whole dataset. A more compact subset with higher accuracy is more desirable. So points in the right bottom are preferable to the ones in the upper left. The graph clearly shows that with the help of the approximate model, FEDA can find a more compact classifier with higher accuracy.

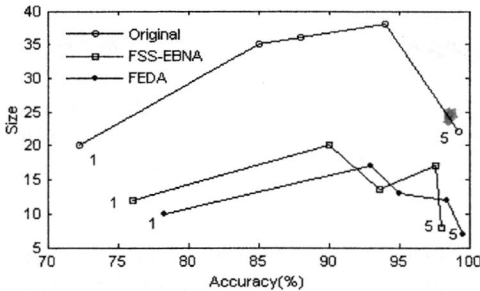

Fig. 2. Performance Comparison between FEDA and FSS-EBNA for the five dataset

4 Summary

This paper presents a fitness approximation strategy in EDA for FS. To exploit all of the cumulated knowledge about the search process, the conditional probability tables of the BNs are extended to incorporate contributions of each bit under different states. Individual control strategy and model management strategy are proposed to find those informative individuals and limit the number of actual fitness evaluations to a minimum. Experimental results show that the algorithm can get a more accurate, more compact subset with less computational cost.

References

1. Inza, I., Larranaga, P.., Etxeberria, R. and Sierra, B.. Feature Subset Selection by Bayesian Network-based Optimization. Artificial Intelligence 123 (2000) 157-184
2. Kohavi, R., John, G. H.. Wrappers for Feature Subset Selection. Artificial Intelligence 97 (1997) 273-324
3. Bengoetxea, E., Larranaga, P., Bloch, I., Perchant, A., Boeres, C.. Inexact Graph Matching by means of Estimation of Distribution Algorithms. Pattern Recognition 35 (2002) 2867-2880
4. Chen, H. X., Yuan, S. M., Jiang, K.. Bayesian Network Optimization Algorithm Based on Holding Strategy. Computer Engineering and Application 14 (2005) 61-65
5. Jin, Y. A Comprehensive Survey of Fitness Approximation in Evolutionary Computation. Soft Computing (2003)
6. Pelikan, M., Sastry, K.. Fitness Inheritance in the Bayesian Optimization Algorithm. IlliGAL Report No. 2004009 (2004)
7. Blake, C. L. and Merz, C. J.. UCI Repository of Machine Learning Databases. http://www.ics.uci.edu/~mlearn/MLRepository.html, Irvine, CA: University of California, Dept. of Information and Computer Science (1998)

Automatic Feature Selection for Classification of Health Data*

Hongxing He, Huidong Jin, and Jie Chen

CSIRO Mathematical and Information Sciences,
GPO Box 664, Canberra ACT 2601, Australia
{Hongxing.He, Warren.Jin, Jie.Chen}@csiro.au

Abstract. For classification of health data, we propose in this paper a fast and accurate feature selection method, FIEBIT (Feature Inclusion and Exclusion Based on Information Theory). FIEBIT selects the most relevant and non-redundant features using Conditional Mutual Information (CMU) while excluding irrelevant and redundant features according to the comparison among Individual Symmetrical Uncertainty (ISU) and Combined Symmetrical Uncertainty (CSU). Small feature subsets are selected before classification without compromising the classification accuracy. In addition, the size of the feature subset is determined automatically. Our preliminary empirical results on health data with hundreds of features suggest FIEBIT is efficient and effective in comparison with representative feature selection methods.

1 Introduction

Excessive numbers of features in health data is commonplace. There are usually many features which either provide little information in deciding the classification or are redundant due to the strong correlations between features. In theory, more features may provide more discriminating power. However in practice like health data mining, there are usually limited amount of training data. The excessive features will not only significantly slow down the learning process, but also cause a learning algorithm, say, a classifier, to over-fit the training data, since the irrelevant or redundant features may confuse the learning algorithm.

A Redundancy Based Filter (RBF) methodology on microarray data has been proposed [1]. The RBF has successfully removed large number of features but has not compromised the accuracy of the classifiers. On each iteration, the method selects one feature simply based on Individual Symmetrical Uncertainty (ISU) followed by a feature removal procedure based on the comparison among symmetrical uncertainty [1]. However, its feature selection based on symmetrical uncertainty considers little about the correlations between features conditional on classification, and sometimes could not generate very accurate results.

In this paper, we combine existing Conditional Mutual Information Maximisation (CMIM) [2,3] and RBF methods to propose FIEBIT (Feature Inclusion

---

* The authors would like to acknowledge Dr H. Altay Guvenir of Bilkent University for donating the Cardiac Arrhythmia Database for public usage.

and Exclusion Based on Information Theory) for health data. It has several interesting characteristics as follows:

- FIEBIT combines forward-selection and backward selection methods. The former is used to include discriminative features and the later to exclude irrelevant or redundant features.
- FIEBIT does not need to specify the optimal number of features. FIEBIT can terminate automatically when all features are processed.
- FIEBIT efficiently generates a small feature subset on health data and leads to more accurate classification.

2 Proposed Feature Selection Method: FIEBIT

We use CMIM in features selection. Conditional Mutual Information (CMI) (Equation 2) based on Mutual Information (Equation 1) is used as criteria in feature inclusion.

$$I(y;x) = H(y) - H(y \mid x) \tag{1}$$

$$I(y;x_n|x_m) = H(y \mid x_n) - H(y \mid x_n, x_m) \tag{2}$$

Equation 3 is used to select the $(k+1)^{th}$ feature when k features have been selected.

$$f(k+1) = \arg\max_{n}(\min_{1 \leq l \leq k} I(y; x_n \mid x_{f(l)})) \tag{3}$$

Input: All Features
Output: Selected Subset of Features, // indicated by Selected

1. UnSelected = All
2. Selected = NULL
3. **for** $n = 1, \cdots, N$ // $1, 2, \cdots, N$ are feature index
4. $\quad s(n) = I(c, n)$
5. **while** UnSelected Not Empty
6. $\quad Selected[k] = \arg\max_n s(n)$ (n in UnSelected)
7. $\quad$ Remove it from UnSelected
8. $\quad$ Remove all features j from UnSelected if
9. $\quad\quad ISU(k;c) \geq ISU(j;c)$ and $ISU(k;c) \geq CSU(k,j;c)$
10. $\quad s^* = 0$
11. $\quad$ **for** n in UnSelected
12. $\quad\quad$ **if** $s(n) > s^*$:
13. $\quad\quad\quad s(n) = \min(s(n), I(c; n \mid Selected[i])), i = last, \ldots, k-1$
14. $\quad\quad\quad s^* = s(n)$

Fig. 1. The FIEBIT Algorithm

Following [1], we use Individual Symmetrical Uncertainty (ISU, Equation 4) and Combined Symmetric Uncertainty (CSU, Equation 5) as the criteria in feature exclusion.

$$ISU(x;y) = 2\frac{I(y;x)}{H(x)+H(y)}. \tag{4}$$

$$CSU(x_j, x_i; y) = 2\frac{I(y; x_j, x_i)}{H(x_j, x_i) + H(y)}. \tag{5}$$

Feature Inclusion and Exclusion Based on Information Theory (FIEBIT) combine CMIM and RBF methods. RBF has the merit of being very efficient and automatically determining the number of features. CMIM has a more discriminating feature selection scheme to select features with maximum relevance and least redundancy on each iteration. FIEBIT takes advantage of merits of both methods. The algorithm implementing FIEBIT is described by Fig. 1.

3 Preliminary Results

C4.5 [4] is used to create pruned and un-pruned decision trees. The decision trees are then used to predict the accuracy of training and test data. We use the *leave-one-off* approach in dividing data into training and test datasets. In the *leave-one-off* approach we use one data record in turn as the test data. All other data records are used to train the C4.5 decision tree. The default C4.5 parameter setting are used. C4.5 gives training and test errors using decision tree (pruned and un-pruned). The average error rates are then calculated on N runs (N is the total number of data records).

We use a computer with Intel(R) Xeon(TM) CPU (3.20 GHz) running the Linux operation system. Procedural language Python is used for programming.

The cardiac arrhythmia dataset [5] from the UCI machine learning data repository is used to test FIEBIT and compare it with other methods. The data consists of 452 records and 279 features. There are sixteen classes. Class 1 refers to 'normal' ECG, classes 2 to 15 refer to different classes of arrhythmia and class 16 refers to unclassified ones. We take the two largest classes (class 1 and 10). This left 295 data records and 238 features. The average error rate is then calculated and listed in Table 1. Note that the run time in the table includes

Table 1. Performance comparison using *leave one off* approach on the cardiac arrhythmia dataset with two classes

	No Selection	CMIM	RBF	FIEBIT
Number of Feature Selected	238	7	7	7
Run Time	1m45s	16.5s	17.6s	17.6s
Error(%), Training, Un-pruned	1.76	3.08	6.05	5.00
Error(%), Training, Pruned	2.15	3.42	6.05	5.02
Error(%), Testing, Un-pruned	9.15	9.15	8.13	**5.76**
Error(%), Testing, Pruned	9.15	9.50	8.13	**6.78**

preprocessing (feature selection) and C4.5 run time. The number of features selected in CMIM is predefined.

Table 1 can be summarised as follows:

- FIEBIT and RBF achieve the same savings in computation time.
- RBF and FIEBIT both lead to better classification accuracy than the case where all features are used.
- FIEBIT select seven features automatically. Six of them are also selected by RBF. One of them is different from the subset selected by RBF. Due to the superior feature selection criteria of FIEBIT, the classification accuracy is improved (error rate improved from about 8% to about 6%).

4 Conclusions

The Feature Inclusion and Exclusion Based on Information Theory (FIEBIT) method has been developed for classification on health data. FIEBIT adopted the novel inclusion method by CMIM and the efficient feature exclusion method of RBF. Therefore it has the following useful characteristics.

- The FIEBIT enables the selected feature on each iteration to have the highest discriminating power when the values of features selected-so-far are given with reasonable efficiency.
- It uses the efficient feature deletion algorithm used by RBF to remove a large number of unimportant features effectively. As a result, the algorithm can determine the number of features automatically.

The method has been tested on a publicly available health dataset. The classification accuracy using selected small fraction of features is improved in comparison with existing methods.

In the future, we will conduct a more comprehensive empirical study to compare FIEBIT with RBF and CMIM. This includes test on other types of classifiers (SVM, NN etc) and especially on large health datasets. How to further reduce the size of the selected feature subset while keeping or improving the classification accuracy is our another research topic.

References

1. Lei Yu and Huan Liu. Redundancy based feature selection for microarray data. In *Proceedings of KDD'04*, pages 737–742, Seattle, WA, USA, 2004.
2. Francois Fleuret. Fast binary feature selection with conditional mutual information. *Journal of Machine Learning Research*, 5:1531–1555, 2004.
3. Gang Wang, Frederick H. Lochovsky, and Qiang Yang. Feature selection with conditional mutual information maxmin in text categorization. In *Proceedings of CIKM'04*, pages 8–13, Washington, US, November 2004.
4. J. Quinlan. *C4.5: Programs for Machine Learning*. Morgan Kaufmann, 1993.
5. S. Jack, D. Heckerman, and C. Kadie. *ftp://ftp.ics.uci.edu/pub/machine-learning-databases/arrhythmia/*, 1998.

BP Learning and Numerical Algorithm of Dynamic Systems

Jiuzhen Liang and Hong Jiang

College of Information Science and Engineering, Zhejiang Normal University,
Jinhua 321004, China
liangjz@zjnu.cn, 01190405@zjnu.net

Abstract. This paper deals with relationship between BP learning for neural networks and numerical algorithm of differential equations. It is proposed that the iteration formula of BP algorithm is equivalent to Euler method of differential dynamic system under certain conditions, and the asymptotic solutions of the two formulas are consistent. It is also proved in theoretic that asymptotic solutions given by BP algorithm are equivalent to that computed by any numerical method for differential dynamic systems under certain conditions. Also, an example to train the BP network by modified numerical method is presented.

1 Introduction

Since the BP algorithm is invented[1], neural networks receive lots of applications and focus[2,3]. Because BP algorithms are the gradient descent search algorithms; the gradient information of the objective function at the searching dot is the key factor. Moreover, because the iteration formula of BP algorithm can be regarded as a discrete dynamic system, which is similar to the differential dynamic system, it counts much to research the characters of the iteration formula of BP algorithm resorting to the differential dynamic system. There are few papers on it except the literatures [4,5].

This paper deals with the relationship between BP algorithm for neural networks and differential dynamic systems. It is proposed that the iteration formula of BP algorithm is a special form of Euler method of differential dynamic system. It is proposed that the neural network learning can be converted to computing numerical solution of differential dynamic systems under some conditions, in order to create more neural networks learning algorithm. Finally, an example is provided to train neural network by Euler method.

2 Problem Proposing

Consider the multi-layer BP neural networks. Consume W is the weight of any multi-layer BP networks including threshold value, that is $W = (w_1, w_2, ..., w_n)$. The sample space is (X, D), that X is the sample input, and D is the desired value. Error energy function is defined as

$$E = \parallel Y - D \parallel^2 \qquad (1)$$

When the sample space is fixed, E is the function of the weight vector W. So the formula above can be rewritten as

$$E = E(W) \tag{2}$$

In most cases, the standard form of BP algorithm used to train multi-layer neural networks is

$$W^{(k+1)} = W^{(k)} - h \nabla E(W^{(k)}) \tag{3}$$

$$W^{(0)} = W_0 \tag{4}$$

Here $h > 0$ is the learning step.

Consider the following dynamic system

$$\frac{dW(t)}{dt} = - \nabla E(W(t)) \tag{5}$$

In the numerical analysis the first order Euler method for solving the differential dynamic systems is as follows

$$W^{(k+1)} = W^{(k)} - (t_{k+1} - t_k) \nabla E(W^{(k)}) \tag{6}$$

Here, $W^{(0)} = W(t_0)$ is the initial value. Assume that $t_{k+1} - t_k = h$, when $k = 0, 1, 2, ...$, then Formula (6) can be transformed into the form of Formula (3). From the above, the standard BP algorithm (3) is a particular example of solving the differential dynamic systems (5) by the Euler method whose step is its learning speed h. Otherwise, it's an attempt to study the character of solution sequence of BP algorithm (3) through considering the characters of dynamic system (5).

3 Existence, Exclusiveness and Consistency for the Solutions

Lemma 1. The sufficient and necessary condition under which the solution of the BP learning algorithm (3) exists with exclusiveness is that the following formula holds up.

$$\lim_{k \to \infty} \nabla E(W^{(k)}) = \lim_{t \to \infty} \nabla E(W(t)) \tag{7}$$

Definition 1. Assume that $S \subset R^n$ is an open set and $S \subset R$, the function $F(t, W)$ is the continuous mapping over $T \times S \to R^n$, then say F respecting for W is provided with local Lipschitz condition. Namely, to any bounded close set $\Omega \subset T \times S$ there is a constant $K(\Omega) > 0$, such that

$$\|F(t, W_1) - F(t, W_2)\| \leq K(\Omega)\|W_1 - W_2\|, \forall (t, W_1), (t, W_2) \in \Omega \tag{8}$$

Here $T \subset R$. Then mark $F(t, W) \in L_\Omega(T \times S)$ which means that F is provided with local Lipschitz condition over $T \times S$, if $K(\Omega)$ can be chosen independently of Ω, then say $F(t, W)$ is provided with Lipschitz condition over $T \times S$, and denote $F \in L(t, W)$. Known from the literature [6], the following conclusions are established for the dynamic system (5).

Lemma 2. If $\nabla E(W) : T \times S \to R^n$, $S \subset R^n$, and also $\nabla E(W(t)) \in C(T \times S) \cap L_\Omega(T \times S)$, then for the initial value problem $W(t_0) = W_0, F(t_0, W_0) \in L_\Omega(T \times S)$, there is only a unique solution for the differential dynamic system (5) called $W(t; t_0, W_0)$ that is the solution for (5), and $W(t_0; t_0, W_0) = W_0$.

Lemma 3. There is only a unique solution for the dynamic system (5), if Ω is a bounded close set, S is an open set with $E(W(t)) \in C^{(2)}(T \times S)$.

Theorem 1. If Ω is a bounded close set, S is an open set, moreover $E(W(t)) \in C^{(2)}(T \times S)$, $\lim_{k \to \infty} \nabla E(W^{(k)}) = \lim_{t \to \infty} \nabla E(W(t)) = 0$, the solutions of the learning algorithm (3) and the dynamic system (5) exist and are exclusive. Let $e(t) = W^{(t)} - W(t)$, namely $e(t)$ is the deviation of solutions of BP algorithm (3) and dynamic system (5). Now consider the properties of the limitation $\lim_{t \to \infty} e(t)$.

Theorem 2. If the Formula (5) is computed by the Euler method, when the step $h < 1$, and $\lim_{t \to \infty} \nabla E(W(t)) = 0$, there is the following formula.

$$\lim_{t \to \infty} W^{(t)}) = \lim_{t \to \infty} W(t) \tag{9}$$

4 BP Algorithm and the Numerical Solutions of Dynamic System

Assume the solution sequence worked out by a numerical method for the differential dynamic system (5) is $\{\overline{W}^{(k)}\}$. Clearly

$$\lim_{k \to \infty} \overline{W}^{(k)} = \lim_{k \to \infty} W^{(k)} \tag{10}$$

$$\lim_{k \to \infty} \overline{W}^{(k)} = \lim_{t \to \infty} W(t) \tag{11}$$

Here $W(t)$ is the solution of the dynamic system(5). Therefore, here is the following theorem for the relationship between BP learning algorithm and the numerical solutions of differential dynamic system.

Theorem 3. Assume the solution sequence of the differential dynamic system (5) obtained by certain numerical method is $\{\overline{W}^{(k)}\}$, the solution sequence computed by BP learning algorithm (3) is $\{W^{(k)}\}$ and the learning speed of the BP algorithm(3) is $0 < h < 1$. If $\lim_{t \to \infty} \nabla E(W(t)) = 0$ and the Formula (11) is satisfied, the Formula (10) holds true. Namely, this numerical solution and that of BP algorithm are asymptotic consistent.

5 Training Neural Network by Modified Euler Method

Next consider the modified Euler method, which is one of the numerical methods for the differential dynamic system (5), and use it for the learning of multi-layer

Table 1. Learning results of Euler method and standard BP algorithm for nine-mode problem

Precision	Iteration number of standard BP algorithm	Iteration number of Euler method	Iteration number of BP-Euler method
0.1	5038	761	333
0.05	14011	2012	1943

neural networks. Table 1 is the learning results of three algorithms (namely the BP algorithm, modified Euler method, BP-Euler combined method) experimented by the nine mode classification problem [7].

6 Conclusions

This paper announces that asymptotic solutions given by BP algorithm are equivalent to that computed by any numerical method for differential dynamic systems under certain conditions. There are many numerical solutions for differential dynamic system. Theoretically these algorithms can be used to train multi-layer neural networks.

References

1. Rumelhart D. E., Hinton G. E. and Williams R. J. Learning internal representations by error propagation. Parallel Distributed Proceeding, Cambridge MA: MIT Press, 1986, 318 362.
2. Reyneri L.M. and Filippi E. Modified backpropagation algorithm for fast learning in neural networks, Electronics letters, 1990, 26(19):1564-1566.
3. Qiu G., Varley M. R. And Terrell T. J. , Accelerated training of backpropagation neural networks by using adaptive momentum step, Electronics letters 1992, 28(4): 377-379.
4. Pinaki Roychowdhury, Y. P. Singh, and R. A. Chansarkar, Dynamic Tunneling Technique for Efficient Training of Multilayer pecoptron, IEEE transactions on neural networks, 1999,10(1): 48-55.
5. Liang J.Z.; He X.G.; Zhou J.Q., Dynamic analysis of BP algorithm for neural networks,Acta Automatica Sinica, 2002,28(5):729-735.
6. Huang L., Stability Theory, Beijing University Press, Beijing, 1992.
7. Liang J.Z., He X.G., Research on approximation theory of fuzzy neural networks and learning algorithm, Beijing University of Aeronautics and Astronautics, Beijing, PhD dissertation, 2001.6

Ant Colony Optimization Combining with Mutual Information for Feature Selection in Support Vector Machines

Chunkai Zhang and Hong Hu

Department of Mechanical Engineering and Automation, Shenzhen Graduate School,
Harbin Institute of Technology, Shenzhen 518055, China
ckzhang@hotmail.com

Abstract. An effective feature selection scheme is proposed, which utilizes the combination of wrapper and filter: ant colony optimization (ACO) and mutual information (MI). By examining the modeling based on SVMs at the Australian Bureau of Meteorology, the simulation of three different methods of feature selection shows that the proposed method can reduce the dimensionality of inputs, speed up the training of the network and get better performance.

1 Introduction

Although support vector machines (SVMs) is an effective classifier for the problems of high dimension, the curse of dimensionality arises when a number of irrelevant and redundant features are recorded [1]. There are two techniques for feature selection: filters and wrappers. Filters, such as mutual information (MI) [2], are based on the statistical tools, which assume the inputs are independent and the objective function disregards the SVMs with which the selected features are to be used. Wrappers, assess subsets of features according to their usefulness to a given SVM. In contrast with filters, wrappers incorporate the inductive bias of the SVMs and the combinatorial optimization process involves no user selectable parameters, such as the final feature size etc., but they require massive amounts of computation [3, 4].

In this paper, an effective feature selection scheme for SVMs is proposed, which is the hybrid of wrapper and filter: ant colony optimization (ACO) combining with mutual information (MI). The objective function of ACO for feature selection is the performance measure of SVMs, and mutual information between input and output is employed as the inherent ability of an ant to exploit a food source with some probability.

2 Ant Colony Optimization(ACO) and Mutual Information(MI)

Ant colony optimization (ACO) is a combinatorial optimization algorithm, which is derived from the foraging behavior of real ants in nature [5]. The main idea of ACO is to model the problem as the search for a minimum cost path in a graph. Artificial ants walk through this graph, looking for good paths. Each ant has a rather simple behavior so that it will typically only find rather poor-quality paths on its own. Better paths are found as the emergent result of the global cooperation among ants in the colony. In this paper, we utilize mutual information as some problem-specific local heuristics, which is similar to the inherent self-exploiting ability of every ant in real ants.

Mutual information (MI) is one of most important heuristic feature selection methods. With the entropy defined by Shannon [6], the MI between X and C, $I(X;C)$ is:

$$I_s(X;C) = -\sum_{c \in C} \int_x p(c,x) \log \frac{p(c,x)}{P(c)p(x)} dx \tag{1}$$

The MI of independent variables is zero, but is large between two strongly dependent variables with the maximum possible value depending on the size of the data set. And this assumes that all the inputs are independent and that no output is in fact a complex function of two or more of the input variables.

3 The Proposed Feature Selection Method

In real ant system, besides the cooperation among ants by exchanging the pheromone trails, every ant has the self-exploiting ability to exploit a food source. In ACO, this ability is determined by random. In this paper, we substitute the mutual information for random as some problem-specific local heuristics. It is following:

1) Every candidate feature in ACO is mapped into a binary ant where a bit "1" denotes the corresponding feature is selected and a bit of "0" denotes the feature is eliminated.
2) The selected features are used to train SVMs, and the accuracy rates of SVMs tested by the test set are the objective function of ACO.
3) The global optimal solution from the beginning of a trial is reserved, and the pheromone intensities of its features are enhanced.
4) The pheromone intensity of each feature becomes:

$$\tau_{i,0} = (1-\rho)\tau_{i,0} + \Delta\tau_{i,0}/N_0 \tag{2}$$

$$\tau_{i,1} = (1-\rho)\tau_{i,1} + \Delta\tau_{i,1}/N_1 \tag{3}$$

where ρ represents evaporation rate in order to avoid unlimited accumulation of trails; $\Delta\tau_{i,0}$ and $\Delta\tau_{i,1}$ are respectively defined as the sum of the pheromone intensities of no-selected and selected features laid by all ant agents; N_0 and N_1 are respectively the sum of the ants in which the feature i is not selected and the sum of the ants in which the feature i is selected.

5) Generating a random, and comparing with the exploitable probability parameter *Exploit*. If this random is greater than or equal to the parameter *Exploit*, whether the feature *i* is selected or not is decided by the pheromone trails; otherwise, self-exploiting ability of an ant. If belongs to the former, the feature *i* is chosen from the larger between the two following probability parameters:

$$P_1 = [\tau_{i,1}]^{\alpha}[d_i + 1]^{\beta} \qquad (4)$$

$$P_0 = [\tau_{i,0}]^{\alpha}[d_i]^{\beta} \qquad (5)$$

where $d_i = \sum_{j=1}^{i-1} Solution_{k,j,1}$, the sum of selected features in which is equal to 1 if the feature is selected, otherwise 0; α, β factors respectively governing the influence of pheromone intensity and the number of selected features on this feature's selection.

If belongs to the latter, whether the feature selected or not is determined by self-exploiting ability of every ant. There are the probabilities: P_1, P_3 and random. If the mutual information of *i* th candidate input is large, it means it is a highly correlated input for each output, so include it into input feature subset with large probability P_1; if the mutual information of *i* th candidate input is moderate, it means it is a general correlated input for each output, so randomly include it into input feature subset; If the mutual information of *i* th candidate input is little, it means it is little correlated input for each output, so exclude it from input feature subset with large probability P_3.

4 Experimental Studies

The temperature data set for Australia was taken from the TOVS instrument equipped NOAA12 satellite in 1995 [7], which is used to evaluate the techniques for selecting the input subset. The input set of TOVS readings to be used by these networks was extracted using each of the three techniques: GA, MI and the proposed method.

In MI method, a common input vector length of 8 was used as initial experimentation had proved this to be a suitable value. In GA, $N = 50$, $T = 60$, $P_c = 0.6$ and $P_m = 0.02$. In the proposed method, $N = 50$, $\alpha = 1$, $\beta = -1$, $\rho = 0.1$, $Q = 8.0$, $P_1 = P_3 = 0.9$, *Exploit*=0.7, 0.9 and 0.1, the initial pheromone intensity of each features is equal to 10.0. And a SVMs with *m* inputs evolves for 10,000 iterations, where *m* represents the number of inputs. And the fitness function is defined to be $1/RMSE$.

Table 1. Mean of *RMSE* (K) derived from all 3 techniques and using all inputs

Method	RMSE (Level 1)	RMSE (Level 3)	Time(s)
Full	2.9	2.7	*
GA	2.6	2.9	286
MI	2.7	3.6	*
The proposed method(*Exploit* =0.7)	2.4	2.8	185
The proposed method (*Exploit* =0.9)	2.5	2.9	243
The proposed method(*Exploit* =0.1)	2.7	3.4	117

For level 1, GA selects the features 1, 3, 7, 15, 17, 18, 19, 21; MI selects the features 22, 20, 14, 1, 2, 4, 13, 12; The proposed method (*Exploit* =0.7) selects the features 3, 8, 14, 20, 22, 4, 2; The proposed method (*Exploit* =0.1) selects the features 22, 20, 14, 1, 2, 4, 13, 12; The proposed method (*Exploit* =0.9) selects the features 3, 15, 17, 18, 19,22,20;

5 Conclusions

Table 1 indicates that the proposed method (*Exploit* =0.7) exhibited better performance at level 1 and 3. Level 3 is interesting, it seems to indicate that the predictive capability at this level is spread more across the inputs – there is less redundancy of information. The proposed method (*Exploit* =0.1) costs least time, but the proposed method (*Exploit* =0.7) cost moderate time in case of the best performance. Although there is considerable similarity between GA and the proposed method (*Exploit* =0.9), there are substantial differences between the inputs selected, and they select the different number of inputs for level 1. The result also indicates that the different value of the parameter *Exploit* have important effect on the performance and cost time of the proposed method, which adjust the balance between the ACO and MI.

References

1. V. N. Vapnik: The Nature of Statistical Learning Theory. Springer-Verlag, New York, (1995).
2. N. Kwak, C-H. Choi, "Input feature selection by mutual information based on parzen window", IEEE Trans. PAMI 24 (12), (2002) 1667–1671.
3. W. Siedlechi and J. Sklansky, "A note on genetic algorithms for large-scale feature selection", Pattern Recognition Letters, 10, (1989) 335–347.
4. C. Emmanouilidis, A. Hunter, J. Macintyre and C. Cox, "Selecting features in neurofuzzy modeling by multiobjective genetic algorithms",Artificial Neural Networks,(1999) 749–754.
5. M. Dorigo and T. Stützle, "Ant Colony Optimization", IEEE TRANSACTIONS ON EVOLUTIONARY COMPUTATION, Vol. 8, No. 4, AUGUST, (2004) 422 - 423.
6. T.M. Cover, J.A. Thomas: "Elements of Information Theory", Wiley, New York, 1991.
7. J. LeMarshall, "An Intercomparison of Temperature and Moisture Fields Derived from TIROS Operational Vertical Sounder Data by Different Retrieval Techniques". Part I: Basic Statistics. Journal of Applied Meteorology, V. 27, (1988) 1282 – 1293.

A Preliminary MML Linear Classifier Using Principal Components for Multiple Classes

Lara Kornienko, David W. Albrecht, and David L. Dowe

School of Computer Science and Software Engineering,
Monash University, Clayton, Victoria 3800, Australia
{Lara.Kornienko, David.Albrecht}@csse.monash.edu.au

Abstract. In this paper we improve on the supervised classification method developed in Kornienko et al. (2002) by the introduction of Principal Components Analysis to the inference process. We also extend the classifier from dealing with binomial (two-class) problems only to multinomial (multi-class) problems.

The application to which the MML criterion has been applied in this paper is the classification of objects via a linear hyperplane, where the objects are able to come from any multi-class distribution. The inclusion of Principal Component Analysis to the original inference scheme reduces the bias present in the classifier's search technique. Such improvements lead to a method which, when compared against three commercial Support Vector Machine (SVM) classifiers on Binary data, was found to be as good as the most successful SVM tested. Furthermore, the new scheme is able to classify objects of a multiclass distribution with just one hyperplane, whereas SVMs require several hyperplanes.

Keywords: Machine Learning, Knowledge discovery and data mining.

1 Introduction

This paper extends the binary linear classification method presented by the authors in [9] by introducing Principal Component Analysis to the inference process. Furthermore, the capability of dealing with multinomial distributions is also developed.

The original method, named the Spikey method [10, Chapter 5] [9,11], used a Linear classifier in conjunction with the Bayesian 'Minimum Message Length' (MML) principle [18,19,20,21] as an objective function to infer the correct distributions of a given binary-labelled data set. We have developed a new scheme named PCA-Spikey, which takes advantage of any biases in the spread of the data by using the Principal Components as an initial set of axes on which to begin the search for the separating hyperplane. Furthermore, rather than just discriminate between two classes of data, as most linear classifiers do, PCA-Spikey allows for any kind of multinomial distribution either side of the hyperplane.

As a benchmark, we have used an implementation in Statistical Learning Theory, namely the Support Vector Machine (SVM) [17].

2 The PCA-Spikey Codes

The primary aim of introducing Principal Components Analysis (PCA) to the Spikey program was to improve the inference technique by obtaining a set of axes on which to perform the inference that were more representative of the natural spread of the data. Doing this would, in theory, enable inherent biases in the data to be recognised - thus producing hyperplanes that were a better fit at a cheaper MML cost. One reason for the belief that introducing PCA would produce cheaper hyperplanes is due to the search technique used in the Spikey scheme: hyperplanes in the direction of or perpendicular to the major axes are given the cheapest encoding costs. Thus, by transforming the original axes to the directions and scales of greatest spread in the data, the cheapest hyperplanes are going to be amongst those which split the data perpendicular to these directions. This suggests the following process to obtain a Linear classifier:

1. The Principal Components are found for the skewed data and the points projected into the Principal Component space.
2. The data in the Principal Component space is then normalised so that it falls within a hyper-cubed region (a square in two dimensions).
3. Inference is performed in the normalised Principal Component space via the Spikey program [10, Chapter 5] [9].
4. The hyperplane found was transformed back into the original coordinates.

3 Results

Four PCA-Spikey methods were developed in [10, Chapters 6,7,8]. These were PCA-MML$_{NU}^{WT}$, PCA-MML$_{NUR}^{WT}$, PCA-MML$_{SR}^{WT}$ and PCA-MML^{ANG}. The SVMs used to test the PCA-Spikey methods against are SVM^{light} [8], the Lagrangian SVM [13] and SMOBR [15].

As with the Spikey methods, all the PCA-Spikey methods were compared to a true hyperplane, if known, using the Kullback-Leibler distance [12] or if the true hyperplane was not known (as for real data), using 10-fold cross-validation in conjunction with Probabilistic Scoring [5,14,4] [16, Section 3.1] [3, Section 11.4.2] and the Right/Wrong Predictive Accuracy scoring metric [10, Section 4.5]. We tested the PCA-Spikey methods on both real and artificial data having both binomial and trinomial distributions.

The boldface entries in the table columns highlight those methods that performed the best for those data sets with a 95% significance level using Student's t distribution on the population mean.

Data. The artificial binary data sets were simply the original uniformly distributed data sets as input to the Spikey methods, but skewed according to two linear translation matrices (TM). In this paper, we present the Kullback-Leibler distances from the second Translation Matrix [10, Section 7.6] [11].

The data presented here is distributed relative to a true hyperplane, $y = 1.6x + 10.0$, where points were generated randomly having 95% of the points

Table 1. Kullback-Leibler distances ($\mu \pm \sigma$) between the true hyperplane ($y = 1.6x + 10.0$) and inferred hyperplanes for TM2 - on **95/05** data, N = 10, 100, 1000 points. The 'n' in $\mu \pm \sigma$ ^{*n} denotes the number of data sets on which SVM^{light} did not converge.

	N = 10	N = 100	N = 1000
PCA-MML$^{WT}_{NU}$	0.2081 ± 0.0527	0.0844 ± 0.0462	0.0303 ± 0.0264
PCA-MML$^{WT}_{SR}$	0.2038 ± 0.0535	0.0547 ± 0.0469	**0.0056 ± 0.0050**
PCA-MML$^{WT}_{NUR}$	0.2110 ± 0.0464	0.0837 ± 0.0441	0.0679 ± 0.0124
PCA-MML^{ANG}	0.1801 ± 0.0735	0.0767 ± 0.0502	0.0122 ± 0.0122
MML^{WT}_{NU}	0.1805 ± 0.0450	0.1139 ± 0.0258	0.1055 ± 0.0029
MML^{WT}_{SR}	0.2167 ± 0.0409	0.3679 ± 0.0109	0.3902 ± 0.0010
SVM^{light}	0.1884 ± 0.0280	0.2609 ± 0.0432	0.1597 ± 0.0136 ^{*2}
Lagrangian	**0.0573 ± 0.0434**	**0.0690 ± 0.0349**	0.0296 ± 0.0156
SMOBR	0.1411 ± 0.0673	0.1093 ± 0.0501	0.1282 ± 0.0236

Table 2. Real Data Set - Wisconsin Prognostic Breast Cancer Database. Probabilistic prediction bit score error results and "right/wrong" predictive accuracy results using 10-fold cross-validation ($\mu \pm \sigma$).

Wisconsin Breast Cancer	Prob. (bit score) error	Right/Wrong Acc'y
PCA-MML$^{WT}_{NU}$	14.0531 ± 13.6865	0.905714 ± 0.160809
PCA-MML$^{WT}_{SR}$	10.1341 ± 7.52156	0.957143 ± 0.0349927
PCA-MML$^{WT}_{NUR}$	9.97667 ± 7.52561	0.957143 ± 0.0368856

Table 3. Real Data Set - Iris, 2D. Probabilistic prediction bit score error results and "right/wrong" predictive accuracy results using 10-fold cross-validation (mean ± standard deviation).

Iris 2D	Prob. (bit score) error	Right/Wrong Acc'y
$PCA - MML^{WT}_{NU}$	8.2333 ± 1.5605	0.6567 ± 0.0568
$PCA - MML^{WT}_{SR}$	7.8656 ± 1.1779	0.6667 ± 0.0544
$PCA - MML^{WT}_{NUR}$	7.3257 ± 1.6426	0.6667 ± 0.0685
$PCA - MML^{ANG}$	8.0853 ± 1.6950	0.6600 ± 0.0717

positive on one side of the hyperplane and 5% positive on the other side (see [10, Section 7.7] for elaboration). 'N' refers to the size of the data sets. All Kullback-Leibler scores presented in the tables are of the form 'Mean ± Standard Deviation', or $\mu \pm \sigma$. Table 1 shows the results for this data.

The real data sets used are the Wisconsin Prognostic Breast Cancer Database, January 8, 1991 [1] and the trinomial Iris data set [7].

The Wisconsin Prognostic Breast Cancer data set consists of 699 data, each having 10 input attributes plus a binary class attribute. The first attribute is the sample code number, which was ignored. The Iris data set contains 150 data points, where each of the three classes contains 50 points and each point consists of four numeric attributes and a class specification. However, we just report here the test on the last two attributes. Tables 2 and 3 refer to the results for the Breast Cancer and Iris data respectively. The first column of each table refers to the results obtained using Probabilistic Scoring and the second column refers to the Right/Wrong Predictive Accuracy score [5,14,4] [16, Section 3.1] [3, Section 11.4.2] [10, Section 4.5]. No SVMs have been tested on the Iris data set as how SVM classifiers deal with multinomial data sets is still an open question.

4 Discussion and Conclusion

It has been shown that the original Spikey encoding scheme described in [10, Chapter 5] [9] could be improved by the introduction of Principal Component Analysis, as results indicate that the PCA-Spikey methods out-performed the original Spikey methods on skewed data. It was also found that the PCA-Spikey methods performed significantly better than the SVMs on the larger artificial Binomial data sets tested, while the SVMs tended to dominate the smaller data sets. On the real Binomial data sets, due to the fact that the data was not highly skewed, the PCA-Spikey methods performed similarly to the original Spikey methods, and they were as good as the best SVM on that data. The PCA-Spikey methods are also flexible enough to deal with multinomial data without any major changes to their implementation. It was found that the PCA-Spikey methods, when run on the trinomial 'Iris' data set, were able to separate the one separable class from the remaining two inseparable classes.

Overall, several improvements can be made to the PCA-Spikey methods in terms of the search procedures and coding schemes used, particularly for smaller data sets. A possible alternative is the encoding of data points to geometrically define a hyperplane, similar to the Support Vectors in SVMs (for an alternative MML approach to a related problem, which does not use Principal Components, see [16]). Furthermore, the type of distribution used for the input data may be varied to non-uniform distributions. Another recent development in MML that may be looked into has been in Comley and Dowe [2,3], where a concrete application of Dowe's abstract notion of inverse learning [6] to generalised Bayesian networks including a mix of both continuous and discrete variables is given.

References

1. C.L. Blake and C.J. Merz (1998), *UCI Repository of machine learning databases*. http://www.ics.uci.edu/~mlearn/MLRepository.html, Irvine, CA: University of California, Dep. of Information and Computer Science.
2. J.W. Comley and D.L. Dowe (2003). General Bayesian Networks and Asymmetric Languages, in Proc. Hawaii Int. Conf. on Stats. and Related Fields, 5-8 June, 2003.
3. J.W. Comley and D.L. Dowe (2005). Minimum Message Length, MDL and Generalised Bayesian Networks with Asymmetric Languages, Chap. 11 in P. Grunwald, I. J. Myung and M. A. Pitt (Eds.), Advances in Minimum Description Length: Theory and Applications, M.I.T. Press, April 2005, ISBN 0-262-07262-9. Final Camera Ready copy submitted October 2003.

4. D.L. Dowe, G.E. Farr, A.J. Hurst and K.L. Lentin (1996). Information-theoretic football tipping, in N. de Mestre (ed.), Third Australian Conference on Mathematics and Computers in Sport, Bond University, Qld, 233-241, 1996.
5. Dowe, D.L, & Krusel N. (1993). A decision tree model of bushfire activity, (Technical report 93/190) Dept Computer Science, Monash University, Melbourne, 7pp, 1993
6. Dowe, D.L. and Wallace, C.S. (1998). Kolmogorov complexity, minimum message length and inverse learning, abstract, page 144, 14th Australian Statistical Conference (ASC-14), Gold Coast, Qld, 6-10 July, 1998.
7. R.A. Fisher (1936), The use of multiple measurements in taxonomic problems, in Annals of Eugenics, Volume 7, pp. 179-188.
8. Joachims, T. (1998). Making Large-Scale SVM Learning Practical. In B. Scholkopf, C. J. C. Burges & A. J. Smola (Eds.), *Advances in Kernel Methods: Support Vector Learning*. MIT Press, Cambridge, USA, 1998.
9. L. Kornienko and D.L. Dowe and D.W. Albrecht (2002), Message Length Formulation of Support Vector Machines for Binary Classification - A Preliminary Scheme in Lecture Notes in Artificial Intelligence (LNAI) 2557, 15th Aust. Joint Conf. on A.I., Canberra, Australia. Springer-Verlag. pp 119-130.
10. L. Kornienko (2005), Implementing a Support Vector Machine in a Message Length Framework. Masters Thesis, School of Information Technology, Monash University, Clayton, Australia.
11. L. Kornienko and D.L. Dowe and D.W. Albrecht (2005), A Preliminary MML Linear Classifier using Principal Components for Multiple Classes. Tech.Report .School of Information Technology, Monash University, Clayton, Australia.
12. Kullback, S. (1959) *Information Theory and Statistics*. John Riley and Sons, Inc.
13. Mangasarian, O. L., & Musicant, D. R. (2000). *Lagrangian Support Vector Machines*. (Tech. Report 00-06). Data Mining Institute.
14. Needham, Scott L., & Dowe, David L. (2001). Message Length as an Effective Ockham's Razor in Decision Tree Induction. Proc. 8th International Workshop on Artificial Intelligence and Statistics (AI+STATS 2001), pp 253-260, Key West, Florida, U.S.A., Jan. 2001.
15. Platt, J. (1999). *Sequential minimal optimization: A fast algorithm for training support vector machines* in *Advances in Kernel Methods - Support Vector Learning*, Bernhard Scholkopf, Christopher J. C. Burges and Alexander J. Smola, Eds. 1999, pp. 185-208, MIT Press.
16. P.J. Tan and D.L. Dowe (2004), MML Inference of Oblique Decision Trees in Lecture Notes in Artificial Intelligence, G.I.Webb and X.Yu, Eds., 17th Australian Joint Conf. on Advances in A.I., Cairns, Australia. pp. 1082-1088, Springer-Verlag. ISSN:0302-9743, ISBN:3-540-24059-4, Vol 3339.
17. Vapnik, V. (1995). The Nature of Statistical Learning Theory. Springer, New York.
18. C.S. Wallace (2005), Statistical and Inductive Inference by Minimum Message Length, Springer. ISBN: 0-387-23795-X
19. Wallace, C. S., & Boulton, D.M. (1968). An information measure for classification. *Computer Journal*, 11, 185-194.
20. Wallace, C .S., & Dowe, D. L. (1999). Minimum Message Length and Kolmogorov Complexity. *Computer Journal*. 42(4), 270-283.
21. Wallace, C. S., & Freeman, P.R. (1987). Estimation and Inference by Compact Coding, *J Royal Stat. Soc. B*. 49, 240-252.

Content-Based Classification of Music Using VQ-Multifeature Clustering Technique

Won-Jung Yoon and Kyu-Sik Park

Dankook University,
Division of Information and Computer Science,
San 8, Hannam-Dong, Yongsan-Ku, Seoul, Korea 140-714
{helloril, kspark}@dankook.ac.kr

Abstract. A new content-based music genre classification algorithm using VQ-Multifeature clustering method is proposed in this paper. In order to alleviate the system uncertainty problem due to the different query patterns and query lengths, a new robust feature extraction method so called VQ-Multifeature clustering with feature selection is proposed. Effectiveness of the proposed system is verified in terms of the system stability and the classification results with SVM pattern classifier.

1 Introduction

Music genre classification based on content-analysis has been a growing area of research in the last few years. All content-based classification methods have three common stages of a pattern recognition problem: feature extraction, training of the classifier based on the sample music, and classification. Depending on different combinations of these stages, several strategies are employed in these studies [1-4].

In this paper, a new robust feature extraction method so called VQ-Multifeature clustering with feature selection is proposed to overcome the system uncertainty problem due to the different query patterns and query lengths. It obviously has gained relatively little attention in the literature. The proposed algorithm is applied to classify the musical genre into the Classical, Hiphop, Jazz, and Rock and effectiveness of the system is verified in terms of the system stability and the classification accuracy with SVM (Support Vector Machine) pattern classifier.

2 Feature Extraction, Selection and VQ-Multifeature Clustering

Two types of features are computed from each frame: One is the timbral features such as spectral centroid, spectral roll off, spectral flux and zero crossing rates. The other is coefficient domain features such as thirteen mel-frequency cepstral coefficients (MFCC) and ten linear predictive coefficients (LPC). The means and standard deviations of these six original features are computed over each frame for each music file to form a total of 54-dimensional feature vector.

In order to reduce the computational burden and so speed up the search process, an efficient feature selection method is desired. As described in paper [5], two different types of feature selection procedures, called sequential forward selection (SFS) and the sequential backward selection (SBS) are tested and compared in terms of the classification success rate.

The classification results corresponding to different input query patterns and lengths within the same music file or same class may be much different. In order to overcome this problem, a new robust feature extraction method called VQ-Multifeature clustering with feature selection is implemented. Key idea is to extract features over the full-length music signal in a step of 20 sec large window and then cluster these features in four disjoint subsets (centroids) using LBG-VQ technique.

3 Experiments on Music Classification

The proposed algorithm has been implemented and used to classify music data from a database of about 240 music files. 60 music samples were collected for each of the four genres in Classical, Hiphop, Jazz, and Rock, resulting in 240 music files in database. 240 music files are partitioned randomly into a training set of 168 (70%) sounds and a test set of 72 (30%) sounds. The overall classification accuracy was obtained as the arithmetic mean of the success rate of the individual iterations.

Nine excerpts with fixed duration of 5 sec were extracted from every other position in same query music- at 10%, 20%, 30%, 40%, 50%, 60%, 70%, 80% and 90% position after the beginning of music signal.

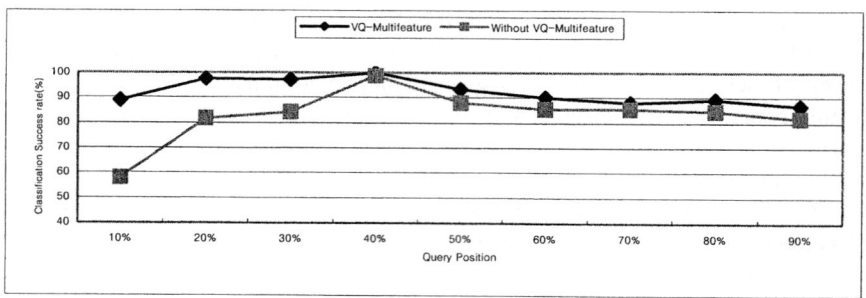

Fig. 1. Genre classification results at different query portions with VQ-Multifeature

Fig. 1 shows the classification results with nine excerpts at the prescribed query position. As we expected, the classification results without VQ-Multifeature clustering greatly depends on the query positions and it's performance is getting worse as query portion towards to two extreme cases of beginning and ending position of the music signal. This is no wonder because, in general, the musical characteristics are not rich enough at those extreme intervals of music signal. On the other hand, we can find quite stable classification performance with VQ-Multifeature clustering method

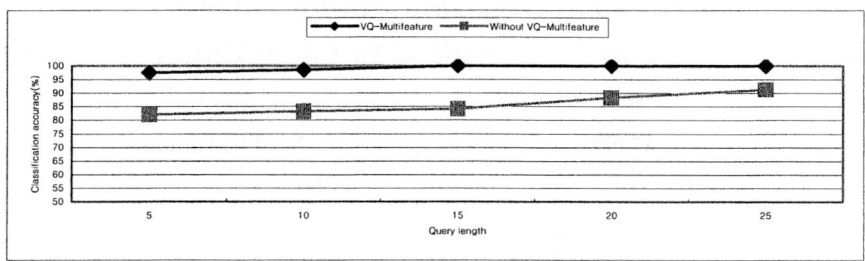

Fig. 2. Genre classification results at different query lengths with VQ-Multifeature

and it yields higher accuracy rate in the range of 87% ~ 98.7%. This is a consequence of good VQ-Multifeature property which helps the system to build robust musical feature set over the full-length music signal.

Fig. 2 explains an importance of the query length to the overall system performance. Again, we see the desirable characteristics of VQ-Multifeature with stable classification performance and more than 20% improvement over the one without VQ-Multifeature.

4 Conclusion

In contrast to previous works, this paper focuses on the uncertainty of the system performance due to the different query patterns and query lengths. The effectiveness of the proposed system is verified in terms of the system stability and the classification accuracy with SVM pattern classifier.

Acknowledgment

This work was supported by grant No. R01-2004-000-10122-0 from the Basic Research Program of the Korea Science & Engineering Foundation.

References

1. G. Tzanetakis and P. Cook, "Musical genre classification of audio signals," *IEEE Trans. on Speech and Audio Processing*, vol. 10, no. 5, pp. 293-302, July 2002.
2. T. Li, M. Ogihara and Q. Li, "A comparative study on content-based music genre classification," in *Proc. of the 26th annual internal ACM SIGIR*, pp. 282-289, ACM Press, July 2003.
3. J. J. Burred and A. Lerch, "A hierarchical approach to automatic musical genre classification," in *Proc. DAFx03*, 2003, pp. 308-311.
4. E. Wold, T. Blum, D. Keislar, and J. Wheaton, "Content-based classification, search, and retrieval of audio," *IEEE Multimedia*, vol.3, no. 2, 1996.
5. Anil K. Jin, Robert P.W. Duin, Jianchang Mai, "Statistical Pattern Recognition: A Review" IEEE Trans. Pattern Analysis and Machine Intelligence, vol. 22, no. 1, Jan. 2000.

Individual Clustering and Homogeneous Cluster Ensemble Approaches Applied to Gene Expression Data

Shirlly C.M. Silva, Daniel S.A. de Araujo, Raul B. Paradeda,
Valmar S. Severiano-Sobrinho, and Marcilio C.P. de Souto

Department of Informatics and Applied Mathematics,
Federal University of Rio Grande do Norte,
Campus Universitario, 59072-970 Natal-RN, Brazil
Phone: +55-84-3215-3815
Fax: +55-84-3215-3813
{shirlly, paradeda}@ppgsc.ufrn.br, marcilio@dimap.ufrn.br
{danielsa, xantho}@lcc.ufrn.br

Abstract. Exploratory data analysis and, in particular, data clustering can significantly benefit from combining multiple data partitions - cluster ensemble. In this context, we analyze the potential of applying cluster ensemble techniques to gene expression microarray data. Our experimental results show that there is often a significant improvement in the results obtained with the use of ensemble techniques when compared to those based on the clustering techniques used individually.

1 Introduction

One of the major challenges for current clustering (unsupervised learning) algorithms is the robustness of the derived solutions. Ensemble techniques have been successfully applied in supervised learning to improve the accuracy and stability of classification algorithms [1]. However, only recently have attempts been made to apply this type of combination to unsupervised algorithms, such as clustering techniques [1,2,3]. In this paper, we analyze the potential of applying cluster ensemble techniques to gene expression microarray data. As pointed out by [4], this type of unsupervised analysis is of increasing interest in the field of functional genomics and gene expression data analysis. One of the reasons for this is the need for molecular-based refinement of broadly defined biological classes, with implications in cancer diagnosis, prognosis and treatment [4].

2 Material and Methods

We develop experiments with the successful cluster ensemble methods described in [3,2]. In order to do so, the results of two clustering algorithms, representative of different clustering paradigms, are selected as input for building the ensembles: k-means and the Expectation-Maximization (EM) algorithm. These individual (base) algorithms have been widely used in the gene expression literature [4].

Table 1. Description of the dataset

Dataset	c	s	f	Class distribution
Leukemia	3	38	999	11 AML, 8 T-ALL, 19 B-ALL
Multi-tissues	4	103	1000	16 breast, 26 prostate, 28 lung, 23 colon
St. Jude	6	248	985	15 BCR, 27 E2A, 64 Hyp, 20 MLL, 43 T-ALL, 79 TEL

With respect to the ensembles methods, in [3], all the clusters in the ensemble partitions can be represented as hyperedges on a graph with N vertices. Each hyperedge describes a set of objects belonging to the same clusters. A consensus function is formulated as a solution to k-way min-cut hypergraph partitioning problem. Each connected component after the cut corresponds to a cluster in the consensus partition.

The other cluster ensemble algorithm analyzed is based on a voting scheme [2]. In the voting scheme, the algorithm tries to find a correspondence between the cluster labels across the different partitions. Once this correspondence is found, the clusters with the same label are fused.

In terms of data for the experiments, we consider three broadly used datasets for which multi-class distinction (a phenotype) is available: Leukemia, Novartis multi-tissue, and St. Jude leukemia [4]. Table 1 summarizes the main properties of these datasets - the letters **c**, **s**, **f** stand, respectively, for number of classes, samples (instances), and attributes (genes) describing an instance.

3 Evaluation Methodology

The cluster composition can be evaluated by measuring the degree of agreement between two partitions (U and V), where partition U is the result of a clustering method and partition V (the gold standard) is formed by an a priori information independent of partition U, such as a class label. There are a number of external indices defined in the literature, such as Hubbert, Jacard, Rand and corrected Rand (or adjusted Rand) that can be used for this measurement [1]. In this work, we will use the corrected Rand index - CR, for short. Such an index can take values from -1 to 1, with 1 indicating a perfect agreement between the partitions, and the values near 0 or negatives corresponding to cluster agreement found by chance.

In order to compare the performance of the clustering algorithms, we calculate the mean of the CR via a unsupervised k-fold cross-validation procedure [5]. The objective of the procedure is to obtain k observations of the accuracy of the clustering methods with respect to the gold standard partition, all this with the use of independent test folds. Next, based on such a result, the means are compared two by two using a paired t-test, as described in [1].

4 Experimental Results

The experiments were accomplished by presenting the three datasets (Leukemia, Norvatis multi-tissue, and St. Jude Leukemia) to the individual clustering methods: k-means

Table 2. Mean of the CR for all Datasets

Algorithm	Leukemia		Multi-tissue		St. Jude	
	Mean CR	St. Dev.	Mean CR	St. Dev.	Mean CR	St. Dev
k-means	0.3637	0.2783	0.7485	0.1970	0.8244	0.1049
Voting k-means	0.6568	0.2216	0.8718	0.1582	0.7667	0.1289
Ensemble k-means	0.6182	0.3446	0.9614	0.0266	0.7759	0.0560
EM	0.3427	0.2779	0.7764	0.18833	0.7903	0.1239
Voting EM	0.5919	0.2216	0.9573	0.0413	0.7470	0.0998
Ensemble EM	0.4512	0.2500	0.9614	0.0266	0.8676	0.0885

and the EM algorithm (all of them implemented with the Euclidian distance). Initially, a five replication of the 2-fold cross-validation of each dataset was applied such that 10 samples of each dataset was formed.

In terms of parameter settings, the number of clusters for the k-means and the EM algorithm was set to the number of class in dataset being considered. Furthermore, as these algorithms are dependent on the choice of the initial conditions (e.g., initial centers and means), for them we repeated each run 10 times, each one with a distinct random initialization. Based on this, the ensembles were formed as follows. We created 10 ensembles, where each ensemble was formed by combining the 10 runs of the k-means (or the EM algorithm) for a given cross-validation partition (10 samples in total - 2x5 cross-validation). That is, we built *homogeneous ensembles* in that the partitions used to form the consensus come from the same type of algorithm.

Table 2 illustrates the mean (and standard deviation) of the Corrected Rand index (CR) for the test sets for, respectively, the Leukemia, Novartis multi-tissue and St. Jude Leukemia datasets. The rows of these tables represent, respectively, the results for the k-means, the cluster ensembles built with k-means by the voting method in [2] and the ensemble approach in [3], the EM algorithm, the cluster ensembles built with the EM algorithm by the voting method in [2] and the ensemble approach in [3].

5 Discussion and Final Remarks

In the case of Leukemia dataset, the use of the ensemble methods did not imply in a great decrease of the standard deviation of the accuracy mean with respect to the individual methods. One of the reasons for this is the fact that such a dataset is composed by few instances (38 instances of three different classes), what makes learning harder in most contexts.

Nevertheless, for a larger dataset like the Novartis multi-tissue dataset, the use of the ensemble methods in most cases led to a great decrease of the standard deviation of the accuracy mean with respect to the individual methods. From this perspective, the ensemble techniques have successfully improved, not only the accuracy, but also the stability of the individual clustering algorithms.

For the case of the St. Jude Leukemia dataset, there was no significant performance gain by combining the partitions produced by individual clustering algorithms, although the standard deviation of accuracy means for the ensembles were usually smaller than those for the individual methods.

A possible explanation for the performance obtained by the ensembles methods for the St. Jude Leukemia dataset could be the following. As pointed out in [6], when this dataset was applied to the k-means and the SOTA with the number of clusters set to exactly the number of classes (six), the partitions generated usually did not separate the patterns of the classes BCR and hyperdip.

For example, the partitions consistently presented a small cluster containing only a few hyperdip and BCR patterns grouped together with patterns of three other classes, and a larger cluster with most of the hyperdip and BCR patterns. In this case, most partitions would show the same type of error. Consequently, no extra information would be present to the ensemble methods.

A solution for this problem could be the construction of the input partitions, for example, by using not only the different random initializations of the same algorithm, but also by varying the number of clusters. For instance, the authors in [6] showed that clustering algorithm were able to correctly separate the classes hyperdip and BCR when the number of cluster was to set to 15. Another possibility is building the input partitions from different clustering algorithms (*heterogeneous ensembles*) [1].

Acknowledgment

This work is partially supported by CNPq via grant 505716/2004-6. We would like to thank Evgenia Dimitriadou for providing her code for the voting-merging clustering algorithm.

References

1. Kuncheva, L.I.: Combining Pattern Classifiers. Wiley (2004)
2. Dimitriadou, E., Weingessel, A., Hornik, K.: A combination scheme for fuzzy clustering. International Journal of Pattern Recognition and Artificial Intelligence **16** (2002) 901–912
3. Strehl, A., Ghosh, J.: Cluster ensembles – a knowledge reuse framework for combining multiple partitions. Journal on Machine Learning Research (JMLR) **3** (2002) 583–617
4. Monti, S., Tamayo, P., Mesirov, J., Golub, T.: Consensus clustering: a resampling-based method for class discovery and visualization of gene expression microarray data. Machine Learning **52** (2003) 91–118
5. Costa, I.G., de Carvalho, F.A.T., de Souto, M.C.P.: Comparative study on proximity indices for cluster analysis of gene expression time series. Journal of Inteligent and Fuzzy Systems (2003) 133–142
6. Faceli, K., de Carvalho, A.C.P.L.F., de Souto, M.C.P.: Evaluation of the contents of partitions obtained with clustering gene expression data. In: Proc. of the Brazilian Symposium on Bioinformatics - Lecture Notes on Bioinformatics. Volume 3594., Spring-Verlag (2005) 65–76

Joint Spatial and Frequency Domains Watermarking Algorithm Based on Wavelet Packets

Yinghua Lu[1,2], Wei Wang[1], Jun Kong[1], Jialing Han[1], and Gang Hou[1,3]

[1] Computer School, Northeast Normal University, Changchun, Jilin Province, China
[2] Computer School, Jilin University, Changchun, China
[3] College of Humanities and Science, Northeast Normal University, Changchun, China
{luyh, wangw680, kongjun, hanjl147, houg007}@nenu.edu.cn

Abstract. A novel Feature-Watermarking algorithm based on wavelet packet decomposition was presented in this paper. We first propose the concept of Feature-Watermark. Dither modulation embedding scheme in wavelet packet coefficients promises the hiding of large capacity of robust information and fulfills watermark blind-extraction. Experimental results show that our method successfully fulfills the compromise between the robustness and capacity.

1 Introduction

As an effective means for the protection of digital property rights, the technique of digital watermarking has lately been well developed. Digital watermarking is a technique that embeds copyright information imperceptibly into multimedia data. Recently, the algorithms of using combinational image watermarking in spatial and frequency domains [1, 2] have been getting wide concern. The algorithms make the watermarks robust but have limitation in capacity of frequency domain information.

In order to embed more information into the host image without decreasing visual effect, we present a novel watermarking technique. The paper is organized as follows: Section 2 introduces Feature-Watermark extraction algorithm and Section 3 exhibits the watermark embedding and extraction algorithm respectively. Experimental results are presented in Section 4 and conclusions are given in Section 5.

2 Feature-Watermark Extraction

The definition of Feature-Watermark is given below:
Feature-Watermark (FW): Feature-Watermark is a new image being composed of small image blocks extracting from the original watermark and representing the essential meaning of the original watermark well.

Traditional ways of watermark splitting just select the central area of the original watermark as the most important area. In this paper, according to the content of original watermark, we first split the watermark, and then construct FW, which is considered as the most essential information. Fig. 1 shows the detail content of FW. Watermarks (b) (c) were extracted from (a) as FWs, and then the Arnold Transform (AT) [3] is adopted to scramble the FWs.

Fig. 1. (a) Original watermark of size 128×128. (b) FW1. (c) FW2. (d) Less important part of (a), W3. (e) Result image of (b) after the 2nd iteration of Arnold Transform.

3 Watermark Embedding and Extraction Algorithm

3.1 Host Image Block-Wise Analysis and Re-composition

In the first stage, sub-images of host image are analyzed to classify into active or inactive regions based on texture features. Traditional ways for looking for texture-active regions include FTM method [4] which demands more time expense. In this paper, we employ the block-variance based method to detect texture-active regions. The two methods do not have significant difference in effect, but the block-variance method is more efficient than FTM method. The process is described as follows:

1. Divide the host image into un-overlapped 8×8 sub-blocks in spatial domain.
2. Compute each sub-block's variance and the host image's average variance.
3. Compare each sub-block's variance with average variance. If sub-block's variance is greater than average value, the sub-block is classified as the texture-active region.

In the second stage, taking texture-active region's sub-blocks' variances as feature value, according to the magnitude of them, we classify the sub-blocks into texture-most-active region or texture-median-active region and then construct the new corresponding sub-images. The left sub-blocks constitute a new smooth sub-image.

Finally, we embed FWs as shown in Fig. 1(b) (c) into the frequency domain of the texture-active sub-images and insert the watermark of Fig. 1(d) into the smooth sub-image in spatial domain.

3.2 Watermark Embedding Algorithm

In our study, watermark embedding algorithm contains spatial domain embedding and frequency domain embedding algorithm.

3.2.1 Spatial Domain Watermark Embedding Algorithm

In order to improve robustness in spatial domain, we modify the less significant bits (LSB) [5] of pixels to embed watermark signals. The exact bit to be modified will be fixed by secret keys. When choosing embedding position, we first divide the smooth sub-image into small blocks, then embed one bit watermark signal into each block.

3.2.2 Frequency Domain Watermark Embedding Algorithm

For the texture-active region sub-images, the full wavelet packet (WP) decomposition is adopted in frequency domain to embed watermarks. We name texture-active region sub-images *H-wavelet*. Algorithm is described as follows:

1. Transform *H_wavelet* by WP decomposition to obtain $H\_wavelet^{wp}$.
2. Select coefficients of $H\_wavelet^{wp}$ to embed watermark $W^{frequency}$.

3. Use dither modulation scheme to insert watermark signal at coefficients WPC_i and get the watermarked coefficients matrix $H\_wavelet^F$.

$$WPC_i^w = \begin{cases} n\Delta & n\Delta < WPC_i \leq (n+0.5)\Delta \\ (n+1)\Delta & (n+0.5)\Delta < WPC_i \leq (n+1)\Delta \end{cases} \quad w_i = 1$$
$$WPC_i^w = (n+0.5)\Delta \qquad n\Delta < WPC_i \leq (n+1)\Delta \qquad w_i = 0 \qquad (1)$$

where w_i is the watermark signal, Δ is the quantize step, n is an integer and WPC_i^w is used to represent wavelet packet coefficients after embedding watermarks.

4. Use the modified $H\_wavelet^F$ to reconstruct the texture-active region sub-images.
5. Embed the watermarked sub-images back into the original host image.

3.3 Watermark Extraction Algorithm

Watermark extraction algorithm is the exact inverse process of embedding algorithm. Owing secret keys, we can extract watermark without original host image.

4 Experimental Results

In our simulation, we take 'Lena' image of size 256×256 as test image. Fig. 2 shows the result image of 'Lena' and the extracted watermarks of size 128×128. In the experiment we first extract three sub-images according to image texture. The watermarks as shown in Fig. 1(b) (c) (d) are scrambled and embedded into sub-images correspondingly using embedding algorithm in frequency domain and spatial domain respectively. In frequency domain, we perform 2-level WP decomposition using 'Haar' wavelet function on both texture-active region sub-images, and embed FWs into the (2, 0) (2, 8) sub-bands coefficients. The quantize steps are 40, 30 in texture-most-active sub-image and 30, 20 in texture-median-active sub-image.

Free of any attacks, *PSNR* of the watermarked image 'Lena' is 42.5179, *NC* is 1. Fig. 2(d) displays the result watermark after cropping attack. Table 1 shows the experimental results. From Table 1, we can make the conclusion that our algorithm is robust to the attacks usually encountered in image processing and transmission.

Fig. 2. (a) Original host image 'Lena'. (b) Watermarked result image. (c) Extracted watermark from Fig. 2(b). (d) Extracted watermark from Fig. 2(b) after cropping attack.

Table 1. *NC* of extracted watermarks from 'Lena' under different attacks

Attack Type	FW1	FW2	OW
JPEG Compression (QF=80)	0.8030	0.9050	0.6762
Cropping (CR=50%)	0.8194	0.8275	0.9221
Pepper and Salt Noise (D=0.02)	0.9318	0.9478	0.9738

where 'OW' denotes 'Original Watermark', 'QF' denotes the JPEG compression quality factor, 'CR' denotes the ratio of cropping and 'D' denotes the noise density.

5 Conclusions

In this paper, a novel technique of digital image watermarking was presented. Our method employs WP to embed FWs in frequency domain. The un-overlapped positions of embedded spatial and frequency domains watermarks decrease the influence of the two types of watermarks. The proposed technique shows excellent performance on both robustness and capacity. Nevertheless, we should improve the spatial domain watermarking algorithm to obtain better performance.

References

1. Yi-Ta Wu, Frank Y. Shih: An adjust-purpose Digital Watermarking Technique. Pattern Recognition 37(2004) 2349-2359
2. Frank Y. Shih, Scott Y. T. Wu: Combinational Image Watermarking in the Spatial and Frequency domains. Pattern Recognition 36(2003) 969-975
3. Tao Kong, Dan Zhang: A New Anti-Arnold Transformation Algorithm (in Chinese). 2004 Journal of Software. China, Vol. 15, No. 10
4. Xu-Dong Zhang, Jian Feng, Kwok-Tung Lo: Image Watermarking using Tree_based Spatial-frequency Feature of Wavelet Transform. Journal of Visual Communication and Image Representation 14(2003) 474-491
5. N. Nikolaidis, I. Pitas: Robust Image Watermarking in the Spatial Domain. Signal Proc. 66(3) (1998) 385-403

Hybrid Agglomerative Clustering for Large Databases: An Efficient Interactivity Approach

Ickjai Lee[1] and Jianhua Yang[2]

[1] School of Information Technology,
James Cook University, Townsville, QLD4811, Australia
[2] School of Computing and Information Technology,
University of Western Sydney, Campbelltown, NSW2560, Australia

Abstract. This paper presents a novel hybrid clustering approach that takes advantage of the efficiency of k-MEANS clustering and the effectiveness of hierarchical clustering. It employs the combination of geometrical information defined by k-MEANS and topological information formed by the Voronoi diagram to advantage. Our proposed approach is able to identify clusters of arbitrary shapes and clusters of different densities in $O(n)$ time. Experimental results confirm the effectiveness and efficiency of our approach.

1 Introduction

This paper attempts to bridge the gap between efficiency-ineffectiveness of k-MEANS clustering and effectiveness-inefficiency of hierarchical clustering. We propose a hybrid agglomerative clustering approach that combines k-MEANS clustering and hierarchical clustering in order to overcome the ineffectiveness of the former and the inefficiency of the latter while keeping the efficiency of the former and the effectiveness of the latter. It initially partitions a given dataset into several temporary clusters based on geometrical information and then merges them into final clusters based on topological information defined by the Voronoi diagram. Our proposed approach is able to identify clusters of non-globular shapes and clusters of different densities in $O(n)$ time. Experimental results confirm the effectiveness and efficiency of our approach.

2 Related Work

A classification of various clustering methods into partitioning clustering and hierarchical clustering is a well-known distinction [1]. In partitioning clustering, k-MEANS [2] is the most widely used technique. It uses the mean (centroid) as the representative of a cluster and improves an initial clustering (with random seeds) by iteratively improving an optimization function. Hierarchical clustering reveals the nested decomposition using a tree diagram (dendrogram) that can either be top-down (divisive) or bottom-up (agglomerative). Its capability of revealing the nested structure makes it effective and popular despite of its computational inefficiency. Algorithms of this type may easily require of $O(n^2)$ [3] time, since they typically need $O(n)$ merging or splitting operations where the decision on what to merge or split is proportional to the current number of parts. The merge is based on some similarity measures (similarly the split is based on some dissimilarity measures). Four widely used similarity measures are single-linkage ($S_{sing}(C_i, C_j)$), complete-linkage ($S_{comp}(C_i, C_j)$), average-linkage ($S_{aveg}(C_i, C_j)$) and mean-linkage ($S_{mean}(C_i, C_j)$) where C_i and C_j are clusters. Recently, cohesion-linkage ($S_{cohe}(C_i, C_j)$) [4] has been proposed in the data mining community. Several hybrid approaches [4,5,6] have been proposed to combine the two clustering approaches to achieve the efficiency of partitioning clustering and the effectiveness of hierarchical clustering. These hybrid approaches start from partitioning the input data into l initial clusters and then use one of the linkage criteria above to merge to find final k clusters. Although CURE [5] achieved a certain level of effectiveness, it suffers from its expensive computational inefficiency requiring $O(n^2 \log n)$ which makes it problematic in data-rich environments. On the other hand, others [4,6] achieved a fast linear time complexity, but still suffer from their ineffectiveness.

3 Hybrid Agglomerative Clustering

Minimizing the optimization function of k-MEANS has the following nice property. For $1 \leq i \leq k$, C_i is contained in the region of the Voronoi diagram [7]. The Voronoi diagram is obtained by assigning every location in the space to the closet $x_i \in X$ with respect to a certain metric for a given set $X = \{x_1, x_2, \ldots, x_n\}$ of distinct objects (typically, point vectors) where $\|X\| \geq 2$ and $x_i \neq x_j$ for $i \neq j$ in the $\mathbb{R}^D$ Euclidean space. If a location happens to be equally close to two or more members of X then assign the location to those members. As a result, the set of locations assigned to each member forming its own region called Voronoi region. The set of the regions is collectively exhaustive and mutually exclusive except for boundaries.

Definition 1. *Neighbouring clusters* of a cluster C_i are clusters whose Voronoi regions share a common boundary with the Voronoi region of C_i.

Definition 2. *Total interactivity* between clusters C_i and C_j, denoted by $S_{tiact}(C_i, C_j)$, is measured by $\frac{n_{ij}}{\|C_i\|} \cdot \frac{n_{ji}}{\|C_j\|}$, where n_{ij} is the number of points satisfying $d(x - C_j) - d(x - C_k) \leq 0$ for $\forall C_k \in C \setminus \{C_i\}$, and n_{ji} is the number of points that satisfying $d(x - C_i) - d(x - C_k) \leq 0$ for $\forall C_k \in C \setminus \{C_j\}$.

Definition 3. *Buffered interactivity*, denoted by $S_{biact}(C_i, C_j)$, between clusters C_i and C_j is measured by $\frac{n^b_{ij}}{\|C_i\|} \cdot \frac{n^b_{ji}}{\|C_j\|}$, where n^b_{ij} is the number of points satisfying $|d(x - C_j) - d(x - C_k)| \leq \epsilon$ for a positive value ϵ and $\forall C_k \in C \setminus \{C_i\}$, and n^b_{ji} is the number of points that satisfying $|d(x - C_i) - d(x - C_k)| \leq \epsilon$ for $\forall C_k \in C \setminus \{C_j\}$.

Algorithmic procedure of our approach, named **BHC**, is described as follows:
Algorithm **BHC**(X, k, l, ϵ)
Input: A set $X = \{x_1, x_2, \ldots, x_n\}$ of points, the targeted number k of clusters, the initial number l of clusters, and the buffer size ϵ.
Output: A hierarchical bottom-up structure of X starting from l clusters to k clusters.

1) **begin**
2)   Construct initial set of l representatives arbitrarily.
3)   Initial Partition
        a) Classification
            Assign each $x \in X$ to its nearest representative.
        b) Minimization
            For each cluster, find a new centroid.
4)   Repeat Step 3) until no change.
5)   Compute S_{biact} between clusters.
6)   **BHC** l-to-k Merge
        a) Retrieval
            Retrieve the maximal S_{biact}.
        b) Merge
            Merge two clusters unless they belong to the same cluster.
7) **end** *Algorithm* **BHC**(X, k, l, ϵ)

BHC consists of three phases: initial partition (Step (3)), computation of S_{biact} (Step (5)), and finally merge (Step (6)). During initial partitioning, it iteratively refines a partition alternating a minimization step and a classification step. In the minimization step, for each cluster in the partition, a new representative is computed. Next, using the new representatives, a classification step obtains new initial l clusters. These steps are repeated until an iteration occurs in which the clustering does not change.

4 Experimental Results

We have performed various experiments for efficiency and effectiveness analysis. Due to the space limit, we provide efficiency analysis only. We compare CPU

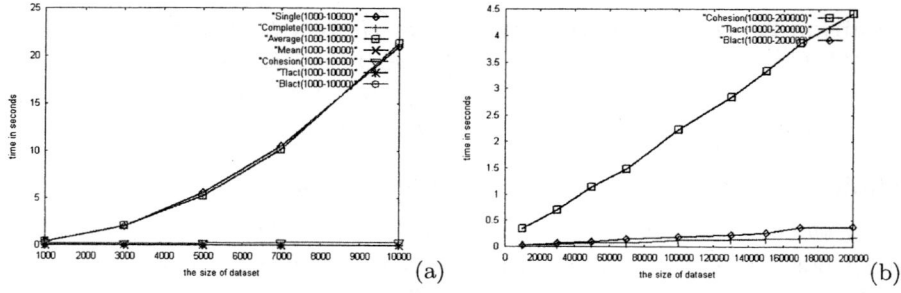

Fig. 1. Comparison of CPU times

times of **BHC** with other linkages. We generated 20 datasets with the number of points ranging from 1000 to 200,000 based on a simple mixture model. Each dataset has 10 randomly distributed cluster seeds within the unit square $[0, 1] \times [0, 1]$ and 10 percent noise of total number of points. All the experiments were performed on a 1700Mhz Pentium III workstation with 1GB memory. Fig. 1(a) confirms that time grows quadratically with the single-linkage, the complete-linkage and the average-linkage. Thus, they are computationally very expensive and not well suited for data-rich environments. On the other hand, the cohesion-linkage and our approach linearly grow and no significant difference found for small datasets. However, the difference becomes obvious as the size of data grows as illustrated in Fig. 1(b). Our approaches S_{tiact} and S_{biact} outperform the cohesion-linkage by a large margin.

5 Final Remarks

In this paper, we proposed a general purpose fast and robust clustering pattern spotter that provides an interactive method especially useful for large databases. The proposed hybrid approach employs the combination of geometrical information defined by k-MEANS and topological information modelled by the Voronoi spatial tessellation. This combination makes our approach to detect clusters of arbitrary shapes, different densities and various sizes in $O(n)$ time. Experimental results confirm the virture of our approach.

References

1. Jain, A.K., Dubes, R.C.: Algorithms for Clustering Data. Prentice-Hall (1988)
2. MacQueen, J.: Some Methods for Classification and Analysis of Multivariate Observations. In: Proceedings of the 5th Berkeley Symposium on Maths and Statistics Problems. Volume 1. (1967) 281–297
3. Murtagh, F.: Comments on Parallel Algorithms for Hierarchical Clustering and Cluster Validity. IEEE Transactions on Pattern Analysis and Machine Intelligence **14** (1992) 1056–1057
4. Lin, C.R., Chen, M.S.: Combining Partitional and Hierarchical Algorithms for Robust and Efficient Data Clustering with Cohesion Self-Merging. IEEE Transactions on Knowledge and Data Engineering **17** (2005) 145–159
5. Guha, S., Rastogi, R., Shim, K.: CURE: An Efficient Clustering Algorithm for Large Databases. In Haas, L.M., Tiwary, A., eds.: Proceedings of the ACM SIGMOD'98 International Conference on Management of Data, Seattle, Washington, ACM Press (1998) 73–84
6. Murty, N.M., Krishna, G.: A Hybrid Clustering Procedure for Concentric and Chain-like Clusters. International Journal of Computer and Information Sciences **10** (1981) 397–412
7. Boros, E., Hammer, P.L.: On Clustering Problems with Connected Optima in Euclidean Spaces. Discrete Mathematics **75** (1989) 81–89

Constructing Multi-resolution Support Vector Regression Modelling

Hong Peng, Zheng Pei, and Jun Wang

School of Mathematics & Computer Science, School of Electrical Information,
Xihua University, Chengdu, Sichuan 610039, China
ph66@tom.com

Abstract. Inspired by the theory of multi-resolution analysis of wavelet transform, combining advantages of multi-resolution theory and support vector machine, a new regression model that is called multi-resolution support vector regression (MR-SVR) for function regression is proposed in this paper. In order to construct MR-SVR, the scaling function at some scale and wavelets with different resolution is used as kernel of support vector machine, which is called multi-resolution kernel. The MR-SVR not only has the advantages of support vector machine, but also has the capability of multi-resolution which is useful to approximate nonlinear function. Simulation examples show the feasibility and effectiveness of the method.

1 Introduction

The support vector machine (SVM) is a new universal learning machines proposed by Vapnik et al.[1], [2], which is successfully applied to function regression [3], [4]. SVM use support vector kernel to map the data from input space to a high-dimensional feature space in which the problem becomes linearly separable. The SVM based on structure risk minimum principle have better generalization capability than other approximate method of nonlinear function. By combining advantages of multi-resolution theory and support vector machine, a new regression model that is called multi-resolution support vector regression (MR-SVR) for function regression is proposed in this paper. In MR-SVR, the basis functions are composed by scaling function at some scale and wavelets functions with different resolution, imposing on multi-kernel decomposition technique, the multi-resolution kernel, which include scaling kernel and wavelets kernel, can be obtained and used to construct MR-SVR.

2 Multi-resolution Analysis (MRA)

Based on multi-resolution Analysis theory, the space V_0, $i.e.$, $L^2(R)$ can be decomposed as

$$V_0 = V_1 \bigoplus W_1 = V_2 \bigoplus W_2 \bigoplus W_1 = V_3 \bigoplus W_3 \bigoplus W_2 \bigoplus W_1$$
$$= \ldots = V_L \bigoplus W_L \bigoplus \ldots \bigoplus W_2 \bigoplus W_1 \tag{1}$$

and
$$V_m = span\{\varphi_{m,k}(x) = 2^{-m/2}\varphi(2^{-m}x - k)\}, \quad (m \in Z) \quad (2)$$

$$W_m = span\{\psi_{m,k}(x) = 2^{-m/2}\psi(2^{-m}x - k)\}, \quad (m \in Z) \quad (3)$$

Traditionally, $\psi(x)$ and $\varphi(x)$ are called mother wavelet function and scaling function, respectively. It should be noted here that the subspace $W_1, W_2, \ldots, W_L, V_L$ are mutually orthogonal.

Decompose $f(x) \in V_0$ successively such that

$$f(x) = f_W^1 + f_W^2 + \ldots + f_W^L + f_V^L \quad (4)$$

where $f_W^m \in W_m (m = 1, 2, \ldots, L), f_V^L \in V_L$. Eq.(4) shows that $f(x)$ can be represented as a low-pass approximation at scale L plus the sum of L detail (wavelet) components at different resolutions.

3 Support Vector Regression

The linear programming support vector regression is commonly achieved by explicit enforcement of sparsity via a linear regularizer [5], [6], [7], i.e., minimize

$$R_{reg} = \frac{1}{n}\sum_{i=1}^{n}|\alpha_i| + \frac{C}{n}\sum_{i=1}^{n}|y - f(x)|_\varepsilon \quad (5)$$

where α_i is Lagrange multiplier. Minimizing (5) can be expressed as a linear programming problem:

$$minimize \quad \frac{1}{n}\sum_{i=1}^{n}(\alpha_i + \alpha_i^*) + \frac{C}{n}\sum_{i=1}^{n}(\xi_i + \xi_i^*) \quad (6)$$

$$with \quad \sum_{j=1}^{n}(\alpha_i - \alpha_i^*)K(x_i, x_j) + b - y_i \leq \varepsilon + \xi_i$$

$$y_i - \sum_{j=1}^{n}(\alpha_i - \alpha_i^*)K(x_i, x_j) - b \leq \varepsilon + \xi_i$$

$$\alpha_i \geq 0, \alpha_i^* \geq 0, \xi_i \geq 0, \xi_i^* \geq 0, \quad i = 1, \ldots, n \quad (7)$$

Hence, regression estimation of f is obtained as follows:

$$f(x) = \sum_{i=1}^{n}(\alpha_i - \alpha_i^*)K(x, x_i) + b \quad (8)$$

Remark 1. 1) For the linear programming approach, its kernel needn't to satisfy the Mercer's condition, and only be any functions of $L^1(R)$ [7]. This property helps us to select kernel functions widely. 2) From function approximation point of view, all $K(x, x_i)$ of Eq.(8) construct a set of basis functions. In real world practice, it can be noticed that all $K(x, x_i)$ are not complete. Hence, Eq.(8) can not approximate every function of an subspace of $L^2(R^d)$. It is a problem that find a set of complete basis. On the other hand, $\{\varphi_{L,k}(x)\}$ and $\{\psi_{m,k}(x)\}(m = 1, \cdots, L)$ can provide a set of complete basis of $L^2(R^d)$.

4 Multi-resolution Kernel and MR-SVR

For estimating $f(x) \in L^2(R^d)$ based on support vector machine, firstly, according to Eq.(4), $f(x)$ is decomposed. Then, $f_W^m(m = 1, \cdots, L)$ and f_V^L are estimated via expressions Eq.(8), $i.e.$,

$$f_W^m(x) = \sum_{i=1}^{n}(\alpha_i^W(m) - \alpha_i^{W*}(m))K_m^W(x, x_i) + b_m^W, \quad m = 1, \ldots, L$$

$$f_V^L(x) = \sum_{i=1}^{n}(\alpha_i^V - \alpha_i^{V*})K^V(x, x_i) + b^V \qquad (9)$$

Hence, it is needed to find $L+1$ kernel functions, $i.e.$, $K_1^W(x, x_i)$, $K_2^W(x, x_i)$, ..., $K_L^W(x, x_i)$, $K^V(x, x_i)$. According to multi-resolution Analysis, the multi-resolution kernels expressed by the scaling function at scale L and the group of L wavelet functions at different resolution are constructed as follows:

$$K_m^W(x, x') = K_m^W(x - x') = \psi(2^{-m} \cdot (x - x')), \quad m = 1, \ldots, L \qquad (10)$$
$$K^V(x, x') = K^V(x - x') = \varphi(2^{-L} \cdot (x - x')), \qquad (11)$$

According to (10) and (11), the estimate function of $f(x)$ is obtained as follows

$$f(x) = \sum_{i=1}^{n}\sum_{m=1}^{L}(\alpha_i^W(m) - \alpha_i^{W*}(m))\psi(2^{-m} \cdot (x - x_i'))$$
$$+ \sum_{i=1}^{n}(\alpha_i^V - \alpha_i^{V*})\varphi(2^{-L} \cdot (x - x_i')) + b, \qquad (12)$$

5 Simulation Results

In this Section, three examples are given to demonstrate the learning capability of the presented MR-SVR. In every example, Meyer scaling function and wavelets are selected as our multi-resolution kernels. For the purpose of comparing our MR-SVR with other methods, the measure J proposed in [8] is adopted as the performance index for all examples.

Example 1. (Approximation of Piecewise) The follows piecewise function was studied in [8], $i.e.$,

$$f(x) = \begin{cases} -2.18x - 12.86 & -10 \leq x < -2 \\ 4.246x & -2 \leq x < 0 \\ 10e^{-0.05x-0.5}\sin[(0.03x + 0.7)x] & 0 \leq x \leq 10 \end{cases} \qquad (13)$$

Here, we sampled 200 points distributed uniformly over $[-10, 10]$ as training data. The approximation errors J using our MR-SVR, SVR with Gaussian kernel and WNN[8] are 0.04925, 0.08467 and 0.05057, respectively. Obviously, the performance of our MR-SVR is superior to that of other methods.

Example 2. (Approximation of Two Variable Function)

$$F(\boldsymbol{x}) = (x_1^2 - x_2^2)\sin(0.5x_1) \quad -10 \le x_1, x_2 \le 10. \tag{14}$$

A data set of 400 input-output pairs was collected by using random inputs being distributed uniformly over the domain $D = [-10, 10] \times [-10, 10]$. The approximation errors J for the MR-SVR is 0.01646. The simulation results show that MR-SVR has good approximation capability.

Example 3. (Nonlinear Dynamic Modelling) The nonlinear dynamical system to be identified is defined as follows:

$$y(t+1) = \frac{[y(t)y(t-1)y(t-2)x(t-1)(y(t-2)-1) + x(t)]}{[1 + y^2(t-1) + y^2(t-2)]} \tag{15}$$

The input signal $x(t)$ is selected as

$$x(t) = \begin{cases} \sin(2\pi t/250) & t \le 500 \\ 0.8\sin(2\pi t/250) + 0.2\sin(2\pi t/25) & t > 500 \end{cases} \tag{16}$$

data on-line for 800 time steps are collected to form input-output sample pairs for constructing the MR-SVR. The approximation errors J for MR-SVR is 0.05872. The simulation results show that MR-SVR has good identification capability for nonlinear dynamic system.

References

1. Vapnik, V.: The Nature of Statistical Learning Theory. Springer-Verlag, New York (2001)
2. Cortes, C., Vapnik, V.: Support Vector Networks. Machine Learning, **20** (1995) 273-297
3. Smola, A., Schölkopf, B.: A Tutorial on Support Vector Regression. NeuroCOLT Technical Report NC-TR-98-030, Royal Holloway College, University of London, UK, (1998)
4. Schölkopf, B., Smola, A., Williamson, R.C., Bartlett, P.L.: New Support Vector Algorithms. Neural Computation, **20** (2000) 1207-1245
5. Bennett, K.: Combining Support Vector and Mathematical Programming Methods for Induction. In: Schölkopf, B., Burges, C.J.C., Smola, A. (eds.), Advances in Kernel Methods - SV Learning, Cambridge, MA, MIT Press, (1999) 307-326.
6. Smola, A.: Learning with Kernels [PhD thesis]. Technische Universitat Berlin (1998)
7. Weston, J., Gammerman, A., Stitson, M., Vapnik, V., Vork, V., Watkins, C.: Support Vector Density Estimation. In: Schölkopf, B., Burges, C.J.C., Smola, A. (eds.), Advances in Kernel Methods - SV Learning, Cambridge, MA, MIT Press (1999) 293-306
8. Zhang, Q., Benveniste, A.: Wavelet Networks. IEEE Trans. Neural Networks, **3** (1992) 889-898

Revised Entropy Clustering Analysis with Features Selection

Ching-Hsue Cheng[1], Jing-Rong Chang[1], and I-Ni Lei[2]

[1] Department of Information Management, National Yunlin University of Science and Technology, 123, Section 3, University Road, Touliu, Yunlin 640, Taiwan
`{chcheng, g9120806}@pine.yuntech.edu.tw`
[2] Graduate School of Resources Management, National Defense Management College, Chung-Ho, Taipei 235, Taiwan

Abstract. Clustering analysis is used to analyze the clustering phenomenon occurred to the data structure. However, there are some problems when the decision maker attempts to use clustering analysis. For solving these existing problems, this paper proposes a revised Entropy Clustering Analysis method requiring no prior setting of clusters, which is based on the mean distance between the data points and the cluster center. Through using several experiments and comparing different clustering analysis methods with proposed method, the results show that the proposed clustering method could achieve reasonable clustering effect. The experiment also proves that using the attributes with high correlation coefficient in clustering can achieve higher clustering accuracies.

1 Introduction

Clustering analysis has been a fundamental research area in data mining and performs un-supervised work in the primary data mining tasks [2, 4]. Unsupervised Clustering analysis has been a fundamental research area in data mining and performs basic work in the primary data mining tasks. Clustering helps find natural boundaries in the data and separate the data set into some clusters. Because different geometry characteristic of the data set, the suitable clustering analysis is not the same.

When the decision maker (DM) attempts to use clustering analysis, the following problems may occur. Firstly, the DM will not be able to choose the right type of clustering analysis, because he may suffer insufficient understanding the nature of the data. The Second problem is that DM does not know how to set the parameters for the clustering analysis, the accurate number of clusters, and the cluster centers locations, etc.

In this work, we focus on clustering of continuous (numerical) data. As for nominal data, it is more suitable to be handled by other kinds of algorithms such as conceptual clustering [1]. This paper proposes a new method to solve the above problems and the proposed methods require no prior setting of clusters. We use some databases for experiment and compare the results of proposed clustering analysis with other clustering analysis.

2 Revised Entropy Clustering Analysis Algorithm

Yao et al. [6] proposed an Entropy-based Fuzzy Clustering (EFC). They calculated entropy values and implemented clustering analysis based on the degree of similarity. After some experiments, we find that using different formula to execute clustering analysis may get the same cluster center but the degrees of similarity are different, and the degrees of similarity may change when the number of dimension increases. This problem may lead to setting the proper clustering threshold is hard. For example, in Yao et al. [6], α is calculated automatically by assigning similarity of 0.5 in equation (2), i.e., it is given as $\alpha = -\ln 0.5/\overline{D}$, where $\overline{D}$ is the mean distance among the pairs of data points in a hyper-space.

Therefore, this paper proposes a Revised Entropy Clustering Analysis method to avoid setting inappropriate threshold. The proposed threshold (equation (5)) is calculated by the half of the mean distance between the data point and the cluster center added with standard deviation. Our method can take the centralization ($\overline{D}$) and distribution (S.D.) trends of data into consideration.

This paper calculates the entropy values of data points and selects the data point having least entropy value as the cluster center. Then, we implement clustering analysis based on the mean distance between the data points and the standard deviation of total distances from each point to the cluster center. We then group the data points having the distance smaller than the threshold (i.e. the half of the mean distance between the data point and the cluster center added with standard deviation) into a cluster. Other points continue implementing clustering analysis. Consider a set T of N data points in an M-dimensional hyper-space, where each data point $x_i, i = 1...N$, is represented by a vector of M values (i.e., $x_{i1}, x_{i2}, \cdots x_{im}$). The algorithm is as follows:

Step 1. Calculate the mean distance ($\overline{D}$) and standard deviation of distance (S.D.) among cluster center and data points.

$$\overline{D} = \frac{\sum_{i,j} d(X_i, X_j)}{N}, \text{ where } i,j = 1,2,....,N, i \neq j \tag{1}$$

$$\text{S.D.} = \sqrt{\frac{\sum (d(X_i, X_j) - \overline{D})^2}{N-1}} \tag{2}$$

Step 2. Calculate entropy for each x_i in T for $i = 1...N$ by equation (5).

$$E_i = -\sum_{\substack{j \in x \\ j \neq i}} (S_{ij} \log_2 S_{ij} + (1 - S_{ij}) \log_2 (1 - S_{ij})), \tag{3}$$

where S_{ij} is the similarity between two data points normalized to [0.0-1.0]. The similarity between two data points, S_{ij} is given by

$$S_{ij} = e^{-D_c} \tag{4}$$

where the threshold D_c is

$$D_c = (\overline{D}+S.D.)/2 \qquad (5)$$

Step 3. Select $x_{i_{min}}$ with least entropy.
Step 4. Gather the cluster center and the data points having the distance with cluster center smaller than $\overline{D}$ to a cluster.
Step 5. If T is not empty go to Step 2.
Step 6. When a data point belongs to different clusters at the same time, we assign this point to the cluster having the shortest distance with this cluster center.

3 Experiments and Comparison

In this section, this paper will follow the proposed clustering analysis method and compare with other clustering analysis methods for examining the robustness of proposed method. The three actual data sets are summarized in Table 1 [7].

Table 1. Summary of data sets

Data set	No. of data points	No. of attributes	No. of clusters	No. of data points in each cluster
WINE	178	13	3	59, 71, 48
IRIS	150	4	3	50, 50, 50
THYROID	215	5	3	150, 35, 30

Table 2. Results of different clustering analysis methods for WINE, IRIS, and THYROID

		Clustering Method			
		K-Means [2, 5]	Fuzzy C-Means [3]	EFC [6] ($\beta = 0.70$)	Revised Entropy Clustering Analysis
WINE	No. of clusters	3	3	3	3
	Accuracy	94.9%	94.9%	92.7%	94.9%
IRIS	No. of clusters	3	3	3	3
	Accuracy	89.3%	87.3%	96.7%	96.7%
THYROID	No. of clusters	3	3	3	3
	Accuracy	88.8%	80%	65.6%	90.2%

Although the clustering analysis is a technique used for agglomerative observations into clusters, and the number of cluster and clustering results are unknown [2, 5], the data points in three data sets are all definitely classified and make it easily to compare the results of proposed methods with other methods. To show that proposed methods can find the natural clusters we follow the procedure in Yao et al. [6].

There are 13 attributes and three actual clusters in WINE. After executing some experiments, we find that to delete the variables with correlation values less than 0.5

can achieve better clustering results. So, we delete three low correlation attributes (Var3, Var4, and Var5).

This paper compares the results of K-Means [2, 5], Fuzzy C-Means [3], and Entropy-based Fuzzy Clustering analysis [6] with proposed Entropy Clustering Analysis (see Table 2). The results in Table 2 show that the performances of our method are best and the clustering accuracies are highest in each data set. Moreover, the proposed method does not need to optimize parameters and can save a lot of execution time, and the number of clusters is automatically determined.

4 Conclusions

This paper proposes a new clustering method requiring no prior setting of clusters, which is revised Entropy Clustering Analysis. Through experiments and comparisons of different clustering analyses on database, the results show that the proposed method could achieve satisfactory clustering effect to confirm the superiority of the proposed clustering methods. Based on the concept of features selection, the paper uses correlation analysis to select appropriate attributes. The experiment results show that using the attributes with high correlation coefficient as the attribute in clustering can achieve higher clustering accuracy and the number of clusters is automatically determined. Applying our method to mixed data with both nominal and continuous attributes is another interesting issue. It is challenging to find an effective similarity measure for mixed data, which is one of future research directions [6].

References

1. D.H. Fisher, Knowledge acquisition via incremental conceptual clustering, Machine Learning (2)(1987) 139-172.
2. J. Han, M. Kamber, Data Mining: Concepts and Techniques, Morgan Kaufmann (2001).
3. F. Hoppner, F. Klawonn, R. Kruse, T. Runkler, Fuzzy Cluster Analysis, John Wiley & Sons, New York, 1999.
4. L. Kaufman, P.J. Rousseeuw, Finding Groups in Data: An Introduction to Cluster Analysis, John Wiley & Sons, New York, 1990.
5. S. Sharma, Applied multivariate techniques, John Wiley & Sons, Inc., NJ, 1996.
6. J. Yao, M. Dash, S.T. Tan, and H. Liu, Entropy-based Fuzzy Clustering and Fuzzy Modeling, Fuzzy sets and system (113)(2000) 381-388.
7. ftp://ftp.ics.uci.edu/pub/machine-learning-databases/

IC^2: An Interval Based Characteristic Concept Learner

Pramod K. Singh*

School of Computer Science and Engineering,
University of New South Wales, Sydney, NSW - 2052, Australia

Abstract. Most classification algorithms suffer from an inability to detect instances of classes which are not present in the training set. A novel approach for characteristic concept rule learning called IC^2 is proposed in this paper.

1 Introduction

Most learning systems, which learn from examples, deliver discriminant description and ignore the problem of the classification of an instance of an unknown category. Unfortunately, in many application domains it cannot be assumed that the collected examples in the training set represent all relevant categories because the number of these categories can be quite large. There is likely to be misclassification of instances of unknown classes by such classifiers unless the training data is fully comprehensive. In some problem domain e.g. medical diagnosis, the misclassification of any instance may cost a lot. What we need under such situations is the ability to reject instances of the categories that the system has not been trained on.

Holte et al. [1] have shown that the CN2 algorithm can be modified to learn characteristic descriptions. Hence it learns the most specific descriptions. On the other end, AQ11 [3] is able to learn the most general descriptions. In most applications these extreme approaches are inadequate due to being static and having no scope of controlling the degree of generalization. To overcome this problem an algorithm called ID3-SD was proposed by Davidsson [2]. However, it needs examples of other classes as negative data to select the features and their class boundaries. In this paper we propose an interval based algorithm for learning characteristic concepts using positive only examples and synthetically generated uniform data as negative examples for each class.

2 Interval Rule Concept

Interval concept proposed here is defined as a set of rules, where each rule has a conjunct of conditions for a feature set. A condition is a numeric value range also

---

* Author acknowledges the financial support in part by the Australian Research Council through a Linkage grant (No LP0212081), with Medical Imaging Australasia as clinical and Philips Medical Systems as Industrial partners. Special thanks to Prof Paul Compton for his valuable suggestions.

called an interval limit with a lower bound and an upper bound for a numerical feature. The interval limits for a numerical feature of a class is created by decomposing the range of values of that feature in a given dataset into k intervals. The value of k is determined separately for each feature of the class using statistical method. Out of k intervals, if any two adjacent intervals are having non zero allocation of instances would be merged to produce a larger size interval.

2.1 Simple Interval Rules

Simple interval rules are defined on single feature of the data set.

Definition 1. *Let feature f of the class C with values $f_1...f_n$, where n is the number of objects in class C. The minimum and maximum values of the feature f in the data set are: $f_{min} = Min(f_i)$, $f_{max} = Max(f_i)$. Further, mean value f_{mean} and the standard deviation f_{SD} of the feature f are calculated. The numver of interval k is:*

$$k = \frac{(f_{max} + \frac{f_{SD}}{2}) - (f_{min} - \frac{f_{SD}}{2})}{\sigma * f_{SD}} \quad (1)$$

where, f_{SD} determines the number of k and width of range in each interval. Here σ is specificity factor for increasing the effect of f_{SD} and generated algorithmically. The specificity of the rules increases monotonically with the increment of σ.

Definition 2. *Let the values of feature f be divided into k intervals and number of the objects in class C be n. The objects are allocated to the k intervals based on the respective values of the feature f for each object. Suppose O_j indicate the number of objects allocated to the jth interval, where $j = 1..k$. The operators of interval merger $Merg$ for obtaining the disjunct interval rules are defined as:*

$$k_{merg} = Merg(k_j, k_{j+1}), \text{ if } O_j \text{ and } O_{j+1} \text{ are non zero}$$

where k_{merg} is an interval produced after merger of the intervals k_j and k_{j+1}. Note that k_j and k_{j+1} are adjacent intervals and O_j and O_{j+1} are the numbers of allocated objects in these intervals, respectively. Intervals with zero allocation are ignored.

2.2 Composite Interval Rules

The composite interval rules are the rules defined using more than one feature by applying cartesian products among the simple interval rules derived for each feature.

Definition 3. *Let features f_1 and f_2 be involved in the definition of the classifier and assume that the set of disjunct interval rules produced using the simple interval rules method defined above for f_1 and f_2 to be $S(f_1)$ and $S(f_2)$, respectively. Then the composite interval rules are the rules produced by the cartesian* product operator $Cart$ on $S(f_1)$ and $S(f_2)$. Furthermore, the created cartesian rule set C_{rules} is used for the allocation of training objects. Finally the reduced cartesian rule set C^r_{rules} is defined as follows:

$$C_{rules} = Cart(S(f_1), S(f_2)) \qquad (2)$$

$$C^r_{rules} = \{\forall rule | rule \in C_{rules} \land cover(rule) \neq 0\} \qquad (3)$$

where $cover(rule)$ is the number of objects covered by the rule.

3 IC^2 Generation Algorithm

The IC^2 generation algorithm consists two main steps - rule generation and feature selection. In the first step a function interval rules are generated. A feature selection method based on a *wrapper model* [4] is used. A goodness measure is used for selection of promising features. The goodness of the interval rules of a feature or a set of features uses two statistics: *precision* and *recall* of the rules. An accuracy factor *f_accuracy* combines *recall* and *precision* statistics as follows:

$$f\_accuracy = \frac{\beta + 1}{\frac{\beta}{recall} + \frac{1}{precision}} \qquad (4)$$

where β is a generalization parameter. *f_accuracy*, with a value of β greater than 1, favors *recall* and more generalization of concepts, whereas with a value smaller than 1, it favors *precision* and more specific rules.

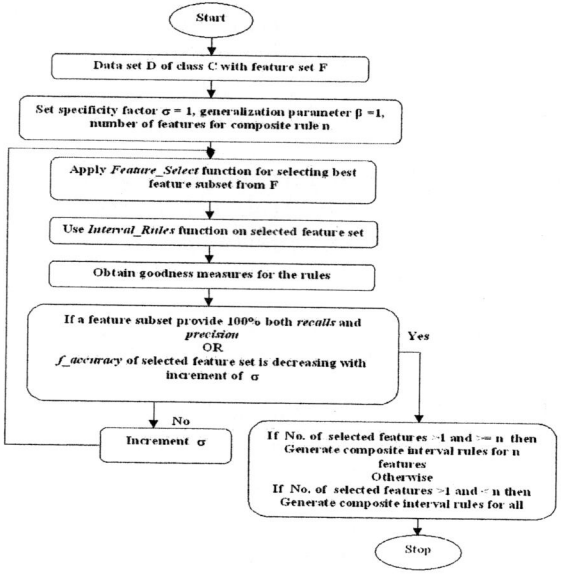

Fig. 1. IC^2 Generation Algorithm

For computation of *precision* of rules negative examples required. Similar to [5] uniformly distributed negative examples are generated synthetically for each target class to be learned. Unlike Mitchell's *Polar*[5] algorithm Interval learner uses the generated negative examples for testing the rules coverage only. Fig.3 summarizes the IC^2 generation algorithm; for ease of exposition we have omitted various details from the presentation.

4 Experimental Results

Since there were no characteristic concept rule learner using only positive instances at our disposal, we use the extended version of ID3-SD [2] for comparison. To use ID3-SD algorithm we add uniformly distributed negative data to produce the characteristic concept rules on positive only data. The extended algorithm is termed as *PolarID3 − SD*. Due to shortage of space, only results of one experiment is presented here. The dataset is generated from the labelled regions in HRCT lung images. The regions of the images are labelled by the radiologist as the region of interest (ROI) for the diagnosis of lung diseases. We selected ROIs of 4 lung disease types; 63 ROIs of Emphysema, 48 of Honey Combing, 59 of GGO, and 27 of Consolidation. Each ROIs are converted into a vector of 20 numerical features. Table 3 shows the results of the classification of disease ROIs. In general the IC^2 performed much better than the *PolarID3 − SD* learner. The misclassification of instances in IC^2 is significantly reduced. Note that the generalization factor β is set 1 in this experiment.

Table 1. % Accuracy of Classification of HRCT Lung ROIs Classes

	Emphysema			Honey Combing			Ground Glass Opacities			Consolidation		
	corr.	miss	reject	corr.	miss	reject	corr.	miss	reject	corr.	miss	reject
PolarID3-SD	93.2±1.3	1.7±.3	5.1±.7	87.4±2.4	4.1±2.2	8.5±.5	83.7±1.8	6.3±1.5	10.0±1.3	95.9±1.2	.9±.2	3.2±.4
IC^2	99.8±0.8	0	1.2±.3	94.7±1.9	.3±0	5.0±.7	90.5±2.2	1.3±.5	8.2±.7	100±0	0	0

5 Conclusion

A characteristic concept classifier based on an interval rule concept using instances of only one class is proposed. The current version of IC^2 handles numerical features only in the rule induction.

References

1. R.C. Holte, L.E. Acker, and B.W. Porter, *Concept of Learning and the Problem of Small Disjoints*, IJCAI, 1989, pp.813-818.
2. Paul Davidsson, *Integrating Models of Discrimination and Characterization for Learning from Examples in Open Domains*, IJCAI, 1997, pp.840-845.
3. R.S. Michalski, and, J.B. Larson, *Selection of Most Representative Training Examples and Incremental Generation of VL Hypotheses: The Underlying Methodology and the Description of Programs ESEL and AQ11*, Tecnical Report 877, Computer Science Department, University of Illinois, Urbana, 1978.
4. G. John, R. Kohavi and K. Pfleger, *Irrelevent Features and the Subset Selection Problem*, Proc. Int. Conf. on Machine Learning, 1994.
5. A.R. Mitchell, *"Boosting" a Positive-Data-Only Learner*, ICML, 2000, pp.607-714.

A Comparative Study for Assessing the Reliability of Complex Networks Using Rules Extracted from Different Machine Learning Approaches

Douglas E. Torres D.[1,2] and Claudio M. Rocco S.[1]

[1] Facultad de Ingeniería, Universidad Central de Venezuela, Venezuela
[2] UNEFA, Núcleo Caracas
douglastd@cantv.net, crocco@reacciun.ve

Abstract. In this paper three machine learning approaches, Neural Networks (NN), Support Vector Machines (SVM) and Neural Fuzzy Networks (FuNN) are used to extract rules and assess the reliability of complex networks. For NN and SVM models the TREPAN approach is proposed as a valid tool for extracting rules whereas the Adaptive Neuro-Fuzzy Inference System (ANFIS) is used for tuning a previous set of rules derived by a fuzzy inference system and neural network approach.

1 Introduction

Hybrid Intelligent Systems (HIS) [1] is the combination of different intelligent techniques as neural networks, genetic algorithms, decision trees, systems based on fuzzy rules, among other. HIS seeks to improve the efficiency, reasoning power and comprehensibility of the integrand systems [2,3].

This paper presents an approach for the extraction of knowledge from different machine learning models: Neural Networks (NN), Support Vector Machines (SVM) and Neural Fuzzy Networks to be used as a tool for the reliability assessment of complex networks. To this aim, empirical models induced by two techniques TREPAN [4,5] and ANFIS [6] are compared.

The paper is organized as follows: Section 2 presents the scope of network reliability assessment. Section 3 presents the proposed approach. Section 4 presents the experimental results. Finally Section 5 presents the conclusions.

2 Network Reliability Assessment

A convenient way of modeling any system is to represent it through Reliability Block Diagram (RBD) [7], in which every block is associated with a system component. Each block in an RBD can be considered to assume one of two possible states, operating (with probability P_i) or failed (with probability $1-P_i$); therefore, a binary variable x_i (1 or -1) can be associated with each connection in the system. In this way, the whole system can be described by a Boolean vector x, having as many components as the number of edges in the RBD. Typical RBDs include series and parallel components. If a network has components neither in series nor in parallel, it is considered as a complex network [8].

The state of a system with d components can be operating or failed, and is therefore described by a binary variable y (1 or -1)[8]. The Boolean mapping that associate every input vector x to its corresponding output y is called Structure Function (*SF*) [9]. The procedure employed to retrieve the value of y that corresponds to a given x is usually referred to as an Evaluation Function (*EF*) [10], that is y=*EF*($\mathbf{x}$). For example, the s-t reliability measure assumes that the system is operating if there exists at least one working path from the source node s to the terminal node t. So the *EF* is equivalent to a depth-first procedure [11,12].

3 Hybrid Intelligent Systems Models

In this paper three machine learning approaches, Neural Networks (NN), trained using the Levenberg-Marquardt optimization method combined with Bayesian optimization of the regularization parameters [13], Support Vector Machines (SVM) [14] and Neural Fuzzy Networks (FuNN) [15,16] are used to extract rules and assess the reliability of complex networks. For SVM and NN, the Extraction of Knowledge is performed using the well-known TREPAN approach, proposed by Craven [4]. In this study, the TREPAN system developed by the Centre for Molecular Design at the University of Portsmouth [17] was selected. The program is a Matlab [18] implementation of the original TREPAN for classification problems. Figure 1 presents the data flow for the extraction of knowledge from a machine learning trained model, with the TREPAN approach.

Two different oracles were implemented in TREPAN: NN-TREPAN and SVM-TREPAN to produce a decision tree for ANN and SVM models respectively.

In the case of the FuNN procedure [19] the rules obtained by FuNN are of linguistic type. The optimization was performed using the back-propagation method as implemented by ANFIS, within the Matlab Fuzzy Logic Toolbox [18].

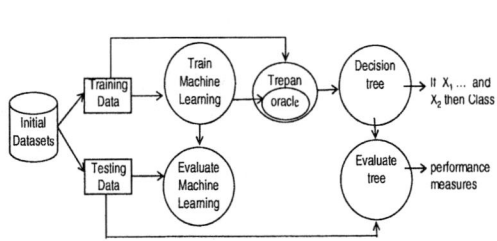

Fig. 1. Knowledge extraction data flow with TREPAN

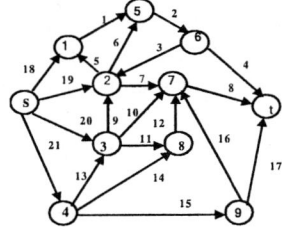

Fig. 2. Complex Network to be evaluated [20]

4 Experimental Results

To evaluate the proposed approach, the complex network shown in Fig. 2 has been considered [20]. It is assumed that each link has reliability P_i and the goal is to obtain models that approximate the s-t reliability metrics. To this aim, 2000 system states

Table 1. Average performance results for NN, SVM, TREPAN and ANFIS models

Model	Rules	Sensitivity %		Specificity %		Accuracy %	
		Training	Testing	Training	Testing	Training	Testing
NN	65[1]	100	94.6	100	95.1	100	94.9
NN-TREPAN	39.6	95.2	93.5	94.3	92.2	94.7	92.9
SVM	621.1[2]	100	95.4	100	95.2	100	95.3
SVM-TREPAN	39.9	95.6	95	94	92.6	94.7	93.8
ANFIS	58.3	93.5	91.9	94.4	93.5	93.9	92.8

[1] number of neurons. [2] number of support vectors.

Table 2. Network reliability results using RE and AREs

P_i	RE	ARE NN-TREPAN	Relative Error (%)	ARE SVM-TREPAN	Relative error (%)
0.7	0.8517	0.8295	2.61	0.8313	2.39
0.8	0.9537	0.9413	1.30	0.9404	1.39
0.9	0.9941	0.9917	0.24	0.9913	0.29

(out of 2^{21} possible states) have been randomly generated without replacement and for each of them the corresponding value of the *EF* has been performed, by a depth-first procedure [11,12]. To select the appropriate model a 10-fold cross-validation (CV) was performed. The performance of each method is measured using sensitivity, specificity and accuracy indexes [21].

The Matlab NN Toolbox was used to train the network [18]. The trained NN (21:65:1) is then integrated to the TREPAN model. The fidelity, that is the percentage of predictions made by the extracted tree that agrees with the predictions made by the network, was 94.7% during the training and 91.7% during the testing.

The Matlab SVM Toolbox [22] was used to train the SVM and to evaluate the oracle of SVM-TREPAN. To select the best set of parameters (γ,C) for the Gaussian kernel, the grid-search and cross-validation approach proposed by Hsu et al. [23] with $\gamma=[2^4,2^3,...,2^{-10}]$ and $C=[2^{12},2^{11},...,2^{-2}]$ was used. The best (γ,C) was (2^{-5}, 2^7) with an average accuracy of 95.4 % during testing and 100 % during training and 621.1 average support vectors (SV). The average fidelity index was 94.7% during the training and 92.4 % during testing phases.

Table 1 shows the average number of rules along with the average performance results obtained using the 10-fold cross-validation. The performance indexes of the SVM-TREPAN model during testing are superior to the NN-TREPAN and ANFIS models. The average performance indexes of the trees extracted by TREPAN are very similar to SVM and NN indexes. However the average number of rules is less than the number of neurons, support vectors and ANFIS rules.

Since the extracted rules from NN-TREPAN and SVM-TREPAN are in disjoint form, they can be used to build the Approximate Reliability Expression (ARE), that is an expression which allows to assess the network reliability as a function of the element reliability, by replacing each element state by its probability. Table 2 shows the network reliability for different values P_i of component reliability, evaluated using the AREs generated by NN-TREPAN and SVM-TREPAN, along with the exact Reliability Expression (RE), as found in [24]. Results for ANFIS are not presented since the rules it provides are not disjoint and then an additional procedure is required to make them disjoint.

The fold with the best accuracy was selected to analyze the physical meaning of the rules derived. For NN-TREPAN, 13 out of the 43 rules derived correspond to true cut sets while 10 correspond to true minimal paths. For SVM-TREPAN, 9 out of the 36 rules correspond to true cut sets and 7 correspond to true minimal paths. For ANFIS, only 3 out of 57 rules correspond to true cut sets and 6 correspond to true minimal paths. NN-TREPAN and SVM-TREPAN are able to extract all of the 6 third-order cuts of the network and 3 and 7of the 8 fourth-order cuts, respectively.

5 Conclusions

In this paper the application of Hybrid Intelligent Systems for the reliability assessment of complex networks has been presented, based on a comparison among two approaches for extracting rules from SVM and NN trained models and from neural fuzzy networks. The average performance indexes of the trees extracted by TREPAN are very similar to the obtained by SVM and NN models, but the average number of rules is significantly less than the support vectors and number of neurons.

References

[1] Jacobsen H.A. (1998): A Generic Architecture for Hybrid Intelligent Systems. IEEE Fuzzy Systems IEEE Fuzzy Systems. Anchorage, Alaska.
[2] Jain L.C, Martin N. M.(1998): Fusion of Neural Networks, Fuzzy Sets, and Genetic Algorithms, Industrial Applications. Ed. CRC Press.
[3] http://www.comp.nus.edu.sg/~pris/HybridSystems/DescriptionDetailed1.html
[4] Craven M.W. (1996): Extracting Comprehensible Models from Trained Neural Networks. Ph.D. Thesis. University of Wisconsin- Madison.
[5] http://www.biostat.wisc.edu/~craven/
[6] Jang J.S, Sun C.T., (1997): Neuro-Fuzzy and Soft Computing. A Computational Approach to Learning and Machine Intelligence. Ed. Prentice Hall, NJ
[7] Lynn, N., Singpurwalla, N. (1998): Bayesian assessment of network reliability. SIAM Review, 40: 202-227.
[8] Billinton R., Allan R. (1992): Reliability Evaluation of Engineering Systems, Concepts and Techniques, 2nd ed. Plenum Press, New York
[9] Marseguerra M., Zio E.(2002): Basics of the Monte Carlo Method with Application to System Reliability, LiLoLe-Verlag GmbH (Publ. Co. Ltd.).
[10] Grimaldi R.P., Shier D.R.: Redundancy and reliability of communication networks. www.math.clemson.edu/ ~shierd/ Shier/abstracts/randr.html.
[11] Reingold E., Nievergelt J., Deo N. (1977): Combinatorial Algorithms: Theory and Practice. Prentice Hall, New Jersey.
[12] Papadimitriou C. H., Steiglitz K. (1982): Combinatorial Optimization: Algorithms and Complexity, Prentice Hall, New Jersey.

[13] Foresee F.D., Hagan M.T. (1997): Gauss-Newton Approximation to Bayesian Regularization Proc. of IJCNN'97
[14] Cortes C., Vapnik V. (1995): SVM. Machine Learning, 20: 273-297.
[15] Lin C.T, Lee C.S.G. (1996): Neural Fuzzy Systems: A Neuro-Fuzzy Synergism to Intelligent Systems. Prentice Hall, NJ
[16] http://divcom.otago.ac.nz/infoscie/kel/cbiis.htm
[17] Trepan – Matlab. Available at www.cmdmport.ac.uk /biomine
[18] MathWorks (2002) MatLab 6.5 R13
[19] Kasabov N. (1996): Investigating the Adaptation and Forgetting in Fuzzy Neural Networks Through a Method of Training and Zeroing. ICNN'96. 118-123
[20] Yoo Y.B, Deo N. (1988): A Comparison of Algorithm for Terminal-Pair Relia- bility, IEEE Transaction on Reliability, 37(2): 210-215
[21] Veropoulos K, Camppbell, Cristianini N. (1999): Controlling the Sensitivity of Support Vector Machines. Proceedings of the IJCAI99
[22] Cawley G.C., MATLAB Support Vector Machine Toolbox v. 0.54. University of East Anglia, Norwich, U.K. Available at: http://theoval.sys.uea.ac.uk/~gcc/svm/toolbox
[23] C. –W Hsu, C.-C Chang, and C.-J. Lin "A Practical Guide to Support Vector Classification.", Available at www.csie.ntu.edu.tw/~cjlin/papers/guide/guide.pdf.
[24] Rocco C., Muselli M (2004): Empirical models based on machine learning techniques for determining ARE. Reliability Engineering and Safety S., 83:301-309

Machine Learning for Time Interval Petri Nets

Vadim Bulitko[1] and David C. Wilkins[2]

[1] Department of Computing Science,
University of Alberta, Edmonton, AB T6G 2E8, Canada
bulitko@ualberta.ca
[2] Center for the Study of Language and Information,
Stanford University, Stanford, CA 94306
dwilkins@stanford.edu

Abstract. Creating Petri Net domain models faces the same challenges that confront all knowledge-intensive AI performance systems: model specification, knowledge acquisition, and refinement. Thus, a fundamental question to investigate is the degree to which automation can be used. This paper formulates the learning task and presents the first machine learning method for Time Interval Petri Net (TIPN) domain models. In a preliminary evaluation within a damage control domain, the method learned a nearly perfect model of fire spread augmented with temporal and spatial data.

Keywords: domain model learning, Petri net learning, spatial-temporal data series learning, real-time decision-making, automated damage control.

1 Introduction

Petri Nets and their extensions, such as Time Interval Petri Nets (TIPNs), have been applied to artificial intelligence reasoning processes, in planning, uncertainty reasoning, intelligent systems [1], qualitative simulation and modelling [2]. TIPNs are especially suitable as fast qualitative-level models for concurrent temporally and spatially referenced processes such as the ones in real-time strategy games, traffic control, and crisis decision making. One example of a TIPN application is a decision-making system for the DC-Train real-time shipboard damage control training environment [2]. On 160 simulated difficult scenarios that involved fire, smoke, flooding, and machinery failure, the TIPN-based decision-making system saved 117 ships (73.1%) [2]. This is a substantial improvement over the performance of human experts, who saved 28 of 160 (17.5%) ships. The system employed TIPNs for qualitative simulation of effects of the proposed crisis responses and used them to select the most appropriate course of action.

At the present, Time Interval Petri Net based models need to be hand-crafted by subject matter experts. Thus, the ability to learn TIPNs automatically from historical data and domain theory would greatly improve applicability of the formalism. To illustrate: records of past scenarios are available in the domain of shipboard damage control. Likewise, microarray time series data can be used for TIPN learning in the study of biological genetic regulatory networks.

2 ML-TIPN Learning Method

In light of difficulties with the use of existing methods, we have developed a novel approach specifically for learning TIPN-based domain models. The method (i) takes a user-supplied domain theory, (ii) refines it using noisy and inconsistent historical data, (iii) allows the user to control the properties of the model produced, (iv) learns fully fledged TIPNs including the temporal and spatial causality, and (v) produces more than one TIPN model should the user so request. We will refer to the algorithm as ML-TIPN.

ML-TIPN's input consists of domain theory P_0 and historical data $\{e_i\}, \{e'_j\}$. Domain theory is encoded as one or more *incomplete* Time Interval Petri Nets. Such representation enables the user to specify the lexicon and known causality information (if any) while leaving the unknown parts for ML-TIPN to learn. Technically, an incomplete TIPN is a Time Interval Petri Net where certain arcs are labeled "unknown" and can be of any standard type (e.g., inhibitory or enabling). ML-TIPN will "refine" such possible arcs into one of the basic types. Additionally, operators on the output arcs can be left open. ML-TIPN will then attempt to fill such an operator with a table of records of the type "input token label $\rightarrow$ output token label" (as illustrated in the bottom boxes of Figures 1 and 2). Temporal delay intervals can be left for ML-TIPN to fill in as well.

Historical data are represented as a series of event records. Each record describes an actual event in terms of token introduction or removal from a particular place in the TIPN model. Specifically, an event is represented as a 5-tuple <place, token, time interval, +/-, ext/int/unknown> where place is the TIPN place the token was put in or removed from, time interval indicates when token is believed to acquire its current attributes and place, '+' denotes token introduction and '-' stands for removal, and finally ext/int/unknown indicates whether the event is *external* (i.e., the token came from outside of the TIPN), or *internal* (i.e., the token introduction/removal is a result of TIPN operation), or *unknown* which may be either of the two. As an example, consider the following event: <fire_fighting, [compartment, 'A'], [team, R5], [3:27, 3:45], +, ext>. It represents the fact that the token [compartment, 'A'], [team, R5] with the timestamp of [3:27,3:45] was *introduced* into the place fire_fighting and it came from *outside* of the given TIPN. In English the record reads: "A firefighting team R5 started to fight fire in compartment A sometime between 3:27 and 3:45".

Usually TIPN models are used within larger AI systems. Therefore, one of the most important attributes is whether the model learned by ML-TIPN improves the system performance. While being conceptually simple, such a wrapper approach would not be practically feasible as frequent evaluations of candidate TIPN models via running the entire performance element are cost-prohibitive. Therefore, we adopt a filter approach and assess the quality of a TIPN model with the following computationally less expensive scoring metric. ML-TIPN's score of a Time Interval Petri Net is inversely proportional to a weighted sum of the following five terms: (i) the total number of known arcs in the TIPN, (ii) the total duration of all transition delays, (iii) the total size of all output arc operator tables, (iv) the total number of false positives (i.e., the events that the TIPN predicts but which were not recorded as a part of the historical data),

(v) the total number of false negatives (i.e., the events that the TIPN does not predict but which were indeed recorded as a part of the historical data). According to the scoring metric, larger TIPN models are penalized more as well as the models that are less accurate with respect to the validation set of historical data. Additionally, the user has control over the weights of the individual terms in the scoring metric. This provides a way of specifying the learning bias. For instance, increasing the weight of component (i) above will encourage ML-TIPN to seek more compact models even if they are less accurate.

3 Learning Process

ML-TIPN learns by conducting a beam search in the space of all TIPNs that are refinements of the domain theory (i.e., of the incompletely specified initial TIPNs P_0). The learning process is carried out in N iterations where N is the number of events in the training data $e_1, \ldots, e_N$. At each iteration t, event e_t is retrieved from the historical data in chronological order. Then the population P_{t-1} of B_t partially specified TIPN models is refined into the new population P_t.

Specifically, if event e_t is external (i.e., is not to be modeled by the TIPN being learned) then ML-TIPN merely updates the marking of every TIPN in population P_{t-1} and copies them all to the new population P_t. If the event e_t is internal (i.e., is to be modeled by the TIPN being learned) then ML-TIPN uses the set of the refinement operators to modify each TIPN in the population P_{t-1} in an attempt to make them able to model the event. Specifically, four types of refinement operators can be applied to a TIPN: (i) converting arc's type from 'unknown' to one of the standard types, (ii) extending the time delay of a transition, (iii) adding a record to an output arc operator table, and (iv) leaving the TIPN intact.

For instance, if an event indicates a fire spread from compartment A to compartment B, all TIPNs in the population that model fire spread can get their output arc operator updated with the record $A \rightarrow B$. Another example: suppose there is an unknown-type arc from the place "Hot" to transition "Engulfment" and the latter leads to the place "On Fire". Suppose also that compartment C is known to be hot (i.e., there is a corresponding token in place "Hot"). Then if ML-TIPN observes an internal event of compartment C catching on fire, it can refine the arc's type from unknown to enabling.

Note that there may be several ways of refining a particular TIPN so that it models the event at hand. All such refinements will be performed, each producing a refined TIPN. All of these refinements are put in the new population P_t. Then ML-TIPN will sort the new population P_t using the scoring metric and the validation set $e'_1, \ldots, e'_{N'}$ and retain B_t top-ranked ones. The beam search width B_t is then updated. Similar to simulated-annealing search, the beam width is gradually decreased as higher quality TIPNs are expected to reside in P_t.

After N iterations, the training data $e_1, \ldots, e_N$ will be exhausted. ML-TIPN will then refine the final population P_N in all possible ways, sort the resulting TIPNs on the validation set using the scoring metric, and output the M top-ranked of them. Note that the number M is supplied by the user giving him/her an opportunity to hand-pick from several learned TIPNs.

4 Empirical Evaluation

The first test of the ML-TIPN learning algorithm illustrates learning a TIPN model of greatly simplified fire spread in the domain of ship damage control. The input scenario involves a fire spread in five adjacent compartments (A, B, C, D, E). The corresponding event record ($e_i = e'_i$ for all i), which is the input to the ML-TIPN algorithm, is shown in Table 1. For the sake of simplicity and space, we will start with the prior domain theory P_0 in the form of the two-element TIPN set shown in Figure 1. Additionally, we will set the beam width B_t to ∞ for all t. The left TIPN in the figure represents the hypothesis that fire boundaries have no effect on fire spread while the right TIPN supposes that they disable fire spread. Note that both candidates are incompletely specified in terms of the temporal information and arc operators. Namely, the arc operator is extendable and already has one record in it: B $\rightarrow$ E meaning that the user knows *a priori* that fire can spread from compartment B to compartment E.

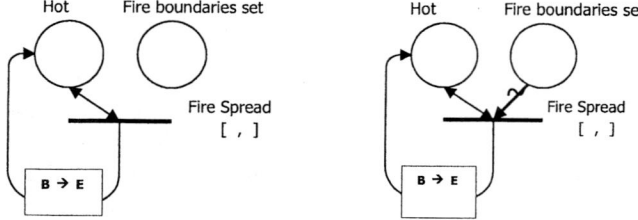

Fig. 1. Prior domain theory used for the ML-TIPN demonstration shown encoded as two TIPNs. Note that the TIPNs are incomplete as their delay intervals are empty and the output arc table contains one record only.

Table 1. Event record for the simple fire spread scenario

Event	Description
<hot,A,[1,1],+,external>	primary damage in compartment A
<fbs,B,[2,2],+,external>	fire boundaries set on B prevent fire spread from B to E
<hot,B,[2,2],+,internal>	fire spreads from A to B with a 1-min delay
<hot,C,[3,3],+,internal>	fire spreads from A to C with a 2-min delay
<hot,D,[5,5],+,internal>	fire spreads from A to D with a 4-min delay

The first two external events e_1 = <hot,A, [1,1],+, external>, e_2 = <fbs,B, [2,2],+, external> and one internal event e_3 = <hot,B, [2,2],+, internal> result in four TIPNs in the population P_3. Then ML-TIPN processes the internal event e_4 = <hot,C, [3,3],+, internal> thereby generating nine TIPNs in P_4. After the final event e_5 = <hot,D, [5,5],+, internal>, the total number of TIPNs in the population becomes 27. The two TIPNs ranked highest with respect to $e_1, \ldots, e_5$ are shown in Figure 2.

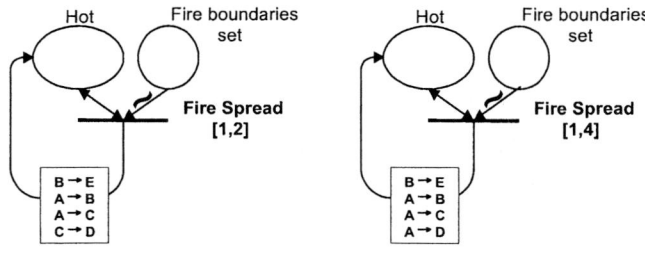

Fig. 2. Two top-ranked models learned by ML-TIPN. The TIPN on the right is accurate.

The second experiment involved larger test and training sets, and the goal was to learn a more complex fire spread model. *Primary damage* ignitions were randomly set in one or more of 476 ship compartments, and physical and intelligent agent simulators propagated the fire to other compartments. Fire would spread to a neighbor compartment if the firefighting efforts were delayed by more than five minutes. Otherwise, a *fire out* event was recorded.

Chain fires were defined as fires in compartments other than the ones with primary damage. Table 1 shows a primary damage event in compartment A, and three chain fires of length 1 in compartments B, C, and D. If the fire spreads to compartment E, then this would create a chain fire of length 2 (A to B to E). Chain fires are particularly challenging to learning as mispredicting one fire usually renders the rest of the fire spread chain causally inexplicable.

Each output event of the simulation became a part of the historical data with a 10% probability of one of the following three errors (i.e., training data noise): (i) its time interval was randomly altered, (ii) the compartment identifier was randomly modified, and (iii) the event was left out of the event record completely. Below is a small fragment of an actual event log $\{e_i\}$:

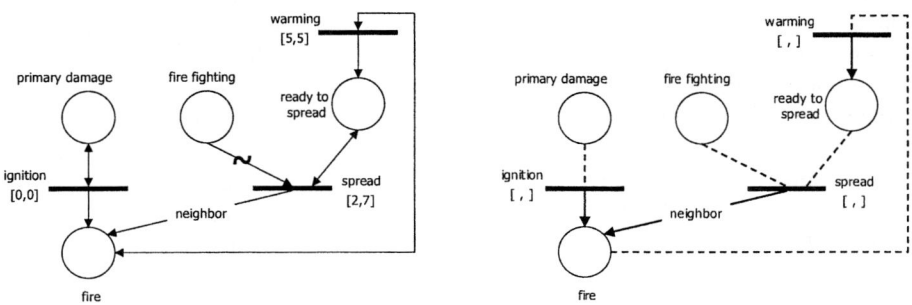

Fig. 3. Left: manually designed TIPN. **Right:** Prior domain theory P_0 expressed as an incomplete TIPN. Dashed lines represent possible/unknown arcs. Temporal interval delays, arc directionality, and enablement/disablement conditions are left to be learned by ML-TIPN.

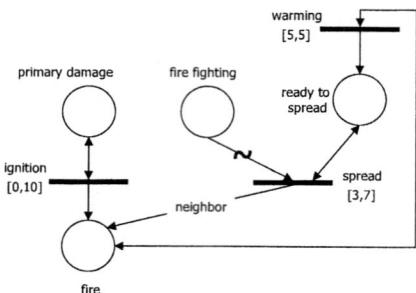

Fig. 4. Time Interval Petri Net learned by ML-TIPN from 30 training events

```
primary_damage('3-142-1',[9,9]).
fire_detected('3-142-1',[9,9]).
fire_fighting('3-142-1',[16,17]).
fire_detected('3-142-0',[19,19]).
primary_damage('1-54-2',[32,32]).
fire_detected('1-54-2',[32,32]).
fire_fighting('1-54-2',[36,37]).
fire_out('1-54-2',[40,41]).
```

Here [t1,t2] represents the time interval of the event and 'D-F-P' is the deck-frame-position compartment identifier. For instance, the first two lines indicate a fire in compartment '3-142-1' at time 9 caused by primary damage there at the same time.

The machine learning objective of the ML-TIPN algorithm was to produce a model for fire events in terms of primary_damage, fightfire, fire_out, and other fire events. Figure 3 shows a TIPN manually designed to model the simulated crisis phenomena *without the noise*. The initial domain theory P_0 given to ML-TIPN is shown in Figure 3 as an incomplete TIPN. We then generated eight training and eight testing data sets of 2, 5, 7, 10, 15, 20, 30, and 50 events. A cross-validation study was carried out by training the algorithms on each of the eight training sets and testing them on each of the eight testing sets. ML-TIPN was run with an initial beam width B_1 of 150. It was decreased by the factor of 0.9 at each iteration until it reached 5 after which it was kept constant. The scoring metric weights were fixed at $(3, 1, 2, 7, 10)$.

The three types of noise in the data present a considerable difficulty to learning as many events cannot be causally explained. Figure 4 shows the TIPN model learned from the training scenario of 30 events. Similar models were learned from 50-event scenarios. Comparing it to the hand-engineered TIPN in Figure 3, we note that all causal conditions are properly learned and the transition delay intervals have only minor differences. This is a result of noise as well as small size of the training data set.

5 Summary

This paper presents results of the first attempt to apply machine learning to the construction of Time Interval Petri Nets (TIPNs) for an AI task. Using an incomplete domain theory and noisy training data, an algorithm called ML-TIPN successfully constructed a fire spread TIPN in the domain of ship damage control. Petri net models of concurrent processes have been widely used in computer science because they have the advantages of providing an intuitive graphical representation of the processes being modeled and because of their strong theoretical foundation. This paper strengthens their relevance to AI problems by demonstrating that parts of TIPN construction can be automated.

We appreciate programming by Tony Czupryna. Feedback from anonymous reviewers, KBS members, Valeriy K. Bulitko, Dan Roth, and Stefan Wrobel has been invaluable. The research was supported in part by ONR Grant N00014-95-1-0749, ARL Grant DAAL01-96-2-0003, NRL Contract N00014-97-C-2061, and the National Science and Engineering Research Council.

References

1. Costa Miranda, M.: Modeling and analysis of a multi-agent system using colored Petri nets. In Portinale, L., Valette, R., Zhang, D., eds.: Proceedings of the Workshop on Application of Petri Nets to Intelligent System Development, Williamsburg, USA (1999) 59–70
2. Bulitko, V., Wilkins, D.: Qualitative simulation of temporal concurrent processes using Time Interval Petri Nets. Artificial Intelligence **144** (2003) 95 – 124

Model Based Abnormal Acoustic Source Detection Using a Microphone Array

Heungkyu Lee[1], Jounghoon Beh[2], June Kim[3], and Hanseok Ko[2]

[1] Dept. of Visual Information Processing,
Korea University, Seoul, Korea
[2] Dept. of Electronics and Computer Engineering,
Korea University, Seoul, Korea
[3] Dept. of Information and Communication Engineering,
Seokyeong University

Abstract. This paper proposes the model based detection method of abnormal acoustic source using a microphone array. General source location algorithm using a microphone array can be used to locate a dominant acoustic source, while this does not verify whether the detected source is permitted one or not on outdoor environments. It is difficult to discern it among a natural environmental sound. Thus, to cope with this problem, we propose the out-of-normal acoustic rejection method based on N-best likelihood ratio test using natural environmental sound models. In order to evaluate the proposed algorithm, a real-time DSP was constructed, and experimental evaluation is described.

1 Introduction

This paper is motivated by the need of abnormal acoustic source detection capability to compensate the detection performance of image sensor [1][2]. When the image sensor rotates between left to right or vice versa, specific boundary region that is out of camera view is not covered for security monitoring. Thus, abnormal intrusion of suspicious person can be occurred using such a small defect. To cope with this issue, microphone array technology can be used to locate an abnormal acoustic source and obtain its coordinates. The abnormal acoustic source is defined as speech signal and manually made acoustic signal. Using the microphone array technology, a Time Difference Of Arrival (TDOA) computation between the signals of array is done as a fist step. Because the accuracy of estimation for direction of arrival angle (DOA) is especially poor on noisy outdoor environment, we employ the end-point detection algorithm to detect the acoustic source greater than the pre-defined and adapted threshold value. In this point, we can not know whether the detected acoustic source is valid one or not. There are sounds of wind, rain, bird's singing, thunder, and a breaking wave as a natural one on outdoor environments. Meanwhile, manually made acoustic source is various like sounds of speech, a footstep of the person, breaking a steel barred window, and so on. Thus, to resolve this issue, we model the sounds of natural environments using HMM (Hidden Markov Model), and then we verify the detected acoustic source. By using the environmental sound models as anti-models, we propose the out-of-normal acoustic rejection method based on N-best likelihood ratio test (LRT). Figure 1 describes the overall process flow.

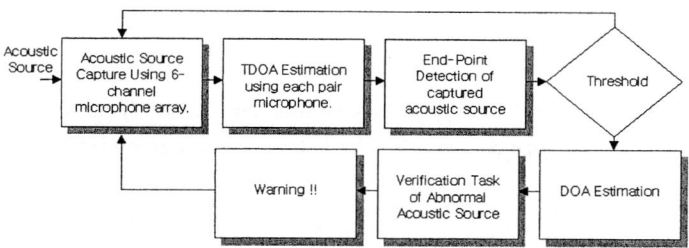

Fig. 1. System block-diagram for detecting abnormal acoustic source

2   Detection and Verification of Abnormal Acoustic Source

For abnormal acoustic source detection as shown in Figure 1, six-channel microphone array is used to locate a dominant acoustic source in a given environment. The distance between microphones is 10 *Cm* and we use the microphone pair. To reduce the false acceptance of normal acoustic source and estimation error of the DOA, we apply the DOA computation procedure just to the detected source using end-point detection algorithm [3] that is the most widely utilized in speech recognition technology. Among various end-point detection approaches, we apply the energy-based methods that are most widely applied solutions to this problem using some parameters: signal energy, zero-crossing rate, duration, and linear prediction error energy. This method is applied after a time difference of arrival computation is done using delay-and-sum beam-forming. Next, to estimate the DOA, a time difference of arrival computation for source location is used using the cross-power spectrum phase (CPSP) method [2]. We use only the phase information in the crosspower spectrum of the two signal because an effective approach is to whiten the input signals if no a priori knowledge about the statistics of the involved signals is available.

To verify whether the detected acoustic source is valid one or not, we apply the HMM decoding module, and then LRT test is performed. Because the manually made acoustic sources have lots of sounds, we utilizes the environmental sounds database as reverse models. That is, we make the acoustic models using environmental sounds database. And then, we employ the *N*-Best out-of-normal acoustic (OONA) rejection method for the final decision-making. If the detected acoustic source is decided as one of the employed acoustic models made by environmental sound database, the acoustic type is decided on the valid one. Otherwise, all of detected acoustic sources are considered as the abnormal acoustic type. The natural sound models of wind, rain, bird's sing, and the sound of waves breaking on the beach are made using Continuous Hidden Markov Model with 24 state, 16 mixture left-right HMM as a discriminate function. First, the verification procedure of abnormal acoustic source is computed by

$$W_k = \arg\max_k \left(L(O / \overline{\lambda}_{1,\ldots,k}) \right) \tag{1}$$

where O is the observation sequence, W_k is the most likely acoustic type, and $\overline{\lambda}$ is environmental sound models. Then, *N*-Best OONA rejection method based on subwords induced by likelihood ratio test (LRT) [4] as follows;

$$LRT(X) = \frac{P(X/H_0)}{P(X/H_1)} = \frac{P(O_n/\lambda_n)}{P(O_n/\overline{\lambda}_n)} \geq \eta \qquad (2)$$

where H_0 and H_1 means that hypothesis is true and false. η is a given threshold value. This equation can be changed for the N-best models given by

$$LRT(O_n) = \frac{1}{l_n}\left[\log P(O_n/\overline{\lambda}_0) - \frac{1}{nBest}\sum_{m=1}^{nBest}\log P(O_n/\overline{\lambda}_m)\right] \qquad (3)$$

where the model $\overline{\lambda}_0$ is an environmental sound model that has maximum likelihood scores and $\overline{\lambda}_m$ is environmental sound models that have N-best high likelihood scores. The variable, $nBest$ is the number of most likely sequences. Finally, the likelihood ratio is compared with given threshold value for verification task. If its value is below the threshold, the candidate is considered as abnormal one because it proves that the overall likelihood scores are similar and there is no corresponding model in given acoustic model. Thus, we decide that the detected acoustic source is abnormal one.

3 Experimental Results

For acoustic source input to detect an occurred acoustic sound, the sampling rate is 11Khz PCM. Acoustic signals are analyzed within 125ms frame with 10ms lapped into 39th order feature vector that has 13th order MFCCs including log energy and their 1st and 2st derivatives. The training data set is collected from the natural scene and previously recorded waves. The total number of classes is five, and total recording time is about 3 hours. It is composed of sounds of wind, rain, bird's singing, rain and thunder, and a breaking wave. For testing a data, Aurora2 speech DB is used.

The sound model is constructed using the left-to-right Continuous Hidden Markov Model (CHMM) having 50 states and 16 mixtures. First, we evaluate the recognition performance when we apply the environmental sound waves to the proposed system in order to verify the training accuracy. In addition, this is to verify that the constructed acoustic model is robust even when the false alarm (environmental sounds) is detected because the false alarm should be discarded. The result according to the number of mixtures is shown in Table 1.

Table 1. Recognition performance to verify the training accuracy

No. of mixture	1	2	4	8	16	32
Recognition rate (%)	86.02	94.37	95.26	96.20	96.84	96.08

To evaluate the OONA rejection rate, the speech data using Aurora 2 DB is applied. In the proposed system, speech signal is considered as abnormal acoustic source. As shown in Table 2, all of speech data is classified as speech data. That is, all of speech data is decided as an abnormal acoustic sound. Some of environmental sound type is considered as other type. But, this result does not affect the final result because the all of environmental sounds are classified as valid class. From the result, abnormal acoustic verification rate showed good performance when a speech signal is detected. This result is due to the fact that feature vectors of speech signals using MFCCs are very different with the one of environmental sounds. In addition, the manually made acoustic signals also showed that that they are very different with the environmental sounds even if the test data are not enough to evaluate.

Table 2. Confusion matrix (TND: Total Number of Data, ACC:Accuracy, %)

	Speech	Beach	Bird	Rain	Thunder	Wind	TND	ACC
Speech	1064	0	0	0	0	0	1064	100
Beach	0	268	1	0	0	0	269	99.6
Bird	0	5	18	0	0	0	23	78.3
Rain	0	2	0	178	0	0	180	98.9
Thunder	0	1	0	26	3	0	30	10.0
Wind	0	0	0	0	0	15	15	100

4 Conclusions

In order to verify whether the detected source is valid or not, we proposed the out-of-normal acoustic rejection method based on the N-best likelihood ratio test using natural environmental sound models. From the result, the verification rate of abnormal acoustic source showed good performance when the speech signal is detected.

Acknowledgements

This work was supported by grant No. 10012805 from the Korea Institute of Industrial Technology Evaluation & Planning Foundation.

References

[1] J.A. Cadzow, "Multiple source location-the signal subspace approach," IEEE Trans. On Signal Processing, Vol. 38, Issue 7, pp. 1110-1125, July 1990.
[2] C.H. Knapp, and G.C. Carter, "The Generalized Correlation Method for Estimation of Time Delay", IEEE Trans. On Speech and Signal Processing, Vol. ASSP-24, n.4, August 1976.
[3] C.E. Mokbel and G. F. A. Chollet, "Automatic word recognition in cars," IEEE Trans. Speech and Audio Processing, vol 3, pp. 346-356, Sept 1995.
[4] E. Lleida, and R.C. Rose, "Utterance verification in continuous speech recognition," IEEE Trans. On Speech and Audio Processing, Vol. 8, March 2000.

Improving the Mobile Phone Habitat - Learning Changes in User's Profiles

Robert Bridle and Eric McCreath

Department of Computer Science, Faculty of Engineering and Information Technology, The Australian National University

Abstract. Mobile phones are becoming a popular platform for a range of applications. However, due to size restrictions, the interfaces of these applications can be difficult to use. Customising an interface for a particular user offers the potential to improve an interface's efficiency. In this paper, we propose customising a mobile phone's Profile application. We apply a machine learning approach to discover concepts that describe a user's profile-activations in terms of their scheduled appointments. We found that it is possible to learn useful concepts, which maybe used to improve the users interaction with mobile phone devices.

1 Introduction

More Australians have access to mobile phones than desktop computers[1]. However, as noted by Amant, Horton and Ritter[6], user interfaces on such devices are often difficult to use. In this paper we focus on a small but important application, the Profiles application. The profile of a mobile includes attributes such as: ringing tones, ringing volume, vibration on/off, keypad tones, and SMS alerts. These profiles enable users to quickly change the setting of the phone depending upon the context they find themselves in. Yet it is easy to forget to change the profile of the phone for the current context. e.g. your phone rings in the middle of a movie, or you miss a number of important calls because you left the phone in *Silent* mode. In this paper we investigate how a direct application of a standard Bayesian learning approach may be used to learn when and how a user changes their profile over time. This domain provides a number of interesting challenges for machine learning because the training data involves temporal attributes, and the training set size is very small. These challenges have been touched on briefly in previous work, most notable that of on-line command-line prediction[2,4] and in Mitchell's calendar apprentice system[5].

2 The Profiles Application and Learning Approach

The Profiles application exists on nearly all mobile phones. The Profile application consists of a set of profiles. Each profile defines properties including: ring tone, ring volume, SMS alert tone, keypad tones and warning tones. The Profiles application is used to change which profile is active. The Profiles application we investigated included the default profiles: *General, Meeting, Silent, Outdoors, Offline* and *Pager*. Each profile defines properties consistent with the activity that their name suggests. Other user-defined profiles may be added. A problem with the Profiles application is that a user has to select which profile they want active every time their situation changes. However, often the profile required by a user is dependent upon the activity they are undertaking. We propose a learning approach that can determine the relationship between a user's activities and the profile they want active. Automating profile-activations would save the user from specifying rules and reduce interactions with their mobile phone.

We investigated using a mobile phone's *Calendar* application, to gather information on a user's scheduled appointments. We considered determining a concept that would describe the relationship between a user's appointments and the profile they activated. An obvious example of a user's schedule determining the profile they activate, would occur when a user schedules a meeting. It is likely a user will select the *Silent* profile for the duration of the scheduled meeting and the *General* profile afterwards. In addition, it is unlikely that a user will activate the *Silent* profile exactly on an appointment's scheduled start-time or select the *General* profile exactly on an appointment's scheduled finish-time. Any learning approach must not only determine which appointments govern which profile-activations, but also the amount of time appropriate between when a profile activates and when an appointment starts or finishes.

We implemented a profile monitoring application on a Nokia^{TM}Series 60 mobile phone. Whenever a user activated a profile a training example was generated. Each training example was represented by a set of attributes and a class label. The attributes consisted of: the time, the location (nearest cell-tower) and the details (subject and location) of appointments scheduled for that day. The class label represented the profile that was activated, either: *General, Meeting, Silent, Outdoors, Offline* or *Pager*. A probabilistic approach was used to generate a concept for each class[3]. From all training examples gathered over a week, a user's week-long calendar schedule was constructed. For each class, we considered every possible model of profile-activations about the user's schedule. We also considered minute time-periods, that ranged from 20 minutes before to 20 minutes after appointment start or finish times. The most likely model became the target concept. We assumed that the likelihood of each of model was given by:

$$L(model) = \lambda^k (1-\lambda)^{n-k} \tag{1}$$

where n is the number of times the model could correspond to a training instance, and k is the number of times the model does correspond to a training instance. The value λ represents the probability that the profile activation is carried out for the appropriate scheduled item. For each model, and for all possible values of λ, we determine the model and λ values of highest likelihood. For each class, we present the user with the most likely models for each appointment subject. These models are the induced hypotheses.

The probabilistic approach described has a number of properties that make it suitable for the intended learning task. Firstly, we assumed that users would sometimes forget to activate a profile. A probabilistic model makes the learning approach robust to this kind of noise. Secondly, a probabilistic model allows us to quantify the uncertainty in learnt concepts. We can make decision on the usefulness of concepts based on this measure of uncertainty. Finally, probabilistic models can be highly parameterised, enabling us to place a strong bias on the learner's hypothesis language. This allows us to restrict the possible concepts considered by the learner.

3 Experimental Results and Discussion

We gave 4 users a Nokia™ phone. The phone was installed with our profile monitoring application. The profile monitoring application ran unobtrusively in the background and was used to gather training examples (as described in Section 2). We monitored each user's profile-activations over a period of one week. The learning approach described in Section 2 was then invoked off-line on the training examples collected over the week. Table 1, shows the concepts generated for each user. Interpreting these parameters we find that User 1 is expected to activate the *Silent* profile 3 minutes after the start of appointments with the subject [Pathology], 5 minutes after the start of appointments with the subject [Movie] and so on. An important question, is whether the concepts generated would be of future use to the user. We asked each user whether they would accept or reject the generated concepts. For those concepts that were rejected, we also asked the user to indicate the reason for the rejection. Table 2 shows the rejected concepts.

Table 1 and Table 2 show that at least one of the concepts generated for each user is accepted. Given the limited amount of data provided to the learner,

Table 1. The concepts identified for the 4 users after a week of training examples

User 1				User 2			
Profile	Subject	Time	λ	Profile	Subject	Time	λ
Silent(start)	[Pathology]	3.0	0.99	Silent(start)	[Auscc]	-2.0	0.90
Silent(start)	[Movie]	5.0	0.99	Silent(start)	[Gym]	-5.0	0.90
Silent(start)	[TeamLunch]	0.0	0.99	Silent(start)	[Seminar]	-5.0	0.90
Silent(start)	[Pds]	-6.0	0.99	Silent(start)	[Sam farewell]	-2.0	0.90
Silent(start)	[JavaTraining]	-20.0	0.99	General(finish)	[Auscc]	6.0	0.90
General(finish)	[Pathology]	-9.0	0.99	General(finish)	[Gym]	8.0	0.90
General(finish)	[TeamLunch]	0.0	0.99	General(finish)	[Seminar]	2.0	0.90
General(finish)	[Pds]	8.0	0.99				
General(finish)	[TeamMeeting]	7.0	0.99				

User 3				User 4			
Profile	Subject	Time	λ	Profile	Subject	Time	λ
Meeting(start)	[AI]	-10.0	0.80	Silent(start)	[Lunch]	-7.0	0.99
Meeting(start)	[OS]	-10.0	0.80	General(finish)	[Lunch]	11.0	0.99
General(finish)	[AI]	10.0	0.80				

Table 2. The concepts rejected by the 4 users, reason are given below each concept. Note, User 3 and User 4 did not reject any of their concepts.

User 1 - Rejected the Following Concepts.

Profile	Subject	Parameters Time	λ
Silent(start)	[Pathology]	3.0	0.99
Silent(start)	[Movie]	5.0	0.99
Silent(start)	[TeamLunch]	0.0	0.99
General(finish)	[Pathology]	-9.0	0.99
General(finish)	[TeamLunch]	0.0	0.99

Reason: *Silent* profile should occur before and not 3 minutes after the start of [Pathology].
Reason: *Silent* profile should occur before and not 5 minutes after the start of [Movie].
Reason: *Silent* profile should occur before and not 0 minutes after the start of [TeamLunch].
Reason: *General* profile should occur after and not 9 minutes before the finish of [Pathology].
Reason: *General* profile should occur after and not 0 minutes before the finish of [TeamLunch].

User 2 - Rejected the Following Concepts.

Profile	Subject	Parameters Time	λ
Silent(start)	[Sam farewell]	-2.0	0.90

Reason: The appointment [Sam farewell] will not occur again.

this is a promising result. It is important to note that the concepts learnt do not completely capture all of the user's profile-activation intentions. For instance, for User 1, User 2 and User 3 in Table 1, the set of appointment subjects in the *Silent* profile concept is different from the set of appointment subjects in the *General* profile concept. If these concepts formed a rule-base, then the *Silent* profile would activate before some appointment subjects and then remain active until the user intervened. A user can not entirely rely on the generated concepts to describe their intentions. Instead, the generated rules would be of most use augmenting a manually defined rule-base.

4 Conclusion

This paper has investigated a method for learning the concepts that govern profile-activations on a mobile phone. The Profile application learning environment posed several interesting challenges. These included training data with temporal attributes, and a very small training set. Despite this, we demonstrated a learning approach that could find useful concepts.

References

1. Australian Bureau of Statistics. Measures of a knowledge-based economy and society. *Australia, Australia Now*, (Cat. no. 8146.0), 2003.
2. B. Davison and H. Hirsh. Probabilistic online action prediction. In *Intelligent Environments: Papers from the AAAI 1998 Spring Symposium, Technical Report SS-98-02.*, pages 148–154, 1998.

3. R. Duda, P. Hart, and D. Stork. *Pattern Classification*. John Wiley and Sons, 2nd edition, 2001.
4. B. Korvemaker and R. Greiner. Predicting unix command lines: Adjusting to user patterns. In *Proceedings of the Seventeenth National Conference on AI and Twelfth Conference on Innovative Applications of AI*, pages 230–235, 2000.
5. T. Mitchell, R. Caruana, D. Freitag, J. McDermott, and D. Zabowski. Experience with a learning personal assistant. *Communications of the ACM*, 37(7):80–91, 1994.
6. R. St. Amant, T. Horton, and F. Ritter. Model-based evaluation of cell phone menu interaction. In *Proceedings of the Conference on Human Factors in Computing Systems*, pages 343–350, 2004.

A Stigmergy Based Approach to Data Mining

Manu De Backer[1], Raf Haesen[1], David Martens[1], and Bart Baesens[1,2]

[1] Department of Applied Economic Sciences, K.U.Leuven, Belgium,
Naamsestraat 69, B-3000 Leuven, Belgium
{Manu.Debacker, Raf.Haesen, David.Martens, Bart.Baesens}@econ.kuleuven.be
[2] University of Southampton, School of Management, United Kingdom,
Highfield Southampton, SO17 1BJ, United Kingdom
Bart@soton.ac.uk

Abstract. In this paper, we report on the use of ant systems in the data mining field capable of extracting comprehensible classifiers from data. The ant system used is a $\mathcal{MAX}$-$\mathcal{MIN}$ ant system which differs from the originally proposed ant systems in its ability to explore bigger parts of the solution space, yielding better performing rules. Furthermore, we are able to include intervals in the rules resulting in less and shorter rules. Our experiments show a significant improvement of the performance both in accuracy and comprehensibility, compared to previous data mining techniques based on ant systems and other state-of-the-art classification techniques.

1 Introduction

In this paper we focus our attention on the use of an ant system capable of extracting comprehensible, accurate rules from categorical data that is competitive with state-of-the art classification techniques. Artificial ant systems are inspired on the behavior of real ant systems. The general idea of the system is the following [1]: a number of computational concurrent and asynchronous agents (ants) move through their environment and by doing so incrementally construct a solution for the problem at hand. Ants move by applying a stochastic local decision policy based on two parameters, called the trail value (pheromone value) and a problem dependent value (heuristic value). Ant systems have shown to be a viable method for attacking hard combinatorial optimization problems. Stützle et al. [6] advocate that improved performance can be obtained by a stronger exploration of the best solutions. According to them, the key to achieve best performance is to combine an improved exploitation of the best solutions found with an effective mechanism for avoiding early search stagnation. A $\mathcal{MAX}$-$\mathcal{MIN}$ ant system ($\mathcal{MMAS}$) differs from a normal ant system in three aspects. First of all, after each iteration only the best ant adds pheromone to its trail. Secondly, the range of possible pheromone trails on each solution component is limited to an interval $[\tau_{min}, \tau_{max}]$. Finally, each trail is initialized with a pheromone value of τ_{max}.

2 AntMiner+

The first application of ant systems for data mining was reported in [4], where the authors described the AntMiner algorithm for the discovery of classification rules. Extensions and optimizations of the AntMiner are described in AntMiner2 and AntMiner3 [3]. The aim is to extract simple **if-then-else** rules from data. We build further on the work introduced before and try to resolve some issues. First of all, we define the environment as a directed, acyclic construction graph which allows a clear representation of the problem domain and considerably improves the performance of the ant system. Furthermore, we introduce the better performing $\mathcal{MAX}$-$\mathcal{MIN}$ ant system for mining rules.

The construction graph is defined as follows: each 'column' or node group corresponds to a variable and every 'row' corresponds to a value. Each ant going from node $n_{i,j}$ to node $n_{i+1,k}$ adds the term $< V_{i+1} = Value_k >$ to its rule. To allow for rules where not all the variables are involved, an extra *dummy node* is added whose value is undetermined, meaning it can take any of the values available. Although only categorical variables can be used in our implementation, we make a distinction between nominal and ordinal variables. Each nominal variable has one node group, but for the ordinal however, we build two node groups to allow for intervals to be chosen by the ants. The first node group corresponds to the lower bound of the interval and should thus be interpreted as $< V_{i+1} \geq Value_k >$, the second node group determines the upper bound, giving $< V_{i+2} \leq Value_k >$. This allows to have less, shorter and actually better rules. Figure 1 gives a general view of the construction graph with the first variable being nominal and the second one ordinal, hence having two node groups.

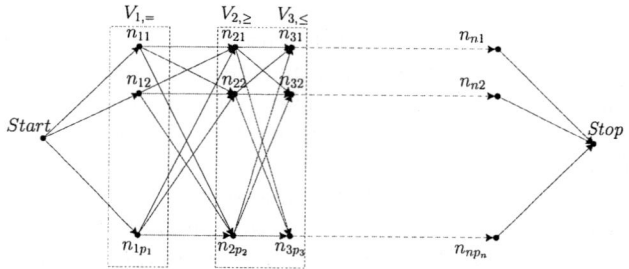

Fig. 1. AntMiner+ construction graph

The edge probability $P_{(n_{i,j}, n_{i+1,k})}$ is the probability that an ant which is in node $n_{i,j}$ (node for which variable V_i is equal to its jth value) will go to node $n_{i+1,k}$. This probability is defined as follows:

$$P_{(n_{i,j}, n_{i+1,k})} = \frac{[\tau_{(n_{i,j}, n_{i+1,k})}]^\alpha \cdot [\eta_{n_{i+1,k}}]^\beta}{\sum_{l=1}^{|V_{i+1}|} [\tau_{(n_{i,j}, n_{i+1,l})}]^\alpha \cdot [\eta_{n_{i+1,l}}]^\beta} \quad (1)$$

Notice that this probability is dependent on two values: the heuristic value and the pheromone value. The importance of these values is determined by the α and β parameters. The heuristic value gives for each node a notion of its importance in the problem domain. For data mining, the importance is measured by the number of data points that are covered (described) by a value. Since we extract rules for the $class = 1$ case, we define the heuristic value for node $n_{i,k}$ as follows:

$$\eta_{n_{i,k}} = \frac{|V_i = Value_k \text{ \& } class = 1|}{|V_i = Value_k|} \quad (2)$$

Generally, updating the pheromone trail of an ant system is accomplished in two phases, viz evaporation and reinforcement. Applying the ideas of $\mathcal{MAX}$-$\mathcal{MIN}$ ant systems has direct consequences for the pheromone updating rule. First of all, evaporation in an ant system is accomplished by diminishing the pheromone level of each trail according to the following rule, with ρ the evaporation factor:

$$\tau_{(n_{i,j}, n_{i+1,k})}(t+1) = \rho \cdot \tau_{(n_{i,j}, n_{i+1,k})}(t) \quad (3)$$

Secondly, in a $\mathcal{MAX}$-$\mathcal{MIN}$ ant system, reinforcement of the pheromone trail is only applied to the best ant's path. Taking into account the evaporation factor as well, the update rule for the best ant's path can be described as:

$$\tau_{(n_{i,j}, n_{i+1,k})}(t+1) = \rho \cdot \tau_{(n_{i,j}, n_{i+1,k})}(t) + \Delta^{best} \quad (4)$$

Clearly, the reinforcement of the best ant's path should be proportional to the quality of the path. For data mining we define the quality of a rule by the sum of its *confidence* and its *coverage*, as defined by equation 5. Confidence is an indication of the number of correctly classified data points by a rule compared to the total number of data points covered by that rule. The coverage gives an indication of the overall importance of the specific rule by looking at the number of correctly classified data points over the total number of data points.

$$\Delta^{best} = \underbrace{\frac{|rule_{best-ant} \text{ \& } Class = 1|}{|rule_{best-ant}|}}_{\text{confidence}} + \underbrace{\frac{|rule_{best-ant} \text{ \& } Class = 1|}{|Cov = 0|}}_{\text{coverage}} \quad (5)$$

An additional restriction imposed by the $\mathcal{MAX}$-$\mathcal{MIN}$ ant systems is that the pheromone level of the edges is restricted by an upper-bound (τ_{max}) and a lower-bound (τ_{min}).

3 Experiments and Results

We applied AntMiner+ to several publicly available datasets. We conducted 10 runs for each dataset where the data is randomized and the first $\frac{2}{3}$ of the data is taken as training data and the remaining $\frac{1}{3}$ as test data. Experiments are conducted on the tic-tac-toe and Breast Cancer Wisconsin datasets [2], and Ripley's dataset [5]. The results are shown in Table 1, also included are the

Table 1. Average out-of-sample performance

	tic-tac-toe		BCW		Ripley	
	inst	attr	inst	attr	inst	attr
	958	9	699	9	1250	2
Technique	Acc	#R	Acc	#R	Acc	#R
AntMiner+	**99.75**	8	**95.58**	1	**89.41**	3.9
AntMiner1	70.99	16.5	92.63	10.1		
AntMiner3	76.58	18.6	94.32	13.2		
C4.5	76.96	23	94.38	6	89.04	6

results for C4.5 and the results published for the tic-tac-toe and Breast Cancer Wisconsin datasets from AntMiner1 and AntMiner3 [3]. For each dataset, the number of instances (inst) and attributes (attr) as well as the accuracy and number of generated rules are displayed. The best performance measure for each dataset is shown in boldface.

The better results of AntMiner+ can be attributed to our $\mathcal{MAX}$-$\mathcal{MIN}$ approach, our simple construction graph with the inclusion of dummy nodes, as well as our ability to include intervals in our rules.

4 Conclusion

Ant systems are a nature inspired technique where ants communicate through the principle of stigmergy. Although ants have a limited memory and perform actions based on local information only, the ants are able to come to complex behavior due to self-organization and indirect communication. We defined our environment as a simple, though complete construction graph so that the ants can construct rules while going from source to sink. The solution provided by AntMiner+ provides comprehensible, accurate classifiers and performs better than or competitive with state-of-the-art classification techniques.

References

1. M. Dorigo, V. Maniezzo, and A. Colorni. Positive feedback as a search strategy. Technical Report 91016, Dipartimento di Elettronica e Informatica, Politecnico di Milano, IT, 1991.
2. S. Hettich and S. D. Bay. The uci kdd archive [http://kdd.ics.uci.edu], 1996.
3. B. Liu, H. A. Abbass, and B. McKay. Classification rule discovery with ant colony optimization. *IEEE Computational Intelligence Bulletin*, 3(1):31–35, 2004.
4. R. S. Parpinelli, H. S. Lopes, and A. A. Freitas. An ant colony based system for data mining: Applications to medical data. In *Proceedings of the Genetic and Evolutionary Computation Conference (GECCO-2001)*, pages 791–797, San Francisco, California, USA, 7-11 2001. Morgan Kaufmann.
5. B. D. Ripley. Neural networks and related methods for classification. *J. Roy. Statist. Soc. B*, 56:409–456, 1994.
6. T. Stützle and H. Hoos. $\mathcal{MAX}$-$\mathcal{MIN}$ ant system. *Future Generation Computer Systems*, 16(8):889–914, 2000.

Mining Domain-Driven Correlations in Stock Markets

Li Lin[1,2], Dan Luo[1], and Li Liu[1]

[1] Faculty of Information Technology, University of Technology, Sydney,
NSW 2007, Australia
{Linli, Dluo, Liliu}@it.uts.edu.au
http://www-staff.it.uts.edu.au/~linli
[2] Capital Market CRC, Sydney,
NSW 2000, Australia

Abstract. There have been many technical trading rules in stock market since the first stock exchange founded. Along with the developing of computer technology, the technical trading rules are playing more and more important roles in the stock market trading system. However, there are many problems also occurred, such as the huge database, inefficiency, etc. So, the in-depth data mining technology is becoming a powerful tool to overcome the shortage of the current technologies. In this paper, we give some applications of in-depth data mining method: to find the optimal range, to find the stock-rule pair and find the relationship between the number of pair and investment. This method can improve both efficiency and effectiveness.

1 Introduction

In the stock market or any other asset trading market, computer becomes a very powerful tool to do more and more work instead of manually. So, the technical trading rule, which is based on the historical data to predict the trading signals in the future data, is the very practicable and convenient method when the users want to get trading alert signals, to compute the return and risk, to decide the investment amount, and so on. Most current research is about how to find the new trading rules [2, 5], How to generate signals for one rule one stock [3]. But, which rule is suitable for some special stocks? Which parameter value is better for the rule to make more profit or higher return? How many stocks are suitable for a large amount investment? To solve these problems, the in-depth data mining method is applied to find the best solutions for the above questions.

The paper is organized as follows: In section 2, three in-depth technical applications are introduced: (1) finding an optimal sub-range; (2) finding the stock-rule pairs; and (3) finding the number of pairs for a large amount investment. Finally, the conclusion and future work are summarized in section 3.

2 Applications of In-Depth Method

Technical trading rules are some mathematics formulas, which can be very easily implemented by computer program. So it is very useful and popular used in stock trading systems. But, they also have some problems, such as: when the data base is too huge, the efficiency is lower; and, the stocks are quite different, so one trading rule is not suitable for any different kind stocks. So, in the following sections, we introduced two methods to solve the problems: sub-range and stock-rule pair method. Both of them are the in-depth [1, 6] applications.

Definition 1 In-Depth Pattern. [1, 6] Referring to patterns which are highly interesting and actionable in business decision-making. These patterns are created through refining model or tuning parameters to optimize generic patterns; they may also be directly discovered from data set with sufficient consideration of business requirement and constraints.

In-depth pattern is different from the previous generic pattern definition for it not only finds the inner rules, but also considers the business requirement and interesting.

2.1 Optimal Sub-range

If we use the technical trading rule to get the alert signals, it will cost a lot of running time because for a parameter of a trading rule, the possible combination is a very large number. But, sometimes the one value does not work because it will be influenced by a noisy signal. To deal with the problem, we should use a sub-range, in which almost every value combination works well, to replace the single value.

In this paper, we use Robust Genetic Algorithm (RGA) to get the sub-range. The target is not a single value, but a range in which every value is better. (See Fig. 1)

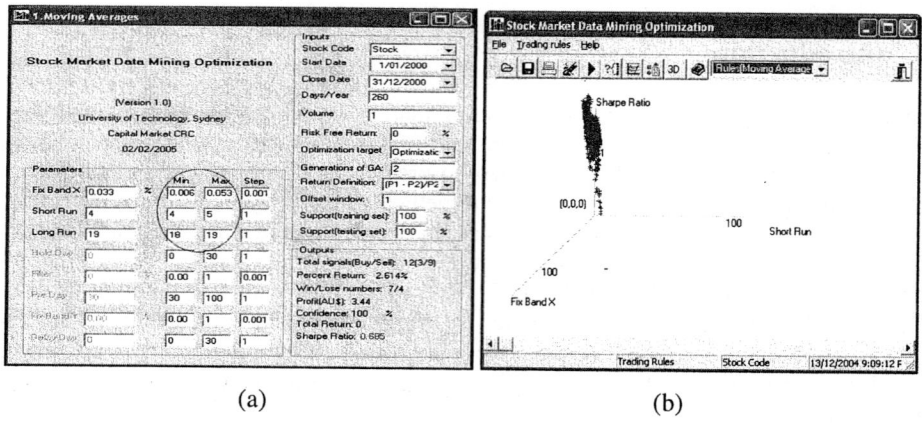

(a)   (b)

Fig. 1. The result is a sub-range (a), in which every combination works well, they can give a positive Sharpe Ratio [4] (b)

2.2 Stock-Rule Pairs

For a single stock and a single rule, we can easily find the "best" robust result through the RGA and domain knowledge, but, if there is one stock and more rules, which stock-rule pair is the best? And, how about if there is one rule and more stocks? More stocks more rules? Which stock-rule pair is the better to make a higher return and take lower risk?

To simulate the real stock market, we divide the historical data into two parts: in-sample data (training set) and out-of-sample data (testing set). Both sets are one month intraday order book data. In the training set, we sort the stock-rule pairs by Sharpe Ratio decreased. And in testing set, the confidence is about 80 percent that means more 80 percent pairs are still better in testing set.

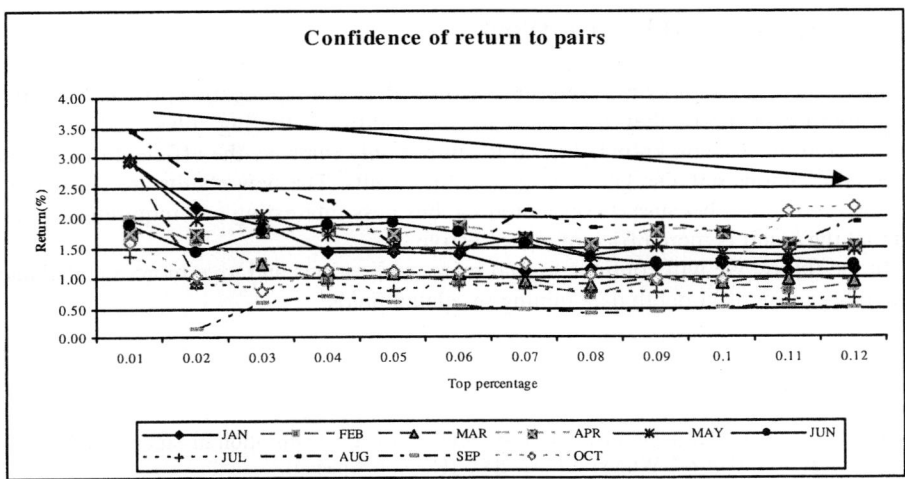

Fig. 2. The Sharpe Ratio to the percent top pairs. It shows that the top pair is better for making more profit and taking less risk because the line decreases when the number of pair increases. (Every line stands for the in-sample data range, and the out-of-sample data is just the continued one month).

2.3 Determining the Investment

For the different amount investment, the return should be different if all the other conditions keep the same. One question is how to find the best number of pair so that the return is the highest when the investment changed. This is the third application of

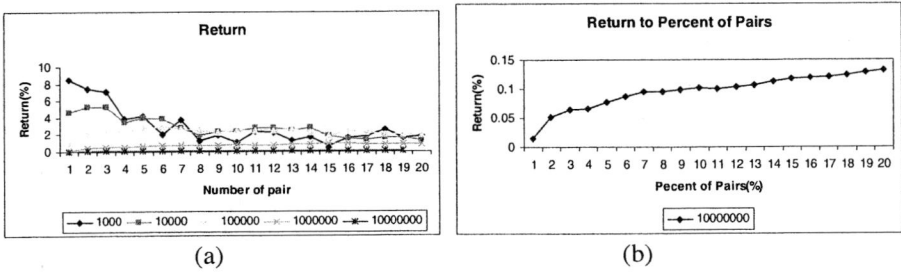

Fig. 3. The relationship among the return, the investment and the number of pairs. (a) is all the lines for different investment; (b) when the investment is $10,000,000.

in-depth pattern discovery. And we have done the experiment for two years 2000 and 2001. (See Fig. 3) Firstly, we get the pairs from the training set (see Section 2.2) and get the signals from the testing set. Secondly, we compute the return from the sorted signals by time. The return result shows the relationship of investment and the number of pair.

3 Conclusion and Future Work

In this paper, the authors have presented some ideas and applications on the in-depth data mining methods, they are based on the traditional trading rules, and, we also considered the domain knowledge, so it can not only improve the efficient of the real time applications but also get more actionable results. The new results are better than the previous ones, because it considered the business interesting and requirement, too, so that the result is more efficient and effective.

In the future, we will continue to find more applications and give more detailed and solid definition of in-depth data mining in related fields.

References

1. C. Q. Zhang, S. C. Zhang, In-Depth Data Mining and Its Application in Stock Market. *Proceedings of ADMA-04,* Wuhan, China, 2005 (Keynote Speech).
2. Sullivan, Ryan, Allan Timmermann, et al: Data-Snooping, Technical Trading Rule Performance, and the Bootstrap. *Journal of Finance*, 54 (1999), pp: 1647-1692.
3. Kin Lam, K.C. Lam: Forecasting for the Generation of Trading Signals in Financial Markets. *Journal of Forecasting*, 19(2000), pp. 39-52.
4. Dowd, Kevin. Adjusting for risk: An Improved Sharpe Ratio, *International Review of Economics & Finance*, Elsevier, vol. 9(3), pages 209-222. 2000.
5. R. Levich and L. Thomas. The Significance of Technical-Trading Rules Profits in the Foreign Exchange Market: A Bootstrap Approach, *Journal of International Money and Finance*, 12(5), 451-474. 1993.
6. L. B. Cao, L. Lin, C. Q. Zhang. Domain-Driven In-Depth Pattern Discovery: A Practical Methodology. *Proceedings of the 18th Australian Joint Conference of Artificial Intelligence*. Sydney, Australia, December 2005.

Selective Data Masking Design in Intelligent Knowledge Capsule for Efficient Data Mining

JeongYon Shim

Division of General Studies, Computer Science, Kangnam University,
San 6-2, Kugal-ri, Kihung-up, YongIn Si, KyeongKi Do, Korea
Tel: +82 31 2803 736
`mariashim@kangnam.ac.kr`

Abstract. Adopting one of human brain'sfunction ,we designed Intelligent Knowledge Capsule with Selective Masking Matrix for efficient data selection which has the hierarchical structure, learning, perception and knowledge retrieval mechanism. This system was applied to the virtual memory and tested.

1 Introduction

According to the brain study, it is known that human being does not see the real objects in the world but sees the virtual image created by his brain. The brain takes the stimuli selectively and composes the new virtual image with the stimuli from the outside and previous knowledge stored in memory. It is one of surviving strategy for small creatures to be adapted in the huge complex world. During this processing, human being receives the data selectively according to necessity or preference. The criteria of accepting data depends on his previous knowledge and necessary data for maintaining the balancing point of whole system. The brain controls the reaction of incoming data through the sensory organ.

As the computer technology is developing quickly and information society is getting complex and full of huge data, the requirement for automatic intelligent system for processing the huge data and mining the important data is getting higher. Especially for the purpose of processing the huge data in the information society efficiently, the system adopting the selecting strategy of human brain would be very useful.

Accordingly, in this paper we design intelligent knowledge capsule as a frame for processing data selection from outside, learning, inference and knowledge retrieval. The mechanism of Selective data masking which can control the degree of reaction was also designed. This system was applied to the virtual memory and tested.

2 The Structure of Intelligent Knowledge Capsule

As shown in Fig. 1, This system consists of Learning memory, Rule base, and Episode memory. They are related to the others according to their association. The memory is constructed by information acquisition process. The obtained data from the knowledge environment come into Input Interface and are temporarily stored in Temporary memory. They are selected and distributed by the basic mechanism. For autonomous learning mechanism. Learning engine receives the training data of the special domain and process its learning mechanism. Episode memory stores the event oriented facts with the information of time and location and memorize them according to the flow of events sequentially. Memory Index which composed of Short term memory Index and Long term memory Index is used for efficient knowledge retrieval.

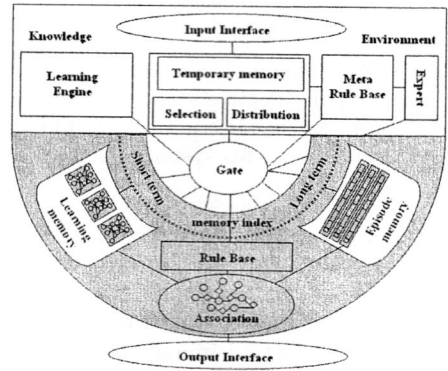

Fig. 1. The structure of Intelligent Knowledge Capsule

3 Selective Data Masking Design

3.1 Data Selection by Selective Masking Matrix

One of important functions of proposed Intelligent Knowledge Capsule is data selection from the outside. In this system the function of data selection was implemented by designing Selective Masking Matrix.

Figure 2 shows the detail structure for selective data masking and learning in Intelligent Knowledge capsule. The part for data selection and learning is composed of four layers, i.e, Input layer, Reaction layer, NN(neural network) layer and Associative layer. Reaction layer is specially designed for data selection. Reaction layer is put on Masking plate connected to Masking Matrix plate in Central part of the system. The nodes of Reaction layer is connected to the switches of Masking plate and controlled by the signal of reaction degree from Masking Plate. This control structure makes this system available to select the data and control the strength of incoming stimuli.

Data flow for processing in this mechanism is : Incoming input data are selected or their strength were changed by the Masking Plate during they pass Reaction layer. Then selected categories by activating criteria of group activates the corresponding NNs in NN layer which process learning mechanism. In learning step, NN takes the training data of corresponding category and processes

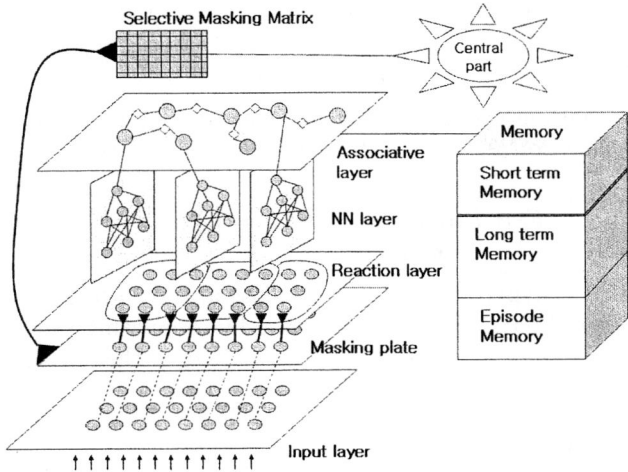

Fig. 2. Selective Data masking

the learning mechanism by BP(Back propagation) algorithm. In perception step, NN classifies the group using stored weight values through passing the incoming data. The passed data from NN layer propagate to the nodes in the next layer because the output nodes of NNs are connected to the nodes in Associative layer vertically. The nodes in Associative layer are connected to other nodes by associative relation in higher conceptual level. This system provides the memory which consists of Long term memory, short term memory and Episode memory. The stored memory is connected to Associative layer in the left side of figure and used for deep knowledge extraction. This structure is used for retrieving the associative knowledge connected to the searching node.

3.2 Selective Masking Matrix

Selective Masking Matrix,M, consists of values of the nodes,m_{ij}, used for controlling the reaction rates.

$$M = [m_{ij}]$$

$$m_{ij} = P(s|r)$$

where m_{ij} is represented by conditional probability of present signal given past related event,r.

For example, m_{ij} is represented by the following matrix. The number and position of matrix is correspondent to the nodes of Masking plate.

$$A = \begin{bmatrix} 1.0 & 1.0 & 1.0 & 0.0 & 0.0 & 0.8 & 0.7 & 0.0 & 0.3 \\ 0.5 & 1.0 & 0.9 & 0.3 & 0.0 & 0.2 & 0.1 & 0.0 & 0.9 \\ 1.0 & 0.6 & 0.4 & 0.2 & 0.0 & 0.9 & 0.0 & 1.0 & 0.4 \end{bmatrix}$$

The incoming input data I_{ij} is changed to I'_{ij} affected by Masking matrix:

$$I'_{ij} = I_{ij} * m_{ij}$$

The masked data are propagated to the corresponding NN activated by criteria. Filtering function F_i is the criteria for determining the state of firing.

$$F_i = P(C_i|e_1, e_2, \ldots, e_n) = \prod_{k=1}^{n}(C_i|e_k) \qquad (1)$$

where C_i denotes a hypothesis for disease class and $e_k = e_1, \ldots, e_n$ denotes a sequence of observed data. F_i can be obtained by calculating the belief in C_i. If filtering factor F_i is over the threshold, q_i, $(F_i \geq q_i)$, the corresponding class and NN is fired.

3.3 Association

Association layer consists of nodes and their relations. These nodes are connected to their neighbors according to their associative relations horizontally and connected to NN of the previous layer vertically. Their relations are represented by the relational graph[1].

The relational graph is transformed to the forms of AM(Associative Matrix) in order to process the knowledge retrieval mechanism. AM has the values of associative strengths in the matrix form.

The matrix, A, has the form of $A = [R_{ij}]$. The associative strength,R_{ij}, between C_i and C_j is calculated by equation (2).

$$R_{ij} = P(a_i|a_j)D \qquad (2)$$

where D is the direction arrow, $D = 1 or - 1$, $i = 1, \ldots, n$, $j = 1, \ldots, n$.

Using this Associative Matrix A, this system can extract the related facts by following knowledge retrieval algorithm.

3.4 Knowledge Retrieval from Associative Memory Controlled by Masking Switch

In this section the Knowledge retrieval mechanism using Selective Masking Matrix is described.

Given the facts or keyword for searching, this system starts Knowledge retrieval mechanism and produces the found extracted knowledge. The knowledge retrieval algorithm is as follows.

Algorithm 1 : knowledge retrieval algorithm using Selective Masking Matrix

Step 1: Input the data to Input Interface.
Step 2: Data Selection by Selective Masking Matrix

$$I'_{ij} = I_{ij} * m_{ij}$$

Step 3: Calculate the reaction value by filtering function
Step 4: Select the activated class.
Step 5: IF (learning) Then perform BP algorithm Else (Perception) Output the results of NN
Step 6: Data Extraction in Association level: Search the associated nodes connected to the inferential output node of NN in the row of the activated node in AM.
Step 7: IF((not found) AND (found the initial activated node))
Goto Step 8.
ELSE
Output the found fact.
Add the found fact to the list of inference path.
Goto Step 6
Step8: STOP

When the class, C_i, in the relational graph is assumed to be activated, from the node, C_i, the inferential paths can be extracted using the knowledge retrieval algorithm. The inferential path, I_i has the following form.

$$I_i = \begin{bmatrix} C_i & (R_{ij}) & C_j \end{bmatrix}$$

where C_i is i-th class node, R_{ij} is the associative strength between C_i and C_j.

4 Experiments

This system is applied to the Virtual memory with Associative layer as Figure 3 and tested. Figure 4 shows the retrieved knowledge from Associative layer and Figure 5 shows the variation of result according to Selective Masking Matrix.

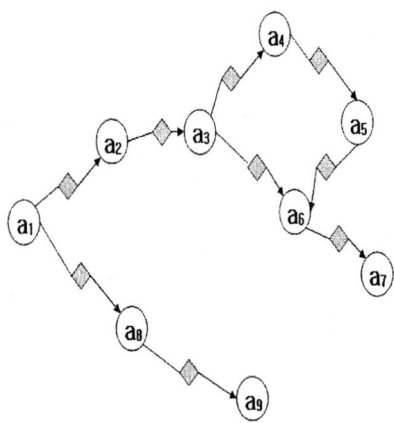

Fig. 3. Knowledge graph in Associative Layer

```
Knowledge Retrieval step...

Inferential pass

a1 0.9 a2 0.8 a3 0.4 a4 0.7 a5 0.9 a6 0.8 a7 0.0 null
a1 0.9 a2 0.8 a3 0.3 a6 0.8 a7 null
a1 0.7 a8 0.2 a9
```

Fig. 4. Retrieved Knowledge from Associative layer

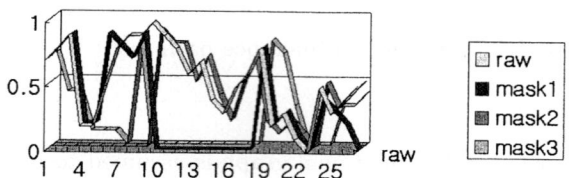

Fig. 5. The variation of output by Selective Masking Matrix

It was found that the reactive result was changed by Selective Masking Matrix and the related knowledge was successfully retrieved.

5 Conclusion

we designed Intelligent Knowledge Capsule and the concept of Selective Masking matrix for data selection. It can learn and perceive the things and has the associative knowledge retrieval function according to the associative keywords. As a result of experiment tt was found that data selection by Selective Masking Matrix and the related knowledge was successfully retrieved. It is expected that this study will contribute to the intelligent system design.

References

1. Jeong-Yon Shim, Knowledge Retrieval Using Bayesian Associative Relation in the Three Dimensional ModularSystem, pp630-635, *Lecture Notes in Computer Science(3007), 2004*.
2. John R. Anderson Learning and Memory, *Prentice Hall*.
3. Laurene Fausett Fundamentals of Neural Networks, *Prentice Hall*.

On a Mathematical Relationship Between the Fixed Point and the Closed Itemset in Association Rule Mining[*]

Tian-rui Li[1,2], Da Ruan[2], Tianmin Huang[1], and Yang Xu[1]

[1] Department of Mathematics, School of Science,
Southwest Jiaotong University, Chengdu 610031, P.R. China
{trli, tmhuang, xuyang}@swjtu.edu.cn
[2] The Belgian Nuclear Research Centre (SCK•CEN),
Boeretang 200, B-2400 Mol, Belgium
{tli, druan}@sckcen.be

Abstract. Association rule mining is one of important research topics in knowledge discovery and data mining. Recent promising direction of association rule mining is mainly to mine closed itemsets. Based on the Galois closed operators, a mathematical relationship between the fixed point and closed itemset in association rule mining is discussed and several properties are obtained. To mine all frequent closed itemsets is equal to build the fixed point lattice and mine its all points that satisfy support constraints. A new method for visualization of association rules based on the generalized association rule base is also proposed.

1 Introduction

Data mining is mainly concerned with methodologies for extracting patterns from large data repositories. Association rule mining, since its introduction in [1], has become an active research topic in knowledge discovery and data mining. Unfortunately, extensive studies in the field have been only focused on algorithms and methodologies for mining frequent itemsets, speeding up of existing algorithms, evaluation of discovered knowledge and applications in many domains such as retail industry for analysis of customer buying behavior as well as extending its algorithms for mining other type of knowledge, e.g., sequential pattern, frequent subtrees and subgraphs. There is very little attention being paid to its theoretical foundations. However, the latter is also important since it can help to use existing theories and methods to support more effective mining tasks.

In this paper, a mathematical relationship between the closed itemset and the fixed point is built and several properties are proved, which provides a theoretical foundation of association rule mining. It is different from Pasquier et al. [2], mainly concentrates on the discovery of frequent closed itemsets, and Zaki [3], specifically interested in generating a smaller non-redundant rule set after

---

[*] This work was partially supported by the National Natural Science Foundation of China (NSFC) under the grant No. 60474022.

mining the frequent closed itemsets, but all based on the elegant mathematical framework of formal concept analysis [5].

2 Preliminaries

The model of mining association rule was firstly introduced in [1]. An itemset, X, is a *closed itemset* if there exists no itemset Y such that Y is a proper superset of X and every transaction containing X also contains Y [4].

A triple (G, M, R) is called a *context* if G and M are two sets and $R \subseteq G \times M$ is a binary relation between G and M. We call the elements of G objects, those of M attributes, and R the incidence of the context (G, M, R). For the object g and the attribute m, $(g, m) \in R$ or more commonly, gRm implies that 'the object g possesses the attribute m' [5].

Theorem 1. *[5] Let (G, M, R) be a context, then the following mappings are Galois connections between $P(G)$ and $P(M)$:*

$$s : G \mapsto M, s(X) = \{m \in M \,|\, (\forall g \in X) gRm\},$$

$$t : M \mapsto G, t(Y) = \{g \in G \,|\, (\forall m \in Y) gRm\},$$

where $P(G)$ and $P(M)$ are the power sets of G and M, respectively.

Obviously, $s \circ t$ and $t \circ s$ are closed operators, also called as Galois closed operators. Let Q be a partial order set, $\Phi: Q \to Q$ is a mapping, $a \in Q$. If $\Phi(a) = a$, then a is called as a *fixed point* of Φ [6].

Theorem 2. *[6] Let Q be a partial order set, $\Phi: Q \to Q$ is a mapping, satisfying that for every $a \in Q, a \leq \Phi(a)$, then Φ has fixed points.*

Theorem 3. *[6] Let Q be a partial order set, $\Phi: Q \to Q$ is an order-preserving mapping, then Φ has fixed points and the minimum fixed point.*

Theorem 4. *[6] Let Q be a complete lattice, $\Phi: Q \to Q$ is an order-preserving mapping, then $\vee \{a \in Q \,|\, a \leq \Phi(a)\}$ is a fixed point of Φ.*

3 The Closed Itemset *vs.* the Fixed Point

In this section, a mathematical relationship between the closed itemsets and the fixed point is built by using the theory of formal concept analysis [2,5], which can serve as a theoretical foundation of association rule mining.

Let an identifier set, ID, a set of all items, I, in a transaction database D be G and M of a context (G, M, R), a binary relation between ID and I be R, then (ID, I, R) becomes a context. By Theorem 1, their Galois connections are as follows:

$$s : ID \mapsto I, s(X) = \{m \in I \,|\, (\forall g \in X) gRm\}$$

$$t : I \mapsto ID, t(Y) = \{g \in ID \,|\, (\forall m \in Y) gRm\}$$

Then, $t(Y)$ denotes the set of the id that includes the itemset Y. Moreover, $s \circ t$ and $t \circ s$ are Galois closed operators.

Theorem 5. $FPS = \{Y \in P(I) \,|\, s \circ t(Y) = Y\}$ *is the set of all closed itemsets of a transaction database* D.

Proof. ($\Rightarrow$) Suppose that an itemset Y, satisfying $s \circ t(Y) = Y$ and it is not a closed itemset. Then there exists an itemset Z, satisfying $Y \subset Z$ and $support(Y) = support(Z)$. Namely, $t(Y) = t(Z)$ and thus $s \circ t(Z) \supseteq Z$. It is concluded that $Y = s \circ t(Y) = s \circ t(Z) \supseteq Z$, which contradicts that $Y \subset Z$. Therefore, Y is a closed itemset.

($\Leftarrow$) Suppose that an itemset Y is a closed itemset of D. Since $s \circ t$ is a closed operator, $s \circ t(Y) \supseteq Y$. If $s \circ t(Y) \supset Y$, according to the definition of s and t, every itemset contains Y also contains $s \circ t(Y)$. Thus, $support(s \circ t(Y)) = support(Y)$, which contradicts the assumption that Y is a closed itemset. Therefore, we have $s \circ t(Y) = Y$.

Hence, every itemset in FPS is a fixed point of the mapping $s \circ t$. To mine all closed itemsets is equal to find all fixed points of $s \circ t$. The existence of the fixed point of the mapping is confirmed by Theorems 2 and 3.

Theorem 6. *There exist fixed points of the mapping* $s \circ t : P(I) \to P(I)$.

Proof. Obviously, $P(I)$ is a partial order set. Since $s \circ t : P(I) \to P(I)$ is a closed operator. Then, for every $Y \in P(I)$, $Y \subseteq s \circ t(Y)$ and $s \circ t$ is an order-preserving mapping. Therefore, there exist fixed points of $s \circ t$.

Since $(P(I), \subseteq)$ is a complete lattice and the closed operator is an order-preserving mapping, then a concrete fixed point (namely, the closed itemset) can be obtained by Theorem 4, which also supplies an inspiring example of the fixed point from mathematical point of view. Moreover, $(FPS, \subseteq)$ is a complete lattice, called as a fixed point lattice.

Let $FFPS = \{Y \in P(I) \,|\, s \circ t(Y) = Y, support(Y) \geq minimum\ support\}$. Obviously, all the elements in $FFPS$ are all frequent closed itemsets. $(FFPS, \subseteq)$ is a meet semi-lattice, called as a frequent fixed point lattice.

Since the closed itemsets keep all the support information of all itemsets of transaction database [4], so does the fixed point lattice. Therefore, to mine all frequent closed itemsets is equal to establish the fixed point lattice and mine its all points that satisfy support constraints.

In addition, according to the definition of the generalized association rule base (GARB) and its properties [7], the frequent fixed point lattice includes all information of association rules. Therefore, we can directly visualize association rules in the lattice. Just move the mouse to the closed itemsets or the line between two closed itemsets, the rules in the GARB will appear in the screen and all rules generating from them [7], namely all association rules, can also appear in screen.

Example 1. Visualization of GARB as well as all association rules of a transaction database is shown in Fig. 1, where the *minimum support* is 60%.

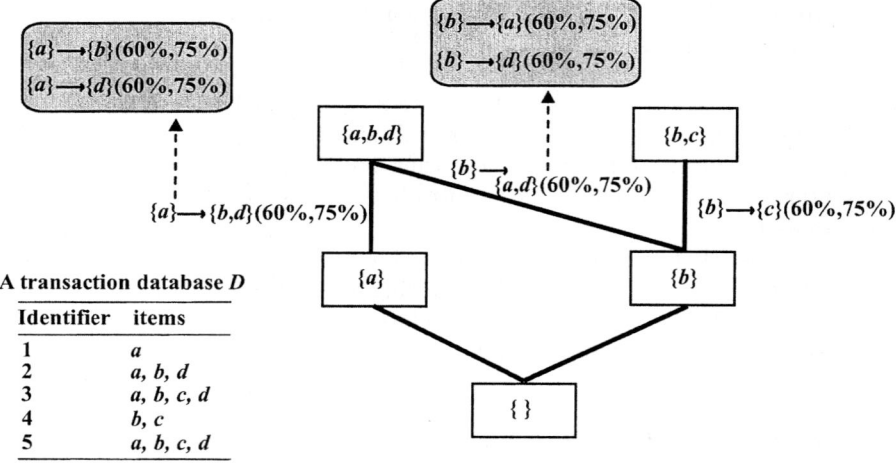

Fig. 1. Visualization of GARB

4 Conclusions

Based on the Galois closed operator, identifier set, itemset in transaction database together with their binary relation constituted a context, the relationship between the fixed point and the closed itemset was established. The task of mining all frequent closed itemsets was thus transferred to build the fixed point lattice in a transaction database which not only serves as a theoretical foundation of association rule mining, but also is useful for visualization of association rules. However, how to use the fixed point and lattice theories to really support more effective association rule mining's tasks, and especially how to build the fixed point lattice effectively, still needs to be carefully explored in the future.

References

1. Agrawal, R., Imielinski, T., Swami, A.: Mining association rules between sets of items in large databases. SIGMOD'93. Washington DC, USA. (1993) 207-216
2. Pasquier, N., Bastide Y., Taouil, R., Lakhal, L.: Efficient mining of association rules using closed itemset lattices. Information Systems. **24** (1999) 25-46
3. Zaki, M.: Mining non-redundant association rules. Data Mining and Knowledge Discovery: An International Journal. **9** (2004) 223-248
4. Han, J., Kamber, M.: Data Mining: Concepts and Techniques. Morgan Kaufmann (2000)
5. Ganter, B., Wille, R.: Formal Concept Analysis: Mathematical Foundations. Springer. Berlin Heidelberg, NY. (1999)
6. Smart, D.: Fixed Point Theorems. Cambridge University Press. Cambridge, UK. (1974)
7. Li, T., Qing, M., Ma, J., Xu, Y.: An algorithm for mining lower closed itemsets. Lecture Notes in Computer Science. **3320** (2004) 21-24

A Data Mining Approach in Opponent Modeling

Remedios de Dios Bulos, Conirose Dulalia, Peggy Sharon L. Go,
Pamela Vianne C. Tan, and Ma. Zaide Ilene O. Uy

College of Computer Studies, De La Salle University,
2401 Taft Avenue, Manila, Philippines
bulosr@dlsu.edu.ph

Abstract. In offline opponent modeling, large datasets can be utilized as training data to model the opponent. In the Coach competition of RoboCup Soccer, offline opponent modeling can be adopted to train the coach learn about the opponent's behavior patterns. Data-mining techniques, particularly decision-tree construction can be applied in identifying interesting behavior patterns of the opponent. This research explores the use of the decision-tree algorithm C4.5 to generate classification rules that will embody the offensive and defensive strategies (plans) of the coach against its opponent(s). To achieve this objective, the SimSoccer Coach system is built.

1 Introduction

A recent addition to the RoboCup League is the "Coach" competition [6, 7]. The online coach is a privileged client that connects to the server in official games and communicates with the players via CLANG (coach language). Its intended role is to observe the game and then provide strategic advice to the team. It receives global and noise-free information, has less real-time demands (since it is not required to execute actions in every time cycle), has access to logs of previous matches and is expected to spend more time deliberating over strategy formulation.

Opponent modeling may be implemented in two ways: online and offline. In game theory [1, 9, 10], it is mostly implemented online, that is, in every turn of a play, a model of the opponent is constructed based on the previous turns; the model is used to predict the move of the opponent for the current turn and then an action is selected based on that prediction. However, according to [1, 2] a problem arises with this approach because the last step is not trivial, as it incorporates the exploration vs. exploitation dilemma. Offline opponent modeling, on the other hand, allows an agent to acquire a model of its opponent based on the history of the play, and then uses the model on the next play.

Data Mining (DM) is a research area that may provide useful solutions to offline opponent modeling. In opponent modeling, data-mining techniques such as decision-tree construction can be applied in identifying interesting behavior patterns of the opponent. In the Coach competition, offline opponent modeling can be adopted to train the coach learn about the opponent's behavior patterns. Particularly, this research explores the use of the decision-tree algorithm C4.5 to generate classification rules that will embody the offensive and defensive strategies (plans) of the coach against its opponent(s). To achieve this objective, the SimSoccer Coach system is built.

2 SimSoccer Coach: Structural Framework

SimSoccer Coach [4, 5] is a learning agent, which is designed to provide advice through detailed analysis of the fixed opponent's (which is the team that the coach's team is scheduled to play against in the future) play patterns in previous games (against other teams). It uses supervised, offline learning in generating offensive and defensive strategies. The SimSoccer Coach System consists of six main modules namely, the *LogFile Reader, Game Analyzer, Rule Translator, CLANG Generator, CLANG Communicator* and *Game Evaluator*.

Before a game is played between the coach's team and the fixed opponent, logfiles generated by the Soccer Server [7] from previous matches are fed into to the Logfile Reader. The Logfile Reader performs data sub-processing to derive additional information that cannot be directly obtained from the logfiles. It creates two sets of training data; the first set consists of data from matches that the opponent lost; and it is used to generate offensive strategy. The second set contains data from matches that the opponent won; and it is used to formulate defensive strategy. Using the C4.5 algorithm, the Game Analyzer module processes the training data sets to construct a decision tree. Once the decision-tree is constructed, the Rule Translator converts the decision tree into production rules, which are then processed and transformed into CLANG format [7] by the CLANG Generator. The CLANG rules are then stored into a Knowledge Base. Before a match starts, the CLANG Communicator is invoked. It connects to the Soccer Server, retrieves the rules stored in Knowledge Base and sends them to the coach's team. After a match has been played, the logfile created for the match is fed into the Game Evaluator module. The Game Evaluator computes the game's statistics and then checks the rules that were activated or fired during the game.

3 Results and Observations

To evaluate the SimSoccer Coach system, system testing and domain testing were conducted. In system testing, several matches were played against three fixed opponent teams. The evaluation criterion used for this test is the comparison of the game statistics with the coach and without the coach. For the domain testing, the system was evaluated based on the testing standards used for the RoboCup 2003 Coach Competition. The results from the experimental games (tests) were then compared to the results from the competition.

For system testing, the SimSoccer Coach was evaluated by comparing the coach's team's performance with and without the use of a coach. The coach's team played against three teams for ten games for each data set. The number of datasets used was: 2, 5, 10, 15 and 20. The three teams used in the experiments were SIRIM, BoldHearts and Caspian. The experiments were repeated for three different rule accuracy thresholds of 0%, 50% and 75%.

Table 1. Performance Improvement (SimSoccer Coach vs CASPIAN)

Data Sets	Offensive Advice (%)	Defensive Advice(%)	Offense + Defense (%)
2	37.54%	6.71%	23.54%
5	43.22%	9.58%	18.58%
10	27.58%	17.17%	32.77%
15	41.06%	10.86%	26.71%
20	32.06%	10.21%	20.14%

These rule accuracy thresholds determine which production rules generated by the C4.5 rule generator will be filtered out. The coachable team that was used in the experiments is the one provided for in the RoboCup Coach competition, WrightEagle for the players and UTA for the goalie.

Table 2. Performance Improvement (SimSoccer Coach vs SIRIM)

Datasets	Offensive Advice(%)	Defensive Advice(%)	Offense+Defense(%)
2	5.00%	4.27%	5.48%
5	20.02%	5.00%	6.11%
10	-11.14%	0.99%	5.42%
15	-15.53%	1.17%	-3.28%
20	-5.88%	6.02%	10.67%

Table 3. Performance Improvement (SimSoccer Coach vs BOLDHEARTS)

Datasets	Offensive Advice(%)	Defensive Advice(%)	Offense + Defense (%)
2	-23.19%	5.59%	8.03%
5	-24.84%	8.96%	11.15%
10	-30.88%	5.64%	12.51%
15	4.92%	6.04%	-5.98%
20	18.27%	2.94%	5.54%

Table 1 (vs Caspian), Table 2 (vs SIRIM), and Table 3 (vs Boldhearts) show the improvement of the coach's team when: (1) the coachable team is given offensive advice (2) the coach's team is given defensive advice and (3) the coachable team is given both offensive advice and defensive advice. Based on these tables, the coachable team has generally improved its performance given the different sets of advice. Sets in which the percentage improvement is negative are caused by the low shoot success rate of the games in these sets.

3.1 Experiment II: Domain Testing

For domain testing, the system was evaluated based on the standards used in the RoboCup 2003 Coach competition [7, 8]. After the first round, SimSoccer Coach system ranked 4th; In the competition this ranking is enough to qualify for the 2nd round of the competition. For the 2nd round the SimSoccer Coach was only able to rank 6th out of 9 coach entries in the competition; only the top 4 ranking teams qualify for the last round. Overall, the SimSoccer Coach would have been in 6th place if it had entered in the competition. This result is fairly good for the system considering that from all the coach entries, only UT Austin and SimSoccer Coach used machine learning methods in generating strategies. Furthermore, unlike UT Austin, SimSoccer Coach is purely based on the machine learning approach used. The UTA coach system has hand coded advice and formations which were manually adjusted based on previous experiment games [6].

4 Conclusions and Future Work

Generally, tests results show that the C4.5 generated advice given by the coach had improved the team's performance against various opponents. It can be said that the variance in the rate of improvement in the performance of the team is caused by the combined effect of the total rule accuracy and the frequency of the rules were fired. To improve the system, the following are recommended. First, explore the possibility of modifying the training data (e.g. adding more attributes) in order to improve the learning process. Second, another aspect that could be further studied is the understanding and analysis of own team to improve weaknesses. Third, the SimSoccer Coach System dealt with simple scenarios or single event. Complex events that form patterns or strategies can be analyzed in the future.

References

1. Carmel, D. 1 and Markovitch, S.: Model-based learning of interaction strategies in multi-agent systems. Journal of Experimental and Theoretical Artificial Intelligence, (1998), 10(3):309.332.
2. Rogowski, C.: Model-based Opponent Modelling in Domains Beyond the Prisoner's Dilemma. Proceedings of Modeling Other Agents from Observations (MOO 2004). Workshop W3 at the International Joint Conference on Autonomous Agents and Multi-Agent Systems. Columbia University, NY, USA, (2004).
3. Chen, M. et. al.: RoboCup Soccer Server: User's Manual.[online]. Available: http://sserver.sourceforge.net/ (February, 2003).
4. Dulalia, C., Go, P. S., Tan, P.V., Uy, M.Z. and Bulos R. D.: " Learning in Coaching" in Advances in Software Computing, The Fourth IEEE International Workshop on Soft Computing as Transdisciplinary Science and Technology, (Eds), Springer-Verlag. (2005).
5. Dulalia, C., Go, P. S., Tan, P.V., Uy, M.Z. and Bulos R. D.: "SimSoccer Coach", in the Proceedings of the 2nd International Conference on Humanoid, Nanotechnology, Information technology, Communication and control, Environment, and Management (2005).
6. Kuhlmann, G., Stone, P., & Lallinger, J.: The Champion UT Austin Villa 2003 Simulator Online Coach Team. Available: www.cs.utexas.edu/ (2003)
7. RoboCup 2003 Coachable Teams . Available: http://www-2.cs.cmu.edu/~pfr/soccer/coachable2003.html (July 25, 2003).
8. RoboCup2003 Simulation League Organizing Committee.: RoboCup2003 Official Rules for the Online Coach Competition. Available: www.cs.cmu.edu/~pfr/ coach_rules.pdf (June, 2003).
9. Steffens, Timo.: Feature-based declarative opponent modelling in multi-agent systems, Timo Steffens, Master thesis, Universität Osnabrück, (2002).
10. Steffens, Timo.: Feature-based declarative opponent modeling, in Daniel Polani, Brett Browning, Andreas Bonarini and Kazuo Yoshida (Eds.) RoboCup 2003: Robot Soccer World Cup VII, Springer, Berlin, (2003) pp. 125-136.

Automated Design and Knowledge Discovery of Logic Circuits Using a Multi-objective Adaptive GA*

Shuguang Zhao, Licheng Jiao, and Min Tang

School of Electronic Engineering, Xidian University,
Xi'an 710071 P. R. China
Sgzhao@xidian.edu.cn

Abstract. Both automated design and knowledge discovery of electronic circuits are challenging tasks for artificial intelligence. A genetic algorithm (GA) based approach to them was proposed in this paper, which features an array-based encoding scheme, a multi-objective evaluation mechanism and an adaptation strategy for GA parameters. It was validated by the experiments on arithmetic circuits of gradually increasing scales, which evolved multi-objective optimized circuits and revealed some novel and generalized principles.

1 Introduction

Evolvable Hardware (EHW) [1,2] promises to realize automated design of circuits by applying evolutionary computing techniques especially GA to circuit design tasks. So far, most relevant works reported were concentrated on gate-level evolution of combinational circuits especially arithmetic circuits, mainly for the sake of finding out novel or efficient building-blocks [1-5]. Among them, the results obtained by Koza [3], Miller [4] and Coello Coello [5] are outstanding, but they were weak in meeting the demand of multi-objective optimization involving circuits' operating speed.

We studied a novel method for multi-objective gate-level evolution of larger scale circuits. As introduced below, it can deal with multiple design objects involving function, speed and efficiency of circuits, and it was validated by some experiments that obtained some optimized circuits and revealed some new knowledge.

2 Outline of the Method

As depicted in Fig. 1, the circuit model adopted is an array of interconnected gate-level multifunctional logic units. Each unit is assigned a sequence number CN and an encoding string [$IS1_{CN}, IS2_{CN}, TS_{CN}$]. Where $IS1_{CN}$ and $IS2_{CN}$ are respectively the sequence numbers of the two units output to it, and TS_{CN} is the index number of its function selected. The array's encoding or a chromosome of GA is formed by linking all units' encoding strings with the encoding string of array's outputs, [$OS_1,...,OS_q$]

$$[IS1_1, IS2_1, TS_1]\cdots[IS1_G, IS2_G, TS_G][OS_1,\cdots,OS_q] \qquad (1)$$

---

* This work was partially supported by National Natural Science Foundation of China under grant 60374063, and granted financial support from China Postdoctoral Science Foundation.

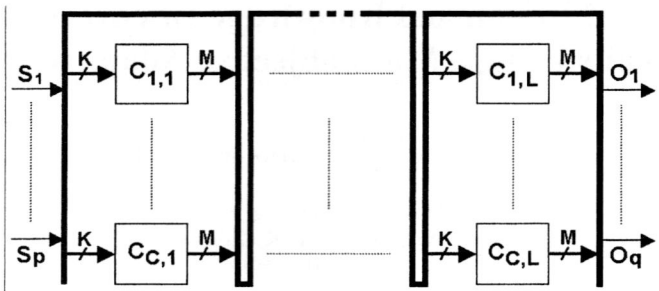

Fig. 1. The model for gate-level evolution

To solve problems of gate-level evolution simply and efficiently, a well-known fitness function in the form of 'sum of weights' was adopted, as shown below

$$\text{Maximize } Fit(X) = \sum_{i=1}^{n} w_i \bullet Fit_i(X) \tag{2}$$

Where w_i is the weight factor corresponding to the ith normalized objective $Fit_i(X)$, and $\sum w_i = 1$. To let the GA give attention to all objectives, the weight factors $\{w_i\}$ is allowed to change in a way similar to that of Back-Propagation Learning Algorithm

$$w_i(t+1) = \alpha \bullet w_i(t) + (1-\alpha) \bullet [2/N - \overline{Fit_i(t)} / \sum_{j=1}^{N} \overline{Fit_j(t)}] \tag{3}$$

Thus, the more an objective is optimized, the less its weight factor and consequent optimizing pressure on it would be, and vice versa. But the initial values of weight factors are still meaningful to express user-preferences.

As to gate-level evolution, the first objective is to maximize a circuit's conformity to the expected behaviors, which was measured by a ratio of its Number of Matched Operations (*NMO*) to the Total Number of defined Operations (*TNO*)

$$Fit_1 = NMO/TNO \tag{4}$$

The 2nd objective is to maximize the efficiency of resource usage estimated by using the Number of *Unused Gates* (*NUG*) that have no effect on the circuit's behavior

$$Fit_2 = \exp(-k_1 \bullet NUG) \tag{5}$$

The 3rd objective is to maximize the operating speed of a circuit, estimated with its Maximal Propagation-Delay (MPD) derived from the simulation results

$$Fit_3 = \exp(-k_2 \bullet MPD) \tag{6}$$

Then, the fitness function to synthetically evaluate the candidate was formed as

$$Fit(t) = \sum_{i=1}^{3} w_i(t) \bullet Fit_i(t) \tag{7}$$

To improve the GA's performances, its crossover probability P_c and mutation probability P_m were allowed to self-adapt to the individuals' diversity and the genetic-procedure. The individuals' concentration degree was estimated as

$$f_d(t) = \overline{f}(t)/[\varepsilon + f_{max}(t) - f_{min}(t)] \qquad (8)$$

Where $f_{max}(t)$, $f_{min}(t)$ and $\overline{f}(t)$ are maximal, minimum and average fitness of all current individuals respectively. Because $f_d(t)$ will vary with individuals distribution or diversity in a reverse direction, P_c and P_m were commanded to adapt as follows

$$P_c = \begin{cases} P_{c0}/f_d(t) & t < t_0 \\ P_{c0} \bullet e^{-k_3 \bullet (t-t_0)/t_{max}}/f_d(t) & t_0 \leq t \leq t_1 \\ P_{c0} \bullet e^{-k_3 \bullet (t_1-t_0)/t_{max}}/f_d(t) & t_1 \leq t \leq t_{max} \end{cases} \qquad (9)$$

$$P_m = \begin{cases} P_{m0} \bullet f_d(t) & t < t_0 \\ P_{m0} \bullet e^{-k_4 \bullet (t-t_0)/t_{max}} \bullet f_d(t) & t_0 \leq t \leq t_1 \\ P_{m0} \bullet e^{-k_4 \bullet (t_1-t_0)/t_{max}} \bullet f_d(t) & t_1 \leq t \leq t_{max} \end{cases} \qquad (10)$$

Where t_{max} is the maximal generation number allowed; P_{c0}, P_{m0}, t_0, t_1, k_3 and k_4 are user-defined constants. In this way, P_c and P_m will slowly decrease during the evolution process while responding to the changes of individuals' diversity.

3 Experimental Results and Discussions

With the approach combining the ideas introduced above with an EGA framework, evolutionary design experiments on some benchmark problems including even-parity checkers and multipliers [3-5], have been implemented successfully. A 3-bit multiplier evolved features GN (gate number) =25 and DN (delay number) =9. It is 10.7% more efficient and 20% faster than the best one designed by human experts, and it is actually as good as the best one evolved by Miller et al[4]. The evolved 4-bit depicted in Fig. 2 is much better than that designed by human experts and that evolved by Miller et al[4]. All evolved circuits feature wondrous reuses of inner outcomes, arguing that our approach is effective and it surpassed its congeners and human experts.

Moreover, we have inferred some novel principles from the circuits evolved for problems of increasing scales by using Case-Based Reasoning (CBR) techniques. For a binary addition that is the core of a binary multiplication, a set of expressions that efficiently derive the carry from addends have been identified as

$$CF_{n+1} = CF_n \oplus [I_{n+1} \bullet (I_1 \oplus \ldots \oplus I_n)] \qquad (11)$$

$$CS_n = \begin{cases} 0 & n < 4 \\ CS_4 = I_1 I_2 I_3 I_4 & n = 4 \\ CS_5 = CS_4 \oplus \{I_5[I_1 I_2(I_3 \oplus I_4) \oplus I_3 I_4(I_1 \oplus I_2)]\} & n = 5 \\ CS_6 = CS_5 \oplus \{I_6\{I_1 I_2(I_3 \oplus I_4) \oplus I_3 I_4(I_1 \oplus I_2) \\ \quad \oplus I_5\{I_1 I_2 \oplus I_3 I_4 \oplus [(I_1 \oplus I_2) \bullet (I_3 \oplus I_4)]\}\}\} & n = 6 \end{cases} \qquad (12)$$

Where CF_n and CS_n are respectively the least-bit and the secondary least-bit of the carry derived from n bits of addend, $I_1,...,I_n$; CF_{n+1} is the n+1 version of CF_n; $CF_1=0$. Some similar results have also been obtained from evolved even-parity checkers.

Although the extracted principles are easy to prove with knowledge of Boolean algebra, they are difficult for human experts to dig out with conventional approaches, arguing our approach is helpful to acquisition and discovery of relevant knowledge.

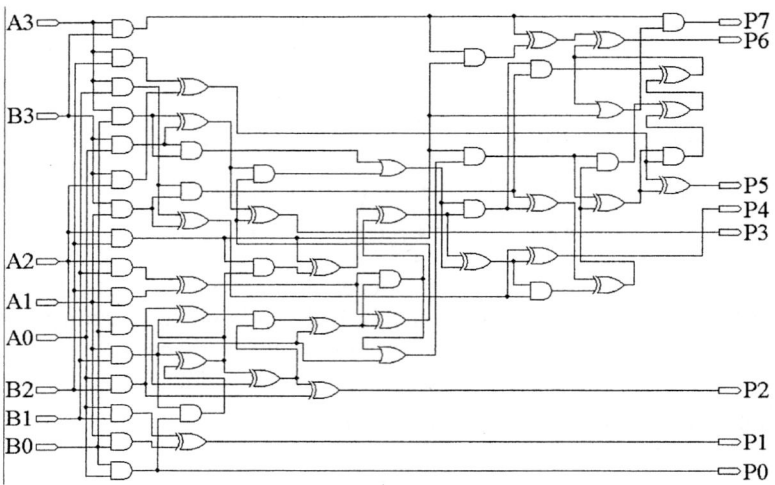

Fig. 2. A 4-bit multiplier evolved (GN=58, DN=18. In Miller's term, GN=55)

References

1. Yao X.: Promises and Challenges of Evolvable Hardware. IEEE Trans. SMC, 1(1999) 87-97
2. Zhao, S.G.: Study of the Evolutionary Design Methods of Electronic Circuits. PhD. dissertation, Xidian University, Xian, China (2003)
3. Koza, J. R.: Genetic Programming: On the Programming of Computers by Means of Natural Selection, Cambridge, MA: MIT Press (1992)
4. Miller, J. F., et al: Principles in the Evolutionary Design of Digital Circuits: Part I. Journal of Genetic Programming and Evolvable Machines, 1 (2000) 8-35
5. Coello Coello, A. C., et al: Use of Evolutionary Techniques to Automate the Design of Combinational Circuits. Int. Journal of Smart Engineering System Design, 4 (2000) 299-314

Mining with Constraints by Pruning and Avoiding Ineffectual Processing

Mohammad El-Hajj and Osmar R. Zaïane

Department of Computing Science, University of Alberta,
Edmonton AB, Canada
{mohammad, zaiane}@cs.ualberta.ca

Abstract. It is known that algorithms for discovering association rules generate an overwhelming number of those rules. While many new very efficient algorithms were recently proposed to allow the mining of extremely large datasets, the problem due to the sheer number of rules discovered still remains. In this paper we propose a new way of pushing the constraints in dual-mode based from the set of maximal patterns that is an order of magnitude smaller than the set of all frequent patterns.

1 Introduction

Frequent pattern discovery has become a common topic of investigation in the data mining research area. Its main theme is to discover the sets of items that occur together more than a given threshold value defined by the decision maker. In most cases when the support threshold is low and the number of frequent patterns "explodes", the discovery of these patterns becomes problematic. To reduce the effects of such problem new methods need to be investigated such as fast traversal techniques to reduce the search space or using constraints that lessen the output size whilst directly discovering patterns that are of interest to the user.

In short, our contributions in this paper is presenting the DPC-COFI (**D**ual-**P**ushing of **C**onstraints in COFI) algorithm that is based on our previous work COFI* where we push both types of constraints at the same time starting from the set of maximal patterns that is much smaller than the set of all frequent patterns. The algorithm does not only focus on the candidate itemset search space reduction, but also the elimination of pointless processing and the lessening of constraint predicate testing. The remainder of this paper is organized as follows: The types of constraints are explained in Section 2. We illustrate in Section 3 how we can integrate the constraint checking in our COFI approach to produce the DPC-COFI algorithm. Experimental results are given in Section 4.

2 Category of Constraints

Let $I = \{i_1, i_2, ...i_m\}$ be a set of literals, called items. Let $\mathcal{D}$ be a set of transactions, where each transaction T is a set of items such that $T \subseteq I$. A transaction

T is said to contain X, a set of items in I, if $X \subseteq T$. An itemset X is said to be *frequent* if its *support* s is greater or equal than a given minimum support threshold σ. An itemset $\mathcal{M}$ is also called maximal if there is no other frequent pattern that is a superset of $\mathcal{M}$. In addition to the transactions, other tables could describe the items in the transactions in terms of attributes such as price, weight, etc. A constraint ζ is a predicate on itemset X that yields either *true or false* and is typically expressed in terms of the items' attributes. An itemset X satisfies a constraint ζ if and only if $\zeta(X)$ is *true*. A constraint ζ is *anti-monotone* if and only if an itemset X violates ζ, so does any superset of X. That is, if ζ holds for an itemset S then it holds for any subset of S. A constraint ζ is *monotone* if and only if an itemset X holds for ζ, so does any superset of X. That is, if ζ is violated for an itemset S then it is violated for any subset of S. The conjunction of all *anti-monotone* constraints forms the predicate $P()$, and the conjunction of all *monotone* constraint forms the predict $Q()$.

3 Pushing Constraints

Our strategy to discover the frequent patterns that satisfy the given constraints is depicted in Figure 1. The major idea is that we first discover the set of maximal patterns, which generalizes the set of all frequent patterns and is significantly smaller than the set of all frequent itemsets, but can be used to straightforwardly generate them all. Initially, we only consider the anti-monotone constraint $P()$ to keep the singleton items that satisfy $P()$. We use $P()$ and $Q()$ to prune the COFI-trees [3] and reduce the search space. When generating the frequent itemsets from the maximals, we consider again both the monotone ($Q()$) and the anti-monotone constraints ($P()$). Before presenting the details, let us introduce the necessary preliminaries. The COFI* algorithm that we use in this work is an extension of our COFI algorithm [3] and consists of two main stages. Stage one is the construction of the Frequent Pattern tree (FP-tree) and stage two is the actual mining for this data structure by successively building other smaller tree structures (COFI-trees) that generate the set of maximal patterns with special data structures that encode the supports of all the subsets of these maximal patterns which are indeed the set of all frequent patterns. For lack of space, we refer the reader to our work in [4] for more details on how we can generate the set of maximals and consequently the set of all frequent patterns with their support using the COFI* algorithm that makes use of the COFI-trees.

3.1 Mining COFI-Trees with Constraints: The DPC-COFI Algorithm

We adapted our COFI* algorithm by considering P() and Q() to reduce the sizes of the trees. Pushing P() early is adopted in COFI* as follows: **1.** Remove individual items that do not satisfy P() (i.e from the FP-tree). **2.** For each A-COFI-tree, remove any locally frequent item B, where AB does not satisfy P(). This reduces the A-COFI-tree size. **3.** There is no need for constraint checking

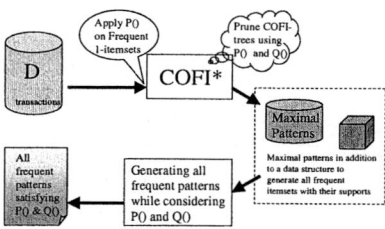

Fig. 1. Pushing P() and Q() using the COFI* approach

for any A-COFI-tree if the itemset X, representing all locally frequent items with respect to A, satisfies P() constraint. Similarly pushing Q() in COFI* is done as follows: **1.** No need to create an A-COFI-tree, if all its local items X with the A itemset violate Q(). This reduces the number of COFI-trees to mine. **2.** No need for constraint checking for any A-COFI-tree if the item A satisfies Q(), since any item with A in the A-COFI-tree will also satisfy this constraint. These strategies allow the pruning of the search space, the reduction of the data structures to mine and the direct pinpointing of patterns that satisfy the constraints without testing for those constraints (i.e. less checking is done). COFI* generates the set of Maximals with a special data structure to encode the supports of all frequent patterns. DPC-COFI is a framework built on top of COFI* during the subset generation. In DPC-COFI not all subset are part of the answer set as in COFI*, only those subsets that satisfy P() and Q(). Because of this we do not have to find the support for any frequent item unless we verify that it satisfies both P() and Q(). In Summary, during the subset generation of DPC-COFI, the following rules are tested: **1.** If an itemset satisfies both P() and Q() then generate its support and add it to the results sets. **2.** if an itemset satisfies P(), then there is no need to test P() for any of its subsets as all will satisfy P(). **3.** If an itemset does not satisfy P() then generate its subsets but do not add it (the initial itemset) to the results set. **4.** If an itemset does not satisfy Q() then prune it from the subset generation process. (i.e. none of its subsets will satisfy Q()).

4 Performance Evaluation

To evaluate our DPC-COFI algorithm, we conducted a set of experiments to test the effect of pushing monotone and anti-monotone constraints separately, and then both in combination for the same datasets. To quantify scalability, we experimented with datasets of varying size. We also measured the impact of pushing versus post-processing constraints on the number of evaluations of P() and Q(). Due to the lack of space we could not depicts all our results in this work. We compared our algorithm with Dualminer [1] which is the only known algorithm to effectively mine both types of constraints at the same time. Based on its authors' recommendations, we built the Dualminer framework on top of the MAFIA [2] implementation provided by its original authors. Our experiments were conducted on a 3GHz Intel P4 with 2 GB of memory running

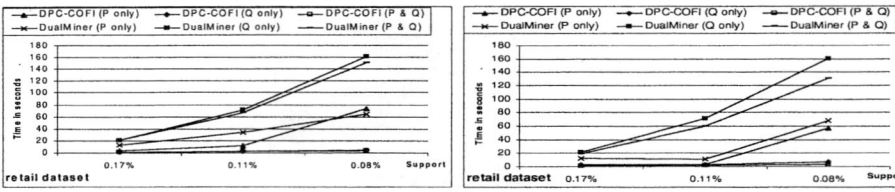

Fig. 2. (A)Pushing $P()$, $Q()$, and $P() \wedge Q()$. (B) Pushing more selective constraints.

Linux 2.4.25, Red Hat Linux release 9. We have tested these algorithms using both real datasets provided by [5] and synthetic datasets generated using [6]; we used 'retail' as our primary real dataset reported here. A dataset with the same characteristics as the one reported in [1] was also generated.

4.1 Impact of P and Q Selectivity on DPC-COFI and Dualminer

To differentiate between our novel DPC-COFI algorithm and Dualminer, we experimented against the retail dataset. In the first experiment (Figure 2.A), we pushed $P()$, then $Q()$, and finally $P() \wedge Q()$. We used the zipf distribution to assign prices to items. Figure 2.B presents the same experiment with more selective constraints.

5 Conclusion

In this paper we introduced an efficient approach allowing the consideration of both monotone and anti-monotone constraints during the mining process. It uses a new strategy of finding first the set of maximals that satisfy the constraints and applying later the constraints again during the subset generation of these maximals. Our experiments show significant performance gains compared to dualminer.

References

1. C. Bucila, J. Gehrke, D. Kifer, and W. White. Dualminer: A dual-pruning algorithm for itemsets with constraints. In *SIGKDD-2002*, pages 42–51, August 2002.
2. D. Burdick, M. Calimlim, and J. Gehrke. Mafia: A maximal frequent itemset algorithm for transactional databases. In *ICDE*, pages 443–452, 2001.
3. M. El-Hajj and O. R. Zaïane. Non recursive generation of frequent k-itemsets from frequent pattern tree representations. In *(DaWak'2003)*, September 2003.
4. M. El-Hajj and O. R. Zaïane. Cofi approach for mining frequent itemsets revisited. In *(DMKD-04)*, pages 70–75, June 2004.
5. B. Goethals and M. Zaki. Advances in frequent itemset mining implementations: Introduction to fimi03. In *(FIMI'03) in conjunction with IEEE-ICDM*, 2003.
6. IBM_Almaden. Quest synthetic data generation code.http://www.almaden.ibm.com/cs/quest/syndata.html.

Rough Association Mining and Its Application in Web Information Gathering

Yuefeng Li[1] and Ning Zhong[2]

[1] School of Software Engineering and Data Communications,
Queensland University of Technology, Brisbane,
QLD 4001, Australia
y2.li@wut.edu.au
[2] Department of Systems and Information Engineering,
Maebashi Institute of Technology, Japan
zhong@maebashi-it.ac.jp

Abstract. It is a big challenge to guarantee the quality of association rules in some application areas (e.g., in information gathering) since duplications and ambiguities of data values (terms). This paper presents a novel concept of rough association rules to improve the quality of discovered knowledge. The precondition of a rough association rule consists of a set of terms (items) and a weight distribution of terms (items). The distinct advantage of rough association rules is that they contain more specific information than normal association rules.

1 Introduction

One of the important issues for Web information gathering is to apply data mining techniques in Web documents to discover some interesting patterns for user information needs [4]. The association discovery approaches for text mining discuss relationship between terms in a broad-spectrum level. They pay no attention to the duplications of terms in a transaction (e.g., a document) and labeled information in the training set. The consequential result is that the precision of the systems is not satisfactory. Multidimensional association rules [2] could be used to consider the duplications of terms if we view terms as attributes and frequencies of terms as values. However, current approaches for multidimensional association rule mining regard only the treatment of quantitative attributes. They do not consider the correlation between attributes.

The objective of this paper is to improve the effectiveness of association discovery by presenting the concept of rough association rules, where the premise (precondition) of a rough association rule consists of a set of terms and also a weight distribution of terms as well. There are two advantages of using rough association rules. The first one is that correlations between attributes are considered as weight distributions. The second one is that the form of rough association rules is the same as patterns defined in [3], that is, negative information can be used to update rough association rules. This research is significant since it takes one more step further to association discovery for text mining.

2 Information Tables and Decision Rules

Formally the association discovery can be described as an information table ($\mathcal{D}$, $V^{\mathcal{D}}$), where $\mathcal{D}$ is a set of documents in which each document is a set of terms (may include duplicate terms); and $V^{\mathcal{D}} = \{t_1, t_2, \ldots, t_n\}$ is a set of selected terms for all documents in $\mathcal{D}$.

A set of terms X is referred to as a *termset* if $X \subseteq V^{\mathcal{D}}$. Let X be a termset, we use $[X]$ to denote the *covering set* of X, which includes all documents d such that $X \subseteq d$, i.e., $[X] = \{d \mid d \in \mathcal{D}, X \subseteq d\}$.

If we view each document as a transaction, *an association rule* between *termset X* and *termset Y* is a rule of the form $X \rightarrow Y$. Its support degree is $|[X \cup Y]|$, and its confidence is $|[X \cup Y]| / |[X]|$, where $|A|$ denotes the number of elements in A.

Two important factors are missed in the information table: the duplications of terms in a document and labeled information. To consider both factors, we use a decision table to replace the information table.

We now assume that $\mathcal{D}$ consists of a set of positive documents, $\mathcal{D}^+$; and a set of negative documents, $\mathcal{D}^-$. Table 1 demonstrates a decision table ($\mathcal{D}$, A_C, A_D), where the set of objects (documents) $\mathcal{D} = \{d_1, d_2, d_3, d_4, d_5, d_6\}$; the set of *condition attributes* (terms) $A_C = \{t_1, t_2, t_3, t_4, t_5, t_6, t_7\}$; the set of *decision attributes* $A_D = \{positive\}$; and N_d is the frequency of the document citied for a specified topic.

Table 1. An example of labeled documents

Doc	t_1	t_2	t_3	t_4	t_5	t_6	t_7	positive	N_d
d_1	2	1	0	0	0	0	0	yes	80
d_2	0	0	2	1	0	1	0	yes	140
d_3	0	0	3	1	1	1	0	yes	40
d_4	0	0	1	1	1	1	0	yes	450
d_5	1	1	0	0	0	1	1	yes	20
d_6	2	1	0	0	0	1	1	yes	200
d_7	0	0	1	1	0	0	0	no	50

Every object (document) in the decision table can be mapped into a decision rule [5]: either a *positive* decision rule (*positive=yes*) or a *negative* decision rule (*positive=no*). So we can obtain 7 positive decision rules in Table 1, e.g., d_1 in Table 1 can be read as the following rule: $(t_1, 2) \wedge (t_2, 1) \rightarrow yes$, where $(t_1, 2)$ denotes a term frequency pair in the corresponding object.

Let $termset(d) = \{t_1, \ldots, t_k\}$, formally every document d determines a sequence: $(t_1, f(t_1, d)), \ldots, (t_k, f(t_k, d)), positive(d)$. The sequence can determine a decision rule: $(t_1, f(t_1, d)) \wedge \ldots \wedge (t_k, f(t_k, d)) \rightarrow Positive(d)$ or in short $d(A_C) \rightarrow d(A_D)$.

We can obtain a lot of decision rules as showed in the above example. However there exists ambiguities whist we use the decision rules to determine relevance of Web pages for a specified topic. For example, give an instance of a piece of information that it contains only four terms t_3, t_4, t_5 and t_6; but we can found two rules' premises (d_3 and d_4) which match this instance. To remove such ambiguities, we present the concept of rough association rules in next section.

3 Rough Association Rules

For every attribute $a \in A_C$, its domain is denoted as V_a; especially in the above example, V_a is the set of all natural numbers. Also A_C determines a binary relation $I(A_C)$ on $\mathcal{D}$ such that $(d_i, d_j) \in I(A_C)$ if and only if $(a(d_i)>0$ and $a(d_j)>0)$ for every $a \in A_C$, where $a(d_i)$ denotes the value of attribute a for object $d_i \in \mathcal{D}$.

It is easy to prove that $I(A_C)$ is an equivalence relation, and the family of all equivalence classes of $I(A_C)$, that is a partition determined by A_C, is denoted by $\mathcal{D}/I(A_C)$ or simply by $\mathcal{D}/A_C$. The classes in $\mathcal{D}/A_C$ are referred to A_C-granules (or called the set of condition granules). The class which contains d_i is called A_C-granule induced by d_i, and is denoted by $A_C(d_i)$. We also can obtain an A_D-granules $\mathcal{D}/A_D$ (or called the set of decision granules) in parallel.

We also need to consider the weight distribution of terms for the condition granules in order to consider the factor of duplications of terms in documents. Let cd_i be $\{d_{i1}, d_{i2}, ..., d_{im}\}$, we can obtain a weigh distribution about the terms in these documents using the following equation: $weight(a_j) = \dfrac{a_j(cd_i)}{\sum_{a \in A_C} a(cd_i)}$, where we use a *merge* operation to assign a value to condition granules' attributes: $a(cd_i) = a(d_{i1}) + a(d_{i2}) + ... + a(d_{im})$ for all $a \in A_C$.

Table 2 illustrates the set of condition granules for positive documents in Table 1, where each condition granule consists of a *termset* and a weight distribution. For example, $cd_1 = <\{t_1, t_2\}, (2/3, 1/3, 0, 0, 0, 0, 0)>$ or in short $cd_1 = \{(t_1,2/3), (t_2, 1/3)\}$.

Table 2. Condition granules

Condition granule	t_1	t_2	t_3	t_4	t_5	t_6	t_7
cd_1	2/3	1/3					
cd_2			1/2	1/4		1/4	
cd_3			2/5	1/5	1/5	1/5	
cd_4	1/3	2/9				2/9	2/9

Formally we represent the association as a mapping $\Gamma: \mathcal{D}/A_C \rightarrow 2^{(\mathcal{D}/AD) \times [0,1]}$ where $\Gamma(cd_i)$ is the set of conclusions for premise cd_i ($i = 1, ..., |\mathcal{D}/A_C|$), which satisfies: $\sum_{(fst,snd) \in \Gamma(cd_i)} snd = 1$ for all $cd_i \in \mathcal{D}/A_C$. We also consider the support degree for each condition granule. The obvious way is to use the cited numbers in the decision table, that is, $NC(cd_i) = \sum_{d \in cd_i} N_d$ for every condition granule cd_i. By normalizing, we can get a support function sup on $\mathcal{D}/A_C$ such that

$$sup(cd_i) = \dfrac{NC(cd_i)}{\sum_{cd_j \in \mathcal{D}/A_C} NC(cd_j)} \text{ for all } cd_i \in \mathcal{D}/A_C.$$

Given a condition granule cd_i, let $\Gamma(cd_i) = \{(fst_{i,1}, snd_{i,1}), ..., (fst_{i,|\Gamma(cd_i)|}, snd_{i,|\Gamma(cd_i)|})\}$ We call "$cd_i \rightarrow fst_{i,j}$" a *rough association rule*, its *strength* is $sup(cd_i) \times snd_{i,j}$ and its *certainty factor* is $snd_{i,j}$, where $1 \leq j \leq |\Gamma(cd_i)|$.

From the above definitions, we have $snd_{i,j} = \frac{|cd_i \cap fst_{i,j}|}{|cd_i|}$ which proves the above definitions about strengths and certainty factors are the generalization of Pawlak's definitions about decision rules.

Table 3 illustrates how to use the negative rule (cd_5) to update positive rules, where we use the reshuffle operation defined in [3].

Table 3. Shifting weights in some condition granules

Condition granule	t_1	t_2	t_3	t_4	t_5	t_6	t_7
cd_1	4/7	3/7					
cd_2			1/4	1/8		5/8	
cd_3			1/5	1/10	7/20	7/20	
cd_4		1/3	2/9			2/9	2/9
cd_5				1/2	1/2		

4 Related Work and Conclusions

Data mining has been used in Web text mining, which refers to the process of searching through unstructured data on the Web and deriving meaning from it. One of main purposes of text mining is association discovery, where the association between a set of terms and a category (e.g., a term or a set of terms) can be described as association rules. The current association discovery approaches include maximal patterns [1], sequential patterns [6] and closed sequential patterns [7].

In this paper, we present a novel concept of rough association rules to improve of the quality of association discovery for text mining. To compare with the traditional association mining, the rough association rules include more specific information and can be updated dynamically in order to produce more effective results.

References

1. R. Feldman, et. al., Maximal association rules: a new tool for mining for keyword co-occurrences in document collection, *3rd International conference on knowledge discovery* (KDD), 1997, 167-170.
2. J. Han and M. Kamber, Data mining: concepts and techniques, Morgan Kaufmann Publishers, 2001.
3. Y. Li and N. Zhong, Capturing evolving patterns for ontology-based, *IEEE/WIC/ACM International Conference on Web Intelligence*, 2004, Beijing, China, 256-263.
4. Y. Li and N. Zhong, Web mining model and its applications on information gathering, *Knowledge-Based Systems*, 2004, Vol. 17, 207-217.
5. Z. Pawlak, In pursuit of patterns in data reasoning from data, the rough set way, *3rd International Conference on Rough Sets and Current Trends in Computing*, 2002, USA, 1-9.
6. F. Sebastiani, Machine learning in automated text categorization, *ACM Computing Surveys*, 2002, Vol. 34, 1-47.
7. S.-T. Wu, Y. Li, Y. Xu, B. Pham and P. Chen, Automatic pattern taxonomy exatraction for Web mining, *IEEE/WIC/ACM International Conference on Web Intelligence*, 2004, Beijing, China, 242-248.

Intrusion Detection Using Text Mining in a Web-Based Telemedicine System

J.J. García Adeva, J.M. Pikatza, S. Flórez, and F.J. Sobrado

Department of Languages and Computer Systems,
Faculty of Computer Science,
The University of the Basque Country,
San Sebastián, Spain
{jjga, jm.pikatza, sh.florez, fj.sobrado}@ehu.es

Abstract. Security in telemedicine systems might be considered a particularly sensitive subject due to the type of confidential information generally handled and the responsibilities consequently derived. In this work we focus on detecting attempts of gaining unauthorised access to a telemedicine web application. We introduce a new Text Mining module that by using Text Categorisation of the web application server log entries is capable of learning the characteristics of both normal and malicious user behaviour. As a result, the detection of misuse in the web application is achieved without the need of explicit programming hence improving the system maintainability.

Keywords: Web Intrusion Detection, Machine Learning, Text Mining, Telemedicine.

1 Introduction

Arnasa [1] is a web-based Decision Support System for asthma treatment. Its main feature consists of integrating the implicit knowledge from Clinical Practice Guidelines (CPG) in order to sustain the decision support to health professionals [2].

Nowadays there is a large number of Governments, including the European Union [3] and the Spanish Authorities [4], that consider health-related data to have a very high security risk. In consequence, the owner of this type of data must comply with severe security measures to guarantee its confidentiality, including password-based access control, activity logging, secure data storage, etc. Medical software systems, such as Arnasa, are affected and have to take the necessary steps to fulfill these legal directives. The present work pays attention to the security of the access control module by detecting intrusion attempts.

There are two main types of intrusion detection methods: *anomaly detection* and *misuse* (also known as *signature detection*). For this work, we are interested in the misuse detection technique as it has the advantages of discovering intrusions with a low number of false positives. The distinctive characteristic of our approach when compared to some related work [5,6] is that the log information created by the web server is not necessarily structured. In other words, while some of the log entries do always keep the same structure, some others do not. Besides, some log entries may contain additional information expressed in one or several natural languages. In view of this requirement, it is clear that a regular Data Mining approach, relying on structured information, is not enough. For this reason, we decided to make use of Text Mining techniques, particularly Text Categorisation, which relies upon non-structured text information.

2 System Description

2.1 Arnasa Overview

Arnasa has three well defined parts that include the client side, the server side, and an external Data Server that belongs to the Health institution system. Our application was developed using Java Enterprise Edition (J2EE), while Hibernate was employed for the object/relational persistence, Apache Tomcat as the web container, and JBoss as the web application server. The main functionalities include the role-based System Access, Management of Asthma-specific Data strongly relying on the external Data Server, Support Decision Requests to provide recommendations using common knowledge from guidelines, and Guidelines Editing for experts to create new CPG.

2.2 Access Control Activity

Access control and administration in Arnasa is based on filters and the application of Java Authentication and Authorisation Service (JAAS). This type of implementation is independent of the application server used, as no configuration files specific to the application server are needed whatsoever. The basic structure is based on two filters: `LoggedInFilter` for authorisation and `LogonActionFilter` for authentication. The execution permissions for the different system functionalities are defined in a database table. Each type of permission is defined as the URL that corresponds to the system functionality. This approach is particularly aimed at avoiding malicious direct GET requests using URLs instead of the proper execution order through menu options. Furthermore, all the traffic between the client web browser and the web server is carried out over Secure Socket Layer (SSL).

Three different levels of logging are used: *info*, *debug*, and *error*. The entries found in the web application log file are interlaced and include which user was logged in, which functionality was requested, what execution exceptions or errors took place, what web pages were requested or served, the click-streams, and other relevant incidents related to the execution of the web application. Fig. 1 shows an example of two log entries. As it can be regarded by lines 3 and 8, many of the log entries do not have a fixed structure as they include some natural language text. Most of these text messages are written in Spanish with some in Basque.

```
1  2005-05-30 09:51:53,218 DEBUG [net.sf.hibernate.impl.Printer]
2  com.erabaki.arnasa.model.bd.jaas.dto.Permisos{rolesSet=uninitialized,
3  descripcion=Permiso para lee un enlace, treeSet=uninitialized,
4  idPermiso=89, tipo=DYNAPATH,
5  pathUri=/educ_m/links/enlaces/Leer_enlace.do}
6  2005-05-30 09:51:53,218 DEBUG [net.sf.hibernate.impl.Printer]
7  com.erabaki.arnasa.model.bd.jaas.dto.Permisos{rolesSet=uninitialized,
8  descripcion=Permiso para visualizar en 3D, treeSet=uninitialized,
9  idPermiso=43, tipo=PATH,pathUri=/ped_m/informes/visualizacion/
10 Elegir_periodoEstudio.do?modo=3d&tipoInforme=4}
```

Fig. 1. Example of Log Entries

2.3 Text Mining Module

Both the Text Mining module of Arnasa and the experiments covered in this paper are based on our own Text Mining framework, which was developed using Java Standard Edition (J2SE). It includes functionalities for Text Categorisation, Language Identification, Text Summarisation, and Text Clustering. Regarding the Text Categorisation functionality used in this project, it includes several learning algorithms such as Naïve Bayes [7] (multinomial and complement), Rocchio [8], and kNN [9]. These algorithms can also be used as the base binary learners for ensembles using the decomposition methods One-to-All, Pairwise Coupling, and Error-Correcting Output Codes (ECOC). The documents to categorised can be provided in English, German, French, Spanish, and Basque and they may belong to one or several categories. There is also complete evaluation of results including the category-specific measures TP_i, FP_i, FN_i, π_i, ρ_i, F_{1_i} and the averaged measures π^μ, ρ^μ, F_1^μ, π^M, ρ^M, F_1^M, as well as partitioning of the testing space using n-fold Cross Validation.

2.4 Intrusion Detection Component

The Intrusion Detection Component is an independent process that can run on either the same server or remotely a different one from where Arnasa is installed. As it can be observed in Fig. 2, this component exposes a Web Service that receives both log entries and control instructions from the Application Server. The Intrusion Analyser component transforms the log entries into text documents that are sent to the Text Categoriser. There is a Document Repository handled by the Text Categoriser to store these text documents. In cosequence, when the system is restarted there is no need to process those documents again. When the Intrusion Analyser detects a possible intrusion attempt, it notifies the Application Server that takes the appropriate action, usually involving raising a severe alarm with the system administrator and blocking the last action requested by the suspicious user.

From the Text Categoriser point of view, we defined the two categories (or labels) *normal* and *misuse* for the text documents to be handled by this module.

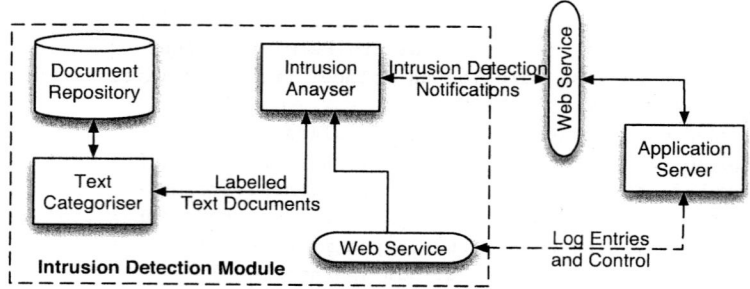

Fig. 2. General Overview of the Intrusion Detection Module

In this particular application of text categorisation, a text document is defined by a number of log entries previously generated by the web application server. In order for a machine learning algorithm to learn the classification models of the *normal* and *misuse* categories, it needs to be previously supplied with a set of training instances. We experimentally determined that using a few thousand entries for each category is enough to properly train the classifier. It is after training the system that it is then prepared to classify new log entries as belonging to the category *normal* or *misuse*. Since a text document with just a single log entry does not contain enough information to be categorised accurately, we decided to use a sequence of log entries to assemble each text document. We experimentally determined that text documents with around 15 log entries provided the best results. Another important decision at this point is regarding when to consider that an intrusion attempt has taken place. We experimentally determined that a number around 7 produced good results.

3 Experimental Results

In order to evaluate the performance of the Intrusion Detection module in terms of detection accuracy, we carried out some off-line tests. These experiments involved using the system for a week under both normal and deliberate malicious use. In this scenario, the Access Control component generated a sufficient number of log entries that allowed to properly train and test the Text Categoriser within the Intrusion Detection component. After we had collected enough information, we employed around 5,000 log entries of each one of the two categories to train the learning algorithms of the Text Categoriser. The rest of the log information, consisting of 16,995 *normal* log entries and 2,235 items categorised as *misuse* were left for testing.

Feature selection was performed using the function $\chi^2(t_i, c_j)$ that measures the dependence of the category c_j on the occurrence of the term t_i. Using χ^2 produced better results than other feature selection functions such as Term Frequency, Document Frequency, or Information Gain. We used a reduction factor

Table 1. Experimental Classification Accuracy Measurements

Classification Algorithm		Category-specific					Averaged	
		TP	FP	FN	F_1	category	F_1^M	F_1^μ
	Bayes	149	75	0	0.7989	misuse	0.8834	0.9447
		1133	0	75	0.968	normal		
	kNN	132	91	7	0.77	misuse	0.865	0.927
		1127	7	91	0.96	normal		
	Rocchio	148	87	1	0.7708	misuse	0.8665	0.9352
		1121	1	87	0.9622	normal		

$\xi = 0.7$ that left around 300 different features. The feature vectors were built using a sparse representation for the sake of memory usage efficiency. Each feature was weighted by means of the function TF/IDF(t_i, d_j).

We display several measurements of classification accuracy in Table 1, which is divided into three sections, each one corresponding to a classification algorithm. For each one of them, there are both category-specific and averaged measurements. On the one hand, the category-specific measures displayed in this table include the number of TP (i.e. true positives or number of correctly classified instances), FP (i.e. false positives or number of instances incorrectly classified in the category in question), FN (i.e. false negatives or number of instances incorrectly classified not in the category in question), and F_1 to indicate the average correctly classified instances. On the other hand, F_1^M is the macro-averaged measure that provides a performance indication of uncommon categories while F_1^μ is the micro-averaged measure that favours the most frequent categories.

The three text categorisation algorithms provided a high rate of classification success, always above 90%. Naïve Bayes was particularly interesting, not only for being the most accurate, but also the fastest in training and classification time as well as the most efficient in terms of system memory usage. Although kNN was almost equally efficient as Naïve Bayes in terms of memory usage, its accuracy and execution time is worse than the other two algorithms. Rocchio offered intermediate results between Naïve Bayes and kNN.

4 Conclusions

We have introduced an Intrusion Detection component integrated into a web-based Decision Support System for asthma treatment. The novelty of this approach is the use of Text Mining, and particularly Text Categorisation, to detect misuse attempts of the web application, focusing mainly on the access control aspect. The advantage of this approach over others often based on Data Mining is that the log information generated by the system does not need any structure-based processing while it can contain text in natural language. When compared to other methods such as pattern matching of deductive inference (i.e. expert systems), our technique based on machine learning offers the advantage of not requiring any explicit programming while offering very good performance in terms of classification accuracy.

Acknowledgements

This project was funded by the Department of Industry, Commerce and Tourism of the Basque Government (grant SAIOTEK S-PE04UN18), the Spanish Ministry of Education and Science (grant MEC TIN2004-06689-C03-01), and the University of the Basque Country (grant 1/UPV 00141.226-T-15436/2003). The authors are thankful to José I. Rubio for generating the log files and Nick Carroll for his useful comments on the draft.

References

1. J., S.F., J.M., P., I.U., L., J.J., G.A., de Ipiña D., L.: Towards a clinical practice guideline implementation for asthma treatment. Lecture Notes in Artificial Intelligence **3040** (2004) 587–596
2. Pikatza, J.M., Larburu, I.U., Sobrado, F.J., Adeva, J.J.G.: Arnasa: una forma de desarrollo basado en el dominio en la construcción de un DSS para la gestión del proceso de tratamiento del asma vía Web. In: 7th Software Engineering and Data Bases Conference (JISBD), Madrid, Spain (2002)
3. Parliament, E.: Directives 97/46/CE and 97/66/CE (1997)
4. de Administraciones Públicas, M.: Ley orgánica 15/1999, de 13 de diciembre, de protección de datos de carácter personal (1999)
5. Lee, W., Stolfo, S.: Data mining approaches for intrusion detection. In: Proceedings of the 7th USENIX Security Symposium, San Antonio, TX (1998)
6. Barbara, D., Couto, J., Jajodia, S., Wu, N.: Adam: a testbed for exploring the use of data mining in intrusion detection. In: Special section on data mining for intrusion detection and threat analysis. Volume 30-4., New York, NY, USA, ACM Press (2001) 15–24
7. Lewis, D.D.: Naive (Bayes) at forty: The independence assumption in information retrieval. In Nédellec, C., Rouveirol, C., eds.: Proceedings of ECML-98, 10th European Conference on Machine Learning, Chemnitz, DE, Springer Verlag, Heidelberg, DE (1998) 4–15
8. Moschitti, A.: A study on optimal parameter tuning for Rocchio Text Classifier. In: Proceedings of the 25th European Conference on Information Retrieval Research. (2003)
9. Yang, Y., Chute, C.G.: An example-based mapping method for text categorization and retrieval. ACM Trans. Inf. Syst. **12** (1994) 252–277

Web Usage Mining Using Evolutionary Support Vector Machine

Sung-Hae Jun

Department of Statistics, Cheongju University,
360-764 Chungbuk, Korea
shjun@cju.ac.kr

Abstract. The web logs contain the information of the user's access record to a web site. The recommender system of the web site is improved by analyzing web log file including user's duration time at each web page. The web usage mining is the application of data mining techniques to large web data repositories in order to extract usage patterns. Many algorithms have been proposed to construct recommender system in web usage mining. In general, the size of web log records is large. So we have difficulties to analyze web log data. To make matter worse, the web log data are very sparse. It is very hard to estimate the dependencies between the web pages. Therefore, we solved these problems of web usage mining using combined evolutionary computing into support vector machine. In this paper, we proposed a new mining model for web usage mining. We verified the performance of proposed model using two data sets from KDD Cup 2000 and our web server.

1 Introduction

The web log records contain much collection of hyperlink information and the usage transactions of web page access. The size of web log data is very large, but web log data are very sparse. So we have serious difficulties for web mining. It is very difficult to estimate the dependencies of all web pages from spare web log data. We have found that the statistical learning theory was a good approach for analyzing the sparse data because of its ε-insensitive loss function[18]. Using statistical learning theory as a missing value imputation, the spare data set is changed to complete data set[10]. Our previous research provided a useful strategy for analyzing sparse data like web log data. Our work was to use SVR(support vector regression) among statistical learning models[10]. The SVR is the regressive version of SVM(support vector machine) by Vapnik[7],[17]. The SVM can be applied to the case of regression, maintaining all the main features that characterize the maximal margin. Using SVR, he made an efficient missing value imputation model to analyze sparse web log data[14]. But, including statistical learning theory, the learning approaches based on minimizing objective function of errors have local minima problems. The recent evolving researches have played an important role for constructing optimal models without minimizing training errors. In this paper, combining the evolutionary computing into SVM, we proposed an evolutionary SVM for web usage mining.

2 Evolutionary Support Vector Machine for Web Usage Mining

In this section, we proposed our ESVR(evolutionary SVM for regressive model). Biological evolution by the way of natural selection is a theory that has changed the way scientists view the world. Distinguished from traditional GA(genetic algorithm), co-evolving approach is evolutionary mechanism of the natural world with competition or cooperation[4],[13]. The organism and the environment including it evolve together. We applied the approach of not cooperation but competition to our proposed co-evolutionary model. In our competitive co-evolving approach, host-parasites co-evolution was used. The host and parasites were used for modeling ESVR and training data set respectively. In ESVR, the model and training data set were considered as the organism and the environment including it. In other words the evolving ESVR model was followed the evolution of host. The initial parameters for ESVR model were determined as uniform random numbers from -1 to 1. The fitness function of ESVR was the inverse form of the squared errors between real and predict values as following.

$$f_{host}(x) = \frac{C}{\sum_{i=1}^{F}\sum_{j=1}^{N_{out}}(o_{ij}(x)-t_{ij})^2} \qquad (1)$$

In the above equation, t was the value of known target variable and o was computed output value for prediction. C was a constant. F and N_{out} were the numbers of patterns and items respectively. Next, the training of given data set was performed by evolving parasites. The evolution of training data was performed to retain larger training errors. So, the fitness function for training data set was inverse of the fitness function of ESVR model as the following.

$$f_{parasites}(x) = \sum_{i=1}^{D}\sum_{j=1}^{N_{out}}(o_{ij}(x)-t_{ij})^2 \qquad (2)$$

D and N_{out} were the numbers of patterns and items respectively in the above equation. The evolutionary approaches of ESVR and training data set were competitive. In other words, proposed model was a competitive co-evolving between two different groups. One was the parasites' evolution of given training data set. The other was the host's evolution of ESVR. Therefore, the ESVR process was consisted of two parts which were parasite's evolution for training data and host's evolution for ESVR model. They were connected by competitive co-evolving approach. The detailed process of ESVR was shown in the following figure.

In the below figure, the ESVR model and training data set were respectively evolved. During evolution for weight optimization of ESVR, the competitive co-evolving was occurred between evolving ESVR model and evolving training data set. In this place our model used co-evolutionary computation instead of Lagrange multipliers of traditional SVM for parameter optimization. The following is a pseudo-code of ESVR.

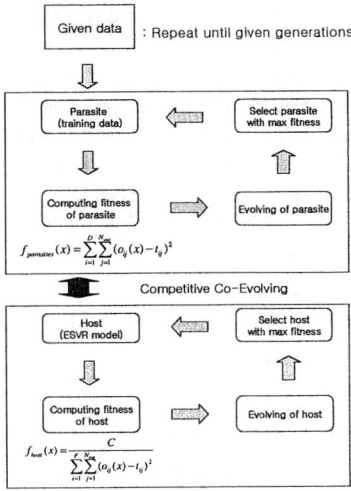

Fig. 1. ESVR process

BEGIN
  INITIALIZE population, $(\underset{\sim}{w}, C) \in R^{p+1}$;
      p: the dimension of weights, l: a regularization parameter
  EVALUATE
      1. ESVR model by $f_{host}(x)$;
      2. Training data set by $f_{parasites}(x)$;
  REPEAT UNTIL (*TERMINATION CONDITION* is satisfied) **DO**
      1. *SELECT* parents;
      2. *MUTATE* the resulting offspring;
          Draw z_i from N(0,1); $y_i^t = x_i^t + z_i$ for all $i \in \{1, \cdots, n\}$;
      3. *EVALUATE* new candidates;
          If ($f(\underset{\sim}{x^t}) \leq f(\underset{\sim}{y^t})$) then $\underset{\sim}{x^{t+1}} = \underset{\sim}{x^t}$; else $\underset{\sim}{x^{t+1}} = \underset{\sim}{y^t}$;
          End if
      4. *SELECT* individuals for the next generation;
          Set $t=t+1$;
  Loop
END

3 Experimental Results

In this first, we showed the experimental results using KDD Cup 2000 data[20]. The data set contained web log file of real internet shopping mall(gazelle.com). After data cleaning, the data set had 13,109 cookie-ids(users) and 269 assortment-ids(web pages). The value of each instance was duration time(0~1,000 second(s)). In this experiment, the P-score(propensity score), MCMC(Markov Chain Monte Carlo), and general SVR methods were compared with our ESVR. The P-score and MCMC methods have been good techniques for web usage mining as multiple missing value imputation[2],[8],[11],[12],[15],[16]. We used MSE(mean squared error) in the following for evaluating performance[6].

$$MSE = \frac{1}{N}\sum_{i=1}^{N}(T_i - O_i)^2 \qquad (3)$$

where, T_i is the target variable(known) and O_i is the predictive variable(unknown). The smaller the value of MSE is, the better the performance of the method is. The following Table shows the result of this experiment.

Table 1. Result of evaluation: KDD Cup

Methods		MSE (total)	MSE (upper 50%)
Multiple Imputation	P-score	3.10	2.38
	MCMC	2.36	1.98
SVR		1.69	1.21
ESVR		1.42	0.98

In this result, the MSE values of total and upper 50% of testing data were computted. The MSE of SVR was smaller than propensity score and MCMC. But, the MSE of ESVR was the smallest in the comparative models. Therefore, we found the ESVR had a good performance. Also, we made an experiment on the performance of ESVR by comparing with SVR, Pearson's correlation, and collaborative filtering methods[1],[3],[14]. For this experiment, the 150 users, those who accessed more than 20 web pages, were used. On the assumption that 10 pages of above given data were already visited, the other 10 pages were used for estimating the preference of each web page. The preferences of web pages were computed by ESVR. According to the order of preference value, the web pages standing a high 50% rank of given data were defined 'High' and the others were defined 'Low'.

Table 2. Accuracy evaluation of recommendation

Confidence	ESVR	SVR	Pearson's correlation	Collaborative filtering
P(High|High)	0.53	0.41	0.35	0.33
P(Low|Low)	0.43	0.38	0.31	0.29
P(High|Low)	0.09	0.16	0.16	0.19
P(Low|High)	0.08	0.12	0.13	0.18

In the above table, we used following confidence measure for the evaluation of recommendation system[6].

$$Confidence(X \Rightarrow Y) = P(Y \mid X) \qquad (4)$$

The equation is the conditional probability of Y given that X has occurred. The X and Y were the web pages in our experiment. In the experimental result, P(High|High) was showed the probability of visited High(web pages) after visited High(web pages). So we wanted that the values of P(High|High) and P(Low|Low) were large and the values of P(High|Low) and P(Low|High) were small. We compared ESVR with Pearson's correlation and collaborative filtering models. Because they have been good models for recommender systems[5],[9],[14]. We knew that the confidence of ESVR was the best in the comparative methods in the above table. In the next we used the web log data of our web server for another experiment[19]. It contained members' profiles, lecture notes, research information, and so forth. Its contents structure was showed as the following figure.

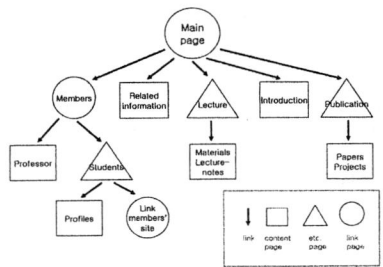

Fig. 2. Contents structure of our web server

After data preprocessing, our data set had 513 cookie-ids(users) and 115 assortment-ids(web pages). The value of each instance was duration time(0~1,000 second(s)). We compared our method with nonlinear regression, SVR with polynomial learning machine kernel, SVR with radial basis function networks kernel, and SVR with two layer perceptron kernel[7]. The following table shows the experimental result.

Table 3. Result of evaluation: our web server

Methods		MSE
SVR	Polynomial	2.15
	RBF	1.98
	Two-layer	2.50
Nonlinear Regression		3.16
ESVR		1.32

We found the MSE of ESVR was the smallest in the comparative methods. In traditional SVR methods, the SVR with RBF kernels was smaller than any other SVR.

4 Conclusion

In this paper, we proposed ESVR model for an effective web usage mining. The evolutionary computing and SVM have been mainly used in machine learning. But, we combined the evolutionary computing into SVM for applying to recommender system of web usage mining. In our work, we verified the performance of ESVR by the MSE and the confidence of recommendation in web usage mining. Compared with popular methods, we knew that the performance of ESVR was improved. Our future works will be to develop the ESVC(evolutionary SVM for clustering) for web documents clustering in the web mining.

References

1. Agrawal, R., Imielinski, T., Swami, A.: Mining association rules between sets of items in large databases, Proceeding of the ACM SIGMOD International Conference on Management of Data, (1993)
2. Conversano, C., Cappelli, C.: Missing data incremental imputation through tree based methods, 14th Conference on Computational Statistics, pp. 24-28, (2002)
3. Cooley, R., Mobasher, B., Srivastava, J.: Web Mining: Information and Pattern Discovery on the World Wide Web, Proceeding of the 9th IEEE International Conference on Tools with Artificial Intelligence, (1997)
4. Eiben, A. E., Smith, J. E.: Introduction to Evolutionary Computing, Springer, (2003)
5. Fisher, D., Hildrum, K., Hong, J., Newman, M., Thomas, M., Vuduc, R.: SWAMI: A Framework for Collaborative Filtering Algorithm Development and Evaluation, Proceeding of SIGIR 2000, ACM Press, (2000)
6. Han, J., Kamber, M.: Data Mining Concepts and Techniques, Morgan Kaufmann, (2001)
7. Haykin, S.: Neural Networks, Prentice Hall, (1999)
8. Hoaglin, D. C., Mosteller, F., Tukey, J. W.: Understanding robust and exploratory data analysis, John Wiley & Sons, (2000)
9. Jang, J. S., Jun, S. H., Oh, K. W.: Fuzzy Web Usage Mining for User Modeling, International Journal of Fuzzy Logic and Intelligent Systems, vol. 2, no. 3, pp. 204-209, (2002)
10. Jun, S. H.: Web Usage Mining Using Support Vector Machine, Lecture Note in Computer Science, vol. 3512, pp. 349-356, (2005)
11. Lavori, R. J. A., Dawson, R., Shera, D.: A Multiple Imputation Strategy for Clinical Trials with Truncation of Patent Data, Statistics in Medicine, vol. 14, 1913-1925, (1995)
12. Little, R. J. A., Rubin, D. B.: Statistical Analysis with Missing Data, Wiley Inter-Science, (2002)
13. Mitchell, T. M.: An introduction to Genetic Algorithms, MIT Press, (1998)
14. Resnick, P.,Lacovou, N., Suchak, M., Berfstrom, P., Riedl, J.: GroupLens: An Open Architecture for collaborative filtering of Netnews, Proceedings of ACM 1994 Conference on Computer Supported Cooperative Work, (1994)
15. Rubin, D. B.: Multiple Imputation for Nonresponse in Surveys, John Wiley & Sons, (1987)
16. Schafer, J. L.: Analysis of Incomplete Multivariate Data, Chapman and Hall, (1997)
17. Smola, A.J.: Regression estimation with support vector learning machines, Master's thesis, Technische University, (1996)
18. Vapnik, V. Z.: Statistical Learning Theory, John Wiley & Sons, Inc. (1998)
19. http://delab.cju.ac.kr
20. http://www.ecn.purdue.edu/KDDCUP

Optimization of Genetic Algorithm Parameters for Multi-channel Manufacturing Systems by Taguchi Method

A. Sermet Anagun[*] and Feristah Ozcelik

Osmangazi University, Department of Industrial Engineering,
Bademlik, 26030, Eskisehir, Turkey
{sanagun, fdurmaz}@ogu.edu.tr

Abstract. An important issue in multi-channel manufacturing (MCM) design is the *channel formation* process. In this study, the control parameters that affect the performance of genetic algorithms (GAs) developed to solve channel formation problem, are examined and the optimum values of such parameters are explored using Taguchi method. Two types of problems were taken into account in terms of machines, parts, and channels. Experimental results show that the performance of a GA significantly dependent on the levels of the design factors for the problem being solved. The results also show that Taguchi method is a powerful approach for identifying design factors suitable for the GA comparing to time consuming and possibly impractical trial-error tests.

1 Introduction

Genetic Algorithms (GAs) are stochastic search techniques for approximating optimal solutions within complex search spaces [1]. A GA is an iterative procedure that consists of a constant-size population of individuals, encoding a possible solution in a given problem space. An initial population of individuals is generated as randomly or heuristically [2]. Every evolutionary step, known as a generation, the individuals in the current population are decoded and evaluated according to some predefined quality criterion, referred to as the fitness, or fitness function. To form the next generation, individuals are selected according to their fitness by reproduction.

The choice of parameters in GAs, such as population size, crossover and mutation rates, is a major difficulty when it comes to their utilization. In recent years, much attention has been paid to the optimization of GA's control parameters [1,3,4]. In general, since the values of the GAs' parameters significantly dependent upon the problem considered, the investigation significant parameters that affect the performance of the GAs and the determination the optimum values of such parameters become an important issue. With these considerations, the Taguchi method has been applied not only to select the critical parameters, but also to determine the appropriate values of such parameters in terms of better solutions for the channel formation problem in MCM systems.

---

[*] Corresponding author.

2   MCM and Proposed GA

MCM is based on the simple observation that in an effective manufacturing system multiple channels (or paths) are provided for each manufactured product as it flows through the system [5]. While traditional manufacturing systems provide a single route for each product in general, MCM furnishes alternative routes for significant parts. This allows the product to flow through the facility by choosing the channel that allows for the greatest manufacturing system efficiency at that time. If a certain line is busy or a machine in the line is out of order or in maintenance, the part can be produced at another channel, which is impossible in a flow shop or in classical cellular manufacturing environment.

MCM is built upon cellular manufacturing and incorporates the advantages of the small-cell focus of cellular manufacturing but modifies it by expanding the capabilities of the cells to handle multiple products. Thus, MCM is a conceptual manufacturing system design approach in the manner that job shop, flow shop, and cellular manufacturing are also conceptual manufacturing system design approaches [5]. An important issue in MCM design is the channel formation process - grouping parts into channels and machine sequencing in channels. This problem is identical with cell formation process in cellular manufacturing systems. Cell formation techniques identify part families and machine cells according to information on available machines and processing requirements of the parts [6]. This problem is NP-complete; therefore, most of the proposed algorithms are heuristic in nature. In this study a GA is used to solve channel formation problem. Each channel is depicted as a certain length of sub strings to represent the layout. The internal ordering of these sub strings resembled the sequence of the machines within channels in turn. An initial population of strings up to the specified population size is generated at random. The objective function of the developed model by [7] is adopted as the fitness function of the proposed GA. A modified roulette wheel method where individuals are selected by randomized fitness value is applied. A two-point crossover operator is used and a mutation threshold is applied to decide the mutation time. If the difference between fitness value of the best parent and the worst parent in a population is less than or equal to mutation threshold, a mutation would be performed. Then a random number is generated to determine the gene that has been mutated. The process is terminated, when the best performing chromosomes remain unchanged with 100 generations.

3   Taguchi Method

Taguchi method may be applied to determine the best combination of design factors and to reduce the variation caused by the noise factors [8]. Experimental design using orthogonal arrays (OAs), recommended by Taguchi, not only minimize the number of treatments for each trial, but also keep the pair-wise balancing property. The selection of which OA to use predominantly depends on these items in order of priority [9]: (1) the number of factors and interactions of interest, (2) the number of levels for the factors of interest, and (3) the desired experimental resolution or cost limitations.

Once the levels of design factors have been settled, the analysis of means (ANOM) is conducted to find affection of each factor on the objective value. Hence, the optimum level of each design factor can be found by means of response graph. The analysis of variance (ANOVA) is then performed to determine the significant factors for the selected criterion. Finally, a prediction model consisting of the significant factors is built and confidence interval for estimated mean is formed.

4 The Experimental Design and Results

In order to investigate how GAs behave for different channel formation problems, two types of problems were tested: 7-machine 6-part problem *[7M_6P]* with three channels introduced by [5] and 24-machine 50-part problem *[24M_50P]* with four channels introduced by [7]. Based on the preliminary tests, three design factors were identified as potentially important for performance of GAs developed for *[7M_6P]* problem: (1) population size, (2) crossover rate, and (3) mutation rate. For each of the design factors, based on the related research, three possible levels were considered: (60, 80,100) for population size, (0.3, 0.6, 0.9) for crossover rate and (0.001, 0.005, 0.01) for mutation rate, respectively. L_{27} (3^{13}) OA was selected since it is the most suitable plan for the conditions being investigated, which allows for examining 13 three-level design factors and/or interactions with 27 trials. Using the experiment setups, the mean responses of the design factors are calculated and used the plot response graph.

Based on the response graph, the optimum levels of the design factors of GA designed for *[7M_6P]*, $A_1B_2C_3$ can be found based on the performance criterion which is defined as maximization. It was observed that factor B has the largest effect on the performance criterion in regard with the ANOVA. Factor A and factor C have the next largest effects, respectively. On the other hand, since the interaction effects of AxB and AxC are significant, they are taken into account to calculate the predicted average.

5 Performance Evaluation for Taguchi Method

In the study of [5] manufacturing cells are formed using the trial-and-error approach. They produced a three-cell design with a total budget equal to $1,640,000 and reached the ideal channel coefficients. After applying the Taguchi method to identify appropriate values of the factors of GA for *[7M_6P]*, $A_1B_2C_3$ combination is selected and the predicted average of 12.42411 for fitness value is obtained. The combination represents not only the same channel coefficients, but also lower total budget, $1,520,000, required for the MCM concerned as the ones given by [5].

The problem of *[24M_50P]* problem is studied to test whether the levels of the design factors of GA are dependent to the problem. Optimum design factors' levels for *[7M_6P]* are then used to solve *[24M_50P]*. The results obtained from the Taguchi method is compared with the solution of [7]. The investment cost is decreased from $484,363 to $278,474. Since the channel coefficients of the 50 parts may be represented using a long string, instead of these, the relative channel coefficients are determined. The relative channel coefficients showed that 33 of the 50 parts, regarding to the study of [7], will be produced in previously determined number of the channel at least. Similarly, the solution of the experimentation conducted with the optimum levels obtained for *[7M_6P]* showed that the 29 of the 50 parts will be reached to their ideal channel coefficients. An experimental design is conducted to investigate the levels of the design factors that are suitable for *[24M_50P]*. With respect to ANOM and ANOVA, the combination of $A_2B_1C_1$ should be selected to improve the performance criterion for *[24M_50P]*. Thus the additional machines to configure these channels brought an investment burden of \$417,494. The investment cost is decreased by approximately 13.8%, the number of parts whose ideal channel coefficients are reached is increased from 33 to 39 comparing with the solution of [7].

6 Conclusion

In contrast to the study of [5], the Taguchi based solution provided not only valid channel coefficients, but also lower total budget. On the other hand, for the problem of *[24M_50P]*, it was found that the best results occurred with the combination of $A_2B_1C_1$. Even though the nature of the problems concerned is similar, the appropriate levels of the design factors needed to be separately investigated depending upon the size of the problems. The optimum levels of the design factors were changed in the following fashion; the population size is increased from low level to medium level, the crossover rate is decreased from high level to low level, and the mutation rate is decreased from medium level to low level, as the size of the problem is increased in terms of the parts being produced with the machines available.

References

1. Pongcharoen, P., Hicks, C., Braiden, P.M., Stewardson, D. J.: Determining Optimum Genetic Algorithm Parameters for Scheduling the Manufacturing and Assembly of Complex Products. International Journal of Production Economics. 78 (2002) 311-322
2. Rajasekharan, M., Peters, B.A., Yang, T.: A genetic algorithm for facility layout design in flexible manufacturing systems. International Journal of Production Research. 36 (1998) 95-110
3. Cavory, G., Dupas, R., Goncalves, G.: A Genetic Approach to the Scheduling of Preventive Maintenance Tasks on a Single Product Production Line. International Journal of Production Economics. 74 (2001) 135-146
4. Grefenstette, J.J.: Optimization of Control Parameters for Genetic Algorithms. IEEE Transactions on Systems, Man and Cybernetics. 16 (1986) 122-128
5. Meller, R.D., DeShazo, R.L.: Manufacturing System Design Case Study: Multi-Channel Manufacturing at Electrical Box & Enclosures. Journal of Manufacturing Systems. 20 (2001) 445-456
6. Arzi, Y., Bukchin, J., Masin, M.: An efficiency frontier approach for the design of cellular manufacturing systems in a lumpy demand environment. European Journal of Operational Research 134 (2001) 346-364.
7. Ozcelik, F., Islier, A.A.: Novel Approach to Multi-Channel Manufacturing System Design. International Journal of Production Research. 41 (2003) 2711-2726
8. Taguchi, G.: Systems of Experimental Design. Unipub Kraus International Publishers, New York (1987)
9. Ross, P.J.: Taguchi Techniques for Quality Engineering. 2nd Edn. McGraw-Hill, New York (1996)

UAV Controller Design Using Evolutionary Algorithms

Sergey Khantsis and Anna Bourmistrova

School of Aerospace, Mechanical and Manufacturing Engineering,
RMIT University, GPO Box 2476V, Melbourne, VIC 3001, Australia
s3007192@student.rmit.edu.au,
anna.bourmistrov@rmit.edu.au

Abstract. Design and optimization of the flight controllers is a demanding task which usually requires deep engineering knowledge of intrinsic aircraft behavior. In this study, EAs are used to design a controller for recovery (landing) of a small fixed-wing UAV (Unmanned Aerial Vehicle) on a frigate ship deck. This paper presents an approach in which the whole structure of the control laws is evolved. The control laws are encoded in a way common for Genetic Programming. However, parameters are optimized independently using effective Evaluation Strategies, while structural changes occur at a slower rate. The fitness evaluation is made via test runs on a comprehensive 6 degree-of-freedom non-linear UAV model. The results show that an effective controller can be designed with little knowledge of the aircraft dynamics using appropriate evolutionary techniques. An evolved controller is demonstrated and a set of reliable algorithm parameters is identified.

1 Introduction

Practical engineering problems are often characterized by significant amount of uncertainty, non-linearity and structural complexity. This is especially common in the areas such as system control and automated modeling. Evolutionary computation is an attractive alternative to conventional design and optimization process for many real world systems.

To date, different evolutionary methods have been successfully applied in the area of system control, from synthesis of the linear optimal controllers [1] to complex automated controller design and optimization [2]. However, most of the works were focused rather on optimization part of the design. Meanwhile, a fixed design structure limits controller's functionality and, on the other hand, requires (to some extent) a priori knowledge of the controlled system.

To circumvent this problem, an adaptive design representation has been proposed and applied in different areas of design [3-5]. The idea of such a representation is that the optimization starts on a simple, low dimensional representation, which leads to a fast convergence to a preliminary solution. Subsequently, new dimensions are added and the representation becomes more refined and the search space more complex. For example, in [4] this approach has been used for the representation of the control laws. The search starts from the simplest possible form of the control law: $y=const$ with new parameters introduced through a stochastic procedure called *structure mutation*.

In many engineering problems, the cost of objective function evaluation is extremely high. In addition all EAs are computationally intensive and require high number of objective function evaluations. One of the ways to keep the computational cost of optimization as low as possible is the use of a surrogate evaluation tool, the so called metamodel, which points to potentially good regions which are then examined with the actual evaluation tool [6]. Another, rather more general approach is to employ an effective evolutionary strategy which uses, somewhat similarly to the above metamodel-assisted evolution strategies (MAES), the previous evolution history [7].

In this research, a problem of moderate computational complexity is considered. A control law is executed thousands of times during each simulation run, which limits the possible length of control equations and requires an extremely fast and effective encoding and interpretation. Therefore, a novel approach has been developed, which combines the power and flexibility of both GP and ES. Some knowledge of basic aircraft control allows modification of the structure of the control laws judiciously (yet stochastically) while continuously evolving the numerical parameters of the laws.

2 UAV Recovery Problem

The problem being addressed is landing of a small fixed-wing UAV on a confined space such as frigate-size ship deck. The proposed recovery method involves capture of a damped arresting wire, stretched over the deck between two poles or in a similar manner, by an onboard flexible trailing line with a self-locking hook attached at the end.

The controller being designed guides the UAV to the recovery point, set 1.5 m above the middle of the arresting wire. There are several challenges involved. First, the requirements to the precision are quite high: 2.5--3 m for elevation and ±2.5 m for sideways displacement.

Second, the whole system is affected by different types of disturbances, such as the random starting point, wind turbulence, the ship airwake, and noise of sensor measurements. However, this study presents only the first stage of controller design, and, for simplicity, only one type of disturbances is considered, namely a random initial state. As the proposed design approach is multi-staged as such, gradual inclusion of more and more details, following control laws elaboration, poses no problem.

The aircraft chosen as a prototype for the research is the UAV *Ariel* [14], which is an unmanned aircraft developed by the UAV group in the Department of Aeronautical Engineering at the University of Sydney. The UAV has three main control surfaces (elevator, ailerons and rudder), plus flaps and throttle control.

The following measurements are available for the controller: airspeed V; three body accelerations n_x, n_y, n_z (along the longitudinal, normal and lateral axis respectively); three body angular velocities ω_x, ω_y, ω_z; three Euler angles γ, ψ, θ (roll, yaw, pitch); angle of attack α, and sideslip angle β. Additionally, several relevant values, which may be important for the control, are calculated on the basis of available measurements. Altogether, 36 parameters are fed to the controller.

To provide flexibility in the usage of the inputs for the genetic algorithm and to increase the relevance of their selection, these inputs are organized in three groups: longitudinal control values, lateral control values and common parameters. At the initial stage of the design, only the values from the appropriate group or the common group are allowed being used for a control law. Later in the design process, greater degree of coupling may be allowed by unrestricted usage of the inputs.

The controller directly links the input signals, measured by onboard sensors, with control surface deflections:

$$\delta_i = f_i(u), \quad (1)$$

where δ_i is the ith control surface deflection and u is the vector of input signals.

3   Adaptive Encoding of the Control Laws

For simplicity of description, only one of the control equations (1) will be considered in this section. The adaptive control representation is aimed at combining the advantages of fast low dimensional search with those of increasing the degrees of freedom when needed. The idea is to use a low parametric encoding in the beginning of the conceptual design. This leads to a fast convergence to the regions in the low dimensional search space where good solution can be found. If the progress stagnates due to the limitations in the variability of the encoding, the new parameters can be introduced. A similar idea has been successfully applied in various engineering fields, such as structure optimization of neural networks [5] and turbine blade aerodynamic shape optimization [4].

All physically sensible combinations were included in the list of 36 input parameters. This allowed to manage with only two mathematical operations of addition and multiplication. The only exception is that any parameter can be raised to the power of 2 before applying any other operation.

Conceptually, the representation is a recursive tree-like expression, in which any numeric coefficient k_i can be replaced with another expression. Each variable u_j is accompanied by a coefficient. The product of the coefficient and the variable is always added to the result, producing an expression like $y = k_1u_1 + (k_2u_2 + k_3)u_3^2 + k_4$.

The encoding should allow a simple way of inserting a new parameter in any place of the equation without disrupting its correctness and in a way that this insertion initially does not affect the result. The condition that such a mutation should be neutral is shown to be useful for evolutionary strategies [4, 9].

In a mathematical form, a realization of the evolution could be

$$k_0 \rightarrow k_1u_1 + k_0 \rightarrow (k_2u_2 + k_1)u_1 + k_0. \quad (2)$$

The algorithm is implemented in MATLAB and is linked with the Simulink model of *Ariel* UAV. The main loop of the algorithm realizes conventional strategy (μ, λ)-ES with individual step size adaptation, which uses deterministic selection of the best μ individuals from the population of size λ.

Two control laws, for elevator and ailerons, are evolved simultaneously; each individual consists of a pair of laws. In a simple crossover operation, two offspring individuals from different parents exchange one of the control laws. The crossover, performed with the probability 0.2 to 0.4, noticeably increased the performance of the algorithm. However, at later stages, the optimal crossover rate is presumed to be lower due to increasing degree of coupling and mutual dependency.

The structure mutation is performed every k_s-th generation with the probability p_s. k_s is fixed, while p_s may be either fixed or changing; the best results were obtained when p_s is steadily reduced from $p_{s\ max} = 1$ to $p_{s\ min} = 0.5$ as $p_s = p_{s\ min} + (p_{s\ max} - p_{s\ min}) \cdot 0.98^g$, where g is the generation number. This scheme showed significantly better results than constant application of the structure mutation with accordingly reduced probability p_s / k_s.

Optionally, protection of the individuals after structure mutation can be applied to let the new controller to develop its potential.

The initial control laws $y_a = c_{a0}$ and $y_e = c_{e0}$ (trim settings) were obtained for the middle (reference) initial point ($V_0 = 30$ m/s, distance $\Delta X = 300$ m, elevation $\Delta H = 9$ m) in a similar manner using (2, 10)-CMA-ES. This required only 20--25 generations. These settings, once calculated, were used as a starting point of all subsequent experiments.

Fitness evaluation procedure is a multi-stage process. Fitness value is based on the analysis of the flight data, recorded during a simulated test flight with the controller in the control loop. Not only successful completion of the mission (the UAV enters the target window) is taken into account, but also the common aspects of the flight quality, such as control surfaces usage, oscillations of the accelerations (both transnational and angular) and the flight trajectory. A penalty is assigned for inappropriate behavior as well as for missing the target. The weights and flight parameters to be taken into account for each of these variants are chosen so that it facilitates fast 'learning.' For example, if the aircraft is crashed, the achieved flight time is rewarded; in other cases it is ignored.

Unless the UAV crashes, each fitness value is averaged over three runs. Although this requires three objective function evaluations, it appears to be more effective than a single run with an unbiased starting point. This approach results in a peculiar behavior of the current-best fitness graph Figure 1: if one (or two) of the points is 'hard' for the controller so that it fails often when started from it, the graph will 'jump' periodically from very good values (three successful consecutive runs) to mediocre level (a rather high penalty for failure is added). However, without averaging over three runs, the consequences of a single failure could be fatal, leading to perishing of a potentially good individual.

4 Results

During the experiments, a huge number of different algorithm settings has been tried. A reliable convergence within 100,000 objective function evaluations was observed in approximately 70% of all runs. However, as each run takes up to 24 hr of computation, only potentially effective combinations have been rechecked multiple times to obtain a reliable statistics. Nevertheless, as it can be seen from Figure 1, even within good settings the convergence behavior varies sufficiently. Apparently, this is due to stochastic nature of the objective function and thus ruggedness of the fitness landscape. Temporary deterioration of both average and current-best values is normal and is not a sign of failure.

Best results were observed for mild selection pressure ($\lambda/\mu = 2$). However, for larger population sizes ($\lambda = 48$), a tougher $\lambda/\mu = 4$ gives comparable outcome. On the whole, the best results were obtained using $\lambda = 24$, $\mu = 12$, structure mutation at every

10th generation with the probability gradually reducing from 1.0 to 0.5. However, even for these settings one of the six runs did not converge within 60,000 function evaluations, although some progress is observable. On the other hand, three runs (50%) produced very well performing controllers after less than 35,000 function evaluations. The control laws of one of these controllers are presented in Figure 2.

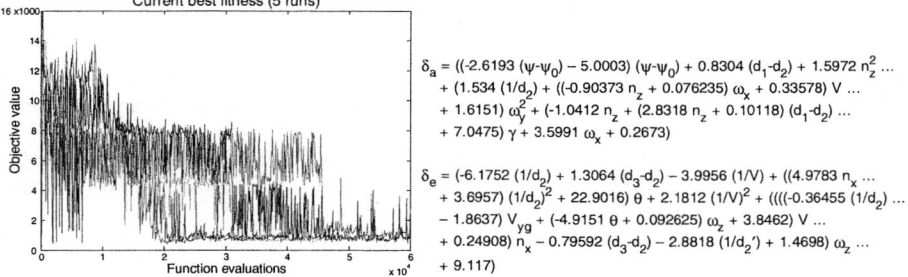

Fig. 1. Current best fitness for five independent runs

Fig. 2. Example of control laws

5 Conclusions

Evolutionary Algorithms are a valuable and effective engineering tool, including the area of system control. Despite being computationally expensive, they allow to use the models of the controlled system in out-of-the-box fashion, without specific knowledge of the system's internals and behavior. In particular, third party models can be easily integrated in an EA.

It is natural and convenient to evolve the control laws as mathematical expressions (or, in general, programs.) However, employing classical Genetic Programming is not always desirable. When knowledge of the basic flight control is available, a more effective adaptive scheme may be used than random shuffling of operations and input values. Reducing the number of operations via including the physically sensible parameter combinations in the terminal set appeared to be effective. Not only it gives better algorithm performance, but also produces more parsimonious and comprehensible control laws.

In addition, flight controllers usually require fine tuning of numeric coefficients, which is better done with Evolution Strategies or other real-coded EAs. Therefore, a combination of ES and GP methods has been applied. Structure mutations introduce new dimensions to the control laws, while ES finds the optimal usage of the new parameters. This scheme allowed evolving a number of high performance controllers.

Stochastic nature of the objective function significantly impedes the evolution. However, gradual complication of the control laws and complying with the principle of strong casualty allows including stochastic components progressively, adding new disturbances as the controller 'learns' to cope with the present ones. Nevertheless, the convergence behavior of the algorithm may be sufficiently different from run to run, although in general the algorithm is robust to change of its parameters, as long as selection pressure is not too high.

References

1. Hunt, K.J.: Polynomial LQG and Hinf controller synthesis: A genetic algorithm solution. In: 31st IEEE CDC. Volume 4., Tucson, AZ (1992) 3604–3609
2. Li, Y., Ng, K.C., Murray-Smith, D.J., Gray, G.J., Sharman, K.C.: Genetic algorithm automated approach to design of sliding mode control systems. Technical Report CSC-94002, Centre for Systems and Control, University of Glasgow (1994)
3. Altenberg, L.: Genome growth and the evolution of the genotype-phenotype map. Evolution as a Computational Process (1995) 205–259
4. Olhofer, M., Jin, Y., Sendhoff, B.: Adaptive encoding for aerodynamic shape optimization using evolution strategies. In: Congress on Evolutionary Computation. Volume 1., Seoul, South Korea (2001) 576–583
5. Sendhoff, B., Kreuz, M.: Variable encoding of modular neural networks for time series prediction. In Porto, V.W., ed.: Congress on Evolutionary Computation, IEEE Press (1999) 259–266
6. Emmerich, M., Giotis, A., ¨Ozdemir, M., Bäck, Th., Giannakoglou, K.: Metamodelassisted evolution strategies. In Merelo Guerv´os, J., et al, eds.: Parallel Problem Solving from Nature VII. Springer-Verlag, Berlin Heidelberg (2002) 361–370
7. Hansen, N., Ostermeier, A.: Completely derandomized self-adaptation in evolution strategies. Evolutionary Computation 9 (2001) 159–195
8. Newman, D.M., Wong, K.C.: Six Degree of Freedom Flight Dynamic and Performance Simulation of a Remotely-Piloted Vehicle. The University of Sydney (1993)
9. Toussaint, M., Igel, C.: Neutrality: A necessity for self-adaptation. In: IEEE Congress on Evolutionary Computation. (2002) 1354–1359
10. Sendhoff, B., Kreuz, M., von Seelen, W.: A condition for the genotype-phenotype mapping: Casualty. In Bck, T., ed.: 7th International Conference on Genetic Algorithms, Morgan Kaufmann (1997) 73–80

River Flow Forecasting with Constructive Neural Network

Mêuser Valença[1], Teresa Ludermir[2], and Anelle Valença[2]

[1] Chesf/UNIVERSO, Rua Gaspar Peres 427/104,
CEP 5670-350, Recife, Brazil
meuser@chesf.gov.br, meuserv@yahoo.com.br
[2] UFPE – Universidade Federal de Pernambuco, Recife, Brazil
tbl@cin.ufpe.br, anellevalenca@yahoo.com.br

Abstract. In utilities using a mixture of hydroelectric and non-hydroelectric power, the economics of the hydroelectric plants depend upon the reservoir height and the inflow into the reservoir for several months into the future. Accurate forecasts of reservoir inflow allow the utility to feed proper amounts of fuel to individual plants, and to economically allocate the load between various non-hydroelectric plants. For this reasons, several companies in the Brazilian Electrical Sector use the linear time-series models such as PARMA (Periodic Auto regressive Moving Average) models. This paper provides for river flow prediction a numerical comparison between constructive neural networks and PARMA models. The results obtained in the evaluation of the performance of Neural Network were better than the results obtained with PARMA models.

1 Introduction

The present Neural networks provide an attractive technology for inflow forecasting, because of (1) their success in power load forecasting, and (2) because of the availability of relevant measurements, including historical data[1][2][3][4].

In this paper, the constructive neural network model [5] is applied to seasonal streamflow forecasting using a database of average monthly inflows of 37 Brazilian hydroelectric plants located in different river basins.

This paper compares models based on Constructive Neural Networks performance with models based on Box-Jenkins methods [6], currently used on the Brazilian Electrical Sector.

The paper is organized as follows. Section 2 brings an overview of the neural network algorithms, followed by a brief presentation of PARMA models in the section 3. Section 4 shows an evaluation of our results. Finally, section 5 concludes the paper.

2 The Constructive Neural Network

2.1 Network Architecture

The goals here are to present practical methods to realize compact networks using the model with hidden units with sigmoidal blocks activation functions. The activation function is [5]

$$Actv_h(x) = (\sigma_{net(h)} + \theta_h) \qquad (1)$$

where h *is* the order of the block (= number of hidden units), θ_h is a bias and $\sigma_{net(h)}$ is the hyperbolic tangent function. The first design step is to divide f (x) up into blocks of equal-degree terms, as in Figure 1. That is

$$f(x) = f_1(x) + f_2(x) + \ldots + f_d(x) \qquad (2)$$

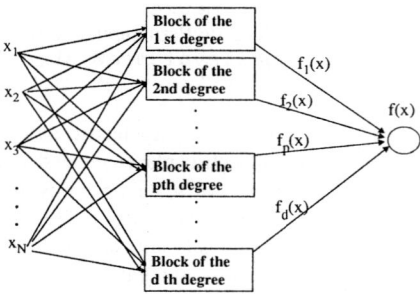

Fig. 1. Network architecture (NSBRN)

The block approach is to realize all terms in $f_p(x)$ functions at the same time, as in Figure 2.

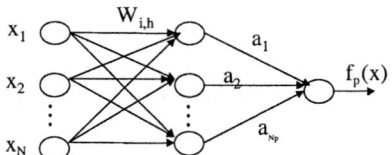

Fig. 2. Block of degree p architecture

The input **x** is an N dimensional vector and x_i is the i-th component of **x**. The inputs are weighted and fed to a layer of h hidden units, where h is the order of the block. Let $f_p(x)$ be the output of the block of degree p. Then,

$$f_p(x) = a_1.(Actv_1(x))^1 + a_2.(Actv_2(x))^2 + +a_3.(Actv_3(x))^3 + \ldots + a_p.(Actv_p(x))^p \qquad (3)$$

and a_h is the weight between h-th hidden unit to output unit and h=1,2,...,p.

3 The PARMA Model

Let us consider the periodic series $z_{v,\tau}$, where v denotes the year, $\tau = 1,\ldots,\omega$ and ω is the number of time intervals in the year. Then the periodic PARMA model for $z_{v,\tau}$ can be written as

$$z_{v,\tau} = \sum_{j=1}^{p} \phi_{j,\tau} \cdot z_{v,\tau-j} - \sum_{i=1}^{q} \theta_{i,\tau} \cdot \varepsilon_{v,\tau-i} + \varepsilon_{v,\tau} \qquad (7)$$

where $\phi_{j,\tau}$ and $\theta_{i,\tau}$ are autoregressive and moving average coefficients, respectively, and $\varepsilon_{v,\tau}$ is an normal random variable.

4 Simulation Results

This experiment made use of data related to the monthly inflow values of 37 hydroelectric plants of the Brazilian electrical energy sector. The data sets were divided into two subsets: the first, with 720 patterns, corresponding to the period from January 1931 to December 1990, was selected for training; the second subset, with 96 patterns, corresponding to the period from January 1991 to December 1998, was selected for testing the forecasting with one-step-ahead.

4.1 Evaluation of the Performance of the Neural Network Model

In order to evaluate the forecasting performance of the NeuroInflow model, a few metrics associated with prediction errors were used: the **MAPE** (*"Mean Absolute Percentage Error"*) and the **RMSE** (*"Root Mean Square Error"*).

$$\text{MAPE}(\%) = \frac{1}{N} * \{\sum_{i=1}^{N}[|Zp - Zo|/Zo\} * 100 \qquad (8)$$

$$\text{RMSE} = \frac{1}{N}[\sum_{i=1}^{N}(Zp - Zo)^2]^{0.5} \qquad (9)$$

where: Z_p – forecast value ; Z_o – measured value and N – number of values.

4.2 The Constructive Neural Network Software

This model was used for training of all the points of interest to the monthly program of operation, having been divided in four modules for bigger easiness of use and maintenance. The NORDESTE that makes forecast for 3 plants, the NORTE that makes forecast for 3 plants the SUL that makes forecast for 15 plants and the SUDESTE that makes forecast for 74 plants. Figure 3 presents a vision of the initial screen of this software.

4.2.1 Election of the Region
The access to the subsystems of the system is made through a click on the button that possesses the name of the desired region. For example: after this click in the Southeastern region appears the following screen (Figure 4):

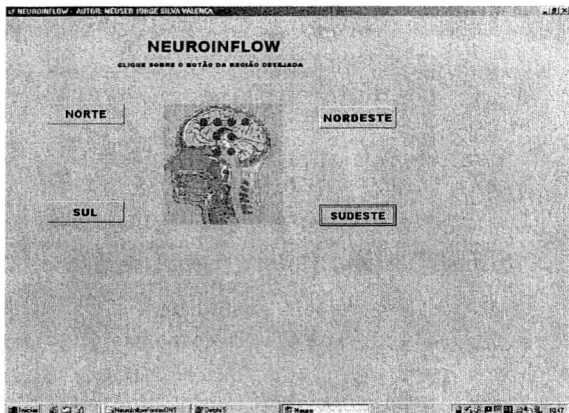

Fig. 3. Initial screen of the software

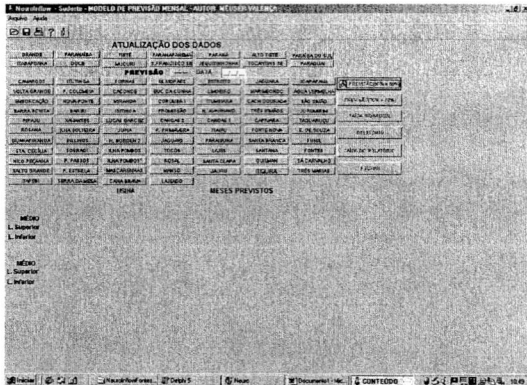

Fig. 4. Screen of the software for the Southeastern region (74 plants)

4.2.2 Election of the Plant

Select the button that possess the name of the plant and click on this. Immediately the forecast carried through for 12 months to the front will be presented in the screen and also a text archive will be generated for impression.

4.2.3 Confidence Intervals

Select the button for which is desired to define the intervals reliable and click on this. You will only be able to define the intervals reliable after you have selected a plant for forecast. For example: selecting the button Forecast (95% and 70%) and giving a click on this the new values will be shown in screen. The screen is of the following form (Figure 5):

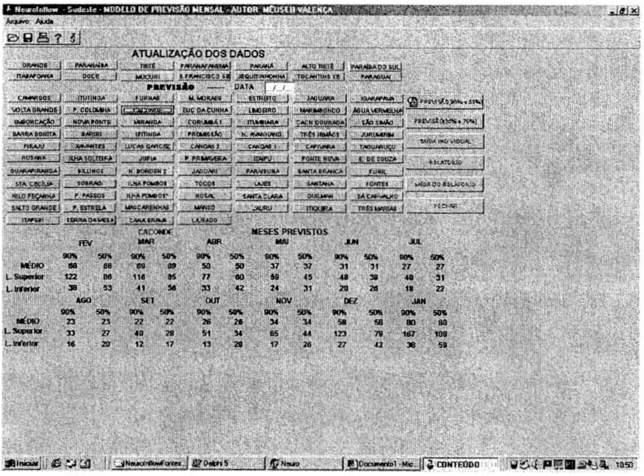

River Flow Forecasting with Constructive Neural Network   1035

Fig. 5. Screen after election of the plant (Plant of Caconde)

This software allows the generation of an only report with the forecast for all the plants of each subsystem with the intervals reliable (Figure 6).

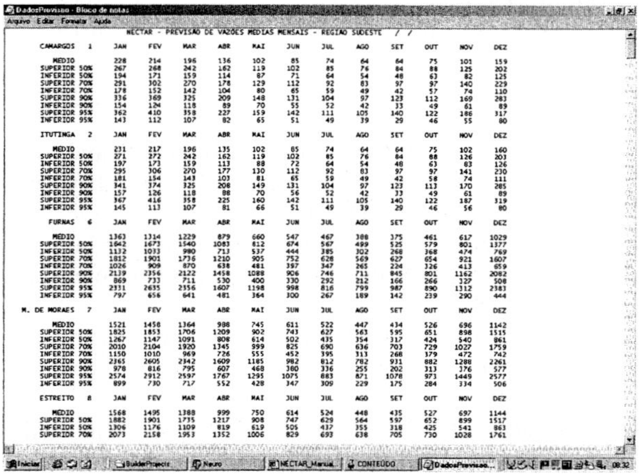

Fig. 6. Screen of the report (Southeastern region)

Table 1 shows, for example, a comparative study of the better results obtained with PARMA models and the results obtained with Constructive Neural Network, one month ahead for six hydroelectric plants.

Table 1. Comparative results one-step-ahead

Hydroelectric plant	PARMA		Constructive Neural Network	
	MAPE	RMSE	MAPE	RMSE
INCR.3M/SBD	19,2	1245	17,9	1230
TUCURUI	15,4	4180	13,5	3604
FOZ DO AREIA	47,6	461	38,0	410
ILHA SOLTEIRA	21,0	1560	17,6	1580
JUPIA	19,0	2000	16,8	1920
TRÊS MARIAS	26,0	544	22,0	538

5 Conclusions

The paper has presented a constructive neural network model (NSRBN) for seasonal streamflow forecasting, called NeuroInflow model. The NeuroInflow model presents a constructive learning, with neurons added to the network whenever new knowledge is necessary. The results obtained with this model were compared to those obtained with PARMA models. The results show a more accurate prediction using the Neuro-Inflow, with a reduction in forecasting error of at least 50%. Constructive neural network model provide good results because the well-known problems of an optimal choice of the neural network architecture are solved in the neural network algorithms by means of an adaptive synthesis of the architecture to provide a parsimonious model for the particular desired function.

References

1. Valença, M. J. S and Ludermir T. B. Multiplicative-Additive Neural Networks with Active Neurons. International Joint Conference on Neural Networks (IJCNN), IEEE, Book of Summaries (2073), Washington, DC, July 1999.
2. Valença, M. J. S and Ludermir T. B. Self-organizing modeling in forecasting daily river flows. V Brazilian Symposium on Neural Networks-Brazilian Computer Society, IEEE, **1**: 210-214, Belo Horizonte 1998.
3. Valença, M. J. S and Ludermir T. B. Uma Rede Neural Construtiva com Atualização dinâmica dos Pesos. IV Congresso Brasileiro de Redes Neurais, pages 114-117, ITA, São José dos Campos, Julho 1999.
4. Valença, M. J. S and Ludermir T. B. Uma nova rede neural polinomial com aplicação na previsão de vazões. V Simpósio Brasileiro de Redes Neurais, . **2**: 273-278, Belo Horizonte 1998.
5. Valença, M. J. S. Analysis and Design of the constructive neural networks for complex systems modeling (in portuguese). Ph.D Theses, UFPE, Brazil, 1999.
6. G.E.P Box & G.M. Jenkins, Time Series Analysis - Forecasting and Control. Holden-Day Inc, California, 1976.

A Novel License Plate Location Method Based on Neural Network and Saturation Information

Yinghua Lu[1,2], Lijie Yu[1], Jun Kong[1], and Canghua Tang[1]

[1] Computer School, Northeast Normal University, Changchun, Jilin Province, China
[2] Computer School, Jilin University, Changchun, Jilin Province, China
{Luyh, yulj774, kongjun, tangch564}@nenu.edu.cn

Abstract. In this paper, a novel license plate location algorithm for color image is presented. Firstly the neural networks are used as filters for analyzing within small windows for an image and deciding whether each window contains a license plate or not coarsely. And then we use the information which the license plate's saturation value is different from the background's, so it can be used to locate license plate finely. At last, color pairs method is presented to prove whether the region we found is the license plate region or not. The experimental results show that proposed algorithms are robust in dealing with the license plate location in complex background.

1 Introduction

The purpose of our research is the automatic recognition of car license plate. As we known, the license plate location is most important stage in the LPR (license plate recognition) systems, which directly affects the system's accuracy. A lot of methods were proposed to locate license plate in recent years, for example edge based detection [1], and morphology based operations [2] [3] [4], and so on. These methods are almost based on gray images, but the color information is an important factor to locate the license plate. In this paper, the location method is based on color images.

This paper is organized as follows: In Section 2, we give two methods to locate the license plate, and give a method to validate that the candidate region is the real plate region or not. We illustrate experimental results obtained on test sets to access the robustness of these methods in Section 3.

2 License Plate Location

2.1 Image Preprocessing

Some images used in our study are captured in different environments and scenes, so the luminance compensation is necessary [5]. This step maps the values in intensity image I to new values in J. It increases the contrast in the output image J. After adjusted operation, the image is brighter and clearer than before. The next work is the saturation adjustment. The color information is very important to license plate location. We can choose an appropriate threshold to adjust the saturation in HIS color space.

2.2 Neural Networks License Plate Location

The next work is license plate location coarsely. In our study, the SOM neural network (Self-Organizing Feature Map) is adopted to do it [6].

The proposed method first applies two SOM neural network-based filters to color image, and then the method uses a post-processor to combine these two filtered images in order to locate license plate.

The main steps are summarized as follows:

Step 1: Convert the original image into gray image. Detect the edge of the gray image using LOG operator. Let I denote the original image and J denote the result image. Partition J and I into small blocks in size of 10×100 and 40×10 respectively.

Step 2: Let a matrix denote the position corresponding of the blocks in I. Each block recorded X and Y matching subscript of an element in the matrix. We calculate median, variance of R in I to all pixels in one block. The same operations are applied to G and B. At last we choose the maximum of the three medians. For every block, we calculate the ratio of the number of the edge pixels whose value is 1 and the whole pixels in J.

Step 3: These seven values (X, Y, three variances, the maximum of three medians, the ratio of the number of the edge pixels whose value is 1 and the whole pixels in J) that were obtained in Step 2 are used as the input for the neural networks training.

Step 4: Combine results that are gotten using two SOM networks. The plate candidate regions are obtained from two filtered images. Intersections of these horizontal and vertical candidate blocks indicate the plate candidate regions, and then we remove isolated blocks and merge neighboring candidate regions. This method can locate the license plate coarsely.

The neural networks are trained with 100 samples that collected under various weather conditions and lighting conditions. And there is one car in each image.

2.3 The License Plate Locating Using Saturation Information

After using the SOM neural networks, we can get several candidate regions. So we need a method to locate the real plate accurately. In our study, the saturation information is adopted to do it.

The license plate's saturation is often different from rest areas of the car. We utilize the saturation to convert the color image into the gray image in HIS color space. The next works are selecting corresponding threshold and get a binarization image. This operation can result in some connected regions. But there are some holes and lines in

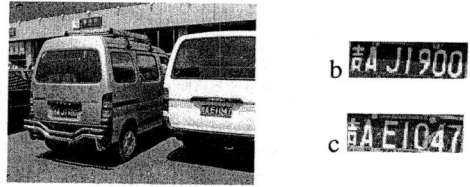

Fig. 1. (a) Original image. (b) The license plate region 1. (c) The license plate region 2.

these regions and it must be removed. The closing operation [4] of morphological operations is used.

After using the closing operation, thin lines and characters strokes on the license plate can be removed. Following step is to remove the isolated point. The fill operation is used to solve this problem.

After using the SOM neural networks to locate coarsely, we use the saturation information method to locate finely. Fig. 1 shows an example of license plate location combining neural network and saturation information.

2.4 Color Pairs Validation

After fine locating stage, our next task is to validate the candidate region that we found is the real region or false. In this paper, the color pairs validation was presented to do it. The color of the characters and the background is fixed in only some types in China. The color pair validation method is scanning the image line by line. For the image of the similar size, the ratio of the color pairs and the number of the background might be within some range.

3 Experimental Results and Conclusions

3.1 Experimental Results

In order to test our algorithm, we performed experiments with three sets of Chinese vehicle images that are distinct from the training sets. Test set 1 consists 200 images of vehicles in a car park. Test set 2 consists 150 images of vehicles traveling on a road. Test set 3 consists 75 images of vehicles that include multiple cars on the road. The sizes of these images are 800×640 and the sizes of the plates in these images range is from100×25 to 300×100. Table 1 descripts the results details in test set 1 and test set 2 respectively.

Table 1. Location results

Test set	Location rate	Missed plate	False location
1	97%	4	1
2	95%	6	4
3	90%	14	7

Table 2. Results of sensitivity test

Gaussian noise	2%	5%	10%
Location rate (%)	97	93.2	81.5
Missed plates	4	14	37
False locations	1	6	25

To show the robustness of the proposed method, we performed a noise sensitivity test [4]. The new test set was created by adding Gaussian noise which variance at 2%, 5%, and 10% respectively. The results show that the noise has lightly effect to the correct location rate. Table 2 descripts the results in test set 1 with noise.

3.2 Conclusions

A method for location license plates in our study uses neural networks and saturation information. The proposed method can get license plates correct location rate at 97 %, 95% and 90% from three test sets respectively. The advantage of this method is that it provides robustness in dealing with slant problems, shadowing problems and noisy, and the speed is very fast.

References

1. M.Yu and Y.D. Kim, "An approach to Korean license plate recognition based on vertical edge matching." IEEE Int. conf. On SMC, vol, 4,pp. 2957-2980.2000.
2. Jun-Wei Hsieh, Shih-Hao Yu, Yung-Sheng Chen, "Morphology-based License Plate Detection from Complex Scenes", 16th International Conference On Pattern Recognition, pp.176-179, 2002
3. D.M..Ha, J.-M.Lee,Y.-D.Kim "Neural-edge- based vehicle detection and traffic parameter extraction" image and vision computing 22, pp. 899-907. 2004
4. S.H. Park, K.I Jung, H. J. Kim "Locating car license plates using neural networks" IEEE electronics letters 19th 1475-1477. 1999.
5. R.C.Gonzalez,R.E. Woods,Digital Image Processing(Reading:Addison-Wesley,1992).
6. S.H.ong, N.C.Yeo, K.H.Lee, Y.V.Venkatesh, D.M.Cao "Segmentation of color images using a two-stage self-organizing network" Image and vision computing, 20, pp.279-289.2002

Verification and Validation of Artificial Neural Network Models*

Fei Liu and Ming Yang

Control and Simulation Center, Harbin Institute of Technology,
150001 Harbin, China
liuf_2005@yahoo.com.cn

Abstract. The increased dependence on artificial neural network (ANN) models leads to a key question – will the ANN models provide accurate and reliable predictions? However, this important issue has received little systematic study. Thus this paper makes general researches on verification and validation (V&V) of ANN models. Basic problems for V&V of ANN models are explicitly presented, a new V&V approach for ANN models is developed, V&V methods for ANN models are deeply discussed, further research areas for V&V of ANN models are recommended, and an example is given.

1 Introduction

During the recent past, the interest in research and application of artificial neural network (ANN) models has increased substantially. The increased dependence on ANN models leads to a key question –Will these models provide accurate and reliable predictions? The reliability of ANN models is built up through verification and validation (V&V).

Often, because of the complex mathematical routines and nature of the training data, the neural network is considered a "black box" and its response may not be predictable. In most instances, traditional testing techniques prove adequate for the acceptance of ANN models. However, in current more complex safety- and mission-critical systems, the standard neural network training-testing approach is not able to provide a reliable method for certification. This V&V challenge is further compounded by adaptive neural network systems, for which traditional testing methods fail to account [1].

V&V of ANN models has been proved extremely difficult, and the lack of well-established techniques and methods to support V&V of ANN models further exacerbates the difficulty of these problems. This important issue has, surprisingly, received little systematic study and most references to ANN model V&V take an ad hoc approach. Thus this paper makes general researches on V&V of ANN models. Basic problems for V&V of ANN models are explicitly presented, a new V&V approach for ANN models is developed, V&V methods for ANN models are deeply discussed, further research areas for V&V of ANN models are recommended, and an example is given.

---

* **Foundation Item:** Project supported by Natural Science Foundation of China (grant No. 60434010).

2 What Is Meant by V&V of ANN Models

V&V is essential to assure that ANN models produce accurate and reliable predictions. Respectively, verification answers the question: "Is an ANN model built rightly?" and validation answers the question: "Is a right ANN model built?" In summary, V&V of ANN models should deal with the following problems:

- Has the ANN model learned the correct data?
- Are the types of networks and learning algorithm appropriate for the goals or requirements of the ANN model?
- Has the ANN model converged to the global minimum or a local minimum?
- How will the ANN model handle data outside of the training set?
- Will the ANN model produce acceptable prediction regions?

Understanding the concerns of V&V is the beginning of V&V study for ANN models. Furthermore, V&V need to be applied to all phases of the ANN model development cycle with these problems above in mind.

3 V&V Approach for ANN Models

Current ANN models have some new characteristics, e.g., more complex network structure, and much more noisy input parameters. For such uncertain and complex models, traditional model V&V approaches are no longer applied to them, and a new V&V approach for ANN models is needed, which should follow the steps [2]: (1) Sensitivity analysis, (2) Uncertainty analysis, (3) Prediction comparison.

3.1 Sensitivity Analysis

ANN models are usually non-linear models, representing a highly complex fabric of effects coupled over many orders of magnitude, a property shared by chaotic systems. Small situation changes often create wildly different responses in the same system. Therefore sensitivity analysis is essential to assess how small changes in the weights affect the error function (and thus how fast and well the network can be trained) during training, and to assess the ANN model's behavior with respect to changes in the input values during testing. Therefore we can strengthen the knowledge base for the sensitive input parameters or weights, thereby increasing model reliability. An example of sensitivity analysis for ANN models is performed in reference [3].

3.2 Uncertainty Analysis

For ANN models, their predictions suffer uncertainties due to (a) inaccuracies in the training data, (b) limitations of the model structures [5], and (c) inaccuracies in the real output measurement. Herein, an ANN model is denoted by $m(\bullet)$, which defines the activity of determining prediction of y from those of x. Denote the ANN model prediction by y^M, and the real output by y^R, and then the model prediction can be expressed as $y^R = y^M + u_i + u_s$, where u_i is input data uncertainty, and u_s is model structural uncertainty. Another uncertainty affecting model prediction is measurement uncertainty. Denote measurement output by y^F, and then the measurement output can be expressed as $y^F = y^R + u_f$, where u_f is measurement uncertainty. Combining the above two expressions, the total uncertainty associated with a model prediction is expressed as $u = y^F - y^M = u_i + u_s + u_f$. The three sources of uncertainty above are main factors that affect the ANN model predictions, and quantifying the sources of uncertainty is important to assure the reliability of ANN models. At present, the existing methods for uncertainty analysis include maximum likelihood, approximate Bayesian and bootstrap [4].

3.3 Prediction Comparison

Denote an ANN model prediction by y, and the corresponding real prediction by r, and then prediction comparison should answer the following questions [5]:

- How close to y can r be expected; and what is the magnitude of $\| y - r \|$?
- How close is the probability distribution F_y of y to F_r of r?
- In what ways do different input values and model variables affect $\| y - r \|$?

Comparing the ANN model prediction and the real output determines accuracy and reliability of ANN models, and this comparison can be realized using the following V&V methods for ANN models.

4 V&V Methods for ANN Models

An ANN model is in essence a numerical method to approximate a function, but it has its own features that distinguish it from conventional models, e.g., uncertainty, complexity, adaptability, training, convergence, and generalization [3], [6]. Therefore, for V&V of ANN models, we not only need to make full use of conventional model V&V methods, but also investigate specific ANN model V&V methods according to ANN model characteristics. After reviewing relevant references [1] and according to our experience, we suggest potential V&V techniques that can be applied to ANN models (see Table 1).

Table 1. Potential V&V methods for ANN models

Classification	Potential V&V methods for ANN models
Informal methods	Inspection, walkthrough, Turing test, face validation, visualization, FMEA, and risk analysis
Formal methods	Error theory, statistical methods, logic methods, optimization methods, testing methods, nonlinear methods, stability analysis, sensibility analysis, confidence interval, and cross validation

It's noted that because of the importance of the confidence interval method, we make a deep research on it. The confidence interval method can be further divided into confidence interval method based on nonlinear regression, and confidence interval method based on Bayesian statistics.

The former considers ANN models as nonlinear equations containing many parameters to be estimated, and calculates prediction intervals using the standard method of nonlinear regression. Let $y_i = f(x_i;u) + \varepsilon_i$ ($i=1, 2,\ldots, n$), represent the ANN model, where the ε_i is i.i.d $N(0,\sigma^2)$. A prediction interval for y_0 can then be given [7] by: $y_0 \pm t_{n-p}^{\alpha/2} s [1 + f_a^{'}(F^T F)^{-1} f_a^{'}]^{1/2}$, where $f_a^{'}$, F, $t_{n-p}^{\alpha/2}$, and s can be seen in [7].

The latter calculates confidence interval by Bayesian statistics. Suppose θ are unknown parameters. During the estimation phase, one uses observation $z=\{x, y\}$ to update the prior distribution of θ, and to compute the posterior density of θ:

$$p(\theta \mid z) = \frac{p(z \mid \theta) p(\theta)}{\int p(z \mid \theta) p(\theta) d\theta},$$ where $p(\theta \mid z)$ is the posterior, $p(z \mid \theta)$ is the likelihood,

$p(\theta)$ is the prior, and $\int p(z \mid \theta) p(\theta) d\theta$ is the evidence [8]. From $p(\theta \mid z)$, one can get the confidence interval of an ANN model. Bayesian method can be applied to not only usual ANN models, but also on-line learning ANN models [3].

In future, how to apply the potential V&V methods to ANN models will center the continuation of this work.

5 Recommendations

Despite rapid and wide application of ANN models, V&V techniques have far to go to reach the level of assurance that ANN models can achieve. To change this situation, thereby increasing V&V capabilities of ANN models, we give below general recommendations.

- Explore the feasibility and practicality of adapting existing V&V theory, tools and techniques to V&V of ANN models,
- Promote the development of new V&V methods that take advantage of the existing V&V techniques and tools,
- To different kinds of ANN models, develop suitable V&V methods.

Besides, we present the following research areas for V&V of ANN models and their recommendations (see Table 2).

Table 2. Research areas for V&V of ANN models

Areas of research	Recommendations
V&V process model	Develop proper approaches to V&V of ANN models learning, trained data selection, layer design, and activation function selection
Evaluation indices	Develop proper evaluation indices for V&V of ANN models, e.g. reliability and validity
V&V tools	Develop automatic testing tools, visualization tools, and runtime monitor tools to aid to verify and validate ANN models
V&V methods	See section 4

6 Case Study

To demonstrate the V&V approach for ANN models presented in this paper, a hypothetical example is given below. This example is to estimate a single-input, single-output function given by: $y(x) = \sin(\pi x) + \varepsilon$, where x is the independent variable, y is the dependent variable and ε is Gaussian noise. 200 training samples and 48 test samples were generated. A feed forward neural network with one hidden layer was used to build the model, the structure was 1-5-1, and the activation function was sigmoidal function.

Fig. 1 (a) shows the plot of the predictions from the ANN model predictions trained from accurate data. From the figure, four of the 40 (10%) outputs lie outside the confidence intervals. Fig. 1 (b) shows the plot of the predictions from the ANN model predictions trained from noisy data. From the figure, twelve of the 40 (30%) outputs lie outside the confidence intervals. From the above analysis, the ANN model trained from accurate data gives expected results, while the ANN model trained from noisy data doesn't give expected results. Therefore, due to uncertainties in training data, model structures and output measurements, the V&V approach for ANN models presented in this paper is reasonable.

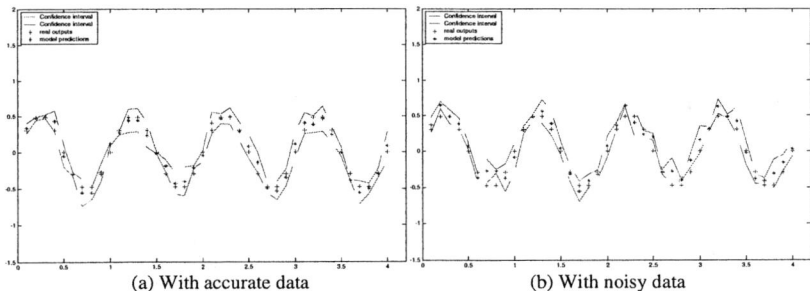

(a) With accurate data   (b) With noisy data

Fig. 1. 85% confidence intervals predictions trained from (*a*) accurate data and (*b*) nosy data

7 Conclusions

It is clear that V&V of ANN models introduces a new level of difficulty. The lack of well established V&V techniques and methods exacerbates the difficulty of this problem. The V&V approach, methods, and recommendations for ANN models that this paper presents provide an effective way to solve this problem. Although this is the beginning of a systematic V&V methodology for ANN models, it provides a basis for further study.

References

1. Pullum, L. L., Darrah, M. A., Taylor, B. J.: Independent Verification and Validation of Neural Networks–Developing Practitioner Assistance. www.isr.us/pdfs/publishedpapers/ivvnn%20stn%20article1.pdf (2003)
2. Liu, F., Yang, M.: Verification and Validation of AI Simulation Models. Proceedings of the Fourth International Conference on Machine Learning and Cybernetics. Guangzhou China (2005) 4083-4088

3. Schumann, J., Gupta, P., Nelson, S.: On Verification and Validation of Neural Network Based Controllers. Proceedings of Engineering Applications of Neural Networks. Malaga Spain (2003)
4. Papadopoulos, G., Edwards, P.J., Murray A.F.: Confidence Estimation Methods for Neural Networks: A Practical Comparison. European Symposium on Artificial Neural Networks. Bruges Belgium (2000) 75-80
5. Morrison, J. D., McKay, M. D.: A Statistical Framework for Simulation Model Design and Validation. Proceedings of 1998 Fall Simulation Interoperability Workshop. Orlando FL (1998)
6. Menzies, T.: Verification and Validation and Artificial Intelligence. Proceedings of Foundations '02, a Workshop on Model and Simulation Verification and Validation for the 21st Century. Laurel Mississippi (2002)
7. Seber, G. A. F., Wild, C. J.: Nonlinear Regression. Wiley, New York (1989)
8. MacKay, D. J. C.: A Practical Bayesian Framework for Back propagation Networks. Neural computation, No. 4. (1992) 448-472

A Simulation Based Multi-criteria Scheduling Approach of Dual-Resource Constrained Manufacturing Systems with Neural Networks

Ozlem Uzun Araz

Dokuz Eylul University, Department of Industrial Engineering, 35100, Izmir, Turkey
`ozlem.uzun@deu.edu.tr`

Abstract. This paper presents a multicriteria DRC scheduler in order to select appropriate dispatching rules. This scheduler integrates several tools, namely; a simulation model, a backpropagation neural network (BPNN) and a Multicriteria decision aid (MCDA) method. Simulation is used to collect predefined performance measures corresponding to decision rule set and system state variables. Because of the time consuming nature of simulation, BPNN is used to obtain the performance measures for each alternative schedule. In order to compare the system performance between all alternatives, the evaluation of each alternative is performed by PROMETHEE, which is a well-known MCDA method. By means of a realistic numerical example, the proposed methodology is proved to be an effective method in a DRC manufacturing system.

1 Introduction

Scheduling is one of the most important functions in a manufacturing firm. Many researchers have developed numerous scheduling approaches for machine-constrained manufacturing systems. However, workers, besides machines, may also be considered as additional resource constraints. This type of system, where both machines and workers represent potential resource constraints, is referred to as a Dual-Resource Constrained (DRC) manufacturing system.

In DRC systems, the number of workers is typically less than the number of available machines, and workers are cross-trained so that they can process jobs in different departments. Consequently, the scheduling decisions in such environments must consider both machine capacity and worker availability. Thus, scheduling of these systems is more complex than the others. During the last few decades, researchers have addressed the DRC scheduling problems using simulation and dispatching heuristics [1, 2, 3, etc]. However, the use of simulation is time consuming and not practical due to the combinatorial nature of the problem. In order to overcome these limitations of simulation, Artificial Neural Network (ANN) based metamodeling approaches have been used. A neural network is a proven tool in providing excellent response predictions in many application areas and it outperforms regression analysis for a wide array of applications [4]. Up to date, many researchers have used ANN based metamodeling to test the performances of dispatching rules for the machine-constrained systems [5, 6, etc.]. There are only few studies for scheduling of DRC systems by using metaheuristics and AI [7, 8].

In spite of its effectiveness in scheduling problems, the applicability of the ANN based metamodeling approaches to DRC systems have not been fully explored in the literature. This is one of the reasons why an ANN based methodology was developed in this study. Furthermore, multicriteria decision aid (MCDA) methods that evaluate the alternatives according to multiple, generally conflicting, criteria have not been extensively studied in the scheduling literature. Cha and Jung [9] presented a methodology for a satisfaction assessment of multi-objective schedules for flexible manufacturing systems which is based on ANN and TOPSIS techniques. To the best of our knowledge, multicriteria decision aid methods have not yet been applied to the DRC scheduling problems. This is another reason to develop a multi-criteria scheduling methodology. In the literature, there are numerous MCDA methods ahich have different propoperties. In the earlier eighties a MCDA outranking method, called PROMETHEE [10], was created. It was designed for ranking alternatives from the best to the worst option. Although it was applied to a large variety of real-world decision making problems, PROMETHEE methods have not been applied to scheduling problems for both of machine constrained and DRC manufacturing.

This paper presents a multicriteria DRC scheduler in order to select appropriate dispatching rules. This scheduler integrates several tools, namely; a simulation model, a backpropagation neural network (BPNN) and PROMETHEE method. The proposed methodology is tested in a hypothetical manufacturing system to prove its effectiveness for DRC manufacturing systems. The rest of the paper is organized as follows. In section 2, brief description of proposed methodology is given. Section 3 is devoted to a numerical application. Finally the conclusions and further research will be given in section 4.

2 The Proposed Multicriteria DRC Scheduler

There are three steps in developing the proposed scheduler: Data collection, training ANN, and Multicriteria evaluation of the alternatives.

- *Data collection:* This step gathers input data using simulation for training the neural network. Firstly, decision variables and system state variables are decided. Decision variables represent the dispatching rule set which includes when-rules, where-rules, part selection by machine and machine selection by part. Combinations of these decision variables generate schedule of the system. To simulate a specific DRC system, random experimental design is applied and some combinations are selected. Each selected combination is simulated for a long simulation period. Finally, the predefined performance measures, which are selected by decision maker, are obtained for each alternative.
- *Training and Testing Neural Network:* In this step, a backpropagation neural network is trained and tested using the input data which provided in the data collection step for each selected performance measures. Then, backpropagation neural network is used to obtain the performance measures for each shop configuration. A shop configuration considers various decision variables such as dispatching rule sets. BPNN generates performance measures for all possible shop configurations.
- *Multicriteria Evaluation of the Alternatives:* In order to evaluate the performance of given schedules, the schedules must be compared in an objective and

quantifiable way. Due to the conflicting nature of the performance measures, it is difficult to assess the quality of a schedule. A schedule, which gives superior performance on some performance indicator (criteria), can perform poorly in another performance indicator. Different schedules may be the best performers on different criteria. However, to find a satisfactory compromise solution between objectives is more important than to find the best solution for only one objective. In order to obtain a satisfactory compromise solution, generally an aggregated cost function is used as a comparison measure. However, in real life, construction of the cost function is a difficult task because of incommensurable nature of some performance measures such as number of tardy jobs, mean tardiness, mean flow time, average machine utilization etc. In this study, we propose an aggregation methodology that uses the PROMETHEE method to evaluate the alternative schedules. The use of the PROMETHEE method enables the methodology to deal with qualitative and quantitative variables, to manage compensatory effects, to understand relations between criteria and to compare the alternatives in an objective and quantifiable way.

3 Numerical Example

In this paper, a DRC scheduling problem with 24 departments and 10 jobs is considered for illustration of the methodology. Each work center has different number of identical parallel machines. There are 25 workers to operate 43 available machines. Each part type can be processed by several flexible routing sequence. Arrival time and processing time of job for each machine are generated from the exponential and normal distribution with a mean different for each type product, respectively. Transfer delays from one work center to another are generated randomly from the uniform distribution. In this study, four decision variables are considered for scheduling of the system:

- *When labor assignment rules:* When should be labor can be considered for reassignment. Centralized and decentralized rule are selected to determine time that is related to assignment of the worker another station.
- *Where labor assignment rules:* Once eligible for reassignment, where should labor be reassigned. The work center with the most jobs in queue (LNQ), The work center with job which has longest waiting time in the queue (LWT), The work center with job, which has shortest processing time and traveling time (MSPT) rules are selected to schedule of the worker.
- *Queue disciplines:* Which job should labor select for operation at the station it has been assigned to. Seven different type dispatching rule are considered: as First in system first service (FIFO), Shortest Processing Time (SPT), Earliest due date (EDD), Shortest remaining processing times (SRPT), Critical Ratio (CRT), (Ratio-selects the job that has the lowest ratio of due date minus current date to total estimated remaining processing time). Minimum Slack Time (MST), Critical ratio/ shortest processing time (CR/SPT).
- *Alternative routing selection:* Part has to select which machine is processed it according to flexible routing using by some decision rules. In this study, three route selection rules are used : Fewest waiting jobs for a machine (SNQ), shortest flow time at an operation (SFT), lowest average utilization first (LAUF).

The three system state variables are conducted with three different levels: *i)* flow allowance factor which measures due date tightness (F: 2-3-4), *ii)* arrival rate (A: 3.5-3.75-4), *iii)* number of part type in the system (NTYPE: 5-8-10).

The best dispatching rule set will be selected according to the following 10 criteria: Throughput rate (TR), Mean Lateness (MLT), Mean tardiness (MT), Number of Tardy Job (NTJ), Mean Flow Time (MFT), Mean Queue Time (MQT), Mean Number of Alternative Route Selection (MRS), Maximum Utilization of Machine (MUTI_M), Average Utilization of Operator (AUTI_OPR), Maximum Utilization of Operator (MUTI_OPR). Five criteria (C1, C7, C8, C9, and C10) are wanted to maximize, while other five criteria to be minimize.

The proposed methodology was performed step by step to select the best schedule for the hypothetical DRC manufacturing system as follows:

- **Data Collection:** In the first step, the set of all possible dispatching rule set and system state combinations is identified. Selection a set of combinations is made by using randomized experimental design. Out of 3402 possible combinations, 180 combinations are selected randomly. The simulation model of the DRC system is constructed with ARENA 2.2 Simulation Software and run for each combination. The replication length is chosen 50.000 minutes with a warm-up period of 2500 minutes. A total of 10 runs were made for each combination and the values of performance measures were obtained.

- **Training and Testing Neural Networks:** After obtaining the corresponding performance measures for 180 combinations, a multilayer feed-forward neural network model is built using Neuro Solution 4.24 for each performance criteria. Each decision rule and system state variable was introduced as input nodes. Decision rule set was coded using binary numbers. Output layer consists of one node that estimates the performance measure considered. Both input and output variables are normalized to increase the efficiency of the neural network models.

  Design parameters of NN such as number of hidden layers, the number of nodes in the hidden layer, etc. are determined by trial and error. Learning rate and momentum rate for each BPNN was used 0.01 and 0.70 respectively. Sigmoid transfer function was used for backpropagation learning algorithm. For neural network model 180 input-output pairs are randomly taken and 135 pairs are used for training and cross validation. When the number of learning epochs is larger than 2000 or the mean square error is less than 0.001 the learning process stops. Remaining 45 combinations are used for testing. The mean square error, mean absolute error, means percentage error is used as the measure of accuracy of the neural network. The normalized values of the performance measures are obtained for 126 dispatching rule combinations using the NN models.

- **Multicriteria Evaluation of the Alternatives:** In order to determine which dispatching rule set performs the best for the selected performance criteria, PROMETHEE is used. In the experiment, the system state variables are assumed as F=2, ARR=3.5 and NTYPE=5. Before the multicriteria evaluation of alternatives, prequalification is performed for some dispatching rule sets which show too poor (unacceptable) performances on some criteria. 99 alternatives are eliminated in the prequalification phase. The evaluation matrix for the remaining 28 alternatives can be seen in Table 1.

Table 1. The Evaluation Matrix

Alternatives	TR	MLT	MT	NTJ	MFT	MQT	MRS	MUTI_M	AUTI_OPR	MUTI_OPR
Action1	0.7584	0.4479	0.0530	0.7712	0.6236	0.5455	0.3147	0.7452	0.8841	0.9148
Action2	0.6058	0.6291	0.0254	0.8109	0.6407	0.5661	0.2845	0.7758	0.8780	0.9103
Action3	0.6381	0.3931	0.0618	0.6874	0.6323	0.5335	0.2201	0.7471	0.8841	0.9143
Action4	0.8101	0.4434	0.1123	0.8438	0.6393	0.4916	0.6738	0.6079	0.8909	0.9260
Action5	0.9082	0.6171	0.0747	0.6442	0.6436	0.4942	0.7144	0.6675	0.8997	0.9227
Action6	0.6855	0.4490	0.1061	0.5898	0.6229	0.5095	0.1628	0.7004	0.8723	0.9213
Action7	0.7918	0.0356	0.0363	0.8478	0.6288	0.5531	0.0329	0.7159	0.8884	0.9093
Action8	0.8289	0.3798	0.0275	0.7557	0.6449	0.5704	0.1304	0.7507	0.8831	0.9100
Action9	0.8246	0.2670	0.0725	0.3603	0.6193	0.4604	0.0388	0.7368	0.8803	0.8838
Action10	0.7227	0.4607	0.0175	0.1908	0.5975	0.4368	0.0008	0.7597	0.8848	0.8967
Action11	0.6054	0.2540	0.0754	0.7388	0.6346	0.5252	0.1153	0.7971	0.8866	0.8943
Action12	0.7845	0.1244	0.0144	0.5584	0.6174	0.4707	0.1493	0.7730	0.8805	0.8965
Action13	0.6686	0.4240	0.1043	0.4576	0.6101	0.4368	0.1954	0.7403	0.8798	0.8937
Action14	0.6925	0.5577	0.0897	0.7410	0.6402	0.4568	0.5757	0.6897	0.8878	0.8885
Action15	0.7772	0.0427	0.0680	0.1900	0.6224	0.3715	0.3495	0.7287	0.8919	0.9212
Action16	0.7536	0.4711	0.0191	0.7455	0.6397	0.5162	0.1620	0.7603	0.8902	0.8931
Action17	0.7690	0.0450	-0.0109	0.6654	0.6456	0.5260	0.0557	0.7692	0.8987	0.8906
Action18	0.9933	0.1014	0.1417	0.2655	0.4467	0.1336	0.0781	0.8012	0.5428	0.9381
Action19	0.8933	0.0636	0.0945	0.5318	0.4450	0.1506	0.0961	0.8026	0.5339	0.9270
Action20	0.9765	0.0930	0.1474	0.3655	0.4398	0.1310	0.0741	0.8372	0.5584	0.9399
Action21	0.8467	0.0739	0.1205	0.3780	0.4717	0.2112	0.6243	0.6428	0.6533	0.9335
Action22	0.6028	0.2567	0.1336	0.8367	0.4918	0.1995	0.6128	0.7418	0.6594	0.9223
Action23	0.7949	0.1458	0.0932	0.8004	0.4705	0.1980	0.4628	0.6532	0.6378	0.9454
Action24	0.8182	0.2046	0.1171	0.5343	0.4629	0.1965	0.5722	0.6773	0.6723	0.9406
Action25	0.9544	0.1423	0.1035	0.5240	0.4987	0.2276	0.1519	0.7182	0.5624	0.9314
Action26	0.8824	0.0549	0.1256	0.1795	0.5110	0.1867	0.1401	0.7758	0.5509	0.9265
Action27	0.8117	0.1626	0.1363	0.4897	0.4701	0.1664	0.2334	0.7457	0.5346	0.9375

It can be seen that no alternative is optimal on the ten criteria. For each criterion, a specific Preference Function, with its thresholds, and weights are determined by the decision maker. If we use PROMETHEE in order to rank remaining 27 alternatives form the best to the worst, we obtain following ranking:

$$a_{18}, a_{20}, a_{19}, a_{26}, a_{21}, a_{25}, a_{15}, a_{24}, a_{27}, a_{12}, a_{23}, a_{10}, a_{17}, a_9, a_5, a_8, a_7,$$
$$a_{22}, a_{16}, a_{13}, a_1, a_3, a_{11}, a_6, a_{14}, a_4, a_2$$

If the tardiness were assumed as sole criterion, alternative 17 should be selected. However, because of the poor performance of the alternative 17 on other criteria, it is ranked in 13th order in the PROMETHEE rankings. According to the PROMETHEE results, alternatives 18, 20 and 19 are the best three performers. It should also be noted that although the alternative 19 is better than alternatives 18 and 20 in terms of lateness and tardiness criteria, it is outranked by other because of the worse performance on throughput and number of tardy job criteria. In the light of the results, we can say that the best compromise solution is the 18th alternative, which represents the following dispatching rules: when labor assignment rule is *Centralized Rule,* where labor assignment rule is LWT, selection of machines by part is SNQ, Selection of parts by machine is SPT.

It is obvious that a decision maker can find different solutions by using different weight and preference function structure that reflect her/his preferences. As mentioned before, the scheduling of DRC manufacturing systems is a complex problem due to the variations in the system state variables. The results showed that the proposed methodology can solve this problem effectively and efficiently.

4 Conclusion

This paper presents a multicriteria DRC scheduler. This scheduler tries to select appropriate dispatching rules by integrating a simulation model, BPNN and PROMETHEE. By means of a realistic numerical example, it is demonstrated that the proposed methodology is an effective tool for scheduling of DRC systems. In this study, determination of parameters of neural network was determined based on the trial and error. It should be noted that such an approach is sometimes cumbersome. To develop a methodology for obtaining appropriate parameters of the neural network should be the future research.

References

1. Bobrowski, P.M, Park, P.S.: An evaluation of labor assignment rules when workers are not perfectly interchangeable. Journal of Operation Management 11 (1993) 257-268.
2. Kher H.V., Fry, T.D.: Labor flexibility and assignment policies in a job shop having incommensurable objectives. Int. J. of Production Research 39 (2001) 2295-2311.
3. Treleven, M.D.: A comparison of flow and queue time variances in machine-limited versus dual-resource-constrained systems. IIE Transactions 1 (1988) 63-67.
4. Chen, M.-C., Yang, T.: Design of manufacturing systems by a hybrid approach with neural network metamodelling and stochastic local search. Int. J. of Production Research 40 (2002) 71-92.
5. Pierreval, H.: Training a neural network by simulation for dispatching problems.Proceedings of the Third Rensselaer International Conference on Computer Integrated Engineering (1992) 332-336.
6. Fonseca, D.J., Navaresse, D., Moynihan, G.P.: Simulation metamodeling through artificial neural networks. Engineering Applications of Artificial Intelligence 16 (2003) 177-183.
7. Lee, Y.: Adaptive and artificial-intelligence based scheduling methodologies applied to dual-resource constrained assembly systems. PhD. Dissertation, Northeastern University, Boston, Massachusetts, (1997).
8. Patel, V., Elmaraghy, H.A., Ben-Abdallah, I.: Scheduling in dual-resource constrained manufacturing systems using genetic algorithms. IEEE (1999) 1131-1139.
9. Cha, Y., Jung, M.: satisfaction assessment of multi-objective schedules using neural fuzzy methodology. Int. J. of Production Research 41 (2003) 1831-1849.
10. Brans, J.P., Vincke, P.H., Mareschal, B.: How to select and how to rank projects: The PROMETHEE method. European Journal of Operational Research 24 (1986) 228-238.

Quantitative Analysis of the Varieties of Apple Using Near Infrared Spectroscopy by Principal Component Analysis and BP Model

Yong He, Xiaoli Li, and Yongni Shao

College of Biosystems Engineering and Food Science,
Zhejiang University, Hangzhou, 310029, China
yhe@zju.edu.cn

Abstract. Artificial neural networks (ANN) combined with PCA are being used in a growing number of applications. In this study, the fingerprint wavebands of apple were got through principal component analysis (PCA). The 2-dimensions plot was drawn with the scores of the first and the second principal components. It appeared to provide the best clustering of the varieties of apple. The several variables compressed by PCA were applied as inputs to a back propagation neural network with one hidden layer. This BP model had been used to predict the varieties of 15 unknown samples; the recognition rate of 100% was achieved. This model is reliable and practicable. So a PCA-BP model can be used to exactly distinguish the varieties of apple.

1 Introduction

The processing of apple post-harvest has been one of the important topic in the agricultural product processing. Now the research of species discrimination is still seldom, but a simple, fast and non-destructive way of species determination of fruit needs to be developed. The discrimination of the tuber dioscoreae [1], the species of capsicums [2] and the species of rhodiola [3] were be studied. Back propagation neural network (BPNN) model is a powerful learning system. Principle component analysis (PCA) is a way of data mining. The principle information of spectrum can be reserved after PCA, and then the analysis of spectrum datum became easy. The species discrimination model of apple was built based on the PCA and BPNN.

2 Material and Methods

In the research, a spectrophotometer (FieldSpec Pro FR (325–1075 nm)) and a 150W halogen lamp were used. The sensitivity is 3.5 nm. The visual angle of the spectrograph is 20°. The software were ASD View Spec Pro, Unscramble V9.1 and DPS. A total of 90 apples which were Fuji apple (from shanxi of China), Red Delicious apple (from American) and Copefrut Royal Gala apple (from American) were purchased at a local market. The number of each species was 30. All samples were separated randomly into two parts, one part that contained 75 apples was used as reality validation samples, and the other was used as predicting samples. From each fruit, three reflection spectra were taken at three equidistant positions around the equator (approximately 120°); for each reflection spectra the scan number were 10 at exactly the same position.

To reduce the noise, the smoothing way of Savitzky [4] was used. The segment size of smoothing was 9. The second type of preprocessing was the use of the multiplicative scatter correction (MSC). The pre-process and calculations were carried out using Unscrambler V9.1. To avoid low signal-noise ratio, only the wavelength ranging from 400 to 960 nm was used in this investigation [5].

3 Results and Discussion

Fig.1 shows the reflectance spectra of three varieties of apples, obtained from the spectrograph. It can be found that the reflectance spectrum of each species is particular.

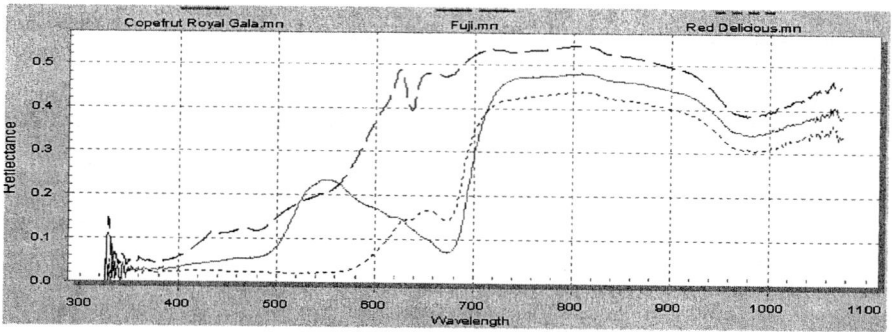

Fig. 1. Near infrared reflect ance spectra of three different varieties apples

3.1 Principal Components Analysis on the Full Wavelength Region

PCA was performed on the reflectance spectra of the 75 apples. If the scores of one certain principal component were organized according to the number of the apples, a new apple plot could be created. The new image is then called 'PCA scores image' just as figure 2. The advantage of using PCA scores image is that it can display the clustering information of species from multiple wavebands. The calculated result shown that reliabilities of principal components PC1,PC2 and PC3 were 68%, 30% and 1.298% respectively. It means the first two components can explain 98% of the variables. They appear to provide the best discrimination of the species.

The scatter plot of PC1×PC2 is shown in Fig.2. It shows the differences among Fuji, Red Delicious and Copefrut Royal Gala. In short, Copefrut Royal Gala samples mostly cluster in the quadrant where PC1 was negative and PC2 was positive, while Red Delicious samples were always in the negative direction of PC1 and PC2. In contrast, the Fuji samples are almost scattered over the quadrant where PC1was positive and PC2 was negative.

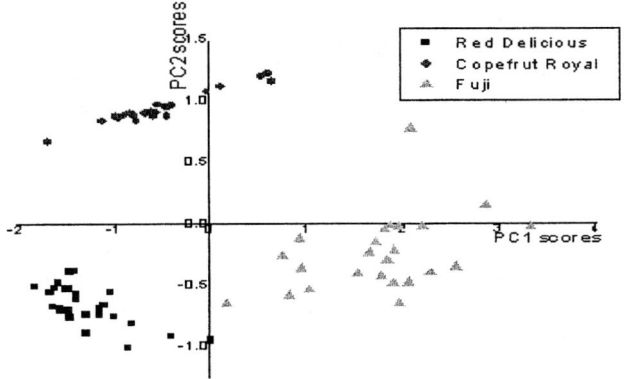

Fig. 2. PCA scores plots (PC1×PC2) for samples

3.2 Selection of Optimal Wavebands

The loadings of the first and second principal components of 75 samples across the entire spectral region were obtained. It is called loading image. As described above, the cumulative reliabilities of PC1 and PC2 were very high, so the loadings of PC1 and PC2 should be considered as the basis to select optimal wavebands for discriminating the species. It can be found that the loading of PC1 has a strong positive correlation at 649-680 nm, and has a strong negative correlation at 555 nm. The loading of PC2 has a strong positive correlation at 555-565 nm, and has a strong negative correlation at 680 nm. Therefore, characteristic wavebands are chosen, which are 649-689 nm and 555-565 nm.

3.3 ANN Model

The training of the ANN is done with a basic error back propagation algorithm [6]. The transfer function of each layer was sigmoid function. The goal error was set as 0.0001. The time of training was set as 1000. The total wavebands were replacing by the 52 characteristic wavebands after PCA. A three-layers ANN was built, 52 input

Table 1. Prediction result for unknown samples by BP-ANN model

No.	SV	CV	No.	SV	CV	No.	SV	CV
(1)	1	1.0087	(6)	2	2.00843	(11)	3	2.98856
(2)	1	1.01031	(7)	2	2.0068	(12)	3	2.9882
(3)	1	1.00866	(8)	2	2.00971	(13)	3	2.98834
(4)	1	1.00908	(9)	2	2.00948	(14)	3	2.98883
(5)	1	1.00932	(10)	2	1.99663	(15)	3	2.98785

Note: 1. SV-standard value; CV-calculate value; 2. (1)-(5), Red Delicious apple; (6)-(10), Copefrut Royal Gala apple; (11)-(15), Fuji apple.

neurons were arbitrarily connected with 39 hidden neurons, which transmitted their output to one single output neuron producing the final measure of resemblance as a number between 1 and 3 (1-Red Delicious apple, 2-Copefrut Royal Gala apple, and 3-Fuji apple). Residual error was 9.94365×10^{-5}. 15 samples were predicted by this model, the recognition is 100% (seen Table 1).

4 Conclusion

Quantitative analysis model of varieties of apple was set up. The recognition rate of 100% was achieved. The results indicate that it is possible to develop a non-destructive technique for discriminating of varieties apple. With the use of principal components analysis (PCA), the fingerprint wavebands to discrimination of varieties were obtained. This study lays a foundation for later developed of a facility apparatus to discriminate the species with sensitive wavebands. Further research will focus on establishing a more optimize, standardize and implement multi-spectral system.

Acknowledgements

This study was supported by the Teaching and Research Award Program for Outstanding Young Teachers in Higher Education Institutions of MOE, P. R. C., Natural Science Foundation of China, Specialized Research Fund for the Doctoral Program of Higher Education and Natural Science Foundation of Zhejiang Province.

References

1. Sun Suqin, Tang Junming, Yuan Zimin.: FTIR and Classification Study on Trueborn Tuber Dioscoreae Samples. Spectroscopy and Spectral Analysis. Vol. 23,No. 2, (2003) 258-261
2. Yu Wei, Yong Kelan.: Study on the Characteristic and Significance of Capsaicinoid. Food Science.Vol. 24, No. 11, (2003) 105-108
3. Wang Sihong, Yin Qifan, Fan Yanling.: Identification Studies of Wild and Cultivated Rhodiola Saccharinensis A. Bor and Rhodiola Angusta Nakai Taken from Changbai Mountains by Fourier Transform Infrared Spectrometry. Spectroscopy and Spectral Analysis. Vol. 24, No. 8, (2004) 957-959
4. Savitzky,A., and M.J.E.Golay.: Smoothing and Differentiation of Data by Simplified Least Squares Procedures. Analytical Chem. (1964)1627-1639
5. Qi Xiaoming, Zhang Luda, Du Xiaolin.: Quantitative Analysis Using NIR by Building PLS-BP Model. Spectroscopy and Spectral Analysis. Vol. 23, No. 5, (2003) 870-872
6. Rich, E., and Knight K.: Connectionist Models. In: Shapiro,D.M., Murphy, J.F. (Eds.), Artificial Intelligence. McGraw HillBook Co., Singapore, (1991)487–519

Identification and Control of ITU Triga Mark-II Nuclear Research Reactor Using Neural Networks and Fuzzy Logic

Ramazan Coban[1] and Burhanettin Can[2]

[1] Turkish Standards Institution, Electronics Laboratory, Gebze, Kocaeli, Turkey
rcoban@kampus.tse.org.tr
[2] Department of Electronics and Computer Education,
Faculty of Technical Education, Marmara University,
34046, Istanbul, Turkey
bcan@marun.edu.tr

Abstract. In this paper, an artificial neural networks identifier and a fuzzy logic controller for ITU Triga Mark-II Nuclear Research Reactor is presented. Three parted control function is used as a reference trajectory that the fuzzy logic controller tracks. The nonlinear behavior of the reactor is identified by using generalized neural networks. The validity of the proposed identification model is tested by comparing these results with the ones obtained by YAVCAN code. The effectiveness of the controller is demonstrated on the neural network model.

1 Introduction

Intelligent methods such as artificial neural networks (ANN) and fuzzy logic control (FLC) are currently used in nuclear reactor identification and control systems by using the decision-making property of fuzzy systems and learning ability of neural networks. Many interesting FLC's are carried out in the area of nuclear reactor control [1-4] and into the power control of ITU Triga Mark-II Nuclear Research Reactor [5-11]. In a research, a self-tuning control algorithm with generalized minimum variance strategy is employed [5]. In another work, the authors aim at designing neural net controller based on plant linearization at each operating point [6]. In [7] and [8], optimal controller is designed for the reactor by using trajectory. The controller consists of two parts: a main and auxiliary controller. The main controller is based on Pontragyn's Maximum Principle and the auxiliary controller is based on PID approach. In [9], a FLC whose variables such as period, rod position, reactivity, fuel temperature, and rule base are defined in separate domains. In addition to these, initial power and demanded power are also subjected to fuzzy rules [10]. In [11], a trajectory tracking fuzzy controller for Triga Mark-II Research Reactor is suggested. In that work, error and change in error between trajectory and reactor power are selected as control variables of the reactor. Many network architectures have been employed in the modeling of the dynamic systems with artificial neural networks (ANN) in the literature [4], [12], [13]. Can et al. [14] developed YAVCAN simulation code for the mathematical model of the nonlinear dynamic behavior of ITU TRIGA MARK-II nuclear research reactor. Besides many researches have been carried out into the modeling and control of ITU TRIGA MARK-II nuclear research reactor [5-11], [14], for the first time, the modeling and control of this reactor by using ANN and FLC is realized in this paper. This ANN model is used for the proposed controller design. So firstly, identification of the reactor is described. Afterwards the designing procedures of the controller and simulation results are presented.

2 Physical Model

Among various TRIGA reactor types, ITU TRIGA MARK-II research reactor is the first Mark-II reactor with stainless steel clad fuel rods which has a steady state power of 250 kW and a peak power of 1200 MW in pulsing operation [15]. The equation representing neutronic-thermal-hydraulic behavior of reactor core can be written in vectorial form as [14]:

$$\frac{dY(t)}{dt} = AY(t) + B \tag{1}$$

where Y is a representative vector of prompt neutron density, precursor concentration, fuel temperature, coolant temperature, coolant velocity, and coolant density. A and B are related matrixes. Power of the reactor is determined by the reactivity inserted into the reactor, ρ_{ex}. In this paper it is assumed that coolant velocity and coolant density are constant and precursor concentration is neglected. The control system of the reactor should be able to predict the amount of reactivity to be inserted. The reactivity inserted into the reactor is determined by the movements of the control rod.

3 Modeling of the Reactor with ANN

In the modeling problem under consideration, the dynamic behavior of the reactor is modeled by using generalized neural networks. Any nonlinear discrete-time dynamic system can be expressed as [12]:

$$y(k+1) = f[y(k), y(k-1), \ldots y(k-q+1); u(k), u(k-1), \ldots u(k-p+1))] \tag{2}$$

where [u(k), y(k)] represents the input-output pair of the system at time step k. The positive integers q and p are the number of past outputs (also called the order of the system) and the number of the past inputs, respectively. A nonlinear continuous function, $f(.)$ shows the characteristic of the system dynamics. The series-parallel structure as shown in Fig. 1a is used at training phase. After training, since $y(k) \cong \hat{y}(k)$, the parallel structure whose output is fed back into its input as shown in Fig. 1b is used in the operating phase [12]. TDL shown in Fig. 1a denotes a tapped delay line.

The system used to model the dynamic behavior of the reactor has one external input ρ_{ex} (p=0) and three internal inputs which are the past information of P, T_f, and T_m (q=1) as shown in Fig.2. At the beginning, the reactor is operated at low power levels. For the transient regime the initial conditions of the fuel temperature $T_f(0)$ and coolant

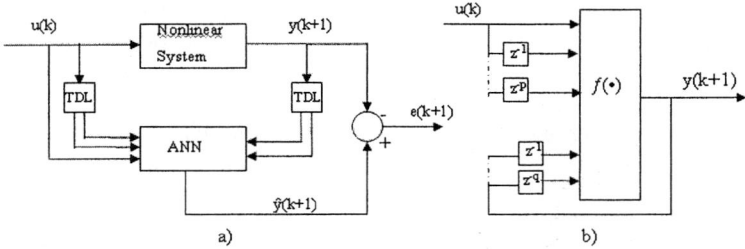

Fig. 1. Block representation of the system in the training and operating phase : a) training phase (series-parallel structure), b) operating phase (parallel structure)

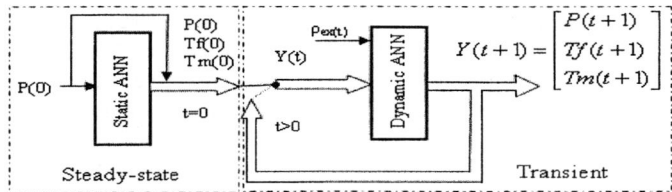

Fig. 2. Selection of variables as inputs and outputs of the ANN for modeling of the reactor

temperature $T_m(0)$ must be determined relating to the desired initial power, $P(0)$. After the steady-state operation the reactor is started up for a desired power.

The static back propagation algorithm and pattern learning method is used in order to train the identification networks. The hyperbolic tangent function is employed as an activation function. The sum squared error function is used here as an error criterion. Network parameters such as the initial weights, the momentum, the learning rate, the number of neurons at the hidden layer are determined by trial and error. A data set employed in the ANN training process is obtained randomly in the range of the reactivity between 0.1 \$ and 0.9 \$ by running YAVCAN code at the sampling periods (T) of collecting the data 0.05 s and 2.5 s. All the data are normalized into the interval [-0.9, 0.9]. After the logarithm to the base 10 of the power (P) is taken, the process mentioned above is performed due to the significant difference between its minimum and maximum values.

To improve the identification networks, the dynamic of the reactor is considered as dividing into sub-regions with respect to the reactivity and the sampling period. The dynamic model is realized by connecting 4 ANN's where sampling period is 2.5 s and 12 ANN's where sampling period is 0.05 s into the parallel structure.

4 Trajectory Tracking Fuzzy Logic Controller

Fuzzy control systems consist of a plant and a fuzzy logic controller in a feedback loop. A fuzzy controller is designed based on the knowledge of the process operator. This knowledge is represented as a collection of If-Then rules that relate imprecise relationships through linguistic variables. For the process under consideration input variables are error (e) and change in error (ė) between a trajectory and the reactor output power. In order to be able to follow the reference trajectory, the fuzzy controller should generate control signals. For a certain power demand, the control system of the reactor inserts the proper amount of reactivity. So, output variable of the controller is the control signal. A simplified block diagram of the control system is shown in Fig. 3. Error (e) has five membership functions: negative big (NB), negative small (NS), zero (ZE), positive small (PS), and positive big (PB). Error in change (ė) has three membership functions: negative (N), zero (Z), and positive (P). As there are two input variables of the FLC and one of them (e) has five and the other (ė) has three different values within its rage, there could be a total of 5 x 3 = 15 rules in the rule base of the FLC. The input variables of the FLC are assumed to have second-order polynomial membership function distributions. Fifteen rules used in the controller are shown in Table 1. It is clear that this rule table is more understandable than that in the reference [11]. The proposed controller has less rules (15) than that controller (23).

For determining the control signal, it is need to combine the control rules. Measuring the reactor power, error and change in error are calculated between the power and the reference trajectory at every time step. The fuzzy labels to which the variables belong are determined. Afterwards the degrees of fulfillment (DOF) of the rules are computed. The final control signal, taking into account the weight of each rule such as -0.85, is computed by using Center of Area method (COA). The discrete form of the COA is presented in Eq. (3):

$$U = \frac{\sum_{i=1}^{n} u(i).DOF(i)}{\sum_{i=1}^{n} DOF(i)} \quad (3)$$

where U is the discrete control signal, u(i) is the weight of the ith rule, n is the number of the rules, and DOF(i) is the degree of fulfillment of the ith rule.

Table 1. Fuzzy controller rule table

e \ ė	N	Z	P
NB	-1	-0.85	-0.7
NS	-0.5	-0.4	-0.3
ZE	-0.1	0	0.1
PS	0.3	0.4	0.5
PB	0.7	0.85	1

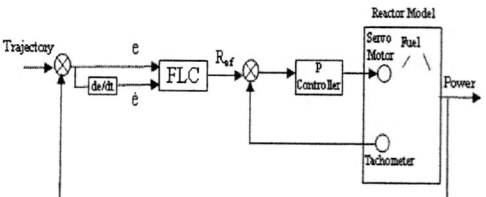

Fig. 3. Block diagram of the control system

As a reference path that is followed by the reactor output power, three parted trajectory is chosen. For the first and third parts, third degree and for the second part, a second degree function is assumed [8].

5 Simulation Results

Modeling of the reactor by using ANN is validated by comparing with YAVCAN code respecting to the step input function. In case of the initial power 100 W, sampling period 0.05 s, and step function input (ρ_{ex}=0.75 $), the obtained ANN results for power, fuel temperature, and coolant temperature are compared with YAVCAN results as seen in Fig. 4. There are only some small deviations between the results of YAVCAN and ANN. The proposed model can be used to capture the behavior of the reactor.

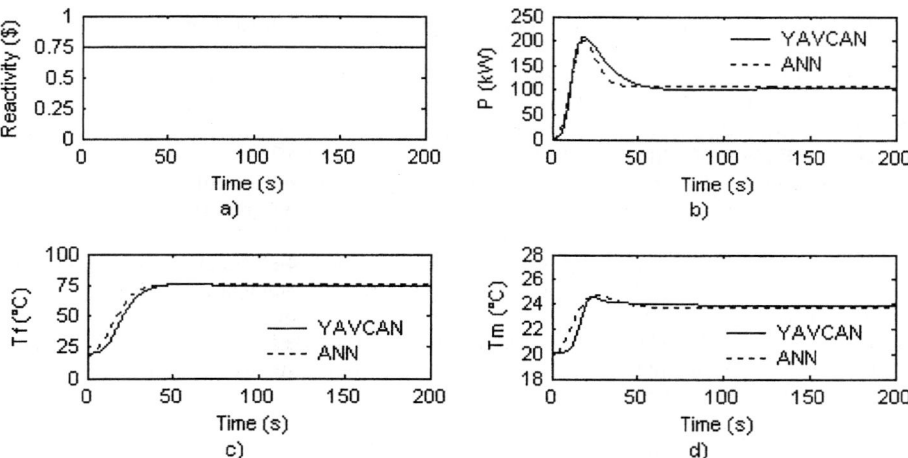

Fig. 4. Results of the simulation: a) reactivity, b) P, c) Tf, and d) Tm (where P(0)=100 W, T is 0.05 s, and the reactivity is the form of step function)

In order to demonstrate the effectiveness of the proposed FLC, some simulation tests are carried out by using ANN model. The reactor is started up for desired power levels 250 kW and 150 kW. As seen in Fig. 5a and Fig 5b for both power demands FLC controls the reactor successfully.

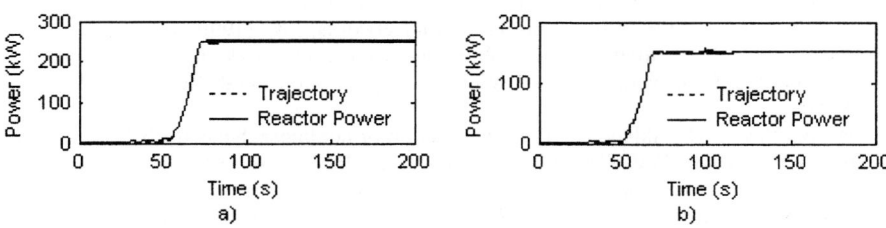

Fig. 5. Simulation results: a) Power demand 250 kW, b) Power demand 150 kW

6 Conclusions

In this paper, the nonlinear behavior of ITU TRIGA MARK-II nuclear research reactor is identified by using generalized neural networks. With the aid of the ANN model of the reactor a fuzzy logic controller is designed and tested on the ANN model. It can be concluded that the proposed ANN model can be employed in absence of the exact mathematical model of the plant.

References

1. Bernard, J.A.: Use of a rule-base system for process control. IEEE Control System Magazine, 8 (5) (1988) 3-13
2. Akin, H.L., Altin, V.: Rule-based fuzzy logic controller for a PWR-type nuclear power plant. IEEE Trans. Nucl. Sci. 38 (2) (1991) 883-890
3. Marseguerra, M., Zio, E.: Model-free fuzzy tracking control of a nuclear reactor. Annals of Nuclear Energy, 30 (2003) 953-981
4. Boroushaki, M., Ghofrani, M.B., Lucas, C.: Identification and control of a nuclear reactor core (VVER) using recurrent neural networks and fuzzy systems. IEEE Transaction on Nuclear Science, vol.50, No.1, February (2003)
5. Erkan, K., Butun, E., Can, B.: Triga Mark-II Reactor controller design using genetic algorithm. Fuzzy Logic and Intelligent Technologies for Nuclear Science and Industry, World Scientific, Singapore (1998)
6. Erkan, K., Unal, M.: Neural net controller for ITU Triga Mark-II Reactor. Proceedings of the First Trabzon International Energy and Environment Symposium, July 29-31, Karadeniz Technical University, Trabzon, Turkey (1996)
7. Can, B.: The Optimal control of ITU Triga Mark II Reactor. The Twelfth European Triga User's Conference, NRI Bucuresti-Pitesti, Romania, 22-25, September (1992)
8. Can, B., Baba, A.F., Erdal, H.: Optimal controller design by using three zones trajectory for ITU Triga Mark-II Reactor. Journal of Marmara University for pure and applied sciences, vol. 15, Istanbul, Turkey (1999) 187-196
9. Baba, A.F., Can, B., Gok, I., Akbay, E.: Design of a fuzzy logic controller for the ITU Triga Mark-II Reactor. Proceedings of the Nuclear Plant Instrumentation Control and Human-Machine Interface Technologies, The Pennsylvania State University, USA, May 6-9 (1996).
10. Akbay, E., Can, B., Baba, A.F.: Fuzzy logic control for ITU TRIGA Mark-II Reactor. 3rd Int. Sym. on Intelligent Manufac. Systems, 2001, Sakarya, Turkey, August 30-31 (2001)
11. Baba, A.F.: Fuzzy logic controller. Nuclear Engineering Int., Vol. 49, (2004) 36-38
12. Narendra, K.S., Parthasarathy, K.: Identification and control of dynamical systems using neural Networks. IEEE Transactions on Neural Networks, 1 (1) (1990) 4-27
13. Adali, T., Bakal, B., Sonmez M.K., Fakory, R. Tsaoi, C.O.: Modeling core neutronics by recurrent neural networks. Proc.of World Congress on Neural Networks, 2, (1997) 504-508
14. Can, B., Yavuz, H., Akbay, E.: The investigation of nonlinear dynamics behavior of ITU TRIGA MARK-II REACTOR. Eleventh European TRIGA Users Conference Papers and Abstracts, the Germen Cancer Research Institute Heidelberg, Germany, (1990) 39-49
15. Safety analysis report for the TRIGA Mark-II Reactor, for the Institute of Nuclear Energy, Technical University of Istanbul, Turkey (1978)

Differential Evolution Algorithm for Designing Optimal Adaptive Linear Combiners

Nurhan Karaboga and Canan Aslihan Koyuncu

Department of Electric Electronics Engineering, Erciyes University,
Melikgazi, 38039, Kayseri, Turkey
{nurhan_k, 1030215054}@erciyes.edu.tr

Abstract. This paper presents the application of Differential Evolution (DE), an Evolutionary Computation method, for the optimization of adaptive FIR filter weights. This method is robust and easy to use and requires a few control variables. Since the algorithm uses differential property, it has a good convergence speed and also quite robust in the case of noise due to parallel structure. In the simulation study three well-known error functions are used to test the performance of proposed method in the Adaptive Linear Combiner (ALC) design.

1 Introduction

Common to most filter design procedures is the fact that the designer has to specify a filter structure beforehand, compute the filter coefficients and then decide if the chosen filter fulfills the requirements [1]. If the statistical characteristic of the input data varies with respect to time or the required knowledge about input data is not satisfactory, adaptive filters are needed. For the design of adaptive FIR filters, namely ALCs, there exist several methods. Computer performance improvement allows solving some technical problems by using a new class of optimization methods based on the so-called 'evolution' algorithm. One of these algorithms, named Differential Evolution (DE), was chosen to proof its ability for solving adaptive FIR filter design.

DE algorithm has been presented for the first time in 1995 by K. Price [2]. The advantage of DE application is the unconstrained objective function, where any requests are not required for function continuity or style. The disadvantage of DE is the stochastic kernel, it means that the rate of convergence is impossible to determine accurately. However, the process of minimal searching is goal directed and by the correct setting of minimization parameters converge quickly [3-4].

In this paper we present a method based on DE algorithm for ALC. In the method, the weights of ALC are adaptively tuned when some noise exists. In the simulation study three different error functions are employed to test the method. This paper is organized as follows. Section 2 contains a brief review of DE Algorithm. Section 3 describes the application of DE algorithm for designing ALC and presents the simulation results.

2 Differential Evolution

An optimization task consisting of D parameters can be represented by a D-dimensional vector. In DE, a population of NP solution vectors is randomly created at the start. This population is successfully improved by applying mutation, crossover and selection operators. The main steps of the DE algorithm are given below:

Initialization
Evaluation
Repeat
  Mutation
  Recombination
  Evaluation
  Selection
Until (*termination criteria are met*)

DE differs from other Evolutionary Algorithms in the mutation and recombination phase. Unlike stochastic techniques such as Genetic Algorithms and Evolutionary Strategies, where perturbation occurs in accordance with a random quantity, DE uses weighted differences between solution vectors to perturb the population at each generation G as expressed in Equation (1).

$$\mathbf{u}_{i;G+1} = x_{i,G} + K \cdot (x_{r3};G \_ x_{i,G}) + F \cdot (x_{r1,G} - x_{r2,G})$$

Randomly select $r_1; r_2; r_3 \in \{1, 2, ..., n\}$; $r_1 \neq r_2 \neq r_3 \neq i$ (1)

Three unique individuals, or solution vectors denoted by **x**, are randomly selected from the population. The coefficient K represents the level of combination that occurs between $\mathbf{x}_{r3,G}$ and the current individual $\mathbf{x}_{i,G}$. The coefficient F represents scaling the step size resulting from the vector subtraction $\mathbf{x}_{r1,G} - \mathbf{x}_{r2,G}$. Typically in the single-objective case, if the new individual $\mathbf{u}_{i,G+1}$, is better than the currently selected individual $\mathbf{x}_{i,G}$, then the current individual is replaced with the new one. The algorithm iterates over i from 1 to n, where n is the size of the population. The DE variant used in this work is known as DE/current-to-rand/1 (Equation 1), and is rotationally invariant [5].

3 Simulation Results

In the DE Algorithm, to improve the fitness value of adaptive filter, the MAE, LMS and MSE functions are used and compared. These are $MSE = 1/N \sum_{n=1}^{N} [\ d(n) - y(n)\ ]^2$, $LMS = 1/N \{ \sum_{n=1}^{N} [\ d(n) - y(n)\ ]^2 \}^{1/2}$, $MAE = 1/N \sum_{n=1}^{N} |d(n) - y(n)|$. The single-input ALC with 15 coefficients is as shown in Figure 1. The input and desired signals are sampled sinusoids at the same frequency, with 5 samples per cycle. These signals are given in Equation 2.

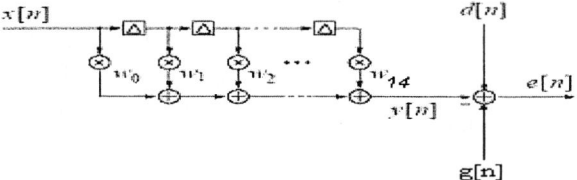

Fig. 1. ALC with 15 weights

$d(n)=2\cos(2\pi n/5)$, $x(n)=\sin(2\pi n/5)$, $d_1(n)=d(n)+g(n)$, $\quad n=1,2,\ldots,50$ (2)

We add g(n) to d(n). g(n) is a Gaussian noise signal. $d_1(n)$ has a value of SNR=10dB. Where MAE, LMS and MSE are the errors to be driven to zero, y is the actual signal to be tracked and d_1 is the desired signal. For the filter design, the parameters of the filters are successively adjusted by DE algorithm until the error between the output of the filter and the desired signal is minimized [6]. Control parameter values of DE used in this work are: population size: 100, crossover rate: 0.8, combination factor: 0.2, scaling factor: 0.2, generating number: 20000. The weights obtained are presented in Table 1. As shown in Figure 2, 3, the input signal is sine and the desired signal is Gaussian noise signal. Figure 4 shows the output signals obtained with the ALC using these three error functions. It can be seen that the output signals with these functions are similar to each other. Figure 5 shows the error performances with generation. As seen from the Figure 4(a), (b), (c), and Figure 5 the most appropriate function is LMS.

Table 1. Control parameters of DE used in this work

Weights	Error values obtained by DE		
	MAE	LMS	MSE
w_0	0.3893	0.2265	0.2115
w_1	-0.0950	-0.9679	-0.0214
w_2	0.4523	-0.2007	-1.2133
w_3	0.8859	1.0126	1.8632
w_4	0.4383	0.8830	1.1143
w_5	0.3041	-0.2301	0.7383
w_6	-0.0046	1.3069	0.8456
w_7	0.1377	-0.2368	1.6929
w_8	0.9226	1.0239	0.9356
w_9	0.6957	0.7194	0.8868
w_{10}	0.7897	0.7222	1.0466
w_{11}	0.6015	1.3647	0.7508
w_{12}	0.2947	-0.1921	0.9741
w_{13}	-0.0339	0.5619	-0.0638
w_{14}	0.8265	0.0610	1.0089

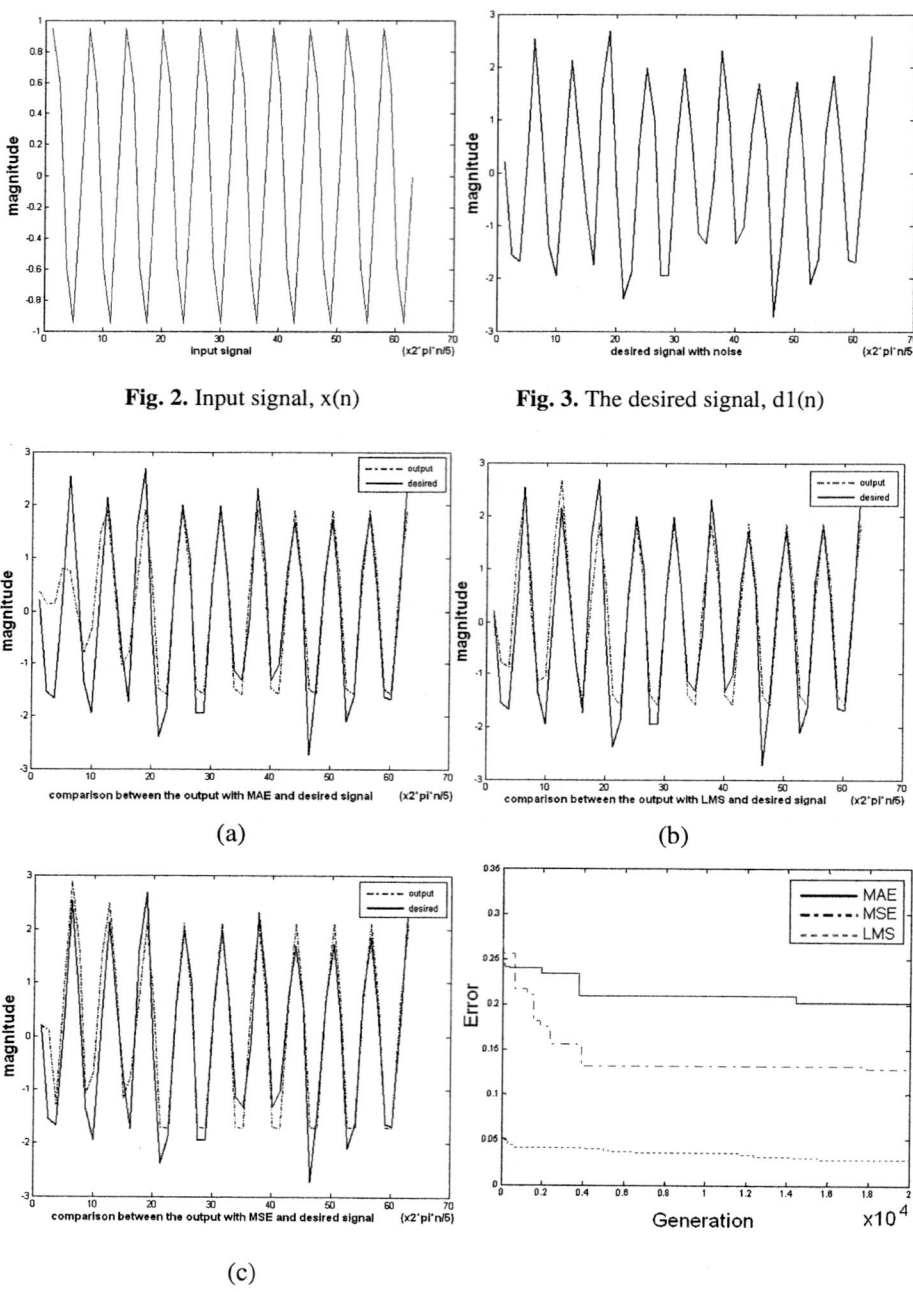

Fig. 2. Input signal, x(n)

Fig. 3. The desired signal, d1(n)

Fig. 4. The output signal obtained with (a) MAE (b) LMS (c) MSE

Fig. 5. The evolution of MAE, MSE and LMS errors

4 Conclusion

In this work DE algorithm has been applied to the design of ALC by using different error functions. As seen from the simulation results, the proposed method is able to design ALCs and can be efficiently used for this type filters even when noise exists. As seen from the figures, the ALC designed by DE algorithm nearly detects the desired signal after a short time. From evolution of the errors, LMS error function has the best performance for designing ALC.

References

1. Nurhan Karaboga, Canan Aslihan Koyuncu: Optimal Determination of Adaptive Linear Combiner Weights Using Differential Evolution Algorithm. INISTA, Yildiz Technical University, Istanbul (2005) 71-74
2. Storn, R. - Price, K.: Differential Evolution - a Simple and Efficient Heuristic for Global Optimization over Continuous Spaces. Journal of Global Optimization, Vol. 11. Kluwer Academic Publishers (1997) 341 – 359
3. Storn, R.: On the Usage of Differential Evolution for function Optimization. NAFIS 1996 Berkeley (1996) 519-523.
4. Price K. V.: Differential Evolution: a Fast and Simple Numerical Optimizer. In: Smith, M., Lee, M., Keller, J., Yen., J. (eds.): Biennial Conference of the North American Fuzzy Information Processing Society, NAFIPS. IEEE Press, New York (1996) 524-527
5. Price, K V.: An Introduction to Differential Evolution. In: Corne, D., Dorigo, M., and Glover, F. (eds): New Ideas in Optimization McGraw-Hill, London UK (1999) 79-108
6. Nurhan Karaboga,: Digital IIR Filter Design Using Differential Evolution Algorithm. EURASIP Applied Signal Processing Vol.2005 No.8 (2005) 1269-1276

A Comparison of Evolutionary Methods for the Discovery of Local Search Heuristics

Stuart Bain, John Thornton, and Abdul Sattar

Institute for Integrated and Intelligent Systems,
Griffith University,
PMB 50, GCMC 9726, Australia
{s.bain, j.thornton, a.sattar}@griffith.edu.au

Abstract. Methods of adaptive constraint satisfaction have recently become of interest to overcome the limitations imposed on "black-box" search algorithms by the no free lunch theorems. Two methods that each use an evolutionary algorithm to adapt to particular classes of problem are the CLASS system of Fukunaga and the evolutionary constraint algorithm work of Bain et al. We directly compare these methods, demonstrating that although special purpose methods can learn excellent algorithms, on average standard evolutionary operators perform even better, and are less susceptible to the problems of bloat and redundancy.

1 Introduction

Problems involving constraints are ubiquitous in both theoretical and applied computer science, and as many real-world problems can be easily formulated as boolean satisfiability problems, the development of algorithms for satisfiability testing remains an important area of research. Consider however, the problem of choosing the most appropriate algorithm for a particular class of constraint problems. Are algorithms with favourable benchmark performance most suited to the specific problems of interest?

According to the no free lunch theorems [1], the short answer to this question is "no". Not only is an algorithm's performance on some problem classes not indicative of its performance on others, unless the algorithm exploits some hidden structure of a problem class then above-average performance on that class must necessarily be balanced by below-average performance on other classes. Given this, the challenge becomes the development and matching of the most appropriate algorithm for a particular class of problem.

As algorithm development is a time-consuming task, methods of adaptive problem solving that can automatically adapt to the specific problems of interest, without the necessity of human problem-solving experience, have started to receive attention [2,3,4]. One method that has proved successful is to treat constraint algorithms as expressions to be modified by some form of evolutionary procedure. Such a procedure applies one or more genetic operators to the "fittest" algorithms in order to breed the next generation of algorithms.

The contribution of this paper is a direct comparison of the various genetic operators that may be used to breed successive generations of algorithms.

2 Evolving Algorithms

When considering methods of algorithm adaptation, there are a number of features crucial to the expressiveness and performance of an adaptive system [5].

1) The ability to represent both complete and local search routines; 2) Unrestricted complexity; 3) Appropriateness for satisfiable and over-constrained problems; 4) The ability to learn from failure; and 5) The ability to recognise synergies, subexpressions that perform well together but poorly individually.

Both complete and local search algorithms for constraint satisfaction can be viewed as iterative procedures that repeatedly assign (in the case of complete search) or reassign (in the case of local search) domain values to variables. Procedures of either type usually rank potential variable-value instantiations according to heuristic merit. This heuristic can be viewed as an expression composed from functions and terminals (constants) describing the nature of the constraint problem and the state of the search. The specific functions and constants used will determine whether the possible expressions lead to heuristics suited for complete or local search. Provided that a sufficiently expressive set of functions is chosen, such expressions do not place an *a priori* bound on the complexity of possible heuristics.

Furthermore, evolutionary methods of adaptation exhibit characteristics 3, 4 and 5 above. Evolutionary algorithms rely on a measure of fitness to rank candidate algorithms, and can include metrics appropriate to satisfiable problems (such as success rate); or to over-constrained problems (such as best solution cost); and that distinguish between algorithms even when they fail to find a solution (such as measures of depth, mobility and coverage for local search [6]). Synergies may also be identified, as the probabilistic nature of evolutionary algorithms does not automatically exclude poor performing individuals from participating in the creation of subsequent generations.

It is not surprising then, that in a number of previous works evolutionary techniques have been applied to the problem of automatically adapting constraint satisfaction algorithms, specifically, the CLASS system of Fukunaga [7,8] and the evolutionary constraint algorithm work of Bain et al. [4,5].

CLASS constructs algorithms composed mainly of *if..then* style production rules and relies heavily on measures that have been used in the GSAT, WALKSAT and NOVELTY families. New algorithms are developed exclusively using the *composition* operator, which works by taking two existing heuristics H_1 and H_2 and a boolean condition C to create a new heuristic of the form "*if C then H_1 else H_2*". Ten different conditions were explicated for use with CLASS [7].

The evolved constraint algorithm work of Bain et al. also considers an algorithm to be an expression but in contrast to CLASS its expressions are mathematical: functions and terminals are added and multiplied together to produce a numeric value for each candidate variable. The variable exhibiting the "best" value of this expression (according to a further metric, such as "maximum" or "minimum") is selected as the variable to modify. Genetic programming [9] was selected as an appropriate method of adaptation for such expressions.

The approaches of Bain and Fukunaga are similar in a number of respects. They both can be considered evolutionary algorithms, with the primary difference between the two systems being the genetic operators used to create subsequent generations of algorithms. A discussion of the various merits of these two approaches must consider why evolutionary methods work. The efficacy of genetic methods is often premised on the existence of *building blocks*, i.e. small clusters of genetic material that imbue an individual with above average performance in the phenotype space [10]. By generating new algorithms, the genetic operators are permitting these building blocks to be tried in new chromosomal contexts. Over a number of generations, repeated selections of above average individuals cause building blocks to proliferate within the population.

In the standard genetic algorithm with a fixed-length chromosome, evaluating genetic material in new chromosomal contexts necessitates some disruption to an existing chromosome. However, when a chromosome is an expression without a predetermined size or structure, disruption is not necessary and it becomes possible to incorporate all of a parent's genetic material into its children. This is the main difference between the two approaches being considered: the possibility of disruption to a parent's genetic material.

The composition operator used in CLASS does not result in any disruption to a parent's genetic material when forming a child. The two parents are included in the new child in their entirety (along with a boolean condition as outlined previously). Whilst it is advantageous to prevent disruption to (and hence removal of) above-average building blocks from the population, there are a number of associated disadvantages with such a method. Of prime importance is the exponential growth in the size of each new child resulting from combining two entire parents. Secondly, as no genetic material is ever removed from a candidate expression, redundant genetic information that might once have exhibited coincidental above-average performance will remain present for all time.

One alternative is to use genetic operators, such as crossover and mutation, that can remove some genetic material from candidate expressions. As crossover works by replacing an existing subtree of an expression with a different one, it does not result in as rapid growth in expression size as occurs with composition. Similarly, the problem of redundant information in expressions is also solved by crossover and mutation, as both operators will probabilistically replace some (potentially redundant) parts of an expression with alternate genetic material. Both of these features are at the expense of potential disruption to building blocks that might be responsible for a parent algorithm's above-average performance. The larger the building block, the greater the probability of disruption.

Whether disruption of building blocks will be significant in a particular domain is a difficult question to answer analytically, as it depends on many factors: the fitness landscape of the domain, the composition of the population, and the parameters of the evolutionary algorithm. Without a definitive, analytical answer, the efficacy of genetic operators that preserve the integrity of parent expressions becomes an empirical question.

3 Experimental Study

The purpose of this experimental study is to compare two different genetic operators (crossover and composition) within a common experimental framework. The UBCSAT package was selected as this framework, as it provides a widely recognised environment for satisfiability testing and evaluating constraint satisfaction algorithms.

Algorithm expressions are constructed from a set of functions and terminals (constants) that describe properties of the constraint system and the current state of the search. The functions and terminals are based on those explicated for use with the CLASS system in [7], which were derived from the material necessary to implement such well-known algorithms as GSAT, WALKSAT and NOVELTY. This representation is strongly-typed to ensure that algorithms constructed from it are functional.

The parameters for the evolutionary procedures are as follows. Both procedures will generate 50 new algorithms each generation (using crossover and composition respectively), with 250 algorithms directly copied from the preceding generation. When duplicating elements, the fittest are selected first, making both experiments "elitist" since the fittest elements can never be lost. This population size was selected to match that used in Fukunaga's original study [7]. Whilst no explicit reason was given for this choice, one plausible explanation concerns the exponential increase in expression size caused by the composition operator. By conveying the majority of the population to the succeeding generation as is, many small algorithms remain to participate in future compositions.

Algorithm expressions are selected to participate in crossover and composition based on their observed fitness value. The raw score of each is taken to be the mean number of flips required to solve 50 randomly generated, phase-transition region, 3-SAT problems: uf100-01 through uf100-050 from the SATLIB benchmark set. Each algorithm expression is permitted 25 tries on each problem, giving a total of 1250 evaluations for each. The cutoff value of 5000 flips is taken as the result of any try for which a solution was not found. The evolutionary procedures were each executed for 50 generations.

Two different fitness equations were considered. As a smaller raw score means a better algorithm, these equations also serve to "standardise" the observed performance so that a smaller score translates into a higher fitness. The first is quite egalitarian, $fitness_i = Best + Worst - score_i$, providing even badly performing algorithms a reasonable chance of being selected. The other equation, $fitness_i = Worst - score_i$, severely punishes the worst performing algorithms so that they are almost never selected. A further option is whether to consider perceived duplicate algorithms eligible for selection (these are truly duplicates or they failed 100% of the time). In both experiments, parent algorithms are selected uniformly at random according to fitness, subject also to whether duplicates are being ignored. If the two algorithms selected would result in a tree exceeding the size bound of 40 nodes, the random choice is repeated up to 1000 times, after which the experiment is terminated.

4 Results and Analysis

The results of experiments conducted with the different selection methods are tabulated in Table 1. These three methods (strict, egalitarian and egalitarian with duplicates) give increasing probability of selection to poorly performing algorithms respectively. In each experiment, the same initial populations were used for crossover as for composition.

Performance: The 4 best algorithms were all evolved using the strict fitness function, suggesting that it is advantageous to give little consideration to poor performing algo-

Table 1. Performance of the best evolved algorithms from each experiment, evaluated using a further 1000 runs on each of 100 problems: uf100-01 through uf100-0100

Selection Method	Run #	Composition					Crossover				
		Tree Size	Success Rate %	Mean Flips	Mean Time	Rank	Tree Size	Success Rate %	Mean Flips	Mean Time	Rank
Strict	1	37	98.79	1186.09	4.80	1	10	98.68	1186.18	1.99	2
	2	34	98.57	1360.69	4.74	3	37	98.50	1236.28	2.83	4
	3	24	97.47	1494.48	2.77	18	14	98.11	1301.99	1.99	7
	Mean	32	98.28	*1347.09*	*4.10*	2	20	98.43	*1241.48*	2.26	*1*
Egalitarian	1	39	98.08	1243.72	3.05	12	17	98.17	1264.89	2.46	6
	2	39	97.82	1358.00	3.63	15	39	98.10	1264.55	3.98	9
	3	38	97.81	1325.15	3.29	16	38	97.84	1394.73	3.27	14
	Mean	39	97.90	*1308.96*	*3.32*	6	31	98.04	*1308.06*	*3.24*	*3*
+Duplicates	1	36	98.09	1247.17	3.78	10	22	98.22	1187.21	2.22	5
	2	36	98.09	1298.19	3.01	11	26	98.11	1456.52	3.79	8
	3	38	97.92	1405.50	3.36	13	22	97.69	1434.38	2.45	17
	Mean	37	98.03	*1316.95*	*3.38*	4	23	98.01	*1359.37*	2.82	*5*
Overall Mean		36	98.07	*1324.33*	*3.60*	2	25	98.16	*1302.97*	2.77	1

rithms. On average, the algorithms generated using crossover were marginally more successful in terms of success, flips and time.

The best individual algorithm was created by the composition operator, solving 98.79% of test runs, slightly more than the best algorithm evolved using crossover, which achieved 98.68% success. The striking difference between these two algorithms is their time performance though, with the crossover algorithm averaging only 1.99 seconds to solve each problem, less than half of the 4.80 seconds required by the composition algorithm. This is due to the their tree size: only 10 versus 37 nodes respectively.

Bloat: Bloating is a problem associated with evolutionary methods that don't use a fixed-length representation, occurring when an increasingly complex solution doesn't produce a fitness benefit over that of a simpler solution. One method to control bloating is to incorporate the measure adversely affected by bloat into the fitness function, in this case, run-time. Unfortunately, this transforms the problem into a multi-criteria optimisation problem, introducing additional challenges to balance the use of two disparate fitness measures.

Although not immune from bloat, algorithms generated with crossover exhibited less bloat on average than those generated using composition, having smaller tree sizes (25 versus 36 nodes on average) and a slightly better average performance. This was to be expected by the nature of the composition operator.

Redundancy: In this context, redundancy is considered to be genetic material that does not improve or that worsens performance but has remained present in an algorithm. As composition is unable to remove genetic material from an algorithm, it is plausible that some redundant material is present.

Given the *if..then* nature of the expressions being learned, redundancy may be tested for by replacing an entire *if* conditional with one of its *then* or *else* branches. For example, to test whether the H_1 branch is redundant in the statement "*if C then H_1 else H_2*", the entire statement would be replaced by H_2.

The above rewriting rule was applied to the best algorithm of both methods. Only the algorithm evolved using composition exhibited redundancy, on 6 of its subtrees. The best of these 6 modified algorithms had a success rate of 98.89%.

5 Conclusion

This work has examined within a common experimental framework two different evolutionary operators for discovering new local search heuristics for satisfiability testing. These two operators are the composition operator, a specialised operator for evolving local search heuristics and a standard crossover operator which has been widely used in the genetic programming community. Additionally, three selection methods were examined, each of which gave a different probability of selecting poorer algorithms to participate in recombination.

Although the best performing algorithm was derived using the composition operator, on average algorithms evolved using standard crossover were found to perform better in terms of success, flips and time. Whilst this superior performance was only marginal in the case of success and flips, it was substantial in terms of time, due to the smaller size of the algorithms learned using crossover.

The larger size of the algorithms evolved using composition, without an appreciable fitness benefit, demonstrates the susceptibility of this method to bloat. Crossover was also found to be less susceptible to redundancy, with its best algorithm containing no redundancy whereas a number of redundant subtrees were present in the best algorithm evolved using composition.

In conclusion, giving less consideration to poorly-performing algorithms resulted in the best evolved algorithms. Although composition was able to evolve a number of excellent algorithms for local search, algorithms evolved using a standard crossover recombination operator were found to be superior on average, in terms of success rate, flips and especially time. They were similarly found less susceptible to bloat and redundancy than the corresponding algorithms evolved using composition.

An appendix is available on the author's homepage at http://stuart.multics.org

References

1. David H. Wolpert and William G. Macready. No free lunch theorems for optimization. *IEEE Transactions on Evolutionary Computation*, 1(1):67–82, April 1997.
2. Steven Minton. Automatically configuring constraint satisfaction programs: A case study. *Constraints*, 1(1):7–43, 1996.
3. Susan L. Epstein, Eugene C. Freuder, Richard Wallace, Anton Morozov, and Bruce Samuels. The adaptive constraint engine. In *CP '02*, pages 525–540, 2002.
4. Stuart Bain, John Thornton, and Abdul Sattar. Evolving variable ordering heuristics for constrained optimization. In *CP'05.*, page to appear, 2005.
5. Stuart Bain, John Thornton, and Abdul Sattar. Methods of automatic algorithm adaptation. In *PRICAI 2004, LNAI 3157*, pages 144–153, 2004.
6. Dale Schuurmans and Finnegan Southey. Local search characteristics of incomplete SAT procedures. *Artificial Intelligence*, 132(2):121–150, 2001.

7. Alex Fukunaga. Automated discovery of composite SAT variable-selection heuristics. In *Proceedings of AAAI 2002*, pages 641–648, 2002.
8. Alex Fukunaga. Evolving local search heuristics for SAT. In *GECCO-04*, 2004.
9. John Koza. *Genetic Programming: On the programming of computers by means of natural selection*. MIT Press, Cambridge, Massachusetts, 1992.
10. John H. Holland. *Adaptation in natural and artificial systems, 2nd Edition*. MIT Press, Cambridge, Massachusetts, 1992.

Evolutionally Optimized Fuzzy Neural Networks Based on Fuzzy Relation Rules and Evolutionary Data Granulation

Sung-Kwun Oh[1], Hyun-Ki Kim[1], Seong-Whan Jang[2], and Yong-Kab Kim[2]

[1] Department of Electrical Engineering, The University of Suwon, San 2-2 Wau-ri, Bongdam-eup, Hwaseong-si, Gyeonggi-do, 445-743, South Korea
ohsk@suwon.ac.kr
[2] Department of Electrical Electronic and Information Engineering, Wonkwang University, 344-2, Shinyong-Dong, Iksan, Chon-Buk, 570-749, South Korea

Abstract. In this paper, we introduce new architectures and comprehensive design methodologies of Evolutionally optimized Fuzzy Neural Networks (EoFNN). The proposed dynamic search-based GAs leads to rapidly optimal convergence over a limited region or a boundary condition. The proposed EoFNN is based on the Fuzzy Neural Networks (FNN) with the extended structure of fuzzy rules being formed within the networks. In the consequence part of the fuzzy rules, three different forms of the regression polynomials such as constant, linear and modified quadratic takes into consideration. The structure and parameters of the EoFNN are optimized by the dynamic search-based GAs.

1 Introduction

CI computing technique becomes hot issue of IT (Information technology) and abilities of that interest. The omnipresent tendency is the one that exploits techniques of CI [1] by embracing neurocomputing imitating neural structure of a human [2], fuzzy modeling using linguistic knowledge and experiences of experts [3], and genetic optimization based on the natural law [4,5]. Especially the two of the most successful approaches have been the hybridization attempts made in the framework of CI. Neuro-fuzzy systems are one of them [6]. A different approach to hybridization leads to genetic fuzzy systems [5,7].

In this paper, new architectures and comprehensive design methodologies of Evolutionally optimized Fuzzy Neural Networks (EoFNN) with the aid of dynamic search-based GAs are introduced for effective analysis and solution of nonlinear problem and complex systems. This methodology can effectively reduce the number of parameters and improve the performance of a model. To assess the performance of the proposed model, we exploit a well-known numerical example.

2 Polynomial Fuzzy Inference Architecture of FNN

The network structure of the consequence part of the fuzzy rules involves simplified (Type 0), linear (Type 1), and polynomial (Type 2)-based type. And the fuzzy inference structure of pFNN can be defined by the selection of Type (order of a polynomial) mentioned previously.

[Layer 1] Input layer
[Layer 2] Computing activation degrees of linguistic labels
[Layer 3] Computing firing strength of premise rules
[Layer 4] Normalization of a degree activation (firing) of the rule
[Layer 5] Multiplying a normalized activation degree of the rule by connection weight

$$f_i = \bar{\mu}_i \times Cy_i \quad \text{where,} \quad \begin{cases} \text{Type 0}: Cy_i = w_{0i} \\ \text{Type 1}: Cy_i = w_{0i} + w_{1i} \cdot x_1 + \cdots + w_{ki} \cdot x_k \\ \text{Type 2}: Cy_i = w_{0i} + w_{1i} \cdot x_1 + \cdots + w_{k+1i} \cdot x_1 \cdot x_2 + \cdots \end{cases} \quad (1)$$

[Layer 6] Computing output of pFNN

$$\hat{y} = \sum_{i=1}^{n} f_i = \sum_{i=1}^{n} \bar{\mu}_i \cdot Cy_i = \sum_{i=1}^{n} \frac{\mu_i \cdot Cy_i}{\sum_{i=1}^{n} \mu_i} \quad (2)$$

The learning of the proposed pFNN is realized by adjusting connection weights w, which organize the consequence networks of pFNN. The standard Back-propagation (BP) algorithm is utilized as the learning method in this study.

The proposed pFNN can be designed to adapt a characteristic of a given system, also, that has the faculty of making a simple structure out of a complicated model for a nonlinear system, because the pFNN comprises consequence structure with various orders (Types) for fuzzy rules.

3 Evolutionally Optimized Fuzzy Neural Networks

We introduce new architectures and comprehensive design methodologies of genetic algorithms (GAs [4,5]) based evolutionally optimized Fuzzy neural networks (EoFNN). For the evolutionally optimized architecture, the dynamic search-based GAs is proposed, and also the efficient methodology of chromosomes application of GAs for the identification of architecture and parameters of EoFNN is discussed.

we introduce the dynamic search-based GAs. This methodology discovers an optimal solution through adjusting search range. Adjustment of a range is based on the moving distance of a basis solution. A basis solution is previously determined for sufficiently large space.

In order to generate the proposed EoFNN, the dynamic search based GAs is used in the optimization problems of structures and parameters. From the point of fuzzy rules, these divide into the structure and parameters of the premise part, and that of consequence part. The structure issues in the premise of fuzzy rules deal with how to use of input variables (space) influencing outputs of model. The selection of input variables and the division of space are closely related to generation of fuzzy rules that determine the structure of FNN, and govern the performance of a model. Moreover, a number of input variable and a number of space divisions induce some fatal problems such as the increase of the number of fuzzy rules and the time required. Therefore, the relevant selection of input variables and the appropriate division of space are required. The structure of the consequence part of fuzzy rules is related to how represents a fuzzy subspace. Universally, the conventional methods offer uniform types to each subspace. However, it forms a complicated structure and debases the output quality of a model, because it does not consider the correlation of input variables and reflect a feature of fuzzy subspace. In this study, we apply the various forms in expressions of a fuzzy subspace. The form is selected according to an influence of a fuzzy subspace for an output criterion and provides users with the necessary information of a subspace for a system analysis.

4 Experimental Studies

In this experiment, we use three-input nonlinear function as in [3]. This dataset was analyzed using Sugeno's method [3]. We consider 40 pairs of the original input-output data. The performance index (PI) is defined by (3). 20 out of 40 pairs of input-output data are used as learning set and the remaining part serves as a testing set.

$$E(PI \text{ or } EPI) = \frac{1}{n}\sum_{p=1}^{n}\frac{|y_p - \hat{y}_p|}{y_p} \times 100(\%) \tag{3}$$

Table 1 summarizes the results of the EoFNN architectures. This table includes the tuning methodologies using dynamic search based GAs. Ⓐ$_k$ case includes two auto-tuning processes, namely, structure and parameter tuning processes. In first process, structure of a given model is tuned, that is input variables of premise and consequence, membership function, and order of polynomial are set. And then, parameters of the identified structure are tuned in second process. Ⓑ$_k$ case includes structure and parameter tuning processes, however, two tuning processes is not done separately but done at the same time. That is, input variables of premise and consequence, parameters of membership function, and order of polynomial are tuned.

Table 1. Performance index of EoFNN for the nonlinear function

Case	Premise			Consequence		PI	E_PI
	Inputs	MFs	Para.	Inputs	Order		
Ⓐ$_2$	≤2 GAs	2×2	Min-Max	GAs	GAs	2.068	5.164
	Tuned (x$_2$,x$_3$)	2×2	GAs	Tuned	Tuned	0.232	1.013
Ⓑ$_2$	≤2 GAs (x$_2$,x$_3$)	2×2	GAs	GAs	GAs	0.224	0.643

The preferred EoFNN results from Ⓑ$_2$. This architecture consists of 2 inputs, x_1 and x_3, in premise part, and 4 fuzzy rules such as (4). The proposed EoFNNs come with a more compact network of higher accuracy and improved prediction capabilities in comparison to other conventional intelligent models.

R^1 : If x_2 is A_{21} and x_3 is A_{31} then $Cy_1 = w_{01} + w_{11}x_1 + w_{31}x_3 + w_{51}x_1x_3$

R^2 : If x_2 is A_{21} and x_3 is A_{32} then $Cy_2 = w_{02} + w_{12}x_1 + w_{22}x_2 + w_{32}x_3 + w_{42}x_1x_2 + w_{52}x_1x_3 + w_{62}x_2x_3$ (4)

R^3 : If x_2 is A_{22} and x_3 is A_{31} then $Cy_3 = w_{03} + w_{13}x_1 + w_{23}x_2 + w_{33}x_3$

R^4 : If x_2 is A_{22} and x_3 is A_{32} then $Cy_4 = w_{04} + w_{14}x_1 + w_{34}x_3$

5 Concluding Remarks

New architectures and comprehensive design methodologies of Evolutionally optimized Fuzzy Neural Networks (EoFNN) has discussed for effective analysis and solution of nonlinear problem and complex systems. Also, the dynamic search-based GAs has introduced to lead to rapidly optimal convergence over a limited region or a boundary condition. This methodology can effectively reduce the number of parameters and improve the performance of a model. The proposed EoFNN with much more compact fuzzy rules can be efficiently carried out both at the structural as well as parametric level for overall optimization.

Acknowledgements. This work was supported in part by BK21 in Wonkwang University.

References

1. W. Pedrycz and J. F. Peters, *Computational Intelligence and Software Engineering*, World Scientific, Singapore, 1998.
2. L. W. Chan and F. Fallside, "An Adaptive Training Algorithm for Back Propagation Networks", *Computer Speech and Language*, Vol. 2, pp. 205-218, 1987.
3. G. Kang and M. Sugeno, "Fuzzy Modeling", *Transactions of the Society of Instrument and Control Engineers*, Vol. 23, No. 6, pp. 106-108, 1987.
4. David E. Goldberg, *Genetic Algorithms in search, Optimization & Machine Learning*, Addison-wesley, 1989.
5. O. Cordon, et al., Ten years of genetic fuzzy systems: current framework and new trends, *Fuzzy Sets and Systems*, Vol. 141, Issue 1, pp.5-31, 2004.
6. H. S. Park and S. K. Oh, "Rule-based Fuzzy-Neural Networks Using the Identification Algorithm of GA Hybrid Scheme", *International Journal of Control, Automation, and Systems*, Vol. 1, No. 1, pp. 101- 110, 2003.
7. H. S. Park and S. K. Oh, "Multi-FNN Identification Based on HCM Clustering and Evolutionary Fuzzy Granulation", *International Journal of Control, Automation and Systems*, Vol. 1, No. 2, pp. 194-202, 2003.

Evolving While-Loop Structures in Genetic Programming for Factorial and Ant Problems*

Guang Chen[1,2,3] and Mengjie Zhang[1]

[1]School of Mathematics, Statistics & Computer Science,
Victoria University of Wellington, P.O. Box 600, Wellington, New Zealand
[2]Computer Center, Peking University, Beijing, 100871, P.R. China
[3]School of Mathematical Sciences, Peking University, Beijing, 100871, P.R. China
ccchen@pku.edu.cn, mengjie@mcs.vuw.ac.nz

Abstract. Loop is an important structure in human written programs. However, it is seldom used in the evolved programs in genetic programming (GP). This paper describes an approach to the use of while-loop structure in GP for the factorial and the artificial ant problems. Two different forms of the while-loop structure, count-controlled loop and event-controlled loop, are investigated. The results suggest that both forms of the while-loop structure can be successfully evolved in GP, the system with the while-loop structure is more effective and more efficient than the standard GP system for the two problems, and the evolved genetic programs with the loop-structure are much easier to interpret.

1 Introduction

Iteration is an important structure in programming. It provides a mechanism to execute a sequence of instructions repeatedly and many real world problems require iteration as part of a solution. Two major types of the iteration structure have been used for different kinds of problems. The first type is *count-controlled loops*, which execute the loop body a specified number of times and can be implemented by either a *for-loop* or a *while-loop*. The second is *event-controlled loops*, which repeat the loop body until something happens within the loop to signal that the loop should be exited. In this case, the repeat number of loop body is unknown in advance, and this kind of loop can generally be implemented by *while-loops* only.

Genetic programming (GP) [1] is a relatively new technique which employs the Darwinian principle of survival of the fittest to automatically generate computer programs for a particular task. Since the 1990s, GP has been successfully applied to many applications [2,3].

Compared with the standard arithmetic operators which are commonly used in GP, loops are more complex and usually require different types of input variables and boolean conditions.In addition, the infinite loop problem often occurs

---

* The work is partially supported by VUW-URF 6/9 and the NNSFC under grant Nos 60473056.

and illegal solutions can be easily generated. Accordingly, the loop structures are relatively difficult to evolve in GP due to the complexity of the loop structures.

The evolution of iteration using GP was first explored by Koza [1], where the Do Until (DU) operator is introduced to allow the evolution of loops for the block stacking problem. To avoid infinite loops, Koza applies both a limit to the total number of loops (100) in a program and a limit to the number of cycles in each loop (25).

In evolving a sorting algorithm, Kinnear used an iterative function (dobl start end work) [4,5]. The system used an index variable for the loop to control the execution of the loop body work, ranging from value start, to the value end. To avoid infinite loops, Kinnear used the same approach as Koza, but with larger limits (2000 and 200).

Recently, Ciesielski and Xiang used for-loop structures to evolve programs for controlling an agent in the modified Santa Fe Ant problem and sorting a 7-element array [6]. In their implementation, strongly typed genetic programming [7] was used to ensure that the generated programs were syntactically correct, and semantics was restricted to avoid infinite loops.

Most of the previous work on evolving loop structures in GP has been focused on the count-controlled loops. Although Koza used event-controlled loop, he did not guarantee the correctness of the program, and there were many ill-formed programs. The goal of this paper is to investigate the evolution of programs with explicit while-loop structures to implement both the count-controlled and the event-controlled loops and compare this approach to the basic GP approach and the approach with for-loops. We have chosen to work with a factorial problem and an artificial ant problem for this investigation.

2 The GP Approach with While-Loop Structures

In this approach and the basic GP approach, we used the tree-structure to represent genetic programs [1]. The ramped half-and-half method was used for generating programs in the initial population and for the mutation operator. The proportional selection mechanism and the reproduction, crossover and mutation operators were used in the learning and evolutionary process. In particular, we used strongly typed genetic programming [7] in experiments.

To implement the count-controlled loops, we define the first form of while-loop as WhileLoop1(start end body), where a counter is initialised to the value of start. When the counter is not greater than end, the body is executed and the counter incremented. The process is repeated until the value of the counter is greater than end.

For event-controlled loops, we define the second form of while-loop as WhileLoop2 (condition body). If the condition is true, then the body will be executed. The process is repeated until the condition becomes false.

In [6], two forms of for-loop were defined as ForLoop1(start end body) and ForLoop2(num-iterations body). In fact, ForLoop1 is the same as the form of WhileLoop1. In ForLoop2, the body is executed num-iterations times. Clearly, both the two forms of for-loop are actually count-controlled loops.

In this paper, we regard the factorial problem as a count-controlled loop and use WhileLoop1 to solve it. The artificial ant problem can be regarded as both a count-controlled loop and an event-controlled loop, so we investigate and compare both WhileLoop2 and ForLoop2 on this problem.

3 Count-Controlled While-Loop for Factorial Problem

3.1 The Factorial Problem

The factorial of any number greater than 0, expressed with the symbol n!, means the product of consecutive numbers 1 through n.

```
fac(n) = n! = 1 * 2 * ... * (n-2) * (n-1) * n
```

This problem is a kind of regression problem, whose target outputs of a set of inputs can be calculated and obtained by the above function. We expect our GP system with a count-controlled loop structure to successfully solve the problem.

3.2 Experiment Design and Configuration

The terminal set is {i, n, y}. i is the loop control variable whose initial value is 0. n is the number to be evaluated for the factorial. y is a settable global variable which is initialized to 1. It is associated with the operator SetY.

The function set is {SetY, MultInt, WhileLoop1}. SetY(arg1) evaluates arg1, sets the value to y and returns that value. MultInt, represented by the symbol *, returns the multiplication of its two arguments. To avoid infinite loops, in WhileLoop1, we restrict the value of end is less than 50.

Fifteen fitness cases are used in this problem. Input values are integers from 1 to 15. We use the number of mismatches as the fitness function.

In the GP system, we used a population size of 150, a crossover rate of 70%, a mutation rate of 28%, and a reproduction rate of 2%. The individual programs start with a depth of 1, and can increase to a maximum depth of 5. The evolution is terminated at generation 100 unless a perfect solution is found.

3.3 Results and Discussion

Effectiveness. we did 50 runs for both the new approach with the WhileLoop1 and the basic approach using the same set of parameters. The basic GP approach uses the four arithmetic operators in the function set without loops. While the new GP approach resulted in an ideal program that successfully found a perfect solution in 25 out of the 50 runs, none of the runs in the basic GP approach gave a successful solution. In another experiment, we increased the program depth to a maximum of 9 from 5 for the basic approach, but solutions still could not be found. These results suggest that our new GP approach with loops is more effective for this problem than the basic GP approach.

Comprehensibility. Compared with the basic approach, the new approach evolved genetic programs that are more comprehensible and easier to interpret for this task. For example, one evolved program from the 25 successful runs

```
(WhileLoop1 (WhileLoop1 y (* n y) y) y (WhileLoop1 y n (SetY (* i y))))
```

can be simplified as (WhileLoop1 y n (SetY (* i y))), which can be easily interpreted as C code [y = 1; i = y; while (i <= n) { y = i * y; i++;}]. Clearly, this program can successfully solve the factorial problem.

However, the programs evolved by the basic GP approach for this task are typically very long and the behaviour of them are generally very hard to interpret, even though some programs contain useful fragments for this task.

4 Event-Controlled While-Loop for the Ant Problem

4.1 The Artificial Ant Problem

The artificial ant problem is described in [1]. The problem is an artificial ant to find all the food lying along irregular trail. The ant can execute three actions: turnRight, turnLeft (the ant turns to left or right without moving), and move (the ant moves one square forward in the direction it is facing. If there is food on the square, the ant will eat the food). Each move or turn operation costs one step. Eating food cost another one step. The ant's goal is to eat all the food within some reasonable amount of time. The time is measured with steps.

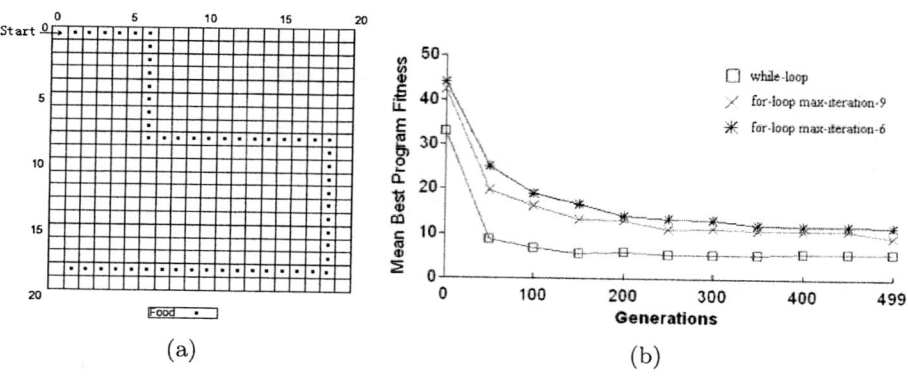

Fig. 1. (a) Food layout: the modified ant problem. (b) Mean best program fitness.

In previous work on the ant problem [1], the evolved programs do not explicitly use any loop. Loop is accomplished implicitly in the environment by invoking the program as many times as necessary to eat all the food or until some maximum number of steps (400) has been reached.

In order to simplify the problem, in our experiment, the size of the grid is set to 20×20 and 53 pieces of food are placed on the grid as shown in figure 1(a). The ant starts at position (0,0), facing east. The ant's goal is to traverse the entire trail and eat all of the food with no restricted time. We expect our GP system to evolve a program with an entire event-controlled loop structure for this problem, rather than the body of a loop only.

4.2 Experiment Design and Configuration

GP Approach with While-Loop2. The terminals set is {move, turnLeft, turnRight, foodAhead}. foodAhead means it is true if there is food in the forward square of current facing, and false otherwise. The function set is {Prog2, Prog3, WhileLoop2}. Prog2 takes two arguments executed sequentially. Prog3 takes three arguments executed sequentially. To avoid infinite loops, we allow a maximum of 20 iterations in each WhileLoop2. The fitness of an evolved genetic program is calculated as the number of food grids left. In the GP system, we used a population size of 200. The evolution is terminated at generation 500 unless a perfect solution is found. The other parameters are the same as the factorial problem.

GP Approach with ForLoop2. The GP system with the ForLoop2 structure used the same fitness function, the same set of parameters, and the same termination criteria as the new GP approach with the WhileLoop2. The terminal set is {turnLeft, turnRight, move, timesn}. timesn generates a random integer n between 0-9 or 0-6, depending on the maximum number of iterations allowed. The function set is {Prog2, Prog3, IfFoodAhead, ForLoop2}. IfFoodAhead (arg1 arg2) executes arg1 if there is food in the forward square of current facing, or executes arg2 otherwise. Notice that the value of num-iterations in function ForLoop2 will be obtained from terminal timesn.

The Basic GP Approach. The basic GP system used a similar set of parameters to the new approach with loops, except that the maximum program depth was increased to 6 to help find possible solutions. The terminal set is {turnLeft, turnRight, move}. The function set is {Prog2, Prog3, IfFoodAhead}.

4.3 Results and Discussion

Effectiveness. For all the three GP approaches, we run 50 independent experiments. Of all the 50 experiments, 43 found a perfect program to enable the ant to successfully take all the food in the two GP systems with either the WhileLoop2 or the ForLoop2 with a maximum iteration of nine. This number was decreased to 32 for the ForLoop2 when the maximum iteration was set to six. For the basic GP approach without loops, only two out of the 50 experiments generated a perfect program that successfully solved the problem. These results suggest that the GP approaches with loops are much more effective than the basic GP method without loops for this problem.

To further investigate and compare the effectiveness, figure 1(b) shows a comparison of the best fitness over the generations. As can be seen from figure 1(b), the GP approach with while-loop resulted in a much better average fitness over different generations than the GP system with the two for-loops, suggesting that the GP approach with while-loop is more effective for this problem than the GP approach with for-loops for a maximum iteration of either nine or six.

Comprehensibility. To investigate the comprehensibility of the genetic programs evolved by the different GP approaches, we check one typical evolved program with while-loops and for-loops that successfully solve the problem.

```
------------ (a) A Sample Evolved Program with While-Loop2 -----------
(WhileLoop2 foodAhead
    (Prog3 (Prog2 (WhileLoop2 foodAhead move) turnLeft)
           (Prog3 (WhileLoop2 foodAhead move)(Prog2 turnRight turnRight)
                  (WhileLoop2 foodAhead turnRight)) turnLeft))
------(b) A Sample Evolved Program with For-Loop2 max-iteration-9-------
(ForLoop2 times9 (Prog2 (ForLoop2 times7 (IfFoodAhead move turnLeft))
                        (ForLoop2 times8 turnLeft)))
```

In program (a), the outmost operator is a while-loop. Clearly, this is a nested while-loop which includes three inner loops. The program can be easily interpreted. Program (b) includes nested for-loops. This program is also relatively easy to understand. Unlike program (a) where each loop can be exited immediately when the condition becomes false, the loops in program (b) will always need to execute the body nine times. Accordingly, the programs with for-loops often need to take more steps to solve the problem than those with the while-loops. In our experiment, the average steps the programs took are 129, 163 and 159 when using the while-loop, for-loops with a max-iteration of nine and six, respectively. In addition, compared with these programs, the programs evolved by the basic GP approach are enormous and are very hard to understand.

Clearly, programs evolved with loops are more comprehensible than those without loops for this problem. In addition, the programs with while-loops usually takes fewer steps to solve the problem than those with the for-loops, suggesting that the GP approach with event-controlled loops is generally more efficient than that with the count-controlled loops for this task.

5 Conclusions

The goal of this paper was to investigate the evolution of programs with explicit while-loop structures in GP to implement both the count-controlled and the event-controlled loops. By defining two different forms of while-loop structures in the function set, genetic programs with loop structures have been successfully evolved for solving the factorial and the artificial ant problems. The results show that, compared to the basic GP approach without using loops, the new approach with while-loops was more effective and more efficient to these problems, and the genetic programs evolved by this new approach were much easier to interpret. Both this new GP approach with while-loops and the GP approach with for-loops found perfect programs to solve the modified artificial ant program and the programs evolved by both approaches were quite understandable, but the new GP approach with while-loops seemed more effective in improving the fitness and needed fewer steps to solve the problem.

References

1. Koza, J.R.: Genetic Programming: On the Programming of Computers by Natural Selection. MIT Press, Cambridge, MA, USA (1992)
2. Zhang, M., Ciesielski, V.: Genetic programming for multiple class object detection. Proceedings of the 12th Australian Joint Conference on Artificial Intelligence (1999) 180–192
3. Zhang, M., Smart, W.: Multiclass object classification using genetic programming. Applications of Evolutionary Computing **3005** (2004) 367–376
4. Kenneth E. Kinnear, J.: Evolving a sort: Lessons in genetic programming. In Proceedings of the 1993 International Conference on Neural Networks **2** (1993) 881–888
5. Kenneth E. Kinnear, J.: Generality and difficulty in genetic programming: Evolving a sort. In Stephanie Forrest, editor, Proceedings of the 5 International Conference on Genetic Algorithms, ICGA-93 (1993) 287–294
6. Ciesielski, V., Li, X.: Experiments with explicit for-loops in genetic programming. In Congress on Evolutionary Computation (2004) 494–501
7. Montana, D.J.: Strongly typed genetic programming. technical report bbn 7866. Technical report, Bolt Beranek and Newman, Inc. (1994)

Evolutionary Optimisation of Distributed Energy Resources

Ying Guo, Jiaming Li, and Geoff James

CSIRO Information and Communications Technology Centre,
Locked Bag 17, North Ryde, NSW 1670, Australia
{firstname.lastname}@csiro.au

Abstract. Genetic optimisation is used to minimise operational costs across a system of electrical loads and generators controlled by local intelligent agents and connected to the electricity grid at market rates. Experimental results in a simulated environment show that coordinated market-sensitive behaviours are achieved. A large network of 500 loads and generators, each characterised by different randomly selected parameters, was optimised using a two-stage genetic algorithm to achieve scalability.

1 Introduction

Many countries including Australia are experiencing a growing gap between electricity supply and demand, and distributed electricity generation technologies alongside improved demand-side management techniques have been identified as one set of solutions to this challenge [1]. Significant reductions in greenhouse gases can also be achieved by the large-scale deployment of clean, efficient distributed generation in place of increased investment in centralised generation.

We are developing multi-agent technology for the management and control of distributed energy resources [2], aimed at deployment in the Australian National Electricity Market within the next five years, and a component of this work is the development of intelligent coordination algorithms agents controlling distributed energy resources (DERs). Agent-based coordination is used in a range of fields including computing, manufacturing, and energy [3-5]. The purposes of coordination of DER agents are to achieve local efficiency goals and to aggregate sufficient quantities of distributed capacity to be of strategic value to market participants. Retailers exposed to volatile wholesale prices and network businesses making infrastructure investment decisions would be significant beneficiaries of such aggregates.

In this paper we tackle the problem of cost minimisation across a set of loads and generators controlled by local agents and connected to the electricity grid at market rates. In contrast to [3] we wish to investigate non-market algorithms. Our approach permits a cap on the power drawn from the grid that can be a local offering to a large-scale aggregation of distributed capacity. We consider systems of small to moderate scale, comprising up to 500 load and generator agents, and our simulated experimental results show that coordinated market-sensitive behaviours are achieved.

The remainder of this paper is organised as follows. Section 2 outlines our approach and Section 3 describes the optimisation process. In Section 4, we present experimental results in a simulated environment. Finally, conclusions based on these experiments are discussed in Section 5.

2 Distributed Energy Management

We assume that each resource has a corresponding agent which is the decision maker and controller of the resource. Resource agents have local objectives. They also have knowledge of their resource's behaviour, and information inputs about the physical environment and the electricity market. Resource agents have the collective objective of contributing to a network benefit; in our case the objective is reduced demand for a group of resources, including loads and generators, during a period of high overall demand. The challenge addressed in this paper is to meet local and collective objectives simultaneously.

Our example system corresponds to a hardware demonstration system at the CSIRO Energy Centre in Newcastle, Australia. It consists of microturbine, photovoltaic, and wind generators, a heating, ventilation, and air-conditioning (HVAC) load, and two cool-room loads, all connected to the electricity network which is treated as another generating resource. Results reported in Section 4.1 refer to this system of 6 resource agents. To study scalability in Section 4.2 we allow there to be any number of each kind of resource with different randomly selected parameters describing thermal mass, power capacity, temperature set-points, and so on.

3 Algorithm Design

Our aim is to find agent strategies that minimise the total cost to the customer while satisfying all load and generator constraints and any constraints on the total power $p_0(t)$ that the customer draws from the electricity network. We obtain solutions using an evolutionary algorithm of a kind that has previously achieved successful multi-agent coordination [5, 6] and strategies for electricity markets [7]. The genetic algorithm (GA) evolves a colony of resource actions for a number of generations, improving the performance of the colony. Techniques of fitness determination, selection, cross-over, reproduction, and mutation are applied to the resource actions and their chromosomal representation. Because there are several agents in the system, we use the "all against best" evolutionary tournament. This has been identified as a useful approach to analysing similar problems [5, 6]. In each round, each agent is chosen in turn and its population is evolved for a number of generations. This evolutionary strategy continues for all agents over numerous generations as they coevolve to each other's changing behaviours.

3.1 Individual Representation

Generators and loads are represented by their physical model and a sequence of states due to switching actions. The physical model for a cool room, for example, must include the thermal mass and the heat-transfer capacity of the compressor, and for this we use discrete time steps and a linear recursive relationship relating internal temperature to internal and external temperatures and heat transferred in the previous time step. There can be two kinds of action as illustrated in Figure 1:

- Resources can be continuously variable between fully on and off, represented as a fraction $\tau_i(t) \in [0,1]$ of fully on. The real-valued sequence $\tau_i(1), \tau_i(2), ..., \tau_i(\Pi)$ contains the parameters to be optimised for generator or load i.

- They can switch only fully on or off, represented as $\tau_j(t) \in \{0,1\}$, and the integer-valued sequence $\tau_j(1), \tau_j(2), ..., \tau_j(\Pi)$ contains the parameters to be optimised for generator or load j.

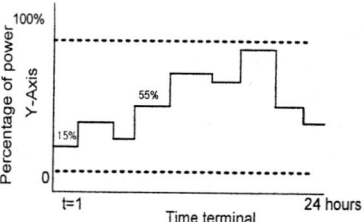 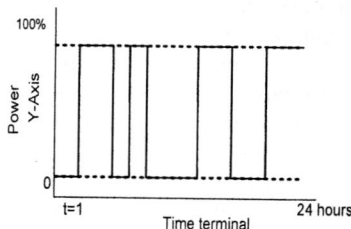

Fig. 1. Generator or load actions during one day as parameterised for the GA, a continuously variable resource on the left and a switched resource on the right

3.2 Fitness Function Design

After every generated population, every individual of the population must be evaluated to distinguish between good and bad individuals. This is done by mapping the objective function to a "fitness function", which is a well-behaved measure of relative fitness. Larger fitness values signify resource actions that can achieve better system performance. Since there are system constraints and resource constraints, the fitness of an individual should depend on both groups of constraints. The fitness function that is used in our experiments has this form:

$$f = \sum_{t=1}^{T} \left(\gamma_{\text{system}} f_{\text{system}} + \gamma_{\text{local}} f_{\text{local}} + \gamma_{\text{load}} f_{\text{load}} \right)$$

Other fitness functions are possible and will be investigated in further work. There are three parts in the fitness function, each with its own weight γ_{system}, γ_{local}, and γ_{load}, to allow their relative importance to be adjusted. The first part is the penalty when the electrical power drawn from the grid beyond the limit imposed by a demand cap for the site. The second part is the reward or penalty based on the operating costs of local generators. The third part is the reward or penalty on loads which do or do not satisfy the local constraints. The third part is defined in terms of temperature constraints for each heating/cooling load and is non-zero when, at some time during the time interval of the optimisation, the internal temperature is predicted to go outside preset limits.

4 Experimental Results

In this section, we will show some of the experimental results in the simulation environment. Firstly, the genetic algorithm results for a system of 6 resource agents are presented in Section 4.1. The results show, through a comparison with resources optimised independently of each other, that cooperative behaviour between resources is achieved. Secondly, we examine the collective behaviour of a set of several hundred heating/cooling loads and distributed generation sources including photovoltaics and microturbines using the "all against best" optimisation strategy.

These experiments optimise load and generator operation during a planning interval based on predicted environmental and market conditions. Predicted outdoor temperature determines the behaviour of heating/cooling loads, predicted solar intensity and wind speed determine the capacity of photovoltaic and wind generators, and predicted market price determines the most cost-effective mix of generation technologies.

4.1 Performance Comparison

In order to judge the improvement due to cooperative performance, we need to compare the optimised solution for the system against individual planning by independent resources. To obtain the independent resources' behaviour we apply the genetic

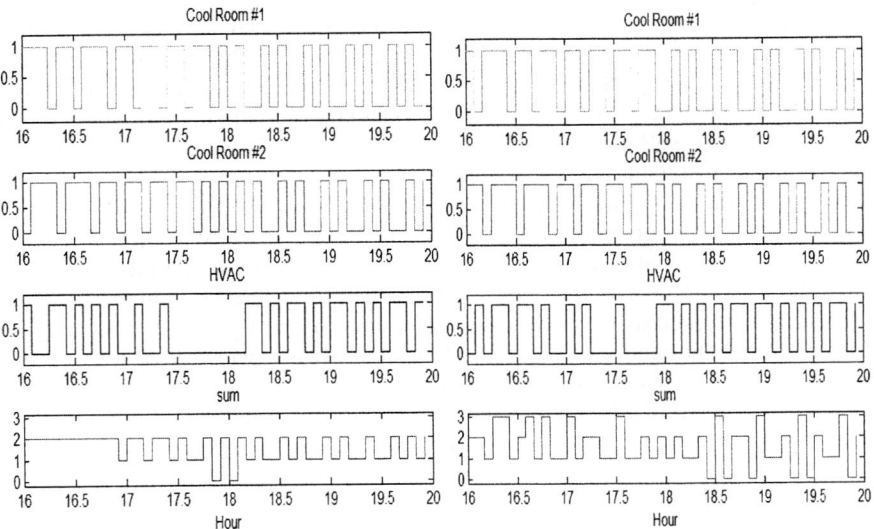

Fig. 2. Performance comparison of cooperative optimisation (left) against independent resource optimisation (right)

algorithm on each of them separately; each generator's action is optimised according to the predicted market price and running cost; each load's action is optimised considering only its own temperature constraints. We chose a four-hour planning interval between 16:00 and 20:00 to investigate the effect of a sharp rise in market price when a demand cap is in place.

Figure 2 shows a comparison between GA results with and without cooperation. The load actions for cool room #1, cool room #2, and HVAC agents are shown, as well as the sum of these actions. Both GA results satisfied the individual resources' constraints, but the three loads were never turned on at the same time with cooperative optimisation in the left-hand side of Figure 2, while this is not true with independent resource optimisation on the right-hand side. The bottom graphs in Figure 2 are the summed of actions and this difference is clearly visible.

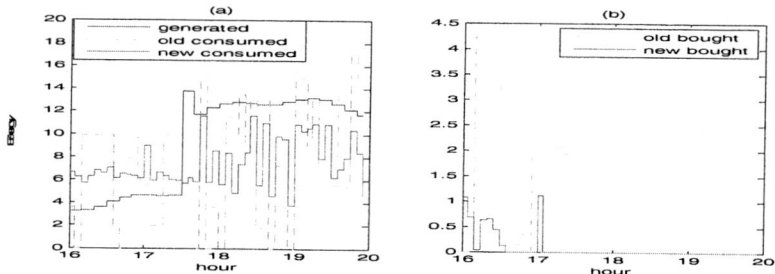

Fig. 3. Scalability using two-stage genetic algorithm

4.2 Scalability

In the following experiments, there are 100 resources in each category, including microturbines, photovoltaic generators, wind generators, HVAC plants, and cool rooms, totalling 500 resources. In order to accelerate what would otherwise be a very slow calculation, genetic optimisation occurs in two stages, the first determining average properties of loads and generators divided into categories, and the second refining properties of individual loads and generators.

The left-hand side of Figure 3 shows the total supply across this set and the total demand after each stage of optimisation. Two observations can be made about this example system: the variability of total demand is reduced as the optimisation proceeds, and the total supply exceeds demand during two long periods of higher market prices. During these periods the excess supply may be sold to the grid through a suitable broker. The right-hand side Figure 3 shows the periods when demand exceeds available generation across this set of resources, partly due to the unavailability of photovoltaics during the night, and thus power must be purchased from the grid. The second stage of optimisation reduces the amount that must be purchased.

5 Conclusions

A genetic optimisation approach has been applied to a simulated set of distributed energy resources. The "all against best" evolutionary tournament was used, and experimental results show coordinated market-sensitive behaviours for a set of 6 loads and generators. Each category of load and generator in the simulator was replicated up to 100 times with random variation, and a two-stage development of the evolutionary tournament coped well with optimisation at this scale. The technique shows promise, therefore, for "soft" real-time application which determines optimal resource behaviour for a period of one to several hours into the future based on market and environmental predictions. As reality differs from predictions the resource agents' behaviours must eventually differ from their optimised power functions and the optimisation should then be repeated.

Further work is being undertaken in two directions: testing genetically optimised behaviours alongside other algorithms on a hardware test platform, and developing large-scale aggregation techniques based on demand capping by such groups of resources as are described here.

References

1. United States D.O.E.: "Report of the US Department of Energy's Power Outage Study Team", Final report, March 2002.
2. Jones, T.E., and James, G.C.: "The Management and Control of Distributed Energy Resources," Proceedings, CIGRE Symposium on Power Systems with Dispersed Generation, Athens, April 2005.
3. Kok, J,K., Warmer, C.J., and Kamphuis, I.G., "PowerMatcher: Multiagent Control in the Electricity Infrastructure", Proceedings, 4th international joint conference on Autonomous Agents and Multi Agent Systems, Utrecht, July 2005.
4. Varga, L.Z., Jennings, N.R., and Cockburn, D.: "Integrating Intelligent Systems into a Cooperating Community for Electricity Distribution Management", *Expert Systems with Applications*, vol. 7, no. 4, 1994, pp. 563-79.
5. MacGill, I. F.: "Optimising Decentralised Power System Operation Using Dual Evolutionary Programming", Ph.D. Thesis, UNSW, Australia, 1998.
6. Poulton, G., Guo, Y., James, G., Valencia, P., Gerasimov, V., and Li, J.: "Directed Self-assembly of 2-Dimensional Mesoblocks using Top-down/Bottom-up Design", *Lecture Notes on Computer Science*, vol. 3464, p. 154, Springer-Verlag, May 2005.
7. Tully, F.R., and Kaye, R. J.: "Unit Commitment in Competitive Electricity Markets Using Genetic Algorithms", *Trans. of the Institute of Electrical Engineers of Japan*, vol. 117-B, no. 6, 1997, pp. 815-21.

Can Evolutionary Computation Handle Large Datasets? A Study into Network Intrusion Detection

Hai H. Dam, Kamran Shafi, and Hussein A. Abbass

The Artificial Life and Adaptive Robotics Laboratory,
School of ITEE, Univ. of New South Wales @ ADFA,
Canberra ACT 2600, Australia
{z3140959, abbass}@itee.adfa.edu.au, k.shafi@student.adfa.edu.au
http://www.itee.adfa.edu.au/~alar/

Abstract. XCS is currently considered as the state of the art Evolutionary Learning Classifier Systems (ELCS). XCS has not been tested on large datasets, particularly in the intrusion detection domain. This work investigates the performance of XCS on the 1999 KDD Cup intrusion detection dataset, a real world dataset approximately five million records, more than 40 fields and multiple classes with non-uniform distribution. We propose several modifications to XCS to improve its detection accuracy. The overall accuracy becomes equivalent to that of traditional machine learning algorithms, with the additional advantages of being evolutionary and with $O(n)$ complexity learner.

1 The Traditional XCS

XCS was introduced by Wilson [8,9] as an enhanced version of the traditional ELCS proposed by Holland [6]. It is widely accepted as one of the most reliable Michigan-style ELCS for machine learning [2,4]. The two major changes of XCS are: a fitness based on the accuracy of the reward prediction instead of the strength (or reward directly received from the environment) using a reinforcement learning approach; and a niche Genetic Algorithm (GA) to improve the spread of the state-action table. Many studies showed that XCS performs at least as well as other traditional machine learning techniques on several small data mining problems [1,7].

Current intrusion detection techniques fall into one of two categories; misuse detection and anomaly detection. The former looks for well known patterns of bad behaviors in network traffic and audit data, while the latter models the normal behavior of the system and flags any deviating event as anomalous. Our work is in the context of misuse detection using XCS. Most traditional algorithms require training in batch mode before exposure to the test data which implies multiple passes through the training data. In domains like intrusion detection it might not be desirable, especially in a real time implementation. XCS can learn in a stream mode thus avoiding the need of multiple passes through the training data. XCS is rule-based and the version we use has a linear $O(n)$ complexity in the number of instances (n).

We chose 1999 the KDD Cup intrusion detection dataset [5] that has a large number of records with non uniform class distribution, rare classes and novel test instances. The symbolic values were first mapped to numeric values and then normalized to a range of 0 to 1. Our results show that the new XCS improves considerably especially on three of the four classes in the dataset i.e. Probe, DOS and U2R.

Table 1. Mean and standard deviation of prediction accuracy of Conventional XCS in 30 runs

Class Prediction	Accuracy
NORMAL	0.572 ± 0.250
DOS	0.000 ± 0.000
PROBE	0.000 ± 0.000
U2R	0.002 ± 0.005
R2L	0.637 ± 0.293

Table 1 presents the prediction accuracy of the conventional XCS on the KDD dataset. The table shows that conventional XCS gets high accuracy on the R2L class, lower accuracy on class Normal and close to 0% accuracy on all other classes.

2   The Modified XCS

- **The Mutation effect:** XCS uses macro-mutation, where it mutates every attribute of a rule's body and rule's class at a certain rate. Mutating the body of a rule generalizes it beyond its locally covered area. XCS also mutates the predicted class. This is somehow less intuitive because: (1) if only the predicted class of a rule is mutated, it will increase conflict within the rule set; and (2) if the condition component is also mutated, it is more likely that by generalizing the rule to cover its immediate neighborhood, the class will remain unchanged. Overall, we believe in many real life problems, allowing the rule to mutate the predicted class will cause harms to the classifier most of the time. Hence, we decided to apply mutation only to the body of the rule. In so doing, we still allow the system to explore a new area without disrupting the rule.
- **Allowing the Deletion operator to handle minority classes:** After we carefully tested the behavior of XCS (please refer to [3]), we found that minority classes cause problems. We decided to include the class distribution factor of the current population into consideration during the deletion scheme. Before deleting a rule, we estimate a class distribution of the population based on the amount of instances of each class the system received up to this point, the more rules predicting to a class in the population, the higher the chance of their being eliminated. Hence, we maintain the diversity

in the population despite the fact of unbalanced sample distribution in the training set.
- **Distance Metric:** As being mentioned in the previous section, in order to apply XCS to the KDD dataset, we modified the traditional XCS by first training it on the training dataset, then using the obtained model to predict the attacks in the test set. Traditional XCS is trained and tested alternatively. In both cases, the covering technique is utilized if the system fails in recognizing an input. In the modified model, we decided not to call the covering technique for unseen instances in the testing phase. It is because the model does not learn in the testing phase and therefore doing it can result in deleting useful rules and leaving the population with random rules. We use a distance metric instead to choose rules which are close to the unseen input. The distance is measured based on the Euclidean distance from the input to each rule in the population in all dimensions (41 attributes). We introduced a new parameter called DISTANCE_THRESHOLD to decide when a rule can be called *close match* the input. The rules with an Euclidean distance less than this threshold are considered to *close match* the input. The decision of the system is then based on voting between these *close match* rules.
- **Post Processing:** In order to make a compact and more precise population, we also decided to post process the final population obtained from the training phase before using it for classification in the testing phase. In this process, we filter out rules with no or less *experience*. It is believed that the more *experience* a rule has, the more it was evaluated or learned from the environment's feedback, and therefore the more accurate it becomes. Remember the fitness of XCS is based on the reward prediction, therefore accuracy in this sense means predicting the reward received from the environment. Normally, rules without evaluation by interacting with the environment might mislead the decision of the system and therefore it is inefficient to keep these rules.

Table 2 shows the prediction accuracy of the modified XCS for normal and attacks. It can be easily seen that the modified XCS outperforms the conventional XCS in all classes except the R2L class. As explained in the previous section, the high accuracy on R2L class is achieved due to default class for unseen instances. Therefore, the prediction accuracy of the modified XCS is lower than the conventional XCS, but it is based on the system's experience not on the default value.

Table 2. Mean and standard deviation of prediction accuracy in 30 runs

Class Prediction	Accuracy
NORMAL	0.957 ± 0.043
DOS	0.491 ± 0.229
PROBE	0.930 ± 0.144
U2R	0.085 ± 0.121
R2L	0.039 ± 0.022

We have calculated the cpu time for running the original and modified XCS. During the initial training phase, XCS was able to process 39,000 instances a minute while during the testing phase (no GA takes place), it was able to process 46,800 instances a minute. There was no differences in the runtime between the original and modified one. These calculations show the power of XCS and the potential to break the barrier to finally adopt evolutionary techniques for real-life data mining problems.

3 Conclusions

This paper showed that our modified XCS is very competitive on the network intrusion detection domain, achieving equivalent accuracy to the literature and linear complexity.

References

1. J. Bacardit and M. V. Butz. *Data Mining in Learning Classifier Systems: Comparing XCS with GAssist*. Illinois Genetic Algorithms Laboratory, University of Illinois at Urbana-Champaign, June 2004. IlliGAL Report No. 2004030.
2. E. Bernadó, X. Llorà, and J. M. Garrell. XCS and GALE: a comparative study of two learning classifier systems with six other learning algorithms on classification tasks. In *Proceedings of the 4th International Workshop on Learning Classifier Systems (IWLCS-2001)*, pages 337–341, 2001.
3. H. H. Dam, K. Shafi, and H. A. Abbass. Can evolutionary computation handle large dataset? Technical Report TR-ALAR-2005070001, http://seal.tst.adfa.edu.au/~alar/techrep.html, 2005.
4. P. W. Dixon, D. Corne, and M. J. Oates. A preliminary investigation of modified XCS as a generic data mining tool. In *Advances in Learning Classifier Systems: 4th International Workshop, IWLCS*, pages 133–150. Berlin Heidelberg: Springer-Verlag, 2001.
5. S. Hettich and S. D. Bay. The uci kdd archive. http://kdd.ics.uci.edu/databases/kddcup99/kddcup99.html, 1999.
6. J. H. Holland. Escaping Brittleness: The Possibilities of General-Purpose Learning Algorithms Applied to Parallel Rule-Based Systems. In Mitchell, Michalski, and Carbonell, editors, *Machine Learning, an Artificial Intelligence Approach. Volume II*, chapter 20, pages 593–623. Morgan Kaufmann, 1986.
7. S. Saxon and A. Barry. XCS and the Monk's problems. In *Learning Classifier Systems, From Foundations to Applications*, pages 223–242, London, UK, 2000. Springer-Verlag.
8. S. W. Wilson. Classifier fitness based on accuracy. *Evolutionary Computation*, 3(2):149–175, 1995.
9. S. W. Wilson. Generalization in the XCS classifier system. In *Genetic Programming 1998: Proceedings of the Third Annual Conference*, pages 665–674, University of Wisconsin, Madison, Wisconsin, USA, 1998. Morgan Kaufmann.

Automatic Loop-Shaping of QFT Controllers Using GAs and Evolutionary Computation

Min-Soo Kim[1] and Chan-Soo Chung[2]

[1] Sejong-Lockheed Martin Aerospace Research Center,
Sejong University, 98 Kunja, Kwangjin,
Seoul, Korea 143-747
mskim@sejong.ac.kr
[2] Electrical Engineering Department,
Soongsil University, 1-1 Sangdo, Dongjak,
Seoul, Korea 156-743
chung@ssu.ac.kr

Abstract. This paper presents a design method of the automatic loop-shaping which couples up manual loop-shaping method to genetic algorithms (GAs) in quantitative feedback theory (QFT). The loop-shaping is currently performed in computer aided design environments manually, and moreover, it is usually a trial and error procedure. To solve this problem, an automatic loop-shaping method based on GAs and evolutionary computation is developed and a benchmark example is used to examine the performance of the proposed automatic loop-shaping compared with that of the manual loop-shaping and similar other research.

1 Introduction

Quantitative Feedback Theory (QFT) has been successfully applied to many engineering systems since it was developed by Horowitz [1]. The QFT method is a robust control design technique that uses feedback of measurable plant outputs to generate an acceptable response considering disturbance and uncertainty. This method uses quantitative information such as the plant's variability, the robust performance requirements, control performance specifications, the expected disturbance amplitude, and attenuation requirements.

Genetic Algorithms (GAs) were invented by John Holland and developed by him and his students and colleagues[2]. GAs are a stochastic global search method that mimics the metaphor of natural biological evolution. At each generation, a new set of approximations is created by the process of selecting individuals according to their level of fitness in the problem domain and breeding them together using operators borrowed from natural genetics.

In this paper, we provide an automatic loop-shaping algorithm that couples up advantages of a classical manual loop-shaping method to those of GAs. From the manual loop-shaping method, the characteristic and/or advantage of the proposed method as follow:

- It is possible to apply to MIMO systems as well as SISO.
- It uses a gain, simple pole/zeros, and complex pole/zeros as optimization variables.

- It diminishes the range of gain values based on computer aided design method.
- It can place optimization variables (i.e. poles, zeros, etc) in a specific region.
- It provides fine tuning.

From GAs, the characteristic and/or advantage of the proposed method are follows:
- It does not need predetermination of the order of the nominator/denominator.
- It can use a constructive design method using termination condition.

2 Genetic Algorithms

We use multiple population method to optimize several variables of QFT controller with real valued representation for the individuals and stochastic universal sampling for selection function. The first step in GAs is to create an initial population consisting of random individuals. Creation of a real-valued initial population produces a matrix containing uniformly distributed random values in its elements. The offspring of a pair of two parents are computed through recombination procedures. Mutation of real-valued populations mutates each population with given probability and returns the population after mutation. Generally, mutation rate μ has within the range [0, 1]. The mutation of a variable x_{new} from x_{old} is computed as $x_{new} = x_{old} + \delta M d_{var}$ where δ specifies the normalized mutation step size, and mutation matrix M produces an internal mask table determining which variable to mutate and the sign for adding +1 or –1 with equal probability based on μ, d_{var} means the half range of the variables domain. Crossover performs migration of individuals between subpopulations in current population when it uses multiple populations.

GA parameters for initialization consist of mutation rate μ_{mut}, maximum number of generations N_{gen}, insertion rate μ_{ins} which specifies that the individuals produced at each generation are reinserted into the population, the number of subpopulations N_{sub}, migration rate μ_{mig} that migrates between subpopulations with probability μ_{mig}, the number of individuals of each subpopulation N_{ind}.

In this paper, we use each parameter in multiple population genetic algorithms with μ_{mut} =1/number of variable, N_{gen} = 150, μ_{ins} = 90 [%], N_{sub} =200, μ_{mig} = 20 [%], and N_{ind} =1000.

3 Automatic Loop-Shaping in QFT

The following algorithm shows procedure of the proposed evolutionary computation method of automatic loop-shaping.

```
Decide variables to optimize;
Initialize controller type G₀(s);
Add frequency array;
Find optimal solution of loop-shaping in GA routine;
   (If termination condition is reached
     Stop program;
   End if)
```

```
For i=1 to M,
    Add variables and decide controller type G_i(s);
    Find optimal solution in GA routine with G_i(s);
    (If termination condition is reached
            Stop program
    End if)
Next i;
```

There is an important factor, termination condition, in the proposed algorithm.

$$\left(\sum_{i=1}^{m} J_{stability_i} = 0\right) \& \left(\sum_{j=1}^{n} J_{tracking\_bound_j} \leq \varepsilon_T\right) \& \left(J_{min\_BW} \leq \varepsilon_{BW}\right) \& \left(\Delta J_{high\_freq} \leq \varepsilon_{high\_freq}\right) \quad (1)$$

where ε_T and ε_{BW} are margin factors, and $\Delta J_{high\_freq} = \left| J_{high\_freq_t} - J_{high\_freq_{t-1}} \right|$.

The controller type of the jth design procedure is as follows, which the variables to be optimized are selected by $\{k, z_1, z_2, \cdots, z_l, p_1, p_2, \cdots, p_m, \zeta_1, \zeta_2, \cdots, \zeta_n, \omega_{n_1}, \omega_{n_2}, \cdots, \omega_{n_n}, \cdots\}$.

$$G_j(s) = k \frac{\left(1 + s/z_1\right)\left(1 + s/z_2\right)\cdots\left(1 + s/z_l\right)}{\left(1 + s/p_1\right)\cdots\left(1 + s/p_m\right)\left(1 + \left(2\zeta_1/\omega_{n_1}\right)s + \left(s^2/\omega_{n_1}^2\right)\right)\cdots\left(1 + \left(2\zeta_n/\omega_{n_n}\right)s + \left(s^2/\omega_{n_n}^2\right)\right)} \quad (2)$$

The fitness in GAs for the QFT design should reflect the stability and performance requirements, and the performance index, given by

$$J = \gamma_S \sum_{i=1}^{m} J_{stability_i} + \gamma_T \sum_{j=1}^{n} J_{tracking\_bound_j} + \cdots + \gamma_{BW} J_{min\_BW} + J_{high\_freq} \quad (3)$$

where γ_S, γ_T and γ_{BW} are a weighting factor. Here m and n denote the number of the sampled frequency of stability bounds (or margin bounds) and tracking bounds respectively. $J_{stability_i}$, $J_{tracking\_bound_j}$, J_{min_BW}, and J_{high_freq} represent performance indexes of the stability specification, tracking bounds, a minimum bandwidth, and a maximum high frequency gain, respectively.

4 Simulations

The proposed method is applied to design a controller for the benchmark example 2 in the QFT Toolbox [3]. The automation of the design of a QFT controller for this example is also investigated by Chait [4] and by Chen [5].

The uncertainty plant is described by $P(s) = \frac{Ka}{s(s+a)}$.

The close-loop specifications are represented as

1. Robust stability: The closed-loop magnitude is satisfied such as

$$\left| \frac{P(j\omega)G(j\omega)}{1 + P(j\omega)G(j\omega)} \right| \leq 1.2 \quad \text{for all } P \in \{p\}, \; \omega > 0 \quad (4)$$

2. Robust tracking: The transfer function $T(j\omega)$ from r to y is bounded by

$$T_L(\omega) \le |T(j\omega)| = \left| F(s) \frac{P(j\omega)G(j\omega)}{1+P(j\omega)G(j\omega)} \right| \le T_U(\omega) \tag{5}$$

where, $T_L(\omega)$ and $T_U(\omega)$ are given in the following:

$$T_L(\omega) = \left| \frac{0.6854(j\omega+30)}{(j\omega)^2 + 4(j\omega) + 19.752} \right|, \quad T_U(\omega) = \left| \frac{120}{(j\omega)^3 + 17(j\omega)^2 + 828(j\omega) + 120} \right| \tag{6}$$

The design objective is to find a controller such that all the closed-loop specifications are satisfied and the cost of feedback is as small as possible.

As in the QFT Toolbox, the QFT bounds on the frequencies $\omega = [0.1, 0.5, 1, 2, 15, 100]$ are calculated. In order to guarantee the specifications at among sampled frequencies, more frequency points $\omega = [5, 50, 60, 70, 80, 90, 300, 500]$ are added to original frequency array. And the nominal values are selected as $a = 1$ and $K = 1$.

The fitness function in GAs for the stability and tracking performance requirements is given by $J = \gamma_S \sum_{i=1}^{m} J_{stability\,i} + \gamma_T \sum_{j=1}^{n} J_{tracking\_bound\,j} + \gamma_{BW} J_{min\_BW} + J_{high\_freq}$

where as a weighting factor, γ_S, γ_T and γ_{BW} are calculated by experimental method. In this example, the parameters $\gamma_S = 10^{10}$ and $\gamma_T = \gamma_{BW} = 10^8$ are used because of $J_{high\_freq} \approx 10^6$. Here m and n denote the number of the sampled frequency of stability bounds (or margin bounds) and tracking bounds, respectively.

We try to design a lower order controller for this plant and specify a second order controller. For a second order controller, there are four parameters $\{k, z, \zeta, \omega_n\}$ assuming that the coefficient of the highest order is 1.

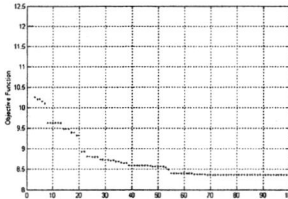

Fig. 1. Object function values

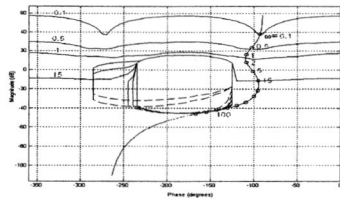

Fig. 2. Automatic loop-shaping using GAs: the proposed method

After 70 generations, the QFT controller is created by the proposed method such as

$$G_1(s) = \frac{2.726622\times 10^6 s + 5.472331\times 10^6}{s^2 + 1100.19s + 674098.47} \tag{7}$$

The proposed loop-shaping result is shown in Fig. 2.

As shown in Fig. 2, all robust stability margin and the performance specifications are satisfied.

To verify the effectiveness of the proposed method, we compare it with the manual loop-shaping and Chen's method. Through the manual loop-shaping, we get the third order controller in the QFT Toolbox such as

$$G_2(s) = \frac{3.0787 \times 10^6 s^2 + 3.5365 \times 10^8 s + 3.8529 \times 10^8}{s^3 + 1.5288 \times 10^3 s^2 + 1.0636 \times 10^6 s + 4.2810 \times 10^7} \tag{8}$$

Next, the second order controller designed by Chen's method is given by

$$G_3(s) = \frac{6.753 \times 10^6 s + 1.3947 \times 10^7}{s^2 + 3.4834 \times 10^3 s + 1.6218 \times 10^6} \tag{9}$$

Comparing with three results, it is clear that the proposed second order controller is smaller the high-frequency gain than the controller designed by Chen's method and QFT Toolbox.

5 Conclusions

This paper presents the new QFT design algorithm which is applied to GAs and evolutionary computation in automatic loop-shaping. The proposed automatic loop-shaping method combines with advantages of a classical manual loop-shaping method and GAs. The proposed method is applied to design a controller of the benchmark example and it is compared with the manual loop-shaping method and Chen's method. The controller generated by the proposed method performed better than others from the viewpoint of the characteristics of frequency domain and the high-frequency gain.

Acknowledgement. This research was supported by the Korea Research Foundation under grant No. D00248.

References

1. Horowitz, I. M., Sidi, M.: Synthesis of Feedback Systems with Large Plant Ignorance for Prescribed Time Domain Tolerance. Int. J. Control 16 (2), (1972) 287-309
2. Goldberg, D. E.: Genetic Algorithms in search, Optimization and machine Learning, Addison Wesley Publishing Company (1989)
3. Borghesani, C., Chait, Y., and Yaniv, O.: Quantitative Feedback Theory Toolbox: For Use with Matlab, Math-Works (1994)
4. Chait Y.: QFT loop-shaping and minimization of the high-frequency gain via convex optimization, Proceedings of the Symposium on Quantitative Feedback Theory and other Frequency Domain methods and Applications (1997) 13-28
5. Chen W-H., Ballance D. J., Feng W., and Li Y.: Genetic Algorithm Enabled Computer-Automated Design of QFT Control Systems, International Symposium on computer Aided Control System Design (1999) 492-497

Investigating the Effect of Incorporating Additional Levels in Structured Genetic Algorithms

Angelos Molfetas

University of Western Sydney,
Locked Bag 1797, Penrith South DC, NSW 1797, Australia
amolfeta@cit.uws.edu.au

Abstract. This paper reports on a study which compared the convergence of different-leveled structured Genetic Algorithms (sGAs) used to generate Neural Networks (NNs). Results suggest that sGAs are more effective at generating NNs compared to simple GAs. Using more than 2 sGA levels does not always yield a better error curve, as each added level provides a diminishing performance increase. The optimum number of sGA levels for NN generation is problem specific, though higher level sGAs tend to produce more efficient NNs. SGAs with more levels seem to perform better for difficult NN problems with complex features and large boundary conditions which create more redundancy. When the emphasis on complexity is increased in the fitness function, the error curve variations between different level configurations become more pronounced.

1 Introduction

Studies have shown that the sGA possesses certain advantages over the simple GA [1,2]. These advantages can be attributed to the sGA's distinguishing characteristic, ie., the incorporation of a gene layer which controls the activation of other genes (see [3]). The next logical step is to investigate the effect that added sGA layers have on convergence. To this end, this study compares the convergence of different-leveled sGAs by implementing experiments which employ sGAs to generate feed forward NNs (see [4,5,6] on sGA generated NNs). This paper builds on previous work [7], which is extended by including a novel 4 level sGA and by examining how convergence variations between different-levelled sGAs change as parameters are altered. This paper has two main objectives. Firstly, it investigates the effect that added levels have on sGA convergence, and secondly, it illustrates the use of a 4 level sGA to generate NNs.

2 Method

The experiments in this paper employ 1 to 4 level sGAs[1]. In the 1 level sGA simulations, the NNs are fully connected. The 2 level sGA utilises an encoding approach which uses the top level to encode NN connectivity and the bottom

---

[1] 1 level sGAs are simple GAs and are referred here as such for convenience.

level for the weights (see [4,5]). The 3 level sGA utilises an added level for neuron activation (as suggested in [5] and implemented in [7]). This paper introduces a novel 4 level sGA encoding structure which extends the 3 level sGA by adding a level for NN hidden layer activation. 2,3,4 level sGAs are capable of producing partially connected NNs. Producing partially connected NNs is beneficial since they offer various advantages such an improved generalization [8].

Two sets of experiments were conducted. The 1st set approximated a relatively simple function, the 4 input XOR, while the 2nd set approximated a relatively hard function, the Mackey-Glass (MG). Each experiment involved running 4 simulations, one for each sGA level configuration. The experiments were averaged over 250 runs. The simulations used a population of 50, crossover/mutation rates of 0.5/0.005, run for 1000 generations and used 16 bits to encode NN weights in a fixed point binary representation. An elitist strategy was used which propagated the two fittest individuals to the next generation. Except for the 2nd XOR experiment, the maximum number of hidden neurons was set to 8.

SGAs were able to derive any NN topology providing they only used feed forward connections and did not connect input neurons to each other. All the hidden neurons were stored as a single group, however, since connections were allowed between them, the sGA was capable of evolving NNs with multiple layers. The mutation rate was increased to 0.5 for invalid NNs (ie., NNs which had no connection path between the inputs and outputs). Other than the code that was related to the sGA levels, the sGAs employed the same code. Consequently, differences in performance cannot be attributed to other incorporated functionality.

3 XOR Experiments

Since this function has 4 binary inputs, the NN has to learn only 16 data sets. This problem is simple, yet it requires a non-trivial topology (a perceptron without hidden layers cannot approximate it as it's not linearibly separable [9]). There were 3 XOR experiments conducted.

The first experiment's FF placed emphasis on only the NN's error. The 2 level sGA convergences to a lower error much faster than the plain GA and it demonstrates a significant improvement in its error sum (ie, total error throughout the simulation's duration) of 67% and a final error (ie, error at the end) improvement of 76% . Much of this improvement is thought to be attributed to the sGA's increased tendency to avoid getting stuck at local minima points. It was observed during the simulations that the simple GA would get stuck at particular error quantities more often compared to the sGAs. This premature convergence state would often persist until the end of the simulation and during that time the algorithm's error would only improve by small increments. Another contributing factor for the increased performance of the 2 level sGA is thought to be its ability to generate partially connected NNs.

All the sGAs outperform the simple GA, however, for each added sGA level above 2 does not improve convergence. Both the error sum and the final error deteriorates with each layer above 2.

Though the 2 level sGA demonstrates the best performance during the 1000 generations, the 4 level sGA exhibits the best performance for approximately the first 25 generations . This suggests that sGAs are focusing more on the NN's topology in the beginning of the simulation, but then shift their focus to the weights as the NN topologies become stable. The 4 level sGA performs better in the beginning because it comes up with a more optimal architecture quicker, as its top level genes are capable of effecting more neurons.

The above observations examined performance over a time frame measured in generational time units. It is important to also examine the effect that the incorporation of added sGA levels have on the algorithm in terms of real time (ie. measured in seconds). This is because it is possible to improve sGA performance over a generational time frame, while at the same time reducing its performance in real time by increasing the run time complexity, meaning each generation may take more time. The average time to complete one generation (in seconds) actually improves with each added level, probably because of a higher incidence of deactivated connections which decreases the computation needed to propagate signals through the NNs.

The 2nd experiment was similar to the 1st, but with a larger search space (hidden node limit was 32 instead of 8). The purpose of this experiment was to establish how added levels affected convergence when expanded NN boundary conditions were used which generated higher connection redudancy. Unlike the 1st experiment, each added level causes an improvement. The 4 level sGA provided the best performance, which is in contrast to the 1st experiment, where the 2 level sGA was the optimum one. As the number of redundant hidden neurons has been increased, higher level sGAs have more spare connections to examine optional regions in the search space. This improvement can also be attributed to the higher computational abilities of top level genes in higher level sGAs, since higher level sGAs are able to create larger topological changes. When dealing with NNs with many redundant connections, genes with an ability to deactivate larger portions of the NN are more likely to be advantageous as they can deactivate more unnecessary connections with one operation. The difference in the results between experiment 1 and 2 suggests that there is a positive correlation between NN potential connection redundancy and the optimum number of sGA levels.

The 3rd experiment was similar to the 1st one, except that the FF placed an emphasis both on NN error (70%) and on NN size (30%). This encouraged the sGA develop smaller NNs. This is similar to the FF strategy used by [5]. The results are similar to the 1st XOR experiment in that the optimum number of sGA levels is 2. However, one distinct difference between the two results is that the divergence between the error curves are signifantly more pronounced in the third experiment. The reason for these more pronounced differences is probably because the higher sGAs are more capable of producing efficient NNs with less connections , but since they are emphasising leaner NNs, the higher level sGAs are underperforming by a greater margin since there is a lesser emphasis on reducing error. It should be noted here that unlike the previous experiments, the individual error curves do not wholy determine the individual's fitness; they only compromise 70% of it. As such, in comparing the performance of different levelled sGAs for the third XOR experiment, the reader is advised to take into consideration both the accuracy and the size of the generated NNs. Of particular note, the 2 level sGA has an error that was almost twice as accurate as the 4 level sGA, however, the 4 level sGA used on average 4.6 times less connections!

4 Chaotic Time Series Experiments

This section reports on two experiments which approximated the MG function [10] (cited by [11]). Gupta and Sexton [11] performed an experiment with the MG which compared gradient descent learning algorithms versus GAs for NN training. Though the research objective of that work is different to this paper's objectives, the MG function was picked for the same reasons that were cited by Gupta and Sexton [op cit] This function being relatively more difficult, provides a good basis for comparison against the much simpler 4 input XOR problem.

The 1st experiment was conducted under similar settings to Gupta and Sexton's experiments. Out of a total of 2000 data sets, the first 200 data sets were used to train the NNs and the last 200 were used to test the NNs performance. This was done to test the NNs' ability to generalise.

Unlike the 1st and 3rd XOR experiments, this one shows a general improvement in accuracy with each added level. As was the case with the XOR experiments, we see here an improvement in the algorithm's training time and a reduction of NN size with each additional sGA level. Each added sGA level alse a demonstrated reduced testing data set error which showed that the algorithm is better at generalisation and learning the underline function, rather than over learning the training data set.

The 2nd exp was similar to the previous one, but it examined the convergence of the algorithm in respect to the time it took to complete the simulation in real time (ie., in seconds). Because of this, the experiment used different terminating conditions to the previous experiment. This experiment terminated when the algorithm reached a target error of 16.0 or when 1000 generations elapsed.

The results show a clear improvement in the time taken to generate suitable NNs with each added layer, though this increase seems to be a diminishing. There is an improvement in the no of connections employed by the NNs, as well as, a decrease in the prediction error of the testing set. These results are in agreement with the previous MG experiment and suggest that the optimum number of sGA levels for this problem is 4.

5 Discussion

Results show that the number of levels does have a significant effect on the convergence of the sGA. This can be a detrimental effect, as was evident in the 1st XOR experiment, or a positive effect, as can be seen in the 2nd MG experiment. In the 2nd XOR experiment, the algorithm incurs a diminishing increase in the performance (time to complete simulation) with each added layer. In the second MG experiment, the 2 level sGA demonstrates an increase in mean time performance of 44% over the 1 level sGA, which is much greater than the performance increases of the 3 and 4 level sGAs. Even if we were to attribute this performance increase to the 1 level sGA's inability to produce partially connected NNs, this diminishing return is still apparent with the next 2 level level configurations.

A similar effect can be observed in the algorithm's ability to produce more efficient NNs, which appears to be approaching a positive asymptotic limit. The ability to produce leaner NNs increases with added levels as there is a lesser probability that each individual connection with be activated. This is because with each new sGA level, the probability that a connection will be active is reduced as it is the product of larger number of probabilities. Therefore, when using sGAs with a high number of levels, it's important to have the FF assign sufficient emphasis on the NN's accuracy to counteract error curve degradation due to the utilisation of unfeasibly small numbers of connections. This is apparent in the 3rd XOR experiment where the number of connections and accuracy for the 4 level sGA decreased significantly compared to the 2 level sGA NNs.

The optimum numbers of sGA levels appears to be problem specific. In the 1st XOR exp, the optimum no. of levels is 2, whereas, in the 2nd XOR and MG exp, the optimum number of levels is 4 (or higher). It seems that difficult problems with larger and/or more complex search space benefit from added levels.

Preliminary results [7] showed that added levels improved the error curves and demonstrated similar diminishing performance that was observed in the new simulation. Importantly, 3 level sGA XOR simulations in that paper demonstrated better performance compared to 2 level sGAs, which is contrast to the results of this paper's 1st XOR exp. The difference can be attributed to the larger search space utilised by the preliminary XOR experiment (its maximum number of neurons was 10) and tighter connectivity restrictions which limited the number of NN topologies that were considered as valid.

6 Conclusions

Experiments reported to by this paper have demonstrated the implementation of a 4 level sGA encoding scheme which allows for the encoding of the activation state of NN hidden layers, neurons, connections and connection weights. The results presented in this paper add further support for the view [4,5] that 2 level sGAs can effectively generate NNs compared to GAs without needing to utilise back propagation or other gradient descent algorithm. Furthermore, the results suggest that sGAs are *more* effective at generating NNs compared to simple GAs. Rresults show that using more than 2 levels in a sGA is not always beneficial. There is also some support for the suggestion that higher level sGAs (in particular ones with 4 levels) may outperform lower leveled sGAs in the beginning of the simulation due to their incorporation of higher level genes which are capable of causing larger topological changes in the beginning of the simulation. All the experiments are in agreement with the view that higher level sGAs have an improved tendency to produce more efficient NNs. Higher level sGAs also seem to become more effective when they are used to generate NNs for difficult problems or when large NN boundary conditions are set which allow for the development for more redundant connections. When the level of emphasis on complexity is increased in the FF, the variations in the error curves of the different-levelled sGAs becomes more pronounced. This is thought to be the case as the higher level sGAs are producing leaner NNs and as such, are sacrificing more accuracy in return for more efficient NNs.

Due to space restrictions for this paper, the reader is advised to refer to the author's soon to be available PhD thesis for a more complete record of this study.

Acknowledgments

The author would like to thank George Bryan, Malcolm Cook, Dieter Merkl and Wayne Moore for their discussions and assistance in the editing of this paper.

References

1. Dasgupta, D.: Optimisation in time-varying environments using structured genetic algorithms. Technical Report IKBS-17-93, University of Strathclyde, Glasgow, UK (1994)
2. Dasgupta, D.: Handling deceptive problems using a different genetic search. In: Proceedings of the First IEEE Conference on Evolutionary Computation. (1994) 807–811
3. Dasgupta, D., McGregor, D.R.: sga: A structured genetic algorithm. Technical Report IKBS-8-92, University of Strathclyde (1992)
4. Dasgupta, D., McGregor, D.R.: Designing neural networks using the structured genetic algorithm. In: Proceedings of International Conference on Artificial Neural Networks (ICANN), Brighton, UK (1992) 263–268
5. Dasgupta, D., McGregor, D.R.: Designing application-specific neural networks using the structured genetic algorithm. In Schaffer, J.D., Whitley, D., eds.: COGANN-92, International Workshop on Combinations of Genetic Algorithms and Neural Networks, USA (1992) 87–96
6. Tang, K.S., Chan, C.Y., Kwong, S.: Genetic structure for NN topology and weights optimization. In: 1st IEE/IEEE International Conference on Genetic Algorithms in Engineering Systems: Innovations and Applications, IEEE (1995) 250–255

7. Molfetas, A.: Comparing structured genetic algorithms for artificial neural network generation. In Hamza, M.H., ed.: Proceedings of the IASTED International Conference on Artificial Intelligence and Applications, IASTED, ACTA Press (2005) 293–299
8. Elizondo, D., Fiesler, E.: A survey of partially connected neural networks. The international journal of neural systems **8** (1997) 535–558
9. Minsky, M., Papert, S.: Perceptrons. MIT Press, Cambridge, Massachusetts (1969)
10. Mackey, M.C., Glass, L.: Oscillation and chaos in physiological control systems. Science **197** (1977) 287–289
11. Gupta, J.N.D., Sexton, R.S.: Comparing backpropagation with a genetic algorithm for neural network training. Omega **27** (1999) 679–684

Accelerating Real-Valued Genetic Algorithms Using Mutation-with-Momentum

Luke Temby, Peter Vamplew, and Adam Berry

School of Computing, University of Tasmania, Private Bag 100, Hobart,
Tasmania 7001, Australia
Peter.Vamplew@utas.edu.au

Abstract. Directed mutation has been proposed for improving the convergence speed of GAs on problems involving real-valued alleles. This paper proposes a directed mutation approach based on the momentum term used in gradient descent training of neural networks. Mutation-with-momentum is compared against gaussian mutation and is shown to regularly result in improvements in performance during early generations. A hybrid of momentum and gaussian mutation is shown to outperform either individual approach to mutation.

1 Introduction

For real-valued genetic algorithms (GAs) gaussian mutation is commonly used. When a gene is mutated, a random value from a gaussian distribution is added to the gene value. This means the mutated value is likely to be close to the original value but allows larger changes, preventing the operator from being overly disruptive whilst still being able to escape from local optima. Gaussian mutation is random, being equally likely to increase or decrease the gene value. In contrast [1] showed that bacteria demonstrated a bias towards beneficial mutations. Whilst the validity of biological directed mutation has been questioned [2], it inspired new techniques in evolutionary computation. Early approaches were based on exploiting constraints within specific problems [3-9]. Whilst useful in these domains, the need for domain knowledge limits their general applicability. More recent dynamic techniques [10-14] allow the direction of mutation to evolve within the system and carry greater general applicability. However, they require an increase in the number of system parameters.

In PoD mutation [15] each gene stores an additional bit, which determines the sign of the half-gaussian mutation operator applied to that gene. Each gene and its direction bit are indivisible during crossover, whilst the direction bits are subject to bit-flipping mutation, allowing the search direction to evolve. PoD is simpler than previous dynamic directed mutation methods in terms of parameter count and computational cost, and has been shown to outperform gaussian mutation.

2 Mutation-with-Momentum

This paper proposes a new dynamic directed mutation algorithm based on the concept of explicit momentum, which has been used in gradient-descent training of neural networks [16]. Momentum involves adding a fraction of the change from the previous time-step onto the change calculated at the current step, allowing increased convergence speed in flat regions of the error-space by enabling larger weight changes, whilst also reducing the likelihood of becoming trapped in local minima.

As with PoD, mutation-with-momentum requires additional data to be stored for each gene in an individual. This momentum term records the change in that gene at its most recent mutation. Each gene and its momentum term are treated as indivisible during the crossover operation. When a gene is mutated, both gaussian mutation and a fraction of the momentum term are added to it, and the momentum term is then updated as in equations 1 and 2 ($g_{i,o}$ is the original value of gene i, $g_{i,m}$ is the value after mutation, $M_{i,o}$ is the momentum value, $M_{i,m}$ is the momentum value after mutation, α controls the amount of momentum ($0 \leq \alpha \leq 1$) and $G(x)$ is the gaussian function). To prevent the momentum term from becoming overly large it can be capped to a maximum magnitude - in these experiments a bound equal to half the range of the allele was used.

$$g_{i,m} = g_{i,o} + \alpha M_{i,o} + G(x) \qquad (1)$$

$$M_{i,m} = g_{i,o} - g_{i,m} \qquad (2)$$

A hybrid system was also developed. This system initially uses mutation-with-momentum, switching to gaussian mutation once a specified level of performance is achieved. For these experiments a simple switching criteria was used - momentum was not used after the best individual had achieved a fitness below a threshold of 0.1.

3 Experimental Method, Results and Discussion

The GAPlayground system [17] was modified to implement gaussian, momentum and hybrid mutation. The same settings were used for all three operators (population size of 30; single-point crossover; a per-gene mutation probability of 0.06). As the range of alleles varies, the gaussian function's width was set to 1/15 of the range of each allele. The momentum parameter α was fixed at 1. For each of the three mutation systems, 100 trials were run on each benchmark. A trial was treated as converged if the best individual in any generation bettered a threshold of 0.001. In addition a maximum number of generations was specified for each benchmark - trials which failed to converge within this limit were stopped at that point.

Seven benchmarks were chosen from the GA literature. The first three (De Jong's Sphere and Step functions, and the Rosenbrock function) are relatively simple tasks. The other four functions (Griewangk, Ackley, Rastrigin and Schwefel) are more challenging tasks, as all exhibit local optima of varying complexity. Table 1 summarises the results achieved by each mutation operator on the test problems.

Momentum results in small improvements on the Sphere and Rosenbrock functions, but slightly poorer results on the Griewangk and Ackley functions. The results on the Rastrigin function are unclear - gaussian mutation is more likely to converge to a solution, but performs very poorly on those trials which do not converge. The most significant variations between the two operators occur on the Steps and Schwefel functions. For Steps the momentum system converges in less than a third of the time required by gaussian mutation. On the Schwefel function gaussian mutation never converges, whilst the momentum system always converges. Across all seven problems, the momentum operator outperforms the gaussian in the early generations, but often struggles to 'fine-tune' the genes in later generations.

The hybrid system successfully merges the early speed of the momentum operator with the fine-tuning capability of gaussian mutation. The hybrid approach equals or outperforms the other systems across all of the benchmark problems except for the Schwefel function where it is faster than the momentum system on those trials which do converge, but fails to converge in a small percentage of trials.

Table 1. Summary of results achieved across 100 trials on each of the benchmark problems

		Gaussian	Momentum	Hybrid
Sphere	% of trials converged	100	100	100
	Mean generations to convergence	108	106	71
Steps	% of trials converged	100	100	100
	Mean generations to convergence	174	54	54
Rosenbrock	% of trials converged	82	85	87
	Mean generations to convergence	25,029	22,041	21,912
Griewangk	% of trials converged	0	0	0
	Mean generations to convergence	-	-	-
	Mean error	0.030	0.056	0.031
Ackley	% of trials converged	0	0	0
	Mean generations to convergence	-	-	-
	Mean error	0.007	0.015	0.007
Rastrigin	% of trials converged	7	1	18
	Mean generations to convergence	34,003	47,351	9,405
	Mean error	10.86	0.067	0.008
Schwefel	% of trials converged	0	100	93
	Mean generations to convergence	-	4,450	2,514
	Mean error	786.29	<0.001	3.65

4 Conclusion and Future Work

In the majority of the problems mutation-with-momentum produced beneficial results, Where performance is impeded the impairment is minor. It should also be noted that the convergence criteria is quite stringent - a more generous choice of threshold would further emphasise the benefits of momentum.

The hybrid system further improved performance by exploiting the relative strengths of momentum and gaussian mutation. It significantly outperformed gaussian mutation on five benchmarks, and produced comparable results on the other two problems. This was achieved at little computational cost and with no tuning of additional parameters.

The major limitation of this work is the global nature of the switching test used in the hybrid system. A single fit solution will cause the whole system to cease using momentum when most individuals are still far from optimal. An algorithm that switches the mutation method on an individual basis may provide more reliable results. We also intend to investigate switching strategies which do not rely on static fitness thresholds, to reduce the need for a priori knowledge of the problem domain.

References

1. Cairns, J, Overbaugh, J, and Miller, S (1988), The Origin of Mutants, *Nature*, no. 335, pp. 142-5.
2. Hall, B (1990), Spontaneous point mutations that occur more often when advantageous than when neutral, *Genetics*, no. 126, pp. 5-16.
3. Craenen, B.G.W. (1998), *An Experimental Comparison of Three Different Heuristic GAs for Solving Constraint Satisfaction Problems*, Internal Report 98-21, Department of Computer Science, Leiden University.
4. Burke, E.K. and Petrovic, S. (2002), *Recent Research Directions in Automated Timetabling*. European Journal of Operational Research.
5. Ross, P., Corne, D., and Fang, H. (1994), *Improving Evolutionary Timetabling with Delta Evaluation and Directed Mutation*. PPSN III.
6. Paechter, B., Ranking, R.C., Cumming, A., Fogarty, T.C. (1998), *Timetabling the Classes of an Entire University with an Evolutionary Algorithm*. PPSN V, LNCS, 1998. p. 865-874.
7. Wiggins, G.A., *The Use of Constraint Systems for Musical Compositions*. ECAI98 Workshop on Constraints and Artistic Applications.
8. Li, L., Louis, S.J., and Brune, J.N. (1995), *Application of Genetic Algorithms to 2D Velocity Inversion of Seismic Refraction Data*. Proceedings of the Third Golden West International Conference on Intelligent Systems.
9. Baron, P.J., Fisher, R.B., Mill, F., Sherlock, A., Tuson, A.L. (1997), *A Voxel-Based Representation for the Evolutionary Shape Optimisation of a Simplified Beam: A Case-Study of a Problem-Centred Approach to Genetic Operator Design*. Soft Computing in Engineering Design and Manufacturing.
10. Schwefel, H.-P. (1994), *Evolution and Optimum Seeking*, New York: John Wiley & Sons.
11. Hilderbrand, L. (2002), *Asymmetrische Evolutionsstrategien*. PhD Thesis, Department of Computer Science, University of Dortmund.
12. Berlik, S. (2003), *A Polymorphical Mutation Operator for Evolution Strategies*. In Proceedings of the International Conference EUSFLAT, p. 502-505.
13. Berlik, S. (2004), *A Directed Mutation Framework for Evolutionary Algorithms*. Proceedings of the International Conference on Soft Computing, MENDEL.
14. Berlik, S., (2004), *Directed Mutation by Means of the Skew-Normal Distribution*. International Conference on Computational Intelligence, FUZZY DAYS.
15. Berry, A. and Vamplew, P. (2004), 'PoD Can Mutate: A Simple Dynamic Directed Mutation Approach for Genetic Algorithms', Proceedings of AISAT2004: International Conference on Artificial Intelligence in Science and Technology, Hobart, Tasmania.
16. Plaut, D. C., Nowlan, S. J., and Hinton, G. E. (1986). Experiments on learning by back propagation (Technical Report CMU-CS-86-126), Computer Science Department, Carnegie-Mellon University, Pittsburgh, PA.
17. Dolan, A (1998), *Artificial Life and Other Experiments*, viewed April 2005, <http://www.aridolan.com/default.aspx>.

A Fuzzy Inference Method for Spam-Mail Filtering

Jong-Wan Kim[1], Sin-Jae Kang[1], and Byeong Man Kim[2]

[1] School of Computer and Information Technology, Daegu University,
Gyeonsan, Gyeongbuk 712-714, South Korea
{jwkim, sjkang}@daegu.ac.kr
[2] School of Computer Engineering, Kumoh National Institute of Technology,
Gumi, Gyungbuk, South Korea
bmkim@se.kumoh.ac.kr

Abstract. This paper gives a comparative study of feature selection methods in spam-mail filtering. In our experiment, the fuzzy inference method showed about 6% and 10% improvements over information gain and χ^2-test as a feature selection method in terms of the average error rate which is more important than typical information retrieval measures. Since it is not easy to reduce error rate, our work can be regarded as a meaningful research for email users suffering from unsolicited emails flooding indiscriminately.

1 Introduction

Spam mails or unsolicited commercial emails flood mailboxes, exposing minors to unsuitable content, and wasting network bandwidth. The spam filtering problem can be seen as a particular case of the text categorization problem. Several information retrieval (IR) techniques are well suited for addressing this problem, in addition it is a two-class problem: spam or non-spam. A variety of machine learning algorithms have been used for email categorization task on different metadata. Sahami et al. [1] focuses on the more specific problem of filtering spam mails using a Naïve Bayesian classifier and incorporating domain knowledge using manually constructed domain-specific attributes such as phrasal features and various non-textual features. In most cases, support vector machines (SVM) developed by Vapnik outperforms conventional classifiers and therefore has been used for automatic filtering of spam mails as well as for classifying email text [2]. In particular, the best result was obtained when SVM was applied to the header with feature selection. Accordingly, we can conclude that SVM classifier is slightly better in distinguishing the two-class problem.

For selection of important features or terms representing documents such as mails or news well, assigning them weights are the same problem that the existing linear classifiers such as Rocchio and Widrow-Hoff algorithms [3] find centroid vectors of an example document collection. Both of these algorithms use TF (Term Frequency) and IDF (Inverse Document Frequency) for re-weighting terms but they do not consider term co-occurrence relationship within feedbacked documents. To resolve this drawback, the computation of term co-occurrences between these representative keywords and candidate terms within each example document is required. Three factors of TF, DF (Document Frequency), and IDF have essentially inexact characteristics, which are used to calculate the importance of a specific term. Since fuzzy logic is more adequate to handle intuitive and uncertain knowledge, we combine the three factors by the use of fuzzy inference. We calculate weights of candidate terms by using the method [4] that it is known to give superior performance to the existing representative keyword extraction methods and assign a priority to select representative keywords with the weights of candidate terms. In this paper, we propose a feature selection by fuzzy inference is a little superior to the conventional methods such as information gain and χ^2-test in pornography or porn mails filtering.

2 Feature Selection

Feature selection involves searching through all possible combination of features in the candidate feature set to find which subset of features works best for prediction. A few of the mechanisms designed to find the optimum number of features are document frequency threshold, information gain, mutual information, term strength, and χ^2-test. In comparing learning algorithms, Yang and Petersen found that, except for mutual information, all these feature selection methods had similar performance and similar characteristics [5]. To select features, which have high discriminating power, we compared the fuzzy inference method [4] with information gain and χ^2-test because information gain and χ^2-test were known effective in text categorization. Information gain measures the number of bits of information obtained for category prediction by knowing the presence or absence of a term in a document. The χ^2-test measures the lack of independence between a term t and a category c and can be compared to the chi-squared distribution with one degree of freedom to judge extremeness.

In the fuzzy inference, TF, DF, and IDF of each term are calculated from the preprocessed emails and are normalized. Since the NTF, NDF, and NIDF values calculated for each term should have been fuzzified for fuzzy inference, we used normal triangular membership function. NTF variable has {S (Small), L (Large)}, NDF and NIDF variables have {S (Small), M (Middle), L (Large)} as linguistic labels or terms. The fuzzy output variable, term weight TW which represents the importance of each term, has six linguistic labels. Table 1 gives 18 fuzzy rules to inference TW, where NTF is considered as primary factor, NDF and NIDF as secondary ones. See in [4] to refer explanation in detail. Finally, the terms with higher TW values are selected as feature vectors to classify mail messages by fuzzy inference.

Table 1. Fuzzy inference rules are composed of 2 groups according to NTF value

NDF \ NIDF	S	M	L
S	Z	Z	S
M	Z	M	L
L	S	L	X

NTF = S

NDF \ NIDF	S	M	L
S	Z	S	M
M	S	L	X
L	M	X	XX

NTF = L

3 Experiments

The email corpus used in the experimental evaluation contained a total of 4,792 emails and 4 categories: 2,218 for legitimate mail, 1,100 for porn spam, 1,077 for financing spam, and 397 for shopping spam. To select important features, we used the *weka.attributeSelection* package provided by WEKA [6]. WEKA is a workbench designed to aid in the application of machine learning techniques to real world data sets. WEKA contains a number of classification models. The SVM classifier used in this experiment was also provided by WEKA. SVM is tested with its default parameters settings within the WEKA. To evaluate the filtering performance on the email document corpus, we use the recall, precision, and F-measure commonly employed in IR field. In email filtering, it is extremely important that legitimate emails are not filtered out. In comparison, a user may be satisfied if some spam-email was not filtered, in order not to miss any good email. To evaluate this kind of reliability, we calculate misclassification error rate which represents the ratio of the incorrect predictions over total mails.

Table 2. Experimental results according to the feature selection methods (for porn spam)

Feature selection method	No. of selected features	Recall	Precision	F-measure	Error rate
Information gain	200	63.7	84.5	72.6	11.0
	338	65.3	92.2	76.4	9.2
	485	75.5	91.7	82.9	7.2
	681	76.2	91.3	83.1	7.1
	838	77.0	91.1	83.4	7.0
Chi-squared test (χ^2-test)	200	49.3	92.6	64.3	12.5
	338	63.5	74.6	76.0	9.2
	485	72.8	92.2	81.4	7.7
	681	75.2	93.6	83.4	6.9
	838	76.5	91.7	83.4	7.0
Fuzzy inference	200	68.7	87.3	76.9	9.5
	338	75.3	87.2	80.8	8.2
	485	76.5	89.1	82.3	7.5
	681	76.9	90.9	83.3	7.1
	838	79.3	91.3	84.9	6.5

In our experiments, we used ten-fold cross validation to reduce random variation. E-mail corpus was randomly partitioned into ten parts, and each experiment was repeated ten times, each time reserving a different part for testing, and using the remaining nine parts for training. Results were then averaged over the ten runs. Table 2 shows the performance of the fuzzy inference and the conventional ones such as information gain and χ^2-test in selecting features for filtering pornography spam. Almost 7,600 morphemes were extracted by eliminating stop words and redundant ones.

These morphemes are the candidate features to be used training porn mails. In this work, we selected 200, 338, 485, 681, and 838 features for information gain and χ^2-test by the WEKA and for the fuzzy inference by our system among these 7,600 morphemes. When compared with the experimental results by Yang [5], it gave almost same results. As shown in Table 2, the fuzzy inference method improved only 2% and 5% over information gain and χ^2-test in terms of the average F-measure. However, the proposed method showed about 6% and 10% improvements over the others in terms of the average error rate which is more important than F-measure for email users. That is a meaningful result because it is not easy to reduce error rate. Therefore, the proposed fuzzy inference is regarded as a good and stable feature selection method regardless of the number of selected features.

4 Conclusion

In this paper, a fuzzy inference approach as a feature selection method in spam mails filtering system was presented. We performed a comparative experiment on feature selection in pornography mails categorization. Though the performance improvement by fuzzy inference is not significant, the proposed fuzzy inference approach could be a slightly better feature selection method than information gain and χ^2-test. Especially the fuzzy inference method showed about 6% and 10% improvements over the conventional ones in terms of the average error rate which is more important than IR measures such as precision, recall, and F-measure for email users, respectively. Therefore, the proposed method is regarded as a reliable feature selection method. We will do further research on how to find more features having high differential power and improve the filtering performance.

References

1. Sahami, M., Dumais, S., Heckerman, D., and Horvitz, E., "A bayesian approach to filtering junk e-mail," In AAAI-98 Workshop on Learning for Text Categorization (1998) 55-62
2. Drucker, H., Wu, D. and Vapnik, V., "Support Vector Machines for Spam Categorization," IEEE Trans. on Neural Networks, Vol.10(5) (1999) 1048-1054
3. Lewis, D. D., Schapire, R. E., Callan, J. P., and Papka, R., "Training algorithms for linear text classifier," Proc. of SIGIR-96, 19th ACM International Conference on Research and Development in Information Retrieval (1996) 298-306
4. Kim, J. W., Kim, H. J., Kang, S. J., and Kim, B. M., "Determination of Usenet News Groups by Fuzzy Inference and Kohonen Network," Lecture Notes in Artificial Intelligence, Vol.3157, Springer-Verlag (2004) 654-663
5. Yang, Y, and Pedersen, J. P., "A comparative study on feature selection in text categorization," in Fourteenth International Conference on Machine Learning (1997) 412-420
6. Witten, I. H. and Frank, E., Data Mining: Practical machine learning tools and Techniques with java implementations, Morgan Kaufmann (2000)

Genetically Optimized Hybrid Fuzzy Polynomial Neural Networks Based on Polynomial and Fuzzy Polynomial Neurons

Sung-Kwun Oh and Hyun-Ki Kim

Department of Electrical Engineering, The University of Suwon, San 2-2 Wau-ri,
Bongdam-eup, Hwaseong-si, Gyeonggi-do 445-743, South Korea
ohsk@suwon.ac.kr

Abstract. We investigate a new category of fuzzy-neural networks-Hybrid Fuzzy Polynomial Neural Networks (HFPNN). These networks consist of genetically optimized multi-layer with two kinds of heterogeneous neurons that are fuzzy set based polynomial neurons (FSPNs) and polynomial neurons (PNs). The augmented genetically optimized HFPNN (namely gHFPNN) results in a structurally optimized structure and comes with a higher level of flexibility in comparison to the one we encounter in the conventional HFPNN. The GA-based design procedure being applied at each layer of gHFPNN leads to the selection leads to the selection of preferred nodes (FSPNs or PNs) available within the HFPNN. The performance of the gHFPNN is quantified through experimentation using a benchmarking dataset–synthetic and experimental data already experimented with in fuzzy or neurofuzzy modeling.

1 Introduction

Lately a lot of researchers on system modeling have been interested in the multitude of challenging and conflicting objectives such as compactness, approximation ability, generalization capability and so on which they wish to satisfy. It is common practice to use various forms of neural networks and fuzzy systems in designing nonlinear system with good predictive abilities as well as approximation capabilities. In particular, when dealing with high-order nonlinear and multivariable equations of the model, we require a vast amount of data for estimating all its parameters that is an important key to determine the model performance. As one of the diverse approaches[2,3,4,7], we study a genetic optimization-driven new neurofuzzy topology, called genetically optimized Hybrid Fuzzy Polynomial Neural Networks (gHFPNN) and discuss a comprehensive design methodology supporting their development. gHFPNN is a network resulting from the combination of fuzzy inference system and PNN algorithm driven to genetic optimization. Each node of the first layer of gHFPNN, that is a fuzzy polynomial neuron (FSPN) operates as a compact fuzzy inference system. The networks of the second and higher layers of the gHFPNN come with a high level of flexibility as each node (processing element forming a PN). The determination of the optimal values of the parameters available within an individual PN and FSPN (viz. the number of input variables, the order of the polynomial, a collection of preferred nodes, and the number of membership functions (MFs)) leads to a structurally and parametrically optimized network.

2 The Architecture of the Hybrid Fuzzy Polynomial Neural Networks Based on FSPN and PN

The FSPN encapsulates a family of nonlinear "if-then" rules. When put together, FSPNs results in a self-organizing Fuzzy Polynomial Neural Networks (FPNN). The FSPN consists of two basic functional modules. The first one, labeled by F, is a collection of fuzzy sets (here denoted by $\{A_k\}$ and $\{B_k\}$) that form an interface between the input numeric variables and the processing part realized by the neuron. The second module (denoted here by **P**) refers to the function – based nonlinear (polynomial) processing that involves some input variables This nonlinear processing involves some input variables (x_i and x_j), which are capable of being the input variables (Here, x_p and x_q), or entire system input variables. Each rule reads in the form

$$\begin{aligned} &\text{if } x_p \text{ is } A_k \text{ then } z \text{ is } P_{pk}(x_i, x_j, a_{pk}) \\ &\text{if } x_q \text{ is } B_k \text{ then } z \text{ is } P_{qk}(x_i, x_j, a_{qk}) \end{aligned} \quad (1)$$

where a_{qk} is a vector of the parameters of the conclusion part of the rule while $P(x_i, x_j, a)$ denoted the regression polynomial forming the consequence part of the fuzzy rule which uses several type of high order polynomials besides the constant function forming the simplest version of the consequence.

When developing the FSPN-based layer, we use genetic algorithms to produce the optimized network, which is realized by selecting such parameters as the number of input variables, the order of polynomial, and choosing a specific subset of input variables. Especially for the polynomial type of the consequent part, we consider two kinds of input vector formats in the conclusion part of the fuzzy rules. The PNN algorithm in the PN based layer of gHFPNN is based on the GMDH method and utilizes a class of polynomials such as linear, quadratic, modified quadratic, etc. to describe basic processing realized there. The detailed PN involving a certain regression polynomial is shown in Table 1.

Table 1. Different forms of the regression polynomial building a PN

Order	No. of inputs	1	2	3
1	(Type 1)	Linear	Bilinear	Trilinear
2	(Type 2)	Quadratic	Biquadratic-1	Triquadratic-1
	(Type 3)		Biquadratic-2	Triquadratic-2

3 Genetic Optimization of gHFPNN

For the optimization of the gHFPNN model, GA[5] uses the serial method of binary type, roulette-wheel used in the selection process, one-point crossover in the crossover operation, and a binary inversion (complementation) operation in the mutation operator. To retain the best individual and carry it over to the next generation, we use elitist strategy [6].

As mentioned, when we construct PNs and FSPNs of each layer in the conventional HFPNN, such parameters as the number of input variables (nodes), the order of polynomial, and input variables available within a PN and a FSPN are fixed (selected) in advance by the designer. This could have frequently contributed to the difficulties in the design of the optimal network. To overcome this apparent drawback, we resort ourselves to the genetic optimization.

4 The Algorithm and Design Procedure of Genetically Optimized HFPNN (gHFPNN)

The framework of the design procedure of the HFPNN based on genetically optimized multi-layer perceptron architecture comprises the following steps.

[Step 1] *Determine system's input variables.*
[Step 2] *Form a training and testing data.*
[Step 3] *Decide initial information for constructing the gHFPNN structure.*
[Step 4] *Decide a structure of the PN and FSPN based layer of gHFPNN using genetic design.*
[Step 5] *Estimate the coefficient parameters of the polynomial in the selected node (PN or FSPN).*
[Step 6] *Select nodes (PNs or FSPNs) with the best predictive capability and construct their corresponding layer.*
[Step 7] *Check the termination criterion.*
[Step 8] *Determine new input variables for the next layer.*

The HFPNN algorithm is carried out by repeating steps 4-8 of the algorithm.

5 Simulation Study

We demonstrate how the gHFPNN can be utilized to predict future values of a chaotic Mackey-Glass time series [4, 7]. The time series is generated by the chaotic Mackey-Glass differential delay equation [2] comes in the form

$$\dot{x}(t) = \frac{0.2x(t-\tau)}{1+x^{10}(t-\tau)} - 0.1x(t) \tag{2}$$

To obtain the time series value at each integer point, we applied the fourth-order Runge-Kutta method to find the numerical solution to (2). From the Mackey-Glass time series $x(t)$, we extracted 1000 input-output data pairs in the following format:
$$[x(t-24), x(t-18), x(t-12), x(t-6), x(t) ; x(t+6)]$$
where, t=118 to 1117. The first 500 pairs were used as the training data set while the remaining 500 pairs formed the testing data set. To come up with a quantitative evaluation of the network, we use the standard RMSE performance index.

The optimal topologies of gHFPNN are given as the following: for 3 layers and Max=5 in case of Type T*, those are quantified as PI=4.28e-4, EPI=4.05e-4 for triangular MF, and PI=2.30e-4, EPI=2.80e-4 for Gaussian-like MF.

6 Concluding Remarks

The GA-based design procedure of Hybrid Fuzzy Polynomial Neural Networks (HFPNN) along with its architectural considerations has been investigated. The design methodology comes as a hybrid structural optimization (based on GMDH method and genetic optimization) and parametric learning being viewed as two fundamental phases of the design process. The comprehensive experimental study involving well-known datasets quantify a superb performance of the network in comparison to the existing fuzzy and neuro-fuzzy models.

Acknowledgements. This work has been supported by KESRI(I-2004-0-074-0-00), which is funded by MOCIE(Ministry of commerce, industry and energy).

References

1. A.G. Ivahnenko.: Polynomial theory of complex systems. IEEE Trans. on Systems, Man and Cybernetics. SMC-12 (1971) 364-378
2. S.-K. Oh and W. Pedrycz.: The design of self-organizing Polynomial Neural Networks. Information Science. 141 (2002) 237-258
3. Oh, S.K., Park, B.J., Kim, H.K. : Genetically Optimized Hybrid Fuzzy Neural Networks Based on Linear Fuzzy Inference Rules. International journal of Control, Automations, and Systems. 3(2) (2005) 183-194
4. S.-K. Oh, W. Pedrycz, and D.-W. Kim.: Hybrid Fuzzy Polynomial Neural Networks. Int. J. of Uncertainty, Fuzziness and Knowledge-Based Systems. 10 (2002) 257-280
5. Z. Michalewicz.: Genetic Algorithms + Data Structures = Evolution Programs. Springer-Verlag, Berlin Heidelberg. 1996
6. D. Jong, K. A.: Are Genetic Algorithms Function Optimizers?. Parallel Problem Solving from Nature 2, Manner, R. and Manderick, B. eds., North-Holland, Amsterdam
7. S.-K. Oh, W. Pedrycz, T.-C. Ahn.: Self-organizing neural networks with fuzzy polynomial neurons. Applied Soft Computing. 2 (2002) 1-10
8. M. C. Mackey and L. Glass.: Oscillation and chaos in physiological control systems. Science. 197 (1977) 287-289

Multi-item Fuzzy Inventory Model with Three Constraints: Genetic Algorithm Approach

Jafar Rezaei[1] and Mansoor Davoodi[2]

[1] Vali-e-Asr University of Rafsanjan, Department of Industrial Management,
Rafsanjan, Kerman, Iran
Rezaei@vru.ac.ir

[2] Vali-e-Asr University of Rafsanjan, Department of Computer Sciences,
Rafsanjan, Kerman, Iran

Abstract. In this paper a multi-item fuzzy inventory model under total production cost, total storage space and number of orders constraints is solved with a Genetic Algorithm. In this model, the production cost and set up cost are directly proportional to the respective quantities, unit production cost is inversely related to the demand and set up cost is assumed to vary directly with lot size. Also Shortages are allowed. However this approach has been applied to solve the model under fuzzy objective of cost minimization and imprecise constraints on storage space, number of orders and production cost with imprecise inventory costs. This model has been formulated as FNLP problem and then converted to equivalent crisp decision making problems and solved by a Genetic Algorithm. Finally the model is illustrated with a numerical example.

1 Introduction

Recently, GAs have been applied in different areas like scheduling (Davis [1]), numerical optimization (Michalewicz and Janikow [2]), inventory classification (Guvenier [3]), multi criteria flow shop scheduling (Bagchi [4]), inventory control (Mondal and Maiti [5]) etc. But, till now, just one work(Mondal and Maiti [5]) has applied it in the field of inventory control. This paper is different from Mondal and Maiti's work [5] from different aspect on model and methodology.

One of the most important of inventory models is multi-item inventory model. Multi-item classical inventory models under resource constraints such as budgetary cost, limited storage area, number of orders, available set-up times, etc. are presented in well-known books (Silver and Peterson [6],Hadely and Whitin [7],Lewis [8]).

In an inventory system, we consider inventory costs which may be imprecise. On the other hand, the resources may be vaguely defined in a different way. Similar may be the cases for total investment and number of production runs. Hence, there is a scope of formulating the inventory control problems with imprecise parameters, resources and objective. Till now, only a very few fuzzy inventory models (Park [9], Vujosevic et. al [10], Lee et. al [11], Yao et. al [12], Fatemi Ghomi and Rezaei [13] are available in the literature.

In this paper, GAs have been developed for non-linear programming problems with fuzzy objective function and resources. Membership function of the fuzzy optimal solution is taken as the fitness function of the algorithm. The individuals with higher membership degree have more probability to reproduce offspring around them. To make the offspring better than their parent, mutation is made along the weighted gradient direction using the random step lengths. A whole arithmetic crossover is also done before getting a new generation. These methodologies have been applied to solve the multi-item EOQ model under three constraints. The inventory model first has been formulated as FNLP problems and then converted to equivalent crisp decision making problem and solved by above GAs.

2 Structure of Genetic Algorithms

Genetic algorithms mimic the selective and evolutionary phenomena that occur in nature by the reproduction and recombination of highly fit chromosomes or solution strings within a string population to form better individuals and hence develop increasingly desirable generations. A solution is represented by a string of characters, each character representing a solution parameter with the ability to assume different values. The coding method used to describe the solution in this way may have a significant influence on the performance of the GA, as does the objective function, which is the mathematical model used to assign a fitness value to the solution string.

The structure of a simple GA consists mainly of three operators. A selection operator and a crossover operator act on the population of strings to perform the required reproduction and recombination, while the mutation operator randomly alters character values, usually with very low probability. The effect of these random alterations is to maintain diversity within the population, thereby preventing early convergence of the algorithm to a possibly false peak. In this respect, mutation is widely viewed as a secondary operator. A fourth operator, the inversion operator, was also suggested by the inventor of the GA, Holland, when the first algorithms were designed [14-17]. The function of this operator is to alter the order in which string characters are arranged, with the intention of creating better linkage within the string. There are many variations of each of these operator types, with the effectiveness of a particular type of operator depending on the nature of the problem [18].

Current GA literature contains many useful guidelines as to which type of operator is best suited to certain circumstances, and these guidelines have been used within the current research insofar as is possible. However, the operations management decision areas investigated required highly problem-specific algorithms. Hence, further research was necessary in order to identify appropriate and efficient operators [15].

3 Mathematical Model

In general the classical inventory problems are designed by considering that the demand rate of an item is constant and deterministic and that the unit price of an item is considered to be constant and independent in nature [6, 7, 19]. But in practical situation, unit price and demand rate of an item may be related to each other. When the demand of an item is high, an item is produced in large numbers and fixed costs of production are spread over a large number of items. Hence the unit cost of the item decreases, i.e., the unit price of an item inversely relates to the demand of that item. So, demand rate of an item may be considered as a decision variable. Cheng [20], Jung and Klein [21] formulated the economic order quantity problem with this idea.

It is often difficult to determine the actual inventory costs. They depend upon different aspects. So the inventory costs are assumed to be flexible, i.e., fuzzy in nature. The inventory problem is controlled by some constraints. Restrictions on storage space, number of orders and production cost affect the optimal inventory cost. But, in real life problems, it is almost impossible to predict the total cost and resources precisely. These may be imprecise in nature. Hence these quantities may be assumed uncertain in non stochastic sense but fuzzy in nature. In this situation, the inventory problem along with constraints can be developed with the fuzzy set theory.

Bellman and Zadeh [22] used the fuzzy set theory to the decision-making problem. Zimmermann [23] gave the concept to solve multi-objective linear programming problem. Fuzzy set theory now has made an entry into the inventory control systems. In this section we first formulated the model as follow:

Assumptions and Notations

W	storage space goal	S_i	shortage level
Pw	the tolerance of W	C_{1i}	holding cost per unit
t	number of orders goal	C_{2i}	shortage cost per unit
Pt	the tolerance of t	C_{3i}	set up cost
u	production cost goal	W_i	storage space
Pu	the tolerance of u	TC_i	total average cost
n	number of items	$SS(Q)$	total available storage
D_i	demand per unit item	$NO(D,Q)$	total number of orders
Q_i	lot size	$PC(D)$	total production cost

Production rate is instantaneous. Unit production cost is taken here as inversely related to the demand of the item. For ith item, unit, price $C_{4i} = \alpha_i D_i^{-\beta_i}$ where scaling constant of C_{4i} be $\alpha_i (>0)$ and degree of economies of scale be $\beta (>1)$.

Formulation

The total cost = production cost + set up cost + holding cost + shortage cost

$$TC_i(D_i, Q_i, S_i) = \alpha_i D_i^{1-\beta_i} + \tilde{c}_{3i} Q_i^{\gamma-1} D_i + \tilde{c}_{1i} \frac{(Q_i - S_i)^2}{2Q_i} + \tilde{c}_{2i} \frac{S_i^2}{2Q_i}$$

There are some restrictions on available resources in inventory problems that cannot be ignored to derive the optimal total cost.

- Limitation on the available total storage space
$$SS(Q) \equiv \sum_{i=1}^{n} W_i Q_i \leq \tilde{W}$$

- Upper limit on the number of orders
$$NO(D,Q) \equiv \sum_{i=1}^{n} \frac{D_i}{Q_i} \leq \tilde{t}$$

- Total production cost
$$PC(D) \equiv \sum_{i=1}^{n} \alpha_i D_i^{-\beta_i} Q_i \leq \tilde{u}$$

The problem is to find demand levels, the lot size, the shortage amount so as to minimize the total cost function subject to restrictions and boundary conditions:

$$\text{Min} \quad TC_i(D_i, Q_i, S_i) = \alpha_i D_i^{1-\beta_i} + \tilde{c}_{3i} Q_i^{\gamma-1} D_i + \tilde{c}_{1i} \frac{(Q_i - S_i)^2}{2Q_i} + \tilde{c}_{2i} \frac{S_i^2}{2Q_i}$$

s.t.

$$SS(Q) \equiv \sum_{i=1}^{n} W_i Q_i \leq \tilde{W}$$

$$NO(D,Q) \equiv \sum_{i=1}^{n} \frac{D_i}{Q_i} \leq \tilde{t}$$

$$PC(D) \equiv \sum_{i=1}^{n} \alpha_i D_i^{-\beta_i} Q_i \leq \tilde{u}$$

$$L_{D_i} \leq D_i \leq U_{D_i}, \quad L_{Q_i} \leq Q_i \leq U_{Q_i}, \quad L_{S_i} \leq S_i \leq U_{S_i}, \quad \text{for } i = 1, 2, \ldots, n.$$

Where $\tilde{C}_i$ is a fuzzy cost coefficient vector with components $\tilde{C}_{1i}$, $\tilde{C}_{2i}$ and $\tilde{C}_{3i}$. These components are fuzzy numbers. Also, $\tilde{W}$, $\tilde{t}$ and $\tilde{u}$ are fuzzy numbers.

Following Zimmerman [23], the above fuzzy model reduces to:

Max α

s.t.

$$\alpha_i D_i^{1-\beta_i} + (c_{3i} - (1-\alpha) Pc_{3i}) Q_i^{\gamma-1} D_i + (c_{1i} - (1-\alpha) Pc_{1i}) \frac{(Q_i - S_i)^2}{2Q_i}$$

$$+ (c_{2i} - (1-\alpha) Pc_{2i}) \frac{S_i^2}{2Q_i} \leq C_0 + (1-\alpha) Pc_0$$

$$SS(Q) \equiv \sum_{i=1}^{n} W_i Q_i \leq W + (1-\alpha) Pw_0$$

$$NO(D,Q) \equiv \sum_{i=1}^{n} \frac{D_i}{Q_i} \leq t + (1-\alpha) Pt_0$$

$$PC(D) \equiv \sum_{i=1}^{n} \alpha_i D_i^{-\beta_i} Q_i \leq u + (1-\alpha) Pu_0$$

where Pc_0, Pw_0, Pt_0, Pu_0, Pc_{1i}, Pc_{2i} and Pc_{3i} are tolerances of C_0, W, t, C_{1i}, C_{2i} and C_{3i}, u respectively, C_0 being the investment target.

4 Numerical Example

In this section we solved a numerical example of the above fuzzy model using GAs (illustrated in section 2). We consider three items with input data as follow:

$W = 280$, $Pw = 100$, $t = 4$, $Pt = 2$, $C_0 = 400$, $Pc_0 = 100$, Production cost of items 1, 2 and 3 are $15000D_1^{-2.7}$, $18000D_2^{-2.1}$, $14000D_3^{-2.2}$ respectively, $C_{11} = 0.2$, $Pc_{11} = 0.7$, $C_{12} = 0.3$, $Pc_{12} = 0.7$, $C_{13} = 0.2$, $Pc_{13} = 0.7$, $C_{21} = 8$, $Pc_{21} = 5$, $C_{22} = 9$, $Pc_{22} = 5$, $C_{23} = 11$, $Pc_{23} = 7$, $C_{31} = 10$, $Pc_{31} = 3$, $C_{32} = 3$, $Pc_{32} = 1$, $C_{33} = 7$, $Pc_{33} = 2$, $\gamma_1 = \gamma_2 = \gamma_3 = 0.5$, $40 \le D_1 \le 100$, $180 \le D_2 \le 250$, $100 \le D_3 \le 200$, $40 \le Q_1 \le 150$, $70 \le Q_2 \le 200$, $80 \le Q_3 \le 200$, $1 \le S_1, S_2, S_3 \le 8$.

The results are shown in Table 1.

Table 1. Result for model by GA

Items	D_i^*	Q_i^*	S_i^*	TC^*
1	56.2	51.4	3.1	
2	249	197	2.1	464.62
3	163.7	85.8	3.3	

5 Conclusion

In this paper we have applied GAs to solve the multi item fuzzy inventory model with three constraints. In fuzzy method, only one optimum solution is obtained, whereas, GAs give a series of alternatives along with the optimum one to the decision maker. In all cases, exact optimum solution is not always wanted. As the model has been formulated with vague parameters and imprecise conditions, the decision maker may choose that solution which suits him best with respect to resources, which will have to be augmented with difficulty. In this respect, GAs are the most suitable methods for a decision maker. In this paper the cost components are considered TFNs. The constraint goals are flexible and to some extent allow tolerance values. Consequently, the objective function is fuzzy and defined by fuzzy ranking function with respect to total integral values. The model can be easily extended to generic inventory problems with other constraints. The method presented here is quite general and can be applied to the real inventory problems faced by the practitioners in industry or in other areas.

References

1. Davis, L. (Ed.).: Handbook of Genetic Algorithms. Van Nostrand Reinhold New York (1991)
2. Michalewicz, Z., Janikow, C. Z.: Genetic Algorithms for Numerical Optimization. Statistics and Computing, 1 (1991) 75–91.

3. Guvenir, H. A.: A Genetic Algorithm for Multicriteria Inventory Classification in Artificial Neural Nets and Genetic Algorithms, Proceedings of the International Conference, Ales, France, D. W. Pearson, N. C. Steele, and R. F. Albrecht (Eds), Springer-Verlag, Wien, (1995) 6-9
4. Bagchi, T.: Multi Objective Scheduling by Genetic Algorithm. Kluwer Academic Publishers. Boston (1999)
5. Mondal, S., Maiti, M.: Multi-item Fuzzy EOQ Models Using Genetic Algorithm. Computers & Industrial Engineering 44 (2002) 105–117
6. Silver, E.A., Peterson, R.: Decision Systems for Inventory Management and Production Planning Wiley New York (1985)
7. Hadley, G., Whitin T.M.: Analysis of Inventory Systems. NJ: Prentice-Hall Englewood Cliffs(1963)
8. Lewis, C.D.: Scientific Inventory Control. Butterworth's London (1970)
9. Park, K. S.: Fuzzy Set theoretic Interpretation of Economic Order Quantity. IEEE Transactions on Systems, Man and Cybernetics 17 (1987) 1082–1087
10. Vujosevic, M., Petrovic, D., and Petrovic, R.: EOQ Formula when Inventory Cost is Fuzzy. Production Economics 45 (1996)499–504
11. Lee, H.M., and Yao, J.Sh, Economic Order Quantity in Fuzzy Sense for Inventory without Backorder Model. Fuzzy Sets and Systems 105(1999)13-31
12. Yao, J.Sh., Lee, HM.:Fuzzy Inventory with or without Backorder for Order Quantity with Trapezoid Fuzzy Number. Fuzzy Sets and Systems 105(1999)311-337
13. Fatemi Ghomi, S.M.T., Rezaei, J.: Development of a Fuzzy Inventory Control Model with a Real Application. Amirkabir 14(55-D)(2003)924-936
14. Holland, J. H.: Hierarchical Descriptions of Universal Spaces and Adaptive Systems. Technical Report, University of Michigan, Ann Arbor, Michigan (1968)
15. Stockton, D.J., Quinn, L., Khalil, R.A.: Use of Genetic Algorithms in Operations Management Part 1: Applications, Proc. Instn Mech. Engrs Vol. 218 Part B: J. Engineering Manufacture(2004)
16. Goldberg, D. E.: Genetic Algorithms in Search, Optimization, and Machine Learning. Addison-Wesley New York (1989)
17. Holland, J. H.: Genetic Algorithms and the Optimal Allocations of Trials. SIAM J. Computing, 2(2)(1973) 88-105
18. Goldberg, D. E. Deb, K.: A Comparative Analysis of Selection Schemes Used in Genetic Algorithms. Foundations of Genetic Algorithms (Morgan Kaufmann, San Diego, California) (1991)
19. Raymond, F.E.: Quantity and Economic in Manufacture. McGraw-Hill Book Co New York (1931)
20. Cheng, T.C.E. : An Economic Production Quantity Model with Demand-Dependent Unit Cost, European J. Operation Research 40 (1989) 252–256
21. Jung, H. Klein, C.M.: Optimal Inventory Policies Under Decreasing Cost Functions via Geometric Programming, European J. Operation Research 132 (2001) 628–642
22. Bellman, R.E., Zadeh, L.A.: Decision-Making in a Fuzzy Environment, Management Sci. 17 (4) (1970) 141–164
23. Zimmermann, H.J.: Description and Optimization off Uzzy Systems, Internat. J. General Systems 2 (4) (1976) 209–215

Fuzzy Attribute Implications: Computing Non-redundant Bases Using Maximal Independent Sets*

Radim Bělohlávek and Vilém Vychodil

Department of Computer Science, Palacký University, Olomouc,
Tomkova 40, CZ-779 00 Olomouc, Czech Republic
{radim.belohlavek, vilem.vychodil}@upol.cz

Abstract. This note describes a method for computation of non-redundant bases of attribute implications from data tables with fuzzy attributes. Attribute implications are formulas describing particular dependencies of attributes in data. A non-redundant basis is a minimal set of attribute implications such that each attribute implication which is true in a given data (semantically) follows from the basis. Our bases are uniquely given by so-called systems of pseudo-intents. We reduce the problem of computing systems of pseudo-intents to the problem of computing maximal independent sets in certain graphs. We outline theoretical foundations, the algorithm, and present demonstrating examples.

1 Introduction and Problem Setting

Fuzzy attribute implications are formulas of a form "if A then B" which describe particular dependencies in data tables. Among all the implications which are true in a given table, there is a lot of them which are trivial and a lot of them which can be removed since they are entailed by the others. Therefore, it is desirable to look for methods for obtaining non-redundant bases, i.e. minimal sets of attribute implications such that all implications which are true in a given data table semantically follow from the basis. In case of data tables with binary attributes (tables containing 0's and 1's), an algorithm for computation of non-redundant bases is known, see [8,10]. For data tables with fuzzy attributes (tables containing degrees, e.g. reals from $[0, 1]$), non-redundant bases of implications determined by so-called systems of pseudo-intents are described in [4,7]. For a particular case when a hedge (a unary logical function used in the definition of validity of attribute implications) is a so-called globalization, there is a unique system of pseudo-intents and an algorithm for the computation of the corresponding non-redundant basis was presented in [4]. The present paper shows an algorithm for getting systems of pseudo-intents for general hedges. Due to the limited scope of this paper, we postpone all proofs to a forthcoming paper.

---

* Supported by grant No. 1ET101370417 of GA AV ČR, by grant No. 201/05/0079 of the Czech Science Foundation, and by institutional support, research plan MSM 6198959214.

2 Fuzzy Attribute Logic (Preliminaries)

In this section we survey notions of fuzzy attribute logic, for more details see [4,5,7]. We use residuated structures of truth degrees [2] and the usual notions of fuzzy logic and fuzzy sets. A residuated structure of truth degrees will be denoted by $\mathbf{L}$. Let Y be a finite set of attributes. A (*fuzzy*) *attribute implication* is an expression $A \Rightarrow B$, where $A, B \in \mathbf{L}^Y$ (A and B are fuzzy sets of attributes). The intended meaning of $A \Rightarrow B$ is: "if it is (very) true that an object has all attributes from A, then it has also all attributes from B". A data table with fuzzy attributes [4,5,7] is a triplet $\mathcal{T} = \langle X, Y, I \rangle$ where X is a set of objects, Y is a finite set of attributes, and $I \in \mathbf{L}^{X \times Y}$ is a binary $\mathbf{L}$-relation (fuzzy relation) between X and Y assigning to each object $x \in X$ and each attribute $y \in Y$ a degree $I(x, y)$ to which x has y. $\mathcal{T}$ can be seen as a table with rows and columns corresponding to objects $x \in X$ and attributes $y \in Y$, respectively, and table entries containing degrees $I(x, y)$. For fuzzy set $M \in \mathbf{L}^Y$ of attributes, we define a *degree* $||A \Rightarrow B||_M$ *to which* $A \Rightarrow B$ *is true in* M by $||A \Rightarrow B||_M = S(A, M)^* \to S(B, M)$, where $\to$ is residuated implication (in $\mathbf{L}$), * is a hedge, and $S(A, M)$ denotes degree of subsethood of A in M, for details see [2,4,5,7,11]. A row of a table $\mathcal{T}$ corresponding to an object $x \in X$ can be seen as a fuzzy set I_x of attributes to which each $y \in Y$ belongs to a degree $I_x(y) = I(x, y)$. Given $\mathcal{T} = \langle X, Y, I \rangle$, we define *degree* $||A \Rightarrow B||_{\langle X,Y,I \rangle}$ *to which* $A \Rightarrow B$ *is true in* (*each row of*) $\mathcal{T}$ by $||A \Rightarrow B||_{\langle X,Y,I \rangle} = \bigwedge_{x \in X} ||A \Rightarrow B||_{I_x}$. Let T be a set of fuzzy attribute implications. $M \in \mathbf{L}^Y$ is called a *model* of T if, for each $A \Rightarrow B \in T$, $||A \Rightarrow B||_M = 1$. The set of all models of T is denoted by $\mathrm{Mod}(T)$. A degree $||A \Rightarrow B||_T$ to which $A \Rightarrow B$ *semantically follows* from T is defined by $||A \Rightarrow B||_T = \bigwedge_{M \in \mathrm{Mod}(T)} ||A \Rightarrow B||_M$. T is called *complete* (*in* $\mathcal{T} = \langle X, Y, I \rangle$) if $||A \Rightarrow B||_T = ||A \Rightarrow B||_{\langle X,Y,I \rangle}$, i.e., if, for each $A \Rightarrow B$, a degree to which T entails $A \Rightarrow B$ coincides with a degree to which $A \Rightarrow B$ is true in $\langle X, Y, I \rangle$. If T is complete and no proper subset of T is complete, then T is called a *non-redundant basis* (*of* $\mathcal{T} = \langle X, Y, I \rangle$). For $A \in \mathbf{L}^X$, $B \in \mathbf{L}^Y$, we define $A^\uparrow \in \mathbf{L}^Y$, $B^\downarrow \in \mathbf{L}^X$ by $A^\uparrow(y) = \bigwedge_{x \in X} \bigl(A(x)^* \to I(x, y)\bigr)$, $B^\downarrow(x) = \bigwedge_{y \in Y} \bigl(B(y) \to I(x, y)\bigr)$. Operators $^\downarrow, ^\uparrow$ form so-called Galois connection with hedge [6], composed operator $^{\downarrow\uparrow}$ is a fuzzy closure operator. The (lattice-ordered) structure of all fixed points of $^{\downarrow\uparrow}$ is called a fuzzy concept lattice (induced by $\mathcal{T}$), see [2,3,6]. Given $\mathcal{T} = \langle X, Y, I \rangle$, a system of fuzzy sets of attributes $\mathcal{P} \subseteq \mathbf{L}^Y$ is called a *system of pseudo-intents* of $\mathcal{T}$ if for each $P \in \mathbf{L}^Y$ we have: $P \in \mathcal{P}$ if and only if $P \neq P^{\downarrow\uparrow}$ and, for each $Q \in \mathcal{P}$ such that $Q \neq P$, $||Q \Rightarrow Q^{\downarrow\uparrow}||_P = 1$. The following property of systems of pseudo-intents was proved is [7]: if $\mathcal{P}$ is a system of pseudo-intents of $\mathcal{T}$ then $T = \{P \Rightarrow P^{\downarrow\uparrow} \,|\, P \in \mathcal{P}\}$ is a non-redundant basis of $\mathcal{T}$. Therefore we focus on computing of systems of pseudo-intents.

3 Computing Non-redundant Bases

For $\mathcal{T} = \langle X, Y, I \rangle$ we define a set V of $\mathbf{L}$-sets (fuzzy sets) of attributes by

$$V = \{P \in \mathbf{L}^Y \,|\, P \neq P^{\downarrow\uparrow}\}. \tag{1}$$

If $V \neq \emptyset$, we define a binary relation E on V by

$$E = \{\langle P, Q\rangle \in V \mid P \neq Q \text{ and } ||Q \Rightarrow Q^{\downarrow\uparrow}||_P \neq 1\}. \tag{2}$$

In this case, $\mathbf{G} = \langle V, E \cup E^{-1}\rangle$ is a graph. For any $Q \in V$ and $\mathcal{P} \subseteq V$ define the following subsets of V: $\mathrm{Pred}(Q) = \{P \in V \mid \langle P, Q\rangle \in E\}$, and $\mathrm{Pred}(\mathcal{P}) = \bigcup_{Q \in \mathcal{P}} \mathrm{Pred}(Q)$.

Theorem. *Let $\mathbf{L}$ be a finite residuated structure of truth degrees, * be any (truth-stressing) hedge, $\mathcal{T} = \langle X, Y, I\rangle$ be a data table with fuzzy attributes (with truth degrees in $\mathbf{L}$), $\mathcal{P} \subseteq \mathbf{L}^Y$, V and E be defined by (1) and (2), respectively. Then the following statements are equivalent.*

(i) $\mathcal{P}$ *is a system of pseudo-intents;*
(ii) $V - \mathcal{P} = \mathrm{Pred}(\mathcal{P})$;
(iii) $\mathcal{P}$ *is a maximal independent set in $\mathbf{G}$ such that $V - \mathcal{P} = \mathrm{Pred}(\mathcal{P})$.* □

The Theorem gives a way to compute systems of pseudo-intents. It suffices to find all maximal independent sets in $\mathbf{G}$ and check which of them satisfy additional condition $V - \mathcal{P} = \mathrm{Pred}(\mathcal{P})$. If * is globalization on finite $\mathbf{L}$, for each $\mathcal{T}$ there is exactly one system of pseudo-intents, see [4,7], which can also be found by the graph procedure but we can take advantage of a special nature of globalization: in order to find the basis, it suffices to traverse through the nodes of a graph in lexical order (details are postponed to the full version of the paper).

4 Example and Conclusions

Let $\mathbf{L}$ be a three-element Lukasiewicz chain with $L = \{0, 0.5, 1\}$. Consider a data table $\mathcal{T}$ given by Fig. 1 (left). The set X of object consists of objects "Mercury", "Venus",...; Y contains four attributes: size of a planet (small / large), distance from the sun (far / near). If * (hedge) is defined so that $1^* = 1$ and $a^* = 0$ for all $a < 1$ (so-called globalization), there is a unique system of pseudo-intents, see [4]. If, for each $a \in L$, $a^* = a$ (i.e., * is identity), we obtain two distinct systems of pseudo-intents (denote the systems by $\mathcal{P}_1$ and $\mathcal{P}_2$), both consist of four elements. Fig. 1 (right) contains the incidence matrix of relation $E \subseteq V \times V$ defined by (2). For brevity, the elements of V are denoted by numbers $0, \ldots, 42$. White box on a position P (row) and Q (column) indicates that $\langle P, Q\rangle \notin E$; gray box means $\langle P, Q\rangle \in E$, "○" ("×") indicates that $Q \in \mathcal{P}_1$ ($Q \in \mathcal{P}_2$) and $P \in \mathrm{Pred}(Q)$. Non-redundant bases T_1 and T_2 given by $\mathcal{P}_1$ and $\mathcal{P}_2$ are the following:

$$T_1 = \{\{n\} \Rightarrow \{^{0.5}/s, n\}, \{f, ^{0.5}/n\} \Rightarrow \{^{0.5}/l, f, ^{0.5}/n\},$$
$$\{l\} \Rightarrow \{l, f, ^{0.5}/n\}, \{s, ^{0.5}/l, ^{0.5}/f\} \Rightarrow \{s, ^{0.5}/l, ^{0.5}/f, ^{0.5}/n\}\},$$
$$T_2 = \{\{n\} \Rightarrow \{^{0.5}/s, n\}, \{f, ^{0.5}/n\} \Rightarrow \{^{0.5}/l, f, ^{0.5}/n\},$$
$$\{l, ^{0.5}/f\} \Rightarrow \{l, f, ^{0.5}/n\}, \{s, ^{0.5}/l, ^{0.5}/f\} \Rightarrow \{s, ^{0.5}/l, ^{0.5}/f, ^{0.5}/n\}\}.$$

If $\mathbf{L}$ is a three-element Gödel chain with identity, we get two distinct systems of pseudo-intents with various sizes. Experiments with randomly generated data have shown that sparse data tables usually lead to larger amount of bases and the bases themselves are greater than in case of tables with average density.

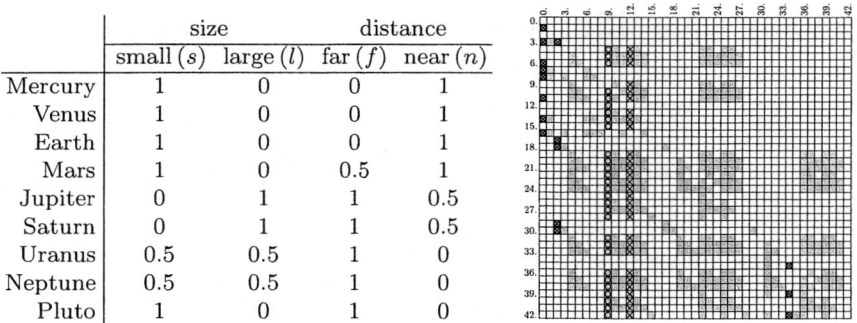

Fig. 1. Data table with fuzzy attributes and the corresponding V and E

References

1. Bělohlávek R.: Similarity relations in concept lattices. *J. Logic Comput.* 10(6):823–845, 2000.
2. Bělohlávek R.: *Fuzzy Relational Systems: Foundations and Principles.* Kluwer, Academic/Plenum Publishers, New York, 2002.
3. Bělohlávek R.: Concept lattices and order in fuzzy logic. *Ann. Pure Appl. Logic* **128**(2004), 277–298.
4. Bělohlávek R., Chlupová M., Vychodil V.: Implications from data with fuzzy attributes. AISTA 2004 in Cooperation with the IEEE Computer Society Proceedings, 2004, 5 pages, ISBN 2-9599776-8-8.
5. Bělohlávek R., Vychodil V.: Implications from data with fuzzy attributes vs. scaled binary attributes. In: FUZZ-IEEE 2005, The IEEE International Conference on Fuzzy Systems, pp. 1050–1055, ISBN 0-7803-9158-6.
6. Bělohlávek R., Vychodil V.: Reducing attribute implications from data tables with fuzzy attributes to tables with binary attributes. *Proceedings of the 8th Joint Conference on Information Sciences*, 2005, pp. 78–81, ISBN 0-9707890-3-3.
7. Bělohlávek R., Vychodil V.: Fuzzy attribute logic: attribute implications, their validity, entailment, and non-redundant basis. In: Y. Liu, G. Chen, M. Ying (Eds.): *Fuzzy Logic, Soft Computing & Computational Intelligence: Eleventh International Fuzzy Systems Association World Congress* (Vol. I), 2005, pp. 622–627. Tsinghua University Press and Springer, ISBN 7-302-11377-7.
8. Ganter B., Wille R.: *Formal Concept Analysis. Mathematical Foundations.* Springer, Berlin, 1999.
9. Gerla G.: *Fuzzy Logic. Mathematical Tools for Approximate Reasoning.* Kluwer, Dordrecht, 2001.
10. Guigues J.-L., Duquenne V.: Familles minimales d'implications informatives resultant d'un tableau de données binaires. *Math. Sci. Humaines* **95**(1986), 5–18.
11. Hájek P.: *Metamathematics of Fuzzy Logic.* Kluwer, Dordrecht, 1998.
12. Hájek P.: On very true. *Fuzzy Sets and Systems* **124**(2001), 329–333.
13. Klir G. J., Yuan B.: *Fuzzy Sets and Fuzzy Logic. Theory and Applications.* Prentice Hall, 1995.
14. Takeuti G., Titani S.: Globalization of intuitionistic set theory. *Annals of Pure and Applied Logic* **33**(1987), 195–211.

Fuzzy Classifier with Bayes Rule Consequent

Do Wan Kim[1], Jin Bae Park[1], and Young Hoon Joo[2]

[1] Yonsei University, Seodaemun-gu, Seoul 120-749, Korea
Tel: +82-2-2123-2773
{dwkim, jbpark}@yonssei.ac.kr
[2] Kunsan National University, Kunsan, Chunbuk 573-701, Korea
Tel: +82-63-469-4706
yhjoo@kunsan.ac.kr

Abstract. This paper proposes a new fuzzy rule-based classifier equipped with a Bayes rule consequent. The main features of our approach are no requirement on the covariance matrices structure and their avoidance of singularity; the expansion in unimodal densities to multimodal ones; and the fuzzy set analysis for measuring the qualities of features. Two tools are exploited in constructing the proposed classifier: the iterative pruning algorithm for removing the irrelevant features and the gradient descent method for training the related parameters.

1 Introduction

This paper aims at improving the classification performance by borrowing some ideas from a fuzzy rule-based approach [2,1,3,5,4]. In specific, we propose a new fuzzy rule-based classifier with a Bayes rule consequent and its design method leads to prune the irrelevant features and train the related parameters. The use of fuzzy rule approach excludes the requirement of the covariance matrices structure, thereby making easily that they are directly constructed from the training data in any case. Instead, adopting the diagonal form of covariance matrices avoids their possible singularity. The fuzzy approach also make possible to expand in the unimodal densities to the multimodal ones through the inference procedure. In addition, by exploiting the both overlapping and categorizing degrees among the fuzzy sets, the relevant features selection issue is well tackled. The proposed classifier is built by removing the irrelevant features and training the related parameters through the fuzzy set analysis and gradient descent method, respectively. It is worthwhile to mention that our proposed method is easily applicable to construct classifiers in the multicategory and high dimensional problem.

2 Preliminaries

Let $\mathcal{W} = \{w_1, w_2, \ldots, w_m\}$ be a set of class labels and $\mathbf{x} = [x_1, x_2, \ldots, x_n]^T \in \Re^n$ be a feature vector. A classifier is any mapping $D : \Re^n \longrightarrow \mathcal{W}$. There are many different ways to represent pattern classifiers. One of the most useful is in terms of a set of m discriminant functions $d_i(\mathbf{x})$, $i \in \mathcal{I}_m = [1, 2, \ldots, m]$, expressing the support for the respective classes. The classifier is said to assign a feature vector $\mathbf{x}$ to the class i if $d_i(\mathbf{x}) > d_j(\mathbf{x}), \forall j \neq i, j \in \mathcal{I}_m$. Both a fuzzy classifier and a Bayes classifier are easily represented in this way. The fuzzy rule-based classifier is a popular counter part of a fuzzy control system and a fuzzy modeling [6], which carries out the pattern classification by using the membership grades of the feature variables [7]. There are various fuzzy models to do pattern classification, but the most general is

$$R_i : \text{IF } x_1 \text{ is } A_{i1} \text{ and } \ldots \text{ and } x_n \text{ is } A_{in},$$
$$\text{THEN the class is } i, \quad (1)$$

where $R_i, i \in \mathcal{I}_m$, denotes the ith fuzzy rule, $x_h, h \in \mathcal{I}_n = [1, 2, \ldots, n]$, is the hth feature, and $A_{ih}, (i, h) \in \mathcal{I}_m \times \mathcal{I}_n$, is the fuzzy set. The conjunction rule to transform the fuzzy sets into a discriminant function is $d_i^F(\mathbf{x}) = \mathcal{A}\{A_{i1}(x_1), A_{i2}(x_2), \ldots, A_{in}(x_n)\}$, where $\mathcal{A}$ means a certain combination with inference engines and fuzzifiers. Using the prior probabilities $P(\mathbf{x})$ and the conditional densities $P(\mathbf{x}|w_i)$, especially, the multivariate Gaussian model, the Bayes classifier is designed by the following discriminant function:

$$d_i^B(\mathbf{x}) = \frac{1}{(2\pi)^{\frac{n}{2}}|\Sigma_i|^{\frac{1}{2}}} \exp\left(-\frac{1}{2}(\mathbf{x} - \mathbf{m}_i)^T \Sigma_i^{-1}(\mathbf{x} - \mathbf{m}_i)\right) P(w_i) \quad (2)$$

where $\mathbf{m}_i = [m_{i1}^B, m_{i2}^B, \ldots, m_{in}^B]^T$ is the n-component mean vector, Σ_i is the $n \times n$ covariance matrix, and $|\Sigma_i|$ and Σ_i^{-1} are its determinant and inverse, respectively.

3 A Fuzzy Approach to the Design of a Bayes Classifier

For a given feature vector $\mathbf{x}$, the proposed fuzzy rule-based classifier is formulated in the following form.

$$R_i : \text{IF } x_1 \text{ is } A_{i1} \text{ and } \ldots \text{ and } x_n \text{ is } A_{in},$$
$$\text{THEN } y_i = f_i(\mathbf{x}) \quad (3)$$

where y_i is the output vector of R_i, and $f_i(\mathbf{x})$ is the discriminant function. Here, we equate the number of the classes to the one of the fuzzy rules. In the premise part of (3), the fuzzy set A_{ih} is characterized by the following Gaussian membership function.

$$A_{ih}(x_h) = \exp\left(-\frac{1}{2}\left(\frac{x_h - m_{ih}^F}{\sigma_{ih}^F}\right)^2\right) \quad (4)$$

In the consequent part, the Bayes classifier (2) is selected as $f_i(\mathbf{x})$. To avoid that the covariance matrix is singular, we assume that the covariance matrix Σ_i takes the following diagonal matrix form:

$$\Sigma_i = \begin{bmatrix} (\sigma^B_{i1})^2 & 0 & \cdots & 0 \\ 0 & (\sigma^B_{i2})^2 & \cdots & 0 \\ \vdots & \vdots & \ddots & \vdots \\ 0 & 0 & \cdots & (\sigma^B_{in})^2 \end{bmatrix} \qquad (5)$$

Then, the Bayes classifier (2) can be described by

$$d^B_i(\mathbf{x}) = \frac{1}{(2\pi)^{\frac{n}{2}} \prod_{h=1}^n \sigma^B_{ih}} \exp\left(-\frac{1}{2} \sum_{h=1}^n \left(\frac{x_h - m^B_{ih}}{\sigma^B_{ih}}\right)^2\right) \qquad (6)$$

The unknown parameters m^F_{ih}, m^B_{ih}, σ^F_{ih}, and σ^B_{ih} are initially identified by using the arithmetic average and the standard deviation for the training data. The ith final output of (3) is inferred as follows: $\hat{y}_i(\mathbf{x}) = d^F_i(\mathbf{x}) d^B_i(\mathbf{x})$, where $d^F_i(\mathbf{x}) = \max_{h \in \mathcal{I}_n} A_{ih}(x_h)$ by using the maximum inference engine and the singleton fuzzifier.

We suggest a pruning algorithm based on the analysis of the fuzzy sets for eliminating the irrelevant features for each fuzzy rule. For this purpose, we define the following equations:

$$C(A_{ih}) = \frac{|A_{ih}|_{(x_h \in w_i) \in \mathcal{R}_{ih}}}{|A_{ih}|_{x_h \in w_i}} \qquad (7)$$

$$\bar{C}(A_{ih}) = \frac{1}{n} \sum_{h=1}^n \frac{\sum_{(x_h \in w_i) \in \mathcal{R}_{ih}} A_{ih}(x_h)}{\sum_{x_h \in w_i} A_{ih}(x_h)} \qquad (8)$$

where $|\cdot|$ denotes the cardinality of a set, and $\mathcal{R}_{ih}$ is one-dimensional fuzzy region according to $d^F_i(x_h) > d^F_j(x_h)$ for all $j \neq i$. The proposed pruning algorithm becomes as follows

Step 1. Select the fuzzy rule in the order of large value of (8).
Step 2. Prune any feature of the selected fuzzy rule that result in improving the recognition rate, where the feature is selected in the order of small value of (7).
Step 3. If no feature of the selected fuzzy rule is pruned, stop the algorithm; otherwise, update (7) and then repeat by going to Step 1.

Applying the gradient descent method to tune the parameters σ^F_{ih}, σ^B_{ih}, m^F_{ih}, and m^B_{ih} of (3) leads the following learning rules: for the class i

$$\Delta m^F_{ih} = \alpha_1 (\max_{j \in \mathcal{I}_m, j \neq i} d^F_j(\mathbf{x}) d^B_j(\mathbf{x}) - d^F_i(\mathbf{x}) d^B_i(\mathbf{x}) + \epsilon) d^B_i(\mathbf{x}) \frac{\partial d^F_i(\mathbf{x})}{\partial m^F_{ih}} \qquad (9)$$

$$\Delta \sigma^F_{ih} = \alpha_2 (\max_{j \in \mathcal{I}_m, j \neq i} d^F_j(\mathbf{x}) d^B_j(\mathbf{x}) - d^F_i(\mathbf{x}) d^B_i(\mathbf{x}) + \epsilon) d^B_i(\mathbf{x}) \frac{\partial d^F_i(\mathbf{x})}{\partial \sigma^F_{ih}} \qquad (10)$$

$$\Delta m^B_{ih} = \gamma_1 (\max_{j \in \mathcal{I}_m, j \neq i} d^F_j(\mathbf{x}) d^B_j(\mathbf{x}) - d^F_i(\mathbf{x}) d^B_i(\mathbf{x}) + \epsilon) d^F_i(\mathbf{x}) \frac{\partial d^B_i(\mathbf{x})}{\partial m^B_{ih}} \qquad (11)$$

$$\Delta \sigma^B_{ih} = \gamma_2 (\max_{j \in \mathcal{I}_m, j \neq i} d^F_j(\mathbf{x}) d^B_j(\mathbf{x}) - d^F_i(\mathbf{x}) d^B_i(\mathbf{x}) + \epsilon) d^F_i(\mathbf{x}) \frac{\partial d^B_i(\mathbf{x})}{\partial \sigma^B_{ih}} \qquad (12)$$

and for the class j

$$\Delta m_{jh}^F = -\beta_1(\max_{j \in \mathcal{I}_m, j \neq i} d_j^F(\mathbf{x})d_j^B(\mathbf{x}) - d_i^F(\mathbf{x})d_i^B(\mathbf{x}) + \epsilon)d_j^B(\mathbf{x})\frac{\partial d_j^F(\mathbf{x})}{\partial m_{jh}^F} \tag{13}$$

$$\Delta \sigma_{jh}^F = -\beta_2(\max_{j \in \mathcal{I}_m, j \neq i} d_j^F(\mathbf{x})d_j^B(\mathbf{x}) - d_i^F(\mathbf{x})d_i^B(\mathbf{x}) + \epsilon)d_j^B(\mathbf{x})\frac{\partial d_j^F(\mathbf{x})}{\partial \sigma_{jh}^F} \tag{14}$$

$$\Delta m_{jh}^B = -\delta_1(\max_{j \in \mathcal{I}_m, j \neq i} d_j^F(\mathbf{x})d_j^B(\mathbf{x}) - d_i^F(\mathbf{x})d_i^B(\mathbf{x}) + \epsilon)d_j^F(\mathbf{x})\frac{\partial d_j^B(\mathbf{x})}{\partial m_{jh}^B} \tag{15}$$

$$\Delta \sigma_{jh}^B = -\delta_2(\max_{j \in \mathcal{I}_m, j \neq i} d_j^F(\mathbf{x})d_j^B(\mathbf{x}) - d_i^F(\mathbf{x})d_i^B(\mathbf{x}) + \epsilon)d_j^F(\mathbf{x})\frac{\partial d_j^B(\mathbf{x})}{\partial \sigma_{jh}^B} \tag{16}$$

where α_1, α_2, β_1, β_2, γ_1, γ_2, δ_1, and δ_2 are the learning rates.

4 Conclusions

In this paper, a new fuzzy approach to the design of the Bayes classifier has been developed. This produces better classification performance as well as lower model complexity. In addition, the proposed approach can make up for the weak points of Bayes classifier, which are about the singularity of covariance matrices, the unimodal densities, and the difficulty of feature selection.

References

1. Leski J. M.: An ε-margin nonlinear classifier based on fuzzy if-then rules. IEEE Trans. Syst., Man, Cybern. B. **34** (2004)68-76
2. Paul S. and Kumar S.: Subsethood based adaptive linguistic networks for pattern classification. IEEE Trans. Syst., Man, Cybern. C. **33** (2003) 248-258
3. Chakraborty D. and Pal N. R.: A neuro-fuzzy scheme for simultaneous feature selection and fuzzy rule-based classification. IEEE Trans. Neural Networks **15** (2004)110-123
4. Roubos H. and Setnes M.: Compact transparent fuzzy models and classifiers through iterative complexity reduction. IEEE Trans. Fuzzy Systems **9** (2001) 516- 524
5. Pal N. R. and Chakraborty S.: Fuzzy rule extraction from ID3-type decision trees for real data. IEEE Trans. Syst., Man, Cybern. B. **31** (2001) 745-754.
6. Joo Y. H., Hwang H. S., Kim K. B., and Woo K. B.: Fuzzy system modeling by fuzzy partition and GA hybrid schemes. Fuzzy Set and Syst. **86** (1997) 279-288
7. Duda R. O., Hart P. E., and Stork D. G.: Pattern classification. A wiley-interscience publishing company, inc. (2001)

Identification of T–S Fuzzy Classifier Via Linear Matrix Inequalities

Moon Hwan Kim[1], Jin Bae Park[1], Weon Goo Kim[2], and Young Hoon Joo[2]

[1] Department of Electrical and Electronic Engineering, Yonsei University,
Seodaemun-gu, Seoul 120-749, Korea
{jmacs, jbpark}@control.yonsei.ac.kr.
[2] School of Electronic and Information Engineering, Kunsan National University,
Kunsan, Chonbuk 573-701, Korea
{wgkim, yhjoo}@kunsan.ac.kr.

Abstract. In this paper a new linear matrix inequality (LMI) based design method for T-S fuzzy classifier is proposed. The various design factors including structure of fuzzy rule and various parameters should be considered to design T-S fuzzy classifier. To determine these design factors, we describe a new and efficient two-step approach that leads to good results for classification problem. At first, LMI based fuzzy clustering is applied to obtain compact fuzzy sets in antecedent. Then consequent parameters are optimized by a LMI optimization method.

1 Introduction

Patten classification plays a crucial role in a large number of applications, including printed and handwritten text recognition [1,2,3], speech recognition [4], human face recognition [5].

In this paper, a new design method for T–S fuzzy classifier via LMI optimization is proposed. The proposed method can optimize structure and all parameters in T-S fuzzy classifier within short time. The proposed method can be described in two-step approach. The membership functions and rule structure are determined in the first by using the proposed LMI based fuzzy clustering method. Then parameters in consequent part are determined via LMI optimization method. The LMI based fuzzy clustering can determine the number cluster automatically and optimize membership function in antecedent part.. After clustering, the parameters in linear polynomial in consequent part are identified with predefined membership function in the antecedent part via LMI optimization method.

The organization of this paper is as follows. Section 2 presents the proposed method to identify T-S fuzzy classifier. Then this paper is concluded in Section 3. Simulation results is omitted by page limitation.

2   Identification T–S Fuzzy Classifier Via LMIs

The T–S fuzzy classifier is consist of T–S type fuzzy rules described as the following form [6]:

$$R_i : \text{IF } x_1 \text{ is } A_{i1} \text{ and } \ldots \text{ and } x_n \text{ is } A_{in} \tag{1}$$
$$\text{THEN } y_i(x) = b_{i1}x_1 + \ldots + b_{in}x_n + c_i, i = 1, \ldots, l$$

where $x_i \in \mathbb{R}$ is the ith feature input, $A_{i1}, \ldots, A_{in}$ are the antecedent fuzzy sets, $y_i(x)$ is the consequent output of the ith rule, $x = [x_1, \ldots, x_n]^T \in F \subset \mathbb{R}^n$ is the input feature vector, F is the feature vector set, b_{ij} and c_i are consequent parameters, and l is the number of fuzzy rule. The output of T–S type fuzzy rule system is inferred by following equations:

$$Y(x) = \frac{\sum_{i=1}^{l} \tau_i(x) y_i(x)}{\sum_{i=1}^{l} \tau_i(x)}, \tau_i(x) = \prod_{k=1}^{n} \mu_{A_{ik}}(x_k) \tag{2}$$

where $\tau_i(x)$ is the firing strength of the ith rule and $\mu_{M_{ij}}(x_j) \in \mathbb{R}[0,1]$ is the membership degree of the jth feature of the ith rule. To compute the degrees of class membership for pattern x, a Gaussian membership function is used.

Fuzzy classifier almost always means arriving at a hard classifier because most pattern recognition systems require hard labels for objects being classified. In order to convert soft label $Y(x)$ to hard label $Y_c(x)$, we use following mapping equation,

$$Y_c(x) = \arg_g \min\{|g - Y(x)|\}, g \in \{1, \ldots, n\} \tag{3}$$

where g is the index of the class and n denotes the number of classes

2.1   Design of Antecedent Part Via LMI Based Fuzzy Clustering

In the proposed clustering method, the number of cluster becomes the number of fuzzy rule and the membership functions in each rule are treated as fuzzy cluster function. This clustering method represents membership degree of cluster as output of firing strength instead of simple fuzzy set.

Consider a finite set of input features $X = \{x^1, x^2, \ldots, x^{N_d}\}, \forall x^k \in F$ as being classification data. N_d means the number of whole data. The problem is to perform a partition of this collection of elements as N_c fuzzy cluster. N_c is a given number of cluster. The end result of LMI based fuzzy clustering can be expressed by as partition matrix $U = [u_{ij}]_{i=1,\ldots,N_c, j=1,\ldots,N_d}$. In addition, we need cluster additional membership matrix $W = [w_{ij}]_{i=1,\ldots,N_c, j=1,\ldots,N_d}$ to determine partition of data. After membership matrix is calculated, the partition matrix is updated by using membership degree

$$u_{ik} = 1, i = 1, 2, \ldots, N_c, \ k = \arg_j \max_{\forall j \in C_i, \sum_{h=1}^{N_c} u_{hj} = 0} w_{ij} \tag{4}$$

where C_i is the set of data belongs to class of the ith cluster.

When partition matrix is updated, the width and center of membership function is updated via LMI optimization method. The center m_k^i is simply update by averaging x_k^j belongs the ith cluster. updating widths can be denoted as identifying membership function satisfying following two constraints,

$$e^{-(e^k)^T V_i(e^k)} = 1, \text{ if } x^k \in C_i, \quad e^{-(e^k)^T V_i(e^k)} = 0, \text{ if } x^k \notin C_i \tag{5}$$

where $V_i = \mathrm{diag}\left(\frac{1}{v_1^i}, \ldots, \frac{1}{v_n^i}\right)$ is the diagonal matrix containing the widthes of the Gaussian membership functions of the ith cluster, and $c_i = [c_1^i, \ldots, c_n^i]$ represents center values of the membership function of the ith cluster. $e^k = (x^k - c_i$ is the error between input and center values.

Theorem 1. *If element x^k belongs to C_i is is given, widths V_i of membership functions of the i th cluster for T–S fuzzy classifier (2) is determined by solving the following GEVPs,*

$$\underset{V_i}{\text{Minimize}} \quad \gamma \quad \text{subject to}$$

$$V_i > 0 \tag{6}$$

$$\begin{bmatrix} \gamma & \star \\ (e^k)^T V_i(e^k) & \gamma \end{bmatrix} > 0, \quad x^k \in C_i \tag{7}$$

$$\begin{bmatrix} \gamma(e^k)^T V_i(e^k) & \star \\ 1 & \gamma \end{bmatrix} > 0, \quad x^k \notin C_i \tag{8}$$

where $\star$ denotes the transposed element matrix for the symmetric position.

Proof. The proof is omitted due to page limitation.

Theorem 1 represents GVEP for ith cluster to identify width of membership functions. After update width of membership function, the distances between clusters are calculated. When distance is short, the two cluster are merged to one cluster. The clustering is iterated until the cluster number and membership function will not change. The detailed cluster merging method and stopping criterion is omitted by page limitation.

2.2 Design of Consequent Part Via LMI

After parameters of membership functions in the antecedent part is determined, the consequent parameters should be identified. For the computational convenience, $Y(x)$ can also be represented as following matrix form,

$$Y(x) = D^T(Bx + C) \tag{9}$$

where $D = [\frac{\tau_1(x)}{\sum_{j=1}^l \tau_j(x)} \cdots \frac{\tau_l(x)}{\sum_{j=1}^l \tau_j(x)}]$ is normalized firing strength. B and C is the consequent parameter matrix. Assume that the parameters of antecedent is completely determined. With Given D and x we could formulated following key equation,

$$Y_d = D^T(Bx + C), \quad \forall x \in F \tag{10}$$

where Y_d is desired output of the class and is determined as one of index of class. Finally, by finding B and C satisfying (10), we could get desired output $Y(x)$. Notice that (10) can be converted LMI optimization problem directly. Theorem 2 shows the GEVP for determining B and C in the consequent part.

Theorem 2. *If x, Y_d, and D are given, B and C of the proposed T–S fuzzy classifier are determined by solving the following GEVP*

$$\underset{B,C}{Minimize} \quad \gamma \quad subject\ to$$

$$\begin{bmatrix} \gamma & \star \\ Y_d - D^T(Bx + C) & \gamma \end{bmatrix} > 0, \quad \forall x \in F. \tag{11}$$

Proof. The proof is omitted due to lack of space.

3 Conclusions

This paper proposes the new linear matrix approach to design T-S fuzzy classifier. Two step design procedure is given to identify T-S fuzzy classifier. First step, the structure and membership function of fuzzy classifier are identified via the proposed LMI based fuzzy clustering method. The consequent parameters is then identified via LMI optimization method.

References

1. Chen M., Kundu A., Zhou J.: Off-line handwritten word recognition using a hidden Markov model type stochastic network. IEEE Trans. Pattern Anal. Mach. Intel. **16** (1994) 481–496.
2. Cohen E.: Computational theory for interpreting handwritten text in constrained domains. Artif. Intell. **67** (1994) 1–31.
3. Partizeau M., Plamondon R.: A fuzzy-syntactic approach to allograph modeling for cursive script recognition. IEEE Trans. Pattern Anal. Mach. Intel. **17** (1995) 702–712.
4. Bourlard H., Morgan N.: Connectionist Speech Recognition-A Hybrid Approach. Boston. MA: Kluwer Academic (1994).
5. Lam K. M., Yan H.: Locating and extracting the eye in human face images. Pattern Recog. **29** (1996) 771–779.
6. Setnes M. and Roubos H.: GA-fuzzy modeling and classification: complexity and performance. IEEE Trans. Fuzzy Syst. **8** (2000) 509–522. raction. Inf.

An Adaptive Fuzzy c-Means Algorithm with the L_2 Norm

Nicomedes L. Cavalcanti Júnior and Francisco de A.T. de Carvalho

Centro de Informática - CIn / UFPE, Av. Prof. Luiz Freire, s/n,
Cidade Universitária, CEP: 50740-540, Recife-PE, Brasil
{fatc, nlcj}@cin.ufpe.br

Abstract. An extension of the fuzzy c-means clustering algorithm based on an adaptive distance is presented. The proposed method furnishes a fuzzy partition and a prototype for each cluster by optimizing a criterion based on an adaptive L_2 distance that changes at each algorithm iteration. Experiments with real and synthetic data sets show the usefulness of this method.

1 Introduction

Cluster analysis seeks to organize a set of items into clusters such that items within a given cluster have a high degree of similarity, whereas items belonging to different clusters have a high degree of dissimilarity [1] . Cluster analysis techniques can be divided into hierarchical and partitional methods [2]. Partitioning a set of data points into a predefined number of clusters is an important topic in data analysis, pattern recognition and image processing [1].

This paper presents an extension of the fuzzy c-means clustering algorithm based on an adaptive L_2 distance. Section 2 introduces an adaptive version of the fuzzy c-means clustering algorithm based on the L_2 Minkowsky distance. Sections 3 and 4 show the usefulness of the method in experiments with real and synthetic data sets. Section 5 gives the concluding remarks.

2 Fuzzy c-Means Clustering Algorithm Based on an Adaptive L_2 Minkowsky Distance

This section presents an adpation of the fuzzy c-means clustering [3] method for quantitative data based on an adaptive L_2 Minkowsky distance. The main idea is that there is a different distance associated to each cluster to compare clusters and their representatives that changes at each iteration with this the clustering algorithm is able to find clusters of different shapes and sizes [4].

This adaptive method looks for a fuzzy partition of a set of patterns in c clusters $\{P_1, \ldots, P_c\}$, the corresponding c prototypes $\{\mathbf{g}_1, \ldots, \mathbf{g}_c\}$ and the square of an adaptive L_2 Minkowsky distance which is different for each class such that a criterion J measuring the fitting between the clusters and their representatives (prototypes) is locally minimized. The criterion J is defined as:

$$J = \sum_{k=1}^{n}\sum_{i=1}^{c}(u_{ik})^m \psi_i(\mathbf{x}_k, \mathbf{g}_i) = \sum_{k=1}^{n}\sum_{i=1}^{c}(u_{ik})^m \sum_{j=1}^{p} \lambda_i^j (x_k^j - g_i^j)^2 \quad (1)$$

where $\psi_i(\mathbf{x}_k, \mathbf{g}_i)$ is the square of an adaptive L_2 Minkowsky distance defined for each class and parameterized by the vectors of weights $\boldsymbol{\lambda}_i = (\lambda_i^1, \ldots, \lambda_i^p)(i = 1, \ldots, c)$. This distance measures the dissimilarity between a pair of vectors of quantitative feature values, $\mathbf{x}_k = (x_k^1, \ldots, x_k^p)$ is the quantitative feature vector describing the kth pattern, $\mathbf{g}_i = (g_i^1, \ldots, g_i^p)$ is the prototype of class P_i, u_{ik} is the membership degree of pattern k in cluster P_i and $m \in]1, +\infty[$ is a parameter that controls the fuzziness of membership for each pattern k.

The algorithm starts from an initial membership degree for each pattern k in each cluster P_i and alternates a representation step and an allocation step until the criterion J reaches a stationary value representing a local minimum.

The representation step has two stages. In the first stage, u_{ik} and $\boldsymbol{\lambda}_i = (\lambda_i^1, \ldots, \lambda_i^p)(i = 1, \ldots, c)$ are fixed and the prototypes $\mathbf{g}_i$ of class $P_i (i = 1, \ldots, c)$, minimizing the criterion J, are updated as follows [3]:

$$g_i^j = \frac{\sum_{k=1}^{n}(u_{ik})^m x_k^j}{\sum_{k=1}^{n}(u_{ik})^m}, j = 1, \ldots, p \quad (2)$$

In the second stage, u_{ik} and $\mathbf{g}_i$ of class $P_i (i = 1, \ldots, c)$ are fixed and the vectors of weights $\boldsymbol{\lambda}_i$, minimizing the criterion J under $\lambda_i^j > 0$ and $\prod_{j=1}^{p} \lambda_i^j = 1$, are updated as follows:

$$\lambda_i^j = \frac{\{\prod_{h=1}^{p} [\sum_{k=1}^{n}(u_{ik})^m (x_k^h - g_i^h)^2]\}}{[\sum_{k=1}^{n}(u_{ik})^m (x_k^j - g_i^j)^2]} \quad (3)$$

In the allocation step, $\mathbf{g}_i$ of class $P_i (i = 1, \ldots, c)$ and $\boldsymbol{\lambda}_i$ are fixed and the membership degree $u_{ik} (k = 1, \ldots, n)$ of each pattern k in each cluster P_i, minimizing the criterion J under $u_{ik} > 0$ and $\sum_{i=1}^{c} u_{ik} = 1$, is updated as follows:

$$u_{ik} = \left[\sum_{h=1}^{c} \left\{ \frac{\sum_{j=1}^{p} \lambda_i^j (x_k^j - g_i^j)^2}{\sum_{j=1}^{p} \lambda_h^j (x_h^j - g_h^j)^2} \right\}^{\frac{1}{m-1}} \right]^{-1} \quad (4)$$

3 Experiments

To show the usefulness of these methods, an image segmentation data set (available at the UCI Repository [5]) and synthetic quantitative data sets in $\mathbb{R}^2$ are considered.

The image data set consists of images that were drawn randomly from a database of 7 outdoor images. This data set presents the following class labels: sky, cement, window, brick, grass, foliage and path. Each class has 330 examples that are represented by 16 real valued attributes.

The synthetic data sets has each four classes, which present different sizes and shapes. Classes 1 and 2 have 150 data points, Class 3 has 50 and Class 4 100. These data were drawn according to a bi-variate normal distribution with vector μ and covariance matrix $\sum$ represented by:

$$\mu = \begin{bmatrix} \mu_1 \\ \mu_2 \end{bmatrix} \text{ and } \sum = \begin{bmatrix} \sigma_1^2 & \rho\sigma_1\sigma_2 \\ \rho\sigma_1\sigma_2 & \sigma_2^2 \end{bmatrix}$$

Data-set 1 were drawn according to the following parameters:

a) Class 1: $\mu_1 = 5$, $\mu_2 = 250$, $\sigma_1^2 = 25$, $\sigma_2^2 = 900$, $\rho = 0.7$;
b) Class 2: $\mu_1 = 35$, $\mu_2 = 320$, $\sigma_1^2 = 25$, $\sigma_2^2 = 900$, $\rho = 0.8$;
c) Class 3: $\mu_1 = 25$, $\mu_2 = 200$, $\sigma_1^2 = 25$, $\sigma_2^2 = 25$, $\rho = -0.7$;
d) Class 4: $\mu_1 = 5$, $\mu_2 = 400$, $\sigma_1^2 = 25$, $\sigma_2^2 = 25$, $\rho = -0.8$.

Data-set 2 were drawn according to the following parameters:

a) Class 1: $\mu_1 = 5$, $\mu_2 = 250$, $\sigma_1^2 = 25$, $\sigma_2^2 = 900$, $\rho = 0.7$;
b) Class 2: $\mu_1 = 25$, $\mu_2 = 320$, $\sigma_1^2 = 25$, $\sigma_2^2 = 900$, $\rho = 0.8$;
c) Class 3: $\mu_1 = 25$, $\mu_2 = 250$, $\sigma_1^2 = 25$, $\sigma_2^2 = 25$, $\rho = -0.7$;
d) Class 4: $\mu_1 = 10$, $\mu_2 = 350$, $\sigma_1^2 = 25$, $\sigma_2^2 = 25$, $\rho = -0.8$.

The normalized Dunn's partition coefficient (DC) and the corrected Rand index (CR) will be considered in order to compare the results of the algorithm proposed in the present paper and the ones of the fuzzy c-means algorithm.

The DC measure how hard is a fuzzy partition [6], when each object has equal memberships in all clusters we have complete fuzziness. The CR index measures the similarity between the a priori hard partition and a hard partition obtained from the fuzzy partition [7]. A CR value ranges from 1 to -1, value 1 indicates perfect agreement between partitions.

For the synthetic data sets, the average of DC and CR indices are estimated in the framework of a Monte Carlo experience with 60 replications for each data set. In each replication a clustering method is run 60 times and the best result, according to the corresponding adequacy criterion is selected. Throughout these experiments parameter m has been set equal 2.

4 Results

Concerning the image segmentation data set, the CR indices were 0.31 and 0.49 for the non-adaptive method (NAM, standard fuzzy c-means) and adaptive method (AM), respectively. The DC indices for the non-adaptive method and for the adaptive method were 0.29 and 0.59, respectively.

Table 1 shows the results for data sets 1 and 2. The suitable hypothesis as well as the observed values for independent Students' t-tests at a 1% significance level are shown. In this Table, μ_1 and μ_2 are the mean of the CR index for the NAM and for the AM, respectively, and μ_3 and μ_4 are the mean of the DC index for the NAM and for the AM, respectively.

It can be observed that the averge CR indices is greater for AM than for NAM meaning that AM correctly classified more patterns than NAM. The average DC indices for AM indicates that it recognized the separation degree on data.

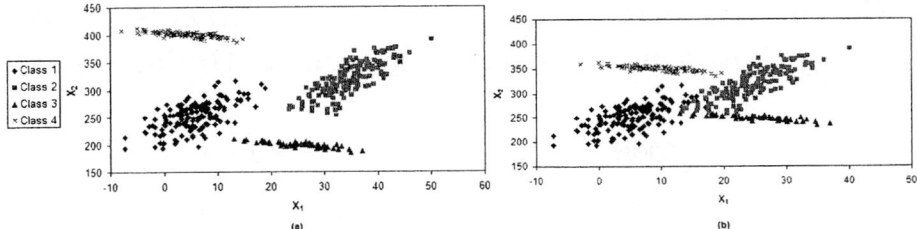

Fig. 1. (a) Data-set 1 showing well-separated classes (b) Data-set 2 showing overlapping classes

Table 1. Comparison of NAM and AM according to CR and DC

Configuration	CR				DC			
	NAM	AM	Test $H_0 : \mu_2 \leq \mu_1$ $H_1 : \mu_2 > \mu_1$	Decision	NAM	AM	Test $H_0 : \mu_4 \leq \mu_3$ $H_1 : \mu_4 > \mu_3$	Decision
Well-separated	0.602	0.909	141.47	Reject	0.715	0.790	89.86	Reject
Overlapping	0.367	0.713	94.95	Reject	0.658	0.421	-284.99	Accept

5 Conclusion

In this paper, an extension of the fuzzy c-means algorithm based on an adaptive L_2 distance was presented. The accuracy of the results furnished by this clustering method is assessed by an external index and compared with the results furnished by the standard fuzzy c-means algorithm. Statistical tests support the evidence that the adaptive method outperforms the non-adaptive method.

Acknowledgments. The authors thank CNPq for its financial support.

References

1. Jain, A.K., Murty, M.N. and Flynn, P.J. Data Clustering: A Review. ACM Computing Surveys, 31, (3), 264-323, 1999
2. Everitt, B. 2001. Cluster Analysis. Halsted, New York.
3. Bezdek, J. C..: Pattern recognition with fuzzy objective function algorithms. Plenum Press, New York, 1981
4. Diday, E. and Govaert, G.: Classification Automatique avec Distances Adaptatives. R.A.I.R.O. Informatique Computer Science, **11** (4) (1977) 329–349
5. Blake, C. L., Merz, C. J.: UCI Repository of machine learning databases [http://www.ics.uci.edu/ mlearn/MLRepository.html]. Irvine, CA: University of California, Department of Information and Computer Science, 1998
6. Dunn, J. C.: Indices of partition fuzziness and the detection of clusters in large data sets, in Fuzzy Automata and Decision Process, edited by M. Gupta, Elsevier, New York, 1976
7. Hubert. L. and Arabie.: Comparing Partitions. Journal of Classification, 2, 193-218, 1985

Design of Information Granules-Based Fuzzy Systems Using Clustering Algorithm and Genetic Optimization

Sung-Kwun Oh[1], Keon-Jun Park[1], Witold Pedrycz[2], and Tae-Chon Ahn[3]

[1] Department of Electrical Engineering, University of Suwon, San 2-2 Wau-ri,
Bongdam-eup, Hwaseong-si, Gyeonggi-do, 445-743, South Korea
ohsk@suwon.ac.kr
[2] Department of Electrical and Computer Engineering, University of Alberta,
Edmonton, AB T6G 2G6, Canada and Systems Research Institute,
Polish Academy of Sciences, Warsaw, Poland
[3] Department of Electrical Electronic and Information Engineering, Wonkwang University,
344-2, Shinyong-Dong, Iksan, Chon-Buk, 570-749, South Korea

Abstract. We introduce information granulation-based fuzzy systems to carry out the model identification of complex and nonlinear systems. The proposed fuzzy model implements system structure and parameter identification with the aid of genetic algorithms (GAs) and information granulation (IG). The design methodology emerges as a hybrid structural optimization and parametric optimization. IG realized with Hard C-Means (HCM) clustering help determine the initial parameters of fuzzy. And the initial parameters are tuned effectively with the aid of the GAs and the least square method (LSM). And we use GAs to identify the structure of fuzzy rules.

1 Introduction

Fuzzy modeling has been studied to deal with complex, ill-defined, and uncertain systems in many other avenues. Linguistic modeling [1] and fuzzy relation equation-based approach [2] were proposed as primordial identification methods for fuzzy models. The general class of Sugeno-Takagi models [3] gave rise to more sophisticated rule-based systems. While appealing with respect to the basic, these models still await formal solutions as far as the structure optimization of the model is concerned, say a construction of the underlying fuzzy sets—information granules being viewed as basic building blocks of any fuzzy model. Some enhancements to the model have been proposed by Oh and Pedrycz [4], yet the problem of finding "good" initial parameters of the fuzzy sets in the rules remains open.

This study concentrates on the central problem of fuzzy modeling that is a development of IG. We propose to cast the problem in the setting of clustering techniques and GAs.

2 Information Granulation Realized with Clustering Algorithm

Roughly speaking, information granules [5] are viewed as related collections of objects drawn together by the criteria of proximity, similarity, or functionality. Granulation of information is aimed at transforming the problem at hand into several smaller and therefore manageable tasks. We partition this problem into a series of well-defined subproblems of a far lower computational.

It is worth emphasizing that the HCM [6] clustering has been used extensively not only to organize and categorize data, but it becomes useful in model identification.

3 Design of Information Granules-Based Fuzzy Systems

The identification of the premise part is completed in the following manner.

Given is a set of data $U=\{x_1, x_2, \ldots, x_l ; y\}$, where $x_k =[x_{1k}, \ldots, x_{mk}]^T$, $y =[y_1, \ldots, y_m]^T$, l is the number of variables and , m is the number of data.

[Step 1] Arrange a set of data U into data set X_k.

$$X_k=[x_k ; y] \qquad (1)$$

[Step 2] Complete the HCM clustering to determine the centers v_{kg} with data set X_k.

$$v_{kg} = \{v_{k1}, v_{k2}, \ldots, v_{kc}\} \qquad (2)$$

[Step 3] Partition the corresponding input space using the prototypes of the clusters v_{kg}.

[Step 4] Set the initial apexes of the membership functions using the prototypes v_{kg}.

We identify the structure considering the initial values of polynomial functions based upon the information granulation realized for the consequence parts.

[Step 1] Find a set of data included in the fuzzy space of the j-th rule.

[Step 2] Compute the prototypes V_j of the data set by taking the arithmetic.

$$V_j = \{V_{1j}, V_{2j}, \ldots, V_{kj}; M_j\} \qquad (3)$$

Where, V_{kj} and M_j are prototypes of input and output data, respectively.

[Step 3] Set the initial values of polynomial functions with the center vectors V_j.

4 Optimization of IG-Based FIS

Genetic algorithms [7] are useful in a global optimization of such problems given their ability to efficiently use historical information to produce new improved solutions with enhanced performance.

To identify the fuzzy model we determine such an initial structure as the number of membership functions standing in premise part and the order of polynomial (Type) in conclusion. The membership parameters of the premise are genetically optimized.

5 Experimental Study

This section includes comprehensive numeric study illustrating the design of the proposed fuzzy model. We consider a nonlinear static system.

$$y = (1 + x_1^{-2} + x_2^{-1.5})^2, \quad 1 \leq x_1, x_2 \leq 5 \tag{4}$$

To evaluate the performance index, we use the standard MSE. We carried out the structure identification on a basis of the experimental data using GAs to design Max_Min-based and IG-based fuzzy model. The number of membership functions assigned to each input of Max_Min-based and IG-based fuzzy model were set up to be 3. At the conclusion part, both models come with the consequence of type 3. Table 1 summarizes the performance index. It is clear that the performance of IG-based fuzzy model is better than that of Max_Min-based fuzzy model. Figure 1 depicts the values of the performance index produced in successive generation of the genetic optimization. We note that the performance of the IG-based fuzzy model is good starting from some initial generations.

Table 1. Performance index of Max_Min-based and IG-based fuzzy model

Model	Identification	No. Of MFs	Type	PI
Max/Min_FIS	Structure	3x3	Type 3	0.014
	Parameters			$3.854e^{-20}$
IG_FIS	Structure	3x3	Type 3	$8.360e^{-22}$
	Parameters			$3.885e^{-26}$

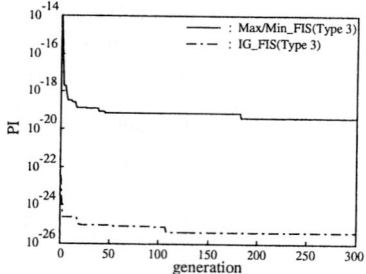

Fig. 1. Optimal convergence process of performance index

Table 2. Comparison of identification error with previous models

Model		No. of rules	PI
Sugeno and Yasukawa[8]		6	0.079
Gomez-Skarmeta et al[9]		5	0.070
Kim et al.[10]		3	0.019
Kim et al.[11]		3	0.0089
Oh et al.[12]	Basic PNN		0.0212
	Modified PNN		0.0041
Park et al.[13]	BFPNN	9	0.0033
	MFPNN	9	0.0023
Our Model		9	$3.885e^{-26}$

The identification error of the proposed model is also compared to the performance of some other models; refer to Table 2. As we know from Table 2, the performance results of the proposed model are quite satisfactory.

6 Conclusions

We have introduced a comprehensive identification framework for fuzzy systems based on information granules using clustering algorithm and genetic optimization in this paper. We used the input space for input variables and defined the fuzzy space by information granule. IG based on HCM clustering helps determine the initial parameters of fuzzy model such as the initial apexes of the membership functions and the initial values of polynomial function being used in the premise and consequence part of the fuzzy rules. The experimental study showed that the model is compact, and its performance is better than some other previous models.

Acknowledgements. This work has been supported by KESRI(R-2004-B-133-01), which is funded by MOCIE(Ministry of commerce, industry and energy).

References

1. Tong, R.M.: Synthesis of fuzzy models for industrial processes. Int. J Gen Syst. **4** (1978) 143-162
2. Pedrycz, W.: Numerical and application aspects of fuzzy relational equations. Fuzzy Sets Syst. **11** (1983) 1-18
3. Takagi, T., Sugeno, M.: Fuzzy identification of systems and its applications to modeling and control. IEEE Trans Syst, Cybern. SMC-**15**(1) (1985) 116-132
4. Oh, S.K., Pedrycz, W.: Identification of fuzzy systems by means of an auto-tuning algorithm and its application to nonlinear systems. Fuzzy Sets and Syst. **115**(2) (2000) 205-230
5. Pderycz, W., Vukovich, G.: Granular neural networks. Neurocomputing. **36** (2001) 205-224
6. Krishnaiah, P.R., Kanal, L.N., editors.: Classification, pattern recognition, and reduction of dimensionality, volume 2 of Handbook of Statistics. North-Holland Amsterdam (1982)
7. Golderg, D.E.: Genetic Algorithm in search, Optimization & Machine Learning, Addison Wesley (1989)
8. Sugeno, M., Yasukawa, T.: A Fuzzy-Logic-Based Approach to Qualitative Modeling. IEEE Trans. on Fuzzy systems. **1**(1) (1993) 7-13
9. Gomez Skarmeta, A. F., Delgado, M., Vila, M. A.: About the use of fuzzy clustering techniques for fuzzy model identification. Fuzzy Sets and Systems. **106** (1999) 179-188
10. Kim, E. T., Park, M. K., Ji, S. H., Park, M. N.: A new approach to fuzzy modeling. IEEE Trans. on Fuzzy systems. **5**(3) (1997) 328-337
11. Kim, E. T, Lee, H. J., Park, M. K., Park, M. N.: a simply identified Sugeno-type fuzzy model via double clustering. Information Sciences. **110** (1998) 25-39
12. Oh, S. K., Pedrycz, W., Park, B. J.: Polynomial Neural Networks Architecture: Analysis and Design. Computers and Electrical Engineering. **29**(6) (2003) 703-725
13. Park, B. J., Pedrycz, W., Oh, S. K.: Fuzzy Polynomial Neural Networks: Hybrid Architectures of Fuzzy Modeling. IEEE Trans. on Fuzzy Systems. **10**(5) (2002) 607-621
14. Ho-Sung Park and Sung-Kwun Oh: Rule-based Fuzzy-Neural Networks Using the Identification Algorithm of the GA Hybrid Scheme. International journal of Control, Automations, and Systems. **1**(1) (2003) 101-110

A Personalized Recommendation System for Electronic Program Guide

Jin An Xu and Kenji Araki

Graduate School of Information Science and Technology,
Hokkaido University,
Kita 14 Nishi 9, Kita-ku, Sapporo, 060-0814 Japan
Phone &. Fax: +81-11-706-7389
{xja, araki}@media.eng.hokudai.ac.jp

Abstract. This paper proposes an idea for constructing a personalized recommendation system for the Electronic Program Guide (EPG). This system would use a basic statistics method with feedback process to predict television programs. We have applied this method to personal prediction of online Internet Electronic Program Guide (IEPG). The system was found to have good accuracy and dynamically adaptive capability.

1 Introduction

With the rapid development of digital television, the digital broadcasting provides a more efficient way to deliver television than analogue transmissions. A multiplex can then be broadcast via a channel. This means that on a channel which would have carried only one program using analogue technology, it is now possible to broadcast six to eight programs for digital broadcasting. With the increasing number of channels being offered, one problem of digital broadcasting is how to offer a convenient and intelligent user interface. It becomes troublesome to select our favorite TV programs by hand, even though we can use EPG navigation systems or other applications.

In related works, some learning theories were used to architect personal recommendation system [1,2,3,4]. In our previous work, an approach using Inductive Learning with N-gram to predict user's habits and preferences, showed good dynamically adaptive capability in small data sets [5].

In this paper, we propose an approach with term extraction method for constructing a personal recommendation system for EPG. The idea is based on a primitive approach of the term extraction method, according to statistical analysis among a compound noun and its components picked up from the history of each user's watched programs, and then to unified feedback process. The objective is to develop a good intelligent user interface between each TV fan and his/her digital television.

This paper includes three sections as follows: Presentation of our system architecture, evaluation of the performance of the present system and a summary of this work.

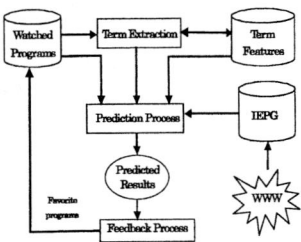

Fig. 1. Outline of the Procedure

2 Outline

The outline of our system consists of term extraction, prediction, feedback and IEPG extraction process, as shown in Figure 1.

Our idea of term extraction is to use bigrams. It is based on the algorithm of Nakagawa [6] et al., which considered both the score using simple noun bigrams as components of compound nouns to calculate score of compound nouns, and the nouns independent frequency to calculate the score of each extracted term. For more details see [6]. Here, we only focus on nouns (single-nouns and compound nouns) and unknown words to acquire the term features.

The IEPG was extracted to XML format from Internet using XMLTV module [7]. IEPG data vector consists of start time, stop time, channel, title, description, Japanese category, English category and so on. In our system, we changed some contents of IEPG, such as time, day of week, channel names and so on.

In feedback process, we have taken into account two factors that cause the dynamics of personalization. The first step is to split the history of user watched programs by time to generate two terms vectors. For prediction of the user's favorite programs, a simple vector space modification model is used as a feedback method as $H^{'} = H_{new} + \gamma \cdot H_{old}$,where, $H^{'}$ is the extracted terms vector for prediction, H_{old} means the extracted terms vector from user watched programs before two weeks ago. H_{new} means the extracted terms vector from the latest user watched programs of two weeks. γ is a coefficient. The second step is to create some tasks for each category according to user watched programs, elements of tasks are start time (including day of week), channel, title, Japanese category, English category and watched frequency. These tasks are extracted from the user watched programs and the frequency is acquired from user watched programs. We use these frequencies, to re-order the acquired categories for improving prediction precision.

The basic idea of prediction is to use extracted terms to evaluate each new TV program. The terms are extracted from watched programs according to the Concurrent Versions System (CVS) of Japanese TV programs. There are 14 categories in IEPG. Using these categories, we can acquire extracted terms of each category. In prediction, using the inner product method between the acquired

Table 1. The Data Size of Each Week

Weeks	1	2	3	4	5	6	7	8	9	10	11	12
Data Num. (A)	30	28	30	27	30	28	28	30	26	28	27	28
Data Num. (B)	32	30	28	32	30	31	28	32	30	28	29	28
Data Num. (C)	28	32	30	30	28	32	30	32	32	30	28	28
Data Num. (D)	36	34	38	36	36	36	38	32	40	36	36	40

terms and the new programs, the credibility of each new program is calculated with the importance of each term. We use the logarithm of accumulation value of all matched terms as the credibility, and then, normalize these measures. We can give some threshold to control the number of recommendations.

3 Experimental Results

As mentioned above, the system based on our proposed approach was developed for experimentation to investigate its validity. In our experiments, we use open data to test the performance of our system. We adopted periodic training to our system. The training data is incremented on weekly basis.

Our experiment datasets were collected based on daily life of four graduate students of engineering over a period of about three months and the total number of data was 1,486. The data size of every week is shown in Table 1. The value of γ was given 0.5, the optimizing value γ will be investigated in future experiments. In order to keep the starting state constant for each user, the file of watched programs and the term features always started from an empty initial state.

We just use rank 10 of predicted results to evaluate precision per day because time used by everyone to watch TV is limited, and TV watchers will judge the prediction results. Figure 2 shows weekly precision of our proposed method.

As a comparison, we performed other experiments, without the feedback method. As reference work, other experiments were performed using a keyword input type TV recorder, named a TV channel server, which is produced by M corporation (Japan).

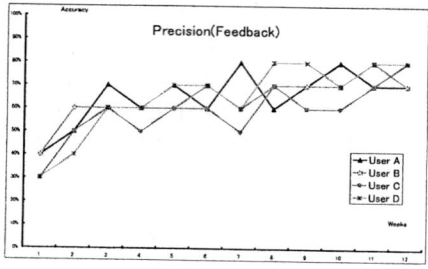

Fig. 2. Precision of Term Extraction with Feedback

In Figure 2 we plot the performance of our proposed method. It is indicated that the average precision is about 65.0% (User A), 64.2% (User B), 58.3% (User C) and 65.0% (User D). With the results of our comparison experiments, the accuracy was improved about 7.0% for both user A and B, 7.5% for user D, and improves by 3.3% for user C, than the method of without feedback.

The average precision of M corporation's TV channel server is about 46.1% (User A), 32.3% (User B), 44.9% (User C) and 40.0% (User D). Comparatively, our proposed method is more effective.

4 Conclusions and Future Work

In this paper, an approach for predicting users' favorite TV programs is described. The system has proven to have better performance than the conventional keyword input method. The system can provide simpler user interface with enhanced functions to TV watchers because they just need to select the recommendation programs rather than to consider any keywords for selection.

Our goal is to develop a personalized system of TV program recommendations with adaptive capability. We will try to test the performance and put our system to practical use for a computer or a digital television.

Experiments on a large scale including languages other than Japanese will be done in the near future to further verify the accuracy of the present system based on term extraction method. Other algorithms, such as reinforcement learning, SVM and neural networks will also be used for comparison.

References

1. Anna B., John Z., and Kaushal K, Improving Ease-of-Use, Trust and Accuracy of a TV show Recommender. *Proc. of 2nd International Conf. on Adaptive Hypermedia and Adaptive Web Based Systems: Workshop on Personalization in Future TV (AH)*, Universidad de Malaga, Spain, 2002, 1-10.
2. L. Ardissono, C. Gena, P. Torasso, F. Bellifemine, A. Chiarotto, A. Difino, B. Negro, Personalized Recommendation of TV Programs. *Lecture Notes in Artificial Intelligence. AI*IA 2003: Advances in Artificial Intelligence*, Pisa, Italy, 2003, 474-486.
3. P. Johansson, Natural language interaction in personalized EPGs. *Proc. of Workshop notes from the 3rd International Workshop on Personalization of Future TV*, Johnstown, Pennsylvania, USA, 2003, 27-31.
4. M. van Setten, M. Veenstra, A. Nijholt, Prediction strategies: Combining prediction techniques to optimize personalization. *Proc. of TV-02: 2nd Workshop on Personalisation in Future TV*, Location Malaga, Spain, 2002, 29-37.
5. J. Xu, T. Itoh and K. Araki, Action Prediction Method Using Recursive Different and Common Parts Extraction Method with N-gram. *Journal of Human Interface Society, Vol.7,No.1,Japan*, 2005, 55-68.
6. Nakagawa H., Mori T., A Simple but Powerful Automatic Term Extraction Method. *Proc.of 2nd International Workshop on Computational Terminology, COLING-2002 WORKSHOP*, Taipei, 2002, 29-35.
7. http://membled.com/work/apps/xmltv/.

An Effective Recommendation Algorithm for Clustering-Based Recommender Systems

Taek-Hun Kim and Sung-Bong Yang

Dept. of Computer Science, Yonsei University,
134 Shinchon-dong, Seadaemun-gu, Seoul, 120-749, Korea
{kimthun, yang}@cs.yonsei.ac.kr

Abstract. In this paper we present an effective recommendation algorithm using a refined neighbor selection and attributes information on the goods. The proposed algorithm exploits the transitivity of similarities using a graph approach. The algorithm also utilizes the attributes of the items. The experiment results show that the recommendation system with the proposed algorithm outperforms other systems and it can also overcome the very large-scale dataset problem without deteriorating prediction quality.

1 Introduction

A recommender system using collaborative filtering which we call it CF, calculates the similarity between the test customer and each of other customers who have rated the items that are already rated by the test customer. Since CF is based on the ratings of the neighbors who have similar preferences, it is very important to select the neighbors properly to improve prediction quality.

With millions of customers and items, a recommender system running on an existing algorithm will suffer seriously the scalability problem. Therefore, there are demands for a new approach that can quickly produce high quality predictions and can resolve the very large-scale problem. Clustering techniques often lead to worse prediction accuracy than other methods. Once clustering is done, however, performance can be quite good, since the size of a cluster that must be analyzed is much smaller. Therefore, the clustering-based method can solve the very large-scale problem in recommender systems[2][3][4].

2 The Clustering-Based CF

In CF, $p_{a,i}$ is used to predict the preference of a customer and computed with Equation (1) in [4]. In the Equation $w_{a,k}$ is the Pearson correlation coefficient which can be computed with Equation (2) in [4].

The k-means clustering method creates k clusters each of which consists of the customers who have similar preferences among themselves. In this method we first select k customers arbitrarily as the initial center points of the k clusters, respectively. Then each customer is assigned to a cluster in such a way that the distance between the customer and the center of a cluster is maximized. The Pearson correlation coefficient can be used as the distance.

If the clustering process is terminated, we choose the cluster with the highest Pearson correlation coefficient from its center to the test customer. Finally, prediction for the test customer is calculated with all the customers in the chosen cluster. The clustering-based neighbor selection method can give a recommendation quickly to the customer when the dataset is quite large, because it selects customers only from the best cluster only as the neighbors[3].

3 The Proposed Recommendation Algorithm

We propose an effective recommendation algorithm for clustering-based recommender systems. It uses a refined neighbor selection algorithm(RNSA) that considers both high and low similarities with respect to the test customer and exploits the transitivity of similarity using a graph approach. The proposed algorithm also utilizes the attributes of the items in the process of prediction for high prediction quality.

We regard a portion of the input dataset a complete undirected graph in which a vertex represents each customer and a weighted edge corresponds to the similarity between two endpoints (customers) of the edge. RNSA creates k clusters from the input dataset with the k-means clustering method. Then it finds the best cluster C with respect to the test customer t among the k clusters. RNSA adds the test customer t into the best cluster C and regard it as v. RNSA then searches the unmarked vertices adjacent to v who have the similarities either larger than δ_H or smaller than δ_L, where δ_H and δ_L are some threshold values for the Pearson correlation coefficients. Note that as the threshold values changes, so does the size of the neighbors. The search is performed in a breadth-first manner. That is, we search the adjacent vertices of v according to δ_H and δ_L to find the neighbors of t, and then search the adjacent vertices of each neighbor of v in turn. The search stops when we have enough neighbors for prediction. The following describes RNSA in detail. When the algorithm is terminated, the test customer t is removed from the set, Neighbors and the set is returned as output.

The Refined Neighbor Selection Algorithm
Input: the test customer t, the input dataset S
Output: **Neighbors**

1. Create k clusters from S with the k-means clustering method;
2. Find the best cluster C for the test customer t;
3. Add the test customer t into the best cluster C and regard it as v;
4. Add v to **Neighbors**;
5. If we have enough neighbors then return Neighbors. Otherwise, traverse C from v in a breadth-first manner when visiting vertices (customers). The sim-

ilarity of the customer is checked to see if it is either higher than δ_H or lower than δ_L. If so, let v = the customer. Go to Step 4;

Note that in Step 5 we terminate the algorithm if the number of levels (depths) we search from the test customer added in Step 3 in a breadth-first manner is greater than a fixed value. This value can be determined through various experiments. The test customer t is removed from the Neighbors before returning the set.

For using the attributes in prediction we use Equation (1) proposed by us in [4] as a new prediction formula in order to predict customer's preferences more accurately. In this equation, $A(\overline{r_{a,i}})$ and $A(\overline{r_{k,i}})$ are the averages of customer a and k's attribute values, respectively.

$$P_{a,i} = A(\overline{r_{a,i}}) + \frac{\sum_k \{w_{a,k} \times (r_{k,i} - A(\overline{r_{k,i}}))\}}{\sum_k |w_{a,k}|} . \tag{1}$$

4 Experimental Results

In order to evaluate the prediction accuracy of the proposed recommendation system, we used the *MovieLens* dataset of the *GroupLens Research Center*[5]. In the *MovieLens* dataset, one of the valuable attributes of an item is the genre of the movies. And we used the mean absolute error(MAE) as the evaluation metrics. MAE is one of the statistical prediction accuracy metrics for evaluating recommender systems[1][2][4].

For the experiment, we have chosen randomly 10% out of all customers in the dataset as the test customers. For each test customer, we have chosen randomly ten movies that are actually rated by the test customer as the test movies. The final experimental results are averaged over the results of ten different test sets for a statistical significance.

We have implemented four recommendation systems for the experiments. The first one is the recommendation system only with the clustering-based CF, called R_{kcf}. The second one is R_{kcf} with the attribute information utilized, called R_{attr}. The third one is R_{kcf} with RNSA, called R_{rnsa}. And the last one is R_{kcf} with both RNSA and the attribute information, called $R_{proposed}$, which is the proposed recommendation algorithm.

The experimental results are given in Table 1. We have tested various number of clusters and have provided the results for typical numbers in multiples of 10. We have determined the threshold values which gave us the smallest MAEs through various experiments. After we have tested extensively, we have obtained that a search depth d is 2 for all the cases. It appears that having many neighbors does not necessarily contribute toward better prediction.

The results show that $R_{proposed}$ outperforms other systems for all the cases. We also found that both R_{rnsa} and R_{attr} are better than R_{kcf} and R_{rnsa} is better

Table 1. The experimental results

k	R_{kcf}	R_{attr}	R_{rnsa}	$R_{proposed}$
2	0.750977	0.700116	0.739342	0.668406
10	0.788403	0.751374	0.739447	0.668461
20	0.814820	0.793039	0.739449	0.668499
30	0.832379	0.811756	0.739440	0.668418
40	0.835119	0.822225	0.739474	0.668445
50	0.841960	0.827376	0.739488	0.668512

than R_{attr}. These fact means that the clustering-based recommender system using both refined neighbor selection and attributes can solve the very large-scale problem without deteriorating prediction quality.

5 Conclusions

In this paper we have proposed an effective recommendation algorithm that finds valuable neighbors using a graph approach along with clustering and exploiting the attribute information of the items. The experimental results show the recommendation system with the proposed algorithm outperforms other systems for all the cases. Therefore, the recommendation system with the proposed system can be a choice to resolve the very large-scale problem while it gives high prediction quality.

Acknowledgements

We thank *the GroupLens Research Center* for permitting us to use the MovieLens dataset. This work was supported by the Brain Korea 21 Project in 2005.

References

1. Jonathan L. Herlocker, Joseph A. Konstan, Al Borchers, and John Riedl: An Algorithmic Framework for Performing Collaborative Filtering. Proceedings of the 22nd International ACM SIGIR Conference on Research and Development in Information Retrieval. (1999)
2. John S. Breese, David Heckerman, and Carl Kadie: Empirical Analysis of Predictive Algorithms for Collaborative Filtering. Proceedings of the Conference on Uncertainty in Artificial Intelligence. (1998)
3. Badrul M. Sarwar, George Karypis, Joseph A. Konstan, John T. Riedle: Recommender Systems for Large-Scale E-Commerce: Scalable Neighborhood Formation Using Clustering. Proceedings of the Fifth International Conference on Computer and Information Technology. (2002)
4. Taek-Hun Kim, Sung-Bong Yang: Using Attributes to Improve Prediction Quality in Collaborative Filtering. Lecture Notes in Computer Science, Vol. 3182. (2004)
5. MovieLens dataset, GroupLens Research Center, url: http://www.grouplens.org/.

An Intelligent Decision Making System to Support E-Service Management

Gülçin Büyüközkan[1,*], Mehmet Şakir Ersoy[2], and Gülfem Işıklar[3]

[1] Galatasaray University, Industrial Eng. Dep., Ortaköy 34357 İstanbul-Turkey
       gbuyukozkan@gsu.edu.tr
[2] Galatasaray University, Management Dep., Ortaköy 34357 İstanbul-Turkey
       msersoy@gsu.edu.tr
[3] Galatasaray University, Computer Eng. Dep., Ortaköy 34357 İstanbul-Turkey
       gisiklar@gsu.edu.tr

Abstract. This paper proposes an intelligent decision support framework for an effective e-service management. The proposed framework integrates case and rule based reasonings and multi criteria decision-making techniques in fuzzy environment for a real-time decision-making, which is dealing with uncertain and imprecise decision situations. The framework potentially leads to more accurate, flexible and efficient retrieval of alternatives that are most similar and most useful to the current decision situation.

1 Introduction

The pervasive spread of the World Wide Web has created a tremendous opportunity for providing services through the Internet. The term electronic (e) service is used for describing a variety of electronic interactions, ranging from the basic services, such as delivery of news and stock quotes, to the smart services, such as delivery of context-aware emergency services [1]. The information-based nature of services mean that the Internet, which offers global reach and multimedia capability, is an increasingly important tool of promoting and distributing various services. Problems in strategic, and frequently operational planning in e-service management, are characterized by their complexity, often being individualistically dynamic and requiring the achievement of multiple goals. The vast amount of information or complex weighting of the different operations can present an insurmountable problem for human resources. For this reason, the aim of this paper is to show how a hybrid intelligent decision support framework can assist in e-service management. The proposed real-time decision-making framework integrates case-based reasoning (CBR), rule base reasoning (RBR) and multi criteria decision-making (MCDM) techniques in a fuzzy environment, which is dealing with uncertain and imprecise decision situations. Common tasks involved in the methodologies are considered and the manner of how to combine the different techniques to build an intelligent decision support model is explored.

---

* Corresponding author. Phone: +90 212 227 4480; Fax: +90 212 259 5557.

2 Used Intelligent Techniques

2.1 Rule and Case Base Reasonings and Fuzzy Logic

RBR and CBR are two of the problem solving methodologies of Artificial Intelligence (AI). CBR enables to make use of the specific knowledge by remembering a previous similar situation and by reusing information and knowledge of that situation [2]. It is an alternative approach to RBR where the knowledge is represented with the rules. As both RBR and CBR have their pros and cons, some researchers have tried to combine them together and form an integrated system [3]. Moreover, data processing procedure is the base of CBR system and directs it to be successful. Fuzzy logic [4] is a formal tool, eminently suited for solving problems with imprecision inherent in empirical data. In conclusion, when different methods are combined in one system, the system stands the chance of inheriting the strengths of all methods. A recent increase in the number of such hybrid systems justifies to the effectiveness of this type integration [5].

2.2 Fuzzy MCDM and the Fuzzy Analytic Hierarchy Process

A CBR method in context-aware systems may not work well because it has more opportunities to have a high number of items or variables to consider. Some supplementary methods to determine weights among the items need to be combined with the CBR method [6]. In fuzzy MCDM, best alternatives are ranked and/or selected according to their degree of preference compared to the other alternatives, instead of degree of partial similarity to just one reference case. In this study, among numerous fuzzy MCDM methods [7], fuzzy Analytic Hierarchy Process (AHP) method is used to determine the criteria weights. Many fuzzy AHP methods are proposed by some authors. In this paper, we use Chang's extent analysis method on fuzzy AHP [8] because of its computational simplicity and effectiveness, and we also integrate the improvement proposed by Zhu et al. [9] to the methodology.

3 Proposed Framework

The proposed system, as given in Figure 1, uses CBR as a mainframe, with fuzzy MCDM and RBR as sub-systems to assist the performance of the intelligent framework. The system initiates by the customer's information request, which is considered as a new case. At the second step, the framework needs the importance weights of case attributes in order to use them in the matching process. Therefore, the linguistic pairwise comparisons made by the sector experts and the customers are used in the fuzzy AHP methodology in order to obtain the final weights of case attributes. The next and maybe the most important step involves the investigation of the case base to see if there are some similar cases to the new one. One of the possibilities to calculate the similarity between two cases in an analytical environment is to calculate the distance between the two cases. For the distance measurement step, so as to reduce search space, a RBR sub-system, which enables to eliminate the inappropriate cases in respect to the certain data belonging to the cases, is introduced. As some attributes may be uncertain in nature, they are represented as linguistic terms in the framework. Then, considering the uncertain data, the system calculates the distances between the new case and each of the case subset. Some authors defined different formula to calculate the distance between fuzzy numbers. We have chosen for this study the area compensation method [10] for its reasonable ordering properties [11] and computational easiness. The solution(s) of the most similar case(s), in other words, case(s) with minimum distance value, can be applied to the new problem if they are accepted. Moreover, if they are confirmed, they are directly inserted into the case base. The intelligent framework in this study is implemented using SWI Prolog, a Prolog environment widely used both for commercial and research applications.

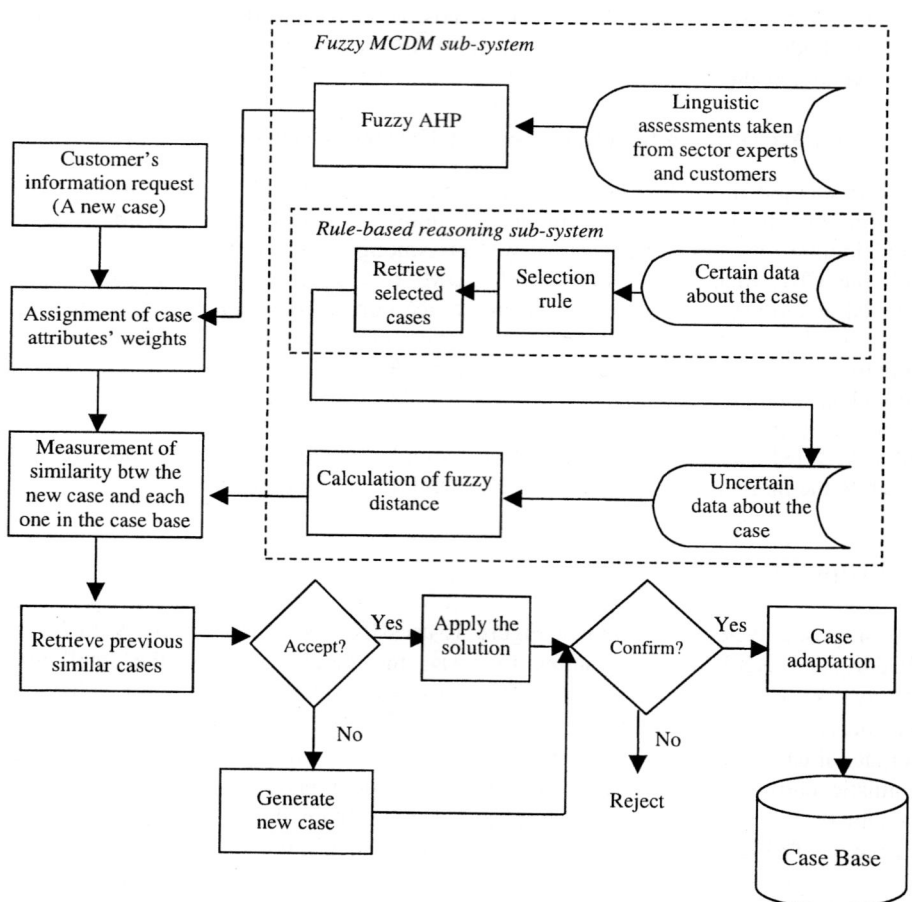

Fig. 1. The proposed system architecture

4 Concluding Remarks

In this paper, we proposed a hybrid intelligent decision support model for e-service management to improve the effectiveness of the decision process. The proposed framework integrated different techniques in order to take advantages of the reasoning power of them. The proposed approach allowed, then, a user to evaluate quickly the filtered set for real-time decision-making under uncertainty and imprecision conditions.

A remarkable aspect of the proposed approach is that the reliability of the obtained result is directly related to the size and up-to-dateness of the case base. Accordingly, it is encountered another notable feature: Although a CBR system may be considered as a learning-based system, which takes the workload from the user and the developers, it necessitates to the developers an amount of time when collecting a sufficient number of old cases. For that reason, this type of systems is preferable when the user traffic is high such as in tourism management. Alongside, they have a short period of refund of initial investment in these cases.

Acknowledgements

The authors acknowledge the financial support of the Galatasaray University Research Fund.

References

1. Chidambaram, L., The editor's column: Why e-Service Journal, e-Service Journal, 1(1) (2001), 1-3.
2. Aamodt, A., Plaza, E., Case-Based Reasoning: Foundational Issues, Methodological Variations, and System Approaches, AI Communications. IOS Press, 7 (1), (1994), 39-59.
3. Chan, F.T.S., Application of a hybrid case-based reasoning approach in electroplating industry. Expert Systems with Applications, 29, (2005), 121-130.
4. Zadeh, L.A., Fuzzy sets. Information and Control, 8, (1965), 338–353.
5. Pal, S.K., Dillon, T.S., Yeung, D.S. eds. Soft Computing in Case-Based Reasoning. London, UK, Springer (2000).
6. Changchien, S.W., Lin, M-C. Design and implementation of a case-based reasoning system for marketing plans. Expert Systems with Applications, 28, (2005), 43–53.
7. Triantaphyllou, E., Multi-criteria decision making methods: A comparative study. Kluwer Academic Publishers, London (2000).
8. Chang, D-Y., Applications of the extent analysis method on fuzzy AHP, European Journal of Operational Research, 95 (3), (1996), 649-655.
9. Zhu, K-J., Jing, Y., Chang, D-Y. A discussion on extent analysis method and applications of fuzzy AHP, European Journal of Operational Research, 116 (2), (1999), 450-456.
10. Fortemps, P., Roubens, M., Ranking and defuzzification methods based on area compensation, Fuzzy Sets and Systems, 82 (1996), 319–330.
11. Wang, X., Kerre, E.E., Reasonable properties for the ordering of fuzzy quantities (I), Fuzzy Sets and Systems, 118 (2001), 375–385.

OWL, Proteins and Data Integration

Amandeep S. Sidhu[1], Tharam S. Dillon[1], Elizabeth Chang[2], and Baldev S. Sidhu[3]

[1]Faculty of Information Technology, University of Technology, Sydney, Australia
{asidhu, tharam}@it.uts.edu.au
[2]School of Information Systems, Curtin University of Technical University, Perth, Australia
Elizabeth.Chang@cbs.curtin.edu.au
[3]State Council of Education Research and Training, Punjab, India
bsidhu@biomap.org

Abstract. In this paper we propose an approach to integrate protein information from various data sources by defining a Protein Ontology. Protein Ontology provides the technical and scientific infrastructure and knowledge to allow description and analysis of relationships between various proteins. Protein Ontology uses relevant protein data sources of information like PDB, SCOP, and OMIM. Protein Ontology describes: Protein Sequence and Structure Information, Protein Folding Process, Cellular Functions of Proteins, Molecular Bindings internal and external to Proteins, and Constraints affecting the Final Protein Conformation. Details about Protein Ontology are available online at **http://www.proteinontology.info/**.

Keywords: Protein Ontology, Biomedical Ontologies, Knowledge Representation, Information Retrieval, Data Integration.

1 Protein Ontology Overview

We defined a Protein Ontology [1, 2, 3, 4, 5] that provides a common structured vocabulary for researchers who need to share knowledge in proteomics domain. It consists of concepts (or type definitions), which are data descriptors for proteomics data and the relations among these concepts. Protein Ontology provides a structured vocabulary description for protein domains that can be used to describe cellular products in any organism. Protein Ontology Framework describes: (1) Protein Sequence and Structure Information, (2) Protein Folding Process, (3) Cellular Functions of Proteins, (4) Molecular Bindings internal and external to Proteins and (5) Constraints affecting the Final Protein Conformation. The Protein Ontology is available online at **http://www.proteinontology.info/**. Complete Documentation about the class hierarchy of Protein Ontology is available at the website. The Class Diagram and UML Diagrams, depicting Protein Ontology are also available at the website. The Ontology is defined by Web Ontology Language (OWL) and the complete OWL file is also available online. The Protein Ontology currently contains 92 *concepts* or classes, 261 *attributes* or properties and 17550 instances, including 17347 instances for Protein Atoms. The XML Representation of the Database of

Human Prion Proteins based on the proposed Protein Ontology is available on the Protein Ontology Website. There are a total of 17550 instances for all of the 10 Major Prion Proteins in the Database for various Protein Concepts defined by the Protein Ontology.

The Main Class of Protein Ontology is ProteinOntology. For each Protein that is entered into the knowledge base of protein ontology, submission information is entered into ProteinOntology Class. ProteinOntologyID has format like "PO000000052". There are six subclasses of ProteinOntology, called Generic Classes that are used to define complex concepts in other Protein Ontology Classes: Residues, Chains, Atoms, AtomicBind, Bind, and SiteGroup. Concepts from these generic classes are reused in various other Protein Ontology Classes for definition of Class Specific Concepts. Details and Properties of Residues in a Protein Sequence are defined by instances of Residues Class. Instances of Chains of Residues are defined in Chains Class. All the Three Dimensional Structure Data of Protein Atoms is represented as instances of Atoms Class. Defining Chains, Residues and Atoms as individual classes has the benefit that any special properties or changes affecting a particular chain, residue and atom can be easily added. Data about binding atoms in Chemical Bonds like Hydrogen Bond, Residue Links, and Salt Bridges is entered into ontology as an instance of AtomicBind Class. Similarly the data about binding residues in Chemical Bonds like Disulphide Bonds and CIS Peptides is entered into ontology as an instance of Bind Class. All data related to site groups of the active binding sites of Proteins is defined as instances of SiteGroup Class. The Root Class for definition of Protein Complexes in the Protein Ontology is ProteinComplex. The Protein Complex Definition defines one or more Proteins in the Complex Molecule. There are six main subclasses within ProteinComplex class: Entry, Structure, StructuralDomains, FunctionalDomains, ChemicalBonds, and Constraints. These classes define sequence, structure and chemical binds present in the Protein Complex.

2 Protein Ontology Implementation

Notions of classification, reasoning, and consistency are applied in the making of Protein Ontology by defining new concepts or classes from defined generic concepts or classes. The concepts derived from generic concepts are placed precisely into class hierarchy of Protein Ontology to completely represent information defining a protein. As the OWL representation used in Protein Ontology is an XML-Abbrev based (Abbreviated XML Notation), it can be easily transformed to the corresponding RDF and XML formats without much effort using the available converters. To understand the reuse of concepts in Protein Ontology, here are some of the examples. ATOMSequence instance is constructed using generic concepts of Chains, Residues, and Atoms. The reasoning is already there in the underlying relationships and hierarchy of Protein Data, as each Chain in a Protein represents a sequence of Residues, and each Residue is defined by a number of three dimensional atoms in the Protein Structure.

```
<ATOMSequence>
    <NumberResidues>244</NumberResidues>
    <chain>
    <ChainID>A</ChainID>
    <Description>A Chain</Description>
    <residue>
    <ResidueID>ILE</ResidueID>
    <Description>ILE Type</Description>
    <ATOM>
    <ATOMID>1</ATOMID>
    <ATOM>N</ATOM>
    <residueSeqnum>16</residueSeqnum>
    <x>60.749</x>
    <y>50.351</y>
    <z>75.583</z>
    <occupancy>1.00</occupancy>
    <temperatureFactor>15.71</temperatureFactor>
    <element>N</element>
    </ATOM>
    7 More Atoms......
</residue> </chain> </ATOM Sequence>
```

Similarly Secondary Structure elements of Protein Structure like helices, sheets, and short loops can also be represented using generic concepts of Chains and Residues. The hierarchy used in a Helices Instance of Protein Ontology differentiates general information about the Helices and the Helix Structure comprising of Chains and Residue Sequences.

```
<Helices>
    <Helix>
    <HelixNumber> 1 </HelixNumber>
    <HelixID> HA </HelixID>
    <HelixLength> 9 </HelixLength>
        <HelixStructure>
        <Chain>
        <ChainID> A </ChainID>
        <intialResidue>GLY</intialResidue>
        <intialResSeqNum>86</intialResSeqNum>
        <endResidue>GLY</endResidue>
        <endResSeqNum>96</endResSeqNum>
    </Chain></HelixStructure></Helix>
... and so on for other helices present in Protein
</Helices>
```

Other secondary structures like sheets and loops are represented using concepts of chains and residues in the similar way. Again the various chemical bonds used to bind various substructures in a complex protein structure are defined using generic concepts of Bind and Atomic Bind. The Chemical Bonds that have Binding Residues reuse the generic concept of Bind. In defining the generic concept of Bind in Protein Ontology we again reuse the generic concepts of Chains and Residues. Similarly the Chemical Bonds that have Binding Atoms reuse the generic concept of AtomicBind. In defining the generic concept of AtomicBind we reuse the generic concepts of Chains, Residues and Atoms. Various other Chemical Bonds in Proteins can be defined in similar way.

```
<ChemicalBonds>
    <ResidueLink>
        <AtomicBind1>
            <AtomicBindResSeqNum>391</AtomicResSeqNum>
            <AtomicBindATOM>MN</AtomicBindATOM>
            <AtomicBindResidue>MN</AtomicBindResidue>
        </AtomicBind1>
        <AtomicBind2>
            <AtomicBindResSeqNum>217</AtomicResSeqNum>
            <AtomicBindATOM>OE2</AtomicBindATOM>
            <AtomicBindResidue>GLU</AtomicBindResidue>
            <AtomicBindSymmetry>2565</AtomicBindSymmetry>
        </AtomicBind2>
    </ResidueLink>
    ... and so on for other chemical bonds in Protein
</ChemicalBonds>
```

3 Conclusion

The explosion of protein data led to increased efforts to logically represent, store and display knowledge. There have been several domains which have successfully created standardized templates for data, and their usefulness is apparent. Protein Ontology improves on these online protein data resources in number of ways. Firstly, it contains templates for all kinds of protein data that is need to understand proteins, their functionality and the proteomics process itself. Previously there is not such integrated and structured data representation format available. Secondly, majority of the values for many attributes unlike previously are not simply text strings, but has been entered into the ontology as instances of other concepts, defined by Generic Classes.

References

[1] Sidhu, A. S., T. S. Dillon, et al. (2005). Ontology-based Knowledge Representation of Protein Data. 3rd International IEEE Conference on Industrial Informatics, Perth, Australia, IEEE CS Press.
[2] Sidhu, A. S., T. S. Dillon, et al. (2005). Protein Ontology: Vocabulary for Protein Data. 3rd IEEE International Conference on Information Technology and Applications. Sydney, Australia, IEEE CS Press.
[3] Sidhu, A. S., T. S. Dillon, et al. (2004). Making of Protein Ontology. 2nd Australian and Medical Research Congress 2004 (Invited Speaker). M. Kavallaris. Sydney, National Heath and Medical Research Council: 151.
[4] Sidhu, A. S., T. S. Dillon, et al. (2004). Protein Knowledge Base: Making of Protein Ontology. HUPO 3rd Annual World Congress 2004 (Invited Speaker). R. A. Bradshaw. Beijing, China, American Society for Biochemistry and Molecular Biology. 3: S262.
[5] Sidhu, A. S., T. S. Dillon, et al. (2004). A Unified Representation of Protein Structure Databases (Book Section). Biotechnological Approaches for Sustainable Development. M. S. Reddy and S. Khanna. Mumbai, India, Allied Publishers Pvt. Ltd.: 396-408.

Web Site Improvements Based on Representative Pages Identification

Sebastían A. Ríos[1], Juan D. Velásquez[2],
Hiroshi Yasuda[1], and Terumasa Aoki[1]

[1] Research Center for Advanced Science and Technology,
University of Tokyo
{srios, yasuda, aoki}@mpeg.rcast.u-tokyo.ac.jp
[2] Department of Industrial Engineering, University of Chile
jvelasqu@dii.uchile.cl

Abstract. Many researchers have successfully shown that web content mining technics and web usage mining techniques can help to find out important patterns on the content and browsing behavior in a site. However, still it is an open problem how to reach a good interpretation of the cluster results after the mining process. We propose a technique called *Reverse Clustering Analysis* (RCA) applied to a Self Organizing Feature Map in order to identify the most representative Web Pages of the Site. Then use this information to perform enhancements in the site. Our mining process is based on the combination of WCM and WUM to find out the content that is most interesting for the visitors. We successfully test our proposal in a real web site.

1 Introduction

To perform improvements in the web site content, first we need to identify which is the most relevant content of the whole web site. Several approaches to do this task have been developed [1]. Techniques like Web Content Mining (WCM), or the use of soft computing to find the representative contents have shown its effectiveness to accomplish such task [1,3].

However, even if we could distinguish the relevant content from the irrelevant content, we have no simple answers to questions like: where should we start making changes to the web site?, which are the most relevant pages of the web site?, should we modify all the web pages?.

The answer to this question is not simple. We propose the *Reverse Clustering Analysis* (RCA) to gather the most relevant web pages from the web site based on a mixed approach of WCM with WUM techniques. These allow us to find out pages which content is not only the most representative from the site but also, the content which is most relevant for the visitors. Then the site owners can use this information for enhance the content of its site.

2 Related Work

Depending on the complexity of the web site, the text content can be written by a professional writer, like a reporter or a linguistic team. Afterwards using a usability test

[2], the final web site text content is checked before the web site goes to production. This process is human dependant, i.e., it is not possible to semi-automatize the text generation process. Moreover, the expert only have an approximate idea of what the correct content is. Therefore it is highly recommendable to establish a guideline on how to create text content based on small sub set of the whole web pages of the site.

2.1 Web Content Mining and Web Usage Mining Process

In order to extract meaning full patterns from the content of the web sites, the web content mining is a widely used technique. On the other hand, the web usage mining process is widely used to discover visitors browsing behavior. The literature mention four steps to accomplish the web content mining and usage mining processes these are: first, data selection; second, data pre-processing; third, web generalization process (automatically discover general patterns) and fourth, analysis of the patterns (validation or interpretation of mined patterns)[1].

We perform a sessionization process, in this process we take the clean logs and re-generate the sessions [3,6,7].

3 Similarity Measure and Reverse Clustering Analysis

If we assume that the degree of importance in some page content is correlated with the time spent on it by the visitors, we can state that those pages where a visitor spends more time are those more interesting to him. This way, we define a similarity measure that allows to combine the content and the usage Eq.(1) [7].

$$IVS(S^i, S^j) = \sum_{k=1}^{\iota} min(\frac{S_\tau^i(k)}{S_\tau^j(k)}, \frac{S_\tau^j(k)}{S_\tau^i(k)}) * PD(S_\rho^i(k), S_\rho^i(k)) \tag{1}$$

The expression shown in Eq.(1) compares the ι-most important pages into the sessions of two different visitors S^i and S^j. The function $PD()$ is the dot product between two vectors.

In the present work we used a SOFM to find patterns of content that is most interesting for the visitors of the site. Then the RCA process [4,5]. allow us to identify the pages which content is the most interesting from the visitors point of view.

We can write formally in a expression that we call the *Page Reference Function*. This is shown in Eq.(2) [4,5], where n_i is the ith neuron in the cluster neurons set and p_j is the jth real page in the whole site.

$$PR(n_i, p_j) = Min\{PD(n_i, p_j)\} \quad \forall j = 1, \ldots, Q \quad \forall i \epsilon \zeta \tag{2}$$

The result of the RCA process is a small set of real web pages whose references are greater than 0. These set of pages is called the *representative real pages set*. We can consider this set, as the set of the real pages that are the most interesting in content to the visitors. This interpretation of the RCA is based on the method used for clustering the web pages. For example, if we only use text for the clustering algorithm then the result of the RCA is also a *representative real pages set* however, in this case, the pages in this set are the pages which contain the content that is most representative from the site (based only on its own text)[4,5].

4 Application in a Real Web Site

The whole process explained before was applied to the web site of the School of Engineering and Sciences of the University of Chile.[1]. This Web Site has 182 web pages. We use the March 2005 version of the web site to work.

In the cleaning stage we reduced the number of different words in the data from more than 11,000 to only about 4,000 words, this is after applying filtering and stemming.

On the other hand, we chose only four weeks of logs to perform the sessionization process. The length of the ι-*most important pages vector* was set in three pages. Therefore, we needed the sessions which contain at least three pages visited to create those vectors in order to apply the *3-most important pages vector*. To do so, we sorted the sessions by time spent on each page and then we only kept the three pages where the visitor spent more time.

We perform two different experiments: first, we use a SOFM of about 100 (10x10) neurons and second, we use a SOFM of 64 (8x8) neurons. The epoch parameter was set in $t = 50$ in both experiments. Then for each network, we use circular and square vicinity with $r = 1$. We use both in order to see the effects of the cluster extraction method in the final results.

4.1 First Experiment: SOFM 10x10 Neurons

The network used in this experiment is a 100 neurons network, about 55% of the size of the original space of documents and near 40% from the sessions space. We applied the RCA to discover the most representative pages using the circular and square vicinity. After applying the *Page Reference Function* in Eq.2 the results were only 18 pages using the square vicinity and 20 pages using the circular vicinity. In both cases, these pages represent almost 11% from the whole web site pages (see Table 1).

Using the square vicinity we discover 8 clusters. On the other hand, using the circular vicinity we discover 49 clusters. As mention before, not all the clusters found using circular vicinity are really clusters. If we consider the clusters found using square vicinity as the real clusters then about 80% of the clusters are not really clusters. The interesting result is that even this high difference in the number of clusters found and also, the high noise of the clusters found with circular vicinity the difference in the final result is only two pages (emovil.htm and escuela.htm) that appeared when using the circular vicinity. Moreover, these pages only has 1 reference that is why the importance of those pages is not so high.

On the other side, although the *representative web pages sets* in the experiments are almost the same, the order of those sets is severely altered depending on the method used.

---

[1] http://escuela.ing.uchile.cl

4.2 Second Experiment: SOFM 8x8 Neurons

We used a network of 64 neurons, this is about 35% of the size of the original space of documents and near 25% from the sessions space. The number of clusters found using circular vicinity was 32 clusters, however, using the square vicinity we only discover 5 clusters. Again, although this huge difference on the number of clusters detected, we can see that the resulting set of web pages are almost the same in both approaches (see Table 2). With square vicinity we detected 16 representative web pages and with circular vicinity we found 19 pages. Once again the order of the representative web pages is severely altered by the vicinity extraction method.

4.3 Comparison Between Experiments and Discussion

If we compare the results of the first and second experiments using square vicinity, we can see that the difference in the number of clusters found is only 3 clusters. However, the final representative web pages sets are almost the same.

The same thing happen when we compare the both experiments using the circular vicinity. Moreover, the page servicios.htm appear in the first experiment but not

Table 1. First experiment results: Most representative real pages from visitors point of view using circular vicinity and square vicinity (fragment of the whole results)

Web Page (Real URL)	Square Vicinity	Web Page (Real URL)	Circular Vicinity
index_home.php	73	novedades/novedad_alumnos.php	243
novedades/novedad_alumnos.php	60	index_home.php	241
novedades.htm	25	novedades.htm	71
mapa.htm	15	mapa.htm	59
escuela/sobrelaescuela.htm	5	departamentos/index.htm	15
departamentos/index.htm	4	escuela/sobrelaescuela.htm	11
servicios/bienestar.htm	4	escuela/a_destacados.htm	10
escuela/a_destacados.htm	3	escuela/LISTA_2003.html	10

Table 2. Second experiment results: Most representative real pages from visitors point of view using circular vicinity and square vicinity (fragment of the whole results)

Web Page (Real URL)	Square Vicinity	Web Page (Real URL)	Circular Vicinity
novedades/novedad_alumnos.php	45	novedades/novedad_alumnos.php	141
index_home.php	37	index_home.php	124
mapa.htm	14	novedades.htm	55
novedades.htm	11	mapa.htm	49
departamentos/index.htm	5	escuela/a_destacados.htm	13
escuela/a_destacados.htm	4	acad_anual.htm	9
escuela/sobrelaescuela.htm	3	reglam.htm	8
baseorganizaciones.htm	2	baseorganizaciones.htm	8

in the second. Besides, the order of the representative web pages is altered in both experiments.

The most impressive result is that the four representative pages sets obtained are very similar. The representative pages are few and are independent form the size of the network and method used for extraction if we analyze the results.

However, we can not say yet which is the best size of neural network to perform the RCA. Even if the first SOFM (100 neurons) took 5 days and the second (64 neurons) took only 3 and the resulting pages are almost the same. In other web site, the results could be severly affected by the size of the SOFM selected.

5 Conclusions

The discovery of meaningful patterns and its good interpretation is a very difficult and challenging task. We propose to combine the web text mining with the usage mining to find the preferred web site content patterns from the visitors point of view.

Once we found these patterns, we realize that it is not straightforward to state which are the pages that are most representative from the clusters found in a SOFM. This information is very important to begin the improvements of the site content or to plan a strategy to focus the resources for the site enhancements.

We propose a technique called by us *Reverse Clustering Analysis* that allow us to discover which are pages that the SOFM patterns are representing.

We perform two experiments using two different SOFMs and then we applied two different clusters extraction techniques to each one (circular and square vicinity). We successfully found small *representative pages sets* which are about 11% of the whole web site documents.

References

1. Kosala, R. and Blockeel, H.:Web mining research: A survey. SIGKDD Explorations: Newsletter of the Special Interest Group (SIG) on Knowledge Discovery & Data Mining, 2(1):1–15 (2000).
2. Nielsen, J.: User Interface directions for the web. Communications of ACM, 42(1):65–72 (1999).
3. Pal, S. K., Talwar, V. and Mitra, P.: Web Mining in Soft Computing Framework: Relevance, state of the art and future directions. IEEE Transactions on Neural Networks, 13(5):1163–1177, Sept. (2002).
4. Ríos, S., Velásquez, J., Vera E., Yasuda, H. and Aoki, T: Using SOFM to Improve Web Site Text Content, Lecture Notes in Computer Science, Volume 3611, Pages 622 - 626, Jul (2005)
5. Ríos, S., Velásquez, J., Vera E., Yasuda, H. and Aoki, T.:Establishing guidelines on how to improve the web site content based on the identification of representative pages. To appear IEEE/WI Int. Conf. on Web Intelligence, France, Sept. (2005).
6. Velásquez, J. D., Yasuda, H., Aoki, T., Weber, R. and Vera, E.: Using self-organizing feature maps to acquire knowledge about visitor behavior in a web site. Lecture Notes in Artificial Intelligence, 2773(1):951–958, Sept. (2003).
7. Velásquez, J. D., Ríos, S., Bassi, A., Yasuda, H. and Aoki, T.: Towards the identification of keywords in the web site text content: A methodological approach. International Journal of Web Information Systems, 1:11–15, March (2005).

Unsupervised Bilingual Word Sense Disambiguation Using Web Statistics

Yuanyong Wang and Achim Hoffmann

School of Computer Science & Engineering,
The University of New South Wales,
Sydney, Australia

Abstract. Word sense disambiguation has sense division and sense selection as its two sub-problems. An appropriate solution to the sense division problem is usually dependent on the application being pursued. In the context of machine translation, picking the correct translation for a word among multiple candidates, is known as target word selection.

The work in this paper uses the Web as the main knowledge source to address the difficulty of making a target word selection based on statistics, which are normally drawn from rather limited corpora. The proposed approach uses simple and easily accessible web statistics–search engine hits (number of document returned for a particular query) to demonstrate the great potential of the Web as a knowledge source for word sense disambiguation. Our experimental results so far are very encouraging.

1 Introduction

Facing the SD problem, most approaches simply take the most convenient collection of sense divisions (dictionaries, thesauri or lexicons) without much analysis and evaluation of the collection. It is found, however, the sense divisions provided by these collections are often too fine and irrelevant in many contexts thus adding unnecessary difficulty. The approaches to the SS problem have developed substantially over time. From the initial dictionary definition based approach to later knowledge-based approaches that use semantic networks and contemporary statistical approaches using large corpora. It is obvious that more and more data have been employed. Web data, due to its enormous quantity and diversity, has come to the attention of many researchers recently.

In this paper, we propose a word sense disambiguation model combining two main elements. The first one is the element of Web statistics. It attempts to use the Web as a text corpus to draw statistics and to reduce the data sparseness problem. The simplest and most easily accessible Web statistics–search engine hits is used as the sole statistics.Bilingual dictionaries, as the second element, transforms the common monolingual word sense disambiguation problem to the target word selection problem of machine translation. The hope is that by using the actual translations instead of the somewhat artificial sense divisions, the problem caused by fine sense division could be eased because some ambiguity is carried over into another language.

2 The WSD Model

The WSD model first extracts phrases in which the target word is involved from the disambiguation context. After POS tagging, the phrase parsing component uses heuristic rules to extract five types of phrases containing the target word. They are NN_NN phrase (two nouns with one modifying another); NN_CC_NN phrase (two nouns connected by a conjunction); JJ_NN phrase (an adjective modifying the noun); NN_IN_NN phrase (two nouns connected by a preposition); NN_VB phrase (a complet subject-verb-object phrase or incomplete subject-verb or verb-object phrase). From these phrases it will choose one that is more likely to be indicative of the sense of the target word. A heuristic rule is used to choose the most indicative one. NN_NN has the highest priority followed by NN_CC_NN, then the JJ_NN and then NN_IN_NN and the last one is NN_VB. Simply put, if there is an extracted phrase with higher priority it will be considered more indicative. In future work multiple phrases could be considered but in this work, only the phrase with top priority will be chosen. For example, the target word "party" is in the context-giving sentence.

> *He was previously imprisoned from June until October 1990 for allegedly organising a political party.*

Phrases extracted are "political party", "organising a party" and "organising a political party". The phrase "political party" is chosen as the most indicative. "Organising a political party" is at least as indicative but more complex in structure. A phrase like "political party" thus extracted is called an *anchor* in this model. All possible translation combinations are enumerated for the words in the anchor. Each translation combination is issued to a search engine as a quoted queriy and the one translation combination that gets the biggest hits contains the correct translation of the target word.

3 Evaluation and Comparison

3.1 Evaluation

Evaluation to the WSD model is limited to 9 selected nouns in this work. It is believed by the author that disambiguation of verb senses involves much more sophisticated syntactic and semantic analysis of the contexts. The selected nouns are summarised in Table 1. As it is shown in Table 1 the number of German translations to a target word is generally smaller than that of its WordNet senses. This is because many WordNet senses can be mapped to the same German translation. Some of the German translations again can be bundled together because they are often used interchangeably. This further reduces the number of choices. The experimental results are summarised in Table 2.

Table 1. Summary of the testing data. WordNet Sense shows the number of senses of the target word in WordNet. German Translation is the number of German translations to the target word. Ambiguity indicates the final number of translations that need to be considered.

Word	WordNet Sense	German Translation	Ambiguity
party	5	5	3
bank	10	2	2
atmosphere	6	2	2
disc	4	4	3
paper	7	4	4
interest	7	3	3
tissue	2	2	2
image	7	5	3
source	9	2	2

Table 2. Summary of the disambiguation results. Precision is defined as the portion of correct judgements in the total number of judgements made. Applicability is defined as the portion of cases where a judgement is made in all tested cases.

Word	Testing data	Precision	Applicability
party	42 instances	82.9%	83.3%
bank	43 instances	90%	70%
atmosphere	51 instances	91.3%	90.2%
disc	50 instances	75%	56%
paper	38 instances	74.2%	81.6%
interest	51 instances	78.5%	93.4%
tissue	38 instances	92%	66%
image	47 instances	76.6%	90%
source	33 instances	73.9%	69.6%

The results in Table 2 show that the average precision is 81.6% and the average applicability is 77.8%. This is roughly equivalent to 63.5% of precision and recall. We used the precision and applicability because it is apparently more informative than precision and recall by showing the level of precision in the cases attempted and the portion of cases attempted.

3.2 Comparison with Related Works

The comparison with related WSD models will focus on three main groups of WSD models corresponding to the three main aspects of our model: unsupervised, using Web statistics, bilingual.

In Senseval-3 (held in 2004) 9 unsupervised systems participated in the lexical sample task [1]. The task included disambiguation of 20 nouns, 32 verbs and 5 adjectives.

The top system called WSDIIT used a Lesk-like similarity between the context of ambiguous words and dictionary definitions (glosses). It obtained a precision of 66.1% and recall of 65.7%. This is comparable to our results. However, it used "densely populated glosses accumulated from the training data for this task" [5]. From past experience, especially the substantially lower performance of unsupervised models compared to supervised models, information from training data should have played a vital role in the better performance of supervised models. We have to be cautious about the contribution of the glosses from the training data. Yarwosky's unsupervised model featuring one sense per discourse and bootstrapping algorithm to expand the sense specific collocations [8]. Ten words are tested in his experiment all with 2-way disambiguation and clear domain distinction between the two senses of the target words. The model obtained a precision as high as 96% and no statistics about applicability is given. It is believed by the author that treating collocations of the target word as a bag of words could seriously limit the applicability of the model to only those words with senses that are in clearly different domains.

Rada proposed a WSD model that utilises WordNet glosses and word pairs from the disambiguation contexts to produce sense specific queries. The hits obtained by a search engine for these queries are used to choose the correct sense of the target word [4]. The model obtained a precision of 80.1% for 384 word pairs manually extracted from Brown corpus, no statistics about applicability is given. This model is one of the first models that attempted to use Web statistics and showed how Web data could be used to overcome data sparseness problem. The extraction of word pairs, however, could be time consuming and the overall applicability could become low when the requirement on the quality of the word pairs are high. Compared with the way Rada's model directly uses search engine hits for WSD, other WSD models such as Turney's supervised machine learning model and Wang&Hoffmann's unsupervised model utilise the Web data or statistics indirectly to facility the WSD task [6,7]. In Turney's model the co-occurrence statistics extracted from Web corpora is used as input to the similarity score computation. It is experimented on Sensevel-3 English lexical sample task and obtained a precision and recall of 69.4% fine grained and 75.9% coarse grained. Wang&Hoffmann's model uses domain constraining words extracted from Web corpora (automatically compiled) as contextual evidence for disambiguation. The experiment obtained a precision of 87% and applicability of 70.6%. The scope of the experiment is however limited to only three selected nouns.

In [2], the authors extracted relations in which the target word is involved from English text and then produce translation enumerations of the relations. The probability of these enumerations are estimated according to the statistics collected from monolingual German corpora, which are not aligned with the English corpora. The model obtained a precision of 78% and applicability of 50% on 54 ambiguous German words [2]. The low applicability shown by the experimental results actually reflects the data sparseness problem. The validity of this model has been confirmed by some later work on a larger scale [3].

Finally a rough but interesting comparison with Altavista's translation engine-Babel Fish is done on the 9 tested nouns. Babel Fish obtained an average precision of 69%

and applicability of 100% (because it gives an anwser for each case). This is equivalent to a precision and recall of 69%, which is 6% higher than our model. But our model has an absolute higher average precision at 81.6% compared to 69% by Babel Fish. From observation, it seems that Babel Fish employs a combination of most frequent sense heuristics and dictionary lookup heuristics, which could be taken as a baseline model. Our system performs substantially better than this baseline model in its average precision.

4 Conclusion and Discussion

By comparing the experimental results of our proposed WSD model with related works, our approach appears very encouraging. Our model has obtained substantially higher applicability than related approaches and has considerably exceeded other competitive unsupervised WSD models in its overall performance. It should be mentioned that the grammatical similarity between English and German does make the anchor extraction and translation enumeration easier. Between other language pairs, more work probably has to be done in producing the proper translation enumerations (especially in correct word order) for the anchors, but this seems a surmountable difficulty. We believe that if properly combined with first sense heuristics and possibly bootstrapping (using labeled data) this model could yield a much wider applicability and even better precision at the same time. We will explore the performance of our approach more thoroughly in the future. We believe that web data and interlingual information are two knowledge sources that, if properly combined, could provide strong support for WSD.

References

1. Timothy Chklovski, Rada Mihalcea, Ted Pedersen, and Amruta Purandare. The senseval-3 multilingual english¡ad¿hindi lexical sample task. In Rada Mihalcea and Phil Edmonds, editors, *Senseval-3: Third International Workshop on the Evaluation of Sys tems for the Semantic Analysis of Text*, pages 5–8, Barcelona, Spain, July 2004. Association for Computational Linguistics.
2. Ido Dagan and Alon Itai. Word sense disambiguation using a second language monolingual c orpus. *Computational Linguistics*, 20(4):563 – 596, 1994.
3. Philipp Koehn and Kevin Knight. Estimating word translation probabilities from unrelated monolingua l corpora using the em algorithm. In *Proceddings of the AAAI/IAAI 2000*. AAAI, Austin, Texas, USA, 2000.
4. Dan I. Moldovan Rada Mihalcea. A method for word sense disambiguation of unrestricted text. In *Proceedings of the 37th annual meeting of the Association for Computational Linguistics on Computational Linguistics*, pages 152–158, College Park, Maryland, 1999.
5. Ganesh Ramakrishnan, B. Prithviraj, and Pus hpak Bhattacharya. A gloss-centered algorithm for disambiguation. In Rada Mihalcea and Phil Edmonds, editors, *Senseval-3: Third International Workshop on the Evaluation of Sys tems for the Semantic Analysis of Text*, pages 217–221, Barcelona, Spain, July 2004. Association for Computational Linguistics.
6. Peter D Turney. Word sense disambiguation by web mining for word co-occurrence probabilities. In *Proceedings Third International Workshop on the Evaluation of Systems for the Semantic Analysis of Text*, pages 239–242, Barcelona, Spain, 2004.

7. Yuanyong Wang and Achim Hoffmann. A new measure for extracting semantically related words. In *Proceedings of Australasian Language Technology Workshop 2004*, pages 117–122, Sydney, Australia, 2004.
8. David Yarowsky. Unsupervised word sense disambiguation rivaling supervised methods. In *Proceedings of ACL 1995*, 1995.

Optimal Production Policy for a Two-Stage Production System Under Lumpy Demand

Ding-zhong Feng[1] and Mitsuo Yamashiro[2]

[1] College of Mechatronics Engineering,
Zhejiang University of Technology,
Hangzhou, 310032, P.R. China
[2] Dept. of Industrial & Information Systems Engineering,
Ashikaga Institute of Technology,
Tochigi Prefecture, 326-8558, Japan
fdz@zjut.edu.cn

Abstract. A two-stage production-delivery system is considered in this research, where raw materials and/or components are procured from outside suppliers and processed into finished products which are delivered to customers periodically at a fixed quantity with a fixed interval of time. A decision-making model is developed for an optimal production policy under lumpy demand. a comprehensive cost function is formulated considering both supplier(of raw materials) and buyer (of finished products) sides. An optimal solution to the problem is derived on basis of the cost model. Also, we examine the sensitivity of raw materials ordering and production lot size to changes in ordering cost, transportation cost and manufacturing cost. A pragmatic computation approach for realistic operation situations is proposed to solve integer approximation solution. Finally, some numerical examples are given to illustrate the optimal solution and computational approach.

1 Introduction

A production-delivery system is not effective if it is operated under excessive inventories, as they denote poor planning behaviors, poor purchasing practices, poor communication, insufficient quality levels, and uneconomical use of resources and funds. In general, inventory management policies are always aimed at lowering holding cost through a higher inventory rotation.

Many researchers have dealt with the inventory management issue [1-6]. Once either a time interval policy or an order point one has been chosen, many works can provide useful indications to determine the principal inventory parameters under different circumstances.

The objective of this research is to model a two-stage production-delivery system which incorporates a fixed quantity supply of finished products to a buyer at a fixed interval of time. It aims at deriving an optimal solution to the problem model, and determining the optimal production lot size for each stage, optimal number of transportation for semi-finished products, and optimal quantity of semi-finished products transported each time to meet the lumpy demand of consumers.

2 Problem Description and Mathematical Modeling

A two-stage production-delivery system in a supply-chain-management (SCM) environment, as shown in Fig.1, is considered in this work. It consists of three distinct entities: suppliers, manufacturers and retailers. In the system, raw materials from outside suppliers are processed at stage 1 and 2 successively, and finally the finished products are delivered to a buyer at a fixed quantity in a fixed interval of time. The annual demand of its buyer is known and fixed. The production rate at each stage is assumed to be larger than finished (or semi-finished) products' demand rate so as to ensure no shortage of products (or semi-finished products) due to insufficient production. The raw materials are nonperishable, and are supplied instantaneously to the two-stage production system. In order to lower inventory-holding cost, raw materials are ordered in small lots and semi-finished products at stage 1 are delivered to the next stage in small lots.

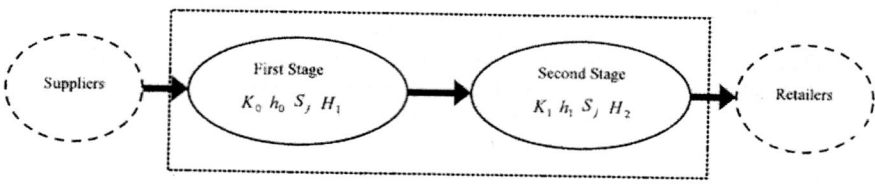

Fig. 1. A two-stage supply chain system of interest

In order to formulate a mathematical model for the problem of interest, some necessary parameters and variables are defined as follows.

Parameters:

D_2 : Demand for finished products, units/year.

x : Fixed quantity of finished products per shipment at a fixed interval of time, units/shipment.

f_j : Conversion factor of raw materials ($j=1$) or semi-finished products ($j=2$) at stage j, $f_j = D_j / D_{j-1}$, $j=1, 2$.

h_0 : Holding cost of raw materials inventory, $/unit/year.

h_1 : Holding cost of semi-finished products inventory at stage 2, $/unit/year.

H_1 : Holding cost of semi-finished products inventory at stage1, $/unit/year.

H_2 : Holding cost of finished products inventory, $/unit/year.

K_0 : Ordering cost of raw materials. $/order.

K_1 : Transportation cost of semi-finished products for each time between two stages, $/time.

S_j : Manufacturing setup cost for each batch at stage j ($j=1, 2$), $/batch.

P_j : Production rate at stage j ($j=1, 2$), units/year.

T_j : Manufacturing period (uptime) at stage j ($j=1,2$), years.

Variables:
m : Number of full shipments of finished products per cycle time.
n_1 : Number of orders for raw materials or component parts during the uptime at stage 1.
n_2 : Number of transportation for semi-finished products between two stages during the uptime at stage 2.
Q_0 : Quantity of raw materials required for each batch, $Q_0 = Q_1 / f_1$, units/batch.
Q_1 : Quantity of semi-finished products manufactured per setup at stage 1, $Q_1 = Q_2 / f_2$, units/batch.
Q_2 : Quantity of finished products manufactured per setup, units/batch.
q_0 : Quantity of raw materials ordered each time, $q_0 = Q_0 / n_1$, units/order.
q_1 : Quantity of semi-finished products transported each time between two stages, $q_1 = Q_1 / n_2$, units/time.

Fig.2 shows on-hand inventory of raw materials, semi-finished products and finished products for a two-stage production system under a lumpy demand. We infer (the details are neglected due to the limit of the paper length) and obtain a total cost function for the problem:

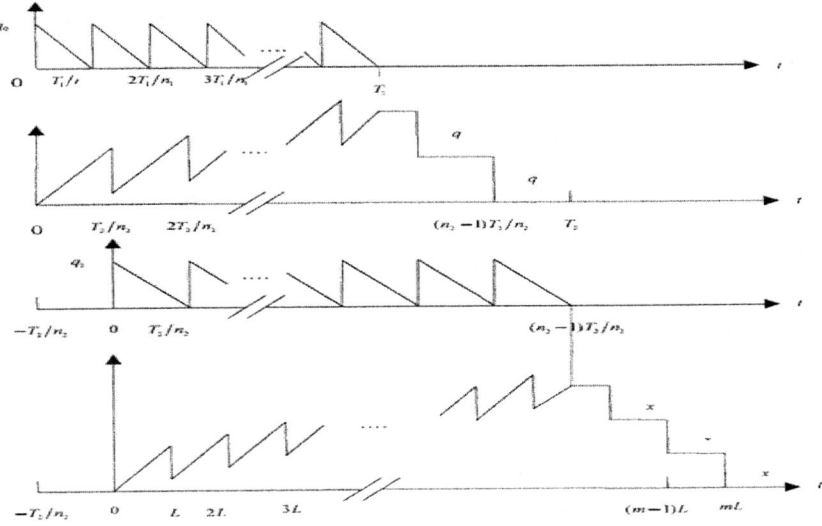

Fig. 2. On-hand inventory of raw materials, semi-finished products and finished products

$$TC(m, n_1, n_2) = \sum_{j=1}^{2} (\alpha_j \cdot \frac{m}{n_j}) + \sum_{j=1}^{2} (\beta_j \cdot \frac{n_j}{m}) + \gamma \cdot \frac{1}{m} + \delta \cdot m + \eta \quad (1)$$

where $\alpha_1 = \dfrac{xD_2^2 h_0}{2f_1 f_2^2 P_1 P_2}$, $\alpha_2 = \dfrac{xD_2(H_1+h_1)}{2f_2 P_2}$, $\beta_1 = \dfrac{D_2 K_0}{x}$, $\beta_2 = \dfrac{D_2 K_1}{x}$,

$\gamma = \dfrac{D_2(S_1+S_2)}{x}$, $\delta = \dfrac{xD_2 H_1}{2f_2 P_2}(1-\dfrac{D_2}{f_2 P_1}) + \dfrac{1}{2}xH_2(1-\dfrac{D_2}{P_2})$, $\eta = \dfrac{1}{2}xH_2$.

The total cost function in Eq.(1), $TC(m, n_1, n_2)$, is a function of three decision variables: m, n_1 and n_2. In order to obtain a solution with a minimum total cost, the following conditions are necessary:

$$\dfrac{\partial TC}{\partial m} = \sum_{j=1}^{2}\dfrac{\alpha_j}{n_j} - \sum_{j=1}^{2}\dfrac{\beta_j n_j}{m^2} - \dfrac{\gamma}{m^2} + \delta = 0 \qquad (2)$$

$$\dfrac{\partial TC}{\partial n_j} = -\dfrac{\alpha_j m}{n_j^2} + \dfrac{\beta_j}{m} = 0, \quad j=1,2 \qquad (3)$$

Hence we have:

$$m^0 = \sqrt{\gamma/\delta} \qquad (4)$$

$$n_j^0 = \sqrt{\alpha_j \gamma/(\beta_j \delta)}, \qquad (5)$$

It is not difficult to prove that the function $TC(m, n_1, n_2)$ attains a minimum solution at the stationary point (m^0, n_1^0, n_2^0). Therefore, we can obtain the following optimal quantities:

$$Q_2^0 = x\sqrt{\gamma/\delta} \qquad (6)$$

$$Q_1^0 = Q_2^0 / f_2 \qquad (7)$$

$$Q_0^0 = Q_1^0 / f_1 \qquad (8)$$

$$q_0^0 = Q_0^0 / n_1^0 = Q_1^0 /(f_1 n_1^0) \qquad (9)$$

$$q_1^0 = Q_1^0 / n_2^0 \qquad (10)$$

$$TC^0 = 2\sum_{j=1}^{2}\sqrt{\alpha_j \beta_j} + 2\sqrt{\gamma \cdot \delta} + \eta \qquad (11)$$

3 Sensitivity Analysis

A manufacturer in SCM environment always expects reducing ordering, transportation and setup costs as much as possible. Hence, the sensitivity of raw material ordering and production lot size to the changes in ordering, transportation and setup costs are examined as follows.

Suppose that the superscript is used to denote the corresponding parameters that have been changed. If $K'_{j-1} = \lambda_j K_{j-1} (0 < \lambda_j < 1, j = 1,2)$ and $\sum S'_j = \lambda \sum S_j$ $((0 < \lambda < 1))$, then $\alpha'_j = \alpha_j$, $\beta'_j = \lambda_j \beta_j$, $\gamma' = \lambda \cdot \gamma$, $\delta' = \delta$. Thus, we have:

$$m'^0 = \sqrt{\gamma'/\delta'} = \sqrt{\lambda \cdot \gamma/\delta} = \sqrt{\lambda} \cdot m^0 \qquad Q'^0_j = \sqrt{\lambda} \cdot Q^0_j, (j = 0,1,2),$$

$$n'^0_j = \sqrt{\lambda/\lambda_j} \cdot n^0_j, (j = 1,2), \qquad \text{and} \qquad q'^0_{j-1} = \sqrt{\lambda_j} \cdot q^0_{j-1}, (j = 1,2)$$

From these expressions, we have some useful observations. The details are neglected here due to the limit of the paper length.

4 Pragmatic Approach for Operational Situations

Since the globally optimal solutions m^0 and n^0_j in Eqs.(4) and (5) are usually treated as real numbers, they are not acceptable from an operational perspective in a real world situation. In other words, m^0 and n^0_j have to be modified into integers for practical us, that is, $m^* = \lfloor m^0 \rfloor$ or $\lceil m^0 \rceil$ and $n^*_j = \lfloor n^0_j \rfloor$ or $\lceil n^0_j \rceil$ where $\{m^*, n^*_j\}$ is a set of modified integer solution.

Once m^0 and n^0_j are modified into m^* and n^*_j, respectively, the corresponding quantities from Eq.(6) to Eq.(10) should be re-calculated. And the minimum integerized total cost should be calculated from Eq.(1) by applying m^* and n^*_j.

Based on the above approximation scheme, a pragmatic algorithm for calculating feasible optimal solution (i.e. optimal integer solution) is presented as follows.

Algorithm:

Step 1: Initialize and store all original parameters;

Step 2: Compute m^0 and n^0_j using Eqs.(4) and (5), respectively;

Step 3: If both m^0 and n^0_j are integers, then go to Step 5; otherwise, go to Step 4;

Step 4: Choose the optimal integer solution (m^*, n^*_j) that gives a minimum integerized total cost using the following model:

$$\min TC(m^*, n^*_j), \forall i,j \ (i=1,2)$$
$$\text{where } m^1 = \lfloor m^0 \rfloor, \ m^2 = \lceil m^0 \rceil, \ n^1_j = \lfloor n^0_j \rfloor, \text{ and } n^2 = \lceil n^0 \rceil$$

Step 5: Compute Q^0_2, Q^0_1, Q^0_0, q^0_0 and q^0_1 using Eqs.(6)-(10), respectively;

Step 6: Compute the minimum total cost TC_{min} using Eq.(1);

Step 7: Stop.

5 Numerical Examples

To illustrate the pragmatic computation approach presented above, a set of ten problems is tested. Using the algorithm proposed above, the corresponding computational results are given in Table 1, where $\delta = (TC^* - TC^0) \div TC^0$.

From Table 1 it can be seen that the deviation of the total costs between at the optimal integer solution and at the optimal solution is extremely small even if the total cost in the former is always higher than that in the latter. It shows that the optimal integer solution is feasible for real industry activities.

Table 1. Computational results by optimization and integer approximation

Problem	Optimum results				Modified results				
	m^0	n_1^0	n_2^0	TC^0	m^*	n_1^*	n_2^*	TC^*	δ
1	11.04	1.64	2.58	2678	12	2	3	2687	0.0034
2	10.32	2.88	3.41	4993	11	3	4	5006	0.0025
3	12.86	1.33	2.66	4413	13	1	3	4442	0.0108
4	6.02	1.44	2.09	7372	6	2	2	7437	0.0144
5	27.24	1.39	2.18	11225	27	1	2	11352	0.0282
6	5.59	1.67	3.29	9103	6	2	4	9147	0.0048
7	13.14	1.94	1.75	7359	14	2	2	7371	0.0016
8	11.89	1.62	2.32	3206	12	2	2	3225	0.0110
9	4.19	1.21	1.71	5825	4	1	2	5892	0.0172
10	12.86	1.63	3.63	5844	13	2	4	5862	0.0031

6 Conclusions

In this research, an optimal batch size and raw material ordering policy for a two-stage production-delivery system under a fixed-interval lumpy demand is developed. Using the presented mathematical model and pragmatic algorithm, one can determine optimal production lot size for each stage, optimal number of orders for raw materials, optimal quantity of raw materials ordered each time, optimal number of transportation for semi-finished products, and optimal quantity of semi-finished products transported each time. The sensitivity analysis shows how the optimal solutions are affected by the changes in ordering cost, transportation cost, and setup cost.

The scope of the solution is limited to a two-stage production system. Future research may be directed to a multi-stage production system.

References

1. Su, C.T., Lin, C.W.: A Production Inventory Model which Considers Dependence of Production Rate on Demand and Inventory. Production Planning & Control. 12 (2001) 69-75
2. Huang, Y.F.: Optimal Retailer's Replenishment Policy for the EPQ Model under the Supplier's Trade Credit Policy. Production Planning & Control, 15 (2004) 27-33
3. Sarker, B.R., Khan, L.R.: An Optimal Batch Size for a Production System Operating under Periodic Delivery Policy. Computers & Industrial Engineering. 37 (1999) 711-730

4. Feng, D.Z., Zhang, L.B.: Optimal Production Policy for a Volume-flexibility Supply-chain System. Lecture Notes in Computer Science. 3645 (2005) 900-909
5. Feng, D.Z., Yamashiro, M.: Optimal Production Policy for a Manufacturing System with Volume Flexibility in a Supply Chain under Lumpy Demand. International Journal of Advanced Manufacturing Technology. 25 (2005) 777-784
6. Feng, D.Z., Yamashiro, M.: A Pragmatic Approach for Optimal Selection of Plant-specific Process Plans in a Virtual Enterprise. Production Planning & Control. 14/6 (2003) 562-570

A Preliminary Investigation of a Linguistic Perceptron

Sansanee Auephanwiriyaku

Computer Engineering Department, Faculty of Engineering,
Chiang Mai University,
Chiang Mai, 50200, Thailand
sansanee@ieee.org

Abstract. For many years, one of the problems in pattern recognition is classification. There are many methods proposed to deal with this type of problem. The data sets are sometimes in the binary form (real number) and represented by vectors of binary numbers (real numbers) although there are uncertainties in the data. This study is concerned with a linguistic perceptron with vectors of fuzzy numbers as inputs. This algorithm is based on the extension principle and the decomposition theorem. A synthetic data set has been utilized to illustrate the behavior of this linguistic version of perceptron. We compare the result from the linguistic perceptron with that from the regular perceptron.

1 Introduction

Data can be in the form of binary values such as +1 and −1, or 0 and 1. Sometimes, it can be in the form of a real number. It can also be represented by a vector of real numbers corresponding to an appropriate linear space. These data can then be analyzed by a numeric mathematical model. The analysis involves finding structures within the data based on their arrangements or connections that can be described by the mathematical model. However, there are numerous times that we encounter uncertainty in the data. This type of data can be produced by the imprecision of an agent who collected the data, or produced by natural language, and can best be modeled by a fuzzy subset, the value of a linguistic variable. We call a vector of fuzzy subsets in the euclidean space a linguistic vector. There have been several studies on fuzzification of neural networks[1–8]. However, some of these works did not developed algorithms using fuzzy weight vectors. Some of these researches did not show any experiment results. There are several other works on fuzzy rule-based systems with fuzzy inputs that is not included in the reference because of the space limitation. The complete list of the references is shown in[9]. It is our belief that developing algorithms that deal with linguistic vectors without using defuzzification methods produces meaningful results. The purpose of this study is to develop a linguistic version of the regular perceptron. We examine the implementation issues of the linguistic perceptron, and demonstrate the application on a synthetic data set since this is only a preliminary report on this algorithm.

2 Background

A fuzzy number A is a normal convex fuzzy set defined on the real line, R[10]. The support of A is bounded in R. A fuzzy number A is called positive if $0 < a_1 \leq a_2$ holds for the support $\Gamma_A = [a_1, a_2]$ of A[11]. Similarly, A is called negative if $a_1 \leq a_2 < 0$ and zero if $a_1 \leq 0 < a_2$[11]. Kaleva [12] also defined a non-negative fuzzy number as follows: a fuzzy number A is called non-negative if $\mu_A(x) = 0$ for all $x < 0$. Suppose that A and B are two fuzzy numbers. Let the symbol $\otimes$ denote any of the algebraic operations +, -, * or /. According to the extension principle[13], the algebraic operation will map fuzzy sets in $\Im(R)$ (the fuzzy power set of R) to a fuzzy subset in $\Im(R)$ producing another fuzzy number Z. The result membership function is given by:

$$\mu_Z(y) = \sup_{x_1 \otimes x_2 = y} \min(\mu_A(x_1), \mu_B(x_2)) \tag{1}$$

where x_1 and x_2 satisfy the mapping constraint. If we discretize the continuous support into finite number of points and approximate the fuzzy set on the discrete domain, the resultant fuzzy set is often irregular and inaccurate compared with the exact result. Therefore, the operation is done based on interval arithmetic[11, 14 – 16] and the decomposition theorem[10]. Klir and Yuan [10] proved that for a fuzzy set $(A \otimes B)$, its α-cut $([A \otimes B]_\alpha)$ equals $[A]_\alpha \otimes [B]_\alpha$ for all $\alpha \in (0, 1]$. Then, by the decomposition theorem,

$$A \otimes B = \bigcup_{\alpha \in [0,1]} [A \otimes B]_\alpha \tag{2}$$

Since, for any of these operations, $[A \otimes B]_\alpha$ is a closed interval for each $\alpha \in (0, 1]$ and A, B are fuzzy numbers, $A \otimes B$ is also a fuzzy number.

For the collection of linguistic vectors (or type 2 fuzzy set) where each component is non-interactive, Mares [17] has shown that with $\vec{0}$ (the vector of singleton fuzzy number **0**), $\vec{1}$ (vector of singleton fuzzy number **1**), and component-wise addition and scalar multiplication, this forms a vector space. Also, with appropriate definitions of distance, these spaces exhibit the properties of metric spaces[12, 18].

3 Proposed Linguistic Perceptron

A linguistic perceptron is an extended version of the perceptron algorithm[19–21]. The perceptron determines a linear decision boundary separating the two given classes by iterative training. It is guaranteed to find a separating hyperplane in a finite number of steps if the vectors in the two classes are linearly separable. Let $X = \{\vec{x}_j | j = 1 \ldots N\}$ be a set of N feature vectors in p-dimensional feature space. Each $\vec{x}_j$ is labeled either class 1 or class 2. If the two classes are linearly separable, then there exists a weight vector $\vec{w} = (w_1, w_2, \ldots, w_{p+1})^t$ such that

$$\vec{w}^t \vec{x}_j > 0 \quad \text{if } \vec{x}_j \text{ is in class 1} \tag{3a}$$

$$\vec{w}^t \vec{x}_j \leq 0 \quad \text{if } \vec{x}_j \text{ is in class 2} \tag{3b}$$

where $\vec{x}_j = (x_{j1}, x_{j2}, \ldots x_{jp}, 1)^t$ is an augmented feature vector j. If all the class 2 feature vectors are multiplied by -1, then $\vec{w}^t\vec{x}_j > 0$ for $j = 1,\ldots N$. (4)

The hyperplane in R^p is defined by $\vec{w}^t\vec{x}_j = 0$ where all class 1 feature vectors lie on one side and all class 2 feature vectors lie on the other side of the hyperplane. The perceptron algorithm is then to find a weight vector as follows:

1. If $\vec{w}^t\vec{x} \leq 0$ then set $\vec{w}$ to $\vec{w} + \eta\vec{x}$ where η is a positive constant.
2. Otherwise, $\vec{w}$ remains the same.

Now, we will extend the algorithm to a linguistic perceptron (LP) for two classes problem. To define the LP, let $\mathbf{X} = \{\vec{X}_j \mid 1 \leq j \leq N\}$ be a set of non-interactive fuzzy vectors in p-dimensional space, $\vec{X}_j = (X_{j1},\ldots,X_{jp})^t \in [\Im(R)]^p$. Suppose there exists a fuzzy weight vector $\vec{W} = (W_1,\ldots,W_{p+1})^t$ such that

$$\vec{W}^t\vec{X}_j = \left(W_1 X_{j1} + W_2 X_{j2} + \ldots + W_p X_{jp} + W_{p+1} X_{jp+1}\right) > 0 \quad \text{if } \vec{X}_j \text{ is in class 1} \quad (5a)$$

$$\vec{W}^t\vec{X}_j = \left(W_1 X_{j1} + W_2 X_{j2} + \ldots + W_p X_{jp} + W_{p+1} X_{jp+1}\right) \leq 0 \quad \text{if } \vec{X}_j \text{ is in class 2} \quad (5b)$$

where $\vec{X}_j = (X_{j1},\ldots,X_{jp}, 1)^t$ is an augmented feature vector j with a singleton fuzzy number $\mathbf{1}$. From the decomposition theorem, the left side of equations (5a) and (5b) is transformed to

$$\vec{W}^t\vec{X}_j = \bigcup_{\alpha \in [0,1]}\left([W_1]_\alpha[X_{j1}]_\alpha + [W_2]_\alpha[X_{j2}]_\alpha + \ldots + [W_p]_\alpha[X_{jp}]_\alpha + [W_{p+1}]_\alpha[1]_\alpha\right) \quad (6)$$

The multiplication between a fuzzy weight vector and fuzzy input vector produces a fuzzy number. In particular, if $\vec{X}_j$ is in class 1, $\vec{W}^t\vec{X}_j$ is a positive fuzzy number and if $\vec{X}_j$ is in class 2 $\vec{W}^t\vec{X}_j$ is a negative or zero fuzzy number. We also multiplied each class 2 linguistic vectors with a numeric number -1, i.e.,

$$\vec{X}_j' = -1 \times \vec{X}_j \quad \text{for all } \vec{X}_j \text{ that are in class 2}. \quad (7)$$

Since the input feature vector is a non-interactive fuzzy vector, this multiplication is done in each dimension separately. For each dimension k and the decomposition theorem,

$$-1 \times X_{jk} = \bigcup_{\alpha \in [0,1]}\left(-1 \times [X_{jk}]_\alpha\right) \quad \text{for all } \vec{X}_j \text{ that are in class 2}. \quad (8)$$

Hence, for all fuzzy input vectors, $\vec{W}^t\vec{X}_j > 0$ for all $j = 1,\ldots, N$ (9)

i.e., the multiplication in equation (9) produces a positive fuzzy number. The fuzzy hyperplane (H) is defined by $\vec{W}^t\vec{X} = 0$ where all class 1 feature vectors lie on one side and all class 2 feature vectors lie on the other side of the hyperplane. In order to understand this definition better, let us first consider the 2-dimensional case. If fuzzy hyperplane is a fuzzy number $\in [\Im(R)]^2$, then it is a fuzzy line[22], i.e.,

$$H = \vee\{\alpha|(x_1, x_2)\in \Omega\} \tag{10}$$

where $\Omega = \{(x_1, x_2) \mid [W_1]_\alpha x_1 + [W_2]_\alpha x_2 + [W_3]_\alpha = 0\} \; \forall \alpha \in [0,1]$ and $(x_1, x_2)\in R^2$. If the fuzzy hyperplane is a fuzzy number $\in [\Im(R)]^p$, then $H = \vee\{\alpha|(x_1,\ldots, x_p)\in \Omega\}$ where $\Omega = \{(x_1,\ldots, x_p) \mid [W_1]_\alpha x_1 + [W_2]_\alpha x_2 + \ldots + [W_p]_\alpha x_p + [W_{p+1}]_\alpha = 0\} \; \forall \alpha \in [0,1]$ and $(x_1,\ldots, x_p)\in R^p$. The perceptron algorithm is then to find a fuzzy weight vector as follows:

1. If $\vec{W}^t\vec{X} \leq 0$ or $\vec{W}^t\vec{X}$ is a negative or zero fuzzy number then

$$\vec{W}(n+1) = \vec{W}(n) + \eta\vec{X}(n) \tag{11}$$

where η is a positive constant (numeric number) and n is a time step. For each dimension k,

$$W_k(n+1) = W_k(n) + \eta X_k(n). \tag{12a}$$

From the decomposition theorem, equation (12a) is transformed to

$$W_k(n) + \eta X_k(n) = \bigcup_{\alpha \in [0,1]} ([W_k(n)]_\alpha + \eta[X_k(n)]_\alpha). \tag{12b}$$

2. Otherwise, $\vec{W}$ remains the same.

We use the similarity [23] of the weight to compute the stopping criteria of our LP algorithm. Let $\overrightarrow{OW}$ be the old weight, $\vec{W}$ be the new weight; $\overrightarrow{OW}$ and $\vec{W} \in [\Im(R)]^p$ and ε be a small positive number. The dissimilarity between the old weight and the new weight is:

$$Q = \max_{1\leq j \leq p+1}\left(1 - \frac{card(OW_j \cap W_j)}{card(OW_j \cup W_j)}\right) \tag{13}$$

The algorithm will stop if: $\quad Q < \varepsilon \tag{14}$

or the weight is not updated for N fuzzy feature vectors. The algorithm of our LP is as following

---

Initial weight fuzzy vector
Do {
　Set Update Flag to false.
　For all vector $\vec{X}_j, j = 1,\ldots,N$
　　If $\vec{W}^t\vec{X}_j$ is negative or zero fuzzy number **Then**
　　　Update weight fuzzy vector using equations (11), (12a) and (12b)
　　　Set Update Flag to true.
　End For
}**Until** weight stabilize using equations (13) and (14) or Update Flag is false.

4 Experiment Results

In this section, we perform an experiment on a numerical example shown in figure 1. We fuzzify each dimension of each data point to be a trapezoid as shown in figure 2. We generate the width on the right and left of the core (w_r, w_l) using Gaussian distribution N(0.1,0.5). The width of the spread (a) is equal to the mean of the distribution that generates w_r and w_l of the core [9]. We apply the regular perceptron on the peaks (the coordinates in figure 1) followed by the LP on the linguistic vectors. We randomly initialize weight to be a singleton fuzzy vector. The learning rate is set to 0.0001 and the maximum iterations is set to 100 for both the LP experiments and the regular perceptron experiments.

For the fuzzified version of this data set, the LP algorithm is stopped after 16 iterations. Figure 3 shows the confusion matrix, while figure 4 shows the final fuzzy weight vector. The centroid of the fuzzy weight vector is $[-0.215\ 0.351\ 0.825]^t$. Because the input fuzzy vector from this data set is $\in [\Im(R)]^2$, the fuzzy hyperplane is a fuzzy line. The support of this fuzzy line and the support of the fuzzy input vectors are shown in figure 5.

The weight vector from the regular perceptron in the data set is $[-0.196\ 0.358\ 0.826]^t$. The decision boundary from the regular perceptron is also shown in figure 5. The weight vector and the bias from numeric case and the centroids of that from fuzzy vectors case are similar. The support of the $\vec{W}^t\vec{X}$ for each fuzzified input vector in this data set is shown in table 1.

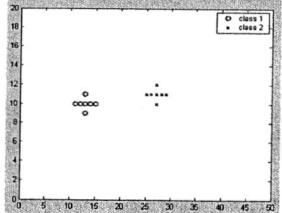

Fig. 1. A Numerical data set

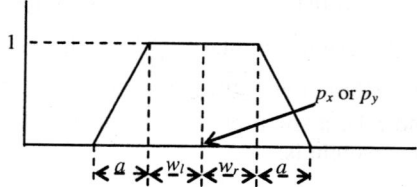

Fig. 2. Data with peak p_x or p_y and (w_r, w_l) generated from normal distribution

		Desired Output	
		Class 1	Class 2
Algorithm's Output	Class 1	7	0
	Class 2	0	7

Fig. 3. Confusion matrix of the linguistic vectors from the second data set

Table 1. Support of fuzzy number $\vec{W}^t\vec{X}$ for the linguistic vectors of the second data set

	Input linguistic vectors						
	1	2	3	4	5	6	7
Class 1	[1.30, 2.29]	[1.29, 2.27]	[0.95, 1.90]	[1.34, 2.38]	[0.89, 1.77]	[0.87, 1.62]	[0.51, 1.59]
Class 2	[-1.35, -0.24]	[-1.86, -0.53]	[-1.79, -0.17]	[-1.35, -0.07]	[-1.81, -0.82]	[-2.30, -0.74]	[-2.13, -1.08]

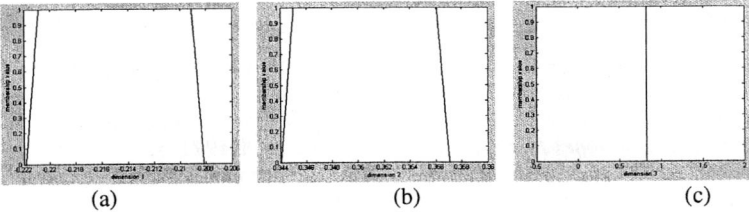

Fig. 4. Weight linguistic vector for the linguistic vectors from the second data set (a) first dimension, (b) second dimension, (c) third dimension (bias)

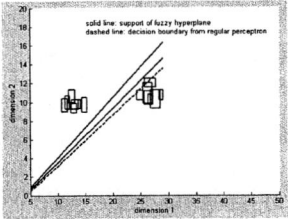

Fig. 5. Supports of input fuzzy vectors from 2 classes and fuzzy hyperplane for the second data set and the decision boundary from the regular perceptron

From the result, we can see that the input lingusitic vectors that are in class 1 yield positive fuzzy numbers from the decision rule. While the input linguistic vectors that are in class 2 yield negative fuzzy numbers from the decision rule.

From figure 5, we can see that the width of the supports of the fuzzy hyperplanes are wider as the value in dimension 1 increases. This is because of the behavior of the multiplication and division of fuzzy numbers as in equation (10).

5 Conclusion

In this paper, we developed a linguistic perceptron (LP) that works with vectors of fuzzy numbers. It employs fuzzy weight update equation that is an extension of the weight update equation from the regular perceptron. The LP also produces a fuzzy hyperplane that is a fuzzy line in the case of the 2-dimensional data set. The supports of the fuzzy hyperplanes are wider as the value in dimension 1 increases. The fuzzy hyperplane is more uncertain as the value in dimension 1 increases. However, the centroids of a fuzzy weight vector and bias from the LP are close to the weights and biases from the regular perceptron. The fuzzy hyperplane and the decision boundary from the LP and the regular perceptron are in similar direction.

Although, the result seems promising, this is only the beginning of the investigation of a linguistic perceptron. We still need to develop a theorem to support the idea of the linguistic perceptron and the idea of linearly separable in the future work. We will utilize this algorithm with several synthetic data sets and real applications as well.

Acknowledgement

This research is supported by the Ministry of Education and the Thailand Research Fund under the contract No. MRG4780053. We thank Prof. Sompong Dhompongsa for his suggestion.

References

1. M. Gupta and J. Qi, "On Fuzzy Neuron Models", *Proceedings of Inter. Joint Conference on Neural Networks (IJCNN91)*, Seattle, 1991, 431-436.
2. Y. Hayashi, J. J. Buckley, and E. Czogala, "Fuzzy Neural Network with Fuzzy Signals and Weights", *International Journal of Intelligent Systems*, 8, 1993, 527-537.
3. H. Ishibuchi, R. Fujioka, and H. Tanaka, "An Architecture of Neural Networks for Input Vectors of Fuzzy Numbers", *Proceedings, FUZZ-IEEE*, San Diego, 1992, 1293-1300.
4. H. Ishibuchi, K. Kwon, and H. Tanaka, "A Learning Algorithm of Fuzzy Neural Networks with Triangular Fuzzy Weights", *Fuzzy Set and Systems*, 71, 1995, 277-293.
5. J. L. Chen and J. Y. Chang, "Fuzzy Perceptron Learning and Its Application to Classifiers with Numerical Data and Linguistic Knowledge", *Proc. IEEE Int. Conf. Neural Networks*, Perth, Australia, 1995, 3129-3133.
6. J. L. Chen and J. Y. Chang, "Fuzzy Perceptron Neural Networks for Classifiers with Numerical Data and Linguistic Rules as Inputs", *IEEE Trans. On Fuzzy Systems*, 8(6), 2000, 730-745.
7. H. M. Lee and W. T. Wang, "Fuzzy Pocket Algorithm: a generalized pocket algorithm for classification of fuzzy inputs", *Proc. IEEE Int. Conf. Neural Networks*, 1993, 2873-2876.
8. H. M. Lee and W. T. Wang, "A Neural Network Architecture for Classification of Fuzzy Inputs", *Fuzzy Sets and Systems*, 63, 1994, 159-173.
9. S. Auephanwiriyakul, J. M. Keller, " Analysis and Efficient Implementation of a Linguistic Fuzzy C-Means", *IEEE Trans on Fuzzy Systems*, 10(5), 2002, 563-583.
10. G. Klir, and B. Yuan, "Fuzzy Sets and Fuzzy Logic: Theory and Application", New Jersey, Prentice Hall, 1995.
11. M. Mizumoto and K. Tanaka, "Some properties of fuzzy numbers in advances in fuzzy sets theory and applications", In: Gupta, M. M. eds., Advances in Fuzzy Set Theory and Applications, Amsterdam, North-Holland, 1979, 153-164.
12. O. Kaleva and S. Seikkala, "On Fuzzy Metric Spaces", *Fuzzy Sets and Systems*, 12, 1984, 215-229.
13. L. Zadeh, "Outline of new approach to the analysis of complex systems and decision processes", *IEEE Trans. Sys. Man Cyb.*, 3(1), 1973.
14. W. Dong, H. Shah, and F. Wong, "Fuzzy computations in risk and decision analysis", *Civ. Eng Syst.*, 2, 1985, 201-208.
15. W. Dong, and F. Wong, "Fuzzy Weighted Averages and Implementation of The Extension Principle", *Fuzzy Sets and Systems*, 21, 1987, 183-199.
16. R. Moore, "Interval Analysis", New Jersey, Prentice-Hall, 1966.
17. M. Mares, " Computation over Fuzzy Quantities", Florida, CRC Press, 1994.
18. I. Kramosil, and J. Michalek, "Fuzzy Metric and Statistical Metric Spaces", *Kybernatika*, 11, 1975, 336-344.
19. F. Rosenblatt, "The perceptron: A perceiving and recognizing automaton", Cornell University, Ithaca, NY, Project PARA, Cornell Aeronaunt Laboratory, Rep., 85-460.1, 1957.
20. T. Tou and R. C. Gonzalez, "Pattern Recognition Principles", Reading, MA: Addison-Wesley, 1974.
21. S. Haykin, "Neural Netrowks: A comprehensive Foundation", New Jersey, Prentice Hall 1999.
22. J. N. Mordeson and P. S. Nair, "Fuzzy Mathematics: An Introduction for Engineers and Scientists", New York, Physica-Verlag 2001.
23. P. H. A. Sneath, "The application of computers in taxonomy", *J. General Microbiology*, 17, 1957, 201-226.

Skeleton Driven Limb Animation Based on Three-Layered Structure

Jiarong Yu, Jiaoying Shi, and Yongxia Zhou

State Key Lab of CAD&CG, Zhejiang University, Hangzhou, 310027, China
{yjr, jyshi, zhou_yongx}@cad.zju.edu.cn

Abstract. In this paper, we present a new model for the skeleton driven limb animation, which is composed of three layers: linear bones, volumetric bones and coarse volumetric control lattice. Volumetric bones are driven by linear bones using geometric method and the coarse volumetric control lattice is driven by volumetric bones using finite element method. In order to compute faster, we perform linearized simulations. The limb is embedded in the volumetric control lattice, and the surface of limb is computed using linear interpolation method. PCG solver is used to solve the large linear system of equations. We can obtain realtime simulations and realize the motions such as bend and torsion of limb.

1 Introduction

Arms and legs play an important role in human character animation. The character should be simulated realistically and fast in film realm or virtual reality. Geometric method is the most common technique for deforming characters. Chadwick et al. [1] presented a deformable model of muscle driven by the articulated skeleton using FFD technique. Recent work in the area of articulated character deformation was done by Sloan et al. [2]. Physical method was introduced by Terzopoulos et al. [3] to achieve more reality. They simulated the elastic objects using Lagrangian equations of motion and finite differences method. To add stability to computations, an implicit solver was proposed by Baraff and Witkin [4].

The technique of combination of physical principle and geometric modeling presented by Capell et al. [5] utilize the advantage of the two methods. Their model is composed of tow layers: linear bones and volumetric control lattice. We present a new model of limb, which is composed of three layers: linear bones, volumetric bones and volumetric control lattice. Volumetric bones are driven by linear bones using geometric method. Finite element method is applied to compute the shape of the volumetric control lattice which is driven by volumetric bones. The limb is embedded in the control lattice and the shape of the limb is computed using linear interpolation method. We can obtain realtime simulations and realize many motions include displacement, bend and torsion of limb conveniently.

2 Three-Layered Structure

Our model is established based on the articulated human character. There are three layers in this model: linear bones, volumetric bones and volumetric control lattice. In this paper, we use arm model to explain our method.

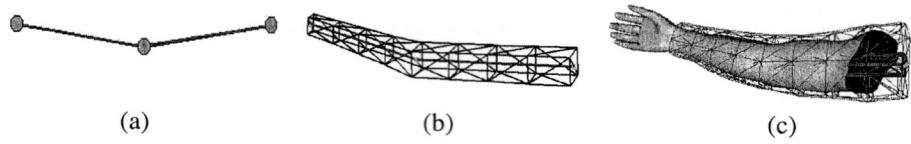

Fig. 1. Three-layered structure

Arm is composed of upper arm and lower arm. The lower arm can perform the motion of torsion. Fig.1 (a) shows the simplified model of arm bones. This is the first layer that we call it as linear bones. The second layer is volumetric bones whose shape is determined by linear bones using geometric method (see Fig.1 (b)). Volumetric control lattice is an elastic deformable body which is the third layer in our model (see Fig.1 (c)). The surface of volumetric bones is constrains of the control lattice. We apply the linear finite element method to the control lattice [6, 7]. The arm is embedded in the control lattice. We use the linear interpolation method to compute the vertices position of the arm. In this paper we don't consider the deformation of the hand.

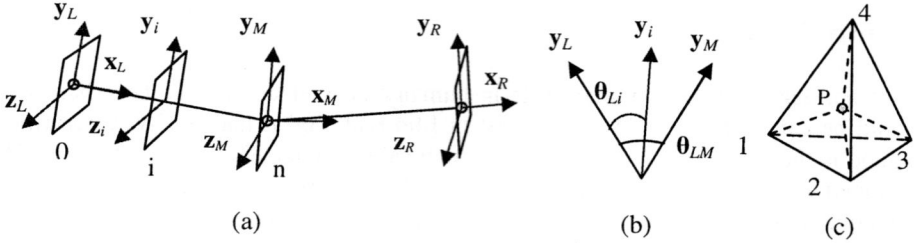

Fig. 2. Calculate the shape of volumetric bones and vertices of the arm

Fig.2 (a) shows how to construct the volumetric bones. For every joint there is a local coordinate system determining the orientation of the arm. Suppose three joints are not collinear at beginning. The axis x_L is along the left bone line and the axis x_R is along the right bone line. The axes z_L and z_R are normal to the plane containing two bone lines. In course of movement, the axis z_M is always parallel to z_R. If the left bone line rotates around the axis z_M, the motion is called bend. If the axes y_L and z_L rotate around the left bone line, the motion is called torsion. Suppose x_L and x_R are unit vectors, then $x_M = x_L + x_R$. Now each local coordinate system has been orientated and we normalize all the axial vectors. There are some rectangles numbered from 0 to n between left and middle joints. The center of rectangle i c_i is calculated using $c_i = c_0 + i(c_n - c_0)/n$. The vectors y_L, y_i, and y_M are in their common plane (see

Fig.2 (b)) and $\theta_{Li} = i \cdot \theta_{LM}/n$. Then we calculate the vector y_i. The same is true of calculating the vector z_i. Given the length of edges along the vector y_i or z_i, the shape of rectangle i is determined. We calculate the shape of rectangles between middle and right joints using the same method. With these rectangles we construct the volumetric bones.

Volumetric control lattice is an elastic body composed of tetrahedral elements. If the body deforms gently, the deformation is computed using the equilibrium equation. After applied finite element method, the equation is expressed as follows:

$$\mathbf{K}\mathbf{q} = \mathbf{f} \qquad (1)$$

where **q** denotes the displacement of the control lattice, **K** is the stiffness matrix, and **f** represents the externally applied forces such as gravity. If the body deforms obviously, we apply linear finite element method to the Lagrangian formulation of the equations of elasticity to solve the system [6, 7]. Then we obtain the dynamic formulation $\mathbf{M}\ddot{\mathbf{q}} + \mathbf{C}\dot{\mathbf{q}} + \mathbf{K}\mathbf{q} = \mathbf{f}$, where **M** is the mass matrix, **C** is the damping matrix. In order to obtain the stable computation with large timestep, we apply the implicit solver presented by Baraff and Witkin [4] to the dynamic formulation. The resulting equations are:

$$\Delta \mathbf{q} = h(\dot{\mathbf{q}} + \Delta \mathbf{v}) \qquad (2)$$

$$(\mathbf{M} - h\mu \mathbf{I} + h^2 \mathbf{K})\Delta \mathbf{v} = h(\mu \dot{\mathbf{q}} - \mathbf{K}\mathbf{q} - \mathbf{f} - h\mathbf{K}\dot{\mathbf{q}}) \qquad (3)$$

where h is the timestep, $\Delta \mathbf{q}$ is the change in displacement **q** during the timestep, $\Delta \mathbf{v}$ is the change in velocity $\dot{\mathbf{q}}$ during the timestep, μ is the damping coefficient, and **I** is the identity matrix. Equations (1) and (3) are large sparse linear systems. In order to compute faster, we apply the Preconditioned Conjugate Gradient (PCG) solver [8].

Suppose there is a vertex of arm surface P in the tetrahedron 1234 (see Fig.2 (c)). The volume of 1234 is V and the volume of 234P is V_1. Then $L_1 = V_1/V$. The same is true of calculating L_2, L_3 and L_4. In course of deformation, the position of P $\mathbf{v}_p$ is calculated as $\mathbf{v}_P = \sum_1^4 L_i \mathbf{v}_i$, where $\mathbf{v}_i$ is the position of the vertex i.

3 Results

Fig.3 shows the results of applying our model to two triangle meshes. Fig.3 (a) shows the bend and torsion of arm solved with dynamic formulation. Fig.3 (b) shows the walk of man solved with equilibrium equation. The control mesh for the man model has 1440 cells and 532 vertices. We obtain realtime simulations on our 1.6 Ghz PC. The table.1 shows that the calculated performance of our algorithm is superior than Capell's.

Table 1. Calculated Performance of Our Algorithm and Capell's

CPU (Ghz)	Model	Num of Cells	Num of vertices	Frames/SEC
1.6 (our)	Man	1440	532	300
1.0 (Capell's)	Cow	572	214	100

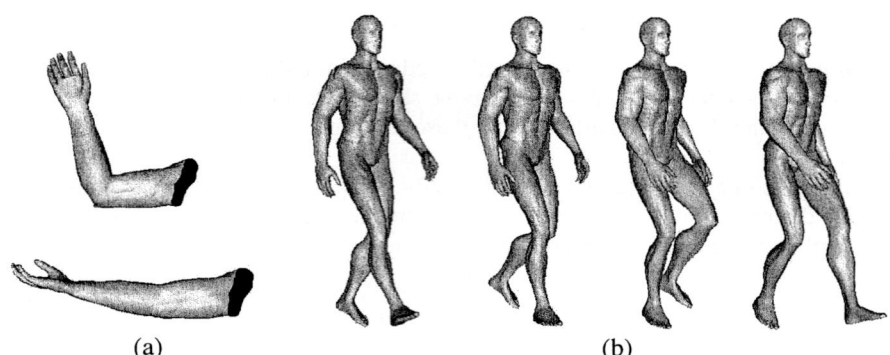

Fig. 3. The bend and torsion of arm and the walk of man

4 Conclusions and Future Work

We introduce a three-layered structure for the animation of limb. The advantage is that it can realize some motions such as bend and torsion of limb. We combine the advantages of geometric method and physical method. The implicit method and PCG solver is applied to accelerate the computation and obtain the realtime simulations.

In our later work, we would like to improve the model of limb and let it has function of muscle. The deformation near the joint should be improved in order to obtain more reality.

References

1. Chadwick, J.E., Haumann, D.R. and Parent, R.E.: Layered Construction for Deformable Animated Characters. In Proceedings of SIGGRAPH 89 (1989) 243-252
2. Sloan, P.P.J., Rose, C.F. and Cohen, M.F.: Shape by Example. In Symposium on Interactive 3D Graphics (2001) 135-144
3. Terzopoulos, D., Platt, J., Barr, A. and Fleischer, K.: Elastically Deformable Models. Computer Graphics (Proceedings of SIGGRAPH 87) 21, 4 (July) (1987) 205-214
4. Baraff, D. and Witkin, A.: Large Steps in Cloth Simulation. In Proceedings of SIGGRAPH 98 (1998) 43-54
5. Capell, S., Green, S., Curless, B., Duchamp, T. and Popović, Z.: Interactive Skeleton-Driven Dynamic Deformations. In Proceedings of SIGGRAPH 2002 (2002) 586-593
6. Zienkiewicz, O. C.: The Finite Element Method. 3rd ed., McGraw-Hill (1977)
7. Shabana, A.: Dynamics of Multibody Systems. Cambridge University Press (1998)
8. Saad, Y.: Iterative Methods for Sparse Linear Systems. PWS Publishing, Boston (1996)

Answer Set Programming for Distributed Authorization: The Language, Computations, and Application

Shujing Wang and Yan Zhang

School of Computing and Information Technology,
University of Western Sydney, Australia
{shwang, yan}@cit.uws.edu.au

Abstract. In this paper, we employ Answer Set Programming to deal with many complex issues associated with the distributed authorization along the trust management approach. Using our approach, we can not only express nonmonotonic delegation policies which have not been considered in previous approaches, but also represent the delegation with depth, separation of duty, and positive and negative authorizations. We also investigate basic computational properties related to our approach and discuss a case study to illustrate the application of our approach in a distributed environment.

1 Introduction

Access control is an important topic in computer security research. The traditional access control process includes identification, authentification and authorization. In a distributed or multi-centralized authorization environment, however, there are more entities in the system, which can be both authorizers and requesters, and probably are unknown to each other. Because the authorizer does not know the requester directly, he/she has to use the information from the third parties who know the requester better. The trust and delegation issues make distributed authorization different from traditional access control scenarios.

In recent years, the trust management approach, which was initially proposed by Blaze *et al.* in [1], has received a great attention in information security community [1,3,4,5]. Several trust management systems such as PolicyMaker [1], Keynote [2], SPKI/SDSI [3], DL [5], and RT [4] have been developed. Although the existing trust management systems may express rich delegation and authorization policies, we observe that an important issue they do not consider is to express nonmonotonic policy (default reasoning) and related issues. Let us consider a scenario. In an large commercial organization, a staff usually can enter the information management system. However, somebody will be denied even though he/she is a staff, if the human resource manager HrM says he/she is on holiday. In this scenario, only the staff for whom there is no information on holiday from hrM are permitted to access the management system.

In this paper, we propose a nonmonotonic language $\mathcal{AL}$, which is based on Answer Set Programming, in which negation as failure is used to implement default reasoning. $\mathcal{AL}$ also enables both positive and negative authorization which make policies more flexible. At the same time, we preserve all desirable properties from existing trust management such as delegation with depth control, structured resources, separation of duty, et al.. We also investigate the computational properties for language $\mathcal{AL}$ and show our approach through a scenario.

2 An Authorization Language $\mathcal{AL}$: Syntax and Semantics

The authorization language $\mathcal{AL}$ consists of *entities, atoms, thresholds, statements, rules* and *queries*. We define the semantics for language $\mathcal{AL}$ through translating it to Answer Set Programming based language $\mathcal{L}_{Ans}$. The *domain description* $\mathcal{D}_{\mathcal{AL}}$ of language $\mathcal{AL}$ is a finite set of rules. We define function $TransRules(\mathcal{D}_{\mathcal{AL}})$ to translate $\mathcal{D}_{\mathcal{AL}}$ into program $\mathcal{P}$ of $\mathcal{L}_{Ans}$, and function $TransQuery(\mathcal{Q}_{\mathcal{AL}})$ to translate query $\mathcal{Q}_{\mathcal{AL}}$ into program Π and ground literals $\varphi(+)$ and $\varphi(-)$. We use $\varphi(+)$ to denote positive right and $\varphi(-)$ to denote negative right. We solve a query based on $\mathcal{P}$, Π and φ via *Smodels*. Here we give the definition about how to answer the query and the detailed information about syntax and semantics of language $\mathcal{AL}$ are referred to [6].

Definition 1. *Given a domain description $\mathcal{D}_{\mathcal{AL}}$ and a query $\mathcal{Q}_{\mathcal{AL}}$ of language $\mathcal{AL}$, there are $TransRules(\mathcal{D}_{\mathcal{AL}}) = \mathcal{P}$ and $TransQuery(\mathcal{Q}_{\mathcal{AL}}) = <\Pi, \varphi(+), \varphi(-)>$. We say that query $\mathcal{Q}_{\mathcal{AL}}$ is permitted, denied, or unknown by the domain description $\mathcal{D}_{\mathcal{AL}}$ iff $(\mathcal{P} \cup \Pi) \models \varphi(+)$, $(\mathcal{P} \cup \Pi) \models \varphi(-)$, or $(\mathcal{P} \cup \Pi) \not\models \varphi(+)$ and $(\mathcal{P} \cup \Pi) \not\models \varphi(-)$ respectively.*

3 Computational Properties of Language $\mathcal{AL}$

In this section, we study basic computational properties of language $\mathcal{AL}$, in which there are four types of statements, *relation statement, assertion statement, delegation statement*, and *auth statement*. To simplify our investigation, we consider each statement as a predicate with n terms, $p(t_1, t_2, \ldots, t_n)$ in which p denotes the statement type, and t_is are terms to denote the variable parts in the statement. For instance, we denote a relation statement, *"local says below(alice, postgraduate)"* using predicate form, $RelStmt(local, below, alice, postgraduate)$. We provide the related definitions, lemmas and theorems in this section, and the detailed descriptions and proofs are referred to [7].

Definition 2. *Term t_1, and t_2 are compatible, denoted by $t_1 \simeq t_2$, if t_1 and t_2 are same type terms, and one of the following conditions holds:*

1. *both of t_1 and t_2 are constant terms with the same name*
2. *at least one of t_1 and t_2 is a variable term, or*
3. *t_1 is a subject constant, t_2 is a subject structure, and t_1 is a member of t_2.*

Definition 3. *Two statements s_1, s_2 are compatible, denoted by $s_1 \simeq s_2$, if s_1 and s_2 have the predicate forms s_1' and s_2' respectively, and*

1. *s_1' and s_2' are the same type predicates,*
2. *all the corresponding terms of s_1' and s_2' are compatible.*

Definition 4. *Let $\mathcal{D}$ be a domain description of $\mathcal{AL}$ and r_p and r_q be two rules in $\mathcal{D}$. We define a set $\mathcal{S}(r_p)$ of statements with respect to r_p as follows:*

$$\mathcal{S}_0 = head(r_p);$$
$$\mathcal{S}_i = \mathcal{S}_{i-1} \cup \{head(r) \mid head(r') \simeq s \text{ where } s \in pos(r) \text{ and }$$
$$\quad r' \text{ are those rules such that } head(r') \in \mathcal{S}_{i-1}\};$$
$$\mathcal{S}(r_p) = \bigcup_{i=1}^{\infty} \mathcal{S}_i.$$

We say that r_q is *defeasible through* r_p in $\mathcal{D}$ if and only if $neg(r_q) \cap^c \mathcal{S}(r_p) \neq \emptyset$ [1].

Definition 5. *Given a domain description $\mathcal{D}_{\mathcal{AL}}$ of $\mathcal{AL}$, we define its* defeasible graph *$\mathcal{DG} = \langle V, E \rangle$, where V is the set of rules r_i in $\mathcal{D}_{\mathcal{AL}}$ as the vertices and E the set of $\langle r_i, r_j \rangle$ which is a directed edge to denote that r_j is defeasible through r_i.*

Lemma 1. *Let $\mathcal{D}_{\mathcal{AL}}$ be a domain description of $\mathcal{AL}$ and $\mathcal{P}$ the translated logic program in language $\mathcal{L}_{Ans}$. If the defeasible graph $\mathcal{DG}$ of $\mathcal{D}_{\mathcal{AL}}$ does not have a cycle, then $\mathcal{P}$ is* locally stratified.

Lemma 2. *Let $\mathcal{D}_{\mathcal{AL}}$ be a domain description of $\mathcal{AL}$ and $\mathcal{P}$ the translated logic program in language $\mathcal{L}_{Ans}$. If the defeasible graph $\mathcal{DG}$ of $\mathcal{D}_{\mathcal{AL}}$ does not have a cycle with an odd number edges, then $\mathcal{P}$ is* call consistent.

Theorem 1. *Let $\mathcal{D}_{\mathcal{AL}}$ be a domain description of $\mathcal{AL}$. If its defeasible graph $\mathcal{DG}$ does not have a cycle, then $\mathcal{D}_{\mathcal{AL}}$ has a unique model that can be computed in polynomial time.*

Theorem 2. *Let $\mathcal{D}_{\mathcal{AL}}$ be a domain description of $\mathcal{AL}$. If its defeasible graph $\mathcal{DG}$ does not have a cycle with an odd number edges, then $\mathcal{D}_{\mathcal{AL}}$ has at lease one model that can be computed in polynomial time.*

4 A Case Study

In this section we represent a specific authorization scenario to demonstrate the application and the computational properties of language $\mathcal{AL}$.

Scenario: A server provides the services including $http$, ftp, $mysql$, and $smtp$. It sets up a group for them, called $services$. The server delegated the right of assigning all the services to the security officer so with depth 3. The security officer so grants the services to $staff$. The service $mysql$ can not be accessed if the staff is on holiday. Officer so can get information of staff from the human resource manager hrM. The policy and credentials are described using language $\mathcal{AL}$ as follows.

$r_0 : local\ says\ below(http, services).$
$r_1 : local\ says\ below(ftp, services).$
$r_2 : local\ says\ below(mysql, services).$
$r_3 : local\ says\ below(smtp, services).$

---

[1] $\cap^c$ is to get a compatible joint set of two statement sets. Formally, $A \cap^c B = \{s_1, s_2 | s_1 \simeq s_2, \text{ where } s_1 \in A, \text{ and } s_2 \in B\}.$

r_4 : *local* delegates $right(\Box, access, services)$ to *so* with depth 3.
r_5 : *so* grants $right(+, access, Y)$ to X if hrM asserts $isStaff(X)$,
       local says $below(Y, services)$, *local says* $neq(Y, mysql)$.
r_6 : *so* grants $right(+, access, mysql)$ to X
       if hrM asserts $isStaff(X)$, *with absence* hrM asserts $onHoliday(X)$.
r_7 : hrM asserts $isStaff(alice)$.
r_8 : hrM asserts $isStaff(bob)$.
r_9 : hrM asserts $onHoliday(alice)$.

The above rules consist of a domain description $\mathcal{D}_{\mathcal{AL}}$, in which r_0, r_1, r_2, r_3, r_7, r_8, and r_9 are facts and only r_6 has a negative body statement. Based on definitions on section 3, r_6 is defeasible through r_9. Because there is no other defeasible rule pair, the defeasible graph of $\mathcal{D}_{\mathcal{AL}}$ is just an arrow from r_9 to r_6. From Theorem 1, this domain description has a unique model and can be computed in polynomial time.

After translating above domain description, we get a logic program that can be run under *Smodels*. Through *Smodels*, we compute one and only one answer set for it. Here we demonstrate part authorization information for *Alice* in the answer set as example,

$grant(alice, right(+, access, http))$,
$grant(alice, right(-, access, mysql))$

5 Conclusion

In this paper, we developed an expressive authorization language $\mathcal{AL}$ to specify the distributed authorization with delegation. We employed Answer Set Programming as a foundational basis for its semantics and investigated the computational properties of language $\mathcal{AL}$. Using an scenario we demonstrated our research.

References

1. M. Blaze, J. Feigenbaum, and J. Lacy. Decentralized Trust Management. In *Proceedings of the Symposium on Security and Privacy*, IEEE Computer Society Press, Los Alamitos,1996, pages 164-173.
2. M. Blaze, J. Feigenbaum, J. Ioannidis, and A. D. Keromytis. The KeyNote Trust-Management System, Version 2, Internet Engineering Task Force RFC 2704, September 1999. http://www.ietf.org/rfc/rfc2704.txt
3. J. Elien. Certificate Discovery Using SPKI/SDSI 2.0 Certificates. Masters Thesis, MIT LCS, May 1998, http://theory.lcs.mit.edu/ cis/theses/elien-masters.ps.
4. N. Li, J. C. Mitchell, and W. H. Winsborough. Design of a role-based trust management framework. In *Proceedings of the 2002 IEEE Symposium on Security and Privacy*, pages 114C130. IEEE Computer Society Press, May 2002.
5. N. Li, B. N. Grosof, and J. Feigenbaum. Delegation Logic: A logic-based approach to distributed authorization. *ACM Transactions on Information and System Security*, 6(1): 128-171.
6. S. Wang and Y. Zhang (2005). A Formalization of Distributed Authorization with Delegation. In *Proceeding of the 10th Australian Conference on Information Security and Privacy*, pp 303-315, LNCS 3574.
7. S. Wang, and Y. Zhang. Handling Distributed Authorization with Delegation through Answer Set Programming (manuscript). 2005.

Multiagent Architecture (BlueAgents) with the Dynamic Pricing and Maximum Profit Strategy in the TAC SCM

David Han

Research School of Information Sciences and Engineering,
The Australian National University,
Acton 2601, Canberra, Australia
David.Han@mail.rsise.anu.edu.au

Abstract. In this paper, we propose a new agent architecture (BlueAgents) with the Dynamic Pricing and Maximum Profit Strategy (DPMPS). BlueAgents we design shows the flow of the trading as request for quotes, offer and order based on the time frame clearly and we describe the function modules that BlueAgents is composed of. One of the main foci of the decision making in a supply chain management for the trading agent competition (TAC SCM) is an optimization of the offer price under the uncertainty. Price is an important factor for maximizing benefit through the bidding process in competition with other agents. DPMPS is a benchmarking model to predict dynamically realistic optimal offer prices for bidding between an estimated offer price and regressed price of current market after estimating an optimized offer price for maximizing profit.

1 Introduction

In this paper, we propose a new agent architecture (BlueAgents) with the benchmarking model as an autonomous agent through the dynamic pricing strategy to predict a realistic optimal offer price for bidding between an estimated offer price and regressed price of current market after estimating an optimized offer price for maximizing profit.

2 Previous Works of the TAC SCM

We briefly surveyed agent strategies of previous works (DeepMaize [8],[9], MinneTAC [7], RedAgent [6], HarTAC [5], PackaTAC [4], Integrated model [1], Machine Learning approach [11], and an algorithm for procurement [3] with a Dynamic Programming (DP) and Markov decision process (MDP), TacTex-03 [10], Botticelli [2], PSUTAC [13], and Jackaroo [14]).

In summarization of the previous works, we have classified problems of the decision makings for the TAC SCM into prices and quantity. Price is important for maximizing benefit through requesting, offering and bidding processes in competing with other agencies. Requested quantities should be procured within a delivery due-date to avoid penalty.

3 Agent Architecture for the TAC SCM

BlueAgents we design is composed of agents with heuristic-based probabilistic function modules under the uncertainty and simple agents. There are three main types of agents: customer agent (**C**), sales manager agent (**A**) and supplier agent (**S**); and four auxiliary ones: bank agent (**B**), market agent (**M**), factory agent (**F**) and warehouse agent (**W**).

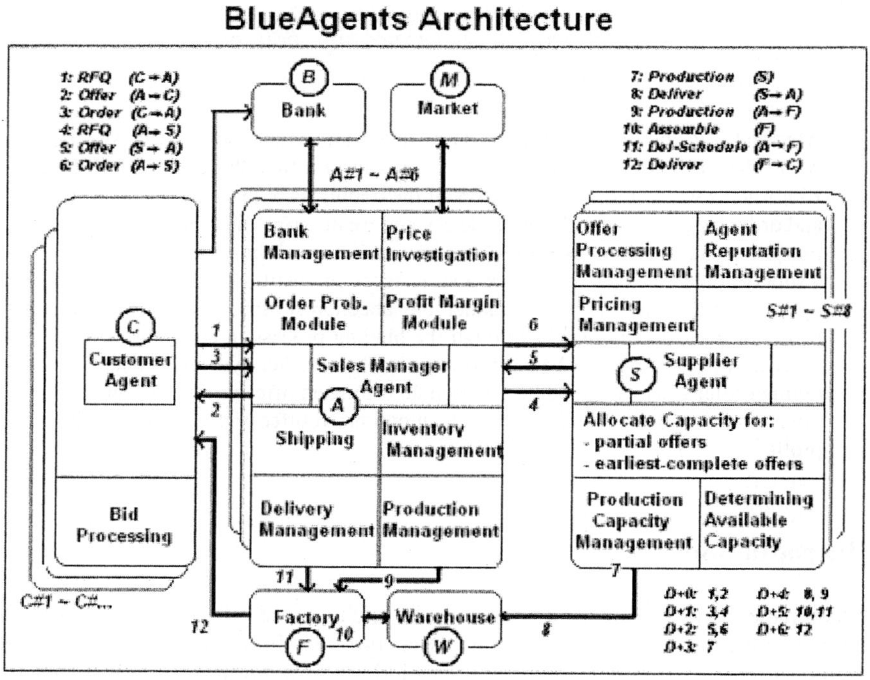

Fig. 1. Overview of the BlueAgents Architecture

4 Strategy for the TAC SCM

Our strategy that price can be changed dynamically in accordance with current market price and can get a maximum profit is introduced. DPMPS is a benchmarking model to predict dynamically realistic optimal offer price for bidding between an estimated offer price and regressed price of current market after estimating an optimized offer price for maximizing profit. An offer price is determined by the agent each day. For this, we should get a linear fitting line from the previous simulated data and we can then estimate offer price for d-day. For maximizing profit, we start from knowing the probability of order by calculating the proportion of demand which actually receives bids.

The agent should estimate the optimal offer price for the maximum benefit from previous data. Firstly, *Prob(Order)* is the estimated probability of winning a customer

Order. Ordered probability at each price is calculated as: *Prob(Order) = No of Orders/ No of Offers*. Additional considerations for the probability of order are quantity, lead time, reserve price, penalty and product type. Next, profit margin should be calculated as: *Prof-margin = simulated price – cost* where *cost* is composed of production cost for components and inventory cost for warehouse. Then we can get the expected profit margin at the simulated price: *E-prof-margin = Prob(Order|Price) * Prof-margin*. With these values, agent should find the maximum point by comparing, the previous point with, the current point that was calculated from every 9 days data. If current data is higher than previous data, increase the offer price. Otherwise, leave the offer price as it is. It takes several cycles to find an optimal offer price. Even though the probability of bidding order is higher, profit is not always higher. One particular example is that the ordered goods should be produced with a loss if the profit margin is less than zero.

Next, we should adjust between estimated point and expected maximum profit point by averaging, and we can then get an adjusted offer price. For the next estimation (d+1 day), we use new ordered price(d day) for new fitting. We repeat this procedure everyday by dynamically updating new data. Implementations of this strategy are very optimistically progressing.

5 Conclusions and Further Study

In conclusion, TAC SCM should be built to meet changing market demands in a timely and cost effective manner for processing bidding through customer order, procurement, production scheduling, and assembly of components, while effective supply management is vital to the competitiveness of manufacturing enterprises. So we need to continuously improve performance of the TAC SCM because the potential impact of supply chain management is tremendous.

Acknowledgements

The author would like to express his gratitude to the team who discussed TAC SCM in the Computer Science Laboratory at the Australian National University, especially Professor John Lloyd and Mr. Joshua Cole.

References

[1] Raghu Arunachalam, The 2003 Supply Chain Management Trading Agent Competition. Electronic Commerce Research and Applications, Volume 4, Spring 2005, Pages 63-81.
[2] Michael Benisch, Amy Greenwald, Victor Naroditskiy, and Michael Tschantz, A Stochastic Programming Approach to Scheduling in TAC SCM. Proceedings of the 5th ACM conference on Electronic commerce 2004, New York, NY, USA   May 17 - 20, 2004 Pages: 152-159
[3] Scott Buffett and Nathan Scott, An Algorithm for Procurement in Supply-Chain Management. Workshop on Trading Agent Design and Analysis Colocated with the Trading Agent Competition at AAMAS'04 July 20, 2004. New York.

[4] Erik Dahlgren and Peter R. Wurman, PackaTAC: A Conservative Trading Agent. SIGecom Exchanges, Vol. 4, No. 3:33-40, Feb 2004.
[5] Rui Dong, Terry Tai and Wilfred Yeung and David C. Parkes, HarTAC – The Harvard TAC SCM '03 Agent. Workshop on Trading Agent Design and Analysis Collocated with the Trading Agent Competition at AAMAS'04 July 20, 2004. New York.
[6] Phillip W. Keller, Felix-Olivier Duguay, Doina Precup. RedAgent - Winner of TAC SCM 2003. ACM Journal Name, Vol. 4. No. 3:1-8, 02, 2004.
[7] Wolfgang Ketter, Elena Kryzhnyaya, Steven Damer and Colin McMillen. Analysis and Design of Supply-Driven Strategies in TAC-SCM. Workshop on Trading Agent Design and Analysis. Collocated with the Trading Agent Competition at AAMAS'04. New York, 2004.
[8] Christopher Kiekintveld, Michael P. Wellman, Satinder singh, and Vishal Soni, Value-Driven Procurement in the TAC Supply Chain Game. ACM SIGecom Exchanges, Vol. 4, No. 3, Feb 2004.
[9] C Kiekintveld, MP Wellman, S Singh, J Estelle, Y Vorobeychik, V Soni, and M Rudary, Distributed Feedback Control for decision Making on Supply Chains. Fourteenth International Conference on Automated Planning and Scheduling (ICAPS), 2004.
[10] David Pardoe and Peter Stone, TacTex-03: A Supply Chain Management Agent. SIGecom Exchanges, Vol. 4, No. 3:19-28, Winter 2004.
[11] David Pardoe and Peter Stone, Bidding for Customer Orders in TAC SCM: A Learning Approach. Workshop on Trading Agent Design and Analysis Collocated with the Trading Agent Competition at AAMAS'04 July 20, 2004. New York.
[12] S. Russel and P. Norvig, Artificial Intelligence: A Modern Approach. Prentice Hall, second edition, 2002.
[13] Shuang Sun, Viswanath Avasarala, Tracy Mullen and John Yen, PSUTAC: A Trading Agent designed from Heuristics to Knowledge. Workshop on Trading Agent Design and Analysis Collocated with the Trading Agent Competition at AAMAS'04 July 20, 2004. New York.
[14] Dongmo Zhang, Kanghua Zhao, Chia-Ming Liang, Gonelur Begum Huq, and Tze-Haw Huang, Strategic Trading Agents via Market Modeling. SIGecom Exchanges, Vol. 4, No. 3:46-55, Feb 2004.

Agent-Based Plot Planning for Automatic Generation of Computer Animation

Wei Tang, Lei Zheng, and Chunnian Liu

Beijing Municipal Key Laboratory of Multimedia and Intelligent Software
Technology, College of Computer Science, Beijing University of Technology,
100022 Beijing, China
wtmaria@gmail.com, {leizheng, ai}@bjut.edu.cn

Abstract. Plot planning is one of the key steps in automatic generation of computer animation, aiming at converting the abstract plots of a story into a series of concrete actions. This paper presents the architecture of plot planning model, in which we employ an agent-based method to develop the abstract plot. In our agent hierarchy, there are two kinds of agents: drama agent and plot agent, both of which can develop the abstract plot according to their knowledge and strategies. Furthermore, to avoid the irrationality of the results, we address a validity checking mechanism to ensure the consistency of the concrete actions.

1 Introduction

To improve the efficiency of animation generation, Ruqian Lu [1] proposed the technique called automatic generation of computer animation which aims to convert the story written in natural language into a cartoon by computer. Plot planning, as one of the key steps in this procedure, converts the abstract plot of the story into a series of concrete actions [2]. For example, the action "wedding" has different forms such as an eastern or western wedding. It is necessary to transform these abstract plots into concrete actions which can be shown directly.

In recent years, there are various attempts in plot or story generation. Thawonmas, R. [3] proposed HTN planning to develop the story while allowing interactions in interactive comedy system. Pablo Gervas [4] described case-based reasoning method to generate story plot. Yunju Shim and Minkoo Kim [5] developed the technology for automatic short story generator based on autonomous agents.

Compared with these work [3][4][5], our research focuses on detailing the abstract plot in light of the context of story. In this paper, we first describe the agent model including drama agent and plot agent. Then, we present the architecture of plot planning module. Finally, we propose a validity checking mechanism to ensure the rationality of the results.

2 The Agent Model

To develop the abstract plot, we propose an agent-based approach which defines the agent into two kinds: plot agent and drama agent [2]. Plot agent contains the concrete knowledge, and drama agent contains the abstract knowledge. The two kinds of agents have the similar syntax:

- both of them have names which indicate the abstract plot they can develop,
- both of them have only one pointer to indicate a father agent,
- both of them have more than one pointer to indicate child agents,
- both of them have a specification part which contains knowledge and strategies about the implementation of an abstract plot.

In our method, we treat agents as entities with knowledge and strategies [1]. When one agent cannot develop a given plot by its own knowledge, it will use its strategies to collaborate with the other agents for further developing. There are four primary strategies inside the agents:

- inheritance: offspring agent can inherit the content of its father agent,
- enrich: offspring agent can add more information to its ancestors before inheriting,
- replace: offspring agent can replace the content of ancestor agent with its own knowledge,
- call: an agent can call the other agents for further developing.

The job of agent is to develop the abstract plot. Based on the agent model, we propose an architecture of plot planning which can develop the abstract plot automatically.

3 The Architecture of Plot Planning Module

In our animation system, the story text is first parsed by the natural language process, and converted into a language representation of GF (Golden Forest) [1]. Then, the action list receiving process selects the abstract plots from GF, and puts them into the queue. After that, the plot planning module gets the abstract plots from the queue and begins to detail them.

3.1 The Performance of the Plot Planning Module

To develop an abstract plot, the plot planning module consists of three submodules coupled with a knowledge base: a plot matching process, a plot developing reasoner, a plot validity checking process, and a plot base which is a collection of agents (see Fig. 1). In plot planning module, the plot matching process first selects one agent whose name matches the semantic of the plot. For example, there is an abstract plot "kidnap" in a story and there is an agent "abduct" in the plot base. Since the two words have the same meaning but different presentation, we erect a synonymous library for each agent. When getting an abstract plot from queue, the plot matching process checks each synonymous library to see if the plot name exists in it. If the answer is true, the agent which owns the synonymous library is chosen to develop the abstract plot.

After finding an agent, the plot developing reasoner gets its content from the plot base, and begins to implement the plot planning algorithm [1]. An

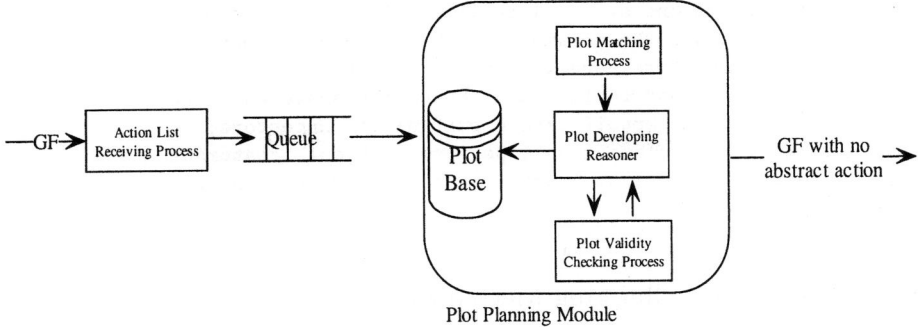

Fig. 1. The Architecture of Plot Planning Module

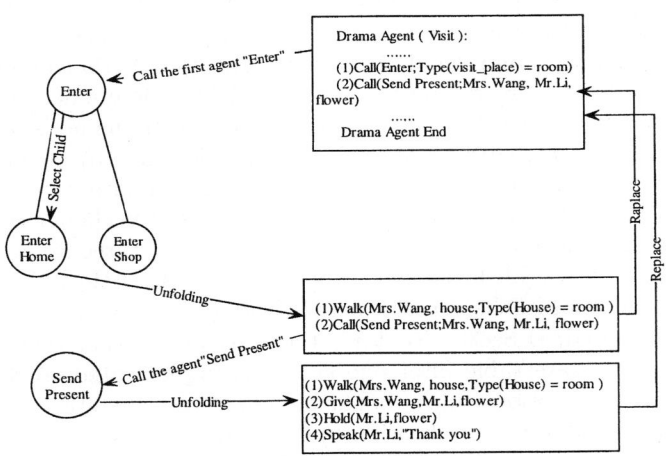

Fig. 2. An example of plot planning

example is given to show the development of the abstract plot "Visit". After being developed, "Visit" is replaced with four concrete actions (see Fig. 2).

```
Plot Planning Algorithm
   {Convert an abstract plot to a call statement: call(hg,x1,x2,...),
   where hg is the name of the agent which is called, x1,x2,... are
   the instances of the roles and objects};
   begin
       1 repeat
           Assign the agent in the call statement to hg. Select
           the child agents of hg which meet the situation as
           given in the story, and call it hg again;
       until no appropriate agent can be found;
```

2 If hg has ancestors, inherit objects and roles of them;
3 Instantiate the parameters of specification part for hg, hg's ancestors, and the agents who call hg;
4 Implement the replace and the enrich statement. Then, inherit the specification part of its ancestors;
5 If hg is a drama agent, perform each call statement according to 1 to 5 until no call statement in hg.
end

3.2 The Validity Checking Mechanism

Though plot planning module can transform the abstract plot into concrete actions, the results may be not rational. For example, suppose Mr. Li's arm is broken, and Mrs. Wang visits him with a bundle of flowers. The abstract plot "Visit" has been developed into four concrete actions (see Sect. 3.1). According to the context of the story, the result is unreasonable. Since Mr. Li's arm is broken, the concrete action "hold" is an unusual action at that moment.

To solve this problem, we must choose the right concrete actions according to the states of the roles and objects. Since the plot planning adds new concrete actions to the story, the changes of the states for roles and objects are unable to be predicted. Though the using of pre-condition is a standard way to ensure the reasonable actions are only included, it cannot describe the changes of the states according to the plot development. In this paper, we use three items to describe the change of state world: P_Section, D_Section, and A_Section. P_Section contains the precondition of the concrete action, and it is used to check if the action can be implemented; D_Section contains the state description which should be deleted from the state table after one action is implemented; A_Section contains the state description which should be added to the state table after one action is implemented. In specification part of plot agent, each concrete action

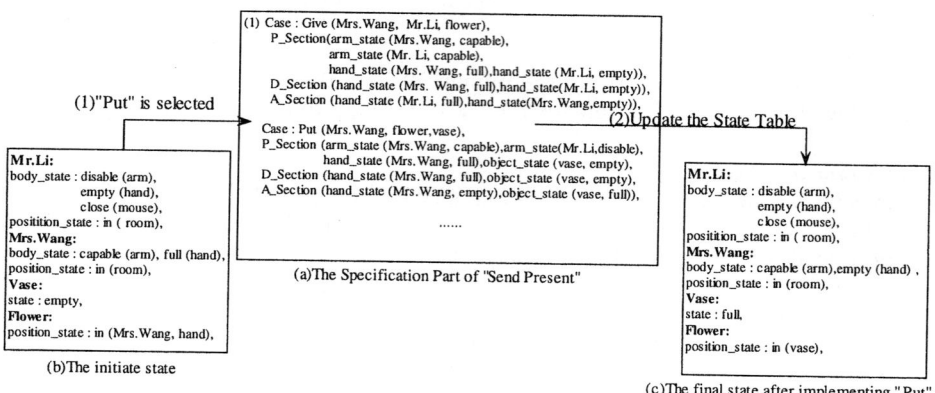

Fig. 3. An example of the validity checking process

contains these three items. For example, we have defined the three items for concrete actions "give" and "put". With the validity checking mechanism, "put" is selected to detail the plot "Send Present", and "give" is the irrational one (see Fig. 3).

4 Conclusion

In this paper, we propose an agent-based method for developing the abstract plot, and present the architecture of plot planning module. In our agent hierarchy, there are two kinds of agents: plot agent and drama agent, both of which can develop the abstract plot according to their knowledge and strategies. Furthermore, we have addressed a validity checking mechanism to ensure the rationality of the planning results. Based on this architecture and mechanism, the plot planning is a flexible and powerful sub-module in our animation system.

In the future, we plan to concentrate on the development of mental state which is also a kind of abstract event. With this improvement, we are convinced that plot planning module will be more effective.

Acknowledgements

This work is partially supported by the NSFC major research program: "Basic Theory and Core Techniques of Non-Canonical Knowledge" (60496322) and the Beijing Municipal Education Commission Project: "Automatic Generation of Computer Animation" (KP0705200384).

References

1. Ruqian Lu, Songmao Zhang: Automatic Generation of Computer Animation. Springer-Verlag, Berlin Heidelberg New York (2002)
2. Ruqian Lu, Songmao Zhang: From Story to Animation-Full Life Cycle Computer Aided Animation Generation. ACTA AUTOMATICA, 1(2002) 321–348
3. Thawonmas, R., Tanaka, K., Hassaky, H.: Extended Hierarchical Task Network Planning for Interactive Comedy. Intelligent Agents and Multi-Agent Systems. Lecture Notes in Computer Science, Vol. 2891. Springer-Verlag, Berlin Heidelberg New York (2003) 205–213
4. Diaz-Agudo, B., Gervas, P., Peinado, F., Hervas, R.: A Case Based Reasoning Approach to Story Plot Generation. In: ECCBR 2004. Lecture Notes in Computer Science, Vol. 3155. Springer-Verlag, Berlin Heidelberg New York (2004) 142–156
5. Yunju Shim, Minkoo Kim: Automatic short story generator based on autonomous agents. In: Proc. 5th Pacific Rim International Workshop on Multi Agents. Lecture Notes in Computer Science, Vol. 2413. Springer-Verlag, Berlin Heidelberg New York (2002) 151–162

Mobile Agent Migration: An Optimal Policy

Salah EL Falou[1,2] and François Bourdon[1]

[1] GREYC UMR 6072,
Campus II, BP 5186 14032 CAEN cedex, France
selfalou@info.unicaen.fr,
francois.bourdon@iutc3.unicaen.fr
[2] CNRS LEBANON

Abstract. The majority of Internet applications requires interaction between various entities through the network, in order to exchange data and to distribute tasks. The client/server model where exchanges are given by distant interactions is the most used model. It has the disadvantage of increasing network traffic by exchanging intermediary information. In this paper we show that in some cases it is better to send the code to the server and to work locally. We study two models of communication (the client/server and the mobile agent) and propose a hybrid one, where agent uses the two models and construct the optimal policy according to the characteristic of the network. The Markov decision processes are used to calculate the optimal policy for agent displacement. This policy is applied by the agent in order to decrease network traffic.

1 Introduction

In distributed application the "client/server" model where exchanges are given by distant interactions is the most used model. This model has the disadvantage of increasing network traffic and it requires a permanent connection. In this paper we propose a new approach that uses the mobile agents' technology. Thus, by sending agents to the server, the exchanged messages become locally and release the load on the network [1].

The advantage of the communication done by one of the two models: "client/server" or "mobile agent" depends on the application (number of distant interactions) it depends also on the network traffic. We study both mode of communication and propose a hybrid model which allows adaptability to the change of the network in order to decrease the network traffic. An intelligent mobile agent is created in order to accomplish the client task. This agent has the capability to use the two models of communication in order to reduce the client waiting delay. In this paper we present a method to learn about interaction and to construct a probabilistic model on the exchanges between various entities. This probabilistic model is used to build a graph that represents the system states. The Markov decision process is used to calculate the optimal policy for agent displacement. This model is applied to the problem of hotels research in a city; the obtained results show the effectiveness of using MDP in this type of applications.

2 Mobile Agent Technology

Mobile agent technology allows distributed system designers and programmers to create autonomous entities on the level of their behaviors and also in space and time. These entities can move from host to another through the network, with their code and execution state. Rather than using remote procedure call (RPC) [4] [7] to interact between entities, we can move codes on a common machine so that they interact locally. In a mobile agent platform [2] [3], agents can move on a common place and perform local interactions. This optimization of the traffic and latency network is not the only motivation. Mobility allows the use of services even in the case of non-permanent connection in particular for mobile devices. In this case, the agent plays the role of the client and transmits to him the results at the time of a new connection.

3 Communication Between n Machines

Distributed applications require interactions between several machines through the network. We consider the case of an application that requires the communications between n machines connected by the TCP/IP network (see Fig.1). In the "client/server" communication model, the client on the first machine will communicate with n machines in order to achieve the requested task. In the mobile agent communication model, we create an agent on the first machine, the agent will move between various machines and it will carry out local interactions in order to accomplish the requested task, this agent returns to the first machine in order to give the assessment.

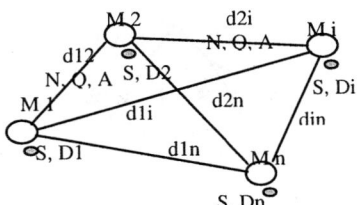

- S: the size of the mobile agent code.
- D_i: the size of the mobile agent data after interaction with the machine M_i.
- Q_{ij}, A_{ij}: the size of a question and response exchanged between M_i and M_j.
- N_{ij}: the number of messages exchanged between M_i and M_j.
- d_{ij}: the rate of link M_i-M_j.

Fig. 1. Communication between n hosts

Before studying the two models, it should be remembered that we do not take into account the treatment cost of a request on each server. This cost remains the same one in the two models of communication.

In the client server model communication time is given by:

$$T_{cs} = \sum_{j=2}^{n} \frac{N_{ij}.(Q_{1j} + A_{1j})}{d_{ij}}$$

For mobile agent model the total time of the communication will be:

$$T_{ma} = \left(\sum_{j=1}^{n-1} \frac{(S + D_i)}{d_{i,i+1}} \right) + \frac{S + D_n}{d_{n1}}$$

Comparison between the two models shows that we don't use the same links. We can also say that communication by "mobile agent" model is more advantageous when the number of intermediary interactions decrease.

In this paper we present a third model of communication, the **hybrid model**. When agent needs to communicate with a distant site, it can choose distant interactions and not to migrate to the host. Thus, mobile agent is not forced to visit all sites. It will choose distant communication when its migration becomes too expensive. The choice of communication mode depends on the link d_{ij} and the number of messages exchanged (N_{ij}) between various machines of the application. The links characteristics (data rate) represent information to be collected permanently; we can use the ping [5] protocol to have this information.

4 Learning About Interaction

Formulas given in paragraph 3 shows that the agent policy displacement depends from links rate, it also depends on interactions (Ni) between various actors of the application. We study the clients' behavior in order to understand interactions between various servers that participate to accomplish the client task. Information about interactions is stored in a table (see Table 1). All clients scenarios are stored in this table; a scenario is represented by a tuple (tuple represents different Ni of a scenario). We calculate the number of appearance and associate a probability Pi for each scenario.

Table 1. Learning phase results

N1	N2	...	Nn	Prob
1	2	...	1	P1
2	3	...	2	P2
...	...	...	...	...
m	10	...	1	Pm

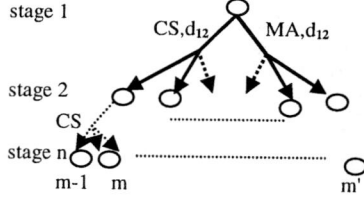

Fig. 2. System states graph

5 Statistical Method for Policy Selection

The learning phase will enable us to better understand the interactions between various entities of the application. The information about interaction is used in order to choose the policy that the agent applies to achieve the task. We consider an application with n sites to be visited. On each machine agent can communicate by two modes: the "mobile agent" and the "client/server". Thus, the agent policy is defined by:

$$\pi = (Ac_1, Ac_2, \cdots, Ac_n) \text{ with } Ac \in \{MA, CS\}$$

In this method we will consider all possible policy for agent displacement and calculate the average communication cost for each one. Agent will choose the policy that minimizes the average communication cost. In the next paragraph we will present another method based on the MDP, this method allows to take account of various states of the system.

6 A MDP Based Solution

Markov decision processes (MDPs) [6] are mathematical formulations of problems in which a decision maker (agent) must choose how to act in order to minimize the total long-term cost over a series of interactions with its environment.
In order to accomplish the client task, mobile agent needs to interact with the n sites of the application. Interaction is given in two ways; agent can choose two types of actions during the construction of our MDP:
 1. Communication by "client/server" mode (CS).
 2. Communication by "mobile agent" mode (MA).

In mobile agent displacement problem, we have uncertainty about the environment and the interaction between several entities of the application. The number of exchanged messages between two machines of the application is represented with a probabilistic model. At stage i, agent is on the machine i and have to communicate with machine (i+1). Ni represents the number of exchanged messages. Knowledge of Ni and the link's rate allows to calculate the communication time for the two actions CS and MA. This time corresponds to the reward that we give to the state in the graph (see Fig.2). This graph does not contain any loop; the optimal policy is calculated by a simple graph traversal. Optimal utility computing is given by upwards graph traversal. MDP can be also used to resolve a problem of agent displacement with a graph that contains loops. The most known algorithms are value iteration and policy iteration. The optimal utility known, we can easily deduce the optimal policy.

7 Application (Searching Hotels in a City)

Searching information is one of the most significant applications to do when using mobile agent technology. In these applications (research hotels in a city, fly reservation ...), agents move on various sites to seek information for their clients. Our example represents a distributed application; the goal is to seek a list of hotels in a given city. Two databases in two different sites must be visited to get this information. In order to present the advantage of the hybrid communication we compared the various models of communication. In the research of hotels example, we obtained the results presented on Figure 3. The x axis represents the evolution of the system in time (implicitly it represents the links rate change of the network). The y axis represents the average time between sending request by the client and receiving of the response by this last one.

To conclude, we note that our method (based on MDP) gives a faster response with reduction of network traffic.

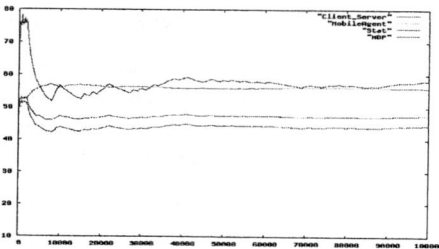

Fig. 3. Hybrid communication

8 Conclusion

The mobile agent communication model is a good model to be used in distributed applications in the case of strong interaction between entities. This communication model allows us to minimize the used bandwidth and to reduce the connection time (the client needs the connection only for sending agent and receiving results). It allows reducing the execution time of the distributed application. This model increases the reliability of the system insofar as the request becomes autonomous agents.

The quantities of information exchanged between various actors, the type of the application and the characteristic of the network are parameters to determine the choice of technology to be implemented. To get benefits from the two models, we propose to communicate by a hybrid one. After a learning stage, information is used to construct a probabilistic model which contains different scenarios. This probabilistic model is used to construct a system states graph. The Markov decision processes are used to calculate the optimal policy for agent displacement. This policy is used by mobile agent in order to reduce the client waiting time. By application on the research of hotels in a city, we can say that our model gives a faster response with reduction of network traffic. Finally, using of mobile agent technology allows adding new personalized web service in a faster way.

References

1. El Falou S., Bourdon F., "Programmation répartie et agents mobiles", SETIT 2004.
2. Kotz D., Robert S. G., "Mobile Agents and the future of the Internet". ACM Operating Systems Review, pp. 7-13, août 1999.
3. White J., "Telescript technology: the foundation for the electronic market place", General Magic White Paper, General Magic, 1994.
4. Bernard G., "Apport des agents mobiles à l'exécution répartie", ISYPAR'00, 2000.
5. H. Lundgren, D. Lundberg, J. Nielsen, E. Nordstrom, and C Tschudin. "A large-scale testbed for reproducible ad hoc protocol evaluations". In Proceedings of the IEEE Wireless Communications and Networking Conference, Orlando, USA, March 2002.
6. Puterman M., " Markov Decision Processes: discrete stochastic dynamic programming". John Wiley &Sons, Inc. New York, NY, 1994.
7. Stamos J. W., Gifford D. D., "Remote Evaluation". ACM Transactions on Programming Languages and Systems, vol. 12, n 4, pp. 537-565, 1990.

Human Action Understanding Using Motion Verbs in WordNet

Miyoung Cho[1], Dan Song[1], Junho Choi[1], and Pankoo Kim[2,*]

[1] Dept. of Computer Science,
Chosun University, 375 Seosuk-dong Dong-Ku Gwangju 501-759, Korea
{irune, spica}@chosun.ac.kr, songdan@stmail.chosun.ac.kr
[2] Dept. of CSE , Chosun University, Korea
pkkim@chosun.ac.kr

Abstract. In this paper, we introduce a novel method about how to recognize the human action/activity in video using motion verbs based on WordNet. We provide a more deterministic mapping, and then we have extended WordNet with a small, fixed vocabulary of highly salient attribute for human motion description.

1 Introduction

Automated understanding of human activity is important for a number of tasks that can be used to augment human capability. Such ability may be used for surveillance to provide security in a home, office or industrial environment. Understanding human activity is also important for enhanced human-computer interaction including advanced video conferencing and for intelligent content-based retrieval of video from digital libraries[3][5]. To bridge the gap between computational models for spatio-temporal relations and people's use of motion verbs in their natural language, we introduce recognition of human action/activity from videos using motion verbs on the ontology of WordNet.

2 Mapping from Low-Level Feature to Semantics

WordNet is a freely available lexical database for English whose design is inspired by current psycholinguistic theories of human lexical memory[6]. We focus on motion verbs which represent the movement of something. For example, we look around structural position of "walk" verb in WordNet. The taxonomy arising from the L+1 verb walk: the superordinate of walk, on level L+2, is {move, travel}; troponyms of walk, on level L0, are march, strut, traipse, amble, mosey, slouch, etc. As shown in the figure 1, we can classify 5 classes {stay_in_place, set, bound, step, speed} about motion in the verbs word net. These classes belong to their corresponding domain, which was distinguished by object attributes such as: non-human or human, direction or speed and so on.

---

* Corresponding author.

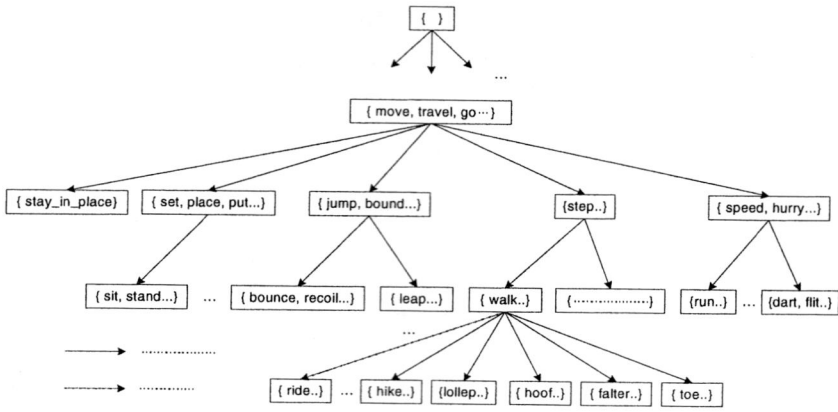

Fig. 1. Hierarchical structure about motion verb in WordNet

Semantic level observable corresponding to objects of interest are mapped directly to general concepts in WordNet, and become elemental terms. This is possible because the semantic meaning of each semantic level observable is clearly defined, and can be mapped directly to a word sense. Moving objects, including moving people, are mapped to verbs. The remaining semantic level information are used as contextual search constraints as described below.

Table 1. Selected mappings from visual information to semantic terms

Visual information	Element	Attribute
object	person(noun)	-
surrounding	-	none, indoor, outdoor
motion	travel / place / (verbs) / sit stand	-
motion speed	-	none, slow, fast
motion direction	-	north→south, south→north, west, east

3 Experiment

In the experiment part, we define hierarchical description about human actions. Figure 2 shows us that 'sit down' and 'stand up' are subclasses of set with IS_A relation. But they are different in direction and speed.

We can closely research hierarchical relation of human actions hierarchical structure of motion verbs on WordNet. In the future works, it can be applied to Semantic

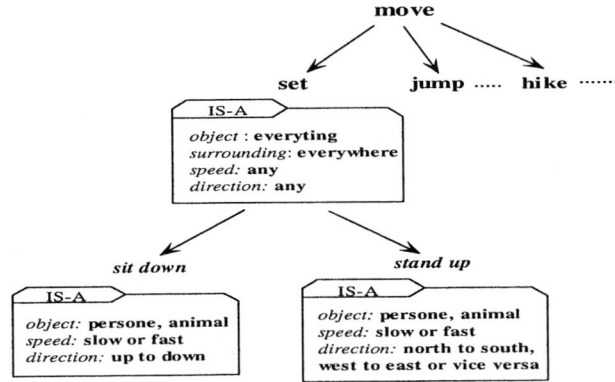

Fig. 2. Hierarchical description for sit_down and stand_up action in Wordnet

retrieval or indexing. So, direction changes create the events person 'goes right side' or 'goes left side', or 'goes away' or 'arrives'. And velocity changes create the events person 'stops' or 'walks' or 'starts running'.

We experiment 5 human action patterns like demonstrated in the table2. Specially, the table shows us "sit down", "stand up" actions example happened in indoor. These figures are snapshots based on time and vector of each figure that indicates direction and velocity[7]. The longer length of vector is, the faster the velocity. Through this example, we can recognize the actions by the simply direction changing and speed accelerating. Not only can we save the time for calculating complex data information of the body moving, but we can get the exact human action recognition.

Table 2. Human action samples by direction and velocity

4 Conclusion

Human action recognition from video streams has a wide range of applications such as human-machine interactions, sports, security surveillance, etc. Depending on the environment, human action may have different forms ranging from simple hand gestures to complex dances which contain a series of actions. We introduce a novel method about how to recognize the human actions/activities in video using motion verbs based on WordNet. Just simply by observing directional relations and velocity, we can identify the activities that take place in a video sequence. Our research result will can be used to resolve the gap of natural language and semantic description by low level features.

In the future work, we will present hierarchy structure about event(human action) like WordNet by using spatio-temporal relations on video.

Acknowledgement

This research was supported by the MIC(Ministry of Information and Communication), Korea, under the ITRC(Information Technology research Center) Support program supervised by the IITA(Institute of Information Technology Assessment). (IITA-2005-C1090-0502-0009)

References

1. Somboon Hongeng, Ram Nevatia, Francois Bremond, "Video-Based event recognition: activity representation and probabilistic recognition methods", Computer Vision and Image Understanding archive Volume 96 , Issue 2, November 2004
2. Jezekei Ben-Arie, Purvin Pandit, "Human Activity recognition Using Multidimensional Indexing", IEEE Transaction on pattern analysis and machine intelligence, Vol.24, No.8, August 2002
3. Ram Nevatia, Tao Zhao, Somboon Hongeng, "Hierarchical Language-based Representation of Events in Video Streams", EVENT(IEEE Workshop on Event Mining)03
4. I. Laptev, T. Lindeberg, "Velocity adapted spatio-temporal receptive fields for direct recognition of activities", IVC, 22(2), 2004
5. Atsuhiro Kojima, Masao Izumi, Takeshi Tamura, Kunio Fukunaga, "Generating Natural Language description of Human Behavior from Video Images", IJCV(50), No 2, November 2002
6. http://wordnet.princeton.edu/
7. Open Source Computer Vision Library-Refrence Manual
8. Mirai Higuchi, Shigeki Aoki, Atsuhiro Kojima, Kunio Fukunaga, "Scene Recognition Based on Relationship between Human Actions and Objects", ICPR'04
9. Nathanael Rota, Monique Thonnat, "Video Sequence Interpretation for Visual Surveillance", Third IEEE International Workshop on Visual Surveillance (VS'2000), p.59-68, 2000

Partitional Approach for Estimating Null Value in Relational Database

Jia-Wen Wang, Ching-Hsue Cheng, and Wei-Ting Chang

Department of Information Management,
National Yunlin University of Science and Technology,
123 University Road, Section 3, Douliou, Yunlin, Taiwan, R.O.C.
{g9220803, chcheng, g9223736}@yuntech.edu.tw

Abstract. In this paper, we propose a partitional approach for estimating null value (1) Firstly, we utilize stepwise regression to select the important attributes from the database. (2) Secondly, we use a partitional approach to build the data category. The data partitioned by the first two important attributes. (3) Thirdly, we apply the clustering method to cluster output data. (4) Fourthly, Calculate the degree of influential between the attributes. There are two ways to calculate the degree of influential. One is correlation coefficient and the other is regression coefficients. (5) To verify our method, this paper utilizes a practical human resource database in Taiwan, and Mean of Absolute Error Rate (MAER) as evaluation criterion to compare with other methods; it is shown that our proposed method proves better than other methods for estimating null values in relational database systems.

1 Introduction

In recent years, relational database systems have been most widely used in a commercial situation, i.e. data mining, but this sort of database system will not operate properly if there are any null values of attributes (incomplete datasets) in the system [2]. Therefore, there are many researchers focused on the issues of incomplete data and null values in relational database systems especially. There are many approaches to deal with missing values [5]: (a) Ignore objects containing missing values; (b) Fill the gaps manually; (c) Substitute the missing values by a constant; (d) Use the mean of the objects; (e) Get the most probable value to fill the missing values. But, these methods are not completely satisfactory to handle null value problems. In this paper, we propose a partitional approach for estimating null values, and use a practical human resource database in Taiwan. For verifying our method, this study utilize mean of absolute error rate (MAER) as evaluation criterion. From the experimental result, we can find the proposed approach can estimate null values in relational database systems more accurately and more efficiently than other methods.

2 Partitional Approach for Estimating Null Value

In this section, we present the algorithm to estimate null values in relational database systems. A relation in a human resource database including six attributes is shown as Table 1. The attributes "AGE", "EXPERIENCE", "SEX" and "DEGREE" are called

Table 1. A relation in a human resource database

EMP_NO	AGE (A)	EXPERIENCE (E)	SEX (X)	DEGREE (D)	SALARY (S)

independent variables (IV) and the attribute "SALARY" is called a dependent variable (DV). The attribute "SALARY" contains a null value ($S_{estimated}$).

Step 1: We use Stepwise Regression [4] to analysis data and select the first two important attributes of the independent variables to build data category.

Step 2: Use k-means [6] and auto-clustering [3] to build clusters by attribute (i.e., null values' variable).

Step 3: Calculate the cluster center c_i

Step 4: Calculate the degree of influential.

(a) Coefficient of determination (r^2; COD)

To calculate the coefficient of correlation (r) and the coefficient of determination (COD) [1] from the attributes between each IV and DV of the cluster C_i, where $1 \leq i \leq k$. In correlation, if there is only one element in C_i, then let $r_i = 0.5$.

(b) Regression coefficient

Calculate the degree of influential $\beta_{c_i, independent\ variable}$ between the attributes IV and DV of the cluster C_i.

Step 5: Calculate the C_i variation

Assume that the jth element of C_i is denoted by $(A_{i,j}, E_{i,j}, X_{i,j}, D_{i,j}, S_{i,j})$, where $1 \leq j \leq m$, m denotes m elements in C_i and ΔIV_DV_i denotes the variation of the DV per unit of the value of the IV of C_i. For example, the "SALARY" and "AGE" (i.e. ΔA_S_i) of C_i can be calculated as follows:

(a) COD (r^2)

$$\Delta A\_S_i = \begin{cases} 0, & if\ m=1 \\ \pm COD_{i,A} \times \dfrac{\sum_{j=1}^{m} |S_{i\_center} - S_{i,j}|}{\sum_{j=1}^{m} |A_{i\_center} - A_{i,j}|}, & if\ 2 \leq m \leq n \end{cases} \quad (1)$$

It must be noted that the sign of the ΔA_S_i are same as the sign of correlation $r_i(A\_S_i)$.

(b) Regression coefficient

$$\Delta A\_S_i = \begin{cases} 0, & if\ m=1 \\ \beta_{i,A} \times \dfrac{\sum_{j=1}^{m} |S_{i\_center} - S_{i,j}|}{\sum_{j=1}^{m} |A_{i\_center} - A_{i,j}|}, & if\ 2 \leq m \leq n \end{cases} \quad (2)$$

Step 6: Calculate the Euclidean distance $Dist_i$ between the tuple containing null value and c_i.

Step 7: Calculate the estimated value S_e of the attribute "SALARY" as follows:

$$S_e = S_{i\_center} + \sum \Delta IV\_DV_i \times (IV_i - IV_{i\_center}) \quad (3)$$

where $1 \leq i \leq k$.

Step 8: Compute MAER to evaluate the estimated accuracy.

$$MAER = \frac{\sum_{i=1}^{n} |(S_{estimated_i} - S_{o_i})/S_{o_i}|}{n} \times 100\% \quad (4)$$

where S_o is the original value, n is denotes the number of tuples in a relation.

3 Verification and Comparison

In order to verify the results of this research, we use a practical human resource database in Taiwan, which contains 609 records. The schema is shown as Table 2. The ordering of the value of the attribute "DEGREE" is (Master)> (Bachelor)> (Junior college)> (Senior high school)> (Junior high school). Hence, "Junior high school" is assigned to 0.0, "Senior high school student" is assigned to 1.0, "junior college" is assigned to 2.0, "Bachelor" is assigned to 3.0, and "Master" is assigned to 4.0, where these assignments can facilitate to estimate null values.

Table 2. The schema of human resource database

EMP_NO	SEX	AGE	EXPERIENCE	DEGREE	SALARY (unit : thousand of dollars)

Table 3. Comparison of the estimated MAER (use Auto-clustering)

EMP NO.	(a) [3]		(b)		(c)		(d)	
	S_e	error	S_e	error	S_e	error	S_e	error
O₁	3.48	-0.31	3.78	-0.24	7.63	0.53	4.66	-0.07
⋮								
O₆₀₉	559.5	0.00	560	0.00	559.5	0.00	560	0.00
MAER (%)	16.57%		14.73%		I:1.64%; II: 6.63%; III: 6.97%; IV: 16.17% 7.85%		I:1.30 %; II: 6.62%; III:6.83%; IV: 15.96% 7.68%	

The attribute "SALARY" contains null value. We utilized stepwise regression to select the first two important attributes (AGE, SEX) from database. There are 8 types of results (2 clustering methods: K-Means and Auto-clustering; 4 types of methods: (a) Overall estimation with COD; (b) Overall estimation with regression coefficient; (c) Partitional approach with COD; (d) Partitional approach with regression coefficient) shown in Table 3~4. The overall estimation is meaning no partition data. In Table 3~4, we can see that the MAER (3.267%) of the partitional approach with regression coefficient is less than other methods.

Table 4. Comparison of the estimated MAER (use K-means)

EMP NO.	(a)		(b)		(c)		(d)	
	S_e	e	S_e	e	S_e	e	S_e	e
O_1	84.2	0.07	83.02	0.05	81.77	81.84	81.8	-0.01
⋮								
O_{609}	283	0.00	283	0.00	283.0	0.0	283.	0.00
MAER (%)	4.01%		3.44%		I: 2.29%; II: 3.04%; III: 4.90%; IV: 4.66% **3.72%**		I: 1.86%; II: 1.93%; III:4.75%; IV: 4.53% **3.27%**	

4 Conclusion

In this paper, we proposed an efficient approach for estimate null values in human resource database. From the result, we can see that the MAER of the proposed approach is better than the other existing methods. That is, the estimated accuracy rate of the proposed method is better than other methods. And the results of partitional approach are better than those without partitional approach. Therefore, we can use partitional approach to increase the accuracy of estimation. In this paper, we need to transfer categorical data into numerical data. In the future, we can add methods of dealing with categorical data in our approach to make the result better.

References

1. Arnold, S.F.: Mathematical Statistics, Prentice-Hall, Englewood Cliffs NJ (1990)
2. Babad, Y. M. & Hoffer, J. A.: Even no data has a value, Vol. 27, Communications of the ACM, (1984)
3. Chen, S.M. & Hsiao, H.R.:A new method to estimate null values in relational database systems based on automatic clustering techniques, Inf. sci., (2004)
4. Draper, N.R., Smith, H.: Applied Regression Analysis, John Wiley and Sons, New York (1998)
5. Han, J. & Kamber, M.: Data Mining: Concepts and Techniques, Morgan Kaufmann (2001)
6. MacQueen, JB.: Some methods for classification and analysis of multivariate observations, Proceedings of the Fifth Berkeley Symposium on Mathematical Statistics and Probability, (1967) 281-297

A Robust Face Recognition System

Ying-Han Pang, Andrew Teoh Beng Jin, and David Ngo Chek Ling

Faculty of Information Science and Technology, Multimedia University,
Jalan Ayer Keroh Lama, 75450 Melaka, Malaysia
{yhpang, bjteoh, david.ngo}@mmu.edu.my

Abstract. This paper proposes a robust face recognition system, by providing a strong discrimination power and cancelable mechanism to biometrics data. Fisher's Linear Discriminant uses pseudo Zernike moments to derive an enhanced feature subset. On the other hand, the revocation capability is formed by the combination of a tokenized pseudo-random data and the enhanced template. The inner product of these factors generates a user-specific binary code, face-Hash. This two-factor basis offers an extra protection layer against biometrics fabrication since face-Hash authenticator is replaceable via token replacement.

1 Introduction

This proposed biometrics system comprises a discriminative feature extractor and biometrics revocable capability. Pseudo Zernike moment, PZM, is a good feature representation, but it may not be an optimal classifier as its discrimination power mainly depends on the image intensity value. Thus, a Moment-Fisher feature extraction is introduced. The introduction of Fisher's Linear Discriminant (FLD) into moment derives an enhanced feature subset by maximizing the between-class scatter, while minimizing the within-class scatter, leads to a better discrimination performance.

The biometrics irrevocability issue is also solved by introducing two-factor basis (pseudo-random data and face template) [1]. Random number is inner product with face feature. The generated random data is then discretized to produce a bitstring, face-Hash. Face-Hash is cancelable- the code can be reissued if it is compromised via token replacement. Besides, users must possess both factors; absence of either one will just handicap the authentication process. Fig. 1 shows our proposed system.

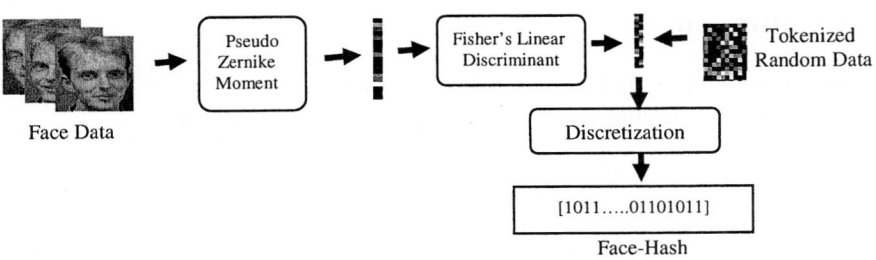

Fig. 1. The overview of the proposed method

2 Pseudo Zernike Moments

The two-dimensional pseudo Zernike moments of order p with repetition q of an image intensity function $f(r,\theta)$ are defined as [2,3],

$$PZ_{pq} = \frac{p+1}{\pi} \int_0^{2\pi} \int_0^1 V_{pq}(r,\theta) f(r,\theta) r dr d\theta \qquad (1)$$

where Zernike polynomials $V_{pq}(r,\theta)$ are defined as,

$$V_{pq}(r,\theta) = R_{pq}(r) e^{-\hat{j}q\theta} ; \quad \hat{j} = \sqrt{-1} \qquad (2)$$

and $r = \sqrt{x^2 + y^2}$, $\theta = \tan^{-1}\left(\frac{y}{x}\right)$, $-1 < x, y < 1$

The real-valued radial polynomials are defined as,

$$R_{pq}(r) = \sum_{s=0}^{p-|q|} (-1)^s \frac{(2p+1-s)!}{s!(p+|q|+1-s)!(p-|q|-s)!} r^{p-s}, \quad 0 \leq |q| \leq p, p \geq 0. \qquad (3)$$

3 Moment-Fisher (MF) Method

FLD is a popular discriminant criterion that measures the between-class scatter normalized by the within-class scatter [4]. Thus, an enhanced moment-fisher-based feature vector (*FPZM*) with high separability can be acquired. In our method, the input of FLD is the moment feature vector. Let us consider a set of Q moment-based facial representations $\{x_j = PZ_{pq,j}, j = 1, 2, \cdots, Q\}$ having l dimension and assume there are C face classes $\{w_1, w_2, \cdots, w_C\}$ and the number of images in each class is Q', $\{x'_{i,Q'}, i \text{ is } i^{th} \text{ class}\}$. Let M_C and M_g be class mean and grand mean, respectively. The within- and between-class scatter matrices, S_w and S_b, are:

$$S_w = \sum_{i=1}^{C} \sum_{x'_{i,k} \in w_i} (x'_{i,k} - M_i)(x'_{i,k} - M_i)^T ; \quad S_b = \sum_{i=1}^{C} Q'_i (M_i - M_g)(M_i - M_g)^T \qquad (4)$$

where $M_i = \frac{1}{Q'_i} \sum_{x'_{i,k} \in w_i} x'_{i,k}$ and $M_g = \frac{1}{Q} \sum_{j=1}^{Q} x_j$. Please refer [4,5,6] for detail.

4 Discretization

The progression of face-Hash is described as below [1],
1. compute x =<feature vector, random data>, where <,> denotes inner product.
2. determine $b(x) = \begin{cases} 0 & ; x < \tau \\ 1 & ; x \geq \tau \end{cases}$, where τ is a threshold for assigning a single bit, which will be used to form face-Hash.

5 Experimental Results and Discussions

The experimental schemes are *PZM* : PZM scheme, *MF* : Moment-Fisher scheme, and *FPZM_d* : the proposed system (with two-factor basis), *d* is the bit length. Table 1 shows the error rates between the *PZM* and *MF* schemes in OVL and PF01 databases [7, 8]. The lowest EER is obtained by *MF* with 10.77% in OVL and 21.56% in PF01. The result indicates that MF features carry discriminating information, leads to better recognition. But, *MF* shows poorer result when higher order moments are included for feature representation. This is because these moments comprise unwanted features, such as noise, and redundant information which seriously affect the feature discrimination.

Table 1. Error rates of *PZM* and *MF* schemes on OVL and PF01 databases

Scheme	Feature length, l	OVL EER (%)	PF01 EER (%)
PZM	100	17.03	25.46
	120	16.60	26.00
	140	16.33	26.39
	160	16.25	26.80
	180	16.38	27.13
	200	16.40	27.29
	400	16.92	28.38
MF	100	10.77	21.81
	120	14.50	21.72
	140	17.26	21.56
	160	29.29	22.76
	180	28.79	22.59
	200	32.95	23.14
	400	48.65	43.69

Note: EER=Equal Error Rate

Table 2 shows the error rates of *FPZM_d*. It can be observed that *FPZM_d* performs much better than *PZM* and *MF*. Besides, we can see that longer bit length produces more impressive result.

Table 2. Error rates of *FPZM_d* in OVL and PF01 databases

FPZM_d scheme	OVL database EER (%)	PF01 database EER (%)
FPZM_10	4.15	8.03
FPZM_20	1.71	2.04
FPZM_30	0.71	1.13

6 Concluding Remarks

A robust face authentication system is proposed in this paper. Two authentication factors are included in this system, which are tokenized pseudo-random pattern and Fisher-moment-based face features. These two factors are used to generate a set of unique private compact binary code, face-Hash, acted as verification key. In this paper, pseudo Zernike moments are chosen as feature extractor due to their superior feature representation capability and prominent orthogonality property. Introduction of Fisher's Linear Dsicriminant onto moments is to strengthen the feature discrimination power. Combination between Fisher-moment-based features and random data enables a cancelable mechanism, in which the verification key can be replaceable once it is compromised via token replacement. Furthermore, the mixing step of both factors even provides higher level security, in which users must possess both authentication factors; absence of either one will just handicap the authentication process.

References

1. Goh, A and Ngo, D: Computation of Cryptographic Keys from Face Biometrics. Communications and Multimedia Security (2003) 1-13.
2. C.H. Teh and R.T. Chin: On Image Analysis by the Methods of Moments. IEEE Trans. Pattern Analysis Machine Intell, vol. 10, (July 1998) 496-512.
3. R. Mukundan and K.R. Ramakrishnan: Moment Functions in Image Analysis – Theory and Applications, World Scientific Publishing (1998).
4. K. Fukunaga: Introduction to Statistical Pattern Recognition, second ed. Academic. New York (1991).
5. D.L. Swets and J. Weng: Using Discriminant Eigenfeatures for Image Retrieval. IEEE Transactions on Pattern Analysis and Machine Intelligence, vol. 18, (1996) 831-836.
6. Y.H. Pang, T.B.J. Andrew and N.C.L. David: A Hybrid Moments and Fisher's Linear Discriminant in face Recognition. International Conference on Robotics, Vision, Information and Signal Processing, ISBN:983-3391-15-X, (2005) 581-585.
7. OVL face database: http://www.uk.research.att.com/facedatabase.html
8. PF01 face database: http://nova.postech.ac.kr/archives/imdb.html

Resampling LDA/QR and PCA+LDA for Face Recognition

Jun Liu and Songcan Chen

Department of Computer Science and Engineering,
Nanjing University of Aeronautics and Astronautics,
Nanjing 210016, P.R. China
{j.liu, s.chen}@nuaa.edu.cn

Abstract. Principal Component Analysis (PCA) plus Linear Discriminant Analysis (LDA) (PCA+LDA) and LDA/QR are both two-stage methods that deal with the Small Sample Size (SSS) problem in traditional LDA. When applied to face recognition under varying lighting conditions and different facial expressions, neither method may work robustly. Recently, resampling, a technique that generates multiple subsets of samples from the training set, has been successfully employed to improve the classification performance of the PCA+LDA classifier. In this paper, stimulated by such success, we propose a resampling LDA/QR method to improve LDA/QR's performance. Furthermore, taking advantage of the difference between LDA/QR and PCA+LDA, we incorporate them by resampling for face recognition. Experimental results on AR dataset verify the effectiveness of the proposed methods.

1 Introduction

Linear Discriminant Analysis (LDA) [1, 2] is a popular feature extraction in pattern recognition. However, when applied to such recognition task as face recognition, LDA may encounter the so-called Small Sample Size (SSS) problem.

Among many existing methods that address this problem, Principal Component Analysis (PCA) plus LDA (PCA+LDA) [1] and LDA/QR [2] are both methods that perform feature extraction in two sequential stages: in PCA+LDA, the face samples are projected to a PCA [3] subspace in the first stage, and then LDA is applied secondly; in LDA/QR, the face samples are firstly projected to the range space of between-class matrix, followed by LDA in the second stage. When applied to face recognition under varying lighting conditions and different facial expressions, neither method may work robustly under relatively great facial variance, due to limited training samples for each class and the resulting biased estimates of both the within-class matrix S_w and the between-class matrix S_b.

To improve the performance of weak classifiers, a number of approaches have been studied in literature, such as the bootstrapping-aggregating (bagging) method [4], the boosting method [5], the random subspace method [6] and the resampling method [7]. Recently, Lu and Jain successfully applied the resampling technique to improve the performance of PCA+LDA and proposed resampling PCA+LDA (R-PCA+LDA) for face recognition [7].

In this paper, we intend to improve the performance of LDA/QR by the resampling technique, and propose the resampling LDA/QR (R-LDA/QR) method. Furthermore, PCA+LDA is quite different from LDA/QR, especially in their corresponding first stages, i.e., face samples are projected to an unsupervised PCA subspace in PCA+LDA, different from the supervised S_b's range space in LDA/QR. As a result, the projection matrices derived respectively by PCA+LDA and LDA/QR may be quite different. Taking advantage of such difference, we can integrate PCA+LDA and LDA/QR by resampling for face recognition, and expect to gain improved classification performance.

The rest of this paper is organized as: we introduce the proposed methods in section 2, give experimental results in section 3 and draw a conclusion in section 4.

2 Proposed Methods

According to [7], the resampling technique generates K subsets from the whole training samples, subject to the following two conditions:

1) The number of sampled images for each subject in the subset is equal or as equal as possible.
2) Sampling within each class is achieved based on a uniform distribution.

2.1 Resampling LDA/QR for Face Recognition

As is stated in [2], LDA/QR may encounter the problem of centroid sensitivity. This will take place in face recognition under great facial variance and lead to a weak classifier. In order to improve the classification performance of LDA/QR classifier, we employ the resampling technique to generate multiple subsets, train a LDA/QR classifier on each subset, and integrate the classification results of these multiple classifiers using majority voting for classification. Note that LDA/QR is much more efficient than PCA+LDA [2], consequently the proposed R-LDA/QR here is much more efficient than R-PCA+LDA.

2.2 Resampling LDA/QR and PCA+LDA for Face Recognition

After applying the resampling technique to improve the classification performance of the LDA/QR, a natural question is, "Can we benefit from integrating R-PCA+LDA and R-LDA/QR for face recognition?" From the theory of classifier combination [8], diversity plays a key factor to boost classification performance of the combined classifiers. As discussed in the introduction, PCA+LDA is quite different from LDA/QR, which means that diversity may exist between them. As a result, we can integrate LDA/QR and PCA+LDA by resampling (R-LDA/QR plus R-PCA+LDA) for face recognition. More specifically, we use the resampling technique to generate multiple subsets, train a LDA/QR and a PCA+LDA respectively on each subset, and integrate the classification results of these multiple classifiers using majority voting for classification.

3 Experiments

To evaluate the effectiveness of the proposed methods, we carry out experiments on AR face dataset [9]. This face dataset consists of over 3200 images of frontal images of faces of 126 subjects. Each subject has 26 different images which were grabbed in two different sessions separated by two weeks, 13 images in each session were recorded. For the 13 images, the first to the fourth are of different facial expressions, the fifth to the seventh under varying light conditions, and the others of occlusions. In our experiments here, we use the 1400 gray level images from 100 objects, where each object has 14 images. More specifically, we use the first seven images from the first session to construct the training set, and the first seven images from the second session for testing. The 1400 images are preprocessed by Martinez [9] with a resolution of 165×120. Here, for computational convenience, we resize them to 66×48 and rescale the gray level values to [0 1].

We set the number of sampled images for each subject to M, where M varies from 3 to 5, and use the resampling technique to generate K (=60) subsets from the whole training set. We dynamically integrate the classification results of the first k (k=1,2, ..., K) classifiers through majority voting, and denote the corresponding classification accuracy as Acc_k. To report the classification accuracy of a given method's final result, the mean result of Acc_{41} to Acc_{60} is used and meanwhile the corresponding standard variance is also reported.

Table 1. Classification accuracies of different methods

	M		
	3	4	5
R-LDA/QR	89.2[a] (2.81[b])	88.0(1.28)	88.0(1.25)
R-PCA+LDA	87.9(1.25)	88.3(2.74)	88.3(1.22)
R-LDA/QR plus R-PCA+LDA	89.8(2.04)	90.6(3.01)	91.0(1.91)
LDA/QR	85.7		
PCA+LDA	84.9		

[a] The classification accuracies (%) reported here are the mean values of Acc_{41} to Acc_{60}
[b] Value in the parenthesis (×10^{-3}) is the according standard derivation of Acc_{41} to Acc_{60}

We list the classification accuracies of all the methods in Table 1, from which we can clearly see that R-LDA/QR achieves significantly better classification accuracy than LDA/QR, and meanwhile comparable to or even better performance than R-PCA+LDA. Moreover, when M=4, R-LDA/QR plus R-PCA+LDA yields a classification accuracy of 90.6%, 2.6, 2.3, 4.9 and 5.7 percentages respectively higher than R-LDA/QR, R-PCA+LDA, LDA/QR and PCA+LDA. Similar observation can also be made when M=3 or 5, which shows that R-LDA/QR plus R-PCA+LDA is a powerful combined framework.

4 Conclusion

In this paper, we introduce the resampling technique to improve the classification performance of LDA/QR classifier, and propose a new R-LDA/QR classifier. Experimental results on AR face dataset with variations on both lighting and facial expression changes show that R-LDA/QR can achieve significantly higher classification accuracy than LDA/QR and meanwhile comparable to or even higher classification accuracy than R-PCA+LDA classifier proposed in [7]. Note that LDA/QR is more efficient than PCA+LDA, hence R-LDA/QR proposed here will offer practitioners a powerful and efficient classifier. Moreover, taking advantage of the difference between LDA/QR and PCA+LDA, we integrate LDA/QR and PCA+LDA by resampling technique for face recognition. Experimental results on the AR face dataset show that R-LDA/QR plus R-PCA+LDA yields higher classification accuracy respectively than R-LDA/QR, R-PCA+LDA, LDA/QR, and PCA+LDA alone.

Acknowledgement

We thank Natural Science Foundation of China under Grant Nos. 60473035 for support.

References

1. Belhumeur, P.N., Hespanha, J.P., and Kriegman, D.J., Eigenfaces vs. fisherfaces: Recognition using class specific linear projection, IEEE Trans. Pattern Analysis and Machine Intelligence, 19(7): 711-720, 1997.
2. Ye, J., Li, Q., A two-stage Linear Discriminant Analysis via QR-Decomposition, IEEE Trans. Pattern Analysis and Machine Intelligence, 27(6): 929-941, 2005.
3. Turk, M.A., and Pentland, A.P., Face Recognition Using Eigenfaces, Proc. of IEEE Conf. on Computer Vision and Pattern Recognition, pp. 586-591, 1991.
4. Breiman, L., Bagging predictors, Machine Learning, 24(2): 123–140, 1996.
5. Freund, Y., and Schapire, R. E., Experiments with a new boosting algorithm, Proc. International Conference on Machine Learning, pp. 148–156, 1996
6. Ho, T. K., The random subspace method for constructing decision forests, IEEE Trans. Pattern Analysis and Machine Intelligence, 20(8):832–844, 1998.
7. Lu, X., and Jain, A. K., Resampling for Face Recognition, Proc. of AVBPA, 2003.
8. Dietterich, T. G., Machine Learning Research: Four Current Directions, AI Magazine, 18(4), 97-136, 1997
9. Martinez, A.M., and Benavente, R., The AR Face Database, CVC Technical Report #24, June 1998.

Curvature Based Range Face Recognition Analysis Using Projection Vector by Subimage

Yeunghak Lee[1] and Ik-Dong Kim[2]

[1] SEECS Yeungnam University, Kyongsan,
Kyongsangbuk-do, Korea, 712-749
annaturu@yumail.ac.kr
[2] Dept. of Computer Engineering, Andong National University,
388 Songcheon-Dong, Andong, Kyungpook, Korea, 760-749
kid7@andong.ac.kr

Abstract. We will present a new practical implementation of a person verification system using the projection vectors based on curvatures for range face images. The combination of the four curvatures according to the curvature threshold and depth values show that proposed method achieves higher recognition rate of the cases for ranked best candidates, respectively, and combined recognition rate also.

1 Introduction

Most human face recognition approaches have centered on feature extraction and using the relationship of these features in face matching process [1]. Lapreste etc. [2] presented a system that identifies facial feature points, such as center of eyes, tip of nose, lips and chin. The authors analyzed the curvature on a human face to extract feature points on profile line images. Lee and Milios [3] tried to detect corresponding regions in two range images. They computed an extended Gaussian image (EGI) for extracted the convex regions in range images of human faces. Gordon [4] presented a detailed study of range images in the human face recognition based on depth and face surface curvature features. The curvatures on a face surface are calculated to find face descriptors: nose ridge and eye features. She proposed two recognition strategies based on template matching and on comparing in the feature space, relying on these descriptor.

In this paper, we propose a new face recognition algorithm using the edge maps which is extracted by the threshold values from each curvature which is analyzed as a curvature-related subimages.

2 Surface Curvature

For each data point on the facial surface, the principal, Gaussian and mean curvatures are calculated and the sign of those (positive, negative and zero) is used to determine the surface type at every point. The $Z(x, y)$ image represents a surface where the individual Z-values are surface depth information. If face surface is a polynomial like as equation (1), we now closely follow the formalism introduced by Peet & Sahota [5] and specify any point on the surface by its position vector:

$$z(x, y) = a_{00} + a_{10}x + a_{01}y + a_{20}x^2 + a_{02}y^2 + a_{11}xy \quad (1)$$

Sahota et al. calculated coefficients of (1) by least square error fit, and calculated minimum and maximum curvature, k_1 and k_2, by finding polynomial into the first and second differential form. And Gaussian (K) and Mean curvature are defined by

$$K = k_1 k_2, \quad M = (k_1 + k_2)/2 \quad (2)$$

Here we have ignored the directional information related to k_1 and k_2 and chosen k_2 to be the larger of the two. For the present work, however, this has not been done.

3 Projection Vectors

In general, the projection executes the role of converting N dimensional coordinate systems into smaller dimensions than N. If it is used as one dimension, the horizontal projection vectors can be obtained by vertical projection. If the curvature image is *I[r, c]*, the projection *H[r]* along the row and the projection *V[c]* along the column of binary image are given by

$$H[r] = \sum_{c=0}^{N-1} I[r,c], \quad V[c] = \sum_{r=0}^{M-1} I[r,c] \quad (3)$$

But there are some problems with indexing database images which include several sizes, using these projections. To solve the problem of projection which is difficult to image indexing, we used grouped projection vectors, as given by

$$V[g_r] = \frac{1}{N} \sum_{g_c=0}^{G-1} I[r,c], \quad H[g_c] = \frac{1}{N} \sum_{g_r=0}^{G-1} I[r,c] \quad (4)$$

where $1 \leq g_r, g_c \leq G$, *I* is curvature image and *G* is the count of the group. In this study, we used 10 groups {WD0(3x3) ~ WD9(12x12)} for horizontal and vertical.

4 Experimental Results

In this study to evaluate the performance of several subspace distance measures for range face images, we used a 3D laser scanner made by a 4D Culture [6]. The used face database was 84 images (42 people). And in our system, the person who wears the spectacles was excluded because of noise.

Using the curvature equations, the measured curvature value displayed between – 1.0 and 1.0 by experiments. In this paper, k_1 is 0.1 (0.0 to 1.0), k_2 is 0.1 (-1.0 to 0.0), K is 0.04 (-0.2 to 0.2) and M is 0.06 (-3.0 to 3.0), as threshold values (TH).

4.1 Face Recognition

The recognition rates are compared by L1 and L2, and D1 and D2 which is proposed distance methods, as given by

$$L1 = |W_q - W_d|, \quad L2 = \|W_q - W_d\|, \quad D1 = \frac{|W_q - W_d|}{1 + W_q - W_d}, \quad D2 = \frac{|W_q - W_d|}{1 + W_q - W_d} * Depth \quad (5)$$

where the weight factor *Depth* is

$$Depth = |Q_{avg} - D_{avg}| \quad (Q_{avg} = Q_{peak} - Q \text{ and } D_{avg} = D_{peak} - D) \quad (6)$$

where W_q and W_d are the projection vector extracted from query and database image. Q_{peak} and D_{peak} are the nose tip value for query image Q and database image D. And we used similarity re-ranking algorithm by the idea of committee machine based on a simple principle, the name referred to as "divide and conquer" [7]. In our system, it is adopted for combining the committee machine, as given by

$$R_i(k) = \max\{D20_i(k), D30_i(k), D40_i(k), D50_i(k)\} \quad (7)$$

Where *k* is the ranking of result for *i* image.

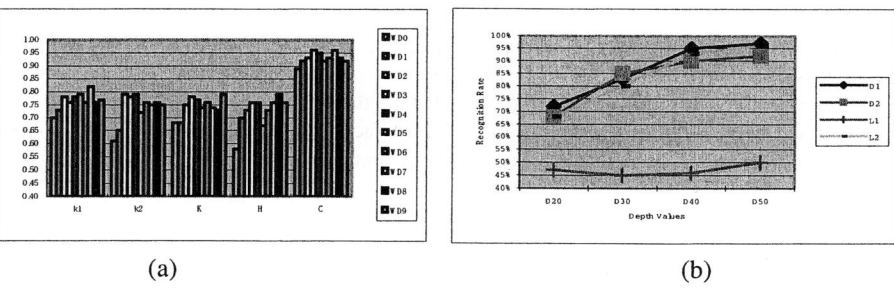

(a)   (b)

Fig. 1. Recognition rate for depth value 50 (a) according to the window (b) each distance method

The experimental results proposed in this paper are shown as Fig. 1. In Fig. 1 (a), the graph is displayed the result of recognition according to the each projection and curvatures by equation (7). It can be seen that in any feature domains dividing images into groups can always attain higher recognition rate than small group images. It can be seen proposed D1 and D2 that is modified by depth value are better performance than L2. D2 is showed more stable for projection windows of each curvature than L2 and D1. The highest recognition rate marked that D1 method is 97%, L2 method is 96% and D2 method is 93%, within ranked best 1.

5 Conclusion

In this paper, a new projection vectors which is reduced dimension and distance weighted by a function based on depth value are proposed. Due to different surface curvature and depth for the face of person, the distance measures proposed to emphasize the depth and the shape of face. The weighting function used in this paper is based on depth values, which have different values according to the people and important facial features such as nose, mouth, eyes and especially face contour. We argues, that even though a large database is constructed, if the statistical features of projection vectors are used, indexing time and complexity will be reduced because of fewer parameters.

References

1. K. W. Bowyer, K. Chang and P. Flynn: A Survey of 3D and Multi-Modal 3D+2D Face Recognition. International Conference on Pattern Recognition 2004.
2. J. T. Lapresté, J. Y. Cartoux, and M. Richetin: Face Recognition from Range Image Data by Structural Analysis. Syntactic and Structural Pattern Recognition, NATO ASI Series (1988), PP. 303-314
3. J. C. Lee and E. Milios: Matching range image of human faces. Third International Conference on Computer Vision (1990), pp. 722-726, 1990.
4. G. G. Gordon: Face Recognition based on depth and curvature feature. Proceeding of the IEEE Computer Society Conference on Computer Vision and Pattern Recognition (1992), pp. 808-810
5. F. G. Peet and T. S. Sahota: Surface Curvaturre as a Measure of Image Texture. IEEE PAMI, Vol. PAMI-7(1985), No.6, pp. 734-738
6. 3D Face Scanner, 4D Culture Co., http:://www.4dculture.com/.
7. Z.Q. Zhao, D. S. Huang and B. Y. Sun: Human face recognition on multi-feature using neural networks committee. Pattern Recognition Letter(2004), Vol. 25, pp.1351-1358

Multiple Face Tracking Using Kalman Estimator Based Color SSD Algorithm

Kyunghwan Baek, Byoungki Kim, Sangbum Park,
Youngjoon Han, and Hernsoo Hahn

School of Electronic Engineering, Soongsil University, Dongjak-ku, Seoul, Korea
{khniki, qsilver, forcepsb, young, hahn}@ssu.ac.kr

Abstract. This paper proposes a new tracking algorithm using the Kalman estimator based color SSD algorithm. The Kalman estimator includes the color information as well as the position and size of the face region in its state vector, to take care of the variation of skin color while faces are moving. Based on the estimated face position, the color SSD algorithm finds the face matching with the one in the previous frame even when the color and size of the face region vary. The features of a face region extracted by the color SSD algorithm are used to update the state of the Kalman estimator. In the experiments, it has been shown that the proposed algorithm traces multiple faces successfully even when they are overlapped for a moment.

1 Introduction

Many methods have been developed to detect and trace faces in surveillance systems. They can be largely categorized in general into two classes: model-based tracking and motion-based tracking. In model-based approach, the performance of these methods depends on how accurately extracts object features and rapidly matches with the object model. So, it requires a large processing time to construct accurate database and extract complex features for including the case where the complete set of object features are not visible[1,2]. In motion-based approach, motion pixels in video sequences are detected using a difference image and then they are grouped using their features to form an object region. Depending on applications, it is segmented by a face and a body, and then either one is traced by using a Kalman filter or mean shift algorithm. Thus, the performance of this approach depends on how accurately detects the motion pixels and groups an object region with less influence of noises[3,4].

This paper proposes a new tracking algorithm using Kalman estimator based color SSD algorithm. It estimates not only the position and size but also the color distribution of faces and uses the color SSD algorithm to find the face regions. The color SSD algorithm is appropriate for the cases where the object's shape changes, since it adaptively updates the template of a model. The matching result from the color SSD algorithm is used as the measurement of Kalman estimator to update the state vector. The predicted state vector including the color distribution allows us to deal with the occlusion problem occurring among multiple faces.

2 Kalman Estimator for Position, Size, and Color

Kalman estimator[5], given in Eq. (1) and Eq. (2) is used in this paper to enhance the accuracy and speed of face detection process

$$S(t) = \Phi(\Delta t)S(t - \Delta t) + W(t) \tag{1}$$

$$m(t) = H(t)S(t) + R(t) \tag{2}$$

Differently from other's approaches, the Kalman estimator proposed in this paper includes the color vector of the face region in its state vector. Therefore, the state $S(t)$ given in Eq. (1) is consisted of the center position(C_x, C_y), width(W), and height(H) of the rectangle including the face area, the average of I, Q color values in the face area, and their first derivatives(V_x, V_y, W', H', $I^{m'}$, $Q^{m'}$). That is, $S(t)$=[C_x, C_y, W, H, I^m, Q^m, V_x, V_y, W', H', $I^{m'}$, $Q^{m'}$]^T. Δt is the sampling time of the state update, and Φ is the state transient matrix which reflects the variation of the state vector to the next frame. $m(t)$ = [C_x, C_y, W, H, I^m, Q^m]^T is the measurement vector and $H(t)$ is the measurement matrix. Here $W(t)$ and $R(t)$ are the system input and measurement error respectively, which are assumed to have the normal distribution and defined as the unit vectors.

3 Measurement Update Based on the SSD Algorithm

In the face detection mode, which is considered as the preprocessing step of the whole system, the face region candidates are searched using the skin color and the motion information. Using a difference image, the motion pixels are obtained and those pixels having the facial features are grouped as the face region. If its size and color and position are out of the acceptable error range from the ones estimated by the Kalman estimator, then it is considered as a new face region appearing first in the current frame and it is registered as a new face region. Otherwise, it is considered as the one moved from the previous frame and the face tracking mode is initiated. In the face tracking mode, the position of the face is estimated by the Kalman estimator and at around the position the face region is searched by the SSD algorithm (Eq. (3)) with the template which is the face region detected in the previous frame.

The position, $^iP(k) = {}^iP(k-1) + \triangle x$, that minimizes the following Eq. (3) is selected.

$$\begin{aligned}&CSSD({}^i\mathbf{P}(k-1), \Delta\mathbf{x}) = \\ &\sum_{m,n \in N} [\{\mathbf{I}_{k-1}({}^ix(k-1)+m, {}^iy(k-1)+n) - \mathbf{I}_k({}^ix(k-1)+m+u, {}^iy(k-1)+n+v)\} \\ &+ \{Q_{k-1}({}^ix(k-1)+m, {}^iy(k-1)+n) - Q_k({}^ix(k-1)+m+u, {}^iy(k-1)+n+v)\}]\end{aligned} \tag{3}$$

where $^iP(k-1) = [{}^ix(k-1), {}^iy(k-1)]$ is the position of the template in the (k-1)th frame, I_{k-1} and Q_{k-1} are the color components of the template in the YIQ color space in the (k-1)th, and $\Delta x=[u,v]^T$ means the offset from the estimated position.

If the SSD algorithm finds the matching region, then the color information predicted by the Kalman estimator is used to exactly confine the face region. Using the size, position, and color information of the refined face region, the measurement vector of the Kalman estimator is determined, from which the state vector of that face region is updated by the following Eq. (4).

$$W = 2 \times \min(w1, w2), \quad H = 2 \times \min(h1, h2)$$
$$I^m = \frac{1}{W \times H} \sum_{x,y \in \text{face region}} I(x,y), \quad Q^m = \frac{1}{W \times H} \sum_{x,y \in \text{face region}} Q(x,y) \quad (4)$$

If the predicted positions of multiple face regions are near enough, then the overlap handling mode begins. When an overlap of multiple faces occurs, only the front one is detected at that moment and the other faces are assumed staying at that position without motion. Tracking is continued when the overlap is released.

4 Experiments

A color camera whose CCD size is 320x240 pixels is used to test the performance of the proposed algorithm. The camera captures twenty images per every second and a Pentium IV PC (3.0GHz) has been used to process the input image and track the multiple face. Prior to the calculation of difference and motion vector, the image sequences were smoothed, both in space and time, by Gaussian filter with $\sigma = 2$.

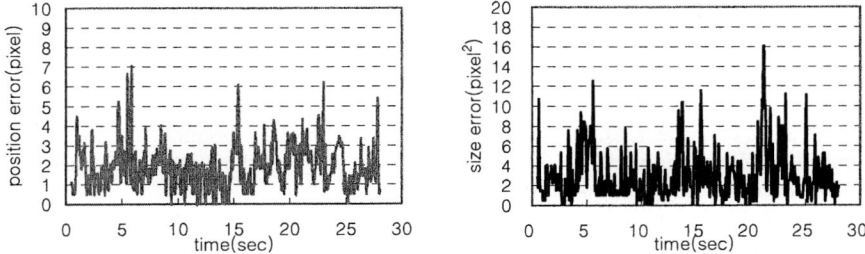

Fig. 1. Position error between the real position and corrected position in pixel

Fig. 1 shows the variations of the position and size errors between the actual one and the corrected one calculated by Kalman estimator in terms of the image coordinate. The errors are measured at every other 0.06 second for 28 seconds. The position error, which is less than 7 pixels and the average error is less than 2 pixels. The average size error is less than 5pixels^2. In Fig. 1, it can be found that the error becomes larger when the face abruptly turns its direction(t=5.9, 15.4, 23.1 and 27.9) or changes its speed (t=1 and 5.5), but the maximum error doesn't deviate from the bound of the search region estimated by Kalman estimator.

5 Conclusions

This paper proposed the Kalman estimator based color SSD algorithm as a new solution to the problems involved in the tracking of multiple faces: one is the variation of the size and color of the face region, another one is the overlap of multiple faces. The Kalman estimator provides the prediction of the color as well as the position and size of a face region, and the color SSD algorithm searches the face region around the predicted position with the template which is adaptively determined as the face region measured in the previous frame. Since the color SSD algorithm uses the template as well as the predicted information of the face region by the Kalman estimator, it can find the occluding face region in the overlapping area. The experimental results have shown that the proposed algorithm works robust in both environments when an overlap among multiple faces occurs and when the color of the face region varies.

Acknowledgement

This work was supported by the Soongsil University Research Fund.

References

1. Strom, J., Jebara, T., Basu, S., Pentland A.: Real time tracking and modeling of faces: an EKF-based analysis by synthesis approach. Modeling People, Proceedings. IEEE International Workshop on 20 Sept. (1999) 55-61
2. Dornaika, F., Ahlberg, J.: Fast and reliable active appearance model search for 3-D face tracking. Systems, Man and Cybernetics, Part B, IEEE Transactions, 34, (2004) 1838 - 1853
3. Jun, Wang., Achanta, R., Kankanhalli, M., Mulhem, P.: A hierarchical framework for face tracking using state vector fusion for compressed video. Acoustics, Speech, and Signal Processing, Proceedings, (ICASSP '03), IEEE International Conference on, 3, (2003) III - 209-12
4. Ce, Wang., Brandstein, M.S.: A hybrid real-time face tracking system. Acoustics, Speech, and Signal Processing, 1998, (ICASSP '98), Proceedings of the 1998 IEEE International Conference, 6, (1998) 3737 – 3740
5. Kalman R. E.: A new approach to linear filtering and prediction problems. Transactions of the ASME, Journal of Basic Engineering, (1960) 35-45

Target Word Selection for Korean Verbs Using a Bilingual Dictionary and WordNet

Kweon Yang Kim[1], Byong Gul Lee[2], and Dong Kwon Hong[3]

[1] Dept. of Computer Engineering, Kyungil University,
Republic of Korea
kykim@kiu.ac.kr
[2] Dept. of Computer Science and Engineering, Seoul Women's University,
Republic of Korea
byongl@swu.ac.kr
[3] Dept. of Computer Engineering, Keimyung University,
Republic of Korea
dkhong@kmu.ac.kr

Abstract. This paper presents an approach of target word selection for Korean verbs based on lexical knowledge contained in a Korean-English bilingual dictionary and WordNet. We focus on deciding which translation of the target word is the most appropriate using the measure of semantic relatedness between possible translations of target word and some indicative clue words. With five Korean ambiguous verbs, we report an average accuracy of 51% that outperforms the default baseline performance and previous works.

1 Introduction

Target word selection is a process of selecting the most appropriate translation word for a given target word in context of source language. The resolution of sense ambiguity and selection of correct translation in non-restricted text are perhaps the great central problem at the lexical level of machine translation.

Dagan and Itai[2] have proposed an approach for resolving word sense ambiguity and selecting a translation word using statistical data from a monolingual corpus of target language. Their method can relieve the knowledge acquisition problem by relying on a monolingual corpus that is sense untagged. However, their method is apt to select an inappropriate translation word because it is based on the simple mapping information between a source word and its possible translation words by using only a bilingual dictionary and a sense untagged target language corpus.

When seeing an occurrence of target language word, their method counts word occurrence as a translation word of all the source language words. This can mislead the selection of correct translation word because the translation word also may have several senses from the view of target language. The source of problem is that this method considers the unnecessary senses of translation words that do not have anything to do with the senses of the original source word.

A possible solution is to use the sense tagged monolingual corpora or bilingual parallel corpora[6]. However, knowledge sources like sense tagged or parallel corpora are generally hard to come by because they need a manual creation. An alternative is dictionary based approaches that take advantage of the information available in machine readable dictionaries or lexical database.

The Lesk algorithm[5] may be identified as a starting point for dictionary based approaches. His algorithm does not require any sense tagged training instances. The main problem of Lesk algorithm is that dictionary definitions tend to be quite short and may not provide sufficient information to measure of relatedness. To overcome the limitation of Lesk algorithm based on short definitions, recently Banerjee and Pedersen[1] presented an extended method of semantic relatedness measurement using WordNet.

In this paper, we present a method of target word selection that attempts to select the most appropriate translation word for Korean verbs using the measure of semantic relatedness that the WordNet similarity package[7] provides.

2 Ranking Senses for Each Possible Translation Word

Our algorithm for target word selection is based on the hypothesis that the correct translation of a target word is highly related to senses of translation words for surrounding context words in the view of target language. The Korean-English dictionary and WordNet provide good information for mapping from the source language word to possible translation words and mapping from the translation word to word senses. The algorithm first identifies a set of possible translation words for the target word and surrounding context words using a Korean-English bilingual dictionary.

Figure 1 shows part of the Korean-English dictionary. Such a bilingual dictionary generally classifies the meaning of an entry word into several senses and groups its translation words and near synonyms by each sense class.

/**gisa^1**/ 技師 *an engineer*; a technician
/**gisa^2**/ 記事 *an article*; an account; news; a statement; description
/**gisa^3**/ 騎士 *a rider*; a horseman

    Fig. 1. A part of the Korean-English dictionary(entry word : 'gisa')

In Korean-English dictionary, each Korean lexical entry word may have multiple senses and there are some corresponding translation words for each sense. In Figure 1, a Korean noun 'gisa' has three senses and has three representative translation words *engineer*, *article*, and *rider* with near synonyms[3] *technician, account, news, statement, description* and *horseman* according to each sense. In order to reduce the weight of application of possibly unwanted senses, our algorithm needs to decide which sense of the representative translation word is more appropriate before we start to compute the score of semantic relatedness between combination pairs of possible senses. The weight of m-th sense t_k^{lm} for translation word t_k^l is computed as follows:

$$w(t_k^{lm}) = \frac{1}{rank(t_k^{lm})}$$

The rank of sense t_k^{lm} is computed using the semantic similarity score between the possible senses of the representative translation word and near synonyms of t_k^1. The measure of semantic similarity is computed by using the method of Jiang and Conrath[4].

3 Target Word Selection

After weighting the senses for each translation word, our algorithm computes the score of semantic relatedness between combination pairs of possible senses for the translation words. This algorithm selects the translation word of target word that has maximum relatedness using the following equation.

$$\arg\max_{i=1}^{x1} \sum_{k \in clues}^{x2,x3,x4} \max_{j,l,m=1} related\ (t_0^{ij}, t_k^{lm}) \bullet w(t_0^{ij}) \bullet w(t_k^{lm})$$

This equation computes a relatedness score of each translation word t_0^i for a target word t_0. t_k^{lm} means m-th sense of translation word t_k^l of t_k that is a surrounding clue word.

While Pedersen and Banerjee[1] used the immediately surrounding context words, we adopt the three major predicate-argument relations such as noun-postposition ('ul'/'rul': objective) + verb, noun-postposition ('ae': locative) + verb, and noun-postposition ('ro'/'uro': instrument) + verb. Figure 2 shows the extended relations between noun and verb we adopt.

{syns; glos; exam}-{syns; glos; exam}
{syns(coor); glos(coor); exam(coor)}-{syns; glos; exam}
{syns; glos; exam}-{syns(coor); glos(coor); exam(coor)}
{syns(hypo); glos(hypo); exam(hypo)}-{syns; glos; exam}
{syns; glos; exam}- {syns(trop); glos(trop); exam(trop)}

Fig. 2. Extended relations (syns : synsets, glos : definitions, exam : examples, coor : coordinate, hypo : hyponyms, trop : troponyms)

4 Experiments and Conclusions

In order to evaluate our algorithm of target word selection, 1.4 milion words Gemong Korean encyclopedia is used as a test data set. Our experiments are performed on five Korean transitive verbs, 'makda', 'ssuda', 'seuda', 'japda', and 'mandulda' that appear with high frequency and ambiguity in our experiment corpus. All the results we report are given as the accuracy performance which means the number of correct translations divided by the number of answers. The results of experiment are summarized in Table 1.

Table 1. Experimental results

	Senses	Instances	Accuracy(%)			
			Baseline	Lesk	P&B	TWS
Average	9	1533	30	17	40	51

The performance of our algorithm was compared with the baseline performance (Baseline) that is achieved by assigning all occurrences to the most frequent translation word. The experimental results show that the accuracy performance of our algorithm(TWS) performs better than the default baseline, original Lesk algorithm(Lesk) and Pedersen and Banerjee's(P&B). While the results are generally lower than the supervised approaches, these results are significant because our approach is based on only a bilingual dictionary and a target language dictionary.

Acknowledgements

This work was supported by grant number (R01-2003-000-10001-0) from the Basic Research Program of Korea Science & Engineering Foundations.

References

1. Banerjee, S. and Pedersen, T.: Extended Gloss Overlaps as a Measure of Semantic Relatedness, Proceedings of the Eighteenth International Joint Conference on Artificial Intelligence (2003) 805-810
2. Dagan, I. And Itai, A.: Word Sense Disambiguation Using a Second Language Monolingual Corpus, Computational Linguistics, Vol. 20, No. 4 (1994) 563-596
3. Inkpen, D. and Hirst, G.: Automatic Sense Disambiguation of the Near-Synonyms in a Dictionary Entry, Proceedings, Fourth Conference on Intelligent Text Processing and Computational Linguistics (2003) 258-267
4. Jiang, J. and Conrath, D.: Semantic Similarity based on Corpus Statistics and Lexicon Taxonomy, Proceedings on International Conference on Research in Computational Linguistics (1997) 19-33
5. Lesk, M.: Automatic Sense Disambiguation Using Machine Readable Dictionaries: how to tell a pine code from an ice cream cone, Proceedings of the Fifth Annual International Conference on Systems Documentations (1986) 24-26
6. Li, H. and Li, C.: Word Translation Disambiguation Using Bilingual Boostrapping, Computational Linguistics, Vol. 30, No. 1 (2004) 1-22
7. Patwardhan, S. and Perdersen, T.: The cpan wordnet::similarity package, http://search.cpan.org/~sid/WordNet-Similarity-0.06/ (2005)

A Color Image Segmentation Algorithm by Using Region and Edge Information

Yuchou Chang[1], Yue Zhou[1], Yonggang Wang[1], and Yi Hong[2]

[1] Institute of Image Processing and Pattern Recognition, Shanhai Jiaotong University,
200030 Shanghai, P.R. China
yuchouchang@yahoo.com.cn
{zhouyue, yonggangwang}@sjtu.edu.cn
[2] Department of Computer Science and Engineering, Shanghai, Jiaotong University,
200030 Shanghai, P.R. China
goodji@sjtu.edu.cn

Abstract. A novel segmentation algorithm for natural color image is proposed. Fibonacci Lattice-based Sampling is used to get the symbols of image so as to make each pixel's label containing color information rather than only as a class marker. Next, Region map is formed based on Fibonacci Lattice symbols to depict homogeneous regions. On the other hand, by applying fuzzy homogeneity algorithm on the image, we filter it to acquire Edge map. To strengthen the ability of discrimination, both the weighted maps are combined to form Region-Edge map. Based on above processes, growing-merging method is used to segment the image. Finally, experiments show very promising results.

1 Introduction

Image Segmentation is an important precondition in image understanding and visual pattern recognition. Deng and Manjunath [1] proposed an unsupervised image segmentation method called JSEG in which a 3-band color image was converted into a scalar map, i.e. color class map, after the color quantization step. Similarly, in [2], an edge map was proposed to indicate the interior of the region or near the boundary. Region growing and merging method was used to get the final segmentation result. In principle, every color quantization method can result in a class map after the pixels' color values are labeled by indices. However, these indices themselves do not typify the true color information and are only used to search quantized colors in the color palette. In our study, we apply a new technique [3] on the color quantization and in turn some features are extracted for image segmentation.

Furthermore, different homogeneous areas always exist in images, which are usually separated by relatively distinct edge lines comparing to the inner part of homogeneous regions. In this paper, we provide a new color image segmentation method through combining advantages of J-map and edge map. The paper is organized as follows. Section 2 depicts the construction of Region map and Edge map respectively. A joint region-edge segmentation method is proposed in Section 3 and some experimental results and summary are given in Section 4.

2 Construction of Region Map and Edge Map

The Fibonacci lattice sampling scheme proposed in [3] provides a uniform quantization of the CIE Lab color space and a way to establish a partial order relation on the set of points, see reference [3] for more details.

In order to achieve as accurate color representation as possible, in our experiment, we use VQ quantization to extract L values. In Fig. 1(b), L component is quantized into {44, 59, 66, 70, 74, 76, 77, 80, 85} and size of palette is 540. Each pixel label not only is the index of the palette, but also typifies the color information to some extent.

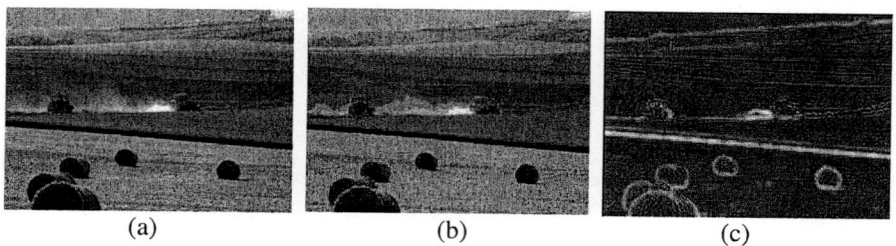

Fig. 1. (a) Original image, (b) color quantized version using 97 valid colors in Fibonacci palette and (c) Fuzzy Homogeneity of image displayed by gray levels

Fibonacci Lattice symbols not only typify the quantized classes, but also denote color information independent of palette. We use following method to form Region map.

Let $I(x, y)$ be the pixel located at the location (x, y) in the image. We construct a new vector to describe variations of homogeneity.

$$h_i = \left(S(x_i, y_i) - S(x_c, y_c)\right) \cdot \frac{vn_i}{\max\left(|x_i - x_c|, |y_i - y_c|\right)} \quad (1)$$

$S(\bullet)$ is Fibonacci Lattice symbol of $I(x, y)$, $vn_i = (x_i - x_c, y_i - y_c)$, $\max\left(|x_i - x_c|, |y_i - y_c|\right)$ is the distance of neighboring pixel to center, which is used to evaluate the influence of different neighboring pixels to center one. Let h be the ultimate vector defined as:

$$h = \sum_{i=1}^{(2N+1)^2} h_i \quad (2)$$

We choose norm of h as the measure of homogeneity, namely:

$$Rmap(x, y) = \|h\| \quad (3)$$

Thereafter, Region map is formed by individual R values. More homogeneous the local area is, less value R is. Fig.2 shows four different patterns derived from parts of the original image.

279	279	279	279	279
279	279	279	279	279
279	279	279	279	279
279	279	279	279	279
279	279	279	279	279

(a) $R = 0$

475	475	475	480	480
540	480	480	480	480
464	472	472	540	540
477	472	472	472	532
472	472	472	532	540

(b) $R = 96.17$

535	535	535	535	535
535	535	535	475	475
535	535	535	475	475
535	475	475	475	475
535	475	475	475	475

(c) $R = 84.85$

233	233	233	233	233
233	233	233	233	233
233	233	233	233	233
61	61	61	61	61
61	61	61	61	61

(d) $R = 243.25$

Fig. 2. Different patterns and their corresponding R values

In order to detect obvious edges, fuzzy homogeneity is used to describe local coarseness, see more details in [4]. Because some unconspicuous lines may be caused by trivial details or textural patterns, in order to resist the interference of these trivial lines, we should filter them and retain major edges. We use the following formula to define Edge map:

$$Emap(x, y) = \begin{cases} FH(x, y), & FH(x, y) > \tau \\ \min FH, & FH(x, y) \leq \tau \end{cases} \quad (4)$$

$FH(x, y)$ is the pixel's fuzzy homogeneity, $\min FH$ is the minimum of all pixels' fuzzy homogeneity, τ is the threshold.

3 Segmentation Using Region Map and Edge Map

As mentioned above, both Region map and Edge map can reflect the distribution of regions' interiors and boundaries. In both maps, if a pixel will be near the boundaries, its value will become large, so their combination may strengthen the ability of discrimination of interiors and boundaries. The final marker map, Region-Edge map, is defined as:

$$REmap(x, y) = \alpha \times Rmap(x, y) + \beta \times Emap(x, y), \quad \alpha > 0, \beta > 0, \alpha + \beta = 1 \quad (5)$$

α and β are coefficients which can be tuned to achieve a well fusion.

In this paper, all pixels are quantified by a predefined quantification level with the acquired RE-map. Next, region growing and splitting algorithm was used to segment the image.

4 Experimental Results

To test the proposed algorithm, we have applied it on a number of real natural images from WWW. A same set of parameters are adopted in all of the experiments: quantization parameter is 120, region merging threshold is 0.4, and other parameters are chosen automatically. Fig. 3 shows the six groups of experimental results of the proposed method and the method of JSEG.

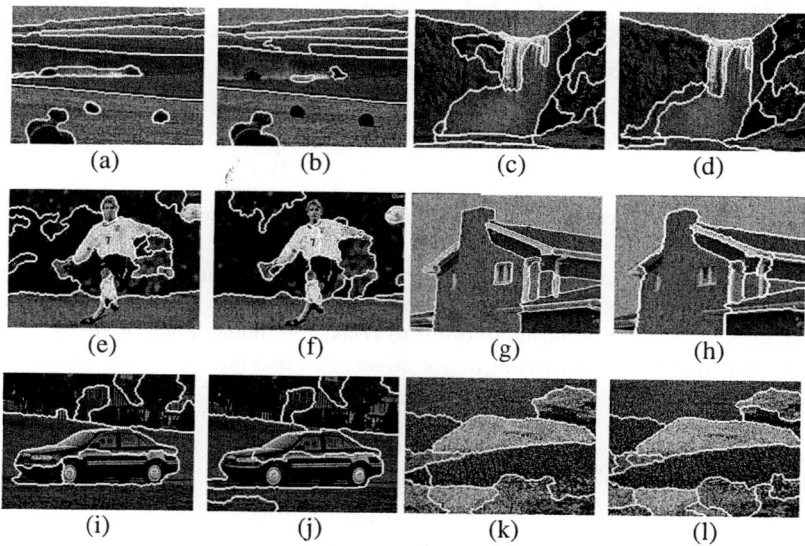

Fig. 3. (a, c, e, g, i, k) Segmentation by proposed method; (b, d, f, h, j, l) Segmentation by JSEG

Homogeneity and edge are two of the most important ingredients in human perception. In this work, using Fibonacci lattice-based quantization helps us calculate local homogeneity and obtain Region map. Fuzzy homogeneity algorithm is used to obtain Edge map. We use region-based method on RE-map to get the final segmentation results. The proposed algorithm can detect small homogeneous regions surrounded by other ones and give effective results.

References

1. Deng, Y., Manjunath, B.S.: Unsupervised Segmentation of Color-Texture Regions in Image and Video, IEEE Transactions on Pattern Analysis and Machine Intelligence, Vol.23 (2001) 800–810
2. Kim, B.G., Park, D.J.: Unsupervised video object segmentation and tracking based on new edge features, Pattern Recognition Letter, Vol.25 (2004) 1731-1742
3. Mojsilovic, A., Soljanin, E.: Color Quantization and processing by Fibonacci Lattices, IEEE Transactions on Image Processing, Vol.10 (2001) 1712–1725
4. H.D.Cheng and J.Li, Fuzzy Homogeneity and Scale Space Approach to Color Image Segmentation, Pattern Recognition, vol. 36, No. 7, pp1545-1562, 2003.

Recognition of Passports Using FCM-Based RBF Network

Kwang-Baek Kim[1], Jae-Hyun Cho[2], and Cheol-Ki Kim[3]

[1] Dept. of Computer Engineering, Silla University, Busan, Korea
gbkim@silla.ac.kr
[2] School of Computer Information Engineering, Catholic University of Pusan, Busan, Korea
jhcho@cup.ac.kr
[3] Div. of Computer Engineering, Miryang National University, Miryang, Korea
ckkim@mnu.ac.kr

Abstract. This paper proposes a novel method for the recognition of passports based on a FCM-based RBF network. First, for the extraction of individual codes for recognizing, this paper targets code sequence blocks including individual codes by applying Sobel masking, horizontal smearing and a contour tracking algorithm on the passport image. As the last step, individual codes are recovered and extracted from the binarized areas by applying CDM masking and vertical smearing. This paper also proposes a FCM-based RBF network that adapts the FCM algorithm for the middle layer. This network is applied to the recognition of individual codes. The results of the experiments for performance evaluation on the real passport images showed that the proposed method has the better performance compared with other approaches.

1 Introduction

The immigration control system authorizes the immigration of travelers by means of passport inspections, which includes the determination of forged passports, the search for a wanted criminal or a person disqualified for immigration, etc. The determination of forged passports plays an important role in the immigration control system, for which automatic and accurate processing is required because of the rapid increase of travelers. We propose a FCM(Fuzzy C-Means) clustering algorithm based RBF network, and by employing these methods, implement a novel system for the preprocessing phase for the determination of forged passports.

For extracting the individual codes from the passport image for recognizing, we extract the code sequence blocks including individual codes using Sobel masking [1], horizontal smearing[2] and 4-directional contour tracking[3]. Then we extract the individual codes from the code sequence blocks using a CDM masking[4] and vertical smearing. Moreover, in this paper a FCM-based RBF network is proposed and applied for the recognition of extracted codes. The network constructs the middle layer using the FCM clustering algorithm for the adjustment of the weight of connections between the input layer and the middle layer. The experiments for performance evaluation of the FCM-based RBF network showed considerable improvement in learning performance and recognition rate.

2 Individual Code Extraction

First, we extract the user code area, and next, extract the picture area to obtain the raw information from passport images. The user code area in the bottom part of passport image has a white background and two code rows containing 44 codes. For extracting the individual codes from the passport image, first, we extract the code sequence blocks including the individual codes by using the feature that the user codes are arranged sequentially in the horizontal direction. The extraction procedure for code sequence blocks is as follows: First, Sobel masking is applied to the original image to generate an edge image[1]. By applying the horizontal smearing to the edge image, the adjacent edge blocks are combined into a large connected block. By successively applying contour tracking to the result of smearing process, a number of connected edge blocks are generated, and the ratio of width to height for all the blocks are calculated. Finally, the edge blocks with the maximum ratio are selected as code sequence blocks.

The individual codes are extracted by applying the CDM (Conditional Dilation Morphology) masking to the areas corresponding to code sequence blocks in the original passport image. We apply CDM(Conditional Dilation Morphology) masking to the result of binarization to recover the information loss caused by the low resolution of input. The CDM masking recovers outer pixels of individual codes by executing only the dilation process without erosion and it is efficient in the images with low resolution[4]. Fig. 1 describes the convergent procedure of CDM mask applied form in the direction of top, bottom, left and right. The CDM mask applied text region is smeared vertically and horizontally. We distinguish the individual codes using vertical coordinates from the vertical smeared text region and define the size of individual codes using horizontal coordinates.

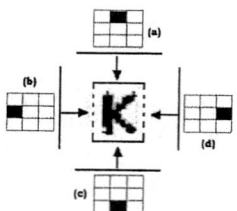

Fig. 1. CDM mask applied form

Finally, we use the vertical smearing and the horizontal projection to extract individual codes form the result of CDM masking. By projecting the vertical smeared areas in the horizontal direction, the horizontal coordinates of individual codes are calculated.

3 Recognition of Passports Using FCM Based RBF Network

Clustering is one of the most fundamental issues in pattern recognition. There are two basic methods of fuzzy clustering. One of the well-known clustering algorithms that allow fuzzy membership function is the fuzzy c-means(FCM) clustering algorithm[5][6]. Therefore, we propose a FCM-based RBF network architecture where the middle layer neurons have RBF (Radial Basis Function) properties and the output layer neurons have a sigmoid function property. By adapting the FCM clustering algorithm for learning structure between the input layer and the middle layer and using the delta rule for training the weights to the output layer neurons, we improve the recognition rate for individual codes.

The FCM-based RBF network performs learning in two phases. The first phase of learning involves competitive learning between the input layer and the middle layer, and the second phase carries out supervised learning between the middle layer and the output layer. This paper enhances a FCM-based RBF network by applying the FCM clustering algorithm to the middle layer, as shown in Fig. 2.

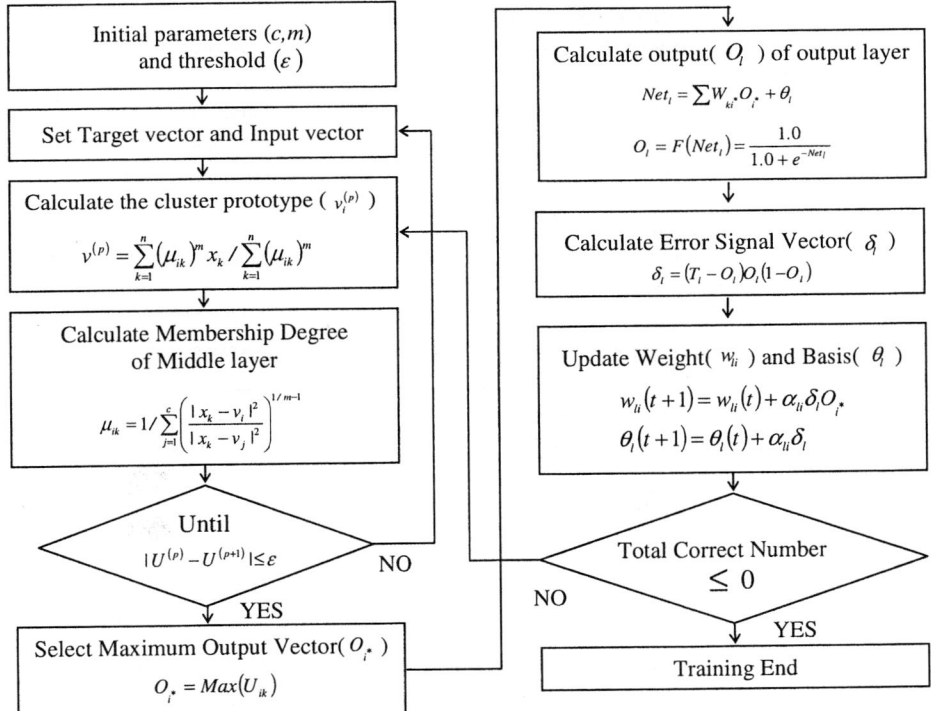

Fig. 2. Learning algorithm of FCM-based RBF network

4 Performance Evaluation

For performance evaluation, we implemented the proposed algorithm and experimented on an IBM-compatible PC with Intel Pentium-IV 2GHz CPU and 256MB RAM. And the 20's passport images of 600x437 pixel size were used in the

(a) Example of passport image

(b) Example of individual code extraction

Fig. 3. Example of individual code and picture extraction

experiments. Fig. 3(a) shows an example of passport image and Fig. 3(b) shows the result of individual code extraction from the passport image in Fig.3(a).

Table 1 shows the number of code sequence blocks and individual codes extracted from the 20 passport images. The extracted individual codes contained 1140 alphabetic codes and 620 numeric codes. In the paper alphabetic codes and numeric ones were used separately in the learning and recognition experiments.

Table 1. Number of extracted for code sequence blocks and individual codes

	Code Sequence Blocks	Individual Codes
The number of extraction (success/target)	40 / 40	1760 / 1760

Table 2. Result of learning and recognition by the FCM-based RBF network

	The number of nodes in middle layer	The number of Epoch	The number of recognition
Alphabetic Codes	60 / 1140	6034	1140 / 1140
Numeric Codes	23 / 620	2418	620 / 620

Table 2 shows the results of the experiment involving FCM-based RBF network for the 20 passport images for recognition. In the FCM-based RBF network, the rate of learning was set to 0.5 and the momentum was set to 0.6. As shown in Table 2, the FCM-based RBF network was able to successfully recognize all of the extracted individual codes.

5 Conclusions

Due to rapid increase of travelers globally, automatic and accurate processing of passports has become a necessity in order to avoid fraud and long waiting time for passengers. In this paper, we discuss an automated system for detection of forgeries in passports.

First, we proposed a novel method for the recognition of passports based on the FCM-based RBF network. In the individual code extraction phase, we extracted the code sequence blocks including individual codes by using Sobel masking, horizontal smearing and the 4-directional contour tracking based on the 2x2 mask. Then we extracted the individual codes form the code sequence blocks by using the CDM masking, and the vertical smearing. In this paper, a FCM-based RBF network was proposed and applied in the code recognition phase. In the experiments for performance evaluation using 20 passport images, it was found that the FCM-based RBF network outperforms traditional approach.

In the future studies, we plan to implement a face authorization module, which can search many databases including driver licenses in order to detect the identity of the perpetrator.

References

1. Jain, A. K.: Fundamental of Digital Image Processing. Englewood Cliffs. New Jersey: Prentice-Hall. (1989)
2. Wang, K. Y., Casey, R. G. and Wahl, F. M. J.: Document analysis system. IBM J. Res. Develop.26. No.6. (1982) 647-656
3. Kim, K. B., Jang, S. W. and Kim, C. K.: Recognition of Car License Plate by Using Dynamical Thresholding Method and Enhanced Neural Networks. Lecture Notes in Computer Science. LNCS 2756. (2003) 309-319
4. Gonzalez, R. C. and Wintz, P.: Digital Image Processing. Addison-Wesley Publishing Company Inc., (1977)
5. George, J. K., Bo, Y.: Fuzzy Sets and Fuzzy Logic Theory and Applications. Prentice Hall PTR. (1995)
6. Kim, K. B., Yun, H. Y., Lho, Y. U.: Developments of Parking Control System Using Color Information and Fuzzy C-Means Algorithm. Journal of Korean Intelligent Information Systems. Vol.8. No.1. (2002) 87-102

A Vision System for Partially Occluded Landmark Recognition

Quoc V. Do[1], Peter Lozo[2], and Lakhmi C. Jain[1]

[1]Knowledge-Based Intelligent Engineering Systems Centre,
School of Electrical and Information Engineering,
University of South Australia,
Mawson Lakes, South Australia, Australia
Quoc.Do@postgrads.unisa.edu.au, Lakhmi.Jain@unisa.edu.au
[2]Weapons Systems Division,
Defence Science and Technology Organisation,
Edinburgh, South Australia, Australia
Peter.Lozo@dsto.defence.gov.au

Abstract. This paper describes a vision system for extracting and recognising partially occluded 2D visual landmarks. The system is developed based on the traditional template matching approach and a memory feedback modulation (MFM) mechanism. It identifies the obscured portions and selectively enhances non-occluded areas of the landmark, while simultaneously suppressing background clutters of the bottom-up edge processed input images. The architecture has been tested with a large number of real images with varying levels of landmark concealment and further evaluated using a vision-based navigating robot in the laboratory environment.

1 Introduction

An essential element in vision-based robot navigation is the ability to recognise visual landmarks, which are salient features along a route. These features serve as navigational references that give rise to space perception. However, the recognition of 2D visual landmarks is a complex and computationally intensive task. Despite the challenge, many successful vision-based robots have been developed. For instance, Mata et al [1] used a genetic algorithm to develop a vision system for recognising quadrangle shapes on walls (doors, windows and posters) to guide the robot along a corridor. Similarly, Li [2], developed a vision system that used a genetic algorithm for detecting numerical signs in an outdoor environment. However, these systems have not addressed the problem of recognising partially occluded landmarks. In the natural environment, it is common that targets are partially covered by other objects or have deteriorated over a period of time. Therefore, it is essential to develop a vision system that is capable of accurately recognising partially obstructed landmarks.

This paper presents a vision system to address the above problem using a simple but effective template matching approach and the memory feedback modulation (MFM) mechanism. The paper is organised as follows: section 2 describes different stages of the vision system, section 3 presents the experimental results and finally the conclusions and future research directions are provided in section 4.

2 The Vision System

The vision system has been implemented based on the traditional template matching approach and recently developed biological artificial neural networks, named selective attention adaptive resonance theory (SAART) [3] and its derivative named complementary SAART [4]. These networks are computationally intensive, thus are not suitable for mobile robot applications. Therefore, the main concepts of these networks are extracted in combination with the template matching approach to develop a fast and sustainable vision system as illustrated Fig. 1.

The major contributions of this paper are the novel means of implementing the memory module, the feature extraction stage and the matching stage. Readers are referred to previous papers for details of other stages. However, it needs to be noticed that, the inputs to the vision system are gray-level images acquired using a CCD camera. The system is edge-based. Thus, the input images are pre-processed using the Prewitt edge detection. The edge processed image is diffused by a Gaussian mask to achieve distortion, small size and view invariant in object recognition using the shape attraction process [5]. The diffused image is fed into the pre-attentive stage. It provides a fast searching mechanism, which attends to regions with abundant edge activity, while discarding regions with minimal activity in the input images. This stage maximises the system's computational resources [6].

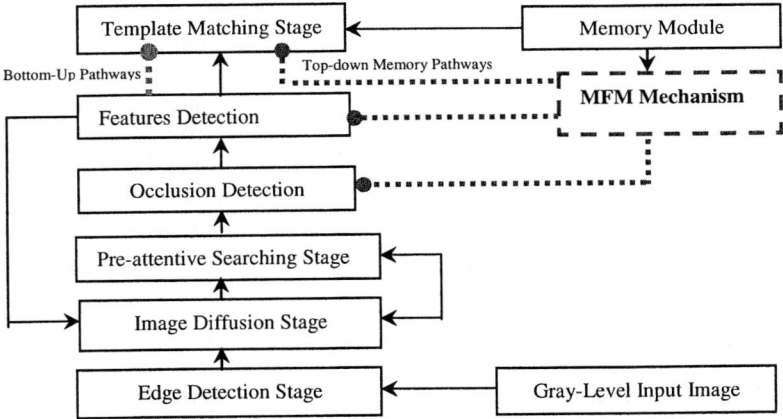

Fig. 1. The vision system for partially occluded visual landmark recognition

The memory module contains a database of memory templates, each template is divided into twenty five smaller sub-memory templates (SMT) as illustrated in Fig. 2.(b). The memory template is further used to create three binary memory filters. The first filter is a 5x5 array with each pixel indicates the status of each STM, which is referred to as the memory active region (MAR) filter, depicted in Fig. 2(d). The second filter is named the memory active edge (MAE) filter, where each high pixel denotes a corresponding active pixel in the memory template, as illustrated in Fig. 2(c). Both MAR and the MAE filters are used to provide memory guidance for the feature extraction stage. The third filter is termed the landmark enclosed area

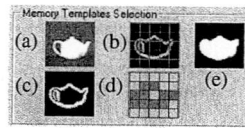

Fig. 2. A Memory template and corresponding binary memory filters. (a) The gray-level image, (b) The memory template, (c) The MAE filter, (d) The MAR filter and (e) The LEA filter.

(LEA), which denotes the entire region that encloses the landmark as shown in Fig. 2(e). This filter is used in the template matching stage.

The feature extraction stage uses the existing knowledge in memory regarding the landmark via the MFM mechanism, to guide the data selection process and mark-out possible regions of occlusions. The MFM mechanism uses the corresponding MAR and MAE binary filter in the memory module, to generate two memory feedback pathways. The MAR filter is used to generate the first pathway that attends to regions containing relevant input data, while ignoring those that are irrelevant. Notice that, each pixel in the MAR filter denotes a corresponding active sub-memory template (SMT) of the current memory template. Thus, only patches in the ROI region that correspond with the active SMT are essential to the template matching stage. Others are regarded as background features.

Similarly, the MAE filter creates the second pathway to further focus the memory guidance feature of the MFM mechanism to the pixel level, which pinpoints pixel locations in the ROI region that correspond to the active pixels in each SMT. Therefore, edges that lie within the second pathway have the potential of belonging to the target landmark. These edges are extracted from the ROI region, by using the first pathway to locate patches that correspond to the active SMT, which is followed by the second pathway to zoom into each patch, analysing its edge pixel's distribution and collecting pixels that correspond to the active edge pixels in the SMT. The extraction of relevant data in each patch is achieved using *eq.1*. Then, pixels in the ROI region are subjected to lateral competition to remove background clutter, which is achieved using L2 normalisation [5].

$$ROI_k(i,j) = ROI_k(i,j)[1 + G * MAE_k(i,j)] \qquad (1)$$

Where $ROI_k(i,j)$ are the active patches in the ROI region - denoted by active cells in the MAR filter, $MAE_k(i,j)$ is the corresponding region in the MAE filter and G is a gain control.

Upon successfully achieving data-background separation, each patch in the ROI region is passed into the occlusion detection stage to determine the possibility of being partially hidden. The evaluation is based on a threshold, which is calculated by analysing the total number of edge pixels in each individual active SMT. Heuristically, for the patch in the ROI region to be non-occluded, it must have at least 75% of the total amount of edge pixels in the corresponding active SMT. Therefore, the patches that are greater than the threshold are marked as non-occluded and conversely others are considered as obstructed areas. The status of these patches is used to create a landmark occluded area (LOA) filter, to provide a bottom-up pathway to the template matching stage, for taking hidden portions into consideration in the matching process.

The matching stage uses a simple but effective template matching algorithm that has multiple guided pathways obtained from the MFM mechanism and the feature extraction stage. These pathways selectively govern the matching between the ROI region and the current memory template, using the MAR, MAE and BOR filters. The combination of these filters produces matching channels that exclude the possible occluded areas in the ROI region, where only pixels that lie within the matching channels are considered in the matching process. The matching channels are created using *eq.2* and it is further illustrated in Fig. 3. Prior to the matching process, the matching channel pathways, indicated with bold dashed lines are used to modify both the active memory template and the bottom-up ROI region to discard the hidden areas.

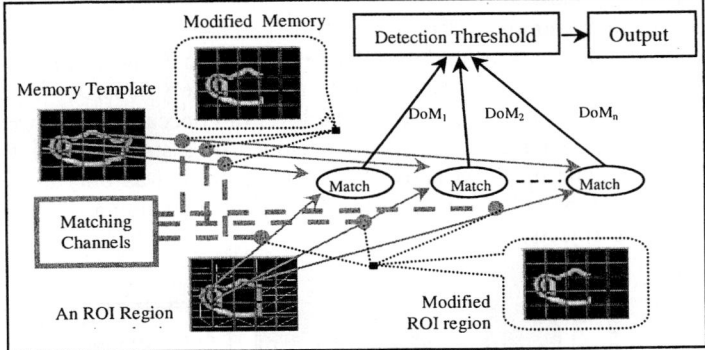

Fig. 3. The matching process between the ROI region and the memory template

The template matching process measures multiple comparisons between each active STM and the corresponding patch in the ROI region – denoted as degree of match (DoM). The matching process is expressed mathematically in *eq.3*. Each DoM has value range from 0 to 1, where 1 represent 100% match. This is evaluated against a matching threshold. The input patch with a DoM value greater than the threshold is regarded as a STM match. If the summation of all the STM matches within the ROI region is greater the detection threshold, then a match is declared.

$$C_k(i,j) = MAE_k(i,j)[MAR(i,j) - LOA(i,j)] \qquad (2)$$

Where $C_k(i,j)$ is the matching channel for each active ROI patch, $MAR(i,j)$ is the memory active region filter, $LOA(i,j)$ is the landmark occluded area filter and $MAE_k(i,j)$ is the corresponding region in the memory active edge filter.

$$DoM = \frac{\sum ROI(i,j) * M(i,j)}{\varepsilon + \sqrt{\sum ROI(i,j)^2} \sqrt{\sum M(i,j)^2}} \qquad (3)$$

Where ROI(i,j) is the patch that corresponds to the active STM and M(i,j) is the STM, ε is a small constant to prevent equation from dividing by zero.

3 Results

The developed vision system has been evaluated in two separate stages. In the first stage, a large number of real images of partially covered landmarks, which simulate six different levels of occlusions, where the landmark is partially occluded at the following locations: in front; left; right; left and right; left and right and in front; and no occlusion, as shown in Fig. 4(a) to Fig. 4(e). Twenty four images comprising of four different landmarks were processed by the vision system, and the final result is recorded in Table 1, showing the best DoM value between the ROI region and the corresponding memory template for each landmark. These DoM values were evaluated against the evaluation threshold of 85%. In contrast to Table.1, all non-occluded landmarks resulted in a very high DoM value, approximately 97%. As expected, this value was diminished with the increases in the level of concealment. However, in all of the cases where the landmark is partially occluded by a single object, the system was capable of maintaining DoM above 90%. However, it was only able to obtain DoM values over the threshold for some images where the landmark is partially obstructed by multiple objects.

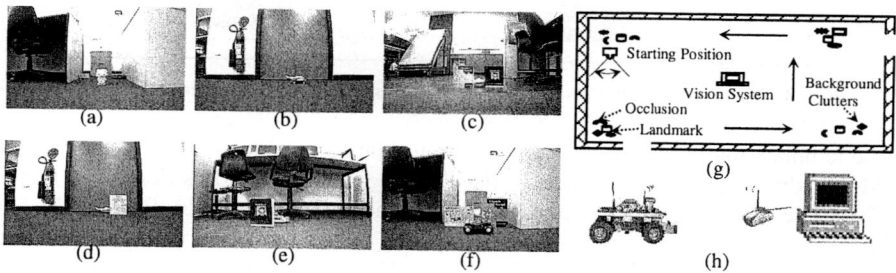

Fig. 4. Different types of partially occluded landmarks. (a) Landmark without occlusion. (b) Occlusion at the centre. (c) Occlusions on both the left and the right. (d) Occlusion on the right. (e) Occlusion on the left. (f), Occlusions on the left, the right and in the front. (g) The topological map of the laboratory. (h) The navigating robot.

In the second stage, a simple navigating robot has been used to evaluate the vision system's real-time, partially occluded landmark recognition capability and applicability in vision-based robot navigation. The robot navigation system is illustrated in Fig. 4(h). The camera is mounted onboard the robot but the visual data is processed on a remote desktop PC, which communities with the robot via wireless RF data and video links. The robot has the following sensors: a wireless video camera, a TCM2 magnetic compass, an odometer and three GP2YA02Yk infrared range sensors. However, navigation is based primarily on the vision system and the compass sensor using a provided topological map. Other sensors were added mainly for safety purposes.

Table 1. The DoM between the best ROI region and the corresponding memory template

Objects	No Occlusion	Occlusion (Right)	Occlusion (Left)	Occlusion (Centre)	Occlusion (L & R)	Occlusion (R,L&C)
Helicopter	97.3%	94.3	96.1%	90.1	91.7%	76.9%
Clock	97.1%	95.7%	91.1%	95%	77.0%	73.5%
Boat	96.7%	92.2%	91.4%	90.1%	84%	74.5%
Teapot	96.0%	94.7%	92.3%	92.5%	91.5%	74.5%

The robot was initially provided with the topological map of the laboratory environment, consisting of partially occluded landmarks positioned at different locations within the laboratory, as illustrated in Fig. 4(g). The map provides relative distances and directions between landmarks. The aim was for the robot to autonomously traverse the pre-defined path and recognised all partially hidden landmarks along the pathway. The robot successfully traversed the route and recognised all partially occluded landmarks, traveling at a moderate speed, approximately 10cm/s.

4 Conclusions

This paper presents the vision system for recognising partially occluded landmarks. The system has been tested using a number of real images, which represent different levels of obstruction. This system is capable of robustly recognising the landmarks, which are partially hidden behind another object. This has been further demonstrated on the navigating robot, where the vision system is provided with a topological map of the laboratory, to successfully guide it along the pre-defined route and recognise all partially obstructed landmarks. Further research is needed to recognise multiple landmark occlusions - where the target is obstructed by several objects.

Acknowledgements

The financial supported by Weapons Systems Division of the Australian Defence Science and Technology Organisation (Research Contract No. 4500 177 390) is acknowledged.

References

1. M. Mata, J. M. Armingol, A. de la Escalera, and M. A. Salichs, "A visual landmark recognition system for topological navigation of mobile robots," *Proc. The IEEE International Conference on Robotics and Automation, Proceedings 2001 ICRA.*, pp.1124-1129, 2001.
2. H. Li and S. X. Yang, "A behavior-based mobile robot with a visual landmark-recognition system," *IEEE/ASME Transactions on Mechatronics*, vol. 8, pp. 390-400, 2003.
3. P. Lozo, Neural theory and model of selective visual attention and 2D shape recognition in visual clutter, PhD Thesis, Department of Electrical and Electronic Engineering. Adelaide, University of Adelaide,1997.
4. E. W.-S. Chong, A Neural Framework for Visual Scene Analysis with Selective Attention, PhD Thesis, Department of Electrical and Electronic Engineering, University of Adelaide,2001.

5. Q. V. Do, P. Lozo, and L. C. Jain, "Autonomous Robot Navigation using SAART for Visual Landmark Recognition," *Proc. The 2nd International Conference on Artificial Intelligence in Science and Technology*, Tasmania, Australia, pp. 64-69, 2004.
6. Q. V. Do, P. Lozo, and L. Jain, "A Fast Visual Search and Recognition Mechanism for Realtime Robotic Applications," *Proc. The 17th Australian Joint Conference on Artificial Intelligence*, Cairns, Australia, pp. 937-342, 2004.

Diversity Control in GP with ADF for Regression Tasks

Huayang Xie

School of Mathematics, Statistics, and Computer Science,
Victoria University of Wellington, P. O. Box 600, Wellington, New Zealand
hxie@mcs.vuw.ac.nz

Abstract. This paper proposes a two-phase diversity control approach to prevent the common problem of the loss of diversity in Genetic Programming with Automatically Defined Functions. While most recent work focuses on diagnosing and remedying the loss of diversity, this approach aims to prevent the loss of diversity in the early stage through a refined diversity control method and a fully covered tournament selection method. The results on regression tasks suggest that these methods can effectively improve the system performance by reducing the incidences of premature convergence and the number of generations needed for finding an optimal solution.

1 Introduction

There are many studies in preventing or reducing premature convergence in Genetic Programming (GP) and Genetic Algorithms (GAs) [1, 2, 3, 4, 5, 6, 7]. Most of studies on maintaining the population diversity measure the loss of diversity first, then take actions based on diversity diagnosis. There has been limited research on actively reducing the loss of diversity beforehand, for which we believe selection operator is a key mechanism that could be used to minimise the loss of diversity.

This paper introduces a two-phase approach to diversity control in the tree-based GP population for reducing premature convergence and the number of generations without increasing the amount of computing time required to find an optimal solution.

2 Our Approach

Our two-phase approach consists of a refined diversity control (RDC) in the initial population before evolution and a fully covered tournament selection (FCTS) during evolution. Both methods are extended from general diversity control (GDC) [8] and standard tournament selection (STS) [9].

2.1 Refined Diversity Control in Population Initialisation

In GDC, the main tree and ADFs were treated as a whole. If two whole programs are not exactly identical in genotype, they pass the diversity check. In our RDC, main trees and ADFs were treated as individual objects. Both main trees and ADFs need to be unique in the population. Thus the checking overhead of RDC is more than that of GDC. However, unlike GDC which re-creates both main tree and ADFs, RDC only re-creates the object that failed the diversity check, which could reduce recreation overhead.

2.2 Fully Covered Tournament Selection

In STS, the whole population was used as the pool for each selection. Because the selection was random, the individual with bad fitness could be selected multiple times and the individual with good fitness could never be selected. To avoid this, FCTS excludes the individuals that have been selected from the pool for next selection. Thus FCTS ensures every individual has an equal chance to participate tournaments. Therefore the population diversity can be better preserved.

3 Experiment Design and Configuration

Two symbolic regression problems (a simple one and a complex one) were used in our experiments:

$$f(x) = x^6 - 2x^4 + x^2 \tag{1}$$

$$f(x) = \begin{cases} x^2 + x & , x >= 0 \\ sin(x) + \frac{1}{x} & , x < 0 \end{cases} \tag{2}$$

We conducted one experiment for each problem. Within each experiment, total number of independent runs is 2000, which was divided equally into four groups — GDC + STS, GDC + FCTS, RDC + STS and RDC + FCTS.

For each experiment, we used the identical function set $\{+, -, *, /, if, sin, cos, ADF_1, ADF_2\}$ and terminal set $\{x, 1\}$ in the main tree design. We also used the identical function set $\{+, -, *, /, sin\}$ and terminal set $\{a_1, a_2\}$ in the ADF design.

Table 1. Parameters for Two Symbolic Regression Problems

Population size	2000	Mutation probability	5%
Creation type	ramped half and half	Reproduction probability	5%
Tournament size	4	Max. depth for creation	3
Crossover probability	90%	Max. depth for crossover	6

We used 100 fitness cases for each problem. In order to distinguish and emphasis the difficulties between these two problems, we generated the fitness cases for the simple problem by giving integer numbers in [1 ... 100] to x, whereas for the complex problem giving x real numbers in (-10 ... 10] with step 0.2.

The fitness function is the root mean square of the differences between the outputs of a program and the expected outputs. Thus ideally the fitness value is zero when a given problem is solved.

The parameter values used in the two experiments are shown in table 1.

Cut off point was set at the 50th generation for the simple regression problem and 100th generation for the complex problem. If the fitness value is less than 0.00000001 before the cut off point, the run was recorded as "completed" and actual number of generation took to get the solution was recorded. Otherwise the case was recorded as "uncompleted". We also took a measurement of the CPU time used for each run.

4 Results and Analysis

This section discusses the results of four groups on the two symbolic regression problems. Three measurements — completion rate, generations and CPU time — have been analysed.

Table 2 summarises the impact of our approach for both experiments on the completion rate — percentage of runs that successfully returned an optimal solution within the given number of generations. It is treated as the antonymous measurement of premature convergence. The first line of data in the table shows that, using GDC and STS methods, 95.0% runs successfully completed the task within 50 generations in the simple regression experiment and 22.2% runs successfully completed the task within 100 generations in the complex regression experiment. The table shows that: (1)The approaches with either RDC, or FCTS or both significantly improved the completion rate for both simple and complex problems; (2) The approach with FCTS alone outperformed that with RDC alone.

Table 2. Completion rate (%) of different approaches

	Simple Regression	Complex Regression
GDC + STS	95.0	22.2
GDC + FCTS	99.2	33.4
RDC + STS	98.0	25.0
RDC + FCTS	98.8	34.6

Table 3. Number of generations taken in different approaches (sd: standard deviation)

	Simple Regression (mean ± sd)	Complex Regression (mean ± sd)
GDC + STS	32.01 ± 9.25	90.74 ± 20.50
GDC + FCTS	30.58 ± 8.08	87.31 ± 22.14
RDC + STS	28.09 ± 9.75	89.58 ± 21.66
RDC + FCTS	27.44 ± 8.70	86.80 ± 22.62

Table 3 summarises the impact of our approach for both experiments on generations — number of generations required to find an optimal solution. The results show that: (1) The approach with both RDC and FCTS performed the

Table 4. CPU Time (seconds) used in different approaches

	Simple Regression (mean ± sd)	Complex Regression (mean ± sd)
GDC + STS	39.60 ± 15.17	102.53 ± 32.07
RDC + FCTS	38.25 ± 14.02	102.84 ± 33.13

best and the approach with GDC and STS performed the worst; (2) The approach with RDC alone performed slightly better than that with FCTS alone for the simple problem, but did slightly worse for the complex problem.

As analysed in section 2.1, RDC has bigger overhead than GDC in terms of time. However, from table 4, we are pleased to see that the overall time including initialisation spending on finding an optimal solution is rather even between GDC+STS and RDC+FCTS. The two-phase approach, which has large overhead in the first phase, did not noticeably increase the time measurement in the complex regression experiment and even reduced the time in the simple regression experiment. Accordingly, the overhead of RDC is paid off by the efficiency of itself and FCTS in preventing the loss of population diversity, which reduced the number of generations required for finding an optimal solution.

5 Conclusions and Future Work

The results of the two experiments suggest that our two-phase diversity control approach can effectively reduce premature convergence and the number of generations required for finding an optimal solution in GP with ADF for symbolic regression tasks, without increasing computing time.

In the future, we will extend RDC and FCTS to more complicated problems, such as image recognition problems. We will investigate an optimal diversity measurement and apply it in the population initialisation to further enhance diversity control. We will also consider more precise diversity measurement in order to improve the efficiency.

References

1. Banzhaf, W., Francone, F.D., Nordin, P.: The effect of extensive use of the mutation operator on generalization in genetic programming using sparse data sets. In: Proceedings of the fourth International Conference on Parallel Problem Solving from Nature. (1996) 300–309
2. Eshelman, L., Schaffer, D.: Preventing premature convergence in genetic algorithms by preventing incest. In: Proceedings of the Fourth International Conference on Genetic Algorithms. (1991) 115–122
3. Ryan, C.: Pygmies and civil servants. In: Advances in Genetic Programming. MIT Press (1994) 243–264
4. Spears, W.: Simple subpopulation schemes. In: Proceedings of the 4th Ann. Conf. on Evolutionary Programming. (1995) 296–307

5. Ciesielski, V., Mawhinney, D.: Prevention of early convergence in genetic programming by replacement of similar programs. In: Proceedings of the 2002 Congress on Evolutionary Computation CEC2002, IEEE Press (2002) 67–72
6. Levenick, J.R.: Swappers: Introns promote flexibility, diversity and invention. In: Proceedings of the 1999 Genetic and Evolutionary Computation Conference. (1999) 361–368
7. Keller, R.E., Banzhaf, W.: Explicit maintenance of genetic diversity on genospaces. Technical report, University of Dortmund (1995)
8. Weinbrenner, T.: GPC++ - Genetic Programming C++ Class Library. http://www.cs.ucl.ac.uk/staff/W.Langdon/ftp/weinbenner/gp.html (1997)
9. Koza, J.R.: Genetic Programming — On the Programming of Computers by Means of Natural Selection. MIT Press (1992)

Some Propositions of Information Fusion for Pattern Recognition with Context Task

Michal Wozniak

Chair of Systems and Computer Networks, Wroclaw University of Technology,
Wybrzeze Wyspianskiego 27, 50-370 Wroclaw, Poland
michal.wozniak@pwr.wroc.pl

Abstract. Paper deals with the concept of information fusion and its application to the contextual pattern recognition task. The concept of the recognition based on the probabilistic model are presented. The machine learning algorithm based on statistical tests for the recognition of controlled Markov chains is shown. Some experimental results of obtained methods are shown.

1 Introduction

In many pattern recognition problems there exist dependencies between patterns to be recognized. This situation is typical for character recognition, image classification and medical diagnosis, to name only a few.

Among the different concepts and methods of using "contextual" information in pattern recognition, the approach through Bayes compound decision theory[1, 2] is both attractive and efficient from the theoretical point of view. This situation is typical for character recognition where the probability of character appearance depends of previous recognized sign.

The content of the work is as follows. Section 2 provides the problem statement and we present pattern recognition algorithms using "contextual" information. Section 3 presents results of the experimental investigations of the algorithms. Last section concludes the paper.

2 The Problem Statement

The Bayes decision theory consists of assumption [1] that the feature vector x and number of class j are the realization of the pair of the random variables X, J. The formalisation of the recognition in the case under consideration implies the setting of an optimal Bayes decision algorithm $\Psi(x)$, which minimizes probability of misclassification for 0-1 loss function[5]:

$$\Psi(x) = i \text{ if } p(i|x) = \max_{k \in \{1, ..., M\}} p(k|x). \tag{1}$$

In the real situation the *posterior* probabilities for each classes are usually unknown. Instead of them we can used the rules and/or the learning set for the constructing decision algorithms[4].

The analysis of different practical examples leads to the following form of rule $r_i^{(k)}$:

IF $x \in D_i^{(k)}$ **THEN** state of object is i **WITH** posterior probability $\beta_j^{(k)} = \int_{D_i^{(k)}} p(i|x)dx$

greater than $\underline{\beta}_i^{(k)}$ and less than $\overline{\beta}_i^{(k)}$.

Lets note the rule estimator will be more precise if rule decision region and differences between upper and lower bound of the probability given by expert will be smaller. For the logical knowledge representation the rule with the small decision area can be overfitting the training data [3]. For our proposition we respect this danger for the rule set obtained from learning data. For the estimation of the *posterior* probability from rule we assume the constant value of for the rule decision area. Therefore lets propose the relation "more specific" between the probabilistic rules pointed at the same class.

Definition. Rule $r_i^{(k)}$ is "more specific" than rule $r_i^{(l)}$ if

$$\left(\overline{\beta}_i^{(k)} - \underline{\beta}_i^{(k)}\right)\left(\int_{D_i^{(k)}} dx \Big/ \int_X dx\right) < \left(\overline{\beta}_i^{(l)} - \underline{\beta}_i^{(l)}\right)\left(\int_{D_i^{(l)}} dx \Big/ \int_X dx\right) \quad (2)$$

Hence the proposition of the *posterior* probability estimator $\hat{p}(i|x)$ is as follow: from subset of rules $R_i(x) = \{r_i^{(k)} : x \in D_i^{(k)}\}$ choose the "most specific" rule $r_i^{(m)}$ and $\hat{p}(i|k) = \left(\overline{\beta}_i^{(m)} - \underline{\beta}_i^{(m)}\right) \Big/ \int_{D_i^{(m)}} dx$

When only the set S is given, the obvious and conceptually simple method is to estimate *posterior* probabilities $\hat{p}(i|x)$ for each classes via estimation of unknown conditional probability density functions (CPDFs) and *prior* probabilities.

For the considered case, i.e. when we have s different rules bases or learning sets we propose two decision algorithms:

$$\psi_n^{(C)}(\overline{x}_n, \overline{u}_{n-1}) = i_n \text{ if } \sum_{l=1}^{s} \alpha_l \times p^{(l)}(i_n|\overline{x}_n, \overline{u}_{n-1}) = \max_{k \in M} \sum_{l=1}^{s} \alpha_l \times p^{(l)}(k|\overline{x}_n, \overline{u}_{n-1}), \quad (3)$$

The $p^{(l)}(k|\overline{x}_n, \overline{u}_{n-1})$ denotes estimator of the *posterior* probability. obtained on base of the l-th information source (learning set or rule base). α_l is the weight of l-th learning set of rule base obtained on base of the following procedure:

```
Let LS be the set of testing examples consists of t
elements and we have s information sources (learning sets
or rule bases) and we construct s classifiers
Let α₁ = α₂ = ... = αₛ = 1.
for v:=1 to t do:
   for l:=1 t  do:
```

```
if l-th classifier recognized the v-th testing element
    correctly then α_l = α_l +1;   fi
end; end
```

Let $SUM_s = \sum_{l=1}^{s} \alpha_l$

for $l:=1$ to s do: $\alpha_l = \dfrac{\alpha_l}{SUM_s}$ end.

3 Experimental Investigation

In order to compare the proposed concept of recognition algorithm and to investigate the quality of recognition for various sizes of learning sets and for various probabilistic characteristics of features, several experiments were made on the computer-generated data[6]. We have only one learning set and one rules base. We have restricted our considerations to the case of rules for with the upper and lower bounds of the *posterior* probabilities are the same, rule defined region for each (i,j), $i,j \in M$ cover the whole feature space X. Furthermore we have considered first-order Markov chains without control. In all experiments we considered a two-class recognition task with set of 10 expert rule, Gaussian CPDFs of scalar feature x ($f_1(x) = N(0,1)$, $f_2(x) = N(2,1)$) and with parameters presented in Table 1 and results of tests on Fig.1.

Table 1. Parameters of simulation

Experiment A	Experiment B	Experiment C
$p_1 = 0.417$, $p_2 = 0.583$	$p_1 = 0.430$, $p_2 = 0.570$	$p_1 = 0.333$, $p_2 = 0.667$
$p_{11} = 0.650$, $p_{12} = 0.250$	$p_{11} = 0.600$, $p_{12} = 0.300$	$p_{11} = 0.400$, $p_{12} = 0.300$
$p_{21} = 0.350$, $p_{22} = 0.750$	$p_{21} = 0.400$, $p_{22} = 0.700$	$p_{21} = 0.600$, $p_{22} = 0.700$

In each experiment we calculate the frequency of correct classification for different learning set sizes and for following recognition algorithms:(A1) $k(N)$-Nearest Neighbors algorithm, (A2) Rule-based algorithms, (A3) Combined algorithm with the same value of α-factor (0.5). The following conclusion may be drawn from experiments:

1. The algorithm (A3) leads to better or similar results compared to algorithms (A1) and (A2). Advantage of algorithms (A3) over algorithm (A1) grows simultaneously with growing dependencies between successive states.
2. Frequency of correct classification for algorithms (A2-A3) grows simultaneously with growing dependencies between successive states.
3. The algorithms based on the unified information achieves the constant frequency of correct classification quickly, but algorithms based on the unified information leads to worse results compared to the algorithms A2 and A3.

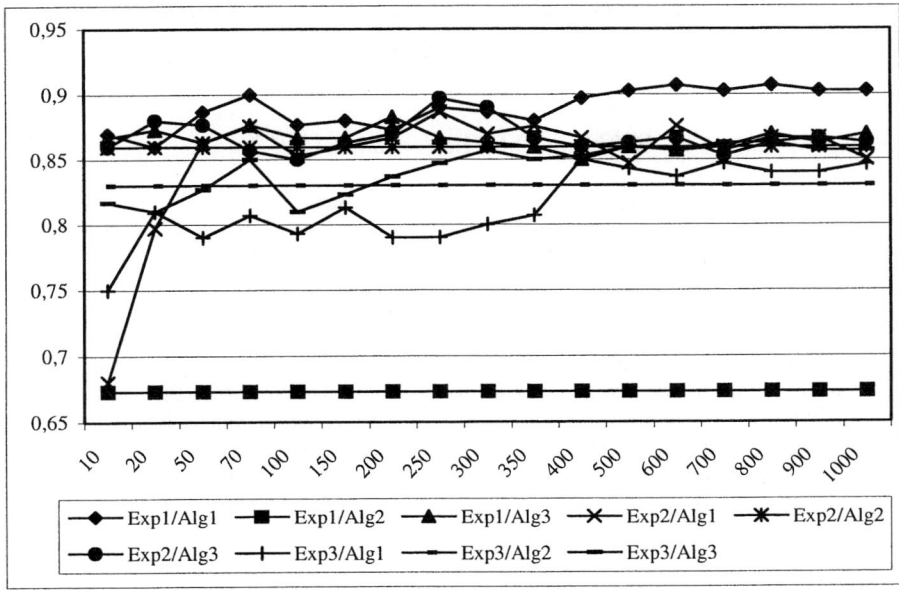

Fig. 1. Frequency of correct classification, versus the learning set size. Exp$m$/Alg$n$ denotes results obtained in experiment m for algorithm n.

4 Conclusion

The original methods information fusion for the pattern recognition with context problem are presented. It must be emphasized that in the experiments performed the scope of possible distributions and rules sets is quite limited. Therefore drawing a general conclusion from presented experiments is of course risky.

This work is supported be The Polish State Committee for Scientific Research under the grant which is realizing in years 2005-2007.

References

1. Devijver P., Kittler J., *Pattern Recognition- A Statistical Approach*, Prentice Hall, London (1982)
2. Haralick R. M., Decision Making in Context, *IEEE Trans. on Pattern Anal. Machine Intell.*, vol. PAMI-5, (1983)
3. Mitchell T.M., *Machine Learning*, The McGraw-Hill Co. Inc., New York (1997)
4. Giakoumakis E., Papakonstantiou G., Skordalakis E., Rule-based systems and pattern recognition, *Pattern Recognition Letters*, No 5, 1987.
5. Puchala E., A Bayes Algorithm for the Multitask Pattern Recognition Problem – direct and decomposed approach, *Lecture Notes in Computer Science*, vol. 3046, 2004, pp. 39-45.
6. Koszalka L., Skworcow P., Experimentation system for efficient job performing in veterinary medicine area, *Lecture Notes in Computer Science*, vol. 3483, 2005, pp. 692-701.

A Personal Locating System Using the Vision-Based Augmented Reality

J.B. Kim[1], J.M. Lee[2], and H.S. Jun[2]

[1] DMITRC, University of Ulsan, Ulsan, S. Korea
[2] School of Computer Eng. and Information Tech., University of Ulsan, Ulsan, S. Korea
{kimjb, neokt1, hsjun}@ulsan.ac.kr

Abstract. This paper describes the personal locating system in image sequence using a vision-based augmented reality technique which allows the user to navigate an unfamiliar and unknown place in an office environment. For identifying personal location in image sequences, the system uses a color histogram matching method and location model. The results are overplayed on the user's view through AR technique. This system is applicable to guide an application.

1 Introduction

A navigation system can provide a location directly, such as in the case of Global Position System (GPS) receivers. A location device can also take the form of a tag, attached to a user or device which periodically communicates with a fixed receiver infrastructure [1]. Navigation systems based on GPS exist to help guide users in outdoor environments where GPS works. However, in case of indoor environment such as an office, room, inside building, etc, a location device cannot be provided the location information directly. If a location information in unknown indoor environments is provided, a visitor or first coming person can navigate easily. As we know, we already know the structural information of an office. If this information can be installed in the environment, a user more easily navigate the unknown or unfamiliar places. In this paper, our approach is real time personal location using a wearable computer [2]. It will be adapted the personal locating system. For identifying personal location, the system uses the color histogram matching method [3]. By comparing the histogram of captured image characteristic features with the histogram of previously stored image sequences, similar location can be identified.

2 Proposed System

2.1 System Overview

The proposed system has employed a combination of a small USB camera and mobile PC with wireless communication to remote PCs. The system consists of a mobile computer, wearable camera and remote PC with wireless LAN. The system captures input image sequence via the wearable camera, and transmits them to the remote PC via the wireless network. The remote PC processes to identify and detect a place in the received image sequences. Then the remote PC sends the results back to the wearable PC. Finally, the result is displayed in the user's view. Given an input of an image sequence taken from a camera mounted mobile PC, the system outputs the result images using Augmented Reality [4, 5]. Fig. 1(a) shows a diagram of the proposed method.

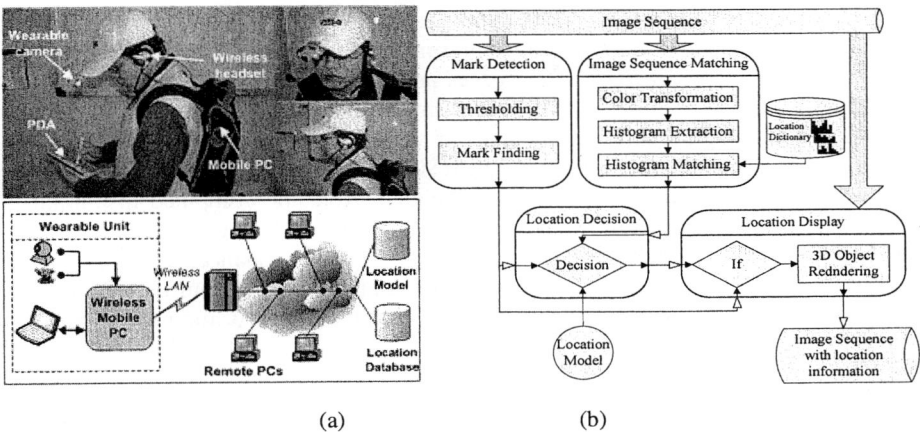

Fig. 1. Flowchart of the proposed method (a) and the block diagram of personal location (b)

2.2 Personal Location

The input data of the system consists of image sequences taken from a single camera. The frame rate is 5 frames per second. The images show the environment in front of the person vision–the wall, hallway, office furniture and office workers. The primary task of the system is to identify the location from previously recorded image sequences. In the system, the personal locator process consists of four stages (as shown Fig. 1(b)).

Mark Detection. This step detects mark image from currently captured image sequences. The mark consist the black color of boundary of 15cm x 15cm rectangle and white color in rectangle. The inside of mark means the predefined patters. For detecting mark in image sequences, the stage performs the image binarization via thresholding and mark finding via pattern matching. The image binarization converts an image of up to 256 gray levels to a black and white image. The simplest way to used image binarization is to choose a threshold value, and classify all pixels with values above this threshold as white, and all other pixels as black. The problem then is how to select the correct threshold. In many cases, finding on threshold compatible to the entire image is very difficult, and in may case even impossible. So, in our system, we adapt an adaptive threshold method [6]. This method is a histogram-based approach to thresholding for image binarization and can be used to discard temporal variations due to illumination of original image. The method for threshold selection was derived under the assumption that the histogram generated from the difference between two gray-level images contains two values combined with additive Gaussian noise. At the end of this phase, a binary image is obtained where changing pixels are set to one and background pixels set to zero. Next, a chain-code-based approach is able to separate loosely connected pixels. Then, we apply the morphological operation on the binary image to remove the noise. After image binarization via thresholding, the binary image finds a mark patterns using the template matching.

Image Sequence Matching. The captured image sequences are identified from the previously stored image sequences using image features similarity. This image feature is the color information. A *RGB* color representation includes not only color but also brightness. Therefore, all *RGB* color spaces are not necessarily the best color representation for identifying images from stored image sequences. The brightness may be removed by dividing the three components of a color pixel, (R, G, B) by the intensity. Image sequence matching is performed in HSI space. After RGB to HSI conversion, the histogram of the hue component is computed. And, the computed histogram is normalized in 64-bin. Therefore, every image has the hue histogram. The similarity between input image sequences (x) and pre-stored image sequences (y) is computed the distance measure $d(d(x,y)=|x-y|^2)$ of image features. The system uses 25 frames which is the currently input images and pre-stored images. And, the total location is 12 places. Therefore, the number of computations is 12 times of the 25x25 matrix. By this calculation, the place of input image sequence will be identified the place with the most small difference value [3].

Location Decision and Display. This stage decides a location information of current personal location using the information results of previous two stages. For deciding a personal location, the stage refers a location model. The location model is a graph of indoor environment. It is consist of nodes and lines. The node means a location information, and the lines means a movement of user. And, the 3D virtual sign objects using Artoolkit[7] are displayed in the user's view. In our system, the camera position and orientation relative to physical marks in image sequence is calculated through the Artoolkit. The overlaid objects are the direction signs, arrows, and texts. These objects help to a personal about unfamiliar or unknown office environment.

3 Experimental Results

The proposed system has been implemented on a Samsung Sens ST10-JB542 Mobile PC (OS: Window 2000, CPU: Pentium IV- 2.2GHz, RAM: 768MB) with a USB digital camera (Samsung SNC-35) and a wireless LAN card (11-Mbps IEEE 802.11b). In order to evaluate the performance of the proposed method, the system has been tested in unconstrained office environment under different lighting conditions. For all experimental sequences, the average frame rate we obtained is about 5 frames per second. The image size is 320×240 pixels. All image sequences are captured by walking around the third floor of DMITRC building in our university.

Fig. 2 and 3 shows examples of personal location. Fig. 2 images are lobby environment image sequences and Fig. 3 images are a walkway in office. Each image sequence have different illumination because Fig. 2 image sequence is captured daytime and Fig. 3 image sequence is captured nighttime. The system overlay a virtual

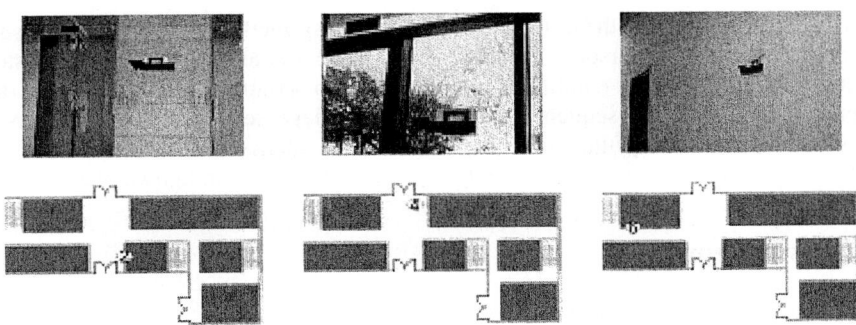

Fig. 2. The results of personal location in day-time

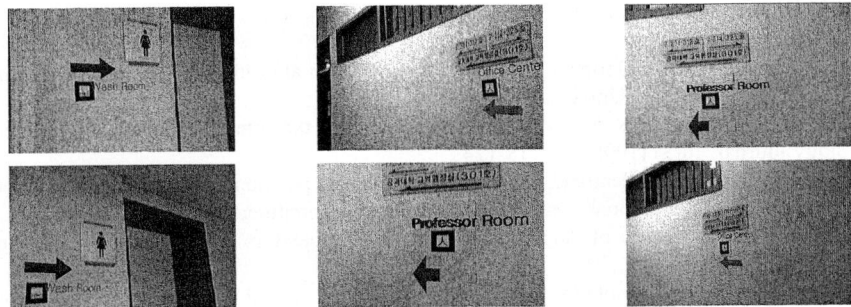

Fig. 3. The results of personal location system in night-time

sign objects in real image sequence according to mark. Each mark has the different virtual object. After place recognition, the information layout of office environment is displayed in a mark. For testing the number of pre-stored image sequences is 12 and each image sequence has 25 frames. Continually the current images are captured by mobile PC with camera, and the captured images are transmitted to a remote PC. The results of the identified personal location information are overlaid to the user's view. To evaluate the personal locating process, several indoor image sequences have been looked for. To recognize a personal location in real time, the proposed system used the histogram matching method. For testing, we used video sequences that included the several locations. The location recognizer has been performed every detected predefined location image by the image sequence matching, and it outputs the final recognition result when the most similar location ID determined by the location table. In the personal locating process, the accuracy rate is about 78.2%.

4 Conclusions

In this paper, the personal locating system using a wearable computer for vision-based augmented reality is described. For identification of personal location in image sequences, the system uses the color histogram matching method. Experimental results demonstrate real-time personal location over image sequences, unless the system encounters uncooperative conditions, e.g., too variant contrast and illumination between the current image sequence and pre-stored image sequence, which occurs at lobby wall or office furniture. In future works, the system will be used for a guide application, which helps the user to navigate an unfamiliar and unknown place.

Acknowledgement

This research was supported by the MIC(Ministry of Information and Communication), Korea, under the ITRC(Information Technology Research Center) support program supervised by the IITA(Institute of Information Technology Assessment).

References

1. Sikking, L. J.: The development of an indoor navigation algorithm for an autonomous mobile robot, Ph.D Thesis, University of Waikato (2004)
2. Crabtree, B. and Rhodes, B.: Wearable computing and the remembrance agent, BT Technology Journal, 16(3) (1998) pp. 118-124
3. Aoki, H., Schiele, B., Pentland, A.: Realtime personal positioning system for a wearable computers, 3rd International Symposium on Wearable Computers, (1999) pp. 37-43
4. Azuma, R. T.: A survey of Augmented Reality, Teleoperators and Virtual Environments, 6(4) (1997) pp. 355-385
5. Kim, J. B.: A person annotation overlay system using a wearable computer for augmented reality, IEEE Proc. International Conference on Consumer Electronics. (2003) pp.244-245
6. Kim, J. B. and Kim, H. S.: Efficient region-based motion segmentation for a video monitoring system, Pattern Recognition Letter, 24(1) (2003) pp.113-128
7. http://www.hitl.washington.edu/artoolkit/

Fast Candidate Generation for Template Matching Using Two 1-D Edge Projections

Jong-Eun Ha[1] and Dong-Joong Kang[2]

[1] Automotive Engineering, Seoul National University of Technology,
172, Gongneung 2-dong, Nowon-gu, Seoul, Korea
jeha2002@hotmail.com
[2] Mechatronics Engineering, Tongmyong University of Information Technology,
535, Yongdang-dong, Nam-gu, Busan, Korea
djkang@tit.ac.kr

Abstract. In machine vision, template matching is key component and used usefully in various tasks such as pick and place, mark identification, and alignment. In this paper, we propose fast template matching algorithm using edge projection. Proposed algorithm reduces the search problem from 2D into 1D using edge projection within the 2D template area. By this, it could effectively reduce the computational burden. Also, it gives comparable discriminating power compared to template matching using intensity. In this paper, rotation and translation search is implemented to cope with typical machine vision application where the height between camera and target object is fixed.

1 Introduction

Template matching is widely used in machine vision application. Typical applications are finding predefined model in the current investigation image such as pick and place, mark identification, and alignment. Model images are usually acquired from the image of object itself. In machine vision, camera and lighting systems are fixed and objects are usually located in predefined location such as on the conveyor transport system. In this case, template matching could be reduced into the search of the translation and rotation while scale is usually fixed.

Several commercial systems such as PatMat of Cognex [1] and Geometric Model Finder of Matrox Imaging [2] are widely used in machine vision application. PatMat is one of the most powerful commercial tools and it uses pixels as their geometric features. PatMat [1] uses geometric information instead of intensity. It first identifies and isolates features such as shape, dimension, angle, arcs, and shading. Then it finds the spatial relationships between key features of model image and target image. Ulrich [3] compares various approaches of template matching such as shape-based matching, the modified Hough transform, PatMat and the normalized cross correlation. In computer vision, more general approaches named as invariant feature descriptors [4,5,6] are investigated under various transform such as projective and affine.

Lowe [4] proposed Scale Invariant Feature Transform (SIFT) that solves scale problem through the scale space analysis and rotation using the local peak of the gradient. SIFT gives high dimensional descriptors such as 126 dimensions and Lowe showed various applications using this descriptor such as mobile robot navigation and object recognition. Also, these approaches [4,5,6] could be used successfully in the machine vision application, but in the machine vision real-time issue is also important and we can control the environment so that the resulting problem becomes much more simpler. In typical machine vision application, the height between camera and object is fixed, so that rotation and translation search covers most applications. In the point of real-time, these approaches require heavy processing hardware.

2 Target and Model Preparation Using Accumulative Edge Map

We use edge as the matching source and we apply Sobel edge operator on the target image and model image. For the horizontal edge projection, we accumulate edge magnitude in the row direction and for the vertical edge projection we accumulate edge magnitude in the column direction. After this accumulation of edge value along horizontal and vertical direction, we can simply obtain the edge projection value of arbitrary location by just subtracting two values accumulated edge values.

Let $E(i, j)$ as the edge magnitude at the pixel location of (i,j).

$$E(i, j) = |I_x(i, j)| + |I_y(i, j)| \tag{1}$$

where $|I_x(i, j)|$ and $|I_y(i, j)|$ represents the edge magnitude by Sobel operator in x and y direction. In this paper, 3X3 mask size is used. Accumulative edge magnitude of horizontal and vertical direction can be defined as

$$\begin{aligned} AE_x(i, j) &= \sum_{k=0}^{i} E(k, j) \\ AE_y(i, j) &= \sum_{k=0}^{j} E(i, k) \end{aligned} \tag{2}$$

where $AE_x(i, j)$ and $AE_y(i, j)$ is accumulative edge magnitude along x and y direction. Using this accumulative edge, we can simply calculate the edge projection of ROI (Region Of Interest).

$$\begin{aligned} EP_x(i, j) &= AE_x(i+h, j) - AE_x(i-h, j) \\ EP_y(i, j) &= AE_y(i, j+h) - AE_y(i, j-h) \end{aligned} \tag{3}$$

where $EP_x(i, j)$ is edge projection along row direction with height of $2h+1$ and $EP_y(i, j)$ is edge projection along column direction with width of $2h+1$. As shown in (2), the edge projection of interesting points with arbitrary width can be obtained by simply subtracting accumulative edge of two points.

This process is applied to the model and target image. To cope with rotation, we constructed rotated model's edge projection separately at each rotation. At each rotated model, we only use two edge projections of x and y directions. At the search, these two 1D values are compared to the target image. Through this, it is possible to reduce the template matching with 2D window into template matching with two 1D windows. Also, edge projection values have a similar discrimination power comparable to the brightness values of 2D template window.

3 Matching Using Edge Projection

Matching is done by finding the minimum cost of the SAD (Sum of Absolute Difference) between model and target image's edge projection. For each step, horizontal and vertical edge projections of predefined rectangular area are compared.

$$SAD\_EP(i,j) = \sum_{k=-n}^{n} \left| EP_x^T(i+k,j) - EP_x^M(k) \right| + \sum_{k=-n}^{n} \left| EP_y^T(i,j+k) - EP_y^M(k) \right| \quad (4)$$

where $SAD\_EP(i,j)$ is SAD of edge projection, $EP_x^T(i,j)$ and $EP_y^T(i,j)$ is target image's value of edge projection along x and y direction, and $EP_x^M(i)$ and $EP_y^M(i)$ is model image's value of edge projection along x and y direction. $2n+1$ is the size of the correlation window between model and target.

To reduce the computation time, we also adopt coarse-to-fine search using pyramid of images. For the construction of pyramid image, Gaussian convolution is employed from the lower level to the upper level of the pyramid. Some predefined portions of image points with higher matching score are propagated into the fine level of pyramid. At the top level of pyramid, all positions are scanned and matching values are calculated. After sorting these matching values, we obtain threshold values corresponding to the predefined percentages of pixels. We could achieve high computational efficiency through the combined usage of edge projection and coarse-to-fine search on the pyramid image.

4 Experimental Results

The same value of parameters is applied in all experiments. We used three level of pyramid. In the top level of pyramid, portions corresponding to the highest 5 percent of matching score are propagated into the next level and in the middle level the highest 10 percent of sorted matching score are propagated into the bottom level. In the highest level of pyramid, all position is searched. In the bottom level, position with highest matching score is selected as the target position. For the search of rotation, we employ 36 level of rotation. So we construct 36 rotated models and this step could be done in off-line so that it is possible to reduce the computational time.

Fig. 1 shows the model image used in the experiment. Model image is obtained from the image itself. Fig. 2 represents the target images used in the experiment and it all has size of 640x480 pixel. During the acquisition of the target image, we target is translated and rotated while keeping scale fixed by keeping height between camera and target plane constant. We implemented sum of absolute brightness difference as the conventional template matching. For the search of rotation, at each pixel location 36 rotated model images are compared, and among these results the minimum cost is selected for the cost of matching of that position. Also the same procedure is applied for the selection of matching candidates in each pyramid level. Computation is done under Intel Pentium 4 CUP 2.00 GHz with 448MB RAM.

Fig. 1. Model images used in the experiment (from left to right: tobacco, mobile phone, and semiconductor)

Fig. 2. Target images used in the experiment (tobacco, mobile phone, and semiconductor)

Table 1. Comparison of the processing time between proposed and conventional template matching (T: Tobacco P: Phone S: Semiconductor, target image size is 640x480 pixel, [sec])

Target	Model Size	Proposed				Conventional Template Matching				B/A
		Level 0	Level 1	Level 2	Sum (A)	Level 0	Level 1	Level 2	Sum (B)	
T1	142x92	0.15	0.116	0.281	0.56	30.488	6.631	9.206	46.325	82.7
P1	128x80	0.126	0.12	0.288	0.53	8.17	4.479	8.019	20.768	39.2
P2		0.157	0.109	0.27	0.547	9.922	4.574	8.013	22.509	41.1
P3		0.15	0.109	0.276	0.535	21.204	5.962	8.019	35.185	65.8
S1	240x240	0.149	0.126	0.389	0.664	34.872	16.962	21.113	72.947	109.9
S2		0.151	0.132	0.386	0.669	40.661	16.081	21.443	78.185	116.9
S3		0.149	0.126	0.389	0.664	33.613	17.021	21.142	71.776	108.1

Table 2. Comparison of the estimated translation error between proposed and conventional template matching

Target	true value		Proposed				Conventional Template Matching			
			estimated value		error		estimated value		error	
	x	y	x	y	x	y	x	y	x	y
T1	422.9	183.5	409	173	-13.9	-10.5	429	186	6.1	2.5
P1	408.8	165.7	409	162	0.19	-3.7	405	164	-3.8	-1.7
P2	449.7	208.9	451	214	1.3	5.1	450	202	0.3	-6.9
P3	385.3	167.4	420	158	34.7	-9.4	599	138	213.7	-29.4
S1	332.5	91.6	388	160	55.5	68.4	541	94	208.5	2.4
S2	233.4	204.1	238	201	4.6	-3.1	236	196	2.6	-8.1
S3	322.0	157.9	319	158	-3.0	0.1	330	164	8.0	6.1

Table 1 shows the comparison of processing time of proposed and conventional gray image-based template matching. Table 2 shows the error of location found by proposed and conventional template matching. True values were set by hand. When intensity based template matching fails, also proposed edge projection based algorithm fails. From Table 2, we can see that proposed edge projection based matching algorithm gives comparable discriminating power to that of intensity based template matching. Proposed approach could be used efficiently in the fast generation of matching candidates and it could be implemented very simply. Further refinement of matching could be done using other approaches on these candidate points.

5 Conclusion

In this paper, we proposed a new simple and fast template matching algorithm using edge projection. We reformulated inherent two dimensional search problem of conventional brightness based template matching problem into one dimensional through the usage of horizontal and vertical edge projection within 2D search window. Edge projections of horizontal and vertical direction within the interesting region also give comparable result to that of using brightness values. Current implementation can cope with the translation and rotation of the model under fixed scale, but it could be used successfully in the typical machine vision application where the distance between the camera and the object has small variation.

Acknowledgement. This research was supported by the KOSEF (Korea Science and Engineering Foundation) under the Grants for Interdisciplinary Research Program.

References

1. www.cognex.com
2. www.matrox.com
3. Ulrich, M., and Steger, C.: Empirical performance evaluation of object recognition methods. Empirical Evaluation Methods in Computer Vision, IEEE Computer Society Press, Los Alamitos, CA, (2001) 62-76
4. Lowe, D.G.: Object Recognition from Local Scale-Invariant Features. Proc. Seventh Int'l Conf. Computer Vision, (1999) 1150-1157
5. Mikolajczyk, K. and Schmid, C.: An Affine Invariant Interest Point Detector. European Conference on Computer Vision, (2002) 128-142
6. Belongie, S., Malik, J. and Puzicha, J.: Shape Matching and Object Recognition Using Shape Contexts. IEEE Trans. on Pattern Recognition and Machine Intelligence, Vol. 24 (2002) 509-522

Finding Similar Patterns in Microarray Data

Xiangsheng Chen[1], Jiuyong Li[1], Grant Daggard[2], and Xiaodi Huang[3]

[1] Department of Mathematics and Computing,
Department of Biological and Physical Sciences,
The University of Southern Queensland, Australia
firstName.lastName@usq.edu.au
[2] Department of Mathematics, Statistics and Computer Science,
The University of New England, Armidale, NSW, 2350

Abstract. In this paper we propose a clustering algorithm called s-Cluster for analysis of gene expression data based on pattern-similarity. The algorithm captures the tight clusters exhibiting strong similar expression patterns in Microarray data, and allows a high level of overlap among discovered clusters without completely grouping all genes like other algorithms. This reflects the biological fact that not all functions are turned on in an experiment, and that many genes are co-expressed in multiple groups in response to different stimuli. The experiments have demonstrated that the proposed algorithm successfully groups the genes with strong similar expression patterns and that the found clusters are interpretable.

Keywords: data mining, bioinformatics, Microarray data analysis, clustering.

1 Introduction

Many clustering techniques in bioinformatics have been applied to analyze gene expression data. Most clustering models [4, 1, 8, 10, 7, 9] are distance based clusterings such as Euclidean distance and cosine distance. However, these similarity functions are not always sufficient in capturing correlations among genes or conditions. To remedy this problem, the bicluster model [2] uses a similarity score to measure the coherence of genes and conditions in a sub matrix of Microarray data. Wang et al. [11] proposed an algorithm to find all (maximum) submatrices such that they are δ-pClusters. Liu et al. [5] introduced a u-Cluster model to capture the general tendency of objects across a subset of dimensions in a high dimensional space. In reality, errors are unavoidable in biological experiments and perfect pattern matching in Microarray data may not occur even among known coordinately regulated genes. In this paper, we will present a model which tolerates such possible errors in the data. Our proposed algorithm is simple, interpretable, and deterministic. The proposed algorithm is distinct from δ-pClustering model in that it is a full space clustering model and allows dissimilarities, possibly caused by experimental errors, in clusters while δ-pClustering does not.

2 s-Clusters

We define *s*-clusters by a threshold as the minimum proportion of conditions in which genes have the similar express. Our model does not cluster all genes and allows clusters to overlap. The resulting clusters are tight. A tight cluster is better for refining a hypothesis.

2.1 Model

The original gene data matrix is first normalized. Gene-condition expression data is represented as a n-by-p matrix where each entry x_{ij} denotes the expression level of the ith gene in the jth condition (where $i = 1,...,n$ and $j = 1,...,p$).

The new standardized data matrix Z is obtained by converting the raw values to *z-scores*, and it will be used for the following clustering analysis. The mean of *z-scores* in each row is zero.

Definition 1. *Let N be the set of genes and P be the set of conditions in a standardized data set Z. Given $x, y \in N$, Z_x and Z_y denote the vectors of the xth gene and yth gene, respectively. We define the sScore of two genes under the jth condition as*

$$sScore_{x,y,j} = |z_{xj} - z_{yj}| \tag{1}$$

With two given thresholds $0 < \alpha \leq 1$ and $\delta > 0$, we say two genes x and y are similar, if at least in a α fraction of conditions, $sScore \leq \delta$ for the two genes.

Definition 2. *Let $S = \{Z_1, Z_2, ..., Z_k\}$ be a set of genes, $S \subset N$. Z_k denotes a vector of a gene. We say S forms an s-Cluster if every pair of genes in S is similar by definition 1.*

In the s-Cluster model, one gene can be in several different clusters. In other words, the clusters are not exclusive. This is very meaningful in the underlying biological processes in which many individual genes are co-expressed in multiple function groups in response to different stimuli.

2.2 Algorithm

The algorithm contains three phases: (1) preprocess the data into a normalized data matrix. The mean and mean absolute deviation are calculated for each row, and are then converted the raw data into *z-scores*;(2) find similar gene pairs. We go through the *z-scores* data and identify all similar gene pairs according to Definition 1; (3) form all s-Clusters. construct a graph where every gene is represented as a vertex, and two similar genes as an edge. s-Clusters can be viewed as the cliques in this graph according to Definition 2. We design an algorithm similar to Bierstone's algorithm [6] to generate all maximum cliques, interesting s-Clusters.

In general, finding all maximal cliques in a graph is NP-complete. The algorithm can enumerate all maximal cliques efficiently only when the equivalent graph is sparse, i.e. edge density is low. Edge density of a gene graph is usually very low since there are not many genes expressing similarly across most conditions. Therefore, this method produces good results with high efficiency in Microarray data.

A simple heuristic to set δ is outlined as follows. It is set high initially, and then is reduced gradually. When the visual inspection of similarity of gene expression patterns in clusters is unacceptable, the process stops. The setting of α is straightforward since its meanings is clear.

The definition of similarity in this model is more strict than that in most other clustering models. As a result, the clusters of this model are usually very tight, including much fewer genes than clusters from other models. We do not intend to find regular clusters to group all genes, but to find small groups of genes that exhibit strong similar expression patterns. We find that these clusters are very interpretable.

3 Experiments

We apply the s-Cluster algorithm to yeast *Saccharomyces cerevisiae* cell cycle expression data from Cho *et al.* [3]. The yeast data contains expression levels of 2,884 genes under 17 conditions. The data set is organized in a matrix where each row corresponds to a gene and each column represents a condition. Each entry

Gene	System Name	Description
58	YAR007C	69 kDa subunit of the heterotrimeric RPA (RF-A) single-stranded DNA binding protein, binds URS1 and CAR1
216	YBR088C	Profilerating cell nuclear antigen (PCNA) accessory factor for DNA polymerase delta, mRNA increases in G1, peaks in S in mitosis, and increases prior to DNA synthesis in meiosis"
217	YBR089W	Unknown
448	YDL003W	Unknown
526	YDL164C	DNA ligase
616	YDR097C	Homolog of the human GTBP protein, forms a complex with Msh2p to repair both single-base and insertion-deletion mispairs, redundant with Msh3p in repair of insertion-deletion mispairs"
1022	YFL008W	Coiled-coil protein involved in chromosome structure or segregation
1184	YGR152C	GTP-binding protein of the ras superfamily involved in bud site selection
1286	YHR154W	Establishes Silent omatin
1795	YLR103C	Omosomal DNA replication initiation protein
1836	YLR183C	Unknown
2278	YNL102W	DNA polymerase I alpha subunit, p180
2375	YNL312W	1-7, 116-930" subunit 2 of replication factor RF-A 29% identical to the human p34 subunit of RF-A
2538	YOR074C	Thymidylate synthase
2725	YPL153C	Protein kinase, Mec1p and Tel1p regulate rad53p phosphorylation"

Fig. 1. A list of genes in s-Cluster #111. 12 genes are related to DNA synthesis and replication and 3 are unknown. This raises the possibility that the 3 genes are also DNA synthesis and replication related.

represents the relative abundance values (percentage of the mRNA for the gene in all mRNA) of the mRNA of a gene under a specific condition, which is scaled into an integer in the range of 0 and 600. We conducted the experiment with the parameters of $\delta = 0.8$ and $\alpha = 0.8$. A total of 1764 s-Clusters with a minimum size of 5 was generated by the algorithm. Clusters of four or fewer genes were ignored. The 1764 s-Clusters covered 453 genes, or 15.7% of the 2884 genes. This method only groups some interesting genes, which express coherently with other genes. All clusters are highly overlapping, and this captures a biological fact that some genes participate in a number of functions.

There are 15 members in the s-cluster #111 in Figure 1, 12 genes of which are related to DNA synthesis and replication, and 3 genes (YBR089W, YDL003W, ULR183C) are unknown. This raises the possibility that the 3 genes are also related to DNA synthesis and replication. Figure 1 shows genes in this s-Cluster in details.

Our findings are interesting when compared with those of Tavazoie et al. [8]. Our 15 members in s-Cluster #111 are all in the cluster #2 discovered by Tavazoie et al.. Their cluster #2 contains 186 genes which are related to four functions: DNA synthesis and replication, cell cycle control and mitosis, recombination and DNA repair, and nuclear organization. Our approach successfully subcategorized Tavazoie's cluster #2 into several smaller sized s-Clusters containing genes which are clearly related to one of the four functional categories. This indicates that the s-Clusters are more tightly grouped and more interpretable than the clusters from the alternative analysis approach.

4 Conclusions

We have proposed a new pattern-similarity clustering model called s-Cluster to capture some tight clusters containing groups of genes with strong coherent expression patterns. Our experimental results show that the proposed algorithm can successfully group genes with similar expression patterns. When compared with the clustering results from a conventional method [8], the clusters found by our algorithm are tighter and more interpretable.

References

1. U. Alon, N. Barlai, D. Notterman, K. Gish, S. Ybarra, D. Mack, and A. Levine. Broad patterns of gene expression revealed by clustering analysis of tumor and normal colon tissues probed by oligonucleotide array. In *Proc. Natl. Acad. Sci. USA*, volume 96(12), pages 6745–6750, 1999.
2. Y. Cheng and G. Church. Biclustering of expression data. In *Proc Int Conf Intell Syst Mol Biol*, pages 93–103, 2000.
3. R. Cho and Team. A genome wide transcriptional analysis of the mitotic cell cycle. *Molecular Cell*, 2:65–73, 1998.
4. M. Eisen, P. Spellman, P. Brown, and D. Botstein. Cluster analysis and display of genome-wide expression patterns. In *Proc. Natl. Acad. Sci. USA*, volume 95, pages 14863–14868, 1998.

5. J. Liu and W. Wang. Op-cluster: Clustering by tendency in high dimensional space. In *Proc of IEEE International Conference on Data Mining (ICDM)*, pages 19 – 22, 2003.
6. G. D. Mulligan and D. G. Corneil. Corrections to Bierstone's algorithm for generating cliques. *Journal of the ACM*, 19(2):244–247, 1972.
7. P. Tamayo, D. Slonim, J. Mesirov, Q. Zhu, S. Kitareewan, E. Dmitrovsky, E. lander, and T. Golub. Interpreting patterns of gene expression with selforganizing maps: methods and application to hematopoietic differentiation. *Proc. Natl. Acad. Sci., USA*, 96:2907–2912, 1999.
8. S. Tavazoie, J. Hughes, M. Campbell, R. Cho, and G. Church. Systematic determination of genetic network architecture. *Natrue Cenetics*, 22:281–285, 1999.
9. P. Toronen, M. Kolehmainen, G. Wong, and E. Castren. Analysis of gene expression data using self-organizing maps. *Federation of European Biochemical Societies FEBS Lett*, 451(2):142–146, 1999.
10. J. Vilo, A. Brazma, I. Jonassen, A. Robinson, and E. Ukkonen. Mining for putative regulatory elements in the yeast genome using gene expression data. In *Proc. 8th Int Conf on Intelligent Systems for Molecular Biology. AAAI Press*, pages 384–394, 2000.
11. H. Wang, W. Wang, J. Yang, and P. Yu. Clustering by pattern similarity in large data sets. In *Proc of the ACM SIGMOD International Conference on Management of Data SIGMOD*, pages 394–405, 2002.

A Stereo Matching Using Variable Windows and Dynamic Programming[*]

Won-Pyo Dong, Yun-Seok Lee, and Chang-Sung Jeong[**]

Department of Electronics Engineering, Korea University,
1-5Ka, Anam-dong, Sungbuk-ku, Seoul 136-701, Korea
{dwp78, leeys}@snoopy.korea.ac.kr, csjeong@charlie.korea.ac.kr

Abstract. In this paper, we present a segment-based stereo matching algorithm using adaptive variable windows and dynamic programming with a robust disparity. We solve the problem of window shape and size using adaptive line masks and adaptive rectangular windows which are constrained by segments and visibility that reduces ambiguity produced by the occlusion in the computation window. In dynamic programming, we also propose the method that selects an efficient occlusion penalty.

1 Introduction

Generally, area-based matching methods measure the similarity between support windows, and an appropriate window should be selected adaptively for each pixel to obtain reliable results. Various algorithms have proposed to overcome this problem [2,3,4]. However, finding an appropriate window with an arbitrary shape and size is still a very difficult problem. Recently, to solve those problems, segmentation-based methods was proposed [5,6]. These methods use segmented regions with arbitrary sizes and shapes, such as support windows. These methods also assume that the depth in each segment region is smooth.

In this paper, we propose a stereo matching algorithm which combines window-based matching and dynamic programming. We solve the problem of window shape and size using line masks and rectangular windows which are constrained by segments and visibility. We also propose the method that selects an efficient occlusion penalty in dynamic programming. Our algorithm first searches initial matching points using adaptive line masks and rectangular windows, then applies dynamic programming.

2 Variable Window Matching

It is assumed that the disparity varies smoothly in a region of homogeneous segments and the depth discontinuity is represented at the boundary of the region. Watershed method for gray images was used for our segmentation [7] with rectified images.

---

[*] This work was partially supported by the Brain Korea 21 Project and KIPA-Information Technology Research Center.
[**] Corresponding author.

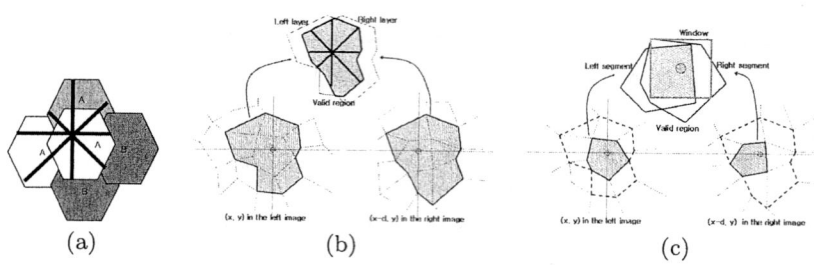

Fig. 1. Variable window. (a) the layer and adaptive line mask, (b) the final line mask which considers visibility, (c) the final valid computation region in window, considering both segment regions.

2.1 Adaptive Line Mask

To determine computation range, each segment is grouped into a layer (layer A, layer B) as shown in Fig. 1(a) according to the similarity between segments in both left and right. The line masks are expanded in accordance with a layer shape (thick solid line in Fig. 1(a)). Consequently, for visibility, we place the left layer upon the right layer to determine the range of the last valid line mask, so that the overlapping region becomes a valid region as thick solid lines shown in Fig. 1(b). Since the range for computation is different according to the disparity, the cost is computed by the mean of absolute difference (MAD). The cost equation is expressed as

$$c(x,d) = \frac{1}{N} \sum_{x \in L} |I_l(x) - I_r(x-d)| \tag{1}$$

where $I(x)$ is the intensity of the point, and d means disparity. L is the region of valid line mask and N is the total number of pixels in L.

2.2 Generalized Cost Function

For generalization, having applied line mask, we sum up the line mask costs using Eq. (1) within a segment-based rectangular window. Then, we use again the segment and visibility constraint in an occluded region. However, contrast to the line mask, only one region will be used instead of layers as shown in Fig. 1(c). The generalized equation can be expressed as follows.

$$G(x,d) = \frac{1}{N} \sum_{x \in R} c(x,d) \tag{2}$$

where R is valid region in a rectangular window, N is the total number of pixels in R. Thus, the generalized equation means the average value of the previous costs at the valid region in a rectangular window (top image in Fig. 1(c)). The initial disparity for each pixel is selected by the winner-takes-all (WTA) method as follows.

$$d_x = \arg \min_{d_{min}<d<d_{max}} G(x,d) \quad (3)$$

where d_x is the disparity of a point x.

Although the initial disparity map given by Eq. (3) is accurate in some measure, there exist several errors. To eliminate the errors, in the first place, disparity smoothness may be used, i.e. disparity jump in one segment is cleared. In the second place, if a point is visible in both images, then bi-directional matching results should be the same. The visibility test confirms the consistency of the bi-directional matching using a visible test of the following equation which is proposed by C. Kim and S.U. Lee [8].

$$d_{x-d_x} = \arg \min_{d_{min}<d<d_{max}} G(x - d_x + d, d) \quad (4)$$

where d_{x-d_x} is the disparity of a position $x - d_x$ in the right image. If the result of Eq. (3) is the same as the result of Eq. (4), the point will be valid.

3 Correspondence by Dynamic Programming

In this section, we will optimize the previous result using dynamic programming and find disparities for undefined regions. The previous result becomes a ground control, and a modified occlusion cost using visibility and maximum difference is used. The occlusion cost should be bigger than the cost of matching; at the same time, it should be small enough to permit occlusion. Thus, we find the maximum cost among correct disparities, then it is used for the occlusion penalty. The occlusion cost is estimated by the following equation.

$$occ = \max_{(x,d) \in V} G(x,d) \quad (5)$$

where V means a group of points which has valid disparity.

We define the following energy function and find a path of disparities that minimizes the following equation,

$$E = \sum_x G(x,d) + \sum_x w_l \cdot occ + \sum_x w_r \cdot occ \quad (6)$$

where w_l is the left occlusion weight and w_r is the right occlusion weight. The weight factor determines whether the disparity jump is permitted or not. The disparity jump is determined by the variation of the segment region, i.e. if the segment region is changed, the disparity jump is permitted. Note that w_l is determined by the variation of the right segment region and w_r is determined by the variation of the left segment region, because there might be occlusion region.

4 Experiments and Results

We evaluated our algorithm with four standard data sets - Tsukuba, Sawtooth, Venus and Map provided by D. Sharstein and R. Szeliski on the web

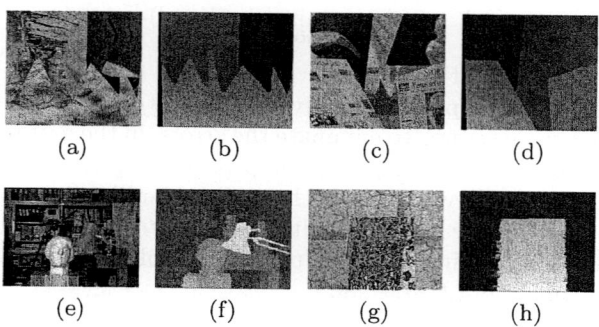

Fig. 2. Disparity maps produced by our method. (a) Sawtooth, (b) the result of Sawtooth, (c) Venus, (d) the result of Venus, (e) Tsukuba, (f) the result of Tsukuba, (g) Map, (h) the result of Map.

(http://www.middlebury.edu/stereo). The quality metric is the percentage of the error of disparity deviated from the ground truth more than 1 pixel [1]. According to test bed, our algorithm had about 1% error in all the test images, and our results are show in Fig. 2. Although our algorithm uses gray images, the performance is not inferior to other algorithms that use color images. In this paper, we have solved the problem of window shape and window size using adaptive line mask and visibility. The visibility constraint can reduce the ambiguities produced by the occlusion in the computation window, and smoothing effects can be reduced by the line mask. Futhermore, the line mask is not only efficient for computation but also easy to extend and apply.

References

1. D. Scharstein, R. Szeliski: A Taxonomy and Evaluation of Dense Two-frame Stereo Correspondence Algorithms. International Journal of Computer Vision. **47** (2002) 7–42
2. T. Kanade, M. Okutomi: A Stereo Matching Algorithm with An Adaptive Window. IEEE Trans. Pattern Analysis and Machine Intelligence. **16** (1994) 920–932
3. G.B. Kim, S.C. Chung: An Accurate and Robust Stereo Matching Algorithm with Variable Windows for 3D Measurements. Mechatronics. **14** (2004) 715–735
4. O. Veksler: Stereo Matching by Compact Windows via Minimum Ratio Cycle. ICCV. (2001)
5. H. Tao, R. Kumar: A Global Matching Framework for Stereo Computation. ICCV. (2001)
6. M. Bleyer, M. Gelautz: A Layered Stereo Algorithm using Image Segmentation and Global Visibility Constraints. ICIP. (2004)
7. A. Bleau, L.J. Leon: Watershed-Based Segmentation and Region Merging. Computer Vision and Image Understanding. **77** (2000) 317–370
8. C. Kim, S.U. Lee: A Dense Stereo Matching Using Two-Pass Dynamic Programming with Generalized Ground Control Points. CVPR. (2005)

Detection of Auto Programs for MMORPGs*

Hyungil Kim, Sungwoo Hong, and Juntae Kim**

Department of Computer Engineering, Dongguk University,
26, 3 Pil-dong, Chung-gu, Seoul, Korea
{hikim, swhong, jkim}@dongguk.edu

Abstract. Auto-playing programs are often used on behalf of human players in a MMORPG(Massively Multi-player Online Role Playing Game). By playing automatically and continuously, it helps to speed up the game character's level-up process. However, the auto-playing programs, either software or hardware, do harm to games servers in various ways including abuse of resources. In this paper, we propose a way of detecting the auto programs by analyzing the window event sequences produced by the game players. In our proposed method, the event sequences are transformed into a set of attributes, and various learning algorithms are applied to classify the data represented by the set of attribute values into human or auto player. The results from experiments with several MMORPGs show that the Decision Tree learning with proposed method can identify the auto-playing programs with high accuracy.

Keywords: Data Mining, Entertainment and AI, Machine Learning, Intelligent Data Analysis.

1 Introduction

The users of the MMORPG(Massively Multi-player Online Role Playing Game) are rapidly increasing. MMORPGs are on-line games in which players use characters with specific roles to interact between game players (communicate, cooperate, or compete) and performs adventure, hunting, etc. [1][2][3].

Auto-playing programs are software or hardware that are used to take the place of human players in a MMORPG. Auto-playing programs automatically produce keyboard or mouse events that control game characters, and continuously perform specific tasks on behalf of human users. Since the auto-playing programs do harm to games servers in various ways including abuse of resources, game service companies have made constant efforts to exterminate the auto programs. However, many kinds of auto programs are still used for various games. Especially the hardware type auto programs that operate between the OS and I/O devices such as mouse, keyboard, joystick, and monitor, can not be easily detected by the server.

In this paper, we propose a way of identifying the auto programs by analyzing the window event sequences produced by the game players. Generally, the auto-playing programs have several goals such as collecting certain objects, and repeatedly

---

* This work has been supported by Dongguk University research fund.
** Corresponding author.

perform specific tasks. Also, the event sequences produced by auto programs have characteristics that are statistically distinguishable from that of human players due to many reasons. In our proposed method, the event sequences produced by human and auto players are transformed into a set of attributes, and various learning algorithms including Decision Tree induction are applied to classify the data represented by the set of attribute values into human or auto player.

The proposed method is applied to the detection of auto programs for various online games including Mu (www.muonline.co.kr), Archlord (archlord.naver.com), GoonZu (www.goonzu.com), and Maple Story (maplestory.nexon.com). The results from experiments with several MMORPGs show that the proposed method can identify the auto-playing programs with high accuracy.

2 Event Sequence Analysis

In this section, we present the method of identifying auto programs in detail by analyzing window event sequences produced by game players. We extract various attributes form the event sequences produced by human and auto players, and a set of those attribute values are used as a training example.

The window events that are produced during game playing include specific key strokes, mouse button clicks, mouse movements, etc. Table 1 shows an example event sequence produced during game playing by an auto program in the hunting scene in Mu game. The messages represent window messages for keyboard and mouse events. The parameters for keyboard messages are values specifying each key, and the parameters for mouse messages represent the x-y coordinate values.

Table 1. Example event sequence

Message	Parameter H	Parameter L	Time
WM_KEYDOWN	57	14624	1540664
WM_KEYUP	57	14624	1540782
WM_KEYDOWN	57	14624	1541076
WM_KEYUP	57	14624	1541186
WM_LBUTTONDOWN	322	503	1541546
WM_LBUTTONUP	322	503	1541716
⋮	⋮	⋮	⋮

Direct comparison between the event sequences is very difficult. To compare the sequences we extract various attributes that possibly characterize the sequence and might be useful to distinguish auto players from human players. The attributes include the total number of events in a given time interval (total_events), ratio of certain events (key_event_ratio, autokey_ratio), average time between mouse and keyboard events (m_stroke_ave, k_stroke_ave), standard deviation of time between mouse and keyboard up and down (m_stroke_dev, k_stroke_dev), average of time interval between specific mouse and keyboard events (ml_kind_ave, mr_kind_ave, sp_kind_ave, etc), average of time interval between specific consecutive mouse and keyboard events (ml_cont_ave, mr_cont_ave, sp_cont_ave, etc.), standard deviation of time between specific consecutive mouse and keyboard events (ml_cont_dev, mr_cont_dev, sp_cont_dev, etc.), existence of specific time series patterns (ml_pattern, mr_pattern, etc.). Total 26 attributes are used.

105, 0.41, 0.08, 0.02, 0.50, 0.28, 0.02, ... , 5.01, 3.99, 0, 0, 0, 0, A

Fig. 1. A sample event sequence data represented in an attribute vector

The example event sequences obtained from human players and auto players are converted into 26 dimensional vectors by using these attributes. Figure 1 shows an example attribute vector generated from an event sequence produced by auto program while playing the Mu game for 1 minute. The first attribute is total_events, the second is key_event_ratio, the third is autokey_ratio, and so on. The attribute vectors like Figure 1 are generated from multiple sample event sequences produced by human players and auto programs, and the set of those attribute vectors are used as a training set for learning. According to the characteristics of various games and the auto play rules specified in auto programs, some of the attributes (or combination of them) can provide clues to distinguish the auto program from human players.

3 Experiments

The experiments of proposed method are performed on 4 different on-line games – Mu, Archlord, GoonZu, and Maple Story. For Mu and Maple Story, a hardware type auto program is used for test, and for Archlord and GoonZu, a software type auto program is used. We use the WEKA machine learning tool, which is a Java implementation of various machine learning algorithms, to classify a game playing event sequence into a human play or auto program play. For classification experiment, sample event sequences are produced from game playing of human players and auto programs.

For each game, 3 human players played the game for 30 minutes and produced 90 example sequences of 1 minute length. The auto programs also played for 90 minutes in the same situation and produced 90 example sequences of 1 minute each. Among the events, simple mouse movements are excluded. Also, for Maple Story, only keyboard events are used because the game is played mainly by keyboard. Those sequences are converted into attribute vectors, and so the total number of training data for classification is 180 for each game. 10-fold cross validation is used for accuracy measurements.

Generally, the auto program produces more events than human players because 1) they are faster than average skilled human players, 2) they are unable to recognized game situations in many cases and produce multiple events to achieve same task. The skilled human players may produce more events because they are faster, but the standard deviation of time between events is generally larger than that of auto programs. According to the information gain analysis, mr_cont_ave in Mu, autokey_kind_dev in Maple Story, sp_kind_ave in Archlord, and ml_cont_ave in GoonZu were the most informative attributes respectively.

Table 2 shows the classification accuracies achieved by using several machine learning methods. For the Mu and the Maple Story, the Decision Tree shows highest accuracy. For the Archlord, the Backpropagation learning with Multilayer Perceptron shows most accurate result, and for the GoonZu, the k-Nearest Neighbor method shows most accurate result. The average accuracies are similar for all cases, but we believe that the Decision Tree learning is a good choice because it can provide the classification rules for detection of the auto players. In all cases, the classification accuracies were above 90%.

Table 2. The classification accuracies of various machine learning methods

Classifier	HW auto program		SW auto program		Average
	Mu	Maple	Archlord	GoonZu	
Decision Tree	**99.4%**	**95.1%**	93.9%	95.9%	96.1%
Multilayer Perceptron	96.1%	91.2%	**98.0%**	97.5%	95.7%
k-Nearest Neighbor	97.2%	90.2%	95.9%	**97.5%**	95.2%
Naïve Bayesian	95.0%	93.1%	96.6%	91.9%	94.2%

4 Conclusion

In this paper, we presented a way of detecting auto programs by analyzing the window event sequences produced by the game players and applying machine learning algorithms to the attributes generated from the sequences. We first collected the keyboard and mouse event sequences produced by the human players and auto programs. Then various attributes such as the average time and standard deviation of time between specific events are extracted. By using those attributes the event sequences are represented as vectors and used as training data for learning.

It is found that, generally the auto program produces more events, and the time interval between the same kinds of event and the standard deviation of consecutive same events is smaller than that of human players. The result of experiments with 4 different on-line games shows that the proposed method can be used to detect auto programs with high accuracy.

References

1. N. Ducheneaut and R. J. Moore, "The social side of gaming: a study of interaction patterns in a massively multiplayer online game," *In Proceedings of the ACM conference on Computer-Supported Cooperative Work*, 2004.
2. G. Robert, Pierre Portier, and Agnes Guillot, "Classifier systems as 'Animat' architectures for action selection in MMORPG," *The Third International Conference on Intelligent Games and Simulation*, 2002
3. S. L. Whang and G. Y. Chang, "Lifestyles of Virtual World Residents, Living in the on-line game, "Lineage"," *International Conference on CYBERWORLDS*, 2003.

Automated Classification of Dementia Subtypes from Post-mortem Cortex Images

David Cornforth[1] and Herbert Jelinek[2]

[1] Australian Defence Force Academy, Northcott Drive, Canberra, ACT, Australia
d.cornforth@adfa.edu.au
[2] Charles Sturt University, PO Box 789, Albury NSW 2640 Australia
hjelinek@csu.edu.au

Abstract. We apply automated classification techniques to determine whether dementia is associated with changes in the physical structure of small blood vessels in the brain. A successful predictive model would imply such an association. The use of measures derived from fractal analysis, and the use of machine learning classification algorithms, allow exploration of highly complex relationships. Results suggest that although physiological differences are difficult to detect, and vary between different areas of brain tissue, there is evidence for such an association. If such changes can be detected from images of post mortem tissue, this implies that investigation of the medical significance of these changes could provide greater understanding of this class of diseases.

1 Introduction

In this work we ask whether dementia subtypes are associated with physiological changes in post mortem cortex. Enumeration of such changes would yield advances in understanding of dementia. To address this, we attempt to build a predictive model that can assign an image of post mortem tissue to one of various classes of diseased or normal. If the model has predictive value, this implies that disease is indeed associated with physical changes. This work continues previous work [1,2] but attempts a fuller range of discrimination problems, providing a more complete assessment of the feasibility of discrimination.

Dementia is a very common disease [3] resulting from degeneration of the brain, and has a number of different subtypes, including Alzheimer's disease (AD) and small vessel disease (SVD). It is believed to be associated with changes in the structure of small blood vessels in the cortex, but there has been little quantitative analysis [4].

Natural objects encountered in pathology, such as these small blood vessels, have complex structural characteristics that are difficult to describe using Euclidean geometry. Some of these complex patterns can be approximated in terms of fractal structures, and encouraging results from work on similar tissue types has prompted us to use fractal analysis [5,6].

To build classification models for this work, we employed a number of algorithms from the Weka toolbox [7], listed in Table 1. We also used an implementation of the

Cerebellar Model Articulation Controller (CMAC) [8] with the *Kernel Addition Training Algorithm* [9] which is not included in the Weka toolbox.

A *Default Classifier* was used as a "straw man" against which to assess the other algorithms. This must take account of cross validation, which was used to assess the other algorithms. Given a dataset containing s samples, to classify an unknown sample we select a record at random from the remaining $s-1$ samples, and choose the class of that record. If the dataset contains k classes, with the number of samples in each class given by $\{n_1 \ldots n_k\}$, the expected number of correct guesses will be:

$$c = \frac{1}{s-1} \sum_{j=1}^{k} n_j - 1 . \tag{1}$$

2 Methods

Fifty images were obtained from postmortem tissue, comprising 18 from the parietal region (side of brain), 20 from the frontal region, and 12 from the occipital region (rear of brain). Images were identified by experts as AD for Alzheimer's disease, SVD for small vessel disease, AD-SVD for both, and CONTROL for normal (non-diseased tissue). In order to perform automated classification, we extracted measures that are free from bias, and were translation, scale and rotation invariant:

- Mean Density – the average gray value within the selection. This is the sum of the gray values of all the pixels in the selection divided by the number of pixels.
- Standard Deviation – the standard deviation of the gray values used to generate the mean gray value.
- Normalised Integrated Density - the sum of the grey values in the image, with background (modal grey value) subtracted, divided by the total number of pixels in the image.

We supplemented these with D_0, D_1 and D_2 from the multifractal spectrum, as well as Lacunarity. We selected features from this set based on their correlation with class labels and with each other. None of the traditional features were highly correlated with disease, while those derived from fractal analysis were more useful.

We prepared four datasets for testing discrimination of: a) all classes, b) AD or no AD, c) SVD or no SVD, and d) disease or no disease. Each experiment involved one classifier algorithm testing one dataset, using leave-one-out cross validation in order to avoid over fitting [10]. Accuracy was measured as number of correctly predicted class labels. Each of the experiments was repeated 20 times, each time altering the order of the data records at random, in order to prevent bias due to data order. A comparative measure of accuracy for the default classifier was calculated manually using equation 1.

3 Results

Table 1 shows the resulting classification accuracy for each problem. Figures shown are averages from 20 runs. Results that are better than the default classifier are shown in bold. There was zero variation in the results of most of the tests, in other words many algorithms displayed no stochastic variation, and the order of records had no effect on the outcome.

Clearly, the results suggest that the nature of change associated with disease is different in the three different areas. The machine learning methods seemed to have the most success with images from the parietal area. The most consistently successful problem was the Disease problem (dataset d), where most classifiers were able to form a successful model for data from the frontal and parietal regions.

Confidence intervals are tabulated in Table 2 for only the best results from Table 1, with $n=20$ for frontal, $n=18$ for parietal and $n=12$ for occipital. The results from parietal region are clearly significant at this level, while the results from the frontal and occipital regions are not significant. This implies that there is evidence for physical changes associated with disease in the parietal region but not in the other regions.

Table 1. Results from the machine learning algorithms, best results shown in bold

Classifier	Frontal				Parietal				Occipital
	4-class	AD	SVD	Disease	4-class	AD	SVD	Disease	Disease
Default	4.4	9.9	9.5	11.2	3.8	8.5	8.6	10.4	5.5
CMAC	**6**	7	10	14	9	**12**	9	13	**7**
Decision Table	0	**12**	0	14	0	0	10	12	0
N.Neigh. k=1	3	8	4	10	4	10	8	13	3
N.Neigh. k=3	0	9	2	10	**9**	13	13	**15**	5
Decision Tree	2	4	0	14	8	**14**	2	13	0
Kernel Density	2	5	5	13	**9**	8	13	14	4
Naïve Bayes	2	9	6	12	**9**	10	**14**	**15**	5

Table 2. Showing 95% confidence intervals for the best results from table 7 to 9. Significant results are shown in bold.

Area	problem	best	min	max	Default classifier
frontal	4-class	6	2.0	10.0	4.4
frontal	AD	10	5.6	14.4	9.9
frontal	SVD	12	7.7	16.3	9.5
frontal	Disease	14	10.0	18.0	11.2
parietal	4-class	9	4.8	13.2	**3.8**
parietal	AD	14	10.5	17.5	**8.5**
parietal	SVD	14	10.5	17.5	**8.6**
parietal	Disease	15	11.9	18.1	**10.4**
occipital	Disease	7	3.7	10.3	5.5

4 Conclusion

In this study, we have made use of measurements and techniques that have not previously been applied to the classification of dementia sub-types. Our main findings are:

- The machine learning algorithms showed evidence of an association between disease and micro-vascular structure.
- This link is not strong, and is strongest in samples from the parietal area.
- Features derived from fractal analysis were clearly superior to the more traditional measures that we examined.

We acknowledge the help of Patricia Waley and Eduardo Fernandez in this work. This work was supported in part by a CSU Early Career Researcher Grant.

References

1. Jelinek, H., Cornforth, D., Waley, P., Fernandez, E., Robinson, W.: A comparison of machine learning approaches for the automated classification of dementia. In: Mckay, Slaney (eds.): Lecture notes in Artificial Intelligence 2557. Springer (2002) 721-722
2. Jelinek, H., Cornforth, D., Waley, P., Fernandez, E. Robinson, W.: Automated Processing of Post-Mortem Cortex Images Reveals Physiological Changes Associated with Dementia Sub-types. In: Mohammadian (ed.): Proc. Int. Conf. Computational Intelligence for Modelling Control and Automation, University of Canberra, Australia, (2004) 646-656
3. Piguet, O., Grayson, D.A., Creasey, H., Bennett, H.P., Brooks, W.S., Waite L.M., Broe, G.A.: Vascular risk factors, cognition and dementia incidence over 6 years in the Sydney Older Persons Study. Neuroepidemiology 22 (3) (2003) 165-171
4. Englund, E.: Neuropathology of white matter changes in Alzheimer's disease and vascular dementia. Dementia & Geriatric Cognitive Disorders, 9 (Suppl.) 1 (1998) 6-12.
5. Fernandez, E., Jelinek, H.F.: Use of fractal theory in neuroscience: methods, advantages and potential problems. Methods, 24 (4) (2001) 309-321
6. Landini, G.: Applications of fractal geometry in pathology, in: Iannaccone, P.M., Khokha, M. (eds.): Fractal Geometry in Biological Systems: an analytical approach. CRC Press, New York, (1995) 205-242
7. Witten, I.H., Frank, E.: Data Mining: Practical Machine Learning Tools and Techniques with Java Implementations. Morgan Kaufmann, (1999)
8. Albus, J.S.: A New Approach to Manipulator Control: the Cerebellar Model Articulation Controller (CMAC), Journal of Dynamic Systems, Measurement and Control 97 (1975) 220-233
9. Cornforth D., Newth, D.: The Kernel Addition Training Algorithm: Faster Training for CMAC Based Neural Networks. In: Proc. Fifth Biannual Conference on Artificial Neural Networks and Expert Systems. Otago University, New Zealand, (2001) 34-39
10. Efron, B.: Estimating the error rate of a prediction rule: improvement on cross-validation. Journal of the American Statistical Association, 78 (382) (1983) 316-330

Metrics for Model Selection in Consumer Finance Problems

Debjit Biswas, Babu Narayanan, and Ramasubramanian Sundararajan*

Computing & Decision Sciences Lab, GE India Technology Centre Pvt. Ltd.,
Plot 122, EPIP Phase 2, Hoodi Village, Bangalore 560066, India
{debjit.biswas, babu.narayanan}@ge.com,
ramasubramanian.sundararajan@geind.ge.com

Abstract. We consider the issue of model selection for some prediction problems in consumer finance. In particular, we look at performance metrics in the context of classification problems. Example areas considered include response modeling, profitability modeling and default prediction in the framework of a customer relationship management (CRM) system. We propose some guidelines for choosing the appropriate performance measure for the predictive model based on the decision framework it is part of.

1 Introduction

A financial institution that offers a portfolio of products (loans, credit cards etc.) to its customers would typically have a database that contains the information pertaining to the history of each customer's relationship with the firm – socio-demographics, account history and transactional information. From a CRM perspective, it is important for the firm to be able to understand response propensity to and profitability (or risk) from its product portfolio at a customer level, and then adapt its marketing and CRM actions based on this knowledge. The key factors that may influence such actions are: propensity to respond to a CRM stimulus (e.g. credit line increase, cross-sell offer), profit potential, risk of default, risk of attrition, and historical lifetime value obtained from products taken since acquisition. Many of these quantities are typically arrived at through predictive models built on existing data about customers. These prediction problems could be broadly classified into two types: classification and regression. In this paper, we shall focus our attention primarily on classification problems, specifically on metrics that address the issue of selection of the right classifier.

Since the CRM action desired drives the model building requirements, it follows that the choice of performance metric to evaluate these models should also be influenced by the decision problem that the model supports. Consider, for instance, the problem of response propensity estimation for cross-selling personal loans to existing cedit card holders. While the primary reason for building a predictive model for this problem is to spend less money on the campaign by not targeting non-responders, it is usually more important to ensure that most of the responders are included in the target list, even at the cost of including non-responders.

---

* Corresponding author.

Now consider two competing models for this problem. Model 1 has better accuracy than Model 2, whereas the latter captures a higher number of respondents while misclassifying a higher number of non-respondents as well. One might argue that Model 2 is the more appropriate choice in this context.

The objective of this paper is to discuss the choice of performance metrics and model selection guidelines for classification problems in consumer finance. The organization of this paper is as follows: Section 2 introduces the problem setting and notation to be used in this paper. Sections 3, 4 and 5 deal with two-class, multiclass and graded multiclass problems respectively. Section 6 briefly touches upon regression problems. Section 7 suggests some directions for further work.

2 Classification

Consider the following generic model of a classification problem wherein examples (vectors $x \in X$) are generated by he environment independently and identically distributed according to some unknown but fixed probability distribution $F(x)$. These vectors are inputs to a supervisor, which returns the output value $y \in \{1, \ldots Q\}$ on the basis of the unknown but fixed conditional distribution $F(y|x)$. (This includes the case where y is a function of x.) The classifier h is one that is provided by the user as an approximation to the joint distribution function $F(x, y)$. Let the output of the classifier h be a Q-tuple of values $(\phi_1, \ldots \phi_Q)$, in which each value ϕ_i indicates the extent of confidence that the given example falls into the class i. This includes, for instance, the case where h outputs a single class label (such as a perceptron), and the case where ϕ_i values represent the posterior probability estimates (such as a Bayesian Belief Network or a logistic regression classifier). The eventual output of the classifier, given an example x, is then defined as: $\hat{y} = h(x) = \arg\max_{i=1 \ldots Q} \phi_i$. The objective of any classification methodology is therefore to arrive at a classifier h_{opt} that optimizes an appropriately defined empirical performance metric In the context of model selection, this implies that the choice of model is determined by their respective empircal loss (or accuracy) values.

The simplest empirical measure of loss $(R_1(S, h))$ for a classifier h on a sample $S = (z_1, \ldots z_\ell)$ (where $z_i = (x_i, y_i)$) is defined as the proportion of misclassified examples in S. However, this metric may not be appropriate for all problems. In the subsequent sections, we shall discuss some alternate choices in the context of some problems in the consumer finance domain. Most of the metrics presented shall be derived from the information present in a confusion matrix $\Sigma_{Q \times Q}$, where σ_{ij}, the $(i, j)^{th}$ element of Σ, gives the proportion of examples in S of class i to be classified as class j by h.

3 Two Class Problems

Two-class problems are a special case of multiclass problems where $Q = 2$. We look at three typical cases of two-class problems in consumer finance to illustrate our ideas.

Response Propensity Prediction

Consider the response propensity prediction problem introduced earlier in Section 1. The business imperatives that drive model selection in this context can be summarized as follows: The firm would like to ensure that a good proportion of the respondents are targeted in a marketing campaign. Once this criterion is met, the secondary issue of misclassification of non-respondents enters the picture, in order to ensure that the firm does not waste its resources targeting potential non-respondents. The key metrics of importance to us in this context are therefore *Sensitivity* and *Positive Predictive Value*, which are defined as follows:

Definition 1. *Sensitivity.* Sensitivity ($Sens(S, h)$) is defined as the proportion of examples of class 1 (respondents in this case) that have been classified correctly.

Definition 2. *Positive Predictive Value.* Positive predictive value ($PPV(S, h)$) is defined as the proportion of examples predicted as class 1 that have been classified correctly.

Both these metrics may be generalized to multiclass problems where one of the classes can be considered a default class (such as non-respondents in a multi-product response propensty model), and the combined accuracy on all the other classes is used instead of simply the accuracy of class 1 above. These generalizations shall be used in Section 4.

The decision rule for model selection for a response propensity problem will have to optimize the trade-off between sensitivity and PPV. This can be viewed as a multiobjective optimization problem.

Default Prediction

Consider the problem of predicting potential defaulters among a set of customers who may be targeted for cross-sell offers. The primary business imperative here is to eliminate potential defaulters so that the respondents among them do not adversely affect the net income from the campaign. However, there is also a secondary objective to minimize the number of customers so eliminated, since the objective in a marketing campaign would still be to target a good percentage of the available customer base.

The model selection in this case has to trade off between eliminating as many defaulters as possible, while not eliminating too many non-defaulters at the same time. Therefore, he choice of optimal model would be the one that achieves a desirable level of both sensitivity and PPV; the definition of "desirable" being dependent on the preference of the decision maker.

Propensity to Take Interest-Free loans

Let us assume that a product at a retail store can be purchased using an interest free loan or an interest bearing loan. The former may be preferred by customers willing to put down a larger down payment, usually required by the interest free loan, while the latter is preferable to those who want a smaller down payment but can afford to pay larger monthly installments.

Now consider the problem of estimating the overall profit from a set of potential respondents. Let us say that we have representative figures for the profit from the two separate types of the loan. A customer level propensity to pick the interest free loan over the interest bearing loan is crucial to estimating population level profitability from the product. Note that we are referring to a propensity score instead of the 0-1 classification problem as it is usually quite hard to solve the classification problem with a satisfactory level of accuracy. Customer level expected profitability can be easily calculated from the propensity score.

Model selection is made by choosing the model with the lowest deviation from the actual profit on a given sample. This deviation may be defined in terms of squared error or any other appropriately defined loss function.

4 Multiclass Problems

A more general form of the two-class problem is a multiclass problem. Multiclass classifiers are often built by combining the results of several binary classifiers, using schemes like One Versus Rest, One versus One etc. (See e.g. [1,2].) Methods that directly build a multiclass classifier include decision trees, Bayesian belief networks, Nearest Neighbour methods, multinomial logit etc.

Consider, for instance, the problem of deciding on the Next Best Offer (NBO) for a customer from among a set of financial products, based on a multiclass response model. Let us assume that there are $Q-1$ products in the portfolio, and a non-respondent class. Let the output tuple therefore be $h(x) = (\phi_1, \ldots, \phi_{Q-1}, \phi_Q)$, and let class Q denote non-respondents, and classes 1 through $Q-1$ denote the various products on offer. The decision rule now has to resolve two issues: Whether or not to offer the customer a product, and which product to offer.

Let us assume that the decision rule for picking a class (and therefore the offer to be made for a customer) is as follows: we pick the product with the highest response propensity, provided that this propensity is greater than a threshold π. Our primary metric of interest is the conversion rate (which is the same as a generalized sensitivity measure as in definition 1) based on the above rule on a sample S. However, since the same business imperatives as in the response propensity problem of Section 3 drive the NBO problem as well, the model selection rule may be defined in a similar manner. For instance, we could first choose the classifiers that have a PPV greater than a predefined threshold α. If none of the classifiers has a PPV greater than α, output the classifier with the highest PPV. Among the classifiers chosen above, output the classifier with the highest conversion rate.

The above rule assumes that there is no difference in the importance between the various products. In case the payoff for the two products is different, metrics used for model selection need to be generalized to include the relative payoff of the various products. We shall assume, for simplicity, that the post-conversion payoff for each product i is given by a representative figure ω_i. The conversion rate above may now be replaced by the expected payoff, given by:

$$EP(S,h) = \frac{\sum_{i=1}^{Q-1} \omega_i \sigma_{ii}}{\sum_{i=1}^{Q-1} \sum_{j=1}^{Q} \omega_i \sigma_{ij}} \qquad (1)$$

5 Graded Multiclass Problems

A graded multiclass classification problem which can be defined as follows: map an input space X into a set of Q classes, $\{1, ..., Q\}$, where $Q > 2$. Here it is also assumed that there is an natural contextual ordering of the classes in the sense that a class value of 1 is better than (worse than) a class value of 2 which is better than (worse than) a class value of 3, and so on. For instance, consider the problem where a financial product (such as a personal loan or credit card) is to be offered by a firm, and a potential customer is to be classified on the basis of credit scores (which may be derived from a set of inputs) as "Credit Risk", "Insufficient Credit Information", "Satisfactory Credit" and "Good Credit", which in turn would determine if the offer is made or not. Thus, for example, only customers classified as "Satisfactory Credit", and "Good Credit" might be offered the product.

Given graded classes, one is not only interested in maximizing the classification accuracy, but also in minimizing the distances between the actual and the predicted classes (see [3]). A metric that summarizes this requirement is described in this section.

Definition 3. Symmetric Band Accuracy. *For a given dataset S, a classifier h and a band size b, the symmetric band accuracy $\theta_h^{Sym}(S, b)$ is defined as the proportion of examples where the observed and predicted class fall within b classes of each other.*

The above definition assumes that our view of accuracy is symmetric in nature, i.e., we are just as concerned about an observation from class i being misclassified as class j as in the opposite case. In some problems, however, this may not be the case (e.g. credit scoring). In this case, the appropriate metric of interest may be of one-sided band accuracy (denoted by $\theta_h^{Asym}(S, b)$).

On the other hand, a naive (random) classifier would select class value j with probability p_j, where $\{p_1, p_2, ..., p_Q\}$ is the empirical distribution, that is the probabilities are assigned according to the observed proportions in the data. The expected confusion matrix Σ^R for a random classifier would therefore be defined as $\sigma_{ij} = p_i p_j$. An illustration of band accuracy of a model versus a naive classifier is given in figure 1. A similar definition is also given in [4].

An average weighted band accuracy metric for a graded multiclass classifier h on a dataset S can be defined as:

$$\psi_h^{Sym}(S) = \frac{\sum_{b=0}^{Q-1} w_b(\theta_h^{Sym}(S, b) - \theta_R^{Sym}(S, b))}{Q \sum_{b=1}^{Q-1} w_b} \tag{2}$$

where $\theta_R^{Sym}(S, b)$ is the band accuracy associated with the naive classifier and w_b can be any non-increasing series of weights that reflects the relative importance of class divergence. Additionally, the quantity $\psi_h^{Sym}(S)$ can be normalized to lie between 0 and 1 by assuming the maximum value to be the output of a perfect classifier (i.e., $\sigma_{ij} = 0$ where $i \neq j$). The definition of $\psi_h^{Sym}(S)$ may also be extended to the asymmetric band case appropriately.

Given the metric described above, the choice of the best model is determined by the average weighted symmetric (or asymmetric) band accuracy $\psi_h(S)$.

6 Regression

Consider the problem where a decision maker wishes to target a subset of customers whose profit potential (given response) is satisfactorily high to warrant the marketing

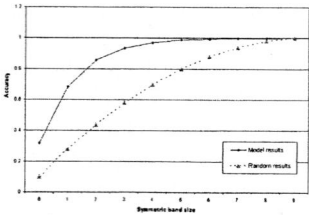

Fig. 1. Illustration: Symmetric band accuracy

effort in a cross-sell campaign. In many cases, the decision is made not on individual customers, but on groups of customers.

For instance, the customer base is divided into quantiles based on the predicted profit score, and a marketing action is targeted at the top 70 percent. This may now be viewed as a two-class problem similar to the response propensity problem addressed in Section 3. Also, if the set of observed values in a sample S are arranged into a set of Q quantiles and the set of predicted values for these customers are also arranged into another set of Q quantiles, one may now construct a confusion matrix Σ where each element represents the percentage of customers who were originally in the ith quantile and were predicted to be in the jth quantile. The problem now becomes analogous to the one discussed in Section 5.

In both cases above, the regression output is transformed to a categorical output before the performance of the model is evaluated. Metrics that preserve the real values have not been dealt with in this paper.

7 Conclusions and Further Work

In this paper, we have suggested various metrics and model selection rules for a cross-section of classification problems in consumer finance. Choosing the right model is in the context of the decision system and all the other models being used. The choice of the right model in this problem setting needs further study. Models that output a distribution (eg. Bayesian Belief Networks) have been dealt with; however, their output has been reduced to a class label based on the mode of the distribution. Metrics that preserve the distribution characteristics while evaluating the model need further study.

References

1. Dietterich, T.G., Bakiri, G.: Solving multiclass learning problems via error-correcting output codes. Journal of Artificial Intelligence Research (1995)
2. Hsu, C., Lin, C.: A comparison of methods for multi-class support vector machines. Technical report, National Taiwan University (2001)
3. Kotsiantis, S.B., Pintelas, P.E.: A cost sensitive technique for ordinal classification problems. In: SETN. (2004) 220–229
4. Van Gestel, T., Baesens, B., Van Dijcke, P.: A support vector machine approach to credit scoring. Bank en Financiewezen 2 (2003)

Microcontroller Based Temperature Control of Oven Using Different Kinds of Autotuning PID Methods

Emine Doğru Bolat, Kadir Erkan, and Seda Postalcıoğlu

Kocaeli University Technical Education Faculty Department of Electronics
and Computer, Kocaeli, Turkey
ebolat@ieee.org, erkan@kou.edu.tr, postalcioglu@ieee.org

Abstract. This paper presents microcontroller based autotuning proportional-integral-derivative (PID) controller for an oven designed as an experiment set. Different types of autotuning PID controller methods have been examined. Proportional, P, control method has been applied first. Relay and integral square time error criterion (ISTE) tuning methods are used as autotuning PID method. For relay tuning method, proportional (P), proportional-integral (PI) and proportional-integral-derivative (PID) and for ISTE disturbance (PI, PID) have been used. These methods have been applied to the experiment set which is an FODPT (First Order Plus Dead Time) system. To be able to control this system a digital signal processing card is designed. PIC17C44 is used as microcontroller and ADS1212 is used as A/D converter. And the results are discussed to define which controller is the best for this experiment set.

Key words: Adaptive control, autotuning PID methods, temperature control.

1 Introduction

PID controllers are standard tools for the industrial applications, because they are simple and robust. But it is difficult to define the PID controller parameters properly. So practicability of the controller is reduced and loss of time occurs. Most of the classical industrial controllers have been provided with special procedures to automate the adjustment of their parameters (tuning and self-tuning) [1,2] and auto-tuning methods are developed. It has autotuning button and by means of this button PID parameters are computed and transferred to the controller. Thus PID controller has been faster, more practical and reliable. Auto-tuning methods used in this study are relay and ISTE method. These methods enable the control, practical and accurately. At the same time, for sensivity and reliability of the controller digital controller has been used. To implement the temperature control, a digital signal processing card and an oven are designed for temperature control. Experiments have been realized on this oven.

2 Proportional (P) Control

Proportional band is an interval where energy can be adjusted from 0% to 100% and proportional control can be applied. In general proportional band is described as percentage of the system's scale value and it is distributed equally around the set value. When the proportional band is got narrow, the gain is increased. Proportional band is presented in Fig. 1. Gain is computed as equation (Gain=100% / proportional band % (1).

Error signal has been acceptable in proportional control. There is always a difference between the system output and the reference value. This is the typical characteristic of proportional controller.

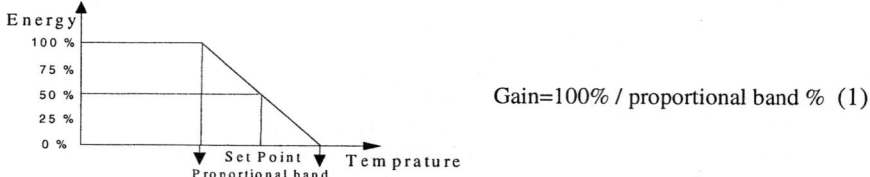

Gain=100% / proportional band % (1)

Fig. 1. Proportional band

3   Relay Tuning Method

The relay method is attractive since a control-relevant excitation signal is generated automatically, and many tuning rules exist to utilize the resulting process information [3]. The relay feedback is an efficient method of obtaining the critical point of a process with the critical point made available. PID types of controllers are easily tuned using classic Ziegler-Nichols rules and variants [4]. The arrangement for a relay feedback autotuner is shown in Fig. 2 a) [5]. The input and output signals obtained when the command signal r is zero are shown in Fig. 2 b).

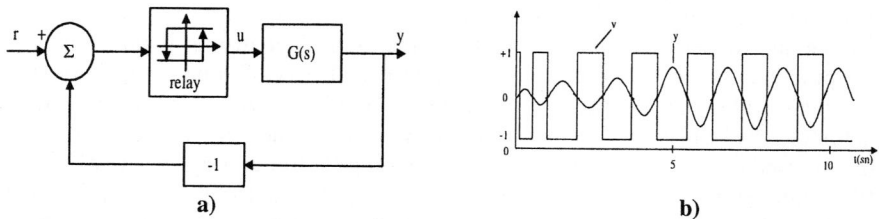

Fig. 2. a) Block diagram of the relay autotuner b) Linear system with relay control

The Fig. 2 b) shows that a limit cycle oscillation is established quite rapidly. The output is approximately sinusoidal, which means that the process attenuates the higher harmonics effectively. Let the amplitude of the square wave be d, then the fundamental component has the amplitude $4d/\pi$. The process output is a sinusoidal with frequency ω_u and amplitude is shown as in equation (2)

$$a = \frac{4d}{\pi}|G(i\omega_u)| \qquad (2)$$

To have an oscillation, the output must also go through zero when the relay switches. We can conclude that the frequency ω_u must be such that the process has a phase lag of 180°. The conditions for oscillation are shown in equation (3).

$$\arg G(i\omega_u) = -\pi \text{ and } |G(i\omega_u)| = \frac{a\pi}{4d} = \frac{1}{K_c} \tag{3}$$

Table 1. PID parameters used in relay tuning method

Controller	K_P	K_I	K_D
P	$0.5\, K_C$	-	-
PI	$0.4\, K_C$	$1.25/T_C$	-
PID	$0.6\, K_C$	$2/T_C$	$0.12 T_C$

K_c can be regarded as the equivalent gain of the relay for transmission of sinusoidal signals with amplitude a. This parameter is called ultimate gain. It is the gain that brings a system with transfer function G(s) to the stability boundary under pure proportional control. The period $T_c = 2\pi/\omega_u$ is similarly called the ultimate period. The controller settings are given in Table 1. These parameters give a closed loop system with quite low damping. Systems with better damping can be obtained by slight modifications of numbers in the table. When a stable limit cycle is established, the PID parameters are computed, and the PID controller is then connected to the process. [6].

4 ISTE Tuning Method

In recent years there has been much interest in the relay autotuning technique for determining the parameters of a PID controller. In this method, the PID controller is replaced by a relay so that the loop has a limit cycle. Tuning parameters of the controller are then calculated from measured values of the amplitude and frequency of the limit cycle. Here, we therefore define the formulate for the FOPDT (First Order Plus Dead Time) plant models which enable the optimum ISTE tuning parameters to be found from these measurements of the oscillation frequency and amplitude. The equations used in this method have been developed based on known critical point data, namely the critical frequency and critical gain. When performing relay autotuning, the approximate critical point data is found from the limit cycle data, namely the oscillation frequency ω_0 and the peak amplitude a_0, which is used to calculate K_o, the approximate critical gain. K_o is found using the describing function for the relay, that is $K_o = 4d/a_o\pi$. For the FOPDT plant, the exact value of ω_c and K_o can be calculated using the Tsypkin method so that their relationship to ω_c and K_c can be found. It is therefore possible to obtain the above formulate in terms of the values of ω_o and K_o which will be found from the limit cycle measurement when using relay autotuning. The normalized gain is calculated by $\kappa_0 = K^*K_0$ [7]. These tuning equations used for disturbance criterion are given in Table 2 and Table 3 in the reference numbered as 7.

5 Experimental Study

Fig. 3 a) and b) present the control system card and block diagram of the control system respectively. In Fig. 3, 1: power supply, 2: RS-232 connection, 3: DSP unit, 4: power block. In Fig. 3 a), digital signal processing unit is designed and a power unit including an IGBT and an IGBT driver is produced. This power unit uses PWM (Pulse Width Modulation) technique. Since the controller is wanted to be flexible, it is achieved by using a computer. The digital signal processing unit gets the temperature data from the experiment set by using a thermocouple temperature sensor and makes the data appropriate for the computer. Then, this unit transmits the data to the computer by using RS-232 protocol. The computer produces control data by using the control method. Afterwards, this control data is transmitted to the digital signal processing unit again. This unit generates a PWM signal from the control data. And,

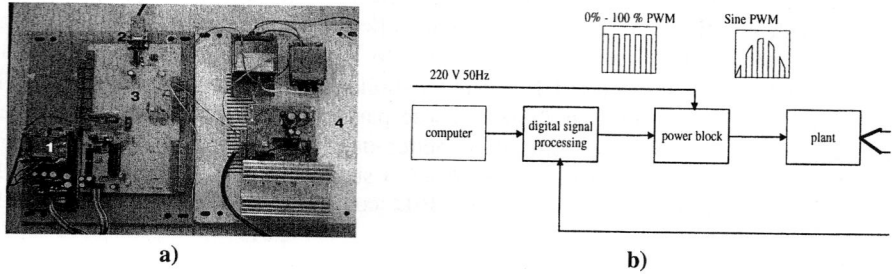

Fig. 3. a) Control system card **b)** The block diagram of the control system

this PWM signal is applied to the power unit. Finally, the PWM signal determines the energy level of the oven. So, the control is achieved by applying necessary amount of energy to the oven. The power unit includes M57959AL Mitsubishi IGBT driver and IXSH45N120 IGBT power transistor. The block diagram of the whole control system is shown in Fig. 3 b).

6 The Experimental Results

In this section, the PID parameters have been calculated for different autotuning methods which are proportional (P) method, relay method (P, PI, PID) and ISTE disturbance (PI, PID) method. So the system responses to these methods are given. For all methods set point is accepted as 100 ^{0}C. First disturbance has been applied at 1300 second that two holes on the top of the oven were open and fan was on during 2

Table 2. Calculated PID parameters of all control methods used in the experiments

	Relay P	Relay PI	Relay PID	ISTE Dist. PI	ISTE Dist. PID
K_p	27.322	21.858	32.786	17.876	21.865
K_I	-	0.021	0.0033	0.007	0.0078
K_D	-	-	71.976	-	95.968

minutes. Second disturbance has been applied at 3280. second that holes were close and fan was on during 6 minutes. Controller parameters for relay (P, PI, PID) and ISTE disturbance (PI, PID) method are presented in Table 2.

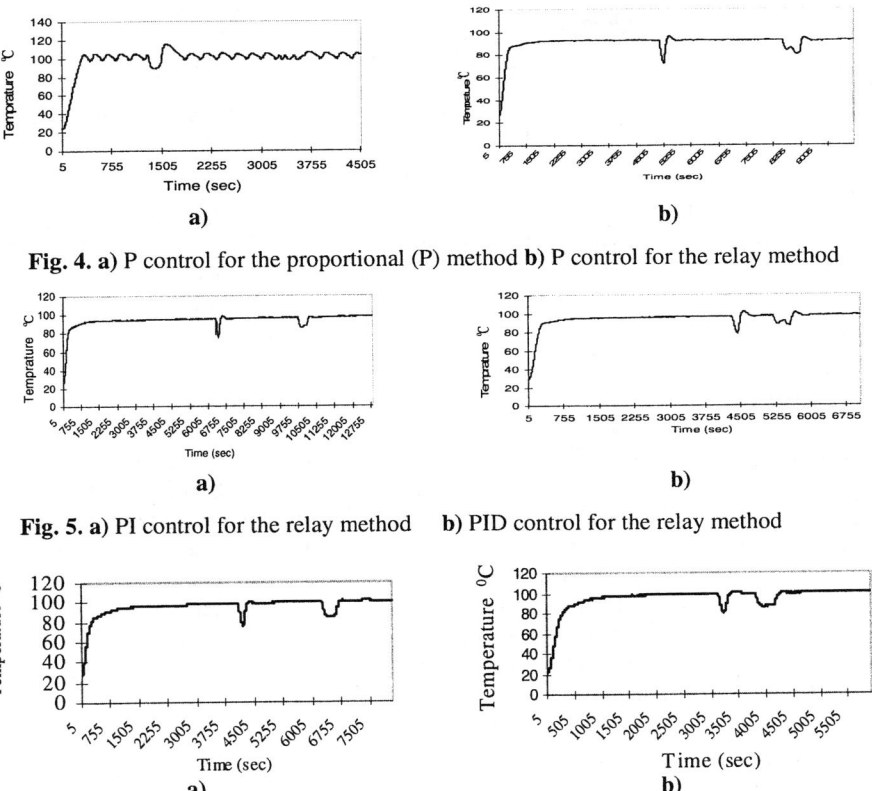

Fig. 4. a) P control for the proportional (P) method b) P control for the relay method

Fig. 5. a) PI control for the relay method   b) PID control for the relay method

Fig. 6. a) PI control for the ISTE disturbance criterion. b) PID control for the ISTE disturbance criterion

For proportional control, proportional band is accepted as 2%. P control for the proportional (P) method is presented in Fig. 4 a). As shown in Fig. 4 a) system has continuous oscillation as 7°C and overshoot as 5°C. P control for the relay method is shown in Fig. 4 b). PI and PID control for the relay method is shown in   Fig. 5 a) and b). After second disturbance, steady state error decreases. Because after distortion, error value increases so effect of the integral increases. System responses for PI and PID control by the ISTE disturbance criterion are presented in Fig. 6 a) and b). Fig. 7 presents that oscillation of system for relay and ISTE tuning method.

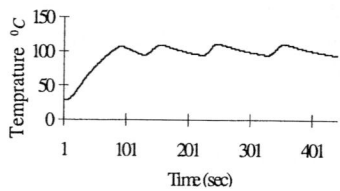

Fig. 7. System oscillation for Relay and ISTE methods

Table 3. The comparison of the applied methods ISE : (the integral of the square of the error)

Controller	Settl. time (s)	ISE	Settl. Temp. (°C)
Relay P	4395	186225.7	92.68
Relay PI.	6350	171729	95.43
Relay PID	4315	139405.8	96.71
ISTE Dist. PI	4095	151147.2	98.47
ISTE Dist. PID	2105	18266.3	99.6

The system responses for applied methods are given in Table 3. In this table, it can easily be understood that the best method for the experiment set used in this study is the PID control for the ISTE disturbance criterion. Because ISTE disturbance PID has got a system response with the smallest settling time, nearest settling temperature and the smallest ISE.

7 Conclusion

This paper presents microcontroller based temperature control of oven using autotuning PID methods. Proportional P, relay (P, PI, PID) and ISTE disturbance (PI, PID) methods have been used for the oven designed as experiment set. Two disturbances have been applied to the oven and system responses have been examined. As a result, for proportional P method, the system has continuous oscillation around the set value and for relay PI and PID method; the system has continuous steady state error. So the ISTE disturbance PID method is the best between these methods. But the most important thing is the system structure and if P method is enough for the system control there is no need to use the other control methods.

References

[1] Reznik,L., Ghanayem, O., Bourmistrov, A. :2000, "PID plus fuzzy controller structures as a design base for industrial applications " Engineering Applications of Artificial Intelligence 13 pp. 419-430.
[2] Tan, K., K., Lee, T., H., Jiang, X. : 2001 "On-line relay identification, assessment and tuning of PID controller", Journal of Process control 11 pp. 483-496.
[3] McCormack, A., S., Godfrey, K., R. : 1998, "Rule-Based Autotuning Based on Frequency Domain Identification " IEEE transactions on control systems technology, vol. 6, no. 1.
[4] Halevi, Y., Palmor, Z., J., Efrati, T. : 1997, "Automatic tuning of decentralized PID controllers for MIMO processes" *J. Proc. Cont.* Vol. 7, No. 2, pp. 119-128.
[5] Tan, K.,K., Wang, Q., G., Lee, T., H., Gan, C., H. :1998, "Automatic tuning of gain-scheduled control for asymmetrical process" Control engineering practice 6 pp. 1353-1363.
[6] Åström, K., J., Wittenmark, B. :1995 "Adaptive Control" Addison-Wesley Publishing Company Inc., ISBN 0-201-55866-1 USA.
[7] Zhuang, M., Atherton, D., P. :1993, "Automatic Tuning of Optimum PID Controllers", IEE Proceedings, Vol. 140, No. 3.

Aggregation of Preferences Based on FSAM

Dae-Young Choi

Dept.of MIS, Yuhan College, Koean-Dong, Sosa-Ku, Puchon,
Kyoungki-Do, 422-749, Korea
dychoi@yuhan.ac.kr

Abstract. We propose a new ε-ASA (Aggregation based on Situation Assessment) algorithm based on the fuzzy situation assessment model (FSAM) to reflect a situation in the process of aggregation. The proposed aggregation algorithm makes an adaptive aggregation result between min and max depending on the value of parameter representing a degree of situation. It is a further step toward situation-based aggregation.

1 Introduction

In a fuzzy environment, existing aggregation operators are, in general, t-norm, t-conorm, mean operators, Ordered Weighted Averaging Operators (OWA) [2] and γ-operator[4]. These aggregation operators have some problems in that they do not properly reflect the situation in the aggregation process. It is tendency that the aggregation of human beings depends on the situation. However, there has been little effort to reflect the situation in the aggregation process. In order to solve these problems we suggest a fuzzy situation assessment model (FSAM) to reflect the situation in the aggregation process. This model generates the parameter representing a degree of situation. We propose a new ε-ASA algorithm based on FSAM to reflect the situation in the aggregation process.

2 Fuzzy Situation Assessment Model (FSAM)

In the FSAM, we assume that a situation has n dimensions. The n dimensions have their own situation factors, respectively. In the FSAM, the values of situation factors are evaluated by decision makers. We utilize fuzzy expected value (FEV) [1] to obtain the representative value of these situation factors of each dimension.

2.1 Fuzzy Expected Value (FEV)

Let χ_A be a B-measurable function such that $\chi_A \in [0,1]$. The FEV of χ_A over the set A, with respect to the fuzzy measure $\mu(\bullet)$ is defined as follows :

$$FEV(\chi_A)=\sup\{\min[t,\mu(\xi_t)]\} \qquad (1)$$

where $\xi_t=\{x|\chi_A(x)\geq t\}$, $t\in[0,1]$, $\mu\{x|\chi_A(x)\geq t\}=f_A(t)$ is a function of the threshold t.
Many explanations and interpretations for FEV are described in [1].

2.2 Determination of Parameter

If there is a n dimensional situation then the n FEVs (i.e., $X_1, X_2, \cdots, X_n$) are obtained. The FSAM generates the parameter, p, using Eq. (2). In this paper, the output of the FSAM, p, will be input to the ε-ASA algorithm as an indicator of current degree of a situation. The parameter, p, is determined as follows :

$$p = [((\sum_{i=1}^{n} X_i)/n) \times 2 - 1] \times k \qquad (2)$$

where $k = (1/\varepsilon)$ (see the ε-ASA algorithm in Appendix).

These FEVs (i.e., $X_1, X_2, \cdots, X_n$) have values between 0 and 1 by the definition of FEV. Hence, $(\sum_{i=1}^{n} X_i)/n$ becomes the value between 0 and 1. Thus, the parameter p representing the current degree of a situation is located between -k and k.

Remark 1. The ε divides the interval [-1, 1] into [-kε (= -1), $\cdots$, -2ε, -ε, **0**, ε, 2ε, $\cdots$, kε (=1)], where $0 < \varepsilon \leq 1$, as in Fig. 2 in Appendix.

Definition 1. Based on Eq. (2), Remark 1, a situation can be parameterized with (2k+1) levels depending on a degree of situation.
   Case 1 : Optimistic situation occurs when 0<p≤ k. Let op = p. (k levels occur)
   Case 2 : Moderate situation occurs when p = 0. (1 level occurs)
   Case 3 : Pessimistic situation occurs when -k≤p<0. Let pp = |p|. (k levels occur)

3 Aggregation of Preferences Based on FSAM

The ε-ASA algorithm uses the output of FSAM as an indicator of situation. The ε-ASA algorithm can be used to aggregate linguistic variables representing human preferences. Let the data aggregated be E^i (i=1, 2, $\cdots$, n) and these E^i are descriptions of linguistic variables [3]. These E^i are characterized by membership functions which associate with each point in a real number in the interval [0, 1]. We assume that min is the value of the most pessimistic data and max is the value of the most optimistic data. Let $E^1 = v_1$, $E^2 = v_2$, $\cdots$, $E^n = v_n$. Based on Eq. (2), Definition 1, the ε-ASA is executed by Algorithm 1 in Appendix :

Remark 2. We show the one case of ELSE in the ε-ASA algorithm : (i-1) < op < i, where $1 \leq i \leq k$ (see Fig. 1 in Appendix). In this case, a situation at op is located between (i-1)ε and iε, (see Fig. 2). Similarly, the other case, i.e., (i-1) < pp < i, can be also explained.

Example 1. We assume that 5 group members express their opinions (preferences) in a group discussion. We consider the case when $v_1 = 0.68$, $v_2 = 0.41$, $v_3 = 0.19$, $v_4 =$

0.57 and $v_5 = 0.42$. That is, let the data aggregated be {0.68, 0.41, 0.19, 0.57, 0.42}. As aforementioned, the output of the FSAM, p, is input to the ε-ASA algorithm as an indicator of the current degree of a situation. We note that Remark 2 cases are omitted in Fig. 2. If we use the ε-ASA algorithm with $\varepsilon = 10^{-2}$, then $k = 10^2$ (see Eq. (2)). In this case, *aggregation_result* in the ε-ASA algorithm is obtained according to the value of parameter, p, as follows : When p is -k, $Agg_{-k\varepsilon}(v_1, v_2, \cdots, v_n) = Agg_{-k\varepsilon}(0.68, 0.41, 0.19, 0.57, 0.42) = M - k[(M - min)/k] = 0.19$ (min). Similarly, when p is -1, $Agg_{-\varepsilon}(v_1, v_2, \cdots, v_n) = 0.4474$. When p is 0, $Agg_0(v_1, v_2, \cdots, v_n) = 0.45$. When p is 1, $Agg_\varepsilon(v_1, v_2, \cdots, v_n) = 0.4523$. When p is k, $Agg_{k\varepsilon}(v_1, v_2, \cdots, v_n) = 0.68$ (max).

4 Conclusions

In Example 1, if we use a smaller ε value, then we can obtain a more sophisticated aggregation result. The ε-ASA algorithm shows the following properties : First, the ε-ASA algorithm makes an adaptive aggregation result between min and max depending on the value of the parameter representing a degree of situation as in Fig. 2. Second, the ε-ASA algorithm makes the stepwise aggregation with directionality according to a degree of situation as in Fig. 2. Third, we note that the aggregation of subjective categories in the framework of human decision almost always shows some degree of compensation [4]. The ε-ASA algorithm makes some degree of compensation between min and max according to a degree of situation. It is a further step toward situation-based aggregation.

Acknowledgement

This work was supported by Korea Research Foundation Grant (KRF-2004-013-D00040).

References

[1] Friedman, M., Henne, M., Kandel, A.: Most Typical Values for Fuzzy Sets, Fuzzy Sets and Systems 87(1997) 27-37.
[2] Yager, R. R.: Families of OWA Operators, Fuzzy Sets and Systems 59(1993)125-148.
[3] Zadeh, L. A.: The Concept of a Linguistic Variable and Its Application to Approximate Reasoning, Information Sciences 8(1975) 199-249.
[4] Zimmermann, H. J., Zysno, P.: Latent Connectives in Human Decision Making, Fuzzy Sets and Systems 4(1980) 37-51.

Appendix

Algorithm 1 : ε-ASA.
/* Let k=(1/ε), where 0<ε≤1, and $M=(v_1+v_2+\cdots+v_n)/n$, i.e., M is an arithmetic mean.*/
Case 1 : When a situation is optimistic, i.e., 0 < p ≤ k.

$aggregation\_value = (v_1+v_2+\cdots+v_n)/n$;
 i = 1; /* In this case, a situation is ε (see Fig. 2) */
 WHILE (i < op) DO /* op is obtained by Definition 1 */
  $aggregation\_value = aggregation\_value + [(max - M)/k]$; i = i + 1 END
IF (i = op) THEN [$aggregation\_result = aggregation\_value + [(max - M)/k]$];
 ELSE /* In case of (i-1)<op< i, i.e., a situation at op is located between (i-1)ε and iε */
  [ε' = op - (i-1) ; $aggregation\_result = aggregation\_value + (ε'/ε)[(max - M)/k]$]
Case 2 : When a situation is moderate, i.e., p = 0.
 $aggregation\_result = M$;
Case 3 : When a situation is pessimistic, i.e., -k ≤ p < 0.
 $aggregation\_value = (v_1+v_2+\cdots+v_n)/n$;
 i = 1; /* In this case, a situation is -ε (see Fig. 2) */
 WHILE (i < pp) DO /* pp is obtained by Definition 1 */
  $aggregation\_value = aggregation\_value - [(M - min)/k]$; i = i + 1 END
IF (i = pp) THEN [$aggregation\_result = aggregation\_value - [(M - min)/k]$]
 ELSE /* In case of (i-1)<pp< i, i.e., a situation at pp is located between (i-1)ε and -iε */
  [ε' = pp - (i-1) ; $aggregation\_result = aggregation\_value - (ε'/ε)[(M - min)/k]$]

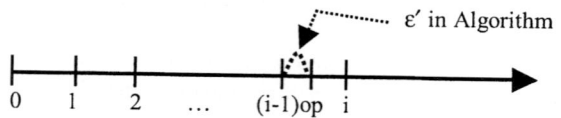

Fig. 1. In case of (i-1) < op < i

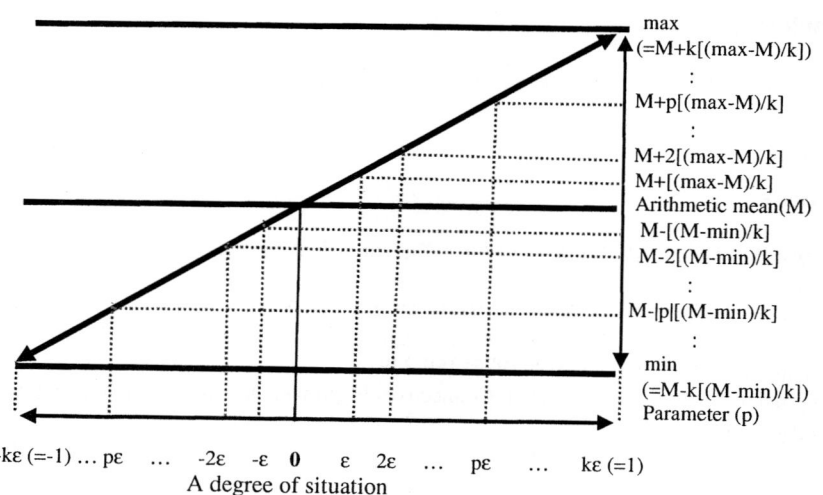

Fig. 2. Aggregation results of the ε-ASA algorithm

A Novel Particle Swarm Optimization for Constrained Optimization Problems

Xiangyong Li, Peng Tian, and Min Kong

Antai School of Management, Shanghai Jiaotong University, Shanghai 200052, China
lixiangyong@163.com, {ptian, kongmin}@sjtu.edu.cn

Abstract. This paper proposes a novel particle swarm optimization (PSO) for solving constrained optimization problems. Based upon the acceptable assumption that any feasible solution is better than any infeasible solution, a new mechanism for constraints handling is incorporated in the standard particle swarm optimization. In addition to the mechanism of constraints handling, a mutation strategy to increase population diversity is added to the proposed algorithm to improve convergence. Experimental results compared with genetic algorithm and a standard PSO show that the proposed algorithm is a desirable and competitive algorithm for solving constrained optimization problems.

1 Introduction

In real world, many application problems can be transformed into constrained optimization problems (COP) such as engineering design etc. In general, a COP can be represented as a linear or nonlinear programming problem with a set of linear or nonlinear constraints. Suppose the set $S \subseteq R^n$ denotes the search space and the set F represents the feasible region of search space S. A constrained minimization problem can be defined as follows:

$$minimize \quad f(X) \tag{1}$$

subject to a set of linear or nonlinear constraints:

$$g_i(X) \leq 0 \quad for \quad i = 1, \ldots, q \tag{2}$$

$$h_i(X) = 0 \quad for \quad i = q+1, \ldots, m \tag{3}$$

where $X = \{x_1, \cdots, x_n\} \in F \subseteq S \subseteq R^n$ is the decision variable. The decision variable X is a n-dimensional vector, each component of which is bounded in an interval $[a_i, b_i]$, $i = 1, \ldots, n$. f is the objective function. It is a common practice to replace an equality constraint $h_i(x) = 0$ by two inequalities $h_i(x) \leq \delta$, and $h_i(x) \geq -\delta$ (δ is a small positive constant) [1]. At any point $X \in F$, the constraint $g_i(x)$ satisfying $g_i(x) = 0$ is called active constraint at X.

The existing algorithms for solving COP can be divided into two categories: deterministic algorithm and metaheuristic. The deterministic algorithm includes

Feasible Direction method, and Gradient Projection method etc. For the deterministic algorithm, the objective function must be differentiable or continuous, or the reasonable region must be convex. Conversely, the metaheuristic needn't the differentiability and continuity of objective functions. Recently, evolutionary algorithm has received considerable attention with respect to its potential as an alternative algorithm for COP. Some algorithms and their variants such as genetic algorithm(GA)etc. have been established to deal with COP[1,2,3]. As a new metaheuristic, particle swarm optimization (PSO) has proved to be a competitive algorithm for unconstrained optimization problems since its introduction. Recently, some work has been done to solve COP by PSO[4,5].

In this paper, a novel PSO combined with a constraints handling mechanism and mutation strategy is proposed to solve COP. The rest of this paper is organized as follows. Section 2 describes the standard PSO briefly. In section 3, the novel PSO for COP is proposed. The experimental results are reported in section 4. Section 5 concludes this paper and discusses some ideas for future research.

2 Standard Particle Swarm Optimization

PSO is a swarm intelligence algorithm inspired by the emergent behavior in socially organized colonies. Since its introduction, PSO has gained rapid popularity as a feasible algorithm for solution of continuous functions. In PSO, the individual manipulate its trajectory toward the best regions of its own previous best performance and toward the locations found by its neighbors dynamically.

In PSO, a population of particles are cooperated to solve the optimization problem by the mutual interaction of individuals. The position of i-th particle is represented as a n-dimensional vector in problem space $x_i = (x_{i1}, x_{i2}, \ldots, x_{in})$, and its fitness is evaluated on the fitness function. The velocity of i-th particle $v_i = (v_{i1}, v_{i2}, \ldots, v_{in})$ is defined as the change of position. The velocity and position of i-th particle at time t is updated according to the following equations:

$$v_i(t+1) = w \cdot v_i(t) + c_1 \cdot rand1 \cdot (p_i - x_i(t)) + c_2 \cdot rand2 \cdot (p_g - x_i(t)) \quad (4)$$

$$x_i(t+1) = x_i(t) + v_i(t+1) \quad (5)$$

where $p_i = (p_{i1}, \ldots, p_{in})$ is the best position found by i-th particle so far, $i = 1, 2, \ldots, N$ (population size); p_g represents the best-found position in the neighborhood of i-th particle; t is iteration counter; c_1 and c_2 are acceleration coefficients, which are the weight of the velocity toward global and local best; $rand1$ and $rand2$ are the random numbers in $[0, 1]$; w denotes the inertia weight.

3 Proposed Particle Swarm Optimization for COP

3.1 The Method of Constraints Handling

Inspired by the basic idea in GA for solving COP[2], we assume that a feasible solution is better than every infeasible solution. Under this assumption, all particles violating constraints will be assigned a bigger fitness value than the ones satisfying constraints(for minimization problems). In the following sections, the particles satisfying all constraints are called feasible particles, otherwise infeasible ones. Except for the above assumption, all infeasible particles at each generation also have bigger fitness than the worst feasible one found over the generations so far. Here, we introduce a variable $Worst\_fit$ to keep track of the fitness value of the worst feasible particle. In the proposed PSO for COP (PSO_CO), all the particles are evaluated by the following objective function:

$$F(X) = \begin{cases} f(X) & \text{if } X \in F \\ f(X) + r\sum_{i=1}^{m} f_i(X) + \varphi(X,t) & \text{if } X \in S - F \end{cases} \quad (6)$$

where, $f_i(X)$ denotes the constraint violation measure of infeasible particles for i-th constraint. In general, it is defined as follows:

$$f_i(X) = \begin{cases} \max\{0, g_i(X)\} & \text{if } 1 \leq i \leq q \\ |h_i(x)| & \text{if } q+1 \leq i \leq m \end{cases} \quad (7)$$

$$\varphi(X,t) = Worst\_fit(t) - \min_{X \in S-F}\{f(X) + r\sum_{i=1}^{m} f_i(X)\} \quad (8)$$

$$Worst\_fit(t) = \max\{Worst\_fit(t-1), \max_{X \in F}\{f(X)\}\} \quad (9)$$

where $f(X)$, $g_i(x)$, and $h_i(x)$ are defined in equation (1)-(3). $\varphi(X,t)$ represents an additional heuristic value for infeasible particles at time t. In other words, an infeasible particle will be assigned with an additional penalty to guarantee that its fitness in current generation is worse than the $Worst\_fit$. r is penalty coefficient. $Worst\_fit(t)$ keeps record of the fitness value of the worst feasible particle until the t-th generation. It is updated dynamically according to equation (9). The method of constraints handling in[2] requires at least one feasible individual to be in the initial population or feasible initial population. Unlike the mechanism in[2], the constraint handling method in the proposed algorithm doesn't require any initial feasible particle in the initial particle swarm. With the variable $Worst\_fit(t)$, the proposed PSO_CO can make all the feasible particles be better than the infeasible ones over the generations. While the initialization of a particle swarm, $Worst\_fit(t)$ is set to a random larger number and updated dynamically over the generations.

3.2 Particle Swarm Optimization with Mutation Strategy

Lack of population diversity, particularly during the latter stage of the optimization, is known as the dominant factor for the convergence of particles to local optimum prematurely. There are many measurement standards and methods of population diversity. The diversity metric used in this paper is as follows:

$$\psi = \frac{1}{N \cdot L} \sum_{i=1}^{N} \sqrt{\sum_{j=1}^{n}(p_{ij} - \overline{p}_j)^2} \quad (10)$$

where ψ is swarm diversity; N is swarm size; L is the length of the longest diagonal in search space; n is the dimensionality of COP; p_{ij} is the value of the j-th component of the i-th particle and $\overline{p}_j$ denotes the average value of the j-th component of all the particles. In order to improve the convergence, a mutation strategy is incorporated in the proposed algorithm on the control of population diversity. When ψ decreases below a predefined threshold ψ_{low}, the algorithm triggers mutation strategy and expands the swarm with high population diversity. With the mutation strategy, a random perturbation is added to the j-th component for the i-th particle by a predefined mutation probability. During the mutation procedure, the j-dimensional position of the i-th particle x_{ij} will be reinitialized if $q < q_m$, otherwise remains invariable. In other words, the value of the j-th component of particle may be changed with a probability p_m.

4 Experiment and Results

Seven testing instances are chosen to investigate the performance of PSO_CO and PSO_COMS for COP[1]. The parameters of PSO_COMS are set as follows: the maximum allowed number of generation T_{max} is set to 3000 for T3 and 2000 for other instances; acceleration coefficients c_1 and c_2 are set to 2; inertia weight w is set to $0.5 + 0.5 \cdot rand$ for T7 and decrease from 1.2 to 0.1 linearly for other instances; the maximum velocity of particles V_{max} is set to 1 for T7, 15 for T3, and 10 for others; the penalty factor r is set to 10; In consideration of computation precision, a violation tolerance ε(a small positive constant) is set for all constraints. For example, for a constraint $g_i(x) \leq 0$, the constraint will be assumed to be violated, only if $g_i(x) > \varepsilon$. Otherwise, we think constraint is satisfied. From T1 to T7, ε is set to 1e-6,7e-5,7e-4,1e-5,7e-6,1e-6,1e-4 respectively.

The PSO_COMS is implemented for 50 runs for each problem. The results in terms of the worst(Worst), average(Avg.), best(Best), and standard deviation(Std.) of optimums are given in Table 1. In the second column of Table 1, the known optimums are given [1]. It is observed clearly that PSO_COMS performs well for all problems and the standard deviation of optimums is almost 0 for all problems except for T3, which can find the optimums of all problems. Table 2 reports comparison results of PSO_COMS, PSO_H[5] and GA[1] over 50 runs. The results show that three methods perform well for six testing problems except for T3. For T3, PSO_H and GA can not find the optimum. However PSO_COMS performs significantly well and a competitive result is observed. Further, PSO_COMS performs better than other algorithms on the average of the optimum, particularly for T3.

The effect of mutation strategy is investigated empirically. Table 3 compares the performance of PSO_COMS and PSO_CO in terms of solution quality and convergence speed. In this simulation, the same parameters above are used except that mutation probability is set to 0.1. It can be concluded that mutation strategy has improved solution quality and PSO_COMS converges significantly faster than PSO_CO for all testing problems. Further, the effect of mutation probability is investigated. The mutation probability is set to change from 0.1 to

Table 1. Summary of results of PSO_COMS on seven testing cases over 50 trials. In this case, the mutation probability is set to 0.1.

Function	Optimum	PSO_COMS			
		Worst	Best	Avg.	Std.
T1	-15	-15	-15	-15	0
T2	-30665.5	-30665.5	-30665.6	-30665.594	0.0189
T3	5126.4981	5178.696	5126.495	5129.298	8.9250
T4	-6961.8138	-6961.6443	-6961.8371	-6961.8143	0
T5	0.095825	0.095825	0.095825	0.095825	0
T6	680.63	680.9084	680.6300	680.6541	0.0517
T7	0.75	0.7499	0.7499	0.7499	0

Table 2. Comparison of performance of PSO_COMS, GA, and PSO_H. A " -" denotes that both GA and PSO_H can not find the optimum.

Function	Optimum	PSO_COMS		GA		PSO_H	
		Best	Avg.	Best	Avg.	Best	Avg.
T1	-15	-15	-15	-14.7864	-14.7082	-15.0	-15.0
T2	-30665.5	-30665.5	-30665.5	-30664.5	-30655.3	-30665.5	-30665.5
T3	5126.4981	5126.495	5129.298	-	-	-	-
T4	-6961.8	-6961.8371	-6961.8143	-6952.1	-6342.6	-6961.7	-6960.7
T5	0.095825	0.095825	0.095825	0.095825	0.089157	0.095825	0.095825
T6	680.63	680.6300	680.6541	680.91	681.16	680.657	680.876
T7	0.75	0.7499	0.7499	0.75	0.75	0.75	0.75

Table 3. Comparison of performance of PSO_COMS and PSO_CO. Std1. and Std2. denote the standard deviation of the optimums and the generation for convergence respectively. C.G. denotes the average of the convergence generation.

Function	PSO_CO				PSO_COMS			
	Avg	Std1.	C.G.	Std2.	Avg	Std1.	C.G.	Std2.
T1	-14.776	0.7710	1648.00	141.6148	-15	0	1662.46	161.1258
T2	-30665.594	-0.0189	1880.88	107.3259	-30665.5	0	764.35	34.11
T3	5129.06	8.8100	2955.4	133.3909	5127.4491	8.7232	2812.54	100.4143
T4	-6961.8143	0.0462	1964.55	41.9203	-6961.8138	0	1989.03	78.9903
T5	0.095825	0	1276.40	142.1174	0.095825	0	1358.25	290.1100
T6	680.666	0.0825	1877.44	251.1106	680.6541	0.0517	1970.75	0.72
T7	0.7499	0	1830.20	261.05	0.7499	0	1635	20.13

0.8 and PSO_COMS is implemented for 50 runs. Table 4 summarizes the results. A slight variation of the average optimum is observed with different mutation probabilities. From the results shown in Table 4, we can see that PSO_COMS is sensitive to mutation probability and it is a good choice to set mutation probability to a small value for all testing problems considered in this paper.

Table 4. The average and standard deviation(in bracket) of optimums over 50 trials for different mutation probabilities for PSO_COMS

Function	Average optimum solution and standard deviation(in bracket)					
	0.1	0.2	0.3	0.4	0.6	0.8
T1	-15 (0)	-14.880 (0.5938)	-14.860 (0.5718)	-14.780 (0.9749)	-14.593 (1.1329)	-14.276 (2.1576)
T2	-30665.594 (0.0189)	-30665.509 (0.0859)	-30665.394 (0.1530)	-30665.133 (0.2732)	-30664.209 (0.9728)	-30663.553 (1.1936)
T3	5127.4491 (8.7232)	5128.5504 (9.3714)	5128.6672 (8.8400)	5129.0641 (10.1246)	5129.4781 (9.8875)	5129.4866 (9.2648)
T4	-6961.814 (0.0462)	-6961.512 (0.2893)	-6959.253 (3.1514)	-6947.562 (10.5464)	-6901.498 (48.7567)	-6814.502 (77.5396)
T5	0.095825 (0)	0.095825 (0)	0.095825 (0)	0.095825 (0.0014)	0.095823 (0.0019)	0.095812 (0.0016)
T6	680.6541 (0.0517)	680.8787 (0.2699)	680.8940 (0.1426)	680.9871 (0.1660)	681.2973 (0.2999)	681.6857 0.3958
T7	0.7499 (0)	0.7502 (0.0283)	0.7515 (0.0081)	0.7507 (0.0044)	0.7514 (0.0096)	0.7512 (0.0040)

5 Conclusions

In this paper, a novel PSO for solving COP is proposed. Based on standard PSO, a new mechanism is introduced to handle constraints, and a mutation strategy is proposed to improve the convergence. The experimental results show the competitiveness of proposed algorithm when compared with GA and standard one. Future empirical analysis of other instances, especially for complex COP will need to be done. It is also important to investigate the effect of other parameters of PSO such as inertia weight on the performance of PSO_COMS.

References

1. S. Koziel and Z. Michalewicz. Evolutionary algorithm, homomorphous mapping, and constrained parameter optimization. *Evolutionary Computation*, 7(1):19, 1999.
2. D. Powell and M.M. Skolnick. Using genetic algorithms in engineering design optimization with non-linear constraints. In *Proceedings of the Fifth International Conference on Genetic Algorithms*, Los Altos, CA, 1993.
3. Z. Michalewicz. Evolutionary computation techniques for nonlinear programming problems. *International Transactions in Operational Research*, 1(2):240, 1994.
4. K. Parsopoulos. Particle swarm optimization method for constrained optimization problems. In P.Sincak, J.Vascak, V.Kvasnicka, and J.Pospicha, editors, *Intelligent Technologies-Theory and Applications: New Trends in Intelligent Technologies*, volume 76, pages 214–220. IOS Press, 2002.
5. X.Hu and R.Eberhart. Solving constrained nonlinear optimization problems with particle swarm optimization. In *Proceedings of the 6th World Multiconference on Systemics, Cybernetics and Informatics 2002*, volume 5, pages 884–889, Orlando, USA, 2002.

A Framework for Relational Link Discovery

Dan Luo[1], Chao Luo[2], and Chunzhi Zhang[3]

[1] Faculty of Information Technology, University of Technology Sydney, Australia
[2] Faculty of Software, Liaoning Technical University, China
[3] Beijing Vocational & Technical Institute of Industry, China

Abstract. Link discovery is an emerging research direction for extracting evidences and links from multiple data sources. This paper proposes a self-organizing framework for discovering links from multi-relational databases. It includes main functional modules for developing adaptive data transformers and representation specification, multi-relational feature construction, and self-organizing multi-relational correlation and link discovery algorithms.

1 Introduction

After the event of September 11, a series of studies have been undertaken on detecting interesting patterns of activities of those hijackers. It is discovered from multiple related databases that the pilots trained together and they only learned how to take off without landing. This actually is quite suspicious and unexplainable behavior. Unfortunately "we had the information but didn't put it together", so that we missed the plot detection in advance. To this end, DARPA has set up a new program called Evidence Extraction and Link Discovery (EELD) [1] aiming at the development of technologies and tools for automated discovery, extraction and linking of sparse evidences contained in large amounts of classified and unclassified data sources.

The above scenarios show that isolated evidences hidden across multiple sources may compensate to indicate a significant event or community. It is critical to develop techniques that allow us to identify/correlate these relevant evidences and links – about linkage between events, activities, people, organizations and places – hidden in the masses of distributed data via joining it together. This is what a newly emergent area in KDD called Link Mining [2] does. Obviously, this is significant in research since it is not an easy task. It brings about challenges to the traditional KDD knowledge base. On the other hand, it is very urgent and practical for real-world applications such as counter-terrorism, fraud detection, compliance program, social network analysis and community finding, asymmetric threats.

The link mining poses new challenges to classic KDD. Some main research tasks [3-8] include feature construction, evidence detection, link-based classification and clustering, link type and strength identification, duplication elimination, and so on. Link discovery is rooted in fields such as multi-relational data mining [8-10], record linkage, discrete mathematics, graph theory, social science, pattern analysis, link analysis and spatial databases, and is relevant to a wide range of research topics that have been developed in past decades. The current directions are on developing stochastic sampling algorithms in large-scale relational data, learning patterns from complex multi-relational data using inductive logic programming [11], developing supervised and unsupervised link discovery methods, and the like. Main nonfunctional research is on scalability, accuracy and efficiency of LM algorithms.

However, the current methods in this area have some major problems in aspects such as not based on real-world case study, focusing on flat relations and single data type rather than multiple-relation and mixed data types, the adaptive capability of algorithms hasn't been paid enough attention. This paper targets these significant problems. We develop a novel and practical self-organizing framework for discovering relational links in multi-relational data with mixed data types.

2 Self-organizing Framework for Link Discovery

This paper investigates data mining techniques for extracting valuable patterns linking together seemingly unrelated items. Three basic tasks consist of evidence extraction, link discovery and pattern learning. A collection of evidences needs to be extracted from multi-relational databases via developing evidence extraction techniques. These evidences are represented in first order ILP signifying entities and links indicating relationships and semantic information. In this evidence base, we need to discover unknown links and build up the set of connections. Fragments of evidence need to be connected into meaningful patterns via developing link discovery techniques. The third step is to learn new patterns through developing pattern learning techniques in order to identify previously unknown patterns of activities.

We build up a multi-layer self-organizing system discovering relational evidences and links in multiple data sources with varieties of data types as shown in Figure 1. The system is composed of three layers: data processor layer, model builder layer, and decision exporter layer. The main functionalities and working mechanism of the three-layer self-organizing system are as follows.

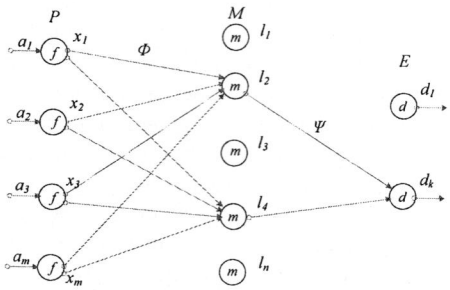

Fig. 1. Multi-layer self-organizing relational link discovery

- Data processor (P) layer: transforming and/or representing data attributes a_i through adaptive algorithms f in terms of data types to features $x_i = f(a_i)$ with values in formats satisfying the model building in an adaptive way; features x_i are presented to model builders as feature candidates.

- Model builder (*M*) layer: self-organizing models and rules *m* to discover potential evidences and links $l_k = m(x_i, \xi)$ in terms of constraints, data sources and types (as presented as ξ), and so on; the discovered evidence candidates l_k are fed into the decision exporter for further assessment.
- Decision exporter (*E*) layer: evidence candidates l_k are assessed and classified into negative or positive evidences d_k in terms of domain-specific factors such as utilities, beliefs and weights.

With respect to the multi-layer self-organizing link discovery framework, we investigate the following points.

(1). Adaptive data transformers and representation specification

An adaptive data transformation and representation specification *f* are developed to look after varieties of data types such as symbolic/categorical, numerical, code, aggregated data. The specification *f*: $x_i = f(a_i)$ may take different forms for those varying data types. We study ILP-based appropriate specification and algorithm *f* to convert/represent data adapting to the types of data feeds. The specific *f* organizes data transformation and representation for the inputs automatically. To this end, proper ILP-based specifications and conversion algorithms are studied to transform/represent mixed data types.

(2). Multi-relational feature construction

In multi-relational situations, it may make sense to use attributes of linked entities across multiple data sources. Further, links, link types (*n*-to-1, 1-to-1, 1-to-*n*), aggregations themselves have attributes which may also be used. We study possible features x_i via capturing local attributes, remote and global attributes distributed in multiple sources, links and semantic information, and categorizing entities based on the categories and other properties of other entities to which it is related. Algorithms and mechanisms are studied for constructing relational features *x*.

x::= *x*(*attributes, keys, links, link types, aggregations, constraints, schemas, ...*)

(3). Self-organizing multi-relational correlation and link discovery algorithms

Self-organizing algorithms *m*: $l_k = m(x_i, \xi)$ are investigated for the multi-layer self-organizing framework, which discover relational evidences and links across multi-relational data. A key issue investigated is how this framework can support adaptive transformation/representation of mixed data feeds, and self-organizing models and rules *m* in terms of feature construction, join paths, nodes, propagation strategies, relationships, metrics and constraints.

A dynamic conceptual structure and model/rule *m* are determined by factors (x_i, ξ), which may include features, keys, paths, nodes, propagation strategies, relationships, metrics and constraints, and so on. Models and rules *m* are dynamically arranged by a self-organizing algorithm in terms of the scenarios and constraints of input multi-relational data and domain-specific knowledge.

In addition, experiments may be conducted to develop suitable transfer functions (Φ) and weight functions (Ψ) between layers for considering domain-specific constraints, requirements, knowledge and weights. Proper multiplier mechanism is researched to build up model output $l_k = x_i \Phi m$ in terms of features x_i, transfer function

Φ, and model m. Furthermore, synthetic mechanism is developed for making decisions in terms of model output l_k, weight distribution Ψ, and decision-making function d.

$l_k = x_i \Phi m$
$d_k = l_k \Psi d$

3 Conclusions and Future Work

This paper introduces a novel system for discovering links and evidences in multi-relational data with mixed data types. It includes a self-organizing framework for discovering relational evidences and links in mixed data types. Appropriate specifications are developed to adaptively transform/represent data with varieties of data types. Inductive logic programming (ILP) based models and rules are studied for identifying, correlating evidences and links across multi-relational sources in a self-organizing manner. Proper metrics and fitness functions are researched to indicate and evaluate the decision-making of discovered evidences and links.

Our further work is performing on enhancing the above framework in terms of efficiency and scalability in a scenario with large distributed databases.

References

[1] T. Senator. DARPA: Evidence Extraction and Link Discovery Program, Speech at DARPATech 2002.
[2] L. Getoor. Link Mining : A New Data Mining Challenge. ACM SIGKDD Explorations Newsletter, 2003.
[3] K. Bharat, B. Chang, M. Henzinger. Who Links to Whom: Mining Linkage between Web Sites, ICDM2001.
[4] B. Kovalerchuk. Correlation of complex evidences and link discovery. The Fifth International Conference on Forensic Statistics, 2002.
[5] J. Adibi, P. Cohenand, T. Morrison. Measuring Confidence Intervals in Link Discovery: A Bootstrap Approach, ACM SIGKDD, 2004.
[6] S. Lin, H. Chalupsky. Using Unsupervised Link Discovery Methods to Find Interesting Facts and Connections in a Bibliography Dataset, SIGKDD Explorations, 2003.
[7] N. Pioch, et al. Multi-Hypothesis Abductive Reasoning for Link Discovery, KDD 2004.
[8] X. Yin, J. Han, J. Yang, P. S Yu. Efficient classification cross multiple database relations: a CrossMine approach, IEEE Transactions on Knowledge and data engineering.
[9] R. Mooney, P. Melville, L. Tang, J. Shavlik. Relational data mining with inductive logic programming for link discovery, National Science Foundation Workshop on Next Generation Data, 2002.
[10] R. Mooney et al. Relational Data Mining with Inductive Logic Programming for Link Discovery. In Data Mining: Next Generation Challenges and Future Directions, H. Kargupta, A. Joshi, K. Sivakumar, and Y. Yesha (Eds.), AAAI Press, 2004.
[11] N. Lavrac, S. Dzerosck. Inductive logic programming: techniques and applications, Ellis Horwood, 1994.

IPQDA: A Software Tool for Intelligent Analysis of Power Quality Disturbances

Aini Hussain[1], Azah Mohamed[1], Mohd Hanif Md Saad[2],
Mohd Haszuan Shukairi[1], and Noor Sabathiah Sayuti[1]

[1] Department of Electrical, Electronic and Systems Engineering,
National University of Malaysia, 43600 UKM, Bangi, Selangor, Malaysia
aini@eng.ukm.my, azah@eng.ukm.my
[2] Department of Mechanical and Materials Engineering,
National University of Malaysia, 43600 UKM, Bangi, Selangor, Malaysia

Abstract. This paper presents the Intelligent Power Quality Disturbance Analysis (IPQDA) software tool that is designed for an automatic analysis of power quality (PQ) disturbance. The main capabilities of the software include analysis of disturbance waveforms, identification of a particular type of disturbance and notification of a disturbance. Another important feature of the program is that it can automatically send email or short messaging notifications upon identification of a disturbance to alert the system operator of a disturbance.

1 Introduction

Various solutions have been proposed in the literature which attempt to solve the problem of detecting automatically power quality disturbances, which include techniques such as FFT, wavelets [1], fractal analysis [2] and time-frequency analysis [3]. For the automatic PQ disturbances classification, various intelligent techniques have been used such as wavelet based artificial neural network, neuro-fuzzy [4], rule-based expert system and event-based expert system [5-7]. To address the issue of automatic recognition of different types of disturbances, this paper presents a software tool for intelligent analysis of PQ disturbances. The objective is to develop an automated disturbance recognition system for use in a real-time power quality monitoring application. The main functions of IPQDA are that it can present measured power quality data graphically, analyze disturbance waveforms, identify automatically a particular type of disturbance and notify a user of a disturbance via SMS or email.

2 Overall Software Structure

The software structure for PQ disturbances intelligent analysis consists of three main modules: a) signal processing and feature extraction module; b) expert system module; and c) result notification module. In general, the detection and classification problem comprises of two steps in which the first step is feature extraction for selecting distinct features of a disturbance using signal processing techniques. The second step is considered as decision making during which, the extracted features are processed by an inference engine to determine the type of disturbance. The output, which is the disturbance type identified is then sent to notify a user of a disturbance. A graphical user interface is developed to provide a friendly environment for using the software.

3 Expert System for Automatic Classification of Disturbances

Three main steps are involved in the detection and classification of PQ disturbances: i) input signal pre-processing, ii) FFT and LPC feature extraction and iii) disturbance classification using expert system approach. Signal pre-processing involves the removal of the fundamental frequency of the single-phase voltage waveform, framing and Hamming windowing the input signals into three separate windows. The Hamming window equation is given as,

$$w[k+1] = 0.54 - 0.46 \cos\left(2\pi \frac{k}{n-1}\right), \quad (1)$$

where, $k = 0, 1, .., n-1$.

Expert system (ES) is used for automating the classifying process of the various types of PQ disturbances. The main components of the ES comprise of the database, knowledge base, inference engine and user interface. The proposed ES uses a built-in component-based forward chaining inference engine module that has been developed by implementing Microsoft Component Object Model (COM) architecture. The Knowledge Base (KB) is the experience based 'intelligence' for the system. A comprehensive analysis and comparison of derived features from each category of disturbance were carried out to formulate the rules. A skill individual meticulous performed visual checking to ensure that the disturbances were correctly classified using the formulated rules. Strict threshold values are then set for each disturbance and incorporated in the KB. The experimental data for training and evaluation of the system are acquired from PQ monitoring. Figure 1 depicts selected samples of the formulated rules.

```
Rule : 1 IF _sum < _c12   THEN Impulsive Transient
Rule : 2 IF _sum > _c12 AND  _k > _c0.04 AND  _result = _result4 THEN
           Sag
Rule : 3 IF _sum > _c12 AND  _k > _c0.04 AND  _result = _result1 THEN
           Oscillatory Transient
    ⋮
Rule : 8 IF _sum > _c12 AND  _k < _c0.04 AND  _resultb = _result3b
           THEN   Repetitive Notch
```

Fig. 1. Selected samples of the formulated rules

Integration of the system was achieved easily due to the fact that all modules were developed using the same programming language, namely the Microsoft Visual Basic 6.0. The modules interconnection for the finished system is as shown in Fig. 2

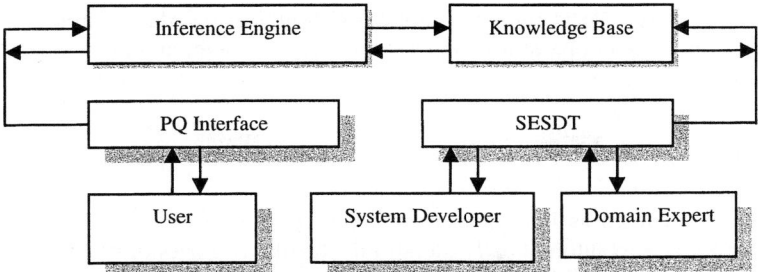

Fig. 2. Integration of the inference engine, KB, user, developer and domain expert interfaces

in which the main modules are the knowledge base (KB), inference engine, PQ database and the user interface using the SESDT.

4 Example of the Software Use

The developed IPQDA software tool is illustrated by an example as can be seen from the user interface shown in Fig. 3. The analysis begins with loading input data by clicking on the 'File' option. From the figure, the data is displayed in terms of event number, monitoring location, date and time of event as well as a display of the voltage waveform. Analysis of the voltage waveform can be done by selecting the 'FFT Plot' or 'LPC Plot' options. The results of the LPC analysis on the voltage waveform are displayed in three frames as shown in Fig. 3.

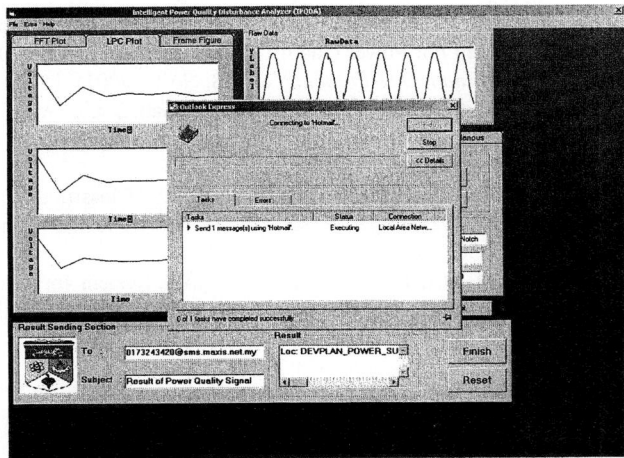

Fig. 3. User interface showing LPC analysis of disturbance waveform & another interface for sending analysis output via short messaging

Automatic detection of the disturbance type can be implemented by choosing the 'Analyze' button. The results of the disturbance type are then displayed in which the disturbance for this case is repetitive notch as shown in the three frames. For the purpose of notifying an operator of the disturbance, notification can be send through email or short messaging.

5 Conclusion

A software tool named as Intelligent Power Quality Disturbance Analysis (IPQDA) has been developed to automatically identify different categories of disturbances such as voltage sag, swell, oscillatory transient, impulsive transient, repetitive and single notch. IPQDA enables its user to analyse disturbance data in the database, view disturbance characteristics through FFT and LPC plots, classify the PQ disturbance type and automatically send email or short messaging notifications upon identification of a disturbance to alert the system operator. Such an analysis tool is useful for customers to manage the growing need for automatic disturbance detection in the digital era.

References

1. Gaouda, M., Salama, M. M. A., Sultan, M. R. and Chikhani, A. Y., "Power Quality Detection and Classification Using Wavelet-Multiresolution Signal Decomposition", *IEEE Transactions on Power Delivery* (1999).
2. Huang, S., Hsieh, C. and Huang, C., "Feasibility of Fractal-based Methods for Visualization of Power System Disturbances", *Electric Power and Energy Systems*, 23, (2000), 31 – 36.
3. Gu, Y. H. and Bollen, M. H. J., "Time-Frequency and Time-Scale Domain Analysis of Voltage Disturbances", *IEEE Transactions on Power Delivery*, Vol.15, No. 4, (2000) 1279 – 1285.
4. Elmitwally, S., Farghal, M., Kandil, Abdelkader S. and Elkateb, M., "Proposed Wavelet-neurofuzzy Combined System For Power Quality Violations Detection and Diagnosis", *IEE Proc. Generation , Transmission, Distribution.* Vol.148, No.1, (2001) 15-20.
5. Santoso, S., Lamoree, J., Grady, W. M., Powers, E. J. and Bhatt, S. C., "A Scalable PQ Event Identification System, *IEEE Transactions on Power Delivery,* Volume 15, Issue 2, (2000) 738 – 743.
6. Dash, P. K., Salama, M. M. A., Mishra, S. and Liew, A. C., "Classification of Power System Disturbances Using A Fuzzy Expert System and a Fourier Linear Combiner", *IEEE Trans on Power Delivery,* 15(2) 2000, 472-477.
7. Styvaktakis, E., Bollen, M. H. and Gu, I. Y. H., "Expert System for Classification and Analysis of Power System Events", *IEEE Trans. On Power Delivery,* 17(2) 2002, 423 – 428.

Bio-inspired Control of Dexterous Manipulation

Rosana Matuk Herrera[1,*] and Fabio Leoni[2]

[1] Department of Computer Science, Facultad de Ciencias Exactas y Naturales,
Universidad de Buenos Aires, Argentina
rmatuk@dc.uba.ar
[2] ARTS Lab, Scuola Superiore Sant'Anna, Pisa, Italy

Abstract. Robots successfully manipulate objects in controlled environments. However, they fail in unknown environments. Few years old children lift and manipulate unfamiliar objects more dexterously than today's robots. Therefore, roboticists are looking for inspiration on neurophysiological studies to improve their robotics control models. We present an artificial intelligence control model for dexterous manipulation, and a grip and load force control algorithm, strongly inspired on neurophysiological studies of the human manipulation process.

Keywords: Robotics, dexterous manipulation, neural networks, reinforcement learning.

1 Introduction

Human dexterous manipulation of objects requires to apply the following fingertip forces to the object of interest:

1. *Load force (LF):* Vertical force required to overcome the force of gravity. It is determined by the weight of the object.
2. *Grip force (GF):* Normal force required to prevent slips. It depends on the force of friction as well as the shape of the finger-object contact area and the distribution of mass [3].

To avoid a slip between the fingers and the object, the grip force has to be greater than the *slip limit*, i.e., the load force divided by the friction coefficient (μ): $GF \geq LF/\mu$. Ideally, the grip force could be tuned in parallel with the load force, so whatever the load force is, the grip force changes accordingly. There are four types of receptors in the glabrous skin of the human hand: FA-I, FA-II, SA-I and SA-II. The SA I and SA II units show a sustained discharge in the presence of ongoing stimuli. The FA I and FA II units fire rapidly when a stimulus is presented (or removed) and then fall silent when the stimulation cease to change.

---

* Postal address: Departamento de Computación, Pabellón 1, Ciudad Universitaria, 1428, Buenos Aires, Argentina. Research partially supported by Universidad de Buenos Aires, Argentina, within the project UBACyT X323. Some of the ideas of this work were developed during the author's stay at the Department of Computer Science, University of Pisa, Italy, supported by an EU *Alpha Cordial 2* grant.

2 Computational Control Model

To design the control system, the first step was to identify the relevant characteristics of the object that are useful for the dexterous manipulation problem. Two relevant characteristics are the *friction* and the *shape* of the object. The friction, together with the shape of the object, influences the slip ratio, that determines the *force ratio*. The term force ratio means the ratio between the grip and load forces. On the other side, the *weight* of the object is the determining factor of the final required load force. The weight is calculated based on the estimated *size* and *density*. Another important factor is the *fragility* of the object, needed to avoid the crash of the object.

The recognition of materials by computer vision is still a complex and unsolved task. We will assume that there is a *visual module* that can recognize different materials. The visual module will give too fuzzy estimated values of the object's shape and size. However, the control system is designed to still work without the visual module outputs, resulting in a performance decrease. It emulates the situation in which humans manipulate objects in the dark.

The human memory remembers the slip ratio and weight of the last manipulated object [2]. Our bio-inspired system will have 2 memory modules:

1. *Recent Memory:* This memory module preserves the force ratio and weight of the last manipulated object. It increases the system's speed response if the robot has to manipulate the same object many times one after the other.
2. *General Memory:* This memory module returns an estimation of the required force ratio, the density and the fragility of the object, based on the material value prediction from the visual module. We upgrade this memory module with the information obtained by the robot for its interaction with the environment, following a reinforcement learning strategy.

Our control system is driven by simulated afferent signals. Israelsson [1] designed a computational simulator of the responses of the afferents from the glabrous skin during human manipulation. The simulation of the signals is based on Israelsson's work. The *force control module* is at the core of the control system. This module sets the actual values of the grip and load forces, detects slips, makes on-line corrections of the forces, and upgrades the memory modules. The strategy used by this module is strongly inspired by the human grasp force strategy during the manipulation process. It divides the manipulation process in different phases, and the same sensory events can be used to elicit different actions appropriate for the accomplishment of each phase, as observed in humans [3].

Inside the force control module, a neural network determines the initial force ratio, studying the initial FA I behavior. When a person touches an object to be manipulated, he/she increments the grip force during a short time. Depending on the friction of the object's material, a specific pattern of FA I signals is received. If the object's material has a great friction coefficient, the FA I signals of the received pattern will have a great intensity. On the other side, if the object's material has a low friction coefficient, the FA I signals will have a low intensity [4]. When the transitional phase is reached, the right force ratio that corresponds with the initial FA I pattern is known. Then, the goal is to create an association between this force ratio, and the initial pattern of the FA I signal received. To achieve this goal, we run a number of experiments with the robotic hand. Next, we create a database of initial FA I signals, with its corresponding right force ratio. With this information, we train a self organized neural network (SOM), which receives as input the pattern of initial FA I signals, and gives as output the corresponding force ratio. We train the SOM continuously, in order to be able to recognize new materials with different friction and correct the existing associations.

Finally, when a slip occurs, there are signals of the FA I, SA I, and FA II mechanoreceptors and a sudden change of the load force [4]. Based on the intensity of these signals, a human being can graduate the force ratio adjustment. To emulate this mechanism, we use inside the force control module another SOM neural network, that receives the simulated signals as input signals, and gives a percentile of force ratio adjustment as output. This neural network uses a reinforcement learning strategy to adjust its weights accordingly with the intensity of the slip.

3 Force Control Algorithms

Algorithms were designed for each one of the manipulation process phases. As a representative example, we present here the algorithm of the loading phase.

```
while LF_t ≤ GF/2 /ρ_t and LF_o ≤ GF/2 /ρ_o and Lift Off = False do
    Do in Parallel(Test Lift-off, Test Slip, Increase LF_t, Increase LF_o)
end
while (LF_t +LF_o) ≤ k_mec*Weight and Lift Off = False do
    if (LF_t +LF_o)≤ (k_mec*Weight)/2 then
        Do in Parallel(Test Lift-off, Test Slip, Parallel increase of GF and
        LF at increasing velocity)
    else
        Do in Parallel(Test Lift-off, Test Slip, Parallel increase of GF and
        LF at decreasing velocity)
    end
end
while Lift Off = False do
    Do in Parallel(Test Lift-off, Test Slip, Burst Parallel increase of GF and
    LF)
end
```

Algorithm 1. Loading Phase Algorithm

References: Thumb load force LF_t, opposing fingers load force LF_o, grip force GF, thumb force ratio ρ_t, opposing fingers force ratio ρ_o, delay of the mechanical motors of the robot to stop the arm k_{mec}.

At this phase, the forces are increased in parallel preserving the force ratio obtained at the preload phase (i.e., $LF_t \leq \frac{GF}{2}/\rho_t$ and $LF_o \leq \frac{GF}{2}/\rho_o$), until the object lifts off. First, the load force is increased to make it proportional with the grip force. Next, the grip and load forces are increased in parallel until the load force reaches the estimated weight value or the object lifts off. The constant $k_{mec} < 1$ is a factor introduced to lower the estimation of the weight, in order to avoid a force overshoot, due to the delay of the robot's mechanical motors to stop the arm. Finally, if the estimated weight is lesser than the actual object's weight, the third cycle is entered. Here, the forces are increased until the object lifts off. We make burst parallel increases of the grip and load forces, as seen in humans.

To detect the lift-off and slip events, we closely follow the neurophysiological methodology observed in the tactile human system. The lift-off and the slip events are signalled by the simulated afferent signals. The lift-off is detected by the intensity of the FA II signal and the absence of FA I and SA I responses. The slips are signaled by sudden changes in the load force between the thumb and the opposing fingers, and by discharges of FA I, SA I, and eventually FA II mechanoreceptors. The slip events fire force ratio corrections. If there are responses of the FA I, SA I and FA II afferents, then the force ratio upgrade will be larger than if there were only responses of the FA I and SA I signals (i.e., a localized slip). A neural network is used to estimate the intensity of the slip and to estimate the force ratio correction. A safety margin is added to the force ratio correction to stop the slip more efficiently.

4 Conclusions and Future Work

An artificial intelligence control model for dexterous manipulation was presented. At present, we are working on building a computer simulator of a robotic hand, to apply and improve our control model and algorithms.

Acknowledgements

The authors acknowledge Antonina Starita for her useful comments.

References

1. A Israelsson. Simulation of responses in afferents from the glabrous skin during human manipulation. Master's thesis, Master thesis in Cognitive Science, Umeå University, Sweden, 2002.
2. R Johansson and BB Edin. Predictive feed-forward sensory control during grasping and manipulation in man. *Biomedical Research*, 14:95–106, 1993.
3. R Johansson and G Westling. Roles of glabrous skin receptors and sensorimotor memory in automatic control of precision grip when lifting rougher or more slippery objects. *Exp Brain Res*, 56:550–564, 1984.
4. R Johansson and G Westling. Signals in tactile afferents from the fingers eliciting adaptive motor responses during precision grip. *Exp Brain Res*, 66:141–154, 1987.

A Lagrangian Relaxation Based Heuristic for Solving the Length-Balanced Two Arc-Disjoint Shortest Paths Problem

Yanzhi Li[1], Andrew Lim[1,2], and Hong Ma[1]

[1] Dept of Industrial Engineering and Logistics Management,
Hong Kong Univ of Science and Technology, Clear Water Bay, Kowloon, Hong Kong
[2] School of Computer Science & Engineering,
South China University of Technology, Guang Dong, PR China

Abstract. We consider a HAZMAT transportation problem, which is modeled as the length-balanced two arc-disjoint shortest paths problem (LB2SP). The objective function of LB2SP is expressed as a weighted sum of two terms, i.e., the sum of the path lengths and the positive length difference between the paths. We demonstrate that LB2SP is NP-Hard, and formulate it as an Integer Programming (IP) model. We develop a Lagrangian relaxation based heuristic (LRBH) for LB2SP. Computational experiments are conducted to compare the performance of LRBH with the CPLEX solver, showing that the LRBH is efficient for LB2SP.

1 Problem Introduction

The U.S. Department of Transportation (DOT) estimates that an average of over 800,000 shipments of hazardous materials (HAZMAT) are made each day in the U.S. [1]. Since September 11, 2001, public concern with transportation security has notably increased. The importance of making HAZMAT transportation more secure is generally recognized. Assume the following situation. A truck carrying HAZMAT is to travel from an origin to a destination. The risk en route is proportional to the tour length, therefore a shortest path from the origin to the destination is prepared for the truck driver. A second alternative path is also required in advance as a backup detour. Thus, the length-balanced two arc-disjoint shortest paths problem (LB2SP) is introduced as follows:

Problem 1 (Length-Balanced Two Arc-disjoint Shortest Paths Problem). In a directed network $G = (V, A)$ with an arc length c_{ij} associated with each arc $(i, j) \in A$. The network has a distinct source node $V = 0$ and a distinguished sink node $V = N$. We need to determine two arc-disjoint paths from the source node to the sink node. Two terms are related to the two paths. One is the the sum of the two path lengths. The other is the difference of the two path lengths. The objective is to minimize the weighted sum of the two terms.

There is no previous research on this particular topic, but the most relevant network problems in literature are the classical shortest path (SP) problem (see [2]) and the K Shortest Arc-disjoint Paths Problem.

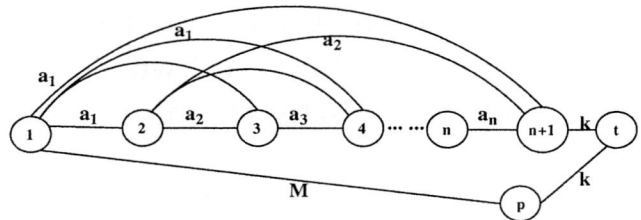

Fig. 1. An Example Network

Theorem 1. *Problem 1 is $\mathcal{NP}$-Hard.*

Proof: We prove our problem to be NP-Hard by reduction from the 2-Partition problem. We construct the above network. For every node i ($i <= n$), there is exactly one outgoing arc that connects node $j(j > i)$ with length a_i. the sum of the arc lengths $a_1, \ldots, a_n$ is $2M$. The arcs $(n+1, t)$ and (p, t) are both equal to k. There exist two arc-disjoint paths from node 1 to node t. One of them must go through node p with the length $M + k$. The other path has to go through node $n + 1$ to node t. In order to minimize path length difference, we need to find a path from node 1 to node $n + 1$, with total length M. It is equivalent to finding a subset from $\{a_1, \ldots, a_n\}$ with sum equal to M. So our problem with objective to minimize length difference of two disjoint paths is NP-Hard.

2 IP Formulation and LRBH

IP Formulation The problem is formulated as follows:

$$z = \min \alpha(\sum_{(i,j) \in A} c_{ij} x_{ij} + \sum_{(i,j) \in A} c_{ij} y_{ij}) + \beta(\sum_{(i,j) \in A} c_{ij} y_{ij} - \sum_{(i,j) \in A} c_{ij} x_{ij})$$

s.t.:

$$\sum_{(i,j) \in A} c_{ij} x_{ij} \leq \sum_{(i,j) \in A} c_{ij} y_{ij} \quad \text{for all } (i,j) \in A \quad (1)$$

$$\sum_{j:(i,j) \in A} x_{ij} - \sum_{j:(i,j) \in A} x_{ji} = \begin{cases} 1 & \text{for } i = 1 \\ 0 & \text{for } i \in N - \{1, n\} \\ -1 & \text{for } i = n \end{cases} \quad (2)$$

$$\sum_{j:(i,j) \in A} y_{ij} - \sum_{j:(i,j) \in A} y_{ji} = \begin{cases} 1 & \text{for } i = 1 \\ 0 & \text{for } i \in N - \{1, n\} \\ -1 & \text{for } i = n \end{cases} \quad (3)$$

$$x_{ij} + y_{ij} \leq 1 \quad \text{for all } (i,j) \in A \quad (4)$$
$$x_{ij} = 0 \text{ or } 1 \quad \text{for all } (i,j) \in A \quad (5)$$
$$y_{ij} = 0 \text{ or } 1 \quad \text{for all } (i,j) \in A \quad (6)$$
$$u_i - u_j + n x_{ij} \leq n - 1 \quad (7)$$
$$w_i - w_j + n y_{ij} \leq n - 1 \quad (8)$$
$$\alpha > 0 \text{ and } \beta > 0 \quad (9)$$

Decision variable x_{ij} and y_{ij} define two s-t paths. The objective function consists of two terms: the sum of the path lengths and length difference of the two paths. Parameter α and β measure the weight of the two terms. Constraints (2) and (3) are the network mass balance constraints corresponding to the SP problem. Constraint (4) states that there is no common arc in the two paths. In a way similar to the IP formulation of TSP [3], constraints (7) and (8) eliminate cycles in the two paths as well as possible subtours.

Lagrangian Relaxation. We transform the above IP formulation into two parallel related network problem models. Model P1 is a SP problem with a set of additional 'arc-disjoint' constraints.

$$z_1 = \min \sum_{(i,j) \in A} c_{ij} x_{ij}$$
s.t.

$$\sum_{j:(i,j) \in A} x_{ij} - \sum_{j:(i,j) \in A} x_{ji} = \begin{cases} 1 & \text{for } i = 1 \\ 0 & \text{for } i \in N - \{1, n\} \\ -1 & \text{for } i = n \end{cases} \quad (10)$$

$$x_{ij} + y_{ij} \leq 1 \qquad \text{for all } (i,j) \in A$$
$$x_{ij} = 0 \text{ or } 1 \qquad \text{for all } (i,j) \in A$$

Model P2 is almost identical except that the decision variables are y_{ij}. If we solve the two models sequentially, the arc-disjoint constraints requires that we delete those arcs appearing in the parallel problem solution. Constraint (1) is automatically satisfied, because the first SP solution must be no worse than the second SP solution. So are constraints (7) and (8). Next we use Lagrangian relaxation in P1 and P2 by associating Lagrange multipliers μ_{ij}^1 and μ_{ij}^2 with the arc-disjoint constraints and relaxing them. The objective function of the Lagrangian subproblems becomes

$$z_1 = \min \sum_{(i,j) \in A} (c_{ij} + \mu_{ij}^1) x_{ij} + \sum_{(i,j) \in A} \mu_{ij}^1 y_{ij} - \sum_{(i,j) \in A} \mu_{ij}^1 \quad (11)$$

$$z_2 = \min \sum_{(i,j) \in A} (c_{ij} + \mu_{ij}^2) y_{ij} + \sum_{(i,j) \in A} \mu_{ij}^2 x_{ij} - \sum_{(i,j) \in A} \mu_{ij}^2 \quad (12)$$

Note that we can dismiss the last terms $\sum_{(i,j) \in A} \mu_{ij}^1$ and $\sum_{(i,j) \in A} \mu_{ij}^2$, and the second last terms $\sum_{(i,j) \in A} \mu_{ij}^1 y_{ij}$ and $\sum_{(i,j) \in A} \mu_{ij}^2 x_{ij}$, all of which can be treated as constants for any fixed choices of Lagrangian multipliers. Hence, this problem turns into two parametric SP problems, which essentially says we solve the SP problem in a new network where the arc costs have been adjusted by the parameter μ_{ij}^1 and μ_{ij}^2. The traditional method is to apply subgradient optimization. In our heuristic approach, we simply set $\mu_{ij} = \mu_{ij}^1 = \mu_{ij}^2$, divide the program into two stages and use an iterative method to find a good μ_{ij} that decreases the length difference $z_2 - z_1$. Meanwhile the SP solutions always provide a reasonably small length sum $z_1 + z_2$.

The Lagrangian relaxation based heuristic (LRBH) is as follows:
1: Set parameter $\mu_{ij} = 0$, solution vectors $\boldsymbol{x} = 0$, $\boldsymbol{y} = 0$;
2: **repeat**
3:    Solve P1 by the Dijkstra algor. Get solution $\boldsymbol{x}$ and objective value z_1;
4:    $\mu_{ij} = \mu_{ij} + stepsize$; $c_{ij} = c_{ij} + \mu$, for all $x_{ij} = 1$;
5: **until** $\boldsymbol{x}$ have changed or maximum number of iteration is reached
6: Delete from the network all arcs in $\boldsymbol{x}$;
7: Solve the second SP problem P2, and get $\boldsymbol{y}$ and objective value z_2;
8: Record $z = z_2 - z_1$ if there is improvement;
9: **go to** step 2 **if** maximum number of iteration is not reached;
10: **terminate**;

Computational Experiments. Non-trivial test cases of geometric graphs with 50, 100, and 150 nodes are generated. Experiments are carried out on a P4 2.4Ghz machine. The average results of 10 cases each are given in the table 1. A simple genetic algorithm(GA) is implemented for comparison. The result shows that The margin between LRBH solutions and CPLEX optimal solutions are quite small. While CPLEX solves the problem with great computational cost, LRBH gets the solution very quickly. In comparison, the GA method is not able to get satisfactory solutions within the time limit of 180 seconds.

Table 1. Comparison between the CPLEX solver, LRBH and GA

	CPLEX		LRBH		GA
Node	obj(180s)	opt(time)	obj(opt%)	time(s)	obj(180s)
50	2555	2361(207.5s)	2527(93.0%)	2.06	4077
100	2663	2047(2367s)	2145(95.18%)	7.65	3535
150	2380	2074(1884s)	2135(97.08%)	14.17	3728

3 Conclusion and Future Work

We have studied LB2SP, which offers the solution to a particular HAZMAT transportation problem. The heuristic LRBH is easy to implement and shown to be efficient. GA's poor performance in the problem could be due to the coding convention and operators. Further research is required before discarding the GA as a viable tool.

References

[1] Hazardous materials shipments. Office of Hazardous Materials Safety, U.S. Department of Transportation, Washington DC, Oct. 1998.
[2] B. V. Cherkassky, A. V. Goldberg, and T. Radzik. Shortest paths algorithms: theory and experimental evaluation. *Mathematical Programming*, 73:129–196, 1996.
[3] C. E. Miller, A. W. Tucker, and R. A. Zemlin. Integer programming formulation of traveling salesman problems. *J. ACM*, 7(4):326–329, 1960.

Optimizing Coupled Oscillators for Stability

David Newth and Markus Brede

CSIRO Centre for Complex Systems Science,
GPO Box 284 Canberra ACT, Australia
{david.newth, markus.brede}@csiro.au

Abstract. Synchronization in chaotic oscillatory systems has a wide array of applications in biology, physics and communication systems. Over the past 10 years there has been considerable interest in the synchronization properties of small-world and scale-free networks. In this paper, we define the fitness of a configuration of coupled oscillators as its ability to synchronize. We then employ an optimization algorithm to determine network structures that lead to an enhanced ability to synchronize. The optimized networks generally have low clustering, small diameters, short path-length, are disassortative, and have a high degree of homogeneity in their degree and load distributions.

1 Introduction

The synchronization of networks of coupled oscillators, in particular synchronization on small-world and scale-free networks, has been widely studied over the past five years [3, 5, 7, 8, 9, 10, 11]. While investigating how the topological properties of certain model networks affect synchronization, several studies have found somewhat conflicting results. For example Hong *et al.* [3] found that increasing degree heterogeneity promoted synchronizability, while Nishikawa *et al.* [5] observed the opposite effect. In this paper we take a different approach. Instead of investigating the synchronizability properties of given classes of networks, we let networks evolve towards a configuration that exhibits superior synchronizability. More precisely, we adopt the framework outlined in [6] to determine the stability of the synchronized state of a set of oscillators coupled by a network. This measure of stability is used as a fitness function in a stochastic hill climber. The hill climber is used to optimize the topology of the coupling scheme of the oscillators. The aim of this paper is to determine the topological features of these networks and identify network characteristics that lead to enhanced synchronizability.

2 Coupled Oscillators

Over the past decade studies of coupled oscillators have shown that certain network properties can enhance or diminish a system's ability to synchronize. Here we follow the framework of Pecora and Carroll [6] for determining synchronizability. We consider a system of N coupled oscillators. Let x_i be the m-dimensional vector of state variables of the ith node. The dynamics of the coupled oscillators are governed by:

$$\dot{x}_i = F(x_i) + \sigma \sum_j G_{ij} H(x_j), \qquad (1)$$

where $F(\cdot)$ determines the dynamics of the individual oscillators without coupling, while $H(\cdot)$ and the matrix G describe the interactions between them. We only consider symmetric connections, which guarantees that all the eigenvalues of G are real. Let the eigenvalues of G be labelled $\lambda_N \geq \lambda_{N-1} \geq \ldots \geq \lambda_2 \geq \lambda_1 = 0$. If G is connected then $\lambda_2 \neq 0$. The stability of the synchronized state $x_1 = x_2 = \ldots = x_N$ is determined by the Jacobian of the functions F, H, and the eigenvalues of G [6]. For a wide array of systems the synchronized state is linearly stable if all except the zero eigenvalue lie in a single parameter interval (α_1, α_2), making the ratio $r = \frac{\lambda_N}{\lambda_2}$ (the largest and smallest non-vanishing eigenvalues) a good indicator of synchronizability. In the remainder of this paper the ratio r defines a network's fitness.

3 Optimization of Coupled Oscillators

To create networks with enhanced synchronizability we make use of the basic optimization scheme known as a stochastic hill-climber. This optimization scheme consists of two stages. First, a small modification to the network is suggested. Essentially an edge is deleted from the network and inserted between two nodes that were not previously connected. Second, if the network is still connected, and is found to have an improved fitness, the suggested rewiring is accepted, otherwise it is rejected. These two steps are then repeated until no improvements are found during $\Delta t = N(N-1)/2$ (such that every edge has on average been probed once) optimization steps.

4 Results and Discussion

As an initial study, we seed our algorithm with three different initial conditions. We consider Erdös and Rényi random graphs, scale free networks and hypercubes. Each of these systems possesses properties thought to promote synchronizability. For each class of networks, we ran the stochastic hill-climber 100 times for 10,000 optimisation steps. Fig. 1 shows the time evolution of $\langle r \rangle$ for the three configurations. It can be seen from this figure that after approximately $1,000$ time steps there is no major improvement in r. Although the networks have the same (average) number of links, the final configurations still differ in their final average ratio $\langle r \rangle$. That is, the optimized networks obtained from scale free and hypercube starting conditions represent suboptimal solutions within the landscape of all possible networks. The search algorithm created networks with better synchronization properties, when seeded with a random network. In the remainder of this paper we will only examine the changes in network topology

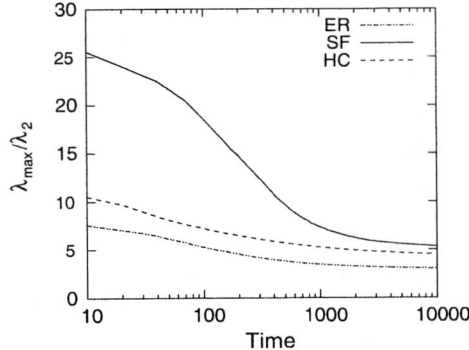

Fig. 1. Time evolution during evolution averaged over an ensemble of SF networks (solid line), a hypercube (dashed line) and an ensemble of ER random graph (dotted line) with the same average number of links and size $N = 128$. The curves represent averages over different optimizations, each time starting with a different member of the ensemble (for ER random graph and SF networks). Because hypercubes represent local optima in network space, an annealing scheme was used in this case.

where the starting condition was an Erdös and Rényi random graph. For the interested reader Brede and Newth [1] provide a systematic analysis of changes in other network types as they evolve.

After building an ensemble of 1,000 optimized networks, we analysed the topological properties of these networks, which are commonly associated with improved synchronization [4]. Fig. 2 shows the eigenvalue ratio against the various topological properties. We found that networks with superior synchronization properties tend to have short average path lengths and exhibit disassortative degree mixing. A reduced cliquishness and a reduced number of small cycles makes them appear locally tree-like. Further analysis of the characteristics of networks with superior synchronizability reveals that their degree distributions have a very small variance in comparison with the initial configurations. This explains the very homogeneous load distributions (distributions of the number of shortest paths running through each node). The above result suggests that the networks explored here may belong to the class of (almost) $\frac{L}{N}$-regular graphs. Studies of random L/N-regular graphs have identified very similar properties [1]. However, a more detailed analysis shows that the optimized networks exhibit properties which are not only a consequence of the collapse of the degree variance. We note that the optimized networks are substantially smaller, more disassortative and even less cliquish then random L/N-regular graphs. This observation allows us to conclude that a small diameter and disassortative degree mixing are features that *per se* improve a networks synchronizability.

Finally, we note that many biological networks show disassortative mixing of node degrees. One example of a system where synchronization may play an important role in the dynamics is the neural network of *C. Elegans*. From our findings we can speculate that apart from enhanced stability against dynamical

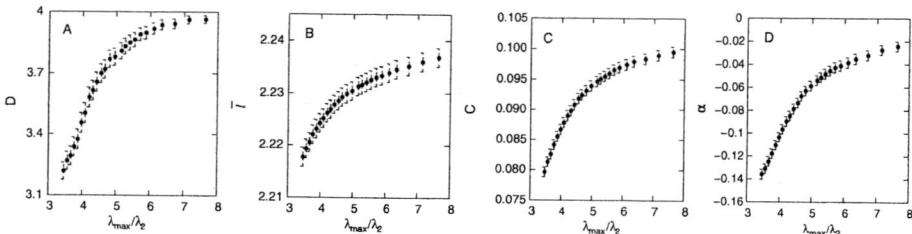

Fig. 2. Evolution of various network statistics as a function of λ_{max}/λ_2. (A) Network Diameter. As the diameter of the network increases the stability of the stable synchronized state decreases. (B) Average Shortest Path-Length. Networks that have enhanced stability properties tend to have on average shorter path-lengths between nodes. (C) Clustering Coefficient. Networks with enhanced synchronizability properties, tend to have reduced clustering than those that have reduced synchronizability. Locally these networks have are very tree like. (D) Assortativity. Network that have high synchronizability tend to be dissasoratative.

perturbations [2], dissasortative mixing could also be the result of the evolution of these networks towards a topology that stabilizes synchronized states.

References

1. Brede, M. and Newth, D. (2005). Evolving networks with optimized synchronization properties. *Physical Review E*. (Under Review).
2. Brede, M. and Sinha, S. (2005) Assortativity reduces stability of degree correlated networks. (in preperation).
3. Hong, H., Kim, B. J., Chio, M. Y., and Park, H. (2004). Factors that predict better synchronizability on complex networks. arXiv:cond-mat/0403745v1.
4. Newman, M. E. J. (2003). Mixing patterns in networks. *Physical Review E*. **67**, 026126.
5. T. Nishikawa, A. E. Motter, Y-C. Lai, and F. C. Hop- pensteadt, (2003) Heterogeneity in Oscillator Networks: Are Smaller Worlds Easier to Synchronize? *Physical Review Letters*. **91**(1), 014101.
6. Pecora, L. M., and Carroll, T. L. (1998). Master stability functions for synchronized coupled systems. *Physical Review Letters*. **80**(10). 2109–2112.
7. Strogatz, S. H. (2000). From Kuramoto to Crawford: exploring the onset of synchronization in populations of coupled oscillators. *Phyica D*. **143**:1–20
8. Strogatz, S. H. (2001). Exploring complex networks. *Nature* **410**:268-276.
9. Strogatz S. H. (2003). *Sync: the emerging science of spontaneous order*. Hyperion, New York Tanner H, Jadbabaie A, Pappas.
10. Watts, D. J. (1999). *Small Worlds*. Princeton University Press, Princeton, NJ.
11. Winfree, A. T. (2000). *The geometry of biological time*. Springer, Berlin Heidelberg New York Wolf JA, Schroeder LF, Finkel LH.

A Novel Approach for Vendor Combination Selection in Supply Chain Management

Ding-zhong Feng[1], Mitsuo Yamashiro[2], and Lei-lei Chen[1]

[1] College of Mechatronics Engineering, Zhejiang University of Technology,
Hangzhou, 310032, P.R. China
[2] Dept. of Industrial & Information Systems Engineering, Ashikaga Institute of Technology,
Tochigi Prefecture, 326-8558, Japan
fdz@zjut.edu.cn

Abstract. To make full use of inside and outside resources in a competitive globalization market, many manufacturers and service providers are seeking a strategic cooperation with suitable vendors to improve their supply chain management (SCM) so that they can concentrate their efforts on their own core business. In this research, a comprehensive evaluation approach is presented for optimal combination selection among candidate vendors and outsourced parts. An evaluation system with a set of vendor selection indices is established. Also, a hierarchical fuzzy model for vendor selection is developed. And thus, a progressively-simplified approach is presented to deal with the vendor combination selection problem in a supply chain system. Finally, an example is given to illustrate the effectiveness of this approach.

1 Introduction

Vendor evaluation and selection has strategic implications that contribute to the operational management of a global supply chain. In order to carry out a long-term cooperative strategy efficiently, a manufacturer has to select a series of right vendors from a large number of potential vendors dispersed geographically. Generally, cost, quality and lead-time are regarded as three most important factors in vendor selection. Layek and Nathapol [1] considered these three factors to be key factors, and pointed out the interaction cost from different order combination. Feng and Yamashiro [2] presented a pragmatic approach for optimal selection of vendor-specific process plans. Others conducted a lot of research activities on vendor evaluation and selection [3-4].

The objective of this paper is to develop a novel approach for optimal combination selection among candidate vendors and outsourced parts in SCM.

2 Problem Description and Prejudgment

Consider a manufacturer that desires to construct its supply chain for its products. Some of components (or parts) of these products are to be outsourced to suppliers or vendors. The problem of interest is how to select right vendors among potential ones.

Suppose that the manufacturer collects enough information for constructing a supply chain to produce a product X. P parts for the product are to be outsourced to vendors. According to the information the core manufacturer owns, there are N potential vendors for these outsourced parts.

The comprehensive vendor selection method presented in this paper is divided into three parts. First, we ignore the vendors who do not possess the capability enough to complete the task. Then, we apply our model based on fuzzy decision theory to evaluate each vendor. Finally, we consider the interaction among different order combinations and decide the corresponding vendors for these outsourced parts.

Treating a large amount of information from potential vendors will result in a waste of resources (such as human resources, financial resources and time) if every piece of information is equally treated. Thus, useless information should and may be filtered by examining vendors' capabilities, process and capacity which assure a vendor can provide right product in right amount and time. By the prejudgment, the number of potential vendors will be reduced from N to M.

3 Hierarchical Fuzzy Model

The evaluation of vendors is a quite complex process involved in many factors or attributions. We investigated the statistical data provided by manufacturing enterprises and searched for relative references. At the same time, as many factors as possible were analyzed affecting vendor selection in supply chain environment. Finally, a set of assessment indices where certain and uncertain factors are comprehensively included, is established.

In the set of indices, C_1, C_2, C_3, Q_1, Q_2 and T can be obtained from certain data: c_1 (production cost of per unit part), c_2 (transportation cost of per unit part), c_3 (business cost of per unit part), q_1 (defect rate in production), q_2 (damage rate in transportation) and t (lead-time), respectively. The other factors (Q_3, E_1, E_2 and E_3) are uncertain or fuzzy. They can be estimated by Delphi method from the values of q_3, e_1, e_2 and e_3, respectively.

Then, a two-level fuzzy assessment model is developed on the basis of fuzzy integration assessment method. The second-level appraisal (S_i) can be obtained by

$$S_i = A_i \cdot R_i = (s_{i1}, \cdots, s_{im}) \qquad (1)$$

where A_i denotes weight vector of index factor i, and R_i denotes appraisal matrix of index factor i. Furthermore, we have the first-level comprehensive appraisal $S = A \cdot R = (s_1, s_2, \cdots, s_m)$, where s_j is integration appraisal value for vendor j.

For $\{c_1, c_2, c_3\}$, their membership function is assigned as:

$$C_{ij} = 1 - \frac{c_{ij}}{\max_{1 \leq j \leq m}\{c_{ij}\}}, \quad (j \in 1, 2, \cdots, m) \qquad (2)$$

And the final appraisal vector (S^p) for part p is obtained by,

$$S^p = A \cdot (C, \ Q, \ E, \ T)^T = (s_1^p, \ s_2^p, \ \cdots, \ s_m^p) \quad (3)$$

4 Optimal Combination Selection

A manufacturer usually out-sources a set of components/parts to several different vendors for a specific product at the same time. That will result in an order-combination problem since different combinations between candidate vendors and outsourced parts bring different interaction costs, such as, different process-collaboration cost, different early/tardiness cost and so on. Due to the complexity of combination problem, we propose a progressively simplified approach based on the characteristics of the combination between vendors and parts. Its algorithm is presented as follows.

Step1: Calculate the appraisal vector of each part by the model in section 3: $S^p = (s_1^p, s_2^p, \cdots, s_m^p)$, $p = 1,2,\cdots P$.

Step2: Assess the impact of interaction cost caused by different order combinations to the whole appraisal. If it is not strong, then the corresponding vendors for these parts are directly determined by the results at Step 1, that is, the vendor with $\max_{1 \leq j \leq m}\{s_j^p\}$ is optimal. Otherwise, turn to the next step.

Step3: Determine importance index ($f^{pp'}$) by Delphi method for those parts (e.g., p and p') that have a strong relationship in process way and/or others.

Step4: For interaction cost, their membership function is assigned as:

$$C_{jj'}^{pp'} = 1 - \frac{c_{jj'}}{\max_{1 \leq j \leq m^p, 1 \leq j' \leq m^{p'}}\{c_{jj'}\}} \quad (4)$$

where j and j' denote the corresponding vendors that supply part p and p', respectively.

Step5: Calculate the total appraisal value for the combination of vendor j and j':

$$S_{jj'}^{pp'} = s_j^p + s_{j'}^{p'} \quad (5)$$

Step6: Calculate final appraisal value:

$$Y_{jj'}^{pp'} = S_{jj'}^{pp'} + f^{pp'} \cdot C_{jj'}^{pp'} \quad (6)$$

5 Illustration Analysis

The case study is based on an important component used in a set of large-size air-separation equipment. The component mainly consists of eight parts. Four of them are found to be worthy of outsourcing (parts 1-4 in Fig.1). After prejudging vendors' process and capacity according to information data, the manufacturer has screened four candidate vendors (A, B, C and D, seen in Fig.1) for possible cooperation.

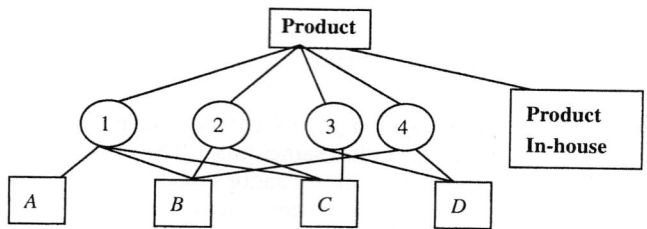

Fig. 1. Product structure and possible vendors

The single part appraisal is conducted by using the above-described model and method. The results are obtained as follows:

$S^1 = (s_A^1 \ s_B^1 \ s_C^1) = (0.473 \ 0.301 \ 0.402)$, $S^2 = (s_B^2 \ s_C^2) = (0.235 \ 0.451)$,

$S^3 = (s_C^3 \ s_D^3) = (0.205 \ 0.312)$, and $S^4 = (s_B^4 \ s_D^4) = (0.375 \ 0.229)$.

After examining the whole production process of this product, it is found that there is a strong relationship and dependence only between part 2 and 3 in production process. Thus, the right vendors for part 1 and 4 can directly be determined. Vendor A is optimal for part 1 since $\max_{1 \leq j \leq 3}\{s_j^1\} = s_A^1$, and vendor B is optimal for part 4.

For part 2 and 3, interaction cost has to be considered, and their importance index $f=0.2$. From Fig.1 it is found that there are four possible vendor combinations: *BC, BD, CC* and *CD*. After assessment, their interaction costs are 5, 4, 0 and 9, respectively. From Eq.(4) it is obtained that their degree of membership is 0.444, 0.556, 1 and 0, respectively. And from Eq.(5) the total appraisal score without considering interaction cost are 0.440, 0.547, 0.656 and 0.763, respectively.

The final appraisal score ($Y_{jj'}^{23}$) is calculated from Eq.(6) and their results are 0.529, 0.658, 0.856 and 0.763, respectively. Therefore, the manufacturer should outsource Parts *1, 2, 3* and *4* to vendors *A, C, C* and *B*, respectively.

References

1. Layek, A.-M., Nathapol, A.: An Analytical Approach for Evaluating and Selecting Vendors with Interdependent Performance in a Supply Chain. International Journal of Integrated Supply Management. 1/1 (2004) 64-78
2. Feng, D.Z., Yamashiro, M.: A Pragmatic Approach for Optimal Selection of Plant-specific Process Plans in a Virtual Enterprise. Production Planning & Control. 14/6 (2003) 562-570
3. Feng, D.Z., Yamashiro, M.: Optimal Production Policy for a Manufacturing System with Volume Flexibility in a Supply Chain under Lumpy Demand. International Journal of Advanced Manufacturing Technology. 25 (2005) 777-784
4. Lin, C.R., Chen, H.S.: A Fuzzy Strategic Alliance Selection Framework for Supply Chain Partnering under Limited Evaluation Resources. Computers in Industry. 55 (2004) 159-179

A Robust SVM Design for Multi-class Classification

Minkook Cho and Hyeyoung Park

Computer Science Dept., Kyungpook National University,
Sankyuk-dong, Buk-gu, Daegu, 702-701, Korea
ucaresoft@paran.com, hypark@knu.ac.kr

Abstract. When we apply support vector machines (SVM) to multi-class classification, some methods of combining the results of independent SVM for each class haven been used, However, the conventional methods may deteriorates generalization performance when the number of data in each class is small. To solve this problem, we proposed a new method, which uses only one SVM and train it to find some similarity measure between data samples. Through an experiment using real data, we confirm that the proposed method can give better classification performance than the conventional one.

1 Introduction

SVM have been successfully applied to diverse pattern recognition problems showing excellent generalization performances[2]. Like other learning system, however, the SVM cannot guarantee good generalization when the number of data is limited due to natures of problem domains. Especially for classification problems with large number of categories, it is often that the whole data set is large but the number of data in each class is very limited, and the conventional design for multi-class classification has a flaw that each SVM is likely to be sensitive to noises in the training set.

There have been two main approaches to multi-class classification using SVM; the OVA(one vs. all)[1] method and the AP(all-pairs)[5] method. The OVA method builds one SVM for each class so that it distinguishes the corresponding class from the others[7]. Thus, this method requires same number of SVM as the number of classes. When the number of class is k, we need to train k SVM. On the other hand, the AP method makes one SVM for each pair of classes. If number of class is k, we need $k(k-1)/2$ number of SVM. Though a number of variations of the original approaches have been developed, all of them basically takes class-based processing[3], and it is hard to expect each SVM to learn statistically stable information of class distribution.

In order to solve this problem, we propose a new design method of SVM for multi-class classification. We use only one SVM and train it to find a similarity measure for each pair of data. With this proposed method, we expect that the SVM can find some essential information for classification, which is also statistically stable information.

2 Proposed Method

In the propose method, we recompose input data. A new input data z_{ij} is composed of a pair of original data x_i and x_j, such as $z_{ij} = (x_i, x_j)$, $(1 \leq i, j \leq n)$ where n denotes the number of training data. The output value y_{ij} for new input z_{ij} is assigned as $y_{ij} = 2\delta_{ij}-1$ where δ_{ij} is the knonecker delta.

When the number of class is k and the number of data in class C_i is n_i, the number of new data generated by the proposed method is $\sum_{i=1}^{k} n_i(\sum_{i=1}^{k} n_i - 1)$. Note that, in OVA case, each SVM can get only n_i data for the corresponding class C_i. With the proposed method, we can expect that it is possible for the proposed method to compose statistically more stable learning machine, so as to improve generalization performance when the number of data in each class is limited.

Using the new data set, a SVM is trained to decide if each data pair are given from same class or not. Since a pair two data from same class gives an positive output, it is possible to regard the output value for input z_{ij} as a measure of similarity $S(x_i, x_j)$. For classification, we add a classification method such as K-NN(K-Nearest Neighbor) to the SVM (See Fig.1). To a new data x_{new}, the classifier assign a class based on the outputs of SVM. Table 1. shows the classification process combining the SVM and K-NN classifier.

Table 1. Classification method using proposed SVM

> 1. For x_i $(i = 1, 2, ..., n)$, compute $S(x_{new}, x_i)$ using SVM.
> 2. From $S(x_{new}, x_i)_{(i=1,...,n)}$, find the set of K nearest neighbors, $N_K(x_{new}) = \{x_{max_1}, ..., x_{max_k}\}$
> 3. For all classes C_i $(i = 1, ..., k)$, compute the value of num_i, num_i = Number of element in $C_i \cap N_K(x_{new})$
> 4. Assigned x_{new} to a class with maximum num_i.

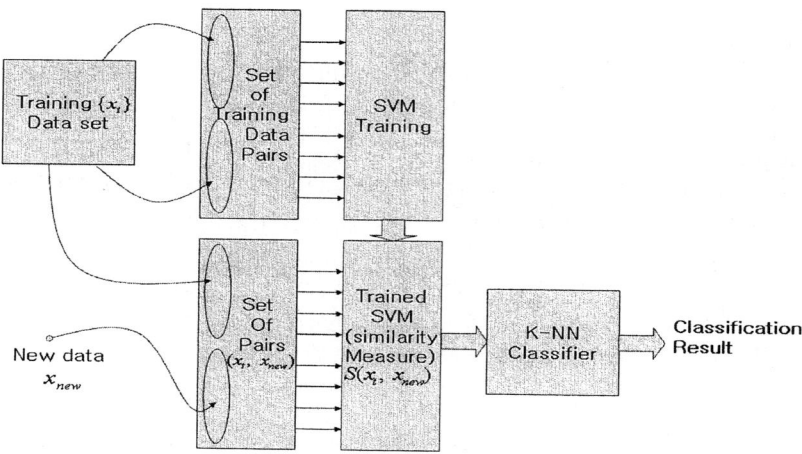

Fig. 1. Overall structure of proposed method

3 Experimental Results

We conducted some experiments with real biometrics data for comparison of performance of proposed method to conventional OVA method. We obtained 260 number of iris image from 14 different individuals. We used 70 data composed of 5 data for each person for traing and used the rest 190 for testing. We first applied the principal component analysis[4] method to reduce the dimensions of iris image, and obtained 70 dimensional feature vectors(See [6] for details).

Table 2. Recognition rates of OVA and proposed method

Kernel (parameter)	Design Method	K = 1	K = 2	K = 3	K = 4	K = 5
Poly (2)	OVA	**93.16%**	**93.16%**	83.68%	83.68%	83.68%
	Proposed	97.37%	**98.95%**	98.42%	98.42%	98.42%
RBF ($\sigma^2 = 20$)	OVA	97.37%	**97.37%**	87.89%	87.89%	87.89%
	Proposed	97.37 %	97.89 %	97.89 %	**98.95%**	98.42 %

Table 2 shows the result of recognition performance. We tried RBF(σ^2=20) and polynomial(parameter=2) as kernel of SVM. At RBF kernel with K=1, two methods show the same recognition rate a 97.37%. The OVA method decreases the recognition rate as K increases, while the proposed method shows the maximum recognition rate a 98.95% at K=4. At the polynomial kernel two methods show maximum recognition rate at K=2, and the proposed method show better recognition rate as 5% than OVA. From the result, we can say that the SVM of proposed method is trained to give appropriate similarity for class pairs based on the class information. In addition, the proposed method does not much depend on the shape of kernels, while the conventional method does. The kernel-dependency may caused by the limited number of data in each class.

4 Conclusion

When we use SVM and the OVA or AP methods for classifying multi-classes with small data set, the decision boundaries found by SVM likely to be spoiled by noisy data. It is emphasized when we use inappropriate kernel functions as shown in the experiment in Section 3. To get good recognition performance with small data set, it is important to reconstruct the input features for training SVM, so that it can keep some core information for classification and be insensitive to noises included in data. The discrepancy in two data pairs in a same class can give good information, and we utilizes it to train SVM to find a similarity measure based on it. From the experimental results, we can see the possibility of the proposed mechanism to various problems with similar properties.

Acknowlegement. This research was supported by Kyungpook National University Research Fund, 2004.

References

1. L. Bottou, C. Cortes, J. Denker, H. Drucker, I. Guyon, L. Jackel, Y. LeCun, U. Muller, E. Sackinger, P. Simard, and V. Vapnik, *Proc. Int. Conf. Pattern Recognition.*, pp.77-87, 1994.
2. C. Campbell, *An introduction to kernel methods, radial basis funtion networks: design and application*, Springer Verlag, Berlin, 2000.
3. C.W. Hsu, C.J. Lin, *IEEE Transcaction on Neural Networks*, Vol 13, No. 2, pp.415-425, 2002.
4. R.O. Duda, P.E. Hart, *Pattern classification and scene analysis*, New York: Wiley, 1973.
5. B. Schölkopf, C.J.C.Burges, and A.J.Smola, *in Advances in Kernel Methods-Support Vector Learning*, Cambridge, MA:MIT Press, pp.255-268, 1999.
6. K. Lee, H. Park, *ETRI Journal*, Vol 25, No. 5, pp.401-406, 2003.
7. B. Schölkopf, A.J. Smola, *Learning with kernels: support vector machines, regularization, optimization, and beyond (Adaptive Computation and Machine Learning)*, MIT Press, 2001.

Author Index

Abbass, Hussein A.   1092
Aguilera, Josep   593
Ahn, Eun-Young   330
Ahn, Sang C.   726
Ahn, Tae-Chon   1142
Albrecht, David W.   922
Aoki, Terumasa   1162
Araki, Kenji   1146
Araz, Ozlem Uzun   1047
Ashrafi, Mafruz Zaman   254
Auephanwiriyaku, Sansanee   1180

Baek, Joon-sik   530
Baek, Joong-hwan   530
Baek, Kyunghwan   1229
Baesens, Bart   975
Bai, Quan   674
Bain, Stuart   1068
Beh, Jounghoon   966
Bĕlohlávek, Radim   1126
Berry, Adam   1108
Billington, David   796, 812
Biswas, Debjit   1289
Bolat, Emine Doğru   1295
Bonnet, Noël   624
Borg, Mark   593
Bourdon, François   1204
Bourmistrova, Anna   1025
Brede, Markus   1327
Brémond, François   593
Bridle, Robert   970
Brzostowski, Jakub   653
Bulitko, Vadim   959
Bulos, Remedios de Dios   993
Burdon, Steve   457
Butaru, Mihaela   875
Büyüközkan, Gülçin   1154

Calbert, Greg   164, 207
Can, Burhanettin   1057
Cao, Minh Duc   143
Cavalcanti Júnior, Nicomedes L.   1138
Chang, Elizabeth   318, 1158
Chang, Jing-Rong   946
Chang, Wei-Ting   1213

Chang, Yuchou   1237
Chee, Marc   17
Chen, Guang   1079
Chen, Haixia   904
Chen, Jie   910
Chen, Jungan   847
Chen, Lei-lei   1331
Chen, Qingfeng   245
Chen, Rong   865
Chen, Songcan   1221
Chen, Xiangsheng   1272
Chen, Yi-Ping Phoebe   245
Cheng, Ching-Hsue   946, 1213
Chew, Eng   457
Chi, Sung-Do   766
Cho, Jae-Hyun   1241
Cho, Jeong-Hoon   746
Cho, Minkook   1335
Cho, Miyoung   1209
Choi, Dae-Young   1301
Choi, Junho   1209
Chung, Chan-Soo   1096
Cleaver, Timothy William   60
Coban, Ramazan   1057
Collins, J.J.   235, 684
Collins, Thomas   235, 684
Compton, Paul   401
Cornforth, David   1285

Daggard, Grant   1272
Dam, Hai H.   1092
Dastani, Mehdi   695
Davoodi, Mansoor   1120
de Araujo, Daniel S.A.   930
De Backer, Manu   975
de Carvalho, Francisco de A.T.   1138
de Souto, Marcilio C.P.   930
Debenham, John   467, 643
Deer, Peter   445
Dib, Lynda   624
Dillon, Tharam S.   318, 1158
Ding, Yulin   5
Do, Quoc V.   1246
Dong, Won-Pyo   1277
Dooley, Laurence   274

Dowe, David L.   922
Dras, Mark   786
Dulalia, Conirose   993

Eaton, Malachy   684
El Falou, Salah   1204
El-Hajj, Mohammad   1001
Erkan, Kadir   1295
Ersoy, Mehmet Şakir   1154

Fan, Yuliang   445
Fayad, Carole   339
Feng, Ding-zhong   1173, 1331
Ferreira Jr., Valnir   70
Ferryman, James   593
Fitch, Robert   164
Flórez, S.   1009
Fogelberg, Christopher   369
Fusier, Florent   593

Gao, Xiaoying   143
García Adeva, J.J.   1009
Ge, Hong-Wei   756, 839
Gilmour, Stephen   786
Go, Peggy Sharon L.   993
Goldberg, David E.   4
Gondal, Iqbal   274
Gossink, Don   207
Governatori, Guido   695
Grant, Kevin   49
Guessoum, Zahia   624
Guo, XiuPing   176
Guo, Xuetao   457
Guo, Ying   1086
Guo, Yunsong   871
Gupta, Gopal   540

Ha, Jong-Eun   1267
Habbas, Zineb   875
Haesen, Raf   975
Hahn, Hernsoo   896, 1229
Hahn, Minsoo   550
Han, David   1195
Han, Hyun Bae   550
Han, Jialing   934
Han, Sang-Hoon   330
Han, Youngjoon   896, 1229
Hawick, K.A.   852
He, Hongxing   910
He, Pilian   892

He, Yong   1053
Hengst, Bernhard   164
Hickmott, Sarah L.   830
Hoffmann, Achim   1167
Hong, Dong Kwon   1233
Hong, Sungwoo   1281
Hong, Yi   1237
Hope, Lucas R.   805
Horsch, Michael C.   49
Hou, Gang   934
Hu, Hong   918
Huang, Tianmin   989
Huang, Xiaodi   1272
Hussain, Aini   1315
Hwang, Chan-Sik   746

Işıklar, Gülfem   1154
Itoh, Hidenori   861
Iwane, Noriyuki   389

Jain, Lakhmi C.   1246
James, Geoff   1086
James, H.A.   852
Jang, Dae-Geun   746
Jang, Kyung Ae   550
Jang, MinSeok   577
Jang, Seong-Whan   1075
Jelinek, Herbert   1285
Jeong, Chang-Sung   1277
Ji, Krystian   17
Jiang, Hong   914
Jiang, Kai   904
Jiang, Yuan   92
Jiao, Licheng   997
Jin, Andrew Teoh Beng   1217
Jin, Huidong   910
Jin, Zhi   39
Joo, Young Hoon   380, 557, 1130, 1134
Jun, H.S.   1262
Jun, Sung-Hae   1015

Kampel, Martin   593
Kang, Byeong Ho   401
Kang, Dong-Joong   1267
Kang, Kyung-Woo   197
Kang, Sin-Jae   1112
Kanoh, Masayoshi   861
Karaboga, Nurhan   1063
Kato, Shohei   861
Kennedy, Paul   360

Khantsis, Sergey   1025
Kim, Byeong Man   1112
Kim, Byoungki   1229
Kim, Byung-Joo   153, 585
Kim, Cheol-Ki   1241
Kim, Do Wan   380, 1130
Kim, Dong Seong   766
Kim, Hyoung-Gon   726
Kim, Hyun-Ki   1075, 1116
Kim, Hyungil   1281
Kim, Ig-Jae   726
Kim, Ik-Dong   1225
Kim, Il Kon   153
Kim, J.B.   1262
Kim, Jae-Won   330
Kim, Jong-Wan   1112
Kim, June   966
Kim, Juntae   1281
Kim, Kwang-Baek   1241
Kim, Kweon Yang   1233
Kim, Min-Soo   1096
Kim, Moon Hwan   557, 1134
Kim, Pankoo   1209
Kim, Sang-Jin   550
Kim, Sang-Woon   614
Kim, Tae Yoon   284
Kim, Taek-Hun   1150
Kim, Weon-Goo   577, 1134
Kim, Yang Sok   401
Kim, Yong-Kab   1075
Ko, Hanseok   966
Kong, Jun   510, 934, 1037
Kong, Min   1305
Korb, Kevin B.   102, 805
Kornienko, Lara   922
Kowalczyk, Ryszard   653
Koyuncu, Canan Aslihan   1063
Kruppa, Michael   225
Kuo, Bor-Chen   567
Kuo, M.H.   633
Kwak, No-Yoon   330
Kwon, Tae-Gyun   746

Lam, Yuk-Hei   664
Laskri, Mohamed T.   624
Lee, Byong Gul   1233
Lee, Chang-Hwan   900
Lee, Chin-Hui   577
Lee, Hakbae   284
Lee, Heungkyu   966

Lee, Hyoung Yong   284
Lee, Ickjai   938
Lee, J.M.   1262
Lee, Jang-Se   766
Lee, Joohun   896
Lee, Kyu Yeul   826
Lee, Kyung Ho   826
Lee, Sang-Yup   726
Lee, Soon-tak   530
Lee, Sungyoung   489
Lee, Yeunghak   1225
Lee, Younjeong   896
Lee, Yun-Seok   1277
Lei, I-Ni   946
Leoni, Fabio   1319
Li, Cheng-Hsuan   567
Li, Chunping   604, 883
Li, Chunsheng   705
Li, Hong-Ru   816
Li, Jiaming   1086
Li, Jiuyong   1272
Li, Lei   133
Li, Li   843
Li, Tian-rui   989
Li, Xiangyong   1305
Li, Xiaoli   1053
Li, Yanzhi   871, 1323
Li, Yongming   308
Li, Yuefeng   1005
Liang, Feng   847
Liang, Jiuzhen   914
Liang, Yan-Chun   756, 839
Lim, Andrew   736, 871, 1323
Lim, Myo-Taeg   726
Lin, Aizhong   405
Lin, Li   979
Ling, David Ngo Chek   1217
Liu, Chuchang   29
Liu, Chunnian   1199
Liu, Enhai   892
Liu, Fei   1041
Liu, Jialiang   498
Liu, Jun   1221
Liu, Li   705, 979
Liu, San-yang   349
Liu, Xinyue   510
Liu, Yuncai   520
Liu, Zhi-Qiang   498
Lozo, Peter   1246
Lu, Chenhui   133

Lu, Ruqian 39
Lu, Wei 133
Lu, YingHua 510, 934, 1037
Ludermir, Teresa 1031
Luo, Chao 1311
Luo, Dan 979, 1311
Luo, Siwei 264
Luo, Yanbin 308

Ma, Hong 1323
Maheshwari, Piyush 405
Mansfield, Mark 235, 684
Martens, David 975
Matuk Herrera, Rosana 1319
McCreath, Eric 970
McLachlan, Geoffrey J. 879
Mendes, Rui 776
Meng, Hong-yun 349
Miao, Yuan 540
Milton, John 360
Min, Kyongho 82
Mitchell, Heather 360
Mohais, Arvind S. 776
Mohamed, Azah 1315
Molfetas, Angelos 1101
Moon, Yoo-Jin 82
Mu, Kedian 39

Naguleswaran, Sanjeev 830
Narayanan, Babu 1289
Newth, David 1327
Ng, Shu-Kay 879
Nguyen, Minh Le 800
Nhat, Vo Dinh Minh 489
Ni, Ailing 123

Oh, Kyong Joo 284
Oh, Sung-Kwun 1075, 1116, 1142
Ollington, Robert 113
Ong, Kok-Leong 664
Oommen, B. John 614
Orgun, Mehmet A. 29
O'Sullivan, Shane 235
Ozcelik, Feristah 1021
Ozols, Maris A. 29

Pan, Jialin 133
Pan, Rong 133
Pang, Ying-Han 1217
Paradeda, Raul B. 930

Park, Gil Cheol 401
Park, Hyeyoung 1335
Park, Hyun-Soo 197
Park, Jin Bae 380, 557, 1130, 1134
Park, Jong Sou 766
Park, Keon-Jun 1142
Park, Kyu-Sik 927
Park, Sangbum 1229
Park, Sung Sik 401
Patnaik, Lalit M. 435
Pedrycz, Witold 1142
Pei, Zheng 942
Peng, Hong 942
Petrovic, Sanja 339
Petrovskiy, Mikhail 186
Phan, Hieu Xuan 800
Pi, Daoying 308
Pikatza, J.M. 1009
Postalcıoğlu, Seda 1295
Posthoff, Christian 776
Pyun, Hye Won 715

Qin, Zhenxing 133

Rezaei, Jafar 1120
Ríos, Sebastían A. 1162
Rocco S., Claudio M. 954
Rodrigues, Brian 871
Rotolo, Antonino 695
Ruan, Da 989
Ruan, J. 790

Saad, Mohd Hanif Md 1315
Sakai, Setsuko 389
Sattar, Abdul 60, 1068
Sayuti, Noor Sabathiah 1315
Schmidt, Stefan 318
Schmitz, Michael 225
Scholz, Jason 164
Schwitter, Rolf 425
Scogings, C.J. 852
Sehgal, Muhammad Shoaib B. 274
Sermet Anagun, A. 1021
Severiano-Sobrinho, Valmar S. 930
Shafi, Kamran 1092
Shao, Chao 264
Shao, Jinyan 857
Shao, Yongni 1053
Sharath, S. 435
Shi, Fanhuai 520

Shi, Jiaoying 1187
Shi, Lukui 892
Shibata, Hiroshi 861
Shim, JeongYon 983
Shimazu, Akira 800
Shukairi, Mohd Haszuan 1315
Sidhu, Amandeep S. 1158
Sidhu, Baldev S. 1158
Sierra, Carles 643
Silva, Shirlly C.M. 930
Simoff, Simeon J. 467
Singh, Pramod K. 950
Skabar, Andrew 888
Smet, Peter 207
Smith, Kate 254
Sobrado, F.J. 1009
Song, Dan 1209
Song, Shaoxu 604
Spassova, Lübomira 225
Srinivasa, K.G. 435
Steele, Robert 318
Šuc, Dorian 164
Sun, Liang 839
Sundararajan, Ramasubramanian 1289

Takahama, Tetsuyuki 389
Tan, Pamela Vianne C. 993
Tang, Canghua 1037
Tang, Jiqing 736
Tang, Min 997
Tang, Wei 1199
Tang, Yongchuan 822
Taniar, David 254
Temby, Luke 1108
Thirde, David 593
Thonnat, Monique 593
Thornton, John 70, 1068
Tian, Peng 1305
Ting, Kai Ming 102
Torres D., Douglas E. 954

Uy, Ma. Zaide Ilene O. 993

Valença, Anelle 1031
Valença, Mêuser 1031
Valentin, Valéry 593
Vamplew, Peter 113, 1108
van der Torre, Leendert 695
van Ditmarsch, H.P. 790
Velásquez, Juan D. 1162

Vengerov, David 477
Venugopal, K.R. 435
Verbrugge, L.C. 790
Vo, Quoc Bao 834
Vychodil, Vilém 1126

Wang, Jia-Wen 1213
Wang, Jun 942
Wang, Kewen 60
Wang, Long 215, 857
Wang, Shujing 1191
Wang, Wei 934
Wang, Yonggang 1237
Wang, Yuanyong 1167
Ward, Christopher 776
Webb, Geoffrey I. 1, 102
White, Langford B. 830
Wilkins, David C. 959
Wilson, William H. 82
Wobcke, Wayne 17
Wotawa, Franz 865
Wozniak, Michal 1258
Wu, Baolin 843
Wu, ZhiMing 176

Xie, Guangming 215, 857
Xie, Huayang 1253
Xu, Guandong 415
Xu, Jin An 1146
Xu, Yang 989
Xue, Xiao-Bing 92

Yager, Ronald R. 3
Yamashiro, Mitsuo 1173, 1331
Yang, Chunjie 308
Yang, Dongyong 847
Yang, GenKe 176
Yang, Jianhua 938
Yang, Ming 1041
Yang, Qiang 133
Yang, Sung-Bong 1150
Yang, Yiming 133
Yang, Ying 102
Yang, Yun 843
Yasuda, Hiroshi 1162
Yavuz, Sırma 297
Yoon, Won-Jung 927
Yu, Jiarong 1187
Yu, Lijie 1037
Yuan, Senmiao 904

Zaïane, Osmar R.   1001
Zhang, Bai-ling   540
Zhang, Chengqi   123
Zhang, Chunkai   918
Zhang, Chunzhi   1311
Zhang, Dandan   215
Zhang, Debbie   467
Zhang, Guangquan   457
Zhang, Jian   883
Zhang, Jing   520
Zhang, Mengjie   369, 1079
Zhang, Minjie   674
Zhang, Weicun   215, 857
Zhang, Wen-Xiu   816
Zhang, Xiao-hua   349
Zhang, Yan   5, 1191
Zhang, Yanchun   415
Zhang, Zili   664
Zhao, Lianwei   264
Zhao, Qiushi   510
Zhao, Shuguang   997
Zhao, Yanchang   264
Zheng, Jiacheng   822
Zheng, Lei   1199
Zhong, Ning   1005
Zhou, Xiaofang   415
Zhou, Xiaofeng   510
Zhou, Yongxia   1187
Zhou, Yue   1237
Zhou, Zhi-Hua   92
Zhu, Xiaofeng   123

Lecture Notes in Artificial Intelligence (LNAI)

Vol. 3835: G. Sutcliffe, A. Voronkov (Eds.), Logic for Programming, Artificial Intelligence, and Reasoning. XIV, 744 pages. 2005.

Vol. 3814: M. Maybury, O. Stock, W. Wahlster (Eds.), Intelligent Technologies for Interactive Entertainment. XV, 342 pages. 2005.

Vol. 3809: S. Zhang, R. Jarvis (Eds.), AI 2005: Advances in Artificial Intelligence. XXVII, 1344 pages. 2005.

Vol. 3789: A. Gelbukh, Á. de Albornoz, H. Terashima-Marín (Eds.), MICAI 2005: Advances in Artificial Intelligence. XXVI, 1198 pages. 2005.

Vol. 3735: A. Hoffmann, H. Motoda, T. Scheffer (Eds.), Discovery Science. XVI, 400 pages. 2005.

Vol. 3734: S. Jain, H.U. Simon, E. Tomita (Eds.), Algorithmic Learning Theory. XII, 490 pages. 2005.

Vol. 3721: A.M. Jorge, L. Torgo, P.B. Brazdil, R. Camacho, J. Gama (Eds.), Knowledge Discovery in Databases: PKDD 2005. XXIII, 719 pages. 2005.

Vol. 3720: J. Gama, R. Camacho, P.B. Brazdil, A.M. Jorge, L. Torgo (Eds.), Machine Learning: ECML 2005. XXIII, 769 pages. 2005.

Vol. 3717: B. Gramlich (Ed.), Frontiers of Combining Systems. X, 321 pages. 2005.

Vol. 3702: B. Beckert (Ed.), Automated Reasoning with Analytic Tableaux and Related Methods. XIII, 343 pages. 2005.

Vol. 3698: U. Furbach (Ed.), KI 2005: Advances in Artificial Intelligence. XIII, 409 pages. 2005.

Vol. 3690: M. Pěchouček, P. Petta, L.Z. Varga (Eds.), Multi-Agent Systems and Applications IV. XVII, 667 pages. 2005.

Vol. 3684: R. Khosla, R.J. Howlett, L.C. Jain (Eds.), Knowledge-Based Intelligent Information and Engineering Systems, Part IV. LXXIX, 933 pages. 2005.

Vol. 3683: R. Khosla, R.J. Howlett, L.C. Jain (Eds.), Knowledge-Based Intelligent Information and Engineering Systems, Part III. LXXX, 1397 pages. 2005.

Vol. 3682: R. Khosla, R.J. Howlett, L.C. Jain (Eds.), Knowledge-Based Intelligent Information and Engineering Systems, Part II. LXXIX, 1371 pages. 2005.

Vol. 3681: R. Khosla, R.J. Howlett, L.C. Jain (Eds.), Knowledge-Based Intelligent Information and Engineering Systems, Part I. LXXX, 1319 pages. 2005.

Vol. 3673: S. Bandini, S. Manzoni (Eds.), AI*IA 2005: Advances in Artificial Intelligence. XIV, 614 pages. 2005.

Vol. 3662: C. Baral, G. Greco, N. Leone, G. Terracina (Eds.), Logic Programming and Nonmonotonic Reasoning. XIII, 454 pages. 2005.

Vol. 3661: T. Panayiotopoulos, J. Gratch, R.S. Aylett, D. Ballin, P. Olivier, T. Rist (Eds.), Intelligent Virtual Agents. XIII, 506 pages. 2005.

Vol. 3658: V. Matoušek, P. Mautner, T. Pavelka (Eds.), Text, Speech and Dialogue. XV, 460 pages. 2005.

Vol. 3651: R. Dale, K.-F. Wong, J. Su, O.Y. Kwong (Eds.), Natural Language Processing – IJCNLP 2005. XXI, 1031 pages. 2005.

Vol. 3642: D. Ślęzak, J. Yao, J.F. Peters, W. Ziarko, X. Hu (Eds.), Rough Sets, Fuzzy Sets, Data Mining, and Granular Computing, Part II. XXIII, 738 pages. 2005.

Vol. 3641: D. Ślęzak, G. Wang, M. Szczuka, I. Düntsch, Y. Yao (Eds.), Rough Sets, Fuzzy Sets, Data Mining, and Granular Computing, Part I. XXIV, 742 pages. 2005.

Vol. 3635: J.R. Winkler, M. Niranjan, N.D. Lawrence (Eds.), Deterministic and Statistical Methods in Machine Learning. VIII, 341 pages. 2005.

Vol. 3632: R. Nieuwenhuis (Ed.), Automated Deduction – CADE-20. XIII, 459 pages. 2005.

Vol. 3630: M.S. Capcarrère, A.A. Freitas, P.J. Bentley, C.G. Johnson, J. Timmis (Eds.), Advances in Artificial Life. XIX, 949 pages. 2005.

Vol. 3626: B. Ganter, G. Stumme, R. Wille (Eds.), Formal Concept Analysis. X, 349 pages. 2005.

Vol. 3625: S. Kramer, B. Pfahringer (Eds.), Inductive Logic Programming. XIII, 427 pages. 2005.

Vol. 3620: H. Muñoz-Ávila, F. Ricci (Eds.), Case-Based Reasoning Research and Development. XV, 654 pages. 2005.

Vol. 3614: L. Wang, Y. Jin (Eds.), Fuzzy Systems and Knowledge Discovery, Part II. XLI, 1314 pages. 2005.

Vol. 3613: L. Wang, Y. Jin (Eds.), Fuzzy Systems and Knowledge Discovery, Part I. XLI, 1334 pages. 2005.

Vol. 3607: J.-D. Zucker, L. Saitta (Eds.), Abstraction, Reformulation and Approximation. XII, 376 pages. 2005.

Vol. 3601: G. Moro, S. Bergamaschi, K. Aberer (Eds.), Agents and Peer-to-Peer Computing. XII, 245 pages. 2005.

Vol. 3596: F. Dau, M.-L. Mugnier, G. Stumme (Eds.), Conceptual Structures: Common Semantics for Sharing Knowledge. XI, 467 pages. 2005.

Vol. 3593: V. Mařík, R. W. Brennan, M. Pěchouček (Eds.), Holonic and Multi-Agent Systems for Manufacturing. XI, 269 pages. 2005.

Vol. 3587: P. Perner, A. Imiya (Eds.), Machine Learning and Data Mining in Pattern Recognition. XVII, 695 pages. 2005.

Vol. 3584: X. Li, S. Wang, Z.Y. Dong (Eds.), Advanced Data Mining and Applications. XIX, 835 pages. 2005.

Vol. 3581: S. Miksch, J. Hunter, E.T. Keravnou (Eds.), Artificial Intelligence in Medicine. XVII, 547 pages. 2005.

Vol. 3577: R. Falcone, S. Barber, J. Sabater-Mir, M.P. Singh (Eds.), Trusting Agents for Trusting Electronic Societies. VIII, 235 pages. 2005.

Vol. 3575: S. Wermter, G. Palm, M. Elshaw (Eds.), Biomimetic Neural Learning for Intelligent Robots. IX, 383 pages. 2005.

Vol. 3571: L. Godo (Ed.), Symbolic and Quantitative Approaches to Reasoning with Uncertainty. XVI, 1028 pages. 2005.

Vol. 3559: P. Auer, R. Meir (Eds.), Learning Theory. XI, 692 pages. 2005.

Vol. 3558: V. Torra, Y. Narukawa, S. Miyamoto (Eds.), Modeling Decisions for Artificial Intelligence. XII, 470 pages. 2005.

Vol. 3554: A.K. Dey, B. Kokinov, D.B. Leake, R. Turner (Eds.), Modeling and Using Context. XIV, 572 pages. 2005.

Vol. 3550: T. Eymann, F. Klügl, W. Lamersdorf, M. Klusch, M.N. Huhns (Eds.), Multiagent System Technologies. XI, 246 pages. 2005.

Vol. 3539: K. Morik, J.-F. Boulicaut, A. Siebes (Eds.), Local Pattern Detection. XI, 233 pages. 2005.

Vol. 3538: L. Ardissono, P. Brna, A. Mitrović (Eds.), User Modeling 2005. XVI, 533 pages. 2005.

Vol. 3533: M. Ali, F. Esposito (Eds.), Innovations in Applied Artificial Intelligence. XX, 858 pages. 2005.

Vol. 3528: P.S. Szczepaniak, J. Kacprzyk, A. Niewiadomski (Eds.), Advances in Web Intelligence. XVII, 513 pages. 2005.

Vol. 3518: T.-B. Ho, D. Cheung, H. Liu (Eds.), Advances in Knowledge Discovery and Data Mining. XXI, 864 pages. 2005.

Vol. 3508: P. Bresciani, P. Giorgini, B. Henderson-Sellers, G. Low, M. Winikoff (Eds.), Agent-Oriented Information Systems II. X, 227 pages. 2005.

Vol. 3505: V. Gorodetsky, J. Liu, V.A. Skormin (Eds.), Autonomous Intelligent Systems: Agents and Data Mining. XIII, 303 pages. 2005.

Vol. 3501: B. Kégl, G. Lapalme (Eds.), Advances in Artificial Intelligence. XV, 458 pages. 2005.

Vol. 3492: P. Blache, E.P. Stabler, J.V. Busquets, R. Moot (Eds.), Logical Aspects of Computational Linguistics. X, 363 pages. 2005.

Vol. 3490: L. Bolc, Z. Michalewicz, T. Nishida (Eds.), Intelligent Media Technology for Communicative Intelligence. X, 259 pages. 2005.

Vol. 3488: M.-S. Hacid, N.V. Murray, Z.W. Raś, S. Tsumoto (Eds.), Foundations of Intelligent Systems. XIII, 700 pages. 2005.

Vol. 3487: J.A. Leite, P. Torroni (Eds.), Computational Logic in Multi-Agent Systems. XII, 281 pages. 2005.

Vol. 3476: J.A. Leite, A. Omicini, P. Torroni, P. Yolum (Eds.), Declarative Agent Languages and Technologies II. XII, 289 pages. 2005.

Vol. 3464: S.A. Brueckner, G.D.M. Serugendo, A. Karageorgos, R. Nagpal (Eds.), Engineering Self-Organising Systems. XIII, 299 pages. 2005.

Vol. 3452: F. Baader, A. Voronkov (Eds.), Logic for Programming, Artificial Intelligence, and Reasoning. XI, 562 pages. 2005.

Vol. 3451: M.-P. Gleizes, A. Omicini, F. Zambonelli (Eds.), Engineering Societies in the Agents World V. XIII, 349 pages. 2005.

Vol. 3446: T. Ishida, L. Gasser, H. Nakashima (Eds.), Massively Multi-Agent Systems I. XI, 349 pages. 2005.

Vol. 3445: G. Chollet, A. Esposito, M. Faúndez-Zanuy, M. Marinaro (Eds.), Nonlinear Speech Modeling and Applications. XIII, 433 pages. 2005.

Vol. 3438: H. Christiansen, P.R. Skadhauge, J. Villadsen (Eds.), Constraint Solving and Language Processing. VIII, 205 pages. 2005.

Vol. 3430: S. Tsumoto, T. Yamaguchi, M. Numao, H. Motoda (Eds.), Active Mining. XII, 349 pages. 2005.

Vol. 3419: B.V. Faltings, A. Petcu, F. Fages, F. Rossi (Eds.), Recent Advances in Constraints. X, 217 pages. 2005.

Vol. 3416: M.H. Böhlen, J. Gamper, W. Polasek, M.A. Wimmer (Eds.), E-Government: Towards Electronic Democracy. XIII, 311 pages. 2005.

Vol. 3415: P. Davidsson, B. Logan, K. Takadama (Eds.), Multi-Agent and Multi-Agent-Based Simulation. X, 265 pages. 2005.

Vol. 3403: B. Ganter, R. Godin (Eds.), Formal Concept Analysis. XI, 419 pages. 2005.

Vol. 3398: D.-K. Baik (Ed.), Systems Modeling and Simulation: Theory and Applications. XIV, 733 pages. 2005.

Vol. 3397: T.G. Kim (Ed.), Artificial Intelligence and Simulation. XV, 711 pages. 2005.

Vol. 3396: R.M. van Eijk, M.-P. Huget, F.P. M. Dignum (Eds.), Agent Communication. X, 261 pages. 2005.

Vol. 3394: D. Kudenko, D. Kazakov, E. Alonso (Eds.), Adaptive Agents and Multi-Agent Systems II. VIII, 313 pages. 2005.

Vol. 3392: D. Seipel, M. Hanus, U. Geske, O. Bartenstein (Eds.), Applications of Declarative Programming and Knowledge Management. X, 309 pages. 2005.

Vol. 3374: D. Weyns, H. V.D. Parunak, F. Michel (Eds.), Environments for Multi-Agent Systems. X, 279 pages. 2005.

Vol. 3371: M.W. Barley, N. Kasabov (Eds.), Intelligent Agents and Multi-Agent Systems. X, 329 pages. 2005.

Vol. 3369: V. R. Benjamins, P. Casanovas, J. Breuker, A. Gangemi (Eds.), Law and the Semantic Web. XII, 249 pages. 2005.

Vol. 3366: I. Rahwan, P. Moraïtis, C. Reed (Eds.), Argumentation in Multi-Agent Systems. XII, 263 pages. 2005.

Vol. 3359: G. Grieser, Y. Tanaka (Eds.), Intuitive Human Interfaces for Organizing and Accessing Intellectual Assets. XIV, 257 pages. 2005.

Vol. 3346: R.H. Bordini, M. Dastani, J. Dix, A.E.F. Seghrouchni (Eds.), Programming Multi-Agent Systems. XIV, 249 pages. 2005.

Vol. 3345: Y. Cai (Ed.), Ambient Intelligence for Scientific Discovery. XII, 311 pages. 2005.